# Computer Desktop Encyclopedia

## Ninth Edition

Alan Freedman

Osborne/**McGraw-Hill**

New York   Chicago   San Francisco
Lisbon   London   Madrid   Mexico City   Milan
New Delhi   San Juan   Seoul   Singapore   Sydney   Toronto

Osborne/**McGraw-Hill**
2600 Tenth Street
Berkeley, California 94710
U.S.A.

To arrange bulk purchase discounts for sales promotions, premiums, or fund-raisers, please contact Osborne/**McGraw-Hill** at the above address. For information on translations or book distributors outside the U.S.A., please see the International Contact Information page at the end of this book.

### Computer Desktop Encyclopedia, Ninth Edition

1234567890 DOC  DOC 901987654321

Book p/n 0-07-219307-7 and CD p/n 0-07-219308-5
parts of
ISBN 0-07-219306-9

| | |
|---|---|
| **Publisher**<br>Brandon A. Nordin | **Computer Designers**<br>Lauren McCarthy, Tabitha Cagan |
| **Vice President & Associate Publisher**<br>Scott Rogers | **Illustrators**<br>Lyssa Wald, Michael Mueller |
| **Editorial Director**<br>Roger Stewart | **Series Design**<br>Peter F. Hancik |
| **Senior Project Editor**<br>Pamela Woolf | **Cover Design**<br>Greg Scott |
| **Proofreaders**<br>Linda Medoff, Paul Medoff | **Cover Illustration**<br>John Bleck |

This book was composed with Corel VENTURA™ Publisher.

To my mother, who had the vision to send me
to "automation school" in 1960.

## About the Author

**Alan Freedman** is president of The Computer Language Company, an organization devoted to computer education training for business and non-technical people. With more than 40 years of experience in the field and 20 years of writing the *Computer Glossary* and *Computer Desktop Encyclopedia*, Freedman is the most noted computer lexicographer in the country. Deemed both "comprehensive and authoritative" by *PC Magazine*, Freedman's work is widely recognized for making abstract computing concepts easily understandable to non-technical people.

# Contents

# Look Up the Acronym!

## Most entries in this book are by acronym only.

# Acknowledgments

It would be impossible to put a book like this together without the help of hundreds of technical engineers and public relations people who work for the hardware and software companies that make up this industry. In addition, many readers of the *Computer Glossary* and previous editions of *Computer Desktop Encyclopedia* have contributed terms, suggestions and comments. For all of you that have graciously helped me, I thank you from the bottom of my heart. For those of you who made the experience akin to pulling teeth, well, thank you too. I do appreciate it.

I'd like to give a special acknowledgement to the following professionals who have continued to help me year after year. Thanks again to

- David Chappell, Chappell Associates
- Thom Drewke, Technical Directions
- James Farrell, III, Motorola, Inc.
- Max Fetzer, Envirotronics
- Steve Gibson, Gibson Research Corporation
- Lynn Thompson, Thompson Associates
- Peter Hermsen, AVC Global Services
- Clive "Max" Maxfield, techBITES INTERactive
- Terry O'Donnel, Adobe Systems
- Jim Stroh, LXD Inc.
- Paul and Jan Witte, Originetics

I would like to thank my editor Roger Stewart and the editorial, design, and production staff at Osborne/McGraw-Hill, including Peter Hancik, Lisa Bandini, Lauren McCarthy, Tabitha Cagan, Lyssa Wald and Pamela Woolf. All of you have shown exceptional enthusiasm for this book, and I am very grateful for your help and expertise.

Most of all, an extra special thank you to Irma Lee Morrison, my wife and partner. Your contribution has always been the most significant. Irmalee, I love you dearly.

**A Note from the Author**    The purpose of *Computer Desktop Encyclopedia* is to provide a meaningful definition of every important computer concept, term and buzzword used in the world of computers from micro to mainframe. Major hardware and software products are included as well as backgrounds on the companies that make them. Many historical photos of the first computers and electronic devices are in this book to remind us of the extraordinary acceleration of the technology of our era, all of which has come about in little more than 100 years. It's a good idea to stop and smell the roses as we race toward the newest and the fastest.

It is also the purpose of this book to make sense out of this industry in general. As impossible a task as that may be, I have been trying for more than two decades. What started out as a 300-term compendium for my computer seminars has now become my life's work. And, for that, I am very grateful, because all the technology fascinates me. I am lucky to have had so much experience in this field, and I am extremely lucky to have expert professionals who are willing to help.

The degree of technical explanation chosen for each term is based on the term. Fundamental terms are explained for the lay person. More technical terms are explained with other technical terms, because, at some point, I have to assume a base knowledge without starting from scratch. However, all the terms used are also defined in the book.

I hope you find this book helpful and enjoyable. If there are concepts or products you feel should be included in the next edition, please let me know. Chances are they may have already been added to the CD-ROM version, which is updated more frequently; however, I would love to hear from you and review your suggestions. Please write, fax, e-mail or call. Thank you very much for purchasing *Computer Desktop Encyclopedia*.

Alan Freedman

The Computer Language Company Inc.
5521 State Park Road
Point Pleasant, PA 18950
phone: 215 297-8082 fax: 8424
e-mail: freedman@computerlanguage.com

# Computer
# Desktop
# Encyclopedia

Edition 9

# Alphabetical Entries

# A

**A:** The designation for the first floppy disk drive in a PC. In PCs that have two floppy drives, the second drive is B:. See *C:*.

**A+ certification**   See *CompTIA*.

**AAC**   (MPEG-2 Advanced Audio Coding) An audio compression technology that is part of the MPEG-2 standard. It provides a greater compression and superior sound quality than MP3, which is also part of the MPEG spec (MPEG Audio Layer 3). AAC is available in three profiles: Main, Low Complexity (LC) and Scaleable Sampling Rate (SSR), with Main providing the highest quality. MPEG-4 includes a superset of MPEG-2 AAC. See *MP3*.

**AAL**   (ATM Adaption Layer) The part of the ATM protocol that breaks up application packets into 48-byte payloads, which become ATM cells when the 5-byte headers are attached. The AAL resides between the higher layer transport protocols and the ATM layer. The AAL is comprised of two layers: Convergence Sublayer (CS) and Segmentation and Reassembly Sublayer (SAR). There are five types of AALs, which are summarized below. See *ATM*.

**AAL-1**   Connection-oriented, Constant Bit Rate (CBR), such as DS1 and DS3.

**AAL-2**   Connection-oriented, Variable Bit Rate (VBR).

**AAL-3/4**   Connection-oriented and connectionless, Available Bit Rate (ABR).

**AAL-5**   Connection-oriented, Unspecified Bit Rate (UBR). Least amount of error checking and retransmission.

**AAL-6**   Connection-oriented, MPEG-2 video streams.

**AAUI**   (Apple AUI) Apple's version of the Ethernet AUI connector. See *AUI* and *10Base5*.

| AAL | CS | SSCS<br>Service Specfiic Convergence Sublayer |
| | | CPCS<br>Common Part Convergence Sublayer |
| | SAR<br>Segmentation & Reassembly | |
| ATM layer | | |

**ATM Adaption Layer**
The SSCS is a service-dependent layer, while the CPCS provides common functions such as CRC checking and padding to fill out a 48-byte payload. The SAR converts the output of the CS into cells for the ATM layer.

**abacus**   One of the earliest counting instruments. Similar devices predate the Greek and Roman days. It uses sliding beads in columns that are divided in two by a center bar. The top is "heaven," where each of two beads is worth 5 when moved to the center bar. The bottom is "earth," where each of five beads is worth 1 when moved toward the center. See *biquinary code*.

**abandonware**   Software that is no longer sold commercially or supported. Games often fall into the abandonware category, and many Web sites that provide links and downloads. Just search on "abandonware" using your favorite search site.

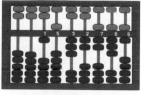

**An Abacus**
The number appearing on this Chinese abacus is 1,532,786.

**ABAP/4**    The Development Workbench part of SAP's R/3 software suite. See *R/3*.

**ABARS**    (1) (Automatic Backup, Archive and Recovery Software) A backup system for UNIX servers from CommVault Systems Inc., Oceanport, NJ, (www.commvault.com). It was introduced in the early 1990s.

(2) (Aggregate Backup And Recovery System) A backup system for MVS S/390 mainframes from IBM. It is part of IBM's DFSMS package.

**ABCs**    See *Win ABCs, MSW ABCs, XL ABCs, DOS ABCs* and *PKZIP ABCs*.

**abend**    (ABnormal END) Also called a "crash" or "bomb," it occurs when the computer is presented with instructions or data it cannot recognize or the program is reaching beyond its protective boundary. It is the result of erroneous software logic or hardware failure.

When the abend occurs, if the program is running in a personal computer under a single-task (one program at a time) operating system, such as DOS, the computer locks up and has to be rebooted. Multitasking operating systems with memory protection halt the offending program, allowing remaining programs to continue.

If you consider what goes on inside a computer, you might wonder why it doesn't crash more often. A large mainframe's memory can easily contain several billion storage cells (bits). Within every second, millions of these cells change their state from uncharged to charged to uncharged. If only one cell fails, the computer can abend. See *GPF*.

**Abilene**    A high-speed backbone network for Internet2 and other research projects developed by the University Corporation for Advanced Internet Development (UCAID) and named after a pioneering railroad outpost in the American West. Announced in April 1998, it is expected to provide an alternate to the vBNS backbone for Internet2 and initially operate at 2.4 Gbps (OC-48). Companies such as 3Com, MCI, Nortel, Cisco and Qwest have donated equipment worth more than $500 million. See *Internet2*.

**ablative WORM**    An optical disk technology in which the creation of the bit permanently alters the recording material, and the data cannot be changed.

**abort**    (1) To exit a function or application without saving any data that has been changed.

(2) To stop a transmission.

**ABR**    (1) (AutoBaud Rate detect) The analysis of the first characters of a message to determine its transmission speed and number of start and stop bits.

(2) (Available Bit Rate) An asynchronous transfer mode (ATM) level of service that adjusts bandwidth according to the congestion levels in the network. ABR is not used for time-critical data such as realtime voice and video.

**absolute**    In programming, a mathematical function that always returns a positive number. For example, ABS(25–100) yields 75, not –75.

**absolute address**    An explicit identification of a memory location, peripheral device, or location within a device. For example, memory byte 107,443, disk drive 2 and sector 238 are absolute addresses. The computer uses absolute addresses to reference memory and peripherals. See *base address* and *relative address*.

**absolute coding**    Writing programming code that refers to fixed locations. See *absolute address*.

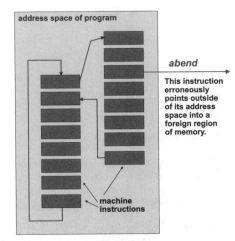

address space of program

*abend*

**This instruction erroneously points outside of its address space into a foreign region of memory.**

**machine instructions**

**Abending**
Abending, or crashing, often occurs when the program points outside of its address space. This diagram depicts the anatomy of a program. "The Data" refers to constants used within the program and the input/output areas that hold the data while it is being processed. "The Processing" refers to the program's logic embodied in the flow chart and physically implemented as thousands of machine instructions (the columns).

**absolute path**    Same as *full path*.

**absolute reference**    An address or pointer that does not change. For example, in a spreadsheet, a cell with an absolute reference does not change, even if copied elsewhere. Contrast with *relative reference*.

**absolute URL**    A URL that specifies the full path to the document page, which includes the domain name. Contrast with *relative URL*.

**absolute vector**    In computer graphics, a vector with end points designated in absolute coordinates. Contrast with *relative vector*.

**absolute zero**    The theoretical temperature at which molecular activity ceases. It is –273.15 degrees Celsius and –459.67 degrees Farhrenheit.

**abstract class**    Also called an "abstract superclass," in object technology, it is a class created as a master structure. No objects of an abstract class are created; rather subclasses of the abstract class are defined with their own variations, and the subclasses are used to create the actual objects.

**abstract data type**    A unique data type that is defined by the programmer. It may refer to an object class in object-oriented programming or to a special data type created in traditional, non-OOP languages. See *abstraction*, *object-oriented programming* and *data type*.

**abstraction**    In object technology, determining the essential characteristics of an object. Abstraction is one of the basic principles of object-oriented design, which allows for creating user-defined data types, known as objects. See *object technology* and *encapsulation*.

**abstraction layer**    A software translation layer that provides a common interface between applications and other programs, typically control programs (OS, DBMS, etc.). An abstraction layer implies that there are two or more implementations of the target program, so that one set of program calls (APIs) works on different platforms or environments. If there is only one target platform and this term is used, then this is just a fancy way of saying "programming interface."

**AC**    (Alternating Current) The common form of electricity from power plant to home/office. Its direction is reversed 60 times per second in the U.S.; 50 times in Europe. Contrast with *DC*.

**AC '97**    (Audio Codec '97) A specification for an audio system within the PC that separates the analog and digital circuits. Formed in 1996 by Intel, Analog Devices, Creative Labs and others, AC '97 enables the digital controller chip to be placed on the motherboard and separated from the "noisy" analog circuits which can be located near the connectors or on a riser card. The two subsystems are interconnected by a 5-wire, TDM interface. The digital controller can support up to four codecs. AC '97 also provides support for modem codecs. See *AMR*.

**AC-3**    (Active Coding-3) Dolby's third digital audio coding technology based on a perceptual coding method. It is more advanced than AC-2 and provides six channels of audio in less space than two-channel stereo CD. AC-3 is used in Dolby Digital. See *Dolby Digital*.

**AC adapter**    Same as *power adapter*.

**ACAP**    (Application Configuration Access Protocol) A protocol for storing configuration information in a central server. It is designed to enhance e-mail functions for remote users by providing a central location for personal address books and client application preferences.

**ACATS**    (Advisory Committee on Advanced Television Service) The FCC committee that was formed in 1987 to recommend a digital TV standard for the U.S. ACATS worked with the ATSC, which refined and finalized ACAT's test results. ACATS recommended the ATSC standards to the FCC in November 1995 and later disbanded. The FCC adopted them on Christmas Eve 1996. During ACAT's reign, more than a thousand people worked on the project in one form or another. See *DTV* and *ATSC*.

**accelerator**    **(1)** A key combination such as ALT-G or CTRL-SHIFT-H that is used to activate a task.
**(2)** An incubator that expects to develop the company considerably faster than normal. See *incubator*.
**(3)** See *accelerator board* and *graphics accelerator*.

**accelerator board**    An add-in board that replaces the existing CPU with a higher performance CPU. See *graphics accelerator*.

**Accelis**    See *LTO*.

**acceptable use policy**    The conduct expected from a person using a computer or service. ISPs, online services and BBSs provide their customers with an acceptable use policy (AUP), which may prohibit spamming or commercial usage. Schools and universities provide AUPs for students using the computer lab, which defines unacceptable behavior.

**acceptance test**    A test performed by the end user to determine whether the system is working according to the specifications in the contract.

**access**    **(1)** To store data on and retrieve data from a disk or other peripheral device. See *access arm*, *access method* and *Microsoft Access*.
**(2)** The entrance to the Internet or other online service or network.

**Access arm**

**platter**

**access arm**    The mechanical arm that moves the read/write head across the surface of a disk similar to a tone arm on a phonograph. The access arm is directed by instructions in the operating system to move the read/write head to a specific track on the disk. The rotation of the disk positions the read/write head over the required sector. The access arm is also called an "actuator arm," because the actuator is the motor and mechanism that moves the arm. See *read/write head*.

**access charge**    The charge imposed by a communications service or telephone company for the use of its network.

**access code**    **(1)** An identification number and/or password used to gain access into a computer system.
**(2)** The number used as a prefix to a calling number in order to gain access to a particular telephone service.

**access concentrator**    See *remote access concentrator*.

**access control**    The management of permissions for logging on to a computer or network. See *access control list* and *security*.

**access control list**    A set of data associated with a file, directory or other resource that defines the permissions that users and/or groups have for accessing it.

**access control protocol**    The technology used to authenticate a user logging onto a computer or network.

**accessibility**    Refers to hardware and software that helps people who are physically or visually impaired. See *screen reader*, *StickyKeys* and *Bat keyboard*. See also *ESD*.

**access line**    The line from a customer site to a telephone company's central office.

**access method**    A software routine that is part of the operating system or network control program that performs the storing/retrieving or transmitting/receiving of data. It is also responsible for detecting a bad transfer of data caused by hardware or network malfunction and correcting it if possible.

**Specialized Keyboard**
This membrane keyboard from IntelliTools provides a 24×24 cell matrix that can be custom programmed. This application uses an oversized keyboard for children with physical disabilities. *(Image courtesy of IntelliTools, Inc., www.intellitools.com)*

**Tape Access Methods**    Tapes use the sequential access method (SAM), which keeps records in order by a key field such as account number. Each record must be compared to find the desired one. Although there is no direct access mechanism to each individual record on a tape, modern drives allow fast forwarding to index points where different groups of records can be stored.

**Disk Access Methods**    For disks, indexed access methods are widely used to keep track of records and files. The index is a table of contents with pointers to the location of each file on the disk or each record within the file. A common approach is the indexed sequential access method (ISAM), which uses an index that is kept in sequential order and points to the records stored in the order that they arrived. The pure sequential method may also be used if direct access is not required. For fastest retrieval, there are various direct access methods that use a formula to convert the record's identifying field, such as account number, into a physical storage address.

**Communications Access Methods**    Local area network (LAN) access methods, such as CSMA/CD (Ethernet) and token passing (Token Ring), transfer data to and from connected computers on the network. These methods reference layers 1 and 2 of the OSI model.

Mainframe access methods, such as IBM's TCAM and VTAM, transfer data between a host computer and remote terminals. These routines prepare the data for transmission by placing the data into frames with appropriate control codes. These methods reference layers 3, 4 and 5 of the OSI model.

**access number**    A telephone number used to dial into the Internet or other online service or network.

**access point**    A base station in a wireless LAN. Access points are typically stand-alone devices that plug into an Ethernet hub or server. Like a cellular phone system, users can roam around with their mobile devices and be handed off from one access point to the other. See *wireless LAN*.

**access provider**    An organization that lets users gain entrance to a network, typically the Internet. It generally refers to a smaller Internet service provider (ISP) rather than a UUNET or MCI, which would be called a "service provider." See *ISP* and *service provider*.

**access rights**    The privileges that are granted to a user, or perhaps to a program, to read, write and erase files in the computer system. Access rights can be tied to a particular server, to directories within that server or to specific programs and data files.

**access router**    See *edge router* and *remote access router*.

**access server**    See *remote access server* and *communications server*.

**access time**    (1) Memory access time is how long it takes for a character in memory to be transferred to or from the CPU. In a personal computer, fast RAM chips have an access time of 70 nanoseconds (ns) or less. SDRAM chips have a burst mode that obtains the second and subsequent characters in 10 ns or less.

(2) Disk access time is an average of the time between initiating a request and obtaining the first data character. It includes command processing, seek time and latency. Fast hard disks have access times of 10 milliseconds (ms) or less. This is a common speed measurement, but disk performance is influenced by channel speed (transfer rate), interleaving and caching. See *cache*, *seek time* and *latency*.

**access token**    In Windows NT, an internal security card that is generated when users log on. It contains the security IDs (SIDs) for the user and all the groups the user belongs to. A copy of the access token is assigned to every process launched by the user.

**account**    See *user account*, *guest account* and *account number*.

**account number**    The number assigned to an employee, customer, vendor or product for identification. Although it may contain only numeric digits, it is often stored as a character field, so that parts of the account number can be searched independently. For example, the number could contain a territory code, and records could be selected by state or region.

**accounts payable software**   Financial software that deals with money owed by the organization to vendors. It summarizes the amounts owed, handles partial payments and vendor credits and also manages vendor terms, sales taxes payable and 1099s.

**accounts receivable software**   Financial software that deals with money owed to the organization. It provides reports on aging (amounts uncollected over time) and collection reports, as well as credit memos and payment history.

**accumulator**   A hardware register used to hold the results or partial results of arithmetic and logical operations.

**accuracy**   How correct an answer is. The accuracy obtained from calculations depends on using bug-free computer chips, as well as the quality of the input. Contrast with *precision*, which refers to the number of digits, or exactness, in an answer.

**ACD**   (Automatic Call Distributor) A computerized phone system that routes incoming telephone calls to the next available operator or agent. ACDs are the electronic heart of call centers, which are widely used in telephone sales and service departments of all organizations. The ACD responds to the caller with a voice menu and connects the call to an appropriate individual. See *IVR*.

**ACF**   (Advanced Communications Function) An official product line name for IBM SNA programs such as VTAM (ACF/VTAM), NCP (ACF/NCP), etc.

**ACH**   (Automated Clearing House) A system of the U.S. Federal Reserve Bank that provides electronic funds transfer (EFT) between banks. It is used for all kinds of fund transfer transactions, including direct deposit of paychecks and monthly debits for routine payments to vendors. The ACH is separate and distinct from the various bank card networks that process credit card transactions. ACH operations are done in a batch mode, which can take up to 72 hours before the money is actually transmitted. A return notification is sent if there are insufficient funds in the account.

**ACK**   (ACKnowledgment code) The communications code sent from a receiving station to a transmitting station to indicate that it is ready to accept data. It is also used to acknowlege the error-free receipt of transmitted data. Contrast with *NAK*.

**ACM**   (Association for Computing Machinery, New York, www.acm.org) A membership organization founded in 1947 dedicated to advancing the arts and sciences of information processing. In addition to awards and publications, ACM also maintains special interest groups (SIGs) in the computer field.

**acoustic coupler**   A device that connects a terminal or computer to the handset of a telephone. It contains a shaped foam bed that the handset is placed in, and it may also contain the modem.

**Acoustic Coupler**

**ACP**   (Associate Computer Professional) The award for successful completion of an examination in computers offered by the ICCP.

**ACPI**   (Advanced Configuration and Power Interface) A power management specification developed by Intel, Toshiba and Microsoft that makes hardware status information available to the operating system. ACPI enables a PC to turn its peripherals on and off for improved power management especially in portables. It also allows the PC to be turned on and off by external devices, so that the touch of a mouse or the press of a key will "wake up" the machine. ACPI support is built into Windows 98. See *OnNow*.

**Acrobat**   Document exchange software from Adobe that allows documents created on one platform to be displayed and printed exactly the same on another no matter which fonts are installed in the computer. The fonts are embedded within the Acrobat document, which is known as a PDF (Portable Document Format) file, thus eliminating the requirement that the target machine contain the same fonts. The PDF Writer in Acrobat turns most DOS, Windows, UNIX and Mac documents to the PDF format by taking the print stream and converting it. The Distiller function takes more complicated PostScript files and creates PDF files.

A

Acrobat Reader is used to display and print PDF files. It is built into Acrobat, but is also available separately as a free download from the Adobe Web site (www.adobe.com). With Acrobat Reader, you can view any Acrobat file, but you cannot edit it or create new ones.

As of Acrobat 3.0, you can make minor text corrections, but you can not cause the text to reflow. In 4.0, you can edit text, tables and graphics, once again as "touch-up," not to make extensive corrections requiring repagination. Version 4.0 also supports digital signatures, HTML to PDF conversion, and the ability to open an Office document and have it be converted to PDF automatically.

Acrobat was first launched in 1993. The PDF Writer was originally marketed as Acrobat Exchange, and Acrobat Pro included PDF Writer and Distiller. Starting with Acrobat 3.0, all functions were packaged together. See *Adobe Document Server*.

**ACS**    (**A**synchronous **C**ommunications **S**erver)  See *remote access server*.

**ACT!**    A popular contact manager from Symantec that runs under DOS, Windows, Mac, Lotus Notes and various PDAs, including the Newton, HP and Psion palmtops. Originally a DOS-only program for contact names, ACT! has evolved into a comprehensive application for the sales professional and includes a full-featured word processor, activity scheduler and report generator. It also provides connectivity to fax and e-mail.

**active addressing**    A variety of techniques that are used to improve the quality of passive matrix LCD screens. See *LCD*.

**The Channel Bar**

This is the default Active Channel Bar on the first Windows 98 desktops. Clicking any item launches the browser so that you can subscribe. The Channel Guide lets you browse through the thousands of offerings from third parties that are made available via Microsoft's Web site.

**An Act! Contact Record**

These screen shots show the typical way Act! is used. Each contact is stored in a name and address record (top) from which activities are scheduled (bottom right). Activity history can be maintained (bottom left) or deleted as required.

**active cell**    The intersection of a row and column in a spreadsheet that is currently selected.

**Active Channel**    An information delivery system from Microsoft that provides a platform for "pushing" information to users from Internet content providers as well as from internal intranets. Active Channels, which are supported starting in Internet Explorer Version 4.0 and Windows 98, are based on Microsoft's Channel Definition Format (CDF). Windows 98 provides a Channel Bar that can be viewed on the desktop. See *Active Desktop* and *CDF*.

**active component**    A device that adds intelligence in some manner to the signal or data that passes through it. For example, in networking, an active hub regenerates fading input pulses into new, strong output pulses. In contrast, a passive hub is just a junction box that does not affect the passing data.

**active content**    A Web page that provides interaction or dynamic changes and contains such "action items" as animated GIFs, Java, JavaScript, streaming audio and video or ActiveX controls.

**Active Desktop**    Enhanced functionality on the desktop that is part of Internet Explorer 4.0 and higher and Windows 98. It enables Web pages to be turned into desktop items that are updated automatically. A Web page can also be turned into wallpaper, allowing a workgroup home page to be readily visible on each user's computer with links to related information on the intranet. Active Desktop supports Active Channels, which are subscriber-based content delivery systems from Internet Web sites or company intranet sites. See *Active Channel*.

**Active Directory**    An advanced, hierarchical directory service that comes with Windows 2000. It is LDAP compliant and built on the Internet's Domain Naming System (DNS). Workgroups are given domain names, just like Web sites, and any LDAP-compliant client (Windows, Mac, UNIX, etc.) can gain access to it. Active Directory can function in a heterogeneous, enterprise network and encompass other directories including NDS and NIS+. Cisco is supporting it in its IOS router operating system. See *ADSI* and *directory service*.

**active hub**    The central connecting device in a network that regenerates signals. Contrast with *passive hub* and *intelligent hub*. See *hub*.

**active matrix**    An LCD technology used in flat panel computer displays. It produces a brighter and sharper display with a broader viewing angle than passive matrix screens. Active matrix technology uses a thin film transistor at each pixel and is often designated as a "TFT screen." See *passive matrix* and *LCD*.

**active monitor**    In a token ring network, the station (network adapter) that controls the token. The active monitor, which is determined through a contention process, maintains clock synchronization and detects and corrects errors in the token framing.

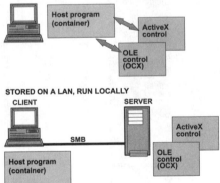

**ActiveMovie**    A video programming interface (API) from Microsoft for Windows 95/98 and NT that provides playback of MPEG, AVI and QuickTime video, as well as WAV audio. It can decode MPEG movies in software and display them full screen at 24 fps on a 90MHz Pentium.

**active window**    The currently-selected window. Contrast with *inactive window*.

**ActiveX**    A brand name from Microsoft that has been used very specifically and very broadly. Today, it refers generally to ActiveX controls. For a short time, it was used to brand Microsoft's entire COM object architecture. See *ActiveX control*, *COM*, *ActiveX Server Component*, *OLE* and *COM automation*.

**ActiveX component**    A software module based on Microsoft's Component Object Model (COM) architecture. Increasingly, Microsoft is using the term ActiveX to refer to a variety of its COM-based technologies. See *ActiveX control*, **ActiveX Documents**, *ActiveX Server Component* and *COM*.

**ActiveX control**    A software module based on Microsoft's Component Object Model (COM) architecture. It enables a program

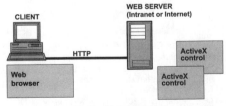

**ActiveX Controls**
ActiveX controls can be stored locally or remotely, but they are run locally.

to add functionality by calling ready-made components that blend in and appear as normal parts of the program. They are typically used to add user interface functions, such as 3-D toolbars, a notepad, calculator or even a spreadsheet.

On the Internet or on an intranet, ActiveX controls can be linked to a Web page and downloaded by an ActiveX-compliant Web browser. ActiveX controls turn Web pages into software pages that can perform just like any program that is launched from a server.

ActiveX controls were originally called "OLE controls" or "OCXs," which were Microsoft's second-generation component architecture (VBXs were the first). OLE controls were renamed ActiveX, and their interface requirements were reduced to speed up downloading from slow-speed Internet connections. See *COM, OLE, COM automation, OCX* and *VBX*.

**ActiveX-enabled browser**    A Web browser that supports Microsoft's ActiveX component technology. It is built into Microsoft's Internet Explorer and is available as a plug-in for Netscape Navigator. See *ActiveX control* and **ScriptActive**.

**ActiveX Server Component**    A server-side software module constructed as an ActiveX component that is stored on a Windows client/server system or a Windows Web site. On a Web site, ActiveX Server Components can be called from Active Server Pages.

**actuator**    A mechanism that causes a device to be turned on or off, adjusted or moved. The motor and mechanism that moves the head assembly on a disk drive or an arm of a robot is called an actuator. See *access arm*.

**actuator arm**    Same as *access arm*.

**Ada**    A high-level programming language developed by the U.S. Department of Defense, along with the European Economic Community and many other organizations. It was designed for embedded applications and process control but is also used for logistics applications. Ada is a Pascal-based language that is very comprehensive.

Ada was named after Augusta Ada Byron (1815-1852), Countess of Lovelace and daughter of Lord Byron. She was a mathematician and colleague of Charles Babbage, who was developing his Analytical Engine. Some of her programming notes for the machine have survived, giving her the distinction of being the first documented programmer in the world.

The following Ada program converts Fahrenheit to Celsius:

```
with Text_IO;
procedure Convert is
package Int_IO is new Text_IO.Integer_IO(Integer);
Fahrenheit : Integer;
begin
 Text_IO.Put_Line("Enter Fahrenheit");
 Int_IO.Get(Fahrenheit);
 Text_IO.Put("Celsius is ");
 Int_IO.Put((Fahrenheit-32) * 5 / 9);
 Text_IO.New_Line;
end Convert;
```

**ADABAS**    A database management systems (DBMS) from Software AG, Reston, VA (www.sagus.com), for IBM mainframes, VAXes, UNIX and Windows. It is an inverted list DBMS with relational capabilities. A 4GL known as NATURAL plus text retrieval, GIS processing, SQL and distributed database functions are also available. Introduced in 1969, it was one of the first DBMSs.

**adapter**    A device that allows one system to connect to and work with another. An adapter is often a simple circuit that converts one set of signals to another; however, the term often refers to devices which are more accurately called "controllers." For example, display adapters (video cards), network adapters (NICs) and SCSI host adapters perform extensive processing, but they are still called "adapters." See *host adapter* and *expansion bus*.

**adapter card**    See *adapter* and *expansion board*.

**adaptive bridge**    A network bridge that remembers destination addresses in order to route subsequent packets more quickly. Most bridges are this type.

**adaptive compression**   A data compression technique that dynamically adjusts the algorithm used based on the content of the data being compressed.

**adaptive equalization**   A transmission technique that dynamically adjusts its modulation method based on the quality of the line.

**adaptive routing**   The ability to select a new communications path to get around heavy traffic or a node or circuit failure.

**adaptor**   An alternate spelling of adapter.

**ADB**   (Apple Desktop Bus) The Macintosh communications port for keyboards, mice, trackballs, graphics tablets and other input devices.

**ad banner**   See *banner ad*.

**ad blocker**   Software that eliminates advertising and other annoyances from Web pages. It detects banner ads by size (typically 60 pixels high) and by the URLs of major advertising sites where the images come from. Such utilities may also be able to eliminate cookies, referrers and animated GIFs, which are time-consuming to download. See *cookie*, *referrer* and *animated GIF*.

**ADC**   (1) See *A/D converter*.
(2) (Advanced Data Connector) See *RDS*.

**ADCCP**   (Advanced Data Communications Control Procedure) An ANSI communications protocol that is similar to the SDLC and HDLC protocols.

**A/D converter**   (Analog/Digital converter) A device that converts continuously varying analog signals from instruments that monitor such conditions as movement, temperature, sound, etc., into binary code for the computer. It may be contained on a single chip or can be one circuit within a chip. See *modem* and *codec*. Contrast with *D/A converter*.

**A/D Converter**

**AD/Cycle**   (Application Development/Cycle) SAA-compliant software from IBM that provides a system for managing systems development. It provides a structure for storing information about all phases of an information system including systems analysis and design, database design and programming.

**add/drop multiplexer**   A device installed at an intermediate point on a transmission line that enables new signals to come in and existing signals to go out. In a typical example, most signals pass through the device, but some would be "dropped" by splitting them from the line. Signals originating at that point can be "added" into the line and directed to another destination.

**Apple Desktop Bus Connector**
ADB plugs and sockets look a lot like PS/2 connectors, but use a different pin configuration.

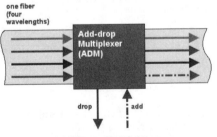

**Blocking Annoyances**
This control panel of options from the interMute utility (www.intermute.com) shows the types of images and privacy intrusions that can be eliminated from downloaded Web pages. The program functions as a proxy server, which acts as an intermediary between your browser and the Web.

**Add/Drop Multiplexer**
Note that the new signal being added can use the same optical channel (wavelength) as the dropped signal. *(Illustration assistance courtesy of Jeff Hecht.)*

Add/drop multiplexing can be done with optical or electronic signals. The device may deal only with wavelengths, or it may convert between wavelengths and electronic TDM signals. The setup in an add/drop multiplexer is generally static, and the device is not reprogrammed very often. See *TDM*, *DWDM*, *digital cross-connect*, *DCS* and *grooming*.

**A**

**adder**   An elementary electronic circuit that adds the bits of two numbers together.

**add-in, add-on**   Refers to hardware modules, such as printed circuit boards, that are designed to be plugged into a socket within the computer.

**address**   (1) The number of a particular memory or peripheral storage location. Like post office boxes, each byte of memory and each disk sector has its own unique address. Programs are compiled into machine language, which references actual addresses in the computer.

(2) As a verb, to manage or work with. For example, "the computer can address 16MB of memory."

(3) The location of a Web site on other Internet facility. See *URL*.

**addressable cursor**   A screen cursor that can be programmed to move to any row or column on the screen.

**address book**   (1) A database of e-mail addresses that is maintained in an e-mail program. See *Web white pages*.

(2) A database of names and addresses that is maintained in a personal information manager (PIM), contact manager or other application that deals with people's addresses.

**address bus**   An internal channel from the CPU to memory across which the addresses of data (not the data) are transmitted. The number of lines (wires) in the address bus determines the amount of memory that can be directly addressed, as each line carries one bit of the address. For example, the 8088 CPU has 20 address lines and can address 1,048,576 bytes. The 68020 has 32 address lines and can address four gigabytes.

Various swapping and switching techniques can be added to the hardware that allow a computer to use more memory than is directly addressable by its address bus. See *EMS*.

**address cleansing**   Converting street addresses to a standard format as set forth by the U.S. Postal Service. For example, standard abbreviations are used, and ZIP codes are converted to 9-digit format. See also *PC Postage*.

**address decoder**   A circuit that converts an address into the electrical signals required to retrieve the data from a memory cell, disk sector, cartridge library or other memory or storage device.

**address mode**   The method by which an instruction references memory. In *indexed addressing*, an instruction address is modified by the contents of an index register before execution. In *indirect addressing*, the instruction points to another address. Ultimately, in order to do any actual processing, the instruction must derive an *absolute address*, which is the real, physical address where the required data is located.

**address register**   A high-speed circuit that holds the addresses of data to be processed or of the next instruction to be executed.

**address resolution**   Obtaining a physical address that is ultimately needed to perform an operation. All instructions executing at the machine level require a physical memory, storage or network node address when referencing the actual hardware. Machine addresses are derived using table lookups and/or algorithms.

In a network, a "where is?" request is broadcast onto the network, and the logical address (name) is turned into a physical address (machine number), either by the recipient node or by a router that maintains a list of address translations.

**address space**   A computer's address space is the total amount of memory that can be addressed by the computer. For example, the Pentium can address 4GB of physical memory and 64TB of virtual memory.

A program's address space is the actual memory used by the program when running. It may refer to physical memory (RAM chips) or virtual memory (disk) or a combination of both.

**address translation**    Transforming one address into another. For example, assemblers and compilers translate symbolic addresses into machine addresses. Virtual memory systems translate a virtual address into a real address. See also *address resolution*.

**adds, moves and changes**    See *moves-adds-changes*.

**ADF**    (Application Development Facility) An IBM programmer-oriented mainframe application generator that runs under IMS.

**ad hoc query**    A non-standardized inquiry. An ad hoc query is composed to answer a question when the need arises.

**ADM**    See *add/drop multiplexer*.

**ADMD**    (ADministrative Management Domain) A public e-mail service. See *X.400*.

**admin**    See *network administrator* and *system administrator*.

**administrator**    See *data administrator*, *database administrator*, *network administrator* and *system administrator*.

**ADO**    (Active Data Objects) A programming interface from Microsoft that is designed as "the" Microsoft standard for data access. First used with Internet Information Server, it is expected to become available for all Microsoft programming languages and applications. ADO is a COM object. See *RDO*, *DAO*, *OLE DB* and *ODBC*.

**Adobe**    (Adobe Systems, Inc., Mountain View, CA, www.adobe.com) The leading graphics and desktop publishing software company. Founded in 1982 by Dr. John Warnock, Adobe helped pioneer desktop publishing with its fonts and applications. Initially developed for the Macintosh, Adobe's PostScript fonts have become the standard among graphics and printing service bureaus. Adobe PhotoShop and Adobe Type Manager are examples of world-class software that spearheaded the industry. With Adobe's 1995 acquisitions of PageMaker and FrameMaker, Adobe has become the preeminent graphics design and desktop publishing software company.

**Adobe Document Server**    Software from Adobe that converts PDF files into GIF or JPEG images so they can be viewed in a browser without requiring Acrobat Reader. It also converts PDF files into HTML text so that they can be read by a screen reader. See *Acrobat* and *screen reader*.

**Adobe fonts**    See *PostScript*.

**Adobe Illustrator**    A full-featured drawing program for Windows and Macintosh from Adobe. It provides sophisticated tracing and text manipulation capabilities, as well as color separations. Included is Adobe Type Manager and a selection of Type 1 fonts. Illustrator was originally developed for the Mac in 1987 and, up until Version 7.0, which was introduced in 1997, the Mac version included more features. The Macintosh version is the most widely used drawing and composition program for the Mac platform.

**Adobe Type Manager**    A PostScript font utility for the Macintosh and Windows from Adobe. It scales Type 1 fonts into screen fonts and prints them on non-PostScript dot matrix and HP laser printers. For printing fonts, current versions of ATM download font bitmaps to the printer. Earlier versions sent a bitmap of the entire page of text to the printer.

ATM technology is built into OS/2 and NeXTstep and was originally developed to provide WYSIWYG screen fonts for the Mac. Since Windows does not render PostScript fonts on screen, ATM is widely used to do so. Both work together. Under Windows, ATM scales Type 1 fonts, while Windows 3.1 scales TrueType fonts. See *ATM.INI* and *PostScript*.

**ADP**    (1) (Automatic Data Processing) Synonymous with data processing (DP), electronic data processing (EDP) and information processing.

(2) (Automatic Data Processing, Inc., Roseland, NJ, www.adp.com) A nationwide computer services organization that specializes in payroll processing.

**ADPCM**    (Adaptive Differential **PCM**)  An advanced PCM technique that converts analog sound into digital data and vice versa. Instead of coding an absolute measurement at each sample point, it codes the difference between samples and can dynamically switch the coding scale to compensate for variations in amplitude and frequency.

ADPCM Levels A and B sample at 37.8 kHz creating 8-bit and 4-bit resolution (size of sample) respectively. Level C is 18.9 kHz, 4-bit. Following is a summary of the G. standards in this database. See *PCM* and *sampling rate*.

| Standard | Method | Kbps |
|----------|--------|------|
| G.711 | PCM | 64 |
| G.721 | ADPCM | 32 |
| G.722 | ADPCM | 64 |
| G.723 | ADPCM | 20, 40 |
| G.723.1 | LD-CELP | 5.3, 6.4 |
| G.726 | ADPCM | 16, 24, 32, 40 |
| G.727 | ADPCM | 16, 24, 32, 40 |
| G.728 | LD-CELP | 16 |
| G.729 | CELP | 8 |

**ADP system**    (Automatic Data Processing system)  Same as *computer system*.

**ad rotation**    See *rotating ad*.

**adserver**    A Web-based server that delivers banner ads to the requesting Web pages. For companies that sell their own ads, the adserver may be an inhouse or co-located machine at an ISP, or it may be owned by an Internet advertising company. See *Internet advertising*.

**ad serving**    The hardware, software and personnel required to deliver advertisements to Web sites and ad supported software. It also includes the monitoring of click throughs and required reporting to the ad purchasers and Web site publishers. See *adserver* and *Internet advertising*.

**ADSI**    (Active Directory Services Interface)  A programming interface from Microsoft for accessing the Microsoft Active Directory (Windows 2000), the directory within Exchange and other directories via providers. For example, an ADSI LDAP provider converts between LDAP and ADSI. Based on COM, ADSI can be used in Visual Basic and other programming languages. See *Active Directory* and *LDAP*.

**ADSL**    See *DSL*.

**ADSL splitter**    See *POTS splitter*.

**ad-supported software**    Software that is paid for by advertisers. It is free software that displays banner ads that come from the Web. Like shareware, you can register ad-supported software for a fee, in which case the ads are eliminated, making more room for data on screen. See *shareware*, *adserver* and *Internet advertising*.

**ADT**    (Asynchronous Data Transfer)  A transmission technique used in ISDN PBXs that dynamically allocates bandwidth. See also *abstract data type*.

**ad view**    Same as *impression*.

**adware**    (AD supported soft**WARE**)  Software that is given away for free because it contains advertising messages. See *adserver*. See also *Free-PC*.

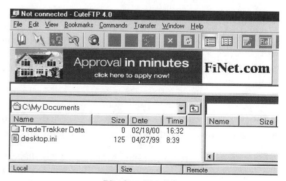

**Placing the Ads**
Conducent's FlexActive software provides the conduit between the source of the ads and their placement in a developer's application, in this case GlobalSCAPE's cuteFTP program. FlexActive keeps track of click-throughs and can also cache ads so they can be rotated when the user is not online. *(Screen shot courtesy of Conducent, Inc.)*

**AES** (Advanced Encryption Standard) A state-of-the-art encryption standard that is being developed by the NIST. It is expected to replace DES. See *NIST* and *DES*.

(2) (Audio Engineering Society, Inc., New York, www.aes.org) A membership association devoted to audio technology research and development, marketing and education. Founded in 1948, technical standards have been continually developed under the its auspices. AES is dedicated to ensuring that audio quality is maintained in the digital world. See *AES/EBU*.

(3) (Automated Export System) A U.S. Customs Service application that tracks goods exported to foreign countries.

**AES/EBU** (American Engineering Society/European Broadcast Union) A serial interface for transferring digital audio between devices such as CD and DVD players and amplifiers. Based on the RS-422 interface, AES/EBU uses 110 ohm shielded twisted pair cable and a 3-pin XLR connector. The consumer version of AES/EBU is S/PDIF, which uses unbalanced coaxial cable for shorter distances, but allows additional information bits to be transmitted. See *S/PDIF*.

**AFAIK** Digispeak for "as far as I know."

**AFC** (Application Foundation Classes) A class library from Microsoft that provides an application framework and graphics, graphical user interface (GUI) and multimedia routines for Java programmers. AFC Enterprise Libraries include support for data access, directory services, transactions and distributed objects. AFC is compatible with AWT and runs in Windows and other JVM environments. See *JFC*, *AWT* and *IFC*.

**AFE** (Apple File Exchange) A Macintosh utility that converts data files between Mac and PC formats. It also includes a file translator between IBM's DCA format and MacWrite; however, MacLink Plus Translators can be used for additional capability.

**affinity group** A special interest group. This is a marketing term for a group of people with similar interests.

**affinity ISP** See *virtual ISP*.

**AFIPS** (American Federation of Information Processing Societies Inc.) An organization founded in 1961 dedicated to advancing information processing in the U.S. It was the U.S. representative of IFIP and umbrella for 11 membership societies. In 1990, it was dissolved and superseded by FOCUS.

**AFM file** (Adobe Font Metrics file) A file that contains font metric information for a Type 1 PostScript font. See *PFA file*, *PFB file* and *PostScript*.

**AFP** (1) (AppleTalk Filing Protocol) The file sharing protocol used in an AppleTalk network. In order for non-Apple networks to access data in an AppleShare server, their protocols must translate into the AFP language. See *file sharing protocol*.

(2) (Advanced Function Presentation) A page description language from IBM introduced in 1984 initially as Advanced Function Printing. It was first developed for mainframes and then brought down to minis and workstations. AFP is implemented on the various platforms by Print Services Facility (PSF) software, which generates the native IBM printer language, IPDS, and depending on the version, PostScript and LaserJet PCL as well. IBM calls AFP a "printer architecture" rather than a page description language.

**AFP printer** A printer that natively accepts the AFP page description language. IBM makes desktop AFP printers, and third parties make network printers that support AFP.

**AFS** A distributed file system for large, widely dispersed UNIX networks from Transarc Corporation, Pittsburgh, PA. It is noted for its ease of administration and expandability and stems from Carnegie-Mellon's Andrew File System.

**AFSMI** (Association For Service Management International, Fort Myers, FL, www.asfmi.org) A membership organization dedicated to the advancement of executives and managers in the high-tech services and support industry. Founded in 1976, benefits include industry studies and publications, education, career placement and an annual conference and exhibition.

**agent** A software routine that waits in the background and performs an action when a specified event occurs. For example, agents could transmit a summary file on the first day of the month or monitor incoming data and alert the user when a certain transaction has arrived. Agents are also called "intelligent agents," "personal agents" and "bots." See *mobile agent*, *bot* and *workflow*.

**A**

**aggregate**    To gather, collect or assemble. For example, "to aggregate data" means to gather separate sets of data. As a noun, "aggregate data" is data that has been collected from two or more sources. See *content aggregator*.

**aggregate function**    A calculation that is made on several records or cells of data. SUM, AVG, MAX, MIN and COUNT are examples of aggregate functions that are used in spreadsheets and database programs.

**aggregator**    See *content aggregator* and *remote access concentrator*.

**Agilent**    The test and measurment subsidiary of HP. In 1999, HP split off the division that started the company into an independent subsidiary named Agilent Technologies. See *HP*.

**AGP**    (**A**ccelerated **G**raphics **P**ort) A high-speed graphics port from Intel that provides a direct connection between the display adapter and memory. AGP is faster than PCI, and only one AGP slot is provided on AGP-equipped motherboards. The PCI slot that would normally hold the display adapter can be used for another device. The brown AGP slot is slightly shorter than the white PCI slot and is located about an inch farther back.

AGP uses a 32-bit bus. The original AGP standard (AGP 1x) provides a data transfer rate of 264 Mbytes/sec. AGP 2x is 528 Mbytes/sec. AGP 4x is 1 Gbyte/sec. AGP 8x is 2 Gbytes/sec. See *PC data buses* and *motherboard*.

**agregator**    See *content aggregator* and *remote access concentrator*.

**AI**    (**A**rtificial **I**ntelligence) Devices and applications that exhibit human intelligence and behavior including robots, expert systems, voice recognition, natural and foreign language processing. It also implies the ability to learn or adapt through experience.

In the future, everything we now know and think about a computer will change. By 2015, you should be able to converse with the average computer. Future systems will ask you what help you need and automatically call in the appropriate applications to aid you in solving your problem.

In the 1990s, the AI buzzword was abused to the hilt as it referred to any and all advancements. However, the acid test of AI was defined in the 1940s by the English scientist, Alan Turing, who said, "A machine has artificial intelligence when there is no discernible difference between the conversation generated by the machine and that of an intelligent person."

Note: The term "intelligence refers" to processing capability; therefore, every computer is intelligent but artificial intelligence implies human-like intelligence. An ironic twist in terminology.

**AIDC**    (**A**utomatic **I**dentification and **D**ata **C**ollection) Capturing data electronically by scanning bar codes or alphanumeric codes (OCR, MICR) by reading magnetic stripes or by wireless means. See *AIM*, *bar code* and *RFID*.

**AIFC file**    See *AIFF file*.

**AIFF file**    (**A**udio **I**nterchange **F**ile **F**ormat) A digital audio file format from Apple that is used on the Macintosh. It uses the .AIF extension and breaks apart the file into chunks. The Common chunk holds file parameters such as sampling rate, and the Sound Data chunk contains the digital sound. AIFC and AIFF-C are compressed versions of the format.

**AI file**    (**A**dobe **I**llustrator file) A vector graphics file created in Adobe Illustrator.

**Shakey the Robot**
Developed in 1969 by the Stanford Research Institute, Shakey was the first fully mobile robot with artificial intelligence. Shakey is seven feet tall and was named after its rather unstable movements. *(Image courtesy of The Computer Museum History Center, www.computerhistory.org)*

**AIIM**    (Association for Information and Image Management International, Silver Spring, MD, www.aiim.org)  A membership organization founded in 1943 devoted to creating industry standards and disseminating information about the document management industry. Its Document Management Alliance (DMA) task group has developed a common programming interface for document management systems (see *DMA*). See also *AIM*.

**AIM**    **(1)** (AOL Instant Messenger)  America Online's instant messenger service which supports text chat, photo sharing, online gaming and PC to PC voice. An AIM list of instant messenger participants is called a "Buddy List." See *instant messaging*.
    **(2)** (Automatic Identification Manufacturers, 634 Alpha Drive, Pittsburgh, PA, www.aimglobal.org)  The trade association for the automatic identification and data collection (AIDC) industry. Established in 1982 as a product division of the Material Handling Institute (MHI), AIM is involved in setting standards for bar codes, magnetic stripes and RFID technology. See also *AIIM*.
    **(3)** (Apple/IBM/Motorola)  The alliance of Apple, IBM and Motorola, which developed the PowerPC chip, Taligent, Kaleida, etc. See *Apple-IBM alliance*.

**AIML**    (AI Markup Language)  An extenstion to XML used for artificial intelligence (AI) applications. See *ALICE*.

**AIN**    (Advanced Intelligent Network)  The Telcordia/Bellcore version of the "intellignet network," which is the public switched telephone system (PSTN). The AIN provides enhanced voice, video and data services and dynamic routing capabilities by using two different networks. The actual voice call is transmitted over a circuit-switched network, but the signaling is done on a separate packet-switched network known as SS7. See *IN* and *SS7*.

**air interface**    The modulation scheme used in a wireless network. It is the wireless counterpart to the physical layer in the OSI model. FDMA, TDMA and CDMA are examples of air interfaces.

**AIS**    **(1)** (Accounting Information System)  The human and machine resources within an organization that are responsible for collecting and processing the daily transactions and preparing financial reports.
    **(2)** (Adobe IntelliSelect)  Software from Adobe that enables a printer to automatically detect the printer language being used (PostScript, PCL, HPGL) and to switch to that mode of operation.

**AIT**    (Advanced Intelligent Tape)  A magnetic tape techology from Sony that uses 8mm cassette-style cartridges that hold up to 50GB (AIT-2) and 100GB (AIT-3). It uses advanced metal evaporated (AME) media and includes a built-in head cleaner and an EEPROM chip that stores tape status and indexing information. This Memory in Cassette (MIC) feature enables fast forwarding to a selected partition. The cartridges are very similar in appearance to Exabyte 8mm tapes, but are not the same. AIT drive numbers have an SDX prefix. See *magnetic tape*.

**AIT Cartridge**
Sony's AIT cartridges contain a memory chip that stores tape status and user information that enables fast forwarding to a selected partition.

**AITP**    (Association of Information Technology Professionals, Park Ridge, IL, www.aitp.org)  Formerly the Data Processing Management Association (DPMA), it is a membership organization founded in 1951 devoted to providing professional development to individuals in the information systems field. It originated the CDP examinations, which were later administrated by the ICCP. It was renamed AITP in 1996.

**AIX**    (Advanced Interactive eXecutive)  IBM's version of UNIX, which runs on 386 and higher PCs, RS/6000 workstations and 390 mainframes. It is based on AT&T's UNIX System V with Berkeley extensions.

**Akamai**    (Akamai Technologies, Inc., Cambridge, MA, www.akamai.com)  A company that provides Internet content delivery with guaranteed peformance using its own worldwide network. Founded in 1998 by a group of MIT scientists and Internet professionals, Akamai licensed routing algorithms developed at MIT to develop a high-performance network that could efficiently route traffic to the most expedient Web server depending on the source of the request and network conditions. Since most of the content of a Web page is graphics, a Web site customer might host the text itself and offload the graphics to Akamai. Akamai (pronounced "AH ka my") is Hawaiian for intellignet, or "cool."

**alarm**    A sound or visual signal that indicates an error condition. The terms alarm and alert are often used synonymously. See *alert.*

**alarm filtering**    In network management, the ability to pinpoint the device that has failed. If one device in a network fails, others may fail as a result and cause alarms. Without alarm filtering, the management console reports all deteriorating devices with equal attention.

**A-Law**    An ITU standard for converting analog data into digital form using pulse code modulation (PCM). A-Law uses a companding technique that provides more quantizing steps at lower amplitude (volume) than at higher amplitude. Europe uses A-Law, while North America and Japan use mu-Law (μ-Law). See *PCM* and *mu-Law.*

**alert**    A sound or visual signal that indicates that some predefined event has occurred or some error condition has occurred. The terms alert and alarm are often used synonymously. See *alarm.*

**alert box**    A dialog box that contains an alert message. See *alert.*

**algebraic expression**    One or more characters or symbols associated with algebra; for example, **A+B=C** or **A/B**.

**ALGOL**    (ALGOrithmic Language) A high-level compiler language that was developed as an international language for the expression of algorithms between people and between people and machines. ALGOL-60 (1960) was simple and widely used in Europe. ALGOL-68 (1968) was more complicated and scarcely used, but was the inspiration for Pascal.
     The following example changes Fahrenheit to Celsius:

```
fahrenheit
 begin
   real fahr;
   print ("Enter Fahrenheit ");
   read (fahr);
   print ("Celsius is ", (fahr-32.0) * 5.0/9.0);
 end
 finish
```

**algorithm**    A set of ordered steps for solving a problem, such as a mathematical formula or the instructions in a program. The terms algorithm and logic are synonymous. Both refer to a sequence of steps to solve a problem. However, an algorithm implies an expression that solves a complex problem rather than the overall input-process-output logic of typical business programs. See *encryption algorithm.*

**algorithmic language**    A programming language that allows complete sets of steps to be written. All major programming languages are algorithmic languages. See *algorithm.*

**alias**    (1) An alternate name used for identification, such as for naming a field or a file. See *CNAME record.*
     (2) A phony signal created under certain conditions when digitizing voice.

**aliasing**    In computer graphics, the stair-stepped appearance of diagonal lines when there are not enough pixels in the image or on screen to represent them realistically. Also called "stair-stepping" and "jaggies." See *anti-aliasing.*

**allocate**    To reserve a resource such as memory or disk. See *memory allocation.*

**allocation unit**    Same as *cluster.*

**all optical**    Refers to the use of optical devices that do not require switching back into the electrical domain. See *all-optical network.*

**Resolutions**
A low-resolution image showing the stair-stepping is on the left. The higher-resolution version is on the right.

**all-optical network**    A communications network that works completely in the optical domain. It uses optical switches connected by optical fibers. See *optical switch*.

**all rights**    Authorization to change the contents of settings and files. See *read-only rights*.

**ALOHA**    A type of TDMA transmission system developed by the University of Hawaii used for satellite and terrestrial radio links. In the traditional ALOHA system, packets are transmitted as required, and, like Ethernet's CSMA/CD method, collisions can occur. A "Slotted ALOHA" system triggers transmission starts by a clock and reduces the number of collisions.

**Alpha**    A family of RISC-based, 64-bit CPUs and computer systems from Compaq. Originally developed by Digital, the first model introduced in early 1992 was the 150MHz 21064-AA, considered equivalent to a Cray-1 on a single chip. Subsequent Alpha models have continued to blaze the trails for high-speed microprocessors. Alpha-based servers and workstations run under Digital Unix, OpenVMS and Windows NT.

**alpha blending**    In computer graphics, the combining of the alpha channel with other layers in an image in order to show translucency. The alpha channel is an additional eight bits used with each pixel in a 32-bit graphics system that can represent 256 levels of translucency. Black and white represent opaque and fully transparent, while various gray levels represent levels of translucency.

More than one layer in a multilayered image may contain a translucent component, thus multiple levels of blending may be required. If the graphics accelerator performs the blending in its own hardware, the results are displayed considerably faster. See *alpha channel* and *translucency*.

**Using the Alpha Channel**
The image on the right shows how translucency can be applied to an object using the alpha channel. *(Image courtesy of Intergraph Computer Systems.)*

**alpha channel**    An additional eight bits in a 32-bit graphics pixel that is used as a separate layer for representing levels of translucency in an object. See *alpha blending*.

**Alpha Four, Five**    A database program from SoftQuad International, Inc., Toronto, that is noted for its ease of use. Alpha programs read and write dBASE files directly. Alpha Four for DOS provides scripts for customizing applications. Alpha Five for Windows includes Xbasic, a BASIC-like programming language that incorporates database commands. These products were developed by Alpha Software, Burlington, MA, which was maintained as SoftQuad's U.S. headquarters.

**alphageometric**    See *alphamosaic*.

**alphamosaic**    A very-low-resolution display technique that uses elementary graphics symbols in its character set.

**alphanumeric**    The use of alphabetic letters mixed with numbers and special characters as in name, address, city and state. The text you're reading is alphanumeric.

**alphanumeric sort**    A reordering of data so that punctuation marks, numeric data and alphabetic data appear as three separate groups. Contrast with *lexicographic sort*.

**alpha test**    The first test of newly developed hardware or software in a laboratory setting. When all the bugs have been fixed, the product next goes into beta test with actual users. See *beta test* and *beta version*.

**alpha version**    Software that has just been compiled and ready for its initial test inhouse. See *alpha test* and *beta test*.

**Altair**    A microcomputer kit introduced in late 1974 from Micro Instrumentation and Telemetry Systems (MITS). It sold for $400 and used an 8080 microprocessor. In 1975, it was packaged with the Microsoft MBASIC interpreter written by Paul Allen and Bill Gates. Although computer kits were advertised earlier by others, an estimated 10,000 Altairs were sold, making it the first commercially successful microcomputer.

**Altair 8800 Computer**
The first successful microcomputer and the first commercial computer that came with a Microsoft product. *(Image courtesy of The Computer Museum History Center, www.computerhistory.org)*

**AltaVista**   (AltaVista Company, Palo Alto, CA, www.altavista.com) The first search engine to index every word on a page and provide a retrieval system to extract revelant information. Developed by Digital's Research Labs in Palo Alto in 1995, the AltaVista search engine is available in more than 25 languages in a variety of versions. See *Web search sites*.

**alternate routing**   The ability to use another transmission line if the regular line is busy.

**ALT key**   A keyboard key that is pressed with a letter or digit key to command the computer. For example, in Windows, holding down the ALT key and pressing F displays the File menu. Pressing ALT+TAB toggles between applications.

**alt newsgroup**   (alternative newsgroup) An Internet newsgroup that is devoted to a very specific topic, often one that is very controversial. Anybody can create an alt newsgroup without any formal voting from other users. See *newsgroup*.

**Alto**   The personal computer from Xerox that pioneered the mouse/icon/desktop environment. Developed at PARC, it was the progenitor of Xerox's Star and Apple's Lisa and Mac. Designed in 1973 with 128K RAM, 608x808 screen, 2.5MB removable hard disk and built-in Ethernet. About 1,000 Altos were in use by 1979.

**ALT text**   (ALTernate text) On a Web page, a text description that can be added to the HTML tag that displays an image. The ALT text is displayed by the browser when the cursor is moved over the picture. If pictures are turned off in the browser, the ALT text is automatically displayed instead.

**ALU**   (Arithmetic Logic Unit) The high-speed CPU circuit that does calculating and comparing. Numbers are transferred from memory into the ALU for calculation, and the results are sent back into memory. Alphanumeric data is sent from memory into the ALU for comparing. The results are tested by GOTOs; for example, IF ITEMA EQUALS ITEMB GOTO UPDATE ROUTINE.

Some chips have multiple ALUs that allow for simultaneous calculations. For example, Chromatic Research's Mpact media processor chip has 450 of them. It allows audio, video and other multimedia processes to be performed simultaneously. See *Mpact chip*.

**always on**   Refers to a system that is online and ready to go 24 hours a day. Nothing has to be turned on or dialed up in order to use it. DSL and cable modems are examples of always-on technologies.

**AM**   (1) (Amplitude Modulation) A transmission technique that blends the data signal into a carrier by varying (modulating) the amplitude of the carrier. Most fiber optic transmission uses amplitude modulation. See *modulate*.

(2) (Application Master) See *QuickBuild*.

**Alto Computer**
The first graphical user interface created for business purposes was working more than 10 years before the Macintosh was introduced.
*(Image courtesy of Xerox Palo Alto Research Center.)*

**An ALU in 1957**
This was an arithmetic logic unit you sit back and admire. It was part of Honeywell's Datamatic 1000 computer. *(Image courtesy of Honeywell, Inc.)*

**Amaya**   A combination Web browser and HTML editor from the W3C. It is considered an experimental product similar to its Jigsaw Web server. Amaya supports multiple views that are synchronized, the PNG graphics format, XHTML and the construction of complex mathematical formulas. See *Jigsaw*.

**Amazon.com**   (Amazon.com, Seattle, WA, www.amazon.com) The largest online shopping site and one of the most controversial e-commerce sites on the Web. Founded by Jeff Bezos in 1995, it had 11 employees by year's end. By 1999, it had more than 1600 employees and 4.5 million customers. Even though the company had never made a profit, the stock soared in 1998, reaching a market cap three times that of K-Mart, a major retailer with more than 2000 physical stores.

Amazon started out as an online bookstore, constantly making news with the number of titles it had to offer: 2.5 million in 1997 and 4.5 million by the end of 1998 after adding CDs, videos, DVDs and games. It continues to add new lines of business including online auctions like eBay, as well as toys and games, consumer electronics, software, power tools and home improvement products.

Amazon has spent considerable time and money getting its name onto AOL's home page, as well as all the major search engines and Web sites and just about any other place imaginable. The company is "the" bellwether of online commerce, as many think the company is only in its infancy and expect it to be the online version of Microsoft. Some attribute this period to the very early years of the automobile industry with the only limitation being the sky. Stay tuned!  See *branding*.

**ambient**    Surrounding. For example, ambient temperature and humidity are atmospheric conditions that exist at the moment. See *ambient lighting*.

**ambient lighting**    Light that comes from all directions. Contrast with *directional lighting*, which is made up of a light source with parallel light rays that do not diminish with distance. Also, contrast with *positional lighting*, in which the rays are not parallel and diminish in intensity from the source.

**AMD**    (Advanced Micro Devices, Inc., Sunnyvale, CA, www.amd.com)  A manufacturer of semiconductor devices including x86-compatible CPUs, embedded processors, flash memories, programmable logic devices and networking chips. Founded in 1969 by W. J. (Jerry) Sanders III and seven other individuals, AMD was the first to produce 386 and 486-compatible CPU chips in 1991 and 1993 respectively and compete head on with Intel.

AMD later introduced its K5 and K6 lines of Pentium-compatible chips and subsequently its Athlon line, which was introduced in 1999 at 700MHz. Athlon chips have since broken the 1GHz range. In the summer of 2000, it introduced its Duron family of lower-priced CPUs for the value market. Over the years, numerous PC vendors, both small and large, have successfully used AMD's CPU chips in their PCs. See *K5*, *K6* and *Athlon*.

**Amdahl**    (Amdahl Corporation, Sunnyvale, CA, www.amdahl.com) A computer manufacturer founded in 1970 by Dr. Gene Amdahl, chief architect of the IBM System/360. In 1975, Amdahl installed its first IBM-compatible mainframe, the 470/V6. Although not the first to make IBM-compatible mainframes, it succeeded where others failed. Today, Amdahl still offers a line of IBM-compatible mainframes along with UNIX-based SPARC servers from Sun. However, more of the company's revenues are derived from software and consulting services.

In 1979, Amdahl left the company he founded to form Trilogy, which tried without success to make the world's largest chip based on wafer scale integration. See *Trilogy* and **CDS**.

**Amdahl's law**    "Overall system speed is governed by the slowest component." By Gene Amdahl, chief architect of IBM's first mainframe series and founder of Amdahl Corporation and other companies. Amdahl's law applied to networking. The slowest device in the network will determine the maximum speed of the network. See *laws*.

**Amiga**    A personal computer series from Amiga, Inc. (www.amiga.com). Originally introduced by Commodore in 1985, the first model was the A1000 with 256KB of RAM, powered by a 7MHz 68000 CPU. Amigas gained a reputation early on as advanced graphics and multimedia machines and NewTek's Video Toaster application brought it to the forefront of economical, high-end video editing.

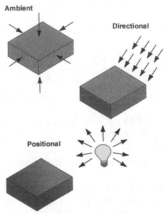

**Primary Light Sources**
Ambient lighting comes from all directions, while directional and positional lighting come from one source. *(Image courtesy of Intergraph Computer Systems.)*

**Amdahl's First Computer**
In 1975, Dr. Amdahl stands beside the Wisconsin Integrally Synchronized Computer (WISC), which he designed in 1950. It was built in 1952. *(Image courtesy of Dr. Gene M. Amdahl.)*

Subsequent machines included the A500, A600 and A1200 home computers and the A2000, A3000 and A4000 models. Commodore went into bankruptcy in 1994, and the technology was purchased by Escom AG, a German PC maker, who created the Amiga Technologies subsidiary. In 1997, Amiga Technologies was purchased by Gateway 2000 and renamed Amiga International. At the end of 1999, the Amiga International was acquired by a private party that continues to sell product and maintain the OS. See *Commodore*.

**AM-LCD**    (Active Matrix-LCD)  See *active matrix*.

**amorphous**    Unorganized or vague. Lacking structure. For example, the amorphous state of a spot on a rewritable optical disk means that the laser beam will not be reflected from it, which is in contrast to a crystalline state which will reflect light. See *crystalline*.

**amorphous silicon**    Silicon that does not have a crystalline structure and which is not conductive. Contrast with *polysilicon*.

**amp**    (AMPere)  A unit of electrical current in a circuit. Contrast with "volts," which is a measure of force, or pressure, behind the current. Multiplying amps times volts derives "watts," the total measurement of power. See *volt* and *watt*.

**amplitude**    The strength or volume of a signal, usually measured in decibels. See *wavelength*.

**AMPS**    (Advanced Mobile Phone Service)  The analog cellular mobile phone system in North and South America and more than 35 other countries. It uses FDMA transmission in the 800Mhz band. The first AMPS system in the U.S. was deployed in Chicago in 1983. See *N-AMPS*, *NMT* and *TACS*.

**AMPS modem**    A wireless modem designed for analog cellular phones. See *wireless modem*.

**AMR**    (Audio/Modem Riser)  A plug-in card for an Intel motherboard that contains audio and/or modem circuits. Specified by Intel, a 46-pin edge connector provides the digital interface between the card and the motherboard. The AMR contains all the analog functions (codecs) required for audio and/or modem operation. The Mobile Daughter Card (MDC) is the equivalent of the AMR for portable computers. The AMR evolved into the Communications and Networking Riser (CNR) card, which added LAN and home networking functions. The CNR uses a 30-pin interface in two formats, and various audio/modem and audio/network combinations are possible.

The AMR and CNR risers are options for the motherboard manufacturer and were not designed for retail interoperability. Rather, they enable the system manufacturer to isolate these functions from the motherboard for faster certification of their products. If audio, modem and networking functions are contained on the motherboard, the risers offer the option of proprietary upgrades; for example, to better audio or a different networking technology.

**analog**    A representation of an object that resembles the original. Analog devices monitor conditions, such as movement, temperature and sound, and convert them into analogous electronic or mechanical patterns. For example, an analog watch represents the planet's rotation with the rotating hands on the watch face. Telephones turn voice vibrations into electrical vibrations of the same shape. Analog implies continuous operation in contrast with digital, which is broken up into numbers.

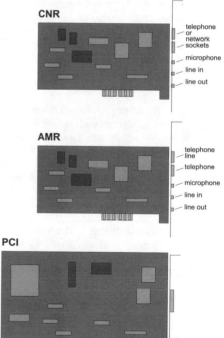

**AMR and CNR Cards**
The AMR and CNR cards are contrasted with a PCI card to show the relative difference in edge connector size but are not meant to be exact pinouts.

### Advantages and Disadvantages of Analog Techniques

Traditionally, audio and video recording has been analog. Sound, which is continuously varying air vibrations, is converted into analogous electrical vibrations. Video cameras scan their viewing area a line at a time and convert the infinitely varying intensities of light into analogous electrical signals.

The ability to capture the subtle nature of the real world is the single advantage of analog techniques. However, once captured, modern electronic equipment, no matter how advanced, cannot copy analog signals perfectly. Third and fourth generations of audio and video recordings show marked deterioration.

By converting analog signals into digital, the original audio or video data can be preserved indefinitely and copied over and over without deterioration. Once continuously varying analog signals are measured and converted into digital form, they can be stored and transmitted without loss of integrity due to the accuracy of digital methods.

The key to conversion is the amount of digital data that is created from the analog signal. The shorter the time interval between samples and the more data recorded from that sample, the more the digital encoding reflects the original signal.

**analog channel**  In communications, a channel that carries voice or video in analog form as a varying range of electrical frequencies. Contrast with *digital channel*.

**analog computer**  A device that processes infinitely varying signals, such as voltage or frequencies. A thermometer is a simple analog computer. As the temperature varies, the mercury moves correspondingly. Although special-purpose, complex analog computers are built, almost all computers are digital. Digital methods provide programming flexibility.

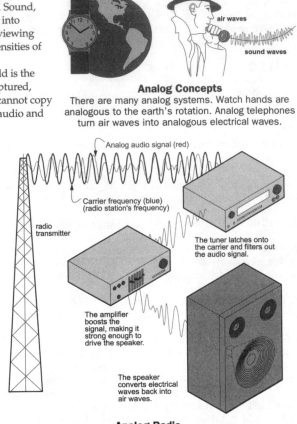

**Analog Concepts**
There are many analog systems. Watch hands are analogous to the earth's rotation. Analog telephones turn air waves into analogous electrical waves.

*Analog audio signal (red)*

*Carrier frequency (blue) (radio station's frequency)*

radio transmitter

The tuner latches onto the carrier and filters out the audio signal.

The amplifier boosts the signal, making it strong enough to drive the speaker.

The speaker converts electrical waves back into air waves.

**Analog Radio**
Radio broadcasting uses analog transmission. The sound waves are wrapped in a carrier frequency unique to each station in the area. The sound is maintained in analog form throughout the entire chain from recording microphone to the listener's speaker.

**analog copy machine**  The traditional copy machine that duplicates the image to be copied with the use of light and lenses. Contrast with *digital copy machine*.

**analog data**  Data that is recorded in a form similar to its original structure. See *analog*.

**analog domain**  The world of analog. When something is done in the analog domain, it implies the manipulation of electronic waveforms. Contrast with *digital domain*.

**analog film**  A plastic sheet with a photosensitive emulsion that comes in various formats for different cameras such as 35mm, 110, 120 and 220. Film was never considered analog until digital cameras came on the scene and stored their images in a digital format in memory. Nevertheless, "old fashioned" plastic-based film is used to create an analog of the actual scene. Analog film has nearly infinite resolution with its resolution quality based on the construction of the lenses. Digital film is based on the number of pixels recorded by the camera. See *digital camera* and *digital photography*.

**analog line**  A wire (cable) that carries an analog signal. See *analog*.

**analog modem**    A common device that converts the computer's digital pulses to tones that can be carried over analog telephone lines. See *modem*.

**analog monitor**    A video monitor that accepts analog signals from the computer (digital to analog conversion is performed in the display adapter). It may accept only a narrow range of display resolutions; for example, only VGA or VGA and Super VGA, or it may accept a wide range of signals including TV. See *multiscan monitor* and *RGB monitor*. Contrast with *digital monitor*.

**analog phone**    The original telephone technology, which converts air vibrations into an analogous electrical frequency. Unless a key telephone system or digital PBX is used, most homes and small offices still use analog phones, and the local loop is mostly analog. Likewise, the first cellular phone systems were analog and are still widely used. All new cellular systems are digital. See *local loop*, *AMPS*, *TDMA*, *CDMA* and *wireless generations*.

**analog signal generator**    A device that creates continuous waveforms for testing analog circuitry.

**analog video**    The original video recording method which stores continuous waves of red, green and blue intensities. In analog video, the number of rows are fixed, but the number of columns are infinite, because the signals are uninterrupted across each row. Contrast with *digital video*. See *analog camera* and *raster*.

**analyst**    See *systems analyst*, *business analyst* and *industry analyst*.

**analytical database engine**    Software that provides multiple views into a database of numerical information. The data is maintained in a nonredundant database, and the views are displayed in a traditional spreadsheet interface. See *spreadsheet* and *TM1*. See also *OLAP*.

**Analytical Engine**    A programmable calculator designed by British scientist Charles Babbage. After his Difference Engine failed its test in 1833, Babbage started the design of the Analytical Engine in 1834. Developed in spurts due to lack of funds and constant redesign, a trial model was finally built in 1871, the year Babbage died. Although never completed, it was a major advance in computing because it contained the principles of the stored program computer. For example, it provided a conditional statement that would branch somewhere else in the program based on the value being tested. The parts of the Engine that were actually built did work however.

Babbage's colleague and close friend, Augusta Ada Byron, the Countess of Lovelace and daughter of the poet Lord Byron, explained the machine's concepts to the public. Her programming notes survived, making her the first official computing machine programmer in the world. The Ada programming language was named after her. See *Difference Engine* and *Mark I*.

**anchor**    In desktop publishing, a format code that keeps a graphic near or next to a text paragraph. If text is added, causing the paragraph to move to a subsequent page, the graphic image is moved along with it. See also *hypertext anchor*.

**Analytical Engine**
Programming the Analytical Engine might have been a bit more tedious than programming one of today's computers. *(Image courtesy of Charles Babbage Institute, University of Minnesota, www.cbi.umn.edu)*

**Andersen**    (Andersen Consulting, Chicago, www.ac.com) The world's largest management and technology consulting firm, which was spun off of Arthur Andersen & Co. in 1989 as a separate entity . The consulting practice, which started out in the 1950s as a secondary area of expertise, grew so rapidly that by 1984 it was more profitable than the company's traditional accounting and tax business. In late 2000, Anderson Consulting changed its name to Accenture. The company has more than 70,000 employees with revenues near $10 billion in 2000.

**AND-OR-NOT**    The fundamental operations of Boolean logic. To learn how they function and how they are wired together to build circuits, see *Boolean logic*.

**angel investor**   An individual that invests his or her own money in a private company, which is typically a startup. An angel investor is not an employee or member of a bank, venture capital firm or other financial institution that normally makes such investments.

**angstrom**   A unit of measurement equal to .1 nanometer, which is approximately 1/250 millionth of an inch. Ten angstroms equal one nanometer. Angstroms are used to measure the wavelengths of light and the elements in a chip. The size of an atom is from three to 10 angstroms.

**ANI**   (Automatic Number Identification) A telephone function that transmits the billing telephone number of the incoming call. ANI is what identifies the calling party for toll call billing and enables the call to be routed to the appropriate long distance service provider. It also enables caller ID and calling name services to be implemented. ISDN supports ANI by carrying the calling telephone number in the D channel. See *caller ID* and *CNAM*.

**animated cursor**   A screen pointer that makes a small amount of movement. In Windows, animated cursors have an .ANI extension.

**animated GIF**   A moving picture in GIF format, which is made up of a series of frames. When displayed, they provide a short animated sequence. Although popular on the Web, animated GIFs are larger than single-frame GIFs and can be annoying when downloaded with a slow analog modem. See *ad blocker* and *GIF*.

**animation**   Moving diagrams or cartoons that are made up of a sequence of images displayed one after the other. Animation files take up much less disk space than a true video sequence.

**anisotropic**   Refers to properties, such as transmission speed, that vary depending on the direction of measurement. Contrast with *isotropic*.

**annoybot**   A bot on an IRC channel that performs some irritating function. For example, the KissServ annoybot sends unessential messages to online users. See *bot*.

**anode**   In electronics, a positively charged receiver of electrons that flow from the negatively charged *cathode*.

**anomaly**   Abnormality or deviation. It is a favorite word among computer people when complex systems produce output that is inexplicable.

**anonymous FTP**   An FTP site on the Internet that contains files that can be downloaded by anyone. The anonymous FTP directory is isolated from the rest of the system and will generally not accept uploads from users.

**anonymous post**   A message that cannot be traced to the person that created it. See *anonymous remailer*.

**anonymous remailer**   An organization that forwards e-mail anonymously stripping out the sender's name and e-mail address. Remailers are used by people that wish to express an opinion to newsgroups or to individuals without fear of excessive responses or retaliation. It is the same as dropping a letter in the post office without a return address. See *Anonymizer*.

**anonymous server**   The software used to perform anonymous remailing. See *anonymous remailer*.

**ANSI**   (American National Standards Institute, New York, www.ansi.org) A membership organization founded in 1918 that coordinates the development of U.S. voluntary national standards in both the private and public sectors. It is the U.S. member body to ISO and IEC. Information technology standards pertain to programming languages, EDI, telecommunications and physical properties of diskettes, cartridges and magnetic tapes.

A

**ANSI character set**   The ANSI-standard character set that defines 256 characters. The first 128 are ASCII, and the second 128 contain math and foreign language symbols, which are different than those on the PC. See *extended ASCII*.

**ANSI lumen**   A measurement of light that has been standardized by ANSI. It is commonly used to rate the brightness of a data projector. An ANSI lumen rating uses an average of several measurements taken across the face of the light source. A small room typically requires from 200 to 300 ANSI lumens, whereas a large room may require from 400 to 600. A large auditorium may need 2000 or more. See *lumen*.

**ANSI terminal**   A display terminal that follows commands in the ANSI standard terminal language. Uses escape sequences to control the cursor, clear the screen and set colors, for example. Communications programs support the ANSI terminal mode and often default to this terminal emulation for dial-up connections to online services and BBSs.

**answer mode**   See *auto answer*.

**answer-only modem**   A modem capable of answering a call, but not initiating one.

**ant**   See *crawler*.

**anti-aliasing**   Smoothing the jagged appearance of diagonal lines in a bitmapped image. The pixels that surround the edges of the line are changed to varying shades of gray or color in order to blend the sharp edge into the background. This technique is also called "dithering," but is usually known as anti-aliasing when applied to diagonal and curved lines.

**anti-blooming**   See *blooming*.

**Antifuse**   A PLD technology from Actel Corporation, Sunnyvale, CA (www.actel.com) that works the opposite of typical programmable chip methods. Instead of creating open circuits (blowing the fuse), closed circuits are created. Two metal layers sandwich a layer of nonconductive, amorphous silicon. When voltage is applied to this middle layer, the amorphous silicon is turned into polysilicon, which is conductive.

**antiglare filter**   A treated glass panel that is placed over a monitor screen to reduce glare. See *antiglare screen*.

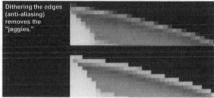

**Anti-aliasing**
This teapot, a famous first example of anti-aliasing, was programmed at the University of Utah. *(Images courtesy of Computer Sciences Department, University of Utah.)*

**antiglare screen**   A monitor screen that is treated to reduce glare from light sources. Non-glare CRTs often use a coating baked onto the screen at the time of manufacture, which provides a significant reduction in glare; however, LCD screens may completely eliminate it. See *antiglare filter*.

**antistatic bag**   A treated plastic bag used to store electronic products in order to reduce static electricity. The inside of the bag provides the protection. See *antistatic device*.

**antistatic device**   Something that reduces static electricity on equipment or on your own body. See *antistatic bag, antistatic mat, antistatic wristband* and *antistatic liquid*.

**antistatic liquid**   A liquid cleaner that does not promote static electricity when used near electronic equipment.

**antistatic mat**    A flat surface that a keyboard or other electronic device can rest on or a person can stand on in order to discharge static electricity. The mat is either grounded or treated in such a manner that it absorbs static electricity. See *antistatic device*.

**antistatic wristband**    A grounded wristband that is worn when working with electronic products in order to discharge static electricity. See *antistatic device*.

**antivirus**    See *virus scanner, behavior blocking, virus* and *virus hoaxes*.

**antivirus program**    See *virus scanner* and *behavior blocking*.

**anycast**    A transmission method for updating routing tables in IPv6. It sends a message to the nearest router within a group. That router in turn sends it to its nearest router. See *IPv6*.

**AO/DI**    (Always On/Dynamic ISDN) A connection between an ISDN customer and an information service provider using the X.25-based D channel, which is a signaling channel that is always active. AO/DI uses 9.6 Kbps of the 16 Kbps D channel and switches to a circuit-switched B channel when more bandwidth is required. It enables low-bandwidth traffic, such as e-mail, newsfeeds, automatic data collection and credit card verifications to be handled quickly and cost effectively. See *ISDN*.

**AOL**    (AOL Time Warner, Inc., Dulles, VA, www.aol.com) The world's largest online information service with access to the Internet, e-mail, chat rooms and a variety of databases and services. AOL has more than 25 million customers. AOL's Windows and Macintosh software combine Web browsing, e-mail and all other functions in one application, which has been appealing for newcomers to online services.

AOL's marketing campaign to freely distribute its trial software in unprecedented numbers in the early days of Internet fever worked well as new members signed on in record numbers. AOL diskettes were distributed with PCs, with software, with virtually anything. They even wound up in dry-ice-frozen packages of filet mignons.

AOL was founded in 1985 as Quantum Computer Services, but changed its name to America Online in 1989. In 1995, AOL acquired ANS CO+RE, a network services provider, and two years later sold ANS to WorldCom in exchange for CompuServe's customer base, which WorldCom had recently acquired. AOL operates its AOL and CompuServe services in 16 countries throughout the world.

In 1999, AOL acquired Netscape and created an alliance with Sun to sell Netscape's Web products. Ironically, AOL's Web browser had actually been Microsoft's Internet Explorer browser and Netscape's primary competition. In the first days of 2001, AOL and Time Warner completed their merger to become the largest online information and entertainment conglomerate in the world. See *AIM, online services* and *ANS*.

**AOL Instant Messenger**    See *AIM*.

**AOLTV**    (America OnLine TV) An Internet TV service from AOL that provides access via a phone line or through the DirecTV satellite from Hughes Electronics. Versions of the AOLTV set-top boxes also include the TiVo technology for digitally recording TV programs. See *PVR* and *WebTV*.

**AON**    (All Optical Network) See *transparent network*.

**Apache**    (1) (A "patchy" server) A widely-used public domain, UNIX-based Web server from the Apache Group (www.apache.org). It is based on, and is a plug-in replacement for, NCSA's HTTPd server Version 1.3. The name came from a body of existing code and many "patch files."

(2) A PowerPC CPU from IBM optimized for commercial processing.

**APCUG**    (Association of Personal Computer User Groups, Washington, DC, www.apcug.org) A non-profit organization dedicated to fostering communication among and between user groups and between user groups and vendors.

**aperture card**    A punched card that holds a frame of microfilm.

**aperture grille**    The technology used for illuminating phosphors in Sony's Trinitron monitors. See *slot mask*.

**API** (Application Program Interface) A language and message format used by an application program to communicate with the operating system or some other control program such as a database management system (DBMS) or communications protocol. APIs are implemented by writing function calls in the program, which provide the linkage to the required subroutine for execution. Thus, an API implies that some program module is available in the computer to perform the operation or that it must be linked into the existing program to perform the tasks.

Understanding an API is a major part of what a programmer does. Except for writing the business logic that performs the actual data processing, all the rest of the programming is writing the code to communicate with the operating system and other software. The APIs for operating systems can be daunting, especially the calls to display and print. There are more than a thousand API calls in a full-blown operating system such as Windows, Mac or UNIX. See *ABI* and *interface*.

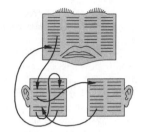
PROGRAMS TALK TO EACH OTHER!

**APL** (A Programming Language) A high-level mathematical programming language noted for its brevity and matrix generation capabilities. Developed by Kenneth Iverson in the mid 1960s, it runs on micros to mainframes and is often used to develop mathematical models. It is primarily an interpreted language, but compilers are available.

APL uses unique character symbols and, before today's graphical interfaces, required special software or ROM chips to enable the computer to display and print them. APL is popular in Europe.

**APM** (Advanced Power Management) A programming interface (API) from Intel and Microsoft for battery-powered computers that lets programs communicate power requirements to slow down and speed up components.

**app** See *application*.

**APPC** (Advanced Program-to-Program Communications) A high-level communications protocol from IBM that allows one program to interact with another program across the network. It supports client/server and distributed computing by providing a common programming interface across all IBM platforms. It provides commands for managing a session, sending and receiving data and transaction security and integrity (two-phase commit).

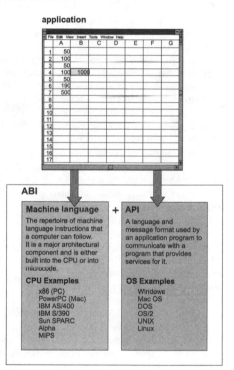

APPC software is either part of, or optionally available, on all IBM and many non-IBM operating systems. Since APPC has only supported SNA, which utilizes the LU 6.2 protocol for session establishment, APPC and LU 6.2 have been considered synonymous.

In the past, APPC commands have differed across platforms. However, the CPI-C interface defines a standard set of APPC verbs.

**Apple** (Apple Computer, Inc., Cupertino, CA, www.apple.com) A manufacturer of personal computers and the industry's most fabled story. Founded in a garage by Steve Wozniak and Steve Jobs and guided by Mike Markkula, Apple blazed the trails for the personal computer industry. Apple was formed on April Fool's Day in 1976. After introducing the Apple I at the Palo Alto Homebrew Computer Club, 10 retail stores were selling them by the end of the year.

In 1977, the Apple II was introduced, a fully-assembled computer with 4K RAM for $1,298. Its open architecture encouraged third-party vendors to build plug-in hardware enhancements. This, plus sound and color graphics, caused Apple IIs to become the most widely used computer in the home and classroom. They were also used in business primarily for the innovative VisiCalc software that was launched on it.

In 1983, Apple introduced the Lisa, the forerunner of the Macintosh. Lisa was aimed at the corporate market, but was soon dropped in favor of the Mac. As a graphics-based machine, the Mac was successful as a low-cost desktop publishing system. Although praised for its ease of use, its slow speed, small monochrome screen and closed architecture didn't excite corporate buyers, but things were to change.

In 1987, the Mac II offered higher speed, larger screens in color and traditional cabinetry that accepted third-party add-in cards. Numerous models were offered and widely accepted. In 1991, Apple surprised the industry by announcing an alliance with IBM to form several companies that would develop hardware and software together. All these eventually folded back into Apple and IBM , but the major product of the alliance was the PowerPC chip (see *Apple-IBM alliance*). In 1994, Apple came out with its first PowerPC-based PowerMacs, which proved very popular. Its PowerBook laptops were an instant success, and all subsequent models departed from the original Motorola 680x0 architecture to the PowerPC.

Apple has stood alone in a sea of IBM and IBM-compatible PCs for more than a decade and a half. It has watched its graphical interface copied more with each incarnation of Windows and watched its market share drop simultaneously. In late 1994, Apple began to license its OS to system vendors in order to create a Macintosh clone industry, which pundits had been suggesting for years. However, a couple of years later, that was discontinued.

In 1997, Apple acquired NeXT Computer, which brought Steve Jobs back to the company he founded and gave it a raft of object-oriented development tools, parts of which filtered down into the Mac OS X operating system.

**The Two Steves**
Wozniak and Jobs (left to right) pioneered the microcomputer revolution. Wozniak's engineering and Job's charisma truly built a legend. Here they hold the motherboard from the Apple I, Apple's first computer. *(Image courtesy of Apple Computer, Inc.)*

**The Apple I**
Rather humble beginnings, yet the Apple I led to the very successful Apple II series, which thrived for many years. *(Image courtesy of Apple Computer, Inc.)*

**A Quarter Century Later**
With a CPU chip 500 times as fast as the Apple I, the PowerBook G4 Cube bears little resemblance to Apple's first offering.

In 1998, Apple introduced the iMac, a low-priced Internet-ready Mac that was the first personal computer without a floppy disk. Self-contained in one unit like the original Mac, Apple sold 800,000 iMacs in a year, making it the fastest-selling computer in its history. Apple's subsequent models, including the G4 Cube and Titanium portable, are in a class by themselves. Apple continues to offer attractive alternatives to the Windows-based PC.

**Apple II**    The personal computer family from Apple that pioneered the microcomputer revolution. It was widely used in schools and home and still made until 1994. Using an 8-bit 6502 microprocessor running at 1MHz and an 8-bit bus, it ran the Apple DOS and ProDOS operating systems. AppleSoft BASIC was built into ROM. With a Z80 microprocessor board plugged in, Apple IIs could run CP/M programs, which were the predominant desktop business software of the time.

APPLE II    Introduced in 1977, the Apple II came with 4KB of RAM and hooked up to a TV and cassette tape recorder. A floppy disk was available in 1978. In 1979, an enhanced II+ came out with 48K and a screen resolution of 280×192×6. In 1983, the "e"nhanced Apple IIe was introduced with four cursor keys (not two) and 128K of RAM. In 1984, the IIc portable was launched with a sleek design.

APPLE III    Introduced in 1980 for the business market, it was not compatible enough with the Apple II to ever catch on.

**Original Apple II**
This was the very first Apple II in 1978. A TV set was often used as a monitor in the beginning. *(Image courtesy of Apple Computer, Inc.)*

**APPLE IIGS** Introduced in 1986 and discontinued in 1992, the faster IIGS added enhanced graphics and sound (GS). It ran Apple II software, but required GS software to use the new features. Specs: 2.8MHz 16-bit 65C816 CPU, 320x200x256 screen, 15 sounds, AppleTalk.

**Apple key** The original name of the CMD (Command) key on Apple keyboards.

**Apple menu** The menu at the upper-left side of a Macintosh screen that is always available to provide access to desk accessories.

**AppleScript** A comprehensive command language used for automating tasks that is part of the Apple operating system from Apple starting with System 7 Pro. AppleScript provides a command-line interface to the Macintosh similar to the way DOS commands are used in a PC.

**AppleShare** Software from Apple that turns a Macintosh into a file server. It works in conjunction with the Mac operating system and can coexist with other Macintosh applications in a nondedicated mode.

**applet** A small application, such as a utility program or limited-function spreadsheet or word processor. Java programs that are run from the browser are always known as applets. See *midlet, crapplet* and *Java applet*.

**AppleTalk** Apple's local area network architecture introduced in 1985. It supports Apple's proprietary LocalTalk access method, as well as Ethernet and Token Ring. The AppleTalk network manager and the LocalTalk access method are built into all Macintoshes and LaserWriters.

With other products from Apple and third parties, AppleTalk can run in PCs, VAXs and UNIX workstations. Since AppleTalk is patterned after the OSI model, it is a routable protocol that contains a network layer (OSI layer 3). See *AFP*.

**AppleWorks** An integrated software package for the Mac and Windows from Apple. Originally ClarisWorks, it includes a word processor, spreadsheet, database and drawing program. It provides compound document creation that lets you, for example, insert a spreadsheet into your text document.

AppleWorks was originally the name for Apple's integrated package for the Apple II, which was introduced in 1983.

**appliance** A device that is dedicated to a specific function in contrast to a general-purpose computer. Many consider the router the first network appliance. See *Internet appliance* and *firewall appliance*.

**application** (1) A specific use of the computer, such as for payroll, inventory and billing. For a list of major application software categories, see *application software*.

(2) Same as *application program* and *software package*.

**application adapter** A layer of software that converts the data from the application into a common form acceptable for integration with other applications. See *application integration* and *integration server*.

**application centric** Focusing on the application as the foundation or starting point. In an application-centric system, the program is loaded first, which in turn is used to create or edit a particular type of data structure (text, spreadsheet, image, etc.). Contrast with *document centric*. See *component software*.

**application developer** An individual that develops a business application and usually performs the duties of a systems analyst and application programmer.

**application development environment** The combination of hardware and software used to develop an application. See *application development system* and *ADE*.

**application development language** Same as *programming language*.

**application development system** A programming language and associated utility programs that allow for the creation, development and running of application programs. Many database management systems (DBMSs) include a complete application development system, along with a query language, report writer and the capability to create and manage database files interactively.

An application development system may also provide a full-scale application generator or various degrees of automatic application generation. An application development system that does not include its own database provides links to other databases via SQL, ODBC and other interfaces.

A client/server application development system is one in which the end product runs on a local area network. A two-tiered system splits the software between client and server. A three-tiered system splits the software between client, application server and database server. The application server provides the business logic in this case. See *client/server development system* and *application generator*.

**application extension**    (1) Microsoft's name for an auxiliary, executable file, which is normally a DLL. See *DLL*.

(2) A supplementary routine that adds capabilities to an application.

(3) A supplementary format that adds options in a data set. See *data set*.

**application framework**    (1) The building blocks of an application.

(2) A class library that provides the foundation for programming an object-oriented application.

**application gateway**    See *proxy server*.

**application generator**    Software that generates application programs from descriptions of the problem rather than by traditional programming. It is at a higher level and easier to use than a high-level programming language. One statement or descriptive line may generate a huge routine or an entire program. However, application generators always have limits as to what they can be used for. Generators used for complex program development allow if-then-else programming to be expressed along with the simpler descriptive entries.

The goal with application generators and computer-aided software engineering (CASE) has always been to create a program by describing it, not programming it. The problem with such high-level systems is that either the resulting code is too slow or certain functions simply cannot be performed at all. As a result, commercial programs are rarely written in these languages; they are used for business information systems and often only for creating prototypes that are later reprogrammed in COBOL or C.

As computers run faster, they are capable of absorbing the excess code generated by higher-level products. In time, it is expected that the machine efficiency demanded of today's hardware may not be as critical, and higher-level development tools may become the norm, relegating lower-level languages to a handful of highly skilled and very highly paid individuals. See *application development system*.

**application integration**    (1) Translating data and commands from the format of one application into the format of another. It is essentially data and command conversion on an ongoing basis between two or more incompatible systems. Implementing application integration has traditionally been done by tedious programming, or occasionally one package might support the interfaces of one or two other packages. However, the trend today is to use message brokers, applications servers and other specialized integration products that provide a common connecting point. Since the advent of the Web, these prepackaged "middleware" solutions have become widely used to Web enable the enterprise. See *messaging middleware*, *middleware*, *application server*, *integration server* and *application adapter*.

(2) Redesigning disparate information systems into one system that uses a common set of data structures and rules.

**application layer**    The software in the OSI protocol stack (layer 7 of 7) that provides the starting point of the communications session. See *OSI* and *TCP/IP ABCs*.

**application-level gateway**    See *proxy server*.

**application management system**    Software that manages the availability of network-centered applications within an organization, such as e-mail, intranets and client/server. It monitors all the components of an application to see if they are up and running. It also checks the traffic load on essential components in order to forecast delays as well as invoke additional processes to handle the overload if possible. See *service level management system* and *event management system*.

**application notes**    Instructions and recommendations from the vendor provided in addition to the normal reference manuals.

**application package**    A software package that is created for a specific purpose or industry.

**application partitioning**    Separating an application into components that run on clients and multiple servers in a client/server environment. Programming languages and development systems that support this architecture, known as *three-tier client/server*, may allow the program to be developed as a whole and then separated into pieces later. Development systems are differentiated by their ability to perform partitioning as a mainstream function in a high-level language or with visual programming (drag and drop) versus having to write chunks of code in C.

Application partitioning is an important capability for migrating legacy systems onto client/server environments. In many business applications, there is a lot of processing that should be done centrally in a server and not in each client machine. Such programs are either too demanding and process intensive for the client or they represent proprietary business logic that should not be replicated all over the enterprise. The centralized mainframe has always made a lot of sense for many applications. Partitioning the logic onto multiple servers emulates this approach in a client/server environment.

**Who's Doing It?**    Application partitioning can always be accomplished by writing 3GL code. However, with today's push for rapid application development (RAD), writing in a traditional programming language takes time. Products such as Forte and DYNASTY were the first to provide application partitioning at the 4GL level, and the capability has been added to other development systems.

The OSF's Distributed Computing Environment (DCE) standard is also used for three-tier client/server because it provides a standard for accessing programs and databases no matter where they are located.

**application processor**    A computer that processes data in contrast with one that performs control functions, such as a front-end processor or database machine.

**application program**    Any data entry, update, query or report program that processes data for the user. It includes the generic productivity software (spreadsheets, word processors, database programs, etc.), as well as custom and packaged programs for payroll, billing, inventory and other accounting purposes. For a list of major application software categories, see *application software*. See also *program*. Contrast with *system program*.

**application programmer**    An individual who writes application programs in a user organization. Most programmers are application programmers. Contrast with *systems programmer*. See *system development cycle*.

**application proxy**    See *proxy server*.

**application server**    **(1)** A computer in a client/server environment that performs the business logic (the data processing). In a two-tier client/server environment, the user's machine performs the business logic, which connects to the database server (DBMS). The bulk of client/server architecture is two-tier. In a three-tier client/server environment, an independent application server performs the business logic. This was the original definition of the term application server. Increasingly, the term refers to the Web-based usage in definition 2 on the following page. See *file server*.

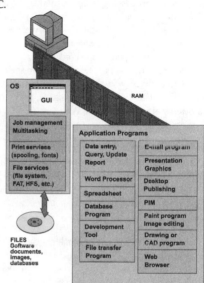

**Application Programs**
This diagram shows the typical application programs that run in a desktop computer. It also shows the major components of the operating system.

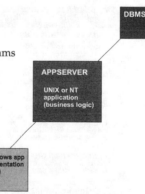

**Three-Tier Client/Server**
An application server in a three-tier client/server environment provides middle tier processing between the user's machine and the database management system (DBMS).

(2) A computer in an intranet/Internet environment that performs the data processing necessary to deliver up-to-date information, as well as process information for Web clients. The application server sits along with or between the Web server and the databases and legacy applications, providing the middleware glue to enable a browser-based application to link to multiple sources of information. With Java-based application servers the processing is performed by Java servlets, JavaServer Pages (JSPs) and Enterprise JavaBeans (EJBs). In a Windows-only environment, the processing is performed by Active Server Pages (ASPs) and ActiveX controls. All environments support CGI scripts, which were the first method for tying database contents to HTML pages.

In large sites, separate application servers link to the Web servers and typically provide load balancing and fault tolerance for high-volume traffic. For small Web sites, the application server processing is often performed by the Web server. Examples of Web application servers are Netscape Application Server, BEA Weblogic Enterprise, Borland AppServer and IBM's Websphere Application Server. See *Web server*.

### application server computing
Citrix's term for its centralized, multiuser technology that runs the application in the server and sends only changes in the user interface to the client machine. See *MetaFrame* and *WinFrame*.

### application sharing
A data conferencing capability that lets two or more users interactively work on the same application at the same time. The application is loaded and running in only one machine; however, keystrokes are transmitted from and screen changes are transmitted to the other participants. Application sharing provides the same capability as remote control software. See *application viewing* and *T.120*.

### application software
Following are the major categories of application programs (software packages). See *application program*.

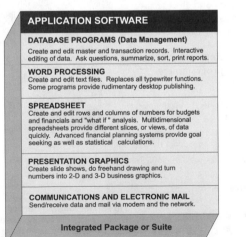

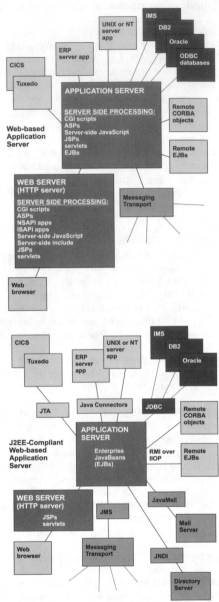

**Web-based Application Servers**
Application servers have become the middleware for the enterprise as they increasingly provide more hooks into legacy applications. The bottom illustration is a J2EE-compliant application server running only Java with services deployed per Sun's recommendation (EJBs being the primary business logic delivery method).

continued from previous page

**DESKTOP PUBLISHING**
Merge text and graphics and provide complete control over page layout for printing. More precise than word processing programs.

**PIM (Personal Information Manager)**
Organize random information for fast retrieval. Includes such features as a telephone list with automatic dialing, calendar, scheduler and tickler.

**PROJECT MANAGEMENT**
Keep track of a project and determine the impact of changes. The "critical path" is computed, which monitors all tasks that will slow down the entire project if delayed.

**CAD (Vector graphics)**
Create drawings for illustration and industrial design.

**IMAGING (Raster graphics)**
Scan documents and paint pictures into TV-like images.

**DIAGRAMMING PROGRAM**
Create drawings of interconnected symbols, such as network diagrams and organization charts. When symbols are moved, the lines stay connected.

**CONTACT MANAGER**
Keep track of prospects, names, addresses, appointments. Similar to a PIM, but specialized for sales activities.

**MATHEMATICAL**
Create, run and print complex mathematical equations.

**SCIENTIFIC**
Analyze real-world events by simulating them on high-speed computers or supercomputers.

**MULTIMEDIA (Games and Education)**
Multimedia adds graphics, sound and video for interactive games, encyclopedias and other references and educational courseware of all kinds.

**VERTICAL MARKETS**
Data entry, query, update and report programs customized for an industry such as banking and insurance. Either off-the-shelf or custom programmed, vertical market software is the most specialized type of information system available.

**WEB BROWSER**
"Surf the Web." Access the largest body of information in the world, shop online and be entertained.

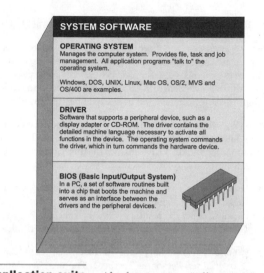

**SYSTEM SOFTWARE**

**OPERATING SYSTEM**
Manages the computer system. Provides file, task and job management. All application programs "talk to" the operating system.

Windows, DOS, UNIX, Linux, Mac OS, OS/2, MVS and OS/400 are examples.

**DRIVER**
Software that supports a peripheral device, such as a display adapter or CD-ROM. The driver contains the detailed machine language necessary to activate all functions in the device. The operating system commands the driver, which in turn commands the hardware device.

**BIOS (Basic Input/Output System)**
In a PC, a set of software routines built into a chip that boots the machine and serves as an interface between the drivers and the peripheral devices.

**application suite**    Also known as an "office suite," it is a set of applications designed to work together. It typically includes word processing, spreadsheet, presentation graphics and database programs. Some of the programs may be available separately, while others come only in the bundle. Microsoft Office, Wordperfect Office and Lotus SmartSuite are the major business application suites for Windows. Sun's StarOffice is a new contender that is expected to become popular.

Although Windows provides integration features such as cut and paste and compound document creation, the suites provide additional tools to move data from one application more easily into another. In addition, common functions such as spell checking can be installed once and shared among all programs.

While no single application suite has the best program in each category, they have become very popular because they come on one CD-ROM, are upgradable as a single unit, and training is available for the entire package.

**application viewing**    A data conferencing capability that lets two or more users view the same application at the same time. All users may be able to highlight different parts of the document, spreadsheet or database, but only the user at the machine where the application is loaded can actually edit it. See *application sharing* and *T.120*.

**APPN**    (Advanced Peer-to-Peer Networking) Extensions to IBM's SNA communications that provide the necessary flexibility to enable direct communication between users anywhere on the network. Features includes improved administration, intermediate node routing and dynamic network services. APPN makes use of LU 6.2 protocols and is implemented in an SNA Node Type 2.1.

**appserver**    See *application server*.

**apps on tap**    Refers to applications that can be quickly "rented" online from an application service provider. See *ASP*.

**APT**    (Automatic Programmed Tools) A high-level programming language used to generate instructions for numerical control machines.

**aptitude tests**   The following organizations provide aptitude and proficiency tests in programming and computer topics.

**Berger Series**   A set of proficiency and aptitude tests from Psychometrics, Inc., Sherman Oaks, CA (www.psy-test.com). Tests are available for many programming languages, including Ada, C, C++, CICS, COBOL, IBM 360/370 Assembler, Xbase and Visual Basic. Tests for MVS and UNIX are also available. Aptitude tests include B-APT for people with no programming experience, B-APT AF for the experienced and B-SYS for systems programming. All tests are paper and pencil, multiple-choice, administered by the recruiting or hiring firm. Psychometrics provides results by phone and by mail.

**Prove It!**   A set of software-based proficiency tests developed by Know It All, Inc., Philadelphia, PA (www.knowitallinc.com). The tests, available on disks, cover a wide range of technical and clerical skills. The company also makes Prove It.Com, a subscription-based, Internet version of 65 tests for assessing various computer programming and related technical skills. Tests are available for one-time or continued use.

**TekCheck**   A series of more than 90 online tests developed by Bookman Consulting, Inc., New York, (www.tekchek.com), to measure programmer proficiency. Companies and employment/recruiting firms administer tests from their locations, send the results to Bookman and receive assessments within a couple of days. The series includes tests for C, C++, COBOL, CICS, DB2, Lotus Notes, Oracle, PowerBuilder, RPG and Visual Basic.

**Wolfe-Spence Programming Aptitude Tests**   A set of tests for programming, systems programming and systems analysis offered by Walden Personnel Testing & Training, Inc., Montreal, Canada (www.waldentesting.com). Completed test booklets are faxed to U.S scoring centers in New Jersey. Walden faxes back detailed evaluation report on each candidate.

**NOCTI**   Technical Skills Tests Developed by the National Occupational Competency Testing Institute, available through Wonderlic Personnel Tests, Inc., Libertyville, IL. Wonderlic offers job-specific tests that assess the candidate's knowledge of a trade or profession. Tests are available for computer programming, computer technology, CAD/CAM and graphics/imaging. The company also offers Hay Aptitude tests to identify candidates who can work quickly and accurately with alphanumeric data.

**arbitrated loop**   A ring topology used in Fibre Channel. Up to 127 devices may be attached in the loop, but only two can communicate at the same time, reflecting the channel nature of Fibre Channel technology. To communicate with a device several hops down the ring, each device repeats the data to its adjacent node. See *Fibre Channel*.

**arbitration**   A set of rules for allocating machine resources, such as memory or peripheral devices, to more than one user or program.

**ARC, ARC+Plus**   (1) PC compression programs from System Enhancement Associates, Inc., Clifton, NJ. ARC was one of the first compression utilities to become popular in the early 1980s. ARC+Plus provides enhanced features and speed.
   (2) The ARC extension was previously used by PKWARE Inc. in its PKARC program.
   (3) (Advanced RISC Computing) An open system specification based on the MIPS R3000 and R4000 CPUs. It includes EISA and TURBOchannel buses.

**Archie**   (ARCHIvE) An Internet utility used to search for file names. There are approximately 30 computer systems throughout the Internet, called "Archie servers," that maintain catalogs of files available for downloading from various FTP sites. Periodically, Archie servers search FTP sites throughout the Internet and record information about the files they find. If you do not have Archie, some Internet hosts let you log on via Telnet as user "archie." See *FTP*.

**architecture**   See *computer architecture*, *network architecture* and *software architecture*.

**architecture neutral**   Refers to software that is designed without regard to the target platform. Software is often written to maximize the performance of a specific hardware platform, but such software must be modified to make it run on other hardware. It is always a tradeoff. The more specialized the software, the faster the performance of the hardware, but the more difficult to make the software work on other platforms. See *intermediate language*.

**architecture police**   The individuals in an organization responsible for enforcing hardware and software standards during the development of systems. The more creative the employees, the more friction between them and the architecture police. See *logo police*.

**archive**    (1) To copy data onto a different disk or tape for backup or data retention purposes. Archived files are normally compressed to maximize storage media, and such compression programs may be called "archiver programs" or "archiving programs."

(2) To save data onto the disk.

**archive attribute**    A file classification that indicates whether the file has been updated since the last backup. A bit is set in the file directory to indicate the archive status.

**archive file**    A file that has been saved in a different location than the original for backup purposes.

**archive formats**    Following are popular data compression and archiving formats.

**.ARC**    Compressed archive. Requires ARC from SEAware, PKARC, or Vernon Buerg's tiny, free ARCE or ARC-E programs to extract. Macintosh program ArcMac and UNIX program arc5521 will also work.

**.ARJ**    A compressed archive requiring the ARJ program to uncompress. Requires UNARJ. No Macintosh equivalent is available.

**.BTOA**    Binary to ASCII. A binary file in text format that must be converted back to binary with the UNIX program BTOA or the Windows/DOS program ATOB. (No Mac equivalent.)  The file extension .atob is, of course, ASCII to binary.

**.CP or .CPIO**    Archives created by UNIX CPIO (copy-in/copy-out) tape archiving program. An early competitor to TAR. UNIX users may use the PAX (Portable Archive Exchange) program to deal with such files or with .TAR files. For DOS/Windows users, the program to get is PAX2EXE. (No Mac equivalent.)

**.CPT**    A Macintosh file created by Compactor. (No DOS/Windows equivalent.)

**.EXE**    Compression programs such as PKZIP and LHA have the ability to create "self-extracting" archive files. These are executable files because they have the decompression program built into them, and that's what you run. When you key in the name or double click the filename, the archive contents are extracted automatically.

**.gz**    A compressed archive requiring a UNIX interpretation of PKZIP, specifically the GZIP (GNU Zip) program from the GNU Project. Get GZIP or GUNZIP for DOS/Windows machines. (No Mac equivalent.)

**.Hqx or .hqx**    A Macintosh compression format. Requires the Mac program BinHex, the DOS/Windows program XBIN or the UNIX program MCVERT to convert.

**.LHA or .LZH**    A DOS compressed archive requiring the use of the public domain program LHA, which can handle archives created by its predecessor if you specify the /O (for "old version") switch. LHA or WinZip are good choices for DOS/Windows users. Mac users should get MacLHarc.

**.PAK**    A DOS compressed archive created by the PAK program. Rarely seen these days. (No Mac equivalent.)

**.PIT**    A file created by the Macintosh program PackIt. DOS/Windows users can use UNPACKIT.

**.SEA**    A Macintosh self-extracting archive. (No DOS/Windows equivalent.)

**.shar, .sh, or .Shar**    A "shell archive" created by the UNIX SHAR program. Use UNSHAR to uncompress. There are versions for both Wintel machines and the Macintosh.

**.SIT**    A compressed archive created with the Macintosh Stuffit or Stuffit Deluxe program from Aladdin Systems, Inc. DOS/Windows users should use UNSTUFF or UNSIT.

**.taz or .tgz**    Short for ".tar.z". Use the GZIP program first on such files, and then TAR. No Mac equivalent for GZIP, but there is one for TAR.

**.tar or -tar**    "Tape ARchive" files are packed into a single file by the UNIX TAR program. Use TAR to unpack. Macintosh users should look for UNTAR.

**.UU or .UUE**    A binary file in ASCII format requiring the UUDECODE program or a clone to convert back into binary form. DOS/Window users should use UUDECODE by Richard Marks since it is the best version. Macintosh users should look for UUTOOL.

**.Z**    Uppercase "Z." A compressed file requiring the UNIX UNCOMPRESS program or a clone, such as the DOS program U16 or the Mac program MacCompress.

**.z**    Lowercase "z." Usually indicates an archive requiring the free GZIP program from GNU Project. To reduce confusion, newer versions of the GZIP program create files ending in .gz instead.

**.ZIP**    Compressed archive created by PKZIP, WinZip, or a similar program. Mac owners may use ZipIt, UnZip or Stuffit Expander.

**.ZOO**    Compressed archive created by the ZOO program, which is required to uncompress it. DOS/Windows users use ZOO. Macintosh users use MaxBooz.

**ARCNET**    (**A**ttached **R**esource **C**omputer **NET**work)  The first local area network (LAN) introduced in 1968 by Datapoint Corporation. It connects up to 255 nodes in a star topology at 2.5 Mbits/sec over twisted pair or coax. A 20 Mbits/sec version was introduced in 1989. Although not as popular as Ethernet and Token Ring, many ARCNET networks were sold due to their lower-cost adapters. Gateways can connect ARCNET to mini and mainframe networks.

ARCNET is a data link protocol and functions at the data link and physical levels of the OSI model (1 and 2). It uses the token passing access method. See *data link protocol* and *OSI*.

**ARC server**    (**AR**Chive server)  A server in a network used to store backup copies of data files.

**ARDIS**    A wireless data network from American Mobile Satellite Corporation, Reston, VA (www.ammobile.com), that covers more than 11,000 cities and towns in the U.S., Puerto Rico and U.S. Virgin Islands. Operating in the 806–824/851–869MHz bands, ARDIS is a packet-switched network that provides a data rate of 19.2 Kbps and is known for its deep penetration into buildings. Primarily used for field service and transportation applications, ARDIS was created by Motorola in the mid-1980s for IBM's field service division and later spun off as a commercial service.

For greater coverage in hard-to-reach locations, ARDIS is used in conjunction with American Mobile's SKYCELL satellite system, created in the mid 1980s for trucking, maritime and emergency use. American Mobile's eLink service offers wireless e-mail over ARDIS and was one of the first to provide mail forwarding from an ISP. ARDIS originally stood for Advanced National Radio Data Service and was the first wireless data network in the U.S.

**areal density**    The number of bits per square inch of storage surface. It typically refers to disk drives, where the number of bits per inch times the number of tracks per inch yields the areal density.

The areal density of disk storage devices has increased dramatically since IBM introduced the RAMAC, the first hard disk computer in 1956. The RAMAC had an areal density of 2000 bits per square inch (2 Kb/sq.in.). Current-day disks have densities exceeding 20,000,000,000 bits per square inch. See *holographic storage* and *atomic force microscope*.

**arg**    See *argument*.

**argument**    In programming, a value that is passed between programs, subroutines or functions. Arguments are independent items, or variables, that contain data or codes. When an argument is used to customize a program for a user, it is typically called a "parameter." See *argc*.

**ARIN**    (**A**merican **R**egistry for **I**nternet **N**umbers, Herndon, VA, www.arin.net)  An organization founded in 1997 to dispense IP addresses in North and South America, the Caribbean and sub-Saharan Africa. This was previous handled by Network Solutions, Inc., (InterNIC), which manages domain names. The European and Asian counterparts of ARIN are Researux IP Europeens (RIPE) and Asia Pacific Network Information Center (APNIC). See *IP address* and *Network Solutions*.

**arithmetic coding**    A statistical data compression method that converts strings of data into single floating point numbers between 0 and 1.

**arithmetic expression**    (1) One or more characters or symbols associated with arithmetic, such as **1+2=3** or **8*6**.
(2) In programming, a nontext expression.

**arithmetic operators**    Symbols for arithmetic functions: + add, – subtract, * multiply, / divide. See *precedence*.

**arithmetic overflow**    The result from an arithmetic calculation that exceeds the space designated to hold it.

**arithmetic underflow**　The result from an arithmetic calculation that is too small to be expressed properly. For example, in floating point, a negative exponent can be generated that is too large (too small a number) to be stored in its allotted space.

**ARJ**　A compression program for backup archiving from ARJ Software, Inc., Norwood, MA (www.arjsoftware.com). Introduced in the early 1990s and created by Robert Jung (the RJ in ARJ), ARJ never achieved the popularity of PKZIP, although it is considered a worthy competitor. See *JAR*.

**ARM chips**　A family of RISC-based microprocessors and microcontrollers from ARM Inc., Los Gatos, CA (www.arm.com). ARM chips are high-speed CPUs that are known for their small die size and low power requirements. They are widely used in PDAs and other handheld devices, including games and phones, as well as a large variety of consumer products. The StrongARM chip is a high-speed version jointly developed with Digital.

　　ARM was formed in 1990 by Acorn Computers, Apple and VLSI Technology as Advanced RISC Machines. Its designs are licensed to various semiconductor manufacturers. See *StrongARM* and *Thumb*.

**ARP**　(Address Resolution Protocol) A TCP/IP protocol used to obtain a node's physical address. A client station broadcasts an ARP request onto the network with the IP address of the target node it wishes to communicate with, and the node with that address responds by sending back its physical address so that packets can be transmitted. ARP returns the layer 2 address for a layer 3 address.

　　Since an ARP gets the message to the target machine, one might wonder why bother with IP addresses in the first place. The reason is that ARP requests are broadcast onto the network, requiring every station in the subnet to process the request. See *RARP*.

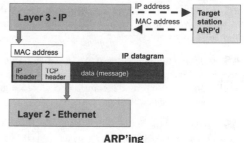

**ARP'ing**
The IP protocol broadcasts the IP address of the destination station onto the network, and the node with that address responds.

**ARPAnet**　(Advanced Research Projects Agency NETwork) The research network funded by the U.S. Advanced Research Projects Agency (ARPA). The software was developed by Bolt, Beranek and Newman (BBN), and Honeywell 516 minicomputers were the first hardware used as packet switches. ARPAnet was launched in 1969 at four sites including two University of California campuses, the Stanford Research Institute and the University of Utah.

　　In late 1972, the ARPAnet was demonstrated at the International Conference on Computers in Washington, DC. This was the first public demonstration of packet switching. Over the next decade, ARPAnet spawned other networks, and in 1983 with more than 300 computers connected, its protocols were changed to TCP/IP. In that same year, the unclassified military Milnet network was split off from ARPAnet.

　　As TCP/IP and gateway technologies matured, more disparate networks were connected, and the ARPAnet became known as "the Internet" and "the Net." Starting in 1987, the National Science Foundation began developing a high-speed backbone between its supercomputer centers. Intermediate networks of regional ARPAnet sites were formed to hook into the backbone, and commercial as well as nonprofit network service providers were formed to handle the operations.

　　Over time, backbones by other federal agencies and organizations were formed and interlinked. In 1995, commercial Internet service providers took control of the major backbones, and the Internet continues to grow every day. See *Internet*.

**ARQ**　(Automatic Repeat reQuest) A method of handling communications errors in which the receiving station requests retransmission if an error occurs.

**array**　An ordered arrangement of data elements. A vector is a one dimensional array, a matrix is a two-dimensional array. Most programming languages have the ability to store and manipulate arrays in one or more dimensions. Multidimensional arrays are used extensively in scientific simulation and mathematical processing; however, an array can be as simple as a pricing table held in memory for instant access by an order entry program. See *subscript*.

| Price list in one-dimensional array | | | | | | |
|---|---|---|---|---|---|---|
| Item | Amount | Item | Amount | Item | Amount | etc. |
| 0001 | 016.43 | 0002 | 005.44 | 0003 | 110.00 | 0004 |

| Sales figures in two-dimensional array | | | | |
|---|---|---|---|---|
| | Jan | Feb | Mar | Apr | etc. |
| Product A | 24484 | 09880 | 45884 | 83304 |
| Product B | 67300 | 12372 | 37461 | |
| Product C | 20011 | 10029 | | |
| etc. | | | | |

**array element**　One item in an array.

**array processor**   A computer, or extension to its arithmetic unit, that is capable of performing simultaneous computations on elements of an array of data in some number of dimensions. Common uses include analysis of fluid dynamics and rotation of 3-D objects, as well as data retrieval, in which elements in a database are scanned simultaneously. See *vector processor* and *math coprocessor*.

**arrow key**   One of four keyboard keys (up, down, left and right) that move the pointer, or cursor, on screen. See *cursor keys*.

**Article 2B**   See *UCITA*.

**artifact**   Some distortion of an image or sound caused by a limitation or malfunction in the graphics and sound hardware or software.

**artificial intelligence**   See *AI*.

**artificial language**   A language that has been predefined before it is ever used. Contrast with *natural language*.

**artificial life**   An evolving computer science that models the behavior of biological systems. The models are used to study evolution as well as to apply the algorithms to a variety of problems in such fields as engineering, robotics and drug research.

**AS**   (1) (Application System) An IBM mainframe 4GL that runs under MVS. It was originally designed for non-computer people and includes commands for planning, budgeting and graphics. However, a programmer can also produce complex applications. It also provides computer conferencing.

(2) See *autonomous system*.

**AS/400**   (Application System/400) An IBM minicomputer series introduced in 1988 that runs under the OS/400 operating system. It is IBM's midrange series of computer systems used primarily for business applications, most of which are written in RPG III and COBOL.

The AS/400 was designed to supersede the System/36 and System/38, IBM's prior midrange computers. The AS/400 is an enhanced version of the System/38, which includes an integrated relational database management system. Since System/38 programs can be run without change in the AS/400, System/38s were readily exchanged for AS/400s. However, in order to run System/36 applications, the programs have to be recompiled.

In 1994, IBM introduced the AS/400 Advanced System/36, a PowerPC-based version of the AS/400 that natively runs the System/36 SSP operating system and its applications.

The AS/400 serves in a variety of networking configurations: as a host or intermediate node to other AS/400s, as a remote system to mainframe-controlled networks and as a network server to PCs. In 2000, IBM changed the name of AS/400s to "iSeries eservers" (see *IBM server series*).

**AS/400**
The AS/400 is used in small to medium-sized businesses, and thousands of applications have been written for it. *(Image courtesy of International Business Machines Corporation. Unauthorized use not permitted.)*

**ascender**   The part of lowercase b, d, f, h, k, l, and t, that extends above the body of the letters. See *typeface*.

**ascending sort**   Arranging data from the normal low to high sequence; for example, from A to Z or from 0 to 9. Contrast with *descending sort*.

**ASCII**   (American Standard Code for Information Interchange) Pronounced "ask-ee." A binary code for text, as well as communications and printer control. It is used for most communications and is the built-in character code in most minicomputers and all personal computers.

ASCII is a 7-bit code providing 128 character combinations, the first 32 of which are control characters. Since the common storage unit is an 8-bit byte (256 combinations) and ASCII uses only 7 bits, the extra bit is used differently depending on the computer.

For example, the PC uses the additional values for foreign language and graphics symbols (see ASCII chart that follows). In the Macintosh, the additional values can be user-defined. See *ASCII chart* for a diagram of all the ASCII characters. See also *hex chart* and *Unicode*.

## ASCII art

Pictures created with normal text characters. This is done by hand or with programs that convert scanned images into ASCII characters. The following image was created by ASCII artist Joan Stark of Westlake, Ohio. ASCII art is very imaginative. For a wide variety of Joan's work as well as that of other artists, visit her gallery on the Web at www.ascii-art.com. See *GIFSCII*.

## ASCIIbetical

(ASCII alpha**BETICAL**) In ASCII order, which is not alphanumeric. In ASCII, upper case letters are grouped separately from lower case (see *ASCII chart*), and special characters are located before, in between and after the letters. If dictionaries and glossaries are maintained in ASCIIbetical order for an electronic version, the terms have to be converted into alphanumeric order for printing, which treats upper- and lowercase letters the same. A lexicographic sort may also be used for printing, although very often, numbers are placed at the beginning or end of the book. See *lexicographic sort*.

**ASCII ART**
ASCII characters may be simple, but used imaginatively, they can create very attractive pictures.
*(Image courtesy of Joan Stark.)*

## ASCII chart

### Standard ASCII
The first 32 characters are control codes.

| | | |
|---|---|---|
| 0 Null | 33 ! | 81 Q |
| 1 Start of heading | 34 " | 82 R |
| 2 Start of text | 35 # | 83 S |
| 3 End of text | 36 $ | 84 T |
| 4 End of transmit | 37 % | 85 U |
| 5 Enquiry | 38 & | 86 V |
| 6 Acknowledge | 39 ' | 87 W |
| 7 Audible bell | 40 ( | 88 X |
| 8 Backspace | 41 ) | 89 Y |
| 9 Horizontal tab | 42 * | 90 Z |
| 10 Line feed | 43 + | 91 [ |
| 11 Vertical tab | 44 , | 92 \ |
| 12 Form feed | 45 - | 93 ] |
| 13 Carriage return | 46 . | 94 ^ |
| 14 Shift out | 47 / | 95 _ |
| 15 Shift in | 48 0 | 96 ` |
| 16 Data link escape | 49 1 | 97 a |
| 17 Device control 1 | 50 2 | 98 b |
| 18 Device control 2 | 51 3 | 99 c |
| 19 Device control 3 | 52 4 | 100 d |
| 20 Device control 4 | 53 5 | 101 e |
| 21 Neg. acknowledge | 54 6 | 102 f |
| 22 Synchronous idle | 55 7 | 103 g |
| 23 End trans. block | 56 8 | 104 h |
| 24 Cancel | 57 9 | 105 i |
| 25 End of medium | 58 : | 106 j |
| 26 Substitution | 59 ; | 107 k |
| 27 Escape | 60 < | 108 l |
| 28 File separator | 61 = | 109 m |
| 29 Group separator | 62 > | 110 n |
| 30 Record separator | 63 ? | 111 o |
| 31 Unit separator | 64 @ | 112 p |
| 32 Blank space | 65 A | 113 q |
| | 66 B | 114 r |
| | 67 C | 115 s |
| | 68 D | 116 t |
| | 69 E | 117 u |
| | 70 F | 118 v |
| | 71 G | 119 w |
| | 72 H | 120 x |
| | 73 I | 121 y |
| | 74 J | 122 z |
| | 75 K | 123 { |
| | 76 L | 124 | |
| | 77 M | 125 } |
| | 78 N | 126 ~ |
| | 79 O | 127 △ |
| | 80 P | |

### Extended ASCII (DOS)

| | | | |
|---|---|---|---|
| 128 Ç | 174 « | 220 |
| 129 ü | 175 » | 221 |
| 130 é | 176 | 222 |
| 131 â | 177 | 223 |
| 132 ä | 178 | 224 α |
| 133 à | 179 | 225 β |
| 134 å | 180 | 226 Γ |
| 135 ç | 181 | 227 π |
| 136 ê | 182 | 228 Σ |
| 137 ë | 183 | 229 σ |
| 138 è | 184 | 230 µ |
| 139 ï | 185 | 231 τ |
| 140 î | 186 | 232 Φ |
| 141 ì | 187 | 233 θ |
| 142 Ä | 188 | 234 Ω |
| 143 Å | 189 | 235 δ |
| 144 É | 190 | 236 ∞ |
| 145 æ | 191 | 237 ø |
| 146 Æ | 192 | 238 ε |
| 147 ô | 193 | 239 ∩ |
| 148 ö | 194 | 240 ≡ |
| 149 ò | 195 | 241 ± |
| 150 û | 196 | 242 ≥ |
| 151 ù | 197 | 243 ≤ |
| 152 ÿ | 198 | 244 ⌠ |
| 153 Ö | 199 | 245 ⌡ |
| 154 Ü | 200 | 246 ÷ |
| 155 ¢ | 201 | 247 ≈ |
| 156 £ | 202 | 248 ° |
| 157 ¥ | 203 | 249 · |
| 158 ₧ | 204 | 250 · |
| 159 ƒ | 205 | 251 √ |
| 160 á | 206 | 252 ⁿ |
| 161 í | 207 | 253 ² |
| 162 ó | 208 | 254 ■ |
| 163 ú | 209 | 255 |
| 164 ñ | 210 | |
| 165 Ñ | 211 | |
| 166 ª | 212 | |
| 167 º | 213 | |
| 168 ¿ | 214 | |
| 169 ⌐ | 215 | |
| 170 ¬ | 216 | |
| 171 ½ | 217 | |
| 172 ¼ | 218 | |
| 173 ¡ | 219 | |

**ASCII Characters (Decimal)**
These are the standard ASCII characters (0–127), plus the extended ASCII characters as implemented in the DOS PC. This chart shows the values in decimal (0–255).

## ASCII file

A file that contains data made up of ASCII characters. It is essentially raw text just like the words you're reading now. Each byte in the file contains one character that conforms to the standard ASCII code (see *ASCII chart*). Program source code, batch files, macros and scripts are straight text and stored as ASCII files. Text editors (Notepad, DOS Editor, Brief, etc.) and a few word processors, such as XyWrite, create ASCII files as their native file format.

ASCII text files become a common denominator between applications that do not import each other's formats. If both applications can import and export ASCII files, you can transfer your files between them. Almost all word processors import and export ASCII files, as well as many database and spreadsheet programs, although the latter may handle only a variation of this format known as comma delimited.

In non-ASCII, proprietary file formats, the actual text (name, address, etc.) is still ASCII, but there are codes in a header at the beginning of the file and codes are often embedded throughout the file. If you were to open a spreadsheet, database or graphics file with a text editor, it will generally display what appears like garble onscreen.

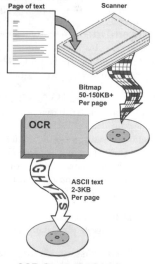

**OCR Creates ASCII Text**
When text documents are scanned, they are "photographed" and stored as pictures in the computer. OCR software analyzes the symbols in the image and converts each letter and digit into an ASCII character.

Users familiar with DOS have often experienced this when using the Type command to display the contents of a file that was not just plain text. For example, if you were to "Type" one of the WMF picture files in this Encyclopedia, such as

`C:\CDE\PICTURES`**type x86.wmf**

you would get an erratic display and lots of beeps, because many of the codes in the file coincidentally contain the same binary patterns as line feeds, returns and the bell character, which are all ASCII control characters (see *ASCII chart*). The terms ASCII file, ASCII text file, text file and TXT file are synonymous. Contrast with *binary file*.

**ASCII protocol**    The simplest communications protocol for text. It transmits only ASCII characters and uses ASCII control codes. It implies little or no error checking.

**ASCII sort**    The sequential order of ASCII data. In ASCII code, lowercase characters follow uppercase. True ASCII order would put the words DATA, data and SYSTEM into the following sequence:

`DATA    SYSTEM    data`

**ASCII terminal**    A simple input/output device that transmits and receives ASCII data. See *dumb terminal*.

**ASCII text**    Alphanumeric characters that are not in any proprietary file format. See *ASCII file*.

**ASCII transfer**    Transmitting ASCII data rather than program files, images and other nontextual data. Contrast with *binary transfer*.

**ASCII value**    The numerical value, or order, of an ASCII character. There are 128 standard ASCII characters, numbered from 0 to 127. Extended ASCII adds another 128 values and goes to 255. The numbers are typically represented in decimal (see *ASCII chart*) or in hexadecimal (see *hex chart*).

**ASF**    (Active Streaming Format) Microsoft's streaming media format, which supports audio, video, slide shows and synchronized events. ASF is used in Microsoft's NetShow, a utility for receiving audio, video and live broadcasts over the Internet. There are two file types associated with this format. An .asx file is used to signal the Web browser to call Windows Media Player and load an .asf file, which contains the streaming content. See *NetShow*, *Windows Media Player*, *streaming audio* and *streaming video*.

**Ashton-Tate**    A software company founded in 1980 by Hal Lashlee and George Tate to market dBASE II, which was created by Wayne Ratliff. The company developed and acquired other products, including Framework, MultiMate and dBASE Mac. In the mid 1980s, Ashton-Tate was one of the hottest software companies in the personal computer business. In 1991, it was acquired by Borland, which dispensed with all products except dBASE.

**ASIC**    (Application Specific Integrated Circuit) Pronounced "A-sick." A chip that is custom designed for a specific application rather than a general-purpose chip such as a microprocessor. The use of ASICs improve performance over general-purpose CPUs, because ASICs are "hardwired" to do a specific job and do not incur the overhead of fetching and interpreting stored instructions. An ASIC chip performs an electronic operation as fast as it is possible to do so, providing, of course, that the circuit design is efficiently architected.

There are many varieties of ASIC manufacturing, including custom built circuits from scratch, which is the most time consuming and complicated, to using gate arrays, standard cells and programmable logic devices. See *gate array*, *standard cell*, *PLD*, *CSIC* and *ASSP*.

**askSam**    A text management system for PCs from askSam Systems, Perry, FL (www.asksam.com). It holds unstructured text as well as standard data fields. The product is noted for its flexible text retrieval and hypertext capabilities.

**ASM**    (1) (Association for Systems Management) An international membership organization based in Cleveland, Ohio. Founded in 1947 and disbanded in 1996, it sponsored conferences in all phases of administrative systems and management.

(2) The file extension for assembly language source programs.

**ASMP**    (ASymmetric MultiProcessing) A multiprocessing design in which each CPU is assigned a particular program or part of a program that it executes for the duration of the session. Contrast with *SMP*, in which all the CPUs function as a single resource pool and take on whatever tasks need to be processed next. See *MPP*.

**ASN** (1) (**A**utonomous **S**ystem **N**umber) A unique identifier of an autonomous system on the Internet. More than 7,000 ASNs have been assigned to ISPs and NSPs. ISPs usually have only one ASN, but NSPs may have more than one. ASNs are maintained in the Routing Arbiter Database (RADB). See *autonomous system*, *ISP* and *NSP*.

(2) (**A**dvance **S**hip **N**otice) A notice sent by the vendor to the customer indicating what merchandise has been shipped. It enables the receiver to identify a package's contents electronically without having to open it.

**ASN.1** (**A**bstract **S**yntax **N**otation.**1**) An international standard for classifying data structures. There are 27 data types with tag values starting with 1; for example, Boolean (1), integer (2), and bit string (3). ASN.1 is widely used in ground and cellular telecommunications and aviation.

ASN.1 uses additional rules to lay out the physical data, the primary set being the Basic Encoding Rules (BERs), which are often considered synonymous with ASN.1. Distinguished Encoding Rules (DER) are used for encrypted applications, and Canonical Encoding Rules (CER) is a DER derivative that is not widely used. Packed Encoding Rules (PER) result in the fewest number of bytes.

**ASP** (1) (**A**pplication **S**ervice **P**rovider) An organization that hosts software applications on its own servers within its own facilities. Customers rent the use of the application and access it over the Internet or via a private line connection. Also called a "commercial service provider." With the advent of the Web browser as the universal client interface, the ASP market is expected to grow rapidly. See *Web-based application* and *service bureau*.

(2) (**A**ctive **S**erver **P**age) A Web server technology from Microsoft that allows for the creation of dynamic, interactive sessions with the user. An ASP is a Web page that contains HTML and embedded programming code written in VBScript or Jscript. It was introduced with Version 3.0 of Microsoft's Internet Information Server (IIS). When IIS encounters an ASP page requested by the browser, it executes the embedded program. ASPs are Microsoft's alternative to CGI scripts and JavaServer Pages (JSPs), which allow Web pages to interact with databases and other programs. Third-party products add ASP capability to non-Microsoft Web servers. The Active Server Page technology is an ISAPI program, and ASP documents use an .ASP extension.

ASP.NET (also ASP+) is an enhanced version of ASP for the .NET platform. It supports executable programs compiled from C#, C++ and other languages and is not backward compatible with regular ASP code. See *CGI script*, *JSP* and *ISAPI*.

(3) (**A**ssociation of **S**hareware **P**rofessionals, Muskegon, MI, www.asp-shareware.org) A trade organization for shareware founded in 1987. Author members submit products to ASP, which are approved, virus checked and distributed monthly via CD to member vendors. CDs are periodically made available to the public.

(4) (**A**nalog **S**ignal **P**rocessing) Processing signals completely within the analog domain. Contrast with *DSP*.

(5) (**A**verage **S**elling **P**rice) The sum of all the prices of a group of products divided by the number of products used in the list.

**ASP+** (**A**ctive **S**erver **P**age **+**) See *ASP*.

**aspect ratio** The ratio of width to height of an object. The aspect ratio of the screen of a standard computer monitor and TV set is 4:3. The high-definition TV (HDTV) format is 16:9.

**ASPI** (**A**dvanced **SCSI** **P**rogramming **I**nterface) An interface specification developed by Adaptec, Inc., Milpitas, CA, that provides a common language between drivers and SCSI host adapters. Drivers written to the ASPI interface can access peripherals that reside on different versions of SCSI host adapter hardware.

**ASP Industry Consortium** (**A**pplication **S**ervice **P**rovider Industry Consortium, Wakefield, MA, www.aspindustry.org) A trade organization founded in 1999 dedicated to research and standards in the application service provider (ASP) industry.

**ASP.NET** See *ASP*.

**assembler** Software that translates assembly language into machine language. Contrast with *compiler*, which is used to translate a high-level language, such as COBOL or C, into assembly language first and then into machine language.

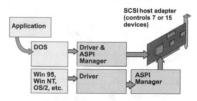

**The ASPI Interface**
The ASPI Manager is the software that supports the ASPI interface. ASPI drivers call ASPI functions to access SCSI peripherals. The ASPI Manager for the SCSI host adapter processes these function calls and generates the appropriate SCSI commands to the SCSI peripherals. In DOS, the driver and ASPI Manager are combined in one module.

---

**assembly language**    A programming language that is one step away from machine language. Each assembly language statement is translated into one machine instruction by the assembler. Programmers must be well versed in the computer's architecture, and, undocumented assembly language programs are difficult to maintain. It is hardware dependent; there is a different assembly language for each CPU series.

In the past, control programs (operating systems, database managers, etc.) were written in assembly language to maximize the machine's performance. Today, C is often used instead. Like assembly language, C can manipulate the bits at the machine level, but it is also portable to different computer platforms. There are C compilers for most computers.

Although often used synonomously, assembly language and machine language are not the same. Assembly language is turned into machine language. For example, the assembly instruction  COMPARE A,B  is translated into COMPARE contents of memory bytes 2340–2350 with 4567–4577 (where A and B happen to be located). The physical binary format of the machine instruction is specific to the computer it's running in.

Assembly languages are quite different between computers as is evident in the example below, which takes 16 lines of code for the mini and 82 lines for the micro. The example changes Fahrenheit to Celsius.

**PC (Intel x86)**

```
cseg    segment para public 'CODE'
        assume  cs:cseg,ds:cseg
start:
        jmp     start1
msgstr  db      'Enter Fahrenheit '
crlf    db      13,10,'$'
nine    db      9
five    db      5
outstr  db      'Centrigrade is $'
start1: push    ds
        push    cs
        pop     ds
        mov     dx,offset cseg:msgstr
        mov     ah,9
        int     21h
sloop:
cent:   call    getnumb
        test    ax,ax
        je      exit
        push    ax
        mov     dx,offset cseg:outstr
        mov     ah,9
        int     21h
        pop     ax
        sub     ax,32
        jns     c1
        push    ax
        mov     dl,'-'
        mov     ah,6
        int     21h
        pop     ax
        neg     ax
c1:     mul     five
        div     nine
        call    putval
        mov     dx,offset cseg:crlf
        mov     ah,9
        int     21h
        jmp     sloop
exit:   pop     ds
        mov     ah,4ch
        int     21h
getnumb:
        xor     bx,bx
```

**HP 3000**

```
begin
intrinsic  read,print,binary,ascii;
array buffer(0:17);
array string(0:3);
byte array b'string(*) = string;
integer ftemp, ctemp, len;
  move buffer:= "Enter Fahrenheit ";
  print (buffer,-30,%320);
  len:=read (string,-4);
  ftemp:= binary(b'string,len);
  ctemp:= (ftemp-32) * 5 / 9;
  len:= ascii(ctemp,1-,b'string);
  move buffer:= "Celsius is ";
  move buffer(14) := string, (-len);
  print (buffer,-32,%0);
end
```

**PC (Intel x86)** *(continued)*

```
llp:     mov     dl,0ffh
         mov     ah,1
         int     21h
         cmp     al,0dh
         je      llr
         sub     al,'0'
         jb      llr
         cmp     al,'9'
         ja      llr
         xor     ah,ah
         shl     bx,1
         add     ax,bx
         shl     bx,1
         shl     bx,1
         add     bx,ax
         jmp     llp
llr:     mov     dx,offset cseg:crlf
         mov     ah,9
         int     21h
         mov     ax,bx
         ret
putval:  xor     bx,bx
         push    bx
         mov     bx,10
llg:     xor     dx,dx
         div     bx
         add     dx,'0'
         push    dx
         test    ax,ax
         jne     llg
bloop:   pop     dx
         test    dx,dx
         je      endx
         mov     ah,6
         int     21h
         jmp     bloop
endx:    ret
cseg     ends
         end     start
```

**assignment statement**  In programming, a compiler directive that places a value into a variable. For example, **counter=0** creates a variable named counter and fills it with zeros. The VARIABLE=VALUE syntax is common among programming languages.

**associative storage**  Same as "content addressable memory." See *CAM*.

**asymmetric**  A difference between two opposing modes. It typically refers to a speed disparity. For example, in asymmetric operations, it takes longer to compress and encrypt data than to decompress and decrypt it. Contrast with *symmetric*. See *asymmetric compression* and *public key cryptography*.

**asymmetric compression**  A data compression technique that typically takes more time to compress than it does to decompress. Some asymmetric compression methods take longer to decompress, which would be suited for backup files that are constantly being compressed and rarely decompressed. Contrast with *symmetric compression*.

**asymmetric encryption**  Same as *public key cryptography*.

**asymmetric modem**  A full-duplex modem that transmits data in one direction at one speed and simultaneously in the other direction at another speed. Contrast with *ping pong*. See *V.90*.

**asymmetric multiprocessing**  See *ASMP*.

**asymmetric system**  (1) A system in which major components or properties are different.
(2) In video compression, a system that requires more equipment to compress the data than to decompress it.

**asynchronous**  Refers to events that are not synchronized, or coordinated, in time. The following are considered asynchronous operations. The interval between transmitting A and B is not the same as between B and C. The ability to initiate a transmission at either end. The ability to store and forward messages. Starting the next operation before the current one is completed. Contrast with *synchronous*.

**asynchronous communications server**  See *ACS*.

**asynchronous I/O**  Overlapping input and output with processing. Both the hardware and the software must be designed for this capability. The peripherals must be able to run independent of the CPU, and the software must be designed to manage it.

**asynchronous protocol**  A communications protocol that controls an asynchronous transmission, for example, ASCII, TTY, Kermit and Xmodem. Contrast with *synchronous protocol*.

**asynchronous transfer mode**  See *ATM*.

**asynchronous transmission**    The transmission of data in which each character is a self-contained unit with its own start and stop bits. Intervals between characters may be uneven. It is the common method of transmission between a computer and a modem, although the modem may switch to synchronous transmission to communicate with the other modem. Also called "start/stop transmission." Contrast with *synchronous transmission*.

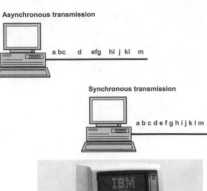

**AT**    (Advanced Technology) IBM's first 286-based PC, introduced in 1984. It was the most advanced machine in the PC line and featured a new keyboard, 1.2MB floppy and 16-bit data bus. AT-class machines run considerably faster than XTs (8088-based PCs). See *PC*.

**AT&T**    (American Telephone & Telegraph Company, New York, www.att.com) The largest long distance carrier in the U.S. It was founded in 1885 and was once the largest corporation in America. On January 1, 1984, it was relieved of its operating telephone companies by Federal court order. AT&T has gone through a major change from the world's largest monopoly to a competitive enterprise. Although it dabbled in the PC market for a while, its ventures with computers were never triumphant. In 1991, it acquired NCR, one of the first computer companies, which it renamed AT&T GIS, only to spin it back off five years later.

In 1996, intentionally this time, AT&T divided itself into three independent companies: (1) AT&T for telecommunications, (2) Lucent Technologies for manufacturing and (3) AT&T GIS for computers, which it renamed back to NCR. See *Lucent* and *NCR*.

**IBM AT**
The fastest PC in 1984. Users were amazed at the extraordinary speed of the 286 with its huge 20MB hard disk. *(Image courtesy of International Business Machines Corporation. Unauthorized use not permitted.)*

**AT&T WorldNet**    One of the world's largest Internet service providers, providing dial-up access to the Net in more than 700 cities and 150 countries. To get started with the service, customers must download an application from the company's Web site at www.att.com/worldnet.

**ATA**    (AT Attachment) The specification for IDE drives. See *IDE*.

**ATA-100**    See *Ultra ATA*.

**ATA-2**    Enhancements to the ATA specification that increased transfer rates. See *IDE*.

**ATA-3**    Enhancements to the ATA-2 specification that added improvements to the interface and included the S.M.A.R.T. monitoring capability. See *IDE* and *S.M.A.R.T.*.

**ATA-33**    See *Ultra ATA*.

**ATA-4**    Enhancements to the ATA-3 specification that increased transfer rates to 33 Mbytes/sec. See *IDE*.

**ATA-66**    See *Ultra ATA*.

**ATA drive**    The formal name for an IDE drive. See *IDE*.

**ATA Flash**    See *flash memory*.

**ATAPI**    (AT Attachment Packet Interface) The specification for IDE tape drives and CD-ROMs. See *IDE*.

**ATA RAID**    Using ATA (IDE) drives in a high-performance and/or fault tolerant configuration. See *RAID*.

**Atari**    Atari Computer was a video game manufacturer founded in 1972 in Sunnyvale, CA, by Nolan Bushnell, who named the company after a word used in the Japanese game of Go. Atari became famous for "Pong," a video game that simulated Ping-Pong on TV. In 1976, Atari was sold to Warner Communications, which came out with a game computer dubbed the Atari Video Computer System. In 1978, the Atari 400 and 800 home computers were introduced and became successful. Later came the 600XL and 1200XL models.

In 1984, Atari was sold to Jack Tramiel and investors, which introduced the ST personal computer line in 1985 to compete with the Macintosh. The STs were advanced machines that were available into the 1990s, but although popular, they received limited application support. Atari made attempts at offering IBM-compatible PCs, but failed in that arena. In late 1992, Atari introduced the Falcon multimedia computer, but soon shut down its R&D. At the end of 1993, it introduced the Jaguar video game, but sales were not sufficient to continue. In 1996, Atari merged with JTS Corporation, a San Jose-based manufacturer of hard disks. In 1998, Hasbro acquired the Atari name and intellectual property rights from JTS.

**AT bus**     Refers to the 16-bit bus introduced with the IBM AT. It was an early term for the ISA bus.

**AT command set**     A series of machine instructions used to activate features on an intelligent modem. Developed by Hayes Microcomputer Products and officially known as the Hayes Standard AT Command Set, it is used entirely or partially by most every modem manufacturer. AT is a mnemonic code for **AT**tention, which is the prefix that initiates each command to the modem. See *Hayes Smartmodem*.

**ATE**     (Automatic Test Equipment) Machines that test electronic systems, primarily chips. See *EDA* and *DTA*.

**Athlon**     A Pentium III-class CPU chip from AMD. The first models were introduced in 1999 with clock speeds from 500MHz to 650MHz. Subsequent models have exceeded 1GHz. Using a 200MHz system bus, the Athlon contains the MMX multimedia instructions used in Pentium MMX and Pentium II CPUs, along with an enhanced version of AMD's 3DNow 3-D instruction set for faster rendering of games and animation.

The Athlon plugs into a slot, known as Slot A, which is similar to the elongated slot used by Pentium II's and III's. The Athlon is the successor to the K6 series and was formerly known as the K7. See *K6* and *Hammer*.

**ATL**     (Active Template Library) A set of software routines from Microsoft that provide the basic framework for creating ActiveX and COM objects. Stemming from the standard template library (STL) that comes with C++ compilers, ATL includes an object wizard that sets up primary structure of the objects very quickly. See *COM* and *ActiveX*.

**ATM**     (1) See also *ATM machine* and *Adobe Type Manager*.

(2) (Asynchronous Transfer Mode) A network technology for both local and wide area networks (LANs and WANs) that supports realtime voice and video and data. The topology uses switches that establish a logical circuit from end to end, which guarantees quality of service (QoS). However, unlike telephone switches that dedicate circuits end to end, unused bandwidth in ATM's logical circuits can be appropriated when needed. For example, idle bandwidth in a videoconference circuit can be used to transfer data.

ATM is widely used as a backbone technology in carrier networks and large enterprises, but never became popular as a local network (LAN) topology. ATM is highly scalable and supports transmission speeds of 1.5, 25, 100, 155, 622, 2488 and 9953 Mbps (see *OC*). ATM is also running as slow as 9.6 Kbps between ships at sea. An ATM switch can be added into the middle of a switch fabric to enhance total capacity, and the new switch is automatically updated using ATM's PNNI routing protocol.

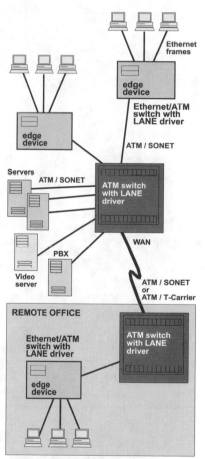

ATM / SONET = ATM cells within SONET frames
ATM / T-Carrier = ATM cells within T1 or T3 frames

**ATM in the Enterprise**
This shows how ATM is used as a network backbone or "switch fabric" within the enterprise. The edge device is an Ethernet workgroup switch with a high-speed ATM link. It converts LAN packets into ATM cells and vice versa.

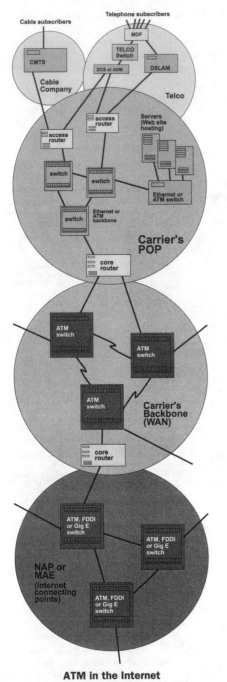

## Cell Switching

ATM works by transmitting all traffic as fixed-length, 53-byte cells. This fixed unit allows very fast switches to be built, because it is much faster to process a known packet size than to figure out the start and end of variable length packets. The small ATM packet also ensures that voice and video can be inserted into the stream often enough for realtime transmission.

ATM works at layer 2 of the OSI model and typically uses SONET (OC-3, OC-12, etc.) for framing and error correction out over the wire. ATM switches convert cells to SONET frames and frames to cells at the port interface.

## Quality of Service (Qos)

The ability to specify a quality of service is one of ATM's most important features, allowing voice and video to be transmitted smoothly. The following levels of service are available:

Constant Bit Rate (CBR) guarantees bandwidth for realtime voice and video.

Realtime variable Bit Rate (rt-VBR) supports interactive multimedia that requires minimal delays, and non-realtime variable bit rate (nrt-VBR) is used for bursty transaction traffic.

**ATM in the Internet**
ATM is widely used as by large carriers and ISPs. It serves as the backbone between points of presence (POPs), and it is also used at the NAP and MAE interconnecting points.

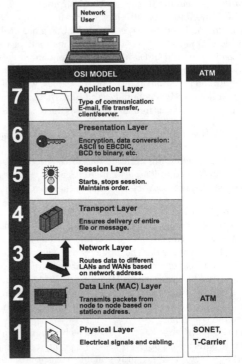

**Where ATM Fits In**
ATM performs its functions at layer 2 of the OSI model and converts its cells into SONET frames (OC-3, OC-12, etc.) or T-carrier frames (DS1, DS3) to go our over the wire.

Available Bit Rate (ABR) adjusts bandwidth according to congestion levels for LAN traffic. Unspecified Bit Rate (UBR) provides a best effort for non-critical data such as file transfers.

**Integration with Legacy LANs**   Network applications use protocols, such as TCP/IP, IPX, AppleTalk and DECnet, and there are tens of millions of Ethernet and Token Ring clients in existence. ATM has to coexist with these legacy protocols and networks. MPOA is an ATM standard that routes legacy protocols while preserving ATM quality of service.

LANE (LAN Emulation) interconnects legacy LANs by encapsulating Ethernet and Token Ring frames into LANE packets and then converting them into ATM cells. It supports existing protocols without changes to Ethernet and Token Ring clients, but uses MPOA route servers or traditional routers for internetworking between LAN segments.

**History of ATM**   When ATM came on the scene in the early 1990s, it was thought to be the beginning of a new era in networking, because it was both a LAN and WAN technology that could start at the desktop and go straight through to the remote office. In addition, ATM's ability to provide quality of service from end to end was highly praised as the perfect transport protocol for multimedia. ATM's roots come from the telephone company, which has delivered the highest quality communications.

However, ATM never become the magic end to end solution. ATM adapters for desktop PCs were expensive, and the standards for interconnecting existing networks to an ATM backbone were confusing and often delayed. When Gigabit Ethernet was announced, providing a 10 times increase in speed and a familiar technology, ATM's demise in the local area network arena seemed assured.

ATM's success has always been in the carrier's network. It has been successfully deployed by major ISPs and telecom carriers and large private enterprises. It continues to be installed for mission critical backbones because of its quality of service (QoS).

**ATM Forum**   A membership organization founded in 1991 to promote ATM networking technology. It works with ANSI and the ITU to set standards. Its first specification in 1992 defined the User-Network Interface (UNI). Technical committees work on various projects in order to accelerate standards.

**ATM machine**   (Automatic Teller Machine machine)  A banking terminal that accepts deposits and dispenses cash. ATMs are activated by inserting a cash or credit card that contains the user's account number and PIN on a magnetic stripe. The ATM calls up the bank's computers to verify the balance, dispenses the cash and then transmits a completed transaction notice. The word "machine" in the term "ATM machine" is certainly redundant, but widely used.

**ATM NIC**   A network interface card (NIC) that transmits and receives Asynchronous Transfer Mode traffic. It is plugged into the bus of a client station or server.

**atom**   In list processing languages, a single element in a list.

**atomic**   Indivisible. An atomic operation, or atomicity, implies an operation that must be performed entirely or not at all. For example, if machine failure prevents a transaction to be processed to completion, the system will be rolled back to the start of the transaction. See *two-phase commit*.

**atomic force microscope**   A device used to detect atoms in a molecule. In 1992, IBM demonstrated a prototype atomic force microscope for recording data. Its pyramid-shaped tip was heated by a laser and pressed against the surface of a disk to form an indentation (a bit). Such a device might be capable of storing 30 billion bits per square inch in the future.

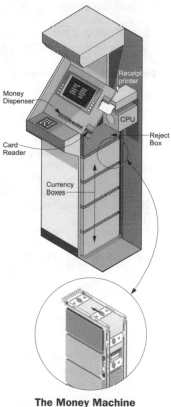

**The Money Machine**
Rubber rollers move one bill at a time from the currency box (each holds about 2,000 bills) to the dispenser area. A sensor determines if two or more bills are stuck together or if the wrong denomination was pulled and causes them to be inserted into the reject box.

**ATRAC3**    An audio compression technology from Sony that provides multiple ratios depending on desired sound quality. At 132 Kbps, the music can be compressed to approximately 10% of the space used by a CD. See *OpenMG*.

**ATSC**    (Advanced Television Systems Committee) An organization founded in 1983 to research and develop a digital TV standard for the U.S. For several years, the ATSC worked closely with ACATS, the FCC's own advisory committee, which later disbanded. In late 1996, the FCC adopted the ATSC standard, which is the digital counterpart of the NTSC standard. For information, visit www.atsc.org. See *ACATS* and *NTSC*.

**at sign**    The at sign (@), which is shorthand for the word "at," has become very popular due to its use in Internet e-mail addresses. It separates the recipient's name from the domain name. See *Internet address*.

**attach a file**    To link a file to an e-mail message so that they travel to their destination together. Any type of file can be attached; for example, a database, spreadsheet, graphics or program file. Even a text file that might elaborate more on the message being sent can be attached. See *how to transfer a file over the Internet*.

**attached document**    See *e-mail attachment*.

**attached processor**    An additional CPU connected to the primary CPU in a multiprocessing environment. It operates as an extension of the primary CPU and shares the system software and peripheral devices.

**attachment**    See *attach a file*.

**attenuation**    Loss of signal power in a transmission.

**atto**    Quintillionth (10 to the –18th power). See *space/time*.

**attribute**    (1) In relational database management, a field within a record.

(2) For printers and display screens, a characteristic that changes a font, for example, from normal to boldface or underlined, or from normal to reverse video.

(3) In an XML document, a subelement defined within an element. In the following example, GENDER and AGE are attributes within the PERSON element:

```
person gender"male" age"36"
   firstNameBob/firstName
   lastNameWhite/lastName
/person
```

(4) See *file attribute*.

**ATV**    (Advanced TV) An early name for the digital TV standard proposed by the Advisory Committee on Advanced Television Service (ACATS). See *digital TV* and *ATV Forum*.

**ATVEF**    (Advanced TeleVision Enhancement Forum, www.atvef.com) A consortium of broadcast, cable and computer companies founded in 1998 that developed the ATVEF Enhanced Content Specification, an HTML and JavaScript-based format for adding content to interactive TV. ATVEF closed at the end of 1999 and turned over the specification to the ATV Forum and SMPTE.

In its short year and a half history, ATVEF compiled a collection of intellectual property from its members about interactive TV that provides a wealth of information about content creation and distribution. After ATVEF's closing, this technology continued to be made available from ATVEF Licensing LLC in Boulder, CO. See *ATV Forum*.

**ATV Forum**    (Advanced TV Forum, Witchita, KS, www.atvf.com) A membership association founded in 2000 that promotes interactive TV. It supports the Enhanced Content Specification originally developed by the Advanced Television Enhanced Forum (ATVEF). Under SMPTE, the specification is known as Declarative Content Standard (DCS). The specification provides an HTML and JavaScript delivery mechanism for adding content to interactive TV programs. It uses IP multicast over the vertical blanking interval for analog TV and data carousels for digital transmission. See *ATVEF*, *Intercast* and *vertical blanking interval*.

**ATX motherboard**   A motherboard that superseded the widely-used Baby AT design. ATX rotates the CPU and memory 90 degrees, allowing full-length boards in all sockets. The power supply blows air over the CPU rather than pulling air through the chassis. The Micro ATX is a smaller version of the ATX with fewer slots. See *Baby AT motherboard*.

**audio**   The range of frequencies within human hearing (approx. 20Hz at the low to a high of 20,000Hz).

Traditional audio devices are analog, because they handle sound waves in an analogous form. Radios maintain the audio signal as rippling waves from antenna to speaker. Sound waves are "carved" into plastic phonograph records, and audio tape records sound as magnetic waves.

Audio is processed in a computer by converting the analog signal into a digital code using various techniques, such as PCM. See *RealAudio*.

**audio adapter**   Same as *sound card*.

**audio board**   Same as *sound card*.

**audio card**   Same as *sound card*.

**audio cassette**   The common 1/8" inch tape module used in portable music players, home stereos and car radio/tape systems. Sound is recorded in analog format on audio cassettes. See *cassette*.

**audiocast**   See *streaming audio*.

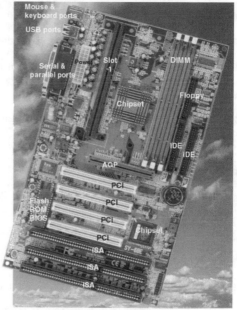

**The ATX Motherboard**
The motherboard glues all the components together via its various slots. Slot 1 is for the CPU. DIMM slots hold memory modules, and the AGP, PCI and ISA slots hold the various adapter cards. Control for the IDE and floppy disk drives as well as the USB, mouse, keyboard and serial and parallel ports are built in.
*(Image courtesy of Soyotek, Inc.)*

**audio CD**   The music compact disc (CD) format that has replaced the phonograph record. Starting in the early 1990s, certain stereo amplifiers and receivers came on the market without a phono input, making the definitive statement that analog phonograph records were history! See *CD* and *Red Book*.

**audio codec**   A hardware circuit (chip) or software routine that converts sound into digital code and vice versa. The first step is to convert the analog sound into digital samples, using PCM or ADPCM. The next step is to use perceptual audio codin to further compress the amount of digital data. If the codec is specialized for human voice, it is known as a speech codec, voice codec or vocoder. See *audio compression*, *speech codec* and *perceptual audio coding*.

**audio compression**   Encoding digital audio data to take up less storage space and transmission bandwidth. Audio compression typically uses lossy methods, which eliminate bits that are not restored at the other end. ADPCM and MP3 are examples of audio compression methods. See *audio codec* and *data compression*.

**audioconferencing**   An audio communications session among three or more people that are geographically dispersed. It is provided by a conference function in a PBX or multiline telephone or by the telephone companies. See *voice chat*, *videoconferencing* and *data conferencing*.

**audio disc**   See *CD*.

**audiographics**   Realtime data conferencing combined with audio capability. See *data conferencing* and *T.120*.

**audio on demand**    The ability to start delivering an audio program to an individual Web browser whenever the user requests it. See *streaming audio*.

**audio response**    See *voice response*.

**audio ripper**    Software that extracts raw audio data from a music CD. See *MP3*.

**audio scrubbing**    Playing back a section of an audio file by highlighting the particular waveforms. The term was coined in the days of audio tape when moving manually moving the reels back and forth looked like the tape was being scrubbed. See *data scrubbing*.

**audio server**    A computer that delivers streaming audio for audio on demand applications. Audio servers may be computers that are specialized for this purpose. The term may just refer to the software that performs this service. See *streaming audio*.

**audio streaming**    See *streaming audio*.

**audiotex**    A voice response application that allows users to enter and retrieve information over the telephone. See *IVR*.

**audio video**    See *A/V*.

**audiovisual**    See *A/V*.

**audit**    An examination of systems, programming and datacenter procedures in order to determine the efficiency of computer operations.

**audit software**    Specialized programs that perform a variety of audit functions, such as sampling databases and generating confirmation letters to customers and vendors. It can highlight exceptions to categories of data and alert the examiner to possible error. Audit software often includes a nonprocedural language that lets the auditor describe the computer and data environment without detailed programming. See *EDP audit*.

**audit trail**    A record of transactions in an information system that provides verification of the activity of the system. The simplest audit trail is the transaction itself. If a person's salary is increased, the change transaction includes the date, amount of raise and name of authorizing manager.

A more elaborate audit trail can be created when the system is being verified for accuracy; for example, samples of processing results can be recorded at various stages. Item counts and hash totals are used to verify that all input has been processed through the system.

An audit trail can contain a record of any activity whatsoever, but a record of routine queries and many other authorized activites is generally not maintained. Such general activity monitoring is very useful when attempting to track a hacker or mischievous employee. See *security*.

**AU file**    (AUdio file) A digital audio file format from Sun that is used on the Internet and can be played by a Java program. It provides toll-quality sound and uses the .AU extension. It generally uses the μ-Law (mu-Law) encoding method, and raw μ-Law files and AU files are the same except for the file header.

**augmented reality**    See *mixed reality*.

**AUI**    (Attachment Unit Interface) The network interface used with standard Ethernet. On the adapter card, it is a 15-pin socket. A transceiver, which taps into the Ethernet cable, plugs into the socket. See *10Base5*.

**AUP**    See *acceptable use policy*.

**authentication**    Verifying the identity of a user that is logging onto a computer system or verifying the integrity of a transmitted message. See *password*, *digital signature*, *IP spoofing* and *biometrics*.

**authentication token**     A security device given to authorized users who keep them in their possession. To log onto the network, the card may be read directly like a credit card, or it may display a changing number that is typed in as a password. See *SecurID card*.

**authoring language**     See *authoring program*.

**authoring program**     Software that allows for the creation of tutorials, CBT courseware, Web sites, CD-ROMs and other interactive programs. Authoring packages generally provide high-level visual tools that enable a complete system to be designed without writing any programming code, although a proprietary authoring language may also be included. See *Web authoring software* and *HTML editor*.

**authorization code**     An identification number or password that is used to gain access to a local or remote computer system.

**Authorware**     A popular multimedia authoring program from Macromedia that is widely used for creating interactive learning programs on Windows and Macintosh.

**auto**     (AUTOmatic) Refers to a wide variety of devices that perform unattended operation.

**auto answer**     (1) A modem feature that accepts a telephone call and establishes the connection. See *auto dial*.
    (2) A cellphone feature that answers the call after some number of rings, allowing you to use a headset and receive a call without manual intervention.

**auto attendant**     The part of an interactive voice response (IVR) system that replaces the human operator and directs callers to the appropriate extensions or voice mailboxes. See *IVR*.

**auto baud detect**     A modem feature that detects the highest speed of the called modem and switches to it.

**auto bypass**     The ability to bypass a terminal or other device in a network if it fails, allowing the remaining devices to continue functioning.

**AutoCAD**     A full-featured CAD program from Autodesk that runs on PCs, VAXs, Macs and UNIX workstations. Originally developed for CP/M machines, it was one of the first major CAD programs for personal computers and became an industry standard. There are countless third-party add-on packages that are available for AutoCAD, and most graphics applications import and export AutoCAD's native DXF file format. AutoCAD LT is an entry-level version of AutoCAD that runs under Win 95/98 and NT. See *AutoSketch*.

**autochanger**     A mechanism that moves disks or tapes from a storage bin to a drive for reading (playing) and writing. See *tape library*, *CD-ROM changer* and *CD-ROM server*.

**autocoder**     An IBM assembly language for 1960s-vintage 1400 and 7000 series computers.

**auto complete**     A feature that lets you fill in the blanks faster when typing names and addresses you routinely use. Auto complete saves your text entries, and compares them with new entries. As soon as you type a few letters, it presents you with a list of possible candidates to choose. Auto complete is very useful for typing in names, addresses, credit card numbers and such when shopping online. Web browsers feature auto complete for typing in Web addresses (URLs).

**AutoCorrect**     A feature that corrects misspellings and makes other grammatical changes on the fly.

**Autodesk**     (Autodesk, Inc., San Rafael, CA, www.autodesk.com) A leading provider of computer-aided design (CAD) software, founded in 1982. It introduced AutoCAD in its first year, and three years later, became the first PC CAD company to go public. The company has since expanded its product line to include design software for multimedia and home improvement. The company has more than three million users in more than 150 countries, and its products are available in more than a dozen foreign languages. See *AutoCAD*.

**auto dial**   A modem feature that opens the line and dials the telephone number of another computer to establish connection. See *auto answer*.

**AUTODIN**   (**AUTO**matic **DI**gital Network) The worldwide communications network of the U.S. Defense Communications System.

**AUTOEXEC.BAT**   (**AUTO**matic **EXEC**ute **BAT**ch) A DOS batch file that is executed when the computer is started. The OS/2 counterpart is STARTUP.CMD. See *DOS AUTOEXEC.BAT*.

**autoflow**   Wrapping text around a graphic image or from one page to the next.

**Auto Insert Notification**   The option in Windows that turns the Autoplay feature on or off. Autoplay runs a program on a CD-ROM or plays a title on an audio CD as soon as the disc is inserted into the drive and the drive door is closed. Users may elect to prevent Autoplay by disabling Auto Insert Notification by double clicking the CD-ROM drive line in Device Manager and selecting the Settings tab. The file on the disc that Autoplay looks for is AUTORUN.INF. See *Device Manager*.

**auto line feed**   A feature that moves the cursor or print head to the next line when a CR (carriage return) is sensed. PCs put a LF (line feed) after the CR and do not use this feature. The Mac uses only a CR for end of line and requires it.

**AutoLISP**   An AutoCAD language used to create customized menus and routines.

**autoloader**   **(1)** A mechanism that inserts disk or tape into a drive sequentially. For example, a diskette duplicator autoloader holds a stack of floppies that are fed to the drive one after the other.
   **(2)** Same as *autochanger*.

**auto logon**   Performing the complete log-on sequence necessary to gain entry into a computer system without user intervention.

**automata theory**   An open-ended computer science discipline that concerns an abstract device called an "automaton," which performs a specific computational or recognition function. Networks of automata are designed to mimic human behavior.

**automate**   To turn a set of manual steps into an operation that goes by itself. See *automation*.

**automated provisioning**   The ability to set up new communications services for customers automatically. Carriers use automated provisioning to set up their network based on customers' requirements. Such systems control all network devices from a central console and greatly speed up deployment time from days to minutes. When automated provisioning is in place, customer self-service (user provisioning) can be implemented, which extends the backoffice interface to the customer. Customers can order, cancel and modify services over the Web. See *provisioning*.

**automatic data processing**   Same as *data processing*.

**automatic design optimization**   Using the computer to achieve the most efficient design of a product. Finite element analysis (FEA) and other methods are used. In the past, design engineers have performed a combination of manual and automated methods to accomplish design optimization. They have applied FEA to parts of a CAD drawing, determined what components needed work and then redrew the object manually. Increasingly, software that is tightly integrated with the CAD program can perform the analysis and automatically redraw the object. See *FEA*.

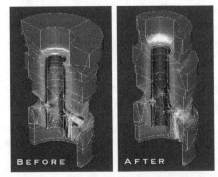

**Automatic Redraw**
PTC's Pro/MECHANICA, which does not use FEA, actually redraws the optimized image when it is used in conjunction with PTC's Pro/ENGINEER CAD software. It can also perform analysis on CAD files from other platforms without the automatic redraw. This picture shows the before and after views of an optimized fuel injector nozzle. *(Image courtesy of PTC.)*

**A**

**automatic feature negotiation**    The ability of a modem to determine and adjust to the speed, error control and data compression method of the modem at the other end of the line.

**automatic provisioning**    See *automated provisioning*.

**automatic vehicle location**    See *mobile positioning*.

**automation**    The replacement of manual operations by computerized methods. Office automation refers to integrating clerical tasks such as typing, filing and appointment scheduling. Factory automation refers to computer-driven assembly lines. See also *COM automation* and *tape library*.

**automation controller**    See *COM automation*.

**automation language**    A programming language, such as JavaScript or VBScript, which is used to automate procedures that might normally be done interactively from menus. See *scripting language*.

**automation product**    See *tape library*.

**automation server**    See *COM automation*.

**automotive systems**    See *embedded system*.

**automounting**    Making remote files available to a client at the time the file is accessed. Remote directories are associated with a local directory on the client ahead of time, and the mounting takes places the first time a remote file is opened by the client.

**A Vision of Automation, Artist Unknown, Circa 1895**
A hundred years ago, the concept of the future lacked one major ingredient... the computer! *(Image courtesy of Rosemont Engineering.)*

**autonegotiate**    To automatically determine the correct settings. The term is often used with communications and networking. For example, Ethernet 10/100 cards, hubs and switches can determine the highest speed of the node they are connected to and adjust their transmission rate accordingly.

**autonomous system**    A network that is administered by a single set of management rules that are controlled by one person, group or organization. Autonomous systems often use only one routing protocol, although multiple protocols can be used. The core of the Internet is made up many autonomous systems. See *ASN*, *routing protocol* and *path vector protocol*.

**Autoplay**    A feature that automatically starts playing an audio CD or runs a program when a disc is inserted into the drive. See *Auto Insert Notification*.

**autopolling**    (AUTOmatic POLLING) See *polling*.

**auto redial**    A modem, fax or telephone feature that redials a busy number a fixed number of times before giving up.

**auto refresh**    To retrieve, scan or display information at predescribed intervals. The term refers to a variety of concepts, but it implies that an operation is performed automatically over and over again such as retrieving the latest data from a news feed every five minutes.

**auto reliable**    A modem feature that enables it to send to a modem with or without built-in error detection and compression.

**autoresponder**    A mail utility that automatically sends a reply to an e-mail message. Autoresponders are used to send back boilerplate information on a topic without having the requester do anything more than e-mail a particular address. They are also used to send a confirmation that the message has been received.

**autorestart**    To be able to automatically restart a computer after a power failure or error condition.

**auto resume**    A feature that lets you stop working on the computer and take up where you left off at a later date without having to reload applications. Memory contents are stored on disk or kept active by battery and/or AC power.

**autorun**    See *Auto Insert Notification*.

**autosave**    Saving data to the disk at periodic intervals without user intervention.

**auto scroll**    To scroll by dragging the mouse pointer beyond the edge of the current window or screen. It is used to move around a virtual screen as well as to highlight text blocks and images that are larger than the current window.

**autosense**    To automatically determine the state or condition of something. See *autonegotiate*.

**autosizing**    The ability of a monitor to maintain the same rectangular image size when changing from one resolution to another.

**autostart routine**    Instructions built into the computer and activated when it is turned on. The routine performs diagnostic tests, such as checking the computer's memory, and then loads the operating system and passes control to it.

**autotrace**    A routine that converts a bitmap into a vector graphics image. It scans the bitmap and turns the dark areas into vectors (lines). Once a bitmap has been turned into vectors, individual components of the drawing can be scaled independently.

This process usually creates many more vectors than if the picture were drawn in a drawing program in the first place. In order to faithfully reproduce the original, the conversion routine will generate a vector for the slightest deviation in a line. However, extraneous vectors can be deleted afterwards.

**autotype**    **(1)** To automatically determine the type or configuration of a hardware model or elements within a program (variables).

**(2)** To automatically fill in the remainder of a name or address. See *auto complete*.

**A/UX**    Apple's version of UNIX for the Macintosh, which is based on AT&T's UNIX System V with Berkeley extensions. A/UX is no longer supported.

**AUX**    (AUXiliary) The DOS name for the first connected serial port. See **DOS device names**. See also *A/UX*.

**auxiliary memory**    A high-speed memory bank used in mainframes and supercomputers. It is not directly addressable by the CPU, rather it functions like a disk. Data is transferred from auxiliary memory to main memory over a high-bandwidth channel. See *auxiliary storage*.

**auxiliary storage**    External storage devices, such as disk and tape.

**A/V**    (Audio/Visual, Audio/Video) Refers to equipment used in audio and video applications, such as microphones, videotape machines (VCRs) and sound systems. See *AV drive*.

**availability**    The measurement of a system's uptime. See *uptime* and *high availability*.

**Avant Stellar keyboard**    A high-quality PC keyboard from Creative Vision Technologies, Inc., Hamel, MN, (www.cvtinc.com). The successor to the popular OmniKey keyboards developed by Northgate Computers, these keyboards have an exceptional feel that is missing on most PC keyboards. The Avant Stellar has function keys on the left and another set above, each of which can be programmed separately for keystroke combinations and macros. All keys can be remapped manually or via software.

**avatar**   An image you select or create to represent yourself in a 3-D chat site on the Web. In order to interact with these sites, you need a VRML plug-in. Avatar is a Sanskrit word that means the incarnation of a god on earth. See *VRML*.

**AVC**   (Audio Visual Connection) Multimedia software from IBM that works in conjunction with IBM's Audio Capture and Video Capture boards for the PS/2. It allows users to integrate sound and pictures into applications and includes an authoring language.

**AV drive**   (Audio Video drive) A hard disk drive that is optimized for audio and video applications. Transferring analog or digital audio and video signals (especially uncompressed video) onto a hard disk in realtime and playing back the data in realtime requires a drive that can maintain continuous reads and writes without interruption. Recording onto high-speed CD-R and similar optical media requires long, sustained transfers, although newer optical drives have a buffer that accomodates a certain amount of underrun.

   AV drives are designed to postpone thermal recalibration when reading and writing so that long data transfers will not be interrupted and frames will not be lost. See *underrun* and *thermal recalibration*.

**AVI**   (Audio Video Interleaved) A Windows multimedia video format from Microsoft. It interleaves standard waveform audio and digital video frames (bitmaps) to provide reduced animation at 15 fps at 160×120×8 resolution. Audio is 11,025Hz, 8-bit samples.

**avionics**   The electronic instrumentation and control equipment used in airplanes and space vehicles.

**AVL**   (Automatic Vehicle Location) See *mobile positioning*.

**Award BIOS**   A PC BIOS from Award Software, Inc., Los Gatos, CA, (www.award.com). Award BIOS chips have been installed in more than 50 million computers.

**AWC**   (Association for Women in Computing, San Francisco, CA, www.awc-hq.org) A membership organization, founded in 1978, dedicated to the advancement of women in computing. It publishes newsletters, hosts seminars and annual conferences and recognizes distinguished women in the field with its Augusta Ada Lovelace award.

**AWG**   (American Wiring Gauge) A U.S. measurement standard of the diameter of nonferrous wire, which includes copper and aluminum. The smaller the number, the thicker the wire. In general, the thicker the wire, the greater the current-carrying capacity and the longer the distance it can span.

   Wire used for communications typically ranges from 18 to 26 AWG. For electric service, number 10, 12 and 14 AWG wires are typically used from the electric panel to the outlets. Number 8 and 10 AWG are used for home appliances such as an electric range or dryer.

**AWGTHTGTTA**   Digispeak for "are we going to have to go through this again?"

**awk**   (Aho Weinberger Kernighan) A UNIX programming utility developed in 1977 by Alfred Aho, Peter Weinberger and Brian Kernighan. Due to its unique pattern-matching syntax, awk is often used in data retrieval and data transformation. Awk is widely used to search for a particular occurrence of text and perform some operation on it. Awk is an interpreted language, which has been ported to other computing environments, including DOS. See *Gawk*.

**AWT**   (Abstract Window Toolkit) A class library from Sun that provides an application framework and graphical user interface (GUI) routines for Java programmers. AWT was the

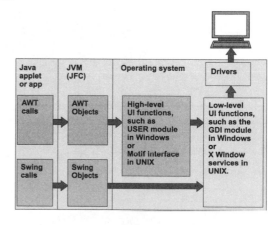

**AWT vs. Swing**
AWT calls the operating system at a higher level than Swing, and the AWT routines use native code. Swing was written entirely in Java and is platform independent.

first user interface development system included in the Java Foundation Classes (JFC). In 1997, Swing was introduced; it provides more capabilities and is written entirely in Java. See *JFC, AFC* and *IFC*.

**aXe**     (An X Editor) A text editor used with the X Window system. By adding widgits, aXe can be customized by the user.

**AYT**     Digispeak for "are you there?"

**azimuth**     The trajectory of an angle measured in degrees going clockwise from a base point. A disk azimuth alignment test checks for the correct positioning of the read/write head to the track.

**B** (**B**yte, **b**it) See *KB*, *MB*, *GB* and *TB*.

**B1** The computer system security level required by the Department of Defense (DOD). See *NCSC*.

**B2B** (**B**usiness to **B**usiness) Refers to one business communicating with or selling to another. See *B2B e-commerce* and *B2C*.

**B2B e-commerce** (**B**usiness to **B**usiness Electronic Commerce) Refers to one business selling to another business via the Web. According to the GarnetGroup, B2B e-commerce is expected to grow from $145 billion in 1999 to more than $7 trillion by 2004, which will represent more than 7% of all sales transactions worldwide. See *e-commerce*.

**B2B Web site** See *vertical portal*.

**B2C** (**B**usiness to **C**onsumer) Refers to a business communicating with or selling to an individual rather than a company. See *B2B*.

**Baan** (Baan Company, Herndon, VA, www.baan.com) A software company that specializes in enterprise wide applications. Founded in the Netherlands in 1978 by Jan and Paul Baan (pronounced "bon"), Baan has become a major ERP vendor operating in more than 80 countries. It supports UNIX, NT and AS/400 platforms.

**BaanERP** An ERP system from Baan that runs on UNIX, NT and the AS/400. It includes modules for manufacturing, financial, project estimating and management and distribution. BaanERP integrates with other Baan modules such as supply chain management. See *manufacturing software*.

**Baan IV** An integrated family of client/server applications from Baan. It included manufacturing, distribution, finance, transportation, service, project and features enterprise modeling via its Orgware modules. Earlier versions of the software were named TRITON. It later evolved into BaanERP, which is more modular and added components for procurement, order management and warehousing.

**Baby AT motherboard** A smaller motherboard (9"×10")

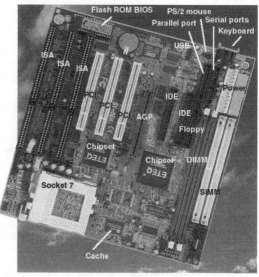

**Baby AT Motherboard**
This is the model SY-5EH motherboard from Soyotek, which is a later version of the original Baby AT. It includes support for DIMM memory, AGP adapters and USB, which came on the scene in the late 1990s. Socket 7 is used for Intel chips and x86 clones from companies such as AMD and Cyrix. *(Image courtesy of Soyotek, Inc.)*

that superseded the one used in the original IBM AT (12"×13.5"). The Baby AT motherboard has been widely used in 386, 486 and Pentium PCs. It was superseded by the ATX motherboard. See *ATX motherboard*.

**backbone**    In communications, the part of a network that handles the major traffic. It employs the highest-speed transmission paths in the network and may also run the longest distance. Smaller networks are attached to the backbone.

A backbone can span a large geographic area or be as small as a backplane in a single cabinet. See *collapsed backbone*.

**backdoor**    See *trapdoor*.

**back end**    The support components of a computer system. It typically refers to the database management system (DBMS), which is the storehouse for the data.

**back-end CASE**    CASE tools that generate program code. Contrast with *front-end CASE*.

**back end processor**    Same as *database machine*.

**backfile conversion**    Scanning older documents that reside in a file cabinet. Service bureaus specialize in this conversion process.

**background**    **(1)** The non-interactive processing in the computer. See *foreground/background*.

**(2)** The base, or backdrop color. In order to distinguish any image on screen, whether text or graphics, there must be a contrasting background color.

**background ink**    A highly reflective OCR ink used to print the parts of the form not recognized by a scanner.

**background noise**    An extraneous signal that has crept into a line, channel or circuit.

**background processing**    Processing in which the program is not visibly interacting with the user. Most personal computers use operating systems that run background tasks only when foreground tasks are idle, such as between keystrokes. Advanced multitasking operating systems let background programs be given any priority from low to high.

**backhaul**    **(1)** To transmit a telephone call or transmit data beyond its normal destination point and then back again in order to utilize available personnel (operators, agents, etc.) or network equipment that is not located at the destination location. For example, depending on distances and service arrangements, it might be cheaper to send a telephone call on a private line to a location way beyond the destination and then dial up the destination, which is back in the other direction.

**(2)** To transmit data from a remote site to a central site.

**backing storage**    Same as *auxiliary storage*.

**backlit**    An LCD screen that has its own light source from the back of the screen, making the background brighter and characters appear sharper.

**BackOffice**    A suite of network server software products from Microsoft that includes Windows NT Server, SQL Server, Systems Management Server (SMS), SNA Server and Mail Server.

**Back Orifice**    A program that installs itself on a Windows machine as a server, allowing a hacker with the client counterpart to manipulate the machine more completely than the user at the keyboard. It can come in the form of a Trojan horse or ActiveX control. Back Orifice 2000 (BO2K) provides access to Windows NT/2000 machines.

Back Orifice was created by "The Cult of the Dead Cow" (cDc), a hacker organization (www.cultdeadcow.com). There are various "BO removers," which are programs that detect and remove it. See **BO remover** and *Trojan horse*. See also *BackOffice*.

**backplane**    An interconnecting device that may or may not have intelligence, but typically has sockets that cards (boards) plug into. Although resistors may be used, a passive backplane adds no processing in the circuit. An intelligent backplane, or active backplane, may have microprocessor or controller-driven circuitry that adds a little or a lot of processing. See *bus*.

**backside bus**    A dedicated channel between the CPU and a level 2 cache. It typically runs at the full speed of the CPU, whereas the frontside bus generally runs slower. See *frontside bus*.

**backside cache**    A level 2 memory cache that has a dedicated channel to the CPU, enabling it to run at the full speed of the CPU. See *inline cache* and *lookaside cache*.

**backsolver**    See *solver*.

**back up**    To make a copy of important data onto a different storage medium for safety. See *backup*.

**backup**    Additional resources or duplicate copies of data on different storage media for emergency purposes. See *backup types* and *back up*.

**backup & recovery**    The combination of manual and machine procedures that can restore lost data in the event of hardware or software failure. Routine backup of databases and logs of computer activity are part of a backup & recovery program. See *checkpoint/restart*.

**backup copy**    A disk, tape or other machine readable copy of a data or program file. Making backup copies is a discipline most computer users learn the hard way—after a week's work is lost.

**backup disk**    A disk used to hold duplicate copies of important files. Floppy disks and disk cartridges are used for backup disks.

**backup power**    An additional power source that can be used in the event of power failure. See *UPS*.

**backup server**    A computer in a network designed to store copies of files from users' machines or other servers. It is generally RAID based with a large number of disk drives. See *RAID* and *SAN*.

**backup tape**    See *tape backup*.

**backup types**    The selection of files for backup purposes.

**Full Backup**    Backs up all selected files.

**Differential Backup**    Backs up selected files that have been changed. This is used when only the latest version of a file is required.

**Incremental Backup**    Backs up selected files that have been changed, but if a file has been changed for the second or subsequent time since the last full backup, the file doesn't replace the already-backed-up file, rather it is appended to the backup medium. This is used when each revision of a file must be maintained.

**Delta Backup**    Similar to an incremental backup, but backs up only the actual data in the selected files that has changed, not the files themselves.

**Backus-Naur form**    Also known as Backus normal form, it was the first metalanguage to define programming languages. Introduced by John Backus in 1959 to describe the ALGOL 58 language, it was enhanced by Peter Naur and used to define ALGOL 60.

**backward chaining**    In AI, a form of reasoning that starts with the conclusion and works backward. The goal is broken into many subgoals or sub-subgoals that can be solved more easily. Known as top-down approach. Contrast with *forward chaining*.

**backward compatible**    Same as *downward compatible*.

**BACP**    (Bandwidth Allocation Control Protocol) An IETF standard for adding and dropping the second B channel during an ISDN session. Working in conjunction with Multilink PPP, it enables sending and receiving devices to negotiate the required bandwidth.

**bad sector** A segment of disk storage that cannot be read or written to because of a physical problem in the disk. Bad sectors on hard disks are marked by the operating system and bypassed. If data is recorded in a sector that becomes bad, file recovery software, and sometimes special hardware, must be used to restore it.

**BAK file** (BAcKup file) A DOS, Windows and OS/2 file extension for backup files.

**balanced line** Refers to a cable design that uses the same wire types for the signal and ground. Twised pair cable is a balanced line. Contrast with *unbalanced line*.

**ballistic gain** A trackball or mouse feature that changes cursor travel relative to hand speed. The faster the ball is moved, the farther the cursor is moved.

**balloon help** Onscreen help displayed in a cartoon-style dialogue box that appears when the pointer (cursor) is placed over the object in question.

**balun** (BALanced UNbalanced) A device that connects a balanced line to an unbalanced line; for example, a twisted pair to a coaxial cable. A balanced line is one in which both wires are electrically equal. In an unbalanced line, such as a coax, one line has different properties than the other.

**Balun**
The BNC connector on the left connects to coaxial cable. The screw connectors on the right connect to telephone style twisted wire pairs. *(Image courtesy of Black Box Corporation.)*

**band** (1) The range of frequencies used for transmitting a signal. A band is identified by its lower and upper limits; for example, a 10MHz band in the 100–110MHz range.

    (2) A contiguous group of tracks that are treated as a unit.

    (3) A rectangular section of a page that is created and sent to the printer. See *band printing*.

    (4) The printing element in a band printer.

**bandgap** In a material, the energy difference between its non-conductive state and its conductive state. There is virtually no bandgap in most metals, but a very large one in an insulator (dielectric). In a semiconductor, the bandgap is small. Technically, the bandgap is the energy it takes to move electrons from the valence band to the conduction band.

**bandpass filter** A communications device that accepts a signal and filters out unwanted frequencies, letting only a particular frequency range (band of frequencies) to reach the output side.

**band printer** A line printer that uses a metal band, or loop, of type characters as its printing mechanism. The band contains a fixed set of embossed characters that can only be changed by replacing the band. The band spins horizontally around a set of hammers, one for each print column. When the required character in the band has revolved to the selected print column, the hammer pushes the paper into the ribbon and against the embossed image of the letter, digit or symbol.

    Band printers can print up to approximately 2,000 lpm and can exist in very harsh industrial environments, although they are mostly used in datacenters. Band printers and line matrix printers are the two surviving line printer technologies.

    Band printer is not to be confused with "band printing," which is a method for sending output to the printer. See *band printing* and *printer*.

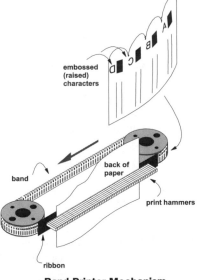

**Band Printer Mechanism**
When the required character in the band has revolved to the selected print column, the hammer pushes the paper into the ribbon and against the embossed image of the letter or digit.

**band printing** Printing a page by creating the output in several rectangular sections, or bands, rather than the entire page. It enables a printer with limited memory to print a full page of text and graphics. Most dot matrix printers and some laser printers benefit from this approach. This is not to be confused with *band printer*, which is hardware.

B

**bandwidth**    The transmission capacity of an electronic line such as a communications network, computer bus or computer channel. It is expressed in bits per second, bytes per second or in Hertz (cycles per second). When expressed in Hertz, the frequency may be a greater number than the actual bits per second, because the bandwidth is the difference between the lowest and highest frequencies transmitted. See *traffic shaping*, *video bandwidth* and *bandwidth junkie*.

**bandwidth junkie**    A person that can't get enough transmission speed, especially when accessing the Internet.

**bandwidth management**    Controlling the traffic flow in a network. See *bandwidth manager*.

**bandwidth manager**    Software that can prioritize communications by allowing high-priority traffic to use more available bandwidth in the network than lower-priority data. For example, realtime video can be given more bandwidth than file transfers. Large file transfers could be given a lower priority than smaller ones.

**bandwidth shaping**    Same as *traffic shaping*.

**bang path**    An address for sending e-mail via UUCP that specifies the entire route to the destination computer. It separates each host name with an exclamation point, which is known as a bang. For example, the bang path **midearth!shire!bilbo!jsmith** would go to the JSMITH user account on the BILBO host, which is reached by first going to MIDEARTH and then SHIRE. See *UUCP*.

**bank**    An arrangement of identical hardware components.

| LAN Technologies | Bandwidth |
|---|---|
| Ethernet | 10 Mbps (shared) |
| Switched Ethernet | 10 Mbps (node to node) |
| Fast Ethernet | 100 Mbps |
| Gigabit Ethernet | 1,000 Mbps |
| 10 Gigabit Ethernet | 10,000 Mbps |
| Token Ring | 4, 16 Mbps |
| Fast Token Ring | 100, 128 Mbps |
| FDDI/CDDI | 100 Mbps |
| ATM | 25, 45, 155, 622. 2488 Mbps + |

| WAN Technologies | Bandwidth |
|---|---|
| **UNSWITCHED PRIVATE LINES (point to point)** | |
| T1 | 24 x 64 Kbps = 1.5 Mbps |
| T3 | 672 x 64 Kbps = 44.7 Mbps |
| Fractional T1 | N x 64 Kbps |
| DSL | 144 Kbps to 52 Mbps |
| **SWITCHED SERVICES** | |
| Dial-up via modem | 9.6, 14.4, 28.8, 33.6, 56 Kbps |
| ISDN | BRI 64-128 Kbps<br>PRI 1.544 Mbps |
| Switched 56/64 | 56 Kbps, 64 Kbps |
| Packet switched (X.25) | 56 Kbps |
| Frame relay | 56 Kbps to 45 Mbps |
| SMDS | 45, 155 Mbps |
| ATM | 25, 45, 155, 622, 2488 Mbps + |

**bank switching**    Engaging and disengaging electronic circuits. Bank switching is used when the design of a system prohibits all circuits from being addressed or activated at the same time, requiring that one unit be turned on while the others are turned off.

**banner ad**    A graphic image used on Web sites to advertise a product or service. Banner ads come in numerous sizes, but are often rectangles 460 pixels wide by 60 pixels high. Also 460 × 55 and 392 × 72 sizes are commonly used. See *interstitial ad*, *SUPERSTITIAL*, *meta ad* and *impression*.

**banner page**    (1) An identification page printed at the beginning of a print job by many print spoolers. It serves as a title page and separator between print jobs.
   (2) A home page on a Web site that serves as an identification screen and launching pad to products, services, etc.
   (3) Same as *splash screen*.

**Banyan**    See *VINES*.

**BAPCo**    (Business Applications Performance Corporation, Santa Clara, CA, www.bapco.com) A non-profit organization founded in 1991 that provides a series of SYSmark brand benchmarks for testing software in the PC client/server and laptop environment. It also has a benchmark for battery life. See *benchmark*.

**BAPI**    (Business API) An interface to one of SAP's R/3 applications. It enables third-party developers to write enhancements that interact with the R/3 modules. See *R/3*.

**bar chart**   A graphical representation of information in the form of bars. See *business graphics*.

**bar code**   The printed code used for recognition by a bar code scanner (reader). Traditional one-dimensional bar codes use the bar's width to encode just a product or account number. Two-dimensional bar codes, such as PDF417, MaxiCode and DataMatrix, are scanned horizontally and vertically and hold considerably more data. PDF417 is widely used for general purposes. MaxiCode is used for high-speed sortation, and DataMatrix is used for marking small parts. See *bar code scanner*, *UPC*, *point of sale*, *AIM* and *PDF417*.

**One-Dimensional Bar Code**
This 1-D bar code is widely used as the universal product code (UPC) on millions of consumer items.

**bar code scanner**   A device specialized for reading bar codes and converting them into either the ASCII or EBCDIC digital character code. Pen scanners, also known as wand scanners, were the first type of bar code scanner developed in the 1970s. In order to be read, the tip of the pen must physically touch the bar code. Later, laser scanners allowed the bar code to be read at a slight distance from the head of the device, enabling supermarkets to read round cans and flexible packages more easily. The most common of that type today is the visible laser diode (VLD) scanner, which emits as many as 50 laser beams simultaneously to capture the image at any angle. See *bar code* and *point of sale*.

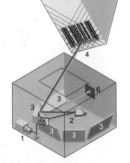

**Laser Diode Mechanism**
A laser diode (1) emits a beam (red) onto a combination of rotating (2) and fixed mirrors (3) that shine multiple beams onto the bar code (4). Although as many as 50 beams may hit the package at different angles, only one is shown in this illustration. The reflected light (yellow) is captured by the collector (5) and aimed at a sensor (6).

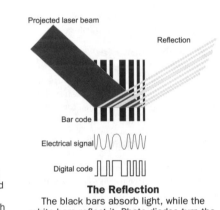

**The Reflection**
The black bars absorb light, while the white bars reflect it. Photo diodes turn the reflected light into an electrical signal, which is converted into digital pulses.

**barebones**   Refers to products that contain only essential elements. Barebones software contains only essential functions. A barebones PC might include just the cabinet, power supply, internal speaker, motherboard, CPU and floppy drive. The CPU chip could be optional. However, a barebones PC intended for resale could also include a low-capacity hard disk, CD-ROM drive, low-end display adapter and sound card, keyboard, mouse and speakers.

**barrel distortion**   A screen distortion in which the sides bow out. Contrast with *pincushioning*.

**barrel printer**   Same as *drum printer*.

**base**   (1) A starting or reference point.

(2) In a bipolar transistor, the line that activates the switch. Same as *gate* in a CMOS transistor.

(3) A multiplier in a numbering system. In a decimal system, each digit position is worth 10x the position to its right. In binary, each digit position is worth 2x the position to its right.

**base64**   An encoding method that converts binary data into ASCII text, and vice versa, and is one of the methods used by MIME. Base64 divides each three bytes of the original data into four 6-bit units, which it represents as four 7-bit ASCII characters. This typically increases the original file by about a third. See *quoted printable encoding*.

**base address**   The starting address (beginning point) of a program or table. See *base/displacement* and *relative address*.

**base alignment**   The alignment of a variety of font sizes on a baseline.

**baseband**    A communications technique in which digital signals are placed onto the transmission line without change in modulation. It is usually limited to a few miles and does not require the complex modems used in broadband transmission. Common baseband LAN techniques are token passing ring (Token Ring) and CSMA/CD (Ethernet).

In baseband, the full bandwidth of the channel is used, and simultaneous transmission of multiple sets of data is accomplished by interleaving pulses using TDM (time division multiplexing). Contrast with *broadband*.

**base/displacement**    A machine architecture that runs programs no matter where they reside in memory. Addresses in a machine language program are displacement addresses, which are relative to the beginning of the program. At runtime, the hardware adds the address of the current first byte of the program (base address) to each displacement address and derives an absolute address for execution.

All modern computers use some form of base/displacement or offset mechanism in order to to run multiple programs in memory at the same time.

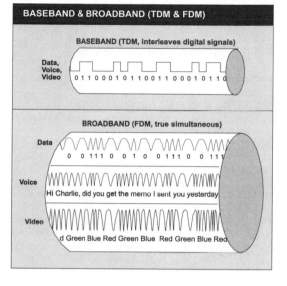

**base font**    The default font used for printing if none other is specified.

**baseline**    The horizontal line to which the bottoms of lowercase characters (without descenders) are aligned. See *typeface*.

**baselining**    Analyzing network traffic to determine the normal traffic flow. Data is collected at various network devices as well as from network analyzers (probes) that are placed at appropriate points throughout the network. See *NRP* and *network analyzer*.

**baselining tool**    A network monitor that analyzes communications usage in order to establish routine traffic patterns. See *network analyzer* and *baselining*.

**base memory**    The amount of RAM that comes with each model of a particular computer. The base memory can usually be ugraded to a significantly higher amount. For example, a desktop machine with 64MB might be upgradable to 768MB.

**base station**    An Earth-based transmitting and receiving station for cellular phones, paging services and other wireless transmission systems. See *earth station*.

**BASIC**    (Beginners All purpose Symbolic Instruction Code) A programming language developed by John Kemeny and Thomas Kurtz in the mid 1960s at Dartmouth College. Originally developed as an interactive, mainframe timesharing language, it has become widely used on small computers.

BASIC is available in both compiler and interpreter form. As an interpreter, the language is conversational and can be debugged a line at a time. BASIC is also used as a quick calculator.

BASIC is considered one of the easiest programming languages to learn. Simple programs can be quickly written on the fly. However, BASIC is not a structured language, such as Pascal, dBASE or C, and it's easy to write spaghetti code that's difficult to decipher later.

The following BASIC example converts Fahrenheit to Celsius:

```
10 INPUT "Enter Fahrenheit "; FAHR
20 PRINT "Celsius is ", (FAHR-32) * 5 / 9
```

**basic cell**    The group of transistors and resistors replicated many times on a gate array chip. See *gate array*.

**bastion host** A computer system in a network that is fortified against illegal entry and attack. It acts as a firewall between the outside world and the internal network. See *firewall*.

**batch** A group, or collection, of items.

**batch data entry** Entering a group of source documents into the computer.

**batch file** (1) A file containing data that is processed or transmitted from beginning to end.
(2) A file containing instructions that are executed one after the other. See *BAT file* and *shell script*.

**batch file transfer** The consecutive transmission of two or more files.

**batch job** Same as *batch program*.

**batch operation** Some action performed on a group of items at one time.

**batch processing** Processing a group of transactions at one time. Transactions are collected and processed against the master files (master files updated) at the end of the day or some other time period. Contrast with *transaction processing*.

Batch and Transaction Processing Information systems typically use both batch and transaction processing methods. For example, in an order processing system, transaction processing is the continuous updating of the customer and inventory files as orders are entered.

At the end of the day, batch processing programs generate picking lists for the warehouse. At the end of some period, batch programs print invoices and management reports.

**batch program** A non-interactive (non-conversational) program such as a report listing or sort.

**batch session** Transmitting or updating an entire file. Implies a non-interactive or non-interruptible operation from beginning to end. Contrast with *interactive session*.

**batch stream** A collection of batch processing programs that are scheduled to run in the computer.

**batch system** See *batch processing*.

**batch terminal** A terminal that is designed for transmitting or receiving blocks of data, such as a card reader or printer.

**batch total** The sum of a particular field in a collection of items used as a control total to ensure that all data has been entered into the computer. For example, using account number as a batch total, all account numbers would be summed manually before entry into the computer. After entry, the total is checked with the computer's sum of the numbers. If it does not match, source documents are manually checked against the computer's listing.

**batch window** The time available for an intensive batch processing operation such as a disk backup.

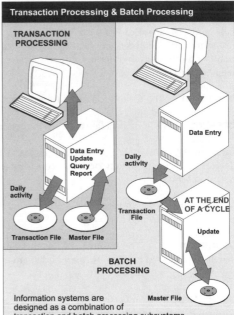

**Transaction Processing & Batch Processing**

TRANSACTION PROCESSING

Data Entry
Update
Query
Report

Daily activity

Transaction File    Master File

Data Entry

Daily activity

Transaction File

AT THE END OF A CYCLE

Update

BATCH PROCESSING

Master File

Information systems are designed as a combination of transaction and batch processing subsystems.

The transaction processing is the daily work. Also called online transaction processing (OLTP), it means that the database is updated as soon as a transaction is received: a sales order depletes inventory, a stock sale updates the last close, a pledge adds to the fund raising balance. Transaction processing keeps business records up-to-date the moment transactions are keyed into or transmitted to the system.

Batch processing is updating or searching an entire table from beginning to end. A month-end report is a batch job as is printing payroll checks. There are many jobs that can be more economically processed at the end of a cycle. For example, the electronic transactions for telephone calls are stored in the computer until month end, when they are matched against the customer table for updating with all the other telephone transactions at the same time.

**BAT file**    (BATch file) A file of DOS or OS/2 commands, which are executed one after the other. It has a .BAT extension and is created with a text editor. See *DOS batch file* and ***DOS AUTOEXEC.BAT***.

**batteries**    See *lead acid, nickel cadmium, nickel metal hydride, lithium ion, lithium polymer, zinc air* and *memory effect*.

**BatteryMark**    A Ziff-Davis benchmark that tests battery life on notebook computers running Windows 95/98. It requires a special hardware device to perform the test. See *ZDBOp*.

**baud**    The signaling rate of a line, which is the number of transitions (voltage or frequency changes) that are made per second. The term has often been erroneously used to specify bits per second. However, only at very low speeds is baud equal to bps; for example, 300 baud is the same as 300 bps. Beyond that, one baud can be made to represent more than one bit. For example, a V.22bis modem generates 1,200 bps at 600 baud.

**baudot code**    Pronounced "baw-doh." One of the first standards for international telegraphy developed in the late 19th century by Emile Baudot. It uses five bits per character.

**baud rate**    A redundant reference to baud. Baud is a rate.

**Bay Networks**    (Bay Networks Division (of Nortel), Santa Clara, CA, www.nortel-bay.com) A division of Nortel Networks, which was formed when Nortel acquired Bay Networks, Inc. in 1998. Before the acquisition, Bay was a communications products company that was formed in 1994 as a merger of SynOptics Communications, Santa Clara, CA and Wellfleet Communications, Billerica, MA. The name was derived from their locations: the California Bay and the Bay State. At the time of the merger, SynOptics was number 1 in hubs, and Wellfleet was number 2 in routers. See *Nortel Networks*.

**bayonet connector**    A plug and socket that uses a connecting mechanism to lock them together. One part is pushed into the other and turned. BNC and ST connectors are examples of bayonet connectors.

**BBN**    (Bolt, Beranek and Newman) A consulting firm that participated in the development of some of the most extensive networks in the world, including ARPANET, which evolved into the Internet. It was founded in 1948 as a consulting service in acoustics by Dr. Richard Bolt and Dr. Leo Beranek. Two years later, Robert Newman became a partner.

In 1997, BBN was acquired by GTE and was merged into its network services organization, which was renamed GTE Internetworking (www.bbn.com).

**BBS**    (1) (Bulletin Board System) A computer system used as an information source and forum for a particular interest group. They were widely used in the U.S. to distribute shareware and drivers and had their heyday before the World Wide Web took off. A BBS functions somewhat like a stand-alone Web site, but without graphics. However, unlike Web sites, each BBS has its own telephone number to dial into.

Today, BBSs are still used throughout the world where there is much less direct Internet access, and many serve as e-mail gateways to the Internet. Some BBSs are still in use in the U.S., and software companies may continue to maintain them as alternatives to their Web sites for downloading drivers.

A general-purpose communications program such as Crosstalk or Qmodem Pro is used to access a BBS. The address list in a communications program stores telephone numbers just like an e-mail program's address list holds e-mail addresses.

(2) (BIOS Boot Specification) A Plug and Play BIOS format that enables the user to determine the boot sequence. See *OPROM*.

**bcc:**    (Blind Carbon Copy) The field in an e-mail header that names additional recipients for the message. It is similar to carbon copy (cc:), but the names do not appear in the recipient's message. Not all e-mail systems support bcc:, in which case the "hidden" names will appear.

**BCD**    (Binary Coded Decimal) The storage of numbers in which each decimal digit is converted into binary and is stored in a single character or byte. For example, a 12-digit number would take 12 bytes. See *binary numbers*.

**BCP documents**   (Best Current Practices documents) Documents that have the technical approval of the IETF. In order to be published, they go through a process similar to an RFC, but they serve as documentation, not official Internet standards. They specify recommended ways to use protocols and configuration options to ensure interoperability. See *Internet Engineering Task Force* and *RFC*.

**BCS**   **(1)** (The British Computer Society, Swindon, Wiltshire, England, www.bcs.org.uk) The chartered body for information technology professionals in the U.K., founded in 1957. It sets standards, conducts exams, advises Parliament and disseminates awards for excellence in computing. The BCS was a founding member of the Council for European Professional Informatics Societies (CEPIS). The BCS is also an Engineering Institution, fully licensed by the Engineering Council to nominate Chartered and Incorporated Engineers and to accredit university courses and training schemes.

**(2)** (The Boston Computer Society) A personal computer users group founded in 1977 by Jonathan Rotenberg and disbanded in 1996. The BCS was one of the first sources for education and technical information about personal computers. At its height in the late 1980s, it had more than 30,000 members, although more than 100,000 were involved at one time or another. The Computer Museum maintains a Web site for some groups that have continued on their own (www.bcs.org).

**(3)** (Binary Compatibility Standard) See *ABI*.

**BDC**   (Backup Domain Controller) In a Windows NT server, a copy of the Primary Domain Controller (PDC). The BDC is periodically synchronized with the PDC. See *PDC*.

**BDPA**   (Black Data Processing Associates, Washington, DC, www.bdpa.org) A membership organization founded in 1975 by Earl A. Pace Jr. and David Wimberly. It is the largest national professional organization representing minorities in the information industry. BDPA provides a forum for exchanging ideas through its monthly meetings, seminars, workshops and annual conferences. Membership is open to members of all races.

**Be**   (Be, Inc., Menlo Park, CA, www.be.com) A software company founded in 1990 by Jean Louise Gassee, former head of R&D at Apple, that specializes in operating systems. BeOS is available for x86-based and PowerPC-based desktop computers, and BeIA is designed for Internet appliances. Be originally developed the PowerPC-based BeBox computer, which ran under BeOS and was designed for digital audio, video and 3-D graphics applications.

**beaconing**   A continuous signaling of error conditions on a LAN. In a token ring network, a beacon frame is sent by the adapter if a failure in the line is detected. See *beacon removal*.

**beacon removal**   In a token ring network that is beaconing, the process of the network adapter removing itself from the network in order to do a self test and then reconnecting if the test is good. See *beaconing*.

**bead**   **(1)** A small programming subroutine. A sequence of beads that are strung together is called a "thread."

**(2)** The insulator surrounding the inner wire of a coaxial cable.

**bearer channel**   One of the data-carrying channels in an ISDN service. See *ISDN*.

**BEA Tuxedo**   A TP monitor from BEA Systems, Inc., San Jose, CA (www.beasys.com), that runs on a variety of UNIX-based computers. Originally developed by AT&T and sold as source code, Novell acquired it, enhanced it and offered it as shrink-wrapped software for various UNIX servers. It was later sold to BEA. BEA Tuxedo and Transarc's Encina are the major TP monitors in the UNIX client/server environment. See *BEA WebLogic*.

**BEA WebLogic**   A family of Java-based application servers from BEA Systems, Inc., San Jose, CA (www.beasys.com). BEA WebLogic Server is the core product that supports the J2EE Java standards. BEA WebLogic Enterprise adds CORBA support and distributed processing. BEA WebLogic Express adds JDBC connectivity and servlet support. See *BEA Tuxedo*.

**BeBop to the Boolean Boogie**   Perhaps the best introductory book written on the fundamentals of digital circuits, *Bebop to the Boolean Boogie* by Clive "Max" Maxfield, is must reading if you are getting into the digital electronics field. It is very informative, understandable and downright enjoyable. (HighText Publishing, 1995, ISBN 1-878707-22-1)

**beep codes**   Some number of short beeps that are sounded by the BIOS upon startup when a memory, cache or processor error is encountered. There are numerous beep code patterns, and Phoenix BIOS codes are long and short beeps delivered in groups. The following beep codes are for AMI BIOSs. There are additional beep codes for this BIOS not included here. See *BIOS* and *POST card.*

**1 Beep — Refresh Failure**   Reseat/replace memory, troubleshoot motherboard.

**2 Beeps — Parity Error**   Reseat/replace memory, troubleshoot motherboard.

**3 Beeps — Memory Error (first 64KB)**   Reseat/replace memory.

**4 Beeps — Timer Failure**   Troubleshoot motherboard.

**5 Beeps — Processor Failure**   Troubleshoot CPU, motherboard.

**6 Beeps — Keyboard Controller Failure**   Troubleshoot keyboard, motherboard.

**7 Beeps — Virtual Mode Exception Error**   Troubleshoot CPU, motherboard.

**8 Beeps — Display Memory Failure**   Trouleshoot display adapter, motherboard.

**9 Beeps — ROM BIOS Checksum Failure**   Replace ROM BIOS, troubleshoot motherboard.

**10 Beeps — CMOS Shutdown Register Failure**   Troubleshoot motherboard.

**11 Beeps — L2 Cache Failure**   Troubleshoot L2 cache, motherboard.

**Continuous Beeps — Memory or Video Failure**   Troubleshoot memory, display adapter, motherboard.

**behavior**   In object technology, the processing that an object can perform.

**behavioral level specification**   See *RTL.*

**behavior blocking**   Also known as "sandboxing," it is software that monitors the executable actions of potentially malicious software and prevents certain operations from taking place. Deleting files and modifying system settings are the kinds of actions that are prohibited. Behavior blocking programs may be more effective than virus scanners, because they monitor the actual functions that are about to take place. In order for a virus scanner to detect a virus, it has to have the actual signature, or fingerprint, of the virus in its database. See *sandbox* and *virus scanner.*

**Bell 103**   An AT&T standard for asynchronous 300 bps full-duplex modems using FSK modulation on dial-up lines.

**Bell 113**   An AT&T standard for asynchronous 300 bps full-duplex modems using FSK modulation on dial-up lines. The 113A can originate but not answer calls, while the 113D can answer but not originate.

**Bell 201**   An AT&T standard for synchronous 2,400 bps full-duplex modems using DPSK modulation. Bell 201B was originally designed for dial-up lines and later for leased lines. Bell 201C was designed for half-duplex operation over dial-up lines.

**Bell 202**   An AT&T standard for asynchronous 1,800 bps full-duplex modems using DPSK modulation over four-wire leased lines as well as 1,200 bps half-duplex operation over dial-up lines.

**Bell 208**   An AT&T standard for synchronous 4,800 bps modems. Bell 208A is a full-duplex modem using DPSK modulation over four-wire leased lines. Bell 208B was designed for half-duplex operation over dial-up lines.

**Bell 209**   An AT&T standard for synchronous 9,600 bps full-duplex modems using QAM modulation over four-wire leased lines or half-duplex operation over dial-up lines.

**Bell 212**   An AT&T standard for asynchronous 1,200 bps full-duplex modems using DPSK modulation on dial-up lines.

**bell character**   The control code used to sound an audible bell or tone in order to alert the user (ASCII 7, EBCDIC 2F).

**The Real Bell**
Alexander Graham Bell was born in Scotland in 1847 and died in 1922. His famous sentence "Mr. Watson. Come here! I want you!" were the first words to travel over a wire, ringing in the birth of electronic communications. *(Image courtesy of AT&T.)*

**Bell compatible**   A modem that is compatible with modems originally introduced by the Bell Telephone System.

**Bellcore**   See *Telcordia*.

**Bell Labs**   The research and development center of Lucent Technologies, formerly AT&T. Bell Labs is one of the most renowned scientific laboratories in the world.

**bells and whistles**   Refers to all the advanced functions that are known to be available in an application or system. Contrast with *plain vanilla*.

**BellSouth Intelligent Wireless Network**   A wireless data network from BellSouth Wireless Data that covers most of the urban population in the U.S. It supports roaming between North America and counterpart networks in some 25 countries in Europe and also stores and forwards messages when the target machine is unavailable. Used for field service, point of sale, public safety and wireless Internet, BellSouth Intelligent Wireless Network is a packet-switched network at 8 Kbps that uses the Mobitex technology.

Mobitex was developed by Ericsson and Swedish Telecom and first put to use in Sweden in 1986. It was later deployed in the U.S. and U.K. by RAM Mobile Data, a joint venture of RAM Broadcasting and BellSouth. In 1998, BellSouth acquired all interest in RAM Mobile Data U.S. and changed its name to BellSouth Wireless Data. See *ARDIS*, *CDPD* and *Ricochet*.

**Bell System**   AT&T and the Bell Telephone Companies before Divestiture. See *Divestiture* and *RBOC*.

**beltware**   Electronic devices carried around the belt, including cellphones, PDAs and pagers. See *wares*.

**benchmark**   A performance test of hardware and/or software. There are various programs that very accurately test the raw power of a single machine, the interaction in a single client/server system (one server/multiple clients) and the transactions per second in a transaction processing system. However, it is next to impossible to benchmark the performance of an entire enterprise network with a great degree of accuracy. See *ZDBOp*, *BAPCo*, *Linpack*, *Dhrystones*, *Whetstones*, *Khornerstones*, *SPEC*, *GPC* and *RAMP-C*.

**benign virus**   A prank virus that does not cause damage. It does such things as randomly displaying a message on screen declaring "Peace on Earth" or causing the computer to make a clicking sound every time a key is pressed on some famous person's birthday. Fortunately, most viruses are benign.

**Bentley**   (Bentley Systems, Inc., Exton, PA, www.bentley.com) A leading CAD software company, founded in 1984 by Keith and Barry Bentley. Its MicroStation CAD software is used by major corporations for engineering large projects, including buildings, airports, hospitals, bridges and industrial plants throughout the world.

**Bento**   A data structure used to store embedded documents in an OpenDoc compound document. Bento, which stands for lunch box in Japanese, provides a "container" to hold the data and a format for defining its contents.

**bent pipe architecture**   The typical way satellites are used to relay information. Data is transmitted to the satellite, which sends it right back down again like a bent pipe. The only processing performed is to retransmit the signals. Newer architectures like the Teledesic project relay the data from satellite to satellite before sending it back down to earth. See *communications satellite* and **Teledesic**.

**BeOS**   See *Be*.

**Beowulf**   Using several smaller computers to provide the computing power of one large computer. A Beowulf cluster uses several off-the-shelf PCs connected via Ethernet to solve problems that would normally be handled by a supercomputer. Beowulf systems are designed for high speed, not redundancy. The first such system was developed by a contractor to NASA in the mid-1990s.

UNIX variants such as Linux and FreeBSD are typically used as the operating system in a Beowulf cluster, and parallel operation is provided by available software in the UNIX community that manages message passing and memory. Access to a particular PC in a cluster is provided by Telnetting to the machine over the network, as most PCs do not contain display adapters. In order to run effectively in a Beowulf cluster, applications must be able to split the data into parallel chunks that can be acted upon simultaneously. See *NOW project* and *Millennium project*.

**BER**    **(1)** (**B**asic **E**ncoding **R**ules) A set of encoding rules for ASN.1 notation, which is a method for defining data structures. See *ASN.1*.

**(2)** (**B**it **E**rror **R**ate) The average number of bits transmitted in error. See *BERT*.

**Berkeley extensions**    See *BSD UNIX*.

**Bernoulli Box**    An early removable disk drive from Iomega. Introduced in 1983 with a SCSI interface and 8" 10MB cartridges, it provided an extremely reliable, transportable storage medium for personal computers at near hard disk speeds. In 1987, 5.25" 20MB disks were introduced, and later 44 and 90MB. The MultiDisk 150 drive accepts 35, 65, 90, 105 and 150MB cartridges. In 1994, the 230MB disk was introduced with backward compatibility to the 44MB disks.

Unlike a hard disk in which the read/write head flies over a rigid disk, the Bernoulli floppy is spun at high speed and bends up close to the head. Upon power failure, a hard disk must retract the head to prevent a crash, whereas the Bernoulli disk naturally bends down. See *Bernoulli principle* and *magnetic disk*.

**Bernoulli Cartridge**
This is an example of a third-generation Bernoulli cartridge. The Bernoulli was the first removable storage for personal computers, which proved very reliable.

**Bernoulli principle**    The Swiss scientist Daniel Bernoulli (1700–1782, demonstrated that, in most cases, the pressure in a fluid (air, water, gas, etc.) decreases as the fluid moves faster. This explains in part why a wing lifts an airplane and why a baseball curves.

**BERT**    (**B**it **E**rror **R**ate **T**est) An analysis of network transmission efficiency that computes the percentage of bits received in error from the total number sent.

**Best Current Practices**    See *BCP documents*.

**best-effort service**    A communications service that makes no guarantees regarding the speed with which data will be transmitted to the recipient or that the data will even be delivered entirely.

**best-of-breed**    The best product of its type. Organizations often purchase software from different vendors in order to obtain the best-of-breed for each application area; for example, a human resources package from one vendor and an accounting package from another. While ERP vendors provide a wealth of applications for the enterprise and tout their integrated system as the superior solution, all modules are rarely best-of-breed. Nobody excels in every niche. See *best-of-class*.

**best-of-class**    A product considered to be superior within a certain category of hardware or software. It does not mean absolute best overall; for example, the best-of-class in a low-priced category may be seriously inferior to the best product on the market, which could sell for ten times as much. See *best-of-breed*.

**Beta**    The first home VCR format, known as Betamax. Developed by Sony, it used 1/2" tape cassettes. Beta Hi-fi added CD-quality audio, and SuperBeta improved the image. The Beta format succumbed to VHS, which is the standard 1/2" VCR format today. See *Betamaxed*.

**Betamaxed**    A superior technology that is overtaken by a lesser one. It comes from Sony's Betamax 1/2" magnetic tape format that was always considered superior to VHS, but did not survive.

**beta release**    See *beta version*.

**beta site**    An organization that is beta testing software. See *beta test*.

**beta test**    A test of hardware or software that is performed by users under normal operating conditions. See *beta version* and *alpha test*.

**beta version**    A pre-shipping release of hardware or software that has gone through alpha test. A beta version of software is supposed to be very close to the final product, but, in practice, it is more a way of getting users to test the software in the first place under real conditions. Given the complexity and ambiguous standards in the PC industry, it is impossible to duplicate the myriad of configurations that exist in the real world. See *alpha test*, *beta test* and *dog-food*.

**betaware**    Software in beta test that has been provided to a large number of users in advance of the formal release.

**BeyondMail**    A Windows-based mail program from Banyan Systems, Inc., Westboro, MA (www.banyan.com) that works with Banyan's own Intelligent Messaging and Novell's MHS messaging systems. It includes a variety of preformatted message forms that can be programmed to access ODBC-compliant databases directly. It provides message distribution into selected folders, automatic filtering and forwarding, and a tickler. An optional calendaring module is available.

**Bezier**    In computer graphics, a curve that is generated using a mathematical formula that assures continuity with other Bezier curves. It is mathematically simpler, but more difficult to blend than a b-spline curve. Within CAD and drawing programs, Bezier curves are typically reshaped by moving the handles that appear off of the curve.

**BFR**    (Big Fast Router)  A routing switch (or switch router). See *layer 3 switch*.

**BFT**    (Binary File Transfer)  An extension to the fax protocol that allows transmission of raw data. A page of text is transmitted faster than a bitmap of the page and is displayed at normal printer resolution at the receiving side.

**BGA**    (Ball Grid Array)  A popular surface mount chip package that uses a grid of solder balls as its connectors. Available in plastic and ceramic varieties, BGA is noted for its compact size, high lead count and low inductance, which allows lower voltages to be used. BGA chips are easier to align to the printed circuit board, because the leads (balls) are farther apart than leaded packages. Since the leads are underneath the chip, BGA has led the way to chip scale packaging (CSP) where the package is not more than 1.2x the size of the semiconductor die itself. See *chip package*, **MicroBGA** and *flip chip*.

**BGA Solder Balls**
These are the undersides of BGA packages showing the solder balls. The small one on the ruler is a µBGA (MicroBGA) chip from Tessera. Using the entire square of the chip package for leads is an advantage of the BGA method. *(Image samples courtesy of Amkor Technology, Inc.)*

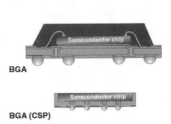

**BGA Package Types**
These cross sections show BGA packages in standard and CSP varieties. *(Illustration courtesy of Joseph Fjelstad.)*

**BGP**    A routing protocol that is used to span autonomous systems on the Internet. It is a robust, sophisticated and scalable protocol that was developed by the Internet Engineering Task Force (IETF). BGP4 supports the CIDR addressing scheme, which has increased the number of available IP addresses on the Internet. BGP was designed to supersede EGP, the orginal exterior gateway protocol. It is also known as a path vector protocol. See *CIDR* and *routing protocol*.

**BHCA**    (Busy Hour Call Attempts)  The number of times a telephone call is attempted during the busiest hour of the day. See *busy hour*.

**BI**    (Business Intelligence)  See *BI software*.

**bias**    A voltage used to control or stabilize an electronic circuit. A forward bias is voltage applied in the direction of the current flow within a transistor, tube or circuit. A reverse bias is voltage applied in the opposite direction.

**bias voltage**    See *bias*.

**BI bus**    A proprietary high-speed bus used in the VAX series.

**BiCMOS**    (**BI**polar**CMOS**) A type of integrated circuit that uses both bipolar and CMOS technologies. The logic gate is primarily made of CMOS, but its output stage uses bipolar transistors, which can handle higher current.

**BICSI**    An international telecommunications association providing education, registration and resources for professionals involved in the design and installation of low-voltage distribution systems in commercial and residential buildings as well as outside plant systems. BICSI publishes technical manuals and offers classroom and distance learning and educational conferences. The Registered Communications Distribution Designer (RCDD) and Installation Registration programs provide professional designations for applicants that demonstrate superior qualifications. BICSI originally stood for Building Industry Consulting Services International.

**bidirectional**    The ability to move, transfer or transmit in both directions.

**bidirectional parallel port**    See *IEEE 1284*.

**bidirectional printer**    A printer that prints alternate lines from right to left.

**bid shielding**    An illegitimate way to preserve a low bid in an online auction. It takes three people. The first places a low bid and the other two immediately bid high and keep bidding higher, which is intended to eliminate all other interested parties. At the last minute, the two high bidders drop out, and the low bidder wins by default. If you recognize the names of bid shielding bandits, the auction site may be able to let you reject their bids. See *online auction*.

**bi-endian**    The ability to switch between big endian and little endian ordering. For example, the PowerPC is a bi-endian CPU. See *byte order*.

**BIFF**    (Binary Interchange File Format) A spreadsheet file format that holds data and charts, introduced with Excel Version 2.2.

**bifurcate**    To divide into two.

**Big Blue**    A nickname for IBM coined from its blue and white logo and the blue covers on most of its earlier mainframes.

**big endian**    The normal order of bytes in a computer word. See *byte order*.

**big iron**    Refers to mainframes.

**BigYellow**    A search facility on the Web that helps you find the addresses of businesses and people. It also includes global directories for names throughout the world. BigYellow was one of the first "yellow page" directories to become popular on the Web. See *Web yellow pages*.

**bilevel display**    A screen that displays only one color (black and white, black and green, etc.). See *bilevel scan*.

**bilevel printer**    The common method used by a printer to dispense ink onto paper. The ink is either fully deposited to form a dot or not at all (two levels). See *contone printer* and *continuous tone*.

**bilevel scan**    Detecting and storing only one level of color on a document page (black or white). Bilevel scanning is typically used to scan text, which may be converted into ASCII or EBCDIC characters using optical character recognition (OCR). Bilevel scans require only one bit per pixel. See *bilevel display* and *OCR*.

**bilinear interpolation**    A texture mapping technique that produces a reasonably realistic image, also known as "bilinear filtering" and "bilinear texture mapping." An algorithm is used to map a screen pixel location to a corresponding point on the texture map. A weighted average of the attributes (color, alpha, etc.) of the four surrounding texels is computed and applied to the screen pixel. This process is repeated for each pixel forming the object being textured.

The term bilinear refers to the performing of interpolations in two dimensions (horizontal and vertical). The top and bottom pairs of each texel quadrant are averaged (horizontal) and then their results are averaged (vertical). This method is often used in conjunction with MIP mapping. See *texture map, MIP mapping, point sampling* and *trilinear interpolation.*

**bill of materials**    The list of components that make up a system. For example, a bill of materials for a house would include the cement block, lumber, shingles, doors, windows, plumbing, electric, heating and so on. Each subassembly also contains a bill of materials; the heating system is made up of the furnace, ducts, etc. A bill of materials "implosion" links component pieces to a major assembly, while a bill of materials "explosion" breaks apart each assembly or subassembly into its component parts.

The first hierarchical databases were developed for automating bills of materials for manufacturing organizations in the early 1960s.

**bill payment**    See *EBPP* and *Web payment service.*

**bill presentment and payment**    See *EBPP.*

**bin**    (BINary) A popular directory name for storing executable programs, device drivers, etc. (binary files).

**binaries**    Executable programs in machine language.

**binaries newsgroups**    A newsgroup hierarchy designed to let people post graphics. Unlike Web sites, no one controls newsgroups, so people use the binaries newsgroups to "express" themselves, and you never know what you will find. Images are typically in .GIF or .JPG format, but because newsgroups can only handle text, images are stored in the text-based UUencoded format. Most browsers have built-in UUcode converters, so you can go to an **alt.binaries** newsgroup, download it in UUencoded format, look at it and save it to disk.

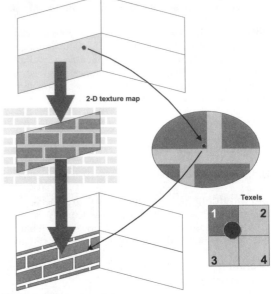

**3-D object before texture is applied**

**2-D texture map**

**Texels**

|  |  |
|---|---|
| 1 | 2 |
| 3 | 4 |

**3-D object after texture is applied**

**Bilinear Mapping**
Each screen pixel of the object is mapped onto the corresponding texel in the texture map. The red dots are an example of one pixel. The attributes of the weighted average of the four nearest texels is applied to the screen pixel. Two horizontal interpolations are made (texels 1-2 and 3-4), and then the results are averaged together for the vertical interpolation. *(Redrawn from illustration courtesy of Intergraph Computer Systems.)*

**binary**    Meaning two. The principle behind digital computers. All input to the computer is converted into binary numbers made up of the two digits 0 and 1 (bits). For example, when you press the "A" key on your personal computer, the keyboard generates and transmits the number 01000001 to the computer's memory as a series of pulses. The 1 bits are transmitted as high voltage; the 0 bits are transmitted as low. The bits are stored as charged and uncharged memory cells in the computer or as microscopic magnets on disk and tape. Display screens and printers convert the binary numbers into visual characters.

The electronic circuits that process these binary numbers are also binary in concept. They are made up of on/off switches (transistors) that are electrically opened and closed. The current flowing through one switch turns on (or off) another switch, and so on. These switches open and close in nanoseconds and picoseconds (billionths and trillionths of a second).

A computer's capability to do work is based on its storage capacity (memory and disk) and internal transmission speed. Greater storage capacities are achieved by making the memory cell or magnetic spot smaller. Faster transmission rates are achieved by shortening the time it takes to open and close the switch. In order to increase computer performance, we keep improving binary devices.

How Binary Numbers Work    Binary numbers are actually simpler than decimal numbers as they use only the digits 0 and 1 instead of 0 through 9.

In decimal, when you add 9 and 1, you get 10. But, if you break down the steps, you find that by adding 9 and 1, what you get first is a result of 0 and a carry of 1. The carry of 1 is added to the digits in the next position on the left. In the following example, the carry becomes part of the answer since there are no other digits in that position.

```
carry—1
         9
     +   1
    _____
        10
```

The following example adds **1** ten times in succession. Note that the binary method has more carries than the decimal method. In binary, **1** and **1** are **0** with a carry of **1**.

| Binary | Decimal | | Binary | Decimal |
|--------|---------|--|--------|---------|
| 0 | 0 | | | |
| + 1 | + 1 | | + 1 | + 1 |
| 1 | 1 | | 110 | 6 |
| + 1 | + 1 | | + 1 | + 1 |
| 10 | 2 | | 111 | 7 |
| + 1 | + 1 | | + 1 | + 1 |
| 11 | 3 | | 1000 | 8 |
| + 1 | + 1 | | + 1 | + 1 |
| 100 | 4 | | 1001 | 9 |
| + 1 | + 1 | | + 1 | + 1 |
| 101 | 5 | | 1010 | 10 |

**binary based**   Using the binary numbering system. The earliest electronic calculating machines did not use the binary system. Contrast with *decimal based*. See *EDSAC*, *Mark I* and *ENIAC*.

**binary code**   A coding system made up of binary digits. See *BCD*, *data code* and ***numbers***.

**binary compatible**   Refers to any data, hardware or software structure (data file, machine code, instruction set, etc.) in binary form that is 100% identical to another. It most often refers to executable programs.

**binary field**   A field that contains binary numbers. It may refer to the storage of binary numbers for calculation purposes, or to a field that is capable of holding any information, including data, text, graphics images, voice and video. See *LOB*.

**binary file**   A file that uses all eight bits of the byte. Machine language programs (executable programs), graphics files, databases, spreadsheets and most word processing files fall into this category. Almost all files except for simple ASCII text files are binary files.

   The distinction is meaningful when transmitting mail over the Internet. SMTP (Simple Mail Transfer Protocol) supports ASCII characters, which use only seven bits. When binary files are attached to e-mail messages, they must be converted into a 7-bit temporary text format, such as MIME, UUcoding or BinHex, and restored to their original 8-bit format at the receiving end. Full-blown e-mail programs (not light versions) support the popular encoding methods.

**binary file transfer**   Sending a file from one location to another in which all eight bits of the byte are transmitted either intact or via some encoding scheme. See *binary file*. See also *BFT*.

**binary format**   (1) Numbers stored in pure binary form in contrast with *BCD* form. See *binary numbers*.

(2) Information stored in a binary coded form, such as data, text, images, voice and video. See *binary file*, *binary field* and *LOB*.

(3) A file transfer mode that transmits any type of file without loss of data.

**binary mode**    A mode of operation that deals with non-textual data. When a "binary" parameter is added to a command, it enables all kinds of data to be transferred or compared rather than just ASCII text.

**binary notation**    The use of binary numbers to represent values.

**binary numbers**    Numbers stored in pure binary form. Within one byte (8 bits), the values 0 to 255 can be held. Two contiguous bytes (16 bits) can hold values from 0 to 65,535. See *numbers* and *binary values*.

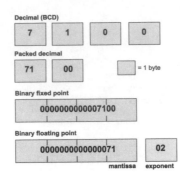

**How Numbers Are Stored**
Binary is one of four primary ways numbers are stored in the computer.

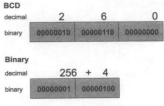

**Binary and Binary Coded Decimal**
The binary method converts the entire decimal number into a binary number. Note that the decimal number "260" takes only nine bits in binary. The 16 bits in the binary example above can hold a decimal number as high as 65,536, using only two bytes instead of five. It also processes faster than binary coded decimal.

**binary search**    A technique for quickly locating an item in a sequential list. The desired key is compared to the data in the middle of the list. The half that contains the data is then compared in the middle, and so on, either until the key is located or a small enough group is isolated to be sequentially searched.

**binary standard**    A standard that has been specified at a working level. Standards organizations often provide specifications that can be interpreted in different ways by vendors. A binary standard implies that there is no possible interpretation, because all the details (fields, variables, messages, etc.) have been defined at the bits and bytes level.

**binary synchronous**    See *bisync*.

**binary transfer**    Transmitting program files, images and other non-textual data. Contrast with *ASCII transfer*.

**Binary Tree**

**binary tree**    A data structure in which each node contains one parent and no more than two children.

**binary values**    This table shows the maximum number of numeric combinations in a binary structure with all bits set to zero equivalent to one combination. For example, in one bit, which can be 0 or 1, there are two possible values.

Just as 99 is the largest decimal number in two decimal digits, 11 is the largest binary number in two binary digits. The decimal equivalent of the largest binary number in a group of bits is one less than the total number of values. For example, in four bits, which provides 16 values, the largest binary number is 1111 or 15 in decimal.

The decimal equivalent of the largest binary numbers as well as the binary numbers themselves are displayed below for up to 16 bits.

**bind**    (1) In programming, to link subroutines. Programs are often built with the help of many standard routines from a library, and large programs may be built as several program modules. Binding

| Bits | | Total Values | Largest Decimal | Binary Number Equivalent | Binary |
|---|---|---|---|---|---|
| 1 | | 2 | 1 | | 1 |
| 2 | | 4 | 3 | | 11 |
| 3 | | 8 | 7 | | 111 |
| 4 | | 16 | 15 | | 1111 |
| 5 | | 32 | 31 | | 1 1111 |
| 6 | | 64 | 63 | | 11 1111 |
| 7 | | 128 | 127 | | 111 1111 |
| 8 | | 256 | 255 | | 1111 1111 |
| 9 | | 512 | 511 | | 1 1111 1111 |
| 10 | 1K | 1,024 | 1,023 | | 11 1111 1111 |
| 11 | 2K | 2,048 | 2,047 | | 111 1111 1111 |
| 12 | 4K | 4,096 | 4,095 | | 1111 1111 1111 |
| 13 | 8K | 8,192 | 8,191 | | 1 1111 1111 1111 |
| 14 | 16K | 16,384 | 16,383 | | 11 1111 1111 1111 |
| 15 | 32K | 32,768 | 32,767 | | 111 1111 1111 1111 |
| 16 | 64K | 65,536 | 65,535 | | 1111 1111 1111 1111 |

links all the pieces together. Before the physical addresses of each routine or module are known, a symbolic address (mnemonic) is used to refer to them. At binding time, the symbolic addresses are substituted with the physical addresses, which point to actual memory or disk locations. See *link editor*.

(2) (**BIND**—**B**erkeley **I**nternet **N**ame **D**omain) The most widely used DNS server software. The Internet Software Consortium (ISC) offers a reference implementation of BIND, which is available at www.isc.org. See *DNS*.

(3) In a communications network, to establish a software connection between one protocol and another. Data flows from the application to the transport protocol to the network protocol to the data link protocol and then onto the network. Binding the protocols creates the internal pathway.

**Binder**     A Microsoft Office workbook file that lets users combine related documents from different Office applications. The documents can be viewed, saved, opened, e-mailed and printed as a group. The Binder is an ActiveX Documents container, and Office applications, such as Excel and Word, are ActiveX Documents servers. The documents are known as ActiveX Documents objects, which were formerly known as DocObjects. See *ActiveX Documents*.

**Binding Protocols in Windows**
This Windows Network control panel shows bindings for the network and the modem. The NetBEUI and TCP/IP protocols are bound to the Ethernet adapter data link protocol for a LAN connection, and TCP/IP is also bound to the dial up adapter for Internet connection via modem.

**bindery**     A NetWare file used for security and accounting in NetWare 2.x and 3.x. A bindery pertains only to the server it resides in and contains the names and passwords of users and groups of users authorized to log in to that server. It also holds information about other services provided by the server to the client (print, modem, gateway, etc.).

NDS (Novell Directory Services) is the bindery counterpart in NetWare 4.x, but NDS is global oriented, manages multiple servers and provides a naming service, which the bindery does not. Bindery emulation software enables NetWare 2.x and 3.x clients to access services on NetWare 4.x servers. See *NDS*.

**bindings**     A set of linkages or assignments. See *bind*.

**binding time**     (1) In program compilation, the point in time when symbolic references to data are converted into physical machine addresses.

(2) When a variable is assigned its type (integer, string, etc.) in a programming language. Traditional compilers and assemblers provide early binding and assign types at compilation. Object-oriented languages provide late binding and assign types at runtime when the variable receives a value from the keyboard or other source.

**BinHex**     A utility and encoding format that originated on the Macintosh that is used to convert binary files into 7-bit ASCII for communications over Internet e-mail. Files formatted in BinHex use the .HQX extension. See *MIME*, *UU coding* and **Wincode**.

**biochip**     See *gene chip*.

**bioinformatics**     Using computers in biological research. Bioinformatics is most prominent in the Human Genome Project, which is recording the three billion chemical base pairs that make up the human DNA system. See *Human Genome Project*.

**biomechanics**     The study of the anatomical principles of movement. Biomechanical applications on the computer employ stick modeling to analyze the movement of athletes as well as racing horses.

**biometrics**    The biological identification of a person, which includes eyes, voice, handprints, voice, fingerprints and handwritten signatures. Biometrics are a more foolproof form of authentication than typing passwords or even using smart cards, which can be stolen. See *authentication* and *biometric signature*.

**biometric signature**    The characteristics of a person's handwritten signature. The pen pressure and duration of the signing process, which is done on a digital-based pen tablet, is recorded as an algorithm that is compared against future signatures. See *biometrics*.

**bionic**    A machine that is patterned after principles found in humans or nature; for example, robots. It also refers to artificial devices implanted into humans replacing or extending normal human functions.

**BIOS**    (Basic Input Output System) An essential set of routines in a PC, which is stored on a chip and provides an interface between the operating system and the hardware. The BIOS supports all peripheral technologies and internal services such as the realtime clock (time and date).

On startup, the BIOS tests the system and prepares the computer for operation by querying its own small CMOS memory bank for drive and other configuration settings. It searches for other BIOSs on the plug-in boards and sets up pointers (interrupt vectors) in memory to access those routines. It then loads the operating system and passes control to it. The BIOS accepts requests from the drivers as well as the application programs.

BIOSs must periodically be updated to keep pace with new peripheral technologies. If the BIOS is stored on a ROM chip (ROM BIOS), it must be replaced. Newer BIOSs are stored on a flash memory chip that can be upgraded via software. See *BIOS upgrades*, *BIOS setup* and *beep codes*.

**A Biometric Mouse**
SecuGen's EyeD Mouse includes a fingerprint reader on the thumb side of the device. It takes less than a second for the EyeD Mouse to verify your fingerprint. *(Image courtesy of SecuGen Corporation, www.secugen.com)*

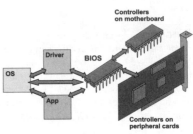

**BIOS Interaction**
On startup, the BIOS searches all peripheral controllers in the system to obtain the current configuration, which it makes available to the software.

**biosensor**    A device that detects and analyzes body movement, temperature or fluids and turns it into an electronic signal. It may be worn (headgear, bracelet, etc.) or used in a handheld or stationary unit. See *data glove*.

**BIOS setup**    A startup routine in a PC that enables users to reconfigure hardware settings that are stored in a small, battery-backed memory bank. Although today's BIOSs can detect new drives and update their settings automatically, older PCs required manual entering of disk parameters after a new drive was installed.

All BIOSs let you get to their settings at startup. Immediately after turning the machine on, a message is displayed that tells you which key to press (typically the DEL or F1 key). If there is no message on screen, refer to your system manual (RTFM!). Many BIOS settings are quite arcane and are only changed by experienced technicians.

The BIOS setup has also been called the "CMOS setup" or the "CMOS RAM," because the settings are held in a tiny CMOS memory bank in the chip. See *BIOS*, **hard disk configuration** and *BIOS Upgrades*.

**BIOS Upgrades**    The following organizations specialize in BIOS upgrades.

**Unicore Software**
N. Andover, MA
800/800-BIOS
www.unicore.com

**American Megatrends, Inc.**
Norcross, GA
800/828-9264
www.megatrends.com

**bipolar**    A category of high-speed microelectronic circuit design, which was used to create the first transistor and the first integrated circuit. The most common variety of bipolar chip is TTL (transistor transistor logic). Emitter coupled logic (ECL) and integrated injection logic (I2L) are also part of the bipolar family.

Today, bipolar and CMOS are the two major transistor technologies. Most all personal computers use CMOS, and even large mainframes that have traditionally used bipolar have given way to CMOS designs. CMOS uses far less energy than bipolar.

However, bipolar transistors are still widely used for high radio frequency (RF) applications that reach into the gigahertz range, which CMOS technology cannot handle.

The bipolar transistor works by pulsing a line called the "base," which allows current to flow from the "emitter" to the "collector," or vice versa, depending on the design. See *bipolar transmission*.

### bipolar transmission
The technique used in T1 transmission, which alternates the 1 bits between positive and negative (+3v, –3v) in order to maintain an average of 0 volts.

### BI portal
See *business intelligence portal*.

### BIPS
(Billion Instructions Per Second) See *MIPS*.

### biquinary code
Meaning two-five code. A system for storing decimal digits in a four-bit binary number. The biquinary code was used in the abacus. See *abacus*.

### birefringence
Using a crystal to split light into two frequencies that travel at different speeds and at right angles to each other. It's used to filter out a color in an LCD display.

### bis
Second version. It means twice in Old Latin, or encore in French. Ter means three. For example, V.27bis and V.27ter are the second and third versions of the V.27 standard.

### B-ISDN
(Broadband-ISDN) A framework for advanced telecommunications from the ITU. Introduced in 1988 as an extension to ISDN, it was designed to provide a blueprint to integrate data, voice and video in the twenty-first century. B-ISDN specifies the use of ATM for switching and SONET for high-speed links. See *ATM* and *SONET*.

### BI software
(Business Intelligence software) Software that enables users to obtain enterprise-wide information more easily. Such products are considered a step up from the typical decision support tools because they more tightly integrate querying, reporting, OLAP, data mining and data warehousing functions.

There are a variety of products that claim BI capabilities, but the bottom line is that they should enable users to obtain "all" the information they desire from their organization's numerous databases. BI software should allow you to derive the transactions and summaries you need without having to know the sources (which databases, which servers, etc.).

Business intelligence is really the 1990s buzzword for the *MIS* (management information system) of the 1970s and the *DSS* (decision support system) of the 1980s. MIS implementations often failed because the hardware wasn't fast enough and the software wasn't sophisticated enough. Countless DSS, EIS and OLAP tools followed, which added functionality, but were often point solutions to the problem. BI implies yet more integration and ease of use. See *business intelligence portal*.

### bison
The Free Software Foundation's version of yacc.

### bistable circuit
Same as *flip-flop*.

### bisync
(BInary SYNCronous) A major category of synchronous communications protocols used in mainframe networks. Bisync communications require that both sending and receiving devices are synchronized before transmission of data is started. Contrast with *asynchronous* transmission.

### bisynchronous
See *bisync*.

### bit
(BInary digiT) The smallest element of computer storage. It is a single digit in a binary number (0 or 1). The bit is physically a transistor or capacitor in a memory cell, a magnetic domain on disk or tape, a reflective spot on optical media or a high or low voltage pulsing through a circuit.

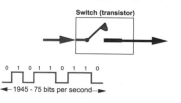

**Transmission—Making It Faster**
The bit is transmitted as a pulse of high or low voltage. Speed is increased by making the transistors open and close faster, which is a combination of making the microscopic elements within the transistor smaller and more durable. Transmitting pulses internally in the computer is much simpler than out over a network, where they are influenced by long distances and interference. The telephone companies have been the pioneers in installing high-speed optical trunks throughout the country.

Groups of bits make up storage units in the computer, called "characters," "bytes," or "words," that are manipulated as a group. The most common is the byte, made up of eight bits and equivalent to one alphanumeric character.

Bits are widely used as a measurement for transmission. Ten megabits per second means that ten million pulses are transmitted per second. A 16-bit bus means that there are 16 wires transmitting the bit at the same time.

Measurements for storage devices, such as disks, files and databases, are given in bytes rather than bits. See *space/time*.

## Bit Alley   See *Bit Valley*.

## bitblt   (BIT BLock Transfer) In computer graphics, a hardware feature that moves a rectangular block of bits from main memory into display memory. It speeds the display of moving objects (animation, scrolling) on screen.

A hardware bitblt provides fastest speed, but bitblts are also implemented in software even in non-graphics systems. For example, text scrolls faster when it is copied as a contiguous block (bitblt) to the next part of the window rather than processing every character on every line. See *stretch blt*.

## bit bucket   An imaginary trash can. The phrase "it went into the bit bucket" means the data was lost.

## bit cell   A boundary in which a single bit is recorded on a tape or disk.

## bit density   The number of bits that can be stored within a given physical area.

## bit depth   (1) The number of bits used to hold a pixel. Also called "color depth" and "pixel depth," the bit depth determines the number of colors that can be displayed at one time. Digital video requires at least 15 bits, while 24 bits produces photorealistic colors.

| Color Depth | Number of Colors |
|---|---|
| 4-bits | 16 |
| 8-bits | 256 |
| 15-bits | 32,768 |
| 16-bits | 65,536 |
| 24-bits | 16,777,216 |
| 32-bits | 16,777,216 + alpha channe |

(2) Bit depth can refer to any coding system that uses numeric values to represent something. The depth, or number of bits, determines how many discrete items can be represented.

## bit diddling   See *bit twiddling*.

## bit flip   Switching a bit from 0 to 1 or 1 to 0. Also refers to changing one's mind 180 degrees. See *bit flipping*.

## bit level device   A device, such as a disk drive, that inputs and outputs data bits. Contrast with *pulse level device*.

**The Bit**

0   1

The bit is the smallest element of computer storage. It is a positive or negative magnetic spot on disk and tape and charged cells in memory.

**Bits on magnetic disk**

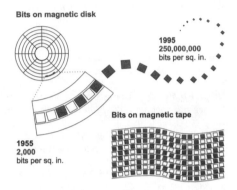

1995
250,000,000
bits per sq. in.

**Bits on magnetic tape**

1955
2,000
bits per sq. in.

**The Byte**

| 0 | 1 | 0 | 0 | 1 | 1 | 0 | 1 |

A byte is 8 binary digits, or cells.

**Bytes in memory**
In a 16 megabyte memory, there are 16 million of these 8-bit structures.

**Storage - Making It Smaller**
Making the spot or cell smaller increases the storage capacity. Our disks hold staggering amounts of data compared to 10 years ago, yet we still want more. Look up *holographic storage* for a look into a fascinating future storage technology.

**A Memory Bit**
This is one storage cell in a 16-megabit dynamic RAM memory chip. There are 16,777,216 of these in the chip, which is about a quarter of an inch square. *(Image courtesy of International Business Machines Corporation. Unauthorized use not permitted.)*

**bit manipulation**    Processing individual bits within a byte. Bit-level manipulation is very low-level programming, often done in graphics and systems programming.

**bitmap**    A binary representation in which a bit or set of bits corresponds to some part of an object such as an image or font. For example, in monochrome systems, one bit represents one pixel on screen. For gray scale or color, several bits in the bitmap represent one pixel or group of pixels. The term may also refer to the memory area that holds the bitmap.

A bitmap is usually associated with graphics objects, in which the bits are a direct representation of the picture image. However, bitmaps can be used to represent and keep track of anything, where each bit location is assigned a different value or condition.

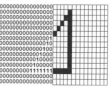

**A Monochrome Bitmap**
The left half of this diagram shows the bits in the bitmap, and the right half depicts what would show on screen. In monochrome systems, one bit is used to represent one pixel. Images that are scanned into the computer are turned into bitmaps, and bitmaps can be created in a paint program.

**bitmap file**    (1) A file that contains an image in one of various bitmap formats such as TIFF, GIF, JPEG and BMP. See *graphics formats*.
(2) A BMP file. See *BMP file*.

**bitmap format**    Referring to any of various picture images such as TIFF, GIF and JPEG. See *bitmapped graphics* and *graphics formats*.

**bitmap graphics**    See *bitmapped graphics*.

**bitmapped font**    A set of dot patterns for each letter and digit in a particular typeface (Times Roman, Helvetica, etc.) for a specified type size (10 points, 12 points, etc.). Bitmapped typefaces either are purchased in groups of pre-generated point sizes, or, for a wide supply of fonts, font generators allow the user to create a variety of point sizes. Bitmapped fonts take up disk space for each point size. Contrast with *scalable font*. See *font* and *font generator*.

**bitmapped graphics**    In computer graphics, a technique for representing a picture image as a matrix of dots. Also known as "raster graphics," it is the digital counterpart of analog TV. However, unlike TV, which uses one standard format in the U.S. known as NTSC, there are dozens of bitmapped graphics formats, including GIF, TIF, BMP, JPG and PCX (see *graphics formats*). See *graphics*. Contrast with *vector graphics*.

**BITNET**    A worldwide communications network founded in 1981 that served higher education and research. Well known for its LISTSERV software for managing electronic mailing lists, for years, BITNET was the world's largest computer-based, higher-education network. It was gradually supplanted by the Internet.

**bit nibbler**    Software that copies data from a file one bit at a time. It functions at a very low level to override any copy protection scheme that the data may be wrapped in.

**bit-oriented protocol**    A communications protocol that uses individual bits within the byte as control codes, such as IBM's SDLC. Contrast with *byte-oriented protocol*.

**bit parallel**    The transmission of several bits at the same time, each bit travelling over a different wire in the cable.

**bit pattern**    A specific layout of binary digits.

**bit plane**    A segment of memory used to control an object, such as a color, cursor or sprite. Bit planes may be reserved parts of a common memory or independent memory banks each designed for one purpose.

**bit rate**    The transmission speed of binary coded data. Same as *data rate*. See *bit time*.

**bit serial**    The transmission of one bit after the other on a single line or wire.

**bit slice processor**    A logic chip that is used as an elementary building block for the computer designer. Bit slice processors usually come in 4-bit increments and are strung together to make larger processors (8 bit, 12 bit, etc.).

**bit specifications**    Everything in the digital world is measured in bits and bytes. Bits are a measurement of different components and functions, depending on what is being referenced. Following are the most common. See also *binary values*.

**(1)** The size of the computer's internal word, or registers, which is the amount of data the CPU can compute at the same time. If the clock rates are the same (50MHz, 100MHz, etc.) and the basic architectures are equal, a 32-bit computer works twice as fast internally as a 16-bit computer.

**(2)** The size of the computer's data bus, which is the pathway over which data is transferred between memory and the CPU and between memory and the peripheral devices. If the bus clock rates are equal, a 16-bit bus transfers data twice as fast as an 8-bit bus.

**(3)** The size of the address bus, which determines how much memory the CPU can address directly. Each bit doubles the number, for example, 20 bits addresses 1,048,576 bytes; 24 bits addresses 16,772,216 bytes. See *binary values*.

**(4)** The number of colors that can be displayed at one time. This is called "bit depth," "color depth" and "pixel depth." Unless some of the memory is used for cursor or sprite movement, an 8-bit display adapter generates 256 colors; 16-bit, 64K colors; 24-bit, 16.8 million colors. See *alpha channel* and *bit depth*.

Bit specifications, such as 64-bit and 128-bit, refer to the display adapter's architecture, which affects speed, not the number of colors. See *64-bit graphics accelerator* and *128-bit graphics accelerator*.

**(5)** The quality of sound based on the number of bits in the samples taken. A 16-bit sample yields a number with 65,536 increments compared to 256 in an 8-bit sample. See *8-bit sample* and *16-bit sample*.

**bitstream**    The transmission, or flow, of binary data (bits).

**bit stuffing**    Adding bits to a transmitted message in order to round out a fixed frame or to break up a pattern of data bits that could be misconstrued for control codes.

**bit time**    The duration of one pulse (one bit). For example, the bit time of Fast Ethernet is 10 nanoseconds (ns). See *bit rate*.

**bit transfer rate**    The amount of bits transmitted over a channel within some defined period of time, typically one second. See *bps*, *Kbps*, *Mbps* and *Gbps*.

**bit twiddling**    Programming at a very low level (manipulating the bits and bytes). Also may refer to spending excessive time on unimportant refinements. See *hacker*.

**Bit Valley**    The Shibuya suburb of Tokyo that is known for its expanding number of Internet companies. See *Silicon Valley*, *Silicon Alley*, *Silicon Forest* and *Silicon Glen*.

**bitwise**    Dealing with bits rather than larger structures such as a byte. Bitwise operators are programming commands or statements that work with individual bits. See *bit manipulation* and *bitwise operators*.

**bitwise operators**    The primary bit manipulation operators are as follows:

```
<<      shift left
>>      shift right
~       flip (0 to 1; 1 to 0)
&       AND
|       OR
^       exclusive OR
```

**BIX**    (Byte Information Exchange, Cambridge, MA, www.bix.com)  An online database of computer knowledge, designed to help users fix problems and obtain info on hardware and software products. BIX was originally a part of *Byte Magazine*, published by McGraw-Hill. BIX was acquired by Delphi in 1992, and a cross promotion of BIX and *Byte Magazine* services ended in 1997. Until the summer of 1998, when CMP Media, Inc., acquired the magazine, BIX informally supported various *Byte* editorial services. See *online services*.

**BizTalk**    An initiative from Microsoft to spearhead XML usage. The "BizTalk Framework" provides a special set of XML tags that provide a common transport envelope for wrapping XML documents for business-to-business and application-to-application interoperability. As part of the BizTalk initiative, Microsoft has defined XDR, an XML schema as a subset of the formal recommendation from the W3C. BizTalk.org, launched in mid 1999, is an XML schema library Web site, that serves as a central repository for publishing and reviewing XML schemas from industry groups and companies. For information, visit www.biztalk.org. See *XML schema repository*.

**BizTalk Server**    An integration product from Microsoft that combines elements of messaging middleware and Web-based application servers. It provides rules-based routing and conversion between data formats, and serves as a protocol bridge between HTTP, SMTP, MQSeries and other applications.

**black box**    A custom-made electronic device, such as a protocol converter or encryption system. Yesterday's black boxes often become today's off-the-shelf products.

**Black Box Corporation**    (Black Box Corporation, Pittsburgh, PA, www.blackbox.com) An organization that specializes in selling communications and LAN products. It offers expert services, custom solutions and hard-to-find products. It also provides free, 24-hour tech support. The company's original name was Expandor, Inc.; it offered manual printer switches known as "black boxes." Its catalog was eventually named the Black Box catalog, and later the company changed its name.

**The Black Box**
A black box doesn't have to look like a box. It can be any contraption that is custom made for an application.

**black box testing**    Testing software based on output requirements and without any knowledge of the internal structure or coding in the program. Contrast with *white box testing*. See also *black box*.

**Black Data Processing Associates**    See *BDPA*.

**Blacklist of Internet Advertisers**    A popular and frequently cited report that describes the offending activities of spammers that routinely distribute large mailings via e-mail or post unwelcome advertising on newsgroups. The Blacklist is updated regularly and can be found by searching for it by name with your favorite search engine. Also visit www.spam.abuse.net. See *spam*.

**blackout**    A complete loss of power. See *brownout*.

**Black Screen of Death**    A Windows 95 error that causes the computer to lock up, and the screen turns black. The solution is to reboot. See *Blue Screen of Death*.

**blank character**    A space character that takes up one byte in the computer just like a letter or digit. When you press the spacebar on a personal computer keyboard, the ASCII character with a numeric value of 32 is created.

**blank squash**    The removal of blanks between items of data. For example, the Trim function in dBASE removes trailing blanks. The expression **trim(city) + ", " + state** concatenates city and state with a blank squash resulting in DALLAS, TX rather than DALLAS        TX.

**BLEC**    (Building Local Exchange Carrier) A network service provider that partners with real estate owners and managers in order to provide broadband services within an apartment house or office building. The BLEC may provide only connectivity or full ISP services including Web hosting and ASP capabilities. See *CLEC* and *MTU*.

**bleed**    Printing at the very edge of the paper. Many laser printers, including all LaserJets up to the 11x17" 4V, cannot print to the very edge, leaving a border of approximately 1/4". In commercial printing, bleeding is generally more expensive, because wider paper is often used, which is later cut to size.

**Blenheim shows**    (The Blenheim Group, Fort Lee, NJ) A major producer of trade shows that organized more than 40 IT expositions around the world, PC EXPO being the largest and most notable. Blenheim was acquired by Miller Freeman in late 1996. See *Miller Freeman*.

**blip**    A mark, line or spot on a medium, such as microfilm, that is optically sensed and used for timing or counting purposes.

**blitting** Using a bitblt to transfer data.

**bloatware** Software that is so overloaded with functionality that its performance suffers. At the very least, it takes a long time to load the program. Software vendors seem to have the perception that more is always better.

**BLOB** (Binary Large OBject) Borland's term for a LOB. See *LOB*.

**block** (1) A group of disk or tape records that is stored and transferred as a single unit.
(2) A group of bits or bytes that is transmitted or processed as a single unit.
(3) A group of text characters that has been marked for moving, copying, saving or other operation.
(4) A rectangular group of pixels that are processed as a unit.
(5) A group of program statements that are treated as a unit based on the results of a comparison.

**block cipher** An encryption method that processes the input in fixed blocks of input, typically 64 or 128 bits. Contrast with *stream cipher*.

**block cursor** An onscreen pointer that is shaped like a rectangular block and covers one character position. It is typically found in command line systems such as DOS and UNIX, where the cursor changes from a block to an underline to indicate the difference between insert and overwrite modes.

**block diagram** A chart that contains squares and rectangles connected with arrows to depict hardware and software interconnections. For program flow charts, information system flow charts, circuit diagrams and communications networks, more elaborate graphical representations are usually used.

**blocking factor** The number of records in a block.

**blocking software** See *Web filtering* and *parental control software*.

**block move** The ability to mark a contiguous segment of text or data and move it.

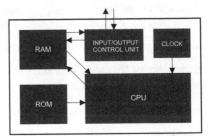

**Block Diagram of a Computer**

**block multiplexor channel** A high-speed mode of operation within IBM's parallel channel. See *parallel channel*.

**blooming** A condition with older CCD devices that causes distortion at the pixel level. It occurs when the electrical charge created exceeds the storage capacity of the device and spills over into adjacent pixels. Newer CCDs incorporate anti-blooming circuitry to drain the excess charge.

**blow** To write code or data into a PROM chip by blowing the fuses of the 0 bits. The 1 bits are left alone.

**Blowfish** A secret key cryptography method that uses a 256-bit key. It uses the block cipher method, which breaks the text into 64-bit blocks before encrypting them. Written by Bruce Schneier, it is considered very fast and secure. See *encryption algorithm*.

**blow up** Same as *crash, bomb* or *abend*.

**Blue Box** A programming interface for the Rhapsody operating system from Apple, which later became Mac OS X. The Blue Box is the Mac Toolbox API, which enables a Mac OS 9 or previous Mac application to run without modification. The Blue Box was renamed the Classic interface in OS X. See *MAC OS X* and *Yellow Box*.

**blue diode laser** A semiconductor laser that emits in the 400–450 nm range. It has been exceedingly more difficult to develop blue lasers than other colors with larger wavelengths. Blue diode lasers will allow for smaller pits to be used in optical discs (CD-ROMs use 780 nm pits; DVDs are 630 nm). Blue LEDs (a related technology) are expected to be used in display screens in the future. See *laser*.

**blue laser**   See *blue diode laser*.

**blue screen**   See *color key*.

**Blue Screen of Death**   A Windows NT error that causes the computer to lock up, and the screen turns blue. The solution is to reboot. The term also refers to a Windows 95 crash where the error message is displayed in a DOS character-mode screen with a blue background. See *Black Screen of Death*.

**Bluetooth**   A wireless personal area network (PAN) technology from the Bluetooth Special Interest Group, (www.bluetooth.com), founded in 1998 by Ericsson, IBM, Intel, Nokia and Toshiba. Bluetooth is an open standard for short-range transmission of digital voice and data between mobile devices (laptops, PDAs, phones) and desktop devices. It supports point-to-point and multipoint applications.

Bluetooth provides up to 720 Kbps data transfer within a range of 10 meters and up to 100 meters with a power boost. Unlike IrDA, which requires that devices be aimed at each other (line of sight), Bluetooth uses omnidirectional radio waves that can transmit through walls and other non-metal barriers. Bluetooth transmits in the unlicensed 2.4GHz band and uses a frequency hopping spread spectrum technique that changes its signal 1600 times per second. If there is interference from other devices, the transmission does not stop, but its speed is downgraded.

The name Bluetooth comes from King Harald Blatan (Bluetooth) of Denmark. In the 10th century, he began to Christianize the country. Ericsson (Scandinavian company) was the first to develop this specification. See *PAN* and *wireless LAN*.

**BMP**   (Batch Message Processor) A facility for producing reports and batch updates to IMS databases. See *BMP file*.

**BMP file**   (BitMaP file) Also known as a "bump" file, it is a Windows and OS/2 bitmapped graphics file format. It is the Windows native bitmap format, and every Windows application has access to the BMP software routines in Windows that support it. BMP files provide formats for 2, 16, 256 or 16 million colors (1-bit, 4-bit, 8-bit and 24-bit color). BMP files use the .BMP or .DIB extensions (DIB stands for Device-Independent Bitmap). See *BMP* and *extension*.

**BNC connector**   (Bayonet Neil-Concelman or British Naval Connector) A commonly used plug and socket for audio, video and networking applications. BNCs connect two-wire coaxial cable (signal and ground) using a bayonet mount. After the plug is inserted, the bayonette mechanism causes the pins to be pinched into the locking groove when the plug is turned. See *A/V ports* and *plugs and sockets*.

**pin**
**lock**
**slot**

**BNC Connector**
BNCs differ from many connectors because of their snap-lock architecture, which keeps the plug firmly in its socket.

**board**   See *card*, *printed circuit board* and *BBS*.

**board level**   Electronic components that are mounted on a printed circuit board instead of in a cabinet or finished housing.

**boardware**   Same as *board level*.

**BOC**   (Bell Operating Company) One of 22 companies that was formerly part of AT&T and later organized into seven regional companies. See *RBOC*.

**body text**   The base font used for text in a paragraph. In many desktop publishing programs, any paragraph that is not tagged separately is assigned the body text style.

**body type**   The typeface and size commonly used for text in paragraph copy. Typically 10 points.

**body-worn computer**   A computer that is worn on the body and accessed via voice recognition and a head mounted display (HMD). The computer is a full PC with hard disk that is ruggedized for the natural abuse it will receive in the work environment. The HMD is worn like goggles and gives the illusion of a floating monitor in front of the user's face. See *HMD*.

**BOF**   (Beginning Of File) The status of a file when it is first opened or when an instruction or command has reset the file pointer.

**boilerplate**   A common phrase or expression used over and over. Boilerplate is stored on disk and copied into the document as needed. See *stationery*.

**boldface**   Characters that are heavier and darker on printed output and brighter than normal on a display screen.

**boldface attribute**   A code that turns normal characters into boldface characters on a printer or display screen.

**boldface font**   A set of type characters that are darker and heavier than normal type. In a boldface font, all characters have been designed as bold characters.

**bomb**   Same as *abend* and *crash*.

**BOMP**   (Bill Of Materials Processor)  One of the first DBMSs used for bill of materials explosion in the early 1960s from IBM. A subsequent version, DBOMP, was used in manufacturing during the 1970s.

**bonded modem**   See *channel bonding*.

**bonding**   Tying two or more devices together to function as one. See *channel bonding* and *ISDN*.

**Bongo**   A visual interface builder for Java from Marimba that includes a variety of ready-to-use controls, known as "interface widgets." Bongo output can be directly published as Castanet channels. See *Castanet*.

**Booch**   An object-oriented analysis and design method developed by Grady Booch, chief scientist of Rational Software. See *object references* and *Rational Rose*.

**bookmark**   A stored location for quick retrieval at a later date. Web browsers provide bookmarks that contain the addresses (URLs) of favorite sites. Most electronic references, large text databases and help systems provide bookmarks that mark a location users want to revisit in the future. See *Favorites* and *bookmark portal*.

**bookmark portal**   A Web site that stores your bookmarks so you can use them from any computer and with any Web browser. Such sites may also allow you to share your bookmarks with others or the world at large, the idea being that these are a more valuable resource than pages randomly located with crawlers.

**Boole & Babbage**   (Boole & Babbage, Inc., San Jose, CA, www.boole.com)  A leader in availability and service-level management software for distributed systems. Founded in 1967, Boole & Babbage is the oldest publicly traded independent software vendor in the systems management industry. Its products are used by large manufacturing companies, government, financial institutions, airlines, IT outsourcers and utilities. In late 1998, it merged with BMC Software, which combined two of the leading providers of enterprise management software. See *BMC*.

**Boolean data**   Yes/no or true/false data.

**Boolean expression**   A statement using Boolean operators that expresses a condition that is either true or false.

**Boolean logic**   The "mathematics of logic," developed by English mathematician George Boole in the mid-nineteenth century. Its rules govern logical functions (true/false). As add, subtract, multiply and divide are the primary operations of arithmetic, AND, OR and NOT are the primary operations of Boolean logic. Boolean logic is turned into logic gates on circuit boards, and various permutations are used, including NAND, NOR, XOR and XNOR. The rules, or truth tables, for Boolean AND, OR and NOT follow. See *logic gate* and *Bebop to the Boolean Boogie*.

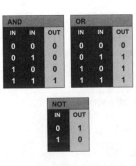

Curious About the Chip?   Wired in patterns of Boolean logic and in less space than a postage stamp, transistors inside one of today's high-speed chips collectively open and close trillions of times every second. If you're curious about how it really works down

B

deep in the layers of the silicon, read the rest of "Boolean logic," then "chip" and, finally, "transistor." It's a fascinating venture into a microscopic world.

The logic of AND, OR and NOT is implemented as transistors, which are electronic switches that are opened and closed by being pulsed. If you don't understand every last detail below, keep on going. It will come together at the end. You can always review.

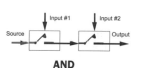

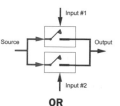

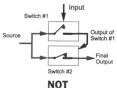

### AND

AND requires both inputs to be present in order to provide output. Because the AND gate is wired in series, both inputs must pulse both switches closed, and current flows from the source to the output.

### OR

OR requires one input to be present in order to provide output. Because the OR gate is wired in parallel, either one or both inputs will generate output.

### NOT

NOT reverses the input. If there is no pulse on the input line, the source goes directly to output, as in the diagram above. If there is a pulse on the input line, switch #1 is closed. The switch #1 current goes to switch #2 and pulses it open (it's a reverse switch), and the source current is impeded.

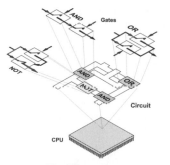

### The Hierarchy

The gates make up circuits, and circuits make a logical device, such as a CPU. We're going to look at a circuit that is present in every computer. It adds one bit to another.

### Adding Two Bits Together

The half-adder circuit adds one bit to another and yields a one-bit result with one carry bit. This circuit in combination with a shift register, which moves over to the next bit, is how a string of binary numbers are added. This diagram shows the four possible binary additions for two bits.

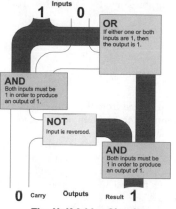

### The Half-Adder Circuit

Trace the current through the example above. See how AND, OR and NOT react to their inputs. The 1 is represented by the red line (flow of current), and the 0 by no line. If it makes sense to you, try it yourself below.

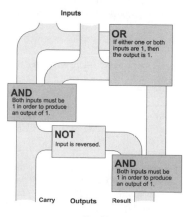

### Try It

Print this diagram and try your Boolean skill. Pick any combination of 0 and 1 and see if you can get the right answer. Review the combinations above.

**Boolean operator**    One of the Boolean logic operators such as AND, OR and NOT.

**Boolean search**    A search for specific data. It implies that any condition can be searched for using the Boolean operators AND, OR and NOT. For example, the English language request: "Search for all Spanish and French speaking employees who have MBAs, but don't work in Sales." is expressed in the following dBASE command:

```
list for degree = "MBA" .and.
  (language = "Spanish" .or. language = "French")
    .and. .not. department = "Sales""
```

**boot**    Cause the computer to start executing instructions. Personal computers contain built-in instructions in a ROM chip that are automatically executed on startup. These instructions search for the operating system, load it and pass control to it. Starting up a large computer may require more button pushing and keyboard input.

The term comes from "bootstrap," since bootstraps help you get your boots on, booting the computer helps it get its first instructions. The term is often used erroneously for application software. You might hear, for example, "let's boot Excel," whereas the correct usage is "launch Excel" or "load Excel." See *cold boot*, *warm boot* and *clean boot*.

**You Need Help
to Get Started**

**bootable CD-ROM**    A CD-ROM that can boot its own operating system. It is used to install the operating system on a brand new machine. See *bootable disk* and *El Torito*.

**bootable disk**    A disk that contains the operating system in a form ready to load into the computer. It usually refers to a floppy disk that contains the operating system in its boot sectors; however, increasingly, CD-ROMs are being made bootable. Desktop computers are usually configured to look for a bootable floppy in the primary floppy drive at startup (A: in a PC). If it is not found, it boots from the hard disk.

It's a good idea to make a bootable disk for your personal computer in case the hard disk doesn't boot some day. That way, you'll be able to start the computer and access important data. In Windows 95/98, select Startup Disk from the ADD/REMOVE PROGRAMS control panel. See also *DOS Sys* and *DOS/Windows format*.

**boot disk**    Same as *bootable disk*.

**boot drive**    A disk drive that is expected to contain the operating system. Most PCs are set to boot from the floppy drive first and the hard drive second. If a diskette is not inserted at startup, the BIOS switches to the hard disk. Although this order can be changed in the BIOS setup, keeping the floppy first provides a way to circumvent loading the operating system on the hard disk and allows another operating system to be loaded for diagnostic purposes or to try out a different one.

**boot failure**    The inability to locate and/or read the operating system from the designated disk.

**booting up**    The process of starting the computer. See *boot*.

**bootleg software**    Software that is illegally copied. See *software piracy*.

**boot manager**    A utility that allows multiple operating systems to be booted from the same computer. IBM's Boot Manager, PowerQuest's BootMagic and V Communications' System Commander are examples. See *dual boot*.

**BOOTP**    (BOOTstrap Protocol) A TCP/IP protocol used by a diskless workstation or network computer (NC) to obtain its IP address and other network information such as server address and default gateway. Upon startup, the client station sends out a BOOTP request in a UDP packet to the BOOTP server, which returns the required information. Unlike RARP, which uses only the layer 2 (Ethernet) frame for transport, the BOOTP request and response use an IP broadcast function that can send messages before a specific IP address is known. See *RARP*.

**boot record**    See *boot sector*.

**boot ROM**    A memory chip that allows a workstation to be booted from the server or other remote station. See *remote boot*.

**boot sector**    Reserved sectors on disk that are used to load the operating system. On startup, the computer looks for the master book record (MBR) or something similarly named, which is typically the first sector in the first partition of the disk. The MBR contains pointers to the first sector of the partition that contains the operating system, and that sector contains the instructions that cause the computer to boot the operating system.

**bootstrap**    See *boot*.

**boot virus**    A virus written into the boot sectors of a floppy disk. If the floppy is booted, it infects the system. For example, the Michelangelo virus, which destroys data on March 6th, Michelangelo's birthday, infects a computer if the virus diskette is left in the drive and booted inadvertently when the computer is turned back on.

**Borland**    (Borland Software Corporation, Scotts Valley, CA, www.borland.com) A software company founded as Borland International in 1983 by Philippe Kahn. The company is noted for its language and development products. It also popularized the desktop accessory for PCs with its DOS-based Sidekick program. Its Turbo Pascal moved Pascal out of the academic halls into a commercial product, and its Turbo C became an industry standard for DOS. Borland C++ and Delphi are widely used for developing Windows applications.

The company acquired the Paradox database in 1987 and dBASE in 1991, making it the leader in PC database software in the early 1990s. It later sold Paradox to Corel. In 1995, Kahn resigned as president, but remained as chairman. In 1998, Borland changed its name to Inprise Corporation in recognition of its focus on "integrating the enterprise." In 2001, it changed the name back to Borland.

**Philippe Kahn**
Borland's founder was a notable personality in the early days of personal computing and led the company into some very successful ventures. *(Image courtesy of Borland Software Corporation.)*

**Borland AppServer**    A Web-based application server for Windows NT and UNIX from Borland that is built on top of the popular VisiBroker CORBA ORB infrastructure. Introduced in late 1998, the product includes its own Web server, but can work with others as well. As of Version 4, it is J2EE compliant and supports EJBs. It fully integrates with Borland's JBuilder Java development environment and AppCenter application management system. See *VisiBroker*.

**Borland C++**    An ANSI C and C++ compiler from Borland for DOS and Windows applications. It is Turbo C-compatible and its debugger supports Windows programs written in Microsoft C. It includes application frameworks for Windows (ObjectWindows) and DOS (Turbo Vision). Borland C++ for OS/2 is also available. See *C++ Builder*.

**boss screen**    A fake business-like screen that can be quickly popped up over a game when the boss walks in.

**bot**    (1) (roBOT) A program used on the Internet that performs a repetitive function such as posting a message to multiple newsgroups or searching for information or news. Bots are used to provide comparison shopping. Bots also keep a channel open on the Internet Relay Chat (IRC). The term is used for all variety of macros and intelligent agents that are Internet or Web related. See *agent*.

(2) BOT—Beginning of tape. Similar to BOF.

**bottleneck**    A lessening of throughput. It often refers to networks that are overloaded, which is caused by the inability of the hardware and transmission lines to support the traffic. It can also refer to a mismatch inside the computer where slower-speed peripheral buses and devices prevent the CPU from being used to its fullest capacity.

**bounced e-mail**    An e-mail message that is returned to the sender. It is generally due to a misspelling of the name or an incorrect address. E-mail can also be returned if the size of the attached file exceeds a set limit by your ISP. See *e-mail*.

**boundary error**    An invalid value entered into an application. For example, if a number is higher or lower than a range of values or there are too many characters in a text entry, a boundary error occurs. See *validity checking*.

**boundary router**    (1) A router that connects the Internet to a company's intranet via a DMZ (demilitarized zone). The boundary router, which may be located at the ISP, is an external firewall that connects to the company's internal firewall and proxy server within the DMZ. See *DMZ*.

(2) Same as *edge router*.

**Boundary Routing**    3Com's trade name for remote office routing, which it pioneered. See *remote-office router*.

**boundary scan**    See *scan technology*.

**Bourne shell**    The original command line processor for UNIX. See *C shell*, *Korn shell*, **bash shell** and *UNIX*.

**box**    Slang for hardware. A box can be a PC or server or any device, although it is typically one that processes information. For example, a "UNIX box" is just another way of saying "UNIX computer."

**bozo filter**    A feature of certain e-mail programs that allows you to delete unread, unwanted mail based on the sender's address or words in the message header or message body. A bozo filter can also be set up using JavaScript on a Web page to block people coming from other Web pages.

**bpi**    (Bits Per Inch) The measurement of the number of bits stored in a linear inch of a track on a recording surface, such as on a disk or tape. After 2000, the bit density on magnetic disks is expected to exceed 500,000 bpi (500 Kbpi). See *track density*.

**bpp**    (1) (Bits Per Pixel) See *bit depth*.
(2) See *brokered private peering*.

**BPR**    (Business Process Reengineering) See *reengineering*.

**bps**    (Bits Per Second) The measurement of the speed of data transfer in a communications system.

**BQFP**    (Bumpered QFP) A earlier QFP package with "bumpers" sticking out from each of its four corners. The bumpers are square plastic protrusions. See *QFP*.

**brain dump**    An unorganized pile of written information quickly put together in an e-mail or newsgroup message in response to a general question. See *memory dump*.

**brains**    A computer's "brains" are its central processing unit. See *CPU*.

**branch**    (1) A machine instruction that switches the CPU to another location in the program (in memory). In assembly languages, branch and jump instructions provide the branch. In high-level languages, the goto statement provides the branch. For example, "IF A EQUALS B GOTO MATCH_ROUTINE." See *branch prediction*.
(2) A connection between two blocks in a flowchart or two nodes in a network.

**branch prediction**    In CPU instruction execution, predicting the outcome of a branch so that those instructions may be executed in parallel with the current instructions. If the CPU guesses the wrong branch, it will take extra machine cycles to go back and execute the correct one; however, on average, if the prediction algorithms are good, overall performance is increased. See *predication* and *branch*.

**BRAS**    (Broadband Remote Access Server) Pronouned "b-raz." A network switch that funnels traffic from DSL and/or cable modem aggregation devices to various carriers' networks based on type of application or type of service required. It supports authentication, traffic accounting, high-level protocols such as IP and MPLS. A BRAS lets carriers fine tune their service offerings as well as charge for traffic on a per-byte basis. See *IP services switch*.

**braze**    To solder using metals with a very high melting point, such as with an alloy of zinc and copper.

**BRB**    Digispeak for "be right back."

**breadboard**    A thin plastic board full of holes used to hold components (transistors, chips, etc.) that are wired together. It is used to develop electronic prototypes or one-of-a-kind systems.

**break**    To temporarily or permanently stop executing, printing or transmitting.

**Breadboard**
Breadboards are nothing more than plastic boards with holes in them. *(Image courtesy of 3M Company.)*

**break key**    A keyboard key that is pressed to stop the execution of the current program or transmission.

**breakout box**    A device inserted into a multiple-line cable for testing purposes that provides an external connecting point to each wire. A small LED may be attached to each line, that glows when a signal is present.

**breakpoint**    The location in a program used to temporarily halt the program for testing and debugging. Lines of code in a source program are marked for break-points. When those instructions are about to be executed, the program stops, allowing the programmer to examine the status of the program (registers, variables, etc.). After inspection, the programmer can step through the program one line at a time or cause the program to continue running either to the end or to the next breakpoint, whichever comes first.

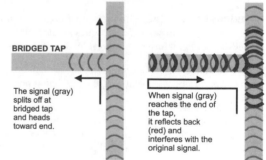

**Breakout Box**

**BRI**    See *ISDN*.

**bricks and mortar**    A store (shop, supermarket, department store, etc.) in the real world. Contrast with *clicks and mortar*.

**bridge**    **(1)** To cross from one circuit, channel or element over to another.

**(2)** A device that connects two LAN segments together, which may be of similar or dissimilar types, such as Ethernet and Token Ring. A bridge is inserted into a network to segment it and keep traffic contained within the segments to improve performance.

Bridges learn from experience and build and maintain address tables of the nodes on the network. By monitoring which station acknowledged receipt of the address, they learn which nodes belong to the segment.

Bridges work at the data link layer (OSI layer 2), whereas routers work at the network layer (layer 3). Bridges are protocol independent; routers are protocol dependent. Bridges are faster than routers because they do not have to read the protocol to glean routing information.

Bridges with more than two ports (multiport bridges) perform a switching function. Today's LAN switches are really multiport bridges that can switch at full wire speed. See *LAN*, *transparent bridge*, *repeater*, *router*, *gateway* and *hub*.

**bridge disc**    See *CD-ROM XA*.

**bridged tap**    In telephone communications, any cable pair spliced into the main pair. Many unused bridged taps remain from the early days when party lines were the norm and two or more taps were made on every line. The extra taps were later cut, taken off the termination block and buried into the wire maze, making them difficult to locate. Bridged taps cause undesirable reflection that can distort the high-frequency signals in modern transmission technologies.

**BRIDGED TAP**

The signal (gray) splits off at bridged tap and heads toward end.

When signal (gray) reaches the end of the tap, it reflects back (red) and interferes with the original signal.

**bridge router**    A communications device that provides the functions of a bridge and router. See *bridge* and *router*.

**bridgeware**    Hardware or software that converts data or translates programs from one format into another.

**Briefcase**    In Windows 95/98, a system folder used for synchronizing files between two computers, typically a desktop and laptop computer. Files to be worked on are placed into a Briefcase, which is then transferred to the second machine via floppy, cable or network. The Briefcase is then brought back to the original machine after its contents have been edited on the second machine, and a special update function replaces the original files with the new ones.

**brightness**    The light level on a display screen. Contrast with *contrast*.

**British Telecom**    The telephone and communications carrier that provides services in Great Britain and Northern Ireland. It used to be a division of the British Post Office, but was privatized in 1984 under Margaret Thatcher's regime.

**broadband**    (1) High-speed transmission. The term is commonly used to refer to communications lines or services at T1 rates (1.544 Mbps) and above. However, the actual threshold of broadband is very subjective and may be well below or well above T1 depending on the situation. For example, on2.com (see *TrueMotion*) offers "broadband streaming video" to users with access to the Internet at 250 Kbps or higher. Other sources claim 45 Mbps is the starting point. In every case however, it implies transmitting at higher speeds than what has been most common up to the current time. See *cable modem*, *DSL* and *T1*.

(2) A method of transmitting data, voice and video using frequency division multiplexing (FDM), such as used with cable TV. Modems are required to modulate digital data streams onto the line. Broadband in this context is used in contrast with baseband, which is all digital transmission and uses time division multiplexing (TDM). However, the term is mostly used in definition #1 above. See *baseband* for illustration.

**broadband access**    Typically refers to using the Internet via a cable modem, DSL or T1 line. See *broadband*.

**Broadband ISDN**    See *BISDN*.

**broadband service provider**    An ISP, telephone company or other carrier that offers high-speed communications to homes and businesses, typically for Internet access. Cable modems, DSL and T1 lines are the common technologies. See *broadband*, *cable modem*, *DSL* and *T1*.

**broadband wireless**    Wireless transmission at high speed. Wireless transmission is slower than wireline speeds, thus, whereas land-based broadband is generally at T1 rates and above, wireless might be considered broadband at 250 Kbps and above. See *broadband*.

**broadcast**    To transmit data to everybody on the network or network segment. Contrast with *narrowcast*. See *multicast*.

**Broadcast.com**    A Webcasting organization that broadcasts live and archived TV and radio shows from its www.broadcast.com Web site, as well as on-demand movies, sports and other audio and video material. It also offers organizations Webcasting for private meetings such as conferences, distance learning and workshops.

**broadcast fax**    The ability to send a fax to multiple recipients, which is very worthwhile when you need to disseminate faxes to several colleagues at once. Not so worthwhile, however, is receiving unsolicited faxes about something that you have no interest in. See *junk faxes*.

**broadcast storm**    Excessive transmission of broadcast traffic in a network. Broadcast storms can be lessened by properly designing and balancing the number of nodes on each network segment.

**broadcast traffic**    In a network, message traffic that is sent out to everybody on a network segment. Broadcasts are issued for address resolution when the location of a user or server is not known. They may occur when clients and servers come online and identify themselves. Sometimes, network devices continually announce their presence. In all cases, the broadcast has to reach all possible networks and stations that might potentially respond. Contrast with *multicast*.

**BroadVision**    A family of e-business applications from BroadVision, Inc., Redwood City, CA (www.broadvision.com) that provide the tools to develop a complete, commercial Web site. BroadVision One-To-One Enterprise is a CORBA and template-based application that runs on HP-UX, Solaris and NT servers and includes Windows-based tools for customizing the site's appearance and programming its functionality.

Other options in the BroadVision family include BroadVision One-To-One Commerce, which provides shopping and transaction capability; One-To-One Knowledge provides channels and publish and subscribe functions, and One-To-One Financial provides financial services. The company was founded in 1993 and initially developed interactive TV applications.

**brochureware**    A Web site that advertises a product but contains only the equivalent of a paper brochure with no interactivity. The Web is not encumbered by the size of paper and offers the ability to show endless views and details of a product, make recommendations based on user input, download demos (of software), compute order totals, even remember what you asked the last time you visited. All this is missing in brochureware.

**broken link**    A hyperlink on a Web page that does not work. It may be due to several things, including the Web server malfunctioning for the moment, or the Web site no longer exists or the page was moved to a different directory or renamed.

**broker**    See *information broker* and *message broker*.

**brokered private peering**    A peering arrangement for the Internet that is proposed by SAVVIS Communications Corporation, St. Louis, MO (www.savvis.com). It defines at least nine exchange points throughout the U.S.. Brokered private peering is more like a private cooperative among several ISPs rather than private peering, which is negotiated between two parties. See *NAP*.

**Brook's law**    "Adding manpower to a late software project makes it later." By Fred Brooks, author of *The Mythical Man-Month*. The extra human communications required to add another member to a programming team is considerably more than anyone ever expects. It, of course, depends on the experience and sophistication of the programmers involved and the quality of the documentation, which is often sparse. See *laws*.

**brouter**    (Bridging **ROUTER**) See *bridge router*.

**brownout**    A lowering of AC power voltage for some period of time. Brownouts can be very harmful to electronic equipment if sustained for long periods. Brownouts can cause flickering or a dimming onscreen, and the computer may experience intermittent problems as a result. See *blackout*.

**browse**    (1) To view the contents of a file or a group of files. Browser programs generally let you view data by scrolling through the documents or databases. In a database program, the browse mode often lets you edit the data. See *Web browser*.

(2) To view and edit a flow chart of a system created in a program specialized for visual system design or to view and edit a class hierarchy of objects in an object-oriented programming language.

(3) In Windows, the Browse button lets you view the file names in your disk folders. Clicking the names of the drives and folders switches you to those locations.

**browser**    A program that lets you look through a set of data. See *Web browser*, *microbrowser*, *class browser* and *browse*.

**browser cache**    Pronounced "browser cash." A temporary storage area in memory or on disk that holds the most recently downloaded Web pages. As you link from page to page on the Web, caching those pages in memory lets you quickly go back to a page without having to download it from the Web again. When you quit the browser session, those pages are stored on disk. The Web browser lets you set the amount of space to use and the length of time to hold them.

**browser compatibility**    The capability of a Web browser to effectively display the HTML code and execute the scripts on Web pages. The changes in HTML features since the mid-1990s, along with the versions of JavaScript and Java languages, combined with the differences between Netscape Navigator, Internet Explorer and other browsers have created an inordinately large number of versions that Web site developers have to deal with.

**browser phone**    A cell phone that includes Web browser capability. See *smart phone* and *microbrowser*.

**browser plug-in**    A third-party software product, such as a multimedia viewer, that extends a Web browser's capabilities. A helper application provides similar capabilities but runs as an external application and typically launches another window for viewing.

**browser safe colors**    See *Netscape color palette*.

**brute force programming**    See *hard coded*.

**BSC**    (Binary Synchronous Communications) See *bisync*.

**BSDL**    (Boundary Scan Description Language) An IEEE language used to describe structures for boundary scan testing. See *scan technology*.

**BSD socket**   A communications interface in UNIX first introduced in BSD UNIX. See *UNIX socket*.

**BSD UNIX**   (Berkeley Software Distribution UNIX) A version of UNIX developed by the Computer Systems Research Group of the University of California at Berkeley from 1979–1993. BSD enhancements, known as the "Berkeley Extensions," include networking, virtual memory, task switching and large file names (up to 255 chars.). BSD's UNIX was distributed free, with a charge only for the media. USL code is contained in most BSD versions, and users require a valid USL license in such cases.

Bill Joy ran the group until 1982 when he co-founded Sun Microsystems, bringing 4.2BSD with him as the foundation of SunOS. The last BSD version released by BSD was 4.4BSD.

Berkeley Software Design, Inc., Colorado Springs, CO (www.bsdi.com), a private company founded in 1991, continues to develop BSD code. See *OpenBSD*.

**BSOD**   See *Blue Screen of Death* and *Black Screen of Death*.

**b-spline**   In computer graphics, a curve that is generated using a mathematical formula that assures continuity with other b-splines. See *spline* and *NURB*.

**BT**   See *British Telecom*.

**BTA**   (Business Technology Association, Kansas City, MO, www.bta.org) A membership association of office equipment dealers founded in 1994. It is a merger of NOMDA (National Office Machine Dealers Association), founded in 1926, with LANDA and AIMED (LAN Dealers Association and Affiliated Independent Mailing Equipment Dealers). Publications, training seminars and annual Business Technology Expos are sponsored by the BTA.

**BTAM**   (Basic Telecommunications Access Method) IBM communications software used in bisynch, non-SNA mainframe networks. Application programs must interface directly with the BTAM access method.

**BTB**   See *B2B*.

**BTLZ**   (British Telecom Lempel-Ziv) A data compression algorithm based on the Lempel-Ziv method that can achieve up to 4x the throughput of 2400 and 9600 bps modems.

**b-to-b**   See *B2B*.

**b-to-c**   See *B2C*.

**B-tree**   (Balanced-tree) A technique for organizing indexes. In order to keep access time to a minimum, it stores the data keys in a balanced hierarchy that continually realigns itself as items are inserted and deleted. Thus, all nodes always have a similar number of keys.

B+tree is a version of B-tree that maintains a hierarchy of indexes while also linking the data sequentially, providing fast direct access and fast sequential access. IBM's VSAM uses this.

**Btrieve**   A database manager for NetWare, Windows 95/98 and Windows NT from Btrieve Technologies, Inc., Austin, TX. It allows for the creation of indexed files, using the b-tree organization method. Btrieve functions can be called from within many common programming languages. Btrieve was originally developed by Novell for NetWare. In 1994, it was sold to Btrieve Technologies, which was founded by former Novell employees. See *Xtrieve*.

**BTW**   Digispeak for "by the way."

**bubble**   A bit in bubble memory or a symbol in a bubble chart.

**BubbleBoy virus**   An e-mail virus launched in November 1999 that affected English and Spanish versions of Microsoft Outlook running with Windows 98 or 2000 and Internet Explorer 5. It did not do any harm, but sent out an e-mail to everyone in the address list, which may have caused a mail storm in certain networks. The virus took advantage of a loophole in Internet Explorer 5 that allows an HTML page or an HTML e-mail message to write files without passing through the required authorization (ActiveX authorization).

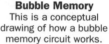

BubbleBoy was a watershed event because it was the first time an e-mail message itself, not an e-mail attachment, was able to execute in the client machine. Adding HTML e-mail to mail readers makes e-mail look just like a Web page; but it becomes subject to virus attacks, because HTML pages can embed or point to Java, JavaScript and ActiveX code, all of which is executable. Our never-ending fixation with making dull text pages glitter and sparkle has created the potential for greater damage, because e-mail is so ubiquitous. See *e-mail virus*.

**bubble chart**     A chart that uses bubble-like symbols often used to depict data flow diagrams.

**Bubble Jet**     Canon's trade name for its thermal drop on demand ink jet printer technology. The ink is heated, which produces a bubble that expands and ejects the ink out of the nozzle. As the bubble cools, the vacuum created draws fresh ink back into the nozzle.

**bubble memory**     A solid state semiconductor and magnetic storage device suited for rugged applications. It is about as fast as a slow hard disk and holds its content without power.

It is conceptually a stationary disk with spinning bits. The unit, only a couple of square inches in size, contains a thin film magnetic recording layer. Globular-shaped bubbles (bits) are electromagnetically generated in circular strings inside this layer. In order to read or write the bubbles, they are rotated past the equivalent of a read/write head.

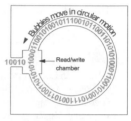

**Bubble Memory**
This is a conceptual drawing of how a bubble memory circuit works.

**bubble sort**     A multiple-pass sorting technique that starts by sequencing the first two items, then the second with the third, then the third with the fourth, and so on, until the end of the set has been reached. The process is repeated until all items are in the correct sequence.

**bucket**     Another term for a variable. It's just a place to store something.

**buckyballs**     A form of carbon expected to have use in a wide variety of applications including computer chips. They are also known as "buckminsterfullerenes," because the 60 atoms that make up their spherical molecule resemble Buckminster Fuller's geodesic domes. Buckyballs were identified in 1985 by three scientists who later received a Nobel prize for the discovery. Buckyballs are used as a building block for many experimental materials. See *buckytubes*.

**buckytubes**     Also called "nanotubes," they are a form of carbon that resembles a cylinder or tube. Accidentally discovered by a Japanese researcher in 1990 while making buckyballs, they have potential for use in a variety of applications including electronic instruments and circuitry. With a tensile strength 100 times greater than steel at about one quarter the weight, buckytubes are considered the strongest material for their weight known to mankind. See *buckyballs*.

**buddy list**     A list of colleagues, workgroup members, friends, etc., that you might wish to communicate with via instant messaging. See *instant messaging*.

**BUF**     (BUFfer gate) A logic gate that generates the same output as the input. It is used as a relay to increase power, to add some delay in the circuit and to isolate signals. See *logic gate*.

| BUF | |
|---|---|
| IN | OUT |
| 0 | 0 |
| 1 | 1 |

**buffer**     A reserved segment of memory used to hold data while it is being processed. In a program, buffers are created to hold some amount of data from each of the files that will be read or written. In a streaming media application, the program uses buffers to store an advance supply of audio or video data to compensate for momentary delays.

With regular computer applications, buffers are allocated and deallocated from the general memory pool. In printers and other hardware devices, buffers can be small memory banks used for just one temporary storage function. See *double buffering*.

**buffer amplifier**     An analog device that is typically used for impedance matching and signal isolation. For example, a sound card typically uses buffer amps at most of its input and output ports.

**buffer flush**     The transfer of data from memory to disk. Whenever you command your application to save the document you're working on, the program is actually flushing its buffer (writing the contents of one or more reserved areas of memory to the hard disk).

**Go Flush Your Cold Buffer!**    Try this one out on your colleagues. A cold buffer is a reserved area of memory that contains data, which hasn't been updated for a while. Cold buffers are flushed at periodic intervals. More important, this phrase sounds as strange as they get. Better yet, try "go flush your cold buffer into your SCSI DASD" (pronounced scuzzy dazdy). Be sure to say this without cracking a smile, and expect quite a grin from a systems professional. If your friend doesn't understand this phrase, be sure to recommend a good computer dictionary!

**buffering**    Currently downloading the first block of data. In streaming audio or video, it refers to bringing in an initial amount of data (filling the buffer) before actually playing or displaying the material. Having more data in the buffer than is necessary for realtime delivery compensates for momentary delays in transmission from the source that would otherwise cause blips in the sound or video.

**buffer pool**    An area of memory reserved for buffers.

**buffer underrun**    See *underrun*.

**bug**    A persistent error in software or hardware. If the bug is in software, it can be corrected by changing the program. If the bug is in hardware, new circuits have to be designed.

Although the derivation of bug is generally attributed to the moth that was found squashed between the points of an electromechanical relay in a computer in the 1940s, the term goes back to the 1800s to refer to flaws in mechanical systems. See *bug fix*, *software bug* and *Web bug*. Contrast with *glitch*.

**A Note from the Author**    On October 19, 1992, I found my first "real bug." When I fired up my laser printer, it printed blotchy pages. Upon inspection, I found a bug lying belly up in the trough below the corona wire. The printer worked fine after removing it!

**bug compatible**    A hardware device that contains the same design flaws as the original.

**bug fix**    A revised program file or patch that corrects a software bug. See *bug*, *patch* and *hot fix*.

**bug inheritance**    Software bugs that are brought down from a higher-level class in an object-oriented system.

**bugrade**    (**BUg** up**GRADE**) A software upgrade that fixes bugs more than it adds functionality. Although new features are touted, the upgrade is purchased to eliminate headaches in the prior version. See *upgrade*.

**build**    (1) A version of a program, typically one still in testing. Although a version number is usually given to a released product, sometimes, a build number is used instead. See *gold code*.

(2) To program (write lines of code).

**buildout**    The construction and implementation of a system. For example, "network buildout" implies constructing the network and going online.

**bulk eraser**    A device that uses electromagnetic energy to erase all the data from magnetic disks and tapes. See *degauss*.

**bulk storage**    Storage that is not used for high-speed execution. May refer to auxiliary memory, tape or disk.

**Bull**    (Bull Worldwide Information Systems, Billerica, MA, www.bull.com) A worldwide computer and information services company with offices in more than 100 countries. It was founded in France in 1933 by Norwegian engineer Fredrik Rosing Bull, who created a revolutionary adding-sorting machine in 1921.

In the 1960s, Bull partnered with GE in computer development in France. When Honeywell took over GE's computer business in 1970, its French division became Honeywell Bull. In 1987, Honeywell turned all its computer business over to Bull. For a while, both Honeywell and NEC had ownership in the company, which was named Bull HN. Today, all operations are under the Bull name.

Bull's smart card distributor, MICRO CARD Technologies, Inc., designs and manufactures IC cards with a wide range of memory and processing power. See *Honeywell*.

**bulletin board**    See *BBS*.

**bulletproof**    Refers to extremely stable hardware and/or software that cannot be brought down no matter what unusual conditions arise. See *industrial strength*.

**bump file**    (BuMP file)  See *BMP file*.

**bump mapping**    In computer graphics, a technique for simulating rough textures by creating irregularities in shading.

**BUNCH**    (**B**urroughs, **U**nivac, **N**CR, **C**ontrol Data and **H**oneywell)  IBM's competitors after RCA and GE got out of the computer business.

**bundle**    To sell hardware and software as a single product or to combine several software packages for sale as a single unit. Contrast with *unbundle*. See also *bundling*.

**bundling**    Combining elements together. Outside the U.S., it is a substitute term for "bonding." For example, "ISDN bundling" and "ISDN bonding" are the same. See *bundle*.

**bunny suit**    The protective clothing worn by an individual in a clean room that keeps human bacteria from infecting the chip-making process. The outfit makes people look like oversized rabbits.

**burn**    To write a write-once optical medium such as a CD-Recordable disc.

**burn in**    To test a new electronic system by running it for some length of time. Weak components often fail within the first few hours of use.

**burn rate**    The speed with which a new, unprofitable company is spending its initial funding whether from investors or from an IPO. In the world of high-speed high tech, the burn rate is carefully monitored to determine how long the company has to live.

**Burroughs**    See *Unisys*.

**burster**    A mechanical device that separates continuous paper forms into cut sheets. A burster can be attached to the end of a collator, which separates multipart forms into single parts.

**burst mode**    A high-speed transmission mode in a communications or computer channel. Under certain conditions, the system sends a burst of data at higher speed for a limited amount of time. For example, a multiplexor channel may suspend transmitting several streams of data and send one high-speed transmission using the entire bandwidth.

**bursty**    Refers to data that is transferred or transmitted in short, uneven spurts. LAN traffic is typically bursty. Contrast with *streaming data*.

**bus**    A common pathway, or channel, between multiple devices. The computer's internal bus is known as the local bus, or processor bus. It provides a parallel data transfer path between the CPU and main memory and to the peripheral buses. A 16-bit bus transfers two bytes at a time over 16 wires; a 32-bit bus uses 32 wires, etc. The bus is comprised of two parts: the address bus and the data bus. Addresses are sent over the address bus to signal a memory location, and the data is transferred over the data bus to that location.

**Bump-mapped Object**
A bump map has been applied to the teapot at the bottom. *(Image courtesy of Intergraph Computer Systems.)*

**Bunny Suit**
Getting into a bunny suit is an elaborate procedure with as many as 100 steps. All workers in a clean room must wear them. *(Image courtesy of VLSI Technology, Inc.)*

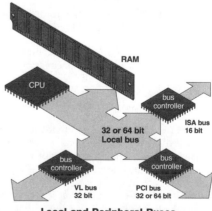

**Local and Peripheral Buses**
Expansion boards (cards, adapters, etc.) plug into the computer's bus and signals and data pass between the peripheral device and memory.

Various buses have been used in the PC, including the ISA, EISA, Micro Channel, VL-bus and PCI bus. Examples of other peripheral buses are NuBus, TURBO-channel, VMEbus, MULTIBUS and STD bus.

Another type of bus is a network bus. For example, some Ethernets use a serial bus, which is a common cable connecting all stations. A data packet, which contains the address of the destination station, is broadcast to all nodes at the same time, and the recipient computer responds by accepting it. Data is transmitted serially (one bit after the other) over the cable. See *local bus* and *software bus*.

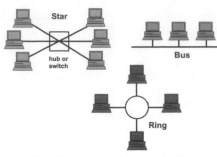

**The Three Network Configurations**
In a network, the bus is one of three primary topologies.

**Why Is It Called a Bus?**    The term was coined after a real bus, the concept being that a bus stops at all the bus stops en route. In an electronic bus, the signals go to all stations connected to it. A weak analog perhaps, but the term will live forever.

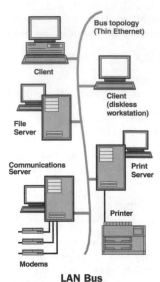

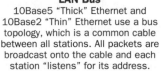

**LAN Bus**
10Base5 "Thick" Ethernet and 10Base2 "Thin" Ethernet use a bus topology, which is a common cable between all stations. All packets are broadcast onto the cable and each station "listens" for its address.

**bus and tag channel**    A common name for the parallel channel between IBM mainframes and peripherals. One set of cables carries the data (the bus), and another set is for control information (the tag). IBM's OEM Information publication (OEMI) is another term for this. See *parallel channel* and *ESCON*.

**bus attached**    Connected directly to the computer's peripheral bus using a hardware interface such as SCSI, IDE, SSA or ESCON.

**bus bridge**    A device that connects two similar or dissimilar busses together, such as two VMEbuses or a VMEbus and a Futurebus. This is not the same as a communications bridge, which connects network segments together. See *bridge*.

**bus card**    An expansion board (card) that plugs into the computer's expansion bus.

**bus/core ratio**    The relationship between the speed of the computer's system bus and the CPU. For example, a 1/4 ratio means that the CPU runs four times as fast as the bus. See *core speed*.

**bus extender**    (1) A board that pushes a printed circuit board out of the way of surrounding boards for testing purposes. It plugs into an expansion slot, and the expansion board plugs into the bus extender.

(2) A device that extends the physical distance of a bus. See *repeater*.

(3) A device that increases the number of expansion slots. It is either an expansion board containing multiple expansion slots, or an expansion board that cables to a separate housing that contains the slots and its own power supply.

**business analyst**    An individual who analyzes the operations of a department or functional unit with the purpose of developing a general systems solution to the problem that may or may not require automation. The business analyst, who is often part of a user department, can provide insights into its operation for the systems analyst that reports to the information systems department.

**Business Basic**    A version of the BASIC programming language derived from the original Dartmouth BASIC created by Kemeny and Kurtz. It was first developed by MAI Systems Corporation with later versions known as Thoroughbred Basic from Thoroughbred Software International, Inc., Somerset, NJ, and BBxPROGRESSION/4 from Basis International, Ltd., Irvine, CA.

**business card CD**     An audio CD or CD-ROM that is cut into the shape of a business card after it is pressed by the manufacturer or recorded on a CD-ROM. Although variations of the full-size 120mm disc may be used, business card CDs are often cut from the smaller 80mm mini CD format, which fits into the slightly indented center circle in the drive tray. They also hold considerably less than a full-size disc, generally from 20–150MB, depending on shape. See *custom-cut CD*.

**business graphics**     Numeric data represented in graphic form. While line graphs, bar charts and pie charts are the common forms of business graphics, there are dozens of others types. The ability to generate business graphics is often included in spreadsheet and presentation graphics programs.

**business intelligence**     Any information that pertains to the history, current status or future projections of an organization. See BI software and *business intelligence portal*.

**business intelligence portal**     A corporate portal that enables users to query and produce reports on enterprise-wide databases. The term was coined by Information Advantage, makers of the MyEureka software, which was the first to combine BI software with a corporate portal. See *MyEureka* and *BI software*.

**business intelligence software**     See *BI software*.

**Business Card CDs**
Note the difference in size to a regular CD. Business card CDs are usually shaped for the inner circle of the drive tray.

Pie Chart     Bar Chart     Graph
**Common Graphics Types**
These are the primary formats of business graphics.

**business logic**     The part of an application program that performs the required data processing of the business. It refers to the routines that perform the data entry, update, query and report processing, and more specifically to the processing that takes place behind the scenes rather the presentation logic required to display the data on the screen (GUI processing). Client applications are made up of a user interface and business logic. Server applications are mostly business logic.

Both client and server applications also require communications links, but the network infrastructure, like the user interface, is not part of the business logic.

**business machine**     Any office machine, such as a typewriter or calculator, that is used in clerical and accounting functions. The term has traditionally excluded computers and terminals.

**Business Objects**     (1) (Business Objects, San Jose, CA, www.businessobjects.com)  The leading software company specializing in decision support tools for the business market. Founded in France in 1990 by Bernard Liautaud and Denis Payre, Business Objects was the first to integrate query, reporting and OLAP into one product, using a patented semantic layer that shields end users from the complexities of making a query. Products include its flagship BusinessObjects software, BusinessQuery for Excel and BusinessMiner data mining program.

The use of the word "objects" refers to "items," not object technology, as the company was founded and its products were created before object-oriented programming became popular. See *BusinessObjects*.

(2) A broad category of business processes that are modeled as objects. A business object can be as large as an entire order processing system or a small process within an information system. See *object technology* and *object-oriented programming*.

**BusinessObjects**     A query, reporting and analysis tool from Business Objects that runs under all versions of Windows and various UNIX clients. It is the leading decision support tool in the business market, providing access to a wide variety of databases, including Oracle, INFORMIX and DB2. As data is extracted from the database, it is stored as multidimensional OLAP cubes that can be easily sliced and diced into different views.

BusinessObjects uses a patented semantic layer that shields users from the complexities of table names and relationships. Once the semantic layer has been defined, users work with familiar "business objects" such as product, customer and revenue.

The use of the word "objects" refers to "items," not object technology, as the company and products were created before object-oriented programming became popular. See *Business Objects*.

**business process reengineering**   See *reengineering*.

**business rule**   A directive, policy or procedure within an organization. Business rules may also come from outside sources such as government regulations and membership association guidelines. See *SME*.

**business software**   Software used to run a company. It specifically excludes games and entertainment products. See *application suite*.

**A BusinessObjects Query**
Once the business objects have been defined, users simply drag and drop the icons from the window on the left into the windows on the right. *(Screen shot courtesy of Business Objects.)*

**bus mastering**   A bus design that allows the peripheral controllers (plug-in boards) to access the computer's memory independent of the CPU. It allows data transfers to take place between the peripheral device and memory while the CPU is performing other tasks.

**bus mouse**   A mouse that plugs into an expansion board instead of the serial port. This type of mouse was somewhat popular in the 1980s. Its connector looks like a PS/2 connector, but the pin configurations are different and not compatible.

**bus network**   A network topology that uses a common pathway between all devices. Ethernet 10Base5 and 10Base2 are examples of bus networks. See *bus* and *Ethernet*.

**bus topology**   See *bus network*.

**busy hour**   The one hour of the day that a telephone system handles the most calls. Most internal PBXs and even the telco systems are not designed to handle 100% of the calls during the busy hour. The actual busy hour changes over time depending on the habits of the population. For example, the Internet has caused the busy hour to be later in the evening when people come home from work and start surfing the Web. See *BHCA*.

**Butterfly Switch**   A parallel processing topology from BBN Advanced Computers Inc., Cambridge, MA, that mimics a crossbar and provides high-speed switching of data between nodes. It can also be used to create a hypercube topology.

**button**   (1) A knob, such as on a printer or a mouse, that is pushed with the finger to activate a function.
(2) A simulated button on screen that is "pushed" by clicking it with the mouse.

**buzzwords**   A term used to refer to what is current or "in" in the field. Buzzwords are hot for a while and then either become mainstream or fade away. Right now, the Web, Java, e-commerce and other Internet-related terms are the hot terms. If the buzzwords are really meaningful, they will make headlines for a couple of years before they blend into the woodwork, making way for the next round.

Some of the major buzzwords in the past were *MIS* in the 1970s, *distributed computing* in the 1980s and *client/server* in the 1990s.

As we cross over into the twenty-first century, some of the latest buzzwords are *e-commerce*, *ASP*, *CRM*, *middleware*, *solutions provider*, *XML* and *business intelligence*.

**Bus mouse connector**
5/16"

**PS/2 connector**
5/16"

**Bus Mouse and PS/2 Connectors Look Alike**
The plug on a bus mouse looks similar to the common PS/2 connector, but it has a different pin structure.

**On-screen Button**
The button on the left is in its normal state. The one on the right has been depressed. When a button is clicked, it simulates the physical depression of a real button by offsetting the icon a few pixels and switching the shadow lines from the right and bottom to the top and left edges.

**BXXP**    (**B**locks **EX**tensible **EX**change **P**rotocol)  An IETF protocol designed to provide an alternate transport to HTTP for the Internet. HTTP has been severely strained by all the various media types it has been forced to carry. BXXP enables simultaneous transmissions to take place, such as chatting and file transfer within the same application, which TCP/IP inherently supports (you use this capability when you run two or more Web applications at the same time).

BXXP also provides the error checking and basic functions necessary in a communications protocol. Writing protocols that support multiple channels is tedious, and having this capability built into a common layer is expected to speed up the development of future Web-based protocols. BXXP was conceived by Marshall Rose, who helped develop the POP3, SNMP and SMTP protocols so widely used on the Internet.

**bypass**    In communications, to avoid the local telephone company by using satellites and microwave systems.

**byte**    (**Binar**Y **T**abl**E**)  The common unit of computer storage from micro to mainframe. It is made up of eight binary digits (bits). A ninth bit may be used in the memory circuits as a parity bit for error checking. The term was originally coined to mean the smallest addressable group of bits in a computer, which has not always been eight.

A byte holds the equivalent of a single character, such as the letter A, a dollar sign or decimal point. For numbers, a byte can hold a single decimal digit (0 to 9), two numeric digits (packed decimal) or a number from 0 to 255 (binary numbers).

Byte Specifications    The primary specifications of hardware are rated in bytes; for example, a 40-megabyte (40M or 40MB) disk holds 40 million characters of instructions and data. A one-megabyte (1M or 1MB) memory allows one million characters of instructions and data to be stored internally for processing.

With database files and word processing documents, the file size is slightly larger than the number of data characters stored in it. Word processing files contain embedded codes for layout settings (margins, tabs, boldface); therefore, a 100,000-byte document implies slightly less than 100,000 characters of text (approx. 30 pages). Database files contain codes that describe the data fields within the records; thus, a 100,000-byte database file holds less than 100,000 characters of data.

Unlike data and text, a 100,000-byte graphics file is not indicative of the size of the image contained within. A 100,000 byte vector graphics file may render a very detailed and elaborate drawing, while a 100,000-byte bitmap file would be considerably smaller. Depending on the format, compression method and number of colors used, bitmapped images can range from a few thousand bytes up into the millions. See *bit*.

**byte addressable**    A computer that can address each byte of memory independent of the others. In today's computers, all of memory is usually byte addressable, which is why memory is used for processing. Units (fields) of data can be worked on independently. Contrast with *word addressable*.

**bytecode**    An intermediate language that is executed by a runtime interpreter. Java and Visual Basic source programs are compiled into bytecode, which is then executed by their respective interpreters. See *Java*.

**byte order**    The order of bytes in a computer word (words are 8, 16, 32 and 64 bits long). "Big endian" is the normal order and the way humans deal with arithmetic: the most significant byte or digits are placed leftmost in the structure. Some CPUs, most notably Intel CPUs, deal with words in "little endian" order, which is the reverse and places the least significant digits on the left. Since numbers are calculated by the CPU starting with the least significant digits, little endian numbers are already set up in the required processing order.

A "bi-endian" machine, such as the PowerPC, supports both big endian and little endian words. In the following example, the decimal number 23,041 (equivalent to 5A01 in hex) is shown in both byte orders.

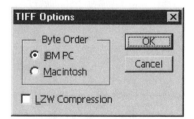

**Choosing Byte Order**
TIFF images store pixel values as words, and byte order makes a difference, witness this Photoshop dialog box asking which platform you're saving to. On the other hand, GIFs and JPEGs are not word oriented, and byte order does not matter.

```
BYTE ORDER FOR 23,041 (5A01 in hex)

Big endian              Little endian
(Such as Motorola 680x0)   (Such as Intel x86)

5A01                    015A
```

**byte-oriented protocol**    A communications protocol that uses control codes made up of full bytes. The bisynchronous protocols used by IBM and other vendors are examples. Contrast with *bit-oriented protocol*.

**byte serving**    Also called "page on demand," it is the ability to retrieve a specific page or set of pages rather than the entire document. For example, if the Web server and browser support byte serving, Acrobat files (PDF files) can be viewed as soon as the first couple of pages have been downloaded. The remainder of the file is retrieved in the background.

**byte sex**    The order of the bits in a byte. See *byte order*.

**bytesexual**    Same as *bi-endian*.

**C**  A high-level programming language developed at Bell Labs that is able to manipulate the computer at a low level like assembly language. During the last half of the 1980s, C became the language of choice for developing commercial software.

C can be compiled into machine languages for almost all computers. For example, UNIX is written in C and runs in a wide variety of micros, minis and mainframes.

C, as well as C++, are written as a series of functions that call each other for processing. Even the body of the program is a function named "main." Functions are very flexible, allowing programmers to choose from the standard library that comes with the compiler, to use third-party functions from other C suppliers, or to develop their own.

Compared to other high-level programming languages, C appears complicated. Its intricate appearance is due to its extreme flexibility. C was standardized by ANSI (X3J11 committee) and ISO in 1989. See *Turbo C*, *Borland C++*, *Microsoft C* and *Visual C++*.

**The Origin of C**  C was developed to allow UNIX to run on a variety of computers. After Bell Labs' Ken Thompson and Dennis Ritchie created UNIX and got it running on several PDP computers, they wanted a way to easily port it to other machines without having to rewrite it from scratch. Thompson created the B language, which was a simpler version of the BCPL language, itself a version of CPL. Later, in order to improve B, Thompson and Ritchie created C.

The following C example converts fahrenheit to centigrade:

```
main()    {
float fahr;
printf("Enter Fahrenheit ");
scanf("%f", &fahr);
printf("Celsius is %f\n", (fahr-32)*5/9);
        }
```

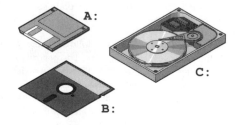

**C:**  The designation for the primary hard disk in a PC. The "C" evolved from the early personal computers that used A: and B: as the labels for two floppy drives. When hard disks became available, they were named C:. Then, for a while, A: and B: were used for the two types of floppies (3.5" and 5.25"). When the 5.25" disk was no longer used, PCs wound up with A: and C: drives. Letters starting with D: and up are used for CD-ROMs, Zip disks, DVDs and other removable media.

**C#**  (C Sharp) An object-oriented programming language from Microsoft that is based on C++ with elements from Visual Basic and Java. For example, like Java C# provides automatic garbage collection, whereas C++ does not. Geared to Microsoft's .NET platform, C# supports XML and SOAP and has access to the .NET class library. See *.NET* and *SOAP*.

**C++**  An object-oriented version of C created by Bjarne Stroustrup. C++ has become popular because it combines traditional C programming with OOP capability. Smalltalk and other original OOP languages did not provide the familiar structures of conventional languages such as C and Pascal. Microsoft's Visual C++ is the most widely used C++ compiler. See *Visual C++*, *Borland C++* and *C++ Builder*.

**C++ Builder**   A C++ compiler and development environment for Windows from Borland. Introduced in 1997, it provides more rapid development tools than Borland C++ and also enables COM and CORBA objects to be built. Its interface is similar to Borland's Delphi and JBuilder products. See *Borland C++*.

**C2**   The minimum security level defined by the National Computer Security Center. See *NCSC*.

**C7**   (Common Channel Signaling 7) See *SS7*.

**CA**   (1) (Computer Associates International, Inc., Islandia, NY, www.cai.com)  The world's largest diversified software vendor offering more than 500 applications from micro to mainframe. Founded in 1976 by Charles Wang and three associates, its first product was CA-SORT, a very successful IBM mainframe utility. Its first personal computer software was SuperCalc, one of the earliest spreadsheets. Computer Associates has grown via numerous acquisitions over the years, and in 1989, was the first independent software company to reach $1 billion in sales. Computer Associates product names generally use a "CA" prefix.

(2) (Certification Authority)  An organization that issues digital certificates (digital IDs) and makes its public key widely available to its intended audience. See *digital certificate*.

(3) (Continuous Availability)  See *fault tolerant*.

**Charles Wang**
Wang developed the world's largest diversified software company that covers all segments of the industry from micro to mainframe.
*(Image courtesy of Computer Associates International, Inc.)*

**CAB file**   (**CAB**inet file) A file format from Microsoft used to hold compressed files on its distribution disks. The Windows 95/98 Extract program is run at the DOS command line to decompress the files. For example, to view the content of the WIN95_02.CAB file in the \WIN95 directory on the E: drive, you would use the **/d** (display) switch as follows:

```
C:\extract e:\win95\win95_02.cab  /d
```

To copy and decompress EDIT.COM from that same CAB file into the current directory, you would type:

```
C:\ANYWHEREextract e:\win95\win95_02.cab edit.com
```

**cable**   A flexible metal or glass wire or group of wires. All cables used in electronics are insulated with a material such as plastic or rubber.

**cable categories**   The following categories are based on their transmission capacity. The majority of new wiring installations use Category 5 UTP wire in order to be able to run or upgrade to the faster network technologies that will require it. Categories 1 through 5 are based on the EIA/TIA-568 standard. Levels 6 and 7 are enhanced Category 5 cables and are not yet standardized. See *twisted pair*.

| Category | Cable Type | Application |
|----------|------------|-------------|
| 1 | UTP | Analog voice |
| 2 | UTP | Digital voice |
|   |     | 1 Mbps data |
| 3 | UTP, STP | 16 Mbps data |
| 4 | UTP, STP | 20 Mbps data |
| 5 | UTP, STP | 100 Mbps data |
| Level 6 | UTP, STP | 155 Mbps data |
| Level 7 | UTP, STP | 1000 Mbps data |

**cable Internet**   Internet access via cable TV. There are two kinds of service. One uses a cable modem to connect to a computer, and the other uses an enhanced cable box that provides Internet

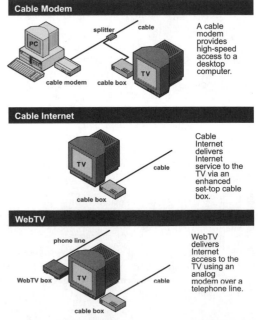

**Cable Modem**

A cable modem provides high-speed access to a desktop computer.

**Cable Internet**

Cable Internet delivers Internet service to the TV via an enhanced set-top cable box.

**WebTV**

WebTV delivers Internet access to the TV using an analog modem over a telephone line.

access directly at the TV. Both of these differ from WebTV, which requires a phone line. See *cable modem*, **WorldGate** and *WebTV*.

**cable matcher**    Same as *gender changer*.

**cable modem**    A modem used to connect a computer to a cable TV service that provides Internet access. Cable modems can dramatically increase the bandwidth between the user's computer and the Internet service provider. Cable modems link to the computer via Ethernet, which makes the service online all the time. However, Ethernet is a shared medium, and the speed will vary depending on how many customers on that cable segment are using the Web at the same time. See *cable Internet*, *Internet appliance* and *WebTV*.

**cable plant**    The wires and connectors used to tie a network together. See *outside plant*.

**cable telephony**    Telephone service provided by a cable TV company.

**cabletext**    A videotex service that uses coaxial cable. See *videotex*.

**Cabletron**    (Cabletron Systems, Inc., Rochester, NH, www.cabletron.com) A holding company for network products and services companies. In early 2000, Cabletron turned itself into four independent companies: Enterasys Networks for enterprise class routers and switches, River Stone Networks for carrier class products, Aprisma Management Technologies for network management and GlobalNetwork Technology Services for consulting.

Cabletron was founded in 1983 by S. Robert Levine and Craig Benson. What began as a part-time venture in a garage evolved into a billion dollar company by 1996. Cabletron has been known for its modular hubs and switches that support Ethernet, Token Ring, FDDI, SNA and ATM. The company also developed a reputation for its advanced SPECTRUM network management software, which is now under the Aprisma umbrella.

**cable TV**    The transmission of TV programs into the home and office via coaxial cable. Cable TV organizations have tremendous potential for new services since they are already wired into so many homes. See *cable Internet*, *data broadcast* and *CATV*.

**cache**    Pronounced "cash." A cache is used to speed up data transfer and may be either temporary or permanent. Memory and disk caches are in every computer to speed up instruction execution and data retrieval. These temporary caches serve as staging areas, and their contents can be changed in seconds or milliseconds (see below).

Browser caches and Internet caches hold popular Web pages long periods of time and even for the duration, because caching servers constantly update the page with the latest version from the Internet (see *Web cache* and *browser cache*). In these cases, the cache database is actually a folder on the disk. See *router cache*.

**Memory Caches**    A memory cache, or "CPU cache," is a memory bank that bridges main memory and the CPU. It is faster than main memory and allows instructions to be excecuted and data to be read at higher speed. Instructions and data are transferred to the cache in blocks, using some kind of look-ahead algorithm. The more sequential the instructions in the routine being accessed, and the more sequential the order of the data being read, the more chance the next desired item will still be in the cache, and the greater improvement in performance.

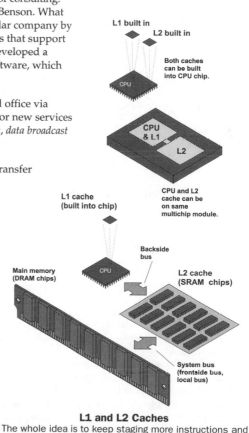

**L1 and L2 Caches**
The whole idea is to keep staging more instructions and data in a high-speed memory closer to the CPU.

A level 1 (L1) cache is a memory bank built into the CPU chip. A level 2 cache (L2) is a secondary staging area that feeds the L1 cache. Increasing the size of the L2 cache may speed up some applications but have no effect on others. L2 may be built into the CPU chip, reside on a separate chip in a multichip package module (see *MCP*) or be a separate bank of chips. Caches are typically static RAM (SRAM), while main memory is generally some variety of dynamic RAM (DRAM). See *SRAM* and *DRAM*.

Disk Caches    A disk cache is a section of main memory or memory on the disk controller board that bridges the disk and the CPU. When the disk is read, a larger block of data is copied into the cache. If subsequent requests for data can be satisfied in the cache, a much slower disk access is not required.

If the cache is used for writing, data is queued up at high speed and then written to disk during idle machine cycles by the caching program. If the cache is built into the hardware, the disk controller figures out when to do it.

Windows 95/98 uses Vcache. DOS and Windows 3.x used the SmartDrive caching program. See *write back cache, write through cache, pipeline burst cache, lookaside cache, inline cache* and *backside cache*.

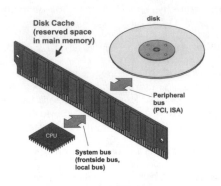

**Disk Cache**
Disk caches are usually just a part of main memory, whereas memory caches (CPU caches) are a special, high-speed memory.

**cacheable content**    Static information that does not change very often and can be cached. Contrast with *non-cacheable content*.

**cache coherency**    Managing a cache so that data is not lost or overwritten. For example, when data is updated in a cache, but not yet transferred to its target memory or disk, the chance of corruption is greater. Cache coherency is obtained by well-designed algorithms that keep track of the cache. It is even more critical in symmetric multiprocessing (SMP) where memory is shared by multiple processors. See *SMP*.

**cache server**    A dedicated network server or a service within a server that caches Web pages in order to speed up access to information that has already been retrieved by a previous user. See *Web cache, origin server, ICP* and *CARP*.

**caching appliance**    A self-contained cache server dedicated to Web caching. See *Web cache* and *NetCache*.

**caching controller**    A disk controller with a built-in cache. See *cache*.

**caching server**    See *Web cache*.

**CA-Clipper**    An application development system from Computer Associates. Originally a dBASE compiler, it evolved into a programming language with many unique features that supports dBASE and non-dBASE databases. Clipper generates DOS programs, but third-party products enable it to create Windows applications. Clipper was originally developed by Nantucket Corporation.

**CAD**    (Computer-Aided Design) Using computers to design products. CAD systems are high-speed workstations or desktop computers with CAD software. A graphics tablet is used for drawing, and a scanner may be attached for additional input. The output of a CAD system is either printed or electronically transmitted to a CAM system, which builds the objects (see *CAD/CAM*).

CAD software is available for generic design or specialized uses, such as architectural, electrical and mechanical. CAD software may also be highly specialized for creating products such as printed circuits and integrated circuits.

More complex forms of CAD are solid modeling and parametric modeling, which allows objects to be created with real-world characteristics. For example, in solid modeling, objects can be sectioned (sliced down the middle) to reveal their internal structure. In parametric modeling, objects have meaningful relationships with each other (a door must be on a wall, not the floor; holes cannot be drilled too close to the edge, etc.). See *wireframe modeling, surface modeling, solid modeling, parametric modeling, graphics* and *CAE*.

**CADAM**    A full-featured IBM mainframe CAD application, which includes 3-D capability, solid modeling and numerical control. Originally developed by Lockheed for internal use, it was distributed by IBM starting in the late 1970s. In 1989, IBM purchased the Lockheed subsidiary, CADAM, Inc.

**CA-DATACOM/DB**    A relational database management system (DBMS) from Computer Associates that runs on PCs, IBM minis and mainframes. There are many options and add-ons that support the product all under the CA-DATACOM umbrella, such as CA-DATACOM/CICS Services and CA-DATACOM/SQL Option.

**CAD/CAM**    (Computer-Aided Design/Computer-Aided Manufacturing) The integration of CAD and CAM. Products designed by CAD are direct input into the CAM system. For example, a device is designed and its electronic image is translated into a numerical control programming language, which generates the instructions for the machine that makes it.

**CADD**    (Computer-Aided Design and Drafting) CAD systems with additional features for drafting, such as dimensioning and text entry.

**caddy**    A plastic container that holds a CD or DVD disc for added protection. The bare disc is placed in the caddy, and the caddy is inserted into the drive. A caddy is not a jewel case. A jewel case protects the disc for transportation. A caddy protects the disc while reading and writing.

**caddy drive**    A disk drive that requires the media to be placed into a cartridge before insertion into the drive. The first CD-ROM and CD R drives were caddy drives, but eventually evolved into tray drives. Contrast with *tray drive* and *feed drive*.

**caddyless**    A tray load drive that does not use a caddy for added protection. See *caddy*.

**caddy load**    Requiring a caddy. See *caddy drive*.

**CADKEY**    An integrated 2-D drafting and 3-D design system for Windows from Baystate Technologies, Marlborough, MA (www.cadkey.com). It offers a total design solution with solids creation and built-in DXF and IGES translators. Over 200 manufacturing systems link to CADKEY through its CADL programming language.

**CADS**    (Computer-Aided Dispatch System) An intelligent vehicle dispatch system that uses mobile data terminals and a GIS.

**CAE**    (1) (Computer-Aided Engineering) Software that analyzes designs that have been created in the computer or that have been created elsewhere and entered into the computer. Different kinds of engineering analyses can be performed, such as structural analysis and electronic circuit analysis.

(2) (Common Application Environment) Software development platform that is specified by X/Open.

**CA-Easytrieve**    An application development system for IBM mainframes, DOS and OS/2 from Computer Associates. It includes 4GL query and reporting capabilities and can access many IBM mainframe and PC database formats. UNIX and Windows versions forthcoming. Easytrieve was originally developed by Pansophic Systems.

**CA-Endevor**    See *Endevor*.

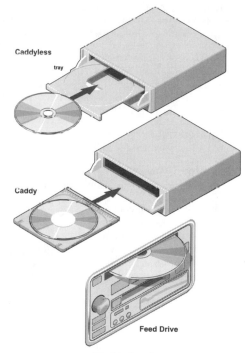

**Caddy Load**
Earlier drives always used a caddy. Today, some drives still require one for added protection.

**Cafe**  A Java development package for Windows and the Macintosh from Symantec. It was Symantec's first development environment for Java, which was superseded by Visual Cafe. See *Visual Cafe*.

**CaffeineMark**  A Java benchmark from Pendragon Software Corporation, Buffalo Grove, IL, (www.webfayre.com). It is used to measure the speed of a Java Virtual Machine (Java interpreter) running on a particular hardware platform. See *Java*.

**CAI**  (1) (Computer-Assisted Instruction)  Same as *CBT*.
(2) See *CA*.

**CA-IDMS**  A relational DBMS from Computer Associates that runs on minis and mainframes. IDMS (Integrated Data Management System) was developed at GE in the 1960s and marketed by Cullinane, later renamed Cullinet and then acquired by CA in 1989. There are a variety of CA-IDMS products, such as CA-IDMS/R for the relational DBMS, CA-IDMS/DDS for its distributed version and so on.

**CA-Ingres**  See *Ingres II*.

**CA-Insight**  A performance monitor from Computer Associates for mainframe DB2 systems running under MVS. Formerly from the Database Utility Group, Inc., it allows searching and selecting of data from system logs and lets you directly view console messages from MVS and DB2.

**CAL**  (1) (Computer-Assisted Learning)  Same as *CBT*.
(2) (Conversational Algebraic Language)  A timesharing language from the University of California.
(3) (Common Application Language)  An object-oriented programming language (EIA-721) for communicating to devices on a home network. It started out as part of the CEBus home network and evolved into an EIA standard. See *CEBus* and **Home Plug & Play**.

**calculated field**  A numeric or date field that derives its data from the calculation of other fields. Data is not entered into a calculated field by the user.

**calculator**  A machine that provides arithmetic capabilities. It accepts keypad input and displays results on a readout and/or paper tape. Unlike a computer, it cannot handle alphabetic data.

**calendaring**  Using an electronic calendar to keep track of events. Calendars can be set up to alert you at a certain time or at recurring times. Group calendaring can alert an entire team as well as let users view each other's calendars. It often includes group scheduling, which allows a user to set up a meeting with project members. Team members are automatically e-mailed, and the program waits for the collective reponses.

**CA-Librarian**  A version control system for IBM mainframes from Computer Associates. Librarian's master files can be simultaneously accessed on shared disks by different operating systems. Librarian was originally developed by ADR, Inc.

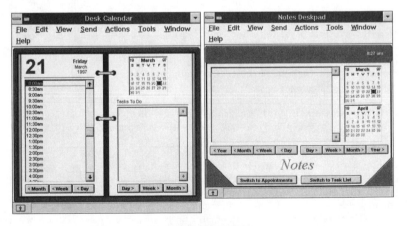

**GroupWise Calendars**
Electronic calendars generally provide multiple views including day, week and month. Fourteen calendar views are available in Novell's GroupWise collaboration system. These are two examples from Version 4.1.

**C**

**calibrate**    To adjust or bring into balance. Scanners, CRTs and similar peripherals may require periodic adjustment. Unlike digital devices, the electronic components within these analog devices may change from their original specification. See *tweak*.

**call**    (1) In programming, a statement that requests services from another subroutine or program. The call is physically made to the subroutine by a branch instruction or some other linking method that is created by the assembler, compiler or interpreter. The routine that is called is responsible for returning control to the calling program after it has finished processing.

(2) In communications, the action taken by the transmitting station to establish a connection with the receiving station in a dial-up network.

**call accounting**    An information system that records and reports on telephone calls. Call accounting is used by most large companies to control expenses and allocate costs to various departments as well as by hotels, hospitals and other organizations that resell calls to its clientele.

**call agent**    See *softswitch*.

**callback**    An authentication technique that calls the sender back. After connection is made, the receiving side breaks the connection and calls the sender to ensure that the logon was made from the authorized computer. Callback prevents a stolen ID and password from being used on a different machine.

**call center**    A company department that handles telephone sales and/or service. Call centers use automatic call distributors (ACDs) to route calls to the appropriate agent or operator. See *ACD* and **Web-enabled call center**.

**call control**    Also known as "call processing," it is the controlling of telephone and PBX functions. It includes connecting, disconnecting and transferring the call, but it does not affect the content of the call. Contrast with *media control*.

**call distributor**    A PBX feature that routes incoming calls to the next available agent or operator.

**called routine**    In programming, a program subroutine that performs a task and is accessed by a call or branch instruction in the program.

**caller ID**    A telephone company service that sends the caller's telephone number to the party that is called. A digital readout on the telephone or other device is required to view the number.

**call pickup service**    An IN (Intelligent Network) service that enables a call to an unanswered telephone to be switched to a pager. After receiving the pager message, the called party can contact the caller by dialing a certain number at any telephone. See **find me service** and *follow me service*.

**call routing service**    An IN (Intelligent Network) service that enables businesses to route calls to another call center if congestion occurs or to another telephone when the store is closed. See *store locator service*.

**CALS**    (Computer-Aided Acquisition and Logistics Support) A DOD initiative for electronically capturing military documentation and linking related information. The CALS bitmap format was developed in the mid 1980s to standardize on graphics data interchange for electronic publishing for the federal government.

**CAM**    (1) (Computer-Aided Manufacturing) The automation of manufacturing systems and techniques, including numerical control, process control, robotics and materials requirements planning (MRP). See *CAD/CAM*.

(2) (Common Access Method) An ANSI standard interface that provides a common language between drivers and SCSI host adapters. It is primarily supported by Future Domain and NCR. See *SCSI*.

(3) (Content Addressable Memory) Also known as "associative storage," it is a memory chip in which each bit position can be compared. In regular dynamic RAM (DRAM) and static RAM (SRAM) chips, the contents are addressed by bit location and then transferred to the arithmetic logic unit (ALU) in the CPU for comparison. In CAM chips, the content is compared in each bit cell, allowing for very fast table lookups. Since the entire chip is compared,

the data content can often be randomly stored without regard to an addressing scheme which would otherwise be required. However, CAM chips are considerably smaller in storage capacity than regular memory chips.

(4) (CAMera) See also *Webcam*.

**CAMA** (Central Automatic Message Accounting) See *AMA*.

**CAMAC** (Computer Automated Measurement And Control) An IEEE standard (IEEE 583) for modular instrumentation systems. CAMAC "crates" are control stations that contain plug-in cards with ports to data acquisition devices. The crates contain a controller that connects via cable to a plug-in card in the computer's bus, known as a "CAMAC coupler." Crates can be daisy chained together for expansion.

**CA-ManMan/X** A comprehensive manufacturing application from Computer Associates that runs under UNIX on VAX and HP platforms. It covers all aspects of manufacturing management including planning, tracking and shop floor control. CA-ManMan/X was originally ManMan (Manufacturing Management), developed by Ask Computer Systems, Inc.

**camera ready** Printed material that serves as original artwork for commercial printing. Camera-ready material is photographed, and the films are made into plates for the printing presses. Camera ready implies high-resolution text and graphics. See *resolution* and *high-resolution*.

**campus** Two or more buildings located in close proximity. For example, a campus backbone implies a high-speed transmission system, such as FDDI or ATM, running between several buildings all within a geographic area that may be only a couple of hundred feet or as much as several hundred yards long.

**Canadian Standards Association** See *CSA*.

**CancelBunny** Also "CancelPoodle." A person that deletes Usenet messages that have been posted to a particular newsgroup.

**candela** A unit of measurement of the intensity of light. An ordinary wax candle generates one candela. See *lumen* and *nit*.

**Candle** (Candle Corporation, Santa Monica, CA, www.candle.com) A leading software company specializing in performance monitoring and systems availability tools for the mainframe environment. It was founded in 1976 by Aubrey Chernick, who developed OMEGAMON, the first realtime performance monitor for MVS. Candle provides a wide variety of products for managing systems and applications, and in 1996, expanded into middleware.

**canned program** A software package that provides a fixed solution to a problem. Canned business applications should be analyzed carefully as they usually cannot be changed much, if at all.

**canned routine** A program subroutine that performs a specific processing task.

**canonical** The standard or authoritative method. The term comes from "canon," which is the law or rules of the church. See *canonical name* and *canonical synthesis*.

**canonical name** The actual name of a resource. For example, a canonical name of a server is its true name rather than an alias. See *CNAME record*.

**canonical synthesis** The process of designing a model of a database without redundant data items. A canonical model, or schema, is independent of the hardware and software that will process the data. See *canonical*.

**CA-OpenIngres** See *Ingres II*.

**CA-OpenROAD** See *OpenROAD*.

**CAP** **(1)** (**C**ompetitive **A**ccess **P**rovider)  An organization that competes with the established telecommunications provider in an area.

**(2)** (**C**arrierless **A**mplitude **P**hase)  A type of ADSL service. See *DSL*.

**Capability Maturity Model**    See *CMM*.

**capacities**    See *space/time*.

**capacitor**    An electronic component that holds a charge. It comes in varying sizes for use in power supplies. It is also constructed as microscopic cells in dynamic RAM chips. See *tantalum capacitor*.

**CA-Panvalet**    A version control system for IBM mainframes from Computer Associates that keeps track of source code, JCL and object modules. Panvalet was originally developed by Pansophic Systems. CA-PAN/LCM is a similar product for PCs, which also provides interfaces to mainframe systems, such as CA-Panvalet and CA-Librarian.

**cap code**    The address assigned to a pager.

**CA-PRMS**    The branding of the PRMS software from 1991 to 1998. See *PRMS*.

**capstan**    On magnetic tape drives, a motorized cylinder that traps the tape against a free-wheeling roller and moves it at a regulated speed.

**capture buffer**    A reserved memory area for holding an incoming transmission.

**CA-Quick Response Engine**    The branding of the Quick Response Engine software from 1996 to 1998. See ***Quick Response Engine***.

**CAR**    (**C**omputer-**A**ssisted **R**etrieval)  Systems that use the computer to keep track of text documents or records stored on paper or on microform. The computer is used to derive the location of a requested item, which must be manually retrieved from a shelf, bin, or microform.

**CA-RAMIS**    A fourth-generation retrieval language for IBM mainframes and PCs from Computer Associates. Originally developed by Mathematica, RAMIS was later acquired by Martin Marietta Data Systems, On-Line Software, then CA in 1991. The earliest version of RAMIS was one of the first database packages with a non-procedural language for IBM mainframes.

**card**    See *expansion board, printed circuit board, magnetic stripe, punched card* and *HyperCard*.

**CardBus**    The 32-bit version of the PC Card. See *PC Card*.

**card cage**    An enclosure that holds printed circuit boards. It differs from a PC cabinet in that the boards (cards) are inserted directly into the cage without pulling off the outer case.

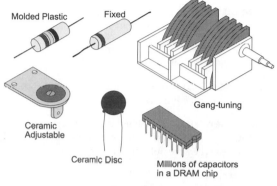

Molded Plastic    Fixed

Ceramic Adjustable

Ceramic Disc

Gang-tuning

Millions of capacitors in a DRAM chip

**Capacitors**

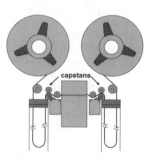

capstans

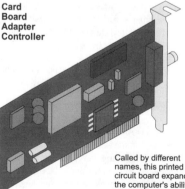

Card
Board
Adapter
Controller

Called by different names, this printed circuit board expands the computer's ability to work with a peripheral device, whose controlling electronics are not built into the motherboard.

In a PC, it plugs into a slot in the ISA, EISA or PCI bus.

**card column**  A vertical column that is used to represent a single character of data by its pattern of punched holes. The common IBM card contains 80 card columns.

**card image**  The representation of punched cards in which each hole in the card is represented by a bit on tape or disk.

**cardinality**  A quantity relationship between elements. For example, one-to-one, one-to-many and many-to-one express cardinality. See *cardinal number*.

**cardinal number**  The number that states how much or how many. In "record 43 has 7 fields," the 7 is cardinal. See *cardinality*. Contrast with *ordinal number*.

**card punch**  (1) An early peripheral device that punches holes into cards at 100 to 300 cards per minute.
(2) Same as *keypunch machine*.

**card reader**  (1) A peripheral device that reads the magnetic stripe on the back of a credit card.
(2) An early peripheral device that reads punched cards at 500 to 2,000 cards/minute. The code is detected by light patterns created by the holes in the card.

**card services**  Software that manages PC Cards. See *PC Card*.

**CA-Realizer**  An application development system for Windows and OS/2 from Computer Associates. It is based on a superset of BASIC and includes visual tools and the ability to incorporate routines written in C, Pascal and other languages. Realizer was originally developed by Within Technologies.

**CARP**  (Cache Array Routing Protocol)  A protocol from Microsoft that is used by one proxy server to query another for a cached Web page without having to go to the Internet to retrieve it. CARP allows arrays of cache servers to be used and managed as a single entity, which avoids redundancy and supports failover and load balancing. See *ICP* and *proxy server*.

**carpal tunnel syndrome**  The compression of the main nerve to the hand due to scarring or swelling of the surrounding soft tissue in the wrist (area formed by carpal bones on top and muscle tendons below). Caused by trauma, arthritis and improper positioning of the wrist, it can result in severe damage to the hands. See *RSI* and *computer vision syndrome*.

**carriage**  A printer or typewriter mechanism that holds the platen and controls paper feeding and movement.

**carriage return**  See *return key*.

**carrier**  (1) An organization that provides communications services. See *common carrier* and *private carrier*.
(2) An alternating current that vibrates at a fixed frequency, used to establish a boundary, or envelope, in which a signal is transmitted. Carriers are commonly used in radio transmission (AM, FM, TV, microwave, satellite, etc.) in order to differentiate transmitting stations. For example, an FM station's channel number is actually its carrier frequency. The FM station merges (modulates) its audio broadcast (data signal) onto its carrier and transmits

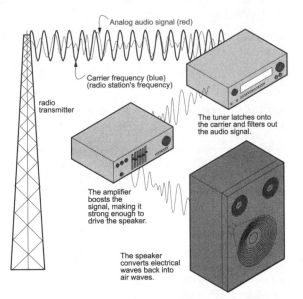

**Carrier Signal**
The radio station transmits its audio signal encased in its carrier frequency. The receiving tuner filters out the audio and sends it to the amplifier. The amplifier increases the signal strength and sends it to the speaker. This diagram depicts an entirely analog system. Notice that the audio signal is maintained as infinitely varying waves throughout all the components. However, digital data is also transmitted in a carrier. Rather than infinitely varying waves, digital signals are made up of two frequencies, one for 0, the other for 1.

the combined signal over the airwaves. At the receiving end, the FM tuner latches onto the carrier frequency, filters out the audio signal, amplifies it and sends it to the speaker.

Carriers can be used to transmit several signals simultaneously. For example, multiple voice, data and/or video signals can travel over the same line with each residing in its own carrier vibrating at a different frequency.

**carrier based**    A transmission system that generates a fixed frequency (carrier) to contain the data being transmitted.

**carrier class**    Refers to hardware or software used in high-speed, high-traffic networks such as used by telcos, ISPs and very large enterprises. See *carrier switch*.

**carrier detect**    A signal that indicates a connection has been made by sensing a carrier frequency on the line. See *RS-232* and *modem*.

**carrier frequency**    A unique frequency used to "carry" data within its boundaries. It is measured in cycles per second, or Hertz. See *carrier* and *FDM*.

**carrier serving area**    A geographic customer area that is consolidated into a single digital transmission by the telephone company. Each carrier serving area (CSA) is served by a digital loop carrier (DLC), which multiplexes hundreds of analog lines into one high-speed digital trunk. The physical size of a CSA is based on the number of lines the DLC supports and the population density. See *central office*.

**carrier switch**    A large-scale computer system that switches telephone calls. It is the type of telco switch used by IXCs such as AT&T, MCI Worldcom and Sprint. The primary vendors of the switches are Lucent and Nortel Networks. Carrier switches provide customer services such as 800 numbers and credit card billing, but not local services such as call forwarding and call waiting. Local telephone companies use end office switches and tandem switches, but all of these digital telephone switches today may use the exact same hardware, the services of which are differentiated by the software that runs in them. See *tandem switch* and *end office switch*.

**carrier system**    A system that uses carrier frequencies to transmit data. See *carrier frequency*.

**Carterfone decision**    The FCC decree in 1968 that permitted users to connect their own telephone equipment to the public telephone system.

**cartridge**    A removable storage module that contains magnetic or optical disks, magnetic tape or memory chips. Cartridges are inserted into slots in the drive, printer or computer. See *font cartridge* and *cassette*. For a summary of removable tape, disk and optical cartridges, see *magnetic tape*, *magnetic disk* and *optical disk*.

**cartridge font**    See *font cartridge*.

**CAS**    (1) (Communications Application Specification) A programming interface from Intel and DCA for activating functions in fax/modems. Introduced in 1988, Intel provides both the boards and the chips. CAS has not been widely used.

(2) (Column Address Strobe) A clock signal in a memory chip used to pinpoint the column of a particular bit in a row-column matrix. See *RAS*.

**cascade**    A connected series of devices or images. It often implies that the second and subsequent device takes over after the previous one is used up. For example, cascading tapes in a dual-tape backup system means the second tape is written after the first one is full. In a PC, a second IRQ chip is cascaded to the first, doubling the number of interrupts.

**cascading menu**    A menu system that displays submenus off to the side when selected. In Windows, the Programs submenu in the Start menu is cascaded to the right side when selected.

**Cascading Style Sheets**    A style sheet format for HTML documents endorsed by the World Wide Web Consortium. CSS1 (Version 1.0) provides hundreds of layout settings that can be applied to all the subsequent HTML pages that are downloaded. CSS2 (Version 2.0) adds support for XML, oral presentations for the visually impaired, downloadable fonts and other enhancements. See *style sheet* and *XSL*.

**cascading windows**    Displaying windows in a progressive order so that all the title bars appear on screen at one time.

**CASE**    (Computer-Aided Software Engineering or Computer-Aided Systems Engineering) Software that is used in any and all phases of developing an information system, including analysis, design and programming. For example, data dictionaries and diagramming tools aid in the analysis and design phases, while application generators speed up the programming phase.

CASE tools provide automated methods for designing and documenting traditional structured programming techniques. The ultimate goal of CASE is to provide a language for describing the overall system that is sufficient to generate all the necessary programs. See also *case statement*.

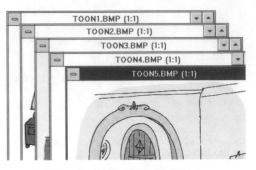

**Cascading Windows**
The Cascade function organizes open documents or images one after the other as in this example.

**case-based reasoning**    An AI problem solving technique that catalogs experience into "cases" and matches the current problem to the experience. Such systems are easier to maintain than rule-based expert systems, because changes require adding new cases without the complexity of adding new rules. It is used in many areas including pattern recognition, diagnosis, troubleshooting and planning.

**case cracker**    A tool used to "crack" open the cases of various laptop computers. The early Macintosh cases and many laptop cases are designed to snap together. The spatula-like ends of the case cracker make it easier to pry open the case without damaging it.

**case sensitive**    Distinguishing lower case from upper case. In a case sensitive language, "abc" is considered different data than "ABC."

**case statement**    In programming, a variation of the if-then-else statement that is used when several ifs are required in a row. The following C example tests the variable KEY1 and performs functions based on the results.

```
switch (key1)   {
  case '+':  add();  break;
  case '-':  subtract();  break;
  case '*':  multiply();  break;
  case '/':  divide();  break;
             }
```

**cash memory**    See *cache*.

**cassette**    A removable magnetic tape storage module that contains supply and takeup reels (hubs) like an audio or videotape. DAT, 8mm and Magstar MP tapes use the cassette-style cartridge (see below). See *single-hub cartridge*.

**Castanet**    Java-based delivery software for the Internet and intranets from Marimba. Castanet automatically pushes application updates and other published content into client machines. Castanet Transmitter is a server program that manages "Castanet channels," which are content streams. Castanet Tuner is client software that looks for selected channels. Castanet Tuner is built into Netscape Netcaster. See *Bongo*.

**casting**    In programming, the conversion of one data type into another. See also *Webcast*, *narrowcast*, *multicast* and *broadcast*.

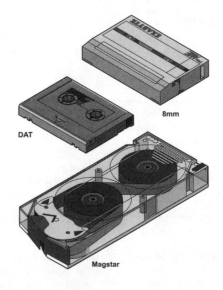

8mm

DAT

Magstar

**cat**   (conCATenate) A UNIX command that displays the contents of a file.

**CAT 5**   See *cable categories*.

**catalog**   A directory of disk files or files used in an application. Also any map, list or directory of storage space used by the computer.

**CA-Telon**   An application generator from Computer Associates that generates COBOL and PL/I code for IBM mainframes and COBOL code for AS/400s. Development can be performed on mainframes or PCs. Telon was originally developed by Pansophic Systems.

**cathode**   In electronics, a device that emits electrons, which flow from the negatively charged cathode to the positively charged anode. Cathodes are used in CRTs and diodes.

(−)    Cathode → Anode    (+)

**CATIA**   A family of 2-D and 3-D CAD programs from IBM. CATIA was one of the first CAD programs to provide 3-D solid modelling. The program was developed by Dassault Aviation, a French aerospace company. CATIA runs on IBM mainframes, RS/6000 and HP 9000 workstations with other platforms expected in the future.

**CAT scan**   (Computer Axial Tomography) A series of X-rays that show the human body in slices. The X-ray mechanism, which surrounds the body, "inches" its way along the area being examined, taking multiple tomograms (slices). The computer is used to turn the tomograms into pictures. See *tomography*.

**CATV**   (Community Antenna TV) The original name for cable TV, which used a single antenna at the highest location in the community.

**CAU**   (Controlled Access Unit) An intelligent hub from IBM for Token Ring networks. Failed nodes are identified by the hub and reported via IBM's LAN Network Manager software.

**CA-Unicenter**   Systems management software from Computer Associates that supports a variety of servers, including Sun, HP, Digital, IBM and NetWare. Unicenter TNG (The Next Generation) manages the global enterprise, including networks, systems, applications and databases regardless of location.

**CAV**   (Constant Angular Velocity) Rotating a disk at a constant speed. Since the length of the inner tracks are smaller than the outer tracks, the same clock frequency for recording causes the innermost track to be the most dense and the outermost track to be the least dense. In order to utilize the space more efficiently, zoned CAV (Z-CAV) breaks the disk into multiple zones and uses a different clock frequency for each zone. The innermost track of each zone is the most dense for that zone.

Partial CAV (P-CAV), also known as CAV/CLV, breaks the disk into only two zones. It varies the disk rotation (CLV) for the inner zone and then switches to constant speed (CAV) for the outer one. Contrast with *CLV*.

**CAVE**   (Computer Automatic Virtual Environment) A virtual reality system that uses projectors to display images on three or four walls and the floor. Special glasses make everything appear as 3-D images and also track the path of the user's vision. CAVE was the first virtual reality system to let multiple users participate in the experience simultaneously. Known as a "spatially immersive display," it was developed by the Electronic Visualization Laboratory at the University of Illinois in the early 1990s. Contrast with *HMD*. See *virtual reality*.

**Training People**
This CAVE system is used to teach people how to operate a Caterpillar bulldozer. The steering wheel you see on the left meets the real steering wheel in virtual space, appearing to the man as the actual wheel he is turning. *(Image courtesy of Fakespace Systems Inc.)*

**CA-Visual Objects** An object-oriented client/server development system from Computer Associates that is used to develop Windows applications. It provides visual programming tools and a programming language that evolved from Clipper. CA-Visual Objects supports ODBC and SQL databases and includes a compiler for generating Windows EXEs and DLLs.

**CA-Warehouse BOSS** The branding of the Warehouse BOSS software from 1991 to 1998. See *Warehouse BOSS*.

**CB** (Citizen's Band) The frequency band of 40 channels for public radio transmission in the 27 MHz range. CB radio uses the same frequencies for sending and receiving on each channel, which is why only one person can talk at the same time (half duplex transmission). CB radios generally have a range of about five miles.

**C-Band** (1) Part of the electromagnetic spectrum used for fixed satellite communications. It uses frequencies in the 4–8GHz range. See *Ka-Band* and *Ku-Band*.
(2) Part of the light spectrum used for fiber optic transmission. See *optical bands*.

**CBEMA** See *ITI*.

**CBR** (1) (Computer-Based Reference) Reference materials accessible by computer in order to help people do their jobs quicker. For example, this database on disk!
(2) (Constant Bit Rate) A uniform transmission rate. For example, realtime voice and video traffic requires a CBR. In ATM, CBR guarantees bandwidth for the peak cell rate of the application.
(3) See *case-based reasoning*.

**CBT** (Computer-Based Training) Using the computer for training and instruction. CBT programs are called "courseware" and provide interactive training sessions for all disciplines. It uses graphics extensively, as well as CD-ROM and LaserDisc.
CBT courseware is developed with authoring languages, such as Adroit, PILOT and Demo II, which allow for the creation of interactive sessions.

**CBX** (Computerized Branch eXchange) Same as *PBX*.

**cc:** (Carbon Copy) The field in an e-mail header that names additional recipients for the message. See *bcc:*.

**CCA** (1) (Common Cryptographic Architecture) Cryptography software from IBM for MVS and DOS applications.
(2) (Compatible Communications Architecture) A Network Equipment Technology protocol for transmitting asynchronous data over X.25 networks.
(3) (Communications Control Architecture) The U.S. Navy network that includes an ISDN backbone is BITS (Base Information Transfer System).

**CCC/Harvest** A software configuration management (SCM) system for client/server environments from Computer Associates. On the server, it runs on all major UNIX platforms and Windows NT. Windows, OS/2 and UNIX are supported on the client. The product was originally developed by Platinum Technology, which was acquired by CA in 1999.

**CCD** (1) (Charge Coupled Device) An electronic memory that can be charged by light. CCDs can hold a variable charge, which is why they are used in cameras and scanners to record variable shades of light. CCDs are analog, not digital, and are made of a special type of MOS transistor. Analog to digital (ADC) converters quantify the variable charge into a discrete number of colors. See *digital camera*.
(2) (Consumer Computing Device) A low-cost consumer-oriented product that contains a computer, such as a PDA, Internet appliance or specialized mobile device.

**CCD camera** See *digital camera*.

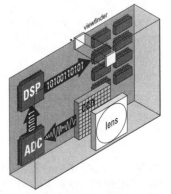

**CCDs Record Light**
In a camera, CCDs work somewhat like film. They are exposed to light, recording the intensities, or shades, of light as variable charges. In digital cameras, such as the one above, the charges are converted to a discrete number by analog to digital (ADC) converter chips.

C

**CCFL**    (Cold Cathode Flurorescent Lamp)  Same as *CCFT*.

**CCFT**    (Cold Cathode Flurorescent Tube)  A type of light source for a backlit screen. It weighs more and uses more power than other backlights.

**CCIA**    (Computer and Communications Industry Association, Washington, DC, www.ccianet.org)  A membership organization composed of computer and communications firms. It represents their interests in domestic and foreign trade, and, working with the NIST, keeps members advised of regulatory policy.

**CCIE**    See *Cisco certification*.

**CCIR 601**    An international standard for digital video designed to encompass both 525-line NTSC and 625-line PAL analog signals. CCIR 601 samples the YCrCb encoding at a 4:2:2 ratio (Y is sampled at 13.5MHz, and Cr and Cb at 6.75MHz each) to produce a 27MB per second component digital data stream. CCIR provides an NTSC-equivalent resolution of 720×486 pixels at 30 fps. CCIR 601 commonly uses the serial digital interface (SDI) for interconnections. CCIR 601 was established in 1987 by CCIR (Consultative Commitee for International Radio), SMPTE and the European Broadcasting Union. See *YUV*.

**CCIS**    (Common Channel Interoffice Signaling)  The signaling technique used in the public switched telephone network that transmits voice conversations and control signals over separate networks. Voice conversations are handled by the traditional telephone switches, while control signals are transmitted over a packet-switched network, providing faster connects and disconnects and allowing data, such as calling number, to be included. CCIS messages can inform switches of network congestion and outages. Previous to CCIS, control signals travelled with the voice (in-band). See *AIN* and *SS7*. See also *CCS*.

**CCITT**    See *ITU*.

**cc:Mail**    An earlier and widely-used messaging system from Lotus that runs on PC LANs. Originally developed by cc:Mail, Inc., Mountain View, CA, Lotus acquired the company in 1991. Mail-enabled applications that are written to the VIM programming interface can use the cc:Mail system.

**CCNA**    See *Cisco certification*.

**CCNP**    See *Cisco certification*.

**CCP**    (Certified Computer Professional)  The award for successful completion of a comprehensive examination on computers offered by the ICCP. See *ICCP*.

**CCS**    (1) (Common Channel Signaling)  A communications system in which one channel is used for signaling and different channels are used for voice/data transmission. Signaling System 7 (SS7) is a CCS system, also known as CCS7. See *SS7*.
   (2) (Common Communications Support)  SAA specifications for communications, which includes data streams (DCA, 3270), application services (DIA, DDM), session services (LU 6.2) and data links (X.25, Token Ring).
   (3) (Common Command Set)  The de facto instruction set between a SCSI-1 adapter and a hard disk.
   (4) (Continuous Composite Servo)  A technique for aligning the read/write head over a track in an optical disk by sensing special tracking grooves in the disk.
   (5) (100 Call Seconds)  A unit of measurement equal to 100 seconds of conversation. One hour = 36 CCS.

**CCS7**    (Common Channel Signaling 7)  See *SS7*.

**CCTA**    (Central Computer and Telecommunications Agency, London, www.open.gov.uk)  An agency of the U.K. government's Cabinet Office that has been providing IT advice and guidance to the public sector for over 25 years. CCTA has also taken a lead in bringing public and private sector organizations together to develop such world-class "best practice" methodologies for IT professionals as SSADM for systems analysis and design, PRINCE 2 for IT and business project management and ITIL for IT service management.

**CCW** (Continuous Composite Write) A magneto-optic disk technology that emulates a WORM (Write Once Read Many) disk. It uses firmware in the drive to ensure that data cannot be erased and rewritten.

**CD** (Compact Disc) See also *carrier detect*. A CD is a digital audio disc that contains up to 74 minutes of hi-fi stereo sound. Introduced in 1982, the disc is a plastic platter 120mm (4.75") in diameter, recorded on one side, with individual selections playable in any sequence.

Sound is converted into digital code by sampling the sound waves 44,056 times per second and converting each sample into a 16-bit number. It requires approximately 1.5 million bits of storage for each second of stereo hi-fi sound. The audio tracks are recorded as microscopic pits in a groove that starts at the center of the disc and spirals outward to the edge.

Other forms of CDs, such as CD-ROM, CD-I and Video CD, all stem from the original audio CD, which is also known as Compact Disc-Digital Audio (CD-DA). See *CD-ROM* for more on how the platters are made.

**The Books** Documentation for various CD formats are found in books commonly known by the color of their covers.

```
Red Book     - Audio CDs (CD-DA)
Yellow Book  - CD-ROM
Orange Book  - Recordable (Photo CD, CD-R, etc.)
Green Book   - CD-I
White Book   - Video CD
Blue Book    - CD Extra
```

**What Happened to the Phonograph?** The audio CD was introduced in the U.S. in 1983. By 1986, CDs and CD players exceeded the sales of LPs and turntables.

Unlike phonograph records, in which the platter contains "carved sound waves," CDs are recorded in binary digital form (microscopic pits) covered by a clear, protective plastic layer. Instead of a needle vibrating in the groove, a laser shines onto the pits and the reflections are decoded. Audio CDs, as well as all variations of the CD (CD-ROM, CD-R, etc.) use a spiral recording track just like the phonograph record, but start at the center, not the edge.

Digital sound is so clear because the numbers are turned into sound electronically. There's no needle pops and clicks as there are with phonograph records (there's also no tape hiss if the original recording was digital). In addition, the CD can handle a wider range of volume (dynamic range), providing more realism. A soft whisper can be interrupted by a loud cannon blast. If a phonograph record were recorded with that much dynamic range, the needle would literally jump out of the groove.

However, pops and clicks aside, from the onset of audio CDs, there are many that believe its sound is harsh and not as realistic as the phonograph record. DVD-Audio and Sony's SACD are two advanced digital sound formats that provide considerably more digital sampling and superior sound quality. See *DVD-Audio* and *SACD*.

**CD+G** (CD+Graphics) An audio CD format that allows images to be stored in subcode channels. It has primarily been used to store lyrics in Karaoke (sing along) discs.

**CD audio** Same as *CD* and *DAD*.

**CD burner** A CD-R machine. See *CD-R*.

**CD business card** See *business card CD*.

**CDC** See *Control Data*, **century date change** and *Back Orifice*.

**CD-DA** (Compact Disc-Digital Audio) The formal designation for the original compact disc format, which was designed for audio only. Since "CD" is used loosely for all compact disc formats, CD-DA differentiates a music disc or player from its data counterparts, such as CD-ROM, CD-R and CD-RW. See *CD*.

**CDDA** (Compact Disc Digital Audio) See *CD*.

**CD database**    See *CDDB*.

**CDDB**    (CD DataBase) A database that contains the track titles from audio CD albums. Developed in 1993 by Ti Kan, it was later turned into an Internet server. Many software audio players support the format by retrieving the data from the CDDB database and displaying album, artist and track titles while the CD is playing. For information, visit www.gracenote.com.

**CDDI**    (Copper Distributed Data Interface) A version of FDDI that uses UTP (unshielded twisted pair) wires rather than optical fiber. The term is a trademark of Crescendo Communications, Sunnyvale, CA. ANSI's standard for FDDI over UTP is officially TP-PMD (Twisted Pair-Physical Media Dependent).

**CD duplication**    Creating CDs and CD-ROMs by writing blank CD-R discs in a CD-R drive on a desktop computer or by using specialized CD duplicating machines with multiple CD-R drives. Contrast with *CD replication*.

**CD-E**    (Compact Disc-Erasable) The original name for rewritable CDs (CD-RWs). See *CD-RW*.

**CDE**    (1) (Common Desktop Environment) A graphical user interface standard for open systems from The Open Group. It is based on Motif with elements from HP, IBM and others and was originally managed by COSE. All the major UNIX vendors support CDE.

CDE also provides remote program launching and the ability to suspend and resume applications in their own workspace. CDE branding is governed by X/Open (The Open Group). See also *CD-E*.

(2) (Cooperative Development Environment) A client/server application development system from Oracle Corporation that evolved into Develper/2000 and Designer/2000.

(3) (Computer Desktop Encyclopedia) What you are reading at this very moment. See *About this product*.

**cdev**    (Control Panel DEVice) Customizable settings in the Macintosh Control Panel that pertain to a particular program or device. Cdevs for the mouse, keyboard and startup disk, among others, come with the Mac. Others are provided with software packages and utilities.

**CD Extra**    Also called "CD Plus," "Enhanced CD" and "Enhanced CD-ROM," it is a compact disc format that contains both audio and data. It uses the multisession capability to store up to 98 audio tracks in the first session and one CD-ROM XA data track in the second session. Audio CD players will play the first session and ignore the second. A multisession CD-ROM drive (all newer drives) will read the last session first, and the software in the data session can cause the audio session to be played. See *Mixed Mode CD*.

**CDF**    (1) (Central Distribution Frame) A connecting unit (typically a hub) that acts a central distribution point to all the nodes in a zone or domain. See *MDF*.

(2) (Channel Definition Format) The file format used in Microsoft's Active Channel technology. Channel providers store CDF files on their Web servers, which contain the URLs to the pages and subpages that make up the channel's offerings. When you select a channel from your desktop, the underlying CDF file is accessed. See *Active Channel*.

**CDFS**    (CD-ROM File System) The 32-bit file system that handles CD-ROMs in Windows 95/98. CDFS uses the Windows Vcache disk cache to buffer data from the CD-ROM in memory to speed up retrieval. CDFS replaced the earlier 16-bit MSCDEX.EXE used in DOS/Windows 3.1.

**CDG**    (CDMA Development Group, Costa Mesa, CA, www.cdg.org) A membership organization founded in 1995 that promotes CDMA wireless systems worldwide. It is involved with developing new features and services and promoting standards that provide global compatibility and interoperability. It also develops system tests that verify performance of cdmaOne systems. See *cdma2000* and *CDMA*.

**CD-I**    (Compact Disc-Interactive) A compact disc format developed by Philips and Sony that holds data, audio, still video and animated graphics. It provides up to 144 minutes of CD-quality stereo, 9.5 hours of AM-radio-quality stereo or 19 hours of monophonic audio.

CD-I includes an operating system standard, as well as proprietary hardware methods for compressing the data further in order to display video images. CD-I discs require a CD-I player and will not play in a CD-ROM player. The standard specification for the CD-I format is contained in a document entitled the Green Book. See *CD, CD-ROM* and *DVD*.

**CDIA**    See *CompTIA*.

**CDIF**    (CASE Data Interchange Format) An EIA standard for exchanging data between CASE tools. See *PCTE*.

**CDIP**    (CERamic Dual In-line Package) A DIP chip made of ceramic materials. It uses gold-plated leads attached to two sides by brazing and a metal lid bonded to the chip with a metal seal. See *DIP, CERDIP, CERQUAD* and *chip package*.

**CD jukebox**    A jukebox for audio CDs. CD-ROM jukeboxes are also called "CD jukeboxes." See *CD-ROM server*.

**CDMA**    (Code Division Multiple Access) A method for transmitting simultaneous signals over a shared portion of the spectrum. The foremost application of CDMA is the digital cellular phone technology from QUALCOMM that operates in the 800MHz band and 1.9GHz PCS band. CDMA phones are noted for their excellent call quality and long battery life.

CDMA is less costly to implement, requiring fewer cell sites than the GSM and TDMA digital cellphone systems and providing three to five times the calling capacity. It provides more than 10 times the capacity of the analog cellphone system (AMPS). CDMA has become widely used in North America and is also expected to become the third-generation (3G) technology for GSM.

Unlike GSM and TDMA, which divides the spectrum into different time slots, CDMA uses a spread spectrum technique to assign a code to each conversation. After the speech codec converts voice to digital, CDMA spreads the voice stream over the full 1.25MHz bandwidth of the CDMA channel, coding each stream separately so it can be decoded at the receiving end. The rate of the spreading signal is known as the "chip rate," as each bit in the spreading signal is called a "chip" (no relation to an integrated circuit). All voice conversations use the full bandwidth at the same time. One bit from each conversation is multiplied into 128 coded bits by the spreading techniques, giving the receiving side an enormous amount of data it can average just to determine the value of one bit.

CDMA transmission has been used by the military for secure phone calls. Unlike FDMA and TDMA methods, CDMA's wide spreading signal makes it difficult to detect and jam. For more information, contact the CDMA Development Group (CDG) at www.cdg.org. See *wireless generations, IS-95, cdma2000, W-CDMA, GSM, FDMA, TDMA, CDPD, CDG* and *spread spectrum*.

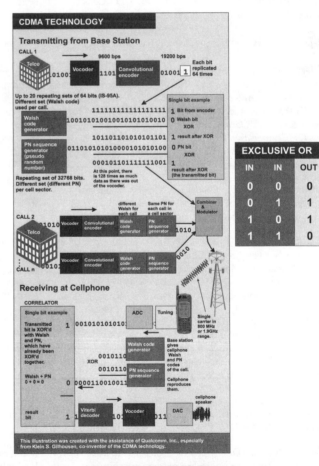

**Follow the Single Bit Example**
This exclusive OR truth table shows you the Boolean algebraic rules if you would like to prove the single bit example in the CDMA illustration above. The example bit is a 1, and the Walsh and PN codes are 0.

**How the Technology Works**  CDMA is a fascinating technology, and the preceding illustration shows you how calls from a base station are encoded and transmitted to a cellphone.

At the base station, each voice conversation is converted into digital code and compressed with a vocoder. The vocoder output is doubled by a convolutional encoder that adds redundancy for error checking. Each bit from the encoder is replicated 64 times and exclusive OR'd with a Walsh code that is used to identify that call from the rest.

The output of the Walsh code is exclusive OR'd with the next string of bits (PN sequence) from a pseudo-random noise generator, which is used to identify all the calls in a particular cell's sector. At this point, there is 128 times as many bits as there were from the vocoder's output. All the calls are combined and modulated onto a carrier frequency in the 800 MHz range.

At the receiving side, the received signals are quantized (turned into bits) and run through the Walsh code and PN sequence correlation receiver to recover the transmitted bits of the original signal. When 20ms of voice data is received, a Viterbi decoder corrects the errors using the convolutional code, and that all goes to the vocoder which turns the bits back into waveforms (sound).

The following illustration shows how bits move from base station to cellphone and a single bit example takes you through the Boolean math. The example bit is a 1, and the Walsh and PN codes are 0.

**cdma2000**  A 3G technology that increases data transmission rates for existing CDMA (cdmaOne) network operators. cdma2000 Phase 1 provides 144 Kbps of data integrated with voice and is known by several names: IS-2000, MC-1X, IMT-CDMA MultiCarrier 1X and 1XRTT.

Phase 2 increases the data rate to 2 Mbps and is based on QUALCOMM's HDR technology. 1XEv-Data Voice (DV) integrates voice and data. 1XEv-Data Only, which is sometimes called Phase 1+, provides 2 Mbps for data only.

Phase 2 may also employ a technology based on 3 times (3X) the carrier rate of Phase 1 (1X). This too is known by several names: MC-3X, IMT-CDMA MultiCarrier 3X and 3XRTT. See *wireless generations* and *W-CDMA*.

**cdmaOne**  The CDMA Development Group's name for cellphone carriers using 2nd-generation CDMA technology. See *IS-95*, *cdma2000* and *CDMA*.

**CDN**  (Content Delivery Network) A system of distributed content on a large intranet or the public Internet in which copies of content are replicated and cached throughout the network. When content is replicated throughout the country, or throughout the world, users have quicker access to it than if it resides on one Web site. CDNs are provided by content delivery organizations such as Akamai, by large ISPs with national coverage or by very large enterprises. See *content peering* and *Content Alliance*.

**CDN peering**  See *content peering*.

**CDO**  (Collaborative Data Objects) A programming interface from Microsoft for accessing MAPI-based e-mail, calendaring and scheduling servers. CDO is an object-oriented extension to Enhanced MAPI that provides the ability to dynamically create Web pages (HTML pages). CDO is server oriented whereas MAPI has a client orientation.

**CDP**  (1) (Certificate in Data Processing) An earlier award for the successful completion of an examination in hardware, software, systems analysis, programming, management and accounting, offered by the ICCP. See *ICCP*.

(2) (Cisco Discovery Protocol) A protocol used by Cisco bridges and routers to inform each other of their existence. It sends frames over the data link layer (Ethernet, frame relay, ATM, etc.) to a multicast address. The content of the CDP message is addresses that SNMP messages can be sent to.

**CDPD**  (Cellular Digital Packet Data) A digital wireless transmission system that is deployed as an enhancement to the existing analog cellular network. Based on IBM's CelluPlan II, it provides a packet overlay onto the AMPS network and moves data at 19.2 Kbps over ever-changing unused intervals in the voice channels. If all the channels are used, the data is stored and forwarded when a channel becomes available. CDPD is used for applications such as public safety, point of sale, mobile positioning and other business services.

CDPD was developed as a wireless extension to an IP network and uses the four octet (0.0.0.0) address for connections. CDPD networks cover most of the major urban areas in the U.S. and has been deployed by AT&T, Ameritech, GTE, BellAtlantic Mobile and other carriers. By the late 1990s, incompatibility issues had been worked out, and roaming agreements and interoperability between carriers is generally nationwide. CDPD modems are available on PC Cards for laptop and handheld computers. See *ARDIS*, *BellSouth Intelligent Wireless Network* and *Ricochet*.

**CD Plus** See *CD Extra*.

**CD-R** (**CD-R**ecordable) A recordable CD-ROM technology using a disc that can be written only once. The drive that writes the CD-R disc is often called a "one-off machine" and can also be used as a regular CD-ROM reader. CD-Rs create the equivalent of pits in the disc by altering the reflectivity of a dye layer. Different dyes can be used, including cyanine (green), pthalo-cyanine (yellow-gold) and metal-azo (blue).

CD-R discs are used for beta versions and original masters of CD-ROM material as well as a means to distribute large amounts of data to a small number of recipients. CD-Rs are also used for archiving data. A major advantage over other media is that they can be read in most CD-ROM drives. "Burning" your own CD-Rs is very efficient for small distributions or when it is vital to create copies immediately. However, when several hundred or more discs must be created, the CD-ROM manufacturing process is generally more efficient. CD-ROMs are made on a pressing machine from a master plate that was derived from a CD-R recording.

To record a full 650MB (74 minute) disc takes as little as six minutes using 12x recorders and as long as an hour with older drives. In 2000, 700MB discs (80 minute) became available, adding only a few minutes for digital audio, but 50MB more for data. See *multisession*, *disc-at-once*, *track-at-once*, *CD UDF* and *optical disk*.

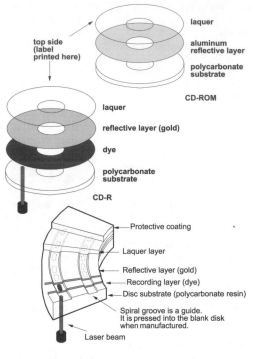

**CD-R and CD-ROM Layers**
Both gold and silver are used for the reflective layer on a CD-R disc. Fresh out of the box, a CD-R disc is entirely reflective lands, because the dye layer is transparent. In order to create the equivalent of a pit, the laser deforms the dye, making it darker and less reflective. On CD-ROMs, the lands and pits are molded into the plastic which is covered by an aluminum reflective coating. To see how a laser reads a CD-ROM, see *CD-ROM*.

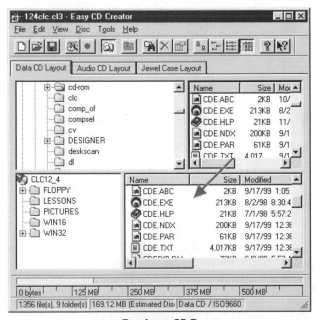

**Burning a CD-R**
It's easy to "burn" a CD-R disc using software such as Adaptec's Easy CD Creator. The required files and folders are simply dragged into the recording window (bottom). The software supports audio and data CDs and also prints the front cover and inside jacket of the jewel case.

**CDRAM** (Cached **DRAM**) A high-speed DRAM memory chip developed by Mitsubishi that includes a small SRAM cache.

**CD-R burner** A CD-R machine. See *CD-R*.

**CD recorder** See *CD-R*.

**CD replication** Manufacturing CDs and CD-ROMs by stamping blank plastic discs from a metal die that contains the predefined pit pattern (binary pattern). Contrast with *CD duplication*.

**C drive** See *C:*.

## CD-ROM

(Compact Disc Read Only Memory) A compact disc format used to hold text, graphics and hi-fi stereo sound. It's like an audio CD with spiral, grooved tracks, but uses a different format for recording data. The audio CD player cannot play CD-ROMs, but CD-ROM players can play audio discs.

CD-ROMs hold 650MB of data, which is equivalent to about 250,000 pages of text or 20,000 medium-resolution images. Sometimes 680MB is used as the capacity, depending on whether the total number of bytes (681,984,000) is divided by 1,000,000 or 1,048,576 (see *binary values*).

A CD-ROM drive (player, reader) connects to a controller card, which is plugged into one of the computer's expansion slots. Earlier drives used a proprietary interface and came with their own card, requiring a free expansion slot in the computer. Today, CD-ROMs use SCSI or EIDE and can be installed without taking up an extra slot.

The first CD-ROM drives transferred data at 150KB per second. Speeds doubled to 300KB and continued upward to more than 40 times the original. Access times range from 80 to 120ms. See *CD-R*, *CD-RW*, *DVD* and *optical disk*.

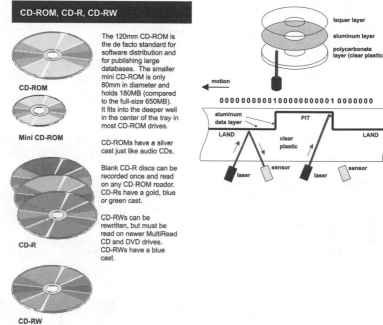

**CD-ROM, CD-R, CD-RW**

**CD-ROM**

**Mini CD-ROM**

**CD-R**

**CD-RW**

The 120mm CD-ROM is the de facto standard for software distribution and for publishing large databases. The smaller mini CD-ROM is only 80mm in diameter and holds 180MB (compared to the full-size 650MB). It fits into the deeper well in the center of the tray in most CD-ROM drives.

CD-ROMs have a silver cast just like audio CDs.

Blank CD-R discs can be recorded once and read on any CD-ROM reader. CD-Rs have a gold, blue or green cast.

CD-RWs can be rewritten, but must be read on newer MultiRead CD and DVD drives. CD-RWs have a blue cast.

laquer layer
aluminum layer
polycarbonate layer (clear plastic)

motion

00000000001000000000010000000

aluminum data layer
PIT
LAND
clear plastic
LAND
laser
sensor
laser
sensor

**Reading a CD-ROM**
Digital data is carved into the CD-ROM as pits (low spots) and lands (high spots). As the laser shines into the moving pits and lands, a sensor detects a change in reflection when it encounters a transition from pit to land or land to pit. Each transition is a 1. The lack of transitions are 0s. There is only one laser in a drive. Two are used here to illustrate the difference in reflection.

## CD-ROM changer

A CD-ROM drive that holds a small number of CD-ROMs for individual use on a desktop computer. Although it can swap discs, it typically contains only one drive and can only read one at a time. See *CD-ROM server*.

## CD-ROM drive

A device that holds and reads CD-ROM discs. CD-ROM drives generally also play audio CD discs by sending analog sound to the sound card via a 4-pin cable. See *CD-ROM*, *CD-ROM changer*, *CD-ROM server* and **CD-ROM audio cable**.

## CD-ROM Extensions

The software required to use a CD-ROM drive on a DOS PC. It allowed CD-ROM drives to be addressed like a hard disk and take the next available drive letter such as D:. Microsoft's CD-ROM Extensions are in the file MSCDEX.EXE. Windows 95/98 includes the CD-ROM File System (CDFS), which is a 32-bit version of MSCDEX.EXE. When upgrading to Windows, MSCDEX.EXE is replaced with CDFS.

## CD-ROM jukebox

See *CD-ROM server*.

**Nakamichi 4-disc Changer**
This Nakamichi MJ-4 changer holds four discs in the same housing as a single-disc unit. The disc is currently at the read head, while the others wait in storage. *(Image courtesy of Nakamichi America Corporation.)*

**CD-ROM reader**    See *CD-ROM drive.*

**CD-ROM server**    A CD-ROM reader designed for network use. It can be configured as a tower or jukebox. Towers contain several drives, and each drive holds one CD-ROM. Jukeboxes hold from a couple dozen to hundreds of discs, but have only a small number of drives. A robotic mechanism moves the discs to the drives as required. See *CD-ROM changer.*

**CD-ROM tower**    See *CD-ROM server.*

**CD-ROM tray**    See *tray drive.*

**CD-ROM XA**    (CD-ROM eXtended Architecture) A CD-ROM format enhancement introduced in 1988 by Philips, Sony and Microsoft that helps to synchronize text, audio and video more accurately on multimedia discs. The original CD-ROM format is known as Mode 1, and XA is known as Mode 2. There are two sector formats in XA: Mode 2 Form 1 contains all the error correction as in Mode 1. This mode is sometimes the default for CD-R authoring programs, because it provides more compatibility with multisession discs. Mode 2 Form 2 eliminates one level of error correction to make more room on the disc for multimedia data.

CD-ROM XA functions as a bridge between CD-ROM and CD-I, as CD-ROM XA discs will play on a CD-I player. CD-ROM XA supports the ADPCM audio compression method and provides up to 9.5 hours of AM-quality stereo or 19 hours of monophonic audio. See *CD-I.*

**CDRS-03**    A modeling and rendering viewset of the Viewperf benchmark, which is used to test OpenGL performance. See *OPC* and *CDRS*.

**CD-RW**    (CD-ReWritable) A rewritable CD-ROM technology. CD-RW drives can also be used to write CD-R discs, and they can read CD-ROMs. But, CD-RW disks have a lower reflectivity than CD-ROMs and CD-Rs, and newer MultiRead CD-ROM drives are required to read them. Initially known as CD-E (for CD-Erasable), a CD-RW disk can be rewritten a thousand times.

CD-RW disks can be used to master CD-ROMs, and the same software used for CD-R creation supports this application. However, unlike CD-Rs, in which the entire disc or an entire track is recorded at once, CD-RWs support UDF (Universal Disk Format), which is similar to the file system on a hard disk. Using variable packet writing, small numbers of files can be appended, and using fixed packet writing, files can be added and deleted. The fixed packet approach requires preformatting like a floppy disk, but takes considerably longer.

CD-RWs use phase change technology to alter the reflectivity of the disk's surface. This is similar to Panasonic's PD (phase change dual) drive, which reads and writes rewritable phase change disks and also reads CD-ROMs. However, the Panasonic phase change disks are only usable in the PD drive. See *phase change*, *DVD* and *optical disk.*

## How a CD-ROM Is Made

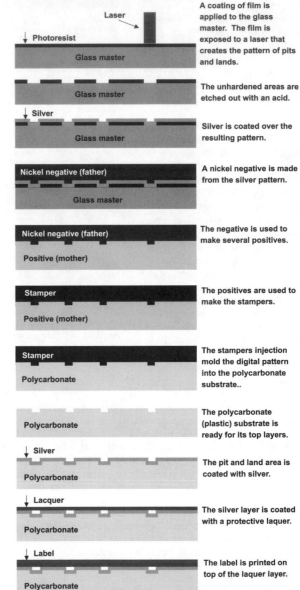

A coating of film is applied to the glass master. The film is exposed to a laser that creates the pattern of pits and lands.

The unhardened areas are etched out with an acid.

Silver is coated over the resulting pattern.

A nickel negative is made from the silver pattern.

The negative is used to make several positives.

The positives are used to make the stampers.

The stampers injection mold the digital pattern into the polycarbonate substrate..

The polycarbonate (plastic) substrate is ready for its top layers.

The pit and land area is coated with silver.

The silver layer is coated with a protective laquer.

The label is printed on top of the laquer layer.

**CDSP**    (Content Delivery Service Provider) A global network that provides faster delivery of Web pages over the Internet. Using servers stationed around the world with duplicate content, the server closest to the user's request is the one that responds. In some cases, the text of the page is maintained on the customer's Web site, and only the graphics are distributed on the CDSP servers, since they are the most time-consuming part of the download. A CDSP network, or "edge network," can reduce the distance these elements travel from 20 to 30 hops down to 3 or 4. See *hop* and *Akamai*.

**CD tower**    See *CD-ROM server*.

**CD track titles**    See *CDDB*.

**CD UDF**    (CD Universal Data Format) A CD-R and CD-RW format introduced in 1996 that allows data to be recorded in packets rather than in a continuous stream. This format is similar to a hard disk and enables small numbers of files to be added. It also eliminates underruns where the computer cannot keep up with the recording process. See *CD-RW*.

**CD writer**    A CD-R machine. See *CD-R*.

**CE**    See *Windows CE, customer engineer* and *consumer electronics*.

**CeBIT**    (www.cebit.de) The world's largest information technology show hosted in Hannover, Germany. In 1996, 6500 exhibitors from around the world drew more than 600,000 attendees. The show is held in March.

**CEBus**    (Consumer Electronic **Bus**) An EIA standard for a control network for the home using a variety of media, including AC power lines, telephone wire, coaxial cable and wireless. CEBus uses the Common Application Language (CAL) to communicate commands over the lines, and the Home Plug & Play specification provides a uniform implementation for using CAL with household objects. The CEbus Industry Council (CIC) supports this effort, and information can be obtained at www.cebus.org.

**CEC**    (Central Electronic Complex) The set of hardware that defines a mainframe, which includes the CPU(s), memory, channels, controllers and power supplies included in the box. Some CECs, such as IBM's Multiprise 2000 and 3000, include data storage devices as well. Also known as "processor complex."

**CE device**    A handheld computer or other device that is managed by the Windows CE operating system. See *Windows CE*.

**Celeron**    A family of lower-cost Pentium II chips from Intel that was introduced in mid 1998. The first models (266 and 300MHz) did not include an external L2 cache and were somewhat sluggish, relegating them to an entry-level or novice rating. However, subsequent models added 128KB of L2 cache that runs at the full speed of the CPU just like the high-end Xeon chips that contain up to 2MB of L2. The chip yields are greater with smaller amounts of cache and can be sold at a better price. Pentium III-based Celerons using the Coppermine technology were introduced in 2000. See *Pentium II* and *Pentium III*.

**cell**    (1) An elementary unit of storage for data (bit) or power (battery).
(2) In a spreadsheet, the intersection of a row and column.

**cell-based IC**    A method for implementing a gate-level design in silicon. Also known as "standard cells," cell-based ICs use standard dimensions for each of the components or gates in order that they can be packed together uniformly. Standard cells are more costly than gate arrays, but are more efficient. Since they are made using blank wafers rather than partially-fabricated ones, they use less silicon real estate. See *gate array* and *ASIC*.

**cellco**    (CELLular phone COmpany) The wireless counterpart of the land-based telephone company. See *telco*.

**Cello**    One of the first Web browsers, introduced by Cornell University in 1993.

**cellphone** (**CELL**ular tele**PHONE**) The first ubiquitous wireless telephone. Originally analog, all new cellular systems are digital, which has enabled the cellphone to turn into a smart phone that has access to the Internet. Digital cellphone systems are also offered in the PCS band, which is radio spectrum that was auctioned off by the U.S. government in the mid-1990s. The major cellular carriers in the U.S. are AT&T Wireless, Verizon Wireless (formerly Bell Atlantic Mobile), CellularONE, Nextel, Sprint PCS and Omnipoint.

The concept behind a cellphone system is that numerous base stations are used, each covering a cell (small geographic area) that only slightly overlaps adjacent cells at the borders. The multiple cells combined with low power transmitters allow the same frequencies to be reused with different conversations in different cells within the same city or locale. The primary cellphone systems are AMPS, GSM, TDMA and CDMA. See *AMPS*, *GSM*, *TDMA*, *CDMA*, *WAP*, *cellspace*, *Internet appliance* and *cordless phone*.

**The Cells**
The cellular system uses multiple base stations to cover a geographic area. As the mobile phone user travels from cell to cell, the call is automatically "handed off" to the next station. The smaller the area covered by the cells, the more the same frequencies can be reused within each cell, thus expanding the total number of concurrent users of the system within a city or metropolitan region.

**Could They Have Imagined?**
As Europeans began to use their new-fangled Ericsson phones in the late 1800s, could they have imagined the wireless world of cellphones 100 years later? Picture taken at Antoni Gaudi's famous "La Pedrera" apartment house in Barcelona.

**cell relay** A transmission technology that uses small fixed-length packets (cells) that can be switched at high speed. It is easier to build a switch that switches fixed-length packets than variable ones. ATM uses a type of cell relay technology.

**cellspace** Using a cellphone or handheld PDA connected to the Internet; that is, being entirely mobile and on the Net at the same time. The term was coined by David Bennahum, publisher of the MEME Electronic Newsletter (www.memex.org).

**cell switch** A network device that switches fixed packets, such as an ATM switch. Contrast with *frame switch*.

**cell switching** Using cell switches to forward fixed-length packets in a network. Contrast with *frame switching*. See *ATM*.

**cellular automata** The plural of *cellular automaton*.

**cellular automaton** A state machine that consists of an array of cells, each of which can be in one of a finite number of possible states. The cells are updated synchronously in discrete time steps, according to a local, identical interaction rule. The state of a cell at the next time step is determined by the current states of a surrounding neighborhood of cells. The transitions are usually specified in the form of a rule table that defines the cell's next state for each possible neighborhood configuration. The cellular array (grid) is typically from one to three dimensions. Highly parallel, locally connected and using simple elemental units, cellular automata can perform so-called cellular computing. See *state machine*.

**Cellular MultiProcessing** See *CMP*.

**CELP** (Code Excited Linear Predictive) A speech compression method that achieves high compression ratios along with toll quality audio. LD-CELP (Low-Delay CELP) provides near toll quality audio by using a smaller sample size that is processed faster, resulting in lower delays. LD-CELP was developed by Dr. Raymond Chen when he was at AT&T. Chen was also involved with CELP.

**CELP socket** (Card Edge Low Profile socket)  A socket from Intel used for plugging in SIMM modules containing cache memory, known as "cache on a stick," or COAST. It replaced the tedious job of adding and removing individual DIP memory chips.

**censorware** Software that blocks certain types of Internet traffic from being retrieved. See *Web filtering* and *parental control software*.

**centering cone** A short plastic or metal cone used to align a 5.25" floppy disk to the drive spindle. It is inserted into the diskette's center hole when the drive door is closed.

**centralized processing** Processing performed in one or more computers in a single location. All terminals in the organization are connected to the central computers. Contrast with *distributed computing* and *decentralized processing*.

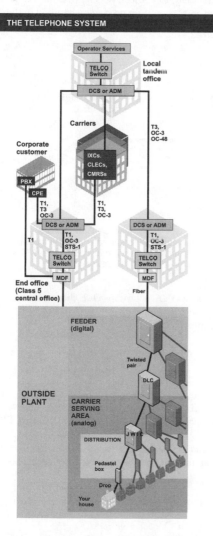

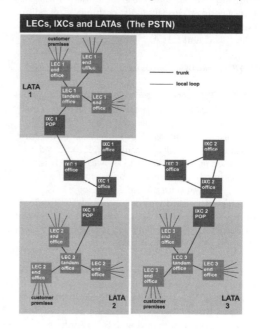

**Central Offices**
End offices provide the local loops directly to customers, while tandem offices carry traffic between end offices. The PSTN is made up of local exchange carriers (LECs) and interexchange carriers (IXCs) that are governed by LATA boundaries.

**Are We Doing a 180?**    The Windows terminal and network computer (NC) are a move towards centralized computing, or thin client computing, once again. This trend towards centralization stems from the high cost of overloaded PCs, which have caused network administration headaches in large organizations.

The Windows terminal works similarly to a mainframe or minicomputer terminal in that all the application processing is done in a central computer (Windows NT server). The NC differs in that it does the processing in the client machine, but keeps nothing locally. All the software is retrieved from the central server. See *Windows terminal, network computer* and *thin client.*

**central office**    A local telephone company switching center. There are two types. The first is called an "end office" (EO) or "local exchange" (LE) and connects directly to the outside plant, which is the feeder and distribution system to homes and offices. The end office (often called a "Class 5 office") provides customer services such as call waiting and call forwarding. The second type is the tandem office (also toll office or tandem/toll office), which is a central office that does not connect directly to the customer. Toll call record generation and accounting used to be handled in the tandem offices. Today, the billing is mostly done in the end offices. There are more than 25,000 central offices in the U.S. See *LEC, IXC* and *LATA.*

**central processor**    Same as *CPU.*

**CENTREX**    PBX services provided by a local telephone company. Switching is done in the telephone company's central office. Some services do the switching at the customer's site, but control it in the central office.

**Centronics**    A standard 36-pin parallel interface for connecting printers and other devices to a computer. It defines the plug, socket and signals used and transfers data asynchronously up to 200 Kbytes/ sec. The plug has 18 contacts each on the top and bottom. The socket contains one opening with matching contacts.

This de facto standard was developed by Centronics Corporation, maker of the first successful dot matrix printers. The printer was introduced in 1970, and the company was bought by Genicom Corporation in 1987. See *printer cable.*

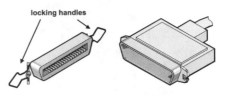

**Centronics Connectors**
Centronics connectors are used on most printers. A larger 50-pin variation is used on SCSI-1 devices.

**Centura**    A high-level development system for 32-bit Windows applications from Centura Software Corporation (formerly Gupta Software), Menlo Park, CA (www.centurasoft.com). It includes a 4GL, a replication facility for OLE clients, Web publishing and three-tier client/server support. Centura is the 32-bit counterpart of the widely-used 16-bit SQLWindows. Code developed with SQLWindows migrates easily to Centura.

**CERDIP**    (CERamic Dual In-line Package) A type of ceramic DIP chip. It uses a ceramic lid that is bonded to the chip with a glass seal. See *DIP, CDIP, CERQUAD* and *chip package.*

**CERN**    (Conseil Europeen pour la Recherche Nucleaire, Geneva, Switzerland, www.cern.ch) CERN is the European Laboratory for Nuclear Research where the World Wide Web was developed to enhance collaboration on research documents pertaining to particle physics. A complete Web server software package is available at no charge from CERN.

**CERQUAD**    (CERamic QUADpack) A square, ceramic, surface mount chip package. It uses a ceramic lid that is bonded to the chip with a glass seal. It has pins on all four sides that wrap under like those of a PLCC package. See *CERDIP, CDIP* and *PLCC.*

**certificate authority software**    The software used by a certification authority (CA) to issue digital certificates. See *CA* and *PKI.*

**certification**   The following certifications are described in this database. See also *aptitude tests*.

- *CISSP*
- *CCP*
- *CNP*
- *CompTIA*
- *Cisco certification*
- *Microsoft certification*
- *NetWare certification*
- *Xplor*

**certification authority**   See *CA*.

**CF card**   (CompactFlash card)  See *CompactFlash*.

**CFG file**   (ConFiGuration file)  A file that contains startup information required to launch a program or operating system. Same as *INI file*.

**CFML**   (ColdFusion Markup Language)  See *ColdFusion*.

**CG**   (Computer Graphics)  See *graphics*.

**CGA**   (Color/Graphics Adapter)  The first video display standard for the IBM PC. This low-resolution system was superseded by EGA and then VGA. CGA required a digital RGB Color Display monitor. See *PC display modes*.

**CGI script**   (Common Gateway Interface script)  A small program written in a language such as Perl, Tcl, C or C++ that functions as the glue between HTML pages and other programs on the Web server. For example, a CGI script would allow search data entered on a Web page to be sent to the DBMS (database management system) for lookup. It would also format the results of that search as an HTML page and send it back to the user. The CGI script resides in the server and obtains the data from the user via environment variables that the Web server makes available to it.

CGI scripts have been the initial mechanism used to make Web sites interact with databases and other applications. However, as the Web evolved, server-side processing methods have been developed that are more efficient and easier to program. For example, Microsoft promotes its Active Server Pages (ASPs) for its Windows Web servers, and Sun/Netscape nurtures its Java roots with JavaServer Pages (JSPs) and servlets. See *ASP*, *JSP*, *servlet* and *FastCGI*.

**CGM**   (Computer Graphics Metafile)  A standard format for interchanging graphics images. CGM stores images primarily in vector graphics, but also provides a raster format. Earlier GDM and VDM formats have been merged into CGM. There are many non-standard varieties of CGM in use.

**chad**   A piece of paper that is punched out on a punched card, paper tape or on the borders of continuous forms. A chadded form is when the holes are cut completely through, which is typical of punched cards. In a chadless form or in chadless paper tape, the chads are still attached to one edge of the hole.

Chads on the Floor!    In the U.S. presidential election of 2000, people were up in arms over the extra chads on the floor where several Florida counties were recounting the vote. The punched holes (chads) are supposed to fall out of the cards when they are punched. The fact that some chads were still hanging but the additional handling caused them

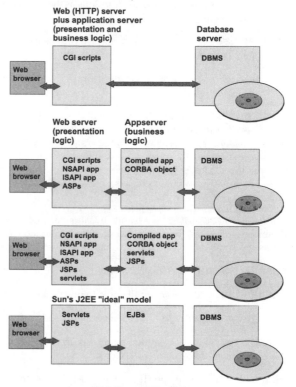

**Web Server Evolution**
Starting at the top and moving down, this illustration shows Web and application server processing as it evolved initially using only CGI scripts and later using Java components. The separation of logic is portrayed here, and the Web server (HTTP server) and application server may reside in the same or different computers.

to fall away is perfectly natural. Why nobody informed the officials that this is normal was as ridiculous as the antiquated voting equipment.

**chained list**    A group of items in which each item contains the location of the next item in sequence.

**chaining**    Linking items or records to form a chain. Each link in the chain points to the next item.

**chain printer**    An early line printer that used type slugs linked together in a chain as its printing mechanism. The chain spins horizontally around a set of hammers. When the desired character is in front of the selected print column, the corresponding hammer hits the paper into the ribbon and onto the character in the chain. Chain and train printers gave way to band printers in the early 1980s.

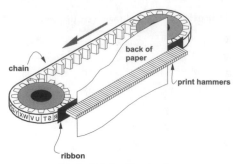

**Chain Printer Mechanism**
When the required character in the chain has revolved to the selected print column, the hammer pushes the paper into the ribbon and against the type slug of the letter or digit.

**challenge/response**    An authentication method used to verify the legitimacy of users logging onto the network. When a user logs on, the server uses account information to send a "challenge" number back to the user. The user enters the number into a credit-card sized token card that generates a response which is sent to the server.

**change control**    See *version control*.

**change file**    A transaction file used to update a master file.

**change management**    See *version control* and *configuration management*.

**change request**    A petition for modifying the behavior of a system due to normal business changes or because there is a bug in the system. See *issue tracking*.

**channel**    (1) A high-speed metal or optical fiber pathway between the computer and the control units of the peripheral devices. Channels are used in mainframes and high-end machines. Each channel is an independent unit that can transfer data concurrently with other channels as well as the CPU. For example, in a 10-channel computer, 10 streams of data are being transmitted to and from the CPU at the same time. In contrast, the bus in a personal computer serves as a common, shared channel between all devices. Each device must wait for its turn on the bus.

(2) In communications, any pathway between two computers or terminals. It may refer to the physical medium, such as coaxial cable, or to a specific carrier frequency (subchannel) within a larger channel or wireless medium.

(3) Information on a particular subject that is transmitted into the user's computer from a Webcast site via the user's browser or push client. It is the Internet's counterpart of the TV or radio channel. See *Webcast, push client* and *push technology*.

(4) The distributor/dealer sales channel. Vendors that sell in the channel rely on the sales ability of their dealers and the customer relationships they have built up over the years. Such vendors may or may not compete with the channel by selling direct to customers via mail order.

**channel bank**    A multiplexor that merges several low-speed voice or data lines into one high-speed digital line and vice versa. Channel banks use TDM (time division multiplexing) to combine the different signals into one by interleaving the bits.

Starting in the 1960s, channel banks converted 24 analog voice lines into digital and multiplexed them onto one T1 line. Toward the late 1980s, they became more sophisticated and accepted plug-in modules that took in a variety of digital signals and multiplexed them onto the T1. See *TDM*.

**channel bonding**    Doubling transmission speed by spreading the data over two lines. ISDN modems use channel bonding to split the data stream into two 64 Kbps channels, which use both lines in an ISDN BRI service. Bonded analog modems use two analog telephone lines to double transmission capacity, splitting data into two streams of 56 Kbps. This "dual analog" method, also known as "modem bonding," uses the Multilink Protocol Plus (MP+), which is supported by most ISPs. With this technique, if one modem fails, the other continues. See *modem teaming*.

**channel coding**    A way of encoding data in a communications channel that adds patterns of redundancy into the transmission path in order to improve the error rate. Such methods are widely used in wireless communications. See *convolutional code* and *Viterbi decoder*.

**channelized**    Refers to an architecture that transmits data in channels. It very often refers to the 64 Kbps channels in T1 lines, which were originally developed to handle digitized voice streams that required 64 Kbps each.

**channel op**    (CHANNEL OPerator)  Also "chanop" and "CHOP." The person who has the highest privileges in an IRC channel. The channel op can expel users and make other users channel ops. See *IRC*.

**channel program**    Instructions executed by a peripheral channel. The channel executes the channel program independently of the CPU, allowing concurrent operations to take place in the computer.

**channel spacing**    The amount of bandwidth alloted to each channel in a communications system that transmits multiple frequencies such as fiber optics. It is measured as the spacing between center frequencies (or wavelengths) of adjacent channels. See *guard band*.

**chaos**    The science that deals with the underlying order of the seemingly random nature of the universe. See *fractals*.

**CHAP**    (Challenge Handshake Authentication Protocol)  An access control protocol that dynamically encrypts the user's ID and password. The logon procedure in the user's machine obtains a key from the CHAP server, which it uses to encrypt the username and password before transmitting it. See *PAP*.

**character**    (1) A single alphabetic letter, numeric digit, or special symbol such as a decimal point or comma. A character is equivalent to a byte; for example, 50,000 characters take up 50,000 bytes.

(2) The term character is also used to describe command-driven systems. For example, in the phrase "it supports Mac, Windows and character interfaces," character refers to the line-at-a-time text entry used with dumb terminals.

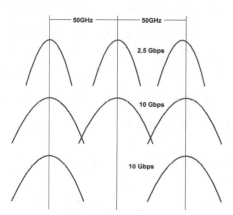

**Channel Spacing in Optical Fibers**
The first 10 Gbps example with 50GHz spacing has a slight signal overlap, but with 100GHz, there is none. The first example provides more bandwidth, but the overlap could be enough to cause significant crosstalk. *(Illustration courtesy of Jeff Hecht.)*

**character based**    Same as *text based*.

**character cell**    A matrix of dots used to form a single character on a display screen or printer. For example, an 8x16 cell is made up of 16 rows each containing eight dots. Character cells are displayed and printed contiguously; therefore the design of each letter, digit or symbol within the cell must include surrounding blank space.

**character code**    A digital coding system for alphanumeric characters. See *ASCII* and *EBCDIC*.

**character data**    Alphanumeric data or text. Contrast with *numeric data*.

**character field**    A data field that holds alphanumeric characters. Contrast with *numeric field*.

**character generator**    (1) Circuitry that converts data characters into dot patterns for a display screen.

(2) A device that creates text characters that are superimposed onto video frames.

**The DOS OEM Font**
The characters at the upper end (extended ASCII) of the character set in the original DOS font allowed elementary forms and bar charts to be printed as in this example.

**character graphics**    A set of special symbols strung together like letters of the alphabet to create elementary graphics and forms, as in the following example:

**character mode** Same as *text mode.*

**character pitch** The measurement of the number of characters per inch. See *cpi.*

**character printer** A printer that prints one character at a time. The typical character printer is the dot matrix printer. See *printer.*

**character recognition** The ability of a machine to recognize printed text. See *OCR* and *MICR.*

**character set** A group of unique symbols used for display and printing. Character sets for languages that use the English alphabet generally contain 256 symbols, which is the number of combinations one byte can hold. Except for special fonts, such as Dingbats and Greek Symbols, the symbols are the same for the first 128 characters. The letters may have different styling due to their typeface, but an "M," for example, is an "M" in the same sequential order in each character set.

The second 128 characters differ depending on the font/character set chosen. See *ASCII chart* for the actual characters in the PC-8 character set, which was defined for the original IBM PC. See *extended ASCII.*

**character string** A group of alphanumeric characters. Contrast with *numeric data.*

**character terminal** A display screen without graphics capability.

**charting program** Software used to create business graphics, charts and diagrams. See *business graphics* and *diagramming program.*

**chassis** Pronounced "chah-see," it is a physical structure that holds everything or that everything is attached to. A computer's cabinet is often called the chassis.

**chat** A realtime conferencing capability between two or more users on a local network (LAN), on the Internet or via a BBS. The chat is accomplished by typing on the keyboard, not speaking. Each keystroke is transmitted as it is pressed. See *Internet Relay Chat* and *instant messenger.*

**chat bot** (CHAT roBOT) A robot designed to talk to humans about various subjects. See *ALICE.*

**chat mode** An option in a communications program that turns on the chat function.

**chat room** An interactive discussion (by keyboard) about a specific topic that is hosted on the Internet or on a BBS. On the Internet, chat rooms are available from major services such as AOL, individual Web sites and the Internet Relay Chat (IRC) system, the Net's traditional computer conferencing. See *3-D chat* and *Internet Relay Chat.*

**chat window** A text window used for conferencing between two or more users. See *chat room.*

**check bits** A calculated number used for error checking. The number is derived by some formula from the binary value of one or more bytes of data. See *parity checking, checksum* and *CRC.*

**check box** A small box onscreen that simulates the equivalent symbol on a paper form. When the box is clicked, the box displays an X or a check mark to indicate that option has been selected.

**check digit** A numeric digit used to ensure that account numbers are correctly entered into the computer. Using a formula, a check digit is calculated for each new account number, which then becomes part of the number, often the last digit.

When an account number is entered, the data entry program recalculates the check digit and compares it to the check digit entered. If the digits are not equal, the account number is considered invalid.

**checkpoint/restart** A method of recovering from a system failure. A checkpoint is a copy of the computer's memory that is periodically saved on disk along with the current register settings (last instruction executed, etc.). In the event of any failure, the last checkpoint serves as a recovery point.

When the problem has been fixed, the restart program copies the last checkpoint into memory, resets all the hardware registers and starts the computer from that point. Any transactions in memory after the last checkpoint was taken until the failure occurred will be lost.

**checksum**    A value used to ensure data is stored or transmitted without error. It is created by calculating the binary values in a block of data using some algorithm and storing the results with the data. When the data is retrieved from memory or received at the other end of a network, a new checksum is computed and matched against the existing checksum. A non-match indicates an error.

Just as a check digit tests the accuracy of a single number, a checksum tests a block of data. Checksums detect single bit errors and some multiple bit errors, but are not as effective as the CRC method. Checksums are also used by the Sophos anitvirus software to determine if a file has changed since the last time it was scanned for a virus. See *ECC memory* and *Sophos*.

**chiclet keyboard**    A keyboard with flat, squared-off keys that resemble chiclets (gum). Used on low-cost devices, it is unsuitable for continuous typing.

**chief technical officer**    See *CTO*.

**child**    (1) In database management, the data that is dependent on its parent. See *parent-child*.
(2) A component that is subordinate to a higher-level component. See *child menu, child program* and *child window*.

**child menu**    A secondary or submenu that is displayed on screen when a certain option in the "parent" menu is selected.

**child program**    A secondary or subprogram called for and loaded into memory by the main program. See *parent program*.

**child window**    A secondary window on screen that is displayed within the main overall window of the application.

**chip**    (2) A bit in a spreading signal. See *chip rate*.
(1) A set of microminiaturized, electronic circuits that are designed for use as processors and memory in computers and countless consumer and industrial products. Chips are the driving force in this industry. Small chips can hold from a handful to tens of thousands of transistors. They look like tiny chips of aluminum, no more than 1/16" square by 1/30" thick, which is where the term "chip" came from. Large chips, which can be more than a half inch square, hold millions of transistors. It is actually only the top one thousandth of an inch of a chip's surface that holds the circuits. The rest of it is just a base. The terms *chip, integrated circuit* and *microchip* are synonymous.

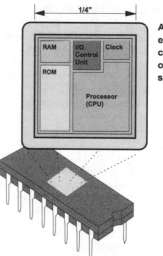

An entire computer on a single chip.

### Types of Chips by Function

**Logic Chip**    A single chip can perform some or all of the functions of a processor. A microprocessor is an entire processor on a single chip. Desktop and portable computers use one microprocessor for their CPU while larger computers may employ several types of microprocessors as well as hundreds or thousands of specialized logic chips.

**Memory Chip**    Random access memory (RAM) chips contain from a couple of hundred thousand to several million storage cells (bits). They are the computer's working storage and require constant power to keep their bits charged. Firmware chips, such as ROMs, PROMs, EPROMs, and EEPROMs are permanent memory chips that hold their content without power.

**Computer on a Chip**    Also called a "microcontroller" or "MCU," it is a single chip that contains the processor, RAM, ROM, I/O control unit, and a timing clock. It is used in a myriad of consumer and industrial products by the hundreds of millions each year.

**Analog/Digital and DSP**    A single chip can perform the conversion between analog and digital signals. A programmable CPU called a "DSP" (digital signal processor) is also used in many analog/digital conversions. It contains fast instructions sequences commonly used in such applications.

**Special Purpose Chip**    Chips used in low-cost consumer items (watches, calculators, etc.) and higher-cost products (video games, automobile control, etc.) may be designed from scratch to obtain economical and effective performance. Today's ASIC chips can be quickly created for any special purpose.

**Logic Array and Gate Array**    These chips contain logic gates that have not been tied together. A final set of steps applies the top metal layer onto the chip stringing the logic gates together into the pattern required by the customer. This method eliminates much of the design and fabrication time for producing a chip.

**Bit Slice Processor**    Bit slice chips contain elementary electronic circuits that serve as building blocks for the computer architect. They are used to custom-build a processor for specialized purposes.

## How the Chip Came About

**Revolution**    In 1947, the semiconductor industry was born at AT&T's Bell Labs with the invention of the *transistor* by John Bardeen, Walter Brattain and William Shockley. The transistor, fabricated from solid materials that could change their electrical conductivity, would eventually replace all the bulky, hot, glass vacuum tubes used as electronic amplifiers in radio and TV and as on/off switches in computers. By the late 1950s, the giant first-generation computers were giving way to smaller, faster and more reliable transistorized machines.

**Evolution**    The original transistors were discrete components; each one was soldered onto a circuit board to connect to other individual transistors, resistors and diodes. Since hundreds of transistors were made on one round silicon wafer and cut apart only to be reconnected again, the idea of building them in the required pattern to begin with was obvious. In the late 1950s, Jack Kilby of TI and Robert Noyce of Fairchild Semiconductor created the *integrated circuit*, a set of interconnected transistors and resistors on a single chip.

Since then, the number of transistors that have been put onto a single chip has increased exponentially, from a handful in the early 1960s to millions by the late 1980s. Today, a million transistors take up no more space than the first transistor.

A byproduct of miniaturization is speed. The shorter the distance a pulse travels, the faster it gets there. The smaller the elements in the transistor, the faster it switches. Transistor speeds are measured in billionths and trillionths of a second. A Josephson junction transistor has been able to switch in 50 quadrillionths of a second.

**Logic and Memory**    In first- and second-generation computers, internal main memory was made of such materials as tubes filled with liquid mercury, magnetic drums and magnetic cores. As integrated circuits began to flourish in the 1960s, design breakthroughs allowed memories to also be made of semiconductor materials. Thus, logic circuits, the "brains" of the computer, and memory circuits, its internal workspace, were moving along the same miniaturization path.

**Drs. Bardeen, Shockley and Brattain**
This picture of the three inventors was taken in 1947. *(Image courtesy of The Computer Museum History Center, www.computerhistory.org)*

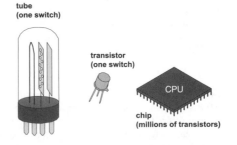

tube
(one switch)

transistor
(one switch)

CPU

chip
(millions of transistors)

**Tube to Transistor to Chip**
A tube was the equivalent of one transistor. Today, you could fit billions of transistors inside one tube.

By the end of the 1970s, it was possible to put a processor, working memory (RAM), permanent memory (ROM), a control unit for handling input and output and a timing clock on the same chip.

Within 25 years, the transistor on a chip grew into the computer on a chip. When the awesome UNIVAC I was introduced in 1951, you could literally open the door and walk inside. Who would have believed the equivalent electronics would some day be built into your watch.

**The Making of a Chip**    Computer circuits carry electrical pulses from one point to another. The pulses flow through transistors (on/off switches) that open or close when electrically activated. The current flowing through one switch effects the opening or closing of another and so on. Transistors are wired together in patterns of Boolean logic. Logic gates make up circuits. Circuits make up CPUs and other electronic systems.

**FROM LOGIC TO PLUMBING**    All circuits were originally designed in some manner by humans. Today, many logic functions reside in libraries, and designers pick and choose modules from a menu. There is always a little bit of "glue logic" necessary to interconnect them however, and this still must be done logic gate by logic gate. If a required function is not predesigned, that part will have to be created gate by gate. In addition, if the purpose of the final chip is to be the "fastest" and "greatest" of all chips of its kind, most likely all the logic will be designed from scratch.

Computers make computers. The computer converts the logical circuit design into transistors, diodes and resistors. From there the whole thing is turned into a plumber's nightmare that connects millions of components together. After inspection by technicians, the electronic images are transferred to machinery that creates glass, lithographic plates, called "photomasks."

The photomask is the actual size of the chip, replicated many times to fit on a round silicon wafer up to 12" in diameter. The transistors are built by creating subterranean layers in the silicon, and a different photomask is created to isolate each layer to be worked on.

**CHIPS ARE JUST ROCKS**    The base material of a chip is usually silicon, although materials such as sapphire and gallium arsenide are also used. Silicon is found in quartz rocks and is purified in a molten state. It is then chemically combined (doped) with other materials to alter its electrical properties. The result is a silicon crystal ingot up to eight inches in diameter that is either positively (p-type) or negatively charged (n-type). Slices of the ingot approximately 1/30th of an inch thick are cut from this "crystal salami." The slices are called "wafers."

**Inspecting the Plumbing**
People are always more flexible than computers and can find flaws that might go undetected by software analysis. *(Image courtesy of Elxsi Corporation.)*

IF (A+B) *AND* (C+D) OCCUR
*OR*
IF (A+B) *AND* (D+E) OCCUR
THEN
F AND G *AND* (H+I) IS...

photomask

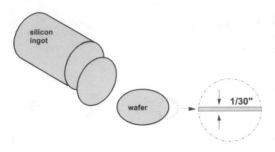

**BUILDING THE LAYERS**    Circuit building starts out by adhering a layer of silicon dioxide insulation on the wafer's surface. The insulation is coated with film and exposed to light through the first photomask, hardening the film and insulation below it. The unhardened areas are etched away exposing the silicon base below. By shooting a gas under heat and pressure into the exposed silicon (diffusion), a sublayer with different electrical properties is created beneath the surface.

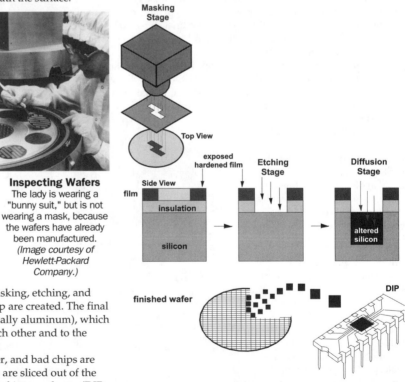

### Drawing the Ingot
The silicon ingot is being drawn from a scalding furnace containing molten silicon. High-speed saws will slice it into wafers about as thick as a dime, which will then be ground thinner and polished like a mirror. *(Image courtesy of Texas Instruments, Inc.)*

### Packaging the Chip
This machine bonds the chips to the metal structure that will be connected to the pins of the chip housing and carry the signals to and from the circuit board. *(Image courtesy of Texas Instruments, Inc.)*

### Inspecting Wafers
The lady is wearing a "bunny suit," but is not wearing a mask, because the wafers have already been manufactured. *(Image courtesy of Hewlett-Packard Company.)*

Through multiple stages of masking, etching, and diffusion, the sublayers on the chip are created. The final stage lays the top metal layer (usually aluminum), which interconnects the transistors to each other and to the outside world.

Each chip is tested on the wafer, and bad chips are marked for elimination. The chips are sliced out of the wafer, and the good ones are placed into packages (DIPs, PQFPs, etc.). The chip is connected to the package with tiny wires, then sealed and tested as a complete unit.

Chip making is extremely precise. Operations are performed in a "clean room," since air particles can mix with the microscopic mixtures and easily render a chip worthless. Depending on the design complexity, more chips can fail than succeed.

The Formation of One Transistor    These illustrations show the stages in the creation of one transistor. Millions of transistors are built on each of several dozen CPU chips on a single wafer. Thus, more than 100 million transistors are typically fabricated simultaneously. The invention of the transistor and its increasing miniaturization is the backbone of computer technology. A run-of-the-mill chip fabrication plant only costs $2 billion.

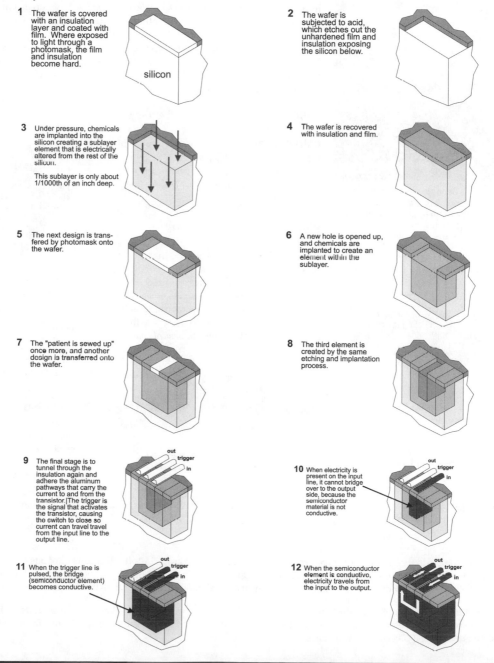

1 The wafer is covered with an insulation layer and coated with film.  Where exposed to light through a photomask, the film and insulation become hard.

silicon

2 The wafer is subjected to acid, which etches out the unhardened film and insulation exposing the silicon below.

3 Under pressure, chemicals are implanted into the silicon creating a sublayer element that is electrically altered from the rest of the silicon.

This sublayer is only about 1/1000th of an inch deep.

4 The wafer is recovered with insulation and film.

5 The next design is transfered by photomask onto the wafer.

6 A new hole is opened up, and chemicals are implanted to create an element within the sublayer.

7 The "patient is sewed up" once more, and another design is transferred onto the wafer.

8 The third element is created by the same etching and implantation process.

9 The final stage is to tunnel through the insulation again and adhere the aluminum pathways that carry the current to and from the transistor. The trigger is the signal that activates the transistor, causing the switch to close so current can travel from the input line to the output line.

out    trigger    in

10 When electricity is present on the input line, it cannot bridge over to the output side, because the semiconductor material is not conductive.

out    trigger    in

11 When the trigger line is pulsed, the bridge (semiconductor element) becomes conductive.

out    trigger    in

12 When the semiconductor element is conductive, electricity travels from the input to the output.

out    trigger    in

**The Future**    There is a never-ending thirst for putting more circuits onto a chip. In order to miniaturize elements of a transistor even more, electron beam lithography will be used to expose the mask patterns directly onto the wafer, eliminating the photomask process entirely.

Just as integrated circuits eliminated cutting apart the transistors only to be reconnected again, eventually *wafer scale integration* will eliminate cutting apart the chips only to be tied together with other chips. All the computer circuitry will be built on one chip.

As we're trying to make the chip wider, we're also trying to make it deeper. Instead of adding more circuits across the surface, we are experimenting with building overlapping layers. Within the next 10 years, today's supercomputer will fit within a cubic inch.

**Dressing for Work**
The fabrication of the tiny transistor is an extremely precise one. The slightest contaminants in the air can render the transistor and chip useless. Putting on the "bunny suit" is an elaborate procedure. *(Image courtesy of Intel Corporation.)*

**chip card**    See *smart card* and *memory card*.

**chip carrier**    (1) The package that a chip is mounted in. See *chip package*.

(2) A chip package with connectors on all sides. See *leaded chip carrier* and *leadless chip carrier*.

**chip cooler**    See *CPU cooler*.

**chip on board**    A bare chip that is mounted directly onto the printed circuit board (PCB). After the wires are attached, a glob of epoxy or plastic is used to cover the chip and its connections. The tape automated bonding (TAB) process is used to place the chip on the board. See *tape automated bonding*.

**The Chip Package**
All chips are packaged in a housing with pins that plug into or are soldered onto a printed circuit board. This is a picture of a Motorola 6801 computer on a chip. It is packaged in a DIP chip which is widely used for memory and small microprocessors.

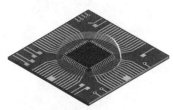

**Chip On Board**
The bare chip is adhered and wire bonded to the board, and an epoxy is poured over it to insulate and protect it. For illustrative purposes only, this picture shows a clear epoxy.

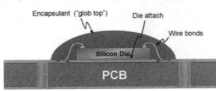

Encapsulant ("glob top")    Die attach

Wire bonds

Silicon Die

PCB

**Side View**
This side view shows how the wires connect the chip to the printed circuit board (PCB). *(Image courtesy of Joseph Fjelstad.)*

**chip on chip**    A 3-D cube of chips, using bare chips mounted one over the other with spacers in between. As this technology matures, it is expected that up to 100 chips can be used in one cube.

**chip package**    The housing that chips come in for plugging into (socket mount) or soldering onto (surface mount) the printed circuit board. See *CDIP, CERDIP, CERQUAD, CLCC, DIP, flatpack, PLCC, QFP, MCM, MCP, SOP, SOIC, SOJ, TSOP* and *ZIP*.

**chip rate**    In direct sequence spread spectrum technologies such as CDMA, it is the number of bits per second (chips per second) used in the spreading signal. A different spreading signal is added to the data signal to code each transmission uniquely. The number of chips (bits) in the spreading signal is significantly greater than the data bits. See *CDMA*.

**chipset**    A group of chips designed to work as a unit to perform a function. For example, a modem chipset contains all the primary circuits for transmitting and receiving. A PC chipset provides the electronic interfaces between all subsystems (see *PC chipset* for illustration).

**CHK file**    (**CHecK**disk file) The file extension applied to unlinked files by the DOS ScanDisk utility and Chkdsk command. See *ScanDisk* and **DOS Chkdsk**.

**CHMOS**    (**H**igh-density **CMOS**) A chip with a high density of CMOS transistors.

**Chooser**    A Macintosh desk accessory that allows the user to select a printer, file server or network device, such as a network modem.

**chroma key**    See *color key*.

**chromatic dispersion**    See *dispersion*.

**chrominance**    The color information in a video signal. See *luminance* for an explanation of chrominance and luminance. See also *saturation* and *hue*.

**CHRP**    (**C**ommon **H**ardware **R**eference **P**latform) A specification intended to make the PowerPC a standard platform. Also known as the PowerPC Reference Platform (PPCP), it defines minimum hardware requirements such as ports, sockets, bootstrap ROM and cache. Introduced in 1995, the first CHRP systems became available from Motorola in 1997. Since OS/2, NT, Solaris and NetWare support for the PowerPC has been halted, CHRP serves as a standard for Macintosh clones.

**cHTML**    (**C**ompact **HTML**) The HTML used by NTT Docomo's i-Mode wireless system. See *i-Mode*.

**churning**    Firing one group of employees and hiring another. As companies move into newer, high-tech ventures, they often eliminate employees with older skills while bringing on new people that have computer programming, networking and Web experience. In short, stay computer literate! It pays to read this publication often.

**CICS**    (**C**ustomer **I**nformation **C**ontrol **S**ystem) A TP monitor from IBM that was originally developed to provide transaction processing for IBM mainframes. It controls the interaction between applications and users and lets programmers develop screen displays without detailed knowledge of the terminals used. It provides terminal routing, password security, transaction logging for error recovery and activity journals for performance analysis.

   CICS has also been made available on non-mainframe platforms including the RS/6000, AS/400 and OS/2-based PCs.

   CICS commands are written along with and into the source code of the applications, typically COBOL, although assembly language, PL/I and RPG are also used. CICS implements SNA layers 4, 5 and 6.

**CICS programmer**    A programmer versed in CICS commands as well as in the programming language used to develop the application.

**CID**    (**C**onfiguration, **I**nstallation and **D**istribution) IBM software for controlling software distribution throughout a network from a central source.

**CIDR**    (**C**lassless **I**nter-**D**omain **R**outing) A method for creating additional addresses on the Internet, which are given to Internet service providers (ISPs) that in turn delegate them to their customers. CIDR reduces the burden on Internet routers by aggregating routes so that one IP address represents thousands of addresses that are serviced by a major backbone provider. All packets sent to any of those addresses are sent to the ISP such as MCI or Sprint. In 1990, there were about 2,000 routes on the Internet. Five years later, there were more than 30,000. Without CIDR, the routers would not have been able to support the increasing number of Internet sites.

   Instead of the fixed 8, 16 and 24 bits used in the Class A-B-C network IDs, CIDR uses a variable network ID from 13 to 27 bits. For example, the CIDR address 204.12.01.42/24 indicates that the first 24 bits are used for network ID. See *IP address*.

**CIE**    (**C**ommission **I**nternationale de l'Eclairage) A color model defined in 1931 that represents all possible colors in a three-dimensional color space. All of the variants of CIE (CIELAB, CIELUV, CIEXYZ, etc.) use values of lightness, red-green and yellow-blue to represent a color. The CIE Chromaticity Diagram is a two-dimensional drawing of this model. Although considered the most accurate color model, RGB is the one widely used for monitors, and CMYK for printers. See *RGB*, *CMYK* and *HSB*.

**CIF**    (1) (Common Intermediate Format) A standard video format used in videoconferencing. CIF formats are defined by their resolution, and standards both above and below the original resolution have been established. The original CIF is also known as Full CIF (FCIF). The bit rates in the chart below are for uncompressed color frames.

| CIF Format | | Resolution | Bit Rate at 30 fps (Mbps) |
|---|---|---|---|
| SQCIF | (Sub Quarter CIF) | 128 x 96 | 4.4 |
| QCIF | (Quarter CIF) | 176 x 144 | 9.1 |
| CIF | (Full CIF, FCIF) | 352 x 288 | 36.5 |
| 4CIF | (4 x CIF) | 704 x 576 | 146.0 |
| 16CIF | (16 x CIF) | 1408 x 1152 | 583.9 |

(2) (Cells In Frames) A networking technology developed by Cornell University that allows ATM backbones to be used with Ethernet LANs. CIF utilizes the inherent quality of service in ATM, which allows for realtime voice and video, all the way to the Ethernet end station by placing the ATM cell within the Ethernet frame. It differs from LAN Emulation, in which Ethernet packets are encapsulated into LAN Emulation packets and then converted into ATM cells.

CIF is implemented by replacing the Ethernet hub with a switch or multiplexor known as a CIF Attachment Device (CIF-AD). CIF drivers are used in the client stations.

**CIFS**    (Common Internet File System) An enhanced version of the SMB file sharing protocol for the Internet. It allows Web applications to share data over the Internet and intranets and is Microsoft's counterpart to Sun's WebNFS. CIFS supports file access only and not printer sharing. See *SMB*, *WebNFS* and *DFS*.

**CIM**    (1) (Computer-Integrated Manufacturing) Integrating office/accounting functions with automated factory systems. Point of sale, billing, machine tool scheduling and supply ordering are part of CIM.

(2) (CompuServe Information Manager) The software provided by CompuServe for installation in a subscriber's computer to access available services.

(3) (Common Information Model) A model for describing management information from the DMTF. CIM is implementation independent, allowing different management applications to collect the required data from a variety of sources. CIM includes schemas for systems, networks, applications and devices, and new schemas will be added. It also provides mapping techniques for interchange of CIM data with MIB data from SNMP agents and MIF data from DMI-compliant systems. See *JMAPI* and *WBEM*.

**Cincom Systems**    (Cincom Systems, Inc., Cincinnati, OH, www.cincom.com) One of the largest and most experienced software companies in the world. Founded in 1968 by Thomas Nies, who has the distinction of being the longest-serving company chief in the industry, Cincom sells manufacturing, financial and sales force automation applications. It was the first U.S. software firm to promote the concept of a database management system, and it provided the first DBMS delivered by an independent software vendor.

**cine-oriented**    A film-image orientation like that of movie film, in which the tops of the frames run perpendicular to the outer edge of the medium. Contrast with *comic-strip oriented*.

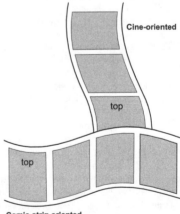

Cine-oriented

top

top

**Comic-strip oriented**

**Cinepak**    A video compression/decompression algorithm from SuperMac Technologies, Sunnyvale, CA, that is used to compress movie files. It is widely used on the Macintosh and is included in Windows 95/98.

**CIO**    (Chief Information Officer) The executive officer in charge of information processing in an organization. All systems design, development and datacenter operations fall under CIO jurisdiction. CIOs have demanding jobs as information systems in an organization are often taken for granted until something breaks down. The CIO is

C

responsible for explaining to executive managment the complex nightmare this industry has gotten itself into over the past 40 years and why equipment must be constantly retrofitted or replaced. Justifying new expenditures can be a difficult part of the job.

Increasingly, CIOs are involved in creating business and e-business opportunities through information technology. Collaborating with other executives, CIOs are often working at the core of business development within the organization. Also known as "MIS Director." See *salary survey*.

**cipher**    An encoded character. See *ciphertext* and *cryptography*.

**cipher strength**    The number of bits in the key used to encrypt data. See *cryptography*.

**ciphertext**    Data that has been coded (enciphered, encrypted, encoded) for security purposes. Contrast with *plaintext* and *cleartext*. See *cryptography*.

**CIR**    (Committed Information Rate) In a frame relay network, the average transmission rate in bits per second (typically Kbps) for a virtual circuit. It defines the maximum rate that the network can handle under normal conditions. The CIR rate plus excess burst rate (Excess Information Rate, EIR) is either equal to or less than the speed of the access port into the network. Frame relay carriers define and package CIRs differently, and CIRs are adjusted with experience. See *UNI*, *DLCI* and *frame relay*.

**circuit**    (1) A set of electronic components that perform a particular function in an electronic system.
(2) Same as *communications channel*.

**circuit analyzer**    (1) A device that tests the validity of an electronic circuit.
(2) In communications, same as *data line monitor*.

**circuit board**    Same as *printed circuit board*.

**circuit breaker**    A protective device that opens a circuit upon sensing a current overload. Unlike a fuse, it can be reset.

**circuit cellular**    The transmission of data over the cellular network using a voice channel and modem similar to using land-based modems. Contrast with *packet cellular*. See *wireless*.

**circuit switching**    A networking technology that provides a temporary, but dedicated, connection between two stations no matter how many switching devices the data is routed through. Circuit switching was originally developed for the analog-based telephone system in order to guarantee steady, consistent service for two people engaged in a phone conversation. Analog circuit switching (FDM) has given way to digital circuit switching (TDM), and the digital counterpart still maintains the connection until broken (one side hangs up). This means bandwidth is continuously reserved and "silence is transmitted" just the same as digital audio. See *connection oriented*. Contrast with *packet switching* and *message switch*.

**circuit trace**    The copper lines (sometimes aluminum) on a printed circuit board (PCB) that allow electricity to flow between electronic components. See *wire trace*.

**CIS**    (1) (CompuServe Information Service) See *CompuServe*.

**Analog Circuit Switched (FDM)**

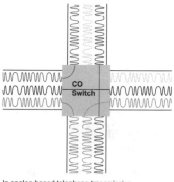

In analog-based telephone transmission systems, a dedicated connection is made between two parties. Multiple voice frequencies are placed on the same line via frequency division multiplexing (FDM) and the connections are maintained by all the switches the signals have to traverse.

**Digital Circuit Switched (TDM)**

The digital equivalent of FDM is TDM (time division multiplexing), in which a digital time slot is reserved for each data stream, and the bits and bytes are interleaved one after the other. In a voice conversation, the time slot is still reserved even though 50% of the time one person is listening and is thus silent, plus there are additional pauses in speech. The two arrows point to two silent time slots (conceptually).

**Digital Packet Switched (IP telephony)**

| 11001011 | 10110010 | 11001011 | 10110110 |

In packet-switched systems, the bits and bytes are still interleaved, but there are no dedicated time slots. If there is silence on the line, no packets are transmitted. When the conversation resumes, codes accompany the data indicating what time the conversation has resumed so the words can be delivered in realtime synchronization.

**Circuit Switched vs. Packet Switched**
Circuit switching can be analog or digital, but it is giving way to the packet-based IP technology as a result of the Internet.

(2) (Card Information Structure) A data structure on a PC Card that contains information about the card's contents. It allows the card to describe its configuration requirements to its host computer.

(3) (Contact Image Sensor) A type of scanning sensor used in low-cost scanners that is smaller than a CCD. Although it allows for smaller, lighter scanners to be built, color fidelity and image quality is not as good as CCD.

**CISC** (Complex Instruction Set Computer) Pronounced "sisk." The traditional architecture of a computer that uses microcode to execute very comprehensive instructions. Instructions may be variable in length and use all addressing modes, requiring complex circuitry to decode them. Contrast with *RISC*.

**Cisco** (Cisco Systems, Inc., San Jose, CA, www.cisco.com) A leading manufacturer of networking equipment, including routers, bridges, frame switches and ATM switches, dial-up access servers and network management software. Cisco was founded in 1984 by Leonard Bosack and Sandra Lerner, a married couple both employed by Stanford University. Initially targeting universities, Cisco sold its first router in 1986.

Today, Cisco is the leading routing vendor and its operating systems and routing protocols are de facto standards. Starting in the early 1990s, Cisco has grown enormous, mostly through acquisitions. In March 2000, it briefly surpassed Microsoft's market cap as the most valued corporation in the world.

**Cisco certification** A series of programs that provide certification of competency in Cisco networking products. Administered throughout the world at authorized Cisco centers, the various certification levels are offered:

**CCNA—Cisco Certified Network Associate** Small office/home office (SOHO) certification for LANs, WANs and dial-up services in networks of 100 nodes or less.

**CCNP—Cisco Certified Network Professional** Certification for LANs, WANs and dial-up services in organizations with networks of 100 to 500 nodes.

**CCIE—Cisco Certified Internetwork Expert** Highest level. Applicants select one of several tracks including "routing and switching," "WAN switching," and "SNA/IP Integration." Hands-on lab work is also required.

**Cisco PIX firewall** A family of network firewalls from Cisco. PIX units are high-performance, stand-alone devices that contain their own embedded operating systems and can support up to 64K simultaneous connections.

**Cisco Resource Manager** A Web-based utility from Cisco that is used for router configuration and status monitoring.

**CISSP** (Certification for the Information Security Professional) The award for successful completion of an examination in computer security administered by the International Information Systems Security Certification Consortium (ISC)2, (www.isc2.org). Subjects covered include access control, cryptography, network security and disaster recovery.

**Citrix** (Citrix Systems, Inc., Ft. Lauderdale, FL, www.citrix.com) A software company founded in 1989 that specializes in multiuser server software. Its ICA-based products enable a wide variety of clients simultaneous access to applications running in the server. See *MetaFrame* and *WinFrame*. See also *Cyrix*.

**CIX** (Commercial Internet eXchange Association, Herndon, VA, www.cix.org) Pronounced "kicks," it is a membership organization that promotes the development of a level playing field for ISPs. Founded in 1991 by Rick Adams, Marty Schofstall and Susan Estrada, it created the first public, commercial interconnect point on the Internet, originally in Santa Clara, California, and later in Palo Alto. Instead of bilateral peering agreements between two parties as is common on other NAPs, CIX is multilateral, whereby all members must exchange traffic with each other. See *NAP* and *peering*.

**CKO** (Chief Knowledge Officer) The executive officer responsible for exchanging knowledge within an organization. CKOs determine how research storehouses and all other expertise throughout the enterprise can be shared by all departments. They work closely with the CIO to provide the necessary information retrieval systems.

The large U.S. accounting firms were the first to develop this position in the mid 1990s. Although more extensive, the CKO's focus is somewhat like that of the data administrator, a popular position in the 1970s and 1980s, whose responsibility it was to model data for the entire enterprise, crossing all departmental lines.

**CL/1**    (Connectivity Language/1) A database language from Apple that lets a Macintosh access an SQL-based database in another computer. CL/1 applications communicate with the CL/1 client program in the Mac, and the client program communicates with the CL/1 server program in the host computer.

**cladding**    The plastic or glass sheath that is fused to and surrounds the core of an optical fiber. The cladding's mirror-like coating keeps the light waves reflected inside the core. The cladding is covered with a protective outer jacket. See *fiber optics glossary*.

**clamping ring**    The part of a 5.25" floppy disk drive that presses the disk onto the spindle. It is usually part of the centering cone.

**clamping voltage**    The voltage at which a surge suppressor performs its suppression tasks such as diverting the power line to ground or absorbing the excessive energy. For 120-volt AC power, the clamping voltage is around 135 volts. For 5 volt DC systems, the clamping voltage is typically 7.5 volts.

**Clarion**    A family of application development systems for DOS and Windows from TopSpeed Corporation, Pompano Beach, FL, (www.topspeed.com). It provides a comprehensive set of tools for development, including a screen builder, 4GL and application generator. It includes a compiler that is known for generating fast executables. It also includes a data dictionary and drivers for popular databases. TopSpeed Corporation was formerly Clarion Software Corporation.

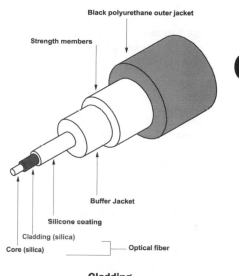

**Cladding**
The cladding covers the inner core of the fiber which is the actual pathway that the light travels through.

**Claris**    (Claris Corporation, Santa Clara, CA) A software subsidiary of Apple that was separated from the corporation (although mostly owned by it) in 1988 and then bought back in 1990. In 1998, Apple turned Claris Corporation into FileMaker, Inc., to focus on database and Web software. FileMaker Pro and Claris Home Page were the products retained by FileMaker.

**Claris CAD**    A full-featured 2-D CAD program for the Macintosh from Claris that is noted for its ease of use. It provides an easy-to-learn path into CAD, while offering most features found in CAD programs.

**ClarisWorks**    See *AppleWorks*.

**Clarke belt**    The geosynchronous (also geostationary) orbit that satellites are placed into. It was named after Arthur C. Clarke who proposed the concept in 1945. See *GEO*.

**class**    (1) In object technology, a user-defined data type that defines a collection of objects that share the same characteristics. An object, or class member, is one instance of the class. Concrete classes are designed to be instantiated. Abstract classes are designed to pass on characteristics through inheritance. See *instantiate*.

(2) In networking, a categorization of a packet based on attributes such as protocol, port and source and destination addresses.

**Class 4 switch**    AT&T's name for the type of switch used in a telephone tandem office. In the past, Class 4 switches dealt only with high-speed, four-wire T1, T3 and OC-3 connections in contrast to two-wire local lines on Class 5 switches. Today, all switches support four-wire lines. See *carrier switch, tandem office, Class 5 switch, echo cancellation, ESS* and *DMS*.

**Class 5 switch**    AT&T's name for the type of switch used in a local telephone end office. It provides customer services such as call waiting and call forwarding. In the past, a Class 5 switch implied two-wire ports from the customer and four-wire ports out the back end. Today, all switches support four-wire lines. See *carrier switch, tandem office, Class 4 switch, echo cancellation, digital cross-connect, ESS, DMS* and *hybrid*.

**Class A, B**    See *FCC Class*.

**class browser**    A software tool in an object-oriented language that lets you scroll through and edit a hierarchical tree of objects. A refactoring browser makes it easier to move routines by ensuring that all linkages are maintained properly. The Smalltalk language pioneered the class browser and has been known for its advanced browsing capabilities. See *browse*.

**Classic**    (1) A modernized remake of the original "hi-rise" Macintosh computer. The Classic came out in 1990.
  (2) The legacy Macintosh programming interface in Mac OS X, originally known as the Blue Box. See *Mac OS X*.

**Classical IP**    An IETF standard for transmitting IP traffic in an ATM network. IP protocols contain IP addresses that have to be converted into ATM addresses, and Classical IP performs this conversion, as long as the destination is within the same subnet. Classical IP does not support routing between networks. The Classical IP-enabled driver in the end station sends out an ARP request to a Classical IP-enabled ARP server, which returns the ATM address.

**class library**    A set of ready-made software routines (class definitions) that programmers use for writing object-oriented programs. For example, a class library is commonly available to provide graphical user interface (GUI) functions such as windowing routines, buttons, scroll bars and other elements. These class definitions also include their inheritance characteristics, if applicable. See *object-oriented programming*.

**class of service**    A classification assigned to users of a network that gives them particular rights and privileges. For an internal telephone system, it can include the ability to make international calls or dial 900 numbers, for example. In the public telephone network, it is used for tariffs and differentiates between categories such as residential or commercial, flat rate or message units, private line or party line. In an enterprise network it differentiates high-priority traffic from lower-priority traffic. See *QoS*.

**class variable**    In object-oriented programming, a variable used by the class definition. Contrast with *instance variable*. See *class*.

**CLCC**    (Ceramic Leadless Chip Carrier) A square, ceramic chip package that uses metal pads for contact and comes in both socket mount and surface mount varieties. See *chip package*.

**clean boot**    Booting the computer without loading anything but the main part of the operating system. See *DOS startup options*.

**clean data**    See *data hygiene*.

**clean install**    An installation of operating system and applications on a new computer or newly-formatted hard disk. On Windows machines especially, a clean install is sometimes the only way to eliminate residual problems that never seem to go away and that cannot be resolved.

**clean room**    A room in which the air is highly filtered in order to keep out impurities. Chip fabrication plants use clean rooms where the air is completely exchanged as much as seven times per minute. Workers go through an elaborate procedure to gown themselves in the "bunny suits" which are required to keep them from contaminating the atmostphere.

**clear box testing**    See *white box testing*.

**clear GIF**    See *invisible GIF*.

**clear memory**    To reset all RAM and hardware registers to a zero or blank condition. Rebooting the computer may or may not clear memory, but turning the computer off and on again guarantees that memory is cleared.

**cleartext**    Same as *plaintext*.

**Taking an Air Shower**
After gowning, this man is taking an "air" shower to purify the outside of his suit before entering the clean room.
*(Image courtesy of Intel Corporation.)*

**CLEC**    (Competitive Local Exchange Carrier) An organization offering local telephone services. Although most CLECs are established as a telecommunications service organization, any large company, university or city government has the option of becoming a CLEC and supplying its own staff with dial tone at reduced cost. It must have a telephone switch, satisfy state regulations, pay significant filing fees and also make its services available to outside customers. This was all sanctioned by the Telecommunications Act of 1996. A Web site that maintains news and information about CLECs is www.clecresouce.com. Contrast with *ILEC*. See *BLEC, ELEC* and *TELRIC*.

**CLI**    (1) (Call Level Interface) A database programming interface from the SQL Access Group, an SQL membership organization. SAG's CLI is an attempt to standardize the SQL language for database access. Microsoft's ODBC conforms to the CLI, but adds its own extensions. Under CLI, SQL statements are passed directly to the server without being recompiled.

(2) (Common Language Infrastructure) A platform independent development system from Microsoft that enables programs written in different programming languages to run on different types of hardware. It is part of Microsoft's .NET platform and is expected to become an ECMA standard. The CLI includes the Common Type System (CTS), which defines the different programming types and operations that the .NET runtime engine supports. It also defines the Common Language Specification (CLS), a subset of CTS that defines minimum compliance.

CLI applications, no matter which programming language they are written in, are compiled into the Common Intermediate Language (CIL), which is further compiled into the target machine language by the Common Language Runtime (CLR) software. See *.NET* and *intermediate language*.

**click**    To select an object by pressing the mouse button when the cursor is pointing to the required menu option, icon or hypertext link.

**Click! disk**    The former name of the *PocketZip disk*.

**clickable image**    Same as *imagemap*.

**click and drag**    Using a pointing device, such as a mouse, to latch onto an icon on screen and move it to some other location. When the screen pointer is over the icon of the object, the mouse button is clicked to grab it. The button is held down while the object is moved ("dragged") to its destination. Then the mouse button is released.

**click potato**    The cyberspace version of the couch potato.

**clicks and mortar**    Also called "bricks and clicks," it refers to businesses that offer online services via the Web as well as the traditional retail outlets (offline) staffed by people. Coined in 1999 by David Pottruck, co-CEO of the Charles Schwab brokerage firm, it refers to running the two divisions in a cooperative and integrated manner where they both support and benefit from each other. Contrast with *bricks and mortar*. See *e-commerce*.

**click speed**    How fast the mouse must be clicked in succession in order to qualify as a double-click.

**clickstream**    The trail of mouse clicks made by a user performing a particular operation on the computer. It often refers to linking from one page to another on the World Wide Web.

**click through**    On the Web, the act of linking to a third party. See *click-through rate*.

**click-through rate**    The number of times an ad on a Web page is clicked compared to the number of times it is displayed, and royalties are often based on the click-through rate. It is also the measure of effectiveness of one site's ability to persuade a visitor to go to another site. See *banner ad*.

**clickwrap**    The equivalent of shrinkwrap on the Internet. A clickwrap contract, or clicktract, is a notice that requires a user to agree to certain conditions before proceeding to the next page.

**client**    (1) A workstation or personal computer in a client/server environment. See *client/server* and *fat client*.

(2) One end of the spectrum in a request/supply relationship between programs. See *X Window* and *OLE*.

**client application**    An application running in a workstation or personal computer on a network. See also *OLE*.

**client based**    Refers to hardware or software that runs in the user's machine (client). Contrast with *server based*.

**client machine**    A user's workstation that is attached to a network. The term can also refer to a portable computer that is plugged into the network. See *client* and *client/server*.

**client program**    Software that runs in the user's PC or workstation. Contrast with *server program*, which resides in a server in the network.

**client/server**    An architecture in which the user's PC (the client) is the requesting machine and the server is the supplying machine, both of which are connected via a local area network (LAN) or wide area network (WAN). Throughout the late 1980s and early 1990s, client/server was the hot buzzword as applications were migrated from centralized minicomputers and mainframes to networks of personal computers.

In client/server, the client processes the user interface (Windows, Mac, etc.) and can perform some or all of the application processing. Servers range in capacity from high-end PCs to mainframes. A database server maintains the databases and processes requests from the client to extract data from or to update the database. An application server provides additional business processing for the clients. See *client/server development system*.

Client/server Versus the Web    Because of the Internet, terms such as "Web based" and "Web enabled" have replaced the client/server buzzword, yet the client/server architecture is conceptually the same. Users' PCs are still clients, and there are tens of thousands of Web servers throughout the Internet delivering Web pages. Nevertheless, client/server is mostly used to refer to "legacy," non-Web based systems.

On the Web, the client runs the browser and just like legacy client/server can perform little or a lot of processing: simple displaying of HTML pages, more processing with embedded scripts or considerable processing with Java applets. A myriad of browser plug-ins provide all sorts of client processing.

The server side of the Web is a multi-tier server architecture with interlinked Web servers, application servers, database servers and caching servers. See *application server*.

**client/server analyst**    A person responsible for performing analysis and design of a client/server system. A knowledge of two-tier and three-tier client/server architectures is required. See *systems analyst* and *client/server*.

**client/server architecture**    An environment in which the application processing is divided between client workstations and servers. It implies the use of desktop computers interacting with servers in a network, in contrast to processing everything in a large centralized mainframe. See *client/server*.

CLIENT PLATFORMS (CPU & OS)

Windows 3.1, 95/98, NT and 2000
DOS
OS/2
Solaris (UNIX)
Interactive UNIX
SCO Open Desktop (UNIX)
SCO UnixWare (UNIX)
AIX ( UNIX)
NeXTStep (UNIX)

Mac OS A/UX (UNIX)

Mac OS AIX (UNIX)

Motorola 680x0

PowerPC

Intel (x86)

HP/UX (UNIX)

Digital UNIX OpenVMS Windows NT

VMS Ultrix (UNIX)

HP 9000 (PA-RISC)

Compaq Alpha

DEC VAX

Solaris (UNIX)

AIX (UNIX)

IRIX (UNIX)

SPARCstation

IBM RS/6000

Silicon Graphics (MIPS)

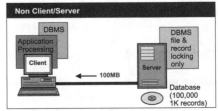

Non Client/Server

DBMS
Application Processing
Client

DBMS file & record locking only
Server

100MB

Database (100,000 1K records)

**Non-Client/Server**
Although there are clients and servers in this scenario, this is not "true" client/server, because the server is nothing more than a remote disk drive, and the client does all the processing. Lengthy searches can bog down the network, because each client has to read the entire database. At 1,000 bytes per record, a database with 100,000 records sends 100MB over the LAN.

## client/server development system

An application development system used to create applications for a client/server environment. A comprehensive system generally includes a GUI builder for creating one or all of the major GUIs: Windows, Mac and Motif, a fourth-generation language for creating the business logic, an interpreter and/or compiler and debugging tools. It provides support for many of the major database management systems (Oracle, Sybase, Informix, etc.), and it may include its own DBMS.

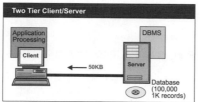

**Two-tier Client/Server**
In two-tier client/server, the application and database processing are done in the file server. A SQL request is generated in the client and transmitted to the server. The DBMS searches for records in the server and returns only matching records to the client. If 50 records met the criteria in our 100,000-record example, only 50K would be transmitted over the LAN.

**Three-tier Client/Server**
In three-tier client/server, the processing is divided between two or more servers, one typically used for application processing and another for database processing. This is common in large enterprises.

For enterprise-wide client/server development, a system may allow for application partitioning, which separates parts of the application onto different machines. Such systems support the major server environments (UNIX, NetWare, NT, etc.) in order to accommodate the dispersion of business logic onto multiple computers. It may also include software configuration management capabilities that provide version control and bug tracking.

Almost any language can be used to develop the client front ends in a client/server application. For example, Visual Basic is very popular for such purposes. However, a client/server system implies that client-to-server connections and application partitioning are written at a higher level than a 3GL programming language. It implies that there is little or no "tweaking" to make things happen. See *client/server* and *application partitioning*. Following is a list of client/server development tools in alphabetical order.

- Axiant
- CA-OpenRoad
- CA-Visual Objects
- Centura
- COOL:Gen
- Corel Paradox
- C/S ELEMENTS
- Delphi Client/Server
- Developer/2000
- DYNASTY
- Enfin/Object Studio

- ESL for Windows
- ESL Workbench
- Forte
- GEMBASE
- INFORMIX-New Era
- JAM
- Key:Enterprise
- ObjectPro
- ObjectView
- OMNIS
- Passport IntRprise

- PowerBuilder
- Progress
- SQLWindows
- Superbase
- Team Enterprise Developer
- UNIFACE
- Unify VISION
- Visual Basic
- Visual dBASE

## client/server environment
A networking environment that is made up of clients and servers running applications designed for client/server architecture. See *client/server*.

## client/server network
(1) A communications network that uses dedicated servers. In this context, the term is used to contrast it with a *peer-to-peer network*, which allows any client to also be a server.

(2) A network that is processing applications designed for client/server architecture. See *client/server*.

## client/server programmer
A person responsible for programming client/server applications in which servers support a body of Windows or Macintosh clients. Such individuals typically write in Visual Basic, C, C++ or 4GL languages and are also experienced in UNIX, NT and NetWare servers. See *client/server development system*, *programmer* and *client/server*.

**client/server protocol**   A communications protocol that provides a structure for requests between client and server in a network. It refers to OSI layer 7.

**client-side**   Refers to any operation that is performed at the client workstation. Contrast with *server-side*.

**client software**   Software that resides in a user's desktop or laptop computer. Contrast with *server software*. See *client/server*.

**CLINKS**   (Connectors are the weakest **LINKS**) The first devices to be checked when the network fails are the plugs and sockets. All networks should be constructed with CLINKS as the golden rule. Coined by American Business Telephones, Inc.

**CLIP**   (**CL**assical **IP**) See *Classical IP*.

**clip art**   A set of canned images used to illustrate word processing and desktop publishing documents.

**clipboard**   A reserved section of memory that is used as a temporary holding area for data that is copied or moved from one application to another using the copy and paste and cut and paste (move) menu options. Each time you transfer something into the clipboard, the previous contents are deleted. Although there are clipboard viewers that let you view the clipboard's current contents, they are seldom used. The clipboard serves as a behind-the-scenes function, holding its contents for pasting (inserting) into another application. See *copy and paste* and *cut and paste*.

**Clipper**   **(1)** See *CA-Clipper*.
   **(2)** A family of 32-bit RISC microprocessors from Intergraph that were used in earlier graphics workstations.
   **(3)** A cryptography chip used by the U.S. government for telephone security that uses the SkipJack algorithm. The federal government has tried to make the Clipper chip a universal method, because it alone can unscramble the data if needed.

**clipping**   Cutting off the outer edges or boundaries of a word, signal or image. In rendering an image, clipping removes any objects or portions thereof that are not visible on screen. See *scissoring*.

**clipping level**   A disk's ability to maintain its magnetic properties and hold its content. A high-quality level range is 65–70%; low quality is below 55%.

**clipping path**   A silhouette of an area that serves as a mask. Only that portion within the clipping path (mask) appears when placed into another application or combined with another image. The area outside the clipping path becomes transparent.

**clobbering memory**   Erroneously writing into an area of memory that contains instructions and data that are still being worked on. See *memory* and *memory allocation*.

**clock**   An internal timing device. Using a quartz crystal, the CPU clock breathes life into the CPU by feeding it a constant flow of pulses. For example, a 200MHz CPU receives 200 million pulses per second. Similarly, in a communications device, the clock synchronizes the data pulses between sender and receiver.
   A realtime clock keeps track of the time of day and makes this data available to the software. A timesharing clock interrupts the CPU at regular intervals and allows the operating system to divide its time between active users and/or applications. See *per clock*.

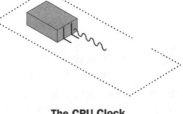

**The CPU Clock**
The quartz crystal generates continuous waves, which are converted into digital pulses.

**clock battery**   See *CMOS battery*.

**clock/calendar**   An internal time clock and month/year calendar that is kept active with a battery. Its output allows software to remind users of appointments, to determine the age of a transaction and to activate tasks at specified times.

**clock cycle**   One "tick" of the clock. For example, a 100MHz clock would have 100 million ticks per second. See *clock*.

**clock doubling**   Doubling the internal processing speed of a CPU while maintaining the original clock speed for I/O (transfers in/out of the chip). Intel popularized the technique with its Speed Doubler chips. See *486* and *clock tripling*.

**clock pulse**   A signal used to synchronize the operations of an electronic system. Clock pulses are continuous, precisely spaced changes in voltage. See *clock speed*.

**clock speed**   The internal heartbeat of a computer, also known as "clock rate." The clock circuit uses fixed vibrations generated from a quartz crystal to deliver a steady stream of pulses to the CPU. See *Mhz*.

**clock tick**   One increment, or pulse, of the CPU clock. See *clock speed*.

**clock tripling**   Tripling the internal processing speed of a CPU while maintaining the original clock speed for I/O (transfers in/out of the chip). See *DX4*.

**clone**   A device that works like the original, but does not necessarily look like it. It implies 100% functional compatibility. See *PC clone*, *cloning software* and *white box*.

**clone PC**   See *PC clone*.

**cloning software**   Software that copies the full image of a hard disk to another machine via direct cable or the network. Cloning saves time setting up new machines by eliminating the installation of the operating system and each individual application. See *image file* and *ghosting server*.

**close**   To disengage a disk or tape file that has been opened for reading and writing. The close procedure generally prompts the user to save any changes made to the disk before it releases the file. Contrast with *open*.

**closed**   With regard to a switch, closed is "on." Open is "off."

**closed architecture**   A system whose technical specifications are not made public. Contrast with *open architecture*.

**closed shop**   An environment in which only data processing staff is allowed access to the computer. Contrast with *open shop*.

**closed system**   A system in which specficiations are kept proprietary to prevent third-party hardware or software from being used. Contrast with *open system*.

**cloud**   See *network cloud*.

**CLR**   (Common Language Runtime) Software for Microsoft's .NET platform that executes the Common Intermediate Language (CIL) or compiles it into machine language. The CLR contains object-oriented services and security services that all .NET applications can utilize. See *CLI* and *.NET*.

**CLS**   (Common Language Specification) A subset of the .NET Common Type System (CTS) that all programming languages must support in order to be interoperable at runtime. See *CLI* and *.NET*.

**CLSID**   (CLaSS ID) The identification of a COM object. Applications that support Microsoft's COM architecture register their objects as class IDs (CLSIDs). See *COM*.

**cluster**   (1) Also called an "allocation unit," it is some number of disk sectors that are treated as a unit. This is the smallest unit of storage the operating system can manage. For example, on a PC with a 200MB hard disk, the smallest cluster is eight sectors (8 × 512 bytes) or 4K. On a 2GB disk, the cluster is 32K. That means a 1K file takes up 32K on the disk, wasting an inordinate amount of space. In mid-1996, the Windows 95 that came with new PCs (Win95B) introduced the FAT32 32-bit file allocation table which decreased the cluster size to 4K. See *FAT32* and *lost cluster*.

Following are the cluster sizes that DOS/Windows uses starting with DOS 4.0. The disk size is the partition size. One physical hard disk may have multiple partitions; for example, C: and D: could be on the same hard disk.

| | **FAT16** |
| Disk Size | Cluster Size |
| --- | --- |
| 0-128MB | 2KB |
| 128-256MB | 4KB |
| 256-512MB | 8KB |
| 512MB-1GB | 16KB |
| 1-2GB | 32KB |

| | **FAT32** |
| | Cluster Size |
| --- | --- |
| 512MB-8GB | 4KB |
| 8-16GB | 8KB |
| 16-32GB | 16KB |
| 32GB+ | 32KB |

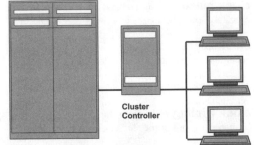

**Computer or Front End Processor**

Cluster
Controller

**Terminals**

**(2)** Two or more systems working together. See *clustering*.

**cluster controller**   A control unit that manages several peripheral devices, such as terminals or disk drives.

**clustering**   Using two or more systems that work together. It generally refers to multiple computer systems that are linked together in order to handle variable workloads or to provide continued operation in the event one fails. Each computer may be a multiprocessor system itself. For example, a cluster of four computers, each with four CPUs, would provide a total of 16 CPUs processing simultaneously.

**Cluster Server**   See *Microsoft Cluster Server*.

**CLUT**   (Color Look Up Table) See *color palette*.

**CLV**   (Constant Linear Velocity) Rotating a disk at varying speeds. By changing speed depending on which track is being accessed, the density of bits in each track can be made uniform. This allows the outer tracks to hold more data than the inner tracks and fully utilizes the disk space. CLV is used on optical media such as CDs and DVDs. In practice, the rotation does not change precisely from every track to the next. A data buffer provides some flexibility for changing speed across some number of tracks.

Zoned CLV (Z-CLV) breaks the disk into several zones (typically 24 on a DVD-RAM disk) and changes the speed within each zone rather than uniformly across the entire platter. Contrast with *CAV*.

**CM**   See *configuration management*.

**CM/2**   (Communications Manager/2) A communications program for OS/2 from IBM that provides terminal emulation to IBM mainframes, AS/400s and VAXes and supports APPN and APPC protocols.

**CMC**   (Common Messaging Calls) A programming interface specified by the XAPIA as the standard messaging API for X.400 and other messaging systems. CMC is intended to provide a common API for applications that want to become mail enabled.

**CMI**   (Computer-Managed Instruction) Using computers to organize and manage an instructional program for students. It helps create test materials, tracks the results and monitors student progress.

**Clustering**
A cluster of computer systems provides fault tolerance and/or load balancing. If one system fails, one or more additional systems are still available. Load balancing distributes the workload over multiple systems.

C

**CMIP**     (**C**ommon **M**anagement **I**nformation **P**rotocol)  Pronounced "C-mip." A network monitoring and control standard from ISO. CMOT (CMIP over TCP) is a version that runs on TCP/IP networks, and CMOL (CMIP over LLC) runs on IEEE 802 LANs (Ethernet, Token Ring, etc.).

**CMIS**     (**C**ommon **M**anagement **I**nformation **S**ervices)  Pronounced "C-miss." An OSI standard that defines the functions for network monitoring and control.

**CMM**     (**C**apability **M**aturity **M**odel)  A process developed by SEI in 1986 to help improve, over time, the application of an organization's supporting software technologies. The process is broken down into five well-defined levels of sequential development: Initial, Repeatable, Defined, Managed and Optimizing.

These five maturity levels provide an ordinal scale for measuring the maturity, and therefore the capacity of, an organization's use of its software technologies. The levels also help prioritize an organization's software improvement efforts. The more an organization depends on formal rules, rather than individual performers, to keep software projects relevant, within budget and on schedule, the more advanced the organization's software development "maturity." See *SEI*.

**CMOS**     (1) (**C**omplementary **MOS**)  Pronounced "C moss." The most widely-used type of integrated circuit for digital processors and memories. Virtually everything is CMOS today. Even mainframe CPUs are CMOS based. CMOS uses PMOS and NMOS transistors wired together in a certain manner that causes less power to be used than PMOS-only or NMOS-only circuits. See *PMOS* and *NMOS*.

(2) See *CMOS memory*.

**CMOS based**     An integrated circuit fabricated using CMOS technology. Most logic chips and CPU chips have been CMOS based for some time. Even mainframes, which have used ultra-fast bipolar chip technology in the past, are giving way to CMOS-based models. See *Parallel Enterprise Server*.

**CMOS battery**     A battery that maintains the time, date, hard disk and other configuration settings in the CMOS memory. See *BIOS setup*.

**CMOS mainframes**     See *Parallel Enterprise Server* and *Multiprise*.

**CMOS memory**     (1) A small, battery-backed memory bank in a personal computer that holds configuration settings. See *BIOS setup*.

(2) Memory made of CMOS. See *CMOS*.

**CMOS RAM**     See *CMOS memory* and *BIOS setup*.

**CMOS setup**     Same as *BIOS setup*.

**CMP**     (1) (CMP Media Inc., Manhasset, NY, www.cmp.com) A leading high-tech media company that offers a huge variety of publications and services in the information technology and electronics fields, including more than 50 news magazines and 100 Web sites. CMP has been at the forefront of the Web. In 1994, it was the first to establish Web sites for its print publications, and it launched TechWeb, the first online technology news service.

(2) (**C**ellular **M**ulti**P**rocessing)  A multiprocessing architecture for Intel CPUs from Unisys. Providing up to 32 processors that are crossbar connected to 64GB of memory and 96 PCI cards, a CMP system provides mainframe-like architecture using Intel CPUs. CMP supports Windows NT and 2000 Server, AIX, NetWare and UnixWare and can be run as one large SMP system or multiple systems with different operating systems. See *SMP*.

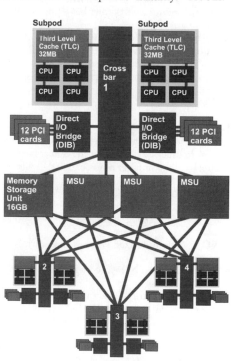

**Eight Subpods, Four Crossbars**
A CMP subpod contains four x86 or Itanium CPUs, which connect through a third-level memory cache to the crossbar. Each crossbar supports two subpods, two direct I/O bridges (DIBs) and can connect to four memory storage units (MSUs). This diagram shows the four crossbars and all eight subpods that make up a complete CMP system.

**CMRS**    (Commercial Mobile Radio Service)  An organization that provides cellular, PCS, mobile radio, paging and other wireless services.

**CMS**    (1) (Conversational Monitor System)  Software that provides interactive communications for IBM's VM operating system. It allows a user or programmer to launch an application from a terminal and interactively work with it. The CMS counterpart in MVS is TSO. Contrast with *RSCS*, which provides batch communications for VM.

(2) (Call Management System)  An AT&T call accounting package for its PBXs.

(3) See *color management system*.

**CMTS**    (Cable Modem Transmission System)  A computerized device that converts cable modem data into data packets for the Internet. The CMTS provides several functions, including routing to contain local data within the cable system, filtering to protect cable operators from unwanted hacking, and traffic shaping to deliver the quality of service a subscriber has signed on for.

**CMYK**    (Cyan Magenta Yellow blacK)  The color model used for printing. In theory, cyan, magenta and yellow (CMY) can print all colors, but inks are not pure and black comes out muddy. Black ink is required for quality printing. See *colors*, *RGB* and *ink coverage*.

**CNA**    (Certified NetWare Administrator)  See *NetWare certification*.

**CNAM**    (Calling NAMe)  An IN (Intelligent Network) service that displays the caller's name on the calling party's digital readout. This is similar to caller ID except that the calling party's name is displayed along with the calling number or instead of the calling number. See *caller ID*.

**CNAME record**    (Canonical NAME record)  A statement in a DNS database (zone file) that assigns an alias to the true (canonical) name of the server. See *canonical*, *canonical synthesis* and *zone file*.

**CNC**    (Computerized Numerical Control)  See *numerical control*.

**CNE**    (Certified NetWare Engineer)  See *NetWare certification*.

**CNG tone**    An 1100Hz tone transmitted by a fax machine when it calls another fax machine. The half-second tone is repeated every 3.5 seconds for approximately 45 seconds. See *fax switch*.

**CNI**    (1) (Certified NetWare Instructor)  See *NetWare certification*.

(2) (Coalition for Networked Information, Washington, DC, www.cni.org)  A partnership of the Association of Research Libraries, CAUSE and EDUCOM, founded in 1990. Its mission is to advance education and intellectual productivity by the use of high-performance networks and computers.

**CNP**    (Certified Network Professional)  The award for successful completion of an examination on networking developed by the Network Professional Association (NPA). It is the leading certification that is not vendor sponsored. Categories in the Core Exam are client operating systems, network operating systems, hardware platforms, protocols and topologies. Additional requirements include work experience, continuing education and adherence to a code of ethics. For information, visit www.inpnet.org/cnpweb. See *NPA*. See also *CMP*.

**CNR**    (Communications and Networking Riser)  A riser card for Intel motherboards that provides expanded audio, modem and networking functions. See *AMR*.

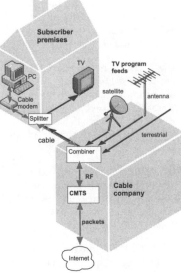

**The Cable Modem System**
The CMTS converts the RF (radio frequency) data from all the cable modems into data packets for the Internet. The combiner merges the TV programming feeds with the RF data from the CMTS.

**CO**    See *central office*.

**coaster**    What a bad CD-R disc is often called. See *CD-R* and *underrun*.

**coax**    Same as *coaxial cable*.

**coaxial cable**    A high-capacity cable used in communications and video, commonly called "co-ax." It contains an insulated solid or stranded wire surrounded by a solid or braided metallic shield, wrapped in a plastic cover. Fire-safe teflon coating is optional.

Although similar in appearance, there are several types of coaxial cable, each designed with a different width and impedance for a particular purpose (TV, baseband, broadband). Coax provides a higher bandwidth than twisted wire pair. See *cable categories*.

**Coaxial Cable**
Coax is a two-wire cable. The inner wire is the primary conductor, and the metal sheath is used for ground.

**COB**    See *chip on board*.

**COBOL**    (COmmon Business Oriented Language) A high-level programming language that has been the primary business application language on mainframes and minis. It is a compiled language and was one of the first high-level languages developed. Officially adopted in 1960, it stemmed from Flomatic, a language in the mid-1950s.

COBOL is a very wordy language. Although mathematical expressions can also be written like other programming languages (see example below), its verbose mode is very readable for a novice. For example, **multiply hourly-rate by hours-worked giving gross-pay** is self-explanatory. COBOL is structured into the following divisions:

```
Division Name     Contains
IDENTIFICATION    Program identification
ENVIRONMENT       Types of computers used
DATA              Buffers, constants, work areas
PROCEDURE         The processing (program logic)
```

The following COBOL example converts a Fahrenheit number to Celsius. To keep the example simple, it performs the operation on the operator's terminal rather than a user terminal.

```
IDENTIFICATION DIVISION.
PROGRAM-ID. EXAMPLE.

ENVIRONMENT DIVISION.
CONFIGURATION SECTION.
SOURCE-COMPUTER.  IBM-370.
OBJECT-COMPUTER.  IBM-370.

DATA DIVISION.
WORKING-STORAGE SECTION.
77 FAHR  PICTURE 999.
77 CENT  PICTURE 999.

PROCEDURE DIVISION.
DISPLAY 'Enter Fahrenheit ' UPON CONSOLE.
ACCEPT FAHR FROM CONSOLE.
COMPUTE CENT = (FAHR- 32) * 5 / 9.
DISPLAY 'Celsius is ' CENT UPON CONSOLE.
GOBACK.
```

IBM COBOLs    In 1994, IBM dropped support of OS/VS COBOL, which conforms to ANSI 68 and ANSI 74 standards and limits a program's address space to 16 bits. IBM's VS COBOL II (1984) and COBOL/370 (1991) conform to ANSI 85 standards and provide 31-bit addressing, which allows programs to run "above the line."

COBOL/370 is more compliant with AD/Cycle, has more string, math and date functions, including four-digit years, allows development through a PC window and provides enhanced runtime facilities.

**CobWeb**    (1) A Web page that has not been updated in a long time.

(2) A Web page that is rarely downloaded because the references to it are obscure or the subject is simply uninteresting.

**COC**    See *chip on chip*.

**COCOMO**    (**CO**nstructive **CO**st **MO**del)  A method for estimating a software project which was conceived by Dr. Barry Boehm in his 1981 book, *Software Engineering Economics*.  The heart of COCOMO is based on the Effort Equation, which applies a value to the tasks at hand based on the scope of the project (ranging from a small, familiar system to a complex system that is new to the organization). The Costar package from Softstar Systems, Amherst, NH, (www.softstarsystems.com) has been using the COCOMO method since 1986. See also *DOCOMO*.

**CODASYL**    (**CO**nference on **DA**ta **SY**stems **L**anguages)  An organization founded in 1959 by the U.S. Department of Defense. It evolved into a variety of volunteer committees and ultimately disbanded by the mid 1990s. CODASYL was widely known for its definition of COBOL, but it was also involved with the network database model and the data description language (DDL) for defining database schemas.

**code**    (1) A set of machine symbols that represents data or instructions. See *data code* and *machine language*.

(2) Any representation of one set of data for another. For example, a parts code is an abbreviated name of a product, product type or category. A discount code is a percentage.

(3) To write a program. See *source code* and **line of code**.

(4) To encode for security purposes. See *cryptography*.

**codec**    (1) (**CO**der-**DEC**oder)  Hardware or software that converts analog sound, speech or video to digital code (analog to digital) and vice versa (digital to analog). Hardware codecs (chips) are built into devices such as digital telephones and videoconferencing stations. Software codecs are used to record and play audio and video over the Web utilizing the CPU for processing. Although hardware codecs are faster than software routines, as desktop machines become more powerful, they can more adequately handle the processing load required for the conversion. See *audio codec*, *speech codec* and *video codec*.

(2) (**CO**mpressor/**DEC**ompressor)  Hardware or software that compresses digital data into a smaller binary format than the original. It generally refers to software routines that compress/decompress and possibly encrypt/decrypt data. However, the codec as described in definition 1 above is also often called a "compressor/decompressor," because compression is an inherent part of the algorithms that produce the digital code. See *data compression*.

**code density**    The amount of space that an executable program takes up in memory. Code density is important in PDAs and handheld devices that contain a limited amount of memory. See *Thumb*.

**code generator**    See *application generator* and *macro recorder*.

**Code Morphing**    See *Crusoe processor*.

**code name**    An internal name given to a product under development. For example, "Chicago" was the code name for Windows 95.

**code page**    A table in Windows (and previously in DOS) that sets up the symbols for the keyboard and screen for all the human languages that are supported.

**coder**    (1) A junior, or trainee, programmer who writes simple programs or writes the code for a larger program that has been designed by someone else. See *codec*.

(2) Person who assigns special codes to data.

**code signing**   A method of ensuring that an executable program is coming from a valid software publisher. Also known as "object signing," the EXEs, DLLs or other executable file types are digitally signed and transmitted along with a digital certificate from a certification authority (CA) such as VeriSign. The end user application such as the Web browser uses the widely-known public key of the CA to decrypt the digital certificate and extract the public key of the publisher. It uses the publisher's public key to decrypt the digital signature, which is a hash, or digest, of the executable files. It computes its own hash from the files and compares the two to ensure they are the same.

A digital signature verifies that the owner of the public key has encrypted the contents, and the digital certificate verifies that the public key is from the entity it says it is. The code signing system conveniently delivers the public key to the verifying application. Although both terms are used interchangeably, object signing refers to any files delivered in the manner, while code signing refers specifically to executables, which is the major concern these days when downloading so many active elements from the Internet. Microsoft uses Authenticode and Netscape uses Object Signing. These code signing systems are not compatible, and publishers have to sign their code using both systems and automatically detect which browser is used in order to transmit the correct package. See *digital certificate* and *digital signature*.

**coercivity**   On magnetic media, the amount of electrical energy required to change the polarization of a bit. The coercivity of hard disks ranges from 500 to 2,000 Oersted. On magneto-optic media, it takes between 5,000 to 10,000 Oersted. See *Oersted*.

**COFF**   (Common Object File Format) A UNIX System V machine language format.

**Cognos**   (Cognos Inc., Ottawa, Canada, www.cognos.com) A leading business intelligence software company specializing in application development and 4GL tools. Founded in 1969 as a consulting firm, its PowerHouse 4GL was introduced in the late 1970s for midrange systems. Numerous products include the PowerPlay OLAP analysis tool, Impromptu report and query language and Axiant client/server development system.

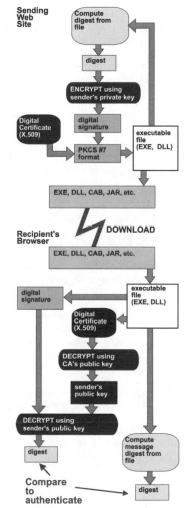

**The Code Signing Process**
The combination of the digitally signed file with the digital certificate ensure that the executable is valid.

**COGO**   (COordinate GeOmetry) A programming language used for solving civil engineering problems.

**Coherent**   A version of UNIX developed by Mark Williams Co., Northbrook, IL, that was noted for its conservative use of resources on Intel-based PCs.

**COLD**   (Computer Output to LaserDisc) Archiving large volumes of transactions on optical media. Instead of printing large paper reports or producing microfilm or microfiche, data is stored on optical disks. The advantage of COLD over COM (Computer Output Microfilm) for high-volume, archival storage is that optical disks can be directly accessed just like a hard disk.

**cold backup**   Backing up a database that is not in active use. The process is performed either on the second or third shift or from a copy of the data. Contrast with *hot backup*.

**cold boot**    Starting the computer by turning power on. Turning power off and then back on again clears memory and many internal settings. Some program failures will lock up the computer and require a cold boot to use the computer again. In other cases, only a warm boot is required. See *boot*, *warm boot* and *clean boot*.

**cold cathode**    A cathode in an gas-filled electron tube that is not heated by a filament in order to excite the electrons and cause current flow. The voltage potential within the tube is sufficient to ionize the gas in the tube and cause current flow. For example, the backlights in many flat panel LCD screens are cold cathode fluorescent tubes.

**ColdFusion**    An application development tool from Allaire Corporation, Cambridge, MA (www.allaire.com), for writing Web pages that interact with databases. Instead of writing tedious CGI and Perl scripts, operations are coded in the ColdFusion Markup Language (CFML) which uses HTML-like tags embedded in the Web pages. The ColdFusion engine, which interfaces with a Windows-based Web server, interprets the codes, accesses the database and delivers the results as HTML pages for the Web browser.

**cold start**    Same as *cold boot*.

**Cole's Law**    A picnic isn't the same without it!  See *laws*.

**collaboration products**    See *e-mail*, *groupware*, *data conferencing* and *videoconferencing*.

**collaborative browsing**    Synchronizing browser access to the same sites. As one user browses the Web, the other users trail along automatically and link to and view the same pages from their browsers.

**collapsed backbone**    A network configuration that provides a backbone in a centralized location, to which all subnetworks are attached. A collapsed backbone is implemented in a router or switch that uses a high-speed backplane that can handle the simultaneous traffic of all or most all of its ports at full wire speed.

**collating sequence**    The sequence, or order, of the character set built into a computer. See *ASCII chart* and **EBCDIC chart**.

**collator**    (1) A punched card machine that merges two decks of cards into one or more stacks.

(2) A utility program that merges records from two or more files into one file.

**collector**    One side of a bipolar transistor. When the base is pulsed, current flows from the emitter to the collector, or vice versa depending on the design. See *drain*.

**collimated**    In a straight line. Collimated light beams are parallel rays of light.

**collision detection**    See *CSMA/CD*.

**co-location**    Placing equipment owned by a customer or competitor in an organization's own facility. Telephone companies often allow co-location in order to provide the best interconnection between devices.

ISPs offer co-location by providing space, power and a link to the Internet for their customers' servers. They do not perform maintenance or troubleshooting, only a repetitive test to make sure the servers are running. The customer will be notified if the server fails. Known as a "ping power pipe" arrangement, "ping" means sending a packet to the server to see if it responds, "power" is electricity, and "pipe" is the line to the Internet.

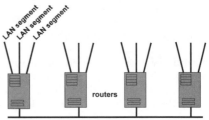

**Distributed Router Backbone**
Many early networks used a series of routers networked together as a LAN backbone.  Typically a router was located on each floor of the building. As more users are added to each segment, traffic can become congested in the shared backbone.

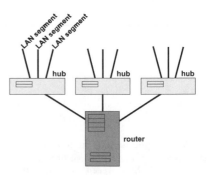

**Collapsed Backbone**
The collapsed backbone router uses a high-speed backplane to move packets quickly from one port to another.  By centralizing the routing in one place, maintenance and troubleshooting is reduced.

Computer distributors and resellers may locate their warehouse within the PC vendor's facility to improve turnaround time to resellers and customers.

**color calibration**    The matching of colors to a base color, such as a Pantone color, or from one device to another; for example, screen and printer output. See *color correction*.

**color correction**    Altering the colors in an image in order to print or display it properly or for special effects. Depending on the application, color correction can be a significant problem if the resulting image must be approved or a purchase is made because of color choice. See *color calibration* and *ICC profile*.

**The SpectroCalibrator**
Light Source's Colortron Color System includes this color calibrator, which is used to accurately determine the color from a sample. Using suction cups, it attaches to the monitor screen to calibrate the monitor so that designers see true representations of the final colors onscreen. *(Image courtesy of Light Source, Inc.)*

**color cycling**    In computer graphics, a technique that simulates animation by continuously changing colors rather than moving the objects. Also called "color lookup table animation."

**color depth**    Same as *bit depth*.

**color gamut**    The entire range of colors available on a particular device such as a monitor or printer. A monitor, which displays RGB signals, has a much greater color gamut than a printer, which uses CMYK inks. See *color management system*.

**color graphics**    The ability to display graphics images in colors.

**colorimeter**    A device that measures the red, green and blue values of color. Contrast with *densitometer*.

**colorimetry**    Using a colorimeter to analyze color. See *colorimeter*.

**color key**    (1) A technique for superimposing a video image onto another. For example, to float a car on the ocean, the car image is placed onto a blue background. The car and ocean images are scanned together. The ocean is made to appear in the resulting image wherever background (blue) exists in the car image. The ocean is cancelled wherever the car appears (no background). If there is a large amount of blue in the image, a green screen can be used as an alternative background to provide the necessary contrast.

(2) In prepress, a high-quality sample of printed output that is used as a comp for the customer and a guide for the printer. It is made by exposing the CMYK negatives onto four acetate films which are developed. When overlaid on top of each other, they simulate the printed results. See *match print*.

**color management system**    Software that translates the colors of an original image into the truest representation obtainable on the output device. Color management works from a profile of the output device, typically a digital printer or offset press, and works backward to the source of the material such as a scanner.

Starting from the colors in real life, the color gamut decreases as it moves to analog film to a digital scanner to a printer. A monitor is also capable of displaying a greater range of colors than the printing process. Color management takes all of these factors into consideration.

**color map**    See *color palette*.

**color mode**    See *bit depth* and *color model*.

**color model**    A system used to represent color for display and printing. It is typically a 3-D model that contains the three attributes of a color, which are hue, value and saturation (chroma). See *RGB, IISB, CIE, CMYK* and *YIQ*.

**color palette**    Also called a "color lookup table," "lookup table," "index map," "color table" or "color map," it is a commonly-used method for saving file space when creating 8-bit color images. Instead of each pixel containing its own red, green and blue values, which would require 24 bits, each pixel holds an 8-bit value, which is an index number into the color palette. The color palette contains 256 predefined RGB values from 0 to 255.

Two or more 256-color (8 bit) images generally cannot display correctly side by side on a 256-color display, because there are too many colors for the system to handle. If the images have very similar colors, there may be little discrepancy, but if they are different, one or more images will suffer. The remedy is to average the palettes in an image editor or to reduce the number of colors to 128 for each (7 bit) image. See *bit depth*.

**colors** The perception of the different wavelengths of light. It is possible to create almost all visible colors using two systems of primary colors. Transmitted colors use red, green and blue (RGB), and reflected colors use cyan (light blue), magenta (purplish-red), yellow and black (CMYK). Color displays use RGB (colors are added to create white) and color printing uses CMYK (colors are subtracted to create white).

**color separation** Separating a picture by colors in order to make negatives and plates for color printing. The four-color process requires four separations: cyan, magenta, yellow and black (CMYK). See *OPI* and *DCS*.

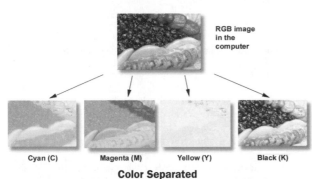

RGB image in the computer

Cyan (C)   Magenta (M)   Yellow (Y)   Black (K)

**Color Separated**

The separations are printed individually in this picture to show how each of the four inks contributes to the total image. Typically, separations are put on film, and the printing plates are made from the film. *(Image courtesy of Intergraph Computer Systems.)*

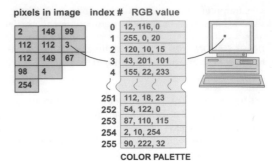

| pixels in image | | | index # | RGB value |
|---|---|---|---|---|
| 2 | 148 | 99 | 0 | 12, 116, 0 |
| 112 | 112 | 3 | 1 | 255, 0, 20 |
| 112 | 149 | 67 | 2 | 120, 10, 15 |
| 98 | 4 | | 3 | 43, 201, 101 |
| 254 | | | 4 | 155, 22, 233 |
| | | | 251 | 112, 18, 23 |
| | | | 252 | 54, 122, 0 |
| | | | 253 | 87, 110, 115 |
| | | | 254 | 2, 10, 254 |
| | | | 255 | 90, 222, 32 |

**COLOR PALETTE**

**Color Palette Index**

The pixels in the image contain an index number, which points to the RGB value in the color palette. The RGB values are the ones use by the display system.

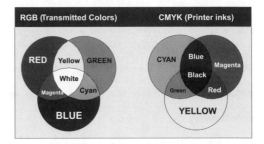

RGB (Transmitted Colors)

RED   Yellow   GREEN
White
Magenta   Cyan
BLUE

CMYK (Printer inks)

CYAN   Blue   Magenta
Black
Green   Red
YELLOW

**Color Mixing Methods**

The two major methods for creating colors are RGB and CMY. RGB uses red, green and blue to create transmitted colors. CMY uses cyan, magenta and yellow to create printed colors. In theory, equal parts of cyan, magenta and yellow ink make black, but the blacks tend to be muddy. Thus, a pure black fourth ink is always used. This is the four color process, called "CMYK" (K for blacK).

**color space** See *color model*.

**color space conversion** Changing one color signal into another. It typically refers to converting YUV analog video into digital RGB video. See *YUV*.

**color table** See *color palette*.

**column move** Relocating a rectangular block of characters within a text document or a column in a spreadsheet.

**COM** (1) (**C**omponent **O**bject **M**odel) A component software architecture from Microsoft, which defines a structure for building program routines (objects) that can be called up and executed in a Windows environment. This capability is built into Windows 95/98 and Windows NT 4.0. Parts of Windows itself and Microsoft's own applications are also built as COM objects. COM provides the interfaces between objects, and Distributed COM (DCOM) allows them to run remotely. COM is used in the following ways:

**COM Objects** COM objects can be small or large. They can be written in several programming languages, and they can perform any kind of processing. A program can call the object whenever it needs its services. Objects can be run remotely (DCOM) over the network in a distributed objects environment.

**Automation (OLE automation)** Standard applications, such as word processors and spreadsheets, can be written to expose their internal functions as COM objects, allowing them to be "automated" instead of manually selected from a menu. For example, a script could be written to extract data from a database, summarize and chart it in a spreadsheet and place the results into a text document. See *COM automation*.

**Controls (OLE controls, ActiveX controls)** Applications can invoke COM objects, called "controls," that blend in and become just another part of the program. An industry of third-party, ready-made controls for the Windows programmer has been created. ActiveX controls can also be downloaded from the Internet to make a Web page perform any kind of processing. See *ActiveX control*.

**Compound Documents and ActiveX Documents** Microsoft's OLE compound documents are based on COM, which lets one document be embedded within or linked to another (see *OLE*). ActiveX Documents are extensions to OLE that allow a Web browser, for example, to view not only Web pages, but any kind of document (see *ActiveX Documents*).

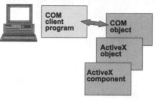

STAND-ALONE MACHINE (CLIENT or SERVER)

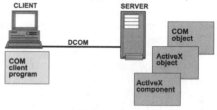

DISTRIBUTED OBJECTS (RUN OVER THE NETWORK)

**COM Objects**
Any kind of program, small or large, can be written as a COM object. It can be run locally or remotely via DCOM. The terms COM object, ActiveX object and ActiveX component are synonymous.

**Programming Interfaces** Increasingly, Microsoft is making its standard programming interfaces conform to the COM object model so that there is continuity between all interfaces. See *DAO*, *ADO* and *OLE DB*.

It's Confusing Microsoft first used the term OLE to refer to its COM-based architecture, then later dropped that designation in favor of ActiveX. Since both OLE and ActiveX are based on COM, the term COM is also used. As a result, any combination of the words COM, OLE and ActiveX followed by the words control, object and component may mean the same thing, or they may not, depending on context.

(2) (Computer Output Microfilm) Creating microfilm or microfiche from the computer. A COM machine receives print-image output from the computer either online or via tape or disk and creates a film image of each page. The leading vendor of COM machines is Anacomp, Inc., San Diego, CA (www.anacomp.com). See *micrographics*.

**COM+** Enhancements to the Microsoft Component Object Model (COM) that enable programmers to develop COM objects more easily. For example, COM+ allows native C++ calls to be translated into the correct COM call. In addition, instead of defining COM interfaces in the traditional IDL language, they can be defined by more familiar programming syntax.

**COM1** In a PC, the logical name assigned to the first serial port. Two serial ports, or COM ports, are provided on a PC to connect a mouse and modem. Typically the mouse is on COM1, and the modem on COM2, but this is not mandatory. Any serial device can be connected to either serial port.

The COM1 and COM2 names are used to inform the operating system of the physical connections that have been made. The term originated before the days of the mouse, when the serial port was primarily used for modem COMmunications.

DOS versions up to 3.2 support COM1 and COM2. Starting with Version 3.3, DOS supports up to COM4, and Windows 95/98 supports COM5 and higher. Contrast with *LPT1*.

**COM2** In a PC, the logical name assigned to the second serial port. See *COM1*.

**COM/ActiveX**    Refers to Microsoft's component software, which is based on COM objects. ActiveX technologies are based on COM; however, in the past, ActiveX has also been used as an umbrella term for COM objects.

**COM automation**    A particular usage of Microsoft's COM-based component software architecture that lets applications expose their internal functions as COM objects. Called "automation" or "OLE automation," it enables tasks that are normally selected from menus to be automatically executed. For example, a small script could be written to extract data from a database, put it into a spreadsheet, summarize and chart it, all without manual intervention.

Virtually any internal routine can be written as a COM object and its interfaces exposed to other programs. Microsoft applications such as Word and Excel are written as COM objects, and not only do they allow their functions to be automated, but they offer programmers a toolbox of functions that can save them the time and effort of writing similar routines themselves.

**combo card**    Typically refers to an Ethernet network adapter that has two or three connectors (twisted pair and/or BNC and/or AUI). See *Ethernet*.

**COMDEX**    (SOFTBANK COMDEX, Needham, MA, www.comdex.com)  A trade show originally created for computer dealers and distributors. COMDEX stands for Computer Dealers Exposition; however, large numbers of end users attend. COMDEX was originally developed by The Interface Group, which was acquired by the Japanese SOFTBANK Corporation in 1995. The first COMDEX/Fall in 1979 had 157 exhibitors and 4,000 attendees. Now, more than 2,000 exhibitors and 200,000 people attend each year.

COMDEX/Spring, which began in 1981 with 237 exhibitors and 11,000 attendees, is about half the size of COMDEX/Fall.

COMDEX/Fall in Las Vegas takes over the entire city and is the largest computer show in the U.S. Housed in both major convention centers and several hotels, shuttle buses escort attendees between sites. Waiting in a long line for a bus can become a welcome relief after walking the massive corridors of COMDEX. COMDEX Las Vegas is exhausting, and fascinating.

**Comdisco**    (Comdisco, Inc., Rosemont, IL, www.comdisco.com)  A technology services company, originally founded as Computer Discount Company in 1969 by Ken Pontikes. It is the largest independent computer and network equipment leasing company and a leader in network services, asset management and business continuity services. By 1997, Comdisco provided help for more than 250 disaster recovery incidents.

**COM file**    (1) (**COM**mand file)  An executable DOS or OS/2 program that takes up less than 64K and fits within one segment. It is an exact replica of how it looks in memory. See *EXE file*.

(2) A VMS file containing commands to be executed.

**comic-strip oriented**    A film-image orientation like a comic strip, in which the tops of the frames run parallel with the edge of the film. Contrast with *cine-oriented*.

**comma delimited**    A record layout that separates data fields with a comma and usually surrounds character data with quotes, for example:

```
"Pat Smith","Main St.","New Hope","PA","18950"
"K. Jones","34 8th Ave.","Syosset","NY","11724"
```

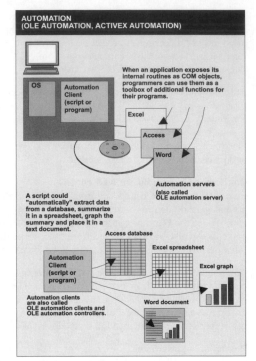

AUTOMATION
(OLE AUTOMATION, ACTIVEX AUTOMATION)

When an application exposes its internal routines as COM objects, programmers can use them as a toolbox of additional functions for their programs.

OS    Automation Client (script or program)

Excel
Access
Word

Automation servers (also called OLE automation server)

A script could "automatically" extract data from a database, summarize it in a spreadsheet, graph the summary and place it in a text document.

Automation Client (script or program)

Access database    Excel spreadsheet    Excel graph

Automation clients are also called OLE automation clients and OLE automation controllers.

Word document

C

**command**  Instruction for the computer. See *command-driven*, *menu-driven* and *function*.

**command and control**  To direct the computer. It typically refers to a capability of voice recognition systems that lets you select menus and other functions by speaking the commands into a microphone. See *voice recognition*.

**COMMAND.COM**  The command processor in DOS and Windows 95/98. COMMAND.COM displays the DOS prompt and executes the DOS commands you type in. The COMMAND.COM in Windows has been expanded to accommodate long file names. See *DOS COMMAND.COM*.

**command-driven**  A program that accepts commands as typed-in phrases. It is usually harder to learn, but may offer more flexibility than a menu-driven program. Once learned, command-driven programs may be faster to use, because the user can state a request succinctly. Contrast with *menu-driven*.

**command interpreter**  Same as *command processor*.

**Command key**  On Apple keyboards, a key with the outline of an Apple, a propeller, or both. It is pressed along with another key to command the computer.

**command language**  A special-purpose language that accepts a limited number of commands, such as a query language, job control language (JCL) or command processor. Contrast with *programming language*, which is a general purpose language.

**command line**  In a command-driven system, the area on screen that accepts typed-in commands. See *command processor*.

**command mode**  An operating mode that causes the computer or modem to accept commands for execution.

**command processor**  A system program that accepts user commands and converts them into the machine commands required by the operating system or some other control program or application. COMMAND.COM is the command processor that accompanies DOS and Windows, and CMD.EXE is the Windows NT/2000 counterpart. The C shell and Bourne shell are examples of command processors in UNIX. See *C shell*, *Bourne shell* and *4DOS*.

**command prompt**  The symbol displayed in a command-driven system that indicates it is ready for user input. For example, in DOS, **C:\BUDGET** would be the command prompt when the working drive is C: and the working directory is BUDGET.

**command queuing**  The ability to store multiple commands and execute them one at a time.

**command set**  Same as *instruction set*.

**command shell**  Same as *command processor*.

**comment**  A descriptive statement in a source language program that is used for documentation.

**comment out**  To disable lines of code in a program by surrounding them with comment-start and comment-stop characters.

**commerce server**  See *merchant server*.

**commercial service provider**  See *carrier*, *ISP* and *ASP*.

**commercial software**  Software that is designed and developed for sale to the general public. See *software package*.

**commit**  To perform an actual update to a record. See *two-phase commit*.

**Commodore**    One of the first personal computer companies. In 1977, Commodore Business Machines, West Chester, PA, introduced the PET computer and launched the personal computer industry along with Apple and Radio Shack. In 1982, it introduced the Commodore 64 (64K RAM) and later the Commodore 128. These were popular home computers, and over 10 million were sold.

In 1985, the Amiga series was introduced, which continued to offer advanced imaging and video capabilities at affordable prices. A line of IBM-compatible PCs were also introduced, but the Amiga series was Commodore's mainstay until May 1994, when it went into bankruptcy. See *Amiga*.

**common carrier**    A government-regulated organization that provides telecommunications services for public use, such as AT&T, the telephone companies, MCI and Western Union. Contrast with *private carrier*.

**Common Desktop Environment**    See *CDE*.

**Common Gateway Interface**    See *CGI script*.

**Common Ground**    Document exchange software from Hummingbird Communications, North York, Ontario, (www.hummingbird.com), that converts a Windows or Macintosh document into a proprietary file format for viewing on other machines. The viewer allows multiple documents to be displayed at the same time. The Common Ground file format is called DigitalPaper.

**Common OS API**    A specification for a standard UNIX programming interface endorsed in 1993 by major UNIX vendors. It led to Spec 1170, which led to the Single UNIX Specification.

**comm port**    May refer to any serial communications port or specifically to the serial ports on a PC. See *COM1*.

**comm program**    See *communications program*.

**communications**    The electronic transfer of information from one location to another. "Data communications" or "datacom" refers to digital transmission, and "telecommunications" or "telecom" refers to a mix of voice and data, both analog and digital. "Networking" refers specifically to LANs and WANs. However, datacom, telecom and networking all fall under the communications umbrella.

**The Protocol**    The way data communications systems "talk to" each other is defined in a set of standards called "protocols." Protocols work in a hierarchy starting at the top with the user's program and ending at the bottom with the plugs, sockets and electrical signals. See *communications protocol* and *OSI*.

**Analog vs. Digital Communications**    The world's largest communications system is the telephone network, which is a mix of analog and digital communications. The system, which used to be entirely analog and transmitted only voice frequencies is now almost entirely digital. The only analog part is the line between your telephone and a digital conversion point (digital loop carrier) within a mile or so of your house. Analog systems are error prone, because the electronic frequencies get mixed together with unwanted signals (noise) that are nearby.

In analog telephone networks, amplifiers were placed in the line every few miles to boost the signal, but they could not distinguish between signal and noise. Thus, the noise was amplified along with the signal. By the time the receiving person or machine got the signal, it may have been impossible to decipher.

**The First Analog Communications**
In 1876, Alexander Graham Bell sent the first electronic communications over a wire when he said, "Mr. Watson. Come here! I want you!"
*(Image courtesy of AT&T.)*

In a "digital" network, only two (binary) distinct frequencies or voltages are transmitted. Instead of amplifiers, repeaters are used, which analyze the incoming signal and regenerate a new outgoing signal. Any noise on the line is filtered out at the next repeater. When data is made up of only two signals (0 and 1), it can be more easily distinguished from the garble. Digital is simple!

**Communications Act**    The establishment of the Federal Communications Commission (FCC) in 1934, the regulatory body for interstate and foreign telecommunications. Its mission is to provide high-quality services at reasonable cost to everyone in the U.S. on a nondiscriminatory basis.

**communications channel**    Also called a "circuit" or "line," it is a pathway over which data is transferred between remote devices. It may refer to the entire physical medium, such as a telephone line, optical fiber, coaxial cable or twisted wire pair, or, it may refer to one of several carrier frequencies transmitted simultaneously within the line.

**communications controller**    A peripheral control unit that connects several communications lines to a computer and performs the actual transmitting and receiving, as well as various message coding and decoding activities.

Communications controllers are typically nonprogrammable units designed for specific protocols and communications tasks. Contrast with *front end processor*, which can be programmed for a variety of protocols and network conditions.

**communications network**    The transmission channels interconnecting all client and server stations, as well as all supporting hardware and software.

**communications parameters**    The basic settings for modem transmission, which include bit rate (14400 bps, 28800 bps, etc.), parity (none, even, odd), number of data bits (7 or 8) and number of stop bits (typically 1). The latter three are often expressed together; for example, N-8-1, which means No parity, 8 data bits and 1 stop bit.

**communications program**    Software that manages the transmission of data between computers, typically via modem and the serial port. Such programs were very popular for connecting to BBSs before the Internet took off. Comm programs include several file transfer protocols and can also emulate dumb terminals for dialing into minis and mainframes. See *communications protocol*.

**communications protocol**    Hardware and software standards that govern transmission between two computers or communications devices. There are several layers, or levels, of functionality in a protocol. Each layer may be available as a separate software component, or several layers may be combined into one. Learning the 7-layer protocol hierarchy, known as the "OSI model," is essential for understanding protocols (see *OSI model*).

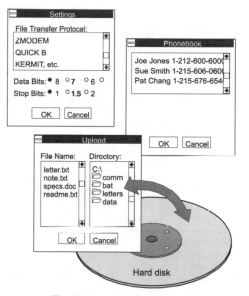

**The Communications Program**
All comm programs have facilities to (1) set the parameters for the transmission, (2) provide a phonebook for frequently dialed calls and (3) select appropriate files for uploading and downloading.

TCP/IP is an example of a major protocol, which provides the fundamental transport for the Internet and UNIX systems. HTTP, FTP, SMTP and others are related protocols (see *TCP/IP*). Before the Web, when users logged onto bulletin boards (BBSs) or dialed up each other's computer to transmit files, communications protocols such as Zmodem, Ymodem and Kermit were widely used.

On local area networks (LANs), mostly Ethernet, but also Token Ring and FDDI, provide the access method (layers 1 and 2) that moves packets from station to station. Higher layer protocols, such as TCP/IP, SPX/IPX and NetBIOS/NetBEUI (layers 3, 4 and 5), are used to control and route the transmission. See *ATM, Ethernet, Token Ring, FDDI, IPX, SPX, NetBIOS, NetBEUI* and *SS7*.

Conceptually Speaking    The following conceptual exchange takes place at protocol layers 2 and 3:

Are you there? **Yes, I am.**  Are you ready to receive? **Yes, I am.**  Here comes the message—bla, bla, bla— did you get it? **Yes, I did.**  Here comes the next part—bla, bla, bla— did you get it? **No, I didn't - resend it.**  Here it comes again— bla, bla, bla— did you get it? **Yes, I did.**  There is no more. Goodbye. **Goodbye.**

**Examples**   The following communications protocols are popular, and you may easily run across them when reading about networking and communications. The protocol in parentheses is the protocol suite. There are a huge number of protocols at all layers. For an exhaustive list with detailed descriptions, visit www.protocols.com.

| Layer | Protocol | | Layer | Protocol | |
|---|---|---|---|---|---|
| 1 | RS-232 | | 4 | SPX | (NetWare) |
| 1 | V.35 | | 4 | TCP | (TCP/IP) |
| 1 | SONET | | 4 | UDP | (TCP/IP) |
| 1-2 | 802.11 wireless | | 4 | NetBEUI | (NetBIOS) |
| 1-2 | Bluetooth wireless | | 5 | NetBIOS | |
| 2 | Ethernet | | 6 | ASN.1 | |
| 2 | Fast Ethernet | | 7 | SMB | (NetBEUI) |
| 2 | Gigabit Ethernet | | 7 | AFP | (AppleTalk) |
| 2 | Token Ring | | 7 | NCP | (NetWare) |
| 2 | FDDI | | 7 | NFS | (TCP/IP) |
| 2 | ATM | | 7 | HTTP | (TCP/IP) |
| 3 | IP | (TCP/IP) | 7 | FTP | (TCP/IP) |
| 3 | IPX | (NetWare) | 7 | SMTP | (TCP/IP) |
| | | | 7 | DNS | (TCP/IP) |

**communications satellite**   A radio relay station in orbit above the earth that receives, amplifies and redirects analog and digital signals contained within a carrier frequency. There are three kinds. Geostationary (GEO) satellites are in orbit 22,282 miles above the earth and rotate with the earth, thus appearing stationary. The downlink from GEOs back to earth can be localized into small areas or cover as much as a third of the earth's surface.

Low-earth orbit (LEO) satellites reside no more than 1,000 miles above the earth and revolve around the globe every couple of hours. They are only in view for a few minutes, and multiple LEOs are required to maintain continuous coverage. Medium-earth orbit (MEO) satellites are in the middle, taking about six hours to orbit the earth and in view for a couple of hours. See *Teledesic*, *Iridium*, *DSS*, *DirecPC* and *bent pipe architecture*.

**communications server**   See *remote access server*, *modem server*, *terminal server* and *communications controller*.

**COM object**   A software component that conforms to Microsoft's Component Object Model (COM). See *COM*.

**CompactFlash**   A flash memory format invented by SanDisk Corporation, Sunnyvale, CA, (www.sandisk.com). At 36.4 x 42.8 x 3.3 mm thick, it is about a third the size of a PC Card. It uses the same PC Card/ATA interface, but has 50 pins instead of 68, and cards support both 3.3 and 5v operation. They can plug into a CompactFlash socket or into a standard Type II PC Card slot with an adapter. Introduced in 1994, CompactFlash has become widely used for handheld digital devices.

A second-generation CompactFlash Type II card increases the thickness from 3 to 5mm allowing for the inclusion of more electronics and a microminiaturized hard disk.

**COMPACT II**   A high-level numerical control programming language used to generate instructions for numerical control (machine tool) devices.

**CompactPCI**   A combination of the PCI bus contained on a Eurocard form factor. The Eurocard provides more rugged packaging and a more secure plug and socket for embedded systems than the standard PCI card used in desktop computers. It supports hot swapping and provides higher performance (32-bit, 33MHz) than the ISA bus in the PC/104 architecture. CompactPCI also provides modularity as Eurocard comes in several sizes. See *Eurocard*.

**Communications Satellite**
There are hundreds of commercial communications satellites in orbit providing services for both industry and consumers. By the 21st century, it is expected that Internet access via satellite will be popular.

**CompactFlash Module**
CompactFlash modules have become very popular as storage for digital film. See *flash memory* for size comparison.

**compact tape**    Refers to magnetic tape technologies that use small cartridges. It includes QIC, DAT, 8mm, Magstar MP, DLT and Ultrium.

**companding**    (1) (**COM**pressing/ex**PANDING**) A compression technique used in pulse code modulation (PCM) that uses a non-linear ruler for the measurement of voice samples. It provides finer spacing at low volume and wider spacing at the loud end. See *mu-Law, A-Law* and *compandor*.

**compandor**    (**COM**pressor/ex**PANDOR**) A device that improves the signal for AM radio transmission. On outgoing transmission, it raises the amplitude of weak signals and lowers the amplitude of strong signals. On incoming transmission, it restores the signal to its original form. See *companding*.

**Compaq**    (Compaq Computer Corporation, Houston, TX, www.compaq.com) The leading PC manufacturer founded in 1982 by Rod Canion, Jim Harris and Bill Murto. In 1983, it shipped 53,000 PC-compatible COMPAQ Portables, which resulted in $111 million in revenues and an American business record. The Portable's success was due to its rugged construction, ability to run all PC software and its semi-portability (it weighed 30 pounds!).

**Compaq's Founders**
Canion, Harris and Murto (left to right) founded one of the most successful computer companies in the industry. *(Image courtesy of Compaq Computer Corporation.)*

**The Compaq Portable**
The Compaq Portable was the first completely IBM-compatible PC. Its rugged construction and "luggability" made it a huge success. *(Image courtesy of Compaq Computer Corporation.)*

In 1984, it introduced its DESKPRO desktop computers and achieved a computer-industry sales record in its second year. In 1986, it was the first to offer a 386-based machine. Throughout its history, Compaq has been well respected for its high-quality computer products and innovations. Maintaining this high profile kept it from initially competing with the mail order houses that were dramatically driving down prices in the 1990s. Compaq later became very competitive, and is now a leading vendor in the mass market chain stores.

In 1997, Compaq acquired Tandem Computers, the first company to build fault-tolerant computers from the ground up. Tandem brings Compaq a strong background in high-availability systems for mission critical applications. In 1998, Compaq acquired Digital Equipment Corporation, one of the oldest computer companies and pioneer of minicomputers in the 1960s. Digital's entree into major companies, plus its large service organization, adds a significant enterprise presence for Compaq.

**comparator**    A device that compares two quantities and determines their equality.

**compatibility mode**    A feature of a computer or operating system that allows it to run programs written for a different system. Programs often run slower in compatibility mode.

**compilation**    Compiling a program. See *compiler*.

**compile**    To translate a program written in a high-level programming language into machine language. See *compiler*.

**compiler**    (1) Software that translates a program written in a high-level programming language (COBOL, C, etc.) into machine language. A compiler usually generates assembly language first and then translates the assembly language into machine language. A utility known as a "link editor" then combines all required machine language modules into an executable program that can run in the computer.

The following example compiles program statements into machine language:

```
Source Code    Assembly Language   Machine Language
IF COUNT=10    Compare A to B      Compare 3477 2883
  GOTO DONE    If equal go to C    If = go to 23883
  ELSE         Go to D             Go to 23343
 GOTO AGAIN
ENDIF
               Actual Machine Code
               10010101001010001010100
               10101010010101001001010
               10100101010001010010010
```

(2) Software that converts a set of high-level language statements into a lower-level representation. For example, a help compiler converts a text document embedded with appropriate commands into an online help system. A dictionary compiler converts terms and definitions into a dictionary lookup system.

### compiler language
See *high-level language* and *compiler*.

### compile time
The time it takes to translate a program from source language into machine language. Link editing time may also be included in compile time.

### complement
The number derived by subtracting a number from a base number. For example, the tens complement of 8 is 2. In set theory, complement refers to all the objects in one set that are not in another set.

Complements are used in digital circuits, because it's faster to subtract by adding complements than by performing true subtraction. The binary complement of a number is created by reversing all bits and adding 1. The carry from the high-order position is eliminated. The following example subtracts 5 from 8.

| Decimal | Binary | Complement |
|---------|--------|------------|
| 8       | 1000   | 1000       |
| -5      | -0101  | +1011      |
|         |        |            |
| 3       | 0011   | 0011       |

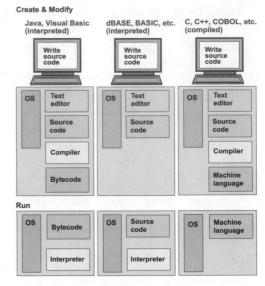

**Create & Modify**

**Compilers and Interpreters**
Compiled programs (right) are translated into the machine language of the target computer. Interpreted programs (left and center) are either kept in their original source code or are precompiled into an intermediate form. In both cases, an interpreter is required to translate the program into machine language at runtime, whereas the compiled program is "ready to go."

### complex data type
Any data that does not fall into the traditional field structure (alpha, numeric, dates) of a relational DBMS. Examples of complex data types are bills of materials, word processing documents, maps, time-series, images and video. In a relational DBMS, complex data types are stored in a LOB, but either the client application or some middleware is required to process the data. In an object DBMS or an object-relational DBMS, complex data types are stored as objects that are integrated into and activated by the DBMS.

### component
One element of a larger system. A hardware component can be a device as small as a transistor or as large as a disk drive as long as it is part of a larger system. Software components are routines or modules within a larger system. See *component software*.

### component digital
The storage and transmission of digital video that keeps the red, green and blue data separate. Contrast with *composite digital*.

### component software
Program modules that are designed to interoperate with each other at runtime. Components can be large or small. They can be written by different programmers using different development environments, and they may or may not be platform independent. Components can be run in stand-alone machines, on a LAN, intranet or the Internet.

The terms component and object are used synonymously. Component architectures have risen out of object-oriented technologies, but the degree to which they comply to all the rules of object technology is often debated.

Component architectures may use a client/component model, in which the client application is designed as the container that holds the other components/objects. The client container is responsible for the user interface and coordinating mouse clicks and other inputs to all the components. A pure object model does not require a container. Any object can call any other without a prescribed hierarchy.

Component software implies the use of small modules that allow applications to be quickly customized. Rather than launch the huge, feature-rich applications in common use today, it is envisioned that users will run smaller, tighter applications in the future, calling in additional features (components) only when needed. See *COM*, *JavaBeans*, *CORBA* and *object technology*.

**component video**    The recording and transmission of video which separates the color information from the synchronization signals. Component video is typically stored in either YUV or RGB formats. See *RGB* and *YUV*. Contrast with *composite video*.

**COM port**    A serial communications port on a PC. See *COM1* and *serial port*.

**composite digital**    The storage and transmission of digital video that combines the red, green and blue data. In practice, composite digital is not used for any broadcast formats, as component digital is easily accommodated with today's equipment. However, composite digital streams can actually exist if NTSC or PAL signals are converted to digital for transmission over a digital network. Contrast with *component digital*.

**composite video**

The recording and transmission of video which mixes the color information and synchronization signals together. The RCA phono connector is commonly used for composite video on VCRs, camcorders and other consumer appliances. Contrast with *component video*.

Left audio (white)   Right audio (red)   Composite video (yellow)

**compound document**    A single document that contains a combination of data structures such as text, graphics, spreadsheets, sound and video clips. The document may embed the additional data types or reference external files by pointers of some kind. SGML and HTML are examples of compound document formats. See *OLE*.

**compress**    **(1)** To compact data to save space. See *data compression*.
   **(2)** A UNIX utility used to compress files. See *archive formats* and *tar*.

**compression**    See *data compression*.

**compression ratio**    The measurement of compressed data. For example, a file compressed into 1/4th of its original size can be expressed as 4:1, 25%, 75% or 2 bits per byte.

**compression utility**    A program such as PKZIP that compresses and decompresses files. See *data compression*.

**compressor**    **(1)** A device that diminishes the range between the strongest and weakest transmission signals. See *compandor*.
   **(2)** A routine or program that compresses data. See *data compression*.

**Compsurf**    A NetWare utility that performs a high-level hard disk format. NetWare servers require their own proprietary format.

**CompTIA**    (Computing Technology Industry Association, Lombard, IL, www.comptia.org) Formerly ABCD:The Microcomputer Industry Association, it is a membership organization of resellers, distributors and manufacturers

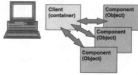

STAND-ALONE MACHINE

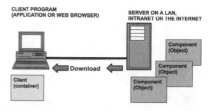

STORED REMOTELY, RUN LOCALLY

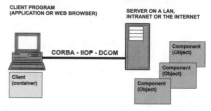

STORED REMOTELY, RUN REMOTELY

**Where Components/Objects Are Run**

dedicated to business ethics and professionalism, founded in 1982. It sets voluntary guidelines and is involved with many issues including product returns, freight and warranty claims and price protection.

CompTIA also provides certification for computer service technicians, known as A+, as well as for document imaging professionals with the Certified Document Imaging Architech (CDIA). Tests are administered worldwide. P.S. Architech is not a typo!

**CompuServe**   An online information service that provides access to the Internet, e-mail, instant messaging and an integrated contact list. Founded in 1969 as a timesharing service, CompuServe is one of the oldest online services, being the first to offer e-mail in 1979 and online chat a year later. The GIF graphics format was developed by CompuServe in 1987 to transfer compressed images over the very low-speed, dial-up lines in common use at that time. GIF images are widely used on Web sites; however, the compression method in GIF is owned by Unisys.

In 1998, CompuServe was acquired by America Online (AOL), and whereas AOL is geared more to the consumer, CompuServe's offerings have been aimed at the professional business user. Specialized versions of CompuServe are also available for the legal, insurance and airline industries. See *online services*.

**compute bound**   Same as *process bound*.

**computer**   A general-purpose machine that processes data according to a set of instructions that are stored internally either temporarily or permanently. The computer and all equipment attached to it are called hardware. The instructions that tell it what to do are called "software." A set of instructions that perform a particular task is called a "program" or "software program."

WHAT A COMPUTER DOES   The instructions in the program direct the computer to input, process and output as follows:

Input/Output   The computer can selectively retrieve data into its main memory (RAM) from any peripheral device (terminal, disk, tape, etc.) connected to it. After processing the data internally, the computer can send a copy of the results from its memory out to any peripheral device. The more memory it has, the more programs and data it can work with at the same time.

Storage   By outputting data onto a magnetic disk or tape, the computer is able to store data permanently and retrieve it when required. A system's size is based on how much disk storage it has. The more disk, the more data is immediately available.

PROCESSING (The 3 Cs*)   Once the data is in the computer's memory, the computer can process it by **calculating**, **comparing** and **copying** it.

Calculate   The computer can perform any mathematical operation on data by adding, subtracting, multiplying and dividing one set with another.

Compare   The computer can analyze and evaluate data by matching it with sets of known data that are included in the program or called in from storage.

Copy   The computer can move data around to create any kind of report or listing in any order.

By **calculating**, **comparing** and **copying**, the computer accomplishes all forms of data processing. For example, records are sorted into a new order by **comparing** two records at a time and **copying** the record with the lower value in front of the one with the higher value.

The computer finds one customer out of thousands by **comparing** the requested account number to each record in the file. The dBASE query statement:  SUM SALARY FOR TITLE = "NURSE" causes the computer to **compare** the title field in each record for NURSE and then add (**calculate**) the salary field for each match.

In word processing, inserting and deleting text is accomplished by **copying** characters from one place to another.

Remember The 3 Cs   If you wonder whether the computer can solve a problem, identify your data on paper. If it can be calculated, compared and copied on paper, it can be processed in the computer.

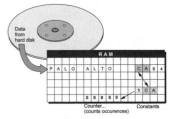

**The 3 Cs—Finding Things**
The example above counts all California records in the database by comparing each record with "CA." Every record in the database is read into memory. The memory locations that state is written into are compared with the letters "CA" in the program. If they are equal, a "1" is added to the California counter. The second record is written into the same memory bytes as the first record, and the field is compared again. This process is performed until the last record has been examined.

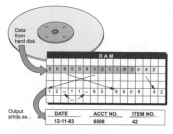

### The 3 Cs—Displaying and Printing

Data is stored as contiguous fields in the database. There are no blanks in between. The data is displayed and printed the way we like to see it by writing the data into memory and copying the characters into the desired order. The date in this example is printed through a "picture," which is a set of characters that acts as a filter. Each character in the date is compared to a corresponding character in the picture, and the one copied as output is determined by the rules. Pictures can be implemented in software or in hardware.

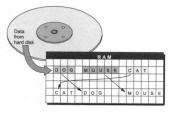

### The 3 Cs—Sorting

Sorting, or resequencing, data is accomplished by comparing each item of data with the others and copying it into the appropriate order. Of course, there's a ton of calculating going on to keep track of what's being compared. Years ago, when databases were stored on tape, the speed of a vendor's sort program was a powerful marketing feature. All transactions had to be sorted into account number sequence in order to be processed. In today's online systems, data is often indexed. Instead of sorting the actual data records themselves, the much smaller indexes are sorted.

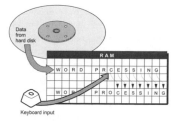

### The 3 Cs—Editing

The magic of word processing is really nothing more than copying the text in memory. In this example, if you want to insert a character into an existing line, the remaining characters are copied one memory location (byte) to the right so there is room for the additional letter. Deleting is just copying in reverse. As in all data processing, there is a whole lot of calculating and comparing going on to keep track of where the text is stored in memory

**THE STORED PROGRAM CONCEPT**    The computer's ability to call in instructions and follow them is known as the "stored program concept." Instructions are copied into memory from a disk, tape or other source before any data can be processed. The computer is directed to start with the first instruction in the program. It copies the instruction from memory into its control unit circuit and matches it against its built-in set of instructions. If the instruction is valid, the processor carries it out. If not, the computer comes to an abnormal end (abend, crash).

The computer executes instructions sequentially until it finds a GOTO instruction that tells it to go to a different place in the program. It can execute millions of instructions per second tracing the logic of the program over and over again on each new set of data it brings in.

As computers get faster, operations can be made to overlap. While one program is waiting for input from one user, the operating system (master control program) directs the computer to process data in another program. Large computers are designed to allow inputs and outputs to occur simultaneously with processing. While one user's data is being processed, data from the next user can be retrieved into the computer.

It can take hundreds of thousands of discrete machine steps to perform very routine tasks. Your computer could easily execute a million instructions to put a requested record onscreen for you.

**GENERATIONS OF COMPUTERS**    First-generation computers, starting with the UNIVAC I in 1951, used vacuum tubes, and their memories were made of thin tubes of liquid mercury and magnetic drums.

Second-generation systems in the late 1950s replaced tubes with transistors and used magnetic cores for memories (IBM 1401, Honeywell 800). Size was reduced and reliability was significantly improved.

Third-generation computers, beginning in the mid 1960s, used the first integrated circuits (IBM 360, CDC 6400) and the first operating systems

**The Beginning of Commercial Computing**
In the early 1950s, the Univac I ushered in the computer age. This picture was taken in Frankfurt, Germany in 1956 and shows the console on the right, a little more than half the CPU on the left and the tape drives in the background.

and DBMSs. Online systems were widely developed, although most processing was still batch oriented using punched cards and magnetic tapes.

Starting in the mid 1970s, the fourth generation brought us computers made entirely of chips. It spawned the microprocessor and personal computer. It introduced distributed processing and office automation. Query languages, report writers and spreadsheets put large numbers of people in touch with the computer for the first time.

The fifth generation is becoming visible in the mid-1990s with more widespread use of voice recognition, natural and foreign language translation, optical disks and fiber-optic networks. Higher-speed machines combined with more sophisticated software will enable the average computer to talk to us with reasonable intelligence sometime after the dawn of the 21st Century.

TYPES OF COMPUTERS    Computers can be as small as a chip or as large as a truck. The difference is in the amount of work they do within the same time frame. Its power is based on many factors, including word size and the speed of its CPU, memory and peripherals. Following is a rough guide to system cost.

**The Installation**
This picture, taken in 1956, shows half the CPU of the UNIVAC I. Imagine yourself watching this awesome sight and someone says to you, "in 20 years, everything you see being wheeled up the ramp will fit on the tip of your finger." Would you have believed it?

```
Computer System Type      Approximate Cost (U.S.$)
Computer on a chip
  (4, 8, 32, 16-bit)          2 - 75
Microprocessor chip
  (4, 8, 16, 32, 64-bit)      5 - 1000
Personal computer client
  (16, 32, 64-bit)          800 - 15,000
Personal computer server
  (32, 64-bit)            6,000 - 30,000
Workstation (32, 64-bit)  6,000 - 100,000
Mini/midrange server
  (32, 64-bit)           25,000 - 1,000,000
Mainframe (32, 64-bit)   500,000 - 10,000,000
Supercomputer (64-bit) 1,000,000 - 10,000,000
```

**computer-aided design**    See *CAD*.

**computer-aided engineering**    See *CAE*.

**computer-aided manufacturing**    See *CAM*.

**computer-aided software engineering**    See *CASE*.

**computer animation**    The creation of animated sequences within the computer. Contrast with *stop-motion animation*.

**computer architecture**    The design of a computer system. It sets the standard for all devices that connect to it and all the software that runs on it. It is based on the type of programs that will run (business, scientific) and the number of them run concurrently.

It specifies how much memory is needed and how it is managed (memory protection, virtual memory, virtual machine). It specifies register size and bus width (16-, 32-, 64-bit) and how concurrency is handled (channels, bus mastering, parallel processing).

Its native language instruction set stipulates what functions the computer performs and how instructions are written to activate them. This determines how programs will communicate with it forever after.

The trend toward large, complicated instruction sets has been reversed with RISC computers, which use simpler instructions. The result is a leaner, faster computer, but requires that the compilers generate more code for complex functions that used to be handled in hardware.

Fault tolerant operation influences every aspect of computer architecture, and computers designed for single purposes, such as array processors and database machines, require special designs.

**computer-assisted learning**   See *CBT*.

**computer-assisted retrieval**   See *CAR*.

**Computer Associates**   See *CA*.

**computer automatic virtual environment**   See *CAVE*.

**computer-based reference**   See *CBR*.

**computer-based training**   See *CBT*.

**computer conferencing**   See *chat*, *videoconferencing* and *data conferencing*.

**computercruiter**   A recruiter that specializes in placing computer professionals. Same as *nerd rustler*.

**computer designer**   A person who designs the electronic structure of a computer. Such individuals are engineers with background in digital circuits.

**computer exchange**   A commodity exchange through which the public can buy and sell used computers. After a match, the buyer sends a check to the exchange and the seller sends the equipment to the buyer. If the buyer accepts it, the money is sent to the seller less commission. Commissions usually range from 10 to 20%.

With the American Computer Exchange, equipment is first sent to the exchange, which inspects it and then sends it to the buyer.

**American Computer Exchange (AmCoEx)**
800/786-0717  FAX 404/250-1399
www.amcoex.com

**National Computer Exchange (NaComEx)**
212/808-3062  FAX 212/681-9211
www.nacomex.com

**Boston Computer Exchange (BoCoEx)**
800/262-6399  FAX 617/542-8849
www.bocoex.com

**United Computer Exchange**
800/755-3033  FAX 770/612-1239
www.uce.com

**computer graphics**   See *graphics*.

**computer language**   A programming language, machine language or the language of the computer industry.

**computer literacy**   Understanding computers and related systems. It includes a working vocabulary of computer and information system components, the fundamental principles of computer processing and a perspective for how non-technical people interact with technical people.

It does not deal with how the computer works (digital circuits), but does imply knowledge of how the computer does its work (calculate, compare and copy). It requires a conceptual understanding of systems analysis and design, application programming, systems programming and datacenter operations.

To be a computer literate manager, you must be able to define information requirements effectively and have an understanding of decision support tools, such as query languages, report writers, spreadsheets and financial planning systems. To be truly computer literate, you must understand all the entries under "standards" in this database. If you can't sleep at night, it's a guaranteed cure for insomnia.

The term computer literacy has been attributed to Andrew Molnar, director of the Office of Computing Activities at the National Science Foundation in 1972.

### Computer Museum

(The Computer Museum History Center, Mountain View, CA, www.computerhistory.org) The home of the largest collection of computer artifacts in the world, which includes more than 3,000 hardware components and 7,000 films, videos and historical photos. The Computer Museum History Center was established in 1996, following its move from The Computer Museum in Boston. Now two separate entities, the original Computer Museum and some of its exhibits live on in Boston's Museum of Science, while the majority of equipment was moved to The Computer Museum History Center at Moffett Field in California. Only a fraction of the equipment is in visible storage, which can be viewed by appointment. The future home of the History Center will be in the California Air & Space Center, a 100,000 square-foot facility expected to be built on the grounds of Moffett Field.

The original Computer Museum was founded in Marlboro, Massachusetts in 1979. Funded by several computer companies and private individuals, it offered the history of the industry, as well as hands-on exhibits for kids and adults. You could literally walk through the world's largest personal computer.

### computer on a chip

A single chip that contains the processor, RAM, ROM, clock and I/O control unit. Hundreds of millions of them are used each year for a myriad of applications from automobiles to toys. A computer on a chip is also called a "microcontroller" or "MCU."

### computerphile

A person that enjoys learning about and using computers. See *technophile*, *hacker* and *dweeb*.

### computer power

The effective performance of a computer. It can be expressed in MIPS (millions of instructions per second), clock speed (10Mhz, 16Mhz) and in word or bus size, (16-bit, 32-bit). However, as with automobile horsepower, valves and cylinders, such specifications are only guidelines. Real power is whether it gets your job done quickly.

A software package is "powerful" if it has a large number of features.

### Computer Press Association

See *CPA*.

### computer readable

Same as *machine readable*.

### computer science

The field of computer hardware and software. It includes systems analysis & design, application and system software design and programming and datacenter operations. For young students, the emphasis in typically on learning a programming language or running a personal computer with little attention to information science, the study of information and its uses.

If students were introduced to data administration, DBMS concepts and transaction and master files, they would have a better grasp of an organization's typical information requirements.

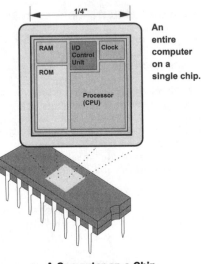

An entire computer on a single chip.

**A Computer on a Chip**
This is the layout of a Motorola 6801, one of the first complete computers on a chip. This category of chip is widely used in automobiles, appliances and toys. Such chips can cost as little as one dollar in quantity.

### Computer Security Act

The first step in improving the security and privacy of information contained in federal computer systems. Signed January 8, 1988 by President Reagan, the Act:

- Establishes a central authority for developing guidelines for protecting unclassified, but sensitive information stored in government computers.

- Requires each agency to formulate a computer security plan, tailored to its own circumstances and based on the guidelines.

- Mandates that each agency provide training for its computer employees on the threats and vulnerabilities of its computer systems.

- Ensures that the National Security Agency and other defense-related government agencies not control computer security standards in civilian agencies of government. See *security*.

**computer services**    Data processing (timesharing, batch processing), software development and consulting services. See *service bureau*.

**computer system**    The complete computer made up of the CPU, memory and related electronics (main cabinet), all the peripheral devices connected to it and its operating system. Computer systems fall into two broad divisions: clients and servers. Client machines fall into three categories from low to high end: laptop, desktop and workstation. Servers range from small to large: low-end servers, midrange servers and mainframes.

A computer system is sized for the total user workload based on (1) number of users sharing the system simultaneously, (2) type of work performed (interactive processing, batch processing, CAD, engineering, scientific), and (3) amount of storage. Following are the components of a computer system and their significance.

**Platform**    The hardware platform and operating system determine which programs can run on the computer. Every application is written to run under a specific CPU and operating system environment. The most widely used platform means more software is available for it. See *platform*.

**Input/Output**    A server's input/output (I/O) capacity determines the number of simultaneous users that it can support at terminals or PCs.

**Number of CPUs**    The more CPUs, the more processing that can take place at the same time. High-end servers often contain multiple processors. See *SMT*.

**Clock Speed**    The megahertz rate of the CPU determines internal processing speed. See *MHz*.

**Disk and Memory**    A computer system's disk capacity determines the amount of information immediately available to all users. Its memory capacity determines how many applications can be efficiently run at the same time.

**Fault Tolerance**    The use of UPS systems as well as redundant processors, peripherals and power supplies provide fault tolerance in the event of power loss or component failure.

**computer telephony**    See *CTI* and *IP telephony*.

**computer-to-plate**    See *CTP*.

**computer-to-press**    See *CTP*.

**Computex**    A Taiwanese trade show for PC manufacturers and PC component buyers promoted by the China External Trade Development Council. For information, call Taiwan 886-2-725-5200, Fax 886-2-757-6653.

**Computing Technology Industry Association**    See *CompTIA*.

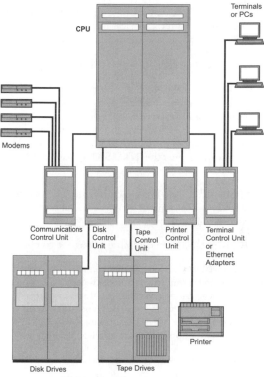

**Multiuser Computer System**
This diagram shows a server with terminals or PCs. All computer systems contain similar components whether in multiple cabinets or one.

| RELATIONSHIP BETWEEN SYSTEMS | |
|---|---|
| **structure (is)** | **function (does)** |
| **Management System** | |
| 1. People<br>2. Machines | Sets organization's goals and objectives, strategies and tactics, plans, schedule and controls. |
| **Information System** | |
| 1. Database<br>2. Application programs<br>3. Procedures | Defines data structures<br>Data entry, updating, queries and reporting.<br>Defines data flow |
| **Computer System** | |
| 1. CPU<br>2. Peripherals<br>3. Operating system | Processes (the 3 C's)<br>Store and retrieve<br>Manages computer system |

**Compuware**    (Compuware Corporation, Farmington Hills, MI, www.compuware.com)  A leading provider of software and consulting services for building, testing and optimizing applications. Founded in 1973, it serves more than 15,000 of the largest companies worldwide. Its products include the UNIFACE development system and EcoSYSTEMS product suite. Initially involved in mainframes, it has since expanded to include client/server. See *UNIFACE*, *XPEDITER*, *Abend-AID* and *File-AID*.

**COMSAT**    (COMSAT Corporation, Clarksburg, MD, www.comsat.com)  Formerly Communications Satellite Corporation, it is a private company that was created by the U.S. Congress in 1962 that provides satellite communications to major carriers and organizations. In 1965, it launched Early Bird, the first commercial satellite in geostationary orbit. COMSAT is the U.S. signatory for INTELSAT and Inmarsat, and its primary business is providing communications over the INTELSAT system. In 2001, COMSAT is expected to become privatized.

**concatenate**    To link structures together. Concatenating files appends one file to another. In speech synthesis, units of speech called "phonemes" (k, sh, ch, etc.) are concatenated to produce meaningful sounds.

**concentration**    In communications, the combining of multiple channels into one.

**concentrator**    A device that combines several communications channels into one. It is often used to tie multiple terminals together into one line. It differs from a multiplexor, which also combines several lines into one, because the total bandwidth of a concentrator's inputs is not equal to its outputs. A concentrator may temporarily store data to allow for this discrepancy, whereas a multiplexor does not.

An Ethernet hub, which is a multiport repeater, is sometimes called a "concentrator."

**The Early Bird**
COMSAT launched the Early Bird in 1965, the first commercial geostationary satellite. Before the end of the century, some 250 more would follow. *(Image courtesy of COMSAT*

**concurrency**    Simultaneous operation within the computer. See *multiprocessing*, *multitasking*, *multithreading*, *SMP* and *MPP*.

**concurrency control**    In a DBMS, managing the simultaneous access to a database. It prevents two users from editing the same record at the same time and is also concerned with serializing transactions for backup and recovery.

**concurrent licensing**    Software licensing that is based on the number of simultaneous users accessing the program. Concurrent licensing is administered by the application itself or via independent software metering tools. See *software metering*. Contrast with *per seat licensing*.

**concurrent operation**    See *multitasking*, *multiprocessing* and *parallel processing*.

**Concurrent PCI**    An enhancement to the PCI bus architecture that allows PCI and ISA buses to transfer data simultaneously. For example, using Concurrent PCI, video performance would be improved with a PCI display adapter and an ISA sound card.

**concurrent processing**    See *multiprocessing*.

**conditional branch**    In programming, an instruction that directs the computer to another part of the program based on the results of a compare. In the following (simulated) assembly language example, the second line is the conditional branch.

```
COMPARE FIELDA with FIELDB

GOTO MATCHROUTINE if EQUAL.
```

High-level language statements, such as IF THEN ELSE and CASE, are used to express the compare and conditional branch.

**conditioning**    Extra cost options in a private telephone line that improve performance by reducing distortion and amplifying weak signals.

**conductor**    A material that can carry electrical current. Contrast with *insulator*.

**CONFIG.SYS**    A DOS and OS/2 configuration file. It resides in the root directory and is used to load drivers and change settings at startup. Install programs often modify CONFIG.SYS in order to customize the computer for their particular use. Windows 95/98 executes the lines in CONFIG.SYS if it contains drivers that it found no counterpart for when it was installed. See **DOS CONFIG.SYS**.

**configuration**    The makeup of a system. To "configure" is to choose options in order to create a custom system. "Configurability" is a system's ability to be changed or customized.

**configuration file**    A file that contains information about a specific user, program, computer or file.

**configuration management**    (1) In a network, a system for gathering current configuration information from all nodes in a LAN.
(2) In software development, a system for keeping track of large projects. Although version control, which maintains a database of revisions, is part of the system, a full-blown software configuration management system (SCM system or CM system) automatically documents all components used to build executable programs. It is able to recreate each build, as well as recreate earlier environments in order to maintain previous versions of a product. It may also be used to prevent unauthorized access to files or to alert the appropriate users when a file has been altered.
Increasingly, parts of version control and configuration management are being added to application development systems. Examples of stand-alone configuration management systems are PVCS, CCC/Harvest and ClearCase.

**congestion**    The condition of a network when there is not enough bandwidth to support the current traffic load.

**connectionless**    A communications architecture that does not require the establishment of a session between two nodes before transmission can begin. The transmission of frames within a local area network (LAN), such as Ethernet, Token Ring and FDDI, is connectionless. UDP packets within a TCP/IP network are also connectionless. Contrast with *connection oriented*.

**Connection Machine**    A family of parallel processing computers from former Thinking Machines Corporation, Cambridge, MA, that contained from 4K to 64K processors. Used in applications such as signal processing, simulation and database retrieval, they were set up as hypercubes and other topologies, which required another computer as a front end.

**connection oriented**    A communications architecture that requires an establishment of the session between two nodes before transmission can begin. When the communications is completed, the session is ended (torn down). All circuit-switched networks are connection oriented because they require a dedicated channel for the duration of the session. The most ubiquitious circuit-switched network is the PSTN. In addition, packet-switched X.25, frame relay and ATM networks are also considered connection oriented, because they require receiving nodes to acknowledge their ability to support the transmission before data can be sent. Contrast with *connectionless*.

**connection pooling**    The ability to open several connections to a database and distribute those connections to the next available request for data. On the Web, connection pooling is performed to improve performance. Otherwise opening a database connection for each user request adds overhead, and maintaining a connection for each user wastes resources.

**connectivity**    (1) Generally, the term refers to communications networks or the act of communicating between computers and terminals.
(2) Specifically, the term refers to devices such as bridges, routers and gateways that link networks together.

**connectoid** A predefined dial-up connection in Windows. Connectoids are created by clicking Make New Connection in the Dial-Up Networking section of My Computer for each type of connection required to ISPs or different services within the same ISP such as landline versus wireless. To view the connectoids, select My Computer/Dial-Up Networking.

**connector** (1) Any plug and socket that links two devices together. Although somewhat bland, connectors are actually a large industry, and the quality of these components is more critical than most people would imagine. When not designed or constructed properly, they often become the weakest element in an electronic system. See *CLINKS*.

(2) In database management, a link or pointer between two data structures.

(3) In flowcharting, a symbol used to break a sequence and resume the sequence elsewhere. It is often a small circle with a number in it.

**connect time** The amount of time a user at a terminal is logged on to a computer system. See *online services* and *service bureau*.

**console** (1) A terminal used to monitor and control a computer or network.

(2) Any display terminal.

**console app** An application that is run from the command line rather than a graphical user interface. For example, a Windows application that runs in the background or has very limited output may be written as a console app. Many DOS utilities were turned into Windows console apps to take advantage of certain 32-bit functions in Windows, but that did not need the graphical userface.

**ConsoleOne** Management console software from Novell for NetWare servers. Introduced with NetWare 5, ConsoleOne is written in Java and runs on the client or server. See *NWAdmin*.

**consolidated server** A multiprocessor computer system. They typically consist of a series of individual, rack-mounted or modularized CPU boards that use fault tolerant components. They generally share common disk storage and SMP versions share a common memory pool. What differentiates them is how efficiently they are controlled by a single administrative console, their degree of fault tolerance and how easily failed components can be replaced without shutting down the entire system. Although typically built on Intel-based motherboards with enhanced features, in effect, the functions of a consolidated server have been employed in mainframes for years. The consolidated server represents the evolution of x86 CPUs for mission critical use.

**constant** In programming, a fixed value in a program. Minimum and maximum amounts, dates, prices, headlines and error messages are examples.

**constant bit rate** See *CBR*.

**constant ratio code** A code that always contains the same ratio of 0s to 1s.

**consultant** A person that acts as an advisor to users or to the technical staff. Consultants are available for all aspects of the computer industry, including electronic circuit design, information systems analysis and software development. In a business environment, consultants are often used to create the functional specifications from which vendors can respond. Consultants typically come from third-party consulting firms, but the title is also used for internal specialists. See *job descriptions*.

**Windows Connectoids**
Clicking on any of the three connectoids shown in this dialog box connects to the Internet through two service providers (AOL and Comcat). Right-clicking a connectoid lets you select Properties in order to see the current dialing and modem configuration.

**Consoles that Were Consoles!**
Up until the late 1970s, computers were designed with panels of blinking lights, which added to their aura of science fiction. The designs gave each computer a personality that is lacking in many of today's machines. *(Top image courtesy of The Computer Museum History Center. Bottom image courtesy of Unisys Corporation.)*

**consumable**    A material that is used up and needs continuous replenishment, such as paper and toner. "The low-tech end of the high-tech field!"

**consumer electronics**    A broad field of electronics that includes devices such as TVs, VCRs, radios, walkie-talkies, hi-fi stereo, home theater, handheld and software-based games, as well as Internet appliances and home computers.

**contact**    A metal strip in a switch or socket that touches a corresponding strip in order to make a connection for current to pass. Contacts may be made of precious metals to avoid corrosion.

**contact manager**    Software that keeps track of people and related activities. It is similar to a personal information manager (PIM), but is specialized for sales and service reps that make repetitive contact with prospects and customers. The foundation of a contact manager is a name and address database, from which phonecalls, meetings and to-do items are scheduled. The contact manager may also link each record to related e-mail messages and text documents.

**container**    (1) Software that acts as a parent program to hold and execute a set of commands or to run other software routines.

(2) A data structure that holds one or more different types of data. See *OLE*.

**content**    On the Internet, content is any information that is available for retrieval by the user, including Web pages, images, music, audio, white papers, driver and software downloads as well as training, educational and reference materials.

**An Act! Contact Record**
These screen shots are from the very popular Act! contact manager. Each contact is stored in a name and address record (top) from which activities are scheduled (bottom right). Activity history can be maintained (bottom left) or deleted as required.

**content aggregator**    An organization that combines information such as news, sports scores, weather forecasts and reference materials from various sources and makes it available to its customers. See *customer aggregator*.

**Content Alliance**    A membership organization founded in 2000 by Cisco, Network Appliance and major service providers to promote open standards for content peering. The alliance is expected to deliver a content peering protocol that enables interoperability between content delivery networks (CDN) so they can expand beyond current borders. The protocol is expected to define such attributes as source of content, quality of service expected and billing details, so that content distributed throughout the network can be billed to the content provider (the customer) after it is delivered. For more information, visit www.content-peering.org. See *content peering* and *CDN*.

**content delivery network**    See *CDN*.

**content filter**    See *Web filtering* and *parental control software*.

**contention**    A condition that arises when two devices attempt to use a single resource at the same time. See *CSMA/CD*.

**contention resolution**    Deciding which device gains access to a resource first when more than one wants it at the same time.

**content peering**    The ability for content delivery networks (CDNs) to interoperate so that smaller CDNs can form alliances and offer national and global service. See *Content Alliance*.

**content provider**   An organization or individual that creates information, educational or entertainment content for the Internet, CD-ROMs or other software-based products. A content provider may or may not provide the software used to access the material. See *content aggregator*.

**content server**   A computer that stores content for the Internet. Content (news, sports, references, etc.) is differentiated from transaction data such as customer records and orders. See *content*.

**context**   The current status, condition or mode of a system.

**context-sensitive help**   Help screens that provide specific information about the condition or mode the program is in at the time help is sought.

**context switching**   Same as *task switching*.

**contextual search**   To search for records or documents based upon the text contained in any part of the file as opposed to searching on a predefined key field.

**contiguous**   Adjacent or touching. Contrast with *fragmentation*.

**continuity check**   A test of a line, channel or circuit to determine if the pathway exists from beginning to end and can transmit signals.

**continuous carrier**   In communications, a carrier frequency that is transmitted even when data is not being sent over the line.

**continuous forms**   A roll of paper forms with perforations for separation into individual sheets after printing. See *pin feed* and *burster*.

**continuous tone**   A printing process that produces photographic-like output. In a continuous tone image, pixel patterns (individual dots) are either not visible or are barely visible under a magnifying glass. Various dye sublimation, CYCOLOR and laser technologies can provide up to 256 intensities of color and even blend the inks. See *contone printer*, *dye sublimation printer* and *CYCOLOR*.

**contone printer**   A laser printer that begins to approach continuous tone quality by varying the dot size. However, unlike continuous tone, which can blend inks more thoroughly, contone has a limited number of dot sizes, and dithering is still used to make up shades. See *continuous tone*.

**contrast**   The difference between the lightest and darkest areas on a display screen. Contrast with *brightness*.

**control**   A program module that enhances the functionality of a program. A control is often a user interface function. In the Windows environment, OLE controls and ActiveX controls are examples. See *OCX* and *ActiveX control*.

**control block**   A segment of disk or memory that contains a group of codes used for identification and control purposes.

**control break**   (1) A change of category used to trigger a subtotal.  For example, if data is subtotalled by state, a control break occurs when NJ changes to NM. See also *CTRL-BREAK*.

**control code**   One or more characters used as a command to control a device. The first 32 characters in the ASCII character set are control codes for communications and printers. There are countless codes used to control electronic devices. See *escape character*.

**Control Data**     (Control Data Systems, Inc., Arden Hills, MN, www.cdc.com) Control Data Corporation (CDC) was one of the first computer companies. Founded in 1957, Bill Norris was its president and guiding force. Its first computer, the 1604, was introduced in 1957 and delivered to the U.S. Navy Bureau of Ships.

For more than 30 years, the company was widely respected for its high-speed computers used heavily in government and scientific installations. Using the CYBER trade name, Control Data produced a complete line from workstations to mainframes. It also manufactured supercomputers.

In 1992, it spun off its military involvement into an independent company called Ceridian Corporation, and Control Data Corporation became Control Data Systems. Soon after, it ceased R&D of its proprietary computers. While providing maintenance for its installed base, it currently specializes in systems integration of UNIX-based computers from HP, Sun and SGI, which includes custom software, consulting services and facilities management.

**William C. Norris**
Norris founded and headed one of the most advanced computer companies in the industry. *(Image courtesy of Control Data Corporation.)*

**control field**     Same as *key field*.

**CONTROL key**     Abbreviated "CTRL" or "CTL." A keyboard key that is pressed with a letter or digit key to command the computer; for example, holding down CONTROL and pressing U, turns on underline in some word processors. The caret (SHIFT-6) symbol represents the CTRL key: ^Y means CTRL-Y.

**controller**     An electronic circuit board or system. In a personal computer, controllers contain the circuitry to run a peripheral device and are either contained on a plug-in expansion board or on the motherboard. Increasingly, plug-in boards for disk control, networking, sound, etc., are being replaced by built-in circuits (chips) on the motherboard. In larger computers, a controller may be contained on one or more boards or in a stand-alone cabinet.

**The 7600**
Control Data's 7600 was open in the middle, and its sides were like walls. You could walk into it from the rear, which is visible in this picture. *(Image courtesy of Control Data Corporation.)*

**controller card**     See *expansion board* and *control unit*.

**control network**     A network of sensors and actuators used for home automation and industrial control.

**control panel**     (1) A program used to change some setting in the operating system or computer. Control panels allow for changing keyboard and mouse sensitivity, speaker volume, display colors and resolution as well as modem, network and printer settings. Control panels are part of most operating systems, but also come with peripheral devices to allow fine tuning of particular features.

(2) A set of switches and dials used to operate a piece of equipment.

**control parallel**     Same as *MIMD*.

**control program**     Software that controls the operation of and has highest priority in a computer. Operating systems, network operating systems and network control programs are examples. Contrast with *application program*.

**control signal**     A pulse or frequency on a wire or fiber that is used to control something in a circuit. Control signals are often carried on dedicated lines that have a singular purpose such as starting or stopping a function.

**control total**     Same as *hash total*.

**control unit**   (1) Within the processor, the circuitry that locates, analyzes and executes each instruction in the program.

(2) Within the computer, hardware that performs the physical data transfers between memory and a peripheral device, such as a disk or screen. See *controller*.

**control variable**   In programming, a variable that keeps track of the number of iterations of a process. Its value is incremented or decremented with each iteration, and it is compared to a constant or other variable to test the end of the process or loop.

**conventional memory**   In a PC, the first 640K of memory. The next 384K is called the "UMA" (upper memory area). The term may also refer to the entire first megabyte (1,024K) of RAM, which is the memory that DOS can directly manage without the use of additional memory managers. See *DOS memory manager*.

**A Rather Large Control Unit**
This is the CPU control unit of the ILIAC IV computer in the 1960s. Today, the equivalent circuitry fits on the head of a pin. *(Image courtesy of The Computer Museum History Center, www.computerhistory.org)*

**conventional programming**   Writing a program in a traditional procedural language, such as assembly language or a high-level compiler language (C, Pascal, COBOL, FORTRAN, etc.).

**converged network**   The integration of the telephone system with IP-based data networks. See *softswitch*.

**convergence**   (1) The intersection of red, green and blue electron beams on one CRT pixel. Poor convergence decreases resolution and muddies white pixels.

(2) See *digital convergence*.

**conversational**   An interactive dialogue between the user and the computer.

**conversion**   (1) Data conversion is changing data from one file or database format to another. It may also require code conversion between ASCII and EBCDIC.

(2) Media conversion is changing storage media such as from tape to disk.

(3) Program conversion is changing the programming source language from one dialect to another, or changing application programs to link to a new operating system or DBMS.

(4) Computer system conversion is changing the computer model and peripheral devices.

(5) Information system conversion requires data conversion and either program conversion or the installation of newly purchased or created application programs.

**converter**   (1) A device that changes one set of codes, modes, sequences or frequencies to a different set. See *A/D converter*.

(2) A device that changes current from 60Hz to 50Hz, and vice versa.

**convolutional code**   A type of channel coding that adds patterns of redundancy to the data in order to improve the signal to noise ratio for more accurate decoding at the receiving end. The Viterbi algorithm is used to decode a particular type of convolutional code. See *Viterbi decoder*.

**COO**   (Cell Of Origin) See *mobile positioning*.

**cooked**   Processed. Said of data that has been manipulated in some manner. Contrast with *raw*.

**cookie**   Data created by a Web server that is stored on a user's computer. It provides a way for the Web site to keep track of a user's patterns and preferences and, with the cooperation of the Web browser, to store them on the user's own hard disk.

The cookies contain a range of URLs (addresses) for which they are valid. When the browser encounters those URLs again, it sends those specific cookies to the Web server. For example, if a user's ID were stored as a cookie, it would save that person from typing in the same information all over again when accessing that service for the second and subsequent time.

You can have your browser disable cookies or warn you before accepting a cookie. Look for the cookie options in your browser in the Options or Preferences menu.

**cookie file**   A file that contains cookies. Netscape saves cookies in a COOKIES.TXT file. Internet Explorer saves cookies in separate files in the Cookies folder. See *cookie* and *COOKIES.TXT*.

**COOKIES.TXT**   The name of the cookie file stored by Netscape Navigator in the Navigator folder (directory). See *cookie file*.

**COOL**   (1) A family of tools from Sterling Software for modeling and developing enterprise applications for every major hardware platform. COOL:Biz is an extensive business and data modeling tool. COOL:Gen is a modeling tool and application generator that turns COOL:Biz and COOL:Gen models into working code. COOL:Jex provides object-oriented analysis and design and program generation as well as UML support, and COOL:Specs is used to define object interfaces. Support only for COOL:Enterprise is provided (see *Key:Enterprise*).

(2) (Cool) Microsoft's code name for an object-oriented programming language that is expected to compete directly with Java.

**cooler**   See *CPU cooler*.

**cooperative multitasking**   Same as *non-preemptive multitasking*.

**cooperative processing**   Sharing a job among two or more computers such as a mainframe and a personal computer. It implies splitting the workload for the most efficiency.

**coopetition**   (**COOPE**ration compe**TITION**) Cooperation between competing companies. In the information field, coopetition means settling on standards and then developing products that compete with each other using those standards.

**coordinate**   Belonging to a system of indexing by two or more terms. For example, points on a plane, cells in a spreadsheet and bits in dynamic RAM chips are identified by a pair of coordinates. Points in space are identified by sets of three coordinates.

**Coordinated Universal Time**   See *UTC*.

**copper chip**   A chip that uses copper rather than aluminum in the top metalization layers, which interconnect all transistors and components together. Copper provides better performance, because it has less resistance than aluminum. Resistance increases as the lines (tracks) get smaller. In order to accomodate ever-decreasing die sizes, materials with inherent less resistance are required. Copper might have been used earlier, but it diffused into the silicon until IBM discovered a way to prevent that from happening. IBM delivered the first copper-based microprocessors in 1998. See *metalization layer*.

**Coppermine**   Intel's code name for Pentium III CPU chips that are the first to use the .18 micron (from .25 micron) manufacturing process. Coppermine chips are not copper chips. Coppermine chips were introduced in late 1999. See *future Intel chips*.

**copper trace**   See *circuit trace*.

**coprocessor**   A secondary processor used to speed up operations by handling some of the workload of the main CPU. See *math coprocessor* and *graphics coprocessor*.

**COPS**   (Common Open Policy Service) An IETF standard for exchanging policy information in a network. COPS allows routers and switches to reserve bandwidth based on organization policy, which stipulates the priority for individual users and groups. The policy data is stored in servers known as "policy decision points" (PDPs). Routers and switches, known as "policy enforcement points" (PEPs), query the PDPs for the required information. COPS supports the RSVP protocol for reserving bandwidth. See *RSVP*.

**copy**    To make a duplicate of the original. In digital electronics, all copies are identical, which is, of course, both a blessing and a curse. The blessing is that data can be maintained and remanufactured accurately forever. The curse is that anyone can duplicate copyrighted material and send it around the world in seconds.

The text in this database takes up approximately four megabytes. During the course of writing and updating it, the text has been copied hundreds of times, causing billions of bits to be transmitted between disk and memory. Just to show that things aren't entirely perfect, a character does get garbled every once in a while. We'll have to settle for 99.999999% instead of 100%!

**copy and paste**    To copy text or an image from one document to another. All graphical-based operating systems (Mac, Windows, etc.) have copy and paste capability that is usually selected from an Edit menu. See *clipboard, cut and paste* and *Win Copy between windows*.

**copy buster**    A program that bypasses the copy protection scheme in a software program and allows normal, unprotected copies to be made.

**copy protection**    The ability to prevent unauthorized copying of software. Copy protection was never a serious issue with mainframes and minicomputers, since vendor support has always been vital in those environments. As personal computer software becomes more complex, technical support becomes just as crucial, requiring users to own valid copies of the product in order to obtain it.

In the early days of floppy-based personal computers, many copy protection methods were used. However, with each scheme introduced, a copy buster program was developed to get around it. When hard disks became the norm, copy protection was abolished. In order to manage a hard disk, files must be easily copied from one part of the disk to another.

This is a constant dilemma for software vendors as well as the publishing and broadcasting industries that transmit their content via digital means. Every recipient of a digitally-distributed medium has the ability to reproduce a perfect copy of the original.

The only copy protection system that works is the hardware key, which is a plug and socket that is attached to the computer's parallel port with a unique serial number that the software identifies. Hardware keys are used to protect high-priced software, but users are generally not fond of them, because it requires unplugging the printer cable, inserting the hardware key, and plugging back the printer.

A system similar to the hardware key designed into the personal computer from day one should have been established. Perhaps some day a solid state software capsule with a digital signature will plug into the computer. In the meantime, anyone who can figure out an economical way to prevent unauthorized duplication of digital material that does not interfere with managing a hard disk or the quality of the original transmission will become a zillionaire overnight!

**copyrights**    See *DRM* and *image protection*.

**CORBA**    (Common Object Request Broker Architecture) A standard from the Object Management Group (OMG) for communicating between distributed objects (objects are self-contained software modules). CORBA provides a way to execute programs (objects) written in different programming languages running on different platforms no matter where they reside in the network. CORBA is suited for three-tier (or more) client/server applications, where processing occurring in one computer requires processing to be performed in another. CORBA is often described as an "object bus" or "software bus," because it is a software-based communications interface through which objects are located and accessed.

Technically, CORBA is the communications component of the Object Management Architecture (OMA), which defines other elements such as naming services, security and transaction services. However, CORBA is the term everybody uses to refer to OMA.

CORBA objects are defined by an Interface Definition Language (IDL) that describes the processing (methods) the object performs and the format of the data sent and returned. There is an IDL compiler for each programming language such as C, C++, Java, Smalltalk and COBOL, which lets programmers use familiar constructs, and both client and

C

server applications talk to each other in their respective programming languages. IDL definitions are stored in the Interface Repository, which can be queried by a client application to determine what objects are available on the bus.

At runtime, a CORBA client makes requests to remote CORBA objects via an Object Request Broker (ORB). The ORB provides a proxy object in the client's address space, which creates the illusion that the remote object is a local one. The client and server communicate by exchanging messages defined by the General Inter-ORB Protocol (GIOP). When a client calls a CORBA operation, the client ORB sends a GIOP message to the server. The server ORB converts the request into a call on the server object and then returns the results in a GIOP reply. Finally, the client ORB converts the reply into a normal object reply (method return) for the client application.

GIOP is independant of any specific network transport. However, when GIOP is sent over TCP/IP, it is called IIOP (Internet Inter-ORB protocol.)

The first version of CORBA provided the IDL and standard mappings to just a few languages such as C. CORBA 2 added more language mappings (in particular C++ and Java) as well as GIOP, which allows ORBs from different vendors to interoperate.

CORBA 3 adds firewall standards for communicating over the Internet, quality of service parameters and CORBAcomponents, which enables programmers to activate fundamental services at a higher level. CORBAcomponents also provides interoperability with Sun's Enterprise JavaBeans (EJBs).

Microsoft's counterpart to CORBA is its COM objects and Distributed COM (DCOM) architecture. The OMG defines interoperability specifications for both COM and DCOM. Great demand for DCOM/CORBA interoperability is not expected, but COM/CORBA interoperability is required to integrate a Windows desktop environment into a CORBA-based enterprise system. There are many vendors of CORBA ORBs on the market. IONA's Orbix and Borland's VisiBroker are popular examples.

**cordless phone**    A portable telephone that transmits to and receives signals from a base station within a range of a few hundred feet. Cordless phones differ from cellphones, which can be moved over vast geographical distances. See *multihandset cordless*, *cellphone*, *DECT* and *PAN*.

**core**    (1) The heart, or central part, of something. The core of a network is its central backbone. The core of a microprocessor chip is its primary processing circuits. A core program would be the primary routines necessary for a larger application (see *kernel*).

(2) A round magnetic doughnut that represents one bit in a core storage system. A computer's main memory used to be referred to as core. See *core storage*.

**core dump**    Same as *memory dump*.

**core frequency**    The clock speed of the CPU, which is generally significantly higher than the speed of the buses that connect to it. See *system bus*.

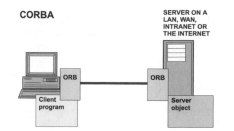

**CORBA**

**One Program Calls Another**
The basic concept is simple: one program calls upon another for its services no matter where it is located. CORBA provides a complete messaging environment for executing remote objects written in multiple languages and running on different platforms.

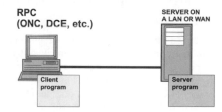

**RPC (ONC, DCE, etc.)**

**Remote Procedure Calls**
RPCs, which have been around for some time, are similar to CORBA, although not as comprehensive. They tend to support one programming language and one platform.

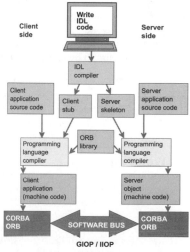

**CORBA Object Creation**
CORBA objects are created by compiling IDL definitions into the client and server code. The resulting applications communicate with each via the CORBA bus using the GIOP or IIOP protocols.

**Corel**   (Corel Corporation, Ottawa, Ontario, Canada, www.corel.com)  Canada's leading software company, founded in 1985 by Dr. Michael Cowpland. For many years, it has been widely known for its award-winning CorelDRAW suite of graphics programs for Windows, Mac and UNIX. Corel offers a variety of business programs, including application suites that include WordPerfect and Quattro Pro. In 1996, it acquired the WordPerfect family of software from Novell. Corel also produces a complete line of publishing tools for the Internet and has invested heavily in the Linux movement.

**CorelDRAW**   A suite of Windows graphics applications from Corel. CorelDRAW was originally a drawing program introduced in 1989, which became popular due to its speed and ease of use. As of CorelDRAW 5, it became a complete suite of applications for image editing, charting and presentations as well as desktop publishing with the inclusion of Corel VENTURA.

**Corel Office**   A suite of applications for Windows from Corel that includes WordPerfect, Quattro Pro, Paradox, Presentations, CorelDRAW, CorelFLOW and a variety of additional applets. Corel Office was superseded by Corel WordPerfect Suite.

**core logic**   The primary processing logic of a component, function or system. For example, a PC chipset provides all the core logic on the motherboard except for the CPU. See *chipset*.

**Corel Paradox**   A relational database management (DBMS) and application development system for DOS and Windows from Corel. It includes the PAL programming language for writing complex business applications. When Paradox was originally released under DOS, it was noted for its visual query by example method, which made asking questions much easier than comparable products of the time. Originally developed by Ansa Corporation, it was later acquired by Borland and then Corel.

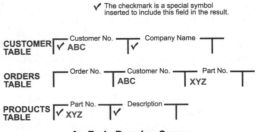

**An Early Paradox Query**
In the mid 1980s, Paradox was the first DBMS on a PC that make linking tables easier. The ability to associate relationships by typing sample words was a breakthrough for that time. The Customer No. and Part No. fields are linked by pressing a function key and typing in the common words "ABC" and "XYZ". Any words suffice as long as they are the same.

**Corel Quattro Pro**   A Windows spreadsheet from Corel that provides advanced graphics and presentation capabilities, including goal seeking, 3-D graphing and the ability to create multi-layered slide shows. It is optionally keystroke compatible with Lotus 1-2-3. Quattro Pro was originally developed by Borland, then purchased by Novell in 1994 and Corel in 1996.

**Corel VENTURA**   A Windows desktop publishing program from Corel. It is a full-featured program suited for producing books and other long documents and includes several graphics functions from CorelDRAW. Corel VENTURA was formerly Ventura Publisher, developed by a company that was later acquired by Xerox. The early versions were available for DOS, Windows, OS/2 and the Mac. In 1993, Corel acquired it and enhanced it.

**Corel WordPerfect**   A full-featured word processing program for Windows from Corel. It is a sophisticated program that has been widely used on many platforms since its inception on the IBM PC in 1982. Under its original developer, WordPerfect became the leading word processor in the late 1980s. The company and product was acquired by Novell and later by Corel. See *WordPerfect Corporation*.

**Corel WordPerfect Suite**   A suite of office applications for Windows from Corel that includes Corel WordPerfect, Corel Quattro Pro, Corel Presentations, Corel Paradox, CorelCENTRAL (PIM, scheduling and integrated Netscape Communicator) and additional utilities. It is the successor to Corel Office.

**core router**   A router that resides within the middle or backbone of the network rather than at its periphery. See *edge router*.

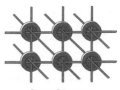

**co-resident**   A program or module that resides in memory along with other programs.

**core speed**   The speed of the CPU, measured in MHz. The term "core" refers to the center, or nucleus, of the computer, which is its CPU. See *bus/core ratio*.

**core storage**   A non-volatile memory that holds magnetic charges in ferrite cores about 1/16th" diameter. The direction of the flux determines the 0 or 1. Developed in the late 1940s by Jay W. Forrester and Dr. An Wang, it was used extensively in the 1950s and 1960s. Since it holds its content without power, it is still used in specialized applications in the military and in space vehicles.

In 1956, IBM paid Dr. Wang $500,000 for his patent on core memories, which he used to expand his company, Wang Laboratories. See *MRAM* and ***early memories***.

**Cores from the Whirlwind**
In 1952, this core plane from the Whirlwind I computer held 256 bits of memory. Today's memory chips occupying the same amount of space hold billions of bits. *(Image courtesy of The MITRE Corporation Archives.)*

**Core Storage**
Core storage is why the internal workspace of the computer is called "memory." Like magnetic disks, magnetic cores hold their content without power.

**Core System**   The first proposed standard for computer graphics, developed by the Graphics Standards Planning Committee of SIGGRAPH and used in the late 1970s and early 1980s. Its objectives were portability of programs between computers and the separation of modeling graphics from viewing graphics. Almost all features of the Core System were incorporated into the ANSI-endorsed GKS standard.

**corona wire**   A charged wire in a laser printer that draws the toner off the drum onto the paper. It must be cleaned when the toner cartridge is replaced.

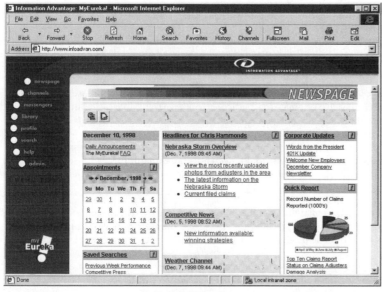

**Portal Software**
Products such as Information Advantage's MyEureka provide out-of-the-box portal software that can be customized. This example is a page that delivers news and links to pages and sites of personal interest. *(Screen shot courtesy of Information Advantage, Inc.)* See *MyEureka*.

**corporate portal**   An internal Web site (intranet) that provides proprietary, enterprise-wide information to company employees, as well as access to selected public Web sites and vertical-market Web sites (suppliers, vendors, etc.). It includes a search engine for internal documents and the ability to customize the portal page for different user groups and individuals. It is the internal equivalent of the general-purpose portal on the Web. See *portal, vertical portal* and *business intelligence portal*.

**Corporation for Open Systems**   An R&D consortium, founded in 1986, that was dedicated to assuring acceptance of worldwide standards. It closed 10 years later.

**correlation**   In statistics, a measure of the strength of the relationship between two variables. It is used to predict the value of one variable given the value of the other.

For example, a correlation might relate distance from urban location to gasoline consumption. Expressed on a scale from –1.0 to +1.0, the strongest correlations are at both extremes and provide the best predictions. See *regression analysis*.

**corrupted file**    A data or program file that has been altered accidentally by hardware or software failure. It causes the bits to be rearranged and renders it either unreadable to the hardware or readable, but indecipherable to the program.

**corruption**    Altering of data or programs due to viruses, hardware or software failure or power failure. See *data recovery*.

**COS**    (1) See *class of service*.
(2) (**C**ray **O**perating **S**ystem) An operating system used in Cray computers.
(3) See *Corporation for Open Systems*.

**cost-based query optimizer**    Software that optimizes an SQL query for the fastest processing, based on the size of the file and other variables.

**cost/benefits analysis**    The study that projects the costs and benefits of a new information system. Costs include people and machine resources for development as well as running the system.

Tangible benefits are derived by estimating the cost savings of both human and machine resources to run the new system versus the old one. Intangible benefits, such as improved customer service and employee relations, may ultimately provide the largest payback, but are harder to quantify.

**COTS**    (**C**ommercial **O**ff-**T**he-**S**helf) Refers to ready-made merchandise that is available for sale.

**counter**    (1) In programming, a variable that is used to keep track of anything that must be counted. The programming language determines the number of counters (variables) that are available to a programmer.
(2) In electronics, a circuit that counts pulses and generates an output at a specified time.

**counter-rotating ring**    See *dual counter-rotating ring*.

**country code**    A two-character component of an e-mail or Web address that identifies a country. Computers read addresses from right to left. Thus, on encountering **sven@univ.oslo.net.se**, the message would first be sent to Sweden, since **se** is the country code for Sweden. Swedish routers would then send the message to **univ.oslo.net** where it will be waiting for Sven the next time he signs on.

Some search engines (AltaVista and Infoseek, among others) let you specify country codes in your search. This comes in handy when you want to locate (or avoid) sites that originate in a particular country. To find Web sites originating in France and devoted to French wines, for example, you might try an AltaVista search for **+wine +domain:fr**. To do the same thing with Infoseek, try **+wine +site:fr**.

If a particular search turns up many sites in a language you can't understand, say Japanese, just do the search again and avoid all sites with the country code **jp**. On AltaVista, that would mean adding **-domain:jp** to your search request. On Infoseek, add **-site:jp**. See *country codes A–E*, *country codes F–M* and *country codes N–Z*. For a unique way to profit from a country code, see *dotTV*.

**Coupling Facility**    The hardware and software that turns an IBM mainframe Base Sysplex system into a Parallel Sysplex. It is comprised of special microcode built into the machine, and the CFCC operating system (Coupling Facility Control Code). It can be implemented as a stand-alone machine, in an LPAR logical partition or in a spare processor that becomes an Internal Coupling Facility (ICF).

The Coupling Facility allows up to 32 coupled systems to communicate using three coupling structures: "list" for simple data, "cache" for data buffering and "lock" for control of access to ensure data integrity. See *Parallel Sysplex*.

**Courier modem**    A modem from U.S. Robotics (now 3Com) that supports standard and proprietary protocols for analog communications. Field upgradable, Courier modems gained a solid reputation for excellence and reliability over the years.

**courseware**    Educational software. See *CBT*.

**covert channel**    A transfer of information that violates a computer's built-in security systems. A covert storage channel refers to depositing information in a memory or storage location that can be accessed by different security clearances. A covert timing channel is the manipulation of a system resource in such a way that it can be detected by another process.

**CP**    **(1)** (Copy Protected)  See *copy protection*.
   **(2)** (Central Processor)  See *processor* and *CPU*.
   **(3)** See *control program*.

**CPA**    (Computer Press Association, Landing, NJ, www.computerpress.org)  An organization founded in 1983 that promotes excellence in computer journalism. Its annual awards honor outstanding examples in print, broadcast and electronic media.

**cPCI**    See *CompactPCI*.

**CPE**    (Customer Premises Equipment)  Communications equipment that resides on the customer's premises.

**CPF**    (Control Program Facility)  The IBM System/38 operating system that included an integrated relational DBMS.

**CPGA**    (Ceramic PGA)  See *PGA*.

**cpi**    **(1)** (Characters Per Inch)  The measurement of the density of characters per inch on tape or paper. A printer's CPI button switches character pitch.
   **(2)** (Counts Per Inch)  The measurement of the resolution of a mouse/trackball as flywheel notches per inch (horizontal and vertical flywheels rotate as the ball is moved). Notches are converted to cursor movement.
   **(3)** (CPI) (Common Programming Interface)  See *SAA* and *CPI-C*.

**CPI-C**    (Common Programming Interface for Communications)  A general-purpose communications interface under IBM's SAA. Using APPC verbs as its foundation, it provides a common programming interface across IBM platforms. See *APPC*.

**CPLD**    (Complex PLD)  A programmable logic device that includes a reprogrammable interconnect between the logic blocks. CPLDs are mostly EEPROM and flash based. See *PLD*.

**CP/M**    (Control Program for Microprocessors)  A single user operating system for the 8080 and Z80 microprocessors from Caldera. Created by Gary Kildall of Digital Research, CP/M had its heyday in the early 1980s; however, as we enter the twenty-first century, it is still being used.

CP/M was an unsophisticated program that didn't instill too much confidence in users, yet it was a major contributor to the personal computer revolution. Because the industry never standardized on a CP/M disk or video format, software publishers had to support dozens of screen displays and floppy disk versions. This chaos helped IBM set the standard with its PC in a very short time.

Although IBM asked Kildall to provide the operating system for its new PC, he didn't agree to certain demands. IBM went to Microsoft, which purchased QDOS from Seattle Computer Products and turned it into PC-DOS and MS-DOS. The rest is history. The irony is that DOS was modeled after CP/M. Digital Research was later acquired by Novell and then Caldera.

**The Otrona Attache**
Introduced in 1982, the Attache was the smallest CP/M portable computer on the market. Weighing 17 pounds and priced at $5,000, the Attache became a kind of cult computer used by prominent people worldwide. *(Image courtesy of Robin Bartlett.)*

**CPM**    **(1)** (Critical Path Method)  A project management planning and control technique implemented on computers. The critical path is the series of activities and tasks in the project that have no built-in slack time. Any task in the critical path that takes longer than expected will lengthen the total time of the project.

**(2)** (Cost Per Milli or Mille) Refers to the cost for a thousand of something. For example, banner ads on the Web, which are also known as "impressions," are typically sold on a CPM basis. See *banner ad*.

**(3)** (Copies Per Minute) The rated speed of a computer printer or copy machine.

**CPO** (Chief Privacy Officer) An individual that manages the privacy issues within an organization. Arising out of the privacy regulations in finance and health care in the late 1990s, the CPO position eventually crossed over to all industries. The CPO, typically an attorney, is involved with setting privacy policy which determines how much information should be collected and how much can be shared both inside and outside of the company. An organization's privacy policy is often stated on its Web site. See *privacy* and *P3P*.

**cps** **(1)** (Characters Per Second) The measurement of the speed of a serial printer or the speed of a data transfer between hardware devices or over a communications channel. CPS is equivalent to bytes per second.

**(2)** (CPS—Certified Product Specialist) See *Microsoft certification*.

**CPU** (Central Processing Unit) The computing part of the computer. Also called the "processor," it is made up of the control unit and ALU. Today, the CPUs of almost all computers are contained on a single chip.

The CPU, clock and main memory make up a computer. A complete computer system requires the addition of control units, input, output and storage devices and an operating system.

**From the Mainframe Point of View** Computer professionals involved with mainframes and minicomputers often refer to the whole computer as the CPU, in which case, CPU refers to the processor, memory (RAM) and I/O architecture (channels or buses).

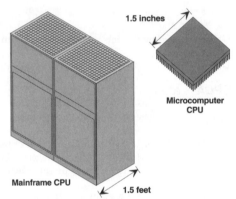

**Microcomputer CPU**

**Mainframe CPU**

1.5 inches

1.5 feet

**CPUs Come in Different Sizes**
Depending on which end of the field you are in, a CPU can mean the processor, memory and everything inside the cabinet, or just the microprocessor itself.

**CPU bound** Same as *process bound*.

**CPU cache** See *cache*.

**CPU chip** Same as *microprocessor*.

**CPU clock** See *clock*.

**CPU cooler** A device that keeps the CPU chip at a cooler temperature. The simplest type is a heat sink, which is a metal cover that provides a larger surface area for heat dissipation. A CPU fan is more effective than a heat sink, because it directs air movement over the chip. The most effective is a refrigeration system that can cause the chip to run at increased performance.

**CPU ID** The identification of a particular CPU. One of Intel's x86 instructions is CPU-ID, which is executed to find out what the capabilities and performance level of the current machine are.

**CPUmark** See *Winbench*.

**CPU speed** See *MHz*.

**CPU time** The amount of time it takes for the CPU to execute a set of instructions and generally excludes the waiting time for input and output.

**CQFP** See *QFP*.

**CR** (Carriage Return) The character code generated when the return (enter) key is pressed. In ASCII and EBCDIC systems, it is a decimal 13 (hex 0D). See *RETURN key*.

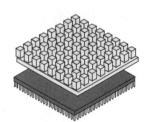

**Heat Sink**
The simplest CPU cooler is an aluminum heat sink. Rather than a flat lump of metal, heat sinks are designed with hills and valleys in order to provide more surface area to make contact with the air.

**cracker**     A person that breaks into a computer system without authorization, whose purpose is to do damage (destroy files, steal credit card numbers, plant viruses, etc.). See *hacker*.

**cramming**     The unauthorized addition of services to your telephone bill such as an 800 number that you never ordered. The charges are usually noted on the bill, but are identified in a cryptic manner and/or are printed in a place that is easy to overlook. See *slamming*.

**crapplet**     A really terrible and useless Java applet. See *applet*.

**crash**     See *abend* and *head crash*.

**crash recovery**     The ability to automatically correct a hardware, software or line failure.

**crawler**     Also known as a "spider," "ant," "robot" ("bot") and "intelligent agent," a crawler is a program that searches for information on the World Wide Web. It is used to locate new documents and new sites by following hypertext links from server to server and indexing information based on search criteria.

**Cray**     (Cray, Inc., Seattle, WA, www.cray.com)  A supercomputer manufacturer founded in 1972 as Cray Research, Inc., by Seymour Cray, a leading designer of large-scale computers at Control Data. In 1976, it shipped its first computer to Los Alamos National Laboratory. The CRAY-1 was a 75MHz, 64-bit machine with a peak speed of 160 megaflops, making it the world's fastest vector processor.

Over the years the company has introduced numerous models of entry-level to high-end supercomputers including the X-MP, Y-MP, C90, T90, J90, T3E, SV1, SV2 and MTA series. All UNIX based, they are used for many different industrial, technical and commercial applications.

In 1989, Seymour Cray left his company to found Cray Computer Corporation, which closed six years later. In 1996, Cray Research was acquired by Silicon Graphics, Inc. (SGI). In 2000, Tera Computer Company acquired the vector processor technology from SGI and changed its name to Cray, Inc.

**The Cray 1**
In the late 1970s, the Cray 1 became synonymous with high-speed computing. It was often photographed for "space-age" computer shots because of its science fiction silhouette.
*(Image courtesy of Cray Research, Inc.)*

**Seymour Cray**
Cray became famous for his supercomputers, and his passion for high-speed computing led to many innovative designs. Cray died in 1996 at the age of 71, due to injuries in an automobile accident. *(Image courtesy of Cray Research, Inc.)*

**Cray Computer**     The Colorado Springs-based supercomputer company founded in 1989 by Seymour Cray after he left Cray Research. Cray developed the Cray-3, an incredibly fast gallium arsenide-based computer that ran at a 1GHz clock rate. With the Cray-4 sitting in the wings, the company was unable to attract customers for the new products and closed its doors in 1995.

**Cray Research**     See *Cray*.

(Cyclical Redundancy Checking)  An error checking technique used to ensure the accuracy of transmitting digital data. The transmitted messages are divided into predetermined lengths which, used as dividends, are divided by a fixed divisor. The remainder of the calculation is appended onto and sent with the message. At the receiving end, the computer recalculates the remainder. If it does not match the transmitted remainder, an error is detected.

**CRC cards**     (Class Responsibility Collaboration card)  An object-oriented design method that uses ordinary 3x5 index cards. Developed by Ward Cunningham at Textronix, a card is made for each class containing responsibilities (knowledge and services) and collaborators (interactions with other objects). The cards provide an informal, intuitive way for group members to work on object design together.

For a book on CRC cards that provides a clear introduction to object concepts and modeling, read *Using CRC Cards* by Nancy Wilkinson, published by SIGS BOOKS, ISBN 1-884842-07-0.

**Creative Labs**    (Creative Labs, Inc., Milpitas, CA, www.creativelabs.com) A leading manufacturer of sound cards and products that was founded in 1988 by Sim Wong Hoo. It introduced the Sound Blaster card in 1989, which has become a de facto standard.

**creative market**    The world of graphics design, which includes artists, illustrators, copywriters, photographers and page layout professionals (compositors) in ad agencies, publishing companies and inhouse corporate design departments. The Macintosh is the preferred computer in this market.

**crippled version**    Software that has certain features disabled because it is used as shareware or as a demo of the full version.

**crippleware**    Demonstration software with built-in limitations; for example, a database package that lets only 50 records be entered.

**criteria range**    Conditions for selecting records; for example, "Illinois customers with balances over $10,000."

**critical ratio**    An index used to determines how much a task is on schedule. A value of 1.0 is "on schedule." A value less than 1.0 is behind, and larger than 1.0 is ahead of schedule. The critical ratio is derived by dividing the time to scheduled completion by the time expected to finish it.

**CR/LF**    (Carriage Return/Line Feed) The end of line characters used in standard PC text files (ASCII decimal 13 10, hex 0D 0A). In the Mac, only the CR is used; in UNIX, the LF.

**CRM**    (Customer Relationship Management) An integrated information system that is used to plan, schedule and control the presales and postsales activities in an organization. Although the dividing lines are not crystal clear, CRM generally does not include the marketing function and could be said to be enterprise relationship management (ERM) without the marketing component. Sales force automation (SFA) evolved into CRM, which became a greatly hyped buzzword by the turn of the century.

The clear objective for CRM is to enable a customer to interact with a company through various means including the Web, telephone, fax, e-mail and snail mail and receive a consistent level of quality service. The integration of all activities means that an order placed by phone can be tracked on the Web and vice versa. See *ERM* and *sales force automation*.

**cron**    A UNIX utility (UNIX daemon) that executes commands in a crontab file at a specified time and date. Cron is used to schedule such functions as backup and maintenance procedures.

**crontab file**    A file of instructions used by the UNIX cron utility. See *cron*.

**crop marks**    Printed lines on paper used to cut the form into its intended size.

**cross assembler**    An assembler that generates machine language for a different type of computer than the one the assembler is running in. It is used to develop programs for computers on a chip or microprocessors used in specialized applications that are either too small or are otherwise incapable of handling the development software.

**crossbar switch**    An earlier telephone switch. First used in the late 1930s, it was a mechanical device that used magnets and metal bars (crossbars) to close connections. Crossbar switches have been replaced with electronic switches (large-scale, specialized computer systems). See *ESS* and *DMS*. See also *crosspoint switch*.

C

**cross compiler** A compiler that generates machine language for a different type of computer than the one the compiler is running in. See *cross assembler*.

**crossfoot** A numerical error checking technique that compares the sum of the columns with the sum of the rows.

**crosshatch** A criss-crossed pattern used to fill in sections of a drawing to distinguish them from each other.

**cross-linked file** A file system error that corrupts the contents of an existing file by writing data from another file into the same cluster. Running ScanDisk or a similar program cleans up the problem, but one of the files is no longer usable. See *ScanDisk* and *cluster*.

**cross media** (1) Advertising in all media including radio, TV, direct mail, magazines, newspapers and the Web.
(2) Same as *cross promotion*.

**cross memory services** The method used by MVS (OS/390) applications for linking to various operating system services. "Cross memory" means that the called routines reside in different address spaces than the calling program. They can even be in another computer. Rather than using a fixed address, cross memory services use a method of indirection whereby the calling program obtains a token that serves as a pointer to the actual routine. Cross memory services adds a more efficient approach than the supervisor call instruction that was initially the only method applications used to call the operating system.

NORMAL CROSSOVER WITHIN HUB OR SWITCH
The transmit line from one node must be accepted by the receive line of the recipient machine. The crossover port (MDI-X port) performs this reversal.

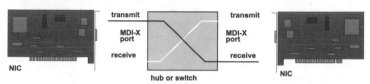

CROSSOVER NOT CORRECTLY MAINTAINED BETWEEN TWO HUBS OR SWITCHES
When two hubs or switches are connected, a regular cable cannot be used. Trace the route below, and note that transmit and receive do not wind up reversed as they should be.

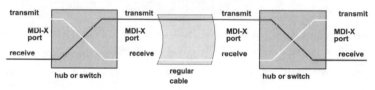

CROSSOVER MAINTAINED CORRECTLY WITH CROSSOVER CABLE
A crossover cable crosses the lines so that it reverses the reversal performed by the MDI-X ports.

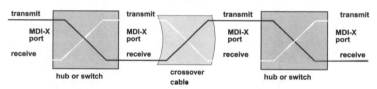

CROSSOVER MAINTAINED CORRECTLY WITH MDI PORT AND REGULAR CABLE
An MDI port (uplink port) does not reverse the lines, allowing two devices to be connected.

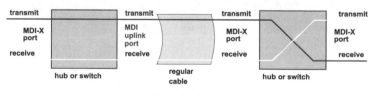

**Crossing Over!**
The whole idea is to put the transmitted data onto the receive line of the receiving machine.

**crossover cable** A network cable that crosses the transmit and receive lines. It is used to connect hubs and switches together using standard MDI-X ports, which are already crossover ports. The crossover cable crosses the lines first so that after the MDI-X crosses the lines, they are effectively back to a non-crossed condition. See *MDI port* and *null modem cable*.

**cross platform** Refers to developing for and/or running on more than one type of hardware platform. It implies two different processes. The first is programming source code that is compiled into different machine environments, each of which has to be supported separately. For example, a software vendor may decide its application should run on a Windows NT and HP server, in which case it would compile once into Windows NT and again for HP/UX. Both environments would be tested separately. While a single set of source code might be the ideal, there are typically differences in the source code to optimize running in the target machine, requiring either two sets of source code or one set with alternate changes embedded within.

The second method is with the use of an interpreter such as the Java Virtual Machine. Java is said to be cross platform, because a program's source code is compiled into an intermediate "bytecode" language. As long as a Java interpreter (Java Virtual Machine) is written for and installed on any computer, the Java bytecode is expected to be executed in the same manner on that computer. The problems arise when the Java interpreter is not as up to date as the Java development system that created the program or the Java interpreters are not faithfully interpreting the bytecode according to the same standard. See *multiple platforms*.

**crosspoint switch**    Also known as a crossbar or NxN switch, it is a switching device that provides for a fixed number of inputs and outputs. For example, a 32x32 switch is able to keep 32 nodes communicating at full speed to 32 other nodes.

**cross post**    To send the same message to several newsgroups.

**cross promotion**    Advertising a Web site using traditional media such as radio, TV and magazines. Same as "offline advertising" and "cross media." See *branding*.

**cross software**    Software that is developed on one type of computer, but used on another. See *cross assembler* and *cross compiler*.

**cross tabulate**    To analyze and summarize data. A common example is summarizing the details from database records and placing them into a spreadsheet. The following example places the details of order records into summary form.

```
Transactions Being Cross Tabbed

Date          Customer        Quantity
1- 7-93       Smith              7
1-13-93       Jones             12
2- 5-93       Gonzales           4
2-11-93       Fetzer             6
3-10-93       Smith             12
3-22-93       Gonzales          15


Results of Cross Tab

Customer      Jan     Feb     Mar     Total
Smith          7              12       19
Jones         12                       12
Gonzales               4      15       19
Fetzer                 6                6

Total         19      10      27       56
```

**crosstalk**    (1) In communications, interference from an adjacent channel.

(2) (Crosstalk) A family of communications programs for DOS and Windows from Attachmate Corporation, Bellevue, WA, (www.attachmate.com). Crosstalk products were originally developed by Microstuf, Inc., later merged with DCA and then Attachmate. It was one of the first personal computer communications programs, originating in the CP/M days. Crosstalk uses the Crosstalk Application Script Language (CASL).

**CRT**    (Cathode Ray Tube) A vacuum tube used as a display screen in a video terminal or TV. The term more often refers to the entire monitor rather than just the tube itself. Years ago, CRT was the popular term for the display screen. Today, monitor is the preferred term. See *monitor*, *VGA* and *flat panel display*.

**CRUD**    (**C**reate, **R**etrieve, **U**pdate, **D**elete) The basic processes that are applied to data.

**crudware**    Derogatory reference to the large amount of free software which is typically handed out at users groups and similar venues. See *wares*.

**crunch**    (**1**) To process data. See *number crunching*.
  (**2**) To compress data. See *data compression*.

**Crusoe processor**    An x86-based CPU chip from Transmeta that is designed for Internet appliances and other handheld devices that require batteries. It consumes significantly less power than mobile x86 chips from Intel, AMD and others because it places more of the processing burden on the software. Designed to run Windows and Linux applications, Crusoe uses a software translation layer known as "Code Morphing" that turns x86 instructions into Crusoe instructions. This translation layer allows the chip to be used for other instruction sets as well. See *Transmeta*.

**cryogenics**    Using materials that operate at very cold temperatures. See *superconductor*.

**cryptography**    The conversion of data into a secret code for transmission over a public network. The original text, or "plaintext," is converted into a coded equivalent called "ciphertext" via an encryption algorithm. The ciphertext is decoded (decrypted) at the receiving end and turned back into plaintext.

The encryption algorithm uses a key, which is a binary number that is typically from 40 to 128 bits in length. The greater the number of bits in the key (cipher strength), the more possible key combinations and the longer it would take to break the code. The data is encrypted, or "locked," by combining the bits in the key mathematically with the data bits. At the receiving end, the key is used to "unlock" the code and restore the original data.

Secret vs. Public Key    There are two cryptographic methods. The traditional method uses a secret key, such as the DES standard. Both sender and receiver use the same key to encrypt and decrypt. This is the fastest method, but transmitting the secret key to the recipient in the first place is not secure.

The second method is public-key cryptography, such as RSA, which uses both a private and a public key. Each recipient has a private key that is kept secret and a public key that is published for everyone. The sender looks up the recipient's public key and uses it to encrypt the message. The recipient uses the private key to decrypt the message.

Owners never have a need to transmit their private keys to anyone in order to have their messages decrypted, thus the private keys are not in transit and are not vulnerable.

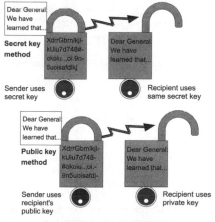

Sometimes, both DES and RSA are used together. DES provides the fastest decryption, and RSA provides a convenient method for transmitting the secret key. Both the DES-encrypted text message and the secret key needed to decrypt it are sent via the RSA method. This is called a "digital envelope."

Cryptography methods change as computers get faster. It has been said that any encryption code can be broken given enough computer time to derive all of the permutations. However, if it takes months to break a code, the war could be won or lost, or the financial transaction has little meaning. As computers get faster, the keys get longer and the algorithms become more complex to stay ahead of the game. See *DES*, *RSA*, *digital signature*, *digital certificate* and *steganography*.

A Little History    The following is reprinted with permission from RSA Data Security, Inc.

In 1518, a Benedictine monk named Johannes Trithemius wrote Polygraphiae, the first published treatise on cryptography. Later, his text Steganographia described a cipher in which each letter is represented by words in successive columns of text, designed to hide inconspicuously inside a seemingly pious book of prayer.

**Secret Key vs. Public Key**
The secret method uses the same key to encrypt and decrypt. The problem is transmitting the key to the recipient in order to use it. The public key method uses two keys. One kept secret and never transmitted, and the other made public. Very often, the public key method is used to safely send the secret key to the recipient so that the message can be encrypted using the faster secret key algorithm.

Polygraphiae and Steganographia attracted a considerable amount of attention not only for their meticulous analysis of ciphers but more notable for the unexpected thesis of Steganographia's third and final section, which claimed that messages communicated secretly were aided in their transmission by a host of summoned spirits.

As might be expected, Trithemius' works were widely renounced as having magical content, by no means an unfamiliar theme in cryptographic history, and a century later fell victim to the zealous flames of the Inquisition during which they were banned as heretical sorcery.

**cryptology**    The science of developing secret codes and/or the use of those codes in encryption systems. See *cryptography*.

**crypto rage**    The online equivalent of "road rage," where people vent their anger by breaking into computer systems and/or writing viruses.

**crystal**    A transparent quartz material that contains a uniform arrangement of molecules. See *crystalline* and *quartz crystal*.

**crystalline**    Like a crystal. It imples a uniform structure of molecules in all dimensions. For example, the crystalline state of a spot on a rewritable optical disk means that the laser beam will be reflected from it, in contrast to an amorphous state that will not reflect light. See *amorphous* and *nematic*.

**Crystal Reports**    Reporting and analysis software for Windows from Seagate Software, Scotts Valley, CA, (www.seagatesoftware.com), that is used to retrieve data from more than 30 types of databases. Using various Web options, queries and reports can be made via a Web browser. Crystal Reports functionality can also be added to proprietary programs written in languages such as C, C++, J++, Delphi and Visual Basic.

**c/s**    See *client/server*.

**CSA**    **(1)** (Canadian Standards Association, Toronto, www.csa.ca) A standards-defining organization founded in 1919. It is involved in many industries, including electronics, communications and information technology.

**(2)** (Client Server Architecture) See *client/server*.

**(3)** (CallPath Services Architecture) An IBM standard that integrates applications with the telephone system, designed for use with AT&T, Northern Telecom and other PBX vendors.

**(4)** See *carrier serving area*.

**CSE**    (Certified Systems Engineer) See *Microsoft certification*.

**C Sharp**    See *C#*.

**C shell**    A command-line processor for UNIX. It provides more interactive control than the original Bourne shell, but is not available for all versions of UNIX. See *Bourne shell*, **bash shell**, *Korn shell* and *UNIX*.

**CSIC**    (Customer Specific Integrated Circuit) Pronounced "C-sick." Another term for ASIC, which was coined by Motorola. Some feel this is a more accurate description of an ASIC chip, since ASICs can be used for a variety of purposes. See also *ASSP*.

**CSID**    **(1)** (Call Subscriber ID) A data field in a fax transmission that identifies the calling party. It can be entered at the fax machine or via software for fax/modems. The CSID can be used by the receiving system to route faxes to the appropriate workgroups and individuals.

**(2)** (Character Set ID) The number of a particular character set.

**CSMA/CA**    A variation of the CSMA/CD method that is used with Apple's LocalTalk and various wireless access methods. Devices are always listening to the network (sensing the carrier) and when the network is quiet, it waits a specified amount of time based on its position in a list before sending. There are different methods used for prioritizing and resetting the list. In some versions, collisions may occur and collision detection is performed. See *CSMA/CD*.

**CSMA/CD**    (Carrier Sense Multiple Access/Collision Detection) The LAN access method used in Ethernet. When a device wants to gain access to the network, it checks to see if the network is quiet (senses the carrier). If it is not, it waits a random amount of time before retrying. If the network is quiet and two devices access the line at exactly the same time, their signals collide. When the collision is detected, they both back off and each wait a random amount of time before retrying. See *CSMA/CA*.

**CSP**    (1) (Certified Systems Professional) An earlier award for successful completion of an ICCP examination in systems development. See *ICCP*.

(2) (Commerce Service Provider) An organization that provides any combination of consulting, software and computer systems for e-commerce Web sites.

(3) (Cross System Product) An IBM application generator that runs in all SAA environments. CSP/AD (CSP/Application Development) programs provide the interactive development environment and generate a pseudo code that is interpreted by CSP/AE (CSP/Application Execution) software in the running computer. For AS/400 applications, CSP/AD generates compiled code. EZ-PREP and EZ-RUN are counterparts for PCs.

(4) (Chip Scale Package or Chip Size Package) A chip housing that is slightly larger than the chip itself. More than 50 CSP formats have been designed, mostly using BGA mounting. See *BGA*.

**CSP BGA**    (Chip Scale Packaging Ball Grid Array) A BGA chip package that is not much larger than the chip itself. See *MicroBGA*, *BGA* and *CSP*.

**CSS**    (1) See *Cascading Style Sheets*.

(2) (Content Scrambling System) The copy protection system used for DVD media. It is implemented in chipsets inside the DVD player. See *DeCSS*.

(3) (Constant Start-Stop) See *load/unload ramp*.

**CSTA**    (Computer Supported Telephony Application) An international standard interface between a network server and a telephone switch (PBX) established by the European Computer Manufacturers Association (ECMA).

**CSTN**    (Color STN) A color passive matrix screen technology developed by Sharp Electronics. CSTN displays have improved dramatically over the years and cost more than half that of an active matrix (TFT) display. See *passive matrix*.

**CSU/DSU**    See *DSU/CSU*.

**CSV**    (1) (Comma Separated Value) Same as *comma delimited*.

(2) (Computer System Validation) See *software validation*.

**CT**    (1) (Certified Trainer) See *Microsoft certification*.

(2) (Computer Telephony) The integration of computers and telephones. See *CTI*.

(3) (cT) A programming language from Carnegie Mellon University that is specialized for multimedia applications. Portable across Windows, the Mac and UNIX, cT combines an algorithmic programming language written in source code with interactive drawing tools that allow for the creation of graphics, animations and video. cT is compiled into an intermediate code (pseudo code) that is executed by an interpreter.

**CTE**    (Coefficient of Thermal Expansion) The difference between the way two materials expand when heat is applied. This is very critical when chips are mounted to printed circuit boards, because the silicon chip expands at a different rate than the plastic board.

**CTFT**    (Color TFT) See *TFT*.

**CTI**    (Computer Telephone Integration) Combining data with voice systems in order to enhance telephone services. For example, automatic number identification (ANI) allows a caller's records to be retrieved from the database while the call is routed to the appropriate party. Automatic telephone dialing from an address list is an outbound example.

**CTIA**    (1) See *CompTIA*.

**(2)** (Cellular Telecommunications Industry Association, Washington, DC, www.ctia.org) A membership organization founded in 1984 that is involved with regulatory and public affairs issues in the cellular phone industry.

**CTL**   See *CONTROL key*.

**CTO**   (**C**hief **T**echnical **O**fficer) The executive responsible for the technical direction of an organization. See *CIO* and *salary survey*.

**CTOS**   An operating system that runs on Unisys' x86-based SuperGen series (formerly the B-series). It was originally developed by Convergent Technologies, which was acquired by Unisys. Designed for network use, its message-based approach allows program requests to be directed to any station in the network.

**CTP**   **(1)** (**C**omputer-**T**o-**P**late) The production of printing plates directly from the computer without requiring film as an intermediate step. Plates are typically made of aluminum, but polyester, polymer and silicon plates are also used. Off-press imaging refers to using a platesetter to create the plates and then manually attaching the plates on the press. On-press imaging, or direct imaging (DI), images plates that are already on the press. In 1988, Presstek, Inc., Hudson, NH, (www.presstek.com), was the first to introduce an on-press system, using spark discharge technology to image the plates. Lasers were used in subsequent models.

**(2)** (**C**omputer-**T**o-**P**ress) Printing directly from digital files. The term is more ambiguous than definition #1. Since all computer printers are computer-to-press, it could refer to a large digital printer. It could also refer to an on-press computer-to-plate machine. It would not refer to off-press computer-to-plate (see above).

**CTRL**   See *CONTROL key*.

**CTRL-ALT-DEL**   In a PC, holding down the CTRL and ALT keys and pressing the DEL key reboots the system.

**CTRL-C**   In a PC under DOS, holding down the CTRL key and pressing the C key cancels the running program or batch file. Same as ***CTRL-BREAK***. See ***DOS Break***.

**CTS**   **(1)** (**C**lear **T**o **S**end) The RS-232 signal sent from the receiving station to the transmitting station that indicates it is ready to accept data. Contrast with *RTS*.

**(2)** (**C**ommon **T**ype **S**ystem) The programming types and operations supported in the Common Language Infrastructure (CLI), which is machine-independent language part of Microsoft's .NET platform. See *CLI* and *.NET*.

**(3)** See *carpal tunnel syndrome*.

**CUA**   (**C**ommon **U**ser **A**ccess) SAA specifications for user interfaces, which includes OS/2 PM and character-based formats of 3270 terminals. It is intended to provide a consistent look and feel across platforms and between applications.

**cube**   See *OLAP cube* and *OLAP*.

**Cuckoo's egg**   A music file that is named erroneously as a joke. For example, you download something you expect to be heavy metal and it is really elevator music. See *Easter Egg*.

**Cu-Cme**   See *CU-SeeMe*.

**CUI**   (**C**haracter-based **U**ser **I**nterface) A user interface that uses the character, or text, mode of the computer, such as DOS and UNIX. In order to instruct the computer, commands are typed in. Contrast with *GUI*.

**CUL**   Digispeak for "see you later."

**Curie point**   The temperature at which the molecules of a material can be altered when subjected to a magnetic field. In optical material, it is approximately 200 degrees Celsius. See *magneto-optic disk*.

**curly brace**     In programming, curly braces (the { and } characters) are used in a variety of ways. In C, they are used to signify the start and end of a series of statements. In the following expression, everything between the { and } are executed if the variable mouseDOWNinText is true.

```
if (mouseDOWNinText)
  {
mouseDOWNinText=0;
CLICK=1;
unHighLightALL();
  }
```

**current**     (1) Present activities or the latest version or model.

(2) The flow of electrons within a wire or circuit, measured in amps.

(3) (Current) A Windows PIM from IBM that includes a calendar, address book, phone dialer, outliner, word processor and Gantt charts for project tracking. It was revised by its developer, Jensen-Jones Inc., Red Bank, NJ, into a new package called Commence.

**current directory**     The disk directory the system is presently working in. Unless otherwise specified, commands that deal with disk files refer to the current directory.

**current loop**     A serial transmission method originating with teletype machines that transmits 20 milliAmperes of current for a 1 bit and no current for a 0 bit. Today's circuit boards can't handle 20mA current and use optical isolators at the receiving end to detect lower current. Contrast with *RS-232*.

**curses**     A programming interface for character-based terminals. Curses provides a terminal-independent method of programming a terminal. It is part of the Single UNIX Specification governed by X/Open.

**cursive writing**     Handwriting.

**cursor**     (1) The symbol used to point to some element on screen. On DOS and other character-based screens, it is a blinking rectangle or underline. On Windows and other graphics-based screens, it is also called a "pointer," and it changes shape as it is moved into different windows. For example, it may turn into an I-beam for editing text, an arrow for selecting menus or a pen for drawing. See *database cursor*.

(2) A pen-like or puck-like device used with a digitizer tablet. As the tablet cursor is moved across the tablet, the screen cursor moves correspondingly. See *digitizer tablet*.

**cursor keys**     The keyboard keys that move the pointer, or cursor, on screen. They include the UP, DOWN, LEFT ← and RIGHT →, HOME, END, PAGEUP and PAGEDOWN keys.

**CU-SeeMe**     Videoconferencing software for the Internet from White Pine Software Inc., Nashua, NH, (www.wpine.com). CU-SeeMe is available for Windows and Mac and allows point-to-point videoconferencing via modem over the Net. White Pine's Reflector software for UNIX and NT servers supports a group videoconference for up to 100 users.

**custom ASIC**     A redundant reference to an ASIC chip. ASICs are already customized for a specific use. See *ASIC*.

**custom control**     A software routine that adds some enhancement or feature to an application. Custom controls are written to provide as little as a few graphical interface improvements to as much as providing full imaging, spreadsheet and text editing extensions to the application. Depending on the development system, custom controls are either linked into the application when it is written or maintained as independent executable files that are called at runtime. DLLs, VBXs and OCXs are examples.

**custom-cut CD** An audio CD or CD-ROM that is cut into a non-round shape after it is pressed by the manufacturer or recorded on a CD-R. To avoid vibration in the drive, the shape is balanced as much as possible. Audio CD drives spin their discs more slowly than CD-ROM drives and can tolerate more out-of-round designs. Custom-cut CDs hold considerably less music, video or data than a full-sized disc. They fit in standard drive trays, but do not work with the feed drives that are used in automobiles. See *business card CD* and *feed drive*.

**customer aggregator** An organization that combines information content geared to a specific audience or community. The customer aggregator may also be the content aggregator. See *content aggregator*.

**customer engineer** An IBM title for systems representative. See *systems representative*.

**customer premises equipment** See *CPE*.

**customer relationship management** See *CRM*.

**customizability** The ability for software to be changed by the user or programmer. See *application programmability*.

**customized toolbar** A toolbar that can be custom configured by the user. Buttons can be added and deleted as required.

**custom software** Software that is specifically designed and programmed for an individual customer. Contrast with *software package*.

**cut and paste** To move text or an image from one document to another. All graphical-based operating systems (Mac, Windows, etc.) have cut and paste capability that is usually selected from an Edit menu. See *clipboard*, *copy and paste* and **Win Copy between windows**.

**CUT mode** (Control Unit Terminal mode) A mode that allows a 3270 terminal to have a single session with the mainframe. Micro to mainframe software emulates this mode to communicate with the mainframe. Contrast with *DFT mode*.

**cut-through switch** A switching device that begins to output an incoming data packet before the packet is completely received. Contrast with *store-and-forward switch*.

**CVS** (1) (Concurrent Versions System) A version control system for UNIX that was initially developed as a series of shell scripts in the mid-1980s. CVS maintains the changes between one source code version and another and stores all the changes in one file. It supports group collaboration by merging the files from each programmer.

(2) See *computer vision syndrome*.

**CWIS** (Campus Wide Information System) An information retrieval system used in colleges and universities before the Web became popular. Students and faculty would Telnet to a CWIS location to find course catalogs and schedules, job openings and the like. Items were selected from a text-based menu.

**cXML** (Commerce XML) A set of XML tags that defines the characteristics of a sale over the Web. It defines tags for purchase orders, changes, payments, order status and shipping information and is designed to provide a common interchange language for sales transactions. cXML has been integrated into Microsoft's BizTalk Framework. See *XML* and *BizTalk*.

**cyber** (1) From cybernetics, a prefix attached to everyday words to add a computer, electronic or online connotation.

(2) (CYBER) An early family of computers from Control Data that ranged from workstations to supercomputers.

**Custom-cut CDs**
Audio CD drives spin slower than CD-ROM drives and can tolerate out-of-round discs such as the four at the top of this image. The snowflake at the bottom is a CD-ROM and is more symmetrical and balanced than the others in order to keep drive vibration to a minimum. *(Image courtesy of Cutting Edge ShapeCD Inc., www.cdshapes.com)*

**cyberage**    The high-tech era that we are living in today.

**CyberAngels**    (CyberAngels Internet Safety Organization, Los Angeles, CA, www.cyberangels.org)  A Web site devoted to education and safety awareness on the Internet. It was founded in 1995 by Gabriel Hatcher along with Guardian Angels' founder Curtis Sliwa.

**CYBERCAFE**    The first Internet cafe in the U.S. Founded in 1995 in New York, the menu is a selection of fine coffees and desserts along with Internet, e-mail, printing, scanning and faxing services. Floppy disks, T-shirts and baseball caps are also available for purchase.

**CyberCash**    A web payment processing service from CyberCash, Inc., Oakland, CA, (www.cybercash.com), that allows merchants to process credit cards and initiate direct transfers from customer checking accounts. Merchant transactions are sent to CyberCash servers, which access the credit card networks and Automated Clearing House (ACH). In addition to its back-end payment processing, CyberCash also provides the InstaBuy digital wallet service that fills in the forms at any online shopping site. CyberCash has been processing credit cards since 1995, making it one of the earliest payment systems on the Internet. See *Web payment service.*

**cybercop**    A criminal investigator of online fraud or harassment.

**cybercrime**    Crime on the information superhighway, typically having to do with online fraud.

**cybercrook**    A person who gains illegal entrance into a computer system or who diverts financial transfers into his or her own account. Same as *hacker*, **computer cracker** and *netopath*.

**cyberjournal**    A personal diary on the Web that contains observations, secrets, frustrations, life stories and offers people a place to document their lives. There are more than a thousand Web Journal services of which Diarist.net (www.diarist.net) is one of the largest. About half of the journals are written under pseudonyms or with only partial disclosure.

**cyberlibertarianism**    The libertarian philosophy applied to the Internet and electronic media. Libertarians believe everyone should have complete and full civil liberties. Organizations such as the Electronic Frontier Foundation promote cyberlibertarianism. See *EFF.*

**cyberlibrarian**    Librarians who do most of their research and information retrieval via the Internet and other online services. The title is often shortened to *cybrarian.*

**cybermall**    A shopping mall on the Internet. Cybermalls are online shopping centers that link a home page to hundreds or thousands of online storefronts. The cybermall generally handles the financial transactions for all the merchants so that a customer does not have to enter duplicate name and address information at each store. Items can literally be placed into an online shopping cart and paid for at once by credit card, ecash or other digital money method. See *digital money.*

**cybernaut**    An electronic astronaut. Avid Net surfers are cybernauts; however, anyone deeply involved in communications networks, online services, and computers in general can assume this handle.

**cybernetics**    The comparative study of human and machine processes in order to understand their similarities and differences. It often refers to machines that imitate human behavior. The term was coined by Norbert Wiener (1894–1964), one of the great mathematicians of the twentieth century. See *AI* and *robot.*

**cyberpunk**    A futuristic, online delinquent: breaking into computer systems; surviving by high-tech wits. The term comes from science fiction novels such as *Neuromancer* and *Shockwave Rider.*

**cyberslacker**    A person at a company location that spends a lot of time on the Internet, but not for work-related activities.

**cybersleuth**     **(1)** A person that searches the Internet for information about a company, both positive and negative, to keep abreast of public opinion. All Internet facilities are used, including the Web, newsgroups and chat rooms.

**(2)** A person that does any kind of detective work using the Internet.

**cyberspace**     Coined by William Gibson in his 1984 novel *Neuromancer*, it is a futuristic computer network that people use by plugging their minds into it! The term now refers to the Internet or to the online or digital world in general. See *Internet* and *virtual reality*. Contrast with *meatspace*.

**cybersquatting**     Registering an Internet name for the purpose of reselling it for a profit. One of the more notable transactions was the domain name wallstreet.com, which was registered in 1994 for $70 and sold for one million in 1999. Some people have registered every common name and name combination they can think of with the hopes of making a fortune some day.

In August 1999, the U.S. government passed the Anti-Cybersquatting Consumer Protection Act, which enables trademark holders to obtain civil damages up to $100,000 from cybersquatters that register their trade names or similar-sounding names as domain names. While not directly outlawing cybersquatting, it is an attempt to improve the situation.

**cyberwar**     Refers to hostile attacks and illegal invasions of computer systems. See *cracker*, *virus* and *denial of service*.

**cyberworld**     The world of computers and communications. It implies today's fast-moving, high-technology world.

**cyborg**     (**CYB**ernetic **ORG**anism)  A being that is part human and machine. See *cybernetics* and *bionic*.

**cybrarian**     See *cyberlibrarian*.

**cycle**     **(1)** A single event that is repeated. For example, in a carrier frequency, one cycle is one complete wave.

**(2)** A set of events that is repeated. For example, in a polling system, all of the attached terminals are tested in one cycle. See *machine cycle* and *memory cycle*.

**cycles per second**     The number of times an event or set of events is repeated in a second. See *Hertz*.

**cycle stealing**     A CPU design technique that periodically "grabs" machine cycles from the main processor usually by some peripheral control unit, such as a DMA (direct memory access) device. In this way, processing and peripheral operations can be performed concurrently or with some degree of overlap.

**cycle time**     The time interval between the start of one cycle and the start of the next cycle.

**CYCOLOR**     A printing technology from Cycolor, Inc., Miamisburg, OH (www.cycolor.com), that is used to produce continuous-tone photographic prints. The technology was originally developed by Mead Imaging and acquired by Yasuhiro Oshima in 1996, a Japanese businessman that specializes in photographic services.

CYCOLOR is more like traditional film than digital printing, because the imaging is in the film itself. CYCOLOR DI film contains billions of light-sensitive microcapsules, called "cyliths." Resembling gel-caps, approximately 20,000 cyliths fit on the head of a pin, and their cyan, yellow and magenta dyes are sensitive to red, green and blue light.

The cylith hardens when exposed to its corresponding color, and the amount of hardness depends on the intensity of the light. The exposed film is then pressed between rollers to release the dyes. If an area was exposed

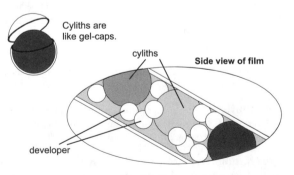

Cyliths are like gel-caps.

cyliths

**Side view of film**

developer

**The Cylith**
As many as 20,000 cyliths can fit on the head of a pin.

heavily to all three colors, the cyliths become hard, do not release any dye and the white film shows. If an area was unexposed, all the cyliths burst under pressure and blend together to become black. All colors in between are based on the degree of hardness of each of the cyan, yellow and magenta capsules.

For commercial high-speed models, the CYCOLOR transfer system adds a second step. The imaging is done on a donor sheet which is pressed onto a receiver sheet, and the donor sheet is peeled away.

**cylinder**    The aggregate of all tracks that reside in the same location on every disk surface. On multiple-platter disks, the cylinder is the sum total of every track with the same track number on every surface. On a floppy disk, a cylinder comprises the top and corresponding bottom track.

When storing data, the operating system fills an entire cylinder before moving to the next one. The access arm remains stationary until all the tracks in the cylinder have been read or written.

**cylinder skew**    The offset distance from the start of the last track of the previous cylinder so that the head has time to seek from cylinder to cylinder and be at the start of the first track of the new cylinder. See *head skew*.

**Cyrix**    (Cyrix Corporation, Richardson, TX, www.cyrix.com) Founded in 1988, Cyrix was a manufacturer of x86-compatible CPU chips. Its first product was a math coprocessor. In 1992, it introduced a line of 486 CPUs, later followed by the 6x86 Pentium-class and 6x86MX Pentium II-class chips. In 1998, Cyrix was acquired by National Semiconductor and operated as a wholly-owned subsidiary. In 1999, National Semi sold its Cyrix processor business to Via Technologies, Inc., a leader in PC chipset design. See also *Citrix*.

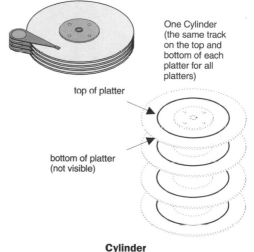

multi-platter hard disk

One Cylinder
(the same track
on the top and
bottom of each
platter for all
platters)

top of platter

bottom of platter
(not visible)

**Cylinder**
The cylinder is the aggregate of the same track
number on every platter used for recording.

**D&B Software** (Dun & Bradstreet Software, Atlanta, GA, division of The Dun & Bradstreet Corporation) D&B Software was formed in 1990 as a merger of Management Science America (MSA), founded in 1963 to provide textile consulting services, and McCormack & Dodge, a packaged financial software firm founded in 1969 and later acquired by Dun & Bradstreet. The company was acquired by Geac Computer Corporation in 1996 and became the Geac Host Technologies and Geac SmartStream divisions of the company. See *Geac*.

**D1** A broadcast-quality digital video format that provides the highest quality recording, using expensive tape decks and metal-particle tape. D1 is a component format at 720×486 resolution and 24-bit color. It is raw, uncompressed digital video that uses 1MB of storage for each frame. At 30 frames per second, it requires a 30MB/sec transfer rate and nearly two gigabytes of storage per minute.

**D2** A broadcast-quality digital video format that integrates well with analog equipment, because the equipment uses composite analog inputs and outputs.

**D2C** The U.S. government's term for the Ampex DD2 format. See *DD2*.

**D3** A broadcast-quality digital video format that provides a lower cost alternative to D1 recording. It is a composite format recorded on half-inch tape. See also *Pick System*.

**D3D** See *Direct3D*.

**D4** A framing format for T1 transmission that places 12 T1 frames into a superframe. See *ESF*.

**D5** A broadcast-quality digital video format that provides a lower cost alternative to D1 recording. It is a component format recorded on half-inch tape.

**DA** See *data administrator*, *desk accessory* and *data acquisition*.

**DAB** (Digital Audio Broadcasting) The broadcasting of radio programs in digital format. iBiquity Digital is the major player in this field, which is a merger of Lucent Digital Radio and USA Digital Radio. iBiquity's iDAB system uses the In Band/On Channel (IBOC) technology that transmits digital signals within the same frequency band and using the same channel number as regular AM and FM analog radio channels. See *satellite radio*.

**DAC** (1) See *D/A converter*.
　　(2) (Discretionary Access Control) A security control that does not require clearance levels. See *NCSC*.

**D/A converter** (Digital/Analog converter) A device that converts digital pulses into analog signals. Contrast with *A/D converter*. See *DSP* and *ladder DAC*.

**DAD**     (1) (Database Action Diagram) Documentation that describes the processing performed on data in a database. (2) (Digital Audio Disc) Same as *CD*.

**daemon**     Pronounced "demon." A UNIX program that executes in the background ready to perform an operation when required. Functioning like an extension to the operating system, a daemon is usually an unattended process that is initiated at startup. Typical daemons are print spoolers and e-mail handlers or a scheduler that starts up another process at a designated time. The term comes from Greek mythology meaning "guardian spirit." See *agent*.

**DAFS**     (Direct Access File System) A high-performance file sharing protocol based on the VI memory-to-memory architecture. Designed for storage area networks (SANs), DAFS provides bulk data transfer directly between the application buffers of two machines without having to packetize the data. It also allows applications to access hardware without operating system intervention. For more information, visit www.dafscollaborative.org. See *VI*.

**daisy chain**     Connected in series, one after the other. Transmitted signals go to the first device, then to the second and so on.

**daisy wheel**     An earlier print mechanism that used a plastic or metal hub with spokes like an old-fashioned wagon wheel minus the outer rim. At the end of each spoke is the carved image of a type character.

When the required character spins around to the print hammer, the image is banged into a ribbon and onto paper. The mechanism is then moved to the next location. Daisy wheel printers print typewriter-like quality from 10 to 75 cps and have been superseded by dot matrix and laser printers.

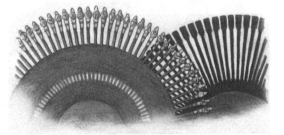

**Daisy Wheel**
In the early 1980s, daisy wheel printers cost $3,000 and more. They clicked and clacked to produce near typewriter-quality output. The technology was popular because you could change the fonts by changing wheels.

**DAL**     (Data Access Language) A database interface from Apple that allows the Mac to access DAL-supported databases on Macs or non-Apple computers. It is a superset of SQL. Database vendors license the specs and translate DAL calls to their database engines.

**damping**     A technique for stabilizing an electronic or mechanical device by eliminating unwanted or excessive oscillations.

**D-AMPS**     (Digital-Advanced Mobile Phone Service) The second generation of TDMA. See *IS-136*.

**DAMS**     (Digital Asset Management System) Software that keeps track of the digital assets of an organization. Companies have come to own a huge amount of digitally-created material that needs to be stored and easily retrieved when necessary.

**Dan Bricklin's demo programs**     See *Demo II*.

**dancing baloney**     Small animated GIF images and other moving objects that are used to quickly and cheaply add "excitement" to a Web page. At best these images are harmless and not too distracting. At worst, they can make a given Web page look like the online equivalent of an animated ransom note. See *cornea gumbo* and *eye candy*.

**dangerous extensions**     Following are potentially dangerous file extensions in e-mail attachments. That means if you launch them (double click them), they will execute instructions in your computer. If a friend sends you an executable attachment in an e-mail and says "this is the coolest thing I've ever seen" or something like that and nothing else… and this is the first time that person ever did this… beware!

It could be a virus sent to you via your friend's address book. The bottom line is you must know why you are launching an .EXE (executable) file. Coming from a "supposed" friend, there are a million clever lines that could trick people into double clicking an attachment that wipes out their hard disks. Have you backed up lately? See *double extension*.

**Executable (know what you are opening!)**
.EXE
.VBS

**Other executables (potentially a problem)**
.BAT
.HTA
.JS
.JSE
.VBE
.WSH

**Text (safe\*\*)**
.TXT

**Images (safe\*\*)**
.GIF  .PCX  .BMP  .PNG  .WMF
.JPG  .EPS  .AI  .TIF  .DXF

The above are common images types. There are numerous others formats used every day. See *graphics formats*.

**Data (potential problem)**
.XLS  (Excel) Can contain macros that execute.
.DOC  (Word) Can contain macros that execute.

**All Other Data (safe\*\*)**
Data is not executable, it is processed. There are hundreds of data file extensions. See *extension*.

*\*\*Data is processed, not executed; thus, all data is theoretically safe. Although virus code can be embedded into data, it would take additional virus code to make it work. Another virus program would have to enter your computer by some other means that would look for new text and image attachments and cause the code in them to run, creating an on-going "you-don't-known-what's-going-to-hit-you-next" situation.*

**DAO**   (Data Access Objects) A programming interface for data access from Microsoft. DAO/Jet provides access to the Jet database, and DAO/ODBCDirect provides an interface to ODBC databases via RDO. DAO is a COM object. See *RDO, ADO, OLE DB* and *ODBC*. See also *disc-at-once*.

**DAP**   (Directory Access Protocol) A protocol used to gain access to an X.500 directory listing. See *LDAP*.

**DAQ**   See *data acquisition*.

**DAR**   (Digital Audio Radio) See *DARS*.

**dark current**   The current that flows in a photodetector when it is not receiving any light. It may increase as the temperature rises.

**darkened datacenter**   Unattended datacenter operation. With printers distributed throughout the enterprise and the use of tape and optical libraries that automatically mount the appropriate disk and tape volume, the datacenter increasingly does not require human intervention.

**dark fiber**   Bulk, raw fiber. Dark fiber is optical fiber that spans some geographic area and is sold to carriers and large businesses without any optical or electronic signaling in its path. The customer is responsible for adding the transmission system at both ends. Contrast with *lit fiber*. See *TONS*.

**Darlington circuit**   An amplification circuit that uses two transistors coupled together.

**DARPA**   (Defense Advanced Research Projects Agency) The name given to the U.S. Advanced Research Projects Agency during the 1980s. It was later renamed back to ARPA. See *ARPAnet*.

**DARS**   (1) (Digital Audio Radio Service) The FCC nomenclature for digital radio. DARS is the landline version that is implemented with the IBOC technology. S-DARS (Satellite DARS) is the satellite version. See *DAB* and *satellite radio*.
(2) (Dow Aviation Reservation System) Dow Chemical's intranet-based reservations system. It lets employees reserve seats on corporate jets scheduled between company locations.
(3) (Disaster Assessment Recovery System) A disaster management application based on Domino from Corporate Workflow Solutions, Inc., Jupiter, FL. It is used to deploy equipment and personnel after natural disasters strike.

**DAS**    See *direct attached storage* and *FDDI*.

**DASD**    (Direct Access Storage Device) Pronounced "dazdee." A peripheral device that is directly addressable, such as a disk or drum. The term is used in the mainframe world.

**Dashboard**    A Windows utility from Starfish Software, Scotts Valley, CA (www.starfishsoftware.com, that provides a centralized control panel for launching applications, finding files and viewing system resources. Dashboard was originally developed by HP, then acquired by Borland.

**DASL**    See *WebDAV*.

**DAT**    (2) (Dynamic Address Translator) A hardware circuit that converts a virtual memory address into a real address.
(1) (Digital Audio Tape) A magnetic tape technology used for backing up data. DAT uses 4mm cartridges that look like thick audio cassettes and conform to the DDS (Digital Data Storage) standard. DAT tape libraries hold from a handful to several hundred cassettes. DAT was initially a CD-quality audio format. It was thought to replace analog audiotapes for consumers, but wound up being used by professional musicians and sound studios. In 1988, Sony and HP defined the DDS format and quality level for computer storage. Like videotapes, DAT uses helical scan recording. See *magnetic tape*.

| Type  | Native Capacity |
|-------|-----------------|
| DDS-1 | 2GB             |
| DDS-2 | 4GB             |
| DDS-3 | 12GB            |
| DDS-4 | 20GB            |

**DAT Cartridge**
DAT provides from one to 20GB of storage in a cartridge that is a little thicker, but smaller overall than an audio cassette.

**data**    (1) Technically, raw facts and figures, such as orders and payments, which are processed into information, such as balance due and quantity on hand. However, in common usage, the terms data and information are used synonymously.
The amount of data versus information kept in the computer is a tradeoff. Data can be processed into different forms of information, but it takes time to sort and sum transactions. Up-to-date information can provide instant answers.
A common misconception is that software is also data. Software is executed, or run, by the computer. Data is "processed." Software is "run."
(2) Any form of information, whether in paper or electronic form. In electronic form, data refers to files and databases, text documents, images and digitally encoded voice and video.
(3) The plural form of datum.

**data abstraction**    See *abstraction*.

**Data Accelerator**    An early utility from BMC used to enhance batch processing operations in IBM mainframes. Its functions were included in IBM's SmartBatch. See *SmartBatch*.

**Data Access Language**    See *DAL*.

**data acquisition**    (1) The automatic collection of data from sensors and readers in a factory, laboratory, medical or scientific environment.
(2) The gathering of source data for data entry into the computer.

**data administration**    The analysis, classification and maintenance of an organization's data and data relationships. It includes the development of data models and data dictionaries, which, combined with transaction volume, are the raw materials for database design.
Although data administration and database administration are separate functions, both are typically combined into one department and are often performed by the same people. However, "data" administration deals with the modeling of the data and treats data as an organizational resource, while "database" administration deals with the implementation of the types of databases that are in use. The person that performs "data" administration functions is a "database analyst" or "data administrator," the latter being an earlier title for the job. The person that handles "database" administration, which is the technical design and management of the database, is the "database administrator."

**Data Is Complex**    The flow of data/information within a company is complex since the same data is viewed differently as it moves from one department to the other.

For example: When a customer places an order, the order becomes a commission for sales, a statistic for marketing, an order to keep track of in order processing, an effect on cash flow for financial officers, picking schedules for the warehouse, and production scheduling for manufacturing.

Users have different requirements for interrogating and updating data. Operations people need detail, management needs summaries. Database design must take this into consideration.

**data administrator**    A person who coordinates activities within the data administration department. Same as "database analyst." See *data administration* and *system development cycle*.

**data aging**    Adding years to a date to bring it into the year 2000 or beyond in order to test applications for year 2000 compliance. See *Y2K problem*.

**data analyst**    See *data administrator*.

**data availability**    Refers to the degree to which data can be instantly accessed. The term is mostly associated with service levels that are set up either by the internal IT organization or that may be guaranteed by a third-party datacenter or storage provider.

**data bank**    Any electronic depository of data.

**database**    A set of related files that is created and managed by a database management system (DBMS). Today, DBMSs can manage any form of data including text, images, sound and video. Database and file structures are always determined by the software. As far as the hardware is concerned, it's all bits and bytes.

**DATABASE 2**    See *DB2*.

**database administrator**    A person responsible for the physical design and management of the database and for the evaluation, selection and implementation of the DBMS.

In most organizations, the database administrator and data administrator are one in the same; however, when the two responsibilities are managed separately, the database administrator's function is more technical. See *system development cycle* and *salary survey*.

**database analyst**    A person responsible for analyzing data requirements within an organization and modeling the data and data flows from one department to another. Formerly called a "data administrator," the database analyst may also perform "database administration" functions, which deal with the particular databases employed. See *data administration*.

**database cursor**    A record pointer in a database. When a database file is selected and the cursor is opened, the cursor points to the first record in the file. Using various commands, the cursor can be moved forward, backward, to top of file, bottom of file and so forth.

**database designer**    See *data administrator* and *database administrator*.

**database driver**    A software routine that accesses a database. It allows an application or compiler to access a particular database format.

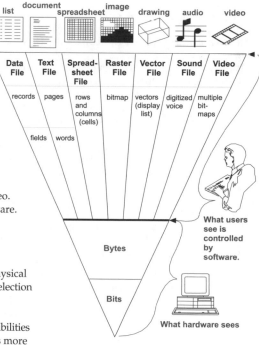

**The Database**
To better understand data and file concepts, learn the hierarchy and terms in this drawing.

**database engine**    Software that stores and retrieves data in a database. It may be a self-contained entity or part of a comprehensive database management system (DBMS). See *database manager*.

**database machine**    A computer system designed for database access. Database machines never caught on until the early 1990s when massively parallel processors (MPPs) from companies such as Teradata (now part of AT&T), nCube, Thinking Machines and Kendall Square Research, proved the concept. Using hundreds and even thousands of microprocessors with database software designed for parallelism, database machines can scan large files much faster than a mainframe.

Dramatic performance increases have been documented. For example, a large financial organization reduced 30 days' worth of month-end analysis and reporting to a single day. In other cases, queries have been speeded up by a factor of 100. Database machines using MPP architecture are expected to grow in popularity for decision support systems in large organizations.

**database management software**    See *DBMS*.

**database management system**    See *DBMS*.

**database manager**    (1) With personal computers, software that allows a user to manage multiple data files (same as *DBMS*). Contrast with *file manager*, which works with one file at a time.

(2) Software that provides database management capability for traditional programming languages, such as COBOL, BASIC and C, but without the interactive capabilities.

(3) The part of the DBMS that stores and retrieves the data.

**database program**    A software application that allows for the management of data and information structured as fields, records and files. Database programs provide a way of creating and manipulating the electronic equivalent of a name and address card that can hold large amounts of information.

Because all data is structured into a one-record-per-subject or -transaction format, it allows for powerful query capabilities, in which you can select records based on any of their content. A database program is the heart of a business information system and provides mainly file creation, data entry, update, query and reporting functions.

The traditional term for a database program is a database management system (DBMS). It is also called a "data management system." For more details on the features of a DBMS, see *DBMS*. Also see *application software* for a breakdown of all major software applications.

User Interaction with a Database Program    The database programs available on personal computers let you perform all the following tasks interactively on one file at a time. However, as soon as you want data in one file to automatically update another, programming has to be done. That's where the faint of heart take their leave, and the hackers take over. Following are the common tasks you need to perform to create and work with a database file.

**Create a File and Set Index Order**    Each field in a record is defined by name, type and length. In order to keep the file in sequence, one or more fields are defined as key fields, upon which indexes are created and maintained. The index is updated whenever new records are added or existing records are deleted, or any data in a key field changes.

**Create Data Entry Forms**    Data entry is accomplished by designing a form to display each record. Data entry forms contain field validation. You decide what data can go in and what must stay out of these fields.

**Update/Edit**    In a single-user, one-file-at-a-time application, there is nothing to predefine here. Changing data is just a matter of opening the file and selecting the EDIT mode. However, in a multiuser system, security must be administered and audit trails must be programmed.

**View/Query**    You can browse an entire file or just selected records. Selected records are usually created as a temporary file that can be saved or abandoned. The temporary file may be sorted into a new sequence if desired. The ease with which a query can be composed determines how much users will ask their own questions or rely on their IS staff to create them. Getting data from two files—for example, customers and orders, or vendors and purchases—requires knowledge of how to link the files for the query. Most database programs have a JOIN function, which creates a new file with data from two existing files. Once a query description has been composed, it can be saved for use again.

**Reporting**    Reports provide details and summaries in a more elaborate fashion than queries. They have page and column headers and can be sorted into order by multiple fields; for example, county within city within state. Once a report description has been composed, it can be saved for use again.

**Modify Structure**    From time to time, it is necessary to add or delete fields, or change their lengths or possibly their names. This function is similar to creating the record structure in the first place, except that you are editing the structure rather than defining it from scratch.

**database publishing**    Using desktop publishing to produce reports of database contents.

**databases**    See *online services*.

**database server**    A computer in a LAN dedicated to database storage and retrieval. The database server is a key component in a client/server environment. It holds the database management system (DBMS) and the databases. Upon requests from the client machines, it searches the database for selected records and passes them back over the network.
  A database server and file server may be one in the same, because a file server often provides database services. However, the term implies that the system is dedicated for database use only and not a central storage facility for applications and files. See *client/server*.

**database system**    See *database program* and *DBMS*.

**database trigger**    See *trigger*.

**data bits**    The number of bits used to represent one character of data. When transmitting ASCII text via modem, either seven or eight bits may be used. Most other forms of data require eight bits.

**DataBlade**    A plug-in to Informix's Universal Server that extends its capability to work with a new type of data. See *Universal Server*.

**DataBolts**    Software components for Web sites from IBM. Available as JavaBeans or ActiveX controls, some of the first products are Cryptolope (encryption), Query and Retrieval (database access) and NewsTicker (scrolling news window). DataBolts are designed to provide all the enhancements necessary to keep visitors from straying off a Web site, such as the ability to search other sites for information and bring those results back to the site.

**data broadcast**    The one-way transmission of digital data directly to TVs and PCs. Using cable, satellite and the unused bandwidth in the VHF TV spectrum, data broadcast can deliver news, weather, stock prices, sports scores, music, video and even Web pages. The user's set-top box functions as a tuner to the desired information.

**data bus**    An internal pathway across which data is transferred to and from the processor or to and from memory. See *local bus*, *system bus* and *peripheral bus*.

**data carousel**    A format that interleaves information streams in a repeating pattern for digital video broadcasting. See *DVB*.

**data carrier**    (1) Any medium such as a disk or tape that can hold machine readable data.
  (2) A carrier frequency into which data is modulated for transmission in a network.

**data cartridge**    (1) A cartridge used to hold computer data. See *cartridge*.
  (2) (Data Cartridge) A 5.25" QIC-style magnetic tape technology that originally used the DC-6000 model designation. Tandberg Data has enhanced the technology in its MLR line for use in medium- to high-end server markets with capacities up to 25MB. See *QIC* and *magnetic tape*.

**The 5.25" Data Cartridge**
Tandberg Data has enhanced the QIC Data Cartridge with capacities up to 25MB.

**data cassette**    A cassette used to hold computer data. See *cassette*.

**Data Cell**    An IBM mass storage device made in the 1960s that used 3" x 15" tape strips which were extracted out of a cartridge and wrapped around a rotating drum for reading. More than 100 of these units were installed worldwide, but the tapes were very susceptible to wear. See *RACE* and *CRAM*.

**datacenter**    The department that houses the computer systems and related equipment, including the data library. Data entry and systems programming may also come under its jurisdiction. A control section is usually provided that accepts work from and releases output to user departments.

**datacenter manager**    A person responsible for the operation of the computer systems in the datacenter. The data entry and data control departments are under this jurisdiction.

**data circuit-terminating equipment**    See *DCE*.

**data cleansing**    See *address cleansing* and *data hygiene*.

**The Datacenter**
No matter how much computers are distributed into the organization, there always seems to be a need for a centralized datacenter in the large enterprise.

**data code**    (1) A digital coding system for data in a computer. See *ASCII* and *EBCDIC*.
(2) A coding system used to abbreviate data; for example, codes for regions, classes, products and status.

**data collaboration**    See *data conferencing*.

**data collection**    Acquiring source documents for the data entry department. It comes under the jurisdiction of the data control or data entry department. See *data acquisition*.

**datacom**    (**DATA COM**munications)    See *communications* and *CA-DATACOM/DB*.

**datacom analyst**    A person responsible for developing and maintaining a data communications network. May be the same as a "network administrator," or could be a higher-level position that does more network planning than device configuration and troubleshooting. See *network administrator*.

**data communications**    Transmitting text, voice and video in binary form. See *communications*.

**data communications equipment**    See *DCE*.

**data compression**    Encoding data to take up less storage space. Digital data is compressed by finding repeatable patterns of binary 0s and 1s. The more patterns can be found, the more the data can be compressed. Text can generally be compressed to about 40% of its original size, and graphics files from 20%–90%. Some files compress very little. It depends entirely on the type of file and compression algorithm used.

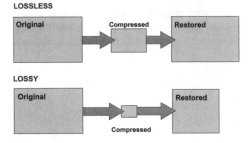

There are numerous compression methods in use. Two major technologies are Huffman coding and Lempel-Ziv-Welch (LZW), representing examples of the statistical and dictionary compression methods.

When a compression algorithm is packaged for use for a specific platform and file format, it is called a "codec" (compressor/decompressor). ADPCM, PCM and GSM are examples of codecs for sound, and Indeo, Cinepak and MPEG are examples of codecs for video.

In the DOS/Windows world, PKZIP is the most widely used compression application. See *archive formats*, *WinZip* and *coder*.

**Lossless versus Lossy**    When text and financial data are compressed, they must be decompressed back to a perfect original, bit for bit. This is known as "lossless compression." However, audio and video can be compressed to as little as 5% of its original size using "lossy compression." Some of the data is actually lost, but the loss is not noticeable to the human ear and eye.

**data conferencing**    Sharing data interactively among several users in different locations. Data conferencing is made up of whiteboards and application sharing. A whiteboard is the electronic equivalent of the chalkboard or flip chart. Participants at different locations simultaneously write and draw on an on-screen notepad viewed by everyone.

Application sharing is the same as remote control software, in which multiple participants can interactively work in an application that is loaded on only one user's machine. Application viewing is similar to application sharing; however, although all users can see the document, only one person can actually edit it.

Whiteboards and application sharing are often used in conjunction with an audio or videoconferencing connection. An audio-only connection can be a separate telephone call or be transmitted with the data using simultaneous voice and data (SVD) modems. See *whiteboard* and *T.120*.

**data control department**    The function responsible for collecting data for input into a computer's batch processing operations, as well as the dissemination of the finished reports. The data entry department may be under the jursidiction of the data control department, or vice versa.

**data conversion**    Changing from one file type to another. There are many data conversion programs on the market that support a wide number of text, database, spreadsheet and graphics formats. If a text document, database or spreadsheet format is not supported in a packaged conversion program, the textual data within the file can be converted if the application that created it is available and it can export its contents to ASCII text; however, page format settings, as well as macros and other attributes, will be lost. If the application or the "export to ASCII" option is not available, the only recourse is to have a custom conversion program written from scratch. If there is no written documentation available for the format, the job will be a tedious one, but it can be done unless the format is inherently encrypted. See *ASCII file* and *conversion*.

**Data D-2**    See *DST*.

**DATA/DAT**    (DATA/Digital Audio Tape) An earlier DAT format that allowed updating in place by dividing the tape into as many as 254 partitions. It gave way to the DDS formats. See *DAT*.

**data declaration**    Same as *data definition*.

**data definition**    (1) In a source language program, the definitions of data structures (variables, arrays, fields, records, etc.).

(2) A description of the record layout in a file system or DBMS.

**data description language**    See *DDL*.

**data dictionary**    A database about data and databases. It holds the name, type, range of values, source, and authorization for access for each data element in the organization's files and databases. It also indicates which application programs use that data, so that when a change in a data structure is contemplated, a list of affected programs can be generated.

The data dictionary may be a stand-alone system or an integral part of the DBMS. Data integrity and accuracy is better ensured in the latter case.

**data dipper**    Software in a personal computer that queries a mainframe database.

**data division**    The part of a COBOL program that defines the data files and record layouts.

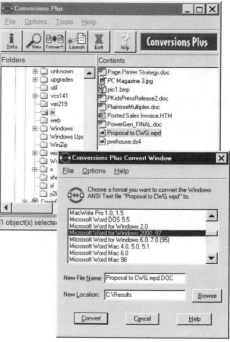

**A Conversion Program**
Conversion programs such as Conversions Plus from DataViz, Inc. (www.dataviz.com) provide conversion between a wide variety of file formats. This example converts a Word Perfect document (.wpd) to a Word document (.doc) by simply highlighting the source file, clicking Convert and selecting the destination format. Packaged conversion programs carry forward all layout settings as long as the target format supports the same feature.

**DataEase**    A relational DBMS for DOS and Windows from MultiWare, Inc., Trumbull, CT (www.multi-ware.com). It provides a menu-driven interface for developing applications without programming and is noted for its ease of use. DataEase was one of the first products on the PC platform to offer an easier way to develop business applications.

**data element**    The fundamental data structure in a data processing system. Any unit of data defined for processing is a data element; for example, ACCOUNT NUMBER, NAME, ADDRESS and CITY. A data element is defined by size (in characters) and type (alphanumeric, numeric only, true/false, date, etc.). A specific set of values or range of values may also be part of the definition.

Technically, a data element is a logical definition of data, whereas a field is the physical unit of storage in a record. For example, the data element ACCOUNT NUMBER, which exists only once, is stored in the ACCOUNT NUMBER field in the customer record and in the ACCOUNT NUMBER field in the order records. See *field*.

**data encryption**    See *cryptography*.

**data entry**    Entering data into the computer, which includes keyboard entry, scanning and voice recognition. When transactions are entered after the fact (batch data entry), they are just stacks of source documents to the keyboard operator. Deciphering poor handwriting from a source document is a judgment call that is often error prone. In online data entry operations, in which the operator takes information in person or by phone, there's interaction and involvement with the transaction and less chance for error. See *data loading*.

**data entry department**    The part of the datacenter where the data entry terminals and operators are located.

**data entry operator**    A person who enters data into the computer via keyboard or other reading or scanning device.

**data entry program**    An application program that accepts data from the keyboard or other input device and stores it in the computer. It may be part of an application that also provides updating, querying and reporting.

The data entry program establishes the data in the database and should test for all possible input errors. See *validity checking, table lookup, check digit* and *intelligent database*.

**data error**    A condition in which data on a digital medium has been corrupted. The error can be as little as one bit.

In DOS, the message "Data error on drive x" means that an area of the disk is unreadable. Press R to retry. Most likely, you'll have to press A to stop (abort). If the data or program is critical and there's no backup, use a utility program to try to reconstruct the damaged area. See **DOS Recover**.

**data field**    See *field*.

**data file**    A collection of data records. This term may refer specifically to a database file that contains records and fields in contrast to other files such as a word processing document or spreadsheet. Or, it may refer to a file that contains any type of information structure, including documents and spreadsheets, in contrast to a program file.

**data flow**    (1) In computers, the path of data from source document to data entry to processing to final reports. Data changes format and sequence (within a file) as it moves from program to program.

(2) In communications, the path taken by a message from origination to destination that includes all nodes through which the data travels.

**data flow diagram**    A description of data and the manual and machine processing performed on the data.

**data fork**    The part of a Macintosh file that contains data. For example, in a HyperCard stack, text, graphics and HyperTalk scripts reside in the data fork, while fonts, sounds, control information and external functions reside in the resource fork.

**data format**    Same as *file format*.

**Edson de Castro**
De Castro founded Data General as the minicomputer market began to flourish. His line of Nova machines helped expand the market for low-priced (under $100,000) computers. This was a time when minicomputers were expected to make mainframes obsolete. *(Image courtesy of Data General Corporation.)*

**Data General**    (Data General Corporation, Westboro, MA, www.dg.com)  A server and storage manufacturer founded in 1968 by Edson de Castro. Product lines include AViiON servers and fault-tolerant CLARiiON storage systems. AViiONs are Intel based and run Windows NT and DG/UX (UNIX). From 1989 to 1995, AViiONs used Motorola 88000 CPUs. CLARiiON storage systems, first introduced in 1992, provide RAID fault tolerance and come in SCSI and Fibre Channel versions. Services make up about a quarter of DG's revenues. In 1999, Data General was acquired by EMC.

Data General was one of the first minicomputer companies. In 1969, it introduced the Nova, the first 16-bit mini with four accumulators, a leading technology at the time. During its early years, the company was successful in the scientific, academic and OEM markets. With its 32-bit ECLIPSE family of computers and its Comprehensive Electronic Office (CEO) software, Data General gained entry into the commercial marketplace in the early 1980s.

The "Eagle project," DG's development of its ECLIPSE and first 32-bit computer, was chronicled in Tracy Kidder's Pulitzer-prize winning novel, "Soul of a New Machine," published by Little, Brown and Company, ISBN 0-316-49170-5. See *Data General One* and *EMC*.

**Data General One**    The first DOS-based laptop. Introduced by Data General in 1984, it was fully IBM compatible and considerably lighter than the 30-pound Compaqs of the time. However, it never caught on, because of its flat panel screen. Although the monochrome LCD panel was very large, it would be considered a joke today. It was almost impossible to see the characters on the display unless lighting conditions and your angle to the screen were perfect. Even then, it was difficult.

**data glove**    A glove used to report the position of a user's hand and fingers to a computer. See *virtual reality*.

**datagram**    The unit of data, or packet, transmitted in a TCP/IP network. Each datagram contains source and destination addresses and data. See *TCP/IP* and *UDP*.

**data hiding**    (1) Secretly embedding data in graphics images and other file types. See *steganography*.

(2) The result of encapsultion in object-oriented programming. See *encapsulation*.

**DataHub**    A database administration tool for DB2 and other database environments from IBM. It functions as a control center for accessing databases located throughout the enterprise.

**data hygiene**    The condition of data in a database. Clean data is error free or has very few errors. Dirty data has errors, including incorrect spelling and punctuation of names and addresses, redundant data in several records or simply erroneous data (not the correct amounts, names, etc.). See *address cleansing*.

**data independence**    Techniques that allow data to be changed without affecting the applications that process it. There are two kinds of data independence. The first type is data independence for data, which is accomplished in an database management system (DBMS). It allows the database to be structurally changed without affecting most existing programs. Programs access data in a DBMS by field and are concerned with only the data fields they use, not the format of the complete record.

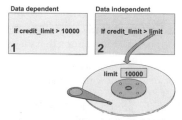

**The Data Glove**
This CyberGlove from Virtual Technologies is an example of a data glove. The wearer is playing a simulated ballgame. As he views the monitor, his hand movements are translated onto the screen via the data gloves. Each of the gloves in the picture contains 18 movement sensors. *(Image courtesy of Virtual Technologies, Inc.)*

**Data Independence for Processing**
Program #1 uses a hard-coded value to test credit limit. To change the limit, the program must be recompiled. Program #2 retrieves the credit limit from a database. To change it, only the database must be updated, a simpler task.

Thus, when the record layout is updated (fields added, deleted or changed in size), the only programs that must be changed are those that use those new fields.

The second type is data independence for processing. This means that any data that can possibly be changed should be stored in a database and not "hard wired" into the code of the program. When values change, only the database item is altered, which is a simple task, rather than recompiling programs.

**data integrity**    The process of preventing accidental erasure or adulteration in a database.

**Data Interchange Format**    See *DIF.*

**data item**    A unit of data stored in a field. See *field.*

**data legibility**    The clear readability of data in a decision support system (DSS). One of the keys to a successful DSS is its ability to provide understandable answers to queries, which conform to the user's business model and use recognizable field and table names.

**data library**    (1) The section of the datacenter that houses offline disks and tapes. Data library personnel are responsible for cataloging and maintaining the media.

(2) A directory on a server that contains files for downloading. BBSs and online services sometimes call these sections data libraries.

**dataline**    An individual circuit, or line, that carries data within a computer or communications channel.

**dataline monitor**    In communications, a test instrument that analyzes the signals and timing of a communications line. It either visually displays the patterns or stores the activity for further analysis.

**data link**    In communications, the physical interconnection between two points (OSI layers 1 and 2). It may also refer to the modems, protocols and all required hardware and software to perform the transmission.

**data link escape**    A communications control character that indicates that the following character is not data, but a control code.

**data link layer**    The services in the OSI protocol stack (layer 2 of 7) that manage node-to-node transmission. See *data link protocol, OSI* and *MAC layer.*

**data link protocol**    In communications, the transmission of a unit of data from one node to another (OSI layer 2). It is responsible for ensuring that the bits received are the same as the bits sent. Following are the major categories:

**Asynchronous Transmission**    Originating from mechanical teletype machines, asynchronous transmission treats each character as a unit with start and stop bits appended to it. It is the common form of transmission between the serial port of a personal computer or terminal and a modem. ASCII, or teletype, protocols provide little or no error checking. File transfer protocols, such as Zmodem and Ymodem, provide data link services and higher-level services, collectively known as transport services.

**Synchronous Transmission**    Developed for mainframe networks using higher speeds than teletype terminals, synchronous transmission sends contiguous blocks of data, with both sending and receiving stations synchronized to each other. Synchronous protocols include error checking. Examples are IBM's SDLC, Digital's DDCMP, and the international HDLC.

**Data Independence for Data**
Program #1 reserves space for the entire record (fields A to K). If the record format is changed, the space must be changed. Program #2 calls the DBMS to deliver just the fields it uses (D G H K). It still reserves space, but unless a field has been resized, it is not affected by other field changes. Program #3 is fully independent of the data structure. It calls for data by field name, and the DBMS allocates the space at runtime.

**LANs**   Developed for medium to high transmission speeds between stations, LANs typically use collision detection (CSMA/CD) or token passing methods for transmitting data between nodes. Common examples are Ethernet, Token Ring and FDDI.

The IEEE 802 specification for LANs breaks the data link layer into two sublayers: the LLC (Logical Link Control) and MAC (Media Access Control). The LLC provides a common interface point to the MAC layers, which specify the access method used. The following compares the data link layer in LANs to IBM's SNA and ISO's OSI model.

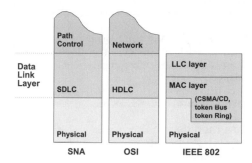

## Data Link Switching   See *DLSw*.

**data loading**   Coping data from one electronic file or database into another. Data loading implies converting from one format into another; for example, from one type of production database into a decision support database from a different vendor. See *data entry*.

**data management**   Refers to several levels of managing data. From bottom to top, they are as follows:

(1) The part of the operating system that manages the physical storage and retrieval of data on a disk or other device. See *access method*.

(2) Software that allows for the creation, storage, retrieval and manipulation of files interactively at a terminal or personal computer. See *file manager* and *DBMS*.

(3) The function that manages data as an organizational resource. See *data administration*.

(4) The management of all data/information in an organization. It includes data administration, the standards for defining data and the way in which people perceive and use it.

## data management system   See *DBMS*.

## data manipulation
Processing data.

## data manipulation language   A language that requests data from a DBMS. It is coded within the application program such as COBOL or C.

## data mart   A subset of a data warehouse for a single department or function. A data mart may have tens of gigabytes of data rather than hundreds of gigabytes for the entire enterprise. See *data warehouse*.

## data migration   See *HSM*.

## data mining   Exploring detailed business transactions. It implies "digging through tons of data" to uncover patterns and relationships contained within the business activity and history. Data mining can be done manually by slicing and dicing the data until a pattern becomes obvious. Or, it can be done with programs that analyze the data automatically. See *OLAP, DSS, EIS, data warehouse and slice and dice*.

**Doing It Automatically**
The goal of this credit card analysis is to determine the most influential factors common to non-profitable customers. In this case, BusinessMiner from Business Objects determined that the credit limit had the greatest effect on profitability and prioritized the results in graphical form. *(Screen shot courtesy of Business Objects.)*

**data mirroring**　　See *replication* and *disk mirroring*.

**data model**　　A description of the organization of a database. It is often created as an entity relationship diagram. Today's modeling tools allow the attributes and tables (fields and records) to be graphically created. The SQL code that defines the data structure (schema) in the database is automatically created from the visual representation. See *entity relationship model*.

**data modem**　　A modem used for sending data and not faxes. See *modem* and *fax/modem*.

**data module**　　A sealed, removable storage module containing magnetic disks and their associated access arms and read/write heads.

**data name**　　The name assigned to a field or variable.

**data network**　　A communications network that transmits data. Contrast with *voice network*. See *communications*.

**data packet**　　One frame in a packet-switched message. Most data communications is based on dividing the transmitted message into packets. For example, an Ethernet packet can be from 64 to 1,518 bytes in length.

**data parallel**　　Same as *SIMD*.

**DataPhone**　　An AT&T trade name for various equipment and services. See *DDS*.

**dataport**　　(1) An RJ-11 telephone socket that provides an outside line for sending data or a fax via modem. In the 1990s, hotels and motels throughout the U.S. started installing dataports in their rooms for customer use. See *RJ-11*.
　　(2) Any socket used for data communications, which can include infrared, serial and parallel ports.

**data processing**　　(1) Processing information by machines. Data processing was the first name used for the information technology business, and it is still used as an umbrella title. In the early days, it meant feeding punched cards into tabulating machines. Then computers followed.
　　(2) Processing data/information. In this context, it refers specifically to processing the actual data of the business (raw number crunching) in contrast to the processing overhead of the operating system and networks. In many instances, the computer does very little data processing compared to the processing required by the operating system, graphical interface and other infrastructure components.

**Data Processing Management Association**　　See *AITP*.

**data processor**　　(1) A person who works in data processing.
　　(2) A computer that is processing data, in contrast with a computer performing another task, such as controlling a network.

**data projector**　　A device that accepts output from a computer and projects it onto a screen or white wall. It accepts VGA output at resolutions typically up to 800×600 or 1024×768 and may also accept standard video output. In the 1980s, the first data projectors used tubes to create the image. They were large and weighed 40 pounds or more. Later, units were made as see-through LCD panels and put on an overhead projector for illumination. In the mid 1990s, projectors combined illumination and imaging in the same device, and have shrunk down to just a few pounds. See *LCD panel*.

**Data Propagator**　　A database administration tool for DB2 and other database environments from IBM. It is used to keep relational databases in sync throughout the enterprise.

**data pump**　　A circuit that transmits pulses in a digital device. It typically refers to the chipset in a modem that generates the bits based on the modem's modulation techniques.

**Dataquest**　　(Dataquest Inc., San Jose, CA, www.dataquest.com) A major market research and analysis firm in the information field. Dataquest offers market intelligence on more than 25 topics and provides conferences, annual subscriptions and custom research. Founded in 1971 as a unit of First Texas, Inc., a Houston-based brokerage firm, it was spun off in 1976. In 1978, it was acquired by A.C. Nielsen Company, which itself was acquired by The Dun & Bradstreet Corporation in 1984. In 1995, Dataquest was acquired by the GartnerGroup. See *GartnerGroup*.

**data rate**    **(1)** The data transfer speed within the computer or between a peripheral and computer.
**(2)** The data transmission speed in a network.

**data recovery**    Restoring data that has been physically damaged or corrupted on a disk or tape. Disks and tapes can become corrupted due to viruses, bad software, and hardware failure, as well as from power failures that occur while the magnetic media is being written. Of course, data can also be damaged by fire and other accidents, and laptop disks are especially vulnerable being bounced around from one location to another.

**data repository**    See *repository*.

**data representation**    How data types are structured; for example, how signs are represented in numerical values or how strings are formatted (enclosed in quotes, terminated with a null, etc.).

**data resource management**    Same as *data administration*.

**data scrubbing**    **(1)** Making data more accurate and consistent; in other words, "cleaning it up". It refers to eliminating duplicate records, correcting misspellings and errors in names and addresses, ensuring consistent descriptions, punctuation, syntax and other content issues. Data scrubbing is often required when data from different databases are combined into one. See *audio scrubbing*.
**(2)** In a RAID disk system, monitoring and correcting parity byte errors that may occur (although infrequently) in order to keep the drives in synchronization.

**Recovered Data**
Since 1985, the DriveSavers service bureau in Novato, CA (www.drivesavers.com), has recovered data from damaged hard disks of all kinds. Even fires and natural disasters cannot keep them from successfully retrieving vital records from computers such as these.
*(Images courtesy of DriveSavers, Inc.)*

**data set**    **(1)** A data file or collection of interrelated data. The term is used in the mainframe community, whereas "file" is used almost everywhere else.
**(2)** A modem in AT&T terminology.

**data set ready**    See *DSR*.

**data sharing**    The ability to share the same data resource with multiple applications or users. It implies that the data is stored in one or more servers in the network, and that there is some software locking mechanism that prevents the same set of data from being changed by two people at the same time. Data sharing is a primary feature of a database management system (DBMS). See *data conferencing* and *groupware*.

**data sheet**    A page or two of detailed information about a product.

**data signal**    Physical data as it travels over a line or channel (pulses or vibrations of electricity or light).

**data sink**    A device or part of the computer that receives data.

**data sizes**    See *space/time*.

**data source**    A device or part of the computer in which data is originated.

**DataStage**    A data extraction and transformation program for Windows NT servers from Ardent. It is used to pull data from legacy databases, flat files and relational databases and convert them into data marts and data warehouses.

**data store**    A permanent storehouse of data. The term is often used to lump the storage of all types of data structures (files, databases, text documents, etc.) into one generic category.

**data stream**　　The continuous flow of data from one place to another.

**data striping**　　See *disk striping*.

**data structure**　　The physical layout of data. Data fields, memo fields, fixed-length fields, variable-length fields, records, word processing documents, spreadsheets, data files, database files and indexes are all examples of data structures.

**data switch**　　A switch box that routes one line to another; for example, to connect two computers to one printer. Manual switches have dials or buttons. Automatic switches test for signals and provide first-come, first-served switching. See *A/B box*.

**data synchronization**　　Keeping data/text/images in different databases up-to-date so that each repository contains the same information. Data in a handheld device or laptop often requires synchronization with a desktop machine or a server. When the same data resides in multiple locations, it must be routinely synchronized. See *replication*.

**data system**　　Same as *information system*.

**data tablet**　　Same as *digitizer tablet*.

**data transfer**　　The movement of data within the computer system. Typically, data is said to be transferred within the computer, but it is "transmitted" over a communications network. A transfer is actually a copy function since the data is not automatically erased at the source.

**data transfer rate**　　Same as *data rate*.

**data transmission**　　Sending data over a communications network.

**data transparency**　　The ability to easily access and work with data no matter where it is located or what application created it.

**data type**　　A category of data. Typical data types are numeric, alphanumeric (character), dates and logical (true/false). Programming languages allow for the creation of different data types.

When data is assigned a type, it cannot be treated like another type. For example, alphanumeric data cannot be calculated, and digits within numeric data cannot be isolated. Date types can only contain valid dates.

**data vaulting**　　Transmitting data to a computer in a different location for backup.

**data visualization**　　See *information visualization*.

**data warehouse**　　A database designed to support decision making in an organization. It is batch updated and can contain enormous amounts of data. For example, large retail organizations can have 100GB or more of transaction history. When the database is organized for one department or function, it is often called a "data mart" rather than a data warehouse.

The data in a data warehouse is typically historical and static and may also contain numerous summaries. It is structured to support a variety of analyses, including elaborate queries on large amounts of data that can require extensive searching. When databases are set up for queries on daily transactions, they are often known as operational data stores (ODSs) rather than data warehouses. See *ODS*, *OLAP*, *DSS* and *EIS*.

**data word**　　See *word*.

**DataWorks**　　(DataWorks Corporation, San Diego, CA, www.dataworks.com) A software company founded in 1977 that develops integrated enterprise resource planning (ERP) systems. The company develops, implements and supports open systems and client/server-based software for midrange manufacturing companies that are primarily in the high technology sector.

**date math**    Calculations made upon dates. For example, March 30 + 5 yields April 4. Date math is the crux of the Y2K problem. In Y2K-compliant systems, calculating dates with the full four-digit year yield the correct results. In non-compliant systems, the year 2000 is interpreted as 1900. See *Y2K problem*.

**date windowing**    Solving the Year 2000 problem without altering the database. The six-digit date remains in the database, but the programs convert it into an eight-digit date for computation, display and reporting.

**datum**    The singular form of data; for example, one datum. It is rarely used, and data, its plural form, is commonly used for both singular and plural.

**daughterboard**    A printed circuit board that plugs into another printed circuit board to augment its capabilities. Although Intel's Pentium II SEC modules are sometimes called daughterboards, it more typically refers to a small board that attaches to a removable expansion board such as a display adapter or sound card.

**daughtercard**    See *daughterboard*.

**DAV**    See *WebDAV*.

**DAVID**    (Digital Audio/Video Interactive Decoder) An operating system for set-top boxes from Microware Systems Corporation, Des Moines, IA (www.microware.com). Based on Microware's OS-9 realtime operating system, it is used for interactive TV, video on demand and Internet applications. See *OS-9*.

**dazdee**    See *DASD*.

**DB**    See *database, decibel* and *DB connector*.

**DB-15**    See *DB connector*.

**DB2**    (DATABASE 2) A relational DBMS from IBM that was originally developed for its mainframes. It is a full-featured SQL language DBMS that has become IBM's major database product. Known for its industrial strength reliability, IBM has made DB/2 available for all of its own platforms, including OS/2, OS/400, AIX (RS/6000) and OS/390), as well as for Solaris on Sun systems and HP-UX on HP 9000 workstations and servers. See *DB2 UDB*.

**DB2/2**    The OS/2 version of DB2 from IBM. Also called DB2 for OS/2, it is a 32-bit DBMS that replaced OS/2's earlier 16-bit Database Manager. See *DB2*.

**DB2/400**    The AS/400 version of DB2 from IBM. See *DB2*.

**DB-25**    See *DB connector*.

**DB2/6000**    The RS/6000 version of DB2 from IBM. See *DB2*.

**DB2 Everywhere**    An embedded version of DB2 designed for cellphones, PDAs and other dedicated devices. It is a slimmed-down version of its flagship database management system (DBMS).

**DB2 UDB**    (DB2 Universal DataBase) An enhanced and very popular version of DB2 that combines relational and object database technology, as well as various query optimization techniques for parallel processing. Also geared for electronic commerce, DB2 UDB provides graphical administration, Java and JDBC support. DB2 UDB runs on mainframes, Windows NT and various versions of UNIX.

**DB-37**    See *DB connector*.

**DB-50**    See *DB connector*.

**DB-9**    See *DB connector*.

**DBA** See *database administrator*.

**dBASE** A relational database management (DBMS) and application development system for Windows from dBASE Inc., Vestal, NY (www.dbase2000.com). dBASE was the first sophisticated database program for personal computers and has been widely used since the early 1980s. dBASE file formats became de facto standards.

dBASE was originally for CP/M and later DOS, but starting with dBASE for Windows and then Visual dBASE, it became a client/server development system with the inclusion of the Borland Database Engine. dBASE has automatic links to the Engine's IDAPI interface, allowing dBASE applications to access remote database servers.

dBASE provides a Pascal-like, interpreted programming language and fourth-generation commands for interactive use. The following dBASE 3GL example converts Fahrenheit to Celsius:

```
INPUT "Enter Fahrenheit  " TO FAHR
? "Celsius is ", (FAHR - 32) * 5 / 9
```

The following dBASE 4GL example opens the product file and displays green items:

```
use products
list for color ='GREEN'
```

**Evolution of dBASE** dBASE II was the first comprehensive relational DBMS for personal computers. Originally named Vulcan, dBASE II was created by Wayne Ratliff to manage a company football pool. It was modeled after JPLDIS, the DBMS at Jet Propulsion Labs in Los Angeles.

Renamed dBASE II when Hal Lashlee and George Tate formed Ashton-Tate to market it (Ashton-Tate was acquired by Borland in 1991), dBASE became a huge success within a couple of years.

dBASE spawned the "Xbase" industry, which included Clipper, FoxBase, FoxPro and other products that provided a dBASE-like programming language and support for dBASE file formats.

**The Versions** Introduced in 1981, dBASE II was the original command-driven dBASE for CP/M and later for DOS. In 1984, dBASE III upgraded the DOS version with more features and support for larger databases. In 1986, dBASE III PLUS added the ability to store queries and relational views. In 1988, dBASE IV added support for SQL.

In 1994, dBASE 5.0 for Windows added objects and visual programming and provided connectivity to a variety of SQL databases using the Borland Database Engine. In 1995, Version 5.5 was renamed Visual dBASE. In 1999, dBASE, Inc., acquired dBASE from Borland to continue the product line and introduce dBASE 2000.

**dBASE compiler** Software that converts dBASE source language into machine language. The resulting programs execute on their own like COBOL or C programs and do not run under dBASE. See *CA-Clipper*, *Force* and *Quicksilver*.

**dBASE Mac** A Macintosh DBMS from Ashton-Tate that never caught on because it was not compatible with dBASE for the PC.

**DB connector** A family of plugs and sockets widely used in communications and computer devices. DB connectors come in 9-, 15-, 25-, 37- and 50-pin sizes. The DB connector defines the physical structure of the connector, not the purpose of each line.

A DB-9 connector is commonly used for the first serial port (COM1) on a PC, which is typically connected to the mouse. A DB-25 connector is used for

**C. Wayne Ratliff**
Ratliff designed and programmed the first successful DBMS for personal computers, dBASE II. *(Image courtesy of Ratliff Software Productions.)*

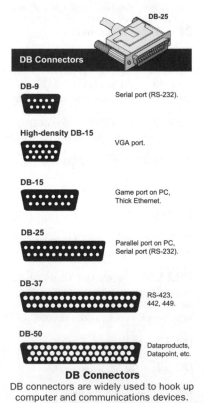

| | |
|---|---|
| **DB-9** | Serial port (RS-232). |
| **High-density DB-15** | VGA port. |
| **DB-15** | Game port on PC, Thick Ethernet. |
| **DB-25** | Parallel port on PC, Serial port (RS-232). |
| **DB-37** | RS-423, 442, 449. |
| **DB-50** | Dataproducts, Datapoint, etc. |

**DB Connectors**
DB connectors are widely used to hook up computer and communications devices.

the second serial port (COM2), often connected to a modem, as well as the parallel port (see *printer cable*). DB-25s are also used in a wide variety of communications devices.

A high-density DB-15 connector is used for the VGA port on a PC, which has 15 pins in the same shell as the 9 pins in the DB-9 connector. See *plugs and sockets*.

**DBCS**    (Double Byte Character Set) See *Unicode*.

**DB/DC**    (DataBase/Data Communications) Refers to software that performs database and data communications functions.

**DBEF**    (Dual Brightness Enhancement Film) A film that increases the brightness of LCD screens from 3M. The film recycles most of the light that is normally lost in the rear polarizer.

**DB EXPO**    A trade show for IT professionals, originally from the Blenheim Group and later Miller Freeman, Inc., that specialized in database and related products. It had become part of IT Forum, which was discontinued after its final show in April 1998.

**DBF file**    The dBASE data file extension. dBASE II and dBASE III files both use DBF, but are not compatible.

**DBLIB**    (DataBase LIBrary) The native, low-level programming interface for Sybase and Microsoft SQL Server databases. In the Microsoft world, much of the interaction between applications and databases is programmed using high-level interfaces such as DAO, RDO and ADO. See *CTLIB*, *ADO*, *RDO*, *DAO* and *high-level interface*.

**DBMS**    (DataBase Management System) Software that controls the organization, storage, retrieval, security and integrity of data in a database. It accepts requests from the application and instructs the operating system to transfer the appropriate data.

DBMSs may work with traditional programming languages (COBOL, C, etc.) or they may include their own programming language for application development.

DBMSs let information systems be changed more easily as the organization's requirements change. New categories of data can be added to the database without disruption to the existing system. Adding a field to a record does not require changing any of the programs that do not use the data in that new field.

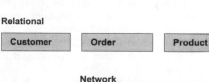

## Major Features of a DBMS

**Data Security**    The DBMS can prevent unauthorized users from viewing or updating the database. Using passwords, users are allowed access to the entire database or a subset of it known as a "subschema." For example, in an employee database, some users may be able to view salaries while others may view only work history and medical data.

**Data Integrity**    The DBMS can ensure that no more than one user can update the same record at the same time. It can keep duplicate records out of the database; for example, no two customers with the same customer number can be entered.

**Interactive Query**    Most DBMSs provide query languages and report writers that let users interactively interrogate the database and analyze its data. This important feature gives users access to all management information as needed.

**Interactive Data Entry and Updating**    Many DBMSs provide a way to interactively enter and edit data, allowing you to manage your own files and databases. However, interactive operation does not leave an audit trail and does not provide the controls necessary in a large organization. These controls must be programmed into the data entry and update programs of the application.

This is a common misconception about personal computer DBMSs. Complex business systems can be developed in dBASE and Paradox, etc., but not without programming. This is not the same as creating lists of data for your own record keeping.

**Data Independence**    With DBMSs, the details of the data structure are not stated in each application program. The program asks the DBMS for data by field name; for example, a coded equivalent of "give me customer name and balance due" would be sent to the DBMS. Without a DBMS, the programmer must reserve space for the full structure of the record in the program. Any change in data structure requires changing all application programs.

**Database Design**    A business information system is made up of subjects (customers, employees, vendors, etc.) and activities (orders, payments, purchases, etc.). Database design is the process of organizing this data into related record types. The DBMS that is chosen is the one that can support the organization's data structure while efficiently processing the transaction volume.

Organizations may use one kind of DBMS for daily transaction processing and then move the detail to another DBMS better suited for random inquiries and analysis.

Overall systems design decisions are performed by data administrators and systems analysts. Detailed database design is performed by database administrators.

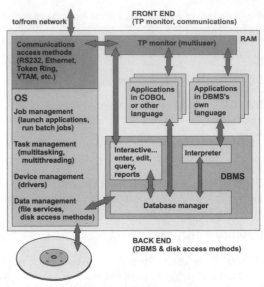

**DBMS and OS Interaction**
This diagram shows the interaction between the DBMS with other system and application software running in memory.

## Hierarchical, Network and Relational Databases

Information systems are made up of related files: customers and orders, vendors and purchases, etc. A key DBMS feature is its capability to manage these relationships.

Hierarchical databases link records like an organization chart. A record type can be owned by only one owner. In the following example, orders are owned by only one  customer. Hierarchical structures were widely used with early mainframe systems; however, they are often restrictive in linking real-world structures.

In network databases, a record type can have multiple owners. In the example on the previous page, orders are owned by both customers and products, reflecting their natural relationship in business.

Relational databases do not link records together physically, but the design of the records must provide a common field, such as account number, to allow for matching. Often, the fields used for matching are indexed in order to speed up the process.

In the preceding example, customers, orders and products are linked by comparing data fields and/or indexes when information from more than one record type is needed. This method is more flexible for ad hoc inquiries. Many hierarchical and network DBMSs also provide this capability.

**Object Databases**    Certain information systems may have complex data structures not easily modeled by traditional data structures. A newer type of database, known as the *object database*, can be employed when hierarchical, network and relational structures are too restrictive. Object databases can easily handle one-to-many relationships combined with many-to-one relationships.

The world of information is also made up of data, text, pictures and voice. Many DBMSs manage text as well as data, but very few manage both with equal proficiency. Throughout the 1990s, DBMSs will begin to integrate all forms of information. Eventually, it will be common for a database to handle data, text, graphics, voice and video with the same ease as today's systems handle data.

The relational DBMS is not suited to storing multimedia data, because there are so many different types of sound and video formats. Although a relational DBMS may provide a LOB (large object) field that holds anything, extensive use of this field can strain the processing.

An object database is often better suited for multimedia. Using the object model, an object-oriented DBMS can store anything or refer to anything. For example, a video object can reference a video file stored elsewhere on some other hard disk and launch the video player software necessary to play it.

**Intelligent Databases**    All DBMSs provide some data validation; for example, they can reject invalid dates or alphabetic data entered into money fields. But most validation is left up to the application programs.

Intelligent databases provide more validation; for example, table lookups can reject bad spelling or coding of items. Common algorithms can also be used, such as one that computes sales tax for an order based on ZIP code.

When validation is left up to each application program, one program could allow an item to be entered while another program rejects it. Data integrity is better served when data validation is done in only one place. Mainframe DBMSs are increasingly becoming intelligent. Eventually, all DBMSs will follow suit.

**DBOMP**    (DataBase Organization and Maintenance Processor) An early DBMS that was derived from BOMP.

**DBQ**    (DataBase for Quality) An RDBMS from Murphy Software, Southfield, MI, that runs on Windows clients and the AS/400. Specialized for quality management, it is used to promote ISO 9000 compliance.

**DBS**    (Direct Broadcast Satellite) A one-way TV broadcast service from a satellite to a small 18" dish antenna. DBS offers every household in the country a cable-like TV service, using a highly compressed digital signal. Prior to DBS, large dishes and costly equipment were required, and multiple satellites made viewing complicated.

Although DBS service existed in other countries, the first DBS satellite in the U.S. was launched in late 1993 by Hughes Communications (DirecTV) and Hubbard Broadcasting (USSB). DirecTV and USSB were offered in 1994 using the DSS standard, with equipment made by RCA and other manufacturers.

Soon after, Primestar introduced its DBS service, which includes installation of its own equipment that is leased along with the monthly programming. In 1995, EchoStar launched its first satellite and offers purchase, finance and lease options for its DISH (DIgital Sky Highway) network.

**DB to DB adapter**    A device that connects one type of DB connector to another. For example, a DB to DB adapter is used to connect a 9-pin mouse to a 25-pin serial port.

**dBXL**    An earlier dBASE III PLUS–compatible DBMS developed by WordTech Systems, Inc., Orinda, CA.

**DC**    (1) (Direct Current) An electrical current that travels in one direction and used within the computer's electronic circuits. Contrast with *AC*.

(2) (Data Communications) See *DB/DC*.

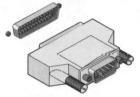

**DB to DB Adapter**
This male DB-9 to female DB-25 adapter is commonly used to attach a 9-pin plug on a mouse cable to a 25-pin serial port.

**DC-2000**    The generic name for the original quarter-inch QIC Minicartridge format. Subsequent to the DC-2000, QIC-Wide, QIC-EX and Travan came onto the market. See *QIC*.

**DCA**    (1) (Document Content Architecture) IBM file formats for text documents. DCA/RFT (Revisable-Form Text) is the primary format and can be edited. DCA/FFT (Final-Form Text) has been formatted for a particular output device and cannot be changed. For example, page numbers, headers and footers are placed on every page.

(2) (Distributed Communications Architecture) A network architecture from Unisys.

(3) (Digital Communications Associates, Inc., Alpharetta, GA) A manufacturer of communications products, known for its famous "Irma" board. In late 1994, DCA merged with and became part of Attachmate Corporation of Bellevue, WA. See *Irma board*.

**D/CAS**    (Data/CASsette) A tape backup technology that uses an upgraded version of the common audio tape cassette. It can hold as much as 600MB of data.

**DCC**    (1) (Direct Cable Connection) A Windows 95/98 feature that allows PCs to be cabled together for data transfer. DCC actually sets up a network connection between the two machines. Even though it is not a dial-up situation, DCC requires that the Dial-Up Networking function be activated.

(2) (Digital Compact Cassette) A digital tape format that used a variation of the common analog audio cassette. DCC never caught on.

(3) (Digital Content Creation) The development of newsworthy, educational and entertainment material for distribution over the Internet or other digital media.

(4) (Distributed Call Center) An automatic call distribution (ACD) system from Teloquent Communications, Billerica, MA (www.teloquent.com), that runs on standard PCs and uses public ISDN lines.

**DCD**   (Document Content Description) An XML schema language from Textuality, Microsoft and IBM that is implemented as an RDF vocabulary. It supports data typing and schema reuse and is the sucessor to XML-Data. A standard XML schema is expected from the W3C in 2000. See *XML schema*, *RDF* and *XML*.

**DCE**   (1) (Data Communications Equipment or Data Circuit-terminating Equipment) A device that establishes, maintains and terminates a session on a network. It may also convert signals for transmission. It is typically the modem. Contrast with *DTE*.

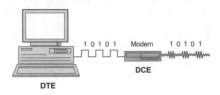

(2) (Distributed Computing Environment) A set of programs from The Open Group that allows applications to be built across heterogeneous platforms in a network. DCE includes security, directory naming, time synchronization, file sharing, RPCs and multithreading services. DCE source code is licensed to major vendors, who sell the executable programs to their customers.

DCE and CORBA, the OMG's distributed, multiplatform implementation, are not mutually exclusive. For example, IBM uses DCE directory and time services in its CORBA-compliant SOM/DSOM implementation. CORBA can use DCE's RPC (remote procedure call) as its communications mechanism.

**DCI**   (Display Control Interface) An Intel/Microsoft programming interface for full-motion video and games in Windows. It allows applications to take advantage of video accelerator features built into the display adapter. DCI requires updated display drivers and the DCI DLL from Microsoft. DCI has been superseded by DirectDraw in Windows 95.

**d-cinema**   See *digital cinema*.

**DCL**   (1) (Digital Command Language) Digital's standard command language for the VMS operating system on its VAX series.

(2) (Data Compression Library) A set of compression routines that allow realtime compression and decompression of data. See *PK software*.

(3) (Data Control Language) A language used to gain access to or manage a database.

**DCLI**   See *DLCI*.

**DCMS**   (Digital Content Management System) See *DAMS*.

**DCOM**   (Distributed Component Object Model) Formerly Network OLE, it is Microsoft's technology for distributed objects. DCOM is based on COM, Microsoft's component software architecture, which defines the object interfaces. DCOM defines the remote procedure call that allows those objects to be run remotely over the network. DCOM began shipping with Windows NT 4.0 and is Microsoft's counterpart to CORBA. See *COM*, *component software* and *CORBA*.

**DC/OSx**   (DataCenter/OSx) Pyramid Technology's UNIX operating system that runs on its Nile series of SMP machines. DC/OSx is the first SMP implementation on UNIX System V Release 4.

**DCS**   (1) (Digital Cross-connect System) A network switching and grooming device used by telecom carriers. See *digital cross-connect*.

(2) (Distributed Communications System) A telephone system that puts small switches close to subscribers making local loops shorter and maximizing long lines to the central office.

(3) (Desktop Color Separation) A graphics format for color separation that uses five Encapsulated PostScript (EPS) files, one for each of the CMYK colors, and one master file, which links the other four and contains a preview image.

(4) (Distributed Control System) A process control system that uses disbursed computers throughout the manufacturing line for control.

(5) (Declarative Content Standard) An HTML and JavaScript-based format for delivering content for interactive TV. See *ATV Forum*.

**DCT**   (Discrete Cosine Transform) An algorithm, similar to Fast Fourier Transform, that converts data (pixels, waveforms, etc.) into sets of frequencies. The first frequencies in the set are the most meaningful; the latter, the least. For compression, latter frequencies are stripped away based on allowable resolution loss. The DCT method is used in the JPEG and MPEG compression.

**DD**    (Double Density) The designation for low-density diskettes, typically the 5.25" 360K and 3.5" 720K floppies. See *double density*. Contrast with *HD*.

**DD2**    (Data D-2) A magnetic tape technology from Ampex that uses the same 19mm, helical scan D2 transport developed for the broadcasting industry. See *DST*.

**D/DAT**    See *DATA/DAT*.

**DDBMS**    (Distributed Database Management System) See *distributed database*.

**DDC**    See *VESA DDC*.

**DDCMP**    (Digital Data Communications Message Protocol) Digital's proprietary, synchronous data link protocol used in DECnet.

**DDE**    (Dynamic Data Exchange) A message protocol in Windows that allows application programs to request and exchange data between them automatically.

**DDL**    (1) (Data Description Language) A language used to define data and their relationships to other data. It is used to create the data structure in a database. Major database management systems (DBMSs) use a SQL data description language.
     (2) (Document Description Language) A printer control language from Imagen that runs on the HP LaserJet series.
     (3) (Direct Data Link) The ability of a supplier to directly interrogate a customer's inventory database in order to manage scheduling and shipping more efficiently. Pioneered by Ford Motor Co. in 1988, Ford lets suppliers check stock levels in assembly plants throughout North America.

**DDM**    (Distributed Data Management) Software in an IBM SNA environment that allows users to access data in remote files within the network. DDM works with IBM's LU 6.2 session to provide peer-to-peer communications and file sharing. See also *distributed database*.

**DDML**    An XML schema language developed by members of the XML-DEV mailing list. Formerly known as XSchema, it supports schema reuse. A standard XML schema is expected from the W3C in 2000. See *XML schema* and *XML*.

**DDN**    (Defense Data Network) An Internet-based global communications network created by the U.S. Department of Defense. In April 1996, users were moved to the more modern Defense Information Systems Network (DISN) made up of NIPRnet (Non-classified IP Router Network) and SIPRnet (Secret IP Router Network).

**DDN NIC**    (Defense Data Network Network Information Center) The organization that originally handled the assignment of Internet network addresses and autonomous system numbers, the administration of the root domain and Internet information and support services. Since the creation of the InterNIC, it performs these functions only for the DDN. See *Network Solutions*.

**DDNS**    (Dynamic DNS) The ability to automatically update a DNS server when an IP address is automatically assigned (typically from DHCP) to a network device. See *DHCP*, *WINS* and *DNS*.

**DDOS**    See *denial of service attack*.

**DDP**    (Distributed Data Processing) See *distributed processing*.

**DDR SDRAM**    (Double Data Rate Synchrous DRAM) See *SDRAM*.

**DDS**    (1) (Digital Data Storage) See *DAT*.
     (2) (Data Dictionary System) See *QuickBuild* and *OpenDDS*.
     (3) (Dataphone Digital Service) A private line digital service from AT&T with data rates from 2.4 to 56 Kbps.
     (4) (Digital Data Service) A private line digital service from carriers other than AT&T.

**DDWG** (Digital Display Working Group) An organization devoted to standardizing a digital interface to flat panel displays. Formed in 1998 by Intel, Compaq, Fujitsu, HP, IBM, NEC and Silicon Image, it introduced its Digital Visual Interface (DVI) in early 1999. See *DVI* and *flat panel display.*

**dead link** A World Wide Web link that turns up a "404 error" if the target page is deleted from the site or moved to another directory. See *404 error.*

**deadlock** See *deadly embrace.*

**deadly embrace** A stalemate that occurs when two elements in a process are each waiting for the other to respond. For example, in a network, if one user is working on file A and needs file B to continue, but another user is working on file B and needs file A to continue, each one waits for the other. Both are temporarily locked out. The software must be able to deal with this.

**dead tree** Paper. Any printed version of reference material or documentation. Contrast with *electronic publishing.*

**deallocate** To release a computer resource that is currently assigned to a program or user, such as memory or a peripheral device.

**DeBabelizer** A graphics processing program for Windows and Mac from Equilibrium, Sausalito, CA (www.debabelizer.com). DeBabelizer is an image editing program similar to Photoshop, but it can perform any of its tasks on multiple images without user intervention. For example, it is widely used to convert a group of images from one format to another.

**debit** A monetary amount that is subtracted from an account balance. A debit from one account is a credit to another. See *credit.*

**deblock** To separate records from a block.

**debug** To correct a problem in hardware or software. Debugging software is finding the errors in the program logic. Debugging hardware is finding the errors in circuit design. See *DOS Debug.*

**debugger** Software that helps a programmer debug a program by stopping at certain breakpoints and displaying various programming elements. The programmer can step through source code statements one at a time while the corresponding machine instructions are being executed.

**DEC** The trade name for Digital Equipment Corporation's earlier products (DECmate, DECnet, etc.). Many people used to refer to the company as DEC. In 1998, Digital was acquired by Compaq. See *Digital Equipment.*

**decay** The reduction of strength of a signal or charge.

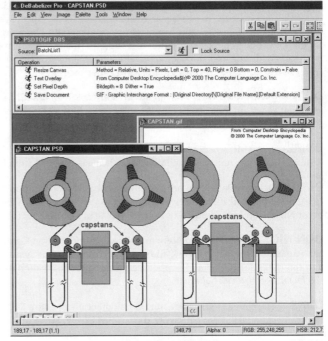

**Adding a Text Overlay**
The PSDTOGIF.DBS script at the top adds a copyright message to a group of PSD files and saves them as GIFs. Note the four steps: (1) add room at top, (2) overlay copyright, (3) reduce colors to 256, (4) save as GIF image.

**decentralized processing** Computer systems in different locations. Although data may be transmitted between the computers periodically, it implies limited daily communications. Contrast with *distributed computing* and *centralized processing.*

**decibel**    (dB) The unit that measures loudness or strength of a signal. dBs are a relative measurement derived from an initial reference level and a final observed level. A whisper is about 20 dB, a normal conversation about 60 dB, a noisy factory 90 dB and loud thunder 110 dB. 120 dB is the threshold of pain.

**decimal**    Meaning 10. The universal numbering system that uses 10 digits. Computers use binary numbers because it is easier to design electronic systems that can maintain two states rather than 10.

**decimal based**    Using the decimal numbering system. The earliest electronic calculating machines were decimal based. Contrast with *binary based*. See *Mark I* and *ENIAC*.

**decipher**    Same as *decrypt*.

**decision box**    A diamond-shaped symbol that is used to document a decision point in a flowchart. The decision is written in the decision box, and the results of the decision branch off from the points in the box.

**decision instruction**    In programming, an instruction that compares one set of data with another and branches to a different part of the program depending on the results.

**decision making**    Making choices. The proper balance of human and machine decision making is an important part of a system's design.

It is easy to think of automating tasks traditionally performed by people, but it is not that easy to analyze how decisions are made by an experienced, intuitive worker. If an improper analysis of human decision making is made, the wrong decision making may be placed into the machine, which can get buried in documentation that is rarely reviewed. This will become an important issue as AI applications proliferate.

From a programming point of view, decision making is performed two ways: algorithmic, a precise set of rules and conditions that never change, or heuristic, a set of rules that may change over time (self-modify) as conditions occur. Heuristic techniques are employed in AI systems.

**DecisionSuite**    A ROLAP engine from Information Advantage, Inc., Eden Prarie, MN (www.infoadvan.com). It was folded into the MyEureka family of portal and BI software and renamed MyEureka ROLAP Server. See *MyEureka*.

**decision support system**    See *DSS*, *EIS* and *OLAP*.

**decision table**    A list of decisions and their criteria. Designed as a matrix, it lists criteria (inputs) and the results (outputs) of all possible combinations of the criteria. It can be placed into a program to direct its processing. By changing the decision table, the program is changed accordingly.

**decision tree**    A graphical representation of all alternatives in a decision making process.

**deck**    The part of a magnetic tape unit that holds and moves the tape reels. See also *DEC*.

**declaration**    In programming, an instruction or statement that defines data (fields, variables, arrays, etc.) and resources, but does not create executable code.

**declarative language**    See *non-procedural language*.

**DECmate**    A family of computer systems from Digital specialized for word processing. Introduced in 1981, DECmates use the PDP-8 architecture.

**DECmcc**    (DEC Managment Control Center) Digital's network management software for DECnet and TCP/IP. DECmcc Management Stations for VMS and ULTRIX support X Window and provide color-coded alarms.

**DECnet**    Digital's communications network, which supports Ethernet-style LANs and baseband and broadband WANs over private and public lines. It interconnects PDPs, VAXs, PCs, Macs and workstations. In DECnet philosophy, a node must be an intelligent machine, and not simply a terminal as in other systems.

DECnet/DOS allows DOS machines to function as end nodes in DECnet networks, and DECnet/OSI is the implementation of DECnet Phase V that supports OSI and provides compatibility with DECnet Phase IV and TCP/IP.

**decode** (1) To convert coded data back into its original form. Contrast with *encode*.
(2) Same as *decrypt*. See *cryptography*.

**decoder** A hardware device or software that converts coded data back into its original form. See *decode* and *MPEG decoder*.

**decollator** A device that separates multiple-part paper forms while removing the carbon paper.

**decompiler** A program that converts machine language back into a high-level source language. The resulting code may be very difficult to maintain, as variables and routines are named generically: A0001, A0002, etc. See *disassembler*.

**decompress** To restore compressed data back to its original size.

**decrement** To subtract a number from another number. Decrementing a counter means to subtract 1 or some other number from its current value.

**decrypt** To convert encrypted data back into its original form. Contrast with encrypt. See *cryptography*.

**DeCSS** (**DE**crypt **CSS**) Software that decrypts the CSS encryption system in DVD movies. The software was engineered through a hacker network known as MoRE (Masters of Reverse Engineering) that obtained some of the CSS code. It was completed by 15-year-old Jon Johansen, a Norwegian student, ostensibly to play DVDs using the Linux operating system, but Johansen released the final version over the Internet in late 1999, causing considerable dismay to the DVD movie industry. See *CSS*.

**DECstation** (1) A series of RISC-based single-user workstations from Digital, introduced in 1989, that run under ULTRIX.
(2) A PC series from Digital introduced in 1989.
(3) A small computer system from Digital, introduced in 1978, used primarily for word processing (DECstation 78).

**DECsystem** (1) A series of RISC-based, 32-bit computers from Digital that run under ULTRIX. Introduced in 1989, the 5400 model is a Q-bus system; the 5800 model uses the XMI bus.
(2) A series of mainframes from Digital that were introduced from 1974 through 1980 and were the successor to the 36-bit PDP-10 computers.

**DECT** (**D**igital **E**nhanced **C**ordless **T**elecommunications) A cordless phone standard widely used in Europe. Based on TDMA and the 1.8 and 1.9GHz bands, it uses Dynamic Channel Selection/Dynamic Channel Allocation (DCS/DCA) to enable multiple DECT users to coexist on the same frequency. DECT provides data links up to 522 Kbps with 2 Mbps expected in the future. Using dual-mode handsets, DECT is expected to coexist with GSM. which is the standard cellphone system in Europe. For more information, contact the DECT Forum at www.dect.ch.

**DECtalk** A voice synthesis system from Digital that accepted serial ASCII text and converted it into audible speech. It was used in Touch-tone telephone response systems, as well as for voice-output for visually handicapped users.

**DECwindows** Digital's windowing architecture, based on X Window, Version 11. It is compatible with X Window while adding a variety of enhancements.

**dedicated channel** A computer channel or communications line that is used for one purpose.

**dedicated line** A phone or other communications line used for one purpose. Synonymous with *leased line* and *private line*.

**dedicated service** A service that is not shared by other users or organizations.

**deep linking** Providing a hyperlink on a Web site or on the results page of a search engine to a page on another Web site that is not the Web site's home page. Many results of a search engine provide deep links to Web sites, because many search engines index any and all pages on the Web.

D

**de facto standard**   A widely used format or language not endorsed by a standards organization.

**default**   The current setting or action taken by hardware or software if the user has not specified otherwise. Application programs have dozens, if not hundreds, of defaults that determine everything from the font size that should be used to the folder a file is saved in. Defaults also imply that the setting or action can be changed.

The term is also used as a verb. For example, in the expression "the program defaults to xxx" means that the program does xxx under these circumstances unless directed to do otherwise.

**default directory**   Same as *current directory*.

**default drive**   The disk drive used if no other drive is specified.

**default font**   The typeface and type size used if none other is specified.

**default gateway**   The router used to forward all traffic that is not addressed to a station within the local subnet.

**default name**   The name initially assigned to a folder or any other resource that comes with or is created in the computer. For example, when you create a new folder in most computers, its default name is "New Folder." Default names can be changed by the user.

**default profile**   The normal default settings assigned to an application or system. See *user default profile*.

**defragger**   Also called an "optimizer program," it is a software utility that defragments a disk. It rewrites the files and stores them in adjacent sectors. Sophisticated defraggers allow frequently used files to be placed at the front of the disk for faster retrieval.

**defragment**   To reorganize the disk by putting files into contiguous order. Because the operating system stores new data in whatever free space is available, data files become spread out across the disk if they are updated often. This causes extra read/write head movement to read them back. Periodically, the hard disk should be defragmented to put files back into order. See *defragger* and **DOS Defrag**.

**degauss**   To remove unwanted magnetism from a monitor or the read/write head in a disk or tape drive. Some monitors have a built-in deguassing function that can be activated by the user. See *gauss* and *bulk eraser*.

**degrees of freedom**   The amount of movement available in a robotics or virtual reality system. See *6DOF*.

**Deja.com**   A Web site that specialized in product ratings and information. Founded in 1995 as Deja News, the site was initially created to archive and search Usenet discussions. In 1999, it rebranded itself as a product decision-making site with consumer opinions and reviews, and product comparisons. In 2000, eBay's Half.com acquired the consumer service, and Google acquired the Usenet archive in 2001.

**DejaNews**   See *Deja.com*.

**de jure standard**   A format or language endorsed by a standards organization.

**delayed binding**   See *TCP splicing*.

**delay equalization**   Compensating for the late arrival of data in one or more channels when multiple channels are used in a transmission. Incoming data is buffered so all streams can be output sequentially when the most tardy channel is finally transmitting.

**delay line**   A communications or electronic circuit that has a built-in delay. Acoustic delay lines were used to create the earliest computer memories. For example, the UNIVAC I used tubes of liquid mercury that would slow down the digital pulses long enough (a fraction of a second) to serve as storage.

**delete**    To remove an item of data from a file, or to remove a file from the disk. See *undelete*.

**delimiter**    A character or combination of characters used to separate one item or set of data from another. For example, in comma-delimited records, a comma is used to separate each field of data.

**deliverable**    The measurable result or output of a process.

**DEL key**    (DELete key) The keyboard key used to delete the character under the screen cursor or some other currently highlighted object.

**Dell**    (Dell Computer Corporation, Austin, TX, www.dell.com) A leading manufacturer of PCs founded in 1984 by Michael Dell. Originally selling under the "PCs Limited" brand, Dell was the first to legitimize mail-order PCs by providing quality telephone support. Dell was also the first major manufacturer to pre-load applications selected by the customer.

Dell's rise throughout the 1990s was extraordinary. It made the Fortune 500 in 1991 with sales of $546 million, and eight years later, sales exceeded $25 billion. With more than 200 patents covering current and future computer systems and related technologies, Dell has become a major force in the industry.

**Michael S. Dell**
From *Inc.* Magazine's
"Entrepreneur of the Year" to
*PC Magazine's* "Man of the
Year," Dell has received
numerous awards for his
management abilities. He
started the company in 1984
with $1,000. *(Image courtesy
of Dell Computer Corporation.)*

**Delphi**    (1) An application development system for Windows from Borland. Introduced in 1995 and based on the object-oriented Object Pascal language, it includes visual programming tools and generates executable programs (.EXE files). Delphi supports all the major databases including Oracle, Sybase and INFORMIX.

(2) (Delphi Consulting Group, Boston, MA, www.delphigroup.com) The leading consulting organization in document management and workflow. Founded in 1987 by Thomas Koulopoulos, it provides consulting services, publications and inhouse and public seminars on the subjects.

(3) See also *Delphi Forums*.

**Delphi Forums**    (Delphi Forums, Cambridge, MA, www.delphi.com) A consumer-oriented Web site that offers self-managed forums on any subject. Similar to UseNet in that messages are posted for subsequent reading at any time, Delphi Forums require all forums to be moderated by the person that originated them or a designated administrator. In the late 1980s, Delphi was an online service, which, in 1992, was the first to offer full Internet access, not just e-mail. In 1998, it switched to the forums model.

The message board and chat engine facilities used in the forums is hosted by Prospero Technologies, Sausalito, CA (www.prospero.com), and available to other Web sites. In 2000, Prospero was formed from the merger of Delphi Forums and Well Engaged, LLC, which was a leading provider of online community services in the B2B sector.

**delta**    A incremental value between one number and another.

**delta backup**    See *backup types*.

**delta frame**    In interframe coding, a frame that provides an incremental change from the key frame. See *interframe coding*.

**delta modulation**    A technique that is used to sample voice waves and convert them into digital code. Delta modulation typically samples the wave 32,000 times per second, but generates only one bit per sample. See *PCM*.

**de-lurk**    To finally type in a comment after "lurking" in a chat room for some time. See *lurk*.

**DEM**    See *digital elevation model*.

**DEMA**    Founded in 1976 as the Data Entry Management Association, it later changed its name to the Association for Input Technology and Management. In 1993, it merged with TAWPI.

**demand dial routing**    The ability to establish a dial-up connection in order to forward data to a destination.

**demand paging**    Copying a program page from disk into memory when required by the program.

**demand printing**    See *POD*.

**demand processing**    Same as *transaction processing*.

**demarc**    See *demarcation point*.

**demarcation point**    The location within a home or office where the lines from the telephone company connect to the customer's lines.

**demilitarized zone**    See *DMZ*.

**Demo Conference**    A computer symposium run by IDG that invites vendors to showcase their newest technologies. Many new companies and products are first launched at Demo. Founded in 1990 by industry pundit Stewart Alsop, the Palm Pilot was introduced at Demo 1996, and 450 units were presold at the conference. For information, visit www.demo.com.

**demodulate**    To filter out the data signal from the carrier. See *modulate*.

**Demo II**    A demonstration, authoring and prototyping program for DOS from Lifeboat Publishing, Shrewsbury, NJ (www.pparadise.com). It was developed by Dan Bricklin, who designed the original VisiCalc spreadsheet. The Windows version is demo-It!

**demon**    See *daemon*.

**demoware**    Demonstration software that shows some or all of the features of a commercial product. See *crippleware*.

**demultiplex**    To reconvert a transmission that contains several intermixed signals back into its original separate signals.

**DEN**    (Directory Enabled Networks) The management of a network from a central depository of information about users, applications and network resources. Originally an initiative from Microsoft and Cisco, DEN was turned over to the DMTF in 1998. A DEN schema is expected for the CIM model. See *WBEM*, *CIM* and *DMTF*.

**denial of service**    A condition in which a system can no longer respond to normal requests. See *denial of service attack*.

**denial of service attack**    An assault on a network that floods it with so many additional requests that regular traffic is either slowed or completely interrupted. Unlike a virus or worm, which can cause severe damage to databases, a denial of service attack interrupts network service for some period. A distributed denial of service (DDOS) attack uses multiple computers throughout the network that it has previously infected. All of these "zombies" work together to send out bogus messages, thereby increasing the amount of phony traffic. See *smurf attack*, *SYN flood attack* and *Ping of Death*.

**denizen**    An inhabitant of a particular place. A "denizen of the Internet" is a person that frequently uses the Web or other Internet facilities.

**dense wavelength division multiplexing**    See *WDM*.

**densitometer**    A device that calibrates the relative strength of a color using complimentary filters. Contrast with *colorimeter*.

**density**    See *packing density* and *bit density*.

**departmental computing**    Processing a department's data with its own computer system. See *distributed computing*.

**dependent segment**    In database management, data that depends on data in a higher level for its full meaning.

**deprecate**    To make invalid or obsolete by removing or flagging the item. See *flagging*.

**dequeue**    Pronounced "d-q." To remove an item from a queue. Contrast with *enqueue*.

**DES**    (Data Encryption Standard) An NIST-standard secret key cryptography method that uses a 56-bit key. DES is based on an IBM algorithm which was further developed by the U.S. National Security Agency. It uses the block cipher method which breaks the text into 64-bit blocks before encrypting them. There are several DES encryption modes. The most popular mode exclusive ORs each plaintext block with the previous encrypted block.

DES decryption is very fast and widely used. The secret key may be kept a total secret and used over again. Or, a key can be randomly generated for each session, in which case the new key is transmitted to the recipient using a public key cryptography method such as RSA.

Triple DES is an enhancement to DES that provides considerably more security than standard DES, which uses only one 56-bit key. There are several Triple DES methods. EEE3 uses three keys and encrypts three times. EDE3 uses three keys to encrypt, decrypt and encrypt again. EEE2 and EDE2 are similar to EEE3 and EDE3, except that only two keys are used, and the first and third operations use the same key. See *encryption algorithm*, *cryptography*, *RSA* and *Fortezza*.

**descender**    The part of lower case characters g, j, p, q and y that fall below the line. Sometimes these characters are displayed and printed with shortened descenders in order to fit into a smaller character cell, making them difficult to read. See *typeface*.

**descending sort**    Arranging data from high to low sequence; for example, from Z to A or from 9 to 0. Contrast with *ascending sort*.

**Deschutes**    See *Pentium II*.

**descriptor**    (1) A word or phrase that identifies a document in an indexed information retrieval system.
(2) A category name used to identify data.

**deserialize**    To convert a serial stream of bits into parallel streams of bits.

**deshoots**    See *Pentium II*.

**DesignCAD**    A family of 2-D and 3-D CAD programs from ViaGrafix, Pryor, OK (www.viagrafix.com), for DOS, Windows and Mac, noted for their ease of use. DesignCAD 3-D for Windows includes such features as texture mapping, reflection mapping with up to eight light sources and keyframe animation.

**Designer**    See *Micrografx Designer*.

**Designer/2000**    See *Developer/2000*.

**design optimization**    See *automatic design optimization*.

**desk accessory**    In the Macintosh, a program that is always available from the Apple menu no matter what application is running. With System 7, all applications can be turned into desk accessories.

**desk checking**    Manually testing the logic of a program.

**DeskJet**    A family of popular desktop ink-jet printers for PCs from HP.

**Deskpro**    A Compaq trade name for various models of its PCs.

**desktop**    (1) When a graphical user interface (GUI) is used to access applications such as with the Macintosh or Windows, the on-screen background is said to be the desktop. Since electronic desktops (computer screens) are generally no more than 15" wide, it is difficult to view more than two pages side by side.
(2) A buzzword attached to applications traditionally performed on more expensive machines that are converted to a personal computer (desktop publishing, desktop mapping, etc.).
(3) Short for *desktop computer*.

**desktop accessory**    Software that simulates an object normally found on an office desktop, such as a calculator, notepad and appointment calendar. See *TSR*.

**desktop application**    See *desktop accessory*.

**Desktop.com**    A Web-based service that provides its own family of applications written in JavaScript, which is supported by all major browsers. The applications are downloaded into any browser on any computer and have more of the look and feel of regular office applications than typical HTML pages. For information, visit www.desktop.com. See *virtual desktop services*.

**desktop computer**    Refers to a personal computer such as a PC or Mac or to a workstation from Sun, IBM, etc. Whether in a horizontal case on top of the desk or in a tower under or to the side of the desk is not the issue. The term refers to a single-user computer in contrast to a server shared by multiple users and in contrast to a laptop, which provides portability.

**desktop conferencing**    See *videoconferencing* and *data conferencing*.

**desktop device**    (1) Any product that is used on the desktop.
(2) A full-blown Windows or Mac machine. The term is used to contrast a desktop personal computer with a handheld device. See *Internet appliance*.

**desktop enhancer**    A utility that adds some non-standard capability to the user's graphical interface. It may provide features such as the ability to customize icons or the cursor, or to change a window's appearance, or to view files and folders in a different way. See *virtual screen*.

**desktop lockdown**    The prevention of changes to configuration settings in a client machine. See *system policy*.

**Desktop Management Interface**    See *DMI*.

**Desktop Management Task Force**    See *DMTF*.

**desktop manager**    The part of a GUI that displays the desktop and icons, that allows programs to be launched from the icon and files to be visually dragged and dropped (copied, deleted, etc.). The desktop manager combined with the window manager make up the GUI. The desktop manager is included with the Mac and Windows. In OSF/Motif and Open Look, products such as IXI's X.desktop and Visix Software's Looking Glass add this capability.

**desktop mapping**    Using a desktop computer to perform digital mapping functions.

**desktop media**    The integration of desktop presentations, desktop publishing and multimedia (coined by Apple).

**desktop organizer**    See *desktop accessory*.

**desktop presentations**    The creation of presentation materials on a personal computer, which includes charts, graphs and other graphics-oriented information. It implies a wide variety of special effects for both text and graphics that will produce output for use as handouts, overheads and slides, as well as sequences that can be viewed on screen. Advanced systems generate animation and control multimedia devices.

**desktop publishing**    Abbreviated "DTP." Using a personal computer to produce high-quality printed output or camera-ready output for commercial printing. It requires a desktop publishing program, high-speed personal computer, large monitor and a laser printer.
A desktop publishing program, also called a "page layout program," provides complete page design capabilities, including magazine style columns, rules and borders, page, chapter and caption numbering, as well as precise typographic aligment. A key feature is its ability to manage text and graphics on screen WYSIWYG style. The program can flow text around graphic objects in a variety of ways.

Text and graphics may be created in the program, but graphics capability is usually very limited. Typically, the work is created in word processing, CAD, drawing and paint programs and then imported into the publishing system.

A laser printer may be used for final text output, but it cannot print line art and shaded drawings respectably unless its resolution is 1,200 dpi or greater. For best results, whether text or graphics, a high-resolution imagesetter at 1,270 or 2,540 dpi is top quality. For electronic transfer to a commercial printer, documents are generally saved as PostScript files, but printing houses are increasingly accepting native documents from popular page layout programs such as PageMaker and QuarkXPress.

Desktop publishing has dramatically brought down the cost of page layout, causing many projects to be done inhouse. Predefined style sheets for newsletters, brochures and other publishing tasks can help rank novices do respectable jobs. But, there is still no substitute for a graphics designer who knows which fonts to use and how to lay out the page artistically.

**desktop switch**   See *frame switch* and *KVM switch*.

**desktop videoconferencing**   Using a PC to videoconference. Contrast with a room system where everyone congregates. See *videoconferencing*.

**deskview**   See *DESQview*.

**DeskWriter**   A family of popular desktop ink-jet printers for the Macintosh from HP. Color models are also available.

**DESQview**   An earlier multitasking, windows environment for DOS from Quarterdeck. In the 1980s, DESQview was the first serious windows program for the DOS PC. Using the included QEMM memory manager, it ran multiple DOS text and graphics programs in resizable windows.

**DESQview/X**   A version of DESQview that adds X Windows to a PC network, allowing each DOS machine to run multiple applications on different PCs in the network. As an integration product, it allows DOS and Windows apps to run in an X Window network under UNIX or any other X-based environment.

**destructive memory**   Memory that loses its content when it is read, requiring that the circuitry regenerate the bits after the read operation.

**detail file**   Same as *transaction file*.

**DETI**   Digispeak for "don't even think it!"

**developer**   A person that designs and writes software for commercial use. Same as *software engineer* and *systems programmer*.

**developer's toolkit**   A set of software routines and utilities used to help programmers write an application. For graphical interfaces, it provides the tools and libraries for creating menus, dialog boxes, fonts and icons. It provides the means to link the application to libraries of software routines and to link it with the operating environment (OS, DBMS, protocol, etc.). See *API*, *development system*, *client/server development system* and *GUI builder*.

**Developer/2000**   A client/server application development system for Windows, Macintosh and Motif from Oracle. Formerly the Cooperative Development Environment, the core programs are Oracle Forms, Oracle Reports and Oracle Graphics. Oracle Procedure Builder provides drag and drop application partitioning. It also includes Discoverer/2000, which is an end user analysis suite made up of Oracle Data Query for reports and queries and Oracle Browser for viewing tables and data dictionaries.

Discoverer replaces Discoverer/2000 and combines several tools into one. Designer/2000 is Oracle's data modeling and repository system.

**development cycle**   See *system development cycle*.

**development environment**   See *development system*.

**development system**    **(1)** A programming language and related components. It includes the compiler, text editor, debugger, function library and any other supporting programs that enable a programmer to write a program. See *developer's toolkit* and *application development system*. For a list of popular client/server development tools, see *client/server development system*.

**(2)** A computer and related software for developing applications.

**development tool**    Software that assists in the creation of new software. Compilers, debuggers, visual programming tools, GUI builders, application generators are examples. See *developer's toolkit*. For a list of popular client/server development tools, see *client/server development system*.

**device**    **(1)** Any electronic or electromechanical machine or component from a transistor to a disk drive. Device always refers to hardware.

**(2)** In semiconductor design, it is an active component, such as a transistor or diode, in contrast to a passive component, such as a resistor or capacitor.

**device adapter**    Same as *interface adapter*.

**device address**    See *address* and *I/O address*.

**Device Bay**    A quick-change peripheral format from Compaq, Intel and Microsoft that enables hard drives, CD-ROM drives and other devices to be easily hot swapped without opening the case. Using the USB and IEEE 1394 FireWire interfaces, it provides three form factors (DB13, DB20 and DB32), which are 13, 20 and 32mm in height. For more information, visit www.device-bay.org. See *USB* and *FireWire*.

**device context**    A data structure in Windows programming that is used to define the attributes of text and images that are output to the screen or printer. The device context (DC) is maintained by GDI. A DC, which is a handle to the structure, is obtained before output is written and released after the elements have been written. See *GDI*.

**device control character**    A communications code that activates a function on a terminal. See *ASCII chart*.

**device dependent**    Refers to programs that address specific hardware features and work with only one type of peripheral device. Contrast with *device independent*. See *machine dependent*.

**device driver**    See *driver*.

**device enumeration**    Identifying all the devices attached to a system and initializing the required routines (drivers) that enable them to function. See *enumerate*.

**device independent**    Refers to programs that work with a variety of peripheral devices. The hardware-specific instructions are in some other program (OS, DBMS, etc.). Contrast with *device dependent*. See *machine independent*.

**device level**    **(1)** In circuit design, refers to working with individual transistors rather than complete circuits.

**(2)** Refers to communicating directly with the hardware at a machine language level.

**Device Manager**    In Windows 95/98/2000, a dialog in the System control panel that shows the status of all the peripheral devices connected to your computer. See *Win Device Manager*.

**device name**    A name assigned to a hardware device that represents its physical address. For example, LPT1 is a DOS device name for the parallel port.

**device resolution**    The resolution of an output device such as a monitor or printer. See *resolution*.

**DFP**    (Digital Flat Panel) A digital interface for a flat panel display as specified by the DFP Group (www.dfp-group.org). Based on TDMS transmission, it uses a 20-pin mini-D ribbon (MDR) connector. Compaq has been the primary supporter of DFP and has put DFP ports on many of its computers; however, the Digital Visual Interface (DVI) is expected to become the standard. DFP was introduced with a limit of 1,024×768 pixels. See *flat panel display*.

**Dfs**　(Distributed File System) An enhancement to Windows NT and 95/98 that allows files scattered across multiple servers to be treated as a single group. With Dfs, a network administrator can build a hierarchical file system that spans the organization's LANs and WANs.

**DFSMS**　(Data Facility Storage Management System) Data management, backup and HSM software from IBM for MVS and OS/390 mainframes. Introduced in 1993, it combines separate backup, copy, HSM and device driver routines into one package, which provides all the I/O management for the operating system. See *SMS* and *ADSM*.

**DFT mode**　(Distributed Function Terminal mode) A mode that allows a 3270 terminal to have five concurrent sessions with the mainframe. Contrast with *CUT mode*.

**DG**　See *Data General*.

**DG/UX**　(Data General UNIX) A UNIX-based operating system developed by Data General. It supports symmetric multiprocessing and is generally used with the Tuxedo TP monitor for transaction processing.

**DHCP**　(Dynamic Host Configuration Protocol) Software that automatically assigns IP addresses to client stations logging onto a TCP/IP network. It eliminates having to manually assign permanent IP addresses. DHCP software typically runs in servers, and is also found in network devices such as ISDN routers and modem routers that allow multiple users access to the Internet. Newer DHCP servers dynamically update the DNS servers after making assignments. See *DNS*, *DDNS* and *WINS*.

**DHCP server**　A server in the network or a service within a server that assigns IP addresses. See *DHCP*.

**Dhrystones**　A benchmark program that tests a general mix of instructions. The results in Dhrystones per second are the number of times the program can be executed in one second. See *Whetstones* and *benchmark*.

**DHTML**　See *Dynamic HTML*.

**DIA**　(Document Interchange Architecture) An IBM SNA format used to exchange documents from dissimilar machines within an LU 6.2 session. It acts as an envelope to hold the document and does not set any standards for the content of the document, such as layout settings or graphics standards.

**Diablo emulation**　A printer that accepts the same commands as the Diablo printer.

**diacritical**　A small mark added to a letter that changes its pronunciation, such as the French cedilla, which is a small hook placed under the letter "c."

**diagnostic board**　An expansion board with built-in diagnostic tests that reports results via its own readout. See *POST card*.

**diagnostics**　(1) Software routines that test hardware components (memory, keyboard, disks, etc.). In personal computers, they are often stored in ROM and activated on startup.

(2) Error messages in a programmer's source code that refer to statements or syntax that the compiler or assembler cannot understand.

**diagnostic tracks**　The spare tracks on a disk used by the drive or controller for testing purposes.

**diagramming program**　Software that allows the user to create flow charts, organization charts and similar diagrams. It is similar to a drawing program, but specialized for creating interconnected diagrams. It comes with a palette of predefined shapes and symbols, and usually keeps the lines connected between them if they are edited and rearranged.

Examples of general flowcharting programs are Visio, FlowCharter, CorelFlow and allClear. Network diagram-specific programs that can link an equipment database to the objects in the diagram are ClickNet and netViz.

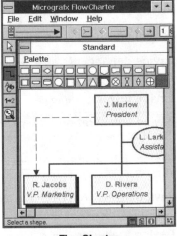

**FlowCharter**
Using a palette of predefined shapes and arrows, FlowCharter allows diagrams and organization charts to be quickly created. One of the features of a flowcharting program is its ability to keep the lines connected to the boxes. If a box is moved, the line is moved with it. *(Screen shot courtesy of Micrografx, Inc.)*

**dialer**    **(1)** The part of a modem that dials a telephone number.
     **(2)** The part of a telephone that is used to manually dial a number.
     **(3)** Software that initiates a dial-up sequence for a modem or telephone. See *dial-up adapter* and *war dialer*.

**DIALOG**    (The Dialog Corporation, Cary, NC, www.dialog.com) The first commercial online service founded in 1972. For years, DIALOG has offered the largest single collection of information available online. There is no charge for searching, but there is a fee for viewing the results. Access is available via the Web or by separate dial-up numbers as was the norm before the Internet became universally popular.

**dialog box**    A window displayed on screen in response to selecting some menu option. It provides the user with the current status and available options for a particular feature in the program. Dialog boxes can be small or large, depending on the amount of information that must be conveyed.

**Dialpad.com**    (Dialpad.com, Inc., Santa Clara, CA, www.dialpad.com) A Web-to-phone service provider founded in 1996 by Dr. Hyunduk Ahn as Serome Technology. In 1999, the company changed its name to Dialpad.com and began to offer the first free, Java-based Web-to-phone service. Using the Internet as the voice transport, and advertiser supported, Dialpad provides free telephone calls from your PC to anyone in the United States. See *Web-to-phone*.

**dialup**    See *dial-up line*.

**dial-up adapter**    Software that dials up a phone number. For example, for Internet connections in Windows, you should see "TCP/IP- Dial-Up Adapter" in the Network control panel. This means the TCP/IP (Internet) protocol has been directed to the Dial-Up Adapter. Although "adapter" implies a card plugged into the computer, this is not the case here.

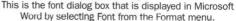

**Sample Dialog Box**
This is the font dialog box that is displayed in Microsoft Word by selecting Font from the Format menu.

**dial-up line**    A two-wire line as used in the dial-up telephone network. Contrast with *leased line*.

**dial-up network**    **(1)** The switched telephone network regulated by government and administered by common carriers.
     **(2)** A computer network that can be accessed remotely via modem. See *remote access server* and **Win Dial-up networking**.

**dial-up networking**    See *dial-up network* and **Win Dial-up networking**.

**dial-up services**    See *online services*.

**diazo film**    A film used to make microfilm or microfiche copies. It is exposed to the original film under ultraviolet light and is developed into identical copies. Copy color is typically blue, blue-black or purple.

**DIB**    **(1)** (Directory Information Base) Also called "white pages," a database of names in an X.500 system.
     **(2)** (Device Independent Bitmap) An internal data structure in Windows for creating graphics that are not tied to a particular output device. DIBs contain more information than a BMP file so that they can be rendered into any display or printer device. When stored on disk however, they become BMP files. See *BMP file*.
     **(3)** (Dual Independent Bus) An enhanced bus architecture from Intel first implemented on the Pentium Pro chip. It provides two buses; one for connecting the CPU to system memory and another for the cache. The DIB enables Pentium II CPU bus speeds to jump from 66MHz to 100MHz.

**dibit**    Any one of four patterns from two consecutive bits: 00, 01, 10 and 11. Using phase modulation, a dibit can be modulated onto a carrier as a different shift in the phase of the wave.

**DIBOL** (DIgital coBOL) A version of COBOL from Digital that runs on the PDP and VAX series.

**dice** The plural of die. See *die*.

**DID** (Direct Inward Dialing) The ability to make a telephone call to an internal telephone extension within an organization without having to go through an operator.

**die** The formal term for the square of silicon containing an integrated circuit. Die (singular) and dice (plural) are used by chip designers and engineers. The popular term is chip.

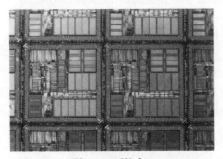

**Dice on a Wafer**
This picture of several dice on the wafer shows the various subsystems on each die (chip). This is known as a "beauty shot," because the areas are colored in for presentation. *(Image courtesy of Texas Instruments, Inc.)*

**dielectric** An insulator (glass, rubber, plastic, etc.). Dielectric materials can be made to hold an electrostatic charge, but current cannot flow through them.

**DIF** **(1)** (Data Interchange Format) A standard file format for spreadsheet and other data structured in row and column form. Originally developed for VisiCalc, DIF is now under Lotus' jurisdiction.

**(2)** (Display Information Facility) An IBM System/38 program that lets users build custom programs for online access to data.

**(3)** (Document Interchange Format) A file standard developed by the U.S. Navy in 1982.

**(4)** (Dual In-line Flatpack) A type of surface mount DIP with pins extending horizontally outward.

**Difference Engine** An early calculator designed by Charles Babbage and subsidized by the British government. Employing wheels and rods, which others had experimented with earlier, the project was started in 1821 but failed its test in 1833. Babbage then turned his attention to the

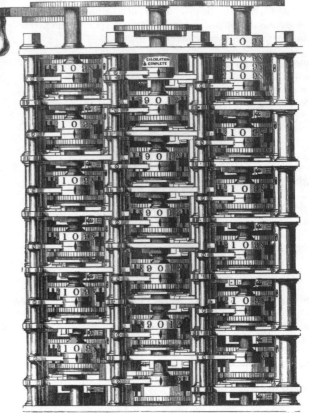

*B. H. Babbage, del.*

Impression from a woodcut ot a small portion of Mr. Babbage's Difference Engine No. 1, the property of Government, at present deposited in the Museum at South Kensington.

It was commenced 1823.
This portion put together 1833.
The construction abandoned 1842.
This plate was printed June, 1853.
This portion was in the Exhibition 1862.

**The Difference Engine**
This impression from a woodcut was printed in 1853 showing a portion of the Difference Engine that was built in 1833. Babbage later turned his attention to the Analytical Engine. It too was never finished. *(Image courtesy of Charles Babbage Institute, University of Minnesota, www.cbi.umn.edu)*

Analytical Engine and completely abandoned the Difference Engine by 1842. Although never completed, it did improve the precision of Britain's machine-tool industry. In 1991, the National Museum of Science and Technology built a working model of the Difference Engine.

In 1879, Babbage's son reassembled a section of the Difference Engine from parts; and in 1995, Christie's auction in London auctioned off that section to the Power House Museum in Sydney for $282,000. The other known sections are owned by Harvard and Cambridge Universities. See *Analytical Engine*.

## difference keying    *See color key.*

## Differential Analyzer    An analog calculator built in the 1930s by
Vannevar Bush at MIT. Designed to solve differential equations, it was used in World War II to calculate ballistics tables that showed the trajectory of a projectile over distance. Containing more than a thousand gears, the machine took up an entire room. It was tediously programmed by physically changing the gears with a screwdriver and wrench, and the output was displayed as graphs. As the gears wore over time, the machine introduced inaccuracies, yet it was a remarkable breakthrough and the fastest computational tool of its kind. No more than a dozen Differential Analyzers were built.

## differential backup    *See backup types.*

## differential configuration    The use of individual wire pairs for each
electrical signal for high immunity to noise and crosstalk. Contrast with *single-ended configuration*.

## differential PCM    *See DPCM.*

## Differential SCSI    *See SCSI.*

## differential updating    Replacing only the files in a software
application that have changed rather than replacing all the files.

## differentiated services    Offerings that can be classified by
type, or quality, of service. For example, a differentiated services network could prioritize realtime traffic for a higher fee.

## Diffie-Hellman    A cryptographic technique that enables
sending and receiving parties to exchange public keys in a manner that derives a shared, secret key at both ends. Using a common number, both sides use a different random number as a power to raise the common number. The results are sent to each other. The receiving party raises the received number to the same random power they used before, and the results are the same on both sides. See *ECC*.

## diffraction    The bending of electromagnetic waves as
they pass around corners or through holes smaller than the wavelengths of the waves themselves. See *diffraction grating* and *refraction*.

## diffraction grating    A device that breaks up an
electromagnetic wave into its different frequencies (wavelengths) by scattering them at different angles. For example, a series of thousands of scored lines in a glass plate diffracts light into a rainbow of colors. Lines of data pits on a CD give the same effect. See *diffraction*.

**Bush with His Differential Analyzer**
Although programmed with a screwdriver and wrench, Bush's Differential Analyzer was a breakthrough in its time. *(Image courtesy of The Computer Museum History Center, www.computerhistory.org)*

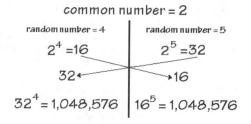

common number = 2

random number = 4 | random number = 5

$2^4 = 16$     $2^5 = 32$

$32$     $16$

$32^4 = 1,048,576$ | $16^5 = 1,048,576$

**It's Rather Clever**
There's more computation in actual practice, but this example, which uses tiny numbers to illustrate the concept, shows a very clever mathematical approach. Each party raises the common number, which is 2 in this example (this has nothing to do with binary—it's just the number 2) to a random power and sends the result to the other. The received number is raised to the same random power. Note that both parties come up with the same secret key, which was never transmitted intact.

**Diffserv** (**DIFF**erentiated **SERV**ices) A method for adding quality of service (QoS) to IP networks from the IETF. Operating at layer 3 only, Diffserv uses the IP type of service (TOS) field as the Diffserv byte (DS byte). Diffserv does not provide traffic engineering or hard quality of service similar to ATM. It is expected that service providers will use MPLS within the network and use Diffserv at the edges of the network for classification and assignment to the right connection. See *MPLS*.

**diffusion** A semiconductor manufacturing process that infuses tiny quantities of impurities into a base material, such as silicon, to change its electrical characteristics. See *chip*.

**digerati** The "digital elite." People that are extremely knowledgeable about computers. It often refers to the movers and shakers in the industry. Digerati is the high-tech equivalent of "literati," which refers to scholars and highly educated individuals. See *jitterati*.

**DigiBoard** A variety of modem and fax boards from Digi International, Minnetonka, MN (www.digi.com) that were used to increase the serial port density on a remote access server. DigiBoards are older products that have been replaced, but users may still refer to remote access products from the company as digiboards or digicards.

**digicam** See *digital camera*.

**DigiCash** See *ecash*.

**digispeak** In online communications, the use of acronyms to make a shorthand out of common phrases. For example, BTW for "by the way" and IMHO for "in my humble opinion." People are doing so much typing these days that they welcome shortcuts, and the shortcuts are turning into a new language.

**digit** A single character in a numbering system. In decimal, digits are 0 through 9. In binary, digits are 0 and 1.

**digital** Traditionally, digital means the use of numbers and the term comes from digit, or finger. Today, digital is synonymous with computer. See also *Digital Equipment*.

Digital Means Original   The 0s and 1s of digital data mean more than than just on and off. They mean perfect copying. When information, music, voice and video are turned into binary digital form, they can be electronically manipulated, preserved and regenerated perfectly at high speed. The millionth copy of a computer file is exactly the same as the original. While this continually drives the software industry crazy protecting its copyrights, it is nevertheless a major advantage of digital processing.

**Digital8** A digital video recording and playback format that uses the same cartridges as 8mm and Hi-8 analog systems, but increases horizontal resolution to 500 lines, similar to MiniDV (8mm is 270 lines; Hi-8 is 400 lines). Digital8 recording uses twice as much tape as analog 8mm or Hi-8 recording. Introduced by Sony, Digital8 camcorders and players compete directly with MiniDV, but have the advantage of playing 8mm and Hi-8 analog tapes. See *Hi-8* and *MiniDV*.

**Digital AMPS** See *IS-136*.

**digital appliance** Any apparatus controlled by a computer. It may refer to an actual household appliance (coffee maker, toaster, etc.) that is computerized, but often refers to a handheld device such as a pager, cellphone or PDA. See *Internet appliance*.

**digital asset** Any material created on the computer by employees of the organization or that has been custom developed for and purchased by the organization. Images scanned into the computer are also a digital asset if the original work is owned by the company.

D

**digital asset management system**   See *DAMS*.

**digital audio**   (1) Sound waves that have been digitized and stored in the computer. Common digital audio formats are music CDs, WAV, AIFF and MP3. Music CDs, which use the Red Book digital audio format, are played in CD players, as well as CD-ROM readers. WAV, AIFF and MP3 files are played by a media player software application. The files can be stored on a hard disk or written onto a CD-ROM as well. Although also in digital form, MIDI music is not considered digital audio. MIDI files contain a coded version of the musical score, not the actual sound. See *CD, WAV file, AIFF file, MP3, MIDI* and *DVD-Audio*.

(2) Broadcasting radio in digital format. See *DARS*.

**digital audio broadcasting**   See *DAB*.

**digital audio disc**   Same as *CD*.

**digital audio encoding system**   See *Dolby Digital, DTS, SDDS* and *THX*.

**digital audio extraction**   A feature of most newer CD-ROM drives that allows the digital data from audio CDs to be passed through the computer's bus (IDE, SCSI) just like CD-ROM data. Without this feature, transferring audio CD tracks to the computer requires using the analog output of the drive and converting it back to digital again, resulting in less sound quality. See *ripper*, **CD-ROM audio cable** and *MP3*.

**digital audio player**   See *MP3 player*.

**digital audio tape**   See *DAT*.

**digital camera**   A video or still camera that records images in digital form. Unlike traditional analog cameras that record infinitely variable intensities of light, digital cameras record discrete numbers for storage on a flash memory card, floppy disk or hard disk. As with all digital devices, there is a fixed, maximum resolution and number of colors that can be represented. The images are transferred to the computer with a serial cable, USB cable or via the storage medium itself if the desktop machine has a counterpart reader.

Digital cameras record color images as intensities of red, green and blue, which are stored as variable charges in a CCD matrix. The size of the matrix determines the resolution, but the analog-to-digital converter (ADC), which converts the charges to digital data, determines the color depth.

TV studio cameras also use CCDs, but may generate traditional analog signals or digital signals depending on the application. Increasingly, TV is going digital, and is expected in time to be digital from end to end. See *flash memory*, *photo scanner* and *optical zoom*.

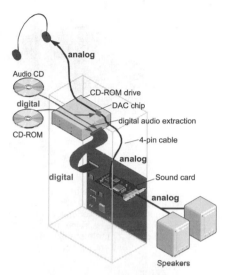

**Digital and Analog Outputs**
CD-ROM drives convert audio CD data to analog and send it to the sound card and headphones. If it also sends audio CD data to the computer's bus, it is known as "digital audio extraction."

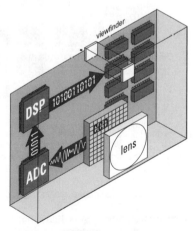

**Digital Camera**
Behind the lens, CCDs pick up the image as charges that are converted to digital data by an A/D converter chip (ADC). The DSP chip adjusts contrast and detail and compresses the digital data for storage.

**Camera and "Film"**
A classic now, the DC50 was one of the first digital cameras from the venerable Kodak company. Holding 24 images in internal memory, it used flash disks for more storage. *(Image courtesy of SanDisk Corporation.)*

**Photo Printer**
FARGO made one of the first printers designed for 4x6" photographic prints. The 1995 introduction of the $595 FARGO FotoFUN! was a breakthrough price for a dye sublimation printer. *(Image courtesy of FARGO Electronics, Inc.)*

**Print Via the Web**
Photo printing companies such as Photoworks, PhotoPoint and Ofoto let you upload your digital pictures to their Web sites so they can be previewed by family and friends from any Internet connection. Clicking on a thumbnail (top) displays a larger, low-res image (bottom). High-resolution prints can be ordered by anyone. Undeveloped analog film can also be sent to the companies for processing. *(Images courtesy of Jim and Karen Clayton.)*

**digital cash**    See *digital money*.

**digital cellphone**    A cellular phone that uses a digital transmission technology. In the U.S., TDMA, CDMA and GSM are the digital cellular standards. See *TDMA*, *CDMA* and *GSM*.

**digital certificate**    The digital equivalent of an ID card used in conjunction with a public key encryption system. Also called "digital IDs," digital certificates are issued by trusted third parties known as certification authorities (CAs) such as VeriSign, Inc., Mountain View, CA (www.verisign.com), after verifying that a public key belongs to a certain owner. The certification process varies depending on the CA and the level of certification. Drivers licenses, notarization and fingerprints are examples of documentation.

The digital certificate is actually the owner's public key that has been digitally signed by the CA's private key. The digital certificate is sent along with the digital signature to verify that the sender is truly the entity identifying itself in the transmission. The recipient uses the widely known public key of the CA to decrypt the certificate and extract the sender's public key. Then the sender's public key is used to decrypt the digital signature. The certificate authorities keep their private keys very secure, because if they were ever discovered, false certificates could be created. See *X.509, digital signature, code signing* and *PKI.*

**digital channel**   A communications path that handles only digital signals. All voice and video signals have to be converted from analog to digital in order to be carried over a digital channel. Contrast with *analog channel.*

**digital cinema**   **(1)** The projection of movies in digital format using digital projectors such as the DLP units from TI. Also known as "d-cinema." See *DLP.*

   **(2)** Refers to any aspect of movie making in the digital domain including capture, editing, distribution and presentation, also known as "d-cinema" and "e-cinema." Computer graphics has greatly enhanced movie making for years, but it will allow for even more spectacular effects in the decades ahead. Although digital dinosaurs and other animals look rather realistic, we are still years away from the man or woman that is nothing more than a digital script (that is, a totally believable human face). In time, it is expected that movie distribution will be all digital, and movies will be beamed to theaters by satellite in realtime.

**digital circuit**   An electronic circuit that accepts and processes binary data (on/off) according to the rules of Boolean logic (AND, OR, NOT, etc.). See *chip* and *Bebop to the Boolean Boogie.*

**digital coins**   See *digital money.*

**digital commerce**   See *e-commerce.*

**digital communications**   Transmitting text, voice and video in binary form. See *communications.*

**digital computer**   A computer that accepts and processes data that has been converted into binary numbers. All common computers are digital. Contrast with *analog computer.*

**digital content**   Products available in digital form. It typically refers to music, information and images that are available for download or distribution on electronic media. See *premium content, DAMS* and *content.*

**digital content creation**   The development of newsworthy, educational and entertainment material for distribution over the Internet or other electronic media. See *DAMS.*

**digital content management system**   See *DAMS.*

**digital convergence**   The integration of computers, communications and consumer electronics. Data and text were converted into digital form for the very first computers years ago; however, since the advent of audio CDs and now DVDs, all forms of information, both for business and entertainment, can be managed together.

   Using cable TV, satellite dish, optical fiber or even the telephone line, music, movies, video games and other interactive programs can be requested on demand along with the Internet's inexhaustible array of offerings.

   The DVD disc is expected to be a major convergence product. It has already replaced LaserDiscs and it is expected to eventually replace VHS tapes for recorded movies. As rewritable DVDs (DVD-RAM) become popular, they are expected to replace videotapes entirely and provide a single medium for home theater, as well as computer storage. See *new media.*

   In addition, the movement toward the IP protocol for not only data, but voice and video, is another major convergence technology. The Internet has upset the applecart from the get-go, and the telecom industry is spending billions to upgrade to IP as the core infrastructure of the future. See *IP on Everything* and *converged network.*

   Another type of convergence is using the Internet as a transport to deliver messages and information to smart cellphones, digital picture frames and Internet radios (the physical ones) rather than interacting with only PCs, and PDAs. See *Internet radio* and *Internet picture frame.*

**digital copy machine**   A copy machine that duplicates the image to be copied by scanning the original into a digital memory and printing from the memory. Contrast with *analog copy machine.*

**digital cross-connect**    A network device used by telecom carriers and large enterprises to switch and multiplex low-speed voice and data signals onto high-speed lines, and vice versa. It is typically used to aggregate several T1 lines into a higher-speed electrical or optical line, as well as to distributed signals to various destinations; for example, voice and data traffic may arrive at the cross-connect on the same facility, but be destined for different carriers. Voice traffic would be transmitted out one port, while data traffic goes out another.

Digital cross-connects (DCSs) are widely used in conjunction with central office telephone switches and may be installed both before and/or after the switch. Cross-connections are established via an administrative process and are semi-permanent, whereas the telephone switch dynamically picks up dialing instructions and routes calls based on telephone number.

Cross-connects come large and small, handling only a few ports up to a couple of thousand. Narrowband, wideband and broadband cross-connects support channels down to DS0, DS1 and DS3, respectively. See *optical cross-connect*.

**digital CRT**    A CRT that accepts digital signals from the display adapter in the computer and converts to analog right before the electron gun stage. Providing sharper images than an analog monitor, they still generate more internal radiation than a flat panel display, which uses digital circuitry and no electron gun. Digital CRTs are expected in the 2000–2001 timeframe. See *analog monitor*.

**digital darkroom**    Using digital hardware to create pictures. With digital cameras, scanners and computer printers, darkroom operations are performed in the light of day.

**digital data**    Data in digital form. All data in the computer is in digital form.

**digital domain**    The world of digital. When something is done in the digital domain, it implies that the original data (images, sounds, video, etc.) has been converted into a digital format and is manipulated inside the computer's memory. Contrast with *analog domain*.

**digital effects**    Special sounds and animations that have been created in the digital domain. Synthetic sounds and reverberation, morphing and transitions between video frames (fades, wipes, dissolves, etc.) are examples.

**digital electronics**    The field of electronics as it pertains to computers and other computer-controlled devices. See *digital circuit*.

**digital envelope**    **(1)** An encrypted message that uses both secret key and public key cryptography methods. The public key method is used to exchange the secret key, and the secret key is used to encrypt and decrypt the message. See *RSA*.

**(2)** A frame, or packet, of data that has been encrypted for transmission over a network.

**(3)** A term occasionally used to describe inserting data into a frame, or packet, for transmission over a network. The envelope metaphor implies a container.

**Digital Equipment**    (Digital Equipment Corporation, Maynard, MA, www.digital.com)  Now merged into Compaq, Digital Equipment, commonly known as DEC or Digital, was founded in 1957 by Kenneth Olsen, who headed the company until he retired in 1992. Digital pioneered the minicomputer industry with its PDP series.

Its early success came from the scientific, process control and academic communities; however, after the VAX was announced in 1977, Digital gained a strong foothold in commercial data processing. The VAX evolved into a complete line from desktop to mainframe, using the same VMS operating system in all models and causing Digital to achieve substantial growth in the 1980s.

Over the years, Digital was widely recognized for its high quality. Its strategy for the 1990s was to embrace open systems with its

**The First "Mini" Computer**
This PDP-1 was Digital's first computer, which was a breakthrough in 1959. Digital spearheaded the minicomputer industry with its PDP series. *(Image courtesy of Digital Equipment Corporation.)*

powerful, RISC-based Alpha architecture introduced in 1992. In addition, Digital had a large services business that provided full project life cycle support from installation to maintenance for Digital and non-Digital products.

In 1997, Digital sold its semiconductor manufacturing facilities to Intel, which will continue to make the Alpha chip until 2007. In 1998, it was acquired by Compaq.

**Kenneth H. Olsen**
Olsen pioneered the minicomputer industry with his PDP computer series. He ran Digital for 35 years until his retirement in 1992. *(Image courtesy of Digital Equipment Corporation.)*

**digital film**     Solid state modules used by digital cameras to store images. They generally are some form of flash memory card such as CompactFlash, SmartMedia or Memory Stick, although Sony has introduced cameras that record onto floppy disks or CD-R discs. Transferring the images to the computer is done by cable to the serial port or USB port as well as by physically moving the film module to a drive attached to the computer. Many cameras offer both methods. See *flash memory* and *digital photography*.

**digital greeting card**     See *e-card*.

**digital home**     A residence that is fully automated. It uses computing devices and home appliances that conform to some common standard for internetworking so that everything can be controlled by computer. The digital home implies network sockets in every room, just like AC power receptacles. See *home network*.

**digital house**     See *digital home*.

**digital ID**     Same as *digital certificate*.

**digital loop carrier**     In telephone communications, a technology that increases the number of channels in the local loop by converting analog signals to digital and multiplexing them back to the end office. Digital loop carriers (DLCs) have increased the capacity of the installed cable plant by enabling several hundred conversations to ride over two twisted wire pairs. A carrier serving area (CSA) is the geographic boundary served by a DLC. Digital loop carrier equipment is either above ground or in small weatherproof, underground rooms, typically within a mile of the final drop to the customer.

The host terminal is the equipment at the end office, and the remote terminal is situated in the outside plant (from end office to customer). The closer the DLC is to the customer, the shorter the analog line and the greater the performance. Analog lines, which used to be three miles long, are now less than a mile in many cases. See *central office* and *pair gain*.

**digitally signed**     Any message or key that has been encrypted with a digital signature. When a user's public key is digitally signed by a certification authority (CA), it is known as a *digital certificate* or *digital ID*. See *digital signature* and *digital certificate*.

**digital mapping**     Digitizing geographic information for a geographic information system (GIS).

**digital media management system**     See *DAMS*.

**digital money**     Electronic money used on the Internet. In order to turn the Internet into a giant cybermall (online shopping center), companies have developed software that provides complete and secure order fulfillment over the Internet. These software packages support a variety of payment schemes, which mostly fall into two categories.

The first category is the traditional credit card. Most Web browsers and Internet Service Providers (ISPs) support one of the major security protocols such as Secure Socket Layer (SSL). For example, on Netscape's browser, if the transmission between browser and server is secure, the key icon at the lower-left side of the screen is connected. Otherwise, it is split in half to signal an unsecure transmission. More elaborate methods, such as CyberCash's credit card system, prevent the merchant from seeing the credit card number.

The second type of digital money is like travelers checks. This digital money either is downloaded as "digital coins" from a participating bank into the user's personal computer, or set up in a digital money account within the bank. Either the digital coins or the transactions that debit the account are transmitted to the merchant for payment. All transactions are encrypted for security.

Many believe that if the cost for processing digital money can be kept down, it will fuel an entirely new online information industry that allows customers to pay for exactly what they use. For example, 5 cents for each information lookup or 10 cents for each applet download, perhaps even a fraction of a cent for certain transactions. Time will tell if the economics allow for this scenario.

In the meantime, although trillions of dollars are routinely transferred around the world via the private banking network, money traversing the public Internet would seem like easy pickings for the dishonest hacker. As with any new system, time, along with a few panics, will bring about the confidence necessary for everyday use. Thus far, traditional credit card transactions are winning out as users become more comfortable buying on the Internet. The forecast for digital coin usage is expected to be considerably less than initially thought.

Other terms for digital money are "e-money," "e-cash" and "digital coins." See *Web payment service*, *First Virtual*, *Open Market*, *cybermall* and *smart card*.

**digital monitor**   (1) A video monitor controlled by a computer circuit that retains settings and resolutions in memory. Subsequent changes in resolutions do not require adjustments. Most computer monitors today are digitally controlled, but still accept analog signals from the display adapter.

(2) A video monitor that accepts a digital signal from the computer and converts it into analog signals to illuminate the screen. Examples are the earlier MDA, CGA and EGA monitors used with PCs. Contrast with *analog monitor*.

**Digital Nervous System**   Microsoft's term for a network and set of enterprise applications that support multimedia for every user. It implies complete integration between intranets and the Internet via landline and wireless communications. In other words, the fully integrated, super-advanced, electronic office of the future.

**digital newscaster**   See *virtual newscaster*.

**digital nonlinear editing**   See *nonlinear video editing*.

**digital offset color press**   See *offset press*.

**digital PABX**   See *digital PBX*.

**digital paper**   (1) A variety of coated and uncoated paper specialized for printing by computer printers.

(2) (Digital Paper Corporation, Alexandria, VA, www.digitalpaper.com) A company that specializes in software that speeds up the distribution of engineering drawings and other large images to users. Supporting a variety of CAD and image formats, Digital Paper's family of docQuest products offer numerous features, including converting high-resolution images to GIFs for collaborative viewing over the Web.

(3) (DigitalPaper) The file format generated by the Common Ground document exchange software. The term implies that the computer file can be used to regenerate the style and format of the original paper form. See *Common Ground*.

(4) An input technology from Anoto AB, Lund, Sweden (www.anoto.com), that turns a paper form into a wireless transmission system. It uses regular paper imprinted with a dot grid that is almost invisible. The dot grid is coded so that when traced with an Anoto-enabled pen, the pen senses the unique dot pattern on this "digital paper" that is associated with a particular application. The pen transmits either ASCII text or the actual written images to a receiving device. The pen discharges regular ink so you can see what you mark or write.

(5) A future e-book technology that uses ultra thin pages, each of which serves as a screen that can be instantly updated. Also known as "e-paper." See *Electronic Paper*.

**digital payment service**   See *Web payment service*.

**digital PBX**   (digital **P**rivate **B**ranch Exchange) A modern PBX that uses digital methods for switching in contrast to older PBXs that use analog methods.

**Digital PC**   (1) An Alpha PC that runs Windows applications. It runs a native Alpha version of Windows NT and uses the FX 32 emulator. See *FX 32*.

(2) An Intel-based PC made by Digital.

**digital phone**    A desktop or cellular phone that uses a digital transmission technology. In-house PBX-based and key telephone systems may use digital phones that convert sound into digital at the handset. Digital cellphones come in several varieties. See *digital cellphone* and *smart phone*.

**digital photography**    Taking pictures with a digital camera, and storing and printing them on digital devices. The "digital film," which is comprised of flash memory modules, floppy disks or CD-Rs, can be transferred to a local computer for printing, or it can be uploaded to a Web site for viewing and printing. See *digital camera* and *digital photography sites*.

**digital picture frame**    An Internet appliance that displays a picture on an LCD screen and uses an always-on cable modem or DSL connection. It lets you upload images over the Internet directly into the digital frames of family members and friends. These "smart" picture frames hold several images and, like a slide projector, can be made to change pictures at prescribed intervals. For a service fee, art of all kinds can also be downloaded into digital picture frames.

**digital postage**    See *PC Postage*.

**digital postcard**    See *e-card*. See also *PC Postage*.

**Digital PowerLine**    See *DPL*.

**digital printing**
All printed output from a computer is technically digital. However, the term refers more to printing finished pages on the computer in contrast to using an offset printing press and commercial printer.

Digital printing eliminates numerous mechanical steps in the conventional printing process, including making films, color proofs, manually stripping the pieces together, making plates and running the paper through the press four or five times.

Instead of cutting and folding printed "signatures" to put the pages in order, software sorts them in memory and prints them in sequence. After printing, the output goes directly to next-stage equipment that can just staple or 3-hole punch the paper, or go all

**Download to the Coffee Table**
Digital picture frames such as this one from Ceiva Logic are online to the Internet. Don't care to show your own pictures? No problem. Ceiva lets you download world-class pictures from Corbis, the leading provider of digital images on the Internet.
*(Image courtesy of Ceiva Logic, Inc., www.ceiva.com)*

**Digital Printing**

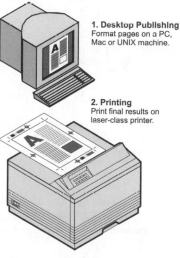

**1. Desktop Publishing**
Format pages on a PC, Mac or UNIX machine.

**2. Printing**
Print final results on laser-class printer.

**Offset Printing**

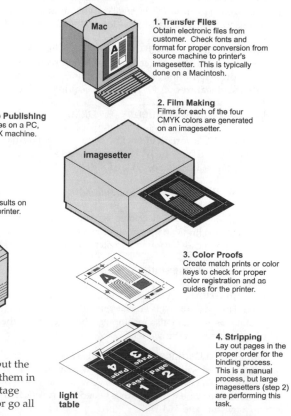

**1. Transfer Files**
Obtain electronic files from customer. Check fonts and format for proper conversion from source machine to printer's imagesetter. This is typically done on a Macintosh.

**2. Film Making**
Films for each of the four CMYK colors are generated on an imagesetter.

**3. Color Proofs**
Create match prints or color keys to check for proper color registration and as guides for the printer.

**4. Stripping**
Lay out pages in the proper order for the binding process. This is a manual process, but large imagesetters (step 2) are performing this task.

light table

the way to turning it into postmarked packages for the mailroom. Millions of invoices, documents and booklets are printed on large digital printer assembly lines every day.

Although digital printer systems do not compete with high-speed newspaper and magazine presses, it is expected that these "analog" monsters will become all digital in time. See *offset press*.

**digital proofing**    Preparing a sample of printed output on a computer printer before the job is printed on a commercial press. Contrast with *match print*.

**digital radio**    Transmitting audio programs (music, news, sports, etc.) in digital format. See *DAB* and *satellite radio*.

**digital recorder**    See *PVR* and *CD-R*.

**digital recording**    See *digital video*, *digital nonlinear editing*, *magnetic recording* and *PVR*.

**digital remaster**    A conversion of music from its original analog master recordings to digital format. In the early days of audio CDs (mid-1980s), many music albums were converted from tapes that were equalized for the smaller dynamic audio range of the LP vinyl record and phonograph player. Some of these songs were later digitally remastered using the original tapes before equalization was applied.

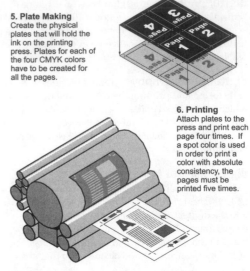

**5. Plate Making**
Create the physical plates that will hold the ink on the printing press. Plates for each of the four CMYK colors have to be created for all the pages.

**6. Printing**
Attach plates to the press and print each page four times. If a spot color is used in order to print a color with absolute consistency, the pages must be printed five times.

**offset press**

**Digital Research**    (Digital Research, Inc., Monterey, CA)  A software company founded in 1976 by Gary Kildall that spearheaded the microcomputer revolution with its CP/M operating system. Other DRI products included the GEM windows environment, FlexOS realtime operating system and DR DOS—a DOS-compatible operating system with advanced features. In 1991, DRI was acquired by Novell. See *Caldera*.

**digital rights management**    See *DRM*.

**Digital-S**    JVC's variant of the DV (Digital Video) format, which provides higher quality by using 1/2" the S-VHS tape format instead of 1/4" DV. It also uses two codecs to double the transfer rate of standard DV. Some Digital-S players play S-VHS tapes as well. See *DV* and *S-VHS*.

**digital satellite radio**    See *satellite radio*.

**digital signal**    (1) An electronic signal transmitted as binary code that can be either the presence or absence of current, high and low voltages or short pulses at a particular frequency.

(2) A common classification for digital circuits established by the telephone companies, such as DS0, DS1, etc. See *DS*.

**digital signal processing**    See *DSP*.

**digital signature**    A digital guarantee that a file has not been altered, as if it were carried in an electronically sealed envelope. The "signature" is an encrypted digest of the file (text message, executable, etc.). The recipient decrypts the digest that was sent and also recomputes the digest from the received file. If the digests match, the file is proved intact and tamper free from the sender.

Signatures and Certificates    A digital signature ensures that the file originated with the entity signing it and that it was not tampered with after the signature was applied. However, the sender could still be an impersonator and not who it claims to be. To verify that the message was indeed sent by the person or organization claiming to send it requires a digital certificate (digital ID), which is issued by a certification authority. See *digital certificate*, *code signing*, *digital envelope*, *electronic signature* and *MAC*.

D

**Example** In the example shown at right, the woman wants to send a secure message to one man. Because he is the only one that should see it, she uses his public key to encrypt the package. To start, she uses a one-way hash function to compute a small digest of her text message. Using her private key, she encrypts the digest, turning it into a digital signature. The signature and the message are then encrypted using his public key and transmitted. The man uses his private key to decrypt the text and derive the still-encrypted signature. Using her public key, he decrypts the signature back into her digest and then recomputes a new digest from the text message. If the digests match, the message is authenticated. In practice, of course, all these processes are automatically done by software, but "he" and "she" are used to illustrate the concept.

**digital subscriber line** See *DSL*.

**Digital SVD** See *DSVD*.

**digital tablet** A flat panel used to display the content of today's newspapers and magazines. Using wireless as well as wireline feeds, such devices are expected to become widely used in the 2005–2010 timeframe. See also *digitizer tablet* and *pen tablet*.

**digital-to-analog converter** See *D/A converter*.

**digital TV** See *DTV*.

**Digital UNIX** See *Tru64 UNIX*.

**digital VCR** See *PVR*.

**digital video** Video recording in digital form. In order to edit video in the computer or to embed video clips into multimedia documents, a video source must originate as digital (digital camera) or be converted to digital. Frames from analog video cameras and VCRs are converted into digital frames (bitmaps) using frame grabbers or similar devices attached to a personal computer.

Uncompressed digital video signals require huge amounts of storage, and high-ratio realtime compression schemes, such as MPEG, are essential for handling digital video in today's computers. See *MPEG*, *DVD*, *digital nonlinear editing* and *HDTV*.

**Digital Video Disc** See *DVD*.

**digital video effects** Visual effects performed by computer that create a more interesting transition from one scene to another, rather than just switching scenes. They include fading or dissolving the frame, wiping one frame over another, flipping the frame and simulating a camera lens opening and closing (iris effect).

**digital video recorder** See *PVR*.

**digital wallet** The electronic equivalent of a wallet for e-commerce transactions. A digital wallet (e-wallet) can hold digital money that is purchased similar to travelers checks, or a prepaid account like an EZPass system, or it can contain credit card information. The wallet may reside in the user's machine or on the servers of a Web payment service. When stored in the client machine, the wallet may use a digital certificate that identifies the authorized card holder. See *digital money* and *Web payment service*.

**digital watermark** A pattern of bits embedded into a file used to identify the source of illegal copies. For example, if a digital watermark is placed into a master copy of an audio CD or a DVD movie, then all copies of that disc are

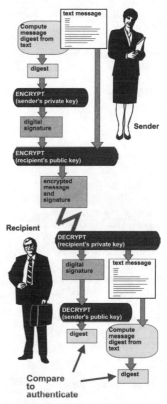

**There Are Many Methods**
This illustration uses one approach. There are others. For example, if the text message is small enough, only the signature needs to be sent. In addition, this uses the public key method for encrypting the text. The public method can also be used to send a secret key, and the text encryption and decryption can be done with the secret key, which is called a "digital envelope."

uniquely identified. If a licensee were to manufacture and distribute them in areas outside of its authorized territory, the watermark provides a trace.

The watermark developer has to find creative ways of altering the file without disturbing it for the user. It is extremely difficult to embed a watermark within an ASCII file, which is just raw text. But it is relatively easy to alter a few bits within audio, video and graphics formats without making a noticeable difference on playback or display.

**digital zoom**    The ability to simulate a range of focal lengths in a digital camera, using dithering and other software techniques. See *optical zoom*.

**digitize**    To convert an image or signal into digital code by scanning, tracing on a graphics tablet or using an analog to digital conversion device. 3-D objects can be digitized by a device with a mechanical arm that is moved onto all the corners.

**digitizer tablet**    A graphics drawing tablet used for sketching new images or tracing old ones. The user makes contact with the tablet with a pen or puck (mistakenly called a mouse) that is either wireless or connected to the tablet by a wire. For sketching, the user draws with the pen or puck and the screen cursor "draws" a corresponding image.

The puck is generally preferred for tracing highly detailed engineering drawings because the crosshairs,

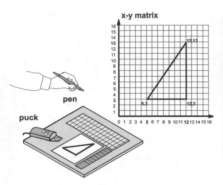

**Digitizer Tablet**
Digitzer tablets are also called "graphics tablets." Objects are drawn using a pen or a puck. The puck is technically a tablet cursor, not a mouse. Drawings created on tablets are stored as mathematical line segments.

**Digitizing Three Dimensions**
The 3DRAW PRO 3-D digitizer system from Polhemus records x, y and z coordinates of an object by touching its surfaces with a pen. It measures the tip position in 3-D space and outputs directly to popular CAD and graphics programs. *(Image courtesy of Polhemus, Inc.)*

visible through a clear glass lens, let you precisely pinpoint ends and corners. Many tablets allow parts of the tablet surface to be customized into buttons that can be tapped to select menus and functions in the program.

When drawing or tracing on the tablet, a series of x-y coordinates (vector graphics) are created, either as a continuous stream of coordinates, or as end points. See *pen tablet* and *digital tablet*.

**dimension**    (1) One axis in an array. In programming, a dimension statement defines the array and sets up the number of elements within the dimension.

(2) In a data warehouse, one side of the dimensional model set up for the department or organization. For example, the product dimension would be a list of the organization's products, the time dimension would be the calendar periods represented, and so on.

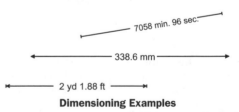

**Dimensioning Examples**

**dimensioning**    In CAD programs, the management and display of the measurements of an object. There are various standards that determine such things as tolerances, sizes of arrowheads and orientation on the paper.

**DIMM**    (**D**ual **I**n-**L**ine **M**emory **M**odule) A printed circuit board that holds memory chips and plugs into a DIMM socket on the motherboard. See *memory module*.

**DIN connector**    (**D**eutsches **I**nstitut fur **N**ormung connector; German Standards Institute connector) A family of plugs and sockets used to connect mice, keyboards and various audio devices. The smaller 6-pin Mini-Din connects today's keyboards and mice, while earlier keyboards used the larger 5-pin variety (the mouse used to connect to the serial port). The 6-pin plug was first used on IBM's PS/2 and was called a "PS/2 connector." Newer keyboards can be plugged into older computers with a 6-pin to 5-pin adapter, and older keyboards can plug into newer computers with 5-pin to 6-pin adapters. See *PC keyboards*.

### Dingbats

A font comprised of symbols (arrows, pointing hands, stars, etc.) that were originally developed by International Typeface Corporation. They are officially called ITC Zapf Dingbats. There are many variations of Dingbats from other font houses. For example, TrueType brings Wingdings and Webdings, offering a wide variety of symbols for numerous purposes.

ABCDEFG

abcdefg

0123456789

**Wingding Examples**
Dingbats, Wingdings and similar fonts provide an easy way of adding graphics by simply typing them as text. However, you have to remember which letters and digits produce which symbols as in the examples above.

**5-pin DIN**
Used on earlier PC keyboards and various audio

**6-pin Mini-DIN**
Used on mouse, keyboard and other devices
(PS/2 connector)

**DIN Connectors**
Adapters switch between these two DIN types so your new keyboard can work with your old PC or your old keyboard can work with a newer PC or laptop, which has always used the 6-pin socket.

### diode

**(1)** An electronic component that acts like a one-way valve. As a discrete component or built into a chip, it is used in a variety of functions. Used as a rectifier, it is a key element in changing AC to DC by limiting current flow to a single direction. Diodes are used as temperature and light sensors and light emitters (LEDs). In communications, they filter out analog and digital signals from carriers and modulate signals onto carriers. In digital logic, they're used as one-way valves and as switches similar to transistors. See *laser diode*.

**(2)** A type of vacuum tube used in electronic circuits as a rectifier or radio frequency detector. Modern applications of tube diodes are generally limited to rectifiers in high-end audio amplifiers and other specialized high-voltage circuits.

The tube diode uses two active elements (cathode and plate) and one passive element (the filament or heater). In typical operation, the cathode is heated by the filament, and the AC voltage is applied to the cathode. The heated cathode releases excited electrons that flow to the plate (anode) and become the rectified current. The diode allows current flow in only one direction. For example, if current were applied to the plate, electron flow could not occur, because the plate's electrons are not heated by the filament.

In some instances, the filament is also the cathode. This is accomplished by connecting the AC voltage source to one of the filament's leads. See *triode*, *tetrode*, *pentode*, **magnetron** and *klystron*.

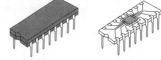

**The DIP**
The DIP package is commonly used to hold small chips, such as main memory, cache memory, A/D and D/A converters.

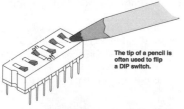

The tip of a pencil is often used to flip a DIP switch.

**Switches on the DIP**
DIP switches provide an inexpensive way to select options on a hardware device and will probably be used for years to come. However, as personal computers become more sophisticated, plug-in boards increasingly contain programmable chips. Instead of opening the case, pulling the board and figuring out which switch to flip, settings are changed using a software control panel.

### diode laser

See *laser diode*.

### DIP

**(1)** (Dual In-line Package) A common rectangular chip housing with leads (pins) on both long sides. Tiny wires bond the chip to metal leads that wind their way down into spider-like feet that are inserted into a socket or are soldered onto the board. See *CDIP*, *CERDIP* and *chip package*.

**(2)** (Document Image Processing) See *document imaging*.

### DIP switch

(Dual In-line Package switch) A set of tiny toggle switches built into a DIP, which is mounted directly on a circuit board. The tip of a pen or pencil is required to flip the switch on or off. Remember! Open is "off." Closed is "on."

**Dir**   (1) (**DIR**ectory) A CP/M, DOS and OS/2 command that lists the file names on the disk. See *DOS Dir*.

(2) (DIR) (**D**igital **I**nstrumentation **R**ecorder) A high-performance magnetic tape technology from Sony that uses 19mm tape and a helical scan transport. Based on the ANSI ID-1 recording format (D1 component digital video), models can provide up to 64 Mbytes/sec data transfer, which is extremely fast and necessary for sonar, radar and other intelligence gathering applications. DIR drives and libraries have become a de facto standard in the U.S. government. Tape cassettes come in 8.7GB, 43GB and 96GB capacities. See *DTF* and *magnetic tape*.

**DIR Tape Storage**
Sony's DIR technology provides extremely high-speed archiving of data. This is an example of the large cassette that holds 96GB of data. The 4mm DAT cassette is shown for size comparison.

**DirecPC**   A satellite Internet service from Hughes Network Systems (www.direcpc.com), that requires installation of a satellite dish cabled to an expansion board plugged into your PC. The uplink is made to your own ISP through whatever medium you currently use, but the downlink is from the satellite to your dish at up to 400 Kbps.

**Direct3D**   A 3-D graphics programming interface (API) from Microsoft for Windows 95/98 and NT. It provides low-level access to the frame buffer and advanced features of the display adapter, and allows game developers to write high-speed animated software. Game programs have stayed mostly in DOS throughout the Windows 3.x life cycle, because DOS programs can access the hardware directly to maximize speed. The Direct3D provides this capability for Windows 95/98 and NT. See *video accelerator* and *DirectDraw*.

**direct access**   The ability to go directly to a specific storage location without having to go through what's in front of it. Memories (RAMs, ROMs, PROMs, etc.) and disks are the major direct access devices.

**direct access method**   A technique for finding data on a disk by deriving its storage address from an identifying key in the record, such as account number. Using a formula, the account number is converted into a sector address. This is faster than comparing entries in an index, but it only works well when keys are numerically close: 100, 101, 102, etc.

**direct access storage device**   See *DASD*.

**direct broadcast satellite**   See *DBS*.

**direct-connect modem**   A modem that connects to a telephone line without the use of an acoustic coupler. Today, almost all modems are of the direct-connect type. See *acoustic coupler*.

**direct current**   See *DC*.

**direct data entry**   Typing text into or drawing an image on the computer in contrast with copying or importing data from another source.

**DirectDraw**   A 2-D graphics programming interface (API) from Microsoft for Windows 95/98 and NT. DirectDraw provides low-level access to the frame buffer and advanced features of the display adapter. See *video accelerator* and *Direct3D*.

**DirectInput**   A programming interface (API) from Microsoft for Windows 95/98 and NT that provides controls for advanced digital input devices for games and virtual reality systems.

**direct inward dialing**   See *DID*.

**directional lighting**   See *ambient lighting*.

**direct memory access**   See *DMA*.

**Director**    A popular multimedia authoring program for Windows and Macintosh from Macromedia. Runtime versions can be run, edited and switched between Windows and Mac platforms. Shockwave is a browser plug-in that lets output from Macromedia's Director, Authorware and Freehand packages be viewed on the Web.

Director was initially introduced as MacroMind Director for the Mac in 1989, and it has been the de facto standard for Macintosh multimedia authoring. Before the Windows authoring version was introduced, a Windows player was available to run Director movies created on the Mac.

**directory**    (1) A simulated file folder on disk. Programs and data for each application are typically kept in a separate directory (spreadsheets, word processing, etc.). Directories create the illusion of compartments, but are actually indexes to the files that may be scattered all over the disk. UNIX and DOS use the term "directory," while the Mac and Windows use the term "folder."

(2) A database of users, hardware devices and applications in a network. See *DSML, directory service* and *metadirectory*.

(3) A search site on the Web that catalogs Web sites by subject and also manually indexes the site, providing a brief description of its content. Yahoo! is the most well-known directory site. See *Web search sites, metasearch sites* and *Yahoo!*.

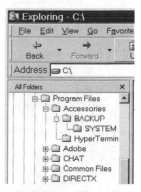

**An Explorer Hierarchy**
This Explorer example in Windows 98 shows various levels of the directory tree stemming from the Program Files folder. This graphical representation shows the folders within folders.

**directory enabled networks**    See *DEN*.

**directory listings**    See *Web white pages* and *Web yellow pages*.

**directory management**    The maintenance and control of directories on a hard disk. Usually refers to menuing software that is easier to use than entering commands.

**directory server**    A network server that provides a directory, or naming service. See *directory service, naming service* and *ULS server*.

**Directory Server Agent**    See *DSA*.

**directory service**    A directory of names, profile information and machine addresses of every user and resource on the network. It is used to manage user accounts and network permissions. When sent a user name, it returns the attributes of that individual, which may include a telephone number as well as an e-mail address. Directory services use highly specialized databases that are typically hierarchical in design and provide fast lookups. See *x.500, LDAP, naming service* and *ULS server*.

**directory tree**    A graphic representation of a hierarchical directory. See *DOS Tree*.

**direct overwrite**    The ability to write a bit on a recording medium without having to erase it first. Magnetic disks and phase change optical disks provide direct overwrite capability. See *LIMDOW*.

**Direct PC**    See *DirecPC*.

**DirectPlay**    A programming interface (API) from Microsoft for Windows 95/98 and NT that provides the communications mechanism that allows multiple users to hook up and play a game with each other via modem, LAN or the Internet.

**Direct Rambus**    See *RDRAM*.

**DirectSound**    See *DirectX*.

**direct thermal printer**    A low- to medium-resolution printer that uses a type of coated paper that darkens when heat is applied to it. The paper is passed by a line of heating elements that burn dots onto the paper. This is typically used in bar code printers and other small specialty printers. It was widely used in early fax machines. See *printer*.

**direct view storage tube**    See *DVST*.

**DirectX**    A set of multimedia programming interfaces from Microsoft for Windows 95/98, NT and 2000 that provide low-level access to the hardware for improved performance. The first DirectX API was introduced in late 1995 to encourage game developers to write their games for Windows. Before DirectX, games were written in DOS in order to activate the graphics and sound directly, but required support for different types of hardware.  DirectX provided a single interface to write to.

DirectDraw and Direct3D provide 2-D and 3-D graphics. DirectSound enables mixing multiple sound sources for sound cards. DirectPlay provides control for multiple users playing the same game via modem, LAN or the Internet. DirectInput provides control for advanced digital input devices for games and virtual reality. In late 2000, DirectX 8 added DirectVoice, which enables players to talk to each other in realtime while they play the game.

**dirty bit**    A bit in a memory cache or virtual memory page that has been modified by the CPU, but not yet written back to storage.

**dirty data**    See *data hygiene*.

**dirty power**    A non-uniform AC power (voltage fluctuations, noise and spikes), which comes from the electric utility or from electronic equipment in the office.

**DirXML**    The code name for directory interchange software from Novell that integrates NDS with other directories in Exchange, Lotus Notes, Windows 2000 (Active Directory) and others. It provides agents that monitor the activity in the directories and uses XML to exchange the updated data. DirXML is not a metadirectory, since it does not create a master directory, rather it keeps all the different directories in synchronization. See *NDS* and *XML*.

**DIS**    (Data Instrumentation Systems) See *DST*.

**disable**    To turn off a function. Contrast with *enable*. See *disabled*.

**disabled**    Turned off. It does not mean broken or in disrepair. Contrast with *enabled*.

**disassembler**    Software that converts machine language back into assembly language. Since there is no way to easily determine the human thinking behind the logic of the instructions, the resulting assembly language routines and variables are named and numbered generically (A001, A002, etc.). Disassembled code can be very difficult to maintain. See *decompiler*.

**disaster recovery**    A plan for duplicating computer operations after a catastrophe occurs, such as a fire or earthquake. It includes routine off-site backup, as well as a procedure for activating necessary information systems in a new location. See *data recovery*.

**disc**    An alternate spelling for disk. Some computer manufacturers use this spelling, but "disc" is usually used with read-only media, such as CDs and CD-ROMs. Rewritable disks are spelled with a "k."  In this database, disc is used for CDs, CD-ROMs, CD-Rs and DVD-Rs, while disk is used for all other disk devices.

**disc-at-once**    To record all the data on a CD-R disc at one time. The lead-in, all the tracks and lead-out are written, the session is closed, and the disc is closed. Earlier CD-R drives used only this method. Subsequent drives added track-at-once, which enabled songs and data to be recorded in multiple sessions. See *track-at-once* for example dialog.

**disc fixation**    A process that ends the current recording session of a CD-R disc. The expression often refers to closing the current track-at-once session, but it may also refer to closing the entire disk in a disc-at-once session. See *disc-at-once* and *track-at-once*.

**Discoverer/2000**    See *Developer/2000*.

**discrete**    A component or device that is separate and distinct and treated as a singular unit.

**discrete component**    An elementary electronic device constructed as a single unit. Before integrated circuits (chips), all transistors, resistors and diodes were discrete. They are widely used in amplifiers and other devices that use large amounts of current. They are also still used on circuit boards intermingled with the chips.

**discrete manufacturing**    Fabricating products by assembling ready-made components and subsystems into larger systems. The computer system, automobile and appliance industries are examples of discrete manufacturing. Contrast with *process manufacturing*.

Diode

Resistor

Transistor

Capacitor

In a chip, there can be millions of transistors, capacitors and other electronic components. However, they cannot handle the power load of discrete components.

**Discrete Components**

**discrete multitone**    See *DSL*.

**discretionary hyphen**    A user-designated place in a word for hyphenation. If the word goes over the margin, it will split in that location.

**discussion thread**    See *threaded discussion*.

**dish**    A saucer-shaped antenna that receives, or transmits and receives, signals from a satellite.

**disintermediation**    The elimination of the middleman. The term has been used to focus on the theoretical advantages of purchasing direct on the Web, such as convenience, cost savings and fast turnaround time. See *reintermediation*.

**disk**    A direct access storage device. See *floppy disk, hard disk, magnetic disk, optical disk, CD-ROM* and *DVD*.

**disk access**    Reading and writing the disk. It generally refers to the most time-consuming part of the operation, which is moving the read/write head. The disk access time is the average of the time it takes to position the head over the requested track. See *defragment* and **32-bit disk access**.

**disk array**    Two or more disk drives combined in a single unit for increased capacity, speed and/or fault tolerant operation. See *RAID*.

**disk-at-once**    See *disc-at-once*.

**disk based**    (1) A computer system that uses disks as its storage medium.
(2) An application that retrieves data from the disk as required. Contrast with *memory based*.

**disk cache**    See *cache*.

**disk cartridge**    A removable disk module that contains a single hard disk platter or a floppy disk. See *cartridge*.

**Old and New Disk Cartridges**
Older cartridges (right) came in a variety of sizes as large as 16" in diameter. Today's cartridges use smaller 5.25" (left) and 3.5" form factors.

**disk cloning**    See *cloning software*.

**disk compression**    See *data compression*.

**disk controller**   A circuit that controls transmission to and from the disk drive. In a personal computer, it is an expansion board that plugs into an expansion slot in the bus. See *hard disk*.

**Diskcopy**   A DOS and OS/2 utility used to copy entire floppy disks track by track. See *DOS Diskcopy*.

**disk crash**   See *head crash*.

**disk drive**   A peripheral storage device that holds, spins, reads and writes magnetic or optical disks. It may be a receptacle for disk cartridges, disk packs or floppy disks, or it may contain non-removable disk platters like most personal computer hard disks. See *magnetic disk*.

**disk dump**   A printout of disk contents without report formatting.

**disk duplexing**   The recording of redundant data for fault tolerant operation. Data is written on two separate disks within the same system. Each disk drive is connected to its own controller. See *disk mirroring* and *RAID*.

**disk duplicator**   A device that formats and makes identical copies of floppy disks for software distribution. Simple units contain two floppy disks and require manual loading. Automated units have hoppers and stackers that can copy 50 or more diskettes without operator intervention. The most comprehensive machines can attach the diskette labels.

**disk emulator**   A solid state replication of a disk drive.

**diskette**   Same as *floppy disk*.

**disk failure**   See *head crash, data error* and **General failure reading drive x.**

**disk farm**   A very large number of hard disks. As more years of computer processing history pile up within the enterprise, databases are reaching staggering proportions. For example, thirty years of sales figures for companies with thousands of products in hundreds of locations result in multiple gigabytes of data. It is not uncommon to need a terabyte disk farm, which would require 250 four-gigabyte drives. See *server farm*.

**disk file**   A set of instructions or data that is recorded, cataloged and treated as a single unit on a disk. Source language programs, machine language programs, spreadsheets, data files, text documents, graphics files and batch files are examples.

**disk format**   The storage layout of a disk as determined by its physical medium and as initialized by a format program. For example, a 5.25" 360KB floppy vs a 3.5" 1.44MB floppy or a DOS disk vs a Mac disk. See *low-level format*, *high-level format*, *DOS/Windows format*, **DOS Format** and *file format*.

**disk grooming**   Deleting old and unnecessary files on a disk.

**disk image**   The contents of a disk drive copied sector by sector from the original and stored in a file. Disk images are used to replicate the entire contents from one disk to another. See *IMG file*.

**diskless workstation**   A workstation without a disk. Programs and data are retrieved from the network server. The network computer (NC) is a diskless workstation.

**disk management**   The maintenance and control of a hard disk. Refers to a variety of utilities that provide format, copy, diagnostic, directory management and defragmenting functions.

**Disk Manager**   A driver from Ontrack Data International, Inc., Eden Prarie, MN (www.ontrack.com), that allows older PCs to support hard disks greater than 528MB. PCs made before 1994 may have a system BIOS that does not support the larger drives. The Disk Manager diskette and instructions are often bundled with new hard disks.

**disk memory**   Same as "disk." In this publication, disks and tapes are called storage devices, not memory devices.

**disk mirroring**    The recording of redundant data for fault tolerant operation. Data is written on two partitions of the same disk or on two separate disks within the same system. Disk mirroring uses the same controller. RAID 1 provides for mirroring, which is usually accomplished with SCSI drives and, increasingly, with IDE drives. See *disk duplexing* and *RAID*.

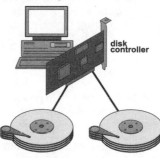
**Disk Mirroring**

disk controller

**disk operating system**    See *DOS*.

**disk optimizer**    A utility program that defragments a hard disk. See *defragment*.

**disk pack**    An early removable hard disk module used in minicomputers and mainframes that contained two or more platters housed in a dust-free container. For mounting, the protective bottom of the unit was removed, and the disk pack was placed into the drive. Then the top part of the disk pack was unscrewed and removed.

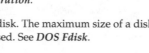
**Disk Duplexing**

disk controllers

**disk parameters**    See *hard disk configuration*.

**disk partition**    A subdivision of a hard disk. The maximum size of a disk partition depends on the operating system used. See ***DOS Fdisk***.

**disks**    See *storage technologies*.

**disk striping**    The spreading of data over multiple disk drives to improve performance. Data is interleaved by bytes or by sectors across the drives. For example, with four drives and a controller designed to overlap reads and writes, four sectors could be read in the same time it normally takes to read one. Disk striping does not inherently provide fault tolerance or error checking. It is used in conjunction with various other methods. See *RAID*.

**DISOSS**    (DIStributed Office Support System) An IBM mainframe centralized document distribution and filing application that runs under MVS. Its counterpart under VM is PROFS. It allows for e-mail and the exchange of documents between a variety of IBM office devices, including word processors and PCs. DISOSS uses the SNADS messaging protocol.

**dispatcher**    Software that determines what pending tasks should be done next and assigns the available resources to accomplish it. It may execute other programs or generate a list for human operators to follow. See *scheduler*.

**dispatch radio**    See *two-way radio*.

**dispersed intelligence**    Same as *distributed intelligence*.

**dispersion**    In optical fibers, the broadening of the waveforms over long distances by the time they reach the receiving end, which makes them difficult to interpret. There are three major causes. One is the multiple transmission paths (modes) possible in large-core multimode fibers where each path results in a different travel distance.

**The Actual Devices**
Taken in the 1970s, this picture shows the disk pack being loaded into the drive. Such disks held only a couple of hundred megabytes. *(Image courtesy of Unisys Corporation.)*

A second has to do with the varying of the refractive index due to changes in frequency (or correspondingly, changes in wavelength). The speed of light in a fiber is based on the frequency of light and the refractive index of the fiber. Thus, different frequencies travel at different speeds. The problem is that there are always multiple frequencies. Analog signals are naturally many frequencies, but digital pulses are also more than one frequency, because it is difficult to create a perfect single frequency.

The third has to do with the random fluctuations of light polarization inside the fiber. Following are the common types of dispersion. See *refractive index, dispersion compensator, step index fiber, graded index fiber, dispersion shifted fiber* and *fiber optics glossary*.

**Modal Dispersion (or Intermodal Dispersion)**   Occurs in multimode fibers, because light travels in multiple modes (reflective paths), and each path results in a different travel distance. Modal dispersion is a major problem with multimode fibers.

**Chromatic Dispersion**   The sum of material dispersion and waveguide dispersion. "Material dispersion" is caused by the variation in refractive index of the glass in the fiber. "Waveguide dispersion" is because of changes in the distribution of light between the core and the cladding of a single-mode fiber.

**Polarization Mode Dispersion (PMD)**   Light travels in two polarization states in singlemode fibers. Over long distances, conditions such as stress and slight irregularites in the fiber core cause random fluctuations in how the two polarizations travel through the fiber. As a result, they gradually spread over the square root of the distance.

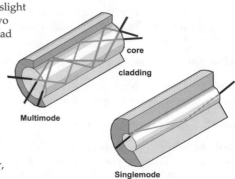

core

cladding

Multimode

Singlemode

**dispersion compensator**   A device that removes pulse distortion in an optical fiber network. It is usually placed near the optical amplifier spaced some 25–50 miles apart. See *dispersion*.

**dispersion shifted fiber**   A single-mode optical fiber that has been designed to reduce chromatic dispersion. The core of the fiber is typically fabricated in a triangular shape with different refractive indices running in parallel throughout its length. See *graded index fiber, step index fiber* and *dispersion*.

**displacement**   Same as *offset*. See *base/displacement*.

**display**   (1) To show text and graphics on a CRT or flat panel screen.
(2) A screen or monitor.

**display adapter**   An expansion board that plugs into a desktop computer that converts the images created in the computer to the electronic signals required by the monitor. It determines the maximum resolution, maximum refresh rate and the number of colors that can be sent to the monitor. The monitor must be equally capable of handling its highest resolution and refresh. In a PC, the display adapter is known by many names (see below).

The display adapter converts the characters or graphic patterns (bitmaps) within the computer's memory into signals used to refresh the display screen. Display adapters also contain their own memory, which is used to build the images before they are displayed (see *frame buffer*).

In earlier PCs, the display adapters (CGA, EGA, etc.) generated digital signals for the monitor, which converted them into analog for the screen. Current display adapters (VGA, Mac, etc.) create the analog signals that are sent to the monitor. Increasingly, display adapters offer digital outputs for flat panel monitors. On a laptop, the equivalent display circuitry, which is digital from end to end, is built into the motherboard. See *graphics accelerator* and *PC display modes*.

**Take Your Pick**   Graphics adapter, graphics board, graphics card, graphics controller, video display adapter, video display board, video display card, video display controller, video adapter, video board, video card, video controller, display board, display card, display controller, VGA adapter, VGA board, VGA card and VGA controller are other terms for the display adapter.

By the way, a video graphics board is something different. It is a combo display adapter and video capture board that accepts analog NTSC video from a videotape player (VCR) or camera. But, guess what. That term is used to refer to a plain old display adapter too.

**display card**   Same as *display adapter*.

**display cycle**     In computer graphics, the series of operations required to display an image.

**Display Data Channel**     See *VESA DDC*.

**display element**     (1) In graphics, a basic graphic arts component, such as background, foreground, text or graphics image.
(2) In computer graphics, any component of an image.

**display entity**     In computer graphics, a collection of display elements that can be manipulated as a unit.

**display font**     Same as *screen font*.

**display frame**     In computer graphics, a single frame in a series of animation frames.

**display list**     In computer graphics, a collection of vectors that are used to display a vector graphic image on screen. The display list is generated from the drawing database.

**display list processor**     In computer graphics, an engine that generates graphic geometry (draws lines, circles, etc.) directly from the display list and independent of the CPU.

**display modes**     See *PC display modes*.

**Display PostScript**     The screen counterpart of the PostScript printer language that translates elementary commands in an application to graphics and text elements on screen. It is designed for inclusion in an operating system to provide a standard, device-independent display language.

**display resolution**     See *how to select a PC display system*.

**display screen**     A surface area upon which text and graphics are temporarily made to appear for human viewing. It is typically a CRT or flat panel technology.

**display terminal**     See *video terminal*.

**DisplayWrite**     A full-featured IBM word processing program for PCs that stems from the typewriter-oriented DisplayWriter word processing system first introduced in 1980. DisplayWrite was widely used in organizations that were mostly IBM oriented.

**distance learning**     Obtaining education and training from a remote teaching site via TV or computer.

**distance vector protocol**     A simple routing protocol that uses distance or hop count as its primary metric for determining the best forwarding path. RIP, IGRP and EIGRP are examples. A distance vector protocol routinely sends its neigboring routers copies of its routing tables to keep them up-to-date. Distance vector protocols date back to the ARPAnet network in the early 1970s. Contrast with *link state protocol* and *path vector protocol*. See *routing protocol*.

**distributed computing**     (1) The use of multiple computers in an organization rather than one centralized system.
(2) The use of multiple computers networked throughout a wide geographical area (or the world via the Internet) to solve a single problem. For example, the Search for Extraterrestrial Intelligence (SETI) employs unused time in millions of home computers to analyze data. See *SETI* and *peer-to-peer computing*.

**Distributed Computing Environment**     See *DCE*.

**distributed database**     A database physically stored in two or more computer systems. Although geographically dispersed, a distributed database system manages and controls the entire database as a single collection of data. If redundant data is stored in separate databases due to performance requirements, updates to one set of data will automatically update the additional sets in a timely manner. See *replication*.

**distributed data processing**    See *distributed processing*.

**distributed file system**    Software that keeps track of files stored across multiple networks. When the data is requested, it converts the file names into the physical location of the file so it can be found.

**distributed function**    The distribution of processing functions throughout the organization.

**distributed intelligence**    The placing of processing capability in terminals and other peripheral devices. Intelligent terminals handle screen layouts, data entry validation and other pre-processing steps. Intelligence placed into disk drives and other peripherals relieves the central computer from routine tasks.

**distributed logic**    See *distributed intelligence*.

**Distributed Management Environment**    See *DME*.

**distributed objects**    Software modules that are designed to work together but reside in multiple computer systems throughout the organization. A program in one machine sends a message to an object in a remote machine to perform some processing. The results are sent back to the calling machine. See *CORBA* and *DCOM*.

**distributed printer**    A computer printer that provides output in a range approximately from 25 to 60 ppm. It is generally considered a higher grade than a network printer and lower than a production printer. IBM typically uses this term. See *network printer* and *production printer*.

**distributed processing**    The first term used to describe the distribution of multiple computers throughout an organization in contrast to a centralized system. It started with the first minicomputers. Today, distributed processing is called "distributed computing." See also *client/server*.

**distribution disk**    A floppy disk or CD-ROM used to disseminate files in a software package.

**Distribution Media Format**    See *DMF*.

**dithering**    Simulating more colors and shades in a palette. In a monochrome system that displays or prints only black and white, shades of grays can be simulated by creating varying patterns of black dots. This is how halftones are created in a monochrome printer.

In color systems, additional colors can be simulated by varying patterns of dots of existing colors. Dithering cannot produce the exact same results as having the necessary color depth (levels of gray or colors), but it can make shaded drawings and photographs appear much more realistic.

Dithering is also used to create a wide variety of patterns for use as backgrounds, fills and shading, as well as for creating anti-aliasing effects.

**Divestiture**    The breakup of AT&T. By federal court order, AT&T divested itself on January 1, 1984, of its 23 operating companies, which became known as the Regional Bell Operating Companies (RBOCs). Bell Labs was renamed AT&T Bell Labs, and its Western Electric manufacturing division became AT&T Technologies. The demarcation point of the physical split was the Class 4 switching center. Except for those that handled large metropolitan regions, all Class 4 offices went to AT&T, and all Class 5 offices went to the RBOCs. It was the switching office class hierarchy within the Bell system that made Divestiture possible, because there were clear borders between long distance and local service. See *Class 4 switch*, *Bellcore* and **Trivestiture**.

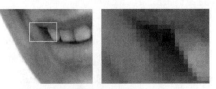

**Dithering a Color Image**
When there aren't enough colors in a display system to render an image properly, an infinite palette can be created by dithering. Quite often, a 24-bit color image is dithered to 256 colors. The right side is a magnification of the white box on the left.

DATABASE
DATABASE

**DATABASE**

**DATABASE**
**Dithering Text**
Text is also dithered. Notice how much softer the word DATABASE is at the top of this example, compared with the undithered word below it. The magnified view shows where lighter blue pixels filled in for the curves. When dithering is performed against the edges of an image, it is called "anti-aliasing."

**divide overflow**    A program error in which a number is accidentally divided by zero or by a number that creates a result too large for the computer to handle.

**Divx**    **(1)** (DIgital Video EXpress) A DVD rental system that was rolled out in June of 1998 and taken off the market one year later due to lack of sales. A joint venture of Circuit City and a Los Angeles entertainment law firm, Divx used special discs and a special DVD machine that played Divx movies and regular DVD movies. Consumers paid a rental charge for the Divx disc, which lasted for two days after the first viewing. Additional playing time or unlimited use could be purchased by credit card via the modem in the Divx player, or the disc was thrown away. One of the problems with the system was that the Divx disc was registered to the specific machine that sent in the registration and could not be played on other Divx players. All remaining Divx discs could not be upgraded to unlimited use, but could be viewed until June 30, 2001.

   **(2)** A copy of the DVD copy protection decryption algorithm that was lifted from a media player and passed around hacker sites. The Divx name was used in honor of a "defunct" system.

**DIX standard**    (DEC-Intel-Xerox standard) An earlier Ethernet standard that has been superseded by IEEE 802.3. Network protocols often use the Ethernet frame from this specification.

**DL/1**    (Data Language 1) An early database from IBM for its DOS/VSE mainframes. DL/1 is a modified version of IMS/DB. See *IMS*.

**DLC**    **(1)** (Data Link Control) See *data link* and *OSI*.

   **(2)** (Data Link Control) The data link layer protocol (layer 2) that is used in IBM's SNA networking. See *SNA*, *data link protocol* and *Microsoft DLC*.

   **(3)** See *digital loop carrier*.

**DLC chip**    Any one of several Intel-compatible CPUs from Cyrix Corporation. See *486DLC*.

**DLCI**    (Data Link Connection Identifier) The number of a private or switched virtual circuit in a frame relay network. Located in the frame header, the DLCI field identifies which logical circuit the data travels over, and each DLCI has a committed information rate (CIR) associated with it. The DLCI number is local to the FRAD and frame relay switch it connects to, and it is generally changed by the switch within the network, because the receiving switch uses a different DLCI for the same connection. See *CIR*, *PVC*, *SVC* and *frame relay*.

**DLL**    (Dynamic Link Library) An executable program module that performs some function. DLLs are widely used in Windows, but they are not launched directly by the user. When needed, they are called for by a running application and are loaded to provide additional functionality. DLLs can be rather simple, such as providing the ability to display a 3-D border around a dialog box (CTL3DV2.DLL), or as complicated as a full-blown language interpreter such as a Visual Basic runtime module (VBRUN400.DLL).

   DLLs are generally written so that their routines are shared by more than one application at the same time (see *reentrant code*). There are many DLLs that come with Windows that applications depend on (look in your \WINDOWS\SYSTEM folder for the .DLL extension). Applications may also include their own DLLs, which may be stored in the application folder or in the \WINDOWS\SYSTEM folder.

   In the DOS world, there was never a formal way to dynamically link and share routines at runtime. ISRs and TSRs were created for this purpose, but they were not sanctioned by Microsoft and often caused conflict. Unfortunately, there are still conflicts in the DLL world (see *DLL hell*).

**DLL hell**    Refers to conflicts with Windows DLLs when the wrong one is installed. A Windows DLL is an extension to the operating system that is shared by any application that calls it. Once a DLL is opened, all programs use that same instance of the DLL when they need its functions. Microsoft is continually adding features to its DLLs; and in order for an application vendor to utilize those features and ensure that the latest DLL is available, it installs the latest DLL along with the application.

   The problem is that the latest DLL can always be superseded by an even later one. If the installation program does not check version numbers or dates and simply installs its shared DLL into the \WINDOWS\SYSTEM directory, it may overwrite a newer version with an older one. This means the installation of a new application can foul up an existing application that depends on functions in the newer DLL that all of a sudden are no longer there.

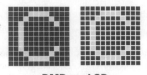

**DMD vs. LCD**
The gap between the mirrors in a DMD pixel (left) is smaller than the gap in an LCD display (right), resulting in a sharper display.

Although Microsoft has published guidelines, there is no way to enforce compliance, and Microsoft itself from time to time has released new versions of DLLs that are incompatible with older ones. One has to remember, however, that this flawed system was set up when 4MB of RAM was the norm and having two instances of the same DLL open was wasteful of precious memory. Today it is a moot point.

Windows 2000 and XP are designed to let software developers install required DLLs in their own application folders and mark them as "not" sharable. Thus, even if a DLL by the same name is already open and in use, the application will use its own version of the DLL instead. These later operating systems also monitor DLLs being replaced and may prevent an erroneous replacement.

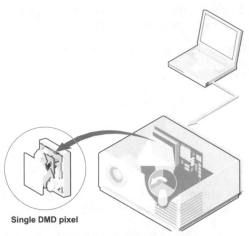

**Single DMD pixel**

**DLP Processing**
The computer's video output is sent to the memory on the DLP chip, which contains millions of microscopic mirrors (DMD pixels). A light is beamed through a color wheel that spins fast enough to display red, green and blue 60 times per second. The mirrors rotate to reflect each color when required. In this drawing, not only is one pixel enlarged (in the circle), but the entire chip is grossly enlarged for illustrative purposes.

**DLP** (Digital Light Processing) A data projection technology from TI that produces clear, readable images on screens in lit rooms. DLP is suitable for all ends of the projection spectrum, from units that weigh under 10 pounds to electronic cinema projectors that are expected to replace large-screen movie projectors some day. The technology uses a Digital Micromirror Device (DMD), a chip with from 400,000 to more than two million light switches that cancel or reflect light. Microelectromechanical mirrors, each 16 micrometers square, are built on top of a CMOS memory chip.

The state of each memory bit (0 or 1) rotates its mirror plus or minus 10 degrees. Gray scale is created by modulating the light, which is accomplished by rotating the mirrors back and forth some number of times within each 16 millisecond video frame. Color is achieved by using color filters with one, two or three DMD chips. See *microdisplay*.

**DLS server** See *ULS server*.

**DLSw** (Data Link SWitching) An IBM method for integrating and forwarding SNA and LAN traffic over wide area networks (WANs) by encapsulating the data in TCP/IP packets. DLSw supports the SDLC (SNA) and LLC2 (Token Ring) data link protocols and is generally employed in routers. Multiprotocol over frame relay (MPOFR) is a later technology designed to move SNA and LAN traffic over frame relay. See *MPOFR*.

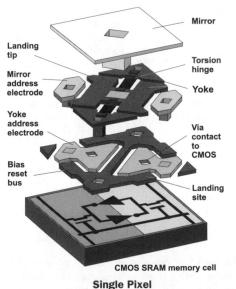

Mirror

Landing tip

Torsion hinge

Mirror address electrode

Yoke

Yoke address electrode

Via contact to CMOS

Bias reset bus

Landing site

**CMOS SRAM memory cell**

**Single Pixel**
Hard to believe, but more than two million of these light switches are fabricated onto one CMOS chip. The state of the memory cell (0 or 1) rotates the mirror sufficiently to cancel or reflect light. Gray scale is achieved by rotating the mirrors back and forth more rapidly. *(Redrawn from original diagram courtesy of Texas Instruments, Inc.)*

**DLT**    (Digital Linear Tape) A magnetic tape technology originally developed by Digital for its VAX line. The technology was later sold to Quantum, which makes it available to other manufacturers. DLT uses half-inch, single-hub cartridges somewhat like IBM's 3480/3490/3590 line. It writes 128 or 208 linear tracks, depending on model, and provides capacities from 10 to 40GB. DLT usage started to grow rapidly in 1995 and has been widely used on medium- to large-scale LANs.

SuperDLT provides native capacities from 50GB to 110GB and transfer rate from 5 to 10MB per second. See *magnetic tape*.

**DLT Cartridge**
Like IBM tapes, DLT use half-inch linear recording in a single-hub cartridge. After insertion, the tape is pulled from the cartridge onto the takeup reel inside the drive.

**DLUR/DLUS**    (Dependent LU Requester/Server) SNA enhancements that enable traditional host connections, such as host to terminal and host to printer, to run over an APPN network. It supports LU sessions other than 6.2. See *LU*.

**DLUS**    See *DLUR/DLUS*.

**DM**    See *document management*.

**DMA**    (1) (Direct Memory Access) Specialized circuitry or a dedicated microprocessor that transfers data from memory to memory without using the CPU. Although DMA may periodically steal cycles from the CPU, data is transferred much faster than using the CPU for every byte of transfer.

On PCs, there are eight DMA channels commonly used as follows. Most sound cards are set to use DMA channel 1.

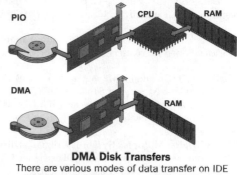

**DMA Disk Transfers**
There are various modes of data transfer on IDE disk drives. The PIO modes use the CPU, and the DMA modes bypass the CPU.

```
DMA      Used For
0        8-bit transfer
1        8-bit transfer
2        Floppy disk controller
3        8-bit transfer
4        Cascaded from 0-3
5        16-bit transfer
6        16-bit transfer
7        16-bit transfer
```

(2) (Document Management Alliance) A specification that provides a common interface for accessing and searching document databases. It is expected to provide interoperability between multivendor document management systems. DMA was released in 1998 by the DMA task group of the AIIM association. See *AIIM*.

**DMA-33**    See *Ultra ATA*.

**DMA-66**    See *Ultra ATA*.

**DMD**    (Digital Micromirror Device) See *DLP*.

**DME**    (Distributed Managment Environment) A network monitoring and control protocol defined by the Open Software Foundation (now The Open Group). DME was not widely used.

**DMF**    (Distribution Media Format) A floppy disk format that Microsoft uses to distribute its software. DMF floppies compress more data (1.7MB) onto the 3.5" diskette, and the files cannot be copied with normal DOS and Windows commands. A utility that supports the DMF format must be used.

**DMI**    (Desktop Managment Interface)  A management system for PCs developed by the Distributed Management Task Force (DMTF). DMI provides a bi-directional path to interrogate all the hardware and software components within a PC. When PCs are DMI-enabled, their hardware and software configurations can be monitored from a central station in the network.

A memory-resident agent resides in the background. When queries are made to the agent, it responds by sending back data contained in MIFs (Management Information Files) and/or activating MIF routines. Static data in a MIF would contain items such as model ID, serial number, memory and port addresses. A MIF routine could report errors to the management console as they occur, or it could read ROM or RAM chips and report their contents, as well.

**DMI LAYERS**

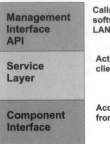

| Management Interface API | Calls to DMI from console software, such as Intel's LANdesk and Novell's NMS. |
| Service Layer | Actual DMI agent in each client machine (DLL, TSR, etc.) |
| Component Interface | Accesses the MIF and provides calls from component back to the console. |

DMI is a complete management system but can co-exist with SNMP and other management protocols. For example, when an SNMP query arrives, DMI can fill out the SNMP MIB with data from its MIF. A single workstation or server can serve as a proxy agent that would contain the SNMP module and service an entire LAN segment of DMI machines.

Data-only MIFs can be created by anyone using a text editor, but it is expected that all hardware and software vendors will eventually include at least a data-only MIF with their products. See *CIM*, *WBEM* and *DTMF*.

**DMPL**    (Digital Microprocessor Plotter Language)  A vector graphics file format from Houston Instruments that was developed for plotters. Most plotters support the DMPL or HPGL standards.

**DMS**    (1) (Document Management System)  See *document management*.

(2) (Defense Messaging System)  An X.500-compliant messaging system developed by the U.S. Dept. of Defense. It is used by all the branches of the armed forces, as well as federal agencies involved with security.

(3) (Desktop Management Suite)  A collection of software administration and backup programs for Windows from Seagate Software.

(4) (Digital Multiplex System)  A digital switch from Nortel Networks that is used in a telephone company central office. It includes the large local/toll exchange DMS-100/200, small local exchange DMS-10, DMS-250 long distance switch, DMS-300 international gateway, DMS-500 local and long distance switch, DMS-100 wireless, DMS-Global Services Platform (GSP), DMS-Programmable Services Architecture (DMS-PSA) and advanced signaling solutions, including the DMS-STP and BroadBand STP.

**DMT**    See *DSL*.

**DMTF**    (Distributed Management Task Force, Inc., Hillsboro, OR, www.dmtf.org)  An industry consortium founded in 1992 that is involved with the development, support and maintenance of management standards for PCs. Its goal is to reduce the cost and complexity of PC management. Focusing initially on the DMI standard, the DMTF is involved with other management technologies, including CIM and DEN. The DMTF was originally the Desktop Management Task Force. See *DMI*, *CIM*, *WBEM* and *DEN*. See also *DTMF*.

**DMZ**    (DeMilitarized Zone)  A middle ground between an organization's trusted internal network and an untrusted, external network such as the Internet. The DMZ is a subnetwork (subnet) that may sit between firewalls or off one leg of a firewall. ISPs typically place their Web, mail and authentication servers in the DMZ. DMZ is a military term that refers to the area between our lines and enemy territory.

**DNA**    (1) See *Windows DNA*.

(2) (Digital Network Architecture)  Introduced in 1978, it was Digital's umbrella term for its enterprise network architecture based on DECnet.

**DNIS**    (Dialed Number Identification Service)  A service that enables a company to track the volume of a telephone number when more than one number is directed to the same PBX port. For example, when several 800 numbers come into the same lines, DNIS data contains the originating number and lets the PBX keep count.

**DNS** (Domain Name System) Name resolution software that lets users locate computers on a UNIX network or the Internet (TCP/IP network) by domain name. The DNS server maintains a database of domain names (host names) and their corresponding IP addresses. In this hypothetical example, if **www.mycompany.com** were presented to a DNS server, the IP address **204.0.8.51** would be returned. DNS has replaced the manual task of updating HOSTS files in an in-house UNIX network, and of course, it would be impossible to do this manually on the global Internet, given its size.

For Windows networks using TCP/IP, the counterpart to DNS is WINS. In a Windows-only network, only WINS needs to be used. In a mixed Windows/UNIX environment, the Microsoft DNS server integrates the two. When a UNIX station wants to resolve the name for a PC, it queries the Microsoft DNS server, which in turn queries the WINS server if it does not already have it. See *reverse DNS*, *HOSTS file*, *ping*, *root server* and *WINS*.

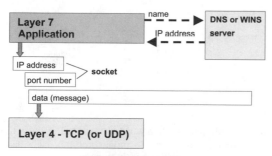

**DNS Name Resolution**
In an IP network, the application queries a DNS or WINS server to turn the name of the machine it wishes to communicate with into its IP address. See **TCP/IP ABCs**.

**doc file** A word processing file created in Word (Microsoft's word processor). It uses a .DOC extension and differs from a text file (.TXT file), because it contains Microsoft's proprietary headers and codes and must be opened in Word or software that reads the Word format. Since Word is used by so many Windows and Mac users, the doc file has become a de facto standard for e-mail attachments over the Internet. Although the page layout is naturally contained in the doc file, if the target computer does not have the same font selected in the original computer, there may be a slight difference in appearance at the other end when another font is substituted. Contrast with *ASCII file*. See *Microsoft Word*.

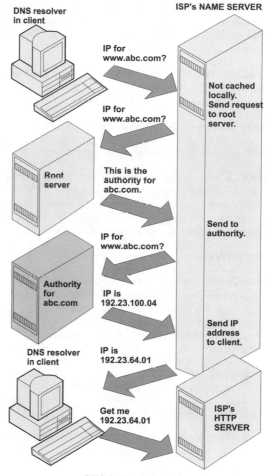

**DNS in the Internet**
Turning a URL into an IP address on the Internet often involves numerous queries starting from the ISP you are connected to through the various name servers. This is a simplified diagram, because the original requester actually talks to each name server in turn, and there can be more name servers in between. PCs running Web browsers almost never talk directly to an authority server, but use a local non-authoritative server as their proxy. *(Illustration assistance courtesy of Paul Vixie.)*

**docking station** A base station for a laptop that turns the portable computer into a desktop system. It uses a large plug and socket to quickly connect the laptop, which duplicates all the cable lines for the monitor, printer, keyboard, mouse, etc. The docking station typically has one or two slots for expansion boards, and may house speakers and other peripherals such as a CD-ROM drive. See *port replicator*.

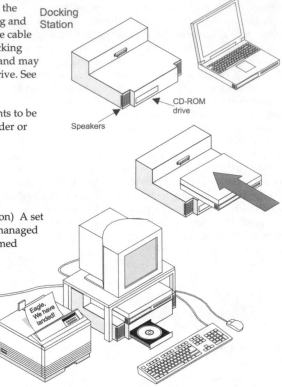

Docking Station

CD-ROM drive

Speakers

**DocObjects** An extension to OLE that allows documents to be placed into OLE containers such as the Microsoft Office Binder or Internet Explorer. See *ActiveX Documents*.

**DoCoMo** See *NTT DoCoMo*. See also *COCOMO*.

**docs** Short for documents or documentation.

**DOCSIS** (**D**ata **O**ver **C**able **S**ervice **I**nterface **S**pecification) A set of standards for transferring data via cable TV. DOCSIS is managed by Multimedia Cable Network System, an organization formed by four major cable operators. DOCSIS is expected to increase the market for cable modems. See *S-CDMA*.

**Doctor Watson** See *Dr. Watson*.

**DocuComp** A Windows program from Adobe that compares two documents and highlights the differences. It is typically used to keep track of revisions by several authors. It was originally developed by MasterSoft, Inc., which was acquired by Adobe.

**document** (1) From the computer perspective, the term initially only referred to a word processing file. Since the advent of the Macintosh, Apple has called virtually any file created on the computer a document, and this usage has migrated to the Windows environment. See *template* and *style sheet*.

(2) From a general office perspective, it is a paper form that has been filled out by typewriter or by hand.

**documentation** The narrative and graphical description of a system. Following are the kinds of documentation required to describe an information system for both users and systems staff. See also *technical writer* and *RTFM*.

Operating Procedures

- Instructions for turning the system on and getting the programs initiated (loaded).
- Instructions for obtaining source documents for data entry.
- Instructions for entering data at the terminal, which includes a picture of each screen layout the user will encounter.
- A description of error messages that can occur and the alternative methods for handling them.
- A description of the defaults taken in the programs and the instructions for changing them.
- Instructions for distributing the computer's output, which includes sample pages for each type of report.

System Documentation

- Data dictionary—Description of the files and databases.
- System flow chart—Description of the data as it flows from source document to report.
- Application program documentation—Description of the inputs, processing and outputs for each data entry, query, update and report program in the system.

Technical Documentation

- File structures and access methods
- Program flow charts
- Program source code listings
- Machine procedures (JCL)

**document centric**    Focusing on the document as the foundation or starting point. In a document-centric system, the document is retrieved and automatically calls the appropriate software required to work with it. Contrast with *application centric*. See *component software*.

**document collaboration**    See *data conferencing*.

**document exchange software**    Software that allows document files to be viewed on other computers that do not have the original application that created it. The software comes in two parts. The first component converts the document into a proprietary format for distribution. The second is a viewer program that displays the files, and viewers are generally free.

Unlike file viewers that rely on the fonts installed in the computer to display file contents accurately, document exchange systems carry the fonts over within the file format to the viewing machine. The fonts are only used for displaying the document, however, not for general use by the system. The viewers may allow sections of the document to be copied to the clipboard. See *Acrobat*.

**document handling**    A procedure for transporting and handling paper documents for data entry and scanning.

**document image management**    See *document imaging*.

**document image processing**    See *document imaging*.

**document imaging**    The online storage, retrieval and management of electronic images of documents. The main method of capturing images is by scanning paper documents.

Document imaging systems replace large paper-intensive operations. Documents can be shared by all users on a network, and document routing can be controlled by the computer (workflow). The systems are often simpler to develop and implement than traditional data processing systems, because users are already familiar with the paper documents that appear on screen.

Document images are stored as bitmapped graphics, and although a small amount of text (keywords) may be associated with the document in order to index it, the meaning of the document content is known only to the human viewer, not the computer. Like microfilm, signatures and other original markings remain intact.

**document management**    The capture and management of documents within an organization. The term used to imply the management of documents after they have been scanned into the computer. Today, the term has become an umbrella under which document imaging, workflow, text retrieval and multimedia fall.

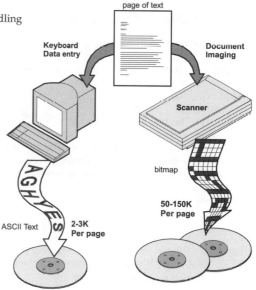

**Document Imaging Takes Storage Space**
When a page of text is scanned, it takes up much more storage space than if the individual characters were typed in. When data is entered on the keyboard, each character uses one byte of storage. When it is scanned, the piece of paper is turned into a digital picture, which is an image of dots. The white space on the paper also takes up storage. Depending on the resolution required for the printed text, a scanned page can take 50 times as much storage as the raw ASCII characters of typed-in data.

The trend toward designing information systems as document centric, where the document becomes the focus, not the application that created it, is expected to bring document management to the forefront of computing.

**document management system**   Software that manages documents for electronic publishing. It generally supports a large variety of document formats and provides extensive access control and searching capabilities across LANs and WANs. A document management system may support multiple versions of a document. It may also be able to combine text fragments written by different authors. It often includes a workflow component that routes documents to the appropriate users. See *workflow*.

**document mark**   In micrographics, a small optical blip on each frame on a roll of microfilm that is used to automatically count the frames.

**Document Objects**   See *ActiveX Documents*.

**document processing**   Processing text documents, which includes indexing methods for text retrieval based on content. See *document imaging*.

**document publishing software**   See *document exchange software* and *desktop publishing*.

**document retrieval**   The ability to search for documents by keywords and other attributes such as date and author. It implies that the documents have been indexed on all pertinent fields, and that keywords have been chosen based upon title and textual content.

**document sharing**   See *data conferencing*.

**document source**   See *page source*.

**document viewer**   See *file viewer* and *document exchange software*.

**docuterm**   A word or phrase in a text document that is used to identify the contents of the document.

**DOD**   (1) (Dial On Demand) A feature that allows a device to automatically dial a telephone number. For example, an ISDN router with dial on demand will automatically dial up the ISP when it senses IP traffic destined for the Internet.

(2) (DoD) (Department Of Defense) The military branch of the U.S. government, which is under the direction of the Secretary of Defense, the primary defense policy adviser to the President. The Annual Report to the President and the Congress (Annual Defense Report) outlines the DoD's capabilities and plans.

**DOF**   See *6DOF*.

**dog bone**   The bone-shaped holographic stickers used to seal CD jewel cases.

**dog-food**   Refers to software as it relates to using one's own products. Developer's are often chastised for not "eating their own dog-food." Phrases such as "we're going to dog-food this really good before we finalize the design" have also turned the word into a verb.

**DOI**   (Digital Object Identifier) A method of appying a persistent name to documents, publications and other resources on the Internet, rather than using a URL, which can change over time. DOI uses the Corporation for National Research Initiatives (CNRI) Handle System technology, which uses a naming system and naming servers to keep track of the location of the resources. To fully implement the system, a browser plug-in is required that will resolve the handle used on a Web page that identifies the resource. Otherwise, a proxy server is required. For more information, visit www.doi.org.

**DOJ**   (Department Of Justice) The legal arm of the U.S. government that represents the public interest of the United States. It is headed by the Attorney General.

**DOLAP**    See *OLAP*.

**Dolby**    (Dolby Laboratories, Wiltshire, England, www.dolby.com)  An audio research laboratory founded in 1965 in London by American engineer and physicist Ray Dolby. The company introduced its noise reduction system for tape recording in that same year, which became known as Dolby A and has been widely used in music recording, as well as movie theater soundtracks. Dolby B and C, introduced in 1968 and 1981, respectively, were geared for consumer audio tapes.

In 1986, Dolby SR (Spectral Recording) added signal processing techniques that doubled the noise reduction of Dolby A for professional use. Its derivative, Dolby S, is found in high-end cassette decks. Dolby circuits have been used in millions of audio tape recorders and players to eliminate the annoying hiss and improve the signal-to-noise ratio of analog tapes. Dolby's digital versions are advancing the art in the digital realm with movie and home theater systems that provide six and seven-channel sound. See *Dolby Digital*.

**Dolby AC-3**    (Dolby Audio Coding-3)  The audio coding technology used in Dolby Digital. See *Dolby Digital*, *AC-1* and *AC-3*.

**Dolby Digital**    A digital audio encoding system from Dolby used in movie and home theaters. First used in 1995, Dolby Digital employs Dolby's AC-3 (Audio Coding-3) coding and compression technology and provides six channels of audio, known as 5.1 for front left, front right, front center, rear left, rear right and subwoofer. Dolby Digital is widely used on LaserDiscs and DVDs, and is the standard for HDTV.

Co-developed with Lucasfilm THX, Dolby Digital Surround EX provides 6.1 channels. The first film to use this enhanced version of Dolby Digital was *Star Wars: Episode I: The Phantom Menace*, which opened in the U.S. in May 1999.

**Dolby Pro Logic**    See *Dolby Surround*.

**Dolby Stereo**    A digital audio encoding system from Dolby that was first used in movie theaters in the mid 1970s. It recorded four channels of audio and provided a breakthrough re-introduction of the optical soundtrack over magnetic tracks on 35mm film. Many noise reduction and equalization techniques were also used on 70mm magnetic-recorded film. Dolby Stereo is now called the Dolby analog format. See *Dolby Digital*.

**Dolby Surround**    A digital audio encoding system from Dolby that provides four channels. Derived from the Dolby Stereo technology, Dolby Surround has been widely used for video soundtracks, audio cassetes, CDs, TV broadcasts, video games and PC software. Dolby Surround Pro Logic is the playback circuit in consumer hardware such as an A/V amplifier or TV.

**Dolch**    (Dolch Computer Systems, Fremont, CA, www.dolch.com)  A manufacturer of high-end, ruggedized portable PCs for industrial use. It introduced the first portable active matrix PC; the first portable 386, 486, Pentium and dual Pentium; and in 1994, the first videoconferencing-equipped portable.

In 1976, Volker Dolch founded Dolch Logic Instruments, which became the largest supplier of logic analyzers in Europe. In 1987, he sold the company and arranged a management buy-out of its American division.

**dollar sign**    The dollar sign ($) is sometimes used to indicate a hexidecimal number. For example, $3E0 is the hex number 3E0.

**do loop**    A high-level programming language structure that repeats instructions based on the results of a comparison. In a DO WHILE loop, the instructions within the loop are performed if the comparison is true. In a DO UNTIL loop, the instructions are bypassed if the comparison is true. The following DO WHILE loop prints 1 through 10 and stops.

```
counter = 0
do while counter 10
  counter = counter + 1
  ? counter
enddo
```

**DOM** (Document Object Model) A common programming interface (API) for accessing HTML and XML documents from a Web browser. It was developed to formalize Dynamic HTML, which allows animation, interaction and dynamic updating of Web pages. DOM provides a language and platform-neutral object model for Web pages, but because it deals with document structures in general, DOM may also be used by any application that accesses documents. In late 1998, the W3C released DOM Level 1. See *Dynamic HTML* and *object model*.

**domain** (1) In a LAN, a subnetwork comprised of a group of clients and servers under the control of one security database. Dividing LANs into domains improves performance and security.

(2) In a communications network, all resources under the control of a single computer system.

(3) On the Internet, a registration category. See *domain name* and *Internet domain name*.

(4) In database management, all possible values contained in a particular field for every record in the file.

(5) In magnetic storage devices, a group of molecules that makes up one bit.

(6) In a hierarchy, a named group that has control over the groups under it, which may be domains themselves.

**domain controller** See *PDC* and *BDC*.

**domain name** The term may refer to any type of domain within the computer field, since there are several types of domains (see *domain*). However, today, it often refers to the address of an Internet site. See *Internet domain name* and *Internet address*.

**Is a Name Already Taken?** To find out if a domain name is taken, visit www.networksolutions.com or www.icann.org.

**domain name address** The unique identification of every entity (company, association, person, etc.) registered on the Internet. See *Internet domain name* and *Internet address*.

**domain namespace** See *namespace*.

**domain name system** See *DNS*.

**domain naming system** See *DNS*.

**domain-specific language** A programming language designed for a particular purpose. For example, Tex is a language used for typesetting, SQL is used to query databases, and Mathematica is used for computations. A domain-specific language (DSL) is more fine tuned to the application environment than a general-purpose programming language.

**domain squatting** See *cybersquatting*.

**dominant carrier** A telecommunications services provider that has control over a large segment of a particular market.

**Domino** See *Lotus Notes*.

**donating old equipment** See *how to donate old equipment*.

**dongle** Same as *hardware key*.

**do nothing instruction** Same as *no-op*.

**door** (1) In a BBS system, a programming interface that lets an online user run an application program in the BBS.

(2) See *drive door*.

**doorway mode** In a communications program, a mode that passes function, cursor, CTRL and ALT keystrokes to the BBS computer in order to use the remote application as if it were on the local machine.

**doorway page** A Web page that is designed to appeal to search engine spiders that continually comb the Web looking for pages to index. Also known as a "bridge page," or a "jump page," the doorway page has the "right phrase" in it so it will become indexed. However, the page itself is not intended to be viewed by people, rather it sends visitors to the real page with either a "Click Here" button or a fast meta refresh. See *meta refresh* and *spamdexing*.

**dopant**    An element diffused into pure silicon in order to alter its electrical characteristics and make it more conductive. Boron, phosphorous, antimony and arsenic are common dopants.

**doping**    Altering the electrical conductivity of a semiconductor material, such as silicon, by chemically combining it with foreign elements. It results in an excess of electrons (n-type) or a lack of electrons (p-type) in the silicon.

**Doppler effect**    The change in electromagnetic frequency that occurs when the source of the radiation and its observer move toward or away from each other. The faster they come together, the higher the frequency. The faster they move away, the lower the frequency. Discovered by Austrian physicist Christian Doppler (1803–1853), this condition has a great effect on low-earth orbit (LEO) satellites as they weave toward and away from the earth. See *Doppler radar*.

**Doppler radar**    A system for measuring speed that is based on the Doppler effect. It is used in police radar systems, as well as for measuring the velocity of hurricanes and tornadoes. See *Doppler effect*.

**Doppler shift**    See *Doppler effect*.

**DOS**    (1) (Disk Operating System) Pronounced "dahss." A generic term for operating system. See *operating system*.

(2) (Disk Operating System) A single-user operating system from Microsoft for the PC. It was the first OS for the PC and is still the underlying control program for Windows 3.1, 95, 98 and ME. Windows NT and 2000 emulate DOS in order to support existing DOS applications.

The DOS version that Microsoft developed for IBM was PC-DOS, and the version that all other vendors used was MS-DOS. However, except for DOS 6, which contains different versions of various utilities, PC-DOS and MS-DOS commands and system functions have been the same. All releases of PC-DOS and MS-DOS are generally called *DOS*. See *DOS ABCs*.

(3) (DOS, DOS/370, DOS/VS, DOS/VSE, VSE/ESA) A series of IBM mainframe "disk operating systems" for System/360, System/370 and System/390. DOS started as a variant of TOS (Tape Operating System), but soon supplanted TOS as disk storage became accepted in the late 1960s. DOS was always the "junior partner" to OS/360 and its progeny. It continues today as VSE/ESA.

(4) (DoS) See *denial of service*.

**DOS backslash**    Backslashes are used to represent the root directory when it precedes the first directory or file name in a path. Used elsewhere in the path, it is a symbol that separates file and directory names. See *DOS ABCs*.

**DOS batch file**    A file of DOS commands that are "batch" processed one after the other. Windows also supports batch files (see *Windows batch file*), which are mostly identical to the DOS commands.

**DOS box**    Slang for a DOS session in Windows or OS/2. The "box" is actually an instance of the Intel x86 Virtual 8086 Mode, which simulates an independent, fully functional PC environment. See *Virtual 8086 Mode*.

**DOS changing directories**    See *DOS Cd* and *DOS directories*.

**DOS command**    An instruction that DOS executes from the command line or from a batch file. A variety of internal commands, such as Dir and Copy, are built into the COMMAND.COM program and are always available as long as DOS is running. Many external commands, such as Format and Xcopy, are individual programs that reside in the DOS directory.

**DOS extender**    Software that is combined with a DOS application to allow it to run in extended memory (beyond 1MB). To gain access to extended memory, it runs the application in Protected Mode. When the application requests DOS services, the DOS extender either handles them itself or, with functions such as disk accesses, resets the machine to Real Mode, lets DOS service the request and then switches back into Protected Mode. Windows 3.0 included a DOS extender; and although it may seem ridiculous today, by breaking the 1MB limit, Windows solved a very thorny issue and became very popular. See *VCPI* and *DPMI*.

**DOS file**    (1) Any computer file created under DOS.
(2) An ASCII text file. See *DOS batch file*.

**DOSmark**    A unit of measurement of DOS benchmarks from Ziff-Davis. Its Windows counterpart is the Winmark. See *ZDBOp*.

**DOS optimizing memory**    See *DOS memory manager* and *DOS Memmaker*.

**DOS SYS files**    .SYS is the file extension commonly used for drivers that are installed in DOS; for example, MOUSE.SYS, COUNTRY.SYS and ASPI.SYS.
The CONFIG.SYS file is the file in which all the .SYS files are specified.

**DOS/VS**    (Disk Operating System/Virtual Storage) One of two operating systems offered on the IBM System/360. The other was OS/360. DOS/VS later evolved into DOS/VSE.

**DOS/VSE**    (Disk Operating System/Virtual Storage Extended) An IBM multiuser, multitasking operating system that was widely used on IBM's 43xx series. It used to be called DOS, but due to the abundance of DOS PCs, was later renamed VSE. It continues today as VSE/ESA. See *DOS*.

**DOS/Win**    Refers to Windows 3.1, which runs under DOS and requires that DOS be installed prior to the Windows installation. It is really just another way of saying Windows 3.1, Windows 3.11 or Windows for Workgroups, all collectively known as Windows 3.1.

**DOS window**    Generally refers to a DOS session under Windows. Windows can run DOS programs full screen or in a resizable window similar to other Windows applications. See *DOS box*.

**DOS/Windows**    (1) Refers to a PC computer environment that uses DOS or Windows in contrast with Mac or UNIX.
(2) Refers specifically to a DOS and Windows 3.1 environment, in contrast with Windows 95/98.

**DOS/Windows format**    DOS and Windows use a file system known as the File Allocation Table (FAT) to keep track of data on a disk. All floppy disks and hard disks must be initialized with the FAT before use. This is known as a high-level format. Windows NT can optionally use its own native format (see *NTFS*).
There is also a low-level format required on every disk. The low-level format creates the original sectors on the disk that hold everything, including the FAT and the data. IDE and SCSI hard disks are low-level formatted at the factory. Floppy disks are not. Thus, when you format a floppy, you are putting both a low-level and high-level format on the diskette at the same time. When you format a hard disk, you are doing only a high-level format.

**dot**    (1) A tiny round, rectangular or square spot that is one element in a matrix, which is used to display or print a graphics or text image. See *dot matrix* .
(2) A period; for example, V dot 22 is the same as V.22.
(3) The dot, or period, is used as a name separator. For example, file names are separated from their extensions with a dot (CDE.ABC, CDE.NDX, etc.). It is used to separate the components of Web addresses, such as www.hotstuff.com.

**dot addressable**    The ability to program each individual dot on a video display, dot matrix printer or laser printer.

**dot bomb**    A dot-com company that went out of business or one that is failing.

**dot chart**    See *scatter diagram*.

**dot-com**    Refers to the period (dot) followed by the abbreviation of the commercial domain (.com) at the end of an Internet e-mail or Web address. Since the .com domain is so widely used, the Internet has become known as the "dot-com" world, and dot-com companies are those that offer their wares on the Web. Since .com addresses are the most popular, Web browsers default to adding the .com to the end of the URL if no other domain, such as .org or .edu, is typed in. See *Internet domain name*, *dot-com company*, *not-com* and *dot-con*.

**dot-com company**    An organization that offers its services or products exclusively on the Internet. Although a company that makes only Web-based software might be in the dot-com industry, it is generally not considered a dot-com company. Amazon.com, Yahoo! and eBay are typical dot-com companies. See *dot-com*.

**dot-con**    A scam on the Internet. The Internet offers crooks and zealous marketers new opportunities to express their creativity. The major dot-con scheme is the online auction scams, where people sell merchandise that is not of the quality advertised. See *Web cramming*.

**dot gain**    An increase in size of each dot of ink when printed due to temperature, ink and paper type.

**dot matrix**    A pattern of dots that forms character and graphic images on printers. Although ink jet and laser printers print in dots, and monitors display dots as well, the term generally refers to images created with serial dot-matrix printers. See *dot-matrix printer*.

**dot-matrix printer**    A printer that uses hammers and a ribbon to form images out of dots. The common desktop dot-matrix printer, also known as a *serial dot-matrix printer*, uses one or two columns of dot hammers that are moved across the paper. The more dot hammers used, the higher the resolution of the printed image. For example, nine pins produces draft quality, and 24-pin heads produce typewriter quality output. Speeds range from 200–400 cps, which is about 90–180 lpm.

A line-matrix printer is a type of dot-matrix printer that attains speeds up to 1,400 lpm and is used in datacenters and industrial environments (see *line-matrix printer*).

Dot-matrix printers are widely used to print multipart forms, address and diskette labels. The tractor and sproket mechanisms used in these printers handle thick media much better than laser and ink jet printers.

| 7 Pin | 9 Pin | 18 Pin | 24 Pin |

**Dot Matrix Mechanism**
Dot matrix printers print columns of dots in a serial fashion. The more dot hammers (pins), the better looking the printed results.

**dot Net**    See *.NET*.

**dot pitch**    The distance between a red (or green or blue) dot and the closest red (or green or blue) dot on a color monitor (typically from .28 to .51mm; large presentation monitors may go up to 1.0mm). The smaller the dot pitch, the crisper the image. A .28 dot pitch means dots are 28/100ths of a millimeter apart. A dot pitch of .31 or less provides a sharp image, especially on text. See *slot pitch*.

**dotTV**    (dotTV Corporation, Pasadena, CA, www.tv) The registrar for Internet addresses that end in .tv. The .tv top-level domain is the country code for the Pacific island of Tuvalu, which has approximately 10,000 inhabitants. For granting exclusive registration rights to dotTV, Tuvalu receives part of the proceeds from registration fees. dotTV provides an auction for bidding on names, and the winning bid becomes the registration fee for two years, which is increased in subsequent years.

**double buffering**    A programming technique that uses two buffers to speed up a computer that can overlap I/O with processing. Data in one buffer is being processed while the next set of data is read into the other one.

In streaming media applications, the data in one buffer is being sent to the sound card and/or display adapter, while the other buffer is being filled with more data from the source of the material (Internet, local server, etc.).

When video is displayed on screen, the data in one buffer is being filled while the data in the other is being displayed. Full-motion video is speeded up when the function of moving the data between buffers is implemented in a hardware circuit rather than being performed by software. See *video accelerator*.

Data is being read into this buffer

48859893293820 0320

while data in this buffer is being processed.

75439948800004880488 40MR88900032342

**Double Buffers**

Two buffers are commonly used to speed up program execution. Data is processed in one buffer while data is written into or read out of the

**double click**    To press the mouse button twice in rapid succession.

**double density**    Twice the capacity of the prior format. Yesterday's double density can be today's low density (see *DD*).

**double extension**    A way to trick users into opening a virus. Many people have learned that text files (.TXT) and image files (.GIF, .JPG, etc.) are safe to launch because they are data and not executable software. They have learned to be leary of .EXE, .VBS and other extensions that are executed immediately. Thus, virus writers try to trick more people using double extensions, so "I LOVE YOU.TXT.vbs" is really not a .TXT file, but a .vbs file, a Visual Basic Script that is executed immediately.

Some mail programs may actually remove the .vbs at the end of the name, leaving users completely helpless to make a determination, even if they know what to look for. As crazy as that sounds, this mentality is pervasive. Most versions of Windows default to showing no extensions in all file name displays, which is beyond absurdity considering the importance of this file designator even under normal operations. See *dangerous extensions* and *Love bug*.

**double precision**    Using two computer words instead of one to hold a number used for calculations, thus allowing twice as large a number for more arithmetic precision. Contrast with *single precision*.

**double quotes**    The double quotes (") symbol is used to delineate a string of text as in the C statement **printf ("Press Enter now.\n");**. They are also used to delineate a phrase for searching. If you enter **"absolute measurement"** in a Web search engine, you are asking for the two-word phrase, not any of the two words. See *single quotes*.

**double scan CGA**    A hardware circuit that improves CGA resolution.

**double twist**    Same as *supertwist*.

**double word**    Twice the length of a single computer word. A double word is typically 32 bits long. See *word*.

**DOW**    (Direct OverWrite) See *magneto-optic disk*.

**down**    Refers to a computer that ceases to operate due to hardware or software failure. A communications line is down when it is unable to transfer data.

**downlink**    A communications channel from a satellite to an earth station. Contrast with *uplink*.

**download**    To receive a file transmitted over a network. In a communications session, download means receive, upload means transmit. Downloads depend on file size and network speed. Via a 28,800 bps modem, small Web pages take seconds when everything is running smoothly, but a 10MB video file takes at least an hour. LAN downloads are much faster. That same 10MB file can fly across a high-speed LAN in one second.

Downloading files from the Internet has become a snap with "click here to download this file" messages on Web pages. The Web browser prompts you where to save the file. Downloading from an online service requires following the menu prompts to find the topics and files of interest. See *download protocol*.

On a network server, downloadable files are placed in public directories (folders) that can be copied using the normal file management procedures of the operating system. On a Windows LAN for example, files are selected by drive letter, directory (folder) and file name. The user could select the J: drive, \PUBLIC directory and NEWDRIVR.SYS file by clicking on the appropriate references to them in File Manager or Explorer.

**D**

**downloadable font**    Same as *soft font*.

**download protocol**    The communications protocol used to transmit a file, also known as a file transfer protocol. For example, the Internet uses HTTP and FTP. UNIX systems use FTP and UUCP. Using a general-purpose communications program to download from a BBS or private site requires selecting a common protocol at both ends. Zmodem has been widely used.

**downsizing**    Converting mainframe and mini-based systems to personal computer LANs.

**downstream**    From the provider to the customer. Downloading files and Web pages from the Internet is the downstream side. The upstream link is from the customer to the provider, such as when requesting the Web page. In cable TV, the downstream signals are the network programs, movies and sports events transmitted over the cable. Unless the cable is used for the Internet, cable TV does not have an upstream. Pay-per-view cable requires an upstream link for requesting an event, which is usually the telephone.

**downtime**    The time during which a computer is not functioning due to hardware or system software failure. That's when you truly understand how important it is to have reliable hardware.

**downward compatible**    Also called *backward compatible*, it refers to hardware or software that is compatible with earlier versions. Contrast with *upward compatible*.

**DP**    See *data processing* and *dot pitch*.

**DPCM**    (Differential **PCM**) An audio digitization technique that codes the difference between samples rather than coding an absolute measurement at each sample point. See *ADPCM*.

**dpi**    (Dots Per Inch) The measurement of the resolution of display and printing systems. A typical CRT screen provides 96 dpi, which provides 9,216 dots per square inch (96×96). Flat panel displays from 110–200 dpi have also been developed.

As the dpi rate doubles, the number of dots within a square inch is quadrupled, because dpi deals with two dimensions. Thus, while 100 dpi produces 10,000 actual dots per square inch, 200 dpi produces 40,000 (see below). We have a long way to go to make the resolution on a screen as dense as a printer. A 1,200 dpi printer produces 157 times as many dots of resolution as a typical 96 dpi screen.

| DPI | Dots per Square Inch |
|-----|----------------------|
| 96 | 9,216 |
| 100 | 10,000 |
| 200 | 40,000 |
| 300 | 90,000 |
| 600 | 360,000 |
| 1,200 | 1,440,000 |

**DPL**    (Digital PowerLine) A technology for transmitting up to a 1 Mbps data signal over electric power lines from Nortel Networks. It has been initially successful in Europe, because a base station deployed at each 220-volt transformer serves from 100 to 200 customers. Since 110-volt transformers in North America serve only a handful of customers, the implementation is more costly, although methods for circumventing the transformers are expected. Technologies such as this enable your electric company to supply you with Internet and local telephone access.

**DPM**    (Documents Per Minute) The number of paper documents that can be processed in one minute.

**DPMA**    (1) (Dynamic Power Management Architecture) Power management features built into Intel chipsets. By monitoring system activity and turning itself off when not required, DPMA chipsets use up to 75% less power than previous chipsets. DPMA supports the ACPI interface. The 430TX was the first DPMA-compliant chipset. See *Intel chipsets* and *ACPI*.

(2) (Data Processing Management Association) See *AITP*.

**DPMI**    (DOS Protected Mode Interface) A programming interface from Microsoft that allows a DOS-extended program to run cooperatively under Windows 3.x. It is not compatible with VCPI, the first DOS extender standard, but Windows 3.1 is more tolerant of VCPI applications than Windows 3.0.

XMS, VCPI and DPMI all deal with extended memory. However, XMS allows data and programs to be stored in and retrieved from extended memory, whereas VCPI and DPMI allow programs to "run" in extended memory.

**DPMS**    See *VESA DPMS*.

**DPOF**    (Digital Print Order Format) A file format for digital film memory cards that stipulates which images are to be printed. At the time of shooting or when reviewing on the camera, it allows the user to specify how many of each image are to be printed. The DPOF file is a built-in order on the "film" for commercial print services. It also enables the images to be printed immediately on desktop printers that accept memory cards without requiring software in the computer to set up the print job. Thumbnails and image rotation can also be specified.

**DPSK**    (Differential Phase Shift Keying) A common form of phase modulation used in modems. It does not require complex demodulation circuitry and is not susceptible to random phase changes in the transmitted waveform. Contrast with *FSK*.

**DQbroker**    Database middleware from Metagon Technologies, LLC., Charlotte, NC (www.metagon.com), that provides enterprise data access to heterogeneous databases. Working with more than 70 relational and hierarchical database systems running under UNIX or NT, DQbroker enables a single SQL statement from any query program on any platform to execute against any number of databases in the network. The DQBroker software resides in each database server and maintains metadata about all the other database servers in the network. The SQL call can be made from the client to any one of the DQbroker-supported databases in the network. DQbroker supports high-speed processing by providing parallel execution of joins between distributed databases, which may even improve performance between databases of the same type. See *DQpowersuite*

**DQDB**    (Distributed Queue Dual Bus) The protocol used to control access to an IEEE 802.6 queued packet synchronous exchange (QPSX) network, used for metropolitan area networks (MANs). This architecture

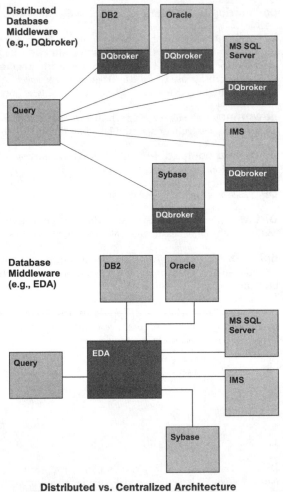

**Distributed vs. Centralized Architecture**
Since DQbroker resides in all the database servers, it enables a query to be sent to any of them. In a hub and spoke architecture, the query goes to a central location.

allows for both circuit and packet switching and supports data, voice and video traffic. Using fixed-length cell relay technology, DQDB is suited to volatile network traffic.

**draft mode**    The highest-speed, lowest-quality printing mode.

**drag**    To move an object on screen such that its complete movement is visible from starting location to destination. The movement may be activated with a stylus, mouse or keyboard keys.

To drag an object with the mouse, point to it. Press the mouse button and hold the button down while moving the mouse. When the object is at its new location, release the mouse button. See *Win Drag and drop*.

**D**

**drag and drop**    A graphical user interface (GUI) capability that lets you perform operations by moving the icon of an object with the mouse into another window or onto another icon. For example, files can be copied or moved by dragging them from one folder to another. Programs can be executed by dragging and dropping. To print a document, an icon of the document is dragged on top of the icon for the printer.

Drag and drop is essential for graphics applications where you need to position text and images on the page or on top of each other. However, there are drag and drop options for copying and moving files, which can be just as easily accomplished with the standard Copy, Cut and Paste functions in the Edit menu. See *Win Drag and drop*.

**drag lock**    The ability to lock onto a screen object so that it can be dragged with the mouse without continuously holding down the mouse (or trackball) button.

**drain**    One side of a field effect transistor. When the gate is pulsed, current flows from the source to the drain, or vice versa, depending on the design. See *collector*.

**DRAM**    See *dynamic RAM*.

**DRAW**    (Direct Read After Write)  Reading data immediately after it has been written to check for recording errors.

**drawing program**    A graphics program used for creating illustrations. It maintains an image in vector graphics format, which allows all elements of the picture to be isolated, moved and scaled independent of the others.

Drawing programs and CAD programs are similar; however, drawing programs usually provide a large number of special effects for fancy illustrations, while CAD programs provide precise dimensioning and positioning of each graphic element in order that the objects can be transferred to other systems for engineering analysis and manufacturing.

Examples of popular drawing programs for Windows are Adobe Illustrator, Macromedia Freehand, Designer and CorelDRAW. Adobe Illustrator and Macromedia Freehand are also available for the Macintosh. Contrast with *paint program*. See *graphics* and *diagramming program*.

**DRDA**    (Distributed Relational Database Architecture)  An IBM architecture for distributing data across multiple heterogeneous platforms. It also serves as a protocol for access to these databases from IBM and non-IBM platforms. DRDA uses LU 6.2 as its transport protocol.

**DRDBMS**    (Distributed Relational DBMS)  A relational DBMS that manages distributed databases. See *distributed database*.

**DR-DOS**    A multitasking DOS-compatible operating system from Caldera. It is used in embedded systems, thin clients and bootable disks for antivirus recovery programs. The embedded version includes display antialiasing so that it can be used in set-top boxes attached to TV sets. DR-DOS also breathes life into older PCs, because it is Y2K compliant and adds a driver that brings old ROM BIOSs up to Y2K compliance. Caldera's DR-WebSpyder provides a graphical browser that makes older 386s usable on the Internet.

DR-DOS was originally developed by Digital Research, the creators of CP/M, as the single-user version of Concurrent DOS. The operating system was extremely popular during the late 1980s and early 1990s, because it added many features lacking in MS-DOS, including memory management and disk compression. In addition, DR-DOS Version 5 was the first retail version of DOS that could be purchased in a computer store.

DR-DOS inspired Microsoft to improve subsequent versions of MS-DOS and to make major efforts to market against it. In 1991, Digital Research was acquired by Novell, which later sold it to Caldera. See *Caldera*.

**D-RDRAM** (Direct Rambus **DRAM**) See *RDRAM*.

**dribbleware** (1) Software that is publicly displayed and previewed well in advance of its actual release. Dribbleware is one stage beyond vaporware.

(2) Software that is released in small increments, especially due to the ease with which updates can be downloaded from a Web site today.

**drift** Change in frequency or time synchronization of a signal that occurs slowly.

**drill down** To move from summary information to the detailed data that created it.

**drive** (1) An electromechanical device that spins disks and tapes at a specified speed. Also refers to the entire peripheral unit such as *disk drive* or *tape drive*.

(2) To provide power and signals to a device. For example, "this control unit can drive up to 15 terminals."

**drive bay** A cavity for a disk drive in a computer cabinet. See *Device Bay*.

**drive mapping** A letter or name assigned to a disk or tape drive. In a PC, the basic drive mappings are A: for the floppy disk (B: used to be the second floppy) and C: for the primary hard disk. When new peripherals are added to the system, additional drive mappings are assigned by the operating system based on the next available letter (D:, E:, etc.).

In a network, drive mappings reference remote drives, and you have the option of assigning the letter of your choice. For example, on your local machine, you might use K: to refer to drive C: and a specific directory on a server in the network. Each time K: is referenced on that local machine, the drive and directory on the remote machine is substituted behind the scenes.

In the days of Windows 3.1, referencing a remote drive required drive mapping. Since Windows 95, UNC (Universal Naming Convention) names have become more popular, because they allow the server to be addressed by its true name (canonical name). See *dynamic drive mapping*, *redirector* and *UNC*.

**driver** (1) A hardware device (typically a transistor) that provides signals or electrical current to activate a transmission line or display screen pixels. See *line driver*.

(2) Also called a "device driver," it is a program routine that links a peripheral device to the operating system. It is written by programmers who understand the detailed knowledge of the device's command language and characteristics. It contains the precise machine language necessary to perform the functions requested by the application.

When a new hardware device is added to the computer, such as a display adapter, its driver must be installed in order to use it. The operating system calls the driver, and

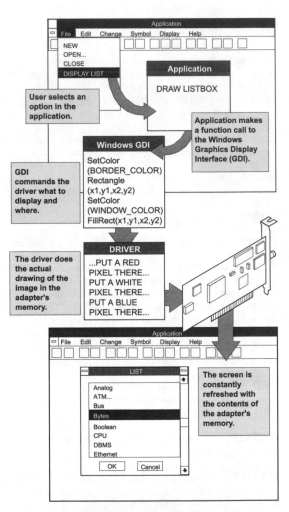

**The Windows Display Driver**

This diagram shows the part the driver plays when an application wants to display something on the screen. The application calls the GDI (Graphics Device Interface) in Windows and tells it to do something. GDI in turn sends commands to the driver supplied with the display adapter to actually draw the image. The display driver draws the image in the display adapter's memory, which is simultaneously being sent to the monitor.

the driver "drives" the device. Routines that perform internal functions, such as memory managers and disk caches, are also called drivers.

**Drivers Can Drive You Crazy!**   If it seems that the solution to every problem is to update a driver, that is often the case. The driver is the link between the operating system and the peripheral device. If the peripheral is changed, the driver must also be changed. If a bug is found in the driver, a new version is released to fix it. New drivers are constantly made available on vendor Web sites for downloading.

In Windows or the Mac, everything you see on screen is the result of the display driver (video driver) drawing the screen according to the commands that the operating system issues to it. A display driver is extremely complex and error prone and is known to cause erratic behavior in Windows.

**There Used to Be Even More Drivers**   The effort required to support different brands of peripheral devices was one of the major reasons DOS gave way to Windows. For example, in the DOS world, in order to provide complete control over the printing of a document, each application had to provide its own drivers for the most popular printers. With Windows and the Mac, the printer driver is installed into the operating system, not into each application. From then on, all applications access the printer through the operating system and the one driver for that printer.

**drive tray**   See *tray drive*.

**DRM**   (Digital Rights Management) A system for protecting the copyrights of digital content that is distributed online. It may also include the accounting for paying royalties to the authors of the material. In the music world, a DRM system provides a container format that includes album and track titles; and a set of rules that enforce copyright compliance that software and hardware players must support in order to play back the material.

**drop cap**   In typography, a large first letter that drops below the first line.

**drop-down menu**   See *pull-down menu*.

**drop in**   An extraneous bit on a magnetic medium that was not intentionally written, due to a surface defect or recording malfunction.

**dropout**   (1) On magnetic media, a bit that has lost its strength due to a surface defect or recording malfunction. If the bit is in an audio or video file, it might be detected by the error correction circuitry and either corrected or not, but if not, it is often not noticed by the human ear or eye.

(2) In data transmission, a momentary loss of signal that is due to system malfunction or excessive noise.

**drop shadow**   A graphics effect that makes elements look more three-dimensional and "pop out" of the picture. The Gaussian Blur filter is widely used to create this effect. Using an image editor, a duplicate of the text is made, changed to black or gray and then passed through the filter. The blurred result is aligned under the original text to create the effect. See *Gaussian Blur*.

**drop ship**   To have your vendor ship directly to your customer. The world of e-commerce has caused a marked increase in the drop shipping business.

**droupie**   (Data gROUPIE) A person who enjoys being with technical people.

**drownloading**   (1) The long time it takes with large downloads over the Internet using a slow analog modem. Web pages full of images can "drownload" your computer.

(2) Starting multiple download sessions concurrently, which winds up crashing the computer. The TCP/IP protocol allows for simultaneous sessions, but less-than-robust implementations of this software will cause the computer to lock up.

**DRP**   (Distribution and Replication Protocol) A W3C protocol for downloading only updated Web information (differential downloads). The Web site maintains an index of its files, including HTML pages, images and applications. The browser downloads the DRP index, which serves as a roadmap to the updated files when compared to the current index.

This is an example of a drop cap in printing.

**Drop Shadow**
Titles such as these are often done with a drop shadow to give them more of a 3-D effect.

**drum**    See *magnetic drum*.

**drum plotter**    A type of pen plotter that wraps the paper around a drum with a pin feed attachment. The drum turns to produce one direction of the plot, and the pens move to provide the other. The plotter was the first output device to print graphics and large engineering drawings. Using different colored pens, it could draw in color long before color ink jet printers became viable. Contrast with *flatbed plotter*.

**The First Drum Plotter**
In 1959, the CalComp Model 565 was the world's first drum plotter. It had one pen and could handle media up to 11" wide. *(Image courtesy of CalComp, Inc.)*

There is a band of letters for each print column

Print Hammer (one for each print column)

Ribbon

Paper

**Drum Printer Mechanism**
The hammer pushes the paper into the type slug when it rotated around to the proper position. Such printer technologies seem ridiculous compared to the quiet, high-speed workings of today's laser printers.

**drum printer**    **(1)** A wide-format ink jet printer. The paper is taped onto a drum for precise alignment to the nozzles.

**(2)** An old line printer technology that used formed character images around a cylindrical drum as its printing mechanism. When the desired character for the selected position rotated around to the hammer line, the hammer hit the paper from behind and pushed it into the ribbon and onto the character.

**drum scanner**    A type of scanner used to capture the highest resolution from an image. Photographs and transparencies are taped, clamped or fitted into a clear cylinder (drum) that is spun at speeds exceeding 1,000 rpm during the scanning operation. A light source that focuses on one pixel is beamed onto the drum and moves down the drum a line at a time.

For transparencies, light is directed from the center of the cylinder. For opaque items, a reflective light source is used. Mirrors filter out the RGB values and send them to the drum scanner's photomultiplier tube (PMT), which is more sensitive than the CCDs used in flatbed and sheet-fed scanners, and can produce resolutions exceeding 10,000 dpi. If one PMT is used, three passes across the image are required. When three PMTs are used, a faster single-pass scan is performed. Contrast with *flatbed scanner*, *sheet-fed scanner* and *handheld scanner*.

**DRV-04**    A 3-D model viewset of the Viewperf benchmark, which is used to test OpenGL performance. See *OPC*.

**Dr. Watson**    A Windows utility that reports extensive details about a crash. It sits in the background and captures the current status of the system at the moment of the abend.

**dry copper**    See *LADS*.

**dry plasma etching**    A method for inscribing a pattern on a wafer by shooting hot ions through a mask to evaporate the silicon dioxide insulation layer. Dry plasma etching replaces the wet processing method that uses film and acid for developing the pattern.

**drystone**    See *Dhrystones*.

**dry wire**    See *LADS*.

**Drum Scanner**
ICG's model 370 provides 12,000 dpi of optical resolution for service bureau–quality scanning. Drum scanners provide the ultimate in scanning quality and resolution and are widely used for commercial graphics production, as well as applications that turn photos into posters and wall-sized images. *(Image courtesy of ICG North America.)*

D

**DS**    (Digital Signal) A classification of digital circuits. The DS technically refers to the rate and format of the signal, while the T designation refers to the equipment providing the signals. In practice, "DS" and "T" are used synonymously; for example, DS1 and T1, DS3 and T3.

**NORTH AMERICA, JAPAN, KOREA, ETC.**

| Service | Voice Channels | Speed (Mbps) | |
|---------|----------------|--------------|---|
| DS0 | 1 | 64 Kbps | |
| DS1 | 24 | 1.544 Mbps | (T1) |
| DS1C | 48 | 3.152 Mbps | (T1C) |
| DS2 | 96 | 6.312 Mbps | (T2) |
| DS3 | 672 | 44.736 Mbps | (T3) |
| DS4 | 4032 | 274.176 Mbps | (T4) |

**SONET CIRCUITS**

| Service | | Speed (Mbps) | |
|---------|---|--------------|---|
| STS-1 | OC1 | 51.84 | (28 DS1s or 1 DS3) |
| STS-3 | OC3 | 155.52 | (3 STS-1s) |
| STS-3c | OC3c | 155.52 | (concatenated) |
| STS-12 | OC12 | 622.08 | (12 STS-1s, 4 STS-3s) |
| STS-12c | OC12c | 622.08 | (12 STS-1s, 4 STS-3c's) |
| STS-48 | OC48 | 2488.32 | (48 STS-1s, 16 STS-3s) |

**EUROPE  (ITU)**

| Service | Voice Channels | Speed (Mbps) |
|---------|----------------|--------------|
| E1 | 30 | 2.048 |
| E2 | 120 | 8.448 |
| E3 | 480 | 34.368 |
| E4 | 1920 | 139.264 |
| E5 | 7680 | 565.148 |

**DS0**    A single 64 Kbps channel, which is the building block of a T1 transmission line. Designed for digital voice (PCM), 24 DS0 channels make up one T1 line. See *DS* and *PCM*.

**DS1**    See *DS*.

**DS2**    See *DS*.

**DS3**    See *DS*.

**DS4**    See *DS*.

**DSA**    (1) (Directory Server Agent) An X.500 program that looks up the address of a recipient in a Directory Information Base (DIB), also known as white pages. It accepts requests from the Directory User Agent (DUA) counterpart in the workstation.

(2) (Digital Signature Algorithm) The algorithm used in the Digital Signature Standard (DSS) by the U.S. government. The de facto standard RSA algorithm is more widely used than DSA.

(3) (Digital Storage Architecture) A disk controller standard from Digital.

(4) (Digital Signal Analyzer) A Tektronix oscilloscope that samples high-frequency signals.

(5) (Distributed Systems Architecture) A Bull HN network architecture.

**DSD AC-3**    (Dolby Stereo Digtal Audio Coding-3) See *Dolby AC-3*.

**DSL**    (2) See *domain-specific language*.

(1) (Digital Subscriber Line) A technology that dramatically increases the digital capacity of ordinary telephone lines (the local loops) into the home or office. DSL speeds are tied to the distance between the customer and the telco central office. DSL is geared to two types of usage. Asymmetric DSL (ADSL) is for Internet access, where fast downstream is required, but slow upstream is acceptable. Symmetric DSL (SDSL, HDSL, etc.) is designed for short haul connections that require high speed in both directions.

Unlike ISDN, which is also digital but travels through the switched telephone network, DSL provides "always-on" operation. At the telco central office, DSL traffic is aggregated in a unit called the DSL Access Multiplexor (DSLAM) and forwarded to the appropriate ISP or data network.

Although DSL only arrived in the very late 1990s, there have been more versions and alphabet soup than most any other new transmission technology. The major DSL flavors are summarized here:

**ADSL**   Asymmetric DSL shares the same line as the telephone, because it uses higher frequencies than the voice band. However, a POTS splitter must be installed on the customer's premises to separate the line between voice and ADSL. A version of ADSL, known as G.lite, Universal ADSL, ADSL Lite and splitterless ADSL, is geared to the consumer. It eliminates the splitter and associated installation charge, but all phones on the line must plug into low-pass filters to isolate them from the higher ADSL frequencies. ADSL is available in two modulation schemes: Discrete Multitone (DMT) or Carrierless Amplitude Phase (CAP). See *ATU-C* and *ATU-R*.

| ASYMMETRIC DSL (Can share line with analog phone.) | | | | |
|---|---|---|---|---|
| Type | Maximum Upstream Speed | Maximum Downstream Speed | Cable Pairs | Maximum Distance |
| ADSL | 1 Mbps | 8 Mbps | 1 | 18000 ft. |
| RADSL | 1 Mbps | 7 Mbps | 1 | 25000 ft. |
| G.Lite | 512 Kbps | 1.5 Mbps | 1 | 25000 ft. |
| VDSL | 1.6 Mbps | 13 Mbps | 1 | 5000 ft. |
| | 3.2 Mbps | 26 Mbps | 1 | 3000 ft. |
| | 6.4 Mbps | 52 Mbps | 1 | 1000 ft. |

| SYMMETRIC DSL (Cannot share line with analog phone.) | | | |
|---|---|---|---|
| Type | Upstream and Downstream Speed | Cable Pairs | Maximum Distance |
| HDSL | 768 Kbps | 2 | 12000 ft. |
| | 1.544 Mbps (T1) | 2 | 12000 ft. |
| | 2.048 Mbps (E1) | 3 | 12000 ft. |
| HDSL-2 | 44 Mbps (T1) | 1 | 18000 ft. |
| | 2.408 Mbps (E1) | 1 | 18000 ft. |
| SDSL | 1.5 Mbps | 1 | 9000 ft. |
| | 784 Kbps | 1 | 15000 ft. |
| | 208 Kbps | 1 | 20000 ft. |
| | 160 Kbps | 1 | 22700 ft. |
| IDSL | 144 Kbps | 1 | 26000 ft. |

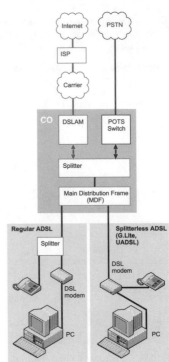

**ADSL Transmission**

Using different frequencies in the line, ADSL allows data to ride over the same wires as voice conversations. The signals are combined and split apart at both sides. At the customer's site, the splitting is done either with an external device that must be installed by the telephone company, or it is built into the DSL modem.

**RADSL**   Rate Adaptive DSL is a version of ADSL that adjusts speeds based on signal quality. Many ADSL technologies are actually RADSL.

**VDSL (also VHDSL)**   Very High Bit Rate DSL is an asymmetric version of DSL that is used as the final drop from a fiber optic junction point to nearby customers. VDSL lets an apartment or office complex obtain high-bandwidth services using existing copper wires without having to replace the infrastructure with optical fiber. Like ADSL, VDSL can share the line with the telephone.

**HDSL**   High Bit Rate DSL is a symmetric technology, which provides the same transmission rate in both directions. HDSL is the most mature DSL, because it has been used to provide T1 transmission over existing twisted pair without requiring the additional provisioning required for setting up T1 circuits. HDSL requires two cable pairs and goes up to 12,000 feet, while HDSL-2 requires only one cable pair and supports distances up to 18,000 feet. HDSL does not allow line sharing with analog phones.

**SDSL**   Symmetric DSL is an HDSL variation that uses only one cable pair and is offered in a wide range of speeds from 144 Kbps to 1.5 Mbps. SDSL is a rate-adaptive technology, and like HDSL, SDSL cannot share lines with analog telephones.

**IDSL**   ISDN DSL offers a rather low speed (144 Kbps) in both directions compared to other symmetric versions, but it does provide 16 Kbps more than standard ISDN, because the 16 Kbps "D" channel is used for data rather than call setup. It also offers the longest distance of 26,000 feet. Unlike standard ISDN, IDSL does not support analog phones, and signals are not switched through the telephone network. Since IDSL uses the same 2B1Q line coding as ISDN, ISDN customers can use their existing equipment (ISDN BRI terminal adapters and routers) when connecting to IDSL.

**DSLAM**   (DSL Access Multiplexor) A central office (CO) device for ADSL service that intermixes voice traffic and DSL traffic onto a customer's DSL line. It also separates incoming phone and data signals and directs them onto the appropriate carrier's network. See *DSL*.

**DSML**   (Directory Services Markup Language) A set of XML tags that defines the contents of a directory. Developed by Bowstreet Software, Portsmouth, NH (www.bowstreet.com), and endorsed by major vendors, it is designed to allow directories to work together. An access protocol such as LDAP is required to request services, and DSML provides a common format for delivering the results. For information on the DSML initiative, visit www.dsml.org. See *LDAP*.

**DSOM**   See *SOM*.

**DSP**   **(1)** (Digital Signal Processor) A special-purpose CPU used for digital signal processing. It provides ultra-fast instruction sequences, such as shift and add, and multiply and add, which are commonly used in math-intensive signal processing applications. DSP chips are widely used in a myriad of devices, including sound cards, fax machines, modems, cellular phones, high-capacity hard disks and digital TVs (see definition 2). The first DSP chip used in a commercial product was believed to be from TI, which was used in its very popular Speak & Spell game in the late 1970s.

**(2)** (Digital Signal Processing) A category of techniques that analyze signals from sources such as sound, weather satellites and earthquake monitors. Signals are converted into digital data and analyzed using various algorithms such as Fast Fourier Transform.

Once a signal has been reduced to numbers, its components can be isolated, analyzed and rearranged more easily than in analog form. DSP is used in many fields, including biomedicine, sonar, radar, seismology, speech and music processing, imaging and communications.

DSP chips are used in sound cards for recording and playback, compressing and decompressing and speech synthesis. Other audio uses are in amplifiers that simulate concert halls and surround sound effects for music and home theater.

**DSR**   (Data Set Ready) An RS-232 signal sent from the modem to the computer or terminal indicating that it is able to accept data. Contrast with *DTR*.

**DSS**   **(1)** (Decision Support System) An information and planning system that provides the ability to interrogate computers on an ad hoc basis, analyze information and predict the impact of decisions before they are made.

DBMSs let you select data and derive information for reporting and analysis. Spreadsheets and modeling programs provide both analysis and "what if?" planning. However, any single application that supports decision making is not a DSS. A DSS is a cohesive and integrated set of programs that share data and information. A DSS might also retrieve industry data from external sources that can be compared and used for historical and statistical purposes. An integrated DSS directly impacts management's decision-making process and can be a very cost-beneficial computer application. See *EIS* and *OLAP*.

**(2)** (Digital Signature Standard) A National Security Administration standard for authenticating an electronic message. See *RSA* and *digital signature*.

**(3)** (Digital Satellite System) A direct broadcast satellite (DBS) system from Hughes Electronics Corporation that delivers more than 175 TV channels. DSS receivers and dishes are made by RCA and other manufacturers. USSB and DirecTV provide the content. See *DBS*.

**DSSS**   (Direct Sequence Spread Spectrum) See *spread spectrum*.

**DSSSL**   (Document Style Semantics and Specification Language) A style sheet and transformation language for SGML documents. It allows an SGML document to be formatted for presentation or converted into another structure. Jade is an example of a DSSSL processor written by James Clark. For information, visit www.jclark.com. See *SGML*.

**DST**   **(1)** (Digital Signal Trust Company, Salt Lake City, UT, www.digsigtrust.com) An organization that sets up and manages PKI systems for companies and industry groups. Using third-party software, it serves as a certification authority (CA), manages the repository and provides a secure location for the private keys. Founded in 1996, Utah-based DST was the first licensed CA in the U.S. and the first PKI service organization. Utah was the first state in the U.S. to pass digital signature legislation. See *PKI*.

**(2)** (Data Storage Technology) A high-capacity magnetic tape technology from Ampex that is based on the digital composite D2 format for the broadcasting industry. It uses the same 19mm, helical scan transport, but provides higher capacities with Ampex's proprietary Data D-2 (DD2) format. DST cartridges range from 50–330GB and are suited for uncompressed digital video (movies, commercials, etc.) and high-resolution images, as well as general data backup for huge databases. Ampex's Data Instrumentation Systems (DIS) tape technology is a counterpart line that provides optional modes and interfaces for data acquisition devices. See *magnetic tape*.

**DSTN** **(1)** (Dual-scan **STN**) An enhanced STN passive matrix LCD display. The screen is divided into halves, and each half is scanned simultaneously, thereby doubling the number of lines refreshed per second and providing a sharper appearance. DSTN is widely used on laptops. See *STN* and *LCD*.

**(2)** (Double layer **STN**) An earlier passive matrix LCD technology that used an extra compensating layer to provide a sharper image.

**DSU/CSU** (Digital (or Data) Service Unit/Channel Service Unit) A pair of communications devices that connect an inhouse line to an external digital circuit (T1, DDS, etc.). It is similar to a modem, but connects a digital circuit rather than an analog one.

The CSU terminates the external line at the customer's premises. It also provides diagnostics and allows for remote testing. If the customer's communications devices are T1 ready and have the proper interface, then the CSU is not required, only the DSU.

The DSU does the actual transmission and receiving of the signal and provides buffering and flow control. The DSU and CSU are often in the same unit. The DSU may also be built into the multiplexor, commonly used to combine digital signals for high-speed lines.

**DSVD** (Digital Simultaneous Voice and Data) An all-digital technology for concurrent voice and data (SVD) transmission over a single analog telephone line. DSVD is endorsed by Intel, Hayes, U.S. Robotics and others, and has been submitted to the ITU for possible standardization. DSVD modems became available in the first half of 1995. See *SVD*.

**DSX-1** (Digital Signal Cross-connect Level 1) A standard that defines the voltage, pulse width and plug and socket for connecting DS-1 (T1) signals.

**DTD** (Document Type Definition) A language that describes the contents of an SGML document. The DTD is also used with XML, and the DTD definitions may be embedded within an XML document or in a separate file. DTDs are expected to be replaced by an XML schema from the W3C. See *XML schema* and *SGML*.

**DTE** (Data Terminating Equipment) A communications device that is the source or destination of signal on a network. It is typically a terminal or computer. Contrast with *DCE*.

**4mm DAT**

**Large (330GB)**

**Medium (150GB)**

**Small (50GB)**

### DST Tape Storage
DST is not exactly for home computer use. The large 330GB tape cassette, which is as big as a laptop computer, could back up the entire neigborhood. The 4mm DAT cassette is shown for size comparison.

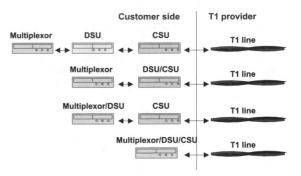

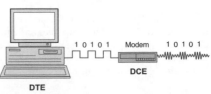

**DTF** (Digital Tape Format) A high-performance magnetic tape technology from Sony that is based on the helical scan transport and cartridge shell of Sony's highly successful 1/2" Digital Betacam. Providing up to 42GB (DTF-1) of storage with a sustained transfer rate of 12 Mbytes/sec, DTF drives are used for general enterprise-wide backup and storage area networks (SANs), as well as archiving video and recording seismic information. The DTF-2 format, introduced in late 1999, increased capacity to 200GB and transfer rate to 24MB/s. See *DIR* and *magnetic tape*.

**DTMF** (Dual-Tone MultiFrequency) The type of audio signals that are generated when you press the buttons on a touch-tone telephone. See also *DMTF*.

**DTP** See *desktop publishing*.

**DTR** (Data Terminal Ready) An RS-232 signal sent from the computer or terminal to the modem indicating that it is able to accept data. Contrast with *DSR*.

**DTS** (1) (Digital Termination Service) A microwave-based, line-of-sight communications provided directly to the end user.

(2) (DeskTop Server) A motorola 68000-based network server from Banyan.

(3) (Developer Technical Support) The tech-support group for developers at Apple.

(4) (Digital Theatre Sound) A digital audio encoding system used in movie and home theaters. Popularized by the movie Jurassic Park, the soundtrack is maintained on CD-ROMs that are synchronized with the DTS timecode in the film, making it compatible with existing theater systems. The conventional stereo optical audio track is still on film for backup. DTS Digital Surround is the home theater counterpart, and many DVD players support DTS 5.1 channel audio. It is the least compressed of digital audio formats, and many claim it is a superior format. See *Dolby Digital*, *SDDS* and *THX*.

**DTV** (Digital TV) A digital television standard for the U.S. approved by the FCC in 1996 and developed by the Advanced Television Systems Committee (ATSC). In November 1998, DTV debuted in major U.S. cities. Canada, South Korea, Taiwan and Argentina have also adopted the ATSC standard.

In order to receive DTV, you need a new digital TV set or a set-top box for an existing analog TV. Digital TV sets will support analog TV transmission, which is expected to be broadcast until at least 2006.

DTV offers 18 formats from SDTV (Standard Definition TV), which is not much more than the digital counterpart of the current NTSC analog standard, except without snow and ghosts, all the way up to HDTV (High Definition TV), which uses a wide screen (16:9 aspect ratio) with up to 1,080 lines of resolution and 5.1 Dolby Digital surround sound.

More SDTV channels can be transmitted within the same bandwidth than HDTV. Therefore, it is up to the broadcasters, cable providers and satellite companies to determine the amount of content versus quality. DTV provides 14 progressive scan and four interlaced formats (see below), but their designations are

4mm DAT

**Large**
**DTF-1: 42GB**
**DTF-2: 200GB**

**Small**
**DTF-1: 12GB**
**DTF-2: 60GB**

**DTF Tape Storage**
Sony's DTF tape drives evolved from its successful Betacam family which has been an industy standard for years. The 4mm DAT cassette is shown for size comparison.

**SDTV vs. HDTV**
The 4:3 aspect ratio on standard TV and computer screens (left) is more square than the 16:9 ratio of HDTV (right). *(Image courtesy of Intergraph Computer Systems.)*

sometimes incomplete. For example, 1080i implies a 1,920×1,080 resolution at 30 fps, because there is only one interlaced frame rate (30i) for this format, but 480p may refer to any of two horizontal resolutions and three progressive scan (p) frame rates. See *HDTV, NTSC, 8-VSB, interlaced* and *progressive scan.*

```
                         Frame Rate (fps)
Resolution     Aspect    i=interlaced
Horiz./Vert.   Ratio     p=progressive scan

DIGITAL HDTV

1920 x 1080    16:9      24p, 30i, 30p
1280 x  720    16:9      24p, 30p, 60p

DIGITAL SDTV

704 x  480     16:9      24p, 30i, 30p, 60p
704 x  480     4:3       24p, 30i, 30p, 60p
640 x  480     4:3       24p, 30i, 30p, 60p

ANALOG (NTSC)

440 x  484     4:3       30i
```

**DUA**    (Directory User Agent) An X.500 routine that sends a request to the Directory Server Agent (DSA) to look up the location of a user on the network.

**dual analog**    Using two analog modems and two phone lines to double transmission speed. See *channel bonding.*

**dual-band headset**    A portable telephone handset that operates in more than one frequency band.

**dual boot**    A computer configuration that allows it to be started with either one of two different operating systems. The dual boot feature is contained in one of the operating systems. There are system programs that can be installed that let you boot from several operating systems. For example, System Commander from V Communications, San Jose, CA, lets you install all the operating systems you will ever need on one PC and choose which one you want at startup.

**dual counter-rotating ring**    A network topology that uses two rings, with transmission in opposite directions in each ring. It is designed for fault tolerance and increased speed. If one of the rings breaks, the devices can reroute traffic on the other ring. Since traffic goes in both directions, packets traveling between two nodes can take the shortest distance between them. See *FDDI* and *Sebring ring.*

**dual-homed**    Connected to two networks or circuits. See *multihomed.*

**dual-mode handset**    A portable telephone handset that supports two types of services. It can switch from analog to digital or from cellular to satellite or from cellular to cordless. See *DECT* and *Globalstar.*

**dual Pentium**    A PC with a motherboard that contains two Pentium CPUs. Such machines are designed for use with an operating system that supports symmetric multiprocessing (SMP), such as Windows NT or 2000. See *SMP.*

**dual ported RAM**    See *video RAM.*

**dual processors**    Using two CPU chips in the same computer. See *SMP.*

**dual-scan LCD**    See *DSTN.*

**dub**    To make a copy of an audio or videotape. See *dub-dub-dub.*

**dub-dub-dub**    A fast way of saying "w-w-w" in a Web address. "3-dub" is an alternate. See *dub.*

**Dublin Core**   A set of metadata descriptions about resources on the Internet. Used for *resource discovery*, it contains data elements such as title, creator, subject, description, date, type, format and so on. Dublic Core descriptions are often included in HTML meta tags. All Dublin Core Metadata Initiative (DCMI) elements are presented in the following structure. See *meta tag*.

```
Name - label
ID - unique identifier (often same as name)
Version - DCMI version
Registration Authority - "DCMI"
Language - written language
Definition - explanation and concept
Obligation - must value be present?
Datatype - value type
Maximum Occurrence - limit to repeatability
Comment - remarks about its application
```

**due diligence**   Research; analysis; your homework. This term has caught on in all industries, because it sounds so "wired." Who would want to do analysis or research when they can do due diligence. See *wired*.

**dumb network**   A network that provides raw wiring from one location to another and introduces either very little or no processing to support the types of signaling that may be used in transmission.

George Guilder, editor of the "Guilder Technology Report," has been calling the Internet a dumb network, and telecom consultant David Isenberg calls it a "stupid network." While the Internet does indeed contain intelligence, these phrases are used to contrast the Internet to the telephone system, which for years has been known as an "intelligent" network. Telephone switches must be programmed for any new type of service that is added, whereas the Internet serves as an oblivious transport, taking bits in and pushing them out the other side. New services and features are added at the periphery by installing new software in users' PCs and in the servers, instead of revamping the network itself.

In order for the Internet to provide the quality of service necessary to effectively deal with interactive voice and video, its routers and switches will have to become even more intelligent in prioritizing traffic. Nevertheless, it is expected that all future networking will be based on Internet-like architectures (IP protocols) that can be upgraded by adding faster hardware as needed, without major upgrades to the architecture, which should be kept as simple (dumb, stupid) as possible. As witness to the concept, both Qwest Communications and multibillion-dollar startup Level 3 Communications are building national voice and data networks based entirely on IP. AT&T has announced that its future infrastructure will be IP based. Times…they are a changin'. See *IP on Everything*.

**dumb terminal**   A display terminal without processing capability. It is entirely dependent on the main computer for processing. Although mainframe and minicomputer terminals (3270, 5150, etc.) are technically smart terminals, because they have a certain amount of built-in screen display capabilities, they are often called dumb terminals. Contrast with *smart terminal* and *intelligent terminal*.

**dump**   To print the contents of memory, disk or tape without any report formatting. See *memory dump*.

**DUN**   (DialUp Networking) The dial-up networking capability in Windows 95/98. See **Win Dial-up Networking**.

**duplex channel**   See *full-duplex*.

**duplexed system**   Two systems that are functionally identical. They both may perform the same functions, or one may be standby, ready to take over if the other fails.

**duplexing**   See *duplex printing*, *duplexed system* and *full-duplex*.

**duplex printing**   The ability to print on both sides of the paper.

**duplicate keys**   Identical key data in a file. Primary keys, such as account number, cannot be duplicated, since no two customers or employees should be assigned the same number. Secondary keys, such as date, product and city, may be duplicated in the file or database.

**Duron**   See *AMD*.

**duty cycle**   A machine's rated capacity to perform work under normal conditions. It generally applies to mechanical devices such as printers, in which case it would indicate the number of pages that can be printed per month without a problem.

**DV**   (**D**igital **V**ideo) A consumer digital video format endorsed by all major video equipment vendors. Using 1/4" (6.35mm) metal evaporated tape, DV is recorded at 25 Mbps (18.8mm/sec) on three-hour standard cassettes or one-hour MiniDV cassettes (sizes are 125×78×14.6 and 66×48×1.2mm, respectively). DV uses a DCT algorithm, similar to Motion JPEG that provides a 5:1 compression ratio. DV tapes can be played back on DV, DVCAM and DVCPRO tape decks; however, MiniDV cassettes require an adapter for DVCPRO machines. See *DVCAM*, *DVCPRO* and *Digital-S*.

**DVB**   (**D**igital **V**ideo **B**roadcasting) An international digital broadcast standard for TV, audio and data. DVB can be broadcast via satellite, cable or terrestrial systems. It has been initially used in Europe and the Far East.

**DVC**   (1) (**D**igital **V**ideo **C**amera) A camcorder that records in digital format. See *DV*.

(2) (**D**igital **V**ideo **C**assette) An earlier term for the DV format. See *DV*.

(3) See *desktop videoconferencing*.

**DV and MiniDV Cartridges**
The full-size DV cartridge holds three hours of digital video. The smaller MiniDV cartridges were designed for today's miniature camcorders, but hold only one hour of video.

**DVCAM**   Sony's variant of the DV (Digital Video) format, which provides professional quality by increasing the tape speed to 28.2mm/sec. It also increases track width from 10 to 15 microns for added reliability. DVCAM uses the same metal evaporated tape as does DV, and DVCAM cassettes can be played in DVCAM, DVCPRO and DVCPRO50 tape decks.

**DVCPRO**   Panasonic's variant of the DV (Digital Video) format, which provides higher quality by increasing tape speed and track width. It uses metal particle tape for added reliability and also adds a cueing track for enhanced editing. DVCPRO50 uses two codecs to double the transfer rate of standard DV. DVCPRO and DVCPRO50 cassettes can be played only in DVCPRO tape decks. See *DV*.

**DVCR**   (**D**igital **VCR**) A VCR that records video in a digital format rather than the original and common analog format. See *D-VHS*.

**DVD**   A family of optical discs that are the same overall dimensions of a CD, but have significantly higher capacities. DVDs are also double sided, whereas CDs are single sided. Dual-layer versions have two distinct data layers per side. DVD drives read most CD media as well.

Both the computer and movie industries worked on DVD, and it is expected to become the next CD-ROM and primary digital movie medium, superseding Video CDs, analog LaserDiscs, and eventually VHS tape.

There are several flavors of DVD. DVD-ROM is like a large CD-ROM, allowing for data and interactive material and audio and video. It requires a DVD-ROM drive installed in a computer, and DVD-ROM drives can play DVD-Video.

DVD-Video is the movie format. It is really DVD-ROM with a slightly different logical format. Players that attach to a TV or home theater system became available at the end of 1996. DVD-Video uses MPEG-2 compression providing approximately 133 minutes of LaserDisc-quality video per side. This is not a fixed length, because the compression rate is based upon the amount of motion taking place. DVD-Video supports Dolby Digital surround sound, which provides five discrete channels of CD-quality audio plus a subwoofer (5.1 channel).

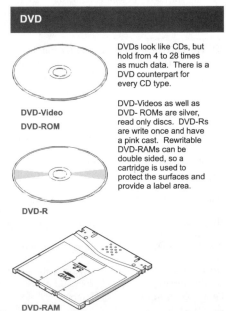

**DVD**

DVDs look like CDs, but hold from 4 to 28 times as much data. There is a DVD counterpart for every CD type.

DVD-Videos as well as DVD-ROMs are silver, read only discs. DVD-Rs are write once and have a pink cast. Rewritable DVD-RAMs can be double sided, so a cartridge is used to protect the surfaces and provide a label area.

DVD-Video
DVD-ROM

DVD-R

DVD-RAM

DVD-R is a write-once version used for creating masters, and DVD-RAM is the official rewritable DVD sanctioned by the DVD Forum. DVD+RW competes with DVD-RAM for the rewritable market, and MMVF is a rewritable version only available in Japan. DVD-R/W is also a rewritable version, but is more an extension to DVD-R than a competitor to DVD-RAM.

DVD-Audio is a second-generation digital music format that provides higher sampling rates than audio CDs. Many have welcomed the new format, believing that the original audio CD was unable to capture the total sound spectrum. See *DVD-Audio*.

**What Does DVD Really Mean?**    DVD originally stood for Digital VideoDisc. Since the technology began to seem as important for the computer world as it did for the video world, the "video" was dropped, and it became simply D-V-D. Later, it was dubbed Digital Versatile Disc, which is the name endorsed by the DVD Forum. For the most part, people refer to the technology as D-V-D.

**Specifications**    Following are the various types of DVDs and their capacities. DVD-Video, DVD-ROM and DVD-Audio use the same physical format and capacity, but have different logical formats due to the differences in their content.

| Type | Sides | Layers | Capacity |
|------|-------|--------|----------|
| **Read-only DVDs** | | | |
| DVD-Video | 1 | 1 | 4.7GB (DVD-5) |
| and | 1 | 2 | 8.5GB (DVD-9) |
| DVD-ROM | 2 | 1 | 9.4GB (DVD-10) |
| | 2 | 2 | 17.0GB (DVD-18) |
| **Write-once DVDs** | | | |
| DVD-R (A) | 1 | 1 | 3.95GB |
| DVD-R (A) | 1 | 1 | 4.7GB |
| DVD-R (G) | 1 | 1 | 4.7GB |
| DVD-R (G) | 2 | 1 | 9.4GB |
| **Rewritable DVDs** | | | |
| DVD-RAM Ver. 1 | 1 | 1 | 2.6GB |
| DVD-RAM Ver. 1 | 2 | 1 | 5.2GB |
| DVD-RAM Ver. 2 | 1 | 1 | 4.7GB |
| DVD-RAM Ver. 2 | 2 | 1 | 9.4GB |
| DVD-RAM (80 mm) | 1 | 1 | 1.46GB |
| DVD-RAM (80 mm) | 2 | 1 | 2.92GB |
| DVD-RW | 1 | 1 | 4.7GB |
| DVD+RW | 1 | 1 | 3.0GB |
| DVD+RW | 2 | 1 | 6.0GB |
| MMVF | 1 | 1 | 5.2GB |
| MMVF | 2 | 1 | 10.4GB |

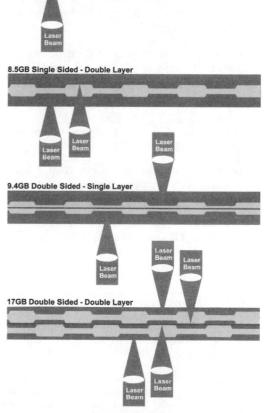

**4.7GB Single Sided - Single Layer**

0.6mm
0.6mm

Laser Beam

**8.5GB Single Sided - Double Layer**

Laser Beam    Laser Beam    Laser Beam

**9.4GB Double Sided - Single Layer**

Laser Beam    Laser Beam    Laser Beam

**17GB Double Sided - Double Layer**

Laser Beam    Laser Beam

**Sides and Layers**
DVDs come in any combination of single or double sided with single or double layers. This shows the laser beam contacting the recorded surface in all of the possibilities.

**DVD+RW**    (DVD+Read Write) A rewritable DVD disk technology endorsed by Sony, HP and Philips. Using phase change technology, the first DVD+RW disks hold 3GB per side instead of the 2.6GB of DVD-RAM. DVD+RW disks can be rewritten 100,000 times and do not require the use of a caddy as do DVD-RAM disks. DVD+RW drives are also expected to write CD-R discs. See *DVD-RW*.

**DVD-A**    See *DVD-Audio*.

**DVD-Audio**    The next-generation music format, which was approved by the DVD Forum in early 1999. It provides for 16, 20 and 24-bit samples at a variety of sampling rates: 44.1, 48,

88.2, 96, 176.4 and 192 kHz, compared to 16 bit samples at 44.1 kHz for CDs. Like CDs, DVD-Audio uses PCM encoding and provides two channels at the highest sampling rates and six channels at lower rates. Channel rates can vary; for example, the channels for the front speakers can be sampled higher than for the rear.

DVD-Audio supports other coding systems such as Dolby Digital, DTS and DSD, but as an alternate track, not stand-alone on the disc. DVD-Audio discs cannot be played on regular DVD-Video players, but combination DVD-Audio/Video players are expected. DVD-Audio discs can also contain video, graphics, text and links to the Web. See *SACD* and *MLP*.

**DVD Forum**   A membership organization devoted to defining DVD standards for read-only, rewritable, video and audio use. Members participate in working groups to develop new standards. Founded in late 1995 as the DVD Consortium, it was renamed in 1997. For more information, visit www.dvdforum.org.

**DVD-R**   (**DVD-R**ecordable) A write-once optical disk used to master DVD-Video and DVD-ROM discs. Pioneer was the first to introduce a drive that records 3.95GB on a DVD-R disc, and later introduced 4.7GB capability in the summer of 2000. DVD-R is not expected to compete with DVD-RAM, which is the rewritable DVD. DVD-Rs are the DVD counterpart to CD-Rs and use the same dye-layer recording technology to "burn" the disc.

In 2000, DVD-R was split into two types to deal with copy protection. The original DVD-R, which uses a 650 nm recording wavelength, was dubbed DVD-R(a) for Authoring. A different format with copy protection that records at 635 nm is called DVD-R(g) for General. Although DVD-R(a) and DVD-R(g) can read each other's format, they cannot write each other's format. See *DVD*, *CD-R* and *optical disk*.

**DVD-RAM**   A rewritable DVD disk endorsed by Panasonic, Hitachi and Toshiba. Using phase change technology, DVD-RAMs are expected to have significant impact on the VHS tape market after the turn of the century, since they provide an erasable, high-capacity optical disk that should become widely accepted. The first DVD-RAM drives with a capacity of 2.6GB (single sided) or 5.2GB (double sided) became available in the spring of 1998. DVD-RAM Version 2 disks with 4.7GB arrived in late 1999, and double-sided 9.4GB disks in 2000. DVD-RAM drives typically read DVD-Video, DVD-ROM and all types of CD media as well. See *DVD+RW*, *DVD-RW* and *optical disk*.

**DVD-ROM**   A read-only DVD disk used for storing data and interactive sequences, as well as audio and video. Expected to become the CD-ROM of the 21st Century, DVD-ROMs run in DVD-ROM or DVD-RAM drives, not DVD-Video players connected to TVs and home theaters. However, most DVD-ROM drives will play DVD-Video movies. See *DVD* and *optical disk*.

**DVD-RW**   (**DVD-R**ead Write) A rewritable DVD disk from Pioneer. Using phase change technology, it holds 4.7GB per side and can be rewritten more than 1,000 times. Unlike DVD-RAM and DVD+RW disks, DVD-RW disks can be read in first-generation DVD-ROM drives. See *DVD+RW* and *optical disk*.

**DVD-Video**   A read-only DVD disc used for full-length movies. DVD-Video discs hold approximately 133 minutes of full-motion video per side using MPEG-2 compression. The first DVD-Video players became available at the end of 1996. See *DVD*.

**DVE**   See *digital video effects*.

**D-VHS**   (**Data-VHS**) A VHS videocassette recorder that is able to store data from a digital satellite system (DSS). A D-VHS machine is a modified S-VHS VCR. See *DVCR*.

**DVI**   (1) (**D**igital **V**isual **I**nterface) A digital flat panel interface from the Digital Display Working Group (www.ddwg.org). The DDWG was formed to create a universal standard for attaching a flat panel monitor, and DVI is expected to become widely used. Based on TMDS signaling, the final draft of DVI was introduced in early 1999. See *flat panel display* and *LVDS*.

(2) (**D**igital **V**ideo **I**nteractive) An earlier compression technique for data, audio and full-motion video from Intel. It provided up to 72 minutes of full-screen video on a CD-ROM with up to 100:1 compression ratio. Intel acquired DVI in 1988 from RCA's Sarnoff Research labs in Princeton, New Jersey, but DVI never caught on.

**D**

**DVMRP**    (Distance Vector Multicast Routing Protocol) The first popular routing protocol to support multicast. Stemming from RIP and used in the Internet's Mbone (multicast backbone), DVMRP allows for tunneling multicast messages within unicast packets. It also supports rate limiting and distribution control based on destination address. Contrast with *MOSPF* and *PIM*.

**Dvorak keyboard**    A keyboard layout designed in the 1930s by August Dvorak, University of Washington, and his brother-in-law, William Dealey. 70% of words are typed on the home row compared to 32% with qwerty, and more words are typed using both hands. In eight hours, fingers of a qwerty typist travel 16 miles, but only one for the Dvorak typist.

```
Qwerty                              Dvorak

52%    Q W E R T Y U I O P          22%    ` , . P Y F G C R L ?
32%    A S D F G H J K L ; `        70%    A O E U I D H T N S -
16%    Z X C V B N M , . /
```

**DVR**    (Digital Video Recorder) See *PVR*.

**DVST**    (Direct View Storage Tube) An early graphics screen that maintained an image without refreshing. The entire screen had to be redrawn for any change.

**DWDM**    (Dense WDM) The term given to wavelength division multiplexing (WDM) when significantly more channels were being added. Since WDM is increasingly more "dense" all the time, both terms are used synonymously. See *WDM*.

**dweeb**    A very technical person. Dweebs sometimes call sales people "slime," anybody interested in technology for profit rather than the art of it. See *nerd* and *geek*.

**dwell software**    For people that have difficulty clicking the mouse, dwell software lets them perform the operation by holding the mouse over an icon or menu option a specified amount of time. To set the default action taken when dwelling, the user dwells over a selection in a dialog box displayed by the software. See *mouse emulator* and *accessibility*.

**DX**    When referencing an Intel 386 CPU, the DX or 386DX is the full 386 with a 32-bit data path, in contrast to the 386SX, which uses a 16-bit data path. In an Intel 486 CPU, the DX or 486DX designation has a different meaning. It refers to the full 486, which contains the math coprocessor, in contrast to the 486SX, which does not.

**DX-03**    A visualization viewset of the Viewperf benchmark, which is used to test OpenGL performance. See *OPC*.

**DXF file**    (Document EXchange Format file) An AutoCAD 2-D graphics file format. Many CAD systems import and export the DXF format for graphics interchange.

**dyadic**    Two. Refers to two components being used.

**dye diffusion**    See *dye sublimation printer*.

**dye polymer recording**    An optical recording technique that uses dyed plastic layers as the recording medium. WORM disks typically use a single layer, and erasable disks use two layers: a top retention layer and a bottom expansion layer. A bit is written by shining a laser through the retention layer onto the expansion layer, which heats the area and forms a bump that expands into the retention layer. The retention layer bumps are the actual bits read by the unit. To erase a bit, another laser (different wavelength) strikes the retention layer and the bump subsides.

**dye sublimation printer**    A printer that produces continuous-tone images that look like photographic film. It uses a ribbon containing an equivalent panel of dye for each page to be printed. Color printers have either three (CMY) or four (CMYK) consecutive panels for each page, thus the same amount of ribbon is used to print a full-page image as it is to print a tenth of the page. Special dye-receptive paper is used, and consumables (ribbon and paper) cost more than other printer technologies.

The paper and ribbon are passed together over the printhead, which contains thousands of heating elements that can produce varying amounts of heat. The hotter the element, the more dye is released. By varying the temperature, shades of each color can be overlaid on top of each other. The dyes are transparent and blend into continuous-tone color.

Thermal wax transfer uses the same transport mechanism as dye sublimation, but uses a wax-based ink, not a transparent dye. Like other color printers, it puts down a solid dot of ink and produces shades of colors by placing color dots side by side (dithering). Wax transfer prints faster than dye sub and consumables (ribbon and paper) are less expensive, but it does not produce photorealistic quality.

Some printers allow swapping of both ribbons so that thermal wax can be used for draft quality and dye sublimation for final output. See *printer*.

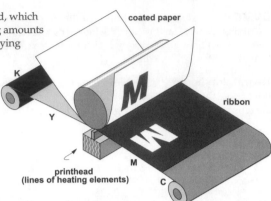

**Dye Sublimation/Thermal Wax Transfer**
The paper and ribbon are passed by the printhead. The ribbon is heated, and shaded dots of dye or solid dots of ink are transferred to the paper. The ribbon contains a panel equivalent in size to the page being printed, with three (CMY) or four (CMYK) panels for each color page to be printed.

**dye transfer**   See *dye sublimation printer*.

**dynamic**   Refers to operations performed "on the fly," which are based on decisions made while the program is running rather than beforehand. The expression, "buffers are dynamically created," means that space is created when actually needed, not reserved ahead of time. The expression, "data is compressed onto the disk dynamically" means that the compression algorithms are being applied when the data is being written rather than before. Contrast with *static*.

**dynamic address translation**   In a virtual memory system, the ability to determine what the real address is at the time of execution. See *dynamic*.

**dynamic binding**   Also called *late binding*, it is the linking of a routine or object at runtime based on the conditions at that moment. Contrast with *early binding*. See *binding time* and *polymorphism*.

**dynamic compression**   The ability to compress and decompress data in realtime; for example, as it's being written to or read from the disk. See *dynamic*.

**dynamic drive mapping**   The ability to automatically assign a drive letter to a remote drive and release the assignment when the application no longer needs it. In the PC world, this was especially useful in the days of Windows 3.1 when applications used multiple CD-ROM drives and all the drive letters were used up. Subsequently, UNC names eliminated the need for drive mapping. See *drive mapping* and *UNC*.

**dynamic HTML**   (1) A general term for Web pages that are customized for each user; for example, returning values from a search. Contrast with a *static HTML* page, which never changes.

(2) (Dynamic HTML) A combination of HTML enhancements, scripting language and interface that are used to deliver animations, interactions and dynamic updating on Web pages. The two major elements are the ECMAScript language and the DOM object model. ECMAScript is a derivative of JavaScript, and DOM is an object model interface that allows HTML elements to be changed. See *DOM* and *ECMAScript*.

**dynamic invocation**   See *dynamic method invocation*.

**dynamic IP address**   An IP address that is automatically assigned to a client station in a TCP/IP network, typically by a DHCP server. Network devices that serve multiple users, such as servers and printers, are usually assigned static IP addresses. See *static IP address*, *IP address* and *DHCP*.

**dynamic link**   The connection established at runtime from one program to another.

**dynamic link library**   A set of program routines that can be called at runtime as needed. See *DLL*.

**dynamic memory allocation**    Allocating memory as needed without having to specify a fixed amount beforehand. All advanced operating systems perform dynamic memory allocation to some extent.

**dynamic method invocation**    In object technology, the activation of a process (method) within an object at runtime.

**dynamic network services**    Realtime networking capabilities, such as adaptive routing, automatically reconfiguring the network when a node is added or deleted and the ability to locate any user on the network.

**dynamic node addressing**    A network technology that dynamically assigns machine addresses to nodes upon startup. For example, when a station is turned on in an AppleTalk network, it identifies itself to the network. If its number has been taken in the meantime by another node, it creates a new one using a random number generator.

**dynamic partitioning**    In a symmetric multiprocessing (SMP) system, the ability to reassign processors, memory and I/O to specific applications on the fly without shutting down the machine. The reassignment can be done by the operator or automatically from a script that monitors conditions, such as time of day or when the traffic to one application becomes excessive.

**dynamic RAM**    The most common type of computer memory, also known as D-RAM or DRAM. It usually uses one transistor and a capacitor to represent a bit. The capacitors must be energized hundreds of times per second in order to maintain the charges. Unlike firmware chips (ROMs, PROMs, etc.) both major varieties of RAM (dynamic and static) lose their content when the power is turned off. Contrast with *static RAM*.

| DYNAMIC RAM (DRAM) MEMORY TECHNOLOGIES | | | | | |
|---|---|---|---|---|---|
| Type | First Used | Clock Rate | Bus** Width | Peak Bandwidth | Volts |
| FPM (60, 70ns) | 1990 | 25MHz | 64 bits | 200 MBps | 5v |
| EDO (50, 60, 70ns) | 1994 | 40MHz | 64 bits | 320 MBps | 5v |
| SDRAM (66MHz) | 1996 | 66MHz | 64 bits | 528 MBps | 3.3v |
| SDRAM (100MHz) | 1998 | 100MHz | 64 bits | 800 MBps | 3.3v |
| SDRAM (133MHz) | 1999 | 133MHz | 64 bits | 1.1 GBps | 3.3v |
| RDRAM (Direct Rambus) | 1999 | 400MHz (x2) | 16 bits | 1.6 GBps | 2.5v |
| DDR SDRAM (100Mhz) | 2000 | 100MHz (x2) | 64 bits | 1.6 GBps | 3.3v |
| DDR SDRAM (133Mhz) | 2000 | 133MHz (x2) | 64 bits | 2.1 GBps | 3.3v |

**\*\*Memory channel width (64 bits started with 75MHz Pentium).**
The specifications in the top half of this chart were obtained from Kingston Technology Company, Fountain Valley, CA (www.kingston.com).

**dynamic range**    A range of signals from the weakest to the strongest.

**dynamic routing**    The ability for a router to forward data via a different route based on the current conditions of the communications circuits. For example, it can adjust for overloaded traffic or failing lines and is much more flexible than static routing, which uses a fixed forwarding path.

**dynamic SQL**    See *embedded SQL*.

**DYNASTY**    An application development system for enterprise client/server environments from Dynasty Technologies, Inc., Lisle, IL (www.dynasty.com). Introduced in 1993, it is a repository-driven system that supports Windows; Mac and Motif clients; and NT, OS/2 and major UNIX servers and databases. It provides partitioning for creating three-tier applications. DYNASTY generates C and SQL code.

**dyne**    A unit of force in the CGS system. It is the force required to accelerate one gram by one centimeter per second squared.

**dynlink**    See *dynamic link*.

**E** See *exponent* and *e-*.

**e-** (Electronic-) The "e" prefix, with or without the dash, may be attached to anything that has moved from the physical world to its electronic alternative, such as e-mail, e-commerce, e-cash, e-cards, etc. "E" words have become synonymous with the Internet.

Although many prefer to write the terms without the dash, the dash is used in this publication wherever possible, because the dash makes it easier to identify the word; for example, e-mail rather than email and e-commerce instead of ecommerce.

**E & M** (Ear & Mouth) Also known as "rEceive & transMit" and "earth & magneto," it is an early telephony term for signaling. For example, PBX operators would signal the long distance operator using E & M. A voltage would be applied to the "mouth" lead of the circuit, which signals the "ear" lead at the other end. There are a variety of two-wire and four-wire E & M signaling methods used between PBXs and PBX to network connections throughout the world.

**E1** The European counterpart to T1, which transmits at 2.048 Mbits/sec. See *DS* for chart.

**EAI** (Enterprise Application Integration) See *application integration*.

**EAM** (1) (Electronic Accounting Machine) Another name for punched card tabulating equipment. EAM equipment (tabulating machines) was the mainstay of data processing for more than 70 years following the advent of Hollerith's card system for the 1890 census.

(2) (Enterprise Asset Management) The management and control of the information technology assets within the enterprise. The asset management repository includes a description of the asset, as well as contract information pertaining to its acquisition. The purpose of enterprise asset management is to keep track of and lower the cost of ownership of technology resources.

**The EAM Room**
This was a typical EAM room in a medium-sized business. Huge rooms full of tabulating machines were common in large companies. *(Image courtesy of International Business Machines Corporation. Unauthorized use not permitted.)*

**EAP** (Extensible Authentication Protocol) A programming interface in Windows 2000 that allows third-party security protocols to be installed and used. It is an extension to the PPP protocol used for dial-up access, and it natively supports the TLS and MD5 protocols. See *TLS*, *MD5*, *PPP* and *RAS*.

**ear & mouth** See *E & M*.

**early binding**    In programming, the assignment of types to variables and expressions at compilation time. Also called "static binding" and "static typing." Contrast with *dynamic binding*. See *binding time*.

**EAROM**    (Electrically Alterable ROM) Same as *EEPROM*.

**Earth station**    A transmitting/receiving station for satellite communications. It uses a dish-shaped antenna for microwave transmission. An earth station is generally made up of a multiplexor, modem, up and downconverters, a high power amplifier (HPA) and a low noise amplifier (LNA).

For digital data transmission to a satellite, data streams are combined in a multiplexing device, whose output goes to a modem for modulation onto a carrier frequency in the 50–180MHz range. An upconverter bumps the carrier up into the gigaHertz range, and the output goes to the HPA and dish.

For receiving, the LNA boost the signals to the downconverter, which lowers the frequency and sends it to the modem. The modem demodulates the carrier, and the digital output goes to the demultiplexing device and then to its destinations. See *base station*.

**Earth Station**
The earth station is no longer only the domain of commercial enterprises, now that millions of homes use small dishes to receive TV signals.

**Easel**    (Easel Corporation) A Burlington, Massachusetts software tools company founded in 1981. It was acquired by VMARK Software in 1995. Easel developed client/server tools based on its ESL technology and its Smalltalk-based ObjectStudio. See *VMARK* and *Ardent*.

**Easel Workbench**    See *ESL Workbench*.

**Easter Egg**    An undocumented function hidden in a program that may or may not be sanctioned by management. Easter Eggs are secret "goodies" found by word of mouth or accident. For example, in Windows applications, pressing some key combination when the About box is open (Help/About) often displays the names of the developers who worked on the software. See *trapdoor* and *Cuckoo's egg*.

**EasyCAD**    Full-featured CAD programs for DOS and Windows from Evolution Computing, Tempe, AZ, (www.fastcad.com), that are noted for their ease of use. EasyCAD users can migrate to FastCAD, which is almost identical on screen, but provides multiple windows and is designed for high-speed operations.

**easy drive**    See *EZFlyer disk*.

**Easy PC**    A simplified PC architecture from Microsoft and Intel introduced in early 1999. It was a design statement for future PCs that no longer contained legacy elements such as DOS, the ISA bus, PS/2 ports, etc..

**easy to learn and use**    Easy to learn refers to software that is well designed and capable of being used right away. If you make the program work with little problem, it's easy to learn.

Easy to learn implies easy to use right away, but it does not imply easy to use after you're familiar with it. The menus that coddled you in the beginning can become tiresome when used constantly. Advanced programs have a macro recorder that lets you store a series of menu selections and execute them automatically.

**Easytrieve**    See *CA-Easytrieve*.

**eBay**    (eBay, Inc., San Jose, CA, www.ebay.com) An auction service on the Web. eBay popularized the concept of buying and selling online, and both individuals and commercial enterprises list items for sale. There is no charge to browse the site or make bids and purchases, but there is a fee to list items. If an item is purchased, the seller pays eBay an additional fee. See *online auction*.

**EBCDIC**     (Extended **B**inary **C**oded **D**ecimal **I**nterchange **C**ode) Pronounced "eb-suh-dick." The binary code for text, as well as communications and printer control from IBM. This data code originated with the System/360 and is still used in IBM mainframes and most IBM midrange computers. It is an 8-bit code (256 combinations) that stores one alphanumeric character or two decimal digits in a byte.

EBCDIC and ASCII are the two codes most widely used to represent data. See *EBCDIC chart*.

**e-beam**     See *electron beam*.

**EBI**     See *electron beam imaging*.

**e-billing**     (Electronic-billing) Paying bills by mail. See *EBPP*.

**EBL**     (Extended **B**atch **L**anguage) A shareware programming language by Frank Canova that allows for more complex programming in DOS batch files.

**e-book**     (Electronic-**BOOK**) A handheld device that is specialized for displaying electronic versions of books. Like its printed counterpart, an e-book lets you set bookmarks and annotate in the margins.

**EBPP**     (Electronic **B**ill **P**resentment and **P**ayment) Sending invoices to customers over the Internet. When payment is due, an e-mail is sent with a link to a Web page that contains the billing information and the payment services that are supported. Customers can "click here" to pay bills via the Web payment service they are enrolled with. The Web page can also provide links to more support and information than would normally be included in a paper bill, as well as offerings for new services. For information and demos from edocs, a major supplier of EBPP software, visit www.edocs.com.

**e-business**     (Electronic-**BUSINESS**) Doing business online. The term is often used synonymously with e-commerce, but e-business is more of an umbrella term for having a presence on the Web. An e-business site may be very comprehensive and offer more than just selling its products and services. For example, it may feature a general search facility or the ability to track shipments or have threaded discussions. In such cases, e-commerce is only the order processing component of the site. See *e-commerce*.

**ebXML**     (Electronic Business XML) An XML-based set of definitions for electronic transactions and business collaboration. Based on work done by the United Nations Centre for Trade Facilitation and Electronic Business (UN/CEFACT), ebXML provides descriptors for modeling business processes that includes the definition of software components. For more information, visit www.ebxml.org. See *XML*.

**EC**     See *e-commerce*.

**e-card**     (Electronic-**CARD**) A digital greeting card or postcard created on the Web and sent to someone via the Web. Most e-card sites are paid for by banner ads which you see while you design your card, while others employ this as a way to attract traffic to the site to sell other products or services. In addition to your own text, e-cards allow different backgrounds, images and music to be used. The cards are sent to you via e-mail with a link to a Web page containing your custom e-card for some period of time. There are numerous sites. Just use your favorite search engine and search on "ecard," "e-card," "digital postcard," "digital greeting card" or "virtual card." The most notable e-card site is Blue Mountain Arts (www.bluemountain.com). See *Flooz*.

**e-cash**     (Electronic-**CASH**) See *Web payment service*, *smart card* and *digital money*.

**eCash**     A Web payment service from eCash Technologies, Inc., Bothell, WA, (www.ecash.com), that requires an active account from an eCash member bank. Digital coins are stored in the eCash Purse digital wallet on the customer's computer, and coins can be deducted from the wallet when purchasing at eCash-compliant sites. Coins can also be transferred directly between eCash users. The system is regulated by adding a serial number to each coin. When the merchant receives the coins from the customer, the coins are sent to the customer's bank for verification. If a coin matches the serial number of a coin that has already been spent, fraudulent activity is detected.

eCash uses a blind signature encryption method that was developed by Amsterdam-based DigiCash, Inc. and acquired by eCash in 1999. This allows the bank to validate the coins without being able to trace them to a particular account. See *Web payment service*.

**ECC** (1) (Error-Correcting Code) A type of memory that corrects errors on the fly. See *ECC memory*.

(2) (Elliptic Curve Cryptography) A public key cryptography method that provides fast decryption and digital signature processing. ECC uses points on an elliptic curve to derive a 163-bit public key that is equivalent in strength to a 1024-bit RSA key. The public key is created by agreeing on a standard generator point in an elliptic curve group (elliptic curve mathematics is a branch of number theory) and multiplying that point by a random number (the private key). Although the starting point and public key are known, it is extremely difficult to backtrack and derive the private key.

Once the public key is computed by ECC, it can be used in various ways to encrypt and decrypt. One way is to encrypt with the public key and decrypt with the private one. Another is to use the Diffie-Hellman method which uses a key exchange to create a shared secret key by both parties. Finally, ECC allows a digital signature to be signed with a private key and verified with the public key. For an in-depth look at elliptic curve cryptography, visit Certicom's Web site at www.certicom.com. There are live examples that show the math and methods. See *Diffie-Hellman*.

**ECC DIMM RAM** ECC memory that is housed in DIMM modules. See *DIMM*.

**ECC memory** (Error-Correcting Code memory) A memory system that tests for and corrects errors on the fly. It uses circuitry that generates checksums, which typically adds seven bits to each 32-bit word. Thus, seven bits of correcting code are computed for every 32 bits of data placed in memory. When data is retrieved from memory, the checksum is recomputed to determine if any of the data bits have been corrupted. Such systems can detect and automatically correct errors of one bit per word and can detect, but not correct, errors greater than one bit. See *checksum*.

**ECCO** A Windows PIM from NetManage, Inc., Bellevue, WA, (www.netmanage.com). ECCO provides a phone book, calendar, to-do list, outlining and notetaking. It is noted for its tightly integrated and sophisticated functions.

**ECC RAM** See *ECC memory*.

**e-centives** (Electronic-in**CENTIVES**) An online service that sends you discount coupons and special offers from the brands of merchandise you are interested in. E-centives (www.e-centives.com) was the first organization to provide this type of e-commerce service.

**ECF** (Enhanced Connectivity Facilities) IBM software that allows DOS PCs to query and download data from mainframes and issue mainframe commands. It also allows printer output to be directed from the PC to the mainframe. It uses the SRPI interface and resides in the PC (client) and mainframe (server). Applications issue SRPI commands to request services.

**eCharge** A Web payment service from eCharge Corporation, Seattle, WA, (www.echarge.com). Initially specializing in digital content and monthly ISP charges, eCharge bills customers via a 900 number on their telephone bills. It later added a revolving line of credit just like a credit card and a prepaid account to support micropayments. Funds can be transferred from the customer's bank via the Automated Clearing House (ACH) system. eCharge uses digital certificates on the user's PC, at the merchant site and at eCharge, and all three are verified before a transaction is completed. See *Web payment service*.

**echo** (1) A repetition of a signal in a communications line. The difference in electrical characteristics at opposite ends can cause the echo.

(2) In communications, to transmit received data back to the sending station allowing the user to inspect visually what was received. A local echo displays what you type on your screen.

(3) A DOS and OS/2 screen command that displays messages and turns off/on screen responses. See *DOS batch file*.

**echo cancellation** The elimination of an echo in a two-way transmission. Echo is created in the telephone company's central office switch when two-wire lines from the customer are converted to four-wire lines for backbone trunks. The echo is exacerbated over longer distances and by certain kinds of network equipment. A delay of 30ms or more is generally noticeable, and 50ms is annoying. To eliminate it, the carriers put echo cancellers on their switch ports and in their long-distance trunks every 500 miles apart.

Echo cancellation is built into high-speed modems. Since telephone system echo cancellation is optimized for voice, the modem emits a 2,100Hz signal to cancel it, allowing the modem's own cancellers to be used, which are more effective.

Echo cancellation is built into a speakerphone to cancel the echo caused by the microphone picking up sound from the speaker. Since echo cancellation is not built into sound cards, making a PC-to-PC voice call using regular speakers and a microphone causes echo. Headsets help eliminate this problem.

Echo cancellation uses extremely sophisticated DSP circuits that are able to isolate the echo and transmit a reverse frequency to cancel it.

**echo check**   In communications, an error checking method that retransmits the data back to the sending device for comparison with the original.

**echo suppressor**   A device that turns off reverse transmission in a telephone line, thus effectively making the circuit one way. It was used to eliminate echo in long-distance circuits before more sophisticated echo cancellation techniques were economical enough to be deployed. See *echo cancellation*.

**e-cinema**   (Electronic-CINEMA) Refers to the digital post production of movies. Movies are shot on film, converted into digital format for editing and then converted back into film for distribution. Also synonymous with "d-cinema" or "digital cinema." See *digital cinema*.

**ECL**   (Emitter-Coupled Logic) A variety of bipolar transistor that is noted for its extremely fast switching speeds.

**ECLIPSE**   A series of 32-bit minicomputers from Data General. The development of the initial 32-bit ECLIPSE MV/8000 was the subject of Tracy Kidders' best-selling book, "Soul of a New Machine" published in 1981 by Little, Brown and Company.

**ECM**   (Error Correcting Mode) A Group 3 fax capability that can test for errors within a row of pixels and request retransmission. It is defined in the T.30 standard.

**ECMA**   (European Computer Manufacturers Association, Geneva, Switzerland, www.ecma.ch) An international association founded in 1961 that is dedicated to establishing standards in the information and communications fields. ECMA is a liaison organization to ISO and is involved in JTC1 activities.

**ECMAScript**   A scripting language that combines Netscape's JavaScript and Microsoft's Jscript with server-side extensions from Borland. See *Dynamic HTML*.

**ECML**   (1) (Electronic Commerce Modeling Language) A common set of field names for online order forms. Supported by the major Web payment services, ECML is designed to provide a standard way of transferring shipping, billing and payment information from digital wallets to merchant sites. See *digital wallet* and *Web payment service*.

(2) (European Conference on Machine Learning) An annual conference devoted to algorithms used in self-learning systems. ECML is held annually unless the International Conference on Machine Learning (ICML) is held in Europe that year. See *ICML*.

**ECN**   (Electronic Communications Network) A computerized, private financial trading system. Terra Nova Trading (www.terranovatrading.com), Island (www.island.com) and Instinet (www.instinet.com) are examples.

**ECNE**   See *NetWare certification*.

**e-commerce**   (Electronic-COMMERCE) Doing business online, typically via the Web. It is also called "e-business," "e-tailing" and "I-commerce." Although in most cases e-commerce and e-business are synonymous, e-commerce implies that goods and services can be purchased online, whereas e-business might be used as more of an umbrella term for a total presence on the Web, which would naturally include the e-commerce (shopping) component.

E-commerce may also refer to electronic data interchange (EDI), in which one company's computer queries and transmits purchase orders to another company's computer. See *m-commerce*, *microcommerce* and *clicks and mortar*.

**The First E-Commerce?** In 1886, a telegraph operator was able to obtain a shipment of watches that was refused by the local jeweler. Using the telegraph, he sold all the watches to fellow operators and railroad employees. Within a few months, he made enough money to quit his job and start his own store. The young man's name was Richard Sears, and his company later became Sears Roebuck.

**e-commerce engineer** A person responsible for developing and maintaining e-commerce applications for a company's public Web site. Experience in database and Web server components (servlets, CORBA, EJB, etc.) is often required. See *Internet engineer*.

**e-commerce service provider** An organization that provides any combination of consulting, software and computer systems for e-commerce Web sites.

**e-content** (Electronic-**CONTENT**) Digital content that can be transmitted over a computer network such as the Internet. See *premium content*.

**ECP** (Enhanced Capabilities Port) See *IEEE 1284*.

**eCRM** (Electronic **CRM**) CRM over the Internet. Most CRM systems have one or more Web-based applications for selling to or supporting the customer, so the terms eCRM and CRM are used interchangeably. See *CRM*.

**ed** (1) (**ED**itor) An early UNIX line editor (text editor) that contained functionality later incorporated into vi. The sed editor (Stream EDitor) supersedes ed and, using ed commands, processes the entire text file instead of one line at a time. See *sed*.

(2) (ED) (Extra high Density) Refers to earlier 2.88MB floppy disks from IBM. The Extra High Density format was never universally adopted, because it did not give enough storage boost to make it worthwhile.

**EDA** (1) (Electronic Design Automation) Using the computer to design and simulate the performance of electronic circuits on a chip. See *ATE*.

(2) (Enterprise Data Access) Popular middleware software from Information Builders that runs on more than 35 platforms and provides a common interface between client requests (typically a SQL query or from FOCUS) to more than 80 different database and file types, as well as to CICS. It allows queries on different types of databases at the same time. Introduced in 1991, EDA was previously known as EDA/SQL. COM, CORBA and EJB capability is also available. See *WebFOCUS*.

(3) (Enterprise Data Access) Providing a uniform way to access data throughout the enterprise. It implies the ability to treat multiple, distributed databases as a single logical entity. See EDA definition (2) above and *DQbroker*.

**EDA/SQL** See *EDA*.

**EDFA** (Erbium-Doped Fiber Amplifier) A device that boosts the signal in an optical fiber. Introduced in the late 1980s, the EDFA was the first successful optical amplifier. It was a major factor in the rapid development of fiber-optic networks in the 1990s, because it extended the distance between costly regenerators. In addition, an EDFA amplifies all the channels in a WDM signal simultaneously, whereas regenerators require optical to electrical conversion for each channel.

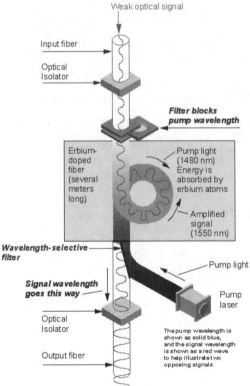

**Erbium-Doped Fiber Amplifier**
EDFAs boost the input regardless of the number of wavelengths. In several meters of doped fiber, the pump laser excites the doped atoms to higher orbits, and the input signal stimulates them to release excess energy as photons in phase and at the same wavelength.
*(Illustration courtesy of Jeff Hecht.)*

Functioning like a laser without mirrors, the EDFA uses a semiconductor pump laser to introduce a powerful beam at a shorter wavelength into a section of erbium-doped fiber several meters long. The pump light excites the erbium atoms to higher orbits, and the input signal stimulates them to release excess energy as photons in phase and at the same wavelength. EDFAs boost wavelengths in the 1550 nm range, and the pump light is typically 1480 nm or 980 nm. See *WDM*, ***Raman amplifier*** and *optical amplifier*.

**EDGAR**     (Electronic Data Gathering, Analysis and Retrieval) A reporting system that public companies must use to send financial data to the Securities and Exchange Commission (SEC). In the latter part of the 1990s, EDGAR was revamped to accept HTML and PDF files. For more information, visit www.edgar-online.com.

**EDGE**     (Enhanced Data rates for Global Evolution) An enhancement to the GSM and TDMA wireless communications systems that increases data throughput to 384 Kbps. See *UWC-136*, *GSM* and *TDMA*.

**edge concentrator**     A device that connects a LAN to a high-speed backbone or switch such as an ATM switch. See *edge device*.

**edge connector**     The protruding part of an expansion board that is inserted into an expansion slot. It contains a series of printed lines that go to and come from the circuits on the board. The number of lines (pins) and the width and depth of the lines are different on the various interfaces (ISA, EISA, PCI, MicroChannel, etc.).

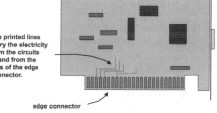

The printed lines carry the electricity from the circuits to and from the pins of the edge connector.

edge connector

**Edge Connector**
Edge connectors are very popular because they are "printed" onto the outer layers of the board in the same process that creates the circuit lines.

**edge device**     **(1)** Any server or other networking device that is located closer to the client machines rather than be in the backbone of the network. For example a cache server is an edge device that sits inside the firewall and holds frequently requested pages. See *cache server* and *edge router*.

**(2)** A network device used to convert LAN frames (Ethernet, etc.) to ATM cells and vice versa. It is typically a switching device with one ATM port and multiple LAN ports. To legacy stations, ports on an edge device look like a router port.

Under MPOA (Multiprotocol Over ATM), the edge device queries a route server for address resolution when the destination station is outside of its attached LANs. It sets up a switched virtual circuit (SVC) in the ATM network, maps LAN frames into ATM frames and forwards the traffic to the ATM backbone. Thus, the edge device performs functions usually associated with a router and becomes a major component in a LAN environment with an ATM backbone.

**edge network**     **(1)** A network located on the periphery of a centralized network. The edge network feeds the central, or core, network.

**(2)** The network provided by a content delivery service provider that duplicates Internet content on many servers around the world. See *CDSP*.

**edge path adapter**     Same as *edge device*.

**edge router**     Also called an "access router," it is a router that sits at the periphery (edge) of a network, in contrast with a core router that is in the middle of a network. Edge routers and core routers are relative terms. They are all just routers, but of different size and capacity. One tier's core router is another tier's edge router.

The ratio of edge routers to core routers is a scalability issue and network design consideration (how much does a service provider want to overbook/oversubscribe the edge to the core). See *router*. See also *edge device*.

**edge switch**     See *edge device*.

**EDI**     (Electronic Data Interchange) The electronic communication of business transactions, such as orders, confirmations and invoices, between organizations. Third parties provide EDI services that enable organizations with different equipment to connect. Although interactive access may be a part of it, EDI implies direct computer to computer transactions into vendors' databases and ordering systems.

The Internet is expected to give EDI quite a boost, but not by using private networks and the traditional EDI data formats (X12, EDIFACT and TRADACOMS). Rather, XML is expected to be the glue that connects businesses together using the Web as the communications vehicle. See *X12*, *EDIFACT*, *TRADACOMS*, *extranet* and *XML*.

**EDI analyst**    A person responsible for the implementation of electronic data interchange systems between companies. The EDI analyst is technical consultant for the trading partners and is involved with deploying systems using the traditional EDI standards and XML-based Web implementations. See *EDI* and *XML*.

**EDID**    See *VESA DDC*.

**EDIFACT**    (**E**lectronic **D**ata **I**nterchange **F**or **A**dministration **C**ommerce and **T**ransport)  An ISO standard for electronic data interchange (EDI) that was proposed to supersede both X12 and TRADACOMS as the worldwide standard. See *EDI*.

**e-disk**    (**E**mulated-**DISK**)  Same as *RAM disk*.

**edit**    To make a change to existing data. See *update*.

**editable PostScript**    A file of PostScript commands that can be edited by a word processor or other program. This allows PostScript documents to be changed without requiring the use of the application that originally created it.

**edit checking**    Same as *validity checking*.

**edit instruction**    A computer instruction that formats a field for display or printing. Using an edit mask, it inserts decimal points, commas and dollar signs into the data.

**edit key**    A key combination or function key that changes the program into edit mode when pressed.

**edit mask**    A pattern of characters that represent formatting codes through which data is filtered for display or printing. See *picture*.

**edit mode**    An operational state in a program that allows existing data to be changed.

**editor**    See *text editor* and *link editor*.

**edit program**    (1) A data entry program that validates user input and stores the newly created records in the file. (2) A program that allows users to change data that already exists in a file. See *update*.

**edit routine**    A routine in a program that tests for valid data. See *validity checking*.

**EDL**    See *nonlinear video editing*.

**EDMS**    (**E**lectronic **D**ocument **M**anagement **S**ystem or **E**nterprise **D**ocument **M**anagement **S**ystem )  See *document management*.

**EDO RAM**    (**E**xtended **D**ata **O**ut **RAM**)  A type of dynamic RAM chip that improved the performance of fast page mode (FPM) memory. As a subset of fast page mode, it can be substituted for page mode chips. However, if the memory controller is not designed for the faster EDO chips, the performance will remain the same as fast page mode.

EDO eliminates wait states by keeping the output buffer active until the next cycle begins. BEDO (Burst EDO) is a faster type of EDO that gains speed by using an address counter for next addresses and a pipeline stage that overlaps operations.

**EDP**    (**E**lectronic **D**ata **P**rocessing)  The first name used for the computer field.

**EDP audit**    An analysis of an organization's computer and information systems in order to evaluate the integrity of its production systems and potential security cracks. See *EDP auditor*.

**EDP auditor**    A person that performs an EDP audit within an organization. Such individuals analyze the existing systems and procedures using audit software that samples databases and generates confirmation letters. See *EDP audit* and *audit software*.

**EDRAM**    (1) (Enhanced **DRAM**) A high-speed DRAM chip developed by Ramtron International Corporation, Colorado Springs, CO. It allows overlap of a read at the trailing end of a write operation to obtain its speed.

(2) (Enhanced **DRAM**) A dynamic RAM memory that contains a small amount of static RAM. Same as *CDRAM*.

**EDS**    (Electronic Data Systems, Plano, TX, www.eds.com) Founded in 1962 by H. Ross Perot (independent challenger for the President of the U.S. in 1992), EDS is the largest outsourcing and data processing services organization in the country. It is the leading services provider to the health care, insurance and banking industries. In 1984, EDS was acquired by General Motors. Within a couple of years, Perot left EDS and later formed Perot Systems Corporation. In 1996, GM spun off EDS as an independent company.

EDS is known for huge contracts. For example, in 1994, Xerox contracted with it for 10 years worth of outsourcing valued at more than $3 billion.

**EDSAC**    (Electronic Delay Storage Automatic Calculator) Developed by Maurice Wilkes at Cambridge University in England and completed in 1949, it was one of the first stored program computers and one of the first to use binary digits. Its memory was 512 36-bit words of liquid mercury delay lines, and its input and output were provided by paper tape. The EDSAC could do about 700 additions per second and 200 multiplications per second. It was in routine use at the university until 1958.

**edu**    See *.edu*.

**education**    Teaching concepts and perspectives. Computer education includes computer systems and information systems. Contrast with *training*.

**education and training**    See *CBT*, *aptitude tests*, *certification*, *distance learning* and *tutorial*.

**edutainment**    Educational material that is also entertaining.

**EE**    See *Extended Edition*.

**The EDSAC**
Using liquid mercury memory, the EDSAC could perform a mind-boggling 700 additions per second. It was one of the first computers to perform calculations in binary. *(Image courtesy of The Computer Museum History Center, www.computerhistory.org)*

**EECMOS**    (Electrically-Erasable Complementary Metal Oxide Semiconductor) A type of semiconductor device used in reprogrammable memory chips such as FPGAs, PALs and GALs. Non-EECMOS devices cannot be changed and must be replaced to incorporate enhancements, but EECMOS chips can be used in prototyping new systems that are rapidly changing as well as in field-upgradeable applications.

EECMOS devices are reprogrammed by applying an erase voltage to specific pins on the chip. The erase voltage clears the existing logic configuration and allows the device to be reprogrammed. See *FPGA*, *PAL* and *GAL*.

**EEMS**    See *EMS*.

**EEPROM**    (Electrically Erasable Programmable Read-Only Memory) A memory chip that holds its content without power. It can be erased, either within the computer or externally and usually requires more voltage for erasure than the common +5 volts used in logic circuits. It functions like non-volatile RAM, but writing to EEPROM is slower than writing to RAM.

EEPROMs are used in devices that must keep data up-to-date without power. For example, a price list could be maintained in EEPROM chips in a point of sale terminal that is turned off at night. When prices change, the EEPROMs can be updated from a central computer during the day. EEPROMs have a lifespan of between 10K and 100K write cycles. See *flash memory*.

**eesa**    See *EISA* and *ESA/370*.

**EFF**    (Electronic Frontier Foundation, San Francisco, CA, www.eff.org)  A non-profit civil liberties organization founded in 1990 by Mitchell Kapor and John Perry Barlow. It works in the public interest to protect privacy and freedom of expression in the arenas of computers and the Internet. The EFF's mission statement is "to help civilize the electronic frontier; to make it truly useful and benefical not just to a technical elite, but to everyone; and to do this in a way which is in keeping with our society's highest traditions of the free and open flow of information and communication." First located in Cambridge, MA, the EFF continually monitors the online community for legal actions that may require its support.

**e-filing**    Filing income tax and other governmental forms online.

**EFNet**    The oldest and largest Internet Relay Chat network. EFNet handles more than 40,000 simultaneous connections daily. For information, visit www.efnet.org. See *Undernet* and *Internet Relay Chat*.

**e-forms**    (Electronic-**FORMS**) See *forms software*.

**EFT**    (Electronic Funds Transfer)  The transfer of money from one account to another by computer. See *ACH*.

**EGA**    (Enhanced Graphics Adapter)  An early IBM video display standard that provided medium-resolution text and graphics. It required a digital RGB Enhanced Color Display or equivalent monitor and was superseded by VGA.

**e-games**    (Electronic-**GAMES**)  A generic term for any amusement or recreation using a stand-alone video game, desktop computer or the Internet with one or more players.

**egosurfing**    Using a search engine such as AltaVista or Yahoo! to see how many times your own name is cited. This is a popular, quasi-competitive sport at Silicon Valley parties and at gatherings of writers, artists, musicians and others who have some expectation of being referred to on the Web or in a newsgroup.

**EGP**    (1) (Exterior Gateway Protocol)  A broad category of routing protocols that are designed to span different autonomous systems. Contrast with *IGP*.

(2) (Exterior Gateway Protocol)  The original exterior gateway routing protocol (see above), which has been widely used in the U.S. Data Defense Network (DDN) and National Science Foundation Network (NSFNet). EGP is a distance vector protocol that uses polling to retrieve routing information. EGP has been superseded by BGP. See *BGP* and *routing protocol*.

**EHLLAPI**    See *HLLAPI*.

**e-hub**    See *Web hub*.

**EIA**    (Electronic Industries Association, Washington, DC, www.eia.org)  A membership organization founded in 1924 as the Radio Manufacturing Association. It sets standards for consumer products and electronic components. In 1988, it spun off its Information & Telecommunications Technology Group into a separate organization known as the TIA.

**EIA-232**    See *RS-232*.

**EIA-422**    See *RS-422*.

**EIA-423**    See *RS-422*.

**EIA-449**    See *RS-449*.

**EIA-485**    See *RS-485*.

**E**

**EIA-568**    An EIA standard for telecommunications wiring in a commercial building. See *cable categories*.

**EIDE**    (Enhanced **IDE**) An extension to the IDE interface that supports the ATA-2 and ATAPI standards. ATA-2 (Fast ATA) provides faster transfer rates (see *IDE* for details) and allows for multiple channels, each connecting two devices. ATAPI supports non-hard disk devices such as CD-ROMs and tape drives. It also specifies a new BIOS for supporting hard disks greater than 504MB. Since mid-1994, PCs have shipped with EIDE interfaces, and most motherboards provide a primary and secondary channel for a total of four devices. In practice, the terms EIDE and IDE are synonymous. See *IDE* and *LBA*.

**Eiffel**    An object-oriented programming language developed by Bertrand Meyer, Interactive Software Engineering Inc., Goleta, CA (www.eiffel.com). It runs on DOS, OS/2 and most UNIX platforms. The Eiffel compiler generates C code, which can be modified and recompiled with a C compiler.

**eight-way server**    See *8-way*.

**EIGRP**    See *IGRP*.

**EIO**    (Enhanced **I/O**) A hardware interface for HP printers that is used for adding an internal print server and network adapter, a hard disk and other plug-in functionality. EIO cards are smaller than previous MIO cards and more energy efficient. They use the PCI bus. See *MIO*.

**EIP**    **(1)** (Enterprise Information Portal) See *corporate portal*.
   **(2)** (Extended Instruction Pointer) The program counter on x86 CPUs.

**EIS**    **(1)** (Executive Information System) An information system that consolidates and summarizes ongoing transactions within the organization. It provides top management with all the information it requires at all times from internal and external sources. If the EIS provides "what if?" manipulation capabilities like that of a DSS (decision support system), they are one in the same. See *DSS*.
   **(2)** (Enterprise Information Services) The back-end layer where the traditional data processing occurs in an organization, which includes the databases, mainframe and ERP applications.
   **(3)** (EIS International, Inc., Herndon, VA, www.eisi.com) Founded in Connecticut in 1980 by Robert Jesurum, EIS is a leading provider of advanced technology solutions for call centers worldwide. The firm's call center workstations are used in a wide variety of industries including finance, telecom and cable, publishing and market research.

**EISA**    (Extended **ISA**) Pronounced "ee-suh." A PC bus standard that extends the 16-bit ISA bus (AT bus) to 32 bits and provides bus mastering. ISA cards can plug into an EISA slot. It was announced in 1988 as a 32-bit alternative to the MicroChannel that would preserve investment in existing boards. However, EISA runs at the slow 8MHz speed of the ISA bus in order to accommodate any ISA cards that may be plugged into it. EISA has been superseded by PCI. See *PC data buses*.

**EJava**    See *PersonalJava* and *Jeliot*.

**EJB**    (Enterprise JavaBeans) A component software architecture from Sun that is used to build Java applications that run in the server. It uses a "container" layer that provides common functions such as security and transaction support and delivers a consistent interface to the applications regardless of the type of server. CORBA is the infrastructure for EJBs, and at the wire level, EJBs look like CORBA components. EJBs are the backbone of Sun's J2EE platform, which provides a pure Java environment for developing and running Web-based applications. See *J2EE*, *JavaBeans*, *distributed objects* and *component software*.

**ELAN**    (Emulated **LAN**) A virtual LAN in the ATM world. See *LANE* and *virtual LAN*.

**elastic body transformation**    A least-squares computer software program run against a raw digitized data source map to produce a geographically true "X" and "Y" coordinate database referenced to any standard map system. Based on the locations of control monuments, a "best fit" is made to the source map's origin, rotation, scale, skew, and stretch. If the source map's systematic errors were small, an accurate "fit" will be made resulting in small residual errors. Also called rubber sheeting and coordinate rotation/translation. (Data West Research Agency definition: See *GIS glossary*.)

**elastomer** (**ELAST**ic p**OlyMER**) A soft, compliant, rubber-like material.

**eldap** See *LDAP*.

**EL display** (ElectroLuminescent **DISPLAY**) A flat panel display technology that provides a sharp, clear image and wide viewing angle. It contains a powdered or thin film phosphor layer sandwiched between an x-axis and a y-axis panel. When an x-y coordinate is charged, the phosphor in that vicinity emits visible light. The phosphors are more like semiconductor materials than those used in a CRT. Most EL displays are monochrome, typically yellow orange.

Although some of the first portable computers used EL displays, they are mostly used today on instrumentation in demanding industrial and medical applications that require long life and crisp images. EL screens range from 3/4" to 10" and larger, but are more cost effective in the smaller sizes. Planar Systems is the leader in this field.

Active matrix EL is an advanced EL technology that uses a transistor at each pixel. It is used to make small head mounted displays (HMDs) that require very sharp images.

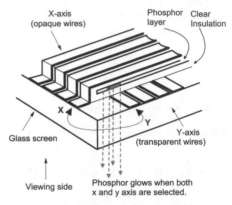

**Electroluminescent Technology**
EL displays contain a powdered or thin film phosphor layer sandwiched between x and y axis panels. When an x-y coordinate is charged, the phosphor in that vicinity emits visible light. *(Redrawn from diagram courtesy of Planar Systems, Inc.)*

**ELEC** (Enterprise **LEC**) An organization that is large enough (about 2,500 or more employees) to file for CLEC status and become its own customer. As a CLEC, it can purchase telephone service at wholesale rates that it can sell to itself and to others to further reduce costs. The Yankee Group coined the term. See *LEC, CLEC* and *ILEC*.

**electricity** The flow of electrons in a circuit. The speed of electricity is the speed of light (approximately 186,000 miles per second). In a wire, it is slowed due to the resistance in the material. Its pressure, or force, is measured in "volts," and its flow, or current, is measured in "amperes" or simply "amps." The amount of work it produces is measured in "watts" (amps X volts).

**electrode** A device that emits or controls the flow of electricity.

**electroluminescence** The generation of light by applying electricity to a material such as a semiconductor or phosphor. LEDs, laser diodes and electroluminescent displays are examples. See *LED, laser diode* and *EL display*.

**electroluminescent** See *electroluminescence* and *EL display*.

**electrolyte** In a battery, the material that allows electricity to flow from one plate to another (between positive and negative electrodes) by conducting ions. Electrolytes are typically liquid, but gelatinous and solid materials are also used. See *lithium polymer*.

**electromagnet** A magnet that is energized by electricity. A coil of wire is wrapped around an iron core. When current flows in the wire, the core generates an energy called "magnetic flux."

**electromagnetic energy** See *electromagnetic radiation*.

**electromagnetic interference** See *EMI*.

**electromagnetic radiation** The energy that radiates from all things in nature and from man-made electronic systems. It includes cosmic rays, gamma rays, x-rays, ultraviolet light, visible light, infrared light, radar, microwaves, TV, radio, cellphones and all electronic transmission systems.

Electromagnetic radiation is comprised of electric and magnetic fields that move at right angles to each other at the speed of light. See *electromagnetic spectrum.*

### electromagnetic spectrum

The range of electromagnetic radiation in our known universe, which includes visible light. The radio spectrum, which includes both licensed and unlicensed frequencies from 3 kHz to 300 GHz has been defined worldwide in three regions: Region 1 is Europe and Northern Asia; Region 2 is North and South America, and Region 3 is Southern Asia and Australia. Certain frequency bands are the same in all three regions while others differ.

Frequencies above 40GHz have not been licensed, but are expected to be made available in the future as the technology is developed to to transmit at these lower wavelengths (higher frequencies). The spectrum can be viewed in excruciating detail from the Federal Communications Commission (FCC) and National Telecommunications and Information Agency (NTIA) by visiting www.fcc.gov/oet/spectrum and www.ntia.doc.gov/osmhome/osmhome.html. See *electromagnetic radiation.*

### electromechanical

The use of electricity to run moving parts. Disk drives, printers and motors are examples. Electromechanical systems must be designed for the eventual deterioration of moving parts.

### electromotive force

The pressure in an electric circuit measured in volts.

### electron

An elementary particle that circles the nucleus of an atom. Electrons are considered to be negatively charged.

### electron beam

A stream of electrons, or electricity, that is directed towards a receiving object.

### electron beam imaging

A technology from Delphax Systems used in high-speed digital printing. It is similar to laser and LED printers in that toner is applied to a charged replica of the image to be printed and then the toned image is transferred to paper and fused. However, instead of using light to create the image, it uses electrons.

### electron beam lithography

Using electron beams to create the mask patterns directly on a chip. The wavelength of an electron beam is only a few picometers compared to the 248 to 365 nanometer wavelengths of light used to create the traditional photomasks.

### electron gun

A device that creates a fine beam of electrons focused on a phosphor screen in a CRT.

### electronic

The use of electricity in intelligence-bearing devices, such as radios, TVs, instruments, computers and telecommunications. Electricity used as raw power for heat, light and motors is considered electrical, not electronic.

Although coined earlier, *Electronics* magazine (1930) popularized the term. The magazine subheading read "Electron Tubes - Their Radio, Audio, Visio and Industrial Applications." The term was derived from the electron (vacuum) tube.

### electronic auction

See *online auction.*

**ELECTROMAGNETIC SPECTRUM**

| TYPE | FREQUENCY RANGE (Hz) | WAVELENGTH RANGE (meters) | |
|---|---|---|---|
| Gamma rays | $10^{20}$ - $10^{24}$ | $<10^{-12}$ m | higher frequencies |
| X- rays | $10^{17}$ - $10^{20}$ | 1 nm - 1 pm | smaller wavelengths |
| Ultraviolet | $10^{15}$ - $10^{17}$ | 400 nm - 1 nm | |
| VISIBLE LIGHT | 4 - 7.5 x $10^{14}$ | 750 nm - 400 nm | |
| Near-infrared | 1 x $10^{14}$ - 4 x $10^{14}$ | 2.5 μm - 750 nm | |
| Infrared | $10^{13}$ - $10^{14}$ | 25 μm - 2.5 μm | |
| Radio waves (AM, FM, radar, TV, amateur radio, aeronautical, martime, cellular phone, taxis, etc.) | 3 kHz - 300 GHz | 3 mm - 25 μm | larger wavelengths lower frequencies |
| | | audible range | |
| Very low frequencies | 0 - 3 kHz | 3x$10^7$ m - 3 mm | |

**Electromagnetic Spectrum**
The radio portion of the electromagnetic spectrum that is used for transmission of voice, video and data starts at the top of the audible range and ends just below infrared light.

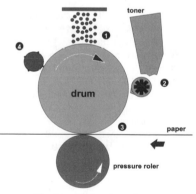

**Electron Beam Imaging**
The image is printed by (1) charging the drum, (2) adhering the toner to the drum, (3) transferring and fusing the toned image to the paper, and (4) cleaning the surface and erasing the residual charge.

**electronic bill presentment and payment**    See *EBPP*.

**electronic book**    See *e-book*.

**electronic cash**    See *e-cash*.

**electronic circuit**    See *circuit* and *digital circuit*.

**electronic commerce**    See *e-commerce*.

**Electronic Computer Glossary**    The predecessor to the disk version of Computer Desktop Encyclopedia. Electronic Computer Glossary was first available for DOS in 1990 and then Windows in 1991. A Macintosh HyperCard stack was also introduced in 1990. All versions were superseded by the Windows-only version of Computer Desktop Encyclopedia in 1996. See *About this product*.

**electronic DMZ**    See *DMZ*.

**electronic forms**    See *forms software*.

**electronic mail**    See *e-mail*.

**electronic messaging**    See *e-mail* and *messaging system*.

**electronic money**    See *e-money*.

**electronic organizer**    See *PDA*.

**Electronic Paper**    A paper-like material, developed by Xerox Palo Alto Research Center (Xerox PARC), Palo Alto, CA (www.parc.xerox.com) which can change its display properties when a voltage is applied. It is made of a thin sheet of gyricon plastic, invented by Xerox, that contains millions of charged beads with black and white hemispheres. When the paper is fed through an "Electronic Paper printer," a voltage pattern is applied, and the beads either show their black or white side. The Electronic Paper can be fed through the printer about a thousand times. See *digital paper*.

**Electronic Paper**
Nick Sheridan, inventor of Electronic Paper, and Fereshteh Lesani show the first roll of paper produced by 3M partners. *(Image courtesy of Xerox PARC.)*

**electronic picture frame**    See *digital picture frame*.

**electronic prepress**    The use of computers to prepare camera-ready materials up to the actual printing stage. It includes drawing, page makeup and typesetting, all performed electronically rather than by drafting or mechanical cut and paste methods.

**electronic printer**    A printer that uses electronics to control the printing mechanism, such as a laser printer and certain line printers.

**electronic publishing**    Providing information in electronic form to internal users or to subscribers via the Internet or an online service. The term also includes the publication of databases on floppy disk and CD-ROM. See *information utility*, *Internet* and **hot topics and trends**.

**electronic signature**    The electronic equivalent of a hand-written signature. There is more to it than just pasting a graphic of your signature into your text document. Electronic signature software binds your signature, or other mark, to a specific document. Just as experts can detect a paper contract that was altered after it was signed, electronic signature software can detect the alteration of an electronically-signed file any time in the future. Montreal-based Silanis Technology (www.silanis.com) is a pioneer of such technology.

An electronic signature is often confused with a digital signature, because it uses digital signature technology for detection alteration. An electronic signature also requires user authentication such as a digital certificate, smart card or biometric method.

In June 2000, the U.S. government passed the E-sign bill, which gives electronic signatures the same legality as hand-written ones. See *digital signature*, *digital certificate* and *biometrics*.

### electronic software licensing   See *ESL*.

### electronic stamp
See *e-stamp*.

### electronic still photography   See *slow scan TV*.

### electronic switch   An on/off switch activated by electrical current.

### electronic typewriter   See *memory typewriter* and *word processing*.

### electronic wallet   See *digital wallet*.

### electron tube   Same as *vacuum tube*.

### electro-optic   Combining electronics and optics. Most photonic systems use electricity as their source. For example, a laser is pulsed with electricity to produce light pulses. See *photonics* and *integrated optics*.

### electrophotographic   The printing technique used in copy machines, laser and LED printers. It uses electrostatic charges, dry ink (toner) and light. A selenium-coated, photoconductive drum is positively charged. Using a laser or LEDs, a negative of the image is beamed onto the drum, cancelling the charge and leaving a positively-charged replica of the original image.

A negatively-charged toner is attracted to the positive image on the drum. The toner is then attracted to the paper, which is also positively charged. The final stage is fusing, which uses heat and pressure, pressure alone or light to cause the toner to permanently adhere to the paper.

Electrophotography was invented by Chester F. Carlson in his Queens, New York laboratory in 1938. His first of 28 patents on the subject was issued in 1940. By 1947, the Haloid Corporation in conjunction with Batelle Development Corporation were working with Carlson on his invention, and xerography was officially announced in 1948.

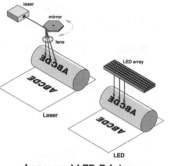

**Laser and LED Printers**
The difference between a laser an LED printer is how the light image is "painted" onto the drum. The laser uses a single light source that is directed by moving mirrors. The LED printer uses an array of hundreds of LEDs that are selectively beamed onto the drum. In a real laser printer, there are many more lenses and parts than in this simple diagram.

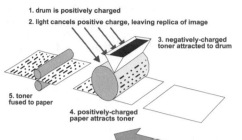

**Electrophotographic Process**
Electrostatic charges are used to create a charged light image on the drum. The toner is attracted to the drum and then to the paper.

**The Model A**
The first electrophotographic copier was sold in 1950. Although manually operated, it provided the experience and revenue to develop automatic xerographic machines. In 1959, Xerox's 914 copier became a huge success. *(Image courtesy of Xerox Corporation.)*

**Chester Carlson**
In this 1965 photo, Carlson enacts his 1938 experiment in which he wrote "10-22-38 ASTORIA" with india ink on a glass slide. The room was darkened and a zinc plate, covered with sulphur, was rubbed vigorously with a handkerchief to apply an electrostatic charge. He put the slide on the plate, exposed it to light for a few seconds, removed the slide, and sprinkled lycopodium powder on the plate. He gently blew off the loose powder and what remained was the first electrophotographic copy. After Xerox became very successful, Carlson was showered with honors and wealth. In 1968, he died of a stroke on a New York street after having left a fortune to charities. *(Image courtesy of Xerox Corporation.)*

Xerography replaced the messy liquid ink of the duplicating machines of the day with a dry, granular ink, which is how the name came about. In Greek, xerography means "dry writing." Xero means "dry," and graphy means "write."

**electrosensitive printer**    A dot-matrix printer that burns away dots on the outer silver coating of a special black paper.

**electrostatic**    Stationary electrical charges in which no current flows. For example, laser printers and copier machines place a positive charge of the image on a drum, and negatively-charged toner is attracted onto the drum. The toner is then transferred to positively-charged paper and fused to the paper by heat.

**electrostatic plotter**    A plotter that uses an electrostatic method of printing. Liquid toner models use a positively-charged toner that is attracted to paper which is negatively charged by passing by a line of electrodes (tiny wires or nibs). Models print in in black and white or color, and some handle paper up to six feet wide. Newer electrostatic plotters are really large-format laser printers and focus light onto a charged drum using lasers or LEDs.

**electrostatic printer**    Same as *electrostatic plotter*.

**elegant program**    A program that is simple in design and uses the least amount of computer resources (memory, disk, etc.).

**elevator**    Also called a "thumb," it is a square box that slides within a scroll bar. The elevator is dragged up and down to position the text or image onscreen.

**elevator seeking**    A disk access technique that processes multiple requests in a priority based upon which ones are closest to the current position of the read/write head.

**ELF**    (Extemely Low Frequency) Electromagnetic radiation in the 30–300 Hz range. Electric power lines and electrical appliances emit radiation in this range. See *low radiation*.

**Eliot**    Software that animates an algorithm written in C. Developed at the University of Helsinki and running under UNIX, a Java version (Jeliot) was later deveoped. See *Jeliot*.

**elipsis**    See *ellipsis*.

**elite**    A typeface that prints 12 cpi.

**ellipsis**    A three-dot symbol used to show an incomplete statement. Ellipses are used in on-screen menus to convey that there is more to come.

**El Torito**    A bootable CD-ROM format developed by Phoenix Technologies and IBM. El Torito is Spanish for "the little bull." See *bootable CD-ROM*.

**em**    In typography, a unit of measure equal to the width of the capital letter M in a particular font.

| |
|---|
| <u>C</u>lear History |
| Clear <u>B</u>ookmarks |
| <u>P</u>icture Paths... |
| <u>W</u>hen a URL is clicked ...   ▶ |
| Display <u>T</u>oolbar |
| <u>Z</u>oom In (Alt-Z, Ctrl-Z) |

**Ellipses Are Used in Menus**
The ellipsis after Picture Paths in this menu indicates that a dialog box will be displayed if selected.

**EMA**    (1) (Enterprise Management Architecture) Digital's stategic plan for integrating network, system and application management. It provides the operating environment for managing a multi-vendor network.

(2) (Electronic Messaging Association, Arlington, VA, www.ema.org) A membership organization founded in 1983 devoted to promoting e-mail, voice mail, fax, EDI and other messaging technologies.

**EMACS**    (Editor MACroS) A text editor developed at MIT by Richard Stallman that is used for writing UNIX programs. It provides a wide variety of editing features including multiple windows. GNU EMACS is maintained by the Free Software Foundation. See *GNU* and *Free Software Foundation*.

**e-mail**    (Electronic-**MAIL**) The transmission of memos and messages over a network. Within an enterprise, users can send mail to a single recipient or broadcast it to multiple users. Mail is sent to a simulated mailbox in the network mail server or host computer until it is interrogated and deleted. You can set up your mail program to query the mail server every so many minutes and alert you if new mail has arrived.

An e-mail system requires a messaging system, which provides the store and forward capability, and a mail program that provides the user interface with send and receive functions. The Web browser can also substitute for the mail program (see *Internet e-mail service*).

The Internet revolutionized e-mail by turning countless incompatible islands into one global system. The Internet initially served its own members, of course, but then began to act as a mail gateway between the major online services. It then became "the" messaging system for the planet. In the U.S., Internet mail is measured in the trillions of messages each year. See *messaging system*, *instant messaging*, *e-mail attachment* and *EDI*.

**E-mail vs. Fax**    Fax documents are scanned images and are thus treated like pictures, even if they contain only text. E-mail messages are raw ASCII text, which can be edited immediately in any mail program, text editor or your favorite word processor.

In order to edit the text in a fax, the images of the characters have to be turned into ASCII text by an OCR (optical character recognition) program, which is error prone. If all you want to do is read a message, either method works well. However, if you are sending text that will be edited and used again, e-mail is the correct choice.

**e-mail address**    See *Internet address*.

**e-mail address search sites**    There are various Web sites that maintain directories of e-mail addresses. Examples of these sites are

```
www.four11.com
www.bigfoot.com
www.whowhere.com
www.infospace.com
```

**e-mail appliance**    A device that is specialized for accessing e-mail. Pocket-sized models are designed for portability, while desktop models are geared for ease of use and eliminate the need to turn a personal computer on and launch an e-mail program just to check mail. Such devices either plug into a standard telephone jack or have a wireless connection to the Internet. See *Internet appliance* and *Internet server appliance*.

**E-Mail Appliance**
The seven-ounce e-Mail Postbox Express fits in your pocket and plugs into a standard telephone jack. *(Image courtesy of Unbound Communications, a VTech company, www.unboundcommunications.com)*

**e-mail attachment**    A file that rides along with an e-mail message. The attached file can be of any type. E-mail programs make it easy to attach a file. For example, in Eudora, all you do is select Attach from the Message menu, browse through the folder hierarchy to find the file you want, and then double-click it. See *how to transfer a file over the Internet*.

**e-mail client**    Same as *mail client*.

**e-mail forwarding**    Sending e-mail to its correct destination. There are Web sites that provide a name service either for a fee or at no cost because they are advertiser supported. These sites let you choose a permanent e-mail address, and all mail sent to that address is forwarded to your currently-active e-mail provider. If you ever change providers, you only have to update your forwarding information at these "name-only" sites. Two such sites are www.four11.com and www.bigfoot.com.

**e-mail header**    The beginning portion of an e-mail message that contains the To, From, Subject, Cc, Bcc and Attached fields. The header uses named fields so that the recipient's address can be quickly extracted by the e-mail system, and the message subject can be easily identified by filters or the user. The rest of the message is unstructured text.

**e-mail program**    Software in the user's computer that can access the mail servers in a local or remote network. Also known as an "e-mail client," "mail client," "mail program," and "mail reader," it provides the ability to send and receive e-mail messages and file attachments. E-mail capability is built into popular Web browsers such as Internet Explorer and Netscape Navigator. Stand-alone programs such as Outlook and Eudora are also popular. See *POP3, IMAP* and *universal client.*

**e-mail reader**    See *e-mail program.*

**e-mail server**    See *mail server.*

**e-mail service**    See *Internet e-mail service.*

**e-mail virus**    A virus that comes within an attached file in an e-mail message. When that file is opened, the virus does its damage. Macro viruses can come in Microsoft Word documents that are sent as e-mail attachments. The macro causes the damage when the document is opened providing macro processing has not been disabled within the Microsoft Word application.

Files with .EXE or .VBS extensions are always suspect, because once the file name is clicked, the program is run, and it can do anything it wants within the computer. SHS files, a somewhat obscure file type, can also contain executable code. Another approach is to attach a Windows link file (.LNK), which is a shortcut, or pointer, to an executable file (.EXE) that is also attached. Since many have been warned not to click an .EXE attachment, the link file is a sneaky way of launching the .EXE file for unaware users. See *virus, Worm.ExploreZip virus, BubbleBoy virus* and *SHS virus.*

**e-market maker**    A developer of a B2B Web site. See *vertical portal.*

**EMBARC**    (EMBARC Communications Service, Boyton Beach, FL, www.espnettogo.com) A Motorola subsidiary that provides wireless broadcasting of mail and news to mobile computers that have a Motorola NewStream, SkyTel SkyStream, PCMCIA NewsCard or similar receiver. EMBARC stands for Electronic Mail Broadcast to a Roaming Computer. It uses a 930–931MHz channel licensed to Motorola and can handle long messages of 30,000 characters and more.

**embedded application**    A program placed into a non-volatile memory such as ROM or flash memory. See *embedded system.*

**embedded command**    (1) A command inserted within text or other codes.

(2) In word processing, a command within the text that directs the printer to change fonts, print underline, boldface, etc. The command is inserted when the user selects a layout change. Commands are often invisible on screen, but can be revealed if required.

**embedded controller**    Controller circuitry built into a device or on the main system board, in contrast with a removable card or module.

**embedded database**    Database software that is used in non-desktop systems such as cellphones, PDAs and other dedicated devices. It may be software built from the ground up for this purpose or a slimmed-down version of a larger, mainstream database management system (DBMS). For example, in 1999, IBM introduced DB2 Everywhere, which is an embedded version of its flagship DBMS.

**EmbeddedJava**    See *PersonalJava.*

**embedded SQL**    SQL statements that are written into a high-level programming language such as C or Pascal. In a preprocessing stage, the SQL code is converted into function calls, which may be optimized to provide the fastest results. If the programmer knows exactly what the query is going to do, and the query does not change, it is called "static SQL." If the query requires user input at runtime, it is called "dynamic SQL." If the client program passes the SQL statements directly to the database server without any intermediate step, it is called "passthrough SQL."

E

## embedded system

A specialized computer used to control devices such as automobiles, home and office appliances, handheld units of all kinds as well as machines as sophisticated as space vehicles. Operating system and application functions are often combined in the same program.

An embedded system implies a fixed set of functions programmed into a non-volatile memory (ROM, flash memory, etc.) in contrast to a general-purpose computing machine. However, sometimes single board computers and rack mounted computers are called "embedded computers" if used to control a single printer, drill press or other such device. See *smart car*.

## embedded Web server

Web server software embedded within a hardware device such as a print server. It is widely used in a myriad of devices, because it allows access to the software via any Web browser, typically for configuring the device or obtaining reports. See *ETI* and *Web server*.

## Embed The Internet

See *ETI*.

| High-Speed Control | Low Speed Control |
|---|---|
| Antilock Braking | Audio |
| Central Electronics | Climate Control |
| Electronic Throttle | Driver's Door |
| Engine Control | Driver Information |
| Steering Wheel | Passenger Door |
| Transmission Control | Phone |
| | Power Seat |
| | Rear Electronics |
| | Sun Roof |
| | Supplemental Restraint System |
| | Upper Electronics |

**Embedded Systems**

In 1968, the Volkswagen 1600 used a microprocessor in its fuel injection system, launching the first embedded system in the automotive industry. Today, more than a dozen systems are monitored and controlled by computers. This list shows the embedded systems in a Volvo S80, which are linked together via two communications networks and controlled by a central module. The car in this picture is not the Volvo S80.

**An Embedded Web Server**

This home page does not come from the Internet, but from the Web server built into i-data's EasyCom print server connected to a printer in the network. Any Web browser can access the EasyCom server via its IP address. *(Screen shot courtesy of i-data International.)*

**EMC** (1) (EMC Corporation, Hopkinton, MA, www.emc.com) The leading supplier of storage products for midrange computers and mainframes. Founded in 1979 by Richard J. Egan and Roger Marino, EMC has developed advanced storage and retrieval technologies for the world's largest companies. It provides a full range of RAID-based file servers and storage networks (SANs) as well as the software and services necessary to implement and manage them. In 1999, EMC acquired Data General Corporation, one of the pioneers in minicomputers in the 1970s. In 1992, Data General introduced its CLARiiON line of RAID storage systems, which became popular. See *SAN*.

(2) (ElectroMagnetic Compatibility) Refers to the use of components in electronic systems that do not electrically interfere with each other. See *EMI*.

**emergency boot** See *remote emergency boot*.

**EMF** (1) (ElectroMagnetic Field) See *electromagnetic radiation*.

(2) (Enhanced MetaFile) The 32-bit version of the Windows Metafile (WMF) format. The original WMF format is simple and cannot completely replicate images created by sophisticated graphics programs. The EMF format enhances the structure and solves most of these deficiencies of the WMF format.

**EMI** (ElectroMagnetic Interference) An electrical disturbance in a system due to natural phenomena, low-frequency waves from electromechanical devices or high-frequency waves (RFI) from chips and other electronic devices. Allowable limits are governed by the FCC.

**EMIF** (ESCON Multiple Image Facility) See *MIF*.

**emitter** One side of a bipolar transistor. See *collector*.

**EMM**   (Expanded Memory Manager) Software that manages expanded memory (EMS). In XTs and ATs, expanded memory boards must also be used. In 386s and up, the EMM converts extended memory into EMS.

**EMM386**   See *DOS EMM386.EXE*.

**e-money**   (1) One of several terms used to describe digital money. See *digital money*.

(2) (E-Money) A Web payment processing service from E-Money, Inc., Washington, DC, (www.emoney.net), that allows merchants to process credit cards and initiate direct transfers from customer checking accounts. Merchant transactions are sent to E-Money servers, which access the credit card networks and Automated Clearing House (ACH). E-Money was the first to provide direct access to the ACH. In addition to its back-end payment processing, the company offers a complete range of merchant e-commerce services, including prepaid micropayments, bill presentment and Web hosting. See *Web payment service*.

**emotag**   A pseudo-HTML tag used in chat rooms, e-mail, and newsgroup postings to express some feeling or emotion. They mimic the format of actual HTML tags; for example, someone might key in the following:

*Wow! I'll bet that hurt a lot!SMIRK. See emoticon.*

**emoticon**   (EMOTional ICON) Also called a "smiley," it is an expression of emotion typed into a message using standard keyboard characters. The following examples are viewed sideways. Tilt your head down toward your left shoulder. See *emotag*.

| Smiley | Meaning |
|--------|---------|
| :) | original smiley face |
| :-) | smile |
| :-( | frown |
| ;-) | wink |
| :-D | big smile |
| :-O | mouth open in amazement |
| :-Q | tongue hanging out in nausea |
| :-{) | smile (user has moustache) |
| :-{)} | moustache and beard |
| 8-) | smile (user wears glasses) |
| (-: | smile (user left handed or Australian) |
| :*) | red nosed smile, suggesting inebriation |
| *<|:{)} | Santa Claus! |
| @:{)=== | sikh with turban and long beard |

**Santa Claus. Of Course!**

For an extensive list of more than 650 emoticons, read *Smileys* by David Sanderson, published by O'Reilly & Associates, Inc., ISBN 1-56592-041-4.

**employment site**   See *How to find a job on the Internet*.

**EMR**   (ElectroMagnetic Radiation) The emanation of energy from everything in the universe. Although the EMR from electrical and electronic devices is typically measured for practical, every-day situations, every object, including humans, emanates energy. Much of it is at levels our equipment is not sensitive enough to detect. See *electromagnetic spectrum*.

**EMS**   (1) (Expanded Memory Specification) The first technique that allowed DOS to go beyond its one megabyte memory limit. It allowed access to 32MB of memory by bank switching it through a 64KB buffer (page frame) in the UMA. Either the application was written to use EMS (Lotus 1-2-3 Ver. 2.x, AutoCAD, etc.) or it was run in an environment that did such as DESQview. The first EMS memory in XTs and ATs required an EMS board and driver. When the 386 came out, it could create EMS memory from extended memory.

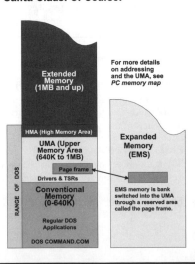

For more details on addressing and the UMA, see *PC memory map*

EMS memory is bank switched into the UMA through a reserved area called the page frame.

There used to be tremendous confusion over EMS. Not only did expanded memory (EMS) and extended memory sound alike, but in the early days, you had to allocate how much EMS you needed. Today, EMS is practically unheard of. Windows manages all the memory in the computer and can allocate whatever EMS it needs on the fly for old DOS applications that require it.

**(2)** (Electronic Message Service) The part of the radio spectrum assigned to electronic messaging over digital satellite circuits.

**(3)** (Enterprise Messaging Server) Original name for Microsoft's Exchange Server. See *Microsoft Exchange*.

**EMS emulator**    Prior to the 386, it was a slow, low-cost software alternative to an EMS board. In XTs and ATs, it simulated EMS memory in extended memory or on disk. On 386s, it referred to a memory manager (EMM) that created EMS from extended memory. Technically, the 386 architecture does not emulate EMS, it maps extended memory into the page frame. See *EMS*.

**EMS memory manager**    See *EMM* and *EMS emulator*.

**emulation mode**    An operational state of a computer when it is running a foreign program under emulation.

**emulator**    A device that is built to work like another. A computer can be designed to emulate another model and execute software that was written to run in the other machine. A terminal can be designed to emulate various communications protocols and connect to different networks. The emulator can be hardware, software or both.

**en**    In typography, a unit of measure equal to one half the width of an em. An en is typically the width of one numeric digit.

**enable**    To turn on. Contrast with *disable*.

**enabled**    Turned on. Contrast with *disabled*.

**Enable/OA**    An earlier integrated software package for PCs from Enable Software, Inc., Ballston Lake, NY. It was a very comprehensive package rivaling many stand-alone programs. Version 4.0 also ran under UNIX.

**Encapsulated PostScript**    See *EPS*.

**encapsulation**    **(1)** In communications, a method for transmitting multiple protocols within the same network. The frames of one type of protocol are carried within the frames of another. For example, SNA's SDLC frames can be encapsulated within TCP/IP and transmitted over a TCP/IP network. See *wrapper*.

**(2)** In object technology, making the data and processing within the object private, which allows the internal implementation of the object to be modified without requiring any change to the application that uses it. This is also known as *information hiding*. See *object technology*.

**Encina**    A UNIX-based TP monitor from Transarc Corporation, Pittsburgh, PA, (www.transarc.com), that is layered over OSF's Distributed Computing Environment (DCE). IBM's CICS/6000 TP monitor is based on Encina, and IBM acquired Transarc in 1994. Encina and BEA Tuxedo are the major TP monitors in the UNIX client/server environment.

**encipher**    Same as *encrypt*.

**encode**    **(1)** To assign a code to represent data, such as a parts code. Contrast with *decode*.

**(2)** To convert from one format or signal to another. See *codec* and *D/A converter*.

**(3)** Same as *encrypt*. See *cryptography*.

**encoder**    A hardware device or software that assigns a code to represent data. See *encode*.

**encoding system**    In a digital system, a method of assigning binary codes to represent characters of data. See *ASCII, 7-bit ASCII, EBCDIC, Unicode, UTF, MIME, BinHex, quoted printable encoding, UUcoding, ASN.1* and *cryptography*.

**Encore**   (Encore Computer Corporation, Ft. Lauderdale, FL, www.encore.com)  A computer company founded in 1983 that specializes in realtime systems and storage products. Its Infinity RT line is an SMP and Alpha-based realtime system that incorporates Encore's Reflective Memory channel, a high-speed memory to memory interconnect. Its Infinity SP disk products are SMP-based UNIX systems that emulate IBM mainframe storage controllers. They provide mainframe storage and also allow UNIX hosts and PC servers access to the same disks as if they were attached SCSI drives.

Encore's products stem back to Systems Engineering Labs, founded in 1961. SEL became a division of Gould, which was acquired by Encore in 1989.

**encrypt**   To encode data for security purposes. See *cryptography*.

**encryption**   See *cryptography* and *encrypt*.

**encryption algorithm**   A formula used to turn data into a secret code. Each algorithm uses a string of bits known as a "key" to perform the calculations. The larger the key (the more bits in the key), the greater the number of potential patterns can be created, thus making it harder to break the code and descramble the contents.

Most encryption algorithms use the block cipher method, which codes fixed blocks of input that are typically from 64 to 128 bits in length. Some use the stream method, which works with the continuous stream of input.

The dialog box below from the ScramDisk encryption program shows the various algorithms offered to encrypt data on your hard disk. ScramDisk is made available free of charge and runs under Windows. For more information, visit www.hertreg.ac.uk/ss. The accompanying descriptions and performance comparisons from the ScramDisk documentation manual are provided because they provide a brief and clear summary of current-day secret key encryption algorithms.

The following is reproduced with permission, courtesy of Sam Simpson and Aman. See *cryptography* and *algorithm*.

**3DES**   This is far better than DES; it uses three applications of the DES cipher in EDE (Encipher-Decipher-Encipher) mode with totally independent keys. Outer-CBC is used. This algorithm is thought to be very secure (major banks use it to protect valuable transactions), but it is also very slow.

**ScramDisk Encryption**
ScramDisk encrypts data on the hard disk, and this dialog box allows for the selection of the encryption algorithm. "Mouse entropy" is the amount of randomness introduced into the creation of the key. The more the mouse is moved around in a random pattern, the more randomness.

**Blowfish**   Blowfish is a high security encryption alogorithm designed by Bruce Schneier, the author of Applied Cryptography and owner of the company Counterpane. It is very fast, is considered secure and is resistant to linear and differential analysis. This is my personal cipher of choice.

**DES**   Data Encryption Standard was designed in the early 1970s by IBM with input from NSA. It is okay, but a single key can be broken in three days by the Electronic Frontier Foundation, a poorly-funded organization. This algorithm was provided for completeness.

**IDEA**   International Data Encryption Algorithm was produced by Xuejia Lai and James Massey. It is fairly fast, is considered secure, and it is also resistant to both linear and differential analysis. To use this for anything other than personal use, a royalty must be paid to Ascom-Systec Ltd.

**Misty1**   Misty1 was designed by M. Matsui of Mitsubishi. It is a reasonably fast cipher that is resistant to both linear and differential analysis. It is fairly new though, so use it with caution.

**Square**    Square is a very fast and reasonably secure block cipher produced by John Daemen and Vincent Rijmen. It hasn't been subject to as much peer review as Blowfish, 3DES, IDEA, etc., so it may be susceptible to attacks.

**Summer**    This is a proprietary stream cipher constructed by the author and is designed for speed alone. It is supplied for backward compatibility with Version 1 of ScramDisk and is not recommended for use on newly created disks. Instead, use TEA or Blowfish, which are both reasonably fast.

**TEA**    Tiny Encryption Algorithm is a very fast and moderately secure cipher produced by David Wheeler and Roger Needham of Cambridge Computer Laboratory. There is a known weakness in the key schedule, so it is not recommended if utmost security is required. TEA is provided in 16 and 32 round versions. The more rounds (iterations), the more secure, but slower.

```
Summary
Block  Key
                          Size    Size    Speed**
Type           Author     Bits    Bits    (m:s)
3DES           Diffie & Hellman    64     168     4:05
Blowfish       Schneier            64     256     0:55
DES            IBM & NSA           64      56     1:42
IDEA           Lai & Massey        64     128     1:07
Misty1         Matsui              64     128     2:50
Square         Daemon & Rijmen    128     128     0:39
Summer         Aman          (stream)     128     0:46
TEA 16         Wheeler & Needham   64     128     0:46
TEA 32         Wheeler & Needham   64     128     1:03
```

*\*\*Speed is time to copy a 50MB file from a normal disk to a ScramDisk on a 166Mhz Pentium.*

**Endeavor**    See *Endevor*.

**Endevor**    A family of configuration management software products from Computer Associates, which are used to keep track of software versions and changes. Products are available for environments such as MVS, UNIX, NT, IDMS and DB2. See *configuration management*.

**endian**    See *byte order*.

**endian problem**    The problem of converting the order of bits when data comes from a machine with one endian type (big or little) that is required by a machine with the opposite type. See *byte order*.

**end key**    A keyboard key commonly used to move the cursor to the bottom of the screen or file or to the next word or end of line.

**endless loop**    A series of instructions that are constantly repeated. It can be caused by an error in the program or it can be intentional; for example, a screen demo on continuous replay.

**endnote**    See *footnote*.

**end office**    A telephone central office that connects directly to the customer. See *central office*.

**end office switch**    A telephone central office switch (telco switch) that connects directly to the customer. Most of the call recording and billing is handled in end office switches today. See *tandem switch* and *carrier switch*.

**end points**    In vector graphics, the two ends of a line (vector). In 2-D graphics, each end point is typically two numbers representing coordinates on x and y axes. In 3-D, each end point is made up of three numbers representing coordinates on X, Y and Z axes.

**end user**    Same as *user*.

**end user computing**    Using personal computers.

**Energy Star**    Power conservation requirements set forth by the Environmental Protection Agency of the U.S. government. In order to display the Energy Star logo, devices (PCs, monitors, printers, etc.) must use less than 30 watts of power when inactive.

**energy technology**    The processes used to create energy. They increasingly are focused on micropower, where individual companies are creating their own power plants for their own use.

**Enfin**    A client/server development system based on the Smalltalk language. It is now part of the ObjectStudio environment. See *ObjectStudio*.

**engine**    **(1)** A specialized processor, such as a graphics processor. Like any engine, the faster it runs, the quicker the job gets done. See *graphics engine* and *printer engine*.
　　**(2)** Software that performs a primary and highly repetitive function such as a database engine, graphics engine or dictionary engine.

**engineer**    See *software engineer*, *systems engineer* and *network engineer*.

**engineering cylinder**    See *diagnostic tracks*.

**engineering drawing sizes**    See also *A4 paper*.

```
A - 8 1/2 x 11
B - 11 x 17
C - 17 x 22
D - 22 x 34
E - 34 x 44
```

**Enhanced BIOS**    See *LBA*.

**Enhanced CD**    See *CD Extra*.

**Enhanced CD-ROM**    See *CD Extra*.

**Enhanced IDE**    See *EIDE*.

**Enhanced keyboard**    A 101-key keyboard from IBM that superseded the PC and AT keyboards. It is the type commonly used on PCs today.

**enhanced resolution**    See *interpolated resolution*.

**enhanced video connector**    See *VESA Enhanced Video Connector*.

**enhancement**    Any improvement made to a software package or hardware device. Sometimes enhancements are really bug fixes in disguise.

**ENIAC**    (**E**lectronic **N**umerical **I**ntegrator **A**nd **C**omputer)  The first operational electronic digital computer developed for the U.S. Army by J. Presper Eckert and John Mauchly at the University of Pennsylvania in Philadelphia. Started in

1943, it took 200,000 man-hours and nearly a half million dollars to complete two years later. Programmed by plugging in cords and settings thousands of switches, the decimal-based machine used 18,000 vacuum tubes, weighed 30 tons and took up 1,800 square feet. It cost a fortune in electricity to run; however, at 5,000 additions per second, it was faster than anything else. Initially targeted for trajectory calculations, by the time it was ready to go, World War II had ended. Soon after it was moved to the army's Aberdeen Proving Grounds in Maryland where it was put to good work computing thermonuclear reactions in hydrogen bombs and numerous other problems until it was dismantled in 1955.

Referring to ENIAC's public introduction in early 1946, The New York Times said "One of the war's top secrets, an amazing machine which applies electronic speeds for the first time to mathematical tasks hitherto too difficult and cumbersome for solution, was announced here tonight." Today, all 1,800 square feet of that machinery fits on the head of a pin.

ENIAC proved that the thinking behind electronic computing was sound, and smaller and faster machines were forecast at the dedication ceremony.

**The First Operational Digital Computer**
Looking a little like a dungeon in an old science fiction movie, this must have been an awesome sight in 1946. The electrical power used could supply thousands of computers today. *(Image courtesy of the Computer Museum History Center, www.computerhistory.org)*

**enqueue**    Pronounced "n-q." To place an item in a queue. Contrast with *dequeue*.

**enquiry character**    In communications, a control character that requests a response from the receiving station.

**enriched ad**    A banner ad that provides user interaction when clicked or when the cursor is rolled over it. There are several variations. For example, the banner may include multiple ads and links, or it might have a scroll bar that can be activated to reveal more information or products. When clicked, the ad might launch another window with a larger ad or a form to be filled out. See *banner ad*.

**enterprise**    The entire organization. See *enterprise networking*.

**enterprise application integration**    See *application integration*.

**enterprise data**    Centralized data that is shared by many users throughout the organization.

**enterprise environment**    The systems used within the organization. Generally refers to the primary architecture. See *enterprise networking*.

**enterprise information portal**    See *corporate portal*.

**enterprise model**    A model of how an organization does business. Information systems are designed from this model.

**enterprise network**    A geographically-dispersed network under the jurisdiction of one organization. It often includes several different types of networks and  computer systems from different vendors.

**enterprise networking**    The networking infrastructure in a large enterprise with multiple computer systems and networks of different types is extraordinarily complex. Due to the myriad of interfaces that are required, much of what goes on has little to do with the real data processing of the payroll and orders. An enormous amount of effort goes into planning the integration of disparate networks and systems and managing them, and, planning again for yet more interfaces as marketing pressures force vendors to develop new techniques that routinely change the ground rules.

Application Development and Configuration Management    There are a large number of programming languages and development tools for writing today's client/server applications. Each development system has its own visual programming interface for building GUI front ends and its own fourth-generation language (4GLs) for doing the business logic. Programmers are always learning new languages to meet the next generation.

Traditional programming has given way to programming for graphical user interfaces and object-oriented methods, two technologies with steep learning curves for the traditional programmer.

Programming managers are responsible for maintaining legacy systems in traditional languages while developing new ones in newer languages and tools for the client/server environment. They must also find ways to keep track of all the program modules and ancillary files that make up an application when several programmers work on a project. Stand-alone version control and configuration management programs handle this, and parts of these systems are increasingly being built into the development systems themselves (see *configuration management*).

**Database Management**    Like all software, a database management system (DBMS) must support the hardware platform and operating system it runs in. In order to move a DBMS to another platform, a version must be available for the new hardware and operating system. The common database language between client and server is SQL, but each DBMS vendor implements its own rendition of SQL, requiring a special SQL interface to most every DBMS.

For certain kinds of applications, relational databases (RDBMSs) are giving way to object-oriented databases (OODBMSs) or unified databases that are both relational and object oriented. This puts a new slant on learning about data structures and the way they are processed.

Database administrators must select the DBMS or DBMSs that efficiently process the daily transactions and also provide sufficient horsepower for decision support. They must decide when and how to split the operation into different databases, one for daily work, the other for ad hoc queries. They must also create the structure of the database by designing the record layouts and their relationships to each other.

**Operating Systems/Network Operating Systems**    Operating systems are the master control programs that run the computer system. Single-user operating systems, such as DOS, Windows and Mac, are used in the clients, and multiuser network operating systems, such as NetWare, Windows NT and all the variations of UNIX, are used in the servers. Windows is the clear winner on the desktop, and Windows NT increasingly gains market share as a server OS.

The operating system sets the standard for the programs that run under it. The choice of operating system combined with the hardware platform determines which ready-made applications can be purchased to work on it.

Systems programmers and IS managers must determine when newer versions of operating systems make sense and plan how to integrate them into existing environments.

**Communications Protocols**    Communications protocols determine the format and rules for how the transmitted data is framed and managed from the sending station to the receiving station. IBM's SNA, Digital's DECnet, Apple's AppleTalk, Novell's IPX/SPX, Microsoft's NetBEUI and the UNIX/Internet's TCP/IP are the major ones. Exchanging data and messages between Macs, PCs, minis, mainframes and UNIX workstations means designing networks for a multiprotocol environment.

**LANs**    Transmission from station to station within a LAN is performed by the LAN access method, or data link protocol, such as Ethernet and Token Ring. As traffic expands within an organization, higher bandwidth is required, causing organizations to plan for Fast Ethernet, switched Ethernet, FDDI and CDDI. At the same time, ATM continues to make inroads, although not as fast as once predicted.

Repeaters, bridges, routers, gateways, hubs and switches are the devices used to extend, convert, route and manage traffic in an enterprise network. Increasingly, one device takes on the job of another (a router does bridging, a hub does routing). Vendor offerings are dizzying.

Network traffic is becoming as jammed as the Los Angeles freeways. Network administrators have to analyze current network traffic in light of future business plans and increasing use of Web pages, images, sound and video files. They have to determine when to increase network bandwidth while maintaining existing networks, which today have become the technical lifeblood of an enterprise.

**WANs**    Transmitting data to remote locations requires the use of private lines or public switched services offered by local and long distance carriers. Connections can be as simple as dialing up via modem or by leasing private lines, such as T1 and T3. Switched 56, frame relay, ISDN, SMDS and ATM offer a variety of switched services in which you pay for the digital traffic you use.

Laptop use has created a tremendous need for remote access to LANs. Network administrators have to design LANs with a combination of remote access and remote control capability to allow mobile workers access to their databases and processing functions.

**Network Management**    Network management is the monitoring and control of LANs and WANs from a central management console. It requires network management software, such as IBM's NetView and HP's OpenView. The Internet's SNMP has become the de facto standard management protocol, but there are many network management programs and options. For example, there are more than 30 third-party add-ons for HP's popular OpenView software.

E

**Systems and Storage Management**    Systems management includes a variety of functions for managing computers in a networked environment, including software distribution, version control, backup and recovery, printer spooling, job scheduling, virus protection and performance and capacity planning. Network management may also fall under the systems management umbrella.

Storage management has become critical for two reasons. First, there is an ever-increasing demand for storage due to document management, data warehousing, multimedia and the World Wide Web as well as increasing daily transaction volume. Secondly, finding the time window in a 7×24 operation to copy huge databases for backup, archiving and disaster recovery is getting more difficult.

**Electronic Mail**    Electronic mail requires a store and forward system so that mail can be safely kept in a "mailbox" until it is retrieved. Although messages and attached files are transmitted using standard transport protocols, the mail system is a high-level application with its own messaging protocols. The major ones are IBM's SNADS, the international X.400, Novell's MHS, Lotus' cc:mail, Microsoft Mail and the Internet's SMTP.

**Formats**    Word processors, DBMSs, spreadsheets, drawing and paint programs generate files in their own proprietary data format. For example, there are more than 75 graphics formats alone. Moving files from one application to another requires conversion (exporting and importing) from one format to another. Dealing with multiple formats and multimedia is why object-oriented databases are being evaluated. They can support any kind of text, picture, sound and video format that exists today or that comes tomorrow.

**The Internet and Intranets**    As if everything mentioned above isn't enough to keep the technical staff busy, the World Wide Web comes along with a force of a nuclear bomb to turn everything in the computing world upside down. Now the Internet sets the standards. The browser becomes an alternate interface for accessing just about everything. Every component of system software from operating system to database management system, as well as every application currently on the market, has been revamped in some manner to be Internet compliant. In Summary...Happy Computing!

**enterprise portal**    See *corporate portal*.

**enterprise storage**    The collection of online, nearline and offline storage within an organization. See *ESM*.

**entity**    In a database, anything about which information can be stored; for example, a person, concept, physical object or event. Typically refers to a record structure.

**entity bean**    An Enterprise JavaBean (EJB) that contains data and is stored on disk or other persistent storage device. For example, an entity bean could be a row in a database table. Contrast with *session bean*. See *EJB*.

**entity relationship model**    A database model that describes the attributes of entities and the relationships among them. An entity is a file (table). Today, ER models are often created graphically, and software converts the graphical representations of the tables into the SQL code required to create the data structures in the database. See *data model*.

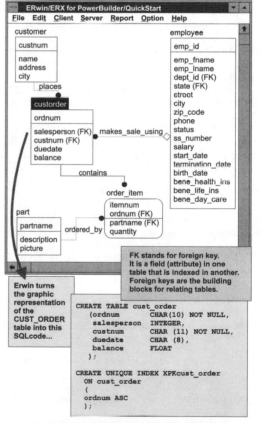

**Building an Entity Relationship Model**
The Erwin modeling program from Logic Works, Princeton, NJ, stands for Entity Relationship for Windows. In this order processing example, the tables for customers and orders are drawn graphically, and Erwin turns the graph into the appropriate SQL code for the target database. *(Example courtesy of Logic Works, Inc.)*

**entity type**    In a database, a particular kind of file; for example, a customer or product file.

**entropy**    Disorder or randomness. In data compression, it is a measure of the amount of non-redundant and non-compressible data in an object (the amount that is not similar). In encryption, it is the amount of disorder or randomness that is added. See *encryption algorithm*.

**entry**    The input of an item or set of items at a terminal. See *data entry*.

**ENUM**    A protocol from the IETF that is used to obtain information about a telephone number. Designed for the Internet, as well as private networks, a record stored in a DNS server contains the telephone number of an individual device, and its particular attributes (can it receive numeric messages or text messages?, Internet capable?, etc.), as well as any pager or fax numbers, IP or e-mail addresses that are associated with it. ENUM is expected to provide a one-stop directory for contacting people and services.

**enumerate**    To count or list one by one. For example, an enumerated data type defines a list of all possible values for a variable, and no other value can then be placed into it. See *device enumeration* and *ENUM*.

**envelope**    (1) A range of frequencies for a particular operation.
(2) A group of bits or items that is packaged and treated as a single unit.

**environment**    A particular configuration of hardware or software. "The environment" refers to a hardware platform and the operating system that is used in it. A programming environment would include the compiler and associated development tools.

Environment is used in other ways to express a type of configuration, such as a networking environment, database environment, transaction processing environment, batch environment, interactive environment and so on. See *platform*.

**environment variable**    An item of data that is updated by the operating system, Web server or other control program. They typically reside in memory and can be read by applications to determine the current status of the system. Environment variables contain data such as time, date, path, version number, login information and so on. See *CGI script* and *DOS Set*.

**EO**    (End Office) See *central office*.

**EOF**    (End Of File) The status of a file when its end has been reached or when an instruction or command resets the file pointer to the end.

**EOQ**    (Economic Order Quantity) The most economical quantity of a product that should be purchased at one time. The EOQ is based on all associated costs for ordering and maintaining the product.

**e-paper**    See *digital paper*.

**EPG**    (Electronic Program Guide) An online listing of TV or other programs. Periodically, EPGs are downloaded into set-top boxes so that viewers can preview offerings by time or category and set reminders.

**EPIC**    (Explicitly Parallel Instruction Computing) The parallel architecture used in Intel's IA-64 chips. It was originally developed by HP. See *IA-64*.

**epitaxial layer**    In chip making, a semiconductor layer that is created on top of the silicon base rather than below it. See *molecular beam epitaxy*.

**EPOC**    A 32-bit operating system for handheld devices from Symbian Ltd., London (www.symbian.com). Used in Psion and other handheld computers, it supports Java applications, e-mail, fax, infrared exchange, data synchronization with PCs and includes a suite of PIM and productivity applications. Symbian was originally the Psion Software division of Psion PLC, (www.psion.com) and was spun off to support EPOC as an independent entity.

**epoch date**    The starting point from which time is measured as the number of days, minutes, etc., from that time.

**EPP**    **(1)** (Enhanced Parallel Port)  See *IEEE 1284*.

**(2)** (Ethernet Packet Processor)  A chip from Kalpana, Inc., Santa, Clara, CA, that doubles speed of Ethernet transmission to 20Mbits/sec.

**EPROM**    (Erasable Programmable **ROM**)  A programmable and reusable chip that holds its content until erased under ultraviolet light. EPROMS have a lifespan of a few hundred write cycles. EPROMS are expected to eventually give way to flash memory. See *EPROM programmer*.

**EPROM programmer**    A device that writes instructions and data into EPROM chips. Some earlier units were capable of programming both PROMs and EPROMs.

**EPS**    (Encapsulated PostScript)  A PostScript file format used to transfer a graphic image between applications and platforms. EPS files contain PostScript code in ASCII text, as well as an optional preview image in TIFF, WMF, PICT or EPSI format (EPSI is also ASCII). Adobe Illustrator has its own variation of EPS, therefore, both Illustrator EPS and standard EPS files are in use.

The typical use of EPS would be to export an illustration created in a drawing program to an EPS file and to import it into a page layout program. Using the preview image, the illustration then could be scaled to fit the page design requirements. The document and embedded EPS images would be saved in the native format of the page layout program (PageMaker, QuarkXPress, etc.) and then printed on a local printer or "printed to disk" as a standard PostScript file for input to an imagesetter.

EPS files are considerably larger than most other graphics file formats; however, since they are text files, they will compress to about a quarter of their original size. See *EPSI*.

**EPSF**    (Encapsulated PostScript File)  The full name of an EPS file. It is used for EPS file extensions in non-DOS and Windows platforms that can handle more than three characters. See *EPS*.

**EPSI**    (Encapsulated PostScript Interchange)  A bitmap format used as a preview image in an EPS file. It contains only 7-bit ASCII data. It has been used in DOS applications that do not support TIFF, WMF and PICT formats. See *EPS*.

**Epson emulation**    Compatible with Epson dot-matrix printers. The command set in the Epson MX, RX and FX printers has become an industry standard. Useful codes are

| ASCII VALUE | COMMAND |
|---|---|
| 12 | Form feed |
| 27 48 | 8 LPI |
| 27 50 | 6 LPI |
| 15 | Condensed on |
| 18 | Condensed off |
| 27 81 1 | Double width on |
| 27 81 0 | Double width off |
| 27 69 | Emphasized on |
| 27 70 | Emphasized off |
| 27 83 1 | Subscript on |
| 27 83 0 | Superscript on |
| 27 84 | Sub/super off |
| 27 45 1 | Underline on |
| 27 45 0 | Underline off |

**EPSS**    (Electronic Performance Support System)  A computer system that provides quick assistance and information without requiring prior training to use it. It may incorporate all forms of multimedia delivery, as well as AI techniques such as expert systems and natural language recognition.

**EQ**    (EQual to)  See *relational operator*.

**equalization**   In communications, techniques used to reduce distortion and compensate for signal loss (attenuation) over long distances.

**equation**   An arithmetic expression that equates one set of conditions to another; for example, $A = B + C$. In a programming language, assignment statements take the form of an equation. The above example assigns the sum of B and C to the variable A.

**ERA**   (Electrically Reconfigurable Array) A programmable logic chip (PLD) technology from Plessey Semiconductor that allows the chip to be reprogrammed electrically.

**erase**   See *delete*.

**erase head**   In a magnetic tape drive, the device that erases the tape before a new block of data is recorded.

**erbium**   A rare earth material used in optical amplifiers. See *optical amplifier*.

**ERD**   (Entity Relationship Diagram) Same as *entity relationship model*.

**ergonomics**   The science of people-machine relationships. An ergonomically-designed product implies that the device blends smoothly with a person's body or actions.

**Erlang**   A unit of traffic use that specifies the total capacity or average use of a telephone system. One Erlang is equivalent to the continuous usage of a telephone line. Traffic in Erlangs is the sum of the holding times of all lines divided by the period of measurement.

**ERM**   (Enterprise Relationship Management) An integrated information system that serves the "front office" departments within an organization, which are sales, marketing and customer service. See *sales force automation* and *ERP*.

**ER model**   See *entity relationship model*.

**ERP**   (Enterprise Resource Planning) An integrated information system that serves all departments within an enterprise. Evolving out of the manufacturing industry, ERP implies the use of packaged software rather than proprietary software written by or for one customer. ERP modules may be able to interface with an organization's own software with varying degrees of effort, and, depending on the software, ERP modules may be alterable via the vendor's proprietary tools as well as proprietary or standard programming languages.

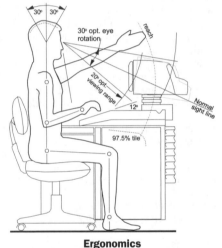

**Ergonomics**
Although ergonomically-designed seats, keyboards and mice are important, perhaps the most beneficial aspect of ergonomics is teaching people to get up periodically and stretch. *(Redrawn from original illustration courtesy of Hewlett-Packard Company.)*

An ERP system can include software for manufacturing, order entry, accounts receivable and payable, general ledger, purchasing, warehousing, transportation and human resources. The major ERP vendors are SAP, PeopleSoft, Oracle, Baan and J.D. Edwards. Lawson Software specializes in back-end processing that integrates with another vendor's manufacturing system. See *ERM* and *NRP*.

**error checking**   (1) Testing for accurate transmission of data over a communications network or internally within the computer system. See *parity checking* and *CRC*.
(2) Same as *validity checking*.

**error control**   Same as *error checking*.

**error detection and correction**   See *error checking* and *validity checking*.

**error-free channel**   An interface (wire, cable, etc.) between devices that is not subject to external interference; specifically not the dial-up telephone system.

**error handling**   Routines in a program that respond to errors. The measurement of quality in error handling is based on how the system informs the user of such conditions and what alternatives it provides for dealing with them.

**error rate**   The measurement of the effectiveness of a communications channel. It is the ratio of the number of erroneous units of data to the total number of units of data transmitted.

**ES**   See *expert system*.

**ES/3090**   A high-end IBM mainframe that incorporates the ESA/370 enhancements.

**ES/9000**   The IBM System/390 computer line introduced in late 1990 that uses 31-bit addressing with maximum memory capacities from 256MB to 9GB. Its 18 models (Model 120 to Model 960) offered the widest range of power in a single introduction at one time with prices ranging from $70K–$23M. Vector processing was optional on high-end water cooled and certain air-cooled models. See *System/390*.

**ESA/370**   (Enterprise System Architecture/370) IBM enhancements that increase the performance of high-end 4381 and 3090 mainframes. Introduced in 1988, it increases virtual memory from 2GB to 16TB and adds techniques for managing it more effectively. This architecture is built into System/390 ES/9000 computers.

**ESA/390**   (Enterprise System Architecture/390) Extensions to ESA/370 for the System/390 series. It includes MVS/ESA, VM/ESA and VSE/ESA operating systems.

**ESC**   See *escape character* and *ESCAPE key*.

**escape character**   A control character that precedes a string of one or more other characters that forms a command to a printer or display device. The escape character can be the Escape character itself (hex 1B in ASCII; hex 27 in EBCDIC) or some arbitrary character. The "escape sequence" causes the device to execute a command rather than print or display the characters. For example, the Escape character followed by **&l10**, sets the LaserJet printer to landscape mode.

The escape character may be used to achieve the opposite effect, causing a command to be displayed rather than executed. For example, in HTML, an ampersand (&) followed by **lt** stipulates that the less than symbol ( should be printed. This is necessary to prevent the browser from executing commands when they are meant to be displayed online for educational purposes.

**ESCAPE key**   A keyboard key commonly used to exit a mode or routine, or cancel some function. It is the key labeled ESC.

**escape sequence**   (1) A machine command that starts with an escape character. Printers are often commanded by escape sequences. See *escape character*.

(2) In a modem, a unique sequence of characters that precedes a command. It allows modem commands (dial, hang up, etc.) to be transmitted with the data. See *TIES* and *Hayes Smartmodem*.

**ESCD**   (Extended System Configuration Data) A format for holding comprehensive data about the peripheral devices plugged into the computer, including ISA cards and Plug and Play cards. ESCD data can be stored in a disk file or non-volatile memory.

**ESCON**   (Enterprise Systems CONnection) An IBM S/390 fiber-optic channel that transfers 17 Mbytes/second over distances up to 60 km depending on connection type. ESCON allows peripheral devices to be located across large campuses and metropolitan areas.

Compared to the copper-based, parallel bus and tag channels, ESCON provides greater speeds and uses a serial interface. An ESCON Director is a hub-and-spoke coupling device that provides 8–16 ports (Model 1) or 28–60 ports (Model 2). See *FICON* and *EMIF*.

**ESD**　**(1)** (Electronic Software Distribution) Distributing new software and upgrades via the network rather than individual installations on each machine. See *ESL*.

**(2)** (ElectroStatic Discharge) Sparks (electrons) that jump from an electrically-charged object to an approaching conductive object.

**(3)** (Entry Systems Division) The IBM division that conceived and developed the original IBM PC.

**ESDI**　(Enhanced Small Device Interface) A hard disk interface that transfers data in the one to three MByte/sec range. ESDI was the high-speed interface for small computers for a while, but has been superseded by IDE and SCSI drives. See *hard disk*.

**ESDL**　(Electronic Software Distribution and Licensing) The combination of ESD and ESL.

**eServer**　See *IBM server series*.

**e-services**　An umbrella term for services on the Internet. E-services include e-commerce transaction services for handling online orders, application hosting by application service providers (ASPs) and any processing capability that is obtainable on the Web. See *e-speak*.

**ESF**　**(1)** (Extended SuperFrame) An enhanced T1 format that allows a line to be monitored during normal operation. It uses 24 frames grouped together (instead of the 12-frame D4 superframe) and provides room for CRC bits and other diagnostic commands.

**(2)** (External Source Format) A specification language for defining an application in IBM's CSP/AD application generator.

**E-sign**　See *electronic signature*.

**e-signature**　See *electronic signature*.

**ESL**　**(1)** A family of client/server development tools for Windows and OS/2 from Ardent (formerly VMARK). It was originally developed by Easel Corporation, which was acquired by VMARK. ESL includes a screen scraper for turning character-based screens into GUI front ends and is often used to develop systems that incorporate the mainframe.

**(2)** (Electronic Software Licensing) Software that keeps track of the number of active users per application in order to comply with the multiuser licensing contracts that have been purchased.

**ESM**　**(1)** (Enterprise Storage Management) Managing the online, nearline and offline storage within a large organization. It includes analysis of storage requirements as well as making routine copies of files and databases for backup, archiving, disaster recovery, hierarchical storage management (HSM) and testing purposes. See *SAN* and *HSM*.

**(2)** (Enterprise Systems Management) Systems management within a large enterprise. See *systems management*.

**ESN**　(Electronic Serial Number) A unique identification number built into a cellphone for security purposes.

**ESP**　**(1)** (Enhanced Service Provider) An organization that adds value to basic telephone service by offering such features as call-forwarding, call-detailing and protocol conversion.

**(2)** (E-Tech Speedy Protocol) A proprietary protocol of E-Tech Research used in its modems.

**(3)** (Electronic Still Photography) Digitizing and transmitting images over a telephone line. See *slow scan TV*.

**(4)** (Emulex SCSI Processor) A proprietary chip used in Emulex's SCSI disk controller.

**e-speak**　A standard interface for e-services from HP. E-speak is designed to let different e-services applications discover and interact with each other over the Internet. See *e-services*.

**ESS**　**(1)** (Electronic Switching System) A large-scale computer from Lucent used to route telephone calls in a telephone company office. The 5ESS is a Class 5 central office switch, and the 4ESS is a Class 4 tandem office switch.

The ESS designation originated with AT&T when it manufactured the machines and was the only telephone company in the U.S. See *SS7*, *Class 4 switch*, *Class 5 switch* and *digital cross-connect*.

(2) (Enterprise Storage Server) A family of RAID-based storage devices for mainframes, UNIX and NT networks from IBM. ESS units are built with a high degree of fault tolerance and connect via Fibre Channel, SCSI, ESCON and FICON interfaces. See *SAN*.

(3) (Executive Support System) See *EIS*.

(4) (Electronic SpreadSheet) See *spreadsheet*.

**Essbase**   A leading decision support tool from Hyperion that is optimized for business planning, analysis and management reporting. It provides an OLAP server that runs on Windows NT, OS/2, AS/400 and major UNIX platforms and supports Windows, Mac and UNIX clients. Data can be extracted from a variety of databases, data warehouses and spreadsheets into Essbase applications. Spreadsheet plug-ins for Lotus 1-2-3 and Excel are available, and the Application Manager is a Windows-based program for building analytical models and providing system management and data loading.

**e-stamp**   (1) (Electronic-STAMP) One of several terms used to refer to the U.S. Postal Service's IBIP program.

(2) (E-Stamp Corporation, Mountain View, CA, www.e-stamp.com) A provider of Web-based shipping and logistics software that determines the most economical carrier to use to ship a package. In 1999, E-Stamp was the first PC Postage service approved by the U.S. Postal Service, but phased out that business in late 2000. E-Stamp's postage system used a hardware key that acted as a vault to store paid postage so that stamps could be printed offline. See *PC Postage* and *Stamps.com*.

**estimating a programming job**   The hardest task in the computer business is estimating the time it takes to create a finished, working program. It always seems to take longer, and sometimes it seems to take forever.

Programmers are an extremely optimistic bunch, and unless they have written a very similar program before with the same programming tools, the new job inevitably takes longer for one reason. Application design is creative work. No matter how much a program is defined on paper, as soon as it starts to take shape, the design flaws become evident. It simply takes multiple iterations to get the design right.

Over the years, some programming estimates have been preposterous. What was thought to take three weeks takes a year. A one year job takes six. In order to improve the accuracy of any estimate, the functional requirements and user interfaces must be carefully designed before the programming begins, the programmers must be experienced, and the users must be involved throughout the project. See *to the recruiter*.

**eSuite**   A Java-based suite of applications from Lotus that includes word processing, spreadsheet, e-mail and presentation graphics. It runs in any NC or PC that has a Java Virtual Machine. Formerly code named Kona, the individual executable programs are considerably smaller than counterpart applications in Microsoft Office and other Windows-based software.

**eSupport**   (Electronic SUPPORT) Providing product support over the Web rather than by telephone. Successful eSupport companies spend an enormous amount of time developing a knowledge base that addresses users' questions in a logical order. However, many do not put in the require effort, and people find wading through the troubleshooting hierarchy or question and answer page as frustrating as waiting on the telephone for a half hour. The bottom line is that eSupport, as well as technical assistance of any kind, is only as good as the education and training given to the support personnel.

To-date, the most beneficial eSupport has been the Internet's capability to offer downloads of drivers, updates and patches from the vendor's Web site. This central source for technical upgrades has been a boon to internal support people and end users alike.

**e-tailer**   (Electronic reTAILER) An online store. See *e-commerce*.

**e-tailing**   (Electronic reTAILING) Selling online. See *e-commerce*.

**etalon**   In optical networking, an etalon is a passive filter that uses a Fabry-Perot cavity. See *Fabry-Perot*.

**etch**    To create a design in a material by digging out the material. The circuit designs on printed circuit boards and chips are etched by acid. See *chip* and *printed circuit board*.

**EtherLoop**    (**ETHER**net Local **LOOP**) A transmission technology from Nortel Networks that combines DSL and Ethernet to deliver up to 6 Mbps between the customer and telco central office (CO). As a point-to-point technology, it elimates the collision detection used in Ethernet, and it also eliminates much of the crosstalk associated with DSL. Unlike asymmetric DSLs, such as ADSL, which provide higher downstream speed, and unlike symmetric DSLs, such as HDSL, which is uniform in both directions, EtherLoop can vary its rates depending on requirements.

At the central office, an EtherLoop multiplexor separates the traffic, sending voice to the voice switch and IP traffic to an Ethernet switch.

**Ethernet**    The most widely-used local area network (LAN) access method, defined by the IEEE as the 802.3 standard. Ethernet has become so popular that a specification for "LAN connection" or "network card" generally implies Ethernet without saying so. All Macs and many PCs come with 10/100 Ethernet ports for home use, not just to create a small home network, but to connect to the Internet via a DSL or cable modem, which requires it. A 10/100 port means that it supports both 10BaseT at 10 megabits per second (Mbps) and 100BaseT at 100 Mbps.

Ethernet is normally a shared media LAN. All stations on the segment share the total bandwidth, which is either 10 Mbps (Ethernet), 100 Mbps (Fast Ethernet) or 1,000 Mbps (Gigabit Ethernet). With switched Ethernet, each sender and receiver pair have the full bandwidth.

Twisted pair Ethernet (10BaseT) uses economical telephone wiring and standard RJ-45 connectors, often taking advantage of installed wires in a building. It is wired in a star configuration and requires a hub or switch. Fast Ethernet (100BaseT) is similar, but uses two different twisted pair configurations (see *100BaseT*). Today's Ethernet network adapters, hubs and switches generally support both 10BaseT and 100BaseT (10/100) and automatically sense and adapt to the transmitted speed. The earlier versions of 10 Mbps Ethernet used coaxial cable (see *10Base5* and *10Base2*).

Fiber-optic Ethernet (10BaseF and 100BaseFX) is impervious to external radiation and is often used to extend Ethernet segments up to 1.2 miles. Specifications exist for complete fiber-optic networks as well as backbone implementations. FOIRL (Fiber-Optic Repeater Link) was an earlier standard that is limited to .6 miles distance.

Ethernet transmits variable length frames from 72 to 1518 bytes in length, each containing a header with the addresses of the source and destination stations and a trailer that contains error correction data. Higher-level protocols, such as IP and IPX, fragment long messages into the frame size required by the Ethernet network being employed (see *MTU*).

Ethernet uses the CSMA/CD technology to broadcast each frame onto the physical medium (wire, fiber, etc.). All stations attached to the Ethernet are "listening," and the station with the matching destination address accepts the frame and checks for errors. Ethernet is a data link protocol (MAC layer protocol) and functions at layers 1 and 2 of the OSI model.

Ethernet was invented by Robert Metcalfe and David Boggs at Xerox PARC in 1973, which first ran at 2.94 Mbps. Metcalfe later joined Digital where he facilitated a joint venture between Digital, Intel and Xerox to collaborate further on Ethernet. Version 1 was finalized in 1980, and products shipped in the following year. In 1983, the IEEE approved the Ethernet 802.3 standard. See *100BaseT*, *Gigabit Ethernet*, *10 Gigabit Ethernet* and *switched Ethernet*.

```
10 Mbps AND 100 Mbps ETHERNET LIMITATIONS
Maximum               Maximum
Type                  Segment  Length      Devices
TWISTED PAIR (star topology)
 10BaseT              328 ft.  (100 m)        1
 100BaseT             328 ft.  (100 m)        1
COAX (bus topology)
 10Base5 "thick"     1640 ft.  (500 m)      100
 10Base2 "thin"       607 ft.  (185 m)       30
FIBER (star topology)
 FOIRL                 .6 mi.  (1 km)         1
 10BaseF              1.2 mi.  (2 km)         1
 100BaseFX multimode  1.2 mi.  (2 km)         1
 100BaseFX single-mode  6 mi.  (10 km)        1
```

**Twisted Pair Ethernet**

Most Ethernets use twisted pair wiring. All cables use RJ-45 connectors between the network adapters in the PC and a central hub or switch.

**Ethernet adapter**    The Ethernet hardware required to attach to an Ethernet network. It typically resides on an expansion board, but is sometimes built into the motherboard. An Ethernet adapter is required in each client and server. See *Ethernet* and *network adapter*.

**Ethernet address**    A unique number assigned to each Ethernet network adapter. It is a 48-bit number maintained by the IEEE. Hardware vendors obtain blocks of numbers that they can build into their cards.

**Ethernet card**    See *Ethernet adapter*.

**Ethernet hub**    A device that all lines on an Ethernet segment are plugged into. 10BaseT and 100BaseT Ethernets are star networks and require a hub for operation. The earlier 10Base5 and 10Base2 Ethernets are bus networks, but are often wired into a star configuration using a central hub for improved troubleshooting. A hub is also known as a "multiport repeater" and is sometimes called a "concentrator." See *hub*.

**Ethernet switch**    See *switched Ethernet*.

**EtherTalk**    Macintosh software from Apple that accompanies its Ethernet Interface NB Card and adapts the Mac to Ethernet networks.

**EtherWave**    An Ethernet adapter from Farallon Communications, Alameda, CA, (www.farallon.com), that supports daisy chaining over 10BaseT. Normally, 10BaseT adapters connect to a central hub. In order to add a station to the network when a hub is out of ports requires adding a hub. EtherWave allows up to seven daisy-chained EtherWave PCs to be connected to a single hub port.

**ETI**    (Embed The Internet) A consortium that is devoted to putting Web servers into microcontrollers used in embedded systems. Using a Web server as a common software engine enables access to the device via any Web browser. See *Web server* and *computer on a chip*.

**E-time**    See *execution time*.

**ETL**    (Extraction, Transformation and Loading) The functions performed when pulling data out of one database and placing it into another of a different type.

**ETSI**    (European Telecommunications Standards Institute, Sophia Antipolis technical park, Nice, France, www.etsi.fr) A non-profit membership organization founded in 1988, dedicated to standardizing telecommunications throughout Europe. It promotes worldwide standards, and its efforts are coordinated with the ITU. Any European organization proving an interest in promoting European standards may represent itself in ETSI.

**Eudora**    A popular Internet mail program from QUALCOMM. A light version is often provided by Internet service providers to its customers. Eudora started out on the Macintosh in 1988 and by 1996 had more than 10 million users. See *stationery*.

**EULA**    (End User License Agreement) The legal agreement between the manufacturer and purchaser of software. It is either printed somewhere on the packaging or displayed on screen at time of installation, the latter being the better method, because it cannot be avoided. The user must click "Accept" or "I Agree" and the license does stipulate the terms of usage, whether the user reads them or not.

The license disclaims all liabilities for what might happen in the user's computer when the software is running. It generally guarantees nothing except that the disk will be replaced if defective. If it sounds like a license to get away with making inferior software, one has to consider that it is impossible for even the largest vendor to test a program in every possible configuration in the PC world. Some combination of hardware and software can always cause a program to crash and cause the loss of whatever data is in the machine at that time.

**Euphoria**    An interpreted programming language developed in 1993 by Robert Craig at Rapid Deployment Software that is noted for its execution speed, flexibility and simplicity. It can simulate any programming method including object-oriented constructs. Euphoria has been used to develop computer games and other applications in DOS, Windows and Linux. For more information, visit www.rapideuphoria.com.

**Eurocard** A family of European-designed printed circuit boards that uses a 96-pin plug rather than edge connectors. The 3U is a 4"×6" board with one plug; the 6U is a 6×12" board with two plugs; the 9U is a 14"×18" board with three plugs. See *CompactPCI*.

**evanescent field** In an optical fiber, the radiation that passes into the cladding, which is the layer that surrounds the core of the fiber.

**Evans & Sutherland** (Evans & Sutherland Computer Corporation, Salt Lake City, UT, www.es.com) A computer graphics and simulation company founded in 1968 by David Evans and Ivan Sutherland. Sutherland's doctoral thesis on computer graphics in 1963 became a cult paper on the subject. They developed many of the first effects at the University of Utah.

In the mid 1970s, the company developed commercial flight simulators in conjunction with Rediffusion Simulation in England. More than a decade later, it dissolved this relationship and began to develop military simulations. The company makes the computer hardware and software, which is then integrated with domes and cockpits into the final product. The simulations are extremely realistic and are output at more than 100 frames per second to eliminate the subliminal flicker produced when scenes are projected inside a dome. The company later created a division that creates special effects for the education and entertainment fields.

**A 3U Eurocard**
CompactPCI boards use the Eurocard form factor. This is a complete PC (sans hard disk) from Xtech. Note the CompactPCI connector at the back of the card (right). *(Image courtesy of Xtech Embedded Computers.)*

**EVC** See *VESA Enhanced Video Connector*.

**even parity** See *parity checking*.

**event driven** An application that responds to input from the user or other application at unregulated times. It's driven by choices that the user makes (select menu, press button, etc.). Contrast with *procedure oriented*.

**event management system** Software that monitors servers, workstations and network devices for routine and non-routine events. For example, routine events such as logons help determine network usage, while unsuccessful logons are warnings that hackers may be at work or that the network access system is failing. Event managers provide realtime information for immediate use and log events for summary reporting used to analyze network performance.

An event management system is typically made up of client agents that reside in the remote devices, a central component for gathering the events, an event database and a reporting system to deliver the results in various formats. See *service level management system* and *application management system*.

**event manager** See *event management system*.

**event monitor** The user interface in an event management system. See *event management system*.

**Evans & Sutherland Flight Simulator**
This 20' dome in the Netherlands has an actual cockpit inside. The simulated scenes are projected onto the dome, and the hydraulics move the unit. *(Image courtesy of Evans & Sutherland Computer Corporation.)*

**evolware** (EVOLvable hardWARE) A future computing architecture that can modify its own circuitry to improve performance for solving the problems it is given. As far fetched as it sounds, self modification of hardware is already possible. For example, FPGAs are a type of logic chip that can be reprogrammed in place. Exactly how that would be done is based on some pretty complicated software. See *wares*.

**e-wallet** See *digital wallet* and *eWallet*.

**eWallet** An electronic wallet originally from LaunchPad Technologies and later integrated into the EntryPoint news and information service. See *digital wallet* and **EntryPoint**.

**eWorld**    An online service from Apple aimed at the consumer market. It was introduced in 1994 and closed in 1996.

**exa**    One quintillion (10 to the 18th power). See *space/time*.

**Exabyte**    (Exabyte Corporation, Boulder, CO, www.exabyte.com) The world's largest independent tape drive manufacturer. Its high-capacity 8mm tape drives, introduced in 1987, are sold direct and through OEMs. With acquisitions made in 1993, Exabyte also makes QIC and DAT drives.

**examinations**    See *CCP, NetWare certification* and *Microsoft certification*.

**Excel**    A full-featured spreadsheet for PCs and the Macintosh from Microsoft. It can link many spreadsheets for consolidation and provides a wide variety of business graphics and charts for creating presentation materials. For a tutorial on the essentials of Excel, see *XL ABCs*.

**exception report**    A listing of abnormal items or items that fall outside of a specified range.

**Exchange**    See *Microsoft Exchange*.

**Exchange administrator**    A person who manages a Microsoft Exchange server. Responsibilities include setting up user accounts and mailboxes, backup and restore operations and security.

**Excite**    (Excite, Inc., Redwood City, CA, www.excite.com) One of the major search sites on the Web. See *Web search sites*.

**exclusive NOR**    See *NOR*.

**exclusive OR**    See *OR*.

**executable**    As an adjective: able to be run in its current format. As a noun: a program file ready to run in a particular environment. See *executable code*.

**executable code**    Machine language, machine code. The native language a computer can follow directly. The source code of a programming language is either compiled directly into executable code or into an intermediate language. For example, C++ is compiled into executable machine code. Java source code is compiled into an intermediate bytecode language that must be turned into executable code at runtime by the Java Virtual Machine software.

   Technically, the compiler creates object code, which is the machine language representation of the source code, and the link editor creates the executable code. The link editor combines program object code, object code from library routines and any other required system code into one addressable machine language file. See *intermediate language*, *machine language* and *Java Virtual Machine*.

**execute**    To run a program (follow instructions in the program). Same as *run*.

**execution time**    The time in which a single instruction is executed. It makes up the last half of the instruction cycle.

**executive**    Refers to an operating system or only to the operating system's kernel.

**executive information system**    See *EIS*.

**EXE file**    (EXEcutable file) The name given to a runnable program in DOS, Windows, OS/2 and VMS. In DOS, if a program fits within 64K, it may be a COM file.

**exit**    (1) To get out of the current mode or quit the program. Contrast with *launch*.
   (2) In programming, to get out of the loop, routine or function that the computer is currently in.

**exit console**    A window that is displayed as soon as a user leaves a Web site. When the user leaves the current Web page that contains the exit console code (typically JavaScript), the browser displays a window that usually contains an advertisement of some type.

**expanded memory**    See *EMS, EMM* and *expanded storage*.

**expanded memory emulator**    A memory manager for 386s and up that converts extended memory into EMS memory. See *EMM*.

**expanded storage**    Additional memory in IBM mainframes that is not normally addressable by applications. Introduced for the 3090 series, the data is usually transferred in 4K pages from expanded storage to central storage (main memory). See *hiperspace*.

**expand the tree**    To display the sublevels of a hierarchical tree.

**expansion board**    A printed circuit board that plugs into an expansion slot and extends the computer's capability to control a peripheral device. All the boards (cards) that plug into a personal computer's bus are expansion boards, such as display adapters, disk controllers, network adapters and sound cards.

Support for additional peripherals can be built into the motherboard. For example, in the early days of the PC, the serial and parallel ports were always contained on an expansion board. Today, they are built into the motherboard. Stereo sound and VGA display may also be built into the motherboard, eliminating the need to plug in separate expansion boards. See *motherboard*. See also *bus extender*.

**expansion bus**    An input/output bus typically comprised of a series of slots on the motherboard. Expansion boards (cards) are plugged into the bus. ISA and PCI are the common expansion buses in a PC. See *expansion board*. See also *bus extender*.

**expansion card**    Same as *expansion board*.

**expansion slot**    A receptacle inside a computer or other electronic system that accepts printed circuit boards. The number of slots determines future expansion. In personal computers, expansion slots are connected to the bus.

**ExperLogo**    A Macintosh version of Logo developed by ExperTelligence, Inc., Goleta, CA. It contains more functions similar to LISP than most versions of Logo.

**expert system**    An AI application that uses a knowledge base of human expertise for problem solving. Its success is based on the quality of the data and rules obtained from the human expert. In practice, expert systems perform both below and above that of a human.

It derives its answers by running the knowledge base through an inference engine, which is software that interacts with the user and processes the results from the rules and data in the knowledge base.

Examples of uses are medical diagnosis, equipment repair, investment analysis, financial, estate and insurance planning, vehicle routing, contract bidding, production control and training. See *EPSS*.

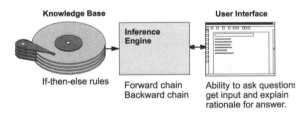

**Expert System**

**expireware**    Software with a built-in expiration date, either by date or number of uses.

**explode**    (1) To break down an assembly into its component pieces. Contrast with *implode*.
(2) To decompress data back to its original form.

**exploded view**    An illustration in which all the elements of an assembly are slightly separated from each other, enabling each element to be viewed independently. Pie charts are a type of business graphic that is also shown in an exploded view, where all pieces of the pie are separated from each other.

**Explorer**    The file manager in Windows 95 and subsequent versions of Windows. Explorer functions are built into Internet Explorer, Microsoft's Web browser. See *file manager*, **Win Explorer** and *Internet Explorer*.

**exponent**    The number written above the line and to the right of a number that indicates the power of a number, or how many zeros there are in it. For example 10 to the 3rd power indicates three zeros. The number 467,000 can be stated as 467 x 10 to the 3rd. On a screen or printout, the number is expressed as 467E3. See *floating point*.

**exponential growth**    Extremely fast growth. On a chart, the line curves up rather than being straight. Contrast with *linear*.

**exponential smoothing**    A widely-used technique in forecasting trends, seasonality and level change. Works well with data that has a lot of randomness.

**export**    To save a copy of the current document, database or image into the file format required by a different application. Mainstream applications typically export (and import) a variety of popular formats. The Save As command in a program gives you access to the export filters in a program. See *import, foreign format, graphics formats* and *Save As*.

**export filter**    The function in a program that saves the document or image onscreen in a different file format that is not native to the application. See *export*.

**expose**    To make available. If software "exposes certain functions," it makes them available to the programmer for use. The company "exposes Web services" means it is making certain services available to users or to other companies on the Web.

**expression**    In programming, a statement that describes data and processing. For example, **VALUE=2*COST** and **PRODUCT="HAT" AND COLOR="GRAY"**.

**extended application**    A DOS application that runs in extended memory under the control of a DOS extender.

**extended ASCII**    The second half of the ASCII character set (characters 128 through 255). Extended ASCII symbols are different for each font. The standard font in DOS uses extended ASCII for foreign language letters, as well as characters that make up simple charts and diagrams (see *ASCII chart*). The Macintosh allows extended ASCII characters to be user defined.

The extended ASCII characters in most Windows fonts are defined by ANSI for foreign languages, and the Character Map utility can be used to view them.

**extended maintenance**    On-call service that is ordered for periods in addition to the primary period of maintenance.

**extended memory**    In Intel 286s and up, it is standard memory above one megabyte. Extended memory is used directly by Windows and OS/2, as well as DOS applications that run with DOS extenders. It is also used under DOS for RAM disks and disk caches. Contrast with expanded memory (EMS), which is specialized memory above one megabyte. See *EMS, XMS* and *DOS extender*.

**extender**    See *bus extender* and *DOS extender*.

**extensible**    Capable of being expanded or customized. For example, with extensible programming languages, programmers can add new control structures, statements or data types.

**extension**  Extensions are file types that are added to the end of DOS, Windows and OS/2 file names. Before Windows 95, an extension could only have up to three letters or digits. However, even after Windows 95, new file formats are generally kept to three characters as a matter of convention.

All programs and almost all data files use extensions, which are separated from the file name with a dot. For example, LETTER.DOC is a Word document. NOTEPAD.EXE is a text editor program that comes with Windows. See *Win Show file extensions* and *graphics formats*. See also *Macintosh extension*.

| Ext. | Type of File |
|------|--------------|
| 3DS | 3D Studio |
| 906 | Calcomp plotter |
| ABC | This program's master index |
| ABK | CorelDRAW auto backup |
| ACL | CorelDRAW keyboard accelerator |
| AD | After Dark image |
| ADM | After Dark MultiModule |
| ADR | After Dark Randomizer |
| AFM | Adobe font metrics (Type 1) |
| AG4 | Access G4 document imaging |
| AI | Adobe Illustrator graphics |
| AI | Encapsulated PostScript header |
| AIF | Digital audio (Mac) |
| AIFC | Digital audio (Mac) |
| ALB | JASC Image Commander |
| ANI | Animated cursor |
| ANN | Windows help annotations |
| ANS | ANSI text |
| ARC | ARC, ARC+ compressed archive |
| ARJ | Compressed archive (Jung) |
| ART | Xara Studio drawing |
| ASA | ASP info |
| ASAX | ASP.NET file |
| ASC | ASCII file |
| ASCX | ASP.NET file |
| ASD | Word temporary document |
| ASF | NetShow file |
| ASM | Assembly source code |
| ASMX | ASP.NET file |
| ASP | Active Server Page |
| ASPX | ASP.NET file |
| ASX | NetShow file |
| ATT | AT&T Group IV fax |
| AU | Digital audio (Sun) |
| AVI | Microsoft movie format |
| AXD | Actrix drawing |
| BAK | Backup |
| BAS | BASIC source code |
| BAT | DOS, OS/2 batch file |
| BFC | Windows briefcase document |
| BIN | Driver, overlay |
| BM1 | Apogee BioMenace file |
| BML | Bookmark library (SyncURL) |
| BMP | Windows & OS/2 bitmap |
| BMK | Windows help bookmarks |
| BMS | BlackMagic script |
| BRK | Brooktrout fax |
| BS1 | Apogee Blake Stone file |
| C | C source code |
| CAB | Microsoft compressed format for distribution |
| CAL | Windows calendar |

| Ext. | Type of File |
|------|--------------|
| CAL | SuperCalc spreadsheet |
| CAL | CALS raster and vector formats |
| CAP | Ventura Pub. captions |
| CCB | Visual Basic animated button |
| CCH | Corel Chart |
| CDA | CD audio track |
| CDR | CorelDRAW vector graphics |
| CDT | CorelDRAW template |
| CDX | CorelDRAW compressed drawing |
| CDX | FoxPro and Clipper index |
| CFG | Configuration |
| CGM | CGM vector graphics |
| CH3 | Harvard Graphics chart |
| CHP | Ventura Pub. chapter |
| CHK | DOS/Windows corrupted file (Chkdsk) |
| CIF | Ventura Pub. chapter info |
| CIT | Intergraph scanned image |
| CK? | iD/Apogee Commander Keen ? |
| COB | COBOL source code |
| COB | Truespace 3-D file |
| CLP | Windows clipboard |
| CLS | Visual Basic class module |
| CMF | Corel metafile |
| CMP | JPEG bitmap, LEAD bitmap |
| CMP | RichLink composed format |
| CMX | Corel clip art |
| CMV | Corel Presentation Exchange |
| CNT | Windows help contents |
| COM | Executable program |
| CPD | Fax cover document |
| CPE | Fax cover document |
| CPI | DOS code page |
| CPL | Windows control panel applets |
| CPL | Corel color palette |
| CPP | C++ source code |
| CPR | Knowledge Access bitmap |
| CPR | Corel Presents presentation |
| CPT | Corel Photopaint image |
| CPX | Corel Presentation Exchange |
| CRD | Cardfile file |
| CRP | Corel Presents runtime presentation |
| CSC | Corel script |
| CSV | Comma delimited |
| CT | Scitex CT bitmap |
| CUR | Cursor |
| CUT | Dr. Halo bitmap |
| CV5 | Canvas 5 vector/bitmap |
| DAT | Data |
| DAT | WordPerfect merge data |
| DB | Paradox table |

| Ext. | Type of File | Ext. | Type of File |
|------|--------------|------|--------------|
| DBF | dBASE database | GDF | GDDM format |
| DBT | dBASE text | GED | Arts & Letters graphics |
| DBX | DATABEAM bitmap | GEM | GEM vector graphics |
| DCA | IBM text | GFI | Genigraphics presentation link |
| DCM | DICOM medical image | GFX | Genigraphics presentation link |
| DCS | Color separated EPS format | GID | Windows help global index |
| DCX | Intel fax image | GIF | CompuServe bitmap |
| DCT | Dictionary | GIM | Genigraphics presentation link |
| DEF | Definition | GIX | Genigraphics presentation link |
| DG | Autotrol vector graphics | GNA | Genigraphics presentation link |
| DGN | Intergraph vector graphics | GNX | Genigraphics presentation link |
| DIB | Windows DIB bitmap | GP4 | CALS Group IV - ITU Group IV |
| DIC | Dictionary | GRA | Microsoft graph |
| DIF | Spreadsheet | GRF | Micrografx Charisma vector graphics |
| DLG | Dialogue script | GRP | Windows ProgMan Group |
| DLL | Dynamic link library | GWX | Genigraphics presentation link |
| DOC | Document (Word and others) | GWZ | Genigraphics presentation link |
| DOT | Word template | GX1 | Show Partner bitmap |
| DOX | MultiMate V4.0 document | GX2 | Show Partner bitmap |
| DPI | Pointline bitmap | GZ | UNIX Gzip |
| DRV | Driver | H | C header |
| DRW | Designer vector graphics (Version 2.x, 3.x) | HED | HighEdit document |
| DS4 | Designer vector graphics (Version 4.x) | HGL | HP Graphics language |
| DSF | Designer vector graphics (Version 6.x) | HLP | Help text |
| DWG | AutoCAD vector format | HPJ | Visual Basic help project |
| DX | Autotrol document imaging | HPP | C++ program header |
| DXF | AutoCAD vector format | HPL | HP Graphics language |
| ED5 | EDMICS bitmap (DOD) | HQX | BinHex format |
| EMF | Enhanced Windows metafile | HT | HyperTerminal |
| EPS | Encapsulated PostScript | HTM | HTML document (Web page) |
| ESI | Esri plot file (vector) | HTML | HTML document (Web page) |
| EVY | Envoy document | HTX | HTML extension file |
| EXE | Executable program | HYC | WordPerfect hypen list |
| FAX | Various fax formats | ICA | IBM MO:DCA - IOCA bitmap |
| FDX | Force index | ICB | Targa bitmap |
| FH3 | Freehand 3 | ICO | Windows icon |
| FLC | Autodesk animation | IDC | Internet Database Connector |
| FLD | Hijaak thumbnail folder | IDD | MIDI instrument definition |
| FLI | Autodesk animation | IDE | Development environment configuration |
| FLT | Graphics conversion filter | IDX | FoxBase index |
| FMT | dBASE Screen format | IFF | Amiga bitmap |
| FMV | FrameMaker raster & vector graphics | IGF | Inset Systems (Hijaak) raster & vector graphics |
| FNT | Windows font | | |
| FOG | Fontographer font | IL | Icon library (hDC Computer) |
| FON | Windows bitmapped font | IMG | ISO 9660 CD-ROM image |
| FON | Telephone file | IMG | Macintosh image file |
| FOR | FORTRAN source code | IMG | GEM Paint bitmap |
| FOT | Windows TrueType font info | INF | Setup information |
| FOX | FoxBase compiled program | INI | Initialization |
| FM3 | Format info for 1-2-3 Version 3 | JFF | JPEG bitmap |
| FP1 | Flying Pigs for Windows data | JIF | JPEG bitmap |
| FPX | FlashPix bitmap | JPG | JPEG bitmap |
| FRM | dBASE report layout | JS | JavaScript file |
| FTG | Windows help file links | JT | JT Fax |
| FTS | Windows help text search index | JTF | JPEG bitmap |
| G4 | GTX RasterCAD (raster into vector) | KDC | Kodak Photo bitmap |
| GAL | Corel Multimedia Manager album | KFX | Kofax Group IV fax |
| GCA | IBM MO:DCA - GOCA vector graphics | KYE | Kye game program data |

E

| Ext. | Type of File | Ext. | Type of File |
|------|-------------|------|-------------|
| LBL | dBASE label | O | UNIX machine language |
| LBM | Deluxe Paint graphics | OAZ | OAZ Fax |
| LEG | Legacy text | OBD | Microsoft Office binder |
| LIB | Function library | OBJ | Machine language, |
| LIT | Microsoft Reader file | OBJ | Wavefront 3-D file |
| LOG | Log file | OBZ | Microsoft Office wizard |
| LNK | Windows 9x/NT shortcut | OEB | Open eBook publication |
| LQT | Liquid Audio | OLB | OLE object library |
| LSN | Topic list (CDE) | OLE | OLE object |
| LST | List | ORG | Organizer file |
| LV | LaserView Group IV | OTF | OpenType font |
| LZH | LHARC compressed | OVL | Overlay module |
| LZS | Skyroads program data | OVR | Overlay module |
| M1V | MPEG file | OZM | Sharp Organizer memo bank |
| M3U | MPEG file | OZP | Sharp Organizer telephone bank |
| MAC | MacPaint bitmap | OUT | Encyclopedia definitions |
| MAK | Visual Basic/MS C++ project | P10 | Tektronic Plot 10 |
| MAP | Link editor map | PAL | Windows palette |
| MB1 | Apogee Moster Bash file | PAS | Pascal source code |
| MBX | Mailbox (e-mail) | PAT | CorelDRAW pattern |
| MCS | MathCAD format | PBD | PowerBuilder dynamic library |
| MCW | Word for Macintosh document | PBK | Microsoft Phonebook |
| MDB | Access database | PBM | Portable Bitmap |
| MEL | Maya script | PCL | HP LaserJet series |
| MET | OS/2 Metafile | PCD | Photo CD bitmap |
| MEU | Menu items | PCM | LaserJet cartridge info. |
| MDX | dBASE IV multi-index | PCS | PICS animation |
| MID | MIDI sound file, | PCT | PC Paint bitmap, |
| MID | Eudora script file | PCT | Macintosh PICT bitmap & vector graphics |
| MIL | Same as GP4 | PCW | PC Write document |
| MIX | PhotoDraw file | PCX | PC Paintbrush bitmap |
| MME | MIME-encoded file | PDF | Portable Document Format (Acrobat) |
| MMF | Microsoft mail file | PDF | Printer driver, |
| MMM | Macromind animation format | PDF | Printer description (QuarkXpress) |
| MOD | Eudora script file | PDV | PC Paintbrush printer driver |
| MOV | QuickTime movie | PDW | HiJaak vector graphics |
| MPA | MPEG file | PFA | Type 1 font (ASCII) |
| MP2 | MPEG file | PFB | Type 1 font (encrypted) |
| MP2V | MPEG file | PFM | Windows Type 1 font metrics |
| MP3 | MPEG-1 Layer 3 audio | PGL | HPGL 7475A plotter (vector graphics) |
| MPE | MPEG file | PIC | Various vector formats: |
| MPEG | MPEG file | PIC | Lotus 1-2-3, |
| MPG | MPEG file | PIC | Micrografx Draw, |
| MPP | Microsoft Project | PIC | Mac PICT format, |
| MRK | Informative Graphics markup file | PIC | IBM Storyboard bitmap |
| MSG | Message file | PIF | Windows info. for DOS programs, |
| MSP | Microsoft Paint bitmap | PIF | IBM Picture Interchange |
| MUS | Music | PIN | Epic Pinball data |
| MVB | Microsoft Multimedia Viewer | PIX | Inset Systems raster & vector graphics |
| M1V | MPEG file | PL | Perl script |
| M3D | Corel Motion 3-D | PLT | AutoCAD plotter file |
| NAP | NAPLPS format | PLT | HPGL plotter file |
| NAV | Eudora script file | PM | PageMaker graphics/text |
| NDX | dBASE index | PMx | PageMaker document (x=ver.) |
| NDX | CDE index | PML | PageMaker library |
| NG | Norton Guides text | PNG | PNG bitmap |
| NLM | NetWare NLM program | POV | POV-Ray ray tracing |
| NTZ | InVircible antivirus blueprint | PP4 | Picture Publisher 4 |

| Ext. | Type of File |
|------|--------------|
| PPD | PostScript printer description |
| PPM | Portable Pixelmap |
| PPS | PowerPoint Slideshow |
| PPT | PowerPoint |
| PRD | Microsoft Word printer driver |
| PRE | Lotus Freelance |
| PRG | dBASE source code |
| PRN | XyWrite printer driver |
| PRN | Temporary print file |
| PRS | WordPerfect printer driver |
| PRS | Harvard Graphics |
| PRT | Formatted text |
| PS | PostScript page description |
| PSD | Photoshop native format |
| PSR | Powersoft report |
| PTx | PageMaker template (x=ver.) |
| PUB | Microsoft Publisher publication |
| PUB | Ventura Publisher publication |
| PUZ | Across puzzle |
| PWL | Windows password list |
| P10 | Tektronix Plot10 plotter (vector graphics) |
| QBW | QuickBooks |
| QLB | Quick programming library |
| QLC | ATM font info |
| QT | QuickTime movie |
| QTM | QuickTime movie |
| RA | Real Audio file |
| RAM | Real Audio file |
| RAS | Sun bitmap |
| RAW | 3-D file (open standard) |
| RC | Resource script |
| REC | Recorder file |
| REG | Registration file |
| RES | Programming resource |
| RFT | DCA/RFT document |
| RGB | SGI bitmap |
| RIA | Alpharel Group IV bitmap |
| RIB | Renderman graphics |
| RIC | Roch FaxNet |
| RIX | RIX virtual screen |
| RLC | CAD Overlay ESP (Image Systems) |
| RLE | Compressed (run length encoded) |
| RLF | RichLink compiled format |
| RM | Real Media file |
| RMI | MIDI music |
| RMM | Real Media file |
| RND | AutoShade rendering format |
| RNL | GTX Runlength bitmap |
| RTF | Microsoft text/graphics |
| R8P | LaserJet portrait font |
| R8L | LaserJet landscape font |
| RV | Real Video file |
| SAM | Ami Pro document |
| SAT | ACIS 3-D model |
| SAV | Saved file |
| SBP | IBM Storyboard graphics/Superbase text |
| SC | Paradox source code |
| SC? | ColoRIX raster (?=res.) |

| Ext. | Type of File |
|------|--------------|
| SC2 | Microsoft Schedule+ 7 |
| SCD | Microsoft Schedule+ 7 |
| SCH | Microsoft Schedule+ 1 |
| SCM | ScreenCam movie |
| SCP | Dial-up Networking script |
| SCR | Windows screen saver |
| SCR | Generic script |
| SCR | Fax image |
| SCR | dBASE screen layout |
| SCT | Lotus Manuscript screen capture text |
| SCT | Scitex bitmap |
| SDL | SmartDraw library |
| SDR | SmartDraw vector graphics |
| SDT | SmartDraw template |
| SET | Setup parameters |
| SFP | LaserJet portrait font |
| SFL | LaserJet landscape font |
| SFS | PCL 5 scalable font |
| SGI | SGI bitmap |
| SHB | Corel Show |
| SHG | HotSpot bitmap |
| SHS | OLE2 package (can contain executables) |
| SHW | Corel Show |
| SLD | AutoCAD slide |
| SLK | SYLK format (spreadsheets) |
| SMI | SMIL multimedia |
| SND | Digital audio |
| SPD | Speedo scalable font |
| STY | Ventura Pub. style sheet |
| SUN | Sun bitmap |
| SVX | Amiga sound file |
| SWF | Shockwave file |
| SY3 | Harvard Graphics symbol |
| SYL | SYLK format (spreadsheets) |
| SYS | DOS, OS/2 driver |
| TAL | Adobe Type Align shaped text |
| TAR | Tape archive |
| TAZ | UNIX Gzip archive |
| TDF | Speedo typeface definition |
| TFM | Intellifont font metrics |
| TGA | TARGA bitmap |
| TGZ | UNIX Gzip archive |
| TIF | TIFF bitmap |
| TLB | OLE type library |
| TMP | Temporary |
| TOC | Table of contents |
| TRM | Terminal file |
| TTC | TrueType font compressed |
| TTF | TrueType font |
| TXT | ASCII text |
| USP | LaserJet portrait font |
| USL | LaserJet landscape font |
| VBP | Visual Basic project |
| VBX | Visual Basic custom control |
| VBS | Visual Basic script |
| VCF | vCard file |
| VDA | Targa bitmap |
| VGR | Ventura Pub. chapter info |

| Ext. | Type of File | Ext. | Type of File |
|------|--------------|------|--------------|
| VOC | Sound Blaster sound | WPT | WordPerfect template |
| VOX | Voxware compressed audio | WQ? | Quattro Pro for DOS (?=version) |
| VP | Ventural Publisher publication | WRI | Windows Write document |
| VSD | Visio drawing | WRK | Sympohony spreadsheet |
| VST | Targa bitmap | WRL | VRML page |
| VUE | dBASE relational view | WS? | WordStar for Windows (?=version) |
| WAV | Digital audio (Windows) | WSD | WordStar 2000 document |
| WAX | WMA metafile (location of WMA file) | WSH | Windows Scrip Host properties |
| WB? | Quattro Pro spreadsheet (?=version) | WVL | Wavelet compressed file |
| WBK | Microsoft Word backup | WVX | WMV metafile (location of WMV file) |
| WBT | WinBatch file | XAR | Corel Xara drawing |
| WCM | WordPerfect macro | XBM | X Window bitmap |
| WDB | Microsoft works data file | XFX | JetFax |
| WGP | Wild Board games data | XLA | Excel add-in |
| WID | Font width table | XLB | Excel toolbar |
| WIF | Wavelet image | XLC | Excel chart |
| WIZ | Microsoft Word wizard | XLD | Excel dialogue |
| WKQ | Quattro spreadsheet | XLK | Excel backup |
| WK1 | Lotus ver. 2.x | XLM | Excel macro |
| WK3 | Lotus ver. 3.x & Windows | XLS | Excel spreadsheet |
| WK4 | Lotus ver. 4.x | XLT | Excel template |
| WKS | Lotus 1-2-3 ver. 1a spreadsheet | XLW | Excel project |
| WMA | Windows Media audio (ASF file) | XPM | X Window pixelmap |
| WMF | Windows Metafile | XWD | X Window dump |
| WMV | Windows Media video (ASF file) | XY? | XyWrite document (?=version) |
| WPD | Corel WordPerfect, | XYW | XyWrite for Windows document |
| WPD | Windows printer description | Z | UNIX Gzip archive |
| WP? | WordPerfect document (?=version) | ZIP | PKZIP compressed |
| WPG | WordPerfect raster & vector graphics | ZOO | Zoo compressed |
| WPM | WordPerfect macro | $$$ | Temporary |
| WPS | Microsoft Works document | | |

**extent**    Contiguous space on a disk reserved for a file or application.

**exterior gateway protocol**    See *EGP*.

**exterior routing protocol**    See *EGP*.

**external bus**    A data pathway between the CPU and peripheral devices that are housed either inside or outside of the computer cabinet. External buses in a PC are the ISA, EISA and PCI buses. Contrast with *internal bus*.

**external cache**    Same as *L2 cache*. See *cache*.

**external command**    (1) In DOS and OS/2, a function performed by a separate utility program that accompanies the operating system. Contrast with *internal command*. See *DOS external command*.
(2) A user-developed HyperCard command. See *XCMD*.

**external drive**    A disk or tape drive that resides in its own case and is cabled to the drive controller (plug-in card) in the computer. SCSI drives are often available as external drives. The external drive derives power from its own internal power supply. Contrast with *internal drive*.

**external function**    A subroutine that is created separately from the main program. See *XFCN*.

**external interrupt**    An interrupt caused by an external source such as the computer operator, external sensor or monitoring device, or another computer.

**external modem**    A self-contained modem that is connected via cable to the serial port of a computer. It draws power from a wall outlet. The advantage of an external modem is that a series of status lights on the outside of the case display the changing states of the modem (off-hook, carrier detect, transmitting, etc.). In varying degrees, the communications program informs the user as well. However, having the indicators on the unit itself is very helpful if a problem occurs. Contrast with *internal modem*.

**external sort**    A sort program that uses disk or tape as temporary workspace. Contrast with *internal sort*.

**external storage**    Storage outside of the CPU, such as disk and tape.

**EXTRA!**    Terminal emulation software from Attachmate Corporation, Bellevue, WA. It is used with 3270 and 5250 emulators to gain access to a mainframe or mini from a personal computer. Versions for Windows and Mac are available.

**Extract**    To decompress. WinZip and other decompression utilities use the term to mean "pulling out" the original files from the compressed archive. See *WinZip* and *data compression*.

**extraction, transformation and loading**    See *ETL*.

**extranet**    A Web site for customers rather than the general public. It can provide access to research, current inventories and internal databases, virtually any information that is private and not published for everyone. An extranet uses the public Internet as its transmission system, but requires passwords to gain entrance. Access to the site may be free or require payment for some or all of the services offered. See *EDI*.

**extremely low frequency**    See *low radiation*.

**eyeball driven**    Refers to a business strategy that is based on obtaining the highest number of visitors to its Web site.

**eyeball hang time**    The length of time a visitor remains on a Web site. See *sticky* and *eyeballs*.

**eyeballs**    The number of users. "There are 110 eyeballs" means there are 110 users currently online. See *eyeball hang time*.

**eye candy**    Images and animated graphics added to Web sites and interactive software that makes the information exciting. In other words, glitz, sizzle and pizzazz. See **cornea gumbo**.

**eZ80**    An 8-bit microprocessor from Zilog that is four times as fast as the Z80. Introduced in 2000, the eZ80 is suited for Internet appliances, PDAs and games and can address up to 16MB of memory. See *Z80*.

**e-zine**    (Electronic magaZINE) A magazine or newsletter published online. See *Webzine*.

**f**   See *farad* and *femto*.

**F1 key**   Function key number one. There are 12 function keys on a PC keyboard. F1 is used for retrieving help in Windows and in most DOS applications.

**F2F**   Digispeak for "face-to-face." For example, "let's meet and work it out F2F."

**fab**   A manufacturing plant that makes semiconductor devices. Be the first on your block to start making chips. All it takes is a couple of billion dollars to build a state-of-the-art facility.

**fabless**   (FABricationLESS) A semiconductor vendor that does not have inhouse manufacturing facilities. Although it designs and tests the chips, it relies on external foundries for their actual fabrication. See *foundry*.

**fabric**   See *switch fabric*.

**Fabry-Perot**   An optical structure containing a pair of mirrors at opposite ends of a cavity. Light reflects back and forth between the mirrors, and one or both transmit a fraction of the resonant frequency. The resonance is created by making the distance of one round trip between mirrors equal to an integral number of wavelengths of the cavity material. Optically speaking, this is an interferometer, because it relies on the interference of light for its operation. A Fabry-Perot device becomes a light generator when a laser medium is used in the cavity, otherwise it is a passive filter. See **distributed feedback laser** and *etalon*.

**FaceLift**   A font scaler for Windows and WordPerfect from Bitstream Inc., Cambridge, MA (www.bitstream.com), that provides on-the-fly font scaling for Bitstream's own Speedo fonts. FaceLift for Windows also supports Type 1 fonts. FaceLift for WordPerfect lets users create a wide variety of custom fonts, including outlines, shadows and fill scaling, for the DOS version of WordPerfect.

**face recognition**   The ability to recognize people by their facial characteristics. The most successful methods use neural networks that learn from their experience and can distinguish the same person with different appearances, such as with and without glasses, changing hair styles and seasonal skin color. See *security*.

**facilities**   A general term for equipment including hardware, software and personnel. It typically refers to equipment in the telecommunications industry and may also include the building or office containing it.

**facilities management**   The management of a user's computer installation by an outside organization. All operations including systems, programming and the datacenter can be performed by the facilities management organization on the user's premises.

**facility area map level**   A map definition level of a virtual map. It describes the street, water, sewer, gas, electric, phone and cable networks together with the cumulated structures developed to meet the needs of the people within the land area. The facility area data files describe and define the street network and street facilities of the area with locational coordinates associated with the facilities and supplemental identifiers. The facility definition (street network), when related to spatial display, uses a base geography area definition.

A GIS provides a framework for data manipulation and display of map data especially for (a) location verification, (b) location correlation, (c) locational relationships. (d) district coding, (e) route analysis, (f) area analysis and (g) mapping/display creation. (Data West Research Agency definition: see *GIS glossary*.)

**facsimile**   See *fax*.

**factorial**   The number of sequences that can exist with a set of items, derived by multiplying the number of items by the next lowest number until 1 is reached. For example, three items have six sequences ($3\times2\times1=6$): 123, 132, 231, 213, 312 and 321.

**failover**   Maintaining an up-to-date copy of a database on an alternative computer system for backup. The alternative system takes over if the primary system becomes unusable. See *replication*.

**fail safe**   Same as *fault tolerant*.

**fail soft**   The ability to fail with minimum destruction. For example, a disk drive can be built to automatically park the heads when power fails. Although it doesn't correct the problem, it minimizes destruction.

**failure horizon**   A future time in which a failure is anticipated. Failure horizons were widely projected for each potential Y2K problem.

**fallback/fall forward**   Features in a modem that allow it to negotiate a lower or higher speed with the other modem as line conditions change.

**fallback system**   Any system of hardware and/or software maintained as a backup to the main system. If a failure occurs in the primary system, the fallback system takes over.

**false drops**   Search results that meet your search criteria but have nothing to do with the information you were trying to find. For example, you want biographical details about Grover Cleveland, but you get information about Cleveland, Ohio. See *full-text search*.

**FAMOS**   (Floating gate Avalanche-injection Metal Oxide Semiconductor)  A type of EPROM.

**fan**   A device that uses motor-driven blades to circulate the air in a computer or other electronic system. Today's CPUs run extremely hot, and large computer cabinets use two and three fans to reduce temperature. See *FanCard*.

**FanCard**   An expansion card for PCs and Macs from T. S. Microtech, Inc., Torrance, CA, that contains twin, counter-rotating fans to reduce heat in a fully-loaded computer.

**fan-fold paper**   Same as *continuous forms*.

**fan in**   To direct multiple signals into one receiver.

**fan out**   To direct one signal into multiple receivers. See *port multiplier*.

**FAQ**   (Frequently Asked Questions)  A group of commonly asked questions about a subject, along with the answers. Vendors may use them to augment the description of their products. FAQs are very popular on the Internet.

**FAQ file**   A text file that contains a number of frequently asked questions and their answers. See *FAQ*.

**farad**    A unit of electrical charge that is used to measure the storage capacity of a capacitor. In microelectronics, measurements are usually in microfarads or picofarads.

**far pointer**    In an Intel x86 segmented address, a memory address that includes both segment and offset. Contrast with *near pointer*.

**Fasgrolia**    (FASt GROwing Language of Initialisms and Acronyms)    The jargon, acronyms and digispeak of the high-tech age. From "Mrs. Byrne's Dictionary of Unusual, Obscure, and Preposterous Words." See *digispeak*.

**Fast**    An asynchronous communications protocol used to quickly transmit files over high-quality lines. Error checking is done after the entire file has been transmitted.

**Fast ATA**    The higher transfer rates used by the EIDE (Enhanced IDE) hardware interface. See *EIDE* and *IDE*.

**FastCAD**    Full-featured CAD program for Windows and DOS from Evolution Computing, Tempe, AZ (www.fastcad.com), that is known for its well-designed user interface. It requires a math coprocessor. Users with less sophisticated requirements can start out with FastCAD's baby brother, EasyCAD.

**FastCGI**    An extension to CGI from Open Market that improves performance by maintaining persistent connections. Regular CGI exits after each request is completed, but FastCGI keeps the connection open and waits for the next request. See *CGI script*.

**FastDisk**    A Windows 3.1 driver that speeds up disk accesses by running in 32-bit mode, bypassing DOS and the BIOS and communicating directly with the disk controller. It works on Western Digital and compatible controllers or on other controllers with upgraded drivers from the manufacturer. To turn this feature on and off, select 386 Enhanced in Control Panel; then click Virtual Memory, Change, Use 32-Bit Disk Access. See *WinDisk*.

**Fast Ethernet**    See *100BaseT*.

**Fast Fourier Transform**    See *FFT*.

**Fast IP**    An IP switching technique from 3Com. The originating machine sends the first packet to the router, which forwards it to its destination. The destination machine sends back a response using the sender's layer 2 address. If the sending machine receives the response, it knows there is a direct connection without going through the router and forwards the remaining packets via layer 2. Fast IP uses a modified version of the NHRP protocol.

**fast page mode**    See *page mode memory*.

**Fast SCSI**    A SCSI interface that transfers at 10 Mbytes/sec rather than 5 Mbytes/sec. The maximum cable length is 9.8 feet. See *SCSI*.

**FastSite**    A Web site develpment program from Lotus that converts batches of documents into HTML pages. Running under Windows, it is part of the SmartSuite Millennium Edition and is also available separately. It is not a full-blown Web authoring program, but allows for quick development of a Web site from existing files.

**FAT**    (File Allocation Table)    The part of the DOS, Windows and OS/2 file system that keeps track of where data is stored on disk. When the disk is high-level formatted, the FAT is recorded twice and contains a table with an entry for each disk cluster.

The directory list, which contains file name, extension, date, etc., points to the FAT entry where the file starts. If a file is larger than one cluster, the first FAT entry points to the next FAT entry where the second cluster of the file is stored and so on to the end of the file. If a

| | |
|---|---|
| Cluster 0 | Cluster 2 |
| Cluster 1 | Cluster 4 |
| Cluster 2 | Cluster 3 |
| Cluster 3 | Cluster 7 |
| Cluster 4 | Cluster 8 |
| Cluster 5 | Damaged |
| Cluster 6 | Damaged |
| Cluster 7 | End |
| Cluster 8 | Cluster 9 |
| Cluster 9 | End |

RESUME.DOC
BUDGET.XLS

**The FAT Table**
The file RESUME.DOC is stored in clusters 0, 2, 3 and 7. The directory entry points to cluster 0 where the file begins. The entry for cluster 0 points to cluster 2 and so on. BUDGET.XLS is stored in clusters 1, 4, 8 and 9.

cluster becomes damaged, its FAT entry is marked as such and that cluster is not used again. The original 16-bit version of the FAT, which is widely used, is limited to 2GB hard drives. The 32-bit version (FAT32) became available with Windows 95 in late 1996 and increases the limit to 2TB. See *VFAT* and *FAT32*.

**FAT16**     Refers to the original FAT after FAT32 was introduced. See *FAT* and *FAT32*.

**FAT32**     The 32-bit version of the file allocation table (FAT) that was added to Windows 95 starting with OEM Service Release 2 (OSR2) in 1996. This version is only installed by PC vendors. FAT32 supports hard disks up to 2TB instead of 2GB. It is able to relocate the root directory on the disk and use the backup copy of the FAT table, providing more safeguards in the event of disk failure. It also reduces cluster waste. On drives up to 8GB, cluster size was reduced from 32K to 4K. See *cluster*.

**fatal error**     A condition that halts processing due to faulty hardware, program bugs, read errors or other anomalies. If you get a fatal error, you usually cannot recover from it. The computer typically locks up, and all data that you have changed that has not yet been saved to disk is lost.

There is no rule of thumb with fatal errors. You may never get one again, or it may manifest until you fix the problem. If you get a fatal error after just adding a new peripheral or installing a new software package, remove or uninstall it and try again.

**fatal exception**     See *fatal error*.

**fat binary**     A Macintosh executable program that contains machine language in one file for both the Macintosh and PowerMac machines (680x0 and PowerPC CPUs). Software distributed in this format will run native on whichever Mac architecture it is loaded on.

**FatBits**     A MacPaint option in the "Goodies" menu that lets a user edit an image a pixel at a time. Any paint or image editing program that lets you zoom down to a single pixel is providing a similar mode of editing.

**fat client**     A client machine in a client/server environment that performs most or all of the application processing with little or none performed in the server. Contrast with *thin client* and *fat server*. See *two-tier client/server*.

**fat finger**     Refers to accidentally pressing the wrong key on a keyboard and entering an erroneous command that causes a serious problem. The term harks back to the very early days when computers were instructed to perform operations by flipping switches on the console.

**father file**     See *grandfather-father-son*.

**fat pipe**     A high-speed communications channel. Contrast with *thin pipe*.

**fat server**     A server in a client/server environment that performs most or all of the application processing with little or none performed in the client. The counterpart to a fat server is a thin client. Contrast with *fat client*. See *two-tier client/server*.

**fault**     An error. A software fault is when the program directs the computer to go outside of its restricted memory boundary (see *abend*). A hardware fault is a failure in one of the circuits (see *fault management*). See also *page fault*.

**fault management**     The monitoring of error indications in a computer system in order to log the occurrences and send alerts to system administrators and field service. Fault management software keeps track of hardware faults such as memory parity errors (see *ECC memory*) and software crashes. The proper analysis of the

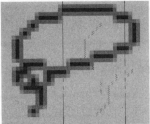

**The Lasso's Fat Bits**
This view zooms in on the lasso button, which is displayed in its normal size in the entry *lasso* in this database. At this depth, you can edit one pixel at a time.

**A Fat Client**

frequency and type of such errors is intended to initiate a repair order before a total breakdown occurs. See *fault* and *fault tolerant*.

**fault resilient**    See *high availability*.

**fault tolerant**    The ability to continue non-stop when a hardware failure occurs. A fault-tolerant system is designed from the ground up for reliability by building multiples of all critical components, such as CPUs, memories, disks and power supplies into the same computer. In the event one component fails, another takes over without skipping a beat.

Many systems are designed to recover from a failure by detecting the failed component and switching to another computer system. These systems, although sometimes called fault tolerant, are more widely known as "high availability" systems, requiring that the software resubmits the job when the second system is available.

True fault tolerant systems are the most costly, because redundant hardware is wasted if there is no failure in the system. On the other hand, fault-tolerant systems provide the same processing capacity after a failure as before, whereas high-availability systems often provide reduced capacity.

Tandem and Stratus are two major manufacturers of fault-tolerant computer systems for the transaction processing (OLTP) market. Stratus computers are used by long distance carriers for 800 routing and other out-of-band services. See *fault management*.

**A RAID Array**
This RAID II prototype in 1992, which embodies principles of high performance and fault tolerance, was designed and built by University of Berkeley graduate students. Housing 36 320MB disk drives, its total storage was less than the disk drive in the cheapest PC only six years later. *(Image courtesy of The Computer Museum History Center, www.computerhistory.org)* See *RAID*.

**Favorites**    Another term for bookmarks, which was popularized by Microsoft's Internet Explorer browser. See *Microsoft Internet Explorer*.

**fax**    (FACSimile) Originally called "telecopying," it is the communication of a printed page between remote locations. Fax machines scan a paper form and transmit a coded image over the telephone system. The receiving machine prints a facsimile of the original. A fax machine is made up of a scanner, printer and modem with fax signaling.

Fax standards were developed starting in 1968 and are classified by Groups. Groups 1 and 2, used until the late 1980s, transmitted a page in six and three minutes respectively. Group 3 transmits at less than one minute per page and uses data compression at 9,600 bps. The Group 3 speed increase led to the extraordinary rise in usage in the late 1980s. Group 3 resolution is 203×98 dpi in standard mode, 203×196 in fine mode and 203×392 in super fine mode.

Group 3 is still the standard today, but Group 4 machines can transmit a page in just a few seconds and provide up to 400×400 resolution. Group 4 requires 56–64 Kbps bandwidth and needs ISDN or Switched 56 circuits. See *fax/modem* and *e-mail*.

**fax board**    Fax capability built onto a printed circuit board. Today, most fax boards are fax/modems, which also provide data transmission. See *fax/modem*.

**fax logging**    Automatically storing copies of incoming and outgoing faxes onto some storage medium.

**fax/modem**    A combination fax board and data modem available as an external unit that plugs into the serial port of the computer or as an expansion board for internal installation. It includes a switch that routes the call to the fax or data modem. Incoming faxes are printed on the computer's printer. Most all modems today are fax/modems.

A fax/modem requires software that generates the fax transmission from typed-in text, a disk file or from a screen image. Fax/modems often transmit a sharper image than a fax machine, which obtains its source material by scanning the page.

Group 3 fax/modems provide various levels of processing based upon their service class. Class 1 devices perform basic handshaking and data conversion and are the most flexible, because much of the work is done by the computer's CPU. Class 2 devices establish and end the call and perform error checking. There are a variety of de facto Class 2 implementations and one Class 2.0 standard. As PCs have become more powerful, future service classes with more features are unlikely.

**fax server**   A computer in a network that provides a bank of fax/modems, allowing users to fax out and remote users to fax in over the next available modem. The fax server may be a dedicated machine or implemented on a file server that is providing other services.

**fax switch**   A device that tests a phone line for a fax signal and routes the call to the fax machine. When a fax machine dials a number and the line answers, it emits an 1100Hz signal (CNG tone) to identify itself. Some devices handle voice, fax and data modem switching and may require keying in an extension number to switch to the modem. See *CNG tone*.

**FBC**   See *fully buzzword compliant*.

**FC**   See *Fibre Channel*.

**FC-AL**   (Fibre Channel-Arbitrated Loop) See *Fibre Channel*.

**FCB**   See *DOS FCB*.

**FCC**   (Federal Communications Commission, Washington, DC, www.fcc.gov) The U.S. government agency that regulates interstate and international communications including wire, cable, radio, TV and satellite. The FCC was created under the U.S. Communications Act of 1934, and its board of commissioners is appointed by the President of the United States.

**FCC Class**   An FCC certification of radiation limits on digital devices. Class A certification is for business use. Class B, for residential use, is more stringent in order to avoid interference with TV and other home reception. See Part 15, Subpart B, of the Federal Register (CFR 47, Parts 0–19).

**FC connector**   A fiber-optic cable connector that uses a threaded plug and socket. For bi-directional transmission, two fiber cables and two FC connectors are generally used. FC is specified by the TIA as FOCIS-4. See *fiber-optic connectors* and *FOCIS*.

**FCFS**   First come, first served.

**fci**   (Flux Changes per Inch) The measurement of polarity reversals on a magnetic surface. In MFM, each flux change is equal to one bit. In RLL, a flux change generates more than one bit.

**FCIF**   See *CIF*.

**F connector**   A two-wire (signal and ground) coaxial cable connector used to connect antennas, TVs and VCRs. F connector cables typically carry NTSC TV signals (audio and video). The plug's shell and socket are threaded. See *A/V ports* and *plugs and sockets*.

**F Connector**
F connectors are commonly used for antennas and other cable TV hookups.

**FCP**   (Fibre Channel Protocol) See *Fibre Channel*.

**FD**   (Floppy Disk) For example, FD/HD refers to a floppy disk/hard disk device.

**FDD**   (1) Abbreviation for Floppy Disk Drive.
   (2) (Frequency Division Duplexing) A transmission method that separates the transmitting and receiving channels with a guard band (some amount of spectrum that acts as a buffer or insulator). Contrast with *TDD*.

**FDDI**   (Fiber Distributed Data Interface) Often pronounced "fiddy," it is a LAN and MAN access method that had its heyday in the mid 1990s. It is an ANSI standard token passing network that uses optical fiber cabling and transmits at 100 Mbits/sec up to 10 kilometers. FDDI provides network services at the same level as Ethernet and Token Ring (OSI layers 1 and 2).

FDDI includes its own Station Management (STM) network management standard. The TP-PMD (CDDI) version runs over copper (UTP), although typically limited to distances up to 100 meters.

FDDI provides an optional dual counter-rotating ring topology that contains primary and secondary rings with data flowing in opposite directions. If the line breaks, the ends of the primary and secondary rings are bridged together at the closest node to create a single ring again.

SAS or DAS    Stations can be configured as Single Attached Stations (SAS) connected to concentrators, or as Dual Attached Stations (DAS), connected to both rings. Groups of stations are typically wired to concentrators connected in a hierarchical tree to the main ring. Large networks may be configured as a "dual ring of trees," in which the dual ring provides the backbone to which multiple hierarchies of concentrators are attached.

FDDI II adds circuit-switched service to this normally packet-switched technology in order to support isochronous traffic such as realtime voice and video.

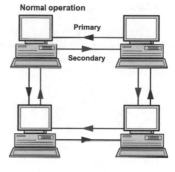

**Normal operation**

**FDISK**    A DOS and Windows utility that is used to partition a hard disk, which is necessary before high-level formatting. See *DOS Format*.

**MIC Connector**
FDDI uses a dual-fiber MIC plug and socket for connection to devices.

**FDIV bug**    (Floating Point **DIV**ision bug) A flaw in early Pentium chips that, in certain cases, caused an erroneous result from the FDIV floating point division instruction. It surfaced in late 1994, and Intel eventually initiated a replacement program for all users of the chip.

**FDM**    (Frequency Division Multiplexing) A technology that transmits multiple signals simultaneously over a single transmission path, such as a cable or wireless system. Each signal travels within its own unique frequency range (carrier), which is modulated by the data (text, voice, video, etc.).

In the 1930s, the telephone companies began to combine multiple analog voice signals over one line using FDM. This was later replaced with digital methods (see *channel bank*). For years, cable TV companies have used FDM to transmit many channels over the same wire. The set-top box or TV tuner locks onto a particular frequency (channel) and filters out the video signal for the TV screen. Contrast with *TDM*. See *circuit switching* and *WDM*.

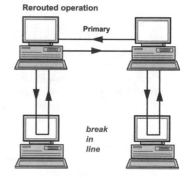

**Rerouted operation**

break
in
line

**FDMA**    (Frequency Division Multiple Access) The technology used in the analog cellular telephone network that divides the spectrum into 30 kHz channels. See *TDMA*, *CDMA* and *CDPD*.

**FD:OCA**    (Formatted Data:Object Content Architecture) An SAA-compliant (CCS) specification for formatting data in fields.

**FDSE**    (Full-Duplex Switched Ethernet) See *full-duplex Ethernet*.

**FDX**    See *full-duplex*.

**FEA**    (Finite Element Analysis) A mathematical technique for analyzing stress, which breaks down a physical structure into substructures called "finite elements." The finite elements and their interrelationships are converted into equation form and solved mathematically.

Graphics-based FEA software can display the model on screen as it is being built and, after analysis, display the object's reactions under load conditions. Models created in popular CAD packages can often be accepted by FEA software. See *automatic design optimization*.

**feasibility study**    The analysis of a problem to determine if it can be solved effectively. The operational (will it work?), economical (costs and benefits) and technical (can it be built?) aspects are part of the study. Results of the study determine whether the solution should be implemented.

**feature connector**    See *VGA feature connector*.

**feature creep**    The continual adding of new functions to an information system while it is in the process of being programmed. Feature creep adds considerable cost to new projects.

**feature negotiation**    See *automatic feature negotiation*.

**feature size**    The size of the elements within a transistor or other electronic device on a chip. The smallest feature size is generally smaller than the number quoted for the manufacturing process. For example, a .18 process might have features as tiny as .13 micron or less.

**FEC**    See *forward error correction*.

**FECN**    (Forward Explicit Congestion Notification) A frame relay message that notifies the receiving device that there is a congestion problem.

**FED**    (Field Emission Display) A flat panel display that provides an image quality equal to or better than a CRT. FED displays provide wide viewing angles and can survive in very harsh temperature environments. Their ultra-fast switching speeds also enables them to support full-motion video.

FEDs are like a thin CRT, using a vacuum-filled chamber and phosphor-coated glass. However, instead of illuminating phosphors with three "guns" that scan the entire screen, FEDs use hundreds of millions of stationary cone-shaped emitters, with some 1,600 of them per pixel. Some FED designs use low voltage emission and high current while others use high voltage and low current, which is more like a standard CRT.

Although FED was invented in the 1970s, it took more than 20 years to realize it. With more than 300 patents on the technology, PixTech is the pioneer in this field with 5" monochrome displays in production in 1998 and 8" mono and color units in 1999. Larger sizes are expected in the future.

**Federal Communications Commission**
See *FCC*.

**federal regulations**    See *NCSC* and *Computer Security Act*.

**feed drive**    A type of drive that grabs the media after it is partially inserted into the slot. All automobile CD players as well as CD-ROM drives in various Macintosh models are feed drives. Contrast with *tray drive* and *caddy drive*. See *custom-cut CD*.

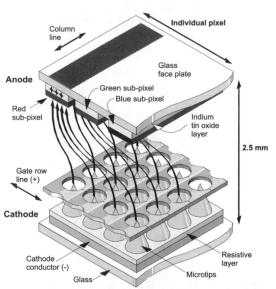

**The FED Technology**
This illustration, which is somewhat conceptual, shows how the energy flows from the microtips to the phosphors (anode). Electrons from the negatively-charged (–) cone column are emitted when the gate row is positively charged (+). The electrons then flow to the phosphors that are momentarily given a larger positive charge (+++), which, in this diagram, are the red ones. The pixels are addressed 180 times per second, providing a very high refresh rate. *(Redrawn from illustration courtesy of PixTech.)*

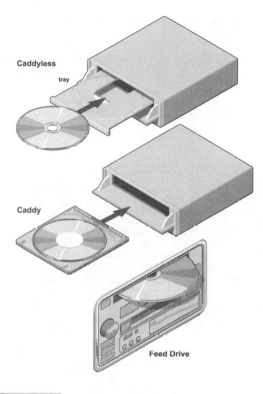

Caddyless

tray

Caddy

**Feed Drive**

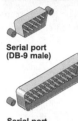

## Serial & Parallel Ports on a PC

**Serial port
(DB-9 male)**

**Serial port
(DB-25 male)**

**Parallel port
(DB-25 female)**

A PC usually comes with two serial ports (COM1, COM2) and one parallel port (LPT1).

On the back of the PC, the serial ports are either two male DB-9 connectors or one DB-9 and one DB-25. The parallel port is a DB-25 female connector.

**feeware**    Commercial software that is sold. Contrast with *freeware*.

**female connector**    A plug or socket that contains receptacles. The male counterpart contains pins.

**femto**    Quadrillionth (10 to the –15th power). See *space/time*.

**femtosecond**    One quadrillionth of a second. See *space/time* and *ohnosecond*.

**FEP**    See *front end processor*.

**Ferranti Mark I**    See *BABY*.

**ferric**    See *ferrous*.

**ferric oxide**    (Fe$_2$O$_3$)  An oxidation of iron used in the coating of magnetic disks and tapes.

**ferromagnetic**    The capability of a material, such as iron and nickel, to be highly magnetized. See *FRAM*.

**ferromagnetic RAM**    See *FRAM*.

**ferrous**    Containing or having to do with iron. The difference between ferrous and ferric is the number of valence electrons they contain (ferrous contains two and ferric contains three), which combine with other atoms to form molecules.

**ferrule**    A ceramic, plastic or stainless steel part of a fiber-optic connector that holds the end of the fiber and precisely aligns it. The fiber is inserted into the ferrule and cemented with an epoxy or adhesive, which gives it long-term mechanical strength and

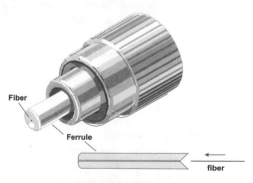

Fiber

Ferrule

fiber

**Fiber-Optic Ferrule**
At a quick glance, you won't see the opening for the optical fiber, because it's so tiny. But if you look at the end of the ferrule assembly under a magnifying glass, you will see it. The epoxy or adhesive is squeezed into the ferrule before the fiber is inserted (bottom right).

prevents contamination from the weather. Connectors are also available with ferrules that are crimped and do not require cement. See *fiber optics glossary*.

**FET**   (Field Effect Transistor) The type of transistor used in CMOS and other types of MOS circuits. The transistor works by pulsing a line called the "gate," which allows current to flow from the "source" to the "drain," or vice versa depending on the design.

**fetch**   To locate the next instruction in memory for execution by the CPU.

**FF**   See *form feed*.

**FFS**   (Flash File System) See *flash memory*.

**FFT**   (Fast Fourier Transform) A class of algorithms used in digital signal processing that break down complex signals into elementary components.

**FHSS**   (Frequency Hopping Spread Spectrum) See *spread spectrum*.

**fiber Bragg grating**   A short length of optical fiber that filters out a particular wavelength. Periodically spaced zones in the fiber core are altered to have different refractive indexes slightly higher than the core. This structure selectively reflects a very narrow range of wavelengths while transmitting others. Fiber Bragg gratings are used to stabilize the output of a laser and to filter out wavelengths in a WDM system.

The name comes from Braggs Law, which is used to create the spacing of the changes. Sir William Lawrence Bragg, noted British physicist (1890–1971) discovered this in his study of x-rays and crystal structures. See *diffraction grating* and *WDM*.

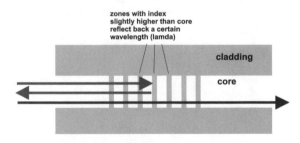

**A Fiber Bragg Grating**
Fiber Bragg gratings such as this one from JDS Uniphase can be customized for a variety of applications covering a range of wavelength bands from 850 to 1650 nm.

**The Gratings Reflect**
In the above example, the red wavelength matches the grating period and is reflected. The blue wavelength is transmitted because it does not match the grating spacings. *(Illustration assistance courtesy of Jeff Hecht.)*

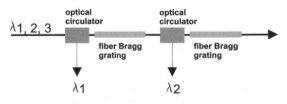

**Optical Circulators**
Since the desired wavelength is reflected back by the grating, another device known as an "optical circulator" detects and switches it. *(Illustration courtesy of Jeff Hecht.)*

**fiber bundle**    (1) A set of adjacent optical fibers running in parallel and adhered together. It is used for transmitting light to brighten an area, as well as whole images, but not for digital communications.

(2) A collection of optical fibers.

**Fiber Channel**    See *Fibre Channel*.

**fiber cut**    An accidental break in an optical fiber, typically due to new construction in the area. The telcos that laid the first fiber are more subject to fiber cuts than the subsequent carriers such as Qwest and Level 3. The newer companies have placed their cables into gas pipelines and other conduits that cannot be easily damaged.

**Fiber Distributed Data Interface**    See *FDDI*.

**fiber exhaust**    Running out of transmission capacity in an optical fiber. See *WDM*.

**Fiber Jack**    A duplex fiber-optic connector standardized by the TIA (FOCIS-6). It allows two fibers to mate in a snap-lock type of plug and socket similar in size and convenience to an RJ-45 connector. See *Opti-Jack*.

**fiber laser**    A laser that is constructed within an optical fiber. It is similar in concept to gas lasers and laser diodes, except that a part of the fiber itself is used as the resonating cavity where the laser action takes place. A laser diode is used as a pump, and mirrors accept the pump wavelength on one side and transmit the lased wavelength on the other.

**fiber loss**    The amount of attenuation of signal in an optical fiber transmission.

**fiber-optic**    Refers to concepts and materials that deal with fiber optics.

**fiber-optic connectors**    There are numerous types of plugs and sockets to connect optical fibers, using threaded, bayonet, push-pull and snap-lock connections. The first fiber-optic connector to be standardized was SMA, which were followed by the SC, ST and FC types. Since most optical transmissions require two cables (one to transmit and the other to receive), smaller form factors such as the snap-lock Fiber Jack are increasingly being developed to make installations as simple as plugging in a telephone.

Attaching a connector to an optical fiber takes more work than copper wire connectors (note the several steps in the following illustrations). The ends of the fiber usually have to be carefully cemented and then polished in order to let the maximum light pass through. Most class time on the subject is "hands on." See *mechanical splice* and *fusion splice*.

**fiber optics**    Communications systems that use optical fibers for transmission. Fiber-optic transmission became widely used in the 1980s when the long-distance carriers created nationwide systems for carrying voice conversations digitally over optical fibers.

Eventually, all transmission systems may become fiber optic-based. Also, in time, the internals of computers may be partially or even fully made of light circuits rather than electrical circuits. See *fiber optics glossary*, *FDDI*, *Fibre Channel* and *optical fiber*.

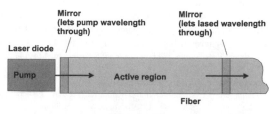

**Fiber Laser**
A fiber laser uses part of the fiber itself to generate the laser light and eliminates coupling problems with external LEDs and laser diodes.

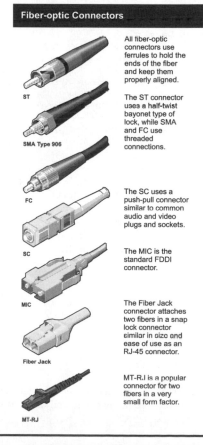

**Fiber-optic Connectors**

ST

SMA Type 906

FC

SC

MIC

Fiber Jack

MT-RJ

All fiber-optic connectors use ferrules to hold the ends of the fiber and keep them properly aligned.

The ST connector uses a half-twist bayonet type of lock, while SMA and FC use threaded connections.

The SC uses a push-pull connector similar to common audio and video plugs and sockets.

The MIC is the standard FDDI connector.

The Fiber Jack connector attaches two fibers in a snap lock connector similar in size and ease of use as an RJ-45 connector.

MT-RJ is a popular connector for two fibers in a very small form factor.

**Fibonacci numbers**   A series of whole numbers in which each number is the sum of the two preceding ones: 1, 1, 2, 3, 5, 8, 13, etc. It is used to speed up binary searches by dividing the search into the two lower numbers; for example, 13 items would be divided into 5 and 8 items; 8 items would be divided into 5 and 3.

**Fibre Channel**   A high-speed transport technology used to build storage area networks (SANs). Although Fibre Channel can be used as a general-purpose network carrying ATM, IP and other protocols, it has been primarily used for transporting SCSI traffic from servers to disk arrays. The Fibre Channel Protocol (FCP) serializes SCSI commands into Fibre Channel frames. IP, however, is used for in-band SNMP network management. Fibre Channel not only supports singlemode and multimode fiber connections, but coaxial cable and twisted pair as well.

Fibre Channel can be configured point-to-point, via a switched topology or in an arbitrated loop (FC-AL) with or without a hub, which can connect up to 127 nodes (see below). It supports transmission rates up to 2.12 Gbps in each direction, and 4.25 Gbps is expected. Fibre Channel uses the Gigabit Ethernet physical layer and IBM's 8B/10B encoding method, where each byte is transmitted as 10 bits. Fibre Channel provides both connection-oriented and connectionless services. Following are the class and functional levels of the architecture. See *IP storage*.

```
Connection-Oriented Services
Class 1    With acknowledgment, full bandwidth
Class 4    Virtual connections, QoS,
              fractional bandwidth
Class 6    Uni-directional

Connectionless Services
Class 2    With acknowledgment
Class 3    Without acknowledgment

Node Levels
FC-4    Translation between Fibre Channel and
           command sets that use it: HiPPI, SCSI, IPI,
           SBCCS, IP, IEEE 802.2, audio, video
FC-3    Common services across multiple ports

Port Levels (FC-PH Standard)
FC-2    Framing and flow control
FC-1    8B/10B encoding, error detection
FC-0    Electrical and optical characteristics
```

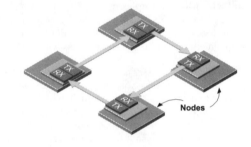

**Arbitrated Loop**
The arbitrated loop is widely used and can connect up to 127 nodes without using a switch. All devices share the bandwidth, and only two can communicate with each other at the same time, with each node repeating the data to its adjacent node. TX means transmit, and RX means receive.

**fiche**   Same as *microfiche*.

**FICON**   (FIber CONnector) An IBM mainframe channel introduced with its G5 servers in 1998. Based on the Fibre Channel standard, it boosts the transfer rate of ESCON's half-duplex 17MB/sec to a full-duplex 100MB/sec. Each FICON channel can support up to 4,000 I/O operations per second and is equivalent to eight ESCON channels. See *ESCON* and *Parallel Enterprise Server*.

**Point-to-Point**
This is the simplest topology connecting two Fibre Channel devices that communicate at full bandwidth.

**Switch Fabric**
A switch fabric is the most flexible topology, enabling all servers and storage devices to communicate with each other. It also provides for a failover architecture in the event a server or disk array ceases to operate.

**fiddy**   See *FDDI*.

**FidoNet**   An e-mail system developed in 1984 by Tom Jennings, creator of the Fido BBS. It was the first popular method of providing e-mail and file transfer across multiple BBSs. FidoNet, as well as all BBS use, has declined dramatically in the U.S., but FidoNet has also grown in other countries. Today, there are more than 25,000 FidoNet nodes in use around the world, many of which are used to provide an e-mail connection to the Internet.

**field**    A physical unit of data that is one or more bytes in size. A collection of fields make up a record. A field also defines a unit of data on a source document, screen or report. Examples of fields are NAME, ADDRESS, QUANTITY and AMOUNT DUE.

The field is the common denominator between the user and the computer. When you interactively query and update your database, you reference your data by field name.

There are several terms that refer to the same unit of storage as a field. A *data element* is the logical definition of the field, and a *data item* is the actual data stored in the field. For each data element, there are many fields in the database that hold the data items.

**field effect transistor**    See *FET*.

**field engineer**    A person who is responsible for hardware installation, maintenance and repair. Formal training is in electronics, although many people have learned on the job.

**field name**    An assigned name for a field (NAME, ADDRESS, CITY, STATE, etc.) that will be the same in every record.

**field separator**    A character used to mark the separation of fields in a record. See *comma delimited* and *tab delimited*.

**field service**    The maintenance and repair of equipment at the customer's location. See *field engineer*.

**field squeeze**    In a mail merge, a function that eliminates extra blank spaces between words when fixed-length fields are inserted into the document text. See *line squeeze*.

**field template**    See *picture*.

**Fiery engine**    A raster image processor (RIP) from Electronics for Imaging, Inc., San Mateo, CA (www.efi.com), that is noted for its high quality color processing and speed. Since 1991, the Fiery Color Server, which is a combination of hardware and software, has been used to transform digital color copiers into color printers. Toward the end of the 1990s, the Fiery components were added to lower-cost color devices such as laser printers and wide format ink jet printers.

**FIF**    (Fractal Image Format) A graphics file format from Iterated Systems, Inc., Norcross, GA (www.iterated.com), that stores fractal images with compression ratios as high as 2,500:1. See *fractals*.

**FIFO**    (First In/First Out) A storage method that retrieves the item stored for the longest time. Contrast with *LIFO*.

**fifth-generation computer**    A computer designed for AI applications. Appearing after the turn of the century, these systems will represent the next technology leap.

**FIGS**    (1) (French, Italian, German, Spanish) The major European languages. This acronym is commonly found in localization circles. See *localization*.

(2) (figs.) Abbreviation of figures; for example, "this process is explained in figs. 3 and 4."

**file**    A collection of bytes stored as an individual entity. All data on disk is stored as a file with an assigned file name that is unique within the folder (directory) it resides in.

To the computer, a file is nothing more than a string of bytes. The structure of a file is known to the software that manipulates it. For example, database files are made up of a series of records. Word processing files contain a continuous flow of text.

**DATA ELEMENTS**

| Product description | Product number |
|---|---|
| FIELD | FIELD |

**DATA ITEMS**

| | |
|---|---|
| manilla folder | M004884 |
| pencil | P3883 |
| rubber band | RB45 |
| copy paper | CP2300 |
| paper clip | PC21-8 |
| envelope | E7600 |

**The Basic Unit of Storage**
Technically, data elements describe the logical unit of data, fields are the actual storage units, and data items are the individual instances of the data elements as in this example. In everyday language, all three terms are used interchangeably. It's only when you read technical documentation on database management that you run across the proper use of these terms.

Except for ASCII text files, which contain only raw text, other files have proprietary structures. Formatting and other types of information are contained in headers or interspersed throughout the file. Following are the major file types. See *file association*.

```
Type                     Contents
data file (table)        data records
document                 text
spreadsheet              rows and columns of cells
image                    rows and columns of bits
drawing                  list of vectors
audio                    digitized sound waves
MIDI                     MIDI instructions
video                    digital video frames
Web page                 text
batch file               text
source program           text
executable program       machine language
```

**File-AID**   A family of mainframe data management tools from Compuware. It lets programmers interactively manipulate databases and readily develop test data for new applications. See *Abend-AID* and *XPEDITER*.

**file and record locking**   A first-come, first-served technique for managing data in a multiuser environment. The first user to access the file or record prevents, or locks out, other users from accessing it. After the file or record is updated, it is unlocked and available. File and record locking is an essential part of every database management system (DBMS), document managment system and any other system that allows data to be updated by multiple users or applications. See also *lock down*.

**file association**   (1) The relationship between the file and the application that created it. In Windows, the association is made by the file extension, which are the last letters of the name preceded by a period, such as .DOC, .GIF and so forth. When a document is double-clicked, the extension identifies which application should be launched to open it.

If you click a file name and there is no association previously registered, the operating system will ask you to set up that relationship. You can also change those associations if you prefer to use a different application to open a text or graphics file, for example. See *Win File Association*.

(2) The relationship of one file to another based on the data it contains.

**file attachment**   See *e-mail attachment*.

**file attribute**   A file access classification that allows a file to be retrieved or erased. Typical attributes are read/write, read only, archive and hidden.

**file compression**   See *data compression*.

**file conversion**   See *conversion*.

**file extension**   See *extension* and *Win Show file extensions*.

**file extent**   See *extent*.

**file find**   A utility that searches all directories for matching file names. See *how to find a file*.

**file format**   The structure of a file. There are hundreds of proprietary formats for database, word processing and graphics files. See *native format, foreign format, graphics formats* and *record layout*.

**file grooming**   Cleaning the files on a computer system. It includes deleting temporary and backup files, as well as defragmenting the disk.

**file handle**    A temporary reference assigned by the operating system to a file that has been opened. The handle is used to access the file throughout the session.

**file handling**    Refers to working with files that are stored on the hard disk. See *file*, *file handle* and *disk management*.

**file layout**    Same as *record layout*.

**file maintenance**    (1) The periodic updating of master files. For example, adding/deleting employees and customers, making address changes and changing product prices. It does not refer to daily transaction processing and batch processing (order processing, billing, etc.).

(2) The periodic reorganization of the disk drives. Data that is continuously updated becomes physically fragmented over the disk space and requires regrouping. An optimizing program is run (daily, weekly, etc.) that rewrites all files contiguously.

**FileMaker**    (1) A database management system (DBMS) for the Macintosh and Windows NT from FileMaker. Originally a file manager from Claris Corporation, it has been a popular program for general data management. It provides a variety of statistical functions, fast search capabilities and extensive reporting features.

(2) (FileMaker, Inc., Santa Clara, CA, www.filemaker.com) A software subsidiary of Apple. Originally Claris Corporation, FileMaker was formed in 1998, retaining the FileMaker Pro line of database software and Claris Home Page for Web development.

**FileMan**    (1) Public-domain MUMPS software that provides a stand-alone, interactive DBMS, as well as a set of utilities for the MUMPS programmer.

(2) Nickname for Windows' file manager, which is precisely named "File Manager."

**file manager**    (1) Software used to manage files on a disk. It provides functions to delete, copy, move, rename and view files as well as create and manage directories. The file manager in Windows 3.x was appropriately named File Manager. In Windows 95/98, NT 4.0 and 2000, the file manager is known as Explorer. See ***Win Explorer***.

(2) Software that manages data files. Often erroneously called "database managers," file managers provide the ability to create, enter, change, query and produce reports on one file at a time. They have no relational capabilty and usually don't include a programming language.

**file name**    A name assigned by the user or programmer that is used to identify a file.

**FileNet**    A document imaging system from FileNet Corporation, Costa Mesa, CA (www.filenet.com). Introduced in 1985, FileNet is the most widely used high-end workflow system. It runs on PCs and a variety of UNIX workstations.

**File Not Found**    A DOS error message that means DOS cannot locate the file you have specified. Use the Dir command to check its spelling. It may be also be in another directory.

**file protection**    Preventing accidental erasing of data. Physical file protection is provided on the storage medium by turning a switch, moving a lever or covering a notch. Writing is prohibited even if the software directs the computer to do so. For example, on half-inch tape, a plastic ring in the center of the reel is removed (no ring-no write).

Logical file protection is provided by the operating system, which can designate files as read only. This allows both regular (read/write) and read only files to be stored on the same disk volume. Files can also be designated as hidden files, which makes them invisible to most software programs.

**If You're Holey, You're Protected!**
On a high-density 3.5" diskette, when both holes are showing, you are "protected."

**file protect ring**    A plastic ring inserted into a reel of magnetic tape for file protection.

**Filer**    A network attached storage (NAS) device. The term was coined by Network Appliance. See *NAS* and *NetApp Filer*.

**file recovery program**   Software that recovers disk files that have been accidentally deleted or damaged.

**file relationships**   See *file association*.

**file server**   A high-speed computer in a network that stores the programs and data files shared by users. It acts like a remote disk drive. The difference between a file server and an application server is that the file server stores the programs and data, while the application server runs the programs and processes the data. See *database server*.

**file sharing protocol**   A high-level network protocol that provides the structure and language for file requests between clients and servers. It provides the commands for opening, reading, writing and closing files across the network and may also provide access to the directory services. Sometimes called a "client/server protocol," it functions at the application layer (layer 7 of the OSI model).

In order for a client to have access to multiple servers running different operating systems, either the client supports the file sharing protocol of each operating system or the server supports the file sharing protocol of each client. Software that adds this capability is very common and allows interoperability between Windows, Macintosh, NetWare and UNIX platforms.

| Operating System | Transport Protocol | File Sharing Protocol |
|---|---|---|
| DOS | NetBIOS | SMB |
| Windows | NetBEUI | SMB, CIFS |
| NetWare | IPX | NCP |
| Macinotosh | AppleTalk | AFP |
| UNIX | TCP/IP | NFS |

**file size**   The length of a file in bytes. See "Byte Specifications" in the term *byte*.

**file spec**   (FILE SPECification)  A reference to the location of a file on a disk, which includes disk drive, directory name and file name. For example, in DOS, Windows and OS/2, **c:\wordstar\books\chapter** is a file spec for the file CHAPTER in the BOOKS subdirectory in the WORDSTAR directory on drive C.

**file system**   (1) A method for cataloging files in a computer system. HPS, FAT, FAT32, NTFS and HPFS are common file systems used on personal computers. See *hierarchical file system*.

(2) A data processing application that manages individual files. Files are related by customized programming. Contrast with *relational database*.

**file transfer program**   A program that transmits files from one computer to another such as Travelling Software's LapLink or the Direct Cable Connection utility that comes with Windows 95/98. The computers can be cabled together via the serial or parallel ports or be in different locations. See *FTP*, *null modem cable* and ***how to transfer a file***.

**file transfer protocol**   A communications protocol used to transmit files without loss of data. A file transfer protocol can handle all types of files including binary files and ASCII text files. Common examples are Xmodem, Ymodem, Zmodem and Kermit. See *FTP*.

**file type**   The kind of file. All computer files are categorized by their contents, such as program files, text files, image files and so on. See *file*, *extension* and ***Win File Association***.

**file viewer**   Software that displays the contents of a file as it would be normally displayed by the application that created it. A single file viewer program is generally capable of displaying a wide variety of document, database and spreadsheet formats. See *graphics viewer* and *document exchange software*.

**fill**   (1) In a graphics program, to apply color to a graphics objects such as a rectangle, circle or polygon. In a paint program, the fill function is depicted as a paint bucket icon. It is used to "paint" objects or the entire canvas.

(2) In a spreadsheet, to enter common or repetitive values into a group of cells.

**filler app**     A well-written application that performs reasonably well. Many filler apps are bundled with PCs and other software combos. Contrast with *killer app*.

**fill pattern**     **(1)** A color, shade or pattern used to fill an area of an image.

**(2)** Signals transmitted by a LAN station when not receiving or transmitting data in order to maintain synchronization.

**fill scaling**     The ability to change a fill pattern from light to dense. For example, if polka dots were used, the fill pattern could range from thick dots widely separated to very thin dots tightly packed together.

**film recorder**     A device that takes a 35mm slide picture from a graphics file, which has been created in a CAD, paint or business graphics package. It generates very high resolution, generally from 2,000–4,000 lines.

It typically works by recreating the image on a built-in CRT that shines through a color wheel onto the film in a standard 35mm camera. Some units provide optional Polaroid camera backs for instant previewing. Film recorders can be connected to personal computers by plugging in a controller board cabled to the recorder.

**filter**     **(1)** A process that changes data, such as a sort routine that changes the sequence of items or a conversion routine (import or export filter) that changes one data, text or graphics format into another. See also *image filter*.

**(2)** A pattern or mask through which only selected data is passed. For example, certain e-mail systems can be programmed to filter out important messages and alert the user. In dBASE, **set filter to file overdue** compares all data to the matching conditions stored in OVERDUE.

**financial planning language**     A language used to create data models and command a financial planning system.

**financial planning system**     Software that helps the user evaluate alternatives. It allows for the creation of a data model, which is a series of data elements in equation form; for example, **gross profit = gross sales – cost of goods sold**. Different values can be plugged into the elements, and the impact of various options can be assessed (what if?).

A financial planning system is a step above a spreadsheet by providing additional analysis tools; however, increasingly, these capabilities are being built into spreadsheets. For example, sensitivity analysis assigns a range of values to a data element, which causes that data to be highlighted if it ever exceeds that range.

Goal seeking provides automatic calculation. For example, by entering **gross margin = 50%** as well as the minimums and maximums of the various inputs, the program will calculate an optimum mix of inputs to achieve the goal (output).

**financial software**     A broad category of software that deals with accounting and monetary transactions. It includes payroll, accounts receivables and payables, general ledger, spreadsheets, financial planning, check writing and portfolio management.

**Finder**     The part of the Macintosh operating system that gives it the Mac "look and feel." It also provides file management (copy, delete, rename files) and control of the desktop icons, windows, Clipboard and Scrapbook, as well as the application startup interface. The Finder resides in the System folder. See *MultiFinder*.

**finger**     A UNIX command widely used on the Internet to find out information about a particular user, such as telephone number, whether currently logged on or the last time logged on. The person being "fingered" must have placed his or her profile on the system. Profiles can be very elaborate either as a method of social introduction or to state particular job responsibilities. Fingering requires entering the full **user@domain** address.

**finger mouse**     Same as *touchpad*.

**fingerprint reader**     A scanner used to identify a person's fingerprint for security purposes. After a sample is taken, access to a computer or other system is granted if the fingerprint matches the stored sample. A PIN may also be used with the fingerprint sample.

**Fingerprint Reader**
Fingerprint readers such as this machine from Identix provide significantly more security than an ID and password. It is extremely difficult to fake a fingerprint.
*(Image courtesy of Identix, Inc.)*

**finite element**   See *FEA*.

**finite state machine**   See *state machine*.

**FIO**   See *Future I/O*.

**FIR**   (Fast InfraRed) A high-speed IrDA protocol with data rates up to 4 Mpbs. See *IrDA*.

**firewall**   A method for keeping a network secure from intruders. It can be a single router that filters out unwanted packets or may comprise a combination of routers and servers each performing some type of firewall processing. Firewalls are widely used to give users secure access to the Internet as well as to separate a company's public Web server from its internal network. Firewalls are also used to keep internal network segments secure; for example, the accounting network might be vulnerable to snooping from within the enterprise.

While much effort has been made excluding unwanted input to the internal network, less attention has been paid to monitoring what goes out. Spyware are applications that keep track of your habits and send those statistics to a Web site (see *spyware*). Following are the techniques used in combination to provide firewall protection. See *firewall appliance* and *honeypot*.

**Packet Filter**   Blocks traffic based on a specific Web address (IP address) or type of application (e-mail, ftp, Web, etc.), which is specified by port number. Also known as a "screening router."

**Proxy Server**   Serves as a relay between two networks, breaking the connection between the two. Also typically caches Web pages (see *proxy server*).

**Network Address Translation (NAT)**   Allows one IP address, which is shown to the outside world, to refer to many IP addresses internally; one on each client station. Performs the translation back and forth.

**Stateful Inspection**
Tracks the transaction to ensure that inbound packets were requested by the user. Generally can examine multiple layers of the protocol stack, including the data, if required, so blocking can be made at any layer or depth.

**firewall appliance**   A device that provides firewall protection for a network. It includes all the necessary hardware and software in a self-contained package that plugs in between the two networks being isolated. Most firewall appliances are entirely solid state and include a stripped down operating system kernel, making the entire system less vulnerable to head crashes and other failures. See *firewall*.

**Firewall Management**
Elron Firewall, which runs under NT as well as its own proprietary OS, uses Elron's Stateful MultiLayer Inspection (SMLI) technology, which combines stateful inspection, multilayer analysis of IP and IPX packets and network address translation to secure a network. The window on the left can scroll down to more than 70 user services, including Telnet, Lotus Notes and CU-SeeMe. *(Screen example courtesy of Elron Software, www.elron.com)*

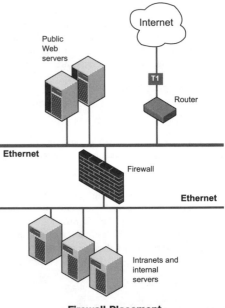

**Firewall Placement**
An organization's public Web sites reside outside the firewall, but intranet servers and all internal computing resources are inside the firewall.

**FireWire**    A high-speed serial bus developed by Apple and Texas Instruments that allows for the connection of up to 63 devices. Also known as the IEEE 1394 standard, the i.Link connector and the High Performance Serial Bus (HPSB), the original spec calls for 100, 200 and 400 Mbits/sec transfer rates. IEEE 1394b provides 800, 1,600 and 3,200 Mbits/sec speeds.

FireWire supports hot swapping, multiple speeds on the same bus and isochronous data transfer, which guarantees bandwidth for multimedia operations. It is expected to be widely used for attaching digital cameras and other video devices to the computer. See *Tailgate*.

**FireWire Connectors**
The 6-pin socket is commonly found on desktop computers. A 4-pin version is used on laptops.

**Firey engine**    See *Fiery engine*.

**firmware**    A category of memory chips that hold their content without electrical power and include ROM, PROM, EPROM and EEPROM technologies. Firmware becomes "hard software" when holding program code.

**first-generation computer**    A computer that used vacuum tubes as switching elements; for example, the UNIVAC I.

**first-level cache**    Same as *L1 cache*. See *cache*.

**First Virtual**    A system of digital money from First Virtual Holdings, Inc., San Diego, CA (www.fv.com). Customers have to establish an account with First Virtual using a credit card. When they want to purchase something online, they send their First Virtual ID number to the participating vendor, who in turn e-mails First Virtual and the customer for confirmation. Money is then transferred to the vendor via the Automated Clearing House (ACH).

**five nines**    Refers to 99.999% uptime that telephone companies are fond of stating as the reliability of their networks. It is often debated whether, in fact, that is truly what is delivered.

**fixate**    To close. The term often refers to closing a track-at-once session on a CD-R disc. See *disc fixation*.

**fixed data user**    An individual with a stationary computer or terminal that requires data transmission to and from a network. Contrast with *mobile data user*.

**fixed disk**    A non-removable hard disk such as is found in most personal computers. Programs and data are copied to and from the fixed disk. See *hard disk* and *magnetic disk*.

**fixed-frequency monitor**    A monitor that accepts one type of video signal, such as VGA only. Contrast with *multiscan monitor*.

**fixed-head disk**    A direct access storage device, such as a disk or drum, that has a read/write head for each track. Since there is no access arm movement, access times are significantly improved.

**fixed-length field**    A constant field size; for example, a 25-byte name field takes up 25 bytes in each record. It is easier to program, but wastes disk space and restricts file design. Description and comment fields are always a dilemma. Short fields allow only abbreviated remarks, while long fields waste space if lengthy comments are not required in every record. Contrast with *variable-length field*.

**fixed-length record**    A data record that contains fixed-length fields.

**fixed point**    A method for storing and calculating numbers in which the decimal point is always in the same location. Contrast with *floating point*.

**fixed satellite**    Refers to point-to-point transmission via satellite between stationary devices. Contrast with *mobile satellite*. See *GEO* and *LEO*.

**fixed wireless**    Refers to point-to-point transmission through the air between stationary devices. Contrast with *mobile wireless.*

**FJ connector**    Panduit's brand name for its Fiber Jack connector. It also uses the Opti-Jack brand. See *Fiber Jack.*

**FK**    See *foreign key.*

**Fkey**    (Function **KEY**) A Macintosh command sequence using CMD, SHIFT and OPTION key combinations. For example, Fkey 1 (CMD-SHIFT 1) ejects the internal floppy.

**F keys**    See *function keys.*

**flag**    (1) In communications, a code in the transmitted message which indicates that the following characters are a control code and not data.

(2) In programming, a "yes/no" indicator built into certain hardware or created and controlled by the programmer.

(3) A UNIX command line argument. The symbol is a dash. For example, in the command **head -15 filex**, which prints the first 15 lines of the file FILEX, the **-15** flag modifies the Head command.

(4) To identify an element of data or a process by embedding a code (flag) in it.

**flagging**    Identifying data or a process by embedding a code (flag) in it. See *flag.*

**flame**    To communicate emotionally via e-mail. Just as people might differ about what is polite behavior and what is not, whether an e-mail message is flaming is also in the eye of the beholder. Vulgar cursing would definitely be flaming, however. See *netiquette* and *holy war.*

**flame bait**    A subject posted to an Internet newsgroup that is designed to produce an emotional reaction and start a flame war.

**flame war**    In an Internet newsgroup, an ongoing tirade of contrasting opinions about a topic.

**flapping**    A condition in which a route in a network becomes unavailable and available over and over again. See *route dampening.*

**Flash**    Animation software for Windows and the Mac from Macromedia. It is used to develop interactive graphics for Web sites, as well as desktop presentations and games. Flash sequences on the Web are displayed by a Web browser plug-in and offline presentations are run by a Flash player that can be included on a floppy or CD-ROM. Flash is used to draw vector-based graphics in one or more timelines that provide a sequential path for describing actions and interactions. See also *flash memory.*

**flash adapter**    See *flash card adapter.*

**flash BIOS**    A PC BIOS that is stored in flash memory rather than in a ROM. A flash BIOS chip can be updated in place, whereas a ROM BIOS must be replaced with a newer chip. See *BIOS.*

**flash card**    A small module that contains flash memory such as a PC Card, CompactFlash, SmartMedia or similar format. Contrast with *socket flash.* See *flash memory* for a variety of flash card formats.

**flash card adapter**    A device that enables flash memory cards to be read without specialized drives. PC Card adapters for all the major flash media are widely available for laptops, and floppy-based adapters are used for desktop machines that do not have PC Card readers.

**Laptop Adapter**
PC Card adapters are widely available to adapt CompactFlash, SmartMedia and other flash memory modules to a laptop's PC Card slot. This adapter is for SmartMedia.

**flash crowd**    An unexpected surge in visitors to a Web site, which is typically because of some newsworthy event that just took place. It may also be due to the announcement of a new service or free software download.

**flash disk**    A solid state disk made of flash memory chips. Flash disks are housed in Type II PC Cards for laptops, but handhelds and digital cameras use smaller flash memory cards such as CompactFlash and SmartMedia. See *flash memory* and *solid state disk*.

**flash fusing**    See *fusing*.

**flash memory**    A memory chip that can be rewritten and hold its content without power. It is also called a "flash RAM" or "flash ROM" chip and is widely used for digital camera film and as storage for many consumer and industrial applications. Flash chips replaced earlier ROM BIOS chips in a PC so that the BIOS could be updated in place instead of being replaced. Flash chips generally have lifespans from 100K to 300K write cycles.

Unlike DRAM and SRAM memory chips, in which a single byte can be written, flash memory must be erased and written in fixed blocks, typically ranging from 512 bytes up to 256KB. Evolving out of the EEPROM chip technology, which can be erased in place, flash memory is less expensive and more dense. The term was coined by Toshiba for its ability to be erased "in a flash."

Flash memory chips are conveniently packaged as "flash cards" and come in several formats, including the full-size PC Card (ATA PC Card) and the smaller CompactFlash, SmartMedia and similar formats.

There are two types of flash interfaces. The first is the ATA interface, which has the same 512-byte block size as the standard hard disk sector. The second is the earlier linear flash, which is also used to execute a program directly from the chip (XIP). It requires Flash Translation Layer (FTL) or Flash File System (FFS) software to make it look like a disk drive. See *CompactFlash*, *SmartMedia* and *Memory Stick*. See also *Flash*.

**FlashPix**    A bitmapped-graphics file format that maintains the image in several resolutions. It uses more storage space than a comparable TIFF file, but when viewed by a Web browser, only the resoultion required for the current screen resolution is transmitted, saving download time. FlashPix files use the .FPX extension and conform to Microsoft's structured storage format which provides multiple "streams" within the file. Descriptive text may also be stored in an FPX file that identifies the image and how it was photographed or scanned.

**flat address space**    A memory that is addressed starting with 0. Each susequent byte is referenced by the next sequential number (0, 1, 2, 3, etc.) all the way to the end of memory. Except for PCs, which are based on the Intel CPU architecture, most computers use a flat address space.

A PC running in 16-bit mode (Real Mode) uses a segmented address space. Memory is broken up into 64KB segments, and a segment register always points to the base of the segment that is currently being addressed. The PC's 32-bit mode is considered a flat address space, but it too uses segments. Since one 32-bit segment addresses 4GB, one segment covers all of memory.

**Flash Memory Cards**

**Type II PC Card**

**CompactFlash**

**SmartMedia**

**Memory Stick**

**MultiMediaCard**

Flash memory cards have become very popular storage devices.

Type II PC Cards provide auxiliary storage for laptops, but the CompactFlash, SmartMedia and Memory Stick cards are expected to become the digital film of the 21st century.

The MultiMediaCard is designed for the smallest handhelds such as cellular phones and pagers.

**Digital Film**
Flash memory cards make the perfect digital camera "film." This Canon Elph uses CompactFlash.

**flatbed plotter**    A graphics plotter that contains a flat surface that the paper is placed on. The size of this surface (bed) determines the maximum size of the drawing. Contrast with *drum plotter*.

**flatbed scanner**    A scanner that provides a flat, glass surface to hold pages of paper, books and other objects for scanning. The scan head is moved under the glass across the page. Sheet feeders are usually optionally available that allow multiple sheets to be fed automatically. Contrast with *sheet-fed scanner*, *handheld scanner* and *drum scanner*.

**An Early Flatbed Plotter**
In the 1970s, this CalComp Model 738 large-format, flatbed plotter was an offline device. Data was delivered to it via magnetic tape.
*(Image courtesy of CalComp, Inc.)*

**flat file**    A data file that is not related to or does not contain any linkages to another file. It is generally used for stand-alone lists. When files must be related (customers to orders, vendors to purchases, etc.), a relational database manager is used, not a flat file manager. Flat files can be related, but only if the applications are programmed to do so.

Years ago, flat files were the very type used in a relational database. Before relational databases, files were related with built-in pointers that could not be dynamically changed. The relational database eliminated the hardwired linkages, resulting in "flat files." Today, flat files do not relate; just the opposite. Another example of how the terminology in this industry can drive you nuts.

**flat network**    A network in which all stations can reach other without going through any intermediary hardware devices, such as a bridge or router. A flat nework is one network segment. Large networks are segmented to contain broadcast traffic and to improve traffic within a workgroup. Contrast with *segmented network*. See *broadcast traffic* and *LAN segment*.

**flatpack**    A plastic, square surface mount chip package that contains leads (pins) on all four sides that extend straight outward. The leads are bent and cut for the specific application. See *QFP* and *chip package*.

**flat panel display**    A thin display screen that uses any of a number of technologies, such as LCD, plasma, EL and FED, with LCD being the most popular. Traditionally used in laptops, flat panel displays are slowly beginning to replace desktop CRTs. With their low power consumption, low radiation and space-saving footprint, flat panels are expected to eventually become the standard. See also *flat screen*.

**Analog vs. Digital**    Unlike CRTs, flat panel displays are entirely digital. In order to work with existing PCs, the first round of desktop flat panels have been designed to accept the standard analog VGA signal from the PC's display adapter. This means that the display adapter converts the digital data to analog, and the flat panel converts the analog signals back to digital. Eliminating the analog stage improves image quality and reduces cost.

Several digital flat panel interfaces have been competing for prime time, including the Compaq-backed Digital Flat Panel (DFP), VESA's Plug and Display and OpenLDI. However, the Digital Visual Interface (DVI) from the Digital Display Working Group (DDWG) is expected to become the standard.

**Beware Flat Panel Resolutions**    The way flat panel displays support resolutions is different than CRTs. No matter what selected resolution is sent to a CRT (800×600, 1,024×768, etc.), the image is spread across the entire screen. Conceptually, the CRT's gun "paints" the screen using larger or smaller globs of paint for the pixels depending on the resolution selected.

**Flat Panel vs CRT**
The L66 is Eizo's first 18" desktop LCD display. Sitting next to its CRT counterpart, the flat panel not only takes up less space, but uses less energy, emits much less radiation and is completely resistant to glare. Formerly selling In the U.S. under the Nanao brand, Eizo is known for its high-quality monitors. *(Image courtesy of EIZO Nanao Technologies Inc.)*

Flat panels use a precise matrix of rows and columns based on the highest resolution supported, and that highest resolution is the only one that fills the entire screen perfectly. For example, if you send an 800×600 image to a flat panel rated at 1,280×1,024, it will either display as a rectangle in the middle of the screen or be scaled up to 1,280×1,024. The quality of scaling differs dramatically between brands, so be sure to test a flat panel at the resolution you are going to use before you buy it. See *DVI, DFP, VESA Plug and Display, OpenLDI, TMDS, LVDS, LCD, plasma display, EL display* and *FED*.

**flat screen**  A CRT in which the viewing surface is flatter than earlier CRTs, which are slightly rounded. The flat screen provides less distortion at the edges and is the preferred design. Note that "flat screens" are not "flat panels." A flat "screen" is a CRT; a flat "panel" is an LCD screen on a laptop computer or a thin, stand-alone (typically LCD) desktop monitor. In time, flat panels are expected to replace all CRTs. See *flat panel display*.

**flat shading**  In computer graphics, a technique for computing a one-tone shaded surface to simulate simple lighting. See *Gouraud shading*.

**flatten layers**  To bring all levels of a multi-layered image down to one plane. High-end graphics programs such as Photoshop provide a native file format that supports multiple layers. It enables image elements to be placed into different layers so they can be moved independently of each other. In order to save the layered image in a common format such as TIFF, BMP or GIF, which support only one layer, the image is said to be "flattened."

**FLC file**  An animation file format from Autodesk, Inc., Sausalito, CA, that is commonly known as a "flick" file. It uses the .FLC file extension and provides a 640×480 resolution. An earlier .FLI format provides 320×200 resolution. Both FLC and FLI files provide animated sequences, but not sound. FLI and FLC formats were introduced respectively with Autodesk's Animator and Animator Pro programs for DOS.

**flex circuit**  See *flexible circuit*.

**flexible circuit**  A pattern of conductors created on a bendable film, which acts as an insulating (dielectric) base material. The top is coated with an dielectric cover layer. A flexible circuit is a pliable counterpart to a rigid printed circuit board. Flexible circuits, or "flex circuits," are often required to enable a more rapid construction of a device rather than their ability to turn and twist in normal operation.

**flexible disk**  Same as *floppy disk* and *diskette*.

**flex print**  See *flexible circuit*.

**flicker**  A fluctuating image on a video screen. See *interlaced*.

**flick file**  See *FLC file*.

**FLI file**  See *FLC file*.

**flip chip**  A chip packaging technique in which the chip is "flipped over" facing downward. Instead of facing up and bonded to the package leads with wires from the outside edges of the chip, any surface area of the flip chip can be used for interconnection, typically through "bumps" that are soldered onto the substrate and underfilled with epoxy. The flip chip allows for a large number of interconnects with shorter distances than wire, which greatly reduces inductance.

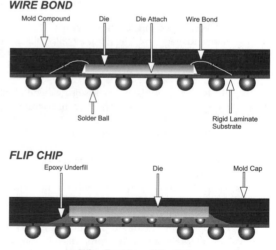

**Wire Bond vs. Flip Chip**
In the wire bond method at top, the chip (die) faces up and is attached via wires. The flip chip on the bottom faces down and is typically attached via solder bumps similar to the larger solder balls that attach BGA packages to the printed circuit board. *(Image courtesy of Amkor Technology, Inc.)*

**flip-flop**  An electronic circuit that alternates between two states. When current is applied, it changes to its opposite state (0 to 1 or 1 to 0). Made of several transistors, it is used in the design of static memories and hardware registers.

**flippy board** A PC expansion board that connects to both ISA/EISA and MicroChannel buses. ISA/EISA connectors are on one edge of the board; MCA on the other.

**flippy-floppy** A single-sided 5.25" floppy converted to double-sided use by punching a second notch into the disk so that it can be flipped over and inserted upside down. This is not recommended as the disk's rotation is alternated.

**float** In programming, a declaration of a floating point number.

**floating point** A method for storing and calculating numbers in which the decimal points do not line up as in fixed point numbers. The significant digits are stored as a unit called the "mantissa," and the location of the radix point (decimal point in base 10) is stored in a separate unit called the "exponent." Floating point methods are used for calculating a large range of numbers quickly.

Floating point operations can be implemented in hardware (math coprocessor), or they can be done in software. In large sysems, they can also be performed in a separate floating point processor that is connected to the main processor via a channel. See *numbers*.

```
FLOATING POINT EXAMPLES

Mantissa  Exponent  Value
71        0            71
71        1           710
71        2          7100
71        -1          7.1
```

**floating point processor** An arithmetic unit designed to perform floating point operations. It may be a coprocessor chip in a personal computer, a CPU designed with built-in floating point capabilities or a separate machine, often called an "array processor," which is connected to the main computer.

**Flooz** A Web-based gift certificate system. The sender prepays for some amount of Flooz, and the recipient spends it on sites that accept Flooz. The gift is e-mailed along with an electronic greeting card selected from available options. A free reminder service is also provided so one will not forget birthdays, anniversaries and other important dates. For information, visit www.flooz.com. See *Flooz* and *e-card*.

**floppy disk** A reusable magnetic storage medium introduced by IBM in 1971. The floppy was the primary method for distributing personal computer software until the mid-1990s when CD-ROMs became the preferred medium. The floppy disk used today is the rigid 3.5" microfloppy that holds 1.44MB. The reason it's called a floppy is that the first varieties were housed in bendable jackets. Floppies are terribly undersized for today's use, and their future is uncertain.

Also called a "diskette," the floppy is a flexible circle of magnetic material similar to magnetic tape, except that both surfaces are used for recording. The drive grabs the floppy's center and spins it inside its housing. The read/write head contacts the surface through an opening in the plastic shell or envelope. Floppies spin at 300 rpm, which is from 10 to 30 times slower than a hard disk. They are also at rest until a data transfer is requested.

The following lists the three types of floppies that have been developed (from oldest to newest) and the amount of raw, uncompressed data they have held.

3 1/2"

5 1/2"

**Floppy Formats**
Although quite ubiquitous in its heyday, the 5.25" diskette gave way to the 3.5" format in the mid-1990s. Although costing less than a quarter, the 3.5" floppy is woefully undersized for today's applications.

```
Housing                   Capacity      Creator
8" flexible envelope      100-500KB     IBM
5.25" flexible envelope   100KB-1.2MB   Shugart
3.5" rigid case           400KB-2.8MB   Sony
```

Although floppy disks look the same, what's recorded on them determines their capacity and compatibility. Every new floppy must be "formatted," which records the sectors on the disk that hold the data. See *format program*, *magnetic disk* and *high-capacity floppy*.

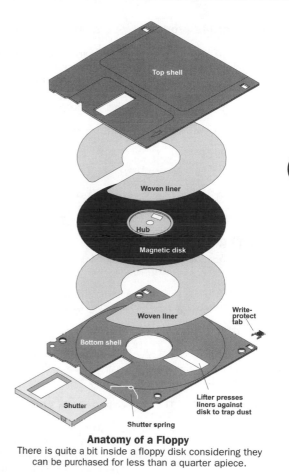

**Anatomy of a Floppy**
There is quite a bit inside a floppy disk considering they can be purchased for less than a quarter apiece.

## Floppy drive's days numbered

In an ever-changing industry, the portable plastic disk has tenaciously held on. But Apple may have sealed its fate.

In an industry where products and components seem to metamorphose overnight, the floppy drive is an anomaly. Since IBM featured it with its PS/2 computers in 1987, the 1.44-megabyte floppy drive has remained virtually unchanged, and it still comes bundled with

Rumor has it that Apple left out the floppy drive because the popular iMac was originally designed as a network computer without local storage, a market that never fully developed.

Apple still expects peo-

drives are available for Macs, come standard with some Compaq PCs, and are offered as options with new PCs from Dell, Gateway, and a number of other vendors.

SuperDisk and Zip drives are the floppy's heirs apparent. "Both the SuperDisk and the Zip have a lot of momentum," says Fara Yale, principal analyst for data storage at market-research firm Dataquest.

But other products could emerge

**Handwriting on the Wall**
This headline from the summer of 1999 foretells the uncertain future of the floppy. Although the floppy may still come with most PCs for the next couple of years, its value as a storage and distribution medium has declined enormously. *(Excerpted article courtesy of the* Philadelphia Inquirer.*)*

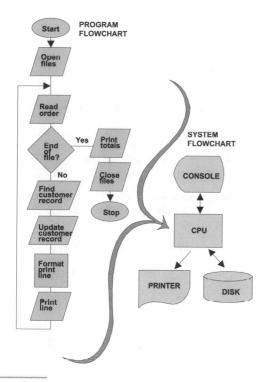

**FLOPS** (FLoating point Operations Per Second) The measurement of floating point calculations. For example, 100 megaflops (mflops) is 100 million floating point operations per second.

**Floptical** (FLoppy OPTICAL) An earlier type of floppy disk that stored 21MB and used optical alignment and magnetic recording. Introduced in 1989 by Insite Peripherals of San Jose, it did not become popular most likely because it did not offer a substantial enough increase in storage capacity. Similar technology is used in the LS-120 drive that was introduced in 1996 with 120MB. See *LS-120*.

**flowchart** A graphical representation of the sequence of operations in an information system or program. Information system flowcharts show how data flows from source documents through the computer to final distribution to users. Program flowcharts show the sequence of instructions in a single program or subroutine. Different symbols are used to draw each type of flowchart.

**flowcharting program**    See *diagramming program*.

**flow control**    (1) In communications, the management of transmission between two devices. It is concerned with the timing of signals and enables slower-speed devices to communicate with higher-speed ones. There are various techniques, but all are designed to ensure that the receiving station is able to accept the next block of data before the sending station sends it. See *xon-xoff*.

(2) In programming, the if-then and loop statements that make up the program's logic.

**flush**    To empty the contents of a memory buffer onto disk.

**flush center**

```
          The centering,
        of text uniformly
between the left and right margins.
```

**flush left**    The alignment of text uniformly to the left margin. All text is typically set flush left as is this paragraph.

**flush right**

```
The alignment of text uniformly to the right
            margin while the left margin is
                        set ragged left.
```

**flux**    The energy field generated by a magnet.

**flux transition**    The change of magnetic polarity from 0 to 1 or 1 to 0 on a magnetic disk or tape.

**flying head**    A read/write head that "flies" over a magnetic disk. The heads are attached to a slider, which is a block of material that acts as an airfoil. The slider's shape and contour, which is designed for a particular disk speed, determine how high it flies. See *flying height*.

**flying height**    The distance between the surface of a disk platter and the read/write head. See *flying head*.

**FM**    (1) (Frequency Modulation) A transmission technique that blends the data signal into a carrier by varying (modulating) the frequency of the carrier. See *modulate*.

(2) (Frequency Modulation) An earlier magnetic disk encoding method that places clock bits onto the medium along with the data bits. It has been superseded by MFM and RLL.

**FM synthesis**    A MIDI technique that simulates the sound of musical instruments. It uses operators, typically four of them, which create wave forms or modulate the wave forms. FM synthesis does not create sound as faithfully as wave table synthesis, which uses actual samples of the instruments.

**FN key**    (FuNction key) A keyboard key that works like a SHIFT key to activate the second function on a dual-purpose key, typically found on laptops to reduce keyboard size. It is different than the function keys F1, F2, etc. It is also a real nuisance when the PAGEUP and PAGEDN keys are placed on the UP and DOWN ARROW keys and have to be activated by pressing the FN key.

**FOCA**    (Font Object Content Architecture) See *MO:DCA*.

**FOCIS**    (Fiber-Optic Cable Intermatability Standard) Specifications for cable connectors from the TIA that define the requirements for interconnection between fiber-optic plugs and sockets. Following are some of the common FOCIS standards.

```
FOCIS-1   SMA
FOCIS-2   ST
FOCIS-3   SC
FOCIS-4   FC
FOCIS-6   Fiber Jack
```

**FOCUS**    (1) A DBMS from Information Builders that runs on more than 35 different platforms. FOCUS has been widely known for its 4GL and report writing capabilities and is the product that built the company. It included a hierarchical database in its first release in 1975 and has evolved to support more than 80 database and file types including Information Builders' own multidimensional database (FOCUS Fusion). See *EDA, WebFOCUS* and *FOCUS Fusion.*

(2) (Federation **On** Computing in the United States, www.acm.org/focus) The U.S. representative of the International Federation of Information Processing (IFIP). FOCUS was founded in 1991 by the ACM and the IEEE Computing Society (IEEE-CS).

**FOCUS Desktop**    Software from Information Builders that extends WebFOCUS capabilities to client machines. It enables a desktop or laptop machine to continue processing the database disconnected from the network. See *WebFOCUS.*

**FOCUS Fusion**    A multidimensional (OLAP) database from Information Builders that runs on mainframes, NT and major UNIX platforms. Introduced in 1996, it supports SQL and ODBC queries, as well as links to front-end tools such as WebFOCUS and EDA. See *WebFOCUS* and *EDA.*

**fogging**    In computer graphics, simulating the effects of fog, smoke and haze. Similar to alpha blending, fogging is very computational. If the operation is performed in the graphics accelerator, the results are displayed considerably faster. See *alpha blending.*

**FOIA**    (Freedom **Of** Information **Act**) A U.S. Government rule that states that public information shall be delivered within 10 days of request.

**FOIRL**    (Fiber Optic Inter Repeater Link) An IEEE standard for fiber-optic Ethernet. FOIRL and 10BaseF are compatible, but FOIRL is an earlier standard generally used to extend a backbone beyond the 328 foot limitation of 10BaseT. FOIRL is limited to .6 miles distance per segment, whereas 10BaseF segments can extend to 1.2 miles. 10BaseF is a more comprehensive standard for complete fiber-based installations.

**fold**    The amount of information that can be viewed on screen without scrolling. This is an important design consideration when laying out a Web page so that the impact can be viewed all at once. The actual area cannot be determined exactly, because a higher screen resolution will show more than a lower one. For example, there will be more data visible in the fold if the monitor is set to 1,024×768 than at 800×600. See *resolution.*

**folder**    In a graphical user interface (GUI), a simulated file folder that holds data, applications and other folders. Folders were introduced on the Xerox Star, then popularized on the Macintosh and later adapted to Windows and UNIX. In DOS and Windows 3.1, a folder is known as a directory, and a subfolder (folder within a folder) is a subdirectory. See *Win Folder organization.*

**folder hierarchy**    The organization of folders (directories) on a hard disk, which is drive-folder-file. See *Win Folder organization.*

**foldering**    Using folders to store and manipulate documents on screen.

**Folio**    (1) Text management software for PCs from the Folio division of Open Market, Inc., Cambridge, MA (www.folio.com). It provides storage, retrieval and hypertext capability for text databases. It can import text from over 40 file formats. Folio files are called "Infobases." Open Market acquired Provo, Utah-based Folio Corporation in 1997.

(2) (folio) In typography, a printed page number. For example, folio 3 could be the 27th physical page in a book.

**A Fogged Image**
The original image (top) is shown with fogging applied to it (below). *(Image courtesy of Intergraph Computer Systems.)*

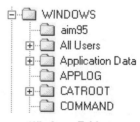

**Windows Folders**
Folders on the hard disk are pictured as manilla file folders, but they are not fixed in size and can hold as much data as there is room on the entire disk.

**follow me service**   An IN (Intelligent Network) service that provides call forwarding based on a time schedule. See *find me service* and *call pickup service*.

**FON file**   (FONt file) In Windows 3.1 and 95/98, a file that contains a font used for onscreen displays (menus, buttons, etc.) by Windows and Windows applications, as well as by DOS applications running under Windows. Most .FON files contain bitmapped fonts. Contrast with *TTF file*.

**fong shading**   See *Phong shading*.

**font**   A set of type characters of a particular typeface design and size. Usually, each typeface (Times Roman, Helvetica, Arial, etc.) is made available in four variations: normal weight, bold, italic and bold italic. Thus, for bitmapped fonts, which are fully generated ahead of time, four fonts would be required for each point size used in each typeface. For scalable fonts, which are generated in any point size on the fly, only four fonts would be required for each typeface.

Fonts come built into the printer, as plug-in cartridges or as soft fonts, which reside on the computer's hard disk or a hard disk built into the printer. See *bitmapped font* and *scalable font*.

**font cartridge**   A set of bitmapped or outline fonts for one or more typefaces contained in a plug-in module for the printer. The fonts are stored in a ROM chip within the cartridge. Contrast with *soft font* and *internal font*.

**font characteristics**   The attributes and properties of a font. In HP LaserJet, font selection is made by sending a coded command to the printer with the following criteria:

| Code | Characteristic |
|---|---|
| Typeface | Courier, Times Roman, etc. |
| Orientation | Portrait or landscape |
| Symbol set | Country or special characters |
| Spacing | Proportional or fixed |
| Pitch | Characters per inch (fixed) |
| Point size | Height |
| Style | Upright or italic |
| Stroke weight | Light, medium, bold |

**font compiler**   Same as *font generator*.

**font editor**   Software that allows fonts to be designed and modified.

**font family**   A set of fonts of the same typeface in assorted sizes, including bold, italic and bold italic variations.

**font generator**   Software that converts an outline font into a bitmap (dot pattern required for a particular font size). Font generation is not linear, simply expanding a letter to any size. As fonts get bigger, their characteristics must change in order to make them attractive.

Font generation is used to create bitmapped fonts, which are fully generated and stored on disk before use. Contrast with *font scaler*, which generates the font in any point size the instant it is needed for display or printing.

**font manager**   See *font scaler*.

**font metric**   Typographic information (width, height, kerning) for each character in a font.

**font number**   An identification number assigned to a font. A program references the font by this number.

**font rasterizer**   See *font scaler*.

**font scaler**   Software that converts scalable fonts into bitmaps on the fly as required for display or printing. Examples are TrueType, Adobe Type Manager and Bitstream's Facelift. See *scalable font* and *font generator*.

**font style**   A typeface variation (normal, bold, italic, bold italic).

**font utility**    Software that provides functions for managing fonts, including the ability to download, install, design and modify fonts.

**Fontware**    A font generator for various DOS applications from Bitstream Inc., Cambridge, MA (www.bitstream.com), which includes a library of typeface outlines in normal, italic, bold and bold italic weights. FontWare has been discontinued in favor of newer scalable font technogies. See *font scaler*.

**font weight**    The thickness of characters (light, medium or bold).

**foo**    A popular name for a temporary file, function or variable, or example of same. Often used with "bar" to create "foobar," which also comes from Fouled Up Beyond All Recognition (FUBAR).

**footer**    In a document or report, common text that appears at the bottom of every page. It usually contains the page number.

**footnote**    Text that appears at the bottom of a page that adds explanation. It is often used to give credit to the source of information. When accumulated and printed at the end of a document, they are called "endnotes."

**footprint**    The amount of geographic space covered by an object. A computer footprint is the desk or floor surface it occupies. A satellite's footprint is the earth area covered by its downlink.

**Force**    A earlier dBASE compiler developed by Sophco, Inc., Boulder, CO, which combined C and dBASE structures. It was noted for generating very small executable programs.

**foreground/background**    The priority assigned to programs running in a multitasking environment. In a multiuser environment, foreground programs have highest priority, and background programs have lowest. Online users are given the foreground, and batch processing activities (sorts, updates, etc.) are given the background. If batch activities are given a higher priority, terminal response times may slow down considerably.

In a personal computer, the foreground program is the one the user is currently working with, and the background program might be a print spooler or communications program.

**foreign exchange service**    A telephone service that provides a local telephone number to a location outside of the customer's calling area. The telephone company creates a private line between the local telephone central office and the remote central office (foreign exchange). When customers dial the local number, they get a dial tone in the foreign exchange.

**foreign file**    See *foreign format*.

**foreign format**    A file format that is different than the native format used by an application. Contrast with *native format*. See *import*, *export* and *file format*.

**foreign key**    In relational database, it is a field in one table that is indexed in another. Foreign keys provide the building blocks for relating tables. For example, in a customer order table, the salesperson field might contain an employee number. That field would be a foreign key in the table, because the employee table would be indexed on employee number. See *entity relationship model*.

**foreign language characters**    See *unicode*.

**ForeRunner**    A family of ATM adapters from Fore Systems, Warrendale, PA.

**Forest & Trees**    A data analysis program for Windows from Platinum Technology, Inc., Oakbrook Terrace, IL (www.platinum.com), that integrates data from a variety of applications. It provides a control room interface that lets users monitor important business information.

**FORE Systems**    See *Marconi*.

**fork**    **(1)** In UNIX, to make a copy of a process for execution.

**(2)** In the Macintosh, a part of a file. See *data fork* and *resource fork*.

**form**    **(1)** A paper form used for printing.

**(2)** A formatted screen display designed for a particular application. See *forms software*.

**formant information**    The structure of speech formation. It deals with how the mouth and vocal tract move to make sounds. See *phoneme*.

**format**    The structure, or layout, of an item.

Screen formats are the layout of fields onscreen.

Report formats are the columns, headers and footers on a page.

Record formats are the fields within a record.

File formats are the structure of data and program files, word processing documents and graphics files (vectors and bitmaps) with all their proprietary headers and codes. See *format program*, *disk format*, *DOS/Windows format* and *style sheet*.

**format program**    Software that initializes a disk. There are two formatting levels. The low-level format initializes the disk surface by creating the physical tracks and storing sector identification in them as required by the particular drive technology used. Today's IDE and SCSI drives are all low-level formatted at the factory.

The high-level format creates the indexes used by the operating system's file system to keep track of data stored on the disk. HFS, FAT, FAT32, NTFS and HPFS are examples of such file systems used on personal computers.

Floppy disk format programs perform both levels of formatting on the diskette at the same time. See ***DOS Format***.

**formatted text**    Text that contains codes for font changes, headers, footers, boldface, italics and other page and document attributes. Word processors create formatted text, but all the major ones use their own coding systems. See *ASCII file*.

**form factor**    The physical size of a device as measured by outside dimensions. With regard to a disk drive, the form factor is the overall diameter of the platters and case, such as 3.5" or 5.25", not the size in terms of storage capacity.

**form feed**    Advancing a printer form to the top of the next page. It is done by pressing the printer's form feed (FF) button or by sending the form feed code (ASCII 12) to the printer from the computer.

**forms software**    **(1)** Workflow software used to create on-screen data entry forms and provide e-mail routing and tracking of the resulting electronic documents.

**(2)** Program development tools that build applications by designing the on-screen forms for data entry, update and so on. The forms are generally designed with visual programming tools that allow fields, buttons and logos to be drawn directly on screen. The business logic is either selected via menus and/or written in behind each field or button with lines of 4GL or 3GL programming code.

**formula**    **(1)** An arithmetic expression that solves a problem. For example, **(fahrenheit–32)*5/9** is the formula for converting Fahrenheit to Celsius.

**(2)** In spreadsheets, an algorithm that identifies how the data in a specific number of cells is to be calculated. For example, **+C3*D8** means that the contents of cell C3 are to be multipled by the contents of cell D8 and the results are to be placed where the formula is located.

**form view**    A screen display showing one item or record arranged like a preprinted form. Contrast with *table view*.

**for statement**    A high-level programming language structure that repeats a series of instructions a specified number of times. It creates a loop that includes its own control information. The following BASIC and C examples print "Hello" 10 times:

```
BASIC                 C
for x = 1 to 10       for (x = 0;  x 10;  x++)
 print "hello"          printf ("hello\n");
next x
```

**Forte**    An application development system for enterprise client/server environments from Sun. Introduced in 1994, it is a repository-driven system that supports Windows, Mac and Motif clients and all the major UNIX servers as well as VMS. It supports Oracle, Sybase and Rdb databases and provides partitioning for creating three-tier applications. Testing and debugging is done in an interpreted mode while production programs are compiled into C++ code. Forte was developed by Forte Software, which was acquired by Sun in 1999.

**Forte for Java**    A family of Java development environments from Sun. The products include an editor, compiler, debugger, object browser and JavaBean creator plus the ability to edit and view HTML files. Forte for Java Community Edition is the entry level version that is available free. The Internet Edition adds database connectivity, and the Enterprise Edition is the complete J2EE development environment. The Community Edition was formerly NetBeans Developer, and the Enterprise Edition was SynerJ. See *Forte*.

**Forte Fusion**    Application integration software that runs on UNIX, Windows NT, VMS and mainframes from Sun. It provides a process engine that interacts with heterogeneous applications via XSL-based rules. Data is transferred between Forte Fusion and the applications in XML or via connector interfaces that convert to and from XML. See *Forte*.

**Fortezza**    An authentication system endorsed by the National Security Agency that uses a PC Card as the authentication token. Fortezza is part of the U.S. Government's GOSIP policy, and vendors must supply Fortezza-compliant products in order to win contracts. Fortezza uses a 56-bit key based on the DES encryption method. The term means "fortress" in Italian.

**FORTH**    (FOuRTH-generation language)  A high-level programming language created by Charles Moore in the late 1960s as a way of providing direct control of the computer. Its syntax resembles LISP, it uses reverse polish notation for calculations, and it is noted for its extensibility.

It is both compiler and interpreter. The source program is compiled first and then executed by its operating system/interpreter. It is used in process control applications that must quickly process data acquired from instruments and sensors. It is also used in arcade game programming as well as robotics and other AI applications. The following polyFORTH example converts Fahrenheit to Celsius:

```
: CONV ( n) 32 - 5 9 * / . ." Celsius
: USER_INPUT  ." Enter Fahrenheit " CONV ;
```

**FORTRAN**    (FORmula TRANslator)  The first high-level programming language and compiler, developed in 1954 by IBM. It was originally designed to express mathematical formulas, and although it is used occasionally for business applications, it is still the most widely used language for scientific, engineering and mathematical problems.

FORTRAN IV is an ANSI standard, but FORTRAN V has various proprietary versions. The following FORTRAN example converts Fahrenheit to Celsius:

```
WRITE(6,*) 'Enter Fahrenheit '
READ(5,*) XFAHR
XCENT = (XFAHR - 32) * 5 / 9
WRITE(6,*) 'Celsius is ',XCENT
STOP
END
```

**forum**    An information interchange regarding a specific topic or product that is hosted on an Internet newsgroup, online service or BBS. It can include the latest news on the subject, a conferencing capability for questions and answers by participants and files for downloading fixes, demos and other related material.

**forward bias**    See *bias*.

**forward chaining**    In AI, a form of reasoning that starts with what is known and works toward a solution. Known as bottom-up approach. Contrast with *backward chaining*.

**forward compatible**    Same as *upward compatible*.

**forward error correction**   A communications technique that can correct bad data on the receiving end. Before transmission, the data is processed through an algorithm that adds extra bits for error correction. If the transmitted message is received in error, the correction bits are used to repair it.

**forward link**   The transmission from a base station to a mobile phone. The reverse link is from the mobile phone to the base station.

**forward slash**   The forward slash, or slash, character (/) is the divide symbol in programming and on calculator keyboards. For example, **10 / 7** means 10 divided by 7. The slash is also often used in command line syntax to indicate a switch. For example, in the DOS Xcopy statement **xcopy \*.\* d: /s**, the **/s** is a switch that tells the program to copy all subdirectories. In UNIX paths, which have become popular due to Internet addresses, the slash separates the elements of the path as in **www.hotstuff.com/news/previous/abc.html**. See *backslash.*

**FOT file**   (FOnt TrueType file) In Windows 3.1, a TrueType font file that points to the location of the TTF file, which contains the actual mathematical outlines of the font. See *TTF file.*

**foundry**   A semiconductor manufacturer that makes chips for third parties. It may be a large chip maker that sells its excess manufacturing capacity or one that makes chips exclusively for other companies. As of 1995, it costs at least a billion dollars to construct a high-production semiconductor manufacturing plant that produces standard chips. See *fabless.*

**fountain fill**   In computer graphics, a painted area that smoothly changes its color or pattern density. A radial fountain fill starts at the center of an area and radiates outward.

**Four11**   See *Web white pages.*

**fourth-generation computer**   A computer made up almost entirely of chips with limited amounts of discrete components. We are currently in the fourth generation.

**fourth-generation language**   Also known as a *4GL*, it is a computer language that is more advanced than traditional high-level programming languages. For example, in dBASE, the command **List** displays all the records in a data file. In second- and third-generation languages, instructions would have to be written to read each record, test for end of file, place each item of data on screen and go back and repeat the operation until there are no more records to process.

First-generation languages are machine languages; second-generation are machine-dependent assembly languages; third-generation are high-level programming languages, such as FORTRAN, COBOL, BASIC, Pascal, and C.

Although many languages are called fourth-generation languages, they are actually a mix of third and fourth. For example, the List command in dBASE is a fourth-generation command, but applications programmed in dBASE are third-generation. The following command examples show the difference between third- and fourth-generation syntax to open a customer file and display all names and addresses onscreen.

```
dBASE 3GL                dBASE 4GL
use customer             use customer
do while .not. eof()     list name, address
  ? name, address
  skip
enddo
```

Query language and report writers are also fourth-generation languages. Any computer language with English-like commands that doesn't require traditional input-process-output logic falls into this category.

Many fourth-generation language functions are also built into graphical interfaces and activated by clicking and dragging. The commands are embedded into menus and buttons that are selected in an appropriate sequence.

**four-way server**   See *4-way.*

**FoxBASE**   An earlier Xbase development system for the Macintosh from Microsoft. It was succeeded by FoxPro. Originally developed by Fox Software for DOS, FoxBASE gained a reputation early on for its speed and compatibility with dBASE. See *Visual FoxPro.*

**FoxPro**    See *Visual FoxPro*.

**FPD**    **(1)** (Flat Panel Display)  See *LCD*, *plasma display*, *EL display*, *FED* and *flat panel display*.
**(2)** (Field Programmable Device)  See *PLD*.

**FPGA**    (Field Programmable Gate Array)  A programmable logic chip (PLD) with a high density of gates. There are a variety of FPGA architectures, some of which can be very sophisticated, including not only programmable logic blocks, but programmable interconnects and switches between the blocks. FPGAs are mostly reprogrammable (EEPROM or flash based) or dynamic (RAM based). See *PLD*.

**FPM RAM**    See *page mode memory*.

**FPO**    (For Position Only)  A low-resolution image used to mark the placement of the final image. When the storage of high-resolution images in a publication present a problem in the draft, or preview, stages, FPOs are used instead. When the publication is finally printed, FPOs are replaced with high-resolution images.

**fps**    (Frames Per Second)  The measurement of full-motion video performance. See *frame*.

**FPU**    (Floating Point Unit)  A computer circuit that handles floating point operations.

**FPX file**    See *FlashPix*.

**FQDN**    (Fully Qualified Domain Name)  The complete domain name for a specific computer (host) on the Internet. It provides enough information so that it can be converted into a physical IP address. The FQDN consists of host name and domain name. For example, **www.computerlanguage.com** is the FQDN on the Web for the publisher of this database. The WWW is the host. That's right. There are millions of hosts named WWW in order to maintain uniformity. COMPUTERLANGUAGE.COM is the domain name, with .COM being the top level domain (TLD) name. See *DNS* and *Internet domain name*.

**FQFP**    See *QFP*.

**FR4**    (Flame Retardant 4)  A widely-used insulating material for making printed circuit boards. It is constructed of woven glass fibers (fiberglass) that are epoxied together.

**Fractal Design Painter**    See *Painter*.

**fractals**    A lossy compression method used for color images. Providing ratios of 100:1 or greater, fractals are especially suited to natural objects, such as trees, clouds and rivers. Fractals turns an image into a set of data and an algorithm for expanding it back to the original.

The term comes from "fractus," which is Latin for broken or fragmented. It was coined by IBM Fellow and doctor of mathematics Benoit Mandelbrot, who expanded on ideas from earlier mathematicians and discovered similarities in chaotic and random events and shapes.

**fractional T1**    A service that provides less than full T1 capacity. Increments of 64 Kbps are provided.

**fractional T3**    A service that provides less than full T3 capacity. Increments of 3 Mbps are typically provided.

**FRAD**    (Frame Relay Access Device or Frame Relay Assembler/Disassembler)  A communications device that formats outgoing data into the format required by a frame relay network. It strips the data back out at the other end. It is the frame relay counterpart to the X.25 PAD. See *frame relay*.

**fragmentation**    **(1)** Storing data in non-contiguous areas on disk. As files are updated, new data is stored in available free space, which may not be contiguous. Fragmented files cause extra head movement, slowing disk accesses. A defragger program is used to rewrite and reorder all the files.

**(2)** In an IP network, breaking a data packet into smaller pieces in order to accomodate the maximum transmission unit of the network. See *MTU*.

**fragments**     The pieces into which a packet is broken when the packet is too large to be sent over a particular network as a single unit. See *fragmentation* and *MTU*.

**FRAM**     **(1)** **(Ferroelectronic RAM)** A non-volatile semiconductor memory that retains its content without power for up to 10 years.

   **(2)** **(Ferromagnetic RAM)** A non-volatile memory that records microscopic bits on a magnetic surface.

**frame**     **(1)** In computer graphics, one screenful of data or its equivalent storage space. In full-motion video, it requires approximately 24 consecutive frames in one second (24 fps) to simulate real, continuous motion.

   **(2)** In communications, a fixed block of data transmitted as a single entity. In local area networks (LANs), the terms frame and packet are used synonymously. See *packet* and *Ethernet*.

   **(3)** In a Web browser, a separate, scrollable window on screen. See *frames*.

   **(4)** In desktop publishing, a movable, resizable box that holds a graphic image.

   **(5)** In telephony, a rack for holding equipment, typically 23" wide by eight feet high. See *rack mounted*.

   **(6)** In AI, a data structure that holds a general description of an object, which is derived from basic concepts and experience.

**frame buffer**     An area of memory used to hold a frame of data. A frame buffer is typically used for screen display and is the size of the maximum image area on screen. It is a separate memory bank on the display adapter that holds the bitmapped image while it is being "painted" on screen. Sophisticated graphics systems are built with several memory planes, each holding one or more bits of the pixel.

**frame grabber**     A device that accepts standard TV signals and digitizes the current video frame into a bitmap image. Frame grabbers can be stand-alone units or a function built into video graphics boards.

**FrameMaker**     A desktop publishing program from Adobe that runs on UNIX platforms, Macintosh and Windows. It is noted for its large number of advanced features, including full text and graphics editing capabilities. Optional viewers let documents run on machines without FrameMaker, providing a way to distribute hypertext-based help systems.

**frame relay**     A high-speed packet switching protocol used in wide area networks (WANs). Providing a granular service of up to DS3 speed (45 Mbps), it has become very popular for LAN to LAN connections across remote distances. Services are offered by all the major carriers. Frame relay is much faster than X.25 networks, the first packet-switching WAN standard, because frame relay was designed for today's reliable circuits and performs less rigorous error detection. Although X.25 was never widely used in the U.S., frame relay has become a major wide area technology. The name comes from the fact that frame relay does not do any processing of the content of the packets; rather, it relays them from the input port of the switch to the output port.

   Voice over frame relay enables voice to be packetized and travel over a frame relay network, often providing significant cost savings but at some sacrifice in voice quality, depending on the network configuration. In 1998, the Frame Relay Forum finalized its voice over frame relay specfication. FRF.11 defines the frame formats, and FRF.12 defines the ability to divide large frames into smaller ones so that realtime voice can be interleaved with data on slower connections.

   Frame relay provides permanent and switched logical connections, known as Permanent Virtual Circuits (PVCs) and Switched Virtual Circuits (SVCs). These are logical connections provisioned ahead of time (PVCs) or on demand (SVCs). The connections are identified by a Data Link Connection Identifier (DLCI) number that is significant to the local frame relay switch, which will change the number as it passes the packet on to its destination, because the receiving switch uses a different DLCI for its end of the same connection. Every DLCI requires a Committed Information Rate (CIR), which is a pledge on the part of the network to provide a certain amount of transmission capacity for the connection. CIRs are adjusted with experience.

   A customer attaches to the frame relay network via a frame relay access device (FRAD) which resides on the customer's premises. The FRAD may be a separate device or software built into the router. The FRAD connects to a port on a frame relay switch on the service provider's network via an interface known as the User-to-Network Interface (UNI). This line/port is typically some multiple of 64 Kbps, and all traffic for one customer generally travels through the same port. The frame relay switches may interconnect via point-to-point lines, but they often use an ATM backbone.

   A Superb Resource     The book *Frame Relay for High-Speed Networks* by Walter Goralski is must reading, not only to learn about frame relay, but to learn about wide area networking in general. Surely the primer on this subject, Goralski factors in history, current and future trends and all related networking technologies. Published by John Wiley & Sons, Inc., ISBN 0-471-31274-6.

**frames**    A Web browser feature that enables a Web page to be displayed in a separate scrollable window on screen. Older browsers do not support the frames feature, and many Web sites have a frames and non-frames version of the site to accomodate them.

**frame switch**    A network device that switches variable-length packets from sender to receiver. Ethernet, Token Ring and FDDI switches are examples. Contrast with *cell switching*. See *LAN switch* and *frame switching*.

**frame switching**    Using frame switches to speed up network traffic. For example, when a 10BaseT Ethernet hub is replaced with an Ethernet frame switch, each sending and receiving pair of stations obtains the full bandwidth of the network. See *frame switch*.

**framework**    (1) See *application framework*.
(2) (FrameWork) One of the first integrated software packages for PCs that included a programming language. It was developed by Ashton-Tate, later acquired by Borland.

**framing bit**    Same as *start bit* and *stop bit*.

**FRED**    (**F**riendly **R**ollabout **E**ngineered for **D**octors)  A mobile medical conferencing unit. See *videoconferencing*.

**Freedman's law**    "Every 18 months, more novices are programming." By Alan Freedman, author of *The Computer Glossary* and *Computer Desktop Encyclopedia*. The job of programming is very misunderstood. It is actually easier to write a program than most people would think. However, the lack of experience causes programmers to create a maze that cannot easily be traversed later. For more details, see *programmer*. See also *user interface* and *laws*.

**free e-mail**    See *Internet e-mail service*.

**free-form data**    Data that does not reside in fixed locations. Unstructured text in a word processing document is a typical example. Contrast with *structured data*. See *free-form database*.

**free-form database**    A database system that allows entry of unstructured text without regard to length or order. Although it accepts text input like a word processor, it differs by providing better methods for searching, retrieving and organizing the data.

**free-form language**    A language in which statements can reside anywhere on a line or even cross over lines. It does not imply less syntax structure, just more freedom in placing statements. For example, any number of blank spaces are allowed between symbols. Most high-level programming languages are free-form.

**free-form text**    Unstructured text (words, sentences, etc.) such as the input to a word processor or text editor. See *free-form database*.

**FreeHand**    See *Macromedia FreeHand*.

**free Internet service**    An ISP that provides access to the Internet without charge to the user. The service is supported by advertising which appears on a special version of the user's browser and cannot be eliminated. NetZero (www.netzero.com) is an example of a free Internet service provider.

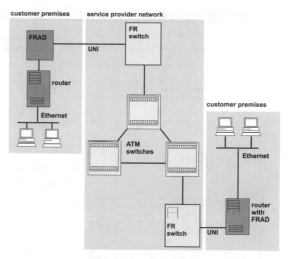

**A Frame Relay Network**
This illustration depicts the customer and service provider sides of a frame relay network. An ATM backbone is shown, because it is a common method of interconnecting frame relay switches. The FRAD may be a separate device (left side of illustration) or software built into the router (right).

**Create Address**

| | | |
|---|---|---|
| Title | First name | Last name |
| ▾ | John | Sensza |

Business \ Home \

| | |
|---|---|
| Job title | |
| Company | Information Sciences Corporation |
| Street | 4723 Alma |
| City | Palo Alto | State | CA |
| Zip | 94302 | Country | USA |
| Tel 1 | 415 494-3920 | Ext | |
| Fax | 415 494-3921 | E-mail | sensza@isc.com |
| Tel 2 | | Assistant | |
| Notes | Reviewed 12/96 proposal for Panasonic DBS 3400 phone system |

Categories  Prospect  ▾

☐ Confidential

OK  Cancel  Add  Help

---

**3/29/97**

Prospect

**John Sensza**
Information Sciences Corporation
4723 Alma
Palo Alto, CA 94302

**415 494-3920**, fax 3921
sensza@isc.com

Reviewed 12/96 proposal for Panasonic DBS 3400
phone system

---

**Structured vs. Unstructured**
The Info Select window at top provides a free-form approach to recording an address. The Lotus Organizer dialog at the bottom provides fixed fields for common data. Usually, people strongly prefer one method over the other if there is a choice.

**free ISP**    See *free Internet service*.

**Freelance Graphics**    A presentation graphics program for Windows from Lotus that is also part of Lotus' SmartSuite set of applications.

**free mail**    See *Internet e-mail service*.

**Free-PC**    An organization that offers free PCs to individuals that promise to use them at least 10 hours per month. The PCs are sponsored by advertisers, and the ads are visible at all times. More than 30,000 units were shipped in the summer of 1999 to qualified applicants. Free-PC was created by idealab!, which was founded by Bill Gross in 1996 and which launched more than 20 Internet businesses in its first two years of operation. In 1999, Free-PC stopped offering free machines and merged with eMachines. For more information, visit www.e4me.com.

**Free Software Foundation**    (Free Software Foundation, Inc., Boston, MA, www.gnu.org) A non-profit organization founded in 1985 by Richard Stallman, dedicated to eliminating restrictions on copying and modifying programs by promoting the development and use of freely redistributable software. It oversees the development of more than 150 software products for its GNU computing environment and provides online and CD-ROM distribution of GNU and other programs. See *GNU* and *League for Programming Freedom*.

**free space optics**    Transmitting optical signals through the air using infrared lasers. Also known as "wireless optics," free space optics provides point-to-point and point-to-multipoint transmission at very high speeds without requiring a government license for use of the spectrum.

Because weather conditions such as fog can reflect light signals, redundant paths can be created by sending multiple signals to reflectors on different buildings.

While free space optics is being deployed for last mile connectivity, in time, it is expected for short distances for use within high-speed buses in computers and switches, even within the chip itself.

**free-text**    See *free-form text*.

**freeware**    Software distributed without charge. Ownership is retained by the developer who has control over its redistribution, including the ability to change the next release of the freeware to payware. See *shareware* and *public domain software*. Contrast with *feeware*.

**freeze**    See *abend*.

**freeze-frame video**    Video transmission in which the image is changed once every couple of seconds rather than 30 times per second as is required in full-motion video.

**frequency**    The number of oscillations (vibrations) in one second. Frequency is measured in Hertz (Hz), which is the same as "oscillations per second" or "cycles per second." For example, the alternating current in a wall outlet in the U.S. and Canada is 60Hz. Electromagnetic radiation is measured in kiloHertz (kHz), megaHertz (mHz) and gigaHertz (gHz). See *wavelength*, *frequency response*, *audio*, *carrier* and *space/time*.

**frequency division multiplexing**    See *FDM*.

**frequency hopping**    A wireless modulation method that rapidly changes the center frequency of a transmission. See *spread spectrum* and *802.11*.

**frequency modulation**    See *FM*.

**frequency range**    In a communications system, the range of frequencies from the lowest to the highest. In a high-fidelity audio system, this would be typically from 20Hz to 20,000Hz.

**frequency response**    In an audio system, the accuracy of sound reproduction. A totally flat response means that there is no increase or decrease in volume level across the frequency range. Measured in decibels (dB), this would be plus or minus 0 dB from 20Hz to 20,000Hz. A high-end audio system can deviate by +/– 0.5 dB, but a CD-ROM drive should not be off by more than +/– 3 dB.

**frequency shift**    See *FSK*.

**fresnel zone**    Pronounced "fraynel zone." The pattern of electromagnetic radiation that is created by a transmitting station from its antenna to receiving antennas. It is in the shape of an ellipsoid, or 3-D ellipse, which looks like an elongated football.

**FRF.11**    See *VoFR*.

**FRF.12**    See *VoFR*.

**friction feed**    A mechanism that allows cut paper forms to be used in a printer. The paper is passed between the platen and a roller that presses tightly against it. Contrast with *tractor feed*.

**frob**    To manipulate and adjust dials and buttons for fun. From the term "frobnicate," of course.

**front end**    The head, starting point or input side in a system. For example, it may refer to the graphical interface on a user's workstation where all data is entered or to a communications system, such as a front-end processor or TP monitor that accepts incoming transactions and messages. See *back end*.

**front-end CASE**    CASE tools that aid in systems analysis and design. Contrast with *back-end CASE*.

**front-end processor**    A computer that handles communications processing for a mainframe. It connects to the communications lines on one end and the mainframe on the other. It transmits and receives messages, assembles and disassembles packets and detects and corrects errors. It is sometimes synonymous with a communications controller, although the latter is usually not as flexible.

**front office automation**    See *sales force automation* and *ERM*.

**FrontPage**    A popular Web authoring program from Microsoft for Windows and the Mac. FrontPage Editor is the graphical editor for designing the pages and FrontPage Explorer is the management tool that lets you construct and maintain the entire site. It also includes WebBots, which generate code for complex functions such as searching and password protection.

**frontside bus**    See *system bus*.

**frontware**   Same as *screen scraper*.

**FS**   See *flat screen*.

**FSB**   (**F**ront**S**ide **B**us) See *system bus*.

**FSIOP**   See *AS/400 Integrated PC Server*.

**FSK**   (**F**requency **S**hift **K**eying) A simple modulation technique that merges binary data into a carrier. It creates only two changes in frequency: one for 0, another for 1.

**FSM**   See *finite state machine*.

**FSN**   (**F**ull-**S**ervice **N**etwork) A communications network that provides shopping, movies on demand and access to databases and a variety of online, interactive services. Telephone, cable and TV companies are positioning themselves to provide FSN services that are expected to evolve throughout the 1990s.

**FSO**   See *free space optics*.

**FSR**   (**F**ree **S**ystem **R**esource) In Windows 3.x, the amount of unused memory in various 64K blocks reserved for managing current applications. Every open window takes some space in this area. See *Windows memory limitation*.

**FSTN**   (**F**ilm Compensated **STN**) A passive matrix LCD technology that uses a film compensating layer between the STN display and rear polarizer for added sharpness. It was used in laptops before the DSTN method became popular. See *DSTN* and *LCD*.

**FT1**   See *fractional T1*.

**FTAM**   (**F**ile **T**ransfer **A**ccess and **M**anagement) A communications protocol for the transfer of files between systems of different vendors.

**FTG file**   See *Windows help system*.

**FTL**   (**F**lash **T**ranslation **L**ayer) See *flash memory*.

**FTMS**   See *Fusion FTMS*.

**FTP**   (**F**ile **T**ransfer **P**rotocol) A protocol used to transfer files over a TCP/IP network (Internet, UNIX, etc.). For example, after developing the HTML pages for a Web site on a local machine, they are typically uploaded to the Web server using FTP.

FTP includes functions to log onto the network, list directories and copy files. It can also convert between the ASCII and EBCDIC character codes. FTP operations can be performed by typing commands at a command prompt or via an FTP utility running under a graphical interface such as Windows. FTP transfers can also be initiated from within a Web browser by entering the URL preceded with **ftp://**.

Unlike e-mail programs in which graphics and program files have to be "attached," FTP is designed to handle binary files directly and does not add the overhead of encoding and decoding the data.

The term is also used as a verb; for example, "let's FTP them the file." See *FTP commands*, *anonymous FTP* and *TFTP*.

**FTP Utility**
Ipswitch's WS_FTP Pro makes FTP'ing easy under Windows. After logging on and switching to the appropriate folders on the local and remote systems, transferring files requires only highlighting, dragging and dropping.

**FTP site**   A computer system on the Internet that maintains files for downloading. See *anonymous FTP*.

**FTS 2000** (Federal Telecommunications System 2000) A digital fiber-optic network providing voice, video, e-mail and high-speed data communications for the U.S. government. AT&T and Sprint are the major equipment providers. FTS 2000 expired in 1998 and will be superseded by FTS 2001.

**FTS file** See *Windows help system.*

**FTTC** (Fiber To The Curb) The installation of optical fiber to within a thousand feet of the home or office. See *FTTH.*

**FTTH** (Fiber To The Home) The installation of optical fiber from the carrier directly into the home or office. See *FTTC.*

**FTX** (Fault Tolerant UNIX) Stratus Computer's version of UNIX System V for its XA/R fault tolerant computer systems.

**FUBAR** (Fouled Up Beyond All Recognition) See *foo.*

**FUD factor** (Fear Uncertainty Doubt factor) A marketing strategy used by a dominant or privileged organization that restrains competition by introducing suspicion and uncertainty into the marketplace. It is usually done by not revealing future plans or by changing them frequently, which presents a moving target for competitors. Thus, customers cannot trust that the competing vendors' products will interface properly with the dominant player's hardware or software.

**full backup** See *backup types.*

**full bleed** See *bleed.*

**full-duplex** Transmitting and receiving simultaneously. In pure digital networks, this is achieved with two pairs of wires. In analog networks or in digital networks using carriers, it is achieved by dividing the bandwidth of the line into two frequencies, one for sending, the other for receiving.

**full-duplex Ethernet** An extension to 10BaseT Ethernet that is implemented in a switched Ethernet environment, which has a dedicated line between the station and switch. It is built into the network adapter (NIC) and switch, providing bi-directional transmission that boosts bandwidth from 10–20 Mbps.

**full featured** Hardware or software that provides capabilities and functions comparable to the most advanced models or programs of that category.

**full-height drive** A 5.25" disk drive that measures 3.25" in height. It was the size of first-generation drives in desktop computers, but high-capacity hard drives are still made in this size. A full-height drive bay allows for the installation of one full-height drive or two half-height drives. Contrast with *half-height drive.*

**full-motion video** Video transmission that changes the image 30 frames per second (30 fps). Motion pictures are run at 24 fps, which is the minimum frequency required to eliminate the perception of moving frames and make the images appear visually fluid to the eye.

TV video generates 30 interlaced frames per second, which is actually transmitted as 60 half frames per second.

Video that has been digitized and stored in the computer can be displayed at varying frame rates, depending on the speed of the computer. The slower the computer, the more jerky the movement. Contrast with *freeze-frame video.*

**full path** A path name that includes the drive (if required), starting or root directory, all attached subdirectories and ending with the file or object name. Contrast with *relative path.* See *path.*

**full project life cycle** A project from inception to completion.

**full-rate ADSL** Refers to the standard ADSL technology in contrast to the slower-speed G.lite version. See *DSL.*

**full-screen mode** A programming capability that allows data to be displayed in any row, column or pixel location onscreen. Contrast with *teletype mode.*

**full-service network**   See *FSN*.

**full-text search**   A search that compares every word in a document, as opposed to searching an abstract or a set of keywords associated with the document. Full-text searching is the type performed by most Web search engines. Although it is very thorough, it often results in too many false drops. See *false drops*.

**full user mobility**   Refers to a wireless service that lets you be completely mobile such as in a car, train, etc.

**fully buzzword compliant**   Said of software that contains the same features and functions of its competitor.

**fully populated**   A circuit board whose sockets are completely filled with chips.

**fully qualified domain name**   See *FQDN*.

**function**   In programming, a self-contained software routine that peforms a job for the program it is written in or for some other program. The function performs the operation and returns control to the instruction following the calling instruction or to the calling program. Programming languages provide a set of standard functions and may allow programmers to define others. For example, the C language is built entirely of functions.

**functional decomposition**   Breaking down a process into non-redundant operations. In structured programming, it provides a hierarchical breakdown of the program into the individual operations, or routines, that are required.

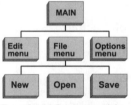

**functional requirements**   See *information requirements* and *functional specification*.

**functional specification**   The blueprint for the design of an information system. It provides documentation for the database, human and machine procedures, and all the input, processing and output detail for each data entry, query, update and report program in the system. See *information requirements*.

**Functional Decomposition of a Program**
This example is ultra simplistic, but shows the hierarchical breakdown of the program into its constituent components.

**functional stovepipe**   See *stovepipe application*.

**function call**   A request by a program to use a subroutine. The subroutine can be large and perform a significant amount of processing, or it can be as small as computing two numbers and returning the result. When applications are running, they make millions of function calls to the operating system.

A function call written in a program states the name of the function followed by any values or parameters that have to be passed to it. When the function is called, the operation is performed, and the results are returned as variables or pointers with new values.

The function may be written within the program, be part of an external library that is combined with the program when it is compiled or be contained in another program, such as the operating system or DBMS.

**function keys**   A set of keyboard keys used to command the computer (F1, F2, etc.). F1 is often the help key, but the purpose of any function key is determined by the software currently running.

**function library**   A collection of program routines. See *function*.

**function overloading**   In programming, using the same name for two or more functions. The compiler determines which function to use based on the type of function, arguments passed to it and type of values returned.

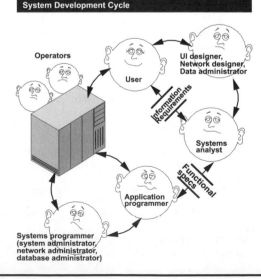

System Development Cycle

Operators

User

UI designer,
Network designer,
Data administrator

Information Requirements

Systems analyst

Functional specs

Application programmer

Systems programmer
(system administrator,
network administrator,
database administrator)

**function prototyping**    In programming, it refers to the defining of each function in the program with the number and types of parameters passed to it and its return values. The compiler can then report an error if a function is not written to conform to the prototype.

**fuse**    (1) A protective device that is designed to melt, or blow, when a specified amount of current is passed through it. PROM chips are created as a series of fuses that are selectively blown in order to create the binary patterns of the data or machine language.

(2) To bond together.

**fusible link**    A line in a PROM or PLD chip that is designed to be blown apart to program the circuit. It functions like a fuse, which, when blown, does not conduct current. See *PROM programmer* and *PLD*.

**fusing**    In electrophotography, making the toner adhere permanently to the paper. Heat fusing melts the toner, which is pressed into the paper. Cold fusing presses the toner into the paper without applying any heat. Flash fusing melts the toner with light, and no heat or pressure is used. The latter is more flexible with all types of media.

**Fusion**    See *ColdFusion, NetObjects Fusion* and *FOCUS Fusion*.

**Fusion FTMS**    (Fusion File Transfer Management System) A mainframe to LAN file transfer program from Proginet Corporation, Garden City, NY (www.proginet.com). It provides file transfer between MVS and Windows desktops and servers. Part of the software resides in the mainframe, another part in the Windows server and client. Support for additional server platforms is expected.

**fusion splice**    A type of fiber-optic splice that melts the two ends of the fiber together using heat. Contrast with *mechanical splice*.

**Futurebus+**    An IEEE standard multisegment bus that can transfer data at 32, 64, 128 and 256-bits and can address up to 64 bits. Clock speeds range from 25 to 100MHz. At 100MHz and 256 bits, it transfers 3.2 Gbytes/sec.

**future Intel chips**    Following are the CPU chips expected from Intel in the future. The 0.18 and 0.13 processes refer to the size of the elements of the semiconductor die. The following information is a best guess only and has been culled from reports and rumors. Since Intel has serious competition in the x86 space, it goes out of its way to keep details of its future products under wraps, releasing fact and fiction as it deems necessary to protect its interests (as do all leading companies in all industries). See *micron*.

IA-32

**Foster (32-bit, 0.13 process)**    1.7GHz Pentium 4 expected in 2001 with 0.13 architecture, new socket and 860 chipset.

**North Wood (32-bit, 0.13 process)**    2.2GHz version of Pentium 4 expected in 2001.

IA-64

**McKinley (64-bit, 0.18 process)**    Expected in 2001, higher performance CPU than Itanium with less or no x86 compatibility. Running at 1GHz+ with advanced I/O. See *Itanium* and *IA-64*.

**Madison (64-bit, 0.13 process)**    Expected in 2003, a .13 micron version of McKinley. Clock speeds of 1.5GHz expected.

**Deerfield (64-bit, 0.13 process)**    Expected in 2003, a lower-end version of the IA-64 family.

**Future I/O**    An input/output architecture developed by IBM, HP and Compaq that evolved into InfiniBand. Future I/O was expected to replace the PCI bus in high-end servers with a switching matrix, providing a high-speed data path between each pair of nodes. In 2000, Future I/O and NGIO and merged into one technology, originally called "System I/O" and later "InfiniBand." See *InfiniBand*.

**future proof**    Not obsolete in the future. As much as the computer field drives the future, there are very few future-proof products within it. One exception might be optical fiber, which seems capable of handling more bandwidth than we can ever imagine. However, we also said 640K would be all the memory we would ever need in a desktop computer.

**fuzzy computer**    A specially-designed computer that employs fuzzy logic. Using such architectural components as analog circuits and parallel processing, fuzzy computers are designed for AI applications.

**fuzzy logic**    A mathematical technique for dealing with imprecise data and problems that have many solutions rather than one. Although it is implemented in digital computers which ultimately make only yes-no decisions, fuzzy logic works with ranges of values, solving problems in a way that more resembles human logic.

Fuzzy logic is used for solving problems with expert systems and realtime systems that must react to an imperfect environment of highly variable, volatile or unpredictable conditions. It "smoothes the edges" so to speak, circumventing abrupt changes in operation that could result from relying on traditional either-or and all-or-nothing logic.

Fuzzy logic was conceived by Lotfi Zadeh, former chairman of the electrical engineering and computer science department at the University of California at Berkeley. In 1964, while contemplating how computers could be programmed for handwriting recognition, Zadeh expanded on traditional set theory by making membership in a set a matter of degree rather than a yes/no situation.

**Fuzzy Computer**
Since the whole computer industry seems fuzzy much of of the time, how about a really fuzzy computer!

**fuzzy logician**    An individual who is involved in developing fuzzy logic algorithms.

**fuzzy search**    An inexact search for data that finds answers that come close to the desired data. It can get results when the exact spelling is not known or help users obtain information that is loosely related to a topic.

**FW**    See *firewall*.

**FWD**    (Fast Wide Differential) Refers to a Fast Wide SCSI implementation that uses differential signaling. See *SCSI*.

**FWIW**    Digispeak for "for what it's worth."

**FWSE**    (Fast Wide Single Ended) Refers to a Fast Wide SCSI implementation that uses the common single ended signaling. See *SCSI*.

**FX**    See *foreign exchange service*.

**FX 32**    An emulator from Digital that allows 32-bit Windows programs to run on Alpha machines. It emulates x86 machine language instructions. It also performs a translation of a program the first time it is run so that it will run faster the second and subsequent times.

**FYI**    Digispeak for "for your information."

# G

**G**   See *giga*.

**G1**   The first generation of IBM's CMOS-based mainframes (Parallel Enterprise Servers). When introduced in 1994, there was no G1 designation, which was later added to clarify the evolution of the line. See *IBM mainframes* and *Parallel Enterprise Server*.

**G2**   (1) The second generation of IBM's CMOS-based mainframes (Parallel Enterprise Servers). When introduced in 1995, there was no G2 designation, which was later added to clarify the evolution of the line. See *IBM mainframes* and *Parallel Enterprise Server*.

   (2) (Generation 2)  See *RealPlayer*.

**G3**   (1) The third generation of IBM's CMOS-based mainframes (Parallel Enterprise Servers), introduced in 1996. See *IBM mainframes* and *Parallel Enterprise Server*.

   (2) A series of Macintosh desktop machines and PowerBook portables from Apple that use the PowerPC 750 chip. Models were introduced in 1997 starting at 233MHz.

   (3) (3G)  See also *wireless generations*.

**G4**   (1) The fourth generation of IBM's CMOS-based mainframes (Parallel Enterprise Servers), introduced in 1997. See *IBM mainframes* and *Parallel Enterprise Server*.

   (2) A series of Macintosh desktop machines and PowerBook portables from Apple that use the PowerPC G4 chip. Introduced in 1999, G4 models are the successor to the Macintosh G3 series. The G4 chips include the "Velocity Engine," a vector processor that provides sustained floating point capability up to one gigaflop. See *G3* and *Apple*.

**G5**   The fifth generation of IBM's CMOS-based mainframes (Parallel Enterprise Servers). Introduced in 1998, G5 doubles the performance of G4 servers, debuts the FICON channel and adds hardware-based Triple DES cryptography and numerous internal improvements. Memory was increased to 24GB. See *IBM mainframes* and *Parallel Enterprise Server* and *FICON*.

**G6**   The sixth generation of IBM's CMOS-based mainframes (Parallel Enterprise Servers). Introduced in 1999, the G6 was the first enterprise server line to use IBM's copper chip technology. See *IBM mainframes* and *Parallel Enterprise Server*.

**G.711**   An ITU standard for speech codecs that provides toll quality audio at 64 Kbps using either A-Law or mu-Law PCM methods. This uncompressed digital format is a required codec for H.323 audio and videoconferencing in order to allow easy connections to legacy telephone networks. Following is a summary of the G. specifications listed in this database. See *PCM*.

| Standard | Method | Kbps |
|----------|--------|------|
| G.711    | PCM    | 64   |
| G.721    | ADPCM  | 32   |

```
Standard   Method    Kbps
G.722      ADPCM     64
G.723      ADPCM     20, 40
G.723.1    LD-CELP   5.3, 6.4
G.726      ADPCM     16, 24, 32, 40
G.727      ADPCM     16, 24, 32, 40
G.728      LD-CELP   16
G.729      CELP       8
```

**G.721**   An ITU standard for speech codecs that uses the ADPCM method and provides toll quality audio at 32 Kbps. See *G.726* and *ADPCM*.

**G.722**   An ITU standard for speech codecs that uses the ADPCM method and provides high-quality audio at 64 Kbps. See *ADPCM*.

**G.723**   An ITU standard for speech codecs that uses the ADPCM method and provides toll quality audio at 20 or 40 Kbps. See *G.726* and *ADPCM*.

**G.723.1**   An ITU standard for speech codecs optimized for modems. It uses the LD-CELP method and provides toll quality audio at 5.3 or 6.4 Kbps. The higher rate requires less processing power. It also provides a mode where one person speaks at a time and uses the extra bandwidth for the talking party.

**G.726**   An ITU standard for speech codecs that uses the ADPCM method to compress 64 Kbps PCM into 40, 32, 24 or 16 Kbps depending on available channel bandwidth. G.726 generally replaces G.721 and G.723. See *G.727* and *ADPCM*.

**G.727**   An ITU standard for speech codecs that uses the ADPCM method to compress 64 Kbps PCM into 40, 32, 24 or 16 Kbps to accomodate the available network. G.727 is a specialized version of G.726 intended for packet-based systems using the Packetized Voice Protocol (PVP). See *G.726* and *ADPCM*.

**G.728**   An ITU standard for speech codecs that uses the LD-CELP method and provides near toll quality audio at 16 Kbps.

**G.729**   An ITU standard for speech codecs that uses the CELP method and provides toll quality audio at 8 Kbps. See *G.729.A*.

**G.729.A**   An ITU standard for speech codecs that is less complex than G.729 and is designed for simultaneous voice and data.

**gain**   The amount of increase that an amplifier provides on the output side of the circuit.

**GAL**   (Generic Array Logic) A programmable logic chip (PLD) technology from Lattice Semiconductor.

**gallium arsenide**   An alloy of gallium and arsenic compound (GaAs) that is used as the base material for chips. It is several times faster than silicon.

**Game Blaster**   A sound card from Creative Labs that included a stereo 12-voice MIDI synthesizer. Originally introduced in 1987 as the Creative Music System (C/MS), it was renamed Game Blaster shortly thereafter. Game Blaster cards evolved into the Sound Blaster standard.

**game port**   An I/O connector used to attach a joy stick. It is typically a 15-pin socket on the back of a PC. See *serial port*.

**gamma**   The relationship between the input and output of a device, expressed as a number, with 1.0 being a perfect linear plot (the output is increased in the exact same proportion as the input).

**gamma correction**   An adjustment to the light intensity of a scanner, monitor or printer. It generally refers to the adjustment of the brightness of a display screen in order to compensate for a CRT's irregularity. A gamma correction plot is a curve, not a straight line as is the standard brightness control. Gamma correction is also used to make the monitor display images more closely in appearance with the laser printer that creates the output.

**gamut**   See *color gamut*.

**gang punch**   To punch an identical set of holes into a deck of punched cards.

**Gantt chart**   A type of floating bar chart usually used in project management to show resources or tasks over time.

**gap**   (1) The space between blocks of data on magnetic tape.
   (2) The space in a read/write head over which magnetic flux (energy) flows causing the underlying magnetic tape or disk surface to become magnetized in the corresponding direction.

**gapless**   A magnetic tape that is recorded in a continuous stream without interblock gaps.

**garbage collection**   A software routine that searches memory for areas of inactive data and instructions in order to reclaim that space for the general memory pool (the heap). Operating systems may or may not provide this feature. For example, Windows does not do automatic garbage collection which requires that the programmer specifically deallocates memory in order to release it. If a program continues to allocate memory for data buffers and eventually exceeds the physical memory capacity, the operating system then has to place parts of the program in virtual memory (on disk) in order to continue, which slows down processing. Deallocating memory after a routine no longer needs it is a tedious task and programmers often forget to do it or do not do it properly. Java performs automatic garbage collection without programmer intervention, which eliminates this coding headache. See *heap* and *Java*.

**garbage in...**   See *GIGO*.

**GARP**   (**G**eneral **A**ttributes **R**egistration **P**rotocol) A standard for registering a client station into a multicast domain. See *802.1p*.

**GartnerGroup**   (GartnerGroup, Stamford, CT, www.gartner.com) The largest information technology consulting firm that specializes in research and analysis. Founded in 1979 by Gideon Gartner, it has grown through acquisitions, including Dataquest in 1995. It offers more than 2000 management reports on every topic in the IT world and hosts the annual GartnerGroup Symposium/ITxpo in the U.S. and abroad. See *Dataquest*.

**GAS**   See *gallium arsenide*.

**gas discharge display**   See *plasma display*.

**gas plasma**   See *plasma display*.

**gate**   (1) An open/closed switch.
   (2) A pattern of transistors that makes up an AND, OR or NOT Boolean logic gate. See *gate array*.
   (3) In a field effect transistor (CMOS), the line that activates the switch. Same as *base* in a bipolar transistor.

**gate array**   An unfinished chip with electronic components that have not been connected. The chip is completed by designing and adhering the top metal layers which provide the interconnecting pathways. This final masking stage is less costly than designing the chip from scratch.
   The gate array is made up of basic cells, each cell containing some number of transistors and resistors depending on the vendor. Using a cell library (gates, registers, etc.) and a macro library (more complex functions), the customer designs the chip, and the vendor's software generates the masks that connect the transistors. See *PLD*, *ASIC*, *hard macro* and *soft macro*.

**gated**   Switched "on" or capable of being switched on and off.

**gatekeeper**    A server that translates user names into physical addresses for H.323 conferencing. It can also be used to provide call authorization and accounting information.

**gate level specification**    A specification for a digital circuit that defines the electronic components and their interconnects. See *RTL*.

**gateway**    (1) A computer that performs protocol conversion between different types of networks or applications. For example, a gateway can convert a TCP/IP packet to a NetWare IPX packet and vice versa or from AppleTalk to DECnet, from SNA to AppleTalk and so on.

Gateways function at layer 4 and above in the OSI model. They perform complete conversions from one protocol to another rather than simply support one protocol from within another, such as IP tunneling. Sometimes routers can implement gateway functions.

An electronic mail, or messaging, gateway converts messages between two different messaging protocols. See *LAN* and *IP gateway*.

(2) A computer that acts as a go-between two or more networks that use the same protocols. In this case, the gateway functions as an entry/exit point to the network. Transport protocol conversion may not be required, but some form of processing is typically performed. See *proxy server*.

(3) An Earth station and computer complex that switches data and voice signals between satellites and terrestrial networks.

(4) An earlier name for router. See *router* and *layer 3 switch*.

**Gateway 2000**    (Gateway 2000, N. Sioux City, SD, www.gw2k.com) A major PC manufacturer founded in 1985 by Ted Waitt and Mike Hammond. Gateway first sold peripherals to owners of Texas Instrument computers. In 1987, it began to offer complete systems and has continued to drive down the cost of quality PCs by mail. In 1997, it acquired ALR (Advanced Logic Research), a PC company founded in 1984 and noted for its high-end machines.

**gateway address**    The default address of a network or Web site. It provides a single domain name and point of entry to the site. See *proxy server*.

**gateway host**    A router that serves as an entry point into and exit point out of a network.

**gather write**    To output data from two or more noncontiguous memory locations with one write operation. See *scatter read*.

**gauss**    A unit of measurement of magnetic intensity named after Karl F. Gauss (1777–1855), considered to be one of the greatest mathematicians of all time. See *degauss*.

**Gaussian blur**    A type of image filter commonly used to blur an object. It may be used to blur the entire image or to produce a drop shadow effect. See *image filter*.

**Gaussian distribution**    A random distribution of events that is often graphed as a bell-shaped curve. It is used to represent a normal or statistically probable outcome.

**Gaussian noise**    In communications, a random interference generated by the movement of electricity in the line. You can actually see and hear Gaussian noise when you tune your TV to a channel that is not operating. Also called "white noise."

**Gawk**    A version of the awk pattern matching language from the GNU foundation. See *awk* and *GNU*.

**GB**    (1) (GB) (GigaByte) One billion bytes (technically 1,073,741,824 bytes). See *giga* and *space/time*.

(2) (Gb) (GigaBit) One billion bits (technically 1,073,741,824 bits). Lowercase "b" for bit and "B" for byte are not always followed and often misprinted. Thus, Gb may refer to gigabyte. See *giga* and *space/time*.

**GbE**    See *Gigabit Ethernet*.

**GBIC** (GigaBit Interface Converter) An interface used to attach network devices to fiber-based transmission systems such as Fibre Channel and Gigabit Ethernet. The GBIC converts the serial electrical signals to serial optical signals and vice versa. GBIC modules are hot swappable and contain ID and system information that a switch can use to determine the network device's capabilities.

**Gbits/sec** (GigaBITS per SECond) Billion bits per second.

**Gbps** (GigaBits Per Second) Billion bits per second. We're not quite up to using GBps (gigaBYTES per second) on a regular basis, but we will some day.

**Gbs** (GigaBits per Second) Same as *Gbps*.

**G-byte** See *gigabyte*.

**Gbytes/sec** (GigaBYTES per SECond) Billion bytes per second.

**GCOS** (General Comprehensive OS) An operating system from Bull used in its minis and mainframes. GCOS was orginally developed by GE in the early 1970s as GECOS (GE Comprehensive OS), then changed to General Comprehensive OS when Honeywell took over GE's computer division. Later, Bull acquired Honeywell's computer products.

**GCR** (1) (Group Code Recording) An encoding method used on magnetic tapes and Apple II and Mac 400K and 800K floppy disks.

(2) (Gray Component Replacement) A method for reducing the amount of printing ink used. It substitutes black for the amount of gray contained in a color, thus black ink is used instead of the three CMY inks. See *UCR* and *dot gain*.

**GD&R** Digispeak for "grinning, ducking and running," said after a snide remark. Another variation is GD&WVVF, which stands for "grinning, ducking and walking very, very fast."

**GDDM** (Graphical Data Display Manager) Software that generates graphics images in the IBM mainframe environment. It contains routines to generate graphics on terminals, printers and plotters, as well as accepting input from scanners. Programmers use it for creating graphics, but users can employ its Interactive Chart Utility (ICU) to create business graphics without programming.

GDDM/graPHIGS is a programming environment that combines graphics capability with a user interface similar to the Presentation Manager in OS/2.

**GDI** (Graphics Device Interface) The graphics display system in Microsoft Windows. When an application needs to display or print, it makes a call to a GDI function and sends it the parameters for the object that must be created. GDI in turn "draws" the object by sending commands to the screen and printer drivers, which actually render the images. See *DirectX* and *device context*.

**GDI printer** A printer designed to work only from Windows. It uses Windows' internal graphics display system (GDI) to rasterize the image. GDI printers are lower-cost printers that place a greater demand on the host processor than traditional printers. See *host-based printer*.

**GDM** (Global DOS Memory) The first megabyte of memory that DOS supports. It consists of conventional memory (0-640K), the UMA (640-1,024K) and the HMA (1,024–1,088K).

**GDMO** (Guidelines for Definition of Managed Objects) The rules for defining the elements (objects) that are managed in a LAN (workstations, servers, switches, etc.). Supported by the CMIP and TMN management standards, the resulting descriptions are used in MIBs for network management. GDMO provides a strict inheritance hierarchy for object classes and a tree structure for object names. ASN.1 is used for syntax. See *CMIP*, *TMN*, *MIB* and *ASN.1*.

**GE** (Greater than or Equal to) See *relational operator*.

**geek**   A technically-oriented person. It has typically implied a "nerdy" or "wierd" personality, someone with limited social skills that likes to tinker with scientific or high-tech projects. Today, however, it has become quite fashionable to be a geek, since countless technical people have become very successful starting with PCs in the 1980s and then the Internet in the 1990s. A geek can be the CEO of a billion dollar company. See *nerd* and *Geekonics*.

**Geekonics**   (GEEK phONICS) Computer English, or more precisely "computer sounds," which are the acronyms and buzzwords spoken by computer people. Geekonics is the high-tech counterpart to Ebonics (ebony and phonics), which is Black English. A whole lot of Geekonics is in this database. Same as *geekspeak* and *nerdspeak*.

**geekspeak**   Technical language. Same as *nerdspeak* and *Geekonics*.

**GEM**   (Graphics Environment Manager) A graphical user interface from Digital Research that was similar to the Mac/Windows environment. It was built into ROM in several Atari computers. The DOS version of Ventura Publisher came with a runtime version of GEM.

**GEMBASE**   A client/server application development system from Ross Systems, Inc., Atlanta, GA (www.rossinc.com), that is noted for its high transaction performance and scalability. It runs on Windows NT, OpenVMS and UNIX servers that support dumb terminals and Windows clients. Its proprietary 4GL programming language can access Oracle, Rdb and Sybase databases as well as provide application partitioning.

GEMBASE's largest customer is Ross Systems itself, which develops the Renaissance CS applications for the process manufacturing industry. GEMBASE was originally developed by Pioneer Computing.

**GEMMS**   (Global Enterprise Manufacturing Management System) An ERP system from Oracle that runs on a variety of UNIX-based computers. It provides more than a dozen integrated modules for research & development, manufacturing, distribution, customer service and financial activities. GEMMS was developed by Datalogix, which was acquired by Oracle in 1997. See also *GEMS*.

**GEMS**   See *Legato*. See also *GEMMS*.

**GENA**   (Generalized Event Notification Architecture) A method for communicating events over the Web. It is an architecture for transmitting notifications between HTTP resources such as buddy lists, distribution lists and print jobs. GENA provides both notification and subscription. Notification sends information as needed, whereas a subscription initiates a relationship so that notification is made automatically when an event occurs.

**gender changer**   A coupler that reverses the gender of one of the connectors in order that two male connectors or two female connectors can be joined together.

**gene chip**   A chip that is used to detect the DNA makeup of a cell. The chip contains hundreds of thousands of tiny squares designed to mate with a particular gene. They react to the liquified human cells poured over it and are detectable by a laser. Gene chips are expected to revolutionize medicine by being able to pinpoint a very specific disease or the susceptibility to it.

**generalized program**   Software that serves a changing environment. By allowing variable data to be introduced, the program can solve the same problem for different users or situations. For example, the electronic versions of this database could be programmed to read in a different title and thus be used for any type of dictionary.

**Gender Changer**
The unit in the middle is the gender changer.

**General Magic**   (General Magic, Inc., Sunnyvale, CA, www.genmagic.com) A company founded in 1990 as a spinoff of Apple Computer. It was established to create personal communications products and services by developing and licensing technology to a wide variety of manufacturers and service providers. See *Telescript* and *Magic Cap*.

**General MIDI**   A standard set of 128 sounds for MIDI sound cards and devices (synthesizers, sound modules, etc.). By assigning instruments to specific MIDI patch locations, General MIDI provides a standard way of communicating MIDI sound.

MIDI's small storage requirement makes it very desirable as a musical sound source for multimedia applications compared to digitizing actual music. For example, a three-minute MIDI file may take only 20 to 30K, whereas a WAV file (digital audio) could consume up to several megabytes depending on sound quality.

**General Protection Fault**   See *GPF*.

**General Public License**   See *GNU General Public License*.

**general-purpose computer**   Refers to computers that follow instructions, thus virtually all computers from micro to mainframe are general purpose. Even computers in toys, games and single-function devices follow instructions in their built-in program. In contrast, computational devices can be designed from scratch for special purposes (see *ASIC*).

**general-purpose controller**   A peripheral control unit that can service more than one type of peripheral device; for example, a printer and a communications line.

**general-purpose language**   A programming language used to solve a wide variety of problems. All common programming languages (C, C++, Java, COBOL, etc.) are examples. Contrast with *special-purpose language*.

**general-purpose machine**   See *general-purpose computer*.

**generation X**   Refers to individuals roughly between the age of 25 and 34. "Generation Y" pertains to ages 18 to 24, and "baby boomers" are people 35 to 54. By the time older gen-Xers became teenagers, the personal computer revolution had begun. Younger gen-Xers and all generation Ys were brought up in the thick of it. In contrast, older baby boomers were certainly raised without desktop computers, but many did not even have TVs as a child.

**generation Y**   See *generation X*.

**generator**   **(1)** Software that creates software. See *application generator* and *macro generator*.
**(2)** A device that creates electrical power or synchonization signals.

**Generic CADD**   A full-featured CADD package for DOS from Autodesk, Inc., Sausalito, CA (www.autodesk.com), that offers levels for beginner, intermediate and advanced users. It was originally developed by Generic Software of Bothell, WA.

**generic top-level domain**   See *Internet domain name*.

**genetic programming**   A type of programming that imitates genetic algorithms, which uses mutation and replication to produce algorithms that represent the "survival of the fittest." While genetic algorithms yield numbers, genetic programs yield ever-improving computer programs. Written in languages such as LISP and Scheme, genetic programming requires the determination of a fitness function, which is a desired output (result). The degree of error in the fitness function determines the quality of the program. For more information, visit www.geneticprogramming.com.

**Genie**   An online information service from Yovelle Renaissance Corporation (www.genie.com), that provides Internet access, chat lines, roundtable discussions and games. It was originally the General Electric Network for Information Exchange. See *online services*. See also *Jini*.

**genlock**   (**gen**erator **lock**) Circuitry that synchronizes video signals for mixing. In personal computers, a genlock display adapter converts screen output into an NTSC video signal, which it synchronizes with an external video source.

**GEO**   (Geostationary Earth Orbit) A communications satellite in orbit 22,282 miles above the equator. At this orbit, it travels at the same speed as the earth's rotation, thus appearing stationary. GEOs are excellent for TV broadcasting, but produce distracting, half-second delays in interactive voice conversations, because of the long round trip from earth and back. LEOs and MEOs, which are closer to the earth, are being deployed for interactive services. See *LEO* and *MEO*.

## geographic information system    See *GIS* and *GIS glossary*.

## geometry accelerator    A high-performance graphics engine that performs geometry calculations. See *graphics accelerator*.

## geometry calculations
In 3-D graphics rendering, the computation of the base properties for each point (vertex) of the triangles forming the objects in the 3-D world. These properties include X-Y-Z coordinates, RGB values, alpha translucency, reflectivity and others. The geometry calculations involve transformation from 3-D world coordinates into corresponding 2-D screen coordinates, clipping off any parts not visible onscreen and lighting. See *graphics accelerator*.

**GEO**
Geostationary satellites are 22,282 miles high and rotate with the earth.

**LEO**
Low-earth orbit satellites are from 400 to 1600 miles high and revolve around the earth.

**GEOs Appear Stationary**
GEOs rotate at earth speed and thus appear stationary. LEOs and MEOs are closer to earth and revolve around the planet.

## geometry transformation    In 3-D graphics rendering, the translation of the X-Y-Z coordinates for each point (vertex) of the triangles forming the objects in the 3-D world into their corresponding 2-D screen coordinates. Animating 3-D objects requires enormous numbers of calculations. See *geometry calculations*.

## GeoPort    A serial port from Apple designed for voice and video applications. With an adapter, it can be used to dial an analog phone. Standard on various Macintosh models, GeoPort provides a 2 Mbps bandwidth, suitable for very high-quality videoconferencing. The GeoPort is endorsed by Versit.

## geostationary    Earth aligned. Refers to satellites (GEOs) that travel at the same speed as the earth and are always a uniform distance from the earth. See *GEO*.

## geosynchronous    Earth aligned. May refer to earlier satellites that travelled at the same speed as the earth, but with orbits that were not continuously the same distance from the earth. See *geostationary*.

## Geoworks Ensemble    An earlier graphical environment for DOS from Geoworks Corpoation, Alameda, CA (www.geoworks.com), that included a basic suite of applications and provided a launching pad for all others.  Later marketed by New Deal, Inc., Cambridge, MA (www.newdealinc.com), as New Deal Office, it is used in older, refurbished computers for education and third-world countries. See *GEOS*.

## germanium    (Ge) The material used in making the first transistors. Although still used in very limited applications, germanium was replaced by silicon years ago.

## gesture recognition    **(1)** The ability to interpret simple hand-written symbols such as check marks and slashes. See *PDA* and *tablet PC*.
   **(2)** The ability to recognize hand signals. In 1998, Toshiba introduced a device that uses infrared light reflected from a user's hand to sense its motion.

**get**   (1) In programming, a request for the next record in an input file. Contrast with *put*.

(2) An FTP command to copy a file or to display the contents of a text file.

**Gflops**   See *gigaflops*.

**ghost**   (1) A faint second image that appears close to the primary image on a display or printout. On a printer, it is caused by bouncing print elements as the paper passes by.

(2) To make an exact copy of an operating system or the complete contents of a hard disk. See *ghosting server*.

(3) In transmission, a secondary signal that arrives ahead of or later than the primary signal.

(4) To display the text of a menu option or the elements on a toolbar button in a grayed or fuzzy manner, indicating that the operation is not currently selectable.

**A Ghosted Button**
The button on the left is ghosted, indicating that the function is not available at that moment. When it is usable, the elements are restored as in the example on the right.

**ghost image**   See *ghosting server*.

**ghosting server**   A server that contains a group of programs to be duplicated verbatim onto other PCs. It typically contains the operating system and a selected set of applications that are preconfigured. See *cloning software*.

**ghost site**   A Web site that is not updated anymore, but is still maintained for public viewing. See *ghost server*.

**GHz**   (GigaHertZ) One billion cycles per second. High-speed radio frequency applications transmit in the gigahertz range. See *RF*.

**giant magnetoresistive**   See *magnetoresistive*.

**GID file**   See *Windows help system*.

**GIF**   (Graphics Interchange Format) A popular bitmapped graphics file format developed by CompuServe. It supports 8-bit color (256 colors) and is widely used on the Web, because the files compress well. GIFs include a color table that includes the most representative 256 colors used. For example, a picture of the forest would include mostly greens. This method provides excellent realism in an 8-bit image.

There are two versions of GIF. The original GIF87a was created in 1987, and GIF89a in 1989. GIF89a allows one of the colors to be made transparent and take on the background color of the underlying page or window. GIF89a also supports animated GIFs, which are GIF sequences displayed one after the other to simulate movement.

Macintosh users call GIF files "giff" files, while PC users call them "jiff" files. See *LZW*, *interlaced GIF* and *PNG*.

**GIFSCII**   (1) (GIF ASCII) A program that converts images into ASCII art or the image that was created in such a manner. See *ASCII art*.

(2) Converting ASCII text into a GIF image for the Web in order to preserve the original fonts and formatting.

**gig**   Same as *giga*.

**giga**   Billion. Abbreviated "G." It often refers to the precise value 1,073,741,824 since computer specifications are usually binary numbers. See *GB*, *binary values* and *space/time*.

**gigabit**   One billion bits. Also Gb, Gbit and G-bit. See *giga* and *space/time*.

**Gigabit Ethernet**   An Ethernet technology that raises transmission speed to 1 Gbps. It is used primarily for backbones. The first IEEE standard (802.3z) for Gigabit Ethernet defined its use over multimode optical fiber providing full-duplex operation from switch to end station or to another switch and half-duplex using CSMA/CD in a shared environment. The 802.3ab standard (1000BaseTX) provides for Gigabit Ethernet over copper cable. The maximum distance between Gigabit Ethernet (GigE) nodes is based on the type of transceiver and cable used as outlined below.

**FIBER**

| Fiber Diameter (microns) | Modal Bandwidth (MHz-km) | Range (meters) |
|---|---|---|
| **1000BaseSX** | | |
| 62.5 multimode | 160 | 220 |
| 62.5 multimode | 200 | 275 |
| 50 multimode | 400 | 500 |
| 50 multimode | 500 | 550 |
| | | |
| **1000BaseLX** | | |
| 62.5 multimode | 500 | 550 |
| 50 multimode | 400 | 550 |
| 50 multimode | 500 | 550 |
| 9 singlemode | -- | 5000 |

**COPPER**

| | | |
|---|---|---|
| **1000BaseTX** | | |
| Category 5 UTP | | 100 |

**Gigabit Switch Router**    Cisco's trade name for its high-end layer 3 switch routers.

**gigabyte**    One billion bytes. Also GB, Gbyte and G-byte. See *giga* and *space/time*.

**gigaflops**    (**GIGA FL**oating point **OP**erations per **S**econd) One billion floating point operations per second. See *FLOPS*.

**gigahertz**    See *GHz*.

**GigaPOP**    (**GIGA**bit **P**oint **O**f **P**resence) A high-speed switching point being developed by universities across the U.S. as part of the Internet2 project. See *Internet2*.

**GigE**    See *Gigabit Ethernet*.

**GIGO**    (**G**arbage **I**n **G**arbage **O**ut) "Bad input produces bad output." Data entry is critical. All possible tests should be made on data entered into a computer.

**"Garbage In, Gospel Out"**    An alternate meaning. Many people have complete faith in computer output!

**GIMP**    (**G**NU **I**mage **M**anipulation **P**rogram) An open source paint and image editing program for UNIX and X Window that originated as an undergraduate project by Peter Mattis and Spencer Kimball at the University of California, Berkeley. Numerous programmers have contributed to the project, turning GIMP into a serious image manipulation tool that supports layers, alpha channels, third-party plug-ins and three scripting languages. Using Python, Perl or Script-Fu scripts, GIMP can be used for batch processing and the automation of tasks such as the interpolation of frames for animation sequences.

The GIMP source code is distributed under the GNU General Public License (GPL). For more information, visit www.gimp.org and www.gimp-savvy.com, the latter providing the entire contentof the book, *Grokking the GIMP* by Carey Bunks.

**GIOP**  (General Inter-Orb Protocol) The protocol used by CORBA to communicate between ORBs. GIOP defines the messages and format that are passed over the ORB between the client and the object. GIOP is a high-level protocol that rides on top of a transport protocol such as TCP/IP. The combination of GIOP running on TCP/IP is IIOP. See *IIOP* and *CORBA*.

**GIS**  (1) (Geographic Information System) A digital mapping system used for exploration, demographics, dispatching and tracking. Using satellites and aerial photography, the United States Geological Survey and other organizations have developed digital maps of most of the world. These maps are processed via software into images that are used for a myriad of explorations and analyses. See *digital elevation model* and *GIS glossary*.

(2) (Generalized Information System) An early IBM mainframe query and data manipulation language.

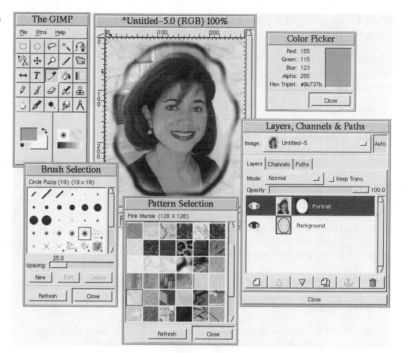

**GIMP In Action**
GIMP provides sophisticated paint and editing functions as is evident in these various dialogs and palettes. *(Image courtesy of Carey Bunks, www.gimp-savvy.com)*

**GKS**  (Graphical Kernel System) A device-independent graphics language for 2-D, 3-D and bitmapped graphics images. It allows graphics applications to be developed on one system and easily moved to another with minimal or no change. It was the first true standard for graphics applications programmers and has been adopted by both ANSI and ISO.

**G/L**  (General Ledger) G/L is often the acronym for the general ledger application in an organization. The general ledger maintains a summary of financial accounts for the business.

**glare filter**  A fine mesh screen that is placed over a CRT screen to reduce glare from overhead and ambient light.

**glass box testing**  See *white box testing*.

**glass house**  The large datacenter, which typically contains one or more mainframes and is often constructed with windows to the inside. Glass houses may contain raised floors for underground wiring and are generally very well air conditioned.

**The Big Glass House**
Mainframes have typically resided in the "glass house" due to stringent air conditioning requirements. Although newer machines dissipate less heat than older models, many units in one room still require substantial cooling. *(Image courtesy of International Business Machines Corporation. Unauthorized use not permitted.)*

**GLINT**    A family of 2-D and 3-D processors from 3D Labs, Inc., San Jose, CA (www.3dlabs.com) that are widely used in high-end display adapters.

**glitch**    A temporary or random hardware malfunction. It is possible that a bug in a program may cause the hardware to appear as if it had a glitch in it and vice versa. At times it can be extremely difficult to determine whether a problem lies within the hardware or the software.

**G.lite**    See *DSL*.

**global**    Pertaining to an entire file, database, volume, program or system.

**global search and replace**    Replacing one set of data or text with another throughout the entire document of file.

**Globalstar**    (Globalstar, San Jose, CA, www.globalstar.com) A satellite-based communications company that offers voice and short messaging services throughout 80% of the world's surface. Globalstar is the second satellite system to use LEO satellites and handheld phones (Iridium was the first), but Globalstar is the first to use QUALCOMM's CDMA technology, which is known for its high quality. Globalstar phones support one or two cellular modes as well as satellite, letting you use standard facilities when possible and switch to the satellites in remote areas. The Globalstar service was rolled out in late 1999.

**global variable**    In programming, a variable that is used by all modules in a program.

**global village**    (1) A term coined by Marshall McLuhan who envisioned the world interconnected via electronic communications.
    (2) (Global Village Communications, Inc., Sunnyvale, CA, www.globalvillage.com) A manufacturer of communications products for the Macintosh and Windows PCs founded in 1989.

**Global Virtual Private Network**    See *GVPN*.

**glocalization**    (GLObal loCALIZATION) Specializing a Web site for a particular country by translating everything into that language. It also refers to targeting the site contents to the culture of the country.

**glossaries in this publication**    See *fiber optics glossary*, *GIS glossary*, *power supply glossary* and *wireless glossary*.

**GLP**    See *MGCP*.

**GLperf**    (OpenGL PERFormance) A benchmark developed by the OPC group for measuring the raw performance of an OpenGL system. See *OPC*.

**glue**    Refers to software that provides some conversion, translation or other process that makes one system work with another. For example, an application adapter reformats the data into a form available to another application and vice versa. A CGI script sits between the browser and the database, enabling search requests to be passed to the database. "Glue" or "glue software" are terms that can be widely used to reference small programs or scripts needed to integrate applications or tie subsystems together. See *application integration* and *integration server*. See also *glue chip*.

**glue chip**    A support chip that adds functionality to a microprocessor, for example, an I/O processor or extra memory.

**glue logic**    A small amount of digital circuitry (logic gates) used to interconnect ready-made circuits. See *standard cell*.

**GMR**    (Giant Magnetoresistive) See *magnetoresistive*.

**Gnapster**    See *Napster*.

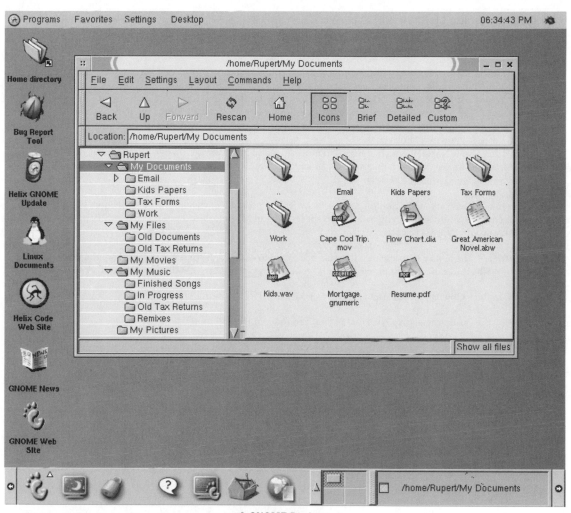

**A GNOME Desktop**
Similar to other graphical interfaces such as on the Mac and Windows, this is a sample GNOME desktop with an open application. *(Screen shot courtesy of Helix Code, Inc.)*

**GNOME**     (GNU Network Object Modeling Environment) A GUI-based user interface for Linux and other UNIX environments that grew out of the GNU project. Providing an alternative to the KDE interface, GNOME is either pronounced "guhnome" or "nome." Companies such as Red Hat Software (www.redhat.com) and Helix Code, Inc., (www.helixcode.com), support the GNOME environment. For more information, visit www.gnome.org. See *Linux*, *KDE* and *GNU*.

**GNU**     (Gnu's Not UNIX) A project sponsored by the Free Software Foundation that develops and maintains a complete software environment including operating system kernel and utilities, editor, compiler and debugger. Many consultants and organizations provide support for GNU software, and more than 150 software products are available online or on CD-ROM. For information, visit www.gnu.org. See *Linux*, *GNU General Public License* and *Free Software Foundation*.

**GNU General Public License**   The license that accompanies the GNU software. Also known as a "copyleft," it gives everyone the right to use and modify the material as long as they make it available to everyone else with the same licensing stipulation.

**Gnutella**   A file sharing system on the Internet that lets you search for software and documents on the GnutellaNet, a loose federation of users and organizations that make a wide variety of information available to the world at large. Software for Windows, Mac, Linux/UNIX and BeOS turns your machine into a search client so you can access the GnutellaNet, as well as a server for offering files to others. In order to do a search, you have to connect to one or more computers on the network directly by IP address, which in turn connect to other computers within a limited domain of about 10,000 hosts, known as a "horizon."

Gnutella differs from Napster, which is geared to music files and provides a centralized listing, whereas the GnutellaNet is a peer-to-peer network that contains all kinds of files. For more information, visit www.gnutellanews.com and http://gnutella.wego.com. See *Napster*.

**go**   A command used on a BBS or online service to switch the user to a particular forum or section. For example, typing **go macintosh** would switch you to a section specializing in Macintosh computers. Like any command language, you have to know what words to enter.

**goal seeking**   The ability to calculate a formula backward to obtain a desired input. For example, given the goal **gross margin = 50%** and the range of possible inputs, goal seeking attempts to obtain the optimum input.

**GOCA**   (Graphics Object Content Architecture)  See *MO:DCA*.

**gold code**   Programming source code that is finalized for commercial duplication. See *build*.

**GoLive**   Web authoring software for Window and Macintosh from Adobe that includes numerous visual design and site managment tools. GoLive Dynamic Link for ASP enables the development of Active Server Pages (ASPs) that are run on Microsoft Web servers. GoLive is used by professional Web developers whereas Adobe's PageMill is more for the first-time site designer. See *ASP* and *PageMill*.

**Good Times virus**   An e-mail virus that contained "Good Times" in the subject field which supposedly would damage the data in your computer if you opened the message. This was a famous hoax first encountered in 1994 and repeated over the next several years. See *virus hoaxes*.

**gooey**   (GUI) The acronymn for graphical user interface. See *GUI*.

**gooey builder**   See *GUI* builder.

**Google**   A search site on the Web noted for its fast retrieval speed as well as its lack of ads and frills. Users claim it gets the job done faster than most other search sites. The Google index of Web pages is over a billion and counting. Visit www.google.com.

**Gopher**   A program that searches for file names and resources on the Internet and presents hierarchical menus to the user. As users select options, they are moved to different Gopher servers on the Internet. Where links have been established, Usenet news and other information can be read directly from Gopher. There are more than 7,000 Gopher servers on the Internet. See *Veronica*, *Archie*, *Jughead*, *WAIS* and *World Wide Web*.

**Gopherspace**   The collective information made available on Gopher servers throughout the Internet.

**GOPS**   (Giga [billion] Operations Per Second)  The measurement of instructional performance of a chip or system. It typically refers to DSP operations. See *MOPS*.

**GOSIP**   (Government Open Systems Interconnection Profile)  A U.S. government mandate that after August 15, 1990, all new network procurements must comply with OSI. Testing is performed at the NIST, which maintains a database of OSI-compliant commercial products. GOSIP also allows TCP/IP protocols to be used.

Since broad adoption of OSI standards never came to fruition, GOSIP evolved into POSIT (Profiles for Open Systems Internetworking Technologies), which is a set of non-mandatory standards that acknowledge the widespread use of TCP/IP.

**goto**     **(1)** In a high-level programming language, a statement that directs the computer to go to some other part of the program. Low-level language equivalents are *branch* and *jump*.

**(2)** In dBASE, a command that directs the user to a specific record in the file.

**(3)** In word processing, a command that directs the user to a specific page number.

**GoTo.com**     (GoTo.com, Inc., Pasadena, CA, www.go2.com) A Web search site founded in 1997 that enables advertisers to prepare their own descriptive summaries and bid on their placement in the results list. If there are no advertisers for the search words, GoTo.com returns results similar to other search sites. However, if advertisers have selected the search words, their summaries appear at the beginning of list.

The results list displays the amount the advertiser bid for that placement, so other advertisers can easily identify how much it would cost to move higher in the list, at least until someone else bids a greater amount. GoTo.com is different than Go2Net.com, which is a search site that uses the MetaCrawler engine (see *MetaCrawler*).

**goto-less programming**     Writing a program without using goto instructions, an important rule in structured programming. A goto instruction points to a different part of the program without a guarantee of returning. Instead of using goto's, structures called "subroutines" or "functions" are used, which automatically return to the next instruction after the calling instruction when completed.

**Gouraud shading**     In 3-D graphics, a technique developed by Henri Gouraud in the early 1970s that computes a shaded surface based on the color and illumination at the corners of every triangle. Gouraud shading is the simplest rendering method and is computed faster than Phong shading. It does not produce shadows or reflections. The surface normals at the triangle's points are used to create RGB values, which are averaged across the triangle's surface. See *flat shading* and *Phong shading*.

Flat          Gouraud          Phong

**Types of Shading**
Flat, Gouraud and Phong shading are the three most common types of shading used on 3-D objects. *(Image courtesy of Intergraph Computer Systems.)*

**GPC**     (GPC Group) Originally the Graphics Performance Characterization committee of the NCGA, the GPC Group is now part of Standard Performance Evaluation Corporation (SPEC) and oversees the following graphics performance benchmarks: APC, MBC, OPC, PLB and XPC. APC tests applications, MBC tests multimedia, OPC tests OpenGL, XPC tests X Window, and PLB tests wireframe and surface modeling. See *APC*, *MBC*, *OPC*, *XPC*, *PLB* and *SPEC*.

**GPCmark**     See *PLB*.

**GPF**     **(1)** (General Protection Fault) The name of an abend, or crash, in a Windows application, starting with Version 3.1. When the GPF occurs, an error message is displayed, and the program is generally unable to continue. See *Application Error* and *abend*.

**(2)** (GUI Programming Facility) An OS/2 application generator from GPF Systems, Inc., Moodus, CT.

**GPI**     (Graphical Programming Interface) A graphics language in OS/2 Presentation Manager. It is a derivative of the GDDM mainframe interface and includes Bezier curves.

**GPIB**     (General Purpose Interface Bus) An IEEE 488 standard parallel interface used for attaching sensors and programmable instruments to a computer. Using a 24-pin connector, up to 15 devices can be daisy-chained together. HP's version is the HPIB.

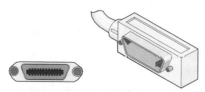

**GPIB (IEEE-488) Connectors**
GPIC connectors are used to attach sensors and programmable instruments to computer systems.

**GPL**    See *GNU General Public License.*

**gppm**    (**G**raphics **P**ages **P**er **M**inute) The measurement of printer speed based on printing graphics, which takes considerably longer to print than text. A gppm rating is more meaningful to the graphics designer than ppm (pages per minute), which usually rates the speed of printing text.

**GPRS**    (**G**eneral **P**acket **R**adio **S**ervice) An enhancement to the GSM mobile communications system that supports data packets. GPRS enables continous flows of IP data packets over the system for such applications as Web browsing and file transfer. GPRS differs from GSM's short messaging service (GSM-SMS) which is limited to messages of 160 bytes in length. See *GSM.*

**GPS**    (**G**lobal **P**ositioning **S**ystem) A system of 24 satellites for identifying earth locations, launched by the U.S. Department of Defense. By triangulation of signals from three of the satellites, a receiving unit can pinpoint its current location anywhere on earth to within a few meters.

With GPS, the "James Bond" style of on-screen, mobile map reading become a reality by the mid-1990s. By 2000, in-the-dash GPS-based navigation systems were standard equipment or at least an option in most luxury cars, and third-party systems are available for all cars. They include a CD-ROM reader or hard disk that reads the digital maps, which can guide you to your destination city or street address and even take you to the nearest gas station, hotel, restaurant and many other points of interest. See *GIS glossary.*

**GPS in the Car**
Although common today on most luxury cars, Sony's NVX-F160 was one of the first navigation systems for the road. It can direct you to the nearest restaurant, hotel or other points of interest. *(Image courtesy of Sony Corporation.)*

**GPSS**    (**G**eneral **P**urpose **S**imulation **S**ystem) A programming language for discrete event simulation, which is used to build models of operations such as manufacturing environments, communications systems and traffic patterns. Originally developed by IBM for mainframes, PC versions are available, such as GPSS/PC by Minuteman Software and GPSS/H by Wolverine Software.

**GQL**    (**G**raphical **Q**uery **L**anguage) A family of query and reporting tools used to access databases on client/server systems from Andyne Computing, Ltd., Ottawa, Ontario, Canada (www.andyne.com).

**GR-2837**    See *SONET.*

**grabber**    See *frame grabber, screen grabber* and *grabber hand.*

**grabber hand**    A screen tool that is shaped like a hand and is used to move objects within a window. For example, if the image is larger than the current window size, the grabber hand lets you scroll the image. When the tool is selected, the screen pointer turns into the hand. When clicked on an image, it "grabs" it so it can be moved.

**The Grabber Hand**
This tool was widely used on the Macintosh before it found its way into the Windows world.

**graceful degradation**    A system that continues to perform at some reduced level of performance after one of its components fails.

**graceful exit**    The ability to get out of a problem situation in a program without having to turn the computer off.

**grade**    The transmission capacity of a line. It refers to a range or class of frequencies that it can handle; for example, telegraph grade, voice grade and broadband.

**graded authentication**    An authentication procedure that determines access not only by username and password, but by the available security protocols users have in their software when logging on to the network.

**graded index fiber**    A multimode optical fiber in which the refractive index of the core gradually decreases toward the outer edges of the core. It enables the reflective paths (modes) that travel more in the center of the core to slow down and those that travel more in the outer area to speed up, thus attempting to reduce modal dispersion. See *step index fiber*, *dispersion shifted fiber* and *dispersion*.

**gradient**    A smooth blending of shades from light to dark or from one color to another. In 2-D drawing programs and paint programs, gradients are used to create colorful backgrounds and special effects and to simulate lights and shadows. In 3-D graphics programs, lighting can be rendered automatically by the software. See *3-D graphics*.

**GRAFCET**    (GRAPHe de Commande Etape-Transition - stage transition command graph)  A PLC specification and programming language.

**GrafPort**    See *graphics port*.

**gram**    See *metric system*.

**grammar checker**    Software that checks the grammar of a sentence. It can check for and highlight incomplete sentences, awkward phrases, wordiness and poor grammar.

**Grammatik**    A popular grammar checking program for DOS, Windows, Macintosh and UNIX that was developed by Reference Software, San Francisco, and acquired by WordPerfect Corporation in 1993. Novell later acquired WordPerfect, and then sold it to Corel. U.S. government versions check for usage according to the Government Printing Office and other military and civilian guides.

**grandfather-father-son**    A method for storing previous generations of master file data that are continuously updated. The son is the current file, the father is a copy of the file from the previous cycle, and the grandfather is a copy of the file from the cycle before that one.

**granularity**    The degree of modularity of a system. More granularity implies more flexibility in customizing a system, because there are more, smaller increments (granules) from which to choose.

**graph**    A pictorial representation of information. See *business graphics*.

**graphical user interface**    See *GUI*.

**graphic character**    See *character graphics*.

**graphics**    The creation and manipulation of picture images in the computer. In such cases, the subject is typically called "computer graphics," but it is defined here under "graphics" to keep the term next to other "graphics" entries for users of our books and software.

A fast desktop computer is required for graphics work, and although a mouse can be used for drawing, graphics tablets are widely used for CAD (computer-aided design) applications. A scanner is also typically used.

Vector Graphics and Bitmapped Graphics    Two methods are used for storing and maintaining pictures in a computer. The first method, called "vector graphics," maintains the image as a series of points, lines, arcs and other geometric shapes.

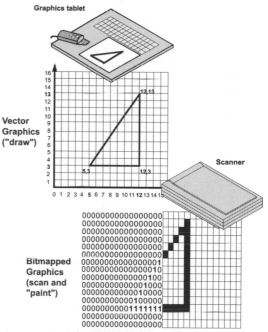

**Drawing, Scanning and Painting**
Pictures are "drawn" into vector graphics images using a digitizer tablet or mouse. Pictures are turned into bitmaps with scanners and digital cameras. Using a paint program, bitmaps can also be "painted" freehand, using the screen as a canvas.

The second method, called "bitmapped graphics" and also known as "raster graphics," resembles television, where the picture image is made up of dots. Understanding these two methods and how they intertwine is essential.

**Vector Graphics for CAD and Drawing**  Vector graphics is the method employed by computer-aided design (CAD) and drawing packages. As you draw, each line of the image is stored as a vector, which is two end points on an x-y matrix. For example, a square becomes four vectors, one for each side. A circle is turned into dozens or hundreds of tiny straight lines, the number of which is determined by the resolution of the drawing. The entire image is commonly stored in the computer as a list of vectors.

A vector graphics image is a collection of graphic elements, such as lines, squares, rectangles and circles. Although grouped together, each element maintains its own integrity and identity and can always be selected and erased or resized independent of all the others.

Vector graphics can be transmitted directly to X-Y plotters that "draw" the images from the list of vectors. Older CAD systems used vector screens that also drew the vectors. Today, all monitors are raster displays made up of dots, and the vectors are "rasterized" into the required dot patterns by hardware or software. In addition, most plotters have given way to ink jet printers.

**3-D Graphics**  3-D images use vector graphics, but 3-D CAD and drawing programs are significantly different than 2-D programs. Objects are created in 3-D form in a 3-dimensional workspace. They can be viewed at any angle by simply rotating them, whereas in 2-D programs, the object would have to be redrawn entirely. 3-D programs can render the drawing with lights and shadows, and camera angles and light sources are used to depict the objects as real-world elements.

**Bitmapped Graphics for Imaging and Painting**  Bitmapped graphics is the TV-like method that uses dots to display an image on screen. Bitmapped images are created by scanners and cameras and are also generated by paint packages. A picture frame is divided into hundreds of horizontal rows, with each row containing hundreds of dots, called "pixels."

Unlike TV, which uses one standard (NTSC) for the country, there are dozens of bitmapped graphics standards. Also, unlike TV, which records and displays the dots as infinitely variable shades and colors (analog), computer graphics have a finite number of shades and colors (digital).

Viewing Frustum

Viewplane

Viewpoint

**The 3-D Stage**
In 3-D graphics, objects are created on a 3-dimensional stage where the current view is derived from the camera angle and light sources, similar to the real world. *(Image courtesy of Intergraph Computer Systems.)*

When you scan an image or paint an object into the computer, the image is created in a reserved area of memory called a "bitmap," with some number of bits corresponding to each dot (pixel). The simplest monochrome bitmap uses one bit (on/off) for each dot. Gray scale bitmaps (monochrome shades) hold a number for each dot large enough to hold all the gray levels. Color bitmaps require three times as much storage in order to hold the intensity of red, green and blue.

The image in the bitmap is continuously transmitted to the video screen, dot for dot, a line at a time, over and over again. Any changes made to the bitmap are instantly reflected on the screen.

Since colors are designated with numbers, changing red to green is simply searching for the red number and replacing it with the green number. Animation is accomplished by continuously copying new sequences from other areas in memory into the bitmap, one after the other.

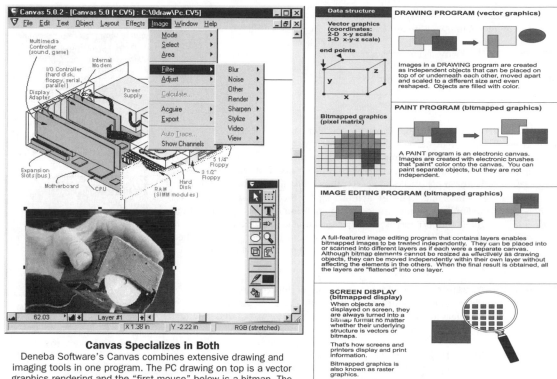

**Canvas Specializes in Both**
Deneba Software's Canvas combines extensive drawing and imaging tools in one program. The PC drawing on top is a vector graphics rendering and the "first mouse" below is a bitmap. The open menus show image editing tools that are not normally found in a drawing program.

Bitmapped images may take up more space on disk than their vector graphics counterpart, because storage for each pixel is required even if it's part of the background. A small object in vector graphics format will take up only a few vectors in the graphics database.

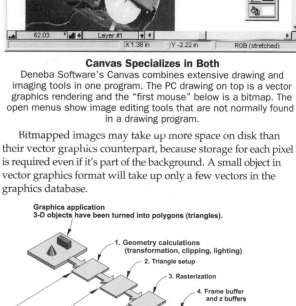

**3-D Graphics Generation**
Rendering an image requires each of the four stages above. The more work done in hardware, the faster the results. *(Redrawn from illustration courtesy of Intergraph Computer Systems.)*

**DRAWING PROGRAM (vector graphics)**

Images in a DRAWING program are created as independent objects that can be placed on top of or underneath each other, moved apart and scaled to a different size and even reshaped. Objects are filled with color.

**PAINT PROGRAM (bitmapped graphics)**

A PAINT program is an electronic canvas. Images are created with electronic brushes that "paint" color onto the canvas. You can paint separate objects, but they are not independent.

**IMAGE EDITING PROGRAM (bitmapped graphics)**

A full-featured image editing program that contains layers enables bitmapped images to be treated independently. They can be placed into or scanned into different layers as if each were a separate canvas. Although bitmap elements cannot be resized as effectively as drawing objects, they can be moved independently within their own layer without affecting the elements in the others. When the final result is obtained, all the layers are "flattened" into one layer.

**SCREEN DISPLAY (bitmapped display)**
When objects are displayed on screen, they are always turned into a bitmap format no matter whether their underlying structure is vectors or bitmaps.

That's how screens and printers display and print information.

Bitmapped graphics is also known as raster graphics.

**Drawing vs. Painting**
Although more painting tools are added to drawing programs and vice versa, their inherent structure is different. Drawing programs (vector graphics) allow for the creation of objects that can be manipulated independently. Paint programs (bitmapped graphics) provide a canvas that can be covered with electronic paint.

**graphics accelerator**    A high-performance display adapter that provides hardware functions to speed up 2-D, 3-D or video operations or all three. When functions are built into the chips on the display adapter, there is less work for the host CPU to do to render the images on screen.

There are many functions that can be built into hardware, including line draw and pixel block moves (bitblt) for 2-D operations, texture mapping and Gouraud shading for 3-D and color space conversion and hardware scaling for video. Much of the performance improvements on new PCs and workstations are due to speeding up the display systems. See *geometry accelerator* and *triangle setup*.

**graphics adapter**    Same as *display adapter*.

**graphics based**   The display of text and pictures as graphics images; typically bitmapped images. Contrast with *text based*.

**graphics board**   Same as *display adapter*.

**graphics card**   Same as *display adapter*.

**graphics character**   See *character graphics*.

**graphics conversion**   Changing one graphics format to another. There are two problems associated with this. One is that the target format may not have the inherent capabilities of the original. For example, if the original supports 24-bit color, such as a TIFF, and the target format only supports 8-bit color, such as GIF, there will be a loss of color depth. Another example would be a vector illustration that supports gradients, and the target format does not. These are all limitations of the file formats themselves.

The second problem is that graphics conversion requires tedious programming, and the graphics filters (import and export functions) in an application do not always work perfectly, witness the following example. The top one is the original, and the bottom was created using the JPEG export filter in the application. They may be similar, but are by no means identical.

**graphics coprocessor**   Graphics hardware that performs various 2-D and 3-D geometry and rendering functions, offloading the main CPU from performing such tasks. This typically refers to a very high-end graphics subsystem, but may also refer to a graphics accelerator. See *graphics accelerator* and *geometry accelerator*.

**graphics engine**   (1) Hardware that performs graphics processing tasks independently of the computer's CPU. See *graphics accelerator* and *graphics coprocessor*.

(2) Software that accepts commands from an application and builds images and text that are directed to the graphics driver and hardware. Macintosh's QuickDraw and Windows' GDI are examples.

**graphics file**   A file that contains only graphics data. Contrast with *text file* and *binary file*.

**graphics formats**   There is a wide variety of graphics formats in use today. The following list contains most of them. The formats are in order by extension name under bitmapped or vector category. Some formats appear in both categories because they can hold both raster and vector images. See *graphics conversion*.

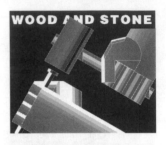

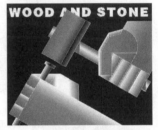

**Original (top) and JPEG Equivalent (bottom)**
Export filters don't always work perfectly. If exact replication is required, be sure to test your application's export filters long before you are on deadline to finish the job. *(Original image courtesy of Cedar Waxwing Design.)*

**BITMAPPED FORMATS (RASTER GRAPHICS)**

| | |
|---|---|
| AG4 | Access G4 document imaging |
| ATT | AT&T Group IV |
| BMP | Windows & OS/2 |
| BRK | Brooktrout fax |
| CAL | CALS Group IV |
| CIT | Intergraph scanned images |
| CLP | Windows Clipboard |
| CMP | Photomatrix G3/G4 scanner format |
| CMP | LEAD Technologies |
| CPR | Knowledge Access |
| CT | Scitex Continuous Tone |
| CUT | Dr. Halo |
| DBX | DATABEAM |
| DCM | DICOM medical image |
| DCX | Intel fax |
| DX | Autotrol document imaging |
| ED5 | EDMICS (U.S. DOD) |
| ED6 | EDMICS (U.S. DOD) |
| EPS | Encapsulated PostScript |
| FAX | Fax |
| FMV | FrameMaker |
| FPX | FlashPix |
| GED | Arts & Letters |
| GDF | IBM GDDM format |
| GIF | CompuServe |
| GP4 | CALS Group IV - ITU Group IV |
| GX1 | Show Partner |
| GX2 | Show Partner |
| ICA | IBM IOCA (see *MO:DCA*) |
| ICO | Windows icon |
| IFF | Amiga ILBM |
| IGF | Insct Systems (HiJaak) |
| IMG | GEM Paint |
| JFF | JPEG (JFIF) |
| JPG | JPEG |

| BITMAPPED FORMATS (RASTER GRAPHICS) (continued) | | VECTOR GRAPHICS FORMATS (continued) | |
|---|---|---|---|
| KFX | Kofax Group IV | CMX | Corel Metafile Exchange |
| LV | LaserView Group IV | DG | Autotrol |
| MAC | MacPaint | DGN | Intergraph drawing format |
| MIL | Same as GP4 extension | DRW | Micrografx Designer 2.x, 3.x |
| MSP | Microsoft Paint | DS4 | Micrografx Designer 4.x |
| NIF | Navy Image File | DSF | Micrografx Designer 6.x |
| PBM | Portable bitmap | DXF | AutoCAD |
| PCD | PhotoCD | DWG | AutoCAD |
| PCX | PC Paintbrush | EMF | Enhanced metafile |
| PIX | Inset Systems (HiJaak) | EPS | Encapsulated PostScript |
| PNG | Portable Network Graphics | ESI | Esri plot file (GIS mapping) |
| PNM | UNIX portable bitmap | FMV | FrameMaker |
| PPM | UNIX portable bitmap | GCA | IBM GOCA |
| PSD | Photoshop native format | GEM | GEM proprietary |
| RAS | Sun | G4 | GTX RasterCAD - scanned images into |
| RGB | SGI | | vectors for AutoCAD |
| RIA | Alpharel Group IV document imaging | HPGL | HP graphics language |
| RLC | Image Systems | IGF | Inset Systems (HiJaak) |
| RLE | Various RLE-compressed formats | IGS | IGES |
| RNL | GTX Runlength | MCS | MathCAD |
| SBP | IBM StoryBoard | MET | OS/2 metafile |
| SGI | Silicon Graphics RGB | MRK | Informative Graphics markup file |
| SUN | Sun | P10 | Tektronix plotter (PLOT10) |
| TGA | Targa | PCL | HP LaserJet |
| TIF | TIFF | PCT | Macintosh PICT drawings |
| WPG | WordPerfect image | PDW | HiJaak |
| XBM | X Window bitmap | PGL | HP plotter |
| XPM | X Window pixelmap | PIC | Variety of picture formats |
| XWD | X Window dump | PIX | Inset Systems (HiJaak) |
| | | PLT | HPGL Plot File (HPGL2 has raster format) |
| **VECTOR GRAPHICS FORMATS** | | PS | PostScript Level 2 |
| 3DS | 3D Studio | RIS | AUCOTEC CAD format |
| 906 | Calcomp plotter | RLC | Image Systems "CAD Overlay ESP" vector files |
| AI | Adobe Illustrator | | overlaid onto raster images |
| CAL | CALS subset of CGM | SSK | SmartSketch |
| CDR | CorelDRAW | SVG | Scalable vector graphics (XML) |
| CGM | Computer Graphics Metafile | WMF | Windows Metafile |
| CH3 | Harvard Graphics chart | WPG | WordPerfect graphics |
| CLP | Windows clipboard | WRL | VRML |

**graphics interface**   See *graphics language* and *GUI*.

**graphics language**   A high-level language used to create graphics images. The language is translated into images by software or specialized hardware. See *graphics engine*.

**graphics mode**   A screen display mode that displays graphics. Contrast with *text mode* and *character mode*.

**graphics port**   (1) A socket on the computer for connecting a graphics monitor.
(2) Also called "GrafPort," it is a Macintosh graphics structure that defines all the characteristics of a graphics window.

**graphics primitive**   An elementary graphics building block, such as a point, line or arc. In a solid modeling system, a cylinder, cube and sphere are examples.

**graphics processing**   See *DeBabelizer*.

**graphics processor**   Same as *graphics engine*.

### graphics program

See *paint* program, *drawing* program, *presentation* graphics, *image* editor and *image* processing.

### graphics tablet

Same as *digitizer tablet*.

### graphics terminal

A terminal or personal computer that displays graphics.

### graphics viewer

An application that displays graphics file formats. Although such programs provide basic image editing, their main purpose is to quickly preview and organize images. They also detail a file's attributes such as file size, resolution in dpi and inches and so on. See *file viewer*.

### graPHIGS

See *GDDM*.

### gratings    See *diffraction grating* and *fiber Bragg grating*.

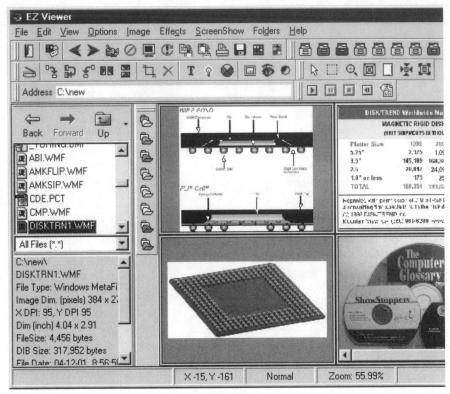

**EZ Viewer**
This gem of a program from GJC Software (www.gjcsoftware.com) does everything a graphics viewer should do. The column of eight folder icons in the middle are preset by the user in order to quickly jump to an application. Providing a raft of image editing tools and supporting more than 25 file formats, images can be displayed as thumbnails or full size.

**Graybar**    (Graybar, Clayton, MO, www.graybar.com)  An international distributor of electrical and voice and data communications equipment. In 1869, the company was founded in Cleveland as Gray and Barton by Elisha Gray and Enos Barton. It initially manufactured Gray's telegraph equipment, the most successful of which was his printing telegraph.

Gray and Barton was later renamed Western Electric Company when Western Union, its major customer, became an investor. Although Elisha Gray and Alexander Graham Bell had battled in the courts over patent rights to the telephone, and Bell had won, Western Electric became the manufacturer of Bell's telephones. Western Electric also supplied electrical products to the telephone companies and to other organizations as the electrical business flourished in the country.

In 1926, Western Electric spun off its electrical distribution as Graybar Electric Company. In 1929, Graybar was the first large company to be bought out by its own employees.

In the mid-1980s, after the breakup of AT&T, Graybar added more voice communications suppliers and got heavily involved in data communications. Today, it handles tens of thousands of products from more than 250 major suppliers.

**Gray's Printing Telegraph**
The printing telegraph was Gray's most successful invention in the late 1800s.
*(Image courtesy of Graybar.)*

**grayed out**  See *ghost*.

**gray hairs**  Experienced people. In other words, what is generally lacking in most Internet startups.

**gray mail**  Another term for *spam*.

**gray scale**  A series of shades from white to black. The more shades, or levels, the more realistic an image can be recorded and displayed, especially a scanned photo. Scanners differentiate typically from 16 to 256 gray levels.

Although compression techiques help reduce the size of graphics files, high-resolution gray scale requires huge amounts of storage. At a printer resolution of 300 dpi, each square inch is made up of 90,000 pixels. At 256 levels, it takes one byte per pixel, or 90,000 bytes per square inch of image. See *halftone*.

**grayware**  The human brain. See *wetware* and *wares*.

**greek**  In desktop publishing, to display text in a representative form in which the actual letters are not discernible, because the screen resolution isn't high enough to display them properly. The software lets you set which font sizes should be greeked.

The term comes from typography and graphics design, in which Greek or Latin letters and words are placed into layouts to hold the position for and represent the real text that was forthcoming. Foreign words and letters were used to quickly identify them as a mockup.

**Green Book**  See *CD-I*.

**green PC**  An energy-saving personal computer or peripheral device. Green computers, printers and monitors go into a low-voltage "suspend mode" if not used after a certain period of time. Laser printers especially waste a lot of energy when not in use, because of their heat-induced fusing mechanism.

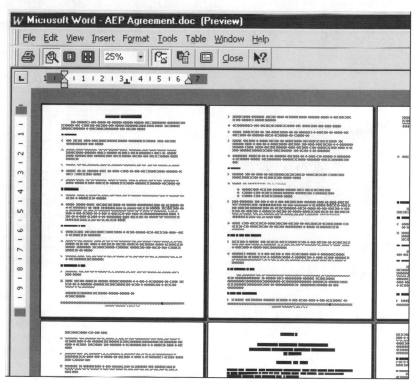

**Greeking**
These pages are greeked in this print preview mode, because there is not enough resolution on screen to display them correctly.

Many contemporary CPUs can run at variable clock rates and can idle at very low speeds, to save current. When input is detected, they revert to full-power. The green concept includes using less packaging materials, recycling toner cartridges, providing a return location for used batteries and sending e-mail rather than paper mail.

**green screen**    A computer terminal that displays green characters on a dark background. Widely used with mainframes and minicomputer systems, the green screen has mostly given way to the Windows, Mac or Motif graphical user interface.

**grep**    (**G**lobal **R**egular **E**xpression and **P**rint) A UNIX pattern matching utility that searches files for a string of text and outputs any line that contains the pattern. Grep came from ed, the UNIX text editor, in which the expression **g/re/p** means "display all text in the file that matches this." That single function became a utility program itself. See *ed*.

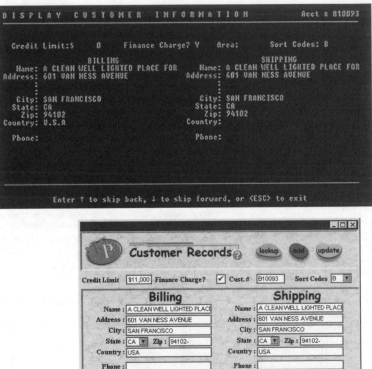

**From Green Screen to the Web**
Computer Associates' Opal software transforms legacy applications (top) into graphics-based documents (bottom) that can be accessed via a Web browser. *(Screen examples courtesy of Computer Associates International, Inc.)*

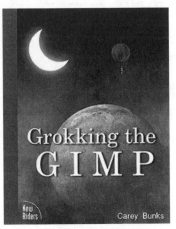

**Grokking the GIMP**
The GIMP is a sophisticated paint and image editing program in the UNIX environment (see *GIMP*). This book, *Grokking the GIMP* by Carey Bunks is a title that means "Completely Understand the GIMP." *(Image courtesy of New Riders Publishing, www.newriders.com)*

**grid**    (1) Any interconnected set of nodes such as the electric power network or a communications network.

(2) "The Grid" is a nickname for Internet2. See *Internet2*.

(3) In a vacuum tube or gas-filled electron tube, the grid is a perforated electrode through which electrons may pass. The term typically refers to the control grid in a triode, tetrode or pentode vacuum tube. In these cases, the grid is used to control the amount of current flow between the cathode and plate (anode). As the voltage potential is varied on the control grid, the amount of current allowed to pass through also varies. Relatively small fluctuations in the grid's potential can control substantially larger amounts of current flow through the tube. This phenomenon is referred to as "gain." Tetrodes and pentodes use additional grids to regulate current flow and effect gain. See *screen grid* and *suppressor grid*.

**grok**    To have a thorough understanding of a subject. The word comes from Robert Heinlein's "Stranger in a Strange Land," and it means "to drink" in Martian. Of course. But more specifically in the book, it meant to take something in so thoroughly that it becomes part of you.

**grooming**    Combining, consolidating and segregating network traffic using devices such as digital cross-connects, add/drop multiplexers and SONET switches. Grooming is a telephone term that typically refers to managing high-capacity lines between central offices, carriers, ISPs and very large corporations rather than subscriber lines (local loops). See *digital cross-connect* and *add/drop multiplexer*.

**ground**    An electrically conductive body, such as the earth, which maintains a zero potential (not positively or negatively charged) for connecting to an electrical circuit.

**ground current**    The current found in a ground line. It may be caused by imbalanced electrical sources; for example, the ground line in a communications channel between two computers deriving power separately.

**ground fault**    The temporary current in the ground line, caused by a failing electrical component or interference from an external electrical source such as a thunderstorm.

**ground loop**    An unwanted ground current flowing back and forth between two devices that are grounded at two or more points.

**ground noise injection**    An intentional insertion of unwanted noise by a power supply into the ground line.

**group collaboration products**    See *e-mail*, *groupware*, *data conferencing* and *videoconferencing*.

**group scheduling**    See *calendaring*.

**groupware**    Software that supports multiple users working on related tasks. Groupware is an evolving concept that is more than just multiuser software which allows access to the same data. Groupware provides a mechanism that helps users coordinate and keep track of ongoing projects together.

The heart of groupware is a messaging system, because e-mail is used to notify team members, obtain responses and send alerts. E-mail messages increasingly include live links to databases, intranets and the Internet. Other applications include document sharing and document management, group calendaring and scheduling, group contact and task management, threaded discussions, text chat, data conferencing and audio and videoconferencing. Workflow, which allows messages and documents to be routed to the appropriate users, is often part of a groupware system.

Lotus Notes is often considered the father of groupware, because it was the first to popularize a multifunction groupware system and development environment. There are a myriad of programs that provide a single groupware function; however, Lotus Notes, GroupWise and Microsoft Exchange are examples of products that provide multiple groupware functions. Communicator and Internet Explorer/NetMeeting are also examples.

The Internet/intranet explosion has focused attention on groupware, because of the ease with which HTML pages can

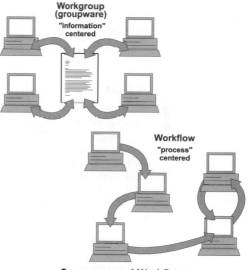

**Groupware and Workflow**
Groupware focuses on the information being processed and enabling users to share it. Workflow emphasizes the process, which acts as a container for the information. Groupware is "information centered." Workflow is "process centered."
*(Illustration courtesy of Delphi Consulting Group, Inc.)*

be created and shared. However, as documents become widely used and distributed throughout the enterprise, security and synchronization problems surface. Document management becomes a problem, and access control and replication become issues. Thus, what starts out as a simple way to electronically publish information, winds up becoming as strategic as the client/server systems that have been distributed throughout the enterprise. Groupware is becoming a critical issue in computing. See *workflow*.

## GroupWise

Messaging and groupware software from Novell that provides a universal inbox for calendaring, group scheduling, task management, document sharing, workflow and threaded discussions. Whiteboards and application sharing are available through third parties. GroupWise clients run on Windows, Mac and UNIX, and the GroupWise server runs on NetWare, NT and UNIX. GroupWise supports a wide variety of mail systems as well as Novell's NDS directory. Text-to-speech and speech-to-wave files lets mobile users hear and create e-mail by telephone. Although entirely revamped, GroupWise stems back to WordPerfect Office, acquired by Novell in 1994.

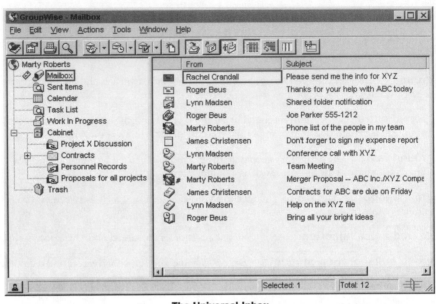

**The Universal Inbox**
GroupWise provides a universal interface to a variety of collaboration functions that team members perform throughout the day. *(Screen shot courtesy of Novell, Inc.)*

**GSA**    **(1)** (Global Mobile Suppliers Association, Sawbridgeworth, U.K., www.gsacom.com)  A membership organization comprised of suppliers of GSM products and services. Its goal is to promote GSM as the worldwide mobile communications standard. See *GSM Association* and *GSM*.

**(2)** (**G**eneral **S**ervices **A**dministration)  The department within the U.S. government that is responsible for procurement of goods and services.

**GSAM**    (**G**eneralized **S**equential **A**ccess **M**ethod)  A batch processing access method for IMS that allows sequential files to be treated as IMS databases. See *sequential access method* and *IMS*.

**GSM**    (**G**lobal **S**ystem for **M**obile Communications)  A digital cellular phone technology based on TDMA that is the predominant system in Europe, but is also used around the world. Developed in the 1980s, GSM was first deployed in seven European countries in 1992. Operating in the 900MHz and 1.8GHz bands in Europe and the 1.9GHz PCS band in the U.S., GSM defines the entire cellular system, not just the air interface (TDMA, CDMA, etc.). As of 2000, there were more than 250 million GSM users, which is more than half of the world's mobile phone population.

GSM phones use a Subscriber Identity Module (SIM) smart card that contains user account information. Any GSM phone becomes immediately programmed after plugging in the SIM card, thus allowing GSM phones to be easily rented or borrowed. SIM cards can be programmed to display custom menus for personalized services.

GSM provides a short messaging service (SMS) that enables text messages up to 160 characters in length to be sent to and from a GSM phone. It also supports data transfer at 9.6 Kbps to packet networks, ISDN and POTS users. GSM is a circuit-switched system that divides each 200 kHz channel into eight 25 kHz time slots. See *GPRS*, *W-CDMA*, *EDGE*, *HSCSD*, *GSM Association*, *GSA*, *TDMA*, *CDMA* and *PCS*.

**Vive la Cellphone!**    When GSM phones were first introduced, they were reported to produce a deafening sound for hearing aid wearers and to interfere with electronic devices such as pacemakers. Swedish hospitals banned them. An

Australian newspaper claimed a motorist set off his airbag with one, and most curious, in Paris, they were said to occasionally reset taxi meters to zero.

**GSMP** (General Switch Management Protocol) The call setup protocol used in the IP Switch. See *IP Switch*.

**GSM-SMS** (GSM-Short Messaging Service) See *GSM*.

**GSOS** (GS Operating System) A graphical operating system for the Apple IIGS that also accepts ProDOS applications.

**GSTN** (General Switched Telephone Network) Same as *PSTN*.

**GT** (Greater Than) See *relational operator*.

**GTK+** (GUI ToolKit+) A library of object-oriented graphical interface elements for developing X Window applications. It is open source software that is available free of charge. For more information, visit www.gtk.org. See *X Window*.

**gTLD** (Generic Top-Level Domain) A general-purpose domain name on the Internet. In 1997, the IAHC created seven new gTLDs (.firm, .store, .web, .arts, .rec, .info & .nom) and recommended that the international TLDs .com, .net & .org be redefined as gTLDs.

**guard band** A frequency that insulates one signal from another. In an analog telephone line, the low band is 0-300; the high band is 3300-4000Hz.

**guest** A person that logs into a network or service that does not have a user account. Guests are given a default set of privileges until they officially register with the service. See *guest account*, *guest privileges* and *user account*.

**guest account** A default set of permissions and privileges given to non-registered users of a system or service. See *guest* and *guest privileges*.

**guest privileges** The rights and permissions given to a non-registered user of a system or service. See *guest*.

**GUI** (Graphical User Interface) A graphics-based user interface that incorporates icons, pull-down menus and a mouse. The GUI has become the standard way users interact with a computer. The three major GUIs are Windows, Macintosh and Motif, the latter being used in the UNIX world. See *drag and drop*, *desktop manager*, *window manager* and *Star*. Contrast with *CUI*.

**GUI accelerator** See *graphics accelerator*.

**GUI builder** Visual programming software that lets a user build a graphical user interface by dragging and dropping elements from a toolbar onto the screen. It may be a stand-alone program or part of an application development system or client/server development system. See *application development system* and *client/server development system*.

**GUID** (Globally Unique IDentifier) A unique number used to identify a COM object. It is computed by adding the time and date to the network adapter's internal serial number. See *COM*.

**guiltware** Shareware that makes a poignant plea to the user to purchase the product and support the developers, because they worked so hard making it.

**The SIM Card**
The back of a GSM phone opens up, and the little SIM card is inserted, in this case from Europe's Amena cellphone service. The bottom view is the card out of the socket showing contact points.

**The First Commercial GUI**
Xerox's Star workstation was the first commercial implementation of the graphical user interface. The Star was introduced in 1981 and was the inspiration for the Mac and all the other GUIs that followed. *(Image courtesy of Xerox Corporation.)*

**GUI painter**  Same as *GUI builder*.

**GUI widget**  A small element used in a graphical user interface (GUI) such as a button or scroll bar.

**gull-wing lead**  A pin on a chip package that extends slightly out, down and then out again. Gull wing leads are used on surface mount chips such as QFPs and SOICs. See *QFP, SOIC* and *J-lead*.

**gulp**  An unspecified number of bytes.

**guru**  An advisor or teacher. The term, which comes from Hinduism, refers to a spiritual teacher. "Gu" means darkness, and "ru" means light; thus a guru turns ignorance into enlightenment. In the west, the term has been interpreted quite often as simply an expert in a field whether that person helps you learn or understand anything or not.

**gutter**  In typography, the space between two columns.

**GVIF**  (Gigabit Video InterFace)  A transmission method for sending digital information to a flat panel display. Developed by Sony, it differs from LVDS and TMDS by offering a longer cable length and using only one wire for RGB signals. See *flat panel display*.

**GVPN**  (Global Virtual Private Network)  A service from cooperating carriers that provides international digital communications for multinational companies.

**GVRP**  (GARP VLAN Registration Protocol)  A standard for registering a client station into a VLAN. See *802.1p*.

**GW-BASIC**  (Gee Whiz-BASIC)  A BASIC interpreter that accompanied MS-DOS in versions prior to 5.0. See *QBasic*.

**GXC**  (Global Exchange Carrier, Inc., Abingdon, VA, www.gxc.com)  A provider of IP voice services via the Internet, intranets and private WANs. GXC provides gateways to the Internet that offer long distance telephony to customers at prices lower than the long distance carriers. See *IP telephony*.

**GZIP**  A UNIX-based program that compresses files using the PKZIP format. See *archive formats*.

**h** (Hexadecimal) A symbol that refers to a hex number. For example, 09h has a numeric value of 9, whereas 0Ah has a value of 10. See *hex chart*. See also *henry*.

**H1B** A category under the U.S. Immigration and Nationality Act by which aliens can enter the U.S. for three years if they work in a specialized field and their employers cannot fill the position locally. The three years may also be extended to six years. Programmers and other technicians in the computer field enter the U.S. under this status.

In 2000, there were estimates of between 420,000 and 460,000 H1B employees in the U.S. Also in 2000, the cap for H1B visas was raised from 115,000 to 195,000 per year until the end of 2003, at which time more than a million H1B workers are expected to be employed. It also allows an extension of H1B beyond six years if the person is in the process of securing a green card.

**H.221** An ITU standard for the framing structure of a videoconferencing transmission over a 64 to 1920 Kbits/sec channel. See *H.230*.

**H.230** An ITU standard for controlling the synchronization of videoconferencing frames. See *H.221*.

**H.231** An ITU standard for multipoint control units for videoconferencing. See *MCU*.

**H.245** An ITU standard protocol for making an audio and videoconferencing call. It defines flow control, encryption and jitter management, as well as the signals for initiating the call, negotiating which features are to be used and terminating the call. It also determines which side is the master for issuing various commands.

**H.261** An ITU standard for compressing an H.320 videoconferencing transmission. The algorithm can be implemented in hardware or software, and uses intraframe and interframe compression. It uses one or more 64 Kbps ISDN channels (Px64). H.261 supports CIF and QCIF resolutions. See *CIF*.

**H.262** An ITU standard for compressing a videoconferencing transmission. It uses the MPEG-2 compression algorithm.

**H.263** An ITU standard for compressing a videoconferencing transmission. It is based on H.261 with enhancements that improve video quality over modems. H.263 supports CIF, QCIF, SQCIF, 4CIF and 16CIF resolutions. See *CIF*.

**H.310** An ITU standard for videoconferencing over ATM and Broadband ISDN networks using MPEG compression.

**H.320** An ITU standard for videoconferencing over digital lines. Using the H.261 compression method, it allows H.320-compliant videoconferencing room and desktop systems to communicate with each other over ISDN, switched digital and leased lines. A counterpart standard for data conferencing is T.120.

**H.321**    An ITU standard for videoconferencing over ATM and Broadband ISDN networks.

**H.322**    An ITU standard for videoconferencing over local area networks (LANs) that can guarantee bandwidth, such as Isochronous Ethernet.

**H.323**    An ITU standard for realtime, interactive voice and videoconferencing over LANs and the Internet. Widely used for IP telephony, it allows any combination of voice, video and data to be transported. H.323 specifies several video codecs, including H.261 and H.263, and audio codecs, including G.711 and G.723.1. Gateways, gatekeepers and multipoint control units (MCUs) are also covered. See *MGCP* and *SIP*.

**H.324**    An ITU standard for videoconferencing over analog telephone lines (POTS) using modems.

**H5**    Refers to models of IBM's water-cooled mainframes that use the bipolar chip technology.

**hack**    Program source code. You might hear a phrase like "nobody has a package to do that, so it must be done through some sort of hack." This means someone has to write programming code to solve the problem, because there is no pre-written routine or function that does it.
   The purist would say that doing a hack means writing in languages such as assembly language and C, which are low level and highly detailed. The more liberal person would say that writing any programming language counts as hacking. See *hacker*.

**hacker**    A person who writes programs in assembly language or in system-level languages, such as C. Although it may refer to any programmer, it implies very tedious "hacking away" at the bits and bytes.
   Since it takes an experienced hacker to gain unauthorized entrance into a secure computer to extract information and/or perform some prank or mischief at the site, the term has become synonymous with "cracker," a person that performs an illegal act. This use of the term is not appreciated by the overwhelming majority of hackers who are honest professionals. See *hack*, *samurai* and *cracker*.

**Hailstorm**    The code name for a centralized user contact and information service on the Internet from Microsoft. Based on its .NET initiative and the Passport wallet service, Hailstorm hosts user data in secure Microsoft servers and makes it accessible to all Hailstorm-enabled applications that require it. The user is expected to have complete control over the distribution of the data, which includes name and address, shopping information, geographic locations, computer hardware and software preferences, favorite Web sites and other personal data. Hailstorm is expected to be in full force by 2002.

**half-adder**    An elementary electronic circuit in the ALU that adds one bit to another, deriving a result bit and a carry bit.

**half-duplex**    The transmission of data in both directions, but only one direction at a time. Two-way radio was the first to use half-duplex, for example—while one party spoke, the other party listened. Contrast with *full-duplex*.

**half-height drive**    A 5.25" disk drive that takes up half the vertical space of first-generation drives in desktop computers. Measuring 1 5/8" in height, it is commonly used for 5.25" floppy disks and hard disks. Contrast with *full-height drive*.

**half-inch tape**    A magnetic tape format that has been in use since the 1950s.
Second generation computers used 7-track, half-inch tape in open reels that were threaded by hand. Third-generation computers used 9-track open reels. Although the maximum storage is little more than 250MB per reel, new open-reel drives have been manufactured and sold all the way to the year 2000. However, the market for such hardware is expected to dwindle to nil shortly thereafter.

## Hackers hit two more major sites, rock market

INQUIRER WIRE SERVICES

WASHINGTON — Attorney General Janet Reno announced a criminal investigation yesterday into the latest wave of hacker attacks on major Internet sites, as law enforcement officials conceded that they had little idea of who or what they

**Hackers Targeted the Internet**
Computers with high-speed connections to the Internet were hacked and planted with illicit programs that, when activated, sent out an unending number of requests and caused a denial of service at Yahoo!, eBay, Amazon.com and other Web sites during the second week of February 2000. *(Excerpted article February 10, 2000, courtesy of the* Philadelphia Inquirer.*)*

Half-inch reels evolved into half-inch, self-threading tape cartridges, including IBM's 3490/3490/3590 line, Quantum's DLT and StorageTek's Redwood, which hold from 800MB to 50GB. See *Magstar*, *DLT*, **Redwood** and *magnetic tape*.

**halftone**    In printing, the simulation of a continuous-tone image (shaded drawing, photograph) with dots. All printing processes, except for Cycolor, print dots. In photographically generated halftones, a camera shoots the image through a halftone screen, creating smaller dots for lighter areas and larger dots for darker areas. Digitally composed printing prints only one size of dot.

In order to simulate variable-sized halftone dots in computer printers, dithering is used, which creates clusters of dots in a "halftone cell." The more dots printed in the cell, the darker the gray. As the screen frequency gets higher (more cells per inch), there is less room for dots in the cell, reducing the number of shades of gray or color that can be generated.

In low-resolution printers, there is always a compromise between printer resolution (dpi) and screen frequency (lpi), which is the number of rows of halftone cells per inch. For example, in a 300 dpi printer, the 8x8 halftone cell required to create 64 shades of grays results in a very coarse 38 lines per inch of screen frequency (300 dpi divided by 8). However, a high-resolution, 2,400 dpi imagesetter can easily handle 256 shades of gray at 150 lpi (2,400/16).

**Open Reel Tape**
Although organizations have migrated to cartridge formats, legacy applications remain that still use open reels.

PRINTER RESOLUTION & MAXIMUM SCREEN FREQUENCY

| Cell size | Shades of gray or cols | At Printer Resolutions: 300 dpi | 1,200 dpi | 2,400 dpi |
|-----------|------------------------|------------------|-----------|-----------|
| 4x4   | 16  | 150 lpi | 300 lpi | 600 lpi |
| 8x8   | 64  | 38 lpi  | 130 lpi | 300 lpi |
| 16x16 | 256 | 19 lpi  | 75 lpi  | 150 lpi |

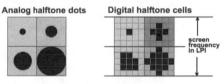

**Analog vs. Digital**
The analog world of commercial printing prints dots in varying sizes. The digital world prints in grids of dots. Increasingly, digital printers use techniques that overlap dots to achieve greater variability in dot sizes.

**hammer**    (1) In a printer, the mechanism that pushes the typeface onto the ribbon and paper or pushes the paper into the ribbon and typeface.

(2) (Hammer) The code name for AMD's next-generation, 64-bit CPU chips. Expected in 2001, the Sledgehammer is one of the CPU models in the line. See *Athlon* and *Itanium*.

**Hamming code**    An error correction method that intersperses three check bits at the end of each four data bits. At the receiving station, the check bits are used to detect and correct one-bit errors automatically.

**hand coding**    Writing in a programming language. Hand coding in assembly language or in a third-generation language, such as COBOL or C, is the traditional way programs have been developed. In contrast, visual programming tools allow full applications or parts of an application to be developed without writing lines of programming code.

**handheld computer**    A computing device that can be easily held in one hand while the other hand is used to operate it. The Palm devices are a popular example. See *Palm*, *smart phone* and *palmtop*.

**handheld scanner**    A scanner that is moved across the image to be scanned by hand. Handheld scanners are small and less expensive than their desktop counterparts, but rely on the dexterity of the user to move the unit across the paper. Trays are available that keep the scanner moving in a straight line. Contrast with *flatbed scanner*, *sheet-fed scanner* and *drum scanner*.

**handle**    (1) In computer graphics, a tiny, square block on an image that can be grabbed for reshaping.

**(2)** A temporary name or number assigned to a file, font or other object. For example, an operating system may assign a sequential number to each file that it opens as a way of identifying it.

**(3)** A nickname used when conferencing like a "CB handle" used by a truck driver.

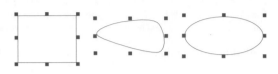

**handler**    A software routine that performs a particular task. For example, upon detection of an error, an error handler is called to recover from the error condition.

**handoff**    Switching a cellular phone transmission from one cell to another as a mobile user moves into a new cellular area. The switch takes place in about a quarter of a second so that the caller is generally unaware of it.

**handset**    The part of the telephone that contains the speaker and the microphone. See *multihandset cordless*.

**hands-free computer**    See *body-worn computer*.

**handshaking**    Signals transmitted back and forth over a communications network that establish a valid connection between two stations.

**hang**    To have the computer freeze or lock up. When a personal computer hangs, there is often no indication of what caused the problem. The computer could have crashed, or it could be something simple such as the printer running out of paper.

**hanging paragraph**    Also called "hanging indent," it is a paragraph in
which the first line is set to the left
    margin, but all subsequent lines are
    indented as is this paragraph.

**haptic interface**    Communicating with the computer via some tactile method. Haptic devices sense some form of finger, hand, head or body movement.

**hard boot**    Same as *cold boot*.

**hard coded**    Software that is programmed to get the job done quickly, which means programmed to do a fixed number of tasks without regard to future flexibility. It is very easy to do this kind of "brute force programming," and it is the ideal kind of programming for one-time jobs. Such programs typically use a fixed set of values and may only work with certain types of devices. The problem is that one-time programs often become widely used, even in day-to-day operations, but they are difficult to change, because the routines have not been generalized to accept change. Such "elegant" programs require much more thought to write, and everybody is in such a hurry that hard-coded, in-elegant programs are written a thousand times a day. Hard-coded solutions may run faster, but programming speed is far more important than processing speed these days. See *data independence*.

**hard copy**    Printed output. Contrast with *soft copy*.

**hard disk**    The primary computer storage medium, which is made of one or more aluminum or glass platters, coated with a ferromagnetic material. Most hard disks are fixed disks, which are permanently sealed in the drive. Removable cartridge disks such as Iomega's Jaz disks enable the disk to be removed from the computer and used as backup or transferred to another machine with the same drive.

Most desktop hard disks are either IDE (also known as EIDE or ATAPI) or SCSI. The advantage of IDE is their lower cost. The advantage of SCSI is that up to seven or more devices can be attached to the same controller board. SCSI drives are typically used in high-end servers, because SCSI is available as a fault tolerant disk subsystem (RAID systems), while IDE drives are found in most desktop and laptop machines. Increasingly, IDE drives are available in RAID configurations (see *RAID*).

Hard disks provide fast retrieval because they rotate constantly at high speed, from 5,000 to 15,000 rpm. In laptops, they can be turned off when idle to preserve battery life.

Back in the 1950s, the very first hard disks held just a few hundred thousand bytes and used platters 12" in diameter. In the 1980s, the first personal computer hard disks started at 5MB (see *ST506*). Today's hard disks start around 20 gigabytes and generally use 3.5" platters for desktop computers and 2.5" platters for notebooks. Smaller disks are also used (see *Microdrive*).

Hard disks are usually low-level formatted from the factory, which records the original sector identification on them. See *floppy disk*, *magnetic disk* and *format program*.

```
TYPES OF HARD DISKS
Interface     Encoding    Transfer Rate
Type          Method*     (Per sec)       Capacities

SCSI***       RLL         5 - 160MB       20MB - 75GB
EIDE**        RLL         3 - 100MB       500MB - 80GB

IPI           RLL         10 - 25MB       200MB - 3GB
ESDI          RLL         1 - 3MB         80MB - 2GB
SMD           RLL         1 - 4MB         200MB - 2GB
IDE           RLL         3 - 8MB         40MB - 1GB

ST506 RLL     RLL         937KB           30MB - 200MB
ST506         MFM         625KB           5MB - 100MB
```

```
* Most disks use RLL, but encoding methods are
  not prescribed by all interfaces.
** For details on EIDE (ATA) modes, see IDE.
*** For details on SCSI rates, see SCSI.
```

**Internal Hard Disk**
Hard disks use one or more metal or glass platters covered with a magnetic coating.

**Hard Disk Measurements**    Capacity is measured in bytes, and speed is measured by transfer rate in bytes per second (see above) and access time in milliseconds (ms). Hard disk access times range from 3 ms to about 15 ms, whereas CDs and DVDs range from 80 ms to 120 ms.

**hard disk recorder**    See *PVR*.

**hard drive**    The mechanism that reads and writes a hard disk. The terms hard drive and hard disk are used interchangeably.

**hard error**    (1) A permanent, unrecoverable error such as a disk read error. Contrast with *soft error*.

(2) A group of errors that requires user intervention and includes disk read errors, disk not ready (no disk in drive) and printer not ready (out of paper).

**hard failure**    Same as *hardware failure*.

**hard hyphen**    A hyphen that always prints. Contrast with *soft hyphen*.

**hard macro**    The design of a logic function that specifies how the required logic elements are interconnected and specifies the physical pathways and wiring patterns between the components. Also called a "macro cell." Contrast with *soft macro*.

**hard return**    A code inserted into a text document by pressing the ENTER key. If the hard return does not display as a symbol on screen, it can usually

**First Hard Disk**
Part computer, part tabulator, in 1956, IBM's RAMAC was the first machine with a hard disk, which was extraordinary technology of the times. Each of its 24" diameter platters held a whopping 100,000 characters (they weren't bytes then) for a total of five million characters. *(Images courtesy of International Business Machines Corporation. Unauthorized use not permitted.)*

be revealed along with other layout codes in an expanded mode. DOS, Windows and OS/2 insert a CR/LF combo: Carriage Return and Line Feed. Mac uses only a CR, and UNIX only an LF. Contrast with *soft return*.

**hard sectored**   A sector identification technique that uses a physical mark. For example, hard sectored floppy disks have a hole in the disk that marks the beginning of each sector. Contrast with *soft sectored*.

**hard space**   A special space character that acts like a letter or digit, used to prevent multiple-word, proper names from breaking between lines.

**hardware**   Machinery and equipment (CPU, disks, tapes, modem, cables, etc.). In operation, a computer is both hardware and software. One is useless without the other. The hardware design specifies the commands it can follow, and the instructions tell it what to do. See *instruction set*.

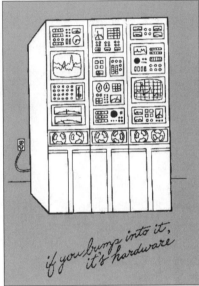

if you bump into it,
it's hardware

### Hardware Is

**Storage and Transmission**   The more memory and disk storage a computer has, the more work it can do. The faster the memory and disks transmit data and instructions to the CPU, the faster it gets done. A hardware requirement is based on the size of the databases that will be created and the number of users or applications that will be served at the same time. How much?  How fast?

### Software Is

**Logic and Language**   Software deals with the details of an ever-changing business and must process transactions in a logical fashion. Languages are used to program the software. The "logic and language" involved in analysis and programming is generally far more complicated than specifying a storage and transmission requirement.

**hardware circuit**   A system made up of electronic components such as transistors, resistors and capacitors. For computers and other digital devices, almost all hardware circuits are built into a chip, with a single chip containing an entire subsystem, such as a CPU, controller or codec. The exceptions are power supplies and other devices that use transformers and discrete components too large for chip fabrication.

**hardware dependent**   See *machine dependent*.

**hardware engineer**   A person involved with the design, implementation and testing of hardware (circuits, components, systems, etc.). See *software engineer*.

**hardware failure**   A malfunction within the electronic circuits or electromechanical components (disks, tapes) of a computer system. Recovery from a hardware failure requires repair or replacement of the offending part. Contrast with *software failure*.

**hardware independent**   Same as *machine independent*.

**hardware interface**   An architecture used to interconnect two pieces of equipment. It includes the design of the plug and socket, the type, number and purpose of the wires and the electrical signals that are passed across them. See *bus, local bus, ISA, VL-bus, RS-232, PCI, IDE, SCSI* and *channel*.

**hardware interrupt**   An interrupt caused by some action of a hardware device, such as the depression of a key or mouse movement. See *IRQ* and *interrupt*.

**hardware key** Also called a "dongle," it is a copy protection device supplied with software that plugs into a computer port, often the parallel port on a PC. The software sends a code to that port, and the key responds by reading out its serial number, which verifies its presence to the program. The key hinders software duplication, because each copy of the program is tied to a unique number, which is difficult to obtain, and the key has to be programmed with that number.

The key also acts as a pass-through to the printer or other peripheral. Multiple hardware keys can be used, each plugged in one after the other.

**hardware monitor** A device attached to the hardware circuits of a computer that reads electronic signals directly in order to analyze system performance.

**hardware platforms** Each hardware platform, or CPU family, has a unique machine language. All software presented to the computer for execution must be in the binary coded machine language of that CPU. Following is a list of the major hardware platforms in existence today.

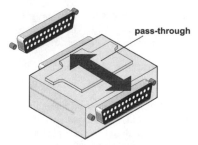

**The Hardware Key**
Hardware keys provide a pass-through so that a peripheral cable can be plugged into the key just as if it were plugged into the back of the computer. Multiple keys can be plugged together as well.

pass-through

H

| CISC Chips | | RISC Chips | |
|---|---|---|---|
| Platform | Developed By and Usage | Platform | Developed By and Usage |
| x86 | Intel, AMD, Cyrix (all PCs) | 88000 | Motorola, DG, Encore |
| 680x0 | Motorola, mostly earlier Macintoshes | MIPS | SGI, Pyramid, Tandem, NEC, Siemens |
| VAX | Digital's mini series, VMS OS | SPARC | Sun and SPARC-licensed clones |
| S/370 | IBM mainframes | PA-RISC | HP workstations, servers |
| S/390 | IBM mainframes | Alpha | Compaq workstations, servers |
| AS/400 | IBM midrange, formerly System/38 | PowerPC | Apple, IBM, Motorola |
| S/36 | old IBM mini, System/36 | i860 | Intel, Stratus systems |
| Tandem | fault tolerant systems, Non-Stop | ARM | Arm, Ltd., embedded systems, NCs |
| Unisys | Unisys mainframes | | |
| PDP/11 | Digital's 1st mini | | |

**hardware profile** Settings that define a specific configuration of peripherals and drivers. Multiple profiles let you set up more than one hardware configuration, which is commonly done when a laptop also serves as a desktop computer. The desktop profile activates one set of peripherals, the laptop profile another.

A separate hardware profile is also used as a last resort when an application conflicts with one of the drivers that is routinely loaded. A special profile is created that boots the computer without the problem driver so the application can run. In order to run the rest of the programs, the machine must be rebooted with the regular profile.

**hardware scaling** Enlarging a video frame by performing the operation within the circuits of the display adapter. Putting the function in a chip speeds up the process. See *video accelerator*.

**hardware T&L** See *T&L*.

**hardware virtual memory** Virtual memory management built into a chip. Although virtual memory can be performed by software only, it is far more efficient to do it in hardware. See *DAT* and *PMMU*.

**hardwired** (1) Electronic circuitry that is designed to perform a specific task. See *hard coded*.

(2) Devices that are closely or tightly coupled. For example, a hardwired terminal is directly connected to a computer without going through a switched network.

**harmonic adapter** A device that converts a 50-pin Telco connector into an RJ-45 connector.

**harmonic distortion** In communications, frequencies that are generated as multiples of the original frequency due to irregularities in the transmission line.

**Harvard Graphics**    Popular presentation graphics programs for DOS and Windows from Software Publishing Corporation, Fairfield, NJ (www.spco.com). Its DOS version was one of the first business graphics packages to allow for the creation of columnar and free form text charts.

**hash function**    An algorithm that turns a variable-sized amount of text into a fixed-sized output (hash value). Hash functions are used in creating digital signatures. See *digital signature* and *one-way hash function*.

**hash total**    A method for ensuring the accuracy of processed data. It is a total of several fields of data in a file, including fields not normally used in calculations, such as account number. At various stages in the processing, the hash total is recalculated and compared with the original. If any data has been lost or changed, a mismatch signals an error.

**hash value**    The fixed-length result of a one-way hash function. See *hash function* and *hash total*.

**HASP**    (Houston Automatic Spooling Program)  A mainframe spooling program that provides task, job and data management functions.

**Hayes**    A company that specialized in modems and remote access products. Based in Atlanta, GA, and founded in 1977 by Dennis Hayes, the company pioneered personal computer communications with the design of its Smartmodem and shipped its first 300 baud model in 1978. Initially Hayes Microcomputer Products, Inc., it became Hayes Corporation in 1997 when it merged with Access Beyond, a spin-off of Penril Data Communications. Hayes filed for Chapter 11 in October 1998 and later ceased operations. Almost all modems use the Hayes command language (see *AT command set*).

   ModemExpress, Inc., Minneapolis, MN, obtained the Hayes domain name (www.hayes.com) and provides service and support of Hayes products. See *Hayes Smartmodem*.

**Hayes compatible**    Refers to modems controlled by the Hayes command language. See *AT command set*.

**Hayes Smartmodem**    A family of intelligent modems for personal computers from Hayes. Hayes developed the "intelligent modem" for first-generation personal computers in 1978, and its command language (Hayes Standard AT Command Set) for modem control became an industry standard.

The Intelligent Modem    An intelligent modem has a command state and an online state. In the command state, it accepts instructions. In the online state, it dials, answers, transmits and receives.

   Once connected, it performs the handshaking with the remote modem, which is similar to the opening exchange of a telephone call. The called party says "hello," the calling party says "hello, this is..." After this, the real conversation begins. If the modem's speaker is on, you can hear the whistles and tones used in the handshake.

   Once the handshake is completed, you are online with the other computer, and data can be transmitted back and forth.

   An important part of the Hayes standard is the escape sequence, which tells the modem to switch from online to the command state. It usually consists of three plus signs in sequence (+++) with a Hayes-patented, one-second guard time interval before and after it, which prevents the modem from mistaking a random occurrence of the escape sequence. The escape sequence and guard time interval can be programmed in the modem's Status registers.

   To issue an escape sequence, hold down the SHIFT key and press + + +. Pause one second before and after the sequence. The modem will return the OK result code, indicating it is ready to accept commands.

**HBA**    (Host Bus Adapter)  See *host adapter*.

**HBL**    (Hue Brightness Luminosity)  A color model that is similar to the HSB and HSV models. See *HSB*.

**HC**    See *high color*.

**HD**    (1) (High Density)  The designation for high-density diskettes; for example, the 5.25" 1.2MB and 3.5" 1.44MB floppies. Contrast with *DD*.
   (2) (Hard Disk)  For example, FD/HD refers to a floppy disk/hard disk device such as a controller.
   (3) (High Definition)  See *HDTV*.

**HD15**    (High Density DB 15)  See *DB connector*.

**HDA**    (Head Disk Assembly)  The mechanical components of a disk drive (minus the electronics), which include the actuators, access arms, read/write heads and platters.

**HDD**    (Hard Disk Drive)  See *hard disk*.

**HDF**    (Hierarchical Data Format)  A file format for scientific data that is developed and maintained by NCSA. Governments and research organizations around the world use HDF for archiving and distributing collected data.

**HDL**    (Hardware Description Language)  A language used to describe the functions of an electronic circuit for documentation, simulation or logic synthesis (or all three). Although many proprietary HDLs have been developed, Verilog and VHDL are the major standards. The first book to provide side-by-side examples of subsets of both languages that can be simulated and synthesized is "HDL Chip Design" by Douglas J. Smith, published by Doone Publications (www.doone.com), ISBN 0-9651934-3-8. See *Verilog* and *VHDL*.

**HDLC**    (High-level Data Link Control)  An ISO communications protocol used in X.25 packet-switching networks. It provides error correction at the data link layer. SDLC, LAP and LAPB are subsets of HDLC. See *SDLC*.

**HDML**    (Handheld Device Markup Language)  A specialized version of HTML designed to enable wireless pagers, cellphones and other handheld devices to obtain information from Web pages. HDML was developed by Phone.com (formerly Unwired Planet) before the WAP specification was standardized. It is a subset of WAP with some features that were not included in WAP. AT&T Wireless launched the first HDML-based service in 1996. See *WAP*.

**HDR**    (High Data Rate)  A wireless data technology from QUALCOMM that provides up to a 2.4 Mbps data rate in a standard 1.25MHz CDMA voice channel. HDR can be used to enhance data capabilities in existing cdmaOne networks or in stand-alone data networks. With existing CDMA networks, some number of channels are changed from voice to data. Using a combination of TDM and CDMA, HDR shares each channel among several users, but on an as-needed basis rather than a fixed time slot as in TDMA. Optimized for IP packets and Internet access, the HDR data rate will vary depending on the distance from the mobile phone to the base station.

HDR is being used as the 3G technology for cdmaOne network carriers, known as cdma2000. A data-only version (1XEv-Data Only) and an integrated voice-data version (1XEv-Data Voice) are available (see *cdma2000*). See *wireless generations*.

**HDSL**    See *DSL*.

**HDTV**    (High Definition TV)  A high-resolution TV standard, which is part of the group of digital TV standards introduced in the U.S. in late 1998 (see *DTV*). Now that HDTV is broadcast in the U.S., it is expected that consumers will become very familiar with it; however, HDTV has been around for many years. Japan was the first to develop and broadcast an 1125-line signal picked up on large-screen TV sets. Both Japan and Europe's initial HDTV used analog signaling.

For many years in the U.S., high-definition formats (HD) in both analog and digital form were used for creating videos that were superior to regular TV/video (NTSC). HD has been used to shoot videos for closed circuit presentations in corporate theaters and board rooms, trade shows and similar events. See *DTV* and *aspect ratio*.

**HDX**    See *half-duplex*.

**head**    See *read/write head* and *HDA*.

**head crash**    The physical destruction of a hard disk. Misalignment or contamination with dust can cause the read/write head to collide with the disk's recording surface. The data is destroyed, and both the disk platter and head have to be replaced.

The read/write head touches the surface of a floppy disk, but on a hard disk, it hovers above its surface at a

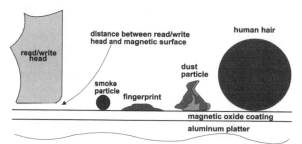

**Read/Write Head and Disk Surface**
Head crashes used to be much more common years ago. When you realize the distance between the head and platter is about 20 millionths of an inch, today's reliability is truly a feat of engineering. However, it can happen, and when it does, it is a literal crash. The head collides into and destroys the magnetic coating of the disk. Your bits go bye-bye.

distance that is less than the diameter of a human hair. It has been said that the read/write head flying over the disk surface is like trying to fly a jet plane six inches above the earth's surface.

**head end**   The originating point in a communications system. In cable TV, the head end is where the cable company has its satellite dish and TV antenna for receiving incoming programming. In online services, the head end is the service company's computer system and databases.

**header**   (1) The first record in a disk or tape file. It may be used for identification only (name, date of last update, etc.), or it may describe the structural layout of the contents, as is common with many document and database formats.

(2) In a document or report, common text printed at the top of every page.

(3) In communications, the first part of the message, which contains controlling data, such as originating and destination stations, message type and priority level.

(4) Any caption or description used as a headline.

**header label**   A record used for file identification that is recorded at the beginning of the file.

**head skew**   The offset distance from the start of the previous track so that the head has time to switch from top of platter to bottom of platter and be at the start of the new track. See *cylinder skew*.

**health problems**   See *carpal tunnel syndrome* and ***computer vision syndrome***.

**heap**   In programming, the common pool of free memory available to the program.

**heat sink**   A material that absorbs heat. Typically made of aluminum, heat sinks are commonly used in amplifiers and other electronic devices that build up heat, and are the most economical method for cooling a semiconductor device (chip). See *CPU cooler* and *thermal grease*.

**helical scan**   A tape recording method that uses a spinning read/write head and diagonal tracks. Although it uses a rather complex transport mechanism, it is very gentle on the tape. After the cassette is inserted into the drive, the tape is pulled out and wrapped around the read/write head. While the head rotates as much as 30 meters per second, the tape travels as little as 1 inch per second (ips), compared to linear technologies where the tape travels at more than 100 ips.

Helical scan was invented by Ampex in 1956. It was the only method that provided fast-enough transfer rate and sufficient storage capacity to record video on tape so that TV programs could be recorded. Using two-inch tape and running at 15 ips, the going rate for tape recorders of the time, the rotating head created an effective rate of 1,500 ips. The helical scan method is used in videotapes, camcorders, 4mm DAT (DDS), Exabyte's 8mm and Mammoth lines, Sony's AIT and StorageTek's Redwood.

**help**   On-screen instruction regarding the use of a program. On PCs, pressing F1 is the de facto standard for getting help. With graphics-based interfaces (Mac, Windows, etc.), clicking a **?** or HELP button gets help. See *context-sensitive help*.

**help compiler**   Software that translates text and compiler instructions into an online help system. See ***Windows help system***.

**help desk**   A source of technical support for hardware or software. Help desks are staffed by people that can either solve the problem directly or forward the problem to someone else. Help desk software provides the means to log in problems and track them until solved. It also provides the management information regarding support activities.

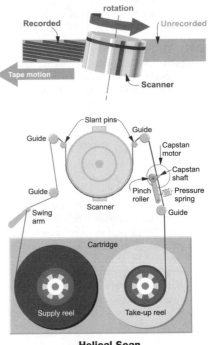

**Helical Scan**

The helical scan method uses a rotating head and diagonal tracks, which allows a slow-traveling tape to provide a very fast transfer rate. The tape is pulled out of the cartridge and wrapped around the read/write head.

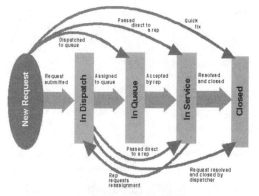

**The Help Desk Process**
Help desk software must be able to effectively support all the possible paths that a service request may follow from start to completion, as diagramed here. *(Illustration courtesy of Help Desk Technology Corporation, www.helpstar2000.com)*

**help desk analyst**   A person that provides technical support for any aspect of the information systems department, including computer hardware, operating systems, applications and networks. Requires troubleshooting and good human communications skills. See *help desk*.

**helper application**   An application that adds additional capabilities to the program that is running. See *browser plug-in*.

**henry**   A unit of measurement of the strength of a magnetic field in an inductor. See *inductor*.

**Hercules Graphics**   The de facto standard monochrome display adapter for PCs, which provides a graphics and text resolution of 720x348 pixels. IBM's monochrome display adapter displayed only text, and Hercules Computer Technology introduced its product in 1982 to fill the void.

**HERMSEN**   (Homogeneous Emergency Recovery Managed Storage Enterprise Network) A distributed storage network from AVC Global Services, Elberon, NJ (www.avcglobal.com), that splits an individual RAID system across geographic boundaries. By distributing live data across multiple sites, it adds disaster recovery to the fault tolerance built into RAID without doubling storage server costs. Also known as a D-SEN (Distributed Storage Enterprise Network).

**Hertz**   The frequency of electrical vibrations (cycles) per second. Abbreviated "Hz," one Hz is equal to one cycle per second. In 1883, Heinrich Hertz detected electromagnetic waves. See *MHz*.

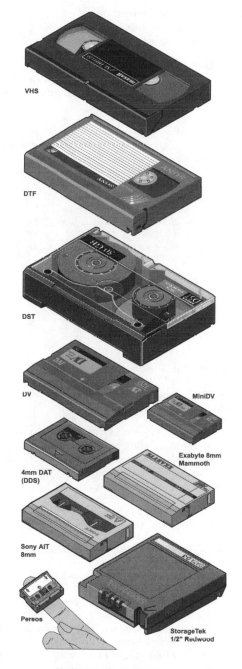

**Helical Scan Formats**
There are numerous helical scan formats used for digital storage. The predecessors to VHS tape (top) were the reason for helical scan in the first place. Although mostly used for analog recording, there have been digital applications of VHS tape as well.

**heterogeneous environment**   Using hardware and system software from different vendors. Organizations often use computers, operating systems and databases from a variety of vendors. Contrast with *homogeneous environment*.

**heuristic**   A method of problem solving using exploration and trial-and-error methods. Heuristic program design provides a framework for solving the problem in contrast with a fixed set of rules (algorithmic) that cannot vary.

**hex**   (HEXadecimal) Hexadecimal means 16. The base 16 numbering system is used as a shorthand for representing binary numbers. Each half byte (four bits) is assigned a hex digit as shown in the following chart, with its decimal and binary equivalents. Hex values are identified with an "h" or dollar sign, thus $3E0, 3E0h and 3E0H all stand for the hex humber 3E0. See *hex chart*.

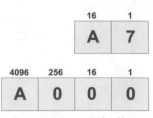

**How to Interpret the Hex**
As decimal digits increment by 10, hex digits increment by 16. Two hex digits make up one byte; for example, A7 is equivalent to one byte containing the binary number 10100111, or 167 in decimal. A is 10, thus 160 (10x16) plus 7 (7x1). The hex number A000 (pronounced "A thousand") is 40,960 in decimal (10x4096); however, for PC addressing, hex addresses are interpreted uniquely (see *table at left*).

| Base 16 Hex | 10 Dec | 2 Binary | Base 16 Hex | 10 Dec | 2 Binary |
|---|---|---|---|---|---|
| 0 | 0 | 0000 | A | 10 | 1010 |
| 1 | 1 | 0001 | B | 11 | 1011 |
| 2 | 2 | 0010 | C | 12 | 1100 |
| 3 | 3 | 0011 | D | 13 | 1101 |
| 4 | 4 | 0100 | E | 14 | 1110 |
| 5 | 5 | 0101 | F | 15 | 1111 |
| 6 | 6 | 0110 | | | |
| 7 | 7 | 0111 | | | |
| 8 | 8 | 1000 | | | |
| 9 | 9 | 1001 | | | |

**hexadecimal**   See *hex*.

**hex chart**   The chart on the right  is ASCII code in hexadecimal.

**HFC network**   (Hybrid Fiber-Coax network) A communications network (typically a cable TV network) that uses a combination of optical fiber and coaxial cable. The fiber provides the high-speed backbone, and the coax is used to connect end users to the backbone.

**HFS**   (Hierarchical File System) The file system used in the Macintosh. See *hierarchical file system*.

**HHOK**   Digispeak for "ha ha only kidding."

**Hi-8**   An analog video recording and playback format for camcorders that uses enhanced 8mm video cassettes (metal evaporated or metal particle tape). With 400 lines of horizontal resolution, Hi-8 provides superior quality to the original 270-line 8mm format. Hi-8 cartridges sizes are 30, 60 and 120 minutes. If a Hi-8 tape player is not available, the camcorder is cabled directly to the VCR or TV for larger-screen display. See *Digital8*.

**HID**   (Human Interface Device) A class of peripheral device that enables people to input data or interact directly

**ASCII Characters (Hexadecimal)**
These are the standard ASCII characters (0–127), plus the extended ASCII characters as implemented in the DOS PC. This chart shows the values in hexadecimal (00–FF).

with the computer, such as with a mouse, keyboard or joystick. The HID specification is a part of the USB standard, thus USB mice and other USB user input devices are HID compliant. Windows 2000 defines HID standards that enable drivers to be written for such devices no matter which connection is used (USB, serial port, etc.).

**hidden file**   A file classification that prevents a file from being accessed. It is usually an operating system file; however, utility programs let users hide files to prevent unauthorized access.

**hidden surface removal**   See *z buffer*.

**hierarchical**   A structure made up of different levels like a company organization chart. The higher levels have control or precedence over the lower levels. Hierarchical structures are a one-to-many relationship; each item having one or more items below it.

**hierarchical communications**   A network controlled by a host computer that is responsible for managing all connections. Contrast with *peer-to-peer communications*.

**hierarchical database**   A database organization method that is structured in a hierarchy. All access to data starts at the top of the hierarchy and moves downward; for example, from customer to orders, vendor to purchases, etc. Contrast with *relational database* and *network database*.

**hierarchical file system**   A file organization method that stores data in a top-to-bottom organization structure. All internal access to the data starts at the top and proceeds throughout the levels of the hierarchy.

Most all operating systems use hierarchical file systems to store data and programs, including DOS, OS/2, Windows NT and 95/98, UNIX and the Macintosh. See *root directory, path* and *HFS*.

**hierarchy**   A structure that has a predetermined ordering from high to low. In object technology, the hierarchy is an ordering of objects. All files and folders on the hard disk are organized in a hierachy (see **Win Folder organization**).

**high availability**   Also called "RAS" (reliability, availability, serviceability) or "fault resilient," it refers to a multiprocessing system that can quickly recover from a failure. There may a minute or two of downtime while one system switches over to another, but processing will continue. This is not the same as fault tolerant, in which redundant components are designed for continuous processing without skipping a heartbeat.

High availability also refers to being able to service a component in the system without shutting down the entire operation. See *clustering* and *hot fix*.

**high color**   The ability to generate 32,768 colors (15 bits) or 65,536 colors (16-bit). 15-bit color uses five bits for each red, green and blue pixel. The 16th bit may be a color, such as XGA with 5-red, 6-green and 5-blue, or be an overlay bit that selects pixels to display over video input. See *true color*.

**high density**   Refers to increased storage capacity of bits and/or tracks per square inch. See *HD*.

**high-level format**   A set of indexes on the disk that the operating system uses to keep track of the data stored on the disk. See *format program*.

**high-level interface**   A programming interface (API) that provides more functionality within one command statement than a lower-level interface. High-level interfaces are designed to enable the programmer to write code in a shorter amount of time and to be less involved with the details of the software module or hardware that is provided the required services. Contrast with *low-level interface*.

**high-level language**   A machine-independent programming language, such as FORTRAN, COBOL, BASIC, Pascal and C. It lets the programmer concentrate on the logic of the problem to be solved rather than the intricacies of the machine architecture such as is required with low-level assembly languages.

There are dramatic differences between high-level languages. Look up the terms C, BASIC and COBOL, and review the sample code. What is considered high level depends on the era. There were assembly languages thirty years ago that were easier to understand than C.

**highlight**     To select an icon or group of icons or some part of a text document or image in order to perform an operation on it, such as moving it, deleting it or copying it. Highlighting is typically done by pointing to the object with the mouse and clicking the left mouse button. See *Win Highlighting icons*.

**highlight bar**     The currently highlighted menu item. Choice is made by moving the bar to the desired item and pressing ENTER or clicking the mouse. The bar is a different color on color screens or reverse video on monochrome screens.

**high memory**     **(1)** The uppermost end of memory.

**(2)** In PCs, it may refer to any of three areas of memory: (1) the Upper Memory Area (UMA) between 640K and 1M, (2) extended memory above 1M or (3) the High Memory Area (HMA), a 64K region between 1,024K and 1,088K. Real straightforward, isn't it?  See *PC memory*, *UMA*, *HMA* and *extended memory*.

**high-pass filter**     A filter that blocks low frequencies and allows higher frequencies to pass through. Such filters are used in devices such as POTS splitters that direct phone and DSL signals to different lines. Contrast with *low-pass filter*.

**high-performance computing**     High-speed computing, which typically refers to supercomputers used in scientific research.

**high resolution**     **(1)** A large amount of information per square inch on a display screen or printed form. Measured in dots per inch (dpi), the more dpi, the higher the resolution and quality. Monitors (both CRTs and flat panels) are in the 70–120 dpi range, whereas printers are in the 300–1,200 dpi range. Imagesetters typically print at 1,270 or 2,540 dpi. See *resolution*.

**(2)** A large amount of information on screen. This is technically "screen resolution."  For example, a 1,600×1,200 screen resolution shows more information than 800×600. See *PC display modes* and *resolution*.

**(3)** A large amount of information per second in a digital audio recording. Measured in samples per second, as well as the size of each sample—the more of either one or both, the higher the quality. See *sampling rate*, *DVD-Audio* and *SACD*.

**High Sierra**     The first CD-ROM file format, named for an area near Lake Tahoe where it was developed in 1985. High Sierra evolved into ISO 9660.

**high technology**     Refers to the latest advancements in computers and electronics, as well as to the social and political environment and consequences created by such machines.

**HIMEM.SYS**     An extended memory manager that is included with DOS and Windows, starting with DOS 5 and Windows 3.0. It allows programs to cooperatively allocate extended memory in 286 and higher PCs. HIMEM.SYS is an XMS driver. In Windows 95/98, HIMEM.SYS is automatically loaded at startup. See *XMS* and *DOS HIMEM.SYS*.

**hints**     Font instructions that make a character uniform and legible at small point sizes and lower resolutions. They also ensure that serifs and accents appear in proper proportion. When there are not enough pixels in the print or display image, smaller fonts can sometimes translate into patterns that are not recognizable as the characters they represent. Hints ensure that both sides of an H, for example, must be of uniform width, and that certain elements of the character cannot be left out.

Hints are not necessary when printing at 600 dpi or more, but are required when printing characters 13 points or less at 300 dpi. When displaying those same characters on a screen with a 96 dpi or lower resolution, hints are also needed.

**HIPERLAN**     A wireless LAN protocol developed by ETSI that provides a 23.5 Mbps data rate in the 5GHz band. It is similar to Ethernet, but unlike 802.11a, the wireless Ethernet standard at the same rate, HIPERLAN/1 provides quality of service (QoS), which lets critical traffic be prioritized. Other versions of HIPERLAN are expected, including HiperLAN/2 and HIPERAccess for wireless ATM and wireless local loop in the 20 Mbps range, and HIPERlink for wireless point-to-point in the 155 Mbps range. See *wireless LAN*.

**hiperspace**     An IBM MVS/ESA feature that allows applications to access expanded storage. See *expanded storage*.

**HIPO**     (**H**ierarchy plus **I**nput-**P**rocess-**O**utput)  Pronounced "hy-po."  An IBM flow-charting technique that provides a graphical method for designing and documenting programs.

**HiPPI**    (HIgh Performance Parallel Interface) An ANSI-standard high-speed communications channel that uses a 32-bit or 64-bit cable and transmits at 100 or 200 Mbytes/sec. It is used as a point-to-point supercomputer channel or, with a crosspoint switch, as a high-speed LAN.

**hi res**    Same as *high resolution*.

**histogram**    A chart displaying horizontal or vertical bars. The length of the bars are in proportion to the values of the data items they represent.

**hit rate**    The chief measurement of a cache, which is the percentage of all accesses that are satisfied by the data in the cache. See *cache* and *hits*.

**hits**    The number of times a program or item of data has been accessed or matches some condition. For example, when you download a page from the Web, the page itself and all graphic elements that it contains each count as one hit to that Web site. If a search yields 100 items that match the searching criteria, those 100 items could be called 100 hits. See *hit rate* and *page view*.

**HLLAPI**    (High Level Language Application Program Interface) An IBM programming interface that allows a PC application to communicate with a mainframe application. The hardware hookup is handled via normal micro to mainframe 3270 emulation. An extended version of the interface (EHLLAPI) has also been defined.

**HLS**    (Hue Lightness Saturation) A color model that is closely related to HSB, except that Brightness is called Lightness and is measured from 0 to 1 rather than from 0 to 100%. See *HSB*.

**HMA**    (High Memory Area) In PCs, the first 64K of extended memory from 1,024K to 1,088K, which can be accessed by DOS. It is managed by the HIMEM.SYS driver. It was discovered by accident that this area could be used by DOS, even though it was beyond the traditional one-megabyte barrier.

**HMD**    (Head Mounted Display) A display system built and worn like goggles that gives the illusion of a floating monitor in front of the user's face. The HMD is a critical component of a body-worn computer (wearable computer). Single-eye units are used to display hands-free instructional material, and dual-eye, or stereoscopic, units are used for virtual reality applications. See also *CAVE*.

**HMI light**    (Hydrargyrum Medium arc Iodide) A flicker-free light source recommended for digital cameras that require long periods of exposure.

**HMOS**    (High-density MOS) A chip with a high density of NMOS transistors.

**hog**    A program that uses an excessive amount of computer resources, such as memory or disk, or takes a long time to execute.

**Hollerith machine**    The first automatic data processing system. It was used to count the 1890 U.S. census. Developed by Herman Hollerith, a statistician who had worked for the Census Bureau, the system used a hand punch to record the data as holes in dollar-bill–sized punched cards and a tabulating machine to count them. The tabulating machine contained a spring-loaded pin for each potential hole in the card. When a card was placed in the reader and the handle was pushed down, the pins that passed through the holes closed electrical circuits causing counters to be incremented and a lid in the sorting box to open.

It was estimated that, with manual methods, the 1890 census wouldn't be completed until after 1900. With Hollerith's machines, it took less than three years to count 62 million people, and it saved the government $5 million.

**Single-Eye HMD**
These Xybernaut HMDs connect to voice-activated, body-worn Pentium computers, allowing the technician to review instructions while working with both hands. *(Images courtesy of Xybernaut Corporation.)*

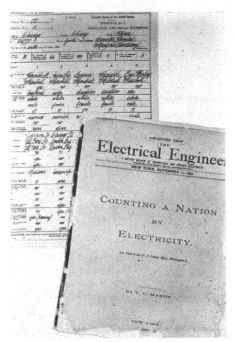

**What a Concept in 1891**
Imagine. Using electricity to count. The date on this issue of "Electrical Engineer" was November 11, 1891. The page at the top is a census form filled out by a census taker.

**High Tech, 1890 Style**
The beginning of data processing made the August 30, 1890 cover of *Scientific American*. The binary concept. A hole or no hole! *(Image courtesy of* Scientific American Magazine.*)*

Hollerith formed the Tabulating Machine Company and sold his machines throughout the world for a variety of accounting functions. In 1911, his company was merged into the company that was later renamed IBM.

**holographic storage**    A future technology that records data as holograms that fill up the entire volume of a small optical cylinder no larger than one millimeter by one centimeter. The hologram is created by two lasers. One laser is beamed into the lithium niobate optical material through a matrix of LCD shutters, called a "spatial light modulator." The shutters are opened or closed based on the binary pattern of the page of data being stored. For example, using a matrix of 1,024 pixels on each side, the page could hold a million bits.

A reference laser is angled into and intersects with the data laser at the storage unit. If the angle and/or frequency is changed, another hologram can be created overlapping and filling the same space as the first hologram. In fact, 10,000 holograms (pages) can overlap each other.

**Hollerith's Keypunch Machine**
All 62 million Americans were counted by punching holes into a card from the census forms. *(Image courtesy of International Business Machines Corporation. Unauthorized use not permitted.)*

**Hollerith and His Tabulator**
Herman Hollerith looks out over the invention that brought data processing to the world. Sixty-two million cards were placed in the readers of these machines and then dropped into the sorting box (right) when the appropriate lid opened. *(Image courtesy of The Computer Museum History Center, www.computerhistory.org)*

The page is read by directing just the reference laser back into the hologram. The light is diffracted into an original copy of the data that is sensed by a matrix of CCD sensors.

Although research in this area stems back to the 1960s, it is expected that holographic storage will begin to make inroads after the turn of the century. Such devices could hold 50 million images or 10 billion pages of text and deliver them instantaneously. It is expected that holographic storage will be first used for high-speed imaging and video requirements. See *PRISM* and *optical disk*.

**Holy Grail**    A very desired object or outcome that borders on a sacred quest. There are several Holy Grails in the computer business. Standards tend to be high on the list; for example, having "one" standard that everybody uses and is happy with for each required area. Writing software once and having it run on every computer platform is also desired by many. Another is a software component architecture that allows software modules to "plug together" like hardware components, no matter the platform they run on or which programming language they were written in.

The term's original meaning is the chalice that Joseph of Arimathea used to collect drops of Jesus' blood at the Crucifixion. Legends of the quest for the Holy Grail, which would bring healing and eternal life, have been recounted in various ancient treatises.

**holy war**    An ongoing dialogue on an Internet newsgroup about some controversial subject. See *flame*.

**home brew**    Products that are developed at home by hobbyists.

**home button**    An icon that represents the beginning of a file or a set of basic or starting functions.

**home computer**    In the 1980s, a home computer was the lowest priced computer of the time, such as an Apple II, Commodore 64 or 128, Tandy Color Computer or Atari ST. Today, the term generally refers to a PC or Mac used in the home.

**home directory**    A disk directory assigned to each user on a UNIX system attached to the Internet. It is the directory you start out in when you log on. It can be used to store temporary or permanent files, a user profile that can be "fingered," as well as lists of newsgroups that have been subscribed to.

**HOME key**    A keyboard key used to move the cursor to the top of the screen or file or to the previous word or beginning of line. See *home button*.

**home network**    (1) A network used within the home to control devices such as lights and appliances, as well as to synchronize clocks. It typically uses the AC power lines as the transmission medium. See *CEBus* and *digital home*.

(2) A communications network for all the computers in the home. The term may refer to a standard Ethernet setup or to specialized networks that use existing phone lines or power lines. See *HomeRF*, *HomePNA*, *DPL* and *Bluetooth*.

**home page**    The first page retrieved when accessing a Web site. It serves as a table of contents to the rest of the pages on the site or to other Web sites. See *World Wide Web* and *URL*.

**HomePNA**    (HOME Phoneline Network Alliance)  A communications network for the home that is based on Ethernet and uses existing phone lines. Version 2.0, introduced at the end of 1999, provides 10 Mbps of bandwidth and is backward compatible with the original 1 Mbps technology introduced the year before. HomePNA allows devices to be up to 1,000 feet apart and supports a huge household area of up to 10,000 square feet. For more information, visit www.homepna.org.

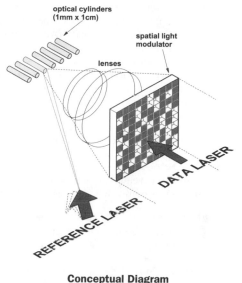

**Conceptual Diagram**
This simplistic drawing shows the data and reference lasers intersecting at the optical material, creating the holographic page. The spatial light modulator creates the data pattern. The reference laser determines the optical location of the page.

**HomeRF**   (HOME Radio Frequency)  A wireless personal area network (PAN) technology from the HomeRF Working Group, Portland, OR (www.homerf.org), founded in 1998 by Compaq, IBM, HP and others. HomeRF uses the Shared Wireless Access Protocol (SWAP) and provides an open standard for short-range transmission of digital voice and data between mobile devices (laptops, PDAs, phones) and desktop devices. Transmitting in the unlicensed 2.4GHz range, up to 127 devices can be addressed within a range of 150 feet at a data rate of 1 or 2 Mbps. Derived from the Digital European Cordless Telephone (DECT) standard, HomeRF uses a frequency hopping technique that changes 50 times per second. Each 20 ms frame contains one CSMA/CA slot (typically for data) and six full-duplex TDMA slots (typically for voice). HomeRF also supports the TCP/IP specification in 802.11. See *wireless LAN*.

**home run**   A cable that begins at a central distribution point, such as a hub or PBX, and runs to its destination station without connecting to anything else. Home runs are used in star topologies.

**homogeneous environment**   Hardware and system software from one vendor; for example, an all-IBM or all-Digital shop. Contrast with *heterogeneous environment*.

**homologation**   Certification, confirmation or approval. Data communications equipment is often subject to the homologation requirements of various countries.

**The Datamatic 1000**
Introduced in 1957, the Datamatic 1000 was a monstrous, tube-driven computer that was very sophisticated for its time. One of them was still in commercial use up until the late 1960s. *(Image courtesy of Honeywell, Inc.)*

**Honeywell**   In 1927, the Minneapolis Honeywell Regulator Company was formed as a merger of Alfred Butz' temperature control company (1885) and Mark Honeywell's water heater company (1906). In 1957, Honeywell, along with Ratheon, introduced one of the first computers in the U.S., the Datamatic 1000. Two years later, Honeywell's 800 and 400 models earned a solid reputation for advanced features.

In the mid 1960s, Honeywell's 200 series gave IBM serious competition. It outperformed IBM's very successful 1401 computer, which it emulated, causing IBM to accelerate its introduction of its System/360. In 1966, Honeywell acquired Computer Control Company's minicomputer line, and in 1970, it acquired the assets of GE's computer business. The computer division was renamed Honeywell Information Systems, Inc.

Through Honeywell's association with Groupe Bull in Europe and Bull's association with NEC in Japan, research and development were mutually explored and products were jointly developed. In the late 1980s, the three companies formed Honeywell Bull, and later Bull acquired the majority interest, renaming the organization Bull HN. The famous Honeywell name, having been identified with the most advanced computers, remained only as the "H" in Bull HN.

**hook**   In programming, instructions that provide breakpoints for future expansion. Hooks may be changed to call some outside routine or function, or may be places where additional processing is added.

**hooked vector**   A trapped interrupt in a PC. The pointer for a particular interrupt in the interrupt vector table has been modified to jump to a new routine to service that interrupt.

**hookemware**   Free software that contains a limited number of features designed to entice the user into purchasing the more comprehensive version.

**hop**   The link between two network nodes. See *hop count*.

**hop count**   The number of point-to-point links in a transmission path. Since each link is terminated at a network device such as a router or gateway, the processing performed within the device to determine how to forward the packet adds

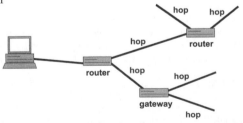

**Hops in a Network**
Electrical signals may travel near the speed of light in a wire, but each junction point (router, gateway, etc.) adds processing overhead.

overhead to the transmission. Although each point-to-point link is technically a hop, the hop count is the number of network devices between the starting node and the destination node. An IP packet traveling from coast to coast via the Internet can "hop" through more than a dozen routers.

**hopper**    A tray, or chute, that accepts input to a mechanical device, such as a disk duplicator or printer. In the days of punched cards, millions of cards were numerically or alphabetically organized by placing them into the hopper of a card sorter, taking them out of all the stackers and putting them back into the hopper for the next card column.

**horizontal market**    Refers to the entire marketplace that crosses all industry boundaries. See *horizontal market software*. Contrast with *vertical market*.

**horizontal market software**    Software packages, such as word processors and spreadsheets, that are used in all industries (banking, insurance, etc.). Such products are also called "productivity software." Contrast with *vertical market software*

**horizontal resolution**    The number of elements, or dots, on a horizontal line (columns in a matrix). Contrast with *vertical resolution*.

**horizontal retrace**    See *raster scan*.

**horizontal scaling**    In multiprocessing, adding more computer systems to the environment. Contrast with *vertical scaling*.

**Sorter Hopper**
In the 1940s and 1950s, millions of punched cards were placed into hoppers on IBM sorters such as this one. The hoppers were also fitted with two-foot extensions that held more cards. *(Image courtesy of The Computer Museum History Center, www.computerhistory.org)*

**horizontal scan frequency**    The number of lines illuminated on a video screen in one second. For example, a resolution of 400 lines refreshed 60 times per second requires a scan rate of 24 kHz plus overhead (time to bring the beam back to the beginning of the next line). Same as horizontal sync frequency in TV. Contrast with *vertical scan frequency*.

**HOS**    (Higher Order Software) A design and documentation technique used to break down an information system into a set of functions that are mathematically correct and error free. It uses a rigid set of rules for the decomposition of the total system into its elementary components. The resulting specifications are complete enough to have machine language programs generated directly from them.

**host**    A computer that acts as a source of information or signals. The term can refer to almost any kind of computer, from a centralized mainframe that is a host to its terminals, to a server that is host to its clients, to a desktop PC that is host to its peripherals. In network architectures, a client station (user's machine) is also considered a host, because it is a source of information to the network, in contrast to a device such as a router or switch that directs traffic. See *host adapter* and *host name*.

**host adapter**    Also called a "controller" or "host bus adapter," it is a device that connects one or more peripheral units to a computer. It is typically an expansion card that plugs into the bus. IDE and SCSI are examples of peripheral interfaces that call their controllers host adapters. See *host*.

**host address**    The physical address of a computer in a network. On the Internet, a host address is the IP address of the machine. See *IP address* and *host name*.

**host attached**    Connected directly to the computer using a peripheral interface such as SCSI, IDE, SSA or ESCON.

**host based**    (1) A system controlled by a central or main computer. A host-based system typically refers to a hierarchical communications system controlled by a central computer.
    (2) Refers to an operation that is performed by software in the computer rather than in a peripheral device. See *host-based printer* and *host-based modem*.

**host-based modem**    A modem that relies on the CPU to perform some of the communications processing. It enables less costly modem circuits to be used. See *soft modem* and *host based*.

**host-based printer**    A printer that relies on the computer's CPU to do the rasterization of the pages. Non-host–based printers accept a command language from the computer, such as PostScript and PCL, and perform the rasterization internally. GDI printers are an example of host-based printers, which rely on the CPU's processing power to do the work. See *GDI printer* and *host based*.

**host card**    (1) A plug-in card that adapts one type of card to another. For example, it might serve as a bridge between a PMC card and VMEbus-based hardware. See *mezzanine card*.

(2) A plug-in card that contains a CPU.

**host-centric**    Designed to run only in a centralized host computer rather than in a client/server-oriented LAN. See *client/server, LAN-centric* and *server-centric*.

**hostid**    See *IP address*.

**hosting**    Maintaining a computer system and its applications at a third-party site. See *Web hosting*.

**host ISP**    The Internet service provider (ISP) that runs a Web site for a person or organization. The host ISP is responsible for the proper identification and administration of the domain name at the site.

**host mode**    A communications mode that allows a computer to answer an incoming telephone call and receive data without human assistance.

**host name**    The logical name assigned to a computer. On the Web, most hosts are named WWW; for example, **www.mycompany.com**. If a site is composed of several hosts, they might be given different names such as **support.mycompany.com** and **sales.mycompany.com**. SUPPORT and SALES are the host names, MYCOMPANY the subdomain name, and COM is the top-level domain name. See *HOSTS file, IP address* and *TLD*.

**HOSTS file**    A text file in a UNIX network that provides name resolution of host names to IP addresses. HOSTS files, which contain host names and IP addresses, are manually updated and replicated onto all the servers in the enterprise. Except in small networks, HOSTS files have given way to the DNS system. See *DNS* and *LMHOSTS file*.

**hot backup**    Backing up a database that is in active use. Contrast with *cold backup*.

**hot desking**    Using a set of cubicles for mobile workers that come into the office from time to time. It is similar to hoteling, but reserverations are not required. People come in and sit down at the next available seat, plug into the network and go to work, which means a vice president might sit next to a junior trainee at any given time. See *hoteling*.

**hot docking**    The ability to place a laptop computer into its docking station without having to turn it off first. After insertion, all the peripheral devices attached to the docking station are actvie. See *hot swap*.

**hoteling**    Using office space on an as-needed basis like a hotel room. Telecommuters reserve office space ahead of time for trips to the office. See *hot desking, virtual company* and *telecommuter*.

**hot fix**    (1) To make a repair during normal operation. It often refers to marking sectors in poor condition as bad and remapping the data to spare sectors. Some SCSI drives can automatically move the data in sectors that are becoming hard to read to spare sectors without the user, operating system or even the SCSI host adapter being aware of it. See *hot swap*.

(2) Microsoft's term for a bug fix, which is accomplished by replacing certain existing files in the application with revised versions.

**hot group**    A collection of motivated employees that work on a project above and beyond the call of duty.

**HotJava**   A Web browser from Sun that supports the Java programming language, which was also developed by Sun. HotJava executes Java programs embedded directly within Web documents.

**hotkey**   The key or key combination that causes some function to occur in the computer, no matter what else is currently running. It is commonly used to activate a memory resident (TSR) program.

**hot link**   A predefined connection between programs so that when information in one database or file is changed, related information in other databases and files are also updated. See *hypertext, hypergraphic, compound document* and *OLE.*

**hotlist**   A listing of the best of something. It typically refers to the most popular Web sites.

**Hotmail**   A free, advertiser-supported e-mail service from Microsoft Network (MSN) that provides you with a permanent e-mail address that can be accessed from any Web browser. Hotmail, originally developed by Hotmail Corporation and acquired by Microsoft in 1998, Hotmail became the fastest growing e-mail service on the Web. For information, visit www.hotmail.com. See *Internet e-mail service* and *viral marketing.*

**hot plug**   See *hot swap.*

**hot potato routing**   (1) In communications, rerouting a message as soon as it arrives.
    (2) On the Internet, routing a message from one backbone to another at the nearest exchange point (NAP) to eliminate as much traffic as possible. See *NAP.*

**hot spare**   A spare disk drive in a RAID configuration that is put into action when another drive fails. Using the RAID algorithms, the missing data from the faulty drive is reconstructed and written to the hot spare. When the bad drive is replaced, it then becomes the hot spare. See *RAID* and *hot swap.*

**hot spot**   (1) An icon or part of a larger image used as a hyperlink to another document or file. When the hot spot is clicked, the linked material is searched for and displayed.
    (2) The exact part of an icon or screen pointer that is sensitive to selection. A hot spot may be part of a larger image. For example, an image may have several hot spots, one for each of its components. When clicked, a greater explanation of the component is produced. Where hot spots begin and end determine how easy they are to select.
    The screen pointer also has a hot spot, which is a small number of pixels that make contact with the icon's hot spot. For example, the tip of an arrow or finger pointer or the crosspoint of an X-shaped pointer may be the pointer's hot spot.
    (3) A network node that is processing at its maximum or is backlogged due to an excessive number of transactions.
    (4) The instructions in a program that are executed the most in actual operation. To improve execution performance, the hot spots are the routines that should be refined.
    (5) (HotSpot) A Java compiler from Sun that optimizes the parts of the program that are executed most frequently (the hot spots).

**hot swap**   To pull out a component from a system and plug in a new one while the power is still on and the unit is still operating. Redundant systems can be designed to swap drives, circuit boards, power supplies, virtually anything that is duplexed within the computer. See *warm swap, hot fix* and *hot spare.*

**hourglass**   A centuries-old device for counting time. It consists of two sand-filled glass chambers attached to each other with a tiny opening. When the hourglass is turned over, the sand falls to the bottom side for a specific amount of time. An hourglass symbol is commonly used on graphical interfaces to mean "wait until finished." When the hourglass icon appears, you cannot do anything within this application until the current task has been completed.

**housekeeping**   A set of instructions that are executed at the beginning of a program. It sets all counters and flags to their starting values and generally readies the program for execution.

**Hover**   An option in Microsoft Internet Explorer that removes the permanent underline from hypertext links. The underline displays automatically and only when the cursor is placed over (hovers over) the link. Hover is available in Tools/Internet Options/Advanced/Underline links.

### how to find things on the Net    See *Web search sites* and *how to access the Internet*.

### how to look up someone on the Net    See *Web white pages* and *Web yellow pages*.

### how to register a domain name    If you are setting up your own Web server, you have to register directly with Network Solutions or one of the other accredited registration organizations. If an Internet service provider (ISP) is hosting your site, it may handle the registration for you. See *Network Solutions* and *ICANN*.

Is a Name Already Taken?    To find out if a domain name is taken, visit www.networksolutions.com or www.icann.org.

### how to search the Web    See *Web search sites*.

### how to spoof your technical friend    To have a light-hearted joke with your technical colleagues, take the highest clock rate of an Intel CPU chip and double or triple it. Then, say something like "did you hear about Intel's three-gigaHertz Pentium? They've kept it a secret, but they're shipping it now!" Expect a "wow" reaction, or "that's impossible!"

Be careful. You have to stay on top of the numbers. Years ago, 100MHz (100 megaHertz) sounded unbelievable. Today, chip speeds are nearing 2GHz. See also *buffer flush* and *Stringy Floppy*.

**HP**    (Hewlett-Packard Company, Palo Alto, CA, www.hp.com) The second largest computer company in the U.S. HP was founded in 1939 by William Hewlett and David Packard in a garage behind the Packard's California home. Its first product, an audio oscillator for measuring sound, was the beginning of a line of electronics that made HP an international supplier of electronic test and measurement instruments. Walt Disney Studios, HP's first big customer, purchased eight oscillators to develop and test a new sound system for the movie *Fantasia*.

HP entered the computer field in 1966 with the 2116A, the first of the HP 1000 series designed to gather and analyze the data produced by HP instruments. HP 1000 computers are used for CIM applications, such as process monitoring and control, alarm management and machine monitoring.

In 1972, HP branched into business computing with the 3000 series, a multiuser system that became well known for its high reliability, especially for that time. The successful 3000 family has continued to be one of HP's major computer series. Also in 1972, HP introduced the first scientific handheld calculator, the HP-35, obsoleting the slide rule and ushering in a new age of pocket-sized calculators. In 1982, the first HP 9000 workstation was introduced.

HP's first personal computer was the Touchscreen 150, a non-standard MS-DOS personal computer that gained only modest acceptance. In 1985, it introduced its first completely IBM-compatible PC, the 286-based Vectra. As of the 1990s, the Vectra has become a very successful part of HP's business.

In 1984, HP revolutionized the printer market with its desktop LaserJet printer, which has set the standard for the industry. HP continues its leadership in this area with routine advances in resolution, speed and price. It has become a formidable contender in desktop and network printers.

In 1986, it introduced Precision Architecture, a RISC-based architecture for its 3000 and 9000 series product lines, which has proven very successful. In 1989, HP acquired Apollo Computer, a workstation manufacturer, and combined technologies to become a leader in the field of UNIX-based workstations.

HP sells over 10,000 different products in the electronics and computer field and has gained a worldwide reputation for its quality

**Hewlett and Packard**
Dave Packard (left) and Bill Hewlett (right) develop their innovative audio oscillator in Packard's Palo Alto garage in 1939. Perhaps they didn't realize they were starting one of the largest and most-respected high-technology companies in the world. *(Image courtesy of Hewlett-Packard Company.)*

**Hewlett and Packard 50 Years Later**
Nearly 50 years after the picture above, this photo was taken in 1988 at an awards ceremony at corporate headquarters. *(Image courtesy of Hewlett-Packard Company.)*

**The 2116A**

The 2116A was HP's first computer designed for the process control industry. It was the beginning of a long line of computers for this niche, as well as for scientific and commercial applications. *(Image courtesy of Hewlett-Packard Company.)*

**HP's First Product**

This is the advertisement for the original audio oscillator, HP's first product in 1939. *(Image courtesy of Hewlett-Packard Company.)*

engineering. In 1999, HP spun off its test and measurement divisions into a new company named Agilent Technologies. The business units involved grossed nearly eight billion in 1998 and employed 45,000 people worldwide. The new company is headquartered at 395 Page Mill Road, the site where Hewlett and Packard constructed their first building in 1943.

**HP 1000**    A family of realtime computers from HP introduced in 1966. They are sensor-based computers used extensively in laboratory and manufacturing environments for collecting and analyzing data.

**HP 3000**    A family of business-oriented servers from HP that run under the MPE/iX operating system. Models are available from entry level to mainframe class. Introduced in 1972, the HP3000A was HP's first business computer. With 128KB of RAM and costing about $250,000, it set a standard for reliability that was unmatched for that era.

In 1986, the line began to migrate to HP's PA-RISC chips, while maintaining compatibility with the original CPUs. Over the years, HP 3000s have migrated from the central minicomputer architecture to client/server, in which intelligent workstations and PCs have replaced the dumb terminal.

**HP 9000**    A family of high-performance workstations and servers from HP that are based on HP's PA-RISC architecture and run under the HP/UX operating system. Both workstations and servers are available in a wide range of machines from entry level to supercomputer class. HP VISUALIZE models are workstations with high-performance graphics capabilities. In the 1980s, the first HP 9000s used Motorola 680x0 CPUs.

**HPA**    (1) (**H**igh **P**erformance **A**ddressing)  Refers to a variety of addressing techniques that improve the quality of a passive matrix (LCD) screen. Passive matrix screens have improved steadily and are getting much closer to the quality of active matrix displays.

(2) (**H**igh **P**ower **A**mplifier)  An amplifier used to transmit signals from a satellite dish to a satellite transponder. The received signals are picked up with a low noise amplifier (LNA).

**HPC**    (Handheld **PC**) A palmtop computer that weighs less than one pound and runs specialized versions of popular applications. Microsoft coined the term for its Windows CE operating system, which is an abbreviated version of Windows 95/98. See also *High-Performance Computing*.

**HP-compatible printer**    A printer that accepts the PCL printer commands used in HP LaserJet printers. Most non-HP laser printers support PCL. However, PCL capabilities evolve over the years, and an HP-compatible printer may not support the latest version of PCL.

**HPFS**    (High Performance File System) The file system introduced with OS/2 Version 1.2 that handles large disks (2TB volumes; 2GB files) and long file names (256 bytes). It coexists with the existing FAT system.

**HPGL**    (Hewlett-Packard Graphics Language) A vector graphics file format from HP that was developed as a standard plotter language. Most plotters support the HPGL and DMPL standards.

**HPIB**    (Hewlett-Packard Interface Bus) HP's version of the IEEE 488 standard GPIB.

**HPNA**    See *HomePNA*.

**HP PA-RISC**    See *PA-RISC*.

**HPR**    (High-Performance Routing) Extensions to IBM's APPN networking that enable SNA data to be sent over frame-based (Ethernet, etc.) and cell-based (ATM) networks. HPR improves routing performance and reliability and is designed to eliminate congestion on network backbones.

**HPSB**    (High Performance Serial Bus) See *FireWire*.

**HP-UX**    HP's version of UNIX that runs on its 9000 family. It is based on SVID and incorporates features from BSD UNIX along with several HP innovations.

**HREF**    (Hypertext REFerence) The mnemonic used to assign a hypertext address to an HTML document. The **HREF=** is followed by the name or URL of the target document. The HREF resides within a hypertext anchor. See *hypertext anchor*.

**HSB**    (Hue Saturation Brightness) A color model that is similar to the way an artist mixes colors by adding black and white to pure pigments. The pigments are the hues (H), measured in a circle from 0 to 359 degrees (0=red, 60=yellow, 120=green, 180=cyan, 240=blue, 300=magenta). The saturation (S) is the amount of black, and the brightness (B) is the amount of white, each measured from 0 to 100%.

**HSCSD**    (High Speed Circuit Switched Data) An enhancement to the GSM mobile communications system that enables up to four 14.4 Kbps channels to be combined to provide 57.6 Kbps data transfer. Part of GSM Phase 2, HSCSD is suited for videoconferencing and multimedia transmission.

**HSI**    (Hue Saturation Intensity) A color model similar to HSB. See *HSB*.

**HSL**    (Hue Saturation Luminosity) A color model similar to HSB. See *HSB*.

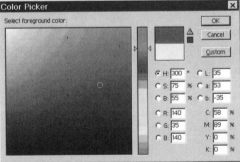

**HSB Colors**
This Photoshop dialog box shows the current color as measured by the HSB, RGB, CMYK and CIE L*a*b color models. The current hue (H) is magenta at 300 degrees. The circle pointer in the color swatch is moved to a selected saturation (S) and brightness (B). S changes from 0 to 100% from left to right, and B changes from 0 to 100% from bottom to top.

**HSM**    (Hierarchical Storage Management) The automatic movement of files from hard disk to slower, less-expensive storage media. The typical hierarchy is from magnetic disk to optical disk to tape. HSM software constantly monitors hard disk capacity and moves data from one storage level to the next based on age, category and other criteria as specified by the network or system administrator. HSM often includes a system for routine backup as well.

When a file is moved off the hard disk, it is replaced with a small stub file that indicates where the original file is located.

**HSP** (Hosting Service Provider) An organization that specializes in hosting Web sites. There are various levels of offerings from sharing a Web server with several other companies to having a dedicated Web server or to providing co-location services. See *co-location*.

**HSRP** (Hot Standby Router Protocol) A protocol from Cisco for switching to a backup router in the event of failure.

**HSSI** (High-Speed Serial Interface) A serial interface with transmission rates up to 52 Mbps. It is often used to connect one or more LAN routers and network devices to a T3 line, which provides 44.736 Mbps. A T3 multiplexor using HSSI can divide the T3 bandwidth into the appropriate speeds of the various devices.

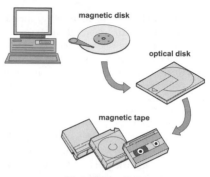

**Data Migration**
A data migration path in an HSM system might be from high-speed hard disk to slower speed optical disk to offline tape. In time, optical disks will almost surely replace magnetic media, but there will still be a need to take data off premises for protection against fire and accidents.

**HST** (1) An asymmetrical modem protocol from U.S. Robotics that includes error control and compression, and transmits from 4,800 to 14,400 bps in one direction and from 300 to 400 bps in the other. HST was the first reliable, high-speed modem protocol before the V.32bis and V.42 standards became widely used.

(2) (Hubble Space Telescope) Launched in April 1990, it views star material some 10 to 12 billion light years from earth.

**HSV** (Hue Saturation Value) A color model similar to HSB. See *HSB*.

**HTM file** An alternate file extension for HTML files. HTML files originated with UNIX, where Web pages are commonly identified with an .HTML extension. The .HTM is an alternate in the Windows world, because three-byte extensions (.EXE, .DOC, etc.) are so commonly used.

**HTML** (HyperText Markup Language) The document format used on the World Wide Web. Web pages are built with HTML tags (codes) embedded in the text. HTML defines the page layout, fonts and graphic elements, as well as the hypertext links to other documents on the Web. Each link contains the URL, or address, of a Web page residing on the same server or any server worldwide, hence "World Wide" Web.

HTML 2.0 was defined by the Internet Engineering Task Force (IETF) with a basic set of features, including interactive forms capability. Subsequent versions added more features, such as blinking text, custom backgrounds and tables of contents. However, each new version requires agreement on the tags used, and browsers must be modified to implement those tags.

HTML is not a programming language like Java or JavaScript (if this, do that), rather it could be considered a "presentation language." HTML is derived from SGML, the Standard Generalized Markup Language, which is widely used to publish documents. HTML is an SGML document with a fixed set of tags that, although change with each new revision, are not flexible.

A subset of SGML, known as XML, allows the developer of the page to define the tags, and HTML 4.0 and XML 1.0 have been combined into a single format called "XHTML," which is expected to become the standard format for Web pages. XHTML also enables Web pages to be developed with different sets of data so that handheld devices, with limited screen sizes, can download abbreviated pages. See *HTML tag*, *CGI script*, *VRML* and *XML*.

**HTML bug** See *Web bug*.

**HTML editor** A low-level Web site authoring tool that is essentially a text editor, specialized for writing HTML code. It assists the HTML author by cataloging all HTML tags and common structures in menus, and by being able to catch certain syntax errors. It often displays tags and contents in colors so they pop out for easy reference. See *Web authoring software*.

**HTML e-mail** An e-mail message formatted as a Web page (HTML document). It allows the publishing of more elaborate newsletters and reports, and sending them via e-mail. In order to view an HTML e-mail message, the e-mail program must support it. See *BubbleBoy virus*.

**HTML extension file** An HTML file that is filled with data from a database by the Internet Database Connector (IDC) component of Microsoft's Internet Information Server (IIS) Web server. The HTML extension file (.HTX file), which uses specific tags for IDC, is returned to the user's browser. See *IDC*.

**HTML table** An HTML structure for creating rows and columns. It is used for lists, specifications, and other tabular data as well as to locate elements on the page. The table command gives the HTML designer reasonably precise control over placement of text and images. HTML tables are built using the <TABLE> tag to define the overall table and then the Table Row <TR> tag to build each row. The Table Data <TD> tag defines the actual data.

**HTML tag** A code used in HTML to define a format change or hypertext link. HTML tags are surrounded by the angle brackets, < and >.

**HTTP** (HyperText Transport Protocol) The communications protocol used to connect to servers on the World Wide Web. Its primary function is to establish a connection with a Web server and transmit HTML pages to the client browser. Addresses of Web sites begin with an **http://** prefix;

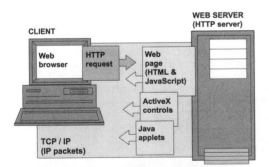

**Web Server Fundamentals**
Web browsers communicate with Web servers via the TCP/IP protocol. The browser sends HTTP requests to the server, which responds with HTML pages and possibly additional programs in the form of ActiveX controls or Java applets.

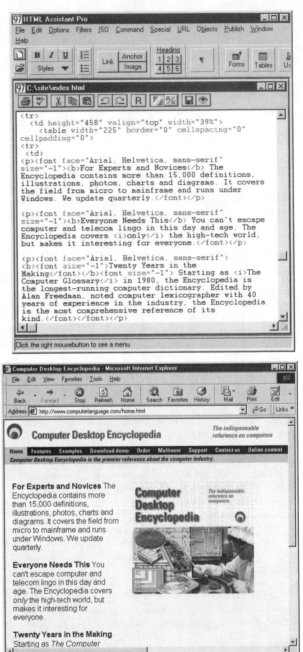

**HTML Tags**
The HTML (top) shows how the text paragraphs on the home page below it are coded. All HTML tags are surrounded by the <and> symbols. HTML Assistant Pro from Exit 0 digital systems Inc., (www.exit0.com), is the HTML editor used to view this source code.

however, Web browsers typically default to the HTTP protocol. For example, typing **www.yahoo.com** is the same as typing **http://www.yahoo.com**.

Version 1.0 of HTTP adds considerable overhead to a Web download. Each time a graphic on the same page or another page on the same site is requested, a new protocol connection is established between the browser and the server. In HTTP Version 1.1, a persistent connection allows multiple downloads with less overhead. Version 1.1 also improves caching and makes it easier to create virtual hosts (multiple Web sites on the same server).

It is expected that the HTTP protocol will undergo several revisions in an attempt to manage the escalating traffic on the Internet. However, many believe that only entirely new protocols will be able to meet the demand. Stay tuned! See *HTTP-NG* and *HTTP request header*.

### HTTP/1.0 404 Object Not Found   See *404 error*.

**HTTPd**   (**HTTP D**aemon) A Web server (HTTP server) available from the NCSA for various versions of UNIX. HTTPd was the first Web server and has been adapted to other implementations. See *NCSA* and *Apache*.

**HTTP–NG**   (**H**yper**T**ext **T**ransport **P**rotocol–**N**ext **G**eneration) An enhanced version of the HTTP protocol that enables it to meet the increasing performance demands of the 21st Century. It is expected to become a layered protocol that is more streamlined and to provide for remote invocation of services resident on Web servers. For technical information, visit the HTTP-NG Working Group of the IETF at www.w3.org. See *Jigsaw*.

**HTTP proxy**   A proxy server that specializes in HTML (Web page) transactions. See *proxy server*.

**HTTP request header**   A set of data at the beginning of an HTTP request that is sent by the Web browser to the Web server. It includes the type, version and capabilities of the Web browser being used. See *user agent* and *HTTP response header*.

**HTTP response header**   A set of data at the beginning of an HTTP response that is sent by the Web server back to the Web browser. It includes the date, size and type of file being sent. See *HTTP request header*.

**HTTPS**   (1) (**H**yper**T**ext **T**ransport **P**rotocol **S**ecure) The protocol for accessing a secure Web server. Using HTTPS in the URL instead of HTTP directs the message to a secure port number rather than the default Web port number of 80. The session is then managed by a security protocol. See *security protocol*.

(2) (**H**yper**T**ext **T**ransport **P**rotocol **S**erver) A Web server that runs under Windows NT, developed by the European Microsoft Windows Academic Centre.

**HTTP server**   Software that services HTTP requests, which is the protocol of the Web. See *Web server* and *HTTP*.

**hub**   (1) A central connecting device in a network that joins communications lines together in a star configuration. Passive hubs are just connecting units that add nothing to the data passing through them. Active hubs, also sometimes called "multiport repeaters," regenerate the data bits in order to maintain a strong signal, and intelligent hubs provide added functionality.

Hubs are widely used in Ethernet and Token Ring networks. In Token Rings, the hub is known as a "Multi-station Access Unit" or MAU. Multiple media hubs interconnect different types of Ethernets

**Intelligent Hub**
Cabletron's MMAC line of hubs is an example of a highly scalable and flexible multiple media hub, supporting Ethernet, Token Ring, FDDI, ATM and WAN connections. This type of device provides a backbone and centralized management for a heterogeneous network. *(Image courtesy of Cabletron Systems, Inc.)*

(twisted pair, coax and optical fiber) and can bridge between Ethernet, Token Ring, FDDI and ATM topologies. Switching hubs provide Ethernet and ATM switching.

Hubs have become intelligent and modular, allowing for the insertion of bridging, routing and switching modules within the same unit. A hub can even host a CPU board and network operating system, turning the hub into a file server or network control processor. See *LAN*.

**(2)** See *Web hub*.

**hub and spoke**    Any architecture that uses a central connecting point. It is the same as a star topology in a network. A network hub is hardware that functions as a central hub to all nodes. See *hub*.

**hub ring**    A flat ring pressed around the hole in a 5.25" floppy disk for rigidity. The drive's clamping ring presses the hub ring onto the spindle.

**hue**    The dominant wavelength of a color. A color system, or model, measures color by hue, saturation and luminance. The hue is the predominant color, the saturation is the color intensity, and the luminance is the brightness. See *HSB*.

**Huffman coding**    A statistical compression method that converts characters into variable-length bit strings. Most-frequently ocurring characters are converted to shortest bit strings; least frequent, the longest. Compression takes two passes. The first pass analyzes a block of data and creates a tree model based on its contents. The second pass compresses the data via the model. Decompression decodes the variable-length strings via the tree. See *LZW*.

**Human Genome Project**    A bioinformatics project that has identified the 30,000 genes in human DNA. Coordinated by the U.S. Department of Energy and the National Institutes of Health, the U.S. Human Genome Project started in 1990 and released its findings in February 2001, along with findings from a separate project by Celera Genomics Group. There are similar projects in other countries as well. The purpose is to store the three billion chemical base pairs (the DNA sequence) derived from these analyses in databases for use in biomedical research.

This information is not a blueprint of the human being, rather it is a dictionary of components. Once believed that each gene made only one protein, it is now believed that each gene creates numerous proteins, although this information is expected to take years to determine. Part of the U.S. government project is to study the ethical and legal impact that this information will have on society.

**Hungarian notation**    In programming, the use of standard prefixes in naming variables. For example, "p" means pointer, hence, pTEXTBUF is a pointer to a buffer called TEXTBUF.

**hunt**    A telephony term for switching to a second line if the first one is busy. The system can "hunt" in a preset order from line 1 to 2, and then from 2 to 3, and so on.

**h/w**    See *hardware*.

**Hub and Spoke Architectures**
Messaging middleware is always configured in a hub and spoke configuration, and most database middleware is also available in this topology. See *EDA* and *DQbroker*.

**hybrid**    Also known as a *termination* or **term set**, it is a device that adapts a two-wire telephone line from a home or business into a four-wire trunk at the telco central office. A hybrid also exists within the telephone set, converting the two-wire line into the four wires required by the handset (two for the speaker; two for the microphone). See *echo cancellation*.

**hybrid circuit**    A circuit that contains different types of circuitry or chips. See *mixed signal* and *hybrid microcircuit*.

**hybrid computer**    A digital computer that accepts analog signals, converts them to digital and processes them in digital form. It is used in process control and robotics.

**hybrid file**    Sometimes refers to a graphics file that contains vector graphics and bitmaps. See *metafile*.

**hybrid microcircuit**    An electronic circuit composed of different types of integrated circuits and discrete components, mounted on a ceramic base. Used in military and communications applications, it is especially suited for building custom analog circuits including A/D and D/A converters, amplifiers and modulators. The hybrid microcircuit evolved into the multichip module (MCM) and, later, the multichip package (MCP). See *MCM, MCP* and *chip package*.

**hybrid network**    In communications, a network made up of equipment from multiple vendors.

**Hydra**    **(1)** The code name for Windows Terminal Server. See *Windows Terminal Server*.

**(2)** (HYDRA) (**HY**brid **D**ocument **R**eproduction **A**pparatus) A printer, photocopier, scanner and fax built into one machine.

**(3)** A device that converts analog signals to ISDN Basic Rate Interface (BRI).

**Hybrid Microcircuits**
The picture shows a variety of hybrid circuits. The tiny, square white spots are the actual chips.
*(Image courtesy of Circuit Technology, Inc.)*

**HyperCard**    A Macintosh application development system from Apple that was one of the first visual tools for building hyperlinked applications. "Stacks" of "cards" are built that hold text, graphics, sound and video with links between them. Complex routines can be embedded in the cards using the HyperTalk programming language.

Until HyperCard 2.1, the HyperCard program had to be resident in the computer to run the stack. Although HyperCard compilers have been available from third parties, as of HyperCard 2.1, a runtime engine is included in the stack so that HyperCard does not have to be on the target machine.

**hypercube**    A parallel processing architecture made up of binary multiples of computers (4, 8, 16, etc.). The computers are interconnected so that data travel is kept to a minimum. For example, in two eight-node cubes, each node in one cube would be connected to the counterpart node in the other.

**Hyper-G**    An enhanced version of Web server technology that provides many advanced features, including link consistency and the ability to search multiple servers. Regular Web browsers can access Hyper-G servers, and Hyper-G browsers can access other Web servers as well as Gopher servers. Hyper-G browsers, such as Harmony and Amadeus, also allow for editing. Hyper-G is a superset of the Internet Gopher technology and was developed at the Graz University of Technology in Austria in the early 1990s. See **Hyperwave Information Server**.

**hypergraphic**    A linkage between related information by means of a graphic image. It is the graphics counterpart of hypertext. Instead of clicking on a word, you click on an icon to jump to the related section, document or file. See *hypertext* and *hot spot*.

**hyperlink**    A predefined linkage between one object and another. The link is displayed either as text or as an icon. On Web pages, a text hyperlink displays as underlined text, while a graphical hyperlink is a small graphics image of any size and shape. The terms "hyperlink" and "hypertext" are used synonymously. See *hypertext* and *hypergraphic*.

**hypermedia**    The use of data, text, graphics, video and voice as elements in a hypertext system. All the various forms of information are linked together so that a user can easily move from one to another.

**HyperPAD**    An earlier application development system from Brightbill-Roberts & Company, that brought the HyperCard paradigm to PCs. See *HyperCard*.

**HyperScript**    An advanced macro (scripting) language that is provided with the WINGZ spreadsheet.

**HyperTalk**    The programming language used in HyperCard.

**hypertext**    A linkage between related text. For example, by selecting a word in a sentence, information about that word is retrieved if it exists, or the next occurrence of the word is found. In the Windows version of this software, you can hypertext to the definition of any term you encounter by clicking on the word or highlighting the phrase.

Hypertext is the foundation of the World Wide Web. Links embedded within Web pages are addresses to other Web pages either stored locally or on a Web server anywhere in the world. Links can be text only, in which case they are underlined, or they can be represented as an icon of any size or shape.

The hypertext concept was originally coined by Ted Nelson in the mid 1960s as a method for making the computer respond to the way humans think and require information. The terms "hypertext" and "hyperlink" are used synonymously. See *hyperlink*.

**hypertext anchor**    In an HTML document, the codes used to define a hypertext link to another page or to a location elsewhere in the document. The following anchor points to the EXAMPLES.HTML Web page located in the same directory on the same server. The word "Examples" is the link text, the text the user sees and clicks on. In the example to the right, the full path to the page is implied.

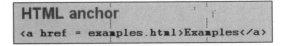

**HTML anchor**
`<a href = examples.html>Examples</a>`

**hypervisor**    A generic mainframe term for a facility that provides and manages multiple virtual machines. Examples include VM/370 and VM/ESA (both are software with hardware assists), MDF, MLPF and PR/SM, as well as the System/390 Integrated Facility for Linux, which supports multiple instances of Linux. See *PR/SM* and *MDF*.

**hyperware**    Software that uses *hypertext*.

**hyphenation**    Breaking words that extend beyond the right margin. Software hyphenates words by matching them against a hyphenation dictionary or by using a built-in set of rules, or both. See *discretionary hyphen*.

**hyphenation dictionary**    A word file with predefined hyphen locations.

**hyphenation zone**    The distance from the right margin within which a word may be hyphenated.

**hyphen ladder**    Hyphens on two or more consecutive lines, which causes distraction to the reader.

**hypotenuse**    In a right triangle, the side opposite the right angle. See *sine*.

**hysteresis**    The lag between making a change, such as increasing or decreasing power, and the response or effect of that change.

**Hz**    (HertZ) See *Hertz*.

**I18N** (I + 18 letters + N) See *internationalization* and *L10N*.

**I2** See *Internet2*.

**i2O** See *i2O*.

**I2O** (Intelligent I/O) A standard for offloading input and output to an auxiliary processor. The auxiliary processor (I/O processor) manages the data transfer while the CPU does something else. Although I2O is being implemented in small systems, it embodies the principle behind mainframe channels, which can have several hundred data transfers occurring simultaneously.

The I2O special interest group (SIG) was formed in early 1996 to promote the technology. For more information, visit www.i2osig.org.

**i2 Technologies** (i2 Technologies, Inc., Irving, TX, www.i2.com) A software company specializing in supply chain management. Its RHYTHM software helps manufacturers plan and schedule production and related operations such as raw material procurement and product delivery. Founded in 1988 by Sanjiv Sidhu, the company provides support for both inter-enterprise and intra-enterprise supply chains.

**i386** A folder on the Windows NT distribution CD-ROM that contains files for PC (Intel x86) use. There is also an Alpha directory for Digital Alpha files. See also *386*.

**i486** See *486*.

**i750** A programmable compression chip from Intel that supports a variety of techniques including DVI, MPEG and JPEG.

**i860** A 64-bit RISC-based microprocessor from Intel that included floating point applications. Although it could serve as a general-purpose CPU, it was used mostly in DSP and 3-D graphics applications. The i860 had its heyday in the early 1990s.

**i960** A general-purpose 32-bit RISC-based microprocessor from Intel that is used in a variety of devices including laser printers and networking equipment. The first i960s were the KA/KB models introduced in 1988.

**IA-32** (Intel Architecture-32) The 32-bit architecture used in Intel's Pentium chips. See *IA-64* and *future Intel chips*.

**IA-64** (Intel Architecture-64) The 64-bit architecture used in Intel's next-generation family of CPU chips. It is designed for fast parallel instruction execution and was designed at the end of the 20th Century, whereas x86 chips (IA-32) hark back to the early 1970s when designs were based on a fraction of the number of transistors that can be built into a chip today.

Jointly designed by Intel and HP, the first model in the line is the Itanium. Formerly code named "Merced" and introduced in May 2001, the Itanium contains 25 million transistors in the CPU and 300 million in the cache using .18 micron technology. The operating systems expected to run on IA-64 are Windows 2000, Compaq's Tru64 (UNIX), Sun's Solaris, SCO's Monterrey, Novell's Modesto and HP's HP-UX.

Although x86-based software (IA-32 software) will run intact on IA-64 machines, programs have to be recompiled in order to take full advantage of the new architecture. HP's PA-RISC applications will run on IA-64 using a software-based translation layer, which is expected to be extremely efficient, since the IA-64 instruction set architecture is very close to PA-RISC. HP's "dynamic translator" will be bundled with all versions of HP-UX (HP's UNIX) that are sold for IA-64 hardware.

The IA-64 architecture differs from IA-32 in several ways. Rather than variable-length instructions, it uses fixed-length, four-byte instructions bundled in sets of three "long instruction words." It uses 256 registers for integer and floating point operations compared to 16 in IA-32. IA-64 employs a technique known as predication, where both sides of a branch instruction are executed in parallel. When the correct branch is determined, the results for the incorrect side are discarded. With IA-64, compilers have to be more intelligent, placing codes into the instruction bundles that tell the CPU how to execute instructions in parallel. They also have to place instructions in interleaved order for predication.

If predication is not set up, the CPU will perform traditional branch prediction, whereby it attempts to guess the outcome of a branch and executes those instructions in parallel. IA-64 also supports speculative loading, which loads data into its registers before the instructions actually need to process it. Explicitly Parallel Instruction Computing (EPIC) is Intel's brand name for its new parallel architecture. See *Itanium* and *future Intel chips*.

**IAB**   See *Internet Architecture Board*.

**IAC**   **(1)** (InterApplication Communications) The interprocess communications capability in the Macintosh starting with System 7.0. Many IAC events take place behind the scenes. For example, when you drag and drop an object onto an icon, the Finder may send an IAC message to the application, or an application may send a message to another application, to perform a function.

**(2)** (Internet Access Coalition) A consortium of vendors including Microsoft, Intel and IBM, whose mission is to keep the Internet affordable and promote high-speed access. They oppose any regulations that would enable a telephone company to charge a customer more for a data call than a voice call.

**IAD**   (Integrated Access Device) A device that multiplexes a variety of communications technologies in the customer's premises onto a single telephone line for transmission to the carrier. It also demultiplexes the incoming streams into their respective channels. Devices supporting various combinations (analog voice, DSL, ISDN, T1, etc.) are available. The term often refers to a device that deals only with DSL, mixing both voice and data over the DSL line. See *VoDSL*.

**IAHC**   See *Internet Ad Hoc Committee*.

**IANA**   (Internet Assigned Numbers Authority, www.iana.org) The Internet body that was responsible for managing Internet addresses, domain names and protocol parameters. It has been superseded by ICANN (Internet Corporation for Assigned Names and Numbers), which was formed in 1998.

IANA was chartered by the Internet Society (ISOC) and Federal Network Council (FNC), and has been located at and operated by the Information Sciences Institute at the University of Southern California. See *how to register a domain name* and *ICANN*.

**IANAL**   Digispeak for "I am not a lawyer, but..."

**IAP**   (Internet Access Provider) See *internet service provider*.

**IAS**   See *iPlanet Application Server*.

**IAW**   Digispeak for "in accordance with."

**IB**   See *InfiniBand*.

**IBI**    See *Information Builders*.

**IBIP**    (Information Based Indicia Program) See *PC Postage*.

**IBIS**    (I/O Buffer Information Specification) A format for defining the analog characteristics of the input and output of integrated circuits. IBIS models are ASCII files that provide the behavioral information required to model the device without divulging the proprietary design of the circuit. IBIS supports complex devices such memory modules and MCMs.

**IBM**    (International Business Machines Corporation, Armonk, NY, www.ibm.com) The world's largest computer company. IBM's product lines include the S/390 mainframes (zSeries), AS/400 midrange business systems (iSeries), RS/6000 workstations and servers (pSeries), and Intel-based servers (xSeries), as well as desktop PCs and notebook computers. All of its product families have been very successful.

It all started in New York in 1911 when the Computing-Tabulating-Recording Company (CTR) was created by a merger of The Tabulating Machine Company (Hollerith's punched card company in Washington, DC), International Time Recording Company (time clock maker in NY state), Computing Scale Company (maker of scales and food slicers in Dayton, Ohio), and Bundy Manufacturing (time clock maker in Auburn, NY). CTR started out with 1,200 employees and a capital value of $17.5 million.

**The Man Who Built an Empire**
This photo of Thomas J. Watson, Sr., was taken in 1920, four years before he renamed the company IBM. *(Image courtesy of International Business Machines Corporation. Unauthorized use not permitted.)*

In 1914, Thomas J. Watson, Sr., became general manager. During the next 10 years, he dispensed with all non-tabulating business and turned it into an international enterprise renamed IBM in 1924. Watson instilled a strict, professional demeanor in his employees that set IBMers apart from the rest of the crowd.

IBM achieved spectacular success with its tabulating machines and the punched cards that were fed them. From the 1920s through the 1960s, it developed a huge customer base that was ideal for conversion to computers, and Watson's son, Thomas J. Watson, Jr., was an enthusiastic supporter of computers.

IBM launched its computer business in 1953 with the 701 and introduced the 650 a year later. By the end of the 1950s, the 650 was the most widely used computer in the world with 1,800 systems installed. The 1401, announced in 1959, was its second computer winner; and by the mid-1960s, an estimated 18,000 were in use.

In 1964, it announced the System/360, the first family of compatible computers ever developed. The 360s were enormously successful and set a standard underlying IBM mainframes to this day.

During the 1970s and 1980s, IBM made a variety of incompatible minicomputer systems, including the System/36 and System/38. Its highly successful AS/400, introduced in 1988, provides a broad family of compatible machines in this segment.

In 1981, IBM introduced the PC into a chaotic personal computer field and set the standard almost overnight. IBM is still one of the largest PC manufacturers, but the majority of PC sales come from the PC industry at large, from companies such as Compaq, Dell and HP to mom and pop shops by the thousands.

Although like everyone else, IBM includes Windows on its PCs, but it still maintains its OS/2 operating system for PC desktops and servers. OS/2 is highly praised, but never gained significant market share.

Although IBM is a company with over $80 billion in sales, the early 1990s were gut-wrenching years. IBM experienced major losses due mainly to slowing sales of high-profit mainframes as companies embraced PCs and small servers by the millions. As a result, IBM reduced its workforce by more than 100,000.

In 1991, IBM teamed up with Apple and Motorola to produce the PowerPC chip, a single-chip version of IBM's RS/6000 workstations (see *Apple-IBM alliance*). Introduced in 1995, the PowerPC systems had little impact as stand-alone PCs, but the chips breathed new life into IBM's RS/6000 and AS/400 lines. In 1995, IBM purchased Lotus Development Corporation, publisher of Lotus 1-2-3 and the popular Notes groupware.

IBM is not a company to be underestimated. Although it does not control the PC market, it rebounded and returned to the profits it had been accustomed to. IBM sells an enormous number of mainframes, workstations, servers and desktop and laptop PCs. Next to Microsoft, it is the second largest software company in the world.

In addition, the bulk of the data in most large enterprises still resides in IBM mainframes. As each year goes by, more electronic history piles up, creating massive databases that mainframes handle with ease. The universe runs in cycles. See *Microsoft and IBM*.

### IBM and Microsoft See *Microsoft and IBM*.

### IBM-Apple alliance See *Apple-IBM alliance*.

### IBM-compatible mainframe
A mainframe that is compatible with an IBM mainframe and that runs mainframe operating systems, such as OS/390. In the late 1960s, RCA's computer division produced the Spectra 70, the first line of machines compatible with the System/360. Later, Amdahl, National Semiconductor (marketed through Itel) and Hitachi entered this segment. Today, Hitachi Data Systems and Amdahl are the major IBM-compatible mainframe vendors. See *HDS* and *Amdahl*.

### IBM-compatible PC
A personal computer that is compatible with the IBM PC and PS/2 standards. Although this term is still used, it had validity in the early days when PC makers were trying to copy the IBM PC, and many PCs were not compatible. Today, PCs conform to standards set by Intel, Microsoft and the PC industry at large.

### IBMDOS.COM
One of two hidden system files that make up IBM's PC-DOS. The other is IBMBIO.COM. These two system files are loaded into memory when the computer is booted. They process the instructions in CONFIG.SYS, and then load COMMAND.COM and, finally, process the instructions in AUTOEXEC.BAT. The MS-DOS counterparts of these system files are IO.SYS and MSDOS.SYS.

### IBM format
Generally refers to applications and files for a PC.

### IBM mainframes
Following are the mainframe architectures used in IBM mainframes since the original System/360 introduced in 1964.

**IBM Office, London, 1935**
"Dayton Money Making Machines" were sold all across the world. IBM became an international enterprise in the late 1930s. *(Image courtesy of International Business Machines Corporation. Unauthorized use not permitted.)*

**Hitachi's Skyline**
Used in the largest companies, Hitachi's Skyline series offers high-speed, IBM-compatible mainframe processing. With up to 512 channels per system and 16 ports into main memory, these machines provide enormous transaction processing throughput. *(Image courtesy of Hitachi Data Systems.)*

| Year | Architecture | Model Numbers |
|------|--------------|---------------|
| **System/360** | | |
| 1964 | System/360 | 2xxx (2020 to 2195) |
| **System/370** | | |
| 1970 | System/370 | 3xxx (3115 to 3168) |
| 1977 | System/370 | 303x (3031, 3032, 3033) |
| 1979 | System/370 | 43xx series |
| 1980 | System/370 | 308x series (3081, 3083, 3084) |
| 1981 | XA/370 | 308x series (3081, 3083, 3084) |
| 1986 | XA/370 | 3090 series (120 to 600) |
| 1986 | XA/370 | 9370 series |
| 1988 | ESA/370 | ES/3090 and ES/4381 |
| **System/390** | | |
| 1990 | ESA/390 | ES/9000, 120 to 9X2 |
| 1994 | ESA/390 | 9672 Exx & Pxx, G1 |
| | | Parallel Transaction Server |

| Year | Architecture | Model Numbers |
|------|--------------|---------------|
| **System/390 (cont'd)** | | |
| 1994 | ESA/390 | 9672 Rx1, G1 |
| | | Parallel Enterprise Server |
| 1995 | ESA/390 | 9672 Rx2, Rx3, G2 |
| 1996 | ESA/390 | Multiprise 2000 (2003-xxx) |
| 1996 | ESA/390 | 9672 Rx4, G3 |
| 1997 | ESA/390 | 9672 Rx5, G4 |
| 1998 | ESA/390 | 9672 Rx6-Yx6, G5 |
| 1998 | ESA/390 | 9672 Y56-YX6, G5 Turbo |
| 1999 | ESA/390 | 9672 X17-XZ7, Z17-ZZ7, G6 |
| 1999 | ESA/390 | 7060-xxx Multiprise 3000, G5 |
| **zSeries** | | |
| 2000 | z/Architecture | 2064 100-116, 1C1-1C9, z900 |

**IBM minicomputers**    Following is a list of the different series of minicomputers IBM has offered over the years. For information about a series, look up the individual term.

```
Year
Intro.      Series Name
1969        System/3
1975        System/32
1976        Series/1
1977        System/34
1978        System/38
1978        8100
1983        System/36
1985        System/88
1988        AS/400
1990        RS/6000
1993        RS/6000 (PowerPC based)
1995        AS/400 (PowerPC based)
```

**The IBM PC**
This was the original IBM PC with two floppy disks. This machine spawned the largest market for computers in the world. *(Image courtesy of International Business Machines Corporation. Unauthorized use not permitted.)*

**IBM or Mac**    Refers to applications and file formats used on a PC versus a Macintosh. The IBM nomenclature is a carry-over from the first PCs made by IBM and cloned by third parties. It is more accurate to say "DOS or Mac" or "Windows or Mac."

**IBM PC**    A PC made by IBM. IBM created the PC industry and is still one of its largest vendors. Introduced in 1981, IBM's first PCs were named PC, XT, etc., while subsequent PS/2 machines were given model numbers. For historical purposes, early IBM models are in the table in the following topic. See *PC, IBM-compatible PC, personal computer* and *ThinkPad*.

**IBM server series**    In late 2000, IBM renamed its major product lines under the eServer brand. The "e" in eServer is a stylized e-in-a-circle logo like IBM's rendering of "eBusiness."

```
Old Series              eServer Series

Intel-based server      xSeries eserver
AS/400 server           iSeries eserver
RS/6000 server          pSeries eserver
S/390 mainframe         zSeries eserver
```

**IBM workstation**    See *RS/6000*.

**IBOC**    (In Band/On Channel) The technology used for terrestrial digital audio broadcasting (DAB). It transmits digital signals in the same frequency band as the analog signals, and uses the same channel number so listeners can tune into the same radio station. See *DAB*.

**iBook**    A consumer-based laptop computer from Apple that is the portable counterpart to the iMac desktop machine. It was introduced in July 1999 with a 300MHz G3 processor. The iBook offers an "AirPort" option, which allows wireless connectivity for an analog modem, cable modem or DSL modem up to 150 feet away from the phone line. With the antenna built into the iBook's case, the AirPort includes a plug-in card for the machine and a base station (AirPort Hardware Access Point). See *iMac*.

**IBT**    **(1)** (Instructor Based Training) Training courses conducted by human teachers.
      **(2)** (Internet Based Training) Training courses provided via the Internet.

**IC**    See *integrated circuit, information center* and *Interoperability Clearinghouse*.

**ICA**   (Independent Computing Architecture) The core of Citrix's MetaFrame and WinFrame software that enables a Windows or UNIX server to run an application for multiple users simultaneously while sending only the changes in the user interface to the client machine. This is similar to the days of mainframes, but with a graphical interface rather than character based. ICA client support includes Windows, DOS, Macintosh, UNIX, Java and Web browsers. Numerous embedded devices are ICA enabled as well.

Originally known as the Intelligent Console Architecture, ICA provides a presentation services protocol that governs input/output between the server and clients. ICA also supports local ports for printing and other interconnections. The timeshared, multiuser processing that allows this all to take place is provided by the native capabilities of UNIX and the Terminal Server options in Windows NT and Windows 2000, the latter being the MultiWin kernel originally developed by Citrix and acquired by Microsoft. ICA is also used in WinFrame, Citix's first implementation of this architecture. See *MetaFrame*, *WinFrame* and *Windows Terminal Server*.

**ICANN**   (Internet Corporation for Assigned Names and Numbers, www.icann.org) A non-profit, international association founded in 1998 and incorporated in the U.S. It is the successor to IANA (Internet Assigned Numbers Authority), which manages Internet addresses, domain names and the huge number of parameters associated with Internet protocols (port numbers, router protocols, multicast addresses, etc.). ICANN provides a list of accredited registrars in addition to Network Solutions that accept domain registrations. See *how to register a domain name*, *IANA* and *Network Solutions*.

**iCAP**   (1) (Internet Content Adaptation Protocol) A high-level protocol for requesting services from an Internet-based server. iCAP provides a common format for requesting services using standard HTTP messaging. It provides a remote procedure call (RPC) capability, allowing iCAP clients to invoke services on iCAP servers for a variety of services, including ad insertion, virus scanning and foreign language translation. iCAP is expected to provide the interoperability so that value-added services can "plug and play" on the Internet. For more information, visit the iCAP Forum at www.i-cap.org.

(2) (Internet Calendar Access Protocol) An interface for group calendaring and scheduling over the Internet that is expected to be endorsed by the IETF.

**I-CASE**   (Integrated CASE) CASE systems that generate applications code directly from design specifications. Features include support for rapid prototyping, modeling the data and processing and drawing logic diagrams.

**ICCA**   (Independent Computer Consultants Association, St. Louis, MO, www.icca.org) A membership organization of independent consultants in the information technology field. It is devoted to helping members improve their professional services capabilities. Chapters are in major metropolitan areas throughout the U.S.

**IC card**   See *PC card* and *memory card*.

**ICCP**   (Institute for Certification of Computer Professionals, Des Plaines, IL, www.iccp.org). An organization founded in 1973 that offers industry certification and worldwide test centers. The Associate Computer Professional (ACP) exam is open to all, but the Certified Computing Professional (CCP) requires four years of experience, although academic credit may substitute for two.

The CCP combines the former Certified Computer Programmer (CCP), Certified Data Processor (CDP) and Certified Systems Professional (CSP).

**ICC profile**   (International Color Consortium profile) A color management standard for specifying the attributes of imaging devices such as scanners, digital cameras, monitors and printers so that the color of an image remains true from source to destination. A profile can be embedded within the image itself. For more information, visit the International Color Consortium Web site at www.color.org.

**ICE**   (1) (In-Circuit Emulator) A chip used for testing and debugging logic circuits typically in embedded systems. The chip emulates a particular microprocessor and contains breakpoints and other debugging functions. See *ROM emulator*.

(2) (Information and Content Exchange) A data-sharing specification that allows one Web site to obtain data from another Web site. Using meta tags, ICE provides a standard way of defining a company's data. ICE is based on XML and OPS. See *XML*, *OPS* and *meta tag*.

**(3)** (Ice) A Lotus 1-2-3 add-on program from Baler Software Corporation, Rolling Meadows, IL, that adds extensions to Lotus macros. It is used for developing customized macro-driven 1-2-3 programs.

**ICL** (International Computers Ltd., London, U.K. www.icl.com) A leading European computer systems and services organization. ICL was formed in 1968, following a decade of frantic mergers by major British electronics firms, largely in response to increasing U.S. dominance of global IT markets (primarily IBM) and by the lack of funding at home for competitive R&D. The dominant survivor of the 10-year scramble was International Computers and Tabulators (ICT), which later merged with Elliott-Automation, English Electric (EE), Lyons Electronic Office (LEO), and Marconi, to become ICL.

Designs and products inherited from so many different companies gave ICL a strong position in the British computer market. In 1964, ICT introduced its Series 1900 mainframes, which were based on the earlier Ferranti Mark I computer. ICL followed these in the 1970s with its highly successful Series 2900, marking the introduction of the company's flagship VME (Virtual Machine Environment) operating system.

**Early Mainframe**
This was a typical ICL mainframe installation in the mid-1960s. The 1904 mainframe cabinets are on the extreme left.
*(Image courtesy of Chris P. Burton.)*

From 1968 to 1985, however, ICL was plagued by recurring financial crises resulting from a major economic recession in Britain in 1980–1981. Profits declined sharply; the company underwent drastic restructuring; the work force was chopped almost in half, and R&D was greatly reduced.

Following a takeover by STC (Standard Telephones and Cables) in 1984, ICL entered a more prosperous period. A series of joint ventures with Fujitsu enabled the company to update its aging 2900 machines and develop the new Series 39 (introduced in 1985) with state-of-the-art semiconductor technology. Later, Fujitsu acquired more than 90% of the company.

Series 39 introduced the use of optical fiber interconnects and, subsequently, won three UK Queen's Awards for Technological Achievement. In 1997, Series 39 was superseded by the Trimetra systems, using a combination of CMOS and Intel processors to support VME, UnixWare and Windows NT on a single system.

In 1998, the company formed an alliance with Microsoft to develop models for community-based learning, part of the UK National Grid for Learning Project. Under the alliance, ICL is developing and marketing new systems running on Windows NT.

ICL is involved in many systems integration projects, helping organizations develop new generation, customer-centered applications and systems. These include solutions for major retailers in the U.S., where ICL (trading as ICL Retail Systems, Inc.) has a major presence in the retail sector with more than 600,000 point-of-sale machines installed worldwide.

**ICL Retail Systems** (ICL Retail Systems, Inc., Dallas, TX, www.iclretail.com) The retail subsidiary of ICL, which manages the point-of-sale business throughout the world and the ATM machine business within the U.S.

**ICML** (Intenational Conference on Machine Learning) An annual conference devoted to algorithms used in self-learning systems. ICML is held in North America or Europe. See *ECML*.

**ICMP** (Internet Control Message Protocol) A TCP/IP protocol used to send error and control messages. For example, a router uses ICMP to notify the sender that its destination node is not available. A ping utility sends ICMP echo requests to verify the existence of an IP address.

**ICMP storm attack** See *smurf attack*.

**I-commerce** (Internet-commerce) Transacting business over the Internet. See *e-commerce*.

**iCOMP** (Intel COmparative Microprocessor Performance) An index of CPU performance from Intel. iCOMP Version 1.0 tests a mix of 16-bit and 32-bit integer, floating point, graphics and video operations. Versions 2.0 and 3.0 are geared for 32-bit processors, and indexes are not compatible with each other.

**icon**    In a graphical user interface (GUI), a small, pictorial, on-screen representation of an object, such as a document, program, folder or disk drive.

**IconAuthor**    A multimedia development system from Asymetrix Learning Systems, Inc., Bellevue, WA (www.asymetrix.com). It is used to combine database and multimedia elements to form interactive training applications. IconAuthor runs on several platforms including Windows, Mac, OS/2 and various UNIX systems.

**iconic interface**    A user interface that uses icons.

**ICP**    (1) (Internet Cache Protocol) A protocol used by one proxy server to query another for a cached Web page without having to go to the Internet to retrieve it. See *CARP* and *proxy server*.

(2) (Internet Content Provider) An organization that provides news, reference, audio or video content for Web sites.

**IC package**    See *chip package*.

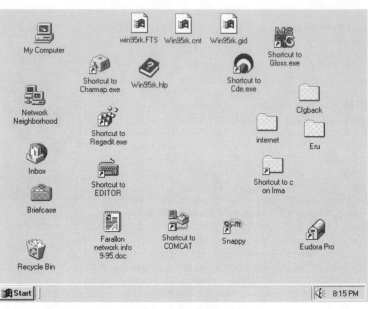

**Icons on the Desktop**
This Windows desktop shows icons of files, folders, programs and other resources. Icons are everywhere these days.

**ICQ**    ("I Seek You") A conferencing program for the Internet from Mirabilis, Tel Aviv, Israel (www.mirabilis.com). It provides interactive chat, e-mail and file transfer and can alert you when someone on your predefined list has also come online. The chat rooms and alerts are managed by the Mirabilis servers. In 1998, Mirabilis and ICQ were acquired by AOL.

**ICR**    (Intelligent Character Recognition or Image Character Recognition) The machine recognition of hand-printed characters, as well as machine printing that is difficult to recognize.

**ICS**    (1) (Internet Connection Sharing) A feature in Windows 98 Second Edition that enables two or more computers to share an Internet connection. See *Windows Second Edition*.

(2) (Internet Chess Server) A server that allows people to play chess over the Internet. Input and output is normally text, but XCIS provides a graphical interface.

**ICSA**    (International Computer Security Association, Carlisle, PA, www.icsa.net) A membership organization founded in 1989 with the purpose of providing education and a clearing house for computer security issues. Formerly NCSA (National Computer Security Association) and renamed ICSA in 1998, it sells all the major books written on the subject. An annual conference is hosted in Washington, DC.

**ICT**    (International Computers and Tabulators) See ICL.

**IDA**    (Intelligent Drive Array) A high-performance hard disk interface from Compaq that controls a disk array via the EISA bus.

**iDAB**    See *DAB*.

**IDAPI**    (Independent Database API) The programming interface to the Borland Database Engine. IDAPI calls are made from dBASE, Paradox and C++ applications to access data in one of the supported databases. See *Borland Database Engine*.

**IDB**    (ITS Data Bus) An interface between devices in an automobile endorsed by the Society of Automotive Engineers (SAE). Designed to fulfill the goal of Intelligent Transportation Systems (ITS), the ITS Data Bus enables engine diagnostic equipment, GPS navigation systems, wireless phones, radios, TVs, games and other mobile devices to interoperate over a standard bus. For example, an IDB-compliant display screen could accept text and/or graphics output from an IDB-compliant navigation system, CD changer, cellphone or video game. For more information, visit www.sae.org and search on "IDB."

**IDC**    (1) (International Data Corporation, Framingham, MA, www.idcresearch.com) A major market research, analysis and consulting firm in the information field. Founded in 1964, it provides annual briefings and in-depth reports on all aspects of the industry.

(2) (Internet Database Connector) A component of Microsoft's Internet Information Server (IIS) Web server that is used to access ODBC-compliant databases. IDC uses two file types. The .IDC file contains the query statement that is sent to the database. The results of the query are placed into an HTML extension file (.HTX file) and returned to the user's browser via IIS. IDC is an ISAPI DLL named HTTPODBC.DLL.

**i.d.Centric**    A family of programs for UNIX and Windows platforms from Firstlogic, Inc., La Crosse, WI (www.idcentric.com) that enhances data quality in existing databases. It includes programs that standardize address conventions and make names and addresses consistent across databases, as well as add demographic information to customer records and other databases. See *Postalsoft*.

**IDE**    (1) (Integrated Development Environment) A set of programs run from a single user interface. For example, programming languages often include a text editor, compiler and debugger, which are all activated and function from a common menu.

(2) (Integrated Drive Electronics) A type of hardware interface widely used to connect hard disks, CD-ROMs and tape drives to a PC. IDE is very popular because it is an economical way to connect peripherals. Starting out with 40MB capacities years ago, 20GB IDE hard disks have become entry level, costing less than half a cent per megabyte. To learn about the other major hardware interface used for disks, see *SCSI*.

With IDE, the controller electronics are built into the drive itself, requiring a simple circuit in the PC for connection. IDE drives were attached to earlier PCs using an IDE host adapter card. Today, two Enhanced IDE (EIDE) sockets are built onto the motherboard, and each socket connects to two devices via a 40-pin ribbon cable.

The IDE interface is officially known as the ATA (AT Attachment) specification. ATAPI (ATA Packet Interface) defines the IDE standard for CD-ROMs and tape drives. ATA-2 (Fast ATA) defined the faster transfer rates used in Enhanced IDE. ATA-3 added interface improvements, including the ability to report potential problems (see *S.M.A.R.T.*). Starting with ATA-4, either the word "Ultra" or the transfer rate was added to the name in various combinations. For example, at 33 Mbytes/sec, terms such as Ultra ATA, Ultra DMA, UDMA, ATA-33, DMA-33, Ultra ATA-33 and Ultra DMA-33 have all been used. Following are the transfer rates for the various ATA modes. See *Cable Select*.

| IDE Drive Type | PIO Mode | Transfer Rate MBytes/sec | DMA Mode | Transfer Rate MBytes/sec |
|---|---|---|---|---|
| ATA | 0 | 3.3 | 0 | 4.2 |
| ATA | 1 | 5.2 | | |
| ATA | 2 | 8.3 | | |
| ATA-2, 3 | 3 | 11.1 | 1 | 13.3 |
| ATA-2, 3 | 4 | 16.6 | 2 | 16.6 |
| ATA-4 (ATA-33) | | | 2 | 33.3 |
| ATA-5 | | | 0 | 16.6 |
| ATA-5 | | | 1 | 25.0 |
| ATA-5 (ATA-33) | | | 2 | 33.3 |
| ATA-5 | | | 3 | 44.4 |
| ATA-5 (ATA-66) | | | 4 | 66.6 |
| ATA-6 (ATA-100) | | | 5 | 100.0 |

**IDEA** (International Data Encryption Algorithm) A secret key cryptography method that uses a 128-bit key. Introduced in 1992, its European patent is held by Ascom-Tech AG, Solothurn, Switzerland. Written by Xuejia Lai and James Massey, it uses the block cipher method that breaks the text into 64-bit blocks before encrypting them.

**IDE controller** (1) The controlling electronics built into an IDE drive.

(2) The adapter on the plug-in card or motherboard that connects to the IDE controller. This is technically the IDE host adapter, but is often called the IDE controller.

**IDE file** A virus identity file used to update the Sophos antivirus program. It is written in Sophos' Virus Description Language (VDL) as ASCII text, which can be e-mailed and faxed. See *Sophos*.

**IDE host adapter** An earlier expansion board that plugs into a PC and contains the connection for up to four IDE hard disks. It generally also provides control for two floppies, two serial, one parallel and one game port. Today, all of this is built into the motherboard. See *IDE*.

**iDEN** (Integrated Digital Enhanced Network) A wireless communications technology from Motorola that provides support for voice, data, short messages (SMS) and dispatch radio (two-way radio) in one phone. Operating in the 800MHz and 1.5GHz bands and based on TDMA, iDEN uses Motorola's VSELP (Vector Sum Excited Linear Predictors) vocoder for voice compression and QAM modulation to deliver 64 Kbps over a 25 kHz channel. Each 25 kHz channel can be divided six times to transmit any mix of voice, data, dispatch or text message. Used by various carriers around the globe, Nextel Communications provides nationwide coverage in the U.S.

**IDE RAID** Using ATA (IDE) drives in a high-performance and/or fault tolerant configuration. See *RAID*.

**IDF** (Intermediate Distribution Frame) A wiring rack located between the MDF (main distribution frame) and the intended end user devices (telephones, routers, PCs, etc.). Cables run from the outside world to the MDF and then to the IDFs. See *MDF* and *wiring rack*.

**IDL** (1) (Interface Definition Language) A language used to describe the interface to a routine or function. For example, objects in the CORBA distributed object environment are defined by an IDL, which describes the services performed by the object and how the data is to be passed to it.

(2) (Interactive Data Language) An interpreted programming language from Research Systems, Inc., Boulder, CO (www.rsinc.com), that runs on Windows, Mac and various UNIX platforms. It is used to write image processing and visualization applications. Some of Research Systems' own software products, such as ENVI and RiverTools, are written in it. Initially created for astronomers by David Stern, founder of the company, IDL provides high-level commands for accessing images, performing data analyses and displaying 3-D objects. IDL includes a complete development environment, and also comes as an ActiveX control so that its routines can be accessed from user interfaces written in other languages, such as Visual Basic.

**idle character** In data communications, a character transmitted to keep the line synchronized when there is no data being sent.

**idle interrupt** An interrupt generated when a device changes from an operational state to an idle state.

**idle time** The duration of time a device is in an idle state, which means that it is operational, but not being used.

**IDMS** See *CA-IDMS* and *IDMSX*.

**IDMS/X** See *IDMSX*.

**IDMSX** (Integrated Data Management System Extended) A database management system (DBMS) from ICL that is widely used on its VME mainframes. It supports journaling, recovery and locking options. A single IDMSX database can contain up to a terabyte of data. See *TPMS*.

**IDSL** See *DSL*.

**IDX**    (IDX Systems Corporation, South Burlington, VT, www.idx.com)  One of the largest health care information systems company in the country. Founded in 1969, it provides a broad range of products for integrated delivery networks, group practices, management service organizations, hospitals and health plans. The company's software automates patient registration, billing, scheduling and data management functions. IDX also sells hardware and provides installation, maintenance, and services.

**IE**    See *Microsoft Internet Explorer* and *information engineering*.

**IEC**    (International Electrotechnical Commission, Geneva, Switzerland, www.iet.ch)  An organization that sets international electrical and electronics standards founded in 1906. It is made up of national committees from over 40 countries.

**IEEE**    (Institute of Electrical and Electronics Engineers, New York, www.ieee.org)  A membership organization that includes engineers, scientists and students in electronics and allied fields. Founded in 1963, it has more than 300,000 members and is involved with setting standards for computers and communications.

The Computer Society of the IEEE is a separate entity that has more than 100,000 members. It holds meetings and technical conferences on computers (visit www.computer.org).

**IEEE 1284**    An IEEE standard for an enhanced parallel port that is compatible with the Centronics port commonly used on PCs. Instead of just data, it can send addresses, allowing individual components in a multifunction device (printer, scanner, fax, etc.) to be addressed independently. IEEE 1284 also defines the required cable type that increases distance to 32 feet.

EPP (Enhanced Parallel Port) mode increases bi-directional transfer from the Centronics 150 Kbytes/sec to between 600 Kbytes/sec and 1.5 Mbytes/sec. Nibble and byte modes provide slower rates. ECP (Enhanced Capabilities Port) mode is designed for printers. It uses DMA channels, which reduces CPU overhead, and also provides a FIFO buffer. The peripheral driver determines which mode to use.

**IEEE 1394**    See *FireWire*.

**IEEE 488**    See *GPIB*.

**IEEE 802**    IEEE standards for local area networks (LANs) and metropolitan area networks (MANs). The IEEE specification for LANs breaks the data link layer into two sublayers: the LLC (Logical Link Control) and MAC (Media Access Control). The LLC provides a common interface to the MAC layers, which specify the access method used.

**IEEE P1394**    See *FireWire*.

**IEF**    (Information Engineering Facility)  A fully integrated set of CASE tools from Sterling Software that runs on PCs and MVS mainframes. It generates COBOL code for PCs, MVS mainframes, VMS, Tandem, AIX, HP-UX and other UNIX platforms. IEF was developed by TI and later renamed Composer. It was acquired by Sterling Software in 1997, which renamed it COOL:Gen. See *COOL*.

**IESG**    See *Internet Engineering Task Force*.

**IETF**    See *Internet Engineering Task Force*.

**I/E time**    See *instruction cycle*.

**IEW**    (Information Engineering Workbench)  CASE software from Sterling Software that runs on DOS PCs and generates COBOL, CICS and IMS code for MVS mainframes. IEW was developed by Knowledgeware, which Sterling acquired in 1984. IEW migrated to ADW for OS/2, which was then renamed Key:Enterprise and later COOL:Enterprise. See *COOL*.

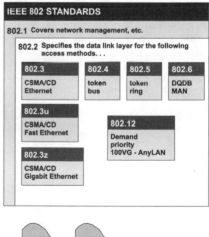

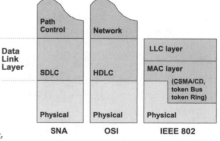

**IFC**   (Internet Foundation Classes) A class library from Netscape that provides an application framework and graphical user interface (GUI) routines for Java programmers. IFC was later made part of the Java Foundation Classes (JFC). See *JFC, AFC* and *AWT*.

**iFCP**   (Internet FCP) A protocol that converts Fibre Channel frames into TCP enabling native Fibre Channel devices to be connected via an IP network. mFCP (Metro FCP) is the metropolitan area network (MAN) counterpart, which uses UDP instead of TCP for high-performance datacenters and metro networks. See *IP storage*.

**IFIP**   (International Federation of Information Processing, Geneva, Switzerland) A multinational affiliation of professional groups concerned with information processing, founded in 1960. There is one voting representative from each country, and the U.S. representative is FOCUS. See *FOCUS*.

**IFMP**   (Ipsilon Flow Management Protocol) The protocol used in Nokia Telecommunication's IP Switch for flow redirection. IFMP is also used in third-party devices, and interoperability is supported by many vendors. See *IP Switch*.

**I-frame**   A keyframe used in MPEG compression. See *MPEG*.

**IFS**   (Installable File System) An OS/2 feature that supports multiple file systems. Different systems can be installed (UNIX, CD-ROM, etc.) just like drivers are installed for new peripherals.

**IFSHLP.SYS**   See *IFSMgr*.

**IFSMgr**   (Installable File System ManaGeR) The driver that provides the 32-bit file system for Windows for Workgroups and Windows 95/98. It also suppotrs IFSHLP.SYS, a "helper" file which, among other things, translates 16-bit to 32-bit calls. See *installable file system*.

**if-then-else**   A high-level programming language statement that compares two or more sets of data and tests the results. If the results are true, the THEN instructions are taken; if not, the ELSE instructions are taken. The following is a BASIC example:

```
10  IF ANSWER = "Y"   THEN PRINT "Yes"
20  ELSE PRINT "No"
```

In certain languages, THEN is implied. All statements between IF and ELSE are carried out if the condition is true. All instructions between ELSE and ENDIF are carried out if not true. The following dBASE example produces the same results as above:

```
IF ANSWER = "Y"
    ? "Yes"
  ELSE
    ? "No"
ENDIF
```

**IGES**   (Initial Graphics Exchange Specification) An ANSI file format that is system independent and also intended for human interpretation. Evolving out of the U.S. Air Force's Integrated Computer Automated Manufacturing (ICAM) program in 1979, IGES was designed as a neutral format for the exchange of CAD models. IGES has been superseded by STEP. See *STEP* and *PDES*.

**IGP**   (Interior Gateway Protocol) A broad category of routing protocols that support a single, confined geographic area such as a local area network (LAN). Contrast with *EGP*. See *routing protocol*.

**iGrafx**   Micrografx's brand name for its graphics software products. Introduced in 1999, iGrafx Designer Suite includes new versions of Micrografx's flagship Designer drawing program and Picture Publisher image editing program. Other iGrafx products include flowcharting, business graphics, network diagramming and other graphics tools. See *Micrografx Designer*.

**IGRP**    (Interior Gateway Routing Protocol) A proprietary routing protocol from Cisco that was developed in 1988 to overcome the shortcomings of RIP. IGRP takes bandwidth, latency, reliability and current traffic load into consideration. It is typically used within an autonomous system, such as an Internet domain. IGRP was superseded by Enhanced IGRP (EIGRP), which provides enhancements such as the ability to detect a loop in the network.

**IHA**    See *Intel Hub Architecture*.

**IHV**    (Independent Hardware Vendor) An organization that makes electronic equipment. It implies a company that specializes in a niche area, such as display adapters or disk controllers, rather than a computer systems manufacturer. Contrast with *ISV*. See *VAR* and *systems integrator*.

**IIA**    **(1)** (Information Industry Association, Washington, DC) In 1999, IIA merged with SPA (Software Publishers Association) to become the Software & Information Industry Association. See *SIIA*.
    **(2)** (Information Interchange Architecture) IBM formats for exchanging documents between different systems.

**IIe**    See *Apple II*.

**IIOP**    (Internet Inter-ORB Protocol) The CORBA message protocol used on a TCP/IP network (Internet, intranet, etc.). CORBA is the industry standard for distributed objects, which allows programs (objects) to be run remotely in a network. IIOP links TCP/IP to CORBA's General Inter-ORB protocol (GIOP), which specifies how CORBA's Object Request Brokers (ORBs) communicate with each other.
    IIOP was built into Netscape's browser starting with Version 4.0. When a user accesses a Web page that uses a CORBA object, a small Java applet is downloaded into Netscape, which invokes the ORB to pass data to the object, execute the object and get the results back. See *CORBA*.

**IIS**    See *Microsoft Internet Information Server*.

**IIXNET**    (Internet-Intranet-EXtraNET) Refers to all uses of Web-based technology.

**IL**    See *intermediate language*.

**ILD**    (Inter Layer Dielectric) The insulation used between layers of aluminum or copper wire that interconnect the transistors in a chip. There are three to four layers in a memory chip and five to seven in a logic chip with hundreds of meters of wiring. Polymer-based dielectrics, which emerged at the start of the twenty-first century, are expected to have a tremendous impact in chip design, as plastic insulating material dramatically reduces the crosstalk associated with glass-based dielectrics. See *SiLK*.

**ILE**    See *RPGLE*.

**ILEC**    (Incumbent Local Exchange Carrier) A traditional local telephone company such as one of the Regional Bell companies (RBOCs). Contrast with *CLEC*. See *ELEC* and *TELRIC*.

**i.Link**    Sony's name for the IEEE 1394 "FireWire" port. See *FireWire*.

**ill-behaved**    See *well-behaved*.

**illegal operation**    An operation that is not authorized or understood. The Windows 95/98 error message that reports an illegal operation means the application crashed. See *abend*.

**illustration program**    Same as *drawing program*.

**Illustrator**    See *Adobe Illustrator*.

**ILS server**   See *ULS server*.

**IM**   See *instant messaging* and *information management*.

**IMA**   (Interactive Multimedia Association, Annapolis, MD, www.ima.org) A trade association founded in 1988 originally as the Interactive Video Industry Association. The IMA provides an open process for adopting existing technologies and is involved in subjects such as networked services, scripting languages, data formats and intellectual property rights.

**iMac**   A Macintosh computer from Apple introduced in 1998. It is a low-priced, self-contained, Internet-ready Mac with a new look aimed at the consumer. In their first incarnation, iMacs came with 32MB RAM, 4GB hard disk, CD-ROM drive and 33.6 Kbps modem. Only the memory could be upgraded. The iMac was also the first personal computer to come without a floppy disk drive. By 2001, 5,000,000 iMacs were shipped. See *iBook*.

**image**   (1) A picture (graphic).
    (2) See *system image*.

**image editing**   Changing or improving graphics images. Using an image editor, images can be interactively modified by an artist using pen, brush, airbrush and other "painting" tools. Or, a filter can be applied to an image that uses an algorithm to automatically alter the appearance without user intervention. See *image editor*, *image filter* and *anti-aliasing*.

**image editing program**   See *image editor*.

**image editor**   Software that allows scanned images to be altered and enhanced. They are designed to read and convert a wide variety of graphics formats and may include a native file format for special features. Image editors include many image filters, but run the gamut from just a few to an abundance of painting tools. They allow images to be scaled and altered in many different ways and may allow plug-ins for infinite expansion.
    If the image editor supports layers, it enables images to be placed into or scanned into different layers as if each were a separate canvas. The bitmap elements can be moved around independently within their layers, and elements can be placed above or below each other temporarily to find the best design. When the final result is obtained, all the layers are "flattened" into one.
    Examples of full-featured image editors are Adobe Photoshop, Picture Publisher and Fractal Design Painter. High-end image editors are sometimes called "photo illustration programs." See *image filter*, *paint program* and *graphics*.

**image enhancement**   See *image editing*.

**image file**   (1) A file that contains graphics data. See *graphics formats*.
    (2) A compressed file that contains all the files required to populate a hard disk with applications and/or operating system. The image file is sent to multiple PCs and decompressed to their original state. See *cloning software*.

**An iMac Displaying an iMac**
iMacs are available in a variety of cabinet colors and designs so users can put a little personality into their computing. The iMacs reflect back to the first Mac, which was all self contained.

**Applying a Filter to an Image**
This Photoshop screen shot shows the lens flare filter being applied to the image on the left. The type of camera lens, amount of brightness and position of the light can be adjusted. *(Screen shot courtesy of Adobe Systems, Inc.)*

**Original**
The original painting was photographed and scanned into the computer. The following images were created in Photoshop by applying a filter to the original. *(From "Moonlit Gladiolas" by Barbara Postel. Image courtesy of Pyramid Studios, www.artistexpo.com)*

**Gaussian Blur Filter**

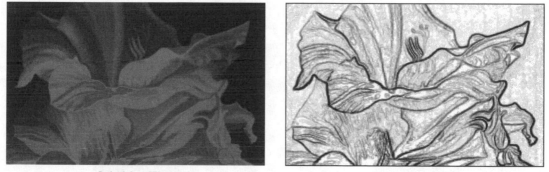

**Solarizing Filter**

**Find Edges Filter**

**image filter**    A routine that changes the appearance of an image or part of an image by altering the shades and colors of the pixels in some manner. Filters are used to increase brightness and contrast, as well as to add a wide variety of textures, tones and special effects to a picture.

**ImageLock**    (ImageLock, Inc., San Francisco, CA, www.imagelock.com) A subscription service that searches for copies of images on the Web. Used by organizations that want to protect their intellectual property, ImageLock routinely sends out a spider to "fingerprint" images (logos, banners, icons, etc.) all over the Web and then matches them to the fingerprints of the subscriber's images.

**imagemap**    A single picture image that is logically separated into areas, each of which is used to select a different option or display a different message when clicked. It is widely used on the Web to provide a navigation bar to link to other topics (pages) on the site. See *navigation bar*.

**image processing**    (1) The analysis of a picture using techniques that can identify shades, colors and relationships that cannot be perceived by the human eye. It is used to solve identification problems, such as in forensic medicine or in creating weather maps from satellite pictures, and deals with images in bitmapped graphics format that have been scanned in or captured with digital cameras.

(2) Any image improvement, such as refining a picture in a paint program that has been scanned or entered from a video source.

(3) Same as *imaging*.

**image protection** Safeguarding copyrighted images in an electronic format, especially the Internet. The Web has made it very easy to save an image that appears on a Web site. All you have to do is right click the image and select Save Picture As or Save Image As and give it a file name. Due to the fact that high-resolution images are not as necessary for screen display as they are for print, most Web images are low resolution and thus provide a form of automatic copy protection for print purposes. Printing a low-res image will not produce a high-quality picture.

However, in order to provide image protection, there has to be cooperation between the browser and the Web server. For example, Alchemedia's Clever Content system lets you download a browser plug-in that will display images from a Clever Content server, but will not let you save them or do a print-screen.

**image scaler** The circuit that translates the image resolution coming from the display adapter (video card) into the maximum resolution of the display screen or flat panel. This is how different resolutions (640×480, 800×600, etc.) fill up the entire width and height of the screen. See *LVDS*.

**imagesetter** A machine that generates output for the printing process, which is either a film-based paper that is photographed or the actual film for making the printing plates. Input comes from the keyboard, or via disk, tape or modem. Earlier machines handled only text and were called "phototypesetters." Most imagesetters today support the PostScript language.

Modern imagesetters use lasers to generate the image directly onto the film. Older machines passed light through a spinning font photomask, then through lenses that created the point size and onto film. Others created images on CRTs and exposed the film.

The typesetter was originally the only machine that could handle multiple fonts and text composition such as kerning. Today, desktop laser printers are used for many typesetting jobs and are quickly advancing in resolution, although the 1,270 and 2,540 dpi resolutions of the imagesetter combined with the high quality of film still provide the finest printing for photographs and halftones. See *CTP*.

**image viewer** See *viewer*.

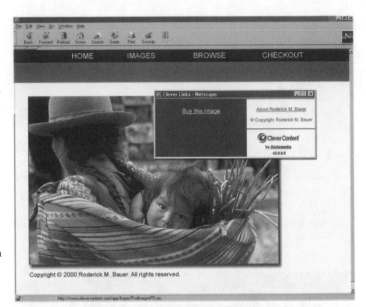

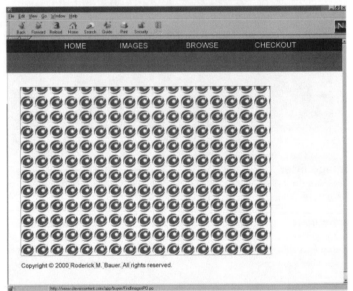

**Clever Content System**
If you try to save the Clever Content picture (top), the blue dialog box appears directing you to another site or to pay for the image. If you try to print the screen, the image will be blanked out (bottom) when you paste it into an image editor. *(Images courtesy of Alchemedia, www.alchemedia.com)*

**imaging**    Creating a film or electronic image of any picture or paper form. It is accomplished by scanning or photographing an object and turning it into a matrix of dots (bitmap), the meaning of which is unknown to the computer, only to the human viewer. Scanned images of text may be encoded into computer data (ASCII or EBCDIC) with page recognition software (OCR). See *micrographics*, *image processing* and *document imaging*.

**imaging model**    A set of rules for representing images.

**imaging system**    See *document imaging*, *image processing* and *image enhancement*.

**IMAP**    (Internet Messaging Access Protocol) A standard mail server expected to be widely used on the Internet. It provides a message store that holds incoming e-mail until users log on and download it. IMAP4 is the latest version.

IMAP is more sophisticated than the Post Office Protocol (POP3) mail server. Messages can be archived in folders, mailboxes can be shared, and a user can access multiple mail servers. There is also better integration with MIME, which is used to attach files. For example, users can read only the headers in the message without having to automatically accept and wait for attached files that they don't want to download.

Both IMAP and POP accept SMTP-formatted messages that have been routed across the Internet. See *POP3*, *SMTP* and *messaging system*.

**IMAP4**    See *IMAP*.

**imbedded system**    See *embedded system*.

**IMCO**    Digispeak for "in my considered opinion."

**IMDB**    See *in-memory database*.

**IMG file**    IMaGe file) A Macintosh file created by Diskmaker that is used to make a sector-by-sector copy of a disk or to turn selected files and folders into a self-contained volume with its own directory. For example, an IMG file can be stored on the desktop and have it function like an additional disk.

**IMG tag**    An HTML tag that defines the location of a graphic image such as a GIF or JPEG file.

**IMHO**    Digispeak for "in my humble opinion." See *IMO*.

**immediate access**    Same as *direct access*.

**immersive visualization**    See *virtual reality* and *CAVE*.

**IMO**    Digispeak for "in my opinion." See *IMHO*.

**i-Mode**    A packet-based information service for mobile phones from NTT DoCoMo (Japan). i-Mode provides Web browsing, e-mail, calendar, chat, games and customized news. It was the first smart phone system for Web browsing and grew very quickly after its introduction in 1999. i-Mode is a proprietary system that uses a subset of HTML, known as cHTML, in contrast to the global WAP standard, which uses a variation of HTML known as WML. The i-Mode transfer rate is 9,600 bps, but is expected to increase to 384 Kbps in 2001, using W-CDMA. See *WAP* and *NTT DoCoMo*.

**IMP**    (Interface Message Processor) The first router used in the ARPAnet. It was a Honeywell 516 minicomputer with special interfaces and software written by BBN.

**impact printer**    A printer that uses a printing mechanism that bangs the character image into the ribbon and onto the paper. See *printer* for examples.

**impedance**    The resistance to the flow of current in a circuit.

**imperative language**    Same as *procedural language*.

**implementation**    The carrying out or physical realization of something. The phrase "there are various implementations of the protocol" means that there are several software products that execute that protocol. A computer system implementation would be the installation of new hardware and system software. An information system implementation would be the installation of new databases and application programs, and the adoption of new manual procedures.

**implode**    To link component pieces to a major assembly. It may also refer to compressing data using a particular technique. Contrast with *explode*.

**import**    To read a file in a format that is not native to the application in use. Mainstream applications typically import (and export) a variety of popular formats. See *import filter*, **Place** and *export*.

**import filter**    The function in a program that reads a non-native file format. In some applications, you have to specify the file type before you can select the file by name. Others let you open the file by name and will use the appropriate import filter automatically. See *import* and *export*.

**imposition**    The printing of pages on a single sheet of paper in a particular order so that they come out in the correct sequence when cut and folded.

**impression**    An advertisement on a Web page. Advertising on the Web is typically sold on a cost per thousand (CPM) basis, and one impression is essentially one banner ad. See *banner ad* and *interstitial ad*.

**Impromptu**    A Windows query and reporting tool from Cognos with support for a large variety of databases. It is capable of generating cross tabs for spreadsheets such as Excel, Lotus for Windows and Quattro Pro for Windows.

**Improv**    A multidimensional Windows spreadsheet from Lotus that allows for easy switching to different views of the data. Data is referenced by name as in a database, rather than the typical spreadsheet row and column coordinates. Improv was originally developed for the NeXt computer.

**IMS**    (Information Management System) An IBM hierarchical DBMS for IBM mainframes running under MVS. It was widely implemented throughout the 1970s and continues to be used. IMS/DB (IMS/DataBase) is the database, which functions in a batch processing environment. IMS/DC (IMS/Data Communications) is the component required when running in an online environment such as CICS. IMS/DC is also used to access DB2 databases.

**IMT-2000**    A framework from the ITU for third-generation (3G) wireless phone standards throughout the world that deliver high-speed multimedia data as well as voice. Formerly known as the Future Public Land Mobile Telecommunications System (FPLMTS), IMT-2000 supports various technologies that increase data rates, such as W-CDMA and cdma2000. Technical specifications for IMT-2000 are developed by 3GPP. See *wireless generations*, *3GPP* and *UMTS*.

**IMTC**    (International Multimedia Teleconferencing Association, San Ramon, CA, www.imtc.org) An international membership organization founded in 1993 as Consortium for Audiographics Teleconferencing Standards (CATS). IMTC contributes to the development of and implements the standards recommendations of the ITU for data and videoconferencing.

**IMUnified**    A coalition of instant messaging companies including Yahoo!, Microsoft, AT&T and Prodigy that was founded in 2000. Its goal is to develop open standards for instant messaging text and buddy lists. See *instant messaging*.

**imux**    See *inverse multiplexor*.

**IN**    (Intelligent Network) The public switched telephone network architecture of the 1990s, which was developed by Bellcore (now Telcordia) and the ITU. It was created to provide a variety of advanced telephony services such as 800 number translation, local number portability (LNP), call forwarding, call screening and wireless integration. While

Bellcore named its version AIN (Advanced Intelligent Network) for use in North America, there are a variety of proprietary versions throughout the world based on the ITU standard.

The IN uses the SS7 signaling protocol in which voice calls (or modem data) travels through circuit-switched voice switches, while control signals travel over an SS7 packet-switched network. See *SS7* and *converged network*.

**inactive window**   A window on screen that is not currently selected. Its title bar is typically grayed out. In Windows, pressing ALT-TAB switches between all active and inactive windows. Contrast with *active window*.

**INAP**   (Intelligent Network Application Part) An IN (Intelligent Network) protocol used in a European SS7 network to query databases for a variety of functions not related to call setup and tear down. INAP uses the ASN.1 standard for defining message content. See *SS7* and *ASN.1*.

**in band**   Inside the primary frequency or system. See *signaling in/out of band*.

**in-betweening**   See *tweening*.

**inboard**   Built in. Inboard devices are built into the main unit. Contrast with *outboard*. See *onboard*.

**inbox**   An area in memory or on the disk that holds received messages that have not been read or processed. Contrast with *outbox*.

**incident light**   In computer graphics, light that strikes an object. The color of the object is based on how the light is absorbed or reflected by the object.

**in-circuit emulator**   See *ICE*.

**Incorrect DOS version**   A DOS error message that means the command you are using belongs to another version of DOS. Somehow an earlier or later version of a command is on your hard disk. Commands from one DOS version often do not work in other versions.

**increment**   To add a number to another number. Incrementing a counter means adding 1 to its current value.

**incremental backup**   See *backup types*.

**incremental spacing**   See *microspacing*.

**incubator**   An organization that fosters the growth of new ideas or companies. An incubator generally acquires small companies and provides them with financing, management expertise, office services and possibly office space. Incubators may adopt a think tank approach and look for synergies between the ideas, products and technologies they are developing in order to grow faster. Many Internet incubators arose in the latter 1990s with the intention of creating more dot-com success stories.

**IND$FILE**   An IBM mainframe program that transfers files between the mainframe and a PC functioning as a 3270 terminal.

**indent**   To align text some number of spaces to the right of the left margin. See *hanging paragraph*.

**Indeo**   A video compression/decompression algorithm from Intel that is used to compress movie files.

**index**   (1) In data management, the most common method for keeping track of data on a disk. Indexes are directory listings maintained by the OS, DBMS or the application.

An index of files contains an entry for each file name and the location of the file. An index of records has an entry for each key field (account no., name, etc.) and the location of the record.

**(2)** In programming, a method for keeping track of data in a table. See *indexed addressing* and *color palette*.

**indexed addressing**   A technique for referencing memory that automatically increments the address with the value stored in an index register. See *subscript*.

**indexed color**   See *color palette*.

**indexed sequential access method**   See *ISAM*.

**index hole**   A small hole punched into a hard sectored floppy disk that serves to mark the start of the sectors on each track.

**INDEX.HTML**   The default name for a home page in a Web server. The page is appropriately named, because the home page is an index to the entire Web site. When you type in a URL such as www.computerglossary.com, it is the same as entering www.computerglossary.com/index.html.

**indexing**   **(1)** Creating indexes based on key data fields or keywords.
**(2)** Creating timing signals based on detecting a mark, slot or hole in a moving medium.

**index map**   See *index* and *color palette*.

**index mark**   A physical hole or notch, or a recorded code or mark, that is used to identify a starting point for each track on a disk.

**index register**   A high-speed circuit used to hold the current, relative position of an item in a table (array). At execution time, its stored value is added to the instructions that reference it.

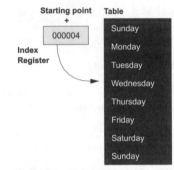

**Disk Index**

| Key | Location |
|-----|----------|
| Smith Corporation | Sector 54 |
| J & D, Inc. | Sector 238 |
| Ames Company | Sector 102 |
| Federated Metals | Sector 755 |
| General Container | Sector 28 |

**Programming Index**

Starting point
+

Index Register    000004

Table
Sunday
Monday
Tuesday
Wednesday
Thursday
Friday
Saturday
Sunday

**Types of Indexes**
An index is a data table that points to some location just like an index in a book. Indexes are widely used to keep track of the physical location of data on the disk, as well as the logical location of data within a database. On the other hand, an index register is a hardware circuit whose content is combined with a value in the program to point to a position in a table.

**Indigo**   An earlier family of desktop graphics computers from SGI. The low end are the Indy machines, which include their own digital video camera. The high end includes a variety of Indigo workstations, with models specialized for graphics functions such as accelerated texture mapping and image procesing. See *SGI*.

**indirect addressing**   An address mode that points to another pointer rather than the actual data. This mode is prohibited in RISC architecture. See *indirection*.

**indirection**   Not direct. Indirection provides a way of accessing instructions, routines and objects when their physical location may constantly be changing. The initial routine points to some place, and, using hardware and/or software, that place points to some other place. There can be multiple levels of indirection. For example, point to A, which points to B, which points to C. See *indirect addressing*.

**inductance**   The magnetic field that is generated when a current is passed through an inductor.

**induction**   The process of generating an electric current in a circuit from the magnetic influence of an adjacent circuit as in a transformer or capacitor.
Electrical induction is also the principle behind read/write heads on magnetic disks. To create (write) the bit, current is sent through a coil that creates a magnetic field, which is discharged at the gap of the head onto the disk surface as it spins by. To read the bit, the magnetic field of the bit "induces" an electrical charge in the head as it passes by the gap.

**inductive device**    A device that acts like a mini surge protector. It uses a core of magnetic material that chokes off any fast frequency shift. The tiny donuts placed on the end of signal cables and the load coils placed into telephone networks are examples.

**inductor**    A coil of wire that generates a magnetic field when current is passed through it. The strength of the magnetic field is measured in henrys. When the current is removed, as the magnetic field disintegrates, it generates a brief current in the opposite direction of the original.

**industrial, scientific and medical band**    See *ISM band*.

**industrial strength**    Refers to software that is designed for high-volume, multiuser operation. It implies that the software is robust and that there are built-in safeguards against system failures. For example, an industrial-strength operating system runs its applications in protected address spaces and does not lock up or stop if one of them crashes. Industrial-strength features in a DBMS are referential integrity and two-phase commit.

The term is used to refer to any solid, sound program that has been thoroughly tested in live user environments for extensive periods, whether system software (OS, DBMS, etc.) or application software (order entry, desktop publishing, etc.). See *bulletproof*.

**industry analyst**    An individual that follows the computer industry and writes about on-going topics and trends. Analysts are made up of individuals in the trade press, as well as in market research organizations such as Dataquest and IDC.

**IndustryPack**    The first popular mezzanine card that was adapted to VMEbus, CompactPCI and PCI cards. IndustryPack (IP) cards are 3.9 x 1.8" and provide a 16-bit data path (double-wide 32-bit cards are specified, but not widely used). IP cards use two 50-pin connectors, one at each end of the card. See *mezzanine card*.

**Industry Standard Architecture**    See *ISA*.

**Indy**    See *Indigo*.

**I-net**    See *Internet*.

**inetd**    (INternET Daemon) A UNIX function that manages many common TCP/IP services. It is activated at startup and waits for various connection requests (FTP, Telnet, etc.) and launches the appropriate server components. See *daemon*.

**inference engine**    The processing program in an expert system. It derives a conclusion from the facts and rules contained in the knowledge base using various artificial intelligence techniques.

**INF file**    (INFormation file) A Windows file that contains installation information. The SETUP.INF file is used to install Windows itself, and other INF files are used for installing other programs and hardware devices.

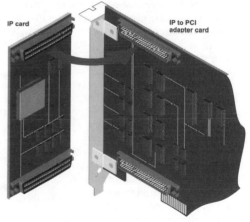

**IP Card and PCI Adapter**
This illustration was drawn from products from Dynamic Engineering. The IP card is a serial I/O card used for data acquisition, and the PCI card is an IP to PCI adapter. The PCI card holds three IP cards, although only one set of sockets is shown. *(Drawn from donated products courtesy of Dynamic Engineering, www.dyneng.com)*

**InfiniBand**    An input/output architecture that is expected to replace the PCI bus in high-end servers. Supporting both copper wire and optical fibers and originally known as "System I/O," InfiniBand is a combination of Intel's NGIO (Next Generation I/O) and Future I/O from IBM, HP and Compaq. Unlike the PCI's bus technology, InfiniBand is a point-to-point switching architecture, providing a data path of from 500 MBps to 6 GBps between each pair of nodes. For more information, visit the InfiniBand Trade Association at www.infinibandta.org. See *NGIO* and *Future I/O*.

**infix notation**    The common way arithmetic operators are used to reference numeric values. For example, **A+B/C** is infix notation. Contrast with *Polish notation* and *reverse Polish notation*.

**infobahn**    (**INFO**rmation **BAHN**) A nickname for the information superhighway. It comes from the German "Autobahn," or automobile superhighway.

**Infobase**    A database created in Folio. See *Folio*.

**infomediary**    (**INFO**rmation inter**MEDIARY**) An information provider that gathers content from several sources and functions as a data aggregator for a target audience.

**infopreneur**    A person who is in business to gather and disseminate electronic information.

**InfoPump**    Software from Trinzic Corporation, Palo Alto, CA, that is used to synchronize data in different types of databases by moving the data and converting it to the destination format. It supports Lotus Notes documents, ASCII files, mainframe file formats and most of the popular databases. A Windows-based client component controls the InfoPump Server. Data movement can be performed on a scheduled or event-driven basis.

**informate**    To dispense information, as coined by Harvard Professor Shoshana Zuboff.

**informatics**    Same as information technology and information systems. The term is more widely used in Europe.

**information**    Information is the summarization of data. Technically, data are raw facts and figures that are processed into information, such as summaries and totals. But since information can also be the raw data for the next job or person, the two terms cannot be precisely defined, and both are used interchangeably.

It may be helpful to view information the way it is structured and used, namely, data, text, spreadsheets, pictures, voice and video. Data are discretely defined fields. Text is a collection of words. Spreadsheets are data in matrix (row and column) form. Pictures are lists of vectors or frames of bits. Voice is a continuous stream of sound waves. Video is a sequence of image frames. See *universal server*.

**Turn your data into information.**

**Information Has "Meaning"**
This excerpt from an R&R Report Writer ad exemplifies the idea that information is more usable for the manager than raw data. *(Image courtesy of Concentric Data Systems, a subsidiary of Wall Data, Inc.)*

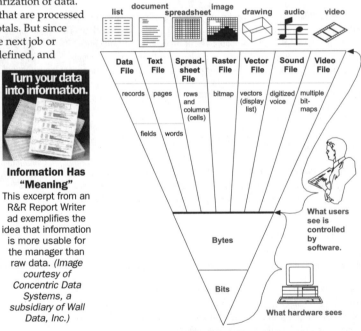

**Information Structures**
When information is stored electronically, it is structured according to the way it is used. Databases support all kinds of information.

**information appliance**
See *Internet appliance*.

**information architect**
See *Web designer* and *systems analyst*.

**information broker**    An individual that searches for information for its client. Information brokers use various resources including the Internet, online services that specialize in databases, public libraries, books and CD-ROMs. They also make plain old-fashioned telephone calls. The word "broker" is a misnomer. "Information retrieval consultant" would be more accurate. Sue Rugge and Alfred Glossbrenner wrote an excellent book on the subject, *The Information Broker's Handbook*, published by McGraw-Hill (ISBN 0-07-057870-2). See *Web search sites* and *online services*.

**Information Builders**    (Information Builders, Inc., New York, www.ibi.com) A software company founded in 1975 by Gerald Cohen that specializes in middleware and reporting software. The company introduced its FOCUS database management system in its first year, which became known for its 4GL reporting capabilities. It was made available on a wide variety of hardware platforms and eventually supported a huge number of database and file types. All this interface experience became a natural for later developing its Enterprise Data Access (EDA) middleware tool, which opened all these databases to a larger variety of client applications than just via FOCUS. EDA has been widely used and became the foundation for WebFOCUS, which, as before, made all this data access available via a Web browser. See *FOCUS*, *EDA* and *WebFOCUS*.

**information center**    A division within the IS department that supports end-user computing. It is responsible for training users in applications and solving related personal computer problems. The term was widely used when personal computers exploded onto the scene in the 1980s. Today, the term may refer to any type of information source, which is precisely what it sounds like.

**information collaboration**    See *data conferencing*.

**information engineering**    An integrated set of methodologies and products used to guide and develop information processing within an organization. It starts with enterprise-wide strategic planning and ends with running applications.

**information hiding**    Keeping details of a routine private. Programmers only know what input is required and what outputs are expected. See *encapsulation* and *abstraction*.

**information highway**    See *information superhighway*.

**information industry**    (1) Organizations that publish information via online services or through distribution by diskette or CD-ROM.

(2) All computer, communications and electronics-related organizations, including hardware, software and services.

**Information Industry Association**    See *IIA*.

**information management**    The discipline that analyzes information as an organizational resource. It covers the definitions, uses, value and distribution of all data and information within an organization whether processed by computer or not. It evaluates the kinds of data/information an organization requires in order to function and progress effectively.

Information is complex because business transactions are complex. It must be analyzed and understood before effective computer solutions can be developed. See *data administration*.

**information overload**    A symptom of the high-tech age, which is too much information for one human being to absorb in an expanding world of people and technology. It comes from all sources, including TV, newspapers, magazines and now the Internet, as well as wanted and unwanted mail, e-mail and faxes. It also includes the excessively intricate and mostly indecipherable manuals that must be read to operate everything from a handheld device to a software application. It boils down to this: the volume of information that crosses our brains in one week at the end of the 20th Century is more than a person received in a lifetime at the beginning of it.

**information processing**    Same as *data processing*.

**information requirements**    The information needed to support a business or other activity. Requirements are typically defined as lists of detailed items, as well as summarized data

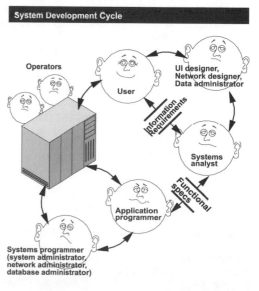

**System Development Cycle**

Operators

User

UI designer,
Network designer,
Data administrator

Information
Requirements

Systems
analyst

Functional
specs

Application
programmer

Systems programmer
(system administrator,
network administrator,
database administrator)

from business transactions, such as orders and purchases, and master records, such as customers and vendors. How frequently this information must be made available is also part of the requirement.

Information requirements (the what and when) are turned into functional specs (the how) of an information system by systems analysts. The information is defined as a collection of data elements that are obtained by running query and report programs against a particular database or group of databases. The data and information that is stored in the databases in the first place is also derived from the information requirements. See *functional specification*.

**information resource management**    See *Information Systems* and *information management*.

**information resources**    (1) The data and information assets of an organization, department or unit. See *data administration*.

(2) Another name for the Information Systems (IS) or Information Technology (IT) department. See *IT*.

**information science**    See *information management*.

**information service**    Any information retrieval, publishing, timesharing or BBS facility. See *online services*.

**Information Services**    See *Information Systems*.

**information sharing**    See *data conferencing*.

**information superhighway**    A proposed high-speed communications system that was touted by the Clinton/Gore administration to enhance education in America in the 21st Century. Its purpose was to help all citizens regardless of their income level. The Internet was originally cited as a model for this superhighway; however, with the explosion of the World Wide Web, the Internet became the information superhighway whether it was ready for it or not.

**information system**    A business application of the computer. It is made up of the database, application programs, manual and machine procedures, and encompasses the computer systems that do the processing.

The database stores the subjects of the business (master files) and its activities (transaction files). The application programs provide the data entry, updating and query and report processing. The manual procedures document how data is obtained for input and how the system's output is distributed. Machine procedures instruct the computer how to perform the batch processing activities, in which the output of one program is automatically fed into another program.

The daily processing is the interactive, realtime processing of the transactions. At the end of the day or other period, the batch processing programs update the master files that have not been updated since the last cycle. Reports are printed for the cycle's activities.

The periodic processing of an information system is the updating of the master files, which adds, deletes and changes the information about customers, employees, vendors and products.

| RELATIONSHIP BETWEEN SYSTEMS | |
|---|---|
| **structure (is)** | **function (does)** |
| **Management System** | |
| 1. People<br>2. Machines | Sets organization's goals and objectives, strategies and tactics, plans, schedule and controls. |
| **Information System** | |
| 1. Database<br>2. Application programs<br>3. Procedures | Defines data structures<br>Data entry, updating, queries and reporting.<br>Defines data flow |
| **Computer System** | |
| 1. CPU<br>2. Peripherals<br>3. Operating system | Processes (the 3 C's)<br>Store and retrieve<br>Manages computer system |

**Information Systems**    The formal title for a data processing, MIS, or IS department. Other titles are Data Processing, Information Processing, Information Services, Management Information Systems, Management Information Services and Information Technology.

**information technology**    Processing information by computer.

**Information Technology Association of America**    See *ITAA*.

**information theory**    The study of encoding and transmitting information. From Claude Shannon's 1938 paper, "A Mathematical Theory of Communication," which proposed the use of binary digits for coding information.

**information utility**    (1) A service bureau that maintains up-to-date databases for public access. (2) A central source of information for an organization or group.

**information visualization**    Representing data in 3-D images in order to navigate through it more quickly and access it in a more natural manner. Although the term was coined at Xerox's Palo Alto Research Center, which has developed very advanced techniques, multidimensional cubes, or pivot tables, are a simpler form of information visualization that is widely used today. See *OLAP* and *slice and dice*.

**information warehouse**    The collection of all databases in an enterprise across all platforms and departments.

**information warfare**    (www.infowar.com) Creating havoc by disrupting the computers that manage stock exchanges, power grids, air traffic control and telecommunications. While the term often refers to warring nations, it also refers to the disruption of individual organizations. Devastating viruses such as the Worm.Explore.Zip virus unleashed in the summer of 1999 can also be considered information warfare. Since the virus deleted Microsoft-only files, it was war against Microsoft in the mind of its creator, even though everybody else suffered. See *Worm.ExploreZip virus*.

**A 3-D Cone Tree**
Data represented in this form provides faster navigation and allows more information to be seen at one time. The Cone Tree shows the structure of an entire hierarchy all at once, and the cones spin around to retrieve occluded data. *(Image courtesy of Xerox Palo Alto Research Center; Brian Tramontana, photographer.)*

**INFORMIX**    A relational database management system (DBMS) from Informix Software, Inc., Menlo Park, CA (www.informix.com), that runs on most UNIX platforms, including SCO UNIX for x86 machines and NetWare. Development tools from Informix include INFORMIX-4GL, a fourth-generation language, and INFORMIX-New Era, a client/server development system for Windows clients that supports INFORMIX and non-INFORMIX databases.

**InfoSeek**    One of the first major search sites on the Web. In 1999, it became Go.com (www.go.com). See *Web search sites*.

**infowar**    See *information warfare*.

**infoware**    Information sold electronically, such as the electronic versions of this database.

**InfoWindow**    The trade name for IBM display screens.

**infrared**    An invisible band of radiation at the lower end of the electromagnetic spectrum. It starts at the middle of the microwave spectrum and goes up to the beginning of visible light. Infrared transmission requires an unobstructed line of sight between transmitter and receiver. It is used for wireless transmission between computer devices, as well as almost all handheld remotes for TVs, video and stereo equipment. Contrast with *ultraviolet*. See *IrDA*.

**Infrared Data Association**    See *IrDA*.

**infrared port**    A transmitter/receiver for infrared signals. See *IrDA*.

**infrastructure**    The fundamental structure of a system or organization. The basic, fundamental architecture of any system (electronic, mechanical, social, political, etc.) determines how it functions and how flexible it is to meet future requirements.

**Ingres**    See *Ingres II*.

**Ingres II**    A relational database management system (DBMS) from Computer Associates that runs on Windows NT, OpenVMS and most UNIX platforms, including Linux. Ingress is an industrial-strength DBMS that is ODBC compliant and e-commerce enabled, and uses the OpenROAD application development environment. Ingress II is an enhanced version of CA-Ingres and CA-OpenIngres.

Years ago, Ingres was one of the first heavyweight DBMSs noted for its advanced features such as triggers and stored procedures. It was originally developed by Relational Technology, which was founded in 1980 to market a commercial version of "INteractive Graphics and REtrieval System," developed at the University of California at Berkeley in the early 1970s. The company was renamed Ingres Corporation, and then later acquired by the Ask Group, and eventually Computer Associates.

**in hardware**   Refers to logic that has been placed into the electronic circuits of the computer.

**inheritance**   In object technology, the ability of one class of objects to inherit properties from a higher class.

**in-house**   An operation that takes place on the user's premises.

**INI file**   (INItialization file) A file that contains startup information required to launch a program or operating system. Same as *CFG file*. See *WIN.INI* and *SYSTEM.INI*.

**IN-IP convergence**   See *converged network*.

**INIT**   (INITiate) A Macintosh routine that is run when the computer is started or restarted. It is used to load and activate drivers and system routines. Many INITs are memory resident and may conflict with each other like TSRs in the PC environment.

**initialization string**   Same as *setup string*.

**initialize**   To start anew, which typically involves clearing all or some part of memory or disk.

**initial program load**   See *IPL*.

**injection loss**   The attenuation of signal strength that occurs right at the point the laser or LED connects to the fiber. Also called "insertion loss." See *fiber optics glossary*.

**ink jet cartridge**   A replaceable unit that holds ink and the print nozzles for ink jet printers. A separate cartridge for each of the four CMYK colors is the most efficient. Low-cost printers include cyan, magenta and yellow inks in one cartridge, requiring the entire unit be replaced when one color is empty. The least efficient is a single cartridge that contains all four colors. See *ink coverage*.

**ink jet printer**   A printer that propels droplets of ink directly onto paper. Today, almost all ink jet printers produce color, or at least have a color option. Low-end ink jets use three ink colors (cyan, magenta and yellow), but produce a composite black that is often muddy. Four-color ink jets (CMYK) use black ink for pure black printing.

Ink jet printers are affordable, quiet and popular, but they do not provide the color quality or text resolution of color laser printers. Notable exceptions are high-end ink jets, such as Tektronix's laser-class solid ink printer and the IRIS printers, which produce extraordinary color quality. Most printers are ink jet; and according to Dataquest, in 1999, more than 50 million ink jets were shipped out of 71 million total worldwide printer sales.

The cost for ink cartridges in some low-priced ink jets can make the less-expensive model more costly in the long run. For example, if the black ink does not come in a separate cartridge, you have to replace the entire four-color unit when you run out of black. Also, for resolution quality, look at text, not graphics. For color quality, be sure that samples from different models are printed on the same kind of paper. Clay-coated and other specialty papers greatly improve the

**Eight Ink Jet Cartridges**
ColorSpan's Giclee PrintMakerFA printer uses standard cartridges that are tethered to larger reservoirs via the tubes that are visible in this picture. The four additional cartridges (light and medium cyan and magenta), combined with ColorSpan's software, produce 1,200 dpi images with very subtle gradations. *(Image courtesy of ColorSpan Corporation.)*

printed results, because they do not absorb the ink like regular copy paper, but they cost more. Ink and paper costs are on-going expenses, which must be taken into consideration.

Large-format ink jet printers are used to produce final output for commercial posters and banners. Using special coated paper, their output is quite extraordinary. Such devices have almost entirely replaced the older pen plotters used to "draw" engineering and architectural renderings.

Continuous Ink vs. Drop on Demand    The first ink jet mechanism that was developed sprays a continuous stream of droplets that are aimed onto the paper. Although still used, most ink jets use the drop on demand method, which forces a drop of ink out of a chamber by heat or electricity. The thermal method used by HP, Canon and others heats a resistor that forces a droplet of ink out of the nozzle by creating an air bubble in the ink chamber. Epson and others use a piezoelectric technique that charges crystals that expand and "jet" the ink. See *solid ink printer*, *IRIS printer*, *printer* and *ink coverage*.

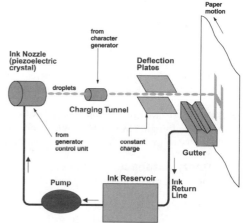

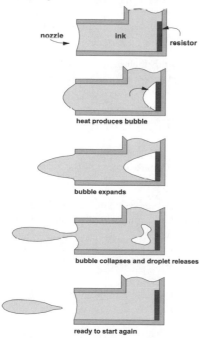

### Continuous Ink Jet Technology
This method sprays continuous droplets of ink that either reach the paper or wind up in the return gutter. The nozzle uses a piezoelectric crystal to synchronize the chaotic droplets that arrive from the pump. The charging tunnel selectively charges the drops that are deflected into the gutter. The uncharged droplets make it to the paper. The diagram depicts a single nozzle.

### Thermal Drop on Demand Method
The thermal drop on demand ink jet technology is very popular. Used by HP, Canon and others, droplets of ink are forced out of the nozzle by heating a resistor, which causes an air bubble to expand. When the bubble collapses, the droplet breaks off and the system returns to its original state.

**Inktomi**    (Inktomi Corporation, Foster City, CA, www.inktomi.com) A company that specializes in high-performance software for Internet service providers (ISPs), carriers and large Web sites. Founded in 1996, its family of products are used for caching Web pages and cataloging and searching the Web, as well as providing comparison shopping.

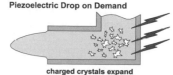

### Drop on Demand Printheads
There are two ways to "jet" the ink in drop on demand systems. The thermal method heats a resistor and expands an air bubble. The piezoelectric method charges crystals that expand.

**inline cache**　A memory cache that resides next to the CPU, but shares the same system bus as other subsystems in the computer. It is faster than lookaside cache, but slower than a backside cache. See *backside cache* and *lookaside cache*.

**inline code**　Source code of a different type that is written into the body of a program. For example, assembly language instructions can be embedded within a C program.

**inline graphics**　Graphics images that are embedded within a text document. Inline graphics on the Web are actually HTML pages with links to graphics files stored on the Web server. The browser displays the text and images as if they were physically on the same page.

**inline routine**　A routine that is written into the program rather than being called externally as a separate subroutine or program module. Inline routines run faster, but add more size to the executable file.

**Inmarsat**　(Inmarsat, London, U.K., www.inmarsat.org) Formerly International Maritime Satellite, it is an international organization founded in 1979 to provide global satellite communications to the maritime industry. Today, it provides satellite service to ships, planes, trains, offshore rigs and mobile phones. COMSAT is the U.S. signatory to Inmarsat.

**in-memory database**　A database that keeps all active records in main memory rather than on disk. Accessing in-memory records is considerably faster than retrieving them from the disk.

**INN**　(InterNet News) A complete Usenet system written by Rich Salz that includes an NNTP server and components for newsreading. INN is available from the Internet Software Consortium (www.isc.org). See *Usenet* and *ISC*.

**inner join**　See *join*.

**innoculate**　To store characteristics of an executable program in order to detect a possible unknown virus if the file is changed.

**i-node**　(Identification **NODE**) An individual entry in a directory system that contains the name of and pointer to a file or other object.

**inorganic semiconductor**　A semiconductor made from a non-carbon–based material such as silicon, gallium or arsenide. Inorganic semiconductors are used in all logic and memory chips. Contrast with *organic semiconductor*.

**Inprise**　See *Borland*.

**Inprise Application Server**　See *Borland AppServer*.

**in-process server**　An executable program that runs as a service to another program rather than stand alone. COM objects and DLLs are examples. Contrast with *out-of-process server*.

**input**　(1) Data that is ready for entry into the computer.
　(2) To enter data into the computer.

**input area**　A reserved segment of memory that is used to accept data from a peripheral device. Same as *buffer*.

**input device**　A peripheral device that generates input for the computer, such as a keyboard, scanner, mouse or digitizer tablet.

**input/output**　See *I/O*.

**input program**　Same as *data entry program*.

**input queue**　A reserved segment of disk or memory that holds messages that have been received or job control statements describing work to be done.

**input stream**    A collection of job control statements entered in the computer that describe the work to be done.

**inquiry program**    Same as *query program*.

**insertion loss**    The amount of loss attributed to a particular device being used in (inserted into) the system. For example, a circuit added to filter out unwanted frequencies may reduce the output current by some amount.

**insert mode**    A data entry mode that causes new data typed on the keyboard to be inserted at the current cursor location on screen. Contrast with *overwrite*.

**inside plant**    The facilities within a telephone company's central office (CO). It includes the main distribution frames (MDFs), switches, digital cross-connects, add/drop multiplexers and other networking equipment. Contrast with *outside plant*. See *central office*.

**Insight**    See *CA-Insight* and *Lawson Insight*.

**in situ**    In place. When something is "in situ," it is in its original location.

**INS key**    (INSert key) A keyboard key that is used to switch between insert and overwrite mode or to insert an object at the current cursor location.

**in software**    Refers to logic in a program. For example, "that routine is done in software."

**insomnia**    The inability to sleep. If you suffer from it, the solution is to look up all the entries under "standards" in this database. Dozing should occur shortly. If it doesn't work, well, at least you'll become a computer guru!

**installable file system**    A file system that can be added to an operating system that is designed to handle multiple file systems. Multiple file systems allow different types of file structures to be accessed. See *IFSMgr*.

**installation spec**    Documentation from an equipment manufacturer that describes how a product should be properly installed within a physical environment.

**installed base**    The number of people using a software package or hardware device.

**install program**    Also called a "setup program," it is a program that prepares an application (software package) to run in the computer. It creates a folder with a default name on the hard disk and copies the files from the distribution CD-ROM or diskettes to that folder. Files are typically compressed on the distribution medium, and the install program decompresses them into their original format.

   With Windows applications, the install program often adds or updates extensions to Windows that reside in the Windows folder (see *DLL hell*). It is also customary for the install program to deposit an uninstall option so the application can be easily removed later on.

   Install programs are also widely used to attach a new peripheral device to the computer. The install program may add the device's driver to the operating system, or it may be used to set or reset parameters in an updatable memory (flash memory, EEPROM, etc.) on the expansion board that was just plugged in. See *how to install a program* and *BIOS setup*.

**InstallShield**    A popular install program from InstallShield Software Corporation, Schaumburg, IL, (www.installshield.com). Versions are available for the Windows, Alpha and Java platforms, as well as for Internet distribution.

**instance**    (1) A single copy of a running program. Multiple instances of a program mean that the program has been loaded into memory several times.

   (2) In object technology, a member of a class; for example, "Lassie" is an instance of the class "dog." When an instance is created, the initial values of its instance variables are assigned.

**instance variable**    In object-oriented programming, a variable used by an instance of a class. It holds data for a particular object. Contrast with *class variable*. See *class*.

**instantiate**    In object technology, to create an object of a specific class. See *instance*.

**instant messaging**    A computer conference using the keyboard (a keyboard chat) over the Internet between two or more people. Instant messaging is not a dial-up system like the telephone; it requires that both parties be online at the same time. You have to put the names of people you want to instant message with in a list, and when any of those individuals log on, you are "instantly" notified so that you can begin an interactive chat session. AOL's Instant Messenger (AIM), Microsoft Network Messenger Service (MSNMS), ICQ and Yahoo! Messenger are the major instant messaging services.

In the business world, instant messaging is often used to avoid telephone tag, or to find out if a person is available to take a phone call. Many instant messaging sessions wind up as traditional telephone calls. However, instant messaging is expected to be the catalyst for IP-based phone calls initiated directly from the computer to provide a seamless move from typing to talking. See *IMUnified* and *Jabber*.

**instant messenger**    The software that provides instant messaging services. See *instant messaging* and *AIM*.

**instant print**    The ability to use the computer as a typewriter. Each keystroke is transferred to the printer.

**instant replay**    See *PVR*.

**Institute for Certification**    See *ICCP*.

**instruction**    (1) A statement in a programming language.
(2) A machine instruction.

**instruction cycle**    The time in which a single instruction is fetched from memory, decoded and executed. The first half of the cycle transfers the instruction from memory to the instruction register and decodes it. The second half executes the instruction.

**instruction mix**    The blend of instruction types in a program. It often refers to writing generalized benchmarks, which requires that the amount of I/O versus processing versus math instructions, etc., reflects the type of application the benchmark is written for.

**instruction register**    A high-speed circuit that holds an instruction for decoding and execution.

**instruction repertoire**    Same as *instruction set*.

**instruction set**    The repertoire of machine language instructions that a computer can follow (from a handful to several hundred). It is a major architectural component and is either built into the CPU or into microcode. Instructions are generally from one to four bytes long.

**instruction time**    The time in which an instruction is fetched from memory and stored in the instruction register. It is the first half of the instruction cycle.

**insulator**    A material that does not conduct electricity. Contrast with *conductor*.

**int**    A programming statement that specifies an interrupt or that declares an integer variable. See *interrupt* and *integer*.

**int 13**    A DOS interrupt used to activate disk functions, such as seek, read, write and format.

**int 14**    A DOS interrupt used to activate functions on the serial port (COM1, COM2, etc.). See *NASI*.

**int 21**     A multipurpose DOS interrupt used for various functions including reading the keyboard and writing to the console and printer. It was also used to read and write disks using the earlier File Control Block (FCB) method.

**integer**     A whole number. In programming, sending the number 123.898 to an integer function would return 123. See *integer arithmetic*.

**integer arithmetic**     Arithmetic without fractions. A computer performing integer arithmetic ignores any fractions that are derived. For example, 8 divided by 3 would yield the whole number 2. See *integer*.

**Integer BASIC**     Apple's version of BASIC for the Apple II that handles only fixed point numbers (non-floating point). Because of its speed, many games are written in it.

**integrated**     A collection of distinct elements or components that have been built into one unit.

**integrated CASE**     See *I-CASE*.

**integrated circuit**     The formal name for the chip. In 1958, TI inventor Jack Kilby demonstrated the first electronic circuit in which more than one transistor was fabricated on a single piece of semiconductor material. It was about half the size of a paper clip.

**integrated injection logic**     A type of bipolar transistor design known for its fast switching speeds.

**integrated network**     A network that supports both data and voice and/or different networking protocols. See *converged network* and *new public network*.

**The First Integrated Circuit**
Only 7/16" wide and containing two transistors, this unassuming integrated circuit was nevertheless the first. It was mounted on a bar of germanium and was demonstrated by TI on September 12, 1958. *(Image courtesy of Texas Instruments, Inc.)*

**integrated optics**     Combining electrical and optical components on the same semiconductor substrate as a chip. In a fiber-optic communications system, numerous devices, including lasers, photodetectors, beam splitters, isolators, filters, prisms, modulators and switches, fall into this category. See *electro-optic*.

**integrated software package**     Software that combines several applications in one program, typically database management, word processing, spreadsheet, business graphics and communications. Such programs (Microsoft Works, AppleWorks, etc.) provide a common user interface for their applications, plus the ability to cut and paste data from one to the other.

   User interfaces, such as found on the Macintosh and Windows, provide this capability with all applications written for their environments.

**integration broker**     See *integration server*.

**integration server**     Software that enables one application to communicate with another on an on-going basis. The foundation of an integration server is a message transport system such as MQSeries. Higher layers of the services an integration server provides are routing and reformatting of the data. Also known as a "message broker." See *message broker*, *messaging middleware*, *application integration* and *application adapter*.

**integrator**     (1) In electronics, a device that combines an input with a variable, such as time, and provides an analog output; for example, a watt-hour meter.
   (2) See *systems integrator*.

**integrity**     See *data integrity*.

**Intel**   (Intel Corporation, Santa Clara, CA, www.intel.com)  The predominant manufacturer of the CPU chips for the PC world. It was founded in 1968 by Robert Noyce, Gordon Moore and Andy Grove in Mountain View, CA. A year later it introduced its first product, a 64-bit bipolar static RAM chip. By 1971, its very successful memory chips began to obsolete magnetic core storage.

In that same year, Intel developed the microprocessor. In response to a calculator chip order from Japanese manufacturer Busicom, Intel engineer Marcian E. "Ted" Hoff decided it would make more sense to design a general-purpose machine. The resulting 4004 chip was the world's first microprocessor.

Although known for its x86 family of chips, over the years, Intel has developed a wide variety of chips and board-level products, including the MULTIBUS bus used in industrial applications. Intel started with 12 people and its first year revenues were less than $3,000. In 1996, it had 49,000 employees with revenues of more than $21 billion. See *future Intel chips*.

**Intel Founders**
The founders of Intel posing with a rubylith of the 8080 CPU in 1978. From left to right: Andy Grove, Robert Noyce and Gordon Moore. *(Image courtesy of Intel Corporation.)*

**Intel chips**   See *x86* and *future Intel chips*.

**Intel chipsets**   A set of chips that provides the interfaces between all of the PC's subsystems. It provides the buses and electronics to allow the CPU, memory and input/output devices to interact. Most Intel chipsets, which are contained on two to four chips, also include built-in EIDE support. In the past, Intel used the name "Triton" for its chipsets. It also used the name PCIset for PCI-based chipsets.

Intel used 420 designations for its 486 chipsets (420EX, 420TX and 420ZX). Following is a brief summary of Pentium chipsets.

## Pentium Chipsets

**430LX**   Mercury - First Pentium chipset (1993) for 60 and 66MHz models. Supports PCI and FPM memory.

**430NX**   Neptune - Supports 90 and 100MHz Pentiums.

**430FX,**   (formerly Triton) -  Supports EDO RAM, Plug and Play.

**430MX**   Version of 430FX designed for portable computers.

**430TX**   Desktop and mobile use. First mobile chipset to support Concurrent PCI. Supports USB, DPMA, Ultra DMA, SMBus.

**430HX**   (formerly Triton II) - Geared for business market. Supports EDO RAM, Concurrent PCI, BGA packaging.

**430VX**   (formerly Triton VX) - Geared for home market. Supports USB, SDRAM, Concurrent PCI.

**440FX**   Optimized for Pentium Pro and Pentium II. Supports USB, EDO RAM, ECC memory, dual processors, Concurrent PCI.

**440LX**   Optimized for Pentium II. Supports LS-120, 33MHz Ultra DMA, AGP, USB, SDRAM, ECC RAM, PC 97 power management, Concurrent PCI.

**440LXR**   Low-end version of 440LX.

**440BX**   Optimized for Pentium II. Supports 100MHz bus, FireWire, ACPI, Concurrent PCI.

**440GX**   For midrange workstations. Supports two CPUs, 2GB SDRAM, dual AGP.

**450GX, 450KX**   Optimized for Pentium Pro. Supports  FPM memory only. KX supports dual processors, 1GB RAM. GX supports quad processors, 8GB RAM.

**450NX**    For high-end workstations and servers. Supports four CPUs, 2MB L2 cache, Intelligent I/O, 8GB EDO memory, two 32-bit or one 64-bit PCI.

**460GX**    For high-end workstations and servers. Supports four CPUs, Slot M and 4xAGP.

**810**    For value PCs. Includes integrated 3-D graphics (AGP) with video out and hardware motion compensation for MPEG-2 software playback. Supports 100MHz system bus and 2 USB ports. Employs Intel Accelerated Hub with 266 MBps between memory and peripherals (2xPCI).

**810e**    Based on 440BX chipset intended for mainstream PCs. Same as 810, but supports 133MHz system bus and ATA-66.

**820**    For high-end desktops and workstations. Provides 2-way multiprocessing (SMP), ATA-66, 4xAGP, and a 133MHz system bus, and was the first to support RDRAM memory. Introduced hub architecture that uses a memory controller hub chip (MCH) for AGP and RDRAM, which is connected to an I/O controller hub chip (ICH) at 266 MB/sec for PCI, sound, hard disk and USB.

**815, 815e**    Uses hub architecture like the 820, but supports PC100 and PC133 SDRAM. Also provides dual ATA-100 control and integrated Ethernet. Second generation of I/O controller hub (ICH2).

**840**    Similar to 820, but adds support for 64-bit PCI and dual RDRAM channels. A prefetch cache increases performance.

**850**    Advanced 800 series chipset designed for Pentium 4. Supports second generation I/O controller hub (ICH2), 4 port USB, 6-channel AC97 sound, dual ATA-100, integrated Ethernet and CNR slot.

**Intel future chips**    See *future Intel chips*.

**Intel Hub Architecture**    A chipset architecture from Intel starting with the 820. It uses a memory controller hub (MCH) chip and an I/O controller hub (ICH) chip that are connected via a 266 MB/sec bus. The memory controller supports the AGP and memory, while the I/O controller provides connectivity for PCI, USB, sound, hard disk and LAN. See *Intel chipsets*.

**Intellect**    A natural language query program for IBM mainframes developed by Artificial Intelligence Corporation, which was later acquired by Trinzic Corporation.

**intellectual property**    See *IP*.

**intelligence**    Processing capability. Every computer is intelligent, which is more than can be said for all humans!

**intelligent agent**    See *agent*.

**intelligent cable**    Same as *smart cable*.

**intelligent controller**    A peripheral control unit that uses a built-in microprocessor for controlling its operation.

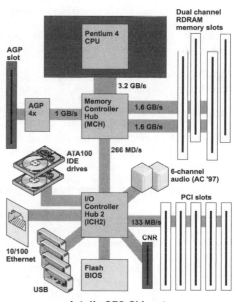

**Intel's 850 Chipset**
Intel introduced its hub architecture starting with the 820 chipset, which divides control between a memory controller chip (MCH) and an I/O controller chip (ICH).

**intelligent database**   A database that contains knowledge about the content of its data. A set of validation criteria are stored with each field of data, such as the minimum and maximum values that can be entered or a list of all possible entries. See *DBMS*.

**intelligent form**   A data entry application that provides help screens and low levels of AI in aiding the user to enter the correct data.

**intelligent hub**   A central connecting device in a network that performs a variety of processing functions such as network management, bridging, routing and switching. Contrast with *passive hub* and *active hub*. See *hub*.

**Intelligent Messaging**   A messaging system from Banyan Systems, Inc., Westboro, MA (www.banyan.com), that runs on NetWare and VINES servers and incorporates Banyan's popular Streettalk directory service. It includes a basic mail program, which can be upgraded to Banyan's more advanced BeyondMail system.

**intelligent modem**   A modem that responds to commands and can accept new instructions during online transmission. It was originally developed by Hayes.

**intelligent network**   A network that is not passive. It contains built-in diagnostics, management, fault tolerance and other capabilities that keep it running smoothly. See *IN*.

**intelligent paper**   Same as *intelligent form*.

**intelligent terminal**   A terminal with built-in processing capability, but no local disk or tape storage. It may use a general-purpose CPU or may have specialized circuitry as part of a distributed intelligence system. Contrast with *dumb terminal*.

**Intelligent Transportation System**   See *ITS* and *IDB*.

**IntelliMirror**   A feature of Windows 2000 (NT 5.0) that stores fundamental configuration data about a user's machine on the server, including a copy of the user's desktop. It allows a crashed PC to be more easily restored, and also enables mobile users to access their applications from a different client machine.

**IntelliMouse**   Microsoft's brand name for its scroll mouse, which popularized the concept. The moving wheel in the center of the mouse scrolls the content of the current window. See *scroll mouse*.

**IntelliSense**   Features in Microsoft applications that help the user by making decisions automatically. By analyzing activity patterns, the software can derive the next step without the user having to explicitly state it. Automatic typo correction and suggesting shortcuts also fall under the IntelliSense umbrella.

**Intel motherboard**   A motherboard manufactured by Intel. Not only does Intel make the CPU chips, it makes motherboards and other printed circuit boards, as well as complete systems that have been sold under third-party logos.

**INTELSAT**   (INTELSAT, Washington, DC, www.intelsat.int)   An international cooperative of more than 135 member nations. It is the world's largest supplier of commercial satellite services with more than 20 satellites in orbit. It was created in 1964, with 11 countries participating. COMSAT is the U.S. signatory of INTELSAT. By mid 2001, INTELSAT is expected to become a private company.

**Intentia**   (Intentia International AB, Schaumburg, IL, www.intentia.com)   Founded in Sweden in 1984, Intentia is an international software company that produces a complete, integrated enterprise management system for the management and control of business operations in manufacturing and distribution industries. As the third largest enterprise management supplier in Europe, and one of the eight largest in the world, Intentia's main product, Movex, links software expertise and industry knowledge into solutions for business processes.

**inter**   To cross over boundaries; for example, internetwork means from one network to another. Contrast with *intra*.

**interactive**    Back-and-forth dialogue between the user and a computer.

**interactive cable TV**    See *interactive TV*.

**interactive fiction**    An adventure game that has been created or modified for the computer. It has multiple story lines, environments and endings, all of which are determined by choices the player makes at various times.

**interactive session**    Back-and-forth dialogue between user and computer. Contrast with *batch session*.

**interactive TV**    Two-way communications between the TV viewer and service providers. Although various experiments have taken place throughout the 1980s, interactive TV has yet to take off. The closest thing to it on a widescale basis is pay TV, which dedicates an entire channel to the same movie so that the viewer can begin to watch it with reasonably short notice.

Internet TV, which began in 1996 with WebTV, is a latest attempt at interaction between the home user and the provider. With the Internet's momentum and the vast amounts of information and interaction available on it, Internet TV may succeed where interactive TV did not. Stay tuned! See *Internet TV* and *digital convergence*.

**Interactive UNIX**    A UNIX-based operating system from SunSoft that runs on x86 machines. It has been widely used to connect character-based terminals or process control devices, such as bar code readers in a supermarket, to a central computer.

**interactive video**    The use of CD-ROM and videodisc controlled by computer for an interactive education or entertainment program. See *CD-ROM* and *videodisc*.

**InterBase**    A relational DBMS from InterBase Software Corporation (a subidiary of Borland), Scotts Valley, CA (www.interbase.com), that runs on UNIX workstations and VAXes. Designed to handle online complex processing (OLCP), InterBase is used in centralized, small- to medium-size businesses. It is also the database engine in various third-party packages from independent vendors.

**Interblock gap**    Same as *interrecord gap*.

**Intercast**    Broadcasting Web pages and other information via TV, using the unused portion of the video signal known as the vertical blanking interval (VBI). Developed by Intel, Intercast data is transmitted in 10 of the 45 lines of the VBI and can provide up to 10.5KBytes/sec of data. Requirements are a TV channel that transmits Intercast data and an Intercast-compliant TV board for the PC or set-top box for the TV. See *TV board*.

**interconnect**    **(1)** To attach one device to another.
    **(2)** A physical port (plug or socket) or wireless port (transmitter or receiver) used to attach one device to another.

**Interdev**    See *Visual Interdev*.

**interexchange carrier**    See *IXC*.

**interface**    The connection and interaction between hardware, software and the user.
    Hardware interfaces are the plugs, sockets, wires and the electrical pulses traveling through them in a particular pattern. Also included are electrical timing considerations. Examples are RS-232 transmission; the Ethernet and Token Ring network topologies; and the IDE, ESDI, SCSI, ISA, EISA and Micro Channel interfaces.
    Software, or programming, interfaces are the languages, codes and messages programs use to communicate with each other and to the hardware. Examples are the applications that run under the Mac, DOS and Windows operating systems, as well as the SMTP e-mail and LU 6.2 communications protocols.
    User interfaces are the keyboards, mice, commands and menus used for communication between you and the computer. Examples are the command lines in DOS and UNIX, and the Mac, Windows and Motif graphical interfaces.
    Interfacing is a major part of what engineers, programmers and consultants do. Users "talk to" the software. The software "talks to" the hardware and other software. Hardware "talks to" other hardware. All this is interfacing. It has

to be designed, developed, tested and redesigned; and with each incarnation, a new specification is born that may become yet one more de facto or regulated standard.

**Format and Function**    Every interface implies a structure. Electrical signals are made up of voltage levels, frequencies and duration. The data passed from one device or program to another has a precise format (header, body, trailer, etc.).

Every interface implies a function. At the hardware level, electronic signals activate functions; data is read, written, transmitted, received, analyzed for error, etc. At the software level, instructions activate the hardware (access methods, data link protocols, etc.). At higher levels, the data transferred or transmitted may itself request functions to be performed (client/server, program to program, etc.).

**Language and Programming**    An interface is activated by programming language commands. The complexity of the functions and the design of the language determine how difficult it is to program.

**User Interface, Protocol, API and ABI**    The design of the interaction between the user and the computer is called a "user interface." The rules, formats and functions between components in a communications system or network is called a "protocol." The language and message formats between routines within a program or between software components is called an "API." The specification for an operating system working in a specific machine environment has been known as an "ABI," but this term is not widely used.

All the above interactions are interfaces. Regardless of what they're called, they all create rules that must be precisely followed in a digital world.

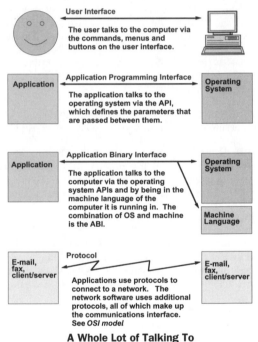

**A Whole Lot of Talking To**
No matter what they're called, interfaces boil down to a format and language that defines the services one system is capable of delivering to another.

**interface adapter**    In communications, a device that connects the computer or terminal to a network.

**interface designer**    See *GUI builder*.

**interferometer**    An instrument that measures the wavelengths of light and distances. It transmits two radio signals or beams of light and uses the interference principal (how they reinforce or neutralize each other) to determine the measurement.

**interframe coding**    In video compression, the coding of only the differences between frames. A video sequence is made up of keyframes, which contain the entire image, and subsequent delta frames, which encode only the incremental differences from the keyframe. When a certain amount of image material changes in the sequence, a new keyframe is generated.

Interframe coding allows very high compression ratios to be achieved, but the compression varies according to the amount of changes in the video content. The amount of action in the scenes has a direct effect on the compression. For example, a car chase will not compress as well as a person sitting in a chair and talking. See *intraframe coding*.

**Intergraph**    (Intergraph Corporation, Huntsville, AL, www.intergraph.com) A graphics computer systems company founded in 1969 as M&S Computing by Jim and Nancy Meadlock, Keith Schonrock, Bob Thurber and Terry Schansman. Initially a computer consulting firm to government agencies, it specialized in computer graphics and changed its name to Intergraph in 1980.

Intergraph developed expertise on Digital PDP and VAX computers and later developed proprietary UNIX workstations based on its own Clipper chip technology. In 1992, it migrated to Windows NT and became the world's leader in NT-based graphics workstations. In 1996, it introduced the first 28" HDTV-format computer monitor. The company's hardware and software is divided into Intergraph Computer Systems and Intergraph Software Solutions.

**interior gateway protocol**   See *IGP*.

**interior routing protocol**   See *IGP*.

**interlaced**   Illuminating a CRT by displaying odd lines first and then the even lines. Interlacing provides a way of displaying more information on screen using a less-sophisticated circuit, but at a penalty of producing an annoying flicker visible on small elements such as icons and buttons. It is less noticeable with motion than a still image, which is why traditional analog television, which uses an interlaced signal, is fine until you have to read still text (see *NTSC*).

Earlier computer displays were often interlaced at the highest resolution. For example, 640x480 and 800x600 might have been non-interlaced, but 1024x768 was interlaced. Today, computer displays are non-interlaced at all resolutions.

A related issue is the vertical scan frequency, or refresh rate, which is the number of times the entire screen is redisplayed within one second. For a flicker-free image, 70 times per second (70 Hz) is required. Most monitors are not designed to support the highest resolution and the highest refresh rate together, and there is typically a compromise. The higher the resolution, the lower the refresh rate. See *interlaced GIF*.

**interlaced GIF**   A GIF image that comes into focus while it is being displayed. Instead of rendering the image a line at a time, the whole frame is displayed looking very pixelated somewhat like a venetian blind and gradually becomes sharper as the lines fill in. It gives the illusion that the whole page has been downloaded faster even though you have to wait the same amount of time for the GIFs to become sharp. The interlaced GIF is created in four passes (scans): every eighth row starting with row 0, every eighth row starting with row 4, every fourth row starting with row 2 and every second row starting with row 1. See *progressive JPEG*, *GIF* and *interlaced*.

**interlaced JPEG**   See *progressive JPEG*.

**Interleaf**   Desktop publishing software for DOS, Windows 95/98, NT and a variety of UNIX-based computers from Interleaf, Inc., Waltham, MA (www.interleaf.com). Interleaf is a full-featured program that supports a large number of document and image types. It is used for creating compound documents, as well as extremely long documents (hundreds of thousands of pages).

It includes built-in word processing and graphics tools, and provides a number of optional components for enhanced document control and workgroup operation. Interleaf used to be known as Interleaf TPS (Technical Publishing Software). In 1990, it became Interleaf5, and later, Interleaf6, etc.

Interleaf RDM (Relational Document Manager) is another product that provides distribution and tracking of documents. Interleaf WorldView provides runtime viewing with customizable searches for Interleaf and other document types.

**interleave**   See *sector interleave* and *memory interleaving*.

**interlock**   A device that prohibits an action from taking place.

**Interactive Graphics**
Realistic flight simulation is an example of the interactive graphics provided by Intergraph's workstations and graphics subsystems. *(Image courtesy of Intergraph Computer Systems.)*

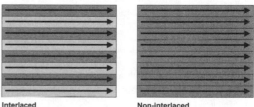

Interlaced                    Non-interlaced

**intermediate language**   A language that is generated from a programming source language, but that is not directly executable by a CPU. The intermediate language, also called "bytecode," "p-code," "pseudo code" or "pseudo language," must be interpreted or compiled into machine language for execution. This method allows the same source language to be used for different types of computers.

An intermediate language supports architecture neutrality, as does an interpreted language. However, the intermediate language is usually faster, because some of the program has been precompiled, whereas the interpreted language remains in source code and must be fully converted to machine code at runtime.

Visual Basic and Java are notable examples of programming languages that generate an intermediate language. They are compiled into bytecode, which is then converted into machine code at runtime.

**intermediate node routing**   Routing a message to non-adjacent nodes; for example, if three computers are connected in series A-B-C, data transmitted from A to C can be routed through B.

**intermittent error**   An error that occurs sporadically, not consistently. It is the most difficult type of problem to diagnose and repair.

**intermodal dispersion**   See *modal dispersion*.

**internal bus**   A pathway between the CPU and memory. Contrast with *external bus*. See *local bus*.

**internal command**   In DOS and OS/2, a command, such as Copy, Dir and Rename, which may be used at all times. Internal commands are executed by the command processor programs COMMAND.COM in DOS and CMD.EXE in OS/2. The command processor is always loaded when the operating system is loaded. Contrast with *external command*.

**internal disk**   See *internal drive*.

**internal drive**   A disk or tape drive that fits inside a drive bay in the computer cabinet. It derives its power from the main power supply. Most computers come with internal hard disk, floppy disk and CD-ROM drives. Contrast with *external drive*.

**internal font**   A set of characters for a particular typeface that is built into a printer. Contrast with *font cartridge* and *soft font*.

**internal interrupt**   An interrupt that is caused by processing, for example, a request for input or output or an arithmetic overflow error. Contrast with *external interrupt*.

**internal memory**   Refers to the memory chips (RAM), which is the internal workspace in the computer. Some people refer to memory and storage as internal memory (chips) and external memory (disk). Memory (chips) and storage (disk) is the preferred usage.

**internal modem**   A modem that plugs into an expansion slot within the computer. Unlike an external modem, an internal modem does not provide a series of display lights that inform the user of the changing modem states. The user must rely entirely on the communications program. Contrast with *external modem*.

**internal sort**   Sorting that is accomplished entirely in memory without using disks or tapes for temporary files.

**Internal stack failure**   A DOS error message that means DOS has gotten completely confused. Turn off the computer and restart.

**internal storage**   Same as *memory*.

**internationalization**   Sometimes abbreviated "I18N," it is support for the display of monetary values, time and date for many countries. See *localization*.

**Internaut**   A person that uses the Internet.

**internet**   **(2)** A large network made up of a number of smaller networks.

**(1)** (Internet) "The" Internet is made up of more than 65 million computers in more than 100 countries covering commercial, academic and government endeavors. Originally developed for the U.S. military, the Internet became widely used for academic and commercial research. Users had access to unpublished data and journals on a huge variety of subjects. Today, the Internet has become commercialized into a worldwide information highway, providing information on every subject known to humankind.

The Internet's surge in growth in the latter half of the 1990s was twofold. As the major online services (AOL, CompuServe, etc.) connected to the Internet for e-mail exchange, the Internet began to function as a central gateway. A member of one service could finally send mail to a member of another. The Internet glued the world together for electronic mail, and today, the Internet mail protocol is the world standard.

Second, with the advent of graphics-based Web browsers such as Mosaic and Netscape Navigator, and soon after, Microsoft's Internet Explorer, the World Wide Web took off. The Web became easily available to users with PCs and Macs rather than only scientists and hackers at UNIX workstations. Delphi was the first proprietary online service to offer Web access, and all the rest followed. At the same time, new Internet service providers rose out of the woodwork to offer access to individuals and companies. As a result, the Web has grown exponentially, providing an information exchange of unprecedented proportion. The Web has also become "the" storehouse for drivers, updates and demos that are downloaded via the browser.

Although daily news and information is now available on countless Web sites, long before the Web, information on a myriad of subjects was exchanged via Usenet (User Network) newsgroups. Still thriving, newsgroup articles can be selected and read directly from your Web browser. See *Usenet.*

Chat rooms provide another popular Internet service. Internet Relay Chat (IRC) offers multiuser text conferencing on diverse topics. Dozens of IRC servers provide hundreds of channels that anyone can log onto and participate in via the keyboard. See *Internet Relay Chat.*

**The Original Internet**   The Internet started in 1969 as the *ARPAnet.* Funded by the U.S. government, the ARPAnet became a series of high-speed links between major supercomputer sites and educational and research institutions worldwide, although mostly in the U.S. A major part of its backbone was the National Science Foundation's NFSNet. Along the way, it became known as the "Internet" or simply "the Net." By the 1990s, so many networks had become part of it and so much traffic was not educational or pure research that it became obvious that the Internet was on its way to becoming a commercial venture.

In 1995, the Internet was turned over to large commercial Internet providers (ISPs), such as MCI, Sprint and UUNET, who took responsibility for the backbones and have increasingly enhanced their capacities ever since. Regional ISPs link into these backbones to provide lines for their subscribers, and smaller ISPs hook either directly into the national backbones or into the regional ISPs.

Internet computers use the TCP/IP communications protocol. There are more than 20 million hosts on the Internet, a host being a mainframe or medium- to high-end server that is always online via TCP/IP. The Internet is also connected to non-TCP/IP networks worldwide through gateways that convert TCP/IP into other protocols.

Although most new users interact with the Internet via their Web browsers, for years, command-line UNIX utilities were used. For example, an FTP (File Transfer Protocol) program allows files

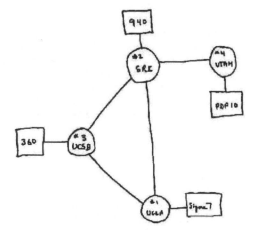

**Modest Beginnings**
These four nodes were drawn in 1969 showing the University of California at Berkeley and Los Angeles, SRI International and the University of Utah. This modest network diagram was the beginning of the ARPAnet, and eventually, the Internet. *(Image courtesy of The Computer Museum History Center, www.historycenter.org)*

to be downloaded, and the Archie utility provides listings of these files. Telnet is a terminal emulation program that lets you log onto a computer in the Internet and run a program. Gopher provides hierarchical menus describing

Internet files (not just file names), and Veronica lets you make more sophisticated searches on Gopher sites. See *FTP, Archie, Telnet, Gopher* and *Veronica*.

Ironically, some of the original academic and scientific users of the Internet are developing their own network once again. The Internet is so jammed these days that they no longer enjoy the quick access they were used to (see *Internet2*).

See *World Wide Web, how to search the Web, intranet, NAP, **hot topics and trends**, IAB, information superhighway* and *online services*.

**The Internet Explosion**    There has been more activity, excitement and hype over the Internet than any other computer or communications topic that was ever conceived. Using the World Wide Web, thousands of companies, from conglomerates to mom and pop shops, are trying to figure out how to make the Internet a worldwide shopping mall. Will it become "the" model for commerce in the 21st Century?  Will traffic bog down like the Los Angeles freeway?  Or, will it just become one more option for doing business in a world rich with choices?  Stay tuned!

**Getting Started?**    For a list of good books on the Internet, see *Internet references*.

**Internet2**    A high-speed network for government, academic and research use administered by UCAID, and being developed by more than 100 universities with assistance from private companies and the U.S. government. It is not intended for commercial use or to replace the Internet, but is, in fact, the reincarnation of it. However, whereas the first Internet was designed to primarily exchange text, Internet2 is being developed to exchange realtime, multimedia data at high speed, something today's commercial Internet does not do well. Resulting technological advancements should eventually migrate to the global Internet.

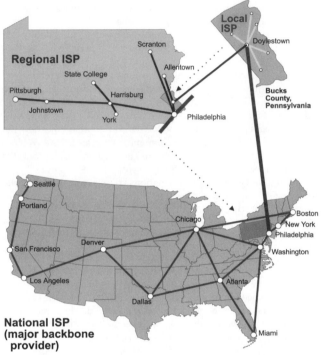

**National ISP (major backbone provider)**

**How the Internet Is Connected**
Small Internet service providers (ISPs) hook into regional ISPs, which themselves link into major backbones that traverse the U.S. connecting major metropolitan areas. This diagram shows what a typical national backbone might look like, as well as a county and state provider. While local ISPs may offer services only within their county, regional providers often span state lines.

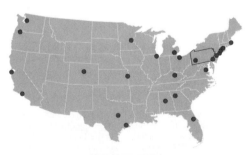

**GigaPOP Sites**
GigaPOPs are being created at these locations by Internet2 member universities in collaboration with affiliate members. *(Image courtesy of UCAID.)*

Universities are developing different techniques for providing high-speed points of presence known as "GigaPOPs," which serve as switching points for the network. The first GigaPOP was deployed in Research Triangle Park, North Carolina, in late 1997. High-bandwidth applications, such as full-motion video and 3-D animations, are being developed and tested to determine the transport designs necessary to carry them in realtime.

UCAID works closely with Clinton's Next-Generation Internet (NGI), which is funding research on high-speed networks for federal agencies. Internet2 uses existing networks such as the vBNS backbone of the National Science Foundation. The Abilene network is expected to provide another backbone. Related Web sites are www.ucaid.org, www.ngi.gov, www.ccic.gov and www.vbns.net. See *vBNS*, *Abilene* and *tele-immersion*.

**Internet access**   See *how to access the Internet*.

**Internet Access Coalition**   See *IAC*.

**Internet access provider**   Same as *Internet service provider*.

**Internet access router**   A router that provides access to the Internet. It is typically connected to the LAN and forwards IP packets destined for the Internet to the WAN ports (modem, ISDN, T1, etc.).

**Internet Adapter**   See *TIA*.

**Internet address**   There are two kinds of addresses that are widely used on the Internet. One is a person's e-mail address, and the other is the address of a Web site, which is known as a URL. Following is an explanation of Internet e-mail addresses. For more on URLs, see *URL* and *Internet domain name*.

The format for addressing a message to an Internet user is *username@domainname*. For example, the address of the author of this database is **freedman@computerlanguage.com**. There are no spaces between any of the words. FREEDMAN is the user name and COMPUTERLANGUAGE.COM is the domain name. The .COM stands for the commercial top-level domain category (see *Internet domain name*). For the actual structure of an Internet address, see *IP address*.

How to Get Your Own Address   You get your e-mail address from your Internet service provider (ISP). However, if you change your service, your Internet address changes. To obtain a permanent e-mail address, you can register your own domain name or you can use an e-mail service. See *how to register a domain name* and *Internet e-mail service*.

How to Find Someone Else's Address   There are Web sites that maintain directories, or white pages, of e-mail addresses. New sites are coming online all the time. You may have to try several sites to find someone, and there's no guarantee. See *Web white pages* and *Web Yellow pages*.

Sending to Old E-Mail Addresses   Before the Internet became mainstream, online services had their own proprietary e-mail addressing schemes. If you happen to have an old account name or number of someone you wish to reach, that address can be translated into the Internet e-mail address that is used today.

To reach CompuServe users, change the comma in their CompuServe account numbers to a period. For example, 71020,1560 becomes 71020.1560@compuserve.com.

The following examples show how the name "jmorrison" would be used in addresses to other online services. If the acount name were "j morrison," you would remove the blank space.

```
jmorrison@aol.com           America Online
jmorrison@genie.geis.com    GEnie
jmorrison@mcimail.com       MCI Mail
jmorrison@prodigy.com       PRODIGY
jmorrison@delphi.com        DELPHI
```

**Internet Ad Hoc Committee**   (www.iahc.org) A coalition of participants from the Internet community that was formed to generate new top-level domain names. See *Internet domain name*.

**Internet advertising**   Delivering ads to Internet users via Web sites, e-mail, ad-supported software and Internet-enabled cellphones. Organizations that provide Internet advertising either sell the ads and pay the Web or software publisher to display them, or they provide software tools and/or adservers that enable an organiztion to deliver the ads it generates itself. See *banner ad*.

**Internet appliance**   Also called "information appliance," "smart appliance," and "Web appliance," it is a device specialized for accessing the Web and/or e-mail. Designed for ease of use, it plugs into a telephone jack or LAN connection for Internet hookup. Portable Internet appliances use a wireless connection to the Internet. Internet TV services, such as WebTV, are sometimes called Internet appliances as well. The term is rather encompassing, and innovative products are expected all the time. See *digital picture frame, network appliance, server appliance, Internet TV, network computer* and *smart phone.*

**Internet Architecture Board**   (www.iab.org) Founded in 1983 as the Internet Activities Board, it is a mostly volunteer organization that provides architectural guidance to and adjudicates conflicts for the Internet Engineering Task Force (IETF). It appoints the IETF Chair and all other Internet Engineering Steering Group (IESG) candidates. It also advises the Internet Society (ISOC) relating to technical and procedural matters.

**Internet audio**   See *RealAudio.*

**Internet backbones**   A group of communications networks managed by several commercial companies that provide the major high-speed links across the country. ISPs are either connected directly to these backbones or to a larger regional ISP that is connected to one. The backbones themselves are interconnected at various access points called "NAPs." The major backbone providers are MCI, Sprint, UUNET, AGIS and BBN. See *NAP.*

**The New Internet Computer**
This Linux-based computer is a pure Web appliance that was introduced in 2000. Designed for browser access to the Web, it contains no disk drives, and files must be stored on an Internet storage service such as Xdrive or I-drive. *(Image courtesy of The New Internet Computer Company.)*

**Internet-based payment service**   See *Web payment service.*

**Internet box**   See *Internet appliance.*

**Internet browser**   See *Web browser.*

**Internet cable**   See *cable Internet.*

**Internet cache**   See *Web cache.*

**Internet cafe**   The high-tech equivalent of the coffee house. However, instead of playing chess or having heated political discussions, you browse the Internet and discuss the latest technology. CD-ROMs, games and other "cyber" stuff is also generally available. They started in Europe, and the CYBERCAFE was the first in the U.S. See *CYBERCAFE.*

**InternetCash**   A Web payment service from Spendcash.com, New York, (www.spendcash.com), that provides a payment method for people without credit cards. Prepaid InternetCash cards are purchased in retail establishments and activated at a participating Web site. See *Web payment service.*

**Internet computer**   See *Internet appliance* and *network computer.*

**Internet content provider**   See *content provider.*

**Internet directories**   See *Web white pages* and *Web yellow pages.*

**Internet domain name**   An organization's unique name on the Internet. As of early 2001, there were more than 20 million registered domain names. The name chosen by the organization combined with a top-level domain (TLD) makes up the Internet domain name. For example, **computerlanguage.com** is the domain name for the publisher of this Encyclopedia.

In order to access the Computer Language site, you have to type in **www.computerlanguage.com**, because the "www" is the name given to the computer that actually hosts the site. WWW is commonly used for uniformity on the Web, but different names are also used.

Technically, computerlanguage.com is a "second-level domain," because the top-level domain is .com. Computerlanguage.com is also known as a "root domain." In practice, both computerlanguage.com and www.computerlanguage.com are called domain names.

Internet domain names are registered with any of several dozen registrars. To find out if a name is already taken, visit www.networksolutions.com or www.icann.org. See *DNS, IP address* and *FQDN*.

**Generic TLDs**     Following are the "generic" top-level domains. The .com is the most desired because all major U.S. corporations adopted it early on, and it became trendy. The .com, .net and .org TLDs are not restricted. If a .com name is already taken, a .net or .org TLD is often chosen instead.

```
.com    commercial
.net    network
.org    organization

.edu    U.S. educational only
.gov    U.S. government only
.mil    U.S. military only

.int    international treaties between
            governments only
```

**New Domain Names**     In November 2000, the Internet Corporation for Assigned Names and Numbers (ICANN) announced the following new top-level domains. Top-level domains are not added at Internet speed. The last time new domains were introduced was in 1989. Stay tuned! More TLDs are expected.

```
.biz     a business
.aero    aerospace
.coop    cooperative
.pro     professional
.museum  museum
.info    information service
.name    individual/personal
```

**Country Codes**     Country codes such as .ca for Canada and .uk for the United Kingdom are widely used top-level domains. The U.S. country code (.us) is also used but not widespread. See *country codes A–E* for the complete list. See also *dotTV*.

## Internet e-mail service

There are two ways to get e-mail over the Internet. One is by using a mail program that is installed in your computer, and the other is a mail service on the Web, which is accessible from any browser.

**The Mail Client**     The use of a mail program (also known as a "mail client" or "e-mail client") such as Eudora or Outlook is the traditional approach. This requires configuring the program to your ISP's service by typing in the names of its incoming and outgoing mail servers (for example, mail.my_isp.com). If you're dialing in via analog modem, you also need local telephone numbers. Your mail access is then tied to that machine and telephone number, which can be costly to dial if you travel to other countries. To use another computer for mail, you have to set up the mail program in that machine. However, mail programs are rich in features compared with Web-based mail and are generally preferred by serious mail users.

**Web-Based E-Mail**     The Web-based e-mail is newer and has two advantages. First, you can get your e-mail from any browser. That means you can go to a computer anywhere in the world with access to the Web and send and receive e-mail. All you have to type in is the username and password you used to subscribe to the service. The Web approach is ideal for people that do not carry laptops to remote offices. Most ISPs offer both methods and synchronize the two so you can get your mail by whichever method is more convenient at the time.

Second, many Web-based e-mail services are supported by advertising and are free. An advantage to free e-mail, which is really due to it being a separate service, is that if you switch ISPs for Web browsing, your e-mail address stays the same. If however you switch your e-mail service, you have to notify everyone that your address has changed. Your old ISP will generally not do it for you. For a directory of e-mail sites, visit www.emailaddresses.com. Some of the major sites are

```
www.coolemail.com     (e-mail by phone)
www.hotmail.com       (Web based)
www.juno.com          (Web based and non-Web)
```

```
www.mail.com            (Web based)
www.netscape.com        (Web based)
www.yahoo.com           (Web based)
www.zdnet.com           (Web based)
www.four11.com          (forwarding)
www.bigfoot.com         (forwarding)
www.emailaddresses.com  (directory of sites)
```

**Internet engineer**    A person responsible for developing and maintaining the infrastruture that supports the public Web site, intranet and associated LANs and WANs. May be involved in developing transaction-based applications for e-commerce. See *e-commerce engineer*.

**Internet Engineering Steering Group**    See *Internet Engineering Task Force*.

**Internet Engineering Task Force**    (c/o Corporation for National Research Initiatives, Reston, VA, www.ietf.org) Founded in 1986, the IETF is a mostly volunteer organization of working groups dedicated to identifying problems and proposing technical solutions for the Internet. It facilitates transfer of ideas from the Internet Research Task Force (IRTF) to the Internet community and is supported by efforts of the Internet Society (ISOC). The Internet Architecture Board (IAB) provides architectural guidelines for the IETF, and the Internet Engineering Steering Group (IESG) provides overall direction.

**Internetese**    See *digispeak*.

**Internet Explorer**    See *Microsoft Internet Explorer*.

**Internet explosion**    The period of tremendous growth of the Internet in the latter half of the 1990s. In the 1994–1996 timeframe, it changed from a scientific and governmental research network to a commercial and consumer marketplace.

**Internet fax**    Using the Internet to send faxes. Fax servers accept an incoming fax message and route it to a fax server in the same locality as the destination fax machine. The fax server then makes a local telephone call to send the fax.

**Internet filter**    See *Web filtering* and *firewall*.

**Internet firewall**    A firewall that is used to shield users from the Internet. See *firewall*.

**Internet gateway**    A computer system that converts messages back and forth between TCP/IP and other protocols. Internet gateways connect the Internet to all the other communications networks in the world.

**Internet II**    See *Internet2*.

**Internet keyboard**    A computer keyboard with buttons for common Internet functions such as launching the Web browser and e-mail applications, and controlling sound volume.

**Internet mail**    See *Internet e-mail service*.

**Internet management software**    See *Internet monitoring*.

**Internet marketplace**    See *vertical portal* and *Web hub*.

**Internet monitoring**    Analyzing traffic on the Internet. Monitoring is performed to determine packet volume for network configuration, as well as to find out how employees are spending their time on the Internet. This is the first step in determining whether or not filtering should be added to the network. See *Web filtering*.

**Internet payment service**    See *Web payment service*.

**Internet PC**   See *network computer*.

**Internet phone**   **(1)** A device or software application that provides the client part of an Internet telephone call.

**(2)** (Internet Phone) An Internet telephony client program for Windows from VocalTec Communications, Ltd., Northvale, NJ (www.vocaltec.com). It allows voice calls to be placed over the Internet or to a standard telephone via an ITSP in the destination city. Video capability is also included. Introduced in early 1995, Internet Phone was the first IP telephony software on the market. See *IP telephony* and *ITSP*.

**Internet picture frame**   See *digital picture frame*.

**Internet postage**   See *PC Postage*.

**Internet Protocol**   See *Internet* and *TCP/IP*.

**Internet protocols**   Refers to all the standards that keep the Internet running. The foundation protocol is TCP/IP, which provides the basic communications mechanism, as well as ways to copy files (FTP) and send e-mail (SMTP). The Web added the HTTP protocol for downloading Web pages and HTML, XML and XHTML for formatting them. There are many others and many more are expected, as the Internet has become "the" arena for global standards. See *TCP/IP*, *FTP*, *SMTP*, *HTTP* and *HTML*.

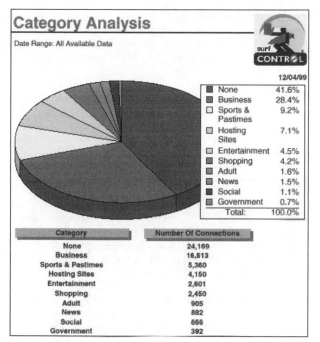

**An Internet Analysis**
This report from the surfCONTROL free evaluation software could be a day's worth of analysis on a network of 2,000 users. The "none" category comprises unrecognizable sites in this test and would be much smaller were the software to be fully configured and put into production. *(Image courtesy of JSP Corporation, www.surfcontrol.com)*

**Internet radio**   Listening to radio broadcasts via the Internet. Using streaming techniques, high-quality audio can be delivered to users at their PCs and Macs. There are more than 4,000 audio broadcasts on the Internet sponsored by all types of organizations, as well as traditional radio stations. Audio is played using a multimedia plug-in to your browser that supports audio formats such as those from RealNetworks and Microsoft. In 2000, Kerbango introduced a physical Internet radio that plugs into your Internet connection. See *RealAudio* and *ASF*.

**Internet references**   A well-written and excellent book for people getting started on the Internet is *Internet Slick Tricks* by Alfred and Emily Glossbrenner, published by Random House, ISBN 0-679-75611-6.

Another book by Alfred Glossbrenner, but more in depth, is *Internet 101*, published by Osborne/McGraw-Hill, ISBN 0-07-024054-X. While aimed at the college market, this is a must-have for anyone interested in the Internet. Glossbrenner is a superb author.

To learn what information is available on the Internet, read *Internet Yellow Pages* by Harley Hahn and Rick Stout, published by Osborne/McGraw-Hill, ISBN 007-882023-5.

Joshua Eddings' *How the Internet Works*, published by Ziff-Davis Press, ISBN 1-56276-192-7, provides a delightful and colorful guide to the inner-workings of the Internet.

**Internet Relay Chat**   Computer conferencing on the Internet. There are hundreds of IRC channels on numerous subjects that are hosted on IRC servers around the world. After joining a channel, your messages are broadcast to everyone listening to that channel. IRC client programs, such as mIRC, provide a graphical interface for all functions, including logging onto popular servers and obtaining a list of their active channels. See *MUD* and *netsplit*.

## Internet Research Task Force

(www.irtf.org) An organization of working groups involved in researching future Internet tecnologies. The IRTF is managed by the IRTF Chair in conjunction with the Internet Research Steering Group (IRSG). The IRTF Chair is appointed by the Internet Architecture Board (IAB). When the technologies are deemed ready for development, they are transferred to the Internet Engineering Task Force (IETF). See *Internet Engineering Task Force.*

## Internet roaming

Accessing your own ISP locally when traveling abroad. Organizations such as GRIC and iPass have alliances with ISPs around the world that enable international travelers to obtain their e-mail without making long distance calls.

## Internet Router

**(1)** A router in the Internet that forwards packets of Internet traffic between local, regional and national providers.

**(2)** (InterNet Router) Macintosh software from Apple that internetworks different access methods (LocalTalk, EtherTalk, TokenTalk, etc.) and can reside in any network station. Each Router can connect up to eight networks with a maximum of 1,024 networks and 16 million nodes.

## Internet server appliance

A self-contained computer system specialized for Internet or intranet use with primary access to setup and configuration through a browser. See *server appliance.*

## Internet service provider

An organization that provides access to the Internet. Small Internet service providers (ISPs) provide service via modem and ISDN, while the larger ones also offer private line hookups (T1, fractional T1, etc.). Customers are generally billed a fixed rate per month, but other charges may apply. For a fee, a Web site can be created and maintained on the ISP's server, allowing the smaller organization to have a presence on the Web with its own domain name.

Large Internet services, such as America Online (AOL) and Microsoft Network (MSN), also provide proprietary databases, forums and services in addition to Internet access. To keep up-to-date, look for *Boardwatch Magazine's* "Internet Service Providers" bimonthly directory at your local bookstore or visit www.boardwatch.com.

## Internet Society

(Internet Society, Reston, VA, www.isoc.org) An international membership organization dedicated to extending and enhancing the Internet, founded in 1992. It supports Internet bodies such as the IETF and works with governments, organizations and the general public to promote Internet research, information, education and standards. It also helps developing nations design their Internet infrastructure.

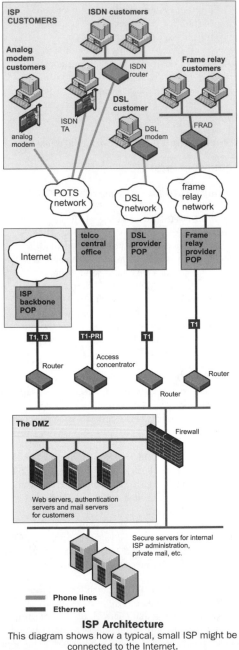

**ISP Architecture**
This diagram shows how a typical, small ISP might be connected to the Internet.

**Internet speak**    See *digispeak* and *geekspeak*.

**Internet storage provider**    An organization that provides free and/or paid storage on the Web. Companies such as Xdrive and I-drive let you back up, store and share files using their storage facilities.

**Internet Talk Radio**    Audio coverage of news events digitized into Internet files at the National Press Building in Washington, DC. ITR files are distributed to FTP sites for users with computers that have sound capabilities.

**Internet telephony**    Using the Internet for a voice call. See *IP telephony*.

**Internet time**    Refers to the fast-paced Internet industry. Companies have scrambled at breakneck speed to be the first to offer their wares on the World Wide Web, ready or not.

**Internet Trojan**    An virus-like program that comes from the Internet. See *Trojan horse*.

**Internet TV**    An Internet service for home TV use. It uses a set-top box that connects the TV to a modem and telephone line. The user interface has been specialized for viewing on an interlaced TV screen rather than a computer monitor. WebTV was the first such service to obtain widespread distribution. See *WebTV* and *net-top box*.

**Internet Usage Policy**    The guidelines and instruction given to employees concerning the use of Internet facilities such as the Web, e-mail and chat conferences. It stipulates all prohibitions, such as access to pornographic sites, conducting illegal activities and sexual harassment. It authorizes who may communicate with members of the press, competitors and other organizations. Employees may be required to sign such a policy statement as a pledge to honor its principles or otherwise be dismissed. See *policy management*.

**Internet utility**    Software used to search the Internet. See *Archie, Gopher, Veronica, WAIS* and *Web browser*.

**internetwork**    (1) To go between one network and another.

(2) A large network made up of a number of smaller networks. Same as *internet* (small "i," not the Internet). See *internet*.

**InterNIC**    The domain name registration project that was formed by agreements between Network Solutions, the National Science Foundation, General Atomics and AT&T. See *Network Solutions*.

**interoperability**    The capability of two or more hardware devices or two or more software routines to work together. For example, routers and switches in a network require interoperability. The term is more often used with hardware than with software.

Although there is interoperability between all software and the computers they are running in, as well as between all applications and the operating system, interoperability is generally not used to describe this kind of standard interaction. See *interoperable*.

**Interoperability Clearinghouse**    An organization supported by the U.S. government and private companies to ensure interoperability between information systems. Formed in late 1998, its goal is to provide a mechanism that validates the interoperability of software, including applications, programming languages, databases, object technology and network protocols. For information, visit www.ichnet.org.

**interoperable**    The ability for one system to communicate or work with another. See *interoperability*.

**Interpedia**    (INTERnet encycloPEDIA)    A proposed public domain encyclopedia to be created for and maintained on the Internet.

**interpolate**    To estimate values that lie between known values.

**interpolated resolution**    An enhanced resolution of a scanning device that is computed using a software algorithm. It makes an image appear as if it were scanned at a higher resolution. An interpolated resolution is considerably greater than the optical resolution, which is the inherent physical resolution of the device. Depending on the contents of the image and the scanning algorithm, an interpolated, or enhanced, resolution can improve or degrade the original. See *optical resolution* and *scanner*.

**Interpress** A page description language from Xerox used on the 2700 and 9700 page printers (medium- to large-scale laser printers). Ventura Publisher provides output in Interpress.

**interpret** To run a program one line at a time. Each line of source language is translated into machine language and then executed.

**interpreted** Translated from source code into machine code one line at a time. See *interpreted language* and *interpreter*.

**interpreted language** A programming language that requires an interpreter program to run it. See *interpreter* and *interpreted*.

**interpreter** A high-level programming language translator that translates and runs the program at the same time. It translates one program statement into machine language, executes it, and then proceeds to the next statement. This differs from regular executable programs that are presented to the computer as binary-coded instructions. Interpreted programs remain in the same source language format the programmer wrote in: as text files, not machine language files.

Interpreted programs run slower than their compiler counterparts. Whereas the compiler translates the entire program before it is run, interpreters translate a line at a time while the program is run. However, it is very convenient to write an interpreted program, since a single line of code can be tested interactively.

Interpreted programs must always be run with the interpreter. For example, in order to run a BASIC or dBASE program, the BASIC or dBASE interpreter must be in the target computer.

If a language can be both interpreted and compiled, a program may be developed with the interpreter for ease of testing and debugging and later compiled for production use.

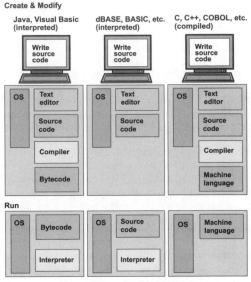

**Interpreters and Compilers**
Unlike compiled languages that have been translated into machine language (right), interpreted languages must be translated at runtime. With languages such as dBASE and BASIC (middle), the interpreter translates the orginal source code. Languages such as Java and Visual Basic (left) use an intermediate language. The source code is compiled into "byte code," and the bytecode is interpreted at runtime.

**interpretive language** See *interpreted language*.

**interprocess communication** See *IPC*.

**interrecord gap** The empty space generated between blocks of data on early magnetic tapes, which was created by the starting and stopping of the reel. Today's drives do not use erase heads and write the entire tape, filling stop and start areas with padded blocks or special frequencies for synchronization.

**interrogate** (1) To search, sum or count records in a file. See *query*.
(2) To test the condition or status of a terminal or computer system.

**interrupt** A signal that gets the attention of the CPU and is usually generated when I/O is required. For example, hardware interrupts are generated when a key is pressed or when the mouse is moved. Software interrupts are generated by a program requiring disk input or output.

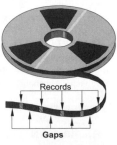

**Interrecord Gaps**
In the old days, the gaps between the records were often larger than the blocks of data.

An internal timer may continually interrupt the computer several times per second to keep the time of day current or for timesharing purposes.

When an interrupt occurs, control is transferred to the operating system, which determines the action to be taken. Interrupts are prioritized; the higher the priority, the faster the interrupt will be serviced.

**interrupt-driven**   A computer or communications network that uses interrupts.

**interrupt latency**   The time it take to service an interrupt. It becomes a critical factor when servicing realtime functions such as a communications line. See *UART overrun*.

**interrupt mask**   An internal switch setting that controls whether an interrupt can be processed or not. The mask is a bit that is turned on and off by the program.

**interrupt priorities**   The sequence of importance assigned to interrupts. If two interrupts occur simultaneously, the interrupt with the highest priority is serviced first. In some systems, a higher-priority interrupt can gain control of the computer while it's processing a lower-priority interrupt.

**Interrupt Request**   See *IRQ*.

**interrupt vector**   In the PC, one of 256 pointers that reside in the first 1KB of memory. Each vector points to a routine in the BIOS or elsewhere in memory, which handles the interrupt.

**intersect**   In a relational database, to match two files and produce a third file with records that are common in both. For example, intersecting an American file and a programmer file would yield American programmers.

**INTERSOLV**   A software company that specialized in software configuration management products for managing large software projects. Its PVCS line has been widely used. INTERSOLV was acquired by Micro Focus Group in mid 1998, which later changed its name to MERANT. See *PVCS* and *MERANT*.

**interstitial**   In a separate window. See *interstitial ad*.

**interstitial ad**   An advertisement on a Web site that is more like a TV commercial, which takes center stage. Meaning "in between," interstitial ads display in a separate window while you download the next Web page. Contrast with a *banner ad*, which is a more passive form of advertising.

Introduced in 1997 by San Francisco–based Streamix, HyperStitial was software that resided in your computer and enabled your browser to display interstitial ads. See *SUPERSTITIAL*.

**in the clear**   Without encryption. See *cleartext* and *plaintext*.

**in the wild**   Refers to viruses that have been not contained. Although tens of thousands of viruses have been unleashed, most of them have been eradicated and exist only in computer labs for research purposes. However, at any given time, there may be a couple hundred viruses that are still "in the wild" contaminating computer systems of unsuspecting users.

**intra**   Within a boundary; for example, intraoffice refers to operations that take place within the office. Contrast with *inter*.

**intraframe coding**   Compressing redundant areas within a video frame. See *interframe coding*.

**Intranet**   (1) An inhouse Web site that serves the employees of the enterprise. Although intranet pages may link to the Internet, an intranet is not a site accessed by the general public.

Using programming languages such as Java, client/server applications can be built on intranets. Since Web browsers that support Java run under Windows, Mac and UNIX, such programs also provide cross-platform capability.

Intranets use the same communications protocols and hypertext links as the Web, and thus provide a standard way of disseminating information internally and extending the application worldwide at the same time. See *network computer* and *extranet*.

(2) The term as originally coined in the preceding definition has become so popular that it is often used to refer to any in-house LAN and client/server system.

**intranet computer**   A computer dedicated for intranet use only. See *network computer*.

**intranet server**   A computer dedicated to providing intranet services to users on the network. See *intranet toaster*.

**intranet toaster**   A self-contained intranet server designed for small departments or businesses. It plugs into the network and is configured via the Web browser. It is not as powerful as a full-blown UNIX or NT server, but provides for a convenient and fast installation.

**IntranetWare**   A network operating system and intranet server from Novell. In late 1996, Novell combined NetWare 4.11, its Web server, TCP/IP support and the Netscape browser into a single package named IntranetWare. NetWare still retained its name as the operating system, but became part of the IntranetWare package. In NetWare 5, the IntranetWare branding was dropped. See *NetWare*.

**inverse addressing**   To perform the opposite of the normal addressing function. For example, inverse addressing in DNS servers converts the IP address into the URL, instead of the URL into the IP address.

**inverse kinematics**   In 3-D animation, a technique that provides automatic movement of objects. It allows elements of an object to be linked, such as the parts of an arm or leg, and causes them to move in a prescribed, realistic manner.

**inverse multiplexor**   In communications, a device that breaks up a high-speed transmission into several low-speed transmissions, and vice versa. It is used to transmit LAN and videoconferencing traffic over lower-speed digital channels. For example, to transmit Ethernet over a T3 link, the 10 Mbps Ethernet channel would be inverse multiplexed into multiple 64 Kbps channels of the T3 line. A 336 Kbps videoconferencing transmission could be split into six 56 Kbps channels to transmit over a Switched 56 service. Contrast with *multiplexor*.

**inverse video**   Same as *reverse video*.

**inverted file**   In data management, a file that is indexed on many of the attributes of the data itself. For example, in an employee file, an index could be maintained for all secretaries, another for managers. It's faster to search the indexes than every record. Inverted file indexes use lots of disk space; searching is fast, updating is slower.

**inverted list**   Same as *inverted file*.

**inverter**   (1) A logic gate that converts the input to the opposite state for output. If the input is true, the output is false, and vice versa. An inverter performs the Boolean logic NOT operation.

(2) A circuit that converts DC current into AC current. Contrast with *rectifier*.

**invisible GIF**   A tiny GIF file comprised of a single, transparent pixel. Also known as a "1-by-1 GIF" or "clear GIF," it is used to monitor a user's activity. See *Web bug*.

**invoke**   To activate a program, routine, function or process.

**I/O**   (Input/Output) Transferring data between the CPU and a peripheral device. Every transfer is an output from one device and an input into another.

**I/O address**   (1) On PCs, a three-digit hexadecimal number (2AB, 2A0, etc.) used to identify and signal a peripheral device (serial port, parallel port, sound card, etc.). Address assignments must be unique; otherwise, conflicts will occur. There are usually a small number of selectable addresses on each controller card. Since Plug and Play was introduced in Windows 95, most of the conflicts have been resolved by the computer. See *PC I/O addressing*.

(2) The identifying address of a peripheral device.

**I/O area**   A reserved segment of memory used to accept data from an input device or to accumulate data for transfer to an output device. See *buffer*.

**I/O bound**   Refers to an excessive amount of time getting data in and out of the computer in relation to the time it takes for processing it. Faster channels and disk drives improve the performance of I/O bound computers. See *I/O intensive*.

**I/O bus**   Same as *peripheral bus*.

**IOCA**   (Image Object Content Architecture) See *MO:DCA*.

**I/O card**   See *expansion board* and *PC card*.

**I/O channel**   See *channel*.

**IOCS**   (Input Output Control System) An early, rudimentary IBM operating system (1950s). It was a set of I/O routines for tapes and disks. Today's counterpart in the PC is the BIOS.

**I/O device**   Same as *peripheral device*.

**I/O intensive**   Refers to an application that reads and/or writes a large amount of data. The performance of such an application depends on the speed of the computer's peripheral devices and can cause a computer to become I/O bound. See *I/O bound*.

**I/O interface**   See *port* and *expansion slot*.

**Iomega**   (Iomega Corporation, Roy, Utah, www.iomega.com) A mass storage company founded in 1980 that made the Bernoulli Box famous. More recently, it introduced the Zip and Jaz drives, which have become very popular. See *Zip disk, Jaz disk, **Ditto drive**, click! disk* and *Bernoulli Box*.

**ion deposition**   A printing technology used in high-speed page printers. It is similar to laser printing, except instead of using light to create a charged image on a drum, it uses a printhead that deposits ions. After toner is attracted to the ions on the drum, the paper is pressed directly against the drum fusing toner to paper.

Quality approaches that of a laser printer; however, the ink has not been embedded as deeply, and the paper can smear more easily.

**I/O port**   (1) (Input/Output port) A pathway into and out of the computer. See *port*.
(2) (Input/Output port) In a PC, an address used for input or output. See *PC I/O addressing*.

**I/O processor**   Circuitry specialized for I/O operations. See *front end processor*.

**IOS**   (1) (Internetwork Operating System) An operating system from Cisco that is the primary control program used in its routers. IOS is widely used, robust system software that supports the common functions of all products under Cisco's CiscoFusion architecture.
(2) (Integrated Office System) See *office automation*.

**I/O statement**   A programming instruction that requests I/O.

**IOW**   Digispeak for "in other words."

**IP**   (1) (Internet Protocol) The IP part of the TCP/IP communications protocol. IP implements the network layer (layer 3) of the protocol, which contains a network address and is used to route a message to a different network or subnetwork. IP accepts "packets" from the layer 4 transport protocol (TCP or UDP), adds its own header to it and delivers a "datagram" to the layer 2 data link protocol. It may also break the packet into fragments to support the maximum transmission unit (MTU) of the network. See *TCP/IP*, ***TCP/IP ABCs**, datagram, IP address* and *IP on Everything*.

**(2)** (Intellectual Property) A broad category of intangible materials that are legally recognized as proprietary to an organization. In the computer field, hardware circuits, software and text is copyrightable. Depending on the situation, the algorithms used within hardware circuits and software may also be patentable, and most brand names can be trademarked. However, IP covers more than just copyrights, trademarks and patents; for example, customer databases, mailing lists, trade secrets and other business information are also included.

**(3)** See *image processing*.

**(4)** See *IndustryPack*.

**IP address**    (Internet Protocol address) The address of a computer attached to a TCP/IP network. Every client and server station must have a unique IP address. Client workstations have either a permanent address or one that is dynamically assigned to them each dial-up session. IP addresses are written as four sets of numbers separated by periods; for example, 204.171.64.2.

The TCP/IP packet uses 32 bits to contain the IP address, which is made up of a network and host address (netid and hostid). The more bits used for network address, the fewer remain for hosts. Certain high-order bits identify class types and some numbers are reserved. The following table shows how the bits are divided. The Class Number is the decimal value of the high-order eight bits, which identifies the class type.

| Class | Class Number | Maximum Networks | Maximum Hosts | Bits in... NetID | Bits in... HostID |
|-------|--------------|------------------|---------------|-------|--------|
| A | 1-127 | 127 | 16,777,214 | 7 | 24 |
| B | 129-191 | 16,383 | 65,534 | 14 | 16 |
| C | 192-223 | 2,097,151 | 254 | 21 | 8 |

Class C addresses have been expanded using the CIDR addressing scheme, which uses a variable network ID instead of the fixed numbers shown above. Network addresses are supplied to organizations by ARIN (previously by InterNIC). See *CIDR, ARIN, InterNIC, IPv6,* **TCP/IP ABCs** and *IP on Everything*.

**Logical or Physical?**    An IP address is somewhat of a hybrid, which can be thought of as either logical or physical depending on how you view it. It is a unique number assigned to a node, which makes it seem physical, especially because there is so much name-to-IP address resolution going on in the network. Yet, there is also the Ethernet address that is built into the network adapter. That is indeed physical, and it does not change, which is very typical of physical device names. However, since IP addresses can be dynamically assigned, causing the same client workstation to have a different IP address every day, the IP address seems more like a logical address. Regardless of what it is, it would make a great debate in a computer science class. See *logical vs physical*.

**IP block**    (Intellectual Property block) See *semiconductor IP*.

**IPC**    (InterProcess Communication) The exchange of data between one program and another either within the same computer or over a network. It implies a protocol that guarantees a response to a request. Examples are OS/2's Named Pipes, Windows' DDE, Novell's SPX and Macintosh's IAC.

IPCs are performed automatically by the programs. For example, a spreadsheet program could query a database program and retrieve data from one of its databases. A manual example of an IPC function is performed when users cut and paste data from one file to another using the clipboard.

**IP card**    (IndustryPack card) See *IndustryPack*.

**IPCS**    See *AS/400 Integrated PC Server*.

**IPDC**    (Internet Protocol Device Control) A protocol for controlling media gateways developed by the Technical Advisory Committee, which was convened by Level 3 and others. It analyzes incoming data signals, in band control signals and tones, and sets up and controls the appropriate gateways. It also handles management and reporting. See *media gateway controller*.

**IPDS**    (Intelligent Printer Data Stream) The native format built into IBM laser printers, which accepts fonts and formatted raster images. One of its major functions is its communications protocol that negotiates printer transfers from servers in the network that perform the rasterization. IBM used to make only IPDS printers. Today, many of its printers natively support PostScript and PCL (LaserJet) as well. See *PSF* and *AFP*.

**IP fax**    See *Internet fax*.

**IP gateway**    A device that converts data into the IP protocol. It often refers to a voice-to-IP device that converts an analog voice stream, or a digitized version of the voice, into IP packets. See *ITSP*, *ITXC*, *H.323* and *Nacchio's law*.

**IPI**    (Intelligent Peripheral Interface) A high-speed hard disk interface used with minis and mainframes that transfers data in the 10 to 25 MBytes/sec range. IPI-2 and IPI-3 refer to differences in the command set that they execute. See *hard disk*.

**iPIN**    A Web payment service from iPIN, San Francisco, CA (www.ipin.com). It specializes in premium digital content that is billed to third-party accounts. Internet service providers (ISPs) and Internet content providers (ICPs) provide the billing mechanism from iPIN-generated purchases. See *Web payment service*.

**IPL**    (Initial Program Load) Same as *boot*.

**iPlanet**    The brand name for software from the Sun-Netscape Alliance. Most Netscape products were renamed iPlanet after the joint venture was organized. See *Sun-Netscape Alliance*.

**iPlanet Application Server**    A J2EE-compliant, Web-based application server from the Sun-Netscape Alliance. It supports C, C++ and Java applications, Java servlets, JavaServer Pages (JSPs) and Enterprise JavaBeans. iPlanet Application Server was formerly Netscape Application Server.

**iPlanet Web Server**    A Web server from the Sun-Netscape Alliance that runs under NT, Solaris and HP-UX. It supports JavaServer Pages (JSP) technology, Java servlets and Server-Side JavaScript (SSJS). The Enterprise Edition is the complete package, and the Developers Edition is a lighter-weight version for development only. iPlanet Web Server was formerly Netscape Enterprise Server. See *Java Web Server*.

**ipm**    (1) (Impressions Per Minute) See *ppm*.
    (2) (IPM) (Intel Power Monitor) A utility from Intel that monitors power usage in notebook computers.

**IP multicast**    Transmitting data to a group of selected users at the same time on a TCP/IP network (internal, intranet or Internet). It is used for streaming audio and video over the network, but is also good for downloading a file to multiple users. IP multicast saves network bandwidth, because the files are transmitted as one data stream over the backbone and only split apart to the target stations by the router at the end of the path. See *DVMRP*, *MOSPF* and *PIM*.

**IP network**    A network that uses the TCP/IP protocol, which includes the Internet, intranets and private UNIX networks. See *TCP/IP*.

**IPng**    (IP Next Generation) See *IPv6*.

**I-PNNI**    (Integrated-Private Network-to-Network Interface) An extension to the PNNI routing protocol used in ATM networks that enables IP routers to select paths through the network based on quality of service (QoS). I-PNNI was never completed by the ATM Forum and was superseded by MPLS. See *PNNI*, *MPLS* and *QoS*.

**IPO**    (Initial Public Offering) The first time a company offers shares of stock to the public. While not a computer term per se, many founders, employees and insiders of computer companies have found this acronym more exciting than any tech term they ever heard.

**IP on Everything**    A while back, Vinton Cerf, Senior VP at MCI, who is often called the "Father of the Internet," printed "IP on Everything" on a T-shirt and wore it under his regular shirt to a conference. Meant as a tongue-in-cheek forecast of the future, IP has indeed turned the telecommunications industry upside down. Since the mid-1990s, we've been trying to turn the Internet into a global communications system. However, until the Internet's infrastructure can handle quality of service (QoS), which allows traffic to be prioritized, it cannot support voice and video like a dedicated telephone connection. Reducing the costs of a phone call to zero might justify the jerks and blips, but for routine communications, we still want to "hear a pin drop."

What makes the Internet most attractive is that, once upgraded for QoS, all future innovations come at the edge of the network. In contrast to the public switched telephone network, which must be reprogrammed for each type of new service that is offered, all that is necessary to launch an Internet service is to install the software in the servers, add the client piece to the user's machine and let 'er rip. If it works, more users put the software in their PCs, and another Netscape is born. If not, the Internet keeps on transporting the bits and bytes, and nobody knows any different (see *dumb network*). What's more, the packet switching nature of IP maximizes every microsecond of bandwidth. Circuit-switched voice does not. Half the time, only one person is talking, and pauses between speech go wasted on dedicated circuits.

IP has become the latest religion of the telecom industry, not only by the newer carriers, such as Quest and Level 3, but AT&T, WorldCom and all the incumbents. Almost every telecom carrier has integrated IP in order to provide converged voice and data services. The major carriers control their own Internet backbones and can implement voice over IP with the telephone quality people expect.

The Internet (underscored by IP) has not only affected every business, information systems department and software publisher, but it is changing world communications forever.

**IP over SONET**   See *packet over SONET*.

**IPP**   (Internet Printing Protocol) A printing protocol for the Internet from the IETF. Initially conceived by Novell, Xerox and others, it was moved to the IETF Printer Working Group in order to develop a standard for submitting jobs over the Internet based on the HTTP protocol. It is expected that IPP will interoperate with LPR/LPD. See *printing protocol* and *LPR/LPD*.

**IP phone**   A digital telephone that uses the Internet Telephony (IP) protocol for packets, and a telephony protocol such as H.323 or SIP. See *IP telephony*.

**IP router**   A router that is set up to route IP packets. See *router* and *IP*.

**ips**   (Inches Per Second) The measurement of the speed of tape passing by a read/write head or paper passing through a pen plotter.

**IP SAN**   (Internet Protocol Storage Area Network) See *IP storage*.

**IPSec**   (IP SECurity) A security protocol from the IETF that provides authentication and encryption over the Internet. Unlike SSL, which provides services at layer 4 and secures two applications, IPSec works at layer 3 and secures everything in the network. IPSec is also supported by IPv6. Since IPSec was designed for the IP protocol, it has wide industry support and is expected to become the standard for virtual private networks (VPNs) on the Internet. See *IPv6* and *security protocol*.

**IP Security**   See *IPSec*.

**IP services switch**   A network switch that funnels traffic from DSL and/or cable modem aggregation devices to various carriers' networks based on type of application or type of service required. It supports authentication, traffic accounting, high-level protocols such as IP and MPLS. An IP services switch lets carriers fine tune their service offerings, as well as charge for traffic on a per-byte basis. Also known as an "IP services router," it is the successor to the broadband remote access server (BRAS), and supports greater bandwidth and more functionality such as support for the IPSec security protocol.

**IP space**   A group of IP addresses. See *namespace*.

**IP spoofing**   Inserting the IP address of an authorized user into the transmission of an unauthorized user in order to gain illegal access to a computer system. Routers and other firewall implementations can be programmed to identify this discrepancy. See *firewall*.

**IP storage**    (Internet Protocol storage)  Using IP and Gigabit Ethernet to build storage area networks (SANs). Traditional SANs were developed using the Fibre Channel transport, because it provided gigabit speeds compared to 10 and 100 Mbps Ethernet used to build messaging networks at that time. Fibre Channel equipment has been costly, and interoperability between different vendors' switches was not completely standardized. Since Gigabit Ethernet and IP have become commonplace, IP storage enables familiar network protocols to be used, and IP allows SANs to be extended throughout the world. Network management software and experienced professionals in IP networks are also widely available.

iSCSI, iFCP and mFCP are protocols that turn SCSI and Fibre Channel Protocol commands into TCP/IP. Native iSCSI and iFCP host adapters and storage arrays are expected in late 2001.

**IP Switch**    A high-speed routing and switching system from Nokia IP Routing, a business unit of Nokia Telecommunications, Inc., Sunnyvale, CA (www.ipsilon.com). Originally developed by Ipsilon Networks of Palo Alto, CA, the IP switch routes IP traffic over ATM switches using a proprietary control protocol.

The IP Switch Controller analyzes the first frame of a message and lets short-lived traffic, such as DNS and SNMP queries, flow through the Controller back to the switch. When long-duration traffic is encountered, it sets up a virtual circuit in an ATM switch, and remaining packets flow at high speed. IP Switch uses the General Switch Management Protocol (GSMP) for call setup and the Ipsilon Flow Management Protocol (IFMP) for flow redirection. See *IP switching*.

**IP switching**    Switching TCP/IP packets at high speed. Ipsilon's IP Switch started the trend and various vendors followed suit with different approaches, including Cisco's tag switching and 3Com's Fast IP. The goal was to switch IP packets faster than traditional router-based layer 3 forwarding. Subsequent routers have improved immensely and can forward packets at even faster speeds while inspecting each and every packet. See *layer 3 switch*, *IP Switch* and *tag switching*.

**IP telephony**    The two-way transmission of audio over a packet-switched IP network (TCP/IP network). When used in a private intranet or WAN, it is generally known as "voice over IP," or "VoIP." When the transport is the public Internet or the Internet backbone from a major carrier, it is generally called "Internet telephony." However, the terms IP telephony, Internet telephony and VoIP are often used interchangeably.

IP telephony over controlled Internet backbones or an enterprise's own private network can provide quality matching that of the PSTN. All major carriers have implemented IP telephony behind the scenes, especially for international calls. Over the public Internet, voice quality varies considerably; however, protocols that support quality of service (QoS) are expected in time, and this may improve.

Starting in the mid-1990s, advertiser-supported, free telephone service from PC to PC or between phones and PCs using the public Internet became popular, especially for international calls. However, the quality was often erratic, and regular international and domestic rates have dropped significantly since then.

The integration of packet-switched IP with the traditional SS7-based telephone system is a complex undertaking with numerous protocols competing for attention. However, the Internet and its TCP/IP protocol suite have turned the telecom industry upside down starting in the late 1990s. IP is expected to become the universal transport for all voice, data and video communications worldwide. Packet networks are considered more scalable than traditional circuit-switched telephone networks, and they naturally integrate with all Internet-based applications. Clicking a button to speak with a customer rep while on that company's Web site is a perfect example. See *ITSP*, *ITXC* and *IP on Everything*.

**Not Quite IP Telephony**
We can be certain that they didn't have the IP protocol in mind when they set up this telephone switchboard in 1882. It was used to switch phone calls between all the lawyers in Richmond, Virginia. *(Image courtesy of AT&T.)*

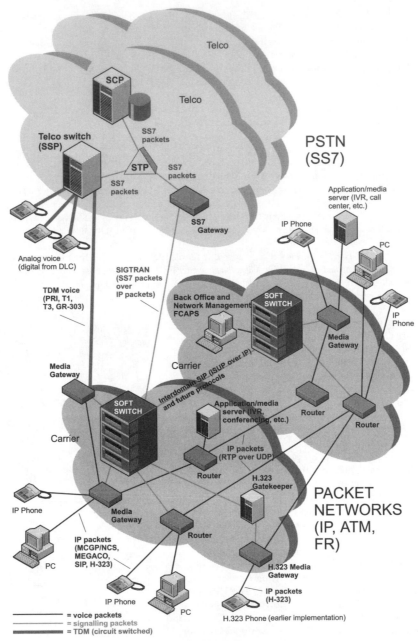

**IP Telephony**

This illustration shows the interaction between the traditional telco system and IP carriers, which are often one in the same. In order to understand the flow between these devices, it is important to note the difference between voice packets (blue lines) and signaling (red lines). *(Illustration assistance courtesy of GNP Computers and Pulver.com.)*

**IP tunneling**    Carrying a foreign protocol within a TCP/IP packet. For example, IPX can be encapsulated and transmitted via TCP/IP.

**IPv4**    (Internet Protocol Version 4) The current version of the IP protocol. See *IPv6*.

**IPv6**    (Internet Protocol Version 6) The next generation IP protocol. Started in 1991, the specification was completed in 1997 by the Internet Engineering Task Force (IETF). IPv6 is backward compatible with and is designed to fix the shortcomings of IPv4, such as data security and maximum number of user addresses.

IPv6 increases the address space from 32 to 128 bits, providing for an unlimited (for all intents and purposes) number of networks and systems. It also supports quality of service (QoS) parameters for realtime audio and video. The draft version of IPv6 was originally called "IP Next Generation" (IPng).

**IP voice**    See *IP telephony*.

**IPX**    (Internetwork Packet EXchange) A NetWare communications protocol used to route messages from one node to another. IPX packets include network addresses and can be routed from one network to another. An IPX packet can occasionally get lost when crossing networks, thus IPX does not guarantee delivery of a complete message. Either the application has to provide that control or NetWare's SPX protocol must be used.

IPX provides services at layers 3 and 4 of the OSI model (network and transport layers). See *SPX*.

**IQ/Objects**    A family of business intelligence products (viewer, query and report tool) from IQ Software. The company was acquired by Information Advantage in 1998, and IQ/Objects products were absorbed into the MyEureka product line. See *MyEureka*.

**IQ/SmartServer**    A reporting tool from IQ Software, which was acquired by Information Advantage in 1998 and turned into MyEureka Report Server. See *MyEureka*.

**IR**    (1) (Industry Remarketer) Same as *VAR* or *VAD*.
(2) See *infrared*.
(3) See *information resources*.

**IRC**    See *Internet Relay Chat*.

**IrDA**    (Infrared Data Association, Walnut Creek, CA, www.irda.org) A membership organization founded in 1993 and dedicated to developing standards for wireless, infrared transmission systems between computers. With IrDA ports, a laptop or PDA can exchange data with a desktop computer or use a printer without a cable connection. IrDA requires line-of-sight transmission like a TV remote control. IrDA products began to appear in 1995. The LaserJet 5P was one of the first printers with a built-in IrDA port.

IrDA is comprised of the IrDA Serial IR physical layer (IrDA-SIR), which provides a half-duplex connection of up to 115.2 Kbps. This speed allows the use of a low-cost UART chip; however, higher non-UART, high-speed extensions up to 4 Mbps for Fast Infrared (FIR) have also been defined. IrDA uses the Infrared Link Access Protocol (IrLAP), an adaptation of HDLC, as its data link protocol. The Infrared Link Management Protocol (IrLMP) is also used to provide a mechanism for handshaking and multiplexing of two or more different data streams simultaneously.

**IrDA port**    A transmitter/receiver for infrared signals. See *IrDA*.

**IRG**    (1) (InterRecord Gap) See *interrecord gap*.
(2) (Internet Research Group, Los Altos, CA, www.irgintl.com) A research and consulting firm founded in 1993 that specializes in developing business stategies for Internet-related companies. In 1997, its research and publishing division was formed to provide in-depth reports and analyses of the market.

**Iridium**    Washington, DC–based Iridium World Communications was the world's first satellite-based phone and paging service. Using a handheld phone and a combination of low-earth orbit (LEO) satellites and cellular partners, Iridium customers could access the satellites or local cellular facilities. Announced in 1990 and completed in 1998 at a cost of $6 billion, Iridium went into Chapter 11 in August 1999. In late 2000, Iridium Satellite was formed by new investors to resurrect the system and offer services once again. See *LEO* and *Globalstar*.

**IRIS printer**    A large-format color printer from the Iris Graphics division of CreoScitex (www.creoscitex.com) that is used for digital proofing. Iris printers use a patented continuous ink jet technology to produce consistent, continuous-tone, photorealistic output on several varieties of paper, canvas, silk, linen and other low-fiber textiles. Iris prints are widely noted for their color accuracy and ability to match printing and proofing standards. They are also known for their low-cost consumables compared to other technologies.

**IRIX**    A UNIX-based operating system from SGI that is used in its computer systems from desktop to supercomputer. It is an enhanced version of UNIX System V Release 4. IRIX integrates the X Window system with OpenGL, creating the first realtime 3-D X environment.

**IrLAP**    See *IrDA.*

**IrLMP**    See *IrDA.*

**IRM**    (1) (Information Resource Management) See *Information Systems* and *information management.*
    (2) (Inherited Rights Mask) In NetWare 3.x and 4.x, a filter that defines the access rights that have been passed down from the parent directory.

**Irma**    An earlier trade name for a variety of host connectivity hardware and software products originally developed by Digital Communications Associates (DCA) and later acquired by Attachmate Corporation. Irma was not an acronym, rather it was the lady's name. Although the Irma line no longer exists, its technology was absorbed into many of Attachmate's subsequent terminal emulation products for mainframes and AS/400s. See *Irma board.*

**Irma board**    The first 3270 emulator for PCs. Introduced in 1982, it was the first product to provide PC to IBM host connectivity. Irma was originally spelled all caps (IRMA) and was developed by Digital Communications Associates (DCA), which later merged with and became part of Attachmate Corporation.

**Irmalan**    An earlier family of gateway programs from Attachmate Corporation, Bellevue, WA (www.attachmate.com) that allowed PCs to connect to NetWare, NetBIOS and VINES networks to access an SNA host. Irmalan gateways supported IEEE 802.2, SDLC (via modem) and DFT environments.

**iron oxide**    The material used to coat the surfaces of magnetic tapes and lower-capacity disks.

**IRQ**    (Interrupt ReQuest) A hardware interrupt on a PC. There are 16 IRQ lines used to signal the CPU that a peripheral event has started or terminated. Except for PCI devices, two devices cannot use the same line. If a new expansion board is preset to the IRQ used by an existing board, one of them must be changed. This was an enormous headache in earlier machines.
    Starting with the 286 (introduced in 1982), two 8259A controller chips have been cascaded together for a total of 16 IRQs (the first PCs had only one chip and eight IRQs). However, IRQ 2 is lost because it is used to connect to the second chip. IRQ 9 may be available for general use, as most VGA cards do not require an IRQ.

PCI to the Rescue    The PCI bus allows IRQs to be shared, which helps solve the problem of limited IRQs available on a PC. For example, if there were only one IRQ left over after ISA devices were given their required IRQs, all PCI devices could share it. In a PCI-only machine, there cannot be insufficient IRQs, as all can be shared.

| IRQ | Assignment | IRQ | Assignment |
|-----|------------|-----|------------|
| 0 | System timer | 9 | VGA, 3270 emulation** |
| 1 | PS/2 port | 10 | ** |
| 2 | Connects to IRQ 9 | 11 | ** |
| 3 | COM2, COM4 | 12 | PS/2 port |
| 4 | COM1, COM3 | 13 | Math coprocessor |
| 5 | Sound | 14 | IDE primary |
| 6 | Floppy disk | 15 | IDE secondary |
| 7 | LPT1 | | |
| 8 | Realtime clock | ** | *For general use.* |

**IRQ steering** See *PCI steering*.

**IRTF** See *Internet Research Task Force*.

**IS** See *Information Systems*.

**IS-41** (Interim Standard-41) The protocol for passing cellular subscriber information from one carrier to another. IS-41 allowed mobile travelers to roam across the country. Prior to IS-41, calling mobile phone users outside of their home territory meant knowing what area they were in at that moment and dialing a special number to reach them.

**IS-54** (Interim Standard-54) The first generation of the TDMA digital cellular system that was released in early 1991. See *IS-136*.

**IS-95** (Interim Standard-95) The CDMA standard for digital cellular in the U.S. Operating in the 800MHz band and the 1.9GHz PCS band, IS-95 is also known as cdmaOne by the CDMA Development Group (CDG)—although network operators use their own brands, such as Sprint PCS.

IS-95B adds data capability up to 64 Kbps that is integrated with voice. IS95C was an earlier designation for cdma2000, the 3G path for cdmaOne systems. See *cdma2000* and *CDMA*.

**IS-136** (Interim Standard-136) The second generation of the TDMA digital cellular system. TDMA operates in North America in the 800MHz band and 1.9GHz PCS band. First introduced in 1994, IS-136 is also known as "Digital AMPS" and "D-AMPS." See *TDMA* and *IS-54*.

**ISA** (1) (Industry Standard Architecture) Pronounced "eye-suh." An expansion bus commonly used in PCs. It accepts plug-in boards that control the sound, video display and other peripherals. Most PCs today have a combination of ISA and PCI slots; however, many no longer support ISA, and it is expected to be obsolete by the mid 2000s.

Originally called the "AT bus," it was first used in the IBM AT, extending the 8-bit bus to 16 bits. Earlier ISA PCs provided a mix of 8 and 16-bit slots. Today, PCs have only 16-bit ISA slots. See *PC data buses*.

(2) (Interactive Services Association, Silver Spring, MD, www.isa.net) A trade group for the online industry originally founded in 1981 as the Videotex Industry Association (VIA). Members are online services, service bureaus and hardware and software companies, all providing products for users with a computer and modem.

**ISAM** (Indexed Sequential Access Method) A common disk access method that stores data sequentially, while maintaining an index of key fields to all the records in the file for direct access. The sequential order would be the one most commonly used for batch processing and printing (account number, name, etc.).

**ISAPI** (Internet Server API) A programming interface on Internet Information Server (IIS), Microsoft's Web server. Using ISAPI function calls, Web pages can invoke programs that are

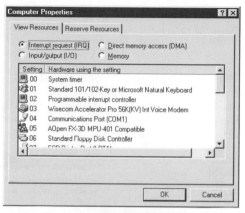

**IRQ Settings**
This display shows the typical IRQ settings on most modern-day PCs. To obtain such details, see **Win Technical details**.

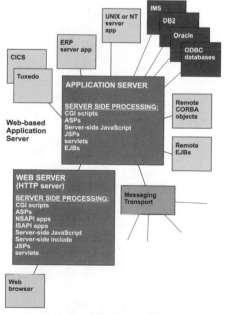

**Server-Side Processing**
This illustration shows the various methods used to deploy server-side processing. ISAPI applications are only one technique used in Web servers.

written as DLLs on the server, typically to access data in a database. IIS comes with a DLL that allows embedded queries to access ODBC-compliant databases. ISAPI is an alternative to using CGI scripts on Microsoft Web servers. The counterpart to ISAPI on the client side is WinInet. See *WinInet*.

**ISC**    (Internet Software Consortium, Redwood City, www.isc.org) An organization founded by Paul Vixie and Rick Adams in 1994 and later sponsored by UUNET and other Internet companies. ISC is devoted to supporting and disseminating key Internet protocols, such as BIND, DHCP and INN, and its reference implementations are used by major ISPs. See also *CISSP*.

**iSCSI**    (Internet SCSI) A protocol that serializes SCSI commands and converts them to TCP/IP. See *IP storage*.

**ISDN**    (Integrated Services Digital Network) An international telecommunications standard for providing a digital service from the customer's premises to the dial-up telephone network. ISDN turns one existing wire pair into two channels and four wire pairs into 23 channels for the delivery of voice, data or video. Unlike an analog modem, which converts digital signals into an equivalency in audio frequencies, ISDN deals only with digital transmission. Analog telephones and fax machines are used over ISDN lines, but their signals are converted into digital by the ISDN modem.

ISDN uses 64 Kbps circuit-switched channels, called "B channels" (bearer channels), to carry voice and data. It uses a separate D channel (delta channel) for control signals. The D channel signals the carrier's voice switch to make calls, put them on hold and activate features such as conference calling and call forwarding. It also receives information about incoming calls,

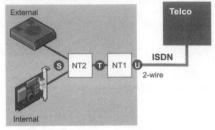

Terminal Adapter (U.S.)

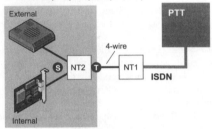

Terminal Adapter (Europe, Japan, etc.)

**The Terminal Adapter**
TAs in the U.S. generally have a built-in NT1 and attach via a two-wire "U" interface. In Europe and Japan, the NT1 is installed by the telephone company and attaches to the TA via a four-wire "T" interface. The NT2 component, which is built into most devices, is a logical interface for multiple access and attaches via the "S" interface.

**ISDN SERVICES**

**Basic Rate Interface (BRI)**
Two 64 Kbps B Channels, one 16 Kbps D Channel

( B )        ( B )        ( **D** )

64 Kbps    64 Kbps    16 Kbps

Bonded ( B ) + ( B ) = 128 Kbps

**Primary Rate Interface (PRI)**
23 64 Kbps B Channels, 1 64 Kbps D Channel

( D )( B )( B )( B )( B )( B )( B )( B )( B )( B )( B )( B )

( B )( B )( B )( B )( B )( B )( B )( B )( B )( B )( B )( B )

**Typical ISDN SOHO Hookup**

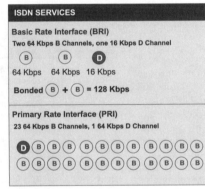

**Typical SOHO Installation**
An ISDN terminal adapter with phone support (ISDN modem) allows a telephone, fax machine and PC to communicate via the ISDN service.

**Typical ISDN LAN Hookup**

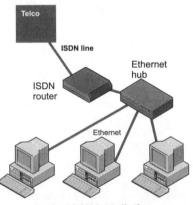

**Typical LAN Installation**
LANs typically connect to ISDN via a router, which enables multiple users to share the available channels. For Internet access, the router supplies temporary IP addresses to each of the nodes. Routers may also provide analog phone support.

such as the identity of the caller. Since the D channel connects directly to the telephone system's SS7 signaling network, ISDN calls are dialed much faster than regular telephone calls.

ISDN's basic service is BRI (Basic Rate Interface), which is made up of two 64 Kbps B channels and one 16 Kbps D channel (2B+D). If both channels are combined into one, called "bonding," the total data rate becomes 128 Kbps and is four and a half times the bandwidth of a V.34 modem (28.8 Kbps).

ISDN's high-speed service is PRI (Primary Rate Interface). It provides 23 B channels and one 64 Kbps D channel (23B+D), which is equivalent to the 24 channels of a T1 line. When several channels are bonded together, high data rates can be achieved. For example, it is common to bond six channels for quality videoconferencing at 384 Kbps. In Europe, PRI includes 30 B channels and one D channel, equivalent to an E1 line. See *SS7*.

**Connecting an ISDN Device**     Connecting ISDN to a personal computer requires a network terminator (NT1) and ISDN terminal adapter (TA). The NT1 plugs into the two-wire line from the telephone company with an RJ-11 connector and provides four-wire output to the TA. Within the U.S., the NT1 is typically built into the TA; but in Europe and Japan, they are separate devices.

Often called an "ISDN modem" because the device may support an analog telephone or fax machine, the TA itself is technically not a modem, because it provides a digital to digital connection. External TAs plug into the serial port while internal TAs plug into an expansion slot. Some TAs hook into the parallel port for higher speed. The TA may also include an analog modem and automatically switch between analog and digital depending on the type of call.

TAs support bonding for Internet operation, which links the channels together for higher speed, but the ISP must provide the Multilink PPP protocol (MPPP) to support this operation.

Although announced in the mid-1980s, it took more than a decade before ISDN usage became widespread. When people asked when would it arrive, the answer was ISDN: "I Still Don't Know."

**ISDN adapter**     See *ISDN terminal adapter*.

**ISDN bonding**     The bridging of two or more ISDN channels to achieve higher data rates. See *ISDN*.

**ISDN modem**     An alternative name for ISDN terminal adapter. The term is widely used, because the unit looks like a modem, connects to the same serial port as a modem and may support analog phones. See *ISDN terminal adapter*.

**ISDN router**     A device that enables several users on a network to access the Internet via ISDN. Also known as an ISDN LAN modem, it contains a BRI ISDN port and an Ethernet port. It may also provide several Ethernet ports, which lets it serve as a central Ethernet hub for a small workgroup. Access to the unit for configuration and monitoring is typically done via a Telnet connection or Web browser or both. See *modem router* and *ISDN*.

**ISDN TA**     See *ISDN terminal adapter*.

**ISDN terminal adapter**     A device that adapts a computer to a digital ISDN line. Like a modem, it plugs into the serial port of the computer or into an expansion slot. Some terminal adapters use the parallel port for higher speed. The adapter may also include a regular data or fax/modem and switch automatically between analog and digital depending on the type of call.

**ISEB**     (Information Systems Examination Board, UK, www.bcs.org.uk/iseb/) A subsidiary of the British Computer Society (BCS) that provides industry-recognized professional training and qualifications for IS competency, ability and performance. ISEB works with Netherlands-based Stichting NLnet and EXIN to develop ITIL and ISO 9000–based products and services. See *ITIL*, *BCS* and *ISO 9000*.

**I Seek You**     See *ICQ*.

**iSeries**     The renaming of IBM's AS/400 under the eserver brand. An AS/400 server is an iSeries eserver. Prices for the iSeries ranged from $20,000 to $100,000 in 2000, when the name change occurred. See *IBM server series* and *AS/400*.

**IS-IS**   (Intermediate System to Intermediate System)  An ISO protocol that provides dynamic routing between routers. IS-IS is an interior gateway protocol (IGP) and link state protocol. See *IGP* and *link state protocol*.

**ISM band**   (Industrial, Scientific and Medical band)  A part of the radio spectrum that can be used by anybody without a license in most countries. The most commonly used ISM bands and their applications and wattage follow:

```
902 to 928MHz
Spread spectrum      1 W
Microwave ovens      750 W
Industrial heaters   up to 100 kW
Military radar       up to 1000 kW

2.4 to 2.4835GHz
Spread spectrum      1 W
Microwave ovens      900 W

5.725 to 5.850GHz
Spread spectrum      1 W
```

**ISO**   (The International Organization for Standardization, Geneva, www.iso.ch)  An organization that sets international standards, founded in 1946. The U.S. member body is ANSI. ISO deals with all fields except electrical and electronics, which is governed by the older International Electrotechnical Commission (IEC). With regard to information processing, ISO and IEC created JTC1, the Joint Technical Committee for information technology.

It carries out its work through more than 160 technical committees and 2,300 subcommittees and working groups, and is made up of standards organizations from more than 75 countries, some of them serving as secretariats for these technical bodies.

**ISO 13346**   A standard format for a rewritable optical disk from the International Standards Association. It specifies the logical format of the disk so that removable cartridges can be interchanged among different platforms.

**ISO 9000**   A family of standards and guidelines for quality in the manufacturing and service industries from the International Standards Association. ISO 9000 defines the criteria for what should be measured. ISO 9001 covers design and development. ISO 9002 covers production, installation and service, and ISO 9003 covers final testing and inspection. ISO 9000 certification does not guarantee product quality. It ensures that the processes that develop the product are documented and performed in a quality manner.

Initially popular in Europe, ISO 9000 certification began to increase in the U.S. in the early 1990s. Certification requires exacting documentation and demonstrations in practice over time. The process, which can take up to a year, involves two major players in addition to the company being certified. A consultant provides (and may help implement) a plan for documenting the company's ISO system. Once documented, a registrar interviews the company's management and line staff to make sure that the new system, as documented, has been effectively implemented. Only a few dozen companies worldwide are authorized to conduct such audits for the issuance of ISO 9000 certificates. See *ISO* and *ISO 9000-3*.

**ISO 9000-3**   The ISO 9000 standards can be applied to the design and development of software, just as they do to the manufacture of hard goods and the delivery of services. In such instances, these standards have to be appropriately interpreted because of the more complex nature of the software design, development, distribution and installation process. In 1987, the ISO 9000-3 guidelines were published by the ISO Technical Committee 17 (TC 176) to address these needs of the IT community. See *ISO 9000*.

**ISO 9660**   A standard CD-ROM file format from the International Standards Association (ISO). Evolving from the High Sierra format, ISO 9660 specifies the directory format of the disc, while the physical format is defined in the Yellow Book. ISO 9660 provides for read-only interoperability between different computer platforms, allowing for example Macs and Windows PCs to read from the same disc. See *UDF*.

**ISOC**   See *Internet Society*.

**isochronous**    Time dependent. Realtime voice, video and telemetry are examples of isochronous data.

**Isochronous Ethernet**    National Semiconductor's enhancement to Ethernet for handling realtime voice and video. It adds 96 ISDN channels to standard 10 Mbps Ethernet and runs over the same Category 3 UTP that most 10BaseT networks use. Each ISDN B channel is 64 Kbps, providing a total bandwidth of 6.144 Mbps that can be used for videoconferencing. A D channel and maintenance channel are also provided.

Isochronous Ethernet can be integrated into an existing network by adding an Isochronous Ethernet hub in the wiring closet and replacing standard Ethernet with Isochronous Ethernet adapters.

**isometric view**    In computer graphics, a rendering of a 3-D object that eliminates the distortion of shape created by true perspective. In isometric views, all lines on each axis are parallel to each other, and the lines do not converge. Such drawings are commonly used in technical illustrations because of their clarity, simplicity and speed of creation.

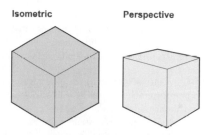

**Isometric            Perspective**

**Isometric View**
Isometric views of objects are made to show as much detail as possible, typically with technical drawings. In the normal perspective, all lines converge in a vanishing point, and detail at the farthest ends can be difficult to see.

**isotropic**    Refers to properties, such as transmission speed, that are the same regardless of the direction that is measured. Contrast with *anisotropic*.

**ISP**    See *Internet service provider*.

**ISP-based payment service**    A Web payment service that uses third-party ISPs to provide the billing for customer purchases. The advantage to an ISP-based service is that as soon as the ISP supports it, all of its customers can make purchases on the Web. See *iPIN*, **WISP** and *Web payment service*.

**ISPF**    (Interactive System Productivity Facility) A full-screen editor from IBM for writing application programs. It is also used to develop dialogs for interactive terminal sessions. Program Development Facility (PDF) provides enhancements to ISPF, including interfaces to languages such as REXX.

**ISR**    (Interrupt Service Routine) Software routine that is executed in response to an interrupt.

**issue tracking**    The management of change requests. It might be a stand-alone system or part of a help desk system that tracks bug reports.

**ISV**    (Independent Software Vendor) A person or company that develops software. It implies an organization that specializes in software only and is not part of a computer systems or hardware manufacturer. ISVs generally create application software rather than system software such as operating systems and database management systems. Contrast with *IHV*.

**IT**    (Information Technology) Processing information by computer. The latest title for the information processing industry.

**ITAA**    (Information Technology Association of America, Arlington, VA, www.itaa.org) Formerly the Association of Data Processing Service Organizations (ADAPSO). A membership organization founded in 1960 that defines performance standards, improves management methods and monitors government regulations in the computer services field.

**Itanium**    The first model of Intel's next-generation IA-64 CPU architecture. Code named Merced and expected in 2001, Itanium is also expected to run x86 and PA-RISC software natively with clock speeds at 700MHz and beyond. See *IA-64*, *future Intel chips* and *Sledgehammer*.

**item**    One unit or member of a group. See *data item*.

**iteration**    One repetition of a sequence of instructions or events. For example, in a program loop, one iteration is once through the instructions in the loop. See *iterative development*.

**iterative development**    A discipline for developing systems based on the Spiral Model introduced in 1988 by Professor Barry Boehme at the University of Southern California. Each of the four project stages (inception, elaboration, construction and transition) is broken down into a number of iterations. Each iteration, consisting of requirements, analysis and design, implementation and testing, results in the release of an executable subset of the final product, which grows incrementally from iteration to iteration to become the final system.

**iterative operation**    An operation that requires successive executions of instructions or processes.

**ITI**    (Information Technology Industry Council, Washington, DC, www.itic.org) Formerly the Computer and Business Equipment Manufacturers Association (CBEMA), founded in 1916. ITI is a membership organization composed of approximately 30 large companies. Its mission is to produce market-driven voluntary standards for information technology in the U.S. and abroad. It sponsors several dozen committees that used to be given alphabetic names such as X3J4, but now fall under the NCITS (National Committee for Information Technology Standards) umbrella.

**ITIL**    (Infrastructure Technology Information Library, www.itil.co.uk) One of the more comprehensive as well as non-proprietary and publicly-available sets of guidelines for "best practice" IT services management. Each library module provides a code of practice intended to improve IT efficiencies, reduce risks and increase the effectiveness and quality of IT services management and infrastructure.

In the late 1980s, the library was conceived by the Central Computer and Telecommunications Agency (CCTA), a U.K. government agency. Although ITIL services and training were popular in Europe, it took more than a decade before they were introduced to the U.S. private sector by a number of consulting firms such as Andersen Consulting, Ernst & Young, Hewlett-Packard (HP), Pink Elephant and Price Waterhouse Coopers.  ITIL certification examinations are available through EXIN in the Netherlands.

**I-time**    See *instruction time*.

**ITMS (AICPA)**    (Information Technology Membership Section, American Institute of Certified Public Accountants, New York, www.aicpa.org) A membership group of the AICPA whose mission is to provide value to their clients and employers through effective application of information technologies. Volunteers serve on committees supported by the Information Technology Team professional staff.

The ITMS provides a forum for all AICPA members, including public practice, industry, education and government, to exchange ideas and benefit from each other's experiences. It helps CPAs improve their competency in technology and keep abreast of the latest changes.

**ITR**    See *Internet Talk Radio*.

**ITS**    (Intelligent Transportation Systems) An umbrella term for advanced automation in mobile vehicles. See *IDB*.

**ITSEC**    See *NCSC*.

**ITSP**    (Internet Telephony Service Provider) An organization, such as an ISP or telephone company (CLEC, LEC, etc.), that supports IP telephony. Using the Internet as the primary backbone, it allows customers to make phone-to-phone calls or PC-to-phone calls. The majority of customers use an ITSP to save money on international calls, and the quality can vary substantially due to the inconsistency of the Internet. The ITSP uses IP gateways to convert between voice and IP packets. See *IP gateway* and *ITXC*.

**ITU**    (International Telecommunications Union, Geneva, Switzerland, www.itu.ch) Formerly the CCITT (Consultative Committee for International Telephony and Telegraphy), it is an international organization founded in 1865 and headquartered in Geneva that sets communications standards. The ITU is comprised of more than 150 member countries. The Telecommunications Standards Section (TSS) is one of four organs of the ITU. Any specification with an ITU-T or ITU-TSS designation refers to the TSS organ.

**ITU-T**    See *ITU*.

**ITU-TSS**    See *ITU*.

**ITV**   See *interactive TV*.

**ITXC**   (Internet Telephony Exchange Carrier Corporation, Princeton, NJ, www.itxc.net) An Internet telephony communications organization that provides routing, authorization and settlement (billing) services to ITSPs (Internet Telephony Service Providers) throughout the world. It provides routing information to ITSPs that enable the call to be received by a cooperating ITSP at the other end. The majority of ITXC traffic is international phone calls. Its group of affiliations form ITXC.net, a telephony network dynamically managed over the public network with more than 100 POPs worldwide. See *ITSP* and *SNARC*.

**IV**   See *interactive video*.

**IVD**   (Interactive VideoDisc) See *interactive video*.

**IVDS**   (Interactive Video and Data Services) The wireless implementation of interactive TV. In 1994, an additional part of the VHF television spectrum (218–219 MHz), which was divided into 1450 licenses, was auctioned to the highest bidders by the U.S. government. Organizations that own these licenses will be able to provide interactive television services to subscribers in their jurisdictions. See *interactive TV*.

**Iverson notation**   A set of symbols developed by Kenneth Iverson for writing statements in APL.

**IVR**   (Interactive Voice Response) An automated telephone answering system that responds with a voice menu and allows the user to make choices and enter information via the keypad. IVR systems are widely used in call centers, as well as a replacement for human switchboard operators. The system may also integrate database access and fax response. See *ACD*, *CTI* and *V-Commerce*.

**iWARP**   A systolic-array microprocessor from Intel that was originally funded by DARPA and developed by Carnegie-Mellon.

**I-way**   (Information SuperhighWAY) Slang for the *Internet*.

**IWS**   See *iPlanet Web Server*.

**IX**   (Internet eXchange) See *NAP* and *CIX*.

**IXA**   (Internet EXchange Architecture) A family of chips from Intel that are designed to enable network device manufacturers to build custom systems. Introduced in 1999, the first models are the StongARM-based IXP 1200 (Internet Exchange Processor) designed for general packet handling with six processors around its core. The IXE 2412 (Internet Exchange Engine) is a core component for building workgroup switches, and the IXF 6400 (Internet Exchange Forwarder) is designed for building carrier-class switches with port speeds up to OC-48. See *StrongARM*.

**IXC**   **(1)** (IntereXchange Carrier) An organization that provides interstate (long distance) communications services within the U.S., which includes AT&T, MCI WorldCom, Sprint and more than 700 others. See *LATA*.

**(2)** (IXC Communications Inc., Austin, TX, www.ixc-comm.com) A wholesale telecommunications provider that offers private line, long-distance, frame relay and ATM services over its nationwide fiber-optic network. IXC is an IXC.

**IXE**   (Internet EXchange Engine) See *IXA*.

**IXF**   (Internet EXchange Forwarder) See *IXA*.

**IXP**   **(1)** (Internet eXchange Point) See *NAP* and *CIX*.
**(2)** (Internet EXchange Processor) See *IXA*.

**IZE**   A DOS text management system that was noted for its flexible searching capabilities. Originally developed by Persoft Corporation, it was acquired by Retrieval Dynamics in 1990, which later closed its doors.

**J** A high-level mathematical programming language developed by Kenneth Iverson, the author of APL. J is the successor to APL and runs on a variety of platforms, including DOS, Windows, OS/2 and the Macintosh. The Windows version can be used as a calculating engine for Visual Basic, in which Visual Basic is used to write the file handling and user interface portions, and J is used to program the math.

**J++** See *Visual J++*.

**J2EE** (Java 2 Platform, Enterprise Edition) A platform from Sun for building Web-based enterprise applications. J2EE services are performed in the middle tier between the user's browser and the enterprise's databases and legacy information systems. J2EE comprises a specification, reference implementation and set of testing suites. Its core component is Enterprise JavaBeans (EJBs), followed by JavaServer Pages (JSPs) and Java servlets and a variety of interfaces for linking to the information resources in the enterprise. The J2EE interfaces include JDBC for databases, JNDI for directories, JTA for transactions, JMS for messaging, JavaMail for e-mail systems and JavaIDL for CORBA connectivity. In December 1999, J2EE Version 1.2 was introduced as the first formal release of the specification. Java Connectors are interfaces to a variety of legacy applications. See *EJB, JSP, servlet, Java Connector, Java 2* and *J2ME*.

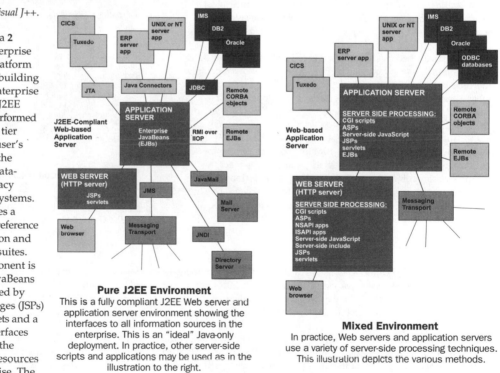

**Pure J2EE Environment**
This is a fully compliant J2EE Web server and application server environment showing the interfaces to all information sources in the enterprise. This is an "ideal" Java-only deployment. In practice, other server-side scripts and applications may be used as in the illustration to the right.

**Mixed Environment**
In practice, Web servers and application servers use a variety of server-side processing techniques. This illustration depicts the various methods.

**J2ME**　　(Java 2 Platform, Micro Edition) A version of Java 2 for small devices such as PDAs and consumer appliances. The Connected Limited Device Configuration (CLDC) provides the programming interface for wireless applications. The Mobile Information Device Profile (MIDP) provides support for a graphical interface, networking and storage. J2ME uses the K Virtual Machine (KVM), a specialized virtual machine for devices with limited memory. See *midlet*.

**J2SE**　　(Java 2 platform, Standard Edition) See *Java 2*.

**Jabber**　　An open source instant messaging system based on XML with client software available for Windows, Mac, Linux and Palm. In order to use Jabber, users must register with a Jabber server either from Jabber.org or some other provider. Access to the AOL, ICQ, MSN and Yahoo! instant messaging services is available with Jabber, providing you have IM accounts with those services and that the appropriate software "Transports" are running the Jabber server. Jabber.org (www.jabber.org) provides open source support for Jabber, and Jabber.com (www.jabber.com) provides commercial products for the system. See *instant messaging*.

**jack**　　A receptacle into which a plug is inserted. Same as *socket*.

**jacket**　　A plastic housing that contains a floppy disk. The 5.25" disk is built into a flexible jacket; the 3.25" disk uses a rigid jacket.

**Jacquard loom**　　An automated loom that transformed the 19th century textile industry and became the inspiration for future calculating and tabulating machines. Developed by the French silk-weaver, Joseph-Marie Jacquard (1752–1834), it used punched cards to control its operation.

Although punched cards were used in earlier looms and music boxes, Jacquard's loom was a vast improvement and allowed complex patterns to be created swiftly. The loom was inspiration to Charles Babbage and, later, to Herman Hollerith who developed the first commercial punched card equipment.

**JAD**　　(Joint Application Development) An approach to systems analysis and design introduced by IBM in 1977 that emphasizes teamwork between user and technician. Small groups meet to determine system objectives and the business transactions to be supported. They are run by a neutral facilitator who can move the group toward well-defined goals. Results include a prototype of the proposed system.

**The Jacquard Loom**
The binary principle embodied in the punched-card operation of the loom was inspiration for the data processing machines to come. *(Image courtesy of The Computer Museum History Center, www.computerhistory.org)*

**jaggies**　　See *aliasing*.

**JAM**　　(JYACC Application Manager) An application development system for client/server environments from JYACC, Inc., New York (www.jyacc.com). It supports Windows, Mac and Motif clients and most all UNIX servers and VMS. It supports over 20 databases and includes its own database (JDB) for prototyping. JAM/CASE allows CASE information to be moved into JAM. JAM/TPi integrates JAM with the Tuxedo and Encina TP monitors.

**JAR**　　(1) (Java ARchive) A file format used to distribute a Java application. It contains all the resources required to install and run a Java program in a single compressed file. JARs are also used to distribute JavaBeans.

(2) A compression program for backup archiving from ARJ Software, Inc., Norwood, MA (www.arjsoftware.com). JAR is similar to ARJ, but files are not compatible. See *ARJ*.

**Java**　　A programming language designed to generate applications that can run on all hardware platforms, small, medium and large, without modification. Developed by Sun, it has been promoted and geared heavily for the Web, both for public Web sites and intranets. Developed by Sun, Java was modeled after C++, and Java programs can be called from within HTML documents or launched stand alone. When a Java program runs from a Web page, it is called a "Java applet." When it is run on a Web server, it is called a "servlet."

Java is an interpreted language. The source code of a Java program is compiled into an intermediate language called "bytecode," which cannot run by itself. The bytecode must be converted (interpreted) into machine code at runtime. Upon finding a Java applet, the Web browser invokes a Java interpreter (Java Virtual Machine), which translates the bytecode into machine code and runs it. This means Java programs are not dependent on any specific hardware and will run in any computer with the Java Virtual Machine software. On the server side, Java programs can also be compiled into machine language for fastest performance, but they lose their hardware independence as a result.

The first Web browsers to run Java applications were Sun's HotJava and Netscape's Navigator 2.0. Java was designed to run in small amounts of memory and provides enhanced features for the programmer, including the ability to release memory when no longer required. This automatic "garbage collection" feature has been lacking in C and C++ and has been the bane of C and C++ programmers for years.

Like other programming languages, Java is royalty free to developers for writing applications. However, the Java Virtual Machine, which executes Java applications, is licensed to the companies that incorporate it in their browsers and Web servers.

**Java and JavaScript**    Java is a full-blown programming language and is not intended for the casual programmer and certainly not the end user. JavaScript is a scripting language that uses a similar syntax as Java, but it is not compiled into bytecode. It remains in source code embedded within an HTML document and must be translated a line at time into machine code by the JavaScript interpreter. JavaScript is very popular and is supported by all Web browsers. JavaScript has a more limited scope than Java and primarily deals with the elements on the Web page itself.

**Java: A Revolution?**    Java was originally developed in 1991 as a language for embedded applications, such as those used in set-top boxes and other consumer-oriented devices. It became the fuel to ignite a revolution in thinking when Sun transitioned it to the Web in 1994. Unlike HTML, which is a document display format that is continually beefed up to make it do more, Java is a full-blown programming language like C and C++. It allows for the creation of sophisticated applications. Thus far, Java applications have been mildly successful at the client side, but server-side Java applications have become very popular.

Java's "write once-run anywhere" model has been one of the Holy Grails of computing for decades. As CPU speeds increase, they can absorb the extra layer of translation required to execute an interpreted language, and Java is expected by many to become a major computing platform in the twenty-first century. See *Java platform, servlet, JSP, Java 2, J2EE, Jini, network computer, CaffeineMark* and **caffeine based**.

The following Java example of changing Fahrenheit to Celsius is rather wordy compared to the C example in this database. Java is designed for GUI-based applications, and several extra lines of code are necessary here to allow input from a terminal.

```
import java.io.*;
class Convert {
  public static void main(String[]args)
    throws IOException {
    float fahr;
    StreamTokenizer in=new StreamTokenizer(new
                 InputStreamReader(System.in));
    System.out.print("Enter Fahrenheit ");
    in.nextToken();
    fahr = (float) in.nval;
    System.out.println ("Celsius is " +
                                (fahr-32)*5/9);
  }
}
```

**Java 2**    The second version of Java from Sun that adds numerous enhancements, including a GUI library (Swing), accessiblity and 2-D libraries, drag and drop capabilities, and support for several audio files and digital certificates, as well as enhanced security tools. Java 2 also provides a JIT compiler and a CORBA ORB. This version is known as the Java 2 Standard Edition, which was followed by the Java 2 Enterprise Edition (J2EE). See *Swing* and *J2EE*.

**Java applet**    A Java program that is downloaded from the server and run from the browser. The Java Virtual Machine built into the browser is interpreting the instructions. Contrast with *Java application*.

**Java application**    A Java program that is run stand alone. The Java Virtual Machine in the client or server is interpreting the instructions. Contrast with *Java applet*. See *servlet*.

**JavaBeans**    A component software architecture from Sun that runs in the Java environment. JavaBeans are independent Java program modules that are called for and executed. They have been used primarily for developing user interfaces at the client side. The server-side counterpart is Enterprise JavaBeans (EJBs). See *EJB* and *component software*.

**Java Card**    A smart card that contains Java applets. Several applets can be stored in the card, and new ones can be added after issuance to the customer. See *Java*.

**Java chip**    A CPU chip from Sun that executes Java bytecode natively. It is based on Sun's picoJava architecture and is expected to be used in a wide range of devices from small, handheld appliances to desktop network computers. The picoJava chip contains the core architecture of the Java Virtual Machine and can be built into cellphones and other handheld devices. The microJava chip includes the picoJava core plus memory, I/O and other control functions, and is targeted toward controllers, network-based devices and consumer products. The first model was introduced in late 1998. The UltraJava chip is targeted for desktop use and incorporates some of Sun's 3-D graphics processing capabilities used in its UltraSPARC machines.

**Java Community Process**    Sun's system for allowing third parties to submit requests for new features to Java. JCP is a formal process that must be adhered to, and fees are involved. In 1999, Sun submitted Java to the ECMA standards body, but withdrew its J2SE specfication later in the year. It has continued to promote its own JCP methodology for further enhancing the language. For more information, visit http://java.sun.com/aboutJava/communityprocess.

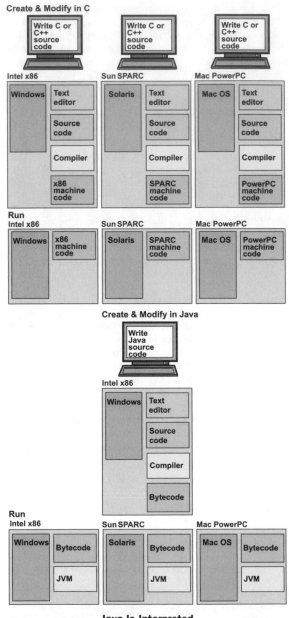

**Java Is Interpreted**
Java is not compiled into machine language for a specific hardware platform like programs written in C or C++ (top). It is compiled into an intermediate language called "bytecode." The bytecode program can be run by any hardware that has a Java Virtual Machine (Java interpreter) available for it. That's the "write once-run anywhere" model that makes Java so appealing.

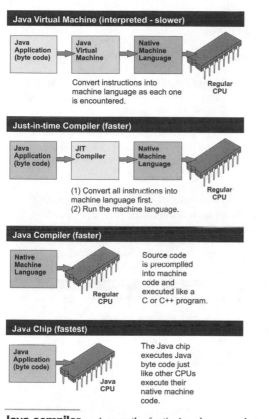

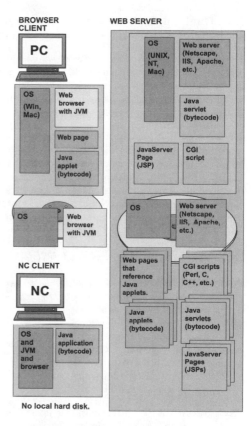

**Java Runs on Clients and Servers**
When a Java program has been called by a Web page from the client machine, it is called an "applet." When it runs on the server, it's known as a "servlet." When running stand alone in a network computer (NC), it is known as a Java application rather than an applet.

**Java compiler**    A compiler for the Java language that converts source code into native machine code. Although this makes the program platform dependent since it only runs in one CPU family, it also runs the fastest when compiled into native machine language. The term may also refer to a Java just-in-time compiler (JIT compiler), which compiles all the Java bytecode downloaded from the server just before running the application. This is faster than interpreting the bytecode one line at a time, but it also takes time to compile the program. See *Java*.

**Java Connector**    A programming interface (API) that provides an interface between a Java program and a legacy application such as CICS and R/3. Java Connectors, which are part of the J2EE platform, make legacy applications look like an Enterprise JavaBean (EJB) to the Java program. See *J2EE*.

**JavaOS**    A Java operating system from Sun that requires minimal hardware requirements and is intended for network computers and embedded systems. It includes the Java Virtual Machine, which, combined with the kernel, is written in the native machine language of the target CPU. Network and graphical user interface components are mostly written in Java.

**Java platform**    Running Java programs under the Java Virtual Machine (JVM). Java "platform" refers to the running of Java programs versus Java itself, which is a programming language. Java programs are machine independent and run intact on any hardware platform that has a Java interpreter (JVM). This "write once, run anywhere" concept is what makes Java so appealing.

    Java has its own graphical user interface routines that are normally contained in the operating system. Since only a small OS is required to run the Java interpreter, Java is closer to its own complete operating environment than other programming languages, hence, "Java, the platform" is often heard.

**Java Runtime Environment**   The combination of the Java Virtual Machine, core classes and supporting files, all of which are required to run a Java program. See *Java* and *Java Virtual Machine*.

**Java sandbox**   A constrained arena within which Java applications can be made to run, preventing, for example, access to the local hard disk or to the network. While this restricts the program's capabilities, it provides security for downloading Java applets from the Internet and running them from the Web browser. Sun has evolved its sandbox policy. Depending on Java VM version, trusted code can be allowed to do any task or only certain tasks, depending on user and configuration. In Java 2, even unsigned code can be given full access to the system if the company policy so dictates. See *object signing*.

**JavaScript**   A popular scripting language that is widely supported in Web browsers and other Web tools. It adds interactive functions to HTML pages, which are otherwise static, since HTML is a display language, not a programming language. JavaScript is easier to use than Java, but not as powerful, and deals mainly with the elements on the Web page. On the client, JavaScript is maintained as source code embedded into an HTML page. On the server, it is compiled into bytecode (intermediate language), similar to Java programs.

JavaScript evolved from Netscape's LiveScript language. First released with Navigator 2.0, it was made more compatible with Java. JavaScript does not have the programming overhead of Java, but can be used in conjunction with it. For example, a JavaScript script could be used to display a data entry form and validate the input, while a Java applet or Java servlet more thoroughly processes the information. JavaScript is also used to tie Java applets together. See *JScript*, *Java*, *Java applet*, *servlet* and *VBScript*.

**JavaScript rollover**   Using JavaScript to change the appearance of a graphic when the pointer is moved (rolled) over it. JavaScript rollovers are used to highlight elements in navigation bars and produce other graphics effects. They have been supported in browsers starting with IE 4, Netscape 3 and Opera 3.1.

| Home | Features | Examples | Download demo | Order | Multiuser | Support | Contact us | Online |

*Computer Desktop Encyclopedia is the premier reference about the computer industry.*

**JavaScript Code Changes the Image**
As the screen pointer is moved across the options in a navigation bar, the elements change color, indicating that they can be selected if you click now. JavaScript is often used to control such changing elements, as in this example where the pointer is over Download Demo.

**Java Servlet API**   An extension to Java from Sun that provides a programming interface (API) for implementing server-side programs written in Java (Java servlets). See *servlet*.

**JavaSoft**   The division within Sun that supports the Java programming language and licenses the Java Virtual Machine.

**JavaSpaces**   An application that provides a unified environment for sharing, communicating and coordinating within a Jini network. It functions like a virtual bulletin board, enabling information to be posted and responded to by the appropriate (object-based) application. For example, sellers could post items for sale, and buyers could respond. See *Jini*.

**JavaStation**   A family of network computers from Sun that comply with the NC Reference Profile. Introduced with the same 100MHz MicroSPARC CPU used in Sun's SPARC 4 and 5 workstations, JavaStations are expected to migrate to the Java chip. JavaStations can also run Windows applications on an NT server using software from Insignia Solutions or Citrix that turns NT into a timeshared central computer.

**Java Virtual Machine**   A Java interpreter. The Java Virtual Machine (JVM) is software that converts the Java intermediate language (bytecode) into machine language and executes it. The original JVM came from the JavaSoft division of Sun. Subsequently, other vendors developed their own; for example, the Microsoft Virtual Machine is Microsoft's Java interpreter. A JVM is incorporated into a Web browser in order to execute Java applets. A JVM is also installed in a Web server to execute server-side Java programs. A JVM can also be installed in a client machine to run stand-alone Java applications. See *Java* and *Java Runtime Environment*.

**Java Web Server**   A Web server from Sun that runs under Solaris and NT. It supports Java servlets and JavaServer Pages (JSP) technology. Version 2.0 is the latest release of the product and was created to provide an upgrade path to servlet processing (Servlet API 2.1) for prior Java Web Server customers. The Web server was superseded by iPlanet Web Server. See *iPlanet Web Server*.

**Javelin Plus** A spreadsheet for DOS that can simulate multidimensional views of data. Introduced in 1985 by Javelin Software, it was more a modeling program than a spreadsheet and was the forerunner of today's OLAP databases, which are inherently designed for multiple dimensions. It was later acquired by Information Resources, Inc. and Javelin Plus 3.5 in 1993 was the last version marketed. The technology, along with IRI's Express software, was acquired by Oracle in 1995.

**Jaz disk** A high-capacity removable hard disk system from Iomega. Introduced in late 1995, Iomega startled the industry with its breakthrough price of $99 for a 1GB removable disk cartridge. The Jaz has been very popular. In 1997, 2GB drives were introduced, which support 1GB and 2GB cartridges. See *magnetic disk*.

**JBOD** (Just a Bunch Of Disks) A group of hard disks in a computer that are not set up as any type of RAID configuration. They are just a bunch of disks.

**Jaz Cartridge**
Iomega introduced its 1GB cartridge at 10 cents per megabyte in late 1995, which was a breakthrough price for that year.

**JCL** (Job Control Language) A command language for mini and mainframe operating systems that launches applications. It specifies priority, program size and running sequence, as well as the files and databases used.

**JDBC** (Java DataBase Connectivity) A programming interface that lets Java applications access a database via the SQL language. Since Java interpreters (Java Virtual Machines) are available for all major client platforms, this allows a platform-independent database application to be written. In 1996, JDBC was the first extension to the Java platform. JDBC is the Java counterpart of Microsoft's ODBC. See *ODBC*.

**J/Direct** (Java/DIRECT) An extension to Microsoft's Java Virtual Machine that lets Java programs access Windows routines directly. Java programs talk to the Win32 API.

**JDK** (Java Development Kit) A Java software development environment from Sun. It includes the JVM, compiler, debugger and other tools for developing Java applets and applications. Each new version of the JDK adds features and enhancements to the language. When Java programs are developed under the new version, the Java interpreter (Java Virtual Machine) that executes them must also be updated to that same version. See *JFC*.

**JEDEC** (Joint Electronic Device Engineering Council) An international body that sets integrated circuit standards.

**JEIDA** (Japanese Electronic Industry Development Association) A Japanese trade and standards organization. JEIDA joined with PCMCIA to standardize the PC card in 1991. The PC card specifications JEIDA 4.1 and PCMCIA 2.0 are the same.

**Jeliot** (Java ELIOT) A visualization environment developed at the University of Helsinki that enables a Java algorithm to be animated on the Web. It uses the EJava language, which is a version of Java intended for embedded systems. Jeliot is the successor to Eliot, which animates algorithms written in C. See *PersonalJava*.

**JES** (Job Entry Subsystem) Software that provides batch communications for IBM's MVS operating system. It accepts data from remote batch terminals, executes them on a priority basis and transmits the results back to the terminals. The JES counterpart in VM is RSCS.

**Jet** (Joint Engine Technology) The database engine used in Microsoft Access and that accompanies Visual Basic and C++. Jet is typically used for storing data in the client machine. Developers using Access and Visual Basic access Jet via the DAO/Jet interface, which is a COM object. See *DAO*.

**JetDirect** A print server for LaserJet printers from HP, available as an internal card or external unit. It supports its own proprietary printing protocol and, depending on model, Novell's QMS and NDPS, LPR/LPD and Apple's PAP. The JetDirect servers use the JetAdmin printer management software to configure and control the unit. See *printing protocol*.

**jewel case**    The plastic container used to package an audio CD or CD-ROM disc. See *tray card*.

**JFC**    (Java Foundation Classes) A class library from Sun that provides an application framework and graphical user interface (GUI) routines for Java programmers. Sun, Netscape, IBM and others contributed to JFC, which combines Sun's Abstract Windowing Toolkit (AWT) and Netscape's Foundation Classes (IFC). See *JDK*, *AFC*, *IFC* and *AWT*.

**JFIF**    See *JPEG*.

**JFS**    See *journaled file system* and *Joliet file system*.

**JHTML**    (Java HTML) A proprietary dynamic page technology from BEA Systems, Inc., San Jose, CA (www.beasys.com). Starting in 1999, BEA's application servers also supported the Java standards for dynamic Web content, including JavaServer Pages (JSPs) and Enterprise JavaBeans (EJBs). See *BEA WebLogic*.

**jiff**    See *GIF*.

**Jigsaw**    A Web server from the W3C that incorporates advanced features that are expected to become mainstream in the future. It uses a modular design similar to the Apache Web server. Jigsaw supports HTTP 1.1 and provides an experimental platform for HTTP-NG. See *HTTP-NG* and *Amaya*.

**Jini**    Pronounced "gee-nee." A Java-based distributed computing environment from Sun in which devices can be plugged into the network and automatically offer their services and make use of other services on the network. Jini creates a "network dialtone" allowing, for example, any PDA or laptop to be plugged in and immediately be able to use printers and other resources. It turns "peripherals into services," so that when a disk drive is plugged in, it becomes a storage service rather than just another disk drive. See *JavaSpaces*.

**JIT compiler**    (Just-In-Time compiler) A compiler that converts all the source code into machine code just before the program is run. In the case of Java, JIT compilers convert Java's intermediate language (bytecode) into native code. See *Java compiler*.

**jitter**    A flicker or fluctuation in a transmission signal or display image. The term is used in several ways, but it always refers to some offset of time and space from the norm. For example, in a network transmission, jitter would be a bit arriving either ahead or behind a standard clock cycle, or, more generally, the variable arrival of packets. In computer graphics, to "jitter a pixel" means to place it offside of its normal placement by some random amount in order to achieve a more natural antialiasing effect.

**jitterati**    A variation of digerati that refers to stressed-out personnel in the fast-paced, high-tech industry. See *digerati*.

**J-lead**    A pin on a chip package that extends down and around under the housing like a reverse "J." J-leads are used on SOJs chips. See *SOJ* and *gull-wing lead*.

**JMAPI**    (Java Management API) A programming interface from Sun for managing network and systems via the Web. It uses the Common Information Model (CIM) schema for storing information about the node. See *WBEM*.

**JML**    (Java HTML) A method for producing dynamic Web pages by embedding Java in an HTML page. Java is embedded in the page with JML tags, and the Java is executed on the server before the HTML page is returned to the user.

**JMS**    (Java Messinging Service) A programming interface (API) from Sun for connecting Java programs to messaging middleware such as IBM's MQSeries and TIBCO's Rendezvous. JMS is part of Sun's J2EE platform. See *J2EE*.

**JNDI**    (Java Naming and Directory Interface) A programming interface (API) from Sun for connecting Java programs to naming and directory services such as DNS, LDAP and NDS. The application is written to the JNDI API, and the directory drivers are written to the JNDI SPI (Service Provider Interface). JNDI is part of Sun's J2EE platform. See *J2EE*.

**JNI**    (Java Native Interface) A programming interface (API) in Sun's Java Virtual machine used for calling native platform elements such as GUI routines. RNI (Raw Native Interface) is the JNI counterpart in Microsoft's Java Virtual Machine.

**job**    A unit of work running in the computer. A job may be a single program or a group of programs that work together. See also *job descriptions* and *salary survey*.

**job class**    The descriptive category of a job that is based on the computer resources it requires when running.

**job descriptions**    Following is a summary of the job titles in this database. In most cases, there is more information under the individual entries.

**business analyst**    An individual who analyzes the operations of a department or functional unit. See *business analyst*.

**CIO**    (Chief Information Officer) The executive officer in charge of information processing in an organization. See *CIO*.

**client/server analyst**    A person responsible for performing analysis and design of a client/server system. See *client/server analyst*.

**client/server programmer**    A person responsible for programming client/server applications. See *client/server programmer*.

**computer designer**    A person who designs the electronic structure of a computer. Such individuals are engineers with background in digital circuits.

**consultant**    A person that acts as an advisor to users or to the technical staff. See *consultant*.

**CTO**    (Chief Technical Officer) The executive responsible for the technical direction of an organization. See also *CIO*.

**datacenter manager**    A person responsible for the operation of the computer systems in the datacenter. The data entry and data control departments are under this jurisdiction.

**datacom analyst**    A person responsible for developing and maintaining a data communications network. See *datacom analyst*.

**data entry operator**    A person who enters data into the computer via keyboard or other reading or scanning device.

**database administrator**    A person responsible for the physical design and management of the database and for the evaluation, selection and implementation of the DBMS. See *database administrator*.

**database analyst**    A person responsible for analyzing data requirements within an organization and modeling the data and data flows from one department to another. See *database analyst*.

**e-commerce engineer**    A person responsible for developing and maintaining e-commerce applications for a company's public Web site. See *e-commerce engineer*.

**EDI analyst**    A person responsible for the implementation of electronic data interchange systems between companies. See *EDI analyst*.

**EDP auditor**    A person that performs an EDP audit within an organization. See *EDP auditor* and *EDP audit*.

**field engineer**    A person responsible for hardware installation, maintentance and repair. Formal training is in electronics, although many people have learned on the job.

**help desk analyst**    A person that provides technical support for any aspect of the information systems department. See *help desk analyst*.

**Internet engineer**    A person responsible for developing and maintaining the infrastructure that supports the public Web site, intranet and associated LANs and WANs. See *Internet engineer*.

**knowledge engineer**    A person who translates the knowledge of an expert into the knowledge base of an expert system. See *expert system*.

**librarian**    A person who works in the data library. See *data library*.

**mainframe programmer**    A person that writes mainframe applications in programming languages such as COBOL, CICS and various 4GLs. See *programmer*.

**mainframe programmer/analyst**    A person responsible for the design and programming of a mainframe application. Programming languages typically include COBOL, CICS and 4GLs. See *programmer analyst*.

**mainframe systems analyst**    A person responsible for the design of a mainframe application. See systems analyst.

**midrange programmer**    A person that writes applications in programming languages such as COBOL, RPG and 4GLs, typically for IBM AS/400s. See *programmer*.

**midrange programmer/analyst**    A person responsible for the design and programming of a medium-sized business application. Programming languages include COBOL, RPG and 4GLs, typically for IBM AS/400s. See *programmer analyst*.

**MIS director**    See *CIO*.

**network administrator**    A person who manages a local area communications network (LAN) within an organization. See *network administrator*.

**network engineer**    A person who designs, implements and supports LANs and WANs. See *network engineer*.

**operator**    A person who operates a computer in a datacenter. See *operator*.

**PC software specialist**    A person who manages personal computer hardware and software. See *PC software specialist*.

**PC technician**    A person responsible for the maintenance of desktop computers within an organization. See *PC technician*.

**programmer**    A person who writes a computer program. See *programmer*.

**programmer analyst**    A person who performs both systems analysis and programming tasks. See *programmer analyst*.

**project leader**    A person that heads an information systems project. See *project leader*.

**project manager**    A person that keeps track of an information systems project. See *project manager*.

**QA analyst**    A person responsible for maintaining software quality within an organization. See *QA analyst*.

**software engineer**    A person that designs and programs system-level software (OS, DBMS, etc.). See *software engineer*.

**system administrator**    A person who manages a multiuser computer system (server). See *system administrator*.

**systems analyst**    The person responsible for the development of an information system. See *systems analyst*.

**systems engineer**    Refers to a variety of jobs in the industry. It may refer to a system-level programmer or to pre-sales and post-sales programming for a hardware or software vendor. See *software engineer*.

**systems integrator**    An individual or organization that builds systems from a variety of diverse components. See *systems integrator*.

**systems programmer**    A person who is the technical expert on some or all of the computer's system software (operating systems, networks, DBMSs, etc.) or a person who designs and writes system software. See *systems programmer*.

**technical writer**    A person responsible for writing hardware and software documentation. See *technical writer*.

**UI designer/specialist**    A person responsible for designing the user interface. See *UI specialist*.

**voice analyst**    A person responsible for designing telephony systems, including PBXs, interactive voice response (IVR) systems and call centers.

**WAN administrator**    A person who manages a wide area communications network (WAN). See *WAN administrator*.

**Web designer**    A person that creates a Web site. See *Web designer*.

**Web programmer**    A person that writes in any of the Web programming languages. See *Web programmer*.

**Webmaster**    A person responsible for the implementation of a Web site. See *Webmaster*.

**job processing**    Handling and processing jobs in the computer.

**job queue**    The lineup of programs ready to be executed.

**job scheduling**    In a large computer, establishing a job queue to run a sequence of programs over any period of time such as a single shift, a full day, etc.

**job stream**    A series of related programs that are run in a prescribed order. The output of one program is the input to the next program, and so on.

**join**    In relational database management, to match one table (file) against another based on some condition creating a third table with data from the matching tables. For example, a customer table can be joined with an order table creating a table for all customers who purchased a particular product.

The default type of join is known as an "inner" join. It produces a resulting record if there is a matching condition. For example, matching shipments with receipts would produce only those shipments that have been received. On the other hand, an "outer" join using that example would create a record for every shipment whether or not it was received. The data for received items would be attached to the shipments, and empty, or null, fields would be attached to shipments without receipts. See also *DOS Join*.

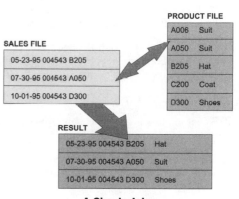

**A Simple Join**
This example matches the sales table against the product table based on product number to derive the product description.

**Joliet file system**    An extension to the ISO 9660 CD-ROM file format from Microsoft that supports long file names used in Windows 95 and subsequent versions of Windows. The original 8.3 naming convention is also included for compatiblity with Windows 3.1 and DOS.

**JOOTT**    Digispeak for "just one of those things."

**Josephson junction**    An ultra-fast switching technology that uses superconductor materials, originally conceived by Brian Josephson. Circuits are immersed in liquid helium to obtain near-absolute zero degrees required for operation. Switching takes place in a few picoseconds. Although Josephson junctions have not materialized for computer circuits, they have been used thus far in medical instruments that sense brain waves.

**joule**    A unit of energy in the MKS system. It is equal to 10,000,000 ergs in the CGS system. Surge protectors are often given joule ratings, but this refers only to the amount of energy they can absorb, not what gets through. See *CGS system*.

**journal**    Same as *log*.

**journaled file system**    A file system that contains its own backup and recovery capability. Before indexes on disk are updated, the information about the changes is recorded in a log. If a power or other system failure corrupts the indexes as they are being rewritten, the operating system can use the log to repair them when the system is restarted.

**journaling**    Keeping track of events by recording them in a journal, or log.

**JOVIAL**    (Jules' Own Version of the International Algebraic Language)    An ALGOL-like programming language developed by Systems Development Corp. in the early 1960s and widely used in the military. Its key architect was Jules Schwartz.

**joy stick**    A pointing device used to move an object on screen in any direction. It employs a vertical rod mounted on a base with one or two buttons. Joy sticks are used extensively in video games and in some CAD systems.

**A Joystick**
Joysticks are used in video games, and similar devices are used in some CAD systems and other electronic control systems. The term came from the main control stick in a small airplane.

**JPEG** (Joint Photographic Experts Group) Pronounced "jay-peg." An ISO/ITU standard for compressing still images that is becoming very popular due to its high compression capability. Using discrete cosine transform, it provides lossy compression (you lose some data from the original image) with ratios up to 100:1 and higher.

It depends on the image, but ratios of 10:1 to 20:1 may provide little noticeable loss. The more the loss can be tolerated, the more the image can be compressed. Compression is achieved by dividing the picture into tiny pixel blocks, which are halved over and over until the ratio is achieved.

JPEG is implemented in software and hardware, with the latter providing sufficient speed for realtime, on-the-fly compression. C-Cube Microsystems introduced the first JPEG chip.

JPEG++ is an extension to JPEG from Storm Technology, Mountain View, CA, that allows picture areas to be selectable for different ratios. For example, the background could be compressed higher than the foreground image.

JPEG uses the JPEG File Interchange Format, or JFIF. File extensions are .JPG or .JFF. M-JPEG and MPEG are variations of JPEG used for full-motion digital video. See *MPEG*.

**JPIG** (1) Misspelling of JPEG. See *JPEG*.

(2) The authorities that patrol the Internet for images of child pornography, which are typically in JPEG format.

(3) Anyone against all pornography on the Internet. Such images are often in JPEG format.

**JRMI** (Java RMI) See *RMI*.

**JRP** (Joint Requirements Planning) Systems planning performed cooperatively by a team of users and technicians. Functions should be prioritized and related to the organization's goals and business opportunities.

**JScript** Microsoft's implementation of JavaScript. It is similar to JavaScript, but has extensions specifically for the Windows environment. Internet Explorer natively supports JScript and VBScript, and both scripting languages have their strengths and weaknesses for Web page programming. See *JavaScript* and *VBScript*.

**JSP** (JavaServer Page) An extension to the Java servlet technology from Sun that provides a simple programming vehicle for displaying dynamic content on a Web page. The JSP is an HTML page with embedded Java source code that is executed in the Web server or application server. The HTML provides the page layout that will be returned to the Web browser, and the Java provides the processing; for example, to deliver a query to the database and fill in the blank fields with the results. The JSP is compiled into bytecode (into a servlet) when first encountered by the server. The JSP can also call Enterprise JavaBeans (EJBs) for additional processing. JSPs are the Sun/Java counterpart to Microsoft's ASPs (Active Server Pages). See *servlet*, *J2EE*, *ASP* and *CGI script*.

**JSQL** (Java SQL) An implementation of the SQL query language for database applications written in Java. It provides a common way of using SQL from within Java to access a database.

**JTA** (Java Transaction API) A programming interface (API) from Sun for connecting Java programs to transaction monitors such as IBM's CICS and BEA's Tuxedo. JTA is part of Sun's J2EE platform. See J2EE.

**JTAG** (Joint Test Action Group) An IEEE standard for boundary scan technology. See *scan technology*.

**jukebox** A storage device for multiple sets of CD-ROMs, tape cartridges or disk modules. Using carousels, robot arms and other methods, a jukebox physically moves the storage medium from its assigned location to an optical or magnetic station for reading and writing. Access between modules usually takes several seconds.

**Julian date** The representation of month and day by a consecutive number starting with Jan. 1. For example, Feb. 1 is Julian 32. Dates are converted into Julian dates for calculation.

**jump** Same as *goto*.

**jumper** The simplest form of an on/off switch. It is just a tiny, plastic-covered metal block, which is pushed onto two pins to close that circuit. It is used to select a myriad of

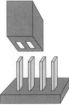

**Jumper**
Jumpers are used to select options on countless printed circuit boards. The more sophisticated the board, the fewer the jumpers. Having no jumpers is best if changes have to be made by the user, otherwise the board has to be pulled out of the case.

functions on a printed circuit board or on a peripheral device. For example, on a PC, jumpers are used to select I/O addresses and IRQs. On an IDE drive, a jumper selects between master and slave. A jumper can be used in place of a more costly DIP switch. See *jumperless*.

**jumperless**    Without the use of jumpers. It means that configuration settings on the hardware are done via software rather than by setting jumpers. See *jumper*.

**junction**    The point at which two elements make contact. In a transistor, a junction is the point where an N-type material makes contact with a P-type material.

**junctor**    In a telephone junction box, a small section of twisted wire pair that is used to attach incoming lines with outgoing lines.

**junk e-mail**    Transmitting e-mail to unsolicited recipients. U.S. federal law 47USC227 prohibits broadcasting junk faxes and e-mail, allowing recipients to sue the sender in Small Claims Court for $500 per copy.

**junk faxes**    Transmitting faxes to unsolicited recipients. U.S. federal law 47USC227 prohibits broadcasting junk faxes and e-mail, allowing recipients to sue the sender in Small Claims Court for $500 per copy.

**Juno**    (Juno Online Services, L.P., www.juno.com, 800 654-JUNO) A free, advertiser-supported e-mail service that provides you with an Internet e-mail address. Juno started out as a non-Web based service, and mail was accessed only via a dial-up connection to the Juno computer. Later, Juno added Web-based e-mail as well as Internet access. See *Internet e-mail service*.

**justification**    In typography, the alignment of text evenly between left and right margins. Contrast with *ragged right*.

**justify**    (1) To shift the contents of a field or register to the right or left.
(2) To align text evenly between left and right margins.

**just-in-time compiler**    See *JIT compiler*.

**JVM**    See *Java Virtual Machine*.

**JWI**    (Junctor Wire Interface) A mechanical cross connect that serves as a junction box in the telephone company outside plant. It is a cabinet full of punch blocks which sits between the digital loop carrier and junction points that provide the final drop to the customer. Often known as a JWIC for Junctor Wire Interface Cabinet. Increasingly, the digital loop carrier is being moved farther down the loop to the JWIC location.

**K**  See *kilo*.

**K&R C**  (**K**ernighan and **R**itchie **C**)  A version of C defined by Brian Kernighan and Dennis Ritchie that preceded the ANSI standard.

**K5**  A Pentium-class CPU chip from AMD. K5 chips are available in models that rival a 166MHz Pentium chip. See *K6*.

**K56Flex**  See *V.90*.

**K6**  A Pentium II–class CPU chip from AMD. The first models were introduced in 1997 at 166MHz, 200MHz and 233MHz clock speeds. The K6 chip contains the MMX instruction set used in Pentium MMX and Pentium II CPUs, and plugs into the Socket 7 processor socket on Pentium motherboards. The K6 was originally engineered by NexGen, which AMD acquired in 1966.

The second-generation K6 2 chip, introduced in 1998, improves performance and adds AMD's 3DNow 3-D instructions for faster rendering of games and animation. The K6-3 was introduced in 1999 with improved performance and greater onboard cache. The K6 series has been superseded by the Athlon. See *Athlon*.

**K7**  See *Athlon*.

**Ka-Band**  Part of the electromagnetic spectrum used for fixed and mobile satellite communications. It uses frequencies in the 18-31GHz range. See *Ku-Band*.

**Kanban**  Meaning "visible record" in Japanese, it is a system of notification from one process to the other in a manufacturing system. Kanban cards, which may be multicolored based on priority, are stored in a bin or container that holds the items. They describe the parts, supplier and quantity. When the bin is emptied, the Kanban is used to order more. A two-card Kanban system uses "move" cards to relocate items from one workplace to another, and "production" cards to replace the material when it is used or sold.

**KB**  (1) (KB) (**K**ilo**B**yte)  One thousand bytes (technically, 1,024 bytes). See *kilo* and *space/time*.

(2) (Kb) (**K**ilo**B**it)  One thousand bits (technically, 1,024 bits). Lower case "b" for bit and "B" for byte are not always followed and often misprinted. Thus, Kb may refer to kilobyte. See *kilo* and *space/time*.

**Kbit**  See *kilobit*.

**Kbits/sec**  (**K**ilo**BITS** per **SEC**ond)  One thousand bits per second. See *kilo*.

**KBM**    (Knowledge Based Manufacturing) A full-featured custom manufacturing ERP system from Acacia for the AS/400. It was originally developed by Data3, which was acquired by the ASK Group and then by Computer Associates (CA) in 1994. See *Acacia*.

**Kbps**    (KiloBits Per Second) One thousand bits per second. Kbps is used as a rating of relatively slow transmission speed compared to the common Mbps or Gbps ratings. Upper case "B" in KBps means kilobytes per second, but "b" for bit and "B" for byte are not always followed and often misprinted. KBps or KB/s would be used for earlier disk and tape transfer ratings as data is transferred in parallel, not serial.

A variation of the term is "K bps," with a space between the K and bps. In this case, it may mean 1,000 bps exactly in constrast to "Kbps" without the space, which would be the binary 1,024 bps. This usage is not widely known or adhered to, and most modem ratings use Kbps. For example, 56 Kbps means 56,000 bps and not 56 times 1024 bps. See *kilo* and *space/time*.

**KB/s**    See *Kbits/sec* and *Kbytes/sec*.

**Kbs**    (KiloBits per Second) Could also be KBs for kilobytes. See *Kbps* and *kilo*.

**K-byte**    See *kilobyte*.

**Kbyte**    One thousand bytes. See *kilo*.

**Kbytes/sec**    (KiloBYTES per SECond) One thousand bytes per second. See *kilo*.

**KDE**    (K Desktop Environment) A GUI-based user interface for UNIX workstations. It provides a complete desktop environment like Windows and the Mac with its own unique style and features. The source code is freely distributed and is maintained by developers around the world. Widely used with Linux, which is also freeware, information can be found at www.kde.org. See *GNOME*.

**Kensington lock**    A security system from Kensington Microware, Ltd, San Mateo, CA (www.kensington.com) that discourages the theft of portable computers and other devices. Officially known as the Universal Notebook Security Cable, the locking slot for this cable is built into many notebook computers. The cable is looped through some permanent object in the room, and then looped through itself and locked into the slot.

**Kerberos**    A security system developed at MIT that authenticates users. It does not provide authorization to services or databases; it establishes identity at logon, which is used throughout the session.

**Kermit**    An asynchronous file transfer protocol developed at Columbia University, noted for its accuracy over noisy lines. Several extensions exist, including SuperKermit, a full-duplex, sliding window version. Kermit is popular on minis and mainframes and can also handle byte-oriented transfers over 7-bit ASCII systems.

**kernel**    The fundamental part of a program, typically an operating system, that resides in memory at all times and provides the basic services. It is the part of the operating system that is closest to the machine and may activate the hardware directly or interface to another software layer that drives the hardware. See *microkernel*.

**kerning**    In proportional spacing, the tightening of space between letters to create a visually appealing flow to the text. Letter combinations, such as WA, MW and TA, are routinely kerned for better appearance. See *tracking*.

**Kerr effect**    A change in rotation of light reflected off a magnetic field. The polarity of a magneto-optic bit causes the laser to shift one degree clockwise or counterclockwise.

**key**    (1) A keyboard button.

(2) In *cryptography*, a numeric code that is combined in some manner with the text to encrypt it for security purposes. See *cryptography*.

(3) See *key field* and *sort key*.

**KEY:Assemble**   A Windows-based client/server application development system from Byteback Computer Solutions Ltd., Lower Earley, Reading, England. KEY:Assemble applications can access multiple databases, including Oracle and Sybase. Business graphics and spreadsheet capabilities can be included. KEY:Assemble was originally ObjectView from Knowledgeware, which was acquired by Sterling Software. Byteback acquired KEY:Assemble in 1998.

**keyboard**   A set of input keys. On terminals and personal computers, it includes the standard typewriter keys,and several specialized keys and features outlined here. See *PC keyboards*.

**ENTER (RETURN) KEY**   In text applications, it ends a paragraph or short line. In data applications, it signals the end of the input for that field or line.

**CURSOR KEYS**   The four arrow keys move the cursor on screen. They are used in conjunction with SHIFT, ALT and CTRL to move the cursor in bigger jumps; for example, CTRL ARROW might scroll the screen. Some earlier keyboards didn't have cursor keys, in which case, CTRL or ALT was used with some letter key.

**CTRL, ALT, COMMAND and OPTION KEYS**   Used like a SHIFT key, these keys are held down while another key is pressed to command the computer in a variety of ways.

**ESCAPE (ESC) KEY**   Commonly used to exit or cancel the current mode, such as exiting from a menu. Also used to clear an area or repeat a function, such as redrawing the screen.

**NUMERIC (NUM) LOCK**   Locks a combination number/cursor keypad into numeric mode only.

**HOME & END KEYS**   Commonly used to move the cursor to the extreme left or right side of the current line. Often used in conjunction with SHIFT, CTRL and ALT; for example, CTRL HOME and CTRL END usually move the cursor to the beginning and end of file.

**PAGE UP/PAGE DOWN KEYS**   Used to move the cursor up and down a page, screen or frame. Often used in combination with SHIFT, CTRL and ALT.

**FUNCTION KEYS**   Used to call up a menu or perform a function, they are located in a cluster on the left side or in a row across the top of the keyboard (F1, F2, etc.). They are often used with the SHIFT, CTRL and ALT keys to extend the number of options.

**BACKSPACE KEY**   Used to delete the character to the left of the cursor (erase typos) and may be used with the SHIFT, CTRL and ALT keys to erase segments of text. The extra-wide, typewriter-style key is preferred.

**DELETE KEY**   Used to erase the character at the current cursor location. Used in conjunction with the SHIFT, CTRL and ALT keys, it is used to erase any segment of text, such as a word, sentence or paragraph.

**INSERT KEY**   Usually, a toggle switch to go back and forth between insert and overwrite mode. Also used to "paste" a segment of text or graphics into the document at the current cursor location.

**REPEATING KEYS**   Most computer keys repeat when held down, a phenomenon first-time computer users must get used to. If you hold a key down that is used to command the computer, you'll be entering the command several times.

**AUDIBLE FEEDBACK**   Keyboards may cause a click or beep to be heard from the computer when keys are pressed. This is done to acknowledge that the character has been entered. It should be adjustable for personal preference.

**All Keyboards Are Not Equal**   Keyboards feel different, and touch typists should spend a few hours with any keyboard, especially on a laptop, before purchasing it. Key placement is extremely important. Even the most popular

**Keys Too Small for Your Fingers?**
Try these for size. A young boy has fun on the giant keyboard in the Walk-Through Computer that opened at The Computer Museum in Boston at the end of 1995. *(Image by FAYFOTO/John Rich; courtesy of The Computer Museum History Center.)*

laptop keyboards can have awkward cursor, PAGE UP/DOWN, HOME and END key placements. It is not uncommon to have ridiculous designs, such as the DELETE key next to a cursor key. For slow typists, all this means little. For fast typists, it is critical. See *Avant Stellar keyboard.*

**keyboard buffer**   A memory bank or reserved memory area that stores keystrokes until the program can accept them. It lets fast typists continue typing while the program catches up.

**keyboard commands**   Using the keyboard to navigate menus and buttons and select options. See *Win Keyboard commands.*

**keyboard connector**   See *DIN connector.*

**keyboard controller**   A circuit that monitors keystrokes and generates the required data bits when pressed.

**keyboard drawer**   A sliding drawer that holds a keyboard under the desk when not in use.

**keyboard enhancer**   Same as *macro processor.*

**keyboard interrupt**   A signal that gets the attention of the CPU each time a key is pressed. See *interrupt.*

**keyboard macro processor**   See *macro processor.*

**keyboard processor**   See *keyboard controller* and *keyboard enhancer.*

**keyboard template**   A plastic card that fits over the function keys to identify each key's purpose in a particular software program.

**key cap**   A replaceable, top part of a keyboard key. To identify commonly used codes, it can be replaced with a custom-printed key cap.

**key click**   An audible feedback provided when a key is pressed. It may be adjustable by the user.

**key command**   A key combination (ALT-G, CTRL-B, CMD-M, etc.) used as a command to the computer.

**key driven**   Any device that is activated by pressing keys.

**KEY:Enterprise**   Formerly Application Development Workbench (ADW), it is an integrated CASE-based application development system that runs under OS/2 from Sterling Software. It includes a variety of tools for designing and developing client/server, AS/400 and IBM mainframe applications. KEY:Enterprise was renamed COOL:Enterprise. See *COOL.*

**key entry**   Data entry using a keyboard.

**key escrow**   A security technique that places a cryptographic key into the hands of a trusted third party.

**key field**   A field in a record that holds unique data that identifies that record from all the other records in the file or database. Account number, product code and customer name are typical key fields. As an identifier, each key value must be unique in each record. See *sort key.*

**keyframe**   In video compression, a frame with a complete image. See *interframe coding.*

**keyframe animation**   Animating a graphics object by creating smooth transitions between various keyframes.

**key in**   To enter data by typing on a keyboard.

**key management**    In cryptography, the creation, transmission and maintenance of a secret key.

**keypad**    A small keyboard or supplementary keyboard keys; for example, the keys on a calculator or the number/cursor cluster on a computer keyboard. See *macro keypad*.

**keypunch**    To punch holes in a punched card. Although punched cards are obsolete, some people still say "keys are punched" on a keyboard.

**keypunch department**    Same as *data entry department*.

**keypunch machine**    A punched-card data entry machine. A deck of blank cards is placed into a hopper, and, upon operator command, the machine feeds one card to a punch station. As characters are typed, a series of dies at the punch station punch the appropriate holes in the selected card column.

**key recovery**    The ability to uncover the secret key to a cryptographic message. See *key escrow*.

**keystroke logger**    A program or hardware device that captures every key depression on the computer. Also known as "keystroke cops," they are used to monitor an employee's activities. Keystroke loggers record every single keystroke, including typos, backspacing and retyping. See *Keystroke Cops*.

**key telephone system**    An in-house telephone system that is not centrally connected to a PBX. Each telephone has buttons for outside lines that can be dialed directly without having to "dial 9."

**key-to-disk machine**    An early stand-alone data entry machine that stores data on magnetic disk for computer entry.

**key-to-tape machine**    An early stand-alone data entry machine that stores data on magnetic tape for computer entry. Introduced by Mohawk Data Sciences in the mid-1960s, it was the first advancement in data entry since the card keypunch. Mohawk's stock went from $2–$200 in a couple of years.

**keyword**    (1) A word used in a text search.
(2) A word in a text document that is used in an index to best describe the contents of the document.
(3) A reserved word in a programming or command language.

**keyword advertising**    See *meta ad*.

**Khornerstones**    A benchmark program that tests CPU, I/O and floating point performance. See *benchmark*.

**kHz**    (KiloHertZ) One thousand cycles per second. See *horizontal scan frequency*.

**kicks**    See *CICS* and *CIX*.

**kill**    To cancel. Kill, as well as "abort" and "cancel," all mean to end or exit the current process.

**killer app**    An application that is exceptionally useful or exciting. When new operating systems are on the horizon, people wish for one or two killer apps that run under the new system in order to justify the migration effort and expense. Contrast with *filler app*.

**Calculator**    **Telephone**

**Really Now**
Couldn't we have agreed on the same key placement for the keypads we use time and time again?

**IBM Keypunch**
This is the type of IBM keypunch machine used in the 1960s and 1970s. Operators by the tens of thousands would spend a full shift keypunching orders, time cards and a host of other transactions. *(Image courtesy of International Business Machines Corporation. Unauthorized use not permitted.)*

K

**killer bit stream**    A demanding section of compressed video data. Interframe compression codes only the differences between frames; thus, when there is a lot of moving objects in view, it takes more computing power to decompress the video stream.

**kilo**    Thousand (10 to the 3rd power). Abbreviated "K." For technical specifications, it refers to the precise value 1,024 since computer specifications are based on binary numbers. For example, 64K means 65,536 bytes when referring to memory or storage (64x1024), but a 64K salary means $64,000. The IEEE uses "K" for 1,024, and "k" for 1,000. See *KB*, *binary values* and *space/time*.

**kilobit**    (thousand bits). For technical specifications, it refers to 1,024 bits. In general usage, it sometimes refers to an even one thousand bits (see *kilo*). Also Kb, Kbit and K-bit. See *space/time*.

**kilobyte**    (thousand bytes). For technical specifications, it refers to 1,024 bytes. In general usage, it sometimes refers to an even one thousand bytes (see *kilo*). Also KB, Kbyte and K-byte. See *space/time*.

**kilogram**    See *metric system*.

**kiosk**    A small, self-standing structure, such as a newstand or ticket booth. Unattended multimedia kiosks dispense public information via computer screens. Either a keyboard, touch screen or both are used for input. See *self-service application*.

**Kittyhawk**    A hard disk used in laptops and portable applications from HP. It was the world's first 1.3" hard disk, introduced in 1992.

**KLOC**    (Kilo Lines Of Code) One thousand lines of programming source code. See *lines of code*.

**kludge**    Also spelled "kluge" and pronounced "klooj." A crude, inelegant system, component or program. It may refer to a makeshift, temporary solution to a problem, as well as to any product that is poorly designed or that becomes unwieldy over time.

**klystron**    A type of vacuum tube used as an amplifier and/or oscillator for UHF and microwave signals. It is typically used as a high-power frequency source in such applications as particle accelerators, UHF TV transmission and satellite earth stations. The klystron was invented at Stanford University in 1937 and originally used as the oscillator in radar receivers during World War II.

A klystron tube makes use of speed-controlled streams of electrons that pass through a resonating cavity. Electrons in a klystron are accelerated to a controlled speed by the application of several hundred volts. As the electrons leave the heated cathode of the tube, they are directed through a narrow gap into a resonating chamber, where they are acted upon by an RF signal. The electrons bunch together and are directed into one or more additional chambers that are tuned at or near the tube's operating frequency. Strong RF fields are induced in the chambers as the electron bunches give up energy. These fields are ultimately collected at the output resonating chamber. See *magnetron* and *diode*.

**The Kiosk**
The software in kiosks must be designed for ease of use. Touch screens make the interface simple and straightforward.

**KNI SSE**    See *SSE*.

**knockout software**    See *masking software*.

**Knowbot**    (KNOWledge roBOT) A UNIX-based system for software agents that roam a distributed network, such as the Internet, in order to gather or distribute information. Developed by the Corporation for National Research Initiatives, Reston, VA (www.crni.com) and written in Python, the Knowbot Operating System is server software that hosts and interacts with the Knowbot mobile agents

**knowledge acquisition**    The process of acquiring knowledge from a human expert for an expert system, which must be carefully organized into IF-THEN rules or some other form of knowledge representation.

**knowledge base**    A database of rules about a subject used in AI applications. See *expert system*.

**knowledge-based system**    An AI application that uses a database of knowledge about a subject. In time, it is expected that everyday information systems will increasingly become knowledge based and provide users with more assistance than they do today. See *expert system*.

**knowledge domain**    A specific area of expertise of an expert system.

**knowledge-driven process management**    The automation of process management using a rule-based expert system that invokes the appropriate tools and supplies necessary information, checklists, examples and status reports to the user.

**knowledge engineer**    A person who translates the knowledge of an expert into the knowledge base of an expert system. See *expert system*.

**KnowledgeMan**    An application development system for DOS, OS/2, VMS and UNIX environments from Micro Data Base Systems, Inc., Lafayette, IN (www.mdbs.com). It includes an RDBMS, object-based 4GL programming and integrated functions, allowing, for example, database queries to update spreadsheets or results to be embedded in text documents.

**knowledge management**    An umbrella term for making more efficient use of the human knowledge that exists within an organization. Knowledge management is the 21st Century equivalent of information management. It is essentially an industry trying to distinguish itself with specialized groupware and business intelligence (BI) products that offer a wide range of solutions.

  The major focus of knowledge management is to identify and gather content from documents, reports and other text and data sources, and derive meaningful relationships from the data. See *data mining*, *information management*, *groupware* and *BI software*.

**knowledge representation**    A method used to code knowledge in an expert system, typically a series of IF-THEN rules (IF this condition occurs, THEN take this action).

**known good die**    Chips that have been fully tested before being placed into their packages. Chips used in ceramic-based multichip modules (MCMs) are typically fully tested beforehand, because the ceramic substrates are costly to replace if the final package is faulty because of a bad chip. See *MCM*.

**Korn shell**    A command line processor for UNIX that adds extensions to the Bourne shell. It includes many C shell functions, but is supported by more versions of UNIX than C shell. See *Bourne shell*, **bash shell**, *C shell* and *UNIX*.

**Kovar**    An inert metal alloy that does not oxidize.

**Kruegerapp**    A term for a downloaded application that, instead of enhancing performance, "kills" your system. The reference is to Freddy Krueger, the gruesome character from the horror series *Nightmare on Elm Street*.

**KSDS**    (Keyed Sequence DataSet) A VSAM structure that uses an index to store records in available free space. Retrieval is by key field or by address. Contrast with *ESDS*.

**KSR terminal**    (Keyboard Send Receive terminal) Same as *teleprinter*. Contrast with *RO terminal*.

**KSU**    (Key Service Unit) The cabinet that contains the electronics for a key telephone system. See *key telephone system*.

**Ku-Band**    Part of the electromagnetic spectrum used predominantly for fixed satellite communications. It uses frequencies in the 10–17GHz range. See *Ka-Band* and *C-Band*.

**KVA**    (Kilo Volt-Amps) One thousand volt-amps. See *volt-amps*.

**KVM**    (K Virtual Machine) A version of the Java Virtual Machine for small devices with limited memory. See *J2ME*. See also *KVM switch*.

**KVM cable**    See *KVM switch*.

**KVM switch**    (Keyboard Video Mouse switch) A device used to connect one keyboard, one mouse and one monitor to two or more computers. KVM switches are used to save space on a desktop when two or more computers are routinely used. They are also widely used to control server farms, where it is only necessary to gain access to each machine periodically. Switches often use special cables that combine keyboard, monitor and mouse cables into one port at the switch end. See *KVM over IP*. See also *KVM*.

# L

**L10N** (L + 10 letters + N) See *localization* and *I18N*.

**L1 cache** A memory cache built into the CPU chip or packaged within the same module as the chip. See *cache*.

**L2 cache** A memory cache that is external to the CPU chip. See *cache*.

**L2F** (Layer 2 Forwarding) A protocol from Cisco for creating virtual private dial-up networks over the Internet. It has been combined with PPTP in the L2TP protocol. See *L2TP*.

**L2TP** (Layer 2 Tunneling Protocol) A protocol from the IETF for creating virtual private networks (VPNs) over the Internet. It supports non-IP protocols such as AppleTalk and IPX, as well as the IPSec security protocol. It is a combination of Microsoft's Point-to-Point Tunneling Protocol and Cisco's Layer 2 Forwarding (L2F) technology. See *VPN*, *PPTP* and *IPSec*.

**L3_PDU** (Level 3_Protocol Data Unit) See *SIP*.

**label** (1) In data management, a made-up name that is assigned to a file, field or other data structure.
(2) In a spreadsheet, any descriptive text that is entered into a cell as a page, column or row heading.
(3) In programming, a made-up name used to identify a variable or a subroutine.
(4) In computer operations, a self-sticking form attached to the outside of a disk or tape in order to identify it.
(5) In magnetic tape files, a record used for identification at the beginning or end of the file.

**label prefix** In a spreadsheet, a character typed at the beginning of a cell entry. For example, in 1-2-3, a single quote (') identifies what follows as a descriptive label even if it's a number.

**ladder DAC** (ladder Digital to Analog Converter) Circuitry used to convert digital sound back into analog form for amplification. An individual resistor is associated with each bit of the digital sample, typically 16 bits. The resistors are weighted to the mathematical value of the bit they represent. The 16-bit sample is read passed to all 16 resistors at the same time, and the sum total of the current passing through the resistors represents the analog value of the digital sample.
Ladder DACs represent a parallel conversion of the sample. See *1-bit DAC*.

**LADDIS test** See *SPEC*.

**LADS** (Local Area Data Service) A point-to-point, private line service from the telephone company that is not connected to internal equipment. The wire pairs have no conditioning or loading coils and are not processed in any way. Also called "dry wire" or "dry copper," and originally intended for burglar alarms, the circuits are also leased for high-speed data transmission with transceivers of the same type placed at both ends.

**LAMA** (Local Automatic Message Accounting) See *AMA*.

**lamda**   The Greek letter "L," which is used as a symbol for "wavelength." A lamda is a particular frequency of light, and the term is widely used in optical networking. Sending "multiple lamdas" down a fiber is the same as sending "multiple frequencies" or "multiple colors." See *WDM* and *wavelength*.

**lamda switching**   See *MPLS*.

**lamer**   A technophobic person or neophyte to computers and technology, as viewed by the technically competent who have little empathy for the novice. See *technophobic*.

**LAN**   (Local Area Network) A communications network that serves users within a confined geographical area. It is made up of servers, workstations, a network operating system and a communications link.

Servers are high-speed machines that hold programs and data shared by network users. The workstations (clients) are the users' personal computers, which perform stand-alone processing and access the network servers as required (see *client/server*).

Diskless and floppy-only workstations are sometimes used, which retrieve all software and data from the server. Increasingly, "thin client" network computers (NCs) and Windows terminals are also used. A printer can be attached locally to a workstation or to a server and be shared by network users.

Small LANs can allow certain workstations to function as a server, allowing users access to data on another user's machine. These peer-to-peer networks are often simpler to install and manage, but dedicated servers provide better performance and can handle higher transaction volume. Multiple servers are used in large networks.

The controlling software in a LAN is the network operating system (NetWare, UNIX, Windows NT, etc.) that resides in the server. A component part of the software resides in each client and allows the application to read and write data from the server as if it were on the local machine.

The message transfer is managed by a transport protocol such as TCP/IP and IPX. The physical transmission of data is performed by the access method (Ethernet, Token Ring, etc.), which is implemented in the network adapters that are plugged into the machines. The actual communications path is the cable (twisted pair, coax, optical fiber) that interconnects each network adapter. See *WAN*.

**LAN adapter**   Same as *network adapter*.

**LAN administrator**   See *network administrator*.

**LAN analyzer**   See *network analyzer*.

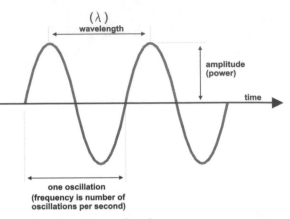

**Lamda**
The symbol above the word "wavelength" in this diagram is the Greek Lamda.

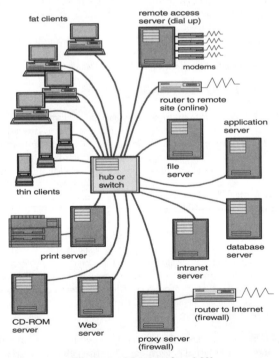

**Clients and Servers in a LAN**
This illustration shows one server for each type of service on a LAN. In practice, several functions can be combined in one machine and, for large volumes, multiple machines can be used to balance the traffic for the same service. For example, a large Internet Web site is often comprised of several computer systems (servers).

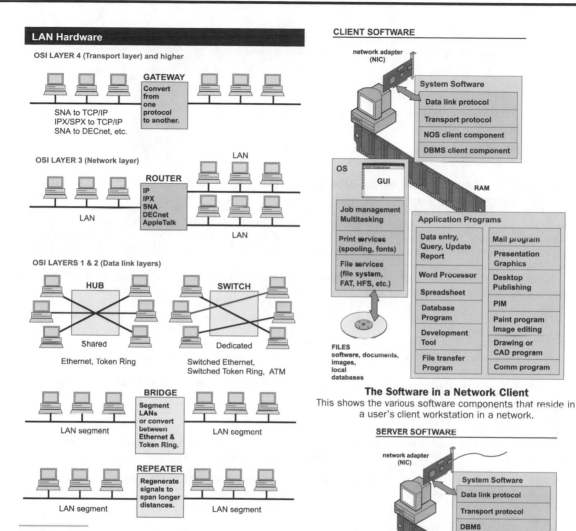

## LAN Hardware

**OSI LAYER 4 (Transport layer) and higher**

**GATEWAY**
Convert from one protocol to another.

SNA to TCP/IP
IPX/SPX to TCP/IP
SNA to DECnet, etc.

**OSI LAYER 3 (Network layer)**

LAN

**ROUTER**
IP
IPX
SNA
DECnet
AppleTalk

LAN

LAN

LAN

**OSI LAYERS 1 & 2 (Data link layers)**

**HUB**
Shared
Ethernet, Token Ring

**SWITCH**
Dedicated
Switched Ethernet,
Switched Token Ring, ATM

**BRIDGE**
Segment LANs or convert between Ethernet & Token Ring.

LAN segment            LAN segment

**REPEATER**
Regenerate signals to span longer distances.

LAN segment            LAN segment

---

### CLIENT SOFTWARE

network adapter (NIC)

**System Software**
Data link protocol
Transport protocol
NOS client component
DBMS client component

**OS**
GUI
RAM

Job management
Multitasking

Print services (spooling, fonts)

File services (file system, FAT, HFS, etc.)

**Application Programs**

| | |
|---|---|
| Data entry, Query, Update Report | Mail program |
| Word Processor | Presentation Graphics |
| Spreadsheet | Desktop Publishing |
| Database Program | PIM |
| Development Tool | Paint program Image editing |
| File transfer Program | Drawing or CAD program |
| | Comm program |

**FILES**
software, documents, images, local databases

**The Software in a Network Client**
This shows the various software components that reside in a user's client workstation in a network.

---

### SERVER SOFTWARE

network adapter (NIC)

**System Software**
Data link protocol
Transport protocol
DBMS
Mail/messaging system

**NOS**
GUI (or CUI)
RAM

Communications Services

Print services

File services

**FILES**
software, databases, shared files

**The Software in a Network Server**
This shows the network operating system and various system software components in a network

---

**LAN-centric**  Designed to run in a LAN in contrast to a centralized host computer. See *client/server, host-centric* and *server-centric*.

**land**  A non-indented area on an optical medium such as a CD-ROM or DVD disc. Contrast with *pit*.

**LANDA**  (**LAN D**ealers **A**ssociation) An association that merged with NOMDA to become the Business Technology Association. See *BTA*.

**landing zone**  A safe non-data area on a hard disk used for parking the read/write head. See *load/unload ramp*.

**landline**  Land based. Refers to standard telephone and data communications systems that use in-ground and telephone pole cables in contrast to wireless cellular and satellite services.

**Landmark rating**   An earlier PC performance test from Landmark Research International, Clearwater, FL, that measured CPU, video and coprocessor speed. It ran under DOS and was widely used. In 1995, Landmark was acquired by Quarterdeck.

**LAND Rover**   See *LANRover*.

**landscape**   A printing orientation that prints data across the wider side of the form. Contrast with *portrait*.

**landscape monitor**   A monitor that is used to display facing text pages. It is wider than it is high.

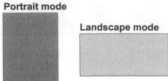

Portrait mode

Landscape mode

**LANE**   (LAN Emulation) The ability to connect Ethernet and Token Ring networks together via ATM. LANE makes the process transparent, requiring no modification to Ethernet and Token Ring stations. LANE allows common protocols, such as IP, IPX, AppleTalk and DECnet, to ride over an ATM backbone.

The LANE driver provides the encapsulation of Ethernet and Token Ring packets into LANE packets and then converts the packets into ATM cells. It performs the reverse functions on the other end. The driver resides in an edge device, which sits between the LAN and the ATM switch. The driver is also required in each ATM client station that communicates with Ethernet and Token Ring.

LANE is also used to create emulated LANs (ELANs) that logically combine users by workgroup traffic (ELANs are the same as VLANs). With LANE, broadcast domains can be larger than with other network technologies, because LANE can manage broadcast traffic within ELANs and keep it under control.

LANE is implemented in an ATM switch or stand-alone server and is made up of two software components: the LANE Configuration Server (LECS), which provides address resolution, and the Broadcast and Unknown Server (BUS), which manages multicast and broadcast traffic within the ELAN.

The ATM Forum governs the LANE User-to-Network Interface (LUNI), which defines how an end station communicates with the ATM network.

With LANE, in order to communicate between one subnet and another, a router is required. This is eliminated with MPOA. See *MPOA*.

**LAN Emulation**   See *LANE*.

**LAN fax**   A fax service provided in a local area network (LAN). The LAN fax software is installed on a server and turns it into a LAN fax server. It provides a centralized service for network users to send and receive faxes.

**language**   A set of symbols and rules used to convey information. See *machine language, programming language, graphics language, page description language, fourth-generation language, standards* and *user interface*.

**LanguageAccess**   An SAA-compliant query language from IBM that translates a user's English-language request into SQL language for QMF. QMF retrieves the data.

**language processor**   Language translation software. Programming languages, command languages, query languages, natural languages and foreign languages are all translated by software.

**LAN Manager**   (1) A network operating system from Microsoft that runs as a server application under OS/2. It supports DOS, Windows and OS/2 clients. LAN Manager was superseded by Windows NT Server, and many parts of LAN Manager are used in NT. See *LAN Server*.

(2) Same as *network administrator*.

**LAN Network Manager**   IBM Token Ring network management software.  LAN Station Manager is the workstation counterpart that collects data for LAN Network Manager.

**LAN Requester**   The client part of LAN Server.

**LANRover**   A remote access server from Shiva that provides modem and ISDN access to remote users on a network. The LANRover is a proprietary device that connects to the LAN and supports the PPP protocol, as well as standard dial-up ANSI terminal connections.

**LAN segment**    A section of a local area network that is used by a particular workgroup or department and separated from the rest of the LAN by a bridge, router or switch. Networks are divided into multiple segments for security and to improve traffic flow by filtering out packets that are not destined for the segment. See *subnet mask*.

**LAN Server**    (1) A network operating system from IBM that runs as a server application under OS/2 and supports both DOS, Windows and OS/2 clients. Originally based on LAN Manager when OS/2 was jointly developed by IBM and Microsoft, starting with LAN Server 3.0, it runs only under IBM's version of OS/2.

LAN Server provides disk mirroring, CID capability and Network Transport Services/2 (NTS/2) for concurrent access to NetWare servers. Options are LAN Server for the Macintosh for Mac client access and System Performance/2 (SP/2), a series of network management utilities.

(2) (LAN server) Generically, a file server in a network.

**LAN station**    (1) A workstation in a local area network.
(2) See *LAN Network Manager*.

**LAN switch**    A network device that cross connects stations or LAN segments. Also known as a "frame switch," LAN switches are available for Ethernet, Fast Ethernet, Token Ring and FDDI. ATM switches are generally considered in a category by themselves.

Network switches are increasingly replacing shared media hubs in order to increase bandwidth. For example, a 16-port 100BaseT hub shares the total 100 Mbps bandwidth with all 16 attached nodes. By replacing the hub with a switch, each sender/receiver pair has the full 100 Mbps capacity. Each port on the switch can give full bandwidth to a single server or client station or it can be connected to a hub with several stations. See *switched Ethernet*.

**LANtastic**    A peer-to-peer LAN operating system for DOS, Windows and OS/2 from Artisoft, Inc., Tucson, AZ (www.artisoft.com). It supports Ethernet, ARCNET and Token Ring adapaters, as well as its own twisted pair adapter at two Mbits/sec. Artisoft also makes Ethernet adapters. Included are e-mail and chat functions. Voice mail and conversation are optional. Simply LANtastic is an entry-level version designed for easy installation and use.

Multiple protocols are supported starting with LANtastic 6.0, allowing a LANtastic client station to access a NetWare, LAN Manager, LAN Server or Windows NT server. LANtastic was very popular before Windows came along with its own networking built in. See *CorStream*.

**HUBS AND SWITCHES**

**Hub versus Switch**

With a hub, the bandwidth is shared among all stations. When the hub is replaced with a switch, each sender and receiver pair has the full wire speed. For example, a 16-port 10BaseT switch would have an 80 Mbps bandwidth to support eight pairs.

**Hub and Switch Used Together**

Hubs are used in combination with switches, because not all users may need the speed of an individual switching port.

**10/100 Switch (10BaseT and 100BaseT)**

A 10/100 Ethernet switch provides a Fast Ethernet 100 Mbps link to the server and 10 Mbps links between user stations.

**LAN Workplace**    A family of software products from Novell that allows DOS, Windows, Macintosh and OS/2 clients in a NetWare environment to access resources on a TCP/IP network. LAN Workplace for DOS can also encapsulate NetWare protocols and run NetWare-dependent applications entirely within a TCP/IP network.

**LAP**    (1) (Link Access Procedure) An ITU family of error correction protocols originally derived from the HDLC standard.

```
LAP-B (Balanced)       Used in X-25 networks.
LAP-D (D channel)      Used in ISDN data channel.
LAP-M (Modem)          Defined in ITU V.42, which
                         uses some LAPD methods and
                         adds additional ones.
LAP-X (Half-dupleX)    Used in ship to shore
                         transmission.
```

**(2)** (Link Access Protocol)  The data link protocol in an Appletalk network. Support for the various data link types are known as ELAP (Ethernet LAP), TLAP (Token Ring LAP), FLAP (FDDI LAP) and LLAP (LocalTalk LAP).

**LapLink**    A file transfer program for Windows from LapLink.com, Inc., Bothell, WA (www.laplink.com). This veteran product, noted for its ease of use, has been so widely used that people often refer to "laplinking" as a general term for file transfer. LapLink 2000 provides file transfer over the Internet. Earlier versions supported transfer between PCs and Macs. LapLink.com was formerly Travelling Software, Inc. See *LapLink cable* and **how to transfer a file**.

**LapLink cable**    A serial cable used to connect two computers together for file transfer. This type of cable is technically a "null modem cable," but is often called a LapLink cable due to the popularity of the LapLink program. The LapLink cable simulates two modems using the telephone system. It crosses the receiving line with the sending line. A special parallel port cable is also available for higher transfer speeds.

**laptop**    See *laptop computer*.

**laptop computer**    A portable computer that has a flat screen and usually weighs less than a dozen pounds. It uses AC power and/or batteries. Most have connectors for an external monitor and keyboard transforming them into desktop computers. Most laptop computers today fall in the notebook computer category (see "Weight" in the following list). Following are the major features of a laptop.

**Keyboard**    Keyboard layout is often sacrificed. The HOME, END, PAGEUP and PAGEDN keys may not be dedicated keys, requiring that you hold down the FN key in conjunction with them. This is cumbersome. Function keys and cursor keys are often made smaller. There's only one rule—test drive the keyboard carefully.

**Screen Quality**    Active matrix LCD screens (TFT) provide a sharper image and wider viewing angle than dual scan or HPA passive matrix.

**Screen Resolution and Acceleration**    Unlike a desktop computer, you cannot replace the display adapter for one with a higher resolution. The built-in display system also feeds an external monitor, so be sure it has the maximum resolution you require.

**External Display and Keyboard Connectors**    Connect a full-size CRT and keyboard for home/office. Even if you like your laptop keyboard, you may want to use an external keyboard with your external monitor, because the laptop screen usually doesn't lie back flat to get out of the way from straight-on viewing of the external monitor. A full-size keyboard can be connected through the external keyboard connector on most laptops. Keyboards can be attached to earlier laptops with an adapter via the serial or parallel port.

**Built-in Pointing Device**    There are a wide variety of pointing devices built into laptops, including trackballs and tracksticks, but each one has a different feel. Try it first. The best option is always an external mouse port that lets you connect your favorite desktop mouse if the built-in device becomes cumbersome.

**Expansion**    Expansion is critical on a laptop. All laptops have PC Card (PCMCIA) slots, and newer laptops have USB ports. For desktop use, a docking station may provide ISA or PCI slots.

**Auto Resume**    Lets you return to the computer and pick up where you left off without having to reload your applications.

**Dual Display**    Using an external monitor and laptop display at the same time. For presentations with a data projector, it may be difficult to look at a projected image off in the distance. Most laptops provide this capability.

**Batteries**    Nickel metal hydride and lithium ion batteries do not suffer from the "memory effect" of older nickel cadmium batteries.

**Removable Hard Disk**    A removable hard drive is the best bet. If you run out of space, you can replace the old disk with a larger one.

**Multimedia**    All laptops today have built-in sound, speakers and CD-ROMs that are either built in or swappable with the floppy drive.

**Weight**    Seven pounds doesn't sound like much until you lug it around all day. Some subnotebooks use an external floppy disk to reduce poundage. Also, check the transformer weight (also called the AC adapter or power adapter). They never mention this, but it can add one or two pounds, and it is an item you will always carry in the computer case. Following is a rough guide to current-day weights and terminology:

| Type | Weight (pounds) Without Transformer |
|------|-------------------------------------|
| Portable | 4-20 |
| Laptop | 4-10 |
| Notebook | 4-7 |
| Subnotebook | 2-4 |
| Pocket | 1 |

---

**large-format printer**    See *wide-format printer*.

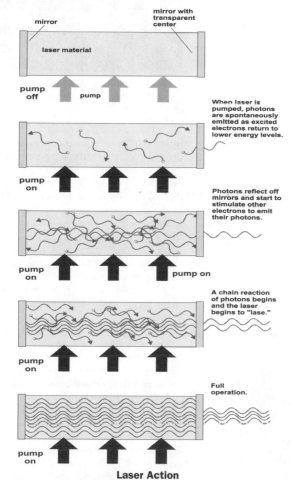

**Laser Action**
The combination of spontaneous emission first, and then stimulated emission, causes the laser to "lase," which means it generates a coherent beam of light at a single frequency.

Labels within figure:
- mirror
- mirror with transparent center
- laser material
- pump off    pump
- When laser is pumped, photons are spontaneously emitted as excited electrons return to lower energy levels.
- pump on
- Photons reflect off mirrors and start to stimulate other electrons to emit their photons.
- pump on    pump on
- A chain reaction of photons begins and the laser begins to "lase."
- pump on
- Full operation.
- pump on

**One of the First**
In 1983, Tandy's Radio Shack division launched the Model 100 Micro Executive Workstation. It weighed only four pounds and included a built-in word processor, name and address list and modem. The Model 100 was inspiration for the huge portable market that followed. *(Image courtesy of Tandy Corporation.)*

**laser**    (Light Amplification by the Stimulated Emission of Radiation) A device that creates a uniform and coherent light that is very different from an ordinary light bulb. Many lasers deliver light in an almost-perfectly parallel beam (collimated) that is very pure, approaching a single wavelength. Laser light can be focused down to a tiny spot as small as a single wavelength.

Laser output can be continuous or pulsed and is used in a myriad of applications. Gas lasers are used to cut steel and perform delicate eye surgery, while solid state lasers create the ultra-high-speed, miniscule pulses traveling in optical fibers traversing the backbones of all major communications networks. Light traveling in an optical fiber is impervious to external interference, a constant problem with electrical pulses in copper wire. See *optical fiber*.

How Does It Work?    A laser is an optical oscillator, which is made out of a solid, liquid or gas with mirrors at both ends. To make the laser work, the material is excited or "pumped," with light or electricity. The pumping excites the electrons in the atoms, causing them to jump to higher orbits, creating a "population inversion." A few of the electrons drop back to lower energy levels spontaneously, releasing a photon (quantum of light). These photons stimulate other excited electrons to emit more photons with the same energy, and thus the same wavelength as the original. These light waves build in strength as they pass through the laser medium, and the mirrors at both ends keep reflecting the light back and forth creating a chain reaction and causing the laser to "lase."

In simple laser cavities, one mirror has a small transparent area that lets the laser beam out. In semiconductor lasers, both mirrors often transmit a beam, the second one being used for monitoring purposes.

**Who Invented It?**    In 1957, the laser was conceived by Gordon Gould, a graduate student in physics at Columbia University. When Gould filed for patents in 1959, he found that Columbia professor Charles Townes and Arthur Schawlow of Bell Labs had already filed for them. The year before, AT&T had, in fact, demonstrated a working laser at Bell Labs. In 1977, after years of litigation, a court awarded Gould rights to the first of three patents and later to all of them. He finally reaped millions in royalties.

### laser-class printer
A category of computer printers that produces output with the same resolution and color quality of a laser printer. Output from LED, solid ink, dye sublimation and Iris printers is in the same class as laser printers.

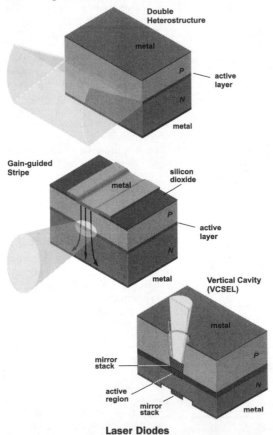

**Laser Diodes**
Laser diodes such as these are all fabricated using semiconductor processes just like CPU and memory chips. Note that the VCSELs (vixels) produce a circular beam that couples well with a fiber.

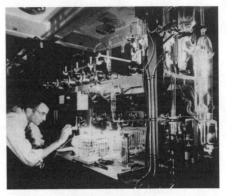

**Developing the Laser**
This photo of the development of the helium-neon laser was taken at AT&T's Bell Laboratories in 1964. *(Image courtesy of AT&T.)*

### laser diode
A semiconductor-based laser used to generate analog signals or digital pulses for transmission through optical fibers. Both laser diodes and LEDs (light-emitting diodes) are used for this purpose, but the laser diode generates a smaller beam that is easier to couple with the smaller core of singlemode fibers. Laser diodes are designed to emit light either from their edge or their surface, the latter providing a circular beam that couples better with the round core of the fiber.

Laser diodes work on the same principle as the bigger gas lasers. They function as an optical oscillator by stimulating a chain reaction of photon emission inside a tiny chamber. In edge-emitting lasers, the semiconductor waver is cleaved, and the inherent properties of the semiconductor create reflective ends that may or may not be enhanced with additional reflective films. With vertical cavity surface emitting lasers (VCSELs), the reflectivity has to be added.

The most common semiconductors used in laser diodes are compounds based on gallium arsenide (750 to 900 nm in the infrared), indium gallium arsenide phosphide (1,200–1,700 nm in the infrared) and gallium nitride (near 400 nm in the blue). See *laser* and *solid state laser*.

**LaserDisc**    An optical disc used for full-motion video and interactive training that stems back to the late 1970s, but which became obsolete in the 1990s. Although several videodisc systems were introduced, only the Philips LaserVision survived until CD-ROMs and DVDs arrived. Even before its demise, it was never very popular.

LaserDisc movies used the CLV format, recording an analog composite video signal on a continuous, spiraling track. Each side of a 12" platter held one hour of video in 108,000 frames. For interactive training and games, the CAV format was used with each circular track holding one video frame. The 54,000 frames allowed 30 minutes of video per side.

Early LaserDiscs recorded only analog sound, but subsequent discs contained analog and digital soundtracks. Newer players defaulted to the digital sound if available. Some players let the user select the soundtrack, supporting multiple languages and other annotations on the same disc. See *CLV* and *CAV*.

**LaserJet**    A family of laser printers from HP. Introduced in 1984 at a price of $3,495, the first LaserJet revolutionized the desktop laser printer market. LaserJets print from 600–1,200 dpi, and PCL is HP's native printer command language.

LaserJets have built-in scalable fonts and also accept bitmapped fonts from the computer (soft fonts). They also come with PostScript emulation. Earlier models used plug-in cartridges, and PostScript was an option until native models were introduced in 1992 (LaserJet 4).

In 1994, HP launched its first color LaserJet, using an enhanced PCL 5 language. At $7,295, it printed 2 ppm in color and 10 ppm in black and white. Subsequent models are higher speed and lower priced as color lasers have begun to make a presence. See *laser printer* and *PCL*.

**laser printer**    A printer that uses a laser and the electrophotographic method to print a full page at a time. The laser is used to "paint" a charged drum with light, to which toner is applied and then transferred onto paper (see *electrophotographic* for more details). Desktop laser printers use cut sheets like a copy machine. Large machines use cut sheets or paper rolls that are cut after printing.

In 1975, IBM introduced the first laser printer, the model 3800. Later, Siemens came out with the ND 2 and Xerox with the 9700. These self-contained printing presses were online to a mainframe or offline, accepting print image data on tape or disk.

In 1984, HP introduced the LaserJet, the first desktop laser printer, which rapidly became a huge success and a major part of the company's business. Desktop lasers obsoleted the clackety daisy wheel printers, but did not eliminate the dot matrix printers that are still widely used for labels and multipart forms.

**The LaserJet**
Noisier than today's models, but built like a tank, HP created a revolution in desktop printing with its 1984 introduction of the LaserJet. The LaserJet's reliability became legendary and caused HP to become the world leader in desktop laser printers. *(Image courtesy of Hewlett-Packard Company.)*

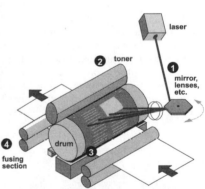

**The Laser Mechanism**
The laser printer uses electrostatic charges to (1) create an image on the drum, (2) adhere toner to the image, (3) transfer the toned image to the paper, and (4) fuse the toner to the paper. The laser creates the image by "painting" a negative of the page to be printed on the charged drum. Where light falls, the charge is dissipated, leaving a positive image to be printed.

Low-end laser printers print in the 4–8 ppm range, while typical office workgroup units print 17–32 ppm. HP is the major vendor, and many quality companies compete, such as Lexmark, IBM and Okidata. Midrange units print in the 40 to 60 ppm range, with a large jump to high-end printers that print from 150 to more than 1,000 ppm.

Laser printer resolution is typically from 300–1,200 dpi, but specialty printers can reach imagesetter resolution of 2,400 dpi. Some units offer paper-handling functions found on copy machines, such as collation, stapling and three-hole punching.

Color laser printers are slower than their monochrome counterparts, typically in the 4–10 ppm range. At the other end of the spectrum, high-end "digital printing presses" can print 70 or more duplexed color pages per minute, producing finished booklets and manuals (see *digital printing*).

There are several printer technologies that fall into the laser class category, but do not actually use a laser. LED printers use an array of LEDs to beam the image onto the drum, and electron beam imaging (ion deposition) creates the image with electricity rather than light. Solid ink printers propel a waxlike ink onto the drum.

**laser pump**    (1) A laser used as the pump for an optical amplifier or other laser. Typically known as a "pump laser." See *EDFA* and *laser*.

(2) The part of a laser that excites the atoms in the laser medium. See *laser*.

**LaserWriter**    A family of desktop laser printers from Apple, introduced in 1985. Most models support PostScript and built-in networking.

**lasso**    An image editing tool that enables you to select an irregular object by dragging the mouse around it (while the mouse button is held down) and letting go. You do not have to join the ends together. When the mouse button is released, the two ends are connected automatically.

**last mile**    The connection between the customer and the telephone or cable company. The last mile has traditionally used copper-based telephone wire or coaxial cable, but wireless technologies offer alternative options in some locations. See *local loop*.

**LAT**    (Local Area Transport) A communications protocol from Digital for controlling terminal traffic in a DECnet environment.

**LATA**    (Local Access and Transport Area) The geographic region set up to differentiate local and long distance telephone calls within the U.S. Telephone calls between parties within a LATA (intraLATA) are handled by the local telephone companies and are under the jurisdiction of the state's public utility commission. Calls between LATAs are handled by interexchange carriers (IXCs) and are governed by the FCC. See *PUC* and *FCC*.

**latch**    An electronic circuit that maintains one of two states. See *flip-flop*.

**late binding**    Same as *dynamic binding*.

**latency**    The time between initiating a request for data and the beginning of the actual data transfer. On a disk, latency is the time it takes for the selected sector to come around and be positioned under the read/write head. Channel latency is the time it takes for a computer channel to become unoccupied in order to transfer data. Network latency is the delay introduced when a packet is momentarily stored, analyzed and then forwarded.

**latent image**    An invisible image, typically of electrical charges. For example, in a copy machine, a latent image of the page to be copied is created on a plate or drum as an electrical charge.

**LaTeX**    (LAmport TeX) A document preparation system based on the TeX language developed by Leslie Lamport at SRI International. LaTex lets the user concentrate on the logical structure of the document rather than the format codes.

**The Lasso Button**
The lasso tool is found in many paint and image editing programs both in the Mac and Windows.

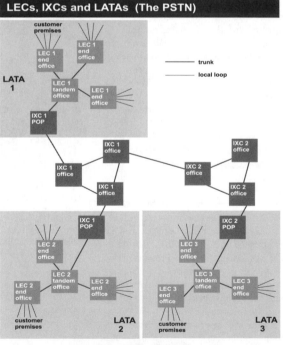

**LATAs, LECs and IXCs**
The PSTN is made up of local exchange carriers (LECs) and interexchange carriers (IXCs) that are governed by LATA boundaries. Although this illustration shows one LEC within one LATA, state regulations may allow multiple LECs within the same LATA. Note that IXC 2 does not have POPs in LATAs 1 and 2, and must have a reselling agreement with IXC 1 in order to gain access to those areas.

**launch**     To cause a program to load and run. Contrast with *exit*.

**laws**     See *Amdahl's law*, *Brook's law*, *Cole's law*, *Freedman's law*, *Metcalfe's law*, *Moore's law* and *Nacchio's law*.

**Lawson Insight**     A family of ERP applications from Lawson Software. It integrates with non-Lawson MRP (manufacturing) systems and provides the back-end processing for industries such as health care, retail, public sector, and professional and financial services. It supports Windows, UNIX, Notes and browser clients, as well as NT, UNIX, AS/400, Domino and Alpha servers. Lawson Insight provides modules that can be used intact or be highly customized with various Lawson-supplied tools and standard programming languages. A set of published interfaces (APIs) allows for integration with other applications.

**Lawson Software**     (Lawson Software, Minneapolis, MN, www.lawson.com) A software company that specializes in ERP for vertical markets including health care, retail, public sector, professional and financial services. The company was founded in 1975 by Bill Lawson, Richard Lawson and John Cerullo to do consulting on Burroughs computers. Its custom software efforts turned into packaged products that eventually led to client/server applications in the mid-1980s. In 1996, all of its applications were converted to work on the Internet. See *Lawson Insight*.

**layer**     (1) In computer graphics, one of several on-screen "drawing boards" for creating elements within a picture. Layers can be manipulated independently, and the sum of all layers make up the total image. See *layers* and *PSD file*.

(2) In communications, a protocol that interacts with other protocols to provide all the necessary transmission services. See *OSI*.

**layer 2**     In networking, the communications protocol that contains the physical address of a client or server station. It is called the "data link layer" or "MAC layer," and contains the address inspected by a bridge or switch. Layer 2 processing is faster than layer 3 processing, because less analysis of the packet is required. See *MAC layer* and *OSI*.

**layer 2 switch**     A network device that forwards traffic based on MAC layer (Ethernet or Token Ring) addresses. See *LAN switch* and *layer 3 switch*.

**layer 3**     In networking, the communications protocol that contains the logical address of a client or server station. It is called the "network layer" and contains the address (IP, IPX, etc.) inspected by a router that forwards it through the network. Layer 3 contains a type field so that traffic can be prioritized and forwarded based on message type as well as network destination. Since layer 3 provides more filtering capabilities, it also adds more overhead than layer 2 processing. See *layer 3 switch*, *router* and *OSI*.

**layer 3 switch**     A network device that forwards traffic based on layer 3 information at very high speeds. Traditionally, routers, which inspect layer 3, have been considerably slower than layer 2 switches. In order to increase routing speeds, many "cut-through" techniques have been used, which "inspect the first packet at layer 3 and send the rest at layer 2" type of processing. Ipsilon's IP Switch and Cabletron's SecureFast switches were pioneers in cut-through switching; however, the MPLS protocol is expected to standardize this technique.

As more routing lookup functions were moved from software into the ASIC chips, layer 3 switches could inspect each packet just like a router at high speed without using proprietary cut-through methods. If a layer 3 switch supports packet-by-packet inspection and supports routing protocols, it is called a "routing switch" or "switch router," which simply means "fast router." For example, Cisco calls its high-end routers Gigabit Switch Routers.

The more deeply a packet is examined, the more forwarding decisions can be made based upon type of traffic, quality of service and so on. To get to this information means digging into the packet's headers to ferret out the data, which takes processing time. To understand how the packets are formed, see *TCP/IP ABCs*. The following shows what is examined at each layer. See *layer 3*, *layer 2 switch*, *Web switch* and *virtual LAN*.

```
        Forwarding
        Decision
Layer   Based on          Examples
2       MAC address       Ethernet, Token Ring, etc.
3       Network address   IP, IPX, etc.
3       Service quality   IP, IPX, etc.
3       Application       IPX socket
4       Application       IP socket
```

**layer 4**   See *transport protocol*.

**layer 4 switch**   A network device that integrates routing and switching by forwarding traffic at layer 2 speed using layer 4 and layer 3 information. When packets are inspected at layer 4, the sockets can be analyzed and decisions can be made based on the type of application being serviced. See *layer 3 switch* and *Web switch*.

**layered architecture**   An architecture in which data moves from one defined level of processing to another. Communications protocols are a primary example. See *OSI model*.

**layers**   In a CAD drawing or image editing program, the ability to maintain elements on separate "canvases" for greater control and enhanced editing. Layers provide different capabilities depending on the program. For example, paint and image editing programs deal with bitmapped images, which are matrices of pixels. When one element is finally placed on top of another, it cannot be removed without leaving a blank space in its stead. When such programs use layers, elements can be freely moved under and over each other, because each complete, original element is maintained within its own layer. A composite of the layers is used as a final image, but the original layered images can always be maintained for further editing.

CAD and drawing programs automatically allow any number of graphic elements to be placed on top of or below others. However, such programs also use layers to separate groups of related elements so that elements in one layer can be easily worked on together. For example, all the elements in a layer can be quickly selected and changed without affecting the rest of the drawing.

**layout setting**   A value used to format a printed page. Margins, tabs, indents, headers, footers and column widths are examples.

**lazy write**   Refers to the effect caused by using a write back cache. Data is written to the cache first and, later, during idle machine cycles or at some specified time, is written to disk if it is a disk cache or to memory if it is a CPU cache.

**LBA**   (Logical Block Addressing) A method used to support IDE hard disks larger than 504MB (528,482,304 bytes) on PCs. LBA provides the necessary address conversion in the BIOS to support drives up to 8GB. BIOSs after mid 1994, which are sometimes called "Enhanced BIOSs," generally provide LBA conversion. LBA support is required for compatibility with the FAT32 directory.

**LBRV**   (Low Bit Rate Voice) A voice sampling technique that analyzes each 15–30 millisecond speech segment independently and converts it into a 30-byte frame.

**LCC**   (Leadless Chip Carrier, Leaded Chip Carrier) See *leadless chip carrier*, *CLCC* and *PLCC*.

**LCD**   (Liquid Crystal Display) A display technology that uses rod-shaped molecules (liquid crystals) that flow like liquid and bend light. Unenergized, the crystals direct light through two polarizing filters, allowing a natural background color to show. When energized, they redirect the light to be absorbed in one of the polarizers, causing the dark appearance of crossed polarizers to show. The more the molecules are twisted, the better the contrast and viewing angle.

Because it takes less power to move molecules than to energize a light-emitting device, LCDs replaced LEDs in digital watches years ago. The LCD was developed in 1963 at RCA's Sarnoff Research Center in Princeton, NJ.

TYPES OF LCDs

**Passive Display (TN and STN)**   Called "passive matrix" when used for computer screens and "passive display" when used for small readouts, all the active electronics (transistors) are outside of the display screen. Passive displays have improved immensely, but do not provide a wide viewing angle, and submarining is noticeable. The passive display types are listed here.

■ **TN — Twisted Nematic — 90° twist**   Low-cost displays for consumer products and instruments. Black on gray/silver background.

■ **STN—Supertwisted Nematic—80–270° twist** Used extensively on laptops for mono and color displays. DSTN and FSTN provide improvements over straight STN. 180° - green/blue on yellow background 270° - blue on white/blue background.

■ **Dual Scan STN** Improves STN display by dividing the screen into two halves and scanning each half simultaneously, doubling the number of lines refreshed. Not as sharp as active matrix.

**Active Display (TFT)** Typically used for laptop color screens and, increasingly, for flat desktop screens. Known as "active matrix" displays, transistors are built into each pixel within the screen. For example, 640×480 color VGA screen requires 921,600 transistors: one for each red, green and blue dot. Provides a sharp, clear image with good contrast and eliminates submarining, but fabrication costs are high. Uses a 90° (TN) twist. Also called "TFT LCD" (thin film transistor LCD).

**Reflective vs. Backlit** Reflective screens used in many consumer appliances and some lightweight laptops require external light and only work well in a bright room or with a desk lamp. Backlit and sidelit screens have their own light source and work well in dim lighting.

**LCD monitor** A flat panel display that uses liquid crystals. Although almost exclusively used in laptops, the LCD technology is also the most popular thus far for flat panel desktop monitors. See *flat panel display* and *LCD*.

**LCD panel** Also called a "projection panel," it is a data projector that accepts computer output and displays it on a see-through liquid crystal screen that is placed on top of an overhead projector. See *data projector*.

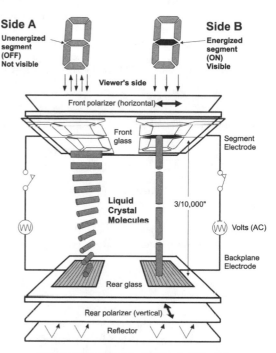

**Twisted-Nematic Liquid Crystal Display**
On side A, the unenergized segment causes the crystals to line up with the front and rear polarizers. The segment appears light gray, which is actually the light traveling down and reflected back up the crystals. On side B, the energized segment causes the crystals to become perpendicular to the polarizers. The segment appears dark, which is the effect of crossed polarizers. Most LCDs use a translucent reflector with light behind it, which makes the background brighter and the characters sharper.
*(Redrawn from illustration courtesy of LXD, Inc.)*

**LCD Panel**
An LCD panel requires an overhead projector. They were the interim stage between the big and bulky tube projectors and today's slim, self-contained units that use LCD or DLP technology for creating the image.

**LCD printer** An electrophotographic printer that uses a single light source directed by liquid crystal shutters.

**LCD projector** See *data projector* and *LCD panel*.

**LCM** (Liquid Crystal Monitor) A flat panel display that uses the liquid crystal (LCD) technology. See *flat panel display*.

**L-commerce**    (Location-**COMMERCE**) Using location services such as GPS tracking for business purposes. See *mobile positioning*.

**LD**    See *LaserDisc*.

**LDAP**    (Lightweight Directory Access Protocol) A protocol used to access a directory listing. LDAP support is being implemented in Web browsers and e-mail programs, which can query an LDAP-compliant directory. It is expected that LDAP will provide a common method for searching e-mail addresses on the Internet, eventually leading to a global white pages. LDAP is a sibling protocol to HTTP and FTP, and uses the ldap:// prefix in its URL.

LDAP is a simplified version of the DAP protocol, which is used to gain access to X.500 directories. It is easier to code the query in LDAP than in DAP, but LDAP is less comprehensive. For example, DAP can initiate searches on other servers if an address is not found, while LDAP cannot in its initial specification. See *DSML* and *ADSI*.

**LDDS**    See *WorldCom*.

**LDI**    See *OpenLDI*.

**LE**    (1) (Less than or Equal to) See *relational operator*.
(2) (Local Exchange) See *central office*.

**lead**    A metal pin that extends out from a chip that plugs into a socket or is soldered onto a circuit board. See *pin*, *socket mount*, *surface mount* and *lead frame*.

**lead acid**    A rechargeable battery technology widely used in portable gardening tools and some earlier portable computers. It uses lead plates and an acid electrolyte. It provides the least amount of charge per pound of the rechargeable technologies. See *batteries*.

**leaded chip carrier**    A surface mount chip package that uses pins that extend out of the chip. Contrast with *leadless chip carrier*. See *PLCC*.

**leader**    (1) A length of unrecorded tape used to thread the tape onto the tape drive.
(2) A dot or dash used to draw the eye across the printed page, such as in a table of contents.

**lead frame**    A common type of chip package that uses metal leads that extend outside the housing. Lead frame technology goes back to the early days of DIP chips, but is still widely used in many package varieties. See *chip package*.

**Lead frame**

**Lead frame (CSP)**

**Lead Frame Packages**
These cross sections show the differences between lead frame chip packages in both standard and CSP varieties. *(Illustration courtesy of Joseph Fjelstad.)*

**lead-in**    A group of 4,500 sectors written at the beginning of a CD-R recording session. When the session is closed, the table of contents is written into the lead-in area, as well as the location where the next session can be recorded. Contrast with *lead-out*.

**leading**    In typography, the vertical spacing between lines of type (between baselines). The name comes from the early days of typesetting when the space was achieved with thin bars of lead. Leading is measured in points and includes the point size of the typeface and the actual space between the lines. Thus, 15 points of leading using 12 point type really means three points of space in-between lines. See *typeface*.

**leading edge**    (1) The edge of a punched card or document that enters the reading station first.
(2) In digital electronics, a pulse as it changes from 0 to 1.

**(3)** In programming, a loop that tests a condition before the loop is entered.

**(4)** (Leading Edge Products, Inc., Westborough, MA) A PC manufacturer founded in 1980. Its Model M (for Mitsubishi) in 1982 was the first PC from overseas. Korean Daewoo Corporation supplied it with products since 1984 and acquired it in 1989. Leading Edge computers are no longer sold in the U.S.

**leading zeros**    Zeros used to fill a field that do not increase the numerical value of the data. For example, all the zeros in 0000006588 are leading zeros.

**leadless chip carrier**    A chip package that uses flat metal pads that make contact with the socket or circuit board. Contrast with *leaded chip carrier*. See *CLCC*.

**lead-out**    A group of sectors written at the end of a CD-R recording session that indicates the end of the data. The first lead-out is 6,750 sectors, and all subsequent ones are 2,250 sectors. Contrast with *lead-in*.

**leaf**    In database management, the last node of a tree.

**League for Programming Freedom**    (League for Programming Freedom, Cambridge, MA, http://lpf.ai.mit.edu) An organization founded in 1989 that is dedicated to preventing software monopolies. Its major tenet is that software copyrights and patents jeopardize the industry, specifically when they pertain to user interfaces.

**leaky bucket**    A technique used in ATM networks at the switch level that applies a sustained cell flow rate to bursty traffic. Incoming data flows into a buffer (the "bucket"), then "leaks" out at a steady rate, which is designated as constant bit rate (CBR) traffic. In the event the in-flow exceeds the negotiated rate for a certain time, the buffer will overflow. At that point, the switch examines the Cell Loss Priority (CLP) bit in each cell, and low-priority cells are discarded and retransmitted by the originating device.

**leapfrog test**    A storage diagnostic routine that replicates itself throughout the storage medium.

**leased line**    A private communications channel leased from a common carrier. Most digital lines require four wires (two pairs) for full-duplex transmission.

**leased-line modem**    A high-speed modem used in private lines. It may have built-in lower speeds for alternate use in dial-up lines.

**least significant digit**    The rightmost digit in a number.

**LEC**    **(1)** (Local Exchange Carrier) An organization that provides local telephone service within the U.S., which includes the RBOCs, large companies such as GTE and more than a thousand smaller and rural telephone companies (approximately 1,300 in total). A LEC provides service from the customer premises to its local exchange (central office) within a local geographic area. See *LATA, CLEC* and *ILEC*.

**(2)** (LAN Emulation Client) A software driver that provides LAN emulation (LANE) in an ATM network. It resides in an ATM end station or in a computer system that provides the LAN to ATM conversion, often known as a LAN access device. See *LANE*.

**LECS**    See *LANE*.

**LED**    (Light Emitting Diode) A display technology that uses a semiconductor diode that emits light when charged. It usually gives off a red glow, although other colors can be generated. It is used in readouts and on/off lights in a myriad of electronic appliances. It was the first digital watch display, but was superseded by LCD, which uses less power.

LEDs are also used as a light source for fiber-optic transmission. They are typically used with lower-bandwidth multimode fibers. See *fiber-optics glossary*.

**LED printer** An electrophotographic printer that uses a matrix of LEDs as its light source. The LED mechanism is much simpler than its laser printer counterpart. A stationary array of LEDs is used instead of numerous moving parts, and the LEDs are selectively beamed onto the drum. LED printers are available from very low-end 4 ppm personal printers to huge digital printing presses that can print more than 700 ppm.

**left click** To press the left button on the mouse. If there are two or three buttons on the mouse, "click the mouse" means click the left button.

**left justify** Same as *flush left*.

**legacy application** An application that has been in existence for some time. It often refers to mainframe and ERP applications; however, as users abandoned DOS and Windows 3.1 for Windows 95/98 and NT, they, too, are called legacy applications. In today's world of the Internet, virtually anything not Web related is often thought of as a legacy app.

**legacy card** In a PC, an expansion card that does not have the ISA Plug and Play capability built into it. Up until late 1994, all cards were legacy cards.

**legacy data** Critical organizational data stored in mainframes and minis (legacy systems). See *legacy system*.

**legacy-free PC** A PC that does not contain ISA bus cards, a serial port or a floppy disk drive. It uses the USB bus for expansion through ports in the front and/or back of the unit. A modem and/or network adapter is typically built in. Some legacy-free PCs have available PCI slots, others do not. Legacy-free PCs intended for company use omit the parallel port and rely on the network for printing. Should an older device need to be plugged into a legacy-free PC, there are adapters for serial and parallel ports to USB.

**legacy LAN** A LAN topology, such as Ethernet or Token Ring, that has a large installed base.

**legacy protocol** A proprietary communications protocol such as DECnet, AppleTalk or SNA. With IP having become the universal protocol, everything but IP is often said to be a legacy protocol.

**legacy system** An older computer system such as a mainframe or minicomputer. It may also refer to only the software (see *legacy application*).

**Lempel Ziv** A data compression algorithm that uses an adaptive compression technique. See *LZW*.

**LEN** (Low Entry Networking) In SNA, peer-to-peer connectivity between adjacent Type 2.1 nodes, such as PCs, workstations and minicomputers. LU 6.2 sessions are supported across LEN connections.

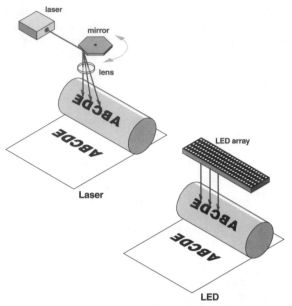

**LED vs. Laser Printing**
The LED mechanism is much simpler, because it is a stationary array of light emitting diodes (LEDs) rather than a number of moving parts.

**The Legacy**
A lot of data still exists on half-inch open reel tapes. Each standard that is widely used in the computer field hangs around for many years after it is no longer popular.

**LEO** (Low-Earth Orbit) A communications satellite in orbit 400 to 1600 miles above the earth. Being much closer than 22,282 mile-high geosynchronous satellites (GEOs), LEO signals make the round trip from earth much faster. Thus, low-powered pizza dishes and handheld devices can be used. LEOs are also better suited to interactive conferencing. Unlike GEOs, which travel at earth speed, LEOs revolve around the globe every couple of hours, and any single LEO is in view for only a few minutes. In order to maintain continuous communications, multiple LEOs must be used. From 48 to 66 LEOs are needed to cover the earth. See *Iridium*, *Teledesic*, *GEO* and *MEO*.

**LEP** (Light Emitting Polymer) An organic polymer that glows (emits photons) when excited by electricity. LEP screens are used to make organic LED (OLED) displays and are expected to compete with LCD screens in the future. See *OLED*.

**LES** See *LANE*.

**less than (<) symbol** The "less than" symbol ( is used to express a lower value. For example, **if (x <10)** means "if x is less than 10." See *greater than symbol*.

**letter bomb** An e-mail or word processing document that contains active code intended to cause damage to the recipient's computer, such as erasing the hard disk. See *macro virus* and *mail bomb*.

**letterbox format** See *16:9*.

**letter quality** The print quality of an electric typewriter. Laser printers, ink jet printers and daisy wheel printers provide letter quality printing. 24-pin dot-matrix printers provide near letter quality (NLQ), but the characters are not as dark and crisp.

**level 1 cache** See *L1 cache*.

**level 2 cache** See *L2 cache*.

**Level 3** (Level 3 Communications, Louisville, CO, www.l3.com) A telecommunications carrier founded in 1985 as Kiewit Diversified Group (KDG). KDG was a wholly owned subsidiary of Peter Kiewit Sons', Inc., a prominent construction company that was founded in 1884. KDG changed its name to Level 3 and spun itself off as a public company.

Level 3 is building a nationwide, optical fiber network based on IP with eventual links to networks in Europe and Asia. Its intentions are to provide fiber access directly into office buildings and provide businesses with end to end voice and data services. With nearly three billion in capital from Pieter Kiewit Sons' and expertise from many people who previously worked for MFS (created under Kiewit and later sold to WorldCom), Level 3 packs a huge wallop as a startup. Private line and co-location services were first offered in the latter part of 1998.

**Level 6** See *cable categories*.

**Level 7** See *cable categories*.

**lex** See *yacc*.

**lexicographer** A person that writes dictionaries. See *computer lexicographer*.

**lexicographic sort** Arranging items in alphabetic order like a dictionary. Numbers are located by their alphabetic spelling, not in a separate group. Today, most technical dictionaries and glossaries place numeric entries at the beginning or back of the book, not in interspersed lexicographic order. Contrast with *alphanumeric sort*. See *ASCIIbetical*.

**LEXIS-NEXIS** A service that provides online legal and business information. LEXIS was the first full-text information service for the legal profession. NEXIS provides the archives of the *New York Times*, as well as Wall Street industry analysis, public records, tax information, political analysis, SEC filings and more. See *online services*.

**Lexmark**    (Lexmark International, Inc., Lexington, KY, www.lexmark.com) A manufacturer of desktop and network printers that was spun off from IBM in 1991. For five years, IBM and Lexmark agreed not to compete with each other, and IBM continued to market printers to its own mainframe and minicomputer customers. During those five years, Lexmark built itself into a $2 billion company selling quality printers at affordable prices. Lexmark makes its own printer engines and was the first to bring a 600 dpi laser printer to market, as well as a true 1,200 dpi printer.

**LF**    See *line feed*.

**LHA**    A popular freeware compression program developed by Haruyasu Yoshizaki that uses a variant of the LZW (LZ77) dictionary method followed by a Huffman coding stage. It runs on PCs, UNIX and other platforms as its source code is also free. LHA performs compression and decompression and creates self-extracting executables.

**LHARC**    An earlier name for LHA. See *LHA*.

**Liberate**    (Liberate Technologies, Redwood Shores, CA, www.liberate.com) A software company that specializes in the information appliance field. Formerly Network Computer, Inc. (NCI), a spin-off from Oracle in 1996, it changed its name in 1999. The company initially promoted the NC Reference Profile specification, later turned over to The Open Group. Liberate provides client and server software for satellite, cable, telco, ISP and corporations to deliver thin computing services. See *network computer*.

**librarian**    (1) A person who works in the data library.
  (2) See *CA-Librarian*.

**library**    (1) A collection of programs or data files.
  (2) A set of ready-made software routines (functions) for programmers. The routines are linked into the program when it is compiled. See *class library*.
  (3) A storage device that handles multiple units of media and provides one or more drives for reading and writing them. For example, a tape library holds multiple tape cartridges and includes a robotic mechanism that moves them in and out of the drive(s).
  (4) See *data library*.

**library function**    A subroutine that is part of a function library. Same as *library routine*.

**library management**    See *version control*.

**library routine**    A subroutine that is part of a macro or function library.

**license agreement**    See *EULA*.

**life cycle**    See *system life cycle*.

**LIFO**    (Last In/First Out) A queueing method in which the next item to be retrieved is the item most recently placed in the queue. Contrast with *FIFO*.

**ligature**    Two or more typeface characters that are designed as a single unit (physically touch). Fi, ffi, ae and oe are common ligatures.

**Light-01**    A radiosity visualization viewset of the Viewperf benchmark, which is used to test OpenGL performance. See *OPC*.

**light bar**    Same as *highlight bar*.

**light guide**    A transmission channel that contains a number of optical fibers packaged together.

**light pen**    A light-sensitive stylus wired to a video terminal used to draw pictures or select menu options. The user brings the pen to the desired point on screen and presses the pen button to make contact. Contrary to what it looks like, the pen does not shine light onto the screen; rather, the screen beams into the pen. Screen pixels are constantly being refreshed. When the user presses the button, the pen senses light, and the pixel being illuminated at that instant identifies the screen location.

**LightShip**    A family of client/server tools for analyzing data from multidimensional databases from Pilot Software, Cambridge, MA (www.pilotsw.com), a pioneer in the OLAP database field. LightShip includes tools for financial modeling, budgeting and consolidation of large databases. It provides Windows-based point-and-click reporting, a full programming language for advanced users, and support for all the popular databases.

**light source**    In computer graphics, the implied location of a light source in order to simulate the visual effect of a light on a 3-D object. Some programs can compute multiple light sources.

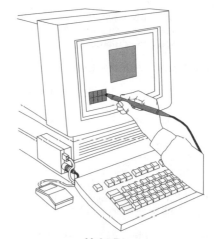

**Light Pen**
Light pens provide a very precise pointing capability directly on the screen.

**light version**    An abbreviated version of an application that is either given away free or bundled with other software. It is a marketing approach used to gain market share and entice users to upgrade to the full version, which has more features. In most cases, light versions are very usable products.

**lightwave**    Light in the infrared, visible and ultraviolet ranges, which falls between x-rays and microwaves. Wavelengths are between 10 nanometers and one millimeter.

**lightwave system**    A device that transmits light pulses over optical fibers at extremely high speeds (Gbits/sec range). Many intercity telephone trunks have been converted to lightwave systems.

**lightweight protocol**    A communications protocol designed with less complexity in order to reduce overhead. For example, it uses fixed-length headers because they are faster to parse than variable-length headers. To ensure compatibility, it eliminates optional subsets of the standard so that both sides are always equipped to deal with each other.

**li-ion**    See *lithium ion*.

**LIMDOW**    (Light Intensity Modulation Direct OverWrite) An enhancement of the magneto-optic technology that improves writing speed by allowing a bit to be written in one pass instead of two. The LIMDOW media is more costly than standard non-direct overwrite MO media. Many MO drives support both types. See *direct overwrite*.

**limited-distance modem**    See *line driver*.

**Linda**    A set of parallel processing functions added to languages, such as C and C++, that allows data to be created and transferred between processes. It was developed by Yale professor David Gelernter, when he was a 23-year old graduate student.

**line**    (1) A communications channel. See *line card* and *port*.
    (2) In text-based systems, a row of characters.
    (3) In graphics-based systems, a row of pixels.

**The First Lines**
This photo, taken at Broadway and Courtlandt Streets in New York in 1883, shows a nation exploding with its first communications. The very same thing is happening today with the Internet, only the infrastructure is not visible. *(Image courtesy of AT&T.)*

**line adapter**   In communications, a device similar to a modem, that converts a digital signal into a form suitable for transmission over a communications line, and vice versa. It provides parallel/serial and serial/parallel conversion, modulation and demodulation.

**line analyzer**   A device that monitors the transmission of a communications line.

**linear**   Sequential or having a graph that is a straight line.

**linear address space**   See *flat address space*.

**linear density**   See *bpi*.

**linear editing**   See *linear video editing*.

**linear programming**   A mathematical technique used to obtain an optimum solution in resource allocation problems, such as production planning.

**line art**   A graphic image drawn only as lines without any color filling or shading.

**linear video**   Continuous playback of videotape or videodisc. It typically refers to analog video technology.

**linear video editing**   Editing analog videotape. Before digital editing (nonlinear video editing), video sequences were edited by inserting new frames and reconstructing the balance of the tape by adding the remainder of the frames. Contrast with *nonlinear video editing*.

**line bonding**   See *channel bonding*.

**line break**   A code that signifies the end of the line. When word processing documents are saved as ASCII text files, some word processors insert a hard return at the end of each line. If the text file is opened up in a word processor or text editor with different margins than the original document, the text will not wrap like the original paragraphs.

**line card**   A printed circuit board that provides a transmitting/receiving port for a particular protocol. Line cards plug into a telco switch, network switch, router or other communications device. A network adapter (NIC) in a PC provides a similar function, but there is typically only one adapter in a client machine. Line card implies a modular chassis that supports multiple transmission ports. See *modular chassis*.

**line concentration**   See *concentrator*.

**line conditioning**   See *conditioning*.

**line dot matrix printer**   See *line matrix printer*.

**line drawing**   A graphic image outlined by solid lines. The mass of the drawing is imagined by the viewer. See *wireframe modeling*.

**line driver**   A device that extends the transmission distance between terminals and computers connected via private lines or networks. Also called a "short-haul modem" or "limited-distance modem," line drivers can extend a signal that is normally limited to a few dozen or a few hundred feet up to several miles. Line drivers are used to connect POS terminals, machine tools, sensors and a myriad of other digital devices to a host computer. Speeds typically range up to 128 Kbps.

**line editor**   An outmoded editing program that allows text to be created and changed one line at a time. Edlin was a line editor included with earlier versions of DOS, and ed was the original UNIX line editor.

**line feed**  (1) A character code that advances the screen cursor or printer to the next line. The line feed is used as an end-of-line code in UNIX. In DOS and OS/2 text files, the return/line feed pair (ASCII 13 10) is the standard end-of-line code.

(2) A printer button that advances paper one line when depressed.

**line frequency**  The number of times each second that a wave or some repeatable set of signals is transmitted over a line. See *horizontal scan frequency*.

**line level**  In communications, the signal strength within a transmission channel, measured in decibels or nepers.

**line load**  (1) In communications, the percentage of time a communications channel is used.

(2) In electronics, the amount of current that is carried in a circuit.

**line matrix printer**  An impact printer that prints a line at a time. Printronix pioneered this technology in 1974. Line matrix and band printers are the surviving line printer technologies, but line matrix can print graphics, whereas band printers cannot. Line matrix resolution is in the 70–140 dpi range and speeds range from 400–1,400 lpm.

Line matrix printers offer medium resolution, monochrome printing with a very low ribbon cost. They also provide high speed; for example, printing a three-part form at 1,200 lpm is equivalent to a 65 ppm page printer. Line matrix printers can exist in harsh conditions and are often found in warehouses and other industrial environments.

The print mechanism is a row of dot hammers that is almost as wide as the page. The hammers are mounted on a shuttle that oscillates back and forth approximately two inches in a track. The hammers are magnetically released at the appropriate time and bang into a ribbon and onto the paper. See *printer*.

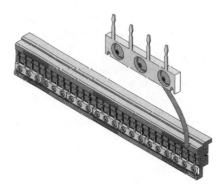

**Printronix Printhead**
This printhead contains seven sets of print hammers that oscillate back and forth to cover 16"-wide paper. The hammers are held back by magnets. The hammer is demagnetized and springs forward onto the ribbon. As it recoils, it is remagnetized back in place. *(Original drawing courtesy of Printronix, Inc.)*

**line number**  (1) A specific line of programming language source code.

(2) On display screens, a specific row of text or row of dots.

(3) In communications, a specific communications channel.

**line of sight**  An unobstructed view from transmitter to receiver.

**line printer**  An impact printer that prints one line at a time. The two surviving line printer technologies are band printers and line matrix printers. Line printers are still widely used in datacenters and in industrial environments, and can print multipart forms at a very rapid rate. For example, a 1,000 lpm line printer printing on three-part forms is the equivalent of a 50 ppm laser printer. See *band printer*, *line matrix printer* and *printer*.

**line segment**  In vector graphics, same as *vector*.

**lines of code**  The statements and instructions that a programmer writes when creating a program. One line of this "source code" may generate one machine instruction or several depending on the programming language. A line of code in assembly language is typically turned into one machine instruction. In a high-level language such as C++ or Java, one line of code may generate a series of assembly language instructions, resulting in multiple machine instructions.

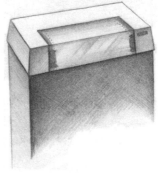

**Line Printer**
The line printer is typically enclosed in a cabinet that completely seals the unit from the outside world. This used to be essential when line printers were extremely noisy. Today's line printers are even quieter than laser printers.

One line of code in any language may call for the inclusion of a subroutine that can be of any size; so, while used to measure the overall complexity of a program, they are not an absolute. Comparisons can also be misleading if the programs are not in the same language or category. For example, 20 lines of code in Visual Basic might require 200 lines of code in assembly language.

In addition, a measurement in lines of code says nothing about the quality of the code. A thousand lines of code written by one programmer can be equal to three thousand lines by another. See *KLOC*.

**lines of resolution**    In television, the number of pixels that make up one horizontal scan line. In an analog NTSC TV broadcast, 440 lines of resolution are transmitted. VHS recording uses from 240 to 260 lines while DVD uses from 704 to 720.

The term can be confusing, because TV is rated at 525 horizontal scan lines per frame, 483 of which are used for the picture (the rest are the vertical blanking interval). However, lines of resolution do not refer to scan lines, but to vertical columns. On computer screens, resolution is given by both horizontal and vertical numbers. See *resolution*.

**line speed**    See *data rate*.

**line squeeze**    In a mail merge, the elimination of blank lines when printing names and addresses that contain no data in certain fields, such as title, company and second address line. See *field squeeze*.

```
Without Line Squeeze        With Line Squeeze
Pat Smith                   Pat Smith
                            10 South Main
                            Bearcat, OR 80901
10 South Main
Bearcat, OR 80901
```

**lingua franca**    It implies a common, or standard, language. The term is used in the information industry to refer to the most widely used format, protocol or command language for a particular pupose. Its actual meaning is "Frankish language," which is spoken in various Mediterranean ports and is a combination of Italian, Spanish, French, Greek, Arabic and Turkish. Its original meaning also implies a hybrid or mixture of languages.

**link**    (1) In communications, a line, channel or circuit over which data is transmitted.

(2) On the World Wide Web, an address (URL) to another document on the same server or on any remote server. See *hypertext*.

(3) In data management, a pointer embedded within a record that refers to data or the location of data in another record.

(4) In programming, a call to another program or subroutine.

**linkage**    See *hypertext* and *link editor*.

**linkage editor**    See *link editor*.

**link analysis**    See *link consistency*.

**link block**    In CD-R recording, a sector of extraneous bits that is written by the laser immediately after it is turned on and once again when it is turned off.

**link consistency**    The assurance that a link on a Web page points to a valid document. See *link rot*, *404 error* and *Hyper-G*.

**link edit**    To use a linkage editor to prepare a program for running. See *link editor*.

**link editor**    A utility program that links a compiled or assembled program to a particular environment. It unites references between program modules and libraries of subroutines. Its output is a load module, which is executable code ready to run in the computer. See *executable code* and *bind*.

**linked list**    In data management, a group of items, each of which points to the next item. It allows for the organization of a sequential set of data in noncontiguous storage locations.

**linker**    See *link editor*.

**link rot**    Refers to hypertext links and bookmarks that point to Web pages that have moved or been deleted. The more the Web matures, the more link rot. See *404 error*, *link consistency* and *Web rage*.

**link state protocol**    A complex routing protocol that shares information with other routers in order to determine the best path. OSPF, NLSP and IS-IS are examples. Rather than continuously broadcast its routing tables, as in a distance vector protocol, a link state protocol router only notifies its neighboring routers when it detects a change. Contrast with *distance vector protocol* and *path vector protocol*. See *routing protocol*, *OSPF*, *NLSP* and *IS-IS*.

**link text**    A word or short phrase on a Web page that provides the visual hypertext link to another page or to somewhere else on that same page. Link text is typically underlined. See *hypertext anchor*.

**Linpack**    A package of FORTRAN programs for numerical linear algebra that is commonly used to create benchmark programs for testing a computer's floating point performance. See *benchmark*.

**Linux**    A version of UNIX that runs on a variety of hardware platforms including x86 PCs, Alpha, PowerPC and IBM's product line. Linux is open source software, which is freely available; however, the full distribution of Linux along with technical support and training are available for a fee from vendors such as Red Hat Software (www.redhat.com) and Caldera (www.caldera.com). The distribution CD-ROMs include the complete source code, as well as hundreds of tools, applets and utilities.

Due to its stability, Linux has gained popularity with ISPs as the OS for hosting Web servers. Its usage is expected to grow as a server OS, as well as for the desktop (see *KDE* and *GNOME*). IBM is supporting Linux for all of its hardware platforms in order to have a common OS for all product lines.

In 1990, Finnish computer science student Linus Torvalds turned Minix, a popular classroom teaching tool, into Linux, which is closer to the real UNIX. Torvalds created the kernel, and most of the supporting applications and utilities came from the GNU project of the Free Software Foundation. Many programmers have contributed to the Linux/GNU system. VA Linux Systems provides a Web site devoted entirely to Linux (www.linux.com).

As for the pronunciation of the word, if you live in Finland, you would say "lee-nooks," because Linus is pronounced "lee-noose." Since the English pronunciation of Linus is "line-us," many call it "line-ucks." Also quite common is "lin-ucks," which is somewhere in between. No matter how you say it, Linux is growing rapidly. See *GNU*, *open source*, *OSDL*, *Trinux*, *Caldera* and *Red Hat*.

**LIPS**    (Logical Inferences Per Second) The unit of measurement of the thinking speed of an AI application. Humans do about 2 LIPS. In the computer, one LIPS equals from 100 to 1,000 instructions.

**Liquid Audio**    A music distribution service from Liquid Audio, Inc., Redwood City, CA (www.liquidaudio.com). Supporting its own SDMI-compliant digital rights managment (DRM) system, as well as those from Microsoft and IBM, Liquid Audio offers content hosting and a large distribution network of retail and music Web sites to bands and record labels for promoting and selling their music via the Web. Liquid Audio tracks, which include album art, liner notes and track titles, are played with Liquid Player, RealPlayer and RealJukebox software. The Liquid Audio system supports AAC, ATRAC3, MP3 and AC-3 recording formats. The company was a founding member of the SDMI initiative in early 1999.

**liquid crystal display**    See *LCD*.

**liquid crystal shutters**    A method of directing light onto the drum in an electrophotographic printer. A matrix of liquid crystal dots function as shutters that are opened and closed. See *LCD*.

**Lisa**    The first personal computer to include integrated software and use a graphical interface. Modeled after the Xerox Star and introduced in 1983 by Apple, it was ahead of its time, but never caught on due to its $10,000 price and slow speed. It gave way to the Macintosh, which was developed by a separate group within Apple. In fact, the final production units of the Lisa were modified into a somewhat-compatible version of the Macintosh.

**LISP** (**LIS**t Processing) A high-level programming language used for developing AI applications. Developed in 1960 by John McCarthy, its syntax and structure is very different than traditional programming languages. For example, there is no syntactic difference between data and instructions.

LISP is available in both interpreter and compiler versions and can be modified and expanded by the programmer. Many varieties have been developed, including versions that perform calculations efficiently. The following Common LISP example converts Fahrenheit to Celsius:

**Lisa**
It was as slow as molasses, but users were entranced by its graphical interface and ability to cut and paste between applications. *(Image courtesy of Apple Computer, Inc.)*

```
(defun convert ()
  (format t "Enter Fahrenheit ")
  (let ((fahr (read)))
  (format t "Celsius is ~D"
    (truncate (*(-fahr 32)
      (/ 5 9))))))
```

**list** (1) An arranged set of data, often in row and column format.

(2) In fourth-generation languages, a command that displays/prints selected records. For example, in dBASE, **list name address** displays all names and addresses in the current file.

**list box** An on-screen display of text items in a scrollable window. For example, in the Windows version of this database, the index on the left side of the screen is a list box.

**listing** Any printed output.

**listproc** See *mailing list*.

**list processing language** A programming language, such as LISP, Prolog and Logo, used to process lists of data (names, words, objects). Although operations such as selecting the next to first or next to last element, or reversing all elements in a list, can be programmed in any language, list processing languages provide commands to do them. Recursion is also provided, allowing a subroutine to call itself over again in order to repetitively analyze a group of elements.

**LISTSERV** Mailing list management software from L-Soft international, Inc., Landover, MD (www.lsoft.com), that runs on mainframes, VMS, NT and various UNIX machines. LISTSERV scans e-mail messages for the words "subscribe" and "unsubscribe" to automatically update the list. See *mailing list*.

**literal** In programming, any data typed in by the programmer that remains unchanged when translated into machine language. Examples are a constant value used for calculation purposes, as well as text messages displayed on screen. In the following lines of code, the literals are 1 and VALUE IS ONE.

```
if x = 1
  print "the value is one"
endif
```

**lite version** See *light version*.

**lit fiber** Optical fiber that is regularly being used to transmit data. Contrast with *dark fiber*.

**lithium ion** A rechargeable battery technology that provides about a 10–15% improvement in charge per pound over nickel metal hydride. In 1993, Toshiba introduced the first notebook in the U.S. with lithium ion batteries. Ever since, lithium ion has become the most popular battery technology for notebooks, and it is widely used in cellphones and other handheld devices. See *lithium polymer* and *batteries*.

**lithium polymer** A rechargeable battery technology introduced in 1998 that is similar to lithium ion in power rating. The difference is that lithium polymer uses a gelatinous electrolyte rather than liquid. Thus, instead of requiring a steel can, lithium polymer cells can be manufactured in various shapes and sizes for custom requirements.

**lithography** A printing technology that dates back to 1798 when Alois Senenfelder developed a method of imaging limestone from which a print was produced. Based on the principle that oil and water do not mix, an aluminum or plastic plate is coated with a photopolymer film that is exposed to light through a photographic mask. The exposed areas are chemically "hardened," and the unexposed areas are dissolved when the plate is put through a chemical process, which is the next stage. When printing a page, the plate is dampened, and the water adheres only to the unexposed, non-image areas, which repel the greasy ink that is applied to the plate immediately thereafter.

The most common lithographic printing uses the offset method, in which the ink is "offset" onto a rubber-coated cylinder that is pressed against the paper. See *offset press*.

**little endian** The reverse order of bytes in a computer word. See *byte order*.

**live link** A reference to a document or image that is active. Clicking on the icon or text that symbolizes the link causes the document to be displayed. Web pages contain hypertext links to other Web pages, this feature being the one that made the World Wide Web explode onto the scene. Live links are also placed into e-mail, allowing users to quickly open an attached document, access a database or go to a Web site.

**LiveMotion** Software from Adobe that is used to develop animated sequences and interface elements for Web sites. Running under Windows or the Mac, LiveMotion supports all popular Web graphics formats, as well as Illustrator and native Photoshop (.PSD) files. It also supports the major sound formats.

**LiveScript** The original name of JavaScript. See *JavaScript*.

**liveware** Quite simply... human beings. See *wetware*, *grayware* and *wares*.

**LIW** See *VLIW*.

**LLC** (Logical Link Control) See "LANs" under *data link protocol*.

**LLCC** See *leadless chip carrier*.

**LMDS** (Local Multipoint Distribution Service) A digital wireless transmission system that works in the 28GHz range in the U.S. and 24–40GHz overseas. It requires line of sight between transmitter and receiving antenna, which can be from one to four miles apart depending on weather conditions. LMDS provides bandwidth in the OC-1 to OC-12 range, which is considerably greater than other broadband wireless services.

LMDS can be deployed in asymmetric and symmetric configurations. It is designed to provide the "last mile" from a carrier of data services to a large building or complex that is not wired for high-bandwidth communications. In areas without gas or steam pipes or other underground conduits, it is less costly to set up LMDS transceivers on rooftops than to dig up the ground to install optical fiber. See *MMDS*.

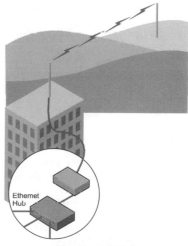

**The "Last Mile"**
LMDS and similar systems are used to span the last mile to the user's facilities. LMDS transmits at an extremely high data rate, but is limited to from two to four miles. MMDS, which operates at lower frequencies, can span 30 or more miles.

**LMHOSTS file** A text file in a Windows network (NetBIOS protocol) that provides name resolution of host names to IP addresses. LMHOSTS files, which contain host names and IP addresses, are manually updated and replicated onto all the servers in the enterprise. Except in small networks, LMHOSTS files have given way to the WINS system. The LM in LMHOSTS came from LAN Manager, Microsoft's earlier network operating system (NOS). See *WINS* and *HOSTS file*.

**LNK file** A Windows shortcut. See **Win Shortcuts** and *extension*.

**LNP** (Local Number Portability) The ability to keep your local phone number when you switch to another telephone service. See *NP*.

**load** (1) To copy a program from some source, such as the hard disk or CD-ROM, into memory for execution. In the early days, programs were loaded first and then run. Today, when referring to applications, loading implies load and run. Thus, "load" the program, "run" the program and "launch" the program mean the same thing.

Many people also use the term to refer to installing an application, so "load the program" may mean "install the program."
(2) To fill up a disk with data or programs.
(3) To insert a disk or tape into a drive.
(4) In programming, to store data in a register.
(5) In performance measurement, the current use of a system as a percentage of total capacity.
(6) In electronics, the flow of current through a circuit.
(7) In a network, the volume of traffic.

**load balancing** The fine tuning of a computer system, network or disk subsystem in order to more evenly distribute the data and/or processing across available resouces. For example, in clustering, load balancing might distribute the incoming transactions evenly to all servers, or it might redirect them to the next available server.

**load coil** A device placed into a telephone circuit between the end office and the subscriber to step up the voltage and compensate for signal loss due to bridged taps. The load coil is an inductive device that acts as a high-frequency choke and must be removed if the line is converted to high-speed digital use. As digital service (digital loop carrier) is moved closer to the customer and the analog lines become shorter, load coils are no longer required. See *bridged tap*.

**loaded** Brought into the computer and ready to go. See *load*.

**loaded line** A telephone line from customer to central office that uses loading coils to reduce distortion.

**loader** A program routine that copies a program into memory for execution.

**loader routine** Same as *loader*.

**load module** A program in machine language form ready to run in the computer. It is the output of a link editor.

**LoadRunner** A load testing tool from Mercury Interactive, Sunnyvale, CA (www.merc-int.com). It simulates thousands of users interacting online in order to test how well a system stands up under a heavy load.

**load sharing** Sharing the workload in two or more computers.

**load test** A test of a computer system and its applications by running under a full complement (full load) of transactions or users. A load test can be real or simulated by testing software. See *load testing software*.

**load testing software** Software that tests a system's ability to handle a heavy workload. The software simulates multiple transactions or users interacting with the computer at the same time, and provides reports on response times and system behavior.

**LOB** (Large OBject) A database field that holds any digitized information including text, images, audio and video.

**lobe length** In a Token Ring network, the length of cable between the MAU and the workstation.

**local access**    Retrieving something from a nearby source. See *LEC, CLEC, local loop* and *local drive*.

**local access carrier**    See *LEC* and *CLEC*.

**local bus**    Also called the "system bus," it is the pathway between the CPU, memory and peripheral devices. In the early 1990s, when the higher-speed VL-bus and PCI bus were introduced, they were called local buses, because they ran at the then-current speed of the local bus. Since then, local buses have gone beyond the speeds of VL-bus and PCI. For example, the local bus in many Pentium PCs is 100MHz, three times as fast as PCI's 33MHz. See *bus* and *PC data buses*.

**local bypass**    An interconnection between two facilities without the use of the local telephone company.

**local console**    A terminal or workstation directly connected to the computer or other device that it is monitoring and controlling.

**local drive**    A disk or tape drive connected to the user's computer. Contrast with *network drive*.

**local echo**    In communications, to display on screen what is being transmitted.

**local exchange**    See *central office*.

**localization**    Customizing software for a particular country. It includes the translation of menus and messages into the native spoken language, as well as changes in the user interface to accomodate different alphabets and culture. See *internationalization*.

**local loop**    The lines between a customer and the telephone company's central office, often called the "last mile." Local loops use copper-based telephone wire. See *last mile, DLC* and *FTTH*.

**local memory**    The memory used by a single CPU or allocated to a single program or function.

**local resource**    A peripheral device, such as a disk, modem or printer, that is directly connected to a user's personal computer. Contrast with *remote resource*.

**local storage**    The disk storage used by a single CPU.

**LocalTalk**    A LAN access method from Apple that uses twisted pair wires and transmits at 230,400 bps. It runs under AppleTalk and uses a daisy chain topology that can connect up to 32 devices within a distance of 1,000 feet. Third party products allow it to hook up with bus, passive star and active star topologies. Apple's LocalTalk PC Card lets a PC gain access to an AppleTalk network. See *LAP*.

**local variable**    In programming, a variable used only within the routine or function it is defined in.

**location-based services**    See *mobile positioning*.

**location broker**    Software that directs a user query to the server that has sufficient resources to search for and provide the answer. A location broker is middleware.

**location services**    See *mobile positioning*.

**lock down**    To restrict the functionality of a system. For example, network administrators can lock down client desktops so that users can perform only certain operations.

**locking**    See *file and record locking, lock down* and *lockup*.

**lock manager**    Software that provides file and record locking for multiple computer systems or processors that share a single database.

**lockup**    Refers to a computer's inability to respond to user input. See *abend* and *hang*.

**log**    A record of computer activity used for statistical purposes, as well as backup and recovery. Log files are created for such purposes as storing incoming text dialog, error and status messages and transaction detail.

**logic**    The sequence of operations performed by hardware or software. It is the "intelligence" built into everything. Hardware logic is contained in the electronic circuits, following the rules of *Boolean logic*. Software logic, or program logic, is contained in the patterns of instructions written by the programmer. Software logic is also called *business logic* when it specifically refers to the transactions of the business and not the operating system or network infrastructure.

Note: Logic is not the same as logical. See *logical vs physical* and *logical expression*.

**logical**    (1) A reasonable solution to a problem.

(2) A higher level view of an object; for example, the user's view versus the computer's view. See *logical vs physical*.

**logical data group**    Data derived from several sources. Same as *view*.

**logical design**    See *logic design*.

**logical drive**    An allocated part of a physical disk drive that is designated and managed as an independent unit. For example, drives C:, D: and E: could represent three physical drives or one physical drive partitioned into three logical drives. Contrast with *physical drive*.

**logical expression**    An expression that results in true or false. Same as *Boolean expression*.

**logical field**    A data field that contains a yes/no, true/false condition.

**logical lock**    The prevention of user access to data that is provided by marking the file or record through the use of software. Contrast with *physical lock*.

**logical operator**    One of the Boolean logical operators (AND, OR and NOT).

**logical partition**    See *LPAR*.

**logical record**    A reference to a data record that is independent of its physical location. It may be physically stored in two or more locations.

**Logical Unit**    See *LU* and *LU 6.2*.

**logical vs physical**    High-level versus low-level. Logical implies a higher view than the physical. Users relate to data logically by data element name; however, the actual fields of data are physically located in sectors on a disk. For example, if you want to know which customers ordered how many of a particular product, your logical view is customer name and quantity. Its physical organization might have customer name in a customer file and quantity in an order file cross-referenced by customer number. The physical sequence of the customer file could be indexed, while the sequence of the order file could be sequential.

A message transmitted from Phoenix to Boston logically goes between two cities; however, the physical circuit could be Phoenix to Chicago to Philadelphia to Boston.

When you command your program to change the output from the video screen to the printer, that's a logical request. The program will perform the physical change of address from, say, device number 02 to device number 04.

**logic analyzer**    (1) A device that monitors computer performance by timing various segments of the running programs. The total running time and the time spent in selected program modules is displayed in order to isolate the least efficient code.

(2) A device used to test and diagnose an electronic system, which includes an oscilloscope for displaying various digital states.

**logic array**    Same as *gate array* or *PLA*.

**logic board**    A printed circuit board that contains logic circuits. Apple calls the motherboard in its Macintoshes the main logic board. See *logic circuit* and *logic gate*.

**logic bomb**    A program routine that destroys data; for example, it may reformat the hard disk or insert random bits into data files. It may be brought into a personal computer by downloading a corrupt public-domain program. Once executed, it does its damage right away, whereas a virus keeps on destroying.

**logic chip**    A processor or controller chip. Contrast with *memory chip*.

**logic circuit**    A circuit that performs some processing or controlling function. Contrast with *memory*.

**logic controller**    See *PLC*.

**logic design**    The architecture of software. See *logic*.

**logic diagram**    A flow chart of hardware circuits or program logic.

**logic error**    A program bug due to an incorrect sequence of instructions.

**logic function**    An elementary processing function in a digital circuit. Logic function and logic circuit are used synonymously. See *logic circuit* and *digital circuit*.

**logic gate**    A collection of transistors and resistors that implement Boolean logic operations on a circuit board. Transistors make up logic gates. Logic gates make up circuits. Circuits make up electronic systems. The truth tables for logic gates follow. See *Boolean logic*.

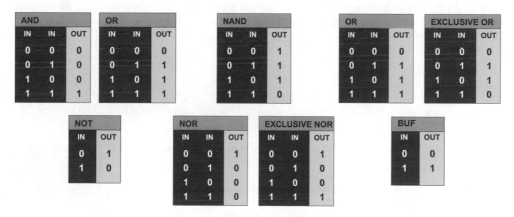

**logic operation**    An operation that analyzes one or more inputs and generates a particular output based on a set of rules. See *AND-OR-NOT* and *Boolean logic*.

**logic-seeking printer**    A printer that analyzes line content and skips over blank spaces at high speeds.

**logic synthesis**    The conversion of a high-level electronic circuit description into a list of logic gates and their interconnections, called the "netlist." Every logic synthesis program understands some subset of Verilog and VHDL. The market leader in logic synthesis software is Synopsis, Mountain View, CA (www.synopsis.com). See *silicon compiler*.

**login**    Same as *logon*.

**Logo**    A high-level programming language noted for its ease of use and graphics capabilities. It is a recursive language that contains many list processing functions that are in LISP, although Logo's syntax is more understandable for novices.

Turtle Graphics is the graphics language built into Logo, which allows complex graphics images to be created with a minimum of coding. The turtle is a triangular-shaped cursor, which is moved on screen with commands that activate the turtle as if you were driving it, for example, go forward 100 units, turn right 45 degrees, turn left 20 degrees.

Stemming from a National Science Foundation project, Logo was created by Seymour Papert in the mid-1960s along with colleagues at MIT and members of Bolt Beranek & Newman. Originally developed on large computers, it has been adapted to most personal computers.

The following Object Logo example converts Fahrenheit to Celsius:

```
convert
local [fahr]
print "|Enter Fahrenheit |
make "fahr ReadWord
print "|Celsius is |
print (:fahr - 32) * 5 / 9
end
```

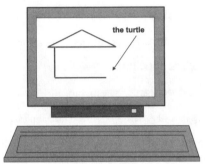

the turtle

**The Logo Turtle**
Logo's Turtle Graphics provides a simple, intuitive way to learn about and program graphics. The commands cause the triangular pointer (the turtle) to draw the image onscreen.

**logoff**    The process of quitting from, or signing off of, a computer system. The noun is generally "logoff," while the verb is "log off."

**logon**    The process of gaining access, or signing in, to a computer system. The noun is generally "logon," while the verb is "log on." If access is restricted, the logon requires users to identify themselves by entering an ID number and/or password. Service bureaus often base their charges for the time between logon and logoff.

**logo police**    The individuals in an organization responsible for the proper use of the company logo (identifying symbol and company name) in print and online. They may also be involved with searching the Web to find unauthorized uses of the logo. See *architecture police*.

**logout**    Same as *logoff*.

**LOL**    Digispeak for "laughing out loud."

**long**    In programming, an integer variable. In C, a long is four bytes and can be signed (–2G to +2G) or unsigned (4G). Contrast with *short*.

**long card**    In PCs, a full-length controller board that plugs into an expansion slot. Contrast with *short card*.

**long file names**    File names that exceed the common eight plus three (8.3) character limitation used in DOS and Windows 3.1. UNIX, Mac and Windows 95/98 support long file names. See *DOS file names*.

**long haul**    Long distance. Long haul implies traversing a state or a country. Contrast with *short haul*.

**long lines**    In communications, circuits that are capable of handling transmissions over long distances.

Short card

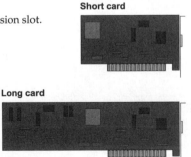

Long card

**LonWorks**    A control network from Echelon Corporation, Palo Alto, CA (www.lonworks.echelon.com), that uses the Echelon's LonTalk protocol and Neuron chip, made by Motorola and Toshiba. Each chip uses a 48-bit number for identification. Modules containing the chip and transceivers for RS-485, twisted pair, coax and AC power lines are available on credit card–sized boards. The LonWorks Interoperability Association was formed to maintain open standards for LonWorks products.

**look and feel** Generally refers to the user interface of a program, especially with regard to its similarity to other programs. This issue has been and will continue to be hotly contested in the courts, because some programs look and function like others, and the original developer sometimes gets upset about it.

Oddly enough, programming languages have never been copyrighted or patented, which allows a developer to write a compiler that translates a language identical to one already in use. However, when a vendor sells a software package that looks and feels like another, it is subject to litigation, and look and feel cases have been won in the U.S. courts.

**lookaside cache** A memory cache that shares the system bus with main memory and other subsystems. It is slower than inline caches and backside caches. See *inline cache* and *backside cache*.

**lookup** A data search performed within a predefined table of values (array, matrix, etc.) or within a data file.

**lookup table** An array or matrix of data that contains values that are searched. See *index* and *color palette*.

**loop** In programming, a repetition within a program. Whenever a process must be repeated, a loop is set up to handle it. A program has a main loop and a series of minor loops, which are nested within the main loop. Learning how to set up loops is what programming technique is all about.

The following example prints an invoice. The main loop reads the order record and prints the invoice until there are no more orders to read. After printing date and name and addresses, the program prints a variable number of line items. The code that prints the line items is contained in a loop and repeated as many times as required.

Loops are accomplished by various programming structures that have a beginning, body and end. The beginning generally tests the condition that keeps the loop going. The body comprises the repeating statements, and the end is a GOTO that points back to the beginning. In assembly language, the programmer writes the GOTO, as in the following example that counts to 10.

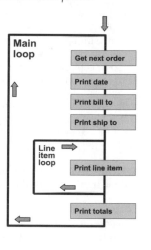

```
        MOVE      "0" TO COUNTER
LOOP    ADD       "1" TO COUNTER
        COMPARE   COUNTER TO "10"
        GOTO      LOOP IF UNEQUAL
        STOP
```

In high-level languages, the GOTO is generated by the interpreter or compiler; for example, the same routine as above using a WHILE loop.

```
COUNTER = 0
DO WHILE COUNTER  <> 10
   COUNTER = COUNTER + 1
ENDDO
STOP
```

For a more detailed look at a loop, look at the end of the C definition. The main event loop of the DOS version of this database is presented.

**loop back** To send the outgoing signals back to the receiving side for testing purposes. See *loopback plug*.

**loopback plug** A connector used for diagnosing transmission problems. It plugs into a port, such as a serial or parallel port, and crosses over the transmit line to the receive line so that outgoing signals can be redirected back into the computer for testing.

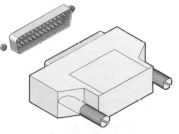

**Looping Back**
This loopback plug is designed for a 25-pin serial port. It crosses the sending pin over to the receiving pin so that outgoing signals come right back in.

**loop carrier**   See *DLC*.

**loosely coupled**   Refers to stand-alone computers connected via a network. Loosely coupled computers process on their own and exchange data on demand. Contrast with *tightly coupled*.

**lo-res**   See *low resolution*.

**lossless compression**   A compression technique that decompresses data back to its original form without any loss. The decompressed file and the original are identical. Contrast with *lossy compression*.

**lossy compression**   A compression technique that does not decompress data 100% back to original. Lossy compression provides high degrees of compression and results in very small compressed files, but there is a certain amount of loss when they are restored.

Audio, video and some imaging applications can tolerate some loss, and in many cases, it may not be very noticeable to the human eye. In other cases, it may be noticeable, but it is not that critical to the application. The more tolerance for loss, the smaller the file can be compressed.

Lossy compression is never used for business data and text, which demand a perfect restoration, or lossless compression.

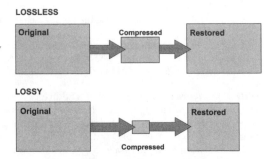

**Lossless vs. Lossy Compression**
Business data requires lossless compression, while audio and video applications can tolerate some loss, which may not be very noticeable.

**lost cluster**   Disk records that have lost their identification with a file name. This can happen if a file is not closed properly, which can sometimes occur if the computer is turned off without quitting the application first. See *DOS Chkdsk*.

**lost packet**   A packet of data that never reaches its destination. For example, if the network becomes congested and the traffic exceeds the momentary holding capacity (buffer space) of the router, packets will be lost.

**Lotus**   (Lotus Development Corporation, Cambridge, MA, subsidiary of IBM, www.lotus.com) A major software company founded in 1981 by Mitch Kapor. It achieved outstanding success by introducing Lotus 1-2-3, the first spreadsheet for the IBM PC. Over the years, it developed a variety of applications and helped set industry standards. In 1989, it introduced Lotus Notes, the first major groupware product, which continues to be a strong contender in this arena. In 1990, it acquired Samna Corporation, developers of the popular, Windows-based Ami word processors. Lotus was acquired by IBM in 1995.

**Lotus 1-2-3**   A popular spreadsheet for Windows and OS/2, which is part of the Lotus SmartSuite package. 1-2-3 was introduced for DOS in 1983 and later on many other platforms, including minis and mainframes.

The 1-2-3 name was chosen because it integrated spreadsheet, database and graphics. It was the first innovative spreadsheet for the PC and was launched with a superior marketing campaign. Its ability to function like a simple database was unique, and turning data into a chart with a single keystroke was dazzling for its time. The Lotus macro language was the first to be widely used in a spreadsheet. It has since been supplemented with LotusScript, a BASIC-like language that supports Notes manipulation.

**Mitchell D. Kapor**
Mitch Kapor was the founder of Lotus and co-programmer of Lotus 1-2-3. The Lotus spreadsheet helped make the IBM PC an outstanding success within a few years of its introduction. Later, Kapor founded the Electronic Frontier Foundation (EFF). *(Image courtesy of ON Technology, Inc.)*

**Lotus menu**   The menu introduced with Lotus 1-2-3 that became a de facto standard. It is a row of words, each of which is an option that can be selected by

```
DISK  Erase  Mono  Hotkey  Search  Quit
Add definition to file GLOSS.OUT. (F1 for more help.)
```

**A Lotus Menu**
The explanations of menu options on this DOS-based Lotus menu were directly below the menu item that was selected, making them easier to read than today's interfaces with the menu at the top and the explanation at the bottom of the screen.

highlighting it and pressing ENTER or by pressing the first letter of the word. When the word is highlighted, an explanation line is displayed directly above or below it.

**Lotus Notes**   Messaging and groupware software from Lotus that was introduced in 1989 for OS/2 and later expanded to Windows, Mac, UNIX, NetWare, AS/400 and S/390. Notes provides e-mail, document sharing, workflow, group discussions and calendaring and scheduling. It also accepts plug-ins for other functions. The heart of Notes, and what makes it different from other groupware, is its document database. Everything, including mail and group discussions, are maintained in a Notes database, which can hold data fields, text, audio and video.

Notes provides strong replication capability, which synchronizes databases distributed in multiple locations and to mobile users. The Notes Name & Address Book provides a central directory for all resources. Many applications have been built with Notes using its macro language and LotusScript, a Visual Basic–like programming language.

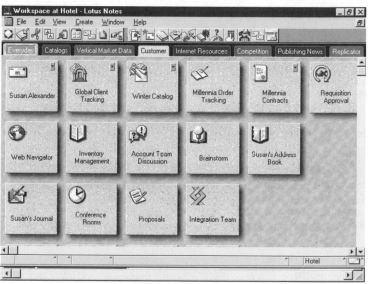

**The Notes Client**
The Notes interface can be customized according to users' individual needs. The square blocks are the databases that are organized by the tabs. The "Workspace at" on the title bar (top left) indicates the location of the user for synchronization purposes. *(Screen shot courtesy of Lotus Development Corporation.)*

In 1996, the Notes client was decoupled from the Notes server, which was renamed Domino. Domino is Internet compliant and can be accessed by a Web browser, converting Notes database contents into HTML pages on the fly. The Notes client also contains a browser, which can download Web pages and maintain them as Notes documents.

Notes is often considered the father of groupware, because it was the first to popularize a development environment around groupware functions.

**Lotus Notes Visual Programmer**   Also known as Notes ViP, it is a graphical development system for Windows from Lotus that is used to create custom Lotus Notes applications.

**LotusScript**   A scripting language from Lotus used to automate tasks in Notes/Domino and SmartSuite applications. LotusScript is similar to Visual Basic. See *Lotus Notes*.

**Loudcloud**   (Loudcloud, Inc., Sunnyvale, CA, www.loudcloud.com) A management service provider (MSP) that specializes in Web site hosting. Founded in 2000 by Marc Andreesen, Ben Horowitz, Tim Howes and In Sik Rhee, Loudcloud's "Cloud" services offer infrastructure for Web and application serving, databases and e-mail, as well as providing procedures for testing and stress testing. Its Opsware technology automates numerous tasks that are often done manually.

**Love Bug**   A famous virus that arrived as an e-mail attachment using the "double extension trick." The file name was "I LOVE YOU.TXT.vbs." The .vbs extension slipped by users who thought it was a safe text (.TXT) file. Victims using Microsoft Outlook spread the virus to everyone in their address book. In May 2000, the Love Bug replicated itself very quickly to countless users worldwide causing more than $6 billion worth of damage. See *double extension* and *virus*.

**low density**   Refers to an earlier version of a storage device with less bits per inch than today's version. See *DD* and *double density*.

**low frequency**   An electromagnetic wave that vibrates in the range from 30 to 300,000 Hertz.

**low-level access**   Close to the hardware. It refers to writing software that drives the hardware directly without going through a software translation layer and its associated overhead. An operating system can provide both low- and high-level APIs, the high-level ones being capable of very elaborate processing. The low-level APIs make programmers do more work, but allow them access to hardware features. For example, Microsoft's DirectDraw and Direct3D APIs allow directly manipulation of the frame buffer in the display adapter.

**low-level format**   The sector identification on a disk that the drive uses to locate sectors for reading and writing. Today's IDE and SCSI hard disks are low-level formatted at the factory. See *format program.*

**low-level interface**   A programming interface (API) that is the most detailed and enables the programmer to manipulate the functions within the software module or hardware at their most granular level. Contrast with *high-level interface.*

**low-level language**   A programming language that is very close to machine language. All assembly languages are low-level languages. Contrast with *high-level language.*

**low memory**   **(1)** The lower end of a computer's memory starting at 0. See *conventional memory.*
   **(2)** Refers to a small amount of memory in a computer. For example, 16MB in a desktop machine is considered low memory.

**low-pass filter**   A filter that blocks high frequencies and allows lower frequencies to pass through. Such filters are used in devices such as POTS splitters that direct phone and DSL signals to different lines. Contrast with *high-pass filter.*

**low radiation**   Refers to video terminals that emit less VLF (Very Low Frequency) and ELF (Extremely Low Frequency) radiation. This level of radiation cannot be shielded by office partitions. It must be canceled out from the CRT. Health studies on this are not conclusive and are very controversial. See *MPR II.*

**low resolution**   A low-grade display or printing quality due to a lower number of dots or lines per inch.

**LPAR**   (Logical **PAR**tition)   A logical segmentation of a mainframe's memory and other resources that allows it to run its own copy of the operating system and associated applications. LPARs are caused by special hardware circuits and allow multiple system images to run in one machine. This can be multiple instances of the same operating system or different operating systems. In the IBM world, this is known as a "virtualized System/390 processor complex."
   LPARs are implemented in hardware extensions: IBM's PR/SM ("prism"), Hitachi's MLPF and Amdahl's MDF. MDF was the first to provide in hardware the equivalent of IBM's VM operating system, which supports multiple system images in software. Interestingly enough, an LPAR can host VM, which itself can host multiple operating systems. See *PR/SM.*

**lpi**   (Lines Per Inch)   The number of lines printed in a vertical inch.

**lpm**   (Lines Per Minute)   The number of lines a printer can print or a scanner can scan in a minute.

**LPR/LPD**   (Line **PR**inter/Line **P**rinter **D**aemon)   The primary UNIX printing protocol used to submit jobs to the printer. The LPR component initiates commands such as "print waiting jobs," "receive job," and "send queue state," and the LPD component in the print server responds to them. LPR/LPD is also used by Windows NT and OS/2 running TCP/IP. LPR/LPD is unidirectional only. See *printing protocol.*

**LPT1**   In a PC, the logical name assigned to parallel port #1. The parallel port is typically used for the printer. A second parallel port, if installed, is assigned to LPT2. Contrast with *COM1.*

**LPX**   An Intel motherboard used for low-profile (space-saving) PCs. It provides more space on the motherboard for I/O ports, because expansion cards are plugged into a riser card.

**LQ**   See *letter quality.*

**LQFP**   See *QFP*.

**LRC**   (**L**ongitudinal **R**edundancy **C**heck) An error checking method that generates a parity bit from a specified string of bits on a longitudinal track. In a row and column format, such as on magnetic tape, LRC is often used with VRC, which creates a parity bit for each character.

**LS-120**   (**L**aser **S**ervo-**120**) A floppy disk technology that holds 120MB, developed by 3M, Compaq, Matsushita and O.R. Technology. LS-120 drives use a dual-gap head that reads and writes 120MB disks, as well as standard 3.5" 1.44MB and 720KB floppies. The technology records data magnetically, but uses optical tracks in the disk to align the heads. LS-120 disks have 2,490 tracks per inch, compared to 135 tpi for the 1.44MB floppy. See *SuperDisk* and *magnetic disk*.

**LS-120 Cartridge**
LS-120 media look very similar to floppy disks, but hold more than 80 times as much.

**LSAPI**   (**L**icensing **S**ervice **API**) A programming interface from Microsoft that allows a licensing server to track applications in use for managing multiuser software licenses.

**LSI**   (**L**arge **S**cale **I**ntegration) Between 3,000 and 100,000 transistors on a chip. See *SSI*, *MSI*, *VLSI* and *ULSI*.

**LSI-11**   A family of board-level computers from Digital that uses the micro version of the PDP-11. Introduced in 1974, it was the first to use the Q-bus.

**LSL**   (**L**ink **S**upport **L**ayer) A common interface for network drivers. It provides a common language between the transport layer and the data link layer and allows different transport protocols to run over one network adapter or one transport protocol to run on different network adapters.

Instead of directly calling a particular data link protocol, the transport protocol calls the LSL library. Thus, any LSL-compliant network driver can provide data link services in that protocol stack. LSL is part of UNIX System V. It is also the basis of Novell and Apple's ODI specification. See *ODI* and *STREAMS*.

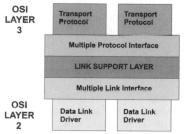

**LT**   (**L**ess **T**han) See *relational operator*.

**LTO**   (**L**inear **T**ape **O**pen) A family of open magnetic tape standards developed by HP, IBM and Seagate that are licensed to third-party vendors. In 1998, LTO introduced the Accelis and Ultrium formats that share common components such as read/write head, track layout and servo technology. LTO cartridges contain a memory that stores historical usage data.

Accelis uses a dual-hub, cassette-style cartridge with a midpoint load similar to Magstar MP and a native 25GB capacity. Ultrium uses a single hub and wider tape like regular Magstar and its initial native capacity is 100GB. To date, none of the LTO licensees have a plan for the Accelis format. For information, visit www.lto-technology.com.

**Ultrium Cartridge**
This is the high-end LTO format that starts at 100GB native capacity. Its single-hub cartridge is similar to Magstar.

**LU**   (**L**ogical **U**nit) In SNA, one end of a communications session. The complete LU to LU session is defined by session type. Common types are

```
1   Host to 3770 RJE terminal
2   Host to 3270 mainframe terminal
3   Host to 3270 printer
6.2 Program-to-program
7   Host to 5250 midrange terminal
```

**LU 6.2**    An SNA protocol that establishes a session between two programs. It allows peer-to-peer communications, as well as interaction between programs running in the host with PCs, Macs and midrange computers.

Before LU 6.2, processing was done only in the mainframe. LU 6.2 allows processing to take place at both ends of the communications, necessary for today's distributed computing and client/server environment. See *APPC* and *CPI-C*.

**Lucent**    (Lucent Technologies, Murray Hill, NJ, www.lucent.com)  A major manufacturer of telecommunications equipment. Lucent makes telephones and telephone systems, large telephone switching computers and integrated circuits and optoelectronics components for communications and computer applications.

The company has a long history in the telecom arena. Its roots go back to 1869 when Elisha Gray and Enos Barton founded Gray and Barton in Cleveland, Ohio, a company that provided parts and models for inventors such as Gray himself. Gray and Barton was later renamed Western Electric Company when Western Union, its major customer, became an investor.

In 1881, American Bell Telephone purchased controlling interest in Western Electric, which became the manufacturing arm of the Bell companies. In 1899, AT&T, which was created 14 years earlier, took over American Bell and Western Electric. In 1925, the already-combined engineering departments of Western Electric and AT&T were turned into Bell Labs, which has become world famous for its research. A year later, Western Electric spun off its electrical distribution operations as Graybar Electric Company, which became the first large company to be bought out by its own employees.

**Lucent Has History**
Although a new company in 1996, Lucent goes way back, spawning Bell Labs and Graybar Electric, and inventing and/or developing some of the most important technologies in the western world. *(Image courtesy of Lucent Technologies.)*

Over the years, the company ushered in the electronic age by developing the vacuum tube. It also invented the loudspeaker, brought sound to motion pictures and introduced mobile communications, the forerunner of today's cellular system. When AT&T was divested of its Bell operating companies in 1984, Western Electric remained with AT&T, but was soon split up into a variety of divisions, including Network Systems, which builds the major switching and telecom equipment. When spun off from AT&T in 1996, Lucent retained all of AT&T's manufacturing units, as well as Bell Labs.

**Luddite**    An individual that is against technological change. Luddite comes from Englishman Ned Lud, who rose up against his employer in the late 1700s. Subsequently, "Luddites" emerged in other companies to protest and even destroy new machinery that would put them out of a job. A neo-Luddite is a Luddite in the Internet age.

**luggable**    A portable computer that weighs more than you want it to. This was said of many of the first portables such as Compaq's famous, first machine that weighed 30 pounds and catapulted the company to prosperity. Today, any laptop that weighs more than 10 pounds could be called a "luggable."

**lumen**    A unit of measurement of the flow (rate of emission) of light. A wax candle generates 13 lumens; a 100 watt bulb generates 1,200. See *ANSI lumen* and *candela*.

**luminance**    The amount of brightness, measured in lumens, that is given off by a pixel or area on a screen. It is the black/gray/white information in a video signal. Color information is transmitted as luminance (brightness) and chrominance (color). For example, dark red and bright red would have the same chrominance, but a different luminance. Bright red and bright green could have the same luminance, but would always have a different chrominance. See *YUV*.

**LUN**    (Logical Unit Number)  The physical number of a device in a daisy chain of drives. See *SCSI*.

**LUNI**    See *LANE*.

**lurk**    To view the interaction in a chat room or online forum without participating by typing in any comments. See *de-lurk*.

**LUT**    (LookUp Table)  An array or matrix of values that contains data that is searched. See *index* and *color palette*.

**lux**    A unit of measurement of the intensity of light. It is equal to the illumination of a surface one meter away from a single candle. See *candela*.

**LVD**    (Low Voltage Differential)  A type of signaling used in SCSI devices that supports cable lengths up to 39.4 feet. Sometimes the term LVDS is used to refer to this method as well. See *SCSI* and *LVDS*.

**LVDS**    (Low Voltage Differential Signaling)  A transmission method for sending digital information to a flat panel display. LVDS has been widely used in laptops because it enables fewer wires to be used between the motherboard and the panel. The technology is also used between the image scaler and the panel in some stand-alone flat panel displays such as SGI's popular 1600SW flat panel. Contrast with *TMDS*. See *flat panel display*, *OpenLDI* and *LVD*.

**LX chipset**    See *Intel chipsets*.

**Lycos**    (www.lycos.com)  One of the major search sites on the Web. See *Web search sites*.

**Lynx**    A text-based Web browser created at the University of Kansas. Though largely supplanted by graphical browsers such as Netscape Navigator and Internet Explorer, Lynx is still popular among people with visual disabilities and those with very slow modem connections. See also *Linux*.

**LZW**    (Lempel-Ziv-Welch)  A compression method that stems from two techniques introduced by Jacob Ziv and Abraham Lempel. LZ77 creates pointers back to repeating data, and LZ78 creates a dictionary of repeating phrases with pointers to those phrases. Unisys researcher Terry Welch created an enhanced version of these methods, and Unisys holds patents on the algorithm until 2004. LZW is one of the most widely licensed patents in history with some 2,500 licensees. LZW is widely used in many hardware and software products, including V.42bis modems; GIF, TIF and PDF files; and PostScript Level 2. See *PNG*.

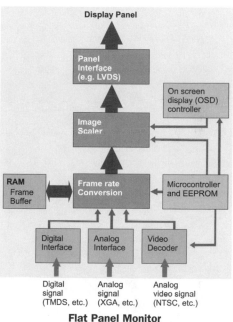

**Flat Panel Monitor**
This diagram of a typical flat panel monitor shows where LVDS is used as the last interface to the panel itself. *(Redrawn from original courtesy of Analog Devices, Inc.)*

**M** (1) See *mega*.

(2) Formerly known as MUMPS, it is a high-level programming language and integrated database that is widely used in the health-care field. Its extensive string handling capabilities make it suitable for storing vast amounts of free text. It was originally developed in 1966 at Massachusetts General Hospital as the Massachusetts Utility MultiProgramming System. The MUMPS Development Committee has maintained the language since 1973, and it became an ANSI standard in 1977.

M has unique features including the ability to store both data and program statements in its database, a fundamental property of object-oriented programming. In addition, formulas written in a program can be stored and used by other programs. See *M Technology Association*.

The following M example converts Fahrenheit to Celsius:

```
READ "Enter Fahrenheit ",FAHR
SET CENT=(FAHR-32)*5/9
WRITE "Celsius is", CENT
```

**ma** See *milliamp*.

**MAC** (1) (Message Authentication Code) A number computed from the contents of a text message that is used to authenticate the message. The MAC is a checksum that is computed using an algorithm and secret key and then sent with the message. The recipient recomputes the MAC at the other end using the same algorithm and secret key and compares it to the one that is sent. If they are the same, the message has not been tampered with. A MAC is like a digital signature, except that a secret key was used in its creation rather than a private key. See *digital signature* and *cryptography*.

(2) (Mandatory Access Control) A security control that requires clearance levels. See *NCSC*.

(3) See *Macintosh*, *MAC address* and *MAC layer*.

**MAC address** The unique serial number burned into Ethernet and Token Ring adapters that identifes that network card from all others. See *OUI* and *MAC layer*.

**MacAPPC** LU 6.2-compliant software from Apple that allows a Macintosh to be a peer to an IBM APPC application.

**MacDFT** Software that provides 3270 emulation for the Macintosh from Apple. It accompanies Apple's TwinAx/Coax board and supports CUT and DFT modes and DFT multiple sessions under SNA.

**MacDraw Pro** A Macintosh drawing program from Claris that is an enhanced version of the original MacDraw from Apple and includes full on-screen slide presentation capability. It is used for illustrations and elementary CAD work. MacDraw files are a subset of the Claris CAD file format.

**Mac emulator**    Software that allows Mac applications to run in a foreign environment. For example, Software Hut's FUSION (www.softhut.com) lets you run Mac applications in a Windows PC, providing you have a copy of the Mac operating system and a real Macintosh. FUSION includes a utility that lets you copy the contents of your Mac's ROM chip so that real Mac system software is running in the PC. Both the Mac OS and Windows cannot run simultaneously. You have to quit one in order to use the other.

**Mach**    A UNIX-like operating system developed at Carnegie-Mellon University. It is designed with a microkernel architecture that makes it easily portable to different platforms.

**machine**    Any electronic or electromechanical unit of equipment. A machine is always hardware; however, "engine" refers to hardware or software.

**machine address**    Same as *absolute address*.

**machine code**    Same as *machine language*.

**machine cycle**    The shortest interval in which an elementary operation can take place within the processor. It is made up of some number of clock cycles.

**machine dependent**    Also called "platform dependent" or "hardware dependent," it refers to software that is designed to run in only one computer or family of computers derived from the same architecture. Machine-dependent software has been compiled into the machine language of that specific hardware platform. Contrast with *machine independent*. See *device dependent*.

**machine independent**    Also called "platform independent" and "hardware independent," it refers to software that runs in a variety of computers. The hardware-specific instructions are in some other program (operating system, DBMS, interpreter, etc.). For example, interpreted programs are machine independent, providing there are interpreters for more than one machine. Contrast with *machine dependent*. See *device independent* and *interpreter*.

**machine instruction**    An instruction in machine language. Its anatomy is a verb followed by one or more nouns:

```
OP CODE    OPERANDS (one or more)
(verb)     (nouns)
```

The op code is the operation to be performed (add, copy, etc.), while the operands are the data to be acted upon (add a to b). There are always machine instructions to INPUT and OUTPUT, to process data by CALCULATING, COMPARING and COPYING it, and to go to some other part of the program with a GOTO instruction. See *hardware platforms* and *computer*.

**machine language**    The native language of the computer. In order for a program to run, it must be presented to the computer as binary-coded machine instructions that are specific to that CPU model or family. Although programmers are sometimes able to modify machine language in order to fix a running program, they do not create it. Machine language is created by programs called "assemblers," "compilers" and "interpreters," which convert the lines of programming code a human writes into the machine language the computer understands.

**SOURCE CODE TO MACHINE LANGUAGE**

**SOURCE CODE TO MACHINE LANGUAGE**

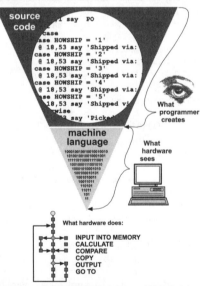

A computer only understands machine language, which is a set of instructions built into its circuits and is specific to that CPU model or family. The programs that it executes are made up of binary-coded instructions in that machine language, which were generated by software translators called assemblers, compilers and interpreters. Every program, whether it is a business application programmed inhouse or a commercial program purchased outside, must be available in the machine language of the computer you want to run it on, or you can't use it.

Programmers write in a programming language, which may be close to the machine or many levels removed from it. For years, the goal of the business organization has been to describe the problem and have that description turned into

Machine language tells the computer what to do and where to do it. When a programmer writes: **total = total + subtotal**, that statement is converted into a machine instruction that tells the computer to add the contents of two areas of memory (where TOTAL and SUBTOTAL are stored).

A programmer deals with data logically, "add this, subtract that," but the computer must be told precisely where this and that are located.

Machine languages differ substantially. What may take one instruction in one machine can take 10 instructions in another. See *hardware platforms*, *assembly language* and *interpreter*.

**machine readable**    Data in a form that can be read by the computer, which includes disks, tapes and punched cards. Printed fonts that can be scanned and recognized by the computer are also machine readable.

**Macintosh**    A family of personal computers from Apple, introduced in 1984. It was the first computer to popularize the graphical user interface (GUI), which, along with its hardware architecture, has provided a measure of unmatched consistency and ease of use. The Macintosh family is the largest non-IBM compatible personal computer series in use. Macs run Mac applications only, but with the aid of a Windows emulator such as SoftWindows, they can run DOS and Windows applications as well. Running the Mac as a combo Mac/Windows machine has never been popular, and it remains essentially a Mac versus PC world for desktop and laptop machines.

**The First Macintosh**
The original Mac was a self-contained unit with a 9" monochrome screen and a unique silhouette. *(Image courtesy of Apple Computer, Inc.)*

The first Mac had only a floppy disk and 128K of memory, and its "high-rise" cabinet and built-in 9" monochrome screen were unique. Maintained for a number of years and streamlined in its Classic model, the high-rise machine gave way to more traditional cabinetry for a while. Starting in the late 1990s, Apple returned to its roots by introducing the iMac and later the G4 Cube, bringing back its unique flair for cabinet design.

The first Macs were powered by Motorola's 32-bit 680x0 family of CPUs. In 1994, Apple introduced the PowerMacs, which used the higher-performance PowerPC chip designed by Apple, Motorola and IBM. PowerMacs run native PowerPC applications and emulate traditional Mac 680x0 applications. PowerPC chips have enjoyed substantial increases in performance. Introduced in 1999, the G4 chip enables a Macintosh to perform one billion floating point operations per second, which provides an extremely fast machine for imaging and graphics-based applications such as Photoshop. See *Apple*.

**The Mac User Interface**    The Macintosh popularized the graphical user interface (GUI) and simulated desktop. It was the first system in wide use that enabled users to perform file management by dragging icons of documents from one folder to another and literally dumping them into an on-screen trashcan for deletion. When introduced, it was immediately favored by non-technical people.

The Mac interface used consistent menus on screen and Apple provided guidelines for application design, all of which were absent in the DOS world. In operation, the operating system and applications were almost indistinguishable, and Apple kept technical jargon to a minimum.

The graphical user interface was actually developed by Xerox and introduced on its Star workstation in 1981. Apple borrowed heavily from the Star, and subsequently, others copied the Mac, moving the graphical interface down the line to Windows, OS/2 and UNIX.

**Why Aren't There More Macs?**    The Macintosh has millions of loyal users that would do anything to avoid switching to a PC. Just ask them. The Mac has always been easier to use. Back in the days of DOS and Windows 3.x PCs, having a Mac meant there were no IRQ, I/O address and upper memory block

**The First Mac GUI**
This is a screen shot of MacPaint on the first Macintosh. The Mac's graphical ability made it a natural for graphics shops and desktop publishing. It might have been sluggish, but it was far more affordable than the workstations used for such purposes in the 1980s. *(Image courtesy of Apple Computer, Inc.)*

**Today's Macintosh**
Apple has always been an innovator. With its HDTV-like screen to its 5-pound titanium body, the Titanium PowerBook G4 keeps up the tradition.

**M**

settings to deal with when you wanted to add a peripheral device. Just plug it in and go, compared to a technical quagmire on the PC. The Mac was introduced only a couple of years after the PC. Why then didn't the Mac take the world by storm?

There are several reasons. DOS PCs had definite advantages, especially in the corporate world. The first was speed. It takes much more computation to display graphics than text, and text-based DOS programs were much faster than the Mac. Second, professional programmers enjoy using commands such as found in DOS and UNIX. The batch languages and command sequences that can automate a myriad of tasks were woefully absent in the Mac's early days, and in many cases still are. There was sound reason for the early expression, "real programmers don't use mice."

Third, Apple emphasized the mouse so much in its introduction that it gave little thought to intelligent keyboard alternatives for text entry. This was hardly a way to gain market share in a world where word processing was the single largest application. Corporate users laughed at the idea of a Mac replacing their DOS word processor.

In time, of course, smart keyboard commands were added and CPU speeds increased dramatically, but the DOS world was simply too entrenched by the time these improvements came about. Windows 3.0, which offered a graphical interface with some of the Mac's advantages, was a natural successor to DOS, since it ran as an extention to DOS. Windows 95 added almost all of the graphical attributes of the Mac, and by this time, it was no contest. The world was buying Windows.

Fourth, for many years the Mac was pricier than a PC, which purchasing agents found hard to justify. Although many corporate users even purchased their own Macs due to their aversion to PCs, IT personnel were not fond of supporting them. They sweated bullets dealing with DOS and Windows. Supporting yet another environment was not met with enthusiasm.

Last, but perhaps most important, Apple kept its technology proprietary. Except for a brief period, it prevented a Macintosh clone industry from developing and growing (see *Macintosh clone*). Apple maintained its sole source vendor status compared to thousands of PC vendors.

As a result, the Macintosh followed its natural bent and became popular in desktop publishing and graphics design, literally pioneering the use of personal computers for these applications. The Mac is the de facto standard in the graphics arts industry. It is used sporadically in other businesses and is popular with home users. However, with about 5% of the desktop market, the Mac still remains, as Apple put it in earlier ad campaigns, "the computer for the rest of us."

**Macintosh clone**     A Power Macintosh from a company other than Apple. In late 1994, Apple began to license its operating system and hardware technologies to third parties. The first models appeared in the spring of 1995 from Radius, Power Computing and DayStar Digital. In late 1996, Apple ceased all future licensing, and the clone business was to become history. Apple paid Power Computing to acquire some of its personnel and to end their agreements.

**Macintosh extension**     Additional software functions for the Macintosh, which include drivers and other enhancements to the operating system. In System 7, system extensions reside in the Extensions folder. Mac extensions are the counterpart to the CONFIG.SYS file for DOS.

**Macintosh Toolbox**     Software routines that perform the graphical user interface functions in the Macintosh. Apple has licensed the Mac Toolbox to vendors developing a version of PowerOpen. This is the first time Apple has licensed the Toolbox. See *MAS*.

**Macintosh User Group**     See *MUG*.

**MacIRMA**     A 3270 emulator board for the Macintosh from Attachmate Corporation, Bellevue, WA (www.attachmate.com). See *Irma*.

**MAC layer**     (Media Access Control layer) The protocol that controls access to the physical transmission medium on a LAN. MAC layer functionality is built into the network adapter and includes a unique serial number that identifies each card (see *OUI*). Common MAC layer standards are the CSMA/CD architecture used in Ethernet and the token passing methods used in Token Ring, FDDI and MAP. The MAC layer is synonymous with the data link layer in the OSI model.

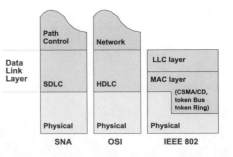

**MacLink Plus**    A Macintosh file transfer program from DataViz Corporation, Trumbull, CT (www.dataviz.com), that provides document conversion for a wide variety of Mac and PC formats. Versions are also available for Sun, NeXT and Wang systems.

**Mac OS**    (**MA**Cintosh **O**perating **S**ystem)  In late 1994, Apple officially renamed its System 7 operating system Mac OS and introduced the Mac OS logo. However, the term has been used for years to refer to all versions of Mac operating systems.

**Mac OS X**    (Mac OS 10)  Apple's next-generation operating system that is the successor to Mac OS 9. OS X runs legacy Mac applications (OS 9 and previous) as well as applications written for OS X. OS X Server was introduced in 1999, and the client version came out in 2001. OS X Server includes WebObjects, a development system for creating server applications accessible by any Web browser. OS X's new user interface is called "Aqua."

Entirely UNIX based and POSIX compliant, OS X adds protected memory, pre-emptive multitasking, multithreading and symmetric multiprocessing (SMP) to the Mac world. The rich set of UNIX commands also becomes available to Mac users. The heart of OS X is the open source "Darwin" kernel, which includes an enhanced BSD 4.4 operating system and Mach 2.5 microkernel.

Mac OS X natively supports three programming interfaces: (1) Classic (previously known as Blue Box) is the Mac Toolbox, which is the legacy Mac API (OS 9 and previous), (2) Cocoa (previously known as Yellow Box) is an enhanced version of the OpenStep API from NeXT, and (3) Carbon is an enhanced version of the Mac Toolbox for OS X. See *Rhapsody* and *NeXT*.

**MacPaint**    A full-featured Macintosh paint program from Claris that was originally developed by Apple and bundled with every Mac up until the Mac Plus. MacPaint's PICT file format is used for printing the screen. By pressing COMMAND-SHIFT-3, the current screen is stored in a PICT file for printing either in MacPaint or other program.

**macro**    (1) A series of menu selections, keystrokes and/or commands that have been recorded and assigned a name or key combination. When the macro name is called or the macro key combination is pressed, the steps in the macro are executed from beginning to end.

(2) A special-purpose command language within an application. See *macro language*.

(3) In assembly language, a prewritten subroutine that is called for throughout the program. At assembly time, the macro calls are substituted with the actual subroutine or instructions that branch to it. The high-level language equivalent is a function.

(4) See *hard macro* and *soft macro*.

**macro assembler**    An assembly language that allows macros to be defined and used.

**macro call**    Same as *macro instruction*.

**macro cell**    See *hard macro*.

**macro generator**    See *macro recorder*.

**macro instruction**    An instruction that defines a macro. In assembly language, MACRO and ENDM are examples that define the beginning and end of a macro. In C, the #DEFINE statement is used.

**macro keypad**    An auxiliary keypad that can be programmed to enter strings of text and commands with one keystroke. It connects between the keyboard and the computer and is entirely self contained without using software.

**macro language**    (1) A special-purpose command language used to automate sequences within an application such as a spreadsheet or word processor. Macro languages often include programming controls (IF THEN, GOTO, WHILE, etc.), but rarely have the capabilities of a full-blown programming language. See *macro recorder*, *batch file* and *shell script*.

(2) Commands used by a macro processor. Same as *script*.

(3) An assembly language that uses macros. See *macro*.

**Macromedia**    (Macromedia, Inc., San Francisco, CA, www.macromedia.com)  A software company specializing in multimedia authoring tools. It was founded in 1992 by the merger of Aurhorware, Inc., which was founded in 1984, and MacroMind-Paracomp. Macromind was founded in 1984 and merged with Paracomp in 1991. Its primary products are Authorware Professional and Macromedia Director, both for Macintosh and Windows.

**Macromedia Freehand**    A full-featured drawing program for Windows and Macintosh from Macromedia. It combines a wide range of drawing tools with special effects. FreeHand was first available on the Mac and was originally Aldus Freehand from Aldus Corporation.

**MacroMind**    See *Macromedia*.

**macro processor**    (1) Software that creates and executes macros from the keyboard. See also *macro language*.
(2) The part of an assembler that substitutes the macro subroutines for the macro calls.

**macro recorder**    A program routine that converts menu selections and keystrokes into a macro. A user turns on the recorder, calls up a menu, selects a variety of options, turns the recorder off and assigns a key command to the macro. When the key command is pressed, the selections are executed. See *macro*.

**macro virus**    A virus that is written in a macro language and placed within a document. Viruses have to be "run" in order to do things. When the document is opened and the macro is executed, commands in the macro language do the destruction or the prank. Thankfully, the overwhelming majority of viruses are harmless. Let's pray they stay that way! See *Word macro virus*, *letter bomb* and *virus*.

**Macster**    See *Napster*.

**MacTerminal**    Macintosh terminal emulation software from Apple that allows a Mac to function as an IBM 3278 Model 2 (when used with an AppleLine Protocol Converter) or Digital VT 52 or VT 100 terminal.

**Mac to PC**    The following DOS and Windows software packages are designed for transferring Macintosh files from the Mac to the PC via floppy disk. These programs read the Mac disks in the PC's 3.5" floppy drive.

**MacAccess**    Syncronys Softcorp, Culver City, CA 800/691-7981, www.syncronys.com

**MacDisk**    Insignia Solutions, Mountain View, CA 800/848-7677, www.insignia.com

**Mac-In-DOS (Windows)**    Pacific Microelectronics, Mountain View, CA 800/628-3475, www.netusa.com/pacmicro

**MacOpener (Windows)**    DataViz, Inc., Trumbull, CT 800/733-0030, www.dataviz.com

**TransferPro for Windows**    Digital Instrumentation Technology, Los Alamos, NM 800/467-1459, www.dit.com

**MacWrite**    A full-featured Macintosh word processing program from Claris Corporation. MacWrite was originally packaged with every Mac.

**MAE**    (1) (**M**acintosh **A**pplication **E**nvironment)  Software from Apple that allows Macintosh programs to run on UNIX workstations under the X Window system. MAE supports AppleTalk and MacTCP, allowing UNIX users to share printers, files and e-mail with other Macintosh users on the network.
(2) (**M**etropolitan **A**rea **E**xchange)  Originally known as Metropolitan Area Ethernets, MAEs are major network access points (NAPs) on the Internet. See *NAP*.

**Maestro**    (1) (Maesto NT)  Scheduling software for Windows NT from Tivoli Systems, Inc., Austin, TX, (www.tivoli.com).
(2) (Business Maestro)  Business planning and analysis software for Windows from Planet Corporation, Worcester, MA (www.planet-corp.com).
(3) (NFS Maestro Gateway)  Software from Hummingbird Communications, Ltd., North York, Ontario, Canada (www.hummingbird.com) that lets Windows clients access files on UNIX servers via NFS.

**mag**     Abbreviation for "magnetic."

**magazine style columns**     Text that is displayed in side-by-side columns. The text flows from the bottom of one column to the top of the next column on the same page.

**Magic Cap**     (Magic Communicating Applications Platform) An object-oriented control program from General Magic for personal intelligent communicating devices (PDAs, handheld units, etc.) that includes the Telescript language. See *Telescript* and *PersonaLink*.

**Magic Link**     A PDA from Sony that uses the Magic Cap operating system and includes an infrared port, fax/modem and PC Card slot. It has a built-in PIM and direct connection to AT&T's PersonaLink service, which requires a phone jack for communication.

**magnetic card**     (1) See *magnetic stripe*.
    (2) Magnetic tape strips used in early data storage devices and word processors. See *CRAM*, *RACE* and *Data Cell*.

**magnetic coercivity**     The amount of energy required to alter the state of a magnet. The higher a magnetic disk's coercivity index, the more data it can store.

**magnetic disk**     The primary computer storage device. Like tape, it is magnetically recorded and can be recorded over and over. Disks are rotating platters with a mechanical arm that moves a read/write head between the outer and inner edges of the platter's surface. It can take as long as one second to find a location on a floppy disk to as little as a couple of milliseconds on a fast hard disk. See *floppy disk* and *hard disk*.

Tracks and Sectors     The disk surface is divided into concentric tracks (circles within circles). The thinner the tracks, the more storage. The data bits are recorded as tiny magnetic spots on the tracks. The tinier the spot, the more bits per inch and the greater the storage. Most disks hold the same number of bits on each track, even though the outer tracks are physically longer than the inner ones. Some disks pack the bits as tightly as possible within each track.

    Tracks are further divided into sectors, which hold the least amount of data that can be read or written at one time; for example, READ TRACK 7 SECTOR 24. In order to update the disk, one or more sectors are read into the computer, changed and written back to disk. The operating system figures out how to fit data into these fixed spaces.

Magnetic Disk Summary     The following magnetic disk technologies are summarized below. Several have been discontinued, but drives and media continue to be used long after they have been officially discontinued. See also *magnetic tape* and *optical disk*.

| | |
|---|---|
| Floppy disk | SyJet |
| Zip | SparQ |
| LS-120 | EZFlyer |
| Fixed hard disk | SyQuest |
| Jaz | PocketZip |
| ORB | Bernoulli |

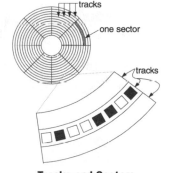

**Magazine Columns**
Nothing is as easy to read as magazine column text on a busy commuter train with standing room only.

**Tracks and Sectors**
Tracks are concentric circles on the disk, broken up into storage units called "sectors." The sector, which is typically 512 bytes, is the smallest unit that can be read or written.

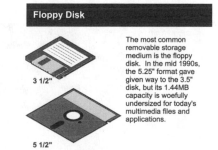

**Floppy Disk**

3 1/2"

5 1/2"

The most common removable storage medium is the floppy disk. In the mid 1990s, the 5.25" format gave given way to the 3.5" disk, but its 1.44MB capacity is woefully undersized for today's multimedia files and applications.

**M**

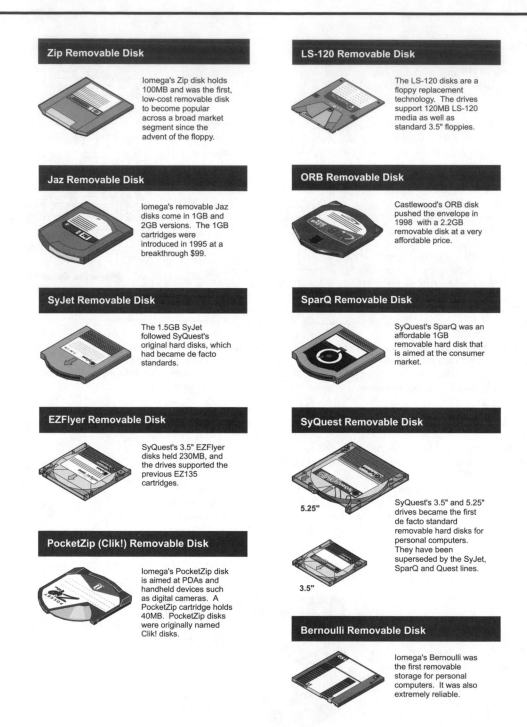

### Zip Removable Disk

Iomega's Zip disk holds 100MB and was the first, low-cost removable disk to become popular across a broad market segment since the advent of the floppy.

### Jaz Removable Disk

Iomega's removable Jaz disks come in 1GB and 2GB versions. The 1GB cartridges were introduced in 1995 at a breakthrough $99.

### SyJet Removable Disk

The 1.5GB SyJet followed SyQuest's original hard disks, which had became de facto standards.

### EZFlyer Removable Disk

SyQuest's 3.5" EZFlyer disks held 230MB, and the drives supported the previous EZ135 cartridges.

### PocketZip (Clik!) Removable Disk

Iomega's PocketZip disk is aimed at PDAs and handheld devices such as digital cameras. A PocketZip cartridge holds 40MB. PocketZip disks were originally named Clik! disks.

### LS-120 Removable Disk

The LS-120 disks are a floppy replacement technology. The drives support 120MB LS-120 media as well as standard 3.5" floppies.

### ORB Removable Disk

Castlewood's ORB disk pushed the envelope in 1998 with a 2.2GB removable disk at a very affordable price.

### SparQ Removable Disk

SyQuest's SparQ was an affordable 1GB removable hard disk that is aimed at the consumer market.

### SyQuest Removable Disk

5.25"

3.5"

SyQuest's 3.5" and 5.25" drives became the first de facto standard removable hard disks for personal computers. They have been superseded by the SyJet, SparQ and Quest lines.

### Bernoulli Removable Disk

Iomega's Bernoulli was the first removable storage for personal computers. It was also extremely reliable.

| DISK/TREND Worldwide Market Projection | | | | |
| --- | --- | --- | --- | --- |
| **MAGNETIC RIGID DISK DRIVES** (UNIT SHIPMENTS IN THOUSANDS) | | | | |
| Platter Size | 1999 | 2000 | 2001 | 2002 |
| 5.25" | 2,175 | 1,095 | 400 | 0 |
| 3.5" | 145,189 | 168,385 | 193,330 | 220,330 |
| 2.5 | 20,817 | 24,090 | 27,740 | 31,850 |
| 1.8" or less | 173 | 250 | 475 | 750 |
| TOTAL | 168,354 | 193,820 | 221,945 | 252,930 |

Reprinted with permission of DISK/TREND Inc.,
a consulting firm specializing in the disk drive industry.
(c) 1999 DISK/TREND Inc.
Mountain View, CA, (650) 961-6209, www.disktrend.com

| DISK/TREND Worldwide Market Projection | | | | |
| --- | --- | --- | --- | --- |
| **MAGNETIC RIGID DISK DRIVES** (DRIVE CAPACITY AND PRICING HISTORY) | | | | |
| | 1988 | 1993 | 1998 | 2002 |
| Sales $ million | 20,424 | 21,730 | 30,077 | 50,318 |
| Total bytes shipped (terabytes) | 1.77 | 14,856 | 694,339 | 16,600,654 |
| Average price per megabyte | $11.54 | 1.46 | .043 | .003 |

Reprinted with permission of DISK/TREND Inc.,
a consulting firm specializing in the disk drive industry.
(c) 1999 DISK/TREND Inc.
Mountain View, CA, (650) 961-6209, www.disktrend.com

**magnetic disk and tape**     The primary computer storage media. The choice depends on accessing requirements. Disk is direct; tape is sequential. Locating a program or data on disk takes a fraction of a second. On tape, it can take several seconds or even minutes. Tapes have traditionally been used for backup and archival storage, and they are easier to transport than removable disk modules. Although tape backup was popular for a while for personal computers, today, backup is usually made on removable media such as Zip and Jaz disks or CD-Rs and CD-RWs. Backup over the Internet is also popular.

In time, magnetic media will no doubt be as obsolete as punched cards. Optical technologies, or perhaps some other yet-to-be-known derivative, that employ no moving parts should eventually supersede them all. Considering the magical technology within the chip, moving chunks of metal and plastic past a read/write head seems archaic by comparison. See *magnetic disk, magnetic tape, optical disk* and *HSM*.

**magnetic drum**     An early high-speed, direct access storage device that used a magnetic-coated cylinder with tracks around its circumference. Each track had its own read/write head. Magnetic drums were used in the 1950s and 1960s.

**magnetic field**     An invisible energy emitted by a magnet. Same as *flux*.

**magnetic ink**     A magnetically detectable ink used to print the MICR characters that encode account numbers on bank checks.

**magnetic oxide**     See *ferric oxide*.

**magnetic recording**     With regard to computers, the technique used to record, or write, digital data in the form of tiny spots (bits) of negative or positive polarity on tapes and disks. A read/write head discharges electrical impulses onto the moving ferromagnetic surface. Reading is accomplished by sensing the polarity of the bit with the read/write head.

**magnetic stripe**     A small length of magnetic tape adhered to ledger cards, badges and credit cards. It is read by specialized readers that may be incorporated into accounting machines and terminals. Due to heavy wear, the data on the stripe is in a low-density format that may be duplicated several times. See *ATM machine*.

**magnetic tape**     A sequential storage medium used for data collection, backup and historical purposes. Like videotape, computer tape is made of flexible plastic with one side coated with a ferromagnetic material. Tapes come in reels and cartridges of many sizes and shapes. Although still used in legacy systems, open reels have been mostly superseded by cartridges with enhanced storage capacities.

Locating a specific record on tape requires reading every record in front of it or searching for markers that identify predefined partitions. Although most tapes are used for archiving rather than routine updating, some drives allow rewriting in place if the byte count does not change. Otherwise, updating requires copying files from the original tape to a blank tape (scratch tape) and adding the new data in between.

M

Tracks either run parallel to the edge of the tape (linear recording) or diagonally (helical scan). A variation of linear recording is serpentine recording, where sets of tracks are duplicated and the data "snakes" back and forth from the end to the beginning.

Open reel tapes use nine linear tracks (8 bits plus parity), while modern cartridges use up to 128 or more (Magstar). Data is recorded in blocks of contiguous bytes, separated by a space called an "interrecord gap" or "interblock gap." Tape drive speed is measured in inches per second (ips). Over the years, storage density has increased from 200 to 38,000 bpi.

Tape is more economical than disks for archival data. However, if tapes are stored for the duration, they must be periodically recopied or the tightly coiled magnetic surfaces may contaminate each other. See *helical scan*.

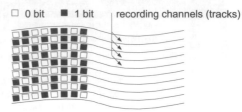

□ 0 bit   ■ 1 bit   recording channels (tracks)

**Tracks on Magnetic Tape**
Except for helical scan recording, most tracks on magnetic tape run parallel to the length of the tape.

## Magnetic Tape Summary
The following magnetic tape technologies are summarized below. See also *magnetic disk* and *optical disk*.

| | |
|---|---|
| QIC, Travan | Redwood |
| DAT 4mm | DV and MiniDV |
| Exabyte 8mm | DST |
| Sony AIT | DTF |
| DLT | DIR |
| 3480/3490/3590 | Open reel |
| Magstar MP | Pereos |

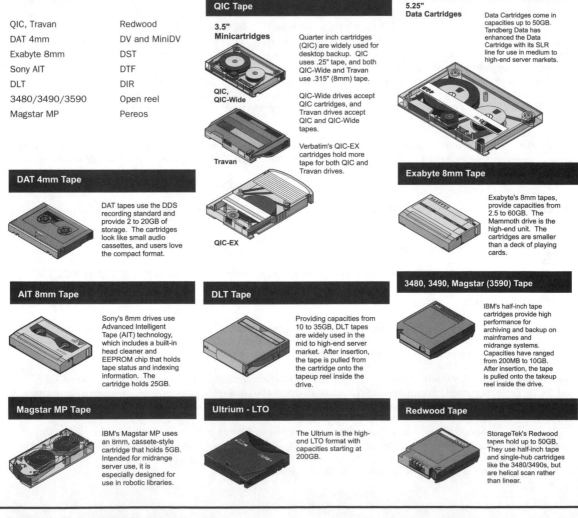

**QIC Tape**

**3.5" Minicartridges**

QIC, QIC-Wide

Travan

QIC-EX

Quarter inch cartridges (QIC) are widely used for desktop backup. QIC uses .25" tape, and both QIC-Wide and Travan use .315" (8mm) tape.

QIC-Wide drives accept QIC cartridges, and Travan drives accept QIC and QIC-Wide tapes.

Verbatim's QIC-EX cartridges hold more tape for both QIC and Travan drives.

**5.25" Data Cartridges**

Data Cartridges come in capacities up to 50GB. Tandberg Data has enhanced the Data Cartridge with its SLR line for use in medium to high-end server markets.

**DAT 4mm Tape**

DAT tapes use the DDS recording standard and provide 2 to 20GB of storage. The cartridges look like small audio cassettes, and users love the compact format.

**Exabyte 8mm Tape**

Exabyte's 8mm tapes, provide capacities from 2.5 to 60GB. The Mammoth drive is the high-end unit. The cartridges are smaller than a deck of playing cards.

**AIT 8mm Tape**

Sony's 8mm drives use Advanced Intelligent Tape (AIT) technology, which includes a built-in head cleaner and EEPROM chip that holds tape status and indexing information. The cartridge holds 25GB.

**DLT Tape**

Providing capacities from 10 to 35GB, DLT tapes are widely used in the mid to high-end server market. After insertion, the tape is pulled from the cartridge onto the tapeup reel inside the drive.

**3480, 3490, Magstar (3590) Tape**

IBM's half-inch tape cartridges provide high performance for archiving and backup on mainframes and midrange systems. Capacities have ranged from 200MB to 10GB. After insertion, the tape is pulled onto the takeup reel inside the drive.

**Magstar MP Tape**

IBM's Magstar MP uses an 8mm, cassette-style cartridge that holds 5GB. Intended for midrange server use, it is especially designed for use in robotic libraries.

**Ultrium - LTO**

The Ultrium is the high-end LTO format with capacities starting at 200GB.

**Redwood Tape**

StorageTek's Redwood tapes hold up to 50GB. They use half-inch tape and single-hub cartridges like the 3480/3490s, but are helical scan rather than linear.

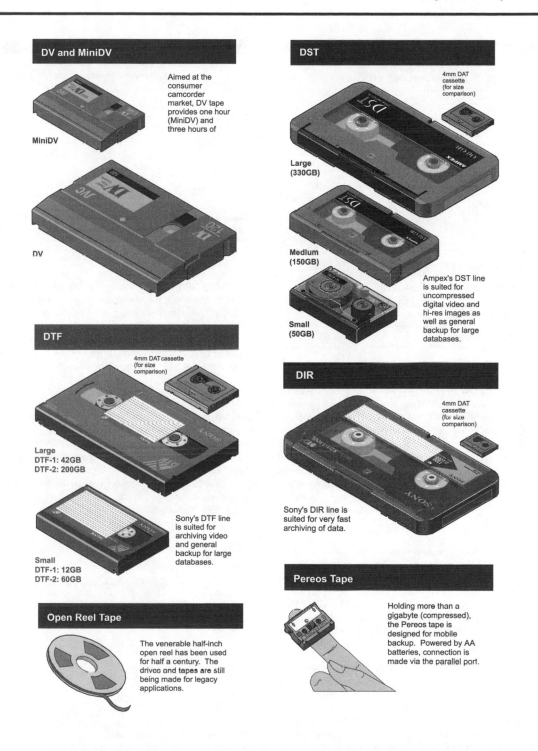

### DV and MiniDV

**MiniDV**

Aimed at the consumer camcorder market, DV tape provides one hour (MiniDV) and three hours of

**DV**

### DTF

4mm DAT cassette (for size comparison)

**Large**
DTF-1: 42GB
DTF-2: 200GB

Sony's DTF line is suited for archiving video and general backup for large databases.

**Small**
DTF-1: 12GB
DTF-2: 60GB

### Open Reel Tape

The venerable half-inch open reel has been used for half a century. The drives and tapes are still being made for legacy applications.

### DST

4mm DAT cassette (for size comparison)

**Large**
**(330GB)**

**Medium**
**(150GB)**

**Small**
**(50GB)**

Ampex's DST line is suited for uncompressed digital video and hi-res images as well as general backup for large databases.

### DIR

4mm DAT cassette (for size comparison)

Sony's DIR line is suited for very fast archiving of data.

### Pereos Tape

Holding more than a gigabyte (compressed), the Pereos tape is designed for mobile backup. Powered by AA batteries, connection is made via the parallel port.

**M**

| Worldwide Market Projection | | |
| --- | --- | --- |
| **COMPACT TAPE DRIVES** <br> (UNIT SHIPMENTS IN THOUSANDS) | | |
| | 1999 | 2005 |
| QIC 3.5" | 1,462 | 300 |
| QIC 5.25" | 469 | 122 |
| DAT | 1,944 | 1,685 |
| 8MM | 149 | 449 |
| Magstar MP | 8 | 0 |
| DLT | 483 | 636 |
| Ultrium | 0 | 504 |
| TOTAL SHIPMENTS | 4,346 | 3,865 |
| INSTALLED BASE | 20,351 | 21,623 |

Reprinted with permission of Freeman Reports,
a market research firm specializing in tape storage.
(c) 2000 Freeman Reports, www.freemanreports.com
Ojai, CA, (805) 649-5135

| Worldwide Market Projection | | |
| --- | --- | --- |
| **PERFORMANCE TAPE DRIVES** <br> (UNIT SHIPMENTS IN THOUSANDS) | | |
| | 1999 | 2005 |
| 1/2" CARTRIDGE <br> (3490, 3590, 9840/9940) | 54.5 | 72.8 |
| 1/2" REEL | 6.4 | 0 |
| HELICAL SCAN <br> (Redwood, DTF/DIR, DST) | 1.5 | 0.6 |
| TOTAL SHIPMENTS | 62.4 | 73.4 |

Reprinted with permission of Freeman Reports,
a market research firm specializing in tape storage.
(c) 2000 Freeman Reports, www.freemanreports.com
Ojai, CA, (805) 649-5135

**magnetographic**   A non-impact printer technology that prints up to 90 ppm. A magnetic image is created by a set of recording heads across a magnetic drum. A toner is applied to the drum to develop the image, which is transferred to paper by light pressure and an electrostatic field. The toner is then fused by heat. The print quality is not as good as a laser printer, but the machines require less maintenance.

**magneto-optic disk**   A rewritable optical disk that uses a combination of magnetic and optical methods. MO disks use removable cartridges and come in two form factors. The 3.5" disks hold 128MB, 230MB and 640MB, and the 5.25" disks hold 650MB, 1.3GB, 2.6GB and 5.2GB. The latter are double sided, but must be removed and flipped over to use the other side. Pinnacle Micro introduced a proprietary 4.6GB drive in 1995 that also supports 2.6GB cartridges.

MO disks disks are very robust and are typically used in high-end disk libraries. They have a 30-year shelf life and can withstand a million rewrites. MO access times are in the sub-25ms range, compared to more than 100ms for phase change disks, the pure optical technology used in CD-RW, DVD-RAM and PD disks.

Data is written on an MO disk by both a laser and a magnet. The laser heats the bit to the Curie point, which is the temperature at which molecules can be realigned when subjected to a magnetic field. Then, a magnet changes the bit's polarity. The laser is focused on one side of the platter, and the magnet is used on the opposite side, which is why double-sided media must be flipped over to access the other side.

Reading is accomplished with a lower-power laser that reflects light from the bits. The light is rotated differently depending on the polarity of the bit, and the difference in rotation is sensed. Writing takes two passes. The existing bits are set to zero in one pass, and data is written on the second pass. A direct overwrite method (LIMDOW) was later added that erases and writes in one rotation. Many drives support the LIMDOW disks, which is more costly than standard MO media. See *Kerr effect* and *optical disk*.

**magnetoresistive**   A technology used for the read element of a read/write head on a high-density magnetic disk. As storage capacity increases, the bit gets smaller and its magnetic field becomes weaker. MR heads are more sensitive to weaker fields than the earlier inductive read coils.

Magnetoresistive means that a material's electrical resistance changes when brought in contact with a magnetic field. Unlike inductive heads in which the bit on the medium induces the current across a gap, the

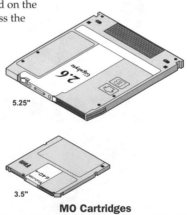

**MO Cartridges**
The 5.25" cartridges are double sided and must be flipped to reach the other side. The 3.5" cartridges are single sided.

MR mechanism is an active element with current flowing through it. The magnetic orientation of the bit increases the resistance in a thin-film, nickel-iron layer, and the difference in current is detected by the read electronics. MR heads use the traditional inductive coil for writing.

Although this technology was used earlier in analog tape recorders, in 1991, IBM was the first to use it in computer disk drives. In 1998, IBM introduced drives with giant magnetoresistive (GMR) heads, which are sensitive to even weaker fields. GMR heads use additional thin film layers in the sensing element to boost the change in resistance. MR disks are expected to reach 5 Gbits/sq.in., while GMR is expected to go beyond 10 Gbits/sq.in.

**Magstar**    A high-performance magnetic tape technology from IBM. The Magstar is the latest model in the half-inch, single-hub cartridge line that comprises the 3480, 3490 and 3490e. Designated the 3590, the Magstar boosts capacity to 20GB and provides ESCON and SCSI connectivity to IBM mainframes and midrange systems. Tape libraries are available that hold from a handful to thousands of cartridges. See *Magstar MP* and *magnetic tape*.

**Magstar Cartridges**
Magstar and Magstar MP are very different tape technologies. Magstar uses a half-inch, single-hub cartridge, while Magstar MP uses an 8mm cassette-style cartridge that starts in the middle for faster retrieval. Both use linear recording.

| Type | Year | Tracks | Length | Raw Capacity | Raw tfr Rate |
|------|------|--------|--------|--------------|--------------|
| 3480 | '84 | 18 | 160 m | 200MB | 3MB/sec |
| 3490 | '89 | 18 | 160 m | 400MB | 3MB/sec |
| 3490e | '91 | 36 | 300 m | 800MB | 3MB/sec |
| 3590 B11 | '95 | 128 | 300 m | 10GB | 9MB/sec |
| 3590 E11 | '99 | 256 | 300 m | 20GB | 14MB/sec |

**Magstar MP**    (Magstar MultiPurpose) A magnetic tape technology from IBM for midrange systems. Except for the use of linear recording, Magstar MP is completely different than the Magstar line. It uses a 5GB cassette-style cartridge rather than a single-hub unit, and it uses 8mm tape rather than half inch. The Magstar MP cartridge was especially designed for picking in a robotic library. Instead of at the beginning, the starting point is in the middle of the tape for faster retrieval. See *magnetic tape*.

**mail API**    See *messaging API* and *MAPI*.

**mail bomb**    A huge number of e-mail messages sent to one destination or an e-mail with an extremely large attached file. Mail bombs are sent to antagonize their recipients and/or to cause them problems by filling up their disks and overloading the system. See *spam* and *letter bomb*.

**mailbot**    (MAIL roBOT) An e-mail server that automatically returns to the sender a fixed e-mail message, typically a description about a service or product or the status of some situation.

**mailbox**    A simulated mailbox on disk that holds incoming electronic mail.

**mail client**    See *e-mail program*.

**mail enabled**    Refers to an application that has built-in, although typically very limited, mail capabilities. For example, it can send or send and receive a file that it has created over one or more messaging systems. See *messaging API*.

**mailer**    (1) An e-mail program. See *e-mail program*.
(2) A message sent by an e-mail program.
(3) A person or organization sending e-mail.

**mailing list**    An automated e-mail system on the Internet, which is maintained by subject matter. There are more than 10,000 such lists. New users generally subscribe by sending an e-mail with the word "subscribe" in it and subsequently receive all new postings made to the list automatically. Mailing lists are also called "listprocs" and "listservs," the latter coming from the popular LISTSERV package. Majordomo is a popular public domain mailing list program.

**mail merge** Printing customized form letters. A common feature of a word processor, it uses a letter and a name and address list. In the letter, Dear A: Thank you for ordering B from our C store..., A, B and C are merge points into which data is inserted from the list. See *variable data printing*, *field squeeze* and *line squeeze*.

| Letter | Database | | |
|---|---|---|---|
| | **A** | **B** | **C** |
| Dear A:<br>Thank you for<br>ordering B<br>at our C store.<br>Sincerely,<br>The Management | Mr. Smith | 1 Widgit | New York |
| | Ms. Gomez | 2 Dingits | Chicago |
| | Mr. Jones | 1 Frabbits | Los Angeles |
| | Mr. Gold | 3 Widgits | Atlanta |
| | Ms. Chang | 2 Frabbits | Philadelphia |
| | Mr. Russo | 4 Dingits | Boston |

**The Mail Merge**
The mail merge inserts the fields from the database into the predefined merge points in the form letter.

**mail program** See *e-mail program*.

**mail protocol** See *messaging protocol* and *messaging system*.

**mail proxy** A proxy server that specializes in e-mail transactions. See *proxy server*.

**mail reader** Software that retrieves and displays e-mail messages from a mail server. Mail readers generally send messages as well. See *e-mail program*.

**mail server** A computer in a network that provides "post office" facilities. It stores incoming mail for distribution to users and forwards outgoing mail through the appropriate channel. The term may refer to just the software that performs this service, which can reside on a machine with other services. See *messaging system*.

**mail system** See *e-mail* and *messaging system*.

**mail virus** See *e-mail virus*.

**mainboard** Same as *motherboard*.

**mainframe** A large computer. In the "ancient" mid 1960s, all computers were called mainframes, since the term referred to the main CPU cabinet. Today, it refers to a large computer system.

There are small, medium and large-scale mainframes, handling from a handful to tens of thousands of online terminals. Large-scale mainframes support multiple gigabytes of main memory and terabytes of disk storage. Large mainframes use smaller computers as front-end processors that connect to the communications networks.

The original mainframe vendors were Burroughs, Control Data, GE, Honeywell, IBM, NCR, RCA and Univac, otherwise known as "IBM and the Seven Dwarfs." After GE and RCA's computer divisions were absorbed by Honeywell and Univac respectively, the mainframers were known as "IBM and the BUNCH."

IBM has the lion's share of the mainframe business, and Hitachi Data Systems and Amdahl are its major competitors, making System/390-compatible computers (see *IBM-compatible mainframe*). Unisys, Sun and others make mainframe-class machines, but run under proprietary or UNIX-based operating systems, not IBM's OS/390.

There Is a Difference! One might wonder why mainframes cost up to several millions of dollars when their raw megahertz (MHz) or MIPS rates are no higher than a PC costing 1,000 times less. There are reasons. Firstly, in a small computer such as a PC, the CPU does almost all the processing. Unless direct memory transfer (DMA) is used, the CPU is also involved with getting data to and from the peripherals, the most time-consuming part of the operation.

A mainframe provides enormous amounts of throughput by offloading its input/output processing to a peripheral channel, which is a computer in itself. Mainframes can support hundreds of channels, up to 512 in some models. Mainframes also have multiple ports into memory and especially into high-speed caches, which can be 10 times faster than main memory. Additional computers may act as I/O traffic cops between the CPU and the channels and handle the processing of exceptions (what happens if the channel is busy, if it fails, etc.). All these subsystems handle the transaction overhead, freeing the CPU to do real "data processing" such as computing balances in customer records and subtracting amounts from inventories, the purpose of the computer in the first place.

Second, the internal bus transfer rates of mainframes are also higher than small computers. A 800MHz Pentium has a data bus that runs at 100MHz, but a 200MHz mainframe may have a data bus that also runs at 200MHz, twice as fast. The multipliers add up. Twice the bus speed, 10 times the cache speed, perhaps 32 or 64 overlapped data transfers. Multiply one times the other, and the combination of fast buses, fast caches, multiple memory ports and independent channels and subsystems produces a powerful machine.

Third, much of the hardware circuitry in a mainframe is designed to detect and correct errors. Every subsystem is continuously monitored for potential failure, in some cases even triggering a list of parts to be replaced at the next scheduled maintenance. As a result, mainframes are incredibly reliable. The mean time between failure (MTBF) is generally 20 years!

In addition, mainframes are highly scalable. Based on symmetric multiprocessing (SMP), mainframes can be expanded by adding CPUs to a system or by adding systems in clusters.

**They're Here to Stay**    Once upon a time, mainframes meant "complicated" and required the most programming and operations expertise. That is no longer. Networks of client/server-based PCs make mainframes look easy. Nothing is more complicated than the Windows environment. Add NetWare, throw in a little UNIX for good measure, and you have enterprise computing at its most complex ever.

With more than two trillion dollars worth of mainframe applications in place, mainframes are here to stay, and their centralized architecture, which is the easiest to manage, may just be the wave of the future!

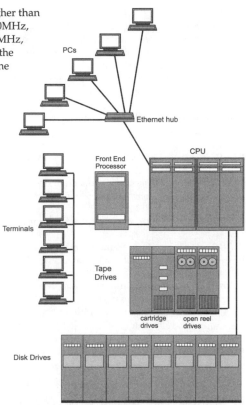

**Mainframe System**

**mainframe analyst**    See *mainframe systems analyst*.

**mainframe programmer**    A person that writes mainframe applications in programming languages such as COBOL, CICS and various 4GLs. See *programmer*.

**mainframe programmer/analyst**    A person responsible for the design and programming of a mainframe application. Programming languages typically include COBOL, CICS and 4GLs. See *programmer analyst*.

**mainframe systems analyst**    A person responsible for the design of a mainframe application. See *systems analyst*.

**main loop**    The primary logic in a program. It contains the instructions that are repeated after each event or transaction has been processed. See *loop*.

**main memory**    Same as *memory*.

**main storage**    Same as *memory*.

**maintenance**    (1) Hardware maintenance is the testing and cleaning of equipment.

**UNIVAC Mainframe**
Mainframes have provided the computing power for major corporations for more than 40 years. Sperry Rand (Univac), IBM, GE, RCA, NCR, Burroughs, Honeywell and Control Data were the first companies that made mainframes in the U.S. This picture was taken in the mid-1970s. *(Image courtesy of Unisys Corporation.)*

**(2)** Information system maintenance is the routine updating of master files, such as adding and deleting employees and customers and changing credit limits and product prices.

**(3)** Software, or program, maintenance is the updating of application programs in order to meet changing information requirements, such as adding new functions and changing data formats. It also includes fixing bugs and adapting the software to new hardware devices.

**(4)** Disk or file maintenance is the periodic reorganizing of disk files that have become fragmented due to continuous updating.

**maintenance credits**   Monetary credits issued to a customer by the vendor for qualified periods during which the vendor's products are not functioning properly.

**maintenance service**   A service provided to keep a product in good operating condition.

**Majordomo**   A mailing list program on the Internet made up of a series of Perl scripts and C source code. It runs in most all UNIX environments. See *mailing list*.

**major key**   The primary key used to identify a record, such as account number or name.

**make**   To compile a program made up of several independent software modules. The make utility recompiles only those modules that have been updated since the last compilation. See *makefile*.

**makefile**   A file of commands that are executed by a compiler's "make" utility or function. The makefile lists the program modules that are part of the project and associated libraries that must be linked in. It also includes special directives that enable certain modules to be compiled differently if required. Unless otherwise specified, generally only the source modules that have changed are actually recompiled.

**male connector**   A plug or socket that contains pins. The female counterpart contains receptacles.

**Maltron keyboard**   A keyboard that uses independent left- and right-hand modules shaped to conform to the natural position of the hands, designed to prevent strain (RSI).

**malware**   (**MAL**icious **WARE**) Software designed to destroy, aggravate and otherwise make life unhappy. See *virus, macro virus, Word macro virus* and *Trojan horse*.

**Mammoth tape**   See *8mm tape*.

**MAN**   (Metropolitan Area Network) A communications network that covers a geographic area such as a city or suburb. See *LAN* and *WAN*.

**managed hub**   A network hub that has intelligence built into firmware. Typically an Ethernet hub, it responds to management queries for statistics and to commands for setting the configuration. Contrast with *unmanaged hub*. See *intelligent hub*.

**management console**   A terminal or workstation used to monitor and control a network.

**management information system**   See *MIS*.

**management science**   The study of statistical methods, such as linear programming and simulation, in order to analyze and solve organizational problems. Same as *operations research*.

**management support**   See *DSS* and *EIS*.

---

**Serial & Parallel Ports on a PC**

Serial port
(DB-9 male)

Serial port
(DB-25 male)

Parallel port
(DB-25 female)

A PC usually comes with two serial ports (COM1, COM2) and one parallel port (LPT1).

On the back of the PC, the serial ports are either two male DB-9 connectors or one DB-9 and one DB-25. The parallel port is a DB-25 female connector.

---

map 583

**management system** The leadership and control within an organization. It is made up of people interacting with other people and machines that, together, set the goals and objectives, outline the strategies and tactics, and develop the plans, schedules and necessary controls to run an organization.

**ManageWise** Network management software from Novell that manages NetWare and Windows NT servers and all supported clients.

**Manchester Code** A self-clocking data encoding method that divides the time required to define the bit into two cycles. The first cycle is the data value (0 or 1) and the second cycle provides the timing by shifting to the opposite state.

**man machine interface** Same as *user interface*.

**ManMan** See *CA-ManMan/X*.

**man page** (**MAN**ual Page) A page of online documentation in a UNIX system. The command **man** followed by the command name retrieves the appropriate page from the online manual.

**MANTIS** An application development language from Cincom Systems, Inc., Cincinnati, OH, (www.cincom.com), that runs on IBM mainframes, VAXs and other mainframes. It provides procedural and non-procedural languages for developing prototypes and applications and works with Cincom's SUPRA database, DB2 and IMS.

**mantissa** The numeric value in a floating point number. See *floating point*.

**manufacturing software** The following list of software modules are the manufacturing components of Baan's ERP (BaanERP) system. It is listed here because it provides a comprehensive overview of the required software.

| | |
|---|---|
| Bills of material | Project control |
| Cost price calculation | Repetitive manufacturing |
| Engineering change control | Routings |
| Engineering data management | Shop floor control |
| Hours accounting | Tool requirements, planning & control |
| Product classification | Capcity requirements planning |
| Product configuration | Master production scheduling |
| Production planning | Material requirements planning (MRP II) |
| Project budgeting | |

**map** (1) A set of data that has a corresponding relationship to another set of data.

(2) A list of data or objects as they are currently stored in memory or disk.

(3) To assign a path or drive letter to a disk drive. See *drive mapping*.

(4) To transfer a set of objects from one place to another. For example, program modules on disk are mapped into memory. A graphic image in memory is mapped onto the video screen. An address is mapped to another address. A logical database structure is mapped to the physical database. Mapping typically requires a conversion of one format to another.

(5) To relate one set of objects with another. For example, a vendor's protocol stack is mapped to the OSI model. An alias is mapped to the true name of the object. See *alias*.

(6) (MAP) (**M**anufacturing **A**utomation **P**rotocol) A communications protocol introduced by General Motors in 1982. MAP provides common standards for interconnecting computers and programmable machine tools used in factory automation. At the lowest physical level, it uses the IEEE 802.4 token bus protocol.

MAP is often used in conjunction with *TOP*, an office protocol developed by Boeing Computer Services. TOP is used in the front office and MAP is used on the factory floor.

---

**RELATIONSHIP BETWEEN SYSTEMS**

| structure (is) | function (does) |
|---|---|
| **Management System** | |
| 1. People | Sets organization's goals |
| 2. Machines | and objectives, strategies |
| | and tactics, plans, |
| | schedule and controls. |
| **Information System** | |
| 1. Database | Defines data structures |
| 2. Application | Data entry, updating, |
| programs | queries and reporting. |
| 3. Procedures | Defines data flow |
| **Computer System** | |
| 1. CPU | Processes (the 3 C's) |
| 2. Peripherals | Store and retrieve |
| 3. Operating system | Manages computer system |

M

**MAPI**   (**M**ail **API**) A programming interface from Microsoft that enables a client application to send to and receive mail from Exchange Server or a Microsoft Mail (MS Mail) messaging system. Simple MAPI is an enhanced version of the Common Messaging Calls (CMC) X.400 standard. Enhanced MAPI adds full calendaring and workgroup capabilities. MAPI has evolved into CDO. See *CDO*.

**MAPICS**   (**M**anufacturing **A**ccounting and **P**roduction **I**nformation **C**ontrol **S**ystem) A comprehensive and widely-used ERP system from Marcam Corporation, Newton, MA (www.marcam.com), that includes more than 45 different software modules. Originally developed by IBM in 1978 and purchased by Marcam in 1993, MAPICS runs on Windows clients and AS/400 servers.

**MAPI method**   Procedures for equipment replacement analysis and capital investment analysis from the Machinery and Allied Products Institute.

**MAPPER**   (**MA**intaining, **P**reparing and **P**rocessing **E**xecutive **R**eports) A Unisys mainframe fourth-generation language. In 1980, it was introduced as a high-level report writer and was later turned into a full-featured development system used successfully by non-technical users.

**mapping**   See *map* and *digital mapping*.

**MAPS**   (**M**ail **A**buse **P**revention **S**ystem) A California-based non-profit organization dedicated to eliminating spamming by maintaining the RBL (Realtime Blackhole List). The RBL contains the IP addresses of spammers, and companies and ISPs can use the list to reject incoming mail. If an offending spammer cannot be shut down, the spammer's ISP may contact MAPS with the subnet addresses allocated to the spammer so those specific addresses may be used instead of the IP address of the entire ISP. For information, visit http://mail-abuse.org. See *Blacklist of Internet Advertisers*.

**Marconi**   (Marconi Communications, Warrendale, PA, www.marconi.com) A leading manufacturer of networking equipment. Founded in 1990 as FORE Systems by four Carnegie Mellon University faculty members, the company name was derived from its founders' first names: Francois, Onat, Robert and Eric. FORE commercialized the ATM market and its products were widely deployed by large enterprises and carriers alike. In late 1999, the company was acquired by Marconi plc of London and became its Marconi Communications division. See *ATM*.

**The Founding Four**
The founders of Marconi Communications (FORE Systems) start with Onat Menzilcioglu at the top left and go clockwise to Eric Cooper, Robert Sansom and Francois Bitz. *(Image courtesy of Marconi Communications.)*

**Far Out**
Everyone does a double take when they arrive at Marconi Communications headquarters, thinking that an earthquake just hit Western Pennsylvania. Having been used as the set for TV spots and movies, the architecture is just as "far out" on the inside. *(Image courtesy of Marconi Communications.)*

**marginal test**    A system test that introduces values far above and far below the expected values.

**Marimba**    (Marimba, Inc., Palo Alto, CA, www.marimba.com)  A software company founded in 1996 by four key members of Sun's original Java development team. In 1996, it introduced Castanet, a family of Java-based delivery systems for publishing and automatically distributing application updates and other published materials via the Internet and intranets.

**mark**    (1) A small blip printed on or notched into various storage media used for timing or counting purposes.
(2) To identify a block of text in order to perform some task on it such as deletion, copying and moving.
(3) To identify an item for future reference.
(4) In digital electronics, a 1 bit. Contrast with *space*.
(5) On magnetic disk, a recorded character used to identify the beginning of a track.
(6) In optical recognition and mark sensing, a pencil line in a preprinted box.
(7) On magnetic tape, a *tape mark* is a special character that is recorded after the last character of data.

**market cap**    (MARKET CAPitalization)  The value of a company based on the current stock price times the number of shares outstanding. The market caps of some computer and computer-related companies is nothing short of astronomical. For example, for years, Microsoft has had the highest market cap of any company in the world, no matter what industry. By the end of 1998, Amazon.com had a market cap three times that of K Mart, and it had never been profitable.

**Mark I**    A programmable, electromechanical calculator designed by professor Howard Aiken. Built by IBM and installed at Harvard in 1944, it strung 78 adding machines together to perform three calculations per second. It was 51 feet long, weighed five tons and used paper tape for input and typewriters for output. Made of 765,000 parts, it sounded like a thousand knitting needles according to Admiral Grace Hopper. The Mark I worked in decimal arithmetic, not binary, but it could go for hours without intervention. At its dedication ceremony, Aiken asserted that the Mark I was the modern embodiment of Babbage's Analytical Engine, although it did not have a conditional statement in its programming repertoire. The experience helped IBM develop its own computers a few years later. See *Analytical Engine*.

**M**

**marking engine**    See *printer engine*.

**mark sensing**    Detecting pencil lines in predefined boxes on paper forms. The form is designed with boundaries for each pencil stroke that represents a yes, no, single digit or letter, providing all possible answers to each question. A mark sense reader detects the marks and converts them into digital code.

**mark up**    To define the layout and certain content within a document by inserting tags and format codes into the appropriate locations. See *markup language*.

**markup language**    A set of labels that are embedded within text to distinguish individual elements or groups of elements for display or identification purposes. The labels are typically known as "tags." Markup languages identify elements within a continuous stream of text rather than more structured data in a database. However, XML is a markup language that turns text streams into the equivalent of database records. SGML is the foundation markup language from which HTML and XML were devised. See *SGML, HTML* and *XML*.

**MAS**    (1) (Multiple Address System)  A radio service in the 932–932.5 and 941–941.5Mhz frequency that covers a 25-mile radius from the antenna. It is used for sensor-based and transaction systems (ATMs, reservations, alarms, traffic control, etc.).
(2) (Multiple Award Schedule)  A list of approved products available for purchase by U.S. government agencies.
(3) (Macintosh Application System)  Software that allows a Macintosh 680x0 application to run in a PowerPC. It includes a 680x0 emulator and the Macintosh Toolbox, which contains the Mac's graphical functions. The Macintosh graphical user interface runs native in the PowerPC while only the Motorola 680x0 instructions are emulated.

**mask**    (1) A pattern used to transfer a design onto an object. See *photomask*.

**(2)** A pattern of bits used to accept or reject bit patterns in another set of data. For example, the Boolean AND operation can be used to match a mask of 0s and 1s with a string of data bits. When a 1 occurs in both the mask and the data, the resulting bit will contain a 1 in that position.

Hardware interrupts are often enabled and disabled in this manner with each interrupt assigned a bit position in a mask register.

**maskable interrupts**   Hardware interrupts that can be enabled and disabled by software.

**mask bit**   A 1 bit in a mask used to control the corresponding bit found in data.

**masked**   A state of being disabled or cut off.

**masked ROM**   Refers to a ROM chip. It is a redundant expression, since all ROMs are created by masks in their manufacture, as well as all other chips. However, the term may be used to strongly differentiate between fixed ROMs and user-programmable memories such as PROMs and FPGAs. See *ROM, PROM* and *FPGA*.

**masking software**   Software that is able to cut out or "knock out" one part of an image. An image editor can be used, but requires that the user trace the object with extreme precision, which may be impossible if it is very complicated. With masking software, the user still has to trace a line around the area, but it can be done much more casually, letting the algorithms in the software figure out every last pixel.

**MASM**   See *macro assembler*.

**massage**   To process data.

**massively parallel**   See *MPP*.

**mass storage**   High-capacity, external storage such as disk or tape.

**master**   Primary, controlling. See *master-slave communications* and *master file*.

**master boot record**   The first sector on the hard disk, which directs the computer to the location of the operating system. See *boot sector*.

**master card**   A master record in punched card format.

**master clock**   A clock that provides the primary source of internal timing for a processor or stand-alone control unit.

**master console**   The main terminal used by the computer operator or systems programmer to command the computer.

**master control program**   The program in control of the machine. See *operating system*.

**master file**   A collection of records pertaining to one of the main subjects of an information system, such as customers, employees, products and vendors. Master files contain descriptive data, such as name and address, as well as summary information, such as amount due and year-to-date sales. Contrast with *transaction file*.

Following are the kinds of fields that make up a typical master record in a business information system. There can be many more fields depending on the organization. The "key" fields below are the ones that are generally indexed for matching against the transaction records as well as fast retrieval for queries. The account number is usually the primary key, but name may also be primary. There can be secondary indexes; for example, in an inverted file structure, almost all the fields could be indexed. See *transaction file* for examples of typical transaction records.

```
    EMPLOYEE MASTER RECORD
key Employee account number
key Name (last)
    Name (first)
    Address, city, state, zip
```

```
       EMPLOYEE MASTER RECORD
       Hire date
       Birth date
       Title
       Job class
       Pay rate
       Year-to-date gross pay

       CUSTOMER MASTER RECORD
key    Customer account number
key    Name
       Bill-to address, city, state, zip
       Ship-to address, city, state, zip
       Credit limit
       Date of first order
       Sales-to-date
       Balance due

       VENDOR MASTER RECORD
key    Vendor account number
key    Name
       Address, city, state, zip
       Terms
       Quality rating
       Shipping method

       PRODUCT MASTER RECORD
key    Product number
key    Name
       Description
       Quantity on hand
       Location
       Primary vendor
       Secondary vendor
```

**master record**    A set of data for an individual subject, such as a customer, employee or vendor. See *master file*.

**master-slave communications**    Communications in which one side, called the "master," initiates and controls the session. The "slave" is the other side that responds to the master's commands.

**match print**    In prepress, a high-quality sample of printed output that is used as a comp for the customer and a guide for the printer. It is made by exposing the CMYK negatives onto four acetate films which are developed and laminated together. See *color key* and *press proof*.

**material dispersion**    See *dispersion*.

**Mathcad**    Mathematical software for PCs and Macs from Mathsoft, Inc., Cambridge, MA (www.mathsoft.com). It allows complicated mathematical equations to be expressed, performed and displayed.

**math coprocessor**    A mathematical circuit that performs high-speed floating point operations. It is generally built into the CPU chip. In older PCs, such as the 386 and 486SX, the math coprocessor was an optional and separate chip. Floating point capability is very important to computation-intensive CAD work, and many CAD programs will not operate without it. A spreadsheet may use it if available, but it is not mandatory. See *array processor* and *vector processor*.

**Mathematica**    Mathematical software for the Macintosh, DOS, Windows, OS/2 and various UNIX platforms from Wolfram Research, Inc., Champaign, IL (www.wolfram.com). It includes numerical, graphical and symbolic computation capabilities, all linked to the Mathematica programming language. Its use requires a math coprocessor.

**mathematical expression**    A group of characters or symbols representing a quantity or an operation. See *arithmetic expression*.

**mathematical function**    A rule for creating a set of new values from an existing set; for example, the function $f(x) = 2x$ creates a set of even numbers (if x is a whole number).

**MATLAB**    (**MAT**rix **LAB**oratory) A programming language for technical computing from The MathWorks, Natick, MA (www.mathworks.com). Used for a wide variety of scientific and engineering calculations, especially for automatic control and signal processing, MATLAB runs on Windows, Mac and a variety of UNIX-based systems. Developed by Cleve Moler in the late 1970s and based on the original LINPACK and EISPACK FORTRAN libraries, it was initially used for factoring matrices and solving linear equations. Moler commercialized the product with two colleagues in 1984. MATLAB is also noted for its extensive graphics capabilities. The following MATLAB commands generate the 3-D graph below:

```
x=(0:2*pi/20:2*pi)';
y=(0:4*pi/40:4*pi)';
[X,Y] = meshgrid(x,y);
z= cos(X).*cos(2*Y);
surf (x,y,z);
```

**matrix**    An array of elements in row and column form. See *x-y matrix*.

**matrix printer**    See *dot-matrix* and *printer*.

**matrix router**    A device used to switch audio or video signals to multiple destinations. It provides a one-to-one or one-to-many distribution, but not many-to-one. Matrix routers are typically designed for either analog or digital and either audio or video signals; however, sophisticated units can support all types, but on different ports.

**MAU**    (**M**ultistation **A**ccess **U**nit) A central hub in a Token Ring local area network. See *hub*.

**maximize**    In a graphical environment, to enlarge a window to full size. Contrast with *minimize*.

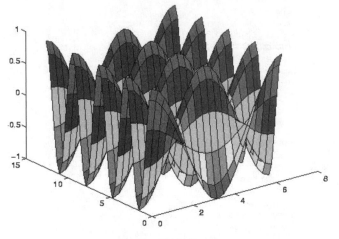

**The Resulting Graph**
This graph was computed from the lines of code above and is an example that might be used in multivariate calculus. *(Image courtesy of Dr. Mark S. Gockenbach, Michigan Technological University, www.math.mtu.edu/~msgocken/intro/intro.html)*

**Maya**    3-D animation and visual effects software for Windows NT and IRIX workstations from the Alias | Wavefront subsidiary of SGI (www.aw.sgi.com). Maya is known for its special character animation capabilities that enables human characters to be simulated with flesh tones, wrinkles and folds in clothing. Maya uses the MEL (Maya Embedded Language) scripting language to define sequences.

**MB**    **(1)** (MB) (**M**ega**B**yte) One million bytes (technically 1,048,576 bytes). See *mega* and *space/time*.
    **(2)** (MB) (**M**other**B**oard) On references to basic hardware components, MB often means motherboard or mainboard.
    **(3)** (Mb) (**M**ega**B**it) One million bits (technically 1,048,576 bits). Lowercase "b" for bit and "B" for byte are not always followed and often misprinted. Thus, Mb may refer to megabyte. See *mega* and *space/time*.

**MBC**    (**M**ultimedia **B**enchmark **C**ommittee) A graphics benchmark that provides MPEG-2 and other tests. See *GPC*.

**Mbits/sec**    (**M**ega**BITS** per **SEC**ond) One million bits per second. See *space/time*.

**Mbone** (Multicast backBONE) A collection of sites on the Internet that support the IP multicast protocol (one-to-many) and allow for live audio and videoconferencing.

**Mbps** (MegaBits Per Second) One million bits per second. Mbps is commonly used as a rating of transmission speed. Uppercase "B" in MBps means megabytes per second, but using "b" for bit and "B" for byte is not always followed and often misprinted. MBps or MB/s would be used for disk and tape transfer ratings as data is transferred in parallel, not serial. See *space/time*.

**MBR** (Master Boot Record) See *boot sector*.

**MB/s** (MegaBytes per Second) One million bytes per second. MB/s would be used for disk and tape transfer ratings. Lowercase "b" in Mb/s means megabits per second and would be used for transmission speeds in a network, but using "b" for bit and "B" for byte is not always followed and often misprinted. See *Mbps*.

**M-byte** See *megabyte*.

**Mbytes/sec** (MegaBYTES per SECond) One million bytes per second. See *space/time*.

**MC68000** See *68000*.

**MCA** See *Micro Channel*.

**McAfee** See *Network Associates*.

**McAfee Office** A suite of utilities for maintaining the health of a Windows PC from Network Associates. It includes 10 stand-alone programs that provide antivirus, diagnostics and repair, encryption, system optimization, automatic driver updating and a host of other functions.

**MCB** (Memory Control Block) An identifier (16 bytes) that DOS places in front of each block of memory it allocates.

**MCC** (The Microelectronics and Computer Technology Corporation, Austin, TX, www.mcc.com) An industrial research and development consortium chartered in 1982. Its membership comes from a wide variety of companies, and its hardware and software projects are just as wide ranging. MCC services include newsletters, seminars and workshops.

**MCDBA** See *Microsoft certification*.

**MCGA** (Multi Color Graphics Array) An IBM video display standard built into low-end PS/2 models. It was never widely supported. See *PC display modes*.

**MCI** (Media Control Interface) A high-level programming interface from Microsoft and IBM for controlling multimedia devices. It provides commands and functions to open, play and close the device.

**MCI decision** An FCC decree in 1969 that granted MCI the right to compete with the Bell System by providing private, intercity telecommunications services.

**McIntosh** See *Macintosh*.

**MCIS** (Microsoft Commercial Internet System) A family of Web server software products from Microsoft that runs on Windows NT and works with Internet Information Server (IIS). Intended for ISPs and other online services, it includes Web, chat, news and search servers and a variety of development tools. It also includes support for NetMeeting and provides an Internet-based messaging system that is different than Microsoft Exchange. MCIS was originally code named "Normandy."

**McKinley** See *future Intel chips*.

M

**MCM**    (MultiChip Module or MicroChip Module) A chip package that contains two or more raw chips closely connected with high-density lines. This method saves space and speeds processing due to short leads between chips. A ceramic base has been widely used with chips wire bonded together (MCM-C) or with thin film interconnects deposited on the ceramic substrate (MCM-D). MCMs have been mounted onto silicon substrates (MCM-S) and resin-based, laminated printed circuit boards (MCM-L), the latter, less-costly version evolving into the multichip module (MCP).

MCMs were originally called "microcircuits" or "hybrid microcircuits," since this technique was suited for mixing analog and digital components together. See *MCP, chip package* and *Trilogy.*

**m-commerce**    (Mobile-COMMERCE) Using smart phones and handheld computers with wireless connections to place orders over the Web. See *e-commerce.*

**MCP**    (1) See *Microsoft certification.*

(2) (MultiChip Package) A chip package that contains two or more chips. It is essentially a multichip module (MCM) that uses a laminated, printed-circuit-board-like substrate (MCM-L) rather than ceramic (MCM-C). MCPs are also tested after packaging, whereas the bare die of ceramic-based MCMs were tested before packaging so as not to waste the more costly ceramic substrate if the chips were no good. See *MCM.*

**MCS**    (1) See *Microsoft Cluster Server.*

(2) (Microsoft Consulting Services) The consulting arm of Microsoft which offers support for installation and maintenance of Microsoft applications and operating systems.

(3) (Multivendor Customer Service) The consulting arm of Digital Equipment that was founded in 1993. It provides hardware, software and network services for a variety of platforms.

(4) (Multimedia Conference Server) A family of video-conferencing servers from VideoServer, Inc., Lexington, MA. The MCS was the first multipoint control unit to comply with H.320.

(5) A family of microcontroller units (MCUs) from Intel. In 1995, Intel introduced its 8-bit MCS 251 chips which are binary compatible with its older MCS 51 series.

**Multichip Packages**
These are examples of multichip packages with stacked chips (top) and side-by-side chips (bottom). The chips are wire bonded to the resin-based substrate which is attached to the printed circuit board using a ball grid array (BGA). *(Illustration courtesy of Joseph Fjelstad.)*

**MCSD**    See *Microsoft certification.*

**MCSE**    See *Microsoft certification.*

**MCT**    See *Microsoft certification.*

**MCU**    (1) (MicroController Unit) A computer on a single chip. See *computer on a chip.*

(2) (Multipoint Control Unit) A device that connects multiple sites and stations for videoconferencing. The MCU joins the lines and switches the video either automatically depending on who is speaking or manually under the direction of a moderator.

**MD**    See *MiniDisc.*

**MD2**    See *MD5.*

**MD4**    See *MD5.*

**MD5**    (Message Digest 5) A popular one-way hash function developed by Ronald Rivest (the "R" in RSA) which is used to create a message digest for digital signatures. MD5 is faster than SHA-1, but is considered less secure. MD5 is similar to the previous MD4 method as both were designed for 32-bit computers, but MD5 adds more security since MD4 has been broken. The earlier MD2 function was designed for 8-bit computers. See *one-way hash function.*

**MDA** **(1)** (**M**onochrome **D**isplay **A**dapter) The first IBM PC monochrome video display standard for text only. Due to its lack of graphics, MDA cards were often replaced with Hercules cards, which provided both text and graphics. See *PC display modes*.

**(2)** (**M**odular **D**igital **A**rchitecture) A snap-together, building-block approach for adding peripherals to a PC from NeoSystems, Inc.

**(3)** (**M**echanical **D**esign **A**utomation) Refers to applications that help automate the design and engineering processes from concept to manufacturing. Automotive, aerospace and discrete manufacturing are examples of industries that use MDA.

**MDAC** (**M**icrosoft **D**ata **A**ccess **C**omponents) A collection of software modules from Microsoft that provide access to databases. MDAC includes ODBC, OLE DB, ADO, and RDS. See *ODBC*, *OLE DB*, *ADO* and *RDS*.

**MDBS IV** A DBMS from that runs on DOS, OS/2, UNIX, MPE and VMS servers from Micro Data Base Systems, Inc., Lafayette, IN (www.mdbs.com). Noted for its performance and maturity (in 1984, MDBS III was the first client/server DBMS), it provides a superset of hierarchical, network and relational storage concepts. M/4 for Windows is a single-user Windows version.

**MDC** (**M**obile **D**aughter **C**ard) See *AMR*.

**MD DATA** The data storage counterpart of Sony's MiniDisc drive. See *MiniDisc*.

**MDDB** (**M**ulti**D**imensional **D**ata**B**ase) See *OLAP*.

**MDF** **(1)** (**M**ain **D**istribution **F**rame) A wiring rack that connects outside lines with internal lines. It is used to connect public or private lines coming into the building to internal networks. In a telco central office (CO), the MDF is generally in close proximity to the telephone switch. See *IDF*, *CDF* and *wiring rack*.

**(2)** (**M**ultiple **D**omain **F**acility) Hardware and microcode supplied by Amdahl that allows the running of multiple system images on a single processor complex. MDF was the first such implementation that did not depend on software such as VM/370 or VM/ESA.

**MDI port** (**M**edium **D**ependent **I**nterface port) Also called an "uplink port," it is a port on a network hub or switch used to connect to other hubs or switches without requiring a crossover cable. The MDI port does not cross the transmit and receive lines, which is done by the regular ports (MDI-X ports) that connect to end stations. The MDI port connects to the MDI-X port on the other device. There are typically one or two ports on a device that can be toggled between MDI (not crossed) and MDI-X (crossed). See *crossover cable*.

**MDIS** See *Metadata Coalition*.

**MDI-X port** (**M**edium **D**ependent **I**nterface-crossed) A port on a network hub or switch that crosses the transmit lines coming in to the receive lines going out. See *MDI port* and *crossover cable*.

**MDRAM** (**M**ultibank **DRAM**) A type of dynamic RAM chip from MoSys, Inc., Sunnyvale, CA (www.mosys.com), that is available in 256KB increments. It enables embedded applications with fixed memory requirements to have exactly the amount of RAM they need. MDRAM uses an internal bus connected to independent 32KB banks of DRAM, which provides a bandwidth of 666 MBytes/sec.

**MDU** **(1)** (**M**ultiple **D**welling **U**nit) A commercial or residential building with multiple offices or apartments. The term comes up when referring to inhouse networks that support multiple tenants. ISPs and carriers increasingly offer specialized systems for such facilities. See *BLEC*.

**(2)** (**M**ultiply-**D**ivide **U**nit) A high-speed circuit that performs multiplication and division within the CPU.

**meatspace** The physical world. Contrast with *cyberspace*.

**mechanical mouse** A mouse that uses a rubber ball that rolls against wheels inside the unit. Contrast with *optical mouse*.

M

**mechanical splice**    A type of fiber-optic splice that uses a connector to bridge between the two ends. Contrast with *fusion splice.*

**media**    Materials that hold data in any form or that allow data to pass through them, including paper, transparencies, multipart forms, hard, floppy and optical disks, magnetic tape, wire, cable and fiber. Media is the plural of "medium."

**media access method**    See "LANs" under *data link protocol.*

**media bus**    A high-speed channel designed for transferring audio and video data. See *VESA Media Channel.*

**media control**    Also called "media processing," in computer telephony it refers to some processing or altering of the call; for example, digitizing the content. Contrast with *call control.*

**media conversion**    See *media converter, data conversion* and *conversion.*

**media converter**    A device that converts from one type of media to another. It typically refers to a hardware device that connects different transmission media; for example, from twisted pair to coax or from twisted pair to optical fiber.

**media failure**    A condition of not being able to read from or write to a storage device, such as a disk or tape, due to a defect in the recording surface.

**media gateway**    A device that converts multimedia input into a backbone network and vice versa. A media gateway can be an IP gateway, a circuit switch (telephone switch) or a modem bank. See *IP telephony.*

**media gateway controller**    See *media gateway* and *softswitch.*

**Media GX**    A CPU from Cyrix that includes sound, display, memory control and PCI bus circuits on the same chip.

**MediaMap**    (MediaMap, Cambridge, MA, www.mediamap.com) A public relations information source for the high-tech industry that maintains editorial lists and schedules for every major computer media organization, including trade and national press, TV and radio, user groups and syndicated columns. Its MediaManager software for PCs and Macs provides a complete media contact management system and allows searches based on editorial niche and scheduled story opportunities.

**media player**    (1) Software that "plays" audio, video or animation files. See *Web player.*
    (2) (Media Player) A Windows multimedia utility that is used to play sound and video files. See *Windows Media Player.*

**media processing**    See *media control.*

**media processor**    A controller or chip that is used to build a multimedia subsystem that processes any combination of audio, video, graphics, fax and modem operations. See *Mpact chip.*

**media rich**    See *rich media.*

**Media Vision**    A former manufacturer of Sound Blaster-compatible multimedia products for PCs founded in 1990. Media Vision was the first to introduce a 16-bit sound card (Pro Audio line) and multimedia upgrade kit. In 1995, it refocused its attention to 3-D chips and later sold its retail business to an Indian company. In 1996, the company was renamed Aureal Semiconductor, Inc.

**medium**    The singular form of *media.*

**medium frequency**    An electromagnetic wave that oscillates in the range from 300,000 to 3,000,000 Hz. See *electromagnetic spectrum.*

**MEDLINE**     The online database of the U.S. National Library of Medicine (NLM). The data is available for a fee on the Internet, CompuServe and directly from the NLM. MEDLINE contains millions of articles from thousands of medical publications.

**meg**     Same as *mega*.

**mega**     **(1)** Million (10 to the 6th power). Abreviated "M." It often refers to the precise value 1,048,576 because computer specifications are based on binary numbers. See *MB*, *binary values* and *space/time*.
　　**(2)** (MEGA) A personal computer series from Atari that was Motorola 68000 based, ran under GEM and the TOS operating system and included a MIDI interface. It was ST compatible.

**megabit**     One million bits. Also Mb, Mbit and M-bit. See *mega* and *space/time*.

**megabyte**     One million bytes, or more precisely 1,048,576 bytes. Also MB, Mbyte and M-byte. See *mega* and *space/time*.

**MEGACO**     (MEdia GAteway COntrol) An IP telephony protocol that is a combination of the MGCP and IPDC protocols. It is simpler than H.323. See *MGCP*, *IPDC* and *H.323*.

**megaflops**     (mega FLoating point OPerations per Second) One million floating point operations per second. See *FLOPS*.

**megahertz**     One million cycles per second. See *MHz*.

**megapel**     (MEGA PixEL) See *megapixel*.

**megapixel**     (Million Pixels) Refers to the resolution of a graphics device (display, scanner, digital camera, etc.). For example, a four-megapixel digital camera takes a picture that is divided into four million pixels, which would be a 2,000×2,000 resolution. See *megapel*.

**meltdown**     The total cessation of operation of a computer system or network. A system meltdown can be caused by hardware or software. A network meltdown can be caused by hardware, software or excessive traffic.

**MEM**     (MicroElectroMechanical) See *MEMS*.

**membrane keyboard**     A dust and dirtproof keyboard constructed of two thin plastic sheets (membranes) that contain flexible printed circuits made of electrically conductive ink. The top membrane is the printed keyboard and a spacer sheet with holes is in the middle. When a user presses a simulated key, the top membrane is pushed through the spacer hole and makes contact with the bottom membrane, completing the circuit. Membrane keyboards, which are much hardier than normal key switch keyboards, offer the advantage of complete customization by programming the cell matrix for any application.

**memo field**     A data field that holds a variable amount of text. The text may be stored in a companion file, but it is treated as if it were part of the data record. For example, in the dBASE command **list name, biography**, name is in the data file (DBF file) and biography could be a memo field in the text file (DBT file).

**memory**     The computer's workspace (physically, a collection of RAM chips). It is an important resource, since it determines the size and number of programs that can be run at the same time, as well as the amount of data that can be processed instantly.

**Customizable Membrane Keyboard**
IntelliKeys uses a membrane base unit divided into a 24×24 cell matrix. Removable 13×8" overlays come with specialized applications, or for custom use, the Overlay Maker software lets you program the keyboard and print the overlay. Developed for children and adults with visual and other impairments, IntelliKeys are also used for regular business applications.
*(Image courtesy of IntelliTools, Inc., www.intellitools.com)*

All program execution and data processing takes place in memory. The program's instructions are copied into memory from disk or tape and then extracted from memory into the control unit circuit for analysis and execution. The instructions direct the computer to input data into memory from a keyboard, disk, tape or communications channel.

As data is entered into memory, the previous contents of that space are lost. Once the data is in memory, it can be processed (calculated, compared and copied). The results are sent to a screen, printer, disk, tape or communications channel.

Memory is like an electronic checkerboard, with each square holding one byte of data or instruction. Each square has a separate address like a post office box and can be manipulated independently. As a result, the computer can break apart programs into instructions for execution and data records into fields for processing. See *early memories*.

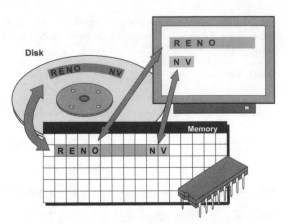

**Memory Is an Electronic Checkerboard**
Each checkerboard square of memory holds one byte. The contents of any single byte or group of bytes can be calculated, compared and copied independently. That's how fields are put together to form records and broken apart when read back in. On the disk, data is stored in sectors, which hold a chunk of data (typically 512 bytes) and are the smallest unit that can be read or written.

**Memory Doesn't Usually Remember**     Oddly enough, the computer's memory doesn't remember anything when the power is turned off. That's why you have to save your files before you quit your program. Although there are memory chips that do hold their content permanently (ROMs, PROMs, EPROMs, etc.), they're used for internal control purposes and not for the user's data.

"Remembering" memory in a computer system is its disks and tapes, and although they are sometimes called "memory devices," many prefer to call them storage devices (as we do) in order to differentiate them from internal memory. Perhaps in time, memory will refer to disks exclusively and RAM will refer to working memory. Until then, its usage for both RAM and disk only adds confusion to the most confusing industry on earth.

**Memory Can Get Clobbered!**     Memory is such an important resource that it cannot be wasted. It must be allocated by the operating system, as well as applications, and then released when not needed. Errant programs can grab memory and not let go of it even when they are closed, which results in less and less memory available as you load and use more programs.

In addition, if the operating system is not advanced, a malfunctioning application can write into memory used by another program, causing all kinds of unspecified behavior. You discover it when the system freezes or something wierd happens all of a sudden. If you were to really look into memory and watch how much and how fast data and instructions are written into and out of it in the course of a day, it's truly a miracle that it works.

Other terms for memory are RAM, main memory, main storage, primary storage, read/write memory, core and core storage. See also *memory module*.

**memory allocation**     Reserving memory for specific purposes. Operating systems and applications generally reserve fixed amounts of memory at startup and allocate more when additional functions must be executed. If there is not enough free memory to load the core kernel of an application, it cannot be launched. Although a virtual memory function will simulate an almost unlimited amount of memory, there is always a certain amount of "real" memory that is needed.

**memory bank**     **(1)** A physical section of memory. See *memory interleaving*.
     **(2)** Refers generically to a computer system that holds data.

**memory based**     Programs that hold all data in memory for processing. Almost all spreadsheets are memory based so that a change in data at one end of the spreadsheet can be instantly reflected at the other end.

**memory cache**     See *cache*.

**memory card**    A removable module used for additional storage in laptops or as film in digital cameras. Typically comprised of non-volatile flash memory chips, they are available in various formats such as CompactFlash, SmartMedia, MultiMediaCard and Memory Stick. See *flash memory*.
(2) A removable module for laptops and palmtops that contains memory chips (RAM). See *memory module*.

**memory cell**    One bit of memory. In dynamic RAM memory, a cell is made up of one transistor and one capacitor. In static RAM memory, a cell is made up of about five transistors. See *memory chip*.

**memory chip**    A chip that holds programs and data either temporarily (RAM), permanently (ROM, PROM) or permanently until changed (EPROM, EEPROM, flash memory). See *memory types*.

**memory compression**    Encoding the contents of memory to take up less space. Similar to data compression, memory compression works with the live contents of memory as it executes instructions and processes data. It works at the lowest levels of the system.

**memory cycle**    A series of operations that take place to read or write a byte of memory. For destructive memories, it includes the regeneration of the bits.

**A Wafer Full of Memory Chips**
Each of the rectangles on this silicon wafer is a four-megabit RAM chip. The wafer is the structural unit that all chips are fabricated on. The chips are cut out and placed into their individual housings. *(Image courtesy of Motorola, Inc.)*

**memory cycle time**    The time it takes to perform one memory cycle.

**memory dump**    A display or printout of the contents of memory. When a program abends, a memory dump can be taken in order to examine the status of the program at the time of the crash. The programmer looks into the buffers to see which data items were being worked on when it failed. Counters, variables, switches and flags are also inspected. See *brain dump*.

**M**

**memory effect**    A condition of a rechargeable nickel cadmium battery in which it continues to hold less and less of a charge over time. It appears to "remember" how full it was when last charged, and it doesn't charge past that point the next time. The solution is to completely drain nickel cadmium (NiCD) batteries before recharging them. See *batteries*.

**memory hierarchy**    The levels of memory in a computer. From fastest to slowest speed, they are

    1. CPU registers            4. Main memory
    2. L1 cache                 5. Virtual memory
    3. L2 cache                 6. Disk

**memory interleaving**    A category of techniques for increasing memory speed. For example, with separate memory banks for odd and even addresses, the next byte of memory can be accessed while the current byte is being refreshed.

**memory leak**    A condition caused by a program that does not free up the extra memory it allocates. In programming languages, such as C and C++, the program must be written to allocate additional memory to hold data and variables as required. When the routine is exited, it is supposed to deallocate the memory. A serious memory leak will eventually usurp all the memory, bringing everything to a halt. In other environments, such as Java, the operating system allocates and deallocates memory automatically, which is the way it should work. See *garbage collection*.

**memory management**    Refers to a variety of methods used to store data and programs in memory, keep track of them and reclaim the memory space when they are no longer needed. In also includes virtual memory, bank switching and memory protection techniques.

It Used to Be a Nightmare    In the days of the first PCs, memory management used to be a major consideration. The PC had more confusing memory types than any computer in history as its architecture was pushed, patched and expanded to meet the increasing demand for more capabilities. DOS was the operating system of the 1980s, and it was first designed to address only one megabyte (1MB) of memory. Today, we take 64MB or 128MB for granted, and

Windows uses up every available drop. But in its first decade of existence, PC technicians had to deal with conventional memory, upper memory, high memory, extended memory and expanded memory in order to support ever-larger applications. Countless books were written on PC memory management. There were even three-day courses on the subject. Eventually, subsequent versions of DOS, and especially Windows, added the necessary memory management functions to eliminate the manual, time-consuming tweaking and configuring of how much memory should be reserved for this and how much for that. See *memory allocation*, *virtual memory*, *garbage collection*, *memory protection*, *EMS*, *EMM* and **DOS memory manager**.

**memory manager**    Software that manages memory in a computer. See *memory management*.

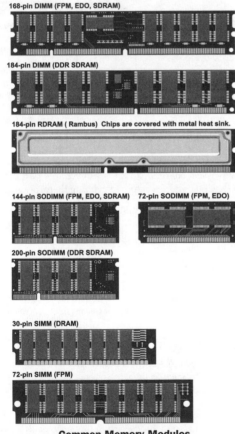

**Common Memory Modules**

DIMMs are widely used in desktop computers and servers. The smaller SODIMMs (Small Outline DIMMs) are used in laptops, while SIMMs are typically found in older PCs. For identification purposes, look at the pattern of the pins on the edge connector (bottom) and the various notches between the pins and on the sides. The layout of the chips is not important, as they can differ signficantly.

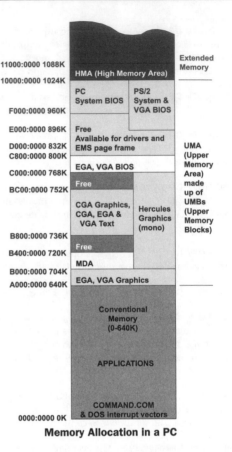

**Memory Allocation in a PC**

**memory map**    The location of instructions and data in memory. See *PC memory map* for a digaram of the PC's upper memory area.

**memory-mapped I/O**    A peripheral device that assigns specific memory locations to input and output. For example, in a memory-mapped display, each pixel or text character derives its data from a specific memory byte or bytes. The instant this memory is updated by software, the screen is displaying the new data.

**memory module**    A narrow printed circuit board that holds memory chips, typically dynamic RAM (DRAM) or synchronous dynamic RAM (SDRAM). Earlier computers used SIMM modules. Current-day machines use DIMMs for desktop computers and SODIMMs for laptops. PCs use either nine-bit memory (eight bits and parity) or eight-bit memory without parity. Macs use eight-bit memory without parity.

SIMMs (single in-line memory modules) evolved into DIMMs (dual in-line memory modules), which double the number of paths between the module and motherboard by using each side of the edge connector independently. SIMMs are generally used in pairs, whereas DIMMs can be used one at a time. Rambus modules must be used in pairs.

Upgrading Memory—RTFM!    To upgrade memory, read your motherboard or system manual. It should show you all possible combinations of different-sized modules that can be used in the available slots. With DIMMs and SODIMMs, there are numerous chip configurations that yield the same total capacity. In some cases, the motherboard is not sensitive to this; in other cases, it is. The bottom line: read the documentation.

**memory protection**    A technique that prohibits one program from accidentally clobbering another active program. Using various different techniques, a protective boundary is created around the program, and instructions within the program are prohibited from referencing data outside of that boundary.

When a program does go outside of its boundary, DOS, Windows 3.x and earlier personal computer operating systems simply lock up (crash, bomb, abend, etc.). Operating systems such as UNIX, OS/2 and Windows NT are more robust and generally allow the errant program to be closed without affecting the remaining active programs.

**memory resident**
A program that remains in memory at all times. See *TSR*.

**memory sniffing**
Coined by Data General, a diagnostic routine that tests memory during normal processing. The processor uses cycle stealing techniques that allow it to test memory during unused machine cycles. A memory bank can be "sniffed" every few minutes.

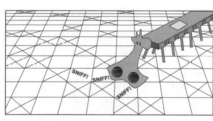

**Memory Sniffing**
Sniffing a memory bank may not look exactly like this, but it does the job of testing memory while the computer is running the daily work.

**Memory Stick**    A flash memory card from Sony designed for handheld digital appliances such as cameras and camcorders. Introduced in 1998 with 4 and 8MB capacities, the tiny modules are less than $1 \times 2$" and about a tenth of an inch thick ($.85 \times 1.97 \times .11$"). Transfer to a computer is made via a PC Card adapter or Memory Stick drive, as well as by direct cable attachment from the camera to the computer's USB port.

**memory typewriter**    An early typewriter that held a few pages of text in its memory and provides limited word processing functions. With a display screen of only one or two lines, editing was tedious.

**Desktop Memory**
To change memory on desktop computers, you have to open the cabinet and locate the slots. These three DIMM slots on this Macintosh motherboard are easy to find and reach.

**Laptop Memory**
To change memory on laptops, you have to unscrew a plate on the bottom of the machine to get to the SODIMM slots.

**Memory Stick Module**
Sony's Memory Sticks are very compact and convenient for digital film storage. See *flash memory* for size comparison.

**One of the First Memory Typewriters**
Its memory wasn't made of magnetic cores or
semiconductors. Text were first punched into player piano-like
rolls with a typewriter/perforator. As the rolls passed over
slots in a bar in this machine, a valve opened and negative
pressure in a hose collapsed a small bellows that pulled down
the typewriter key. *(Image courtesy of TMC/Compco, Inc.)*

**MEMS**    (MicroElectroMechanical Systems)
Semiconductor chips that have a top layer of mechanical
devices such as mirrors or fluid sensors. In the research
labs since the 1980s, MEMS devices began to materialize as
commercial products in the mid-1990s. They are used to make
pressure, temperature, chemical and vibration sensors, light
reflectors and switches as well as accelerometers for airbags,
vechice control, pacemakers and games. They are also used in
the construction of microactuators for data storage as well as
read/write heads, and they are used in all-optical switches
to forward light beams by reflecting them to the appropriate
output port. See *DLP* and *optical switch*.

**menu**    An on-screen list of available functions, or
operations, that can be performed currently. Depending on
the type of menu, selection is accomplished by (1) highlighting
the menu option with a mouse and releasing the mouse, (2)

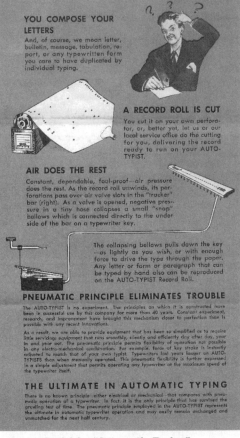

**An Ad for "Automatic Typing"**
This explains the fabulous AUTO-TYPIST procedure for the
prospective customer. Throughout the 1940s and up until
the mid-1970s, AUTO-TYPIST machines like this one from the
American Automatic Typewriter Company provided reliable
document processing. *(Image courtesy of TMC/Compco, Inc.)*

pointing to the option name with the mouse and clicking it, (3) highlighting the option with the cursor keys and pressing
ENTER, or (4) pressing the first letter of the option name or some designated letter within the name. See *Lotus menu* and
*pull-down menu*.

**menu bar**    A row of on-screen menu options.

**menu-driven**    Using menus to command the computer. Contrast with *command-driven*.

**menuing software**    Software that provides a menu for launching applications and running operating system
commands.

**MEO**    (Medium-Earth Orbit) A communications satellite in orbit some 6,000 miles above the earth, which is higher
than a LEO and lower than a GEO. MEOs take six hours to orbit the earth and are in view for a couple of hours. See
*LEO* and *GEO*.

**MERANT**    (MERANT plc, Newbury, England, www.merant.com)  Formerly Micro Focus Group, it changed its name in early 1999 after acquiring INTERSOLV, Inc., a development tools company in 1998. Founded in the U.K. in 1976, it later opened a major facility in California. The company became known for its COBOL programming tools that enabled both migrating from mainframe to client/server and developing on client/server platforms for the mainframe.

**Merced**    See *Itanium*.

**merchant account**    An agreement between a credit card processor and a seller that establishes the rules for accepting credit card purchases and transferring funds. See *card not present account*.

**merchant server**    Also known as a "commerce server," it is a server in a network that handles online purchases and credit card transactions. It implements an electronic commerce protocol that ensures a secure transmission between the clients and cooperating banks. The term may refer to the entire computer system or just the software that provides this service.

**Mercury chipset**    See *Intel chipsets*.

**merge**    See *mail merge* and *concatenate*.

**merge purge**    To merge two or more lists together and eliminate unwanted items. For example, a new name and address list can be added to an old list while deleting duplicate names or names that meet certain criteria.

**mesa**    A semiconductor process used in the 1960s for creating the sublayers in a transistor. Its deep etching gave way to the planar process.

**mesh**    A term often used to describe an interconnect architecture that cross connects several devices. It is synonymous with *fabric*. Contrast with *point-to-point*. See *mesh network*.

**mesh network**    A net-like communications network in which there are at least two pathways to each node. Since the term network means net-like as well as communications network, the term mesh is used to avoid saying "network communications network."

A fully-meshed network means that every node has a direct connection to every other node, which is a very elaborate and expensive architecture. Most mesh networks are partially meshed and require traversing nodes to go from each one to every other.

**message**    (1) In communications, a set of data that is transmitted over a communications line. Just as a program becomes a job when it's running in the computer, data becomes a message when it's transmitted over a network.

(2) In object technology, communicating between objects, similar to a function call in traditional programming.

**message based**    An interface that is based on a set of commands. A message-based system is a type of client/server relationship, in which requests are made by a client component, and the results are provided by a server component. It implies greater flexibility and interoperability in contrast with a hard coded operation, which would have to be modified by reprogramming the source code.

**message broker**    A messaging system for applications that includes a message transport, rules engine and formatting engine. See *messaging middleware*.

**message digest**    A condensed text string that has been distilled from the contents of a text message. Its value is derived using a one-way hash function and is used to create a digital signature. See *digital signature* and *MD5*.

**message handling**    (1) An electronic mail system. See *messaging system*.

(2) In communications, the lower level protocols that transfer data over a network, which assemble and disassemble the data into the appropriate codes for transmission.

**message handling system**    Same as *messaging system*.

**message header**   The identification lines at the beginning of an e-mail message, such as To:, From:, Subject: and Date:.

**MessagePad**   A family of PDAs from Apple that use the Newton operating system. See *Newton*.

**message queue**   A storage space in memory or on disk that holds incoming transmissions until the computer can process them. See *messaging middleware*.

**message switch**   A computer system used to switch data between various points. Computers have always been ideal switches due to their input/output and compare capabilities. It inputs the data, compares its destination with a set of stored destinations and routes it accordingly. Note: A message switch is a generic term for a data routing device, but a messaging switch converts mail and messaging protocols.

**message thread**   A running commentary by one user in a threaded discussion.

**message transfer agent**   The store and forward capability in a messaging system. See *messaging system*.

**messaging API**   A programming interface that enables an application to send and receive messages and attached files over a messaging system. VIM, MAPI and CMC are examples. Novell's SMF-71, although also called an API, is actually the message format that mail must be placed into for submission to Novell's MHS. There are no functions associated with it.

**messaging gateway**   A computer system that converts one messaging protocol to another. It provides an interface between two store and forward nodes, or message transfer agents (MTAs).

**messaging middleware**   Software that provides an interface between applications, allowing them to send data back and forth to each other asynchronously. Data sent by one program can be stored in a queue and then forwarded to the receiving program when it becomes available to process it. Without using a common message transport and queueing system such as this, each application must be responsible for ensuring that the data sent is received properly. Maintaining communications between different types of applications as they evolve, change and are replaced combined with the ever-increasing requirement to exchange data between them creates an enormous programming burden in the large enterprise.

A message broker is either a complete messaging system or software that works with existing messaging transports in order to add routing intelligence and data conversion capabilities. A rules engine analyzes the messages and determines which application should receive them, and a formatting engine converts the data into the structure required by the receiving application. Examples are MQSeries Integrator which extends MQSeries, e-Biz Integrator and Rendezvous (see *MQSeries Integrator*, *NEON e-Biz Integrator*, *TIB/Rendezvous* and *ActiveWorks*).

Messaging middleware and e-mail messaging systems provide similar transport functionality. The primary difference is that messaging middleware deals with transactions between programs, whereas e-mail messaging deals with memos between people. See *messaging system* and *publish and subscribe messaging*.

**messaging-oriented middleware**   See *messaging middleware*.

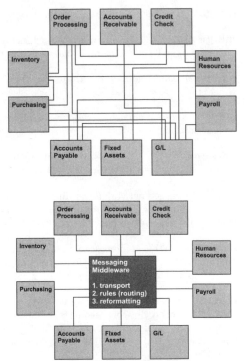

**Messaging Middleware**
Messaging middleware provides a hub and spoke architecture that serves as a central point of communication between all applications. Without a messaging system, each application must be custom programmed to call the other and ensure the data arrives. Once an enterprise conforms to a common messaging interface, future connections between applications are more easily developed, and the message queue can hold transactions that are currently not deliverable due to system or network failure or overload.

**messaging protocol**    The rules, formats and functions for exchanging messages between the components of a messaging system. The most widely used messaging protocol is the Internet's Simple Mail Transfer Protocol (SMTP). Other messaging protocols are IBM's SNADS, Novell's MHS, Lotus' cc:Mail, Microsoft's MS Mail and the international X.400. See *messaging system*.

**messaging switch**    A messaging hub that provides protocol conversion between several messaging systems. Examples of switches include Soft-Switch's EMX, HP's OpenMail and Digital's MAILbus. A messaging switch differs from a messaging gateway in that it supports more than two protocols and connections, as well as providing management and directory integration.

**messaging system**    Software that provides an electronic mail delivery system. It is comprised of the following functional components, which may be packaged together or independently. The mail user agent (MUA or UA) is the client e-mail program, such as Eudora or Outlook, that submits and receives the message. The message transfer agent (MTA) forwards the message to another mail server or delivers it to its own message store (MS). Sendmail is the most widely-used MTA on the Internet. In a large enterprise, there may be several MTA servers (mail servers) dedicated to Internet e-mail while others support internal e-mail.

The message store (MS) holds the mail until it is selectively retrieved and deleted by an access server. In the Internet world, a delivery agent writes the messages from the MTA to the message store, and typical access servers are either POP or IMAP servers.

Internet e-mail, the most ubiquitous messaging system in the world, is based on the SMTP protocol. Prior to the Internet's enormous growth in the late 1990s, numerous proprietary messaging systems were widely used including cc:Mail, Microsoft Mail, PROFS and DISOSS. See *messaging middleware* and *SMTP*.

**meta**    One definition of this Greek word is transcending, or going above and beyond. In the computer field, it defines things that embrace more than the usual. For example, a metafile contains all types of data. Metadata describes other data. See *metafile*, *metadata* and *meta tag*.

**meta ad**    A banner ad that appears on the results page of a search engine which is related to the subject of the search. Also known as "keyword advertising," it targets the advertisement to the interests of the user based on the words in the search text. See *banner ad*.

**MetaCrawler**    A metasearch engine from Go2Net, Inc., Seattle, WA (www.go2net.com), that was developed at the University of Washington and released on the Internet in 1995. Go2Net acquired the technology in 1997 and later changed the www.metacrawler.com site address to www.go2net.com. See *Web search sites*.

**metadata**    (1) Data that describes other data. Data dictionaries and repositories are examples of metadata. The meta tag that describes the content of a Web page is called metadata. The term may also refer to any file or database that holds information about another database's structure, attributes, processing or changes. See *data dictionary*, *repository* and *meta tag*.

(2) (Metadata) A trade name of Metadata Information Partners, Long Beach, CA. A consulting firm providing custom information systems to the health care industry.

**Metadata Coalition**    An organization of database and data warehouse vendors founded in 1995. Within a year, it introduced the Metadata Interchange Specification (MDIS) as a standard for defining metadata.

**MetaDirectory**    (1) A data warehousing tool from Information Builders that captures and associates metadata from the company's different applications. Formerly SmartBase, it was renamed MetaDirectory in 1998. See *SmartMart* and *Information Builders*.

(2) (metadirectory) A directory that contains information about other directories. It functions as a master directory gleaning information from all the other directories. See *DirXML*.

**metafile**    A file that contains other files. It generally refers to graphics files that can hold vector drawings and bitmaps. For example, a Windows Metafile (WMF) can store pictures in vector graphics and bitmap formats, as well as text. A Computer Graphics Metafile (CGM) also stores both types of graphics.

M

**MetaFrame**    Software from Citrix that supports "application server computing," in which the application runs in the server for multiple users and only screen changes in the user interface are sent to the individual client machines. The core technology in MetaFrame is the ICA (Independent Computing Architecture) protocol, which governs the input/output between client and server. The timeshared, multiuser processing that takes place is provided by the native capabilities of UNIX or the Terminal Server options in Windows NT and 2000. See *NFuse*, *ICA* and *WinFrame*.

**MetaFrame for Windows NT and MetaFrame for Windows 2000**
Adds the ICA presentation protocol to Windows NT 4.0, Terminal Server Edition, or to the Terminal Services option in Windows 2000, expanding the number of client types to Windows, DOS, UNIX, Macintosh, Java and Web browsers. Citrix's NFuse feature enables Windows applications to be run from a Web browser.

**MetaFrame for UNIX**    Adds ICA presentation services protocol to the X Window system in Solaris, AIX and HP-UX, enabling UNIX, Windows, DOS, Macintosh, Java and Web browser client access to an application. In UNIX, the X Window system provides this same type of server-based computing. As a result, MetaFrame for UNIX sets up an X Window partition in the server for each user and converts between X and ICA. Citrix's NFuse feature enables UNIX applications to be run from a Web browser. See *X Window*.

**MetaFrame for Windows**

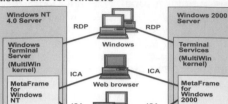

Windows, Mac, DOS, OS/2, UNIX, Linux, Java, Windows CE, embedded devices, etc.

**MetaFrame for UNIX**

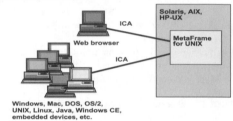

Windows, Mac, DOS, OS/2, UNIX, Linux, Java, Windows CE, embedded devices, etc.

**MetaFrame**
MetaFrame adds the ICA protocol to Windows Terminal Server and UNIX environments enabling a wide variety of clients to participate in "application server computing."

**metalanguage**    A language used to describe another language.

**metalization layer**    The top layers of a chip that interconnect the transistors and resistors. There are usually two to four such layers made of aluminum that are separated by a silicon dioxide insulation layer. See *copper chip*.

**metamail**    A public-domain UNIX utility that composes and decomposes a MIME message on the Internet.

**metamerism**    The quality of some colors that causes them to appear differently under different light sources. For example, two color samples might appear the same in natural light, but not in artifical light.

**metaphor**    The derivation of metaphor means "to carry over." Thus the "desktop metaphor" as so often described means that the office desktop has been brought over and simulated on computers.

**meta refresh**    An HTML command that switches you to a different Web page within a specified amount of time. It is used to briefly display an outdated page and send the visitor to the new page. Fast meta refreshes are used to quickly switch doorway pages to the page the user is supposed to see. See *doorway page*.

**metasearch engine**    Software that is used on a Web site to search other Web search sites. See *Web search sites*.

**metasearch sites**    Web sites that search other Web search sites. See Web search sites.

**metasite**    (1) A Web search site that searches other search sites. See *MetaCrawler*.
(2) A Web site that functions as a directory to other Web sites.

**MetaStream**    A streaming 3-D format for the Web from MetaCreations Corporation, Carpinteria, CA (www.metacreations.com), and Intel. With the MetaStream plug-in installed in your browser, you can zoom, pan and rotate objects downloaded from the Web.

**meta tag**   An HTML tag that identifies the contents of a Web page. Meta tags contain such things as a general description of the page, keywords for search engines and copyright information. See *Dublin Core*.

**Metcalfe's law**   "The value of a network increases exponentially with the number of nodes." By Bob Metcalfe, founder of 3Com Corporation and major designer of Ethernet. A network becomes more useful as more users are connected. A primary example is the Internet. It fostered global e-mail, which becomes more valuable as more users are connected. See *laws*.

HTML meta tag example

```
<meta name="distribution"

content = "global">
```

**meter**   The basic unit of the metric system (39.37 inches). A yard is about 9/10ths of a meter (0.9144 meter). See *metric system*.

**method**   In object technology, a method is the processing that an object performs. When a message is sent to an object, the method is implemented.

**methodology**   The specific way of performing an operation that implies precise deliverables at the end of each stage.

**metric**   Measurement. Although metric generally refers to the decimal-based metric system of weights and measures, software engineers often use the term as simply "measurement." For example, "is there a metric for this process?" See *software metrics*.

**metric system**   A system of weights and measures that uses the gram, meter and liter as its primary units of weight, distance and capacity.

```
Metric                            English
1 gram                             .0022046 lb. (.03527 oz.)
1 decagram (10 gr)                 .022046 lb. (.3527 oz.)
1 hectogram (100 gr)               22046 lb. (3.527 oz.)
1 kilogram (1000 gr)               2046 lbs. (35.27 oz.)

1 meter                            39.37 in.
1 decameter (10 m)                 32.8 ft.
1 hectometer (100 m)               328.08 ft.
1 kilometer (1000 m)               3280.8 ft.
1 decimeter (1/10 m)               3.937 in.
1 centimeter (1/100 m)             .3937 in.
1 millimeter (1/1,000 m)           .03937 in.
1 micrometer (1/1,000,000 m)       .00003937 in.
1 nanometer  (1/1,000,000,000 m)   .00000003937 in.

1 liter                            1.0567 liquid quart
```

**metropolitan area network**   See *MAN*.

**mezzanine card**   A printed circuit board that plugs directly into a another plug-in card. For example, a mezzanine card might plug into a VMEbus, CompactPCI or PCI card, which may be peripheral controller or CPU board or just an adapter card that connects the mezzanine card to the target bus. Smaller than standard PCI and ISA cards, mezzanine cards are designed for rugged industrial use, because they are typically bolted down after being plugging in. IndustryPack, PMC, PC*MIP and PC/104+ are commonly-used mezzanine cards. See *IndustryPack, PMC, PC*MIP* and *PC/104*.

**MFC**   See *Microsoft C* and *Visual C++*.

**MF-COBOL**    (Micro Focus **COBOL**)  See *MERANT*.

**MFD**    (**M**ulti**F**unction **D**evice)  Hardware that combines several functions into one unit; for example, the combination fax, copier, printer and scanner. Such devices save money and room on crowded desktops.

**Mflops**    See *megaflops*.

**MFM**    (**M**odified **F**requency **M**odulation)  A magnetic disk encoding method used on most floppy disks and most hard disks under 40MB. It has twice the capacity of the earlier FM method, transfers data at 625 Kbytes per second and uses the ST506 interface. See *hard disk*.

**MFP**    (**M**ulti**F**unction **P**roduct, **M**ulti**F**unction **P**eripheral)  Same as *MFD*.

**MGA**    **(1)** (**M**onochrome **G**raphics **A**dapter)  A display adapter that employs Hercules Graphics, combining graphics and text on a monochrome monitor.
**(2)** (**M**atrox **G**raphics **A**ccelerator)  A trade name used by Matrox Graphics Inc., Dorval, Quebec, on its graphics adapters; for example, the MGA Millennium.

**MGCP**    (**M**edia **G**ateway **C**ontrol **P**rotocol)  A protocol for IP telephony from the IETF. Working in conjunction with the Gateway Location Protocol (GLP), it enables a caller with a PSTN phone number to locate the destination device and establish a session. It provides the gateway-to-gateway interface for the Session Initialization Protocol (SIP). SIP is a less-complex alternative to the H.323 protocol. See *SIP* and *H.323*.

**MGP**    (**M**onochrome **G**raphics **P**rinter port)  A display adapter that employs Hercules Graphics and a parallel printer port on the same expansion board.

**MHS**    **(1)** (**M**essage **H**andling **S**ervice)  A messaging system from Novell that supports multiple operating systems and other messaging protocols, including SMTP, SNADS and X.400. It uses the SMF-71 messaging format. Standard MHS runs on a DOS machine attached to the server. Global MHS runs as a NetWare NLM. Under NetWare, MHS runs on top of IPX. With NetWare 4, MHS was discontinued and superseded by GroupWise. See *GroupWise*.
**(2)** See *messaging system*.

**MHz**    (**M**ega**H**ert**Z**)  One million cycles per second. It is used to measure the transmission speed of electronic devices, including channels, buses and the computer's internal clock. Megahertz is generally equivalent to one million bits per second or to one million times some number of bits per second.

When it refers to the computer's clock, it is used to measure the speed of the CPU. For example, a 133MHz Pentium processes data internally (calculates, compares, copies) twice as fast as a 66MHz Pentium. However, this does not mean twice as much finished work gets done in the same time frame, because cache design, disk speed and software design all contribute to the computer's actual performance, not just CPU speed. See *MIPS* and *Hertz*.

**MHz Is the Heartbeat**    When referencing CPU speed, the megahertz rating is really the heartbeat of the computer, providing the raw, steady pulses that energize the circuits. If you know any German, it's easy to remember this. The word "Herz," pronounced "hayrtz," means heart. This was not the derivation. In 1883, Heinrich Hertz identified electromagnetic waves.

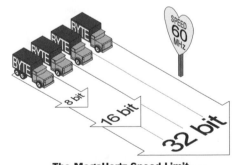

**The MegaHertz Speed Limit**
MegaHertz is analogous to a highway speed limit. The higher the speed, the faster the traffic moves. In a CPU, the higher the clock rate, the quicker data gets processed. The 8-, 16- and 32-bit designation is the CPU's word size and can be thought of as the number of lanes on the highway. The more lanes, the more traffic. The combination of speed and number of paths determines the total processing speed or channel bandwidth.

**MIB**    (**M**anagement **I**nformation **B**ase)  An SNMP structure that describes the particular device being monitored. See *SNMP*.

**MIC**    (**M**emory **I**n **C**assette) A storage chip inside a magnetic tape cassette used to enhance read/write operations. See *AIT*.

**MIC connector**    (**M**edium **I**nterface **C**onnector) A fiber-optic cable connector that handles a pair of cables. The design of the plug and socket ensures that the polarity is maintained (transmit and receive cables are in correct order). It is used in FDDI and a variety of LANs and wiring hubs. See *fiber-optic connectors*.

**mickey**    A unit of mouse movement typically set at 1/200th of an inch.

**MICR**    (**M**agnetic **I**nk **C**haracter **R**ecognition) The machine recognition of numeric data printed with magnetically-charged ink. It is used on bank checks and deposit slips. MICR readers detect the characters and convert them into digital data. Although optical methods (OCR) became as sophisticated as the early MICR technology, magnetic ink is still used. It serves as a deterrent to fraud, because a photocopied check will not be printed with magnetic ink.

**micro**    (**1**) A microcomputer or personal computer.
(**2**) Millionth (10 to the −6th power). See *space/time*.
(**3**) Microscopic or tiny.

**Micro ATX**    See *ATX motherboard*.

**microbrowser**    A Web browser designed for small display screens on smart phones and other handheld wireless devices. See *smart phone* and *WAP*.

**MicroChannel**    Also known as MCA (MicroChannel Architecture), it was a proprietary 32-bit bus from IBM used in PS/2, RS/6000 and certain ES/9370 models. It supported 15 levels of bus mastering and transferred data from 20 to 80MBytes/sec. The boards had a unique, built-in ID that allowed for easier installation than ISA devices. In late 1996, IBM discontinued its use in favor of PCI. See *PC data buses* and *PCI*.

**microchip**    Same as *chip*.

**microchip art**    Graphic images that are drawn into the chip by the chip designer. These images are rarely discovered unless somebody happens to be looking at the chip under a microscope.

**MIC Connector**
MIC is a dual-fiber connector
that is the standard for FDDI
connections.

**MICR Font**
The E13B standard font is
used for MICR digits and
symbols on bank checks and
deposit slips. There are only
14 characters in the font.

**Microchip Art Examples**
The duck was embedded in a Siemens 8-bit
microprocessor, while the windmill comes from a
Music Semiconductors content addressable memory
(CAM) chip. *(Images courtesy of Chipworks Inc.)*

**Early MICR Machine**
The "football field-long" machine from Recognition
Equipment was used in the 1970s to process checks
and credit card slips. *(Image courtesy of BancTec, Inc.)*

**microchip module**    See *MCM*.

**microcircuit**    A miniaturized, electronic circuit, such as is found on an integrated circuit. See *chip* and *MCM*.

**microcode**    A permanent memory that holds the elementary circuit operations a computer must perform for each instruction in its instruction set. It acts as a translation layer between the instruction and the electronic level of the computer and enables the computer architect to more easily add new types of machine instructions without having to design electronic circuits. Microcode is used in CISC architecture. See *microprogramming*.

**microcommerce**   Low-value transactions in electronic commerce. The ability to charge pennies for a transaction enables pay-per-view services such as selling a single article from a newspaper or magazine or providing invidivual lookups from a resource such as a dictionary or encyclopedia for example. Microcommerce enables services that are too small to be paid by a single credit card transaction. See *micropayment*.

**Microcom Protocol**   See *MNP*.

**microcomputer**   Generally synonymous with personal computer, such as a Windows PC or Macintosh, but it can refer to any kind of small computer. When the term was first introduced, it meant a computer with a single microprocessor chip as its CPU, namely, the personal computer. Today, most every computer uses at least one microprocessor CPU, including desktop PCs, high-end workstations, small, medium and large servers and even mainframes.

**Microcomputer Industry Association**   See *CompTIA*.

**microcontroller**   See *computer on a chip*.

**microdisplay**   A microminiaturized display, typically with a screen size less than 1.5" diagonal. They are used in head-mounted displays (HMDs), in data projectors and in the traditional viewfinders of digital cameras. Reflective displays bounce light off the displayed image into the viewer's lens or the projection lens. Transmissive displays are similar to backlit, portable computer screens using LCD and EL technologies.

Although microdisplay research goes back to the mid 1980s, commercial products emerged in the latter 1990s. The microdisplay is expected to be widely used in viewfinders of handheld Internet appliances and cellphones for Web surfing and videoconferences, because a full computer screen can be viewed. See *DLP*.

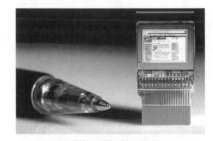

**A Microdisplay Unit**
This amazing screen from Colorado MicroDisplay, (www.comicro.com) is used in HMDs and digital camera viewfinders. This reflective LCD display provides an 800×600 resolution in a half-inch screen that uses only 45 milliwatts of energy, as much as ten times less than transmissive displays. *(Image courtesy of Colorado MicroDisplay, Inc.)*

**Microdrive**   An ultra-miniature hard disk from IBM that was introduced in 1998. Using a single platter the size of a quarter that holds 340MB (at time of introduction) and either one or two GMR heads, the Microdrive is built into a Type II CompactFlash form factor. The tiny elements inside a drive of this size are quite an advantage. For example, since the actuator has 50 times less inertia than one in a larger drive, it can ramp up to full speed in half a second. As a result, the drive can stop spinning when data is not being accessed, which conserves power in handheld devices. See *actuator* and *CompactFlash*.

**microelectomechanical systems**   See *MEMS*.

**microelectronic**   The miniaturization of electronic circuits. See *chip*.

**microfiche**
Pronounced "micro-feesh." A 4×6" sheet of film that holds several hundred miniaturized document pages. See *micrographics*.

**microfilm**   A continuous film strip that holds several thousand miniaturized document pages. See *micrographics*.

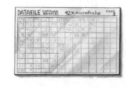 

**Microfilm and Microfiche**
Billions of pages have been recorded on film and fiche, but optical methods are replacing this old imaging method.

**The Microdrive**
While all-electronic, solid state devices continue to amaze us, the Microdrive is a marvel of electromechanical technology. The platter stops rotating to conserve power, but it can ramp back up to full speed in half a second.

**microfloppy**    The formal name for the standard 3.5" floppy disk, which was developed by Sony.

**Micro Focus**    See *MERANT*.

**microform**    In micrographics, a medium that contains microminiaturized images such as microfiche and microfilm.

**Micrografx**    (Micrografx, Inc., Richardson, TX, www.micrografx.com) A software company founded in 1982 by Paul and George Grayson that specializes in graphics software. With its award-winning Designer drawing program, Microfgrafx was the first company to bring the graphics tools commonly found on the Macintosh to the Windows platform. Micrografx provides very full-featured and sophisticated graphics products.

**Micrografx Designer**    A full-featured Windows drawing program that is part of the Micrografx Graphics Suite. Designer is a very sophisticated vector graphics program providing many features of a CAD program, including layers and dimensioning. It creates its own file formats (DRW, DS4 and DSF) and supports PIC files compatible with other Micrografx products. See *iGrafx*.

**Micrografx Graphics Suite**    A suite of graphics applications for Windows 95/98 and NT from Micrografx. It includes the Designer drawing program, Picture Publisher image editor, FlowCharter diagramming tool and Simply 3D 3-D modeling and animation program. See *Micrografx Designer*.

**micrographics**    The production, handling and use of microfilm and microfiche. Images are created by cameras or by COM units that accept computer output directly. The documents are magnified for human viewing by readers, some of which can automatically locate a page using indexing techniques.

Microfiche and microfilm have always been an economical alternative for high-volume data and picture storage. Although optical disks have superseded fiche and film for most archival storage, film is still the only medium that can survive continual upgrading of electronic technologies. Storage devices generally remain compatible with only one or two generations of media. At some point, new drives cannot read older cartridges. However, film is an analog image that can always be read by future readers. See *COM* and *COLD*.

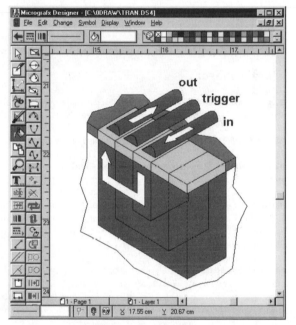

**Micrografx Designer**
Most of the illustrations in this publication were drawn in Micrografx Designer, which offers a huge assortment of drawing tools for the illustrator. This picture is one of the elements in the drawing under "transistor" in this database.

**microimage**    In micrographics, any photographic image of information that is too small to be read without magnification.

**microinstruction**    A microcode instruction. It is the most elementary computer operation that can take place; for example, moving a bit from one register to another. It takes several microinstructions to carry out one machine instruction.

**microjacket**    In micrographics, two sheets of transparent plastic that are bonded together to create channels into which strips of microfilm are inserted and stored.

**microJava**    One of Sun's implementations of its Java chip. See *Java chip*.

**microkernel** (1) The part of an operating system that is specialized for the hardware it is running in. The other components of the OS interact with the microkernel in a message-based relationship and do not have to be rewritten when the OS is ported to a new platform. Only the hardware-dependent microkernel has to be reprogrammed. See *kernel*.
(2) A small control program that is designed to perform a limited set of functions in one type of computer.

**microlithography** Using X rays instead of light rays to form the patterns of elements on a chip. This technology is expected to emerge by the twenty-first century. AT&T Bell Labs has speculated that by the year 2001, a dynamic RAM chip with one billion bits (1 gigabit) will be built using .18 micron microlithography.

**micro machine** Same as *MEMS*.

**micro machining** Making microminiaturized devices using the same manufacturing techniques employed by the semiconductor industry. See *MEMS*.

**micromainframe** A personal computer with mainframe or near mainframe speed.

**micro manager** See *PC software specialist*.

**micromechanics** The microminiaturization of mechanical devices (gears, motors, rotors, etc.) using similar photomasking techniques as in chip making.

**micrometer** One millionth of a meter. See *metric system*.

**micromini** An earlier term for a personal computer that ran at minicomputer or near minicomputer speed. See *minicomputer*.

**micron** One millionth of a meter, or one micrometer, which is approximately 1/25,000 of an inch. The tiny elements that make up a transistor on a chip are measured in microns. For example, the 486 started out at 1.0 micron technology. See *process technology*.

**micropayment** An electronic commerce transaction of very low value. It may refer to charging just a few cents or even a fraction of a cent for a transaction such as an information lookup. It may also refer to aggregating several small-value purchases and charging a credit card at the end of the day or some other period for the total amount. See *microcommerce*.

**Micro PDP-11** The microcomputer version of the PDP-11 from Digital introduced in 1975. Uses the Q-bus and serves as a stand-alone computer or is built into other equipment.

**Micropolis** A manufacturer of disk drives that was known for its high-quality products. Founded in 1976 and based in Chatsworth, CA, it produced its first floppy drive in 1977 and its first hard drive in 1981. Acquired by Singapore Technologies in 1996, Micropolis closed its doors in 1997.

**Magnified 800 Times**
This is an 800× magnification of a few bits of RAM from an early Motorola computer on a chip. Although the actual size of what you see in this picture would fit on a pinhead, the elements in the devices on this chip are several microns wide, which is quite large by today's standards.

**micropower** Electrical power that comes from a company-owned generating plant. Increasingly, large enterprises are developing their own power sources as the demand for energy increases and the sources of supply decrease. In addition, the enterprise has greater control over the consistent quality of the power, which is critical for the efficient operation of huge datacenters.

**microprocessor** A CPU on a single chip. In order to function as a computer, it requires a power supply, clock and memory. The first-generation microprocessors were Intel's 8080, Zilog's Z80, Motorola's 6800 and Rockwell's 6502. The first microprocessor was created by Intel. Today's popular microprocessor families are the x86, PowerPC, Alpha, MIPS and SPARC.

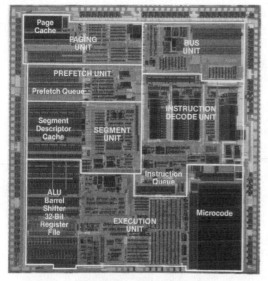

**386 Microprocessor**
The chip is overlayed with the names of its subsystems. No computer technology industry is more incredible than the microprocessor. Every second, trillions of switch openings and closings occur all within a thousandth of an inch below the surface. The older 386 chip is shown because it contains only 275,000 transistors. You can see some slight detail here, which would otherwise be impossible with comtemporary chips that contain tens of millions of transistors. *(Image courtesy of Intel Corporation.)*

**microprocessor based**   A computer that uses a single microprocessor chip as its CPU.

**microprogram**   Same as *microcode*.

**microprogramming**   Programming microcode.

**micropublishing**   In micrographics, the issuing of new or reformatted information on microfilm for sale or distribution.

**microrepublishing**   In micrographics, the issuing of microfilm that has been previously or is simultaneously published in hardcopy for sale or distribution.

**microsecond**   One millionth of a second. See *space/time* and *ohnosecond*.

**microsegmentation**   In networking, the ability to manage a smaller number of nodes as a single segment or domain. Total microsegmentation is accomplished with a switch, which treats each node as a segment.

**Microsoft**   (Microsoft Corporation, Redmond, WA, www.microsoft.com) The world's largest software company, founded in 1975 by Bill Gates and Paul Allen. Its Windows operating system is the de facto standard on the desktop and a major contender in the server arena. Microsoft Office is the most successful application suite in history. Microsoft also has a thriving business in programming languages, which are its roots, as well as in numerous other software categories.

Gates and Allen were two college students when they wrote the first BASIC interpreter for the Intel 8080 microprocessor. MBASIC was licensed to Micro Instrumentation and Telemetry Systems to accompany its Altair 8800 kit. By the end of 1976, more than 10,000 Altairs were sold, and versions were licensed to Radio Shack, Apple and others. Later. Although the company became a leader in microcomputer programming languages, its outstanding success was caused by fitting IBM PCs with DOS in 1981 and non-IBM PCs with MS-DOS. In 1990, its third attempt at creating Windows was enormously popular, and Windows 3.0, and later Windows 95, cemented Microsoft's leadership.

Since the explosion of the Web, Microsoft has worked feverishly to gain a foothold. By giving away its Internet Explorer browser and then fully integrating it into Windows 98, Internet Explorer is now the leading on-ramp to the Internet. Its Microsoft Network (MSN) ISP division is also a growing part of the company.

Microsoft's position as the supplier of the major operating systems and applications to the world's largest computer base has given it considerable advantage. With a market cap that earlier exceeded half a trillion dollars, it has made thousands of people wealthy and enabled the industry to grow immense because of Windows. However, the company used its dominance in the operating system arena to induce PC makers, which could not survive without Windows, into favoring other Microsoft products, most notably its Office applications and Web browsers. In 1998, the U.S. Government and 19 states sued Microsoft for antitrust violations. In June 2000, the court ordered Microsoft be broken into two companies, which is currently under appeal. A year later, the appeals court stopped the breakup and sent the case back to the lower court. The final outcome is still pending as of this writing. Nevertheless, whether one Microsoft or two, the company will remain a major force for years to come. See *Microsoft and IBM*, *Windows*, *DOS*, *Microsoft Office*, *Microsoft Internet Explorer*, *Microsoftie* and *Altair*. See also **hot topics and trends**.

**William H. Gates, III**
Bill Gates has become the most widely known business entrepreneur in the world, regardless of industry. *(Image courtesy of Microsoft Corporation.)*

**Microsoft Access**   A database program for Windows, available separately or included in the Microsoft Office suite. Access is programmable using Visual Basic for Applications (VBA). Access can read Paradox, dBASE and Btrieve files, and using ODBC, Microsoft SQL Server, SYBASE SQL Server and Oracle data.

**Microsoft and IBM**   Many people are too new to the computer industry to remember that IBM once occupied the lofty position that Microsoft currently enjoys. Today, it's a Microsoft versus The Rest of the World computer industry. Yesterday, it was IBM versus everybody else.

From the early 1960s to the mid-1980s, because of its size and power, just like Microsoft, IBM took the blame for everything wrong with the computer industry. Like Microsoft, countless articles and even books were written about how evil IBM was, and how, if not restrained, it was going to destroy the industry and dominate the world order. There was anti-IBM sentiment everywhere. And what seems inevitable when there is absolute power, the government has to step in as it did with both companies: slapping a consent decree on IBM for trying to take over the service bureau industry and on Microsoft for heavy-handed licensing.

IBM may have given Microsoft the keys to the kingdom with DOS, but, in so doing, it shed a lot of bad press. In the process of losing control of the PC to Microsoft (as well as Intel), IBM turned itself into something akin to a giant, benign bear that still controls the heart and soul of corporate data processing, but is no longer in the crosshairs of everybody's daily wrath.

**Microsoft Bob**   An alternative Windows interface from Microsoft that was introduced in early 1996, but never caught on. It let you decorate your own "rooms" with familiar objects, and various animated guides, such as Rover the dog, provided online help. It also came with a word processor, checkbook and other home-oriented utilities.

**Microsoft C**   A C compiler and development system for DOS and Windows applications from Microsoft. Windows programming requires the Windows Software Development Kit (SDK), which is included.

Version 7.0 includes C++ capability and Version 1.0 of the Microsoft Foundation Class Library (MFC), which provide a base framework of object-oriented code to build an application upon. See *Visual C++*.

**Microsoft certification**   A series of programs that provide certification of competency in Microsoft products. Administered throughout the world at Microsoft centers as well as colleges and universities, it provides various certification levels, including the following:

**MCP—Microsoft Certified Professional**   Umbrella term for individuals passing exams in Microsoft certification categories.

**MCSE—Microsoft Certified Systems Engineer**   For the technical specialist involved with advanced Microsoft products. Candidates are required to pass exams on NT or 2000, plus electives.

**MCSD—Microsoft Certified Solution Developer**   For the VAR or software developer. Candidates must pass exams on Windows architecture and services plus programming languages of their choice.

**MCDBA—Microsoft Certified Database Administrator**   For the administrator involved with Microsoft's SQL Server database management system.

**MCT—Microsoft Certified Trainer**   For the person that trains others in these subjects through Microsoft authorized education sites.

**MOUS—Microsoft Office User Specialist**   For the user that requires proficiency with Office applications, including Word, Excel and PowerPoint.

**Microsoft Certified Professional**   See *Microsoft certification*.

**Microsoft Cluster Server**   Clustering software from Microsoft for Windows NT. It provides rudimentary load balancing and two-node failover, which allows a second server to take over if the first one fails. More sophisticated load balancing is expected. Cluster Server was formerly code named Wolfpack.

**Microsoft Consulting Services**    The consulting arm of Microsoft which offers support for installation and maintenance of Microsoft applications and operating systems.

**Microsoft DLC**    (Microsoft **D**ata **L**ink **C**ontrol) A communications protocol for Windows clients that supports terminal connections to IBM mainframes and AS/400s. HP printers that are attached via the network using HP's JetDirect internal print servers may optionally use or even require this protocol. See *SDLC, DLC* and *3270 emulator.*

**Microsoft Exchange**    Messaging and groupware software for Windows from Microsoft. Exchange Server is an Internet-compliant messaging system that runs under Windows NT/2000 and can be accessed by Web browsers, the Windows Inbox, Exchange client or Outlook. Exchange Server is also a storage system that can hold anything that needs to be shared.

The Exchange client includes an e-mail client with server based rules, forms design, threaded discussions and group calendaring and scheduling. The Inbox is a limited version of the Exchange client that comes on Windows 95 and NT desktops.

Microsoft's Outlook can also be used as the Exchange client, adding features such as richer forms design, group contact and task management, journaling (tracking hourly billing), message recall (unread messages can be pulled back), shared folders and freeform notes.

**Microsoftie**    A person that works for Microsoft.

**Microsoft Internet Explorer**    Microsoft's Web browser, also known as "IE." Versions for Windows, Mac and UNIX are available. Internet Explorer was developed after Netscape began to turn the computer world upside down with its Navigator browser, and both companies went head to head on enhancements and features. Although Netscape's browser was a purchased product, Microsoft made Internet Explorer free, forcing Netscape to do the same. Since Microsoft integreted the browser into Window 98, Internet Explorer has become the market leader. Internet Explorer has also been the browser in AOL's online software.

**M**

**Microsoft Internet Information Server**    Web server software from Microsoft that runs under Windows NT. It supports Netscape's SSL security protocol and turns an NT-based PC into a Web site. Microsoft's Web browser, Internet Explorer, is also included.

**Microsoft Mail**    An earlier and simple messaging system from Microsoft that runs on PC and AppleTalk networks. Gateways are available to a variety of mail systems including X.400, PROFS and MHS. Microsoft Mail-enabled applications are written to the MAPI programming interface. See *Microsoft Exchange.*

**Microsoft Management Console**    Network management software from Microsoft for Windows NT and Windows 2000 that provides a hierarchical view of resources similar to an Explorer view. Microsoft Management Console (MMC) provides the software framework, and "snap-in" components from Microsoft and third parties add the actual device management.

**Microsoft Message Queue Server**    Messaging middleware for Windows NT from Microsoft. Code named Falcon, and abbreviated MSMQ, it allows programs to send messages to other programs. It can be used to queue up transactions in a transaction processing system, for example. MSMQ is optionally used with Microsoft Transaction Server, Microsoft's COM-based TP monitor. See *messaging middleware* and *Microsoft Transaction Server.*

**Microsoft.NET**    See *.NET.*

**Microsoft Network**    An online service from Microsoft that was launched with Windows 95. It initially caused much furor in the industry, because people thought Microsoft was taking undue advantage of its position. Originally intended as a general-purpose service similar to America Online (at that time), MSN evolved into an Internet provider (ISP) with added functions. See also *Windows network.*

**Microsoft Office**    A suite of Microsoft's primary desktop applications for Windows and Macintoshes. Depending on the package, it includes some combination of Word, Excel, PowerPoint, Access and Schedule along with a host of

Internet and other related utilities. The applications share common functions such as spell checking and graphing, and objects can be dragged and dropped between applications. Microsoft Office is the leading application suite on the market.

Office 4.x was the last 16-bit version, and the first 32-bit version of Office (Office 95) was released in 1995. Office 97 (1997) added Internet integration and Outlook, a personal information manager (PIM) and e-mail client. The file formats in Excel 97, PowerPoint 97 and Word 97 changed from Office 95. An Office 97 option allows saving files in a dual 95/97 format for backward compatibility. A new Access 97 file format is not backward compatible.

Office 2000 is a major upgrade with numerous enhancements and changes. It is thoroughly integrated with the Web, providing several Web-based collaboration features, as well as being able to open HTML documents and save to the HTML format. It even doubles as an HTML editor. A new menu system displays only the most-frequently used commands.

Office XP, introduced in 2001, adds document sharing over the Web and also integrates Microsoft's Web-based Hotmail e-mail service. See *Binder* and *MSW ABCs*.

**Microsoft Plus!**     A set of utilities from Microsoft that augment the Windows 95/98 operating system, including visual enhancements for the desktop, improved disk compression and the ability to dial up your computer from a remote location.

**Microsoft SQL Server**     A relational DBMS from Microsoft that runs on Windows NT servers. It is Microsoft's high-end client/server database and a key component in its BackOffice suite of server products. SQL Server was originally developed by Sybase and also sold by Microsoft for OS/2 and NT. In 1992, Microsoft began development of its own version. Today, Microsoft SQL Server and Sybase SQL Server are independent products with some compatibility.

**Microsoft SQL Server OLAP Services**     OLAP extensions to Microsoft's flagship database software than enable users to perform "what if" analyses on their data. Formerly code named "Plato," OLAP Services was introduced with Version 7.0 of SQL Server in late 1998. See *OLAP*.

**Microsoft TechNet**     A CD-ROM subscription service from Microsoft that contains technical documentation, drivers and patches for all of Microsoft's products. It includes two updated CD-ROMs every month and contains the Microsoft Knowledge Base with more than 30,000 questions and answers.

**Microsoft Transaction Server**     A TP monitor for Windows NT servers from Microsoft that supports transaction-based applications on LANs, the Internet and intranets. It also serves as the infrastructure for a multitier system. It is used in the middle tier between the client and the database server. Microsoft Transaction Server (MTS) supports two-phase commit with its included Distributed Transaction Coordinator (DTC).

Based on Microsoft's component software architecture (COM), MTS hosts business logic written as ActiveX Server Components. A component is written for a single user, and MTS scales the process for many users. The server components access the required data via any of several interfaces including ADO, OLE DB and ODBC. In Windows 2000, MTS is not a separate component, but is part of the operating system. See *Microsoft Message Queue Server*.

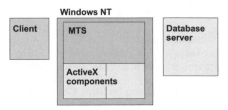

**Middle Tier Processing**
Microsoft Transaction Server provides the infrastructure for the middle tier in a transaction environment. It serves as the container for ActiveX components.

**Microsoft Virtual Machine**     The Java interpreter (Java Virtual Machine) that works with Microsoft's Internet Explorer Web browser. It can be downloaded from Microsoft's Web site. See *Java Virtual Machine* and *Java*.

**Microsoft Wallet**     A digital wallet capability built into Internet Explorer. The client-based wallet has been superseded by the server-based wallet in Microsoft's Passport service. See *Passport*.

**Microsoft Windows**     See *Windows*.

**Microsoft Windows network**     See *Windows network*.

**Microsoft Word**    A full-featured word processing program for Windows and the Macintosh from Microsoft. It is a sophisticated program with rudimentary desktop publishing capabilities that has become the most widely-used word processing application on the market. The first versions of Word came out under DOS and provided both graphics-based and text-based interfaces for working with a document. For a tutorial on the essentials of Microsoft Word, see *MSW ABCs*.

**Microsoft Works**    An integrated software package for Windows and the Macintosh from Microsoft. It provides file management with relational-like capabilities, word processing, spreadsheet, business graphics and communications capabilities in one package.

**microspacing**    Positioning characters for printing by making very small horizontal and vertical movements. Many dot matrix printers and all laser printers have this ability.

**MicroStation**    A full-featured 2-D and 3-D CAD program for DOS, Windows, Mac and UNIX workstations from Bentley Systems, Inc., Exton, PA (www.bentley.com). Created in 1984, MicroStation is a high-end package used worldwide in environments where many designers work on large, complex projects. MicroStation Modeler is a superset of MicroStation that provides solid modeling, and MasterPiece is MicroStation's rendering and animation program.

   MicroStation has also been marketed by Intergraph as the software for its proprietary workstations. See *solid modeling*.

**micro to mainframe**    An interconnection of personal computers to mainframes. See *3270 emulator*.

**MicroVAX**    A series of entry-level VAXs introduced in 1983 that run under VMS or ULTRIX. Some models use the Q-bus architecture.

**microwave**    An electromagnetic wave that vibrates at 1GHz and above. Numerous transmission systems use microwaves including line-of-sight between buildings and across vast distances, communications satellites, PCS cellular systems and wireless LANs. See *wireless local loop* and *electromagnetic spectrum*.

**Microwindows**    An open source graphical windowing environment for small devices typically running under Linux. Similar to the X Window system, it is designed for limited amounts of memory and storage. Microwindows supports the Win32 programming interface and Nano-X, an X-like interface, which enables Windows and X Window applications to be ported over rather easily. For information, visit http://microwindows.org.

**middle tier**    (1) Generally refers to the processing that takes place in an application server that sits between the user's machine and the database server. The middle tier server performs the business logic. See *application server* and *client/server*.

   (2) A level or step between two others. May refer to an infinite variety of situations.

**Early Microwave Tower**
Microwaves were first used to transmit across long distances that were difficult to wire as long as line-of-sight was possible. This tower was installed in 1969 in Boulder Junction, Colorado.
*(Image courtesy of AT&T.)*

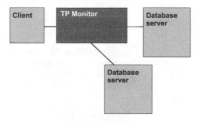

**TP Monitors**
The TP monitor (transaction monitor) was perhaps the first product to be called middleware. Sitting between the requesting client program and the databases, it ensures that all databases are updated properly (see *TP monitor*).

**middleware**    Software that functions as a conversion or translation layer. It is also a consolidator and integrator. Custom-programmed middleware solutions have been developed for decades to enable one application to communicate with another that either runs on a different platform or comes from a different vendor or both. Today, there is a diverse group of products that offer packaged middleware solutions as outlined in the following examples. See *application integration*.

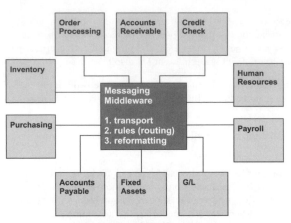

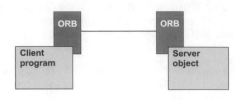

### Distributed Processing
Distributed object systems such as CORBA, DCOM and EJB enable processes to be run anywhere in the network. They differ from messaging middleware in that they cause processes (components/objects) to be executed in realtime rather than sending data.

### Messaging Middleware
Messaging middleware provides a common interface and transport between applications. If the target machine is down or overloaded, it stores the data in a message queue until it becomes available. The messaging system may contain business logic that routes messages to the appropriate destinations and reformats the data as well. Messaging middleware is similar to an e-mail messaging system, except that it is used to send data between applications. (see *messaging middleware*).

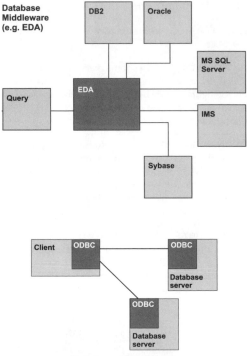

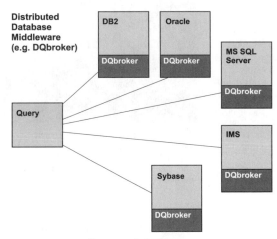

### Common Interfaces
Common programming interfaces between applications are considered middleware. For example, Open Database Connectivity (ODBC) enables applications to make a standard call to all the databases that support the ODBC interface.

### Database Middleware
Middleware provides a common interface between a query and multiple, distributed databases. Using either a hub and spoke architecture (top) or a distributed architecture (bottom), it enables data to be consolidated from a variety of disparate data sources (see *EDA* and *DQbroker*).

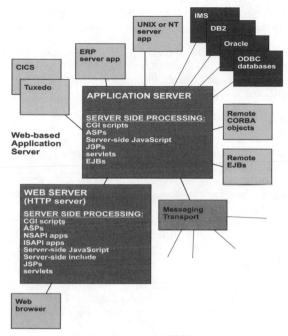

**Application Server Middleware**

A Web-based application server that provides interfaces to a wide variety of applications is used as middleware between the browser and legacy systems. The browser can be used at desktops or on laptops when travelling. A wide range of server-side processing has been supported by appservers (see *J2EE*).

**MIDI** (Musical Instrument Digital Interface) A standard protocol for the interchange of musical information between musical instruments, synthesizers and computers. It defines the codes for a musical event, which includes the start of a note, its pitch, length, volume and musical attributes, such as vibrato. It also defines codes for various button, dial and pedal adjustments used on synthesizers.

MIDI is commonly used to synchronize notes produced on several synthesizers. Its control messages can orchestrate a series of synthesizers, each playing a part of the musical score.

A computer with a MIDI interface can be used to record a musical session, but instead of recording the analog sound waves as in a tape recorder, the computer stores the music as keystroke and control codes. The recording can be edited in an entirely different manner than with conventional recording; for example, the rhythm can be changed by editing the timing codes in the MIDI messages. In addition, the computer can easily transpose a performance from B major into D major. MIDI files also take up much less disk space than sound files that contain the actual digitized music.

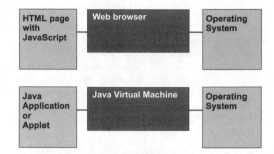

**Universal Computing**

These two examples link an application to an operating environment and are the Holy Grail of computing. They enable the same program to run on any hardware platform without modification. HTML pages written in JavaScript can execute on any JavaScript-enabled Web browser running under any operating system. Java applications and applets are executed by a Java Virtual Machine, which can be created for any operating system. Thus, the browser and Java negate the requirement for a single operating system and hardware environment.

**MID file** See *MIDI file*.

M

MIDI (digital notes)

10011101 10010011 10010010 00110010 10010100

Digital Audio (digitized sound waves)

100111001010001110111011001101011001101010111100110
001011100010101110100010101101110001100111010101101
010111010111010101010000100101011101000010101010101
100010110111010101011010000100101001110101110101000
101001010010001011010110101100001010101010001011101
001011011011010010010010011101010110110111011110100
010111010010110101101011010010010010011001000010101

**MIDI vs. Digitized Sound**

This shows musical notes stored in MIDI compared to digital audio. MIDI is musical notation, whereas digital audio is a sample of the actual waveforms. This is a conceptual example. The binary coding is not accurate.

The objective of MIDI was to allow the keyboard of one synthesizer to play notes generated by another. However, since Version 1.0 in 1983, MIDI has brought electronic control of music to virtually everybody, benefiting musicians and teachers alike.

MIDI makes an ideal system for storing music on digital media due to its small storage requirement compared with digitizing actual music. Since the advent of General MIDI, a standard for defining MIDI instruments, MIDI has become widely used for musical backgrounds in multimedia applications. See *General MIDI*, *MIDI sequencer*, *MIDI patch*, *MIDI voices*, *MPU-401*, *wave table synthesis*, *FM synthesis* and *sound card*.

**midicomputer**   An earlier term for a computer with performance and capacity between a minicomputer and a mainframe.

**MIDI file**   A MIDI sound file that contains MIDI messages. MIDI files used in DOS and Windows have a .MID extension. A variation of this format is the RIFF MIDI file, which uses the .RMI extension.

The format for MIDI files, or Standard MIDI File (SMF), contains a header "chunk" at the beginning of the file, which defines the format type, followed by one or more track chunks. Type 0 files store all tracks in one track chunk. Type 1 files use a separate chunk for each track, with the first chunk storing the tempo.

Type 0 files use less memory and run faster than type 1. Thus, original MIDI music is maintained in type 1 format and frequently distributed in type 0. MIDI files distributed for editing are usually in type 1 format, since it is difficult to convert from type 0 to type 1 using a MIDI sequencer.

A less-widely used type 2 file can contain several type 0 files.

**MIDI Mapper**   A Windows application that converts MIDI sound sequences (MIDI messages) to conform to a particular MIDI sound card or module. The keyboard map is used to assign values to non-standard keyboard keys. The patch map assigns sounds to an instrument number (see *MIDI patch*). The channel map assigns input channels to output channels.

**MIDI messages**   A series of MIDI notes for a musical sequence. Since MIDI data is a set of musical note definitions rather than the actual sound of the music, the contents of a MIDI file are called MIDI messages.

**MIDI patch**   One of 16 channels in a MIDI device. Many keyboard synthesizers and MIDI sound modules can handle several waveforms per patch, mixing different instruments together to create synthetic sounds. Each waveform counts as a MIDI voice. Some sound cards can support two or more waveforms per patch.

Before General MIDI, which standardized patches, MIDI vendors assigned patch numbers to their synthesizer products in an arbitrary manner. See *MIDI voices*.

**MIDI sequencer**   A hardware device or software application that allows for the composition, editing and playback of MIDI sound sequences. Media player applications can play MIDI sound files, but creating and modifying MIDI files requires a sequencer.

**MIDI sound module**   A stand-alone device that generates MIDI sound. Other MIDI sound-generating devices are synthesizers with keyboards and sound cards for personal computers.

**MIDI voices**   The number of musical notes that can be played back simultaneously in a MIDI sound device. MIDI provides up to 16 channels of simultaneous playback. The number of voices is the total number of notes from all the instruments played back through all the channels.

For example, if one of the channels (patches) is a piano, up to 10 fingers could strike the keyboard at the same time, generating 10 notes, assuming that particular piano patch triggers only one waveform (see *MIDI patch*). Typically, a MIDI sound card will support from 24 to 32 voices. Keyboard synthesizers and sound modules can handle up to 64.

**midlet**   A cellphone or pager application written in the Java 2 Platform, Micro Edition version (J2ME). See *MIDP* and *J2ME*.

**MIDP**   (Mobile Information Device Profile) A programming interface (API) for cellphones and pagers for the Java 2 Platform, Micro Edition (J2ME). It provides support for a graphical interface, networking and storage of persistent data for "MID Profile" applications, also known as "midlets." See *J2ME*.

**midpoint load**    A dual-hub magnetic tape cartridge that is positioned at the middle of the tape to start. It enables faster searching than a single hub, where all searches must start at the beginning. Magstar MP and the LTO Accelis formats use this method.

**midrange computer**    A medium-sized computer system or server. Midrange computers encompass a very broad range between high-end PCs and mainframes and cost from $25,000 to more than $1 million. IBM's AS/400s, HP's 3000s and Compaq's Alpha families are examples. Formerly called "minicomputers," which used dumb terminals connected to centralized systems, most midrange computers today function as servers in a client/server configuration.

**midrange programmer**    A person that writes applications in programming languages such as COBOL, RPG and 4GLs, typically for IBM AS/400s. See *programmer*.

**midrange programmer/analyst**    A person responsible for the design and programming of a medium-sized business application. Programming languages include COBOL, RPG and 4GLs, typically for IBM AS/400s. See *programmer analyst*.

**MIF**    **(1)** (Maker Interchange Format) An alternative file format for a FrameMaker document. A MIF file is ASCII text, which can be created in another program and imported into FrameMaker.

**(2)** (Management Information File) A DMI file format that describes a hardware or software component used in a PC. It can contain data, code or both. See *DMI*.

**(3)** (Machine Interface Format) A proprietary language for configuring Ascend networking devices. Instead of setting up via menus one option at a time, a MIF file can be created with all the changes and uploaded to the unit.

**(4)** (Multiple Image Facility) The management of ESCON and FICON mainframe channels so that multiple LPARs (Logical PARtitions) may share it concurrently. See *ESCON*, *FICON* and *LPAR*.

**migration**    A change from one hardware or software technology to another. Migration is a way of life in the computer industry. For example, once known only to those in the glass-enclosed datacenter, users today understand the meaning of migrating from one operating system to another.

**M**

**migration path**    A series of conversion steps that allow an organization to evolve smoothly to newer hardware and software in order to keep pace with changing technology.

**mil**    An Internet address domain name for a military agency. See *Internet address*.

**mill**    A very old term for processor (number crunching!).

**Millenium Bug**    See *Y2K Problem*.

**millennium**    **(1)** One thousand years. As it pertains to the calendar, we recently passed through the second millennium (January 1, 1901 to December 31, 2000), and the third millennium began January 1, 2001.

**(2)** (Windows Millennium) See *Windows ME*.

**Millennium Bug**    See *Y2K Problem*.

**Millennium project**    A parallel computing project at the University of California at Berkeley. Using nearly a thousand computers donated by Intel, its focus is on developing a multi-level "system of systems" that uses local clusters of SMP machines called a "CLUMP." The CLUMPs use technology from the earlier NOW (Network of Workstations) project at Berkeley. See *NOW project* and *Beowulf*.

**Miller Freeman**    An earlier subsidiary of United News & Media (www.unm.com). Miller Freeman was a leading trade show organizer and publisher serving a variety of industries. In 1996, it acquired the Blenheim Group, producers of the popular PC EXPO trade show, and in 1999, it acquired the CMP publishing company, a leading publisher of high-tech magazines. In 2000, United News & Media acquired Miller Freeman and subsequently folded all IT-related products into the CMP name and sold off the rest.

**milli**   Thousandth (10 to the –3rd power). See *space/time*.

**milliamp**   One thousandth of an amp. See **ampere**.

**Millicent**   (MILLI CENT) A microcommerce application from Digital that allows transactions of very small monetary value to be contracted on the Internet. The term stands for "one thousandth of a cent." See *microcommerce*.

**millimeter**   One thousandth of a meter, or 1/25th of an inch. See *metric system*.

**millisecond**   One thousandth of a second. See *space/time* and *ohnosecond*.

**MIL STD**   (MILitary STandarD) A detailed technical specification for a product that is purchased by a U.S. military agency.

**MIMD**   (Multiple Instruction stream Multiple Data stream) A computer architecture that uses multiple processors, each processing its own set of instructions simultaneously and independently of the others. Contrast with *SIMD*.

**MIME**   (Multipurpose Internet Mail Extensions) A common method for transmitting non-text files via Internet e-mail, which was originally designed for ASCII text. MIME encodes the files using one of two encoding methods and decodes it back to its original format at the receiving end. A MIME header is added to the file which includes the type of data contained and the encoding method used. S/MIME (Secure MIME) is a version of MIME that adds RSA encryption for secure transmission. See *base64*, *quoted printable encoding*, *UUcoding*, *BinHex* and **Wincode**.

**MIME type**   A file identification derived from the MIME encoding system that identifies the content of a file. In order to define the content of attachments, MIME types are embedded in e-mail messages. Web servers send the MIME type to the requesting browser so that it can launch the appropriate helper application or plug-in.

The MIME "Content Type" has a type and subtype separated by a slash; for example, text/plain and image/gif. The major types are application, audio, image, text and video. Application refers to a variety of formats; for example, application/x-pdf refers to Adobe Acrobat documents, and application/octet-stream refers to an .EXE file.

**mini**   See *minicomputer*.

**Miniature Card**   A flash memory card used in some consumer devices for a while, but later replaced by CompactFlash and other memory technologies due to its problematic connector design.

**minicartridge**   See *QIC*.

**mini CD**   A CD disc 80mm in diameter. It holds 20 minutes of music (audio) compared to the 74 minutes of the standard 120mm CD and fits into the deeper well in the center of the tray of most CD players. See *mini CD-ROM* and *business card CD*.

**mini CD-ROM**   A CD-ROM disc 80mm in diameter. It holds 180MB compared to the 650MB of the standard 120mm CD-ROM and fits into the deeper well in the center of the tray of most CD-ROM drives. See *mini CD* and *business card CD*.

**minicomputer**   (1) An earlier medium-scale, centralized computer that functioned as a multiuser system for up to several hundred users. The minicomputer industry was launched in 1959 after Digital Equipment Corporation introduced its PDP-1 for $20,000, an unheard-of low price for a computer in those days. Subsequently,

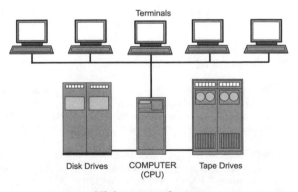

Terminals

Disk Drives    COMPUTER    Tape Drives
                (CPU)

**Minicomputer System**
The minicomputer was a centralized computer that served from a handful to several hundred "dumb" terminals.

a variety of systems became available from HP, Data General, Wang, Tandem, Datapoint and Prime Computer. The single-user mini evolved into a centralized system with dumb terminals for departmental use.

During the 1980s and early 1990s, most centralized minicomputers migrated from their dumb terminal architecture into servers for PC networks. The terms "midrange computer" and "server" replaced the venerable minicomputer designation. See *midrange computer*.

(2) An earlier term for a high-end, single-user workstation, typically for CAD use.

**MiniDisc**   A compact digital audio disc from Sony that comes in read-only and rewritable versions. Introduced in late 1993, the MiniDisc has been popular in Japan. The read-only 2.5" disc stores 140MB compared to 650MB on a CD, but holds the same 74 minutes worth of music due to Sony's Adaptive Transform Acoustic Coding (ATRAC) compression scheme, which eliminates inaudible signals. MD discs store disc and track titles displayed by the player. Used for music recording, rewritable MiniDiscs employ magneto-optic technology and come in 60 and 74-minute cartridges. The MiniDisc drive for computers (MD DATA) never caught on.

**MiniDV**   See *DV*.

**minifloppy**   The formal name for the once-ubiquitous, black floppy disk encased in a 5.25"-wide plastic jacket. Introduced by Shugart in 1978, it superseded IBM's 8" floppy. Although used extensively, it gave way to the 3.5" floppy (microfloppy) in the mid 1990s.

**minimize**   In a graphical environment, to hide an application that is currently displayed on screen. The window is removed and represented with an icon on the desktop or taskbar.

**mining**   See *data mining*.

**mini notebook**   Same as *subnotebook*.

**M**

**Mini PCI**   An extension of the PCI bus used in portable computers. Designed for peripherals such as modems and network adapters, Mini PCI cards are credit-card sized modules that snap onto the motherboard; they are not inserted into slots like PC Cards. Using the standard PCI signaling that is found in PCI-based desktop computers, Mini PCI allows high-speed transfer peripheral connections in small form factor devices such as laptop computers. See *PCI*.

**mini-phone connector**   A plug and socket widely used for audio connections. Walkmans, headphones, CD players, speakers and all variety of audio equipment use stereo (three wire) and monaural (two wire) mini-phone connectors. See *A/V ports* and *plugs & sockets*.

**mini-supercomputer**   A computer that is 25% to 100% as fast as a supercomputer, but costs less. Note: A mini-supercomputer is not the same as a supermini.

**Mini-Phone Connectors**
Stereo plugs are identified by the three divisions in their prong, while monaural plugs have only two.

**Minitel**   An online service of the French government that is used to look up phone numbers, pay bills, purchase merchandise and chat. Introduced in the early 1980s, the videotex-based terminals have been freely distributed by France Telecom. Access to the services, known as the Teletel network, is free except for telephone charges. Because it was quite advanced for the 1980s and widely used, Minitel has slowed France's acceptance of the Web.

**MINIX**   A version of UNIX for the PC, Mac, Amiga and Atari ST developed by Andrew Tannenbaum and published by Prentice-Hall. It comes with complete source code.

**minor key**   A secondary key used to identify a record. For example, if transactions are sorted by account number and date, account number is the major key and date is the minor key.

**minus sign**   The minus sign (–) is the subtract symbol in programming and on calculator keyboards. For example, 10 – 7 means subtract 7 from 10. It is also used in command line syntax for a switch. For example, in the PKUNZIP statement **pkunzip lotstuff -d**, the **-d** is a switch that tells the program to create the original Directory structure that is stored in the .ZIP file. See *forward slash*.

**MIO** (Modular I/O) A hardware interface for HP printers that is primarily used to plug in an internal print server and network adapter. MIO has been superseded by EIO. See *EIO*.

**MIP mapping** A texture mapping technique that uses multiple texture maps, or MIP maps. Each MIP map is half the size of the first one, providing several texture maps for various levels of depth. MIP mapping is combined with various other techniques to produce different amounts of realism. It is typically used with bilinear interpolation and always used with trilinear interpolation. MIP stands for "multum in parvo," which is Latin for "many in a small place." See *bilinear interpolation*, *trilinear interpolation*, *texture map* and *point sampling*.

**MIPS** (Million Instructions Per Second) The execution speed of a computer. For example, .5 MIPS is 500,000 instructions per second. High-speed personal computers and workstations perform at 200 MIPS and higher. Digital's Alpha chip has a peak rate of over 1,200 MIPS (that's 1.2 BIPS!). Inexpensive microprocessors used in toys and games may be in the .05–.1 MIPS range.

MIPS rates are not uniform. Some are best-case mixes while others are averages. In addition, it takes more instructions in one machine to do the same thing as another (RISC vs CISC, mainframe vs micro). As a result, MIPS has been called "MisInformation to Promote Sales" as well as "Meaningless Interpretation of Processor Speed."

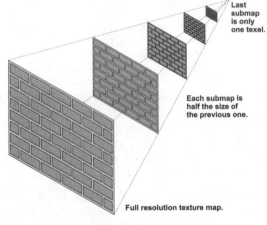

Last submap is only one texel.

Each submap is half the size of the previous one.

Full resolution texture map.

**MIP Maps**
MIP maps provide more depth realism to objects, because texture maps for varying levels of depth have been prepared. *(Redrawn from illustration courtesy of Intergraph Computer Systems.)*

MIPS rate is just one factor in overall performance. Bus and channel speed and bandwidth, memory speed, memory management techniques and system software also determine total throughput. See also *MIPS Computer*.

MIPS and MHz There is a mathematical relationship between MIPS and MHz. You can derive MIPS from MHz if you know how many machine cycles it takes to execute an instruction in the CPU. For example, a 486 takes 1.9 cycles on average. To obtain MIPS on a 50MHz 486, you would divide 50 by 1.9, yielding 26 MIPS.

**MIPS Computer** (MIPS Technologies, Inc., Sunnyvale, CA, subsidiary of SGI). Founded in 1984 as MIPS Computer Systems Inc., the company merged with SGI in 1992. MIPS is the designer of RISC-based microprocessors, which are made under license by NEC, Toshiba, Philips and others. They are widely used in the industry and cumulative shipments exceeded 100 million units in 1997. SGI computers are all powered by MIPS CPUs as well as computers from Pyramid, Tandem, NEC and Siemens.

The MIPS 32-bit R3000 and 64-bit R4000 families are very popular in embedded systems (handheld PDAs and computers, games, consumer products, etc.). Additional 64-bit chips include the R5000, R8000 and R10000 lines, each increasing in performance. MIPS also licenses its compilers and RISC/OS system software. See *SGI*.

**mIRC** A popular Internet Relay Chat program developed by Khaled Mardam-Bey. mIRC runs under Windows and provides a graphical interface for logging onto IRC servers and listing, joining and leaving channels.

**mirrored** Duplicated. See *mirroring* and *disk mirroring*.

**Mirror III** A DOS communications program from Softklone Distributing Corporation, Tallahassee, FL, that supports a variety of terminals and protocols and provides a learn mode for recording common sequences and the PRISM scripting language.

**mirroring**    Duplicating data onto another computer at another location. Mirroring is performed for backup purposes or to be in closer proximity to the user. See *disk mirroring* and *replication*.

**Mirrors**    Software from Micrografx that allows Windows programs to be converted to OS/2 with minimal modification.

**mirror site**    An alternative site that contains the same information. Many software vendors have mirror sites on the Web due to the high volume of requests they get for drivers and beta copies of programs.

**MIS**    (1) (Management Information System) An information system that integrates data from all the departments it serves and provides operations and management with the information they require.

It was "the" buzzword of the mid to late 1970s, when online systems were implemented in all large organizations. See *DSS*.

(2) (Management Information Services) See *Information Systems*.

**MIS director**    See *CIO*.

**missing links**    See *link rot*.

**mission critical**    Vital to the operation of an organization. In the past, mission critical information systems were implemented on mainframes and minicomputers. Increasingly, they are being designed for and installed on personal computer networks. See *client/server*.

**mitso**    See *MTSO*.

**Mixed Mode CD**    A compact disc format that contains both data and audio. Data is stored in track 1, and audio is stored in the remaining tracks. Newer audio CD players will skip the first track upon encountering the data, while earlier players will attempt to play the non-audio data, causing a loud, raucous sound that can damage the speakers. Since Mixed Mode recording is done in a single session, old non-multisession CD-ROM drives will support it.

**mixed object**    Same as *compound document*.

**mixed reality**    A type of virtual reality that combines real and imagined images. In "augmented reality," most of the images are real. For example, using transparent headsets, you could see how that new sofa would look in your own living room, or view the 3-D schematic of a jet engine while you work on the engine itself.

With "augmented virtuality," most of the imagery is computer-generated. For example, you might see something real, perhaps even yourself, projected into an imaginary environment. See *virtual reality*.

**mixed signal**    The combination of analog and digital processing. It typically refers to the capabilities of a chip.

**MKS**    (Mortice Kern Systems Inc., Waterloo, Ontario, www.mks.com) A software company that specializes in programming tools and utilities for a variety of platforms. For example, its RCS system for Windows, OS/2 and UNIX is a version control software package.

**MKS system**    (Meter-Kilogram-Second system) A metric system of measurement that uses the meter, kilogram, gram and second for length, mass and time. The units of force and energy are the "newton" and "joule." See *newton* and *joule*. Contrast with *CGS system*.

**ML**    A symbolic programming language developed in the 1970s at the University of Edinburgh, Scotland. Although similar to LISP, its commands and structures are like Pascal.

**MLPF**    (Multiple Logical Processor Feature) Hardware features on Hitachi mainframes that support the running of multiple system images (multiple virtual machines) on a single processor complex. Each such image has a full complement of CPUs (dedicated or shared), central storage, expanded storage and channels. MLPF is the equivalent of IBM's PR/SM. See *PR/SM*, *LPAR* and *hypervisor*.

M

**MLPPP**    See *MPPP*.

**MM**    See *Multiple Master* and *millimeter*.

**MMA**    (Microcomputer Managers Association, Inc.) A membership organization with chapters throughout the U.S. that was devoted to educating personnel responsible for personal computers. It disbanded in 1996.

**MMC**    See *MultiMediaCard* and *Microsoft Management Console*.

**MMCD**    (MultiMedia CD) A high-capacity CD specification from Sony and Philips that was merged with the Super Density (SD) format to become DVD. See *DVD*.

**MMDS**    (Multichannel Multipoint Distribution Service or Microwave Multipoint Distribution Service) A digital wireless transmission system that works in the 2.2–2.4GHz range. It requires line of sight between transmitter and receiver, which can be 30 or more miles apart. It was designed initially as a one-way service for bringing cable TV to subscribers in remote areas or in locations that are difficult to install cable. MMDS supports approximately 33 analog channels and more than 100 digital channels of TV. In late 1998, the FCC opened up the technology for two-way transmission, enabling MMDS to provide data and Internet services to subscribers. See *LMDS* and *DBS*.

**MME**    See *Multimedia Extensions*.

**MMF**    See *multimode fiber*.

**MMI**    (Man Machine Interface) Same as *user interface*.

**MMU**    (Memory Management Unit) A virtual memory circuit that translates logical addresses into physical addresses.

**MMVF**    (MultiMedia Video File) A proposed rewritable DVD format from NECT. It holds 5.2GB per side. MMVF is initially only available in Japan and is not expected to be a branded product in the U.S. See *DVD*.

**MMX**    (MultiMedia EXtensions) A set of 57 additional instructions built into Intel CPU chips that are used for faster audio, video, graphics and modem operations. MMX is found in Pentium MMX and Pentium II chips, but not in Pentiums and Pentium Pros. MMX instructions allow operations to be performed simultaneously on multiple units of data; for example, eight 8-bit units or four 16-bit units can be added or multiplied at the same time. In addition, MMX includes a multiply-add instruction that allows most of the capabilities of a DSP chip to be provided at very high speed. MMX provides these capabilities on integer data only.

Intel's competitors (AMD, Cyrix and Centaur) have extended their MMX-compliant chips with proprietary floating point instructions for performing the geometry calculations required to move 3-D objects on screen. In order to allow 3-D applications to run on computers with different instruction sets, the chip vendors have helped Microsoft modify its Direct3D graphics system to support their variations. Similar to the way 3-D accelerator cards work that have specialized functions built in, if Direct3D finds special instructions in the CPU, it uses them. If not, it uses regular instructions.

Intel added floating point geometry on the Pentium III with the addition of 70 new instructions known as the Katmai New Instructions. See *future Intel chips*, *DSP* and *SIMD*.

**mnemonic**    Pronounced "nee-monic." Means memory aid. A name assigned to a machine function. For example, in DOS, COM1 is the mnemonic assigned to serial port #1. Programming languages are almost entirely mnemonics.

**MNP**    (Microcom Networking Protocol) A family of communications protocols from Microcom, Inc., Norwood, MA, that have become de facto standards for error correction (classes 2 though 4) and data compression (class 5).

**Class 1:**    Half-duplex asynchronous transmission. This is an earlier mode that is no longer used.

**Class 2:**    Full-duplex asynchronous transmission.

**Class 3:**    Full-duplex synchronous transmission using HDLC framing techniques and 64-byte blocks. Start/stop bits are stripped.

**Class 4:** Increased throughput. Shorter headers,frames up to 256 bytes. Some vendors adjust frame size based on line quality.

**Class 5:** Compresses data up to two times.

**Class 6:** Starts at V.22bis modulation and switches to V.29 if possible. Uses pseudo-duplexing ping-pong method for faster turnaround of V.29 transmission.

**Class 7:** Compresses data up to three times.

**Class 8:** Not in use.

**Class 9:** Adds Piggy-back Acknowledgement** and selective retransmission for more efficient data transport. Provides better performance over variety of links.

**Class 10:** Adds Adverse Channel Enhancements** for better transmission on rural, cellular and other noisy lines.

** *Proprietary Microcom techniques.*

**M-O** See *magneto-optic disk.*

**MO7** (Magneto-Optic7) See *ASMO.*

**mobile** A mobile phone. A "mobile" is wireless parlance for a cellphone; for example, "we're transmitting from the base station to several mobiles."

**mobile agent** A software module that moves from host to host in a network. See *Knowbot* and *agent.*

**mobile computing** Using a computing device while in transit. See *wireless data.*

**mobile data** See *wireless data.*

**mobile data user** A roving individual with a smart phone, pager, PDA or other handheld device that requires wireless data transmission. Contrast with *fixed data user.*

**Mobile Daughter Card** See *AMR.*

**Mobile IP** An IP enhancement that provides forwarding of traffic to moving users. It uses agents in the user's home network and in all foreign networks. When logging on to a remote network, users register their presence with the foreign agent, and the home agent forwards the packets to the remote network.

**mobile positioning** The ability to pinpoint the location of a mobile caller or vehicle in transit. These location-based services are used for emergency purposes, as well as enhanced business applications such as location sensitive billing, traffic updates, fleet management and asset and people tracking.

There are various techniques starting with the simplest cell of origin (COO) method, which identifies the cell the call is made from and requires no infrastructure changes to implement, all the way to the use of GPS coordinates, which are the most accurate.

Enhanced Observed Time Difference (E-OTD), Time of Arrival (TOA) and Angle of Arrival (AOA) are all methods that require reference beacons or antennas stationed within the network and provide accuracy somewhere between COO and GPS.

**mobile processor** A CPU chip designed for portable computers. It is housed in a smaller chip package and features lower voltage than its desktop counterpart in order to run cooler.

**mobile satellite** Refers to transmission via satellite from non-stationary transmitters and receivers. Iridium and Globalstar are examples of mobile satellite communications systems. Contrast with *fixed satellite.* See *Iridium, Globalstar, GEO* and *LEO.*

M

**mobile wireless**   Refers to transmission through the air from a base station to a moving device such as a carphone. Contrast with *fixed wireless*.

**Mobitex**   See *BellSouth Intelligent Wireless Network*.

**mobo**   Slang for motherboard.

**mod**   See *modulo*.

**modal**   Mode oriented. A modal operation switches from one mode to another. Contrast with *non-modal*.

**modal bandwidth**   The capacity of an optical fiber measured in MHz-km (megahertz over one kilometer). One MHz-km equals approximately .7 to .8 Mbps. Thus, a 100 MHz-km fiber can carry about 70 to 80 Mbps of data.

**modal dispersion**   See *dispersion*.

**MO:DCA**   (Mixed Object:Document Content Architecure)   An IBM compound document format for text and graphics elements in a document. It supports Revisable Documents, which are editable like revisable-form DCA; Presentation Documents, which provide specific output formatting similar to DCA final-form; and Resource Documents, which hold control information such as fonts.

Formats for specific objects are specified in OCAs (Object Content Architectures): PTOCA for Presentation and Text that has been formatted for output, GOCA for vector Graphics objects, IOCA for bitmapped Images and FOCA for Fonts. MO:DCA is implemented as IBM's AFP page description language.

**mode**   (1) An operational state that a system has been switched to. It implies at least two possible conditions. There are countless modes for hardware and software. With regard to modes on a hard drive (Mode 2, Mode 3, etc.), see *IDE*. See *Real Mode*, *Protected Mode*, *burst mode*, *insert mode*, *supervisor state* and *program state*.

(2) In fiber optics, the reflective path taken by a light beam through the fiber. The mode is a actually a standing wave that propagates down the fiber. In multimode fiber, several reflective paths (modes) are taken. See *multimode fiber* and *fiber optics glossary*.

**model**   (1) A style or type of hardware device.

(2) A mathematical representation of a device or process used for analysis and planning. See *data model*, *data administration*, *financial planning system* and *scientific application*.

**model-based expert system**   An expert system based on fundamental knowledge of the design and function of an object. Such systems are used to diagnose equipment problems, for example. Contrast with *rule-based expert system*.

**modeling**   Simulating a condition or activity by performing a set of equations on a set of data. See *data model*, *data administration*, *financial planning system* and *scientific application*.

**modem**   (MOdulator-DEModulator)   A device that adapts a terminal or computer to an analog telephone line by converting digital pulses to audio frequencies and vice versa. The term usually refers to 56 Kbps modems (V.90), the current top speed, or to older 28.8 Kbps modems (V.34). The term may also refer to higher-speed cable or DSL modems or to ISDN terminal adapters, which are all digital and technically not modems. See *ISDN terminal adapter*.

A modem is an analog-to-digital and digital-to-analog converter. It also dials the line, answers the call and controls transmission speed. Modems have evolved at 300, 1,200, 2,400, 9,600, 1,4400, 28,800, 33,300 and 56,000 bps. Whatever the top speed, some number of lower speeds are always supported so the modem can accomodate earlier modems or negotiate downward on noisy lines.

For hookup to a personal computer, an internal modem needs a free expansion slot, while an external modem requires a free serial port or USB port. The software required to drive a modem is included in the operating system. In Windows, the Dial-up Networking "Make New Connection" wizard takes you through setting up your modem to dial your Internet provider.

Modems have built-in error correction (V.42) and data compression (V.42bis, MNP 5). On files that are already compressed, the hardware data compression adds little value, because it cannot make compressed files smaller. Modems also have automatic feature negotiation, which adjusts to the other modem's speed and hardware protocols.

Most modems use the Hayes AT command set (machine instructions for modem control). The term modem is also used as a verb; for example, "I'll modem you later." See *modem status signals* and *AT command set*.

**modem bonding**    See *channel bonding*.

**modem eliminator**    A device that allows two close computers to be connected without modems. For personal computers, it is the same as a null modem cable. In synchronous systems, it provides active intelligence for synchronization.

**modem lights**    See "Modem Status Signals" under *modem*.

**modem PC Card**    A modem for use in a laptop or other computer with a PC Card (PCMCIA) slot. Modem PC Cards come in landline and wireless varieties, the latter enabling you to connect to a specific cellular or data service. See *wireless modem*.

**modem pool**    A collection of modems and software that let users dial out and remote users dial in on the next available modem. The modem pool may be internal or external to the remote access server. See *remote access server*.

**modem router**    A device that enables several users on a network to access the Internet. It contains an RJ-11 port for the telephone line and an Ethernet port. It may also provide several Ethernet ports, which lets it serve as a central Ethernet hub for a small workgroup. Access to the unit for configuration and monitoring is typically done via a Telnet connection or Web browser or both. Some models support dual modems for increased bandwidth. See *channel bonding*.

**modem server**    Same as *modem pool*.

**modem teaming**    Using two modems to double transmission rate. Modem teaming splits the download into two parts and sends each part over a different modem. Thus, teaming is not good for streaming or isochronous media. Modem teaming differs from modem bonding (channel bonding), in which the same stream is multiplexed over two modems. See *channel bonding*.

**moderated newsgroup**    A newsgroup that is managed by a human referee who keeps the discussion focused and prevents it from getting out of hand.

**Modesto**    The code name for Novell's next-generation operating system that runs on the IA-64 platform. It includes Novell's popular NDS directory services. See *IA-64*.

**modify structure**    A database command that changes a file's structure. Field lengths and field names can be changed, and fields can be added or deleted. It may convert the old data file into the new structure without data loss, unless fields have been truncated or deleted.

**MODKA**    See *MO:DCA*.

**Modula-2**    (MODUlar LAnguage-2) An enhanced version of Pascal introduced in 1979 by Swiss professor Nicklaus Wirth, creator of Pascal. It supports separate compilation of modules, allowing it to be used for large projects. The following example changes Fahrenheit to Celsius:

```
    MODULE FahrToCent;
FROM InOut IMPORT ReadReal,WriteReal,
WriteString,WriteLn;
```

**The Sportster**
The Sportster was one of the hottest-selling products in the 1990s as people went online in record numbers. External units have the advantage of status lights, which help troubleshoot connections. Internal modems have since become the norm. *(Image courtesy of 3Com Corporation.)*

M

```
VAR Fahr:REAL;
BEGIN
WriteString("Enter Fahrenheit ");
ReadReal(Fahr);
WriteLn;
WriteString("Celsius is ");
WriteReal((Fahr - 32) * 5 / 9);
    END FahrToCent
```

**Modula-3**    (MODUlar LAnguage-3) The successor to the Modula-2 language. Developed by Digital and Olivetti, it adds object-oriented extensions, automatic garbage collection and improved exception handling. It is considered an excellent teaching language.

**modular chassis**    A hardware device that is designed for expansion and accepts a variety of plug-in modules of different types. Network switches and routers are typically built with a modular chassis. See *line card*.

**modular hub**    A network hub that is configured by adding different modules, each supporting a topology, such as Ethernet, Token Ring, FDDI, etc. See *hub*.

**modularity**    The characteristic of a system that has been divided into smaller subsystems which interact with each other.

**modular programming**    Breaking down the design of a program into individual components (modules) that can be programmed and tested independently. It is a requirement for effective development and maintenance of large programs and projects.

Modular programming has evolved into object-oriented programming, which provides formal rules for developing self-contained software modules. See *object-oriented programming*.

**modulate**    To vary a carrier wave. Modulation blends a data signal (text, voice, etc.) into a carrier for transmission over a network. The most common methods are (1) amplitude modulation (AM), which modulates the height of the carrier wave, (2) frequency modulation (FM), which modulates the frequency of the wave, and (3) phase modulation (PM), which modulates the polarity of the wave. Contrast with *demodulate*. See *carrier*.

**module**    A self-contained hardware or software component that interacts with a larger system. Hardware modules are often made to plug into a main system. Program modules are designed to handle a specific task within a larger program. See *memory module, ROM card, MCM* and *modular programming*.

**modulo**    A mathematical operation (modulus arithmetic) in which the result is the remainder of the division. For example, 20 MOD 3 results in 2 (20/3 = 6 with a remainder of 2).

**MOF**    (1) (Managed Object Format) An ASCII file that contains the formal definition of a CIM schema. See *CIM*.

(2) (Meta Object Facility) An object model from the Object Management Group (OMG) for defining metadata in a distributed CORBA environment. Its four levels define the meta-meta model, meta model, model and instance data. See *CORBA* and *OMG*.

**moire**    Pronounced "mor-ray" and spelled "moiré." In computer graphics, a visible distortion. It results from a variety of conditions; for example, when scanning halftones at a resolution not consistent with the printed resolution or when superimposing curved patterns on one another. Internal monitor misalignment can also be a cause.

**MOLAP**    See *OLAP*.

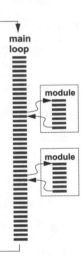

**Modular Programming**
Building a program in modules, or independent routines, is common practice. The module performs a function and then returns control back to the program or instruction that called it. Modular programming has evolved into object-oriented programming, which provides stricter rules for developing self-contained routines.

**molecular beam epitaxy**    A technique that "grows" atomic-sized layers on a chip rather than creating layers by diffusion.

**molecular memory**    A potential future memory technology that stores data at the molecular level. Using lasers and the bacteriorhodopsin protein molecule, the W. M. Keck Center for Molecular Electronics has built a molecular memory device holding several hundred megabytes. The advantage of such a memory is its small size and stability. It holds its content without power.

**MOM**    (Messaging-Oriented Middleware) See *messaging middleware*.

**monadic**    One. A single item or operation that deals with one item or operand.

**Monarch**    A data capture program from Datawatch Corporation, Wilmington, MA (www.datawatch.com), that is used to transfer data from mainframe and minicomputer reports to the PC. It uses report files that contain data ready to print. Users identify the data directly from the report format on screen, and the program copies the data into the fields of various database or spreadsheet formats for the PC.

**monaural**    Same as *monophonic*.

**Monday Morning Webmaster**    The fellow worker that was totally uninterested in helping you with your Web site, but who has plenty of comments to make the day after you put it online.

**moniker**    A COM object that is used to create instances of other objects. Monikers save programmers time when coding various types of COM-based functions such as linking one document to another (OLE). See *COM* and *OLE*.

**monitor**    (1) A display screen used to present output from a computer, camera, VCR or other video generator. A monitor's clarity is based on video bandwidth, dot pitch, refresh rate and convergence. See *VGA*, *analog monitor*, *digital monitor* and **how to select a PC display system**.

     (2) Software that provides utility and control functions such as setting communications parameters. It typically resides in a ROM chip and contains startup and diagnostic routines.

     (3) Software that monitors the progress of activities within a computer system.

     (4) A device that gathers performance statistics of a running system via direct attachment to the CPU's circuit boards.

**monitor calibrator**    A handheld device that is placed over the screen of a monitor and "reads" the colors.

**monitor profile**    A file of attributes about a specific monitor, which includes information about its gamma, white point and phosphors. It is used to produce accurate color conversion from the display to some other destination such as a printer.

**monitor size**    Monitor size is measured by the distance from one corner of the screen's viewable area to the diagonally-opposite corner. With CRTs, the number is generally about an inch greater than the actual area. Starting in the late 1990s, the real number is included in the specs. For example, you might see a 17" monitor state 16.1" viewable. See *resolution*.

**mono**    See *monochrome* and *monophonic*.

**monochrome**    Also called "mono." The display of one foreground color and one background color; for example, black on white, white on black and green on black. Monochrome screens have been widely used on mini and mainframe terminals. Non-color laptop screens on PCs are often said to be "monochrome VGA" screens, but they are actually gray-scale screens, not monochrome.

**monolithic**    Single object. Self contained. One unit.

**monolithic integrated circuit**    The common form of chip design, in which the base material (substrate) contains the pathways as well as the active elements that take part in its operation.

**M**

**monophonic**    Also called "mono" and "monaural." Sound reproduction using a single channel. Contrast with *stereophonic*.

**monospaced font**    A font in which each character is the same width. The "i" takes up the same horizontal space as an "m." Courier is a common monospaced font. Contrast with *proportional spacing*.

**Monte Carlo method**    A technique that provides approximate solutions to problems expressed mathematically. Using random numbers and trial and error, it repeatedly calculates the equations to arrive at a solution.

**Monterey**    A UNIX operating system from IBM, SCO and Sequent that is expected to run on Intel Pentium and Itanium (IA-32 and IA-64) and PowerPC machines. Also backed by Intel, it combines parts of SCO's UnixWare, IBM's AIX and Sequent's DYNIX/ptx.

**MOO**    (MultiUser Dimension Object-Oriented Technology) Same as *MUD*.

**Moore's law**    "The number of transistors on a chip doubles every 18 months." By Intel co-founder Gordon Moore regarding the pace of semiconductor technology. It has proven fairly accurate. More recently, he said that the cost of a semiconductor manufacturing plant doubles with each generation of microprocessor. See *laws*.

**mopier**    A machine that makes mopies. See *mopy*.

**MOPS**    **(1)** (Mega million Operations Per Second) The measurement of instructional performance of a system. It often refers to DSP operations. See *GOPS*.

**(2)** (Millionaires On Paper) Refers to people that have wealth tied up in their company's stock, which cannot be sold until a certain date. The high tech industry has created thousands of MOPS.

**mopy**    (Multiple Original Prints + Y) To print multiple copies of a document on a computer printer. As more information is created digitally and printers become faster, it is increasingly easier to print multiple originals than to use a copy machine later. In other words, "mopy... don't copy!"

**morphing**    Transforming one image into another; for example, a car into a tiger. The term comes from metamorphosis. Morphing programs work by marking prominent points, such as tips and corners, of the before and after images. The points are used to mathematically compute the movements from one object to the other. See *tweening*.

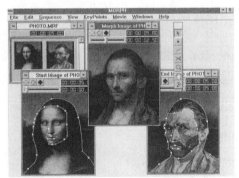

**Plotting the Points**
The prominent points of both the before and after images are marked in Gryphon's Morph software, which computes all the in-between stages. (*Image courtesy of Gryphon Software Corporation.*)

**Morris worm**    A famous occurrence of Internet sabotage. On November 2, 1988, Robert Morris, a Cornell University graduate student, unleashed a worm on the Internet that infected hundreds of thousands of computers, overloading the entire Internet and causing many servers to fail as a result. As a computer science student, he was interested in determining how far and how quickly the worm could spread throughout the network, but he did not anticipate that it would cause as much trouble as it did due to his own misjudgment in coding the program's logic. Morris was convicted and sentenced to three years of probation and 400 hours of community service and a $10,000 fine. This was a seminal incident in the history of Internet security. See *worm* and *denial of service attack*.

**Morse code**    A character code represented by dots and dashes, developed by Samuel Morse in the mid-nineteenth century. A dot can be a voltage, carrier wave or light beam of one duration, while a dash is a longer duration. It was used to send telegraph messages before the telephone and was used in World War II for signaling by light. See *telegraph*.

**Mortice Kern**    See *MKS*.

**MOS**    (**M**etal **O**xide **S**emiconductor) Pronounced "moss." One of two major categories of chip design (the other is bipolar). It derives its name from its use of metal, oxide and semiconductor layers. There are several varieties of MOS technologies, including PMOS, NMOS and CMOS.

**Mosaic**    A Web browser created by the University of Illinois National Center for Supercomputing Applications (NCSA) and released on the Internet in early 1993. Mosaic was "the" application that caused interest in the World Wide Web to explode. Originally developed for UNIX, it was soon ported to Windows. An enhanced version of NCSA Mosaic is offered by Spyglass, Inc., Naperville, IL. See *Netscape Navigator*.

**MOSFET**    (**M**etal **O**xide **S**emiconductor **F**ield **E**ffect **T**ransistor) A common type of transistor fabricated as a discrete component or into MOS integrated circuits.

**MOSPF**    (**M**ulticast extended **OSPF**) Extensions to the OSPF routing protocol that support multicast. MOSPF allows unicast and multicast routers to interoperate, but does not support tunneling as does DVMRP. Contrast with *DVMRP* and *PIM*.

**most significant digit**    The leftmost, non-zero digit in a number. It is the digit with the greatest value in the number.

**MOT**    (**O**penView **M**anaged **O**bject **T**oolkit) An OpenView toolkit from HP for developing network management applications based on CMIS. The toolkit contains library routines that handle the transmission and receipt of CMIS requests and responses.

**motherboard**    Also called the "system board," it is the main printed circuit board in an electronic device, which contains sockets that accept additional boards. In a personal computer, the motherboard contains the bus, CPU and coprocessor sockets, memory sockets, keyboard controller and supporting chips.

Chips that control the video display, serial and parallel ports, mouse and disk drives may or may not be present on the motherboard. If not, they are independent controllers that are plugged into an expansion slot on the motherboard.

**M**

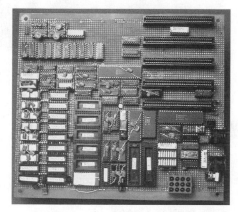 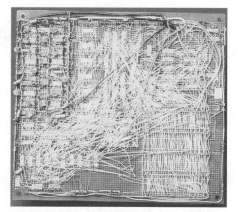

**The Mother of All Motherboards**
This is the front and the back of the prototype of the first IBM PC motherboard in 1981. The chips are wired together on a "breadboard" designed for making new system boards. *(Images courtesy of International Business Machines Corporation. Unauthorized use not permitted.)*

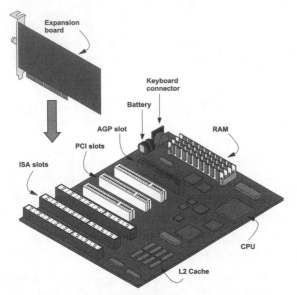

Expansion
board

Keyboard
connector

Battery

AGP slot

RAM

PCI slots

ISA slots

CPU

L2 Cache

**Motherboard**
This is a Baby AT style motherboard for a PC. The adapter cards
(expansion boards) plug into the expansion slots on the motherboard.

**The Motif GUI**
Motif is the de facto standard graphical interface for the UNIX world today.
*(Screen shot courtesy of The Santa Cruz Operation, Inc.)*

**mother glass**    A large, fabricated glass substrate that is cut into individual units for LCD and gas plasma flat panel displays.

**Motif**    The graphical user interface (GUI) endorsed by the Open Software Foundation. It has become the standard graphical interface for UNIX. Motif, Windows and Mac are the three major GUIs. See *Open Group*.

**motion capture**    The entering of a movement pattern into the computer. For example, if a person, hooked up to sensors, goes through the act of batting a ball, that motion trail can be used to simulate a more realistic baseball player in the computer.

**Capturing Live Motion in Realtime**
The ULTRATRAK PRO system from Polhemus provides a series of wearable sensors that captures motion in six degrees of freedom (6DOF). The sensors connect via Ethernet, and the ULTRATRAK PRO software interfaces with 3-D animation programs to provide realtime capture of the person's movements. *(Image courtesy of Polhemus, Inc.)*

**motion path**    In computer graphics, the path to be followed by an animated object.

**motion video**    Refers to moving video images, but does not imply a frame rate. Full-motion video refers to fluid, TV-like images displayed at a rate of 24 to 30 frames per second.

**Motorola**    (Motorola, Inc., Schaumburg, IL, www.motorola.com) A leading manufacturer of semiconductor devices, electronics, telecommunications and satellite systems. Founded in Chicago, IL in 1928 by Paul V. Galvin as Galvin Manufacturing Corporation, its first product allowed radios to operate from household current instead of batteries. In the 1930s, the company commercialized car radios under the Motorola brand suggesting "sound in motion." In 1937, it introduced a line of home radios and its first two-way radio products. By 1947, its Motorola brand became so popular that the company changed its name to match.

Motorola's first semiconductor plant was operating in 1953, and by the 1960s, the company was a leader in semiconductors, communications and consumer electronics. It produced its first integrated circuits in 1960 and its first microprocessor in 1974, the same year that it sold its color TV business.

In the computer industry, Motorola is widely known for its 68000 and PowerPC microprocessor families. It is also one of the world's largest suppliers of microcontrollers (computers on a single chip). The company has more than 40,000 items in its product line used in a myriad of radio, communications, automotive, industrial and consumer applications.

**The Galvin Brothers**
This picture of Paul Galvin (left) and his brother Joseph was taken circa 1930. *(Image courtesy of Motorola Museum of Electronics.)*

**America Was Driving to Music**
In 1930, Motorola produced the first commercially-successful car radio, which had to be installed by the dealer. By the early 1940s, Motorola was becoming a household word. *(Images courtesy of Motorola Museum of Electronics.)*

**mount** To cause a file on a remote workstation or server to be available for access locally. For example, in NFS (Network File System), a server maintains a list of its directories that are available to clients. When a client mounts a directory on the server, that directory and its subdirectories become part of the client's directory hierarchy. See *automounting.*

**MOUS** See *Microsoft certification.*

**The First Mouse**
Invented by Doug Engelbart in the early 1960s while at Stanford Research Institute (now SRI), the device employed two moving wheels 90 degrees apart. This is how most mice are still made except that the wheels are inside, and the ball moves the wheels. *(Image courtesy of The Bootstrap Institute.)*

**mouse** The most popular pointing device. It was called a mouse because it more or less resembled one, with the cord being the mouse's tail. Graphical interfaces (GUIs) are designed to be used with pointing devices, but key commands may be substituted. However, graphics applications, such as CAD and image editing, demand a mouse-like device. On a PC, the mouse generally connects to a serial port via a 9-pin DB or PS/2 connector.

Mouse movement is relative. The cursor moves from its existing location. The mouse could be moved across your arm, and the screen cursor would move as well. The mouse-like object on a graphics tablet, which is correctly called the "tablet cursor" or "puck" is not relative. It contacts the tablet with absolute reference. Placing it on the upper-left part of the tablet moves the screen cursor to the corresponding location.

After years of use by millions of users, it is now widely known that mice can be hazardous to your health. Many applications require endless clicking and dragging to accomplish tasks. Continuous use puts enormous stress on the wrist, and constant double-clicking can be the most strenuous function. See *pointing device, mechanical mouse, optical mouse, serial mouse, bus mouse, mickey* and *carpal tunnel syndrome.*

**mouse emulator**    Hardware or software for the disabled that simulates mouse movement and/or clicking. Various devices are available that let head and body movement perform operations. See *dwell software* and *accessibility*.

**mouse miles**    The distance your mouse travels when using the computer. You might be amazed at the number of miles you can rack up especially when surfing the Web. There are programs on the market that track mouse miles.

**mouse pad**    A fabric-covered rubber pad roughly 9" square that provides a smooth surface for rolling a mouse. There are also mouse pads than provide a better surface; for example, 3M makes the Precise Mousing Surface, an ultra-thin mouse pad that is engineered to reduce friction.

**mouse port**    A socket in the computer into which a mouse is plugged. The mouse port on a laptop PC uses a PS/2 connector, which is a 6-pin Mini-DIN socket. On desktop PCs, the serial port is typically used for the mouse, not a mouse port. On a Macintosh, the ADB connector is used.

### Apple Desktop Bus Connector (ADB)

5/16"

The Apple Desktop Bus (ADB) is used to connect keyboards, mice, trackballs, tablets and other devices to the computer.

**mouse potato**
See *click potato*.

**mouse trails**    The creation of repeating, trailing images of the pointer when it moves across the screen in order to make it more visible on passive matrix screens. See *submarining*.

### Mouse Trails
On a passive matrix screen, mouse trails are left when an object, such as this pointer, is moved quickly across the screen.

**MOV**    **(1)** (Metal Oxide Varistor) A discrete electronic component that diverts excessive voltage to the ground and/or neutral lines. See *MOV surge suppression*.

**(2)** An assembly language instruction that moves (copies) data from one location to another. See *move*.

**move**    **(1)** In programming, to copy data from one place in memory to another. At the end of the move, source and destination data are identical. For example, MOV is an assembly language instruction for move.

**(2)** In word processing and graphics, to relocate text and images to another part of the document or drawing. Also an operating system function that relocates files and folders on the hard disk.

**moved to Atlanta**    Slang for a 404 error on the Web, which is a link to a missing page. The area code for Atlanta, Georgia is 404. See *404 error*.

**moves-adds-changes**    Typically refers to the network administration necessary when users or network components are added to, removed from or change their location in the network.

**movie file**    A file that contains full-motion, digital video, such as an AVI file.

Odometer [MILES]    0.0094

Odometer [INCHES]    474

Odometer [FEET]    57.9

### Mileage Statement
**Mileage Statement for 102 Feet**
*You've traveled the following distances*
**Landmarks**
* You are on climb 1 of **The Brooklyn Bridge**. You have traveled 102 feet of the 1,595 feet total. You're 6.39 percent of the way.
* You are on climb 1 of **The Grand Canyon**. You have traveled 102 feet of the 5,280 feet total. You're 1.93 percent of the way.
* You are on jump 1 of **The Hoover Dam**. You have traveled 102 feet of the 726 feet total. You're 14.05 percent of the way.

### Mouse Odometer
Introspect Software's Mouse Odometer lets you keep track of your mouse miles (or feet, inches, etc.) and also lets you know how you fare compared to a whole bunch of distance landmarks. The "I Want To" button takes you to all the options. *(Screen shot courtesy of Introspect Software, www.introspectsoftware.com)*

### PC Mouse Connectors

DB-9

5/16"

6-pin Mini-DIN
(PS/2 connector)

Mice are generally attached to PCs via the serial port using a 9-pin DB connector or via the PS/2 port, which uses a 6-pin Mini-DIN connector.

**MOV surge suppression**    The most common type of surge suppression technology in which the surge energy is diverted to neutral and/or ground. The metal oxide varistor (MOV) is the component that shunts the surge to the neutral and ground lines. Contrast with *series mode surge suppression*.

**Mozart**    A screen scraper from Mozart Systems Corporation, Burlingame, CA, (www.mozart.com), that is used to turn a character-based mainframe screen into a Windows or DOS front end via 3270 emulation. It is noted for being able to easily combine multiple terminal screens into one. Mozart was originally named "Enter 3270".

**Mozilla**    The code name for Netscape Navigator and Netscape's first alligator-like mascot. It stood for "Mosaic Killer." Mosaic was the Web browser that caused the Web to become popular, which was created by the same people that later founded Netscape.

In early 1998, Netscape Communicator was made free of charge, and its source code was also made available to the developer world. An internal group within Netscape, entitled "mozilla.org," was created to act as a central clearing house for improvements made to Communicator by third parties. For more information, visit www.mozilla.org.

**MP**    See *multiprocessing* and *PPP*.

**MP3**    (MPEG Audio Layer 3) An audio compression technology that is part of the MPEG-1 and MPEG-2 specifications. Developed in Germany in 1991 by the Fraunhofer Institute, MP3 uses perceptual audio coding to compress CD-quality sound by a factor of 12, while providing almost the same fidelity. MP3 music files are played via software or a physical player that cables to the PC for transfer.

MP3 has made it feasible to download quality audio from the Web very quickly, causing it to become a worldwide auditioning system for new musicians and labels. Established bands post sample tracks from new albums to encourage CD sales, and new bands post their music on MP3 sites in order to develop an audience.

Copyrighted music is also offered for a fee, or sometimes for free, creating a major legal issue. MP3 has revolutionized music distribution, since an hour of near CD-quality audio can be downloaded in five minutes. Major publishers are trying to cope with this phenomenon by introducing copyright protection (see *SDMI* and *Windows Media Rights Manager*).

There are numerous MP3 "rippers" and encoders on the market that pull out raw audio data from a music CD and encode it into the MP3 format. For more information, visit www.mp3.com. See *AAC*, *perceptual audio coding* and *Napster*.

**The Rio MP3 Player**
Diamond Multimedia pioneered the handheld MP3 market with its Rio player, which debuted with a maximum of 32MB of flash memory in September 1998. Numerous MP3 devices have since been developed by a variety of companies. *(Image courtesy of SONICblue.)*

**MP3 file sharing**    See *Napster*.

**MP3 player**    A software utility or hardware device that plays audio files encoded in MPEG Audio Layer 3. See *MP3*.

**Mpact chip**    A programmable media processor from Chromatic Research, Sunnyvale, CA (www.mpact.com), that provides parallel processing of audio, video and graphics. Introduced in 1997, software from Chromatic enables the chip to perform DVD control, video (MPEG-1 and 2), Dolby Digital audio, wavetable audio, 2-D and 3-D graphics and modem operations. In the Mpact 2, 3-D functions are hard-wired into the chip. Mpact is licensed to semiconductor manufacturers for implementation.

**MPC**    (Multimedia PC) Earlier hardware requirements for running multimedia and obtaining certification in order to use the MPC insignia on a product. Specified by the Multimedia PC working group of the Software Publishers Association, three levels were developed, all of which seem archaic by today's standards. For example, the minimums for MPC and MPC2 levels were a 3MB 386SX and 4MB 486SX. Dell was the first to be MPC3 certified in 1997. Since then, PCs have become much more powerful, and the specification has no relevance today.

**MPEG**    (Moving Pictures Experts Group) Pronounced "em-peg." An ISO/ITU standard for compressing video. MPEG is a lossy compression method, which means that some of the original image is lost during the compression stage, which cannot be recreated. MPEG-1, which is used in CD-ROMs and Video CDs, provides a resolution of 352x288 at 30 fps with 24-bit color and CD-quality sound. Most MPEG boards also provide hardware scaling that boosts the image to full screen. MPEG-1 requires 1.5 Mbps bandwidth.

MPEG-2 supports a wide variety of audio/video formats, including legacy TV, HDTV and five channel surround sound. It provides the broadcast-quality image of 720×480 resolution that is used in DVD movies. MPEG-2 requires from 4 to 15 Mbps bandwidth. MPEG-3 never came to fruition.

MPEG-4 is the next-generation MPEG that goes far beyond compression methods. Instead of treating the data as continuous streams, MPEG-4 deals with audio/video objects (AVOs) that can be manipulated independently, allowing for interaction with the coded data and providing considerably more flexibility in editing. MPEG-4 supports a wide range of audio and video modes and transmission speeds. It also deals with intellectual property (IP) and protection issues.

For the best playback, MPEG-encoded material requires an MPEG board, and the decoding is done in the board's hardware. It is expected that MPEG circuits will be built into future computers. If the computer is fast enough (400MHz Pentium, PowerPC, etc.), the CPU can decompress the material using software, providing other intensive applications are not running simultaneously.

MPEG uses the same intraframe coding as JPEG for individual frames, but also uses interframe coding, which further compresses the video data by encoding only the differences between periodic key frames, known as I-frames.

A variation of MPEG, known as Motion JPEG, or M-JPEG, does not use interframe coding and is thus easier to edit in a nonlinear editing system than full MPEG. MPEG-1 uses bandwidth from 500 Kbps to 4 Mbps, averaging about 1.25 Mbps. MPEG-2 uses from 4 to 16 Mbps. See *MP3, JPEG* and ***DVx chip***.

**MPEG decoder**   Software or hardware that decompresses MPEG data into viewable form. The results are not exactly the same as the orginal video image, because MPEG is a lossy compression method. See *MPEG*.

**MPE/iX**   (MultiProgramming Executive/POSIX) A POSIX-compliant multitasking operating system that runs on HP's 3000 series, the models of which are now known as e3000 midrange servers. The earlier non-POSIX version of the OS was called MPE. See *HP 3000*.

**MPG**   The extension used on the MPEG file format. See *MPEG*.

**MPK**   (MultiProcessor Kernel) The kernel in Netware starting with NetWare 5, which is natively SMP based. An SMP-based NLM can run in the MPK no matter whether the computer has one or multiple CPUs. See *NetWare* and *NetWare 5*.

**MPLamdaS**   See *MPLS*.

**MPLS**   (1) (MultiProtocol Label Switching) A specification for layer 3 switching from the IETF. Similar to Cisco's tag switching, MPLS uses labels, or tags, that contain forwarding information, which are attached to IP packets by a router that sits at the edge of the network known as a label edge router (LER). The routers in the core of the network, known as label switch routers (LSRs), examine the label more quickly than if they had to look up destination addresses in a routing table.

When fully implemented on the Internet, MPLS is expected to deliver the quality of service (QoS) required to adequately support realtime voice and video, as well as service level agreeements (SLAs) that guarantee bandwidth. Following in the tradition of the "dumb network," MPLS enables more decisions to be made at the periphery of the network. See *dumb network* and *Diffserv*.

(2) (MultiProtocol Lamda Switching) In a WDM optical networking system, it is the ability to route a data transmission based on the wavelength of light that carries it. The routing device only analyzes wavelengths (light frequencies) to make its forwarding decision rather than inspecting fields within each packet. The correct spelling of this term is with the Greek "L" for Lamda. See *lamda* and *WDM*.

**MPOA**   (MultiProtocol Over ATM) An ATM Forum standard that provides routing of legacy protocols (IP, IPX, etc.) over ATM networks. MPOA separates the routing processing from the actual forwarding. A route server performs the routing calculations and sends its results to the ATM switches and edge devices which perform high-speed forwarding of the packets. See *virtual routing, I-PNNI* and *IP Switch*.

**MPOFR**     (MultiProtocol Over Frame Relay) A standard for forwarding SNA and LAN traffic over a wide area frame relay network. MPOFR (also known as RFC 1490) followed DLSw, which was a de facto standard; however, MPOFR was widely adopted at the onset.

**MPP**     (Massively Parallel Processing or Massively Parallel Processor) A multiprocessing architecture that uses up to thousands of processors. Some might contend that a computer system with 64 or more CPUs is a massively parallel processor. However, the number of CPUs is not as much the issue as the architecture. MPP systems use a different programming paradigm than the more common symmetric multiprocessing (SMP) systems used as servers.

In an MPP system, each CPU contains its own memory and copy of the operating system and application. Each subsystem communicates with the others via a high-speed interconnect. In order to use MPP effectively, an information processing problem must be breakable into pieces that can all be solved simultaneously. In scientific environments, certain simulations and mathematical problems can be split apart and each part processed at the same time. In the business world, a parallel data query (PDQ) divides a large database into pieces. For example, 26 CPUs could be used to perform a sequential search, each one searching one letter of the alphabet.

To take advantage of more CPUs in an MPP system means that the specific problem has to be broken down further into more parallel groups. However, adding CPUs in an SMP system increases performance in a more general manner. Applications that support parallel operations (multithreading) immediately take advantage of SMP, but performance gains are available to all applications, simply because there are more processors. For example, four CPUs can be running four different applications. See *SMP*.

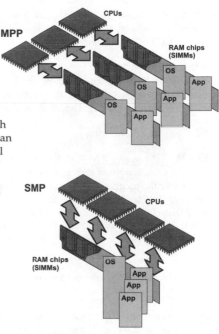

**MPP and SMP Architecture**
In MPP operation, the problem is broken up into separate pieces, which are processed simultaneously. In SMP, CPUs are assigned to the next available task or thread that can run concurrently.

**MPPC**     (Microsoft Point-to-Point Compression) A data compression method from Microsoft that is used to reduce the amount of data sent over a virtual private network (VPN) and thus speed up transmission. See *MPPE*.

**MPPE**     (Microsoft Point-to-Point Encryption) An encryption method from Microsoft that is used to secure virtual private network (VPN) transmissions. See *MPPC*.

**MPPP**     (MultiLink **PPP**) An extension to the point-to-point protocol that enables two channels to be linked together to double the throughput. It is used for ISDN transmission and channel bonding. See *PPP*, *ISDN* and *channel bonding*.

**MPR**     (MultiProtocol Router) Software from Novell that provides router capabilities for its NetWare servers. It supports IPX, IP, AppleTalk and OSI protocols, as well as all the major LANs and WANs.

**MPR II**     The Swedish government standard for maximum video terminal radiation. The earlier MPR I is less stringent. See *TCO*.

**MPS**     (MultiProcessing Specification) A specification from Intel for designing SMP-based PCs using its Pentium processors. It defines how memory and interrupts are shared.

**MPU**     (MicroProcessor Unit) Same as *microprocessor*.

**MPU-401**     A MIDI standard from Roland Corporation that has become the de facto interface for connecting a personal computer to a MIDI device.

**MQ**    (Message Queue) See *MQSeries* and *messaging middleware*.

**MQFP**    See *QFP*.

**MQSeries**    Messaging middleware from IBM that allows programs to communicate with each other across all IBM platforms, Windows, VMS and a variety of UNIX platforms. Introduced in 1994, it provides a common programming interface (API) that programs are written to. The MQ stands for Message Queue. See *messaging middleware*.

**MQSeries Integrator**    Extensions to IBM's MQSeries from New Era of Networks, Inc., Englewood, CO (www.neonsoft.com). It adds routing and formatting to IBM's messaging transport system. NEONrules evaluates the content of messages and routes them to the approriate application. NEONformatter restructures the data into the format required by the target application. See *NEON e-Biz Integrator*.

**MR**    See *magnetoresistive*.

**MRAM**    (Magnetic **RAM**) A non-volatile memory technology that uses magnetic, thin film elements on a silicon substrate. Data is written and read by pulsing wires that are perpendicular to each other with one set above and the other below the magnetic bits. In most MRAM designs, the magnetic orientation is linear (north or south). In VMRAM (Vertical MRAM) designs, the magnetic elements are washer-shaped like the early magnetic cores, and the magnetic direction is clockwise or counter clockwise.

In the development stages by IBM, Intel, HP and others, MRAM is expected to become commercially viable in the mid-2000s. It is expected to initially replace flash memory, but has the potential of replacing SRAM and DRAM chips in the future. See *core storage*.

**MRCI**    (Microsoft Realtime Compression Interface) The programming interface for Microsoft's DoubleSpace technology used in DOS 6.

**MRP**    (Material Requirements Planning) An information system that determines what assemblies must be built and what materials must be procured in order to build a unit of equipment by a certain date. It queries the bill of materials and inventory databases to derive the necessary elements. See *MRP II*.

**MRP II**    (Manufacturing Resource Planning II) An information system that integrates all manufacturing and related applications, including decision support, material requirements planning (MRP), accounting and distribution. See *MRP* and *ERP*.

**ms**    (1) (MilliSecond) See *space/time*.
     (2) (MS) See *Microsoft* and *messaging system*.

**MSA**    (Metropolitan Service Area) An urban area with at least 50,000 people plus surrounding counties. There are 306 MSAs and 428 RSAs in the U.S. MSAs and RSAs are used to allocate cellular licenses.

**MSAA**    (MicroSoft Active Accessibility) A software interface that lets a Windows application be designed for the visually impaired. It enables each object (window, dialog box, etc.) in the user interface to identify itself so a screen reader can be used. See *screen reader*.

**MS Access**    See *Microsoft Access*.

**MSAP**    (MultiService Access Platform) An integration device located on a carrier's premises that supports a variety of protocols. It acts like a central switch between all of the customer's communications technologies and the carrier side, which is the PSTN, the Internet and other available data networks. An MSAP supports a variety of copper (DS1-DS3) and optical (OC3-OC192) connections.

**MSa/s**    (MegaSAmples per Second) A measurement of sampling rate in millions of samples per second.

**MSAudio**    A compression method from Microsoft for delivering high-quality audio over the Internet. MSAudio competes with the MP3 method. See *MP3*.

**MSC**    **(1)** (MacNeal-Schwendler Corporation, Los Angeles, CA www.macsch.com). Founded in 1963 by Richard H. MacNeal and Robert G. Schwendler, MSC is the world's largest provider of mechanical computer aided engineering (MCAE) strategies, software and services. It is the largest single provider of finite element analysis (FEA) products and a leader in FEA pre- and post-processing. MSC products have played a key role in the design of almost every major automobile, aircraft and space vehicle developed in the 1990s.

**(2)** (**M**obile **S**witching **C**enter) The GSM equivalent of an MTSO (Mobile Telephone Switching Office). See *MTSO*.

**(3)** (**M**essage **S**equence **C**hart) A diagramming technique used to describe the message interchange between entities in a system. The MSC language is the Z.120 Recommendation from the ITU. An MSC is similar to a UML Sequence Diagram. See *UML*.

**MSCDEX**    (**M**icro**S**oft **CD**-ROM **EX**tensions) See *CD-ROM Extensions*.

**MSCS**    See *Microsoft Cluster Server*.

**MSD**    (**M**icro**S**oft **D**iagnostics) A utility that accompanies Windows 3.1 and DOS 6 that reports on the internal configuration of the PC. A variety of information on disks, video, drivers, IRQs and port addresses is provided.

**MSDN**    (**M**icro**S**oft **D**eveloper **N**etwork) A subscription service from Microsoft for software developers. It includes technical documentation and news, patches and fixes for existing products and beta copies of upcoming releases.

**MS-DOS**    (**M**icro**S**oft-**D**isk **O**perating **S**ystem) A single user operating system for PCs from Microsoft. It is functionally identical to IBM's PC-DOS version, except that starting with DOS 6, MS-DOS and PC-DOS each provide different sets of auxiliary utility programs. Both MS-DOS and PC-DOS are called DOS. See *DOS*.

**MSDOS.SYS**    One of two hidden system files that make up Microsoft's MS-DOS. The other is IO.SYS. These two system files are loaded into memory when the computer is booted. They process the instructions in CONFIG.SYS, then load COMMAND.COM and finally process the instructions in AUTOEXEC.BAT. The PC-DOS counterparts of these system files are IBMBIO.COM and IBMDOS.COM.

In Windows 95/98, MSDOS.SYS is a text configuration file rather than an executable program. It determines among other things whether the computer boots into DOS or into Windows 95/98. IO.SYS is still a binary executable that is loaded when the computer is booted.

**MSI**    (**M**edium **S**cale **I**ntegration) Between 100 and 3,000 transistors on a chip. See *SSI, LSI, VLSI* and *ULSI*.

**MSIE**    See *Microsoft Internet Explorer*.

MSC BasicSequence

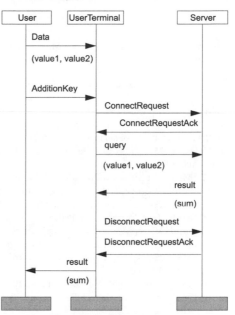

**Message Sequence Chart**
This MSC shows the simple sequence of adding two values and summing the results. This chart was created in the Telelogic Tau SDL suite. *(Diagram courtesy of Telelogic, AB, www.telelogic.com)*

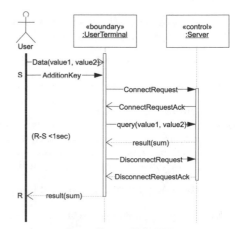

**Same Example in UML**
This is the Sequence Diagram in UML, which is very similar to the MSC example. See *UML* for more diagrams. *(Diagram courtesy of Telelogic, AB, www.telelogic.com)*

**MS Mail**   See *Microsoft Mail*.

**MSMQ**   See *Microsoft Message Queue Server*.

**MSN**   See *Microsoft Network*.

**MS-Net**   (MicroSoft Network) Microsoft's version of PC-Network introduced in 1985. It was not widely used. See *PC Network*.

**MSO**   (Multiple System Operator) A major cable TV organization that has franchises in multiple locations.

**MSP**   (1) (Management Service Provider or Managed Service Provider) An organization that manages a customer's computer systems and networks which are either located on the customer's premises or at a third-party datacenter. MSPs offer a variety of service levels from just notifying the customer if a problem occurs to making all necessary repairs itself. MSPs may also be a source for hardware and staff for its customers. For information, visit www.mspassociation.org.

(2) (Microsoft Solution Provider) A Microsoft certification for qualifying resellers that sell and provide training and support on Microsoft products. A certain number of employees must be Microsoft Certified Professionals.

(3) A Microsoft Paint graphics file format.

(4) (Multi-Tech Supervisory Protocol) A simultaneous voice and data (SVD) protocol from Multi-Tech Systems, Inc., Mounds View, MN. When a telephone handset is picked up, the modem switches to packet mode, digitizes the voice and interleaves the voice packets with the data packets. See *SVD*.

(5) (Media Suite Pro) A popular Macintosh-based nonlinear video editing system from Avid Technologies, Tewksbury, MA.

(6) An operating system used in Fujitsu IBM-compatible mainframes.

(7) (Multiprocessing Server Pack) A utility that enables LAN Manager to utilize a computer's multiprocessing capabilities.

**mSQL**   (Mini SQL) A relational DBMS that runs on a variety of UNIX servers as well as Windows and OS/2. It uses a subset of ANSI SQL as the query language in order to keep it compact and provide rapid access. Scripting languages such as W3-mSQL (which comes with mSQL), PHP and MsqlPerl are used to access the database from Web pages, and programming languages such as C can be used as well. The database can also be accessed using the mSQL prompt via Telnet.

mSQL was developed in 1994 by David J. Hughes for a Ph.D. research project. It was later commercialized by his Queensland, Australia-based company, Hughes Technologies, (www.hughes.com.au). See *PHP*.

**MS SQL**   See *Microsoft SQL Server* and *mSQL*.

**MS SQL Server**   See *Microsoft SQL Server*.

**MSVBVMxx.DLL**   (MicroSoft Visual Basic Virtual Machine [xx=version #].DLL) The Visual Basic runtime module starting with VB 5. MSVBVMxx contains necessary runtime functions and also provides the interpreter for Visual Basic applications that are compiled to bytecode rather than native machine code. All Visual Basic applications prior to VB 5, and optionally in VB 5, are compiled into an intermediate "bytecode" language, which the runtime module turns into machine language on the fly. See *VBRUNxxx.DLL* and *Visual Basic*.

**MS Virtual Machine**   See *Microsoft Virtual Machine*.

**MSW**   (MicroSoft Word) See *Microsoft Word*.

**MS-Windows**   (MicroSoft Windows) See *Windows*.

**MS Word**   See *Microsoft Word*.

**MS-Works**   See *Microsoft Works*.

**MTA**    **(1)** (Message Transfer Agent) The store and forward part of a messaging system. See *messaging system*.
**(2)** See *M Technology Association*.

**MTBF**    (Mean Time Between Failure) The average time a component works without failure. It is the number of failures divided by the hours under observation.

**MTBSO**    (Mean Time Between Service Outages) The average time a network is working without failure. It is the number of failures divided by the hours under observation.

**M Technology Association**    (M Technology Association, Silver Spring, MD, www.mtechnology.org) Formerly the MUMPS Users Group, it is an organization that supports the M community through training, meetings and distribution of publications and software.

**MTF**    **(1)** (Modulation Transfer Function) A measurement of monitor sharpness. MTF compares the contrast ratio between alternating black and green lines that are one pixel thick.
**(2)** (Microsoft Tape Format) A backup tape format developed by Seagate Software and Microsoft. It is able to identify operating system-specific data.

**MTOPS**    (Million Theoretical Operations Per Second) A measurement of a computer's cryptographic performance in decoding a secret message. For example, a 600MHz Pentium III yields approximately 1,400 MTOPS. Although widely used, MTOPS is a rather imprecise measurement, as are MIPS, FLOPS and other such gauges of performance.

**MTS**    **(1)** See *Microsoft Transaction Server*.
**(2)** (Modular TV System) The stereo channel added to the NTSC standard, which includes the SAP audio channel for special use.

**MTSO**    (Mobile Telephone Switching Office) An operations center that connects the landline PSTN system to the mobile phone system. It is also responsible for compiling call information for billing and handing off calls from one cell to another.

**MTTR**    (Mean Time To Repair, Mean Time To Restore) The average time it takes to repair a failed component.

**MTU**    **(1)** (Maximum Transmission Unit, Maximum Transfer Unit) The largest frame size that can be transmitted over the network. Messages longer than the MTU must be divided into smaller frames. The layer 3 protocol (IP, IPX, etc.) extracts the MTU from the layer 2 protocol (Ethernet, FDDI, etc.), fragments the messages into that frame size and makes them available to the lower layer for transmission.
**(2)** (Multi-Tenant Unit) A building with multiple offices or apartments. MTUs are more economical to target for installing DSL and other broadband links than single-occupancy offices or houses. See *MDU* and *BLEC*.

**MUA**    (Mail User Agent) See *messaging system*.

**MUCK**    See *MUD*.

**MUD**    (MultiUser Dungeon, MultiUser Dimension, MultiUser Dialogue) Interactive games played by several people on the Internet. Originally dungeons and dragon games with demons, elves and magicians, MUDs have been created for science fiction themes, cartoon characters and other types of games. MUDs have also evolved into 3-D virtual reality sites.
There are many variations and permutations of MUDs. MOOs are object-oriented MUDs, and MUSEs (Multiuser Shared Environments) are generally designed for elementary and secondary students. A MUSH (MultiUser Shared Hallucination) allows new rooms and situations to be created. A MUCK (MultiUser Chat Kingdom) is a text-based MUD system similar to MUSH, and there is yet another MUCK (MultiUser Construction Kit), heavy on fantasy and myth. See *avatar* and *VRML*.

**MUG**    (Macintosh User Group) There are many Macintosh user groups throughout the world.

M

**mu-Law**   A North American standard for converting analog data into digital form using pulse code modulation (PCM). Mu-Law uses a companding technique that provides more quantizing steps at lower amplitude (volume) than at higher amplitude. North America and Japan use mu-Law, while Europe uses A-Law. Mu-Law comes from μ-Law, which uses the Greek letter μ, pronounced "myoo." See *PCM* and *A-Law*.

**Multibank DRAM**   See *MDRAM*.

**MULTIBUS**   An advanced bus architecture from Intel used in industrial, military and aerospace applications. It includes message passing, auto configuration and software interrupts. MULTIBUS I is 16-bits; MULTIBUS II is 32-bits.

**multicast**   **(1)** In communications networks, to transmit a message to multiple recipents at the same time. Multicast is a one-to-many transmission similar to broadcasting, except that multicasting implies sending to a list of specific users, whereas broadcasting implies sending to everybody. Contrast with *unicast*. See *IP multicast*.

**(2)** In digital television broadcasting, to send multiple channels of programming over the allotted bandwidth for digital transmission rather than one high-definition TV (HDTV) signal.

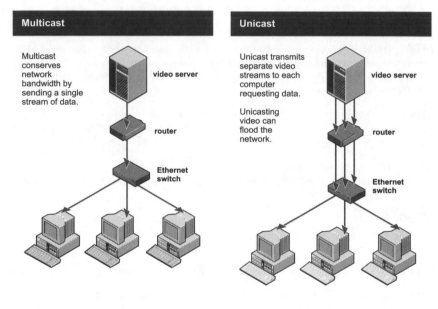

**multicast backbone**   See *Mbone*.

**multicast IP**   See *IP multicast*.

**multicast routing protocol**   A routing protocol that supports multicast packets (one to many). See *DVMRP*, *MOSPF* and *PIM*.

**multichip module**   See *MCM*.

**multicomputer**   A computer made up of several computers. The term generally refers to an architecture in which each processor has its own memory rather than multiple processors with a shared memory. See *parallel computing*.

**MULTICS**   (**MULT**iplexed **I**nformation and **C**omputing **S**ervice)  Developed at MIT and Bell Labs in the mid-1960s, MULTICS was the first timesharing operating system. It was used on GE's mainframes, which were absorbed into the Honeywell product line, later acquired by Bull.

**multidimensional database**   See *OLAP*.

**multidimensional query**   Asking for a multidimensional view of data.

**multidimensional spreadsheet**   See *spreadsheet*.

**multidimensional views**    Looking at data in several dimensions; for example, sales by region, sales by sales rep, sales by product category, sales by month, etc. Such capability is provided in numerous decision support applications under various function names. For example, in a spreadsheet or database, a pivot table provides these views and enables quick switching between them. See *OLAP*.

**multidrop line**    See *multipoint line*.

**MultiFinder**    The part of earlier Macintosh operating systems that allowed multiple programs to be open at the same time and cooperatively multitasked. Its use was optional as many earlier Macs had limited memory. MultiFinder was prevalent in System 6 and became part of Finder in System 7, at which time it lost its identity as a separate element. See *Finder*.

**multifrequency monitor**    A monitor that adjusts to all frequencies within a range (multiscan) or to a set of specific frequencies, such as VGA and Super VGA.

**multifunction drive**    A storage drive that reads and writes more than one type of storage medium. For example, a magneto-optic disk drive can be used for rewritable disks as well as write-once disks. A Floptical drive can read and write floppy disks as well as Floptical disks.

**multifunction printer**    See *MFD*.

**multihomed**    Connected to two or more networks or having two or more network addresses. For example, a network server may be connected to a serial line and a LAN or to muliple LANs. A Web server might be connected to two different ISPs for fault tolerance.

**multilaunch**    To open the same application that is stored in a server simultaneously in two or more clients.

**multilayer optical disk**    See *multilevel optical disk*.

**multilayer switch**    See *layer 3 switch*.

**multilevel optical disk**    An optical disk technology that uses multiple platters sandwiched together with a tiny spacer between them. The different layers are accessed by moving the lens up and down and focusing on one of the disk surfaces. IBM demonstrated this technology in 1994 at its Almaden Research Center in San Jose, CA, and showed its feasibility with various optical technologies. It is expected that, in time, all optical disks, including audio CDs and CD-ROMs, will employ multilevel technology to increase storage capacity.

**multiline**    A cable, channel or bus that contains two or more transmission paths (wires or optical fibers).

**Multilink PPP**    See *PPP*.

**multilocation extension dialing**    An IN (Intelligent Network) service that allows an extension number to be assigned to individuals so they can be reached no matter where they are.

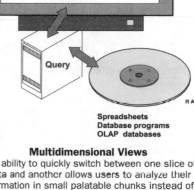

Multidimensional views (pivot table)

By product

By region

By sales rep

Query

RAM

Spreadsheets
Database programs
OLAP databases

**Multidimensional Views**
The ability to quickly switch between one slice of data and another allows users to analyze their information in small palatable chunks instead of a giant report that is confusing.

M

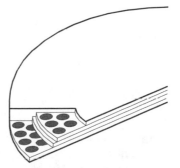

**Multilevel Optical Disk**
Using multiple layers of recording within the disc's surface yields higher capacities. Using two layers, the DVD disc provides the equivalent storage of 14 CD-ROMs per side.

**multimastering**   See *bus mastering*.

**MultiMate**   A DOS word processing program that was popular during the 1980s. It was noted for its similarity to the Wang word processing system. Developed by MultiMate International Corporation, it was acquired by Ashton-Tate in 1985.

**multimedia**   Disseminating information in more than one form. It includes the use of text, audio, graphics, animated graphics and full-motion video. Multimedia programs are typically games, encyclopedias and training courses on CD-ROM. However, any application with sound and/or video can be called a multimedia program. See *hot topics and trends* and *MPC*.

**MultiMediaCard**   A flash memory card from SanDisk that provides storage for small handheld devices such as cellphones and pagers. The ultra-small (32×24×1.4mm) MultiMediaCard, which weighs less than two grams, was introduced in late 1997 with a 4MB capacity. The card is also made with ROM chips for storing static information. See *SD Memory Card*.

**MultiMediaCard Module**
MultiMediaCard modules are tiny and can provide storage for the smallest handheld devices. See *flash memory* for size comparison.

**multimedia conferencing**   See *videoconferencing* and *data conferencing*.

**Multimedia Extensions**   Windows routines that support audio recording and playback, animation playback, joysticks, MIDI, the MCI interface for CD-ROM, videodiscs, videotapes, etc., and the RIFF file format. See also *MMX*. See *MPC*.

**multimedia monitor**   A monitor that contains built-in speakers. In time, multimedia monitors are expected to contain a built-in camera for videoconferencing.

**multimedia PC**   A PC that includes stereo sound and a CD-ROM or DVD drive. See *MPC* and *multimedia upgrade kit*.

**multimedia upgrade kit**   A package of hardware and software that turns a standard PC into a multimedia PC. It includes a CD-ROM drive, sound card, speakers and cable, the appropriate software drivers and may contain multimedia applications. See *CD-ROM audio cable*.

**multimode fiber**   An optical fiber with a core diameter of from 50 to 100 microns. It is the most commonly-used optical fiber for short distances such as LANs. Light can enter the core at different angles, making it easier to connect the light source to broader light sources such as LEDs. However, light rays travel down multiple reflective paths in multimode fiber, causing modal dispersion, which is a broadening of the pulses at the receiving end. Contrast with *singlemode fiber*. See *dispersion* and *fiber optics glossary*.

**multipath**   Refers to a radio signal that winds up taking two or more paths because the signal is reflected off buildings or other obstructions. Ghosts on a TV channel are an example of multipath.

**MultiPlan**   One of the first spreadsheets. Developed by Microsoft, it was first used on CP/M machines, which predated the IBM PC.

**multiple inheritance**   In object-oriented programming, a class that can contain more than one parent. Contrast with *single inheritance*.

**Multiple Master**   A font technology from Adobe that allows a typeface to be generated in different styles, from condensed to expanded and from light to heavy. Multiple Master can generate fonts that are more optically correct at both extremes in size from very small to very large than standard Type 1 fonts.

**multiple platforms**    Two or more operating environments, which typically include the CPU family and operating system. For example, if versions of a program run on Windows and the Macintosh, the software is said to support multiple platforms. That application is also known as a cross platform application.

A program that runs on all versions of Windows (3.1, 95, 98 and NT) is sometimes said to support multiple platforms. Although Windows operating systems all stem from the same core, 32-bit Windows programs (95, 98 and NT) will not run under Windows 3.1, and many Windows 3.1 programs behave poorly under 95, 98 and NT. See *cross platform*.

**multiplexer**    See *multiplexor* and *multiplexing*.

**multiplexing**    Transmitting multiple signals over a single communications line or computer channel. The two common multiplexing techniques are FDM, which separates signals by modulating the data onto different carrier frequencies, and TDM, which separates signals by interleaving bits one after the other.

**multiplexor**    In communications, a device that merges several low-speed transmissions into one high-speed transmission and vice versa. Contrast with *inverse multiplexor*.

**multiplexor channel**    A computer channel that transfers data between the CPU and several low-speed peripherals (terminals, printers, etc.) simultaneously. It may have an optional burst mode that allows a high-speed transfer to only one peripheral at a time.

**multiple zone recording**    See *ZBR*.

**multiplier-accumulator**    A general-purpose floating point processor that multiplies and accumulates the results of the multiplication. Newer versions also perform division and square roots.

**multiplier lock**    A feature built into a CPU chip that prevents it from being overclocked (run at a higher speed). See *overclock*.

**M**

**multipoint**    Refers to a communications line (network) that provides a path from one location to many. A cell phone is an example of a multipoint system. See *multipoint line*. Contrast with *point-to-point*.

**multipoint conferencing**    Same as *teleconferencing*. This is a rather redudant phrase, because conferencing implies three or more participants, rather than point-to-point between two people.

**multipoint control unit**    See *MCU*.

**multipoint line**    In communications, a single line that interconnects three or more devices.

**multiport bridge**    A bridge with more than two ports. There is little difference between a multiport bridge and a switch, such as used to switch Ethernet packets, except that the multiport bridge may introduce some overhead. The switch must be able to maintain the full wire speed of the medium between any two ports.

**multiported memory**    A type of memory that provides more than one access path to its contents. It allows the same bank of memory to be read and written simultaneously. See *video RAM*.

**multiport repeater**    A hub in a 10BaseT network is often known as a multiport repeater, because it sends any input signal to all outputs. See *10BaseT*.

**multiport serial card**    A circuit board that contains multiple serial ports for connection to modems or other serial devices. The serial port is used as an interface by a many different kinds of sensors and data collection terminals in a variety of industrial and medical applications.

**Multiprise**    A family of System/390 entry-level to medium-scale mainframes from IBM that use microprocessor-based CMOS technology. They house the control units, channels and hard disks in the same cabinet similar to midrange servers. The first Multiprise models were introduced in 1996. See *IBM mainframes*.

**multiprocessing**  Simultaneous processing with two or more processors in one computer, or two or more computers processing together. When two or more computers are used, they are tied together with a high-speed channel and share the general workload between them. If one fails, the other takes over.

It is also accomplished in special-purpose computers, such as array processors, which provide concurrent processing on sets of data. Although computers are built with various overlapping features, such as executing instructions while inputting and outputting data, multiprocessing refers specifically to concurrent instruction executions. See *parallel processing*, *SMP*, *MPP*, *CMP*, *bus mastering* and *fault tolerant*.

**multiprocessor**  Multiple processors. A multiprocessor machine uses two or more CPUs for routine processing. See *multiprocessing*.

**multiprogramming**  Same as *multitasking*.

**multiprotocol router**  A router that supports two or more communications protocols, such as IPX, TCP/IP and DECnet. It is used to switch network traffic between different LANs located throughout the enterprise as well as to switch LAN traffic to WANs.

**multipurpose cadastre system**  An integrated land information system containing legal (e.g., property ownership or cadastre), physical (e.g., topography, man-made features), and cultural (e.g., land use, demographics) information in a common and accurate reference framework. The reference framework typically is established with rigorous geodetic and survey control standards, such as the state plane and latitude/longitude coordinate systems. The Cadastre is made up of multiple independent, interrelated layers commonly used to describe the graphic component of a GIS database. Each layer contains a set of homogeneous map features registered positionally to other database layers through a common coordinate system. Data is separated into layers based on logical relationships and the graphic portrayal of sets of features. (Data West Research Agency definition: see **GIS glossary**.)

**MultiRead drive**  A drive that can read CD-DA, CD-ROM, CD-R and CD-RW disks.

**multiscan monitor**  A monitor that adjusts to all frequencies within a range. See *multifrequency monitor*.

**multiscanning**  See *multifrequency monitor*.

**multiservice switch**  A network switch that not only handles data, but adequately supports the realtime transmission of voice and video.

**multisession**  A compact disc capability in which data is recorded in more than one session. Each subsequent recording session can be linked to the previous so that they all appear as one. Each session adds overhead on the disc, because lead-in and lead-out sectors must be recorded each time, which take up from 13 to 15MB. See *multivolume*, *multisession drive*, *track-at-once*, *disc-at-once* and *CD Extra*.

**multisession drive**  A CD-ROM drive that can read a multisession compact disc. All current CD-ROM drives have this capability. See *multisession*.

**MultiSync monitor**  A family of multiscan monitors from NEC. NEC popularized the multiscan monitor.

**multitapping**  Selecting alphabetic letters on a telephone keypad by pressing the key from one to three times depending on the placement of the letters. For example, the 2 key is also a-b-c. To enter "a," you would press once; for "b," twice, and for "c," three times. See *T9*.

**multitasking**  The running of two or more programs in one computer at the same time. The number of programs that can be effectively multitasked depends on the type of multitasking performed (preemptive vs cooperative), CPU speed and memory and disk capacity.

Programs can be run simultaneously in the computer because of the differences between I/O and processing speed. While one program is waiting for input, instructions in another can be executed. During the milliseconds one program waits for data to be read from a disk, millions of instructions in another program can be executed. In interactive programs, thousands of instructions can be executed between each keystroke on the keyboard.

In large computers, multiple I/O channels also allow for simultaneous I/O operations to take place. Multiple streams of data are being read and written at the exact same time.

In the days of mainframes only, multitasking was called "multiprogramming," and multitasking meant "multithreading."

**multitenant**   See *MDU*.

**multithreading**   Multitasking within a single program. It allows multiple streams of execution to take place concurrently within the same program, each stream processing a different transaction or message. In order for a multithreaded program to be of any value, it must be run in a multitasking or multiprocessing environment, which allows multiple operations to take place.

Certain types of applications lend themselves to multithreading. For example, in an order processing system, each order can be entered independently of the other orders. In an image editing program, a calculation-intensive filter can be performed on one image, while the user works on another. In a symmetric multiprocessing (SMP) operating system, its multithreading allows multiple CPUs to be controlled at the same time. It is also used to create synchronized audio and video applications.

Multithreading generally uses reentrant code, which cannot be modified when executing, so that the same code can be shared by multiple programs.

**multitier application**   An application, in which one part runs on one server and another part runs on another. See *three-tier client/server*.

**multitimbral**   The ability to play multiple instrument sounds (patches) simultaneously. See *MIDI patch* and *timbre*.

**multiuser**   Two or more users.

**Multiuser DOS**   **(1)** A multiuser DOS-compatible operating system from Caldera that supports multiple terminals from a single PC (386 and up). It is distributed mainly through VARs that have modified it for their own purposes. Multiuser DOS evolved out of Concurrent DOS from Digital Research, which was acquired by Novell and later sold to Caldera.

**(2)** (multiuser DOS - generic) A DOS-compatible operating system that supports multiple terminals from a single PC.

**multiuser NT**   Using Windows NT like a central, timeshared computer. Citrix developed this method with its WinFrame software and subsequently worked with Microsoft to create Windows Terminal Server. Since NT is a network operating system (NOS), it already services multiple users (file server, Web server, etc.); however, multiuser NT refers to Windows Terminal Server and Winframe. See *Windows Terminal Server* and *WinFrame*.

**multivariate**   The use of multiple variables in a forecasting model.

**multivolume**   Refers to multiple, independent entities that reside on the same disk or cartridge. For example, using software that supports the feature, a CD-R disc can be recorded in multiple sessions that are retrieved independently of each other and not linked as one. See *multisession*.

**MultiWin**   A multiuser kernel for Windows from Citrix that enables its MetaFrame and WinFrame products to timeshare an application for multiple users. See *MetaFrame* and *WinFrame*.

**MUMPS**   See *M*.

**MUSE**   **(1)** (MultiUser Simulation Environment, MultiUser Shared Environment) See *MUD*.
**(2)** See *BABY*.

**MUSH**   (MultiUser Shared Hallucination) See *MUD*.

**Musicam**   See *5.1 channel*.

**music CD**    Generally refers to an audio CD, otherwise known as "Red Book audio." However, the term could refer to a CD-ROM that contains sound files, such as WAV and MID files.

**music titles**    See *CDDB*.

**Mustang**    The code name for an Athlon CPU chip from AMD that is expected to have large amounts of L2 cache and be introduced in 2001. The core of this CPU may be used in other chips instead.

**mutex**    **(1)** (**MUT**ually **EX**clusive)  A programming flag used to grab and release an object. When data is acquired that cannot be shared or processing is started that cannot be performed simultaneously elsewhere in the system, the mutex is set to "lock," which blocks other attempts to use it. The mutex is set to "unlock" when the data is no longer needed or the routine is finished. See *flag*.

**(2)** (**MU**sic **TEX**)  A package of macros for the TeX typesetting system that supports musical notation.

**mutter machine**    An audio device that plays a background garble for open office spaces. It sounds like a whole bunch of people chatting, but the words are indistinguishable. The constant noise level allows people to feel more privacy on the phone and also helps them feel less isolated when fewer office workers are at their desks. It has also been used by small offices to fake a large, busy company for incoming telephone callers. See *prairie dogging*.

**MUX**    (**MU**ltiple**X**or)  See *multiplexor*.

**MVGA**    (**M**onochrome **VGA**)  The designation is sometimes used for a non-color laptop screen. It should more accurately be called "gray scale VGA," since monochrome means two colors; for example, black and white and no shades in between.

**MVIP**    (**M**ulti**V**endor **I**ntegration **P**rotocol)  A voice bus and switching protocol for PCs originated by a number of companies, including Natural Microsystems of Natick, MA, its major supporter. It provides a second communications bus within the PC that is used to multiplex up to 256 full-duplex voice channels from one voice card to another.

Digital voice, fax, video (any digital data) is bussed over a ribbon cable connected at the top of each ISA, EISA or MicroChannel card. For example, several fax boards could be cabled to a board that multiplexes their lines onto a T1 channel. Using the high bandwidth of this second bus, video conferencing systems are built around MVIP.

MVIP products can make the PC perform like a small-scale PBX. For example, an interactive voice response system on one card could pass incoming voice conversations to a card that switches the lines to live agents in a call center.

The ability to plug a card into a standard AT bus and perform voice and video processing is opening up a whole new world to vendors. It allows far more flexible and affordable systems to be built, and it helps solve worldwide interface problems. A variety of interface cards from different countries can be plugged in, allowing MVIP products to connect to telephone systems all around the world.

**MVP**    (**M**ultimedia **V**ideo **P**rocessor)  A high-speed DSP chip from TI introduced in 1994. Officially introduced as the TMS320C80, it combines RISC technology with the functionality of four DSPs on one chip.

**MVS**    (**M**ultiple **V**irtual **St**orage)  Introduced in 1974, the primary operating system used on IBM mainframes (the others are VM and DOS/VSE). MVS is a batch processing-oriented operating system that manages large amounts of memory and disk space. Online operations are provided with CICS, TSO and other system software.

MVS/XA (MVS/eXtended Architecture) manages the enhancements, including 2GB of virtual memory, introduced in 1981 with IBM's 370/XA architecture.

MVS/ESA (MVS/Enterprise Systems Architecture) manages the enhancements made to large scale mainframes, including 16TB of virtual memory, introduced in 1988 with IBM's ESA/370 architecture. MVS/ESA runs on all models of the System/390 ES/9000 product line introduced in 1990.

In 1996, MVS/ESA was packaged with an extensive set of utilities and renamed OS/390. The name MVS is still used to refer to the base control program in OS/390. See *OS/390*.

**My Computer**    The source of all resource information in a Windows computer, including the drives, printers and control panels. See *Win My Computer*.

**MyEureka**　Corporate portal software from Information Advantage, Inc., Eden Prarie, MN (www.infoadvan.com). MyEureka provides HTML templates and Java-based server applications for developing a corporate intranet. It includes a search engine and repository for linking enterprise-wide information as well as agents that can deliver custom Web pages to different user groups as well as individual news pages to each user.

MyEureka supports Information Advantage's own OLAP and ROLAP products (MyEureka Cube Server and MyEureka ROLAP Server) as well as databases from SAP, PeopleSoft and others. Information Advantage coined the term "business intelligence portal" to define this product family, because it was the first to integrate BI software (query, reporting, OLAP) with the portal framework.

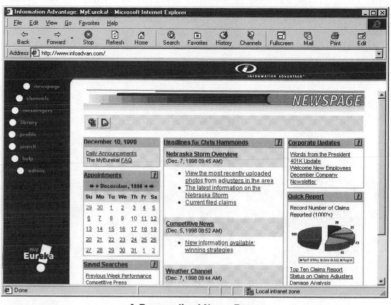

**A Personalized News Page**
MyEureka lets users create a custom Intranet page that delivers news and links to pages and sites of personal interest. Out of the box, MyEureka provides many portal templates that can be readily adapted to your needs. *(Screen shot courtesy of Information Advantage, Inc.)*

**My Network Places**　The source of network information in Windows 2000 and Windows ME. It was previously known as Network Neighborhood. See *Win My Network Places*.

**MYOB**　Digispeak for "mind your own business."

**MySQL**　A version of mSQL. See *mSQL*.

**NACCB** (National Association of Computer Consultant Businesses, Greensboro, NC, www.naccb.resourcecenter.com) An organization representing companies that provide temporary, high-level professional help in the information technology field. Founded in 1987, it is concerned with legislation that affects computer consultants.

**Nacchio's law** "The number of ports and price per port of an IP gateway (analog voice to digital IP) improve by two orders of magnitude every 18 months." By Joseph Nacchio, president and CEO of Qwest Communications and former head of long distance service at AT&T. Economical IP gateways are essential to enable voice over IP to become commonplace. See *Qwest*.

**NACOMEX** (NAtional COMputer EXchange) See *computer exchange*.

**NADN** (Nearest Active Downstream Neighbor) In a token ring network, the station following this station. Contrast with *NAUN*.

**NAEC** See *NetWare certification*.

**nag screen** An advertisement in a shareware program that routinely asks the user to register and pay for the software. Although it generally pops up at the beginning or end of the program, it can appear at certain intervals as it is being used. See *nagware*.

**nagware** Software that periodically prompts the user to register the product. Similar to a nag screen for shareware, nagware is built into a commercial product. See *nag screen*.

**nailed up** In communications, it refers to a permanent connection rather than one that is dynamically created and released. For example, a leased, private, point-to-point line is a nailed-up connection.

**NAK** (Negative AcKnowledgement) A communications code used to indicate that a message was not received, or that a terminal does not wish to transmit. Contrast with *ACK*.

**name delivery** See *CNAM*.

**Named Pipes** An IPC facility in LAN Manager that allows data to be exchanged from one application to another either over a network or running within the same computer. The use of the term pipes for interprocess communication was coined in UNIX.

**name resolution** Converting a name into the address required by a machine or network. In a TCP/IP network, HOSTS and LMHOSTS files are examples of manually keeping host names and IP addresses updated. DNS and WINS are examples of systems that automatically convert names to IP addresses. See *naming service*, *DHCP*, *DNS*, *WINS*, *HOSTS file* and *LMHOSTS file*.

**name server**   A network server that provides a naming, or directory, service. See *DNS*, *naming service* and *directory service*.

**name service**   See *naming service*.

**namespace**   A name or group of names that are defined according to some naming convention. A flat namespace uses a single, unique name for every device. For example, a small Windows (NetBIOS) network requires a different, made-up name for each computer and printer. The Internet uses a hierarchical namespace that partitions the names into categories known as top level domains such as .com, .edu and .gov, etc., which are at the top of the hierarchy. See *Internet domain name* and *XML namespace*.

**naming service**   Software that converts a name into a physical address on a network, providing logical-to-physical conversion. Names can be user names, computers, printers, services or files. The transmitting station sends a name to the server containing the naming service software, which sends back the actual address of the user or resource. The process is known as name resolution.

A naming service functions as a Yellow Pages for the network, which is precisely what Sun's NIS system was originally called. In AppleTalk, the naming service is embedded within the protocol. In the case of the Internet or other IP network, DNS servers and WIN servers return the IP address for the submitted name. See *DNS*, *WINS* and *directory service*.

**N-AMPS**   (Narrow-bandwidth **AMPS**) A version of the analog cellular mobile phone system that uses a narrower bandwidth and provides more calling capacity. See *AMPS* and *D-AMPS*.

**NAND**   (Not **AND**) A Boolean logic operation that is true if any single input is false. Two-input NAND gates are often used as the sole logic element on gate array chips, because all Boolean operations can be created from NAND gates.

| NAND | | |
|------|------|------|
| IN | IN | OUT |
| 0 | 0 | 1 |
| 0 | 1 | 1 |
| 1 | 0 | 1 |
| 1 | 1 | 0 |

**nanny software**   See *parental control software*.

**nano**   Billionth (10 to the –9th power). See *space/time*.

**nanojet**   A tiny nozzle with an orifice only a couple dozen molecules wide. Such tiny "spray guns" are expected to etch circuits some day and could become a major component of *nanotechnology*.

**nanometer**   One billionth of a meter. Nanometers are used to measure the wavelengths of light. See *angstrom* and *metric system*.

**nanosecond**   **(1)** One billionth of a second. Used to measure the speed of logic and memory chips, a nanosecond can be visualized by converting it to distance. In one nanosecond, electricity travels about nine inches in a wire.

Even at 186,000 miles per second, electricity is never fast enough for the hardware designer who worries over a few inches of circuit path. The slightest delay is multiplied millions of times, since millions of pulses are sent through a wire in a single second. In addition, today's chips contain more than a quarter mile of wire traces (current-carrying pathways). Future chips are expected to contain several miles of circuit paths. See *space/time* and *ohnosecond*.

**(2)** The time between a traffic light turning green and a New York City cab driver blowing his horn.

**nanotechnology**   A science that experiments with building devices at the molecular and atomic level. For example, a bit might be represented by only one atom some time in the future. Nanotechnology could be used to build anything, not just computers and communications devices. See *nanojet*.

**nanotubes**   See *buckytubes*.

**NAP**   (Network Access Point) A junction point where major Internet service providers interconnect with each other. Also known as Internet Exchanges (IXs), connection at one or more of these NAPs means "connected to the Internet."

When the Net went commercial in 1995, four official NAPs were created: three run by the telephone companies in San Francisco, Chicago and New York (actually Pennsauken, NJ), and the fourth in Washington, D.C., run by Metropolitan Fiber Systems (MFS) and known as MAE-East (Metropolitan Area Exchange-East). Four more MAEs have become de facto NAPs, plus three historical exchanges (two Federal plus CIX) add up to about a dozen major exchange points within the United States. National ISPs generally connect at all four of the original ones and all MAEs. This is known as public peering.

In addition, due to the congestion at these exchanges, large ISPs agree to peer privately and interconnect with each other at many other points throughout the country where equipment at both companies is conveniently located. Dropping the packet off earlier to the destination backbone eliminates considerable traffic. In late 1995, UUNET, MCI and GTE were the first to begin private arrangements. See *brokered private peering* and *CIX*.

**NAPLPS**    (North American Presentation-Level Protocol Syntax) An ANSI-standard protocol for videotex and teletext. It compresses data for transmission over narrow-bandwidth lines and requires decompression on the receiving end. PRODIGY uses this format for transmitting and displaying some of its graphics.

**Napster**    A music indexing service from Napster, Inc., San Mateo, CA (www.napster.com), that includes an MP3 player (software), chat capability and MP3 file sharing. The application works in conjunction with Napster's Web site, which provides an index to MP3 music files residing on other computers currently logged onto the Internet. The digital music itself is not located on Napster servers, only the directory service. The Napster software is for Windows, and Macster and GNapster are versions for Mac and Linux.

Napster has been quite a controversial venture. The music industry sued the company, claiming it is losing millions in royalties from copyrighted material being shared around the world. Napster lost the case in July 2000 and was about to be shut down, except for a last minute stay from the Circuit Court of Appeals. Subsequently, Napster and Bertelsmann, parent of BMG music, agreed to partner so that Napster could be developed into a paid subscription service that would monitor all transfers and pay royalties to the record label companies. In February 2001, the Appeals Court decided that Napster had to remove the titles of all copyrighted material from its service. Stay tuned! See *Gnutella*.

**narrowband**    In communications, transmission rates from 50 bps 64 Kbps. Earlier uses of the term referred to 2,400 bps or less or to sub-voice grade transmission from 50–150 bps. Contrast with *wideband* and *broadband*.

**narrowcast**    To transmit data to selected individuals. Contrast with *broadcast*.

**NAS**    (1) (Network Attached Storage) A specialized file server that connects to the network. A NAS device contains a slimmed-down (microkernel) operating system and file system and processes only I/O requests by supporting popular file sharing protocols such as NFS (UNIX) and SMB (DOS/Windows). Using traditional LAN protocols such as Ethernet and TCP/IP, the NAS enables additional storage to be quickly added by plugging it into a network hub or switch. As network transmission rates have increased from Ethernet to Fast Ethernet to Gigabit Ethernet, NAS devices have come up to speed parity with direct attached storage devices.

Some general-purpose computers using a full-blown operating system such as Windows or UNIX are labeled as NAS products, but the true NAS is built from scratch as a dedicated file I/O device. See *SAN* and *NetApp Filer*.

(2) See *network access server* and *Netscape Application Server*.

(3) (Network Application Support) Digital's umbrella term for its open systems support that enabled a wide variety of workstations and PCs to interface to VAX and ULTRIX servers.

**A NAS Box**
Network Appliance popularized the network attached storage (NAS) device. Sophisticated units such as this one can hold terabytes of storage and provide mission-critical reliability for large enterprises. *(Image courtesy of Network Appliance, Inc.)*

**NASI**    (1) (NetWare Asynchronous Service Interface) A protocol from Novell for connecting to modems in a communications server. It was derived from the NCSI protocol. NASI provides more advanced features than the common int 14 (interrupt 14) method. It allows a specific modem or line to be chosen. It frees the call more quickly, and it transfers data more efficiently.

(2) (National Association of Systems Integrators, Falmouth, MA, www.nasi-info.com) An organization of more than 10,000 members founded in 1991, dedicated to exchanging up-to-date information on members' products and services. Its annual Computer Industry Buying Guide in print and on disk includes suppliers and services.

**NAT**   (Network Address Translation) An IETF standard that allows an organization to present itself to the Internet with one address. NAT converts the address of each LAN node into one IP address for the Internet, and vice versa. It also serves as a firewall by keeping individual IP addresses hidden from the outside world. See *proxy server*.

**National Cristina Foundation**   (National Cristina Foudation, Stamford, CT, www.cristina.org) A not-for-profit public charity that seeks donations of used or excess computers. Founded in 1984 by Yvette Marrin and Bruce McMahan, it was named in honor of McMahan's daughter, Cristina, who has cerebral palsy. Donations are directed to programs that rehabilitate people with disabilities, students at risk of failing and the economically disadvantaged. The foundation has helped hundreds of thousands of individuals in the U.S. and abroad. See *how to donate old equipment*.

**National Office Machine Dealers Association**   See *BTA*.

**National Semiconductor**   (National Semiconductor Corporation, Santa Clara, CA, www.national.com) A major semiconductor manufacturer that provides system-level products for telecommunications, desktop computers, automobiles, consumer products and the military. Founded in 1959 in Danbury, CT, National Semiconductor was in the forefront of the first transistors and integrated circuits. Over the years, it has become known for its analog and mixed mode signaling devices. In 1987, it acquired Fairchild Semiconductor, which it sold in 1997, the same year it merged with Cyrix Corporation.

**native application**   An application designed to run in the computer environment (machine language and OS) being referenced. The term is used to contrast a native application with an interpreted one, such as a Java application that is not native to a single platform. The term may also be used to contrast a native application with an emulated application, which was originally written for a different platform.

**native capacity**   The raw capacity of a device. The storage capacity of many backup tapes is published as compressed storage in order to sound larger. It is typically expressed as twice the native capacity. The actual capacity may be less than or exceed the published figure, because different data compress at different rates. Text files generally compress to about 40% of their original size, but other files may not compress nearly as well.

**native format**   The file format that an application normally reads and writes. The native format of a Microsoft word document is different than a WordPerfect document, etc. The problem is that there are tons of et ceteras. Even image editing programs, which are designed to read and convert a raft of different graphics file types, have their own built-in native format. For example, in order to build an image in layers, Photoshop converts foreign images into its native, layered file format (.PSD extension). Contrast with *foreign format* and *file format*.

**native language**   Same as *machine language*. See *native mode*.

**natively**   See *native mode*.

**native mode**   (1) The normal running mode of a computer, executing programs from its built-in instruction set. Contrast with *emulation mode*.

(2) The highest performance state of a computer, such as a 486 or Pentium running in Protected Mode.

**NATURAL**   A fourth-generation language from Software AG, Reston, VA, that runs on a variety of computers from micro to mainframe.

**natural language**   English, Spanish, French, German, Japanese, Russian, etc.

**natural language query**   A query expressed by typing English, French or any other spoken language in a normal manner. For example, "how many sales reps sold more than a million dollars in any eastern state in January?" In order to allow for spoken queries, both a voice recognition system and natural language query software are required.

**natural language recognition**   Same as *voice recognition*.

**NAU**   (1) (Network Access Unit) An interface card that adapts a computer to a local area network.

**English Wizard Query Builder**

How many customers buy both meat and dairy products?

Dictionary Construct | Dictionary Map | Dictionary Editor | Show SQL | Show Echo | Set Date

**Common Words...**
how many
how much
in
in each
is
list
maximum
minimum
not
of
of each
or
over
print
show
sort

**Tables and Columns:**
Categories
Customers
Employees

**Values:**

Query    OK

**English Wizard's Interpretation**

Show SQL | Show Echo | Pause | Copy | Close

```
SELECT count(*) as "Count"
FROM "CUSTOMERS"
WHERE (exists(SELECT
"CATEGORIES"."Category_Name",
"CUSTOMERS"."LAST_NAME",
"CUSTOMERS"."FIRST_NAME",
"CUSTOMERS"."COMPANY_NAME",
"PRODUCTS"."Product_Name" FROM "ORDERS",
"LINE_ITEMS", "PRODUCTS", "CATEGORIES" WHERE
("Category_Name"='Meat') and "CUSTOMERS"."CUST_ID"
= "ORDERS"."CUST_ID" and "ORDERS"."ORDER_ID" =
"LINE_ITEMS"."ORDER_ID" and
"PRODUCTS"."Product_ID" =
"LINE_ITEMS"."PRODUCT_ID" and
"CATEGORIES"."Category_ID" =
"PRODUCTS"."Category_ID")) and exists(SELECT
"CATEGORIES"."Category_Name",
"CUSTOMERS"."LAST_NAME",
"CUSTOMERS"."FIRST_NAME",
"CUSTOMERS"."COMPANY_NAME",
"PRODUCTS"."Product_Name" FROM "ORDERS",
"LINE_ITEMS", "PRODUCTS", "CATEGORIES" WHERE
("Category_Name"='Dairy') and "CUSTOMERS"."CUST_ID"
= "ORDERS"."CUST_ID" and "ORDERS"."ORDER_ID" =
"LINE_ITEMS"."ORDER_ID" and
"PRODUCTS"."Product_ID" =
"LINE_ITEMS"."PRODUCT_ID" and
"CATEGORIES"."Category_ID" =
"PRODUCTS"."Category_ID"))
```

**A Natural Language Example**
EasyAsk's English Wizard generated the SQL code in the window at the bottom from the English sentence at the top. It is amazing how much SQL is necessary to ask what looks like a simple question.
*(Screen shot courtesy of EasyAsk, Inc.)*

**(2)** (**N**etwork **A**ddressable **U**nit) An SNA component that can be referenced by name and address, which includes the SSCP, LU and PU.

**NAUN** (**N**earest **A**ctive **U**pstream **N**eighbor) In a token ring network, the station that precedes this station. When the network beacons, the NAUN initiates the beacon removal process. Contrast with *NADN*. See *beacon removal*.

**navigable database** The database designed and prepared for Intelligent Vehicle Highway Systems to support such systems for "smart cars" and "smart highways." These databases contain first the geometry element layer of the roadway that contains links, nodes, shape points, relative elevations, and connectivity. The second navigation element layer contains physical and logical classification of the roadway environment, directionality, dividers, barriers, turn restrictions, freeway exit numbers, exact freeway sign text speed limits, and others. Additional element layers include points of interest, path, geopolitical, cartography, geocoding, and special commercial/business listings. (Data West Research Agency definition: see *GIS glossary*.)

**navigate** "Surfing the Web." To move from page to page on the Web.

**navigation bar** A set of buttons or graphic images typically in a row or column used as a central point that link you to major topic sections on a Web site. If the navigation bar is a single graphic image with multiple selections, it is known as an imagemap. See *imagemap*.

**navigation key** A keyboard key used to move the pointer around on the screen. They include the four arrow keys, PAGEUP, PAGEDOWN, HOME and END keys.

**N**

**navigation system** A GPS-based system in a car for automatic directions to a programmed destination. See *GPS*.

**Navigator** See *Netscape Navigator* and *Norton Navigator*.

**Naviken** A format used for geographic databases that originated in Japan. Naviken CD-ROMs have become a de facto standard for car navigation maps. See *GPS*.

Home  Features  Examples  Download demo  Order  Multiuser  Support  Contact us  Online
*Computer Desktop Encyclopedia is the premier reference about the computer industry.*

**A Typical Navigation Bar**
As the screen pointer is moved across the bar, the individual elements typically change color or shading. In this example, the pointer is over Download Demo. Clicking each element of the bar switches you to a different page on the Web site.

**NB card**    (NuBus card)  See *NuBus*.

**NBS**    (National Bureau of Standards)  See *NIST*.

**NC**    See *network computer* and *numerical control*.

**NCA**    (Network Computing Architecture)  An architecture from Oracle for developing applications within a networked computing environment. It provides a three-tier distributed environment based on CORBA that uses program components known as "cartridges."  NCA is managed by Oracle Enterprise Manager software that integrates clients with processes running in application and database servers.

**NCB**    (Network Control Block)  A packet structure used by the NetBIOS communications protocol.

**NCF file**    (NetWare Command File)  A file of NetWare commands that are executed one at a time, similar to a DOS batch (.BAT) file. The NetWare AUTOEXEC.NCF file is executed in the server at startup, just like the DOS AUTOEXEC.BAT file.

**NCGA**    (National Computer Graphics Association)  A Fairfax, Virginia–based organization dedicated to developing and promoting the computer graphics industry. It maintained a clearinghouse for industry information. NCGA closed its doors in 1996.

**NCI**    See *Liberate*.

**NCITS**    See *ITI*.

**NC machine**    See *network computer* and *numerical control*.

**NCOS**    (Network Computer Operating System)  The operating system in Oracle's network computer. See *Network in a Box*.

**NCP**    **(1)** (Network Control Program)  See *SNA* and *network control program*.

**(2)** (NetWare Core Protocol)  The file sharing protocol used in a NetWare network. It is the internal NetWare language used to communicate between client and server and provides access to files and the NDS and bindery directory services. See *file sharing protocol*.

**(3)** (Not Copy Protected)  Software that can be easily copied.

**NCR**    (NCR Corporation, Dayton, OH, www.ncr.com)  A major manufacturer of computers and financial terminals. It was founded in 1884 when John Henry Patterson purchased National Manufacturing Company of Dayton, Ohio, and renamed it National Cash Register. It became the leading cash register company and, by 1911, had sold its one-millionth machine.

Starting in the 1930s, NCR made accounting machines that posted customer accounts and became successful in the banking and retail industries, in which it has remained ever since.

In 1957, it introduced the "304" transistorized computer. It accepted data from NCR cash registers and banking terminals via paper tape. The 304 was very reliable and widely accepted.

NCR computer lines have included the Century series (1960s), Criterion series (1970s) and the V and

**John H. Patterson**
Patterson was the consumate salesman and built a small empire as machinery was first introduced into the commercial world at the end of the nineteenth century. *(Image courtesy of NCR Corporation.)*

**An Early Cash Register**
These were marvelous machines when first introduced, because they could tally the day's receipts automatically. *(Image courtesy of NCR Corporation.)*

I series (1980s). Starting in 1982 with the UNIX- and Motorola 68000–based Tower series, NCR embraced open systems and industry standards. In 1990, the x86-based System 3000 series was introduced, a complete line from desktops to massively parallel machines running DOS, Windows and OS/2 at the low end and UNIX at the high end. The desktop line was later dropped.

In 1991, AT&T acquired the company and ran it as a wholly owned subsidiary, renaming it AT&T Global Information Systems (AT&T GIS) in early 1994. The NCR name did remain on ATM and POS terminals, as well as microelectronics and business forms. In 1996, AT&T GIS was spun off of AT&T and renamed NCR, and it became an independent company once again.

**The NCR 304**
Introduced in 1957, the 304 was NCR's first computer. Using paper tape from NCR cash registers as input, it was very reliable and widely accepted. *(Image courtesy of NCR Corporation.)*

**NC Reference Profile**    (Network Computer Reference Profile) See *network computer*.

**NCRP**    (Network Computer Reference Profile) The specification for network computer compliance established by Oracle and endorsed by Sun, IBM and others. The first version of this specification was known as the NC1 Reference Profile. See *network computer*.

**NCR paper**    (No Carbon Required paper) A multiple-part paper form that does not use carbon paper. The ink is adhered to the reverse side of the previous sheet.

**NCSA**    **(1)** (National Center for Supercomputer Applications, Urbana-Champaign, IL, www.ncsa.uiuc.edu) A high-performance computing facility located at the University of Illinois at Urbana-Champaign. Founded in 1985 by a National Science Foundation grant, the NCSA provides supercomputer resources to hundreds of universities and organizations engaged in scientific research. It was also the birthplace of the first Web server (HTTPd) and the Mosaic browser.

**(2)** (National Computer Security Association) See *ICSA*.

**NCSC**    (National Computer Security Center) The arm of the U.S. National Security Agency that defines criteria for trusted computer products. Following are the Trusted Computer Systems Evaluation Criteria (TCSEC), DOD Standard 5200.28, also known as the Orange Book, and the European equivalent. The Red Book is the Orange Book counterpart for networks.

Level D is a non-secure system. Level C provides discretionary access control (DAC). The owner of the data can determine who has access to it.

**C1:**  Requires user log-on, but allows group ID.

**C2:**  Requires individual user log-on with password and an audit mechanism.

Levels B and A provide mandatory access control (MAC). Access is based on standard DOD clearances. Each data structure contains a sensitivity level, such as top secret, secret and unclassified, and is available only to users with that level of clearance.

**B1:**  DOD clearance levels.

**B2:**  Guarantees path between user and the security system. Provides assurances that system can be tested and clearances cannot be downgraded.

**B3:**  System is characterized by a mathematical model that must be viable.

**A1:**  System is characterized by a mathematical model that can be proven. Highest security. Used in military computers.

**European Ratings** The European Information Technology Security Evaluation Criteria (ITSEC) is similar to TCSEC, but rates functionality (F) and effectiveness (E) separately.

```
Orange
Book
TCSEC    ITSEC
D        E0
C1       F-C1, E1
C2       F-C2, E2
B1       F-B1, E3
B2       F-B2, E4
B3       F-B3, E5
A1       F-B3, E6
```

**NCSI** (Network Communications Services Interface) Also called "nixie," it is a protocol used to handle serial port communications on a network. NCSI applications talk to the NCSI driver rather than directly to the COM port, which allows redirection of the data to a communications server on the network. See *NASI*.

**NCTP** (Next Compatible Tape Product) A tape drive from Philips Laser Magnetic Storage, Colorado Springs, CO, (www.philipslms.com), that supports legacy 3480 and 3490e cartridges, as well as 18GB NCTP cartridges. The NCTP cartridges, which use the same housing, are bright green on the bottom for easy recognition.

**NDA** (Non Disclosure Agreement) An agreement signed between two parties that have to disclose confidential information to each other in order to do business. In general, the NDA states why the information is being divulged and stipulates that it cannot be used for any other purpose. NDAs are signed for a myriad of reasons, including when source code is handed to another party for modification or when a new product under development is being reviewed by the press, a prospective customer or other party.

**n-dimensional** Some number of dimensions. See *multidimensional views*.

**NDIS** (Network Driver Interface Specification) A network driver interface from Microsoft. See *network driver interface*.

**NDMP** (Network Data Management Protocol) An initiative from Network Appliance and IntelliGuard Software to develop an open standard for backing up data in a heterogeneous environment. NDMP uses a common data format that is written to and read from drivers for the specific disk and tape devices. NDMP also provides for control of libraries.

**NDPS** (Novell Distributed Print Services) A full-featured printing protocol co-developed by Novell, Xerox and HP that provides print services on NetWare file servers. NDPS supports bi-directional capability with sophisticated features, enabling, for example, a low-toner situation to e-mail the toner supplier before the toner runs out. NDPS relies on NetWare's bindery or NDS directories to identify printer resources on the network. It is the successor to Novell's Queue Management Services (QMS) printing protocol (see *QMS*).

Based on the SNMP and ISO 10175 open standards, NDPS runs as an NLM on a NetWare server, and the client part runs under Windows. It supports QMS and LPR/LPD, plus a third-party "gateway" to interface with other printing protocols. Starting with NetWare 5, JetDirect and Xerox protocols are included in NDPS. NDPS first shipped as an option for NetWare 4 in late 1997.

**nDRAM** See *RDRAM*.

**NDS** (Novell Directory Services) Novell's flagship directory service that is included in NetWare beginning with Version 4. It is also available for Windows NT and Solaris. NDS maintains a hierarchical database of information about the network resources within a global enterprise, including networks, users, subgroups, servers, volumes and printers. Unlike the bindery, which was the directory service in NetWare 3.x, NDS users log onto the network as a whole, not a specific server, and NDS determines their access rights.

NDS is based on the X.500 directory standard and is LDAP compliant. Novell provides the NDS source code free of charge to developers that wish to integrate it into their products. In NDS, every network resouce is called an "object," and each object contains properties (fields). For example, a user object would contain login ID, password, name, address, telephone and node address.

**NE1000**    An 8-bit Ethernet network adapter from Novell that became a de facto standard. Many earlier Ethernet adapters were NE1000 compatible. The NE2000 is the 16-bit version.

**nearest neighbor**    See *point sampling.*

**near field optics**    An optical recording technology in which the distance between the read/write head and the bit (spot, pit, etc.) is less than the diameter of the bit (wavelength of light). See *Terastor.*

**near letter quality**    See *NLQ.*

**nearline**    (NEAR onLINE) Available within a short amount of time, but not instantly. Tape and disk libraries are considered nearline devices, because it takes several seconds to retrieve the appropriate cartridge before it can be read. Contrast with *online.*

**near online**    See *nearline.*

**near pointer**    In an x86 segmented address, a memory address within a single segment (the offset). Contrast with *far pointer.*

**NEAT chipset**    (New Enhanced AT chipset) A chipset used to build AT-class machines from Chips and Technologies, Inc.

**NEBS compliant**    (Network Equipment Building Systems compliant) Adhering to standards from Bellcore for equipment used in telco central offices (COs). It provides stringent specifications for durability, grounding, cables and hardware interfaces.

**NECT**    (NEC Technologies, Inc., Itasca, IL, www.nec.com) The North American subsidiary of NEC that specializes in imaging peripherals, including monitors, data projectors, printers and CD-ROM drives. In 1986, NECT introduced its MultiSync line, the first multifrequency monitors, which have become very popular. In 1996, the CromaClear line of monitors was introduced that combines the aperture grille and shadow mask into a new CRT technology for improved resolution.

NECT's parent company was founded in Tokyo in 1899 as Nippon Electric Company, Ltd., which was renamed NEC Corporation in 1983. NEC was the first Japanese company to joint venture with a foreign enterprise, which was Western Electric Company, then part of AT&T. Throughout the twentieth century, NEC has been involved with electrical, communications, electronics and computer products worldwide.

**negative logic**    The use of high voltage for a 0 bit and low voltage for a 1 bit. Contrast with *positive logic.*

**nematic**    The stage between a crystal and a liquid that has a threadlike nature; for example, a liquid crystal. See *crystalline* and *LCD.*

**nemonic**    See *mnemonic.*

**neo-Luddism**    Having a Luddite philosophy in the Internet age. See *Luddite.*

**neo-Luddite**    A Luddite in the Internet age. See *Luddite.*

**NEON e-Biz Integrator**    An application integration system from New Era of Networks, Inc., Englewood, CO (www.neonsoft.com). It includes a messaging transport (messaging middleware), business rules software that determines how to route transactions between applications and a formatting module that rearranges the data as required. e-Biz Integrator provides application adapters for a variety of legacy systems and also supports XML and EDI. See *MQSeries Integrator* and *messaging middleware.*

**NeoPlanet**    A Web browser from NeoPlanet Inc., New York (www.neoplanet.com), that uses certain core modules from Internet Explorer. IE Version 3.02 or greater must be installed in your computer to use it. NeoPlanet is noted for its complete customizability, allowing you to change the look and sound of the interface. A version that requires Netscape is also expected. The browser may be downloaded from NeoPlanet's Web site.

**neper**    The unit of measurement based on Napierian logarithms that represents the ratio between two values, such as current or voltage.

**Neptune chipset**    See *Intel chipsets*.

**nerd**    A person typically thought of as dull socially. Nerds are often bookworms that like technical work and are generally introspective. Synonymous with *geek*, *nerd bird* and **entreprenerd**.

**nerd bird**    An airplane that regularly flies a high-tech route, such as between San Jose, California, and Seattle, Washington. See *nerd*.

**nerd rustler**    A recruiter that specializes in placing computer people. Same as *computercruiter*.

**nerdspeak**    Same as *geekspeak* and *Geekonics*.

**NEST**    (Novell Embedded Systems Technology) Extensions to NetWare 4.x that provide networking to office machines and consumer products. Originally touted as a connectivity protocol for everything from a VCR to a TV, NEST has been primarily used in millions of print servers and some fax servers, implementing Novell's QMS printing protocol.

**nesting**    **(1)** In programming, the positioning of a loop within a loop. The number of loops that can be nested may be limited by the programming language. See *loop*.

**(2)** In a folder hierarchy, it refers to storing a folder inside another folder. You can nest folders inside of folders ad infinitum, but it becomes more unwieldy to retrieve them. See **Win Folder organization**.

**net**    Abbreviation of network. "The Net" generally refers to the Internet.

**Net2phone**    (Net2phone, Inc., Newark, NJ, www.net2phone.com) A Web-to-phone service that provides Internet telephony around the globe. It also provides PC-to-PC telephony and PC-to-fax service using a browser-based Java applet or stand-alone software for Windows or Mac. Advertisements, which appear on the dialpad, supplement the low domestic and international rates. Net2phone was introduced in 1996 as a division of IDT, a Hackensack, NJ–based telephone reseller and ISP, and then spun off in 1999 as a separate company.

**NET Act**    (No Electronic Theft Act) U.S. Federal legislation passed in December 1997 that covers illegal distribution of software over the Internet. Anybody uploading copyrighted software to a Web site and posting its availability is liable for prosecution. ISPs are also liable if they have been warned to close down a Web page and do not comply. Penalties include up to 10 years in prison and a $250,000 fine.

**First Web-to-Phone**
Launched in 1996, Net2phone was the first Web-to-phone service, which uses advertisers to support its low domestic and international rates. Calls are sent over Net2phone's own Internet backbone for the long haul, adding a large degree of control over the service.
*(Image courtesy of Net2phone, Inc., www.net2phone.com)*

In August 1999, a 22-year-old university student was the first person convicted under the NET Act of making copyrighted software, music recordings and movies available to the general public. See *software piracy* and *SIIA*.

**net address**    See *Internet address*.

**netadmin**    See *network administrator*.

**NetApp**    See *Network Appliance* and *NetApp Filer*.

**NetApp Filer**    A family of network attached storage (NAS) appliances from Network Appliance that are highly scalable to terabytes of data. NetApp Filers are high-performance, mission-critical products used by large enterprises and service providers. Filers use Network Appliance's innovative Data ONTAP microkernel OS and Write Anywhere File Layout file system (WAFL). See *NAS* and *SAN*.

**Net appliance**    See *Internet appliance*.

**NetBeans**    A Java-based development environment (IDE) from Sun that is noted for its features and ease of use. The product is NetBeans Developer, which runs on Windows NT and Solaris. Sun acquired NetBeans in 1999 and rebranded it under the Forte name (Sun acquired Forte in 1999). NetBeans Developer became Forte for Java Community Edition. See *Forte for Java*.

**NetBench**    A benchmark from Ziff-Davis Media that tests the performance of a file server handling requests from Windows clients. NetBench computes the average throughput based on all the client requests. See *ZDBOp*.

**NetBEUI**    (NetBIOS Extended User Interface) Pronounced "net-booey." The transport layer for NetBIOS. NetBIOS and NetBEUI were originally part of a single protocol suite that was later separated. NetBIOS sessions can be transported over NetBEUI, TCP/IP and SPX/IPX protocols. See *NetBEUI network* and *NetBIOS*.

**NetBEUI network**    Pronounced "net-booey." A local area network (LAN) made up of Windows PCs. NetBEUI is the transport protocol supported natively by all versions of Windows, including Windows 3.1. Since NetBEUI is part of the NetBIOS protocol, the terms NetBEUI network, NetBIOS network and Windows network are usually synonymous. Except for HP's JetDirect print servers, almost all other print servers support the NetBEUI protocol for printer sharing over the LAN. See *NetBIOS* and *NetBEUI*.

**NetBIOS**    The native networking protocol in DOS and Windows networks. Although originally combined with its transport layer protocol (NetBEUI), NetBIOS today provides a programming interface for applications at the session layer (layer 5). NetBIOS can ride over NetBEUI, its native transport, which is not routable, or over TCP/IP and SPX/IPX, which are routable protocols.

NetBIOS computers are identified by a unique 15-character name, and Windows machines (NetBIOS machines) periodically broadcast their names over the network so that Network Neighborhood or My Network Places can catalog them. For TCP/IP networks, NetBIOS names are turned into IP addresses via manual configuration in an LMHOSTS file or a WINS server.

There are two NetBIOS modes. The Datagram mode is the fastest mode, but does not guarantee delivery. It uses a self-contained packet with send and receive names, usually limited to 512 bytes. If the recipient device is not listening for messages, the datagram is lost. The Session mode establishes a connection until broken. It guarantees delivery of messages up to 64KB long. See *WINS* and *LMHOSTS file*.

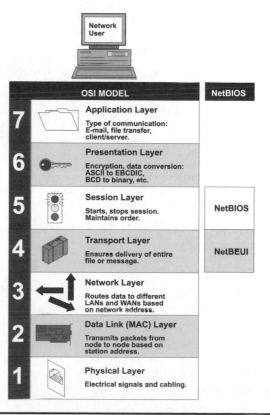

**netbooey**   See *NetBEUI*.

**NetBurst**   The technology used in Intel's Pentium 4 chips. It doubles the instruction pipeline to 20 stages, runs the ALU at twice the core frequency and improves performance in the Level 1 and 2 caches. It provides a 400MHz system bus (frontside bus), which is three times as fast as the bus in the Pentium III. An additional 144 instructions were also added to the instruction set, known as SSE2 (Streaming SIMD Extension 2). See *Pentium 4*.

**NetBus**   A Trojan horse on the Internet that sneaks in under the guise of a game entitled "Whack-A-Mole." It sets up software in your computer that acts as a server to the cracker at a remote client. It informs the client when you are online and enables the charming fellow (it's almost always a male) to take control of your computer and do pretty much anything he wants. See *Trojan horse*.

**NetCache**   A family of Web cache servers from Network Appliance that come in a wide range of sizes for use in branch offices to large service providers. NetCache devices support video on demand and broadcast streaming and use Network Appliance's innovative Data ONTAP microkernel OS and Write Anywhere File Layout file system (WAFL). NetCache supports "split streaming," which, like multicasting, provides a one-to-many transmission enabling one video stream from the Internet to be sent to multiple users at the same time.

**NetCam**   See *WebCam*.

**netcast**   See *Webcast* and *Netscape Netcaster*.

**Netcaster**   See *Netscape Netcaster*.

**Netcenter**   (www.netcenter.com) Netscape's home page and Web portal. It provides Web search facilities, news, white and yellow pages directories, classified ads, free e-mail and a variety of features. There were so many visitors to Netscape's home page that it was later turned into a full-service Web portal.

**NetCool**   A suite of network management tools from Micromuse Inc., San Francisco, CA (www.micromuse.com), that gathers information from a huge variety of network applications and devices. Supporting SNMP and non-SNMP products, NetCool enables organizations to monitor large, heterogeneous networks.

**Netdocs**   (1) The code name for a hosted application suite from Microsoft. Based on its .NET architecture, Netdocs includes e-mail, instant messaging and document creation.
   (2) (NETDOCS) The online documentation for the National Center for Supercomputer Applications (NCSA) networks. See *NCSA*.

**NetDynamics**   (NetDynamics, Menlo Park, CA, www.netdynamics.com) A software company founded in 1995 that specializes in Java-based application servers and development tools. Development products include NetDynamics Studio (integrated environment for developing Java client and server applications) and NetDynamics Java Object Framework (foundation classes and methods). Its NetDynamics Application Server is its core application server, and NetDynamics Command Center provides local and remote administration and control. In 1998, NetDynamics was acquired by Sun.

**netfilter**   See *Web filtering*.

**Netfinity**   A family of Intel-based servers from IBM that run Windows and Linux. In 2000, IBM changed the name of these servers to "xSeries eservers." See *IBM server series*.

**Nethead**   A person involved with data networks or someone that thinks about networking from a packet-switched point of view. Contrast with *Bellhead*.

**netid**   See *IP address*.

**netiquette**   (**NET**work et**IQUETTE**)  Proper manners when conferencing between two or more users on an online service or the Internet. Emily Post may not have told you to curtail your cussing via modem, but netiquette has been established to remind you that profanity is not in good form over the network.

Using UPPER CASE TO MAKE A POINT all the time and interjecting emoticons throughout a message is also not good netiquette. See *flame*.

**Netizen**   A user of the Internet. A Net "citizen."

**Netlib**   A repository of free software, documents and databases of scientific and mathematical interest. Information can be obtained from the Web, via FTP and gopher, and on CD-ROM. The Netlib collection is maintained by the University of Tennessee and Oak Ridge National Labs and is mirrored at sites around the world. For information, visit www.netlib.org.

**netlist**   A list of logic gate and their interconnections which make up a circuit. See *logic synthesis*.

**netmask**   See *subnet mask*.

**NetMeeting**   Collaboration and conferencing software that comes with Internet Explorer and is available separately from Microsoft's Web site. NetMeeting includes point-to-point telephony and videophone capability over the Internet, as well as multipoint whiteboard and application sharing. Starting with Version 2.0, it supports the H.323 standard.

When NetMeeting is started and stopped, it sends messages to one of Microsoft's ILS directory servers. Other NetMeeting users wishing to establish a connection with someone can view the directory to determine who is currently online and available.

**NetNews**   See *Usenet*.

**NetObjects Fusion**   A popular Windows-based Web authoring system from NetObjects, Inc., Redwood City, CA (www.netobjects.com). It provides a visual environment for designing Web pages and can import an existing site. It was one of the first Web authoring programs to apply desktop publishing tools to an entire site. It is also noted for its ability to generate a complex site without writing any lines of code.

**netopath**   (**NET** psych**OPATH**)  Refers to individuals that display a variety of deviant behavior over the Internet, especially hackers that write and unleash damaging viruses. See *cybercrook*.

**NetPC**   (**NET**work PC)  Introduced in 1997, it is a Windows PC that downloads all installations of Windows and applications from the server. The software remains on the hard disk, but program versions are monitored by a management server. Floppy and/or CD-ROM drives are optional and may be restricted to prevent user installations.

NetPCs can alternatively be configured as thin clients, in which case the OS is booted from the network each time it is turned on, and all applications and data come from the server. The local hard disk is used for caching parts of the application during the day to improve performance.

NetPCs must conform to the NetPC Design Guidelines, which include the management capabilities of Intel's Wired for Management Baseline Specification (see *WfM*). Intel's LANDesk Configuration Manager was the first management server to support NetPCs. See *network computer*.

**Net phone**   See *Internet phone*.

**net processor**   See *network processor*.

**Net-savvy**   Knowledge of the Internet. It implies more than being able to occasionally surf the Web and use e-mail. Net-savvy means having the next level or next several levels of Internet/Web skills, which includes downloading files and updating applications, as well as being extremely aware of potential viruses.

**Netscape**   (1) (Netscape Communications Corporation, Mountain View, CA, www.netscape.com)  Part of America Online (AOL), Netscape specializes in World Wide Web software, including the Netscape Navigator Web browser. Founded in 1994 by James Clark, former patriarch of SGI, and Marc Andreessen, who, along with Eric Bina, created the

Mosaic browser at the University of Illinois, Netscape quickly became the number one topic of conversation as Internet and Web fever enveloped the nation in the mid-1990s.

Netscape seriously impacted the status quo. Its stock was catapulted to a market cap of more than two billion before the company ever made a dime, making it one of the most successful public offerings in stock market history. Netscape forced Microsoft into restructuring its entire product line to become Internet compliant. Microsoft reacted so strongly to Netscape that it developed a browser and Web server that it gave away for free and then built it into Windows 98. As a result, Netscape was forced to give away its browser, which resulted in the Microsoft antitrust trial. In 1999, while the trial was still taking place, Netscape was acquired by AOL. See *AOL*.

**(2)** Netscape's Web browser, which is Netscape Navigator. Most people refer to Navigator as simply "Netscape." For example, the phrase "IE and Netscape" means Internet Explorer (Microsoft's browser) and Netscape Navigator, the two most-popular browsers.

**Netscape Application Builder**   A development environment for Netscape Application Server that allows for the creation of multi-tiered applications and the automatic generation of Enterprise JavaBeans, servlets and SQL queries, etc. See *Netscape Application Server*.

**Netscape Application Server**   A Web-based application server from the Sun-Netscape Alliance that supports C, C++ and Java applications, Java servlets, JavaServer Pages (JSPs) and Enterprise JavaBeans. In 2000, Netscape Application Server was superseded by iPlanet Application Server. See *iPlanet Application Server*, *Netscape Application Builder* and *Netscape Extension Builder*.

**Netscape color palette**   A palette of 216 colors that Netscape displays the same on its Windows and Mac browsers. If other colors are used in images, Netscape will dither them, and the results will differ between the platforms.

**Netscape Communicator**   A suite of Web browsing and groupware tools from Netscape that were packaged as a bundle starting with Navigator 4.0. Communicator includes the Navigator browser, Netscape Messenger e-mail client, Netscape Collabra threaded discussions, Netscape Composer HTML editor and Netscape Conference—which provides audio and videoconferencing, whiteboard, text chat and collaborative browsing. The Professional version adds group calendaring and scheduling, remote administration and 3270 emulation. See *Netscape Navigator* and *Netscape Netcaster*.

**Netscape Composer**   See *Netscape Communicator*.

**Netscape Conference**   See *Netscape Communicator*.

**Netscape Constellation**   See *Netscape Netcaster*.

**Netscape Enterprise Server**   A Web server from Netscape that runs under NT, Solaris and HP-UX. It supports JavaServer Pages (JSP) technology, Java servlets and Server-Side JavaScript (SSJS). It was superseded by iPlanet Web Server. See *iPlanet Web Server*.

**Netscape Extension Builder**   A toolkit that enables developing extensions to Netscape Application Server that integrate with enterprise applications and Internet services. Prebuilt extensions are provided for BEA Tuxedo, SAP, PeopleSoft, CICS, IMS and MQSeries. See *Netscape Application Server*.

**Netscape LiveWire**   A suite of management and development tools from Netscape for creating Netscape Web sites. It includes a site manager for maintaining HTML links, a compiler for developing server-side JavaScript applications and a library that provides SQL connectivity to a variety of databases. Initially a separate product, LiveWire was included starting with Version 3.0 of Netscape Enterprise Server. LiveWire Pro includes an Informix database and the Crystal Reports report and analysis program.

**Netscape Messenger**   The e-mail client in Netscape Communicator. See *Netscape Communicator*.

**Netscape Navigator**   A Web browser for Windows, Macintosh and X Windows from Netscape that provides secure transmission over the Internet. Soon after its introduction in 1994, Navigator, or just "Netscape," as it is commonly called, quickly became the leading Web browser on the Web. Initially a purchased product, Netscape was forced to give it away after Microsoft developed Internet Explorer and offered it free of charge. After Microsoft integrated Internet Explorer into Windows 98, Microsoft's browser became the market leader. See *Netscape Communicator*.

**Netscape Netcaster**    A component of Netscape Communicator that provides a push model delivery system based on Marimba's Castanet Tuner. Users can subscribe to content channels on the Internet and receive information updates in the background while working on other applications. See *Netscape Communicator*.

**Netscape palette**    See *Netscape color palette*.

**Netscape plug-in**    See *browser plug-in*.

**NetShow**    Client and server software from Microsoft for streaming audio and video over the Internet. It uses the Active Streaming Format (ASF) and provides utilities for translating common audio, video and image formats into ASF. Using IP multicast, NetShow provides ActiveX extensions to NT Server. NetShow On-Demand provides transmission of static data. NetShow Live handles live broadcasts.

The NetShow client has been superseded by Windows Media Player, which supports streaming media and popular audio and video file formats. See *RTSP* and *Windows Media Player*.

**netsourcing**    Outsourcing applications that run on the Web. Since the browser provides universal access to Web content and applications, an application can run on a third-party Web server as easily as it can on an internal Web server (intranet). See *outsourcing*.

**netspeak**    The vocabulary associated with the concepts, functions and features of the Internet.

**netsplit**    A failure in an IRC link or server that divides online users into two groups. IRC servers are often linked in series; thus, a break in the line or failure in one computer causes a separation, and all of a sudden, a whole group of users sign off at once. See *Internet Relay Chat*.

**Net surfer**    An individual that regularly accesses the Internet.

**net-top box**    The set-top box used with Internet TV. See *Internet TV*.

**Net TV**    See *Internet TV*.

**NetView**    IBM SNA network management software that provides centralized monitoring and control for SNA, non-SNA and non-IBM devices. NetView/PC interconnects NetView with Token Ring LANs, Rolm CBXs and non-IBM modems, while maintaining control in the host. See also *NetVue*.

**netViz**    A network diagramming program for Windows from Quyen Systems, Inc., Rockville, MD (www.quyen.com). It keeps the lines connected to the objects when they are moved and also allows a database to be linked to diagram objects for equipment and network documentation. More than 400 predefined symbols are included.

**NetVue**    Web server software from AccuSoft Corporation, Westborough, MA (www.accusoft.com), that provides Web access to stored documents and ODBC-compliant databases. See also *NetView*.

**netwar**    See *information warfare*.

**NetWare**    A family of network operating systems from Novell that support DOS, Windows, OS/2 and Macintosh clients. UNIX client support is available from third parties. In the early 1990s, NetWare was the largest installed base of LAN operating systems.

Except for the earlier Personal NetWare and NetWare ELS peer-to-peer versions, NetWare is a stand-alone operating system that runs in the server. Until NetWare 5, which natively supports TCP/IP and Java, NetWare always used its own proprietary protocols (IPX, SPX and NCP). Its hard disks are formatted with the NetWare format; and although DOS and Windows applications reside in the server, they cannot be run in the server unless they have been compiled into NetWare Loadable Modules (NLMs) using Novell libraries.

**N**

Introduced in 2001, NetWare 6 adds disk pooling and Novell Internet Printing (NIP), which enables documents to be printed over the Internet. NetWare 5 (1998) fully supports TCP/IP and Java and includes a kernel that natively supports symmetric multiprocessing (SMP). NetWare 4 (1993) was the first NetWare version to use the much-acclaimed Novell Directory Services (NDS), which provides directory services for a global enterprise.

Introduced in 1989 as NetWare 386 and then again in 1992 as NetWare 3.11, it was the first 32-bit version of NetWare with a limit of 250 concurrent users. It used the Novell bindery, which provides directory services for a single server, unlike the global NDS directory. NetWare 2.x (originally Advanced NetWare 286 in 1985) ran in a 286 supporting up to 100 concurrent users. See *IPX*, *SPX*, *NCP* and *MHS*.

**NetWare certification**    Novell provides certification for technical competence with self-study tests and courses given at National Authorized Education Centers (NAECs). Certificates include CNA (Certified NetWare Administrator), CNE (Certified NetWare Engineer), ECNE (Enterprise CNE, which includes WAN expertise) and CNI (Certified NetWare Instructor).

The ECNE program has been replaced with a Master CNE, which includes an area of specialization. ECNEs can become Master CNEs by passing a single examination.

**NetWare client**    The software in a desktop client machine that supports the IPX and NCP protocols required to access a NetWare server. Microsoft and Novell provide NetWare clients for Windows, and UNIX and Macintosh support is also available. As of NetWare 5, which fully supports IP, NetWare clients include the IP protocol. The NetWare client used to be known as the NetWare shell.

**NetWare for Small Business**    A network operating system from Novell for up to 50 users. Based on NetWare 4, it also includes GroupWise messaging, and groupware and Border Manager FastCache software for caching Web pages.

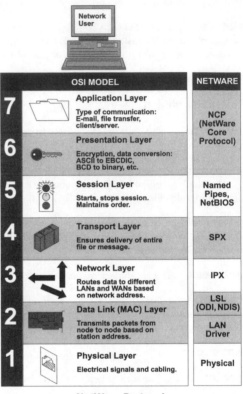

**NetWare Protocols**
This chart compares the NetWare protocol stack with the OSI model. One difference is the LSL layer, which provides a common interface to network drivers. ODI and NDIS are the two most commonly used LSL implementations.

**NetWare Global Messaging**    E-mail software from Novell for NetWare 3.x that includes directory synchronization across distributed servers and provides optional interfaces to X.400, SMTP and SNADS. See *SMF*.

**NetWare Lite**    See *NetWare peer-to-peer network*.

**NetWare Management System**    Also known as *NMS*, it is an SNMP-based network management software from Novell for monitoring and controlling NetWare networks. NMS was superseded by ManageWise.

**NetWare NFS**    Software from Novell that implements the NFS distributed file system on NetWare servers. It allows UNIX and other NFS client machines to access files on a NetWare server. See *LAN Workplace*.

**NetWare peer-to-peer network**    Software from Novell that allows DOS and Windows 3.1 machines to share resouces over the network. NetWare ELS (Entry Level System) was introduced in 1987, followed by NetWare Lite in 1991. NetWare Lite was renamed Personal NetWare in 1993.

**NetWare shell**    Same as *NetWare client*.

**NetWare SMP**     An extension to NetWare 4 that added SMP support. NLMs have to be written for SMP to take advantage of it. In NetWare 5, the Multiprocessor Kernel (MPK) natively supports SMP and can run an SMP-based NLM even if only one processor is used.

**NetWare Users International**     (www.novell.com/nui) A voluntary organization of more than 250 NetWare user groups worldwide.

**network**     (1) A system that transmits any combination of voice, video and/or data between users. The network includes the network operating system in the client and server machines, the cables connecting them and all supporting hardware in between, such as bridges, routers and switches. In wireless systems, antennas and towers are also part of the network. See *LAN*, *WAN*, *client*, *server*, *enterprise networking* and *communications*.

(2) Any arrangement of elements that are interconnected. See *network database*.

**network access server**     A server in a network dedicated to authenticating users that log on. It may refer to a dedicated server or to the software service within a server.

**network accounting**     The reporting of network usage. It gathers details about user activity, including the number of logons and resources used (disk accesses and space used, CPU time, etc.).

**network adapter**     A printed circuit board that plugs into both the clients (personal computers or workstations) and servers, and controls the exchange of data between them. The network adapter provides services at the data link level of the network, which is also known as the "access method" (OSI layers 1 and 2).

A transmission medium, such as twisted pair, coax or fiber optic, interconnects all adapters to network hubs or switches, or—in the case of a bus network—to each other. A network adapter is also commonly called a "NIC" (network interface card). Ethernet, Token Ring and Apple's LocalTalk are common network adapters. The equivalent circuitry may be built directly into the motherboard. See *LAN*.

**network administrator**     A person who manages a local area communications network (LAN) within an organization. Responsibilities include network security, installing new applications, distributing software upgrades, monitoring daily activity, enforcing licensing agreements, developing a storage management program and providing for routine backups. See *system administrator*, *WAN administrator*, *system development cycle* and *salary survey*.

**network analyzer**     Software only or a combination of hardware and software that monitors traffic on a network. It can also read unencrypted text transmitted over the network.

**network appliance**     (1) A specialized device for use on a network. For example, Web servers, cache servers and file servers can be implemented as general-purpose computers with the appropriate software or as network appliances, which are computers dedicated to a single function that cannot do anything else. See *server appliance*, *Internet appliance* and *Web cache*.

(2) (Network Appliance, Inc., Sunnyvale, CA, www.netapp.com) A leading provider of network file storage and content delivery systems. Founded in 1992, it pioneered the network attached storage (NAS) device as an extension of the industry trend toward single-function products. It developed storage, content distribution and reporting software and content delivery platforms under the Filer and NetCache brands. Network Appliance products use the innovative Data ONTAP operating system and WAFL file system, support multiple protocols and provide transparent integration between UNIX and Windows. See *NAS*, *WAFL*, *ICAP*, *DAFS*, *NetApp Filer*, *NetCache* and *Content Alliance*.

**network architecture**     (1) The design of a communications system, which includes the hardware, software, access methods and protocols used. It also defines the method of control; for example, whether computers can act independently or are controlled by other computers monitoring the network.

(2) The access method in a LAN, such as Ethernet and Token Ring.

**Network Associates**     (Network Associates, Inc., Santa Clara, CA, www.nai.com) The number-one provider of antivirus, network security and management software. Formed in 1997 from the acquisition of Network General by McAfee Associates, the company offers a family of products that protect, manage, and monitor computer networks. Via acquisitions, it has entered the hardware sales and encryption technology sectors.

**network attached storage**   See *NAS*.

**network card**   See *network adapter*.

**network cloud**   A cloud-like symbol in a network diagram used to reduce an entire communications network into points of entry and exit. It infers that although there may be any number of switches, routers, trunks, and other network devices within the cloud, the point of interconnection to the cloud (network) is the only technical issue in the diagram. Clouds are often used to depict a WAN (wide area network).

**network computer**   **(1)** A computer in the network.

**(2)** A desktop computer that provides connectivity to intranets and/or the Internet. It is designed as a "thin client" that downloads all applications from the network server, and obtains all of its data from and stores all changes back to the server. The network computer (NC) is similar to a diskless workstation and does not have floppy or hard disk storage.

The attraction of NCs is twofold. Since everything is maintained at the server side, software is installed and upgraded in one place rather than at each client station. NCs have thus been touted as "the way" to lower the cost of computer maintenance. NCs are designed to run Java applets from a browser or stand-alone Java applications. Java programs are interpreted, so that once a Java application is written, it can be run on any NC with a Java interpreter (Java Virtual Machine), regardless of the CPU type (x86, PowerPC, SPARC, etc.).

Several varieties of NCs have been developed, mostly running a compact operating system that is booted from the server. The OS hosts the Java Virtual Machine (JVM), which is launched when a stand-alone Java application is downloaded or when a browser is used and encounters a Java applet. Like any Web browser, it also supports HTML pages from the intranet/Internet. NCs may include slots for smart cards for user login verification.

In order to support existing Windows applications, NCs may use software from Citrix or other licensees of Citrix, which turns a Windows NT or 2000 Server into a timeshared, central computer. In this mode, the NCs function similar to dumb terminals connected to a centralized system.

Oracle subsidiary, Network Computer, Inc. (now Liberate Technologies), established a specification for ensuring compliance to a minimum set of capabilities. Vendors that licensed its Network Computer Reference Profile (NCRP) and built compliant machines were able to brand them with the NC logo. The NCRP was later turned over to The Open Group.

Network computers are designed for business use and have standard computer monitors, whereas Web set-top boxes connect to a TV set. Such devices are aimed at the home user and may or may not conform to the NC standard. See *NetPC*.

**Network Cloud**
The cloud symbol represents communications services without specific details of the network architecture. The user is only responsible for getting data into and out of the network.

**The Panacea?**   When NCs were first introduced, they were touted as the death knell for all Windows PCs. NCs may lower the cost of ownership compared to a PC, but control is placed squarely in the hands of the IT department, and all new software must be implemented by the IT staff. Users can no longer experiment with new software on their own.

Althouh the network computer has not taken the world by storm, its usage is expected to grow, as there are countless computing applications that do not require full-blown desktop PCs. With network computers, the cost of ownership and maintenance can definitely be controlled. The New Internet Company, co-founded by Oracle magnate Larry Ellison, introduced an Internet appliance that is similar to the network computer (see *NIC*).

**network control center**   Refers to a single point of network control, which could be as small as a single software application, to a single workstation with various network monitoring tools, all the way to a "war room" that controls a network in a large enterprise, ISP or communications carrier.

**Sun JavaStation NC**
Since Sun developed Java, it was one of the first to introduce a Java-based NC that conforms to the NC Reference Profile. *(Image courtesy of Sun Microsystems, Inc.)*

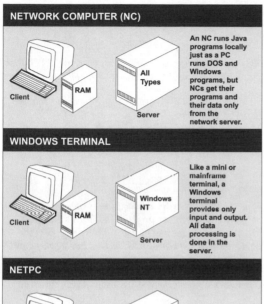

**NETWORK COMPUTER (NC)**

An NC runs Java programs locally just as a PC runs DOS and Windows programs, but NCs get their programs and their data only from the network server.

Client — RAM — All Types — Server

**WINDOWS TERMINAL**

Like a mini or mainframe terminal, a Windows terminal provides only input and output. All data processing is done in the server.

Client — RAM — Windows NT — Server

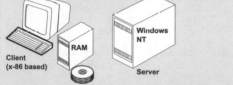

**NETPC**

Client (x-86 based) — RAM — Windows NT — Server

NetPCs can be configured as fully-loaded PCs (fat clients) or as network computers (thin clients).

As fat clients, the installation of Windows and applications and all subsequent software upgrades are obtained from the server.

As thin clients, they function like a network computer (NC) and obtain OS, apps and data from the server. The difference is that parts of the application may be cached on the local hard disk during the day to improve performance.

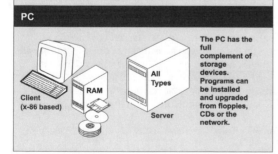

**PC**

The PC has the full complement of storage devices. Programs can be installed and upgraded from floppies, CDs or the network.

Client (x-86 based) — RAM — All Types — Server

**network control program**  Software that manages the traffic between terminals and the host mini or mainframe. It resides in the communications controller or front end processor. In a personal computer LAN, it is called a "network operating system" (NOS), and resides in the server and manages requests from the workstations. IBM's SNA network control program is called "NCP."

**network database**  (1) A database that runs in a network. It implies that the DBMS was designed with a client/server architecture.

(2) A database that holds addresses of other users in the network.

(3) A database organization method that allows for data relationships in a net-like form. A single data element can point to multiple data elements and can itself be pointed to by other data elements. Contrast with *relational database* and *hierarchical database*.

**network drive**  A disk or tape drive connected to a server in the network that is shared by multiple users. Contrast with *local drive*.

**network driver**  Software that activates the actual transmission and receipt of data over the network. It provides the data link protocol (Ethernet, Token Ring, etc.) that controls the specific brand of network adapter installed in the computer.

**network driver interface**  A software interface between the transport protocol and the data link protocol (network driver). The interface provides a protocol manager that accepts requests from the transport layer and activates the network adapter. Network adapters with compliant network drivers can be freely interchanged.

This method allows multiple protocol stacks to run over one network adapter. For example, a PC can connect to a NetWare network running SPX/IPX and a UNIX network running TCP/IP. It also allows one transport protocol to run over different network adapters; for example, SPX/IPX over Ethernet and Token Ring.

In PC LANs, the two primary network driver interfaces are Novell's ODI and Microsoft's NDIS. Novell provides an ODI interface utility that allows NDIS and ODI protocols to work in the same computer.

**network effect**  The resulting increased value of a product because more and more people use it. Telephones, fax machines and computer operating systems are examples.

Its success is due to compatibility and conformity issues, not that the product or technology may be superior or inferior to the competition. For more on the subject, read *Winners, Losers & Microsoft* by Stan J. Liebowitz and Stephen E. Margolis, published 1999 by The Independent Institute, Oakland, CA (ISBN 094599980-1).

**network engineer**  A person who designs, implements and supports local area and wide area networks within an organization. Network engineers are high-level technical analysts specializing in networks. See *network administrator* and *salary survey*.

**network externality**    A situation in which the price somebody is willing to pay to gain access to a network is based solely on the number of other people that are currently using it. Fax machines and the Internet are prime examples. The more people used the service, the more others were willing to buy in.

**Network in a Box**    An earlier turnkey network computer (NC) solution from Network Computer, Inc. (NCI) that included an x86-based server with the NCOS operating system, Oracle Web server, Oracle Interoffice messaging and various bundled applications. See *Liberate*.

**networking**    Dealing with networks. See *network*, *LAN* and *enterprise networking*.

**network interface card**    Same as *network adapter*.

**network layer**    The services in the OSI protocol stack (layer 3 of 7) that provide internetworking for the communications session. See *OSI*.

**network management**    Monitoring an active communications network in order to diagnose problems and gather statistics for administration and fine tuning. Examples of network management products are IBM's NetView, HP's OpenView, Sun's SunNet Manager and Novell's NMS. Almost all network management software supports the SNMP network management protocol. Other management protocols are CMIP and DME. See *systems management* and *configuration management*.

**network management console**    The client component of network management software that provides the user interface and "control room" view of the network.

**network manager**    See *network administrator*.

**network meltdown**    A condition in which the network barely ceases to function due to excessive traffic. It can be caused by a legitimate overload of valid traffic or by malicious or erroneous conditions. See *broadcast storm*.

**network modem**    A modem shared by all users in a network. See *remote access server*.

**Network Neighborhood**    The source of network information in Windows 95/98/NT4. See **Win Network Neighborhood**.

**network operating system**    An operating system that is designed for network use. It may be a completely self-contained operating system, such as UNIX, NetWare and Windows, or as with some earlier products, may be a separate component that requires an existing OS in order to function (LAN Server requires OS/2; LANtastic requires DOS, etc.).

A network operating system (NOS) manages multiple requests concurrently and provides the security necessary in a multiuser environment. One piece of the NOS resides in each client and another resides in each server. It allows the remote drives on the server to be accessed as if they were local drives on the client machine. It allows the server to handle requests from the client to share files and applications, as well as network devices such as printers, faxes and modems.

In a peer-to-peer network, the NOS allows each station to be both client and server. Users can access files on other users' machines by setting up the appropriate permissions. The Mac and all versions of Windows are widely used for peer-to-peer networks. In a non-peer-to-peer network, servers are stand-alone and dedicated to the network. Windows NT, Windows 2000, NetWare and UNIX are examples.

Along with file and print services, the NOS may include or optionally offer a Web server, directory services, messaging system, network management and multiprotocol routing capabilities. See *LAN*.

**network operator**    An organization that provides carrier services in the wired or wireless arena. See also *network administrator*.

**network PC**    See *NetPC* and *network computer*.

**network printer**    A computer printer connected to the network. Network printers are typically in the range of 25 ppm and under. See *distributed printer* and *production printer*.

**network processor**    A programmable CPU chip that is optimized for networking and communications functions. It offers network equipment vendors an off-the-shelf alternative for building routers, switches and access devices much faster than by designing a custom ASIC chip. The network processor is programmed to perform the packet processing supported by the device and is expected to be widely used in all but the highest-end products. MMC Networks coined the term in 1997. See *ASIC*. See also *network computer*.

**network protocol**    A communications protocol used by the network. There are many layers of network protocols. See *OSI*.

**network ready**    Software designed to run in a network. It implies that multiple users can share databases without conflict.

**network security**    The authorization of access to files and directories in a network. Users are assigned an ID number and password that allows them access to information and programs within their authority. Network security is controlled by the network administrator.

**network segment**    See *LAN segment*.

**network server**    A computer system that serves as a central repository of data and programs shared by users in a network. See *server*.

**Network Solutions**    (Network Solutions, Inc., Herndon, VA, www.networksolutions.com) The first private organization to register Internet domain names. Founded in 1979 as a consulting company, it continues to be a major registrar along with others accredited by the Internet Corporation for Assigned Names and Numbers (ICANN). In 1993, agreements between the National Science Foundation, General Atomics and AT&T formed the InterNIC project, which turned the government's name registration over to Network Solutions. The company initially provided the service for free, but began charging in 1995. In late 1998, it began to develop interfaces to its business systems to accomodate multiple registrars and still hosts the master database of registrations that all registrars use. See *ICANN* and *ARIN*.

Is a Name Already Taken?    To find out if a domain name is taken, visit www.networksolutions.com or www.icann.org.

**network switch**    See *LAN switch* and *softswitch*.

**network time protocol**    See *NTP*.

**network transparency**    Reading and/or writing to resources on the network (folders, files, printers, etc.) as if they were attached locally. Either built into the operating system or a separate file sharing component, network transparency implies that there is no additional effort required by the user or by the application to access a remote device than a local one. They all appear as one pool of resources. See *file sharing protocol*.

**network vulnerability probe**    Software that tests for potential security breaches on the network.

**Neugents**    (NEUral aGENTS) Neural network agents from Computer Associates that are included in several of its products and available separately for predictive management. Using pattern recognition techniques, Neugents are used to predict system failures before they occur. See *neural network*.

**neural network**    A modeling technique based on the observed behavior of biological neurons and used to mimic the performance of a system. It consists of a set of elements that start out connected in a random pattern, and, based upon operational feedback, are molded into the pattern required to generate the required results. It is used in applications such as robotics, diagnosing, forecasting, image processing and pattern recognition.

**newbie**    The first-time user of computers or of a particular environment, such as Windows or UNIX. The term is often used for newcomers to the Internet.

**New Era**    See *INFORMIX*.

**newline**  End of line code. See *CR/LF*.

**new media**  **(1)** The forms of communicating in the digital world, which includes electronic publishing on floppy disk, CD-ROM, DVD, digital television and—perhaps most significantly—the Internet. It implies the use of desktop and portable computers, as well as wireless, handheld devices. Most every company in the computer industry is involved with new media in some manner. See *digital convergence*.

**(2)** The concept that new methods of communicating in the digital world allow smaller groups of people to congregate online and share, sell and swap goods and information. It also allows more people to have a voice in their community and in the world in general.

**new public network**  The next-generation, IP-based telephone network that supports voice, video and data.

**NeWS**  (**N**etwork **E**xtensible **W**indowing **S**upport)  A networked windowing system (similar to X Windows) from SunSoft that renders PostScript fonts on screen the way they print on a PostScript printer.

**news and weather**  See *Usenet* and *online services*.

**newsfeed**  The actual news being routed from its sources to news servers or end users.

**newsgroup**  A message board on the Internet. Also known as Internet discussion groups, they are like player-piano rolls of messages devoted to a particular topic. It all starts by someone posting an initial query or comment, and other members reply. Still others reply to the replies, and so the "discussion" forms a chain of related postings called a "message thread."

Newsgroups were popular long before the World Wide Web exploded onto the scene. By the end of 1997, there were more than 50,000. Some are moderated; some are not, and no single server or online service hosts them. They originate from many sources and are hosted on many systems, known collectively as the Usenet network, the original name given to this service. It is the system administrator at any given ISP or online service such as AOL or CompuServe that decides which newsgroups will be offered and how long postings will be available, typically about two weeks.

Newsgroups are organized into topical hierarchies, which include alt (alternative), biz (business), comp (computing), misc (miscellaneous), rec (recreational), and others. As you move to the right in a newsgroup name, the subject focus becomes more limited. For example, the group **alt.music** might discuss every aspect of music, while **alt.music.baroque** and **alt.music.jazz** are more specific.

Newsgroup postings amount to what noted computer author Alfred Glossbrenner has called the "collective consciousness." Newsgroup postings represent the wisdom, experiences, and opinions of millions of people around the world on just about any topic imaginable. Unlike a Web site, which is owned by someone or some organization, nobody controls or filters what appears in a newsgroup. Although everything should be taken with a grain of salt, newsgroups can nevertheless be extremely valuable.

In the early days, Internet users would hear about a group of interest and then "subscribe" to it with a UNIX-based newsreader program. This made it possible to automatically retrieve all the postings you had not yet seen whenever you accessed a group. You could read postings and prepare queries and replies to given messages offline, and then upload them to your favorite groups in a batch.

That can still be done today with the newsreaders built into Netscape Navigator and Internet Explorer. But the feeling of community within most groups no longer exists, and many are clogged with spam. However, if newsgroups are treated as a vast database of potentially useful information on a subject, they can be quite worthwhile. Try Deja News (www.dejanews.com), a search engine devoted to newsgroups that not only archives years' worth of postings, it also aggressively filters out spam.

**newsreader**  An Internet utility, such as nn, rn or tin, that is used to read the messages in a newsgroup.

**news server**  A Usenet server on the Internet that hosts newsgroups.

**Newton**  **(1)** A set of mobile computing technologies from Apple introduced in 1993 with its MessagePad PDA, more commonly known as "Newton." In 1997, Apple spun it off into Newton, Inc., but folded it back in early 1998, when it announced that the Newton OS would no longer be enhanced. See *PDA*.

**(2)** (newton) A unit of force in the MKS system. It is the force required to accelerate one kilogram by one meter per second squared.

**NexGen**   See *Nx586*.

**NeXT**   A computer company that became a software company and then merged into Apple. NeXT Computer was founded in Redwood City, California, in 1985 by Steven Jobs, co-founder of Apple. In 1988, it introduced a high-resolution workstation housed in a black cube that used the Motorola 680x0 CPU and ran under the NextStep operating system.

The computer was discontinued in 1993, at which time NeXT became NeXT Software and focused on OpenStep, the object-oriented development environment of NextStep, which was made available on x86, Sun and HP machines. In 1996, NeXT Software was acquired by Apple and Steve Jobs returned to the company he helped create.

**Nextel**   (Nextel Communications, Inc., Reston, VA, www.nextel.com) A wireless communications carrier founded in New Jersey in 1987 as Fleet Call, a two-way radio service. Throughout the late 1980s and 1990s, the company acquired a large number of SMR (Specialized Mobile Radio) operators and turned them into a nationwide system. In 1996, it introduced Motorola's iDEN technology, which incorporates dispatch radio, cellphone, data and text messaging into one phone. Branded as Nextel's Direct Connect, the iDEN two-way radio service provides an always-on connection between mobile workers similar to a walkie talkie. Nextel was one of the first cellular carriers to institute a nationwide, no roaming charge service.

**next generation Internet**   See *Internet2*.

**NextStep**   A UNIX-based operating system originally designed by NeXT for the NeXT computer. It was also ported to x86, Sun and HP workstations. Later, after Apple acquired the company, the Mach microkernel used in NextStep became the heart of Mac OS X. See *OpenStep*, *NeXT* and *Mac OS X*.

**NFS**   (Network File System) The file sharing protocol in a UNIX network. This de facto UNIX standard, which is widely known as a "distributed file system," was developed by Sun. See *file sharing protocol* and **WebNFS**.

**NFuse**   A major feature of Citrix's MetaFrame products that enables Windows or UNIX applications to be launched from an ICA-enabled browser. NFuse includes the ALE (Application Launching & Embedding) functionality combined with its Program Neighborhood feature, which assigns applications to users. NFuse can automatically create an HTML page for users with links to the applications they are authorized to use.

**NGI**   (Next Generation Internet) A project of the U.S. government for researching high-speed network technologies for use by federal agencies. See *Internet2*.

**NGIO**   (Next Generation Input Output) An input/output architecture developed by Intel that evolved into InfiniBand. NGIO was expected to replace the PCI bus with a switching matrix, providing a 2.5 GBps data path between each pair of nodes. In 2000, NGIO and Future I/O merged into one technology, originally called "System I/O," and later "InfiniBand." See *InfiniBand*.

**NGM**   See *NetWare Global Messaging*.

**NGWS**   (Next Generation Web Services) An earlier name for the Microsoft's .NET platform. See *.NET*.

**NHRP**   (Next Hop Resolution Protocol) A protocol for layer 3 switching that routes a request through traditional routers to obtain the destination address and sends the data packets via layer 2 switches. An NHRP request is dropped if it is not recognized by an intermediate router.

**NI**   See *non-interlaced*.

**nibble**   Half a byte (four bits).

**nibble mode memory**   A type of dynamic RAM that outputs four consecutive bits (nibble) at one time.

**NIC**    **(1)** (Network Interface Card)  Same as *network adapter*. See also *InterNIC*.

**(2)** (New Internet Computer)  A Linux-based computer from The New Internet Computer Company (NICC), San Francisco, CA (www.thinknic.com). The NIC is a pure Web appliance that does not contain a hard drive or floppy. The OS, Java Virtual Machine, browser and browser plug-ins all reside on a CD-ROM, which allows for easy upgrading. An Internet storage service is required to save files, but bookmarks are saved in flash memory. In order to use e-mail, a Web-based e-mail service is required. Co-founded in 2000 by Oracle magnate Larry Ellison, the NIC is a new incarnation of the network computer. See *network computer* and *Internet appliance*.

**NICAD**    A trademark of SAFT America Inc., Valdosta, GA, for nickel cadmium products. See *nickel cadmium*.

**nickel cadmium**    (NiCd) A rechargeable battery technology that has been widely used in portable applications, including portable computers. It provides more charge per pound than lead acid batteries, but less than nickel metal hydride. Its major problem is a so-called "memory effect," in which the battery seems to remember how full it was when you last charged it, and it doesn't go past that point the next time. Nickel cadmium batteries should be completely drained periodically to maintain the longest charge. It uses a nickel and cadmium plate and potassium hydroxide as the electrolyte. See *batteries*.

**nickel hydride**    See *nickel metal hydride*.

**nickel metal hydride**    (NiMH) A rechargeable battery technology that provides approximately 50% more charge per pound than nickel cadmium and does not suffer from the "memory effect." It uses nickel and metal hydride plates with potassium hydroxide as the electrolyte. See *batteries*.

**nickname**    **(1)** An alternate name used to identify yourself in a chat room.

**(2)** A shortcut for identifying a recipient in an e-mail address book.

**Nifty Serve**    A Japanese online service. Nifty Serve and PC-VAN are the major online services in Japan.

**NIH**    Digispeak for "not invented here."

**NII**    (National Information Infrastructure)  The U.S. government's policy for managing advanced technology in the country. The Clinton/Gore administration was very enthusiastic about the Internet and proposed that it should be funded by private industry and be made available to rich and poor alike.

**Nile**    A family of MIPS R4400–based servers from Siemens Pyramid that provide high availability by connecting multiple units in clusters. The machines run an SMP version of UNIX.

**NiMH**    See *nickel metal hydride*.

**NIP**    (Novell Internet Printing)  See *NetWare 6*.

**NIS**    (Network Information Services)  A naming service from SunSoft that allows resources to be easily added, deleted or relocated. Formerly known as Yellow Pages, NIS is a de facto UNIX standard. NIS+ is a redesigned NIS for Solaris 2.0 products. The combination of TCP/IP, NFS and NIS comprises the primary networking components of UNIX.

**NIST**    (National Institute of Standards & Technology, Washington, DC, www.nist.gov)  The standards-defining agency of the U.S. government, formerly the National Bureau of Standards.

**nit**    A measurement of luminance. One nit is equal to one candela per square meter (1cd/m2). Ten thousand nits are equal to one stilb. See *candela*.

**Nixdorf**    See *Siemens Nixdorf*.

**nixie**    See *NCSI*.

**NJE**    (Network Job Entry) An IBM mainframe protocol that allows two JES devices to communicate with each other.

**N-key rollover**    An essential keyboard circuit built into most keyboards, that is vital for fast typing. To test this capability, press four adjacent keys in sequence without removing any finger from any of the keys. If all four letters appear on screen, it has this feature.

**NLB**    (Network Load Balancing) A clustering technology developed by Microsoft for Windows 2000 Advanced Server. This software-scaling technology spreads client requests among a group of servers linked together to support a particular application. Client requests are routed to the least-busy server for processing. As client load increases, additional servers can be added to share the load.

**NLI**    (1) (Natural Language Interface) An English language interface for database queries. Using inference engines, combined with database interfaces and other tools, an NLI system lets anyone access database information without the need for traditional query tools such as SQL. For example, the sentence, "Show me the sales of widgets over the last year in the northeast" could translate to the SQL code: SELECT Sales FROM Products WHERE Region = "Northeast" AND SalesDate "Nov 7 1999." See *natural language query* and *inference engine*.

(2) (Natural Language Interface) Derived from experiments in artificial intelligence, NLI systems provide alternatives for people with severe disabilities to communicate and manage their surroundings more effectively. Such systems include speech assistive devices, device control and voice recognition systems.

**NLM**    Software that runs in a NetWare server. Although NetWare servers store DOS and Windows applications, they do not execute them. All programs that run in a NetWare server must be compiled into the NLM format. They are typically written in C and use Novell's libraries. NLMs began with NetWare 3.x. The earlier NetWare 2.x counterpart was known as a Value Added Process (VAP). See *NetWare*.

**NLQ**    (Near Letter Quality) The print quality that is almost as sharp as an electric typewriter. The slowest speed of a dot-matrix printer often provides NLQ.

**NLSP**    (NetWare Link Services Protocol) A routing protocol from Novell that is used in NetWare networks. NLSP is a link state protocol that was designed to reduce the wasted bandwidth associated with the RIP routing protocol. See *routing protocol*, *link state protocol* and *distance vector protocol*.

**NLX motherboard**    An Intel motherboard used for NetPCs and other low-profile (space-saving) systems. Introduced in 1997, NLX supports the AGP and uses a riser card for expansion boards.

**nm**    See *nanometer*.

**NMI**    (NonMaskable Interrupt) A high-priority interrupt that cannot be disabled by another interrupt. It is used to report malfunctions such as parity, bus and math coprocessor errors.

**NMOS**    (N-Channel MOS) Pronounced "N moss." A type of microelectronic circuit used for logic and memory chips. NMOS transistors are faster than their PMOS counterpart and more of them can be put on a single chip. It is also used in CMOS design.

**NMS**    See *NetWare Management System*.

**NMT**    (Nordic Mobile Telephone) An analog cellular phone system deployed in more than 40 countries in Europe. Launched in the Scandinavian countries in 1979, NMT was the first analog cellphone system. Both 450MHz and 900MHz versions are available. See *wireless generations*.

**nn**    (NetNews) A newsreader for Usenet newsgroups that maintains a database of article headers for keeping track of subjects. Nn was developed in Denmark. See *Usenet*.

**NNI**    (Network-to-Network Interface) In ATM networking, the interface between two ATM devices (typically ATM switches). In frame relay networking, the interface between two separate frame relay networks. Contrast with *UNI*.

**NNTP**   (**N**etwork **N**ews **T**ransfer **P**rotocol)  The protocol used to connect to Usenet groups on the Internet. Usenet newsreaders support the NNTP protocol.

**NNTP client**   A Usenet newsreader that connects to a news server via the NNTP protocol. NNTP clients include command-line UNIX newsreaders such as rn and trn to GUI-based newsreaders built into Web browsers.

**NOC**   (**N**etwork **O**perations **C**enter)  A central location for network management. It functions as a control center for network monitoring, analysis and accounting.

**NOCTI**   See *aptitude tests*.

**nodal**   Having to do with nodes. See *node*.

**nodal processing delay**   The time it takes to process a packet in a network node (router, switch, hub, etc.), which is dependent on the speed of the device and congestion in the network. Contrast with *propagation delay*.

**node**   (1) In communications, a node is a network junction or connection point. For example, a personal computer in a LAN is a node. A terminal connected to a minicomputer or mainframe is a node.

(2) In database management, a node is an item of data that can be accessed by two or more routes.

(3) In computer graphics, a node is an endpoint of a graphical element.

(4) In multiprocessing systems, a node can be a single processor or system. In MPP, it is one processor. In SMP, it is one computer system with two or more processors and shared memory.

**node address**   The identification of a host, workstation, server, printer or other device in a network. See *physical address* and *Internet address*.

**noise**   An extraneous signal that invades an electrical transmission. It can come from strong electrical or magnetic signals in nearby lines, from poorly fitting electrical contacts, and from power line spikes.

**NOMAD**   A relational DBMS for IBM mainframes, PCs and VAXes from Thomson Software Products, Norwalk, CT (www.thomsoft.com). Introduced in the mid-1970s, it was one of the first database systems to provide a non-procedural language for data manipulation. NOMAD can also access data on Oracle, Sybase, DB2 and other databases.

**NOMDA**   (**N**ational **O**ffice **M**achine **D**ealers **A**ssociation)  An association that merged with LANDA to become the Business Technology Association. See *BTA*.

**NOME**   See *GNOME*.

**non-blocking**   The ability of a signal to reach its destination without interference or delay. In a non-blocking switch, all ports can run at full wire speed without any loss of packets or cells.

**non-breaking space**   See *hard space*.

**non-cacheable content**   Dynamic information that changes regularly or for each user request and serves no purpose if it were cached. Web pages that return the results of a search are non-cacheable, because their contents are unique almost all the time. Contrast with *cacheable content*. See *Web switch*.

**non-desktop device**   Refers to handheld devices such as a PDA, cellphone or pager.

**non-document mode**   A word processing mode used for creating source language programs, batch files and other text files that contain only text and no proprietary headers and format codes. All text editors output this format.

**non-glare screen**   See *anti-glare screen*.

**non-impact printer**   A printer that prints without banging a ribbon onto paper. Laser, LED, ink jet, solid ink, thermal wax transfer and dye sublimation printers are examples of non-impact printers. See *printer*.

**non-interlaced**   Illuminating a CRT by displaying lines sequentially from top to bottom. Non-interlaced monitors eliminate annoying flicker found in interlaced monitors, which illuminate half the lines in the screen in the first cycle and the remaining half in the second cycle. Contrast with and see *interlaced* for a diagram.

**nonlinear**   A system in which the output is not a uniform relationship to the input.

**nonlinear editing**   See *nonlinear video editing*.

**nonlinear video editing**   Storing video in the computer for editing. It is much easier to edit video in the computer than with earlier analog editing systems. Today's digital nonlinear editing systems provide high-quality, post-production editing on a personal computer. However, lossy compression is used to store digital images, and some detail will be lost.

Depending on the purpose for the video presentation, output is either the final video turned back into analog or an edit decision list (EDL) that describes frame sources and time codes in order to quickly convert the original material into the final video in an editing room. For commercial production, the latter allows editing to be done offline rather than in a studio that costs several hundred dollars per hour.

Prior to digital, a system using several analog tape decks was considered a nonlinear video editing system. Contrast with *linear video editing*.

**nonmaskable interrupt**   See *NMI*.

**non-modal**   Not mode oriented. A non-modal operation moves from one situation to another without apparent mode switching.

**non-numeric programming**   Programming that deals with objects, such as words, board game pieces and people, rather than numbers. Same as *list processing*.

**non-parity memory**   Memory chips that do not have a ninth bit used for parity checking. See *parity checking*.

**non-parity RAM**   See *non-parity memory*.

**non-preemptive multitasking**   A multitasking environment in which an application is able to give up control of the CPU to another application only at certain points, such as when it is ready to accept input from the keyboard. Under this method, one program performing a large number of calculations, for example, can dominate the machine and cause other applications to have limited access to the CPU.

Non-preemptive multitasking is also called "cooperative multitasking," because programs must be designed to cooperate with each other in order to work together effectively in this environment.

A non-preemptive multitasking operating system cannot guarantee service to a communications program running in the background. If another application has usurped the CPU, the CPU cannot process the interrupts from the communications program quickly enough to capture the incoming data, and data can be lost. Contrast with *preemptive multitasking*.

**nonpreemptive multitasking**   See *non-preemptive multitasking*.

**non-procedural language**   A computer language that does not require writing traditional programming logic. Also known as a "declarative language," users concentrate on defining the input and output rather than the program steps required in a procedural language such as C++, COBOL or Visual Basic. For example, a command, such as LIST, might display all the records in a file on screen, separating fields with a blank space. In a procedural language, all the logic for inputting each record, testing for end of file and formatting each column on screen has to be explicitly programmed.

Query languages, report writers, interactive database programs, spreadsheets and application generators are examples of non-procedural languages. Contrast with and see *procedural language* for an example.

**non-repudiation**   Unable to deny the validity of a document.

**non-routable protocol**    A communications protocol that contains only a device address and not a network address. It does not incorporate an addressing scheme for sending data from one network to another. Examples of non-routable protocols are NetBIOS and DEC's LAT protocols. Contrast with *routable protocol*.

**non-text file**    A file that contains more than simple text. See *binary file*.

**non trivial**    A favorite word used among programmers for any task that isn't simple.

**non-volatile memory**    Memory that holds its content without power. ROMs, PROMs, EPROMs and flash memory are examples. Disks and tapes may be called non-volatile memory, but they are usually considered storage devices. Sometimes the term refers to memory that is inherently volatile, but maintains its content because it is connected to a battery at all times. See *solid state disk*.

**no-op**    (NO OPeration)  An instruction that does nothing but hold the place for a future machine instruction or fill up the space of a very large instruction word (VLIW). See *VLIW*.

**NOP**    (NO oPeration)  See *no-op*.

**no parity**    Not using a parity bit to check for errors. For example, an 8-N-1 communications setting means each character transmitted contains (8) eight bits, (N) "no" ninth parity bit and (1) one additional stop bit to mark the end. See *non-parity memory*.

**NOR**    (Not OR)  A Boolean logical operation that is true if all inputs are false, and false if any input is true. An exclusive NOR (XNOR) is true if both inputs are the same.

| NOR | | | EXCLUSIVE NOR | | |
|---|---|---|---|---|---|
| IN | IN | OUT | IN | IN | OUT |
| 0 | 0 | 1 | 0 | 0 | 1 |
| 0 | 1 | 0 | 0 | 1 | 0 |
| 1 | 0 | 0 | 1 | 0 | 0 |
| 1 | 1 | 0 | 1 | 1 | 1 |

**normalization**    In relational database management, a process that breaks down data into record groups for efficient processing. There are six stages. By the third stage (third normal form), data is identified only by the key field in the record. For example, ordering information is identified by order number, and customer information by customer number.

**normal wear**    Deterioration due to natural forces that act upon a product under average, everyday use.

**Nortel Networks**    (Northern Telecom Limited, Brampton, Ontario, Canada, www.nortel.com)  A world leader in telecommunications products, which includes switching, wireless and broadband systems for service providers and carriers, telephones and systems for residential and business users, computer telephony integration, multimedia and telephone network management systems.

With an international history that goes back more than a century, Nortel Networks was a true pioneer in telecom. After Alexander Graham Bell's father sold his share in his son's telephone patent to National Bell Telephone of Boston in 1880, a former sea captain, Charles Fleetford Sise, was sent to Montreal to create Bell Telephone Company of Canada. Within two years, the company began to make its own telephones. By 1895, the manufacturing branch was spun off into Northern Electric and Manufacturing and later renamed Northern Electric when it merged with a wire and cable subsidiary of Bell in 1914.

Over the next decades, Northern Electric manufactured equipment tied to designs from Western Electric, which had owned as much as 46% of the company at one time. It also made a raft of other products including radios, TVs, amplifiers, Hammond organs, sound equipment and police and fire call boxes. After the 1956 consent decree that caused AT&T to eliminate some of its partnerships, the company gained technical independence from Western Electric and established its own R&D labs in Ottawa.

In 1971, Northern Electric merged its research and development with Bell Canada to form BNR (Bell Northern Research). A year later, it introduced its first line of computerized PBXs, which evolved into digital PBXs and digital switches.

In 1976, Northern Electric was renamed Northern Telecom. Its DMS line of digital central office telephone switches, introduced a year later, provided explosive growth for the company especially after the breakup of AT&T in the U.S. in 1984. Nortel became the first non-Japanese supplier to Nippon Telegraph & Telephone, and the company took advantage of opportunities in Europe and China. In 1995, it presented a new look to the world by adopting a new logo and a new name: Nortel. In 1998, it added Networks to its name, because it merged with Bay Networks, a major manufacturer of hubs and routers. From its roots back to Alexander Graham Bell, Nortel Networks is today one of the world's largest suppliers of digital network solutions.

**The Creation of Northern Electric**
In 1914, this dinner at St. Lawrence Hall in Montreal celebrated the merger of Northern Electric and Manufacturing Company and Imperial Wire and Cable Company.

**Northbridge**   Intel's earlier chipset architecture. The Northbridge is the controller for the frontside bus that interfaces between the CPU and all high-speed components such as memory, the AGP bus and the PCI bus. Some Northbridge chips also include the display controller, obviating the need for a separate display adapter (video card).

The Southbridge, which stems from the PCI bus, is the controller for IDE drives and lower-speed ports (USB, serial port, audio, etc.). Starting with the 8xx series chipsets, the Northbridge/Southbridge design was superseded by the Intel Hub Architecture (IHA), which uses a Memory Controller Hub (MCH) and I/O Controller Hub (ICH). Similar to the Northbridge, the MCH does not include PCI, however. The ICH, like the Southbridge, supports input/output, but also the PCI bus. The IHA architecture is much faster and optimizes data transfer depending on type of data. See *Intel Hub Architecture*.

**Northgate**   (Northgate Computers, Inc., Eden Prarie, MN) A PC manufacturer founded in 1987 by Arthur Lazere that was known for its quality systems and keyboards. Its PCs were sold through direct marketing, and its highly praised line of OmniKey keyboards was also sold through dealers. Northgate closed its doors 10 years after it began, but its keyboards were available from different sources for a while, and with some enhancements, later offered by a different company. See *Avant Stellar keyboard*.

**Norton Utilities**   Widely used utility programs for DOS, Windows and Macintosh from Symantec. It includes programs to search, edit and undelete files; restore damaged files; defragment the disk, and more. Originally from Peter Norton Computing, these programs were the first to popularize disk utilities for the PC.

**NOS**   See *network operating system*.

**NOS/VE**   (Network Operating System/Virtual Environment) A multitasking, virtual memory operating system from Control Data that runs on its medium- to large-scale mainframes.

**NOT**   A Boolean logic operation that reverses the input. If 0 is input, 1 is output, and vice versa. See *AND-OR-NOT*.

**Nota Bene**   A Windows word processor with enhanced features for writers from Nota Bene Associates, Inc., New York (www.notabene.com). The Scholar's Workstation package includes the Nota Bene word processor, Ibidem bibliographic manager and Orbis text retrieval system. Lingua Workstation is Scholar's Workstation plus an advanced multi-lingual module that adds support for Greek, Hebrew, Cyrillic, the International Phonetic Alphabet (IPA) and additional characters in the Roman alphabet. Based on the XyWrite word processing engine, Nota Bene was originally developed in 1983 for DOS by Dragonfly Software.

**notation**   How a system of numbers, phrases, words or quantities is written or expressed. Positional notation is the location and value of digits in a numbering system, such as the decimal or binary system.

**not-com**   A domain name from a country that coincidentally has commercial appeal. For example, the .TV domain for the island country of Tuvalu is used to promote TV stations and other television and video-related organizations. See *dotTV* and *dot-com*.

**notebook computer**    A laptop computer that weighs approximately five to seven pounds. A notebook that weighs under five pounds is usually called a "subnotebook." For features of a portable computer, see *laptop computer*.

**Notepad**    The text editor that comes with Windows. It is a very elementary utility, but gets the job done most of the time. See *text editor* and *WordPad*.

**Notes**    See *Lotus Notes*.

**notwork**    A network that is not functioning.

**Nova**    A minicomputer series from Data General. When introduced in 1969, it was the first 16-bit mini to use four CPU accumulators, quite advanced for its time. Novas and its RDOS operating system were used extensively in the OEM marketplace.

**NovaNET**    A satellite-based network for educational services created by the Education Research Lab of the University of Illinois. It includes over 10,000 hours of lesson material from third grade to post graduate work, in over a hundred subject areas.

**Novell**    (Novell Inc., Provo, UT, www.novell.com)  Novell was founded as Novell Data Systems in 1981 by Jack Davis and George Canova. It initially manufactured terminals for IBM mainframes. In 1983, Ray Noorda became CEO and president of a restructured Novell, Inc., which would concentrate on the development of its NetWare operating system. In the early 1990s, NetWare became the most widely used server operating system for PC networks.

With the acquisition of AT&T's UNIX in 1993 and WordPerfect and Quattro Pro in 1994, Novell extended its system software products and branched into applications. It planned to integrate UnixWare and NetWare into a "super" network operating system, but instead sold UNIX to the Santa Cruz Operation (SCO) in 1995, and WordPerfect and Quattro Pro to Corel Corporation in 1996. From that point, it continued to concentrate on NetWare, its highly acclaimed NetWare Directory Services (NDS), as well as related products for the Internet. See *NetWare* and *NDS*.

**Novell DOS**    The name Novell gave to DR-DOS after it acquired it from Digital Research in 1991. Novell added NetWare client support to the product and released it as Novell DOS 7 in 1994. It was later dropped from the product line and then sold to Caldera. See *DR-DOS* and **Caldera**.

**Novell network**    A LAN controlled by one of Novell's NetWare operating systems. See *NetWare*.

**no wait state memory**    Memory fast enough to meet the demands of the CPU. Idle wait states do not have to be introduced.

**NOW project**    (Network Of Workstations)  A parallel computing project at the University of California at Berkeley. Developed in the mid-1990s with support from DARPA and NSF, its focus was on exploring high-speed interconnects between multiple computers. Some of the clustering technology developed for NOW was handed down to the subsequent Millennium system. See *Millennium project* and *Beowulf*.

**NP**    (Number Portability)  The ability to keep your 800 telephone number when you switch to another service provider. NP later led to LNP (Local Number Portability), offering the same ability for regular local numbers. NP sometimes refers to both services. See *LNP*.

**NPA**    (Network Professional Association, Naperville, IL, www.npa.org)  A membership organization founded in 1994 that is dedicated to advancing computer professionals that specialize in networking. It developed and funded the Certified Network Professional examination, the leading non-vendor examination in network technology. The NPA evolved out of the CNE Professional Association (CNEPA), which was formed in 1990. See *CNP*.

**NPA/Nxx**    (Numbering Plan Area/Nxx)  Area codes within the U.S. that use 0–9 as a center digit. The first area codes used only 0 or 1.

**NPN**    See *new public network*.

**nroff**     (**N**ontypesetting **RunOFF**) A UNIX utility that formats documents for terminals and dot-matrix printers. Using a text editor, troff codes are embedded into the text and the nroff command converts the document into the required output. Complex troff codes are ignored. See *troff*.

**NRP**     (**N**etwork **R**esource **P**lanning) The planning, scheduling and control of a computer network. It includes documentation writing and network diagramming, analyses of traffic and congestion, analyses of application behavior and demand, procedures for failsafe and disaster recover operation, forecasting requirements and redesign. See *baselining* and *ERP*.

**nrt-VBR**     (**N**on **R**eal**T**ime-**VBR**) See *VBR*.

**NRZ**     (**N**on-**R**eturn-to-**Z**ero) A data transmission method in which the 0s and 1s are represented by different polarities, typically positive for 0 and negative for 1. See *NRZI*.

**NRZI**     (**N**on-**R**eturn-to-**Z**ero **I**nverted) A magnetic recording and data transmission method in which the polarity of the bit is reversed when a 1 bit is encountered. All subsequent 0s following the 1 are recorded at the same polarity.

**ns**     (**N**ano**S**econd) See *space/time*.

**NSAPI**     (**N**et**S**cape **API**) A programming interface on Netscape's Web Server. Using NSAPI function calls, Web pages can invoke programs on the server, typically to access data in a database. NSAPI is an alternative to using CGI scripts on Netscape Web servers.

**NSBD**     (**N**ot **S**o **B**ad **D**istribution) An open source system for distributing free software and software updates over the Web. Running on UNIX servers, NSBD uses the PGP encryption method to manage digital signatures in order to prevent tampering with the software. NSBD is available at www.bell-labs.com/nsbd.

**NSFnet**     (**N**ational **S**cience **F**oundation **NET**work) The network funded by the U.S. National Science Foundation, which linked five supercomputer sites across the country in the mid-1980s. Universities were also allowed to connect to it. In 1988, it was upgraded from its original 56 Kbps lines to T1 circuits. By the early 1990s, NSFnet was using a T3 backbone and served as the primary Internet backbone until 1995, when the Net became commercialized. See *ARPAnet*.

**NSI**     See *Network Solutions*.

**NSM**     (**N**etwork and **S**ystem **M**anagement) Running and controlling the networks and computer systems in an enterprise. See *network management*.

**NSP**     (1) (**N**etwork **S**ervice **P**rovider) An organization that provides a high-speed Internet backbone to ISPs and other service providers. Sprint, MCI and UUNET are examples of NSPs. See *Internet backbones*.

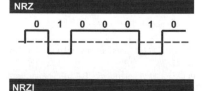

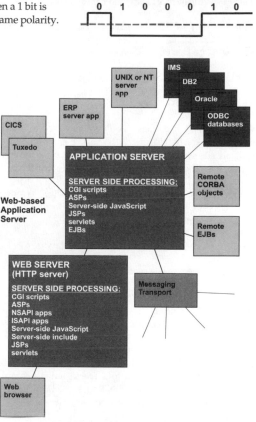

**Server-Side Processing**
This illustration shows the various methods used to deploy server-side processing. NSAPI applications are only one technique used in Web servers.

**(2)** (Native Signal Processing) Enhancements to Pentium CPUs proposed by Intel that later evolved into the MMX CPU. See *MMX*.

**NSS**   (Novell Storage Services) A 64-bit file system introduced with Netware 5 that can support terabyte-sized files. NSS files and standard Netware files can be used in the same server. See *Netware 5*.

**NSTL**   (National Software Testing Lab, Philadelphia) An independent organization that evaluates computer hardware and software. It adheres to controlled testing methods to ensure objective results and publishes its findings in Software Digest Ratings Report and *PC Digest*.

**NT**   See *Windows NT*.

**NT1**   (Network Terminator 1) A device that terminates an ISDN line at the customer's premises. See *ISDN*.

**NT 4**   (Windows **NT 4**.0) See *Windows NT*.

**NT4**   (Windows **NT 4**.0) See *Windows NT*.

**NTAS**   (**NT A**dvanced Server) The server version of Windows NT. See *Windows NT*.

**NT Cluster Server**   See *Microsoft Cluster Server*.

**NTED**   See *TED*.

**NT File System**   See *NTFS*.

**NTFS**   (**NT F**ile **S**ystem) A file system used in Windows NT that uses the Unicode character set and allows file names up to 255 characters in length. The NTFS is designed to recover on the fly from hard disk crashes. Windows NT supports multiple file systems. It can run with a DOS/Windows FAT, an OS/2 HPFS and a native NTFS, each in a different partition on the hard disk. NT's security features require that the NTFS be used.

**NTFSDOS**   A redirector that enables DOS/Windows clients to access drives on UNIX servers (NTFS drives). NTFS drives can be accessed via the DOS command line, File Manager or Explorer. For more information, visit http://www.ntinternals.com.

**n-tier**   Some number of tiers (servers, layers, elements, etc.). See *two-tier client/server* and *three-tier client/server*.

**NT multiuser**   See *multiuser NT*.

**NTP**   (Network Time Protocol) A protocol used to synchronize the realtime clock in a computer. There are numerous primary and secondary servers in the Internet that are synchronized to the Coordinated Universal Time (UTC) via radio, satellite or modem. For more information, visit www.eecis.udel.edu/~ntp. See *UTC*.

**NTSC**   (National TV Standards Committee) A color TV standard that was developed in the U.S. Administered by the FCC, NTSC broadcasts 30 interlaced frames per second (60 half frames per second, or 60 "fields" per second in TV jargon) at 525 lines of resolution. The signal is a composite of red, green and blue and includes an audio FM frequency and an MTS signal for stereo. NTSC is used throughout the world, including the U.S., Canada, Japan, South Korea and several Central and South American countries. See *PAL*, *SECAM* and *ATSC*.

**NTSC port**   An analog video connection. An NTSC port on a computer is typically an input connector for an analog video source such as a standard VCR or camcorder.

**NTT DoCoMo**   (NTT Mobile Communications Network, Inc., Japan) Founded in 1991, NTT DoCoMo is a spinoff of Japan's NTT (Nippon Telegraph and Telephone Corporation), which provides wireless services, including cellular, paging, satellite and maritime and in-flight telephone services. DoCoMo means "anywhere" in Japanese. See *i-Mode*.

**NTVDM** (NT Virtual DOS Machine) See *Windows on Windows*.

**NuBus** A bus architecture (32 bits) originally developed at MIT and defined as a Eurocard (9U). Apple has changed its electrical and physical specs for its Macintosh series. Many Macs have one or more NuBus slots for peripheral expansion.

**NUI** (1) (Network User Interface) A user interface for a computer attached to the network. The NUI is designed to work with remote applications and files as easily as local files.

(2) (Notebook User Interface) A term coined by Go Corporation for its PenPoint pen-based interface.

(3) (Network User Identifier) A code used to gain access into local European packed-switched networks.

(4) See *NetWare Users International*.

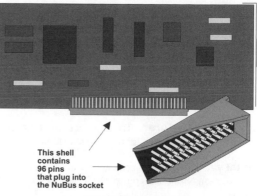

This shell contains 96 pins that plug into the NuBus socket

**The NuBus Card**
The plugs on NuBus cards use pins rather than the edge connectors found on ISA, EISA and PCI cards.

**nuke** To erase.

**null** The first character in ASCII and EBCDIC, also known as the "NUL" character. In hex, it prints as 00; in decimal, it prints as a blank. It is naturally found in binary numbers when a byte contains no 1 bits. It is also used to pad fields and act as a delimiter; for example, in C, it specifies the end of a character string.

**null modem cable** An RS-232 cable used to connect two personal computers together in close proximity for file transfer. It attaches to the serial ports of both machines and simulates what would occur naturally if modems and the phone system were used. It crosses the sending wire with the receiving wire. A counterpart special cable is also available that uses the parallel port for higher transfer speed. See *LapLink cable*.

**null pointer** In programming, a reference to zero. It may be the starting value in the pointer, or may be used as the response to an unsuccessful search function.

**null string** In programming, a character string that contains no data.

**null value** A value in a field or variable that indicates nothing was ever derived and stored in it. For example, in a decimal-based amount field, a null value might be all binary 0s (null characters), but not a decimal 0. The decimal 0 would imply no dollars and cents, and could in fact be a valid derived value. See *null*.

**NUMA** (Non-Uniform Memory Access) A multiprocessing architecture in which memory is separated into close and distant banks. NUMA is similar to SMP, in which multiple CPUs share a single memory. However, in SMP, all CPUs access a common memory at the same speed. In NUMA, memory on the same processor board as the CPU (local memory) is accessed faster than memory on other processor boards (shared memory), hence the "non-uniform" nomenclature. As a result, NUMA architecture scales much better to higher numbers of CPUs than SMP. "Cache coherent NUMA" means that caching is supported in the local system.

**NUMA-Q** A family of Intel-based servers from IBM that use a non-uniform memory access architecture (NUMA). The NUMA-Q line was developed by Sequent Computer Systems, which IBM acquired in 1999. See *NUMA*.

**number cruncher** A computer that is either specialized for or capable of high-speed calculations. See *number crunching*.

**number crunching** Refers to computers running mathematical, scientific or CAD applications, which perform large amounts of calculations. See *number cruncher*.

**Number Nine** (Number Nine Visual Technology Corporation, Lexington, MA, www.nine.com) A manufacturer of PC display adapters founded in 1982 as Number Nine Computer Corporation by Andrew Najda and Stan Bialek. Over the years, Number Nine display adapters have been highly praised for advancing the state of the art. Products have often begun with a #9 prefix, such as #9GXe and #9FX. In 1999, the assets of Number Nine were acquired by S3. See *SONICblue*.

**number sign** In some programming languages, the number sign (#), also called the "pound sign," is used as a not-equals symbol. For example, the expression **if amount # 500** means "if amount not equal to 500."

**numerical aperture** The amount of light that can be coupled to an optical fiber. The greater the aperture, the easier it is to connect the light source to the fiber.

**numerical control** A category of automated machine tools, such as drills and lathes, that operate from instructions in a program. Numerical control (NC) machines are used in manufacturing tasks, such as milling, turning, punching and drilling.

First-generation machines were hardwired to perform specific tasks or programmed in a very low-level machine language. Today, they are controlled by their own microcomputers and programmed in high-level languages, such as APT and COMPACT II, which automatically generate the tool path (physical motions required to perform the operation).

The term was coined in the 1950s when the instructions to the tool were numeric codes. Just like the computer industry, symbolic languages were soon developed, but the original term remained.

**numeric data** Refers to quantities and money amounts used in calculations. Contrast with *string* or *character data*.

**numeric field** A data field that holds only numbers to be calculated. Contrast with *character field*.

**numeric keypad** A four-row keyboard of digits used on calculators, computer keyboards and telephones. See *keypad*.

**NUM Lock** (NUMeric Lock) A keyboard key used to toggle a combination number/cursor keypad between number keys and cursor keys.

**NUON** An interactive video platform from VM Labs, Mountain View, CA (www.vmlabs.com) that is used for interactive games, educational content and movies. VM Labs provides the design for the NUON Media Processor, which is embedded in the DVD player or set-top box, and can decode digital video and provide interaction at the same time. It also licenses the tools for developing the games and software.

**NURB** (NonUniform Rational B-spline) A type of b-spline that is very flexible. NURB curves can represent any shape from a straight line to a circle or ellipse with very little data. They can also be used for guiding animation paths, for approximating data and for controlling the shapes of 3-D surfaces. NURBs are known for their ability to control the smoothness of a curve. See *spline* and *b-spline*.

**NutCRACKER** A software porting tool for converting UNIX applications to Windows 95 and Windows NT from DataFocus, Inc., Fairfax, VA (www.datafocus.com). It includes MKS Toolkit, which is a comprehensive set of UNIX utilities from Mortice Kern that can be used in the Windows environment.

**Nutella** See *Gnutella*.

**Nuts & Bolts** A set of Windows utilities from Network Associates that provides crash protection, disk repair, optimization, data security and performance enhancements.

**NVRAM** (Non-Volatile RAM) See *non-volatile memory*.

**NWAdmin** (NetWare ADMINistrator) Management console software from Novell for NetWare networks. NWAdmin runs under Windows and is used to configure network resources via NDS. NWAdmin was introduced with NetWare 4 and supports third party plug-ins that add functionality. See *ConsoleOne*.

**NWLink**    NetWare **LINK**)  Microsoft's implementation of Novell's IPX/SPX transport and network layer protocols. NWLink comes with Windows NT and Windows 9x and enables Windows clients to access NetWare servers, and NetWare clients to access Windows NT servers. See *NetWare*.

**Nx586**    A family of Pentium-class CPUs from NexGen, Inc. The line was dropped after AMD acquired NexGen.

**Nx686**    A Pentium Pro–class CPU from NexGen, Inc. With AMD's acquisition of the company in 1996, the Nx686 became AMD's K6 chip.

**NxN switch**    See *crosspoint switch*.

**nybble**    See *nibble*.

**Nyquist law**    See *Nyquist rate*.

**Nyquist rate**    The minimum sampling rate required to turn an analog signal into an accurate digital representation. The sampling rate is twice that of the analog frequency; therefore, a 4MHz frequency requires an 8MHz sampling rate.

**NZ**    (Non Zero)  A value greater or less than 0.

N

# O

**OA**   See *office automation*.

**OADG**   (Open Architecture Development Group) An organization founded by IBM Japan in 1991 to promote PC standards in Japan. See *DOS/V*.

**OAI**   (Open Application Interface) A computer to telephone interface that lets a computer control and customize PBX and ACD operations.

**OASIS**   (Organization for the Advancement of Structured Information Standards, Billerica, MA, www.oasis-open.org) A membership organization that is involved in promoting public information standards including XML, SGML and CGM. OASIS sponsors seminars, conference panels, exhibits and other educational events.

**object**   (1) A self-contained module of data and its associated processing. Objects are the software building blocks of object technology. See *object technology* and *object-oriented programming*.

(2) In a compound document, an independent block of data, text or graphics that was created by a separate application.

**object-based**   Having to do with object technology. See *object technology*.

**object browser**   A utility that provides a hierarchical view of the Java classes in a Java application. It typically comes in an integrated development environment (IDE). See *IDE*.

**object bus**   The communications interface through which objects are located and accessed. An object bus is a high-level protocol which rides on top of a lower-level transport protocol. See *CORBA* and *DCOM*.

**object code**   The machine language representation of programming source code. Object code is created by a compiler and is then turned into executable code by the link editor. This is an early term that has no relationship to object technology. See *executable code*, *machine language* and *object-oriented programming*.

**object computer**   Same as *target computer*. This is an early term that has no relationship to object technology.

**object database**   See *object-oriented database*.

**Object Database Management Group**   (Object Database Management Group, Burnsville, MN, www.odmg.org) An organization founded in 1991 to promote standards for object databases. The ODMG standard adds programming extensions to C++ and Smalltalk for accessing an object-oriented database. It also includes a superset of SQL 92 Entry Level, the most widely supported version of SQL.

The Object Database Management Group (ODMG) defines an interface to the database, whereas the Object Management Group (OMG) defines an interface for using objects in a distributed environment. The ODMG object model complies with the core model of the Object Management Architecture (OMA) of the OMG. See *OMA* and *CORBA*.

**Objective-C**   The first commercial object-oriented version of the C programming language. It runs on PCs, Macs and various UNIX workstations. Originally developed by the Stepstone Corporation, it was acquired by NeXT Computer.

**object language**   (1) A language defined by a metalanguage.
   (2) An object-oriented programming language.
   (3) Same as *machine language* or *target language*.

**Object Management Architecture**   A definition of a standard object model from the Object Management Group. It defines the behavior of objects in a distributed environment. The communications component of the Object Management Architecture, or OMA, is the Common Object Request Broker, or CORBA. CORBA is often referenced more than OMA, but it is part of OMA and thus implies OMA. See *CORBA*.

**Object Management Group**   (Object Management Group, Framingham, MA, www.omg.org) An international organization founded in 1989 to endorse technologies as open standards for object-oriented applications. The OMG specifies the Object Management Architecture (OMA), a definition of a standard object model for distributed environments, more commonly known as CORBA. See *CORBA*. Also see *Object Database Management Group*.

**object model**   (1) A description of an object architecture, including the details of the object structure, interfaces between objects and other object-oriented features and functions.
   (2) An object-oriented description of an application.

**object module**   The output of an assembler or compiler, which must be linked with other modules before it can be executed. This is an early term that has no relationship to object technology.

**object oriented**   See *object technology* and *object-oriented programming*.

**object-oriented analysis**   The examination of a problem by modeling it as a group of interacting objects. An object is defined by its class, data elements and behavior. For example; in an order processing system, an invoice is a class, and printing, viewing and totalling are examples of its behavior.  Objects (individual invoices) inherit this behavior and combine it with their own data elements.

**object-oriented database**   A database that holds abstract data types (objects) and is managed by an object-oriented database management system (DBMS). See *object-oriented DBMS*.

**object-oriented DBMS**   A database management system (DBMS) that manages objects, which are abstract data types. An object-oriented DBMS (ODBMS) is suited for data with complex relationships that are difficult to model and process in a relational DBMS. It is also capable of handling multimedia data types (images, audio and video).

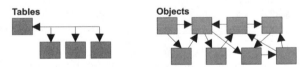

**Structural Flexibility**
Object-oriented information systems provide more flexibility than systems designed for relational databases. While relational databases easily provide one-to-many and many-to-one relationships, object databases allow for many to many. Information systems that require complex relationships can be more easily modeled with object technology, rather than being "shoehorned" into the row and column format of relational tables.

A relational DBMS is designed to handle numbers, alphanumeric text and dates. It may also support a LOB field, which holds any binary data (image, video, etc.), but the database program does not manipulate the LOB directly. Another application has to be written or some middleware has to be used to process the LOB. In an object database, a picture or video clip object can include the routine to display it which is dynamically invoked by the DBMS.

Some ODBMSs are entirely object oriented and are accessed from an application program written in an object-oriented programming language. Others allow access via an SQL-like language or derivative.

Examples of pure object-oriented DBMSs are Servio Corporation's Gemstone, Object Design's Object Store and Ontos' ONTOS DB. Increasingly, object databases (ODBMSs) are being merged with relational databases (RDBMSs),

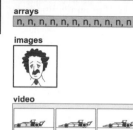

**Relational format: rows and columns**

**Object format: any structure**
rows and colums

arrays
n, n, n, n, n, n, n, n, n, n, n, n

images

video

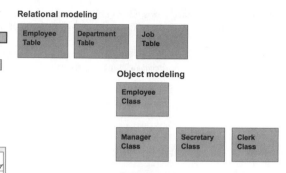

**Relational modeling**

| Employee Table | Department Table | Job Table |
| --- | --- | --- |

**Object modeling**

Employee Class

| Manager Class | Secretary Class | Clerk Class |
| --- | --- | --- |

**Multimedia Ready**
Relational databases store everything in rows and columns. Although they may support large binary object (LOB) fields that can hold anything, an object database can support any type of data combined with the processing to display it.

**Object Modeling**
When information systems are modeled as objects, they can employ the powerful inheritance capability. Instead of building a table of employees with department and job information in separate tables, the type of employee is modeled. The employee class contains the data and the processing for all employees. Each subclass (manager, secretary, etc.) contains the data and processing unique to that person's job. Changes can be made globally or individually by modifying the class in question.

providing a single environment for traditional business transactions, multimedia data and complex structures. UniSQL was one of the first vendors to provide both capabilities in one product, and all major RDBMS vendors eventually followed suit. See *universal server* and *ODMG*.

**object-oriented design**    Transforming an object-oriented model into the specifications required to create the system. Moving from object-oriented analysis to object-oriented design is accomplished by expanding the model into more and more detail.

**object-oriented graphics**    Same as *vector graphics*.

**object-oriented interface**    A graphical interface that uses icons and a mouse, such as Mac, Windows and Motif.

**object-oriented operating system**    An operating system that is based on objects.

**object-oriented programming**    Abbreviated "OOP," programming that supports object technology. It is an evolutionary form of modular programming with more formal rules that allow pieces of software to be reused and interchanged between programs. Major concepts are encapsulation, inheritance, and polymorphism.

**Encapsulation** is the creation of self-sufficient modules that contain the data and the processing (data structure and functions that manipulate that data). These user-defined, or abstract, data types are called "classes." One instance of a class is called an "object." For example, in a payroll system, a class could be defined as Manager, and Pat and Jan, the actual objects, are instances of that class.

Classes are created in hierarchies, and **inheritance** allows the knowledge in one class to be passed down the hierarchy. That means less programming is required when adding functions to complex systems. If a step is added at the bottom of a hierarchy, then only the processing and data associated with that unique step needs to be added. Everything else about that step is inherited.

Object-oriented programming allows procedures about objects to be created whose exact type is not known until runtime. For example, a screen cursor may change its shape from an arrow to a line depending on the program mode. The routine to move the cursor on screen in response to mouse movement would be written for "cursor," and **polymorphism** would allow that cursor to be whatever shape is required at runtime. It would also allow a new shape to be easily integrated into the program.

The SIMULA simulation language was the original object-oriented language. It was used to model the behavior of complex systems. Xerox's Smalltalk was the first object-oriented programming language and was used to create the graphical user interface whose derivations are so popular today. C++ has become the major commercial OOP language, because it combines traditional C programming with object-oriented capabilities. ACTOR and Eiffel are also meaningful OOP languages.

The following list compares some fundamental object-oriented programming terms with traditional programming terms and concepts. See *object-oriented DBMS* and *object technology*.

```
Object-Oriented    Traditional
Programming        Programming
class              data type + characteristics
instance           variable
instantiate        declare a variable
method             processing code
message            call
object             data type + processing
```

**object-oriented technology**    Same as *object technology*.

**Object Packager**    A Windows utility that embeds a document as an icon inside another document. It is part of Windows' OLE (object linking and embedding). It also allows objects created by non-OLE-compliant applications to be embedded. When the icon is double-clicked, the application that created it is opened to view and edit it. See *OLE*.

**ObjectPro**    An object-oriented client/server development system from Platinum Technology, Inc., Oakbrook Terrace, IL (www.platinum.com). It includes its own programming language and generates executable programs for Windows, HP/UX and Solaris. It supports the major databases and also provides an interpreted mode for development.

**object program**    A machine language program ready to run in a particular operating environment. It has been assembled, or compiled, and link edited. This is an early term that has no relationship to object technology.

**object references**    To learn about object technology, two excellent easy-to-read books on the subject are David Taylor's *Object-Oriented Technology: A Manager's* Guide (Addison-Wesley ISBN 0-201-56358-4) and *Business Engineering with Object Technology* (Wiley ISBN 0-471-04521-7). These are excellent starter books.

For more in-depth analysis, also read *Object-Oriented Analysis and Design* by Grady Booch (Benjamin Cummings ISBN 0-8053-5340-2) and *Object-Oriented Modeling and Design* by James Rumbaugh, et al (Prentice-Hall, ISBN 0-13-629841-0).

**object-relational database**    See *universal server*.

**object-relational DBMS**    See *universal server*.

**objects**    See *object technology* and *object-oriented programming*.

**object signing**    (1) Digitally signing a file to ensure its integrity and authenticity. See *code signing*.

(2) The ability to assign access privileges to Java applications that lets them work outside of their normally-constrained arena. See *Java sandbox*.

**ObjectStudio**    An object-oriented client/server development system  that supports Windows, OS/2, UNIX and the major databases from Cincom Systems, Inc., Cincinnati, OH (www.cincom.com). Its Synchronicity module is used to graphically diagram the data and business logic and generate Enfin Smalltalk code. A visual programming tool is used to create the user interfaces. ObjectStudio was originally developed by Easel Corporation, which was acquired by VMARK Software. ObjectStudio was then sold to Cincom.

**object technology**    The use of objects as the building blocks for applications. Objects are independent program modules written in object-oriented programming languages. Just as hardware components are routinely designed as modules to plug into and work with each other, objects are software components designed to work together at runtime without any prior linking or precompilation as a group.

The ultimate goal of objects is that it should not matter which source language they were programmed in or which computer on the network they are running in. They are designed to interoperate strictly through the messages passed between them. CORBA and SOAP come closest to that goal, while COM and JavaBeans are more platform and language specific. See *object-oriented DBMS, object-oriented programming, component software, CORBA, COM, SOAP* and *JavaBeans*.

**ObjectView**    See *KEY:Assemble*.

**ObjectVision**    An earlier development package from Borland for creating Windows and OS/2 2.0 applications. It used visual techniques for user interface design and programming logic. It also provided links to spreadsheets and databases.

**ObjectWindows**    See *OWL*.

**ObjectWorks**    See *VisualWorks*.

**Obsydian**    See *Synon/2E*.

**OC**    (Optical Carrier) The transmission speeds defined in the SONET specification. OC defines transmission by optical devices, and STS is the electrical equivalent.

```
Service                Speed (Mbps)
OC-1      STS-1           51.84 (28 DS1s or 1 DS3)
OC-3      STS-3          155.52 (3 STS-1s)
OC-3c     STS-3c         155.52 (concatenated)
OC-12     STS-12         622.08 (12 STS-1, 4 STS-3)
OC-12c    STS-12c        622.08 (12 STS-1, 4 STS-3c)
OC-48     STS-48        2488.32 (48 STS-1, 16 STS-3)
OC-192    STS-192       9953.28 (192 STS-1, 64 STS-3)
OC-768    STS-768      38813.12 (768 STS-1, 256 STS-3)
```

**OC-1**    The SONET transmission rate of 51.84 Mbps. See *OC*.

**OC-12**    The SONET transmission rate of 622.08 Mbps. See *OC*.

**OC-192**    The SONET transmission rate of 9953.28 Mbps. See *OC*.

**OC-3**    The SONET transmission rate of 155.52 Mbps. See *OC*.

**OC-48**    The SONET transmission rate of 2488.32 Mbps. See *OC*.

**occam**    A parallel processing language designed to handle concurrent operations. The INMOS Transputer executes occam almost directly. In the following statements, two items of data are read and incremented at the same time. PAR specifies that following statements are to be executed concurrently, and SEQ indicates that the following statements are executed sequentially.

```
PAR
  SEQ
    chan1 ? item1
    item1 := item1 + 1
  SEQ
    chan2 ? item2
    item2 := item2 + 1
```

**OCE**    See *AOCE*.

**OCF**    (OpenCard Framework) A smart card specification from the OpenCard Consortium. Introduced in early 1998, it is designed to standardize smart cards for use in ATM machines, set-top boxes and merchant readers.

**OCR**    (Optical Character Recognition)  The machine recognition of printed characters. OCR systems can recognize many different OCR fonts, as well as typewriter and computer-printed characters. Advanced OCR systems can recognize hand printing.

When a text document is scanned into the computer, it is turned into a bitmap, which is a picture of the text. OCR software analyzes the light and dark areas of the bitmap in order to indentify each alphabetic letter and numeric digit. When it recognizes a character, it converts it into ASCII text. Hand printing is much more difficult to analyze than machine-printed characters. Old, worn and smudged documents are also difficult. Scanning documents and processing them with OCR is sometimes as much an art as it is a science.

**octal**    A numbering system that uses eight digits. It is used as a shorthand method for representing binary characters that use six-bits. Each three bits (half a character) is converted into a single octal digit.  Okta is Greek for 8.

| Decimal | Binary | Octal |
|---------|--------|-------|
| 0 | 000 | 0 |
| 1 | 001 | 1 |
| 2 | 010 | 2 |
| 3 | 011 | 3 |
| 4 | 100 | 4 |
| 5 | 101 | 5 |
| 6 | 110 | 6 |
| 7 | 111 | 7 |

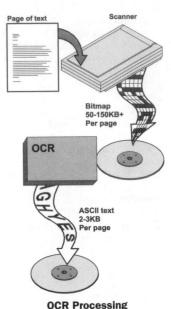

**OCR Processing**
When text documents are scanned, they are "photographed" and stored as pictures in the computer. OCR software converts the pictures into actual text characters, which take up considerably less room on disk.

**octet**    An eight-bit storage unit. In the international community, octet is often used instead of byte.

**octopus cable**    A cable that is spliced into several branches. There is one connector on one end and multiple connectors on the other.

**OCX**    (OLE Control EXtension)  A component software technology from Microsoft that enables a Windows program to add funtionality by calling ready-made components. Generally called "OLE controls" or "OLE custom controls," they appear to the end user as just another part of the program.

OCXs are Microsoft's second-generation component architecture. Unlike first-generation 16-bit Visual Basic controls (VBXs), which were only written in Visual Basic, OCXs can be written in several languages and come in 16-bit and 32-bit versions. The interface requirements for OCXs were reduced to speed up interaction via the Web, and they turned into ActiveX controls. See *VBX* and *ActiveX control*.

**ODAPI**    (Open Data API)  A database programming interface from Borland that was rewritten and turned into the IDAPI interface. See *Borland Database Engine*.

**ODBC**    (Open DataBase Connectivity)  A database programming interface from Microsoft that provides a common language for Windows applications to access databases on a network. ODBC is made up of the function calls programmers write into their applications and the ODBC drivers themselves.

For client/server database systems such as Oracle and SQL Server, the ODBC driver provides links to their database engines to access the database. For desktop database systems such as dBASE and FoxPro, the ODBC drivers actually manipulate the data. ODBC supports SQL and non-SQL databases. Although the application always uses SQL to communicate with ODBC, ODBC will communicate with non-SQL databases in its native language. See *JDBC*.

**ODBCDirect**    See *DAO*.

**ODBMS**    See *object-oriented DBMS*.

**odd parity**   See *parity checking*.

**ODI**   (Open Data-Link Interface) A network driver interface from Novell. ODI is based on the LSL interface developed by AT&T for its UNIX System V operating system. See *network driver interface* and *LSL*.

**Odin**   An open source emulator for OS/2 that runs 32-bit Windows applications. There are add-ons to OS/2 that support emulation of 32-bit Windows applications up to Windows 95, thus some programs will run, while others will not. Odin supports the full Win32 Windows NT/2000 interface. The Odin project team is based in Germany, hence, the name Odin, which means "chief god" in Norse and Teutonic mythology. For more information, visit http://en.os2.org/projects/odin.

**ODMA**   **(1)** (Open Document Management API) A programming interface used to allow client programs to communicate with document management systems on a server.
   **(2)** (Optical Disc Manufacturing Association, Milford, PA, www.odma.com) A membership organization that addresses various issues in the manufacturing, testing, labeling and packaging of CD and DVD media.

**ODMG**   See *Object Database Management Group*.

**ODS**   (Operational Data Store) A database designed for queries on transactional data. An ODS is often an interim or staging area for a data warehouse, but differs in that its contents are updated in the course of business, whereas a data warehouse contains static data. An ODS is designed for performance and numerous queries on small amounts of data such as an account balance. A data warehouse is generally designed for elaborate queries on large amounts of data. See *data warehouse*.

**ODSI**   (Open Directory Services Interface) A programming interface from Microsoft for gaining access to network naming services and directory services.

**ODT**   See *SCO Open Desktop*.

**Oe**   See *Oersted*.

**OEB**   (Open eBook) An open standard for e-book content from the Open eBook Forum, Boulder, CO (www.openebook.org). OEB publications are not read directly by the e-book. They must be compiled into the proprietary format of the e-book, which applies encryption and other optimization techniques required by the hardware. OEB supports the unique features of e-books such as different window sizes and unlimited scrolling lengths, requirements that are not addressed in page description languages intended for paper output. Any publication formatted in OEB can be readily converted for use by a vareity of e-book hardware.
   Introduced in mid-1999 and based on HTML, XML, CSS and other standards, Microsoft and Gemstar are major contributors. OEB is officially known as the Open eBook Publication Structure Specification. It defines the format for description and content files. The OEB File Format from NuvoMedia and SoftBook Press (both acquired by Gemstar) is another format expected to consolidate all the files into a single MIME file type. See *e-book*.

**OEM**   (Original Equipment Manufacturer) A manufacturer that sells equipment to a reseller for rebranding or repackaging. However, the term has evolved to refer to the reseller itself. Thus, an OEM either adds value to the product before reselling it, private labels the merchandise under its own name or bundles it with its own products. OEM generally refers to most everthing that does not have to do with direct sales to the end user via normal wholesale/retail distribution. See *VAR*.

**OEM font**   A font that uses the extended ASCII characters as defined by IBM for the original PC. The OEM, or DOS/OEM character set contains line draw and other symbols commonly used by DOS programs to create charts and simple graphics. Also known as the PC-8 symbol set as well as Code Page 437, the OEM character set is built into every display adapter. It is also the character set used by Windows in order to display DOS applications properly. See *ASCII chart* for the actual characters.

**OEMI**   (OEM Information)  An IBM publication that describes the parallel channel interface. See *parallel channel*.

**OEO**   (Optical in Electrical processing Optical out)  Refers to network devices that convert photonic transmission signals to electronic signals in order to analyze the traffic content for switching purposes. It then reconverts the signal to light for output. Contrast with *OOO*.

**Oersted**   Pronounced "ers-ted." The measurement of magnetic energy. The higher the Oe rating in a material, the more current is required to changes its magnetic polarity. Named after the Danish scientist, Hans Cristian Oersted (1777–1851), it is used, for example, to measure the coercivity point on magnetic media. See *coercivity*.

**OFDM**   (Orthogonal **FDM**)  The modulation technique used for digital TV in Europe, Japan and Australia. It was first promoted in the early 1990s as a wireless LAN technology. OFDM's spread spectrum technique distributes the data over a large number of carriers that are spaced apart at precise frequencies. This spacing provides the "orthogonality" in this technique which prevents the demodulators from seeing other frequencies than their own. Coded OFDM (COFDM) adds forward error correction to the OFDM method. Contrast with *8-VSB*.

**offboard**   Refers to a chip or other hardware component that is not directly attached to the printed circuit board (motherboard). Contrast with *offboard*.

**off-hook**   The state of a telephone line that allows dialing and transmission but prohibits incoming calls from being answered. The term stems from the days when a telephone handset was lifted off of a hook. Contrast with *on-hook*.

**Office**   See *Microsoft Office*.

**Office 2000**   See *Microsoft Office*.

**office application**   Any of the typical applications that come bundled in a suite of applications, such as word processing, spreadsheet and database management. See *application suite*.

**office automation**   The integration of office information functions, including word processing, data processing, graphics, desktop publishing and e-mail.

The backbone of office automation is a LAN, which allows users to transmit data, mail and even voice across the network. All office functions, including dictation, typing, filing, copying, fax, Telex, microfilm and records management, telephone and telephone switchboard operations, are candidates for integration.

**Office document**   (1) Any file created in a Microsoft Office application, such as a Word text document or an Excel spreadsheet.

(2) (office document) A document created in a business environment. See *application suite*.

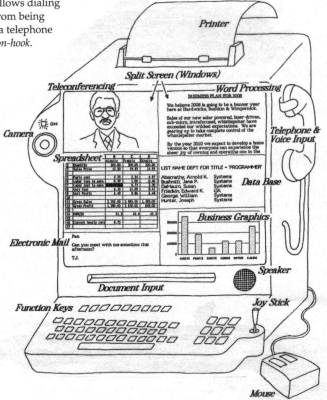

**Office Automation**
This drawing was made by the author in 1981 to depict an integrated terminal in the office of the future. Most of the features have been incorporated into today's desktop computers, except for the telephone, which still remains a separate device in most cases.

**OfficeJet**    A combination ink jet printer, copier and fax machine from HP. The first OfficeJet was introduced in 1994.

**Office:Mac**    Microsoft's suite of business applications for the Macintosh. See *Microsoft Office*.

**office suite**    See *application suite*.

**Office Vision**    Integrated office automation applications from IBM that run in all IBM computer families. Introduced in 1989, it includes e-mail, scheduling, document creation and distribution as well as decision support and graphics capabilities. It was the first major implementation of SAA and incorporates the Presentation Manager interface across OS/2 networks, AS/400s and mainframes.

**Office XP**    See *Microsoft Office*.

**offline**    (1) Not connected to the Internet, online service or internal network.

(2) Not connected to or not installed in the computer. If a terminal, printer or other device is physically connected to the computer, but is not turned on or in ready mode, it is considered offline.

Disks and tapes that have been demounted and stored in the data library are considered offline. Contrast with *online*.

(3) "Not with it." A situation where a person is uninformed about something. See *404*.

**offline advertising**    Advertising a Web site and its URL in traditional media such as radio, TV and magazines. Same as *cross promotion*.

**offline browser**    See *offline reader*.

**offline navigator**    See *offline reader*.

**offline reader**    Software that downloads e-mail and selected data from an online service or the Internet, allowing the user to browse the captured material after disconnecting. It automates retrieving routine data and saves online fees by shortening the connect time.

**offline storage**    Disks and tapes that are kept in a data library.

**offload**    To remove work from one computer and do it on another. See *cooperative processing*.

**offset**    (1) The distance from a starting point, either the start of a file or the start of a memory address. Its value is added to a base value to derive the actual value. An offset into a file is simply the character location within that file, usually starting with 0; thus "offset 240" is actually the 241st byte of the file. See *relative address*.

(2) In word processing, the amount of space a document is printed from the left margin.

**offset lithography**    See *offset press*.

**offset press**    A printer that uses an intermediate rubber-coated cylinder known as a "blanket" to transfer the image onto the paper. Instead of transferring the image from a metallic drum onto paper as is done with most digital printers, the image is "offset" onto the blanket and then to paper. The blanket creates a smoother image on most types of paper and can print on rough or heavy stock as well as other media. Most offset presses use the lithographic method.

Since offset presses use the intermediate blanket as the transfer mechanism, the original negative image on the drum is right-reading. It becomes wrong-reading on the blanket and then back to the original on the paper.

Indigo USA, Woburn, MA (www.indigonet.com), combines laser printing and offset printing. It makes a "digital offset color press," which is an electrophotographic printer that offsets to a blanket instead of imaging directly from the drum. It also uses a special liquid toner instead of dry toner, enabling it to print on polyester, PVC, films and other media as well as coated and uncoated paper. See *lithography*, *digital printing* and *right-reading*.

**off site**    In another location. It is common practice to store copies of important data off site as part of a disaster recovery program. See *disaster recovery*.

**O**

**off-the-shelf**   Refers to products that are packaged and available for sale.

**OH**   See *off-hook* and *modem.*

**ohm**   A unit of measurement for electrical resistance. One ohm is the resistance in a circuit when one volt maintains a current of one amp.

**ohnosecond**   (**Oh No! second**)  That tiny fraction of a second it takes for you to realize you've just made a big mistake on the computer. For example, you just clicked "No" when prompted to save the document you've been composing all day. Or, you just clicked "Send," and forgot to delete the profanity you wrote at the bottom of the e-mail message to your boss.

**OIC**   Digispeak for "oh, I see."

**Oil Change**   A software update service for Windows 95/98 from CyberMedia, Inc., Santa Monica, CA (www.cybermedia.com). The Oil Change software analyzes the applications in your PC and, after connection to the CyberMedia Web site, alerts you to bug fixes, free enhancements and other "goodies" you might want to download from the Internet.

**OJI**   (**O**pen **J**ava VM **I**nterface)  A programming interface from Netscape that enables third-party Java VMs to be used instead of the default JVM in its browser.

**OK**   The common on-screen button that must be clicked to confirm some process that is about to take place. If the process can be cancelled, then there is a Cancel (or similarly named) button next to the OK button. The OK button is also displayed on information messages when no further action is required simply to keep the message on screen until you click OK and it goes away. In these cases, there is no Cancel option.

**Okidata**   (Okidata, Mount Laurel, NJ, www.okidata.com)  A manufacturer of fax machines and dot matrix, laser-class and ink jet printers, founded in 1972. Okidata's printers are known for their durability. For years, its dot matrix line has been considered the workhorse of desktop impact printers. Starting in 1982, it introduced the first of its LED-based, laser-quality printers, which are widely used.

The company is a division of Oki America, Inc., which is a subsidiary of Tokyo-based Oki Electric Industry Company, Ltd. Oki Electric began making telephones in 1881 and developed the first thermal fax machine in 1976.

**OLAP**   (**O**n**L**ine **A**nalytical **P**rocessing)  Decision support software that allows the user to quickly analyze information that has been summarized into multidimensional views and hierarchies. For example, OLAP tools are used to perform trend analysis on sales and financial information. They can enable users to drill down into masses of sales statistics in order to isolate the products that are the most volatile.

Traditional OLAP products, also known as multidimensional OLAP, or MOLAP, summarize transactions into multidimensional views ahead of time. User queries on these types of databases are extremely fast, because the consolidation has already been done. OLAP places the data into a cube structure that can be rotated by the user, which is particularly suited for financial summaries.

Relational OLAP (ROLAP) tools extract data from traditional relational databases. Using complex SQL statements against relational tables, ROLAP is able to create multidimensional views on the fly. ROLAP tends to be used on data that has a large number of attributes, where it cannot be easily placed into a cube strucutre. For example, customer data with numerous descriptive fields are typically ROLAP candidates, rather than financial data.

A database OLAP, or DOLAP, refers to a relational DBMS that is designed to host OLAP structures and perform OLAP calculations.

A Web OLAP, or WOLAP, refers to OLAP data that is accessible from a Web browser.

**OLAP cube**   A multidimensional database that holds data more like a 3-D spreadsheet rather than a relational database. The cube allows different views of the data to be quickly displayed. See *OLAP* and *multidimensional views.*

**OLAP Services** See *OLAP* and *Microsoft SQL Server OLAP Services*.

**olay** See *OLE*.

**OLCP** (OnLine Complex Processing) Processing complex queries, long transactions and simultaneous reads and writes to the same record. Contrast with *OLTP*, in which records are updated in a more predictable manner.

**OLE** A compound document technology from Microsoft that is based on its Component Object Model (COM). OLE allows an object such as a spreadsheet or video clip to be embedded into a document, called the "container application." When the object is double-clicked, the application that created it, called the "server application," is launched in order to edit it.

An object can be linked instead of embedded, in which case the container application does not physically hold the object, but provides a pointer to it. If a change is made to a linked object, all the documents that contain that same link are automatically updated the next time you open them. An application can be both client and server. See *Object Packager*.

OLE was originally known as "Object Linking and Embedding." However, with version 2.0, OLE's infrastructure was built on a new component architecture known as COM (Component Object Model) that went beyond compound documents. New capabilities such as OLE automation and Network OLE were widely promoted. Later, Microsoft dropped the term OLE for all COM operations except compound documents; however, the old usage still lingers. See **ActiveX Documents** and *COM*.

**OLE automation** See *COM automation*.

**OLE container** In OLE compound document technology, it is the OLE client application, which holds the linked or embedded objects. See *OLE*.

**OLE custom control** See *OCX*.

**OLED** (Organic Light Emitting Device, Organic Light Emitting Diode) Also known as an Organic Electroluminescent Device (OEL), it is a thin-film, light-emitting device that typically consists of a series of organic layers between two electrical contacts (electrodes). OLEDs can be made using small-molecular weight organic materials (SM-OLEDs) or polymer-based materials (PLEDs, LEPs). Unlike LCDs and FEDs, which are constructed of layered materials, OLEDs are monolithic devices, because each layer is deposited on the other, creating a single unit.

Initially developed for display applications, OLEDs offer bright, colorful images with a wide viewing angle and low power. They do not need backlights as do LCD screens. OLEDs are commonly constructed on glass, but can also be fabricated on plastic and other flexible substrate films, such as Universal Display's Flexible OLED (FOLED). Display screens of this type are expected to have a dramatic impact on handheld devices in the future.

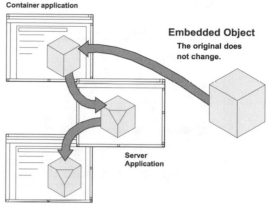

**Embedded Object**
The original does not change.

**OLE Embedding**
If an object is embedded, the document contains a copy of it. Changes made to the object affect only the document that contains it.

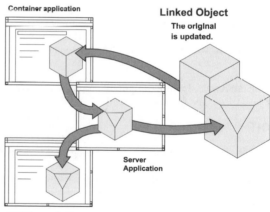

**Linked Object**
The original is updated.

**OLE Linking**
If an object is linked, the document contains a pointer to the original file. When you change a linked object, you are changing the original, and all the documents that link to that object are automatically updated.

NOT DRAWN TO SCALE

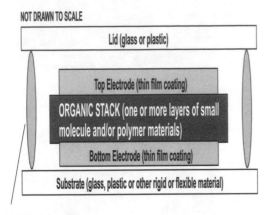

**OLED Cross Section**
This is a cross section of a simple OLED device. Depending on construction type, the user's view can be through the lid, through the substrate or from both sides. *(Illustration courtesy of Universal Display Corporation, www.universaldisplay.com)*

**The Future**
This OLED display screen unrolled out of a pen may seem far fetched, but such products are expected to be commercialized in a few years. *(Image courtesy of Universal Display Corporation, www.universaldisplay.com)*

**OLE DB**    (OLE DataBase) A programming interface for data access from Microsoft. It functions in a similar manner as ODBC, but for every type of data source not just SQL databases. Applications can use OLE DB to access ODBC databases as well. OLE DB for OLAP is used to access OLAP databases. OLE DB is a COM object. See *ODBC, DAO, RDO* and *ADO*.

**OLE server**    In OLE compound document technology, it is the application that is called upon to display and process a linked or embedded object. See *OLE*.

**OLR**    See *offline reader*.

**OLTP**    (OnLine Transaction Processing) See *transaction processing* and *OLCP*.

**OM1**    (Open MPEG-1) A programming interface developed by the Open PC MPEG Consortium for interactive MPEG-1 titles. It provides a common set of commands for programming interactive games that are compressed under MPEG. OM1 is based on Sigma Design's RealMagic MPEG-1 board and has become a de facto standard.

**OMA**    See *Object Management Architecture*.

**OME**    (Open Messaging Environment) An open messaging system from Novell. It is based on Microsoft's MAPI and is a superset of Novell's MHS and WordPerfect Office's messaging systems.

**OMEGAMON**    A family of performance tools for S/390 environments from Candle that monitor processing activities of major systems programs such as MVS, CICS and DB2. OMEGAMON was the first realtime performance monitor for MVS.

**OM-Express**    An offline browser for the Internet from Open Market, Inc., Cambridge, MA. It can automatically dial up and download selected Web pages automatically, storing them on the hard disk for reading at a later date.

**OMG**    See *Object Management Group*.

**OMI**    (1) See *Open Market*.

**(2)** (Open Microprocessor Initiative, Brussels, Belgium) An organization that functions under the umbrella of the European Commission. It funds projects that research and develop advanced microcontroller technologies. There are more than 400 organizations working in joint ventures.

**(3)** (Open Messaging Interface) A messaging protocol developed by Lotus, later included in VIM.

**omnidirectional**   In all directions. For example, an omnidirectional antenna can pick up signals in all directions.

**OmniKey keyboard**   A high-quality PC keyboard originally offered by Northgate Computers of Eden Prarie, MN. See *Avant Stellar keyboard* and *Northgate*.

**OmniPage**   Character recognition software for PCs and the Macintosh from ScanSoft, Inc., Los Gatos, CA (www.scansoft.com). It was the first personal computer software that could distinguish text from graphics and convert a wide variety of fonts into text. Originally developed by Caere Corporation, which merged with ScanSoft in 2000.

**OMNIS 7**   A client/server development system for creating Windows and Mac applications from Blyth Software, Foster City, CA (www.blyth.com). It includes its own database manager for local and laptop use and supports a wide variety of databases. OMNIS includes visual programming tools and a 4GL for application development.

**OmniTRACS**   A fleet management system from QUALCOMM. Introduced in the late 1980s, it includes two-way mobile communications hardware, fleet management software and satellite tracking through its San Diego-based network management center.

**OMR**   (Optical Mark Reader) A scanner that reads marks on specific areas of the page. See *mark sensing*.

**OMT**   (Object Modeling Technique) An object-oriented analysis and design method developed by James Rumbaugh. See *Rational Rose*.

**OM-Transact**   See *Transact*.

**ONA**   (Open Network Architecture) An FCC plan that allows users and competing enhanced service providers (ESPs) equal access to unbundled, basic telephone services. The Open Network Provision (ONP) is the European counterpart.

**onboard**   Refers to a chip or other hardware component that is directly attached to the printed circuit board (motherboard). Contrast with *offboard*. See *inboard*.

**ONC**   (Open Network Computing) A family of networking products from SunSoft for implementing distributed computing in a multivendor environment. Includes TCP/IP and OSI protocols, NFS distributed file system, NIS naming service and TI-RPC remote procedure call library. ONC+ adds Federated Services, which is an interface for third-parties to connect network services into the Solaris environment.

**on-demand printing**   The ability to print a pamphlet, manual or book in small quantities as required. It implies printing from a computer rather than the traditional offset printing process. On-demand printing is environmentally sound, because hundreds of thousands of unsold, new books are destroyed annually, and even books that had a run go out of print when interest declines. On-demand allows every book ever published to be available for the future, and it allows new authors to be published more easily. A complete, finished hardcover book can be created from scratch in less than 20 minutes using on-demand equipment. See *digital printing*.

**on die**   Refers to circuits that are on the same chip. For example, the phrase "the L2 cache is on die" means that the level 2 cache is fabricated on the same silicon as the processor.

**one-chip computer**   See *computer on a chip*.

**one-click buying**   The ability to purchase on the Web by clicking a single button on a Web page after selecting your merchandise. Your name, address and credit card information are stored on the vendor's Web server or extracted from a cookie on your computer so you don't have to enter the same information each time you make a purchase from the site. One-click buying also implies that the quantities, shipping and taxes are automatically computed and totalled. See *digital wallet* and *cookie*.

**one-off**   (1) One at a time. CD-ROM recorders (CD-R drives) are commonly called one-off machines because they write one CD-ROM at a time.

(2) Only once. Software that is written to solve a specfic problem only one time is sometimes called a one-off.

**one-way hash function**   In cryptography, an algorithm that generates a fixed string of numbers from a text message. The "one-way" means that is extremely difficult to turn the fixed string back into the text message. One-way hash functions are used for creating digital signatures for message authentication. See *digital signature*.

**on-hook**   The state of a telephone line that can receive an incoming call. Contrast with *off-hook*.

**onion diagram**   A graphical representation of a system that is made up of concentric circles. The innermost circle is the core, and all outer layers are dependent on the core.

**online**   Available for immediate use. It typically refers to being connected to the Internet or other remote service. When you connect via modem, you are online after you dial in and log on to your Internet provider with your username and password. When you log off, you are offline. With cable modem and DSL service, you are online all the time.

A peripheral device (terminal, printer, etc.) that is turned on and connected to the computer is also online. For example, if your data is on a disk attached to your computer, the disk and the data are said to be online. If your data is on a removable disk cartridge in your desk drawer, it is offline. A printer can be taken offline by simply pressing the ONLINE, GO or SEL button. The printer is still attached and connected, but is internally cut off from receiving data from the computer. Pressing the button turns it back online.

In the 1960s and 1970s, the ancient days of computers, systems were designed as either online or batch. Online meant terminals were connected to a central computer, and batch meant entering batches of transactions (from punched cards or tape) on a second or third shift. Other terms, such as *realtime* and *transaction processing* evolved from online processing. See also *nearline*.

**Want to Impress Your Friends?**   Although somewhat overkill, it is not incorrect to say that one has an online, realtime, transaction processing system (that is, providing you do). In this day and age of buzzwords, this phrase still sounds pretty high tech. But if you say this at your next cocktail party, watch out. Your friends will start asking you how to get their printers to work right and their programs not to crash. An experienced systems analyst will probably chuckle.

online means happiness!

**online advertising**   See *Internet advertising*.

**online auction**   Using the Web to match buyers and sellers around the globe. eBay pioneered this marketplace and Amazon.com, Yahoo! and others quickly followed. Variations of the theme are also available from priceline.com and Microsoft's Expedia, which ask the buyers to name their prices and see if the sellers will match it. Group buying is also available from Mercata.com and others that enable several people to pool their interests and pay for a bulk purchase. There are even "haggling" sites from HaggleZone.com and NexTag.com, which let you negotiate the price. See *eBay*, *Amazon.com*, *priceline.com* and *bid shielding*.

**online complex processing**   See *OLCP*.

**online coupons**   See *e-centives*.

**online help**    On-screen instruction that is immediately available. See *user interface* and *RTFM*.

**online industry**    The collection of service organizations that provide dial-up access to databases, shopping, news, weather, sports, e-mail, etc. See *online services*.

**online marketplace**    See *vertical portal* and *Web hub*.

**online postage**    See *PC Postage*.

**online services**    An organization that provides access to the Internet as well as proprietary content. Before the Internet became widely used by the general public, all online services were self-contained organizations known for their unique mix of databases and resources. If e-mail was provided, it was only within the same service.

After the Internet became popular, all the services either provided Web access to their specialized databases or added general-purpose Internet access such as AOL and CompuServe. Proprietary e-mail system were either switched to Internet e-mail protocols (SMTP) or their formats were routinely converted back and forth to the Internet format. The following online services predate the Internet explosion of the mid 1990s. See *portal*.

**America Online, Inc. (AOL)**    Internet access, variety of databases www.aol.com

**CompuServe Information Service, Inc.**    Internet access, variety of databases www.compuserve.com

**DataTimes Corporation**    Newspapers, magazines, financial www.datatimes.com

**DIALOG**    Largest collection of databases www.dialog.com

**Dow Jones Interactive**    Finance, daily news & news searching http://bis.dowjones.com

**Genie**    Internet access, BBSs, roundtables www.genie.com

**LEXIS-NEXIS**    Legal and news information www.lexis-nexis.com

**National Library of Medicine**    MEDLINE and MEDLARS databases www.nlm.nih.gov

**Prodigy**    Internet access, variety of databases www.prodigy.com

**Questel - Orbit**    Patent, trademark, scientific, chemical, business and news information www.questel.orbit.com

**West Publishing/WESTLAW**    Legal databases www.westpub.com

**online stalker**    An individual that attempts to gain the respect of another in chat rooms or by e-mail in order to eventually harass or stalk the victim.

**online stamps**    See *PC Postage*.

**online storefront**    A store on the Internet that offers items for sale and is capable of handling the financial transaction online. See *cybermall* and *digital money*.

**online transaction processing**    See *transaction processing* and *OLCP*.

**OnNow**    A feature that allows a PC to be turned on by external devices. Implementing the Advanced Configuration and Power Interface (ACPI) in newer PC motherboards, the PC can be placed into a sleep mode that uses virtually no power until it is "awakened." See *ACPI*.

**on the fly**    Same as *dynamic*.

**Onyx** A family of graphics supercomputers from SGI that use the MIPS R10000 CPU and range from single-processor workstations to rack-mounted systems with 24 CPUs. They use SGI's InfiniteReality graphics subsystem which processes geometry, imaging and video data in realtime.

**OO** Object oriented.

**OOA** See *object-oriented analysis*.

**OOAD** (Object-Oriented Analysis and Design) See *object-oriented analysis* and *object-oriented design*.

**OOB bug** See *WinNuke*.

**OOB data** See *out-of-band data*.

**OOBE** (Out Of Box Experience) The experience of setting up and using a new computer or software package.

**OOD** See *object-oriented design*.

**OODB** See *object-oriented database*.

**OODBMS** See *object-oriented DBMS*.

**OOO** (Optical in Optical processing Optical out) Refers to network devices that maintain the photonic transmission signal without converting back to electrical signals. Contrast with *OEO*. See *optical switch*.

**OOOS** See *object-oriented operating system*.

**OOP** See *object-oriented programming*.

**OOPL** (OOP Language) An object-oriented programming language.

**OOPS** (Object-Oriented Programming System) See *object-oriented programming*.

**OORDBMS** (Object-Oriented Relational DBMS) A relational database management system that has object-oriented capabilities.

**OOSE** (Object-Oriented Software Engineering) An object-oriented analysis and design method developed by Ivar Jacobsen. OOSE is known for its high-level design capabilities. See *Rational Rose*.

**OOT** (Object-Oriented Technology) See *objects* and *object-oriented programming*.

**Opal** Software from Computer Associates that converts legacy output from mainframes and minicomputers into a graphical-based format. Opal Integrator provides the development environment and supports 3270, 5250 and VT220 terminals and ODBC-compliant databases. Development can be done by drag and drop or by scripting in OpalScript or VBScript. Opal Server provides a Telnet connection to the mainframe or mini and maintains a connection to the desktop allowing the Web browser or a Windows client with the Opal Player to have access to the newly-formatted data. See *green screen*.

**op amp** (Operational Amplifier) A device that amplifies analog signals. It uses two inputs; one for power and one for data. It is used in a myriad of applications from communications to stereo.

**OPC** (OpenGL Performance Characterization) A project group within GPC that manages OpenGL benchmarks. OPC endorses the Viewperf and GLperf benchmarks. Viewperf was created by IBM and OPC provides viewsets for it, which are combinations of tests using specific applications to test OpenGL performance. PTC's CDRS (CDRS-03) is used for modeling and rendering. IBM's Data Explorer (DX-03) is used for visualization. Intergraph's DesignReview

(DRV-04) is used for 3-D models. Alias/Wavefront's Advanced Visualizer (AWadvs-01) is used for animation, and Lightscape Technology's Lightscape Visualization System (Light-01) is used for radiosity visualization.

Developed by the OPC, the GLperf benchmark measures low-level OpenGL 2-D and 3-D graphics primitives. The results are the raw performance of a system rather than the application performance as provided by the Viewperf benchmarks. Viewperf results are in frames per second, and GLperf results are in primitives per second. See *GPC*.

**op code**　　See *operation code*.

**open**　　(1) To engage a disk or tape file for reading and writing. The open procedure "locks on" to an existing file. Contrast with *close*.

(2) With regard to a switch, open is "off."

(3) Made to operate with other products. See *open architecture* and *open systems*.

**OpenAir**　　A wireless LAN protocol endorsed by the Wireless LAN Interoperability Forum (WLIF). It uses a frequency hopping spread spectrum (FHSS) air interface in the unlicensed 2.4GHz band and is based on Proxim's RangeLAN2 architecture. See *RangeLAN* and *wireless LAN*.

**open architecture**　　A system in which the specifications are made public in order to encourage third-party vendors to develop add-on products. Much of Apple's early success was due to the Apple II's open architecture. The PC is open architecture.

**Open Blueprint**　　IBM's architecture and strategy for enterprise computing. It is a comprehensive set of documentation available to customers and prospects for integrating mainframes, client/server and network computing into a cohesive, distributed computing environment. It provides building blocks and checklists for the systems analyst and technical staff. For more information, visit www.software.ibm.com/openblue.

**OpenBSD**　　An open-source UNIX operating system that was originally developed by the University of California at Berkeley. It is designed to be an industrial-strength Internet server with strong cryptographic techniques for resisting attacks from criminal hackers. OpenBSD runs on x86, Sun, Alpha and other platforms. For more information, visit www.openbsd.org. See *BSD UNIX*.

**open computing**　　See *open systems*.

**Open Database Connectivity**　　See *ODBC*.

**OpenDDS**　　(**Open**VME **D**ata **D**ictionary **S**ystem) A central repository for administering databases and systems from ICL for its OpenVME environment. OpenDDS provides an enhanced interface to DDS and supports the CDIF format for data interchange with CASE tools.

**Open Desktop**　　See *SCO OpenServer*.

**OpenDoc**　　An object-oriented compound document and component architecture. Documents and images can be embedded within or linked to documents set up as containers. OpenDoc is a superset of OLE, and OLE objects can be placed into OpenDoc documents and behave like OLE objects. OpenDoc components (Live Objects) are CORBA compliant and can be called up on a remote computer. OpenDoc was governed by Component Integration Labs (CI Labs), a vendor consortium in Sunnyvale, CA. In June 1997, CI Labs dissolved, and OpenDoc became history.

**OpenDoc parts**　　The original name for OpenDoc components, which were renamed Live Objects. See *OpenDoc*.

**Open eBook**　　See *OEB*.

**open file**　　A file, typically a disk file, that has been made available to the application by the operating system for reading and/or writing. All files must be "opened" before they can be accessed and "closed" when no longer required.

**OpenGL** (OPEN Graphics Language) A 3-D graphics language developed by SGI, which has become a de facto standard endorsed by many vendors. OpenGL can be implemented as an extension to an operating system or a window system and is supported by most UNIX-based workstations, Windows and X Window. Most high-end 3-D accelerators support OpenGL. See *OPC*. See *graphics accelerator*.

**Open Group** (The Open Group, Cambridge, MA, www.opengroup.org) Formed in 1966 as the merger of the Open Software Foundation (OSF) and X/Open organizations, The Open Group is dedicated to promoting open standards. The OSF side is responsible for research and development and licensing of source code, while X/Open is responsible for certification and registration.

Founded in 1988, OSF is a coalition of worldwide vendors and users that delivers technology innovations in all areas of open systems. Founded in 1984, X/Open is dedicated to developing specifications and tests for open system compliance. X/Open also manages the UNIX trademark on behalf of the industry. Following are the major products from the OSF side. See also *ANDF*.

**OSF/1** The OSF/1 operating system uses Carnegie Mellon's Mach kernel. It is a B1-secure, symmetric multiprocessing system that is compliant with POSIX, XPG4 and SVID base and kernel extensions. IBM, HP, DEC and Hitachi use OSF/1 in full or in part.

**Motif** Motif is a graphical user interface (GUI) for applications running on any system with X Window Version 11. Compliant with POSIX, ANSI C and XPG, Motif is the de facto standard graphical interface for UNIX.

**DCE** The Distributed Computing Environment is a set of programs that allows applications to be built across heterogeneous platforms in a network. DCE has been adopted by many organizations.

**DME** The Distributed Management Environment is a set of programs for system and network management. DME was not widely used.

**OpenLDI** (OPEN LVDS Digital Interface) A digital interface for a flat panel display based on LVDS and endorsed by SGI, Number Nine, National Semiconductor and others. The first flat panel monitor to use this interface is SGI's award-winning 1600SW with a 1,600×1,024×16M resolution. OpenLDI is expected to be superseded by DVI. See *DVI*, *flat panel display* and *LVDS*.

**OPEN LOOK** An X Window-based graphical user interface for UNIX developed by Sun. It has been widely used by Sun and was defined and distributed by AT&T when it was still involved with UNIX. OPEN LOOK has given way to Motif, which has become the standard user interface in the UNIX world.

**OpenMail** An electronic mail system from HP that runs on UNIX servers. It complies with the X.400 messaging and X.500 directory standards and supports all major mail programs that run on the client.

**Open Market** (Open Market, Inc., Cambridge, MA, www.openmarket.com) A software company founded in 1994 by Shikar Ghosh and David Gifford that specializes in electronic commerce on the Internet. Open Market's Transact system enables Web servers to conduct secure order fulfillment using credit cards, ecash and other payment systems. Open Market was the first company to provide a software package that provided a single point of access control, user authentication and financial processing to multiple content servers (online storefronts, cybermalls, internal Web sites, etc.). See *digital money*.

**OpenMG** An SDMI-compliant digital rights management (DRM) system from Sony. Once the data is downloaded to the user's hard disk, it cannot be distributed onto the network. OpenMG Jukebox is the software component that downloads and encrypts the files. Supporting ATRAC3, WAV and MP3 formats, OpenMG Jukebox lets you check out music files to the VAIO Music Clip portable player. "Checking out" and then "checking in" the files transfers them temporarily to the Music Clip without violating copyrights. See *ATRAC3* and *DRM*.

**OpenNT** A software subsystem that adds UNIX capability to Windows NT from Softway Systems, Inc., San Francisco, CA. A developer's kit allows UNIX applications to be recompiled into POSIX and X/Open-compliant applications that can run under NT.

**OpenPIC**    (OPEN Programmable Interrupt Controller) An SMP chip architecture endorsed by AMD and Cyrix Corporation that provides symmetric multiprocessing (SMP) for x86 and PowerPC systems It can support up to 32 processors. See *APIC*.

**open pipe**    A continuous path from sender to receiver, such as found in a circuit-switching network or leased line. Transmitted data is not broken up into packets.

**open reel**    A reel of magnetic tape. It typically refers to half-inch open reels that still remain in the archives of many data libraries. In the 1950s, before the 8-bit byte, 7-track tapes (seven parallel tracks) were used to accomodate a 6-bit character plus parity. Starting in the 1960s, 9-track tapes were used to support the byte. See *half-inch tape* and *magnetic tape*.

**The Venerable Open Reel**
Practically extinct today, open reels were the common means of computer storage from the 1950s to the 1970s. The earlier drives required manual threading of the tape onto the empty takeup reel.

**OpenROAD**    A client/server development system from Computer Associates that runs on Windows, X terminal and OS/2 clients. It supports the major SQL databases including Ingres. OpenROAD was originally Windows 4GL from Ingres, but supported only the Ingres database. See *Ingres II*.

**Open Server**    See *SCO OpenServer*.

**open shop**    A computing environment that allows users to program and run their own programs. Contrast with *closed shop*.

**Open Software Foundation**    See *Open Group*.

**open source**    Free source code of a program, which is made available to the development community at large. The rationale is that a broader group of programmers will utlimately produce a more useful and more bug-free product for everyone, especially because more people will be reviewing the code. Peer review is considered one of the most important safeguards to prevent buggy code, but is often not given enough, if any, attention by software companies. Peer review is a natural byproduct of open source projects.

In addition to having better code, open source software allows an organization to modify the product for its own use rather than hope that the vendor of a proprietary product will implement its suggestions in a subsequent release. Examples of popular open source programs are the Apache Web server, sendmail mail server and Linux operating system. Netscape Communicator was made open source in 1998 (see *Mozilla*). For more information, visit www.opensource.org.

**open source UNIX**    Refers to the versions of UNIX that are distributed as open source products, primarily Linux and BSD UNIX. Solaris and SCO UnixWare are examples of proprietary UNIX versions. See *open source*.

**OpenStep**    An object-oriented development environment from Apple, which runs on Windows, Sun and HP machines. OpenStep was originally developed by NeXT Computer as part of its NextStep operating system. OpenStep was incorporated into Rhapsody and later Mac OS X as the Yellow Box programming interface (now known as Cocoa). See *NeXT* and *Rhapsody*.

**open storage**    Disk and tape systems that connect via standard interfaces such as SCSI and IDE.

**open systems**    For years, open systems and UNIX-based computing have been synonymous, because UNIX runs on more different kinds of computers than any other operating system. The goal of open systems is interoperability between hardware and software that is defined by the industry at large and not one or two vendors.

Open systems includes database management systems (DBMSs) that run on many different platforms as well and any other tools that are used across multiple platforms. While this provides a certain freedom for future changes, it is by no means a problem free environment and never will be. Whenever several hardware platforms are used, a version of each software product must be available for that platform.

For example, in order to migrate an application from one UNIX system to another, all the system software components (DBMSs, TP monitors, compilers, etc.) that are currently linked to that application must also be available for the new system. Otherwise, custom conversion programs must be developed and more conversion effort is required.

The goal of open systems is a beautiful one, very much akin to world peace. Everyone pledges allegiance to it, but getting there seems to take forever.

Increasingly, the term also refers to the Wintel PC. Technically, the PC is an open architecture, not an open system, since Intel and Microsoft control the primary hardware and software standards. However, countless third-party vendors have been encouraged to write software for the platform as well as make hardware add-ons and interoperable products, which is why the PC became the largest segment of the computer industry.

Many in the industry also use the term to refer to everything other than proprietary IBM S/390, AS/400 and RS/6000 environments. Contrast with *closed system*. See *OSI*, *Open Group* and *X/Open*.

**Open Transport**   The subsystem in the Macintosh operating system that implements AppleTalk, TCP/IP and serial communications protocols. Macintosh developers creating network applications interact with the network by writing to the same Open Transport programming interface (API), regardless of the underlying transport mechanism. Open Transport is a superset of X/Open's Transport Interface.

**OpenType**   A font technology from Microsoft and Adobe that is an extension to the TrueType format with support for Type 1 fonts, which it contains within a TrueType wrapper. It provides more support for glyphs and ligatures than previous formats and is expected to ease cross-platform operations between Windows and the Mac. Like TrueType fonts, OpenType fonts use only one font file rather than two as with Type 1 fonts. OpenType is also unicode based.

**OpenView**   Network management software from HP. It supports SNMP and CMIP protocols, and third-party products that run under OpenView support SNA and DECnet network management protocols. OpenView is an enterprise-wide network management solution.

**OpenVME**   An operating system from ICL that was introduced in 1994 for its Series 39 mainframes and carried forth on its Trimetra systems. OpenVME is the open systems version of the VME operating system, which includes all the open interfaces previously available as an option. In late 1992, VME had already achieved XPG4 branding for its conformance to open systems standards. See *VME*.

**OpenVMS**   A later version of the VMS operating system from Digital that is POSIX and XPG3-compliant and runs on VAX and Alpha systems.

**Opera**   A Web browser for Windows, EPOC, BeOs and Linux from Opera Software, Oslo, Norway, (www.opera.com). Developed at Telenor (Norwegian Telecom) in 1994 and commercialized by Opera in 1995, it is noted for its unique features, including fast rendering of Web pages and built-in zoom. Opera can display multiple windows with only one instance of the program running, which allows for example, a Web page with many links to be kept in view in one window while retrieving the linked pages in another. Opera can import bookmarks from Netscape and Internet Explorer.

**operand**   The part of a machine instruction that references data or a peripheral device. In the instruction, **ADD A to B**, A and B are the operands (nouns), and ADD is the operation code (verb). In the instruction **READ TRACK 9, SECTOR 32**, track and sector are the operands.

**operating system**   The master control program that runs the computer. The first program loaded when the computer is turned on, its main part, the "kernel," resides in memory at all times. The operating system sets the standards for all application programs that run in the computer. The applications "talk to" the operating system for all user interface and file management operations. Also called an "executive" or "supervisor," an operating system performs the following functions.

**User Interface**   All graphics based today, the user interface includes the windows, menus and method of interaction between you and the computer. Prior to the Mac, Windows and Motif (UNIX) interfaces, all interaction was based on commands entered by the user. Operating systems may support optional interfaces and allow a new shell, or skin, to be used instead.

**Job Management** Job management controls the order and time in which programs are run and is more sophisticated in the mainframe environment where scheduling the daily work has always been routine. IBM's job control language (JCL) was developed decades ago. In a desktop environment, batch files can be written to perform a sequence of operations that can be scheduled to start at a given time.

**Task Management** Multitasking, which is the ability to simultaneously execute multiple programs, is available in all operating systems today. Critical in the mainframe and large server environment, applications can be prioritized to run faster or slower depending on their purpose. In the desktop world, multitasking is necessary just for keeping several applications open at the same time so you can bounce back and forth between them. See *multitasking*.

**Data Management** Data management keeps track of the data on disk, tape and optical storage devices. The application program deals with data by file name and a particular location within the file. The operating system's file system knows where that data is physically stored (which sectors on disk) and interaction between the application and operating system is through the programming interface. Whenever an application needs to read or write data, it makes a call to the operating system (see *API*).

**Device Management** Device management controls peripheral devices by sending them commands in their own proprietary language. The software routine that knows how to deal with each device is called a "driver." The operating system contains all the drivers for the peripherals attached to the computer. When a new peripheral is added, that device's driver is installed into the operating system. See *driver*.

**Security** Multiuser operating systems provide password protection to keep unauthorized users out of the system. Large operating systems also maintain activity logs and accounting of the user's time for billing purposes. They also provide backup and recovery routines for starting over in the event of a system failure.

**History** The earliest operating systems were developed in the late 1950s to manage tape storage, but programmers mostly wrote their own I/O routines. In the mid-1960s, operating systems became essential to manage disks, complex timesharing and multitasking systems.

Today, all multipurpose computers from micro to mainframe use an operating system. Special-purpose devices (appliances, games, toys, etc.) generally do not. They usually employ a single program that performs all the required I/O and processing tasks.

**Common Operating Systems** The primary operating systems in use are the many versions of Windows (95, 98, NT, ME, 2000, XP), the many versions of UNIX (Solaris, Linux, etc.), the Macintosh OS, IBM mainframe OS/390 and the AS/400's OS/400. DOS is still used for some applications, and there are other special-purpose operating systems.

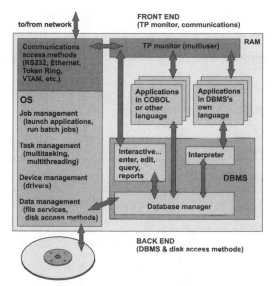

**System and Application Software**
This diagram shows how the major system software interacts with applications in memory. System software comprises the programs that support the running of applications (operating system, DBMS, TP monitor and access methods).

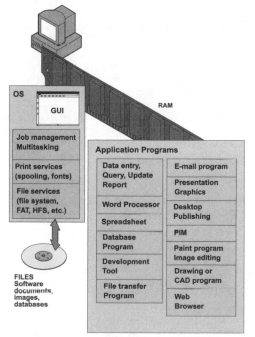

**Operating System and Application Software**
This diagram shows the components of the operating system and typical application programs that run in a desktop computer.

**operation code** The part of a machine instruction that tells the computer what to do, such as input, add or branch. The operation code is the verb; the operands are the nouns.

**operations** See *datacenter*.

**operations manager** See *datacenter manager*.

**operations research** See *management science*.

**operator** (1) A person who operates a typically large computer in a datacenter and performs such activities as commanding the operating system, mounting disks and tapes and placing paper in the printer. Operators may also write the job control language (JCL), which schedules the daily work for the computer. See *system development cycle* and *salary survey*. See also *network operator*.

(2) In programming and logic, a symbol used to perform an operation on some value. See *arithmetic operators* and *Boolean operator*.

**operator overloading** In programming, the ability to use the same operator to perform different operations. For example, arithmetic operators such as +, –, * and / could be defined to perform differently on certain kinds of data.

**operator services** A variety of telephone services that require human intervention, including person-to-person calls, collect calls, credit card billing and directory and dialing assistance. Such services are performed by LECs, IXCs and alternative operator services (AOS) organizations that are used by small telephone resellers and aggregators as well as the larger companies.

**OPI** (Open Prepress Interface) An extension to PostScript that provides color separations. It was developed by Aldus Corporation, which was later acquired by Adobe.

**OPROM** (Option ROM) Firmware on adapter cards that control bootable peripherals. The system BIOS interrogates the option ROMs to determine which devices can be booted. See *BBS*.

**OPS** (Open Profiling Standard) A specification for sharing data and ensuring privacy of a user's data. The OPS provides a standard way of identifying which data can be transferred from the user to a Web site and how it can and cannot be used. See *ICE*.

**optical amplifier** A device that boosts light signals in an optical fiber network. Unlike regenerators, which have to convert light to electricity in order to amplify it and then convert it back again to light, the optical amplifier amplifies the light signal itself. Developed in the late 1980s, the erbium-doped fiber amplifier (EDFA) was the first successful optical amplifier. See *EDFA*.

**optical bands** The spectrum for transmission in singlemode optical fibers has been broken into the following wavelength ranges, or bands. Typically, the wavelengths transmitted in multimode fibers are around 850 and 1310 nm, known originally as first window and second window.

| Band | Name | Wavelength Range in Nanometers (nm) |
|------|------|-------------------------------------|
| O-band | Original | 1260–1360 |
| E-band | Extended | 1360–1460 |
| S-band | Short | 1460–1530 |
| C-band | Conventional | 1530–1565 |
| L-band | Long | 1565–1625 |
| U-band | Ultra-long | 1625–1675 |

**optical cross-connect** A network device used by telecom carriers to switch high-speed optical signals (OC-3, OC-12, OC-48, etc.). It differs from a digital cross-connect in that it deals with mulitple high-speed signals that are switched in their entirety and not multiplexed together. Optical cross-connects work entirely at the optical layer and may be able to operate without having to convert to electrical and back again. Bellcore spin-off Tellium, Inc., Oceanport, NJ (www.tellium.com), introduced the first optical cross-connect in 1998. See *digital cross-connect*.

**optical disk**    A direct access disk written and read by light. CD, CD-ROM, DVD-ROM and DVD-Video are read-only optical disks that are recorded at the time of manufacture and cannot be erased. CD-R, DVD-R, WORM and magneto-optic (in WORM mode) disks are write-once. They are recorded in the user's environment, but cannot be erased. CR-RW, DVD-RAM, DVD-RW and MO disks are rewritable.

Rewritable disks use either magneto-optic (MO) or phase change technology. Used in libraries that hold multiple cartridges, magneto-optic (MO) disks are extremely robust. Phase change disks (CD-RW, DVD-RAM, etc.) are lower cost consumer-oriented products, and DVD-RAM is expected to become very popular.

Optical disks have some advantages over magnetic disks. They have higher capacities as removable modules. They are not subject to head crashes or corruption from stray magnetic fields. They have a 30-year life and are less vulnerable to extremes of hot and cold. See *holographic storage, ISO 13346, multilevel optical disk* and ***legality of optical storage***. See also *magnetic disk* and *magnetic tape*.

| Writability | Optical Disk Types |
|---|---|
| Read-only | CD, CD-ROM, DVD-ROM, DVD-Video |
| Write once | CR-R, DVD-R, WORM |
| Rewrite | CD-RW, DVD-RAM, DVD-RW, MO |

### Magneto-optic (MO) Disk

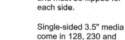

MO disks provide robust online and archival storage (30-year life).

**5.25"**

Double-sided 5.25" disks come in 650MB, 1.3, 2.6 and 5.2GB capacities and must be flipped for each side.

**3.5"**

Single-sided 3.5" media come in 128, 230 and 640MB formats.

### PD Optical Disk

Panasonic's PD is a phase change optical disk that holds 650MB. PD drives support both phase change cartridges and CD-ROMs.

### CD-ROM, CD-R, CD-RW

**CD-ROM**

**Mini CD-ROM**

The 120mm CD-ROM is the de facto standard for software distribution and for publishing large databases. The smaller mini CD-ROM is only 80mm in diameter and holds 180MB (compared to the full-size 650MB). It fits into the deeper well in the center of the tray in most CD-ROM drives.

CD-ROMs have a silver cast just like audio CDs.

**CD-R**

Blank CD-R discs can be recorded once and read on any CD-ROM reader. CD-Rs have a gold, blue or green cast.

CD-RWs can be rewritten, but must be read on newer MultiRead CD and DVD drives. CD-RWs have a blue cast.

**CD-RW**

### DVD

**DVD-Video**
**DVD-ROM**

DVDs look like CDs, but hold from 4 to 28 times as much data. There is a DVD counterpart for every CD type.

DVD-Videos as well as DVD-ROMs are silver, read only discs. DVD-Rs are write once and have a pink cast. Rewritable DVD-RAMs can be double sided, so a cartridge is used to protect the surfaces and provide a label area.

**DVD-R**

**DVD-RAM**

**O**

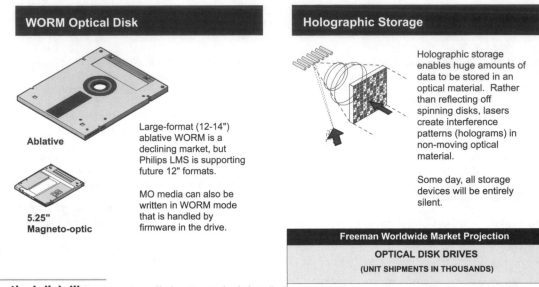

## WORM Optical Disk

**Ablative**

**5.25"
Magneto-optic**

Large-format (12-14") ablative WORM is a declining market, but Philips LMS is supporting future 12" formats.

MO media can also be written in WORM mode that is handled by firmware in the drive.

## Holographic Storage

Holographic storage enables huge amounts of data to be stored in an optical material. Rather than reflecting off spinning disks, lasers create interference patterns (holograms) in non-moving optical material.

Some day, all storage devices will be entirely silent.

**optical disk library**   Also called an "optical jukebox," it is an optical disk storage system that houses multiple disk platters. It is similar to a music jukebox, except that instead of "playing one tune," more than one drive can be used to read and write several disks simultaneously. Such devices are made for rewritable optical disks, write once disks and CD-ROMs, and can hold from a handful to several thousand disks or cartridges.

**optical fiber**   A thin glass strand designed for light transmission. A single hair-thin fiber is capable of transmitting trillions of bits per second. In addition to their huge transmission capacity, optical fibers offer many advantages over electricity and copper wire. Light pulses are not affected by random radiation in the environment, and their error rate is significantly lower. Fibers allow longer distances to be spanned without repeaters that regenerate fading signals. Fibers are more secure, because taps in the line can be detected, and finally, fiber installation is streamlined due to the dramatically lower weight and smaller size of the material compared to copper cables.

For years, the telephone companies have used fibers extensively to rebuild their communications infrastructure. According to KMI Corporation, specialists in fiber optic market research, by the end of 1990 there were approximately eight million miles of fiber laid in the U.S. (this is miles of fiber, not miles of cable which can contain many fibers). By the end of 2000, there were more than 80 million miles in the U.S. and more than 225 million worldwide. Copper cable is increasingly being replaced with fibers for LAN backbones as well, and this usage is expected to increase substantially.

An optical fiber is constructed of a transparent core made of nearly pure silicon dioxide ($SiO2$), through which the light travels. The core is surrounded by a cladding layer that reflects light, guiding the light along the core. A plastic coating covers the cladding to protect the glass surface. Cables also include fibers of Kevlar and/or steel wires for strength and an outer sheath of plastic or Teflon for protection.

For glass fibers, there are two "optical windows" where the fiber is most transparent and efficient. The centers of these windows are 1,300 nm and 1,550 nm, providing approximately 18,000GHz and 12,000GHz respectively, for a total of 30,000GHz. This enormous bandwidth is potentially usable in one fiber. Plastic is also used for short-distance fiber runs, and their transparent windows are typically 650 nm and in the 750–900 nm range.

| Freeman Worldwide Market Projection | | |
|---|---|---|
| **OPTICAL DISK DRIVES** (UNIT SHIPMENTS IN THOUSANDS) | | |
| | 1997 | 1998 | 2003 |
| **REWRITABLE** | 3,573 | 7,435 | 16,449 |
| **WRITE ONCE** | 1,670 | 1,187 | 0 |
| **READ-ONLY** | 82,331 | 96,944 | 139,700 |
| **TOTAL SHIPMENTS** | 87,574 | 105,566 | 156,149 |

Reprinted with permission of Freeman Associates, Inc., a management consulting firm specializing in data storage. (c) 1999 Freeman Associates, Inc., www.freemaninc.com Santa Barbara, CA, (805) 963-3853

There are two primary types of fiber. Multimode fiber is very common for short distances and has a core diameter of from 50 to 100 microns. For intercity cabling and highest speed, singlemode fiber with a core diameter of less than 10 microns is used. See *laser*, *WDM*, **fiber optics glossary** and *cable categories*.

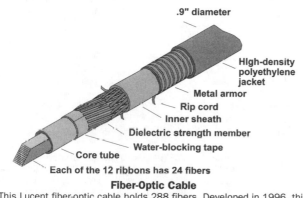

.9" diameter

High-density polyethylene jacket

Metal armor

Rip cord

Inner sheath

Dielectric strength member

Water-blocking tape

Core tube

Each of the 12 ribbons has 24 fibers

**Fiber-Optic Cable**
This Lucent fiber-optic cable holds 288 fibers. Developed in 1996, this was a record-high fiber count for the time. Cables with more than a thousand fibers have since been developed.

**Fiber vs. Copper**
Not only does optical fiber provide enormous transmission bandwidth, but it takes a lot less room. The single strand of fiber in the center is equivalent in capacity to any one of the copper bundles in the picture. *(Image courtesy of Corning Incorporated.)*

**optical isolator**   A device used to prevent lightwaves from reflecting backward (the optical counterpart to an electrical diode). It is a one-way filter for a range of light frequencies.

**optical jukebox**   See *optical disk library*.

**optical library**   See *optical disk library*.

**optical mouse**   A mouse that uses light to get its bearings. It is rolled over a small desktop pad that contains a reflective grid. The mouse emits a light and senses its reflection as it is moved. Contrast with *mechanical mouse*.

**optical networking**   Communications between computers, telephones and other electronic devices using light. An optical network is far more reliable and has far greater potential transmission capacity than networking in the electrical domain. See *optical fiber*.

**optical reader**   An input device that recognizes typewritten or printed characters and bar codes and converts them into their corresponding digital codes.

**optical recognition**   See *OCR*.

**Laying Optical Fiber**
Embedding thousands of miles of fiber in the ground has been a herculean feat undertaken by many companies. Nevertheless, in time, all copper wires are expected to give way to fiber. *(Image courtesy of Metromedia Fiber Network.)*

**optical resolution**   The built-in resolution of a scanning device. Contrast with *interpolated resolution*, which enhances an image by software. Both resolutions are given as dots per inch (dpi), thus a 2,400 dpi scanner can be the true resolution of the machine or a computed resolution. See *interpolated resolution* and *scanner*.

**optical scanner**   See *scanner*.

**optical storage**    See *optical disk* and *legality of optical storage*.

**optical storage library**    See *optical disk library*.

**optical switch**    An all-optical fiber-optic switching device that maintains the signal as light from input to output. Traditional switches that connect optical fiber lines are electro-optic. They convert photons from the input side to electrons internally in order to do the switching and then convert back to photons on the output side.

Although some vendors call electro-optical switches "optical switches," true optical switches support all transmission speeds. Unlike electronic switches, which are tied to specific data rates and protocols, optical switches direct the incoming bitstream to the output port no matter what the line speed or protocol (IP, ATM, SONET) and do not have to be upgraded for any such changes. Optical switches may separate signals at different wavelengths and direct them to different ports.

Using tiny mirrors that reflect the input signal to the output port, MEMS technology is expected to be the prevailing method for building optical switches, also known as "photonic switches." There are various fabrication methods for building MEMS mirrors. See *MEMS* and *transparent network*.

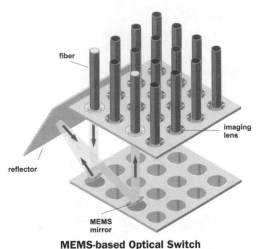

**MEMS-based Optical Switch**
MEMS mirrors reflect the input signal to an output port without regard to line speed or protocol. This technology is expected to be the dominant method for building photonic switches.

**optical wireless**    See *free space optics*.

**optical zoom**    The use of lenses to change the focal length of a digital camera. It is the same as a zoom lens on a traditional 35mm analog film cameras. Digital cameras have both optical and digital zoom. The digital zoom is performed in software. Nothing is better than the optical zoom, because it sees the real objects being photographed. A digital zoom augments the optical zoom, and, depending on subject matter, the results can be quite acceptable or mediocre.

**Opti-Jack**    A Fiber Jack fiber-optic connector from Panduit Corporation, Tinley Park, IL (www.panduit.com), that provides a snap-lock plug and socket for a pair of fiber cables. It enables fibers to be quickly plugged and removed in a manner similar to RJ-45 connectors. See *fiber-optic connectors*.

**optimizer**    Hardware or software that improves performance. See *defragger* and *disk management*.

**Opti-Jack**
The Opti-Jack can be used to quickly plug and unplug fiber-optic cables for any type of application.

**opt-in**    To purposefully accept some situation or condition ahead of time. For example, to opt-in to an e-mail campaign means that you want to receive the specific information being sent even though it may be advertising and your name may be sold to an advertising agency because you expressed interest in a certain topic. You can always unsubscribe to opt-in e-mail, which is not the same as spam. See *spam*.

**option ROM**    See *OPROM*.

**Options menu**    See *Tools menu*.

**optoelectronics**    Combining light and electronics technologies. See *integrated optics*.

**opt-out**    To cancel some situation or condition. See *opt-in*.

**OQL** (Object Query Language) A query language that supports complex data types (multimedia, spatial, compound documents, etc.) that are stored as objects. Defined by the ODMG, it is a superset of the SQL-92 query language. Standard SQL queries can still be used, and the OQL server process converts the objects into relational views.

OQL also supports the OMG's object model (OM), allowing queries to be made against CORBA objects. In addition, OQL commands can be embedded in URL links that are sent to an OQL gateway by the HTTP server. The results are converted back into Web pages for the user.

**OR** A Boolean logic operation that is true if any of the inputs is true. An exclusive OR (XOR) is true if only one of the inputs is true, but not both. See *AND-OR-NOT*.

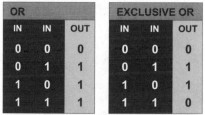

| OR | | | EXCLUSIVE OR | | |
|---|---|---|---|---|---|
| IN | IN | OUT | IN | IN | OUT |
| 0 | 0 | 0 | 0 | 0 | 0 |
| 0 | 1 | 1 | 0 | 1 | 1 |
| 1 | 0 | 1 | 1 | 0 | 1 |
| 1 | 1 | 1 | 1 | 1 | 0 |

**Oracle** (Oracle Corporation, Redwood Shores, CA, www.oracle.com) The world's largest database and application development software vendor founded in 1977 by Larry Ellison. The Oracle database was the first DBMS to incorporate the SQL language and to be ported to a wide variety of platforms. Oracle offers a variety of application development tools and is a major promoter of the network computer. Its Network Computer subsidiary defines the specifications for a compliant platform.

**Oracle8** Oracle's relational database managment system (DBMS). This is the current version of Oracle's flagship product, which includes such features as replication and high availability. Oracle8 runs on more than 80 platforms and includes object-oriented extensions. See *Oracle8i*.

**Oracle8i** A version of the Oracle DBMS that added Internet enhancements. Introduced in 1999, noteworthy features are increased performance and support for XML and Java. A JVM (Java interpreter) is built into the DBMS so that triggers and stored procedures can be written and executed in Java rather than PL/SQL. It enables Internet developers to write applications and database procedures in the same language. In addition, the JVM can also execute Enterprise JavaBeans (EJBs), turning the DBMS into an application server. See *PL/SQL*.

**Oracle Browser** See *Developer/2000*.

**Oracle Data Query** The query function in Discoverer/2000. See *Developer/2000*.

**Oracle Documents** An earlier name for a variety of Oracle software products, including a messaging system, text database and document management system. Each of the products was later offered separately.

**Oracle Express Server** An Oracle database that provides multidimensional views of data. It is Oracle's OLAP product offering, which allows views to be created ahead of time (MOLAP) or directly from relational databases (ROLAP). Oracle Express also lets users gain access to their data from an Excel spreadsheet. See *OLAP*.

**Oracle Forms** See *Developer/2000*.

**Oracle Media Server** An multimedia system for interactive TV delivery from Oracle Corporation that runs on nCUBE, HP and other hardware platforms. The client software runs on Macs, PCs and set-top boxes. It is designed to store and disseminate multiple streams of text (news), images, audio and video on demand.

**Oracle Parallel Server** A version of the Oracle database system designed for massively parallel processors (MPPs). It allows multiple CPUs to access a single database.

**Oracle Rdb** (Oracle Relational DataBase) A relational DBMS that runs under OpenVMS on Digital's VAX and Alpha systems. Rdb was originally developed by Digital and widely used on VAX systems. Oracle acquired it in 1994 and has enhanced the product.

**Oracle Reports** See *Developer/2000*.

**Oracle Universal Server**    Oracle's object-relational version of the Oracle7 DBMS. Object-relational databases store multimedia data as well as the traditional row and column tables of relational data.

**Orange Book**    See *NCSC* and *CD*.

**ORB**    (Object Request Broker) Software that handles the communication of messages from the requesting program (client) to the object as well as any return values from the object back to the calling program. See *CORBA* and *DCOM*. See also *ORB disk*.

**ORB disk**    A high-capacity removable hard disk system from Castlewood Systems, Inc., Pleasanton, CA (www.castlewood.com). Introduced in late 1998 with a capacity of 2.2GB and a 12MB transfer rate, ORB drives use magnetoresistive (MR) read/write head technology. Castlewood is a private company founded by Syed Iftikar, the founder of SyQuest and co-founder of Seagate. See *magnetic disk*.

**ORB Cartridge**
Castlewood is pushing the removable storage envelope further with its ORB drive, which was introduced at $199. Its $29.95 cartridges are considerably lower than the competition.

**ORB gateway**    Software that translates messages between two different ORBs.

**Orbix**    A CORBA-compliant ORB from IONA Technologies Inc., Dublin, Ireland (U.S. office, Marlboro, MA). Founded in 1991, IONA is a leading member of the OMG, and Orbix has become a popular CORBA-based system due to its multiplatform support and OLE integration. This combination made it the first distributed solution for OLE automation.

   OrbixWeb is IONA's Java implementation of Orbix. When users retrieve OrbixWeb-based Java applets, OrbixWeb is downloaded into their machines, providing them with CORBA connectivity.

**ORDBMS**    (Object Relational DBMS) See *universal server*.

**order**    See *precedence* and *byte order*.

**ordering upgrades**    The Encyclopedia is available in several options for individuals and organizations. To find out about them, press F1 and click "Ordering upgrades and licenses."

**order of magnitude**    A change in quantity or volume as measured by the decimal point. For example, from tens to hundreds is one order of magnitude. Tens to thousands is two orders of magnitude; tens to millions is three orders of magnitude, etc.

**ordinal number**    The number that identifies the sequence of an item, for example, record #34. Contrast with *cardinal number*.

**org**    See *.org*.

**organic chemistry**    The molecular science that deals primarily with materials constructed of carbon and hydrogen atoms. See *organic compound*.

**organic compound**    In physics, a material that contains carbon and hydrogen and usually other elements such as nitrogen, sulfur and oxygen. Organic compounds can be found in nature or they can be synthesized in the laboratory. An organic substance is not the same as a "natural" substance. A natural material means that it is essentially the same as it was found in nature, but "organic" means that it is carbon based. See *organic chemistry*.

**organic LED**    See *OLED*.

**organic semiconductor**    A semiconductor made from a carbon-based material. For example, light-emitting polymers (LEPs) are organic semiconductors. Contrast with *inorganic semiconductor*. See *LEP*.

**organizer**    See *PIM* and *PDA*.

**orientation**    In typography, the direction of print across a page. See *portrait*.

**origin server**    A Web server that contains the original Web page. The term is used to identify the Web server from the cache server. Since there is no physical difference between a digital original and a digital copy, the term implies that the origin server is the one that is maintained and updated by the enterprise. See *Web cache*.

**orphan**    See *widow* and *orphan*.

**orthogonal**    At right angles. The term is used to describe electronic signals that appear at 90 degree angles to each other. It is also widely used to describe conditions that are contradictory, or opposite, rather than in parallel or in sync with each other.

**orthophotograph**    An aerial photograph in which the displacement of images has been removed and that has the distortion due to tilt, curvature, and ground relief corrected. It is a "scale corrected" aerial image, depicting ground features in their exact ground positions, in which distortion caused by camera and flight characteristics and relief displacement have been removed using photogrammetric techniques. (Data West Research Agency definition: see *GIS glossary*.)

**OS**    See *operating system*.

**OS 10**    See *Mac OS X*.

**OS/2**    A family of multitasking operating systems for x86 machines from IBM. The client version is OS/2 Warp, and the server version is Warp Server for e-Business. There are add-ons to OS/2 that run DOS and Windows applications (see *Odin*). The server version includes advanced features such as the journaled file system (JFS) used in IBM's AIX operating system. OS/2 provides both a graphical user interface as well as a command line interface similar to DOS. See *OS/2 Warp* and *Warp Server*.

OS/2 is highly regarded as a robust operating system and, although it never became widely used, it is still strong in the banking industry, especially in Europe. In the U.S., many ATM machines run OS/2 due to it stability.

OS/2 provides a dual boot feature. When you turn the computer on, you can boot either OS/2 or DOS. Adobe Type Manager is included for rendering Type 1 fonts on screen and providing PostScript output on non-PostScript printers.

OS/2's Workplace Shell graphical user interface is similar to Windows and the Macintosh. Originally known as Presentation Manager (PM) before Version 2.0, the term still refers to the programming interface for writing GUI-based applications.

The first versions of OS/2 were single-user operating systems written for 286s that were jointly developed by IBM and Microsoft. Subsequent releases, starting with Version 2.0, were written for 32-bit 386s and up and are solely the product of IBM. Following is some of the evolution:

**OS/2 16-bit Version 1.x**    The first versions (1.0, 1.1, etc.) were written for the 16-bit 286. DOS compatibility was limited to about 500K. Version 1.3 (OS/2 Lite) required 2MB RAM instead of 4MB and included Adobe Type Manager. IBM's Extended Edition version included Communications Manager and Database Manager.

**OS/2 32-bit Version 2.x - IBM**    Introduced in April 1992, this 32-bit version for 386s from IBM multitasked DOS, Windows and OS/2 applications. Data could be shared between applications using the clipboard and between Windows and PM apps using the DDE protocol. Version 2.x provided each application with a 512MB virtual address space that allowed large tasks to be easily managed. Version 2.1 supported Windows' Enhanced Mode and applications could take full advantage of Windows 3.1. It also provided support for more video standards and CD-ROM drives. Communications and database management for OS/2 were provided by Communications Manager/2 (CM/2) and Database Manager/2 (DB2/2). CM/2 replaced Communications Manager, which was part of OS/2 2.0's Extended Services option.

**OS/2 32-bit Version 3 - IBM**    In late 1994, IBM introduced Version 3 of OS/2, renaming it OS/2 Warp. The first version ran in only 4MB of memory and included a variety of applications, including Internet access.

**Windows NT - Microsoft**    Originally to be named OS/2 Version 3.0, this 32-bit version from Microsoft was renamed "Windows NT" and introduced in 1993. See *Windows NT*.

O

**OS/2 for Windows**    A special edition of OS/2 Version 2.1 for PCs that already have DOS and Windows 3.1 installed. It is less expensive than the full OS/2, because it does not include the Windows code. This was superseded by OS/2 Warp. See *OS/2*.

**OS/2 PM**    (OS/2 Presentation Manager) The graphical user interface in OS/2 Version 1.x. It was later renamed Workplace Shell starting with Versions 2.0. See *OS/2*.

**OS/2 Warp**    The client version of the OS/2 operating system. It includes peer-to-peer networking, fax and communications programs, multimedia viewing and editing applications and IBM Works (word processing, spreadsheet, database and other office tools).

Introduced in late 1994 as Version 3.0 of OS/2, it was the successor to OS/2 for Windows and OS/2 Version 2.1. When first introduced, it could run in 8MB of memory, which was important for its time.

There were originally two versions of OS/2 Warp. One required Windows 3.1 to be installed, the other included a modified version of Windows 3.1. See *OS/2*.

**OS/2 Warp Connect**    The first version of OS/2 Warp to provide peer-to-peer networking to OS/2 and Windows machines. These networking functions were later added into the regular product line. See *OS/2*.

**OS/360**    The operating system for the IBM System/360, which was introduced in 1964. It was later released in two versions. OS/MFT (Multiple Fixed Transactions) supported multiple programs that used fixed memory regions, and OS/MVT (Multiple Variable Transactions) supported varying program sizes. OS/MFT and OS/MVT were later enhanced for virtual storage and became OS/VS1 and OS/VS2. OS/VS2 evolved into MVS.

**OS/390**    The primary operating system used in IBM mainframes. OS/390 was originally the MVS/ESA operating system renamed and repackaged in 1996 with an extensive set of utilities. Although the name MVS is still used to refer to the base control program of OS/390, enhancements in usability and workload balancing have made OS/390 stand apart from its MVS heritage. OS/390 is upward compatible from MVS/ESA 5.2.2, but downward compatibility is not ensured.

**OS/400**    The operating system designed for the AS/400 minicomputer from IBM.

**OS/8**    A single user, multitasking operating system from Digital for its PDP-8 computers. Variants run on DECstation and DECmate systems.

**OS-9**    A UNIX-like realtime operating system from Microware Systems Corporation, Des Moines, IA (www.microware.com), that is widely used in embedded systems such as pagers and cellular phones. OS-9 runs on Motorola 68000 and PowerPC CPUs. Originally developed for the 6809 chip, a version of OS-9 was created for CD-I players. See *DAVID*.

**OS/9000**    A portable version of OS-9, written in C, which runs on x86 and Motorola 68000 CPUs.

**Osborne I**    The first portable computer, developed by Adam Osborne and introduced in 1981. Floppy disk based with 64K of memory, it used the CP/M operating system and a modified version of the WordStar word processor that would display only 40 characters at a time across its tiny 4.5" CRT. It cost $1,795, which was considerably inexpensive for a computer of that era. Weighing in at nearly 30 pounds and requiring AC power, the Osborne was really more "transportable" than a true portable.

**oscillate**    To swing back and forth between the minimum and maximum values. An oscillation is one cycle, typically one complete wave in an alternating frequency.

**oscillator**    An electronic circuit used to generate high-frequency pulses. See *crystal oscillator*, *VCO* and *clock*.

**oscilloscope**    A test instrument that displays electronic signals (waves and pulses) on a screen. It creates its own time base against which signals can be measured, and displayed frames can be frozen for visual inspection.

**OSD** (1) (**O**n-**S**creen **D**isplay) An on-screen control panel for adjusting monitors and TVs. The OSD is used for contrast, brightness, horizontal and vertical positioning and other monitor adjustments.

(2) (**O**pen **S**oftware **D**escription) A data format for describing a software package, module or component. Based on XML, OSD is designed for distributing and updating software via push technology. Initially introduced for Windows, it is expected to be adopted for other platforms.

**OSF/Motif** See *Motif* and *Open Group*.

**OSI** (**O**pen **S**ystem **I**nterconnection) An ISO standard for worldwide communications that defines a framework for implementing protocols in seven layers. Control is passed from one layer to the next, starting at the application layer in one station, proceeding to the bottom layer, over the channel to the next station and back up the hierarchy.

At one time, most vendors agreed to support OSI in one form or another, but OSI was too loosely defined and proprietary standards were too entrenched. Except for the OSI-compliant X.400 and X.500 e-mail and directory standards, which are widely used, what was once thought to become the universal communications standard now serves as the teaching model for all other protocols.

Most of the functionality in the OSI model exists in all communications systems, although two or three OSI layers may be incorporated into one. See *OSI model*.

## OSI model

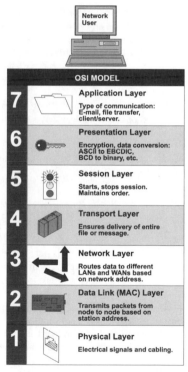

**Application—Layer 7** This top layer defines the language and syntax that programs use to communicate with other programs. The application layer represents the purpose of communicating in the first place. For example, a program in a client workstation uses commands to request data from a program in the server. Common functions at this layer are opening, closing, reading and writing files, transferring files and e-mail messages, executing remote jobs and obtaining directory information about network resouces.

**Presentation—Layer 6** When data is transmitted between different types of computer systems, the presentation layer negotiates and manages the way data is represented and encoded. For example, it provides a common denominator between ASCII and EBCDIC machines as well as between different floating point and binary formats. Sun's XDR and OSI's ASN.1 are two protocols used for this purpose. This layer is also used for encryption and decryption.

**Session—Layer 5** Provides coordination of the communications in an orderly manner. It determines one-way or two-way communications and manages the dialogue between both parties; for example, making sure that the previous request has been fulfilled before the next one is sent. It also marks significant parts of the transmitted data with checkpoints to allow for fast recovery in the event of a connection failure.

In practice, this layer is often not used or services within this layer are sometimes incorporated into the transport layer.

**Transport—Layer 4** The transport layer is responsible for overall end to end validity and integrity of the transmission. The lower data link layer (layer 2) is only responsible for delivering packets from one node to another. Thus, if a packet gets lost in a router somewhere in the enterprise internet, the transport layer will detect that. It ensures that if a 12MB file is sent, the full 12MB is received.

"OSI transport services" include layers 1 through 4, collectively responsible for delivering a complete message or file from sending to receiving station without error.

**Network—Layer 3** The network layer establishes the route between the sending and receiving stations. The node to node function of the data link layer (layer 2) is extended across the entire internetwork, because a routable protocol contains a network address in addition to a station addresses.

This layer is the switching function of the dial-up telephone system as well as the functions performed by routable protocols such as IP, IPX, SNA and AppleTalk. If all stations are contained within a single network segment, then the routing capability in this layer is not required. See *layer 3 switch*.

**Data Link—Layer 2**   The data link is responsible for node to node validity and integrity of the transmission. The transmitted bits are divided into frames; for example, an Ethernet, Token Ring or FDDI frame in local area networks (LANs). Layers 1 and 2 are required for every type of communications. For more on this layer, see *data link protocol*.

**Physical—Layer 1**   The physical layer is responsible for passing bits onto and receiving them from the connecting medium. This layer has no understanding of the meaning of the bits, but deals with the electrical and mechanical characteristics of the signals and signaling methods. For example, it comprises the RTS and CTS signals in an RS-232 environment, as well as TDM and FDM techniques for multiplexing data on a line. SONET also provides layer 1 capability.

**OSI stack**   The protocol stack in the OSI model. See *OSI*.

**OSP**   (Online Service Provider) See *online services*.

**OSPF**   (Open Shortest Path First) A routing protocol that determines the best path for routing IP traffic over a TCP/IP network. OSPF is an interior gateway protocol (IGP), which is designed to work within an autonomous system. It is also a link state protocol that provides less router to router update traffic than the RIP protocol (distance vector protocol) that it was designed to replace. See *RIP* and *routing protocol*.

**OSS**   (Open Source Software) Software that can be modified and recompiled by the user. See *open source*.

**OSTA**   (Optical Storage Technology Association, Santa Barbara, CA, www.osta.org) A membership organization composed of major optical drive manufacturers. Its purpose is to endorse standards and promote the use of optical media in computing.

**OSU**   (Open Source UNIX) Refers to the UNIX variants that are maintained as open source, which are primarily BSD UNIX and Linux.

**OSX**   See *Mac OS X*.

**OT**   (Object Technology) The use of objects.

**OTDR**   (Optical Time Domain Reflectometer) A test instrument that analyzes the light loss in an optical fiber. Used to find faults, splices and bends in the line, it works by sending out a light pulse and measuring its reflection. Such devices can measure fiber lines that are longer than 150 miles.

**OTG**   (The OBJECTive Technology Group, Ltd., Alexandria, VA, www.theotg.com) An organization devoted to distributed computing and object technology. Founded in 1994, it augments the object and Internet standards community and serves as an intermediary between them and ISVs and users. The OTG hosts the Object Oriented Technology & Symposium (OOTS) conferences for communications and media, the financial industry and the Federal Government.

**OTOH**   Digispeak for "on the other hand."

**OTP**   (1) (One Time Programmable) Refers to programming the content into chips such as ROMs and EEPROMs, which cannot be altered.
   (2) (One Time Pad) A cryptography method that uses a random number to generate a unique encryption key, which is stored on a smart card. See *SwapCrypt*.
   (3) (Open Trading Protocol) A framework for Internet commerce that provides a consistent purchasing experience regardless of the hardware and software used.

**OTPROM**    (One Time **PROM**) A PROM chip that can be programmed only once.

**OUI**    (**O**rganizational **U**nique **I**dentifier) The part of the MAC address that identifies the vendor of the network adapter. The OUI is the first three bytes of the six-byte field and is administered by the IEEE. See *MAC layer*.

**outboard**    Not built in. Outboard devices are external to the main unit. Contrast with *inboard*. See *offboard*.

**outbox**    An area in memory or on the disk that holds messages or files that have not yet been sent to their destination. Contrast with *inbox*.

**outdent**    Same as *hanging paragraph*.

**outer join**    See *join*.

**outline font**    A type of font made from basic outlines of each character. The outlines are scaled into actual characters (bitmaps) before printing. See *scalable font*.

**outline processor**    Software that allows the user to type in thoughts and organize them into an outline form.

**Outlook**    Microsoft's mail client and personal information manager. Outlook Express is a lite version for e-mail only that comes with Windows. The full version includes a PIM, calendaring, to-do list and groupware functions. It also provides a journaling capability for keeping track of hourly billing. Outlook can be used as the client end to Microsoft's Exchange Server or as the e-mail client with any ISP account. See *Microsoft Office* and *Microsoft Exchange*.

**out-of-band**    Outside the primary frequency or system. See *signaling in/out-of-band* and *out-of-band data*.

**out-of-band data**    Data transmitted with the primary data stream that is considered a control signal and which demands immediate attention. The receiving side must pass the OOB data to the appropriate software routine in front of any other data that has been buffered and not yet processed, because the command must be executed as soon as possible.

**out of box**    See *out of the box* and *outside the box*.

**out-of-process server**    An executable program that is launched as an independent application. For example, an EXE file is an out-of-process server. Contrast with *in-process server*.

**out of the box**    Hardware that has just been removed from its original carton and plugged in or software just removed from its original package and installed. See *OOBE*. See also *outside the box*.

**output**    (1) Any computer-generated information displayed on screen, printed on paper or in machine-readable form, such as disk and tape.
    (2) To transfer or transmit from the computer to a peripheral device or communications line.

**output area**    A reserved segment of memory used to collect data to be transferred out of the computer. Same as *buffer*.

**output bound**    Excessive overall slowness due to moving data out of the computer to low-speed lines or devices. See *printer buffer*.

**output device**    Any peripheral that presents output from the computer, such as a screen or printer. Although disks and tapes receive output, they are called "storage devices."

**outside plant**    The facilities that link a telephone company's central office (CO) to the subscriber. The outside plant is essentially the local loops and all their associated equipment, which includes the cables, junction boxes, load coils and other structures. Contrast with *inside plant*.

**outside the box**     To think differently. One thing the computer industry has always fostered is newness, and thinking outside the box implies change and doing away with old methods in research, design and implementation. See also *out of the box.*

**outsourcing**     Contracting with outside consultants, software houses or service bureaus to perform systems analysis, programming and datacenter operations. See *netsourcing, ASP, SSP* and *facilities management.*

**overclock**     To speed up the computer beyond the manufacturer's specifications in order to it run faster. This is accomplished by changing a jumper on the motherboard or by changing the clock crystal. The motherboard and CPU may or may not be able to handle the increased speed. See *multiplier lock.*

**OverDrive CPU**     Intel's trade name for its CPU upgrade chips. For the 486, there are 486 and Pentium OverDrives. Depending on the motherboard, the old chip is either replaced or the new one is installed in the upgrade socket, leaving the old chip intact or removing it. Pentium Overdrive chips install in the original socket.

**overflow error**     An error that occurs when calculated data cannot fit within the designated field. The result field is usually left blank or is filled with some symbol to flag the error condition.

**overflow server**     A standby Web server that accepts excess traffic from the primary Web servers. It typically contains the identical software of the Web server (100% mirrored server). See *Web server.*

**overhead**     (1) The amount of processing time used by system software, such as the operating system, TP monitor or database manager.

(2) In communications, the additional codes transmitted for control and error checking, which take more time to process.

**overlay**     (1) A preprinted, precut form placed over a screen, key or tablet for indentification purposes. See *keyboard template.*

(2) A program segment called into memory when required. When a program is larger than the memory capacity of the machine, parts of the program not in constant use can be set up as overlays. Each overlay called in overwrites the existing overlay in memory. Virtual memory provides for automatic overlays. See *virtual memory.*

**overlay card**     A controller that digitizes NTSC signals from a video source for display in the computer.

**overloading**     In programming, the ability to use the same name for more than one variable or procedure, requiring the compiler to differentiate them based on context.

**overload server**     A server in a network that stands by waiting to handle additional traffic. Additional Web servers and application servers can be made into overload servers on a large Web site. See *Web server* and *application server.*

**oversampling**     Creating a more accurate digital representation of an analog signal. In order to work with real-world signals in the computer, analog signals are sampled some number of times per second (frequency) and converted into digital code. Using averaging and different algorithms, samples can be generated between existing samples, creating more digital information for complex signals, "smoothing out the curve" so to speak.

Sampling requires at least twice the bandwidth of the frequency being sampled. For example, with regard to sound, 20 kHz is the highest frequency perceptible to the human ear, and sampling is done at 44.1 kHz for high quality audio playback. A 2x oversampling means that the CD player runs at twice the rate, or 88.2 kHz, and inserts a made-up sample in between each real sample on the disc. An 8x oversampling runs eight times faster and so on. See *sampling rate.*

**overscan**     Outside of the normal rectangular viewing area on a display screen. Contrast with *underscan.*

**overstrike**     (1) To type over an existing character.

(2) A character with a line through it.

**oversubscribed**     Refers to connecting more users to a system than can be fully supported if all of them were using it at the same time. Networks and servers are almost always designed with some amount of oversubscription, counting on the fact that everybody does not need the service simultaneously. If they do, delays are certainly the result, and outages may also occur.

An oversubscription of 8 to 1 is not uncommon for Internet access, which means that only 1 out of 8 users can be supported at sustained, maximum speed. However, with the Internet's TCP/IP packet switching architecture, all 10 users could be online at the same time without noticing delays, because there is so much idle time while people read the pages they retrieve.

**overwrite** (1) A data entry mode that writes over existing characters on screen when new characters are typed in. Contrast with *insert mode*.

(2) To record new data on top of existing data such as when a disk record or file is updated.

**OWL** (ObjectWindows Library) A class library of Windows objects from Borland that serves as application frameworks for developing Windows applications in C++. It is the Borland counterpart of the Microsoft Foundation Class Library (MFC).

**ownership tag** An encrypted string of text displayed at startup on Compaq computers. It is designed for identification in the event of loss or theft.

O

**P1394**   See *FireWire*.

**P2P**   See *peer-to-peer*.

**P3P**   (Platform for Privacy Preferences) A protocol for sharing private information over the Internet. It enables the browser to transparently transmit sensitive data such as a credit card number to a P3P-enabled Web site.

**P4**   (Pentium 4) See *Pentium*.

**P6 class**   Refers to a Pentium Pro, Pentium II, Pentium III or Celeron CPU chip or to a PC that uses the chip. See *P6*.

**P7**   The Intel code name for the IA-64 CPU architecture. P7 was later known as Merced, and then officially named Itanium. See *IA-64* and *Itanium*.

**P75, P90, P100, etc.**   Generally refers to Pentium CPUs or Pentium systems running at 75, 90, 100MHz, etc.

**PABX**   (Private Automatic Branch eXchange) Same as *PBX*.

**PAC**   See *perceptual audio coding*.

**PACBASE**   Integrated CASE software for mainframes and UNIX systems from CGI Systems, Malvern, PA, subsidiary of IBM (www.cgisystems.com). It supports a wide variety of databases including DB2 and Oracle. PACLAN is the version for PC servers running OS/2 and Windows NT. PACBASE generates COBOL code for the servers. Visual Age for PACBASE is used to create the client side.

**pack**   (1) To compress data in order to save space. Unpack refers to decompressing data. See *data compression*.
   (2) An instruction that converts a decimal number into a packed decimal format. Unpack converts a packed decimal number into decimal.
   (3) In database programs, a command that removes records that have been marked for deletion.

**packaged software**   See *software package*.

**Packard Bell NEC**   (Packard Bell NEC, Inc., Westlake Village, CA, www.packardbell.com) A major PC manufacturer that pioneered sales into the mass-market retail chains in the late 1980s. The first to offer toll-free support to end users, it is a major supplier of PCs to the retail channel.
   The original Packard Bell was founded in 1926 as a consumer radio manufacturer and later entered the defense electronics industry. It was acquired by Teledyne in 1968. In 1986, Beny Alagem and a group of partners acquired the Packard Bell name from Teledyne and formed Packard Bell Electronics.

In 1995, Packard Bell acquired Zenith Data Systems and, in 1996, merged with NEC's personal computer operations to become Packard Bell NEC.

**packed decimal**    A storage mode that places two decimal digits into one byte, each digit occupying four bits. The sign occupies four bits in the least significant byte.

**packet**    A block of data used for transmission in packet switched systems. The terms frame, packet and datagram are often used synonymously. See *TCP/IP ABCs*.

**packet cellular**    The transmission of data over the cellular network. Data is divided into packets, or frames, for error checking. Contrast with *circuit cellular*. See *CDPD* and *wireless*.

**packet classification**    The identifying of packets for quality of service (QoS). Packets can be classified by source and destination ports and address and protocol type. See *TOS*.

**packet filtering**    Discarding unwanted network traffic based on its originating address or range of addresses or its type (e-mail, file transfer, etc.). Packet filtering is generally performed in a router. See *firewall*, *Web filtering* and *router*.

**packetized voice**    The transmission of realtime voice in a packet switching network.

**packet loss**    The discarding of data packets in a network when a device (switch, router, etc.) is overloaded and cannot accept any incoming data at a given moment. High-level transport protocols such as TCP/IP ensure that all the data sent in a transmission is received properly at the other end. See *packet switching*.

**packet overhead**    Refers to the time it takes to transmit data on a packet-switched network. Each packet requires extra bytes of format information, which, combined with the assembly and disassembly of packets, reduces the overall transmission speed of the raw data.

**packet over SONET**    A metropolitan area network (MAN) or wide area network (WAN) transport technology that carries IP packets directly over SONET transmission without any data link facility such as ATM in between. Packet over SONET is intended to transmit data at the highest rates possible, because SONET has a smaller packet header overhead than ATM (28 bytes out of an 810-byte frame compared with 5 out of a 53-byte ATM cell). However, ATM has traditionally provided proven management and quality of service (QoS) for long haul transport.

**LAN**

| Data, voice, video |
| --- |
| IP (layer 3) |
| Ethernet (layer 2) |
| Copper |

**WAN**

| Data, voice, video | Data, voice, video | Data, voice, video |
| --- | --- | --- |
| IP (layer 3) | IP (layer 3) | IP (layer 3) |
| ATM (layer 2) | SONET (layer 1) | Fiber |
| SONET (layer 1) | Fiber | |
| Fiber | | |

**Transporting IP**
In a LAN, IP generally runs over Ethernet. In a WAN, it typically is transported by ATM, which rides over SONET, and increasingly, directly over SONET. In the future, it is expected that IP will run directly over DWDM fiber (rightmost diagram).

**packet radio**    The wireless transmission of data, which is divided into packets, or frames, for error checking. See *ARDIS* and *BellSouth Intelligent Wireless Network*.

**packet switching**    A networking technology that breaks up a message into smaller packets for transmission and switches them to their required destination. Unlike circuit switching, which requires a constant point-to-point circuit to be established, each packet in a packet switched network contains a destination address. Thus all packets in a single message do not have to travel the same path. They can be dynamically routed over the network as lines become available or unavailable. The destination computer reassembles the packets back into their proper sequence.

Packet switching efficiently handles messages of different lengths and priorities. By accounting for packets sent, a public network can charge customers for only the data they transmit. Packet switching has been widely used for data, but not for realtime voice and video. However, this is beginning to change. IP and ATM technologies are expected to enable packet switching to be used for everything (see *IP on Everything* and *ATM*).

The first international standard for wide area packet switching networks was X.25, which was defined when all circuits were analog and very susceptible to noise. Subsequent technologies, such as frame relay and SMDS were designed for today's almost-error-free digital lines.

ATM uses a cell-switching technology that provides the bandwidth-sharing efficiency of packet switching with the guaranteed bandwith of circuit switching.

Higher-level protocols, such as TCP/IP, IPX/SPX and NetBIOS, are also packet based and are designed to ride over packet-switched topologies.

Public packet switching networks may provide value added services, such as protocol conversion and electronic mail. Contrast with *circuit switching*.

**packet telephony**    Another term for IP telephony, in which continuous voice is broken up into packets and transmitted over a packet-switched network. See *IP telephony*.

**packing density**    The number of bits or tracks per inch of recording surface. Also refers to the number of memory bits or other electronic components on a chip.

**pad**    (1) To fill a data structure with padding characters.

(2) (PAD) (**Packet Assembler/Disassembler**)  A communications device that formats outgoing data into packets of the required length for transmission in an X.25 packet switching network. It also strips the data out of incoming packets.

**padding**    Characters used to fill up unused portions of a data structure, such as a field or communications message. A field may be padded with blanks, zeros or nulls.

**paddle**    An input device that moves the screen cursor in a back-and-forth motion. It has a dial and one or more buttons and is typically used in games to hit balls and steer objects. See *joy stick*.

**page**    (1) In virtual memory systems, a segment of the program that is transferred into memory.

(2) In videotex systems, a transmitted frame.

(3) In word processing, a printed page.

(4) On the Web, a single HTML document. See *HTML*.

**page break**    In printing, a code that marks the end of a page. A "hard" page break, inserted by the user, breaks the page at that location. "Soft" page breaks are created by word processing and report programs based on the current page length setting.

**page description language**    A device-independent, high-level language for commanding a printer to print text and graphics on a page. The two major languages are Adobe's PostScript and HP's PCL.

Much of the character and graphics shaping is done within the printer rather than in the user's computer. Instead of downloading an entire font from the computer to the printer, which includes the design of each character, a command to build a particular font is typically sent, and the printer creates the characters from font outlines. Likewise, a command to draw a circle is sent to the printer rather than sending the actual bits of the circle image. However, bitmaps can also be used when necessary. See *PostScript* and *PCL*.

**page fault**    A virtual memory interrupt that signals that the next instruction or item of data is not in physical memory and must be swapped back in from the disk. If the required page on disk cannot be found, then a page fault error occurs, which means that either the operating system or an application has corrupted the virtual memory. If such an error occurs, the user has to reload the application.

**page header**    Common text that is printed at the top of every page. It generally includes the page number and headings above each column.

**page hijacking**     Refers to numerous ways in which Web pages are copied or redirected covertly. It may refer to making copies of popular Web pages and posting them on a third-party site so they become indexed by search engines. When the user retrieves one of the pages, it has been altered to go to another Web site.

Page hijacking may also refer to copying source code of a well-designed page and using it on another site. "Home page" hijacking refers to clandestinely changing the default address of the home page in the browser, so that when you launch it, that Web site is immediately retrieved.

URL hijacking takes advantage of a user's inadvertent typo by using a Web address with a misspelled version of a well-known company. For example, www.micrsoft.com could be a site offering products that a user going to the Microsoft site might be interested in.

**page layout program**     A desktop publishing program such as PageMaker and QuarkXPress. See *desktop publishing*.

**PageMaker**     A full-featured desktop publishing program for Windows and Macintosh from Adobe. PageMaker is the de facto standard in the graphics arts industry. It is used to create ads, brochures, newsletters and books of all sizes and kinds. Originally introduced for the Mac in 1985 by Aldus Corporation, it set the standard for desktop publishing. In fact, Paul Brainerd, president of Aldus, coined the term. The PC version was introduced in 1987 for Windows 1.0 and was the first non-Microsoft Windows application.

**page makeup**     Formatting a printed page, which includes the layout of headers, footers, columns, page numbers, graphics, rules and borders.

**PageMill**     Web authoring software for Windows and Macintosh from Adobe. It provides a visual environment for creating Web pages. SiteMill is an additional program that works with PageMill for managing the entire site. See *GoLive*.

**page mode memory**     An earlier speed enhancement to dynamic RAM (DRAM) chips. Also known as "fast page mode" (FPM) memory, the row of bits is selected only once for all columns within the row. Previously, each bit was accessed by pulsing its row and column. EDO, SDRAM, DDR and RDRAM memory technologies followed page mode memory. See *dynamic RAM*.

**page on demand**     See *byte serving*.

**page printer**     A printer that prints a page at a time. Laser, LED and solid ink printers are examples. The first page printers were huge, floor-standing devices, and although such "digital printing presses" today print much faster and even in color, the ubiquitous page printer is the desktop laser printer. See *laser printer*, *LED printer*, *solid ink printer*, *digital printing* and *printer*.

**The Page Printer**
Whenever you need to print a million forms in a hurry, use a high-speed page printer.

**page recognition**     Software that recognizes the content of a printed page which has been scanned into the computer. It uses OCR to convert the printed words into computer text and should be able to differentiate text from other elements on the page, such as pictures and captions.

**page source**     Also known as "source" and "document source," it is the HTML code (source code) of a Web page (HTML document). See *HTML*.

**page view**     A Web page, which can be of any length and can contain any number of graphic images. The HTML page itself and every image are each considered a hit. Thus, one page view is one hit only if there are no graphics on the page. See *hits*.

**pagination**     (1) Page numbering.

(2) Laying out printed pages, which includes setting up and printing columns, rules and borders. Although pagination is used synonymously with *page makeup*, the term often refers to the printing of long manuscripts rather than ads and brochures.

**paging**　　(1) In a virtual memory computer, paging is the transfer of program segments (pages) into and out of memory. Although paging is the primary mechanism for virtual memory, excessive paging is not desired. See *thrashing*.

　　(2) A communications service that is evolving from a one-way beeper service to a one-way text service, and eventually, to a two-way text and voice service. It is expected that the paging industry will undergo several changes as new handheld devices and wireless services mature. See *PCS*.

**paint**　　(1) In computer graphics, to "paint" the screen using a tablet stylus or mouse to simulate a paintbrush.

　　(2) To transfer a dot matrix image as in the phrase "the laser printer paints the image onto a photosensitive drum."

　　(3) To create a screen form by typing anywhere on screen. To "paint" the screen with text.

**Painter**　　A full-featured paint program for Macintosh and Windows from MetaCreations Corporation, Carpinteria, CA (www.metacreations.com), formerly Fractal Design Corporation. Painter is the most sophisticated paint program on the market with an array of tool palettes that is simply remarkable. It can simulate natural painting styles, such as oil, watercolor and charcoal, on almost every kind of paper texture. Painter's packaging used to be as unique as the product... a paint can!

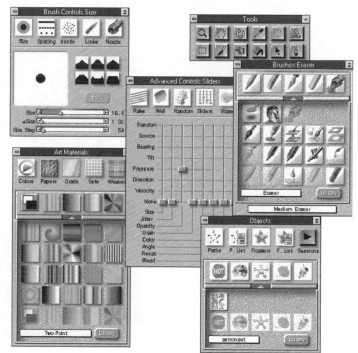

**paint program**　　A graphics program that allows the user to simulate painting on the computer with a mouse or tablet. The images that are generated in a paint program, which are made up of dots, are called "bitmapped graphics" or just plain "bitmaps."

　　Unlike drawing programs, which generate vector graphics images, the picture objects created in a paint program cannot be easily isolated and scaled independently. Bitmapped graphics are much like a painted canvas as objects are "painted" together. However, colors can be changed and parts or all of an image can be run through image filters to create a wide variety of special effects.

　　Full-featured paint programs are called "image editors." They include a variety of image editing capabilities for enhancing scanned images, which are also created as bitmaps. If the image editor contains layers, then bitmap elements can be placed into different layers and treated independently like drawing programs. See *graphics*, *image editor* and *Painter*.

**An Electronic Paintbox**
Painter offers the most amazing variety of painting tools on the market. You can fine tune your brushes, felt pens, ink pens and chalk and even simulate different types of paper. The number of settings is staggering, and the tools shown here offer only a glimmer of this program's amazing repertoire.

**pair gain**　　The number of additional wire pairs that may be served by applying some technology to existing telephone lines (wire pairs). For example, with the installation of digital loop carrier equipment at the telco office and at the customer site, one cable pair can be turned into two phone lines. Two cable pairs can be turned into many more lines using T1 and other technologies. Every channel bank, digital loop carrier and DSLAM is a pair gain system. See *channel bank*, *digital loop carrier* and *DSLAM*.

**PAL** (1) (Programmable Array Logic) A type of programmable logic chip (PLD) that contains arrays of programmable AND gates and predefined OR gates. PALs outlived PLA chips, which were their counterpart, and eventually evolved into CPLDs. See *PLD*.

(2) (Phase Alternating Line) A color TV standard that was developed in Germany. It broadcasts 25 interlaced frames per second (50 half frames per second) at 625 lines of resolution. Brazil uses PAL M, which broadcasts 30 fps. PAL is used throughout Europe and China as well as in various African, South American and Middle Eastern countries. PAL's color signals are maintained automatically, and the TV set does not have a user-adjustable hue control. See *NTSC* and *SECAM*.

(3) (Paradox Application Language) Paradox's programming language.

**palette** (1) In computer graphics, a range of colors used for display and printing. See *color palette*.

(2) A collection of on-screen painting tools.

(3) A toolbar that contains a set of functions for any kind of application.

**Palm** The leading handheld electronic organizer from Palm, Inc., Santa Clara, CA (www.palm.com). The first Palm was the PalmPilot introduced in April 1996, which sold more than 350,000 units by year end. Later renamed simply the "Palm," these devices fit into a shirt pocket, contain an address book, scheduler and to-do list, and newer versions can download e-mail.

The Palm uses a pen interface and "Graffiti" handwriting recognition for entering data. Its HotSync technology lets you synchronize data between the Palm and a PC. Palm supports an open architecture operating system, and third-party developers have created a huge variety of software for it. See *PDA*.

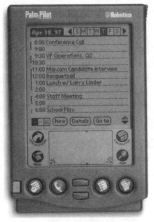

**The PalmPilot**
PalmPilot started a revolution in handheld organizers that store thousands of names, appointments, to-do items, memos and e-mail messages. The rectangle at the bottom is where you hand print your input. *(Image courtesy of Palm, Inc.)*

**PalmPilot** See *Palm*.

**palmtop** A computer small enough to hold in one hand and operate with the other. Palmtops may have specialized keyboards or keypads for data entry applications or have small qwerty keyboards.

**One of the First Palmtops**
This was one of the first fully-functional 486 palmtops. Weighing less than a pound and a half, it used a CompactFlash card (shown on right) and had a PC Card (not visible) for storage. *(Image courtesy of SanDisk Corporation.)*

**PAM** (1) (Pulse Amplitude Modulation) The conversion of audio wave samples to pulses (voltages). PAM is the first step in pulse code modulation (PCM), which is followed by converting the pulses to digital numbers. See *PCM*.

(2) (Pluggable Authentication Modules) A programming interface that enables third-party security methods to be used in UNIX. For example, smart cards, Kerberos and RSA technologies can be integrated with various UNIX functions such as rlogin, telnet and ftp.

**pan** (1) In computer graphics, to move (while viewing) to a different part of an image without changing magnification.

(2) To move (while viewing) horizontally across a text record.

(3) (PAN—Personal Area Network) See *WPAN*.

(4) (PAN—Personal Area Network) A transmission technology developed at IBM's Almaden Research Center, San Jose, CA, that lets people transfer information by touch. For example, you could exchange electronic business cards by shaking hands. By touching your pager in one hand, you

**Touch and Transfer**
Reminiscent of the movie *E.T.*, this photo depicts the transfer of business card information by touching fingers. *(Image courtesy of IBM Almaden Research Center.)*

could send the calling telephone number to your cell phone in the other. A PAN-enabled unit worn on the wrist could transmit a user's ID to all variety of check-in or check-out machines (ATMs, security checkpoints, hospital admittance, etc.). The miniscule amount of current is a thousand times less than the electricity generated by combing your hair and is easily conducted through the body.

**panacea**    Some antidote or remedy that completely solves a problem. Most so called panaceas in this industry, if they survive at all, wind up sitting alongside and working with the products they were supposed to replace. In addition, nothing solves a problem without introducing its own new set of problems. See *Systemantics*.

**Panduit**    (Panduit Corporation, Tinley Park, IL, www.panduit.com) A leading manufacturer of wiring and communications products with locations worldwide. Founded in 1955, Panduit has a substantial product line that includes cable ties, connectors, raceways, ducts and all variety of ancillary equipment to support electrical and network wiring installations. See *Opti-Jack* and *fiber optics glossary*.

**Panvalet**    See *CA-Panvalet*.

**PAP**    (1) (**P**assword **A**uthentication **P**rotocol) The most basic access control protocol for logging onto a network. A table of usernames and passwords is stored on a server. When users log on, their usernames and passwords are sent to the server for verification. Contrast with *CHAP*, which encrypts the username and password before transmitting it.

(2) (**P**rinter **A**ccess **P**rotocol) A printing protocol for the Macintosh introduced in 1985 by Apple with the advent of its LaserWriter laser printer. It provides bi-directional capability, sending PostScript commands between the printer and the requesting client or server via AppleTalk or over TCP/IP with third-party software. See *printing protocol*.

**paperless office**    Long predicted, the paperless office is still a myth. Although paper usage has been reduced in some organizations, it has increased in others. Today's PCs make it easy to churn out documents.

As one technology eliminates paper, another comes along to increase its usage. While laptops with gigabyte hard disks help replace paper on the road, the Internet comes along with tons of interesting Web pages that beg to be printed.

Color laser printers, which are slowly being implemented now in the corporate world, are expected to increase dramatically as prices fall. This alone will increase paper usage. Perhaps the only thing that could ever bring about a paperless office is if paper costs went through the roof.

Xplor International predicts that by 2005, 30% of all documents will still be printed with the rest created and maintained electronically. That compares with 90% of all documents being printed in the mid 1990s. However, the amount of information is doubling every three to four years. Therefore, in 2005, there will still be more than twice as much printed output as in the 1990s. As Keith Davidson, Executive Director of Xplor International, so succinctly put it, "the paperless office is as about as realistic as the paperless toilet!"

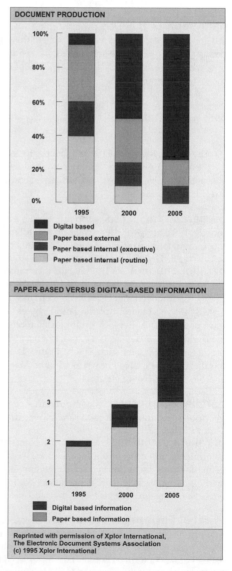

**DOCUMENT PRODUCTION**

- Digital based
- Paper based external
- Paper based internal (executive)
- Paper based internal (routine)

**PAPER-BASED VERSUS DIGITAL-BASED INFORMATION**

- Digital based information
- Paper based information

Reprinted with permission of Xplor International, The Electronic Document Systems Association (c) 1995 Xplor International

**paper tape** (1) A slow, low-capacity, sequential storage medium used on earlier computing and communications devices. Paper tape holds data as patterns of punched holes.

(2) A paper roll printed by a calculator or cash register.

**paradigm** Pronounced "para-dime." A model, example or pattern.

**Paradise** A family of display adapters for PCs from the Paradise subsidiary of Western Digital Corporation, Irvine, CA.

**Paradox** See *Corel Paradox*.

**paragraph** (1) In DOS programming, a 16 byte block. Memory addresses are generated as "segment:offset," where the segment is expressed in paragraphs. To compute an address, the segment register is shifted left four bits, which effectively multiplies it by 16. For example, in the address A000:0100, the A000 becomes A0000, as follows:

```
Segment    A0000    655,360
Offset      0100        256
Result     A0100    655,616
```

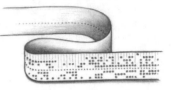

**Paper Tape**
Paper tape was widely used in the early years of computing as a storage medium. Its capacity of only a handful of characters per inch seems pitiful by today's storage standards.

This means there are 4,096 possibilities for expressing each memory byte, a situation that has helped generate confusion.

(2) In word processing and desktop publishing, a collection of words and sentences that contains an end-of-line character (return, line feed or both) at the end of it. From the viewpoint of the software, even a single word followed by a return is a paragraph.

**paragraph tag** In desktop publishing, a code embedded in the text that defines a style for the paragraph that follows it. It defines typeface, tab, indent, letter spacing, alignment and other settings. See *character tag*.

**parallel channel** (1) A channel that transmits data over several wires simultaneously, typically in increments of a byte (8-bit channel, 16-bit, etc.).

(2) A parallel channel for IBM mainframes that transmits up to 4.5MB/sec. In byte multiplexing mode, bytes are interleaved from several low speed devices. In block multiplexing mode, the channel provides full bandwidth to the device, but can disconnect when the device does not require a data transfer such as when a disk is performing a seek. IBM's parallel channel is also known as a bus and tag channel, OEMI channel and block multiplexor channel.

**parallel computer** A computer that can perform multiple processes simultaneously. See *parallel computing*.

**parallel computing** Solving a problem with multiple computers or computers made up of multiple processors. It is an umbrella term for a variety of architectures, including symmetric multiprocessing (SMP), clusters of SMP systems and massively parallel processors (MPPs). See *SMP*, *MPP*, *pipeline processing*, *array processor*, *vector processor* and *hypercube*.

**S/390 G4 Model**
IBM's air-cooled, CMOS-based mainframes hardly resemble the huge water-cooled, bipolar models. *(Image courtesy of International Business Machines Corporation. Unauthorized use not permitted.)*

**Parallel Enterprise Server** A family of S/390 (System/390) mainframes from IBM that are air cooled and use CMOS-based microprocessor technology (CPU on one chip). Introduced in 1994 as the 9672 series, Parallel Enterprise Servers rapidly replaced the earlier water-cooled, bipolar machines that were considerably larger and more power hungry.

Parallel Enterprise Servers employ symmetric multiprocessing (SMP), and up to 32 servers can be tied together in a Parallel Sysplex cluster. See *IBM mainframes* and *Parallel Sysplex*.

**parallel interface**    A multiline channel that transfers one or more bytes simultaneously. Personal computers generally connect printers via a Centronics 36-wire parallel interface, which transfers one byte at a time over eight wires, the remaining ones being used for control signals. Large computer parallel interfaces transfer more than one byte at a time. It is faster than a serial interface, because it transfers several bits concurrently. Contrast with *serial interface*. See *Centronics*.

**parallelism**    An overlapping of processing, input/output (I/O) or both.

**parallelizing**    To generate instructions for a parallel processing computer.

**parallel port**    A socket on a computer used to connect a printer or other parallel device via the computer's parallel interface. Although slower than the IDE or SCSI interfaces, many removable disks and tape backup units come in parallel port options for machines without free slots or for transporting files between machines. Transferring files can also be accomplished by directly cabling two machines together via the parallel ports and using a file transfer program such as LapLink.

On new PCs, the parallel port circuit is built into the motherboard. On earlier PCs, it was contained on a small expansion card along with serial ports and a game port, or it was included on the IDE host adapter, which contained the serial ports and game port as well as floppy disk control.

The IEEE 1284 parallel port provides bi-directional transfer at increased speed and cable length up to 32 feet. See *IEEE 1284*.

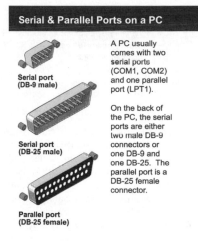

**Serial & Parallel Ports on a PC**

Serial port
(DB-9 male)

Serial port
(DB-25 male)

Parallel port
(DB-25 female)

A PC usually comes with two serial ports (COM1, COM2) and one parallel port (LPT1).

On the back of the PC, the serial ports are either two male DB-9 connectors or one DB-9 and one DB-25. The parallel port is a DB-25 female connector.

**parallel processing**    (1) An architecture within a single computer that performs more than one operation at the same time. See *pipeline processing*, *array processor* and *vector processor*.

(2) An architecture using multiple computers. See *parallel computing*.

**Parallel Query Server**    An early CMOS-based mainframe from IBM, specialized for decision support. It was later replaced by the Parallel Enterprise Server. See *Parallel Enterprise Server*.

**parallel server**    A computer system used as a server that provides various degrees of simultaneous processing. See *SMP*, *MPP* and *multiprocessing*.

**Parallel Sysplex**    IBM's System/390 clustering architecture. It allows multiple System/390 computers to work together as a single system. It supports data sharing with guaranteed integrity, extensive resource sharing and sophisticated workload balancing. A Parallel Sysplex cluster uses one or more Coupling Facilities to connect machines together. See *Sysplex* and *Coupling Facility*.

**Parallel Transaction Server**    An early CMOS-based mainframe from IBM, specialized for transaction processing. It was later replaced by the Parallel Enterprise Server. See *Parallel Enterprise Server*.

**parallel transmission**    Transmitting one or more bytes at a time using a cable with multiple lines dedicated to data (8, 16, 32 lines, etc.). Contrast with *serial transmission*.

**parameter**    (1) Any value passed to a program by the user or by another program in order to customize the program for a particular purpose. A parameter may be anything; for example, a file name, a coordinate, a range of values, a money amount or a code of some kind. Parameters may be required as in parameter-driven software (see below) or they may be optional. Parameters are often entered as a series of values following the program name when the program is loaded.

A DOS switch is a parameter. For example, in the DOS Dir command **dir /p** the DOS switch **/p** (pause after every screenful) is a parameter.

**(2)** In programming, a value passed to a subroutine or function for processing. Programming today's graphical applications with languages such as C, C++ and Pascal requires knowledge of hundreds, if not thousands, of parameters.

In the following C function, which creates the text window for the Windows version of this database, there are 11 parameters passed to the CreateWindow routine. Some of them call yet other functions for necessary information. In order to call this routine in a program, the programmer must decide what the values are for every parameter.

```
hWndText = CreateWindow     (
    "TextWClass",
    NULL,
    WS_CHILD|WS_BORDER|WS_VSCROLL|WS_TABSTOP,
    xChar*23+GetSystemMetrics(SM_CXVSCROLL)+8,
    yChar*4,
    Rect.right-Rect.left+1-xChar*23
       -2*GetSystemMetrics(SM_CXVSCROLL)+5,
    yChar*(Lines+1)+2,
    hWnd,
    IDC_TEXTLIST,
    (HANDLE)hInstance,
    NULL                    ) ;
```

**parameter-driven**    Software that requires external values expressed at runtime. A parameter-driven program solves a problem that is partially or entirely described by the values (parameters) that are entered at the time the program is loaded. For example, typing **bio 6-20-36** might load a program that calculates biorhythms for someone born on June 20, 1936. In this case, the date is a required parameter. The more user-friendly approach is a menu-driven program that would have you select a menu option and present you with a data entry box to type in date of birth.

Parameter-driven software is widely used when a program is called for and loaded by another program rather than by the user. Since the parameters are generated by one program and used by another, any number of parameters can be passed no matter how obscure the codes.

**parameter RAM**    See *PRAM*.

**parametric modeling**    Using the computer to design objects by modeling their components with real-world behaviors and attributes. Typically specialized for either mechanical design or building design, a parametric modeler is aware of the characteristics of components and the interactions between them. It maintains consistent relationships between elements as the model is manipulated. For example, in a parametric building modeler, if the pitch of the roof is changed, the walls automatically follow the revised roof line. A parametric mechanical modeler would ensure that two

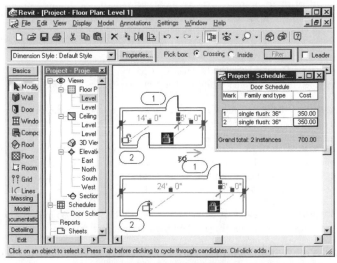

**Using Parametric Modeling**
The door in this room has been "locked" to four feet from the right wall. When the wall is dragged to the right to make the room larger, the door maintains its relationship with the wall. This screen shot is in Revit, the first parametric building modeler to tie together all component views and annotations parametrically for the A/E/C industry. In addition, Revit maintains automatic interaction between graphic and schedule views (note door schedule at right). If either one is changed, its counterpart is updated.
*(Screen shot courtesy of Revit Technology Corporation, www.revit.com)*

holes are always one inch apart or that one hole is always offset two inches from the edge or that one element is always half the size of another.

Parametric modeler software also provides tabular views of the components (parts list, door schedule, window schedule, etc.) and maintains their association with other views of the model. If a component is edited graphically, the list is updated; if a component is edited on the list, the graphic views are updated.

**PARC** (Palo Alto Research Center, Palo Alto, CA, www.parc.xerox.com) Founded in 1970, PARC is Xerox Corporation's research and development center. Although Xerox headquarters are in Stamford, Connecticut, and manufacturing and marketing are in Rochester, New York, PARC is located in the heart of Silicon Valley.

Over the years, PARC has made significant contributions to the computer industry, including the development of the Smalltalk programming language, the mouse and graphical user interface (GUI) and Ethernet. It continues to be on the cutting edge of high technology. See *Xerox*.

**parcel maps** The basic drawings (maps) of the land cadastre (ownership boundaries) for all public and private lands. Parcel maps are typically maintained at a variety of scales, and can be either very precise on very general "cartoon maps" which show only schematic layouts of the basic land cadastre. They are commonly related in some manner to legal description documents, which typically constitute the record for describing boundary ownership for a given parcel (e.g., metes and bounds descriptions). Parcel maps of an area provide more than a representation of ownership. The maps serve a wide range of purposes if they are constructed with a known level of positional accuracy and integrated with other cultural and physical information. Such databases are frequently used as a multipurpose cadastre. (Data West Research Agency definition: see *GIS glossary*.)

**parental control software** A special browser or filtering program designed to reject Web sites not suited for children. Such programs may screen pages by word content, site rating or by URL, using an updated database of objectionable sites, or any combination of these techniques. See *PICS* and *RSAC*.

| | |
|---|---|
| Information | www.netparents.org |
| ChiBrow | www.chibrow.com |
| Cyber Patrol | www.cyberpatrol.com |
| CYBERsitter | www.solidoak.com |
| Net Nanny | www.netnanny.com |
| Net Shepherd | www.netshepherd.com |
| Surfin' Annette | www.spycatcher.com |
| SurfWatch | www.surfwatch.com |
| WebChaperone | www.webchaperone.com |
| WizGuard | www.wizguard.com |

**parent-child** In database management, a relationship between two files. The parent file contains required data about a subject, such as employees and customers. The child is the offspring; for example, an order is the child to the customer, who is the parent.

**parent directory** A disk directory that is one level up from the current directory. In DOS and Windows, two dots (..) refer to the preceding directory level, or parent directory.

**parenthesis** The left parenthesis "(" and right parenthesis ")" are used to delineate one expression from another. For example, in the query **list for size="34" and (color = "red" or color ="green")**, parentheses group the ORs together so they are as a distinct entity from the AND.

In programming, parentheses are used to surround input parameters of a function call. For example, in C, the string compare statement **strnicmp (itemA, itemB, 10)** uses parentheses to group the ITEMA, ITEMB and 10 values handed over to the function.

**parent program** The main, or primary, program or first program loaded into memory. See *child program*.

**PA-RISC**    (Precision Architecture-**RISC**)  A proprietary RISC-based CPU architecture from HP that was introduced in 1986. It is the foundation of HP's 3000 and 9000 computer families. See *IA-64*.

**parity bit**    An extra bit attached to the byte, character or word used to detect errors in transmission.

**parity checking**    An error detection technique that tests the integrity of digital data within the computer system or over a network. Parity checking uses an extra ninth bit that holds a 0 or 1 depending on the data content of the byte. Each time a byte is transferred or transmitted, the parity bit is tested.

Even parity systems make the parity bit 1 when there is an even number of 1 bits in the byte. Odd parity systems make it 1 when there is an odd number of 1 bits.

There are 12% more memory cells in 9-bit parity memory than there are in 8-bit non-parity memory. To shave costs, many desktop computers are built with non-parity memory; however, sometimes you can choose to use either type. See *RAID*.

**parity drive**    A separate disk drive that holds parity bits in a disk array. See *RAID*.

**parity error**    An error condition that occurs when the parity bit of a character is found to be incorrect.

**parity memory**    Memory that uses a ninth bit for parity checking. See *parity checking*.

**park**    To retract the read/write head on a hard disk to its home location before the unit is physically moved in order to prevent damage. Most modern drives park themselves when the power is turned off.

**PARM**    Abbreviation for *parameter*.

**parse**    (1) To analyze a sentence or language statement. Parsing breaks down words into functional units that can be converted into machine language. For example, to parse the expression  **sum salary for title = "MANAGER"**  the word SUM must be identified as the primary command, FOR as a conditional search, TITLE as a field name and MANAGER as the data to be searched.

Parsing breaks down a natural language request, such as **"What's the total of all the managers' salaries"** into the commands required by a high-level language, such as in the example above.

(2) To convert from one format to another. The term is often used as a substitute for the word "convert" when continuous strings of text are scanned to find embedded format codes that must be changed. In contrast, when data is moved between different databases, it is generally known as database "conversion," because the locations of the fields in a database record are usually fixed and easily identified.

**parser**    A routine that performs parsing operations on a computer or natural language.

**partition**    A reserved part of disk or memory that is set aside for some purpose. On a PC, new hard disks must be partitioned before they can be formatted for the operating system, and the Fdisk utility is used for this task. It can make one partition, creating one drive letter for the entire disk, or it can make several partitions sized to your requirements. For example, drives C:, D: and E: could be the same physical disk, but they would act like three separate drives to the operating system and user. See *primary partition* and *DOS Fdisk*.

**partitioning**    To divide a resource or application into smaller pieces. See *partition*, *application partitioning* and *PDQ*.

**PartitionMagic**    A utility from PowerQuest Corporation, Orem, UT (www.powerquest.com), that works on DOS, Windows and OS/2 hard disks. It allows disk partitions to be changed on the fly without destroying existing data. By making multiple smaller drives out of a large one, their cluster sizes are lowered and waste less space. This utility has been highly praised for its convenience. Without a product such as this, the DOS Fdisk utility is used to repartition a hard disk, and all data is lost in the process. See *partition*.

**Pascal**    A high-level programming language developed by Swiss professor Niklaus Wirth in the early 1970s and named after the French mathematician, Blaise Pascal. It is noted for its structured programming, which caused it to achieve popularity initially in academic circles. Pascal has had strong influence on subsequent languages, such as Ada, dBASE and PAL. See *Turbo Pascal*.

Pascal is available in both interpreter and compiler form and has unique ways of defining variables. For example, a set of values can be stated for a variable, and if any other value is stored in it, the program generates an error at runtime. A Pascal set is an array-like structure that can hold a varying number of predefined values. Sets can be matched and manipulated providing powerful non-numeric programming capabilities.

The following Turbo Pascal example converts Fahrenheit to Celsius:

```
program convert;
var
fahr, cent : real;
begin
 write('Enter Fahrenheit ');
 readln(fahr);
 cent := (fahr - 32) * 5 / 9;
 writeln('Celsius is ',cent)
end.
```

**The Pascaline**
We worried three centuries ago about losing our jobs. We worry today about losing jobs. No matter how much technology we develop on this planet, we still worry! *(Image courtesy of The Computer Museum History Center, www.computerhistory.org)*

**Pascaline**    A calculating machine developed in 1642 by French mathematician Blaise Pascal. It could only add and subtract, but gained attention because 50 units were placed in prominent locations throughout Europe. Accountants expressed grave concern that they might be replaced by technology!

**passive backplane**    A backplane that adds no processing in the circuit. See *backplane*.

**passive component**    A device that does not have any impact on the electrical signals or the data that passes through it. See *active component*.

**passive hub**    A central connecting device in a network that joins wires from several stations in a star configuration. It does not provide any processing or regeneration of signals. Contrast with *active hub* and *intelligent hub*. See *hub*.

**passive matrix**    A common LCD technology used in laptops. Passive matrix displays (DSTN, CSTN, etc.) are not quite as sharp and do not have as broad a viewing angle as active matrix (TFT) displays, but they have improved dramatically over the years. Looking head on into a passive matrix screen is not all that different than looking at an active matrix (TFT) screen. The difference is more noticeable with the viewing angle. A person looking from the side sees a dimmer image with passive matrix. See *LCD*.

**passive star**    See *passive hub*.

**Passport**    A single sign-on and digital wallet service for the Web from Microsoft. The Passport Single Sign-in Service (formerly known as the Passport Authentication Service) enables users to enter their IDs and passwords once and be able to log onto all Passport Web sites without having to retype the data. The Passport Digital Wallet service stores credit card, shipping and billing information on Microsoft secure servers, which enables users to make purchases without having to retype the information. When users make a purchase on Passport sites, the merchant sends a request to the Passport server, which returns the appropriate information. This server-based wallet supersedes the client-based wallet in Microsoft Internet Explorer. See *single sign-on* and *digital wallet*.

**Passport IntRprise**    An object oriented client/server development system from Passport Corporation, Paramus, NJ (www.passport4gl.com), that supports Windows, OS/2, Motif and Java clients, VAXes, UNIX servers and all the major SQL databases. It includes visual programming utilities and fully supports event-driven systems that respond to realtime interrupts. Originally developed for the VAX/VMS world in the mid-1980s, Passport generates C source code and is designed to easily integrate with other third-party GUIs and software.

**passthrough SQL**    See *embedded SQL*.

**password**    A secret word or code used to serve as a security measure against unauthorized access to data. It is normally managed by the operating system or DBMS. However, the computer can only verify the legitimacy of the password, not the legitimacy of the user. See *NCSC*.

**password hint**    A reminder to you of how you made up your password. Some systems let you enter a password hint so that if you forget your password, the hint will be displayed to help jog your memory. For example, if your password is your child's birthday, you might use "Karen" or "Jim" as a reminder.

**paste**    See *cut and paste*.

**paste bomb**    A random chunk of data copied from any place on the hard disk and pasted into the text of an online chat. It is done just to irritate or confuse participants.

**patch**    A temporary or quick fix to a program. Too many patches in a program make it difficult to maintain. The term may also refer to changing the actual machine code when it is not convenient to recompile the source program. The term is also used to refer to a general-purpose fix that does not actually patch a piece of the program, but is an entirely new executable module that replaces the old one. See *MIDI patch*.

**patch cord**    A short length of cable used to connect ports in patch panels or in expansion boards and systems that are in close proximity. It is typically a telephone, data communications, audio or video cable that is generally no longer than 10 feet in length. Both ends of the cable are terminated with plugs or sockets.

**patch panel**    A group of sockets used to connect incoming and outgoing lines in communications and electronic systems. Patch panels allow for manually wiring the connections with small cables (patch cords), not automatic switching. Wireless patch panels are also available that provide the cross connections by flipping a switch rather than plugging in wires. See *wiring rack*.

**path**    (1) In communications, the route between any two nodes. Same as line, channel, link or circuit.
(2) In database management, the route from one set of data to another, for example, from customers to orders.
(3) A selected line or area in an image. See *clipping path*.
(4) The route to a file on a disk. In DOS, Windows and OS/2, the path for file MYLIFE located in subfolder STORIES within folder JOE on drive C: looks like this:

```
c:\joe\stories\mylife
```

The equivalent UNIX path follows. UNIX knows which drive is used:

```
/joe/stories/mylife
```

The Macintosh can also use a path in certain command sequences; for example, with "hard disk" as the drive, the same path is this:

```
hard disk:joe:stories:mylife
```

**path determination**    In a network router or switch, the processing that determines which output port the incoming packet or frame is diverted to.

**path vector protocol**    A routing protocol, sometimes known as a policy routing protocol, that is used to span different autonomous systems. EGP and BGP are examples. The routing table maintains the autonomous systems that are traversed in order to reach the destination system. Contrast with *distance vector protocol* and *link state protocol*. See *autonomous system, routing protocol, EGP* and *BGP*.

**PATHWORKS**    A network operating system from Digital that lets a VAX minicomputer function as a server for DOS, Windows, Windows NT, OS/2 and Macintosh clients. DECnet, TCP/IP, AppleTalk and NetWare protocols are supported.

**PATROL**    An application management suite from BMC that uses agents to report on software activities on all the servers within the enterprise. Using the information in "knowledge modules" (KMs) about each system component, agents detect events, collect information and notify system and network administrators to take corrective action.

**PAX**    (1) (Private Automatic Exchange) An inhouse intercom system.

(2) (Parallel Architecture Extended)  A parallel processing environment standard based on Intel's i860 RISC chip, UNIX System V and Alliant Computer's parallel and 3-D graphics technologies.

**payload**    The data-carrying capacity of some structure. It typically refers to a part of a packet or frame in a communications system that holds the message data in contrast to the headers, which are considered overhead.

**payment service**    See *Web payment service*.

**payware**    Software distributed for money. Contrast with *freeware*.

**PB**    See *PowerBuilder*.

**PBX**    (Private Branch eXchange)  An inhouse telephone switching system that interconnects telephone extensions to each other, as well as to the outside telephone network. It may include functions such as least cost routing for outside calls, call forwarding, conference calling and call accounting. Modern PBXs use all-digital methods for switching and may support both digital terminals and telephones along with analog telephones. See *WPBX*.

**An Early PBX**
This PBX began operation in Bangor, Maine in 1883. *(Image courtesy of AT&T.)*

**PC**    (3) (Printed Circuit)  See *printed circuit board*.

(2) (Personal Computer)  Any laptop or desktop computer such as Windows machine or a Macintosh.

(1) (Personal Computer)  A stand-alone laptop or desktop computer running Windows (or DOS for earlier applications). PC hardware and operating systems are primarily governed by Intel and Microsoft respectively. The PC is the world's largest computer base.

PCs are also widely used as clients and servers in a local area network (LAN). PC clients predominantly run under Windows, but PC servers (x86-based servers) run under Windows, NetWare or a variation of UNIX such as Linux or UnixWare. PC servers may use Windows 95/98, but Windows NT and 2000 are more likely choices.

Although there are literally thousands of PC vendors, from mom and pop shops to large mail order houses (Dell, Gateway, etc.) to the major computer companies (Compaq, HP, etc.), and of course IBM, still one of the world's largest PC makers, all PCs use an Intel x86 or compatible CPU.

After IBM introduced the PC in 1981, the first attempts at cloning it were mostly unsuccessful. Except for Compaq's first PC, from 1982 to 1985, there were a lot of "almost compatible" PCs. However, as soon as the part of the operating system known as the BIOS was successfully cloned and made commercially available, true compatibles appeared in abundance.

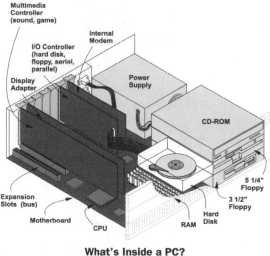

**What's Inside a PC?**

Before Windows 95, adding another peripheral device to a PC was often an exercise in trial and error. Modifying DOS's infamous configuration files (AUTOEXEC.BAT and CONFIG.SYS) caused many a user to give up. Windows 95, 98 and 2000 added Plug and Play, which means for the most part, you can replace hard disks and display adapters, as well as add a scanner, CD-ROM or other device without difficulty.

The PC has become a commodity item, winding its way onto the shelves of retail outlets worldwide. This is a testimonial to the power of a computer standard, even one fraught with loopholes and inconsistencies.

Today, most PCs run most software and work with most plug-in boards. However, with the myriad of adapters and applications available, one device, application or utility can always conflict with another. The way to guarantee that something works is to try it. This has been true since day one in the computer business.

**PC*MIP** A small PCI-based mezzanine card that is adapted to VMEbus, CompactPCI and PCI cards. Smaller than PMC mezzanine cards and similar in size to IndustryPack (IP) cards, Type I PC*MIP cards are 90 × 47mm, and Type II are 99 × 47mm, making them suitable for small-footprint applications. They use 64-pin connectors, the same as PMC cards, and the 32-bit PCI data path. See *mezzanine card*, *PMC* and *IndustryPack*.

**PC100** A specification from Intel for designing memory chips that support the 100MHz system bus in Pentium CPUs. See *PC133* and *PC66*.

**PC/104** A modular system architecture that uses 3.5" square boards that snap together. PC/104 products are widely used, because this "stack through" bus, which uses the ISA technology, provides a compact and rugged design for building process control and embedded systems. PC/104+ are PCI-based boards rather than ISA based.

**PC133** A specification from Intel for designing memory chips that support the 133MHz system bus in Pentium CPUs. See *PC100* and *PC66*.

**PC66** A specification from Intel for designing memory chips that support the 66MHz system bus in Pentium CPUs. See *PC100* and *PC133*.

**PC-8** A symbol set that contains the extended ASCII characters of the IBM PC.

**PC 95** The first PC 9x specification, which required that ISA cards be Plug and Play compliant. See *PC 9x*.

**PC 97** The second PC 9x specification, which was aimed at Windows 97 (now Win 98) and 2000 (NT 5.0). It defines three categories (Basic, Workstation and Entertainment), retains the ISA bus and adds USB and FireWire buses. The minimum requirements are a 120MHz CPU and 16MB of RAM. See *PC 9x*.

**PC 98** **(1)** The third PC 9x specification, which defines five categories (Consumer, Office, Mobile, Entertainment and Workstation). It eliminates the ISA bus and pushes the minimum requirements to a 200MHz CPU with 32MB of RAM and 256K of L2 cache. PC 98 machines must support OnNow, and the BIOS must support booting from a CD-ROM and be Y2K compliant. Systems cannot ship with ISA cards installed, but may have an ISA bus for legacy devices. See *PC 9x*.

**(2)** (PC-98) A personal computer series from NEC. It is the most popular PC in Japan.

**PC 99** The fourth PC 9x specification, which defines the minimum system as a 300MHz machine with 128KB of L2 cache and two USB ports. Consumer PCs must have 32MB of RAM, and office machines must have 64MB. The ISA bus is eliminated.

**PC 9x** Specifications from Microsoft and Intel that define minimum system requirements for Windows-based PCs. Thus far, the PC 95, PC 97, PC 98 and PC 99 specs have been defined, and details change frequently. See *PC 99*.

**pcANYWHERE** Remote control software for Windows from Symantec. It is a popular product that is noted for its variety of features.

**PC/104 Boards**
The top board is a complete PC from Intelec Technologies (www.intelec-tech.com). The bottom one could be a data acquisition board or any other peripheral not part of the primary PC. The pin layouts on a PC/104 board's perimeter depend on its function, and there are a lot of I/O connections required in this example. However, the stacking pins and sockets are common to all PC/104 boards for connecting them through the ISA bus.

**PCard** (1) (Purchasing **CARD**) An enhanced credit card used by business employees. It is similar to a MasterCard or Visa card, but contains more information that can be used to control purchases such as dollar limits and number of transactions within a given period or for an individual or group.

(2) (Processor **CARD**) A PCI adapter from NetGame Cable, Givatayim, Israel (www.netgame.com), that provides realtime processing for cable modems. Supporting NetGame's Elastream scheduling algorithm, one PCard resides in the host computer of the cable company for each head end and supports thousands of cable modem users.

**PCB** See *printed circuit board*.

**PC board** See *printed circuit board*.

**PC bus** The bus architecture used in first-generation IBM PCs and XTs. It refers to the original 8-bit bus, which accepted only 8-bit expansion boards. In 286s and up, it was superseded by the 16-bit AT bus, later known as the ISA bus. See *PC data buses*.

**PC Card** A credit-card sized, removable module for portable computers standardized by PCMCIA. PC Cards are also known as "PCMCIA cards." PC Cards are 16-bit devices that are used to attach modems, network adapters, sound cards, radio transceivers, solid state disks and hard disks to a portable computer. The PC Card is a "plug and play" device, which is configured automatically by the Card Services software (see below).

All PC Cards are 85.6 mm long by 54 mm wide (3.37" × 2.126") and use a 68-pin connector. The original Type I card is 3.3 mm thick and is typically used to hold memory.

Type II cards (5.0 mm thick) are commonly used for memory, modems and LAN adapters in laptops. Type III cards (10.5 mm thick) are used to hold a hard disk, wireless transceiver or other peripheral that needs more space. The Type III slot can hold two Type II cards.

Toshiba introduced a 16 mm Type IV card, but this has not been officially adopted by the PCMCIA. Smaller cards will work in a Type IV slot.

**The PC Card**
The PC Card (left) on laptops is the equivalent expansion mechanism as the printed circuit board (right) is on desktop computers.

*A Card for a PC*

*PC Card*

**Card and Socket Services** In order to use a PC Card slot in the computer, Card and Socket services must be loaded, typically at system startup. Card and Socket Services software is generally included with laptops that have PC Card slots. It also comes packaged with PC Cards.

Card Services manage system resources required by the PC Card, and, on PCs, determines which IRQs and memory and I/O addresses are assigned. They also manage hot swapping and pass changes in events to higher-level drivers written for specific cards.

Card Services talk to Socket Services, which is the lowest level of software that communicates directly with the PC Card controller chips. Socket Services can be built into the system BIOS or added via software.

**CardBus** In early 1995, PCMCIA introduced the 32-bit CardBus standard. Although electrically different, the CardBus is architecturally identical to the PCI bus. The CardBus supports bus mastering and accommodates cards operating at different voltages. Its advanced power managment features allows the computer to take advantage of CardBus cards designed to idle or turn off in order to increase battery life. The CardBus specification allows data transfer up to 132 Mbytes/sec over a 33MHz, 32-bit data path. For more information, visit www.pc-card.com. See *PCMCIA*.

**PC Card adapter** (1) A PC Card used as a drive that accepts a removable module. Typically used for flash memory cards, such as CompactFlash and SmartMedia, the PC Card adapter plugs into the PC Card slot of the computer, and the memory card plugs into the adapter. See *CompactFlash* and *SmartMedia*.

(2) A network adapter for a portable computer contained on a PC Card.

**PC Card Adapter**
This example shows a SmartMedia card being plugged into a PC Card adapter that plugs into a Type II PCMCIA slot on a laptop (or desktop) machine. The card is inserted all the way into the adapter, and the button on the left is used to eject it.

P

**PC chipset**   A set of chips that provides the interfaces between all of the PC's subsystems. It provides the buses and electronics to allow the CPU, memory and input/output devices to interact. Most PC chipsets, which are contained on from one to four chips, also include built-in ATA hard disk (IDE) support. The PC chipset, CPU, memory, clock, buses, keyboard circuit and BIOS make up the PC motherboard. See *Intel chipsets*.

**PC clone**   A PC that is not made by one of the major PC vendors. Years ago, it meant any PC not made by IBM. See *white box* and *PC compatible*.

**PC compatible**   A misguided reference to a PC. The term IBM compatible is more accurate, because IBM made the first PC. Even that has little meaning today, because Intel and Microsoft set PC standards. The correct way to refer to a PC is to call it a "PC." See *PC clone*.

**PC CPU models**   The brains of the PC is a CPU, or processor, from the Intel 8086 family (x86) of microprocessors or from a company that makes x86-compatible CPUs, such as AMD (Advanced Micro Devices) and Cyrix Corporation. IBM also makes its own x86-compatible chips. Following are the major classes of PCs, starting with the most current.

Pentium   In 1993, the Pentium family was introduced, and numerous models have been developed (Pentium, Pentium Pro, Pentium II, Pentium III, etc.). Models of the Pentium chip range in performance from entry-level desktop machines to high-end servers. The Itanium, Intel's next-generation chip, is expected in 2001 and uses a different architecture than the x86 line. See *Itanium* and **PC operating environments**.

386 and 486   First used by Compaq in 1986, the 386 introduced an advanced architecture that has been carrier forth in all subsequent chips, including the 486 and Pentium models. The 386 brought a 32-bit mode of operation and the ability to address four gigabytes of memory, although even today, most PC motherboards cannot hold anywhere near that amount. The 32-bit mode was rarely used until Windows 95 was introduced. The 486 came out in late 1989 and offered faster speed and a built-in math coprocessor, which is required by CAD programs.

AT CLASS—286   First used in the IBM AT in 1984, the 286's 16-bit CPU can address up to 16 megabytes of memory. ATs were just faster XTs, and memory above one megabyte was rarely used for applications until Windows 3.0 became popular. By then, 386s and 486s were widely available. AT-class machines were used under DOS, but were extremely sluggish under Windows.

XT CLASS—8086, 8088   The original PC launched by IBM in 1981 used the 16-bit 8088 CPU. This chip family was designed so that the major installed base of CP/M applications could be easily ported to the new architecture.

Unfortunately, it was limited to one megabyte of memory and was designed with limited flexibility. Nobody knew this would become the world's greatest hardware standard. Although more advanced CPUs (386, 486, Pentium, etc.) came later, they had to build in 16-bit operating modes to conform to the original standard and run all the DOS and Windows 3.x applications on the market.

These first PCs, known as XT-class machines, are sold only at computer flea markets and can still be used with older DOS software.

**PC data buses**   The bus in a PC is the common pathway between the CPU and peripheral devices. Parallel buses use slots on the motherboard and provide multiple lines for data (8 bit, 16 bit, etc.) between the CPU and peripheral card. Cards plug into the bus inside the cabinet. Serial buses have external ports, and the cable that plugs into them can connect to multiple devices. Following are the buses used in the PC:

Parallel Buses (Current)

**ISA—Industry Standard Architecture**   Pronounced "eye-suh," ISA stems from the original PC. It was an 8-bit bus originally known as the PC bus and then the XT bus. It was later extended to 16 bits and became the AT bus and eventually the ISA bus. See *ISA*.

**PCI—Peripheral Component Interconnect**   PCI is the primary bus architecture today and is much faster than ISA with 32 and 64-bit versions. When first introduced along with the VL-bus, which eventually faded, it was called a "local bus." See *PCI*.

**AGP—Accelerated Graphics Port**   The 32-bit AGP bus was introduced to speed up graphics display and was faster than PCI when first introduced. If AGP is used, there is one port for the display adapter only. See *AGP*.

### Serial Buses (Current)

**USB—Universal Serial Bus**    One USB port connects up to 127 peripherals. The first version of USB was designed for all low speed peripherals.

**FireWire (IEEE1394)**    FireWire connects up to 63 peripheral devices and has been mostly used for digital camera connections.

### Parallel Buses (Earlier)

**MicroChannel (MCA)**    IBM switched to the 32-bit MicroChannel with its PS/2 line in 1987, then later added back ISA. Eventually, it gave up MicroChannel for PCI. See *MicroChannel*.

**EISA—Extended ISA**    Pronounced "ee-suh," this bus was a 32-bit extension of ISA created by major vendors to counter IBM's Micro Channel. EISA slots accepted both EISA and ISA cards, but clock speed was still at the slow ISA rate. EISA was used in servers but later abandoned for PCI. See *EISA*.

**VL-bus—VESA Local Bus**    The 32-bit VL-bus was introduced during the 486 era and offered higher speed than ISA. It then gave way to PCI. See *VL-bus*.

**PCD file**    See *Photo CD*.

**PC display modes**    The screen resolution on a PC is determined by a plug-in card called a "display adapter," "video card," "graphics adapter" or "VGA card," the latter term referring only to the base mode of the card. The equivalent circuitry is also built into many motherboards.

The primary screen resolutions are 640×480, 800×600, 1,024×768 and 1,280×1,024. At higher resolutions, more of the document is visible, but the text and images appear smaller. On small monitors, 640×480 and 800×600 are used. On 17" monitors, 1,024×768 is common, and 1,280×1,024 and higher are used on monitors 19" and above. It all depends on your eyesight. Display adapters may provide a 1,600×1,200 mode and even higher resolutions for medical and other demanding applications. In order to use the highest mode of the card, the monitor must be able to support that resolution.

The number of colors that can be displayed jump in large increments from 256, to 65,000 to 16 million. To display more colors at higher resolution requires more memory on the adapter card.

A PC display system supports both text mode and graphics mode. Before Windows, a graphics DOS application had to switch the display to graphics mode. Under Windows, the computer still boots up in text mode, but Windows switches the PC to the graphics mode last set in the display control panel. See *display adapter*, **PC display modes (details)**, *how to select a PC display system* and *virtual screen*.

### Changing Display Adapters

When switching to a different display adapter, set the resolution to VGA (640×480, 16-colors) before you turn the machine off and remove the old one (Settings tab in the Display control panel). Although the Windows installation CD-ROM includes a wide variety of display drivers, display adapters come with their own drivers just in case.

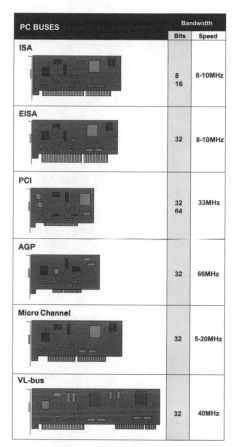

| PC BUSES | Bandwidth | |
| --- | --- | --- |
| | Bits | Speed |
| ISA | 8<br>16 | 8-10MHz |
| EISA | 32 | 8-10MHz |
| PCI | 32<br>64 | 33MHz |
| AGP | 32 | 66MHz |
| Micro Channel | 32 | 5-20MHz |
| VL-bus | 32 | 40MHz |

**Types of Expansion Boards**
EISA, MicroChannel and Vl-bus have all but disappeared in the PC. Eventually ISA will give way to USB. The AGP bus is used for the display adapter only.

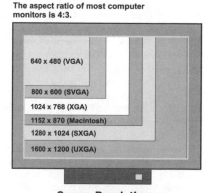

The aspect ratio of most computer monitors is 4:3.

640 x 480 (VGA)
800 x 600 (SVGA)
1024 x 768 (XGA)
1152 x 870 (Macintosh)
1280 x 1024 (SXGA)
1600 x 1200 (UXGA)

**Screen Resolutions**
At higher resolutions, more of the document is visible, but the text and images will appear smaller.

| REQUIRED DISPLAY ADAPTER MEMORY (MB) | | | | |
|---|---|---|---|---|
| | NUMBER OF COLORS | | | |
| RESOLUTION | 16 (4 bit) | 256 (8 bit) | 65K (16 bit) | 16M (24 bit) |
| 640 x 480 | .5 | .5 | 1 | 2 |
| 800 x 600 | .5 | 1 | 2 | 2 |
| 1024 x 768 | 1 | 1 | 2 | 4 |
| 1152 x 870 | 1 | 2 | 2 | 4 |
| 1280 x 1024 | 1 | 2 | 4 | 4 |
| 1600 x 1200 | 2 | 2 | 4 | 8 |

**Memory Requirements**
More memory is required on the display adapter for higher resolutions and more colors.

**PC-DOS** The DOS operating system originally developed by Microsoft and supplied by IBM on its PCs before Windows 95 became the norm. Up until DOS 6, PC-DOS was almost identical to Microsoft's MS-DOS for non-IBM PCs, and both versions are called "DOS." See "IBM's DOS 6" under *DOS 6*.

**PC EXPO** A trade show for resellers and corporate PC buyers from Miller Freeman. It is held in New York in the summer and in Chicago in the fall. It started in New York in 1983 with 120 exhibitors and 9,600 attendees. In 1999, 550 vendors exhibited at the New York show, which drew 86,771 attendees.

**PC floppy disks** Until 1995, there were two kinds of floppy disks routinely used in a PC: the 5.25" disk, housed in a square, flexible envelope, and the 3.5" disk in its rigid plastic case. Today, 5.25" disks are obsolete, and the 3.5" floppy is the standard.

**5.25" DISKETTES** The first floppy, the low-density 360KB 5.25" diskette, was widely used as the distribution medium for software even after the high-density 1.2MB drive came out in 1984. The high-density drive also reads and writes the low-density format.

**3.5" DISKETTES** The 3.5" diskettes were introduced in a low-density 720KB version on IBM's Convertible laptop. Capacity was doubled to 1.44MB with the PS/2 line. The high-density drive also reads and writes the low-density format. You can tell the difference between the 720KB and 1.44MB disks. Looking at it from the label side with the aluminum slider at the bottom, the 1.44MB disk has a hole in the upper-left corner, while the 720KB disk does not.

IBM included its extra-high density 2.88MB floppy drives on selected models. It was compatible with 1.44MB diskettes, but the format never caught on.

**Floppy Disk Formats**

```
 720KB    3.5"   DS/DD   Low density (Double Density)
1.44MB    3.5"   DS/HD   High density
2.88MB    3.5"   DS/ED   Extra-high density (IBM)

 360KB    5.25"  DS/DD   Low density (Double Density)
 1.2MB    5.25"  DS/HD   High density
```

*DS stands for double sided.*

**PC hard disks** See *hard disk*.

**PCI** (Peripheral Component Interconnect) A peripheral bus commonly used in PCs, Macintoshes and workstations. It was designed primarily by Intel and first appeared on PCs in late 1993. PCI provides a high-speed data path between the CPU and peripheral devices (video, disk, network, etc.). There are typically three or four PCI slots on the motherboard. In a Pentium PC, there is generally a mix of PCI and ISA slots or PCI and EISA slots. Early on, the PCI bus was known as a "local bus."

PCI provides "plug and play" capability, automatically configuring the PCI cards at startup. When PCI is used with the ISA bus, the only thing that is generally required is to indicate in the CMOS memory which IRQs are already in use by ISA cards. PCI takes care of the rest.

PCI allows IRQs to be shared, which helps to solve the problem of limited IRQs available on a PC. For example, if there were only one IRQ left over after ISA devices were given their required IRQs, all PCI devices could share it. In a PCI-only machine, there cannot be insufficient IRQs, as all can be shared.

PCI runs at 33MHz, supports 32- and 64-bit data paths and bus mastering. PCI Version 2.1 calls for 66MHz, which doubles the throughput. There are generally no more than three or four PCI slots on the motherboard, which is based on 10 electrical loads that deal with inductance and capacitance. The PCI chipset uses three loads, leaving seven for peripherals. Controllers built onto the motherboard use one, whereas controllers that plug into an expansion slot use 1.5 loads. A "PCI bridge" can be used to connect two PCI buses together for more slots. See *PC data buses*, *PCIx*, *Concurrent PCI*, *CompactPCI*, *Mini PCI*, *PICMG* and *Sebring ring*.

**PCI-ISA Passive Backplane**    An industrial architecture developed by the PICMG that supports the ISA and PCI buses. The backplane contains ISA and PCI slots so that existing ISA and PCI cards can be used. The CPU card has both ISA and PCI edge connectors so it can plug into both slots. See *PICMG*.

**PC input/output**    There are three ways of getting data into and out of the PC. The first is via the keyboard, which plugs into a 6-pin socket on the motherboard. The second is via the data bus, or expansion bus, which is a set of slots on the motherboard for plug-in cards that cable to the peripheral device.

The third is through the input/output pathways built on the motherboard. On the back of the PC, there is either one or two serial ports, one parallel port and two USB ports. The serial ports are used for external modems, digitizer tablets and other devices, and the parallel port is used for the printer. Both serial and parallel ports can be used to transfer data between two computers cabled together. Increasingly, the serial and parallel ports are giving way to the USB ports, which can be used to attach almost any peripheral.

**PC I/O addressing**    This is a method for passing signals from the CPU to the controller boards of peripheral devices on x86 machines. An I/O address, also called a "port address," references a separate memory space on peripheral boards. This is often confused with memory-mapped peripherals, such as video cards, which use a block of upper memory (UMB) in the upper memory area (UMA). Peripheral devices often use both methods: an I/O address for passing control signals and an upper memory block (UMB) for transferring and buffering data to and from the CPU.

There is a 64K address space for I/O addresses, although typically less than 1K is used. Each board that uses an I/O address contains a few bytes of memory (16, 32, etc.) set to a default address range. One or more alternative addresses is also provided to resolve conflicts with other boards. These I/O spaces are a bunch of tiny memory banks scattered over different devices. As long as each one is set to a different address, the CPU can transmit signals to the appropriate boards without conflict.

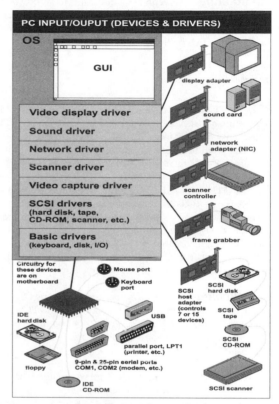

**Input/Output Connections**

A plug-in card is required when the circuitry is not built on the motherboard. This diagram shows the typical devices used. All peripherals require driver software, which enables the operating system to work with each device.

An I/O address operation takes place as follows. If a program needs to send a byte to the serial port, it issues an OUT instruction to the CPU with the address of that serial port. The CPU notifies the address bus to activate the I/O space, not regular memory, and the address bus signals the appropriate byte location on the board. The CPU then sends the data character over the data bus to that memory location.

Following are the default I/O addresses for the serial and parallel ports in a PC.

| Port | PC | PS/2 |
|------|------|------|
| COM1 | 3F8h | |
| COM2 | 2F8h | |
| COM3 | 2E8h | |
| COM4 | 2E0h | |
| LPT1 | 378h | 3BCh |
| LPT2 | 278h | 378h |
| LPT3 | 3BCh | 278h |

**PClset**    A chipset that supports the PCI bus. See *Intel chipsets*.

**PCI steering**    Directing PCI interrupts to an IRQ in the PC. There are four PCI interrupts used by PCI plug-in cards or onboard devices such as the USB. These are directed to one of the available IRQs by the BIOS or operating system. See *IRQ* and *PCI*.

**PCI-X**    See *PCIx*.

**PCIx**    (PCI eXtended) An enhanced PCI bus from IBM, HP and Compaq that is backward compatible with existing PCI cards. It uses a 64-bit bus with a clock speed as high as 133MHz, providing a large jump in speed from the original PCI bus at 132MBytes/sec to as much as 1GBytes/sec.

**PCjr**    (PC JunioR) IBM's first home computer introduced in 1983. It was discontinued two years later, because there was not enough compelling software for the family at that time. In addition, the PCjr was introduced with a chiclet keyboard that was not suitable for touch typing. By the time IBM added a better keyboard, the handwriting was on the wall. It took another decade before the PC became widely used in the home.

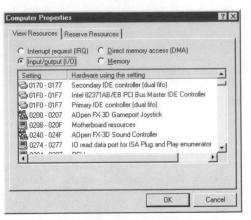

**I/O Addresses**
Windows provides ways to view the details of I/O addresses and other internal settings. This is a Windows 98 screen obtained from the Settings control panel. See ***Win Technical details***.

**PC keyboard**    (1) Any keyboard made for the PC.
   (2) The keyboard introduced with the first IBM PC in 1981 that provided a dual-function keypad for numeric entry and cursor movement. It was severely criticized for its non-standard SHIFT key placement, which was corrected with the AT keyboard in 1984. Regardless of key placement, users have always loved the feel of IBM keyboards. See *PC keyboards* and *Avant Stellar keyboard*.

**PC keyboards**    IBM introduced three generations of keyboards that drove touch typists batty. The original PC keyboard had an awkward RETURN and left SHIFT key placement. Finally corrected on the AT keyboard, the BACKSPACE key was made harder to reach. Then the Enhanced keyboard fixed the BACKSPACE key and relocated the function keys from the side to the top. For a while, it was impossible to assign those keys intelligently. What was easy to reach on one keyboard was difficult on the other.
   The third-generation Enhanced keyboard is the standard today. Manufacturers follow the herd and use the same layout, and only a few have dared to be different. There are some compatibility problems with PC keyboards; however, most keyboards will work on most desktop PCs or as an alternative laptop keyboard. Very old keyboards may have a manual XT-AT switch that changes internal electronics from the first PC keyboard used with XTs to the later AT and subsequent keyboards. Keyboards plug into 6-pin mini-DIN socket on the motherboard. Adapters connect earlier 5-pin DIN plugs to the 6-pin DIN socket.

**PCL**    (Printer Control Language) The page description language for HP LaserJet printers. It has become a de facto standard used in many printers and typesetters. PCL Level 5, introduced with the LaserJet III in 1990, also supports Compugraphic's Intellifont scalable fonts. Starting with the LaserJet 5 in 1996, PCL Level 6 streamlines the graphics and font commands, reducing the amount of information that has to be sent to the printer. See *PJL*.

**PC LAN**    (1) A network of IBM or IBM-compatible PCs.
   (2) A network of any variety of personal computers.

**PCM**    (1) (Pulse Code Modulation) A technique for converting analog signals into digital form that is widely used by the telephone companies in their T1 circuits. Every minute of the day, millions of telephone conversations, as well as data transmissions via modem, are converted into digital via PCM for transport over high-speed intercity trunks. In North America and Japan, PCM samples the analog waves 8,000 times per second and converts each sample into an 8-bit number, resulting in a 64 Kbps data stream (a single DS0 channel). The sampling rate is twice the 4 kHz bandwidth required for a toll-quality conversation. See *ADPCM, A-Law, mu-Law, sampling rate* and *DS0*.

(2) (**P**lug **C**ompatible **M**anufacturer) An organization that makes a computer or electronic device that is compatible with an existing machine.

## PCMCIA

(Personal Computer Memory Card International Association, San Jose, CA, www.pc-card.com) An international standards body and trade association that was founded in 1989 to establish a standard for connecting peripherals to portable computers. PCMCIA created the PC Card. See *PC Card*.

## PC memory

The original PC design was constrained to one megabyte of memory. In addition, certain parts of the operating system were placed into fixed locations in the upper part of memory without any method for cooperatively storing additional drivers and programs. This design gave rise to the most confusing platform in history. Windows 3.0 became very popular because it handled all of the memory types much better than DOS.

Following are the different types of memory in a PC. In other computers, there is just plain memory. In mainframes and supercomputers, there are also large, auxiliary memory banks that function as caches between disk and RAM. See *PC memory map*.

```
Conventional Memory        First 640K
UMA (Upper Memory Area)    Next 384K
HMA (High Memory Area)     Next 64K
Extended Memory            From 1MB up
EMS (Expanded Memory)      Additional memory
                             beyond 1MB
                             bank-switched
                             into the UMA
```

## PC memory card    See *memory card*.

## PCM modem    See *V.90*.

## PC network    (1) A network of PCs or of any variety of personal computers.

(2) (PC Network) The first PC LAN from IBM introduced in 1984. It inaugurated the NetBIOS interface and used the CSMA/CD access method. Token Ring support was later added. See *MS-Net*.

## p-code    See *intermediate language*.

## PC Paintbrush    A DOS paint program developed by the ZSoft Corporation, Marietta, GA. It was the first popular paint program for the PC, and its PCX bitmapped graphics format became a de facto standard for bitmapped images. See *PCX* and *graphics formats*.

## PC Postage    A U.S. Postal Service approved service provided by third parties for producing U.S. postage stamps on a user's own desktop or laptop computer with a laser-class or ink jet printer. In 1999, E-Stamp Corporation (www.e-stamp.com) and Stamps.com (www.stamps.com) were the first PC Postage sites. Postage is paid for and downloaded from the service's Web site, and the stamp and bar code are printed on an envelope or label. The printed stamps are known as "electronic stamps," "Internet postage," "online postage," "online stamps," "digital stamps," and "digital postage." They are also called "e-stamps," however, E-Stamp is a trademark of E-Stamp Corporation (see *E-Stamp*).

The bar code and associated printed elements are based on the Post Office's Information Based Indicia Program (IBIP). The indicia contains numerous data elements, including date, delivery point and digital signature. Some systems rely on software only while others use a hardware key (dongle) that holds the downloaded postal funds. Address cleansing may also be offered by the provider. See *hardware key* and *address cleansing*.

P

**PC printers**   There are hundreds of printer models that work with PCs. Most printers plug into the PC's parallel port, but the USB port is increasingly being used. The most popular printers are ink jet and laser-class printers. Dot-matrix printers are still used for printing labels on continuous forms and for multipart forms.

Ink jet printers provide reasonable text quality and excellent graphics. They are slower than laser printers, but provide the most affordable color printing. Monochrome laser printers provide finer text quality and are suited to business applications. Color laser printers are slower than their monochrome counterparts and more expensive, but generate superb output. See *printer*.

**PCS**   (1) (Personal Communications Services)  Refers to wireless services that emerged after the U.S. government auctioned commercial licenses in 1994 and 1995. This radio spectrum in the 1.8–2GHz range is typically used for digital cellular transmission that competes with analog and digital services in the 800Mhz and 900MHz bands.

(2) (Personal Conferencing Specification)  A videoconferencing technology that uses Intel's Indeo compression method. It is endorsed by the Intel-backed Personal Conferencing Working Group (PCWG). Initially competing against H.320, Intel subsequently announced its videoconferencing products will also be H.320 compliant.

**PC server**   An x86-based computer that is used as a shared machine in the network. PC servers are increasingly more powerful with multiple CPUs and features that heretofore where only found on mainframes and minicomputers. See *server*, *PC* and *SMP*.

**PC software specialist**   A person who manages personal computer operations within an organization and is responsible for the analysis, selection, installation, training and maintenance of personal computer hardware and software. The term was popular in the 1980s as was "information center." Also known as "micro manager." See *MMA*.

**PC subscription service**   An IT outsourcing arrangement where PCs and related equipment are installed in the customer's premises by a third party that owns the equipment. The customer pays a monthly rental to the third party (the PC subscription service provider).

**PCT**   (Private Communications Technology)  A protocol from Microsoft that provides secure transactions over the World Wide Web. See *security protocol*.

**PCTE**   (Portable Common Tool Environment)  An ECMA standard for exchanging data between CASE tools. See *CDIF*.

**PC technician**   A person responsible for the maintenance of desktop computers within an organization. Such individuals troubleshoot problems and may be responisble for some level of software distribution. If required, preventive maintenance may fall under their jurisdiction.

**PC-to-host**   Refers to desktop computers (PCs) communicating with minis and mainframes (hosts). The connections may be direct cabling from the PC to the host or via the network.

**PC Tools**   A popular and comprehensive packages of utilities for DOS and Windows from Symantec (originally Central Point Software). They include a DOS or Windows shell as well as antivirus, file management, caching, backup, compression and data recovery utilities.

**PC troubleshooting**   See *PC conflicts* and *Windows Resource Kit*.

**PC/TV**   A PC with a built-in TV tuner. TV boards that plug into a personal computer typically have standard RCA phono inputs to connect a VCR or camera. Some also have S-VHS inputs.

**PCX**   (1) A bitmapped graphics file format that handles monochrome, 2-bit, 4-bit, 8-bit and 24-bit color and uses RLE to achieve compression ratios of approximately 1.1:1 to 1.5:1. Images with large blocks of solid colors compress best under the RLE method. See *PC Paintbrush*.

(2) (**PC** to the power of **X**)  Introduced in early 2001, this is Intel's concept of the digital home in which the PC is at the center synchronizing with PDAs and cellphones.

**PDA**    (Personal Digital Assistant) A handheld computer that serves as an organizer for personal information. It generally includes at least a name and address database, to-do list and note taker. PDAs are pen based and use a stylus to tap selections on menus and to enter printed characters. The unit may also include a small on-screen keyboard which is tapped with the pen. Data is synchronized between the PDA and desktop computer via cable or wireless transmission.

A PDA is like a palmtop computer except that the PDA typically uses a pen whereas the palmtop uses a small keyboard. Apple's MessagePad, more commonly known as the "Newton," was the first to popularize the concept. See *Palm*.

**PDC**    **(1)** (Primary Domain Controller) A Windows NT service that manages security for its local domain. Every domain has one PDC, which contains a database of usernames, passwords and permissions. See *BDC*.

**(2)** (Personal Digital Communications) A digital cellular phone system widely used in Japan. Based on TDMA, it transmits in the 810–826MHz and 1,477–1,501MHz bands. PDC is a 2G wireless system. See *wireless generations* and *PHS*.

**PD disk**    (Phase change Dual disk) A rewritable optical disk from Panasonic that uses phase change technology. Introduced in 1995, it uses 5.25" cartridges that hold 650MB and can withstand 500,000 rewrites. The PD drive also reads CD-ROMs, and the drive tray accomodates both PD cartridges and CD-ROM discs. The drive does not support Panasonic's earlier 5.25" phase change (PCR) cartridges. Panasonic's DVD-RAM drives also read and write PD disks. See *phase change* and *optical disk*.

**PDES**    (Product Data Exchange using STEP) A standard format for exchanging data between advanced CAD and CAM programs. It describes a complete product, including the geometric aspects of the images as well as manufacturing features, material properties and tolerance and finish specifications. For more information, visit http://pdesinc.aticorp.org. See *IGES*.

**PDF**    (Portable Document Format) The page description language used in the Acrobat document exchange system. See *Acrobat* and *extension*.

**PDF417**    (Portable Data File417) A two-dimensional bar code developed by Symbol Technologies, Inc., Bohemia, NY, (www.symbol.com). Created in the late 1980s, the standard was later placed in the public domain and is governed by the Automatic Identification Manufacturers (AIM) trade association. PDF417 is the most widely used 2-D bar code (more than one row of codes), and it can hold up to 1,800 bytes of any digital data in a printed area about the size of a business card. For bills of lading and applications that require more information, multiple bar codes can be printed. The scanner, which is made by Symbol Technologies and other companies, reads the bar code horizontally and vertically. MicroPDF417 is a denser version of PDF417 that takes up less space. It is used for marking small parts and can hold up to 300 bytes.

**PDIAL**    (Public Dialup Internet Access List) A list of Internet service providers (ISPs) maintained by Peter Kaminsky. The last available PDIAL list is on various Web sites.

**PDIP**    (Plastic DIP) See *DIP*.

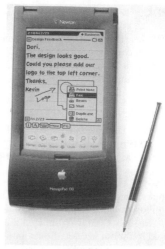

**The Newton**
Although later taken off the market, Apple's Newton pioneered the PDA concept. *(Image courtesy of Apple Computer, Inc.)*

**PD Cartridge**
The PD cartridges look like and use the same technology as DVD-RAM disks. Panasonic's DVD-RAM drives read and write PD cartridges.

**The Gettysburg Address**
This PDF417 image contains the entire Gettysburg address. *(Image courtesy of Symbol Technologies, Inc.)*

**PDL**    See *page description language*.

**PDM**    (Product Data Management) An information system used to manage product development from inception to manufacturing and maintenance. It handles all the data necessary at all stages including plans, geometric models, CAD drawings, images, NC programs as well as all related project data, notes and documents. PDMs are developed for workgroups as well as the entire enterprise.

**PDMS**    (Product Data Management System) See *PDM*.

**PDN**    (1) (Packet Data Network) See *packet switching*.
    (2) (Premises Distribution Network) The network that connects a customer's ADSL transceiver (ATU-R) to the Service Modules (PCs, routers, set-top boxes, etc.). See *DSL*.

**PDP**    (1) (Programmed Data Processor) A minicomputer family from Digital that started with the 18-bit PDP-1 in 1959. Its $120,000 price was much less than the million dollar machines of the time and 50 units were built.
    In 1965, Digital legitimized the minicomputer industry with the PDP-8, which sold for about $20,000. By the late 1970s, the PDP-8 processor was put on a single chip and used in DECmate workstations. Other PDPs were built, including 12-bit, 18-bit and 36-bit machines, the larger ones evolving into DECsystem models.
    In 1970, Digital introduced the 16-bit PDP-11, which became the most widely used minicomputer with more than 50,000 systems sold. The VAX series was introduced in 1977, but PDP machines lingered on for many years.
    (2) (Plasma Display Panel) See *plasma display*.
    (3) (Policy Decision Point) See *COPS*.

**Programmed Data Processor-5**
The PDP-5 was one of Digital's early computers. The PDP series pioneered the minicomputer industry. *(Image courtesy of Digital Equipment Corporation.)*

**PDQ**    (Parallel Data Query) A query optimized for massively parallel processors (MPPs). The software breaks down the query into pieces so that several parts of the database can be searched simultaneously. See *SMP*.

**PDS**    (1) (Processor Direct Slot) In the Macintosh, an expansion socket used to connect high-speed peripherals as well as additional CPUs. It is equivalent to the local bus in the PC. There are different types of PDSs for various Macintosh models and types. Some Macs do not have a PDS, others have both PDS and NuBus slots.
    (2) (Premises Distribution System) The cabling, racks and adapters that connect telephone wires within a building or group of buildings to each other and to external lines of the telephone company.

**PD software**    See *public domain software*.

**PDU**    (Protocol Data Unit) The technical name of a frame of data transmitted over the data link layer (layer 2) in a communications network. Ethernet and Token Ring are examples of this layer. Many people neither use the term PDU nor the term frame, but call every unit of data travelling over a network a "packet." See *OSI model*.

**PE**    (1) (Phase Encoding) An early magnetic encoding method used on 1600 bpi tapes in which a 1 is an up transition and a 0 is a down transition in the center of the bit cell.
    (2) (Processing Element) One of multiple CPUs in a parallel processing system.
    (3) (Professional Engineer) An engineering degree.

**Pearl**    See *Perl*.

**PEBCAK**    Digispeak for a person that does something stupid. It stands for "problem exists between chair and keyboard."

**pedestrian speed**    The pace of people walking. In-home or in-office cordless phones are designed for pedestrian speeds, which have different requirements than cellphones that may be used in a moving vehicle.

**peek/poke**    Instructions that view and alter a byte of memory by referencing a specific memory address. Peek displays the contents; poke changes it.

**peer**    In communications, a functional unit that is on the same protocol layer as another.

**peering**    The act of one national Internet backbone provider accepting and passing traffic from another national provider. See *NAP*.

**peer protocol**    A protocol at the same protocol layer; for example, a layer 2 protocol talking to another layer 2 protocol, layer 3 with layer 3, etc. See also *peer-to-peer communications* and *peer-to-peer network*.

**peer review**    Having one or more programmers review the source code of a program written by someone else. Peer review produces much better code, since others have already tried to understand it. Indecipherable routines are eliminated before they get buried into the fabric of the program. See *open source*.

**peer-to-peer**    From user to user. There are two primary applications. The first is peer-to-peer file sharing in which users access resources on other users' machines as exemplified by Napster and Gnutella. The other is distributed computing, where multiple computers are used to work on a single problem. See *Napster*, *Gnutella* and *peer-to-peer computing*. See also *peer-to-peer network*.

**peer-to-peer communications**    Communications in which both sides have equal responsibility for initiating, maintaining and terminating the session. Contrast with "master-slave communications," in which the host determines which users can initiate which sessions. If the host were programmed to allow all users to initiate all sessions, it would look like a peer-to-peer system to the user. See *peer-to-peer network* and *peer-to-peer computing*.

**peer-to-peer computing**    Sharing the CPU resources across a network so that all machines function as one large supercomputer. It allows unused CPU capacity in any of the machines to be allocated to the total processing job required. In a large enterprise, hundreds of desktop machines are often sitting idle at any given time. The goal is to use this processing potential more efficiently. See *SETI*. See also ***anticiparallelism*** and *peer-to-peer network*.

**peer-to-peer network**    A communications network that allows all desktop and laptop computers in the network to act as servers and share their files with all other users on the network. Peer-to-peer networks are quite common in small offices that do not use a dedicated file server. Peer-to-peer networks also exist on the Internet. For example, Napster and Gnutella allow users to access files in other users' computers. See *Napster* and *Gnutella*.

**PE format**    (Portable Executable format) A Win32 file format for executable programs (EXEs and DLLs) supported under Windows 3.1 Enhanced Mode (Win32s) and Windows NT.

**pel**    Same as *pixel*.

**PEM**    (Privacy Enhanced Mail) A standard for secure e-mail on the Internet. It supports encryption, digital signatures and digital certificates as well as both private and public key methods. Not widely used, work on PEM later evolved into S/MIME. See *MIME*.

**pen computing**    See *gesture recognition* and *tablet PC*.

**penetration test**    A test of a network's vulnerabilities by having an authorized individual actually attemp to break into the network. The tester may undertake several methods, workarounds and "hacks" to gain entry, often initially getting through to one seemingly harmless section, and from there, attacking more sensitive areas of the network. Security experts recommend that an annual penetration test be undertaken as a supplement to a more frequent automated security scan. See *security scan*.

**Penguinhead**    A Linux enthusiast. Since the Linux logo is a penguin, "Penguin Power" is the Linux manifesto.

**pen plotter**    See *plotter*.

**PenPoint**    An operating system developed by Go Corporation, Foster City, CA, that was designed for handwritten input. The direction, speed and order of the user's pen strokes was analyzed for recognition. See *NUI*.

**pen tablet**    A digitizer tablet that is specialized for handwriting and hand marking. LCD-based tablets emulate the flow of ink as the tip touches the surface and pressure is applied. Non-display tablets display the handwriting on a separate computer screen. See *digitizer tablet* and *tablet computer*.

**Pentium**    A family of 32-bit CPU chips from Intel. The term may refer to the chip or to a PC that uses it. Pentium chips and Pentium PCs are the most widely used in the world for general-purpose computing.

The first Pentium chip was introduced in 1993 as the successor to the 486, thus the Pentium began as the fifth generation of the Intel x86 architecture. Numerous variations of the Pentium have been introduced with increased performance. Each new line executes more instructions in the same clock cycle as the previous, and clock speeds increase constantly. The Pentium uses a 64-bit internal bus compared to 32-bits on its 486 predecessor. Intel's next-generation Itanium chip departs from the Pentium architecture (see *Itanium*). See *x86* and *386*.

**Pentium 4—2000 (1.4–1.5GHz)**    Latest Pentium architecture adds a 400MHz system bus and 256KB L2 Advanced Transfer Cache. It contains 42 million transistors, uses the 0.18 micron process and comes in a PGA422 chip package. Intel's i850 chipset for the Pentium 4 supports only dual Rambus memory although DDR supports is expected. See *NetBurst*.

**Pentium III—1999–2001 (500MHz–1.13GHz)**    The Pentium III added 70 additional instructions to the Pentium II. The Pentium III uses a 100 or 133MHz system bus and either a 512KB L2 cache or a 256KB L2 Advanced Transfer Cache. Depending on model, it contains from 9.5 to 28 millions transistors, uses the 0.25 or 0.18 micron process and comess in SECC and SECC2 packages. Mobile units come in BGA and micro PGA packages.

**Pentium III Xeon—1999–2001 (500MHz–933MHz)**    Typically used in 2-way to 8-way servers, Xeon specs are like Pentium III, except both types of L2 cache can go up to 2MB. The Xeon uses the SECC2 and SC330 chip packages.

**Pentium II—1997–1999 (233MHz–450MHz)**    Added MMX multimedia instructions to Pentium Pro and introduced large Single Edge Connector Cartridge (SECC) for Slot 1. The Pentium II uses a 66 or 100MHz system bus. Desktop models have 7.5 million transistors, 512KB L2 cache and are housed in SECC packages. Mobile models have 27.4 million transistors, 256KB L2 cache and are housed in either BGA or Mobile Mini-Cartridge (MMC) packages.

**Pentium II Xeon—1998–1999 (400MHz–450MHz)**    Typically used in high-end and 2-way and 4-way servers, Xeon specs are like Pentium II with L2 cache from 512KB to 2MB and 100MHz system bus.

**Celeron—1998–2001 (266MHz–800MHz)**    Typically used for lower-end PCs. Initially Celerons had no L2 cache, but 128KB on-die cache was added in 1999 making them competitive with Pentium IIs. Celerons use a 66 to 100MHz system bus and 0.25 micron process. Desktop models have from 7.5 to 19 million transistors and use SEPP or PPGA chip packages. Mobile units have 18.9 million transistors and are housed in BGA packages.

**Pentium Pro—1995–1997 (150MHz–200MHz)**    Typically used in high-end desktops and servers, the Pentium Pro increased memory from 4GB to 64GB. The Pentium Pro has L2 cache from 512KB to 1MB, uses a 60 or 66MHz system bus, contains from 5.5 to 62 million transistors. It is made with 0.35 process and is housed in a dual cavity PGA package. When introduced, it was touted as being superior to the Pentium for 32-bit applications.

**Pentium MMX—1997–1999 (233MHz–300MHz)**    Added MMX multimedia instructions to Pentium CPU and increased transistors to 4.5 million. Desktop units used PGA package and 0.35 process while mobile units used TCP and 0.25 process.

**Pentium—1993–1996 (60MHz–200MHz)**    First Pentium CPU models. The Pentium has L2 cache from 256KB to 1MB, uses a 50, 60 or 66MHz system bus and contains from 3.1 to 3.3 million transistors built on 0.6 to 0.35 process. Chips were housed in PGA packages.

| Model | Maximum Memory | Gen** | Multimedia Instructions |
|---|---|---|---|
| Pentium | 4GB | P5 | |
| Pentium MMX | 4GB | P5 | MMX |
| | | | |
| Pentium Pro | 64GB | P6 | |
| Pentium II | 4GB | P6 | MMX |
| Pentium III | 4GB | P6 | MMX, SSE |
| Celeron | 4GB | P6 | MMX |
| | | | |
| Pentium 4 | 4GB | | MMX, SSE, SSE2 |
| | | | |
| Xeon PII | 64GB | P6 | MMX |
| Xeon PIII | 64GB | P6 | MMX, SSE |

*\*\* Code name for generation of architecture*

Multimedia Extensions (MMX) added 57 new instructions and Katmai New Instructions (KNI) added 70 more. See *MMX*.

**Pentium class**    Refers to a Pentium CPU chip or to a PC that uses the chip. The term is also used for non-Intel CPUs that are Pentium compatible, such as the K5 from AMD and the 6x86 from Cyrix. See *P6 class*.

**Pentium clone**    Refers to a Pentium-based computer system that is not made by a top-tier vendor or to a Pentium CPU chip that is not made by Intel.

**Pentium II class**    Refers to a Pentium II CPU chip or to a PC that uses the chip. The term is also used for non-Intel CPUs that are Pentium II compatible, such as the K6 from AMD and the 6x86MX from Cyrix. See *P6 class* and *Pentium*.

**Pentium III class**    Refers to a Pentium III CPU chip or to a PC that uses the chip.

**Pentium IV**    See *Pentium 4*.

**Pentium Pro class**    Refers to a Pentium Pro CPU chip or to a PC that uses the chip. The term is also used for non-Intel CPUs that are Pentium Pro compatible, such as the K6 from AMD. See *P6 class* and *Pentium*.

**Pentium upgradable**    The ability to be upgraded to a Pentium CPU. 486 motherboards designed for Pentium upgrades contain a ZIF socket to make chip changing easy and are, in theory, designed to support the higher speeds of the Pentium chip.

**pentode**    A type of vacuum tube used in high-end audio preamplifiers, ham radios and a variety of other electronic circuits. A pentode is like a tetrode with the addition of a "suppressor grid" between the screen grid and the plate. Typically biased at or near the cathode voltage, the suppressor grid provides additional isolation between the control grid and plate. See *tetrode* and *diode*.

**Pen Windows**    An extension to Windows that allows pen-based computing.

**PeopleSoft**    (PeopleSoft, Inc., Pleasanton, CA, www.peoplesoft.com) A software company that specializes in enterprise-wide applications for client/server environments. Initially specializing in human resources, its package offerings today cover the gamut including financial, distribution, manufacturing and supply chain, plus numerous vertical markets. All major databases are supported. Its products are known for their modularity as well as their ease of modification and customization using the PeopleTools development system.

**PEP**    **(1)** (Packet Exchange Protocol)  A Xerox protocol used internally by NetWare to transport internal Netware NCP commands (NetWare Core Protocols). It uses PEP and IPX for this purpose. Application programs use SPX and IPX.

**(2)** A high-speed modem protocol suited for cellular phone use from Telebit Corporation, Sunnyvale, CA (www.telebit.com).

**(3)** (Policy Enforcement Point)  See *COPS*.

**PEPPER board**    An earlier family of high-resolution display adapters for PCs from Number Nine Visual Technology Corporation, Lexington, MA. Number Nine's assets were acquired by S3 in 1999.

**percent sign**    In certain programming languages, the percent sign (%) is used to indicate a type of variable. For example, in the C statement **printf ("The result is %d\n", amount);**, the %d indicates an integer variable.

**perceptual audio coding**    A technique for further compressing digital sound by eliminating frequencies that cannot be perceived by the human ear. For example, when multiple sounds occur simultaneously, such as with several musical instruments, some cancel out others at any given moment depending on frequency and volume.

Perceptual audio coding uses the psycho-acoustic algorithms developed by Dr. Amar Bose, inventor of the Bose speakers and whose company is known for its quality audio products. MP3 uses perceptual audio coding to dramatically reduce the amount of digital data on a music CD. See *MP3, audio codec* and *speech codec*.

**per clock**    For each clock cycle. The phrase "the CPU does four instructions per clock" means that four machine instructions have been executed within one cycle of the CPU clock, the master clock that synchronizes everything in the computer. For example, in a 200MHz computer, each clock cycle is 5ns long (one billion nanoseconds divided by 200 million). See *clock*.

**percussive maintenance**    Banging on your computer or other electronic device to get it working. Not always recommended.

**Pereos**    The world's smallest magnetic tape technology. The drive, which is about the size of a bar of soap, weighs 10 ounces, runs on AA batteries and connects via the parallel port. Using helical scan technology, the tiny cartridges hold more than 1.25GB compressed. Originally developed by Datasonix and manufactured by Sony, Pereos products later became available from J&J Peripherals, Broomfield, CO (www.jj-peripherals.com). See *magnetic tape*.

**It Doesn't Get Much Smaller**
Helical scan technology crams more than a gigabyte (compressed) on the tiny Pereos cartridges.

**PerfectOffice**    A suite of applications for Windows from Novell that includes WordPerfect, Quattro Pro, Presentations (presentation graphics), InfoCentral PIM, Envoy document exchange software and GroupWise e-mail and calendar. PerfectOffice Professional also includes Paradox and AppWare.

**performance ratings**    See *benchmark*.

**peripheral**    Any hardware device connected to a computer, such as a monitor, keyboard, printer, disk, tape, graphics tablet, scanner, joy stick, paddle and mouse.

**peripheral bus**    Also known as an "input/output bus" or "I/O bus," it is a pathway that connects peripheral devices to the CPU. The ISA, PCI and USB busses are commonly used in PCs. EISA and VL-bus were used previously. Contrast with *system bus*. See *bus*.

**peripheral card**    See *expansion board*.

**peripheral controller**    See *control unit*.

**peripheral device**    See *peripheral*.

**Perl**    (Practical Extraction Report Language) A programming language written by Larry Wall that combines syntax from several UNIX utilities and languages. Introduced in 1987, Perl is designed to handle a variety of system administrator functions and provides comprehensive string handling functions. It is widely used to write Web server programs for such tasks as automatically updating user accounts and newsgroup postings, processing removal requests, synchronizing databases and generating reports. Perl has also been adapted to non-UNIX platforms. See also *PURL*.

**permanent font**    (1) A soft font that is kept in the printer's memory until the printer is turned off.
    (2) Same as *internal font*.

**permanent memory**    Same as *non-volatile memory*.

**permutation**    One possible combination of items out of a larger set of items. For example, with the set of numbers 1, 2 and 3, there are six possible permutations: **12, 21, 13, 31, 23** and **32**.

**perpendicular recording**    See *vertical recording*.

**per seat**    By workstation. See *per seat licensing*.

**per seat licensing**    Software licensing based on a per user basis. For example, a 100-user license means that up to 100 specifically-named users have access to the program. Per seat licensing is administered by providing user-level security to the directory containing the program. Contrast with *concurrent licensing*.

**persistence**    (1) In a CRT, the time a phosphor dot remains illuminated after being energized. Long-persistence phosphors reduce flicker, but generate ghost-like images that linger on screen for a fraction of a second.
    (2) In object technology, the storage of an object on a disk or other permanent storage device.

**persistent data**    Data that exists from session to session. Persistent data is stored in a database on disk or tape. Contrast with *transient data*.

**persistent link**    See *hot link*.

**persistent object**    An object that continues to exist after the program that created it has been unloaded. An object's class and current state must be saved for use in subsequent sessions. In object technology, persistence means storing the object for later use.

**personal agent**    See *agent*.

**personal communicator**    See *PDA*.

**personal computer**    Synonymous with "microcomputer," "desktop computer," and "laptop computer," it is a computer that serves one user in the office or home. A complete personal computer system with printer can cost as little as $1,000 or as much as $8,000 or more. Size is based on memory and disk capacity. Speed is based on the CPU that runs it, and output quality is based on the type and resolution of its monitor and printer.

**Major Suppliers of Personal Computers**    The personal computer world is dominated by Windows-based PCs. There are thousands of vendors that make them, from mom and pop shops to huge companies such as Compaq, HP and IBM. The alternate personal computer standard is Apple's Macintosh, which is only made by Apple. Atari and Commodore once carved out their respective niches, but Atari returned to its gaming roots and Commodore has since closed its doors.

**The History of Personal Computers**    The industry began in 1977, when Apple, Radio Shack and Commodore introduced the first off-the-shelf computers as consumer products. The first machines used an 8-bit microprocessor with a maximum of 64K of memory and floppy disks for storage. The Apple II, Atari 500, and Commodore 64 became popular home computers, and Apple was successful in companies after the VisiCalc spreadsheet was introduced. However, the business world was soon dominated by the Z80 processor and CP/M operating system, used by countless vendors in the early 1980s, such as Vector Graphic, NorthStar, Osborne and Kaypro. By 1983, hard disks began to show up, but CP/M was soon to be history.

In 1981, IBM introduced the PC, an Intel 8088-based machine, slightly faster than the genre, but with 10 times the memory. It was floppy-based, and its DOS operating system from Microsoft was also available for the clone makers (MS-DOS). The 8088 was cleverly chosen so that CP/M software vendors could convert to it easily. They did!

dBASE II was introduced in 1981 bringing mainframe database functions to the personal computer level and launching an entire industry of compatible products and add-ons. Lotus 1-2-3 was introduced in 1982, and its refined interface and combined graphics helped spur sales of the new standard.

The IBM PC was successfully cloned by Compaq and unsuccessfully by others. However, by the time IBM announced the AT in 1984, vendors were effectively cloning the PC and, as a group, eventually grabbed the majority of the PC market.

In 1983, Apple introduced the Lisa, a graphics-based machine that simulated the user's desktop. Although ahead of its time, Lisa was abandoned for the Macintosh in 1984. The graphics-based desktop environment caught on with the Mac, especially in desktop publishing, and the graphical interface (GUI) worked its way to the PC world with Microsoft Windows, and, eventually Ventura Publisher with its GEM interface.

In 1986, the Compaq 386 ushered in the first Intel 386-based machine. In 1987, IBM introduced the PS/2, its next generation personal computer, which added improved graphics, 3.5" floppy disks and an incompatible bus to help fend off the cloners. OS/2, jointly developed by IBM and Microsoft, was also introduced to handle the new machines, but the early versions didn't catch on.

In the same year, more powerful Macintoshes were introduced, including the Mac SE and Mac II, which opened new doors for Apple.

In 1989, the PC makers introduced 486-based computers, and Apple gave us faster Macs, which it has continued to do each year since.

In 1990, Microsoft introduced Windows 3.0, which became a huge success within a couple of years. Software publishers developed Windows versions of almost everything.

In 1991, Microsoft and IBM decided to go it alone each working on their own version of the next operating system (IBM's OS/2 and Microsoft's Windows NT). Although NT gained significant market share, OS/2 quietly disappeared within a few years.

1992 was the year of PC price cuts with all major suppliers slashing prices to keep in line with mail-order vendors, such as Gateway 2000, who along with others, had dramatically driven down the cost.

In 1993, Intel introduced its Pentium CPU to keep pace with the multimedia explosion that has been going on throughout the 1990s. The once text-based PC has become a graphics workstation competing with machines that cost 100 times as much only a few years ago. Within a couple of years, the home market would explode with low-cost, high-performance PCs.

In 1995, the personal computer became a window into the Internet for global e-mail and access to the fastest growing information bank the world has ever witnessed. Although graphical Web browsers such as Mosaic and Netscape were the catalyst, had the desktop personal computer not been in place, the World Wide Web in all of its glory would have never exploded onto the scene.

Inspired by Radio Shack's Model 100 over a decade ago and ignited by companies such as Toshiba and Zenith, the laptop market has had explosive growth throughout the 1990s. More circuits are being stuffed into less space, providing computing power on the go that few would have imagined back in 1977.

The late 1990s were witness to dramatically lower PC prices and much higher speeds. Today, the sub-$1000 PC is incredibly more powerful than the first IBM PC introduced in 1981 at more than three times the cost, and in 1981 dollars as well.

Summary    The personal computer industry sprang up without any planning. All of a sudden, it was there. Machines were bought to solve individual problems, such as automating a budget or typing a letter.

The personal computer has become the desktop appliance in every office throughout the developed world. It has been networked together with the organization's mainframes and departmental computers and is an integral part of the technology infrastructure of every company, small, medium and large. Since 1977, no single device has had more impact on more people and more businesses than the personal computer.

As stand-alone machines, personal computers have placed creative capacity into the hands of an individual that would have cost millions less than 25 years ago. They slowly but surely have shifted the balance of power from the large company to the small, from the elite to the masses, from the wealthy to individuals of modest means. The personal computer revolutionized the computer industry... and the world.

**The First Personal Computer**
In the mid-1970s, Xerox developed the Alto, which was the forerunner of its Star workstation and inspiration for Apple's Lisa and Macintosh. *(Image courtesy of Xerox Corporation.)*

**Commodore PET**
In 1977, this machine along with the Apple II and TRS-80 launched the personal computer industry. The PET sold for $595 and contained its own tape cassette (on the left) and a whopping 12K of memory. *(Image courtesy of Commodore Business Machines, Inc.)*

**PersonalJava**    A version of Java from Sun intended for PDAs and other handheld devices. EmbeddedJava (EJava) is a counterpart set of technologies that provide support for character-based displays or devices without displays rather than graphical interfaces. PersonalJava (PJava) is intended for open systems that require Web browsing, and PJava includes applet support. EJava is intended for closed systems that have severe restrictions on memory. See *Java*.

**personal workstation**    Same as *personal computer* or *workstation*.

**pervasive computing**    See *pervasive workplace*.

**peta**    Quadrillion (10 to the 15th power). See *space/time*.

**petabyte**    One quadrillion bytes. Also PB, Pbyte and P-byte. See *peta* and *space/time*.

**PET computer**    (Personal Electronic Transactor computer) A CP/M and floppy disk-based personal computer introduced in 1977 by Commodore. It was one of the first personal computers along with the Apple II and Radio Shack's TRS-80.

**PEX**    (PHIGS Extensions to X) A set of 3-D extensions to the X Window System. See *PHIGS* and *X Window*.

**PFA file**    (Printer Font ASCII file) A Type 1 font file that contains the mathematical outlines of each character in the font. The codes in this file are in ASCII (raw text). See *PFB file* and *PostScript*.

**PFB file**    (Printer Font Binary file) A Type 1 font file that contains the mathematical outlines of each character in the font. It is an encrypted version of the PFA file. See *Type 1 font*, *PFA file*, *PFM file* and *PostScript*.

**PFM file**    (Printer Font Metrics file) A Type 1 font file that contains the measurements of each character in the font. In a PC, both PFM and PFB files are required. The PFB files are located in the \PSFONTS folder, and the PFM files are in the \PSFONTS\PFM folder. Sometimes \PSFONTS is in the \WINDOWS folder. See *Type 1 font*, *PFB file* and *PostScript*.

P

**PFQ**    (Per-Flow Queuing) A queuing method that forwards traffic based on priority, not the order of arrival into the queue as with first in-first out. See *FIFO*.

**PFS:First Choice**    An earlier integrated software package for PCs from SoftKey International that provided word processing, database, spreadsheet, graphics and communications capabilities. See *Learning Company*.

**PFS:Write**    See *Professional Write*.

**PGA**    (1) (Pin Grid Array) A square chip package with a high density of pins (200 pins can fit in 1.5" square), enabling it support a large amount of I/O. PGAs are typically ceramic (CPGA), but plastic cases are also used (PPGA). The underside of a PGA package looks like a "bed of nails." In a staggered PGA (SPGA), the pins do not line up in perfect rows and columns. See *ZIF socket*.

    (2) (Programmable Gate Array) See *gate array* and *FPGA*.

**Pin Grid Array**
The bottom of PGA packages look like beds of nails.

**(3)** (Professional Graphics Adapter) An early IBM PC display standard for 3-D processing with 640x480x256 resolution. It was not widely used.

**PGP**    (Pretty Good Privacy) Public key cryptography software from Pretty Good Privacy, Inc., San Mateo, CA (www.pgp.com). It was developed by Phil Zimmermann, founder of the company, and it is based on the RSA cryptographic method. A version for personal, non-business use is available on various BBSs and Internet hosts. See *cryptography*.

**PGUP/PGDN keys**    The PAGEUP and PAGEDOWN keys are typically used to move text up and down one screenful, but they can be programmed to do anything.

**phantom call**    A telephone call that the user is not aware of. It may refer to a call made by accidentally pressing a preset on a cellphone to a computer application dialing up the Internet to send data to a Web site. The former causes an inordinate number of erroneous 911 calls each year, and each call must be given serious attention, while the latter may secretly capture behavior patterns for market research.

**phantom lines**    Lines that are made visible as dots or dashes to reveal the edges of objects currently hidden from view. See *wireframe modeling*.

**phase change**    A rewritable optical disk technology developed by Panasonic (Matsushita). Phase change was used in a line of optical drives in the early 1990s. It was later used in Panasonic's PD drive and is also the technology used for writing CD-RWs and DVD-RAMs.

protective layer

0.74 µm

Reflector
Dielectric layer
Phase change layer
Dielectric layer

substrate

Phase change is a pure optical technology and does not rely on any magnetic influence as does magneto-optic and its progeny. A short, high-intensity laser pulse turns a bit in the recording layer from its natural crystalline state (reflective) to an amorphous one (dull), which does not reflect light as well. A medium-intensity pulse restores the crystalline structure, and a low-intensity pulse reads the bit. See *optical disk* and *PD disk*.

**phase change disk**    A rewritable optical disk that uses phase change technology originally developed by Panasonic. Panasonic's earlier PCR disks and its subsequent PD disks as well as CD-R and DVD-RAM disks all use phase change technology. See *phase change*.

**phase change printer**    See *solid ink printer*.

**phase encoding**    See *PE*.

Laser
Beam

**Phase Change Recording**
In rewritable DVDs, different intensities of the laser turns bits in the phase change recording layer between a crystalline state and an amorphous state.

**phase locked**    A technique for maintaining synchronization in an electronic circuit. The circuit receives its timing from input signals, but also provides a feedback circuit for synchronization.

**phase modulation**    A transmission technique that blends a data signal into a carrier by varying (modulating) the phase of the carrier. See *modulate*.

**phase-shift keying**    See *DPSK*.

**PHIGS**    (Programmer's Hierarchical Interactive Graphics Standard) A graphics system and language used to create 2-D and 3-D images. Like the GKS standard, PHIGS is a device independent interface between the application program and the graphics subsystem.

It manages graphics objects in a hierarchical manner so that a complete assembly can be specified with all of its subassemblies. It is a very comprehensive standard requiring high-performance workstations and host processing.

**Phoenix BIOS**    A popular PC BIOS from Phoenix Technolgies Ltd., San Jose, CA (www.phoenix.com). Phoenix was the first company to successfully mass produce the ROM BIOS for the PC, which made the PC industry possible.

**Phone.com**    (Phone.com, Inc., Redwood City, CA, www.phone.com)  A software company that provides an application infrastructure for wireless data. Its microbrowsers (UP.Browser) and server software (UP.Link Server) enable cellphones and other wireless devices to retrieve stock quotes, e-mail and other data from the Web. UP.Smart is a suite of PDA applications that include an address book, calendar and to-do list using the rapid T9 text entry feature. Phone.com also provides software that lets network operators develop their own Internet portals.

Founded in 1994 as Libris, Inc., the company changed its name to Unwired Planet in 1996 and introduced its microbrowser on AT&T's Wireless PocketNet service using the HDML markup language. In 1997, Unwired Planet (UP) launched the WAP Forum with Ericsson, Motorola and Nokia, which turned HDML into WML (Wireless Markup Language) and introduced a complete wireless protocol stack. In 1999, Unwired Planet changed its name to Phone.com. In late 2000, Phone.com merged with Software.com to become Openwave Systems, Inc. See *WAP* and *T9*.

**phone connector**    A plug and socket widely used to connect microphones to amplifiers and for other audio applications. Phone connectors come in stereo (three wire) and monaural (two wire) versions. The prong is .25" thick by 1.25" long. See *RCA connector*, *A/V ports* and *plugs and sockets*. See also *RJ-11*.

**Phone Connector**
Stereo plugs are identified by the three divisions in their prong, while monaural plugs have only two.

**phone hawk**    A person who calls up a computer via modem and either copies or destroys data.

**phone-home**    The ability of a server, PC or other device to directly notify a repair center when it is failing, beginning to fail or for routine maintenance.

**phoneme**    A speech utterance, such as "k," "ch," and "sh," that is used in synthetic speech systems to compose words for audio output. See *formant information*.

**PhoneNET**    Communications products from Farallon Communications, Inc., Emeryville, CA (www.farallon.com), that extend LocalTalk distances to 3,000 feet and use unshielded twisted phone lines instead of shielded twisted pair. Configurations include daisy chain, passive star and active star topologies for both EtherTalk and LocalTalk. Optional Traffic Watch software provides network management and administration.

**Phong shading**    In 3-D graphics, a technique developed by Phong Bui-Tuong in the mid-1970s that computes a shaded surface based on the color and illumination at each pixel. Phong shading is more realistic than Gouraud shading, but requires more computation. It does not produce shadows or reflections. The surface normals at the triangle's points are used to compute a surface normal for each pixel, which in turn creates a more accurate RGB value for each pixel. See *flat shading* and *Gouraud shading*.

**phono connector**    See *RCA connector*.

**phosphor**    A rare Earth material used to coat the inside face of a CRT. When struck by an electron beam, the phosphor emits a visible light for a few milliseconds. In color displays, red, green and blue phosphor dots are grouped as a cluster.

**Photo CD**    An imaging system from Kodak, (www.kodak.com), that digitizes 35mm of Advantix film and stores the pictures in Photo CD (PCD) format in five different resolutions on a CD-ROM. The process is done by a photofinisher using a Kodak Picture Imaging Workstation, which takes about a half hour to put 100 photos (the maximum per disc) onto the CD. Each photographic-quality image (2,048×3,072×24) compresses into 6MB. Thumbnails of each image (contact prints) are also provided.

Other formats include the Photo CD Portfolio, which holds up to 800 TV-quality images (512×768), the Pro Photo CD, which stores images from professional format film (120, 4×5, etc.), the Photo CD Catalog, which holds thousands of pictures and the Photo CD Medical disk for storing film-based images.

Various graphics software packages support the PCD file format. A Kodak Photo CD player is also available that lets you view the Photo CDs on your TV and also play audio CDs. Photo CD did not take off as expected and was followed by the Picture CD system, which is geared more for the consumer. See *Picture CD*.

**photocomposition**    Laying out a printed page using electrophotographic machines, such as imagesetters and laser printers. See *page makeup* and *pagination*.

**photoconductor**    The type of material typically used in a photodetector. It increases its electrical conductivity when exposed to light.

**PhotoDeluxe**    A consumer version of Photoshop that is bundled with a variety of scanners, digital cameras and other software. Although it lacks the myriad of sophisticated features found in Photoshop, it is widely used to add basic enhancements to scanned images. See *Photoshop*.

**photodetector**    A device that senses the light pulses in an optical fiber and converts them into electrical pulses. It uses the principle of photoconductivity, which is exhibited in certain materials that change their electrical conductivity when exposed to light. See *photoelectric*.

**PhotoDraw**    An image editing program from Microsoft that combines painting and drawing tools in one package. PhotoDraw is used for scanning and retouching photos, developing banner ads and images for Web sites and enhancing Microsoft Office graphics. PhotoDraw provides essential vector elements (lines, rectangles, etc.), arrows and other shapes that can be resized and edited. It also includes a wide variety of clip art and templates for business graphics, Web graphics, mailing labels and other purposes.

**photo editing**    See *image editing*.

**photoelectric**    Converting photons into electrons. When light is beamed onto a metal, electrons are released from its atoms. The higher the light frequency, the more electron energy released. Photonic sensors of all kinds work on this principle. They sense light and cause an electric current to flow. Although most people think Einstein won the Nobel Prize because of his Theory of Relativity, it was actually due to his discovery of the photoelectric effect. He theorized that light was made of particles (later called photons) and that it carried an amount of energy exactly proportional to its frequency.

**photo illustration program**    See *image editor*.

**photolithography**    A lithographic technique used to transfer the design of circuit paths onto printed circuit boards, as well as the circuit paths and electronic elements of a chip onto a wafer's surface.

A photomask is created with the design for each layer of the board or wafer (chip). The board or wafer is coated with a light-sensitive film (photoresist) that is hardened when exposed to light shining through the photomask. The board or wafer is then exposed to an acid bath (wet processing) or hot ions (dry processing), and the unhardened areas are etched away. See *chip* and *printed circuit board*.

**photomask**    An opaque image on a transluscent plate that is used as a light filter to transfer an image from one device to another. See *chip*.

**photomicrography**    Photographing microscopic images. Like other photography fields, photomicography is expected to transition to digital imaging. However, since film is analog, it provides infinite resolution compared to digital techniques.

**photomultiplier tube**    A vacuum tube that converts light into electrical energy and amplifies it. Photomultiplier tubes are used in high-end drum scanners, because they are more sensitive to light than the CCD elements used in lower-cost devices.

**photon**    A particle of light. See *photoelectric*, *photonic* and *wave-particle duality*.

**photonic**    Dealing with light (photons). See *photon* and *photonics*.

**photonics**    Systems that generate and transmit light (photons). Most photonic systems use electricty and electronic circuits as their source of energy. See *electro-optic*.

**photonic sensor**    A device that senses light and releases electricity. See *photoelectric*.

**photonic switch**    See *optical switch*.

**photooptic memory**    A storage device that uses a laser beam to record data onto a photosensitive film.

**photo printer**    A printer specialized for printing 3"×5" or 4"×6" prints, typically using dye sublimation technology. See *digital camera* and *photo scanner*.

**photorealistic**    Having the image quality of a photograph.

**photorealistic image synthesis**    In computer graphics, a format for describing a picture that depicts the realism of the actual image. It includes such attributes as surface texture, light sources, motion blur and reflectivity.

**photoresist**    A film used in photolithography that temporarily holds the pattern of a circuit path or microscopic element of a chip. When exposed to light, it hardens and is resistant to the acid bath that washes away the unexposed areas.

**photo scanner**    A scanner specialized for reading photographs up to 4"×6". It uses the same principles as a larger desktop scanner, but is generally a low-cost, consumer-oriented device geared for digitizing home photos into the computer. See *scanner* and *photo printer*.

**photosensitive**    A material that changes when exposed to light. See *photoelectric*.

**photosensor**    A light-sensitive device that is used in optical scanning machinery. See *photoelectric*.

**Photoshop**    A popular high-end image editor for the Macintosh and Windows from Adobe. The original Mac versions were the first to bring affordable image editing down to the personal computer level in the late 1980s. Since then, Photoshop has become the de facto standard in image editing. Although it contains a large variety of image editing features, one of Photoshop's most powerful capabilities

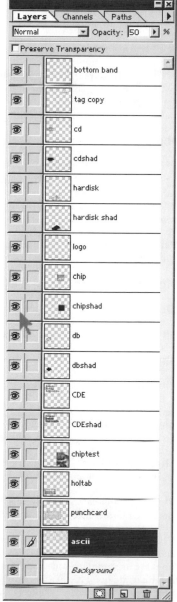

**Photoshop Layers**
The image above is built in 23 layers plus a background layer, enabling the individual elements to be moved independently of the others. The layer window (below) shows the layers. The arrow is pointing to the view option (the "eye") in the chip shadow layer. Clicking the eye toggles between making the layer invisible and bringing it back into view.

is layers, which allows images to be rearranged under and over each other for placement. Photoshop is designed to read and convert to a raft of graphics formats, but it provides its own native format for layers (.PSD extension).

It would be extremely difficult to develop the CD-ROM jewel case cover pictured without layers. If only one layer were available, you would have to locate each and every element perfectly the first time, because it immediately becomes merged into a single bitmapped image overlaying what was previously there. Without having all elements in view and being able to move them around in different ways, it would be virtually impossible to derive the most pleasing effect. See *image editor*.

**Photoshop plug-in**    A third-party software product that extends Photoshop's capabilities. There are countless plug-ins that provide ways to enhance and change an image beyond the already-comprehensive set of tools that comes with Photoshop.

**phototypesetter**    See *imagesetter*.

**PHP**    (PHP Hypertext Preprocessor) A scripting language used to create dynamic Web pages. With syntax from C, Java and Perl, PHP code is embedded within HTML pages for server side execution. It is commonly used to extract data out of a database and present it on the Web page. The major NT and UNIX Web servers support the language, and it is widely used with the mSQL database. PHP was originally known as "Personal Home Page." See *mSQL*.

**phreaker**    A person who makes free long distance phone calls using illegal methods.

**PHS**    (Personal Handyphone System) A TDMA-based cellular phone system introduced in Japan in mid-1995. Operating in the 1880–1930MHz band, PHS uses microcells that cover an area only 100 to 500 meters in diameter, resulting in lower equipment costs but requring more base stations. Using the PHS Internet Access Forum Standard (PIAFS), PHS provides up to 64 Kbps of data transfer. Higher speeds are expected. For more information, visit www.phsmou.or.jp. See *PHS-WLL* and *PDC*.

**PHS-WLL**    (Personal Handyphone System-Wireless Local Loop) Using the PHS cellular technology to provide "last mile" access to subscribers. See *PHS*.

**physical**    Refers to devices at the electronic, or machine, level. Contrast with *logical*. See *logical vs physical*.

**physical address**    The actual, machine address of an item or device.

**physical drive**    Refers to the actual unit of hardware of a disk or tape drive. Contrast with *logical drive*.

**physical format**    See *record layout* and *low-level format*.

**physical layer**    The services in the OSI protocol stack (layer 1 of 7) that provide the transmission of bits over the network medium. See *OSI*.

**physical link**    (1) An electronic connection between two devices.

(2) In data management, a pointer in an index or record that refers to the physical location of data in another file.

**physical lock**    A device that prevents access to data, such as a key lock switch on a computer or a file protection mechanism on a floppy disk. Contrast with *logical lock*.

**pi**    The 16th letter of the Greek alphabet, which is used to represent the number 3.14159265 (ratio of a circle's circumference to its diameter).

**The Pi Symbol**

**PIC**    (1) (PICture) A file extension used for graphics formats. Lotus PIC is a vector format for 1-2-3 charts and graphs. Videoshow PIC is a vector format that is a subset of the NAPLPS standard.

(2) (Programmable Interrupt Controller) An Intel 8259A chip that controls interrupts. Starting with the 286-based AT, there are two PICs in a PC, providing a total of 15 usable IRQs. The PIC has been superseded by an Advanced Programmable Interrupt Controller, or 82489DX chip, that is enhanced for multiprocessing. See *IRQ*.

**(3)** A family of 8-bit microcontrollers from Microchip Technology Inc., Phoenix, AZ (www.microchip.com). Under the brand name of PICmicro Devices, products range from 8 to 68 pins and from 12- to 16-bit instruction words.

**(4)** (Position Independent Code) Instructions that can be placed and executed anywhere in memory.

**pica**　**(1)** In word processing, a monospaced font that prints 10 characters per inch.

**(2)** In typography, about 1/6th of an inch (0.166") or 12 points.

**Pick System**　A multiuser operating environment and database management system (DBMS) from Pick Systems, Inc., Irvine, CA (www.picksys.com), that runs on x86, PowerPC and UNIX platforms. It has been highly praised for its ease of use, flexibility and advanced features. The DBMS portion of the Pick System is widely used in third-party products. R83 is the original Pick System. R93 and Advanced Pick are later versions. D3 is the DBMS, and D3 Pro Plus is a Linux/DBMS package.

The Pick System was originally developed by Richard Pick, who created a system for the U.S. Army while working at TRW Corporation. He later transformed it into the Reality operating system for Microdata and then obtained the right to license it to other vendors.

**PICMG**　(PCI Industrial Computer Manufacturers Group) An industry consortium that develops specifications for PCI-based systems for industrial use. It supports the CompactPCI and PCI-ISA Passive Backplane architectures. See *CompactPCI* and *PCI-ISA Passive Backplane.*

**pico**　Trillionth (10 to the –12th power). See *space/time.*

**picoJava**　The core architecture in Sun's Java chip. See *Java chip.*

**picometer**　One trillionth of a meter. Pronounced "pee-co-meter." See *nanometer.*

**picosecond**　One trillionth of a second. Pronounced "pee-co-second." See *space/time* and *ohnosecond.*

**PICS**　**(1)** (Pantone Internet Color System) The Pantone implementation of the Netscape color palette. See *Netscape color palette.*

**(2)** (Platform for Internet Content Selection) A system for rating the content of Web sites that has been endorsed by the World Wide Web Consortium. PICS is promoted worldwide in order to encourage self regulation and avoid governmental censorship. For information, visit www.w3.org.

**PICT**　(PICTure) The primary Macintosh graphics file format. It holds QuickDraw vector images, bitmapped images and text and is the Mac counterpart to the Windows Metafile (WMF) format. When PICT files are converted to the PC, they use the .PCT file extension.

**picture**　In programming, a pattern that describes the type of data allowed in a field or how it will print. The pattern is made up of a character code for each character in the field; for example, 9999 is a picture for four numeric digits. A picture for a telephone number could be (999) 999-9999. XXX999 represents three alphanumerics followed by three numerics. Pictures are similar but not identical in all programming languages. See also *graphics* and *graphics formats.*

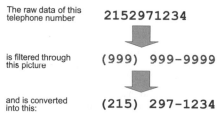

The raw data of this telephone number　**2152971234**

is filtered through this picture　**(999)　999-9999**

and is converted into this:　**(215)　297-1234**

**Picture CD**　An imaging system from Kodak (www.kodak.com) that digitizes 35mm or Advantix film and stores the pictures as JPEG images on a CD-ROM. Like Kodak's Photo CD system, the process is done by a photofinisher, but Picture CD is geared more for the consumer and provides only one high-resolution image of each picture rather than several. Software for Mac and Windows also comes on the CD-ROM (technically a CD-PROM) that lets you zoom, crop and remove red-eye from the pictures. See ***CD-PROM*** and *Photo CD.*

**picture element**　See *pixel.*

**Picturephone**    The proposed video/telephone introduced by AT&T at the 1964 World's Fair in New York. Many thought it would flourish by the end of the 1980s. Realtime video is expected to be widely used after the turn of the century.

**Picture Publisher**    A full-featured image editing program for Windows from Micrografx. It includes a customizable user interface and provides layers for building composite pictures. In Version 5.0, every user action is recorded in a command list that can be edited and used as a macro.

**pictures**    See *graphics* and *graphics formats*.

**PID**    **(1)** (Process IDentifier) A temporary number assigned by the operating system to a process or service.
    **(2)** (Proportional Integral Derivative) A controller used to regulate a continuous process such as grinding or cooking.

**pie chart**    A graphical representation of information in which each unit of data is represented as a pie-shaped piece of a circle. See *business graphics*.

**piezoelectric**    The property of certain crystals that causes them to oscillate when subjected to electrical pressure (voltage). See *ink jet printer* for a diagram of the piezoelectric drop on demand ink jet technology.

**PIF**    (Program Information File) A Windows data file used to hold requirements for DOS applications running under Windows. Windows comes with a variety of PIFs, but users can edit them and new ones can be created with the PIF editor if a DOS application doesn't work properly. An application can be launched by clicking its PIF.

**piggyback board**    A small printed circuit board that plugs into another circuit board in order to enhance its capabilities. It does not plug into the motherboard, but would plug into the boards that plug into the motherboard.

**pigtail**    A cable that has an appropriate connector on one end and loose wires on the other. It is designed to patch into an existing line or to terminate the ends of a long run. Contrast with *patch cord*.

**PII**    See *Pentium II*.

**PIL**    (Publishing Interchange Language) A standard for document interchange that defines the placement of text and graphics objects on the page. It does not address the content of the objects.

**PILOT**    (Programmed Inquiry Learning Or Teaching) A high-level programming language used to generate question-and-answer courseware. A version that incorporated turtle graphics ran on Atari computers.

**PIM**    **(1)** (Personal Information Manager) Software that organizes names and addresses and random notes for fast retrieval. It provides a combination of features such as a telephone list with automatic dialing, calendar, scheduler and tickler. A PIM lets you jot down text for any purpose and retrieve it based on any of the words you typed in. PIMs vary widely, but all of them attempt to provide methods for managing information the way you use it on a daily basis.
    **(2)** (Protocol Independent Multicast) A multicast routing protocol endorsed by the IETF. Used in conjunction with an existing unicast routing protocol, it comes in two flavors: Dense Mode (PIM-DM) is used when recipients in the target group are in a

**Two Schools of Thought**
While both PIMs (above and top of opposite page) provide the ability to generate fixed forms, Lotus Organizer (top) provides a structured way to record addresses. The Info Select window (below) provides a free-form area where you can place text anywhere you wish. The best method is the one that suits your personality. Usually, people strongly prefer one method over the other.

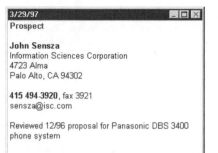

3/29/97
Prospect

**John Sensza**
Information Sciences Corporation
4723 Alma
Palo Alto, CA 94302

**415 494-3920**, fax 3921
sensza@isc.com

Reviewed 12/96 proposal for Panasonic DBS 3400
phone system

concentrated area, while Sparse Mode (PIM-SM) is more efficient when members are scattered. Contrast with *DVMRP* and *MOSPF*.

**pin**    (1) The male lead on a chip or cable connector (serial cable, keyboard cable, etc.). Each pin is plugged into its female counterpart to complete the circuit. The number of pins reflects the number of wires, or pathways, that can carry signals.

(2) (PIN—Personal Identification Number)  A password used for identification. The term came from the banking industry. See *password*.

(3) (PIN—Processor Independent NetWare)  A version of NetWare 4.1 designed for portability to multiple platforms. Development was stopped in early 1995.

**pinch roller**    A small, freely-turning wheel in a tape drive that pushes the tape against a motor-driven wheel (the capstan) in order to move it.

**pin compatible**    Refers to a chip or other electronic module that can be plugged into the same socket as the chip or module it is replacing.

**pincushioning**    A screen distortion in which the sides bow in. Contrast with *barrel distortion*.

**pin feed**    A method for moving continuous paper forms. Pins at both ends of a rotating platen or tractor engage the forms through pre-punched holes at both sides. See *tractor feed*.

**ping**    (1) (Packet INternet Groper) An Internet utility used to determine whether a particular IP address is online. It is used to test and debug a network by sending out a packet and waiting for a response.

Ping also functions like a domain name (DNS) server, because "pinging" a domain name will return its IP address. See *ICMP*.

(2) See also PNG.

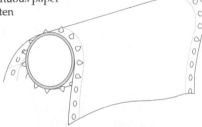

**Pin Feed Platen**
This platen has pins on both ends that engage the continous forms. Pin feed platens and tractors are widely used on dot matrix printers.

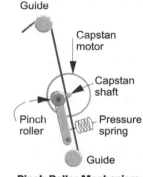

**Pinch Roller Mechanism**
This diagram shows how the pinch roller moves the tape in a helical scan tape drive. The pinch roller is on the right hand side pulling the tape from the supply reel to the take-up reel. See *helical scan*.

**P**

**Ping of Death**    A ping request that crashes the target computer. It is caused by an invalid packet size value in the packet header. There are patches for most operating systems to prevent it. See *denial of service attack*.

**ping pong**    (1) A half-duplex communications method in which data is transmitted in one direction and acknowledgement is returned at the same speed in the other. The line is alternately switched from transmit to receive in each direction. Contrast with *asymmetric modem*.

(2) To go in one direction and then in the other.

**ping-pong buffer**    See *double buffering*.

**pin grid array**    See *PGA*.

**Pink Elephant**    (Pink Elephant, The Netherlands, www.pinkelephant.com, subsidiary of InkRoccade)  A worldwide IT service management provider founded in 1979, with North American offices in Toronto and Chicago. Pink Elephant provides IT service management consulting and certification training in the ITIL and PRINCE 2 methodologies. See *ITIL* and *PRINCE 2*.

**pink noise**    The non-random sounds that occur in nature such as the sound of waterfalls and wind rustling through trees. Contrast with *Gaussian noise*.

**pinouts**    The description and purpose of each pin in a multiline connector.

**PIO mode**    (Programmed Input/Output mode)  The data transfer mode used by IDE drives. These modes use the CPU's registers for data transfer in contrast with DMA, which transfers directly between main memory and the peripheral device. For transfer rates, see *IDE*.

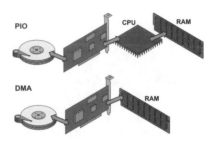

**PIP**    **(1)** (Picture In Picture)  Viewing a small video window in the middle of a full-screen video display. Although widely used for TV, it is also used in videoconferencing to see how you appear to the other members in the conference.

**(2)** (Peripheral Interchange Program)  A CP/M utility program that was used to copy files.

**pipe**    A shared space that accepts the output of one program for input into another. In DOS, OS/2 and UNIX, the pipe command is a vertical line (|). For example, in DOS and OS/2, the statement, **dir | sort** directs the output of the directory list to the sort utility. See *DOS filters & pipes* and *DOS redirection*.

**pipeline burst cache**    A common type of static RAM chip used for memory caches. Access to subsequent memory locations after the first byte is accessed takes fewer machine cycles than previous designs. See *L2 cache* and *static RAM*.

**pipeline processing**    A category of techniques that provide simultaneous, or parallel, processing within the computer  It refers to overlapping operations by moving data or instructions into a conceptual pipe with all stages of the pipe processing simultaneously. For example, while one instruction is being executed, the computer is decoding the next instruction. In vector processors, several steps in a floating point operation can be processed simultaneously.

**Pippin**    A multimedia game and Internet machine from Apple that used the PowerPC architecture and a limited version of the Mac OS. It included a CD-ROM drive and handheld game controller. Introduced in 1994, it was later abandoned due to poor sales in Japan and the U.S.

**piracy**    See *software piracy*.

**piracy investigator**    A person that searches for individuals and organizations that illegally duplicate copyrighted software for resale. The intent of such investigations is to shut down the operation and prosecute the culprits. See *software piracy*.

**pit**    An indentation in an optical medium such as a CD-ROM or DVD. The laser beam is either absorbed in the pit or reflects off the non-indented areas, which are called "lands."  Using various algorithms, the reflections are converted into 0 and 1 bits.

**pitch**    The number of printed characters per inch. With proportionally spaced characters, the pitch is variable and must be measured as an average. See *dot pitch* and *pitch-yaw-roll*.

**pitchware**    See *adware*.

**pitch-yaw-roll**    Movements of an object that are measured as angles. Pitch is up and down like a box lid. Yaw is left and right like a door on hinges, and roll is rotation.

**pivot table**    See *multidimensional views.*

**pixel**    (PIX [picture] ELement) The smallest addressable unit on a display screen. The higher the pixel resolution (the more rows and columns of pixels), the more information can be displayed.

In storage, pixels are made up of one or more bits. The greater this "bit depth," the more shades or colors can be represented. The most economical system is monochrome, which uses one bit per pixel (on/off). Gray scale and color displays typically use from 4 to 24 bits per pixel, providing from 16 to 16 million colors. See *bit depth.*

Onscreen, pixels are made up of one or more dots of color. Monochrome and gray scale systems use one dot per pixel. For monochrome, the dark pixel is energized light. For gray scale, the pixel is energized with different intensities, creating a range from dark to light. Color systems use a red, green and blue dot per pixel, each of which is energized to different intensities, creating a range of colors perceived as the mixture of these dots. Black is all three dots dark, white is all dots light. See *resolution.*

```
0000000000000000
0000000000000000
0000000000000000
0000000000000000
0000000000000000
0000000000000000
0000000000000001
0000000000000010
0000000000000100
0000000000001000
0000000000010000
0000000000100000
0000000001111111
0000000000000000
0000000000000000
```

**A Monochrome Bitmap**
The simplest pixel representation is a monochrome image in which one bit represents a dark or light pixel (black or white, black or amber, etc.).

**pixelated**    The appearance of pixels in a bitmapped image. For example, when an image is displayed or printed too large, the individual, square pixels are discernible to the naked eye where one color or shade of gray blends into another. Sometimes, images are pixelated purposefully for special effects.

**A Pixelated Picture**
The picture on the left was pixelated in Adobe PhotoShop. There are more than a half dozen "Pixelate" options in PhotoShop's Filter menu. The middle picture uses the standard square cell, wich can contain from two to 64 pixels (this one uses nine). The picture on the right uses a crystal cell pattern.

**pixel depth**    Same as *bit depth.*

**pixel graphics**    Same as *bitmapped graphics.*

**PixelPaint**    A Macintosh drawing program from SuperMac Technology, Sunnyvale, CA, that is known for its extensive paint palette and color mixing schemes.

**PIX firewall**    See *Cisco PIX firewall.*

**Pixie**    See *PXE.*

**pJava**    See *PersonalJava.*

**PJL**    (Printer Job Language) A printer command language from HP that adds control for individual print jobs and also includes the ability to set printer default settings. See *PCL.*

**PKI**    (Public Key Infrastructure) The policies and procedures for establishing a secure method for exchanging information within an organization, an industry, a nation or worldwide. It includes the use of certification authorities (CAs) and digital signatures, as well as all the hardware and software used to manage the process. See *CA*, *digital certificate* and *DST.*

**PK Software**     A family of compression utilities for DOS, Windows, OS/2, OpenVMS and UNIX from PKWARE Inc., Brown Deer, WI (www.pkware.com). Years ago, Phil Katz (the PK in PKWARE) developed the Zip standard that is widely used throughout the world. Originally as DOS command line programs, graphics-based versions have been added, and third parties have also developed products that support the format.

Whether command line or GUI based, PK utilities provide these functions. PKZIP compresses, and PKUNZIP decompresses. PKSFX and ZIP2EXE create self-extracting archives that automatically decompress when run. PKLITE compresses only .EXE and .COM files, which decompress and run at the same time. Compression libraries are also available for developers.

PKARC and PKXARC were previous compression programs that are no longer supported. See *PKZIP ABCs* and *PKZIP cross platform*.

**PKZIP**     See *PK software*.

**PKZIP cross platform**     ZIP compression support is available on more than 15 platforms from Ascent Solutions, Inc., Miamisburg, OH (www.asizip.com). This allows files, for example, that are zipped in Windows to be unzipped on a mainframe.

**PL1**     See *PL/I*.

**PLA**     (Programmable Logic Array) A type of programmable logic chip (PLD) that contained arrays of programmable AND and OR gates. PLAs are no longer used. See *PLD*.

**plaintext**     Normal text that has not been encrypted and is readable by text editors and word processors. Contrast with *ciphertext*.

**plain vanilla**     Refers to the bare minimum of functions that are known to be available in an application or system. Contrast with *bells and whistles*.

**planar**     A technique developed by Fairchild Instruments that creates transistor sublayers by forcing chemicals under pressure into exposed areas. Planar superseded the mesa process and was a major step toward creating the chip.

**planar area**     In computer graphics, an object that has boundaries, such as a square or polygon.

**planning system**     See *spreadsheet* and *financial planning system*.

**plasma display**     Also called "gas discharge display," a flat-screen technology that contains an inert ionized gas sandwiched between X- and Y-axis panels. A pixel is selected by charging one X and one Y wire, causing the gas in that vicinity to glow. Plasma displays were initially monochrome, typically orange, but color displays have become increasingly popular with models 40 inches diagonal and greater being used for computer displays, high-end home theater and digital TV.

**platen**     A long, thin cylinder in a typewriter or printer that guides the paper through it and serves as a backstop for the printing mechanism to bang into.

**platesetter**     A machine that generates plates for a printing press. A platesetter is similar in function to an imagesetter, except that instead of producing film from which the plates are made, the plates themselves are made. See *imagesetter* and *CTP*.

**platform**     A hardware or software architecture. The term originally dealt with only hardware, and it is still used to refer to a CPU model or computer family. For example, "the x86, or PC, is the world's largest hardware platform." VAX, AS/400 and SPARC are other examples of hardware platforms (see *hardware platforms* for a complete list).

Platform also refers to an operating system, in which case the hardware may or may not be implied. For example, when a program is said to "run on the Windows platform," it means that the program has been compiled into the Intel x86 machine language and that it communicates with the Windows operating system. If for example Windows were to become extremely popular on Alpha hardware, then "it runs on the Windows platform" would be ambiguous. In order to differentiate, one would have to say "Windows for Alpha" or "Windows for Intel."

This is especially true for UNIX. Since some variation of UNIX runs on almost every hardware platform, the phrase "the program runs on the UNIX platform" is not precise. It generally means that the application runs on the most popular UNIX workstations, but you would have to find out which ones to be sure.

The term also refers to software-only environments. For example, a messaging platform or groupware platform implies one or more programming interfaces that e-mail, calendaring and other client programs are written to in order to communicate with the services provided by the server.

The terms platform and environment are often used interchangeably. See *environment*.

**platform dependent**   See *machine dependent*.

**platform independent**   See *machine independent*.

**Platinum**   (Platinum Technology, Inc., Oakbrook Terrace, IL, www.platinum.com) A major independent software vendor with more than 160 data, systems and application software products. Founded in 1987, Platinum's key business areas were database and systems management, application life cycle, data warehousing, the Internet and Y2K compliance. Key alliances with HP, IBM, Intel, Microsoft and SAP helped the company expand to more than 40 countries. In 1999, Platinum was acquired by Computer Associates.

**PLATO**   (1) (**P**rogrammed **L**ogic for **A**utomatic **T**eaching **O**perations) Developed by Donald Bitzer and originally marketed by CDC, it was the first CBT system to combine graphics and touch-sensitive screens for interactive training.

(2) The code name for Microsoft's OLAP extensions to SQL Server. See *Microsoft SQL Server OLAP Services*.

**platter**   One of the disks in a hard disk drive. Each platter provides a top and bottom recording surface. See *magnetic disk*.

**PLB**   (**P**icture **L**evel **B**enchmark) A benchmark for measuring graphics performance on workstations. The Benchmark Interface Format (BIF) defines the format, the Benchmark Timing Methodology (BTM) performs the test, and the Benchmark Reporting Format (BRF) generates results in PLBmarks (formerly GPCmarks), which are divided into PLBwire93 (wireframe modeling) and PLBsurf93 (surface modeling) ratings. Image quality is not rated. See *GPC*.

**PLBmark**   See *PLB*.

**PLBsurf93**   A graphics benchmark that measures surface modeling performance. See *PLB*.

**PLBwire93**   A graphics benchmark that measures wireframe modeling performance. See *PLB*.

**A Whole Lot of Platters**
It seems that platters will spin for many years to come. This earlier 5.25" drive held 9GB over its 14 platters. Today's drives hold more than five times as much. *(Image courtesy of Singapore Technologies.)*

**PLC**   (**P**rogrammable **L**ogic **C**ontroller) A computer used in process control applications. PLC microprocessors are typically RISC-based and are designed for high-speed, realtime and rugged industrial environments.

**PLCC**   (**P**lastic **L**eaded **C**hip **C**arrier) A plastic, square, surface mount chip package that contains leads on all four sides. The leads (pins) extend down and back under and into tiny indentations in the housing. See *chip package*.

**PLD**   (**P**rogrammable **L**ogic **D**evice) An umbrella term for a variety of chips that are programmable at the customer's site. There are three physical structures. The first is the permanent fuse type which blows apart or fuses together two lines by electrically melting an aluminum trace or an insulator. The second is reprogrammable and uses EEPROM or flash memory. It causes a transistor to open or close depending on the contents of its associated memory cell. The third type is RAM based, which makes it dynamic and volatile. Its contents are loaded each time it starts up.

CPLDs (Complex PGAs) and FPGAs (Field Programmable Gate Arrays) are the most common PLD chips. CPLDs are mostly EEPROM and flash based and are reprogrammable. FPGAs use all three methods.

Unlike gate arrays, which require the final masking fabrication process, PLDs are easily programmable in the field. PLDs are always used for logical functions, but programmable storage chips such as PROMs and EPROMs might also be considered PLDs if they contain program code rather than just data. See *CPLD*, *FPGA*, *gate array* and *ASIC*.

**plenum**   In a building, the space between the real ceiling and the dropped ceiling, which is often used as an air duct for heating and air conditioning. It is also filled with electrical, telephone and network wires. See *plenum cable*.

**plenum cable**   Cable that is suitable for running in air ducts and spaces between the floor and ceiling. It uses a fire retardant coating that must comply with local building codes. See *plenum*.

**plesiochronous**   Almost synchronous. Refers to a transmission where the sending and receiving devices are synchronized, but set to different clocks. Although the bits may not arrive in the same time slot as they were sent, as long as they arrive within a certain, defined range, the transmission is said to be plesiochronous.

**PL/I**   (Programming Language 1) A high-level IBM programming language introduced in 1964 with the System/360 series. It was designed to combine features of and eventually supplant COBOL and FORTRAN, which never happened. A PL/I program is made up of procedures (modules) that can be compiled independently. There is always a main procedure and zero or more additional ones. Functions, which pass arguments back and forth, are also provided.

**PL/M**   (Programming Language for Microprocessors) A dialect of PL/I developed by Intel as a high-level language for its microprocessors. PL/M+ is an extended version of PL/M, developed by National Semiconductor for its microprocessors.

**plot**   To create an image by drawing a series of lines. In programming, a plot statement creates a single vector (line) or a complete circle or box that is made up of several vectors.

**plotter**   A graphics printer that draws images with ink pens. It actually draws point-to-point lines directly from vector graphics files. The plotter was the first computer output device that could print graphics as well as accomodate full-size engineering and architectural drawings. Using different colored pens, it was also able to print in color long before ink jet printers became an alternative.

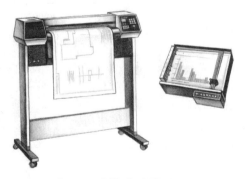

Pen plotters are still the most affordable printing device for CAD use and offer resolution unlike any other printer. The lines are not made up of dots. They are actually drawn, providing infinite resolution. See *drum plotter*, *flatbed plotter*, *electrostatic plotter* and *ink jet printer*.

**Drum and Flatbed Plotters**
Both types of plotters actually "draw" the images. The drum plotter (left) wraps the paper around a drum with pin feeds. It moves the paper back and forth for one direction of the plot. The pens move across the paper, creating the other axis. The bed of the flatbed unit (right) determines the maximum size of the total drawing.

**Plotter in a Cartridge**   HPGL emulation in a cartridge for laser printers from Pacific Data Products, San Diego, CA.

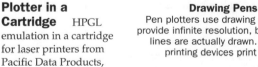

**Drawing Pens**
Pen plotters use drawing pens that provide infinite resolution, because the lines are actually drawn. All other printing devices print dots.

**PLP**   (Presentation Level Protocol) A North American standard protocol for videotex.

**PL/SQL**    (Procedural Language/SQL) A programming language from Oracle that is used to write triggers and stored procedures that are executed by the Oracle DBMS. It is also used to add additional processing (sorting and other manipulation) of the data that has been returned by the SQL query. A PL/SQL program is structured as a "block," which is comprised of a declaration, executable commands and exception handling section. See *SQL, trigger, stored procedure* and *Oracle8i*.

**plug and hope**    Refers to the frustration of installing additional peripheral devices on a PC. See *plug and tell, plug and play* and *how to install a PC peripheral*.

**plug and play**    (1) The ability to add a new component and have it work without having to perform any technical analysis or procedure.

(2) (Plug and Play) Also known as *PnP*, it is an Intel standard for the design of PC expansion boards. Plug and Play is supported directly in Windows 95/98. It eliminates the frustration of configuring the system when adding new peripherals. IRQ and DMA settings and I/O and memory addresses self configure on startup.

Implementing Plug and Play requires a system BIOS on the motherboard that supports Plug and Play as well as Plug and Play expansion cards. Plug and Play can also be retrofitted to older systems by installing the DWCFGMG.SYS driver and using new Plug and Play cards.

A Plug and Play system will also assist with older non-Plug and Play cards. When a non-Plug and Play card is installed, the ISA Configuration Utility, or ICU, will check its list of known card requirements and recommend the appropriate settings. If the card is not in the list, it will also help the user determine the correct settings, providing a "plug and tell" capability.

In time, when all systems and cards are Plug and Play, we can forget the "plug and hope" days of installing PC peripherals. See *how to install a PC peripheral* and *Home Plug and Play*.

**Plug and Play BIOS**    A system BIOS in a PC that supports Plug and Play. Although it ensures effective operation of Plug and Play under all circumstances, it is not vital for general Plug and Play operation.

**plug and pray**    What some people call Plug and Play on the PC. Plug and Play goes a long way to solving the frustration of adding peripherals to a PC, but it is not infallible.

**plug and tell**    Refers to installing new peripheral devices in a PC and using a utility program that helps to configure the device properly. MicroChannel and EISA bus installations, as well as installing a non-Plug and Play card in a Plug and Play machine, are plug and tell because they analyze the system and recommend which settings should be made.

Plug and tell is between the "plug and hope" of installing a legacy ISA card in a PC and the "plug and play" of installing an ISA Plug and Play card in a Plug and Play machine.

**plugboard**    A board containing a matrix of sockets used to program a machine. Plugboards were widely used in punched card tabulating machines and early computers and were the predecessor to software programming. For example, each wire in the board directs a column of data from its source column to its destination which could be a print column or a card column to be punched. A wire could also function as a switch by closing a circuit. Complicated programs looked like "mounds of spaghetti."

**plug compatible**    Hardware that is designed to perform exactly like another vendor's product. A plug compatible CPU runs the same software as the machine it's compatible with. A plug compatible peripheral works the same as the device it's replacing.

**The Author in 1962**
Alan Freedman, the author of this *Encyclopedia*, got his start in programming plugboards of punched card machines. In those "good old days" you learned data processing the hard way, by carrying the data on your back. Trays of cards were heavy, and tons of them were routinely moved from one machine to another. Note the plugboard on the desk and the wiring rack in the back.

**plugfest**    A test of interoperability of network devices by actually plugging them into a running network. A plugfest is more of a down-and-dirty approach in contrast to the tedious process of certification by running a variety of test programs and test equipment. If you plug a device into the plugfest, it either works or it doesn't.

**plug-in**    An auxiliary program that works with a major software package to enhance its capability. For example, plug-ins are widely used in image editing programs such as Photoshop to add a filter for some special effect. Plug-ins are added to Web browsers to enable them to support new types of content (audio, video, etc.). The term is widely used for software, but could also be used to refer to a plug-in module for hardware. See *plug-inless*.

**plug-inless**    Refers to some unique feature on a Web site that does not require a plug-in to be downloaded, installed and associated with the browser in order to use it. Users prefer plug-inless solutions for many reasons. First, everyone is leery of viruses coming from the Web, and second, if you work on several machines, or if you buy a new one, all your browser plug-ins have to be downloaded again and reinstalled. See *plug-in*.

**plugs and sockets**    The physical connectors used to link together all variety of electronic devices. All the plugs and sockets described in this database are summarized below.

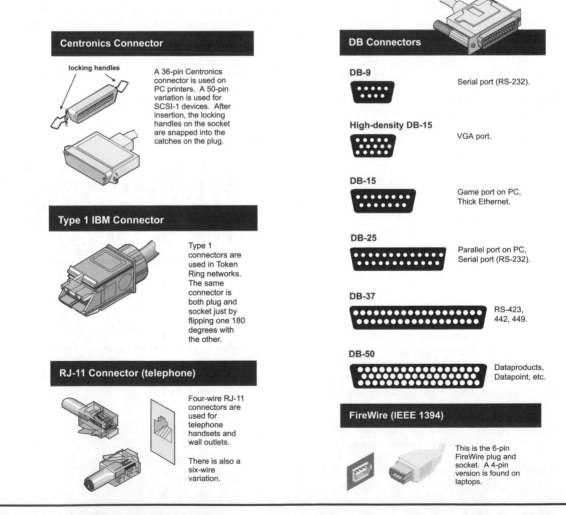

**Centronics Connector**

locking handles

A 36-pin Centronics connector is used on PC printers. A 50-pin variation is used for SCSI-1 devices. After insertion, the locking handles on the socket are snapped into the catches on the plug.

**Type 1 IBM Connector**

Type 1 connectors are used in Token Ring networks. The same connector is both plug and socket just by flipping one 180 degrees with the other.

**RJ-11 Connector (telephone)**

Four-wire RJ-11 connectors are used for telephone handsets and wall outlets.

There is also a six-wire variation.

**DB Connectors**

DB-25

**DB-9**    Serial port (RS-232).

**High-density DB-15**    VGA port.

**DB-15**    Game port on PC, Thick Ethernet.

**DB-25**    Parallel port on PC, Serial port (RS-232).

**DB-37**    RS-423, 442, 449.

**DB-50**    Dataproducts, Datapoint, etc.

**FireWire (IEEE 1394)**

This is the 6-pin FireWire plug and socket. A 4-pin version is found on laptops.

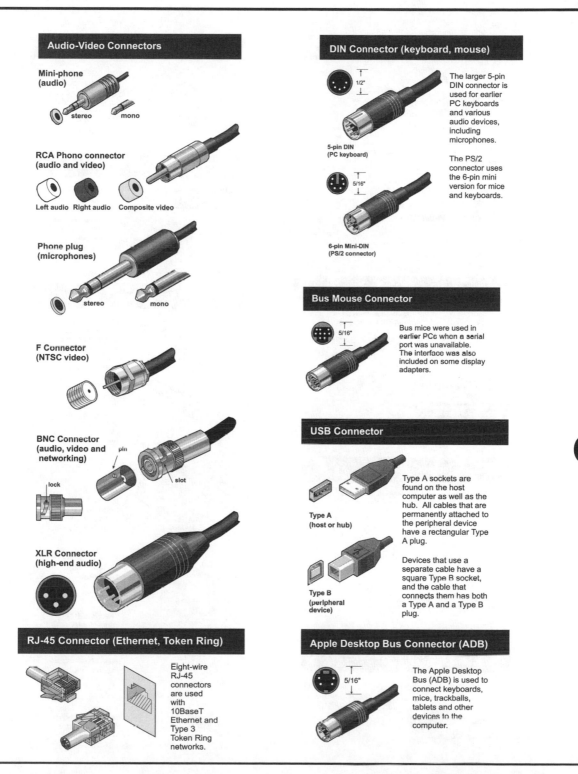

## Audio-Video Connectors

**Mini-phone (audio)**
stereo  mono

**RCA Phono connector (audio and video)**
Left audio  Right audio  Composite video

**Phone plug (microphones)**
stereo  mono

**F Connector (NTSC video)**

**BNC Connector (audio, video and networking)**
pin  slot  lock

**XLR Connector (high-end audio)**

## RJ-45 Connector (Ethernet, Token Ring)

Eight-wire RJ-45 connectors are used with 10BaseT Ethernet and Type 3 Token Ring networks.

## DIN Connector (keyboard, mouse)

1/2"
**5-pin DIN (PC keyboard)**

5/16"
**6-pin Mini-DIN (PS/2 connector)**

The larger 5-pin DIN connector is used for earlier PC keyboards and various audio devices, including microphones.

The PS/2 connector uses the 6-pin mini version for mice and keyboards.

## Bus Mouse Connector

5/16"

Bus mice were used in earlier PCs when a serial port was unavailable. The interface was also included on some display adapters.

## USB Connector

**Type A (host or hub)**

**Type B (peripheral device)**

Type A sockets are found on the host computer as well as the hub. All cables that are permanently attached to the peripheral device have a rectangular Type A plug.

Devices that use a separate cable have a square Type B socket, and the cable that connects them has both a Type A and a Type B plug.

## Apple Desktop Bus Connector (ADB)

5/16"

The Apple Desktop Bus (ADB) is used to connect keyboards, mice, trackballs, tablets and other devices to the computer.

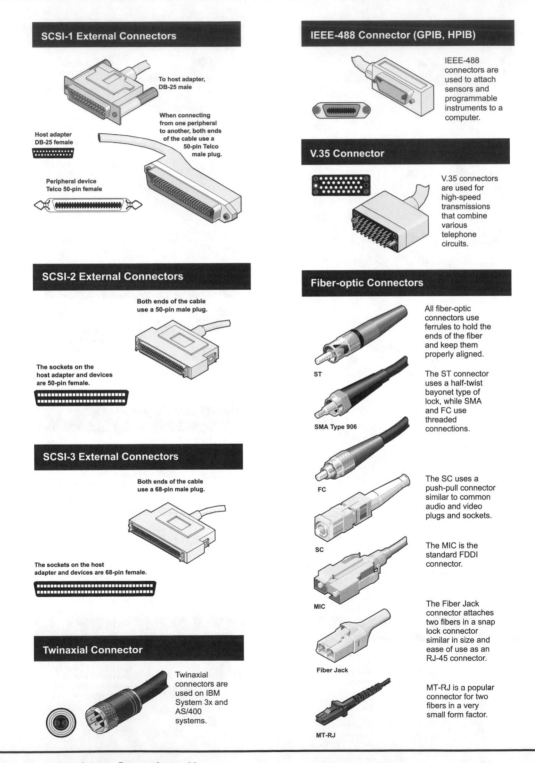

## SCSI-1 External Connectors

To host adapter, DB-25 male

When connecting from one peripheral to another, both ends of the cable use a 50-pin Telco male plug.

Host adapter DB-25 female

Peripheral device Telco 50-pin female

## SCSI-2 External Connectors

Both ends of the cable use a 50-pin male plug.

The sockets on the host adapter and devices are 50-pin female.

## SCSI-3 External Connectors

Both ends of the cable use a 68-pin male plug.

The sockets on the host adapter and devices are 68-pin female.

## Twinaxial Connector

Twinaxial connectors are used on IBM System 3x and AS/400 systems.

## IEEE-488 Connector (GPIB, HPIB)

IEEE-488 connectors are used to attach sensors and programmable instruments to a computer.

## V.35 Connector

V.35 connectors are used for high-speed transmissions that combine various telephone circuits.

## Fiber-optic Connectors

All fiber-optic connectors use ferrules to hold the ends of the fiber and keep them properly aligned.

ST

The ST connector uses a half-twist bayonet type of lock, while SMA and FC use threaded connections.

SMA Type 906

FC

The SC uses a push-pull connector similar to common audio and video plugs and sockets.

SC

The MIC is the standard FDDI connector.

MIC

The Fiber Jack connector attaches two fibers in a snap lock connector similar in size and ease of use as an RJ-45 connector.

Fiber Jack

MT-RJ is a popular connector for two fibers in a very small form factor.

MT-RJ

**plus sign**  The plus sign (+) means add in programming and on calculator keyboards. For example, **10 + 7** means 10 added to 7. It is also used as a concatenation symbol for text fields. For example, **city + ", " + state** combines the CITY field with a comma, blank space and the STATE field.

**PM**  See *preventive maintenance*, *Presentation Manager*, *Program Manager* and *phase modulation*.

**PMC**  (PCI Mezzanine Card)  A PCI-based mezzanine card that is widely adapted to VMEbus, CompactPCI and PCI cards. Small and compact (74mm x 149mm) and providing 32 or 64-bit data paths, PMC cards enable a large variety of PCI products to be retrofitted to other bus environments. PMC cards use 64-pin connectors. See *mezzanine card* and *PC\*MIP*.

**PMD**  (Polarization Mode Dispersion)  The type of dispersion that occurs in singlemode fiber due to a lack of perfect symmetry in the fiber and from external pressures on the cable. Light travels over singlemode fiber in two polarization states. Over long distances, PMD causes each one to arrive at the receiving end at a different time. See *dispersion*.

**Data Acquisition PMC Card**
This BiSerial-IO card from Dynamic Engineering provides 20 bi-directional RS-485 ports on one PMC card. This design provides independent receive and transmit rates up to 12MHz. *(Image courtesy of Dynamic Engineering, www.dyneng.com)*

**PMJI**  Digispeak for "pardon my jumping in."

**PMMU**  (Paged Memory Management Unit)  A virtual memory chip for the 68020 processor (it is built in on the 68030), which is required to run A/UX on the Mac or any 68020 platform running hardware virtual memory.

**PMOS**  (Positive channel MOS)  Pronounced "P moss."  A type of microelectronic circuit in which the base material is positively charged. PMOS transistors were used in the first microprocessors and are still used in CMOS. They are also used in low-cost products (calculators, watches, etc.).

**PMS**  (Pantone Matching System)  A color matching system that has a number assigned to over 500 different colors and shades. This standard for the printing industry has been built into many graphics and desktop publishing programs to ensure color accuracy.

**PMT**  See *photomultiplier tube*.

**PNG**  (Portable Network Graphics)  A bitmapped graphics file format endorsed by the World Wide Web Consortium. It is expected to eventually replace the GIF format, because there are lingering legal problems with GIFs. CompuServe owns the format, and Unisys owns the compression method. In addition, GIF is a very basic graphics format that is limited to 256 colors (8-bit color).

PNG provides advanced graphics features such as 48-bit color, including an alpha channel, built-in gamma and color correction, tight compression and the ability to display at one resolution and print at another.

**PNNI**  (Private Network-to-Network Interface)  A routing protocol used between ATM switches in an ATM network. It lets the switches inform each other about network topology so they can make appropriate forwarding decisions. PNNI is based on the OSPF protocol, but also measures line capacities and delays rather than just simple cost metrics. Thus, ATM switches can dynamically reroute packets based on current line conditions. See *I-PNNI*.

**PnP**  See *Plug and Play*.

**PN sequence**  (Pseudo-random Noise sequence)  A set of bits that are generated to be statistically random. See *pseudo-random*.

**pocket computer**  A handheld, calculator-sized computer that runs on batteries. It can be plugged into a personal computer for data transfer. See *Pocket PC*.

**Pocket Excel**   A version of Microsoft Excel for the Windows CE/Pocket PC operating system.

**Pocket Internet Explorer**   A version of Microsoft Internet Explorer for the Pocket PC operating system.

**Pocket PC**   An operating environment for handheld computers from Microsoft based on the Windows CE operating system. In 2000, Microsoft introduced the Pocket PC platform, which includes a combination of Windows CE Version 3.0, an enhanced user interface, Pocket Office applications (Internet Explorer, Word and Excel), handwriting recognition, an e-book reader, wireless Internet and longer battery life. The Pocket PC was designed to compete more directly with the popular Palm devices.

**Pocket Word**   A version of Microsoft Word for the Windows CE/Pocket PC operating system.

**PocketZip disk**   A low-cost, portable disk drive technology from Iomega. Introduced under the Clik! disk brand name, the PocketZip uses floppy-like, 40MB removable cartridges that are half the size of a credit card and were introduced at less than $10 each. The external drive connects to the computer via the USB port or a PC Card, the latter containing a removable cartridge slot within the card itself. See *magnetic disk*.

**PocketZip Cartridge**
PocketZip drives are aimed at handheld devices that require removable storage, such as PDAs and digital cameras.

**POD**   (Print On Demand)  See *on-demand printing*.

**point**   (1) To move the cursor onto a line or image onscreen by rolling a mouse across the desk or by pressing the arrow keys.

(2) In typography, a unit equal to 1/72nd of an inch, used to measure the vertical height of a printed character.

**point and shoot**   To select a menu option or activate a function by moving the cursor onto a line or object and pressing the return key or mouse button.

**PointCast**   The first major deployment of push technology on the Web. Introduced in 1996 and supported by ad revenues, PointCast provided Internet-based news and customized information to the desktop. In 1999, LaunchPad Technologies acquired the product and turned it into EntryPoint, which later became Infogate. See *Infogate*.

**point code**   The physical address of a node in an SS7 network. Every node must have a unique point code. See *SS7* and *signaling point*.

**pointer**   (1) In database management, an address embedded within the data that specifies the location of data in another record or file.

(2) In programming, a variable that is used as a reference to the current item in a table (array) or to some other object, such as the current row or column onscreen.

(3) A symbol used to point to some element onscreen. See *cursor*.

**The PointCast Screen**
PointCast "pushed" a lot of information into the users machine. Its successor product kept the details on the Web and provided an "entry point" to them. *(Screen examples courtesy of EntryPoint, Inc.)*

**pointing device**    An input device used to move the pointer (cursor) on screen. The major pointing devices are the mouse, trackball, pointing stick and touchpad.

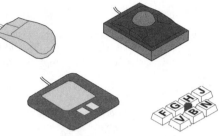

**pointing stick**    A pointing device that looks like a pencil eraser between the G, H and B keys. It is moved with the forefinger, while the thumb is used to press related keys located in front of the space bar. IBM popularized this device by introducing the TrackPoint on its ThinkPad notebooks. See *mouse, trackball* and *touchpad*.

**The Pointing Stick**
Popularized by IBM's TrackPoint, the pointing stick has become a popular pointing device on laptop computers.

**The Major Pointing Devices**
The mouse, trackball, touchpad and pointing stick are the four major pointing devices.

**point of presence**    See *POP*.

**point of sale**    Capturing data at the time and place of sale. Point of sale systems use personal computers or specialized terminals that are combined with cash registers, bar code readers, optical scanners and magnetic stripe readers for accurately and instantly capturing the transaction.

Point of sale systems may be online to a central computer for credit checking and inventory updating, or they may be stand-alone machines that store the daily transactions until they can be delivered or transmitted to the main computer for processing.

**Point of Sale**
Busy supermarkets would be hard pressed to keep up with the traffic if it were not for bar code readers and point of sale systems. Do we even remember the days without them? *(Image courtesy of Sweda International AB.)*

**point product**    Refers to a product that provides a solution to a single problem rather than addressing all the requirements that might otherwise be met with a multipurpose or multiservice product. For example, as telecommunications carriers combine more services, point products that each support one protocol have given way to multiservice products that support several protocols in one device.

**point sampling**    Also called "nearest neighbor," it is the simplest form of texture mapping, which is often associated with low-end games and applications that do not demand much realism. An algorithm is used to map a screen pixel to the corresponding point on the texture map. The attributes (color, alpha, etc.) of the nearest texel are then directly applied to the screen pixel. The process in repeated for each pixel forming the object being textured. See *texture map, bilinear interpolation, trilinear interpolation* and *MIP mapping*.

**point solution**    Solving one particular problem without regard to related issues. Point solutions are widely used to fix a problem or implement a new service quickly. See *point product*.

**point-to-multipoint**    A communications network that provides a path from one location to multiple locations (from one to many).

**point-to-point**    Refers to a communications line that provides a path from one location to another (point A to point B). Contrast with *multipoint*.

**Point-to-Point Protocol**    See *PPP*.

**Poisson distribution**    A statistical method developed by the eighteenth century French mathematician S. D. Poisson, which is used for predicting the probable distribution of a series of events. For example, when the average transaction volume in a communications system can be estimated, Poisson distribution is used to determine the probable minimum and maximum number of transactions that can occur within a given time period.

**poke**   See *peek/poke*.

**polarity**   (1) The direction of charged particles, which may determine the binary status of a bit.
(2) In micrographics, the change in the light to dark relationship of an image when copies are made. Positive polarity is dark characters on a light background; negative polarity is light characters on a dark background.

**polarized**   A one-way direction of a signal or the molecules within a material pointing in one direction.

**policy**   The rules and regulations set by the organization. Policy determines the type of internal and external information resources employees can access, the kinds of programs they may install on their own computers as well as their authority for reserving network resources. Policy is also related to network quality of service (QoS), because it can define priorities by user, workgroup or application with regard to reserving network bandwidth. See *COPS* and *Internet Usage Policy*.

**policy based**   A decision made by any software application that is based on the policy (rules and regulations) of the organization. See *COPS* and *policy*.

**policy management**   Enforcing the policy (rules and regulations) of the organization that pertain to information and computing. See *policy*, *COPS* and *security*.

**policy routing protocol**   See *path vector protocol*.

**Polish notation**   A method for expressing a sequence of calculations developed by the Polish logician Jan Lukasiewicz in 1929. For example, **A(B+C)** would be expressed as
    * A + B C. In reverse Polish notation, it would be **A B C + ***.

**polling**   (1) A communications technique that determines when a terminal is ready to send data. The computer continually interrogates its connected terminals in a round robin sequence. If a terminal has data to send, it sends back an acknowledgement and the transmission begins. Contrast with an interrupt-driven system, in which the terminal generates a signal when it has data to send.
(2) A technique that continually interrogates a peripheral device to see if it has data to transfer. For example, if a mouse button was pressed or if data is available at a communications port. Contrast with event-driven or interrupt-driven techniques, in which the operating system generates a signal and interrupts the system.

**polling cycle**   One round in which each and every terminal connected to the computer or controller has been polled once.

**polycarbonate**   A category of plastic materials used to make a myriad of products, including CDs and CD-ROMs.

**polygon**   In computer graphics, a multi-sided object that can be filled with color or moved around as a single entity. See *triangle*.

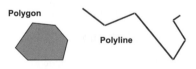

**polygon map**   Defines the borders of homogeneous features as well as the characteristics associated with those features which identify special land related information (e.g., a soils map describes the boundary characteristics of soil types from which the following types of information can be obtained:  areas which have unstable land for construction; areas that may be within a floodplain; wetland areas; areas with high potential productivity for farming, etc.)
    Polygon mapping is the cartographic display of regularly or irregularly shaped polygons and their attributes. Typically, this capability includes shading, symbology and numeric labeling, as well as other map cosmetic functions for generating alphanumeric labeling of polygons. (Data West Research Agency definition: see *GIS glossary*.)

**polyhedron**   A six- or more-sided object. A group of connected polygons.

**polyimide**   Pronounced "poly-ih-mid." A type of plastic (a synthetic polymeric resin) originally developed by DuPont that is very durable, easy to machine and can handle very high temperatures. Polyimide is also highly insulative and does not contaminate its surroundings (does not outgas). Vespel and Kapton are examples of polyimide products from DuPont. See *tape automated bonding.*

**polyline**    In computer graphics, a single entity that is made up of a series of connected lines.

**polymer**    Meaning "many parts," it is a material constructed of smaller molecules of the same substance that form larger molecules. For example, plastic is a synthetic polymer, while protein is a natural polymer.

**polymer diode**    See *OLED.*

**polymer LED**    See *OLED.*

**polymorphic tweening**    See *tweening.*

**polymorphic virus**    A virus that changes its binary pattern each time it infects a new file to keep it from being identified. See *stealth virus.*

**polymorphism**    Meaning many shapes. In object technology, the ability of a generalized request (message) to produce different results based on the object that it is sent to. See *polymorphic virus.*

**polyphonic**    The ability to play back some number of musical notes simultaneously. For example, 16-voice polyphony means a total of 16 notes, or waveforms, can be played concurrently.

**poly-si**    See *polysilicon.*

**polysilicon**    (POLYcrystalline SILICON) Silicon with a crystalline structure, which acts as a conductor of electricity. It is used as the gate in MOS transistors as well as an interconnect between them. Contrast with *amorphous silicon.* See *LTPS TFT LCD.*

**polysilicon LCD**    See *LTPS TFT LCD.*

**PON**    (Passive Optical Network) A passive, point-to-multipoint (one to many) access network based on ATM. Using optical fiber, it connects several hundred homes and/or offices into an optical line termination (OLT) device at a telco office or ISP. The OLT attaches to as many as 32 optical network units (ONUs), which can be on the street or in buildings.

**POP**    (Point of Presence) The point at which a line from a long distance carrier (IXC) connects to the line of the local telephone company or to the user if the local company is not involved. For online services and Internet providers, the POP is the local exchange users dial into via modem. See *POP3, POP-1, Super POP* and *push/pop.*

**POP-1**    (Package for Online Programming) The first of a family of programming languages introduced in England in the mid 1960s. It used reverse polish notation. Successors were POP-2, POP-9X, POP-10, POP-11, POPCORN, POP++, POPLOG and POPLER.

**POP3**    (Post Office Protocol 3) A standard mail server commonly used on the Internet. It provides a message store that holds incoming e-mail until users log on and download it. POP3 is a simple system with little selectivity. All pending messages and attachments are downloaded at the same time. POP3 uses the SMTP messaging protocol. See *IMAP* and *messaging system.*

**pop-down menu**    See *pull-down menu.*

**Popper**    An early UNIX POP server, which was written at the University of California at Berkeley.

**POP server**    A server that implements the Post Office Protocol. See *POP3.*

**populate**   To plug in chips or components into a printed circuit board. A fully populated board is one that contains all the devices it can hold.

**population inversion**   The condition that occurs when a material is radiated with another material at a certain wavelength, causing electrons to jump to a higher orbit (higher shell). When the electrons return to their ground state, they spontaneously emit a photon. Population inversion is the reason a laser works. The spontaneous emission of photons is amplified by mirrors causing a chain reaction and further stimulation of the excited atoms to release photons. See *laser*.

**popup**   **(1)** A type of menu called for and displayed on top of the existing text or image. When the item is selected, the menu disappears and the screen is restored.

   **(2)** Same as *TSR*.

**port**   **(1)** A pathway into and out of the computer or a network device such as a switch or router. For example, the serial and parallel ports on a personal computer are external sockets for plugging in communications lines, modems and printers. Every network adapter has a port (Ethernet, Token Ring, etc.) for connection to the local area network (LAN). Any device that transmits and receives data implies an available port to connect to each line. See *port speed*, *line card*, *serial port*, *parallel port* and *PC input/output*.

   **(2)** To convert software to run in a different computer environment. The phrase "to port the program to UNIX," means to make the necessary changes in the application to enable it to run under UNIX.

   **(3)** A number assigned to an application running in a server. See *port number*.

**port 80**   **(1)** The default port address used to link incoming Web traffic to the appropriate application program. See *port number*.

   **(2)** An input/output address in a PC used for sending POST codes. See *POST* and *PC I/O addressing*.

**portability**   See *portable*.

**portable**   Refers to software that can be easily moved from one type of machine to another. It implies a product that has a version for several hardware platforms or has built-in capabilities for switching between them. However, a program that can be easily converted from one machine type to another is also considered portable.

**portable computer**   A personal computer that can be transported. Portable computing started in 1981, when Adam Osborne introduced his CP/M-based business computer called the Osborne I. It came bundled with a modified version of the WordStar word processor specialized for the machine's pint-sized screen. The Osborne I was soon followed by Kaypro, Hyperion, Otrona and many others. One year after the Osborne, Compaq introduced the first MS-DOS portable. See *laptop computer*, *notebook computer* and *pocket computer*.

**Portable NetWare**   An OEM version (C source code) of Novell's NetWare operating system that can be compiled for a specific vendor's machine.

**port address**   See *I/O address* and *port number*.

**port aggregation**   Using multiple transmission paths between network devices in order to increase transmission speed. Port aggregation between a server and a switch requires multiple network adapters (NICs) in the server or adapters with multiple ports. Each server port hooks up to a switch port, and the port aggregation software is typically in the server. When port aggregation is provided between switches, the software is in the switches.

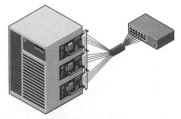

**A Fatter Pipe**
Port aggregation provides a "fatter pipe" between the network device and the server. In this example, three multiport network adapters in the server are connected to a switch. The pipe in the center is conceptual, as each line is connected separately between the devices.

**portal**    A Web "supersite" that provides a variety of services including Web searching, news, white and yellow pages directories, free e-mail, discussion groups, online shopping and links to other sites. Web portals are the Web equivalent of the original online services such as CompuServe and AOL. Although the term was initially used to refer to general purpose sites, it is increasingly being used to refer to vertical market sites that offer the same services, but only to a particular industry such as banking, insurance or computers. See *corporate portal*, *business intelligence portal* and *vertical portal*.

**port configuration hub**    See *port switching hub*.

**port density**    The number of ports on a device, such as a network switch, router or hub. The more ports (the greater the port density), the more devices or lines can be supported by the unit.

**port expander**    A device that connects several lines to one port in the computer. The port may be one interface type that is expanded into several by this device (see *port multiplier*), or it may contain multiple interfaces. For example, a port expander may provide additional serial and parallel ports on a laptop.

**porting**    See *port*.

**port multiplier**    Also called a "fan-out," it is a device that expands one port into several. For example, an Ethernet port multiplier allows multiple stations to be connected to a 10Base5 cable via one transceiver tap. Otherwise, each station requires its own transceiver.

**port number**    In a TCP/IP-based network such as the Internet, it is a number assigned to an application program running in the computer. The number is used to link the incoming data to the correct service. Well-known ports are standard port numbers used by everyone; for example, port 80 is used for HTTP traffic (Web traffic). See *UNIX socket*.

**portrait**    An orientation in which the data is printed across the narrow side of the form. Contrast with *landscape*.

**port replicator**    A device used to connect multiple peripherals to a laptop. The desktop devices are permanently plugged into the port replicator, which connects to the laptop via a large plug and socket that duplicates all the cable lines for the monitor, printer, keyboard, mouse, etc. It serves a similar purpose as a docking station, but does not contain any slots for expansion or speakers or peripherals. See *docking station*.

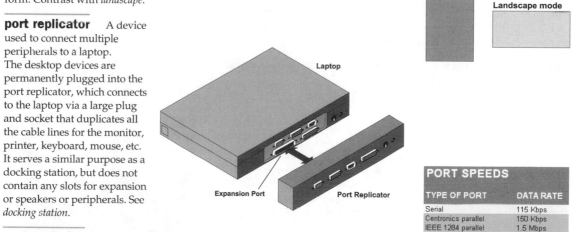

**port scanning**    Sending queries to Internet servers (hosts) in order to obtain information about their services and level of security. On Internet hosts, there are standard port numbers for each type of service. Port scanning is sometimes done to find out if a network can be compromised. See *well-known port*.

**port speed**    The data transmission rate of an input/output channel. The speeds of common ports are listed here. See *port*.

**PORT SPEEDS**

| TYPE OF PORT | DATA RATE |
|---|---|
| Serial | 115 Kbps |
| Centronics parallel | 150 Kbps |
| IEEE 1284 parallel | 1.5 Mbps |
| USB | 12 Mbps |
| USB-2 | 480 Mbps |
| IEEE 1394 FireWire | 400 Mbps |
| IEEE 1394b FireWire | 3,200 Mbps |
| T1 | 1.544 Mbps |
| T3 | 44,736 Mbps |
| 10Base-T | 10 Mbps |
| 10Base-2 | 10 Mbps |
| 10Base-5 | 10 Mbps |
| 100Base-T | 100 Mbps |
| 1000Base-T | 1000 Mbps |

**port switching hub** An intelligent network hub that attaches to multiple LAN segments. Via software, it allows the station ports to be connected to one of the segments. This is a type of virtual LAN, because one LAN segment can be located on different floors or geographic locations.

**POS** See *point of sale* and *packet over SONET*.

**POSIT** (Profiles for Open Systems Internetworking Technolgoies) A set of voluntary standards published by the National Institute of Standards and Technology (NIST) for network equipment purchased by the U.S. government. It is the successor to GOSIP.

**positional lighting** See *ambient lighting*.

**positional sound** See *3-D positional sound*.

**positive logic** The use of low voltage for a 0 bit and high voltage for a 1 bit. Contrast with *negative logic*.

**POSIX** (Portable Operating System Interface for UNIX) An IEEE 1003.1 standard that defines the language interface between application programs and the UNIX operating system. Adherence to the standard ensures compatibility when programs are moved from one UNIX computer to another. POSIX is primarily composed of features from UNIX System V and BSD UNIX.

**POS keyboard** A computer keyboard that contains built-in readers for magnetic stripe cards, bar codes or smart cards or any combination of the three.

**POSSI** (Phoenix OS/2 Society, Inc., Phoenix, AZ, www.possi.org) A membership group founded in 1994 to promote the OS/2 operating system. Through its "extended attributes" magazine and regular meetings, POSSI's primary goal is to educate its members.

**POST** (1) (Power On Self Test) A series of built-in diagnostics performed by the BIOS in a PC when the computer is first started. See *POST card*.
(2) (post) To send a message to an Internet newsgroup or to place an HTML page on the Web or on an intranet. See *Usenet*.

**postage sites** See *PC Postage*.

**Postalsoft** A family of programs for UNIX and Windows platforms from Firstlogic, Inc., La Crosse, WI (www.postalsoft.com) that provides mail automation and management. Since 1984, Postalsoft programs have been used to create mailing labels, correct addresses, assign postal codes and consolidate mailing lists (merge purge). Firstlogic was originally Postalsoft, Inc. See *i.d.Centric*.

**POST card** (Power On Self Test card) A diagnostic board that is plugged into a PC's peripheral bus in order to display the BIOS's POST codes on a built-in readout. The last POST code displayed before the system locks up identifies the problem area. POST codes are different for each BIOS vendor (of course).

**POST code** (Power On Self Test code) A proprietary number generated by each PC BIOS vendor indicating the current diagnostic test being taken at startup. The results are displayed on a small readout on a

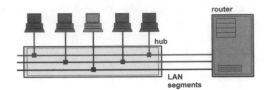

**Port Switching Hub**
Each station attached to a port switching hub can be linked to a different LAN segment via software. In order to forward traffic from one LAN segment to another, a router is required.

**A POST Card**
This POST card from Ultra-X plugs into a PCI slot and displays the POST codes on the readout at the top right side of the board.
*(Image courtesy of Ultra-X, Inc., www.uxd.com)*

POST card that is plugged into the peripheral bus. The last POST code displayed before the system locks up identifies the problem area. One might ask why the video system was not the first test so that the remaining POST codes could be displayed on the computer's monitor. Then again, one might not. See *POST card*.

**post dial delay**  The time between punching in the last digit of a telephone number and receiving a ring or busy signal.

**posterization**  The effect produced when a photographic image is displayed or printed with a small number of colors or shades of gray. For example, displaying color photographs or video with 16 colors produces a visible posterization, but the images are discernible. At 256 colors, the flesh tones on color images are still mildly posterized. For realistic flesh tones, it takes 65K colors. For absolute realism, it requires 16M colors.

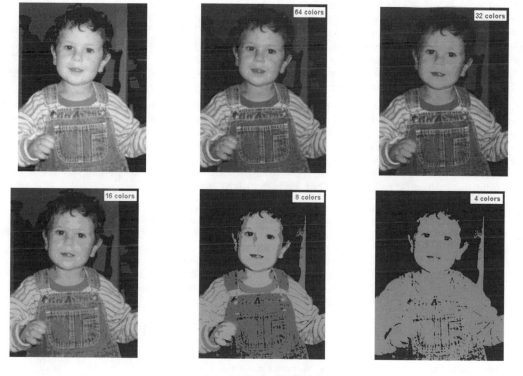

**Posterization—128 Colors**
These examples show how an image posterizes as fewer colors are used to display it. The picture above is displayed with 128 colors, and each of the following pictures is halved.

**postfix notation**  See *reverse Polish notation*.

**Post Office Protocol**  See *POP*.

**post-PC era**  (1) The use of numerous machines each dedicated to a specific application in contrast to the general-purpose desktop or laptop computer.
(2) The use of desktop and laptop computers that run under operating systems other than Windows. Java was expected to be "the" technology that would enable the post-PC era by supporting platform independence. The Java interpreter (Java

Virtual Machine) in each different computer environment would be able to execute the same Java application, and since the Windows PC would not be mandatory, it would no longer be the dominant computer environment.

Java is not the only way to allow multiple computer environments to proliferate. If data standards were widely adopted and supported, any hardware, operating system and application could be used as long as the standard file types were supported. However, given human nature and the state of the industry, it would seem to require a federal government mandate to effect such conformity.

**postprocessor**   Software that provides some final processing to data, such as formatting it for display or printing.

**PostScript**   A page description language (PDL) from Adobe that is used extensively on all computer platforms. It is the de facto standard in commercial typesetting and printing houses. Most all accept and may even require PostScript files as electronic input.

PostScript commands do not drive the printer directly. They are language statements in ASCII text that are translated into the printer's machine language by a PostScript interpreter built into the printer. Fonts are scaled to size by the interpreter, thus eliminating the need to store a variety of font sizes on disk. PostScript Level 2, downward compatible with original PostScript, adds data compression and enhancements, especially for color printing. Level 3 adds more enhancements and native fonts and the ability to directly support more formats, including HTML, PDF, GIF and JPEG.

Encapsulated PostScript (EPS) is a subset of PostScript used to exchange a single graphic image in the PostScript format. See *EPS* and *Adobe Type Manager*.

PostScript Fonts   PostScript fonts come in Type 1 and Type 3 formats. Type 1 fonts are widely used and are made by Adobe and other companies. Type 1 fonts are encrypted and compressed and also allow for hints, which improve the appearance of text at 300 dpi and lower resolutions. Type 1 fonts use a simpler, more efficient command language than Type 3. With Adobe Type Manager, Type 1 fonts can also be used on non-PostScript printers.

Type 3 fonts do not use encryption or hints, but can use the entire PostScript language to create complex designs. They can also be bitmaps. Type 3 fonts are not widely used; however, in order to speed up printing small fonts on PostScript printers, Windows 3.1 creates Type 3 bitmaps from its TrueType outlines.

Type 1 Font Files   Type 1 fonts are distributed by Adobe as two files. One contains the outlines, and the other contains the font metrics, which includes character widths and heights and kerning values.

Type 1 font distribution disks for Windows contain PFB, AFM and INF files. The PFB (Printer Font Binary) outline files are copied to the hard disk, and the AFM (Adobe Font Metric) files are converted into PFM (Printer Font Metric) files on the hard disk. INF files contain information that the font installer requires.

Type 1 font distribution disks for the Mac contain outline and metric files that are copied onto the hard disk. For example, a Helvetica font would have an outline file named "Helve" and a font metrics file named "Helvetica." The icon for the font metrics file looks like a suitcase, and is often called the "suitcase file." A Helve.AFM file may also be included on the distribution disk.

PostScript font distribution disks for UNIX contain both AFM and PFA (Printer Font ASCII) files. The PFA files contain the PostScript ASCII code of the outline.

**PostScript emulation**   Using a PostScript interpreter that is not from Adobe.

**potentiometer**   A device that controls the amount of current that flows through a circuit, such as a volume switch on a radio.

**POTS**   (Plain Old Telephone System or Service)   See *PSTN* and *AMPS*.

**POTS splitter**   A device that uses low-pass and high-pass filters to direct analog voice and DSL signals to different lines. See *DSL*.

**pound sign**   See *number sign*.

**Potentiometer**
It may have a fancy name,
but it is quite often nothing
more than the volume control
on your radio or hi-fi.

**POV-Ray**    (Persistance Of Vision Raytracer) A popular freeware ray tracing program for DOS, Windows, Mac and various UNIX platforms from the Persistance of Vision development team. The program and source code are available at www.povray.org.

**power**    (1) See *computer power*.

(2) (POWER—Performance Optimization With Enhanced RISC) A RISC-based CPU architecture from IBM used in its RS/6000 workstation and parallel computer line. The PowerPC, enhanced by Motorola and Apple, is a single-chip version of the POWER architecture.

**power adapter**    A transformer that converts AC power from a wall outlet into the DC power required by an electronic device.

**PowerBook**    Apple's trade name for its portable computers, which are widely used and very popular. See *Macintosh* and *Titanium*.

**PowerBuilder**    A popular application development system for Windows client/server environments from Powersoft. It supports various databases, including DB2 and Oracle, and is also packaged with the Watcom SQL database. PowerBuilder provides visual programming tools as well as a BASIC-like programming language called PowerScript. Macintosh, Windows NT and UNIX support is also provided.

PowerMaker is a subset of PowerBuilder with a simplified interface for non-programmers and departmental use. PowerViewer is the query, reporting and business graphics generator for both products.

**An Early PowerBook**
PowerBooks were an instant success as soon as they hit the market and have been very popular ever since. *(Image courtesy of Apple Computer, Inc.)*

**PowerCD**    A consumer-oriented CD-ROM player from Apple that connects to a TV for Photo CD use, to a Macintosh for data, audio and Photo CD or to a stereo for audio CDs.

**PowerChip**    A semiconductor-based, high-speed switching device for electrical power. Such products, which open and close at nanosecond speeds, are expected to be widely used to distribute clean, uniform power for computers and electronics. Large units switch electrical feeds in the national power grid, while smaller ones switch at the circuit board level in power supplies and UPS systems.

**power down**    To turn off the computer in an orderly manner by making sure all applications have been closed normally and then shutting the power.

**power good**    A signal transmitted from the power supply to the circuit board indicating that the power is stable. For various power supply definitions, see *power supply*.

**PowerHouse**    A fourth-generation language from Cognos that was introduced in the late 1970s for midrange computers. It supports both character-oriented, terminal-based applications as well as Windows clients. Applications developed under PowerHouse can be imported into Cognos' Axiant client/server environment.

**PowerMac**    A PowerPC-based Macintosh, officially known as the "Power Macintosh." PowerMacs were introduced in 1994 along with more than 100 applications that were ported to the new architecture. Since then, Apple has migrated all of its Macintosh line from the Motorola 680x0 CPU family to the PowerPC RISC chip.

In order to accommodate both platforms, Apple created a "fat binary" disk that allows software to be distributed in both 680x0 and PowerPC formats. Although PowerMacs emulate 680x0 applications, they can run faster on a PowerMac, because Apple's QuickDraw graphics engine runs native. Applications call the graphics engine extensively for screen display.

The first PowerMacs came with 8MB of RAM and used the 601 PowerPC CPU chip with clock speeds from 60 to 80MHz. Over the years, the PowerMacs have dramatically increased in speed and capability. See *Macintosh* and *Apple*.

**Power Macintosh**   See *PowerMac*.

**power management**   Maximizing battery power by using low-voltage CPUs and slowing down components when they are inactive. See *SMM*.

**power margin**   The excess capacity in a UPS system. For example, if a PC uses 400 watts and the UPS provides 600 watts, there is 200 watts of power margin.

**PowerOpen**   A standard for a UNIX-based operating system running on PowerPCs from the former PowerOpen Association. Founded in 1991, the goal was to create shrink-wrapped PowerPC applications, which would run under any PowerOpen-compliant OS. Since IBM's AIX was already a shrink-wrapped UNIX for the PowerPC, the need for different UNIXs became less important, and the association disbanded in 1995. See *UNIX* and ***Apple-IBM alliance***.

**PowerPC**   A family of CPU chips designed by Apple, IBM and Motorola, introduced in 1993. Both IBM and Motorola offer the chips for sale, but IBM owns the architecture. The PowerPC is designed to span a range of computing devices from handheld machines to supercomputers.

To date, PowerPC chips have been used as the CPUs in Apple's PowerMacs, IBM's RS/6000 and AS/400 models as well as in embedded systems. IBM originally offered the PowerPC as a stand-alone AIX or Windows NT machine, but since dropped the models.

**PowerPC CPU Technical Specs**   The PowerPC is a refined version of IBM's RS/6000 single-chip CPU. It is a RISC-based 32-bit multitasking microprocessor that has an internal 64-bit data path to memory similar to the Pentium.

The first PowerPC chip was the 601 (MPC601), which was introduced with clock speeds of 50 and 66MHz. Subsequent models include the 602, 603, 603e, 604 and 604e. The 602 is designed for consumer products, while the 603s are geared for notebooks. The 604 and 604e provide higher speeds, mostly due to increased amounts of built-in cache and higher clock speeds.

In 1997, the PowerPC 750 was introduced, providing a significant increase in performance. Also known as the G3 series, the first chips arrived with clock speeds of 233MHz and 266MHz. In 1999, the G4 chip came out starting at 350MHz. The G4 includes the Velocity Engine vector processor that provides a sustained one billion floating point operations per second. See *Macintosh* and *CHRP*.

**power platform**   Refers to a mature, high-speed computer system.

**PowerPlay**   A decision support system from Cognos that summarizes information for management. It combines EIS and DSS features in an integrated environment, and its Transformer creates multidimensional views of information. It runs on Windows clients and VMS and UNIX servers.

**PowerPoint**   A presentation graphics program from Microsoft for Macintosh and Windows. It was the first desktop presentation program for the Mac and provides the ability to create output for overheads, handouts, speaker notes and film recorders.

**PowerSCSI**   Software from Future Domain Corporation that accompanies its SCSI host adapters for PCs allowing them to control all SCSI peripherals. It translates the popular methods for accessing SCSI devices, including DOS' int 13, Windows FastDisk, ASPI and various CD-ROM methods into industry standard CAM, supported on its host adapter. See *CorelSCSI*.

**PowerShare**   Software from Apple that resides in a Macintosh server and provides messaging store and forward, authentication of network users, encryption of messages and other workgroup/enterprise services.

**Powersoft**   (Powersoft Corporation, Concord, MA, www.powersoft.com) The developer of the popular PowerBuilder application development system. In 1995, the company was acquired by Sybase, creating a software vendor with 4,400 employees and revenues of 700 million. The Powersoft brand has been maintained as a separate tools division of the company.

**power supply**     An electrical system that converts AC current from the wall outlet into the DC currents required by the computer circuitry. In a personal computer, the power supply typically generates multiple voltages. 12 volts is used for drives, and either 3.3 or 5 volts is used for the electronic circuitry.

**power surge**     An oversupply of voltage from the power company that can last up to several seconds. Power surges are the most common cause of loss to computers and electronic equipment. See *spike* and *sag*.

**PowerTalk**     Secure messaging software from Apple that is included in the System 7 operating system (starting with Mac System 7 Pro). PowerTalk provides a unified mail box that holds different types of communications, including e-mail, fax, voice mail and pager. It provides for RSA digital signatures, which guarantees the authenticity of documents electronically signed by other users.

   PowerTalk uses the AppleTalk transport protocol for network transmission. PowerTalk runs on individual Macs, while PowerShare runs on Mac servers.

**PowerToys**     A set of utilities from Microsoft that enhance the Windows 95/98 operating system for the power user. They provide shortcuts for executing functions and various options. However, although written by the Microsoft development team and available from the Microsoft Web site, they are not supported functions.

**power up**     To turn the computer on in an orderly manner.

**power user**     A person who is very proficient with personal computers. It implies knowledge of a variety of software packages.

**PPC**     See *PowerPC*.

**PPCP**     (PowerPC Platform) A term used for CHRP for a while. See *CHRP*.

**PPD file**     (PostScript Printer Description file) A file that contains detailed information about a particular printer. Although PostScript is a device-independent language, the PostScript driver uses information in the PPD file to take advantage of special features in the target printer or imagesetter. The PPD file is an ASCII file that can be transferred between PCs and Macs.

**PPGA**     (Plastic PGA) See *PGA*.

**pph**     (Pages Per Hour) Measures printing speed.

**ppi**     (1) (Pixels Per Inch) The measurement of the display or print elements.
   (2) (Points Per Inch, Pulses Per Inch) The measurement of mouse movement.

**ppm**     (Pages Per Minute) The measurement of printer speed. See *gppm*.

**PPP**     (Point-to-Point Protocol) The communications protocol used to dial up the Internet over a serial link, such as a POTS or IDSN line. Developed by the Internet Engineering Task Force in 1994, it superseded the SLIP protocol. PPP establishes the session between the user's computer and the ISP using the Link Control Protocol (LCP), which also handles authentication (PAP, CHAP, etc.), compression and encryption.

   PPP encapsulates protocols in specialized Network Control Protocol packets and supports other high-level protocols such as IPX, AppleTalk and DECnet. For example, IPCP (IP over PPP) encapsulates TCP/IP packets for the Internet, and IPXCP (IPX over PPP) encapsulates IPX packets for NetWare networks. PPP can multiplex different protocols over the same circuit.

   PPP can run on any full-duplex link from POTS to ISDN to high-speed lines (T1, T3, etc.). It can also be used to replace a network adapter driver, allowing remote users to log on to the network as if they were in-house. PPP can hang up and redial on a low-quality call.

   Over ISDN, PPP uses one 64 Kbps B channel for transmission. The Multilink PPP protocol (MP, MPPP or MLPPP) bridges B channels for higher speed. See *PPPoE*, *PPTP* and *SLIP*.

**PPPoE** (Point-to-Point Protocol Over Ethernet) A method for running the PPP protocol, commonly used for dial-up Internet connections, over Ethernet. Used by DSL and cable modem providers, PPPoE supports the protocol layers and authentication widely used in PPP and enables a point-to-point connection to be established in the normally-multipoint architecture of Ethernet. A discovery process in PPPoE determines the Ethernet MAC address of the remote device in order to establish a session.

**pps** (Packets Per Second) The measurement of transmission speed in a local area network (LAN). In LANs such as Ethernet, Token Ring and FDDI, data is broken up and transmitted in packets (frames), each with a source and destination address. Network devices, such as hubs, bridges, routers and switches are rated for performance by the number of packets they can forward in one second.

**PPTP** (Point-to-Point Tunneling Protocol) A protocol that encapsulates other protocols for transmission over an IP network. For example, it can be used to send NetWare IPX packets over the Internet. Due to its RSA encryption, PPTP is also used to create a private network (VPN) within the public Internet. Remote users can access their corporate networks via any ISP that supports PPTP on its servers.

**PQFP** (Plastic Quad Flat Package) Refers to many varieties of QFP chip packages, which are molded in plastic. See *QFP*.

**pragma** A message written into the source code that tells the compiler to compile the program in some fashion that differs from the default method. For example, pragmas may alter the kinds of error messages that are generated or optimize the machine code in some way.

**prairie dogging** A phenomenon that occurs in cubicle-filled office buildings. Whenever there's a loud sound or other unusual occurrence, everyone pops up to look over the walls to see what's happening. Co-worker conversations and team meetings may also take place via prairie dogging as an alternative to the water cooler or conference room. See *mutter machine*.

**PRAM** (Parameter RAM) Pronounced "P RAM." A battery-backed part of the Macintosh's memory that holds Control Panel settings and the settings for the hidden desktop file. If the COMMAND and OPTION keys are held down at startup, the desktop settings are cleared and a dialog to rebuild the desktop is initiated.

**precedence** The order in which an expression is processed. Mathematical precedence is normally

> 1. unary + and − signs
> 2. exponentiation
> 3. multiplication and division
> 4. addition and subtraction

In order to properly compute the formula that converts Fahrenheit to Celsius, which is **fahrenheit-32*5/9**, the expression

```
(fahrenheit-32)*5/9
```

must be used with parentheses separating the fahrenheit-32 from the multiplication. Since multiplication is evaluated before subtraction, 32 would be multiplied by 5 first, which is not what is wanted.

Logical precedence is normally

> 1. NOT
> 2. AND
> 3. OR

In the dBASE query:

```
list for item = "TIE" .and. color = "GRAY"
  .or. color = "RED"
```

all gray ties and anything red will be selected, since ANDs are evaluated before ORs. Grouping the colors in parentheses as in the example below yields only gray and red ties.

```
(color="GRAY" .or. color="RED")
```

**precision**   The number of digits used to express the fractional part of a number. The more digits, the more precision. See *single precision* and *double precision*. See also *accuracy*.

**precomp**   See *write precompensation*.

**precompile**   To do a preliminary conversion before doing the final conversion. The precompile phase sets up the source code, database, etc., in such a way that the final phase is performed faster.

**preconfigured**   Set up ahead of time. It implies that the device or software application has been modified to suit the customer or situation. See *ghosting server*.

**predicate**   In programming, a statement that evaluates an expression and provides a true or false answer based on the condition of the data.

**predication**   In CPU instruction execution, executing all outcomes of a branch in parallel. When the correct branch is finally known, the results of the incorrect branch sequences are discarded. See *branch prediction*.

**predictive branching**   See *branch prediction*.

**preemptive multitasking**   A multitasking method that shares processing time with all running programs. Preemptive multitasking creates a time-shared environment in which running programs get a recurring slice of time from the CPU. Depending on the operating system, the time slice may be the same for all programs or it may be adjustable to meet the current mix of programs and users. For example, background programs can be given more CPU time no matter how heavy the foreground load and vice versa.

   Preemptive multitasking is vital in a mainframe, but is also useful in a desktop operating system. For example, it ensures that data will not be lost if a transmission is taking place in the background. The OS is able to grab the machine cycles that the modem or network program needs to continue processing the incoming data stream. Contrast with *non-preemptive multitasking*.

**preferences**   Options in a program that can be changed by the user. Preferences usually control the user interface, letting users customize the way they view their data. They may also control routine actions taken by the program. If preferences are not modified by the user, the default settings are used. See *default* and *Tools menu*.

**prefetch**   To bring data or instructions into a higher-speed storage or memory before it is actually processed. See *cache*.

**prefix notation**   See *Polish notation*.

**premises distribution system**   See *PDS*.

**premium content**   Digital content on the Web that is not free. It is downloaded for a charge. See *Web payment service* and *digital content*.

**premium digital content**   See *premium content*.

**PReP**   (PowerPC REference Platform) A common specification for PowerPCs from IBM and Apple that allows them to run a variety of operating systems. PReP was superseded by CHRP. See *CHRP*.

**prepackaged software**   See *software package*.

**prepress**   In typography and printing, the preparation of camera-ready materials up to the actual printing stage, which includes typesetting and page makeup.

**preprocessor**    Software that performs some preliminary processing on the input before it is processed by the main program.

**presence**    The state of knowing that another person is currently online and available. The term is generally used with regard to instant messaging applications. See *buddy list*.

**presentation graphics**    Business graphics, charts and diagrams used in a presentation. Presentation graphics software provides predefined backgrounds and sample page layouts to assist in the creation of complete computer-driven slide shows, which in combination with a data projector, are obsoleting the 35mm slide presentation.

The software also provides a variety of special effects that can be used to fade and wipe one frame into another such as commonly found in the video world. Sound and video can also be merged into the presentation. Examples of Windows presentation graphics programs are Harvard Graphics, Freelance Graphics, PowerPoint and Charisma.

**presentation layer**    The services in the OSI protocol stack (layer 6 of 7) that provide conversion of codes and formats for the communications session. See *OSI*.

**Presentation Level Protocol**    See *PLP*.

**presentation logic**    The processing (instructions, routines, etc.) required to display or print data. It typically refers to the execution of the user interface (GUI). Contrast with *business logic*.

**Presentation Manager**    A graphical user interface (GUI) library used to develop OS/2 applications. Character-based OS/2 applications can be developed similar to DOS applications, but OS/2 PM applications are graphics based like Macintosh, Windows and Motif applications. The term used to be the name of the interface itself, which was later named Workplace Shell.

**presentation services protocol**    A protocol that provides graphical interface screen updates to a client station from an application executing in a multiuser computer system. ICA and T.share are examples for the WinFrame and Windows-based Terminal Server systems. See *WinFrame, Windows Terminal Server, ICA* and *T.share*.

**press proof**    A sample of actual printing on the intended paper stock. It is the most accurate and also the most costly way to preview the output of a commercial print job. It is, in fact, the final job, except that only a small number of units are printed. See *match print*.

**Prestel**    A commercial videotex service of British Telecom (formerly part of the British Post Office).

**Pretty Good Privacy**    See *PGP*.

**PrettyPark**    A Trojan horse that was unleashed in the summer of 1999. Spread as an e-mail attachment, once executed, it causes users to log onto an Internet Relay Chat (IRC) channel when they surf the Web. The IRC channel is capable of downloading files and extracting personal data such as passwords and credit card numbers. See *Trojan horse*.

**preventive maintenance**    The routine checking of hardware that is performed by a field engineer on a regularly scheduled basis. See *remedial maintenance*.

**PRI**    (Primary Rate Interface) An ISDN service that provides 23 64 Kbps B (Bearer) channels and one 64 Kbps D (Data) channel (23B+D), which is equivalent to the 24 channels of a T1 line. The advantage of the D channel is that it sends control signals that can dynamically allocate any number of B channels for different applications. For example, one channel can be used for voice, while another can be used for data, while six more can be used for a videoconferencing channel and so on. PRI lines typically use four wire pairs. PRI lines are often desginated as PRI/T1 or T1/PRI lines, but they are dial-up PRI lines, not T1 lines, which are point-to-point. See *ISDN*.

**priceline.com**    (priceline.com Incorporated, Stamford, CT, www.priceline.com) A Web-based shopping site where buyers submit the price they are willing to pay for airline tickets, hotel rooms, new cars and rentals, groceries and other products and services   If a vendor in the system agrees to the price, the transaction is consummated and priceline.com receives a commission. See *online auction*.

## Primary Domain Controller   See *PDC*.

## primary index   The index that controls the current processing order of a file. It maintains an index on the primary key. See *secondary index*.

## primary key   An indexed field that maintains the primary sequence of the file/table.

## Primary Rate   See *ISDN*.

## primary storage   The computer's internal memory (RAM). Contrast with *secondary storage*.

## primitive   (1) In computer graphics, a graphics element that is used as a building block for creating images, such as a point, line, arc, cone or sphere.

(2) In programming, a fundamental instruction, statement or operation.

(3) In microprogramming, a microinstruction, or elementary machine operation.

## PRINCE 2   (PRojects IN Controlled Environments 2)  A product-based approach for project management that provides an easily tailored and scalable method for managing IT and other business projects. A PRINCE 2 project is defined by its business case, which is regularly reviewed during a project under the assumption that business objectives may well change during the product lifecycle. PRINCE 2 represents the latest version of a project management standard developed by the United Kingdom's CCTA in 1989. Widely used in Europe, it has gained popularity in the U.S. See *Pink Elephant* and *CCTA*.

## print buffer   See *printer buffer*.

## print column   A column of data on a printed report that may be subtotalled or totalled. Print columns are the heart of a report writer's description.

## printed circuit board   A flat board that holds chips and other electronic components. The board is made of layers (typically 2 to 10) that interconnects components via copper pathways. The main printed circuit board in a system is called a "system board" or "motherboard," while smaller ones that plug into the slots in the main board are called "boards" or "cards."

The printed circuit board of the 1960s connected discrete components together. The circuit board of the 1990s interconnects chips, each containing hundreds of thousands or millions of elementary components.

The "printed" circuit is really an etched circuit. A copper foil is placed over the fiberglass or plastic base of each layer and covered with a photoresist. Light is shined through a negative image of the circuit paths onto the photoresist, hardening the areas that will remain after etching. When passed through an acid bath, the unhardened areas are washed away. The finished layers are then glued together. A similar process creates the microminiaturized circuits on a chip (see *chip*). See *motherboard*.

## print engine   See *printer engine*.

## printer   A device that converts computer output into printed images. Following is an overview of the various technologies.

For more details, look up the individual entries.

GENERAL CATEGORIES

**SERIAL PRINTERS (CHARACTER PRINTERS)**   Serial printers print one character at a time moving across the paper. Electrosensitive, direct thermal, older daisy wheel and even ink jet printers could be cataloged in this group; however, the primary desktop serial printer is the serial dot matrix printer, with speeds ranging from 200 to 400 cps, which is about 90 to 180 lines per minute (lpm).

**LINE PRINTERS**   Line printers print a line at a time from approximately 400 to 2,000 lpm and are commonly found in datacenters and industrial environments. Earlier technologies included drum, chain, train and dot band matrix technologies. The surviving technologies use band and line matrix mechanisms.

**PAGE PRINTERS**   Page printers print a page at a time from four to more than 800 ppm. Laser, LED, solid ink and electron beam imaging printers fall into this category. All of these printers adhere toner or ink onto a drum which is transferred to the entire page in one cycle for black and white and multiple cycles for color.

IMPACT PRINTERS

**SERIAL DOT MATRIX**   A desktop printer that uses a moving printhead of wire hammers. It forms characters and graphics by impacting a ribbon and transferring dots of ink onto the paper. See *dot matrix printer*.

**LINE MATRIX**   A type of line printer that uses an oscillating row of print hammers. The hammers form characters and graphics by impacting a ribbon and transferring dots of ink onto the paper. See *line matrix printer*.

**BAND (LINE CHARACTER)**   A type of line printer that uses a fixed set of characters attached to a continuously-revolving metal band. A set of hammers (one for each column) hit the paper, pushing it into the ribbon and against the character image on the band. See *band printer*.

**EARLIER IMPACT TECHNOLOGIES**   Impact printers were developed for the first computers, and several earlier technologies have gone by the wayside. Chain, train and drum printers were precursors to band printers. They all used actual shaped characters, or type slugs, to print a fixed size and style of letter and digit. Daisy wheel printers were desktop impact printers used in the 1970s and 1980s. Dot band matrix printers used a combination of band printer and dot matrix methods. See *chain printer*, *train printer*, *drum printer*, *daisy wheel* and **dot band matrix printer**.

NON-IMPACT PRINTERS

**LASER and LED**   Laser printers and LED printers employ the electrophotographic method used in copy machines. Both technologies are available from small desktop units to high-speed digital printing presses, ranging in speed from four to more than 700 ppm, and color units from three to 75 ppm. See *laser printer*, *LED printer* and *electrophotographic*.

**INK JET**   Ink jets have become the most popular form of desktop, personal printer. Most all units can print in color or have a color option. Ink jets propels droplets of ink directly onto the paper. See *ink jet printer*.

**IRIS**   IRIS printers use ink jet technology, but are in a class by themselves. They achieve a perceived 1,800 dpi resolution and can print on fabric as well as paper. See *IRIS printer*.

**SOLID INK**   Solid ink printers use sticks of wax ink that are melted into a liquid. The ink is directed onto a drum, similar to a laser printer, and then transferred onto the paper to produce high-quality output. See *solid ink printer*.

**ELECTRON BEAM IMAGING**   A technology somewhat similar to a laser printer, except that electricity is used to create the image instead of light. This evolved from ion deposition and is used in very high-speed page printers exceeding 800 ppm. See *electron beam imaging*.

**THERMAL WAX TRANSFER and DYE SUBLIMATION**   Dots of ink or dye are transferred from a ribbon onto paper by passing the ribbon and the paper across a line of heating elements. Thermal wax is used for bar code and other types of labels as well as medium-resolution graphics. Dye sublimation is used for photorealistic color output. See *thermal wax transfer printer* and *dye sublimation printer*.

**ELECTROSENSITIVE**   A dot matrix printhead charges dots on aluminum-coated silver paper, usually in a serial fashion. The charge removes the coating, leaving a black image. See *electrosensitive printer*.

**DIRECT THERMAL**   Used in bar code and other specialty printers as well in earlier fax machines, dots are burned onto a type of coated paper that darkens when heat is applied to it. See *direct thermal printer*.

**ELECTROSTATIC**   Dots are charged onto a coated paper, typically a line at a time. A toner is attracted to the paper and made permanent by pressure or heat. See *electrostatic plotter*.

**printer buffer**    A memory device that accepts printer output from one or more computers and transmits it to the printer. It lets the computer dispose of its printer output at full speed without waiting for each page to print. Printer buffers with automatic switching are connected to two or more computers and accept their output on a first-come, first-served basis.

**printer cable**    A cable that connects a printer to a computer. On a PC, the cable has a 25-pin DB-25 male connector to plug into the computer and a 36-pin Centronics male connector to plug into the printer.

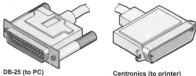

DB-25 (to PC)          Centronics (to printer)

**Printer Control Language**    See *PCL*.

**printer description file**    A configuration file that contains information about a specific printer. See *PPD file*.

**printer driver**    A software routine that converts an application program's printing request into the language the printer understands. For example, PostScript printer drivers create a file that is accepted by PostScript printers. HP printer drivers create PCL files and so on. Drivers for Windows-only printers rasterize the pages (RIP function) and send the actual bit patterns to the printer, which are applied to the drum by the laser or LED array.

**printer engine**    The unit within a printer that does the actual printing. In a laser printer, it includes the laser and mechanism to transfer the toner onto the paper. A printer engine is specified by its resolution and speed. See *electrophotographic*.

**printer file**    (1) A document in print image format ready to be printed. See *print to disk*.
(2) Same as *printer driver*.

**printer font**    A font used for printing. Printer and screen resolutions are not the same, thus fonts generated for the printer will not display accurately on screen. Contrast with *screen font*.

**print head**    A mechanism that deposits ink onto paper in a character printer.

**print image**    A text or graphics document that has been prepared for the printer. Format codes for the required printer have been embedded in the document at the appropriate places. With text files, headers, footers and page numbers have been created and inserted in every page.

**print image format**    See *print image*.

**printing protocol**    The commands and functions used to print a job on a network printer. It manages the submission of print jobs by maintaining queues and controlling the transfer of their contents to the printer. It also enables the user to determine the capabilities of the printer and the status of the job and be able to cancel it. It may provide flow control if the underlying transport protocol does not (UDP, IPX, etc.).

A unidirectional protocol such as LPR/LPD is mainly responsible for job submission. However, full-featured, bi-directional protocols such as PAP and NDPS include sophisticated printer management, responding to messages and alerts from the printer. The primary printing protocols are the LPR/LPD UNIX standard, Apple's PAP, Novell's QMS and NDPS, HP's JetDirect and the Internet's IPP. See *page description language*.

**Print Manager**    In Windows 3.x, the software that prints documents in the background. It is also used if the computer is connected to a network and the printer is shared with other users. Print Manager is the Windows print spooler, which accepts the incoming print jobs, stores them and prints them in the background.

**printout**    (PRINTer OUTput) Same as *hard copy*.

**print queue**    Disk space that holds output designated for the printer until the printer can receive it.

**print screen**    The ability to print the current on-screen image. See *screen dump* and **Win print screen**.

**print server**   (1) A computer in a network that controls one or more printers. It is either part of the network operating system or an add-on utility that stores the print-image output from users' machines and feeds it to the printer one job at a time. The computer and its printers are known as a "print server" or a file server with "print services."

(2) A hardware device that enables a printer to be located anywhere in the network. Available as a plug-in card for printers that have an expansion slot or as an external unit that plugs into the printer's parallel port, print servers have an Ethernet port for network connection. The print server uses the printer's memory to queue the print jobs.

A print server can be used with or without a file server dedicated to print services (definition 1 above). If there is not enough memory in the printer to hold the entire print job, the print server causes the print services machine or the individual client machines to spool the print output in the background. See *print spooler*.

**print spooler**   Software that manages printing in the computer. When an application is requested to print a document, it quickly generates the output on disk and sends it to the print spooler, which feeds the print images to the printer at slower printing speeds. The printing is then done in the background while the user interacts with other applications in the foreground. See *spooling* and *Print Manager*.

**print to disk**   To redirect output from the printer to the disk. The resulting file contains text and graphics with all the codes required to direct the printer to print it. The file can be printed later or at a remote location without requiring the word processor, DTP or drawing program that was originally used to create it. This is actually the first stage of a print spooling operation. See *print spooler*.

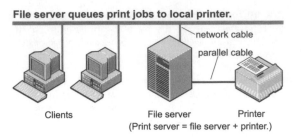

**File server queues print jobs to local printer.**

Clients          File server          Printer
(Print server = file server + printer.)

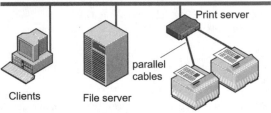

**Using a print server, file server queues print jobs to remote printer.**

Clients          File server

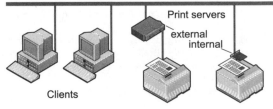

**Using a print server without a file server, clients queue print jobs to remote printer.**

Clients

**Print Servers**
These are all print server configurations. In the top example, the print server is the combination of the file server, which includes print services, and its attached printer. The middle and bottom examples use print servers to allow the printers to reside anywhere on the network.

**PRISM**   (1) (**P**hoto**R**efractive **I**nformation **S**torage **M**aterials Consortium) A collaboration of IBM, Stanford University, GTE, Hughes Research Labs, Optitek, SRI International and Rockwell Science Center that is funded by the U.S. government's Advanced Research Projects Agency for the purpose of researching holographic storage.

(2) (**PR**ogrammable **I**ntegrated **S**cripts for **M**irror) The programming language for the Mirror communications programs.

(3) See *PR/SM*.

**PRI/T1**   See *PRI*.

**privacy**   The authorized distribution of information (who has a right to know?). Although always a concern when users pass confidential information to vendors by phone, mail or fax, the Internet has brought this issue to the forefront. Web sites often have privacy policies that stipulate exactly what will be done with the information you enter. Contrast with *security*, which deals with unauthorized access to data. See *CPO* and *P3P*.

**Privacy Enhanced Mail**    See *PEM*.

**private branch exchange**    See *PBX*.

**private carrier**    An organization that provides communications services. A private carrier can refuse to sell its services to an organization, whereas a "common carrier" is obligated to treat all customers equally. Contrast with *common carrier*.

**private data network**    A communications network that is used by one organization or an industry group. It may be deployed as private lines leased from common carriers and entirely architected by the network owner, or it may be a virtual private network (VPN) cither over the Internet or one that was provisioned within a carrier's network. Contrast with *public data network*. See *VPN*.

**Private Eye**    A headband-mounted LED display system that plugs into a PC from Reflection Technology, Waltham, MA (www.reflection.com). Its 1"×1" screen gives the appearance of a 12" monitor floating in space. See *virtual display*.

**private file**    A file made available only to the user that created it. Contrast with *public file*.

**private key**    The private part of a two-part, public key cryptography system. The private key is kept secret and never transmitted over a network. See *RSA* and *cryptography*.

**private key cryptography**    Same as *secret key cryptography*.

**private label**    See *OEM*.

**private line**    (1) A dedicated line leased from a common carrier.
(2) A line owned and installed by the user.

**private peering**    Peering between two ISPs rather than at a national exchange point. Sec *NAP*.

**private Web site**    An intranet. A Web site available to internal personnel only. See *intranet* and *firewall*.

**privileged mode**    An operational state of hardware or software that has the highest priority. Also called the "supervisor mode" or "supervisor state," it is typically the mode in which the operating system runs.

**PRMD**    (PRivate Management Domain) An inhouse e-mail service. See *X.400*.

**PRML**    (Partial Response Maximum Likelihood) A technique used to differentiate a valid signal from noise by measuring the rate of change at various intervals of the rising waveform. Bits generated by a modem or by reading a hard disk have uniform characteristics, whereas random noise does not. PRML uses digital signal processing (DSP) to reconstruct the data.

On magnetic disks, PRML increases the number of bits that can be recorded over earlier methods. It uses an RLL encoding sequence of 0,4,4 and provides an 8:9 ratio of user data to recorded data. See *RLL*.

**PRMS**    A full featured ERP system from the interBiz Solutions division of Computer Associates for the AS/400. PRMS dates back to 1980 when the PCR company released its Resource Management System (RMS) software. In 1987, Pansophic Systems acquired PCR and added the "P" to the name. In 1991, Computer Associates (CA) acquired Pansophic, which later became the Acacia Technologies division and then interBiz Solutions. See *Acacia*.

**PRN**    (PRiNter) The DOS name for the first connected parallel port. See *DOS device names*.

**Pro\*COBOL**    A precompiler for Windows from Oracle that converts SQL and PL/SQL statements embedded within a COBOL program to normal COBOL statements that can be compiled.

**problem-oriented language**   A computer language designed to handle a particular class of problem. For example, COBOL was designed for business, FORTRAN for scientific and GPSS for simulation.

**procedural language**   A programming language that requires programming discipline, such as COBOL, FORTRAN, BASIC, C, Pascal and dBASE. Programmers writing in such languages must develop a proper order of actions in order to solve the problem, based on a knowledge of data processing and programming. Contrast with *non-procedural language*.

The following dBASE examples show procedural and non-procedural ways to list a file. Procedural and non-procedural languages are also considered third and fourth-generation languages.

```
Procedural (3GL)          Non-Procedural (4GL)
USE FILEX                 USE FILEX
DO WHILE .NOT. EOF        LIST NAME, AMOUNTDUE
  ? NAME, AMOUNTDUE
  SKIP
ENDDO
```

**procedural rendering**   The application of special rendering techniques to selected elements in a 3-D image. See *rendering*.

**procedural texture**   An algorithmic way of describing a texture. Unlike a bitmapped texture, in which the texture is represented as a bitmap, a procedural texture describes the texture mathematically. Although not widely used, because this method is resolution independent, it can create more precise textures especially if there is great and varying depth to the objects being textured. Procedural textures may be 2-D or 3-D. See *texture mapping* and *volumetric texture*.

**procedure**   (1) Manual procedures are human tasks.
(2) Machine procedurs are lists of routines or programs to be executed, such as described by the job control language (JCL) in a mini or mainframe, or the batch processing language in a personal computer.
(3) In programming, a procedure is another term for a subroutine or function.

**procedure oriented**   An application that forces the user to follow a predefined path from step A to step B. Data entry programs are typical examples. Contrast with *event driven*.

**process**   To manipulate data in the computer. The computer is said to be processing no matter what action it is taking upon the data; whether the data is actually being updated in a database or just being displayed on screen.
In order to evaluate a computer system's performance, the time it takes to process data internally is often analyzed separately from the time it takes to get it in and out of the computer. The I/O (input/output) is usually more time consuming than the processing. For an explanation of how the computer processes data, see "Processing" under the term *computer*. See also *process technology*.

**process bound**   An excessive amount of processing in the CPU that causes an imbalance between I/O and processing. In a multitasking system, process-bound applications may slow down other applications and other users, depending on how the operating system slices time (see *preemptive multitasking*). A personal computer can become process bound when it is recalculating a spreadsheet, for example.

**Process Charter**   A flowcharting and simulation program for Windows from Scitor Corporation, Menlo Park, CA (www.scitor.com). It provides the ability to model and simulate a process based on the resources required for each step.

**process color**   A color printed from four separate printing plates. Four-color process printing uses cyan, magenta, yellow and black (CMYK) inks to produce full color reproduction. Contrast with *spot color*.

**process control**   The automated control of a process, such as a manufacturing process or assembly line. It is used extensively in industrial operations, such as oil refining, chemical processing and electrical generation. It uses analog devices to monitor real-world signals and digital computers to do the analysis and controlling. It makes extensive use of analog/digital, digital/analog conversion.

**process identifier**   See *PID*.

**processing**   Manipulating data within the computer. The term is used to define a variety of computer functions and methods. See *centralized processing*, *distributed processing*, *batch processing*, *transaction processing* and *multiprocessing*. For an explanation of "The 3 Cs," or how the computer processes data, see *computer*.

**process management**   The execution and monitoring of repeatable business processes that have been defined by a set of formal procedures. See *knowledge-driven process management*.

**process manufacturing**   Fabricating products from materials that come directly from the earth. The integrated circuit, pharmaceutical and food and beverage industries are examples of process manufacturing. Contrast with *discrete manufacturing*.

**processor**   (1) Same as *CPU*.

(2) May refer to software. See *language processor* and *word processor*.

**processor complex**   See *CEC*.

**processor core**   The processing part of a CPU chip minus the cache. It is made up of the control unit and the arithmetic logic unit (ALU). See *control unit* and *ALU*.

**Processor Direct Slot**   See *PDS*.

**Processor Independent NetWare**   See *PIN*.

**processor unit**   Same as *computer*.

**process printing**   See *process color*.

**process technology**   In the computer industry, it refers to the manufacturing of semiconductor chips. The driving force behind this technology is miniaturization. The smaller the elements of the chip, the faster the transistor switches, the less energy required and the cooler the chip runs. The elements of the chip are measured in microns (micrometers), and the specfications of process technology are given in microns. For example, the 486 CPU chip, which was introduced in 1989 and now a glimmer in most people's memories, used elements that were 1 micron wide. Some features could be less than 1 micron and some slightly larger; however, 1 micron would be the average.

Going from 1.0 micron to .18 micron, which is less than one fifth the size, has taken thousands of man years and billions of dollars worth of research and development. The first Pentium chips used .8 technology. The current state-of-the-art is .18. Chips are expected to be made with .13 elements in a couple of years.

**Procomm Plus**   A communications program for Windows from Quarterdeck that supports a wide number of protocols and terminals. Procomm was originally developed for DOS by Datastorm Technologies and was also available as a shareware program, which was very popular.

**Prodigy**   An online information service that provides access to the Internet, e-mail and a variety of databases. Launched in 1988, Prodigy was the first consumer-oriented online service in the U.S. The original service, which uses proprietary software, is now Prodigy Classic, and Prodigy Internet is a newer all-Internet service that uses a Web browser. Prodigy was founded as a partnership of IBM and Sears. It was acquired by International Wireless in 1996. See *online services*.

**ProDOS**   (PROfessional Disk Operating System) An operating system for the Apple II family that superseded Apple's DOS 3.3. It provided a hierarchical file system and file names up to 15 characters.

**product data management**   See *PDM*.

**production database**   A central database containing an organization's master files and daily transaction files.

**production printer**    A high-speed computer printer used for volume printing, manuals and booklets. Production printers start around 60 ppm, although some vendors claim that printers must produce 100 or 150 ppm to qualify for this designation. See *network printer* and *distributed printer*.

**production system**    A computer system used to process an organization's daily work. Contrast with a system used only for development and testing or for ad hoc inquiries and analysis.

**productivity**    The most overused and abused buzzword in computer advertising. It is truly amazing how every hardware and software product is supposed to make everybody more productive. Of course, the ads never mention the years of training you will need to understand how to use it effectively.

Because of technology, the U.S. is the most productive society on earth, but perhaps we have to ask "what are we producing?" If we're generating more tech support nightmares and technical trivia than the benefits we derive from it, then we have to temper our zeal for technology with wisdom and patience. "Newfangled systems" don't always work the way we expect (see *Systemantics*).

**productivity software**    Refers to word processors, spreadsheets, database management systems, PIMs, schedulers and other software packages that are designed for individual use. Contrast with custom-designed, multiuser information systems, which provide the primary data processing in an organization.

**productivity suite**    A suite of applications that generally includes a word processor, spreadsheet, database program, comm program and perhaps a presentation graphics or charting program.

**Professional Write**    A word processing program for Windows from Software Publishing Corporation, Fairfield, NJ (www.spco.com). It is the successor to PFS:Write, one of the earliest word processors for personal computers.

**Professional YAM**    (Professional Yet Another Modem) A communications program for DOS, Windows, OS/2 and various UNIX platforms from Omen Technology, Inc., Portland, OR (www.omen.com). It is a flexible, full-featured program for the advanced communications user.

**proficiency tests**    See *aptitude tests*.

**PROFS**    (PRofessional OFfice System) IBM office automation software for the VM mainframe environment. It provides an e-mail facility for text and graphics, a library service for centrally storing text, electronic calendars and appointment scheduling, and it allows document interchange with DISOSS users. PROFS uses IBM's proprietary ZIP messaging protocol.

**Profusion chipset**    An Intel chipset designed to allow eight Xeon CPUs run in an SMP-based multiprocessing server. Slowly but surely, more SMP multiprocessing capability is being added to Intel servers. The Profusion chipset was introduced in August 1999. See *SMP*.

**program**    A collection of instructions that tell the computer what to do. A program is called "software" and programs that users work with, such as word processors and spreadsheets, are called "applications" or "application programs." Therefore, the terms software, application and program are synonymous: they tell the computer what to do in precise detail. Although you may think you're telling your computer what to do, what is actually happening is that the program is allowing you to perform only those tasks it has been written to let you do.

A program is written in a programming language, such as Visual Basic, C or C++, and the statements and commands written by the programmer are converted into the computer's machine language by software called "assemblers," "compilers" and "interpreters."

A program is made up of:

- ■ Machine instructions
- ■ Buffers
- ■ Constants and counters

Instructions are the directions that the computer will follow (the program's logic). Buffers are reserved space, or input/output areas, that accept and hold the data while it's being processed. They can receive any kind of information required by the program.

Constants are fixed values used to compare the data against, such as minimums and maximums and dates. Menu titles and error messages are another example of constants.

Counters, also called "variables," are reserved space for summing money amounts, quantities, virtually any calculations, including those necessary to keep track of internal operations, such as how many times a function should be repeated.

The program calls for data in an input-process-output sequence. After data has been input into one of the program's buffers from a peripheral device (keyboard, disk, etc.), it is processed. The results are then output to a peripheral device (screen, printer, etc.). If data has been updated, it is output back onto the disk.

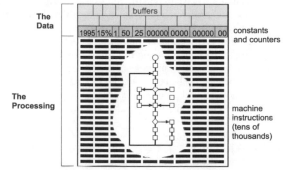

**Anatomy of a Program**
A program is made up of machines instructions, buffers, constants and counters. The program's logic is embedded within the instructional sequence.

The application program, which does the actual data processing, does not instruct the computer to do everything. When it is ready for input or needs to output data, it sends a request to the operating system, which performs those services and then turns control back to the application program.

Above is a conceptual illustration of a program residing in memory. In the physical reality of memory, everything below would be in binary coded form (0s and 1s).

Although represented as small blocks below, machine instructions can be variable in length and they are in some kind of logical sequence. Some of the instructions would be GOTO instructions that point back to the beginning of a routine or to other parts of the program for example.

For an understanding of what the computer does to process data, look up *computer* and read about The 3 Cs (calculate, compare and copy).

**program counter**    A register or variable used to keep track of the address of the current or next instruction. See *address register* and *instruction register*.

**program development**    See *system development cycle*.

**Program Files**    The folder in a Windows computer with the Windows 95 interface that contains application subfolders. Upon installation, most applications create a new folder that is installed within the Program Files folder. The Program Files folder can be easily viewed in Explorer. It is in alphabetical order in the left window pane. See *Programs Menu*.

**program generator**    See *application generator*.

**Program Information File**    See *PIF*.

**program logic**    A sequence of instructions in a program. There are many logical solutions to a problem. If you give a specification to ten programmers, each one may create program logic that is slightly different than all the rest, but the results can be the same. The solution that runs the fastest is usually the most desired, however.

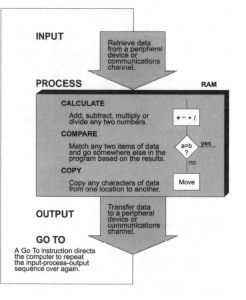

**Program Logic**
This is the overall logic of a business application, which is also defined as the main loop in a program. The logic contained within the process block can however be extremely complicated.

Program logic is written using three classes of instructions: sequential processing, selection and iteration.

1. Sequential processing is the series of steps that do the actual data processing. Input, output, calculate and move (copy) instructions are used in sequential processing.

2. Selection is the decision making within the program and is performed by comparing two sets of data and branching to a different part of the program based on the results. In assembly languages, the compare and branch instructions are used. In high-level languages, IF THEN ELSE and CASE statements are used.

3. Iteration is the repetition of a series of steps and is accomplished with DO LOOPS and FOR LOOPS in high-level languages and GOTOs in assembly languages. See *loop*.

**programmability**    The capability within hardware and software to change; to accept a new set of instructions that alter its behavior. Programmability generally refers to progam logic (business rules), but it also refers to designing the user interface which inclues the choices of menus, buttons and dialogs.

**programmable**    Capable of following instructions. What sets the computer apart from all other electronic devices is its programmability.

**programmable calculator**    A limited-function computer capable of working with only numbers and not alphanumeric data.

**programmable IC**    See *PLD*.

**program maintenance**    Updating programs to reflect changes in the organization's business or to adapt to new operating environments. Although maintaining old programs written by ex-employees is often much more difficult than writing new ones, the task is usually given to junior programmers, because the most talented professionals don't want the job.

**Program Manager**    The control center for Windows 3.x operation. It provided the means to launch applications and manage the desktop. Although the interface changed in Windows 95, Program Manager has been included for those users that prefer this method of launching programs. The file PROGMAN.EXE is included in Windows 95/98, NT 4.0 and 2000. See *File Manager*. See *Win 3.1/9x differences*.

**programmatically**    Using programming to accomplish a task.

**programmatic interface**    Same as *API*.

**programmer**    A person who designs the logic for and writes the lines of codes of a computer program. Programming is the heart and soul of developing computer applications, and programmers are the most misunderstood people in the business. They are constantly being criticized for taking longer to write a program than they initially estimated.

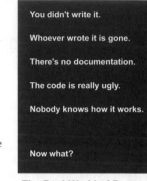

You didn't write it.

Whoever wrote it is gone.

There's no documentation.

The code is really ugly.

Nobody knows how it works.

Now what?

**The Real World of Program Maintenance**
Undocumented programs are a huge problem, and this commentary from PROCASE Corporation gets right to the point. The company's SMARTsystem program created a flowchart from programming source code in order to make it understandable.

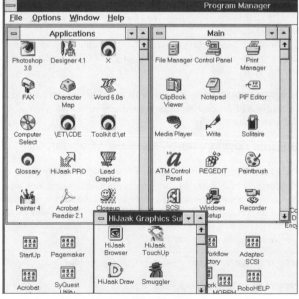

**Program Manager**
Program Manager uses resizable windows so you can group program icons to suit your work style. The individual icons at the bottom of the screen are minimized group windows. Many users find program launching easier with Program Manager that with the Start menu, and Program Manager is still available in Windows 95/98, NT 4.0 and 2000.

It is very difficult for people that have not spent any time programming to understand why programmers are often the world's worst estimators. Programming is very creative, and after a program is put into production, programmers derive a sense of completion that is very satisfying. Thus, the more programs programmers write, the more confidence they have. As a result, they take on what seems like an eternal optimism that the job can be done easily. As their confidence builds with experience, it often seems their estimates are even more absurd. It takes numerous hard knocks to wise up and then double, triple or even quadruple one's initial estimate in order to put reality into it.

It is also very difficult for non-programmers to understand how easy it is to program oneself into a real mess. Programmers love to code and are often in too much of a hurry to dive in instead of sitting back and analyzing the problem carefully on paper. There are a thousand logic solutions for every problem, and it is so easy to pick one that seems to solve the hurdle for the moment, only to find out a month later that the logic is inflexible and making changes is difficult. Even experienced programmers fall into the trap, which compounds over and over as more patches are made until the program becomes unwieldy and nobody can bring it back into stability. Programs are then reworked and reworked, because they were not designed right from the start. This is why projects take longer and why your favorite program sometimes becomes quirkier in its next version.

It would seem that programming is a profession for bright, young whiz kids, and, in fact, there are tons of them creating and maintaining some of the most widely used software in the world. Whiz kids, or any left-brained, intelligent person, for that matter, can program with just a little bit of practice. But, it takes years to become an expert at anything. Masters in all professions have earned their stripes by making their mistakes over the course of 10, 20 or even 30 years. When you consider the average age of programmers in most software houses, it is understandable why programs don't always work well. Too many novices make decisions that even more novices have to live with. In addition, programming is such tedious work that those that would eventually become the experts burn out and take other jobs. There is a constant influx of inexperienced souls to this field. See *Freedman's law*, *application programmer*, *systems programmer* and *salary survey*. See also *to the recruiter*.

## Programmer's Switch

The physical buttons included with the Macintosh (fkey on the LC) that include a System Reset button and a Debugging button that will invoke MacsBug if present or switch to the built in monitor in ROM.

## programmer analyst

A person who analyzes and designs information systems and designs and writes the application programs for the system. In theory, a programmer analyst is both systems analyst and applications programmer. In practice, the title is sometimes simply a reward to a programmer for tenure. Which skill is really dominant is of concern when recruiting people with such titles. See *salary survey*.

## programming

Creating a computer program. The steps are

1. Developing the program logic to solve the particular problem.
2. Writing the program logic in a specific programming language (coding the program).
3. Assembling or compiling the program to turn it into machine language.
4. Testing and debugging the program.
5. Preparing the necessary documentation.

The logic is generally the most difficult part of programming. However, depending on the programming language, writing the statements may also be laborious. One thing is certain. Documenting the program is considered the most annoying activity by most programmers. See *estimating a programming job* and *peer review*.

**CREATING A COMPUTER PROGRAM**

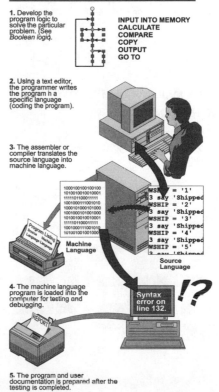

1. Develop the program logic to solve the particular problem. (See *Boolean logic*).

INPUT INTO MEMORY
CALCULATE
COMPARE
COPY
OUTPUT
GO TO

2. Using a text editor, the programmer writes the program h a specific language (coding the program).

3. The assembler or compiler translates the source language into machine language.

Machine Language

Source Language

4. The machine language program is loaded into the computer for testing and debugging.

Syntax error on line 132.

5. The program and user documentation is prepared after the testing is completed.

## PROGRAM LOGIC & CODING

The following three examples use a mailing list print program to show how the programming code and logic become more complicated as more processing is done. Printing one label at a time is rather simple. Printing two across requires a method to keep track of which labels go where. But making the labels print better by eliminating blank lines requires even more planning ahead.

The following examples are written in the dBASE programming language, which has been widely used to develop applications on DOS and Windows PCs.

dBASE is also a database management system (DBMS), and its programming language is tightly integrated with the database, which makes it simpler to program.

The following examples assume that a database table (data file) has already been opened by the user. When a table is opened in dBASE, dBASE points to the first record in the table. The pointer is incremented with the **skip** command, which bumps it to the next record.

| 00001 | | | |
| 00002 | | | |
| 00003 | | | |
| 00004 | | | |

The dBASE record pointer points to the current record in the table. When the table is first opened, it points to record #1.

**The ROWS are the records.**
**The COLUMNS are the fields.**

## PRINT MAILING LABEL - TWO UP
## WITH BLANK SQUASH

NAME
COMPANY
ADDRESS
CITY, STATE, ZIP

NAME
COMPANY
CITY, STATE, ZIP

In order to vertically squash blank lines, both left and right labels must be formatted in memory first. Each data field is tested for blanks. If it is not blank, it is copied into the next unused variable for either the left or right side.

Note the difference between the code here and the first example that printed only one label and did not concern itself about blank fields.

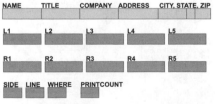

| NAME | TITLE | COMPANY | ADDRESS | CITY, STATE, ZIP |

| L1 | L2 | L3 | L4 | L5 |

| R1 | R2 | R3 | R4 | R5 |

SIDE  LINE  WHERE  PRINTCOUNT

## PRINT MAILING LABELS - ONE UP

NAME
TITLE
COMPANY
ADDRESS
CITY, STATE, ZIP

This program simply inputs a record into memory, prints it and calls for the next record (SKIP command). Any blank fields in the record will be printed as blanks.

| NAME | TITLE | COMPANY | ADDRESS | CITY, STATE, ZIP |

PRINTCOUNT

☐ = Fields in input buffer
■ = Variable
Blue text = Documentation
Black text = dBASE command
Red text = Names of fields and variables
            and literals (constants)

```
*** MAILING LABEL PRINT PROGRAM - ONE UP ***
* Housekeeping
set talk off
set print on
printcount = 0        &&  count of labels printed

* Main Loop
do while .not. eof
    ? name                && ? command prints line
    ? title
    ? company
    ? address
    ? trim(city) + ', ' + state + ' ' + zip
    ?
    ?                     && TRIM drops trailing blanks
    ?
    ?
    printcount = printcount + 1
    skip                  && SKIP gets next record
enddo

* End of Job
set print off
? 'Total labels printed'
?? printcount
set talk on
```

## PRINT MAILING LABELS - TWO UP

NAME

COMPANY
ADDRESS
CITY, STATE, ZIP

NAME
TITLE
COMPANY

CITY, STATE, ZIP

This program reads a record and stores its data for the left label in memory variables L1, L2, etc. It then reads the next record and prints both labels. Once again, blank fields are not tested. The variable SIDE keeps track of which label is being worked on.

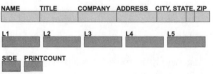

| NAME | TITLE | COMPANY | ADDRESS | CITY, STATE, ZIP |

| L1 | L2 | L3 | L4 | L5 |

SIDE  PRINTCOUNT

```
*** MAILING LABEL PRINT PROGRAM - TWO UP ***
* Housekeeping
set talk off
set print on
x = space(12)              && spacer between labels
printcount = 0
side ='L'

* Main Loop
do while .not. eof
     store space(35) to L1,L2,L3,L4,L5
     if side = 'L'
          L1 = name
          L2 = title
          L3 = company
          L4 = address
          L5 = trim(city) + ', ' state + ' ' + zip
          side = 'R'
          printcount = printcount + 1
          skip
          loop
     endif

* Print Left and Right Labels
     ? L1 + x + name
     ? L2 + x + title
     ? L3 + x + company
     ? L4 + x + address
     ? L5 + x + trim(city) + ', ' + state + ' ' + zip
     ?
     ?
     ?
     side = 'L'
   skip
enddo

* Print Last Odd Label
if side = 'R'
     ? L1
     ? L2
     ? L3
     ? L4
     ? L5
     ?
     ?
     ?
     ?
endif

* End of Job
set print off
? 'Total labels printed'
?? printcount
set talk on
```

```
*** MAILING LABEL PRINT PROGRAM - TWO UP ***
***          SQUASH VERTICAL BLANKS          ***
* Housekeeping
set talk off
set print on
printcount = 0
side = 'L'
store space(35) to L1,L2,L3,L4,L5
store space(35) to R1,R2,R3,R4,R5

* Main Loop
do while .not. eof
     line = 1
     where = side + '1'              && set to line 1

     if name # space(35)            && these routines
          &where = name             && test for non
          line = line + 1           && blank fields and
          where = side + str(line,1) && store them into
     endif                          && the next line

     if title # space(35)           && the expression
          &where = title            && &where means
          line = line + 1           && this variable
          where = side + str(line,1) && contains the
     endif                          && name of
                                    && another
     if company # space(35)         && variable
          &where = company
          line = line + 1
          where = side + str(line,1)
     endif

     if address # space(35)
          &where = address
          line = line + 1
          where = side + str(line,1)
     endif

     &where = space(35)
     &where = trim(city) + ', ' + state + ' ' + zip

* Print Left and Right Labels
     if side = 'R'
          ? L1 + x + R1
          ? L2 + x + R2
          ? L3 + x + R3
          ? L4 + x + R4
          ? L5 + x + R5
          ?
          ?
          ?
          ?
          side = 'L'
          store space(35) to L1,L2,L3,L4,L5
          store space(35) to R1,R2,R3,R4,R5
     else
          side = 'R'
     endif
     printcount = printcount + 1
   skip
enddo

* Print Last Odd Label
     if side = 'R'
          ? L1
          ? L2
          ? L3
          ? L4
          ? L5
          ?
          ?
          ?
          ?
     endif

* End of Job
set print off
? 'Total labels printed'
?? printcount
set talk on
```

**programming interface**    See *API*.

**programming language**    A language used
to write instructions for the computer. It lets the
programmer express data processing in a symbolic
manner without regard to machine-specific details.

The statements that are written by the programmer
are called "source language," and they are translated
into the computer's "machine language" by programs
called "assemblers," "compilers" and "interpreters."
For example, when a programmer writes MULTIPLY
HOURS TIMES RATE, MULTIPLY must be turned
into a code that means multiply, and HOURS and
RATE must be turned into memory locations where
those items of data are actually located.

Like human languages, each programming language has its own grammar and syntax. There are many dialects of
the same language, and each dialect requires its own translating system. Standards have been set by ANSI for many
programming languages, and ANSI-standard languages are dialect free. However, it can take years for new features to
be included in ANSI standards, and new dialects inevitably spring up as a result.

Programming languages fall into two categories: low-level assembly languages and high-level languages. Assembly languages are available for each CPU family, and each assembly instruction is translated into one machine instruction by the assembler program. With high-level languages, a programming statement may be translated into one or several machine instructions by the compiler.

Following is a synopsis of the major high-level languages. Look up each one for more details. For a list of high-level programming languages designed for client/server development, see *client/server development system*.

**Ada**   Comprehensive, Pascal-based language used by the Department of Defense.

**ALGOL**   International language for expressing algorithms.

**APL**   Used for statistics and mathematical matrices. Requires special keyboard symbols.

**BASIC**   Developed as a timesharing language in the 1960s. It has been widely used in microcomputer programming in the past, and various dialects of BASIC have been incorporated into many different applications. Microsoft's Visual Basic is widely used.

**C**   Developed in the 1980s at AT&T. Widely used to develop commercial applications. UNIX is written in C.

**C++**   Object-oriented version of C that is popular because it combines object-oriented capability with traditional C programming syntax.

**COBOL**   Developed in the 1960s. Widely used for mini and mainframe programming. Also available for personal computers.

**dBASE**   Widely used in business applications. Offshoots of dBASE ("Xbase" languages) are Clipper, Quicksilver, FoxBase and FoxPro.

**FORTH**   Developed in the 1960s, FORTH is used in process control and game applications.

**FORTRAN**   Developed in 1954 by IBM, it was the first major scientific programming language. Some commercial applications have been developed in FORTRAN, and it continues to be widely used.

**Java**   The programming language developed by Sun and repositioned for Web use. It is widely used on the server side, although client applications are increasingly used.

**JavaScript**   A scripting language widely used on the Web. JavaScript is embedded into many HTML pages.

**LISP**   Developed in 1960. Used for AI applications. Its syntax is very different than other languages.

**Logo**   Developed in the 1960s, it is noted for its ease of use and "turtle graphics" drawing functions.

**M**   Originally MUMPS (Massachusetts Utility MultiProgramming System), it includes its own database. It is widely used in medical applications.

**Modula-2**   Enhanced version of Pascal introduced in 1979.

**Pascal**   Originally an academic language developed in the 1970s. Borland commercialized it with its Turbo Pascal.

**Perl**   A scripting language widely used on the Web to write CGI scripts.

**Prolog**   Developed in France in 1973. Used throughout Europe and Japan for AI applications.

**Python**   A scripting language used for system utilities and Internet scripts. Developed in Amsterdam by Guido van Rossum.

**REXX**   Runs on IBM mainframes and OS/2. Used as a general purpose macro language.

**Visual Basic**   Version of BASIC for Windows programming from Microsoft that is very popular.

**Web Languages**   Languages such as JavaScript, Jscript, Perl and CGI are used to automate Web pages as well as link them to other applications running in servers.

**programming proficiency**    See *aptitude tests*.

**programming tests**    See *aptitude tests*.

**Program Neighborhood**    A feature in Citrix's MetaFrame products that enables applications to be assigned to users. See *NFuse* and *MetaFrame*.

**Programs menu**    In a Windows computer with the Windows 95 interface, it is a submenu off the Start menu that contains shortcuts (pointers) to the user's applications. When an application is first installed, one or more icons are placed in a group within the Programs menu. If you right-click the Start menu and select Open, Programs will be the first icon. Double-clicking Programs displays a list that corresponds to the Program submenu.

The Programs menu is indirectly related to the Program Files folder, which contains most, but not all, application folders. Shortcuts in the Programs menu can point to programs in Program Files subfolders or in folders on the same level as the Program Files folder. See *Program Files*.

**program state**    An operating mode of the computer that executes instructions in the application program. Contrast with *supervisor state*.

**program statement**    A phrase in a high-level programming language. One program statement may result in several machine instructions when the program is compiled.

**program status word**    See *PSW*.

**program step**    An elementary instruction, such as a machine language instruction or an assembly language instruction. Contrast with *program statement*.

**program-to-program communications**    Communications between two programs. Often confused with peer-to-peer communications, it is a set of protocols a program uses to interact with another program. Peer-to-peer establishment is the network's responsibility. You can have program-to-program communications in a master-slave environment without peer-to-peer capability.

**Progress**    An application development system for client/server environments from Progress Software, Corporation, Bedford, MA (www.progress.com). It supports a variety of clients, including DOS, Windows, OS/2, AIX, HP-UX and Sun. It includes its own relational DBMS, but interfaces to Oracle, Sybase and others. The majority of Progress systems are created by third-party developers. The company was founded in 1984.

**progressive GIF**    See *interlaced GIF*.

**progressive JPEG**    A JPEG image that comes into focus while it is being displayed. Instead of rendering the image a line at a time from top to bottom, the whole image is displayed as very low-quality and fuzzy, which becomes sharper as the lines fill in. It gives the illusion that the page has downloaded faster even though it takes the same time to achieve the final sharpness. The progressive JPEG is created in multiple passes (scans) of the image. See *interlaced GIF* and *JPEG*.

**progressive scan**    Same as *non-interlaced*.

**projection panel**    See *LCD panel*.

**project leader**    A person that heads an information systems project. This is a senior position that typically requires systems analysis and programming experience, although the individual may only act as adviser. Project leaders use project manager software to keep track of the tasks and acts as liaison between the technical staff and users. See *project manager*.

**project life cycle**    See *full project life cycle* and *system life cycle*.

**project manager**   (1) Software used to monitor the time and materials on a project. All tasks to complete the project are entered into the database, and the program computes the critical path, the series of tasks with the least amount of slack time. Any change in the critical path slows down the entire project.

(2) A person that keeps track of an information systems project either from inception to deployment or through a single stage. Project managers have varying levels of responsibilities and authority. See *system development cycle* and *project leader*.

**Project OXYGEN**   A global network that is expected to link 78 countries with more than 100,000 miles of optical fiber (mostly under the sea) at a minimum transmission speed of 1.2 Gbps. Phase 1 is expected to cost more than $10 billion, and the trans-Atlantic link is expected to become operational in 2000. For information, visit www.oxygen.org.

**Prokey**   A keyboard macro processor for DOS and Windows from CE Software, Inc., West Des Moines, IA (www.cesoft.com), that allows users to eliminate repetitive typing by setting up an occurrence of text or a series of commands as a macro.

**Prolog**   (**PRO**gramming in **LOG**ic) A programming language used for developing AI applications (natural language translation, expert systems, abstract problem solving, etc.). Developed in France in 1973, it is used throughout Europe and Japan and is gaining popularity in the U.S.

Similar to LISP, it deals with symbolic representations of objects. The following example, written in University of Edinburgh Prolog, converts Fahrenheit to Celsius:

```
convert:- write('Enter Fahrenheit'),
 read(Fahr)'
 write('Celsius is '),
 Cent is (5 * (Fahr - 32)) / 9,
 write(Cent),nl.
```

**PROM**   (**P**rogrammable **R**ead **O**nly **M**emory) A permanent memory chip that is programmed, or filled, by the customer rather than by the chip manufacturer. It differs from a ROM, which is programmed at the time of manufacture. PROMs have been mostly superseded by EPROMs, which can be reprogrammed. See *PROM programmer*.

**PROM blower**   Same as *PROM programmer*.

**promiscuous mode**   The condition in which a node in a network recognizes and accepts all packets on the line regardless of protocol type or destination. Any software tool that filters out unwanted packets must be in a computer system with a network adapter and driver that supports promiscuous mode.

**PROM programmer**   A device that writes instructions and data into PROM chips. The bits in a new PROM are all 1s (continuous lines). The PROM programmer only creates 0s, by "blowing" the middle out of the 1s. Some earlier units were capable of programming both PROMs and EPROMs.

**PROM Programmer**

**prompt**   A software message that requests action by the user; for example, "Enter employee name." Command-driven systems issue a cryptic symbol when ready to accept a command; for example, the dot (.) in dBASE, the $ or % in UNIX, and the venerable C:\ in DOS. See *DOS prompt*.

**propagation**   The transmission (spreading) of signals from one place to another.

**propagation delay**   The time it takes to transmit a signal from one place to another. Propagation delay is dependent solely on distance and two thirds the speed of light. Signals going through a wire or fiber generally travel at two thirds the speed of light. Contrast with *nodal processing delay*.

**properties**   Attributes that are associated with something. Windows uses the term extensively to refer to the configuration of hardware and the characteristics and features of software and data files. In Windows 3.1, the Properties option in the File menu shows the path of an icon in a Program Group in Program Manager. In Windows 95/98, right-clicking an icon almost always brings up a Properties option that provides details about the file or device.

**property list**   In a list processing language, an object that is assigned a descriptive attribute (property) and a value. For example, in Logo, **PUTPROP "KAREN "LANGUAGE "PARADOX** assigns the value PARADOX to the property LANGUAGE for the person named KAREN. To find out what language Karen speaks, the Logo statement **PRINT GETPROP "KAREN "LANGUAGE** will generate PARADOX as the answer.

**Property Sheet**   A dialog box in Windows 9x that shows the configuration settings of a particular resource. Right-clicking icons and menu items displays a Properties option that can be selected. See *Win Properties*.

**proportional font**   A font that uses proportional spacing. See *proportional spacing*.

**proportional spacing**   Character spacing based on the width of each character. For example, an I takes up less space than an M. In monospacing (fixed), the I and M each take up the same space. See *kerning*.

**proprietary protocol**   A non-standard communications format and language developed by a single organization. It requires that both sending and receiving devices use the same protocol.

**proprietary software**   Software owned by an organization or individual. Contrast with *public domain software*.

**Prospero**   See *Delphi Forums*.

**Protected Mode**   In PCs, starting with the 286, an operational state that allows the computer to address all its memory. It also prevents an errant program from entering into the memory boundary of another. In a 386 and higher machine, it provides access to 32-bit instructions and sophisticated memory management modes.

For example, Windows 95/98 and OS/2 are 32-bit operating systems and their operations are performed in Protected Mode in contrast to the 16-bit Real Mode of DOS and Windows 3.1. See *32-bit processing*, *Real Mode*, *Virtual 8086 Mode* and *memory protection*.

**Protected Mode driver**   A PC driver that is written to the original 32-bit 386 architecture, which allows access to 32-bit instructions and four gigabytes of memory. Protected Mode drivers run in extended memory (above one megabyte).

Windows 95/98 provides Protected Mode, 32-bit drivers for all the popular peripheral devices. If it does not include a driver for a particular device, it loads the 16-bit driver that was used under DOS/Windows 3.x.

**protection**   See *security*, *access control*, *virus* and *file protect ring*.

**protection error**   See *GPF*.

**protocol**   Rules governing transmitting and receiving of data. See *communications protocol* and *OSI*.

**protocol analyzer**   See *network analyzer*.

**protocol-based DRAM**   A memory chip architecture that transfers addresses, control signals and the data over the same multiplexed bus rather than using separate lines (pins) for each category. Rambus DRAM (RDRAM) and SLDRAM are protocol-based DRAM technologies. See *RDRAM* and *SLDRAM*.

**protocol-based RAM**   See *protocol-based DRAM*.

**protocol port**   In TCP/IP networks, a number assigned to different types of data in order to distribute incoming traffic to the appropriate program running in the computer. It is not a physical plug or socket, but a logical assignment. See *well-known port*.

**protocol stack**   The hierarchy of protocols used in a communications network. Network architectures designed in layers, such as TCP/IP, OSI and SNA, are referred to as stacks. See *OSI*.

**protocol suite**   Same as *protocol stack*.

**prototyping**   (1) Creating a demo of a new system. Prototyping is essential for clarifying information requirements. The design of a system (functional specs) must be finalized before the system can be built. While analytically-oriented people may have a clear picture of requirements, others may not.

Using fourth-generation languages, systems analysts and users can develop the new system together. Databases can be created and manipulated while the user monitors the progress. Once users see tangible output on screen or paper, they can figure out what's missing or what the next question might be if this were a production system. If prototyping is carefully done, the end result can be a working system.

Even if the final system is reprogrammed in other languages for standardization or machine efficiency, prototyping has served to provide specifications for a working system rather than a theoretical one.

(2) See *function prototyping*.

**provisioned**   Set up for a particular type of telecommunications service. See *provisioning*.

**provisioning**   Setting up a telecommunications service for a particular customer. Common carriers provision circuits by programming their computers to switch customer lines into the appropriate networks.

**proxy**   See *proxy server*.

**proxy cache**   A facility in a proxy server that caches incoming Web pages on the hard disk. If the next page requested by a browser is already in the proxy cache, the page is retrieved locally instead of from the Internet. With proxy caches, the browsers must be configured to use the proxy server. See *proxy server*, *reverse proxy cache*, *transparent cache* and *Web cache*.

**proxy server**   Also called a "proxy" or "application level gateway," it is an application that breaks the connection between sender and receiver. All input is forwarded out a different port, closing a straight path between two networks and preventing a hacker from obtaining internal addresses and details of a private network.

Proxy servers are available for common Internet services; for example, an HTTP proxy is used for Web access, and an SMTP proxy is used for e-mail. Proxies generally employ network address translation (NAT), which presents one organization-wide IP address to the Internet. It funnels all user requests to the Internet and fans responses back out to the appropriate users. Proxies may also cache Web pages, so that the next request can be obtained locally. Proxies are only one tool that can be used to build a firewall. See *LAN*, *firewall*, *proxy cache* and *SOCKS server*.

**PR/SM**   (Processor Resource/Systems Manager) Hardware circuits and microcode built into IBM System/390 mainframes that support logical partitions (LPARs). LPARs allow the running of multiple system images on a single processor complex. Each such image has a full complement of CPUs (dedicated or shared), central storage, expanded storage and channels. ESCON and FICON channels may be shared across images using the MIF feature. Pronounced "prism," PR/SM was derived from VM, the IBM operating system that provides multiple system images in software. See *LPAR*, *MIF* and *VM*.

**PRT SC**   See *print screen*.

**ps**   (1) (PicoSecond) See *space/time*.
(2) (PS—Personal Services) IBM office automation software for PCs, minis and mainframes, which includes word processing, electronic mail and library services.
(3) (PostScript) See *PostScript*.

**PS/1**   An early IBM home computer series introduced in 1990. The original models featured an integrated monitor and easy-to-open case. The first PS/1 was a 286 with an ISA bus. See *PC*.

**PS/2**   An IBM personal computer series introduced in 1987, superseding the original PC line. It introduced the 3.5" floppy disk, VGA graphics and MicroChannel bus. The 3.5" disks and VGA are common in all PCs, but the MicroChannel has since given way to the PCI bus. See also *PS2*.

**PS2**   (PlayStation 2) An Internet-capable gaming machine from Sony that contains a DVD player. Introduced in the U.S. in the fall of 2000 after its outstanding success in Japan, the first PS2 models came with a 300MHz Emotion 128-bit CPU which exceeded the floating point performance of a 500MHz Pentium III. They also included a MIPS R3000 chip for I/O handling and backward compatibility with the earlier PlayStation. See also *PS/2*.

**PS/2 bus**   Same as *MicroChannel*.

**PS/2 connector**   A 6-pin Mini-DIN plug and socket used to connect a keyboard and mouse to a computer. First introduced on IBM's PS/2 desktop PC, the port was later used by everybody else, first on laptops, then on desktops. See *DIN connector*.

**PS/2 mouse**   See *DIN connector*.

**PS/2 port**   A hardware interface used to connect a mouse or keyboard. See *PS/2 connector*.

**PSC**   (Public Service Commission) Same as *PUC*.

**PSCRIPT.DRV**   The file name of the Microsoft Windows PostScript driver.

**PSD file**   Photoshop's native, layered file format. The layers enable an illustration to be built with individual graphic elements that can be moved over and over to obtain a desired results. When the PSD format is converted into a TIFF, JPEG, GIF or other graphics format, the layering is "flattened" into one bitmapped image. For example, it would be very difficult to build a collage of many images overlapping each other without layers, because the placement of each object would have to be perfect from the start. Without layers, once a small bitmap is placed on top of the large bitmap, it becomes "one with the image" and cannot be altered at all or at least without major effort. See *extension*.

**pSeries**   The renaming of IBM's RS/6000 under the eserver brand. An RS/6000 server is a pSeries eserver. Prices for the pSeries ranged from $150,000 to $600,000 in 2000, when the name change occurred. See *IBM server series* and *RS/6000*.

**pseudo code**   See *intermediate language*.

**pseudo compiler**   A compiler that generates a pseudo language, or intermediate language, which must be further compiled or interpreted for execution.

**pseudo-duplexing**   A communications technique that simulates full-duplex transmission in a half-duplex line by turning the line around very quickly.

**pseudo language**   Same as *intermediate language*.

**pseudorandom**   A set of values or elements that is statistically random, but it is derived from a known starting point and is typically repeated over and over. It creates the necessary values for processes that require randomness, such as creating test signals or for synchronizing sending and receiving devices in a spread spectrum transmission. See *CDMA* and *PN sequence*.

**PS/2 Model 50**
The 286-based Model 50 was one of IBM's early PS/2 models. The PS/2 introduced the Micro Channel bus, VGA graphics and the 3.5" floppy disk. *(Image courtesy of International Business Machines Corporation. Unauthorized use not permitted.)*

**PSF**   (Print Services Facility) Software from IBM that performs the printer rasterization for IBM's AFP and other page description languages. PSF products are available for IBM mainframes, AS/400 and RS/6000 series and output the IPDS format for IBM printers. Various versions also input and output PostScript and PCL (LaserJet) with PSF/AIX for the RS/6000 and SP2 mainframes being the most flexible and providing the most conversion capability.

**PSK**   See *DPSK*.

**PSN**   (Packet-Switched Network) A communications network that uses packet switching technology.

**PSS**   See *EPSS*.

**PSTN**   (Public Switched Telephone Network) The worldwide voice telephone network. Once only an analog system, the heart of most telephone networks today is all digital. In the U.S., most of the remaining analog lines are the ones from your house or office to the telephone company's central office (CO). See *POTS* and *AIN*.

**PSW**   (Program Status Word) A hardware register that maintains the status of the program being executed.

**psycho-acoustic model**   A set of algorithms for analyzing sounds developed by Dr. Amar Bose. The psycho-acoustic model is used by perceptual audio coding methods to analyze audio content to reduce the complexity of the frequencies in order to further compress the digital data. See *perceptual audio coding*.

**PTG&LI**   Digispeak for "playing the game and loving it."

**PTOCA**   (Presentation Text Object Content Architecture) See *MO:DCA*.

**p-to-p**   See *peer-to-peer*.

**PTT**   (Postal, Telegraph & Telephone) The governmental agency responsible for combined postal, telegraph and telephone services in many European countries.

**PU**   (Physical Unit) In SNA, software responsible for managing the resources of a node, such as data links. A PU supports a connection to the host (SSCP) for gathering network management statistics.

**PU 2.1**   (Physical Unit 2.1) In SNA, the original term for Node Type 2.1, which is software that provides peer-to-peer communications between intelligent devices (PCs, workstations, minicomputers). Only LU 6.2 sessions are supported between Type 2.1 nodes (PU 2.1).

**public data network**   A communications network provided by a carrier organization that makes its transport available to many companies. Customers attach to such networks using a variety of protocols including frame relay, ATM, IP, etc., and pay by the month or on a per-byte basis. Contrast with *private data network*.

**public domain software**   Software in which ownership has been relinquished to the public at large. See *freeware* and *shareware*.

**public file**   A file made available to all other users connected to the system or network. Contrast with *private file*.

**public key**   The published part of a two-part, public key cryptography system. The private part is known only to the owner. See *RSA* and *cryptography*.

**public key cryptography**   A cryptographic method that uses a two-part key (code) that is made up of public and private components. To encrypt messages, the published public keys of the recipients are used. To decrypt the messages, the recipients use their unpublished private keys known only to them. See *RSA* and *cryptography*.

**public key infrastructure**   See *PKI*.

**public/private key cryptography**    See *public key cryptography*.

**public Web site**    A site on the World Wide Web which is accessible by anyone with a Web browser and access to the Internet. Contrast with *private Web site*.

**publish and subscribe**    (1) To provide a source of information that users select from and then receive on a regular basis or when certain events occur. The service can be public or private, free or paid, and information can be provided via e-mail and the Web or by means of proprietary applications. For example, a stock trading application lets you select particular stocks, and those quotes are sent to you on either on a regular schedule or when there is a change in price. See *push technology*.

(2) (Publish and Subscribe) A Macintosh capability starting with System 7 that provides hot links between files. All or part of a file can be published into an "edition file," which is imported into a subscriber file. When any of the published files are updated, the subscriber file is also updated.

**publish and subscribe messaging**    An e-mail system or message broker that supports the publish and subscribe model. It enables multiple users or applications to sign up for an event, and when that event occurs, those users or applications are sent the appropriate notification or data. See *messaging system* and *messaging middleware*.

**PUC**    (Public Utility Commission) A regulatory body in every state in the U.S. that governs public utilities within its jurisdiction such as electricity, gas, oil, sewer, water, transportation and telephone service. Some states call it the Public Service Commission (PSC).

**puck**    The mouse-like object used to draw on a digitizer tablet. See *mouse*.

**pull-down menu**    Also called a "drop-down menu" or "pop-down menu," the common type of menu used with a graphical user interface (GUI). A menu title is displayed that, when selected by clicking it, causes the menu to drop down from that position and be displayed. Items are selected by highlighting the line in the menu and either clicking it or letting go of the mouse button.

**pulling glass**    Installing optical fiber by pulling it through pipes and conduits.

**pull model**    See *pull technology*.

**pull technology**    Specifically requesting information from a particular source. Downloading Web pages with a Web browser is an example of pull technology. Contrast with *push technology*.

**pulse code modulation**    See *PCM*.

**pulse dispersion**    In optical fibers, a general term for the broadening of a pulse by the time it reaches the receiving end. It can be the net effect of any or all of modal, chromatic and polarization dispersion. See *dispersion*.

**pulse level device**    A disk drive or other device that inputs and outputs raw voltages. Data coding/decoding is in the controller the device. Contrast with *bit level device*.

**PUMA**    (Programmable Universal Micro Accelerator) A Chips and Technolgies' chipset that accelerates graphics operations for the screen and printer.

**pump laser**    A laser used as the pump for an optical amplifier or other laser. See *EDFA* and *laser*.

**punch block**    Also called a "quick-connect block," it is a device that interconnects telephone lines from remote points. The wires are pushed, or punched, down into metal teeth that strip the insulation and make a tight connection.

**punch card**    An alternate spelling for "punched card." See *punched card*.

**punched card**    A storage medium made of thin cardboard stock that holds data as patterns of punched holes. Each of the 80 or 96 columns holds one character. The holes are punched by a keypunch machine or card punch peripheral and are fed into the computer by a card reader.

From 1890 until the 1970s, punched cards were synonymous with data processing. The concepts were simple: the database was the file cabinet; a record was a card. Processing was performed on separate machines called "sorters," "collators," "reproducers," "calculators" and "accounting machines." Today, the punched card is all but obsolete except for voting systems in some states. Of course, the presidential election of 2000 brought punched cards into infamy and made the U.S. the brunt of jokes worldwide for using such antiquated and error-prone systems.

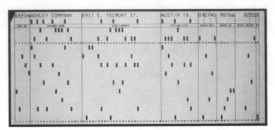

**The Punched Card**
Stemming from Hollerith's punched card tabulating system in 1890, punched cards "were" data processing for more than 70 years. IBM and Sperry Rand were the two major providers of punched card equipment. This 80-column IBM card shows a typical customer master record.

**punch in**    To press the keys of a keyboard in order to enter data.

**pundit**    An expert or knowledgeable person. From "pandit" in Hindi. See *guru*.

**purchasing a personal computer**    See *how to select a personal computer*.

**Pure Java**    Refers to initiatives from Sun that specify 100% compliance with its Java specification. The goal is to maintain a consistent, single interface for Java so that all Java Virtual Machines can run all Java programs. See *Holy Grail*.

**pure play**    Refers to dealing with a specific category of product rather than a mix of products. It is generally used in marketing to indicate that a company is specializing in one area. For example, "xyz is betting on a pure play in desktop PCs" means that xyz sells nothing but desktop PCs.

**PURL**    (Persistent **URL**) A URL that points to another URL. PURLs are used when document pages are expected to be moved to different locations from time to time. The PURL is maintained as the official URL for that resource, and when that PURL is requested, a PURL server redirects the browser to the actual current URL. See also *Perl*.

**push client**    Software that resides in a user's computer which receives transmissions from Webcast servers from the Internet or intranet. It may be a Web browser with built-in push technology, such as Netscape's Netcaster, or a stand-alone program such as PointCast.

**push model**    See *push technology*.

**push/pop**    Instructions that store and retrieve an item on a stack. Push enters an item on the stack, and pop retrieves an item, moving the rest of the items in the stack up one level. See *stack*.

**push/pull tractor**    A printer tractor that can be switched from pushing paper onto the platen to pulling it from the platen. Single-sheet continuous forms can be pushed, but most multipart forms and labels must be pulled to prevent jamming.

**push technology**    A data distribution technology in which selected data is automatically delivered into the user's computer at prescribed intervals or based on some event that occurs. Contrast with *pull technology*, in which the user specifically asks for something by performing a search or requesting an existing report, video or other data type.

Browsing the Web is an example of the pull model, while EntryPoint (originally PointCast) and Castanet are push technologies. PointCast was the first Internet service to become extremely popular by pushing selected news and stock quotes into a user's machine at prescribed intervals. See *PointCast*, *Castanet*, **BackWeb** and *Active Channel*.

**pushware**    Software that uses the push model for delivery of data. See *push technology*.

**put**    In programming, a request to store the current record in an output file. Contrast with *get*.

**PVC**    (Permanent Virtual Circuit) A point-to-point connection that is established ahead of time. A group of PVCs defined at the time of subscription to a particular service is known as a virtual private network (VPN). Contrast with *SVC*.

**PVCS**    A popular system of version control and configuration management software from MERANT that runs on DOS, Windows, OS/2 and various UNIX platforms. It is widely used on PC-based LANs. PVCS was originally developed by INTERSOLV of Rockville, MD, which was acquired by Micro Focus Group in mid 1998. Micro Focus later changed its name to MERANT. See *MERANT*.

**PVGA**    (Paradise VGA) A VGA adapter or VGA chips from the Paradise Division of Western Digital.

**PVM**    (Parallel Virtual Machine) Software that enables multiple UNIX and Windows NT computers to function as one large, parallel machine. It is used to solve scientific, industrial and medical problems around the world. For information, visit www.epm.ornl.gov/pvm.

**PVN**    (Private Virtual Network) See *VPN*.

**PVR**    (Personal Video Recorder) Also known as a "digital video recorder" or "DVR," it is a consumer device that digitizes broadcast TV onto a hard disk and plays it back immediately, allowing the viewer to pause at any time and return later. Using hardware-based MPEG-2 compression like DVD movies, it also records programs for later viewing just like a VCR. Using a phone line, the PVR can call a service provider and download the channel guide updates as well as software updates for the unit itself. The PVR can also be set to periodically record favorite shows whenever they are broadcast. Also built into satellite receivers and set-top boxes, ReplayTV (www.replaytv.com) and TiVo (www.tivo.com) were the first to introduce products in 1999.

**PWB**    (Printed Wiring Board) An alternate term for printed circuit board. See *printed circuit board*.

**Px64**    An ITU standard for transmitting audio and video in 64 Kbits/sec ISDN channels (P represents number of channels used). Although video conferencing can be done in only one or two channels, more channels are required for smooth motion.
    Px64 uses two screen formats. The CIF (Common Intermediate Format) generates a 352×288 resolution, while QCIF (Quarter CIF) is 176×144. CIF transmits at 36.45 Mbits/sec; QCIF is 9.115 Mbits/sec. See *H.261*.

**PXE**    (Preboot EXecution Environment) An Intel Wired for Management (WfM) capability that enables a PC to boot from the server. It enables remote booting (boot the OS), remote emergency booting (boot a diagnostic program) and remote new system startup (boot the installation program to install the OS). PXE is supported in the BIOS. See *BIOS*, *remote boot*, *remote emergency boot* and *remote new system startup*.

**PXP**    (Packet eXchange Protocol) See *PEP*.

**Python**    A popular, object-oriented scripting language used for writing system utilities and Internet scripts. It is also used as a glue language for integrating components in C and C++. Created by Guido van Rossum in Amsterdam in the early 1990s, it was named after the BBC comedy series *Monty Python's Flying Circus*. Python is an interpreted language that compiles to bytecode and requires a "virtual machine" for runtime execution. It uses elements from C, C++ and Modula and supports interfaces to popular functions and libraries such as UNIX sockets, the Tk GUI library, Microsoft Foundation Classes (MFC) and X11.

**Q&A** An integrated file manager and word processor for DOS and Windows from Symantec that includes mail merge capability as well as a programming language for customizing data entry forms and reports. Its Intelligent Assistant feature provides a query language that can learn new words from the user.

**QA** (Quality Assurance) A department, procedure or program within an organization that is involved in testing hardware and/or software. QA ensures that all products and systems perform as originally specified. See *QA analyst*.

**QA analyst** (Quality Assurance analyst) A person that is responsible for maintaining software quality within an organization. Such individuals develop and use stringent testing methods and may also be involved with ISO 9000 and the SEI models. See *SEI* and *ISO 9000-3*.

**QAM** (1) (Quadrature Amplitude Modulation) A modulation technique that generates four bits out of one baud. For example, a 600 baud line (600 shifts in the signal per second) can effectively transmit 2,400 bps using this method. Both phase and amplitude are shaped with each baud, resulting in four possible patterns.
(2) (Quality Assessment Measurement) A system used to measure and analyze voice transmission.

**QBasic** A BASIC interpreter from Microsoft that comes with DOS starting with DOS 5. It supersedes Microsoft's GW-BASIC and includes REMLINE.BAS, a program that helps convert GW-BASIC programs to QBasic.

**QBE** (Query By Example) A method for describing a database query originally developed by IBM for mainframes. A replica of an empty record is displayed and the search conditions are typed in under their respective columns (fields). This visual approach has been adopted by nearly every modern query program. Although there are differences from one to another with regard to expressing complicated queries, everything is selected from a menu by the user. The program turns the visual query into the command language, such as SQL, necessary to interrogate the database.

| City | State | Balance due |
|------|-------|-------------|
|      | PA    | >=5000      |

**Query By Example**
This query selects all Pennsylvania records that have a balance due of $5000 or more.

**Q-bus** A bus architecture used in Digital's PDP-11 and MicroVAX series.

**QCIF** See *CIF*.

**QDOS** (Quick and Dirty Operating System) A CPM-like operating system developed by Seattle Computer Products. Microsoft purchased it for $50,000 and turned it into PC-DOS and MS-DOS. The rest is history.

**QEMM** (Quarterdeck EMM) A popular DOS and Windows memory manager from Quarterdeck. QEMM was very popular in the DOS-only days and continues to be used under Windows to manage memory more efficiently.

**QFP**    (Quad FlatPack)  A square, surface mount chip package that has leads on all four sides and comes in several varieties. PQFP (Plastic QFP) may refer to all of the following QFP types. All quad flatpacks use gull-wing leads, except for the CQFP, which stick straight out. See *flatpack* and *chip package*.

**Plastic**
```
MQFP    Metric QFP
FQFP    Fine pitch QFP
BQFP    Bumpered QFP
LQFP    Low-profile QFP
TQFP    Thin-profile QFP
SQFP    Shrink QFP (same as MQFP)
```

**Ceramic**
```
CQFP    Ceramic QFP
```

**Quad Flatpack**
QFPs come in a variety of sizes and types. Notice the gull-wing leads on both of these chips.

**QIC**    (Quarter Inch Cartridge)  A magnetic tape technology used for backup. Although the largest installed base of backup drives in the world, the QIC format is not expected to last for too many years in the future.

The "quarter inch" is the width of the original tape. QIC comes in two form factors: 3.5" Minicartridges and 5.25" Data Cartridges. Minicartridges have been enhanced with wider and longer tapes (QIC-Wide, QIC-EX and Travan), but Travan has become the most popular. Most drives read and write cartridges one generation back. Minicartridges use a DC-2000 designation, and Data Cartridges use DC-6000. See *Travan*, *QIC-Wide*, *QIC-EX* and *magnetic tape*.

**3.5" MINICARTRIDGE NATIVE CAPACITIES**

| Format | QIC DC-2000 .25" | QIC-Wide .315" | Travan .315" | QIC-EX .25-.315" |
|---|---|---|---|---|
| QIC-40 | 40MB | | | |
| QIC-80 | 125MB | 200MB | 400MB | 500MB |
| QIC-3010 | 340MB | 420MB | 800MB | 1.1GB |
| QIC-3020 | 680MB | 850MB | 1.6GB | 2.2GB |
| QIC-3040 | 840MB | 1GB | | 2.5GB |
| QIC-3050 | 1GB | 1.3GB | | 3.1GB |
| QIC-3080 | 1.6GB | 2GB | | 5GB |
| QIC-3095 | | 2GB | 4GB | 5GB |
| QIC-3210 | | 2.3GB | | 5.1GB |
| QIC-3230 | | 8GB | 10GB | 20GB |

**5.25" DATA CARTRIDGE NATIVE CAPACITIES**

| Format | DC-6000 |
|---|---|
| QIC-150 | 250MB |
| QIC-525 | 525MB |
| QIC-1000 | 1GB |
| QIC-2GB | 2GB |
| QIC-5GB | 5GB |
| QIC-5010 | 13GB |
| QIC-5210 | 25GB |
| SLR100 | 50GB (Tandberg) |

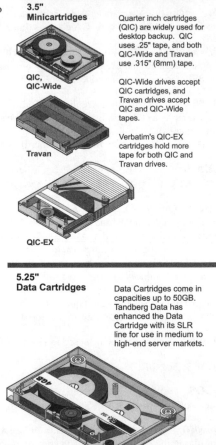

**QIC Tape**

**3.5" Minicartridges**

Quarter inch cartridges (QIC) are widely used for desktop backup. QIC uses .25" tape, and both QIC-Wide and Travan use .315" (8mm) tape.

QIC, QIC-Wide

QIC-Wide drives accept QIC cartridges, and Travan drives accept QIC and QIC-Wide tapes.

Travan

Verbatim's QIC-EX cartridges hold more tape for both QIC and Travan drives.

QIC-EX

**5.25" Data Cartridges**

Data Cartridges come in capacities up to 50GB. Tandberg Data has enhanced the Data Cartridge with its SLR line for use in medium to high-end server markets.

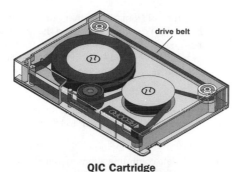

**QIC Cartridge**
QIC cartridges have supply and takeup hubs which are moved by a drive belt that wraps around them. The belt is pinched between the capstan and drive motor when the cartridge is inserted into the drive.

**QIC-EXtra Cartridge**
Verbatim's QIC-EX cartridge, which is physically extended to hold more tape, can be read and written by many QIC and Travan drives.

| Worldwide Market Projection | | |
|---|---|---|
| **COMPACT TAPE DRIVES** | | |
| (UNIT SHIPMENTS IN THOUSANDS) | | |
| | 1999 | 2005 |
| **QIC 3.5"** | 1,462 | 300 |
| **QIC 5.25"** | 469 | 122 |
| **DAT** | 1,944 | 1,685 |
| **8MM** | 149 | 449 |
| **Magstar MP** | 8 | 0 |
| **DLT** | 483 | 636 |
| **Ultrium** | 0 | 504 |
| **TOTAL SHIPMENTS** | 4,346 | 3,865 |
| **INSTALLED BASE** | 20,351 | 21,623 |

Reprinted with permission of Freeman Reports,
a market research firm specializing in tape storage.
(c) 2000 Freeman Reports, www.freemanreports.com
Ojai, CA, (805) 649-5135

**QIC-157**    A QIC specification for increased transfer rates under the ATAPI interface. ATAPI is the interface under Enhanced IDE that supports CD-ROMs and tape drives. See *Enhanced IDE* and *ATA*.

**QIC-EX**    (Quarter Inch Cartridge-EXtra) A QIC cartridge from Verbatim that uses longer tape and extends the cartridge depth to accomodate it. QIC-EX cartridges are available in .25" tape formats for earlier DC-2000 drives as well as in .315" tape for Travan drives. See *QIC, QIC-Wide* and *Travan*.

**QIC-Wide**    (Quarter Inch Cartridge-Wide) An enhanced version of QIC tape from Sony that provides more storage capacity. It increases recording density and uses wider .315" tape in a standard QIC Minicartridge with a redesigned housing. QIC-Wide drives support both QIC-Wide and QIC (DC2000) formats. Travan drives also support QIC-Wide tapes. See *QIC, QIC-EX* and *Travan*.

**QM**    (QueryMaster) See *QuickBuild*.

**QMF**    (Query Management Facility) An IBM fourth-generation language for end-user interaction with DB2.

**Qmodem Pro**    An earlier family of communications programs for DOS and Windows from Mustang Software, Inc., Bakersfield, CA (www.mustang.com). The programs supported a variety of modems, file transfer protocols and terminal emulations. Mustang Software was also the publisher of the popular WILDCAT! BBS software. In 2000, Mustang was acquired by Quintus Corporation.

**QMS**    (1) (Minolta-QMS, Inc., Mobile, AL, www.qms.com) A manufacturer of laser printers founded in 1977 by Jim Busby. Initially involved with controllers for printing bar codes and labels, it entered the laser printer business in the mid-1980s and set numerous records. QMS pioneered PostScript along with Apple and introduced the first auto switching printer and the first Kanji color laser printer. It was also the first to sell a laser printer for under $2,000 in 1985 and a color laser printer for under $1,300 in 1998. In 1998, QMS was acquired by Minolta and changed its name to Minolta-QMS.

**(2)** (Queue Management Services)  Also called "Q-server."  A printing protocol from Novell that provides print services and runs as an NLM on NetWare file servers. The client part runs under Windows, OS/2 and the Macintosh, and it uses the NetWare bindery or NDS to find the queues. QMS code has been embedded in millions of print servers in order to provide printer connectivity to NetWare file servers. QMS has been superseded by NDPS. See *NDPS*.

**(3)** (Quality Management System)  A system that ensures that a manufacturing process or service is performed at a quality level. See *TQM* and *ISO 9000*.

**QNX**    A multiuser, multitasking, realtime operating system for PCs from QNX Software Systems, Ltd., Kanata, Ontario, Canada (www.qnx.com), that is noted for its low-memory requirement and rapid response. Similar to UNIX, it has been in use since the early 1980s.

**QoS**    (Quality Of Service)  The ability to define a level of performance in a data communications system. For example, ATM networks specify modes of service that ensure optimum performance for traffic such as realtime voice and video. QoS has become a major issue on the Internet as well as in enterprise networks, because voice and video are increasingly travelling over IP-based data networks that were not designed for continuous speech or video. Thus, transmissions are broken into packets that can travel different routes and arrive at different times, hardly the design architecture for a system where you want "to continuosly hear a pin drop."

The plain old telephone system (POTS) provides the highest quality of service in the world for voice calls. This circuit-switched system provides a continuous channel between two parties until one hangs up. There is no better quality. The telecommunications industry is now figuring out how to modify IP to make it behave equally as well.

There are those that say, in time, we will have enough bandwidth to have an available circuit between every telephone or video station in every home and office in the world, and we will wind up going back to circuit switching yet again. Very possibly. The universe runs in circles.

**QoS vs. CoS**    QoS (Quality of Service) refers to the mechanisms in the network software that make the actual determination of which packets have priority. CoS (class of service) refers to feature sets, or groups of services, that are assigned to users based on company policy. If a feature set includes priority transmission, then CoS winds up being implemented in QoS functions within the routers and switches in the network. See *class of service*.

**Qpass**    A Web payment service from Qpass Inc., Seattle, WA (www.qpass.com), that specializes in premium digital content. A regular credit card is used to make purchases, and the Qpass servers contain the digital wallet information. Qpass merchant sites look for a cookie in the user's machine to determine compliance and then process the sale using the credit card. Another Qpass service automatically fills in the order form on any Web site by clicking a button that is added to the Web browser. A Java applet or ActiveX control, which must be downloaded, figures out what goes where on the form.

Introduced in 1997, Qpass was the first to provide a full e-commerce system shared by participating merchants and hosted remotely, but that looks like part of the merchant site. See *Web payment service*.

**QppD**    See *TPC*.

**QPS**    (Queries Per Second)  The number of database transactions that can be handled in one second.

**Q-server**    See *QMS*.

**Qt**    A library of widgits used in the open source community (primarily UNIX) for building graphical user interfaces. Qt is written in C++.

**QTAM**    (Queued Telecommunications Access Method)  An early communications program for the System/360 from IBM. It was primarily used to transmit batches of data.

**QthD**    See *TPC*.

**QTW**    (QuickTime for Windows)  See *QuickTime*.

**quadbit**    A group of four bits used in QAM modulation.

**Quadra**    A family of Macintosh computers that were popular in the early 1990s. See *Macintosh*.

**QUALCOMM** (QUALCOMM Incorporated, San Diego, CA, www.qualcomm.com) A wireless communications and software company founded in 1985 by Dr. Irwin Jacobs. Originally involved in satellite tracking and fleet management, QUALCOMM has become widely known for its CDMA technology used in cellphones and satellite phones. CDMA provides high-quality digital communications and is expected to become the third-generation (3G) wireless standard. The popular Eudora e-mail program is also a QUALCOMM product. See *CDMA*, *OmniTRACS* and *Eudora*.

**QUAM** See *QAM*.

**quantization** (1) The division of a range of values into a single number, code or classification. For example, class A is 0 to 999, class B is 1000 to 9999 and class C is 10000 and above.

(2) In analog to digital conversion, the assignment of a number to the amplitude of a wave. The larger the range of numbers, the finer the increments can be measured, and the more the digital sample represents the analog signal. See *sampling rate* and *quantization error*.

**quantization error** The difference between an analog wave and its digital representation. See *quantization*.

**quantization noise** See *quantization error*.

**quantize** To perform quantization. See *quantization*.

**quants** (**QUANT**itative analyst**S**) Financial analysts who use the computer and complex algorithms to develop derivatives and other intricate financial instruments.

**quantum computing** A future technology for designing computers based on quantum mechanics, the science of atomic structure and function. It uses the "qubit," or quantum bit, which can hold an infinite number of values. In 1999, the feasibility of such a computer was demonstrated by a collaboration of scientists at MIT, the University of California at Berkeley and Stanford University, which used a technique similar to MRI scans in hospitals. The computation that was accomplished was an ingenious search algorithm devised by Lov K. Grover of Bell Laboratories.

The concept is that the atoms can be made to peform higher level gating functions rather than just be used to store 0s and 1s. It is believed that such a device could factor large numbers 10,000 times faster than today's computers.

**quantum cryptography** A future technology for encrypting data that draws on inherent properties of photons. It enables a secret key to be transmitted over a fiber-optic channel without detection.

**quantum mechanics** The branch of physics developed in the first part of the twentieth century that was highly successful in explaining the behavior of atoms, molecules and nuclei. Developed between 1900 and 1930 and combined with the general and special theory of relativity, it revolutionized the field of physics. The new concepts, which were the particle properties of radiation, the wave properties of matter, quantization of physicial properties and the idea that one can no longer know exactly where a single particle such as an electron is at any one time were necessary to explain all of the new experimental evidence that was available at the time. For example, quantum mechanics explains the behavior of semiconductors which are used to make the myriad of devices we use every day.

Following are the important contributors to the foundation of quantum mechanics and the principles they uncovered.

| Year | Researcher | Quantum Mechanics Concept |
|------|------------|---------------------------|
| 1901 | Planck | Blackbody radiation |
| 1905 | Einstein | Photoelectric effect |
| 1913 | Bohr | Quantum theory of spectra |
| 1922 | Compton | Scattering of photons off electrons |
| 1924 | Pauli | Exclusion principle |
| 1925 | de Broglie | Matter waves |
| 1926 | Schroedinger | Wave equation |
| 1927 | Heisenberg | Uncertainty principle |
| 1927 | Davison and Germer | Wave properties of electrons |
| 1927 | Born | Interpretation of the wavefunction |

Q

**quarantine**   To move a virus-infected file to a folder that is not easily accessed by regular file management utilities. The quarantine option is available in antivirus software so that companies can keep a record of who has been infected, where the file came from and to possibly send the virus to the antivirus vendor for inspection. See *virus*.

**QuarkImmedia**   An extension to QuarkXPress from Quark, Inc., Denver, CO (www.quark.com), that is used to author multimedia publications on disk, CD-ROM and the Web. Initially offered for the Mac, a Windows version was later introduced.

**QuarkXPress**   A desktop publishing program for the Macintosh and Windows from Quark, Inc., Denver, CO (www.quark.com). Originally developed for and very popular on the Mac, it is noted for its precise typographic control and advanced text and graphics manipulation.

**QuarkXTension**   A third-party enhancement to the QuarkXPress desktop publishing program. There are hundreds of QuarkXTensions on the market.

**Quarterdeck**   (Quarterdeck Corporation, Marina del Rey, CA, www.quarterdeck.com)  A software company, founded in 1983, that offers a variety of utilities, diagnostics, connectivity and Internet products for the PC and Macintosh. In the 1980s, with its popular QEMM and DESQview programs, Quarterdeck was the first software company to offer a serious, alternative operating environment for the DOS PC. Quarterdeck continues to look for innovative software that helps users maintain, repair and maximize the performance of their computers.

**quartz crystal**   A slice of quartz ground to a prescribed thickness that vibrates at a steady frequency when stimulated by electricity. The tiny crystal, about 1/20th by 1/5th of an inch, creates the computer's heartbeat.

**Quattro Pro**   See *Corel Quattro Pro*.

**qubit**   (**QU**antum **BIT**)  A data bit in quantum computing. Such an entity can hold more than two values. See *quantum computing*.

**query**   To interrogate a database (count, sum and list selected records). Contrast with *report*, which is usually a more elaborate printout with headings and page numbers. The report may also be a selective list of items; hence, the two terms may refer to programs that produce the same results.

Defining a query for a relational database can be extremely simple or very complex. If the query is based on one matching condition, such as "retrieve all customers who owe us more than $10,000," it is usually pretty easy to define in a query language or program. However, "retrieve all customers who owe us more than $10,000 from purchasing toasters" is not easy. It requires several steps to determine how many toaster orders make up the balance. In fact, this is actually very complicated to program if it is absolutely necessary that the $10,000 be for toaster orders and nothing else.

In addition, relational databases are designed to eliminate redundancy. The idea is to store a data item in one table and not have it duplicated in others. For example, an order record will contain the product number ordered, but often not its description. The description is stored in a product table. Thus, any printout of products ordered and their descriptions requires that the order table be linked to the product table for that query or report. Linking customer, order and product tables is a common example of relating tables to satisfy a query.

"How may customers in Pennsylvania bought widgits and ower more than $1000?"

Select which databases the data are located in and determine how they are linked.

Select databases

Customers

Orders

Relate by

Account number

Define the matching condition through which the data will be filtered. State which fields are to be in the result.

Filter

| State | = | PA |
| Balance | > | $1000.00 |
| Product | = | Widgit |

Fields

Company

Balance

Product

Quantity

**The Query Statement**
This diagram depicts the typical conditions that have to be stated when querying a relational database.

Most queries require at least the following conditions to be stated. First, which table or tables is the data coming from. If from two or more tables, what is the link between (typically account number or name). Next, define the selection criteria, which is the matching condition or filter. Last, define which fields in the tables are to be displayed or printed in the result.

**query decomposition**    Separating elements of a query so that each can be processed by a different database server.

**query language**    A generalized language that allows a user to select records from a database. It uses a command language, menu-driven method or a query by example (QBE) format for expressing the matching condition.

Query languages are usually included in DBMSs, and stand-alone packages are available for interrogating files in non-DBMS applications. See *query program*.

**Querymaster**    See *QuickBuild*.

**query program**    Software that counts, sums and retrieves selected records from a database. It may be part of a large application and be limited to one or two kinds of retrieval, such as pulling up a customer account on screen, or it may refer to a query language that allows any condition to be searched and selected.

**question mark**    In C programming, the question mark is used as a conditional symbol. For example, in the expression **x1 ? x2 : x3**, if x1 is not zero, then x2 is evaluated, otherwise x3 is evaluated.

**queue**    Pronounced "Q." A temporary holding place for data. See *message queue* and *print queue*.

**QuickApp**    A software tool from Attachmate Corporation, Bellevue, WA (www.attachmate.com), that adds screen scraping capability to client/server development systems. QuickApp scans and records the mainframe terminal screens that are displayed on the PC via a 3270 emulator. QuickApp navigation engines that work within languages, such as PowerBuilder, Visual Basic, SQLWindows, ObjectView and Visual C++, allow developers point-and-click access to on-screen fields.

**Quick B**    A communications protocol for downloading files developed by CompuServe.

**QuickBASIC**    A popular BASIC compiler from Microsoft that adds advanced features to the BASIC language.

**QuickBooks**    A small business accounting system for Windows from Intuit, Inc., Menlo Park, CA (www.intuit.com). It works like the popular Quicken program, but is designed to track a whole business.

**QuickBuild**    An integrated package of tools from ICL for designing and developing business applications for its Series 39 mainframes. It supports batch and transaction processing on IDMSX databases. QuickBuild Pathway is a menu system used to support each step of the QuickBuild development cycle. Application Master (AM) is used to develop business applications. Querymaster (QM) extracts information from IDMSX databases. Automatic System Generator (ASG) creates working prototypes of the application. Data Dictionary System (DDS) is used to model the business structure, information and workflow.

**QuickC**    A C compiler and development system from Microsoft that is compatible with Microsoft C and used by the beginner or occasional programmer. QuickC for Windows is a version that provides a Windows-based environment for developing Windows applications. See *Visual C++*.

**quick-connect block**    See *punch block*.

**QuickDB**    An ODBC driver from Attachmate Corporation, Bellevue, WA (www.attachmate.com), that provides an APPC connection directly from the client to communicate with IBM's DRDA interface.

**QuickDraw**    The graphics display system built into the Macintosh. It accepts commands from the application and draws the corresponding objects on the screen. It provides a consistent interface that software developers can work with.

QuickDraw GX adds capabilities to QuickDraw, including special graphics effects, more sophisticated font kerning and ligature handling and enhanced printer management. Applications must be programmed for GX in order to take advantage of most of its capabilities.

Q

**Quicken**    A popular financial management program for PCs and Macs from Intuit, Inc., Menlo Park, CA (www.intuit.com). It is used to write checks, organize investments and produce a variety of reports for personal finance and small business.

**QuickPascal**    A pascal compiler from Microsoft that is compatible with Turbo Pascal and provides object-oriented capabilities.

**QuickPeer**    A software tool from Attachmate Corporation, Bellevue, WA, that generates the communications code for developing three-tier client/server systems. It works with languages such as PowerBuilder, Visual Basic, SQLWindows, ObjectView and Visual C++. It eliminates writing highly technical code in languages such as C to support the communications protocols.

**QuickSilver**    (1) (QuickSilver Technology, Inc., Santa Clara, CA, www.qstech.com)  A mobile communications company developing a new chip for cellphones and PDAs. Its Adaptive Computing Machine technology enables code to be rapidly paged into the chip as needed. This quick paging method conserves power by making active only those software routines necessary at the moment.

(2) A browser plug-in from Micrografx that allows a variety of vector drawings to be viewed from the Web.

(3) A family of dBASE III PLUS compilers developed by WordTech Systems, Inc. In 1992, the technology was acquired by Borland.

**quick tape**    See *QIC*.

**QuickTime**    Multimedia extensions to the Macintosh starting with System 7 that add sound and video capabilities. A QuickTime file can contain up to 32 tracks of audio, video, MIDI or other time-based control information. Most major Macintosh DBMSs (database management systems) support QuickTime. Apple also provides a version of QuickTime for Windows PCs.

**Quicktime VR**    The virtual reality version of QuickTime. It allows subjects to be viewed on screen in 3-D space. Scenes are compiled from renderings or from multiple still shots taken of all sides.

**QuickWin**    A library of C and FORTRAN routines from Microsoft that allows quick porting of DOS applications to the Windows environment. Character-based apps run in resizable windows.

**quit**    To exit the current program.

**quoted printable encoding**    An encoding method that converts binary data into ASCII text and vice versa and is one of the methods used by MIME. This method is good for text that contains an occasional 8-bit character. The 7-bit text is kept the same, and only the 8-bit text is encoded. See *base64*.

**quotes**    See *laws*.

**qwerty keyboard**    The standard English language typewriter keyboard.

Q, W, E, R, T and Y are the letters on the top left, alphabetic row. Designed in 1868 by Christopher Sholes, who invented the typewriter, the keyboard was organized to slow down a person's typing in order to prevent the keys from jamming. See *Dvorak keyboard*.

**Qwest**    (Qwest Communications International Inc., Denver, CO, www.qwest.com)  A telecommunications company that offers services to telecom carriers, businesses and homes using an extensive fiber-optic network throughout the U.S. and Mexico. It started in 1988 as the SP Construction subsidiary of Southern Pacific Railroad, laying fiber optic cables for other carriers along railroad right-of-ways. In 1991, it became SP Telecom, a subsidiary of Anschutz Corporation (Philip Anschutz owned Southern Pacific).

In the mid-1990s, SP Telecom acquired Qwest Transmission, Inc., a digital microwave carrier and subsequently changed its name. It also began leasing fiber to carriers and has been upgrading its network ever since. In early 1998, it introduced retail long distance service in selected cities at 7.5¢ per minute. Qwest claims its network bandwidth is greater than AT&T, WorldCom and Sprint combined. See *Nacchio's law*.

**R**

**R/2** See *R/3*.

**R/3** An integrated suite of client/server applications from SAP America, Inc., Wayne, PA (www.sap.com). It is the client/server versions of SAP's R/2 mainframe applications. R/3 includes information systems for manufacturing, distribution, order processing, accounting and human resources. It includes the ABAP/4 Development Workbench. See *BAPI*.

**RAB** See *RAID Advisory Board*.

**RACE encoding** A method for encoding foreign languages that use non-English characters (Chinese, Japanese, etc.) in ASCII characters for storage in domain name system servers (DNS servers). RACE codes are made up of digits, letters and dashes. See *DNS*.

**RACF** (Resource Access Control Facility) IBM mainframe security software introduced in 1976 that verifies user ID and password and controls access to authorized files and resources.

**rack mounted** Built into a cabinet that has a standard panel width of 19" or 23". All types of electronics and computing devices come in rack mounted packages, including servers, test instruments, telecommunications components and tape drives. Such units can be bolted into the rack or placed on shelves. The height of a rack-mounted device is specified in a unit (U) measure or rack unit (RU). 1U (or 1RU) is 1.75" from top to bottom.

**rack unit** A unit of measurement of the height of a rack-mounted device. One rack unit, or RU, is 1.75". See *rack mounted*.

**RAD** (1) (Rapid Application Development) Developing systems incrementally and delivering working pieces every three to four months, rather than waiting until the entire project is programmed before implementing it. Over the years, many information projects have failed, because, by the time the implementation took place, the business had changed.

RAD employs a variety of automated design and development tools, including CASE, 4GLs, visual programming and GUI builders, that get prototypes up and running quickly. The term was coined years ago by industry guru James Martin, and focuses on personnel management and user involvement as much as on technology. Joint application development (JAD) is another RAD concept.

(2) (Rapid Application Development) A term applied to development tools to refer to any number of features that make programming easier.

**Rack Mount Cabinet**
This picture from AMCO Engineering shows the variety of shelves that can be used in its 19" rack mount cabinets. Side and rear panels, doors, locks, fans and a host of other accessories are also available. *(Image courtesy of AMCO Engineering Company.)*

**radar** (RAdio Detection And Ranging) A method of determining the location and speed of an object. Radar works by transmitting signals and measuring the time it takes for them to bounce off the targeted object and return. See *Doppler radar*.

**radio** The transmission of electromagnetic radiation (energy) through the air or through a hollow tube called a "waveguide." Although radio is often thought of as only AM and FM, all airborne transmission is radio, including TV, satellite and cellphones. See *electromagnetic spectrum*.

**radio buttons** A series of onscreen buttons that allow only one selection. If a button is currently selected, it will de-select when another button is selected.

**radio signal** The transmission of electromagnetic energy. See *radio*.

**radiosity** A rendering method that simulates light reflecting off one surface and onto another. It is a more accurate method of rendering light and shadows than ray tracing. Radiosity produces the soft shadows from multiple reflections and light sources that exist in the real world. See *reflection mapping* and *ray tracing*.

**radio spectrum** The part of the electromagnetic spectrum used to transmit voice, video and data. It uses frequencies from 3 kHz to 300 GHz. See *electromagnetic spectrum*.

**RADIUS** (Remote Authentication Dial-In User Service) An access control protocol that uses a challenge/response method for authentication. It was developed by Livingston Enterprises. See *challenge/response*.

**radix** The base value in a numbering system. For example, in the decimal numbering system, the radix is 10.

**radix point** The location in a number that separates the integral part from the fractional part. For example, in the decimal system, it is the decimal point.

**RADSL** See *DSL*.

**RAD tool** Any program or utility that speeds up the development and programming of an application. Visual programming tools are widely used to quickly develop graphical front ends.

**ragged right** In typography, non-uniform text at the right margin, such as the text you're reading.

**RAID** (Redundant Array of Independent Disks) A disk subsystem that increases performance and/or provides fault tolerance. RAID is a set of two or more hard disks and a specialized disk controller that contains the RAID functionality. Developed initially for servers and stand-alone disk storage systems, RAID is increasingly becoming available in desktop PCs primarily for fault tolerance. RAID can also be implemented via software only, but with less performance, especially when rebuilding data after a failure.

RAID improves performance by disk striping, which interleaves bytes or groups of bytes across multiple drives, so more than one disk is reading and writing simultaneously. Fault tolerance is achieved by mirroring or parity. Mirroring is 100% duplication of the data on two drives (RAID 1), and parity (RAID 3 and 5) calculates the data in two drives and stores the result on a third drive: a bit from drive 1 is XOR'd with a bit from drive 2, and the result bit is stored on drive 3 (see *OR* for an explanation of XOR). A failed drive can be hot swapped with a new one, and the RAID controller automatically rebuilds the lost data.

RAID systems come in all sizes from floor-standing cabinets to a complete system in one full-size drive bay. Self-contained systems often include large amounts of cache and redundant power supplies.

RAID used to mean arrays of "inexpensive" disks, which was the title of a paper written in 1988 at the University of California at Berkeley. RAIDs were contrasted with SLEDs (Single Large Expensive Disks), which were still popular on

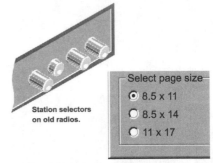

Station selectors
on old radios.

Select page size
- ● 8.5 x 11
- ○ 8.5 x 14
- ○ 11 x 17

**Radio Buttons**
This type of selection is used whenever there is only one choice out of several. Choosing one deselects the others. Pressing a preset station button on old radios pushes out the others.

large computers. Today, all hard disks are inexpensive by comparison, and the RAID Advisory Board (www.raid-advisory.com) changed the name to "independent" disks. For more details, review the white paper from the RAID Advisory Board at www.raid-advisory.com/rabguide.html. See *SAN* and *sector sparing*.

**RAID LEVEL 0**    Level 0 is disk striping only, which interleaves data across multiple disks for better performance. It does not provide safeguards against failure.

**RAID LEVEL 1**    Uses disk mirroring, which provides 100% duplication of data. Offers highest reliability, but doubles storage cost.

**RAID LEVEL 2**    Bits (rather than bytes or groups of bytes) are interleaved across multiple disks. The Connection Machine used this technique, but this is a rare method.

**RAID LEVEL 3**    Data is striped across three or more drives. Used to achieve the highest data transfer, because all drives operate in parallel. Parity bits are stored on separate, dedicated drives.

**RAID LEVEL 4**    Similar to Level 3, but manages disks independently rather than in unison. Not often used.

**RAID LEVEL 5**    Most widely used. Data is striped across three or more drives for performance, and parity bits are used for fault tolerance. The parity bits from two drives are stored on a third drive.

**RAID LEVEL 6**    Highest reliability, but not widely used. Similar to RAID 5, but does two different parity computations or the same computation on overlapping subsets of the data.

**RAID LEVEL 10**    Actually RAID 1,0. A combination of RAID 1 and 0 (mirroring and striping).

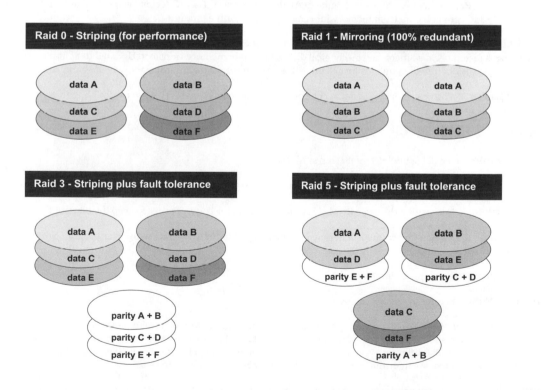

**RAID Advisory Board** (RAID Advisory Board, North Grafton, MA, www.raid-advisory.com) An organization founded in 1992 that is involved with education, standardization and classification of RAID storage systems. See *RAID*.

**RAM** (Random Access Memory) A group of memory chips, typically of the dynamic RAM (DRAM) type, which functions as the computer's primary workspace. See *memory* and *computer* for an explanation of how memory is used in processing data.

The "random" in RAM means that the contents of each byte can be directly accessed without regard to the bytes before or after it. This is also true of other types of memory chips, including ROMs and PROMs. However, unlike ROMs and PROMs, RAM chips require power to maintain their content, which is why you must save your data onto disk before you turn the computer off. See *memory module, dynamic RAM* and *static RAM*.

**RAM... the Old Fashioned Kind**
Before chips, RAM was made of pulsating tubes of mercury and magnetic drums and cores. This magnetic drum unit was the memory in the IBM 650, introduced in 1954. It held two thousand 10-digit words. That much memory today would fit on the head of a pin, and a very thin pin to be sure. See also *core storage* and **early memories**. *(Image courtesy of the Hagley Museum and Library.)*

**Rambus DRAM** See *RDRAM*.

**RAM card** (1) A printed circuit board containing memory chips that is plugged into a socket within the computer.

(2) A credit card–sized module that contains memory chips and battery. See *memory card*.

**RAM chip** (Random Access Memory chip) A memory chip. See *dynamic RAM, static RAM, RAM* and *memory*.

**RAMDAC** (Random Access Memory Digital to Analog Converter) The VGA controller chip that maintains the color palette and converts data from memory into analog signals for the monitor.

**RAM disk** A disk drive simulated in memory. To use it, files are copied from magnetic disk onto the RAM disk. Processing is faster, because there's no mechanical disk action, only memory transfers. Updated data files must be copied back to disk before the power is turned off—otherwise, the updates are lost. Same as *E-disk* and *virtual disk*.

**RAM doubler** A software technique that compresses the contents of memory, thereby doubling (more or less) its available capacity.

**RAMIS** See *CA-RAMIS*.

**RAM Mobile** See *BellSouth Intelligent Wireless Network*.

**RAMP-C** A proprietary benchmark from IBM for measuring the performance of OLAP systems. See *benchmark*.

**RAM refresh** Recharging dynamic RAM chips many times per second in order to keep the bit patterns valid.

**RAM resident** Refers to programs that remain in memory in order to interact with other programs or to be instantly popped up when required by the user. See *TSR*.

**random access** Same as *direct access*.

**random noise** Same as *Gaussian noise*.

**random number generator** A program routine that produces a random number. Random numbers are created easily in a computer, since there are many random events that take place—for example, the duration between keystrokes. Only a few milliseconds' difference is enough to seed a random number generation routine with a different number each time. Once seeded, an algorithm computes different numbers throughout the session.

**range** (1) In data entry validation, a group of values from a minimum to a maximum.

**(2)** With spreadsheets, a series of cells that are worked on as a group. It may refer to a row, column or rectangular block defined by one corner and its diagonally opposite corner.

**(3)** A geographic distance.

**(4)** A group of frequencies.

**RangeLAN**    A series of wireless LAN products from Proxim, Inc., Sunnyvale, CA (www.proxim.com). RangeLAN2 uses Proxim's OpenAir protocol and provides 1.6 Mbps in the 2.4GHz band. RangeLAN2 cards will operate in a Symphony home system, but not with the earlier RangeLAN 900MHz products. RangeLAN802 is a family of 802.11-compliant products at 1 and 2 Mbps. See *OpenAir, Symphony, 802.11* and *wireless LAN*.

**ransom note typography**    Using too many fonts in a document. The term comes from the text in a ransom note that is pasted together from words cut out of different magazines and newspapers.

The ease with which fonts can be selected in a word processor has led many inexperienced people to use too many fonts in a document or newsletter. Typographers and graphics artists know that only two or three fonts are necessary for the most professional appearance.

> rAₙSOm Note tYₚOgraphy
>
> It's great to have all these NEAT fonts.
>
> But sometimes people get carried away!
>
> More than three fonts in an entire page generally become tiresome.
>
> There is elegance in simplicity!
>
> But that is not demonstrated here.

**rapid prototyping**    Turning 3-D models within the computer into actual, physical 3-D objects. Machines are available that build prototypes from various materials, such as paper and liquid polymer. See *rendering*.

**RARP**    (Reverse **ARP**) A TCP/IP protocol used by a diskless workstation to obtain its IP address. Upon startup, the client station sends out a RARP request in an Ethernet frame to the RARP server, which returns the layer 3 address for a layer 2 address (performing the opposite function of an ARP). See *BOOTP*.

**RAS**    **(1)** (**R**emote **A**ccess **S**ervice) A Windows NT Server feature that allows remote users access to the network from their Windows laptops or desktops via modem. See *RRAS* and *remote access server*.

**(2)** (**R**eliability **A**vailability **S**erviceability) Originally an IBM term, it refers to a computer system's overall reliability, its ability to respond to a failure and its ability to undergo maintenance without shutting it down entirely.

**(3)** (**R**ow **A**ddress **S**trobe) A clock signal in a memory chip used to pinpoint the row of a particular bit in a row-column matrix. See *CAS*.

**raster**    A pattern of horizontal lines (scan lines) that are displayed on a TV or computer CRT. This is the origin of the term "raster graphics," which refers to bitmapped images, or images comprised of a matrix of pixels. Technically, a raster refers to rows, not columns and rows, and hardware engineers prefer the term "bitmapped" graphics when referring to the images. See *raster scan* and *analog video*.

**raster display**    A display terminal that uses the raster scan method for creating the image on screen. See *raster scan*. Contrast with *vector display*.

**raster graphics**    See *bitmapped graphics*.

**raster image processor**    See *RIP*. Remember... try the acronym first!

**rasterize**    To prepare a page for display or printing. Rasterization is performed by a raster image processor (RIP), which turns text and images into the matrix of pixels (bitmap) that will be displayed onscreen or printed on the page. Various conversions may take place. For example, the mathematical coordinates of vector and outline fonts, as well as vector drawings, must be converted into bitmaps. Existing bitmaps may have to be scaled into different-sized bitmaps.

Unless output is printed on a vector graphics plotter, which literally draws the illustration with pens, all text and graphics must be rasterized into a bitmap for display or printing. See *RIP, font scaler* and *host-based printer*.

**raster scan**    Displaying or recording a video image line by line. Computer monitors and TVs use this method, whereby electrons are beamed (scanned) onto the phosphor coating on the screen a line at a time from left to right starting at the top-left corner. At the end of the line, the beam is turned off and moved back to the left and down one line, which is known as the horizontal retrace (flyback). When the bottom-right corner is reached, a vertical retrace (flyback) returns the gun to the top-left corner. In a TV signal, this is known as the vertical blanking interval.

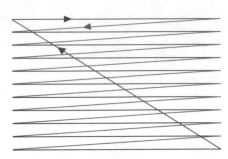

**Raster Scan Tracing**
Raster displays are imaged a line at a time (black lines), starting at the top left of the screen and going to the bottom right. The horizontal lines are the horizontal retraces, and the diagonal line is the vertical retrace.

### raster scan display   Same as *raster display*.

### Rational Apex   A comprehensive Ada development environment for UNIX systems from Rational Software Corporation, Cupertino, CA (www.rational.com). It evolved from the original, proprietary hardware-based Ada environment that the company was founded on in 1980. The tools in this environment are being extended to C and C++.

### Rational Rose   An object-oriented analysis and design tool that runs on Windows and UNIX platforms from Rational Software Corporation, Cupertino, CA (www.rational.com). It supports the Unified Modeling Language (UML), as well as the earlier Booch and OMT notations. With contributions from many large companies, Rational Software was the driving force to unify Booch, OMT, OOSE and others into UML.

The base product is used for modeling applications, but versions of Rose are available that generate C++, Smalltalk, Ada, SQLWindows and ObjectPro code.

### raw   Untouched. See *raw data* and *native capacity*. Contrast with *cooked*.

### raw data   Data that has not been processed in any manner. It often refers to uncompressed text that is not stored in any proprietary format. See *ASCII file* and *native capacity*.

### Raw Iron   The code name for a compact operating system from Oracle that runs the Oracle8i database. The OS is expected for the 64-bit Itanium (Merced) chip and is designed strictly for database processing.

### ray tracing   A rendering method that simulates light reflections, refractions and shadows. It follows a light path from a specific source and computes each pixel in the image to simulate the effect of the light. It is a very process-intensive operation. See *reflection mapping* and *radiosity*.

**Ray-Traced Image**
Many of the first graphics simulations were done at the University of Utah, and this is one of them. The shadows in this picture were created by software algorithms that simulate a beam of light from a designated source. *(Image courtesy of Computer Sciences Department, University of Utah.)*

### R:BASE 2000   A relational DBMS for DOS and Windows from R:BASE Technologies, Inc., Murraysville, PA (www.rbase.com). It provides a complete programming language, as well as an application generator for developing programs. Options include Oterro 2000, which provides connectivity from any ODBC-compliant application to R:BASE, and Tango Enterprise, which provides Web connectivity to R:BASE. Introduced in 1981 and originally developed by Microrim of Bellevue, WA, R:BASE was the first DBMS to compete with dBASE II, the leading personal computer DBMS of that era. R:BASE was acquired by R:BASE Technologies in 1998.

### RBL   (Realtime Blackhole List) A list of the IP addresses of known spammers. See *MAPS*.

### RBOC   (Regional Bell Operating Company) The regional Bell telephone companies that were spun off of AT&T by court order. Although some have since merged with others, the initial seven companies were Nynex, Bell Atlantic, BellSouth, Southwestern Bell, US West, Pacific Telesis and Ameritech. See *Divestiture*.

### RC2   See *RC5*.

### RC4   See *RC5*.

**RC5**    The latest in a family of secret key cryptographic methods developed by RSA Data Security, Inc., Redwood City, CA (www.rsa.com). Algorithms previously developed by RSA were RC2 and RC4, and all use a variable-length key. RC5 is more secure than RC4 but is slower. RSA Data Security is more widely known for its RSA public key method. See *RSA*.

**RCA connector**    A plug and socket for a two-wire (signal and ground) coaxial cable that is widely used to connect audio and video components. Also called a "phono connector," rows of RCA sockets are found on the backs of stereo amplifiers and numerous A/V products. The prong is 1/8" thick by 5/16" long. See *A/V ports* and *plugs & sockets*.

Left audio    Right audio    Composite video
(white)    (red)    (yellow)

**RCA (Phono) Connector**
The red and white for audio and yellow for video are standard colors used throughout the world.

**RCDD**    See *BICSI*.

**RCS**    (1) (Remote Computer Service) A remote timesharing service.
(2) (Revision Control System) A UNIX utility that provides version control.

**Rdb**    See *Oracle Rdb*.

**RDBMS**    (Relational DataBase Management System) See *relational database*.

**RDF**    (Resouce Description Format) A recommendation from the W3C for defining the content of Web pages in XML. It provides common tags for describing data and graphic elements, which provides a structure for metadata. For example, using the RDF descriptor for ZIP code would let systems exchange ZIP code data that use different names for that data element, such as "ZIP" and "ZIPCODE."

**RDO**    (Remote Data Objects) A programming interface for data access from Microsoft. It is used in Visual Basic to access remote ODBC databases. See *DAO*, *ADO*, *OLE DB* and *ODBC*.

**RDP**    (Remote Desktop Protocol) The presentation services protocol that governs input/output between a Windows terminal client and Windows Terminal Server. It is based on the T.share protocol. See *Windows Terminal Server*.

**RDRAM**    (Rambus DRAM) Pronounced "R-D RAM." A dynamic RAM chip technology from Rambus, Inc., Mountain View, CA (www.rambus.com). Rambus licenses its memory designs to semiconductor companies, which manufacture the chips. In 1995, Base RDRAM was introduced with speeds up to 600 MBytes/sec. In 1997, Concurrent RDRAM increased speed to 700 MBps; and in 1998, Direct RDRAM boosted speed to 1.6 GBps. Concurrent RDRAMs have been used in video games, but Direct RDRAMs are used in computers.
Direct RDRAM chips are housed in RIMM modules, which are similar to DIMMs, but have different pin settings. Direct RDRAM chips can also be built with dual channels, doubling the transfer rate to 3.2 GBps. Intel has invested in and has been involved in the design of the Direct Rambus (Direct RDRAM) technology. See *dynamic RAM* and *SLDRAM*.

**R**

**RDS**    (Remote Data Services) A set of programming interfaces from Microsoft that enables users to update data on the Internet or intranets from their ActiveX-enabled browser. Formerly ADC (Advanced Data Connector), it was integrated into ADO (Active Data Objects) and renamed RDS. See *ADO*.

**read**    To input into the computer from a peripheral device (disk, tape, etc.). Like reading a book or playing an audio tape, reading does not destroy what is read.
A read is both an input and an output (I/O), since data is being output from the peripheral device and input into the computer. Memory is also said to be read when it is accessed to transfer data out to a peripheral device or to somewhere else in memory. Every peripheral or internal transfer of data is a read from somewhere and a write to somewhere else.

**read channel**    A circuit in a disk drive that encodes the data bits into flux changes for recording and decodes the magnetic flux changes into bits for reading.

**read cycle**    The operation of reading data from a memory or storage device.

**reader**    A machine that captures data for the computer, such as an optical character reader, magnetic card reader and punched card reader. A microfiche or microfilm reader is a self-contained machine that reads film and displays its contents.

**read error**    A failure to read the data on a storage or memory device. Although it is not a routine phenomenon, magnetic and optical recording surfaces can become contaminated with dust or dirt or be physically damaged, and cells in memory chips can malfunction.

When a read error occurs, the program will allow you to bypass it and move on to the next set of data, or it will end, depending on the operating system. However, if the damaged part of a disk contains control information, the rest of the file may be unreadable. In such cases, a recovery program must be used to retrieve the remaining data if there is no backup.

**readme file**    A text file copied onto software distribution disks that contains last-minute updates or errata that have not been printed in the documentation manual.

**read notification**    A confirmation transmitted back to the sender that an e-mail message has been read.

**read only**    (1) Refers to storage media that permanently hold their content; for example, ROM and CD-ROM.
(2) A file that can be read, but not updated or erased. See *file attribute*.

**read-only attribute**    A file attribute that, when turned on, indicates that a file can only be read, but not updated or erased.

**read only rights**    Authorization to read the contents of files, but not to change them. "All rights" or "read/write rights" let you modify the contents. Rights are assigned to files and folders by the user or the network administrator, and the operating system checks the status during file operations.

**readout**    (1) A small display device that typically shows only a few digits or a couple of lines of data.
(2) Any display screen or panel.

**read rights**    Same as *read only rights*.

**read-while-write**    The ability of a tape drive to write data and read it back for verification immediately so that both operations take place in the same pass.

**read/write**    (1) Refers to a device that can both input and output, or transmit and receive.
(2) Refers to a file that can be updated and erased.

**read/write channel**    Same as *I/O channel*.

**read/write head**    A device that reads (senses) and writes (records) data on a magnetic disk or tape. For writing, the surface of the disk or tape is moved past the read/write head. By discharging electrical impulses at the appropriate times, bits are recorded as tiny, magnetized spots of positive or negative polarity.

For reading, the surface is moved past the read/write head, and the bits that are present induce an electrical current across the gap.

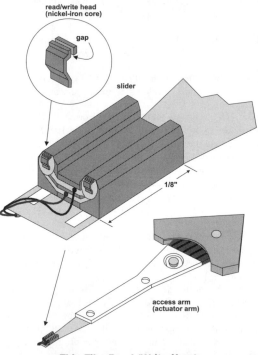

**Thin Film Read/Write Head**
The read/write heads on today's magnetic disks are so tiny you need a microscope to see them. The heads are attached to a pair of aerodynamically designed rails, known as a "slider," that keep the head at the proper distance from the disk platter.

**read/write memory**   Same as *RAM*.

**read/write rights**   Authorization to change the contents of files. See *read only rights*.

**real address**   Same as *absolute address*.

**RealAudio**   The most popular streaming audio technology for the Internet and intranets from RealNetworks, Inc., Seattle, WA (www.real.com). A browser equipped with a RealPlayer or RealAudio plug-in enables news, sports and other programs transmitted from RealAudio servers (RealServers) to be heard on the user's computer. Encoders and plug-ins can be downloaded from RealNetworks' Web site. Server software is available for a variety of platforms. RealNetworks was formerly Progressive Networks. See *RealVideo*.

**Realizer**   See *CA-Realizer*.

**RealMedia**   A streaming media technology for the Internet from RealNetworks, Inc., Seattle, WA (www.real.com). Using the Realtime Streaming Protocol (RTSP), it is designed to handle any type of media, including audio, video, MIDI, text, animation and presentations. The RealMedia Architecture (RMA) allows multiple streams to be synchronized simultaneously—for example, sending images intermixed with audio.

**Real Mode**   An operational state in Intel CPU chips (starting with the 286) in which the computer functions like the first Intel CPU chip (8086/8088), which is limited to accessing one megabyte of memory. DOS applications run in Real Mode, unless they have been enhanced with a DOS extender that allows them to use more memory. See *Protected Mode* and *Virtual 8086 Mode*.

**Real Mode driver**   A PC driver that is written to the original 16-bit 8086/8088 architecture, which is limited to one megabyte of memory. Real Mode drivers must run within the first megabyte. See *Real Mode*.

**RealPC**   A DOS emulator for the Macintosh from FWB Software, San Francisco, CA (www.fwb.com). Known earlier as SoftPC, it was originally developed by Insignia Solutions (www.insignia.com). RealPC is used to run DOS games and other DOS application on the Mac.

**RealPlayer**   A multimedia player and browser plug-in from RealNetworks, Inc., Seattle, WA (www.real.com) that plays RealAudio and RealVideo transmissions. RealPlayer G2 offers more features and enhancements. See *RealAudio* and *RealVideo*.

**real storage**   Real physical memory in a virtual memory system.

**R**

**realtime**   An immediate response. It refers to process control and embedded systems; for example, space flight computers must respond instantly to changing conditions. It also refers to fast transaction processing systems, as well as any electronic operation fast enough to keep up with its real-world counterpart (animating complex images, transmitting live video, etc.).

**realtime audio**   The ability to transmit voice (telephony) digitally without any loss of frames. Realtime audio is "realtime" when it is being listened to at the receiving side. If the audio data is merely transported from one digital system to another, the realtime requirement is not necessary. See *IP telephony*, *UDP* and *ATM*.

**realtime chat**   See *chat*.

**realtime clock**   An electronic circuit that maintains the time of day. It may also provide timing signals for timesharing operations. See *NTP*.

**realtime compression**   The ability to compress and decompress data without any noticeable loss in speed compared to non-compressed data. PC products such as Stacker and SuperStor let you create a separate compressed drive on your hard disk. All data written to that drive is compressed and decompressed when read back. Realtime compression is included in DOS starting with DOS 6. See **DOS DoubleSpace** and **DriveSpace**. See *JPEG*.

**realtime conferencing**   A "live" teleconferencing session that uses communications equipment fast enough to keep up with the speech and movements of all participants. See *teleconferencing*.

**realtime credit card processing**   Obtaining immediate authorization of a credit card purchase when ordering online. The card processing company notifies the merchant, and the merchant confirms or denies the order with the customer.

**realtime image**   A graphics image that can be animated onscreen at the same speed as the real-world object.

**realtime information system**   A computer system that responds to transactions by immediately updating the appropriate master files and/or generating a response in a time frame fast enough to keep an operation moving at its required speed. See *transaction processing*.

**realtime operating system**   A master control program that can provide immediate response to input signals and transactions.

**realtime system**   A computer system that responds to input signals fast enough to keep an operation moving at its required speed.

**realtime video**   The ability to transmit video live without missing any frames. Realtime video implies digital transmission and is "realtime" when it is being viewed at the receiving side. If the video data is merely transported from one digital system to another, the realtime requirement is not necessary. See *UDP* and *ATM*.

**RealVideo**   A streaming video technology for the Internet and intranets from RealNetworks, Inc., Seattle, WA (www.real.com). A browser equipped with a RealPlayer or RealVideo plug-in enables video broadcasts from RealVideo servers (RealServers) to be viewed on screen. The material can be statically stored in the server and viewed in full, or it can be an on-going broadcast like that of TV. Plug-ins can be downloaded from RealNetworks' Web site. Server server software is available for a variety of platforms. See *RealAudio*.

**reasonable test**   A type of test that determines whether a value falls within a range considered normal or logical. It can be made on electronic signals to detect extraneous noise, as well as on data to determine possible input errors.

**reboot**   To reload the operating system and restart the computer. See *boot*.

**receiver**   A device that accepts signals. Contrast with *transmitter*.

**recompile**   To compile a program again. A program is recompiled after a change has been made to it in order to test and run the revised version. Programs are recompiled many times during the course of development and maintenance. See *compile*.

**record**   (1) A group of related fields that store data about a subject (master record) or activity (transaction record). A collection of records make up a file.

Master records contain permanent data, such as account number, and variable data, such as balance due. Transaction records contain only permanent data, such as quantity and product code. See *master file* and *transaction file* for examples of record contents.

(2) In certain disk organization methods, a record is a block of data read and written at one time without any relationship to records in a file.

**record format**   Same as *record layout*.

**record head**   A device that writes a signal on tape. Some tape drives and all disk drives use a combination read/write head.

**record layout**   The format of a data record, which includes the name, type and size of each field in the record.

**record locking**    See *file and record locking*.

**record mark**    A symbol used to identify the end of a record.

**record number**    The sequential number assigned to each physical record in a file. Record numbers change when the file is sorted or records are added and deleted.

**records management**    The creation, retention and scheduled destruction of an organization's paper and film documents. Computer-generated reports and documents fall into the records management domain, but traditional data processing files do not.

**recovery**    See *backup & recovery, checkpoint/restart* and *tape backup*.

**recruiter information**    See *salary survey, to the recruiter, computercruiter, nerd rustler* and *programmer*.

**rectifier**    An electrical circuit used to convert AC into DC current. A rectifier is a diode that causes the current to flow in only one direction. The output of the rectifier is essentially half-AC current, which is then filtered into DC. Contrast with *inverter*. See *diode*.

**recursion**    In programming, the ability of a subroutine or program module to call itself. It is helpful for writing routines that solve problems by repeatedly processing the output of the same process.

**recycle bin**    In Windows 95/98, an icon of a waste can used for deleting files. The icon of a file or folder is dragged to the trash can and released. See *trash can*.

**recycling old computers**    See *National Cristina Foundation*.

**redaction**    The editing done to sensitive documents before release to the public.

**Red Book**    (1) The documentation of the U.S. National Security Agency that defines criteria for secure networks. The volumes are "Trusted Network Interpretation of the Trusted Computer System Evaluation Criteria" (NCSC-TG-005) and "Trusted Network Interpetation Environments Guideline: Guidance for Applying the Trusted Network Interpretation" (NCSC-TG-011). It is the network counterpart of the Orange Book for computers. See *NCSC*.

(2) The documentation for the technical specification of audio CDs (CD-DA), which includes such details as sampling and transfer rates. "Red Book audio" refers to digital sound that conforms to the common standard used in music compact discs. See *CD*.

**Red Hat**    (Red Hat, Inc., RTP, NC, www.redhat.com) A software company founded in 1994 by Marc Ewing and Bob Young that specializes in distributing the open source Linux operating system. Even though the primary program components are available for free, Red Hat commercialized the product to provide training, tech support, certification, on-site consulting, documentation and priority FTP access to updates. See *Linux*.

**redirection**    Diverting data from its normal destination to another—for example, to a disk file instead of the printer, or to a server's disk instead of the local disk. See **DOS redirection** and *redirector*.

**redirector**    In a LAN, software that routes workstation (client) requests for data to the server. In a Windows network, the redirector program is added to the PC to intercept requests for files and printers, and direct them to the appropriate remote device if applicable. Starting with Windows 95 and Windows NT 4.0, the redirector recognizes UNC names, as well as drive letters that have been mapped to remote servers. The counterpart in NetWare is known as the Requester. See *UNC* and *drive mapping*.

**redlining**    Identifying text that has been changed in a word processing document by displaying it in a special color, for example. It allows the original author of the text or other users to see ongoing revisions. The term comes from manual editing where a red pen is used to mark up the pages.

R

**redo**   To reverse an undo operation. See *undo*.

**redraw**   To redisplay an image onscreen, whether text or graphics. The concept is that the first time elements are displayed, they are "drawn," and if something is changed, they are "redrawn." Applications often have a Refresh command that redraws the screen. For example, in the Windows Explorer file manager, the Refresh command redraws the screen with the current directory (folder) structure. In some graphics programs, a Redraw or Refresh command redraws the elements on screen, because artifacts have been left over after numerous changes were made by the illustrator, which the program did not automatically "clean up."

**redundancy**   Refers to peripherals, computer systems and network devices that take on the processing or transmission load when other units fail. See *fault tolerant*, *mirroring*, *RAID* and *backup types*.

**redundancy check**   In communications, a method for detecting transmission errors by appending a calculated number onto the end of each segment of data. See *CRC*.

**reengineering**   Using information technology to improve performance and cut costs. Its main premise, as popularized by the book *Reengineering the Corporation* by Michael Hammer and James Champy, is to examine the goals of an organization and to redesign work and business processes from the ground up rather than simply automate existing tasks and functions.

According to the authors, reengineering is driven by open markets and competition. No longer, can we enjoy the protection of our own country's borders as we could in the past. Today, we are in a global economy, and worldwide customers are more sophisticated and demanding.

In addition, modern industrialization was based on theories of fragmentation and specialization, which have led to the "left eye" specialist with millions of workers doing dreary, monotonous jobs, as well as the creations of departments, functions and business units governed by multiple layers of management. Management has been the necessary glue to control the fragmented workplace.

In order to be successful in the future, the organization will have fewer layers of management and fewer, but more highly skilled workers that do more complex tasks. Information technology, used for the past 50 years to automate manual tasks, will be used to enable new work models. The successful organization will not be "technology driven," rather it will be "technology enabled."

Although reengineering may, in fact, reduce a department of 200 employees down to 50, it is not just about eliminating jobs. Its goals are customer oriented; for example, it's about processing a contract in 24 hours instead of two weeks, or performing a telecommunications service in one day instead of 30. It's about reducing the time it takes to get a drug to market from eight years to four years, or reducing the number of suppliers from 200,000 to 700.

Reengineering is about radical improvement, not incremental changes.

**References**   The primer on the subject is the best-selling book *Reengineering the Corporation* by Michael Hammer and James Champy, (HarperBusiness, 1993, ISBN 0-88730-640-3). It is "must reading" for anybody who wants to gain a basic understanding of the subject.

*BPR Wizdom: A Practical Guide to BPR Project Management* by Dennis E. Wisnosky and Rita C. Feeney (Wizdom Systems, Inc., 1999, ISBN 1-893990-03-6). Considered extremely helpful for top managers, it includes a blueprint for reengineering from start to finish.

*The Great Transition* by James Martin elaborates on seven disciplines for engineering the enterprise, (AMACOM, 1995, ISBN 0-8144-0315-8). Martin is an industry guru and one of the most prolific writers in the information field.

**reentrant code**   A programming routine that can be used by multiple programs simultaneously. It is used in operating systems and other system software, as well as in multithreading, where concurrent events are taking place. It is written so that none of its code is modifiable (no values are changed), and it does not keep track of anything. The calling programs keep track of their own progress (variables, flags, etc.), thus one copy of the reentrant routine can be shared by an any number of users or processes.

Conceptually, it is as if several people were each baking a cake from a single copy of a recipe on the wall. Everyone looks at the master recipe, but keeps track of their own progress by jotting down the step they are at on their own scratchpad so they can pick up where they left off. The master recipe is never disturbed.

**referential integrity**    A database management safeguard that ensures every foreign key matches a primary key. For example, customer numbers in a customer file are the primary keys, and customer numbers in the order file are the foreign keys. If a customer record is deleted, the order records must also be deleted; otherwise, they are left without a primary reference. If the DBMS doesn't test for this, it must be programmed into the applications.

**referrer**    The URL of the Web page you are viewing, which the browser sends along with the request for another page when you click on a hyperlink or when an image is called for on the same page. On a search site, in addition to the URL, the text you are searching for is often sent to an advertising agency that sends back a tailored banner ad or just simply collects demographics. Most ad blocker programs can eliminate referrer data. See *ad blocker*.

**Reflection**    A family of connectivity software from WRQ that runs under Windows. Reflection products include terminal emulation for UNIX, Digital, IBM and X Window, as well as NFS support for clients and NT servers.

**reflection mapping**    A rendering method that simulates light reflecting on an object. It is a much faster method than ray tracing because it maps light over the image rather than actually computing the path the light takes. See *ray tracing* and *radiosity*.

**reflective media**    Opaque materials such as a printed page or photograph that are scanned by shining light onto them, which is then reflected back to the sensors in order to record the image. Contrast with *transparent media*.

**reflective spot**    A metallic foil placed on each end of a magnetic tape. It reflects light to a photosensor to signal the end of tape.

**reflective VGA**    An LCD screen that needs bright ambient light for viewing. Backlit and sidelit screens are much easier to see.

**reformat**    (1) To change the record layout of a file or database.
(2) To initialize a disk over again.

**refraction**    The bending of electromagnetic waves as they pass between materials with different refractive indices. Refraction is an important characteristic of optical systems. As light rays travel at a more perpendicular angle to the edge of a medium, they are refracted outside the medium rather than being reflected inside. See *refractive index*, *total internal reflection* and *diffraction*.

**refractive index**    A property of a material that changes the speed of light, computed as the ratio of the speed of light in a vacuum to the speed of light through the material. When light travels at an angle between two different materials, their refractive indices determine the angle of transmission (refraction) of the light beam. In general, the refractive index varies based on the frequency of the light as well, thus different colors of light travel at different speeds. High intensities also can change the refractive index.

The refractive index of a vacuum is 1.0, and air is a tiny fraction greater than 1.0. The higher the index, the slower the speed of light through the medium, because the speed through the material is the speed of light (c) over the refractive index (n), thus speed = c/n. Following are common refractive indexes. See *fiber optics glossary*.

| Material | Refractive Index (n) |
|----------|----------------------|
| Vacuum | 1.0 |
| Air | 1.0 (tiny fraction more than 1) |
| Water | 1.33 |

**Blocking Referrer Data**
InterMute, Inc.'s interMute program (www.intermute.com) is an example of a utility that can keep referrer data from being transmitted.

| Material | Refractive Index (n) |
|----------|----------------------|
| Glass | 1.45-1.48 |
| Lithium niobate | 2.25 |
| Gallium arsenide | 3.35 |
| Silicon | 3.5 |
| Germanium | 4.0 |

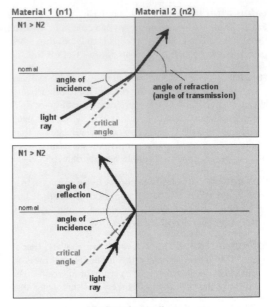

**Refractive Indices**
When light travels at an angle between two materials, light bends according to their refractive indices. The light must be on the more angular side of the critical angle in order to reflect.

**refresh**   (1) To continously charge a device that cannot hold its content. CRTs must be refreshed, because the phosphors hold their glow for only a few milliseconds. Dynamic RAM chips require refreshing to maintain their charged bit patterns. See *vertical scan frequency* and *redraw*.

(2) To download again (reload) the same Web page that is on screen to see if it has changed since the last time it was downloaded. See *reload*.

**refresh rate**   The number of times per second that a device is re-energized, such as a CRT or dynamic RAM chip. See *vertical scan frequency*.

**regenerator**   (1) In communications, the same as a *repeater*.

(2) In electronics, a circuit that repeatedly supplies current to a memory or display device that continuously loses its charges or content.

**ReGIS**   (REmote Graphics InStruction) A graphics language from Digital used on graphics terminals and first introduced on the PDP-11.

**register**   A small, high-speed computer circuit that holds values of internal operations, such as the address of the instruction being executed and the data being processed. When a program is debugged, register contents may be analyzed to determine the computer's status at the time of failure.

In microcomputer assembly language programming, programmers reference registers routinely. Assembly languages in larger computers are often at a higher level.

**register level compatibility**   A hardware component that is 100% compatible with another device. It implies that the same type, size and names of registers are used.

**Registry**   The database of configuration settings in Windows 95/98/NT/2000. It is a database that holds configuration data about the hardware and environment of the PC it has been installed in. It is made up of the SYSTEM.DAT and USER.DAT files. Many settings that were previously stored in WIN.INI and SYSTEM.INI in Windows 3.1 are in the Registry.

The Registry can be edited directly, but that is usually only done for very technical enhancements or as a last resort. Routine access is done via the Control Panels in My Computer and the Properties menu option, which is on the File menu. In addition, right clicking almost every icon brings you the option of selecting Properties. See See *Win Registry*.

**regression analysis**   In statistics, a mathematical method of modeling the relationships among three or more variables. It is used to predict the value of one variable given the values of the others. For example, a model might estimate sales based on age and gender. A regression analysis yields an equation that expresses the relationship. See *correlation*.

**regression testing**   In software development, testing a program that has been modified in order to ensure that additional bugs have not been introduced. When a program is enhanced, testing is often done only on the new features.

However, adding source code to a program often introduces errors in other routines, and many of the old and stable functions must be retested along with the new ones.

**reinstall**    To go through the installation process once again, because files have become corrupted. See *reload*.

**reintermediation**    To provide value as a middleman in order to avoid disintermediation. See *disintermediation*.

**related files**    Two or more data files that can be matched on some common condition, such as account number or name.

**relational algebra**    (1) The branch of mathematics that deals with relations, for example, AND, OR, NOT, IS and CONTAINS.

(2) In relational database, a collection of rules for dealing with tables, for example, JOIN, UNION and INTERSECT.

**relational calculus**    The rules for combining and manipulating relations, for example, De Morgan's law, "the complement of a union is equal to the union of the complements."

**relational database**    A database organization method that links files together as required. In non-relational systems (hierarchical, network), records in one file contain embedded pointers to the locations of records in another, such as customers to orders and vendors to purchases. These are fixed links set up ahead of time to speed up daily processing.

In a relational database, relationships between files are created by comparing data, such as account numbers and names. A relational system has the flexibility to take any two or more files and generate a new file from the records that meet the matching criteria (see *join*).

Routine queries often involve more than one data file. For example, a customer file and an order file can be linked in order to ask a question that relates to information in both files, such as the names of the customers that purchased a particular product.

In practice, a pure relational query can be very slow. In order to speed up the process, indexes are built and maintained on the key fields used for matching. Sometimes, indexes are created "on the fly" when the data is requested.

The term was coined in 1970 by Edgar Codd, whose objective was to easily accommodate a user's ad hoc request for selected data.

```
Relational Terms      Common Terms
table or relation     file
tuple                 record
attribute             field
```

**relational DBMS**    See *relational database* and *DBMS*.

**relational model**    See *relational database*.

**relational operator**    A symbol that specifies a comparison between two values.

```
Relational Operator            Symbol
EQ    Equal to                 =
NE    Not equal to             <> or # or !=
GT    Greater than             >
GE    Greater than or equal to >=
LT    Less than                <
LE    Less than or equal to    <=
```

**relational query**    A question asked about data contained in two or more tables in a relational database. The relational query must specify the tables required and what the condition is that links them; for example, matching account numbers. Relational queries are tricky to specify because even the simplest of questions may require data from two or more tables. Both the knowledge of the query language and the database structure is necessary. Even with graphical interfaces that let you drag a line from one field to another, you still need to know how the tables were designed to be related.

R

**relative address**   A memory address that represents some distance from a starting point (base address), such as the first byte of a program or table. The absolute address is derived by adding it to the base address.

**relative movement**   A change in position that is based on the current position. For example, it doesn't matter where the mouse is on the desk in relation to the pointer on the screen. When you move it, the pointer starts moving, starting from where it was last positioned.

**relative path**   An implied path. When a command is expressed that references files, the current working directory is the implied, or relative, path if the full path is not explicitly stated. Contrast with *full path*.

**relative reference**   An address or pointer that changes when the target item is moved or the relationship to it has changed. For example, in a spreadsheet, a cell with a relative reference changes its formula when copied elsewhere. Contrast with *absolute reference*.

**relative URL**   A URL that specifies only the document name. The full path is implied by the current document. Contrast with *absolute URL*.

**relative vector**   In computer graphics, a vector with end points designated in coordinates relative to a base address. Contrast with *absolute vector*.

**relay**   An electrical switch that allows a low power to control a higher one. A small current energizes the relay, which closes a gate, allowing a large current to flow through.

**release**   Same as *version*.

**reload**   **(1)** To load a program from disk into memory once again in order to run it. Reload is entirely different than reinstall. Reinstall means that you have to run the install program from a CD-ROM or floppy disk and perform the installation procedure over again.

  Reloading is common when the program crashes. Reinstalling is much less common, but necessary if program files have become unreadable due to damaged sectors on the disk or because files were accidentally erased or corrupted. This can also happen due to program error, in which the program erroneously writes incorrect data to some of its own configuration and status files.

  **(2)** To download again the same Web page that is on screen to see if it has changed since the last time it was downloaded. See *refresh*.

**relocatable code**   Machine language that can be run from any memory location. All modern computers run relocatable code. See *base/displacement*.

**remedial maintenance**   A repair service that is required due to a malfunction of the product. Contrast with *preventive maintenance*.

**remmed out**   See *Rem*.

**remote access**   See *remote control software*.

**remote access concentrator**   A remote access server that supports one or more T1/E1 lines, allowing multiple analog and ISDN calls to come in over one port from the telephone company. Remote access concentrators can handle

**An Early Relational Query**
In the mid-1980s, Paradox was the first DBMS on a PC that made linking tables easier. Although not as sophisticated as today's methods, the ability to associate relationships by typing sample words was a breakthrough. The Customer No. and Part No. fields are related by "ABC" and "XYZ." Any words would suffice as long as they are the same.

much higher call densities than remote access servers. They include the dial-up protocols and access control, and the equivalent of a modem pool. See *remote access server, remote access router* and *IAD*.

**remote access router**  A network device used to connect remote sites via private lines or public carriers. The router is required at both ends and provides the protocol conversion between the internal network (LAN) and the external network (WAN). See *remote access concentrator* and *remote access server*.

**remote access server**  A computer in a network that provides access to remote users via analog modem or ISDN connections. It includes the dial-up protocols and access control (authentication), and may be a regular file server with remote access software or a proprietary system such as Shiva's LANRover. The modems may be internal or external to the device. See *remote access concentrator, remote access router* and *IAD*.

**Remote Access Service**  See *RAS*. Remember... try the acronym first!

**remote access software**  See *remote control software*.

**remote batch**  See *RJE*.

**remote boot**  Booting up a client machine from the server. Remote boot capability is necessary for diskless workstations and network computers, but is also helpful for restarting failed desktop machines. See *PXE* and *boot ROM*.

**remote bridge**  A device that connects two LAN segments together that are in geographically dispersed locations. It connects LANs via a WAN. See *bridge*.

**remote call forwarding**  A local telephone service that routes calls from an old number to a new number. It is typically used for an interim period after moving to a new location.

**remote communications**  (1) Communicating via long distances.
(2) See *remote control software*.

**remote console**  A terminal or workstation in a remote location that is used to monitor and control a local computer.

**remote control software**  Software, installed in both machines, that allows a user at a local computer to have control of a remote computer via modem. Both users run the remote computer and see the same screen. Remote control operation is used to take control of an unattended desktop personal computer from a remote location, as well as to provide instruction and technical support to remote users.

Remote control is different than a remote node operation. In remote control, only keystrokes are transmitted from and screen updates are transmitted to the remote machine as all processing takes place in the local computer. All file transfers are done locally or over a high-speed LAN. In a remote node setup, the user is logged onto the network using the phone line as an extension to the network. Thus, all traffic has to flow over a low-speed telephone line.

When working with large files, remote control is faster than remote node, and it gives users the flexibility to do whatever they want on the local machine. However, remote control sessions move screen changes constantly to the remote machine and graphics applications are slow. Remote control usually requires more network ports than remote node for the same number of users. In addition, in remote control, you don't do any local processing in the remote machine, so online sessions are often longer than with remote node. See *application sharing*.

**Remote Control and Application Sharing**  Remote control operation and application sharing are similar if not almost identical in some cases. Application sharing lets two or more users work in

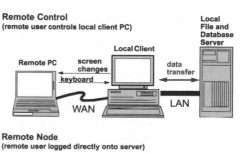

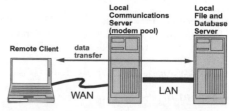

the same application, which is running in one user's machine. If the application sharing program allows another user to take control of the operating system rather than just a single, specific application, then there is really no difference.

**remote echo**    The transmission of received data back to the sending station for visual verification. A local echo displays the typed keystrokes from the local machine, but a remote echo displays the data after it has been sent, received and retransmitted back.

**remote emergency boot**    The ability to boot a diagnostic program into a computer that cannot load its operating system due to hardware or software failure. See *PXE*.

**remote invocation**    To cause a program to be launched on a remote server. See *RMI*.

**remote new system startup**    The ability to install the operating system from the server into a brand new PC with a clean hard disk. See *PXE*.

**remote node**    A remote user or workstation. Access to the company LAN is made via POTS or ISDN modem to a connection at the remote access server. See *remote access server* and *remote control software*.

**remote-office router**    A router specialized to route data to its counterpart in a remote site. Configuring the router is done at the central site, thus network administration is simplified. 3Com pioneered the concept with its Boundary Routing.

**remote resource**    A peripheral device, such as a disk, modem or printer, that is available for shared use in the network. Contrast with *local resource*.

**remote sensing**    Deriving digital models of an area on the earth. Using special cameras from airplanes or satellites, either the sun's reflections or the earth's temperature is turned into digital maps of the area. In order to view the results, the data must be rendered by specialized image processing software. See *digital elevation model*.

**remote startup**    See *remote new system startup*.

**remote wake-up**    The ability for the power in a client station to be turned on by the network. Remote wake-up enables software upgrading and other management tasks to be performed on users' machines after the work day is over. It also enables remote users to gain access to machines that have been turned off. Intel calls remote wake-up "Wake-on-LAN."

**removable disk**    A disk module that is inserted into the drive for reading and writing and removed when not required. Floppy disks, Zip disks, Jaz disks and CD-ROMs are common examples. See *magnetic disk* and *optical disk*.

**render**    To draw a real-world object as it actually appears.

**rendering**    In computer graphics, turning one view of a 3-D model into a 2-D display image that incorporates basic lighting such as Gouraud shading, or more sophisticated effects that silmulate shadows, reflection and refraction. It may also include the application of textures to the surfaces. See *Gouraud shading*, *Phong shading*, *texture mapping* and *rapid prototyping*.

**Removable Zip Disk**
The Zip has been the most popular removable disk since the introduction of the floppies.

**Renderman interface**    A graphics format that uses photorealistic image synthesis from Pixar, Inc., Richmond, CA (www.pixar.com). Developer's Renderman (PCs and UNIX) and Mac Renderman (Macintosh) are Pixar programs that apply photorealistic looks and surfaces to 3-D objects.

**Rendezvous**    See *TIB/Rendezvous*.

**Renovator**    See *ESL Renovator*.

**Rendered Image**
Photorealistic pictures require high-end rendering software. This drawing of downtown Philadelphia was rendered in MicroStation MasterPiece from Bentley Systems. *(Image courtesy of Bentley Systems, Inc.)*

**repeater**    (1) A communications device that amplifies or regenerates the data signal in order to extend the transmission distance. Available for both analog and digital signals, it is used extensively in long distance transmission. It is also used to tie two LANs of the same type together. Repeaters work at layer 1 of the OSI model. See *bridge* and *router*.

(2) The term may also refer to a multiport repeater, which is a hub in a 10BaseT network.

**repetitive brain injury**    A condition that affects tech support and customer service personnel that have to answer the same question over and over again. See *RSI*.

**replication**    In database management, the ability to keep distributed databases synchronized by routinely copying the entire database or subsets of the database to other servers in the network.

There are various replication methods. Primary site replication maintains the master copy of the data in one site and sends read-only copies to the other sites. In a workflow environment, the master copy can move from one site to another. This is called "shared replication" or "transferred ownership replication." In symmetric replication, also called "update-anywhere" or "peer-to-peer replication," each site can receive updates, and all other sites are then updated. Failover replication, or hot backup, maintains an up-to-date copy of the data at a different site for backup. See *distributed database* and *mirroring*.

**report**    A printed or microfilmed collection of facts and figures with page numbers and page headings. See *report writer* and *query*.

**report file**    A file that describes how a report is printed.

**report format**    The layout of a report showing page and column headers, page numbers and totals.

**report generator**    Same as *report writer*.

**R**

**report writer**    Software that prints a report based on a description of its layout. As a stand-alone program or part of a DBMS or file manager, it can sort selected records into a new sequence for printing. It may also print standard mailing labels.

A report is described by entering text for the page header, and stating the position of the print columns (data fields) and which ones are totaled or subtotaled. Once created, the description is stored in a report file for future use.

Developed in the early 1970s, report writers (report generators) were the precursor to query languages and were the first programs to generate computer output without having to be programmed.

**repository**    (1) A database of information about applications software that includes author, data elements, inputs, processes, outputs and interrelationships. A repository is used in a CASE or application development system in order to identify objects and business rules for reuse. It may also be designed to integrate third-party CASE products.

(2) A database of digital certificate information. The repository is maintained by the certification authority (CA) and is queried to find out if a certificate is valid, has expired or has been revoked. See *CA* and *PKI*.

**reproducer**    An early tabulating machine that duplicated punched cards.

**reprographics**    Duplicating printed materials using various kinds of printing presses and high-speed copiers.

**repurpose**    To change the media format, for example, to go from print to online.

**Requester**    See *redirector*.

**resampling**    Reducing or increasing the number of pixels in an image to change its resolution without changing the print size. When resampling is turned off, changing the number of pixels changes the print size.

**reserved word**    A verb or noun in a programming or command language that is part of the native language.

**reset button**    A computer button or key that reboots the computer. All current activities are stopped cold, and any data in memory is lost. On a printer, the reset button clears the printer's memory and readies it to accept new data.

**residential gateway**    (1) A device that connects multiple computers in the home to a single Internet connection. (2) A device that connects all internal home networks (telephone, LAN, cable TV, security, etc.) to their external counterparts.

**resident module**    The part of a program that must remain in memory at all times. Instructions and data that stay in memory can be accessed instantly.

**resident program**    A program that remains in memory at all times. See *TSR*.

**resident protection**    An antivirus or similar program that is currently resident in memory.

**resistor**    An electronic component that resists the flow of current in an electronic circuit.

**resolution**    (1) The degree of sharpness of a displayed or printed character or image. On screen, resolution is expressed as a matrix of dots. For example, the VGA resolution of 640×480 means 640 dots (pixels) across each of the 480 lines. Sometimes the number of colors are added to the spec; for example, 640×480×16 or 640×480×256. The same resolution looks sharper on a small screen than a larger one. See *how to select a PC display system* and *PC display modes*.

For printers and scanners, resolution is expressed as the number of dots per linear inch. 300 dpi means 300×300, or 90,000 dots per square inch. Laser printers and plotters have resolutions from 300 to 1,000 dpi and more, whereas most display screens provide less than 100 dpi. That means jagged lines on screen may smooth out when they print. Scanners have both an optical (physical) resolution and an interpolated resolution, which is computed (see *scanner*). See *lines of resolution*.

(2) The number of bits used to record the value of a sample in a digitized signal. See *sampling rate*.

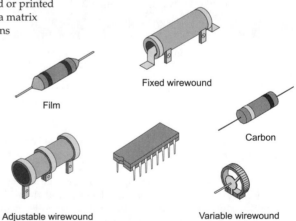

Film

Fixed wirewound

Carbon

Adjustable wirewound

Variable wirewound

**Resistors**
There are a wide variety of resistors in use. They can also be built into the circuits of the chip.

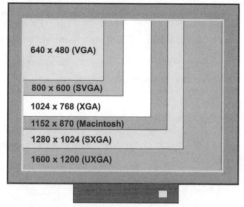

**The aspect ratio of most computer monitors is 4:3.**

640 x 480 (VGA)

800 x 600 (SVGA)

1024 x 768 (XGA)

1152 x 870 (Macintosh)

1280 x 1024 (SXGA)

1600 x 1200 (UXGA)

**Screen Resolutions**
These are common screen resolutions. Higher resolutions are available for demanding applications such as document imaging. The higher the resolution, the more information (pixels) can be displayed on screen at one time.

**Disk Mirroring**

| RESOLUTION | NUMBER OF COLORS | | | |
|---|---|---|---|---|
| | 16 (4 bit) | 256 (8 bit) | 65K (16 bit) | 16M (24 bit) |
| 640 x 480 | .5 | .5 | 1 | 2 |
| 800 x 600 | .5 | 1 | 2 | 2 |
| 1024 x 768 | 1 | 1 | 2 | 4 |
| 1152 x 870 | 1 | 2 | 2 | 4 |
| 1280 x 1024 | 1 | 2 | 4 | 4 |
| 1600 x 1200 | 2 | 2 | 4 | 8 |

REQUIRED DISPLAY ADAPTER MEMORY (MB)

**Memory Requirements**
The higher the resolution and the more colors desired, the more memory required by the display adapter to lay out the image.

**resolve**   To change, transform or solve a problem. The phrase "external references are resolved" refers to determining the addresses that link modules together—that is, solving the unknown links. See *address resolution*.

**resolver**   The client part of a DNS name service. The resolver queries the name server to turn a name into an IP address. See *DNS*.

**resource**   One element of hardware, software or data that is part of a larger system. For example, network resources are the available servers and printers in the network. Software resources can be programs, utilities or even smaller elements within a program. Data resources are the files and databases that can be accessed.

**resource compiler**   In a graphical interface (GUI), software that converts and links a graphical resources (menu, dialog box, icon, font, etc.) into the executable program.

**resource discovery**   The ability for software to automatically determine what a resource is and what it contains. See *Dublin Core* and *XML*.

**resource fork**   The resource part of a Macintosh file. For example, in a text document, it contains format codes with offsets into the text in the data fork. In a program, it contains executable code, menus, windows, dialog boxes, buttons, fonts and icons.

**resource manager**   (1) Software that keeps track of the available hardware and/or software components for a system, project or application. Refers to a variety of applications, all of which are specialized for many different purposes. See *resource*.

(2) The component within a database management system (DBMS) or a third-party utility that manages the state of a transaction. The transaction manager (TP monitor) communicates with the resource managers to apply the transaction. If a part of a transaction fails, the resource managers are informed to restore the previous status of their databases.

(3) Software that manages resources in a network. See *Cisco Resource Manager*.

**R**

**resource requirements**   The components of a system that are required by software or hardware. It refers to resources that have finite limits, such as memory and disk. In a PC, it may also refer to the resources required to install a new peripheral device, namely, IRQs, DMA channels, I/O addresses and memory addresses. See *how to install a PC peripheral*.

**response time**   The time it takes for the computer to comply with a user's request, such as looking up a customer record.

**restart**   To resume computer opertion after a planned or unplanned termination. See *boot*, *warm boot* and *checkpoint/restart*.

**restricted function**   A computer or operating system function that cannot be used by an application program.

**retrieve**   To call up data that has been stored in a computer system. When a user queries a database, the data is retrieved into the computer first and then transmitted to the screen.

**return**   In programming, upon completion of a routine or function, to go back to the point in the program that called this operation. See also *return key*.

**RETURN key**   Also called the ENTER key, the keyboard key used to signal the end of a line of data or the end of a command. In word processing, RETURN is pressed at the end of a paragraph, and a return code is inserted into the text at that point. See *CR*.

**reusability**   The ability to use all or the greater part of the same programming code or system design in another application.

**RETURN (ENTER) Key Placement**
The correct placement of the RETURN key next to the quote key is of considerable importance to the touch typist.

**reverse DNS**   (Reverse Domain Name System)  Name resolution software that looks up an IP address to obtain a domain name. It performs the opposite function of the DNS server, which turns names into IP addresses. Reverse DNS is used by an ISP to log incoming traffic by domain name for statistical purposes, enabling high-level domains (.com, .net, etc.) and specific domains (aol.com, ibm.com, etc.) to be counted. Reverse DNS is also used to determine the authenticity of a domain, for example, whether an e-mail really is coming from the same domain in the from field. See *DNS*.

**reverse engineer**   To isolate the components of a completed system. When a chip is reverse engineered, all the individual circuits that make up the chip are identified. Source code can be reverse engineered into design models or specifications. Machine language can be reversed into assembly langauge (see *disassembler*).

**reverse link**   See *forward link*.

**reverse polish notation**   A mathematical expression in which the numbers precede the operation. For example, $2 + 2$ would be expressed as **2 2 +**, and $10 - 3 * 4$ would be **10 3 4 * −**. See *FORTH*.

**reverse proxy cache**   Also known as a "server accelerator," it is a cache server that resides at the Web site or ISP rather than at the user's site. All Web pages sent back to the browser move through and are stored on the reverse proxy cache. If the next request for a Web page has already been stored in the cache, it is retrieved locally, which eliminates upstream traffic for that file. See *proxy cache* and *Web cache*.

**reverse video**   A display mode used to highlight characters on screen. For example, if the normal display mode is black on white, reverse video would be white on black.

**revision level**   See *version number*.

**rewritable**   Refers to storage media that can be written, erased and rewritten many times. Magnetic disks and tapes and magneto-optic disks are examples. See *write once*.

**REXX**    (REstructured EXtended eXecutor) An IBM mainframe structured programming language that runs under VM/CMS and MVS/TSO. It can be used as a general-purpose macro language that sends commands to application programs and to the operating systems. REXX is also included in OS/2 Version 2.0.

The following REXX example converts Fahrenheit to Celsius:

```
Say "Enter Fahrenheit "
Pull FAHR
Say "Celsius is " (FAHR - 32) * (5 / 9)
```

**RF**    (Radio Frequency) The range of electromagnetic frequencies above the audio range and below visible light. All broadcast transmission, from AM radio to satellites, falls into this range, which is between 30 kHz and 300 GHz. See *RF modulation*.

**RFC**    (Request For Comments) A document that describes the specifications for a recommended technology. RFCs are used by the Internet Engineering Task Force (IETF) and other standards bodies. First used during the creation of the ARPAnet protocols in the 1970s, the IETF has published more than 2,500 RFCs, all of which can be viewed at www.ietf.org/rfc. See *ARPAnet*.

**RFI**    (Radio Frequency Interference) High-frequency electromagnetic waves that eminate from electronic devices such as chips.

**RFID**    (Radio Frequency IDentification) A data collection technology that uses electronic tags to store identification data and a wireless transmission method to capture the data. The tag, which is also known as an electronic label, transponder or code plate, gets its power from the gun used to read the data.

**RF modulation**    The transmission of a signal through a carrier frequency. In order to connect to a TV's antenna input, some home computers and all VCRs provide RF modulation of a TV channel, usually Channel 3 or 4. See *FCC class*.

**RFP**    (Request For Proposal) A document that invites a vendor to submit a bid for hardware, software and/or services. It may provide a general or very detailed specification of the system.

**RFS**    (Remote File System) A distributed file system for UNIX computers introduced by AT&T in 1986 with UNIX System V Release 3.0. It is similar to Sun's NFS, but only for UNIX systems.

**RF shielding**    A material that prohibits electromagnetic radiation from penetrating it. Personal computers and electronic devices used in the home must meet U.S. government standards for electromagnetic interference.

**R**

**RFT**    See *DCA*.

**RGB**    (Red Green Blue) The color model used for generating video on a display screen. It displays colors as varying intensities of red, green and blue dots. When all three are turned on high, white is produced. As intensities are equally lowered, shades of gray are derived. The base color of the screen appears when all dots are off. See *colors*.

**RGB color**    The maximum number of colors that can be used for a color image in the computer, which is typically 24-bit color. Contrast with *color palette*. See *24-bit color*.

**RGB monitor**    (1) A video display screen that requires separate red, green and blue signals from the computer. It generates a better image than composite signals (TV), which merge the three colors together. It comes in both analog and digital varieties.

(2) Sometimes refers to a CGA monitor that accepts digital RGB signals.

**Rhapsody**    The code name given to Apple's next-generation operating system, which eventually turned into Mac OS X. Rhapsody was a UNIX–based operating system that supported the Mac OS (Blue Box) and OpenStep (Yellow Box) from NeXT. See *Mac OS X*, *Yellow Box* and *NeXT*.

**RIAA**    (Recording Industry Association of America, Washington, DC, www.riaa.com)  A membership association of music recording companies. Its goal is to promote the record label industry and protect the rights of copyright owners. It was a major contributor to the SDMI digital distribution system. Spanning decades, RIAA awards (Gold, Platinum, etc.) for successful albums are coveted marks of achievementhas by musical artists. IFPI (International Federation of the Phonographic Industry) is the European counterpart to RIAA (www.ifpi.org). See *SDMI*.

**ribbon cable**    A thin, flat, multiconductor cable that is widely used in electronic systems; for example, to interconnect peripheral devices to the computer internally.

**rich e-mail**    E-mail messages annotated with graphics, audio and video. See *rich media* and *rich text*.

**rich media**    Information that consists of any combination of graphics, audio, video and animation, which is more storage and bandwidth intensive than ordinary text. See *rich text*.

**rich text**    (1) Text that includes formatting commands for page layout such as fonts, bold, underline, italic, etc. It may also refer to a multimedia document that can include graphics, audio and video. See *rich media*.

(2) Text in Microsoft's RTF format. See *RTF*.

**Ricochet**    A wireless Internet service from Metricom, Inc., Los Gatos, CA (www.metricom.com). It uses appoximately 100 small "microcell" radio transceivers attached to utility poles within a 20-square mile cell. Each cell has one wired access point, which is a T1, frame relay connection to the Internet. Each microcell bounces digital signals from the mobile devices to other microcells, and eventually to its wired access point. The transceivers in this MicroCellular Data Network (MCDN) employ 162 frequency-hopping channels in the 902–928MHz band from user to microcell. The 2.4GHz band is used in the rest of the system, and licensed spectrum in the 2.3GHz band is used for its high-speed service. Rocochet modems attach to laptops and other handhelds via the serial port.

Ricochet 1 provides 28.8 Kbps service with access primarily to stationary users; while Ricochet 2, introduced in 2000, offers 128 Kbps for the commuter in transit. First deployed in Washington, DC, Seattle and Silicon Valley, coverage in more than 40 urban areas is expected by 2002. See *CDPD*.

**RIFF**    (1) (Resource Interchange File Format)  A file format from Microsoft that can be used to create composite files from existing AVI, WAV, MIDI and other multimedia formats.

(2) An earlier bitmapped graphics format developed for Letraset's ImageStudio and Ready, Set, Go programs for the Macintosh.

**right click**    To press the right button on the mouse and release it. The right mouse button can be used for anything, but is typically an ancillary function, while the left mouse button is used for primary functions. For example, in Windows, the right mouse button lets you view the properties (defaults, current status, etc.) of a file, folder or other object.

**right justify**    Same as *flush right*.

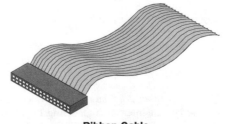

**Ribbon Cable**
Ribbon cables are widely used to connect peripherals and other electronic components internally. They are rarely used outside of the case or cabinet.

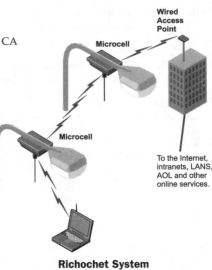

**Richochet System**
The microcells "ricochet" signals from the mobile device to other microcells and eventually to the wired access point that connects to the land-based Internet. There is one wired access point and about 100 microcells within a 20-square mile area.

**right-reading**    In printing, a photographic image that looks the same as the original. See *offset press*. Contrast with *wrong-reading*.

**rightsizing**    Selecting a computer system, whether micro, mini or mainframe, that best meets the needs of the application.

**rigid disk**    Same as *hard disk*.

**RIMM**    See *RDRAM*.

**ring**    One stage or level in a set of prioritized stages or levels. Ring 0 is the lowest level, and system functions and utilities communicate with the operating system kernel at this most privileged ring. Applications access the operating system at the higher ring 3, and fewer instructions are available at this level. Although Intel has defined rings 1 and 2, they are rarely used.

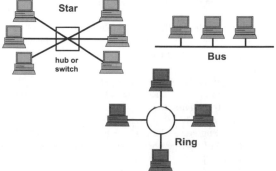

**ring network**    A communications network that connects terminals and computers in a continuous loop.

**RIP**    (1) (Raster Image Processor) The hardware and/or software that rasterizes an image for display or printing. RIPs are designed to rasterize a specific type of data, such as PostScript or vector graphics images, as well as different kinds of raster data. As desktop computers become more powerful, software RIPs become more appealing than hardware RIPs. Software can be upgraded more easily than hardware, and the operation can be speeded up by installing the software RIP in a faster CPU. See *rasterize*.

(2) (Routing Information Protocol) A simple routing protocol that is part of the TCP/IP protocol suite. It determines a route based on the smallest hop count between source and destination. RIP is a distance vector protocol that routinely broadcasts routing information to its neighboring routers and is known to waste bandwidth. AppleTalk, DECnet, TCP/IP, NetWare and VINES all use incompatible versions of RIP. See *routing protocol*.

(3) (Remote Imaging Protocol) A graphics format from TeleGrafix Communications, Inc., Winchester, VA (www.telegrafx.com), designed for transmitting graphics over low-speed lines. Using a communications program that supports RIP enables graphical interfaces to be used on a BBS with respectable performance via modem.

**ripper**    Software that extracts raw audio data from a music CD. See *digital audio extraction* and *MP3*.

**ripping**    (1) Using a raster image processor, which prepares a page for display or printing. See *RIP*.

(2) Extracting the digital data from an audio CD. See *digital audio extraction*.

**RISC**    (Reduced Instruction Set Computer) A computer architecture that reduces chip complexity by using simpler instructions. RISC compilers have to generate software routines to perform complex instructions that were previously done in hardware by CISC computers. In RISC, the microcode layer and associated overhead is eliminated.

RISC keeps instruction size constant, bans the indirect addressing mode and retains only those instructions that can be overlapped and made to execute in one machine cycle or less. The RISC chip is faster than its CISC counterpart and is designed and built more economically.

**RISC System/6000**    See *RS/6000*.

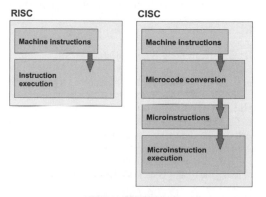

**RISC Versus CISC**
The RISC machine executes instructions faster because it doesn't have to go through a microcode conversion layer. The RISC compiler does more work than the CISC compiler. It has to generate routines using simpler instructions that would normally be performed by a single, complex instruction in the CISC computer.

**riser card**  An expansion card that is used to physically extend a slot for a chip or card in a fully loaded computer to make room to plug it in. It may also refer to a card that contains several slots used in low-profile, space-saving cabinets. The cards are plugged into the riser card and reside parallel with the motherboard.

Intel has used the term to define an expansion card for audio and modem functions that has nothing to do with extending a card or saving space. See *AMR*.

**RJ-11**  (Registered Jack-11) A telephone connector that holds up to four wires. The RJ-11 is the common connector used to plug the handset into the telephone and the telphone into the wall. A six-wire variation of RJ-11 is also used.

**RJ-21**  (Registered Jack-21) An Ethernet cable that uses a 50-pin Telco connector on one end and branches out to 12 RJ-45 connectors on the other. See *50-pin Telco connector*.

**RJ-45**  (Registered Jack-45) A telephone connector that holds up to eight wires. RJ-45 plugs and sockets are used in Ethernet and Token Ring Type 3 devices. See *RJ-48*.

**RJ-48**  (Registered Jack-48) A telephone connector that holds up to eight wires. It uses the same plug and socket as RJ-45 but has different pinouts. RJ-48C is commonly used for T1 lines and uses pins 1, 2, 4 and 5. RJ-48X is a variation of RJ-48C that contains shorting blocks in the jack so that a loopback is created for troubleshooting when unplugged. RJ-48S uses pins 1, 2, 7 and 8, and is commonly used for 56 Kbps digital lines (DDS). See *RJ-45*.

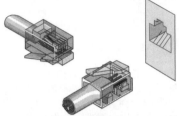

**RJ-11 Connectors**
Four-wire RJ-11 connectors are used for telephone handsets and wall outlets. There is also a six-wire variation.

**Variations of RJ-45**
These are the variations of RJ-45 pins and wire colors.

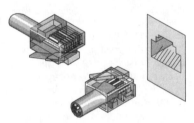

**RJ-45 Connectors**
Eight-wire RJ-45 connectors are used with Ethernet and Type 3 Token Ring networks.

**RJE**  (Remote Job Entry) Transmitting batches of transactions from a remote terminal or computer. The receiving computer processes the data and may transmit the results back to the RJE site for printing. RJE hardware at remote sites can employ teleprinters with disk or tape storage, or complete computer systems.

**RL**  Digispeak for "real life."

**RLE**  (Run Length Encoding) A simple data compression method that converts a run of identical characters into a code. A rough example might be []36*, where [] is a code and 36* means 36 *'s follow. Microsoft includes an RLE codec in Video for Windows; however, other compression methods are far superior for full-motion video.

**RLL**  (Run Length Limited) An encoding method commonly used on magnetic disks, including RLL, IDE, SCSI, ESDI, SMD and IPI interfaces. The actual number of bits recorded on the disk is greater than the data bits. Earlier drives inserted extra bits into the data stream so there was more space between signals when reading the data back. As electronics improve, fewer extra bits are inserted, and the ratio of data bits to recorded bits becomes greater.

The "run length" is the number of consecutive 0s before a 1 bit is recorded. For example, RLL 1,7 means there must be at least one 0 between every 1, and the 7 means a maximum of eight time periods between flux transitions. See *hard disk*.

**rlogin**  (Remote LOGIN) A UNIX command that allows users to remotely log onto a server in the network as if they were at a terminal directly connected to that computer. rlogin is similar to the Telnet command, except that rlogin also passes information to the server about the type of client machine, or terminal, used. See *rsh*.

**RMA**  (RealMedia Architecture) See *RealMedia*.

**RMI** (Remote Method Invocation) A standard from Sun for distributed objects written in Java. RMI is a remote procedure call (RPC), which allows Java objects (software components) stored in the network to be run remotely. Unlike CORBA and DCOM objects, which can be developed in different languages, RMI is designed for objects written only in Java. See *RMI over IIOP* and *EJB*.

**RMI over IIOP** (Remote Method Invocation over Internet Inter-ORB Protocol) An extension to Sun's RMI procedure call that enables Java programs to execute CORBA objects. It allows Java access to non-Java processes via CORBA. See *RMI*.

**RMON** (Remote MONitoring) Extensions to the Simple Network Management Protocol (SNMP) that provide comprehensive network monitoring capabilities. In standard SNMP, the device has to be queried to obtain information. RMON is proactive and can set alarms on a variety of traffic conditions, including specific types of errors. RMON2 can also monitor the kinds of application traffic that flow through the network. The full RMON capabilities are very comprehensive, and generally only portions of it are placed into routers and other network devices. See *SNMP*.

**RMON probe** A network device that analyzes RMON information. The probe can monitor traffic and set an alarm when a certain condition occurs. It can be used to periodically audit traffic, as well as gather statistics that are sent to the management console. RMON probes are often placed permanently into networks.

**RMS** (1) (Record Management Services) A file management system used in VAXs.
(2) (Root Mean Square) A method used to measure electrical output in volts and watts.

**rn** (ReadNews) A newsreader for Usenet newsgroups. An enhanced version of rn that includes threads is trn. See *Usenet*.

**RNI** (Raw Native Interface) A programming interface in Microsoft's Java Virtual Machine used for calling native Windows elements such as GUI routines. RNI is Microsoft's Windows-oriented counterpart of Sun's JNI (Java Native Interface).

**RO** See *read only*.

**road warrior** A person that travels a lot with laptop and cellphone.

**roaming** The ability to use a communications device such as a cellphone or PDA, and be able to move from one cell or access point to another without losing the connection.

**RoboCAD** A CAD program from Robo Systems International, Inc., Newtown, PA, that runs under DOS and includes a wide variety of features and text functions. It provides up to 256 colors and layers, has two drawing pages and a scratch pad, and can transfer data to its solid modeling program. RoboCAD is noted for its performance and ease of use, and is very popular in the education market.

**robot** A stand-alone hybrid computer system that performs physical and computational activities. It is a multiple-motion device with one or more arms and joints that is capable of performing many different tasks like a human. It can be designed similar to human form, although most industrial robots don't resemble people at all.

It is used extensively in manufacturing for welding, riveting, scraping and painting. Office and consumer applications are also being developed. Robots, designed with AI, can respond to

**Huey, Dewey and Louie**
Named after Donald Duck's famous nephews, robots at this Wayne, Michigan plant apply sealant to prevent possible water leakage into the car. Huey (top) seals the drip rails while Dewey (right) seals the interior weld seams. Louie is outside of the view of this picture.
*(Image courtesy of Ford Motor Company.)*

unstructured situations. For example, specialized robots can identify objects in a pile, select the objects in the appropriate sequence and assemble them into a unit.

Robots use analog sensors for recognizing real-world objects and digital computers for their direction. Analog-to-digital converters convert temperature, motion, pressure, sound and images into binary code for the robot's computer. The computer directs the physical actions of the arms and joints by pulsing their motors. See *AIBO*.

**robotics**   The art and science of the creation and use of robots.

**robust**   Refers to software without bugs that handles abnormal conditions well. It is often said that there is no software package totally bug free. Any program can exhibit odd behavior under certain conditions, but a robust program will not lock up the computer, cause damage to data or send the user through an endless chain of dialog boxes without purpose. Whether or not a program can be totally bug free will be debated forever. See *industrial strength*.

**Computers Making Computers**
Robots, whose brains are nothing but chips, are making chips in this TI fabrication plant. *(Image courtesy of Texas Instruments, Inc.)*

**ROFL**   Digispeak for "rolling on the floor laughing."

**rogue site**   A Web site that is set up to spread a virus or collect names for spammers, or for some other illicit or repugnant purpose.

**ROLAP**   See *OLAP*.

**rollback**   A database management system feature that reverses the current transaction out of the database, returning the database to its former state. This is done when some failure interrupts a half-completed transaction.

**roll in/roll out**   A swapping technique for freeing up memory temporarily in order to perform another task. The current program or program segment is stored (rolled out) on disk, and another program is brought into (rolled in) that memory space. See *pitch-yaw-roll*.

**rollover**   A graphic element in an application or on a Web page that changes its color or shape when the pointer is moved (rolled) over it. See *JavaScript rollover*. See also *n-key rollover*.

**ROM**   (Read-Only Memory)   A memory chip that permanently stores instructions and data. Its contents are created at the time of manufacture and cannot be altered. ROM chips are used to store control routines in personal computers (ROM BIOS), peripheral controllers and other electronic equipment. They are also often the sole contents inside a cartridge that plugs into printers, video games and other systems.

When computers are used in handheld instruments, appliances, automobiles and any other such devices, the instructions for their routines are generally stored in ROM chips or some other non-volatile chip, such as a PROM or EPROM. Instructions may also be stored in a ROM section within a general-purpose computer on a chip. See *PROM*, *EPROM* and *EEPROM*. Contrast with *RAM*.

**ROMable**   Machine language capable of being programmed into a ROM chip. Being "read-only," the chip cannot be updated, and ROMable programs must use RAM or disk for holding changing data.

**roman type**   The normal typography style in which the vertical lines of the chracters are upright. Contrast with italics, which uses slanted lines.

**ROM BIOS**   (ROM Basic Input/Output System)   A PC's BIOS stored in a ROM chip. The first BIOSs were put in ROMs, but later BIOSs have come on flash memory chips, which can be updated in place. See *BIOS*.

**ROM card**   A credit card–sized module that contains permanent software or data. See *memory card*.

**ROM emulator**    A circuit that helps debug a ROM chip by simulating the ROM with RAM. The RAM circuit plugs into the ROM socket. Since RAM can be written over, whereas ROM cannot, programming changes can be made easily.

**root**    (1) The top level of a hierarchy. See *root directory* and *root domain*.
(2) A person with unlimited access privileges, who can perform any and all operations on the computer. Also called "superuser."

**root directory**    In hierarchical file systems, the starting point in the hierarchy. When the computer is first started, the root directory is the current directory. Access to directories in the hierarchy requires naming the directories that are in its path.
In DOS and Windows, the command-line symbol for the root directory is a backslash (\). In UNIX, it is a slash (/). See *path*, **DOS Path** and **DOS ABCs**.

**root domain**    The highest level domain name of an organization. For example, **mycompany.com** is the root domain of **www.mycompany.com**, which is a subdomain. Root domain is also synonymous with "second level domain," where the **.com** would be the top-level domain. Which term is used depends on the environment and application being referenced. See *subdomain* and *Internet domain name*.

**root server**    One of 13 domain name servers that contain the top-level domains (TLDs). Located throughout the world, they are maintained by various organizations. See *DNS*.

**ROP**    (1) (Raster Operation) An instruction that manipulates the bits of a bitmapped image in some manner.
(2) (RISC Operation) An instruction in a RISC processor.

**RosettaNet**    (RosettaNet, Santa Ana, CA, www.rosettanet.org) A non-profit organization founded in 1998 that is devoted to standardizing interfaces for electronic commerce between supply chain partners. Its goal is to create Partner Interface Processes, which provide an exchange framework along with the defined fields and labels for different types of transactions.

**rot13**    A simple cryptography system that substitutes each letter with the 13th letter down the alphabet, rotating back to the beginning. The algorithm that encodes also decodes, because there are 26 letters in the alphabet. It is used to keep messages from the casual observer.

**rotating ad**    An advertisement on a Web page that comes from a list of ads and changes each time the page is requested. If you were to reload the same page you are viewing, you would see the next ad in the list. Contrast with *static ad*.

**rotational delay**    The amount of time it takes for the disk to rotate until the required location on the disk reaches the read/write head.

**RO terminal**    (Receive Only terminal) A printing device only (no keyboard).

**rotoscope**    To paint, draw or overlay images onto frames in a movie.

**round robin**    Continuously repeating sequence, such as the polling of a series of terminals, one after the other, over and over again.

**routable protocol**    A communications protocol that contains a network address as well as a device address, allowing data to be routed from one network to another. Examples of routable protocols are SNA, OSI, TCP/IP, XNS, IPX, AppleTalk and DECnet. Contrast with *non-routable protocol*. See *routing protocol*.

**route dampening**    A feature in the BGP router protocol that identifies flapping routes by adding a penalty value to the route each time it flaps (changes between available and unavailable). When the penalty reaches a preset limit, the route is no longer advertised to other routers as a valid path. See *BGP*.

R

**route miles**   The number of miles that are spanned by a telecommunications network. It does not include combined wire mileage due to multiple wires or fibers within a single cable or by overlapping segments, just the total geographic distance between cities or other terminal points.

**router**   A device that forwards data packets from one local area network (LAN) or wide area network (WAN) to another. Based on routing tables and routing protocols, routers read the network address in each transmitted frame and make a decision on how to send it based on the most expedient route (traffic load, line costs, speed, bad lines, etc.). Routers work at layer 3 in the protocol stack,

**Between LANs**
Routers filter traffic from one LAN segment (subnet) to another in order to balance traffic and enforce policy management.

**Remote Access**
Routers are widely used for remote access changing the LAN frames into the data structures required of the wide area transport.

whereas bridges and switches work at the layer 2.

Routers are used to segment LANs in order to balance traffic within workgroups, and to filter traffic for security purposes and policy management. Routers are also used at the edge of the network to connect remote offices. Multiprotocol routers support several protocols such as IP, IPX, AppleTalk and DECnet.

Routers can only route a message that is transmitted by a routable protocol such as IP or IPX. Messages in non-routable protocols, such as NetBIOS and LAT, cannot be routed, but they can be transferred from LAN to LAN via a bridge. Because routers have to inspect the network address in the protocol, they do more processing and add more overhead than a bridge or switch, which both work at the data link (MAC) layer.

Most routers are specialized computers that are optimized for communications; however, router functions can also be implemented by adding routing software to a file server. NetWare, for example, includes routing software. The NetWare operating system can route from one subnetwork to another if each one is connected to its own network adapter (NIC) in the server. The major router vendors are Cisco Systems and Nortel Networks.

Routers serve as an internet backbone, interconnecting all networks in the enterprise. This architecture strings several routers together via a high-speed LAN topology such as Fast Ethernet or Gigabit Ethernet. Routers are also the backbone of "the" Internet, which spans the planet.

Another approach within an enterprise is the collapsed backbone, which uses a single router with a high-speed backplane to connect the subnets, making network management simpler and improving performance.

In older Novell terminology, a router is a network-layer bridge. Routers also used to be called "gateways." For more understanding of how the network layer 3 works within the protocol stack, see *TCP/IP ABCs*. See *LAN, layer 3 switch, route server, router cluster* and *routing protocol*.

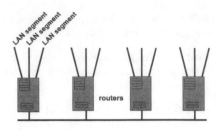

**Distributed Router Backbone**
Many early networks used a series of routers networked together as a LAN backbone. Typically a router was located on each floor of the building. As more users are added to each segment, traffic can become congested in the shared backbone.

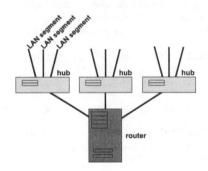

**Collapsed Backbone**
The collapsed backbone router uses a high-speed backplane to move packets quickly from one port to another. By centralizing the routing in one place, maintenance and troubleshooting is reduced.

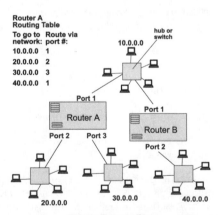

**Route Forwarding**
Routers use routing tables to make forwarding decisions. Although this is about as simplistic an example as it gets, routing tables become very complex. Static routing uses fixed tables, but dynamic routing uses routing protocols that let routers exchange data with each other.

**router cache**    The database of addresses and forwarding information stored in a router. See *router* and *cache*.

**router cluster**    Two or more routers grouped together to provide any combination of hardware redundancy, service redundancy, load balancing and increased speed. The speed enhancement is accomplished by bonding the routers together. For example, three separate routers—such as T1, T3, E1, E3 or wireless—can be combined to provide three times the speed, reliability and redundancy. Although failover can be accomplished in routers through software, all of the features just mentioned either require additional hardware within the router or an external router cluster device.

**router droppings**    The cryptic and somewhat repugnant text that is inserted into e-mail messages that cannot reach their destination.

**router protocol**    See *routing protocol*.

**router table**    See *routing table*.

**route server**    A server that contains a description of a large number of network routes. A route server typically provides a more global view of a geographic area than a router, which is only aware of the destinations that it can reach. See *router* and *routing protocol*.

**routine**    A set of instructions that perform a task. Same as *subroutine*, *module*, *procedure* and *function*.

**routing**    Forwarding data to its destination. See *router*, *intermediate node routing* and *DNS*.

**routing protocol**    A formula used by routers to determine the appropriate path onto which data should be forwarded. The routing protocol also specifies how routers report changes and share information with the other routers in the network that they can reach. A routing protocol allows the network to dynamically adjust to changing conditions; otherwise, all routing decisions have to be predetermined and remain static. See *router*, *routing table*, *RIP*, *OSPF*, *IGRP*, *EGP* and *BGP*.

**routing switch**    See *layer 3 switch*.

**routing table**    A database in a router that contains the current network topology. See *routing protocol*.

**RPC**    (Remote Procedure Call) A programming interface that allows one program to use the services of another program in a remote machine. The calling program sends a message and data to the remote program, which is executed, and results are passed back to the calling program.

This type of interface is designed to allow programs to communicate with each another while freeing the programmer from the nitty gritty networking details. Sun developed the RPC concept as part of its Open Network Computing (ONC) architecture, and a similar type of RPC is used in The Open Group's DCE architecture. Microsoft's DCOM was modeled after the RPC in DCE. CORBA also provides this capability, but provides a comprehensive messaging environment that is designed to support multiple programming languages and platforms.

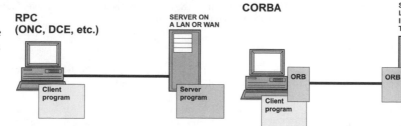

**RPCs vs. CORBA**
The concept may be the same (one program calls another to execute some service), but RPCs function more like a program calling a function in the same machine, only it's done remotely. RPCs also tend to be language and platform specific.
CORBA provides a complete messaging environment that Object Request Broker (ORB) software manages at both ends of the communication.

**RPG**    (Report Program Generator)  One of the first program generators designed for business reports, introduced in 1964 by IBM. In 1970, RPG II added enhancements that made it a mainstay programming language for business applications on IBM's System/3x midrange computers. RPG III and RPG IV added more enhancements and have been widely used on the AS/400. RPGLE added the "Integrated Language Environment (ILE)," which enables C, Java and other modules to be integrated into the program.

Until RPGLE, all processing statements were written in strict columnar format. The following RPGLE example changes Fahrenheit to Celsius. The A lines are Data Description Specs (DDS) code. They define a display file and are compiled separately. The F line links the processing code (C lines) to the A lines:

```
A                                 DSPSIZ(24 80 *DS3)
A    R FHEITR
A                                 CA03(03 'End')
A                         6 18'Enter Fahrenheit:'
A    FRHEIT    3Y  0B     6 42DSPATR(PC)
A                                 EDTCDE(J)
A                         9 18'Celsius is:'
A    CGRADE    3Y  00     9 42DSPATR(PC)
A                                 EDTCDE(J)
A                        23  8'F3=End'


FFheitd   CF   E       Workstn

C    *IN03    DoWEq     *Off
C             ExFmt     Fheitr
C             Eval      CGrade = 0
C             Eval      CGrade = ((Frheit-32)*5)/9
C*            ExFmt     Fheitr
C             EndDo
C             Seton                    LR
```

**RPGLE**    (RPG with Integrated Language Environment)  This later version of RPGLE is sometimes just called "ILE." See *RPG*.

**rpm**    (Revolutions Per Minute)  The measurement of the rotational speed of a disk drive. Floppy disks rotate at 300 rpm, while hard disks rotate from 2,400 to 3,600 rpm and more.

**RPN**    See *reverse polish notation*.

**RPQ**    (Request for Price Quotation)  A document that requests a price for hardware, software or services to solve a specific problem. It is created by the customer and delivered to the vendor.

**RRAS**    (Routing and Remote Access Service)  Software routing and remote access capability in Windows NT. RRAS combines RAS (Remote Access Service) and Multi-Protocol Routing with additional capabilities. including packet filtering, demand dial routing and OSPF support.

**RS-170**    An NTSC standard for composite video signals.

**RS-232**    (Recommended Standard-232)  A TIA/EIA standard for serial transmission between computers and peripheral devices (modem, mouse, etc.). Using a 25-pin DB-25 or 9-pin DB-9 connector, its normal cable limitation of 50 feet can be extended to several hundred feet with high-quality cable.

RS-232 defines the purpose and signal timing for each of the 25 lines; however, many applications use less than a dozen. RS-232 transmits positive voltage for a 0 bit, negative voltage for a 1. In 1984, this interface was officially renamed TIA/EIA-232-E standard (E is the current revision, 1991), although most people still call it RS-232.

**RS-422**    A TIA/EIA standard for serial interfaces that extend distances and speeds beyond RS-232. RS-422 is a balanced system requiring more wire pairs than its RS-423 counterpart and is intended for use in multipoint lines. Both use either a 37-pin connector defined by RS-449 or a 25-pin connector defined by RS-530.

RS-449 and RS-530 specify the pin definitions for RS-422 and RS-423. RS-422/423 specify electrical and timing characteristics. See *RS-530*.

**RS-423**    See *RS-422*.

**RS-449**    Defines a 37-pin connector for RS-422 and RS-423 circuits.

**RS-485**    A TIA/EIA standard for multipoint communications lines. It can be implemented with as little as a wire block with four screws or with DB-9 or DB-37 connectors. By using lower-impedance drivers and receivers, RS-485 allows more nodes per line than RS-422.

**RS-530**    Defines a 25-pin connector for RS-422 and RS-423 circuits. It allows for higher speed transmission up to 2Mbits/sec over the same DB-25 connector used in RS-232, but is not compatible with it. See *RS-422*.

**RS/6000**    (RISC System/6000) A family of RISC-based workstations and servers from IBM that use the AIX (UNIX) operating system. They are widely used in scientific, industrial and commercial applications. Introduced in 1990, the first RS/6000s used IBM's POWER chip. Starting in 1993, the line began to migrate to the PowerPC chip, which is a single-chip version of the POWER architecture. Also initially supporting the MicroChannel bus, it later switched to PCI. In 2000, IBM changed the name of RS/6000 servers to "pSeries eservers" (see *IBM server series*).

**RSA**    (1) (Rural Service Area) See *MSA*.
(2) (Rivest-Shamir-Adleman) A highly secure cryptography method by RSA Data Security, Inc., Redwood City, CA (www.rsa.com). It uses a two-part key. The private key is kept by the owner; the public key is published.

Data is encrypted by using the recipient's public key, which can only be decrypted by the recipient's private key. RSA is very computation intensive, thus it is often used to create a digital envelope that holds an RSA-encrypted DES key and DES-encrypted data. This method encrypts the secret DES key so that it can be transmitted over the network, but encrypts and decrypts the actual message using the much faster DES algorithm.

RSA is also used for authentication by creating a digital signature. In this case, the sender's private key is used for encryption, and the sender's public key is used for decryption. See *digital signature*.

The RSA algorithm is also implemented in hardware. As RSA chips get faster, RSA encoding and decoding add less overhead to the operation. See *cryptography* and *digital certificate*.

**RSAC**    (Recreational Software Advisory Council, Washington, DC, www.rsac.org) A non-profit organization that rates game software and online content. It supports the PICS rating system. See *PICS*.

**An Early RS/6000**
This POWERSERVER 590 was one of the many models introduced in IBM's RS/6000 series, which are used in scientific, industrial and commercial applications. *(Image courtesy of International Business Machines Corporation. Unauthorized use not permitted.)*

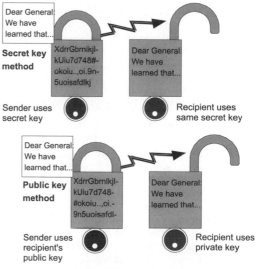

**Secret Key vs. Public Key**
The secret method uses the same key to encrypt and decrypt. The problem is transmitting the key to someone so they can use it. The public key method uses two keys—one kept secret and never transmitted, and the other made public. Sometimes the public key method is used to send the secret key of the private method, and then the message is sent using the private key method.

**RSCS**    (Remote Spooling Communications Subsystem) Software that provides batch communications for IBM's VM operating system. It accepts data from remote batch terminals, executes them on a priority basis and transmits the results back to the terminals. The RSCS counterpart in MVS is called "JES." Contrast with *CMS*, which provides interactive communications for VM.

**RSDL**    (Reverse Spiral Dual Layer) A technique used with dual-layer DVD discs that allows the end of the first layer to seamlessly connect to the second layer. The first layer is recorded from the inside out, and the second layer is recorded from the outside in.

**rsh**    (Remote SHell) A UNIX command that enables a user to remotely log on to a server on the network and pass commands to it. It is similar to the rlogin command, but provides passing of command line arguments to the command interpreter on the server at the same time. rsh can be used within programs as well as from the keyboard.

**RSI**    (Repetitive Strain Injury) Ailments of the hands, neck, back and eyes due to computer use. The remedy for RSI is frequent breaks, which should include stretching or yoga postures. See *carpal tunnel syndrome* and *repetitive brain injury*.

**RSTS/E**    A PDP-11 operating system from Digital.

**RSVP**    (ReSerVation Protocol) A communications protocol that signals a router to reserve bandwidth for realtime transmission. RSVP is designed to clear a path for audio and video traffic, eliminating annoying skips and hesitations. It has been sanctioned by the IETF, because audio and video traffic is expected to increase dramatically on the Internet. See *RTP* and *COPS*.

**RSX-11**    (Resource Sharing eXtension-PDP 11) A multiuser, multitasking operating system from Digital that runs on its PDP-11 series.

**RT**    A RISC-based workstation from IBM introduced in 1986 that was superseded by the RS/6000 family.

**RT-11**    A single user, multitasking operating system from Digital that runs on its PDP-11 series.

**RTC**    See *realtime clock*.

**RTC/BIOS fix**    (RealTime Clock/BIOS fix) Refers to repairing the realtime clock and BIOS in a PC in order to make it Y2K compliant. The repair may be made by hardware or software or both.

**RTCP**    See *RTP*.

**RTF**    (Rich Text Format) A Microsoft standard for encoding formatted text and graphics. It was adapted from IBM's DCA format and supports ANSI, IBM PC and Macintosh character sets.

**RTFM**    (Read The Flaming Manual) The last resort when having a hardware or software problem! The definition of this acronym is rated G. You can figure out what it really means.

This is, of course, a sad but true state of affairs. Most people do not enjoy reading documentation manuals, because they are difficult, if not downright impossible, to understand. The online help is about the same. The reason is that technical documentation is often a last minute rush job with programmers trying to communicate to writers. At times, programmers write the documentation, which is guaranteed to perpetuate the RTFM syndrome.

Some day perhaps, the great minds in the software publishing industry will realize that if they put more time and energy into the design of the menus, buttons and explanations in the first place, they wouldn't be drowning in tech support. User interface design and technical documentation are as difficult as the programming, but this is rarely understood or appreciated.

Until that day arrives, you have several choices for problem resolution if the manual and on-screen help don't help much and all your techy friends are nowhere to be found. You can call tech support and wait on hold, which is usually on your nickel, or you can fax or e-mail your problem and wait a day or more for a reply. Or, you can look it up in one or more good books on the subject. See *user interface* and ***how to find a good computer book***.

**At Least Get a Laugh**    This problem is so pervasive that *InfoWorld* magazine decided to come up with its "Dumpy" (Documentation User's MalPractice) award for the worst documentation. Although hardly coveted, there are always an inordinate number of candidates.

**RTL**    (Register Transfer Level) A specification for a digital electronic circuit that defines how to store circuit state (data) in the registers and how to compute new values in each clock cycle. RTL sits in between behavioral-level and gate level specifications. Behavioral level defines what function the circuit is to perform, and gate level defines the actual components and interconnects. The most popular languages for writing RTL are Verilog and VHDL. See *Verilog* and *VHDL*.

**RTOS**    (RealTime Operating System) An operating system designed for use in a realtime computer system. See *realtime system*, *embedded system*, *process control* and *OS/9*.

**RTP**    (1) (Realtime Transport Protocol) An IP protocol that supports realtime transmission of voice and video. An RTP packet rides on top of UDP and includes timestamping and synchronization information in its header for proper reassembly at the receiving end. Realtime Control Protocol (RTCP) is a companion protocol that is used to maintain QoS. RTP nodes analyze network conditions and periodically send each other RTCP packets that report on network congestion. See *RSVP*, *RTSP* and *UDP*.

(2) (Rapid Transport Protocol) The protocol used in IBM's High Performance Routing (HPR) system.

**RTS**    (Request To Send) An RS-232 signal sent from the transmitting station to the receiving station requesting permission to transmit. Contrast with *CTS*.

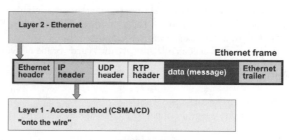

**RTP Packet**
In a UDP/IP stack, the RTP header is created first and then the packet is moved down the stack to UDP and IP. This shows the RTP packet within an Ethernet frame ready for transmission over the network.

**RTSP**    (RealTime Streaming Protocol) A specification for transmitting audio, video and 3-D animation over the Internet. It was developed by Netscape and Progressive Networks. Contrast with *ASF*.

**RTTI**    (RunTime Type Information) A facility that allows an object to be queried at runtime to determine its type. One of the fundamental principles of object technology is polymorphism, which is the ability of an object to dynamically change at runtime.

**RTUA**    See *TAWPI*.

**rt-VBR**    (RealTime-VBR) See *VBR*.

**RU**    (Rack Unit) A unit of measurement of the height of a rack-mounted device, which is equal to 1.75". See *rack mounted*.

**rubber banding**    In computer graphics, the moving of a line or object where one end stays fixed in position.

**rubout key**    A keyboard key on a terminal that deletes the last character that was entered.

**ruggedized PC**    A PC that is designed for rough usage such as police, fire, industrial and other hazardous duty applications. Although they command a price premium over standard machines, a ruggedized portable PC offers an advantage for everyone that uses a laptop computer, because it is designed to work even if accidentally dropped.

In a ruggedized machine, the keyboard is usually showerproof, allowing liquid to be accidentally spilled on it. The hard disk is in a vibration-damped mounting to withstand shock. The screen is typically rubber damped for shock resistance and dropping. The hard drive should be removable, allowing it to be stored in a secure and safe environment during the most severe travel conditions. In addition, its removability allows the data to be more easily reused if the machine is heavily damaged.

**rule-based expert system**     An expert system based on a set of rules that a human expert would follow in diagnosing a problem. Contrast with *model-based expert system*.

**ruler line**     A graphic representation of a ruler on screen that is used for laying out text and graphics.

**rules**     (1) A set of conditions or standards that have been agreed upon.
(2) In printing, horizontal and vertical lines between columns or at the top and bottom of a page in order to enhance the appearance of the page.

**rules based**     Using "if-this, do that" rules to perform actions. Rules-based products implies flexibility in the software, enabling tasks and data to be easily changed by replacing one or more rules.

**RUMBA**     A family of PC-to-host connectivity programs from Wall Data, Inc., Kirkland, WA (www.walldata.com). On desktop computers connected to minis and mainframes, RUMBA provides a window that emulates a terminal session with these hosts. RUMBA supports Windows and OS/2 clients connected to IBM mainframes, AS/400s, VAXes and other hosts via coax adapters, twinax cards or the network.

**Rumbaugh**     See *OMT*.

**run**     (1) To execute a program.
(2) A single program or set of programs scheduled for execution.

**run around**     In desktop publishing, the flowing of text around a graphic image.

**run native**     To "run native" is to execute software written for the native mode of the computer. Contrast with running a program under some type of emulation or simulation.
Running native has traditionally been the fastest way to execute instructions on a computer. However, if, as expected, in the future, machines are so fast they can run emulated programs without any noticeable delay to the user, this will no longer be the important issue it is today.

**run on top of**     To run as the control program to some other program, which is subordinate to it. Contrast with *run under*.

**runt**     The frame that remains after a collision on a CSMA/CD medium such as Ethernet. See *runt filtering*.

**runt filtering**     Discarding runt packets that clog up the network. See *runt*.

**runtime**     Refers to the actual execution of a program.

**runtime version**     Software that enables another program to execute on its own or with enhanced capabilities. For example, Visual Basic programs are interpreted, which means Visual Basic applications cannot be executed natively in the computer. They need the runtime module that interprets the Visual Basic code into the machine language of the computer. That actual module in a Windows PC is named VBRUN300.DLL, VBRUN400.DLL, etc.
A full-featured database management system (DBMS) includes a programming language for developing applications. The language is generally interpreted, and the DBMS software must be loaded into the computer in order to run the programs. A runtime version of the DBMS allows the developer to create the application in that language and to package it for customers that have not purchased the DBMS. The runtime version "runs" the application, but does not allow the user access to all the bells and whistles that the owner of the full DBMS has.
In the book *Dvorak Predicts*, published by Osborne/McGraw-Hill, the well-known computer columnist John Dvorak proposes an interesting runtime version. He says that Apple should create a "runtime Mac." As an example, he uses an automobile tune-up kit, suggesting that its probes to the spark plugs, exhaust pipe, etc., be controlled by a computer using the Mac interface for that application only. He claims that the advantages are lower hardware costs if a full-blown Mac isn't required and that the Mac's interface would become widely known if runtime Macs were used for many specialized jobs.

**run under**     To run within the control of a higher-level program. Contrast with *run on top of*.

**RUP**     (Rational Unified Process) Software from Rational Software Corporation, Cupertino, CA (www.rational.com) that provides guidelines, templates and examples for each team member in the system development process. Supporting the Unified Modeling Language (UML), RUP can be used with other Rational tools to provide a uniform set of best practices for interative development, which was developed in the 1970s. Rational calls its product the "e-coach" for software teams. See *iterative development*.

**RVP**     (RendezVous Protocol) A proposed standard for declaring your presence on the network when you log on. See *instant messenger*.

**RWIN**     (Receive WINdow) A TCP/IP setting in Windows 95/98 that defines the size of the buffer that holds incoming packets. RWIN is set in the Registry.

**RX**     A communications abbreviation for receive. Contrast with *TX*.

**RXD**     (Receiving Data) See *modem*.

R

**S-100 bus**　　An IEEE 696, 100-pin bus standard used extensively in first-generation personal computers (8080, Z80, 6800, etc.). It is still used in various systems.

**S/360**　　See *System/360*.

**S/370**　　See *System/370*.

**S/390**　　Originally an abbreviation for IBM's System/390 machines. Today, IBM's CMOS-based System/390 systems are designated as S/390s.

**S3 chip**　　A graphics accelerator chip used by many manufacturers of PC display adapters. See *SONICblue*.

**S/3x**　　See *System/3x*.

**SAA**　　(System Application Architecture) A set of interfaces designed to cross all IBM platforms from PC to mainframe. Introduced by IBM in 1987, SAA includes the Common User Access (CUA), the Common Programming Interface for Communications (CPI-C) and Common Communications Support (CCS). See *CUA*, *CPI-C* and *CCS*.

**sabermetrician**　　Nickname for a statistician who uses computers to predict future performance of sports teams and players.

**SACD**　　(Super Audio CD) A high-end CD audio format from Sony and Philips. SACD and DVD-Audio (DVD-A) are the two next-generation digital audio formats that provide better quality sound than audio CDs. SACD uses Direct Stream Digital (DSD) audio technology, which provides 1-bit encoding at 2,822,400 samples per second. Each bit sample points up or down, representing the analog sound wave very accurately as it rises and falls.

　　In 1999, Sony's SCD-1 was the first SACD player on the market, which also played audio CDs. Hybrid SACD discs include an SACD layer and an audio CD layer so they can be played in standard CD players. See *DVD-Audio*.

**SAD**　　See *systems analysis and design*.

**Safe Mode**　　The troubleshooting mode in Windows 95/98/2000. It allows the system to boot when it otherwise may not, often due to conflicts from newly-installed hardware. Only the mouse, keyboard and standard VGA drivers are loaded, and all configuration files are bypassed, including the Registry, CONFIG.SYS, AUTOEXEC.BAT and SYSTEM.INI. Windows may automatically boot up in this mode if the previous session was not shut down properly. See *Win Safe Mode*.

**Safe-Tcl**　　A secure version of the Tcl language. See *Tcl/Tk*.

**sag**   (1) A momentary drop in voltage from the power source. Contrast with *spike*.
(2) (SAG) (SQL Access Group)  See *CLI*.

**salary survey**   The following salaries were summarized from kforce.com's 2000 Salary Survey of information technology professionals. The survey is based on the current salaries of more than 75,000 computer professionals nationwide.  For the complete salary survey which includes a breakdown of 46 regions in the U.S. plus Toronto, visit www.kforce.com.

The Average column is the average of all salaries within all regions in the U.S. plus Toronto. Low is the average of all salaries within the lowest region, and High is the average of all salaries within the highest-paying region, thus, there were individual salaries both below and above the Low and High figures. See *job descriptions*.

| PROGRAMMING | Avg. | Low | High | | SPECIALISTS (continued) | Avg. | Low | High |
|---|---|---|---|---|---|---|---|---|
| | (000 U.S. dollars) | | | | | (000 U.S. dollars) | | |
| MAINFRAME | | | | | EDP auditor | 52 | 42 | 63 |
| Jr. programmer | 41 | 31 | 51 | | Sr. EDP auditor | 64 | 50 | 80 |
| Programmer analyst | 52 | 35 | 66 | | | | | |
| Sr. prog/analyst | 63 | 45 | 80 | | Technical writer | 43 | 31 | 57 |
| | | | | | Systems architect | 73 | 40 | 96 |
| MIDRANGE | | | | | QA/Test analyst | 59 | 38 | 78 |
| Jr. programmer | 40 | 32 | 50 | | | | | |
| Programmer analyst | 51 | 41 | 60 | | **MANAGEMENT** | | | |
| Sr. prog/analyst | 62 | 49 | 76 | | | | | |
| | | | | | MIS DIRECTOR/CIO | | | |
| CLIENT/SERVER/GUI | | | | | Small/medium shop | 88 | 70 | 151 |
| Jr. programmer | 42 | 34 | 51 | | Large shop | 122 | 88 | 165 |
| Programmer analyst | 58 | 39 | 70 | | | | | |
| Sr. prog/analyst | 69 | 50 | 84 | | Mgr. business apps | 89 | 68 | 125 |
| | | | | | Applications dev. | 89 | 64 | 117 |
| SYSTEMS ENGINEER | | | | | Technical services | 85 | 66 | 108 |
| Jr. engineer | 44 | 35 | 55 | | VP/Mgr Systems engnr. | 94 | 71 | 111 |
| Engineerer | 55 | 38 | 70 | | VP/Mgr Customer svcs. | 80 | 53 | 101 |
| Sr. engineer | 70 | 49 | 84 | | Project manager | 77 | 59 | 105 |
| | | | | | Project leader | 70 | 53 | 81 |
| **BUSINESS SYSTEMS** | | | | | | | | |
| Business analyst | 60 | 50 | 74 | | **SALES** | | | |
| Consultant | 72 | 60 | 98 | | Account rep. | 85 | 59 | 127 |
| EDI analyst | 59 | 46 | 75 | | Pre/post sales support | 69 | 44 | 100 |
| Systems analyst | 66 | 57 | 75 | | Management | 104 | 74 | 139 |
| | | | | | | | | |
| **SPECIALISTS** | | | | | **DATACENTER** | | | |
| Database analyst | 68 | 54 | 83 | | Datacenter manager | 73 | 39 | 105 |
| Database admin. | 77 | 59 | 90 | | Operations support | 42 | 43 | 50 |
| LAN admin. | 53 | 43 | 66 | | Operator | 39 | 24 | 65 |
| Network engineer | 62 | 36 | 75 | | Sr. operator | 49 | 32 | 62 |
| PC software specialist | 44 | 32 | 56 | | Help desk analyst | 46 | 30 | 69 |
| PC technician | 44 | 30 | 55 | | | | | |
| | | | | | **INTERNET** | | | |
| System admin./mgr. | 61 | 49 | 73 | | Project manager | 78 | 57 | 108 |
| WAN voice analyst | 55 | 45 | 66 | | Engineer | 61 | 44 | 91 |
| Data comm analyst | 63 | 48 | 80 | | Web programmer | 59 | 44 | 75 |
| WAN administrator | 61 | 42 | 79 | | Web graphic designer | 54 | 44 | 70 |
| Systems programmer | 67 | 49 | 78 | | Webmaster | 49 | 38 | 75 |

**sales force automation**   Automating the sales activities within an organization. A comprehensive SFA package provides such functions as contact management, note and information sharing, quick proposal and presentation generation, product configurators, calendars and to-do lists. When sales functions are integrated with marketing and customer service, it is known as "enterprise relationship management."  See *ERM*.

**Salsa** A Windows application development system from Wall Data Inc., Kirkland, WA (www.walldata.com) that uses predefined templates for common business functions. The templates make designing the database more intuitive for non-technical users.

**SAM** **(1)** (Security Accounts Manager) The part of Windows NT that manages the database of usernames, passwords and permissions. A SAM resides in each server as well as in each domain controller. See *PDC* and *trust relationship*.

**(2)** (Symantec AntiVirus for Macintosh) A popular Macintosh antivirus program from Symantec Corporation, Cupertino, CA.

**(3)** See *sequential access method*.

**Samba** (SaMBa) Software that allows a UNIX server to act as a file server to Windows clients. Samba is a free, open source implementation of the SMB file sharing protocol used in DOS/Windows and runs under Linux, FreeBSD and other UNIX variants. Samba can be used with any modern PC as well as other hardware, but its efficiency lends itself to old 486s that can be recycled to serve as inexpensive file, print and backup servers in a Windows environment. See *SMB*.

**Samna** One of the first full-featured word processors for PCs (1983) from Samna Corporation, which was acquired by Lotus.

**sample size** See *sampling rate*.

**sampling** **(1)** In statistics, the analysis of a group by determining the characteristics of a significant percentage of its members chosen at random.

**(2)** In digitizing operations, the conversion of real-world signals or movements at regular intervals into digital code. See *sampling rate* and *oversampling*.

**sampling rate** In digitizing operations, the frequency with which samples are taken and converted into digital form. The sampling frequency must be at least twice that of the analog frequency being captured. For example, the sampling rate for hi-fi playback is 44.1 kHz, slightly more than double the 20 kHz frequency a person can hear. The sampling rate for digitizing voice for a toll-quality conversation is 8,000 times per second, or 8 kHz, twice the 4 kHz required for the full spectrum of the human voice. The higher the sampling rate, the closer real-world objects are represented in digital form.

Another attribute of sampling is quantizing, which creates a number for the sample. The larger the size of the sample, which is also known as resolution or precision, or just sample size, the more granular the scale and the more accurate the digital sampling. See *oversampling* and *quantization*.

**samurai** A technical professional that is paid to break into a computer system in order to test its security. See *hacker* and *cracker*.

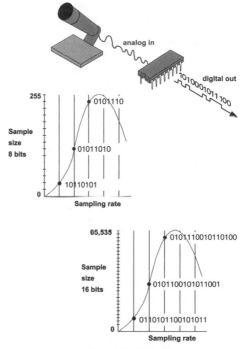

**Sampling Sound**
The faster the sampling rate and the larger the sample size, the more accurately sound can be digitized. An 8-bit sample breaks the sound wave into 255 increments compared with 65,535 for a 16-bit sample.

**Sampling Dialog**
This typical recording dialog from one of Creative Labs' Sound Blaster sound cards shows the sampling options for digitizing sound into Windows WAV files.

**SAN**    (2) (System Area Network)  A high-speed networking architecture used to connect processors and I/O subsystems together. Tandem coined the term with its ServerNet product. See *ServerNet*.

(1) (Storage Area Network)  A back-end network connecting storage devices via peripheral channels such as SCSI, SSA, ESCON and Fibre Channel. There are two ways of implementing SANs: centralized and decentralized. A centralized SAN ties multiple hosts into a single storage system, which is a RAID device with large amounts of cache and redundant power supplies. The cabling distances allow for local as well as campus-wide and metropolitan-wide hookups over peripheral channels rather than an overburdened network. SCSI distances have also been extended. Using fiber, Gigalabs' SCSI switches can communicate over 20 km. This centralized storage topology is commonly employed to tie a server cluster together for failover.

Having data in one place is easier to manage. In addition, some storage systems can copy data for testing, routine backup and transfer between databases without burdening the hosts they serve. The glass house is coming back, not to centralize processing necessarily, but to keep data manageable and safe.

Fibre Channel has been a driving force in the SAN arena, because it supports existing peripheral interfaces, which in most cases is SCSI. Fibre Channel (FC) can be configured point-to-point, in an arbitrated loop (FC-AL) or via a switch (see *Fibre Channel*). IP storage is also coming on strong, which enables peripheral data transfer over IP and Gigabit Ethernet (see *IP storage*), extending the range across the world via the Internet.

If a centralized storage system is not feasible, a SAN can connect multiple hosts with multiple storage systems. Considering the proliferation of file servers in an enterprise, SANs with distributed storage are expected to be widely employed.

Another related storage device is the network attached storage (NAS) system. The NAS is connected to the LAN just like a file server. Rather than containing a full-blown OS, it typically uses a slim microkernel specialized for handling only I/O requests such as NFS (UNIX), SMB/CIFS (DOS/Windows) and NCP (NetWare). Adding or removing a NAS system is like adding or removing any network node. In contrast, the channel-attached storage system must be brought down in order to reconfigure it. However, the NAS is subject to the variable behavior and overhead of the network.

**Channel Attached**
EMC has been a pioneer in channel-attached storage networks, especially in the mainframe arena. Its Symmetrix storage systems support up to 32 ports (channels) and hold up to 6TB. Network-attached options are also available. *(Image courtesy of EMC Corporation.)*

**Network Attached**
It doesn't get much simpler than Meridian Data's Snap! Server. Containing only an on/off switch and Ethernet port, it provides an instant storage boost by simply plugging it into the network hub. *(Image courtesy of Meridian Data, Inc.)*

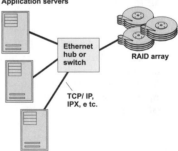

**SAN (Channel attached) Centralized**

Application servers

SCSI, SSA, Fibre Channel

RAID array

ESCON

Mainframe

**SAN (Channel attached) Distributed**

Application servers

FC or SCSI switch

to remote location

RAID array

**NAS (Network attached)**

Application servers

Ethernet hub or switch

RAID array

TCP/ IP, IPX, e tc.

**SANs and NASs**
SANs are channel attached, and NASs are network attached. They all fall under the "storage network" umbrella.

SAN-NAS terminology is confusing (network attached storage vs storage area network). NASs are often contrasted with SANs, but are also included under the "storage network" umbrella. The major difference is that the SAN is channel attached, and the NAS is network attached. See *SNIA*.

**sandbox**   A restricted environment in which certain functions are prohibited. For example, deleting files and modifying system information such as registry settings and other control panel functions may be prohibited. Sandboxes are used when executable code has come from an external source that is not entirely trusted. See *Java sandbox* and *behavior blocking*.

**Sand Hill Road**   A street in Silicon Valley that contains a large number of venture capital firms dedicated to the high-tech industry. It stretches from Sharon Heights to Interstate 280.

**sans-serif**   A typeface style without serifs, which are the short horizontal lines added at the tops and bottoms of the vertical member of the letter. Helvetica is a common sans-serif font.

**Santa Cruz Operation**   See *SCO*.

**SAP**   **(1)** (Service Advertising Protocol) A NetWare protocol used to identify the services and addresses of servers attached to the network. The responses are used to update a table in the router known as the Server Information Table.

   **(2)** (Secondary Audio Program) An NTSC audio channel used for auxiliary transmission, such as foreign language broadcasting or teletext.

   **(3)** (SAP America, Inc., Newtown Square, PA, www.sap.com) The U.S. branch of the German software company, SAP AG. SAP's R/3 integrated suite of applications and its ABAP/4 Development Workbench became popular starting around 1993 and have gained significant market share in the ERP arena. See *R/3*.

**SAPI**   (Speech API) A programming interface from Microsoft for speech recognition and synthesis. It provides a way for developers to enable their applications to receive text from and send text to voice devices.

**SAR**   (Segmentation And Reassembly) The protocol that converts data to cells for transmission over an ATM network. It is the lower part of the ATM Adaption Layer (AAL), which is responsible for the entire operation. See *AAL*.

**SAS**   (SAS Institute Inc., Cary, NC, www.sas.com) A software company that specializes in data warehousing and decision support software based on the SAS System. Founded in 1976, SAS is one of the world's largest privately-held software companies. See *SAS System*.

**SASI**   (Shugart Associates Systems Interface) A peripheral interface developed by Shugart in 1981 that evolved into the ANSI SCSI standard in 1986. It was renamed SCSI because ANSI does not allow corporate names in its standards. See *SCSI*.

**SAS System**   **(1)** Originally called the "Statistical Analysis System," it is an integrated set of data management and decision support tools from SAS that runs on platforms from PCs to mainframes. It includes a complete programming language as well as modules for spreadsheets, CBT, presentation graphics, project management, operations research, scheduling, linear programming, statistical quality control, econometric and time series analysis and mathematical, engineering and statistical applications. It also provides multidimensional data analysis (OLAP), query and reporting, EIS, data mining and data visualization.

   **(2)** See *FDDI*.

**SATAN**   (Security Analysis Tool for Auditing Networks) A utility that analyzes security vulnerabilities on the Internet. In April 1995, it was placed onto the Net as freeware by computer security specialist Dan Farmer.

**satcom**   (SATellite COMmunication) Refers to the field of communications via satellite.

**satellite**   See *communications satellite*.

**satellite channel**   A carrier frequency used for satellite transmission.

**satellite computer**   A computer located remotely from the host computer or under the control of the host. It can function as a slave to the master computer or perform offline tasks.

**satellite link**   A signal that travels from the earth to a communications satellite and back down again. Contrast with *terrestrial link*.

**satellite modem**   A device used to transmit and receive signals from a satellite transponder. For transmission, it modulates digital data signals from a multiplexing device into a carrier frequency for delivery to an upconverter, amplifier and antenna. For receiving, it converts the frquencies from the downconverter into digital pulses for the multiplexor.

Commercial telecom providers use stand-alone satellite modems; however, the satellite receivers and large dishes that were used before DSS became popular contained the demodulator part of the modem. See *earth station*.

**satellite radio**   Broadcasting radio programs in digital format via satellites. XM Satellite Radio (www.xmradio.com) and Sirius Satellite Radio (www.siriusradio.com) are the two major players in this arena with their own satellites. Satellite radio offers 100 channels of digital audio (music, news, sports, etc.), and unlike terrestrial digital radio (DAB), the signal stays tuned no matter where you travel within the U.S.

Initially, both companies have partnered with different auto manufacturers to offer their radios, but a single standard is expected in the future. The two companies use the 2320–2345MHz frequency band, which is split in two so each has exclusive spectrum. See *DAB* and *DARS*.

**Tune by Category**
Satellite radios enable tuning by category or a program guide as envisioned in this AM/FM/XM digital radio from XM Satellite Radio. *(Image courtesy of XM Satellite Radio Holdings Inc.)*

**saturation**   **(1)** On magnetic media, a condition in which the magnetizable particles are completely aligned and a more powerful writing signal will not improve the reading back.

**(2)** In a bipolar transistor, a condition in which the current on the gate (the trigger) is equal to or greater than what is necessary to close the switch.

**(3)** In a diode, a condition in which the diode is fully conducting.

**(4)** In a color, the amount of white contained in it. For example, a fully saturated red would be a pure red. The less saturated, the more pastel the appearance. See *chrominance*, *luminance* and *hue*.

**save**   To copy the document, record or image being worked on onto a storage medium. Saving updates the file by writing the data that currently resides in memory (RAM) onto disk or tape. Most applications prompt the user to save data upon exiting.

All processing is done in memory (RAM). When the processing is completed, the data must be placed onto a permanent storage medium such as disk or tape.

**Save As**   A command in the File menu of most applications that lets you make a copy of the current document or image you are working on. It differs from the regular Save command. Save stores your data back into the folder (directory) it originally came from. Save As lets you give it a different name and/or put it in a different folder on your hard disk or floppy disk.

If the Save as function provides you with a list of optional file formats, it is used to export a file. Exporting is saving a copy of the current document into a foreign file format. See *foreign file*.

**SAX**   (**S**imple **A**PI for **X**ML)  An event-based programming interface (API) between an XML parser and an XML application. An object-based interface is supplied by DOM. See *DOM* and *SOX*.

**SBC**   **(1)** (SBC Communications Inc., San Antonio, TX, www.sbc.com)  A telecommunications company made up of Southwestern Bell, Pacific Bell, Nevada Bell and Cellular One.

**(2)** See *single board computer*.

**Sbus**   Originally a proprietary bus from Sun, the Sbus has been released into the public domain. The IEEE standardized a 64-bit version in 1993.

**SCA** (Single Connector Attachment) An 80-pin plug and socket used to connect peripherals. With a SCSI drive, it rolls three cables (power, data channel and ID configuration) into one connector for fast installation and removal. An SCA to SCSI adapter allows SCA-configured SCSI drives to fit in traditional SCSI enclosures.

**SCADA** (System Control and Data Acquisition, Supervisory Control and Data Acquisition, Security, Control and Data Acquisition). A common process control application that collects data from sensors on the shop floor or in remote locations and sends them to a central computer for management and control.

**SCAI** (Switch-to-Computer Applications Interface) A standard for integrating computers to a PBX. See *switch-to-computer*.

**scalability** Refers to how much a system can be expanded. The term by itself implies a positive capability. For example, "the device is known for its scalability" means that it can be made to serve a larger number of users without breaking down or requiring major changes in procedure.

**scalable** Capable of being changed in size and configuration. It typically refers to a computer, product or system's capability to expand. See *scale* and *scalability*.

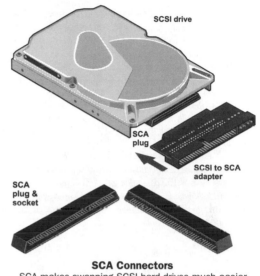

SCSI drive

SCA plug

SCSI to SCA adapter

SCA plug & socket

**SCA Connectors**
SCA makes swapping SCSI hard drives much easier than with the traditional SCSI cables, plugs and sockets. An adapter enables SCA drives to fit into standard SCSI enclosures.

**scalable font** A font that is created in the required point size when needed for display or printing. The dot patterns (bitmaps) are generated from a set of outline fonts, or base fonts, which contain a mathematical representation of the typeface. The two major scalable fonts are Adobe's Type 1 PostScript and Apple/Microsoft's TrueType.

Although a bitmapped font that is designed from scratch for a particular font size will always look the best, scalable fonts eliminate storing hundreds of different sizes of fonts on disk. In most cases however, only the trained eye can tell the difference. Contrast with *bitmapped font*.

**scalar** A single item or value. Contrast with *vector* and *array*, which are made up of multiple values.

**scalar processor** A computer that performs arithmetic computations on one number at a time. Contrast with *vector processor*.

**scalar variable** In programming, a variable that contains only one value.

**scale** (1) To resize a device, object or system, making it larger or smaller. The term is widely used to refer to the expansion capability of hardware or software. See *scalability* and *scaler*.

(2) To change the representation of a quantity in order to bring it into prescribed limits of another range. For example, values such as 1249, 876, 523, –101 and –234 might need to be scaled into a range from –5 to +5.

(3) To designate the position of the decimal point in a fixed or floating point number.

**scaler** Refers to products that can be upgraded to much larger capacities or that will automatically expand to accomodate much greater volume. See *scale* and *scalability*.

**scaling** (1) See *scale*.

(2) In the storage industry, obtaining incremental improvements in new products via traditional methods. Evolutionary rather than revolutionary.

**SCAM** (SCSI Configured AutoMatically) A subset of Plug and Play that allows SCSI IDs to be changed by software rather than by flipping switches or changing jumpers. Both the SCSI host adapter and peripheral must support SCAM. See *SCSI*.

**scan**   (1) In optical technologies, to view a printed form a line at a time in order to convert images into bitmapped representations, or to convert characters into ASCII text or some other data code.

(2) In video, to move across a picture frame a line at a time, either to detect the image in an analog or digital camera, or to refresh a CRT display.

(3) To sequentially search a file for specific content.

(4) To sequentially search for peripheral devices attached to the computer. See *Win Rescan peripherals*.

**scan converter**   A device that changes the video output from a computer to standard TV signals, allowing a regular TV to be used as a computer screen. A VCR can then also be used to record screen output. A scan converter may provide multiple TV formats, such as NTSC and PAL, as well as be able to output digital video such as a D1 signal.

**ScanDisk**   A utility in Windows 95/98 and DOS (as of Version 6.2) that detects and repairs errors on disk. In Windows 95/98, the ScanDisk Standard option searches for files that have been corrupted. The Thorough option checks the condition of each sector on the disk. For good disk maintenance, periodically run ScanDisk and then Defrag.

ScanDisk will find file fragments from applications that were not closed properly and ask you if you want to convert them into files (with a .CHK extension). Most of the time, these files are worthless, and you can choose to ignore them. See *DOS ScanDisk*.

**scan head**   An optical sensing device in an scanner or fax machine that is moved across the image to be scanned.

**scan line**   One of many horizontal lines in a graphics frame.

**scanner**   A device that reads a printed page and converts it into a graphics image for the computer. The scanner does not recognize the content of the printed material it is scanning. Everything on the page (text and graphics objects) is converted into one bitmapped graphics image (bitmap), which is a pattern of dots.

Optical character recognition (OCR) systems perform the same scanning operation, but use software to convert the dots into coded ASCII or EBCDIC characters (see *OCR*). Digital cameras are similar to desktop scanners, except that they focus into infinity, whereas desktop scanners accept paper, one page at a time or in a continuous feed like a copy machine (see *digital camera*).

Scanners are optical devices that use CCDs to record the images. They are rated in dots per inch (dpi) by their optical resolution and interpolated resolution, the former being the actual, physical

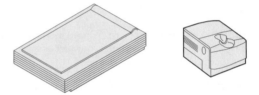

**Desktop Scanners**
The flatbed scanner on the left is the most common type of desktop scanner. With the addition of a transparancy adapter, which provides a light source from the top, it can scan 35mm slides and large transparencies. The slide scanner on the right is specialized for 35mm slides. The slide is inserted into the slot, and the scanner mechanism moves it past the reading sensors.

resolution of the device, the latter being a higher resolution that is computed by software. Most all scanners feature 24-bit color, which is generally the maximum number of colors supported in most digital systems. For example, a 24-bit color, 1,200 dpi scanner means each of the 1,200 pixels uses 24 bits to hold color information. However, the 1,200 dpi is often an "enhanced," or interpolated resolution, not the optical resolution. See *optical resolution, interpolated resolution, flatbed scanner, sheet-fed scanner, handheld scanner, drum scanner, slide scanner, photo scanner* and *digital camera*. See also *virus scanner*.

**scan rate**   The number of times per second a scanning device samples its field of vision. See *horizontal scan frequency*.

**scan technology**   A method for testing chips on the printed circuit board by building the chip with additional input and output pins that are only used for test purposes. Full scan methods test all the registers on the chip. Partial scan tests some of them, and boundary scan tests only the input/output cells. JTAG is the IEEE standard for boundary scan.

**SCART connector**   (Syndicat Français des Constructeurs d'Appareils Radio et Télévision) An audio visual connector used to hook up VCRs and DVD players to TV sets and audio equipment. Developed by Peritel in France and also known as a "EURO connector," the SCART cable uses 21-pin male plugs at both ends, while the devices use female sockets.

**Scart Connector**

**scatter diagram**     A graph plotted with dots or some other symbol at each data point. Also called a "scatter plot" or "dot chart."

**scatter read**     The capability that allows data to be input into two or more noncontiguous locations of memory with one read operation. See *gather write*.

**SCbus**     See *SCSA*.

**SC connector**     A fiber-optic cable connector that uses a push-pull latching mechanism similar to common audio and video cables. For bi-directional transmission, two fiber cables and two SC connectors (Dual SC) are generally used. SC is specified by the TIA as FOCIS-3. See *fiber-optic connectors* and *FOCIS*.

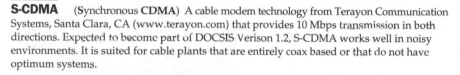

**A Scatter Diagram**

**S-CDMA**     (Synchronous **CDMA**) A cable modem technology from Terayon Communication Systems, Santa Clara, CA (www.terayon.com) that provides 10 Mbps transmission in both directions. Expected to become part of DOCSIS Verison 1.2, S-CDMA works well in noisy environments. It is suited for cable plants that are entirely coax based or that do not have optimum systems.

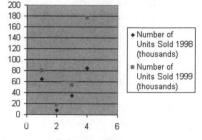

**SC Connector**
SC uses a push-pull connector similar to common audio and video plugs and sockets.

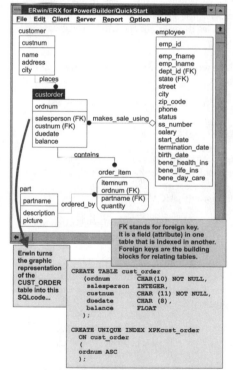

**A Database Schema**
In this order processing example, the tables for customers and orders are drawn graphically, and the Erwin modeling program turns the graph into the appropriate SQL code for the target database.
*(Example courtesy of Logic Works, Inc.)*

**scene description language**     A method for describing graphics objects to be rendered. Unlike a paint program or image editor, which uses graphical tools for creating images, scene description languages are more like programming source code.

**scheduler**     The part of the operating system that initiates and terminates jobs (programs) in the computer. Also called a "dispatcher," it maintains a list of jobs to be run and allocates computer resources as required.

**scheduling algorithm**     A method used to schedule jobs for execution. Priority, length of time in the job queue and available resources are examples of criteria used.

**schema**     Pronounced "skeema." The definition of an entire database. It defines the structure and the type of contents that each data element within the structure can contain. Schemas are often designed with visual modeling tools that automatically create the SQL code necessary to define the table structures. See *subschema* and *XML schema*.

**Scheme**     A LISP dialect developed at MIT and Indiana University. TI developed a personal computer version of Scheme called "PC Scheme." See *Script-Fu*.

**Schottky**     A category of bipolar transistor known for its fast switching speeds in the three-nanosecond range. Schottky II devices have switching speeds in the range of a single nanosecond.

**SCI**     (Scalable Coherent Interface) An IEEE standard for a high-speed bus that uses wire or fiber-optic cable. It can transfer data up to 1GByte/sec.

**scientific application**    An application that simulates real-world activities using mathematics. Real-world objects are turned into mathematical models, and their actions are simulated by executing the formulas.

For example, some of an airplane's flight characteristics can be simulated in the computer. Rivers, lakes and mountains can be simulated. Virtually any objects with known characteristics can be modeled and simulated.

Simulations use enormous calculations and often require supercomputer speed. As personal computers become more powerful, more laboratory experiments will be converted into computer models that can be interactively examined by students without the risk and cost of the actual experiments.

**scientific computer**    A computer specialized for high-speed mathematic processing. See *array processor*, *floating point processor* and *supercomputer*.

**scientific language**    A programming language designed for mathematical formulas and matrices, such as ALGOL, FORTRAN and APL. Although all programming languages allow for this kind of processing, statements in a scientific language make it easier to express these actions.

**scientific notation**    The display of numbers in floating point form. The number (mantissa) is always equal to or greater than one and less than 10, and the base is 10. For example, 2.345E6 is equivalent to 2,345,000. The number following E (exponent) represents the power to which the base should be raised (number of zeros following the decimal point).

**scientific visualization**    Using the computer to display real-world objects that cannot normally be seen, such as the shapes of molecules, air and fluid dynamics and weather patterns. Scientific visualization requires enormous computing resources, and the supercomputer centers and national laboratories throughout the world are always at the forefront of such activity. See *visualization*.

**scissoring**    In computer graphics, the deleting of any parts of an image which fall outside of a window that has been sized and laid over the original image. Also called "clipping."

**SCL**    (1) (Switch-to-Computer Link)  Refers to applications that integrate the computer through the PBX. See *switch-to-computer*.

(2) A file extension used for ColoRIX bitmapped graphics file format (640×400 256 colors).

**SCM**    (1) (Software Configuration Management, Source Code Management)  See *configuration management*.

(2) (Service Control Manager)  The part of Windows NT that launches background tasks. Developers can write executable programs that run under the control of the SCM.

(3) (Single Chip Module)  A chip package that contains one chip. Contrast with *MCM*.

**SCMS**    (Serial Copy Management System)  A copy protection method used for recordable audio CDs that allows one copy of the original to be made.

**SCO**    (The Santa Cruz Operation, Inc., Santa Cruz, CA, www.sco.com)  The leading vendor of the UNIX operating system on the Intel x86 platform, which accounts for about one third of all UNIX servers worldwide. SCO has sold licenses for more than two million nodes of UNIX client and server products. Founded in 1979 as a custom programming house, its first operating system was SCO XENIX in 1984. It ran on the Apple Lisa, PC XT and the DEC Pro 350. Subsequently, all SCO products were developed for Intel machines.

In 1995, SCO purchased UnixWare and all the AT&T source code for UNIX System V from Novell. It merged UnixWare and its OpenServer product into a single operating system, which was released in 1998 as SCO UnixWare 7.

**SCO OpenServer**    A family of client and server operating systems for the Intel platform from SCO. It is based on UNIX System V Release 3.2 and includes the Motif and X Window user interfaces and standard UNIX networking (TCP/IP, NFS and NIS). SCO OpenServer Desktop is the client version. SCO OpenServer Enterprise is the server version, which has optional SMP support for up to 30 processors. SCO OpenServer Host System is used on computers with dumb terminals.

SCO OpenServer Enterprise was formerly SCO Open Desktop Enterprise. SCO OpenServer Desktop was formerly SCO Open Desktop. SCO OpenServer Host System was originally SCO XENIX. See *Gemini*.

**scope** (1) A CRT screen, such as used on an oscilloscope or common display terminal.

(2) In programming, the visibility of variables within a program; for example, whether one function can use a variable created in another function.

(3) See *search scope*.

**SCO UNIX** An enhanced version of UNIX System V Release 3.2 for Intel processors from SCO. In 1989, SCO UNIX was introduced as a major upgrade to SCO XENIX with more security, networking and standards conformance. SCO UNIX servers support dumb terminals, Windows, X terminal and SCO OpenServer clients. The SCO OpenServer line evolved from SCO UNIX.

**SCO UnixWare** A family of client and server operating systems for the Intel platform from SCO. It is based on UNIX System V Release 4.2MP and includes SMP support for two processors with optional support for up to 32. As of UnixWare 2.1, it includes NetWare 4.1 file, print and directory services. UnixWare Personal Edition is the client version which comes with the Mosaic Web browser.

UnixWare was originally developed by Univel, a joint venture of Novell and AT&T's UNIX System Labs (USL). In 1993, Novell purchased USL and UnixWare and sold it to SCO two years later. See *SCO UnixWare 7*.

**SCO UnixWare 7** An enhanced version of UnixWare that combines the UNIX System V Release 5 kernel with the SCO OpenServer graphical front end. Formerly code named Gemini, it was introduced in 1998. UnixWare 7 is intended to provide a smooth migration path to 64-bit computers.

**SCO Wabi** Software from SCO that adds DOS and Windows capability to SCO OpenServer products. SCO Wabi has not been widely used.

**SCP** (Service Control Point) A node in an SS7 telephone network that provides an interface to databases, which may reside within the SCP computer or in other computers. The SCP may also be combined with the SS7 node that routes messages, called a "signal transfer point" (STP).

The local exchange node, which is called the "service switching point" (SSP) send SS7 messages to SCPs to retrieve subscriber and routing information. The databases support such features as 800 and 900 numbers, calling card validation, collect and third-party billing calls. Databases for cellular providers hold subscriber information as well as visitor information (other carrier's customers moving through at this moment). See *SS7*, *SSP* and *AIN*.

**scramble** Same as *encrypt*. The term came from the early days of cryptography which camouflaged analog transmissions with secret frequency patterns. Today, the 0s and 1s are rearranged.

**scrambler** A device or software program that encrypts data for security purposes.

**scrambling** Encoding data to make it indecipherable. See *cryptography*.

**Scrapbook** A Macintosh disk file that holds frequently-used text and graphics objects, such as a company letterhead. Contrast with *Clipboard*, which holds data only for the current session.

**scratch disk** A hard disk used to temporarily store data.

**scratchpad** A register or reserved section of memory or disk used for temporary storage.

**scratch tape** A magnetic tape that can be erased and reused.

**screen** The display area of a video terminal or monitor. It is either a CRT or one of the flat panel technologies.

**screen angle** The angle at which a halftone screen is placed over an image. Generally, 45 degrees produces the best results. In a digital system, the screen angle is simulated by the placement of the dots within the halftone cells. See *halftone*.

**ScreenCam** Screen recording software from Lotus that is used to make "movies" of software actions for demos and training purposes. Voice annotations can be added with a microphone and sound card. A runtime player, which can be freely distributed, plays the .SCM files. The player can also be combined with the file, providing a self-running ScreenCam movie.

**S**

**screen capture**    Transfering the current on-screen image to a text or graphics file. In Windows, programs such as HiJaak make capturing the screen a snap. You can save the capture as a GIF, BMP or other bitmapped format.

**screen dump**    Printing the entire on-screen image. In Windows, you have to save the screen contents to the clipboard first and then paste them into an image editor from which you can print (see **Win Print screen**). On the Macintosh, press CMND-SHIFT-3 to create a MacPaint file of the current screen. On DOS PCs, pressing SHIFT-PRINTSCREEN prints the current text screen. For graphics in DOS, third-party programs work best.

**screen font**    A font used for on-screen display. For true WYSIWYG systems, screen fonts must be matched as close as possible to the printer fonts. Contrast with *printer font*.

**screen frequency**    The resolution of a halftone. It is the density of dots (how far they're spaced apart from each other) measured in lines per inch. In a digital system, the screen frequency is simulated by the placement of the dots within the halftone cells. See *halftone*.

**screen grabber**    A program that saves the current screen image and other screen status information in order for the screen to be restored at a later time.

**screen grid**    A grid used in tetrode and pentode vacuum tubes that reduces the electrostatic influence of the plate on the control grid. A fixed bias voltage is applied to the screen grid, which sits between the control grid and plate (anode). The screen grid's fixed potential helps isolate the control grid from any fluctuations that occur on the plate. See *tetrode* and *pentode*.

**screen name**    America Online's term for username. See *username*.

**screen overlay**    (1) A clear, fine-mesh screen that reduces the glare on a video screen.

(2) A clear touch panel that allows the user to command the computer by touching displayed buttons on screen.

(3) A temporary data window displayed on screen. The part of the screen that was overlaid is saved and restored when the screen overlay is removed.

**screen reader**    Software for the visually impaired that reads the contents of a computer screen, converting the text to speech. Screen readers are designed for specific operating systems and generally work with most applications. See *text-to-speech* and *MSAA*.

**screen resolution**    See *high resolution*, *PC display modes* and **how to select a PC display system**.

**screen saver**    A utility that prevents a CRT from being etched by an unchanging image. After a specified duration of time without keyboard or mouse input, it blanks the screen or displays moving objects. Pressing a key or moving the mouse restores the screen.

It would actually take many hours to burn in an image on today's color monitors. However, the entertainment provided by these utilities (swimming fish, flying toasters, etc.) has made them very popular.

**screen scraper**    Also called "frontware," it is software that adds a graphical user interface to character-based mainframe and minicomputer applications. The screen scraper application runs in the personal computer which is used as a terminal to the mainframe or mini via 3270 or 5250 emulation.

Popular screen scrapers are Star:Flashpoint, Mozart and ESL. Attachmate's QuickApp adds screen scraper capability to development systems such as PowerBuilder, Visual Basic and SQLWindows.

**script**    (1) A typeface that looks like handwriting or calligraphy.

(2) A program written in a special-purpose programming language such as used in a communications program or word processor. See *macro language*.

(3) A program written in an interpreted programming language typically smaller in scope and function than full-blown compiled languages such as C and C++. See *scripting language*.

**scripting host**    The facility within a program that runs another program. For example, a Web browser is a scripting host that can execute instructions in languages such as Java and JavaScript. See *Windows Script Host.*

**scripting language**    A high-level programming, or command, language that is interpreted (translated on the fly) rather than compiled ahead of time. A scripting, or script, language may be a general-purpose programming language or it may be limited to specific functions used to augment the running of an application or system program. Spreadsheet macros and communications scripts are examples of limited-purpose scripting languages. DOS batch files are another example. Microsoft's Visual Basic for Applications (VBA) is a scripting language version of Visual Basic used to automate Microsoft Office applications. Scripting  languages, such as Perl, Tcl and Python, are quite extensive rivaling many programming languages. See *Perl, Tcl/Tk, Python, VBA, DOS batch file* and *COM automation.*

**scriptlet**    A reusable HTML and script element introduced by Microsoft starting with Internet Explorer 4.0. It enables an HTML or script fragment to be downloaded once, maintained in a cache and referenced over and over by different HTML pages and scripts.

**ScriptX**    A multimedia technology from Apple that includes data formats, a scripting language and runtime environment. It is designed for creating applications that can be played on a variety of computers and consumer electronic devices. ScriptX was originally developed by Kaleida, Inc., a joint venture between Apple and IBM, which closed its doors in 1995.

**scroll**    To continuously move forward, backward or sideways through the text and images on screen or within a window. Scrolling implies continuous and smooth movement, a line, character or pixel at a time, as if the data were on a paper scroll being rolled behind the screen. See *auto scroll.*

**scrollable field**    A short line on screen that can be scrolled to allow editing or display of larger amounts of data in a small display space. When you type into Look Up in this software, you can type beyond the end of the input box. That's a scrollable field.

**scrollable window**    A window that contains more data than is visible at one time. Its contents can be scrolled (moved up, down, sideways within the window) in order to view the entire document, image or list of items.

**scroll arrow**    Onscreen arrow that is clicked in order to scroll the screen in the corresponding direction. The screen moves one line, or increment, with each mouse click.

**scroll back buffer**    Reserved memory that holds a block of transmitted data, allowing the user to browse back through it.

**scroll bar**    A horizontal or vertical bar that contains a box that looks like an elevator in a shaft. The bar is clicked to scroll the screen in the corresponding direction, or the box (elevator, thumb) is clicked and then dragged to the desired direction.

**SCROLL LOCK**    On PC keyboards, a key used to toggle between a scrolling and non-scrolling mode. When on, the arrow keys scroll the screen regardless of the current cursor location. This key is rarely used for its intended purpose, if at all.

**scroll mouse**    A mouse with a rubber wheel in the center. Also known as a "wheel mouse," when you move the wheel back and forth, it scrolls the content of the active window. The scroll mouse is very useful for research on the Web where all pages are created with a vertical (portrait) orientation. Some mice have an additional button on the side that can be used to quickly go back to the previous Web page.

**Scroll Mouse**
Popularized by Microsoft's
IntelliMouse, the scroll mouse
has become a standard feature
on many PCs ever since.

**scrubbing**    See *data scrubbing* and *audio scrubbing.*

**SCSA**    (Signal Computing System Architecture)  An open architecture for transmitting voice and video signals from Dialogic Corporation, Parsippany, NJ (www.dialogic.com). Its backbone is the SCbus, a 131 Mbps data path that provides up to 2,048 time slots, the equivalent of 1,024 two-way voice conversations at 64 Kbps.

## SCSI    (Small Computer System Interface)

Pronounced "scuzzy." SCSI is a hardware interface that allows for the connection of up to 15 peripheral devices to a single board called a "SCSI host adapter" that plugs into the motherboard, typically using a PCI slot. SCSI peripherals are daisy chained together. They all have a second port used to connect the next device in line. SCSI host adapters are also available with two controllers that support up to 30 peripherals.

Introduced in 1986 and originally developed by Shugart Associates (see *SASI*), SCSI is widely used from desktop PCs to mainframes, although most desktop PCs come with IDE drives. The advantage of SCSI in a desktop PC is that a scanner and several other drives (CD-Rs, DVD-RAM, Zip drives, etc.) as well as hard drives can be added to one SCSI cable chain. However, this has become less important as alternative interfaces such as USB and FireWire have become popular.

Until the late 1990s, SCSI hard disks were the only ones used in RAID configurations, which provide improved performance and/or fault tolerance. Since the advent of IDE RAID controllers, SCSI and IDE have become more equalized, although SCSI continues to be the drive interface of choice in the server market. See *RAID*.

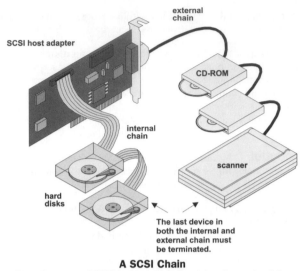

**A SCSI Chain**
The advantage of SCSI is that several peripherals can be daisy chained to one host adapter, using only one slot in the bus.

Windows 95/98/NT/2000 and the Macintosh provide internal support for SCSI, but Windows 3.1 and DOS did not. Installing SCSI in a Win 3.1 or DOS machine required adding the appropriate SCSI driver. See *SCSI switch*.

### ASPI and CAM

Because internal support for SCSI was not provided by DOS and Windows 3.x, there was no benchmark for a standard implementation. As a result, hooking up two SCSI devices often meant plugging in two host adapters, negating SCSI's advantage of connecting multiple peripherals.

ASPI and CAM were created to resolve these differences and provide common interfaces between the drivers and the host adapters. Almost all SCSI products are ASPI and CAM compliant. Windows 95 and higher does support popular SCSI host adapters directly. It also supports the ASPI and CAM standards so that older applications and drivers will run even if Windows does not support that peripheral with a native driver.

### SCSI Is Like a LAN

SCSI is a bus structure itself and functions like a mini-LAN connecting eight or 16 devices. The host adapter counts as one device, thus up to seven or 15 peripherals can be attached depending on the SCSI type. SCSI allows any two devices to communicate at one time (host to peripheral, peripheral to peripheral).

### SCSI SPECIFICATIONS

| Type | Bus Width (bits) | Max Dev | Tfr Rate MB/ Sec | SE | LVD | HVD | Pins |
|------|------------------|---------|------------------|----|-----|-----|------|
| SCSI-1 | 8 | 8 | 5 | 6 | 12* | 25 | 25 |
| SCSI-2 | 8 | 8 | 5 | 6 | 12* | 25 | 50 |
| Fast SCSI | 8 | 8 | 10 | 3 | 12* | 25 | 50 |
| Wide SCSI, aka | | | | | | | |
| Fast Wide SCSI | 8 | 16 | 20 | 3 | 12* | 25 | 68 |
| Ultra SCSI | 8 | 8 | 20 | 3 | - | - | 50 |
| Wide Ultra SCSI | 16 | 16 | 40 | - | 12* | 25 | 68 |
| Wide Ultra SCSI | 16 | 8 | 40 | 1.5 | - | - | 68 |
| Wide Ultra SCSI | 16 | 4 | 40 | 3 | - | - | 68 |
| Ultra2 SCSI | 8 | 8 | 40 | - | 12 | 25 | 50 |

| Type | Bus Width (bits) | Max Dev | Tfr Rate MB/ Sec | SE | LVD | HVD | Pins |
|------|------------------|---------|------------------|----|-----|-----|------|
| Wide Ultra2 SCSI | 16 | 16 | 80 | - | 12 | 25 | 68 |
| Ultra3 SCSI, aka | | | | | | | |
| Ultra160 | 16 | 16 | 160 | - | 12 | - | 68 |
| Ultra4 SCSI, aka | | | | | | | |
| Ultra320 | 16 | 16 | 320 | - | 12 | - | 68 |

12* - LVD was not part of these specs; however,
    if all devices are LVD, 12 meters applies.
    If any device is single ended, then length
    in SE column applies.

Information for this chart was obtained from the
SCSI Trade Association (STA), San Francisco, CA,
(www.scsita.org).

**Version Compatibility**    The different SCSI types provide backward and forward compatibility. If a new SCSI host adapter is used with an older SCSI drive, the drive will run at its maximum speed. If an older SCSI host adapter is used with a newer drive, the drive will run at the host adapter's maximum speed.

**SCSI and IDE Drives**    You can install SCSI hard disk drives in a PC that already contains one or two IDE disk drives. The IDE drive will still be the boot drive, and the SCSI drives will provide additional storage. Follow the instructions in your SCSI host adapter manual carefully to make the correct settings. Some SCSI host adapters provide floppy disk control, which can be disabled.

**IDs and Termination**    SCSI devices are daisy chained together. External devices have two ports, one for the incoming cable and another for the outgoing cable to the next device. An internal device has a single port that attaches to a ribbon cable with multiple connectors. Each device must be set to a unique ID number, which is normally done by flipping rotary switches on external devices or by setting jumpers on internal ones. The SCSI ID determines the device priority, which starts at 7 and goes to 0 and then from 15–8. The host adapter defaults to the highest priority, which is 7.

A subset of Plug and Play, called "SCSI Configured Automatically" (SCAM), allows IDs to be set by software rather than manually. Both the host adapter and peripheral must support this.

The device at the end of a SCSI chain must be terminated by either setting a switch or plugging a resistor module into the open port. Usually, host adapters default to terminated. If devices are connected both internally and externally, the host adapter termination must be removed, and termination must be applied to the ends of both chains.

**Parallel to SCSI**    There are adapters that allow SCSI peripherals to be connected via the parallel port. Although the parallel port's transfer rate is considerably less than the SCSI host adapter, it does provide a means to hook up SCSI devices to laptops without PC Card slots or desktop machines without available bus slots.

**LUNs**    Each SCSI device can be further broken up into eight logical units, identified by logical unit numbers (LUNs) 0–7. Although most SCSI disks contain only one disk inside and are addressed as LUN 0, CD-ROM and optical disk jukeboxes contain multiple units. Each disk in these devices can be addressed independently via LUN numbers; for example, a four-disk jukebox could be assigned LUN 0 to 3.

**Single Ended, Differential, and Low Voltage Differential**
There are three types of SCSI signaling. Single-ended SCSI allows devices to be attached to a total cable length of 6 or 3 meters for Fast and Ultra SCSI. Single-ended SCSI is not defined for Ultra2 SCSI and higher.

Differential SCSI, or High Voltage Differential SCSI (HVD), is used when devices are spread across a room, because the total cable length is increased to 25 meters. Differential devices cost more than single-ended ones.

Ultra2 SCSI introduced Low Voltage Differential signaling (LVD or LVDS) that supports cable lengths up to 12 meters. Single-ended SCSI uses a data line and ground. Both HVD SCSI and LVD SCSI use data low and data high lines to increase transmission distance. However, LVD requires less power and is less costly, because the transceivers are built into the controller chips.

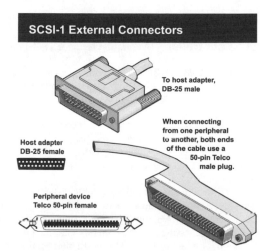

**SCSI-1 External Connectors**

To host adapter,
DB-25 male

When connecting
from one peripheral
to another, both ends
of the cable use a
50-pin Telco
male plug.

Host adapter
DB-25 female

Peripheral device
Telco 50-pin female

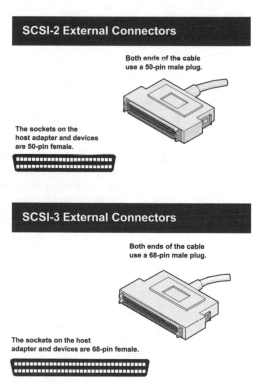

**SCSI-2 External Connectors**

Both ends of the cable
use a 50-pin male plug.

The sockets on the
host adapter and devices
are 50-pin female.

**SCSI-3 External Connectors**

Both ends of the cable
use a 68-pin male plug.

The sockets on the host
adapter and devices are 68-pin female.

S

**SCSI adapter**   See *SCSI host adapter.*

**SCSI controller**   A common term for a SCSI host adapter. See *SCSI.*

**SCSI host adapter**   The controlling electronics for SCSI contained on a printed circuit board that plugs into the computer's motherboard. A SCSI host adapter is often called a "SCSI controller." See *SCSI.*

**SCSI switch**   A device that cross connects computers to SCSI devices and overcomes many SCSI limitations. The regular SCSI interface is a shared bus, but a SCSI switch, pioneered by GigaLabs, Inc., Sunnyvale CA, (www.gigalabs.com), provides the full bandwidth between any two devices, greatly increasing overall throughput.

SCSI switches also double the cable distance between devices and minimize access contention, because the devices are not subject to a priority by their ID numbers. In addition, the 7-device or 15-device limit gives way to any number of devices, because the switches can be cascaded. GigaLabs provides remote access between its switches via ATM or with fiber up to 20 km.

**SCSI termination**   The end of a SCSI chain, which must be identified by placing a resistor module in the open port. See *SCSI.*

**scuzzy**   See *SCSI.*

**S-DARS**   (**S**atellite-**D**igital **A**udio **R**adio **S**ervice) See *DARS.*

**SDBN**   (**S**oftware-**D**efined **B**roadband **N**etwork) A future high-bandwidth service from AT&T for data, voice and video. It uses ATM cell relay technology with speeds up to 600 Mbits/sec.

**SDDS**   (**S**ony **D**ynamic **D**igital **S**ound) A digital audio encoding system used in movie theaters since 1993. The SDDS sound track is recorded optically as microscopic pits similar to a CD along both outer edges of the 35mm film strip. An SDDS reader is mounted on the projector, and red LEDs read the pits and convert them into digital data. Using a 5:1 compression, SDDS supports 6-channel and 8-channel auditoriums. No home theater counterpart is expected. See *Dolby Digital, DTS* and **THX.**

**SDF**   (**S**tandard **D**ata **F**ormat) A simple file format that uses fixed length fields. It is commonly used to transfer data between different programs.

```
SDF
Pat Smith     5 E. 12 St.      Rye        NY
Bob Jones     200 W. Main St.  Palo Alto  CA

Comma Delimited
"Pat Smith","5 E. 12 St.","Rye","NY"
"Bob Jones","200 W. Main St.","Palo Alto","CA"
```

**SDH**   (**S**ynchronous **D**igital **H**ierarchy) The European counterpart to SONET. See *SONET.*

**SDI**   **(1)** (**S**erial **D**igital **I**nterface) A physical interface widely used for transmitting digital video, typically D1. It uses a high grade of coaxial cable and a single BNC connector with teflon insulation. See *D1, BNC connector* and *serial interface.*

**(2)** (**S**witched **D**igital **I**nternational) An AT&T dial-up service providing 56 and 64 Kbits/sec digital transmission to international locations.

**(3)** (**S**ingle **D**ocument **I**nterface) A Windows function that allows an application to display only one document at a time. SDI requires the user to load another instance of the application to work with two or more documents. Contrast with *MDI.*

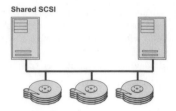

**Shared SCSI**

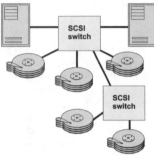

**Switched SCSI**

**Shared versus Switched**
Switched SCSI eliminates many limitations, including bandwidth, cable distance and number of devices. The switch has a backplane capable of handling the full SCSI bandwidth at each of its ports.

**(4) (S**tandard **D**rive **I**nterface) A hard disk interface for VAXs.

**(5) (S**trategic **D**efense **I**nitiative) A high-tech defense system for the U.S. proposed during the Reagan administration.

**S-DIMM**    (SDRAM-DIMM) SDRAM chips housed on a DIMM module. See *SDRAM* and *DIMM*.

**SDIP**    See *Shrink DIP* and *Skinny DIP*.

**SDK**    (**S**oftware **D**eveloper's **K**it) See *developer's toolkit* and *Windows SDK*.

**SDL**    (**S**pecification and **D**escription **L**anguage) A modeling language used to describe realtime systems. It is widely used to model state machines in the telecommunications, aviation, automotive and medical industries. SDL is used to model the details of a system, which can be simulated and proven, whereas UML is used to model at a higher level of abstraction.

There are three parts to an SDL diagram: the system definition, block and process. The system definition defines the major nodes (blocks) of the system such as clients and servers, while the block charts show more details. The process diagram shows the processing steps in each block. See *state machine* and *UML*.

**SDLC**    (**S**ynchronous **D**ata **L**ink **C**ontrol) The primary data link protocol used in IBM's SNA networks. It is a bit-oriented synchronous protocol that is a subset of the HDLC protocol. See *SNA*, *DLC* and *Microsoft DLC*.

**SD Memory Card**    (**S**ecure **D**igital Memory Card) A flash memory card that provides secure storage for handheld devices such as cellphones and PDAs. The SD card extends the MultiMediaCard (MMC) format by adding encryption and using the same 32×24 mm form factor. The SD is slightly thicker (2.1 mm rather than 1.4), but SD readers will accept standard MMC cards. For more information, visit www.sdcard.org. See *MultiMediaCard*.

**SDMI**    (**S**ecure **D**igital **M**usic **I**nitiative) A set of rules for securely distributing digital music over the Internet. Announced in February 1999, it is backed by the Recording Industry Association of America (RIAA) and Sony, Warner, BMG, EMI and Universal, the top five music production companies. SDMI provides the guidelines for developing compliant digital rights management (DRM) systems. See *DRM* and *RIAA*.

**SDP**    (**S**treaming **D**ata **P**rocedure) A MicroChannel mode that increases data transfer from 20MB per second to 40MB per second.

**SDRAM**    (**S**ynchronous **DRAM**) A type of dynamic RAM memory chip that has been widely used starting in the latter part of the 1990s. SDRAMs are based on standard dynamic RAM chips, but have sophisticated features that make them considerably faster. First, SDRAM chips are fast enough to be synchronized with the CPU's clock, which eliminates wait states. Second, the SDRAM chip is divided into two cell blocks, and data is interleaved between the two so that while a bit in one block is being accessed, the bit in the other is being prepared for access. This allows SDRAM to burst the second and subsequent, contiguous characters at a rate of 10ns, compared to 60ns for the first character.

SDRAM provides 800 MBps or 1 GBps data transfer depending on whether the bus is 100MHz or 133MHz. Double Data Rate SDRAM (DDR SDRAM) doubles the rate to 1.6 GBps and 2.1 GBps by transferring data on both the rising and falling edges of the

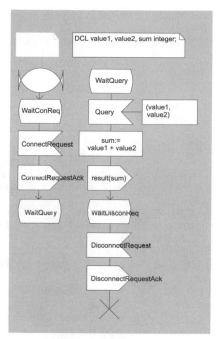

**SDL Process Diagram**
This diagram shows the processing steps within the server of a very simple system that lets the user add two numbers at a terminal. Note that there is more detail in this diagram than their is in the UML counterpart below.
*(Diagram courtesy of Telelogic, AB, www.telelogic.com)*

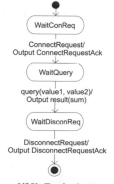

**UML Equivalent**
This is the UML equivalent of the process diagram above. Note the difference in the levels of detail. This UML diagram was turned into the SDL above by Telelogic's UML to SDL Translator (see *UML* for more diagrams). *(Diagram courtesy of Telelogic, AB, www.telelogic.com)*

clock. DDR SDRAM uses additional power and ground lines and requires 184-pin DIMM modules rather than the 168-pin DIMMs used by SDRAM. DDR SDRAM is also known as DSDRAM (Double-Speed DRAM), DDR DRAM (Double Data Rate DRAM) and SDRAM-II. See *SGRAM*.

**SDSL**    See *DSL*.

**SDTV**    (StanDard TV) The digital equivalent of the NTSC television format, which has been the broadcast standard since TV's inception. The digital TV standard (DTV) in the U.S., launched in November 1998, defines the SDTV format. See *DTV*.

**SDX**    (1) See *AIT*.
(2) (**S**torage **D**ata **A**cceleration) A technique from Western Digital that improves performance of IDE-based CD-ROM drives. Instead of cabling the drive to the 40-pin IDE interface on the motherboard, it is connected to the Western Digital IDE hard drive with a 10-pin cable. SDX-compliant CD-ROM drives are required.

**SE**    (1) See *systems engineer*, *service engineer* and **Windows Second Edition**.
(2) (**S**ingle **E**nded) The traditional type of signaling on the SCSI bus. See *SCSI*.

**Seagate**    (Seagate Technology, Inc., Scotts Valley, CA, www.seagate.com) The largest independent manufacturer of disk drives. Founded in 1979 by Alan Shugart, Tom Mitchell and Doug Mahon, it was the first to offer a 5MByte drive using 5.25" platters making it ideal for the burgeoning desktop computer industry. Seagate became the first company to ship 10 million drives.

In 1989, it aquired Imprimis Technology, a CDC subsidiary making workstation and mainframe drives, nearly doubling Seagate's revenue to $2.5 billion. In 1996, it acquired Conner Peripherals bringing combined revenues to more than eight billion dollars. Starting in the mid 1990s, Seagate acquired several software companies and formed Seagate Software subsidiaries in Europe and the U.S. Seagate Software provides products for asset, network, storage and information management.

**The ST506**
Introduced in 1979, Seagate's ST506 was the first hard disk drive for personal computers. This 5.25" full-height drive held 5MB and became an industry standard used in CP/M machines and, later, the IBM PC and its successors. *(Image courtesy of Seagate Technology, Inc.)*

**SEAlink**    A version of Xmodem that uses a sliding window protocol, transmits file name, date and size and provides batch file transfer. Good for delay-introduced transmissions (packet switching, satellites).

**seamless integration**    An addition of a new application, routine or device that works smoothly with the existing system. It implies that the new feature can be activated and used without problems. Contrast with *transparent*, which implies that there is no discernible change after installation.

**search**    To look for specific data in a file or an occurrence of text in a file.

**search and replace**    To look for an occurrence of data or text and replace it with another set of data or text.

**search box**    A rectangular onscreen box, or field, that accepts typed-in text in order to search for matching documents.

**search engine**    Software that searches for data based on some criteria. Although search engines have been around for decades, they have been brought to the forefront since the World Wide Web exploded onto the scene. Every Web search site uses a search engine that it has either developed itself or has purchased from a third party. Search engines can differ dramatically in the way they find and index the material on the Web, and the way they search the indexes from the user's query.

The terms "search engine" and "Web search site" are used synonymously, although the former technically describes the software and methodolgy used, while the latter refers to the site itself. See *Web search sites*.

**search engine optimization**    Designing a Web site so that search engines easily find the pages and index them. The goal is to have your page be in the top 10 results of a search. Optimization includes the choice of words used in the text paragraphs and the placement of those words on the page, both visible and hidden inside meta tags. Search engines use different criteria for indexing, and those criteria may change. Thus, it becomes increasingly difficult to satsify every one equally. Yahoo! and other directory-oriented search sites manually index a Web site, which may provide the best results for the user.

**search key**    In a search routine, the data entered and used to match other data in the database.

**search path**    The route to a particular file. See *path*.

**search scope**    The location that a search should look in. In a search or query, the search scope can refer to a single folder, several folders, a disk or several disks.

**search sites**    See *Web search sites*.

**seat**    See *per seat*.

**Sebring ring**    A network of PCI buses that provides up to 512 slots for PCI boards. It links up to 128 PCI buses via a 16-bit dual counter-rotating ring that operates at 266MHz, which achieves a 4.25 GBytes/sec aggregate throughput.

**SEC**    (Single Edge Contact) See *SECC*.

**SECAM**    (Systeme En Couleur Avec Memoire) A color TV standard that was developed in France. It broadcasts 25 interlaced frames per second (50 half frames per second) at 625 lines of resolution. SECAM is used in France and Russia and many countries in Africa, Eastern Europe and the Middle East. See *NTSC* and *PAL*.

**SECC**    (Single Edge Contact Cartridge) Starting with the Pentium II, a chip module from Intel that contains CPU and L2 cache chips. SECC and SECC2 cartridges plug into Slot 1 on the motherboard. See *Slot 1* and *SEPP*.

**secondary cache**    See *L2 cache*.

**secondary channel**    In communications, a subchannel that is derived from the main channel. It is used for diagnostic or supervisory purposes, but does not carry data messages.

**secondary index**    An index that is maintained for a data file, but not used to control the current processing order of the file. For example, a secondary index could be maintained for customer name, while the primary index is set up for customer account number. See *primary index*.

**secondary storage**    External storage, such as disk and tape.

**Second Edition**    See *Windows Second Edition*.

**second-generation computer**    A computer made of discrete electronic components. In the early 1960s, the IBM 1401 and Honeywell 400 were examples.

**second-level cache**    Same as *L2 cache*. See *cache*.

**second source**    An alternative supplier of an identical or compatible product. A second source manufacturer is one that holds a license to produce a copy of the original product from another manufacturer.

**secret key cryptography**    Using the same secret key to encrypt and decrypt messages. The problem with this method is transmitting the secret key to a legitimate person that needs it. See *cryptography*.

**sector**    The smallest unit of storage read or written on a disk. See *magnetic disk*.

**sector interleave**    Sector numbering on a hard disk. A one to one interleave (1:1) is sequential: 0,1,2,3, etc. A 2:1 interleave staggers sectors every other one: 0,4,1,5,2,6,3,7.

In 1:1, after data in sector 1 is read, the disk controller must be fast enough to read sector 2, otherwise the beginning of sector 2 will pass the read/write head and must rotate around to come under the head again. If it isn't fast enough, a 2:1 or 3:1 interleave gives it time to read all sectors in a single rotation, eliminating wasted rotations. The best interleave is based on the speed of the particular disk drive. Interleaves are created with the low-level format.

**sector map**    See *sector interleave.*

**sector sparing**    Maintaining a spare sector per track to be used if another sector becomes defective. After detecting a bad write, the disk driver or controller writes the data into the spare sector and marks the bad sector as unusable. Existing data can also be moved to the spare sector if the sector is marginal, but the data can be read after several attempts. Sector sparing provides a degree of fault tolerance within the individual disk itself, but RAID provides fault tolerance for the entire disk. See *RAID* and *hot fix.*

**sector tandem**    See *tandem switch.*

**Secure Digital card**    See *SD Memory Card.*

**secure server**    A server that is fortified against attack. See *firewall, bastion host* and *secure Web server.*

**secure transaction**    A transaction that has been encrypted for online transmission. See *secure Web server.*

**secure Web protocol**    See *secure Web server.*

**secure Web server**    (1) A server on the Web that supports one or more of the major security protocols such as SSL, SHTTP and PCT. This means that order form data from your browser is encrypted before being sent (uploaded) to the Web site, making it extremely difficult for a third party to decipher credit card numbers and other sensitive data that it were to fraudulently capture. See *security protocol* and *cryptography.*

(2) An intranet Web server that is fortified against attack from the public Internet. All public Web servers present themselves to the outside world and are more vulnerable than Web servers for internal intranets. See *firewall.*

**SecurID card**    An authentication token from Security Dynamics, Inc., Bedford, MA (www.securid.com), that uses a smart card that authorized users keep in their possession. The card's microprocessor and the host computer are synchronized by a unique number and the time of day. When users log onto a SecurID-enabled host, they type in the number displayed on their cards at that moment as an additional passcode. If the number matches the number that the host computes, the user is presumed to be the valid holder of the card.

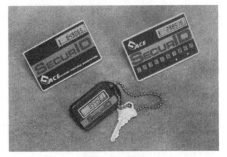

**SecurID Card**
A variety of SecurID authentication tokens are displayed in this picture. *(Image courtesy of Security Dynamics, Inc.)*

**security**    The protection of data against unauthorized access. Programs and data can be secured by issuing identification numbers and passwords to authorized users. However, systems programmers, or other technically competent individuals, will ultimately have access to these codes. In addition, the password only validates that a correct number has been entered, not that it the actual person. Using biometric techniques (fingerprints, eyes, voice, etc.) is a more secure method.

Passwords can be checked by the operating system to prevent logging in. Database (DBMS) software prevents unauthorized access by assigning each user an individual view of the database. Data transmitted over networks can be secured by encryption to prevent eavesdropping.

Although precautions can be taken to detect an unauthorized user, it is extremely difficult to determine if a valid user is purposefully doing something malicious. Someone may have valid access to an account for updating, but determining whether phony numbers are entered requires more processing. The bottom line is that effective security measures are always a balance between technology and personnel management. See *security scan, security audit, audit trail, NCSC, ICSA, access control, share-level security, user-level security* and *social engineer*.

**security audit**    An examination of networks and computer systems by an independent consultant to determine an organization's vulnerability to criminal invasion (hackers, viruses, arson, etc.) and natural disasters (fire, tornados, earthquakes, etc.). See *security scan*.

**security card**    A card used for identification purposes which is typically the size of a credit card. See *magnetic stripe, smart card* and *SecurID card*.

**security ID**    See *security card, SID* and *SecurID card*.

**security kernel**    The part of the operating system that grants access to users of the computer system.

**security levels**    See *NCSC*.

**security protocol**    A communications protocol that encrypts and decrypts a message for online transmission. Security protocols generally also provide authentication. The security protocols that have emerged on the Web are Netscape's SSL, NCSA's SHTTP, Microsoft's PCT and the IETF's IPSec. Web browsers and servers generally support all the popular security protocols. See *HTTPS, SHTTP, SSL, PCT* and *IPSec*.

**Face Recognition**
Face recognition is one of the best ways to authenticate a person. This TrueFace system from Miros uses neural network technology to distinguish a face with different appearances, such as with and without glasses and changing hair styles. *(Image courtesy of Miros, Inc.)*

**security scan**    A test of a network's vulnerabilities. A security scan does not attempt to break into the network illegally, rather it tries to find areas of vulnerability. A security scan uses a variety of automated software tools, typically performing hundreds of routine tests and checks. Security experts recommend that a security scan be undertaken at least quarterly. See *penetration test* and *security audit*.

**sed**    (Stream EDitor) A UNIX text editor that processes an entire file. It executes "ed" commands from an earlier UNIX editor, but instead of interactively editing text one line at a time, sed applies the commands to the entire file. Thus, sed is the stream-oriented version of ed.

**seed**    (1) The starting value used by a random number generation routine to create random numbers.
(2) (SEED) (Self-Electro-optic-Effect Device) An optical transistor developed by David Miller at Bell Labs in 1986.

**seek**    (1) To move the access arm to the requested track on a disk.
(2) An assembly language instruction that activates a seek operation on disk.
(3) A high-level programming language command used to select a record by key field.

**seek time**    The average of the time it takes to move the read/write from its current location to a particular track on a disk. In 1998, Seagate introduced its line of Cheetah hard disks with 5ms seek time. See *access time*.

**segment**    (1) Any partition, reserved area, partial component or piece of a larger structure. See *overlay*.
(2) One of the bars that make up a single character in an LED or LCD display.
(3) For DOS segment addressing, see *paragraph*.

**segmented address space**    Memory addressing in which each byte is referenced by a segment, or base, number and an offset that is added to it.
    A PC running in 16-bit mode (Real Mode) uses a segmented address space. Memory is broken up into 64KB segments, and a segment register always points to the base of the segment that is currently being addressed. The PC's 32-bit mode is considered a flat address space, but it too uses segments. However, since one 32-bit segment addresses 4GB, one segment covers all of memory.

**segmented network**   A network that is broken up into groups in order to contain broadcast traffic and improve performance. Contrast with *flat network*. See *LAN segment*.

**segment register**   A register that points to the base of the current segment being addressed. See *segmented address space*.

**SEI**   (Software Engineering Institute, Pittsburg, PA, www.sei.cmu.edu) A federally funded research and development center that is under contract to Carnegie Mellon University and is devoted to the advancement of software engineering and the quality of software support systems. The SEI carries out its mission through two principal areas of work: Software Engineering Management Practices, and Software Engineering Technical Practices.

The former practice, which employs the use of the Capability Maturity Model (CMM) focuses on improving the management of software acquisition, development and implementation processes. The latter focuses on improving software engineering processes and tools. Together, these two practices are intended to promote the evolution of software engineering from an ad hoc, labor-intensive activity to a well managed discipline that is supported by technology. See *CMM*.

**Sel**   (SELect) A toggle switch on a printer that takes the printer alternately between online and offline.

**selection sort**   (1) A sort that starts by searching for the lowest or highest item (alphanumerically) in the list and moving it to the #1 position. The search is repeated starting with the second item, then the third, and so on, until all of items are in the required order. Selection sorts perform numerous comparisons, but fewer data movements than other methods.

(2) A search for specific data starting at the beginning of a file or list. It copies each matching item to a new file so that the selected items are in the same sequence as the original data.

**selective calling**   In communications, the ability of the transmitting station to indicate which station in the network is to receive the message.

**selector channel**   A high-speed computer channel that connects a peripheral device (disk, tape, etc.) to the computer's memory.

**selector pen**   Same as *light pen*.

**Selectric typewriter**   Introduced in 1961 by IBM, the first typewriter to use a golf-ball-like print head that moved across the paper, rather than moving the paper carriage across the print mechanism. It rapidly became one of the world's most popular typewriters. IBM has always excelled in electromechanical devices. In 1991, IBM's typewriter division was spun off into Lexmark International.

**self-booting**   Refers to automatically loading the operating system upon startup.

**self-checking digit**   See *check digit*.

**self-clocking**   Recording of digital data on a magnetic medium such that the clock pulses are intrinsically part of the recorded signal. A separate timer clock is not required. Phase encoding is a commonly-used self-clocking recording technique.

**self-documenting code**   Programming statements that can be easily understood by the author or another programmer. COBOL provides more self-documenting code than does C, for example.

**self-extracting archive**   An executable program that contains one or more compressed files. The program, which is actually the decompression program itself, decompresses the files automatically (self extracting) when run.

**self-extracting file**   See *self-extracting archive*.

**self healing**   The ability to restore a failure situation such as a broken transmission line or a missing program file that is part of a software application. See *self-healing network*.

**self-healing network**   A network architecture that can withstand a failure in its transmission paths. See *SONET ring*.

**self-service application**    A software application that allows a user to obtain information or complete a business transaction on the computer that has traditionally required the help of a human representative. Voice response systems and Web sites are widely used for self-service applications. See *kiosk*.

**self-subscribing**    Signing up for an online service such as an e-mail newsletter or information service (push technology) at one's own initiative.

**semantic error**    In programming, writing a valid programming structure with invalid logic. The compiler will generate instructions that the computer will execute, because it understands the syntax of the programming statements, but the output will not be correct.

**semantic gap**    The difference between a data or language structure and the real world. For example, in order processing, a company can be both customer and supplier. Since there is no way to model this in a hierarchical database, the semantic gap is said to be large. A network database could handle this condition, resulting in a smaller semantic gap.

**semantic processor**    Software that can extract knowledge (relevance, meaning, etc.) from text. See *knowledge management*.

**semantics**    The study of the meaning of words. Contrast with *syntax*, which governs the structure of a language.

**semaphore**    **(1)** A hardware or software flag used to indicate the status of some activity.
    **(2)** A shared space for interprocess communications (IPC) controlled by "wake up" and "sleep" commands. The source process fills a queue and goes to sleep until the destination process uses the data and tells the source process to wake up.

**semicolon**    In programming, the semicolon (;) is often used to separate various elements of an expression. For example, in the C statement **for (x=0; x; x++)** the semicolons separate the starting value, number of iterations and increment).

**semiconductor**    A solid state substance that can be electrically altered. Certain elements in nature, such as silicon, perform like semiconductors when chemically combined with other elements. A semiconductor is halfway between a conductor and an insulator. When charged with electricity or light, semiconductors change their state from nonconductive to conductive or vice versa. The most significant semiconductor is the transistor, which is simply an on/off switch. See *chip*.

**semiconductor device**    An elementary component, such as a transistor, or a larger unit of electronic equipment comprised of chips.

**semiconductor IP**    (semiconductor Intellectual Property) A collection of pre-designed hardware circuits that are implemented in ASICs or other semiconductor chips. An "IP block" is an individual function or circuit.

**semiconductor laser**    See *laser diode*.

**sendmail**    An SMTP-based mail transport program for UNIX developed at the University of California at Berkeley by Eric Allman in 1981.

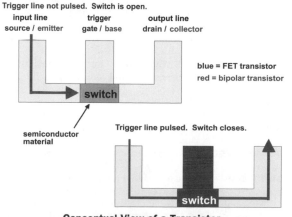

**The Transistor Concept**

The transistor is an electronic switch. The switching element is made of semiconductor material which conducts electricity when it is pulsed.

If there is no pulse on the trigger line, the semiconductor element is in a non-conductive state. When it is pulsed, it becomes conductive and current flows from the input to the output.

Trigger line not pulsed. Switch is open.

| input line | trigger | output line |
| source / emitter | gate / base | drain / collector |

blue = FET transistor
red = bipolar transistor

switch

semiconductor material

Trigger line pulsed. Switch closes.

switch

**Conceptual View of a Transistor**
Semiconductor material normally acts as an insulator. When it is pulsed with electricity, it becomes electrically conductive for that moment. It simply acts as an electrical bridge.

S

Sendmail is the MTA (message transfer agent) which stores and forwards the mail and is the most widely used MTA on the Internet. In 1998, Allman commercialized the product by forming Sendmail, Inc. (www.sendmail.com), which offers a GUI interface for modifying the configuration file instead of dealing directly with more than a thousand lines of text. Sendmail, Inc. also offers a Windows NT version that includes the POP mail server and message store. Examples of mail clients developed for sendmail in the UNIX world are elm, pine, mush and mailx. For information on the open source version, visit www.sendmail.org. See *messaging system* and *BSD UNIX*.

**sensor**    A device that measures or detects a real-world condition, such as motion, heat or light and converts the condition into an analog or digital representation. An optical sensor detects the intensity or brightness of light, or the intensity of red, green and blue for color systems.

**SEPP**    (Single Edge Processor Package) A chip module from Intel that contains CPU and L2 cache chips. Used with Celeron CPUs, the SEPP plugs into Slot 1 on the motherboard. See *Slot 1* and *SECC*.

**sequence check**    Testing a list of items or file of records for correct ascending or descending sequence based on the item or key fields in the records.

**sequencer**    See *MIDI sequencer*.

**Sequent**    (Sequent Computer Systems, Inc., Beaverton, OR, www.sequent.com) A computer company founded in 1983 by 17 ex-employees of Intel that specializes in multiprocessing systems for the client/server environment. Sequent pioneered adapting SMP to UNIX and is a leader in the high-end UNIX market.

Sequent's SMP machines are all Intel based and are scalable up to 30 Pentium processors. Its Symmetry series runs the UNIX-based DYNIX/ptx operating system, and the WinServer series runs Windows NT. Its NUMA-Q 2000 line, introduced in 1996, can scale up to 252 processors. In 1999, Sequent was acquired by IBM.

**sequential**    One after the other in some consecutive order such as by name or number.

**sequential access method**    Organizing data in a prescribed ascending or descending sequence. Searching sequential data requires reading and comparing each record, starting from the top or bottom of file. See *GSAM*.

**sequential scan**    Same as *non-interlaced*.

**serial**    One after the other.

**serial async card**    Same as *multiport serial card*.

**serial bus**    A type of bus that transmits data serially. Ethernet is an example of a serial bus on a network. Serial buses are also expected to become popular for attaching multiple peripherals to computers.

Although both use serial transmission, a serial bus differs from a serial port. The serial port connects the computer to one peripheral device. A serial bus allows for the connection of multiple devices.

**serial computer**    A single-processor computer that executes one instruction after the other. Contrast with *parallel computer*.

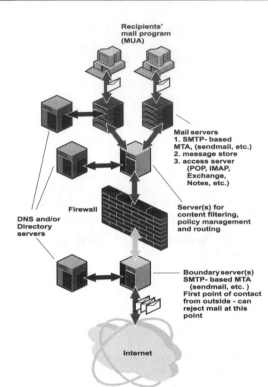

**Enterprise Mail System**
This is a typical architecture of a large enterprise mail system. *(Illustration assistance courtesy of Sendmail, Inc.)*

**serial dot matrix printer**    See *dot-matrix printer*.

**Serial Infrared**    See *SIR*.

**serial interface**    A data channel that transfers digital data in a serial fashion: one bit after the other over one wire or fiber. The serial port on a PC is a serial interface that is used to attach modems and scanners. On earlier PCs, mice also used the serial port. USB and FireWire (IEEE 1394) are other types of serial interfaces. Serial interfaces may have multiple lines, but only one is used for data. Contrast with *parallel interface*. See *serial port*, *RS-232*, *USB* and *FireWire*.

**serialize**    To convert a parallel signal made up of one or more bytes into a serial signal that transmits one bit after the other.

**Serial Line IP**    See *SLIP*.

**serial matrix printer**    See *dot-matrix printer*.

**serial mouse**    A mouse that plugs into the serial port on a PC. Serial mice are the most common type. Contrast with *bus mouse*.

**serial number**    A unique number assigned by the vendor to each unit of hardware or software. See *signature*.

**serial port**    A socket on a computer used to connect a modem, mouse, scanner or other serial device via the computer's serial interface. The Macintosh uses the serial port to attach a printer, whereas the PC uses the parallel port. Transferring files between two personal computers can be accomplished by cabling the serial ports of both machines together and using a file transfer program.

The serial port uses DB-9 and DB-25 connectors. On the back of PCs, either one serial port is provided (9-pin connector) or two (one 9- and one 25-pin or two 9-pin). Serial port #1 (COM1) is typically used for the mouse and serial port #2 (COM2) for the modem.

In a PC, serial port circuits are built into the motherboard (typically two serial ports, one parallel port and one game port). On earlier PCs, they were either on stand-alone expansion cards or on the IDE host adapter card. Contrast with *parallel port*. See *serial interface* and *RS-232*.

**Faster Serial Interfaces Have Arrived!**    The USB and FireWire (IEEE 1394) interfaces finally made it onto PCs in 1998, offering a quantum jump in transfer rate, plus the ability to daisy chain large numbers of devices on the same bus. See *USB* and *FireWire*.

**Serial & Parallel Ports on a PC**

**Serial port (DB-9 male)**

**Serial port (DB-25 male)**

**Parallel port (DB-25 female)**

A PC usually comes with two serial ports (COM1, COM2) and one parallel port (LPT1).

On the back of the PC, the serial ports are either two male DB-9 connectors or one DB-9 and one DB-25. The parallel port is a DB-25 female connector.

**serial printer**    (1) A printer that uses a serial port for connection to the computer.
(2) A printer that prints one character at a time, such as a dot matrix printer.

**Serial SCSI**    Running SCSI on Fibre Channel, SSA or FireWire. SCSI is a parallel bus, and the parallel signals must be converted to serial transmission to ride over different transport systems. See *Fibre Channel*, *SSA*, *FireWire* and *SCSI*.

**serial transmission**    Transmitting data one bit at a time. Contrast with *parallel transmission*.

**Series/1**    An IBM minicomputer series introduced in 1976. It was used primarily as a communications processor and for data collection in process control.

**series mode surge suppression**    A type of surge suppression that absorbs the surge energy either completely or it absorbs most of it, releasing the residue slowly to neutral. Contrast with *MOV surge suppression*.

**serif**    Short horizontal lines added to the tops and bottoms of traditional typefaces, such as Times Roman. Contrast with *sans-serif*.

**serpentine recording**    Tape recording format of parallel tracks in which the data "snakes" back and forth from the end of one track to the beginning of the next track.

**server**    A computer in a network shared by multiple users. The term may refer to both the hardware and software or just the software that performs the service. For example, Web server may refer to the Web server software in a computer that also runs other applications, or, it may refer to a computer system dedicated only to the Web server application. There would be several dedicated Web servers in a large Web site.

The following are the network servers defined in this database.

- Application server
- Audio server
- Database server
- Fax server
- File server
- Intranet server
- Mail server
- Merchant server
- Modem server
- Network access server
- Print server
- Proxy server
- Remote access server
- Telephony server
- Terminal server
- Video server
- Web server

**server appliance**    A self-contained computer system specialized for network use. Its applications are preinstalled, and access to setup and configuration is via a Web browser. Server appliances may provide a single application or several applications; for example, a single device may provide file server, Web server, mail server and firewall capabiliies.

Server appliances are designed to be plugged into the network and configured, loaded with files and begin working immediately with limited or no technical support, at least for a power user or experienced network administrator. The appliance may also include a RAID-based disk system and redundant power supplies to provide an increased level of fault tolerance.

Although not known as such, one might say that the router was the first server appliance. It is a specialized, self-contained system that plugs into the network and is used for the application of packet forwarding. However, routers come in many sizes and complexities, the larger ones requiring significant technical expertise and detailed knowledge of the network. See *Internet appliance*.

**server application**    (1) An application designed to run in a server. See *client/server*.

(2) Any program that is run in the server, whether designed as a client/server application or not.

(3) See *OLE*.

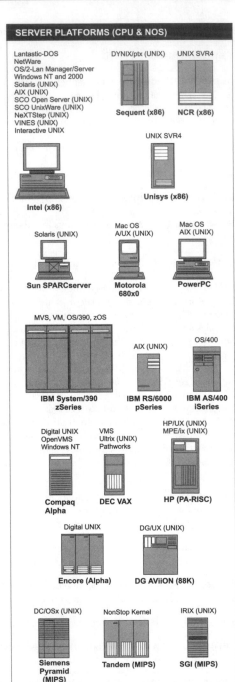

**SERVER PLATFORMS (CPU & NOS)**

Lantastic-DOS
NetWare
OS/2-Lan Manager/Server
Windows NT and 2000
Solaris (UNIX)
AIX (UNIX)
SCO Open Server (UNIX)
SCO UnixWare (UNIX)
NeXTStep (UNIX)
VINES (UNIX)
Interactive UNIX

DYNIX/ptx (UNIX)    UNIX SVR4

**Sequent (x86)**    **NCR (x86)**

**Intel (x86)**

UNIX SVR4

**Unisys (x86)**

Solaris (UNIX)    Mac OS A/UX (UNIX)    Mac OS AIX (UNIX)

**Sun SPARCserver**    **Motorola 680x0**    **PowerPC**

MVS, VM, OS/390, zOS

AIX (UNIX)    OS/400

**IBM System/390 zSeries**    **IBM RS/6000 pSeries**    **IBM AS/400 iSeries**

Digital UNIX
OpenVMS
Windows NT

VMS
Ultrix (UNIX)
Pathworks

HP/UX (UNIX)
MPE/ix (UNIX)

**Compaq Alpha**    **DEC VAX**    **HP (PA-RISC)**

Digital UNIX    DG/UX (UNIX)

**Encore (Alpha)**    **DG AViiON (88K)**

DC/OSx (UNIX)    NonStop Kernel    IRIX (UNIX)

**Siemens Pyramid (MIPS)**    **Tandem (MIPS)**    **SGI (MIPS)**

**server based**     Refers to hardware or software that runs in the server. Contrast with *client based*.

**server-based computing**     Refers to storing applications in a server. The term has two meanings, depending on whether the applications are also run in the server. If the applications are only stored in the server, it refers to the network computer architecture. If the applications are run in the server, it refers to the centralized, timeshared architecture of the mainframe, which is available in the Windows environment with Windows Terminal Server (NT 4.0), Windows Terminal Services (Windows 2000) and Citrix's MetaFrame and WinFrame products. In the UNIX world, it is implemented by X Window systems and Citrix's MetaFrame (see *network computer, thin client, ICA* and *Windows Terminal Server*).

During the late 1980s and early 1990s, the term, although not widely used, would have described client/server architecture in which both client and server participated in the processing (see *client/server*).

**server-based rules**     Procedures that are executed on the server. It often refers to messaging systems that can be programmed to do such things as alerting the user when a certain type of mail arrives or automatically replying to specific kinds of mail.

**server-centric**     Designed to run only in a server rather than in individual workstations. See *LAN-centric* and *host-centric*.

**server farm**     A group of network servers that are housed in one location. They might all run the same operating system and applications and use load balancing to distribute the workload between them. See *clustering*.

**ServerNet**     A clustering technology from Tandem that provides a high-speed interconnect architecture between subsystems. ServerNet I uses switching technology to transfer data at 50 Mbytes/sec in both directions between CPUs, between I/O devices and between CPU and I/O, but not CPU to memory. ServerNet II products transfer at 125 Mbytes/sec. Originally used with Tandem's proprietary fault-tolerant computers, ServerNet is available for NT clusters. See *clustering* and *SAN*.

**server program**     Software that runs in a server in the network. Contrast with *client program*, which is software that resides in the user's PC or workstation.

**server-side**     Refers to any operation that is performed at the server. Contrast with *client-side*.

**server-side include**     An HTML command used to place up-to-date data or boilerplate into a Web page before sending it to the user. For example, it can be used to retrieve the current date and size of downloadable files that are constantly changing. It can be used to insert a boilerplate message where only the boilerplate needs to be changed to bring all the pages up-to-date. HTML pages that contain server-side includes often use the .shtml file extension.

The Include command inserts the contents of another document at the tag location. Echo inserts the contents of an environment variable. Fsize and Flastmod insert size and date of a file, and Config controls the format of the output. The Exec command executes a CGI script. See *SHTML*.

**server-side script**     A small program run on the server that automates or controls certain functions or links one program to another. On the Web, a CGI script is an example of a server-side script.

**server software**     Software that resides in a server and provides services to multiple users on the network. Contrast with *client software*. See *client/server*.

**service**     Functionality derived from a particular software program. For example, network services may refer to programs that transmit data or provide conversion of data in a network. Database services provides for the storage and retrieval of data in a database.

**service-aware switch**     A network switch that forwards traffic based on high-level protocols and with awareness of the services being supplied to users of the network. See *BRAS* and *IP services switch*.

**service bureau**     An organization that provides data processing and online services. It may offer a variety of software packages, batch processing services (data entry, COLD, etc.) and custom programming.

Customers pay for storage of data on the system and processing time used. Connection is made to a service bureau through dial-up connections, private lines, the Internet, frame relay or other WAN services.

Service bureaus also exist that support desktop publishing and presentations and provide imagesetting, color proofing, slide creation and other related services on an hourly or per item basis.

**service discovery**   The automatic identifying of a software-based service in a network. Traditionally, software communicates with other software through predefined linkages. A service discovery infrastructure allows processing functions to be offered throughout the Internet for example and then executed after they have been located.

**service engineer**   A technician that maintains and repairs computers.

**service level management system**   Software that manages the delivery of guaranteed levels of network services and application availability within an organization. An SLM system uses event management and reporting components to gather statistics and notify the appropriate individuals or groups to take action. A comprehensive system enables the administrator to view the status of the network and all running applications in realtime. See *event management system* and *application management system*.

**service pack**   A software patch that is applied to an installed application. It is either downloaded from the vendor's Web site or distributed via CD-ROM. When executed, it modifies the application in place.

**service provider**   An organization that provides some type of communications service such as a telephone company, an Internet service provider (ISP), an application service provider (ASP) or a storage service provider (SSP). See *common carrier* and *Internet service provider*.

**servlet**   A Java application that runs in a Web server or application server and provides server-side processing, typically to access a database or perform e-commerce processing. It is a Java-based replacement for CGI scripts, Active Server Pages (ASPs) and proprietary plug-ins written in C and C++ for specific Web servers (ISAPI, NSAPI).

Because they are written in Java, servlets are portable between servers and operating systems. The servlet programming interface (Java Servlet API) is a standard part of J2EE. If a Web server, such as Microsoft's Internet Information Server (IIS), does not run servlets natively, a third-party servlet plug-in can be installed to add the runtime support. See *Java, application server, JSP, J2EE, ISAPI, NSAPI* and *CGI script*.

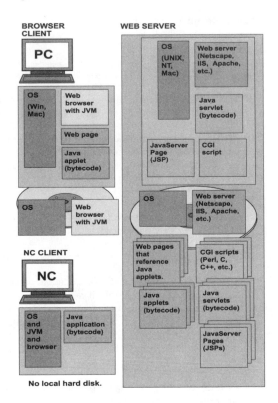

**Servlets Run in the Server**
Servlets, as well as JavaServer Pages (JSPs), are server-side applications. The Web server or application server must support servlet processing, which became available as part of the Java 2 platform.

**servo**   An electromechanical device that uses feedback to provide precise starts and stops for such functions as the motors on a tape drive or the moving of an access arm on a disk.

**session**   (1) In communications, the active connection between a user and a computer or between two computers.

(2) Using an application program (period between starting up and quitting).

(3) One or more tracks of audio or data that were recorded at one time on a compact disc. See *multisession*.

**session bean**   An Enterprise JavaBean (EJB) that implements a service (processing). Contrast with *entity bean*. See *EJB*.

**session layer**    The services in the OSI protocol stack (layer 5 of 7) that initiates and manages the communications session. See *OSI*.

**SET**    (Secure Electronic Transaction) A standard protocol from MasterCard and Visa for securing online credit card payments via the Internet. It is a three-way transaction: the user, merchant and bank must use the SET protocols.

Credit card data and a digital certificate (for authentication) is stored in a plug-in to the user's Web browser. The order is received by a SET-enabled merchant server that passes encrypted payment information to the bank. Approval is electronically sent to the merchant.

**SETI**    (Search for ExtraTerrestrial Intelligence) The search for life on other planets. Numerous programs have been undertaken, and one that involves anyone connected to the Internet is the SETI@home project at the University of California at Berekeley. Using a screen saver to convert idle time into computations, it analyzes radio telescope data and sends the results back to a Web site. For more information, visit www.setiathome.ssl.berkeley.edu. See also www.seti-inst.edu.

**SETL**    (SET Theory Language) A programming language developed by Jack Schwartz in the early 1970s. It is based on set theory and used for mathematical and telecommunications applications. See *ALICE* and *set theory*.

**set theory**    The branch of mathematics or logic that is concerned with sets of objects and rules for their manipulation. UNION, INTERSECT and COMPLEMENT are its three primary operations and they are used in relational databases as follows.

Given a file of Americans and a file of Barbers, UNION would create a file of all Americans and Barbers. INTERSECT would create a file of American Barbers, and COMPLEMENT would create a file of Barbers who are not Americans, or of Americans who are not Barbers. See *fuzzy logic*.

**settlement rate**    The amount charged by the local access carrier for terminating a call from another country.

**set-top box**    The cable TV box that "sits on top" of the TV set. A variety of new set-top boxes are emerging for Internet TV and other interactive services.

**setup**    See *BIOS setup* and *install program*.

**SETUP.INF**    A file that contains information Windows needs to install itself into the PC. See *INF file*.

**setup program**    (1) Same as *install program*.
(2) See *BIOS setup*.

**setup string**    A group of commands that initialize a device, such as a printer. See *escape character*.

**seven dwarfs**    IBM's early competitors in the mainframe business: Burroughs, CDC, GE, Honeywell, NCR, RCA and Univac.

**seven-segment display**    A common display found on digital watches and readouts that looks like a series of 8s. Each digit is formed by selective illumination of up to seven separately addressable bars.

**sex changer**    See *gender changer*.

**SFA**    See *sales force automation*.

**SGI**    (SGI, Mountain View, CA, www.sgi.com) A manufacturer of workstations and servers, founded in 1982 by Jim Clark. The company was founded as Silicon Graphics, Inc., but changed to its acronym in 1999. SGI offers a line of UNIX, Linux and Windows-based workstations and servers that are geared to high-performance computing and

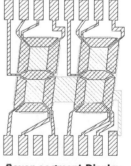

**Seven-segment Display**
Using two seven-segment display units, this readout can show from 00 to 99. Each of the seven segments has its own contact to the outside electronics. *(Image courtesy of LXD, Inc.)*

advanced graphics. SGI workstations are optimized with SGI's proprietary graphics technologies.

SGI shipped its first graphics terminal in 1983 and first workstation in 1984 and has always led the way in computer graphics. Its custom chips and subsystems perform the tedious processing necessary to display objects on screen. Running a flight simulator on an SGI workstation was always far more realistic than any personal computer or video game. In 1992, SGI acquired MIPS Technologies and has used its RISC-based microprocessors in most of its product lines.

SGI computers are used in a variety of commercial and industrial applications. Airplane manufacturers use them to simulate airflow on new aircraft. Auto companies visualize new car designs and simulate crashes. Medical researchers visualize cell structures, and Hollywood creates extraordinary special effects.

**Dr. James H. Clark**
Clark founded SGI in 1982. Clark has a penchant for starting innovative companies. In 1994, he founded Netscape. *(Image courtesy of SGI.)*

**Virtual Reality**
Moving through a 3-D environment in realtime that looks as real as this takes enormous computing power. SGI machines create this kind of visual reality. *(Image courtesy of SGI.)*

**SGML**    (**S**tandard **G**eneralized **M**arkup **L**anguage)  An ISO standard for defining the format in a text document. An SGML document uses a separate Document Type Definition (DTD) file that defines the format codes, or tags, embedded within it. Since SGML describes its own formatting, it is known as a meta-language. SGML is a very comprehensive language that includes hypertext links. The HTML format used on the Web is an SGML document that uses a fixed set of tags. See *HTML*, *XML* and *DSSSL*.

**SGRAM**    (**S**ynchronous **G**raphics **RAM**)  A type of dynamic RAM chip that is similar to the SDRAM technology, but includes enhanced graphics features for use with display adapters. Its Block Write and Mask Write functions allow the frame buffer to be cleared faster and selected pixels to be modified faster.

**sh**    (**SH**ell)  A UNIX command that invokes a different shell. It can be used like a batch file to execute a series of commands saved as a shell.

**SHA-1**    (**S**ecure **H**ash **A**lgorithm-1)  A popular one-way hash algorithm used to create digital signatures. SHA was developed by the NIST, and SHA-1 is a revision to the standard released in 1994. SHA-1 is similar to the MD4 and MD5 algorithms developed by Rivest, but it is slightly slower and more secure. See *one-way hash function*.

**shadow batch**    A data collection system that simulates a transaction processing environment. Instead of updating master files (customers, inventory, etc.) when orders or shipments are initiated, the transactions are stored in the computer. When a user makes a query, the master record from the previous update cycle is retrieved; but before it's displayed, it's updated in memory with any transactions that may affect it. The up-to-date master record is then displayed for the user. At the end of the day or period, the transactions are then actually batch processed against the master file.

**shadow mask**    A thin screen full of holes that adheres to the back of a color CRT's viewing glass. The electron beam is aimed through the holes in the mask onto the phosphor dots. There are generally more holes per inch than the maximum resolution obtainable from that monitor. See *slot mask*.

**shadow RAM**    A RAM copy of a PC's ROM BIOS. In order to improve performance, the BIOS, which is stored in a ROM chip, is copied to and executed from RAM. RAM chips are accessed faster than ROMs.

**shaped CD**    See *custom-cut CD* and *business card CD*.

**share**    A resource such as a file, folder or printer, that is sharable with other users on the network. See *share-level security*.

**shared DASD**    A disk system accessed by two or more computers within a single datacenter. Disks shared in personal computer networks are called "file servers" or "database servers."

**shared Ethernet**    Refers to the traditional Ethernet topology in which all stations share the total bandwidth of the network. Whether connected via a common cable (10Base5, 10Base2) or a hub (10BaseT), transmission is on a first-come, first-served basis. Contrast with *switched Ethernet*, in which each sender and receiver pair has the full bandwidth of the line.

**shared logic**    Using a single computer to provide processing for two or more terminals. Contrast with *shared resource*.

**shared media LAN**    A local area network (LAN) that shares its total available bandwidth with all transmitting stations at any given time. Ethernet, Token Ring and FDDI are examples. When shared media LANs run out of capacity to serve their users effectively, they can often be upgraded by replacing the hub with a switch. See *LAN switch*.

**shared memory**    Memory that can be used by more than one processor. See *SMA, SMP* and *MPP*.

**shared resource**    Sharing a peripheral device (disk, printer, etc.) among several users. For example, a file server and laser printer in a LAN are shared resources. Contrast with *shared logic*.

**shared slot**    Typically refers to two different expansion slots that are physically in line with each other in order to save space. Only one of the slots can be used. For example, there may be a PCI/ISA or PCI/EISA shared slot on a motherboard.

**shared WAP**    See *HomeRF*.

**share-level security**    Access control to a file, printer or other network resource based on knowing the password of that resource. Share-level security provides less protection than user-level security, which identifies each person in the organization. Contrast with *user-level security*.

**share name**    The name of a shared resource such as a file, folder or printer. See *share-level security*.

**shareware**    Software distributed on a trial basis through the Internet, online services, BBSs, mail-order vendors and user groups. Shareware is software on the honor system. If you use it regularly, you're required to register and pay for it, for which you will receive technical support and perhaps additional documentation or the next upgrade. Paid licenses are required for commercial distribution.

There are tens of thousands of shareware programs, some fantastic, some awful. Shareware vendors compile catalogs with hundreds and thousands of products and sell them by mail or at shows for a small fee. That fee is often misunderstood. It is not the registration fee, rather it is the fee for distributing the shareware to you. See *freeware, public domain software, ASP* and *ad-supported software*.

**Sharing Violation**    An attempt to open a file that is being used by another program. In a normal single-user environment, if an application has already called in a file (document, spreadsheet, etc.), and another program tries to read it, a sharing violation occurs. The solution is to close the file in the application that has "locked" it in order to release it for use by another application.

In a network environment, files can be made sharable for multiple users. If the data is only read and not changed, multiple applications (users) can read the file at the same time. If the file can be updated by multiple users, the operating system or DBMS must manage access to the data via file and record locking or other tracking mechanisms.

**Shark disk**    (1) A family of high-end storage servers from IBM. See *ESS*.

(2) A removable disk drive from Avatar Peripherals, Inc., Milpitas, CA, designed for the mobile market. Its compact 250MB cartridges never became popular, and the company closed in 1998. See *magnetic disk*.

**sheet-fed scanner**    A scanner that allows only paper to be scanned rather than books or other thick objects. It moves the paper across a stationary scan head. Contrast with *flatbed scanner, handheld scanner* and *drum scanner*.

**sheet feeder**    A mechanical device that feeds stacks of cut forms (letterheads, legal paper, etc.) into a printer.

**shelfware**    Products that remain unsold on a dealer's shelf or unused by the customer.

**S**

**shell**    The outer layer of a program that provides the user interface, or way of commanding the computer. In UNIX, the Bourne shell was the original command processor, with C shell and Korn shell developed later. In DOS, the shell command typically specifies COMMAND.COM, the command processor that interprets commands such as Dir and Type. DOS also came with an optional user interface with menus, known as the DOS Shell, but was never very popular. See *DOS Shell*.

**shell account**    See *UNIX shell account*.

**shell out**    To temporarily exit an application, go back to the operating system, perform a function and then return to the application.

**shell script**    A file of executable UNIX commands that is created in a text editor. When the file is run, each command is executed until the end of the file is reached. Shell scripts are the UNIX counterpart to DOS batch files and scripts supported by the Windows Scripting Host. Once the shell script is written, it is made usable by changing its file status to "executable" with the UNIX chmode (change mode) command. See *Windows Script Host* and *DOS batch file*.

**Sherlock**    A Macintosh utility starting with Version 8.5 of the operating system that provides a common facility for searching the local hard disk, the local network and the Internet.

**shielded pair**    See *twisted pair*.

**shielded twisted pair**    See *twisted pair*.

**shift register**    A high-speed circuit that holds some number of bits for the purpose of shifting them left or right. It is used internally within the processor for multiplication and division, serial/parallel conversion and various timing considerations.

**Shiva**    The leading remote access server manufacturer. Founded in 1985, Shiva's first products were its NetModem network modems for the Macintosh and later for PCs. Its LANRover is a proprietary remote access server, providing remote users access to LANs via modem. Shiva also developed the remote access software in Windows 95. In 1999, Shiva was acquired by Intel.

**Shlaer-Mellor**    An object-oriented analysis and design method developed by Sally Shlaer and Stephen Mellor. The method is applied by partitioning the system into domains. Each domain is analyzed, and the analysis is verified by simulation. A translation method is specified, and the domain models are translated into the object-oriented architecture of the target system.

**shocked site**    A Web site that contains animations created in Macromedia Director. Users need the Shockwave plug-in for their browser in order to view the files.

**Shockmachine**    Software for Windows and the Macintosh from Macromedia that lets you play Shockwave games, puzzles and other animations offline. You can download your favorite games and play them whenever you wish without being on the Internet. See *Shockwave*.

**Shockwave**    A browser plug-in that lets output from Macromedia's Director, Authorware and Freehand software be viewed on the Web. Shockwave is a popular plug-in for viewing animated sequences. See *Shockmachine* and *shocked site*.

**shopping bot**    A program that searches the Web for the best price for a particular item you wish to purchase. See *bot*.

**shopping cart**    The online equivalent of the supermarket cart. You place your merchandise in the cart and then check out when you are all finished.

**short**    In programming, an integer variable. In C, a short is two bytes and can be signed (–32K to +32K) or unsigned (64K). Contrast with *long*.

**short card**    In a PC, a plug-in printed circuit board that is half the length of a full-size board. Contrast with *long card*.

**shortcut**    In Windows, a shortcut is a pointer to a program or data file. Shortcut icons can be placed on the desktop or stored in other folders. Double-clicking a shortcut is the same as double clicking the original file. However, deleting a shortcut does not remove the original. See *Win Shortcuts*.

**shortcut key**    A keyboard key or combination of keys that performs some function in Windows or in Windows applications. See also *Win Shortcuts*.

**shorthand**    See *digispeak*.

**short haul**    Short distance. Short haul implies traversing a small geographic area such as a few miles at most. Contrast with *long haul*. See *line driver*.

**short-haul modem**    See *line driver*.

**short messaging**    See *SMS*.

**shovelware**    A large amount of "extras" included on a CD-ROM that add little benefit to the user. Shovelware implies that a lot of freeware, shareware and/or public domain software was added to make it look like a great value. With seven times as much capacity, DVD-ROMs are expected to include even more shovelware than CD-ROMs.

**Shortcuts**
Shortcut icons have a northeast-pointing arrow at their bottom left side. Note the difference between the icons on the actual items (left) and the shortcuts that point to them (right). Deleting the shortcut does not delete the original item.

**shows**    See *trade shows*.

**Shrink DIP**    (Shrink Dual In-line Package) A wider, flatter and longer DIP chip that contains a large number of pins on both of its long sides. See *DIP*.

**shrink-wrapped software**    Refers to store-bought software, implying a standard platform that is widely supported.

**SHS virus**    An Internet virus that comes as an e-mail attachment or Web site download with an .SHS extension. SHS files are Windows OLE "scrap files," which act as containers, or packages, for a variety of contents, including executable code. If run, the program or script within the SHS file can do almost anything. The file type fools people because it does not use an obvious, executable extension such as .EXE or .VBS.

**SHTML**    (Server-parsed HTML) A file extension used to identify HTML pages that contain server-side includes. Server-parsed means that the server scans the page for commands that require additional insertion before the page is sent to the user. See *server-side include* and *parse*.

**SHTTP**    (Secure HTTP) A protocol that provides secure transactions over the World Wide Web. It is endorsed by NCSA and a variety of organizations. See *security protocol*.

**shunt**    To divert, switch or bypass.

**shut down**    To quit all applications and turn off the computer.

**SI**    See *systems integrator* and *silicon*.

**SID**    **(1)** (Society for Information Display, Santa Ana, CA, www.sid.org) A membership organization founded in 1962 devoted to the information display industry. With chapters around the world, SID hosts conferences in the U.S. and abroad and publishes a monthly magazine.
   **(2)** (Security ID) In Windows NT and 2000, a unique name assigned to each user and to each workgroup. See *access token*.

**sideband**    In communications, the upper or lower half of a wave. Since both sidebands are normally mirror images of each other, one of the halves can be used for a second channel to increase the data-carrying capacity of the line or for diagnostic or control purposes.

**Sidekick**    A personal information manager (PIM) for Windows from Starfish Software, Scotts Valley, CA (www.starfishsoftware.com). Introduced by Borland in 1984, it was the first popular popup (TSR) program for DOS PCs. It included a calculator, notepad, appointment calendar, phone dialer and ASCII table. Later versions added more notepad commands, calendar alarms, scientific and programming calculators, limited file management and an outliner.

**sidetone**    In a telephone handset, sending a small amount of your voice signal back into your ear through the handset so that you hear yourself talk. It makes the conversation more comfortable when you hear a little bit of your own speech, because you know the line isn't dead. See *hybrid*.

**SIDF**    (System Independent Data Format) A tape format designed as a standard for tape backup systems. If widely used, tapes created by one backup software vendor on one platform would be readable by another vendor's software on another platform.

Using a Field Identifier (FID) that identifies the operating system the data was created on, the SIDF format can be extended to support future file systems. Originating from Novell's Storage Management Services (SMS) and governed by the SIDF Association based in Arlington Heights, IL, SIDF is expected to become an international standard.

**Siebel software**    A family of Web-based enterprise relationship management (ERM) applications from Siebel Systems, Inc., San Mateo, CA (www.siebel.com). A complete range of products for sales, marketing and customer service are provided. For example, Siebel Sales is the sales force automation module for one user, which is available free at the Siebel Web site. Siebel Sales Enterprise is the commercial version which provides global sharing of information. Siebel Systems was founded in 1993 by Tom Siebel and Pat House.

**Sieve of Eratosthenes**    A benchmark program used to test the mathematical speed of a computer. The program calculates prime numbers based on Eratosthenes's algorithm.

**SIG**    (Special Interest Group) A group of people that meets and shares information about a particular topic of interest. It is usally a part of a larger group or association.

**SIGCAT**    (Special Interest Group on CD Applications and Technology, Reston, VA, www.sigcat.org) The world's largest CD-ROM users group, founded by Jerry McFaul in 1986. With more than 10,000 members worldwide, it provides catalogs, publications, regular meetings and conferences.

**SiGe**    See *silicon germanium*.

**SIGGRAPH**    (Special Interest Group on Computer Graphics, www.siggraph.org) The arm of the ACM that specializes in computer graphics. Providing publications, workshops and conferences, it serves technicians and researchers as well as the artist and business community.

**sign**    A symbol that identifies a positive or negative number. In digital code, it is either a separate character or part of the byte. In ASCII, the sign is kept in a separate character typically transmitted in front of the number it represents (+ and − is 2B and 2D in hex).

In EBCDIC, the minus sign can be stored as a separate byte (hex 60), or, more commonly, as half a byte (+ and − is C and D in hex), which is stored in the high-order bits of the least significant byte. For packed decimal, it is in the low-order bits of the least significant byte.

**signal**    Any electrical or light pulse or frequency. The term is often used when a combination of signals are described, such as power, data and control. See *control signal*.

**signal converter**    A device that changes the electrical or light characteristics of a signal.

**signaling**    Sending control signals that start and stop a transmission or other operation. See *signaling in/out of band*.

**signaling in/out-of-band**    In communications, signaling "in-band" refers to sending control signals within the same frequency range or channel as the data signal. For example, a Switched 56 service transmits over a 64 Kbps channel, but uses one out of every eight bits for signaling.

The D channel in an ISDN service, which carries control signals, is often said to use "out-of-band" signaling, but it does not. The D channel is a separate channel which is known as "common channel signaling." See *CCS* and *AIN*.

**signaling point**   A node in an SS7 network. See *SS7* and *point code*.

**signal path**   A wire, or line, that carries an electrical or light pulse or frequency.

**signal processing**   See *DSP*.

**signal to noise ratio**   The ratio of the amplitude (power, volume) of a data signal to the amount of noise (interference) in the line. Usually measured in decibels, it measures the clarity or quality of a transmission channel, audio signal or electronic device. The intent is always to make the ratio greater so that the unwanted noise can be more easily identified and thus eliminated.

**signature**   (1) A unique number built into hardware or software for identification. See *digital signature*.
(2) A group of printed pages, typically 16 or 32, that is bound with other signatures to form a book. The signature was originally printed on one large sheet of paper in a certain "imposition" order that, when cut and folded, results in the right page sequence. Signatures may also be 8, 12, 24, 48 or 64 pages long.

**signature file**   A pre-written text file appended to the end of an e-mail message that is used as a closing or end to the message. It typically contains the sender's name and address, but may contain any kind of text or boilerplate that is repetitively sent.

**signed document**   See *digital signature*.

**significant digits**   Those digits in a number that add value to the number. For example, in the number 00006508, 6508 are the significant digits.

**sign off**   Same as *log off*.

**sign on**   Same as *log on*. See also *Synon/2E*.

**SIIA**   (Software and Information Industry Association, Washington, DC, www.siia.net) A trade organization devoted to the health and welfare of the software and digital content industry by providing support in government relations, business development, education and intellectual property protection. The SIIA sponsors conferences, newsletters and awards and is the 1999 merger of the Software Publishers Association (SPA) and the Information Industry Association (IIA).
SIIA supports the SPA's well-established anti-piracy activities as a separate entity. The SPA Anti-Piracy division of SIIA supports legislation for copyright enforcement and works with the DOJ and FBI to enforce the NET Act. It conducts audits on organizations suspected of illegal copying and files lawsuits against violators. To blow the whistle on a company that has a policy of making illegal copies, call 800/388-PIR8. See *NET Act*.

**silence suppression**   Encoding the start and stop times of silence (lack of voice) in order to eliminate wasted bandwidth when sending voice over a packet-switched system.

**silica**   Same as *silicon dioxide*.

**silica gel**   A highly absorbent form of silicon dioxide often wrapped in small bags and packed with equipment to absorb moisture during shipping and storage.

**silicon**   (Si) The base material used in chips. Next to oxygen, it is the most abundant element in nature and is found in a natural state in rocks and sand. Its atomic structure and availability make it an ideal semiconductor material. In chip making, it is mined from white quartz rocks and put through a chemical process at high temperatures to purify it. To alter its electrical properties, it is mixed (doped) with other chemicals in a molten state. See *silicon germanium*.

**S**

**Silicon Alley**    An area in New York that has become known for its companies devoted to multimedia and the Internet. It is located in Manhattan's "Soho" district, which does not stand for Small Office Home Office, rather it is SOuth of HOuston Street. For job listings in Silicon Alley, visit www.siliconalleyjobs.com. See *Silicon Valley*, *Silicon Forest*, *Silicon Prarie*, *Silicon Glen*, *Bit Valley* and *Siliwood*.

**silicon compiler**    Software that translates the electronic design of a chip into the layout of the logic gates, including the actual masking from one transistor to another. The source of the compilation is either a high-level description or the netlist. See *HDL*, *netlist* and *logic synthesis*.

**silicon dioxide**    ($SiO_2$) A hard, glassy mineral found in such materials as rock, quartz, sand and opal. In MOS chip fabrication, it is used to create the insulation layer between the metal gates of the top layer and the silicon elements below.

**silicon disk**    A disk drive that is permanently simulated in memory. Typically used in laptops for weight reduction, it requires constant power from a battery to maintain its contents.

**Silicon Forest**    An area in Northern Oregon noted for its high-tech companies such as Intel, Fujitsu and Tektronix. Seattle, Washington is also called Silicon Forest. See *Silicon Valley*, *Silicon Prarie*, *Silicon Glen*, *Bit Valley* and *Siliwood*.

**silicon foundry**    See *foundry*.

**silicon germanium**    (SiGe) A semiconductor material made from silicon and germanium. Germanium is very similar to silicon, but when one layer is grown on top of the other to form the base of the transistor, the resulting transistor can switch faster and yield higher performance. SiGe transistors are compatible with standard fabrication processes and are built on the same chip with silicon transistors to create high-frequency circuits. Only a handful of SiGe transistors are used in mobile phones, while tens of thousands are used in optical switches, DACs and ADCs. See *silicon*.

**Silicon Glen**    An area in Scotland that has become known for its growing number of high-tech companies. It is part of central Scotland running east and west between Edinburgh and Glasgow and a bit farther in each direction. See *Silicon Valley*, *Silicon Alley*, *Silicon Prarie*, *Silicon Forest*, *Bit Valley* and *Siliwood*.

**Silicon Graphics**    See *SGI*.

**silicon nitride**    ($Si_3N_4$) A silicon compound capable of holding a static electric charge and used as a gate element on some MOS transistors.

**silicon on insulator**    See *SOI*.

**silicon on sapphire**    See *SOS*.

**Silicon Prarie**    The area around Austin, Texas noted for it high tech companies. Dell Computer headquarters is in Austin. See *Silicon Valley*, *Silicon Alley*, *Silicon Forest*, *Silicon Glen*, *Bit Valley* and *Siliwood*.

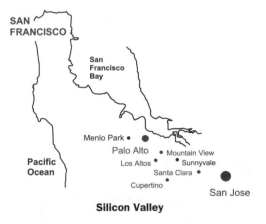

**Silicon Valley**

**Silicon Valley**    An area south of San Francisco, California that is noted for its huge number of computer companies. Initially, Silicon Valley was confined to the Santa Clara valley and started north of Palo Alto stretching 25 miles south to San Jose. With expansion into neighboring towns, the entire San Franciso Bay area can be considered Silicon Valley.

Thousands of hardware, software and related firms have headquarters or offices in Silicon Valley, making it the largest confluence of high tech in the U.S. Throughout the 1970s and 1980s, the number of computer and electronics firms grew exponentially, which is when the area got its nickname. In the 1990s, software and Internet-related companies proliferated. A downside to all this has been high prices for houses and apartments. Real estate goes for two to 10 times prices elsewhere in the country, especially if there is any sizeable land, which is only for the very wealthy. See *Silicon Alley, Silicon Forest, Silicon Glen, Bit Valley* and *Siliwood*.

**Siliwood**    (SILIcon HollyWOOD) A digital convergence term (computers, DVDs, WebTV, etc.). See *digital convergence*.

**SiLK**    A polymer-based, dielectric resin from Dow Chemical, (www.dow.com), that is used to insulate the aluminum or copper wire traces on a chip. See *ILD*.

**SIM**    (1) (Society for Information Management, Chicago, IL, www.simnet.org) Founded in 1968 as the Society for MIS, it is a membership organization comprised of corporate and division heads of IT organizations. SIM provides a forum for exchange of technical information and offers educational and research programs, competitions and awards.

(2) (Subscriber Identity Module) A smart card inserted into GSM phones that contains your telephone account information. It lets you use a borrowed or rented GSM phone as if it were your own. SIM cards can also be programmed to display custom menus on the phone's readout. See *GSM*.

**SIMD**    (Single Instruction stream Multiple Data stream) A computer architecture that performs one operation on multiple sets of data, for example, an array processor. One computer or processor is used for the control logic and the remaining processors are used as slaves, each executing the same instruction. Contrast with *MIMD*.

**SIMM**    (Single In-line Memory Module) An earlier printed circuit board that holds memory chips and plugs into a SIMM socket on the motherboard. See *memory module*.

**SIMM converter**    A printed circuit board that allows older 30-pin SIMMs to be plugged into the newer 72-pin socket. The board contains a 72-pin plug and a number of 30-pin sockets. SIMM converters are also used to expand a single 30-pin or 72-pin socket to multiple SIMM modules.

**simplex**    One way transmission. Contrast with *half-duplex* and *full-duplex*.

**SIMSCRIPT**    A programming language used for discrete simulations.

**SIMULA**    A simulation language originating in the late 1960s that was used to model the behavior of complex systems. SIMULA was the original object-oriented language.

**simulation**    (1) The mathematical representation of the interaction of real-world objects. See *scientific application*.
(2) The execution of a machine language program designed to run in a foreign computer.

**simultaneous voice and data**    See *SVD*.

**sine**    In a right triangle, the ratio of the side opposite an acute angle (less than 90 degrees) and the hypotenuse. The cosine is the ratio between the adjacent side and the hypotenuse. These angular functions are used to compute circular movements.

**sine wave**    A uniform wave that is generated by a single frequency. See *wavelength*.

**A Sine Wave**

**single board computer**    A printed circuit board that contains a complete computer, including processor, memory, I/O and clock.

**single-ended configuration**    Electrical signal paths that use a common ground, which are more susceptible to noise than *differential configuration*.

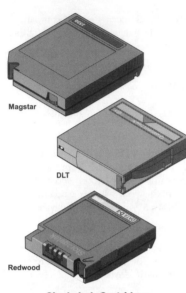

**Single-hub Cartridges**
DLT, Magstar and Redwood all use half-inch, single-hub cartridges in which the tape is fed onto a takeup reel inside the drive. While DLT and Magstar use linear recording, Redwood uses helical scan.

**single-hub cartridge**    A tape cartridge that uses only one spindle and reel. The tape is pulled out of the cartridge and attached to a takeup reel inside the drive. Contrast with *cassette*.

**single inheritance**    In object-oriented programming, a class that has no more than one parent. Contrast with *multiple inheritance*.

**singlemode fiber**    An optical fiber with a core diameter of less than 10 microns. Used for high-speed transmission over long distances, it provides greater bandwidth than multimode, but its smaller core makes it more difficult to couple the light source. Increasingly, singlemode fiber is used for shorter distances. Contrast with *multimode fiber*. See *dispersion* and **fiber-optics glossary**.

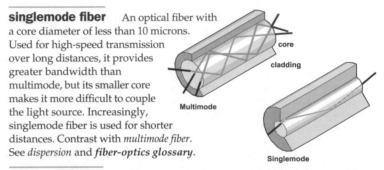

**single precision**    The use of one computer word to hold a numeric value for calculation. Contrast with *double precision*.

**single quotes**    The single quote character (') is sometimes used with double quotes to express quotes within a quoted string. For example, in the dBASE statement **? 'Press the "Enter" key.'**, the single quotes surround the entire string, allowing the double quotes to be used as actual double quotes. See *double quotes*.

**single sign-on**    The ability for users to log on once to a network and be able to access all authorized resources within the enterprise. A single sign-on program accepts the user's name and password and automatically logs on to all appropriate servers. Single sign-on services such as Microsoft's Passport are increasingly being used for Web sites.

**single-system image**    An operational view of multiple networks, distributed databases or multiple computer systems as if they were one system.

**single threading**    Processing one transaction to completion before starting the next.

**Single UNIX Specification**    A common UNIX programming interface governed by X/Open. Formerly known as Spec 1170, it is the latest attempt to unify the UNIX operating system into one set of common programming calls. Products branded by the X/Open organization with the UNIX 95 and UNIX 98 logos conform to Versions 1 and 2 of the specification respectively.

Version 2 of the specfication adds support for realtime processing, threads, Y2K compliance and architecture neutrality. About half of the original APIs were derived from X/Open's XPG4 operating system. Also included are the X/Open Transport Interface (XTI), X and Motif interfaces, UNIX sockets and curses.

**sink**    A device or place that accepts something. See *heat sink* and *data sink*.

**S interface**    The interface used between network terminator 2 (NT2) and an ISDN terminal adapter. This is an internal interface as NT2 is typically built into the terminal adapter. See *ISDN*.

**SIP**    (1) (Single In-line Package) A type of chip module that is similar to a SIMM, but uses pins rather than edge connectors. SIP is sometimes spelled SIPP (Single In-Line Pin Package). See *SIMM*.

**SIP Module**
SIPs use pins to plug the module into the socket whereas SIMMs and DIMMs use edge connectors like ISA and PCI plug-in cards.

**(2)** (System In Package) A complete system packaged in one housing. The SiP term was first used by Amkor Technology in the late 1990s and not trademarked in order to encourage its use worldwide. See *SoC*.

**(3)** (Session Initiation Protocol) A protocol that provides IP telephony services similar to H.323, but is less complex and uses less resources, making it suitable for very small portable devices. See *H.323* and *MGCP*.

**(4)** (SMDS Interface Protocol) The protocol used to support SMDS service. It is composed of the Level 3 Protocol Data Unit (L3_PDU), which contains source and destination addresses and an information field up to 9188 bytes long. See *SMDS*.

**System In Package**
This cross section of an SiP shows a microprocessor (µP), SRAM and flash memory chips packaged together in the same housing. The L,R,C stands for inductor, resistor, capacitor. *(Image courtesy of Amkor Technology, Inc.)*

**(5)** (Software Integration Platform) A specification that provides a common format and interface for storing and retrieving geographic data for the petroleum industry.

**SIPC**    (Simply Interactive PC) An umbrella term from Microsoft and Intel for a PC that works like a home appliance. For example, it has a sealed case, uses external connectors for expansion and boots in just a couple of seconds. The hardware components expected in these machines are the Universal Serial Bus (USB), IEEE 1394 Firewire, DVD drives and Intel's MMX processors and Accelerated Graphics Port (AGP).

**SIPP**    See *SIP*.

**SIR**    (Serial InfraRed) The physical protocol of the IrDA wireless transmission standard. See *IrDA*.

**SISD**    (Single Instruction stream Single Data stream) The architecture of a serial computer. Contrast with *SIMD* and *MIMD*.

**site license**    A license to use software within a facility. It provides authorization to install the software on all or some number of servers for a specified number of users at specified locations as well as make copies of the software for distribution within that jurisdiction. See *SLA, clickwrap* and *UCITA*.

**site management**    See *Web site management*.

**site map**    A hierarchical diagram of the pages on a Web site.

**SiteMill**    See *PageMill*.

**SIT file**    See *StuffIt*.

**six degrees of freedom**    See *6DOF*.

**SIXEL**    A graphics language from Digital that supersedes ReGIS. ReGIS to SIXEL conversion programs are available.

**skew**    **(1)** The misalignment of a document or punched card in the feed tray or hopper that prohibits it from being scanned or read properly.

**(2)** In facsimile, the difference in rectangularity between the received and transmitted page.

**(3)** In communications, a change of timing or phases in a transmission signal.

**(4)** See *cylinder skew* and *head skew*.

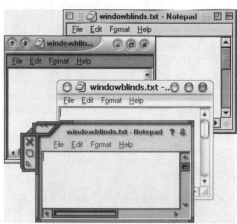

**New Skins for Windows**
Stardock's WindowBlinds lets you create a new skin for Windows. You can design it yourself or get downloads from Stardock's Web site. *(Image courtesy of Stardock.net, Inc., www.stardock.net)*

**skin**    A particular look of a graphical user interface (GUI). For example, Windows enables developers to create an entirely different look for the window frames, scroll bars, buttons and elements on the Windows interface.

**skin effect**   Electrons flowing at the outer edges of a wire rather than through the middle. This occurs at very high frequencies.

**skinning**   Creating a new appearance on a graphical interface (GUI). See *skin*.

**Skinny DIP**   (Skinny Dual In-Line Package)  A narrow, small DIP chip with pins on both of its long sides. See *DIP*.

**SKU**   (StockKeeping Unit)  The number of one specific product available for sale. If a hardware device or software package comes in different versions, there is an SKU for each one.

**skyscraper ad**   An advertisement on a Web site that is vertically oriented on the page and larger than the typical horizontal banner. See *banner ad*.

**SkyTel**   (SkyTel Corporation, Washington, DC, www.skytel.com)  The first nationwide paging service, founded in 1987. It was also the first to integrate voice messaging (dial up and receive the message) as well as alphanumeric text into the pager.

**sky wave**   A radio signal transmitted into the sky and reflected back down to Earth from the ionosphere.

**SLA**   (Service Level Agreement)  A contract between the provider and the user that specifies the level of service that is expected during its term. SLAs are used by vendors and customers as well as internally by IT shops and their end users. They can specify bandwidth availability, response times for routine and ad hoc queries, response time for problem resolution (network down, machine failure, etc.) as well as attitudes and consideration of the technical staff.

   SLAs can be very general or extremely detailed, including the steps taken in the event of a failure. For example, if the problem persists after 30 minutes, a supervisor is notified; after one hour, the account rep is contacted, etc.

**slamming**   The unauthorized switching of your long-distance telephone provider. Unethical marketing organizations contact the local telephone company and claim that certain customers have authorized them to handle their long distance. The company may have obtained your name from a list or spoke to you over the phone with a clever hustle whereby you said yes once to another question. See *cramming*.

**slashdot effect**   The condition in which a Web site is overloaded with traffic because of a positive news article or review published at another Web site. The term comes from Slashdot.com, the "News for Nerds" site that posts articles on technical subjects submitted by users. For information, visit www.slashdot.com.

**slave**   A computer or peripheral device controlled by another computer. For example, a terminal or printer in a remote location that only receives data is a slave. When two personal computers are hooked up via their serial or parallel ports for file exchange, the file transfer program may make one computer the master and the other the slave.

**slave tube**   A display monitor connected to another monitor in order to provide an additional viewing station.

**SLC**   (Subscriber Loop Carrier)  Lucent's designation for its digital loop carrier (DLC) products. See *digital loop carrier*. See also *386SLC*.

**SLDRAM**   (Synchronous Link DRAM)  An enhanced version of SDRAM memory that uses a multiplexed bus to transfer data to and from the chips rather than fixed pin settings. Similar to Rambus DRAM (RDRAM), but not proprietary, SLDRAM never came to fruition. In 1999, the SLDRAM consortium turned itself into Advanced Memory International (www.aim2.com) to support DDR SDRAM. See *RDRAM*, *SDRAM* and *AMI2*.

**SLED**   (Single Large Expensive Disk)  The traditional hard disk drive used in minicomputers and mainframes. Such drives were widely used starting in the mid 1960s through the late 1980s. Today, all hard disks are small and inexpensive by comparison. See *RAID*.

**Sledgehammer**   See *Hammer*.

**sleep**    (1) In programming, an inactive state due to an endless loop or programmed delay. A sleep statement in a programming language creates a delay for some specified amount of time.

(2) The inactive status of a terminal, device or program that is awakened by sending a code to it.

**slew rate**    (1) How fast paper moves through a printer (ips).

(2) The speed of changing voltage.

**slice and dice**    Refers to rearranging data so that it can be viewed from different perspectives. The term is typically used with OLAP databases that present information to the user in the form of multidimensional cubes similar to a 3-D spreadsheet. See *OLAP*.

**slide adapter**    See *transparent media adapter*.

**slider**    A block of material that holds the read/write head of a magnetic disk. See *flying head*.

**slide scanner**    A scanner that is specialized for scanning 35mm slides. The slide is inserted into the slot and the scanner moves the slide past the read sensors. See *transparent media adapter* and *scanner*.

**slideware**    Software that is presented in a vendor's "slide" presentation, but that is not anywhere near completion. See *vaporware*.

**sliding window**    (1) A communications protocol that transmits multiple packets before acknowledgement. Both ends keep track of packets sent and acknowledged (left of window), those which have been sent and not acknowledged (in window) and those not yet sent (right of window).

(2) A view of memory that can be instantly shifted to another location.

**slime**    A dweeb's term for a sales person. See *dweeb* and *suit*.

**SLIP**    (Serial Line IP) A data link protocol for dial-up access to TCP/IP networks. It is commonly used to gain access to the Internet as well as to provide dial-up access between two LANs. SLIP transmits IP packets over any serial link (dial up or private lines). See *CSLIP* and *PPP*.

**slipstream**    To fix a bug or add enhancements to software without identifying such inclusions by creating a new version number.

**SLM**    See *service level management system*.

**slot**    (1) A receptacle for additional printed circuit boards.

(2) A receptacle for inserting and removing a disk or tape cartridge.

(3) In communications, a narrow band of frequencies. See *time slot*.

(4) May refer to reserved space for temporary or permanent storage of instructions, data or codes.

**Slot 1**    A 242-pin slot on the motherboard that holds Intel CPU modules including the Intel Single Edge Contact Cartridge (SECC and SECC2) and Single Edge Processor Package (SEPP). The Pentium II was the first to use Slot 1. Slot 1 is a narrow slot like a PCI bus slot, not a small rectangular chip socket. See *Slot 2*, *SECC* and *Slot A*.

**Slot 2**    A 330-pin slot on the motherboard that holds an Intel Single Edge Contact Cartridge (SECC). Intel's Xeon chips were the first to use Slot 2. Designed for multiprocessing (SMP) systems, Slot 2 motherboards typically come with two slots and require a termination card if only one CPU is plugged in. See *Slot 1*, *SECC* and *SMP*.

**Slice and Dice Dialog**
The BusinessObjects query, reporting and OLAP software provides a Slice and Dice Panel that can be called on at any time to rearrange the data. After dragging and dropping the icons into the appropriate windows, BusinessObjects displays the new perspective onscreen. The "Section" window shows the breakdown of the overall report, and the "Block Structure" shows the required fields.
*(Screen shot courtesy of Business Objects.)*

**Slot A** A receptacle on the motherboard for a K7 CPU chip from AMD. It is physically similar to Slot 1, but has different electrical requirements. See *K7* and *Slot 1*.

**slot loading** Same as *feed drive*.

**slot mask** A type of shadow mask used in CRTs. There are two methods. The first is the aperture grille used in Sony's Trinitron monitors, which uses vertical phosphor stripes and vertical slots in the mask compared to the traditional shadow mask that uses phosphor dots and round holes in the mask.

**Shadow mask**

The second is a combination of traditional shadow mask and aperture grille technologies used in NECT's CromaClear monitors. Sometimes known as a slotted shadow mask, this mask uses elliptical holes and vertical phosphor stripes.

**Aperture grille (slot mask) Sony Trinitron**

**slot pitch** The distance between like-colored phosphor stripes in a CRT that uses a slot mask. This is slightly closer than the dot pitch in traditional shadow mask CRTs, which measures the diagonal distance between dots. See *slot mask*.

**Slot mask NECT CromaClear**

**slow scan TV** The transmission of still video frames over telephone lines. Not realtime transmission, it takes several seconds to transmit one frame. Also called "electronic still photography."

**slug** A metal bar containing the carved image of a letter or digit that is used in a printing mechanism.

**SMA** **(1)** (**S**hared **M**emory **A**rchitecture) Using the computer's memory for video display in order to reduce system cost. Instead of having the required frame buffer memory on the display adapter, a part of regular memory is used, and the total memory available to applications is reduced.

**(2)** (**S**oftware **M**aintenance **A**ssociation) A membership organization from 1985 to 1996. With chapters worldwide, it was dedicated to advancements in software maintenance.

**(3)** (**S**ystems **M**anagement **A**rchitecture) An IBM network management repository.

**(4)** (**S**pectrum **M**anufacturers **A**ssociation) A DBMS standard for application compatibility.

**SMA connector** A fiber-optic cable connector that uses a threaded plug and socket. It was the first connector for optical fibers to be standardized. For bi-directional transmission, two fiber cables and two SMA connectors are generally used. SMA is specified by the TIA as FOCIS-1. See *fiber-optic connectors* and *FOCIS*.

**SMA Connector**
The SMA uses a threaded connection to keep the plug intact in the socket.

**Smalltalk** An operating system and object-oriented programming language that was developed at Xerox PARC. As an integrated environment, it eliminates the distinction between programming language and operating system. It also allows its user interface and behavior to be customized.

Smalltalk was the first object-oriented programming language to become popular. It was originally used to create prototypes of simpler programming languages and the graphical interfaces that are so popular today. Smalltalk was first run on Xerox's Alto computer, which was designed for it. In 1980, Smalltalk-80 was licensed to Tektronix, Apple, HP and TI for internal use. The first commercial release of Smalltalk was Methods from Digitalk in 1983, which later evolved into Visual Smalltalk. In 1997, Smalltalk became an ANSI standard (X3J20). See *VisualWorks*, **Visual Smalltalk**, *VisualAge* and *Alto*.

**S.M.A.R.T.** (**S**elf **M**onitoring **A**nalysis and **R**eporting **T**echnology) A drive technology that reports its own degradation enabling the operating system to warn the user of potential failure. It was included in EIDE drives with the ATA-3 specification.

**SMART** See *S.M.A.R.T.*.

**smart appliance** See *Internet appliance*.

**smart book** A book that has been converted into an electronic format. Its "smartness" comes from being able to search the contents and move between sections more quickly than with the printed form.

**smart browser**    A Web browser that implements smart browsing features. See *smart browsing*.

**smart browsing**    Features in a Web browser that assist the user in obtaining the desired Web site or content. Basic features include automatic entering of the **http://** prefix or **.com** suffix for the URL as well as using previous lookups to complete the URL after the first several characters have been typed in (see *auto complete*). Other features include analyzing what is typed in and determining whether the browser should go to a site with that name or to a search site to search for content.

**smart cable**    A cable with a built-in microprocessor used to connect two devices. It analyzes incoming signals and converts them from one protocol to another.

**smart car**    An automobile with advanced electronics. Microprocessors have been used in car engines since the late 1960s and have steadily increased in usage throughout the engine and drivetrain to improve stability, braking and general comfort. The 1990s added information-oriented enhancements such as GPS navigation, reverse sensing systems and night vision (able to visualize animals and people beyond normal human range). The 2000s are adding Web and e-mail access, voice control, smart card activation instead of keys and systems that keep the vehicle a safe distance from cars and objects in its path. See *embedded system*.

**smart card**    A credit card with a built-in microprocessor and memory used for identification or financial transactions. When inserted into a reader, it transfers data to and from a central computer. It is more secure than a magnetic stripe card and can be programmed to self-destruct if the wrong password is entered too many times. As a financial transaction card, it can be loaded with digital money and used like a travelers check, except that variable amounts of money can be spent until the balance is zero. See *digital money, SIM, Java Card, **UltraCard*** and *contactless smart card*.

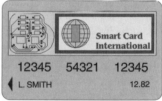

**The Smart Card**
Widely used in Europe, the smart card is rapidly gaining acceptance in North America.

**Smartdrive**    A disk cache program that comes with DOS and Windows. In DOS 4.0 and Windows 3.0, the name of the driver file was SMARTDRV.SYS. Starting with DOS 5 and Windows 3.1, the name of the driver was SMARTDRV.EXE. See *S.M.A.R.T.*.

**SmartFilter**    A Web filtering tool for business from Secure Computing Corporation, San Jose, CA (www.securecomputing.com). SmartFilter adds management control to Internet servers, firewalls and proxy servers. The software uses a URL database that catalogs sites by content (games, investing, sports, sex, cults, etc.), which is updated weekly.

**smart house**    A home that is highly automated. It uses a common network infrastructure for lights, appliances and other devices. See *home network*.

**smart hub**    See *intelligent hub*.

**smart install program**    An install program that configures itself automatically based on the hardware environment.

**SmartMart**    A family of software tools from Information Builders that run on a wide variety of platforms and are used to create and manage data warehouses. Some of the primary products follow:

- SmartModeler (data modeling)
- Copy Manager (ETL tool)
- Site Analyzer (performance monitor)
- SmartMode (performance governor)
- FOCUS Fusion (multidimensional database)
- MetaDirectory (metadata manager)
- WebFOCUS (browser access to databases)

**SmartMedia**  An ultra-compact flash memory format developed by Toshiba. About the size of CompactFlash, but as thin as a credit card, SmartMedia cards are popular storage for digital cameras with capacities up to 128MB. Available in 3.3 and 5 volt variations, SmartMedia cards require no assembly in manufacture as they are actually flash memory chips in a unique chip package. The cards can be plugged into a SmartMedia socket or into a standard Type II PC Card slot with a PC Card adapter.

**smart network**  See *intelligent network.*

**SmartMedia Module**
SmartMedia cards are extremely compact and have become popular for digital film storage. See *flash memory* for size comparison.

**SmartNIC**  A network interface card (network adapter) that performs in hardware processing tasks that the system CPU would normally handle. Using its own on-board processor, the smartNIC may be able to perform any combination of encryption/decryption, firewall, TCP/IP and HTTP  processing. SmartNICs are ideally suited for high-traffic Web servers. See *network adapter.*

**smart pager**  A two-way pager that lets you send short messages using a small keyboard. Units typically contain a built-in address book, and additional software is expected. The Motorola PageWriter and Research in Motion (RIM) pagers provide platforms for third-party software and services. Smart pagers are intended for composing short messages, because typing on the tiny keyboard is tedious, especially for people with large hands.

**smart phone**  A telephone with advanced information access features. It is typically a digital cellular telephone that provides normal voice service as well as any combination of e-mail, text messaging, pager, Web access and voice recognition. Smart phones emerged in the late 1990s and are expected to become widespread. See *WAP* and *Internet appliance.*

**smart picture frame**  See *digital picture frame.*

**smart quotes**  Also called "typographer's quotes" and "smart apostrophes," it is the use of angled single and double apostrophes instead of the ones found on a typewriter. They are considered more stylish for typeset books. Programming source code uses the old-fashioned, straight-up variety.

"Straight-up typewriter quotes"
"Smart stylish quotes"

**SmartSuite**  A suite of applications for Windows and OS/2 from Lotus that includes the 1-2-3 spreadsheet, Word Pro word processor, Freelance Graphics, Approach database, Organizer PIM and ScreenCam screen recorder. Also included is a common toolbar for launching the applications and selecting predefined macros that provide tighter integration between the applications.

**smart terminal**  A video terminal with built-in display characteristics (blinking, reverse video, underlines, etc.). It may also contain a communications protocol. The term is often used synonymously with intelligent terminal. See *intelligent terminal* and *dumb terminal.*

**SMB**  (1) (**S**erver **M**essage **B**lock)  The file sharing protocol in a DOS, Windows or OS/2 network. SMB originated with the NetBIOS protocol used in early DOS networks. See *file sharing protocol*, *CIFS* and *Samba.*

(2) (**S**mall to **M**edium-sized **B**usiness)  A category of user that is generally larger than a SOHO user, but smaller than a major company. See *SOHO.*

**SMBus**  (**S**ystem **M**anagement **Bus**)  A bus used for communicating system requirements. It is used among other things to send charging requirements to the host CPU from the battery.

**SMD**  (1) (**S**torage **M**odule **D**evice)  A high-performance hard disk interface used with minis and mainframes that transfers data in the 1–4 MBytes/sec range (SMD-E provides highest rate). See *hard disk.*

(2) (**S**urface **M**ount **D**evice)  A surface mounted chip.

**SMDS**  (**S**witched **M**ultimegabit **D**ata **S**ervice)  A high-speed, switched data communications service offered by the local telephone companies for interconnecting LANs in different locations. It was introduced in 1992 and became generally available nationwide by 1995.

Connection to an SMDS service can be made from a variety of devices, including bridges, routers, CSU/DSUs as well as via frame relay and ATM networks. SMDS can employ various networking technologies. Early implementations use the IEEE 802.6 DQDB MAN technology at rates up to 45 Mbps.

Data is framed for transmission using the SMDS Interface Protocol (SIP), which packages data as Level 3 Protocol Data Units (L3_PDU). The L3_PDU contains source and destination addresses and a data field that holds up to 9,188 bytes.

**SME** (1) (**S**mall and **M**edium **E**nterprises) Refers to organizations that are larger than SOHOs and smaller than the Fortune 1000. The size is subjective ranging from approximately 25–500 employees. See *SOHO*.

(2) (**S**ubject **M**atter **E**xpert) An individual that is well-versed in the policies and procedures of a particular department or division. Such people are used to derive the business rules for the organization. See *business rule*.

(3) (**S**un **M**icro**e**lectronics) The unit within Sun that develops its chips.

**SMF** (1) (**S**tandard **M**essaging **F**ormat) An electronic mail format for Novell's MHS messaging system. The application puts the data into this format in order to send an e-mail message. NGM (NetWare Global Messaging) is based on SMF-71, which supports long addresses and synchronized directories.

(2) (**S**tandard **MIDI** **f**ile) See *MIDI file*.

(3) See *singlemode fiber*.

**SMI** (1) (**S**imple **M**ail **I**nterface) A subset of functions within the VIM messaging protocol used by applications to send e-mail and attachments.

(2) (**S**tructure of **M**anagement **I**nformation) A definition for creating MIBs in the SNMP protocol.

(3) (**S**ystem **M**anagement **I**nterrupt) A hardware interrupt in Intel SL Enhanced 486 and Pentium CPUs used for power management. This interrupt is also used for virus checking.

**SMIL** (**S**ynchronized **M**ultimedia **I**ntegration **L**anguage) Pronounced "smile." A format for delivering and synchronizing multimedia content on the Web. Introduced in the summer of 1998 by the W3C, it is a document type (DTD) of XML and provides the timing commands that enable audio, video and graphics elements to be executed sequentially or in parallel. SMIL supports multimedia streaming protocols such as RTSP. See *XML*.

**smiley** See *emoticon*.

**S/MIME** See *MIME*.

**SMM** (**S**ystem **M**anagement **M**ode) An energy conservation mode built into Intel SL Enhanced 486 and Pentium CPUs. During inactive periods, SMM initiates a sleep mode that turns off peripherals or the entire system. It retains the computer's status in a protected area of memory called the "System Management RAM" (SMRAM).

**smoke test** A test of new or repaired equipment by turning it on. If there's smoke, it doesn't work!

**smoothed data** Statistical data that has been averaged or otherwise manipulated so that the curves on its graph are smooth and free of irregularities.

**smoothing circuit** An electronic filtering circuit in a DC power supply that removes the ripples from AC power.

**SMP** (**S**ymmetric **M**ulti**P**rocessing) A multiprocessing architecture in which multiple CPUs, residing in one cabinet, share the same memory. SMP systems provide scalability. As business increases, additional CPUs can be added to absorb the increased transaction volume.

SMP systems range from two to as many as 32 or more processors. However, if one CPU fails, the entire SMP system, or node, is down. Clusters of two or more SMP systems can be used to provide high availability, or fault resilience, in case of failure. If one SMP system fails, the others continue to operate.

A single CPU generally boots the system and loads the SMP operating system, which brings the other CPUs online. There is only one instance of the operating system and one

**Smoke Test**
Not the most sophisticated way to tell if something is working properly, but it's a sure guarantee that it isn't.

instance of the application in memory. The operating system uses the CPUs as a pool of processing resources, all executing simultaneously, either processing data or in an idle loop waiting to do something.

SMP speeds up whatever processes can be overlapped. For example, in a desktop computer, it would speed up the running of multiple applications simultaneously. If an application is multithreaded, which allows for concurrent operations within the application itself, then SMP will improve the performance of that single application.

Sequent, Pyramid and Encore pioneered SMP on UNIX platforms. SMP servers are also available from IBM, HP, NCR, Unisys and others. Many versions of UNIX as well as proprietary operating systems, such as Windows NT, OS/2 and NetWare, have been designed for or are being revamped for SMP. SMP usage is expected to grow rapidly, and applications are increasingly being designed to take advantage of the SMP architecture. Contrast with *MPP*. See also *NUMA*.

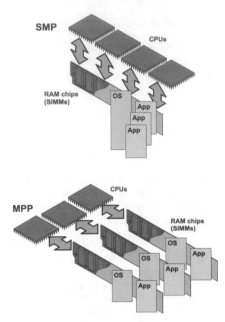

**SMP and MPP Processing**
In SMP, CPUs are assigned to the next available task or thread that can run concurrently. In MPP operation, the problem is broken up into separate pieces, which are processed simultaneously.

**SMPTE**    (Society for Motion Picture and TV Engineers, White Plains, NY, www.smpte.org) A professional society for motion picture and TV engineers with more than 9,000 members worldwide. It prepares standards and documentation for TV production. SMPTE time code records hours, minutes, seconds and frames on audio or videotape for synchronization purposes.

**SMR**    (Specialized Mobile Radio) Communications services used by taxicabs, trucks and other mobile businesses. Throughout the U.S., approximately 3,000 independent operators are licensed by the FCC to provide this service. Nextel Communications is known in this field for acquiring a large number of SMR operators and turning them into a nationwide system. See *Nextel*.

**SMRAM**    See *SMM*.

**SMS**    (1) (Storage Management System) Software used to routinely back up and archive files. See *HSM*.

(2) (Systems Management Server) Systems management software from Microsoft that runs on Windows NT Server. It requires a Microsoft SQL Server database and is used to distribute software, monitor and analyze network usage and perform various network administration tasks. See *SMS Installer*.

(3) (Short Message Service) A text message service that enables short messages of generally no more than 140–160 characters in length to be sent and transmitted from a cellphone. SMS is supported by GSM and other mobile communications systems. Unlike paging, short messages are stored and forwarded in SMS centers. In the GSM system, short messages ride on a separate signaling path so they are transmitted simultaneously with voice, data and fax.

(4) (Storage Management Services) Software from Novell that allows data to be stored and retrieved on NetWare servers independent of the file system the data is maintained in (DOS, OS/2, Mac, etc.). It is used to back up data from heterogeneous clients on the network. Various third-party backup products are SMS compliant. See *SIDF*.

(5) (System-Managed Storage) Enhanced data management software for MVS mainframes from IBM. Introduced in 1988, it provides functions such as automatically allocating data, which prevents most out-of-space errors when disk volumes become full. See *DFSMS*.

**SMS Installer**    A software distribution program from Microsoft that installs applications on client machines throughout the network. It is an add-on to Microsoft's System Management Server.

**SMT**    (1) (Surface Mount Technology) See *surface mount*.

(2) (Station ManagemenT) An FDDI network management protocol that provides direct management. Only one node requires the software.

**SMTP**   (Simple Mail Transfer Protocol) The standard e-mail protocol on the Internet. It is a TCP/IP protocol that defines the message format and the message transfer agent (MTA), which stores and forwards the mail. SMTP was originally designed for only ASCII text, but MIME and other encoding methods enable program and multimedia files to be attached to e-mail messages.

SMTP servers route SMTP messages throughout the Internet to a mail server, such as POP3 or IMAP4, which provides a message store for incoming mail. See *POP3*, *IMAP* and *messaging system*. See also *SNMP*.

**smurf attack**   An assault on a network that floods it with excessive messages in order to impede normal traffic. It is accomplished by sending ping requests (ICMP echo requests) to a broadcast address on the target network or an intermediate network. The return address is spoofed to the victim's address. Since a broadcast address is picked up by all nodes on the subnet, it functions like an amplifier, generating hundreds of responses from one request and eventually causing a traffic overload. See *denial of service attack* and *ICMP*.

**SNA**   (Systems Network Architecture) IBM's mainframe network standards introduced in 1974. Originally a centralized architecture with a host computer controlling many terminals, enhancements, such as APPN and APPC (LU 6.2), have adapted SNA to today's peer-to-peer communications and distributed computing environment. Following are some of SNA's basic concepts.

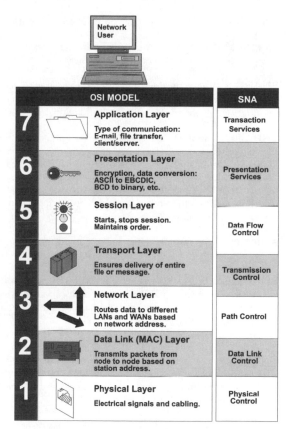

**Nodes and Data Links**   In SNA, nodes are end points or junctions, and data links are the pathways between them. Nodes are defined as Type 5 (hosts), Type 4 (communications controllers) and Type 2 (peripheral; terminals, PCs and midrange computers).

Type 2.0 nodes can communicate only with the host, and Type 2.1 nodes can communicate with other 2.1 nodes (peer-to-peer) without going to the host.

Data links include high-speed local channels, the SDLC data link protocol and Token Ring.

**SSCPs, PUs and LUs**   The heart of a mainframe-based SNA network is the SSCP (System Services Control Point) software that resides in the host. It manages all resources in its domain.

Within all nodes of an SNA network, except for Type 2.1, there is PU (Physical Unit) software that manages node resources, such as data links, and controls the transmission of network management information. In Node Type 2.1, Control Point software performs these functions.

In order to communicate user data, a session path is created between two end points, or LUs (Logical Units). When a session takes place, an LU-LU session is established between an LU in the host (CICS, TSO, user appliction, etc.) and an LU in the terminal controller or PC.

An LU 6.2 session provides peer-to-peer communication and lets either side initiate the session.

**VTAM and NCP**   VTAM (Virtual Telecommunications Access Method) resides in the host and contains the SSCP, the PU for the host, and establishes the LU sessions within the host.

NCP (Network Control Program) resides in the communications controller (front-end processor) and manages the routing and data link protocols, such as SDLC and Token Ring.

**SNA Layers**   SNA is implemented in functional layers starting with the application that triggers the communications down to the bottom layers that transmit packets from station to station. This layering is called a "protocol stack."

The SNA stack is compared with the OSI model in the previous illustration. Although SNA had major influence on the OSI model, there are differences in implementation.

**SNADS**    (SNA Distribution Services) An IBM messaging protocol used by IBM office automation products such as DISOSS and AS/400 Office. Various messaging gateways and messaging switches support SNADS.

**snail mail**    Mail sent via the postal system.

**snap-in**    A software module for the Microsoft Management Console (MMC) that provides administrative capabilities for a particular type of device. See *Microsoft Management Console*.

**snapshot**    The saved current state of memory including the contents of all memory bytes, hardware registers and status indicators. It is periodically taken in order to restore the system in the event of failure.

**snapshot dump**    A memory dump of selected portions of memory.

**snapshot program**    A trace program that provides selected dumps of memory when specific instructions are executed or when certain conditions are met.

**SNARC**    A network device from ITXC that moves telephone calls from a carrier's switch to and from the Internet. Connecting through a T1 or E1 port, the SNARC enables resellers and carriers to become Internet telephony service providers (ITSPs) via ITXC's network affiliations. See *ITXC*.

**SND file**    (SouND file) One of several digital audio file formats that were created by Apple, NeXT and others. It typically refers to an uncompressed sound file used on the Macintosh. SND files use the .SND extension. In the Mac, digitized sounds can be stored as SND and AIFF files, or as resources in the resource fork.

**sneakernet**    Carrying floppy disks, Zip disks, CD-Rs or some other removable recording medium from one machine to another to exchange information when there is no network in place.

**sneezing**    To verbally tell somebody about a new and interesting Web site. See *viral marketing*.

**SNI**    (1) (Subscriber Network Interface) The point of interface between the customer's equipment (CPE) and a communications service from a common carrier.
    (2) (SNA Network Interconnection) Using a mainframe as a gateway between two independent SNA networks.
    (3) See *Siemens Nixdorf*.

**Sneakernet**
The way to transfer data in a workgroup when the network is down. It's a very reliable method.

**SNIA**    (Storage Networking Industry Association, Santa Barbara, CA, www.snia.org) An organization devoted to the advancement of mission critical storage systems. Founded in 1997, its goal is to determine the standards that must be developed to allow hosts and storage systems to interact via common protocols. SNIA was spearheaded by Strategic Research Corporation's Michael Peterson.

**sniffer**    Software and/or hardware that analyzes traffic and detects bottlenecks and problems in a network.

**snippet**    A small amount of something. In the computer field, it often refers to a small piece of program code.

**SNMP**    (Simple Network Management Protocol) A widely-used network monitoring and control protocol. Data is passed from SNMP agents, which are hardware and/or software processes reporting activity in each network device (hub, router, bridge, etc.) to the workstation console used to oversee the network. The agents return information contained in a MIB (Management Information Base), which is a data structure that defines what is obtainable from the device and what can be controlled (turned off, on, etc.). Originating in the UNIX community, SNMP has become widely used on all major platforms.

SNMP 2 provides enhancements including security and an RMON (Remote Monitoring) MIB, which provides continuous feedback without having to be queried by the SNMP console. See *RMON*. See also *SMTP*.

**SNOBOL**    (StriNg Oriented symBOlic Language) One of the first list processing languages, which was developed by Ralph Griswold and associates at Bell Labs in Holmdel, NJ. It was used for text processing and compiler development. The first version was introduced in 1963, with later versions throughout the 1960s.

**snow**    The flickering snow-like spots on a video screen caused by display electronics that are too slow to respond to changing data.

**snowflake structure**    In a data warehouse, the structure that is created when highly repeated fields are placed into separate tables. The resulting diagram has short and long branches extending from the original dimension that resemble the irregularities of a snowflake. Snowflake structures are generally not recommended as they slow down browsing the data.

**SNR**    See *signal to noise ratio*.

**SOAP**    (Simple Object Access Protocol) A protocol from Microsoft, IBM and others for accessing services on the Web. It employs XML syntax to send text commands across the Internet using HTTP. Similar in purpose to the COM and CORBA distributed object systems, but lighter weight and less programming intensive (at least initially), SOAP is expected to become widely used to invoke services throughout the Web. Because of its simple exchange mechanism, SOAP can also be used to implement a messaging system. SOAP is supported in COM, DCOM, Internet Explorer and Microsoft's Java implementation. See *UDDI* and *.NET*.

**SoC**    (System On a Chip) The electronics for a complete, working product contained on a single chip. While a computer on a chip includes all the hardware components required to process instructions, an SoC includes the computer and all required ancillary electronics. For example, an SoC for a telecom application might contain a microprocessor, digital signal processor (DSP), RAM and ROM. See *SiP*.

**social engineer**    A person that illegally enters computer systems by having persuaded an authorized person to reveal IDs, passwords and other confidential information. The social engineer is the "con man" of this business, taking the low-tech road rather than using programming skills and other cracker techniques.

**socket**    (1) A receptacle which receives a plug. Same as *jack*.
(2) See *UNIX socket*.

**Socket 370**    A CPU plug and socket from Intel for Pentium CPUs that is more economical than the elaborate Slot 1 system introduced with the Pentium II. Socket 370 accepts a 370-pin PPGA (plastic pin grid array) chip package, instead of the SEC (single edge cartridge) Slot 1 package. Socket 370 chips and motherboards cost less to manufacture. See *Super7*.

**Socket 7**    The receptacle on the motherboard that holds a Pentium CPU chip. It is also used to hold Pentium-compatible chips such as AMD's K5 and K6 CPUs. See *Slot 1* and *Super7*.

**Socket 8**    The receptacle on the motherboard that holds a Pentium Pro CPU chip. See *Slot 1*.

**socketed**    Temporarily attached. For example, a socketed chip plugs into a receptacle and can be pulled out and replaced with relative ease in contrast to a soldered chip.

**socket flash**    Flash memory that is housed in a standard chip package and plugs into a socket on the circuit board. A flash BIOS is an example. Contrast with *flash card*.

**Socket 7**
Socket 7 uses a zero insertion force (ZIF) assembly. After insertion of the chip, the lever is pulled down and the pins are locked in.

**S**

**socket mount**    A circuit board packaging technique in which a chip or component plugs into a socket. Socket mount devices can be removed and replaced by the user, although the flexible pins on some types of chips make them difficult to insert. Contrast with *surface mount* and *thru-hole*.

**socket services**    Low-level software that manages a PC Card controller. See *PC Card*.

**SOCKS server**    (SOCKetS server) A proxy server that functions as a general-purpose TCP/IP proxy and handles any kind of traffic (HTTP, SMTP, FTP, Telnet, etc.). Major Web browsers support SOCKS, and OS/2 4.0 builds it into its TCP/IP stack, enabling all applications to use it. See *proxy server* and *TCP/IP stack*.

**SODIMM**    (Small Outline-DIMM) A DIMM module with a thinner profile due to the use of TSOP chip packages. SODIMMs are commonly used in laptop computers. See *memory module* and *TSOP*.

**soft**    Flexible and changeable. Software can be reprogrammed for different results. The computer's soft nature is its greatest virtue; however, the reason it takes so long to get new systems developed has little to do with the concept. It is based on how systems are developed (file systems vs database management), the programming languages used (assembly vs high-level), combined with the skill level of the technical staff, compounded by the organization's bureaucracy.

**Softbank**    (Softbank Corporation, Tokyo, www.softbank.com) A computer conglomerate founded in 1981 by Masayoshi Son. The company has backed Yahoo! and more than 50 hardware, software, communications and Internet companies both in the U.S. and Japan. It also acquired COMDEX, the largest computer show in the U.S. Softbank Inc. is a wholly owned subsidiary that handles U.S. operations. See *COMDEX*.

**soft boot**    Same as *warm boot*.

**soft copy**    Refers to data displayed on a video screen. Contrast with *hard copy*.

**soft error**    A recoverable error, such as a garbled message that can be retransmitted. Contrast with *hard error*.

**soft font**    A set of characters for a particular typeface that is stored on the computer's hard disk, or in some cases the printer's hard disk, and downloaded to the printer before printing. Contrast with *internal font* and *font cartridge*.

**soft hyphen**    A hyphen that prints if it winds up at the end of the line, but does not print otherwise. Contrast with *hard hyphen*. See *discretionary hyphen*.

**soft key**    (1) A keyboard-style key that serves multiple purposes on small devices such as cellphones and PDAs with limited room. Soft keys are located adjacent to a screen or readout that displays the function selected when the key is pressed.

(2) A simulated button or keyboard key that is displayed on a touch screen. The soft key is tapped with the finger or stylus for activation. See *touch screen*.

(3) (SoftKey) See *Learning Company*.

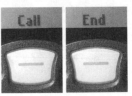

**A Soft Key**
In this cellphone example, the same physical key becomes the Call key after you enter a telephone number and then switches to the End key, the next logical function.

**soft launch**    A Web site that is implemented in stages rather than all at once. Unlike other publishing media, such as a book or CD-ROM, which requires the entire project to be completed before it is distributed, a Web site can easily be deployed in pieces. The Web medium allows for an ever-expanding online publication that can be routinely updated.

**soft macro**    The design of a logic function that specifies how the required logic elements are interconnected, but not the physical wiring pattern on the chip. Contrast with *hard macro*.

**soft modem**    Software that performs modem functions using the computer's main CPU rather than in modem hardware. Instead of using a dedicated data pump, programmable DSP chips are used. For example, the PowerPC and Intel's MMX Pentiums have instructions that allow it to perform modem functions.

Many modems themselves are already built as soft modems rather than using chips hardwired to a particular modulation technique. Such modems may be upgradable to new modulation methods with new software that can be downloaded or purchased from the vendor.

**soft patch**    A quick fix to machine language currently in memory that only lasts for the current session.

**soft return**    A code inserted by word processing software into a text document to mark the end of the line. When the document is printed, the soft return is converted into the end-of-line code required by the printer. Soft returns are determined by the right margin and change when the margins are changed. Soft returns were always a format option determined by the programmer. In most graphics-based environments today, soft returns are not used. Contrast with *hard return*.

**soft sectored**    A common method of identifying sectors on a disk by initially recording sector information on every track with a format program. Contrast with *hard sectored*.

**Softstrip**    An earlier bar code and scanner system from Cauzin that used a unique encoding pattern of from 50 to 600 bytes of data per inch.

**softswitch**    A programmable network switch that can process the signaling for all types of packet protocols. Also known as a "media gateway controller," "call agent" or "call server," such devices are used by carriers that support converged communications services by integrating SS7 telephone signaling with packet networks. Using network processors at its core, softswitches can support IP, DSL, ATM and frame relay in the same unit.

The International Softswitch Consortium says a softswitch should be able to (1) control connection services for a media gateway and/or native IP endpoints, (2) select processes that can be applied to a call, (3) provide routing for a call within the network based on signaling and customer database information, (4) transfer control of the call to another network element, and (5) interface to and support management functions such as provisioning, fault, billing, etc. For more information, visit www.softswitch.org.

The switching technology in a softswitch is in software (hence its name) rather than in the hardware as with traditional switching center technology. This software programmability allows it to support existing and future IP telephony protocols (H.323, SIP, MEGACO, etc.). See *IP telephony*. See also *Soft-Switch*.

**software**    Instructions for the computer. A series of instructions that performs a particular task is called a "program." The two major categories of software are "system software" and "application software." System software is made up of control programs such as the operating system and database management system (DBMS). Application software is any program that processes data for the user (inventory, payroll, spreadsheet, word processor, etc.). See *system software* and *application software*.

A common misconception is that software is data. It is not. Software tells the hardware how to process the data.

> Software is "run."
>
> Data is "processed."

**software administration**    The ongoing management of software applications in an enterprise, which includes the distribution of new software and upgrading of existing software. Improving software administration is one of the main reasons for the creation of the network computer (NC) and NetPC.

**software architecture**    The design of application or system software that incorporates protocols and interfaces for interacting with other programs and for future flexibility and expandability. A self-contained, stand-alone program would have program logic, but not a software architecture.

**software bug**    A problem that causes a program to abend (crash) or produce invalid output. Problems that cause a program to abend are invalid data, such as trying to divide by zero, or invalid instructions, which are caused by bad logic that misdirects the computer to the wrong place in the program.

A program with erroneous logic may produce bad output without crashing, which is the reason extensive testing is required for new programs. For example, if the program is supposed to add an amount, but instead, it subtracts it, bad output results. As long as the program performs valid machine instructions on data it knows how to deal with, the computer will run.

**software bus**    A programming interface that allows software modules to transfer data to each other. Although "bus" is traditionally a hardware term for an interconneting pathway, it is occasionally used in this manner when the focus is on internally transferring large amounts of data from one process to another. See *bus*.

S

**software codec** A compression/decompression routine that is implemented in software only without requiring specialized DSP hardware. See *codec*.

**software distribution program** A program that installs new applications or application upgrades on client machines throughout the network. See *WinInstall* and *SMS Installer*.

**software engineer** A person that designs and programs system-level software, such as operating systems, database management systems (DBMSs) and embedded systems. The title is often used for programmers in the software industry that create commercial software packages, whether they be system level or application level. "Software engineer," "systems programmer" and "systems engineer" titles are often synonymous. See *systems engineer*.

**software engineering** The design, development and documentation of software. See *CASE, systems analysis and design, programming, object-oriented programming, software metrics* and *Systemantics*.

**software failure** The inability of a program to continue processing due to erroneous logic. Same as *crash, bomb* and *abend*.

**software house** An organization that develops custom software for a customer. Contrast with *software publisher*, which develops and markets software packages.

**software interface** Same as *API*.

**software interrupt** An interrupt caused by an instruction in the program. See *interrupt*.

**software metering** Limiting the number of users running an application from a centralized source (server) based on the current license agreement.

**software metrics** Software measurements. Using numerical ratings to measure the complexity and reliability of source code, the length and quality of the development process and the performance of the application when completed.

**software package** An application program developed for sale to the general public. Packaged software is generally designed to appeal to a large audience of users, and although the programs may be tailored to a user's taste by setting various preferences, it is not as individualized as custom-designed and custom-programmed software. Contrast with *custom software*.

**software piracy** The illegal copying of software for distribution within the organization or to friends, clubs and other groups or for commercial duplication and resale. The software industry loses billions of dollars each year to piracy, and although it may seem innocent enough to install an application on a couple of additional machines, it may ultimately shatter the profitability of a small software company. Software piracy is a major issue in the U.S. and Europe, but it is rampant in the rest of the world where major applications are routinely copied for resale. See *piracy investigator, NET Act* and *SIIA*.

**software program** A computer program (computer application). All computer programs are software. Usage of the two words together is redundant, but common.

**software programmer** Same as *systems programmer*.

**software protection** See *copy protection*.

**software publisher** An organization that develops and markets software. It does market research, production and distribution of software. It may develop its own software, contract for outside development or obtain software that has already been written.

**Software Publishers Association** See *SIIA*.

**software reuse**   The ability to use software routines over again in new applications. This is the major purpose of object technology.

**software stack**   A stack that is implemented in memory rather than in hardware registers. See *stack*.

**software tool**   A program used to develop other software. Any program or utility that helps a programmer design, code, compile or debug sofware can be called a tool.

**software validation**   The certification that an information system has been implemented correctly and that it conforms to the functional specifications derived from the original requirements. Such validation is often performed by a third party consulting organization.

**SoftWindows**   A Windows emulator for the Macintosh from FWB Software, San Francisco, CA (www.fwb.com). It allows Windows 3.1, Windows 95/98 and DOS applications to run on the Mac. SoftWindows 98 includes Windows 98 Second Edition. SoftWindows was originally developed by Insignia Solutions.

**SOHO**   (Small Office/Home Office) Refers to the small business or business-at-home user. This market segment demands as much or more than the large corporation. The small business entrepreneur generally wants the latest, greatest and fastest equipment, and this market has always benefited from high technology, allowing it to compete on a level playing ground with the bigger companies. See *SMB*.

**SOI**   (Silicon On Insulator) A chip architecture that increases transistor switching speed by reducing capacitance (build-up of electrical charges in the transistor's elements), and thus reducing the discharge time. The power requirement is also reduced in some designs. The SOI technique creates the transistors on a thin top silicon layer that is separated from the silicon substrate by a thin insulating layer of glass or silicon dioxide. One method of forming this insulating layer is the Separation by Implantation of Oxygen (SIMOX) technique, which implants oxygen into the wafer under intense heat.

**SOIC**   (Small Outline IC) A small-dimension, plastic, rectangular, surface mount chip package that uses gull-wing pins extending outward. See *gull-wing lead*, *SOJ* and *chip package*.

**SoIP**   (Storage Over IP) Nishan Systems' branding of its IP storage products. See *IP storage*.

**SOJ**   (Small Outline package J-lead) A small-dimension, plastic, rectangular surface mount chip package with j-shaped pins on its two long sides. See *J-lead*, *SOP* and *chip package*.

**Solaris**   A multitasking, multiprocessing operating system and distributed computing environment for Sun's SPARC computers from SunSoft. It provides an enterprise-wide UNIX environment that can manage up to 40,000 nodes from one central station. Solaris is known for its robustness and scalability, which is expected in UNIX-based SMP systems. An x86 version of Solaris is available that can also run applications written for Sun's Interactive UNIX. Solaris was available for the PowerPC, but support was dropped as of Version 2.6.

Solaris includes the SunOS UNIX SVR4-based operating system, ONC networking products (NFS, NIS, etc.) and OpenWindows (Sun's version of X Windows). Also provided are Motif and OPEN LOOK graphical interfaces.

**solder**   A metal alloy used to bond other metals together. Tin and lead are used in "soft" solders, which melt rather easily. The more tin, the harder the solder, and the higher the temperature required. Copper and zinc are used in "hard" soldering, or brazing, which requires considerably more heat to melt. See *braze*, *reflow* and *wave soldering*.

**solder bumping**   A technique for attaching chips to a printed circuit board. Solder balls are attached to the bonding pads on the chip and then melted in place on the board. See *BGA* and *flip chip*.

**soldered**   Pronounced "sodderd." Permanently attached by a hard metal bond. In order to replace a chip soldered to a circuit board requires heating the soldering joints until they melt. Contrast with *socketed*.

**solder mask**   An insulating pattern applied to a printed circuit board that exposes only the areas to be soldered.

S

**solenoid**  A magnetic switch that closes a circuit, often used as a relay.

**solid ink printer**  A laser-class printer that uses solid wax inks that are melted into a liquid before being used. Instead of jetting the ink onto the paper directly as ink jet printers do, solid ink printers jet the ink onto a drum. A better registration of color is obtained by transferring the ink to the drum first and then to the printer, because the drum can be more tightly controlled than moving paper.

Tektronix has pioneered the solid ink printer market and is the primary producer of this technology. The color print quality of the Tektronix printer is stunning, and its print speed generally exceeds that of an equivalent-priced color laser printer, because it prints colors in one pass instead of four. With laser printers, each of the four CMYK colors must be applied to a secondary accumulator drum one at a time before the image is transferred to paper. Tektronix applies a four-color solid ink mirror image onto the drum in one pass.

**solid logic**  Same as *solid state*.

**solid modeling**  A mathematical technique for representing solid objects. Unlike wireframe and surface modeling, solid modeling systems ensure that all surfaces meet properly and that the object is geometrically correct. Solid models allow for interference checking, which tests to see if two or more objects occupy the same space.

Solid modeling is the most complicated of the CAD technologies, because it simulates an object internally and externally. Solid models can be sectioned (cut open) to reveal their internal features, and they can be stress tested as if they were physical entities in the real world. See *tessellation*.

**solid state**  An electronic component or circuit made of solid materials, such as transistors, chips and bubble memory. There is no mechanical action in a solid state device, although an unbelievable amount of electromagnetic action takes place within.

For data storage, solid state devices are much faster and more reliable than mechanical disks and tapes, but are more expensive. Although solid state costs continually drop, disks, tapes and optical disks also continue to improve their cost/performance ratio.

The first solid state device was the "cat's whisker" of the 1930s. A whisker-like wire was moved around on a solid crystal in order to detect a radio signal.

**solid state disk**  A disk drive made of memory chips used for high-speed data access or in hostile environments. Solid state disks are used in battery-powered, handheld devices as well as in desktop units with hundreds of megabytes of storage that contain their own UPS systems.

Different types of storage chips are used for solid state disks, both volatile and non-volatile. However a solid state disk looks like a standard disk drive to the operating system, not a proprietary one that requires additional drivers. See *flash disk*.

**solid state laser**  A laser that uses a glass or crystalline laser medium that is excited by light from an external source. A solid state laser is not a semiconductor laser, although articles may erroneously refer to them as such. See *laser*.

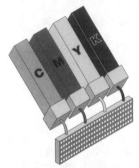

**Solid Ink Printhead**
The solid wax ink is melted and turned into a liquid before it enters the plumbing of the printhead. The inks are typically jetted from the nozzles using the piezoelectric drop on demand method. The printhead in this example is as wide as the paper.

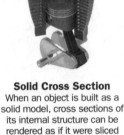

**Solid Cross Section**
When an object is built as a solid model, cross sections of its internal structure can be rendered as if it were sliced down the middle. This two-cycle engine assembly was created in MicroStation Modeler. *(Image courtesy of Bentley Systems, Inc.)*

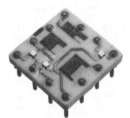

**Solid State Logic in the mid-1960s**
The three transistors in this solid state module (top removed) used in IBM's System/360 computers were advanced technology in the mid-1960s. *(Image courtesy of International Business Machines Corporation. Unauthorized use not permitted.)*

**Solid State Disk**
This MegaRam-3000 solid state disk system from Imperial Technology holds up to 4GB. Access time is virtually non existent. In case of power failure, the battery enables the unit to copy its contents from the memory chips to the hard disk. *(Image courtesy of Imperial Technology, Inc., www.imperialtech.com)*

**solid state memory**    Any transistorized, semiconductor or thin film memory that contains no mechanical parts. See *solid state disk*.

**solid state relay**    A relay that contains no mechanical parts. All switching mechanisms are semiconductor or thin film components.

**soliton**    A laser pulse that retains its shape in a fiber over long distances. By generating the pulse at a certain frequency and at a certain power level, the pulse takes advantage of competing dispersion effects. As it travels, the pulse is lengthened and then shortened back to its original size.

**solutions**    The IT buzzword of the twenty-first century. Nobody makes products anymore; everybody just provides solutions! See *solutions provider*.

**solutions provider**    An organization that provides a mix of consulting services, custom programming and hardware to solve a customer's information problem. The hardware may be manufactured by the company, purchased from a third party or merely recommended. "Solutions" implies a range of custom-tailored services rather than only off-the-shelf packages. See *solutions*.

**solver**    Mathematical mechanisms that allow spreadsheets to perform goal seeking.

**SOM**    (1) (System Object Model) An object architecture from IBM that provides a full implementation of the CORBA standard. SOM is language independent and is supported by a variety of large compiler and application development vendors. DSOM, for distributed SOM, allows objects to be used across the network.

(2) (Self Organizing Map) A two-dimensional map that shows relationships in a neural network.

**SONET**    (Synchronous Optical NETwork) A fiber-optic transmission system for high-speed digital traffic. Employed by telephone companies and common carriers, SONET speeds range from 51 megabits to multiple gigabits per second. SONET is an intelligent system that provides advanced network management and a standard optical interface. It uses a self-healing ring architecture that is able to reroute traffic if a line goes down. SONET backbones are widely used to aggregate lower-speed T1 and T3 lines.

SONET is specified in the Broadband ISDN (B-ISDN) standard. The European counterpart is SDH. Following are the levels of service. OC (Optical Carrier) refers to the optical signal, and STS (Synchronous Transport Signal) refers to the electrical signal, which is the same speed.

SONET uses time division multiplexing (TDM) to send multiple data streams simultaneously. Its smallest increment of provisioning is VT-1.5, which provides 1.7 Mbps of bandwidth. The next increment, STS-1, jumps to 51.84 Mbps. Any data stream that does not fill that channel goes wasted.

Bellcore's GR-2837 standard maps ATM cells onto SONET, turning a SONET pipe into a cell-switched (packet-switched) transmission carrier that utilizes the full bandwidth of the medium without waste.

SONET is built in a self-healing ring architecture which uses at least two transmission paths in the event one fails (see *SONET ring*).

```
SONET CIRCUITS

Service           Speed (Mbps)
        VT-1.5       1.7
OC-1    STS-1       51.84  (28 DS1s or 1 DS3)
OC-3    STS-3      155.52  (3 STS-1s)
OC-3c   STS-3c     155.52  (concatenated)
OC-12   STS-12     622.08  (12 STS-1, 4 STS-3)
OC-12c  STS-12c    622.08  (12 STS-1, 4 STS-3c)
OC-48   STS-48    2488.32  (48 STS-1, 16 STS-3)
OC-192  STS-192   9953.28  (192 STS-1, 64 STS-3)
OC-768  STS-768  39813,12  (768 STS-1, 256 STS-3)
```

**LAN**

| Data, voice, video |
| --- |
| IP (layer 3) |
| Ethernet (layer 2) |
| Copper |

**WAN**

| Data, voice, video | Data, voice, video | Data, voice, video |
| --- | --- | --- |
| IP (layer 3) | IP (layer 3) | IP (layer 3) |
| ATM (layer 2) | SONET (layer 1) | Fiber |
| SONET (layer 1) | Fiber | |
| Fiber | | |

**Transporting IP**
In a WAN or over the Internet, IP traffic is widely carried over SONET lines, either using ATM as a management layer or over SONET directly. In the future, IP is exptected to travel directly over DWDM fiber (rightmost diagram).

S

## SONET ring

**SONET ring** The architecture used in SONET technology. SONET rings, known as "self-healing rings," use two or more transmission paths between network nodes, which are typically digital cross-connects (DCSs) or add/drop multiplexers (ADMs). If there is a break in one line, the other may still be available, providing the second is not in close proximity to the first and also damaged. For the best security against failure, when possible, different physical routes are used for the two lines. The most fault-tolerant architecture is the four-fiber bi-directional ring. See *SONET*.

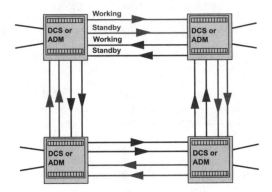

**Two Fiber Unidirectional**
This is the simplest SONET ring topology. All data is transmitted on the working or active path, while the standby path (protection path) lies in waiting. When a failure in the active path occurs, the two network nodes affected immediately switch to the standby line. Four fibers may be used in a unidirectional system, but it is not usually done.

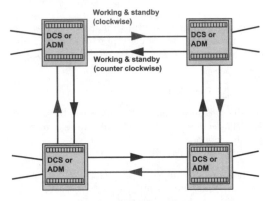

**Two Fiber Bidirectional**
In this architecture, traffic flows in both directions, but half the capacity of the line is used as a data channel and the other half for protection. In the event of failure, the alternate line takes up the slack.

**Four Fiber Bidirectional**
This is the most robust architecture, which can withstand multiple failures providing the lines are routed in different locations. Both active and standby paths are duplicated in this topology, which is common in large carrier networks that cannot afford a breakdown.

## SONICblue

**SONICblue** (SONICblue, Santa Clara, www.sonicblue.com) A digital products company founded in 1989 as S3 Corporation by Dado Banatao and Ronald Yara. SONICblue offers a variety of products including the Rio line of MP3 players, the Diamond brand of organizers, home networking and modems, professional display adapters and other Web appliances.

In its first decade as S3 Corporation, the company was a major player in the graphics chip business, launching the first GUI accelerator in 1991 and the first single-chip 3-D accelerator in 1995. Chip families such as ViRGE, Savage and Trio3D have been used in thousands of third-party display adapters.

In 1999, S3 acquired Diamond Multimedia Systems, a maker of popular PC display adapters and the Rio MP3 player. It also acquired the assets of Number Nine Visual Technology, another high-quality display adapter vendor. In 2000, S3 sold its chip business to Via Technologies and renamed itself SONICblue.

## SOP

**SOP** (**S**mall **O**utline **P**ackage) A small-dimension, plastic, rectangular surface mount chip with gull-wing pins on its two long sides. See *gull-wing lead*, *TSOP*, *SOJ* and *chip package*.

## Sophos

**Sophos** Antivirus software from Sophos Plc, Abingdon, Oxfordshire, England (www.sophos.com), that runs in Windows, Mac, OS/2, UNIX, NetWare and Notes environments. Sophos differs from most antivirus programs because it only scans files that have changed in size. After installing Sophos, it scans every file in the computer no matter what the extension and records a checksum of the file's bytes in its database. Rather than rescanning every file at boot time and each time a file is opened, which takes time, Sophos recomputes the checksum to determine whether the file was altered. Computing the file's checksum is extremely fast compared to virus scanning. A file is only scanned if comparing the two checksums shows the file was changed or if it is new file that was never scanned before. See *virus*.

**sort**    To reorder data into a new sequence. The operating system can typically sort file names and text lists. Word processors typically allow lines of text to be reordered, and database programs sort records by one or more fields, often generating a new file.

**sort algorithm**    A formula used to reorder data into a new sequence. Like all complicated problems, there are many solutions that can achieve the same results. One sort algorithm can resequence data faster than another. In the early 1960s, when tape was "the" storage medium, the sale of a computer system may have hinged on the sort algorithm, since without direct access capability, every transaction had to be sorted into the sequence of the master file.

**sortation**    Identifying objects that are stamped with a bar code and routing them to the appropriate destination. Sortation is typically a high-speed process used in the transportion industry by companies such as Federal Express, UPS and others. See *sort* and *bar code*.

**sorter**    (1) A sort program.
(2) A person who manually puts data into a specific sequence.
(3) An early tabulating machine that routed punched cards into separate stackers based on the content of a card column. The complete operation required passing the cards through the machine once for each column sorted.

**sort key**    A field or fields in a record that dictate the sequence of the file. For example, the sort keys STATE and NAME arrange the file alphabetically by name within state. STATE is the major sort key, and NAME is the minor key.

**An Early Sorting Machine**
This is a sorter from the Computing-Tabulating-Recording Company in 1917. Punched cards were placed into the hopper and sorted into the respective stackers based on the content of one card column. A 10-digit account number required sorting the cards 10 times. This would have been a great year to buy stock in the company. In 1924, it became IBM. *(Image courtesy of International (Image courtesy of International Business Machines Corporation. Unauthorized use not permitted.)*

**SOS**    (1) (**S**ilicon **O**n **S**apphire) An MOS chip-fabrication method that places a thin layer of silicon over a sapphire substrate (base). This technique was used for earlier LSI fabrication, but not considered useful for higher-density VLSI chips. See *SOI*.
(2) (**S**ystems **O**n **S**ilicon) A complete system on a single chip. See *SoC*.
(3) (**S**erver **O**perating **S**ystem) An operating system that resides on the server.
(4) (**S**ophisticated **O**perating **S**ystem) The operating system used on the Apple III. See *Apple III*.

**SOT**    (**S**mall **O**utline **T**ransistor) A surface mount package for electronic components (transistor, resistor, etc.). It was the first type of surface mount packaging.

**sound bandwidth**    A range of sound frequencies. The human ear can perceive approximately from 20–20,000Hz, but human voice is confined to within 3,000Hz.

**Sound Blaster**    A family of sound cards from Creative Labs. The Sound Blaster protocol has become the de facto audio standard for PCs. Monaural versions of Sound Blaster cards were introduced in 1989, and the stereo version, Sound Blaster Pro, in 1992. The Sound Blaster AWE32 and AWE64 are 16-bit sound cards that provide wave table MIDI with 32 and 64 voices respectively.

**sound card**    Also called a "sound board" or "audio adapter," it is a personal computer expansion board that records and plays back sound, providing inputs from a microphone or other sound source and outputs to speakers or an external amplifier. The de facto standard for sound card compatibility in PCs is Creative Labs' Sound Blaster.

**Digital Audio and MIDI**    Sound cards play digital audio files and usually support MIDI. Digital audio files contain the actual soundwaves that have been converted into digital form. Without compression, they take up considerable storage space. The native digital audio format for Windows is the wave file (.WAV extension). The Mac uses AIFF, and Sun's AU format is used on the Internet. See *WAV file, AIFF file, AU file* and *sampling rate.*

MIDI files (.MID extension) differ from digital audio, because they contain a coded representation of the musical notes of the instrument; for example, middle C on the piano. MIDI files take up considerably less space than digital audio files, but require a MIDI synthesizer on the sound card. MPC requires MIDI on the board.

There are two kinds of MIDI sound reproduction methods used in sound cards. FM synthesis simulates musical notes. Wavetable synthesis (or waveform synthesis) actually holds digitized samples of the notes and produces richer sound. Another MIDI feature is the number of voices, or notes, that can be played back simultaneously. High-quality sound cards can have up to 64 MIDI voices.

**source**   (1) One side of a field effect transistor. See *drain.*

(2) (The Source) An online information service in McLean, VA, launched in 1979 and purchased by CompuServe in 1989.

(3) The HTML code (source code) of a Web page.

**source code**   Programming statements and instructions that are written by a programmer. Source code is what a programmer writes, but it is not directly executable by the computer. It must be converted into machine language by compilers, assemblers or interpreters.

In some cases, source code can be machine generated by conversion programs that convert the source code of one programming language or dialect into the source code of another language or dialect. See *lines of code.*

**source code compatible**   Able to run a program on a different platform by recompiling its source code into that machine code.

**source code management**   See *configuration management.*

**source computer**   The computer in which a program is being assembled or compiled. Contrast with *object computer.*

**source data**   The original data that is handwritten or printed on a source document or typed into the computer system from a keyboard or terminal.

**source data acquisition**   Same as *source data capture.*

**source data capture**   Capturing data electronically when a transaction occurs; for example, at the time of sale.

**source directory**   The directory from which data is obtained.

**source disk**   The disk from which data is obtained. Contrast with *target disk.*

**source document**   The paper form onto which data is written. Order forms and employment applications are examples.

**source drive**   The disk or tape drive from which data is obtained. Contrast with *target drive.*

**source language**   The language used in a source program. Contrast with *target language* and *machine language.* See *source code.*

**source program**   A program in its original form, as written by the programmer. See *source code.*

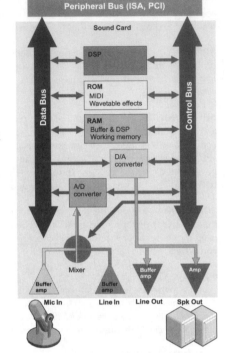

**Anatomy of a Sound Card**
PC sound cards typically have all the components in this picture. Some have only one output, which may be amplified (Amp) or not (Buffer amp). These components may also be built directly into the motherboard. *(Illustration courtesy of Peter Hermsen.)*

**source route bridging**     A communications protocol in which the sending station is aware of all the bridges in the network and predetermines the complete route to the destination station before transmitting. Token Ring uses this method. Contrast with *transparent bridge*. See *SRT*.

**source statement**     An instructional phrase in a programming language (source language).

**Southbridge**     See *Northbridge*.

**SOX**     (Schema for Object-oriented XML) An XML schema developed by Veo Systems and Muzino Communications, which was submitted to the W3C. SOX is based on DTD, but adds data typing and reuse mechanisms. A standard XML schema is expected from the W3C in 2000. See *XML schema, XDR, XML* and *SAX*. See also *SOCKS server*.

**SP**     See *service provider*.

**SP1**     (Service Pack 1) The first service pack introduced to upgrade a major release of software. See *service pack*.

**SP2**     (1) A massively parallel computer system from IBM that supports from two to 512 RS/6000 processors. It runs AIX and uses IBM's POWERparallel architecture, which includes a communications system between processors called the High-Performance Switch. In 1994, the University of New Mexico's Maui High Performance Computing Center installed an SP2 with 400 CPUs, which provides 100 gigaflops of computational power.
     (2) (Service Pack 2) The second service pack introduced to upgrade a major release of software. See *service pack*.

**SP3**     (Service Pack 3) The third service pack introduced to upgrade a major release of software. See *service pack*.

**SP4**     (Service Pack 4) The fourth service pack introduced to upgrade a major release of software. See *service pack*.

**SP5**     (Service Pack 5) The fifth service pack introduced to upgrade a major release of software. See *service pack*.

**SPA**     (Software Publishers Association, Washington, DC) In 1999, SPA merged with the IIA (Information Industry Association) to become the Software & Information Industry Association. See *SIIA*.

**space**     (1) In digital electronics, a 0 bit. Contrast with *mark*.
     (2) Generic for area or field of endeavor. For example, "in the Internet space" means that it pertains to the Internet industry.

**space/time**     The following units of measure are used to define storage and transmission capacities. See *binary values*.

| Space - Bits/bytes | | Power of 10 | |
|---|---|---|---|
| Kilo | (K) | Thousand | 3 |
| Mega | (M) | Million | 6 |
| Giga | (G) | Billion | 9 |
| Tera | (T) | Trillion | 12 |
| Peta | (P) | Quadrillion | 15 |
| Exa | (E) | Quintillion | 18 |
| Zetta | (Z) | Sextillion | 21 |
| Yotta | (Y) | Septillion | 24 |

| Time - Fraction of second | | Power of 10 | |
|---|---|---|---|
| Millisecond | (ms) | Thousandth | -3 |
| Microsecond | (µs) | Millionth | -6 |
| Nanosecond | (ns) | Billionth | -9 |
| Picosecond | (ps) | Trillionth | -12 |
| Femtosecond | (fs) | Quadrillionth | -15 |
| Attosecond | (as) | Quintillionth | -18 |
| Zeposecond | (zs) | Sextillionth | -21 |
| Yoctosecond | (ys) | Septillionth | -24 |

| Storage/Channel Capacity | Measured In: |
|---|---|
| CPU word size | bits |
| Bus size | bits |
| Disk, tape | bytes |
| Overall memory capacity | bytes |
| SIMM and DIMM modules | bytes |
| Individual memory chip | bits |

| Transmission Speed | Measured In: |
|---|---|
| Network line/channel | bits/sec |
| Disk transfer rate | bytes/sec |
| Disk access time | ms |
| Memory access time | ns |
| Machine cycle | µs, ns |
| Instruction execution | µs, ns |
| Transistor switching | ns, ps, fs |

S

**spaghetti code**    Program code written without a coherent structure. The logic moves from routine to routine without returning to a base point, making it hard to follow. It implies excessive use of the GOTO instruction, which directs the computer to branch to another part of the program without a guarantee of returning.

In structured programming, functions are used, which are subroutines that guarantee a return to the instruction following the one that called it.

**spam**    To send copies of the same message to large numbers of newsgroups or users on the Internet. People spam the Internet to advertise products as well as to broadcast some political or social commentary. See *mail bomb*, *letter bomb*, *spamdexing*, *Blacklist of Internet Advertisers*, *MAPS* and *opt-in*.

**spamdexing**    Techniques employed by some Web marketers and site designers in order to fool a search engine's spider and indexing programs. The objective is to ensure that their Web sites always appear at or near the top of the list of search engine results.

There are a variety of methods, but one of the most common is "word stuffing," which embeds a particular word in the site dozens or even hundreds of times. The words may be presented in such a way that people who visit the site cannot see them (as white text on a white background, for example), but search engines can. Or they may be quite obvious: line after line of "make money fast" on a page promoting a marketing opportunity.

Another technique is to combine word stuffing with "bait-and-switch," which loads the page with a popular search word such as sex, free, shareware or Windows, even though the word has nothing to do with the site content.

Major search engines such as AltaVista, Excite, and Lycos use special software to try to outsmart the spamdexers. Lycos, for example, automatically gives a lower ranking in its search results to any page that contains a lot of repeated words. But as soon as one method is successfully dealt with, others emerge that call for new and different approaches by the major engines.

Legitimate techniques that site designers can use to make their site more visible to search engines, such as inserting appropriate keywords in the site's tags, are often provided along with the search engine's "Search Tips" or "Help" information. Another good source is Search Engine Watch (www.searchenginewatch.com), which covers the major search engines. See *doorway page* and *spam*.

**spam relay**    Sending mail to a destination via a third-party mail server in order to hide the address of the source of the mail. For travelling users, it is common to use a local ISP to gain access to the Internet and send their mail to their home ISP, which forwards (relays) it to its destination. Nevertheless, ISPs can take precautions to prohibit spam relay. See *spam*.

**spanning tree algorithm**    An algorithm used in transparent bridges that dynamically determines the best path from source to destination. It avoids bridge loops (two or more paths linking one segment to another), which can cause the bridges to misinterpret results.

The algorithm creates a hierarchical "tree" that "spans" the entire network including all switches. It determines all redundant paths and makes only one of them active at any given time. The spanning tree protocol (STP) is part of the IEEE 802.1 standard. See *BPDU*.

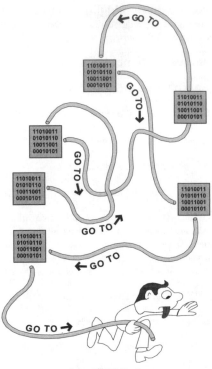

**Spaghetti Code**
There are tons of spaghetti code lurking in the millions of applications that have been written over the years. Spaghetti code is often the result of being in a rush to fix something or change something.

**SPARC**     (Scalable Performance ARChitecture) A family of 32-bit RISC CPUs developed by Sun. The first chip was introduced in 1989 in Sun's SPARCstation 1. Prior to that, Sun used Motorola 680x0 CPUs in its products. The 64-bit UltraSPARC line was introduced in 1995.

**spatial data**     Data that is represented as 2-D or 3-D images. A geographic information system (GIS) is one of the primary applications of spatial data (land maps). See *spatial analysis*, *spatial resolution* and *GIS glossary*.

**spatial light modulator**     A matrix of shutters that represents a page of binary data. It is used modulate a laser beam for holographic storage. See *holographic storage*.

**spawn**     To launch another program from the current program. The child program is spawned from the parent program.

**The First SPARCstation**
In 1989, Sun introduced the SPARCstation 1, the first Sun computer that used the SPARC chip. The SPARC line has been very successful.
*(Image courtesy of Sun Microsystems, Inc.)*

**S/PDIF**     (Sony/Philips Digital InterFace) A serial interface for transferring digital audio between devices such as CD and DVD players and amplifiers. S/PDIF is the consumer version of the AES/EBU interface and uses unbalanced 75 ohm coaxial cable with RCA or BNC connectors. An optical counterpart with a Toslink connector is also part of the specification. See *AES/EBU*.

**speaker recognition**     The ability to recognize a person by his or her spoken voice. This is used for security purposes, not voice recognition. Like voice recognition however, the user is required to train the system by speaking certain phrases. Contrast with *voice recognition*. See *biometrics*.

**spec**     (1) See *specs* and *specification*.
    (2) (SPEC) (Standard Performance Evaluation Corporation, Manassas, VA, www.specbench.org) An organization founded in 1988 to establish standard benchmarks for computers. Its first benchmark was the SPECmark, in which one SPECmark was equivalent in performance to a VAX 11/780. Subsequent SPECint and SPECfp benchmarks measured integer and floating point performance respectively. In 1996, SPEC introduced SPEC CPU95 which includes SPECint95 and SPECfp95, replacing SPECint92 and SPECfp92. A few comparisons of CPU SPEC ratings follow.

| CPU Chip | SPECint95 | SPECfp95 |
|----------|-----------|----------|
| 266MHz Pentium II | 10.8 | 6.8 |
| 250MHz PPC 604e | 11.1 | 7.8 |
| 300MHz UltraSPARC-2 | 10.4 | 14.5 |

    SPEC SFS 1 (System File Server) tests NFS server performance. It is also known as the LADDIS test, which was developed by a team of NFS developers. SPECweb96 and SPECweb97 are benchmarks for Web servers. See *benchmark*.

**Spec 1170**     See *Single UNIX Specification*.

**SPEC CPU92**     See *SPEC*.

**SPEC CPU95**     See *SPEC*.

**SPECfp**     See *SPEC*.

**special character**     Non-alphabetic or non-numeric character, such as @, #, $, %, &, * and +.

**special-purpose computer**     A computer designed from scratch to perform a specific function. Contrast with *general-purpose computer*.

**special-purpose language**     A programming language designed to solve a specific problem or class of problems. For example, LISP and Prolog are designed for and used extensively in AI applications. Even more specific are languages such as COGO, for civil engineering problems, and APT for directing machine tools. Contrast with *general-purpose language*.

**specification**　A definition (layout, blueprint, design) of hardware or software. See *specs* and *functional specification*.

**specs**　(SPECificationS) The details of the components built into a device. See *specification*.

**SPEC SFS 1**　See *SPEC*.

**spec sheet**　A detail listing of the components of a system.

**spectral bands**　See *optical bands* and *electromagnetic spectrum*.

**spectral color**　In computer graphics, the color of a single wavelength of light, starting with violet at the low end and proceeding through indigo, blue, green, yellow and orange and ending with red.

**spectral response**　The variable output of a light-sensitive device that is based on the color of the light it perceives.

**spectral width**　The amount of the electromagnetic spectrum that a laser beam covers. Thus far, it has been impossible to produce light pulses with zero spectral width. For example, a 1540 nm pulse might actually cover 1539.9 to 1540.1 nm, but not 1540.0 dead on. See *optical bands*.

**spectroscopy**　The study of electromagnetic radiation.

**spectrum**　A range of electromagnetic frequencies. See *electromagnetic spectrum* and *radio*.

**speech codec**　Also called a "voice codec" or "vocoder," it is a hardware circuit (chip) or software rouine that converts the spoken word into digital code and vice versa. A speech codec is an audio codec specialized for human voice. By analyzing vocal tract sounds, a recipe for rebuilding the sound at the other end is sent rather than the soundwaves themselves. As a result, the speech codec is able to achieve a much higher compression ratio which yields a smaller amount of digital data for transmission. However, if music is encoded with a speech codec, it will not sound as good when decoded at the other end. See *audio codec*.

**speech compression**　Encoding digital speech to take up less storage space and transmission bandwidth. The PCM, ADPCM, CELP and LD-CELP methods are commonly used for speech compression. See *speech codec* and *data compression*.

**speech recognition**　Same as *voice recognition*.

**speech synthesis**　Generating machine voice by arranging phonemes (k, ch, sh, etc.) into words. It is used to turn text input into spoken words for the blind. Speech synthesis performs realtime conversion without a pre-defined vocabulary, but does not create perfect-sounding human speech. Although individual spoken words can be digitized into the computer, it takes more storage, and the resulting phrases still lack inflection. Spoken phrases that are repetitively used in voice applications are usually digitized whole to provide the most pleasing announcements.

**speed buffering**　A technique that compensates for speed differences between input and output. Data is accepted into the buffer at high speed and transferred out at low speed, or vice versa.

**SPEEDE**　(Standardization of Postsecondary Education Electronic Data Exchange) A standard for electronically transferring transcripts and other records between colleges and universities.

**spell checker**　A separate program or word processing function that tests for correctly-spelled words. It can test the spelling of a marked block, an entire document or group of documents. Advanced systems check for spelling as the user types and can correct common typos and misspellings on the fly.

　　Spell checkers simply compare words to a dictionary of words, and the wrong use of a correctly-spelled word cannot be detected. See *grammar checker*.

---

**MY SPELL CHECKER**

I have a spelling checker,
It came with my PC,
It plainly marks
four my revue
Mistakes I cannot sea.

I've run this poem,
threw it,
I'm sure your
please too no.
It's letter perfect
in its weigh;
My checker
tolled me sew.

---

**spherization**    In computer graphics, turning an image into a sphere.

**SPICE**    (Simulation Program with Integrated Circuit Emphasis) A program widely used to simulate the performance of analog electronic systems and mixed mode analog and digital systems. SPICE solves sets of non-linear differential equations in the frequency domain, steady state and time domain and can simulate the behavior of transistor and gate designs. Developed at the University of California at Berkeley, there are enhanced versions of SPICE provided by several software companies.

**SPID**    (Service Profile IDentifier) A number assigned to an ISDN line by the telephone company that indicates which services the ISDN device can access. The SPID is used by the central office switch, and depending on the type of switch, either one or two SPIDs or none at all are required per line. The SPID is usually the 10-digit ISDN telephone number with a couple of extra digits tacked on. For example, the SPID for the ISDN number (215) 489-2077 might become 21548920770101.

**spider**    See *crawler*.

**spike**    Also called a "transient," it is a burst of extra voltage in a power line that lasts only a fraction of a second. Contrast with *sag*. See *power surge*.

**spindle**    A rotating shaft in a disk drive. In a fixed disk, the platters are attached to the spindle. In a removable disk, the spindle remains in the drive. Laptops use spindle designations to indicate the number of built-in drives. For example, a two-spindle machine contains a hard drive and a second bay for a floppy or CD-ROM drive. A three-spindle machine means that all three drives (hard disk, floppy and CD-ROM) are built in.

**SpinRite**    A popular DOS-based hard disk analysis program for PCs from Gibson Research Corporation, Laguna Hills, CA (www.grc.com). It performs a series of tests to detect defects and causes the drive to move the data in failing sectors to its own hidden, spare sector pool. Supporting all types of drives including IDE, SCSI, Zip and Jaz, SpinRite has been widely used for years. It is written by Steve Givson, noted throughout the world for his technical excellence.

SpinRite can also low-level format old MFM, RLL and IDE drives without erasing data. It rewrites only sector ID, which may have drifted over time.

| Partition C: Information | | | | |
|---|---|---|---|---|
| Partition C: with | 210 megabyte capacity on the 1st physical drive. | | | |
| Info | In use | Marked bad | Free clusters | Total |
| Percent | 84.54% | 0.05% | 15.41% | 100.00% |
| Clusters | 41,756 | 25 | 7,612 | 49,394 |
| Bytes | 171,034,243 | 104,220 | 31,177,969 | 202,316,432 |

| Date | Lev | Most Recent Usage History | Partition Setup | |
|---|---|---|---|---|
| 02/01/93 | 4 | Repaired 12 sectors | volume label : | ZXP DRIVE C |
| 04/05/93 | 1+ | Hit 3 bad sectors | volume serial # : | 3426-6753 |
| 06/20/93 | +2 | 2 Defective Sectors | 512 : | logical sector size |
| 08/01/93 | 7 | Restored 14 Sectors | 8 : | sectors per cluster |
| 10/23/93 | 2 | Refreshed the Surface | 4,096 : | bytes per cluster |

**SpinRite**
Widely used for years, SpinRite provides a wealth of information about your hard disk. The 210MB disk example is used to keep the numbers more readable. *(Image courtesy of Gibson Research Corporation, www.grc.com)*

**SPL**    (1) (Systems Programming Language) The assembly language for the HP 3000 series. See *assembly language* for an SPL program example.

(2) (Structured Programming Language) See *structured programming*.

**splash screen**    An introductory screen displayed by an application after it is loaded and just before it starts. It generally shows the software company's name and logo. Fancy splash screens may provide some kind of animated graphic to entertain you for a few seconds.

**SPLD**    (Simple PLD) A programmable logic device that provides an array of logic blocks that can be programmed. See *PLD*.

**splice**    To permanently fasten two string-like objects together such as copper wires, optical fibers or magnetic tape. See *mechanical splice* and *fusion splice*.

**spline**    In computer graphics, a smooth curve that runs through a series of given points. The term is often used to refer to any curve, because long before computers, a spline was a flat, pliable strip of wood or metal that was bent into a desired shape for drawing curves on paper. See *Bezier* and *B-spline*.

S

**split screen**    The display of two or more sets of data on screen at the same time. It implies that one set of data can be manipulated independently of the other. This was a popular term with DOS applications and other character-based text screens. Today, a window implies the same thing.

**spoofing**    (1) In communications, creating fake responses or signals in order to keep a session active and prevent timeouts. For example, a mainframe or mini  continuously polls its terminals. If the lines to remote terminals are temporarily suspended because there is no traffic, a local device spoofs the host with "I'm still here" reponses.

(2) Faking the sending address of a transmission in order to gain illegal entry into a secure system.

**spoofing your technical friend**    See *how to spoof your technical friend*.

**spooling**    (**S**imultaneous **P**eripheral **O**perations **O**n**L**ine) The overlapping of low-speed operations with normal processing. It originated with mainframes in order to optimize slow operations such as reading cards and printing. Card input was read onto disk and printer output was stored on disk. In that way, the actual business data processing was done at high speed, since all I/O was on disk.

Today, spooling is used to buffer data for the printer as well as remote batch terminals. See *print spooler*.

**spot color**    A color that is printed from one printing plate which contains one matched color of ink. Spot colors are used when only one or two solid colors are needed on a page or when a color has to match perfectly and be consistent such as with a company logo or when colors are the trademark of the organization or message. If spot color is used along with process color, then a four-color print job becomes a five or six-color job. Contrast with *process color*.

**SPP**    (1) (**S**calable **P**arallel **P**rocessor) A multiprocessing computer that can be upgraded by adding more CPUs.

(2) (**S**tandard **P**arallel **P**ort) The parallel port that has been used on PCs since their inception. Contrast with the higher-speed EPP and ECP ports. See *IEEE 1284*.

**spreadsheet**    Software that simulates a paper spreadsheet, or worksheet, in which columns of numbers are summed for budgets and plans. It appears on screen as a matrix of rows and columns, the intersections of which are identified as cells. Spreadsheets can have thousands of cells and can be scrolled horizontally and vertically in order to view them.

The cells are filled with

- Labels
- Numeric values
- Formulas

The labels, can be any descriptive text, for example, RENT, PHONE or GROSS SALES.

The values are the actual numeric data used in the budget or plan, and the formulas command the spreadsheet to do the calculations; for example, SUM CELLS A5 TO A10.

Formulas are easy to create, since spreadsheets allow the user to point to each cell and type in the arithmetic operation that affects it. Roughly speaking, a formula is created by saying "this cell PLUS that cell TIMES that cell."

The formulas are the spreadsheet's magic. After numbers are added or changed, the formulas will recalculate the data either automatically or with the press of a key. Since the contents of any cell can be calculated with or copied to any other cell, a total of one column can be used as a detail item in another column. For example, the total from a column of expense items can be carried over to a summary column showing all expenses. If data in the detail column changes, its column total changes, which is then copied to the summary column, and the summary total changes.

Done manually, each change would require recalculating, erasing and changing the totals of each column. The automatic ripple effect allows users to create a plan, plug in different assumptions and immediately see the impact on the bottom line. This "what if?" capability makes the spreadsheet indispensable for budgets, plans and other equation-based tasks.

The spreadsheet originated with VisiCalc in 1978 for the Apple II, and was followed by SuperCalc, Multiplan, Lotus 1-2-3 and a host of others. See *XL ABCs*.

## Classes of Spreadsheets

**2-D**    Every spreadsheet can create a two-dimensional matrix of rows and columns. In order to summarize data, totals from various parts of the spreadsheet can be summed to another part of the spreadsheet.

**3-D**    Each cell in the spreadsheet has an X, Y and Z reference. For example, a spreadsheet of expense items by month uses two dimensions, but expense items by month by department requires three.

While this method is superior for consolidating and summarizing data, it lacks some of the flexibility required by sophisticated applications. In addition, all data typically resides in one file as with a standard 2-D spreadsheet.

**Multidimensional**    Multidimensional spreadsheets support more than three axes and allow the data and the relationships to be viewed from different perspectives. Data is not stored by cell references (A1, B2, etc.), but by name. Formulas are not placed into cells as in a traditional spreadsheet, but are defined separately as in a modeling language; for example, "gross profit=gross sales–cost of goods."

With name references, data can be used in multiple spreadsheets with greater accuracy, and new spreadsheets can be created more easily. However, since data isn't tied to cell references, this method lacks the flexibility and ease of use that caused the traditional 2-D spreadsheet to revolutionize the computer industry.

**Analytical Databases**    The need for multidimensional views of large amounts of data has given rise to a variety of methods over the years. All sorts of modeling programs have been created, but none have been as easy to use as the spreadsheet. Some combine spreadsheets with traditional database management. For example, TM1 was one of the first programs to provide multiple dimensions and isolate the data from the spreadsheet. This method provides database consistency (the data is not replicated in every spreadsheet) with the ease of use of the spreadsheet for creating the viewing models.

Organizations that analyze large amounts of sales history and other data are increasingly using OLAP (OnLine Analytical Processing) databases. OLAP databases use proprietary algorithms for summarizing data so that multidimensional views can be quickly queried. See *OLAP*.

**spreadsheet compiler**    Software that translates spreadsheets into stand-alone programs that can be run without the spreadsheet package that created them.

**spread spectrum**    A variety of radio transmission methods that continuously change frequencies or signal patterns. Direct sequence spread spectrum (DSSS), which is used in CDMA, multiplies the data bits by a very fast pseudo-random bit pattern (PN sequence) that "spreads" the data into a large coded stream that takes the full bandwidth of the channel (see *CDMA*).

Frequency hopping spread spectrum (FHSS) continuously changes the center frequency of a conventional carrier several times per second according to a pseudo-random set of channels, while chirp spread spectrum changes the carrier frequency. Because a fixed frequency is not used, illegal monitoring of spread spectrum signals is extremely difficult, if not downright impossible depending on the particular method. See *frequency*.

**sprite**    An independent graphic object controlled by its own bit plane (area of memory). Commonly used in video games, sprites move freely across the screen, passing by, through and colliding with each other with much less programming.

**SPS**    (Standby Power System) A UPS system that switches to battery backup upon detection of power failure. See *UPS*.

**SPSS**    A statistical package from SPSS, Inc., Chicago, IL (www.spss.com) that runs on PCs, most mainframes and minis and is used extensively in marketing research. It provides over 50 statistical processes, including regression analysis, correlation and analysis of variance. Originally named Statistical Package for the Social Sciences, it was written by Norman Nie, a professor at Stanford. In 1976, he formed SPSS, Inc.

**spt**    (Sectors Per Track) The number of sectors in one track.

**SPUFI**    (SQL Processing Using File Input) A SQL statement used natively without being embedded in a program.

**SPX**    (Sequenced Packet EXchange) The NetWare communications protocol used to control the transport of messages across a network. SPX ensures that an entire message arrives intact and uses NetWare's IPX protocol as its delivery mechanism. Application programs use SPX to provide client/server and peer-to-peer interaction between network nodes. SPX provides services at layer 4 of the OSI model.

**spyware**    Software that sends information about your Web surfing habits to its Web site. Often built into free downloads from the Web, it transmits information in the background as you move around the Web. The license agreement that you often accept without reading may say that the information is anonymous. Anonymous profiling means that your habits are being recorded, but not you individually. It is used to create marketing profiles; for example, people that like Web sites that feature A often go to Web sites that feature B and so on.

**SQL** (Structured Query Language) Pronounced "SQL" or "see qwill," a language used to interrogate and process data in a relational database. Originally developed by IBM for its mainframes, all database systems designed for client/sever environments support SQL. SQL commands can be used to interactively work with a database or can be embedded within a programming language to interface to a database. Programming extensions to SQL have turned it into a full-blown database programming language.

Some of the major database management systems (DBMSs) that support SQL are DB2, SQL/DS, Oracle, Sybase, SQLbase, INFORMIX and CA-OpenIngres (Ingres).

The following SQL query selects customers with credit limits of at least $5,000 and puts them into sequence from highest credit limit to lowest. The blue words are SQL verbs. See *SPUFI*.

```
SELECT NAME, CITY, STATE, ZIPCODE
FROM CUSTOMER
WHERE CREDITLIMIT 4999
ORDER BY CREDITLIMIT DESC
```

SQL - A Standard? The American National Standards Institute (ANSI) has standardized the SQL language, but it does not cover all the bases. Each database management system (DBMS) has its own enhancements, quirks and tricks that, for all intents and purposes, makes SQL non standard. Moving an application from one SQL database to another generally requires hand tailoring to convert some of the SQL statements. So what's new? See *CLI*, *ODBC* and *IDAPI*.

**SQLBase Server** A relational DBMS for DOS, OS/2, NetWare, NT and Sun servers from Centura. It is one of the leading database programs on servers running OS/2 and NetWare. SQLBase has been Centura's flagship product since the company was founded in 1984. See *SQLWindows*.

**SQL/DS** (SQL/Data System) A full-featured relational DBMS from IBM for VSE and VM environments that has integrated query and report writing facilities.

**SQL engine** A program that accepts SQL commands and accesses the database to obtain the requested data. Users' requests in a query language or database language must be translated into an SQL request before the SQL engine can process it.

**SQL Forms** An earlier version of Oracle Forms, an application development tool for client/server systems. See *Developer/2000*.

**SQLJ** (SQL Java) A programming interface that allows SQL statements to be expressed at a high level in a Java program. SQLJ statements are converted into JDBC commands. See *JDBC*.

**SQL precompiler** Software that turns SQL commands written within a source program into the appropriate function calls for the database management system (DBMS) being used. After the SQL precompiler stage, the resulting program is translated into machine language by the COBOL compiler or the compiler of whatever language the program is written in. See *embedded SQL*.

**SQL Server** A relational DBMS from Sybase that runs on OS/2, Windows NT, NetWare, VAX and UNIX servers. It is designed for client/server use and is accessed by applications using SQL or via Sybase's own QBE and decision support utilities.

SQL Server was also available through Microsoft as Microsoft SQL Server for OS/2 and Microsoft SQL Server for Windows NT. In 1992, Microsoft started to modify the program and eventually rewrote its own version that it sells independently.

**SQLWindows** A high-level application development system for Windows from Centura Software Corporation, Menlo Park, CA (www.centurasoft.com). It is used to write Windows applications that access SQL databases in a client/server environment. SQLWindows Solo is a demonstration version that provides all of the functionality of SQLWindows, but works only on a single machine. See *SQLBase Server* and *Centura*.

**SQR**    Query and reporting software from SQRIBE Technologies, Menlo Park, CA (www.sqribe.com). SQR Workbench runs under Windows 95 and NT and provides a graphical front end for designing and viewing complex reports. SQR Server provides native drivers for all the major databases and runs under Windows and most versions of UNIX. It also provides extensions to SQL for more complicated database processing. Output is available as HTML documents.

**square wave**    A graphic image of a digital pulse as visualized on an oscilloscope. It appears square because it rises quickly to a particular amplitude, stays constant for the duration of the pulse and drops fast at the end of it.

**SQUID**    (Superconducting Quantum Interference Device) An electronic detection system that uses Josephson junctions circuits. It is capable of detecting extremely weak signals.

**SRAM**    See *static RAM*.

**SRAPI**    (Speech Recognition API) A programming interface from Novell for speech recognition. SRAPI has been superseded by Microsoft's SAPI. See *SAPI*.

**SRB**    See *source route bridging*.

**SRI**    (SRI International, Menlo Park, CA, www.sri.com) One of the oldest and largest research, technology development and consulting firms in the U.S. Founded in 1946 in conjunction with Stanford University, SRI (then Stanford Research Institute) was created to "promote the application of science in the development of commerce, trade and industry."

Over the years, SRI scientists and researchers have been involved in such fields as health care, information sciences and technology, national defense, chemical engineering, advanced materials and TV and electronics. See *telepresence surgery*.

**SRPI**    (Server Requester Programming Interface) An IBM programming interface that allows a PC to interact with a mainframe. See *ECF*.

**SRT**    (1) (Source Routing Transparent) An IEEE-standard that provides bridging between Ethernet and Token Ring networks. Ethernet LANs use transparent bridging, and Token Ring LANs use source route bridging (SRB). The SRT method sends Ethernet packets via transparent bridging and Token Ring packets via SRB.

(2) (Speech Recognition Technology) See *voice recognition*.

**SS7**    (Signaling System 7) The protocol used in the public switched telephone system (the "intelligent network" or "advanced intelligent network") for setting up calls and providing services. SS7 is a separate signaling network that is used in Class 4 and Class 5 voice switches.

The SS7 network sets up and tears down the call, handles all the routing decisions and supports all modern telephony services such as 800 numbers, call forwarding, caller ID and local number portability (LNP). The voice switches known as "service switching points" (SSPs) query "service control point" (SCP) databases using packet switches known as "signal transfer points" (STPs).

Accessing databases using a separate signaling network enables the system to more efficiently obtain static information such as the services a customer has signed up for and dynamic information such as ever-changing traffic conditions in the network. In addition, a voice circuit is not tied up until a connection is actually made between both parties.

There is an international version of SS7 standardized by the ITU, and national versions determined by each country. For example, ANSI governs the U.S. standard for SS7, and Telcordia (Bellcore) provides an extension of ANSI for its member companies. See *AIN, Class 4 switch, Class 5 switch* and *CCIS*.

SS7 Protocol Stack    The SS7 protocols do not conform precisely to the OSI model, but showing the comparison helps put them into perspective.

**IN, AIN, INAP and MAP**    IN, AIN and INAP protocols are used to initiate non-circuit related functions throughout the network (not dealing with connect/disconnect). AIN (Advanced Intelligent Network) is used in North America. INAP (Intelligent Network Application Part) is used in Europe, and other countries use proprietary versions of IN (Intelligent Network) standards based on the ITU. These protocols use TCAP to access remote devices.

S

**MAP**    MAP (Mobile Application Part) enables cellular carriers to use the SS7 network and allows the cellphone's telephone number and serial number to be transmitted over the network. See *IS-41*.

**TCAP**    TCAP (Transaction Capabilities Application Part) is used to send database queries to a service control point (SCP). It is also used to send non-circuit related messages between switches. TCAP keeps track of multiple queries that are part of the same session.

**ISUP and TUP**    ISUP (ISDN User Part) is used to connect and disconnect a call in North America, and TUP (Telephone User Part) is the counterpart used elsewhere.

**SSCP**    When TCAP is used to query a database, SSCP (Signaling Connection Control Point) is used in conjunction with TCAP to route the message to the appropriate database subsystem. SSCP also provides guaranteed end to end delivery and thus delivers both OSI layer 3 and 4 capabilities.

**MTP**    MTP-3 (Message Transfer Part-3) provides message routing and network management. The individual data links are continuously monitored. When a link fails, messages are rerouted, and the link is reset and resynchronized, which often solves the problem.

MTP-2 is responsible for error-free transmission between two SS7 nodes (signaling points). Packet sequence numbers are also generated at this level to ensure that everything arrives properly.

MTP-1 supports numerous digital interfaces including DS0A, DS1 and V.35.

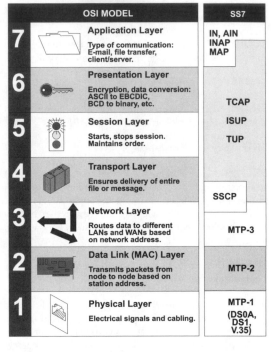

| OSI MODEL | | SS7 |
|---|---|---|
| **7** | **Application Layer**<br>Type of communication:<br>E-mail, file transfer,<br>client/server. | IN, AIN<br>INAP<br>MAP |
| **6** | **Presentation Layer**<br>Encryption, data conversion:<br>ASCII to EBCDIC,<br>BCD to binary, etc. | TCAP |
| **5** | **Session Layer**<br>Starts, stops session.<br>Maintains order. | ISUP<br>TUP |
| **4** | **Transport Layer**<br>Ensures delivery of entire<br>file or message. | SSCP |
| **3** | **Network Layer**<br>Routes data to different<br>LANs and WANs based<br>on network address. | MTP-3 |
| **2** | **Data Link (MAC) Layer**<br>Transmits packets from<br>node to node based on<br>station address. | MTP-2 |
| **1** | **Physical Layer**<br>Electrical signals and cabling. | MTP-1<br>(DS0A,<br>DS1,<br>V.35) |

**SSA**    (Serial Storage Architecture)  A peripheral interface from IBM that transfers data up to 80 Mbytes/sec. SSA 160 increases the rate to 160 MBps. SSA's ring configuration allows remaining devices to function if one fails. SCSI software can be mapped over SSA allowing existing SCSI devices to be used. While distances of SCSI cables are measured in feet, SSA cable can be up to 25 meters over copper and 2.4 kilometers over fiber.

**SSAD**    (Structured Systems Analysis and Design)  See *SSADM*.

**SSADM**    (Structured Systems Analysis and Design Methodology)  A technology widely used for the analysis and design of IT systems. SSADM does not cover strategic information planning (SITP) issues or the construction, testing and implementation of software. Because it is an open standard, many companies offer SSADM support, training and CASE tools.

SSADM was commissioned by the CCTA in 1981 in order to standardize the many and varied IT projects that were then being developed across government departments. The CCTA investigated a number of approaches before accepting a tender from Learmonth & Burchett Management Systems to develop the method. The U.S. government is a major user of SSADM.

**SSCP**    (1) (System Services Control Point)  A controlling program in an SNA domain. It resides in the host and is a component within VTAM.

(2) (Signaling Connection Control Point)  A layer 3 protocol in an SS7 network that routes a message to the appropriate database. SCCP is used in conjunction with the TCAP protocol for sending queries to databases. See *SS7* and *TCAP*.

**SSD**    See *solid state disk*.

**SSE** **(1)** (Single SIMD Extensions) A group of 70 instructions added to the Pentium III chip that improves 3-D graphics performance. It includes floating point capability for 3-D geometry calculations. SSE is the second set of enhancements to the Intel CPU chips for multimedia operations (MMX was the first). The Pentium 4 added 144 more instructions known as SSE2. SSE was originally code named the Katmai New Instructions (KNI), because the Pentium III was code named Katmai. See *Pentium III*, *MMX* and *SIMD*.

**(2)** A Protected Mode full-screen editor in OS/2.

**SSI** **(1)** See *server-side include* and *single-system image*.

**(2)** (Small-Scale Integration) Less than 100 transistors on a chip. See *MSI*, *LSI*, *VLSI* and *ULSI*.

**SSJS** (Server-Side JavaScript) A JavaScript interpreter for running JavaScript programs on the server. It includes a library of objects and functions for accessing databases, sending e-mail and performing other tasks. Contrast with *CSJS*.

**SSL** (Secure Sockets Layer) The leading security protocol on the Internet. When an SSL session is started, the server sends its public key to the browser, which the browser uses to send a randomly-generated secret key back to the server in order to have a secret key exchange for that session. Developed by Netscape, SSL has been merged with other protocols and authentication methods by the IETF into a new protocol known as Transport Layer Security (TLS). See *TLS*, *security protocol* and *public key cryptography*.

**SSP** **(1)** (Service Switching Point) The local exchange node in an SS7 telephone network. The SSP can be part of the voice switch or in a separate computer connected to it. The SSP creates SS7 signaling messages that are sent to a "service control point" (SCP) to query databases for subscriber service and routing information. See *AIN* and *SCP*.

**(2)** (Storage Service Provider) A third party that manages the storage facilities for an enterprise. The storage devices can be on the customer's premises or at the SSP's site connected to the customer's machines via fiber-optic links. See *ASP*.

**(3)** (Switch to Switch Protocol) The protocol used in DLSw that locates resources and routes messages.

**(4)** (System Support Program) A multiuser, multitasking operating system from IBM that is the primary control program for the System/34 and System/36.

**stack** **(1)** A set of hardware registers or a reserved amount of memory used for arithmetic calculations or to keep track of internal operations. Stacks keep track of the sequence of routines called in a program. For example, one routine calls another, which calls another and so on. As each routine is completed, the computer returns control to the calling routine all the way back to the first one that started the sequence. Stacks used in this way are LIFO based: the last item, or address, placed (pushed) onto the stack is the first item removed (popped) from the stack.

Stacks are also used to hold interrupts until they can be serviced. Used in this manner, they are FIFO stacks, in which the first item onto the stack is the first one out of the stack. See *DOS Stacks*.

An "internal stack failure" is a fatal error which means that the operating system has lost track of its next operation. Restarting the computer usually corrects this, otherwise the operating system may have to be re-installed. See *stack dump* and *stack fault*.

**(2)** See *protocol stack* and *HyperCard*.

**stackable hub** A type of Ethernet hub that can be expanded by daisy chaining additional hubs together via dedicated ports for that purpose. They are designed to stack vertically and be treated as a single domain by the network management software.

**stack dump** The contents of a stack. A stack dump is often displayed when an error occurs. See *stack*.

**stacker** **(1)** An output bin in a document feeding or punched card machine. Contrast with *hopper*.

**(2)** (Stacker) A realtime compression program from Stac Electronics, Carlsbad, CA (www.stac.com) that doubles the disk capacity of a DOS, Windows, Mac or OS/2 computer.

**stack fault** An error condition that occurs when the stack is either empty or full. See *stack overflow*.

**stack overflow** An error condition that occurs when there is no room in the stack for a new item. This error condition can also occur when other things go awry; for example, a bad expansion board or one that isn't seated properly in the slot can cause erratic signals eventually leading to a stack overflow error message. Contrast with *stack underflow*. See *stack*.

**stack pointer**    An address that identifies the location of the most recent item placed on the stack.

**stack underflow**    An error condition that occurs when an item is called for from the stack, but the stack is empty. Contrast with *stack overflow*. See *stack*.

**staging server**    A server used to temporarily show certain users new and revised Internet and/or intranet pages before they are put into production.

**stair-stepping**    See *jaggies*.

**standard**    A specification for hardware or software that is either widely used and accepted (de facto) or is sanctioned by a standards organization (de jure). See *standards*.

**standard cell**    See *cell-based IC*.

**standard deviation**    In statistics, the average amount a number varies from the average number in a series of numbers.

**standard mapping**    A formalized way of converting one set of codes into another. See *map*.

**standards**    Standards is the most important issue in the computer field. As an unregulated industry, we have wound up with thousands of data formats and languages, but few standards that are universally used. This subject is as heated as politics and religion to vendors and industry planners. In order to truly understand this industry, it is essential to understand the categories for which standards are created.

No matter how much the industry talks about compatibility, new formats and languages appear routinely. The standards makers are always trying to cast a standard in concrete, while the innovators are trying to create a new one. Even when standards are created, they are violated as soon as one vendor adds a proprietary extension.

**The Future**    After 40 some years of computing, we've managed to create thousands of languages, formats and interfaces in this business. While many become bona fide standards endorsed by recognized standards organizations such as ANSI and the IEEE, some of the most widely used are de facto standards. Intel and Microsoft standards are the most obvious examples.

While the Internet is helping immensely, it will by no means solve all issues. As we forge ahead with new technologies, there is some point where we can no longer cling to the old designs for compatibility. At that time, the new has to break from the past, as the previous infrastructure only holds us back. It's no different than constructing a new building on top of a weak foundation. It seems to be the way of things. See *standards bodies*.

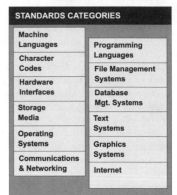

**STANDARDS CATEGORIES**

| | |
|---|---|
| Machine Languages | Programming Languages |
| Character Codes | File Management Systems |
| Hardware Interfaces | Database Mgt. Systems |
| Storage Media | Text Systems |
| Operating Systems | Graphics Systems |
| Communications & Networking | Internet |

**Standards Categories**
These are the major categories of electronic systems that require standards. Developing information systems in today's environment often seems like the Tower of Babel.

**standards bodies**    Following are the standards bodies defined in this database. For CD-ROM users, also review the Associations lesson list as many associations are instrumental in developing specifications that become standards.

| Organization | Covers | Organization | Covers |
|---|---|---|---|
| ANSI | U.S. standards | ETSI | European telecom standards |
| NIST | U.S. standards | IEEE | Electronics standards |
| CCIA | Computer/communications industry | JEDEC | IC standards |
| ITU | International standards | JEIDA | Japanese electronics |
| IEC | International standards | PCMCIA | PC memory card standards |
| ISO | International standards | W3C | Internet |
| EIA | Interface standards; RS-232 | XAPIA | X.400 standards |

## standards—character codes

The character code built into the computer determines how each letter, digit or special character ($, %, #, etc.) is represented in binary code. Fortunately, there are only two methods in wide use: EBCDIC and ASCII. IBM's mainframes and midrange systems use EBCDIC. ASCII is used for most everything else, including all PCs and Macs.

ASCII is a 7-bit code placed into an 8-bit storage unit. The seven bits provide the basic set of 128 ASCII characters. The 8th bit adds storage for another 128 symbols, and these symbols vary from font to font and system to system. For example, the DOS character set contains line drawing and foreign language characters. The ANSI character set uses them for foreign languages and math and publishing symbols (copyright, trademark, etc.). In the Mac, the upper 128 characters can be custom drawn.

When systems are moved from one computer to another, converting between ASCII and EBCDIC is just a small part of the data conversion process. It is done in conjunction with converting file formats from the old to the new systems. The following is a sample of ASCII and EBCDIC code. See *ASCII chart, hex chart* and **EBCDIC chart**.

| Character | ASCII | EBCDIC |
|-----------|----------|----------|
| space | 01000000 | 00100000 |
| period | 01001011 | 00101110 |
| sign | 01001100 | 00111100 |
| + sign | 01001110 | 00101011 |
| $ sign | 01011011 | 00100100 |
| A | 11000001 | 01000001 |
| B | 11000010 | 01000010 |

## standards—communications and networking

Going online to the Internet is relatively simple. All that's required is a modem and a browser, which have become standard fare on PCs and Macs. Communications within the enterprise is far more complex. Over the years, organizations have developed islands of computer systems, each with their own networking protocols and access methods. The enterprise has been faced with tying mainframes, midrange systems and PCs together for file sharing, electronic mail and routine data processing.

It is a daunting task connecting client machines running DOS, Windows, Mac and Motif with servers that run DOS, Windows, Mac, VMS, MVS and UNIX via protocols such as TCP/IP, IPX and NetBIOS over topologies such as Ethernet, Fast Ethernet, Switched Ethernet, Token Ring, FDDI and ATM using devices such as bridges, routers, hubs, switches and gateways, and there you have it. Oh, add interfacing between multiple mail and messaging systems and managing the entire process from one management console.

To understand the layers of protocols required to transmit a message from one machine to another, review the layers of the OSI model. OSI is a seven-layer reference model for worldwide communications defined by the International Standards Organization (ISO). Originally thought to be the future standard for communications, it was never widely supported. However, it does serve as a teaching model to line up other protocols against. See *enterprise networking*, *client/server* and *OSI model*.

## standards—DBMSs

Database management systems (DBMSs) have their own proprietary formats for storing data. For example, a header record with a unique format that contains identification data is typically placed at the beginning of each file. Codes may also be embedded in each record.

Most DBMSs have an import and export capability that converts popular database formats into their proprietary format. If not, the program usually can import and export a plain EBCDIC or ASCII file, which is stripped of all proprietary codes and can be used as a common denominator between both systems. If conversion facilities cannot be found, a custom program can be written to convert one database format into another if documentation describing the old format is available.

The application program "talks" to the database in the SQL language typically. In theory, that means any application program requesting data in SQL would work with any DBMS that supports it. Like everything else however, there are dialects of SQL. Whatever special features exist within the DBMS, proprietary syntax is needed to activate them, thus automatically making one DBMS incompatible with another.

## standards—file management systems

In its simplest form, a data file uses fields of the same length for each item of data, for example, a plain EBCDIC or ASCII file would look like this:

```
Chris Smith    34 Main St.    Bangor      ME18567
Pat Jones      10 W. 45 St.   New York    NY10002
```

A common format stemming from the BASIC programming language is an ASCII comma delimited file; for example, the data above would look like the following:

```
"Chris Smith","34 Main St.","Bangor","ME","18567"
"Pat Jones","10 W. 45 St.","New York","NY","10002"
```

Both file formats above are simple, contain only data (except for quotes and commas) and can be easily manipulated by a word processor. However, data files may also contain special codes that identify the way the data is structured within the file. For example, variable length records require a code in each field indicating the size of the field.

Whether fixed or variable length fields, the data in non-DBMS systems is linked directly to the processing. The program must know the layout of the fields in each record, and it cannot accept records in a different format. In order to process a different file format, the program must be changed.

Incompatible file formats often exist within the same organization because they were developed separately. For example, one record may reserve 40 characters for name, while another holds only 30. As long as a file management system is used rather than a database management system (DBMS), the program that processes the first file structure would have to be changed to process the second.

### standards—graphics systems

There are many formats for storing a picture in a computer; but, unlike text and data files, which are primarily made up of alphanumeric characters, graphics formats are more complex.

To begin with, there are the two major categories of graphics: vector graphics (objects made up of lines) and bitmapped graphics (TV-like dots). Images stored in vector format can be moved to another vector system typically without loss of resolution. There are 2-D vector formats as well as 3-D vector formats.

In transferring raster images among different devices, resolution is a major concern. Such transfers can occur without loss of resolution as long as the new format supports the same or higher resolution as the older one.

Standard graphics formats allow graphics data to be moved from machine to machine, while standard graphics languages let graphics programs be moved from machine to machine. For example, GKS, PHIGS and OpenGL are major graphics languages that have been adopted by high-performance workstation and CAD vendors.

High-resolution graphics has typically been expensive to implement due to its large storage and fast processing requirements. However, as personal computers become more powerful, graphics have become widely used in business applications. The ability to see a person's face or a product's appearance on screen is now as commonplace as text and data.

### standards—hardware interfaces

The hardware interface specifies the plugs, sockets, cables and electrical signals that pass through each line between the CPU and a peripheral device or communications network.

Common hardware interfaces for personal computers are the Centronics parallel interface used for printers and the RS-232 interface, typically used for modems, graphics tablets and mice. In addition, the IDE and SCSI interfaces are commonly used for disks and tapes, and the GPIB IEEE 488 standard is used for process control instruments. See *plugs and sockets*.

The bus in a computer's motherboard, into which additional printed circuit boards are inserted, is a hardware interface. Most PCs have a combination of ISA and PCI slots to accomodate both types of plug-in cards. See *PC data buses*.

LANs, such as Ethernet and Token Ring, dictate the hardware interface as part of their specifications. An Ethernet cable cannot connect to a Token Ring board, and vice versa.

### standards—Internet

One of the Internet's most significant contributions is that it drives worldwide standards. TCP/IP, HTML, POP, IMAP, LDAP and so on are global standards that have become the glue that is binding the world together electronically. However, these standards are continuously being updated to newer versions, thus, nothing is static for long. However, now we have a global focal point for compatibility, which is a major improvement.

### standards—machine languages

Machine language is the fundamental standard for hardware compatibility. It is the language the CPU understands. All programs presented to the computer for execution must be in the machine language of that particular CPU family.

Different machine languages not only exist among different vendors, but are created by the same vendor. For example, IBM's zSeries mainframe family differs from its iSeries midrange family (AS/400), which is also different than its pSeries (RS/6000). Compaq's Alpha line does not understand the machine language of its VAX predecessor. For all the major hardware platforms, see *hardware platforms*.

After a program is written, it must be translated (assembled, compiled or interpreted) into the machine language the computer understands. In order to run in a different machine, the program must be reassembled or recompiled into a different machine language.

Since the late 1960s, companies seeking a chunk of the IBM market have designed computers that run the same machine language as the IBM mainframes. RCA's Spectra 70 was the first IBM-compatible mainframe, and companies, such as Amdahl, Itel, National Advanced Systems, Hitachi and Fujitsu have introduced IBM-compatible mainframes at one time or another.

IBM PC machine language compatibility is achieved by using a processor from Intel's x86 family of microprocessors or a clone chip from AMD and others.

Machine language compatibility can also be achieved by emulation. An emulator is software (or hardware or both) that executes the machine language of another computer directly. With DOS and Windows emulation in a UNIX workstation or a PowerMac, users can run non-native programs in their computer.

Emulation goes back to the 1950s and 1960s when IBM built a 1401 emulator in its System/360 to ease migration from the very popular 1401s to the new 360s. The terms simulator and emulator are used interchangeably.

## standards—operating systems

An operating system is a master control program that manages the running of the computer system. In all environments, except for specialized scientific and process control applications, the operating system interacts with the application programs. The application programs must "talk" to the operating system.

If application programs are moved to a different computing environment, they have to be converted to interface with a different operating system. If a new operating system is installed that is not compatible with the old one, the application programs have to be converted to the new operating system. Before personal computers, the lay person did not have a clue why there was so much conversion going on in the glass-enclosed datacenter. However, the 1990s changed all that as users learned what it meant to upgrade applications from DOS to Windows and then from 16-bit Windows to 32-bit Windows, etc.

## standards—programming langauges

Every software program is written in a programming language, and there is at least one programming language for every major CPU series. There is typically an assembly language and a number of high-level languages for each family. Assembly languages are machine specific, and the machine language they generate runs on only one CPU family. Unless the machine languages are very similar, it is difficult to translate an assembly language program from one CPU series into another.

The high-level programming language was created to eliminate this machine dependency. Programming languages, such as COBOL, FORTRAN and BASIC are designed to run on many different computers. However, due to dialects of each language, compatibility is always an issue. Each compiler vendor keeps adding new features to its language thereby making it incompatible with previous or other versions.

By the time a new feature becomes a standard, a dozen new features have been already implemented. For example, in the early 1980s, dBASE became a de facto standard business programming language. Soon after, dBASE spawned Clipper, QuickSilver, Force III, dbXL, Foxbase and FoxPro, all competitive products and all incomplete versions of dBASE. None of them provided every dBASE command, and they all provided features not found in dBASE.

There's no rule of thumb for translating one dialect of a programming language into another. The job may be difficult or easy. At times, software is written to translate one dialect into another, as well as one programming language into another. If the translation program cannot translate the program entirely, then manual tailoring is necessary. In these cases, it is often easier to rewrite the program from scratch.

Compatibility can be achieved when a programming language conforms to the ANSI (American National Standards Institute) standard for that language. If the same version of an ANSI COBOL compiler is available for two different CPUs, a program written in ANSI COBOL will run on both machines.

Beyond traditional programming languages such as COBOL, C and C++, known as third-generation languages, or 3GLs, there are more than a hundred software environments used to develop client/server applications on LANs (see *client/server development system*). Each of them attempts to provide less programming-like and more English-like syntax, which is considered a *fourth-generation language*, or 4GL.

They also provide visual development tools to build the graphical user interface by "drawing" the screen and dragging and dropping symbols on it. They may provide the ability to point and click and drag and drop symbols to link objects together rather than by writing programming code. These software-building tools are proliferating and producing even more standards to be dealt with. The programming pools are becoming increasingly fragmented. It's no longer just COBOL, BASIC, dBASE, C and C++. Now it's PowerBuilder, SQLWindows, ObjectView, DYNASTY, OMNIS and JAM and many more. See *programming language*.

S

**standards—storage media**     There are many varieties of disk cartridges, floppy disks, reel-to-reel tapes, tape cartridges and tape cassettes. Each one has its own shape and size and can be used only in drives designed to accommodate them. With all storage devices, the physical shape is half the standards issue. The other half is the recording pattern, which is invisible to the human eye and is written onto the tape or disk by the drive. Most of the time, the media cannot be inserted into the wrong drive. See *magnetic disk*, *magnetic tape* and *optical disk*.

**standards—text systems**     Although the basic structure of an English-language text file is standard throughout the world: word, sentence, paragraph, page; word processing, desktop publishing and typesetting programs different codes to set up the layout within a document. The code that turns boldface on in Microsoft Word is entirely different in WordPerfect. Likewise, the codes that define a header, footer, footnote, page number, margin, tab setting, indent and font change are unique to the application. Even the codes to end a line and paragraph are not the same.

Document conversion is accomplished by using import and export filters within the application itself. If a document format is not supported, a separate conversion program is often available. If no automatic conversion is available, manual searching and replacing is sometimes possible if the embedded codes can be displayed and edited and follow the same syntax. For example, Microsoft Word does not reveal its general formatting codes to the user. In addition, while some systems use one code to turn a function on and another to turn it off, other systems use the same code for on and off, requiring manual verification and tailoring when using the search and replace function.

**Star**     The Xerox workstation that officially introduced the graphical user interface and desktop metaphor in 1981. It was the inspiration for Xerox's subsequent computers and for Apple's Lisa and Macintosh. All graphical user interfaces owe their roots to the Star. See *Alto*.

**The Star User Interface**
If the graphical interface and simulated desktop in this picture seems amazingly similar to the Macintosh and Windows, there is a reason why. That's where they both came from.
*(Image courtesy of Xerox Palo Alto Research Center.)*

**star design**     See *star network* and *star schema*.

**Starfire**     The code name for Sun's high-end Ultra Enterprise 10000 server, which was introduced in 1997. It is an SMP-based system that supports up to 64 processors and 64GB of RAM.

**Starlan**     An early local area network from AT&T that used twisted pair wire, the CSMA/CD access method, transmitted at 1 Mbps and used a star or bus topology. In 1988, the original Starlan was renamed Starlan 1, and Starlan 10 was introduced as a 10 Mbps Ethernet product.

**star network**     A communications network in which all terminals are connected to a central computer, controller or hub. PBXs and telephone systems are prime examples as well as Token Ring and 10BaseT Ethernet.

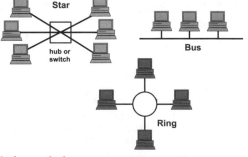

**star schema**     A data warehouse design that enhances the performance of multidimensional queries on traditional relational databases. One fact table is surrounded by a series of related tables. Data is joined from one of the points to the center, providing a so called "star query." See *OLAP*.

**start bit**     In asynchronous communications, the bit transmitted before each character.

**Start menu**     In Windows 95/98/NT4/2000, the Start menu is a launching pad for applications. It contains pointers (shortcuts) to the programs that are stored on the hard disk. Installation programs place an icon in the Start menu's Programs section. You can also drag icons to the Start menu to have favorite programs quickly available for launching. See *Win Start menu*.

**star topology**     See *star network*.

**start/stop transmission**    Same as *asynchronous transmission*.

**STARTUP.CMD**    (STARTUP.CoMmanD) An OS/2 file that is executed immediately upon startup. It contains instructions that can initialize operating system settings and call in a specific application program. The DOS counterpart is AUTOEXEC.BAT.

**StartUp folder**    The folder in Windows 95/98 that contains applications (or pointers to applications) that are to be launched when Windows is started. The StartUp folder can be found in the Programs folder under the Start menu at

`c:\WINDOWS\Start Menu\Programs\StartUp`

**startup routine**    A routine that is executed when the computer is booted or when an application is loaded. It is used to customize the environment for its associated software.

**state**    The current or last-known status, or condition, of a process, transaction or setting. In object-oriented programming, the state of an object is the combination of the original values in the object plus any modifications made to them. "Maintaining state" means keeping track of data for the next time.

This is an issue on the Web, because the HTTP protocol does not maintain state between one page request and the next. A Web site needs to keep track of customers that fill a shopping cart with an item, wander off to another page and then come back to complete the order. Likewise, Webmasters like to analyze the routes users take when visiting their sites. In order to maintain state in a stateless environment, cookie files and server protocols such as NSAPI and ISAPI are used. See *Web bug*, *cookie file*, *NSAPI* and *ISAPI*.

**stateful inspection**    A firewall technology that monitors the state of the transaction so that it can verify that the destination of an inbound packet matches the source of a previous outbound request. See *firewall*.

**stateless**    Refers to software that does not keep track of configuration settings, transaction information or any other data for the next session. When a program "does not maintain state" (is stateless) or when the infrastructure of a system prevents a program from maintaining state, it cannot take information about the last session into the next, such as settings the user made or conditions that arose during processing. For example, the HTTP protocol is stateless, and other schemes are necessary to maintain state in the Web environment. See *state*.

**state machine**    Also called a "finite state machine," it is a computing device designed with the operational states required to solve a specific problem. The circuits are minimized, specialized and optimized for the application. For example, chips in audio, video and imaging controllers are often designed as state machines, because they can provide faster performance at lower cost than a general-purpose CPU. Automatic ticket dispensing machines are another example. There are countless special-purpose devices built as state machines. See *SDL* and *cellular automaton*.

**statement**    In a high-level programming language, a descriptive phrase that generates one or more machine language instructions in the computer. In a low-level assembly language, programmers write instructions rather than statements, since each source language instruction is translated into one machine language instruction.

**static**    Refers to something that is fixed and unchanging. Contrast with *dynamic*.

**static ad**    An advertisement on a Web page that does not change. Contrast with *rotating ad*.

**static binding**    Same as *early binding*.

**static electricity**    A stationary electrical charge that is the result of intentional charging or of friction in low-humidity environments.

**static HTML**    An HTML page that never changes. See *dynamic HTML*.

**static IP address**    A permanent IP address that is assigned to a node in a TCP/IP network. Servers and routers are usually assigned static IP addresses, while client stations are often assigned dynamic IP addresses from a DHCP server each time they come online. Users connected to the Internet via cable modems and DSL either in the office or at home are also assigned long term (static) IP addresses, which makes them more vulnerable to hacker attacks than IP addresses that are dynamically assigned. See *dynamic IP address*, *IP address* and *DHCP*.

**static RAM**    A memory chip that requires power to hold its content, also known as S-RAM or SRAM. Static RAM chips have access times in the 10 to 30 nanosecond range. Dynamic RAMs are usually above 30, and Bipolar and ECL memories are under 10.

A static RAM bit is made up of a pretzel-like flip-flop circuit that lets current flow through one side or the other based on which one of two transistors is activated. Static RAMs do not require refresh circuitry as do dynamic RAMs, but they take up more space and use more power.

**static routing**    Forwarding data in a network via a fixed path. Static routing cannot adjust to changing line conditions as can dynamic routing. See *routing protocol*.

**static SQL**    See *embedded SQL*.

**static typing**    Same as *early binding*.

**station**    A computer, workstation or terminal in a network. Same as *node*.

**stationery**    The term for boilerplate in the Eudora mail client, starting with Version 3.0. Stationery files are stored on disk and brought into new messages or added to replies. See *boilerplate*.

**statistical multiplexor**    In communications, a device that merges several low-speed channels into a single high-speed channel and vice versa. A standard multiplexor is set up for a fixed number of incoming channels regardless of whether every one is transmitting. A statistical multiplexor analyzes the traffic and dynamically changes its pattern of interleaving to use all the available capacity of the outgoing channel.

**stat mux**    (**STAT**istical **MU**ltiple**X**or) See *statistical multiplexor*.

**status line**    An information line displayed on screen that shows current activity.

**STB**    See *set-top box*.

**ST connector**    A fiber-optic cable connector that uses a bayonet plug and socket. It was the first de facto standard connector for most commercial wiring.   For bi-directional transmission, two fiber cables and two ST connectors are generally used. ST is specified by the TIA as FOCIS-2. See *fiber-optic connectors* and *FOCIS*.

**ST Connector**
The ST uses a half-twist bayonet type of lock to keep the connection secure.

**STD bus**    A bus architecture used in medical and industrial equipment due to its small size and rugged design. Originally an 8-bit bus, extensions have increased it to 16 and 32 bits.

**STDM**    (Statistical **TDM**) Fully utilizing the capacity of a time division multiplexing (TDM) channel. Traditional TDM interleaves data into slots, and the slot is wasted if there is no data to send at that moment. Statistical TDM fills all available slots. See *TDM* and *statistical multiplexor*.

**stealth URL**    A Web site that uses a domain name that attracts visitors because they mispelled the name of another site. For example, amazom.com (zoM instead of zoN) will take you to another book store on the Web.

**stealth virus**    A virus that is able to keep itself from being detected. See *polymorphic virus*.

**steganography**    Hiding one type of file within another. It is used as an alternate to encryption and takes advantages of unused areas within a file structure to enclose another. For example, a spreadsheet or graphics file could contain a text message. Unlike encrypted messages, which are easily detected as such, although their content may be undeciperhable, a steganographic message rides secretly to its destination. For a white paper on the subject written by Neil F. Johhnson of George Mason University, visit www.jjtc.com/stegdoc. See *ScramDisk*.

**STEP** (STandard for the Exchange of Product Model Data) An ISO standard for product modeling. It is designed to provide a vendor-neutral and computer readable definition of a product throughout its life cycle. See *PDES* and *IGES*.

**step frame** To capture video images one frame at a time. If a computer is not fast enough to capture analog video in realtime, the video can be forwarded and processed one frame at a time.

**step index fiber** A multimode or singlemode optical fiber with a uniform refractive index throughout the core. The step is the shift between the core and the cladding, which has a lower refractive index. See *graded index fiber*, *dispersion shifted fiber* and *dispersion*.

**stepper motor** A motor that rotates in small, fixed increments and is used to control the movement of the access arm on a disk drive. Contrast with *voice coil*.

**stereophonic** Sound reproduction that uses two or more channels. Contrast with *monophonic*.

**stick model** A picture made of lines, or vectors. For example, in biomedical applications, the limbs of a person or animal are converted into lines so that the motion can be visually observed and graphically plotted and analyzed.

**sticky** Refers to an application or service that keeps you on a Web site. For example, stock quotes, glossaries, educational material, chat rooms and similar offerings give you reason to remain on the site, while it allows the company to show you more banner ads or more of its own messages.

One of the major advantages of the Web is the ability to link elsewhere in an instant, but for the company that is hosting the site, it can also be a major disadvantage. See *sticky connection*.

**sticky connection** A connection between a client and server that is maintained for some period of time. On the Web, streaming audio or video and e-commerce transactions are examples. See *sticky* and *sticky timer*.

**StickyKeys** An accessibility feature that lets users enter key combinations with one hand. When pressing CTRL, ALT or SHIFT and letting go, the computer considers them still depressed so that pressing the next key results in a combination such as ALT-F or CTRL-B.

**sticky timer** A clock that keeps track of non-activity in sticky connections. See *sticky connection* and *sticky*.

**stiction** (STatic frICTION) A type of hard disk failure in which the read/write heads stick to the platters. The lubricant used on certain drives heats up and liquifies. When the disk is turned off, it cools down and can become like a glue.

**STN** (SuperTwisted Nematic) A passive matrix LCD technology that provides better contrast than twisted nematic (TN) by twisting the molecules from 180 to 270 degrees. See *DSTN*.

**stochastic** By guesswork; by chance; using or containing random values.

**stop bit** In asynchronous communications, a bit transmitted after each character.

**stop-motion animation** The original technique used to create an animated sequence. Each frame is created and photographed (or digitized) independently. Contrast with *computer animation*. See **claymation**.

**storage** The semi-permanent or permanent holding place for digital data. Storage means disks and tapes, not memory. Memory, which is made of RAM chips, is a temporary workspace for executing instructions and processing data. See *magnetic disk*, *magnetic tape* and *optical disk* for summaries of all storage technologies.

**storage array** A group of disks that work as a unit. It typically refers to a RAID system. See *RAID* and *storage system*.

**storage capacity** The amount of data a storage device such as a disk or tape can hold. Storage capacity is measured in kilobytes (KB), megabytes (MB), gigabytes (GB) and terabytes (TB). See *space/time*, *magnetic disk*, *magnetic tape* and *optical disk*.

S

**storage device**    A peripheral unit that holds data such as magnetic tape, magnetic disk and optical disk. See *storage* for complete summary.

**storage hierarchy**    The range of memory and storage devices within the computer system. The following list runs from lowest to highest speed. See *storage* for complete summary.

- Punched cards **
- Punched paper tape **
- Magnetic tape
- Floppy disks
- CD-ROM
- Bubble memory
- Optical disks

- Magnetic disks (movable heads)
- Magnetic disks (fixed heads) **
- Low-speed bulk memory
- Main memory
- Cache memory
- Microcode
- Registers

   ** *Obsolete*

**storage management**    The administration of any or all of backup, archival, disaster recovery and hierarchical storage management (HSM) procedures within an organization. See *storage virtualization*, *HSM*, *ESM*, *SAN* and *data management*.

**storage media**    Disks and tapes. See *magnetic disk*, *magnetic tape* and *optical disk*.

**storage network**    See *SAN*.

**storage subsystem**    The part of a computer system that provides the storage. It includes the controller and disk drives. See *storage system*.

**storage system**    A computer system that provides storage for one or more hosts. See *SAN* and *RAID*.

**storage virtualization**    Treating storage as a single logical entity without regard to the hierarchy of physical media that may be involved or that may change. It enables the applications to be written to a single programming interface rather than to the details of the various disk, tape and optical devices that are used. See *storage management* and *SAN*.

   The terms "storage virtualization" and "virtual storage" are not the same. The latter is an earlier term for virtual memory, which extends memory to the disk. See *virtual memory*.

**store and forward**    The temporary storage of a message for transmission to its destination at a later time. Store and forward techniques allow for routing over networks that are not accessible at all times. For example, messages crossing time zones can be forwarded during daytime at the receiving side, or messages can be forwarded at night in order to obtain off-peak rates. See *messaging protocol*.

**store-and-forward switch**    A switching device that stores a complete incoming data packet before it is sent out. Such switches are used when incoming and outgoing speeds differ. Contrast with *cut-through switch*.

**stored procedure**    In a database management system (DBMS), it is an SQL program that is stored in the database which is executed by calling it directly from the client or from a database trigger. When the SQL procedure is stored in the database, it does not have to be replicated in each client. This saves programming effort especially when different client user interfaces and development systems are used. Triggers and stored procedures are built into DBMSs used in client/server environments.

**stored program concept**    The fundamental computer architecture in which the computer acts upon (executes) internally-stored instructions. See *von Neumann architecture*.

**stored-value card**    A smart card that is "loaded" with cash. See *smart card*.

**store locator service**    An IN (Intelligent Network) service for retail outlets that transfers the caller to the nearest store based on the calling telephone number. This allows the business to advertise only one telephone number. See *call routing service*.

**stovepipe application**   A stand-alone program. It implies an application that does not integrate with or share data or resources with other applications.

**STP**   **(1)** (Shielded Twisted Pair) Telephone wire that is wrapped in a metal sheath to eliminate external interference. See *twisted pair*.

**(2)** (Spanning Tree Protocol) See *spanning tree algorithm*.

**(3)** (Signal Transfer Point) A node in the SS7 telephone network that routes messages between exchanges and between exchanges and databases that hold subscriber and routing information. See *SS7, SSP, SCP* and *AIN*.

**(4)** See *straight through processing*.

**straight through processing**   In financial technology, the ability to process a stock transaction by computer from beginning to end without manual intervention at any of the stages.

**stream**   **(1)** A contiguous group of data.

**(2)** The I/O management in the C programming language. A stream is a channel through which data flows to/from a disk, keyboard, printer, etc.

**(3)** The data part of a Structured Storage file. See *Structured Storage*.

**stream cipher**   An encryption method that works with continuous streams of input rather than fixed blocks. Contrast with *block cipher*.

**streaming**   Refers to the continuous transmission of data, typically audio or video. See *streaming audio* and *streaming video*.

**streaming audio**   Audio transmission over a data network. The term implies a one-way transmission to the listener, in which both the client and server cooperate for uninterrupted sound. The client side buffers a few seconds of audio data before it starts sending it to the speakers, which compensates for momentary delays in packet delivery. Audio conferencing, on the other hand, requires realtime two-way transmission for effective results. See *streaming video*.

**streaming data**   Data that is structured and processed in a continous flow, such as digital audio and video. See *streaming audio* and *streaming video*.

**streaming media**   See *streaming audio* and *streaming video*.

**streaming tape**   A high-speed magnetic tape drive that is frequently used to make a backup copy of an entire hard disk.

**streaming video**   Video transmission over a data network. It is widely used on the Web to deliver video on demand or a video broadcast at a set time. In streaming video, both the client and server software cooperate for uninterrupted motion. The client side buffers a few seconds of video data before it starts sending it to the screen, which compensates for momentary delays in packet delivery. Streaming video implies a one-way transmission, whereas videoconferencing requires realtime two-way transmission for effective results. The latter is far more demanding on the network. See *streaming audio*.

**stream-oriented file**   A type of file, such as a text document or digital voice file, that is more openly structured than a database file. Text and voice files contain continuous streams of characters, whereas database files contain many small repeating structures (records).

**STREAMS**   A feature of UNIX System V that provides a standard way of dynamically building and passing messages up and down a protocol stack. STREAMS passes messages from the application "downstream" through the STREAMS modules to the network driver at the end of the stack. Messages are passed "upstream" from the driver to the application. A STREAMS module would be a transport layer protocol such as TCP and SPX or a network layer protocol such as IP and IPX.

STREAMS modules can be dynamically changed (pushed and popped) at runtime, allowing the stack to be used for multiple protocols. Two important STREAMS components are the TLI and LSL interfaces, which provide common languages to the transport and data link layers. See *TLI, LSL, ODI* and *OSI*.

**Streettalk** The directory service used in the VINES network operating system from Banyan Systems Inc., Westboro, MA (www.banyan.com). Streettalk has always been highly regarded and versions are also available for Windows NT. Streettalk Desktop is a 32-bit Windows client program that lets users create folders and keep track of shared documents.

**STRETCH** The code name for IBM's first "supercomputer," the 7030, which was started in 1955 and completed in 1961. The first of eight units was delivered to the Los Alamos Scientific Laboratory and was in use for 10 years. STRETCH was IBM's first attempt at building transistorized computers and was designed to "stretch" the speed of its current vacuum tube models by a factor of 100.

The machine was very sophisticated for its time, providing simultaneous execution of business instructions with floating point arithmetic. It was estimated that IBM lost 40 million dollars in developing STRETCH, but that the knowledge gained led to huge profits with its subsequent computers.

**The STRETCH**
The STRETCH was the first of IBM's transistorized computers. Its style of cabinetry and console were used in many subsequent computers by the company. *(Image courtesy of International Business Machines Corporation. Unauthorized use not permitted.)*

**stretch blt** An enhanced type of bitblt used for resizing video images. The function expands or contracts the number of bits while moving them from main memory to the display memory. See *bitblt*.

**string** In programming, a contiguous set of alphanumeric characters that does not contain numbers used for calculations. Names, addresses and error messages are examples of strings. Contrast with *numeric data*.

**string handling** The abilty to manipulate alphanumeric data (names, addresses, text, etc.). Typical functions include the ability to handle arrays of strings, to left and right align and center strings and to search for an occurrence of text within a string.

**Stringy Floppy** A tape drive developed by Exatron, Sunnyvale, CA, for the Radio Shack TRS-80 personal computer that used a continuous loop cartridge of 1/16" tape. It was faster than the audio cassettes used for data storage on the first TRS-80s, and the company sold several thousand of these "tape wafers." However, soon after, the floppy disk became the norm.

Why not have some fun with such a unique name. Ask your systems people if they've seen the new "Stringy Floppy" on the market, and watch the puzzled expression. Keep a straight face now!

**striping** Interleaving or multiplexing data to increase speed. See *disk striping*.

**stroke** **(1)** In printing, the weight, or thickness, of a character. For example, in the LaserJet, one of the specifications of the font description is the stroke weight from –3 to +3.

**(2)** In computer graphics, a pen or brush stroke. The stroke function lets you set the width of the line being drawn.

**stroke font** Same as *vector font*.

**stroke weight** The thickness of lines in a font character. The HP LaserJet defines stroke weights from Ultra Thin (–7) to Ultra Black (+7), with Medium, or Text, as normal (0).

**stroke writer** Same as *vector display*.

**StrongARM** A family of high-performance RISC-based microprocessors from Intel. StrongARM chips are used in handheld devices such as PDAs and palmtops. The StrongARM technology was jointly developed by Digital Equipment Corporation and Advanced RISC Machines (ARM). In 1997, Intel acquired Digital's chip manufacturing facilities and continues to make the Alpha and StrongARM chips. See *ARM chips*.

**strong encryption** An encryption method that uses a very large number as its cryptographic key. The larger the key, the longer it takes to unlawfully break the code. Today, 128 bits is considered strong encryption. As computers become faster, the length of the key must be increased.

**strong typing**     A programming language characteristic that provides strict adherence to the rules of typing. Data of one type (integer, string, etc.) cannot be passed to a variable expecting data of a different type. Contrast with *weak typing*.

**structured analysis**     Techniques developed in the late 1970s by Yourdon, DeMarco, Gane and Sarson for applying a systematic approach to systems analysis. It included the use of data flow diagrams and data modeling and fostered the use of implementation-independent graphical notation for documentation.

**structured data**     Data that resides in fixed fields within a record or file. Relational databases and spreadsheets are examples of structured data. Contrast with *unstructured data*. See *record, file, database* and *spreadsheet*.

**structured design**     A systematic approach to program design developed in the mid 1970s by Constantine, Yourdon, et al, that included the use of graphical notation for effective documentation and communication, design guidelines and recipes to help programmers get started.

**structured programming**     Techniques that impose a logical structure on the writing of a program. Large routines are broken down into smaller, modular routines. The use of the GOTO statement is discouraged (see *spaghetti code*).

Certain programming statements are indented in order to make loops and other program logic easier to follow. Structured walkthroughs, which invite criticism from peer programmers, are also used.

Structured languages, such as Pascal, Ada and dBASE, force the programmer to write a structured program. However, unstructured languages such as FORTRAN, COBOL and BASIC require discipline on the part of the programmer.

**Structured Storage**     A file structure from Microsoft for storing compound elements, such as compound documents and the persistent data of COM objects. Contained within one file, its structure looks like a miniature disk drive with the Root storage at the top of the hierarchy and Storages (directories) and streams (data files) below.

**STS-1**     See *OC*.

**stub**     A small software routine placed into a program that provides a common function. Stubs are used for a variety of purposes. For example, a stub might be installed in a client machine, and a counterpart installed in a server, where both are required to resolve some protocol, remote procedure call (RPC) or other interoperability requirement.

**stub file**     A data file or program that stands in for the original file. See *HSM*.

**StuffIt**     A Macintosh shareware program from Aladdin Systems, Inc., Watsonville, CA (www.aladdinsys.com) that compresses files onto multiple floppies. A commercial version adds a scripting language, file viewing and supports multiple compression techniques. It was originally developed by Raymond Lau at age 16. StuffIt files use a .SIT extension.

**stupid network**     See *dumb network*.

**style sheet**     A master page layout used in document creation systems such as word processing, desktop publishing and the Web. The style sheet is a file that is used to store margins, tabs, fonts, headers, footers and other layout settings for a particular category of document. When a style sheet is selected, its format settings are applied to all the documents created under it, saving the page designer or programmer from redefining the same settings over and over again for each page. See *Cascading Style Sheets, template* and *document*.

**stylus**     A pen-shaped instrument that is used to "draw" images or point to menus. See *light pen* and *digitizer tablet*.

**subarea node**     In an SNA network, a system that contains network controlling functions. It refers to a host computer or a communications controller and its associated terminals.

**subclass**     In programming, to add custom processing to an existing function or subroutine by hooking into the routine at a predefined point and adding additional lines of code.

**subdirectory**     A disk directory that is subordinate to (below) another directory. In order to gain access to a subdirectory, the path must include all directories above it. See *subfolder*.

**S**

**subdomain**     A smaller component of a domain name. For example, **www.mycompany.com** and **support. mycompany.com** are subdomains of **mycompany.com**, which is either known as a "second level domain" or "root domain." See *zone* and *root domain*.

**subfolder**     A folder that is placed within another folder. See *subdirectory*.

**submarining**     The temporary visual loss of the screen pointer on a passive matrix display screen. See *mouse trails* and *active matrix*.

**submenu**     An additional list of options within a menu selection. There can many levels of submenus.

**subnet**     (SUBNETwork) A division of a network into an interconnected, but independent, segment, or domain, in order to improve performance and security. Before the Internet, the vast majority of traffic within an organization moved within subnets. Today, traffic is increasingly routed across subnets.

**subnet mask**     (SUBNETwork MASK)The technique used by the IP protocol to filter messages into a particular network segment (subnet). The subnet mask is a binary pattern that is stored in the client machine, server or router and is matched up with the incoming IP address to determine whether to accept or reject the packet. The subnet mask below shows a Class C address, which uses the first 24 bits for network ID and the last 8 bits for host ID (see IP address). In the first example, the 0 in the default Class C mask means that all packets to that address are accepted and used to address 254 individual hosts. In the second example, the 224 reserves the three high-order bits of that field for subnets, leaving the remaining 5 bits for host ID. This subnet pattern creates subnets in the range of 001 to 110 (000and 111 are reserved and cannot be used for subnets). As such, 6 subnets of 30 hosts each are created (00000 and 11111 are reserved and cannot be used as host addresses).

```
255.255.255.0
11111111.11111111.11111111.00000000

255.255.255.224
11111111.11111111.11111111.11100000
```

**subnetting**     Dividing a network into smaller subgroups. See *subnet* and *subnet mask*.

**subnetwork**     See *subnet*.

**subnetwork mask**     See *subnet mask*.

**subnotebook**     A laptop computer that weighs less than four pounds. Subnotebooks often use an external floppy drive to reduce weight, which is inconvenient if you need to exchange data via diskettes in remote locations. For features of a portable computer, see *laptop computer*.

**subroutine**     A group of instructions that perform a specific task. A large subroutine might be called a "module" or "procedure." Subroutine is somewhat of a dated term, but it is still quite valid.

**subschema**     Pronounced "sub-skeema." In database management, an individual user's partial view of the database. The schema is the entire database.

**subscribe**     To sign up for a service. Signing up for something is often simpler than getting out of it, or unsubscribing. See *unsubscribe*.

**subscriber line**     The line from the customer site to the local telephone company. Another term for *local loop*.

**subscript**     (1) In word processing and mathematical notation, a digit or symbol that appears below the line. Contrast with *superscript*.

(2) In programming, a method for referencing data in a table. For example, in the table **PRICETABLE**, the statement to reference a specific price in the table might be **PRICETABLE (ITEM)**, ITEM being the subscript variable. In a two-dimensional table that includes price and discount, the statement **PRICETABLE (ITEM,DISCOUNT)** could reference a discounted price. The relative locations of the current ITEM and DISCOUNT are kept in two index registers.

**subset**    A group of commands or functions that do not include all the capabilities of the original specification. Software or hardware components designed for the subset will also work with the original. However, any component designed for the full original specification will not operate with the subset product. Contrast with *superset*.

**substrate**    The base layer of a structure such as a chip, multichip module (MCM), printed circuit board or disk platter. Silicon is the most widely used substrate for chips. Fiberglass (FR4) is mostly used for printed circuit boards, and ceramic is used for MCMs. Disk substrates are typically aluminum, glass or plastic.

**substring**    A subset of an alphanumeric field or variable. The substring function in a programming language is used to extract the subset; for example, the programming expression **substr(prodcode,4,3)** extracts characters 4, 5 and 6 out of a product code field or variable.

**subsystem**    A unit or device that is part of a larger system. For example, a disk subsystem is a part of the computer system. The bus is a part of the computer. A subsystem usually refers to hardware, but it may be used to describe software, although module, subroutine and component are more typically used for software elements.

**subtract**    In relational database, an operation that generates a third file from all the records in one file that are not in a second file.

**suit**    A derogatory term for a corporate employee that wears a suit. See *slime*.

**SuiteSpot**    A suite of programs used for building an Internet or intranet Web site from Netscape. It is based on Netscape's Enterprise Server Web server and runs on Windows NT and various UNIX machines. SuiteSpot includes Proxy Server, Catalog Server (index and search), Calendar Server (scheduling), Mail Server (e-mail), News Server (discussions and newsgroups), Media Server (slide presentations with audio), Directory Server (LDAP directory) and Certificate Server (certificate authority).

Mail Server and News Server are called Messaging Server and Collabra Server as of Version 3.0. See *Communicator*.

**Sun**    (Sun Microsystems, Inc., Mountain View, CA, www.sun.com) A major manufacturer of UNIX-based workstations and servers. In 1981, Bavarian-born Andreas Bechtolsheim was licensing rights to a computer he designed. Named Sun for Stanford University Network and using off-the-shelf parts, it was an affordable workstation for engineers and scientists. In that year, he met Vinod Khosla, a native of India, who convinced him to form a company and expand. Khosla, Bechtolsheim and Scott McNeally, all Stanford MBAs, founded Sun in 1982.

Its first computers, the Sun-1 and subsequent Sun-2 were instant successes in the university market. Sun began to compete against its rival Apollo Computer, an east-coast workstation company, eventually surpassing it in sales (Apollo was later purchased by HP).

Sun has been a major force in open systems. Its computers have always run under UNIX, which was licensed from AT&T and then later purchased outright. Sun and AT&T had formed such a tight alliance for a while that a host of UNIX vendors formed the Open Software Foundation (OSF) in 1988 to keep Sun from dominating UNIX.

In 1984, Bill Joy, head of R&D, designed NFS, which was broadly licensed and became the industry standard for file sharing. Sun later packaged its UNIX components into a complete environment named Solaris, which it later ported to other platforms, including the Intel x86.

Sun used the Motorola 680x0 CPUs in its products until it designed its own RISC-based SPARC chips, which it launched with the SPARCstation 1 in 1989. SPARC technology is also licensed to third parties. The latest version of this architecture is the UltraSPARC, which began shipping in 1995.

**The Founders**
From left to right: Vinod Khosla, Bill Joy, Andreas Bechtolsheim and Scott McNealy. Although Joy was not a founder, he was hired shortly thereafter and became one of Sun's major contributors. *(Image courtesy of Sun Microsystems, Inc.)*

S

**The Sun-1**
Sun's workstations were an instant success primarily in the university market. This led many professionals to the company who helped it grow steadily. *(Image courtesy of Sun Microsystems, Inc.)*

In 1994, Sun introduced the Java programming language and ushered in a new era for application development on the Internet. Sun is one of the major proponents behind network computers, which are leaner client workstations that download all their software from the server. In 1996, it introduced its first network computer for Java applications, appropriately named the JavaStation. Java CPU chips that execute the Java language directly are also available. See *Java*, *network computer* and *Sun-Netscape Alliance*.

**Sun-Netscape Alliance**   (Sun-Netscape Alliance, Mountain View, CA, www.iplanet.com) A joint venture of Sun and Netscape to market Netscape's Web-based software products. The Alliance was formed when AOL acquired Netscape in 1999. It took advantage of the fact that the bulk of Netscape software was already running on Sun hardware. Netscape product names are replaced by the iPlanet brand name.

**SunOS**   Sun's UNIX operating system. SunOS was renamed Solaris. See *Solaris*.

**Super7**   A specification from AMD for PC motherboards or single board computers that allows non-Intel CPU chips to take advantage of faster bus speeds and newer peripheral technologies. It specifies the older Socket 7 CPU receptacle and adds support for AGP, USB, Ultra ATA and the 100MHz bus. See *Socket 7*.

**Superbase**   A relational database management (DBMS) and client/server application development system for Windows from Superbase Developers, Inc., Huntington, NY (www.superbase.com). It includes a database that supports a variety of multimedia types, an object-based Super Basic Language similar to Visual Basic and a suite of visual programming tools. It supports the major SQL databases as well as ODBC-compliant databases.

Superbase has been widely used worldwide. It was originally created in 1984 by Precision Software for the Commodore Amiga and Atari ST. In 1989, it was the first DBMS to run on a Windows computer.

**SuperCalc**   One of the first spreadsheets which followed in the footsteps of VisiCalc in the early 1980s. It was Computer Associates' first personal computer product.

**superclass**   In object technology, a high-level class that passes attributes and methods (data and processing) down the hierarchy to subclasses, the classes below it. Abstract superclasses are used as master structures and no objects are created for it. Concrete superclasses are used to create objects.

**supercomputer**   The fastest computer available. It is typically used for simulations in petroleum exploration and production, structural analysis, computational fluid dynamics, physics and chemistry, electronic design, nuclear energy research and meteorology. It is also used for realtime animated graphics. See *supercomputer sites*.

**supercomputer sites**   A list of the 500 most powerful computers and their installations is updated twice a year and posted on Web servers in the U.S., Germany and Japan. To view the list, visit www.netlib.org/benchmark/top500.html.

**superconductor**   A material that has little resistance to the flow of electricity. Traditional superconductors operate at –459 Fahrenheit (absolute zero).

Thus far, the major use for superconductors, made of alloys of niobium, is for high-powered magnets in medical imaging machines that use magnetic fields instead of x-rays.

Using experimental materials, such as copper oxides, barium, lanthanum and yttrium, IBM's Zurich research lab in 1986 and the University of Houston in 1987 raised the temperature of superconductivity to –59 degrees Fahrenheit. If superconductors can work at reasonable temperatures, they will have a dramatic impact on the future of computing. See *Josephson junction*.

**super floppy**   (1) A high-capacity floppy disk. The Zip disk could be considered a super floppy. In the early 1990s, the Floptical was the super floppy drive for a while, but never caught on. See *Zip disk*.

(2) An earlier 3.5" floppy disk introduced by IBM that held 2.88MB. The drives were compatible with standard floppies, but were not widely used.

**superframe**   A T1 transmission format made up of 12 T1 frames (superframe) and 24 frames (extended superframe). See *D4*.

**supermini**   A large-scale minicomputer. Note: Supermini is not the same as mini-supercomputer.

**Super POP**    (SUPER Point Of Presence) An ISP access point that provides T3 speeds or higher. See *POP*.

**superscalar**    A CPU architecture that allows more than one instruction to be executed in one clock cycle.

**superscript**    Any letter, digit or symbol that appears above the line. Contrast with *subscript*.

**superserver**    A high-speed network server with very large RAM and disk capacity. Superservers typically support multiprocessing.

**superset**    A group of commands or functions that exceed the capabilities of the original specification. Software or hardware components designed for the original specification will also operate with the superset product. However, components designed for the superset will not work with the original. Contrast with *subset*.

**SUPERSTITIAL**    An animated advertisement on the Web delivered by Unicast Communications, New York (www.unicast.com). Unlike the small banner ads that are static, or at most, a short animated GIF image, a SUPERSTITIAL uses Flash animation or video for a complete TV-like experience. It is downloaded "politely" in the background while the user's modem is idle and appears in a separate window only after the entire ad has been sent. If you leave the page that triggered the SUPERSTITIAL before it is fully downloaded, it will not play. See *interstitial ad*.

**supertwist**    An LCD technology that twists liquid molecules greater than 90 degrees in order to improve contrast and viewing angle. See *LCD*.

**superuser**    A person with unlimited access privileges who can perform any and all operations on the computer. See *root*.

**Super VGA**    See *VGA* and *PC display modes*.

**supervisor**    Same as *operating system*.

**supervisor call**    The instruction in an application program that switches the computer to supervisor state.

**supervisor control program**    The part of the operation system that always resides in memory. Same as *kernel*.

**supervisor mode**    See *supervisor state* and *privileged mode*.

**supervisor state**    Typically associated with mainframes, it is a hardware mode in which the operating system executes instructions unavailable to an application program; for example, I/O instructions. Contrast with *program state*.

**supply chain management**    The planning, scheduling and control of the supply chain, which is the sequence of organizations and functions that mine, make or assemble materials and products from manufacturer to wholesaler to retailer to consumer. The driving force behing supply chain management is to reduce inventory.

Dr. Roger D. Blackwell, professor of marketing at Ohio State University and author of the best-selling book, *From Mind to Market*, says it very succinctly. "Supply chain management is all about having the right product in the right place, at the right price, at the right time and in the right condition." See *supply chain system*.

**supply chain system**    A computer system (essentially the software) that is used to reduce inventory and lower costs of assembly and distribution in the supply chain. Traditional supply chain systems supported only two organizations; for example, between the wholesaler and the retailer. Today, more sophisticated systems integrate three or more organizations, so that for example, a retailer can signal a reorder to its wholesaler and to its wholesaler's supplier at the same time.

In the business world, supply chain management and supply chain systems have become the buzzwords of the late 1990s. A whole raft of software has come to market, offering enhanced analysis and scheduling algorithms that can refine the process. See *supply chain management*.

**support**    (1) The assistance provided by a hardware or software vendor in installing and maintaining its product.

(2) Software or hardware designed to include or work with some other software or hardware product. For example, if a computer "supports multiprocessing," it can host more than one CPU internally. If a development system "supports Windows," it is used to create applications for Windows. If a system "supports the major databases," it provides interfaces to those databases.

**S**

**suppressor grid**    A grid used in pentode vacuum tubes that suppresses interference or secondary electron flow caused by electrons that bounce off or are reflected by the plate. The suppressor grid sits between the screen grid and plate (anode). By applying a voltage to the suppressor grid at or near the cathode potential, spurious current flow is contained between the plate and suppressor grid, and leakage to other elements in the tube is limited. See *pentode*.

**surface**    In CAD, the external geometry of an object. Surfaces are generally required for NC (numerical control) modeling rather than wireframe or solids.

**surface modeling**    A mathematical technique for representing solid-appearing objects. Surface modeling is a more complex method for representing objects than wireframe modeling, but not as sophisticated as solid modeling. Surface modeling is widely used in CAD (computer-aided design) for illustrations and architectural renderings. It is also used in 3-D animation for games and other presentations.

Although surface and solid models appear the same on screen, they are quite different. Surface models cannot be sliced open as can solid models. In addition, in surface modeling, the object can be geometrically incorrect; whereas, in solid modeling, it must be correct. See *tessellation*.

**surface mount**    A circuit board packaging technique in which the leads (pins) on the chips and components are soldered on top of the board, not through it. Boards can be smaller and built faster. SMT stands for surface mount technology, and an SMD is a surface mount device. Contrast with *socket mount* and *thru-hole*.

**surface normal**    In 3-D graphics, an imaginary line that is perpendicular to the surface of a polygon. It may be computed at the vertex of a triangle, in which case it is the average of all the vertices of adjoining triangles, or it may be computed for each pixel in the triangle as in Phong shading. Surface normals are used to derive the reflectivity of a light source shining onto an object. See *tessellation*, *triangle*, *Phong shading* and *Gouraud shading*.

**surf control**    See *Web filtering*.

**surfing**    Scanning online material, such as databases, news clips and forums. The term originated from "channel surfing," the rapid changing of TV channels to find something of interest.

**surge**    See *power surge*.

**surge protector**    A device that employs some method of surge suppression to protect electronic equipment from excessive voltage (spikes and power surges) in the power line. The most common method uses a metal oxide varistor (MOV) component to shunt the surge to the neutral and ground lines. Another method is series mode, which actually absorbs the energy. Surge protectors may use both methods. See *surge suppression*, *voltage regulator* and *UPS*.

**surge suppression**    The diversion of power surges from the incoming hot line to the neutral and/or ground lines. The most common method uses metal oxide varistors (MOVs). See *surge protector*.

**suspend and resume**    To stop an operation and restart where you left off. In portable computers, the hard disk is turned off, and the CPU is made to idle at its slowest speed. All open applications are retained in memory.

**SVC**    (1) (Switched Virtual Circuit) A network connection that is established at the time the transmission is required and disconnected when the session is completed. SVCs are normally implemented in connection-oriented systems such as the analog telephone network and ATM networks. Contrast with *PVC*.

(2) (SuperVisor Call) A mainframe instruction that passes control to the operating system.

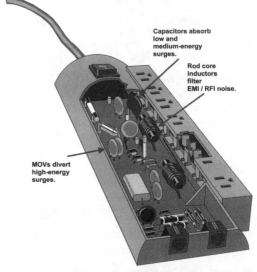

Capacitors absorb low and medium-energy surges.

Rod core inductors filter EMI / RFI noise.

MOVs divert high-energy surges.

**Inside a Surge Protector**
The SurgeArrest Net7T from American Power shows the internal components used to filter line noise and divert the surges. Note that the capacitors absorb some of the energy, while the MOVs divert the high energy. *(Image courtesy of American Power Conversion Corporation.)*

**SVD**    (**S**imultaneous **V**oice and **D**ata) The concurrent transmission of voice and data by modem over a single analog telephone line. The first SVD technologies on the market are MultiTech's MSP, Radish's VoiceView, AT&T's VoiceSpan and the all-digital DSVD, endorsed by Intel, Hayes and others.

**SVG**    (**S**calable **V**ector **G**raphics) A vector graphics file format from the W3C that enables vector drawings to be included in XML pages on the Web. GIFs and JPEGs are the standard bitmapped formats for the Web, and SVG is expected to become the standard vector format for the Web. Vector drawings will scale to the size of the viewing window, whereas bitmaps remain constant. See *graphics* and *XML*.

**SVGA**    (**S**uper **VGA**) A screen resolution of 800×600 pixels. Third-party vendors extended IBM's VGA display standard and were the first to use the term. SVGA has also referred to 1,024×768 resolutions. See *PC display modes*.

**S-VHS**    (**S**uper-**VHS**) A video recording and playback system that uses a higher-quality VHS cassette and the S-video technology. VCRs that support S-VHS can also record and play back normal VHS tapes. See *Digital-S*.

**SVID**    (**S**ystem **V** **I**nterface **D**efinition) An AT&T specification for the UNIX System V operating system. SVID Release 3 specifies the interface for UNIX System V Release 4.

**S-video**    (**S**uper-**VIDEO**) Recording and transmitting video by keeping luminance (Y) and color information (C) on separate channels. S-video uses a special 5-pin connector rather than the common RCA phono plug. It is widely used on camcorders, VCRs and A/V receivers and amplifiers. If S-video connectors are available between the two devices you want to hook up, using an S-video cable will improve transmission quality and the image at the receiving end.

**s/w**    See *software*.

**swap file**    A disk file used to temporarily save a program or part of a program running in memory. See *Windows swap file*.

**swapping**    Replacing one segment of a program in memory with another and restoring it back to the original when required. In virtual memory systems, it is called "paging."

**SWAP protocol**    See *HomeRF*.

**sweet spot**    Refers to almost anything that embodies an optimum combination of characteristics and qualities. As a result, it is most efficient, useful or popular, or even the most lucrative product in the line to sell. See also *SuiteSpot*.

**Swing**    A Java toolkit for developing graphical user interfaces (GUIs). It includes elements such as menus, toolbars and dialog boxes. Swing is written in Java and is thus platform independent, unlike the Java Abstract Window Toolkit (AWT), which provides platform-specific code. Swing also has more sophisticated interface capabilities than AWT and offering such features as tabbed panes and the ability to change images on buttons. Swing is included in the Java Foundation Classes (JFC) which are provided in the Java Developers Toolkit (JDK). See *JFC* and *JDK*.

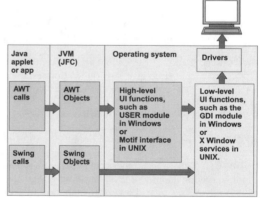

**Swing vs. AWT**
Swing calls the operating system at a lower level than AWT. Whereas AWT routines use native code, Swing was written entirely in Java and is platform independent.

**switch**    (1) A mechanical or electronic device that directs the flow of electrical or optical signals from one side to the other. Switches with more than two ports, such as a LAN switch or PBX, are able to route traffic. See *LAN switch*, *softswitch*, *PBX*, *data switch* and *transistor*.

With regard to a simple on/off switch, remember... **Open is "off." Closed is "on."**

(2) In programming, a bit or byte used to keep track of something. Sometimes refers to a branch in a program.

(3) A modifier of a command. See *DOS switch*.

**Switched 56**    A dial-up digital service provided by local and long distance telephone companies. There is a monthly fee and per-minute charge like the analog voice network. For connection, a DSU/CSU is used instead of a modem. Switched 56 uses a 64 Kbps channel, but one bit per byte is used for in band signaling, leaving 56 Kbps for data.

**switched broadband network**    A communications network that provides connectivity across a large area at high speed.

**switched digital service**    See *Switched 56*.

**switched Ethernet**    An Ethernet network that is controlled by a switch. The switch cross connects two stations and gives each sender-receiver pair the full bandwidth of the network. The total bandwidth is 20 Mbps or 200 Mbps between nodes for full-duplex operation or 10 and 100 for half-duplex. A major advantage in migrating to switched Ethernet is that the existing NICs are still used. See *LAN switch*.

**switched line**    In communications, a link that is established in a switched network, such as the international dial-up telephone system, a Switched 56 digital line or ISDN.

**switched network**    (1) The international dial-up telephone system.

(2) A network in which a temporary connection is established from one point to another for either the duration of the session (circuit switching) or for the transmission of one or more packets of data (packet switching).

**switched SCSI**    See *SCSI switch*.

**switch fabric**    (1) The internal interconnect architecture used by a switching device, which redirects the data coming in on one of its ports out to another of its ports.

(2) The combination of interconnected switches used throughout a campus or large geographic area, which collectively provide a routing infrastructure.

**switching hub**    A device that acts as a central switch or PBX, connecting one line to another. In a local area network (LAN), a switching hub gives any two stations on the network the full bandwidth of the line. Contrast with *shared media LAN*, in which all stations share the bandwidth of a common transmission path. See *hub*.

**switch router**    See *layer 3 switch*.

**SXGA**    (Super **XGA**) A screen resolution of 1280x1024 pixels. See *PC display modes*.

**Sybase**    (Sybase Inc., Emeryville, CA, www.sybase.com) A software company founded in 1984 that specializes in client/server development products. It was originally known for its SQL Server relational DBMS, but expanded its line in 1995 when it acquired Powersoft, makers of the PowerBuilder application development software. Sybase offers a variety of application development tools, compilers, middleware, database and data warehousing products.

**Sybase database**    See *SQL Server*.

**Sybase System**    A family of SQL development tools from Sybase that includes SQL Server, SQL Toolset (design, development and control) and Client/Services Interfaces (distributed database architecture). See *SQL Server*.

**Sybperl**    (SYBase PERL) A set of extensions to Perl that provide access to the Sybase database. Sybperl adds the Sybase database APIs to Perl.

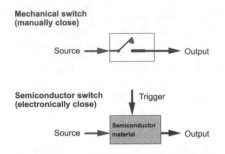

**Mechanical and Semiconductor Switches**
The semiconductor switch (transistor) performs the same function as an on/off light switch on the wall. Instead of being manually closed, the switch is electronically closed by pulsing the semicondutor material, which makes it conduct.

**Symantec**     (Symantec Corporation, Cupertino, CA, www.symantec.com) A software company founded in 1982 by Dr. Gary Hendrix. It was acquired by Gordon Eubanks in 1984 and released its Q&A file manager the following year. In 1990, it merged with Peter Norton Computing, Inc., developer of the well-known Norton Utilities and Norton Desktop programs. Since then, it has acquired more than a dozen other software companies, including Central Point Software, maker of PC Tools, and Zortech, developer of of C++ compilers.

**Symbian**     See *EPOC*.

**symbol**     In data compression, a unit of data (byte, floating point number, spoken word, etc.) that is treated independently.

**symbolic language**     **(1)** A programming language that uses symbols, or mnemonics, for expressing operations and operands. All modern programming languages are symbolic languages.
     **(2)** A language that manipulates symbols rather than numbers. See *list processing*.

**symbol set**     Same as *character set*.

**symmetric**     No difference in opposing modes. It typically refers to speed. For example, in symmetric operations, it takes the same time to compress and encrypt data as it does to decompress and decrypt it. Contrast with *asymmetric*.

**symmetric compression**     A data compression technique that takes about the same amount of time to compress as it does to decompress. Contrast with *asymmetric compression*.

**symmetric encryption**     Same as *secret key cryptography*.

**symmetric multiprocessing**     See *SMP*.

**Symphony**     **(1)** A wireless LAN family from Proxim, Inc., Sunnyvale, CA (www.proxim.com) that transmits 1.6 Mbps in the unlicensed 2.4GHz band. Symphony is geared for the home and small office and covers an indoor range of 150 feet and up to 10 computers. Symphony supports laptops fitted with Proxim's RangeLAN2 cards, but does not support roaming. See *RangeLAN* and *wireless LAN*.
     **(2)** One of the first integrated software packages for the PC. Developed by Lotus, it included word processing, database, speadsheet, business graphics, communications and a macro language.

**sync character**     In synchronous communications systems, a special character transmitted to synchronize timing.

**sync generator**     A device that supplies synchronization signals to a series of cameras to keep them all in phase.

**synchronous**     Refers to events that are synchronized, or coordinated, in time. For example, the interval between transmitting A and B is the same as between B and C, and completing the current operation before the next one is started are considered synchronous operations. Contrast with *asynchronous*.

**synchronous protocol**     A communications protocol that controls a synchronous transmission, such as bisync, SDLC and HDLC. Contrast with *asynchronous protocol*.

**synchronous transmission**     The transmission of data in which both stations are synchronized. Codes are sent from the transmitting station to the receiving station to establish the synchronization, and data is then transmitted in continuous streams.
     Modems that transmit at 1,200 bps and higher often convert the asynchronous signals from a computer's serial port into synchronous transmission over the transmission line. Contrast with *asynchronous transmission*.

**synergy**     The enhanced result of two or more people, groups or organizations working together. In other words, one and one equals three! It comes from the Greek "synergia," which means joint work and cooperative action. The word is used quite often to mean that combining forces produces a better product. However, in the field of software development, synergy is often the goal, but not the result. The more people put on a programming job, the more the quality suffers in many cases. See *Freedman's law*.

**S**

**SYN flood attack**   An assault on a network that prevents a TCP/IP server from servicing other users. It is accomplished by not sending the final acknowledgment to the server's SYN-ACK response (SYNchronize-ACKnowledge) in the handshaking sequence, which causes the server to keep signalling until it eventually times out. The source address from the client is, of course, counterfeit. SYN flood attacks can either overload the server or cause it to crash. See *denial of service attack*.

**Synon/2E**   An integrated development environment for AS/400s from Synon, Inc., Larkspur, CA (www.synon.com). Synon/2E was introduced in the same year as the AS/400 (1988) and is the leading tools product in this market. It provides an upper and lower CASE environment that generates COBOL and RPG code. Synon was founded in England in 1983 by Simon Williams. The name came from and is pronounced "sign on."

Synon's Obsydian is an object-oriented PC-based environment that is used to develop C++ code for Windows clients and RPG code for AS/400 servers.

**SynOptics**   See *Bay Networks*.

**syntax**   The rules governing the structure of a language statement. It specifies how words and symbols are put together to form a phrase.

**syntax error**   An error that occurs when a program cannot understand the command that has been entered. See *parse*.

**synthesis**   A combination, derivation or compilation. See *logic synthesis*.

**synthesize**   To create a whole or complete unit from parts or components. See *synthesis*.

**synthesizer**   A device that generates sound by creating waveforms electronically (FM synthesis) or from stored samples of musical instruments (wave table synthesis). See *MIDI* and *speech synthesis*.

**SyQuest**   (SyQuest Technology, Inc., Fremont, CA, www.syquest.com) A manufacturer of removable disk drives, founded in 1982 by Syed Iftikar (Sy's Quest). It originally made 3.9" drives for the military and introduced its first 5.25" drive in 1986, essentially pioneering the removable, hard disk industry for personal computers. Its drives became de facto standards in the graphics arts and printing industries with more than a million units sold by 1994. SyQuest subsequently introduced several new drives, all of which were incompatible with its first-generation drives and each other.

In late 1998, SyQuest filed for Chapter 11 and later sold its assets to Iomega, its arch rival. The competition in the removable market had been fierce in the late 1990s since Iomega's introduction of its Zip and Jaz drives. See *SyQuest disk*, *EZFlyer disk*, *SyJet disk*, *SparQ disk* and *Quest disk*.

**SyQuest disk**   A removable hard drive from SyQuest. Using the SCSI interface, SyQuest's 5.25" drives support 44, 88 and 200MB cartridges. SyQuest's 3.5" drives support 105 and 270MB cartridges. SyQuest disks became de facto standards for transportable interchange of personal computer data. In the mid 1990s, SyQuest introduced several new 3.5" drives that were not compatible with the original formats. See *EZFlyer disk*, *SyJet disk*, *SparQ disk*, *Quest disk* and *magnetic disk*.

**sysadmin**   See *system administrator*.

**SYSCON**   (SYStem CONfiguration) A comprehensive NetWare utility that is used to configure trustee, login and accounting information on NetWare servers.

**sysgen**   (SYStem GENeration) The installation of a new or revised operating system. It includes selecting the appropriate utility programs and identifying the peripheral devices and storage capacities of the system the operating system will be controlling.

**5.25"**

**3.5"**

**SyQuest Cartridges**
SyQuest hard disks were the first de facto standard removable hard disks for personal computers.

**SYSmark**    See *BAPCo*.

**sysop**    (**SYS**tem **OP**erator) Pronounced "siss-op." A person who runs an online communications system or bulletin board. The sysop may also act as mediator for system conferences.

**Sysplex**    (**SYS**tem com**PLEX**) The multiprocessing capability in IBM MVS/ESA and OS/390 mainframes. Introduced with MVS/ESA 4.3 in 1991, it enables the linking of multiple system images within multiple machines and treating them all as a single image. Sysplex added the external Sysplex Timer to synchronize internal clocks. If a failure occurs in a multiprocessor complex, precise transaction time stamps are required for accurate rollback and recovery. It also added XCF (Cross-system Communications Facility), which is software that manages the interconnections between machines.

The addition of one or more Coupling Facilities creates a Parallel Sysplex system that provides high-level clustering that includes data sharing with guaranteed integrity and extensive resource sharing between the systems. See *Coupling Facility* and *Parallel Sysplex*.

**SYSREQ key**    (**SYS**tem **REQ**uest key) A keyboard key on a terminal keyboard that is used to get the attention of the central computer. The key exists on PC keyboards, but is rarely used by applications.

**system**    (1) A group of related components that interact to perform a task.

(2) A *computer system* is made up of the CPU, operating system and peripheral devices.

(3) An *information system* is made up of the database, all the data entry, update, query and report programs and manual and machine procedures.

(4) "The system" often refers to the operating system.

**System 2000**    A hierarchical, network and relational DBMS that runs on IBM, CDC and Unisys computers from the SAS Institute, Cary, NC (www.sas.com). It has been integrated into the SAS System.

**System/3**    A batch-oriented minicomputer from IBM. Introduced in 1969, it introduced a new punched card about half the size of previous ones. With the addition of the Communications Control Program (CCP), it could handle interactive terminals.

**System/32**    A batch-oriented minicomputer from IBM. Introduced in 1975, it provided a single terminal for operator use. It was superseded by the System/34, which could run System/32 applications in a special mode.

**System/34**    A multiuser, multitasking minicomputer from IBM, introduced in 1977. The typical system had a handful of terminals and could run System/32 programs in a special mode. Most large System/34 users migrated to the System/38, while small users migrated to the System/36.

**System/36**    A multiuser, multitasking minicomputer from IBM that was introduced in 1983. Superseding the System/34, it was mostly compatible with it, and System/34 programs ran in the System/36 after recompilation. The typical system supported from a handful to a couple of dozen terminals. System/36 applications had to be recompiled to run on the AS/400.

**System/36**
This is a small model of the System/36 family. Most System/36 applications were ported to the AS/400. *(Image courtesy of International Business Machines Corporation. Unauthorized use not permitted.)*

**System/360**    IBM's first family of computer systems introduced in 1964. It was the first time in history that a complete line of computers was announced at one time. Although considerable enhancements have been made, much of the 360 architecture is still carried over in current-day IBM mainframes. Since its inception, trillions of dollars worth of information systems have been developed for this platform.

The 360, which took four years to develop and cost $5 billion ($24 billion today) was an enormous and risky undertaking. Thomas Watson, Jr. literally "bet his company" on the project. The 360 has been ranked as one of the major business accomplishments in American history alongside of Ford's Model T and Boeing's 707. See *IBM mainframes*.

**System/370**   The mainframe product line introduced in 1970 by IBM (superseding System/360), which added virtual memory and other enhancements. Subsequent series include the 303x, 43xx, 308x, 309x and 9370, all 370-architecture machines. The 370 architecture was brought down to the PC level in 1983 with the PC XT/370, and then again in 1989 with the VM/SP Technical Workstation. See *IBM mainframes*.

**System/38**   A minicomputer from IBM that included an operating system with an integrated relational database management system. Introduced in 1978, it was an advanced departure from previous System/3x computers. The typical system handled from a dozen to several dozen terminals. It was superseded by the AS/400.

**System/390**   The mainframe product line introduced in 1990 by IBM (superseding System/370) that features ESA/390 architecture and operating systems, ES/9000 hardware (18 models introduced), ESCON fiber-optic channels, Sysplex multiprocessing and SystemView.

In 1994, IBM introduced its next generation of System/390 systems known today as Parallel Enterprise Servers or S/390s. These are SMP machines that contain single-chip CMOS CPUs and use less power and dissipate less heat than the bipolar-based ES/9000 models. In 1995, IBM introduced new models that provide up to 10-way SMP within the same machine. Up to 32 10-way systems can be hooked together providing a multiprocessing system with up to 320 CPUs.

As processing requirements increase, customers are migrating from the ES/9000s to clusters of the CMOS-based machines. In 2000, IBM changed the name of S/390 mainframes to "zSeries eservers" (see *IBM server series*). See *Parallel/Sysplex*.

**System/3x**   Refers to IBM System/34, System/36 and System/38 midrange computers.

**System/360**
The System/360 was a bold move for IBM, because it was the first time in history a family of computers was developed and introduced. *(Image courtesy of The Computer Museum History Center, www.computerhistory.org)*

**System/38**
The System/38 was an advanced system for its time, incorporating a relational database management system as part of its core software. Most System/38 applications are now running on AS/400s. *(Image courtesy of International Business Machines Corporation. Unauthorized use not permitted.)*

**System 7**   (1) A major upgrade of the Macintosh operating system introduced in 1991. It included virtual memory, increased memory addressing, hot links (Publish and Subscribe), multitasking (MultiFinder was no longer optional), TrueType fonts and a variety of user interface enhancements.

System 7 Pro added PowerTalk communications, the AppleScript language and QuickTime for sound, movies and animation. System 7.5 advanced the online help with AppleGuide and more sophisticated graphics with QuickDraw GX.

(2) (System/7) A sensor-based minicomputer from IBM introduced in 1970 and used for process control. It was superseded by the Series/1.

**System 8**   A major upgrade of the Macintosh operating system introduced in 1997. More routines are natively coded for the PowerPC chip. It adds an enhanced 3-D look and provides assistance for connecting to the Internet.

**System/88**   A family of fault-tolerant midrange computers from IBM used for online transaction processing. It uses the System/88 virtual memory and System/88 FTX (Fault Tolerant UNIX) operating systems.

**System 9**   A major upgrade of the Macintosh operating system introduced in 1999. System 9 added more native PowerPC routines in the Toolbox and provides tighter integration with Sherlock.

**system administrator**     A person who manages a multiuser computer system. Responsibilities are similar to that of a network administrator. A system administrator would perform systems programmer activities with regard to the operating system and other network control programs. See *system development cycle* and *salary survey*.

**system analyst**     See *systems analyst*.

**Systemantics**     An insightful book on the systems process by John Gall (1977). The following is copied with permission from Random House.

A Concise Summary of the Field of General Systemantics     Systems are seductive. They promise to do a hard job faster, better, and more easily than you could do it by yourself. But if you set up a system, you are likely to find your time and effort now being consumed in the care and feeding of the system itself. New problems are created by its very presence. Once set up, it won't go away, it grows and encroaches. It begins to do strange and wonderful things. Breaks down in ways you never thought possible. It kicks back, gets in the way, and opposes its own proper function. Your own perspective becomes distorted by being in the system. You become anxious and push on it to make it work. Eventually you come to believe that the misbegotten product it so grudgingly delivers is what you really wanted all the time. At that point encroachment has become complete... **you have become absorbed... you are now a systems person!**

**system BIOS**     The BIOS on a PC motherboard. Contrast with BIOSs on the peripheral cards. See *BIOS*.

**system board**     A printed circuit board that contains the primary CPU. See *motherboard*.

**system bus**     **(1)** The primary pathway between the CPU and memory. The speed is derived from the number of parallel lines (16 bit, 32 bit, etc.) and the clock speed (66MHz, 100MHz, etc.). Also known as a "frontside bus," it is typically faster than the peripheral bus (PCI, ISA, etc.), but slower than the backside bus. See *backside bus*. Contrast with *peripheral bus*.

**(2)** The primary pathway between the CPU and peripherals. See *peripheral bus*.

**system design**     See *systems analysis and design* and *information system*.

**system development cycle**     The sequence of events in the development of an information system (application), which requires mutual effort on the part of user and technical staff.

**1. SYSTEMS ANALYSIS & DESIGN**
feasibility study
general design
prototyping
detail design
functional specifications

**2. USER SIGN OFF**

**3. PROGRAMMING**
design
coding
testing

**4. IMPLEMENTATION**
training
conversion
installation

**5. USER ACCEPTANCE**

**system development methodology**     The formal documentation for the phases of the system development cycle.

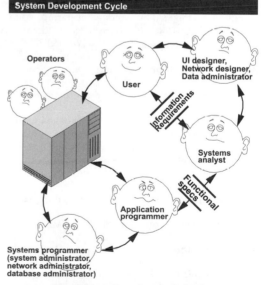

**The System Development Cycle**
From information requirements to final implementation, the system development cycle is an on-going process. As the business changes, information requirements change, and the cycle continues.

It defines the precise objectives for each phase and the results required from a phase before the next one can begin. It may include specialized forms for preparing the documentation describing each phase.

**system disk**    A hard or floppy disk that contains part or all of the operating system or other control program. See *bootable disk*.

**system failure**    A hardware or operating system malfunction.

**system file**    An executable file (in machine language) that is part of the operating system or other control program. The term may also refer to a configuration file used by such programs.

**System folder**    The operating system folder in the Macintosh that contains the System, Finder and MultiFinder, printer drivers, fonts, desk accessories, INITs and cdevs.

**system font**    The primary font used by the operating system or other control program to display messages and menus unless otherwise directed.

**system image**    The current contents of memory, which includes the operating system and running programs. For effective management, a cluster of computer systems may be organized as a single system image, in which all systems appear as one. See *virtual server* and *Sysplex*.

**SYSTEM.INI**    (SYStem INItialization) A Windows configuration file that describes the current state of the computer system environment. It contains hundreds of entries and is read by Windows on startup. It identifies such things as the drivers in the system, how DOS applications are handled and provides immense detail about internal Windows settings.

The information in SYSTEM.INI is updated by Windows when you change various defaults; however, in order to tweak system performance, the file can be edited with a text editor or a word processor that imports ASCII files.

Most of the time, users do not deal with SYSTEM.INI; however, on occasion, a line in the 386 Enhanced section ([386Enh]) may have to be modified. Sometimes an **EMMExclude=** statement is added or changed to exclude a section of upper memory used by a new peripheral from the general pool of memory that Windows uses. WIN.INI is another major configuration file read by Windows at startup.

Although SYSTEM.INI was created in Windows 3.x, it is still used in Windows 95/98 and NT primarily for compatibility with Windows 3.x applications. See *WIN.INI*.

**system integrator**    See *systems integrator*.

**system level**    An operation that is performed by the operating system or some other control program.

**system life cycle**    The useful life of an information system. Its length depends on the nature and volatility of the business, as well as the software development tools used to generate the databases and applications. Eventually, an information system that is patched over and over no longer is structurally sound enough to be expanded.

Tools like DBMSs allow for changes more readily, but increased transaction volumes can negate the effectiveness of the original software later on.

**system management**    See *systems management*.

**System Management Bus**    See *SMBus*.

**system memory**    The memory used by the operating system.

**system policy**    System-wide rules and regulations that override user settings (user profiles). System policies can be assigned to individual users or to workgroups. See *user profile* and *desktop lockdown*.

**system program**    See *system software*.

**system programmer**    See *systems programmer*.

**system prompt**    An on-screen symbol that indicates the operating system is ready for a command. See *DOS prompt*.

**system resources**    **(1)** In a computer system, system resources are the components that provide its inherent capabilities and contribute to its overall performance. System memory, cache memory, hard disk space, IRQs and DMA channels are examples.

**(2)** In an operating system, system resources are internal tables and pointers set up to keep track of running applications. They may be limited by hardware resources, but are often as not arbitrary limitations within the software itself. See *Windows memory limitation*.

**systems**    A general term for the department, people or work involved in systems analysis & design activities.

**systems administrator**    See *system administrator*.

**systems analysis and design**    The examination of a problem and the creation of its solution. Systems analysis is effective when all sides of the problem are reviewed. Systems design is most effective when more than one solution can be proposed. The plans for the care and feeding of a new system are as important as the problems they solve. See *system development cycle, information system* and *Systemantics*.

**systems analyst**    The person responsible for the development of an information system. They design and modify systems by turning user requirements into a set of functional specifications, which are the blueprint of the system. They design the database or help design it if data administrators are available. They develop the manual and machine procedures and the detailed processing specs for each data entry, update, query and report program in the system.

Systems analysts are the architects, as well as the project leaders, of an information system. It is their job to develop solutions to user's problems, determine the technical and operational feasibility of their solutions, and estimate the costs to develop and implement them.

They develop prototypes of the system along with the users, so that the final specifications are examples of screens and reports that have been carefully reviewed. Experienced analysts leave no doubt in users' minds as to what is being developed, and they insist that all responsible users review and sign off on every detail.

Systems analysts require a balanced mix of business and technical knowledge, interviewing and analytical skills, and a good understanding of human behavior. See *system development cycle, salary survey* and *Systemantics*.

**systems disk**    A disk pack or disk drive reserved only for system software, which includes the operating system, assemblers, compilers and other utility and control programs.

**systems engineer**    Refers to a variety of jobs in the industry. It may refer to a system-level programmer or to pre-sales and post-sales programming for a hardware or software vendor. See *software engineer*.

**systems house**    An organization that develops custom software and/or turnkey systems for customers. Contrast with *software house*, which develops software packages for sale to the general public. Both terms are used synonymously.

**systems integration**    Making diverse components work together. See *NASI*.

**systems integrator**    An individual or organization that builds systems from a variety of diverse components. With increasing complexity of technology, more customers want complete solutions to information problems, requiring hardware, software and networking expertise in a multivendor environment.

Some of the major systems integrators are Andersen Consulting, Price Waterhouse, Computer Sciences Corporation, IBM Global Services, HP, Compaq, Ernst & Young, EDS and Deloite Consulting. See *OEM, VAR* and *NASI*.

**systems life cycle**    See *system life cycle*.

**systems management**    **(1)** Software that manages computer systems in an enterprise, which may include any and all of the following functions: software distribution and upgrading, user profile management, version control, backup & recovery, printer spooling, job scheduling, virus protection and performance and capacity planning. Microsoft's Systems Management Server and Novell's ZENworks are examples of systems management applications.

Depending on organizational philosophy, systems management may include network management or come under it. See *network management* and *configuration management*.

**(2)** The management of systems development, which includes systems analysis & design, application development and implementation. See *system development cycle*.

**(3)** The management of the computer systems within an organization. Used in this context, the term may refer to the entire IT organization or just to datacenter management.

### system software
Programs used to control the computer and develop and run application programs. It includes operating systems, TP monitors, network operating systems and database managers. Contrast with *application program*.

The following diagram shows the flow between system software and application software residing in memory in a multiuser computer. The operating system (OS), TP monitor, database manager and interpreter are considered system software. The applications and interactive DBMS query and edit would be considered application software.

### systems person
An umbrella term for an individual that performs systems analysis and consulting in the computer field. See *systems representative, systems analyst, systems engineer* and *software engineer*.

### systems program
See *system program* and *system software*.

### systems programmer
**(1)** In the IS department of a large organization, a technical expert on some or all of the computer's system software (operating systems, networks, DBMSs, etc.). They are responsible for the efficient performance of the computer systems.

They usually don't write programs, but perform a lot of technical tasks that integrate vendors' software. They also act as technical advisors to systems analysts, application programmers and operations personnel. For example, they would know whether additional tasks could be added to the computer and would recommend conversion to a new operating or database system in order to optimize performance.

In mainframe environments, there is one systems programmer for about 10 or more application programmers, and systems programmers generally have considerably higher salaries than application programmers. In smaller environments, users rely on vendors or consultants for systems programming assistance. In fact, end users are actually performing systems programmer functions when they install new software or hardware on their own personal computers. See *system administrator* and *salary survey*.

**(2)** In a computer hardware or software organization, a person who designs and writes system software. In this case, a systems programmer is a programmer in the traditional sense and is often called a "software engineer." See *salary survey*.

### systems representative
An individual that performs presales and post-sales activities for a hardware or software vendor. Depending on the product they represent, systems reps can perform just about any task short of making the actual sale, including systems analysis, programming and general consulting.

---

**SYSTEM SOFTWARE**

**OPERATING SYSTEM**
Manages the computer system. Provides file, task and job management. All application programs "talk to" the operating system.

Windows, DOS, UNIX, Linux, Mac OS, OS/2, MVS and OS/400 are examples.

**DRIVER**
Software that supports a peripheral device, such as a display adapter or CD-ROM. The driver contains the detailed machine language necessary to activate all functions in the device. The operating system commands the driver, which in turn commands the hardware device.

**BIOS (Basic Input/Output System)**
In a PC, a set of software routines built into a chip that boots the machine and serves as an interface between the drivers and the peripheral devices.

**TP MONITOR**
Mainframe/midrange program that distributes input from multiple terminals to the appropriate application. This function is also provided in LAN operating systems.

CICS is widely used in IBM mainframes, and Tuxedo and Encina are widely used in UNIX systems.

**NETWORK OPERATING SYSTEM**
Manage traffic and security between clients and servers in a network. Examples are UNIX, Linux, NetWare, Windows NT and Windows 2000.

**COMMUNICATIONS PROTOCOL**
Set of rules, formats and functions for sending data across the network. There are many protocol layers starting at the top application layer to the bottom physical layer

Popular transport protocols are TCP/IP, NetBEUI and TCP/IP. Popular data link protocols (access methods) used to transmit data from point to point are Ethernet, Token Ring, SDLC and RS-232.

**MESSAGING PROTOCOL**
Set of rules, formats and functions for sending, storing and forwarding e-mail in a network. The major messaging protocols are SMTP (Internet), SNADS, MHS, X.400, cc:Mail and Microsoft Mail.

**DATABASE MANAGEMENT SYSTEM (DBMS)**
Manages the storage, retrieval, security and integrity of the database. A DBMS may provide interactive data entry, updating, query and reporting or rely entirely on the application program for such functions. The DBMS may reside in a mainframe or in a file server in a client/server architecture. Most DBMSs support the SQL language, and many include a complete programming language for application development.

Examples of popular mainframe and client/server DBMSs are DB2, Oracle, Sybase, SQL Server and Informix. Access, dBASE and Paradox are used in PCs.

**PROGRAMMING LANGUAGE**
Translate source language into machine language using assemblers, compilers, interpreters and application generators. All system software and application software must be programmed in a programming language and turned into machine language for execution.

Examples of programming languages are assembly language, BASIC, FORTRAN, C, C++, Pascal, dBASE, Paradox, Visual Basic and COBOL.

---

**systems software**    See *system software*.

**system test**    Running a complete system for testing purposes. See *unit test*.

**system time/date**    The on-going time of day in the computer, which is maintained by a battery when the computer is turned off. It is used to time stamp all newly created files and activate time-dependent processes.

**system unit**    The primary computer equipment. Housed in a desktop or floor-standing cabinet, it contains such components as the motherboard, CPU, RAM and ROM chips, hard and floppy disks and several input/output ports.

**SystemView**    An IBM architecture for computer systems management introduced with System/390 that provides an enterprise-wide approach for controlling multiple systems and networks. It will be implemented in stages through the 1990s. NetView is a major component.

**systolic array**    An array of processing elements (typically multiplier-accumulator chips) in a pipeline structure that is used for applications such as image and signal processing and fluid dynamics. The "systolic," coined by H. T. Kung of Carnegie-Mellon, refers to the rhythmic transfer of data through the pipeline like blood flowing through the vascular system.

S

# T

**T**  See *tera*.

**T&L**  (Transformation **&** Lighting) Moving 3-D objects on screen and changing the corresponding lighting effects. Transforming these 3-D matrices many times per second as the objects move and recomputing their shadows each time takes an enormous amount of processing. Hardware T&L offloads these functions from the system CPU into the display adapter or some other board, which enables a greater number of polygons to be processed to create a more realistic effect. See *graphics accelerator*.

**T+0**  (Transaction plus **0** days) In financial processing, the ability to complete a stock transaction in the same day it was made, which includes settlement, payment and transfer of ownership. This is a long-term goal.

**T1**  **(1)** A 1.544 Mbps point-to-point dedicated, digital circuit provided by the telephone companies. The monthly cost is typically based on distance. T1 lines are widely used for private networks, as well as interconnections between an organization's PBX or LAN and the telco. The first T1 line was tariffed by AT&T in January 1983. However, starting in the early 1960s, T1 was deployed in intercity trunks by AT&T to improve signal quality and make more efficient use of the network.

A T1 line uses two wire pairs (one for transmit, one for receive) and time division multiplexing (TDM) to interleave 24 64 Kbps voice or data channels. The standard T1 frame is 193 bits long, which holds 24 8-bit voice samples and one synchronization bit with 8,000 frames transmitted per second. T1 is not restricted to digital voice or to 64 Kbps data streams. Channels may be combined and the total 1.544 Mbps capacity can be broken up as required. See *DS*, *T-carrier*, *bipolar transmission*, *D4* and *ESF*.

**(2)** See *Type 1 font*.

```
                             64 Kbps
T-Carrier    Total Speed     Channels
T1            1.544 Mbps       24
T2            6.312 Mbps       96
T3           44.736 Mbps      672
```

**T.120**  An ITU standard for realtime data conferencing (sharing data among multiple users). It defines interfaces for whiteboards, application viewing and application sharing. The ITU standard for videoconferencing is H.320. Following are all the elements of T.120.

**T.121—Generic Application Template**  Common structure for T.120 applications.

**T.122—Multipoint Communication Service**  Service definition for T.123 networks (implemented in T.125).

**T.123—Audiovisual Protocol Stacks**  Protocol stacks for terminals and MCUs.

**T.124—Generic Conference Control**   Conference management (establish, terminate, etc.).

**T.125—Multipoint Communication Service**   Protocol implementation of T.122.

**T.126—Still Image & Annotation Protocol**   Whiteboards, graphic display and image exchange.

**T.127—Multipoint Binary Transfer**   Protocol for exchanging binary files.

**T.128—Audio Visual Control**   Interactive controls (routing, identification, remote control, source selection, etc.)

**T.130—Realtime Architecture**   Interaction between T.120 and H.320.

**T.131—Network Specific Mappings**   Transport of realtime data used with T.120 over LANs.

**T.132—Realtime Link Management**   Creation and routing of realtime data streams.

**T.133—Audio Visual Control Services**   Controls for realtime data streams.

**T.RES—Reservation Services**   Interaction between devices and reservation systems.

**T.Share—Application Sharing Protocol**   Remote control protocol.

**T.TUD—User Reservation**   Transporting user-defined data.

**T1/E1**   Refers to the U.S. T1 line or European E1 equivalent.

**T1 font**   See *Type 1 font*.

**T1/PRI**   See *PRI*.

**T.2**   An ITU standard for Group 1 fax machines. It was introduced in 1968.

**T2**   A 6.312 Mbps point-to-point dedicated line provided by the telephone companies. A T2 line provides 96 64 Kbps voice or data channels. See *T-carrier* and *DS*.

**T3**   A 44.736 Mbps point-to-point dedicated line provided by the telephone companies. A T3 line provides 672 64 Kbps voice or data channels. T3 channels are widely used on the Internet. See *T-carrier* and *DS*.

**T.30**   An ITU standard for Group 3 fax machines that specifies the handshaking, protocols and error correction. T.4 and T.30, which were introduced in 1980, make up the complete standard for Group 3 fax.

**T.4**   An ITU standard for Group 3 fax machines that specifies the page dimensions, resolutions and compression scheme. T.4 and T.30, which were introduced in 1980, make up the complete standard for Group 3 fax.

**T.6**   An ITU standard for Group 4 fax machines. Although introduced in 1984, Group 4 has yet to be implemented on any major scale, as it requires high-speed ISDN and DSL technologies for operation.

**T9**   (**T**ext on **9** Keys) A text input system from AOL that adds intelligence to multi-tapping letters on a telephone keypad. For example, instead of typing 8-4-4-3-3 for the word "the," you would type only 8-4-3, and T9 would recognize it as "t-h-e." For words with numerous meanings, the default word is displayed first, and you can select from a list. To enter a proprietary name, you switch to multi-tapping mode to type the name, and then back to T9 mode. T9 was developed by Tegic Communications (www.t9.com), which was acquired by AOL. See *multi-tapping*.

**TA**   (**T**erminal **A**dapter) See *ISDN terminal adapter*.

**tab**   (1) To move the cursor on a display screen or the print head on a printer to a specified column (tab stop). There are both horizontal and vertical tab characters in the ASCII character set. See ***tab stop***.

**(2)** A small flap used for quick access that projects out from the end of a page or file folder. The on-screen equivalent is clicked to display a dialog for the user.

**(3)** (TAB) See *tape automated bonding*.

**tab character**     A control character in a document that represents movement to the next tab stop. In the ASCII character set, a horizontal tab is ASCII 9, and a vertical tab is ASCII 11. See *ASCII chart*.

**tab delimited**     A text format that uses tab characters as separators between fields. Unlike comma-delimited files, alphanumeric data is not surrounded by quotes.

**TAB key**     A keyboard key that moves the cursor to the next tab stop.

**table**     **(1)** In programming, a collection of adjacent fields. Also called an "array," a table contains data that is either constant within the program or is called in when the program is run. See *decision table* and *HTML table*.

**(2)** In a relational database, the same as a file; a collection of records.

**table lookup**     Searching for one item in a matrix of data. It is widely used in data entry validation and numerous operations that must match an item of data to obtain a set of values (ranges, prices, routes, etc.).

**tablet** ·   See *digitizer tablet*.

**tablet computer**     A complete computer contained in a touch screen. Tablet computers can be specialized for only Internet use, or be full-blown, general-purpose PCs with all the bells and whistles of a desktop unit. The distinguishing characteristic is the use of the screen as an input device using a stylus or finger. See *Webpad* and *touch screen*.

**tablet cursor**     The mouse-like object used to draw on a digitizer tablet. See *mouse*.

**tablet PC**     **(1)** Same as *tablet computer*.

**(2)** A tablet computer environment from Microsoft that is based on Windows XP. Designed to function more like a portable writing tablet than previous tablet-based computers, it includes handwriting recognition, as well as the ability to retain handwritten words and annotations without turning them into computer text. This latter ability is known as "rich digital ink," because the inking (writing, drawing, scribbling) is stored as is with algorithms smoothing out any rough edges.

**table view**     A screen display of several items or records in rows and columns. Contrast with *form view*.

**tabular form**     Same as *table view* with respect to printed output.

**tabulate**     **(1)** To arrange data into a columnar format.

**(2)** To sum and print totals.

**tabulator**     A punched card accounting machine that calculates totals and prints the results. Since the late 1800s, tabulators were used to accumulate totals and were later capable of printing. Countless invoices, checks and green-striped reports were printed on tabulating machines all the way up into the 1970s. See *Hollerith machine*.

**TACACS**     (Terminal Access Controller Access Control System) An access control protocol used to authenticate a user logging onto the network. TACACS is a simple username/password system. Extended TACACS

**Dialog Box Tabs**

On-screen tabs are widely used in control panels and other setting dialogs. In this Windows display control panel example, the Appearance tab is currently selected.

**A Tabulator in the 1960s**

Tabulating machines such as this IBM 407 (left) were used throughout the 1960s to print millions of reports, invoices and checks. IBM was the leading tabulating equipment vendor. *(Image courtesy of International Business Machines Corporation. Unauthorized use not permitted.)*

(XTACACS) adds more intelligence in the server, and TACACS+ adds encryption and a challenge/response option. See *challenge/response*.

**TACS**   (Total Access Communication System) An analog cellular phone system deployed mostly in Europe. It was modeled after the AMPS system in the U.S. In the U.K., ETACS (Extended TACS) tramsmits in the 871–904/916–949MHz band. International TACS (ITACS) and International ETACS (IETACS) are versions that operate outside the U.K. Narrowband TACS (NTACS) operates in the 860–870/915–925MHz band, and by using a narrower channel spacing, delivers more channels in the same amount of spectrum. See *AMPS*.

**tag**   **(1)** A set of bits or characters that identifies various conditions about data in a file and is often found in the header records of such files.

    **(2)** A name (label, mnemonic) assigned to a data structure, such as a field, file or paragraph.

    **(3)** The key field in a record.

    **(4)** A format code used in a document language. See *HTML tag*, *character tag* and *paragraph tag*.

    **(5)** A brass pin on a terminal block that is connected to a wire by soldering or wire wrapping.

**tag-based language**   A language that is used to define elements in a document or Web page by embedding codes (tags) surrounded by common start and stop characters. The tags in SGML, HTML, XML and WML all use the less-than symbol (<) to start the tag and a greater-than symbol (>) to end it. See *HTML tag*.

**tag RAM**   A specialized bank of static RAM used to hold addresses. When a stored address matches an input address, a signal is output to perform a function. It is used with hardware devices such as CPU caches to keep track of which memory addresses are stored in the cache.

**tag sort**   A sorting procedure in which the key fields are sorted first to create the correct order, and then the actual data records are placed into that order.

**tag switching**   A layer 3 switching technology from Cisco that is used in large enterprise networks (WANs). It uses tags (labels) containing forwarding information. Tag switching uses routers (Tag Edge Routers) that sit on the periphery of the network and make forwarding decisions for all the routers in the backbone. They append this information to each packet in fixed positions of the header that can be quickly examined by interior backbone routers (Tag Edge Switches), saving the time involved in decoding the packet and its associated table lookups.

**Tailgate**   A conversion layer that lets IDE devices connect to the IEEE 1394 Firewire interface.

**talk-off**   An unintentional command activation when a human voice generates the same tone as a control signal.

**Tandem**   (Tandem Computers, Inc., Cupertino, CA, www.tandem.com) A manufacturer of fault-tolerant computers founded in 1974 by James Treybig. It was the first company to address the transaction processing (OLTP) market for online reservations and financial transfers by providing computers designed from the ground up for fault-tolerant operation. Tandem computers are used in all the major banks, stock exchanges and credit card companies in the world.

    Tandem's flagship fault-tolerant product is its MIPS-based Himalaya series, which runs the NonStop Kernel operating system and is compatible with Tandem's Guardian OS. Tandem also offers a line of UNIX and Windows NT servers. In 1997, Tandem was acquired by Compaq.

**James Treybig**
Treybig founded
Tandem and was at
its helm for more
than 20 years.
*(Image courtesy of
Tandem Computers
Incorporated.)*

**tandem office**   A telephone switching center (central office) that does not connect directly to the customer. It connects offices in the same network or between networks, but always deals with trunks rather than customer lines. After Divestiture, most Class 4 tandem offices moved to AT&T, while Class 5 local tandem offices stayed with the RBOCs where they remain today. RBOCs installed new tandem offices to handle intraLATA toll and provide access to the interLATA toll carriers. Tandem offices and end offices are generally located in the same facility, and may even be serviced by the same switch. See *LATA*, *Class 4 switch* and *end office*.

**tandem processors**   Two processors hooked together in a multiprocessor environment.

**tandem switch**    A central office switch (telco switch) that connects end offices together and does not deal directly with the customer. Most of the call recording and billing used to be handled by tandem switches (also called "toll/tandem switches"), but today is provided in the end offices by the end office switches. A sector tandem switch connects end offices for intraLATA traffic, while an access tandem switch provides the connection between end offices and the POPs for interexchange carriers (IXCs). See *LATA*, *end office switch* and *carrier switch*.

**Tandy**    (Tandy Corporation, Ft. Worth, TX, www.tandy.com)  A manufacturer of PCs and electronics that started as a family leather business in 1919. In 1963, it acquired the nine Radio Shack stores in Boston. Today, it has over 7,000 company-owned stores and franchises.

In 1977, it introduced one of the first personal computers, the TRS-80 Model I. Tandy's Model 100 and 200 lightweight portables were also inspiration to the laptop generation. Its first computers were proprietary, and its initial PCs were non-standard. However, starting with the Model 1000 in 1984, Tandy offered a full line of IBM-compatible PCs.

In 1993, Tandy sold its PC manufacturing facilities to AST and began to eliminate the Tandy brand name on its machines. Radio Shack stores currently offer a variety of desktop and laptop machines from Compaq.

**One of the First Personal Computers**
In 1977, Tandy's Radio Shack division introduced one of the first personal computers, the TRS-80. It became widely used in small business and was a major contributor to the personal computer explosion. *(Image courtesy of Tandy Corporation.)*

**tanstaafl**    Digispeak for "there ain't no such thing as a free lunch."

**tap**    (1) In communications, a connection made on a line. For example, a wire tap is the connecting point where a wire to a recording device is attached to the telephone wire for a particular phone line. See *transceiver* and *bridged tap*.

(2) (TAP) (**T**elocator **A**lphanumeric **P**rotocol)  A paging protocol used to transmit up to a thousand 7-bit characters to an alphanumeric pager. Developed in the early 1980s and also known as IXO and PET, TAP is widely used in the U.S. and throughout Europe.

(3) To press a button displayed on a touch-sensitive screen or press a key on a keypad.

**tape**    See *magnetic tape* and *paper tape*.

**tape automated bonding**    A process that places bare chips onto a printed circuit board (PCB) by attaching them to a polyimide film. The film is moved to the target location, and the leads are cut and soldered to the board. The bare chip is then encapsulated ("glob topped") with epoxy or plastic. See *chip on board*.

**tape automation**    See *tape library*.

**tape backup**    Using magnetic tape for storing duplicate copies of hard disk files. See *magnetic tape*. For a complete summary of tape, disk and optical storage technologies, see *storage*.

**tape cassette**    See *cassette* and *audio cassette*.

**taped out**    Refers to the completion of the design of a chip. The next stage is to put it into production. The term comes from the early days when designs were transferred to the fabricator via magnetic tape.

**tape drive**    A physical unit that holds, reads and writes the magnetic tape. See *magnetic tape*.

**tape dump**    A printout of tape contents without any report formatting.

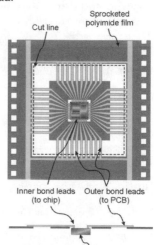

**Tape Automated Bonding**
After the chip leads are cut and soldered to the board, the chip is covered with a glob of epoxy or plastic. *(Illustration courtesy of Joseph Fjelstad.)*

**tape library**    A high-capacity data storage system for storing, retrieving, reading and writing multiple magnetic tape cartridges. Also called a "tape automation system," it contains storage racks for holding the cartridges and a robotic mechanism for moving the cartridge to the drive.

Tape libraries are available for 3480, 3490, Magstar, Magstar MP, DLT, 4mm DAT, 8mm and Travan tape cartridges. Smaller units can have several drives for simultaneous reading and writing and may hold from a handful to several hundred cartridges. Large units support dozens of drives and hold several thousand cartridges.

Accessing data in a tape library can take from 15 seconds to a minute in order to find, retrieve and load a cartridge, making it available for reading and writing.

**A Massive Tape Library**
StorageTek's RedWood SD-3 tape libary is one of the largest in the world and can hold up to 6,000 helical scan cartridges. Each cartridge holds 50GB, which if fully populated would store 300 terabytes of data. *(Image courtesy of Storage Technology Corporation.)*

**tape mark**    A control code used to indicate the end of a tape file.

**tape transport**    The mechanical part of a tape drive.

**TAPI**    (Telephony API) A programming interface from Microsoft and Intel that is part of Microsoft's WOSA architecture. It allows Windows client applications to access voice services on a server. TAPI is designed to provide interoperability between PCs and telephone equipment, including phone systems and PBXs. See *WOSA*.

**tar**    (Tape ARchive) A UNIX utility that is used to archive files by combining several files into one. It is often used in conjunction with the "compress" or "gzip" commands to compress the data. The name came from the days when magnetic tape was the predominant storage medium rather than disk. Tar archives are often called "tarballs." See *archive formats*.

**tarball**    See *tar*.

**target computer**    The computer into which a program is loaded and run. Contrast with *source computer*. See *cross assembler* and *cross compiler*.

**target directory**    The directory into which data is being sent. Contrast with *source directory*.

**target disk**    The disk onto which data is recorded. Contrast with *source disk*.

**target drive**    The drive containing the disk or tape onto which data is recorded. Contrast with *source drive*.

**target language**    The language resulting from a translation process such as assembling or compiling. Contrast with *source language*.

**target machine**    Same as *target computer*.

**tariff**    A schedule of rates for common carrier services.

**task**    An independent running program. See *multitasking*.

**taskbar**    An on-screen toolbar that displays the active applications (tasks). Clicking on a taskbar button restores the application to its previous appearance. Windows 95 popularized this feature. See *Win Taskbar*.

**task management**    (1) The part of the operating system that controls the running of one or more programs (tasks) within the computer at the same time.

(2) Managing personal and office tasks using a to-do list, or task list. This function is typically in a PIM or groupware product.

**task swapping**    Switching between two applications by copying the current running program to disk or other high-speed storage device (auxiliary memory, EMS, etc.) and loading another program into that program space.

**task switching**    Switching between active applications. It generally refers to a user purposefully jumping from one application to another, for example, by pressing ALT-TAB in Windows. Task switching can also be performed by a multitasking operating system that continually switches the CPU from one program to another in the background.

**TAWPI**    (The Association for Work Process Improvement, Boston, MA, www.tawpi.org) A membership organization dedicated to the improvement of work processes in data capture, document and remittance processing. It was originally the OCR Users Association (OCRUA) founded in 1970, which was renamed the Recognition Technology Users Association (RTUA) in 1981. In 1993, RTUA merged with DEMA (Association for Input Technology and Management) and various OCR/Scanner/Fax associations, and changed its name to TAWPI.

**TB**    (1) (TB) (TeraByte) One trillion bytes (technically, 1,099,511,627,776 bytes). See *tera* and *space/time*.
    (2) (Tb) (TeraBit) One trillion bits (technically, 1,099,511,627,776 bits). Lower case "b" for bit and "B" for byte are not always followed and often misprinted. Thus, Tb may refer to terabyte. See *tera* and *space/time*.

**Tbits/sec**    (TeraBITS per SECond) Trillion bits per second.

**TBps, Tbps**    (TeraBytes Per Second, TeraBits Per Second) Trillion bytes per second. Trillion bits per second.

**T-byte**    See *terabyte*.

**Tbytes/sec**    (TeraBYTES per SECond) Trillion bytes per second.

**TC**    See *true color*.

**T-cal**    See *thermal recalibration*.

**TCAL**    See *thermal recalibration*.

**TCAM**    (TeleCommunications Access Method) IBM communications software widely used to transfer data between mainframes and 3270 terminals. See *access method*.

**TCAP**    (Transaction Capabilities Application Part) The protocol used in an SS7 network for sending database queries to a service control point (SCP). The SCP provides the interface to local and remote databases that contain subscriber and routing information. TCAP messages can also be sent from one voice switch to invoke functions in another switch in the network. See *SS7*.

**T-carrier**    A digital transmission service from a common carrier. Although developed in the 1960s and used internally, AT&T introduced it as a communications product to the public in 1983. Initially used for voice, its use for data grew steadily, and T1 and T3 lines are widely used to create point-to-point private data networks. T-carrier lines use four wire cables. One pair is used to transmit, the other to receive.
    The cost of the lines is generally based on the length of the circuit. Thus, it is the customer's responsibility to utilize the lines efficiently. Multiple lower-speed channels can be multiplexed onto a T-carrier line and demultiplexed (split back out) at the other end. Some multiplexors can analyze the traffic load and vary channel speeds for optimum transmission. See *DS*, *DSU/CSU* and *inverse multiplexor*.

**Tcl/Tk**    (Tool Command Language/ToolKit) Pronounced "tickle" or "ticklet," it is an interpreted script language that is used to develop a variety of applications, including GUIs, prototypes and CGI scripts. Created for the UNIX platform by John Ousterhout along with students at the University of California at Berkeley, it was later ported to PCs and Macs. Safe-Tcl is an enhanced Tcl interpreter that provides a secure, virus free environment.
    Tcl also provides an interface into compiled applications (C, C++, etc.). The application is compiled with Tcl functions, which provide a bi-directional path between Tcl scripts and the executable programs. Tcl provides a way to

T

"glue" program modules together. The Tk part of Tcl/Tk is the GUI toolkit, which is used to create graphical user interfaces. Other languages, including Perl, Python and Scheme, have incorporated Tk as well.

**TCM** (1) (**T**rellis-**C**oded **M**odulation/Viterbi Decoding) A technique that adds forward error correction to a modulation scheme by adding an additional bit to each baud. TCM is used with QAM modulation, for example.

(2) (**T**hermal **C**onduction **M**odule) An IBM circuit packaging technique that seals chips, boards and components into a module that serves as a heat sink. TCMs are mostly water cooled, although some are air cooled.

**TCO** (1) (**T**otal **C**ost of **O**wnership) The cost of using a computer. It includes the cost of the hardware, software and upgrades, as well as the cost of the in-house staff and/or consultants that provide training and technical support.

(2) Refers to the Swedish Confederation of Professional Employees, which certifies electronic devices that meet safety standards. TCO'92 certification requires greatly reduced magnetic field emission and energy efficiency, as well as fire and electrical safety. TCO'95 added ergonomic and ecologial requirements dealing with eyestrain and the use of certain materials in the manufacture and packaging. TCO'99 tightened the requirements of TCO'95. For more information, visit www.tco-info.com. See *MPR II*.

**TCP** (1) (**T**ransmission **C**ontrol **P**rotocol) The TCP part of TCP/IP. TCP and UDP (User Datagram Protocol) are the two transport protocols in TCP/IP. TCP ensures that a message is sent accurately and in its entirety. However, for realtime voice and video, there is really no time or reason to correct errors, and UDP is used instead. See *TCP/IP* and *UDP*.

(2) (**T**ape **C**arrier **P**ackage) Another term for *tape automated bonding*.

**TCP/IP** (**T**ransmission **C**ontrol **P**rotocol/**I**nternet **P**rotocol) A communications protocol developed under contract from the U.S. Department of Defense to internetwork dissimilar systems. Invented by Vinton Cerf and Bob Kahn, this de facto UNIX standard is the protocol of the Internet and has become the global standard for communications.

TCP provides transport functions, which ensures that the total amount of bytes sent is received correctly at the other end. UDP, which is part of the TCP/IP suite, is an alternate transport that does not guarantee delivery. It is widely used for realtime voice and video transmissions where erroneous packets are not retransmitted.

TCP/IP is a routable protocol, and the IP part of TCP/IP provides the routing capability. In a routable protocol, all messages contain not only the address of the destination station, but the address of a destination network. This allows TCP/IP messages to be sent to multiple networks within an organization or around the world, hence its use in the worldwide Internet (see *Internet address*). Every client and server in a TCP/IP network requires an IP address, which is either permanently assigned or dynamically assigned at startup. For an explanation of how the various layers in TCP/IP work, see *TCP/IP ABCs*. See also *IP address*, *NFS*, *NIS*, *DNS*, *DHCP*, *dumb network* and *IP on Everything*.

**TCP/IP stack** An implementation of the TCP/IP communications protocol. Network architectures designed in layers, such as TCP/IP, OSI and SNA, are called "stacks."

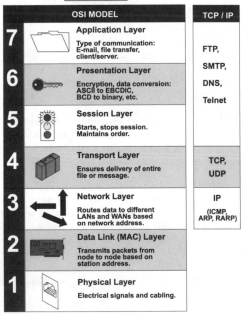

| OSI MODEL | | TCP / IP |
|---|---|---|
| 7 | **Application Layer**<br>Type of communication:<br>E-mail, file transfer,<br>client/server. | FTP,<br>SMTP,<br>DNS,<br>Telnet |
| 6 | **Presentation Layer**<br>Encryption, data conversion:<br>ASCII to EBCDIC,<br>BCD to binary, etc. | |
| 5 | **Session Layer**<br>Starts, stops session.<br>Maintains order. | |
| 4 | **Transport Layer**<br>Ensures delivery of entire<br>file or message. | TCP,<br>UDP |
| 3 | **Network Layer**<br>Routes data to different<br>LANs and WANs based<br>on network address. | IP<br>(ICMP,<br>ARP, RARP) |
| 2 | **Data Link (MAC) Layer**<br>Transmits packets from<br>node to node based on<br>station address. | |
| 1 | **Physical Layer**<br>Electrical signals and cabling. | |

Network User

**TCS** (**T**ransportation **C**ontrol **S**ystem) A widely used integrated information system for railroad transportation developed by the Missouri Pacific Railroad Company in the late 1960s and early 1970s. It was later implemented by Union Pacific when the companies merged. It is very comprehensive and includes traffic scheduling and tracking, maintenance scheduling, yard assignments, inventory control and billing. TCS also became the foundation of Mexico's modern rail system.

**TCSEC**   See *NCSC*.

**TCU**   (Transmission Control Unit) A communications control unit controlled by the computer that does not execute internally stored programs. Contrast with *front end processor*, which executes its own instructions.

**TDD**   (Time Division Duplexing) A transmission method that uses only one channel for transmitting and receiving, separating them by different time slots. No guard band is used. Contrast with *FDD*.

**TDES**   (Triple **DES**) See *DES*.

**TDM**   (Time Division Multiplexing) A technology that transmits multiple signals simultaneously over a single transmission path. Each lower-speed signal is time sliced into one high-speed transmission. For example, three incoming 1,000 bps signals (A, B and C) can be interleaved into one 3,000 bps signal (AABBCCAABBCCAABBCC). The receiving end divides the single stream back into its original signals.

   TDM enabled the telephone companies to migrate from analog to digital on all their long distance trunks. The technology is used in channel banks, which convert 24 analog voice conversations into one digital T1 line. Contrast with *FDM*. See *circuit switching*, *channel bank* and *T1*.

**TDMA**   (Time Division Multiple Access) A satellite and cellular phone technology that interleaves multiple digital signals onto a single high-speed channel. For cellular, TDMA triples the capacity of the original analog method (FDMA). It divides each channel into three subchannels, providing service to three users instead of one. The GSM cellular system is also based on TDMA, but GSM defines the entire network, not just the air interface. See *wireless generations*, *FDMA*, *CDMA* and *CDPD*.

**TEA**   (Tiny Encryption Algorithm) A secret key cryptography method that uses a 128-bit key. It uses the block cipher method, which breaks the text into 64-bit blocks before encrypting them. Written by David Wheeler and Roger Needham of Cambridge Computer Laboratory in the U.K., it is available in 16-round and 32-round versions. The more rounds (iterations), the more secure the results. See *encryption algorithm*.

**Team Enterprise Developer**   A client/server application development system from Symantec that supports Windows clients and a variety of databases, including Access, SQL Server, Oracle and Sybase. It is a fully integrated system that is repository driven. It also includes entity relationship diagrams and version control.

**tear down**   In communications, to free up a circuit that has been established for a particular session. When the session is completed, the circuit is "torn down" and the components and services involved are available for use by someone else.

**tear-off menu**   An on-screen menu or palette that can be moved off of its primary position and relocated to any part of the screen.

**technical writer**   The person responsible for writing the hardware and software documentation you read in manuals and in the online help. Quite often, the technical writer is given the task of documenting an application at the last minute, allowing very little time for a thorough understanding of the myriad of options, let alone time for others to read the material and to revise and edit it.

   Technical writers are often paid much less than other professionals in the field. As a result, almost all of the documentation we read could be better, and much of it is indecipherable. It is hardly a wonder that users and even technical people avoid reading the manuals at all costs. See *RTFM*.

**A Note from the Author**   When the great minds in the computer industry wake up and figure out how critical it is to write good, clear documentation, they might pay more attention to it, because it would keep their companies from drowning in technical support. Describing technical material is as difficult a job as some of the most complex programming.

However, poor programming is invisible. As long as the program works, you have no idea how many resources are being wasted behind the scenes, or if, in fact, the program causes conflicts with your other applications. People are so used to the computer locking up (crashing), they take it in stride. But, poor writing is not invisible. It is up front, staring you in the face. You either understand it or you do not.

If the writing in this publication is reasonably understandable, it is because I have been writing about computers for more than 40 years. In addition, I have revised most of the definitions at least a half dozen times, and in some cases, more times than I can count. And, although it does get easier after a while, writing this material is still the greatest challenge of my life.

**technology transfer**   (1) Sharing technical information by means of education and training.

(2) Using a technical concept or hardware or software product to solve a problem in an industry that is entirely different from the one the technology was developed for.

**technophile**   A person that enjoys learning about and using electronics and computers. See *computerphile*, *hacker* and *dweeb*. Contrast with *technophobic*.

**technophobic**   Afraid of technology. See *lamer* and *Luddite*. Contrast with *technophile*.

**technoscaping**   Sculpting technology into the architecture of a building. For example, rather than bolting a monitor onto the wall, the wall would be built to contain the monitor. The term was coined by Mark J. E. Shapiro.

**tech support**   Technical assistance from the hardware manufacturer or software publisher. Unless you have a simple, straightforward question that has nothing to do with a problem you are encountering with your computer, be sure you are sitting at your computer when you call the tech support line, and the application in question has been launched.

This is a precise business. Whenever you get an error message, be sure to write down exactly what it says. "I don't quite remember" will generally not solve your problem. In addition, in large companies, some of these people take hundreds of calls all day long and may have little patience with you if you cannot describe the circumstances of your problem in detail.

Intermittent problems are extremely difficult to resolve. If you cannot re-create the problem onscreen, there may be very little a tech support person can do to help you.

**tech writer**   See *technical writer*.

**telco**   (TELephone COmpany) A company that provides telephone services. It may refer only to local telephone companies, or to both local and long distance carriers if referring to the telephone industry in general. See *cellco*.

**Telcordia**   (Telcordia Technologies, Morristown, NJ, www.telcordia.com, an SAIC company) A telecommunications software, engineering and consulting organization. Telcordia was originally founded as Bellcore in 1984 by the regional Bell telephone companies (RBOCs) after they were split apart from AT&T due to court order (see *Divestiture*). Bellcore provided the research and development to the RBOCs that was originally within AT&T.

In late 1997, Bellcore was acquired by Science Applications International Corporation (SAIC), which was founded by Dr. J.R. Beyster in 1969. By 1999, SAIC had more than 35,000 employees and was the largest high-tech company in the country that was employee owned.

On March 9, 1999, Bellcore changed its name to Telcordia Technologies, which was required as part of the SAIC acquisition.

**telco switch**   A large-scale computer system that is used to switch telephone calls, which are comprised of digital voice streams. Also called a "voice switch," Lucent and Nortel Networks are the primary vendors of this equipment. Telco switches that are used by long distance IXCs are known as carrier switches. Telco switches used in local telephone company central offices are known as end office switches and tandem switches. See *carrier switch*, *end office switch* and *tandem switch*.

**tele**   ("long distance") Operations performed remotely or by telephone.

**telecom**   Same as *telecommunications*.

**telecom company**    An organization that provides voice or data transmission services, such as AT&T, Bell Atlantic and Qwest. A company that specializes in making carrier-class hardware and software, such as Lucent and Nortel Networks, is often called a telecom company. Manufacturers of networking hardware and software are also sometimes called telecom companies, but are more likely to refer to themselves as data networking or networking companies.

**telecommunications**    Communicating information, including data, text, pictures, voice and video over long distance. See *communications*.

**Telecommunications Act of 1996**    Telecommunications legislation passed by the U.S. Congress in 1996. Although it covers many aspects of the field, the most controversial has been the deregulation of local phone service, allowing competition in this arena for the first time. Long-distance carriers (IXCs) and cable TV companies can get into the local phone business, while local telcos (the LECs) can get into long distance. Some of the major provisions follow.

**Section 251**    Allows states to regulate prices in the local access market.

**Section 254**    Extends universal service to everyone no matter how rural, even if others have to subsidize the expense.

**Section 271**    Provides a 14-point checklist of requirements for RBOCs to offer intrastate long-distance service.

**It Hasn't Been a Picnic**    The RBOCs thought the Act would be a road map for getting into long distance in exchange for ending their local monopolies. What they got were 700 pages of dubious rules that made "deregulating" as complicated as any regulated industry could be. The RBOCs have claimed that the Act discriminates against them and that other large telephone companies have received more favorable treatment. Complaints and lawsuits ensued. Stay tuned.

**telecommunity**    A society in which information can be transmitted or received freely between all members without technical incompatibilities.

**telecommuter**    A person that does telecommuting. See *telecommuting*, *virtual company* and *hoteling*.

**telecommuting**    Working at home and communicating with the office by electronic means. The IT industry was one of the first to implement telecommuting as far back as the 1960s. In those days, a small number of programmers worked at home one or more days a week; however, the only communications link to the office was the telephone. There were no modems attached to desktop computers, because there were no desktop or laptop computers. A few programmers may have had the luxury of a terminal connected to a mainframe or minicomputer, but the majority wrote source code using a pen and paper and created the input (punched the cards) and did the testing at a local datacenter. See *virtual company* and *hoteling*.

**telecon**    (TELEphone CONversation) A plain old voice telephone session with another person.

**teleconferencing**    ("long distance" conferencing) An interactive communications session between three or more users that are geographically separated. See *audioconferencing*, *videoconferencing* and *data conferencing*.

**telecopying**    ("long distance" copying) The formal term for fax.

**teledensity**    The number of telephones in use for every 100 individuals living within an area. A teledensity greater than 100 means there are more telephones than people. Third-world countries may have a teledensity of less than 10.

**telefax**    The european term for a fax machine.

**telegraph**    A low-speed communications device that transmits up to approximately 150 bps. Telegraph grade lines, stemming from the days of Morse code, cannot transmit a voice conversation.

**The Days of the Morse Code**
Data was transmitted at about four to six bits per second in the latter half of the 1800s, which was as fast as a human hand could tap out Morse code. The unit on the right is the telegraph key. A metal bar on the receiver (left) simply banged against another bar when the current passed through, creating a clicking sound.

T

In 1843, the U.S. Congress authorized $30,000 to build a telegraph line between Baltimore and Washington, DC. The wire was strung onto 700 poles, which were placed approximately 300 feet apart. On May 24, 1844, at the U.S. Supreme Court in Washington, Samuel Morse tapped out "What hath God wrought" via telegraph to his assistant Alfred Vail who was waiting at a Baltimore railroad station, some 40 miles away.

**telemanagement**    Management of an organization's telephone and telecommunications systems, which includes maintaining and ordering new equipment and monitoring expenses for usage.

**telematics**    The convergence of telecommunications and information processing. The term has evolved to refer to automobile systems that combine GPS satellite tracking and wireless communications for automatic roadside assistance and remote diagnostics. General Motors was the first to popularize this service with its OnStar system.

**telemedicine**    ("Long distance" medicine) Using videoconferencing for medical diagnosis. With a videoconferencing link to a large medical center, rural health care facilities can perform diagnosis and treatment available only in larger metropolitan areas. A specialist can monitor the patient remotely taking cues from the general practitioner or nurse that is actually examining the patient. A patient's blood can be placed under a microscope in the remote facility and transmitted for examination.

**telemetry**    Transmitting data captured by instrumentation and measuring devices to a remote station where it is recorded and analyzed. For example, data from a weather satellite is telemetered to earth.

**Telenet**    One of the first value-added, packet switching networks that enabled terminals and computers to exchange data. Established in 1975, it was later acquired by Sprint and ultimately integrated into the SprintNet network. See also *Telnet*.

**telephone switch**    A large-scale computer used to route telephone calls in a central office. Such devices are made by Lucent, Nortel and others. See *ESS*, *SS7*, *Class 4 switch*, *Class 5 switch* and *digital cross-connect*.

**telephony**    The science of converting sound into electrical signals, transmitting it within cables or via radio and reconverting it back into sound. It refers to the telephone industry in general.

**telephony server**    A computer in a network that provides telephone integration. The term may refer to the entire system or to just the plug-in boards and software. An Internet telephony server links phone lines to the Internet.

**Telephony Server NLM**    A NetWare NLM that provides an interface between a NetWare server and a PBX. The physical connection is made by cabling the PBX to a card in the server. The NLM provides an open programming interface that allows PBX manufacturers to write drivers for their products.

**teleprinter**    A typewriter-like terminal with a keyboard and built-in printer. In can be a desktop or portable unit. Teleprinters were quite common years ago as input terminals for computers, but have given way to the video screen. Teleprinter-like devices are still used in retail applications where receipts are necessary. As ink jet printers get lighter, they are expected to be built into more notebook computers for sales and similar applications.

**The Teleprinter**
Teleprinters were widely used starting with the very first computers. They lived well into the 1970s as a computer input device. Any keyboard and printing unit can be called a teleprinter.

**teleprocessing**    ("long distance" processing) An early IBM term for data communications.

**teleprocessing monitor**    See *TP monitor*.

**teleservices**    (1) Refers to a variety of enhanced services via telephone, including fax-on-demand, voice mail and computer telephone integration. See *CTI* and *IVR*.

(2) Services by human operators for taking orders and providing customer assistance and other tasks via telephone.

**teleteaching**    See *distance learning*.

**teletext**    A broadcasting service that transmits text to a TV set that has a teletext decoder. It uses the vertical blanking interval of the TV signal (black line between frames when vertical hold is not adjusted) to transmit about a hundred frames. See *videotex*.

**Teletype**    The trade name of Teletype Corporation, which refers to a variety of teleprinters used for communications. The Teletype was one of the first communications terminals in the U.S.

**teletype mode**    Line-at-a-time output like a typewriter. Contrast with *full-screen mode*.

**teletypewriter**    A low-speed teleprinter, often abbreviated "TTY."

**televaulting**    Continuous transmitting of data to vaults for backup purposes. The term was coined by TeleVault Technology, Inc.

**telewebber**    A person that accesses the Web using a personal computer while watching TV.

**The Teletype Machine**
For years, the clicking and clanging of Teletype machines were familiar sounds in the "wire rooms" of many companies.
*(Image courtesy of Honeywell, Inc.)*

**telework**    The work being performed by a telecommuter (teleworker). See *telecommuter*.

**Telex**    An international, dial-up data communications service administered in the U.S. by AT&T, MCI and other providers. In the 1960s, it was the first worldwide, realtime data communications service to use terminals for transmitting and receiving messages. Prior to Telex, telegrams and cablegrams were the primary method for delivering a text message. Although diminishing each year, Telex is still used for commerce in more than 200 countries.

Telex is a low-speed service that transmits Baudot code at 50 bps. It was originally administered worldwide by various carriers and the local PTTs. Western Union handled the U.S., and in 1971, purchased and integrated the Bell System's TXW service. AT&T acquired Western Union's Telex service in 1991.

**Telnet**    A terminal emulation protocol commonly used on the Internet and TCP/IP-based networks. It allows a user at a terminal or computer to log onto a remote device and run a program. Telnet was originally developed for ARPAnet and is an inherent part of the TCP/IP communications protocol.

Although most computers on the Internet that allow Telnet access require users to have an established account and password, there are some that allow the public to run programs such as search utilities (see *Archie*). See also *Telenet*.

**Telon**    See *CA-Telon*.

**TELRIC**    (Total Element Long Run Incremental Cost) A calculation method that ILECs can charge CLECs for interconnection and colocation. See *ILEC* and *CLEC*.

**TEMPEST**    Refers to external electromagnetic radiation from data processing equipment and the security measures used to prevent them. Almost all electronic equipment emanates signals into free space or surrounding conductive objects, such as metal cabinets, wires and pipes. Equipment and cables that meet TEMPEST requirements have extra shielding in order to keep data signals from escaping and being picked up by unauthorized listeners.

```
Telnet - 192.168.1.1                    _ □ X
Connect  Edit  Terminal  Help

Netopia R3100-U v4.3

Easy Setup...

WAN Configuration...

System Configuration...

Utilities & Diagnostics...

Statistics & Logs...

Quick Menus...

Quick View...


Return/Enter goes to Easy Setup -- minimal configuration.
You always start from this main screen.
```

**Telnetting from Windows**
Starting with Windows 95, Windows comes with its own Telnet utility, which is widely used to launch programs on network devices. For example, this Windows Telnet screen is accessing built-in software within a Netopia ISDN router for management and control of its functions. This is the main menu.

**temp folder**   See *temporary folder*.

**template**   **(1)** A pre-designed document or data file formatted for common purposes such as a fax, invoice or business letter. If the document contains an automated process, such as a word processing macro or spreadsheet formula, then the programming is already written and embedded in the appropriate places. It becomes a custom document after filling in the blanks with your data. See *style sheet* and *document*.

   **(2)** A model of an application that is customized by the system designer. See *template-based application*.

   **(3)** A plastic or stiff paper form placed over the function keys on a keyboard to identify their use.

**template-based application**   An application that is customized by filling in predefined fields and/or answering questions. The template provides a basic framework that must be tailored to the requirements of the customer.

**temporary file**   A file created by an application for its own processing purposes. There are numerous reasons for creating such files; for example, when data files are updated, temporary files may be created with the new data. When the operation is completed, the original files are deleted and the temporary files are renamed to the originals. In this way, if a failure occurred during the update process, the originals are still intact. The application is responsible for deleting its temporary files; however, such files often remain on disk when applications are not closed properly. Temporary files generally use a .TMP file extension. See *temporary folder*.

**temporary font**   A soft font that remains in the printer's memory until the printer is reset manually or by software. Contrast with *permanent font*.

**tera**   Trillion (10 to the 12th power). Abbreviated "T." It often refers to the precise value 1,099,511,627,776 since computer specifications are usually binary numbers. See *TB*, *binary values* and *space/time*.

**terabit**   One trillion bits. Also Tb, Tbit and T-bit. See *tera* and *space/time*.

**terabyte**   One trillion bytes. Also TB, Tbyte and T-byte. See *tera* and *space/time*.

**teraflops**   (tera **FL**oating point **OP**erations per **S**econd)  One trillion floating point operations per second.

**terminal**   **(1)** An I/O device for a computer that usually has a keyboard for input and a video screen or printer for output. See *ASCII terminal*.

   **(2)** An input device, such as a scanner, video camera or punched card reader.

   **(3)** An output device in a network, such as a monitor, printer or card punch.

   **(4)** A connector used to attach a wire.

**terminal adapter**   See *ISDN terminal adapter*.

**terminal emulation**   Using a computer to simulate the type of terminal required to gain access to another computer. See *virtual terminal*.

**terminal mode**   An operating mode that causes the computer to act like a terminal; ready to transmit typed-in keystrokes and ready to receive transmitted data.

**terminal server**   **(1)** A computer or controller used to connect multiple terminals to a network or host computer.

   **(2)** See *Windows-based Terminal Server*.

**Terminal Services**   The Windows 2000 counterpart of Windows Terminal Server in Windows NT. See *Windows Terminal Server*.

**terminal session**   **(1)** Interacting with a mainframe, minicomputer or UNIX server from a terminal. When a terminal session is activated in a client machine with a GUI (Windows, Mac, etc.), a window for typing in commands is provided. See *3270 emulator*, *twinax card* and *Telnet*.

   **(2)** The time in which a user is working at a terminal.

**terminal strip**     An insulated bar that contains a set of screws to which wires are attached.

**terminal window**     A dialog box that lets you send commands to your modem. In Windows 95/98 Dial-Up Networking (DUN), you have the option of bringing up a terminal window before or after you dial your number.

**termination**     The point where a line, channel or circuit ends. See *SCSI termination* and *hybrid*.

**terminator**     (1) A character that ends a string of alphanumeric characters.

(2) A hardware component that is connected to the last peripheral device in a series or the last node in a network.

**terminology**     The terminology used in the computer and telecommunications field adds tremendous confusion not only for the lay person, but for the technicians themselves. What many do not realize is that terms are made up by anybody and everybody in a nonchalant, casual manner without any regard or understanding of their ultimate ramifications. Programmers come up with error messages that make sense to them at the moment, and never give a thought that people actually have to read them when something goes wrong. In addition, marketing people turn everything upside down, naming things based on how high-tech and sexy they sound. And, the worst of all is naming specific technologies with generic words. See *naming fiascos* and *technical writer*.

**terrestrial**     Dealing with the earth. See *terrestrial link*.

**terrestrial link**     A communications line that travels on, near or below ground. Contrast with *satellite link*.

**tessellation**     In surface modeling and solid modeling, the method used to represent 3-D objects as a collection of triangles or other polygons. All surfaces, both curved and straight, are turned into triangles either at the time they are first created or in realtime when they are rendered. The more triangles used to represent a surface, the more realistic the rendering, but the more computation is required.

Triangles may also be discarded at the time they are rendered depending on their distance from the camera. Some applications create multiple models with different amounts of triangles and use the best one, depending on distance. The vertices (end points) of the triangles are assigned X-Y-Z and RGB values, which are used to compute light reflections for shading and rendering.

Tessellation is not used in 2-D graphics. Although 2-D graphics may be used to draw 3-D objects, any simulation of depth and shading must be created by the artist using standard drawing tools, color fills and gradients. See *surface normal* and *triangle*.

**test automation software**     Software used to test new revisions of software by automatically entering a predefined set of commands and inputs.

**test data**     A set of data created for testing new or revised programs. It should be developed by the user as well as the programmer and must contain a sample of every category of valid data and many invalid conditions.

**testing**     Running new or revised programs to determine whether they process all data properly. For professional certification testing, see *certification*. For proficiency and aptitude tests, see *aptitude tests*. See also *test data*, *black box testing* and *white box testing*.

**TeX**     A typesetting language used in a variety of typesetting environments. It uses embedded codes within the text of the document to initiate changes in layout, including the ability to describe elaborate scientific formulas.

**texel**     (TEXture ELement) The smallest addressable unit of a texture map. When objects in the image are near, one texel is mapped to one or more screen pixels. When objects are distant, multiple texels are averaged into one screen pixel. See *texture map*.

**text**     Words, sentences and paragraphs. Contrast with *data*, which are defined units, such as name and amount due. Text may also refer to alphanumeric data, such as name and address, to distinguish it from numeric data, such as quantity and dollar amounts. A page of text takes about 2,000–4,000 bytes. See *text field*.

**text based**   Also called "character based," the display of text and graphics as a fixed set of predefined characters. For example, 25 rows of 80 columns. Contrast with *graphics based*.

**text box**   An on-screen rectangular frame into which you type text. Text boxes are used to add text in a drawing or paint program. The flexibility of the text box is determined by the software. Sometimes you can keep on typing and the box expands to meet your input. Other times, you have to go into a different mode to widen the frame, and then go back to typing in more text.

**text editing**   The ability to change text by adding, deleting and rearranging letters, words, sentences and paragraphs.

**text editor**   Software used to create and edit files that contain only text—for example, batch files, address lists and source language programs. Text editors produce raw ASCII or EBCDIC text files and, unlike word processors, do not usually provide word wrap or formatting (underline, boldface, fonts, etc.).

Editors designed for writing source code may provide automatic indention and multiple windows into the same file. They may also display the reserved words of a particular programming language in boldface or in a different font, but they do not embed format codes in the file. See *DOS Editor*.

**text entry**   Entering alphanumeric text characters into the computer. It implies typing the characters on a keyboard. See *data entry*.

**text entry box**   A rectangular on-screen box, or field, that accepts the text you type in.

**text field**   A data structure that holds alphanumeric data, such as name and address. If a text field holds large, or unlimited, amounts of text, it may be called a "memo field." Contrast with *numeric field*.

**text file**   A file that contains only text characters. See *ASCII file*. Contrast with *graphics file* and *binary file*.

**text management**   The creation, storage and retrieval of text. It implies flexible retrieval capabilities that can search for text based on a variety of criteria. Although a word processor manages text, it usually has limited retrieval capabilities.

**text messaging**   Sending short messages to a smart phone, pager, PDA or other handheld device. Text messaging implies sending short messages generally no more than a couple of hundred characters in length. In Europe, text messaging was popularized by the GSM cellphone system's Short Messaging Service (SMS), which supports messages of up to 160 characters. See *GSM* and *SMS*.

**text mode**   (1) A screen display mode that displays only text and not graphics. Before graphical user interfaces were common, the text mode was the primary mode built into display systems, and graphics mode was an optional mode, if available. See *text based*.

(2) A program mode that allows text to be entered and edited.

**text-to-speech**   Converting text into voice output using speech synthesis techniques. Although initially used by the blind to listen to written material, it is now used extensively to convey financial data and other information via telephone for everyone. See *screen reader*.

**texture map**   A two-dimensional image of a surface that is used to cover 3-D objects. See *texture mapping*.

**texture mapping**   In computer graphics, the application of a type of surface to a 3-D image. A texture can be uniform, such as a brick wall, or irregular, such as wood grain or marble.

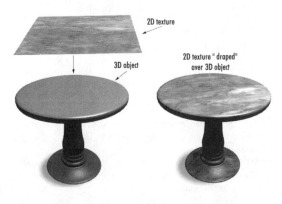

**Applying a Texture Map**
A 2-D texture map is "draped" over a 3-D object to create the required surface. *(Image courtesy of Intergraph Computer Systems.)*

The common method is to create a 2-D bitmapped image of the texture, called a "texture map," which is then "wrapped around" the 3-D object. An alternate method is to compute the texture entirely via mathematics instead of bitmaps. The latter method is not widely used but can create more precise textures, especially if there is great depth to the objects being textured. See *texel, point sampling, bilinear interpolation, trilinear interpolation, MIP mapping, procedural texture* and *volumetric texture.*

**texture memory**    Memory on the display adapter used to hold the texture maps. See *texture mapping.*

**TFT**    (Thin Film Transistor) The term typically refers to active matrix screens on laptop computers. Active matrix LCD provides a sharper screen display and broader viewing angle than does passive matrix. See *LCD* and *thin film.*

**TFT LCD**    (Thin Film Transistor LCD) See *LCD.*

**TFTP**    (Trivial File Transfer Protocol) A version of the TCP/IP FTP protocol that has no directory or password capability.

**theme-based search**    A search for information based on a subject such as sports, automobiles or computers.

**thermal dye transfer**    See *dye sublimation printer.*

**thermal grease**    A conductive substance that is used to transfer heat from one device to another. When a heat sink is attached to a chip, there is a huge number of microscopic gaps between the two surfaces. The thermal grease helps bond the two surfaces and transfer the heat more effectively. See *heat sink.*

**thermal printer**    See *direct thermal printer* and *thermal wax transfer printer.*

**thermal recalibration**    The periodic sensing of the temperature in hard disk drives in order to make minor adjustments to the alignment of the read/write heads. In an AV drive, this process is performed only in idle periods so that there is no interruption in reading and writing long streams of data. See *AV drive.*

**thermal sensor**    A device that detects temperature. Thermal sensors are found in many laptops and desktop PCs in order to sound an alarm when a certain temperature has been exceeded.

**thermal transfer**    See *thermal wax transfer printer* and *direct thermal printer.*

**thermal wax transfer printer**    A printer that adheres a wax-based ink onto paper. It uses a ribbon containing an equivalent panel of ink for each page to be printed. Monochrome printers have an equivalent black panel for each page to be printed. Color printers have either three (CMY) or four (CMYK) consecutive panels for each page, thus the same amount of ribbon is used to print a full-page image as it is to print a tenth of the page. Coated paper is used, and

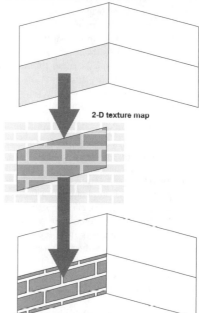

3-D object before texture is applied

2-D texture map

3-D object after texture is applied

**Bitmap Texture Mapping**
Each pixel in the 3-D object is mapped to a corresponding texel in the 2-D texture map.
*(Redrawn from illustration courtesy of Intergraph Computer Systems.)*

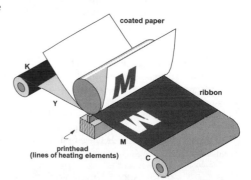

**Thermal Wax Transfer Mechanism**
The paper and ribbon are passed by the printhead. The ribbon is heated, and dots of ink are transferred to the paper. Monochrome ribbons contain a black panel equivalent in size to each page being printed. Color ribbons contain three (CMY) or four (CMYK) panels for each page to be printed.

consumables (ribbon and paper) cost more than other printer technologies, except for dye sublimation printing.

The paper and ribbon are passed together over the printhead, which contains from hundreds to thousands of heating elements. Dots of ink are melted and transferred to the paper. The wax-based ink will adhere to almost any kind of stock, from ordinary paper to complex synthetics and film.

Thermal wax uses the same type of transport mechanism as dye sublimation, but does not produce the same photorealistic output. Like other monochrome and color printers, thermal wax puts down a solid dot of ink, and produces shades of gray and colors by placing dots side by side (dithering). Wax transfer does print faster than dye sub and consumables (ribbon and paper) are less expensive. Some printers allow swapping of both ribbons so that thermal wax can be used for draft quality and dye sublimation for final output. See *dye sublimation printer* and *printer*.

**thick film**    A layer of magnetic, semiconductor or metallic material that is thicker than the microscopic layers of the transistors on a chip. For example, metallic thick films are silk screened onto the ceramic base of hybrid microcircuits. Contrast with *thin film*.

**thin client**    (1) A "thin processing" client in a client/server environment that performs very little data processing. The client processes only keyboard input and screen output, and all application processing is done in the server. Examples are X Window terminals and Windows terminals. See *X Window* and *Windows terminal*. Contrast with *fat client*, which is a typical desktop PC performing all or most of the application processing.

(2) A "thin storage" client in a network computer environment. The client downloads the program from the server and performs processing just like a PC, but does not store anything locally. All programs and data are on the server. This is a new and different definition for thin client created by the NC community.

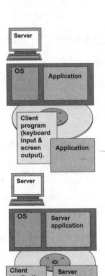

The Only True
Thin Client!

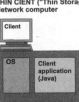

THIN CLIENT ("Thin Processing")
X Window terminal,
Windows terminal,
ICA terminal

THIN CIENT ("Thin Storage")
Network computer

**Thin Clients**
The original thin client (top) performs no application processing. The network computer definition below it refers to not providing storage, but it does the same types of client processing as in a PC.

**thin film**    A microscopically thin layer of semiconductor or magnetic material that is deposited onto a metal, ceramic or semiconductor base. For example, the layers that make up a chip and the surface coating on high-density magnetic disks are called thin films.

**thin film head**    A read/write head for high-density disks that is made from thin layers of a conducting film deposited onto a nickel-iron core.

**ThinkPad**    A family of popular notebook computers from IBM. The ThinkPads include the TrackPoint pointing stick, which IBM introduced and popularized. The ThinkPads were first to offer the largest LCD screens that became available.

**thin pipe**    A low-speed communications channel. Contrast with *fat pipe*.

**thin server**    (1) A network-based computer specialized for some function such as a print server, ISDN router or network attached storage (NAS). Designed for ease of installation, it has little expandability and no keyboard or monitor. Web server software is typically built in, allowing management and control via a Web browser residing on any client platform in the network. See *ETI* and *Web server*.

**The ThinkPad**
IBM's ThinkPad has introduced innovative features, such as the TrackBall pointing stick, TrackWrite keyboard and ever-increasing screen size.

**(2)** A rack-mounted server. 1U and 2U servers can be stacked on top of each other and take up considerably less space than tower cases. See *rack mounted*.

**third-generation computer**    A computer that uses integrated circuits, disk storage and online terminals. The third generation started roughly in 1964 with the IBM System/360.

**third-generation language**    Also known as a *3GL*, it refers to a high-level programming language such as FORTRAN, COBOL, BASIC, Pascal and C. It is a step above assembly language and a step below fourth-generation language (4GL). For an example of the difference between a 3GL and a 4GL, see *fourth-generation language*.

**third normal form**    See *normalization*.

**third party**    An organization that provides an auxiliary product not supplied by the primary manufacturer. Countless third-party add-on and plug-in products keep the computer industry advancing at a rapid pace. It is the third-party vendor that is often the most inventive and innovative.

**thrashing**    Excessive paging in a virtual memory computer. If programs are not written to run in a virtual memory environment, the operating system may spend excessive amounts of time swapping program pages in and out of the disk.

The goal of virtual memory is to increase internal memory capacity, not to waste time reloading program segments over and over. However, a well-designed virtual memory system tracks page usage and prevents the most-often-used modules from being swapped to disk.

**thread**    **(1)** One transaction or message in a multithreaded system. See *multithreading*.

**(2)** A topic or theme in an Internet newsgroup or groupware program that generates on-going e-mail from interested parties. See *threaded discussion*.

**threaded connector**    A plug and socket that uses a threaded mechanism to lock them together. One part is screwed into the other. F and SMA connectors are examples of threaded connectors.

**threaded discussion**    A running log of remarks and opinions about a subject. Users e-mail their comments, and the computer maintains them in order of originating message and replies to that message. Threaded discussions are used in chat rooms on the Internet and on online services, as well as in groupware products.

**threading**    See *multithreading*.

**three degrees of freedom**    See *6DOF*.

**three-state logic element**    An electronic component that provides three possible outputs: off, low voltage and high voltage.

**three-tier client/server**    A three-way interaction in a client/server environment, in which the user interface is stored in the client, the bulk of the business application logic is stored in one or more servers, and the data is stored in a database server. See *two-tier client/server*.

**threshold**    The point at which a signal (voltage, current, etc.) is perceived as valid.

**throughput**    The speed with which a computer processes data. It is a combination of internal processing speed, peripheral speeds (I/O) and the efficiency of the operating system and other system software all working together.

**thru-hole**    A circuit board packaging technique in which the leads (pins) on the chips and components are inserted into holes in the board. The leads are bent 90 degrees under the board, snipped off and soldered from below. Contrast with *surface mount*.

T

**thumb**    (1) Also called an "elevator," it is the square box that slides within a scroll bar. The thumb is dragged up and down to position the text or image on screen.

(2) (Thumb) An extension to the architecture of an ARM chip that provides enhanced code density. It stores a subset of 32-bit instructions as compressed 16-bit instructions and decompresses them back to 32 bits upon execution.

**thumb culture**    Refers to handheld, wireless devices that users often work with their thumbs.

**thumbnail**    A miniature representation of a page or image. A thumbnail program may be stand-alone or part of a desktop publishing or graphics program. Thumbnails take considerable time to generate, but provide a convenient way to browse through multiple images before retrieving the one you need. Programs often let you click on the thumbnail to retrieve it.

**thunk**    In a PC, to execute the instructions required to switch between segmented addressing of memory and flat addressing. A thunk typically occurs when a 16-bit application is running in a 32-bit address space, and its 16-bit segmented address must be converted into a full 32-bit flat address. On the other hand, if a 32-bit program calls a 16-bit DLL, then the thunk is in the opposite direction: from 32 bit to 16 bit.

**THz**    (TeraHertZ) One trillion cycles per second.

**TI**    (Texas Instruments, Inc., Dallas, TX, www.ti.com) A leading semiconductor manufacturer founded in 1930 as Geophysical Service, an independent contractor specializing in petroleum exploration using sound waves (reflection seismograph method). In 1938, it spun off Geophysical Services, Inc., a Delaware subsidiary, to do explorations for others. The parent company was later renamed Coronado Corporation, which ultimately dissolved in 1945.

In 1941, GSI was purchased by three employees and one of the original founders. The next day, the Japanese bombed Pearl Harbor, and the company found itself making equipment that would find enemy submarines, not just oil.

**First Transistor**
In 1954, TI pioneered the commercialization of the silicon transistor. *(Image courtesy of Texas Instruments, Inc.)*

**The First Handheld Calculator**
In 1967, TI introduced this handheld calculator. People were as excited to use this machine as they were when portable computers came on the scene a decade and a half later. *(Image courtesy of Texas Instruments, Inc.)*

In 1951, GSI's name was changed to Texas Instruments, and soon after it began making transistors via a licensing arrangement with Western Electric. In 1954, TI pioneered the first commercial production of transistors made from silicon, and in that same year, introduced the first pocket-sized transistor radio.

In 1958, TI's Jack Kilby demonstrated the first integrated circuit (IC), which incorporated several transistors on a single chip. Three years later, it demonstrated a working computer using ICs that were six cubic inches in size and weighed only 10 ounces. TI produced a complete computer on a chip in 1971.

In the early 1980s, TI made a large number of low-priced 99/4a home computers. It later introduced desktop PCs, but then discontinued them. Offering a line of notebook PCs for several years, it was sold to the Acer Group in 1997.

As the first to commercialize the silicon transistor, pocket radio, integrated circuit, handheld calculator, single-chip computer and the LISP chip, TI has a long history of contributions to the electronics and computer industry.

**TIA**    (1) (Telecommunications Industry Association, Arlington, VA, www.tiaonline.org) A membership organization founded in 1988 that sets telecommunications standards worldwide. It was originally an EIA working group that was spun off and merged with the U.S. Telecommunications Suppliers Association (USTSA), sponsors of the annual SUPERCOMM conferences.

(2) Digispeak for "thanks in advance."

(3) (The Internet Adapter) An earlier utility that emulated a SLIP connection, enabling access to the Internet without a SLIP account.

**TIB/Rendezvous** (The Information Bus/Rendezvous) Messaging middleware from TIBCO Software Inc., Palo Alto, CA (www.tibco.com) that provides the foundation for the TIB/ActiveEnterprise suite of application integration products. TIB/Rendezvous supports request/supply and publish and subscribe models, and connects to SAP, PeopleSoft and other legacy systems via application adapters. There are also interfaces to MQSeries and MSMQ messaging systems and COM.

**tick** One clock cycle, or one "tick" of the clock. See *clock cycle*.

**tickle** See *Tcl/Tk* and *tickle packet*.

**tickle packet** A data packet sent in a communications system in order to keep the line open and prevent a timeout. See *timeout*.

**tickler** A manual or automatic system for reminding users of scheduled events or tasks. It is used in PIMs, contact management systems and scheduling and calendar systems.

**Tier 1** The top level of something. A Tier 1 city is one of the major metropolitan areas in a country. A Tier 1 vendor is one of the largest and most well known in its field. However, the term can sometimes refer to the bottom level or first floor. For example, the U.S. government labels Tier 1 Y2K compliance as the bottom level.

**TIFF** (Tagged Image File Format) A widely used bitmapped graphics file format developed by Aldus and Microsoft that handles monochrome, gray scale, and 8- and 24-bit color. TIFF allows for customization, and several versions have been created, which does not guarantee compatibility between all programs.

TIFF files are compressed using several compression methods. LZW provides ratios of about 1.5:1 to 2:1. Ratios of 10:1 to 20:1 are possible for documents with lots of white space using ITU Group III and IV compression methods (fax). See *JPEG*.

**tight code** Refers to a program that is written very efficiently. A very experienced and intelligent programmer can produce a program with much tighter code than a novice. The difference can be like night and day.

**tightly coupled** Refers to two or more computers linked together and dependent on each other. One computer may control the other, or both computers may monitor each other. For example, a database machine is tightly coupled to the main processor. Two computers tied together for multiprocessing are tightly coupled. Contrast with *loosely coupled*, such as personal computers in a LAN.

**tile** To display objects side by side. The Tile command in a graphical interface squares up all open windows and displays them in a row and column order.

**timbre** A quality of sound that distinguishes one voice or musical instrument from another. For example, MIDI synthesizers are multi-timbral, meaning that they can play multiple instruments simultaneously.

**time base generator** An electronic clock that creates its own timing signals for synchronization and measurement purposes.

**time-of-day clock** See *realtime clock*.

**timeout** In communications, the intentional ending of an incomplete task. If an acknowledgment, carrier, logon, etc., has not occurred in a specified amount of time, the timeout ends the waiting loop so that the request can be retransmitted or the process terminated. Timeouts are common in communications applications in order to free up a line or port that is tied up with a request that has not been answered in a reasonable amount of time. For each type of situation, there is a default length of time before the timeout is initiated, which typically can be adjusted by the user or network administrator. See *tickle packet*.

**timer interrupt** An interrupt generated by an internal clock. See *interrupt*.

**timesharing**   A multiuser computer environment that lets users initiate their own sessions and access selected databases as required, such as when using online services. A system that serves many users, but for only one application, is technically not timesharing.

**time shifting**   Recording a TV program for later viewing. Rather than using a VCR and playing back the tape, personal video recorders (PVRs) have become the most advanced way to time shift as everything you watch can be replayed at a later date. See *PVR*.

**time slice**   A short interval of time allotted to each user or program in a multitasking or timesharing system. Time slices are typically in milliseconds.

**time slot**   Continuously repeating interval of time or a time period in which two devices are able to interconnect.

**time synchronization**   See *realtime clock*, *UTC* and *NTP*.

**timing clock**   See *clock*.

**timing signals**   Electrical pulses generated in the processor or in external devices in order to synchronize computer operations. The main timing signal comes from the computer's clock, which provides a frequency that can be divided into many slower cycles. Other timing signals may come from a timesharing or realtime clock.

   In disk drives, timing signals for reading and writing are generated by holes or marks on one of the platters, or by the way the digital data is actually recorded.

**tin**   (Threaded Internet Newsreader) A newsreader for Usenet newsgroups that maintains message threads. It is based on the tass newsreader, which was derived from Plato Notes. See *Usenet*.

**T interface**   The interface used between network terminator 1 (NT1) and 2 (NT2) in an ISDN connection. This is an internal interface in the U.S., but external in other countries. See *ISDN*.

**Tiny BASIC**   A subset of BASIC that has been used in first-generation personal computers with limited memory.

**tip and ring**   The transmit and receive wires on a telephone. The terms were derived in the early days when operators manually plugged the line into a cord board (manual switchboard). In order to see whether a particular extension was already in use, the operator touched the tip of the plug to the outer ring of the extension socket on the board. Known as "tipping," if static was heard, the line was busy.

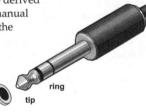

**TI-RPC**   (Transport-Independent-Remote Procedure Call) A set of functions from Sun for executing procedures on remote computers. It is operating system and network independent and allows the development of distributed applications in multivendor environments.

**Tivoli Enterprise Management**   A comprehensive suite of applications from IBM subsidiary Tivoli Systems, Inc., Austin, TX (www.tivoli.com) that provides enterprise-wide network and systems management across all platforms, from IBM mainframes to desktop PCs.

**Tk**   (ToolKit) A graphical user interface (GUI) library originally developed for the Tcl programming language. Tk is also used with the Perl, Python and Scheme languages. See *Tcl/Tk*.

**TLA**   (Three Letter Acronym) The epitome of acronyms! While two-, four- and five-letter acronyms exist, there are more three-letter acronyms. Obviously, three words to describe a concept or product is the most popular.

**TLAN**   See *transparent LAN service*.

**TLD**    (Top-Level Domain) The highest level domain category in the Internet domain naming system. There are two types: the generic top-level domains, such as .com, .org, and .net, and the country codes, such as .ca, .uk and .jp. See *Internet domain name*.

**TLI**    (Transport Level Interface) A common interface for transport services (layer 4 of the OSI model). It provides a common language to a transport protocol and allows client/server applications to be used in different networking environments.

Instead of directly calling NetWare's SPX, for example, the application calls the TLI library. Thus, any transport protocol that is TLI compliant (SPX, TCP, etc.) can provide transport services to that application. TLI is part of UNIX System V. It is also supported by NetWare 3.x. See *STREAMS*.

**TLS**    (1) (Transport Layer Security) A security protocol from the IETF that is a merger of SSL and other protocols. It is expected to become a major security standard on the Internet, eventually superseding SSL. TLS is backward compatible with SSL and uses Triple DES encryption. See *SSL* and *DES*.

(2) (Transparent LAN Service) A communications service from the telephone companies that connects LANs in different locations. The service is provided via copper or fiber lines and is called "transparent," because the customer connects at both ends via the same protocol.

**TM1**    (Tables Manager 1) A multidimensional analysis program for DOS and Windows from Applix, Inc., Westboro, MA (www.applix.com). It allows data to be viewed in up to eight dimensions. The data is kept in a database; and the formulas are kept in a spreadsheet, which is used as a viewer into the database. TM1 makes it easy to display different slices of the data, and it is designed to import and cross tab large amounts of data. TM1 was originally developed by Sinper Corporation.

**TMDS**    (Transmission Minimized Differential Signalling) A transmission method for sending digital information to a flat panel display. TMDS is used in the VESA Plug and Display, DFP and DVI interfaces. TMDS is a variation of LVDS, but converts an 8-bit signal into a 10-bit signal to minimize voltage swings and provide more tolerance. See *DVI*, *LVDS* and *flat panel display*.

**TMN**    (Telecommunications Management Network) A set of international standards for network management from the ITU. It is used by large carriers such as Sprint, MCI WorldCom and AT&T.

**TN**    (Twisted Nematic) The first LCD technology. It twists liquid crystal molecules 90 degrees between polarizers. TN displays require bright ambient light and are still used for low-cost applications. See *STN* and *LCD*.

**TN3270**    (TelNet 3270) A client program that includes the 3270 protocol for logging onto IBM mainframes. Using the TCP/IP networking protocol, it is widely used to connect a desktop computer to a mainframe and emulate a mainframe terminal (3270) session.

**TNT**    (1) (Transparent Network Transport) Services from the telephone companies and common carriers that provide Ethernet and Token Ring transmission over MANs and WANs.

(2) A DOS extender from Phar Lap Software, Cambridge, MA (www.pharlap.com) that allows DOS applications to use various Win32 features, including memory allocation, DLLs and threads.

**toaster**    See *intranet toaster* and *Video Toaster*.

**TOF**    (Top Of Form) The beginning of a physical paper form. To position paper in many printers, the printer is turned offline, the forms are aligned properly and the TOF button is pressed.

**toggle**    To alternate back and forth between two states.

**toggle switch**    A device that opens and closes an electric circuit. It uses a lever that is moved back and forth; a light switch on the wall being a common example. Old computers often had rows of toggle switches on their consoles, making them look very formidable.

**token**    See *token passing* and *authentication token*.

**token bus network**    A LAN access method that uses the token passing technology. Stations are logically connected in a ring but are physically connected by a common bus. All tokens are broadcast to every station in the network, but only the station with the destination address responds. After transmitting a maximum amount of data, the token is passed to the next logical station in the ring. The MAP factory automation protocol uses this method. See *token passing*.

**token passing**    A communications network access method that uses a continuously repeating frame (the token) that is transmitted onto the network by the controlling computer. When a terminal or computer wants to send a message, it waits for an empty token. When it finds one, it fills it with the address of the destination station and some or all of its message.

Every computer and terminal on the network constantly monitors the passing tokens to determine whether it is a recipient of a message, in which case it "grabs" the message and resets the token status to empty. Token passing uses bus and ring topologies. See *token bus network* and *token ring network*.

**Token Ring**    A local area network (LAN) developed by IBM (IEEE 802.5). It uses a token ring access method and connects up to 255 nodes in a star topology at 4 or 16 Mbps. All stations connect to a central wiring hub called the "Multistation Access Unit" (MAU) using a twisted wire cable. The central hub makes it easier to troubleshoot failures than a bus topology. This is a different type of hub than the one used in 10BaseT twisted pair Ethernet networks.

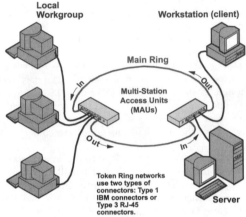
**Token Ring Topology**
Token Ring uses a logical ring topology, which provides more equal opportunity for each station to gain access to the network than the broadcast method used by Ethernet. All nodes connect to the MAU.

Token Ring is more deterministic than Ethernet. It ensures that all users get regular turns at transmitting their data. With Ethernet, all users compete to get onto the network.

There are two types of Token Ring networks. Type 1 Token Ring networks allow up to 255 stations per network and use shielded twisted pair wires with IBM-style Type 1 connectors. Type 3 Token Rings allow up to 72 devices per network and use unshielded twisted pair (Category 3, 4 or 5) with RJ-45 connectors.

Token Ring is a data link protocol (MAC layer protocol) and functions at layers 1 and 2 of the OSI model. See *data link protocol* and *OSI*.

**Token Ring adapter**    A network adapter used in a token ring network. See *network adapter*.

**Token Ring connector**    Called a "Type 1 connector" and developed by IBM, it is a combination plug and socket. Flip any connector 180 degrees with the other and they plug together.

**token ring network**    A LAN access method that uses the token passing technology in a physical ring. Each station in the network passes the token on to the station next to it. Token Ring and FDDI LANs use the token ring access method. See *Token Ring*, *FDDI* and *token passing*.

**TokenTalk**    Software for the Macintosh from Apple that accompanies its TokenTalk NB board and adapts the Mac to Token Ring networks.

**Type 1 IBM Connector**

Type 1 connectors are used in Token Ring networks. The same connector is both plug and socket just by flipping one 180 degrees with the other.

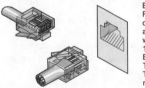
**RJ-45 Connector (Ethernet, Token Ring)**

Eight-wire RJ-45 connectors are used with 10BaseT Ethernet and Type 3 Token Ring networks.

**toll office**   A telephone central office that generates toll call transactions. Toll accounting used to be performed in tandem offices, but today is mostly generated in the end offices. See *tandem office* and *end office*.

**toll quality audio**   Audio transmission at the quality level of an ordinary long distance telephone call. The standard of performance is generally a PCM line. See *PCM*.

**toll switch**   A telephone central office switch (telco switch) that generates toll call transaction. Today, the end office switches provide most of the call accounting. See *end office switch* and *tandem switch*.

**toll/tandem office**   See *toll office*.

**toll/tandem switch**   See *toll switch*.

**tombstoning**   Refers to a discrete component (resistor, capacitor, etc.) that has turned straight up instead of laying flat as it goes through the soldering process. It can be caused by uneven amounts of soldering paste at different ends of the component or by shadows on the board causing different temperatures at the ends.

**tomography**   An X-ray technique that shows a single plane (slice) of the object under examination, typically a part of the human body. See *CAT scan*.

**toneloc**   (TONE LOCator) A program that looks for dial tone by randomly dialing numbers or dialing within a range. It can also look for a carrier frequency of a modem or fax. ToneLoc uses a file that contains the area codes and number ranges to dial. See *war dialer*.

**toner**   An electrically charged ink used in copy machines and laser printers. It adheres to an invisible image that has been charged with the opposite polarity onto a plate or drum, or onto the paper itself.

**TONS**   (Transparent Optical Networking Services) A marketing term for providing dark fiber to a customer. The customer is responsible for generating the transmission signal and interpreting it at the other end. See *dark fiber*.

**tool**   (1) A program used for software development or system maintenance. Virtually any program or utility that helps programmers or users develop applications or maintain their computers can be called a tool. Examples of programming tools are compilers, interpreters, assemblers, 4GLs, editors, debuggers and application generators. See *toolkit* and *Tools menu*.

(2) A program that helps the user analyze or search for data. For example, query and report programs are often called query tools and report tools.

(3) An on-screen function in a graphics program, for example, a line draw, circle draw or brush tool.

(4) Any function that sets up preferences in an application. A "Tools menu" is another way of labeling an "Options menu."

**toolbar**   A row or column of on-screen buttons used to activate functions in the application. Some toolbars are customizable, letting you add and delete buttons as required. See *tool palette*.

**A Toolbar with Tools!**
Most toolbar buttons show only pictures, while some have a text explanation, too. This toolbar from VTEL's videoconferencing software has real tools on it!

**ToolBook**   A courseware development system for Windows from click2learn.com, Bellevue, WA (www.click2learn.com) that uses a "page and book" metaphor analogous to Apple's HyperCard "card and stack." Its OpenScript language is also similar to HyperTalk.

**toolbox**   See *toolkit* and *toolbar*.

**toolkit**   An integrated set of software routines or utilities (tools) that are used to develop and maintain applications and databases. There are toolkits for developing almost anything. See *tool, developer's toolkit, library, class library, Encyclopedia Toolkit* and *CASE*.

**tool palette**   A collection of buttons (icons) grouped on screen that provide a quick way to select available functions by pointing and clicking. Tool palettes were originally used with graphics applications such as paint, drawing and image editing programs. With the advent of graphical interfaces, they migrated to business applications. Some tool palettes can be customized, allowing you to display only the tools you use most often and leaving the rest to be selected by menus. See *toolbar*.

**Tools menu**   A menu of options that let you configure your software to your preferences. Such menus are also called Options menus and Preferences menus. Sometimes, there is a Tools option inside an Options menu, or an Options selection inside a Tools menu. In either case, Tools | Options and Preferences let you customize your application.

**tools vendor**   A publisher of development software used by programmers, which includes compilers, debuggers, visual programming utilities and CASE products. A tools vendor may provide a variety of utilities and routines that assist programmers and systems analysts. See *tool*.

**TOP**   (Technical Office Protocol) A communications protocol for office systems developed by Boeing Computer Services, Seattle, WA (www.boeing.com). It uses the Ethernet access method and is often used in conjunction with *MAP*, the factory automation protocol developed by GM. TOP is used in the front office, and MAP is used on the factory floor. TOP uses the CSMA/CD access method, while MAP uses token bus.

**topdown design**   A design technique that starts with the highest level of an idea and works its way down to the lowest level of detail.

**topdown programming**   A programming design and documentation technique that imposes a hierarchical structure on the design of the program. See *structured programming*.

**top-level domain**   See *TLD* and *Internet domain name*.

**top of file**   The beginning of a file. In a word processing file, it is the first character in the document. In a data file, it is either the first record in the file or the first record in the index. For example, in a dBASE file that is indexed on name, **goto top** might go to physical record #608 if record #608 is AARDVARK.

**topographic map**   A map depicting terrain relief showing ground elevation, usually through either contour lines or spot elevations. The map represents the horizontal and vertical positions of the features represented. It is a graphic representation delineating natural and man-made features of an area or region in a way that shows their relative positions and elevations. (Data West Research Agency definition: see **GIS glossary**.)

**topology**   (1) In a communications network, the pattern of interconnection between nodes, for example, a bus, ring or star configuration.

(2) In a parallel processing architecture, the interconnection between processors, for example, a bus, grid, hypercube or Butterfly Switch configuration.

**TOPS**   (1) A multiuser, multitasking, timesharing, virtual memory operating system from Digital that runs on its PDP-6, DECsystem 10 and DECsystem 20 series.

(2) (Transparent OPerating System) A peer-to-peer LAN from Sitka Corporation, Alameda, CA, that uses the LocalTalk access method and connects Apple computers, PCs and Sun workstations. Its Flashcard plugs LocalTalk capability into PCs.

**top-tier vendor**   A vendor of a product that is highly recognized for its brand name. Examples of top-tier PC vendors are Compaq, HP and IBM.

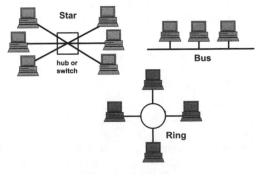

**Network Topologies**
These are the three major topologies used in networks. Ethernet uses bus, hub and switch topologies. Token Ring uses ring and switch.

**TOS** (1) (Terms Of Service) See *acceptable use policy*.

(2) (**Type Of Service**) A field in an IP packet (IP datagram) that is used for quality of service (QoS). The TOS field is 8 bits, broken into five subfields.

**TOTAL** An early network DBMS from Cincom Systems, Inc., Cincinnati, OH (www.cincom.com) that ran on a variety of minis and mainframes.

**total bypass** Bypassing local and long distance telephone lines by using satellite communications.

**total internal reflection** Light that is reflected back from the edge of the medium it is traveling through. When light rays travel at an angle greater than the "critical" angle, which is determined by the medium, the light reflects back into the medium. When they are less than the critical angle (more perpendicular), the light is refracted out of the medium and lost to the outside. See *refractive index*.

**to the recruiter** One of the most important things for a recruiter to understand about the psychology of technical people is the split between systems analysis & design and programming.

The skills required of a systems analyst, or the programmer analyst or business analyst who functions as a systems analyst, are different than a programmer or technical professional.

Analysts with experience in a specific type of vertical application, such as insurance and manufacturing, are more valuable to another company with the same application. Since there are fundamentals that apply to all information systems, analysts ocassionally do cross industry lines. For example, good listening and interviewing skills are as important as technical knowledge in designing information systems. An analyst with an abundance of these skills can work with new applications successfully. However, analysts with moderate listening and interviewing skills are generally more successful in the same niche industry, because they are more familiar, hopefully, with the nuances of the business.

Programmers are also sought with application experience, for example, a COBOL programmer in banking. However, programmers can cross application boundaries much more easily than systems analysts. Programmers often have little allegiance to their company's industry in the first place, being more concerned with the software environment they work with. It can also take years to learn the nuances of a language, and many programmers do not like to learn a new one.

As far as getting work done on time, it is more important that the programmer have experience with the type of functions required in the program than the nature of the business. If the functional specifications have been well designed, then coding the program is based on the kinds of algorithms required and the complexity of the interface.

Coding routine data processing operations is typically much easier than reworking the user interface, especially if some new kind of user interaction is required that is not part of the GUI library and must be "hand coded." All of it depends on the tools being used and the experience level of the programmer. These variables should not be underestimated, because what can take one programmer one month to do can take another one hour. A programmer's experience, skill level and innate analytic ability can make that much of a difference.

The point is that programmers—as well as technical staff at the programming level, such as systems programmers, systems administrators, network administrators and database administrators—can easily cross industry lines as long as they continue to be involved in their niche hardware and software, such as the hardware platform, programming language, operating system and network protocols. See *programmer*, *computercruiter* and *nerd rustler*.

**touchpad** A stationary pointing device that provides a small, flat surface that you slide your finger over using the same movements as you would a mouse. You can tap on the pad's surface as an alternative to pressing one of the touchpad keys. See *mouse*, *trackball* and *pointing stick*.

**touch screen** A display screen that is sensitive to the touch of a finger or stylus. Touch screens are very resistant to harsh environments where keyboards might eventually fail.

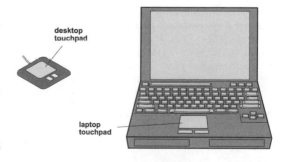

desktop touchpad

laptop touchpad

**Touchpads**
The touchpad has become especially popular on laptops, but external units for desktop computers have also been produced.

They are often used with custom-designed applications so that the onscreen buttons are large enough to be pressed with the finger. Applications are typically very specialized and greatly simplified so they can be used by anyone. However, touch screens are also very popular on PDAs and full-size computers with standard applications, where a stylus is required for precise interaction with screen objects.

There are two primary technologies used for touch screens and both use a clear glass panel overlaid onto the CRT or LCD screen. The resistive method is completely pressure sensitive. It uses a plastic layer on top of a metallic-coated glass layer, separated by spacers. When pressed, it shunts the current in the glass panel, and the X-Y coordinates pick up the location on the screen.

**Pressure Sensitive**
Keytec makes a wide variety of resistive touch screens that can be touched with the finger or any stylus-like object. When the plastic layer is pushed into the glass layer, it diverts the current. *(Image courtesy of Keytec, Inc., www.magictouch.com)*

**Sensitive to a Charge**
The Qbe tablet computer uses a capacitive touch screen that is sensitive to the charge in your finger or a stylus. The stylus is wired and plugged into the unit. *(Image courtesy of Aqcess Technologies, Inc., www.qbenet.com)*

The capacitive method uses a metallic coated glass panel, but without the plastic overlay. It senses the change in current from the charge in your finger or a stylus. The stylus used with this technique must emit a charge and is thus wired to the computer.

**tower**    (1) A floor-standing cabinet taller than it is wide. Desktop computers can be made into towers by turning them on their side and inserting them into a floor-mounted base.

(2) (Tower) Series of UNIX-based single and multiprocessor computer systems from NCR that use the Motorola 68000 family of CPUs.

**TP**    See *twisted pair*, *TPO*, *teleprocessing* and *TP monitor*.

**TP0-TP4**    (Transport Protocol Class 0 to Class 4) The grades of OSI transport layers from least to most complete and specific. TP4 is a full connection-oriented transport protocol.

**TPC**    (Transaction Processing Performance Council, San Jose, CA, www.tpc.org) An organization devoted to benchmarking transaction processing systems. In order to derive the number of transactions that can be processed in a given timeframe, TPC benchmarks measure the total performance of the system, which includes the computer, operating system, database management system and any other related components involved in the transaction processing operation.

Earlier TPC-A and TPC-B benchmarks produced tpsA and tpsB ratings, which were measured in transactions per second. The subsequent TPC-C benchmark yields transactions per minutes expressed in tpmC ratings. The TPC-D benchmark is designed for decision support and tests 17 complex queries. TPC-D results are relative numbers based on the size of the database being queried and yield a single-user Qppd Power metric and a multiple-user QthD Throughput metric.

**TPC-A**    A benchmark that measures overall transaction processing performance. See *TPC*.

**TPC-B**    A benchmark that measures overall transaction processing performance. See *TPC*.

**TPC-C**    A benchmark that measures overall transaction processing performance. See *TPC*.

**TPC-D**    A benchmark that measures decision support performance. See *TPC*.

**TPF**    (Transaction Processing Facility) An operating system for IBM mainframes specialized for large transaction processing systems such as airline reservations. TPF supports thousands of terminals with a typical response time of two to three seconds. It was formerly called Airline Control Program/Transaction Processing (ACP/TP).

**tpi**    (Tracks Per Inch) The measurement of the density of tracks recorded on a disk or tape. See *track density*.

**TPM**    (Transactions Per Minute) The number of transactions processed within one minute. See *TPS*.

**tpmC**    The rating from the TPC-C benchmark, which measures overall transaction processing performance. See *TPC*.

**TP monitor**    (TeleProcessing monitor or Transaction Processing monitor) A control program that manages the transfer of data between multiple local and remote terminals and the application programs that serve them. It may also include programs that format the terminal screens and validate the data entered.

In a distributed client/server environment, a TP monitor provides integrity by ensuring that transactions do not get lost or damaged. It may be placed in a separate machine and used to balance the load between clients and various application servers and database servers. It is also used to create a high availability system by switching a failed transaction to another machine. A TP monitor guarantees that all databases are updated from a single transaction (see *two-phase commit*).

Examples of popular TP monitors are CICS, a veteran TP monitor used on IBM mainframes and the UNIX-based Tuxedo and Encina products. See *BEA Tuxedo* and *Encina*.

**TPMS**    (Transaction Processing Monitor System) A TP monitor from ICL that is used in conjunction with its IDMSX database system. TPMS supports up to 16,000 online users. See *IDMSX*.

**TPO**    (Twisted Pair Only) Refers to the use of twisted pair wire when other options are available. For example, a TPO suffix at the end of 3com Ethernet adapter model numbers indicates the card has only an RJ45 connector. TP means RJ45 and AUI connectors, TPC is RJ45 and BNC, and COMBO cards provide all three.

**TP-PMD**    (Twisted Pair-Physical Medium Dependent) An ANSI standard for an FDDI network that uses UTP instead of optical fiber. See *CDDI*.

**TPS**    (1) (Transactions Per Second) The number of transactions processed within one second. See *TPM*.

(2) (Transaction Processing System) Originally used as an acronym for such a system, it now refers to the measurement of the system (See definition 1 above).

**tpsA**    The rating from the TPC-A benchmark, which measures overall transaction processing performance. See *TPC*.

**tpsB**    The rating from the TPC-B benchmark, which measures overall transaction processing performance. See *TPC*.

**TQFP**    See *QFP*.

**TQM**    (Total Quality Management) An organizational undertaking to improve the quality of manufacturing and service. It focuses on obtaining continuous feedback for making improvements and refining existing processes over the long term. See *ISO 9000*.

**TR**    See *Token Ring*.

**trace**    See *autotrace*.

**Traceroute**    An Internet utility that describes the path in realtime from the client machine to the remote host being contacted. It reports the IP addresses of all the routers in between. Windows comes with its own Traceroue utility (TRACERT.EXE) that is executed from the command line.

**track**    A storage channel on disk or tape. On disks, tracks are concentric circles (hard and floppy disks) or spirals (CDs and videodiscs). On tapes, they are parallel lines. Their format is determined by the specific drive they are used in. On magnetic devices, bits are recorded as reversals of polarity in the magnetic surface. On CDs, bits are recorded as physical pits under a clear, protective layer. See *magnetic disk*.

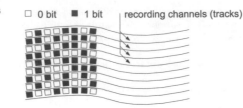

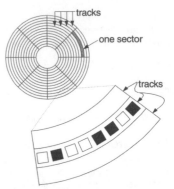

**Tracks and Sectors**
On disk, tracks are concentric circles, as shown at right. On tape, they are generally parallel with the length, although helical scan tracks run diagonal.

### track-at-once
The recording of data on a CD-R disc a session at a time. The track-at-once feature, which was added shortly after the first CD-R drives were introduced, enables songs and data to be written at different intervals. The lead-in sectors that are written at the beginning of each session contain the location where additional data can be placed on the disc.

For audio CDs, the session can be left open in order to mix songs from different sources, but it must be closed in order to play the disc. If the disc is closed, no more songs or data can be written to the medium.

### trackball
A stationary pointing device that contains a movable ball rotated with the fingers or palm. From one to three keys are located in various positions depending on the unit. Years ago, Kensington Microware popularized the trackball with its Turbo Mouse for the Macintosh. See *mouse, pointing stick* and *touchpad*.

**The Turbo Mouse**
The Turbo Mouse popularized the trackball for the Macintosh. Later models were developed for the PC. *(Image courtesy of Kensington Microware, Ltd.)*

**CD-R Options**
This dialog box from Adaptec's EZ CD Creator software provides an excellent example of showing all the disc-at-once, track-at-once options just before "burning" a disc. The "Leave Session Open" option at the top is grayed in this dialog, because a data CD has been selected. Were an audio CD being recorded, it would be an available option.

### track density
The number of parallel recording tracks per inch on a magnetic or optical surface. In 2000, magnetic disk track density reached 30,000 tpi (tracks per inch); but drives using one or more additional systems to position the head, known as "micro positioning," are expected to increase track density, bringing it eventually to 100,000 tpi. See *OAW*.

### tracking
In desktop publishing, the consistent letterspacing of text. Tracking is used to expand or contract the amount of text on a page by expanding or reducing the amount of space between letters. It differs from kerning in that it is applied to an entire font or to a range of text, whereas kerning refers to certain letter pairs.

### TrackPoint
The pointing stick used in IBM laptops. IBM introduced and popularized this type of pointing device on its ThinkPad laptops.

**trackstick** Same as *pointing stick*.

**tractor feed** A mechanism that moves paper forms through a printer. It contains pins on tractors that engage the paper through perforated holes in its left and right borders. A "pull" tractor pulls the forms through the printer mechanism, while a "push" tractor pushes the forms. Contrast with *sheet feeder*.

**TRADACOMS** A European EDI standard developed by the Article Numbering Association. TRADACOMS has been mostly used by the retail industry in the U.K. See *EDI*.

**trademarks** The purpose of this publication is to provide a meaningful definition of computer science and telecommunicaions terms and related products, but it is not meant to be a source of trademark registration information. When we know of an origin of a term, we state it. There are thousands of terms in this database that do not include a lineage, because we either did not know of it at the time of writing or felt it was not pertinent.

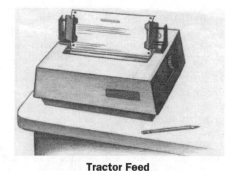

**Tractor Feed**
A tractor feed moves the paper from the bottom of the printer through the top. It contains a sprocket that grabs the perforated holes at both sides of the form and pulls it through uniformly.

We presume that every name of a product is a trademark of its respective organization. If a company creates a name for its product and continues to use it, it is a de facto trademark whether or not it is registered. Among other legal reasons, registration serves to officially document how long a name has been in use.

If a particular technology in this database is attributed to an organization, we do not know if it is a de facto or de jure trademark of that organization. To find out trademark information about a particular item mentioned, please contact the legal counsel of the organization that is mentioned as its creator.

**traffic** Data crossing a network. Traffic is a very general term and can refer to transactions and messages of any kind.

**traffic engineering** The ability to guarantee performance in a network for a certain amount of capacity for a certain amount of time. It implies the ability to analyze the current traffic load and dynamically make the changes necessary to accomodate the new stream of data. ATM is known for its traffic engineering capabilities. See *ATM*.

**traffic shaping** Limiting the amount of bandwidth an interface can accomodate. For example, an OC-3 port (155 Mbps) might be installed on a switch, but it can be limited to DS-3 (45 Mbps) traffic for an existing application.

**traffic surge protection** Preventing an overload of a server due to a sudden burst of traffic. See *overload server*, *flash crowd* and *Web switch*.

**trailer** In communications, a code or set of codes that make up the last part of a transmitted message. See *trailer label*.

**trailer label** The last record in a tape file. May contain number of records, hash totals and other ID.

**training** (1) Teaching the details of a subject. With regard to software, training provides instruction for each command and function in an application. Contrast with *education*.

(2) In communications, the process by which two modems determine the correct protocols and transmission speeds to use.

(3) In voice recognition systems, the recording of the user's voice in order to provide samples and patterns for recognizing that voice.

**train printer** An early line printer that used a mechanism similar to a chain printer, except that the characters were not chained together. They were independent type slugs that were pushed around a track by engaging with a drive gear at one end. Train and chain printers gave way to band printers in the early 1980s. See *chain printer* and *printer*.

**Transact** An e-commerce system for the Web from Open Market that includes order capture and secure order fulfillment using credit cards, ecash and other payment systems. It includes customer service and subscription administration capabilities, as well as an integrated database for reporting and analysis.

**transaction**    An activity or request. Orders, purchases, changes, additions and deletions are typical business transactions stored in the computer. Transactions update one or more master files and serve as both an audit trail and history for future analyses. Ad hoc queries are a type of transaction as well, but are usually just acted upon and not saved. Transaction volume is a major factor in figuring computer system size and speed.

Keeping Transactions in Sync    A major problem in a transaction processing system is ensuring that all master files are updated before the transaction is considered completely processed. For example, if two files must be updated, but a system failure occurs after the first one but before the second one, the software must be able to roll back the first update and start over later. In a distributed environment, this is called "two-phase commit." See *transaction file*.

**transactional software**    Software that guarantees that all appropriate databases are updated from a single transaction. See *two-phase commit* and *TP monitor*.

**transaction environment**    A system that processes transactions by updating various files and returning confirmations. It implies a regular, high-volume stream of records entering the system. See *transaction processing*, *transaction file* and *transaction*.

**transaction file**    A collection of transaction records. The data in transaction files is used to update the master files, which contain the subjects of the organization. Transaction files also serve as audit trails and history for the organization. Where before they were transferred to offline storage after some period of time, they are increasingly being kept online for routine analyses. See *data warehouse*, *transaction processing* and *information system*.

Following are the kinds of fields that make up a typical transaction record in a business information system. There can be many more fields, depending on the organization. The following "key" fields are the ones that are generally indexed for fast matching against the master record. The account number is usually the primary key, but name may also be used as a primary key. See *master file* for examples of typical master records.

```
        EMPLOYEE PAYROLL RECORD                 PURCHASE ORDER
key     Employee account number          key    Purchase order number
        Today's date                            Today's date
        Hours worked                            Department
                                                Authorizing agent
        ORDER RECORD                            Vendor account number
key     Customer account number                 Quantity
        Today's date                            Product number
        Quantity                                Due date
        Product number                          Total cost

        PAYMENT RECORD                          WAREHOUSE RECEIPT
key     Customer number                  key    Purchase order number
        Today's date                     key    Invoice number
        Invoice number                          Today's date
        Amount paid                             Quantity
        Check number                            Product number
```

**transaction monitor**    See *TP monitor*.

**transaction processing**    Processing transactions as they are received by the computer. Also called "online" or "realtime" systems, transaction processing means that master files are updated as soon as transactions are entered at terminals or received over communications lines. It also implies that confirmations are returned to the sender.

If you save receipts in a shoebox and add them up at the end of the year for taxes, that's batch processing. However, if you buy something and immediately add the amount to a running total, that's transaction processing.

Organizations increasingly rely on computers to keep everything up-to-date all the time. A manager might need to know how many items are left on the shelf, what the latest price of a stock is or what the value of a financial portfolio is at any given moment.

Transaction processing is often called "online transaction processing" (OLTP). The OLTP market is a demanding one. If a business depends on computers for its day-to-day operations, the computers must stay up and running during business hours. See *two-phase commit*, *mission critical*, *industrial strength* and *fault tolerant*.

**transceiver**   A transmitter and receiver of analog or digital signals. It comes in many forms; for example, a transponder or network adapter.

**transcode**   **(1)** To convert from one format to another. It implies conversion between very distinct kinds of data, such as from speech into text or from analog video into digital frames, rather than from one digital format into another.

**(2)** To convert a Web page for display on any size screen. Transcoding services rearrange and reformat the elements for smaller screens, such as on PDAs and cellphones. In order that the pages can be quickly transcoded on the fly, some systems require that the Web page be preprocessed so that its elements can be analyzed and annotated ahead of time.

**transcribe**   To copy data from one medium to another—for example, from one source document to another, or from a source document to the computer. It often implies a change of format or codes.

**transducer**   A device that converts one energy into another; for example, a read/write head converts magnetic energy into electrical energy, and vice versa. In process control applications, it is used to convert pressure into an electrical reading.

**transfer**   To send data over a computer channel or bus. "Transfer" generally applies to transmission within the computer system, and "transmit" refers to transmission outside the computer over a line or network.

Transfers are actually copies, since the data is in both locations at the end of the transfer. Input, output and move instructions activate data transfers in the computer.

**transfer protocol**   See *file transfer protocol*.

**transfer rate**   Also called "data rate," it is the transmission speed of a communications or computer channel. Transfer rates are measured in bits or bytes per second.

**transfer time**   The time it takes to transmit or move data from one place to another. It is the time interval between starting the transfer and the completion of the transfer.

**transformer**   A device that changes AC voltage. Also called a "power adapter." It is made of steel laminations wrapped with two coils of wire. The coil ratio derives the voltage change. For example, if the input coil has 1,000 windings, and the output has 100, 120 volts is changed to 12. In order to create direct current (DC), the output is passed through a rectifier.

**transient**   A malfunction that occurs at random intervals, for example, a rapid fluctuation of voltage in a power line or a memory cell that intermittently fails.

**transient area**   An area in memory used to hold application programs for processing. The bulk of a computer's main memory is used as a transient area.

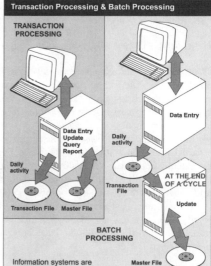

**Transaction Processing & Batch Processing**

Information systems are designed as a combination of transaction and batch processing subsystems.

The transaction processing is the daily work. Also called online transaction processing (OLTP), it means that the database is updated as soon as a transaction is received: a sales order depletes inventory, a stock sale updates the last close, a pledge adds to the fund raising balance. Transaction processing keeps business records up-to-date the moment transactions are keyed into or transmitted to the system.

Batch processing is updating or searching an entire table from beginning to end. A month-end report is a batch job as is printing payroll checks. There are many jobs that can be more economically processed at the end of a cycle. For example, the electronic transactions for telephone calls are stored in the computer until month end, when they are matched against the customer table for updating with all the other telephone transactions at the same time.

**transient data**     Data that is created within an application session. At the end of the session, it is discarded or reset back to its default and not stored in a database. Contrast with *persistent data*.

**transient state**     The exact point at which a device changes modes, for example, from transmit to receive or from 0 to 1.

**transistor**     A device used to amplify a signal or open and close a circuit. In a computer, it functions as an electronic switch or bridge. The transistor contains a semiconductor material that can change its electrical state when pulsed.

In its normal state, the semiconductor material is not conductive. When voltage is applied to it, it becomes conductive and current flows through. The gate, or base, is the triggering line; and the source and drain, or emitter and collector, are the two end points.

Transistors, resistors, capacitors and diodes make up logic gates. Logic gates make up circuits, and circuits make up electronic systems. To learn how the transistor is built, see *chip*.

**translate**     **(1)** To change one language into another; for example, assemblers, compilers and interpreters translate source language into machine language.

**(2)** In computer graphics, to move an image onscreen without rotating it.

**(3)** In telecommunictions, to change the frequencies of a band of signals.

**translating bridge**     A type of bridge that interconnects two different types of LAN protocols, such as Ethernet and Token Ring. Translating bridges are generally very complicated devices. However, source routing transparent (SRT) bridging integrates both bridging methods of Ethernet and Token Ring to solve the problem. See *SRT*.

**TransLISP PLUS**     A version of LISP for PCs developed by Solution Systems, Inc., Wellesley, MA. It provided the ability to link a Microsoft C routine to the LISP library as a function.

**translucency**     The quality of being able to see through a material, whereby the distant image is hazy or foggy. The terms translucency and transparency are often used synonymously; however, translucent would technically mean "seeing through frosted glass," while transparent would mean "seeing through clear glass."

**Transmeta**     (Transmeta Corporation, Santa Clara, CA, www.transmeta.com)  A chip design firm that was founded in 1995 by David Ditzel. The company retained a low profile until 2000 when it announced its Crusoe processor, an x86-based CPU that uses less battery power. Designed for running Windows and Linux applications on handheld devices, Crusoe chips are manufactured by IBM. Linus Torvalds, creator of Linux, later became part of Transmeta. See *Crusoe processor*.

**transmission**     The transfer of data over a communications channel.

**transmission channel**     A path between two nodes in a network. It may refer to the physical cable, the signal transmitted within the cable or to a subchannel within a carrier frequency. In radio and TV, it refers to the assigned carrier frequency.

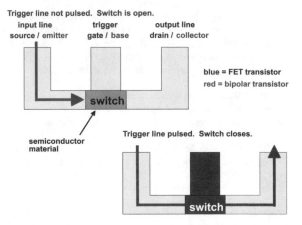

**The Transistor Concept**

The transistor is an electronic switch. The switching element is made of semiconductor material which conducts electricity when it is pulsed.

If there is no pulse on the trigger line, the semiconductor element is in a non-conductive state. When it is pulsed, it becomes conductive and current flows from the input to the output.

Trigger line not pulsed.  Switch is open.

input line            trigger            output line
source / emitter    gate / base    drain / collector

blue = FET transistor
red = bipolar transistor

semiconductor material

Trigger line pulsed.  Switch closes.

**Conceptual View of a Transistor**
Semiconductor material normally acts as an insulator. When it is pulsed with electricity, it becomes electrically conductive for that moment. It simply acts as an electrical bridge.

**transmission multiplexor**    Same as *add/drop multiplexer*.

**transmission speed**    The rate at which data is moved across a communications channel. Following are the transmission speeds of common LAN and WAN technologies. See *bandwidth*.

**transmissive art**    See *transparent media*.

**transmit**    To send data over a communications line. See *transfer*.

**transmitter**    A device that generates signals. Contrast with *receiver*.

**transmogrify**    To change into something completely different.

**transparency**    (1) The quality of being able to see through a material. The terms transparency and translucency are often used synonymously; however, transparent would technically mean "seeing through clear glass," while translucent would mean "seeing through frosted glass." See *alpha blending*.
   (2) A film-based photographic negative or positive. Light is beamed through the film for display, scanning or processing.

**transparency adapter**    A device that allows a flatbed scanner to scan 35mm slides and other film transparencies. It provides a mechanism that shines light through the transparencies. See *reflective media* and *transparent media*.

**transparent**    (1) Refers to a change in hardware or software that, after installation, causes no noticeable change in operation.
   (2) In computer graphics, a color that is treated as background and takes on the color of the underlying window or page. See *transparency* and *alpha blending*.

**transparent bridge**    A common type of network bridge, in which the host stations are unaware of their existence in the network. A transparent bridge learns which node is connected to which port through the experience of examining which node responds to each new station address that is transmitted. Ethernet uses this type of bridge, also called an *adaptive bridge*.   Contrast with *source route bridging*. See *spanning tree algorithm*.

**transparent cache**    A computer system or software within a computer system that determines whether a requested page or file has already been stored in memory or on its hard disk. If it has not, the request is sent upstream to its normal destination. The transparent cache sits between the client and server, and is invisible to either side. There are also no configuration adjustments required in the browser to use a transparent cache. See *Web cache*.

**transparent GIF**    See *GIF*.

**transparent LAN service**    A communications service from a local telephone company or common carrier that links remote LANs together. It is called transparent because the Ethernet, Token Ring or FDDI network is connected directly to the service at both ends regardless of the technology employed by the carrier in between. The network administrator of the LAN is not responsible for dealing with a different protocol. See *VPN*.

**transparent media**    Transparent materials such as 35mm slides, large transparencies and photographic negatives in which the scanner shines light through the objects to the sensors on the other side in order to record the image. Transparent media require a transparency adapter in the scanner, if available. Slide scanners can also be used, and there are scanners that have a transparency tray built into the unit that accomodates slides and larger transparencies. Contrast with *reflective media*.

**transparent media adapter**    See *transparency adapter*.

**transparent network**    An all-optical network from end to end. Expected in the future, such networks add their own complexity when the electrical component is removed. For example, due to switching, the distance a light signal travels one day may be different the next time. This creates a different dispersion characteristic that has to be dealt with, because the lack of photonic to electrical conversion (no more OEO switches) also eliminates the regeneration of the signal. See *optical switch* and *OEO*.

**transponder**    A receiver/transmitter on a communications satellite. It receives a microwave signal from earth (uplink), amplifies it and retransmits it back to earth at a different frequency (downlink). A satellite has several transponders.

**transport layer**    The services in the OSI protocol stack (layer 4 of 7) that provide end-to-end management of the communications session. See *transport protocol* and *OSI*.

**transport protocol**    A communications protocol responsible for establishing a connection and ensuring that all data has arrived safely. It is defined in layer 4 of the OSI model. Often, the term transport protocol implies transport services, which include the lower-level data link protocol that moves packets from one node to another. See *OSI* and *transport services*.

**transport services**    The collective functions of layers 1 through 4 of the OSI model.

**transputer**    (**TRANS**istor com**PUTER**) A computer that contains a CPU, memory and communications capability on a single chip. Chips are strung together in hypercube or gridlike patterns to create large parallel processing machines, used in scientific, realtime control and AI applications.

**trap**    To test for a particular condition in a running program; for example, to "trap an interrupt" means to wait for a particular interrupt to occur and then execute a corresponding routine. An error trap tests for an error condition and provides a recovery routine. A debugging trap waits for the execution of a particular instruction in order to stop the program and analyze the status of the system at that moment.

**trapdoor**    A secret way of gaining access to a program or online service. Trapdoors are built into the software by the original programmer as a way of gaining special access to particular functions. For example, a trapdoor built into a BBS program would allow access to any BBS computer running that software. See *Easter Egg*, *Back Orifice* and *one-way hash function*.

**trash can**    An icon of a garbage can used for deleting files. The icon of a file is dragged to the trash can and released. In the Mac, the trash can is also used to eject a floppy by dragging the icon of the floppy disk onto it. In Windows 95, the equivalent of the trash can is the recycle bin, but it is used only for deleting files and folders, not ejecting floppies.

**trashware**    Software that is so poorly designed that it winds up in the garbage can.

**Travan**    A backup tape technology from Imation Enterprises Corporation, Oakdale, MN (www.imation.com). Travan has evolved from the QIC backup tapes, but uses wider tape, different tape guides and improved magnetic media to yield higher capacities. With Network Series (NS) drives, which provide hardware compression and read-while-write features, Travan tapes are migrating from desktop backup to workgroup server backup. Travan drives may be compatible with QIC, QIC-Wide and QIC-EX cartridges, but it varies from model to model. See *QIC*, *QIC-Wide*, *QIC-EX* and *magnetic tape*.

```
TRAVAN NATIVE CAPACITIES
TR-1              400MB
TR-2              800MB (never took off)
TR-3              1.6GB

HP 5GB (TR-4 with
    less tape)    2.5GB

Travan 8GB (TR-4)   4GB
Travan NS 8         4GB

Travan 20GB (TR-5) 10GB
Travan NS 20       10GB
```

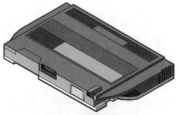

**Travan Cartridge**
Travan is a member of the QIC family of backup tapes. Travan drives may also be capable of reading earlier QIC and QIC Wide, as well as QIC-EX cartridges.

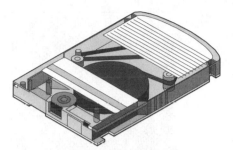

**QIC-EX Extends Travan Capacities**
QIC-EX cartridges from Verbatim extend the cartridge housing to include more tape. Many Travan drives support QIC-EX cartridges.

**tray card**  The printed insert that goes under the tray in a CD jewel case and wraps around both edges. If the printed cover of the jewel case is only a single piece of paper rather than a booklet, it is often known as the front tray card. See *jewel case.*

**tray drive**  A type of drive that uses a flat tray to hold the media. The tray is ejected from the drive for media placement and retracted for playing (reading). CD and CD-ROM drives are common examples of tray drives. Contrast with *feed drive* and *caddy drive.*

**tray load**  Inserting a bare CD or DVD disc into a drive. Contrast with *caddy load.*

**tree**  A hierarchical structure like an organization chart. See *directory tree.*

**treeware**  Products derived from trees, namely, the documentation manuals. See *RTFM.*

**T.RES**  See *T.120.*

**triangle**  A three-sided polygon. In 3-D graphics, the surfaces of 3-D objects are broken down into triangles. Small numbers of triangles are used for flat surfaces, while large numbers are used to mold curved surfaces similar to the way a geodesic dome is constructed. The three points of every triangle (vertices) are computed on an X-Y-Z scale and must be recomputed each time the object is moved. See *triangle setup* and *geometry calculations.*

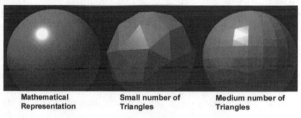

Mathematical Representation    Small number of Triangles    Medium number of Triangles

**Triangles**
The smaller the triangle, the more realistic the curve. It takes an enormous number of triangles to simulate totally round objects.
*(Image courtesy of Intergraph Computer Systems.)*

**triangle setup**  In 3-D graphics rendering, computing the rate of change of RGB color values between the points of each triangle (vertices) so that the triangles can be filled with color properly in the rasterization stage. Triangle setup comes after the geometry calculations and before rasterization. In the 3-D world, each object is represented as a collection of triangles. See *graphics accelerator.*

**trichromatic**  In computer graphics, the use of red, green and blue to create all the colors in the spectrum.

**trigger**  A mechanism that initiates an action when an event occurs, such as reaching a certain time or date, or upon receiving some type of input. A trigger generally causes a program routine to be executed.

In a database management system (DBMS), it is an SQL procedure that is executed when a record is added or deleted. It is used to maintain referential integrity in the database. A trigger may also execute a stored procedure. Triggers and stored procedures are built into DBMSs used in client/server environments. See *intelligent database.*

**trilinear interpolation**  A texture mapping technique that produces the most realistic images and requires the most computations. This technique is used in conjunction with MIP mapping, which provides texture maps in different depths.

An algorithm is used to map a screen pixel location to a corresponding point on the two nearest texture maps (MIP maps). A weighted average of the attributes (color, alpha, etc.) of the four surrounding texels on each MIP map is computed (bilinear interpolation). Then the weighted average of the two results is applied to the screen pixel. This process is repeated for each pixel forming the object being textured.

The term trilinear refers to the performing of interpolations in three dimensions (horizontal, vertical and depth). See *texture map, MIP mapping, bilinear interpolation* and *point sampling.*

**Trilogy**    A company founded in 1979 by Gene Amdahl to commercialize wafer scale integration and build supercomputers. It raised a quarter of a billion dollars, the largest startup funding in history, but could not create its 2.5" superchip. In 1984, it abandoned supercomputer development and later the superchip project. In 1985, Trilogy acquired Elxsi Corporation, a manufacturer of VAX-compatible systems, and eventually merged itself into Elxsi.

**triode**    A type of vacuum tube that is used in audio and radio amplifiers, and oscillator circuits. It is like a diode with the addition of a wire mesh control grid between the cathode and plate (anode) that controls current flow. A filament heats the cathode, enabling it to release electrons. When a small voltage is applied to the grid, the current flow between the cathode and plate is changed accordingly. In some triodes, the filament is the cathode. See *diode* and *magnetron*.

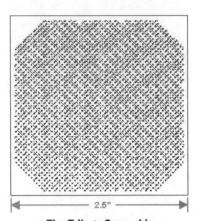

| $\longleftarrow$ 2.5" $\longrightarrow$ |

**The Trilogy Superchip**
The 2.5" square superchip was never completed, because it was too far ahead of its time. Each year however, we make chips larger and larger. In time, Amdahl's vision will become a reality. *(Image courtesy of Elxsi Corporation.)*

**Triple DES**    See *DES*.

**triple precision**    The use of three computer words to hold a number used for calculation, providing an enormous amount of arithmetic precision.

**triple twist**    A supertwist variation that twists crystals to 260 degrees for improved clarity. See *LCD*.

**TRITON**    The name of earlier versions of Baan software, before the release of BAAN IV. See *BAAN IV*.

**Triton chipset**    The name Intel previously used for its chipsets. See *Intel chipsets*.

**trn**    (Threaded ReadNews) A popular newsreader for Usenet newsgroups. It is an enhanced version of rn (ReadNews) that includes threads. See *Usenet*.

**troff**    (Typesetting RunOFF) A UNIX utility that formats documents for typesetters and laser printers. Using a text editor, troff codes are embedded into the text and the troff command converts the document into the required output. See *nroff*.

**Trojan horse**    A program that appears legitimate, but performs some illicit activity when it is run. It may be used to locate password information or make the system more vulnerable to future entry, or simply destroy programs or data on the hard disk. A Trojan horse is similar to a virus, except that it does not replicate itself. It stays in the computer doing its damage or allowing somebody from a remote site to take control of the computer. Trojans often sneak in attached to a free game or other utility. For information about various Trojans that are spread on the Internet, visit Harbor Telco Security's Web site at http://lockdown2000.com. See *Back Orifice*, *NetBus*, *PrettyPark* and *virus*.

**trolling**    (1) Surfing, or browsing, the Web.
   (2) Posting derogatory messages about sensitive subjects on newsgroups and chat rooms to bait users into responding.
   (3) Hanging around in a chat room without saying anything, like a "peeping tom."

**TRON**    (The Realtime Operating System Nucleus) An advanced realtime operating system developed by Japanese universities and corporations. i-TRON is a version that is used for microcontrollers in industrial machinery.

**troubleshoot**    To find out why something does not work and to fix the problem. Troubleshooting a computer often requires determining whether the problem is due to malfunctioning hardware, or buggy or out-of-date software. See *debug*.

**TRS-80**    (Tandy Radio Shack) An early line of personal computers from Tandy. In 1977, the TRS-80, along with the Apple II and the Commodore PET, ushered in the personal computer revolution. The operating system for the TRS-80 was TRS-DOS. See *Tandy* and *personal computer*. See also *TSR*.

**Tru64 UNIX**     A 64-bit UNIX operating system from Compaq that runs on its Alpha line. It was formerly Digital UNIX when Alpha was a product family from Digital Equipment Corporation. Digital UNIX was renamed Tru64 UNIX in 1999.

**True BASIC**     An ANSI-standard structured-programming version of BASIC for the PC, Mac and Amiga from True BASIC, Inc., West Lebanon, NH. Developed in 1984 by BASIC's creators, John Kemeny and Thomas Kurtz, it includes many enhancements over original BASIC. It comes in both interpreter and compiler form.

**true color**     (1) The ability to generate 16,777,216 colors (24-bit color). See *high color*.
    (2) The ability to generate photo-realistic color images (requires 24-bit color minimum).

**TrueType**     A scalable font technology that renders fonts for both the printer and the screen. Originally developed by Apple, it was enhanced jointly by Apple and Microsoft. TrueType fonts are used in Windows, starting with Windows 3.1, as well as in the Mac System 7 operating system.
    Unlike PostScript, in which the algorithms are maintained in the rasterizing engine, each TrueType font contains its own algorithms for converting the outline into bitmaps. The lower-level language embedded within the TrueType font allows unlimited flexibility in the design. See *TTF file* and *TrueImage*.

**truncate**     To cut off leading or trailing digits or characters from an item of data without regard to the accuracy of the remaining characters. Truncation occurs when data is converted into a new record with smaller field lengths than the original.

**trunk**     A communications channel between two points. It typically refers to large-bandwidth telephone channels between switching centers that handle many simultaneous voice and data signals. A circuit from a user's terminal or PC to a network is more appropriately called a line rather than a trunk, although the terms line, trunk and circuit are often used synonymously.

**trusted computer system**     A computer system that cannot be illegally accessed. See *NCSC*.

**trusted domain relationship**     A trust association between two domains. See *trust relationship*.

**trustee**     A user or group of users that has been given access rights to files on a network server. See also *TRUSTe*.

**trust relationship**     In Windows NT, an association between servers in one domain or an association between one domain and another. It allows a user to log on once and have access to all associated resources without having to be authenticated again. In Windows 2000 (NT 5.0), the process of defining trust relationships is automated.

**truth table**     A chart of a logical operation's inputs and outputs. The example on the right is a Boolean NAND truth table.

**TSAPI**     (Telephony Services **API**) A telephony programming interface from Novell and AT&T. Based on the international CSTA standard, TSAPI is designed to interface a telephone PBX with a NetWare server to provide interoperability between PCs and telephone equipment.

| NAND | | |
|------|------|------|
| IN | IN | OUT |
| 0 | 0 | 1 |
| 0 | 1 | 1 |
| 1 | 0 | 1 |
| 1 | 1 | 0 |

**TSAT**     See *VSAT*.

**T.share**     The remote control part of the T.120 realtime data conferencing protocol. T.share is used in Microsoft's NetMeeting, as well as RDP (Remote Desktop Protocol)—the protocol that connects Windows desktops to Windows Terminal Server. See *Windows Terminal Server*, *RDP* and *T.120*.

**TSO**     (Time Sharing Option) Software that provides interactive communications for IBM's MVS operating system. It allows a user or programmer to launch an application from a terminal and interactively work with it. The TSO counterpart in VM is called CMS. Contrast with *JES*, which provides batch communications for MVS.

**TSOP** (Thin Small Outline Package) A very-thin, plastic, rectangular surface mount chip package with gull-wing pins on its two short sides. TSOPs are about a third as thick as SOJ chips. See *gull-wing lead*, *SOP*, *SOJ* and *chip package*.

**T-span** A 24-channel group, which makes up one T1 line. See *T1*.

**TSR** (Terminate and Stay Resident) Refers to a program that remains in memory when the user exits it in order that it be immediately available at the press of a hotkey. TSRs were popular under DOS to quickly pop up a calendar, calculator or other utility, because DOS did not have built-in task switching. Standards for writing TSRs were not codified early on, and TSRs often conflicted with each other and regular applications. After Windows 3.0, TSRs became moot, since any DOS or Windows application could be conveniently task switched in a separate window.

**TSS** See *ITU*.

**TTCN** (Tree and Tabular Combined Notation) A programming language endorsed by ISO that is used to write test suites for telecommunications systems. TTCN is used for "black box testing," which means that all interaction to the system is via messages, rather than by a user with a mouse. Test suites are built in a hierarchical and modular manner, allowing many programmers to be involved in the project. Numerous telecom vendors use TTCN for their products, and organizations such as the ITU, ATM Forum and ETSI, provide TTCN conformance tests for new standards.

**TTFN** Digispeak for goodbye ("ta ta for now").

**TT font** See *TrueType*.

**TTL** **(1)** (Transistor Transistor Logic) A digital circuit composed of bipolar transistors wired in a certain manner. TTL logic has been widely used since the early days of digital circuitry. TTL designations may appear on input or output ports of various devices, which indicates a digital circuit in contrast to an analog circuit.

**(2)** (Time To Live) A set maximum amount of time a packet is allowed to propagate through the network before it is discarded.

**(3)** (Through The Lens) Refers to a single-lens reflex camera that lets the photographer view the scene through the same lens that captures the image.

**T.TUD** See *T.120*.

**TTY protocol** (TeleTYpewriter protocol) A low-speed asynchronous communications protocol with limited or no error checking. See *teletypewriter*.

**tube** See *CRT* and *vacuum tube*.

**tunable laser** A laser that can change its frequency over a given range. In time, tunable lasers are expected to be capable of switching frequencies on a packet-by-packet basis.

**tuner** An electronic part of a radio or TV that locks on to a selected carrier frequency (station, channel) and filters out the audio and video signals for amplification and display.

**tunneling** Transmitting data structured in one protocol format within the format of another protocol. Tunneling allows other types of transmission streams to be carried within the prevailing protocol. See *IP tunneling* and *L2TP*.

**tuple** In relational database management, a record, or row. See *relational database*.

**Turbo C** A C compiler from Borland used to create a wide variety of commercial products. It is known for its well-designed debugger. Borland's object-oriented versions of C are Turbo C++ and Borland C++.

The DOS version of this database is written in Turbo C. The Windows version is written in Microsoft C.

**turbo code** A type of channel coding that uses a convolutional code and a type of Viterbi decoder that outputs a continuous value rather than a 0 or 1. See *convolutional code* and *Viterbi decoder*.

**Turbo Pascal**    A pascal compiler for DOS from Borland used in a wide variety of applications from accounting to complex commercial products. Turbo Pascal for Windows provides an object-oriented programming environment for Windows development. Borland is responsible for moving the Pascal language from the academic halls to the commercial world.

**Turing test**    The "acid test" of true artificial intelligence, as defined by the English scientist Alan Turing. In the 1940s, he said "a machine has artificial intelligence when there is no discernible difference between the conversation generated by the machine and that of an intelligent person."

**turnaround document**    A paper document or punched card prepared for re-entry into the computer system. Paper documents are printed with OCR fonts for scanning. Invoices and inventory stock cards are examples.

**turnaround time**    (1) In batch processing, the time it takes to receive finished reports after submission of documents or files for processing. In an online environment, turnaround time is the same as *response time*.

(2) In half-duplex transmission, the time it takes to change from transmit to receive, and vice versa.

**turnkey system**    A complete system of hardware and software delivered to the customer ready-to-run.

**turnpike effect**    In communications, a lockup due to increased traffic conditions and bottlenecks in the system.

**tutorials in this publication**    See *Win ABCs, MSW ABCs, DOS ABCs, TCP/IP ABCs, XL ABCs* and *PKZIP ABCs*.

**TUV**    (Technischer Überwachungs-Verein) Literally "Technical Watch-Over Association." A German certifying body involved with product safety for the European Community. The "TÜV Rheinland" mark is placed on tested and approved electrical and electronic devices like our UL (Underwriters Laboratory) seal.

**Tuxedo**    See *BEA TUXEDO*.

**TV board**    An expansion board in a personal computer that contains a TV tuner. It derives its source from an antenna or cable TV just like any TV set. The accompanying software is used to change the channel and create a video window that is displayed with other windows on screen. In a PC, the board is generally connected to the VGA adapter via the feature connector. The TV board may also cable directly to the computer's monitor or indirectly through the display adapter. See *feature connector* and *VESA Advanced Feature Connector*.

**TV-out port**    A connection on a computer that allows a standard TV to be used for display. It sends out analog NTSC or PAL signals. See *NTSC* and *PAL*.

**TVPC**    See *PC/TV*.

**TV recorder**    See *PVR*.

**TWAIN**    (Technology Without An Interesting Name) A programming interface that lets a graphics application, such as an image editing program or desktop publishing program, activate a scanner, frame grabber or other image-capturing device.

**tweak**    To make minor adjustments in an electronic system or in a software program in order to improve performance. See *calibrate*.

**Alan Mathison Turing**
One of the pioneers in computing, Turing helped fellow scientists break Germany's Enigma encryption code in World War II. In 1954, barely reaching the age of 42, Turing died of a self-administered dose of potassium cyanide, the motivation for which was unclear. *(Image courtesy of The Computer Museum History Center, www.computerhistory.org)*

T

**tweening**    An animation technique that, based on starting and ending shapes, creates the necessary "in-between" frames. See *morphing*.

**twinax card**    An expansion board in a personal computer that emulates a 5250 terminal, the common terminal on an IBM midrange system (AS/400, System/3x).

**twinaxial**    A type of cable similar to coax, but with two inner conductors instead of one. It is used in IBM midrange (AS/400, System/3x) communications environments.

**TWIP**    (TWentIeth of a Point)  Equal to 1/1440th of an inch.

**twisted pair**    A thin-diameter wire (22 to 26 guage) commonly used for telephone and network cabling. The wires are twisted around each other to minimize interference from other twisted pairs in the cable (Alexander Graham Bell invented this and was awarded a patent for it in 1881). Twisted pairs have less bandwidth than coaxial cable or optical fiber.

**Twinaxial Connector**
Twinax connectors are used on IBM System 3x and AS/400 computer systems.

**UTP, STP, Stranded and Solid**    Twisted pair cables are available unshielded (UTP) or shielded (STP). UTP is the most common. STP is used in noisy environments where the shield protects against excessive electromagnetic inteference. Both UTP and STP come in stranded and solid wire varieties. The stranded wire is the most common and is also very flexible for bending around corners. Solid wire cable has less attenuation and can span longer distances, but is less flexible than stranded wire and cannot be repeatedly bent. Following are the twisted pair categories.

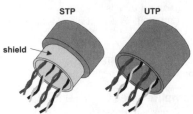

**Shielded and Unshielded Twisted Pairs**
The metal shield on the STP cable adds protection against external interference.

```
Category   Cable Type    Application
1          UTP           Analog voice
2          UTP           Digital voice
                         1 Mbps data
3          UTP, STP      16 Mbps data
4          UTP, STP      20 Mbps data
5          UTP, STP      100 Mbps data
Level 6    UTP, STP      155 Mbps data
Level 7    UTP, STP      1000 Mbps data
```

**two-out-of-five code**    A numeric code that stores one decimal digit in five binary digits in which two of the bits are always 0 or 1 and the other three are always in the opposite state.

**two-phase commit**    A technique for ensuring that a transaction successfully updates all appropriate files in a distributed database environment. All DBMSs involved in the transaction first confirm that the transaction has been received and is recoverable (stored on disk). Then each DBMS is told to commit the transaction (do the actual updating).

Although, traditionally, two-phase commit meant updating databases in two or more servers, the term is also applied to updating two different kinds of databases within the same server. See *transaction*, *transaction file* and *transaction processing*.

**The Twisted Pair**

**two-tier client/server**    A two-way interaction in a client/server environment, in which the user interface is stored in the client and the data is stored in the server. The application logic can be in either the client or the server. See *fat client*, *fat server* and *three-tier client/server*.

**two-way radio**    A voice network that provides an always-on connection enabling the user to just "push the button and talk."  Also called "dispatch radio," two-way radio has traditionally been used by police, fire, taxi and other mobile fleets. Motorola's iDEN system, which is implemented by various carriers around the world, integrates two-way radio capablity with its cellphone systems. See *SMR* and *iDEN*.

**two-wire lines**     A transmission channel made up of only two wires, such as used in the common dial-up telephone network.

**TWX**     (TeletypeWriter eXchange Service) A U.S. and Canadian dial-up communications service that became part of Telex. In 1971, the Bell System sold TWX to Western Union. TWX transmits 5-bit Murray code or 7-bit ASCII code at up to 150 bps. See *Telex*.

**TX**     A communications abbreviation for transmit. Contrast with *RX*.

**TX chipset**     See *Intel chipsets*.

**TXD**     (Transmitting Data) See *modem*.

**TXT file**     See *ASCII file*.

**Tymnet**     A value-added, packet switching network that enables many varieties of terminals and computers to exchange data. It is now part of Concert Communications Services, owned by MCI and British Telecom (BT). See *Concert*.

**type**     (1) In data or text entry, to press the keys on the keyboard.

(2) In programming, a category of variable that is determined by the kind of data stored in it. For example, integer, floating point, string, logical, date and binary are common data types.

(3) (Type) In DOS and OS/2, a command that displays the contents of a text file.

**Type 1 connector**     See *Token Ring connector*.

**Type 1 font**     The primary type of PostScript font. Each font is composed of a .PFB and .PFM file, which are stored in the \PSFONTS and \PSFONTS\PFM folders. Sometimes, \PSFONTS is in the \WINDOWS folder (\WINDOWS\PSFONTS). In Windows 95/98, Adobe Type Manager lets you view the file names under the Properties of each font. For example, the following files make up the Garamond typeface. See *PostScript*.

```
\psfonts\gdrg_____.pfb          normal
\psfonts\gdi_____.pfb          italics
\psfonts\gdsb_____.pfb          bold
\psfonts\gdsbi____.pfb          bold italics

\psfonts\pfm\gdrg_____.pfm       normal
\psfonts\pfm\gdi_____.pfm       italics
\psfonts\pfm\gdsb_____.pfm       bold
\psfonts\pfm\gdsbi____.pfm       bold italics
```

**Type 3 font**     A type of PostScript font that is used to create complex designs. See *PostScript*.

**typeahead buffer**     See *keyboard buffer*.

**Type A plug**     See *USB*.

**Type B plug**     See *USB*.

**type casting**     See *casting*.

**typeface**   The design of a set of printed characters, such as Courier, Helvetica and Times Roman. The terms "typeface" and "font" are used interchangeably; but the typeface is the primary design, while the font is the particular implementation and variation of the typeface, such as bold or italics (or none; the normal, upright style).

A major difference between typefaces is whether there are tiny horizontal lines at the tops and bottoms of any straight lines. The age-old serif typeface is Times Roman while Helvetica is the traditional sans-serif typeface. Since the TrueType fonts have become so ubiquitous, Times New Roman and Arial have become widely used for serif and sans-serif fonts. See *font*.

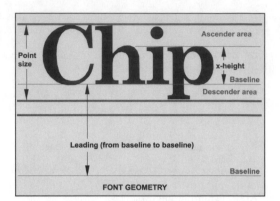

serif    sans-serif

M M

FONT GEOMETRY

Point size · Ascender area · x-height · Baseline · Descender area · Leading (from baseline to baseline) · Baseline

**typeface family**   A group of typefaces that include the normal, bold, italic and bold-italic variations of the same design.

**type family**   See *typeface family*.

**type font**   A set of print characters of a particular design (typeface), size (point size) and weight (light, medium, heavy). See *font*.

**typeover mode**   In word processing and data entry, a state in which each character typed on the keyboard replaces the character at the current cursor location. Contrast with *insert mode*.

**typesetter**   See *imagesetter*.

**typing**   (1) To input data to a typewriter or computer by pressing the keys on the keyboard.

(2) In programming, classifying variables by the kind of data they hold (string, integer, floating point, etc.). Strongly typed languages enforce strict adherance to typing and do not allow data types to be mixed in the same variable. Weakly typed languages provide minimal validation, which can result in processing errors.

**U** (Unit) A unit of measurement of the height of a rack-mounted device that is equal to 1.75". See *rack mounted*.

**UA** See *messaging system*.

**UAE** (Uninterruptible Application Error) The name of an abend, or crash, in a Windows 3.0 application. When the UAE occurs, an error message is displayed, and the program is generally unable to continue. Starting with Windows 3.1, an abend is known as a GPF (General Protection Fault). See *Application Error* and *abend*.

**UART** (Universal Asynchronous Receiver Transmitter) The electronic circuit that makes up the serial port. It converts parallel bytes from the CPU into serial bits for transmission, and vice versa. It generates and strips the start and stop bits appended to each character. Note that in the following paragraphs, dashes have been added after the 16 for readability. Older 8250 and 16-450 UARTs are not fast enough for today's modems. A 16-550 is required for transmission up to 115,200 bps (115 Kbps).

ISDN users running both 64 Kbps channels are losing performance with a 16-550 UART, because the maximum 115 Kbps is reduced further to 92 Kbps when the start/stop bits are removed. Upgrading to a 16-650 or higher UART boosts real data speed from 92 to 128 Kbps. The 16-650 is the more sophisticated UART, providing hardware flow control that reduces the burden on the CPU. See *UART overrun*.

| UART<br>Chip | Buffer<br>Size<br>(Bytes) | Maximum<br>Speed<br>Bits/Sec |
|---|---|---|
| 8250 | None | 9,600 |
| 16450 | 1 | 9,600 |
| 16550 | 16 | 115,200 |
| 16650 | 32 | 430,800 |
| 16750 | 64 | 921,600 |
| 16850 | 128 | 1.5 Mbps |

**UART overrun** A condition in which a UART cannot process the byte that just came in fast enough before the next one arrives.

**UBR** (Unspecified Bit Rate) An asynchronous transfer mode (ATM) level of service that does not guarantee available bandwidth. It is very efficient, but not used for critical data.

**UCAID** (University Corporation for Advanced Internet Development, Washington, DC, www.ucaid.org) A non-profit consortium founded in 1997, dedicated to developing advanced networking technology. It started as the Internet2 project with 34 universities in late 1996, and grew so large in one year (more than 100 universities and 20 companies) that it became necessary to formalize its administration and coordination. See *Internet2* and *Abilene*.

**UCITA** (Uniform Computer Information Transactions Act) A law that deals with software contracts and licensing drafted by the National Conference of Commissioners on Uniform State Laws (NCCUSL). UCITA is designed to favor the software publishers, because it enforces the license agreements and assumptions created by their attorneys. For example, the notion that software is licensed rather than purchased is a major tenet upheld in UCITA. Among other things, it enables the publisher to remotely shut down the customer's application without a court order, to prohibit a customer from transferring ownership of the software to another party and to stipulate under what jurisdiction legal disputes will be resolved.

Initially drafted as Article 2B, an amendment to the Uniform Commercial Code (UCC), the NCCUSL turned it into a non-UCC recommendation in 1999 and adopted it as a proposed uniform act. UCITA has passed in Maryland and Virginia and is being considered by several other states. Numerous industry groups have been vehemently opposed to Article 2B and UCITA, including the Society for Information Management (SIM).

**UCR** (Under Color Removal) A method for reducing amount of printing ink used. It substitutes black for gray color (equal amounts of cyan, magenta and yellow). Thus, black ink is used instead of the three CMY inks. See *GCR* and *dot gain*.

**UDA** (Universal Data Access) An umbrella term from Microsoft for its combined set of standards for file and database access. UDA includes ODBC, ADO, OLE DB and RDS. See *ODBC*, *ADO*, *OLE DB* and *RDS*.

**UDDI** (Universal Description, Discovery and Integration) An XML-based specification for a registry, or catalog, of businesses and the services (transactions, searches, etc.) they provide on their Web sites. Led by Ariba, IBM, Microsoft and others, UDDI is designed to enable software to automatically discover services on the Web and to automatically integrate with them by providing the necessary translations. UDDI capability is expected to be written into software, and a network of UDDI servers, similar to the Domain Name System (DNS) network of servers, is expected to proliferate.

UDDI contains white pages (addresses and contacts), yellow pages (industry classification) and green pages (descriptions of services). The green pages include the XML version, type of encryption and a Document Type Definition (DTD) of the standard. UDDI messages ride on top of the SOAP protocol, which invokes services on the Web. For more information, visit www.uddi.org. See *SOAP* and *DTD*.

**UDF** **(1)** (Universal Disk Format) A file system for optical media developed by the Optical Storage Technology Association (OSTA). It was designed for read-write interoperability between all the major operating systems, as well as compatibility between rewritable and write-once media. DVDs are based on the UDF format, and UDF is an optional second standard for CD-R and CD-RW disks. See *CD UDF*.

**(2)** (User Defined Function) A routine that has been defined or programmed by the user of the system and has been included in a standard library of functions. In these cases, "user" typically means programmer, not end user.

**UDI** (Uniform Driver Interface) A standard programming interface for writing device drivers for UNIX operating systems. Supported by SCO, HP, IBM, Sun and others, once a driver is written to the UDI standard, it can be compiled in and used with each respective version of UNIX. Drivers are complex pieces of code, which normally have to be written for each operating system. Providing a common way to write UNIX drivers helps unify the UNIX community.

**UDMA** (Ultra DMA) See *Ultra ATA*.

**UDP** (User Datagram Protocol) A protocol within the TCP/IP protocol suite that is used in place of TCP when a reliable delivery is not required. For example, UDP is used for realtime audio and video traffic where lost packets are simply ignored, because there is no time to retransmit. If UDP is used and a reliable delivery is required, packet sequence checking and error notification must be written into the applications. See *RTP*.

**UDP/IP** Refers to the use of UDP packets over IP. UDP does not guarantee reliable delivery, whereas TCP does. See *UDP*.

| Layer 2 - Ethernet | | | | | |
|---|---|---|---|---|---|
| | | | | | Ethernet frame |
| Ethernet header | IP header | UDP header | data (message) | | Ethernet trailer |

Layer 1 - Access method (CSMA/CD)
"onto the wire"

**UDP Packet**
A UDP packet is framed just like a TCP packet. This shows a UDP packet in an Ethernet frame ready for transmission over the network.

**ugly code**    Programming source code that is either poorly written or so complex that it is extremely difficult to figure out. See *program maintenance*.

**UHF**    (Ultra High Frequency) The range of electromagnetic frequencies from 300MHz to 3GHz.

**UI**    See *UNIX International* and *user interface*.

**UIDL**    (1) (Unique ID Listing) A POP3 mail server function that assigns a unique number to each incoming mail message. This allows mail to be left on the server after it has been downloaded to the user. Both the mail client and the POP server must support this feature.
   (2) (User Interface Definition Language) A language used to describe the elements in a user interface.

**UIMX**    (User Interface Management System for X Window) Software from Visual Edge Software, Ltd., St. Laurent, Quebec, Canada (www.vedge.com), that allows a user to design and modify Open Look and Motif interfaces.

**U interface**    The interface used to connect a pair of wires from the telephone company to network terminator 1 (NT1), which in the U.S. is typically part of the terminal adapter. See *ISDN*.

**UI specialist**    A person responsible for the design of the user interface. Like the technical writer, this is one of the most critical and least-understood professions in the computer industry. UI design takes years to master, yet is often relegated to the most junior people. See *user interface*.

**u-Law**    See *mu-Law* and *AU file*.

**ULSI**    (Ultra Large Scale Integration) More than one million transistors on a chip. See *SSI*, *MSI*, *LSI* and *VLSI*.

**ULS server**    (User Location Service server) A conferencing directory server on a TCP/IP network (intranet, Internet, etc.) that is used to identify participating users. When an audio or videoconferencing program is launched, it sends its user profile and current IP address to the ULS server, so that others can query the server and find out who is currently logged on. Microsoft renamed its ULS servers to ILS servers (Internet Locator Server), and Netscape Conference uses DLS servers (Dynamic Lookup Service). See *IP telephony*.

**Ultra ATA**    An enhanced version of the IDE interface that transfers data at 33, 66 or 100 Mbytes/sec. These enhancements are also called "Ultra DMA," "UDMA," "ATA-33," "ATA-66," "ATA-100," "DMA-33," "DMA-66" and "DMA-100." See *IDE* for all the ATA types and speeds.

**Ultra DMA**    Same as *Ultra ATA*.

**ultrafiche**    Pronounced "ultra feesh." A microfiche that holds up to 1,000 document pages per 4x6" sheet of film. Normal microfiche stores around 270 pages.

**Ultra IDE**    Same as *Ultra ATA*.

**Ultra SCSI**    The designation for various high-speed SCSI interfaces. The original specification was Ultra SCSI, followed by Ultra2, Ultra3, etc. For details, see *SCSI*.

**UltraSPARC**    An enhanced series of SPARC chips introduced by Sun in 1995. The UltraSPARC chips are 64-bit CPUs that run all 32-bit SPARC applications.

**ultraviolet**    An invisible band of radiation at the high-frequency end of the light spectrum. It takes about 10 minutes of ultraviolet light to erase an EPROM chip.

**Ultrium**    See *LTO*.

**ULTRIX**    Digital's version of UNIX for its PDP-11 and VAX series.

## UM   See *unified messaging*.

## UML   (Unified Modeling
Language) An object-oriented
analysis and design language
from the Object Management
Group (OMG). Many design
methodologies for describing
object-oriented systems were
developed in the late 1980s. UML
standardizes several diagramming
methods, including Grady
Booch's work at Rational
Software, Rumbaugh's Object
Modeling Technique and Ivar
Jacobson's work on use cases.
There are nine kinds of diagrams
that are supported under UML.

### Use Case Diagram
This diagram shows a system's
functions from a user's point of
view, which in this case is pretty
simple. All the following diagrams
were created in the Telelogic Tau
UML suite by Telelogic for this
same example. Five of the nine
possible diagrams available in UML
are shown here. The Component
Diagram (software module
interaction), Deployment Diagram
(hardware nodes) and the Activity
Diagram (tasks) are not included.
The Object Diagram (instantiations
of classes) is rarely used. *(All
diagrams courtesy of Telelogic, AB,
www.telelogic.com)*

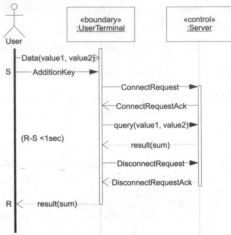

### Sequence Diagram
Like an MSC (Message Sequence Diagram), the
Sequence Diagram depicts the message flow between
entities in the system. The items between double
left/right arrows are UML "stereotypes." See *MSC*.

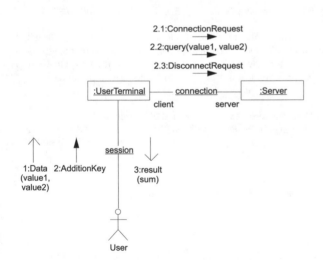

### Collaboration Diagram
This diagram emphasizes the structure of the relationships
between entities. Note that the user is associated with the
user terminal in a session, and the terminal is associated with
the server in a connection. The order of messages can be read
by interpreting the number prefixes.

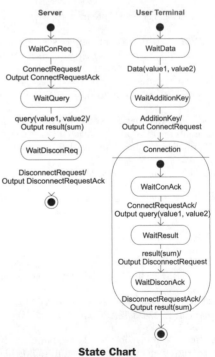

### State Chart
This describes the finite states that take place in the system.
The rectangles are the states, and the lines between them are
the transitions. The connection state shows three substates.
The single circles are starting points, and the double circles
are the ends.

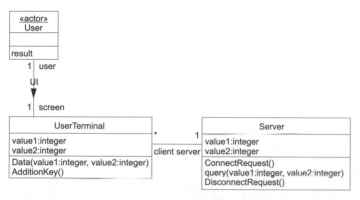

**Class Diagram**
User, User Terminal and Server are three classes, that have attributes and operations. An actor is a UML "stereotype" that is external to the system. Lines between classes are "associations." The asterisk means "many," in this case, a many-to-one relationship between client and server.

**UMTS**    (Universal Mobile Telecommunications System)  The European implementation of the 3G wireless phone system. UMTS, which is part of IMT-2000, provides service in the 2GHz band and offers global roaming and personalized features. Designed as an evolutionary system for GSM network operators, multimedia data rates up to 2 Mbps are expected using the W-CDMA technology. In the meantime, GPRS and EDGE are interim steps that will speed up wireless data for GSM. For more information, visit www.umts-forum.org. See *IMT-2000, GPRS, EDGE* and *W-CDMA*.

**unary**    Meaning one; a single entity or operation, or an expression that requires only one operand.

**unbalanced line**    Refers to a cable design that uses different wire types for the signal and ground. Coaxial cable is an unbalanced line, because the signal wire is a small solid wire, and the ground wire is a braided metal that wraps around the inner wire and insulation. Contrast with *balanced line*.

**unbundle**    To sell components in a system separately. Contrast with *bundle*.

**unbundling**    A regulatory requirement that enables a competing service provider to purchase parts of the incumbent local exchange carrier's network in order to provide service to its customers. See *ILEC*.

**UNC**    (Universal Naming Convention)  A standard for identifying servers, printers and other resources in a network that originated in the UNIX community. A UNC path uses double slashes or backslashes to precede the name of the computer. The path (disk and directories) within the computer are separated with a single slash or backslash, as in the following examples (note that the drive letter is no longer used in the DOS/Windows example):

```
//servername/path      UNIX

\\servername\path      DOS/Windows
```

**uncached speed**    The data transfer rate between devices or components without using any cache in between. See *cache*.

**unchannelized**    Not using channels. See *channelized*.

**unconditional branch**    In programming, a GOTO, BRANCH or JUMP instruction that passes control to a different part of the program. Contrast with *conditional branch*.

**undelete**    To restore the last delete operation that has taken place. There may be more than one level of undelete, allowing several or all previous deletions to be restored. See *DOS Undelete*.

**underflow**    (1) An error condition that occurs when the result of a computation is smaller than the smallest quantity the computer can store.
(2) An error condition that occurs when an item is called from an empty stack.

**Undernet**    One of the largest Internet Relay Chat networks. It serves more than 35 countries and 100,000 users weekly. Its UnderCurrents newsletter covers news and events in the IRC world. For information, visit www.undernet.org. See *EFNet* and *Internet Relay Chat*.

**underrun**    When writing a CD-R disc, the inability for the computer to keep up with the recording process. CD-R discs, prior to using the CD UDF file format, have to be written in one continuous stream that cannot be interrupted. See *CD UDF*, *thermal recalibration* and *coaster*.

**underscan**    Within the normal rectangular viewing area on a display screen. Contrast with *overscan*.

**undo**    To restore the last editing operation that has taken place. For example, if a segment of text has been deleted or changed, performing an undo will restore the original text. Programs may have several levels of undo, including being able to reconstruct the original data for all edits performed in the current session. See *redo*.

**UNI**    (User-to-Network Interface) The interface between the end user and the network. The terms are used in ATM and frame relay networks. Contrast with *NNI*.

**Unibus**    A bus architecture from Digital that was introduced in 1970 with its PDP-11 series. Unibus peripherals can be connected to a VAX through Unibus attachments on the VAXs.

**unicast**    In communications networks, to transmit a message to one receiver, typically from a server to a workstation. In unicast, even though multiple users might request the same data from the same server at the same time, duplicate data streams are transmitted, one to each user. Contrast with *multicast*.

**unicast routing protocol**    A routing protocol that does not support multicast. See *routing protocol* and *multicast*. Contrast with *multicast routing protocol*.

**Unicenter**    See *CA-Unicenter*.

**Unicode**    A superset of the ASCII character set that uses two bytes for each character rather than one. Able to handle 65,536 character combinations rather than just 256, it can house the alphabets of most of the world's languages. ISO defines a four-byte character set for world alphabets, but also uses Unicode as a subset. For information, visit www.unicode.org. See *UTF*.

**unidirectional**    The transfer or transmission of data in a channel in one direction only.

**UNIFACE**    An application development system for e-commerce and client/server environments from Compuware. It is a repository-driven system that integrates with a variety of CASE tools, report writers and version control systems. Supporting all major Web standards and component models, Windows, Mac and OS/2 clients, and VMS and UNIX servers, UNIFACE is known for its scalability and deployment on large enterprise-wide applications. UNIFACE was developed by Uniface International, which was acquired by Compuware.

**unified messaging**    Having access to e-mail, voice mail and faxes via a common interface on the computer or by telephone. Computer-based unified messaging displays e-mail and faxes on screen and plays back voice mail over the speaker. Audio-based systems convert text to speech to deliver messages to any remote user at a desk phone or cellphone.

**UNIFY 2000**    A relational DBMS for UNIX platforms from Unify Corporation, Sacramento, CA (www.unify.com). Introduced in 1982, it was the first commercially available RDBMS for UNIX.

**Unify VISION**    An application development system for client/server environments from Unify Corporation, Sacramento, CA (www.unify.com). Introduced in 1993, it provides visual programming tools and supports a variety of UNIX platforms and databases. It provides automated application partitioning for developing three-tier client/server architectures. Other Unify Corporation products are the ACCELL/SQL 4GL and UNIFY 2000 relational DBMS.

**Unimodem**   A driver from Microsoft that provides common telephony services for Windows applications that access data and fax modems. Unimodem is a Telephony Service Provider (TSP) that accepts calls written to the TAPI interface and commands the modem directly.

**uninstall**   To remove hardware or software from a computer system. In order to remove a software application from a PC, an uninstall program, also called an "uninstaller," deletes all the files that were initially copied to the hard disk and restores the AUTOEXEC.BAT, CONFIG.SYS, WIN.INI and SYSTEM.INI files if they were modified.

Many applications come with their own uninstall utility. Otherwise, a generic uninstall program can be used to uninstall any application. It must be used when the application is first installed, because it works by monitoring and recording all changes made to the computer system.

**uninstaller**   Software that helps uninstall applications from a computer. See *uninstall*.

**union**   In relational database, the joining of two files. See *set theory*.

**uniprocessor**   A single processor. As more and more computers employ multiprocessing architectures, such as SMP and MPP, the term is used to refer to a system that still has only one CPU. Although most desktop computers are uniprocessor systems, it is expected that dual processor systems will become commonplace on the desktop in the coming years.

**unique visitors**   A count of how many different people access a Web site. For example, if a user leaves and comes back to the site five times during the measurement period, that person is counted as one unique visitor, but would count as five "user sessions."

Unique visitors are determined by the number of unique IP addresses on incoming requests that a site receives, but this can never be 100% accurate. Depending on configuration issues and type of ISP service, in some cases, one IP address can represent several users; in other cases, several IP addresses can be from the same user.

**UniSQL**   An object-oriented DBMS from UniSQL, Austin, TX (www.unisql.com). UniSQL/X is a relational and object-oriented DBMS for UNIX servers that provides SQL and object access to the database. UniSQL/M adds object-oriented capability to SQL Server, Oracle, Ingres and other relational DBMSs.

**Unisys**   (Unisys Corporation, Blue Bell, PA, www.unisys.com)  An information technology company that was created in 1986 as a merger of the Burroughs and Sperry corporations. It was the largest merger of computer manufacturers in history. Today, Unisys offers a wide range of consulting and support services, as well as enterprise-class computer systems and software, for a variety of industries.

Unisys' line of Intel–based e-@ction Enterprise Servers utilize many features inherited from the company's vast mainframe experience. Running Windows NT, 2000 or UnixWare, the top-end ES7000 uses a unique crossbar architecture than delivers mainframe performance with 32-way processing on Pentium Xeon or Itanium processors. Its e-@ction ClearPath mainframes continue to support the MCP (Burroughs) and OS 2200 (Sperry) environments by providing both native CMOS-based CPUs and Intel CPUs in the same system. RAID storage systems and desktop PCs are also available.

**Burroughs Adding Machine**
This adding machine was built circa 1895 and was an example of the exciting new machinery at the turn of the twentieth century.
*(Image courtesy of Unisys Corporation.)*

Unisys traces its roots back to the earliest days of computing and data processing. Sperry started in 1933 in navigational guidance and control equipment. In 1955, it merged with Remington Rand, creator of the UNIVAC I, and became Sperry Rand. Sperry became known for its mainframes and for providing communications and realtime systems to the military and NASA. In 1971, it absorbed RCA's computer division and supported the Spectra 70 series until it was phased out. From the 1960s to the 1980s, Sperry's UNIVAC line provided state-of-the-art mainframe processing.

Burroughs started as a maker of calculating machines and cash registers in 1886. It was first involved with computers by supplying memory for the ENIAC in 1952. A decade later, it introduced the B5000 computer, which was hailed for its advanced operating system. Burroughs computers became well established in the banking and finance industries throughout the 1960s and 1970s.

U

**unit test**   Running one component of a system for testing purposes. See *system test*.

**UNIVAC I**   (UNIVersal Automatic Computer) The first commercially successful computer, introduced in 1951 by Remington Rand. Over 40 systems were sold. Its memory was made of mercury-filled acoustic delay lines that held 1,000 12-digit numbers. It used magnetic tapes that stored 1MB of data at a density of 128 cpi. In 1952, it predicted Eisenhower's victory over Stevenson, and UNIVAC became synonymous with computer (for a while). UNIVAC I's were in use up until the early 1960s.

**The UNIVAC I**
In 1951, Remington Rand had the jump on the computer industry when it introduced the UNIVAC I. For a while, the words "Univac" and "computer" were synonymous. There were more than 40 UNIVAC I's installed. *(Image courtesy of Unisys Corporation.)*

**UNIVAC I**
The circuitry that filled up the walk-in CPU of the UNIVAC I, now fits on your finger. The UNIVAC I made history in 1952 when it predicted Eisenhower's victory. This picture is news coverage of that event. *(Image courtesy of Unisys Corporation.)*

**UniVBE**   (UNIveral VESA BIOS Extension) A SciTech Software VESA driver from TR Consulting, San Jose, CA, that supports VGA adapters from more than 20 different vendors. It allows DOS applications that are written to the VESA BIOS Extension standard to work with most of the display adapters on the market.

**universal client**   A computer that can access a wide variety of applications on the network. The Web browser is hailed as a universal client because of its platform-independent ability to reach the Internet and corporate intranets. An e-mail client (mail program) that can access multiple messaging systems could be called a universal client.

**universal port replicator**   A port replicator that works with any notebook computer. It connects to the computer via a PC Card rather than a proprietary connector. See *port replicator* and *docking station*.

**universal server**   (1) A database management system (DBMS) that stores all types of information, including traditional data fields (relational database), as well as graphics and multimedia (object-oriented database). A universal server is an *object-relational DBMS* or *ORDBMS*.

(2) (Universal Server) A universal server from Informix. It supports DataBlades, which are plug-ins designed to manage a particular type of complex data. For example, an image DataBlade might allow a user to search for matching images.

**universal time**   See *UTC*.

**UNIX**   A multiuser, multitasking operating system that is widely used as the master control program in workstations, and especially servers. A myriad of commercial applications run on UNIX servers, and most Web sites run under UNIX. There are many versions of UNIX, and, except for the PC world, where Windows dominates, almost every hardware vendor offers it either as its primary or secondary operating system. Sun has been singularly instrumental in commercializing UNIX with its Solaris OS (formerly SunOS). HP, SCO, IBM and Digital have also been major UNIX vendors and promoters.

UNIX is written in C. Both UNIX and C were developed by AT&T and freely distributed to government and academic institutions, causing it to be ported to a wider variety of machine families than any other operating system. As a result, UNIX became synonymous with "open systems."

UNIX is made up of the kernel, file system and shell (command-line interface). The major shells are the Bourne shell (original), C shell and Korn shell. The UNIX vocabulary is exhaustive, with more than 600 commands that manipulate data and text in every way conceivable. Many commands are cryptic (as you can see in the following table), but just as Windows hid the DOS prompt, the Motif GUI presents a friendlier image to UNIX users.

| Command | UNIX | DOS |
|---|---|---|
| List directory | ls | dir |
| Copy a file | cp | copy |
| Delete a file | rm | del |
| Rename a file | mv | rename |
| Display contents | cat | type |
| Print a file | lpr | print |
| Check disk space | df | chkdsk |
| Change directory | cd | cd |

**The History of UNIX**    UNIX was developed in 1969 by Ken Thompson at AT&T, who scaled down the sophisticated MULTICS operating system for the PDP-7. The name was coined for a single-user version (UNo) of "multIX." More work was done by Dennis Ritchie; and, by 1974, UNIX had matured into an efficient operating system primarily on PDP machines. UNIX became very popular in scientific and academic environments.

Considerable enhancements were made to UNIX at the University of California at Berkeley, and versions of UNIX with the Berkeley extensions became widely used. By the late 1970s, commercial versions of UNIX, such as IS/1 and XENIX, became available.

In the early 1980s, AT&T began to consolidate the many UNIX versions into standards that evolved into System III, and eventually System V. Before Divestiture (1984), AT&T licensed UNIX to universities and other organizations, but was prohibited from outright marketing of the product. After divestiture, it began to market UNIX aggressively.

**A Lot of Bouncing Around**    In 1989, AT&T formed the UNIX Software Operation (USO) division. USO introduced System V Release 4.0 (SVR4), which incorporated XENIX, SunOS, Berkeley 4.3BSD and System V into one UNIX standard. The System V Interface Definition (SVID) was introduced, which defined UNIX compatibility. In 1990, USO became an AT&T subsidiary renamed UNIX System Laboratories, Inc. (USL). In 1993, the UNIX source code was acquired by Novell, and, in 1995, Novell sold it to The Santa Cruz Operation (SCO).

More attempts at unifying UNIX into one standard have been made than for any other operating system. Over the years, various industry consortia have tried to make UNIX a shrink-wrapped standard like DOS, Windows and the Mac. However, since UNIX runs on so many different hardware platforms, the only way the same shrink-wrapped UNIX program could ever run on all of them is by the use of an intermediate language similar to Java. The Open Group's ANDF was an attempt at this.

What UNIX application developers really hope for is a single UNIX programming interface (API) so that they only have to recompile the source code for each platform, rather than maintain different versions of the source code. The latest attempt to do this is the Single UNIX Specification governed by X/Open, which brands compliant software with the UNIX logo. X/Open also governs the Common Desktop Environment (CDE), which is a standard user interface for UNIX based on Motif.

**UNIX Is Popular**    Even with its many versions, UNIX is widely used in mission-critical applications for client/server and transaction processing systems. UNIX components are world class standards. The TCP/IP transport protocol and SMTP e-mail protocol are de facto standards on the Internet. NFS allows files to be accessible across the network, NIS provides a "Yellow Pages" directory, Kerberos provides network security, and X Window lets users run applications on remote servers and view the results on their machines. See *X/Open, Open Group, POSIX, CDE, BSD UNIX, USENIX* and *UDI*.

**UNIX Is Everywhere**    The UNIX versions that are widely used are Sun's Solaris, Digital's UNIX, HP's HP-UX, IBM's AIX and SCO's UnixWare. A large number of IBM mainframes also run UNIX applications, because the UNIX interfaces were added to MVS and OS/390, which have obtained UNIX branding (see *X/Open*). Linux, another variant of UNIX, is also gaining enormous popularity (see *Linux*).

**UNIX 93**   An X/Open brand used on a product that is compliant with a number of UNIX-based specifications, including XPG3, XPG4, SVID and AT&T source code. In early 1996, X/Open closed this branding. See *X/Open* and *UNIX 95*.

**UNIX 95**   An X/Open brand used on a product that is compliant with Version 1 of the Single UNIX Specification. See *Single UNIX Specification* and *X/Open*.

**UNIX 98**   An X/Open brand used on a product that is compliant with Version 2 of the Single UNIX Specification. See *Single UNIX Specification* and *X/Open*.

**UNIX International**   A non-profit industry association founded to provide direction for UNIX System V. It was disbanded in 1993 after Novell purchased UNIX from AT&T.

**UNIX server**   A medium- to large-scale computer system in a network that runs under UNIX. UNIX servers are widely used as application servers and database servers, and are available from a variety of vendors, including Sun, HP, IBM, Digital and others. Sun has been the major proponent of UNIX-based computer systems in the commercial world running on its SPARC processors, and The Santa Cruz Operation (SCO) has been the leading vendor of UNIX on the Intel platform for some time. See *UNIX*, *server* and *SPARC*.

**UNIX shell account**   A customer account with an Internet service provider (ISP) that requires the user to enter UNIX commands to send and receive mail and files. Prior to today's graphical interfaces, Internet access was always a command-line operation performed by researchers and computer buffs.

**UNIX socket**   The method of directing data to the appropriate application in a TCP/IP network. The combination of the IP address of the station and a port number make up a socket. See *port number* and *well-known port*.

**UnixWare**   See *SCO UnixWare*.

**UNIX/X**   See *X Window*.

**unlicensed band**   See *ISM band*.

**unload**   To remove a program from memory or take a tape or disk out of its drive.

**UNMA**   (Unified Network Management Architecture) A network strategy from AT&T for managing multi-vendor networks.

**unmanaged hub**   A network hub that does not support management queries or commands. Typically an Ethernet hub, it serves as a central connecting point only. Contrast with *managed hub*.

**unmark**   (1) In word processing, to deselect a block of text, which usually removes its highlight.
   (2) To deselect an item that has been tagged for a particular purpose.

**unpack**   See *pack*.

**unqualified address**   An incomplete address. For example, a mail program may provide a default name for all recipient addressess that are given without a domain name.

**unscramble**   Same as *decrypt*. See *scramble*.

**unshielded twisted pair**   See *twisted pair*.

**unstructured data**   Data that does not reside in fixed locations. Free-form text in a word processing document is a typical example. Contrast with *structured data*. See *free-form database*.

**unsubscribe**   To cancel a service. It is often possible to unsubscribe to an e-mail service by typing the word "unsubscribe" into a reply message. Contrast with *subscribe*.

**unzip**    To decompress a file in the .ZIP file format. See *Zip file*.

**up**    Refers to a device that is working.

**UPC**    (Universal Product Code) The standard bar code printed on retail merchandise. It contains the vendor's identification number and the product number, which are read by passing the bar code over a scanner. See *bar code scanner*.

**update**    To change data in a file or database. The terms update and edit are often used synonymously, although update is more often used to refer to changes in a database and edit for changes in a text file. The terms "update" and "upgrade" are also used synonymously, although "update" generally refers to adding and deleting elements of data and "upgrade" refers to changing to new software. For example, we revise this *Encyclopedia* database and then release a software upgrade that contains the updated database. See *edit*.

**UPC Codes Everywhere**
You can hardly pick up a retail package anywhere today that does not have a UPC bar code on it.

**upgrade**    To replace existing software with a newer version. See *update*, *upgrade* and ***About this product***.

**uplink**    A communications channel from an Earth station to a satellite. Contrast with *downlink*.

**uplink port**    A port on a network hub or switch that is used to connect to other hubs and switches rather than an end station. See *MDI port*.

**upload**    See *download*.

**UPS**    (Uninterruptible Power Supply) Backup power used when the electrical power fails or drops to an unacceptable voltage level. Small UPS systems provide battery power for a few minutes; enough to power down the computer in an orderly manner. Sophisticated systems are tied to electrical generators that can provide power for days.

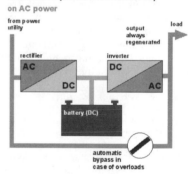

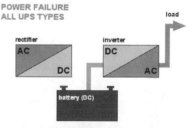

**Three UPS Types**
All UPS systems switch to battery when the power fails. The difference is how they handle the power under normal circumstances. Standby units provide limited attenuation, whereas line interactive systems will adjust the voltage and smooth out bad harmonics. Online systems are constantly regenerating clean power. *(Diagrams courtesy of MGE UPS SYSTEMS.)*

A UPS system can be connected to a file server so that, in the event of a problem, all network users can be alerted to save files and shut down immediately.

An "online UPS" provides a constant source of electrical power from the battery, while the batteries are being recharged from AC power. A "standby UPS," also called an "offline UPS," normally draws current from the AC outlet and switches to battery within a few milliseconds after detecting a power failure.

U

The "line interactive UPS" is a hybrid of the online and standby units. Like the standby, it does not constantly draw from the battery, but it switches to battery faster when required. In addition, the line interactive unit does not use the battery when low voltage is encountered. It uses extra power from the AC source to make up the difference in voltage.

A surge protector filters out surges and spikes, and a voltage regulator maintains uniform voltage during a brownout, but a UPS keeps a computer running when there is no electrical power. UPS systems typically provide surge suppression and may also provide voltage regulation.

**UPS—Now More Than Ever**   In order to improve performance, computers are increasingly using write-back caches, which means that updated data intended for the disk is temporarily stored in RAM. If a power failure occurs, there is more of a chance that new data will be lost; thus, UPS systems are becoming important for all computers.

**upstream**   See *downstream*.

**uptime**   The time during which a system is working without failure. Contrast with *downtime*. See *availability*.

**upward compatible**   Also called "forward compatible." Refers to hardware or software that is compatible with succeeding versions. Contrast with *downward compatible*.

**URI**   (Uniform Resource Identifier) The addressing technology from which URLs are created. Technically, URLs such as HTTP:// and FTP:// are specific subsets of URIs.

**URL**   (Uniform Resource Locator) The address that defines the route to a file on the Web or any other Internet facility. URLs are typed into the browser to access Web pages, and URLs are embedded within the pages themselves to provide the hypertext links to other pages.

The URL contains the protocol prefix, port number, domain name, subdirectory names and file name. Port addresses are generally defaults and are rarely specified. To access a home page on a Web site, only the protocol and domain name are required. For example,

```
http://www.computerlanguage.com
```

retrieves the home page at The Computer Language Company's Web site. The "http" is the Web protocol, and www.computerlanguage.com is the domain name.

If the page is stored in another directory, or if a page other than the home page is required, slashes are used to separate the names. For example, http://www.computerlanguage.com/order.html points to the order page.

If a required page is stored in a subdirectory, its name is separated by a slash. Like path names in DOS and Windows, subdirectories can be several levels deep. For example, the components of the following hypothetical URL are described here:

```
http://www.abc.com/clothes/shirts/formal.html
```

```
http:           protocol
//              separators
www.abc.com/    domain name
clothes/        subdirectory name
shirts/         subdirectory name
formal.html     document name (Web page)
```

Following is a list of the Internet protocols defined by URLs. Most browsers default to HTTP if a prefix is not typed in.

| Prefix | To Gain Access to... | Prefix | To Gain Access to... |
|--------|----------------------|--------|----------------------|
| http:  | World Wide Web server | file:   | file on local system |
| ftp:   | FTP server (file transfer) | ldap:   | directory request |
| news:  | Usenet newsgroups | telnet: | applications on network server |
| mailto: | e-mail | rlogin: | applications on network server |
| wais:  | Wide Area Information Server | tn3270: | applications on mainframe |
| gopher: | Gopher server | | |

**URL hijacking**   See *page hijacking*.

**URL switch**   See *Web switch*.

**usability**   How easy something is to use. Both software and Web sites can be tested for usability. Considering how difficult applications are to use and Web sites are to navigate, one would wish that more designers took this seriously. See *user interface* and *usability lab*.

**usability lab**   A testing facility for software that deals with its ease of learning and ease of use. See *usability*.

**USB**   (Universal Serial Bus) A hardware interface for low-speed peripherals such as the keyboard, mouse, joystick, scanner, printer and telephony devices. It also supports MPEG-1 and MPEG-2 digital video. USB has a maximum bandwidth of 12 Mbits/sec (equivalent to 1.5 Mbytes/sec), and up to 127 devices can be attached. Fast devices can use the full bandwidth, while lower-speed ones can transfer data using a 1.5 Mbits/sec subchannel.

USB's hot swap capability allows everything to be plugged in and unplugged without turning the system off. USB ports began to appear on PCs in 1997, and Windows 98 fully supports it. USB 2.0 dramatically increases capacity to 480 Mbits/sec, which challenges FireWire (IEEE 1394) as the serial interface of the future.

Devices are plugged directly into a four-pin socket on the PC or into a multi-port hub that plugs into the PC or into a device that also functions as a hub for other devices.

The USB bus distributes 0.5 amps (500 milliamps) of power through each port. Thus, low-power devices that might normally require a separate AC adapter can be powered through the cable. Hubs may derive all power from the USB bus (bus powered), or they may be powered from their own AC adapter. Powered hubs with at least 0.5 amps per port provide the most flexibility for future downstream devices. Port switching hubs isolate all ports from each other so that one shorted device will not bring down the others.

USB ports on the PC and hubs use a rectangular Type A socket. All cables that are permanently attached to the device have a Type A plug. Devices that use a separate cable have a square Type B socket, and the cable that connects them has a Type A and Type B plug.

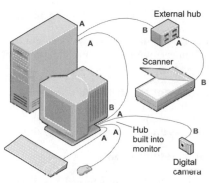

**USB Connections**
Hubs can be stand-alone units or built into the monitor, which makes it easier to connect the keyboard, mouse and other devices. The thin Type A sockets are used on the PC and hubs. Type B sockets are on the input side of hubs and on peripherals that have separate cables.

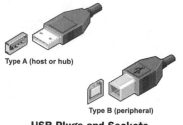

Type A (host or hub)

Type B (peripheral)

**USB Plugs and Sockets**

**USB hub**   A device that increases the number of USB ports on a PC. It cables into the PC's USB port and typically provides four Type A sockets for expansion.

**USB modem**   A modem that plugs into the USB port of a computer. It typically refers to a V.90 analog modem, but might refer to a DSL modem. See *V.90* and *DSL*.

**use-case analysis**   An object-oriented method for designing information systems by breaking down requirements into user functions. Each use case is a transaction or sequence of events performed by the user. Use cases are studied to determine what objects are required to accomplish them and how they interact with other objects. See *UML*.

**used computers**   See *computer exchange*.

**Usenet**   (USEr NETwork) A public access network on the Internet that provides user news and group e-mail. It is a giant, dispersed bulletin board that is maintained by volunteers who provide news and mail feeds to other nodes. All the news that travels over the Internet is called "NetNews," and a running collection of messages about a particular subject is called a "newsgroup." Usenet began in 1979 as a bulletin board between two universities in North Carolina. Today, there are more than 50,000 newsgroups. News can be read with a Web browser or via newsreaders such as nn, rn, trn and tin. See *newsgroup* and *NNTP*.

**USENIX**   (USENIX Association, Berkeley, CA, www.usenix.org) Known officially as the Advanced Computer Systems Association, it is a membership group of UNIX programmers and systems professionals that was founded in 1975. USENIX sponsors workshops and conferences, student programs and awards. The System Administrators Guild (SAGE), which is a special technical group for USENIX members, is devoted to the advancement of system administrators.

**user**   Any individual who interacts with the computer at an application level. Programmers, operators and other technical personnel are not considered users when working in a professional capacity on the computer.

**user account**   An established relationship between a user and a computer, network or information service. User accounts require a username and password, and new user accounts are given a default set of permissions. See *user profile* and *guest account*.

**user agent**   (1) The mail client in a messaging system. See *messaging system*.
(2) A field in the HTTP request header that contains the name and version of the Web browser. See *HTTP request header*.

**user area**   A reserved part of a disk or memory for user data.

**user default profile**   A default set of permissions assigned to new uesrs. See *user account* and *user profile*.

**user defined**   Any format, layout, structure or language that is developed by the user.

**user friendly**   A system that is easy to learn and easy to use. This term has been so abused that many vendors are reluctant to use it.

**user group**   An organization of users of a particular hardware or software product. Members share experiences and ideas to improve their understanding and use of a particular product. User groups are often responsible for influencing vendors to change or enhance their products.

The oldest user group in the U.S. still extant is ACGNJ (Amateur Computer Group of New Jersey). Founded in 1974 by Professor Sol Libes, it was one of the first computer clubs organized around microprocessors. ACGNJ also created the Trenton Computer Festival (TCF) in 1976, which it sponsors every year. TCF was the first personal computer show and flea market in the U.S. See **Trenton Computer Festival**.

For contacts and information about the user groups in the U.S. and Canada, visit the User Group Connection at www.ugconnection.org.

**userid**   (USER IDentification) See *username*.

**user interface**   The combination of menus, screen design, keyboard commands, command language and online help, which creates the way a user interacts with a computer. If input devices other than a keyboard and mouse are required, this is also included. In the future, natural language recognition and voice recognition will become standard components of the user interface.

The user interface is the most important, yet least-understood area in the software industry, as programmers are often the ones responsible for designing everything the user interacts with. This is generally a formula for disaster, because most programmers do not have a clue how to do it. Every application has only a handful of basic functions that users need all the time, yet they are buried in arcane menus and submenus that must be memorized. Worse yet, once bad examples are set by Microsoft, Adobe or some other major vendor, everybody follows it like sheep. Since the most popular applications are often the hardest to learn, users have come to expect that software is just plain difficult, when, in fact, it could be downright simple if educated user interface designers were involved.

Because of the steep learning curves users have gone through, many are afraid to change applications. While the industry touts "productivity gains" for almost every software product, the lost hours frustrating over how to do something, combined with the general reluctance to try something else that could truly be an improvement, all results in lost productivity that cannot be measured. If we are ever to make computers usable for the masses, this issue must be addressed.

For an excellent display of good and bad examples of user interface design, visit www.iarchitect.com. See *RTFM*, **naming fiascos**, *Freedman's law*, *Web rage* and *HCI*.

**A User Interface Can Change World History**    Nothing could better highlight the importance of a user interface than the U.S. national election of 2000. The confusing punched card ballot used in Palm Beach County Florida caused thousands of voters to vote for Buchanan rather than Gore or Bush, and the presidency hinged on the results. Is a ballot a user interface? You bet it is. Any designed interaction between man and machine is a user interface, and this one people will remember in the history books!

| Desired file type | Double-click |
|---|---|
| Still image | "100msdcf" folder |
| Moving image* | "Mom10001" folder |
| Audio* | "Momlv100" folder |
| E-mail image TIFF image | "Imcif100" folder |

**Give Us a Break!**
These delightful folder names were chosen to store pictures on a digital camera's memory card. Wouldn't folder names such as Still, Moving, Audio, and E-mail be slightly more to the point. Hello-o-o-o-o-o! This insanity is perpetrated by countless vendors.

**user-level security**    Access control to a file, printer or other network resource based on username. It provides greater protection than share-level security, because users are identified individually or within a group. User-level permissions are stored in a central server and managed by the network administrator. See *share-level security*.

**username**    The name you use to identify yourself when logging onto a computer system or online service. Both a username (user ID) and a password are required. In an Internet e-mail address, the username is the left part before the @ sign. For example, KARENB is the username in **karenb@mycompany.com**. AOL calls a username a "screen name."

**user profile**    The preferences and current desktop configuration of a user's machine. User profiles enable several users to work on the same computer with their own desktop setup. When stored in a server, user profiles enable users to obtain their desktop configuration when working at a different machine. See *system policy*.

**user provisioning**    The ability for customers to change voice and data services from their carriers online without having to place the order with a human representative. Web-based user provisioning lets you add and delete services and features from your browser. See *automated provisioning*.

**user session**    An encounter between a user and an application, or with the computer in general. One user session is the time between starting the application and quitting. See also *user sessions*.

**user sessions**    A count of how many times all users access a Web site, regardless whether the same person came back several times during the measurement period. If a user leaves and returns within a short time, some systems count those sessions as one. Contrast with *unique visitors*. See also *user session*.

**USOC**    (Universal Service Order Code) An equipment coding system created by AT&T. The number was applied to telephone equipment and to wire termination patterns. See *568A*.

**USR**    See *U.S. Robotics*.

**U.S. Robotics**    (U.S. Robotics, Inc., Skokie, IL, www.usr.com) A modem manufacturer highly regarded for its quality products. The company manufactures its own chipsets (data pumps) and often leads with innovations. Its HST protocol was a high-speed, reliable protocol before V.32bis became a modem standard in 1991. USR's Sportster models have been the best-selling modems in the world. In 1997, the company became part of 3Com in the largest merger in data networking history. See *3Com*.

**USRT**    (Universal Synchronous Receiver Transmitter) An electronic circuit that transmits and receives data on the serial port. It converts bytes into serial bits for transmission, and vice versa, and generates the necessary signals for synchronous transmission.

**UTC**   (Universal Time Coordinated) The international time standard (formerly Greenwich Mean Time, or GMT). Zero hours UTC is midnight in Greenwich England, which is located at 0 degrees longitude. Everything east of Greenwich (up to 180 degrees) is later in time; everything west is earlier. See *NTP*.

**UTF**   (Universal Transformation Format) A method for converting 16-bit Unicode characters into 7- or 8-bit characters. UTF-7 converts to 7-bit ASCII for transmission over 7-bit mail systems, while UTF-8 converts Unicode to 8-bit bytes. See *Unicode* and *7-bit ASCII*.

**UTG**   (UnixWare Technology Group) An organization formed in 1994 to establish UnixWare as an open standard. UnixWare was then owned by Novell who later sold it to SCO. UTG has since folded.

**utility program**   A program that supports using the computer, an application or a development environment. Utility programs, or "utilities," that support everyday use of the computer include file management (creating, moving and renaming folders; copying and deleting files), searching for files and comparing file contents, as well as performing diagnostic routines to check performance and current health of the hardware.

Utilities that support a development environment can perform a myriad of tasks. For example, at the end of each update cycle of this *Computer Desktop Encyclopedia*, custom-programmed utilities are run that test for the proper sequence of terms, and test to make sure all "See this term" references and all picture references are valid, and so on.

**UTP**   (Unshielded Twisted Pair) See *twisted pair*.

**UTP Ethernet**   (1) (Unshielded Twisted Pair Ethernet) See *Ethernet*.
(2) May refer to pre-IEEE standard twisted pair Ethernet networks.

**UTS**   (Universal Timesharing System) Amdahl's version of UNIX System V. Release 4.0 is POSIX compliant.

**UUcoding**   A common method for transmitting non-text files via Internet e-mail, which was originally designed for ASCII text. The UUencode utility encodes the files by converting 8-bit characters into 7-bit ASCII text, and the UUdecode utility decodes it back to its original format at the receiving end. Originating in the UNIX community, UUcoding was one of the first methods for sending binary files as attached files over Internet e-mail. Today, MIME is widely used. See *BinHex*, *MIME* and ***Wincode***

**UUCP**   (UNIX to UNIX CoPy) A UNIX utility that copies a file from one computer to another. It was widely used for mail transfer. Unlike TCP/IP, which is a routable communications protocol, UUCP provides a point-to-point transmission where a user at one UNIX computer dials up and establishes a session with another UNIX computer. See *bang path*.

**UUNET**   (UUNET Technologies, Inc., Fairfax, VA, www.uunet.net) Founded in 1987, UUNET was the first commercial Internet service provider. Originally offering e-mail and news, it is now a full Internet service organization providing dial-up and leased line accounts, as well as archive space for files and Web pages. UUNET stands for UNIX to UNIX Network. In 1996, UUNET was acquired by MFS Communications, which was acquired by WorldCom in that same year. See *Worldcom*.

**UWC-136**   (Universal Wireless Communications-136) Enhancements to the TDMA (IS-136) cellular phone system that increase data rates. EDGE and WIN are key components of UWC-136. See *UWC Consortium*, *wireless generations*, *EDGE* and *WIN*.

**UWC Consortium**   (Universal Wireless Communications Consortium) A membership organization that supports the IS-41 (WIN) information and control system, and EDGE enhancements for increased data rates. See *WIN*.

**UXGA**   (Ultra XGA) A screen resolution of 1,600×1,200 pixels. See *PC display modes*.

**V.110**   An ITU standard (1984) that specifies how data terminal equipment (DTE) with asynchronous or synchronous serial interfaces can be supported on an ISDN network. It uses rate adaption, which involves a bit-by-bit alignment between the DTE and the ISDN B channel.

**V.120**   An ITU standard (1988) that specifies how DTEs with asynchronous or synchronous serial interfaces can be supported on an ISDN network using a protocol (similar to LAP-D) to encapsulate the data to be transmitted. It includes the capability of using statistical multiplexing to share a B channel connection between multiple DTEs.

**V.17**   An ITU fax standard (1991) that uses TCM modulation at 12,000 and 14,400 bps for Group 3. It adds TCM to the V.29 standard at 7,200 and 9,600 bps to allow transmission over noisier lines. It also defines special functions (echo protection, turn-off sequences, etc.) for half-duplex operation. Modulation use is a half-duplex version of V.32bis.

**V.21**   An ITU standard (1964) for asynchronous 0-300 bps full-duplex modems for use on dial-up lines. It uses FSK modulation.

**V.22**   An ITU standard (1980) for asynchronous and synchronous 600 and 1,200 bps full-duplex modems for use on dial-up lines. It uses DPSK modulation.

**V.22bis**   An ITU standard (1984) for asynchronous and synchronous 2,400 bps full-duplex modems for use on dial-up lines and two-wire leased lines, with fallback to V.22 1,200 bps operation. It uses QAM modulation.

**V.23**   An ITU standard (1964) for asynchronous and synchronous 0-600 and 0-1,200 bps half-duplex modems for use on dial-up lines. It has an optional split-speed transmission method with a reverse channel of 0-75 bps (1,200/75, 75/1,200). It uses FSK modulation.

**V.24**   An ITU standard (1964) that defines the functions of all circuits for the RS-232 interface. It does not describe the connectors or pin assignments; those are defined in ISO 2110. In the U.S., EIA-232 incorporates the control signal definition of V.24, the electrical characteristics of V.28 and the connector and pin assignments defined in ISO 2110.

**V.25**   An ITU standard (1968) for automatic calling and/or answering equipment on dial-up lines. It uses parallel circuits and is similar in function to RS-366 and Bell 801 autodialers used in the U.S. The answer tone defined in V.25 is the first thing heard when calling a modem. It serves a dual function of identifying the answering equipment as being a modem and also disabling the echo suppression and echo cancellation equipment in the network so that a full-duplex modem will operate properly.

**V.25bis**   An ITU standard (1968) for automatic calling and/or answering equipment on dial-up lines. It has three modes: asynchronous (rarely used), character-oriented synchronous (bisync) and bit-oriented synchronous (HDLC/SDLC). Both synchronous versions are used in IBM AS/400 and other small-to-medium sized computers that do automatic dialing for remote job entry.

Due to the popularity of the Hayes AT Command Set, V.25bis is not used as widely in North America. It does not perform modem configuration functions and is limited to dialing and answering calls.

**V.26**    An ITU standard (1968) for synchronous 2,400 bps full-duplex modems for use on four-wire leased lines. It uses DPSK modulation and includes an optional 75 bps back channel.

**V.26bis**    An ITU standard (1972) for synchronous 1,200 and 2,400 bps full-duplex modems for use on dial-up lines. It uses DPSK modulation and includes an optional 75 bps back channel.

**V.26ter**    An ITU standard (1984) for asynchronous and synchronous 2,400 bps full-duplex modems using DPSK modulation over dial-up and two-wire leased lines. It includes a 1,200 bps fallback speed and uses echo cancellation, permitting a full-duplex modem to send and receive on the same frequency.

**V.27**    An ITU standard (1972) for synchronous 4,800 bps full-duplex modems for use on four-wire leased lines. It uses DPSK modulation.

**V.27bis**    An ITU standard (1976) for synchronous 2,400 and 4,800 bps full-duplex modems using DPSK modulation for use on four-wire leased lines. The primary difference between V.27 and V.27bis is the addition of an automatic adaptive equalizer.

**V.27ter**    An ITU standard (1976) for synchronous 2,400 and 4,800 bps half-duplex modems using DPSK modulation on dial-up lines. It includes an optional 75 bps back channel. V.27ter is used in Group 3 fax transmission without the back channel.

**V.28**    An ITU standard (1972) that defines the functions of all circuits for the RS-232 interface. In the U.S., EIA-232 incorporates the electrical signal definitions of V.28, the control signals of V.25 and the connector and pin assignments defined in ISO 2110.

**V.29**    An ITU standard (1976) for synchronous 4,800, 7,200 and 9,600 bps full-duplex modems using QAM modulation on four-wire leased lines. It has been adapted for Group 3 fax transmission over dial-up lines at 9,600 and 7,200 bps.

**V.32**    An ITU standard (1984) for asynchronous and synchronous 4,800 and 9,600 bps full-duplex modems using TCM modulation over dial-up or two-wire leased lines. TCM encoding may be optionally added. V.32 uses echo cancellation to achieve full-duplex transmission.

**V.32bis**    An ITU standard (1991) for asynchronous and synchronous 4,800, 7,200, 9,600, 12,000 and 14,400 bps full-duplex modems using TCM and echo cancellation. Supports rate renegotiation, which allows modems to change speeds as required.

**V.32terbo**    An AT&T standard for 19,200 bps modems adopted by some modem manufacturers. See *V.34*.

**V.33**    An ITU standard (1988) for synchronous 12,000 and 14,400 bps full-duplex modems for use on four-wire leased lines using QAM modulation. It includes an optional time-division multiplexor for sharing the transmission line among multiple terminals.

**V.34**    An ITU standard (1994) for 28,800 bps and (1996) 31,200 and 33,600 bps modems using QAM modulation. Before V.34, AT&T's V.32terbo and Rockwell International's V.FC modems came on the market to provide greater speed than the V.32bis 14,400 bps standard. After V.34 was standardized at 28.8 Kbps, subsequent enhancements that raised speeds to 33.6 Kbps were folded back into V.34, and there was no change in number or designation.

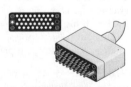

**V.35**    An ITU standard (1968) for group band modems that combine the bandwidth of several telephone circuits to achieve higher data rates. Although not specified in the ITU standard, the V.35 connector has become a de facto standard for a serial interface in the 48 to 64 Kbps range. It is typically used between a modem and a multiplexor.

**V.35 Connector**
V.35 connectors are used for serial transmission between communications devices.

**V.42**    An ITU standard (1989) for modem error checking that uses LAP-M as the primary protocol and provides MNP Classes 2 through 4 as an alternative protocol for compatibility.

**V.42bis**    An ITU standard (1989) for modem data compression. It uses the LZW technique to achieve up to a 4:1 ratio. V.42bis implies the V.42 error checking protocol.

**V.44**    An ITU standard (2000) for modem data compression. Optimized for Web traffic, V.44 provides up to a 6:1 compression ratio, compared to 4:1 in the V.42bis standard. See *V.92*.

**V.54**    An ITU standard (1976) for various loopback tests that can be incorporated into modems for testing the telephone circuit and isolating transmission problems. Operating modes include local and remote digital loopback and local and remote analog loopback.

**V.56**    An ITU standard (1972) for a method of testing modems to compare their performance. Newer procedures are currently under study.

**V.90**    An ITU standard (1998) for a modem that communicates at 56 Kbps downstream and 33.6 Kbps upstream. It is intended for use only with ISPs and online services that are digitally attached to the telephone system. Most service providers are typically connected with high-speed digital T1 or T3 circuits.

In practice, the downstream link isn't generally faster than 45 Kbps in these PCM modems, so called because they use pulse code modulation downstream and standard V.34 upstream. Initially, two incompatible technologies competed in this arena: x2 from U.S. Robotics and K56Flex from Rockwell and Lucent. Such modems can be upgraded to V.90 if they contain software-upgradable memory chips. See *V.92*, *V.34* and *channel bonding*.

**V.92**    An improved version of the V.90 modem that boosts the upstream rate from 33.6 Kbps to 48 Kbps. Introduced in 2000, V.92 reduces connection time (handshaking) by remembering the previous settings negotiated when dialing the same telephone number. It also supports call waiting by allowing the data session to be put on hold while a voice call is taken. See *V.90*.

**VAC**    (Volts Alternating Current)  See *volt* and *AC*.

**vacuum tube**    An electronic device that controls the flow of electrons in a vacuum. It is used as a switch, amplifier or display screen. Used as on/off switches, they allowed the first computers to perform digital computations. Although vacuum tubes have made a comeback in high-end stereo components, most vacuum tubes today are the picture tubes (CRTs) in monitors and TVs. See *vacuum tube types*.

**vacuum tube types**    Following are the different types of vacuum tubes and the elements used to control the flow of current.

**Early Vacuum Tube**
Early vacuum tubes were used to amplify signals for radio and other audio devices. This one was made in 1915. Tubes were not used as switches in calculating machines until 1939. *(Image courtesy of AT&T.)*

| Elements | Diode | Triode | Tetrode | Pentode |
|---|---|---|---|---|
| Cathode | X | X | X | X |
| Plate | X | X | X | X |
| Control grid | | X | X | X |
| Screen grid | | | X | X |
| Suppressor grid | | | | X |

**VAD**    (Value Added Dealer)  Same as *VAR*.

**VADSL**    (Very high bit rate Asymmetric DSL)  An earlier name for VDSL. See *DSL*.

**VAFC**    See *VESA Advanced Feature Connector*.

**validity checking**    Routines in a data entry program that tests the input for correct and reasonable conditions, such as numbers falling within a range and correct spelling, if possible. See *check digit*.

**value**    (1) The content of a field or variable. It can refer to alphabetic as well as numeric data. For example, in the expression, **state = "PA"**, PA is a value.

(2) In spreadsheets, the numeric data within the cell.

**value-added network**    A communications network that provides services beyond normal transmission, such as automatic error detection and correction, protocol conversion and message storing and forwarding. Telenet and Tymnet are examples of value-added networks.

**value market**    The market for low-priced consumer goods. A value PC is intended for the first-time user or as a second or third computer in the household.

**value PC**    A lower priced PC intended for the first-time user or as a second or third computer in the household.

**value proposition**    The essential benefit of a product or service. "What is the value proposition?" means "what problem is this really solving?" A company's value proposition is its primary mission or goal (its reason for being). The term is widely used in the high-tech industry.

**vampire tap**    A cable connection that is made with a unit that clamps onto and "bites" into the cable, hence the vampire name. Vampire taps are often used to attach thick Ethernet transceivers to the coaxial cable. Without a vampire tap, the cable has to be cut and connectors have to be attached to both ends.

**VAN**    See *value-added network*.

**vandal**    A program that performs a clandestine or malicious function such as extracting a user's password or other data or erasing the hard disk. A vandal differs from a virus, which attaches itself to an existing executable program. The vandal is the full executing entity itself which can be downloaded from the Internet in the form of an ActiveX control, Java applet, browser plug-in or e-mail attachment. See *virus*.

**VAP**    (Value Added Process) An executable program in a NetWare 2.x server. Starting with NetWare 3.x, VAPs were replaced by NLMs. See *NetWare*.

**vaporware**    Software that is not completed and shipping to customers, but the announced delivery date has passed. At times, major software vendors are criticized for intentionally producing vaporware in order to keep customers from switching to competitive products that offer more features. However, today's commercial software is more difficult than ever to program, and programmers are notorious for being terrible estimators of project time. As a result, shipping dates often slip over and over again.

There is often just as large a gap between management and technical staff in software companies than there is user organizations, private or public. Dates slip because the project is not managed properly, which can be caused by management's lack of understanding of the scope of the project as well as a lack of knowledge of the technical competence of the systems and programming staff.

A programming verity: as bad as programmers are at estimating the length of a project, they are equally as optimistic about their ability to meet the requirements and deadlines.

**VAR**    (Value Added Reseller) An organization that adds value to a system and resells it. For example, it could purchase a CPU and peripherals from different vendors, graphics software from another and package it all together as a specialized CAD system. Although VARs typically repackage products, they might also include programs they have developed themselves. The terms VAR and ISV are often used interchangeably. See *OEM*, *ISV* and *systems integrator*.

**variable**    In programming, a structure that holds data and is uniquely named by the programmer. It holds the data assigned to it until a new value is assigned or the program is finished.

Variables are used to hold control values. For example, the C statement **for (x=0; x; x++)** performs the instructions following it five times. X is a variable set to zero (x=0), incremented (x++) and tested to reach five (x). Variables also hold data temporarily that is being processed.

Variables are usually assigned with an equal sign; for example, **counter = 1**, places a 1 in COUNTER. Numeric data is unquoted: **counter = 1**, character data requires quotes: **product="abc4344"**. In some languages, the type of data must be declared before it is assigned; for example, in C, the statement, **int counter;** creates a variable that will only hold whole numbers.

A local variable is one that is referenced only within the subprogram, function or procedure it was defined in. A global variable can be used by the entire program.

**variable data printing**    Printing letters, flyers or documents with different data on each one. It can be as simple as a mail merge letter with personalized names to something much more sophisticated such as a catalog with merchandise tailored to your buying history and customer profile. Of course, variable data printing uses computer printers rather than traditional commercial printing presses. See *mail merge* and *digital printing*.

**variable length field**    A record structure that holds fields of varying lengths. For example, PAT SMITH would take nine bytes and GEORGINA WILSON BARTHOLOMEW would take 27 plus a couple of bytes that would define the length of the field. If fixed length fields were used, at least 27 bytes would have to be reserved for both names.

There's more programming with variable length fields, because every record has to be separated into fixed length fields after it is brought into memory. Conversely, each record has to be coded into the variable length format before it is written to disk.

The same storage savings can be achieved by compressing data stored on disk and decompressing it when retrieved. All blank spaces in fixed length fields would be filtered out. For acceptable performance, this method must be well integrated into the operating system. See *realtime compression*.

**variable length record**    A data record that contains one or more variable length fields.

**varname**    (VARiable NAME) An abbreviation for specifying the name of a variable.

**VAX**    (Virtual Address eXtension) A family of 32-bit computers from Digital introduced in 1977 with the VAX-11/780 model. VAXes range from desktop personal computers to mainframes all running the same VMS operating system. Large models can be clustered in a multiprocessing environment to serve thousands of users. Software compatibility between models caused the VAX family to achieve outstanding success during the 1980s. VAXes also provide PDP emulation.

**VAXcluster**    A group of VAXs coupled together in a multiprocessing environment.

**VAXELN**    A realtime operating environment for VAXs from Digital. It runs under VMS and provides application development in Pascal and other languages. Resulting programs are downloaded into the target systems.

**VAXmate**    A partially IBM-compatible PC from Digital introduced in 1986, which has been superseded by the DECstation 200 and 300 series in 1989.

**VAXstation**    A single-user VAX computer that runs under VMS introduced in 1988.

**VB**    See *Visual Basic*.

**The Vax 11/780**
The VAX series was an outstanding success and made Digital a major competitor of computers in all sizes from workstation to mainframe in the 1980s. This is a picture of the first VAX model. *(Image courtesy of Digital Equipment Corporation.)*

V

**VBA**    (Visual Basic for Applications) A subset of Visual Basic that provides a common language for customizing Microsoft applications. VBA supports COM, which allows a VBA script to invoke internal functions within Excel, Word and other COM-based programs or to make use of stand-alone, external COM objects. VBA evolved into a common language to consolidate earlier macro and scripting languages. Since 1996, VBA has been licensed to third parties for use in non-Microsoft applications within the Windows environment. Microsoft encourages Windows developers to put VBA support in their software. See *COM*, *COM automation* and ***application programmability***.

**VBE** See *VESA BIOS Extension*.

**VBE/AI** See *VESA BIOS Extension/Audio Interface*.

**VBI** See *vertical blanking interval*.

**vBNS** (**V**ery high-speed **B**ackbone **N**etwork **S**ervice) A high-speed network backbone developed by the National Science Foundation (NSF) and MCI that interconnects several supercomputer centers at 622 Mbps (OC-12). vBNS was expanded to provide backbone services for Internet2. See *Internet2* and *Abilene*.

**Vbox** (Video **BOX**) A hardware interface from Sony that attaches up to seven VCRs, videodiscs and camcorders to the serial port. Devices must have the Control-L (LANC) connector.

**VBR** (**V**ariable **B**it **R**ate) An asynchronous transfer mode (ATM) level of service that guarantees bandwidth for traffic that is well understood. Realtime variable bit rate (rt-VBR) supports interactive multimedia that requires minimal delays. Non-realtime variable bit rate (nrt-VBR) is used for bursty transaction traffic. See *ATM*.

**VBRUNxxx.DLL** (**V**isual **B**asic **RUN**time [xxx=version #]**.DLL**) The Visual Basic runtime module. A Visual Basic application prior to VB 5 is compiled into an intermediate "bytecode" language, which the runtime module turns into machine language on the fly. It also contains many functions called for by the application. VBRUNxxx.DLL or MSVBVMxx.DLL (VB 5 and higher) are similar to the Java Virtual Machine (JVM) in the Java world, although as of VB 5, native .EXE files can also be created. See *MSVBVMxx.DLL* and *Visual Basic*.

**VBS** See *VBScript*.

**VBScript** (**V**isual **B**asic **SCRIPT**) A scripting language from Microsoft. A subset of Visual Basic, VBScript is widely used on the Web for both client processing within a Web page and server-side processing in Active Server Pages (ASPs). As an ActiveX scripting language, VBScript is also used with the Windows Script Host (WSH) to perform functions locally on a Windows machine. See *JScript* and *ASP*.

**VBX** (**V**isual **B**asic **EX**tension) A component software technology from Microsoft that enables a Visual Basic (Windows) program to add funtionality by calling ready-made components (controls). Also called "Visual Basic Controls," they appear to the end user as just another part of the program. VBXs were Microsofts's first component architecture, and 16-bit VBXs were superseded by 32-bit OCXs. See *OCX* and *ActiveX control*.

**VC** **(1)** (**V**enture **C**apital or **V**enture **C**apitalist) The money or the person or organization that invests money in startup or small companies. A tremendous amount of venture capital has been invested in the computer field, especially in Internet startups.
**(2)** See *virtual circuit*, *videoconferencing* and *Visual C++*.

**Vcache** The disk cache software in Windows 95/98. It is a 32-bit program that dynamically allocates available free memory and replaces the 16-bit Smartdrive cache in DOS/Windows 3.1. Vcache can automatically adjust the size of the cache depending on the current environment and amount of free disk space. See *cache*.

**vCalendar** A standard format for group calendaring and scheduling. Originally developed by the Versit group, it was later turned over to the Internet Mail Consortium (www.imc.org).

**vCard** A standard format for an electronic business card that includes fields for photos, sound and company logos. Information is contained in a file with a .vcf extension. Originally developed by the Versit group, it was later turned over to the Internet Mail Consortium (www.imc.org).

**VCD**   See *Video CD*.

**V-Chip**   An electronic circuit in a TV that parents can use to block TV programs they consider objectionable for their children. The FCC has mandated that after January 1, 2000, all TVs 13" and larger contain the V-Chip. TV programs are rated based on violence and sexual content, and this rating is transmitted in the TV's vertical blanking interval (VBI). The V-Chip is a programmable closed-caption controller chip that decodes the signals. For existing TVs, a V-Chip set-top box can be added.

**V-Commerce**   (Voice Commerce) Voice-enhanced electronic commerce. The term was coined by Nuance Communications, Menlo Park, CA (www.nuance.com), which founded, along with others, the V-Commerce Alliance to promote a framework for this service. V-Commerce uses speech recognition to allow voice transactions such as an order or query to be made over the phone, via a PC using the Internet or any other audio-enabled device that communicates with a network. Although it has a limited, specialized vocabulary for recognition, it implies much more than just saying "yes" or "no" or pronouncing a number. See *IVR*.

**VCPI**   (Virtual Control Program Interface) A programming interface that allowed DOS-extended programs and Real Mode programs to run together in 386s. It was primarily developed by Quarterdeck to allow its DESQview multitasker to run DOS-extended programs. DPMI succeeded VCPI and provided the same capability for Windows.

**VCR**   (Video Cassette Recorder) A videotape recording and playback machine that is available in several formats. One inch tape is used for mastering video recordings. Sony Umatic 3/4" tape was widely used in commercial training. VHS 1/2" tape, first used only in the home, has mostly replaced the 3/4" tape. Sony's 1/2" Beta tape, the first home VCR format, is defunct.

   Although VCRs are analog recording machines, adapters allow them to store digital data for computer backup.

**VCS**   (1) (Verilog Computer Simulator) See *Verilog*.
   (2) (Version Control System) See *version control*.

**VCSEL**   (Vertical Cavity Surface Emitting Laser) Pronounced "vixel." A type of laser diode that emits light from its surface rather than its edge. A VCSEL's circular beam is easy to couple with a fiber, and due to its surface-emission architecture, can be tested on the wafer. VCSELs are also noted for their excellent power efficiency and durability. See *laser diode*.

**VDE**   (1) (Video Display Editor) A WordStar and WordPerfect-compatible shareware word processor written by Eric Meyer.
   (2) (Verband Deutscher Elektrotechniker) The German counterpart of the U.S. Underwriters Lab.

**VDI**   (1) (Video Device Interface) An Intel standard for speeding up full-motion video performance. See *DCI*.
   (2) (Virtual Device Interface) An ANSI standard format for creating device drivers. VDI has been incorporated into CGI.

**VDM**   See *Virtual DOS Machine* and *CGM*.

**V dot**   Refers to the ITU standards for communications that are named starting with a V and followed by a period; for example, V.32bis and V.34.

**VDSL**   See *DSL*.

**VDT**   (Video Display Terminal) A terminal with a keyboard and display screen.

**VDT radiation**   The electromagnetic radiation emitted from a computer display screen. Exhaustive testing so far seems inconclusive, but vendors recommend keeping the face at least 18 to 20 inches from the screen.

**VDU**   (Video Display Unit) Same as *VDT*.

**V**

**vector**    (1) In computer graphics, a line designated by its end points (X-Y or X-Y-Z coordinates). When a circle is drawn, it is made up of many small vectors. See *vector graphics* and *graphics*.

    (2) In matrix algebra, a one-row or one-column matrix.

**vector display**    A display terminal that draws vectors (lines) on the screen. Vector displays, also called "stroke writers," were used in the early days of CAD, but gave way entirely to raster displays. See *raster display*.

**vector drawing**    See *vector graphics*.

**vector font**    A scalable font made of vectors (point-to-point line segments). It is easily scaled as are all vector-based images, but lacks the hints and mathematically-defined curves of outline fonts, such as Adobe Type 1 and TrueType.

**vector graphics**    In computer graphics, a technique for representing a picture as points, lines and other geometric entities. For more details about this technique, see *graphics*. Contrast with *bitmapped graphics*.

**vector processor**    A computer with built-in instructions that perform multiple calculations on vectors (one-dimensional arrays) simultaneously. It is used to solve the same or similar problems as an array processor; however, a vector processor passes a vector to a functional unit, whereas an array processor passes each element of a vector to a different arithmetic unit. See *pipeline processing* and *array processor*.

**vector to raster**    See *rasterize*.

**vendor neutral**    Not a product or specification by one vendor. It is another way of describing open systems. See *open systems*.

**Venn diagram**    A graphic technique for visualizing set theory concepts using overlapping circles and shading to indicate intersection, union and complement.

**Ventura Publisher**    See Corel VENTURA.

**verbose**    Wordy; long winded. The term is often used as a switch to display the status of some operation. For example, a **/v** might mean "verbose mode."

**verify**    In data entry operations, to compare the keystrokes of a second operator with the files created by the first operator.

**Verilog**    A hardware description language (HDL) used to design electronic systems at the component, board and system level. Developed by Phil Morby, it was initially developed as a simulation language that could also be used to describe the stimulus (test factors). By the late 1980s, Verilog was the de facto standard for proprietary HDLs. After Cadence put it into the public domain, it became an IEEE standard. A Verilog simulator is a separate entity, but the term by itself typically refers to the language (HDL). See *VHDL* and *HDL*.

**VERITAS file system**    See *VxFS*.

**Veronica**    A program that searches the Internet for specific resources by description, not just file name. Using Boolean searches (this AND this, this OR this, etc.), users can search Gopher servers to retrieve a selected group of menus that pertain to their area of interest. See *Gopher*.

**VersaCAD**    A family of CAD systems for DOS and Macintosh from Computervision, Bedford, MA (www.cv.com) that features 2-D geometric and construction drafting and 3-D modeling with 16 viewports. The Mac version includes CAD-oriented HyperCard stacks.

**version**    A specific edition or release of a software package. Sometimes the term "release" is used in combination; for example: "Server Version, Release 3.5."

**version control**     The management of source code, bitmaps, documents and related files in a large software project. Version-control software provides a database that is used to keep track of the revisions made to a program by all the programmers and developers involved in it. See *configuration management*, *PVCS* and *CVS*.

**version number**     The identification of a release of software. The difference between Version 2.2 and 2.3 can be night and day, since new releases not only add features, but often correct bugs. What's been driving you crazy may have been fixed!

Numbers, such as 3.1a or 3.11, often indicate a follow-up release only to fix a bug in the previous version, whereas 3.1 and 3.2 usually mean routine enhancements. Version "1.0" drives terror into the hearts of experienced users. The program has just been released, and bugs are still to be uncovered.

**Versit**     A joint venture of Apple, AT&T, IBM and Siemens launched in late 1994 that promoted interoperability between existing and emerging telphony and data comm standards. The primary contribution of this group, which later disbanded, was the vCard and vCalendar formats that were turned over to the Internet Mail Consortium (www.imc.org).

**vertex**     A corner point of a triangle or other geometric image. Vertices is the plural form of this term.

**vertical bandwidth**     See *vertical scan frequency*.

**vertical bar**     The vertical bar character ( | ), located over the backslash (\) key, is used as an OR operator. For example, the C statement **if (x == "a" | | x == "b")** means "if X is equal to A or B." It is also used as a pipe symbol, which directs the output of one process to another. See ***DOS filters & pipes***.

**vertical blanking interval**     The part of a TV signal that is sent between each video frame. In North American TV (NTSC), it takes up the last 45 lines of each 525-line frame. Its purpose is to allow the TV time to reposition its electron beam from the bottom of the current frame (screen) to the top of the next one. This non-viewable part of the signal is used to transmit closed-caption content. See *Intercast*, *V-chip* and *ATV Forum*.

**vertical market**     Refers to a particular industry such as banking, insurance or computers. See *vertical market software*. Contrast with *horizontal market*.

**vertical market software**     Software packages that are designed for a particular industry such as banking, insurance or manufacturing. Contrast with *horizontal market software*.

**VerticalNet**     (VerticalNet Inc., Horsham, PA, www.verticalnet.com) An organization that develops, owns and operates business-to-business Web portals for scientific, industrial and manufacturing industries. In 1995, it introduced Water Online, its first "Web community." It has since developed more than 40 others. See *vertical portal* and *Web hub*.

**vertical portal**     A vertical-market Web site that provides information and services to a particular industry. It is the industry-specific equivalent of the general-purpose portal on the Web. See *portal*, *corporate portal*, *business intelligence portal* and *Web hub*.

**vertical recording**     A magnetic recording method that records the bits vertically instead of horizontally, taking up less space and providing greater storage capacity. The vertical recording method uses a specialized material for the construction of the disk.

**vertical refresh**     See *vertical scan frequency* and *interlaced*.

**vertical resolution**     Number of lines (rows in a matrix). Contrast with *horizontal resolution*.

**vertical retrace**     See *raster scan*.

**vertical scaling**     In multiprocessing, adding more CPUs within the same computer system. Contrast with *horizontal scaling*.

**vertical scan frequency**    Also called "refresh rate," it is the number of times an entire display screen is refreshed, or redrawn, per second. Measured in Hertz, display systems typically range from 56Hz to well over 100Hz. A minimum of 70Hz is recommended to help prevent eye strain. Contrast with *horizontal scan frequency*. See *interlaced*.

**vertical scan rate**    Same as *vertical scan frequency*.

**vertical software**    See *vertical market software*.

**vertices**    The plural of vertex. See *vertex*.

**Vertigo**    Software from Citrix that provides cross platform development for Windows, PDAs and Web phones. The application is constructed of COM objects or Enterprise JavaBeans (EJBs), which are stored in the server, along with an XML description of the user interface. The Vertigo player, which resides in the client device, creates the appropriate user interface based on the XML description.

**verti-port**    See *vertical portal*.

**VESA**    (Video Electronics Standards Association, San Jose, CA, www.vesa.org) A membership organization founded in 1989 that sets interface standards for the PC, workstation and computing environments. Note the following VESA standards following this entry.

**VESA Advanced Feature Connector**    A VESA standard point-to-point channel used to transfer video signals between two video controllers, typically between the display adapter and a video capture or TV board. The Advanced Feature Connector (VAFC) increases the original feature connector from 8 to 32 bits and from 40 to 150 Mbytes/sec. The cable is increased from 26 pins to 80. See *VGA feature connector* and *VESA Media Channel*.

**VESA BIOS**    A BIOS chip on a VGA display adapter that conforms to the VESA BIOS Extension standard.

**VESA BIOS Extension/Audio Interface**    A VESA standard for sound cards. Like the VBE for display adapters (see above), the purpose of the VESA BIOS Extension/Audio Interface (VBE/AI) is to provide a standard sound card interface across all platforms and environments. It also allows sound cards to be programmed using 32-bit instructions.

**VESA DDC**    (VESA Display Data Channel) A VESA standard communications channel between the display adapter and monitor. The DDC is used to pass Extended Display Identification Data (EDID), which is stored in the monitor and describes its characteristics (vendor name, serial number, frequency range, etc.).

DDC requires an additional wire in the cable. The first level implementation (DDC1) provides a unidirectional channel that lets the monitor inform the host of its capabilities. A second bi-directional level (DDC2) allows the host to adjust the monitor. For example, the monitor's switch settings could be put into a software control panel. See *VESA DPMS*.

**VESA DPMS**    (VESA Display Power Management Signaling) A VESA standard for signaling the monitor to switch into energy conservation modes. It provides for two low energy modes: standby and suspend. See *VESA DDC*.

**VESA/EISA**    Refers to an EISA-bus motherboard or system that contains from one to three VL-bus slots.

**VESA/ISA**    Refers to an ISA-bus motherboard or system that contains from one to three VL-bus slots.

**VESA local bus**    See *VL-bus*.

**VESA Media Channel**    A VESA standard bus for transferring video signals between the display adapter and multimedia boards (TV board, audio/video capture, videoconferencing, etc.). The Media Channel (also VM Channel or VMC) was designed as a high-speed multimedia bus to accommodate realtime audio and video traffic. Up to 16 devices can be connected.

Unlike the VESA Advanced Feature Connector, which is a point-to-point channel, the VMC is a sophisticated packet-oriented, timeshared bus, which can guarantee bandwidth for realtime transmission, even more suited for audio and video than PCI. The VMC can handle up to 16 simultaneous streams of data (audio, video, etc.) and can arbitrate between 8, 16 and 32-bit connections.

**VESA Plug and Display**    Also known as "P&D," it is a digital interface for a flat panel display from VESA. Based on TMDS transmission, VESA Plug and Display also supports the analog interface and VGA connector, and it allows for USB and FireWire signals to be carried with the digital video stream. IBM has supported P&D, but the Digital Visual Interface (DVI) is expected to become the standard. See *DVI* and *flat panel display*.

**vesicular film**    A film used to make copies of microforms. It contains its own developer and creates a pink negative or positive copy when exposed to a negative master through ultraviolet light.

**V.Everything**    A modem from U.S. Robotics that supports a wide variety of modem speeds including all the V.34 standards as well as x2. V.Everything modems can be upgraded to future specifications and standards by downloading new software into their flash memory chips.

**VFAT**    (Virtual File Allocation Table)  The file system used in Windows for Workgroups and Windows 95/98. It provides 32-bit Protected Mode access for file manipulation. VFAT is faster than, but also compatible with, the DOS 16-bit File Allocation Table (FAT). In Windows for Workgroups, VFAT was called "32-bit file access." In Windows 95/98, it supports long file names up to 255 characters.

**V.FC**    (V.Fast Class)  A modem technology for 28800 bps from Rockwell International endorsed by many modem vendors before V.34 was finalized. V.FC is very similar to V.34, but V.FC modems required an upgraded chip for full compatibility.

**VFP**    See *Visual FoxPro*.

**VfW**    See *Video for Windows*.

**VG**    See *voice grade*.

**VGA**    (Video Graphics Array)  The minimum standard for PC video display, which originated with IBM's PS/2 models in 1987. It supports earlier CGA and EGA modes and requires an analog monitor. VGA was initially 640×480 pixels with 16 colors, but non-IBM vendors quickly boosted resolution and colors to so-called "Super VGA," which was later standardized by VESA. See *PC display modes* and **how to select a PC display system**.

**VGA adapter**    A display adapter that provides VGA resolution. Most VGA adapters are capable of 640×480, 800x600 and 1,024×768 resolutions with at least 256 colors. Many go up to 1,280×1,024 with color depth to 16M colors (true color). VGA cards include graphics acceleration. See *VGA, graphics accelerator, video accelerator* and **how to select a PC display system**.

**VGA feature connector**    A point-to-point channel used to transfer video signals between two video controllers, typically between the display adapter and a video capture or TV board. Using an 8-bit data path, it provides 40 Mbytes/sec bandwidth. The port is a 26-pin male connector or a 26-pin (13 per side) edge connector at the top of the VGA board.

**VGA HC**    (VGA HiColor)  A VGA board that provides 32K or 64K colors using Tseng Labs' ET4000 chip or equivalent.

**VGA pass through**    A feature of a high-resolution display adapter that is built without standard VGA capability. The standard VGA card in the computer is cabled to the pass through

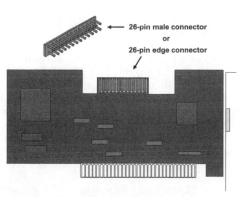

26-pin male connector
or
26-pin edge connector

**Feature Connector**
The VGA feature connector is either a 26-pin male connector on the chip side of the VGA adapter or a 26-pin (13 pins on each side) edge connector on the top edge. All VGA boards do not have the feature connector.

circuit on the high-res adapter. When the high-resolution capability of the adapter is not used, signals from the VGA card pass through the adapter directly to the monitor. The driver that accompanies the high-res adapter turns the pass through circuit on and off.

Pass-through circuits are also built into MPEG boards, allowing both VGA and MPEG signals to go directly to the monitor.

**VHD** (Very High Density) A term applied to storage devices from time to time to indicate a higher capacity.

**VHDCI** (Very High Density Cable Interconnect) A standard 68-pin interface for connecting UltraSCSI and other peripheral devices. It is highly miniaturized and uses a smiliar flat leaf-style pin like the Centronics connector. Up to four VHDCI sockets can be placed on the outside face of a plug-in card.

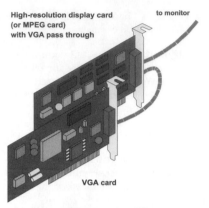

**VGA Pass Through**
The signals go from the VGA card to the high-resolution adapter and then to the monitor.

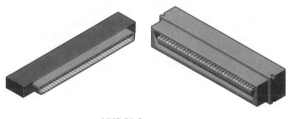

**VHDCI Connector**
The VHDCI 68-pin interface is highly miniaturized and is similar in architecture to the widely-used Centronics connector.

**VHDL** (VHSIC Hardware Description Language) A hardware description language (HDL) used to design electronic systems at the component, board and system level. VHDL allows models to be developed at a very high level of abstraction. Initially conceived as a documentation language only, most of the language can today be used for simulation and logic synthesis. VHDL is an IEEE standard, but was initially developed for the U.S. military's VHSIC program. See *Verilog* and *HDL*.

**VHF** (Very High Frequency) The range of electromagnetic frequencies from 30MHz to 300MHz.

**VHS** A VCR format introduced by JVC in 1976 to compete with Sony's Beta format. VHS has become the standard for home and industry, and Beta is now obsolete. SVHS (Super VHS) is a subsequent format that improves resolution.

**VHSIC** (Very High Speed Integrated Circuit) Pronounced "vizik." Ultra-high-speed chips employing LSI and VLSI technologies.

**vi** (Visual Interface) A UNIX full-screen text editor that can be run from a terminal or the system console. It is a fast, programmer-oriented utility.

(VI) (Virtual Interface) A memory to memory transport protocol that is used for high-speed transfer of data between machines. Used in clusters of two or more computers, VI enables long blocks of data to be sent from one application in one machine directly to another application in a remote machine without the overhead associated with being broken up into packets by a transport protocol. However, the lower data link protocols VI relies on to transmit over a network may or may not break up the data into frames. Another feature is VI's ability to communicate directly from the application's buffer to the network interface and bypass the operating system. Also known as Virtual Interface Architecture (VIA), VI could be considered a "remote DMA." See *DMA* and *DAFS*.

**via** (1) By means of, by way of. From Latin for "way" or "path."

(2) In a printed circuit board, a conducting pathway between two or more substrates (layers). The via is created by drilling through the board at the appropriate place where two or more layers will interconnect and allowing copper to run through the hole. The copper may coat only the the sides of the hole or fill the entire hole. See *printed circuit board*.

(3) (Virtual Interface Architecture) See *VI*.

**video** An audio/visual recording and playback technology used in TV as well in the home and for commercial purposes. In the U.S., the NTSC system is the standard for analog recording, and the DTV system is the standard for digital. The term also refers to computer screens and terminals, but they typically support a variety of computer display standards such as SVGA and XVGA, but not NTSC or DTV. See *NTSC* and *DTV*.

**Video1** A video compression/decompression algorithm from Microsoft and Media Vision that is used to compress movie files.

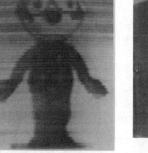

**An Early Recording Star**
Felix the Cat was one of the first images displayed on a television set. *(Image courtesy of RCA Corporation.)*

**The First Video Camera**
This is one of the first video cameras which dates back to the late 1920s. Although some stations were broadcasting TV in the 1930s, RCA began regular transmission in 1939. *(Image courtesy of RCA Corporation.)*

**video accelerator** A hardware component on a display adapter that speeds up full-motion video. The primary video accelerator functions are color space conversion, which converts YUV to RGB, hardware scaling, which is used to enlarge the image to full screen and double buffering which moves the frames into the frame buffer faster. See *graphics accelerator*.

**video adapter** See *video capture board, video graphics board* and *display adapter*.

**video bandwidth** The maximum display resolution of a video screen, measured in MHz, and calculated by horizontal x vertical resolution x refreshes/sec. For example, 800×600×60 = 28.8MHz. Traditional TV studio recording is limited to 5MHz, and TV broadcasting is limited to 3.58Mhz.

**video board** See *display adapter* and *video capture board*.

**videocam** See *Webcam*.

**video camera** A camera that takes continuous pictures and generates a signal for display or recording. It captures images by breaking down the image into a series of lines. The U.S. and Canadian standard (NTSC) is 525 scan lines. Each line is scanned one at a time, and the continuously varying intensities of red, green and blue light across the line are filtered out and converted into a variable signal. Most video cameras are analog, but digital video cameras are also available. See *digital camera*.

**video capture board** An expansion board that digitizes full-motion video from a VCR, camera or other video source. The board may also provide digital to analog conversion for recording onto a VCR.

**video card** Same as *display adapter*.

**Video CD** A compact disc format used to hold full-motion video. Developed by Matsushita, Philips, Sony and JVC, a Video CD holds 74 minutes of VHS-quality video and CD-quality sound. Video CD movies are compressed using the MPEG-1 method and require an MPEG decoder for playback on the computer. They can also be played on certain CD-I and 3DO players. Specifications for this format are defined in the "White Book." See *DVD*.

**video codec** A hardware circuit that converts analog video (NTSC, PAL, SECAM) into digital code and vice versa incorporating one of several compression techniques, such as MPEG, Indeo, Cinepak or Video1. The term may refer to only the compression and decompression processing, which can be done in software or in hardware and is separate from the A/D and D/A conversion.

---

**video compression**    Encoding digital video to take up less storage space and transmission bandwidth. See *video codec* and *data compression*.

---

**videoconferencing**    A video communications session among three or more people that are geographically separated. This form of conferencing started with room systems where groups of people meet in a room with a wide-angle camera and large monitors and conference with other groups at remote locations. Federal, state and local governments are making major investments in group videoconferencing for distance learning and telemedicine.

Although the earliest videoconferencing was done with traditional analog TV and satellites, inhouse room systems became popular in the early 1980s after Compression Labs (now part of VTEL) pioneered digitized video systems that were highly compressed and could be transmitted over leased lines and switched digital facilities available from the telephone companies. Companies such as PictureTel and VTEL produce group systems.

WAN, LAN and POTS    The standard for wide area (WAN) videoconferencing is H.320, which defines the communications handshaking and the compression algorithm for reducing the digital video into a smaller bandwidth. H.320 runs over ISDN, Switched 56 and T1 lines. Multiple ISDN lines can be coupled together providing bandwidth in multiples of 64 Kbits/sec channels.

Desktop videoconferencing over LANs as well as over the plain old telephone system (POTS) is also widely available. Although many proprietary systems were used for first-generation systems, the H.323 (LAN) and H.324 (POTS) standards have made different videoconferencing systems interoperable.

Desktop videoconferencing systems come with a camera and one or two boards for video capture, video compression and ISDN hookup. Some systems are dedicated to videoconferencing, while others can be used for other transmission and video purposes. LAN-based systems attach to an Ethernet instead of an ISDN line, and POTS-based systems use a modem.

As with everything else, the Internet has impacted this field tremendously, causing all videoconferencing vendors to introduce H.323-based products using the IP protocol for their LAN offerings. While the global Internet cannot currently guarantee the quality of service (QoS) required for realtime interaction, videoconferencing over an inhouse, IP-based intranet is much more viable, since most networks have been or are being upgraded to 100Mbps Fast Ethernet, with 1,000Mbps Gigabit Ethernet backbones coming on strong.

At 768Kbps, digital videoconferencing is like analog TV. At 384Kbps, it's more than usable, and even quite respectable at 128Kbps. It takes 24 frames per second (fps) to make the video frames look fluid and fool the eye into believing the motion is continuous. Thus, it's always a tradeoff between the video window size you want on screen and the available network capacity. The bottom line when there is not enough bandwidth is fewer frames per second, and the more we move down from the ideal 24 fps, the jerkier the motion.

Companies such as Datapoint with its MINX system forgo the digital domain and provide full-motion video via an independent analog video network. MINX still uses the LAN for data conferencing (see below), but, since the video is not dependent on the LAN, it will still work if the LAN goes down.

Data Conferencing    A concomitant part of videoconferencing is data conferencing, which allows data and documents to be shared by multiple participants. The ITU's T.120 standard provides the standard for whiteboards, application sharing and application viewing. These data collaboration tools can be used with audio only and even on the Internet, because realtime interaction is not critical. If you paste an image into a whiteboard, and it takes a couple of seconds to register on somebody else's screen, it is not at all as annoying as the delays in audio or video frames.

A whiteboard is the electronic equivalent of the chalkboard where participants at different locations can simultaneously write and draw on an onscreen notepad that is viewed by everyone. A document, drawing or even the screen shot of an application can also be pasted into the whiteboard and annotated by conference members. Application sharing is like remote control software for multiple users, in which participants can all interactively work in an application that is running on one user's machine. Application viewing is similar, but although everybody can see the program running, only one can edit the documents involved.

Point-to-Point and Multipoint    A point-to-point conference between two people is relatively simple. In fact, that's not really conferencing. It's videophoning. A video session between three or more is true videoconferencing, and there are considerations. For example, does everybody hear and see everybody? There's not that much real estate on a large monitor let alone a PC screen to show large numbers of people if they are all in different locations. Does the audio follow the person speaking or is the entire session moderated by one person who is entirely in control of who sees what?

---

A multipoint conference is managed by a multipoint control unit (MCU), which is a specialized device or software in a server that coordinates all of this. The MCU joins the lines and switches the video according to the method required. Multipoint conferences are also achieved by connecting to a conferencing network service from a common carrier.

**Summary**    The explosion of videoconferencing has always been forcast to be right around the corner, but that corner has been farther down the road than expected. When cable modems and digital subscriber line (DSL) technologies become ubiquitous, and the Internet supports true quality of service (QoS), videophoning and videoconferencing will become a major part of every IT budget and many family's personal budgets as well. A Web site that provides a lot of information about videoconferencing is www.gvcnet.com.

**video controller**    **(1)** A device that controls some kind of video function.

**(2)** Same as *display adapter*.

**video digitizer**    Same as *frame grabber*.

**videodisc**    An optical disc used for full-motion video. See *DVD*, *LaserDisc* and *Video CD*.

**video display board**    See *display adapter* and *video graphics board*.

**video editing**    See *nonlinear video editing*.

**video editor**    A dedicated computer that controls two or more videotape machines. It keeps track of frame numbers in its own database and switches the recording machine from playback to record. The video editor reads SMPTE time codes provided on professional tape formats.

**video effects**    See *digital video effects*.

**Video for Windows**    The name of Microsoft's first video playback implementation in Windows. Supporting the AVI movie format, Video for Windows (VfW) had to be installed separately in Windows 3.x, but was later built into Windows 95 and subsequent versions. Initially, the Video 1, RLE and Indeo compression methods were included. Windows 95 added Cinepak compression and provided drivers for Sony ViSCA VCRs and LaserDiscs. Video playback quality was rather jerky on 486s and earlier Pentiums.

**videographer**    A person involved in the production of video material.

**Room System**
Room systems is where videoconferencing got its start. They are still commonly used for small and large business groups. Most systems use ISDN lines and the H.320 standard. *(Image courtesy of VTEL Corporation.)*

**Video Window or Full Screen?**
It's always a tradeoff. The more pixels in the video image, the more network bandwidth required for the transmission. *(Images courtesy of PictureTel Corporation and VTEL Corporation.)*

**Classroom Environment**
Videoconferencing is a natural for classroom training, allowing instructors to teach an audience that would otherwise be impossible to reach. This room system provides digital videoconferencing to remote sites around the country. *(Image courtesy of VTEL Corporation.)*

V

**video graphics board**   A display adapter that has ports for analog video (NTSC, PAL, etc.) from a TV, camera or VCR. The term is also used to refer to a regular display adapter. See *display adapter*.

**video on demand**   The ability to start delivering a movie or other video program to an individual Web browser or TV set whenever the user requests it. See *streaming video*.

**video-out port**   A connection to a TV set. Video out ports are often found on laptop computers so that the screen content can also be displayed on a standard TV or data projector with a video-in jack. The video-out socket is a phono connector which uses a standard RCA phono cable. The signal is either NTSC or PAL composite video.

**Composite video**

**Video-Out Port**
Any yellow phono connector found on a laptop or other audio/visual device is a composite video port. Audio connectors are red and white.

**video overlay**   The placement of a full-motion video window on the display screen. There are various techniques used to display video on a computer's screen, depending on whether the video source has been digitized or is still in analog NTSC format.

**videophone**   **(1)** A telephone with built-in video capability, including a camera and screen. The videophone was expected to happen in the twentieth century, but the communications infrastructure for universal realtime video for everyone was never built.
   **(2)** (VideoPhone) A line of videophones from AT&T. It uses AT&T's Global VideoPhone Standard technology, which is also licensed to other manufacturers. See *PicturePhone*.

**video port**   A socket on a computer used to connect a monitor. On a PC, the standard video port is a 15-pin VGA connector. See *VGA*.

**video RAM**   Also called "VRAM," it is a type of memory used in a display adapter. It is designed with dual ports so that it can simultaneously refresh the screen while text and images are drawn in memory. It is faster than the common dynamic RAM (DRAM) used as main memory in the computer.

**video server**   A computer that delivers streaming video for video on demand applications. Video servers may be computers that are specialized for this purpose. The term may just refer to the software that performs this service. See *streaming video*.

**video streaming**   See *streaming video*.

**videotape**   A magnetic tape used for recording full-animation video images. The most widely used videotape format is the 1/2" wide VHS cassette. VHS has all but obsoleted earlier videotape formats for home and commercial use.

**video teleconferencing**   See *videoconferencing*.

**video terminal**   A data entry device that uses a keyboard for input and a display screen for output. Although the display screen resembles a TV, it usually does not accept TV/video signals.

**videotex**   The first attempts at interactive information delivery for shopping, banking, news, etc. Many trials were made, but it never caught on in the U.S. and was not very successful anywhere except in France (see *Minitel*). Videotex uses a TV set-top box and keyboard. Data is delivered by phone line and stored in the box as predefined frames with limited graphics that are retrieved by menu.

**Video Toaster**   A video production system popular on the Amiga computer from NewTek, Inc., San Antonio, TX (www.newtek.com). The Toaster includes hardware and software that provides video functions such as digital effects, character generation and 3-D animation. It controls professional analog tape decks and is considered the most affordable broadcast-quality video system on the market.

**video window**   The display of full-motion video in an independent window on a computer screen.

**view**   **(1)** To display and look at data on screen.

**(2)** In relational database management, a special display of data, created as needed. A view temporarily ties two or more files together so that the combined files can be displayed, printed or queried; for example, customers and orders or vendors and purchases. Fields to be included are specified by the user. The original files are not permanently linked or altered; however, if the system allows editing, the data in the original files will be changed.

**viewable image**    The actual diagonal image on a monitor screen. For a long time, CRT measurements have been overstated; for example, a 17" CRT is generally between 15" and 15.8" diagonal. On the other hand, flat panel monitors on laptops, and later on desktops, have always provided accurate measurements, which is known as "viewable image." A 15" flat panel is actually 15" diagonal. What a concept!

**viewer**    A program that displays the contents of an electronic (digital) file. Viewers may be stand-alone programs or components within a larger program. They are widely used to display images downloaded from BBSs, online services and the Internet. Viewers for sound and video files are also available.

A viewer typically displays or plays one type of file, whereas a file viewer is a program that supports many different formats. See *file viewer*.

**viewport**    **(1)** In the Macintosh, the entire scrollable region of data that is viewed through a window.

**(2)** Same as *window*.

**vignetting**    **(1)** A defect of an optical system in which light at the edges of images is cut off or reduced. It is caused by an obstruction in its original construction; for example, when the elements used in a lens are too small.

**(2)** A visual effect of darkened corners used to help frame an image or soften the frame outline.

**VIM**    (Vendor Independent Messaging Interface) A programming interface developed by Lotus, Novell, IBM and others. In order to enable an application to send and receive mail over a VIM-compliant messaging system such as cc:Mail, programmers write to the VIM interface.

**VINES**    (VIrtual NEtworking System) A UNIX System V-based network operating system from Banyan Systems Inc., Westboro, MA (www.banyan.com), that runs on DOS and OS/2-based servers. It provides internetworking of PCs, minis, mainframes and other computer resources providing information sharing across organizations of unlimited size.

Incorporating mainframe-like security with a global directory service called Streettalk, VINES allows access to all network users and resources. Options include printer sharing, e-mail, remote PC dial-in, bridges and gateways.

**viral marketing**    A marketing approach that spreads like wildfire and has nothing to do with computer viruses. The term was coined by venture capital firm, Draper Fisher Jurvetson, Redwood City, CA (www.venture-capital.com), after its investment in Hotmail grew dramatically. Hotmail automatically puts an advertisement at the end of everybody's e-mail message suggesting that they sign up for the free service. In a year and a half, more than 12 million people became Hotmail users. See *sneezing*.

**viral programming**    Developing programs that replicate themselves. Although known more as the means to write viruses, viral programming is used to develop software agents that replicate themselves throughout the network or Internet for the benefit of the user. Such programs can detect problems in a network or be used to find the best price for merchandise when replicated and snooping around multiple shopping sites.

**virtual**    An adjective that expresses a condition without boundaries or constraints. It is often used to define a feature or state that is simulated in some fashion. For example, one of the first uses of the term was for "virtual memory," in which memory is saved to disk and swapped back and forth as needed, thus memory is essentially "simulated on disk."

However, the term has become such a fashionable computer word that it may be a prefix to "virtually" any electronic or Internet-related concept or product without regard to the original meaning of the term. See *virtualize*.

**V**

**Virtual 8086 Mode**    An operational mode in Intel CPU chips (starting with the 386) that allows it to perform as multiple 8086 CPUs. Under direction of a control program, each virtual machine (VM) runs as a stand-alone 8086 running its own operating system and applications, thus DOS, UNIX and other operating systems can be running simultaneously. All virtual machines are multitasked together.

This mode divides up the computer into multiple address spaces and maintains virtual registers for each virtual machine. This is not the same as the virtual memory mode, which extends main memory to disk. See *virtual machine* and *Virtual DOS Machine*.

**virtual card**   See *e-card*.

**virtual circuit**   (1) A temporary communications path created between devices in a switched communications system. For example, a message from New York to Los Angeles may actually be routed through Atlanta and St. Louis. Within a smaller geography, such as a building or campus, the virtual circuit traverses some number of switches, hubs and other network devices.

(2) A logical circuit within a physical network. The actual lines may be shared by other users at the same time, but the virtual circuit appears exclusive to the users that are communicating with each other. The terms "permanent virtual circuit" and "virtual private network" also describe this kind of logical circuit. See *packet switching*, *VPN*, *PVC* and *SVC*.

**virtual community**   A group of individuals that share a common interest via e-mail, chat rooms or newsgroups (threaded discussions). Members of a virtual community are self-subscribing. Contrast with *virtual workgroup*.

**virtual companion**   An electronic pet. The most popular virtual companion to come down the pike has been Sony's AIBO pet robot. AIBO simulates instincts and feelings, and you don't have to walk it!

**virtual company**   An organization that uses computer and telecommunications technologies to extend its capabilities by working routinely with employees or contractors located throughout the country or the world. Using faxes, modems, data and videoconferencing, it implies a high degree of telecommuting as well as remote workgroups and facilities.

The extreme virtual company is one that hires only temporary help and whose office facilities are little more than a post office box and answering machine. See **pervasive workplace** and *hoteling*.

**virtual connection**   A temporary connection made between two nodes.

**virtual corporation**   See *virtual company*.

**virtual desktop**   An infinitely-large desktop, which is provided either by a virtual screen capability or a shell program that enhances the user interface. See *virtual screen* and *virtual desktop services*.

**virtual desktop services**   Internet-based applications that can be accessed from any Web browser. They include applications such as a PIM, e-mail client, calendar, to-do list and contact manager, all of which can be accessed remotely from any computer. Some of the virtual desktop service follow. See also *desktop.com*.

```
www.magicaldesk.com
www.storagepoint.com
www.visto.com
www.zkey.com
```

**virtual device**   See *virtual peripheral* and *VxD*.

**virtual device driver**   See *VxD*.

**virtual disk**   See *volume set* and *RAM disk*.

**virtual display**   A display technology that creates a full screen image in a small space. It enables a handheld device, such as a pager or handheld fax machine, to simulate a desktop monitor. See *Private Eye*, *virtual monitor* and *virtual screen*.

**Virtual DOS Machine**   A DOS session created by OS/2 and Windows 95/98/NT/2000 in order to run a DOS or Windows 3.1 application. Depending on the operating system version, an application may run in its own Virtual DOS Machine or all applications run in the same one. It may or may not use the Virtual 8086 mode of the x86 chip. See *Virtual 8086 Mode*.

**virtual function**    In object technology, a function that has a default operation for a base class, but which can be overridden and perform a different operation by a derived class. A derived class inherits the attributes (data) and methods (processing) of a higher-level class.

**virtual host**    On the World Wide Web, a server that contains multiple Web sites, each with its own domain name. As of the first version of the Web protocol (HTTP 1.0), each Web site on a virtual host must be assigned a unique IP address. HTTP Version 1.1 eliminates this requirement. See *virtual server*.

**virtual image**    In graphics, the complete graphic image stored in memory, not just the part of it that is displayed at the current time.

**virtual ISP**    An ISP that uses the facilities and services (servers, switches, backbone, etc.) of a large ISP, but retains its own branding for marketing and billing purposes. Virtual ISPs are often formed to target a specific group, whether by location, profession, language or other subject of common interest. A virtual ISP, also known as an "affinity ISP," might be created for a charity, a church, an entertainer, virtually any group or cause that is popular. After obtaining a sufficient number of customers, a virtual ISP may decided to build its own facilities and operate independently.

**virtualize**    (1) To activate a program in virtual memory.
(2) To create a virtual screen.
(3) To simulate ("make virtual"), which can refer to numerous effects and conditions. See *virtual*.

**virtual LAN**    Also called a "VLAN," it is a logical subgroup within a local area network that is created via software rather than manually moving cables in the wiring closet. It combines user stations and network devices into a single unit regardless of the physical LAN segment they are attached to and allows traffic to flow more efficiently within populations of mutual interest.

VLANs are implemented in port switching hubs and LAN switches and generally offer proprietary solutions. VLANs reduce the time it takes to implement moves, adds and changes.

VLANs function at layer 2. Since their purpose is to isolate traffic within the VLAN, in order to bridge from one VLAN to another, a router is required. The router works at the higher layer 3 network protocol, which requires that network layer segments are identified and coordinated with the VLANs. This is a complicated job, and VLANs tend to break down as networks expand and more routers are encountered. The industry is working towards "virtual routing" solutions, which allows the network manager to view the entire network as a single routed entity. See *802.1q*.

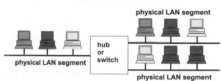

**The VLAN**
Virtual LANs solve the problem of containing traffic within workgroups that are geographically dispersed. They allow moves, adds and changes to be performed via software at a console rather than manually changing cables in the wiring closet.

**virtual library**    The worldwide collection of online books, journals and articles available on the Internet.

**virtual machine**    (1) One system image in a computer that supports multiple system images. Each system image contains the operating system and its associated applications, and each image may have the same operating system or a different operating system. Computers are built with hardware circuits that support virtual machine capability. Years ago, IBM's VM mainframe operating system was the first to provide this capability, and it did it entirely in software. Later, hardware circuits were added to provide virtual partitioning of the computer (see *VM*, *LPAR* and *PR/SM*). The x86 CPU in a PC has a built in virtual machine mode (see *Virtual 8086 Mode*).
(2) The name given to various programming language interpreters. See *Java Virtual Machine* and *Python*.
(3) A computer that has built-in virtual memory capability. See *virtual memory*.

**virtual memory**    Simulating more memory than actually exists, allowing the computer to run larger programs or more programs concurrently. It breaks up the program into small segments, called "pages," and brings as many pages into

**V**

memory that fit into a reserved area for that program. When additional pages are required, it makes room for them by swapping them to disk. It keeps track of pages that have been modified, so that they can be retrieved when needed again.

If a program's logic points back and forth to opposite ends of the program, excessive disk accesses, or "thrashing," can slow down execution.

Virtual memory can be implemented in software only, but efficient operation requires virtual memory hardware. Virtual memory claims are sometimes made for specific applications that bring additional parts of the program in as needed; however, true virtual memory is a hardware and operating system implementation that works with all applications. See *Windows swap file.*

**virtual monitor**    In the Macintosh, the ability to dynamically configure to any monitor type and to use multiple monitors of different types including displaying the same object across two or more screens.

**virtual network**    An interconnected group of networks (an internet) that appear as one large network to the user. Optionally, or perhaps ideally, a virtual network can be centrally managed and controlled.

Banyan Systems, creator of VINES, which stands for VIrtual NEtworking System, defines virtual networking as "the ability for users to transparently communicate locally and remotely across similar and dissimilar networks through a simple and consistent user interface." See *virtual LAN.*

**virtual newscaster**    A machine-created person that broadcasts the news on the Internet. The virtual newscaster is available 24 hours per day to deliver any and all kinds of information and news bulletins. He or she becomes a familiar character that you identify with every time you get the news.

The service behind the virtual newscaster is what really differentiates this 21st Century system. Such newscasters are expected to be the brand logos of personalized news services that can search the Internet 24 hours a day to bring you personalized news and information.

**Ananova—The First Virtual Newscaster**
Launched in the U.K. in the spring of 2000, Ananova delivers breaking news, sports, weather, business news and entertainment gossip. This exotic young lady can also be used to look for entertainment throughout the U.K. and even purchase tickets. She can also provide selected news and information based on your personal profile. *(Image courtesy of Ananova Ltd., www.ananova.com)*

**virtual operating system**    An operating system that can host other operating systems. See *virtual machine.*

**virtual peripheral**    A peripheral device simulated by the operating system.

**virtual printer**    A simulated printer. If a program is ready to print, but all printers are busy, the operating system will transfer the printer output to disk and keep it there until a printer becomes available.

**virtual private network**    See *VPN.* Remember... try the acronymn first!

**virtual processing**    A parallel processing technique that simulates a processor for applications that require a processor for each data element. It creates processors for data elements above and beyond the number of processors available.

**virtual processor**    A simulated processor in a virtual processing system.

**virtual reality**    An artificial reality that projects you into a 3-D space generated by the computer. A virtual reality system uses stereoscopic goggles that provide the 3-D imagery and some sort of tracking device, which may be the goggles themselves for tracking head and body movement, or a "data glove" that tracks hand movements. The glove lets you point to and manipulate computer-generated objects displayed on tiny monitors inside the goggles.

Virtual reality (VR) can be used to create an illusion of reality or imagined reality and is used both for entertainment and training. Flight simulators for training airplane pilots and astronauts were the first form of this technology, which provided a very realistic and very expensive simulation.

Virtual reality has other variants. Spatially immersive displays use multi-sided rooms that you walk into, and an "immersive theater" or "immersive wall" uses a large flat or curved screen (8–24' long) that completely fills your peripheral vision. Desktop virtual reality (desktop VR) uses a personal computer to play games and view environments that you move around in, although they lack the 3-D reality of true VR systems. See *HMD*, *6DOF*, *cyberspace*, *VRML* and *mixed reality*.

**virtual root** A root directory that points to another root directory. It allows one root directory to be consistently named although the physical location may change. See *PURL*. See also *virtual circuit*.

**virtual route** Same as *virtual circuit*.

**virtual routing** An integrated, comprehensive solution to forwarding traffic at high speed in a network. All LAN, WAN and routing protocols are fully supported by all devices in the network so that the entire network can be viewed as a single router at one management console.

It implies the creation of virtual subnets, which are groups of users that are physically located in different areas but are logically treated as a single domain. Virtual subnets combine the logical subdivision provided by layer 2 VLANs with the filtering and firewall benefits of layer 3 routing.

The goal is to provide virtual routing (virtual subnets) in a multivendor environment. Many solutions are expected to tout this capability as ATM is integrated into legacy networks. See *MPOA*, *I-PNNI* and *IP Switch*.

**virtual screen** A viewing area that is larger than the physical borders of the screen. It allows the user to scroll very large documents or multiple documents side by side by moving the mouse pointer beyond the edge of the screen. For example, you might look through an 800x600 screen resolution into a 1600x1200 virtual screen.

**virtual server** (1) Same as *virtual host*.

(2) Multiple servers that appear as one server, or one system image, to the operating system or for network administration. See *system image*.

**virtual storage** (1) Dealing with the storing of data without regard to medium type (disk, tape, etc.). See *storage virtualization* and *VTS*.

(2) An earlier term for *virtual memory*.

(3) Storing data over the Internet, which implies extremely large capacities and the ability to access it from any Web browser.

**virtual store** A retail presence on the Web. See *e-commerce*.

**virtual subnet** See *virtual routing*.

**virtual tape** Simulating an infinite number of tape drives to the host system. See *VTS*.

**virtual terminal** Terminal emulation that allows access to a foreign system. Often refers to a personal computer gaining access to a mini or mainframe.

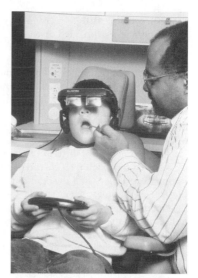

**Virtual Reality at the Dentist**
In this application, the child is looking through the goggles and manipulating the scenes that he sees with a game controller. *(Image courtesy of I-O Display, www.i-glasses.com)*

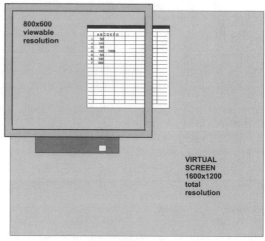

**Virtual Screen**
In this example, the user can see 800x600 pixels at a time and can pan the entire 1,600x1,200 pixels by moving the mouse beyond the edge of the viewable screen.

**virtual toolkit** Development software that creates programs for several computer environments. Its output may require additional conversions or translations to produce executable programs.

**virtual workgroup**    A group of individuals that work on a common project via technologies such as e-mail, shared databases, threaded discussions and calendaring. Virtual workgroups are mandated by company policy and employment requirements. Contrast with *virtual community* and **pervasive workplace**.

**virus**    Software used to infect a computer. After the virus code is written, it is buried within an existing program. Once that program is executed, the virus code is activated and attaches copies of itself to other programs in the system. Infected programs copy the virus to other programs.

The effect of the virus may be a simple prank that pops up a message on screen out of the blue, or it may destroy programs and data right away or on a certain date. It can lie dormant and do its damage once a year. For example, the Michaelangelo virus contaminates the machine on Michaelangelo's birthday.

A common type of virus is a boot virus, which is stored in the boot sectors of a floppy disk. If the floppy is left in the drive when the machine is turned off and then on again, the machine is infected, because it reads the boot sectors of the floppy expecting to find the operating system there. Once the machine is infected, the boot virus may replicate itself onto all the floppies that are read or written in that machine from then on until it is eradicated.

A virus cannot be attached to data. It must be attached to a runnable program that is downloaded into or installed in the computer. The virus-attached program must be executed in order to activate the virus. Macro viruses, although hidden within documents (data), are similar. It is in the execution of the macro that the damage is done.

File attachments in e-mail messages are also suspect. If the attachment is an EXE file, it can do anything when it is run.

In 1996, the National Computer Security Assocation claimed that only about 5% of the more than 6,000 known viruses are harmful. The majority are benign and are more like pranks created for the sheer art of programming. For example, on a certain day of the month, hearing a clicking noise from your speaker every time you press a key is a type of benign virus designed to drive you a little nutty until you figure out what it is. See *antivirus, in the wild, quarantine, macro virus, e-mail virus, polymorphic virus, stealth virus, worm, boot virus, vandal, virus hoaxes* and *crypto rage*.

**Be Careful Out There!**    If you're on the Internet, obtain a virus and vandal detector that looks for rogue files that you might have downloaded. Before you run a shareware, public domain or freeware program, check it with a virus detection program first. In fact, to be 100% safe, every time you insert any new floppy disk or CD-ROM into your computer from an unknown source, it should be checked.

**Who's Keeping Track?**    Since 1993, the WildList Organization has been keeping track of virus attacks all over the world. For the list and more information, visit www.wildlist.org.

**Sample Viruses**    The style and purpose of viruses runs the gamet. The Sophos antivirus company offers these brief synopses. For an exhaustive list of virus explanations, visit www.sophos.com/virusinfo/analyses. See *Sophos*.

**Love Letter**    The fastest spreading virus in history appears to have been written by a resident of Manila in the Philippines. Sent via e-mail in May 2000 with "I LOVE YOU" in the subject field, it replicated itself to everyone in the user's Outlook address book and then destroyed local files. Love Letter forced numerous organizations to shut down their e-mail systems, as computer users were far too willing to let love into their life.

**CIH (a.k.a. Chernobyl)**    This virus, written by Taiwanese student Chen Ing-Hau, triggers on the anniversary of the Chernobyl meltdown. The virus attacks the BIOS chip on the computer, effectively paralyzing your entire PC.

**Melissa**    David L Smith, 31, named his virus after a stripper he knew in Florida. His virus created chaos in March 1999 when it spread around the world in a day, clogging up e-mail systems and inserting quotes from Bart Simpson into documents. Smith has admitted causing over $80 million worth of damage to North American businesses.

**911**    The 911 virus was seen in Houston, Texas. It takes over the computer modem and dials emergency services.

**Kylie**    This virus, fortunately rarely encountered, plays the pint-sized Australian popster's song "Never too late" through your PC speaker.

**SMEG**    "Smoke me a kipper, I'll be back for breakfast! Unfortunately most of your data won't!" The Simulated Metamorphic Encryption Generator viruses, written by the Black Baron, trashed hard disks up and down the country in the mid-1990s. The author, Christopher Pile, was a fan of the Red Dwarf series and ended up being sentenced to 18 months in prison.

**Nuclear**     This word macro virus adds a paragraph to the end of every document you print protesting against French nuclear testing in the South Pacific.

**Coffeeshop**     Written by the Trident virus writing gang based in the Netherlands, the Coffeeshop virus displays a large cannabis leaf on the screen of your PC and urges the government to legalize marijuana.

**Casino**     Casino was written on the island of Malta and plays Russian Roulette with your hard disk. If you get the number wrong, you lose everything.

**virus hoaxes**     Considering the speed with which messages can be copied and sent via e-mail on the Internet, pranksters love to spread phoney warnings just to upset as many people as they can. Virus hoaxes such as the Good Times virus tell people that if they open their e-mail, their hard drives will be erased or some such catastrophe will occur.

The Department of Energy maintains the Computer Incident Advisory Capability Web site which identifies current virus hoaxes. For information, visit http://hoaxbusters.ciac.org.

**VirusScan**     A popular virus scanner from Network Associates for Windows and Mac. Originally developed by McAfee Associates, it is also part of the McAfee Office package. See *McAfee Office*.

**virus scanner**     An antivirus program that searches for binary signatures (patterns) of known viruses that have attached themselves to executable programs. As new viruses are discovered, the signature database has to be updated in order for the antivirus program to be effective. Vendors generally offer downloads via the Web in order to keep current.

There are two ways in which scanners work. One type scans every file each time you boot the computer and each time a file is opened. The other takes a blueprint of all existing executables one time and scans the file only when it has changed. The latter method saves time when starting or rebooting the computer since there is no processing performed. In addition, opening files is quicker, because the antivirus software does not scan the file unless it has been changed, and it can determine if the file has been changed much faster than it can scan it for thousands of viruses.

**virus signature**     The binary pattern of the machine code of a particular virus. Antivirus programs compare their database of virus signatures with the files on the hard disk and removable media (including the boot sectors of the disks) as well as within RAM.

**virus signature file**     A file of virus patterns that are compared with existing files to determine if they are infected with a virus. The vendor of the antivirus software updates the signatures frequently and makes them available to customers via the Web.

**VIS**     (1) (Voice Information Service) A variety of voice processing service applications.

(2) (Visible Image Size) The actual viewing area on a monitor. In the late 1990s, the industry had an honesty attack and began to provide actual viewing size along with the overall designation (14", 15", 17" etc.) which was exaggerated.

**ViSCA**     (VIdeo System Control Architecture) A Sony protocol for synchronized control of multiple video peripherals. A ViSCA-compatible VCR can be controlled very precisely by the computer. ViSCA is the software interface. Control-L is the hardware plug and socket.

**VisiBroker**     An object request broker (ORB) from Borland that fully supports the CORBA standard. VisiBroker for Java is written in Java and can run in any Java environment. VisiBroker for C++ provides ANSI C++ interfaces for maximum source portability. VisiBroker's SmartAgent provides a dynamic, distributed naming and directory service with support for fault tolerance and load balancing. VisiBroker was the first CORBA ORB to support the Java language. See *Borland AppServer*.

**V**

**VisiCalc**     The first electronic spreadsheet. It was introduced in 1978 for the Apple II. Conceived by Dan Bricklin, a Harvard student, and programmed by a friend, Bob Frankston, it became a major success. It launched an industry and was almost entirely responsible for the Apple II being used in business. Thousands of $3,000 Apples were bought to run the $150 VisiCalc.

VisiCalc was a command-driven program that was followed by SuperCalc, MultiPlan, Lotus 1-2-3 and a host of others, each improving the user interface. Spreadsheets have also been implemented on minis and mainframes, and it all started with VisiCalc.

**Visio**   A drawing and diagramming program for Windows from Visio Corporation (formerly Shapeware), Seattle, WA, that includes a variety of pre-drawn shapes and picture elements that can be dragged and dropped onto the illustration. Users can define their own elements and place them onto the Visio palette. Visio Home is a version of Visio designed for personal use and includes elements for landscaping, family trees, decorating, etc.

**Vision Server**   An OLAP engine from IQ Software, which was acquired by Information Advantage in 1998 and turned into MyEureka Cube Explorer and MyEureka Cube Server. See *MyEureka*.

**visit**   To access a Web site. See *visitor* and *unique visitors*.

**visitor**   A person that accesses a Web site. See *unique visitors* and *visit*.

**Visor**   An electronic PDA from Handspring, Mountain View, CA (www.handspring.com) that was introduced in September of 1999 by the people that invented and marketed the PalmPilot. Based on the Palm OS, it is the first handheld to use the USB interface. Visor can be expanded via its Springboard expansion slot to accomodate hardware and software modules for such applications as business software, games, GPS systems, MP3 players and digital cameras.

**VisualAge**   A family of object-oriented application development software from IBM that includes VisualAge for Basic, VisualAge for C++, VisualAge for COBOL, VisualAge for Java, VisualAge for PacBase and VisualAge for Smalltalk. For example, VisualAge for C++ is a multiplatform environment for writing C++ applications for OS/2, Windows, AS/400, MVS/ESA, AIX and Solaris. It is widely used to write an application on one platform that will be used on another.

Today, the skills of a VisualAge programmer are not implicit, as the term refers to several languages. In the past it implied one or two. The VisualAge name was first used in the late 1980s for Smalltalk, then in 1994 for C++ and later for all the others. Nevertheless, all the VisualAge languages are themselves written in IBM's Smalltalk. See *Smalltalk*.

**Visual Basic**   A version of the BASIC programming language from Microsoft specialized for developing Windows applications. When first released in 1991, Visual Basic was similar to Microsoft's QuickBASIC. By the mid 1990s, it became extremely popular. User interfaces are developed by dragging objects from the Visual Basic Toolbox onto the application form.

Visual Basic (VB) is widely used to write client front ends for client/server applications. As of Version 5.0, it is also used to create ActiveX controls for the Web (both EXE's and DLL's). Visual Basic for Applications (VBA) is a subset that provides a common macro language included with many Microsoft applications.

Up until VB 5, the Visual Basic compiler only converted the source code written by the programmer into an intermediate language called "bytecode." Starting with VB 5, native executable programs can be generated. No matter what the version, in order to run a VB program, the VB runtime module, must reside in the target computer. This .DLL file, named VBRUNxxx (up to VB 4) or MSVBVMxx (VB 5 and after), where x is the version number, contains necessary runtime libraries and also converts programs compiled to bytecode into the machine language of the computer. The runtime DLLs are widely available and typically accompany a Visual Basic application. See *compiler* and *VBScript*.

**Visual Basic Control**   See *VBX*.

**Visual C++**   A C and C++ development system for DOS and Windows applications from Microsoft. It includes Visual Workbench, an integrated Windows-based development environment and Version 2.0 of the Microsoft Foundation Class Library (MFC), which provide a basic framework of object-oriented code to build an application upon.

Introduced in 1993, the Standard Edition of Visual C++ replaces QuickC for Windows and the Professional Edition includes the Windows SDK and replaces Microsoft C/C++ 7.0.

**Visual Cafe**   A family of Java development products from the WebGain division of Symantec (www.webgain.com). Versions for Windows and the Macintosh are available that include a host of Java components and features for rapidly building applications. Visual Cafe added visual programming tools and superseded Cafe, which was Symantec's first-generation Java product that was based on its C++ environment.

As of Version 2.0, Visual Cafe was renamed Visual Cafe for Java and includes Symantec's Visual Page HTML authoring package. The Professional edition includes enhanced debugging and development features. The Database edition includes the dbANYWHERE server, which provides native connectivity to many popular databases. See *WebGain Studio*.

**visual computing**  The use of computers for 3-D modelling and animation. See *visualization*.

**Visual FoxPro**  An Xbase development system for Windows from Microsoft. Originally known as FoxPro for Windows, FoxPro for DOS, etc., Visual FoxPro added object orientation and client/server support. Although FoxPro usage is on the decline, the language is highly regarded by the developers that use it. Many business applications, both large and small, have been written in it.

Starting with Version 5.0, Visual FoxPro added support for ActiveX and is a 32-bit Windows only product. Version 3.0 was the last Macintosh version and 2.6 was the last DOS version. Visual FoxPro stems from FoxBASE, which was originally developed for DOS by Fox Software and widely praised for its speed and compatibility with dBASE.

**Visual InterDev**  A Windows-based development system from Microsoft for building dynamic Web applications using Microsoft standards. It is used to write Active Server Pages that can interact with databases and ActiveX-based components in the server.

**visualization**  Using the computer to convert data into picture form. The most basic visualization is that of turning transaction data and summary information into charts and graphs. Visualization is used in computer-aided design (CAD) to render screen images into 3-D models that can viewed from all angles and which can also be animated. See *scientific visualization* and *information visualization*.

**Visual J++**  A Windows-based Java development system from Microsoft. It is used to create Java applications that can run on any platform or to create Windows-specific applications that call ActiveX components or Windows directly. Visual J++ also includes a Java compiler.

**Visual Objects**  See *CA-Visual Objects*.

**Visual Page**  An HTML authoring package for Windows and the Macintosh from Symantec. It is included with the Visual Cafe for Java development kits. See *Visual Cafe*.

**visual programming**  Developing programs with tools that allow menus, buttons and other graphics elements to be selected from a palette and drawn and built on screen. It may include developing source code by creating and/or interacting with flow charts that graphically display the logic paths and associated code.

**Visual Studio**  A suite of development tools from Microsoft that include its major programming languages and Web development package (Visual Basic, Visual C++, Visual FoxPro, Visual J++ and Visual InterDev). The Enterprise Edition includes version control, a database, TP monitor and reference material (Visual SourceSafe, Microsoft SQL Server and Microsoft Transaction Server, Developer Network Library).

**visual tool**  Any program module or program routine used in a visual programming environment for developing a program or used in a graphics environment for creating drawings or images.

**Visual Workbench**  See *Visual C++*.

**VisualWorks**  An application development environment for Smalltalk for Windows, Mac and UNIX from ObjectShare, Inc., Sunnyvale, CA (www.objectshare.com). Introduced in 1991, it includes development tools such as a compiler, debugger, GUI builder and class browser. VisualWorks was originally ObjectWorks from ParcPlace, but was renamed when the GUI builder was added. ParcPlace was spun off of Xerox PARC in 1987 and merged with Digitalk in 1995 to form ObjectShare. See *Smalltalk*.

**VITA** (VMEbus International Trade Association, Scottsdale, AZ, www.vita.com) A trade association that supports the VMEbus and other open standards. Founded in 1984, VITA was accredited as an ANSI standards development organization in 1993. See *VMEbus*.

**Viterbi decoder** A decoding algorithm developed in the late 1960s by Andrew Viterbi that is used to decode a particular convolutional code. Viterbi decoders have been the most effective way to decode wireless voice communications in satellite and cellphone transmissions. Viterbi outputs a 0 or a 1 based on its estimate of the input bit. See *CDMA*, *convolutional code* and *turbo code*.

**vixel** See *VCSEL*.

**VKD** (Virtual Keyboard Device) In Windows, a built-in virtual device driver that manages the keyboard and allows keystrokes to be sent to the appropriate, active application.

**VLAN** See *virtual LAN*.

**VL-bus** (VESA Local-BUS) A peripheral bus from VESA that was primarily used in 486s. It provides a high-speed data path between the CPU and peripherals (video, disk, network, etc.). VL-bus is a 32-bit bus that supports bus mastering and runs at speeds up to 40MHz. It generally provides up to three slots on the motherboard, each slot using one 32-bit MicroChannel connector placed adjacent to the standard ISA, EISA or MicroChannel connector. See *PC data buses*.

**VLDB** (Very Large DataBase) An extremely large database. What consitutes a VLDB is debatable, but databases of 100GB or more are generally considered the starting point. A VLDB is also measured by the number of transactions per second and the type of complex queries that it can support.

**VLD scanner** (Visible Laser Diode scanner) A device that reads bar codes using a laser beam. See *bar code scanner*.

**VLF** (Very Low Frequency) See *low radiation*.

**VLIW** (Very Long Instruction Word) A CPU architecture that reads a group of instructions and executes them at the same time. For example, the group (word) might contain four instructions, and the compiler ensures that those four instructions are not dependent on each other so they can be executed simultaneously. Otherwise, it places no-ops (blank instructions) in the word where necessary.

**VLSI** (1) (Very Large Scale Integration) Between 100,000 and one million transistors on a chip. See *SSI*, *MSI*, *LSI* and *ULSI*.
(2) (VLSI Technology, Inc., Tempe, AZ, www.vlsi.com) A designer and manufacturer of custom chips that was acquired by Philips Semiconductor.

**VM** (1) (Virtual Machine) An IBM mainframe operating system, originally developed by its customers and eventually adopted as an IBM system product (VM/SP). It can run multiple operating systems within the computer at the same time, each one running its own programs. CMS (Conversational Monitor System) provides VM's interactive capability. See *hypervisor*, *Java Virtual Machine* and *Virtual 8086 Mode*.
(2) (Virtual Machine) One instance of a virtual machine in a virtual machine environment. See *virtual machine*.

**v-mail** (Video MAIL) The ability to send video clips along with e-mail messages. This is not the same as videoconferencing, which requires realtime capabilities between sender and receiver, but it does require high-speed computers and networks.

**VMEbus** (VersaModule Eurocard BUS) An expansion bus technology developed by Motorola, Signetics, Mostek and Thompson CSF in the early 1980s. Supporting up to 21 cards in a single backplane, VMEbus is widely used in industrial, telecommunications and military applications with products available from several hundred manufacturers worldwide. VMEbus cards (VME cards) come in 3U, 6U and 9U formats (see *Eurocard*).
In 1995, VME64 was introduced, which increased the data and addressing paths from 32 to 64 bits and added several enhancements. However, VME boards can be VME64 compliant and provide less than 64 bits of data transfer

and/or addressing. In 1997, VME64x (VME64 eXtensions) added features such as new pin connections, support for 3.3 volts and hot swap capability. See *VITA* and *PMC*.

**VML**    **(1)** (Vector Markup Language) An extension to XML that defines images in vector graphics format for the Web. It also defines how the image is displayed and edited. VML graphics can be modified by style sheets that pertain to the page they reside in.

**(2)** (Voice Markup Language) See *VXML*.

**VMM**    **(1)** (Virtual Machine Manager) The underlying operating system component of Windows. It manages the computer's memory and virtual machines. The services in the VMM are not directly called by Windows applictions, but are accessible by virtual device drivers (VxDs).

**(2)** (Virtual Memory Manager) The software that manages virtual memory in a computer.

**VMRAM**    A type of MRAM that uses washer-shaped thin films for the magnetic element. The direction of the current determines the 0 or 1 similar to the early days of magnetic core memory. See *MRAM*.

**VMS**    **(1)** (Virtual Memory System) A multiuser, multitasking, virtual memory operating system for the VAX series from Digital. VMS applications run on any VAX from the MicroVAX to the largest unit. See *OpenVMS*.

**(2)** (Voice Messaging System) See *voice mail*.

**VM/SP**    See *VM*.

**VMTP**    (Virtual Message Transaction Protocol) A datagram communications protocol that provides efficient and reliable transmission across networks.

**VOC**    (Vertical Online Community) See *vortal*.

**vocoder**    (VOice CODER) Same as *speech codec*.

**VOD**    See *video on demand*.

**VoDSL**    (Voice Over DSL) Sending voice over a DSL line. Using compression, a large number of voice channels can be placed on DSL channels, which makes the technology very attractive. For example, up to 150 voice channels can be transmitted over a 1.5 Mbps DSL line. DSL signals at the customer side are delivered into an integrated access device (IAD), which forwards them over twisted pair to the carrier. The signals go to the carrier's DSLAM and then to an access switch that forwards voice to a voice gateway and then the PSTN and data to the appropriate data network.

**VOFDM**    (Vector Orhogonal FDM) A radio frequency technology that enables a wireless connection to provide the same performance as a cable modem. Known to be reliable in areas with a lot of interference, VOFDM is being developed and supported as an open standard for broadband wireless Internet services by Cisco and other communications vendors.

**VoFR**    (Voice Over Frame Relay) Transmitting packetized voice over a frame relay network. In 1998, the Frame Relay Forum finalized its voice over frame relay specfication. FRF.11 defines frame formats, and FRF.12 covers fragmentation (creating smaller packets for more efficient realtime voice transmission). See *frame relay*.

**voice analyst**    A person responsible for designing telephony systems, including PBXs, interactive voice response (IVR) systems and call centers.

**voice channel**    A transmission channel or subchannel that has the bandwidth necessary to carry human voice. See *voice grade*.

**voice chat**    An audioconferencing capability via the Internet. It enables two or more people to use the computer as a telephone conferencing system. While the word "voice" in voice chat seems redundant, "chatting" in the computer field has traditionally meant conferencing via the keyboard, thus the word voice is used to signify a real chat.

**V**

**voice codec**   Same as *speech codec*.

**voice coil**   A type of motor used to move the access arm of a disk drive in very small increments. Like the voice coil of a speaker, the amount of current determines the amount of movement. Contrast with *stepper motor*, which works in fixed increments.

**voice compression**   Same as *speech compression*.

**voice grade**   Refers to the bandwidth required to transmit human voice, which is about four thousand Hertz (4 kHz). The term generally refers to analog lines.

**voice mail**   A computerized telephone answering system that digitizes incoming voice messages and stores them on disk or flash memory. It usually provides auto attendant capability, which uses prerecorded messages to route the caller to the appropriate person, department or mailbox. Voice mail systems may also offer directory lookup by name.

**voice menu**   A series of options and the corresponding number to press that are announced to the listener in an IVR or voice processing system. See *IVR* and *voice processing*.

**voice messaging**   Using voice mail as an alternative to electronic mail, in which voice messages are intentionally recorded, not because the recipient was not available.

**voice navigation**   Using voice recognition to select options from a menu.

**voice network**   A communications network that transmit voice. Contrast with *data network*. See *communications*.

**voice over IP**   See *IP telephony* and *IP on Everything*.

**voiceprint**   A sample of a persons voice to be used for voice recognition or security systems.

**voice processing**   The computerized handling of voice, which includes voice store and forward, voice response, voice recognition and text to speech technologies.

**voice recognition**   The conversion of spoken words into computer text. Speech is first digitized and then matched against a dictionary of coded waveforms. The matches are converted into text as if the words were typed on the keyboard.

Speaker-dependent systems require that users enunciate samples into the system in order to tune it to their individual voices. Speaker-independent systems do not require tuning and can recognize limited vocabularies such as numeric digits and a handful of words. For example, such systems have replaced human operators for telephone services such as collect calls and credit card calls.

There are three types of voice recognition applications. Command systems recognize a few hundred words and eliminate using the mouse or keyboard for repetitive commands. This is the least taxing on the computer. Discrete voice recognition systems are used for dictation, but require a pause between each word. Continuous voice recognition understands natural speech without pauses and is the most process intensive. Speaker-independent continuous systems that can handle large vocabularies are expected to become mainstream in the 2000s. Contrast with *speaker recognition*.

**voice response**   The generation of voice output by computer. It provides pre-recorded information either with or without selection by the caller. Interactive voice response allows interactive manipulation of a database. See *IVR*.

**VoiceSpan**   (1) A proposed satellite communications system from AT&T for interactive, multimedia applications that never came to fruition.

(2) A modem technology for simultaneous voice and data transmission from AT&T. See *SVD*.

**voice store and forward**   The technology behind voice mail and messaging systems. Human voice is digitized, stored in the computer, routed to the recipient's mailbox and retrieved by the user when required.

**voice switch**   See *telco switch*.

**VoiceView**   A modem technology for simultaneous voice and data transmission over the same line from Radish Communications Systems, Inc., Boulder, CO. VoiceView works in different modes. One mode can transmit up to regular V.34 speeds for data only with up to an eight-second delay to change to voice. Another mode, suited for sending small amounts of data, uses 9,600 bps for simultaneous voice and data. See *SVD*.

**VoiceXML**   See *VXML*.

**VoIP**   (Voice Over IP) See *IP telephony*.

**volatile memory**   A memory that does not hold its contents without power. A computer's main memory, made up of dynamic RAM or static RAM chips, loses its content immediately upon loss of power.

**volt**   A unit of measurement of force, or pressure, in an electrical circuit. The common voltage of an AC power line is 120 volts of alternating current (alternating directions). Common voltages within a computer are from 5–12 volts of direct current (one direction only).

**voltage regulator**   A device used to maintain a level amount of voltage in the electrical line. Contrast with *surge suppressor*, which filters out excessive amounts of current, and contrast with *UPS*, which provides backup power in the event of a power failure.

**volt-amps**   The measurement of electrical usage that is computed by multiplying volts times amps. See *watt*.

**volume**   (1) A physical storage unit, such as a hard disk, floppy disk, disk cartridge, CD-ROM disc or reel of tape.
(2) A logical storage unit, which is a part of one physical drive or one that spans several physical drives.

**volume label**   (1) A name assigned to a floppy disk, hard disk or CD-ROM when the volume is first formatted or created.
(2) An identifying stick-on label attached to the outside of a tape reel or disk cartridge. The label is handwritten or printed for human viewing.
(3) See *header label*.

**volume serial number**   A number assigned to a floppy disk or hard disk, which uniquely identifies the volume. It is automatically created by the format program and cannot be modified by the user.

**volume set**   A logical storage unit that spans several physical drives. The operating system sees the volume set as a contiguous group of storage blocks, but the physical data resides on multiple drives, broken up by various methods. See *RAID* and *disk striping*.

**volumetric texture**   A texture that is described in three dimensions. It can be created as a "stack" of 2-D bitmapped textures or as a 3-D procedural texture. When an object with volumetric texture is sliced in half, the texture would still be rendered accurately on the inside. See *procedural texture* and *texture mapping*.

**von Neumann architecture**   The sequential nature of computers: an instruction is analyzed, data is processed, the next instruction is analyzed, and so on. Hungarian-born John von Neumann (1903–1957), an internationally renowned mathematician, promoted the stored program concept in the 1940s.

**Voodoo Graphics**   A family of 3-D graphics accelerator chipsets from 3Dfx. Voodoo Graphics chips are used in a variety of 3-D display adapters from major manufacturers. 3Dfx's Voodoo Rush technology adds 3-D capabilities to 2-D adapters. See *3Dfx*.

**vortal**   (Vertical pORTAL) See *vertical portal*.

**John Luis von Neumann**
Von Neumann's name is perhaps mentioned more than any other early computer pioneer because the subject of sequential operations versus parallel operations is often discussed. *(Image courtesy of The Computer Museum History Center, www.computerhistory.org)*

V

**voxel**   (VOlume piXEL) A three-dimensional pixel. A voxel represents a quantity of 3-D data just as a pixel represents a point or cluster of points in 2-D data. It is used in scientific and medical applications that process 3-D images.

**Voyetra**   (Voyetra Turtle Beach, Inc., Yonkers, NY, www.tbeach.com) A manufacturer of sound cards and music software that is a result of a late-1996 merger of Voyetra Technologies and Turtle Beach Systems. Voyetra was founded in 1975 as Octave Electronics, a synthesizer and repair facility in southern New York state. It introduced the Voyetra synthesizer and later moved into software for MIDI sequencer and music-related applications. Voyetra utilities are bundled with numerous sound cards.

Turtle Beach was founded in 1985 in York, PA, and became known for its award-winning Multisound line of high-end sound cards. Its consumer brands are also popular and are named after beaches from around the world such as Malibu, Montego and Daytona.

**VPC**   (Virtual Processor Complex) An IBM mainframe multiprocessing that uses several computers under tight central control.

**VPN**   (Virtual Private Network) A private network that is configured within a public network. For years, common carriers have built VPNs that appear as private national or international networks to the customer, but physically share backbone trunks with other customers. VPNs enjoy the security of a private network via access control and encryption, while taking advantage of the economies of scale and built-in management facilities of large public networks. VPNs have been built over X.25, Switched 56, frame relay and ATM technologies. Today, there is tremendous interest in VPNs over the Internet, especially due to the constant threat of hacker attacks. The VPN adds that extra layer of security, and a huge growth in VPN use is expected. See *PPTP, L2F, L2TP, IPsec, PVC, security* and *transparent LAN service.*

**VP ratio**   (Virtual Processor ratio) The number of virtual processors that a physical processor is simulating.

**VPS**   (Vectors Per Second) The measurement of the speed of a vector or array processor.

**VR**   See *virtual reality.*

**VRAM**   See *video RAM.*

**VRC**   (Vertical Redundancy Check) An error checking method that generates and tests a parity bit for each byte of data that is moved or transmitted.

**VRML**   (Virtual Reality Modeling Language) A 3-D graphics language used on the Web. After downloading a VRML page, its contents can be viewed, rotated and manipulated. Simulated rooms can be "walked into." The VRML viewer is launched from within the Web browser.

The first VRML viewer was WebSpace from SGI, whose Open Inventor graphics library was the basis for developing VRML. WebFX, WorldView and Fountain are other Windows viewers, and Whurlwind and Voyager are Mac viewers.

**VS**   (1) (Virtual Storage) Same as *virtual memory.*
(2) (Virtual Storage) A family of minicomputers from Wang introduced in 1977, which use virtual memory techniques.

**VSAM**   (Virtual Storage Access Method) An IBM access method for storing data, widely used in IBM mainframes. It uses the B+tree method for organizing data.

**VSAT**   (Very Small Aperture satellite Terminal) A small earth station for satellite transmission that handles up to 56 Kbits/sec of digital transmission. VSATs that handle the T1 data rate (up to 1.544 Mbits/sec) are called "TSATs."

**VSB**   (1) (VME Subsystem Bus) An auxiliary "backdoor" protocol on the VME bus that allows high-speed transfer between devices. It was faster than the main bus before the 64-bit implementation arrived.
(2) (Vestigial SideBand) A digital modulation method developed by Zenith for cable modems and terrestrial transmission for DTV. See *8-VSB.*

**VSE**   See *DOS/VSE.*

**V Series**    A series of of small to medium-scale mainframes from Unisys that were the Burroughs B2500 and B3500 product lines, originally introduced in 1966.

**VSX**    (Verification Suite for X/Open) A testing procedure from X/Open that verifies compliance with their endorsed standards. VSX3 has over 5,500 tests for compliance with XPG3.

**VT100, 200, 300, etc.**    A series of asynchronous display terminals from Digital for its PDP and VAX computers. Available in text and graphics models in both monochrome and color.

**VTAM**    (Virtual Telecommunications Access Method) Also ACF/VTAM (Advanced Communications Function/ VTAM), it is software that controls communications in an IBM SNA environment. VTAM usually resides in the mainframe under MVS or VM, but may be offloaded into a front end processor that is tightly coupled to the mainframe. It supports a wide variety of network protocols, including SDLC and Token Ring. VTAM can be thought of as the network operating system of SNA.

**VTOC**    (Volume Table Of Contents) A list of files on a disk. The VTOC is the mainframe counterpart to the FAT table on a PC.

**VTR**    (VideoTape Recorder) A video recording and playback machine that uses reels of magnetic tape. Contrast with *VCR*, which uses tape cassettes. See *Ampex*.

**VTS**    (Virtual Tape Server, Virtual Tape System) A peripheral unit that combines a disk cache and tape library to improve performance and eliminate cartridge waste. Data intended for tape storage is written to the disk cache and later written to tape in the background. If a tape is read frequently, a certain amount of its data is held in the cache, which greatly improves access times over the slow loading process of a robotic library.

Tape files are typically stored on one cartridge no matter how small they are. A VTS provides volume stacking, which stores multiple files on a single volume. The VTS indexes the files and manages them, dramatically improving cartridge efficiency.

IBM's Virtual Tape Server for MVS uses its own Magstar tape library. Sun-based Scimitar systems from Sutmyn Storage Corporation, Santa Clara, CA (www.sutmyn.com), support the tape library attached to the host.

**VUI**    (Voice User Interface) A voice-controlled application on a computer, PDA or smart phone. A VUI is more sophisticated than an interactive voice response (IVR) system. It implies a wide range of commands rather than just voicing "yes" or "no." Contrast with *GUI*.

**vulnerability**    A security exposure in an operating system or other system software or application software component. Security firms maintain databases of vulnerabilities based on version number of the software. Each vulnerability can potentially compromise the system or network if exploited.

**VX chipset**    See *Intel chipsets*.

**VxD**    (Virtual Device Driver) A special type of Windows driver that allows Windows to perform functions that cannot be done by applications communicating with Windows in the normal manner. VxDs run at the most privileged CPU mode (ring 0) and allow low-level interaction with the hardware and internal Windows functions, such as memory management.

Like DOS TSRs, poorly-written VxDs can conflict and lock up the system. WIN386.EXE (Win 3.1) and VMM32.VXD (Win 95/98) are the VxD files that provide the primary functions (kernel) in Windows.

**VxFS**    (VERITAS File System) A journaled file system for various UNIX systems from VERITAS Software Corporation, Mountain View, CA (www.veritas.com), that provides high performance on large volumes of data and fast recovery from system failure. See *journaled file system*.

**VXML**    (Voice XML) An extension to XML that defines voice segments and enables access to the Internet via telephones and other voice-activated devices. AT&T, Lucent and Motorola created the Voice XML Forum to support this development. For more information, visit www.vxml.org.

V

**W2K**  See *Windows 2000*.

**W3C**  (World Wide Web Consortium, www.w3.org) An international industry consortium founded in 1994 to develop common standards for the World Wide Web. It is hosted in the U.S. by the Laboratory for Computer Science at MIT.

**Wabi**  (Windows **ABI**) Software from SunSoft that emulates Windows applications under UNIX by converting the calls made by Windows applications into X Window calls. Since it executes native code, it runs Windows applications at the same or higher performance level than a Windows machine. Wabi is an option for Sun's Solaris environment as well as for OEM products.

**wafer**  (1) The base material in chip making, which goes through a series of photomasking, etching and implantation steps. It is a slice approximately 1/30" thick from a salami-like silicon crystal up to 12" in diameter (300mm). See *chip*.

(2) A small, thin continuous-loop magnetic tape cartridge that has been used from time to time for data storage and specialized applications.

**The Boule Is Sliced**
The silicon ingot, which is known as a "boule," is sliced into wafers. *(Image courtesy of International Business Machines Corporation. Unauthorized use not permitted.)*

**wafer scale integration**  The evolution in semiconductor technology that builds a gigantic circuit on an entire wafer. Just as the integrated circuit eliminated cutting apart thousands of transistors from the wafer only to wire them back again on circuit boards, wafer scale integration eliminates cutting apart the chips. All the circuits for an entire computer are designed onto one super-sized chip.

Thus far, wafer scale integration has not come to fruition (see *Trilogy*); however, chip packaging such as the multichip module (MCM) and multichip package (MCP), in which several chips are connected closely together in a single housing, has become widely used.

**WAFL**  (Write Anywhere File Layout) A high-performance journaled file system used in Network Appliances's NAS and caching devices. It natively supports RAID implementations and allows for expansion on the fly. Using a clever system of pointers to disk clusters that take up a small amount of extra disk space, WAFL enables up to 31 snapshots of the disk to be scheduled in order to roll back to previous versions of the data. See *Network Appliance*.

**Finished Wafers**
The man in the picture is holding up two wafers that have just come off the assembly line in a Texas Instruments plant in Italy. *(Image courtesy of Texas Instruments, Inc.).*

**WAIS**  (Wide Area Information Server) A database on the Internet that contains indexes to documents that reside on the Internet. Using the Z39.50 query language, text files can be searched based on keywords. Information resources on the Internet are called "sources." See *Archie* and *Gopher*.

**wait state**   The time spent waiting for an operation to take place. It may refer to a variable length of time a program has to wait before it can be processed, or to a fixed duration of time, such as a machine cycle.

When memory is too slow to respond to the CPU's request for it, wait states are introduced until the memory can catch up.

**Wake-on-LAN**   See *remote wake-up*.

**wallet**   See *digital wallet*.

**wallpaper**   A pattern or picture used to represent the desktop surface (screen background) in a graphical user interface. GUIs comes with several wallpaper choices, and third-party wallpaper files are available. You can also scan in your favorite picture and make it wallpaper.

If you wonder why you cover a desktop with wallpaper, don't. Whoever came up with that one had too many sleepless nights programming.

**Walsh code**   Also known as "Walsh-Hadamard code," it is an algorithm that generates statistically unique sets of numbers for use in encryption and cellular communications. Known as "pseudo-random noise codes," Walsh codes are used in direct sequence spread spectrum (DSSS) systems such as QUALCOMM's CDMA. They are also used in frequency hopping spread spectrum (FHSS) systems to select the target frequency for the next hop. See *CDMA*.

```
Walsh Code Algorithm

(a', b') = (a+b, a-b)
```

**WAN**   (Wide Area Network) A communications network that covers a wide geographic area, such as state or country. A LAN (local area network) is contained within a building or complex, and a MAN (metropolitan area network) generally covers a city or suburb. Following is a bandwidth comparison between major LAN and WAN technologies.

**WAN administrator**   A person who manages a wide area communications network (WAN). Such individuals are responsible for the configuration, implementation and monitoring of all networking hardware such as modems, DSU/CSUs, routers and switches. See *network administrator*.

**WAN analyzer**   See *network analyzer*.

**wand**   A handheld optical reader used to read typewritten fonts, printed fonts, OCR fonts and bar codes. The wand is waved over each line of characters or codes in a single pass.

**Wand**
Handheld optical character readers, or wands, are increasingly being used to capture retail product information in point of sale applications.

| LAN Technologies | Bandwidth |
|---|---|
| Ethernet | 10 Mbps (shared) |
| Switched Ethernet | 10 Mbps (node to node) |
| Fast Ethernet | 100 Mbps |
| Gigabit Ethernet | 1,000 Mbps |
| 10 Gigabit Ethernet | 10,000 Mbps |
| Token Ring | 4, 16 Mbps |
| Fast Token Ring | 100, 128 Mbps |
| FDDI/CDDI | 100 Mbps |
| ATM | 25, 45, 155, 622. 2488 Mbps + |

| WAN Technologies | Bandwidth |
|---|---|
| **UNSWITCHED PRIVATE LINES (point to point)** | |
| T1 | 24 x 64 Kbps = 1.5 Mbps |
| T3 | 672 x 64 Kbps = 44.7 Mbps |
| Fractional T1 | N x 64 Kbps |
| DSL | 144 Kbps to 52 Mbps |
| **SWITCHED SERVICES** | |
| Dial-up via modem | 9.6, 14.4, 28.8, 33.6, 56 Kbps |
| ISDN | BRI 64-128 Kbps<br>PRI 1.544 Mbps |
| Switched 56/64 | 56 Kbps, 64 Kbps |
| Packet switched (X.25) | 56 Kbps |
| Frame relay | 56 Kbps to 45 Mbps |
| SMDS | 45, 155 Mbps |
| ATM | 25, 45, 155, 622, 2488 Mbps + |

**Wang**   (Wang Laboratories, Inc., Lowell, MA, www.wang.com) A computer services and network integration company. Wang was one of the major early contributors to the computing industry from its founder's invention that made core memory possible, to leadership in desktop calculators and word processors. Founded in 1951 by Dr. An Wang and specializing in electronics, the company became world famous for its desktop calculators by the 1960s.

In the 1970s, Wang introduced its WPS word processor and VS minicomputers. It became North America's largest supplier of small business computers and the world's leader in word processors. Throughout the 1980s, it developed integrated voice and data networks and imaging systems.

In 1992, Wang declared Chapter 11 and recovered 18 months later. Soon after, it acquired Groupe Bull's federal systems integration business, its European imaging installations and its maintenance operations in North America and Australia. Wang has since sold off its software business to specialize in services.

Dr. Wang came from China in 1945 to study applied physics at Harvard. Six years later, he started Wang Labs. In 1988, two years before he died, he was inducted into the National Inventors Hall of Fame for his 1948 invention of a pulse transfer device that let magnetic cores be used for computer memory. The Hall of Fame has recognized an elite group including Edison, Pasteur and Bell.

## WAP

**WAP** (Wireless Application Protocol) A standard for providing cellular phones, pagers and other handheld devices with secure access to e-mail and text-based Web pages. Introduced in 1997 by Phone.com (formerly Unwired Planet), Ericsson, Motorola and Nokia, WAP provides a complete environment for wireless applications that includes a wireless counterpart of TCP/IP and a framework for telephony integration such as call control and phone book access. WAP features the Wireless Markup Language (WML), which was derived from Phone.com's HDML and is a streamlined version of HTML for small screen displays. It also uses WMLScript, a compact JavaScript-like language that runs in limited memory. WAP also supports handheld input

**The Wang Calculator**
In 1965, Wang's calculator was a major step forward, because it could generate a natural logarithm with only one keystroke. *(Image courtesy of Wang Laboratories, Inc.)*

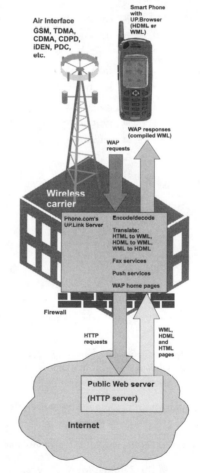

**A WAP Gateway/Application Server**
This diagram depicts Phone.com's UP.Link Server product, which hosts WAP applications and provides numerous services (push, fax, etc.) along with the WAP Gateway, which encodes and decodes WAP pages between the microbrowser in the smart phone and the Web server.

**Dr. An Wang**
Dr. Wang was a major force in the early days of computing. His contribution to the invention of core memory significantly advanced the computer industry in the 1950s. His business and word processing systems were used worldwide by the 1970s. *(Image courtesy of Wang Laboratories, Inc.)*

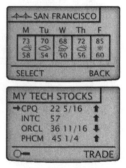

**No Information Overload Here**
Due to the small screen real estate, WAP-based applications get right to the point, because they can't afford to waste your time with unnecessary "eye candy." WAP-based phones may provide a welcome relief from the information overload on most Web home pages. *(Image courtesy of Phone.com, Inc.)*

methods suchas a keypad and voice recognition. Independent of the air interface, WAP runs over all the major wireless networks in place now and in the future. It is also device independent, requiring only a minimum functionality in the unit so that it can be used with a myriad of phones and handheld devices. See *WAP Forum*, *HDML* and *i-Mode*. See also *wired access point*.

**WAP Forum**    (Wireless Application Protocol Forum, Mountain View, CA, www.wapforum.org)  An organization founded in 1997 to promote a wireless standard for delivering e-mail, text-based Web pages and data to cellphones, pagers, PDAs and other mobile terminals. See *WAP*.

**war dialer**    A program that dials up telephone numbers to determine which lines are connected to modems and fax machines. It is used to illegally bust into systems. See *toneloc*.

**wares**    We love "wares" in this industry as noted below. See also *warez*.

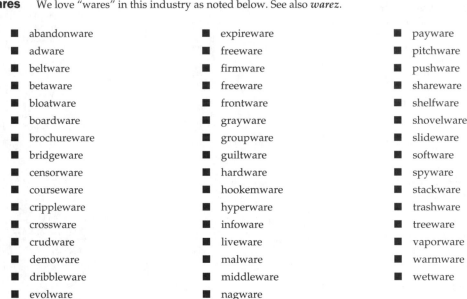

| | | |
|---|---|---|
| ■ abandonware | ■ expireware | ■ payware |
| ■ adware | ■ freeware | ■ pitchware |
| ■ beltware | ■ firmware | ■ pushware |
| ■ betaware | ■ freeware | ■ shareware |
| ■ bloatware | ■ frontware | ■ shelfware |
| ■ boardware | ■ grayware | ■ shovelware |
| ■ brochureware | ■ groupware | ■ slideware |
| ■ bridgeware | ■ guiltware | ■ software |
| ■ censorware | ■ hardware | ■ spyware |
| ■ courseware | ■ hookemware | ■ stackware |
| ■ crippleware | ■ hyperware | ■ trashware |
| ■ crossware | ■ infoware | ■ treeware |
| ■ crudware | ■ liveware | ■ vaporware |
| ■ demoware | ■ malware | ■ warmware |
| ■ dribbleware | ■ middleware | ■ wetware |
| ■ evolware | ■ nagware | |

**warm boot**    Restarting the computer by performing a reset operation (pressing reset, CTRL-ALT-DEL, etc.). See *boot*, *cold boot* and *clean boot*.

**warm swap**    To pull out a component from a system and plug in a new one without turning the power off. Although often used synonymously with *hot swap*, a unit that is warm swapped must not be functioning. For example, a hard disk cannot be reading or writing while it is pulled out. See *hot swap*.

**Warnier-Orr diagram**    A graphic charting technique used in software engineering for system analysis and design.

**WARP**    (1) See *OS/2 Warp*.
   (2) A parallel processor developed at Carnegie-Mellon University that was the predecessor of iWARP.

**Warp Server**    The server version of OS/2 from IBM. Warp Server combines OS/2 and Lan Server into one package that was introduced in 1996. Warp Server is generally highly praised and well suited as a Lotus Notes server. Among other features, the journaled file system (JFS) in AIX was later added, and the product was renamed Warp Server for e-Business in 1999. See *OS/2*.

**watchdog packet**     In a NetWare network, an inquiry packet sent by the server to the client if it has not had any requests from the client for some period of time. If there is no response to the watchdog packets, the server clears the connection.

**watermark**     See *digital watermark*.

**watt**     The measurement of electrical power. One watt is one ampere of current flowing at one volt. Watts are typically rated as AMPS × VOLTS; however, AMPS × VOLTS, or VOLT-AMP (V-A) ratings and watts are only equivalent when powering devices that absorb all the energy such as electric heating coils or incandescent light bulbs. With computer power supplies, the actual watt rating is only 60–70% of the VOLT-AMP rating.

**wave**     A ripple or undulation. All radio signals, light rays, x-rays, and cosmic rays radiate an energy that behaves likes rippling waves. To visualize a wave, take a piece of paper and start drawing an up and down line very fast while pulling the paper perpendicular to the line. See *wave-particle duality* and *wavelength*.

**waveform**     The shape of a wave. See *wavelength*.

**waveguide**     A rectangular, circular or elliptical tube through which radio waves are transmitted.

**wavelength**     The distance between crests of a wave, computed by speed divided by frequency (speed / Hz). For electromagnetic waves, the wavelength in meters is equal to 300,000,000 divided by frequency (Hz). For sound travelling through the air, it is 335 divided by frequency (Hz). See *optical bands*.

**wavelet compression**     A lossy compression method used for color images and video. Instead of compressing small blocks of 8×8 pixels (64 bits) as in JPEG and MPEG, the wavelet algorithms compress the entire image with ratios of up to 300:1 for color and 50:1 for gray scale.

 Wavelet compression also supports nonuniform compression, where specified parts of the image can be compressed more than others. There are several proprietary methods based on wavelet mathematics, which are available in products from Compression Engines, LLC, (www.cengines.com), InfinOp, Inc., (www.infinop.com) and Summus, Ltd., (www.summus.com). See *lossy compression*.

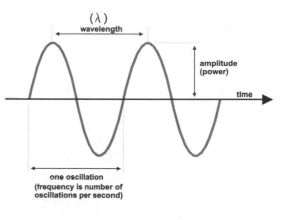

**Length of a Wave**
The wavelength is the distance between crests. The higher the frequency, the shorter the wavelength.

**wave-particle duality**     The inherent contradiction in the way energy behaves. At the turn of the twentieth century, it was believed that light was electromagnetic waves and electrons were particles. By the 1930s, it was determined that light behaves as if it were made up of particles (photons) as well as waves, and electrons also behave like waves. This has driven scientists to drink and is one of the most puzzling phenomena in the universe. See *quantum mechanics*.

**wavetable synthesis**     The technique used by MIDI for creating musical sounds by storing digitized samples of the actual instruments. It provides more realistic sound than the FM synthesis method, which generates the sound waves entirely via electronic circuits. The more notes sampled in the wavetables, the better the resulting sound recreation. See *MIDI* and *FM synthesis*.

**WAV file**     The native digital audio format in Windows. Using the .WAV file extension, 8-bit or 16-bit samples can be taken at rates of 11,025 Hz, 22,050 Hz and 44,100 Hz. The highest quality (16-bit at 44,100 Hz) uses 88KB of storage per second. Windows uses WAV files for general system sounds, and new WAV files can be placed in the Windows Media folder (\windows\media or \winnt\media) and assigned in the Sounds control panel. See *sampling rate*.

**WBEM**     (Web-Based Enterprise Management) An umbrella term for using Internet technologies to manage systems and networks throughout the enterprise. Both browsers and applications can be used to access the information that is made available in formats such as HTML and XML. Built into Windows 98 and 2000, WBEM uses the Common Information Model (CIM) as the database for information about computer systems and network devices. Originally an initiative of Microsoft, Intel and others, WBEM was passed over to the DMTF in 1998. See *CIM* and *JMAPI*.

**WBT**     See *Windows-based terminal*.

**W-CDMA**     (Wideband-CDMA) A 3G technology that increases data transmission rates in GSM systems by using the CDMA air interface instead of TDMA. In the ITU's IMT-2000 3G specification, W-CDMA has become known as the Direct Sequence (DS) mode. See *GSM*, *cdma2000* and *wireless generations*.

**WDM**     (1) (Wavelength Division Multiplexing) A technology that uses multiple lasers and transmits several wavelengths of light (lamdas) simultaneously over a single optical fiber. Each signal travels within its unique color band, which is modulated by the data (text, voice, video, etc.). WDM enables the existing fiber infrastructure of the telephone companies and other carriers to be dramatically increased. Vendors have announced WDM systems, or DWDM (dense WDM) systems, as they are also called, that can support more than 150 wavelengths, each carrying up to 10 Gbps. Such systems provide more than a terabit per second of data transmission on one optical strand, thinner than a human hair. Contrast with *TDM*. See also *FDM*.

     (2) (Win32 Driver Model) A device driver architecture from Microsoft that consolidates drivers for Windows 95/98 and Windows NT. It allows a hardware vendor to write one Windows driver for its peripheral device that works with Windows 95/98 and NT.

**weak typing**     A programming language characteristic that allows different types of data to be moved freely among data structures, as is found in Smalltalk and other earlier object-oriented languages. Contrast with *strong typing*.

**Web**     See *World Wide Web*.

**Web accelerator**     Software that speeds up the retrieval of Web pages. Anticipating that you might click a link on the current page, it downloads the linked pages in the background. Most of these utilities require nothing more than your browser, while others require a counterpart component in the server. See also *CDN*.

**Web address**     The URL of a page on the Web; for example, www.computerlanguage.com. See *URL*.

**Web administrator**     The Web equivalent of a system administrator. Web administrators are system architects responsible for the overall design and implementation of an Internet Web site or intranet. See *Webmaster*.

**Web aggregator**     A content aggregator that uses the Internet as the distribution medium. Most content aggregators are Web aggregators. See *content aggregator*.

**Web app**     See *Web-based application* and *Web application*.

**Web appliance**     See *Internet appliance*.

**Web application**     Software based on the Web. This can refer to almost anything Web related, including a Web browser or other client software that can access the Web. It can refer to software that runs on Web sites or software that is stored on Web sites and downloaded to the user. See *Web-based application*.

**Web application server**     See *application server*.

**Web authoring software**     A Web site development system that allows Web pages to be visually created like a desktop publishing program. It generates the required HTML code for the pages and is able to switch back and forth (in varying degrees) between the page layout and the HTML. At a high level, the software is judged by its GUI tools used for designing the page. At a low level, the clarity of HTML code that is generated determines how easily people can modify and maintain the site.

Comprehensive products can read an entire Web site and display it as a graphical hierarchy of pages, providing a way to manage existing sites. See *Web development software* and *HTML editor*.

**Web based**     Any software that runs on or interacts with a Web site, which may be on the Internet or on an inhouse intranet.

**Web-based application**     An application that is downloaded from the Web each time it is run. The advantage is that the application can be run from any computer, and the software is routinely upgraded and maintained by the hosting organization rather than each individual user. Some envision a future where everything is stored and downloaded from the Web, which is a return to the centralized processing architecture of the 1960s and 1970s. Changes are definitely expected. Stay tuned! See *ASP*.

**Web-based e-mail**     See *Internet e-mail service*.

**Web beacon**     Same as *Web bug*.

**WebBench**     A benchmark from Ziff-Davis Media that tests the performance of Web server software. It is a Windows-based program that can test any server platform and can thus be used to guage a Web package running on different hardware or different Web packages running on the same hardware. See *ZDBOp*.

**Web browser**     The program that serves as your front end to the World Wide Web on the Internet. In order to view a site, you type its address (URL) into the browser's Location field; for example, **www.computerlanguage.com**, and the home page of that site is downloaded to you. The home page is an index to other pages on that site that you can jump to by clicking a "click here" message or an icon. Links on that site may take you to other related sites.

Browsers have a bookmark feature that lets you store references to your favorite sites. Instead of typing in the URL again to visit the site the next time, you select one of the bookmarks.

Although Mosaic was the browser that put the Web on the map, the two major browsers today are Netscape Navigator and Microsoft Internet Explorer. Navigator and Internet Explorer each vie for top recognition by introducing new features and functions that fragment Web sites into competing camps. When a site says "best viewed by Netscape Navigator" or "best viewed by Internet Explorer," it means that the pages were programmed for that particular browser. Using the other browser will

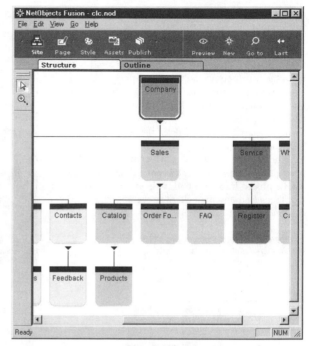

**Sample Site**
Web authoring programs such as NetObjects Fusion will automatically create a hierarchy for a typical public Web site and let you edit it however you wish. Such programs let you place text and images on a page and automatically create the complex navigation bars that let you link to all areas of the site. *(Screen shot courtesy of NetObjects, Inc.)*

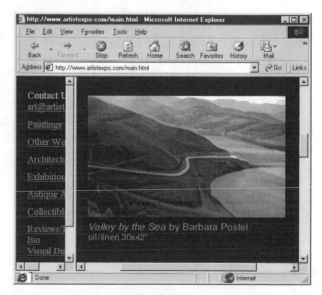

W

ignore some of the page's fancy features until a subsequent release supports them. See *World Wide Web*, *HTML* and *microbrowser*.

**Web bug**    A method for passing information from the user's computer to a third-party Web site. Used in conjunction with cookies, Web bugs enable information to be gathered and tracked in the stateless environment of the Internet. The Web bug is typically a one-pixel, transparent GIF image, although it can be a visible image as well. As the HTML code for the Web bug points to a site to retrieve the image, it can pass along information at the same time. Web bugs can be placed into an HTML page used for e-mail messages as many mail client programs support the display of HTML pages. See *state*.

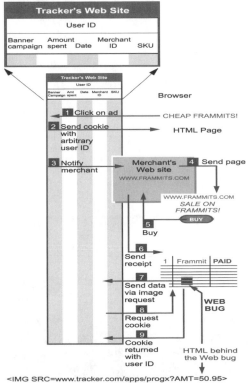

`<IMG SRC=www.tracker.com/apps/progx?AMT=50.95>`

### A Web Bug Scenario

There are a myriad ways in which Web bugs can be used. This example uses a third-party tracking site to determine how much merchandise was purchased for a particular banner ad campaign. In scenarios such as these, the individual users may still remain anonymous, even though their buying habits are disclosed.

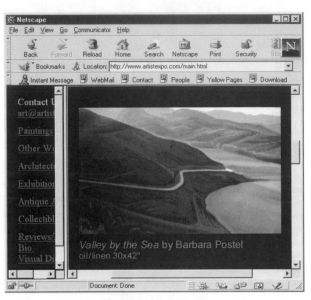

### The Most Well Known

Internet Explorer and Netscape are the two major browsers used to access the World Wide Web. Similar in features and function, each new version includes enhancements that the other generally catches up to in its next release. *(Web page examples courtesy of Pyramid Studios, www.artistexpo.com)*

### There Are Others

Opera is a highly-respected Web browser from Norway that offers many unique features, including the ability to magnify the image as shown here (see *Opera*). *(Web page example courtesy of Pyramid Studios, www.artistexpo.com)*

**Web cache** **(1)** A computer system in a network that keeps copies of the most-recently requested Web pages in memory or on disk in order to speed up retrieval. If the next page requested has already been stored in the cache, it is retrieved locally rather than from the Internet. Web caching servers (or caching servers or cache servers) sit inside the company's firewall and enable all popular pages retrieved by users to be instantly available. Since the content of Web pages can change, the caching software is always checking for newer versions of the page and downloading them. Pages will be deleted from the cache after a set amount of non activity. See *proxy cache*, *reverse proxy cache*, *transparent cache*. See also *Akamai*.

**(2)** The storehouse of pages maintained by your Web browser for a period of time. Options in your browser let you set the amount of disk space used and length of time before pages expire and are deleted. In Internet Explorer, select Tools/Internet Options. In Netscape, select Edit/Preferences.

**WebCam** **(WEB CAM**era**)** A video camera that is used to send periodic images or continuous frames to a Web site for display. WebCam software typically captures the images as JPEG or MPEG files and uploads them to the Web server. There are countless WebCam sites throughout the Internet that have cameras pointed at virtually everything, including people just going about their daily work. WebCams have become popular on sexual-oriented sites providing the electronic rendition of the live "peep show."

**Webcast** **(1)** To send live audio or video programming over the Web. It is the Internet counterpart to traditional radio and TV broadcasting.

**(2)** To send selected Web-based information (text, graphics, audio, video, etc.) to Internet users based on individual requirements. See *push technology*.

**Web-centric** Having to do with the Web. A Web-centric view of something means that the application or system has been designed for the Web. See *Webified*.

**Web client** The client, or user, side of the Web. It typically refers to the Web browser in the user's machine. It may also refer to plug-ins and helper applications that enhance the browser to support special services from the site. The term may imply the entire user machine or to a handheld device that provides Web access. Contrast with *Web server*. See *browser plug-in*.

**Web clipping** **(1)** Extracting a smaller amount from a Web page in order to display effectively on a handheld Web appliance. Web clipping often uses a predefined form, or template, into which the extracted data is placed.

**(2)** An excerpt of information taken from the Web.

**Web cluster** See *Web farm*.

**Web cramming** An offer to start Internet access if you cash the check you just received in the mail. However this scheme generally binds you to a contract you did not expect, such as a long-term agreement with severe penalties for withdrawing. As always... read the fine print! See *dot-con*.

**WebCrawler** **(www.webcrawler.com)** A search site on the Web that searches other search sites. It returns a list of titles first giving you the option of going directly to a specific article or reviewing the summaries of all the hits. See *Web search sites*.

**WebDAV** **(Web** **D**istributed **A**uthoring **A**nd **V**ersioning**)** Enhancements to the HTTP protocol that turn the Web into a document database that enables collaborative creation, editing and searching from remote locations. Standardized by the IETF, WebDAV enables documents to be written via HTTP (HTTP normally only supports reading). It also allows documents to be assigned properties, or attributes, that can be searched using the DAV Searching and Locating (DASL) protocol. WebDAV supports its own file system that stores documents in folders called "collections." See *HTTP*.

**Web designer** A person that creates a Web site. Web designers may use Web authoring software or an HTML editor to create the actual pages, or they may design the overall look and let a Webmaster do the actual coding. See *Webmaster*, *Web authoring software* and *HTML editor*.

**W**

**Web development software**    Software used to develop Web sites. Although often synonymous with "Web authoring software," it implies a more programming-oriented set of tools for linking pages to databases and other software components. It generally includes an HTML editor. See *Web authoring software, HTML editor, CGI script* and *application server*.

**Web e-mail**    See *Internet e-mail service*.

**Web enabled**    Able to connect to or be run on the Web. This is a rather broad term that may refer to an application that outputs HTML for display on the Web or that launches a Web browser to retrieve specific Web pages. It can also refer to an application that must run on a Web server, the output of which could be displayed by a browser or a Java application.

**Web farm**    (1) A group of computer systems and Web server software that collectively provide the Web page delivery mechanism in a company either for internal use (intranet) and/or for the public Internet. It is a server farm made up of Web servers (HTTP servers). See *server farm*.

(2) A group of Web servers that are controlled locally, but centrally managed. Each Web site is administered by its own Webmaster; however, centralized monitoring provides load balancing and fault tolerance. See *server farm*.

**Web filtering**    Blocking the viewing of undesirable Internet content. Businesses can block content based on traffic type. For example, Web access might be allowed, but file transfers may not. Content can also be blocked by site, using lists of URLs cataloged by content that are updated frequently. Parents can restrict their children's access with special browsers and filtering programs. For the anti-censoring, opposing view, visit www.censorware.org. See *Internet monitoring* and *parental control software*.

**WebFOCUS**    A family of information retrieval tools from Information Builders. The foundation is the WebFOCUS query and reporting engine which lets users have Web browser access to more than 80 different database and file types. Introduced in 1997, WebFOCUS is an extension to Information Builder's EDA middleware product with support for the Web. The WebFOCUS Suite provides optional enhancements for report scheduling and distribution and for viewing multidimensional data (OLAP viewing). See *FOCUS Desktop* and *EDA*.

**Webhead**    An enthusiastic and frequent user of the World Wide Web. See *Webhippie*.

**Webhippie**    A person that believes the World Wide Web is ushering in a new culture for the 21st Century and that its primary tenets are "freedom of expression" and "freedom of information." See *Webhead*.

**Web hosting**    Placing a customer's Web page or Web site on a commercial Web server. Many ISPs host a personal Web page at no additional cost above the monthly service fee, but the address is subordinate to the ISP; for example, www.friendlyisp.com/pat_smith. Multi-page, commercial Web sites are hosted at a very wide range of prices, and the customer's registered domain name is used. A single computer can hold dozens to hundreds of small Web sites, while larger Web sites use a dedicated computer or even multiple computers.

Web hosting organizations can provide full service, including site design and programming as well as all e-commerce facilities. If Web site customers wish to use their own servers and software, all their privately-owned equipment can be co-located at the ISP, which provides the power, the on-ramp to the Internet and some level of maintenance.

When a large enterprise runs its own Web site internally with its own equipment, it is not incorrect to say that "it hosts its own Web site" as well. See *ISP, co-location* and *how to register a domain name*.

**Web hub**    A business-to-business Web site for a particular industry. It provides a meeting ground for buyers and sellers in a specific field and rather than being advertising based, may charge a transaction fee for each purchase. Also known as a vertical portal, or "vortal." See *vertical portal*.

**Webified**    Made to operate on the Web using a browser or made to function in a similar manner. For example, the Windows 98 desktop has an option that Webifies its look and feel. See *Web-centric*.

**Webinar** (WEB-based semINAR) A workshop or lecture delivered over the Web. Rather than just a one-way video presentation, a webinar implies a two-way interaction between the audience and the presenters.

**Web integration specialist** A person with experience in melding existing systems with the Web. It requires a knowledge of legacy systems and the latest Web technologies to convert older applications to Web applications or to Web enable existing systems using integration software and programming tools.

**Webisode** (WEB epISODE) A short audio or video presentation on the Web. Webisodes are used to promote a product, preview music, deliver news events and present all sorts of information. Flash animation is often used for Webisodes. See *Flash, streaming audio* and *streaming video*.

**Weblication** An application that runs on the Web. See *netsourcing*.

**Web log** (1) A Web page that contains links to Web sites that cover a particular subject or that are based on some other criterion, such as interesting or entertaining sites. The Web log typically provides a short summary of the referenced sites and may also contain commentary and humor. Web logs have become a new form of artistic expression, enabling one to create an interactive catalog of the parts of the world they find fascinating.

(2) An analysis of traffic on a Web site. It would show the number of visitors, sessions, page views, etc.

**Weblogic** See *BEA Weblogic*.

**WebMail** (1) A free Internet e-mail service available at Netscape's Netcenter portal. See *Netcenter*.

(2) (Webmail) An Internet e-mail service. See *Internet e-mail service*.

**Webmaster** A person responsible for the implementation of a Web site. Webmasters must be proficient in HTML as well as one or more scripting and interface languages such as JavaScript and Perl. They may also have experience with more than one type of Web server. See *Web administrator* and **Webmistress**.

**Web monitoring** See *Internet monitoring*.

**Web objects** (1) The elements on a Web page, which include text, graphics, URLs and scripts.

(2) A sophisticated development environment from Apple for creating Web applications that runs on NT, Solaris, HP/UX and OPENSTEP Mach. Supporting the major databases, WebObjects enables development in Java and a variety of C versions including Objective-C and C++.

**Webpad** (1) A handheld, wireless device designed for Web browsing. A Webpad is like a laptop computer without a fold-down screen and keyboard, which is why it is also called a "Web slate" or "tablet computer." Using a touch screen, Webpads typically weigh under three pounds and are less than an inch thick. See *tablet computer*.

(2) (WebPad) An HTML editor from Rainer Link, (www.webpadpro.com), that provides WYSIWYG design capability and numerous features.

**Web page** A World Wide Web document. A Web page is a text file coded in HTML, which may also contain JavaScript code or other commands. See *HTML, World Wide Web* and *Webmaster*.

**Web page editor** Software used to create and change Web pages (HTML-based documents). Low-level Web page editors are used to write HTML code directly. High-level Web authoring programs provide complete WYSIWYG design with the ability (in varying degrees) to switch back and forth between the page layout and the HTML code. See *HTML editor* and *Web authoring software*.

**Web palette** See *Netscape color palette*.

**Web payment service** A facility that manages the transfer of funds from a customer to a merchant of an e-commerce Web site. The money may come from a digital wallet inside the user's machine, from a credit card stored on a server of a digital wallet service or from a prepaid account stored in the payment service's server. See *digital money*, **Brodia**, *CyberCash, eCash, eCharge, E-Money*, **EntryPoint**, *InternetCash, iPIN, Qpass, Passport*, **WISP** and *1ClickCharge*.

**W**

**Web PC**    **(1)** A PC dedicated to only some form of Internet access such as the Web and/or e-mail. See *Internet appliance*.
**(2)** A desktop computer that derives all of its applications and data from an intranet or the Internet. See *network computer*.

**Web phone**    **(1)** A cellphone with Web access. See *WAP*.
**(2)** Using the Internet for telephone transport either for free or subsidized national or international calling. See *Web-to-phone* and *IP telephony*.

**Web player**    **(1)** Software that "plays" audio, video or animations directly from the Web. It is typically a plug-in for the browser.
**(2)** An organization that embraces the World Wide Web in some manner.

**Web programmer**    A person that writes in any of the formatting or programming languages commonly used on the Web, which includes HTML, XML, JavaScript, Java, Perl, C and C++. See *Web programming*.

**Web programming**    Writing the necessary source code to deliver Web pages to the user. It includes writing in HTML and XML as well as writing in a variety of programming languages such as C, C++, Visual Basic, JavaScript, Java and Perl. See *CGI script*, *Web development software* and *application server*.

**Web publishing**    Creating a Web site and placing it on the Web server. A Web site is a collection of HTML pages with the home page typically named INDEX.HTML. Web sites are designed using Web authoring software which provides a graphical layout capability or by hand coding in HTML or both. Distributing the site requires copying the resulting HTML pages and graphic elements into the appropriate directories on the server. See *Web authoring software* and *HTML editor*.

**Web radio**    See *Internet radio*.

**Web rage**    A user's frustration and anger when accessing the Web. Web rage is caused by such things as slow or overloaded connections, busy servers, missing links, excessive results when doing a search, and very often, poorly-designed Web sites that make you go through hoops to find what you want. See *link rot* and *user interface*.

**Webring**    (www.webring.org) A navigation system that links related Web sites together. Each ring links sites that pertain to a particular topic.

**Web search sites**    There are various Web sites that maintain databases about the contents of other Web sites. Most sites are free and are paid for by advertising banners, while others charge for the service. Yahoo! was the first search site to gain worldwide attention, and it differs from most other search sites because its content is indexed by people who create a hierarchical directory by subject. As a result, Yahoo! and similar sites are technically called "directories" rather than search engines.

Most other sites are highly automated, sending spider programs out on the Web around the clock to collect the text of Web pages. Spiders follow all the links on a page and put all the text into one gigantic database, which is what you search when you use the site. Sometimes, a Web site will offer both search engine and directory capabilities.

There are also sites that do nothing but search other sites. These metasearch engines bring you results from multiple search engines at one time (see below). See *information broker*.

The Portal    Major search sites have evolved into the so-called "portal," which is another term for "we've got everthing you want." Instead of just linking to other sites, they contain the information themselves. Thus, many search sites have evolved into content sites with a host of other features, including free e-mail, chat rooms and shopping.

The Web Site of Search Sites    Be sure to visit www.searchenginewatch.com. The site maintains a list of all major search engines and goes into detail about how they work and explains their significant features.

General-Purpose Sites    Following are popular sites for searching any topic. If you don't find what you want at one site, try another, even if you are using a metasearch engine. The spiders don't always find the same information at the same time.

| | | |
|---|---|---|
| www.altavista.com | www.webcrawler.com | |
| www.askjeeves.com | www.about.com | directory |
| www.directhit.com | www.looksmart.com | directory |
| www.excite.com | www.netcenter.com | directory |
| www.go.com | www.suite101.com | directory |
| www.go2.com | www.yahoo.com | directory |
| www.google.com | | |
| www.hotbot.com | www.dogpile.com | metasearch |
| www.lycos.com | www.go2net.com | metasearch |
| www.northernlight.com | www.mamma.com | metasearch |
| www.opentext.com | www.profusion.com | metasearch |
| www.search.com | www.savvysearch.com | metasearch |
| www.snap.com | www.webinfosearch.com | metasearch |

**Special-Purpose Sites**  Following are popular sites that deal with specific topics. For example, Four11 searches a database of the nation's white pages for phone numbers and addresses. Deja News searches a database of postings to Usenet newsgroups. See also *Web white pages* and *Web yellow pages*.

| | |
|---|---|
| **Authors & Books**  www.amazon.com | **Maps & Driving Directions**  www.mapquest.com |
| **Automobile Buyers Guides**  www.edmunds.com | **Microsoft Support**  www.microsoft.com/support |
| **Book Reviews**  www.nytimes.com/books | **Movies, Actors & Actresses**  www.imdb.com |
| **Business News**  www.wsj.com | **Music & Videos**  www.cdnow.com |
| **Computer Supersite**  www.techweb.com | **Newsgroups (Usenet)**  www.dejanews.com |
| **Computer Supersite**  www.cnet.com | **Package Tracking & Drop Offs**  www.fedex.com |
| **Computer Supersite**  www.zdnet.com | **Package Tracking & Drop Offs**  www.ups.com |
| **Computer Technical**  www.developer.com | **Parenting Library**  www.parentsoup.com |
| **Computer Technical**  www.slashdot.org | **Recipes & Cooking**  www.epicurious.com |
| **Computer Technical**  www.bix.com | **Research**  www.clearinghouse.net |
| **Consumer Info**  www.consumerworld.org | **Research**  www.elibrary.com |
| **Education & Career Info**  www.petersons.com | **Restaurant Menus**  www.menusonline.com |
| **Government (U.S.)**  http://thomas.loc.gov | **Shareware**  www.shareware.com |
| **Health & Medicine**  www.healthatoz.com | **Shareware**  www.softseek.com |
| **Jobs & Careers**  www.occ.com | **Subculture**  www.disinfo.com |
| also see *how to find a job on the Internet* | **Tax Forms**  www.1040.com |
| **Legal Resources**  www.findlaw.com | **White Pages (people)**  www.four11.com |
| **Literature (Great Works)**  www.promo.net/pg | **Yellow Pages (business)**  www.zip2.com |
| **Mailing Lists (Internet)**  www.liszt.com | **ZIP codes**  www.usps.gov |

## Web server

A computer that provides World Wide Web services on the Internet. It includes the hardware, operating system, Web server software, TCP/IP protocols and the Web site content (Web pages). If the Web server is used internally and not by the public, it may be known as an "intranet server."

The term may refer to just the software and not the entire computer system. In such cases, it refers to the HTTP server that manages Web page requests from the browser and delivers HTML documents (Web pages) in response. The Web server also executes server-side scripts (CGI scripts, JSPs, ASPs, etc.) that provide functions such as database searching and e-commerce.

A single computer system used to provide all the Internet services for a department or a small company would include the HTTP server (Web pages), FTP server (file downloads), NNTP server (newsgroups) and SMTP server (mail service). This system with all its services could be called a Web server.

Web servers are also often used for vertical applications. Any network device, such as the print server in the following example,

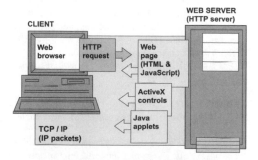

**Web Server Fundamentals**
Web browsers communicate with Web servers via the TCP/IP protocol. The browser sends HTTP requests to the server, which responds with HTML pages and possibly additional programs in the form of ActiveX controls or Java applets.

can contain an internal Web server (HTTP server) as the means for configuring the unit. Contrast with *Web client*. See *application server* and *embedded Web server*.

**Web site**    A server that contains Web pages and other files which is online to the Internet 24 hours a day. See *World Wide Web*, *intranet* and *HTTP*.

**Web site management**    The administration and control of the hardware and software used in a Web site. There are a variety of monitoring and analysis tools that report on usage, missing links and files as well as performance, all of which keeps a site intact and running smoothly.

**Web site name**    See *Internet domain name*.

**Web slate**    See *Webpad*.

**Websphere**    A family of Web application server products from IBM that run on OS/390, OS/400, NT and various UNIX platforms. Websphere Application Server is a Java-based application server that supports servlets, JavaServer Pages (JSPs) and Enterprise JavaBeans (EJBs). It also includes the Apache Web server (HTTP server). Websphere Studio provides a visual development environment running on Windows for writing JSPs and servlets. Websphere Performance Pack adds load balancing, caching, proxy services and replication capabilities.

**Web switch**    A network device that routes traffic to the appropriate Web server based on the URL of the request. Also known as a "URL switch," "Web content switch" and "Layer 7 switch," the Web switch is designed to provide improved load balancing for a Web site, because different requests can be routed to the most efficient source for delivering their content. For example, streaming audio and video, which have long-lived "sticky" connections, might be better served from a dedicated server or from a server that is closer to the user. Search requests that have to be processed would specifically not be directed to a cache server, because the cache would only have to redirect it to the origin server.

Web switches provide more targeted load balancing than layer 4 switches. Although layer 4 switches can examine the TCP/IP port number and differentiate HTTP from FTP and SMTP traffic, Web switches can differentiate HTTP requests and send them to the appropriate servers for processing. For example, requests for HTML pages are switched to one Web server, while searches go to another, and streaming media requests go to yet another. ArrowPoint Communications (later acquired by Cisco) pioneered this technology in 1998. See *Content Smart Web Switch* and *TCP splicing*.

**Web switching**    Using a Web switch to route Web traffic based to the server that can process it most efficiently. See *Web switch*.

**Webtop**    (1) Using a Web browser as the desktop interface in a client machine.
    (2) A specification from Sun, IBM and Oracle for a common interface for Java-based network computers.

**Web-to-phone**    Refers to making a phone call on a computer to a regular telephone using the Internet as the transport. Your PC's speakers and microphone, or optionally a PC headset, are used as the telephone handset. The dialing is done from a Java applet that is launched from your browser or via stand-alone software. Voice-to-IP gateways are used to convert the IP packets into voice streams for the PSTN.

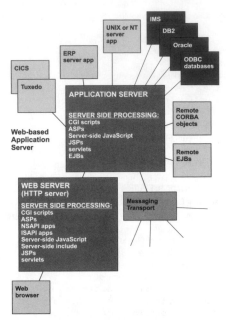

**Web Server Environment**
This shows all the server-side processes that can take place in a Web server and application server. The Web server and application server can be one in the same or individual services within the same computer system or separate services in separate computers.

**WebTV** (WebTV Networks Inc., Palo Alto, CA, www.webtv.net) The first Internet TV service that obtained widespread distribution of its set-top boxes in the retail channel. Acquired by Microsoft in 1997, WebTV uses an analog modem and telephone line to deliver the Web to the TV set. See *Internet TV* and *AOLTV*.

**Web white pages** Web sites that provide searchable databases of invidivual e-mail addresses and other "people-finding" tools. They typically include residential telephone numbers and street addresses. However, unlike phone company white pages, there is no single source for this information, and you may have to try several sources. There's no guarantee that a person's e-mail address is available in any of these directories. Following are some of the popular white pages sites. See *Web yellow pages* and *Web search sites*.

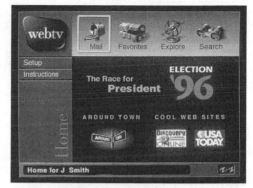

**WebTV Home Page**
This is the WebTV home page in the first year of its introduction. *(Image courtesy of Sony Corporation.)*

```
www.bigfoot.com
www.four11.com
www.go.com
www.infospace.com
www.switchboard.com
www.whowhere.com
www.555-1212.com
www.1800ussearch.com (fee based)
```

**Web yellow pages** Web sites that provide searchable databases of business listings. Some also include additional information such as maps, driving directions, and Web addresses. Following are some of the popular yellow pages sites. See *Web white pages* and *Web search sites*.

```
www.tollfree.att.net
www.bigbook.com
www.bigyellow.com
http://yp.gte.net
www.zip2.com
www.555-1212.com
```

**Webzine** A magazine published on the World Wide Web.

**WECA** (Wireless Ethernet Compatibility Association, San Jose, CA, www.wi-fi.org) A membership organization founded in 1999 to promote the direct sequence (DS) version of the 802.11 wireless Ethernet technology (IEEE 802.11b High Rate). Compatible products receive the "Wi-Fi" (Wireless Fidelity) logo from WECA. See *802.11* and *WLIF*.

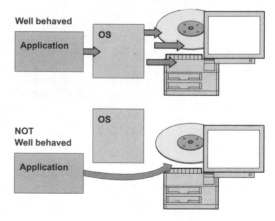

**well-behaved** Refers to programs that do not deviate from a standard. A program that is not well-behaved (ill-behaved) typically bypasses the operating system or some other control program and accesses the hardware directly to improve performance.

**W**

**well-known port** A protocol port number from 0 through 1023 that is widely used for a certain type of data on the network. For example, World Wide Web traffic (HTTP packets) is typically assigned port 80, FTP transfer is port 20, and Kerberos authentication is port 88. For the complete list, visit the following Information Sciences Institute Web site:

```
www.isi.edu/in-notes/iana/assignments/port-numbers
```

The above Web site address is expected to change as IANA is migrating to ICANN. See *protocol port*, *port scanning*, *ICANN* and *IANA*.

**Western Digital**    (Western Digital Corporation, Irvine, CA, www.wdc.com)  Founded originally as a specialty semiconductor company under the name General Digital in 1970, its name was changed to Western Digital in 1971. In 1976, it introduced the first floppy disk controller, and later, hard disk controllers. In the late 1980s, it introduced a line of display adapters for the PC and also entered the disk drive business. Western Digital's line of award-winning Caviar drives, introduced in 1990, have been widely used in PCs.

**wetware**    A biological system. It typically refers to the human brain and nervous system. See *liveware*, *grayware* and *wares*.

**WfM**    (Wired For Management)  A specification from Intel for a PC that can be centrally managed in a network. It must be DMI compliant, be accessible by a management server prior to booting, contain instrumentation for component discovery and identification and include remote wake-up capabilities. See *PXE*, *NetPC* and *DMI*.

**WFW**    See *Windows for Workgroups*.

**wheel mouse**    See *scroll mouse*.

**Whetstones**    A benchmark program that tests floating point operations. Results are expressed in Whetstones per second. Whetstone I tests 32-bit, and Whetstone II tests 64-bit operations. See *Dhrystones* and *benchmark*.

**Whirlwind**    The first electronic digital computer used in a realtime application and the first to use magnetic core memory. The Whirlwind was originally intended to be a general-purpose aircraft simulator for the U.S. Navy, but evolved into a general-purpose computer that became the prototype for the SAGE air defense system (see *SAGE*). Developed at the Massachusetts Institute of Technology, construction began in 1947. It became operational in the early 1950s.

Its first memory used electrostatic storage tubes that proved unreliable, and in 1953, magnetic core memory was added, dramatically improving performance and reliability. The Whirlwind used 2K words of core memory and magnetic drum and tape for storage. The machine was continually enhanced, eventually using 12,000 vacuum tubes and 20,000 diodes and occupying two floors of an MIT campus building.

Whirlwind's circuit design, core memory and use of CRTs contributed greatly in the making of future computers. Project members later worked on IBM's 700 series. One in particular, Kenneth Olsen, founded Digital Equipment Corporation.

**whiteboard**    The electronic equivalent of chalk and blackboard, but between remote users. Whiteboard systems allow network participants to simultaneously view one or more users drawing on an onscreen blackboard or running an application. This is not the same as application sharing, where two or more users can interactively work in the application. Only one user is actually running the application from his or her computer. In many desktop systems, the application is not viewable interactively. A copy of the current application window is pasted into the whiteboard, which then becomes a static image for interactive annotation as in the example to the right.

**white box**    Another term for a PC clone. It refers to the non-branded carton, which is typically white and is the original carton the metal case alone came in. White box marketing refers to the hundreds of small

**Whirlwind I**
In the early 1950s, the Whirlwind was the prototype computer for the U.S. air defense system. It was also the first to use core memory. *(Image courtesy of The MITRE Corporation Archives.)*

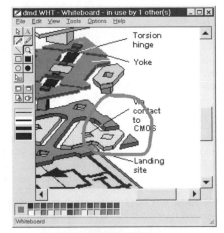

**Collaborating via Whiteboard**
In this example, two people are collaborating on a drawing that one of them pasted into the whiteboard in a NetMeeting conference. Using the whiteboard's marker, a particular area of interest was circled.

companies that assemble and sell PCs; essentially everybody except Compaq, HP, IBM, Dell, Gateway, Packard-Bell, Sony, Toshiba and other vendors with highly-recognizable brand names. See *white box testing*.

**white box testing**   Also "glass box testing" and "clear box testing." Testing software with the knowledge of the internal structure and coding inside the program. Contrast with *black box testing*. See also *white box*.

**white noise**   Same as *Gaussian noise*.

**white pages**   See *Web white pages* and *DIB*.

**white paper**   An authoritative report on a topic. There are countless white papers on technology subjects written by vendors, research firms and consultants. Many are now available on the Web.

**white point**   The measurement of "white" on a color monitor. It can be expressed in degrees Kelvin or as one of the standard illuminants or in X-Y coordinates from the CIE Chromaticity Diagram. For example, the most neutral white point is 6,500 degrees Kelvin or D65 or x=0.3127/y=0.3290.

**whois**   An Internet utility used to query a host and find out if a certain user is registered on that system. Originally developed by the military, others followed with their own whois databases, which provide a white pages directory for the organization. See *finger*.

**wideband**   In communications, transmission rates from 64 Kbps to 2 Mbps. Contrast with *narrowband* and *broadband*.

**wide-format printer**   A printer that prints on very large paper. Such printers typically use ink jet technology to print on a variety of output, including highly coated glossy paper for signs and posters.

**widget**   Pronounced "wih-jit." A popular word for a generic "thing." It is often used to describe examples of made-up products along with other fictitious names; for example, "10 widgets, 5 frabbits and 2 dingits."

**widget set**   A group of screen structures (menu, button, scroll bar, etc.) provided in a graphical interface.

**widow & orphan**   A "widow" is the last line of a paragraph that appears alone at the top of the next page, and an "orphan" is the first line of a paragraph that appears alone at the bottom of a page. Widow and orphan settings are usually set for a minimum of two lines.

**Wide-Format Printer**
This ColorSpan printer prints on matte and glossy paper up to five feet in width. For several years, ColorSpan has been making a line of high-quality, wide-format ink jet printers. *(Image courtesy of ColorSpan Corporation.)*

**width table**   A list of horizontal measurements for each character in a font, used by word processing and desktop publishing programs.

**Wi-Fi**   (WIreless FIdelity) The logo provided by certified cards from the Wireless Ethernet Compatibility Association. See *WECA*.

**wild**   See *in the wild* and *wild cards*.

**wild cards**   Symbols used to represent any value when selecting specific files. In DOS, Windows and UNIX, the asterisk (*) represents any collection of characters, and the question mark (?) represents one single character. Note the following examples:

```
*.exe      All .EXE files
a*.exe     All .EXE files beginning with A
boot.*     All files named BOOT
```

```
*.d*        All files with with D— extensions

?abc        Files such as 1ABC, 2ABC, etc.
??abc       Files such as 10ABC, XXABC, etc.


Windows 95/98 Additional Capability
*t          Files that end in T (HOT, FAT, etc.)
```

**Win16 application**   An application written for Windows 3.x, which runs within the computer's 16-bit mode of operation. A Win32 application is written for Windows 95, Windows NT or the Win32s extensions to Windows 3.1. See *Win32* and *32-bit processing*.

**Win32**   The programming interface (API) for 32-bit Windows operating systems, including Windows NT, 95, 98 and 2000. When applications are written to the Win32 API, they are activating advanced functions not available from the 16-bit API (Win16).

An application written to Win32 can run in all operating systems except where there are OS-specific features that are unavailable in the others. For example, Windows NT provides security features that are not in Windows 95/98. A program written for those features in NT will not run under the other Windows versions.

When Windows 95 came out, many 32-bit functions were made available to Windows 3.1 applications with Win32s, a subset of Win32. Win32s functionality had to be added to Windows 3.1 machines, and applications that used that API generally installed the necessary Win32s DLLs.

```
An Application
Using This
API         Can Be Run In
Win32       95, 98, NT, 2000
Win32s      3.1, 95, 98, NT, 2000
Win32c      95
Win16       3.0, 3.1, 95, 98, NT, 2000
```

**Win32 application**   An application written for 32-bit Windows operating systems. See *Win32* and *32-bit processing*.

**Win95**   See *Windows 95*.

**Win 95/98**   Refers to Windows 95 and 98. See *Win 9x*.

**Win98**   See *Windows 98*.

**Win9x**   Refers to Windows 95 and 98. Same as *Windows 95/98*.

**Winamp**   A popular MP3 player for Windows from Nullsoft, Sedona, AZ (www.nullsoft.com). Winamp also plays MIDI, WAV, CD-audio (CDA), Windows Media Audio (WMA) and other digital music files. See *MP3*.

**Winchester disk**   An early removable disk from IBM that put the heads and platters in a sealed unit for greater speed. Its dual 30MB modules, or 30-30 design, caught the "Winchester rifle" nickname. The term later referred to any fixed hard disk where the heads and platters were not separable.

**WinChip**   A Pentium MMX-class chip from Centaur Technology, Inc., Austin, TX, (www.winchip.com). The WinChip is optimized for Windows business applications

**The Winchester Disk**
IBM's Winchester disk was a removable cartridge, but the heads and platters were built in a sealed unit and were not separable. *(Image courtesy of International Business Machines Corporation. Unauthorized use not permitted.)*

and uses the Socket 7 motherboard socket. The first C6 models were introduced in 1997 at 180MHz and 200MHz. C6+ chips contain enhanced instructions for 3-D graphics. See *MMX*.

**window**    (1) A scrollable viewing area on screen. Windows are generally rectangular, although round and polygonal windows are used in specialized applications. A window may refer to a part of the application, such as the scrollable index window or the text window in the electronic versions of this database, or it may refer to the entire application in a window. Windows were first used in the late 1960s at Stanford Reserach Laboratories (now SRI). See *GUI*. See also *Windows*.

    (2) A reserved area of memory.

    (3) A time period.

**windowing software**    See *window system*.

**window manager**    Software incorporated into all popular GUIs, which displays a window with accompanying menus, buttons and scroll bars. It allows the windows to be relocated, overlapped, resized, minimized and maximized. See *desktop manager*.

**Windows**    The most widely-used operating system for personal computers. Windows provides a graphical user interface and desktop environment similar to the Macintosh, in which applications are displayed in re-sizable, movable windows on screen.

    Windows contains built-in networking, which allows users to share files and applications with each other if their PCs are connected to a network. In large enterprises, Windows clients are often connected to a network of UNIX and NetWare servers. The server versions of Windows NT and 2000 are gaining market share, providing a Windows-only solution for both the client and server. See *Windows versions*.

Advantages of Windows    The single advantage to Windows is the huge wealth of application programs that have been written for it. It is the de facto standard for desktop and laptop computers worldwide with hundreds of millions of users. In many cases, people no longer ask what platform software runs on. If you use a computer, they expect it to be Windows.

    Windows is supported by Microsoft, the largest software company in the world, as well as the Windows industry at large, which includes tens of thousands of software developers. This *network effect* is the reason Windows became successful in the first place.

Disadvantages of Windows    Windows 95, 98, ME, NT, 2000 and XP are complicated operating environments. Certain combinations of hardware and software running together can cause problems, and troubleshooting can be daunting. Each new version of Windows has interface changes that constantly confuse users and keep support people busy.

    Installing Windows applications is problematic. When Windows was first introduced, memory was limited and expensive, and operating system components (DLL files) were designed to be shared by all applications. Microsoft allowed software publishers to install its latest DLLs along with their applications to ensure that the DLL version the application needed would be present on the user's machine. The problem is that some installation programs do not check dates and overwrite a newer DLL with an older one. This causes another application that worked for months to fail just because you installed a new application that has no apparent relationship to it (except for sharing functions in the same DLL).

    Microsoft has worked hard to make Windows 2000 and Windows XP more resilient to installation problems and crashes in general. It takes years to bullet proof an operating system especially when major new versions are constantly developed and rushed to market.

Are There Other Choices?    The primary other choice is the Macintosh. The Mac has always been more consistent and easier to use than Windows. The primary disadvantage of the Mac is that there are fewer Mac applications on the market than for Windows. However, all the fundamental applications are available, and the Macintosh is a perfectly useful machine for almost everybody. Data compatibility between Windows and Mac is an issue, although it is often overblown and readily solved.

    In the latter part of the 1990s, Oracle, Sun, IBM and others launched the network computer (NC), which is a diskless workstation that obtains all data and programs from the network server. Aimed primarily at large corporations, NCs have been struggling to gain acceptance in a Windows-centric world (see *network computer*). However, the confusion and complication of the Windows platform, combined with the explosion of the Internet have caused many to believe

**W**

that the Web browser will become the future user interface to all data and programs whether hosted on intranets internally or at a servce provider on the Web. Since the Web browser runs on all platforms (Windows, Mac, UNIX, etc.), it provides a universal client interface that can run Java applications.

It was expected that Java programs downloaded from a server could replace all the common Windows applications (word processors, spreadsheets, e-mail, etc.). To date, this has not happened, because Java runs slower than native applications, and the Java interpreter (Java Virtual Machine) from Microsoft is specialized for Windows, making interoperability a problem. As a result, although the Web has changed everything else, it has thus far not displaced Windows as the client standard by any stretch.

## Windows 2000

**Windows 2000**   Also known as "Win2K" and "W2K," it is a major upgrade to Windows NT 4. Launched in February 2000, Windows 2000 comes in one client and three server versions. It adds support for Plug and Play, which makes adding peripherals considerably easier than in NT 4. Windows 2000 looks like Windows 95/98, but adds considerably more features, dialogs and options.

Windows 2000 uses Active Directory, which replaces NT's domain system and makes network administration simpler. This is a major redesign of the directory structure for companies. Windows 2000 is more stable than NT and is designed to eliminate erroneous replacement of DLLs when applications are installed (see *DLL hell*).

Windows 2000 Advanced Server is similar to Windows NT Server, Enterprise Edition, which supports clustering and automatic failover in the event of a system failure. Windows 2000 DataCenter Server supports more advanced clustering and is the top end server offering. Windows 2000 was originally thought to be named NT 5.

Although Windows 2000 Professional is the client (workstation) version, Windows XP followed one year later with a redesigned user interface in two flavors. See *Windows NT*, *Windows XP*, *Windows versions*, *Active Directory* and *Plug and Play*.

```
Windows 2000               SMP
Version            Use     Support  RAM
Professional       Client           2GB
Server             Server  4-way    2GB
Advanced Server*   Server  8-way    8GB
DataCenter Server* Server  32-way   64GB
```

*\*Supports clustering, failover and load balancing*

**Windows 3.0**   A complete overhaul of Microsoft Windows introduced in 1990. It was widely supported because of its improved interface and ability to manage large amounts of memory and essentially launched Windows as a real product. Windows 3.0 ran 16-bit Windows and DOS applications and required at least a 286 CPU. Windows 3.0 substituted the clunky MS-DOS Executive in Windows 2.0 with Program Manager and File Manager. See *Windows versions*.

**Windows 3.1**   A major upgrade to Windows 3.0, introduced in 1992. It added support for multimedia, TrueType fonts, compound documents (OLE) and drag and drop and also provided a more stable environment. Windows 3.1 ran 16-bit Windows and DOS applications but was unable to run subsequent 32-bit Windows 95/98 and NT programs.

Most Windows 3.1 applications run well under Windows 95/98 and NT, and some may be used for quite some time. Although Windows 95/98 and NT support long file names, Windows 3.1 applications running in these later environments are still subject to the 8.3 naming convention (file names cannot contain more than eight characters). See *Windows versions*.

**Windows 95**   Released in August 1995, Windows 95 is a 32-bit operating system designed to replace the 16-bit Windows 3.1. Windows 95 boots up in its own version of DOS and automatically loads Windows in one operation. It supports 32-bit Windows 95 applications as well as 16-bit DOS and Windows 3.1 applications.

Windows 95 added a completely redesigned user interface, adding a Start menu and Taskbar and eliminating the earlier Program Manager and File Manager, although both were available as an option. Windows 95 improved networking and added support for long file names and Plug and Play, the latter a welcome relief for users. The memory limitations, which plagued users in Windows 3.1, were greatly expanded. Windows 95 became very popular and within a couple of years, most everybody switched over. See *Windows versions* and **Win 9x/3.1 Differences**.

**Windows 95/98**   Refers to Windows 95 and Windows 98, both of which are close in appearance and functionality. See *Windows versions*.

**Windows 98**    A major upgrade to Windows 95. Introduced in June 1998, it includes numerous bug fixes, performance enhancements and support for more hardware, including the Univeral Serial Bus (USB). It supports two monitors, which helps developers working in one resolution and testing in another. Windows 98 tightly integrates Microsoft's Internet Explorer Web browser into the desktop. For an introductory explanation of Windows 98, see *Win ABCs*. See *Windows versions*, *Active Channel*, *Active Desktop*, **Windows Second Edition** and **Windows ME**.

**Windows 9x**    Refers to Windows 95, 98 and ME.

**Windows accelerator**    A display adapter that provides 2-D functions in hardware. See *graphics accelerator*.

**Windows-based terminal**    A specialized terminal or slimmed-down PC used as a client to Windows Terminal Server. See *Windows terminal*.

**Windows-based Terminal Server**    See *Windows Terminal Server*.

**Windows batch file**    A file of Windows commands that are "batch" processed one after the other. Windows commands are mostly identical to earlier DOS commands, and in Windows 2000, an extensive array of commands have been added, many of which are available only in an optional resource kit. See *Windows Script Host*.

**Windows CE**    Microsoft's version of Windows for handheld devices and embedded systems. Introduced in 1996, it supports multiple CPU architectures. Windows CE-based PDAs use abbreviated version of Word, Excel and other Windows applications, which are known as "Pocket" applications. See *Pocket PC*.

**Windows command line**    A function within Windows that executes individual commands typed in one at a time or one after the other if they are grouped in a text file (batch file). Commands, which are similar to the earlier DOS commands, perform numerous functions including copying, listing folders and executing programs. See *Windows batch file*.

**Windows console app**    See *console app*.

**Windows DNA**    (Distributed InterNet Architecture) An umbrella term for Microsoft's enterprise network architecture built into Windows 2000. It includes all the following components which collectively provide a Web-enabled infrastructure for an organization. The DNA moniker was coined in 1997 for Windows NT.

**Web Server and ASP**    Internet Information Server provides the HTTP processing for the organization and supports Active Server Pages (ASPs) for dynamic processing of content from databases.

**COM Objects**    Microsoft's COM object technology is part of the Windows infrastructure and supported by all of Micrsoft's development tools.

**MTS and MSMQ**    Microsoft Transaction Server (MTS) and Microsoft Message Queue Server (MSMQ) provide the transaction and messaging services to support online transactions between users and programs and between programs.

**AppCenter Server**    AppCenter provides a variety of features for managing a large cluster of Web servers, including load balancing, fault tolerance, replication and testing tools.

**windows environment**    (1) (lowercase "w") Any software that provides multiple windows on screen such as Windows, OS/2, Mac, Motif and X Window. Also any application that provides multiple windows for documents or pictures.
    (2) (uppercase "W") Refers to computers running under a Microsoft Windows operating system.

**Windows for Workgroups**    A version of Windows 3.1 introduced in 1992 that added peer-to-peer networking. See *Windows versions*.

**Windows Media format**    A secure downloadable format from Microsoft for distributing copyrighted material over the Internet. See *Windows Media Rights Manager*.

**W**

**Windows Media Player**    A media player utility from Windows that supports all the popular audio and video file formats including MP3. It also plays Microsoft's own streaming files (.asf, .asx) coming directly from the Web. Windows Media Player combines and supersedes the Media Player utility and NetShow client that come with Windows. NetShow server components are used to host the streaming content played back by Windows Media Player.

**Windows Media Rights Manager**    A digital rights management (DRM) system from Microsoft for securing digital content and distributing it over the Internet. Software components allow for publishing the files in a secure downloadable format, configuring and managing the site and issuing licenses. Starting with Version 6.2, Windows Media Player checks for secured files before playing them. If the files are not authorized, the player sends users to the appropriate Web site for registration.

**Windows Media Technologies**    An umbrella term for Microsoft's streaming audio and video technologies via the Internet or an intranet. It includes the media player and tools for publishing content on a Web site and distributing it. See *Windows Media Player* and *Windows Media Rights Manager*.

**Windows Metafile**    A Windows file format that holds vector graphics, bitmaps and text. It uses the .WMF file extension for 16-bit Windows and the .EMF extension for 32-bit Windows (see *EMF*). The Windows Metafile is Windows' preferred vector format, since it contains actual Windows commands (GDI calls) to draw the images. It is also used by programs to hold data between sessions, and, Windows sometimes uses it for temporary storage.

A Placeable Metafile is a common variation of the WMF format. It includes a 22-byte header that contains X-Y coordinates and resolution. This data is used to compute new coordinates to allow the metafile to be drawn into a display window of any size.

**Windows NT**    (Windows New Technology) A 32-bit operating system from Microsoft for Intel x86 and Alpha CPUs. It is also the core technology in Windows 2000 and Windows XP. NT comes in separate client and server versions, the latter including Microsoft's Web server (IIS). Like Windows 95/98, NT includes built-in networking and preemptive multitasking. It also includes the same user interface, but some dialogs are different and many are exclusive to NT.

Unlike Windows 95/98, NT supports multiprocessing systems (see *SMP*), adds extensive security and administrative features and offers a dual boot capability. Designed for enterprise use, each application can access 2GB of virtual memory. NT does not support Plug and Play, which was later added in Windows 2000 and XP. NT 4 Server, Enterprise Edition supports clustering and failover in the event of system failure.

NT runs 16-bit DOS and Windows applications, but in its own emulation mode (see ***Windows on Windows***). It also provides a command processor that executes DOS commands as have all previous Windows versions. Support for the PowerPC and MIPS platforms was initially planned, but subsequently dropped. See *Windows 2000* and *Windows versions*.

| NT<br>Ver. | Date<br>of<br>Intro. | GUI | Workstation<br>Version<br>Name | Server<br>Version<br>Name |
|---|---|---|---|---|
| 3.1 | Jul 93 | PM* | NT | Advanced Server |
| 3.5 | Sep 94 | PM | NT | Advanced Server |
| 3.51 | Aug 95 | PM | NT | Advanced Server |
| 4.0 | Aug 96 | 95 | Workstation | Server |
| 2000 | Feb 00 | 95 | Professional | Server |
| 2000 | Feb 00 | 95 | Professional | Advanced Server |
| 2000 | Feb 00 | 95 | Professional | DataCenter Server |

*=Program Manager

**Windows Resource Kit**    Windows technical documentation from Microsoft written for support personnel. It is a comprehensive document with more than 1000 pages of technical details that includes flow charts and a chapter on troubleshooting.

**Windows Script Host**    A facility within Windows that executes ActiveX scripting languages including Microsoft's own VBScript and JScript, as well as PerlScript, PScript and others. The scripts can be run from the desktop using the

WSCRIPT.EXE program or from a command line using CSCRIPT.EXE. Windows supports commands and batch files similar to DOS, but the Windows Script Host enables a much more comprehensive set of scripting languages to be run in the Windows environment. Such languages can gain access to many more internal Windows functions than can the batch commands. See *VBScript, JScript*.

### Windows SDK
**(1)** A set of development utilities and programming interfaces for writing Windows applications in C or C++. It provides tools for creating custom cursors, fonts and icons, bitmaps, menus and online help.

**(2)** A set of programming interfaces for Windows applications to link to. There are countless third-party extensions to Windows that add a myriad of functionality.

### Windows shell
An add-on user interface for Windows. Numerous shells were created for Windows 3.x to streamline or replace Program Manager by providing such features as foldering, customized toolbars and quick access to the DOS command line. For example, Norton Desktop for Windows was popular. Fewer products were made available for Windows 95.

### Windows SNA APIs
Programming interfaces that allow Windows applications to communicate with SNA protocols and functions, such as HLLAPI and APPC.

### Windows swap file
A disk file used by Windows for its virtual memory. A virtual memory system temporarily stores segments of the application on disk when there is not enough memory to hold all the programs called for.

### Windows Telephony
See *TAPI*.

### Windows terminal
An input/output terminal for a Windows NT or Windows 2000 server running multiuser

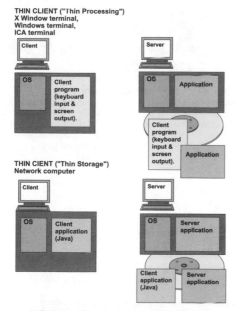

THIN CLIENT ("Thin Processing")
X Window terminal,
Windows terminal,
ICA terminal

THIN CIENT ("Thin Storage")
Network computer

**Windows Terminals Are Thin Clients**
Windows terminals and X Window terminals process only screen display functions. They do not perform the application processing. Network computers are also called "thin clients," but they are "thin storage" clients, since they perform application processing like a PC client.

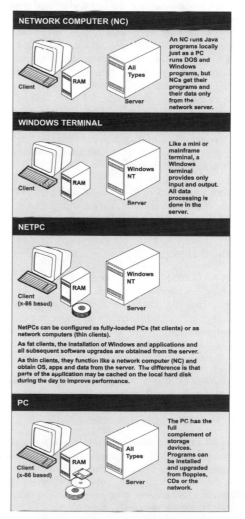

**NETWORK COMPUTER (NC)**
An NC runs Java programs locally just as a PC runs DOS and Windows programs, but NCs get their programs and their data only from the network server.

**WINDOWS TERMINAL**
Like a mini or mainframe terminal, a Windows terminal provides only input and output. All data processing is done in the server.

**NETPC**
NetPCs can be configured as fully-loaded PCs (fat clients) or as network computers (thin clients).

As fat clients, the installation of Windows and applications and all subsequent software upgrades are obtained from the server.

As thin clients, they function like a network computer (NC) and obtain OS, apps and data from the server. The difference is that parts of the application may be cached on the local hard disk during the day to improve performance.

**PC**
The PC has the full complement of storage devices. Programs can be installed and upgraded from floppies, CDs or the network.

software such as Windows Terminal Server, WinFrame or MetaFrame. The terminals function like mini and mainframe terminals, where all the processing is done in a central host and only the input and output is performed at the terminal. A Windows terminal can be a full-blown PC, a slimmed-down PC or a specialized terminal for this purpose, the latter being called a "Windows-based terminal." See *Windows Terminal Server* and *MetaFrame*.

## Windows Terminal Server
Known officially as Windows NT 4.0, Terminal Server Edition, it is an option in NT that enables an application to be run simultaneously by multiple users at different Windows PCs. Windows Terminal Server turns an NT server into a centralized, timeshared computer like the good old days of mainframes and dumb terinals. The difference is that Windows provides a graphical interface, whereas mainframes provided only character-based interfaces. All the data processing (business logic) is performed in the server, and the client PCs display only the user interface and screen changes. Windows Terminal Server uses Citrix's MultiWin technology to provide the timesharing of the application and Microsoft's RDP access protocol for governing screen changes. The Windows 2000 counterpart of Terminal Server Edition is known as the Terminal Services option.

Using Citrix's MetaFrame software on top of Terminal Server adds the ICA protocol, which is supported by a huge number of client types, including Windows, OS/2, DOS, Linux, UNIX, Macintosh, Java-based apps as well as Web browsers. In addition, ICA provides the flexibile, resizable graphical windows that users are accustomed to. See *MetaFrame* and *WinFrame*.

## Windows versions
Following is a summary of all important Windows versions, starting with the most current. Each new version always contains a raft of enhancements and bug fixes.

### Windows NT Lineage

**Windows XP (2001)** A client version of Windows 2000 with a redesigned user interface and .NET capability. XP comes in a Home Edition and Professional version, the latter adding more security and administrative capabilities. XP has improved support for digital photography, gaming, instant messaging and wireless networks. A 64-bit version is also available for Intel's Itanium CPUs.

**Windows 2000 (2000)** An updated version of Windows NT 4.0 (originally thought to be named NT 5.0). It added numerous enhancements including Plug and Play and Active Directory. Windows 2000 comes in one workstation version (Windows 2000 Professional) and three server versions, the latter supporting as much as 64GB of memory and as many as 32 CPUs in a single system.

**Windows NT (1993)** Windows NT 3.5 was introduced two years before Windows 95. It was an entirely different and self-contained operating system and offered separate versions for client and server. Providing greater crash protection than Windows 3.1, its first user interface was the Windows 3.0 Program Manager. In 1996, Version 4.0 was introduced with the Windows 95 interface, but did not include Win 95's Plug and Play capability. Windows NT Server gained significant market share as a server operating system, although the workstation version did not compete very much with other Windows versions.

**MetaFrame for Windows**

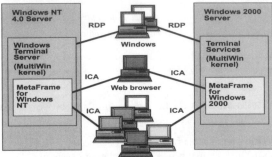

Windows, Mac, DOS, OS/2, UNIX, Linux, Java, Windows CE, embedded devices, etc.

**MetaFrame for UNIX**

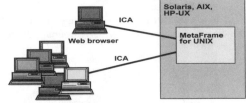

Windows, Mac, DOS, OS/2, UNIX, Linux, Java, Windows CE, embedded devices, etc.

**RDP and ICA Protocols**
Windows Terminal Server's native protocol is Microsoft's RDP (Remote Desktop Protocol), which works only with Windows clients. Citrix's MetaFrame adds the ICA protocol, allowing a huge variety of client types to have timeshared access to the application and providing a look and feel more like a normal Windows application.

## Windows 95 Lineage

**Windows ME (2000)**    An upgrade to Windows 98. ME has a shorter boot time but no longer can be booted into DOS only (DOS sessions can still be run in a Windows window). See *Windows ME.*

**Windows 98 (1998) and Second Edition**    An upgrade to Windows 95 that tightly integrated the Internet Explorer Web browser with the OS.  It added support for the Universal Serial Bus (USB) and dual monitors. In 1999, Windows 98 Second Edition fixed numerous bugs by incorporating Service Pack 1 with upgraded applications including Internet Explorer 5 and Outlook Express 5. See *Windows 98.*

**Windows 95 (1995) and OSR2**    Windows 95 introduced a new user interface that added more Macintosh features. It included preemptive multitasking, which allows programs to be timeshared together more effectively than in Windows 3.1, and Plug and Play, which makes adding new peripherals much easier than Windows 3.1. Unlike Windows 3.1, which was loaded after booting up with DOS, Windows 95 was a self-contained 32-bit operating system that boots with its own version of DOS. Windows 95 ran most Windows 3.x and DOS applications, and within a couple of years, support for earlier 16-bit Windows applications was dropped by most vendors. In 1996, an upgrade known as Win95B or OS Release 2 (OSR2) added support for FAT32 files and 32-bit CardBus PC cards.

## Windows 3.0 Lineage

**Windows 3.1 (1992)**    An upgrade to Windows 3.0 that provided a more stable and faster environment. It added multimedia support, TrueType fonts, drag and drop commands and OLE compound documents. Windows for Workgroups was later introduced with built-in networking, allowing PCs to share data and programs when fitted with network adapters. Windows for Workgroups 3.11 was the last 3.x version. Windows 3.1 is rarely used anymore. See *Windows 3.1.*

**Windows 3.0 (1990) "First Real Windows"**    Windows 3.0 put Windows on the map. Its ability to manage more than one megabyte of memory, which was a serious limitation in DOS. Its built-in DOS extender could manage 16MB of RAM, a huge amount for that time, and its Program Manager user interface was widely accepted. It still required DOS to be booted first, but Windows added multitasking, cut and paste capability between applications and centralized printer and font management, all of which were sorely lacking in DOS. Within a couple of years, Windows would become the major desktop operating system worldwide. See *Windows 3.0.*

**Version 1.0**    Version 1.0 of Windows was introduced in 1985, but barely made a dent in the market. Subsequent versions (Windows 2.0, Windows/386) began to make some inroads, and a handful of companies adopted Windows as their operating environment. However, it wasn't until Version 3.0 that Windows had any impact. The PCs of the time were also terribly underpowered for a graphics-based interface. See *Windows 1.0.*

| Windows Version | Word Size (bits) | Year Intr. | Built-in Networking |
|---|---|---|---|
| **Windows NT Lineage** | | | |
| Windows XP | 32 | 2001 | X |
| Windows 2000 | 32 | 2000 | X |
| Windows NT | 32 | 1993 | X |
| **Windows 95 Lineage** | | | |
| Windows ME | 32 | 2000 | X |
| Windows 98 | 32 | 1998 | X |
| Windows 95 | 32 | 1995 | X |
| **Windows 3.0 Lineage** | | | |
| WfW 3.1 | 16 | 1992 | X |
| Windows 3.1 | 16 | 1992 | |
| Windows 3.0 | 16 | 1990 | |
| **First versions** | | | |
| Windows/386 | 16 | 1987 | |
| Windows 2.0 | 16 | 1987 | |
| Windows 1.0 | 16 | 1985 | |

**Windows XP**    An upgraded client version of Windows 2000. Introduced in 2001, it provides numerous changes to the user interface, including the Start menu, Taskbar and control panels. XP adds improved support for gaming, digital photography, instant messaging and wireless networking. XP Home Edition is designed for the consumer, and XP Professional is aimed at the office worker with added security and administrative options. XP supports the ClearType display technology for improved sharpness on LCD screens. Internet enhancements include Internet Explorer 6, improved connection sharing and a built-in firewall. A 64-bit version is also provided. Originally code named Whistler, Windows XP is .NET enabled. See *.NET.*

**window system**    Software that adds a windows capability to an existing system. See *X Window.*

**Windoze**    A disparaging term for Windows by OS/2, Linux and other non-Windows aficionados. It reflects the long time it takes for Windows to boot up as well as the sluggishness often found in Windows applications most noticeable with earlier, slower PCs.

W

**Wine**  (**WIN**dows Emulator)  Software that emulates Windows applications under certain versions of UNIX (such as Linux) running on an x86 machine. It is made up of two components. The program loader loads and executes Windows binaries, and an emulation library converts Windows calls into X Window calls. See *WABI* and *ODIN*.

**WinFrame**  Software from Citrix Systems that turns a Windows NT 3.51 server into a centralized, timeshared computer. Windows applications are run in the server and only screen changes are sent to the client machines. WinFrame includes a copy of NT 3.51 integrated with Citrix's MultiWin multiuser technology and ICA (Independent Computing Architecture) presentation protocol. MultiWin is the technology used by Microsoft in its Terminal Server options for Windows NT and 2000. See *Windows Terminal Server* and *MetaFrame*.

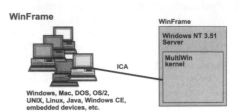

**Windows NT and MultiWin**
WinFrame is made up of a licensed version of Windows NT 3.51 and Citrix's MultiWin technology. It uses the ICA protocol to send input from the client machine to the server and send only screen changes back to the client. A huge variety of client machines support the ICA protocol.

**WinG**  (**WIN**dows **G**ames)  A programming interface (API) that lets Windows application developers access the video frame buffer directly. It allows game programs to be written to run as fast in Windows as they are under DOS.

**WINGZ**  A spreadsheet for the Mac, Windows and various UNIX platforms from Investment Intelligence Systems Group, London (www.newweb.iisc.co.uk). Text, graphs and charts, scanned images, freehand illustration and spreadsheet data can be combined. When data is updated, related graphics and numerical references within the text are changed. WINGZ was originally developed by Informix Software in 1988.

**Win Hardware configuration**  See *Win Device Manager*.

**WinInet**  (**WIN**dows **IN**tern**ET** API)  A Microsoft programming interface for Windows that provides access to the HTTP, FTP and Gopher protocols. It enables Windows programs to be written as clients to Web servers over the Internet or on an intranet. The server counterpart is ISAPI, which is specific to Microsoft's IIS Web server. See *ISAPI*.

**WIN.INI**  (**WIN**dows **INI**tialization)  A Windows configuration file that describes the current state of the Windows environment. It contains hundreds of entries and is read by Windows on startup. It tells Windows such things as which programs to load or run automatically, if any, what the various screen, keyboard and mouse settings are, what the desktop looks like (icon spacing, wallpaper, colors, etc.) and what fonts are used.

Information in WIN.INI is grouped by section headers, which are names enclosed in brackets. For example, the [Colors] section contains the colors selected by the user for window borders, titles, backgrounds and so forth.

The information in WIN.INI is updated by Windows when you change various defaults; however, the file can also be edited with a text editor or a word processor that imports ASCII files. Sections in WIN.INI are added by many application install programs under their own section header and are used to inform the application about the current defaults.

Although WIN.INI was created in Windows 3.x, it is still used in Windows 95 and NT for font substitutions, but primarily for compatiblity with Windows 3.x applications.

SYSTEM.INI is another major Windows configuration file that is read at startup. See *SYSTEM.INI*.

**WINMAIL.DAT**  A file sent by Outlook and Microsoft Office programs that contains e-mail formatting information.

**WinMark**  A unit of measurement of the WinBench benchmarks from Ziff-Davis Media. See *WinBench* and *ZDBOp*.

**WinNT**  See *Windows NT*.

**WinNuke**  (**WIN**dows **NUKE**)  A program that would crash Windows 3.1 and Windows NT computers over the network by sending erroneous out-of-band data packets that Windows was unable to process. Subsequent versions of Windows corrected the weak error checking in the TCP/IP protocol. Also known as the "OOB bug." See *out-of-band data*.

**Win-OS/2** (WINdows-OS/2) The Windows functionality in OS/2 Version 2.x. OS/2 Version 2.x contains the original Windows source code.

**WINS** (Windows Internet Naming Service) Name resolution software from Microsoft that runs under Windows NT Server and converts NetBIOS names to IP addresses. Windows machines are assigned NetBIOS names, which must be converted to IP addresses if the underlying transport protocol is TCP/IP.

Windows machines identify themselves to the WINS server, so that other Windows machines can query the server to find the IP address. Since, the WINS server itself is contacted by IP address, which can be routed across subnets, WINS allows Windows machines on one LAN segment to locate Windows machines on other LAN segments by name.

When a computer is assigned an IP address by DHCP, the WINS database is updated. In a Windows-only network, WINS is queried for name resolution. In a mixed environment, a UNIX machine has to query the Microsoft DNS server, which in turn queries the WINS server, because the DHCP in Windows NT does not update the DNS server. The DHCP in Windows 2000 does however update the DNS server (Dynamic DNS). See *DNS*.

**Winsock** (WINdows SOCKets) The Windows interface to TCP/IP, which is the communications protocol of UNIX networks and the Internet. Windows network applications that communicate via TCP/IP are Winsock compliant, as are the implementations of the TCP/IP protocol (TCP/IP stacks) from Microsoft or from third parties.

The WINSOCK.DLL file is included with all Windows subsequent to Windows 3.1. Early Internet programs often included a WINSOCK.DLL, which could overwrite the one that was present, causing problems with other networking applications. The WINSOCK.DLL was included either to ensure that it was available or that it contained modifications needed by the application. See *DLL hell*.

**Winsock client** A Windows program that communicates to a TCP/IP-based communications network, such as UNIX or the Internet.

**Wintel** (WINdows InTEL) Refers to the world's largest personal computer environment, which is Windows running on an Intel CPU.

**WinZip** A Windows-based utility for zipping and unzipping files from Nico Mac Computing, Bristol, CT (www.winzip.com). Evaluation copies are available from the Web site. See *Zip file*.

**wire center** A location where a large number of network cables terminate. See *central office* and *wiring closet*.

**wired** Connected. Slang for "with it," and "in tune."

**wired access point** A base station that connects a wireless system to a wired land-based system. The acronym "WAP" is used, but WAP is also popular because of the Wireless Application Protocol (see *WAP*).

**wireframe modeling** In CAD, a technique for representing 3-D objects, in which all surfaces are visibly outlined in lines, including the opposite sides

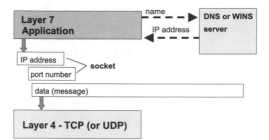

**WINS Name Resolution**
In an IP network, the application queries a WINS or DNS server to turn the name of the machine it wishes to communicate with into its IP address. See *TCP/IP ABCs*.

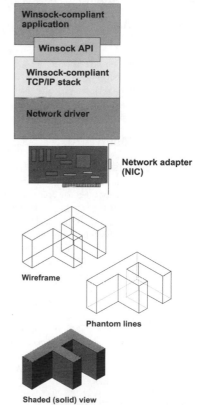

**Wireframe Image**
The wireframe image at the top created in RoboCAD shows all hidden lines. In the middle, the hidden lines are turned into dotted lines, known as "phantom lines." The bottom shaded view could be a surface model or a solid model. *(Redrawn from illustration courtesy of Robo Systems Corporation.)*

**W**

and all internal components that are normally hidden from view. Compared to surface and solid modeling, wireframe modeling is the least complex method for representing 3-D images.

**wirehead**    A person that loves to build, fix and generally tinker with electronics, much like a motorhead enjoys working with cars and engines.

**wireless**    Radio transmission via the airwaves. Various communications techniques are used to provide wireless transmission including infrared line of sight, cellular, microwave, satellite. packet radio and spread spectrum. See *wireless generations*, **wireless glossary**, *CMRS, PCS, FDMA, TDMA, CDMA* and *CDPD*.

**wireless bridge**    A device that connects two LAN segments together via infrared or microwave transmission. A wireless bridge is often used to span buildings and provides a more economical method than laying cable or leasing a private line. Wireless bridges generally require line of sight between transmitter and receiver.

**wireless broadband**    See *broadband wireless*.

**wireless cable**    See *MMDS*.

**wireless data**    The tranmission of data via air waves to a mobile terminal (smart phone, PDA, etc.). Wireless data includes paging, text messaging, e-mail, Web access and other specialized data applications and specifically excludes voice transmission. Also called "mobile data." See *wireless generations*, *wireless LAN* and *mobile computing*.

**Wireless Fidelity**    See *WECA*.

**wireless generations**    The first generation (1G) of mobile cellular communications systems were analog such as AMPS, TACS and NMT. Primarily used for voice, they were introduced in the late 1970s and early 1980s. Starting in the 1990s, second generation (2G) systems used digital encoding and include GSM, TDMA and CDMA. Except for GSM's SMS text message service, 2G systems have been used mostly for voice. Between now and the third generation (3G), which is expected in the 2003–2005 timeframe, a variety of 2G+, or 2.5G, techniques are being employed to improve the speed of data for enhanced e-mail and Internet access. These technologies include packet enhancements for GSM (GPRS), improved data rates for GSM and TDMA (EDGE) and improved data rates for CDMA (IS-95B and HDR).

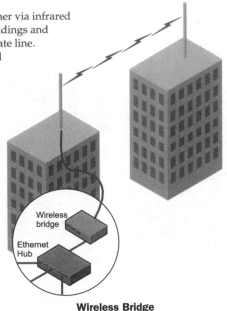

**Wireless Bridge**
A wireless bridge is used to span buildings or areas where laying cable or leasing lines is prohibitive. Although this example shows an outdoor solution, wireless bridges can be used indoors.

    The third generation (3G) is defined by the ITU under the IMT-2000 global framework and is implemented regionally in Europe (UMTS), North America (cdma2000) and Japan (NTT DoCoMo). 3G is designed for high-speed multimedia data and voice. Its goals include high-quality audio and video and advanced global roaming, which means being able to go anywhere and automatically be handed off to whatever wireless system is available (inhouse phone system, cellular, satellite, etc.). See *AMPS, TACS, NMT, UMTS, GPRS, EDGE, IS-95, cdma2000, HDR, 3GPP, wireless LAN* and *wireless glossary*.

**wireless LAN**    A local area network that transmits over the air typically in an unlicensed frequency such as the 2.4GHz band. A wireless LAN does not require lining up devices for line of sight transmission like IrDA. Wireless access points (base stations) are connected to an Ethernet hub or server and transmit a radio frequency over an area of several hundred to a thousand feet that can penetrate walls and other non-metal barriers. Roaming users can be handed off from one access point to another like a cellular phone system. Laptops use wireless modems that plug into an existing Ethernet port or that are self contained on PC cards, while stand-alone desktops and servers use plug-in cards (ISA, PCI, etc.).

There have been numerous proprietary products on the market for home and office, but Proxim's OpenAir and the IEEE 802.11 are two major standards for which numerous products are available. Bluetooth and HomeRF are home and small office technologies that are expected to proliferate in the 2000–2002 timeframe. Such systems have a more limited range and do not support roaming. Small wireless LANs are sometimes called "personal area networks" (PANs) since one of their primary uses is to serve an individual connecting a laptop or PDA to a desktop machine. See *802.11*, *WPAN*, *Bluetooth*, *HomeRF*, *HIPERLAN* and *IrDA*.

**wireless local loop**  Providing communications to the home or office via wireless transmission. It is a "last mile" system that does not use copper cable or even fiber-optic cable. See *last mile* and *local loop*.

**wireless modem**  A modem and antenna that transmits and receives over the air. Wireless modems support several technologies, including CDPD, ARDIS, Mobitex, Ricochet, 802.11 and OpenAir. There are wireless modems for laptops, handhelds and cellphones. Except for only a few analog cellphone models, you cannot plug your cellphone into your laptop's land-based modem, even if you have a cable that fits. You generally need a wireless modem on a PC card and a cable designed for your type of phone. See *wireless glossary*.

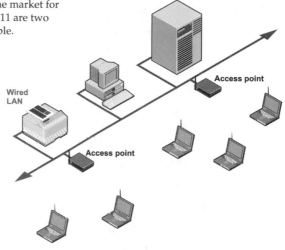

**Wireless LAN**
Wireless LANs function like cellphone systems. Each access point is a base station that transmits over a radius of several hundred feet. In systems designed for office use, users can seamlessly roam between access points without dropping the connection.

**wireless networking**  Transmitting data between personal computers, servers and other network devices without the use of a physical cable or wire. See *wireless LAN* and *free space optics*.

**wireless optics**  See *free space optics*.

**wireless portal**  A Web site that supports a user with a smart phone or alphanumeric pager. It may offer a variety of features, including providing a springboard to other (WAP based) wireless sites, the ability to select content to be pushed to the user's device as well as providing a point of entry for anyone to send the user a message. See *WAP*.

**wireless service provider**  An organization that provides wireless services to its customers, including cellular services, satellite services and ISPs.

**wireless technologies**  See *wireless generations*, *wireless LAN*, *wireless glossary*, MMDS, LMDS, BellSouth *Intelligent Wireless Network*, ARDIS, CDPD, Globalstar, Iridium, *Teledesic* and *Ricochet*.

**wire rate**  See *wire speed*.

**wire speed**  The bandwidth of a particular transmission or networking system. For the example, the wire speed of 10BaseT Ethernet is 10 Mbps. When data is said to run at wire speed or at "wire rate," it implies there is little or no software overhead associated with the transmission and that the data travels at the maximum speed of the hardware.

**wire trace**  A conductive line (pathway) in a printed circuit board or chip that allows electricity to flow from one electronic component to the other. Future chips are expected to have as many as eight miles of wire traces.

**W**

**wire wrap**    An early method of wiring circuit boards to each other. The boards were plugged into a backplane that contained metal prongs, which were wired together using a special tool. The tool stripped the end of the wire and coiled it around the prong. Thousands of computers were made with wire wrapped methods.

**wiring closet**    The central distribution or servicing point for cables in a network. See *MDF* and *wire center*.

**wiring rack**    A self-standing or wall-mounted unit that is used to connect wires to each other. In telephony, wiring racks are called "distribution frames." In local area networks (LANs), wiring racks are called "patch panels." See *MDF* and *patch panel*.

**wizard**    Instructional help that guides the user through a series of steps to accomplish a task.

**WLAN**    See *wireless LAN*.

**WLL**    See *wireless local loop* and *PHS-WLL*.

**WMF**    See *Windows Metafile*.

**WMI**    (Windows Management Instrumentation)  A programming interface (API) in Windows 98 and 2000 that allows system and network devices to be configured and managed. Also available for 95 and NT, WMI is based on WBEM, which stores all definitions in a CIM database. WMI uses a subset of SQL called the "WMI Query Language" (WQL) to access managed objects through VBScripts or Microsoft Managment Console (MMC) snap-ins. WMI can also be used to access the Active Directory. See *WBEM* and *Microsoft Management Console*.

**WML**    (Wireless Markup Language)  A tag-based language used in the Wireless Application Protocol (WAP). WML is an XML document type allowing standard XML and HTML tools to be used to develop WML applications. It evolved from Phone.com's HDML, but WML is not a superset of HDML. Certain HDML features are not found in WML. See *WAP*.

**WOLAP**    See *OLAP*.

**word**    (1) The computer's internal storage unit. Refers to the amount of data it can hold in its registers and process at one time. A word is often 16 bits, in which case 32 bits is called a "double word." Given the same clock rate, a 32-bit computer processes four bytes in the same time it takes a 16-bit machine to process two.

(2) The primary text element, identified by a word separator (blank space, comma, etc.) before and after a group of contiguous characters.

(3) See *Microsoft Word*.

**word addressable**    A computer that can address memory only on word boundaries. Contrast with *byte addressable*.

**WordBASIC**    A subset of Microsoft QuickBASIC with added word processing functions used to customize Microsoft Word word processors.

**Word file**    A Microsoft word file. See *doc file*.

**Word macro**    A script that is executed within a Word document which adds some automatic function for the user. Macros can be created with the Word macro recorder, which stores repetitive keystrokes, or a small program can be written in Visual Basic for Applications (VBA). The macro is executed when the document is opened. See *Word macro virus* and *VBA*.

**Wire Wrapping**
The technician in this picture is wiring circuits together using the wire wrap tool. *(Image courtesy of Digital Equipment Corporation.)*

**Word macro virus**    A virus written into a macro that is stored in a Word document or template. There are more than 30 different kinds of this virus. When the document is opened, the macro is executed and the virus does its damage. It also attaches itself to the Normal template in Word so that subsequent documents are saved with the virus. Questionable documents can always be opened with macros turned off. See *Word macro*, *Melissa virus* and *letter bomb*.

**WordPad**    The word processor that comes with Windows, starting with Windows 95. Superseding Write, which came with Windows 3.1, WordPad supports Microsoft Word, RTF (Rich Text) and standard TXT (text) file formats. It offers rudimentary word processing capabilities and is nowhere near as extensive as Word. See *Notepad*.

**WordPerfect**    See *Corel WordPerfect* and *WordPerfect Corporation*.

**WordPerfect Corporation**    Founded in 1979 as Satellite Software International by Alan Ashton, Bruce Bastian and Don Owens. In 1980, W. E. Pete Peterson, Bastian's brother-in-law, joined the Utah-based company as office manager and later became executive vice president.

Its first product was a word processor for the Data General minicomputer. In 1982, WordPerfect was introduced for the IBM PC. At the time, WordStar was number one, and there were other word processors available for the PC. Yet, over time, WordPerfect outsold them all and the company was later renamed WordPerfect Corporation. In 1994, the company was acquired by Novell and then by Corel in 1996.

For an interesting inside story by Pete Peterson on how the company got started and grew into a software giant without external financing, read his book, *AlmostPerfect*, published by Prima Publishing, Rocklin, CA 95677, 916/786-0426, ISBN 1-55958-477-7.

**WordPerfect Office**    A suite of office applications for Windows from Corel that includes WordPerfect, Quattro Pro, Corel Presentations, Paradox and CorelCENTRAL (PIM, scheduling, etc.). It is the successor to Corel WordPerfect Suite, which was the successor to Corel Office.

**word prediction software**    Software that anticipates the correct word after typing only a couple of characters. Word prediction is used in Web browsers to save typing in a lengthy URL. It is also available for word processors to lower the number of keystrokes required by turning abbreviations into words or by learning a user's word patterns.

**Word Pro**    A full-featured Windows word processing program from Lotus. It provides groupware features that allow documents to be created and edited collaboratively and also includes version control for tracking document updates. Word Pro is the successor to Ami Pro, which was developed by Samna Corporation and was one of the first full-featured word processors for Windows.

**word processing**    The creation of text documents. Except for labels and envelopes, it has replaced the electric typewriter in most offices, because of the ease in which documents can be edited, searched and reprinted.

Advanced word processors function as elementary desktop publishing systems. Although there are still machines dedicated only to word processing, most word processing is performed on general-purpose computers using word processing software such as Microsoft Word and WordPerfect.

Functions of a Full-featured Word Processor

**Text Editing**    Text can be changed by deleting it, typing over it or by inserting additional text within it.

**Word Wrap and Centering**    Words that extend beyond the right margin are wrapped around to the next line. Text can be centered between left and right margins.

**Search and Replace, Move and Copy**    Any occurrence of text can be replaced with another block of text. You can mark a block of text and move it elsewhere in the document or copy it throughout the document.

**Layout Settings**    Margins, tabs, line spacing, indents, font changes, underlining, boldface and italics can be set and reset anywhere within the document.

W

**Headers, Footers and Page Numbering**    Headers and footers are common text printed on the top and bottom of every page. Headers, footers and page numbering can be set and reset anywhere within the doucment. Page numbering in optional Roman numerals or alphabetic letters is common.

**Style Sheets**    After designing a document, its format can be used again. Layout codes (margins, tabs, fonts, etc.) can be stored in a style sheet file and applied to a new document.

**Mail Merge**    Creates customized letters from a form letter and a list of names and addresses. The list can be created as a document or can be imported from popular database formats.

**Math and Sorting**    Columns of numbers can be summed and simple arithmetic expressions can be computed. Lines of text can be reordered into ascending (A–Z) or descending (Z–A) sequence.

**Preview, Print and Group Print**    A document can be previewed before it is printed to show any layout change that may not normally show on screen (page breaks, headers, footers, etc.). Documents can be printed individually or as a group  with page numbers consecutively numbered from the first to the last document.

**Footnotes and Endnotes**    Footnote entries can be made at any place in the document, and the footnotes printed at the end of a page or document.

**Spelling Checker and Thesaurus**    Spelling for an individual word, marked block of text or an entire document can be checked. When words are in doubt, possible corrections are suggested. Advanced systems can correct the misspellings automatically the next time. A thesaurus displays synonyms for the word at the current cursor location.

**File Management**    Documents can be copied, renamed and deleted, and directories, or folders, can be created and deleted from within the program. Advanced systems set up a purge list of names or glimpses of document contents in order to allow a user to easily rid the disk of unwanted files.

Advanced Functions

**Windows**    Allows two or more documents to be worked on at the same time. Text can be moved or copied from one document to the other.

**Columns**    Columns can be created in all word processors by tabbing to a tab stop. However, true column capability wraps words to the next line within each column. Columns are required for writing resumes with employer information on the left and work history on the right. Script writing also requires column capability. Magazine-style columns flow words from the bottom of one column to the top of the next.

**Tables of Contents and Indexes**    Tables of contents and indexes can be generated from entries typed throughout the document.

**Desktop Publishing**    Graphics can be merged into the text and either displayed on screen with the text or in a preview mode before printing. A graphic object can be resized (scaled), rotated and anchored so that it remains with a particular segment of text. Rules and borders can also be created within the text.

Graphics-based vs. Text-based    Graphics-based programs (Windows, Macintosh, etc.) show a close facsimile on screen of the typefaces that will be printed. Text-based programs always show the same type size on screen.

Text-based screens are fine for typing letters and documents with a simple format. They are also very responsive and good for creative writing. Graphics-based systems are necessary for preparing newsletters and brochures that contain a variety of font styles and sizes.

Format Standards    Every major word processing program generates its own proprietary codes for layout settings. For example, in WordStar, ^**PB** turns on and off boldface. In WordPerfect, [**BOLD**] turns boldface on, and [**bold**] turns it off.

Conversion programs are used to translate documents from one format to another. If a conversion program doesn't exist for the two required formats, multiple search & replace commands can be performed on the original document. However, if the same code turns a mode on as well as off, as in the WordStar example above, the codes have to be changed manually one at a time.

**The User Interface** Word processing programs run from the ridiculous to the sublime. Some of the most awkward programs have sold well. As a novice, it's difficult to tell a good one from a bad one. It takes time to explore the nuances. Also, what's acceptable for the slow typist can be horrendous for the fast typist.

Repetitive functions such as centering and changing display attributes (boldface, italic, etc.) should be a snap. Changing margins, tabs, indents and fonts should also be easy.

The most important components in word processing hardware are the keyboard and screen. The feel of a keyboard is personal, but proper key placement is critical. Display screens should have the highest resolution possible, and color screens are better than monochrome as long as the program allows the user to change colors.

**word processor** (1) Software that provides word processing functions on a computer.

(2) A computer specialized for word processing. Until the late 1970s, word processors were always dedicated machines. Today, personal computers have replaced almost all dedicated word processors.

**word separator** A character that separates a word, such as a blank space, comma, period, dash, question mark and exclamation point.

**WordStar** A full-featured word processing program for CP/M and DOS from MicroPro International Corporation, later renamed WordStar International. Introduced in 1978 for the CP/M operating system, WordStar was the first program to give full word processing capabilities to personal computer users at far less cost than the dedicated word processors of the time. Many WordStar keyboard commands became de facto standards for text manipulation (see *WordStar diamond*). WordStar was later acquired by The Learning Company. A Windows version was also created, and all were subsequently disbanded.

**WordStar diamond** The pattern of W-A-Z, E-S-D-X, and R-F-C keys used with the CTRL key in WordStar. It allowed all scrolling functions to be done with the left hand in its normal keyboard position. Although it became a de facto standard, this clever system faded into history after IBM moved the CTRL key on its Enhanced keyboard and the mouse became popular.

**word wheel** A lookup method in which each character that is typed in moves the on-screen index to the closest match. By watching the index move character by character, you can easily tell if you have made a typo. In addition, you can get to the beginning of a word group quickly and then scroll to the word or phrase you are looking for. The DOS and Windows versions of this database use a word wheel.

**word wrap** A word processing feature that moves words to the next line automatically as you type based on the current right margin setting. Some word processing programs allow word wrap to be turned off for writing source code.

**workflow** The automatic routing of documents to the users responsible for working on them. Workflow is concerned with providing the information required to support each step of the business cycle. The documents may be physically moved over the network or maintained in a single database with the appropriate users given access to the data at the required times. Triggers can be implemented in the system to alert managers when operations are overdue.

The manual flow of documents in an organization is prone to errors. Documents can get lost or be constantly shuffled to the

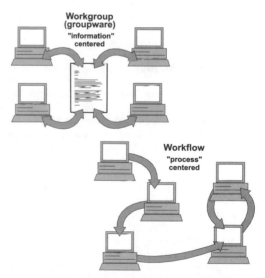

**Groupware (WorkGroup) vs. Workflow**
Groupware, or workgroup computing, focuses on the information being processed and enabling users to share information. Workflow, on the other hand, emphasizes the importance of the process, which acts as a container for the information. Workflow combines rules, which govern the tasks performed, and coordinates the transfer of the information required to support these tasks. This is "process-centered" rather than "information-centered." *(Illustration courtesy of Delphi Consulting Group, Inc.)*

bottom of the in basket. Automating workflow sets timers that ensure that documents move along at a prescribed pace and that the appropriate person processes them in the correct order.

Integrating workflow into existing software applications may require extensive reprogramming, because although independent workflow software can launch a whole application, a workflow system must be able to invoke individual routines within the application. As a result, vendors of application software have teamed up with workflow vendors to provide the appropriate interfaces and/or they have developed their own workflow capability. Workflow standards developed by the Workflow Management Coalition (WFMC) are expected to provide interoperability between workflow software and the applications as well as between different workflow systems.

Workflow software is not the same as workgroup software, otherwise known as *groupware*. Workflow deals with the step-by-step processes, whereas workgroup systems are concerned with information sharing and threaded discussions among users.

For an excellent book on the subject of workflow written by the guru in this field, read *The Workflow Imperative* by Thomas M. Koulopoulos, published by Van Nostrand Reinhold, ISBN 0-442-01975-0.

**work function**    The amount of photon energy required to cause an electron to be emitted from a material.

**workgroup**    Two or more individuals that share files and databases. LANs designed around workgroups provide electronic sharing of required data. In general, products designed for workgroups support up to 50 people, whereas departmental devices support several hundred, and enterprise devices serve several thousand. See *groupware* and *workflow*.

**workgroup switch**    A network switch designed for LAN traffic within an enterprise. Contrast with *carrier-class switch*.

**working directory**    See *current directory*.

**Workplace Shell**    The user interface in OS/2 introduced with Version 2.0. The Workplace Shell is extensible and application developers can use Workplace Shell library functions when developing programs.

**worksheet**    Same as *spreadsheet*.

**worksheet compiler**    Same as *spreadsheet compiler*.

**workstation**    (1) A high-performance, single-user computer used for graphics, CAD, CAE, simulation and scientific applications. It is typically a RISC-based computer that runs under some variation of UNIX. The major vendors of workstations are Sun, HP, IBM, Compaq and SGI. High-end Pentium PCs increasingly provide workstation performance.

(2) A terminal or desktop computer in a network. In this context, workstation is just a generic term for a user's machine (client machine). Contrast with *server* and *host*.

(3) In the telecom industry, a combined telephone and computer.

**WorldCom**    (WorldCom, Inc., Jackson, MS, www.wcom.com) A major, international telecommunications carrier founded in 1983 as Long Distance Discount Service (LDDS), a reseller of AT&T WATS lines to small businesses. It grew by acquiring many small, and eventually, large long distance and networking organizations, including IDB WorldCom, a leading international carrier, WilTel, a major telecom carrier, and MFS Communications, an international phone company and recent parent of UUNET, a prominent Internet provider.

In 1997, the network operations of America Online and CompuServe became part of WorldCom. It also merged with Brooks Fiber and then acquired MCI in 1998 to become the MCI WorldCom powerhouse. While WorldCom may have been a pretentious name for rather modest beginnings, it was very prophetic, because the MCI name was later dropped, leaving WorldCom as the name of the company.

**World Wide Wait**    What many have called the Web while waiting patiently for the next page to download. The World Wide Wait is caused by any combination of a slow modem, overloaded Web server at the site you are accessing or any clog in one of the routers or switches at a national, regional or local ISP. See *Internet service provider*.

**World Wide Web**    An Internet facility that links documents locally and remotely. The Web document, or Web page, contains text, graphics, animations and videos as well as hypertext links. The links in the page let users jump from page to page (hypertext) whether the pages are stored on the same server or on servers around the world. Web pages are accessed and read via a Web browser, the two most popular being Internet Explorer and Netscape Navigator.

In the last half of the 1990s, the Web became "the" center of Internet activity, because the Web browser provided an easy, point-and-click interface to the largest collection of online information in the world. Ever since the Web became the focal point of the Internet, the amount of information has increased at a staggering rate.

The Web has also turned into an online shopping mall as almost every organization has added electronic commerce (e-commerce) capabilities. In addition, the Web has become a multimedia delivery system as new browser features and plug-in extensions allow for audio, video, telephony, 3-D animations and videoconferencing. Most browsers also support the Java language, which allows applications to be downloaded from the Net and run locally.

The fundamental Web format is a text document embedded with HTML tags that provide the formatting of the page as well as the hypertext links (URLs) to other pages. HTML codes are common alphanumeric characters that can be typed with any text editor or word processor. Numerous Web publishing programs provide a graphical interface for Web page creation and automatically generate the HTML codes. Many word processors and publishing programs also export their documents to HTML, thus basic Web pages can be created by users without learning any coding system. The ease of page creation has helped fuel the Web's growth.

Web pages are maintained at Web sites, which are computers that support the Web's HTTP protocol. When you access a Web site, you generally first link to its home page, which is an HTML document that serves as an index, or springboard, to the site's contents. In fact, the default home page for most Web sites is named INDEX.HTML.

Large organizations create their own Web sites, but the actual Web servers (computer systems) that store the Web pages are often housed (co-located) at third-party facilities that provide space, power and access to the Internet. Smaller Web sites are generally hosted on servers run by their Internet service providers (ISPs). Countless individuals have developed personal Web pages, as many ISPs include this service with their monthly access charge. Individuals can post their resumes, hobbies and whatever else they want as a way of introducing themselves to the world at large.

The Web spawned the *intranet*, an inhouse, private Web site for internal users. It is protected from the Internet via a firewall that lets intranet users out to the Internet, but prevents Internet users from coming in.

## Where It Came From Where It's Going

The World Wide Web was developed at the European Center for Nuclear Research (CERN) in Geneva from a proposal by Tim Berners-Lee in 1989. It was created to share research information on nuclear physics. In 1991, the first command-line browser was introduced. By the start of 1993, there were 50 Web servers, and the Voila X Window browser provided the first graphical capability for the Web. In that same year, CERN introduced its Macintosh browser, and the National Center for Supercomputing Applications (NCSA) in Chicago introduced the X Window version of Mosaic. Mosaic was developed by Marc Andreessen who later became world famous as a principal at Netscape.

By 1994, there were approximately 500 Web sites, and, by the start of 1995, nearly 10,000. In 1995, more articles were written about the Web than any other subject in the computer field. Today, there are millions of Web sites, with new ones coming online at an extraordinary rate.

Many believe the Web signifies the beginning of the real information age and envision it as the business model of the twenty-first century. Others consider it the "World Wide Wait" as surfing the Net via analog modem using an ISP scrambling to keep up with demand is often an exercise in extreme patience.

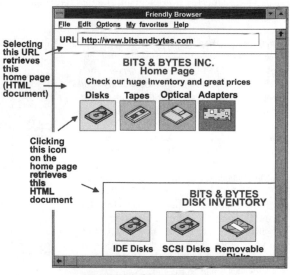

**World Wide Web Linking**
Accessing a Web document requires typing in the URL (Uniform Resource Locator) address of the home page in your Web browser. The home page contains hypertext links to other documents that can be stored on the same server or on a server anywhere in the world.

It seems that everyone has some vested interest in the Web. The telephone and cable companies want to give you high-speed access to it, while the existing ISPs want to gain market share. IS managers are concerned with intranet vulnerability when connected to the Internet. The publishing industry is perplexed over how to manage its copyrighted material on a medium that can send it all over the world in a few seconds. Software vendors make their products more Web compatible every day. Hardware vendors are debating whether network computers (NCs) and handheld Internet devices will eventually replace the desktop PC.

Nothing in the computer/communications field has ever come onto the scene with such intensity. Is it really the marketplace of the twenty-first century? Stay tuned! It will be more than interesting. See *Internet*.

### World Wide Web Consortium   See *W3C*.

**worm**   **(1)** A destructive program that replicates itself throughout disk and memory, using up the computers resources and eventually putting the system down. See *virus*, *logic bomb*, *Worm.ExploreZip virus* and *Morris worm*.

**(2)** A program that moves through a network and deposits information at each node for diagnostic purposes or causes idle computers to share some of the processing workload.

**(3)** (WORM) (**W**rite **O**nce **R**ead **M**any)  An optical disk that can be recorded only once. Updating requires destroying the existing data (all 0s made 1s), and writing new data to an unused part of the disk.

There are two kinds of WORM technologies. Ablative large-format (12–14") WORM is the traditional type, which makes a permanent change in the optical material. Continuous composite write (CCW) WORM is a mode in multifunction 5.25" optical (MO) drives that emulates a WORM drive. The data is not permanently changed, but the drive contains firmware that ensures that recorded areas are not rewritten. See *optical disk*.

Ablative

5.25" MO

**WORM Cartridges**
Large-format 12–14" WORM drives have used the ablative technology. Magneto-optic drives have firmware that turns MO media into write-once disks.

### Worm.ExploreZip virus   A devastating

worm unleashed in the summer of 1999 that works with MAPI-based e-mail servers such as Microsoft Exchange. It automatically sends a stock reply to the sender of each incoming message that says "Hi <name of person>! I received your email and I will send you a reply ASAP. Till then, take a look at the attached zipped DOCs. Bye."  When the attached "ZIPPED_FILES.EXE" file is double-clicked, it decompresses and places EXPLORE.EXE in your \WINDOWS\ SYSTEM directory. It then proceeds to delete the data in Microsoft Word, Excel and PowerPoint files as well as assembly, C and C++ source files. You wind up with file names with 0 bytes. It also spreads to all the machines attached to the network.

```
Directory of C:\karen\NCEFT Horse Show

.               <DIR>         10-29-98 11:15a .
..              <DIR>         10-29-98 11:15a ..
NCEFTM~1 DOC            0     06-11-99  2:53p NCEFT mtg notes 8.4.98.doc
SPONAGR  DOC            0     06-11-99  2:53p SponAgr.doc
CHECKL~1 DOC            0     06-11-99  2:53p checklist.doc
MERRIL~1 DOC            0     06-11-99  2:53p MerrillSponsor.doc
GOLDMA~1 DOC            0     06-11-99  2:53p GoldmanSponsor.doc
GRAYSP~1 DOC            0     06-11-99  2:53p GraySponsor.doc
NCEFTH~1 LNK       51,198     08-20-98  2:43a NCEFT Horse Show.lnk
HORSES~1 XLS            0     06-11-99  2:53p horse show schedule.xls
HORSES~1 DOC            0     06-11-99  2:53p Horse Show Fax.doc
SIEBEL~1 DOC            0     06-11-99  2:53p siebel~1.doc
MERRIL~2 DOC            0     06-11-99  2:53p Merrill Logo in word.doc
MERRIL~1 PPT            0     06-11-99  2:53p Merrill in PowerPoint.ppt
HORSET~1 DOC            0     06-11-99  2:53p horse trials blurb.doc
WELCOM~1 DOC            0     06-11-99  2:53p welcom~1.doc
          14 file(s)        51,198 bytes
           2 dir(s)      3,333.75 MB free
```

**Actual Damage**
This is a small part of the damage done to one machine from the Worm.ExploreZip virus. Note that only the Microsoft files (Word, Excel and PowerPoint) were destroyed. This is one of those unfortunate times when you understand what offline backup really means.

### WOSA   (**W**indows **O**pen **S**ystem **A**rchitecture)  An umbrella term for a variety of programming interfaces from

Microsoft designed to provide application interoperability across the Windows environment. It provides a common denominator for front-end Windows applications to access back-end services from different vendors. For example, any

WOSA-compliant query program from one vendor can gain access to any WOSA-compliant DBMS from any another vendor. See *SPI*.

| WOSA Interface | Provides Access To |
|---|---|
| ODBC | Databases (DBMSs) |
| MAPI | Messaging systems |
| TAPI | Telephone network services |
| LSAPI | Software licensing |
| Windows SNA | IBM SNA networks |
| Windows Sockets | Internet, TCP/IP networks |
| Microsoft RPC | Run remote procedures |
| Financial Services | Banking services |
| WOSA/XRT | News, stock market, etc. |

**WP**   See *word processing* and *WordPerfect*.

**WPAN**   (Wireless Personal Area Network) A wireless network that serves a single person or small workgroup. It has a limited range and is used to transfer data between a laptop or PDA and a desktop machine or server as well as to a printer. Similar to the way a cordless phone works with its base station, technologies such as Bluetooth and HomeRF are expected to be deployed in dual mode smart phones that can download e-mail and Web data while on the road and then exchange that data with a laptop or desktop machine in the office. See *Bluetooth*, *HomeRF* and *wireless LAN*.

**WPcom**   See *write precompensation*.

**wrapper**   A data structure or software that contains ("wraps around") other data or software, so that the contained elements can exist in the newer system. The term is often used with objects (component software), where a wrapper is placed around a legacy routine to make it behave like an object. This is the same as encapsulating data, and you might come across the expression "wrapper encapsulation." But, this is not the same as object encapsulation, a primary concept of object-oriented programming. See *encapsulation* and *tunneling*.

**wrist rest**   A platform used to raise the wrist above keyboard level for typing. The correct height for a wrist rest is several inches higher than the keyboard (even though almost none of them are). The arms and wrist should be level, and the fingers should be pointing down toward the keyboard.

**wrist strap**   A device that grounds the user when making repairs to electronic equipment. It prevents electrostatic discharge (ESD) by channeling static electricity from the person to ground. One end is wrapped around the wrist, and the other is typically attached to the frame of the device being worked on.

**wrist support**   A product that prevents and provides a therapy for carpal tunnel syndrome by keeping the hands in a neutral wrist position. It is like a wrist bandage that is worn.

**writable DVD**   See *DVD-R*, *DVD-RAM*, *DVD-RW* and *DVD+RW*.

**write**   To store data in memory or record data onto a storage medium, such as disk and tape. Read and write is analogous to play and record on an audio tape recorder.

**write access**   Authorization to record or update data stored in the computer.

**write-back cache**   A disk or memory cache that supports the caching of writing. Data normally written to memory or to disk by the CPU is first written into the cache. During idle machine cycles, the data is written from the cache into real memory or onto disk. Write-back caches improve performance, because a write to the high-speed cache is faster than to normal RAM or disk.

A write-back cache for disks adds a degree of risk, because the data stays in memory longer. Although it is generally no more than a few seconds until the data is written to disk, if the computer crashes or is shut down before then, the data is lost. A write-back cache for memory is no more or less risky than normal memory, because all memory loses its data when the power is turned off. See *write through cache.*

**write cycle**   The operation of writing data into a memory or storage device.

**write error**   The inability to store into memory or record onto disk or tape. Malfunctioning memory cells or damaged portions of the disk or tape's surface will cause those areas to be unusable.

**write once**   Refers to storage media that can be written to but not erased. WORM and CD-R disks are examples. See *rewritable.*

**write-once CD**   See *CD-R.*

**write-once run anywhere**   Refers to writing software that can run on multiple hardware platforms. Interpreted languages such as Java allow a program to be written once and run in any computer that supports the same version of the Java interpreter. See *Java platform* and *network computer.*

**write-only code**   Jokingly refers to source code that is difficult to understand.

**write precompensation**   Using a stronger magnetic field to write data in sectors that are closer to the center of the disk. In CAV recording, in which the disk spins at a constant speed, the sectors closest to the spindle are packed tighter than the outer sectors.

One of the hard disk parameters stored in a PC's CMOS memory is the WPcom number, which is the track where precompensation begins. See *BIOS setup.*

**write protect**   A mode that restricts erasing or editing a disk file. See *file protection.*

**write-protect notch**   A small, square cutout on the side of a 5.25" floppy disk used to prevent it from being written and erased. To enable the protection, the notch is covered with self-sticking tape. See *file protection.*

**writer**   See *technical writer* and *coder.*

**write through cache**   A disk or memory cache that supports the caching of writing. Data written by the CPU to memory or to disk is also written into the cache. Write performance is not improved with this method. However, if a subsequent read operation needs that same data, read performance is improved, because the data is already in the high-speed cache. See *write back cache.*

**wrong-reading**   In printing, a photographic image that is the mirror image of the original. See *offset press.* Contrast with *right-reading.*

**WSH**   See *Windows Script Host.*

**WSP**   See *wireless service provider.*

**WTS**   See *Windows Terminal Server.*

**WUGNET**   (Windows Users Group Network, Media, PA, www.wugnet.com)  Founded in 1988, it is the oldest and largest independent organization that supports the Windows environment. It provides technical information, software resources and tools, CompuServe forums and newsletters.

**WWW**   (World Wide Web)  The **www.** prefix used on most Web addresses is actually the mnemonic name of the Web server used at the Web site. Most Webmasters name their servers WWW in order to provide a recognizable address for everyone. Web addresses (URLs) are read from right to left, so that the WWW is the last component of the address, which is the name of the Web server itself. See *World Wide Web* and *URL*.

**WYSIWYG**   (What You See Is What You Get)  Pronounced "wizzy-wig."  It refers to displaying text and graphics on screen the same as they will print. To have WYSIWYG text, there must be an equivalent screen font for each printer font used.

The screen and printed results may look the same, but, in fact, it is impossible to get an exact representation because screen and printer resolutions do not match. The typical monitor may display 75 dpi, whereas a low-end desktop printer prints 300 dpi. That means the screen produces approximately 5,000 dots per square inch compared to the printer's 90,000.

W

**X** In programming, a symbol used to identify a hexadecimal number. For example, "0x0A" and "\x0A" specify the hex number 0A. See also *X Window* and *MDI-X port*.

**x-** The prefix used to describe a MIME type. For example, **x-pdf** and **x-gzip** refer to PDF and Gnu ZIP file formats respectively. See *MIME type*.

**X11** The current version of the X Window System. X11R5 (Version 11, Release 5, Sept. 1991) provides a stable and feature-rich environment.

**X.12** See *X12*.

**X12** Also known as "ANSI X12" and "ASC X12," it is a protocol from the American National Standards Institute (ANSI) for electronic data interchange (EDI). X12 was the primary North American standard for defining EDI transactions. It merged with EDIFACT in 1997. See *EDI*.

**x2** See *V.90*.

**X.21** An ITU standard protocol for a circuit switching network.

**X.25** The first international standard packet switching network developed in the early 1970s and published in 1976 by the CCITT (now ITU). X.25 was designed to become a worldwide public data network similar to the global telephone system for voice, but it never came to pass due to incompatibilities and the lack of interest within the U.S. It has been used primarily outside the U.S. for low speed applications (up to 56 Kbps) such as credit card verifications and automatic teller machine (ATM) and other financial transactions. It has also been used for signaling networks in first-generation cellular systems.

X.25 provides a connection-oriented technology for transmission over highly error-prone facilities, which were more common when it was first introduced. Error checking is performed at each node, which can slow overall throughput and renders X.25 incapable of handling realtime voice and video.

In the U.S., leased T1 lines were favored for internetworking offices together rather than public data networks. However, frame relay, which was modelled after X.25, has been successful as a public data network technology for meeting the high bandwidth demands of today's organizations. See *packet switching*, *frame relay* and *SMDS*.

**X25** See *X.25*.

**X.28** An ITU standard (1977) for exchange of information between a DTE and a PAD; commonly known as PAD commands.

**X.29** An ITU standard (1977) for exchange of information between a local PAD and a remote PAD; procedures for interworking between PADs.

**X.3**    An ITU standard (1977) for a PAD (packet assembler/disassembler), which divides a data message into packets for transmission over a packet-switched network and reassembles them at the receiving side.

**X.32**    An ITU standard (1984) for connecting to an X.25 network by dial up. It defines how the network identifies the terminal for billing and security purposes and how default parameters are negotiated for the connection.

**X.400**    An OSI and ITU standard messaging protocol. It is an application layer protocol (layer 7 in the OSI model). X.400 has been defined to run over various network transports including Ethernet, X.25, TCP/IP and dial-up lines. See *messaging protocol*, *XAPIA* and *CMC*. Following is the format of an X.400 address:

```
/c=  /admd=  /prmd=  /o=  /s=  /g=
```

```
X.400
Code      Purpose
/c=       country
/admd=    administrative management domain
            (public e-mail service)
/prmd=    private management domain
            (inhouse e-mail)
/o=       organization
/s=       surname
/g=       given name
```

**X400**    See *X.400*.

**X.400 API Association**    See *XAPIA*.

**X.445**    An ITU standard for sending X.400 traffic over standard telephone lines. It is also known as the Asynchronous Protocol Specification (APS).

**X.500**    An OSI protocol for managing online directories of users and resources. X.500 can be used to support X.400 and other messaging systems, but it is not restricted to e-mail usage. It provides a hierarchical structure that fits the world's classification system: countries, states, cities, streets, houses, families, etc. The goal is to have a directory that can be used globally.

An X.500 directory is called a "Directory Information Base" (DIB) or white pages. The program that maintains the DIBs is called a "Directory Server Agent" (DSA). A Directory Client Agent (DCA) is used to search DSA sites for names and addresses.

The X.500 specification was published in 1988, and the 1993 edition is interoperable with it. The 1993 edition includes replication and access control. Using the Directory Information Shadowing Protocol (DISP), replication allows a portion of the Directory Information Tree (DIT) to be copied between nodes.

Access control provides a method to allow or deny access to a particular attribute of a directory entry based on the identity of the requesting user.

**X500**    See *X.500*.

**X.509**    A widely used specification for digital certificates that has been a recommendation of the ITU since 1988. Following are its contents. See *digital certificate* and *code signing*.

```
Version number (certificate format)
Serial number (unique value from CA)
Algorithm ID (signing algorithm used)
Issuer (name of CA)
Period of validity (from and to)
Subject (user's name)
Public key (user's public key & name of algorithm)
Signature (of CA)
```

**X.75**   An ITU standard for connecting X.25 networks.

**x86**   Also 80x86. Refers to the Intel 8086 CPU family used in PCs, which includes the 8086, 8088, 80186, 80286, 386, 486, Pentium, Pentium MMX, Pentium Pro, Pentium II, III and 4. This is the largest installed base of computers worldwide.

**x86 based**   Refers to a computer that uses an Intel CPU (486, Pentium, etc.) or an x86 clone chip.

**x86 clone**   A CPU chip that is compatible with various models of the Intel x86 family. Companies such as AMD and Cyrix make x86 clones.

**x86 compatible**   See *x86 clone.*

**x86 emulator**   Software running in a non-x86 machine (non-PC) that runs applications written for an x86 machine. Emulators are typically developed to run 16-bit DOS and Windows and/or 32-bit Windows applications. See *Wine* and *ODIN.*

**XA**   (1) A programming interface from The Open Group that provides bidirectional communications between a transaction manager (TP monitor) and resource managers. It is part of The Open Group's Distributed Transaction Processing model. See *resource manager.*
   (2) See *CD-ROM XA* and *370/XA.*

**XAPIA**   (X 4.00 **API A**ssociation) A consortium dedicated to standardizing X.400 and other specifications, such as the CMC messaging API.

**x86 PROCESSORS (from Intel)**

| | CPU | Clock Speed (MHz) | Bus Size (bits) | Max RAM MB | Floppy Disk | Typical Hard disk | Operating Systems |
|---|---|---|---|---|---|---|---|
| **16-bit CPUs** | 8088 | 5 | 8 | 1 | 5.25" 360K | 10-20MB | DOS DR DOS |
| | 8086 | 5-10 | 16 | | | | |
| | 286 | 6-12 | 16 | 16 | 5.25" 1.2MB | 20-80MB | DOS DR DOS Windows 3.0 OS/2 1.x |
| | | | | Max RAM GB | | | |
| **32-bit CPUs** | 386DX | 16-40 | 32 | 4 | 5.25" 1.2MB 3.5" 1.44MB | 60-200MB | DOS DR DOS OS/2 1.x OS/2 2.x Win 3.x Win 95 Win 98 |
| | 386SX | 16-33 | | | | | |
| | 386SL | 20-25 | | | | | |
| | 486DX | 25-100 | 32 | 4 | | 200-500MD | Win NT Win 2000 UNIX (SCO) Solaris Linux Misc. DOS multiuser |
| | 486SX | 20-40 | | | | | |
| | Pentium | 60-200 | | 4 | | 500MB-80GB | |
| | Pentium MMX | 150-233 | | 4 | | | |
| | Pentium Pro | 150-200 | 64 | 64 | | | |
| | Pentium II | 233-450 | | 4 | | | |
| | Pentium III | 450-1.2GHz | | 4 | | | |
| | Celeron | 266-766 | | 4 | | | |
| | Xeon | 400-850 | | 64 | | | |
| | Pentium 4 | 1.4-1.5 GHz | | 64 | | | |

**Xbase**   Refers to dBASE-like languages such as Clipper and FoxPro. Originally almost identical to dBASE, new commands and features over the years have made Xbase languages only partially dBASE compatible.

**X-based**   See *X Window* and *Xbase.*

**X Bitmap**   A black-and-white bitmapped graphics format used in the UNIX environment. It uses the .XBM extension and is often used as a hypertext icon on a Web page. Many Web browsers treat the white parts of the image as transparent, or background, which takes on the color of the underlying window.

**XBM**   The file extension used by an X Bitmap image. See *X Bitmap.*

**Xbox**   A gaming machine from Microsoft intended to compete with the Sony Playstation. Starting out with a 733MHz Pentium III CPU, 5x DVD drive and custom-designed graphics processor, the Xbox also includes four game controller ports, Ethernet networking and Internet connectivity.

**XCIS**   See *ICS.*

**XCMD**   (eXternal CoMmanD) A user-developed HyperCard command written in a language such as C or Pascal. See *XFCN.*

**XDB Enterprise Server**   A relational database management system (DBMS) for DOS, Windows, Windows NT and OS/2 from XDB Systems, Inc., Columbia, MD, (www.xdb.com). XDB is fully compatible with IBM's DB2 database.

**X**

**XDF**    (EXtended Density Format) A floppy disk format that extends the capacity of a 1.44MB floppy to about 1.86MB.

**XDR**    (1) (EXternal Data Representation) A data format developed by Sun that is part of its networking standards. It deals with integer size, byte ordering, data representation, etc. and is used as an interchange format. Different systems convert to XDR for sending and from XDR upon receipt.

(2) (XML-Data Reduced) An XML schema language from Microsoft. XDR was released in 1999 as a working schema as part of Microsoft's BizTalk initiative. A standard XML schema is expected from the W3C in 2000, and all the structures within XDR are expected to be supported. XDR supports data typing and XML namespaces. See *XML schema*, *XML namespace* and *XML*.

**Xdrive**    A third-party storage facility on the Internet from Xdrive Technologies, Inc., Santa Monica, CA (www.xdrivetechnologies.com). Xdrive enables data to be stored and retrieved from any browser. Xdrive Enterprise is the flagship service, while Xdrive Express provides a limited amount of free storage to everyone.

**xDSL**    Refers to DSL technologies in general, including ADSL, HDSL, SDSL and VDSL. See *DSL*.

**xe file**    See *EXE file*.

**XENIX**    See *SCO XENIX*.

**Xeon**    A Pentium CPU chip designed for server and high-end workstation use. Xeon chips plug into Slot 2 on the motherboard and run the L2 cache at the same speed as the CPU. Xeon was introduced in the summer of 1998 using the Pentium II chip at 400MHz and in the spring of 1999 with the Pentium III at 500MHz. The final Xeon chip was the 900MHz Pentium III in 2001.

Xeon includes additional error checking and system management features and an L2 cache from 512MB to 2MB. It introduced the System Management Bus (SMBus) interface, which includes a Processor Information ROM (PIROM) that contains data about the processor and an empty EEPROM that can be used by manufacturers or resellers to track their own information such as usage and service information. Using Intel's Extended Server Memory Architecture, Xeon chips can address 64GB of memory.

**xerography**    See *electrophotographic*.

**Xerox PARC**    See *PARC*.

**XFCN**    (eXternal FunCtioN) A user-developed HyperCard function that is written in a language, such as C or Pascal. XFCNs usually return a value. See *XCMD*.

**xfr**    Often used as an abbreviation for "transfer" in may electronic and communications terms and phrases.

**XGA**    (EXtended Graphics Array) A screen resolution of 1,024×768 pixels. The term stems from IBM's XGA display standard introduced in 1990, which extended VGA to 132-column text and interlaced 1,024×768×256 resolution. XGA-2 later added non-interlaced 1,024×768×64K. See *PC display modes*.

**x-height**    In typography, the height of the letter "x" in lowercase. Point size includes the x-height, the height of the ascender and the height of the descender. See *typeface*.

**XHTML**    (EXtensible HTML) The combining of HTML 4.0 and XML 1.0 into a single format for the Web. XHTML enables HTML to be eXtended (the X in XHTML) with proprietary tags. XHTML is also coded more rigorously than HTML and must conform to the rules of structure more than HTML. See *HTML*.

**XICS**    (X Window interface to the Internet Chess Server) A graphical interface to the Internet Chess Server (ICS), which allows people to play chess over the Internet. X Window displays the chess board and allows mouse moves rather than typing and receiving text. See *ICS*.

**XIE** (**X** Image Extension) Extensions to the X Window system that enhance its graphics capability. It allows the desktop terminal or PC (the server) to retrieve various types of compressed images from the client and be able to manipulate them.

Remember, in X, the client and server are the opposite of what they are in client/server. See *X Window*.

**XIP** (Execute In Place) The ability to execute a program directly from a memory card.

**Xlib** (**X** LIBrary) Functions in the X Window System. See *X toolkit*.

**X library** See *Xlib*.

**XLISP** A microcomputer version of the LISP programming language that has been in the public domain for a number of years.

**XLL** (XML Linking Language) See *XLink*.

**XLR connector** An audio plug and socket used in professional and high-end audio equipment. It uses a balanced connection and typically locks into the socket. XLR connectors are twice the size of the standard RCA plug and socket. See *A/V ports* and *plugs and sockets*.

**XLR Connector**
This is a high-end plug that you will not find on everyday audio equipment.

**Xmark** See *XPC*.

**XMI** A high-speed bus from Digital used in large VAX machines.

**XML** (EXtensible Markup Language) An open standard for describing data from the W3C. It is used for defining data elements on a Web page and business-to-business documents. It uses a similar tag structure as HTML; however, whereas HTML defines how elements are displayed, XML defines what those elements contain. HTML uses predefined tags, but XML allows tags to be defined by the developer of the page. Thus, virtually any data items, such as product, sales rep and amount due, can be identified, allowing Web pages to function like database records. By providing a common method for identifying data, XML supports business-to-business transactions and is expected to become the dominant format for electronic data interchange (see *EDI*).

Since its introduction, XML has been hyped tremendously as the panacea to e-commerce, but it's only the first step. The human-readable XML tags provide a simple data format, but the intelligent defining of these tags and common adherance to their usage will determine their value. For example, cXML (Commercial XML) from Ariba and CBL (Common Business Library) from Commerce One are some of the first XML vocabularies for business data. DSML is a set of XML tags that defines the items in a directory. XML tags are defined in an XML schema, which defines content type as well as name. XML tags can also be described in the original SGML DTD format, since XML is a subset of the SGML language. There are several Web sites that provide repositories for publishing and reviewing XML schemas (see *XML repository*).

Unlike HTML, which uses a rather loose coding style and which is tolerant of coding errors, XML pages have to be "well formed," which means they must comply with rigid rules. See *XSLT, XML schema, DTD, XHTML, HTML, SGML, SMIL* and *XML-RPC*.

**XML and HTML** To the right are examples of XML and HTML tags. Note that the XML statements define data content, whereas the HTML lines deal with fonts and boldface. XML defines "what it is," and HTML defines "how it looks."

**XML**

```
<firstName>Maria</firstName>
<lastName>Roberts</lastName>
<dateBirth>10-29-52</dateBirth>
```

**HTML**

```
<font size="3">Maria Roberts</font>
<b>October 29, 1952</b>
```

X

**XML-Data**   An XML schema language developed by Microsoft, Arbor Text, Data Channel and others. It was the forerunner of DDML, DCD, SOX and XDR schemas. See *DDML*, *DCD*, *SOX*, *XDR*, *XML schema* and *XML*.

**XML namespace**   A unique name that identifies an organization that has developed an XML schema. It serves as a prefix so that multiple schemas can be used to define tags in an XML document.

**XML parser**   Software that reads an XML document, identifies all the XML tags and passes the data to the application. See *XML processor*.

**XML processor**   Software that reads an XML document, parses the XML tags and validates the tags against an XML schema. See *XML parser*.

**XML repository**   A Web site that serves as a central storehouse for publishing and reviewing XML schemas. Examples are www.xml.org, www.dtd.com, www.biztalk.org and www.xml-schemas.com.

**XML-RPC**   (**XML R**emote **P**rocedure **C**all) A remote procedure call (RPC) that is based on XML syntax. An XML-RPC message is passed to the target server in an HTTP POST request. For more information, visit www.xml-rpc.com. See *XML* and *RPC*.

**XML schema**   The definition of the content used in an XML document. The XML schema is a superset of DTD, which is the standard SGML schema. Various recommendations were submitted to the W3C, and a standard was approved in May 2001 that includes the ability to define data by type (date, integer, etc.).

Unlike DTD, XML schemas are written in XML syntax, which although more verbose than DTD, they can be created with any XML tools. This figure is an example of XML schema statements that define first and last name, followed by tags in actual use within the document. For information, visit www.w3.org/XML/Schema. See *XML repository*, *DTD*, *XDR* and *XML*.

### Schema for the Tags

```
<ElementType name="firstName" content="textOnly"/>
<ElementType name="lastName" content="textOnly/>
```

### Actual Tags in Use

```
<firstName>Pat</firstName>
<lastName>Jones</lastName>
```

**XML schema library**   See *XML repository*.

**XML schema repository**   See *XML repository*.

**XML tag set**   See *XML vocabulary*.

**XML vocabulary**   A set of XML tags for a particular industry or business function. See *XML schema*.

**XML Web site**   See *XML schema repository*.

**Xmodem**   The first widely-used file transfer protocol for personal computers, developed by Ward Christensen for CP/M machines. Xmodem programs supported the earlier checksum method and the subsequent CRC method of error detection. Xmodem transmits 128-byte blocks. Xmodem-1K improves speed with 1KB blocks. Xmodem-1K-G transmits without acknowledgment for error-free channels or when modems are self correcting, but transmission is cancelled upon any error.

**XMP**   (**X/**Open **M**anagement **P**rotocol) A high-level network management protocol governed by X/Open. Network management software written to the XMP interface is shielded from the details of the underlying SNMP or CMIP protocols.

**XMS** **(1)** (eXtended Memory Specification) A programming interface that allows DOS programs to use extended memory in 286s and up. It provides a set of functions for reserving, releasing and transferring data to and from extended memory without conflict, including the high memory area (HMA). See *HIMEM.SYS* and *DOS extender*.

XMS, VCPI and DPMI all deal with extended memory. However, XMS allows data and programs to be stored in and retrieved from extended memory, whereas the VCPI and DPMI interfaces allow programs to "run" in extended memory.

**(2)** See *cross memory services*.

**XMT** In communications, an abbreviation for transmit.

**XNOR** (eXclusive **NOR**) See *NOR*.

**XNS** (Xerox Network Services) An early networking protocol suite developed at Xerox's Palo Alto Research Center (PARC). XNS has been the basis for many popular network architectures including Novell's NetWare, Banyan's VINES and 3Com's 3+.

| XNS Layer | XNS Protocols | OSI Layers | NetWare Protocols |
|---|---|---|---|
| 4 Application | | 7 | |
| 3 Control | | 5 & 6 | |
| 2 Transport | SPP, PEP | 4 | SPX |
| 1 Internet | IDP | 3 | IPX |
| 0 Transmission | Ethernet | 1 & 2 | |

**xon-xoff** In communications, a simple asynchronous protocol that keeps the receiving device in synchronization with the sender. When the buffer in the receiving device is full, it sends a "transmit off" signal to the sending device, telling it to stop transmitting. When the receiving device is ready to accept more, it sends the sending device a "transmit on" signal to start again.

**X/Open** (X/Open, San Francisco, CA, division of The Open Group, www.opengroup.org) A consortium of international computer vendors founded in 1984 to resolve standards issues. Incorporated in 1987 and based in London, North American offices are in San Francisco. In 1996, it merged with OSF into The Open Group. Its purpose is to integrate evolving standards in order to achieve an open environment. XPG are X/Open specifications, and VSK are X/Open testing and verification procedures.

In late 1993, Spec 1170 was announced to provide a common programming interface for UNIX in order to unify all the various versions of the operating system. Containing more than 1,100 APIs, Spec 1170 later evolved into the Single UNIX Specification, which is branded by X/Open.

X/Open is also responsible for governing the Common Desktop Environment (CDE), a standard user interface for UNIX above and beyond X and Motif, which are part of the Single UNIX Specification. The first CDE products were introduced in early 1995. See *Open Group*.

**X/Open Portability Guide** Known as the *XPG*, it is a set of standards that specify compliance with X/Open's Common Application Environment (CAE). XPG3 (1989) and XPG4 (1992) define operating systems, languages and protocols, etc. About half of the Single UNIX Specification (formerly Spec 1170) was taken from XPG4. The term "base" with XPG (XPG3 base, XPG4 base, etc.) refers to a minimum number of required APIs.

**XOR** See *OR*.

**XP** **(1)** See *Windows XP*.

**(2)** (EXtreme Programming) A discipline for developing software that emphasizes customer satisfaction and teamwork. Developed by Kent Beck, it is based on a formal set of rules that govern planning, designing, coding and testing. For more information, visit www.extremeprogramming.org and www.xprogramming.com.

**X**

**XPath** (XML PATH Language) A subset of the XSLT language used to identify input, calculate numbers and manipulate strings. See *XSLT*.

**XPC** (X Performance Characterization) A graphics benchmark that tests X Window performance. In 1993, the XPC project group created Xmark93, which rates a broad set of X functions in Xmarks. See *GPC*.

**XPG** See *X/Open Portability Guide*.

**X Pixelmap** An 8-bit bitmapped graphics format used in the UNIX environment. It uses the .XPM extension and is similar to the X Bitmap format, but provides 256 colors. X Pixelmaps are often used for X Window icons and hypertext icons on Web pages.

**XPM** The file extension used by an X Pixelmap image. See *X Pixelmap*.

**XPointer** (XML POINTER Language) The pointer to an XML document. It enables internal structures to be referenced rather than just the entire page. It was later folded into the Xpath language. See *XSLT*.

**X protocol** The message format of the X Window System.

**xSeries** The renaming of IBM's Intel-based servers under the eserver brand. A Linux or Windows-based server is an xSeries eserver. Prices for the xSeries ranged from $10,000–$50,000 in 2000, when the name change occurred. See *IBM server series* and *Netfinity*.

**X server** The receiving computer in an X Window system. The X server displays the application that is running on a remote machine, which is the X client. See *X Window*.

**XSL** (eXtensible Stylesheet Language) A style sheet format for XML documents. It is the XML counterpart to the Cascading Style Sheets (CSS) language in HTML, although XML supports CSS1 and CSS2 as well. XSLT (XSL Transformations) are extensions to XSL for converting XML documents into XML or other document types and may be used independently of XSL. See *XSLT*, *XML* and *CSS*.

**XSLT** (XML Style sheet Language: Transformations) A language used to convert an XML document into another XML document or into HTML, PDF or some other format. It is widely used to convert XML to HTML for screen display. The conversion is accomplished with an XSLT processor, which transforms the input based on XSLT extensions of the XSL style sheet. XSL statements are also followed. The processor requires an XML parser to separate the XML elements into a tree structure which the processor manipulates. Xpath is a subset within XSLT used for identifying input, calculating numbers and manipulating characters. See *XML* and *SAX*.

**xSP** (1) (X Service Provider) An umbrella term for service provider organizations including ISPs, ASPs, SSPs and MSPs. See *ISP*, *ASP*, *SSP* and *MSP*.

**XT** (1) (EXtended Technology) The first IBM PC with a hard disk, introduced in 1983. It used the same 8088 CPU as the original PC but included a whopping 128KB of RAM and a 10MB hard drive. See *PC*.

(2) (Xt) See *X toolkit*.

(3) (XT) An open source XML parser written in Java by James Clark, a specialist in SGML/XML. For information, visit www.jclark.com. See *XSLT*.

**XTACACS** See *TACACS*.

**XT class** Refers to first-generation PCs, which included the first floppy-disk PC, the actual "XT" PC with a hard disk and all compatibles that used the 8088, 8086 or compatible CPU and an 8-bit bus.

**X terminal** A terminal with built-in X server capability.

**XTI** (X/Open Transport Interface) A common programming interface between the application and the transport layer of the communications protocol. It is governed by The Open Group.

**X toolkit**   Development software for building X Window applications. Typically includes a widget set, X Toolkit Intrinsics (Xt) libraries for managing the widget set and the X Library (Xlib).

**XTP**   (Xpress Transfer Protocol) A research transport protocol designed by Greg Chesson of SGI. It is a type of lightweight protocol designed for high-speed networks and provides services at layers 3 and 4 of the OSI model.

XTP is flexible and can select rate and flow control. In order to handle different traffic; for example, transactions versus realtime video, XTP's "universal receiver" has the transmitting station tell the receiver when to acknowledge. ANSI's version is called "High Speed Transport Protocol" (HSTP).

**XTree**   Introduced in 1985 by the Xtree Company, it was the first program to help DOS users manage hard disks by providing a hierarchical display of directories. Versions for Windows came later, and XtreeGold added file viewers.

**Xtrieve**   A menu-driven query language and report writer from Novell that accesses Btrieve files.

**XVT**   (EXtensible Virtual Toolkit) A C++ developers toolkit for creating user interfaces across multiple environments from XVT Software, Inc., Boulder, CO (www.xvt.com). Programmers design the user interface by calling XVT functions, which are then translated to Windows, OS/2, Motif or the Mac.

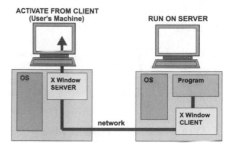

**X Window Servers Run on Clients**
It is correct to say that the X Window server runs on your client, and the X Window client runs on your server. Hey, all's fair in love and computers!

**X Window**   (X Window System) Also called "X Windows" and simply "X," it is a windowing system developed at MIT, which runs under UNIX and all major operating systems. It lets users run applications on other computers in the network and view the output on their own screen.

X Window generates a rudimentary window that can be enhanced with GUIs, such as Open Look and Motif, but does not require applications to conform to a GUI standard. The window manager component of the GUI allows multiple resizable, relocatable X windows to be viewed on screen at the same time.

X client software resides in the computer that performs the processing and X server software resides in the computer that displays it. Both components can also be in the same machine. This seems opposite to today's client/server terminology, but the concept is that the server is "serving up" the image. See *thin client*, *XIE* and *MetaFrame*.

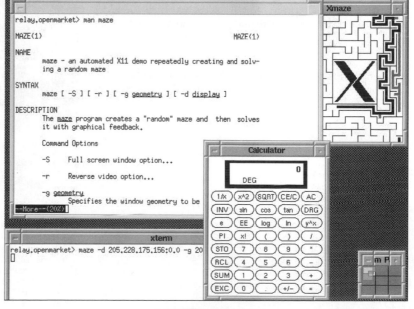

**An X Window Screen**
All the windows in this screen shot are "X" windows displaying output from one or more remote servers (X Window clients). The small window at the bottom right that looks like a puzzle game is a virtual screen indicator. It shows the current windows that are displayed in relation to the whole desktop. *(Screen shot courtesy of Peter Hermsen.)*

**x-y matrix**    A group of rows and columns. The X-axis is the horizontal row, and the Y-axis is the vertical column. An X-Y matrix is the reference framework for two-dimensional structures, such as mathematical tables, display screens, digitizer tablets, dot matrix printers and 2-D graphics images.

**x-y monitor**    In graphics, the display screen of a vector display terminal. The entire vector display comprises the monitor and vector graphics controller.

**xy plotter**    Same as *plotter*.

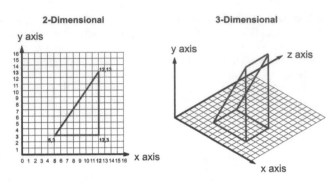

**XyWrite for Windows**    The Windows version of the XyWrite word processor from The Technology Group, Baltimore, MD. It is a full-featured Windows word processor that accepts XyWrite and ASCII files and automatically converts IBM's DCA documents into XyWrite format. XyWrite for Windows maintains the flexibility that made its DOS predecessors popular among writers and editors. It also retains the XyWrite method for displaying format codes on screen. See *XyWrite III Plus*.

**XyWrite III Plus**    Pronounced "zy-write." A word processing program that has been used extensively in the newspaper and magazine business as well as by professional writers. Developed by XyQuest, Inc., Billerica, MA, it was the most customizable DOS word processor ever developed and the first DOS program to provide complete typographic control over the page layout.

    XyWrite generates a pure ASCII file with commands embedded in high-order DOS characters that display as unobtrusive triangles. Their contents can be easily revealed at any time.

**x-y-z matrix**    A three-dimensional structure. The X and Y axes represent the first two dimensions; the Z axis, the third dimension. In a graphic image, the X and Y denote width and height; the Z denotes depth.

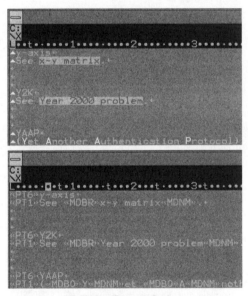

**XyWrite Format Codes**
This database is maintained in XyWrite III Plus, a 10-year old DOS word processor that is fast, flexible and can perform a myriad of text manipulation functions. Old software and methods do stay around in this business. Once time and energy is invested in a method, there is no reason to change if it does a good job. These examples show how the text following this actual paragraph looks when the codes are hidden and then revealed.

# Y

**Y, (R-Y), (B-Y)**  See *YUV*.

**Y2K compliant**  Capable of correctly processing any data that deals with a date beyond the year 1999. See *Y2K problem*.

**Y2K problem**  (Year 2000 problem) The inability of older hardware and software to recognize the century change in a date. The reason they could not was because the year was stored with only two digits; for example, 12-11-42 instead of 12-11-1942. Thus, when the year changed from 1999 to 2000, the date became 01-01-00, and the system thought it was January 1, 1900.

Many financial transactions match dates in database records with today's date or with a future date. If the system does not handle dates correctly, bills do not get paid, notices do not get triggered and actions are not taken. Virtually all software that deals with dates had problems after 2000 in a system that cannot recognize the millennium change.

The solution to this "millennium bug" was mammoth. It required upgrading hardware to support four-digit years, converting files and databases to four-digit years and converting all the software that references dates. Enterprises had large numbers of legacy data files and huge numbers of programs that deal with them. Each reference to a date must be changed in every program, and finding them can be extremely difficult. There are many legacy systems still running, but the programmers that wrote the software are long gone. The programs may lack documentation or even the original source code. Even when the changes could be made, the time it took to test them all was taxing on the IS staff trying to run the daily work and implement new applications.

**How Did It Happen?**  The problem originated with punched cards that go back to the early 1900s. In order to cram an entire order or customer record into typically less than 100 character columns, which was the physical size of the card, the year field was shortened to two digits. Why waste two columns for "19" when it was going to be "19" for such a long time. When punched card systems were converted to magnetic tape during the 1960s, which had ample room for two more digits, the twenty-first century still seemed far off. Likewise, computer systems were built to keep track of dates using two-digit years.

Saving two columns (two bytes) in a punched card was appropriate 50 years ago, but the lack of attention to this over the years cost more than $300 billion worldwide to correct.

**It's Happened Before 2000**  We didn't have to wait until 2000 to experience the problem. For example, how about a company that wanted to delete all customers that had not purchased anything in five years. The program logic would be to add five years to the date of the last order and compare the result to this year. Suppose a customer last ordered in 1995 and this year were 1996. Add five to 1995 in a non-Y2K compliant system and you get 1900. Since 1996 is greater than 1900, the customer would be deleted. See *data aging* and *year 2038 problem*.

**Making the Point**
This ad for Isogon's TICTOC Year 2000 compliance software made a strong point. TICTOC was used to test Y2K compliance for MVS applications by setting fictitious dates on a job-by-job basis. *(Image courtesy of Isogon Corporation, www.isogon.com)*

**YAAP**   (Yet Another Authentication Protocol) A proposed access control protocol from Microsoft designed to replace RADIUS and TACACS+.

**yacc**   (Yet Another Compiler Compiler) A UNIX compiler used to create a compiler. The operators, variables and constants of the program are typically defined in C using lex (LEXical analyzer), which converts them into preprocessed, machine-readable tokens for yacc. The grammar of the new language is written in C and compiled in yacc. The combination of lex (define elements) and yacc (define actions) creates a new compiler. For more information, visit www.epaperpress.com. See *bison*.

**Yahoo!**   (Yahoo! Inc., Santa Clara, CA, www.yahoo.com) The first search site on the Web to gain worldwide attention. Yahoo! differs from most search sites, because its indexes are created manually. Instead of sending out automated spiders that roam the Web and index everything in sight, people decide what categories a Web page belongs in. As a result, Yahoo! belongs to a category called a "directory," rather than just a search engine. Yahoo! has become a major portal on the Web. See *Yahoo! Store* and *Web search sites*.

**Yahoo! Mail**   A free, Web–based e-mail service from Yahoo!. It includes Yahoo! Messenger, which alerts you if you have mail and also provides voice chat. See *Yahoo! Messenger*.

**Yahoo! Messenger**   An instant messenger service from Yahoo! that alerts you if you have e-mail. It includes a voice chat service, which allows two or more people to converse over the Internet. It also allows for regular chat (text) at the same time. See *instant messenger* and *voice chat*.

**Yahoo! Store**   An online storefront for selling merchandise that is hosted by Yahoo!. Templates are available for creating and editing the Web pages directly online. Vendors set up their online stores ahead of time and go live after establishing the licensing arrangements.

**Yankee Group**   (the Yankee Group, Boston, MA, www.yankeegroup.com) A major market research, analysis and consulting firm founded in 1970 by Howard Anderson. It provides general consulting and Planning Services in the computer and communications field. Planning Services are a package of services on a particular topic that includes reports, personal consulting, conference attendance and electronic delivery of material.

**yaw**   See *pitch-yaw-roll*.

**Y-axis**   See *x-y matrix*.

**YCrCb**   Component digital terminology for YUV encoding. See *YUV*.

**Y/C video**   See *S-video*.

**year 2000 problem**   See *Y2K problem*.

**year 2038 problem**   Another date problem, which results from computing dates into the year 2038 and beyond in 32-bit operating systems. UNIX and other C applications represent time as the number of seconds from January 1, 1970. The 32-bit variable (time_t) that stores this number overflows in the year 2038 and becomes January 1, 1970 again. However, even today, any date caculations forecasted beyond that time will be erroneous. Switching to 64-bit computing solves the problem. See *Y2K problem*.

**Yellow Book**   The standard for the physical format of a CD-ROM disk. The ISO 9660 standard defines the logical format for the disk. See *CD*.

**Yellow Box**   A programming interface for the Rhapsody operating system from Apple, which later became Mac OS X. The Yellow Box is an enhanced version of the OpenStep API from NeXT Computer, which was acquired by Apple. The Yellow Box was later renamed Cocoa in OS X. See *MAC OS X* and *Blue Box*.

**Yellow Pages**   See *NIS*, *naming service* and *Web yellow pages*.

**yield**    In semiconductor manufacturing, the percentage of chips that work out of one wafer.

**YIQ**    The color model used for encoding NTSC video. Y is the luminosity of the original black and white TV signal. I and Q are subcarrier axes that are modulated with the color difference signals red minus Y and blue minus Y (R–Y and B–Y). YIQ refers specifically to NTSC video. See *YUV*.

**Ymodem**    A file transfer protocol that adds batch file processing to Xmodem. Multiple files can be sent at the same time. It is faster than Xmodem and sends the file name before sending the data. Ymodem-G transmits without acknowledgment for error-free channels or when modems are self correcting, but transmission is cancelled upon any error.

**yocto**    Septillionth (10 to the –24th power). See *space/time*.

**yotta**    Septillion (10 to the 24th power). See *space/time*.

**youth grinder**    A company that employs a lot of young people so that it can pay low salaries. It tries to compensate by offering gadgets and goodies (free soda, pizza, video games, etc.).

**YUV**    The color model used for encoding video. Y is the luminosity of the black and white signal. U and V are color difference signals. U is red minus Y (R–Y), and V is blue minus Y (B–Y). In order to display YUV data on a computer screen, it must be converted into RGB through a process known as "color space conversion." YUV is used because it saves storage space and transmission bandwidth compared to RGB. YUV is not compressed RGB; rather, it is the mathematical equivalent of RGB. Also known as component video, the YUV elements are written in various ways: (1) Y, R–Y, B–Y, (2) Y, Cr, Cb and (3) Y, Pa, Pb. See *luminance*, *CCIR 601* and *YIQ*.

**YUV Outputs**
Video editing and quality home theater equipment provides YUV component video outputs. This is a typical set of connectors that use standard phono plugs (RCA plugs).

**Z**  A mathematical language used for developing the functional specification of a software program. Developed in the late 1970s at Oxford University, IBM's CICS software is specified in Z.

**Z39.50**  An ANSI standard query language that is a simplified version of SQL. It is used on the Internet to search for documents. See *WAIS*.

**Z80**  A family of 8-bit microprocessors from Zilog. The original Z80 chip was the successor to the Intel 8080 and was widely used in first-generation personal computers that used the CP/M operating system. Subsequent Z180, Z280 and Z380 chips have been widely used in embedded systems, and hundreds of millions of them have been shipped. See *eZ80*.

**Z8000**  A 16-bit microprocessor from Zilog that was the successor to the Z80. Many military-grade units are used in advanced weaponry.

**ZAI**  (Zero Administration Initiative)  A slogan for lower cost network administration using NetPCs. See *NetPC*.

**ZAK**  (Zero Administration Kit)  A series of wizards that assist network administrators in using system policies and user profiles in Windows 95 and NT. See *ZAW, system policy* and *user profile*.

**zap**  A command that typically deletes the data within a file but leaves the file structure intact so that new data can be entered.

**z/Architecture**  The hardware architecture in IBM's zSeries (mainframes). z/Architecture is an evolutionary step beyond ESA/390. The primary difference is the widening of all registers from 32–64 bits and the use of 64-bit addressing for both real and virtual storage. It includes the ability to execute programs using older 24 and 31-bit addressing so that ESA/390 programs run unchanged.

   z/Architecture adds 130 instructions, many of which deal with 64-bit data, and support for Variable Workload License Charges, which allows software to be priced based on usage. See *z/OS*.

**ZAW**  (Zero Administration for Windows)  Features in Windows 2000 that provide central administration of Windows PCs and NetPCs in a network. For example, it provides for more automatic distribution of new software and upgrades. Support for ZAW is also expected in Windows 98. See *ZAK*.

**Z-axis**  The third dimension in a graphics image. The width is the X-axis and the height is the Y-axis.

**ZBR**  See *zone bit recording*.

**z buffer**  A memory buffer in a graphics accelerator that is used to speed up the rendering of 3-D images. It holds the depth of each pixel (Z axis), and as an image is drawn, each pixel is matched against the z buffer location. If the next pixel in line to be drawn is below the one that is already there, it is ignored. This is also known as "hidden surface removal." See *graphics accelerator*.

**Z-CAV**    See *CAV*.

**Z-CLV**    See *CLV*.

**ZDBOp**    (Ziff-Davis Benchmark Operation)  An earlier name for Ziff-Davis Media's software benchmarks, which are available from the ZDNet Web site and can still be directly accessed by the ZDBOp URL (www.zdbop.com). See *Winstone*, *WinBench*, *NetBench*, *BatteryMark*, *i-Bench* and *WebBench*. See *benchmark*.

**ZDNet**    (ZDNet, Cambridge, MA, www.zdnet.com)  Formerly ZiffNet, ZDNet is a shareware and technical information service for PC users from Ziff-Davis Media. It contains a wide of variety of shareware and public domain software that can be downloaded. See *ZDBOp*.

**zebra strip**    A packaging device that allows quick alignment of electronic devices on a printed circuit board. It is a small rubber strip with carbon bands running around it. It allows contact to be made from the pads on the board to the pads on the device by whichever bands happen to line up at both points.

**ZENworks**    A family of directory-enabled system management products from Novell. Using Novell's popular NDS directory service, ZENworks supports Windows clients and NetWare and Windows NT/2000 servers. System administration features allow users to log in from any PC and obtain their custom desktop configuration.

**zeon**    See *Xeon*.

**zepto**    Sextillionth (10 to the −21st power). See *space/time*.

**zero administration**    An umbrella term for improved network administration functions in Windows products. See *ZAW* and *ZAK*.

**zero latency**    (1) Having no delay between the time a request is initiated and the response is given. See *latency*.
   (2) (Zero Latency)  Coined by the GartnerGroup, it is the immediate exchange of information across geographical, technical and organizational boundaries so that all departments, customers and related parties can work together in realtime.

**zero-slot LAN**    Refers to transmitting between computers over a serial or parallel port, thus freeing up an expansion slot normally used by LAN cards (NICs).

**zero suppression**    Eliminating leading zeros for readability. For example, 00000001542 becomes 1542.

**zero wait state**    Refers to a high-speed memory that transfers its data immediately upon being accessed without waiting one or more machine cycles to respond.

**zetta**    Sextillion (10 to the 21st power). See *space/time*.

**ZiffNet**    See *ZDNet*.

**ZIF socket**    (Zero Insertion Force socket)  A type of socket designed for easy insertion of pin grid array (PGA) chips. The chip is easily dropped into the socket's holes, and a lever is pulled down to lock it in. Pulling the lever moves the top plate of the assembly, pushing the pins into their contacts. See *PGA*.

**ZIF Socket**
After insertion of the chip, the lever is
pulled down and the pins are locked in.

**Zilog** (Zilog, Inc., Campbell, CA, www.zilog.com) A semiconductor manufacturer that was founded in 1974. It was a subsidiary of Exxon from 1980–1989 and became a public company in 1991. Zilog's Z80 chip was the CPU in CP/M machines, which helped to create the personal computer industry. Today, Zilog makes a variety of microprocessors and microcontrollers, and the Z80 family is still a major part of it.

**zinc air** A battery technology that provides more charge per pound or size than nickel cadmium or nickel metal hydride and does not suffer from the memory effect. It uses a carbon membrane that absorbs oxygen, a zinc plate and potassium hydroxide as the electrolyte. Zinc air technology dates back to the 1920s, where large batteries were used for remote railroad switches and lights on harbor buoys.

Air causes the chemical reaction and must be allowed into the cell when current is required and kept out when not. Thus, many zinc air batteries are designed for continuous use. For example, widely used for hearing aid batteries, the zinc air battery continuously discharges once it is activated. AER Energy is the pioneer in air management technology, which prevents air from entering the battery when not in use. Its Diffusion Air Manager provides an economical method for generating air flow and keeping the air out when there is no load to power. See *batteries*.

**zine** Pronounced "zeen." See *Webzine* and *e-zine*.

**zip** (1) To compress a file with PKZIP. See *ZIP file*.
(2) (Zip) A removable disk from Iomega. See *Zip disk*.
(3) (ZIP) (**Z**ig-**Z**ag **I**nline **P**ackage) A chip package similar to a DIP, but both rows of pins come out of one side in an alternating pattern. See *DIP* and *chip package*.
(4) (ZIP) A proprietary messaging protocol from IBM. PROFS uses ZIP for its e-mail transport.

**ZipCD** An earlier name for a CD-RW drive from Iomega introduced in 1999. See *Iomega* and *Zip disk*.

**Zip disk** A 3.5" removable disk drive from Iomega. It uses design concepts from Iomega's Bernoulli technology and hard disks to provide 100MB removable cartridges that cost about $15. The drive is bundled with software that can catalog the disks and lock the files for security.

In late 1998, a 250MB version of the Zip drive was introduced which also reads and writes the 100MB Zip cartridges. See *magnetic disk*.

**Zip Cartridge**
Since the introduction of the Zip in 1995, it has become the most popular removable storage medium since the floppy.

**ZIP file** (1) A file that contains one or more files compressed in the .ZIP file format. In the 1980s, Phil Katz developed algorithms for compressing files into smaller amounts of space. His compression and decompression programs became PKZIP and PKUNZIP from PKWARE, Inc. The format became so popular that other companies such as Nico Mac and Netzip developed ZIP and UNZIP utilities. See *PK software* and *WinZip*.
(2) A file on a Zip disk. See *Zip disk*.

**zipped** Compressed into the .ZIP file format. See *ZIP file*.

**zipped file** A file that contains one or more files compressed into the .ZIP file format. See *ZIP file*.

**zipping** The act of compressing one or more files into a .ZIP file. See *ZIP file*.

**Zmodem** A file transfer protocol that has become very popular because it handles noisy and changing line conditions very well, including satellite transmission. It sends file name, date and size first, uses variable length blocks and CRC error correction.

If a transmission is interrupted using Zmodem or Ymodem, Zmodem will transmit only the remainder of the file on the next try. This feature is extremely valuable when sending large files over noisy lines.

**zone** An administrative unit defined in a DNS server. It may refer to a single domain name or a subdomain. See *subdomain*.

Z

**zone bit recording**   Breaking a disk into recording zones using Z-CAV or Z-CLV methods. See *CAV* and *CLV*.

**zoned CAV**   See *CAV*.

**zoned CLV**   See *CLV*.

**zoned constant angular velocity**   See *CAV*.

**zoned constant linear velocity**   See *CLV*.

**zone file**   The database in a DNS server that contains the translations (mappings) between domain names and IP addresses. It also contains timing information and CNAME records. There are typically three zone files in a DNS server: (1) forward lookup (host names to IP addresses), (2) reverse lookup (IP addresses to host names) and (3) host names and IP addresses for name servers on the Internet that maintain the root domains. See *CNAME record*.

**Zoo**   A freeware compression program, including source code, used in UNIX, DOS and other environments.

**zoom**   To change from a distant view to a more close-up view (zoom in) and vice versa (zoom out). An application may provide fixed or variable levels of zoom. A display adapter may also have built-in zoom capability.

**Zoomed Video Port**   See *ZV Port*.

**Zortech compilers**   A series of C and C++ compilers from Zortech Inc., which was acquired by Symantec in 1991. Zortech compilers became Symantec compilers.

**z/OS**   A mission critical mainframe operating system that extends OS/390 to IBM's zSeries eServers. Although in its first release there are few functional enhancements compared to OS/390 Version 2 Release 10, many more are expected. z/OS, Version 1 Release 1 runs on G5 and G6 Parallel Enterprise Servers, Multiprise 3000 Servers and supports 64-bit real memory addressing on the z900 (64-bit virtual storage is expected). On the G5 and G6, z/OS uses 31-bit addressing and is somewhat restricted. See *zSeries*.

**zSeries**   The latest family of IBM mainframes introduced in 2000. It uses the z/Architecture, a major upgrade to the ESA/390 architecture. The zSeries is a major departure in naming for IBM, which has used the System/360, 370 and 390 designations for decades. The first model in the line is the 900, and the operating system is z/OS. All IBM products come under the eServer branding, thus a mainframe is a zSeries eServer. See *z/OS*, *z/Architecture*, *IBM server series* and *System/390*.

**ZV Port**   (Zoomed Video Port) An extension to the PC Card (PCMCIA) standard that provides a high transfer rate for video applications on portable computers. Video data goes directly to the display controller, bypassing the CPU and system bus, allowing full-screen, full-motion playback of digital video. The ZV Port is built into the notebook computer and activated by plugging in an MPEG PC Card that is ZV Port-compliant.

The ZV Port equivalent on a desktop computer is the pass through capability built into the MPEG board. The MPEG board is cabled directly to the monitor and provides a pass through for the VGA signals from the display adapter. See *VGA pass through*.

**ZyIMAGE**   Document management software for Windows from ZyLAB International, Inc., Rockville, MD (www.zylab.com), that provides storage and retrieval for text documents, dBASE files and TIFF images. It provides full indexing on text, spreadsheet and data files and allows keywords to be appended to TIFF files. ZyIMAGE includes the ZyINDEX system.

**ZyINDEX**   Text management software for DOS and Windows from ZyLAB International, Inc., Rockville, MD (www.zylab.com). It indexes the full text of word processing documents, spreadsheets and dBASE files. ZyINDEX works with Calera Recognition Systems WordScan OCR program to provide integrated scanning, optical character recognition and indexing. See *ZyIMAGE*.

**zywrite**   See *XyWrite for Windows* and *XyWrite III Plus*.

# Computer
# Desktop
# Encyclopedia

Edition 9

## Numerical Entries

# Numerals & Symbols

**/**   See *forward slash*.

**! point**   See *bang path*.

**# sign**   See *number sign*.

**\* symbol**   See *asterisk*.

**0x**   In programming, the symbol for a hexadecimal number. See *x*.

**1000Base-TX**   See *Gigabit Ethernet*.

**100BaseFX**   See *100BaseT*.

**100BaseT**   Also called "Fast Ethernet," it is a 100 Mbps version of Ethernet (IEEE 802.3u standard). 100BaseT transmits at 100 Mbps rather than 10 Mbps. Like regular Ethernet, Fast Ethernet is a shared media LAN. All nodes share the 100 Mbps bandwidth. 100BaseT uses the same CSMA/CD access method as regular Ethernet with some modification. Three cabling variations are provided. 100BaseTX uses two pairs of Category 5 UTP, 100BaseT4 uses four pairs of Category 3, and 100BaseFX uses multimode optical fibers and is primarily intended for backbone use. See *100VG-AnyLAN*.

**100BaseVG**   See *100VG-AnyLAN*.

**100BT**   See *100BaseT*.

**100MHz bus**   A bus speed of 100 million cycles per second. See *PC100* and *system bus*.

**100VG-AnyLAN**   A 100 Mbps version of Ethernet developed by HP that was able to transport both Ethernet and Token Ring frames. It was a shared media LAN like Ethernet, but employed the Demand Priority access method rather than CSMA/CD, allowing realtime voice and video to be given high priority. For a while, 100VG-AnyLAN was also called "Fast Ethernet," but the IEEE 802.3u Fast Ethernet became the standard.

**10/100 card**   An Ethernet network adapter (NIC) that supports both 10BaseT (10 Mbps) and 100BaseT (100 Mbps) access methods. Most cards autonegotiate at startup, enabling them to run at the higher speed if supported by the device they are connected to (hub or switch).

**10/100 hub**   An Ethernet hub that automatically senses the speed (10 Mbps or 100 Mbps) of the network adapter connected to it. See *10/100 card*.

**10/100 switch**    An Ethernet switch that automatically senses the speed (10 Mbps or 100 Mbps) of the network adapter connected to it. See *10/100 card*.

**1,024×768**    Standard super VGA resolution of 1,024 columns by 768 rows (lines). In the specification 1024x768x64K, the 64K is the number of colors. See *resolution*.

**10Base2**    An earlier 10 Mbps Ethernet standard that uses a thin coaxial cable. Network nodes are attached to the cable via T-type BNC connectors in the adapter cards. Also called "thin Ethernet," "ThinWire," "ThinNet" and "Cheapernet," 10Base2 has a distance limit of 607 feet. See *Ethernet*.

**10Base5**    The original IEEE 10 Mbps Ethernet standard which uses a thick coaxial cable. Network nodes are attached via transceivers that tap into the cable and provide a line to a 15-pin plug in the adapter card known as the AUI interface. Also called "thick Ethernet," "ThickWire" and "ThickNet," 10Base5 has a distance limit of 1,640 feet without repeaters. See *Ethernet*.

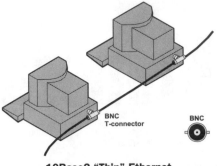

**10Base2 "Thin" Ethernet**
10Base2 uses a thin coaxial cable that is attached to each node using BNC T-connectors.

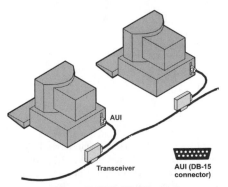

**10Base5 "Thick" Ethernet**
10Base5 was the first Ethernet and uses a bus topology. Transceivers connect the network adapters to a common coaxial cable. They often use a vampire tap that "bites" into the coax.

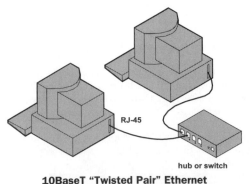

**10BaseT "Twisted Pair" Ethernet**
10BaseT and 100BaseT are the most popular Ethernets. All nodes connect to a central hub or switch using twisted pair wires and RJ-45 connectors.

**10BaseF**    A 10 Mbps Ethernet standard that uses optical fibers. All stations connect in a star configuration to a repeater or to a central concentrator. Connections are made via ST or SMA fiberoptic connectors. Adapter cards with AUI connectors are connected to 10BaseF networks via a fiber-optic transceiver.

The 10BaseFL standard defines the link between the concentrator and a station; 10BaseFP defines a star-coupled network; 10BaseFB defines a fiber backbone. See *Ethernet*.

**10BaseT**    A 10 Mbps Ethernet standard that uses twisted wire pairs (telephone wire). All stations connect in a star configuration to a central hub, also known as a "multiport repeater," or to a central switch. 10BaseT has been widely used due to the lower cost and flexibility of installing twisted pair. It has mostly been superseded by 100BaseT, which is 10 times as fast. See *Ethernet*.

**10BT**    See *10BaseT*.

**10 GbE**    See *10 Gigabit Ethernet*.

**10 Gigabit Ethernet**    An upcoming Ethernet technology that transmits at 10 Gbps. 10 Gigabit Ethernet enables a familiar network technology to be used in LAN, MAN and WAN architectures; however the CSMA/CD method for gaining access to the physical medium is not employed, and half duplex operation is not supported. 10 Gigabit Ethernet uses multimode optical fiber up to 300 meters and singlemode fiber up to 40 kilometers. See *Ethernet*.

**10-way**    Typically refers to a 10-CPU symmetric multiprocessing (SMP) system. See *SMP*.

**1-2-3**    See *Lotus 1-2-3*.

**1280×1024**    Standard super VGA resolution of 1,280 columns by 1,024 rows (lines). In the specification 1,280×1,024×64K, the 64K is the number of colors. See *resolution*.

**1284**    See *IEEE 1284*.

**128-bit**    See *bit specifications*.

**128-bit graphics accelerator**    A display adapter that has a pathway 128 bits wide between its on-board graphics processor and memory (video RAM).

**12-way**    Typically refers to a 12-CPU symmetric multiprocessing (SMP) system. See *SMP*.

**12x CD-ROM**    A CD-ROM drive that spins 12 times as fast as the first CD-ROM. It provides 1.8MB per second data transfer.

**1300 nm**    See *1550 nm*.

**133MHz bus**    A bus speed of 133 million cycles per second. See *PC100* and *system bus*.

**1394**    See *FireWire*.

**1401**    A second-generation IBM computer introduced in 1959 and used until the late 1960s. It had 16K of core memory, six tape drives and used punched cards for input. It was an outstanding success due to its reliability. More than 18,000 units were installed. For migration, 1401 emulators were built into IBM's 360 series.

**14.4**    Refers to the speed of modems that transmit at 14,400 bits per second.

**1.44M**    Refers to the 1.44MB high-density 3.5" disk used in PCs.

**1550 nm**    One of the two optical windows in an optical fiber where the glass is most transparent and efficient for transmission. See *optical fiber*.

**IBM 1401**
The 1401 was very successful. Its architecture and machine language were simple and straightforward. *(Image courtesy of International Business Machines Corporation. Unauthorized use not permitted.)*

**16:9**    The aspect ratio of HDTV (High Definition TV), which is like the wide screen in movie theaters. It is wider than the 4:3 aspect ratio of computer monitors and standard TV. The 16:9 size is also called the "letterbox format." See *HDTV*.

**16-bit**    See *bit specifications*.

**16-bit characters**    See *Unicode*.

**16-bit color**    Using two bytes per pixel in a color image. Up to 65,536 colors can be represented in the color palette. Most graphics formats provide 8-bit color or 24-bit color; however, display adapters generally have an intermediate 16-bit color range and can display 65,536 colors. See *bit depth* and *bit specifications*.

**16-bit computer**   A computer that uses a 16-bit word length. It processes two bytes (16 bits) at a time. See *32-bit processing*.

**16-bit driver**   A driver written for a 16-bit environment. It often refers to drivers written for DOS or Windows 3.x machines, in contrast to 32-bit drivers written for Windows 95/98 or Windows NT. For example, when users upgrade a PC from Windows 3.1 to Windows 95/98, they have to replace the Windows 3.1 display adapter driver with the Windows 95/98 version. In this case, they are replacing the 16-bit driver with a 32-bit driver.

**16-bit sample**   See *sampling rate*.

**16-bit sound**   A sound card that processes 16-bit sound samples. The more data in the sample, the more accurately sound can be digitized. See *sampling rate*.

**16-bit version**   A program that runs in a 16-bit environment. It typically refers to a program that was written for a DOS or Windows 3.1 PC, in contrast with a 32-bit version that was written for Windows 95/98 or Windows NT.

**16CIF**   See *CIF*.

**16 million colors**   See *24-bit color*.

**16x CD-ROM**   A CD-ROM drive that spins 16 times as fast as the first CD-ROM. It provides 2.4MB per second data transfer.

**.18 process**   See *micron*.

**18-track**   See *Magstar*.

**19mm tape**   See *DST*.

**1-bit DAC**   (1-bit **D**igtal to **A**nalog **C**onverter) A serial method of converting digital samples back into analog form for amplification. Each bit of the sample is converted into its analog weight rather than all bits of the sample converted in parallel. See *ladder DAC*.

**1-by-1 GIF**   See *invisible GIF*.

**1ClickCharge**   A Web payment service from 1ClickBrands, LLC., New York (www.1clickcharge.com) that specializes in premium digital content and micropayments. Similar to the E-ZPass system for highway tolls, 1ClickCharge requires prepaid deposits charged on a credit card. It also provides complete back-end credit card processing for the merchant without requiring integration to the merchants Web servers. See *Web payment service*.

**1G wireless**   See *wireless generations*.

**1U**   (1 Unit) See *U*.

**1x1 GIF**   See *invisible GIF*.

**1x DVD-ROM**   A first-generation DVD-ROM drive that provides a transfer rate of 1,350KB per second. It uses the CLV method and reads CD-ROMs at 8x speed, but generally cannot read CD-R and CD-RW disks. See *2x DVD-ROM* and *CLV*.

**216 colors**   See *Netscape color palette*.

**23B+D**   See *ISDN*.

**24-bit color**   Using three bytes per pixel in a color image. Also called "true color" and "RGB color," up to 16,777,216 colors can be represented in the color palette. See *bit depth* and *bit specifications*.

**2.4GHz band**   See ISM band.

**24×7**   Non-stop operation 24 hours a day, 7 days a week. Same as *7×24*.

**24x CD-ROM**   A CD-ROM drive that spins 24 times as fast as the first CD-ROM. It provides 3.6MB per second data transfer.

**256-bit**   See *bit specifications*.

**2.5G wireless**   See *wireless generations*.

**.25 process**   See *micron*.

**2780**   See *3780*.

**286**   The second generation of the Intel x86 family of CPU chips. The term may refer to the chip or to a PC that uses it. Introduced in 1982, it is the successor to the 8088/8086 chips used in the first PCs. The 286 broke the infamous one-megabyte memory barrier, but although faster than the previous generation, it was never capable of supporting Windows and other graphics-based applications. See *AT class* and *x86*.

**286 CPU Technical Specs**   A 16-bit multitasking microprocessor in a 68-pin PGA, PLCC or LCC package. Has 15 16-bit registers including eight general-purpose. Operational modes: "Real Mode" performs as a fast 8086 CPU and addresses 1MB memory. "Protected Mode" addresses 16MB physical and 1GB virtual memory and provides access to memory protection capabilities. Contains 134,000 transistors.

**28.8**   Refers to the transmission speed of a modem that can transmit up to 28,800 bits per second. See *V.34*.

**2B+D**   See *ISDN*.

**2B1Q**   (2 Binary 1 Quaternary) An encoding method used in ISDN in which each pair of binary digits represents four discrete amplitude and polarity values.

**2-D**   (2 Dimensional) Refers to objects that are constructed on two planes (X and Y, height and width, row and column, etc.). Two-dimensional structures are also used to simulate 3-D images on screen.

**2-D accelerator**   See *graphics accelerator*.

**2-D graphics**   The creation, display and manipulation of objects in the computer in two dimensions. Drawing programs and 2-D CAD programs allow objects to be drawn on an X-Y scale as if they were drawn on paper. Although 3-D images can be drawn in 2-D programs, their views are static. They can be scaled larger or smaller, but they cannot be rotated to different angles as with 3-D objects in 3-D graphics programs. They also lack the automatic lighting effects of 3-D programs. Any desired shadows must be created by the artist using color fills or gradients. See *graphics* and *3-D graphics*.

**2G+**   See *wireless generations*.

**2G wireless**   See *wireless generations*.

**2-tier architecture**   See *two tier client/server*.

**2U**   (2 Units) See *U*.

**2xAGP**   See *AGP*.

**2x CD-ROM**   A CD-ROM drive that spins twice as fast as the first CD-ROM. It provides 300KB per second data transfer.

**2x DVD-ROM**   A DVD-ROM drive that spins twice as fast as first-generation DVD-ROMs. It provides 2,700KB per second data transfer. The drives read CD-ROMs at a varying rate (CAV) between 8x and 20x, and they can read CD-Rs and possibly CD-RWs. See *1x DVD-ROM* and *CAV*.

**3+Open**   An OS/2-based network operating system from 3Com that supported DOS, OS/2 and Mac clients. It was discontinued in 1993.

**3+Share**   A DOS-based network operating system from 3Com that supported DOS and Mac clients. It was discontinued in 1993.

**303x**   A series of medium to large-scale IBM mainframes introduced in 1977, which includes the 3031, 3032 and 3033. See *IBM mainframes*.

**308x**   A series of large-scale IBM mainframes introduced in 1980, which includes the 3081, 3083 and 3084. See *IBM mainframes*.

**3090**   A series of large-scale IBM mainframes introduced in 1986. Before the ES/9000 models (System/390), 3090s were the largest mainframes in the System/370 line. Models 120, 150 and 180 are single CPUs. Models 200 through 600 are multiprocessor systems (first digit indicates the number of CPUs). The E, S and J models represent increased speed respectively. See *IBM mainframes*.

**3270**   A family of IBM mainframe terminals and related protocols (includes 3278 mono and 3279 color terminal). See *3270 emulator*.

**3270 Data Stream**   The format for transmitting data from an application to a 3270-type terminal.

**3270 emulator**   A plug-in board that converts a personal computer or workstation into an IBM mainframe terminal. The first 3270 emulator was the Irma board from Attachmate Corporation. The board is sometimes called a "coax adapter" because of its coaxial cable connection to the IBM cluster controller.

**32-bit**   See *bit specifications*.

**32-bit color**   Using 24 bits per pixel to represent a color image in a computer, plus an additional eight bits for an alpha channel. See *24-bit color*, *alpha channel*, *bit depth* and *bit specifications*.

**32-bit computer**   A computer that uses a 32-bit word length. It processes four bytes (32 bits) at a time. See *32-bit processing*.

**32-bit driver**   A driver written for a 32-bit environment. It often refers to drivers written for Windows 95/98 or Windows NT, in contrast to 16-bit drivers written for DOS and Windows 3.x. For example, when users upgrade a PC from Windows 3.1 to Windows 95/98, they have to replace the Windows 3.1 display adapter driver with the Windows 95/98 version. In this case, they are replacing the 16-bit driver with a 32-bit driver.

**32-bit processing**   Refers to programs running in a 32-bit computer. A 32-bit computer processes four bytes at a time, compared with two bytes in a 16-bit computer or one byte in an 8-bit computer. Starting with the 386 chip, Intel CPUs have been built with a split personality for compatibility with earlier models. They have both 16- and 32-bit modes of operation, the 32-bit mode being the native mode with more advanced capabilities.

   In 16-bit mode, or Real Mode, a program executes 16-bit instructions. In Protected Mode, a program has access to both 16- and 32-bit instructions, the maximum amount of RAM, virtual memory and virtual machine capabilities as well as memory protection, which keeps one program from crashing another.

DOS applications run in Real Mode, while Windows 3.1 switches back and forth between Real Mode and Protected Mode. OS/2, UNIX, Windows 95/98, Windows NT and other 32-bit operating systems run in Protected Mode when running 32-bit applications.

The 32-bit mode does not result in two times as much real work getting done as in 16-bit mode, because it relates to internal processing and not every instruction or unit of data takes advantage of the four bytes. In addition, program design as well as disk and bus speed play important roles in a computer's performance. While the speed may improve a little or a lot, depending on the program being run, 32-bit processing for the PC means as much a break from the past architecture as it does faster speed.

**32-bit version**   A program that runs in a 32-bit environment. In the DOS/Windows world, it refers to a program that was written for a Windows 95, 98, NT or 2000 machine in contrast with a 16-bit version that was written for DOS or Windows 3.1.

**32-bit Windows**   Refers to any or all of Windows 95/98/NT and 2000, which use the 32-bit native mode of the Intel CPU. The 32-bit mode became available starting with the 386. The term explicitly excludes Windows 3.1 and earlier Windows versions, all of which relied on 16-bit DOS being installed first. See *Win32*.

**32x CD-ROM**   A CD-ROM drive that spins a maximum of 32 times as fast as the first CD-ROM. It provides a maximum of 4.8MB per second data transfer.

**33.3**   Refers to the transmission speed of a modem that can transmit up to 33,300 bits per second. See *V.34*.

**3.3v**   (3.3 Volts) Refers to the amount of voltage required by the chips on newer personal computer motherboards. See *5v*.

**3480**   See *Magstar*.

**3490**   See *Magstar*.

**3.5"**   (1) Refers to the common 3 1/2 inch microfloppy disk used in personal computers.
(2) Refers to disk drives and other devices with a 3 1/2 inch wide form factor.

**3590**   See *Magstar*.

**360**   See *System/360* and *IBM mainframes*.

**36-track**   See *Magstar*.

**370**   See *System/370*.

**370/XA**   (370 EXtended Architecture) A major enhancement (1981) to System/370 architecture that improved multiprocessing, introduced a new I/O system and increased addressing from 24–31 bits (16MB–2GB). See *IBM mainframes*.

**3770**   The standard communications protocol for batch transmission in an IBM SNA environment. It also refers to early remote batch terminals that used punched cards and floppy disks as input.

**3780**   A standard communications protocol for transmitting batch data (also 2780). The protocols originated with early IBM remote job entry (RJE) terminals that included a card reader and a printer.

**37xx**   IBM communications controllers that includes the 3704, 3705, 3720, 3725 and 3745 models. The 3704 and 3705 are early units, and the 3745 models are newer and more versatile. The 3745 includes a cluster controller that can connect 512 terminals, eight token ring networks and 16 T1 lines.

**386**     The third generation of the Intel x86 family of CPU chips. The term may refer to the chip or to a PC that uses it. Introduced in late 1985, it is the successor to the 286, and although adequate for DOS applications, it is very slow for Windows and other graphics-based programs. The 386 was the first chip in the x86 line to provide 32-bit processing and provides both 16-bit and 32-bit modes. It added enhanced memory management, allowing both extended and expanded (EMS) memory to be allocated on demand. The 386 architecture has been followed in all of Intel's subsequent 486 and Pentium lines. See *PC* and *x86*.

**386 CPU Technical Specs**     A 32-bit multitasking microprocessor in a 132-pin PGA package. Supports 8, 16 and 32-bit data types. Has 32 32-bit registers including eight general-purpose. Operational modes: "Real Mode" performs as a fast 8086 CPU and addresses 1MB memory. "Protected Mode" addresses 4GB physical and 64TB virtual memory and provides access to memory management, paging and memory protection capabilities (see *32-bit processing*). "Virtual 8086 Mode" is a Protected Mode subset that runs tasks as if each were in an individual 8086 CPU. Contains 275,000 transistors and uses 1.5 micron technology (transistor elements average 1.5 microns). See *Virtual 8086 mode*.

**386/25, 386/33...**     The designation of CPU speed for a 386. The second number is the clock rate: 386/25 means 25MHz.

**386 Enhanced Mode**     An operational mode in Windows 3.x. See ***Windows 3.x modes***.

**390**     See *System/390* and *IBM mainframes*.

**3Com**     (3Com Corporation, Santa Clara, CA, www.3com.com) Founded in 1979 by Bob Metcalfe, 3Com is a leading communications hardware vendor, offering a wide variety of network adapters, hubs and related products. The company name was derived from Computer, Communication and Compatibility. In 1997, 3Com and U.S. Robotics agreed to merge. Retaining the 3Com name, it created a $5 billion dollar company with more than 12,000 employees and was the largest merger in the history of the data networking industry.

   3Com used to develop and support a line of network operating systems, which it discontinued in 1993. 3+Share was a DOS-based network operating system for PC and Mac clients. 3+Open was OS/2 based and supported DOS, OS/2 and Mac clients.

**3-D**     (3 Dimensional) Refers to objects that are constructed on three planes (X, Y and Z). A 2-D drawing program can be used to illustrate a 3-D object; however, in order to automatically rotate the object as a self-contained entity, a 3-D drawing program must be used.

**3-D accelerator**     See *graphics accelerator*.

**3-D animation**     Animating objects that appear in a three-dimensional space. They can be rotated and moved like real objects. 3-D animation is at the heart of games and virtual reality, but it may also be used in presentation graphics to add flair to the visuals. See *geometry calculations*, *VRML* and *surface modeling*.

**3-D audio**     Audio reproduction that simulates sounds coming from all directions. Using signal processing techniques as well as multiple speakers, 3-D audio is used in virtual reality and home theater systems. See *Dolby Digital* and *3-D positional sound*.

**3-D chat**     A chat room environment that incorporates 3-D images. See *chat room*, *VRML* and *avatar*.

**3-D digitizer**     A graphics input system that records x, y and z coordinates of a real object. Contact is made with various points on the object's surface by a light sensor, sound sensor, robotic instrument or pen. See *digitizer tablet*.

**3DES**     (Triple **DES**) See *DES*.

**3Dfx**     (3Dfx Interactive, San Jose, CA, www.3dfx.com) A company that specializes in 3-D accelerator chips and arcade game subsystems geared to the entertainment market. Founded in 1994, 3Dfx is known for its Voodoo Graphics processors which are used in a variety of products. See *Voodoo Graphics*.

**3-D graphics**    The creation, display and manipulation of objects in the computer in three dimensions. 3-D CAD and 3-D graphics programs allow objects to be created on an X-Y-Z scale (width, height, depth). As 3-D entities, they can be rotated and viewed from all angles as well as be scaled larger or smaller. They also allow lighting to be applied automatically in the rendering stage. See *graphics, Gouraud shading, Phong shading* and *2-D graphics.*

**3-D modeling**    The ability to create three-dimensional images. See *surface modeling* and *solid modeling.*

**3DNow!**    A technology developed for the K6-2 series of microprocessors from AMD to speed up floating point operations used in graphics-intensive applications. It provides a performance boost that enables more realistic rendering of 3-D graphics, as well as faster multimedia playback. The technology is a combination of execution units and new instructions within the microprocessor. See *K6.*

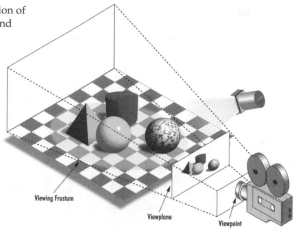

**The 3-D Stage**

In 3-D graphics, objects are created on a 3-dimensional stage where the current view is derived from the camera angle and light sources, similar to the real world. *(Image courtesy of Intergraph Computer Systems.)*

**3DO**    A multimedia and video game technology from 3DO Company, Redwood City, CA (www.3do.com) that is licensed to manufacturers and developers. The first 3DO player was Panasonic's Realistic Entertainment Active Learning (REAL) Multiplayer, which plays audio CDs and can be fitted for Video CDs.

3DO developers are able to create games from a large library of royalty-free sound effects, music, stills, clip art and film. The technology provides very high speeds for animation and can also provide a 3-D capability that is viewed through glasses.

3DO was founded by Trip Hawkins, one of Apple's earliest employees and founder of Electronic Arts software company. In 1990, Hawkins left Electronic Arts to start 3DO.

**3DOF**    See *6DOF.*

**3-D positional sound**    A technique that adds effects to the audio stream to create a three-dimensional space. It enables a pair of speakers to simulate the spatial sound that surround speakers can produce. See *3-D audio.*

**3-D sound**    See *3-D positional sound* and *3-D audio.*

**3D Studio**    A 3-D modeling and animation program from Autodesk, Inc., Sausalito, CA (www.autodesk.com). 3D Studio is the DOS version, and 3D Studio Max is the Windows version. It was the first program to bring professional animation and 3-D rendering from high-end workstations to the PC. Its 2D Shaper module lets you create 2-D shapes that become the cross sections of the 3-D models. 3D Lofter creates the underlying framework of the 3-D model, and 3D Editor is used to prepare the scene for rendering. In Release 4, the Keyframer animation module includes inverse kinematics, which links components so that they move together. See *Character Studio.*

**3GL**    See *third-generation language.*

**3GPP**    (3rd Generation Partnership Project) A cooperation of standards organizations (ARIB, CWTS, ETSI, T1, TTA and TTC) throughout the world that is developing the technical specifications for IMT-2000. 3GPP develops the W-CDMA technology, and 3GPP2 develops the cdma2000 technology, all of which increase data rates for 3G wireless communications. See *IMT-2000.*

**3GSP**    (3G Service Provider) An organization that provides 3G wireless services. See *wireless generations.*

**3G wireless**    See *wireless generations*.

**3-tier architecture**    See *three-tier client/server*.

**3U**    See *U* and *Eurocard*.

**4004**    The first microprocessor. Designed by Marcian E. "Ted" Hoff at Intel in 1971, it was a 4-bit, general-purpose CPU initially developed for the Japanese Busicom calculator.

**404**    Clueless. Not with it. Out to lunch. Said of somebody who is uninformed about something. It comes from the 404 error message commonly found on the Web. See *404 error* and *offline*.

**404 error**    The error message that is commonly displayed when a Web browser cannot locate a Web page or CGI script. The link to a Web page (URL) is static like a telephone number in a telephone book. A Web site can use software to search each link that it references for validity, but there is no program that can automatically find the new address for the missing link. The Webmaster can also replace the 404 message with something more understandable. See *link rot* and *moved to Atlanta*. See also *404*.

**411**    See *Web white pages*.

**4:2:2**    See *CCIR 601*.

**4:3**    The aspect ratio of the standard computer monitor and TV set. See *aspect ratio*.

**430FX**    See *Intel chipsets*.

**430HX**    See *Intel chipsets*.

**430MX**    See *Intel chipsets*.

**430TX**    See *Intel chipsets*.

**430VX**    See *Intel chipsets*.

**43xx**    A series of medium-scale IBM mainframes initially introduced in 1979, which include the 4300, 4321, 4331, 4341, 4361 and 4381.

**440BX**    See *Intel chipsets*.

**440FX**    See *Intel chipsets*.

**440LX**    See *Intel chipsets*.

**450BX**    See *Intel chipsets*.

**450GX**    See *Intel chipsets*.

**486**    The fourth generation of the Intel x86 family of CPU chips. The term may refer to the chip or to a PC that uses it. Introduced in 1989, it is the successor to the 386, and depending on clock speed, can be up to five times as fast. It provides very acceptable performance for DOS applications, but is bare minimum for Windows and other graphics-intensive programs. The 486 has a built-in math coprocessor.

Later versions of the chip offered double and triple the internal speed while maintaining the same external speeds (see *DX2* and *DX4*). See *OverDrive CPU*, *PC* and *x86*.

486 CPU Technical Specs    A 32-bit multitasking microprocessor that uses the same registers and operational modes as the 386 (see *32-bit processing*). It obtains its speed from an internal 8KB memory cache that it quickly fills in burst mode. The chip is housed in a 168- or 169-pin PGA package.

The 486DX chip contains 1.2 million transistors; the 486SX contains 1.1 million. Both use 1.0 micron technology (transistor elements are as small as one micron).

**486/25, 486/33...**    The designation of CPU speed for a 486. The second number is the clock rate: 486/25 means 25MHz. CPUs beyond 33MHz may have different internal and external speeds as noted in the following table. The internal clock speed is the rate at which the CPU processes (calculates, compares, etc.). The external clock speed is the rate at which it communicates with RAM and external bus.

**486DLC**    A 486SX-compatible CPU from Cyrix that is pin compatible with the 386DX. Designed for upgrading 386s, it comes in a variety of speeds including clock doubling versions.

**486DX**    A designation for the 486 CPU to distinguish it from the DX2 and DX4 models. See *486*.

**486DX2**    See *DX2*.

**486SL**    A version of the 486 from Intel designed for laptops. It runs on 3.3 volts (instead of 5) and includes power management features like the 386SL.

**486SLC**    (1) A 486SX-compatible CPU from Cyrix that is pin compatible with the 386SX, has a 1K cache and uses a 16-bit bus. It provides an upgrade path for 386SXs.

(2) The IBM version of the 486SX.

**486SX**    A slower version of the 486 without the math coprocessor. 486SXs can be upgraded to 486DX2s with Intel's OverDrive chip, which includes the coprocessor. The DX2 chip is plugged into the empty coprocessor socket, disabling the original CPU. See *486*.

**487**    The math coprocessor for the 486.

**4CIF**    See *CIF*.

**4GL**    See *fourth-generation language*.

**4mm tape**    See *DAT*.

**4-way**    Typically refers to a 4-CPU symmetric multiprocessing (SMP) system. See *SMP*.

**4xAGP**    See *AGP*.

**4x CD-ROM**    A CD-ROM drive that spins four times as fast as the first CD-ROM. It provides 600KB per second data transfer.

**50-pin Telco connector**    A plug and socket used to attach 25 pairs of telephone wires. It is also used for SCSI-1 connections and is the 50-pin version of the widely used Centronics connector found on the back of PC printers. See *RJ-21*.

**5100**    The first IBM desktop computer (1974). It came with up to 64K of RAM, a built-in tape drive and used APL or BASIC. Eight inch floppy disks became available in 1976.

**5.1 channel**    A digital audio recording and playback system for home theater. It includes five channels (left, right, center, rear/surround left and right) plus a subwoofer channel. The major 5.1 channel standards are Dolby AC-3 and Philips Musicam.

**5.25"**    **(1)** Refers to disk drives and other devices with a 5 1/4 inch wide form factor.

**(2)** Refers to the common 5 1/4 inch floppy disk that was widely used in personal computers. By late 1994, usage dwindled to nil.

**5250**    A family of terminals and related protocols for IBM midrange computers (System 3x, AS/400).

**5250 emulator**    Same as *twinax card*.

**568A**    An EIA/TIA standard for the termination pattern of an 8-wire RJ-45 cable. 568A and 568B (AT&T 268A) are functionally identical, but uses different colors wire identification. They both differ from the older USOC termination pattern that was widely used by AT&T. See *RJ-45*.

**56K modem**    See *V.90*.

**586**    A Pentium-class chip made by a company other than Intel. The 486 was the last numeric designation used by Intel. What was to be the 586 became the Pentium, thus, Pentium-class chips from non-Intel manufacturers were often designated as 586s and Pentium Pro-class chips as 686s.

**5 nines**    See *five nines*.

**5v**    (5 Volts) Refers to the amount of DC electricity required by the chips on most personal computer motherboards. The power supply converts 120v alternating current (AC) into 5v direct current (DC). It also generates 12v for the disk drives. See *3.3v*.

**5x86**    A Pentium-class CPU chip from Cyrix that runs in 486 motherboards. It is similar in power to a 75MHz to 90MHz Pentium chip.

**601**    The first model of the PowerPC chip. See *PowerPC*.

**603**    A low-power PowerPC chip designed for notebooks and portable applications. See *PowerPC*.

**604**    The second model of the PowerPC chip. Depending on clock speed, it runs applications from 50–100% faster than the 601. The 604e is a version of the 604 that has enhanced architecture for improving DOS and Windows emulation. See *PowerPC*.

**615**    An IBM version of the PowerPC that was expected to be able to execute PowerPC and x86 instructions natively.

**620**    A high-end model of the PowerPC chip, expected in 1997, but never came to fruition. See *PowerPC*.

**640K**    (640 Kilobytes) Typically refers to the first 640 kilobytes of memory in a PC, known as *conventional memory*. See *PC memory* and **PC memory map**.

**640×480**    Standard VGA resolution of 640 columns by 480 rows (lines). In the specification 640x480x16, the 16 is the number of colors. See *resolution*.

**64-bit**    See *bit specifications*.

**64-bit graphics accelerator**    A display adapter that has a pathway 64 bits wide between its onboard graphics processor and memory (video RAM).

**650**   IBM's first major computer success. Introduced in 1954, it read data from punched cards and magnetic tapes. It used a fixed-head magnetic drum that rotated at 12,500 rpm for its internal memory of from 1,000–2,000 10-digit words. Magnetic disks, which IBM pioneered on its 305 RAMAC, were made available to the 650 in 1956.

By the end of the 1950s, there were more than 1,500 units installed, making it the most widely used computer in the world. The 650 added high-speed computational ability to punched card data processing shops, which were the norm in those days.

**6502**   An 8-bit microprocessor from Rockwell International Corporation used in the Apple II and earlier Atari and Commodore computers.

**6800**   An 8-bit microprocessor from Motorola. The 6801 is a computer-on-a-chip version.

**68000**   A family of 32-bit microprocessors from Motorola that are the CPUs in Macintoshes and a variety of workstations. It is also known as the 68K or 680x0 series.

**IBM 650**
The 650 was IBM's first successful computer system. This photo taken in 1960 shows the author of this publication, Alan Freedman, sitting at the console. Directly behind him is a punched card reader, and behind that, the magnetic tape drives.

| Model | Bus Size | Max RAM | |
|-------|----------|---------|---|
| 68000 | 16 | 16MB | |
| 68020 | 32 | 4GB | |
| 68030 | 32 | 4GB | (built-in cache) |
| 68040 | 32 | 4GB | (2x fast as 68030) |
| 68060 | 32 | 4GB | (last 680x0 model) |

**680x0**   Refers to the Motorola 68000 family of CPU chips or to applications that are written for that chip. See *68000*.

**686**   A Pentium Pro-class chip made by a company other than Intel. The 486 was the last numeric designation used by Intel. What was to be the 586 became the Pentium, thus, Pentium-class chips from non-Intel manufacturers are often designated as 586s and Pentium Pro-class chips as 686s.

**68K**   See *68000*.

**6DOF**   (6 Degrees Of Freedom)  The amount of motion supported in a robotics or virtual reality system. Six degrees provides X, Y and Z (horizontal, vertical and depth) and pitch, yaw and roll. Three degrees of freedom (3DOF) provides X, Y and Z only. See *pitch-yaw-roll*.

**6U**   See *Eurocard*.

**6-way**   Typically refers to a 6-CPU symmetric multiprocessing (SMP) system. See *SMP*.

**6x86**   A Pentium-class CPU chip from Cyrix that is available in a variety of clock speeds. The 100MHz 6x86 is similar in power to a 133MHz Pentium chip. IBM produces the 6x86 for Cyrix and also sells and uses the chip.

**6x86MX**   A Pentium II-class CPU chip from Cyrix. Initial models run at 200MHz and 233MHz. The 6x86MX was code named "M2."

**6x CD-ROM**   A CD-ROM drive that spins six times as fast as the first CD-ROM. It provides 900KB per second data transfer.

**701**    IBM's first computer which was introduced in 1952. It was designed for scientific work and research, which later led to the development of the high-level FORTRAN language. Nineteen machines were built, a record volume for such a machine in that era. Its internal memory contained 2,048 36-bit words of Williams electrostatic storage tube memory and 8,192 words of magnetic drum memory. It used magnetic tapes for storage and was one of the first machines to use plastic-based tapes instead of metal tapes.

**702**    IBM's first commercial computer designed for business data processing. It was introduced in 1955.

**720K**    May refer to the 720K microfloppy disk used in PCs.

**750**    See *i750*.

**7-bit ASCII**    The original ASCII character code, which provides for 128 different characters. Internet mail as well as certain PBXs support 7-bit ASCII, not the 8-bit byte. In order to transmit proprietary file formats and binary executables over these systems, the 8-bit data must be encoded into a 7-bit format using such encoding methods as MIME, UUcoding and BinHex.

**IBM's First Computer**
At General Electric's Aircraft Jet Engine Plant in Evendale, Ohio, this 1954 photo shows GE manager Herbert Grosch explaining the 701 to Ronald Reagan. Reagan was a TV personality for GE at the time. *(Image courtesy of International Business Machines Corporation. Unauthorized use not permitted.)*

**7-track**    Refers to older magnetic tape formats that recorded 6-bit characters plus a parity bit on seven parallel tracks along the length of the tape. See *half-inch tape*.

**7×24**    Non-stop operation 7 days a week; 24 hours a day. Same as *24×7*.

**800×600**    Standard super VGA resolution of 800 columns by 600 rows (lines). In the specification 800×600×256, the 256 is the number of colors. See *resolution*.

**80186/80188**    An integrated version of the 8086/8088 CPU that includes additional system components, such as the clock, DMA and interrupt controller, on the same chip.

**802.1**    An IEEE standard for network management. See *IEEE 802*.

**802.11**    A family of IEEE standards for wireless LANs first introduced in 1997. 802.11 provides 1 or 2 Mbps transmission in the 2.4GHz band using either a frequency hopping modulation (FHSS) technique or direct sequence spread spectrum (DSSS), which is also known as CDMA. 802.11b defines an 11 Mbps data rate in the 2.4GHz band, and 802.11a defines 24 Mbps in the 5GHz band. See *wireless LAN* and *802.15*.

**802.11a**    See *802.11*.

**802.11b**    See *802.11*.

**802.12**    See *100VG-AnyLAN*.

**802.15**    An IEEE working group that is expected to introduce a wireless personal area network (WPAN) in 2000. A second task group is working on coexistence of 802.11 WLANs and 802.15 PANs. See *802.11*.

**802.1p**    An IEEE standard for providing quality of service (QoS) in 802-based networks. 802.1p uses three bits (defined in 802.1q) to allow switches to reorder packets based on priority level. It also defines the Generic Attributes Registration Protocol (GARP) and the GARP VLAN Registration Protocol (GVRP). GARP lets client stations request membership in a multicast domain, and GVRP lets them register into a VLAN. See *IEEE 802* and *QoS*.

**802.1q**    An IEEE standard for providing VLAN identification and quality of service (QoS) levels. Four bytes are added to an Ethernet frame, increasing the maximum frame size from 1518 to 1522 bytes. Three bits are used to allow eight priority levels (QoS) and 12 bits are used to identify up to 4096 VLANs. See *virtual LAN*.

**802.2**    An IEEE standard that specifies the data link layer for various media access methods. See *IEEE 802*.

**802.3**    An IEEE standard for a CSMA/CD local area network access method, which is widely implemented in Ethernet. The 802.3u standard covers Fast Ethernet, and 802.3ab and 3z cover Gigabit Ethernet. See *IEEE 802*.

**802.3ab**    See *802.3z*.

**802.3u**    See *802.3*.

**802.3z**    An IEEE standard for Gigabit Ethernet over optical fiber. It provides for full-duplex transmission from switch to end station or to another switch and half-duplex over a shared channel using the CSMA/CD access method. 802.3ab is the counterpart standard for Gigabit Ethernet over Category 5 copper wiring. See *Gigabit Ethernet*.

**802.4**    An IEEE standard for a token bus local area network access method, which is used in the MAP factory automation protocol. See *IEEE 802*.

**802.5**    An IEEE standard for a token ring local area network access method, which is widely implemented in Token Ring. See *IEEE 802*.

**802.6**    An IEEE standard for a DQDB metropolitan area network access method. See *IEEE 802*.

**80286**    See *286*.

**80386**    See *386*.

**80486**    See *486*.

**8080**    An Intel 8-bit CPU chip introduced in 1974. It was the successor to the first commercial 8-bit microprocessor (8008) and precursor to the x86 family. It contained 4,500 transistors and other electronic components.

**8086**    Introduced in 1978, the CPU chip that defines the base architecture of Intel's x86 family (XT, AT, 386, 486, Pentium). 8086s are used in some XT-class machines. See *PC* and *x86*.

**8086 CPU Technical Specs**    A 16-bit microprocessor in a 40-pin CERDIP package. Has 14 16-bit registers including eight general-purpose. Addresses 1MB memory using base addresses contained in segment registers. Contains 29,000 transistors.

**8086 emulator**    See *x86 emulator*.

**8088**    The Intel CPU chip used in first-generation PCs (XT class). It is a slower version of the 8086, chosen for migration from CP/M programs, the predominate business applications of the early 1980s. See *PC* and *x86*.

**8088 CPU Technical Specs**    Same as the 8086 CPU except that is uses an 8-bit data bus instead of a 16-bit data bus. Designed to ease conversion from 8-bit, Z80-based CP/M programs. Contains 25,000 transistors.

**80x86**    See *x86*.

**The Intel 8080**
The founders of Intel pose with a rubylith of the 8080 CPU in 1978. From left to right: Andy Grove, Robert Noyce and Gordon Moore. *(Image courtesy of Intel Corporation.)*

**8100**   An IBM minicomputer introduced in 1978 that was designed for departmental computing and used the DPPX/SP operating system.

**810 chipset**   See *Intel chipsets*.

**815 chipset**   See *Intel chipsets*.

**820 chipset**   See *Intel chipsets*.

**82385**   An Intel controller chip that manages the memory cache in 386 and 486 CPUs.

**8250A**   See *UART*.

**8259A**   Known as a Programmable Interrupt Controller, it is the interrupt controller chip used in a PC. It is superseded by the 82489DX chip. See *IRQ* and *PIC*.

**8.3**   Often refers to the method used to name files in DOS and Windows 3.x. The file name is up to eight characters long and the file extension is up to three characters long. See ***DOS file names***.

**840 chipset**   See *Intel chipsets*.

**850 chipset**   See *Intel chipsets*.

**8514**   The IBM monitor used with its 8514/A display adapter.

**8514/A**   An early high-resolution PC display adapter with 2-D graphics acceleration from IBM. Designed for MicroChannel machines and as a second monitor for dual screen display, it provided an interlaced 1,024×768×256 resolution. Third parties provided non-interlaced versions for the ISA bus.

**860**   See *i860*.

**88000**   A family of 32-bit RISC microprocessors from Motorola. The 88100 is the first processor in the 88000 family. Introduced in 1988, it incorporates four built-in execution units that allow up to five operations to be performed in parallel. Although the 88000 processors are very sophisticated chips, they never took off in the marketplace. See *88Open*.

**88K**   See *88000*.

**88Open**   A consortium founded in 1988 that provides information and certification for the Motorola 88000-based platform. Companies such as Data General, Encore and Harris offer products using the 88K chips.

**8-bit**   See *bit specifications*.

**8-bit color**   Using one byte per pixel in a color image. Up to 256 colors can be represented in the color palette. Various graphics formats are limited to 256 colors; for example, GIF images, which are widely used on the Web, are 8-bit color. See *bit depth* and *bit specifications*.

**8-bit sample**   See *sampling rate*.

**8-bit sound**   A sound card that processes 8-bit sound samples. The more data in the sample, the more accurately sound can be digitized. See *sampling rate*.

**8mm tape**   An 8mm-wide magnetic tape technology that is used in analog and digital camcorders (see *Hi-8*) and in data applications. Exabyte enhanced the international 8mm format established in 1984 and turned it into a high-performance digital storage device in 1987. The cartridges held 2.5GB, a breakthrough for the time. Exabyte has sold its products direct and through OEMs.

In 1996, Exabyte introduced the Mammoth drive, a capstanless version of its 8mm line, which initially supported AME-based 20GB cartridges and earlier MP-based cartridges. The lack of capstan reduces wear on the tape, because the capstan has to press against the medium to move it. Mammoth-2 later capacity to 60GB. Tape libraries hold from 500GB to more than 1TB. See *magnetic tape* and *helical scan*.

**8mm video**   See *Hi-8*.

**8-N-1**   (8 bits, No parity, 1 stop bit)  Common parameters for modem transmission.

**8-second rule**   Researchers seem to think that if users have to wait longer than eight seconds to download a Web page, they will go elsewhere. See *information overload*.

**8-VSB**   (8 level Vestigial SideBand)  The modulation technique used for digital TV (DTV) in the U.S. It minimizes interference with analog NTSC signals, which must be transmitted simultaneously with the digital signals until 2006. NTSC uses an analog VSB modulation. See *DTV*. Contrast with *OFDM*.

**8-way**   Typically refers to an 8-CPU symmetric multiprocessing (SMP) system. See *SMP*.

**8x CD-ROM**   A CD-ROM drive that spins eight times as fast as the first CD-ROM. It provides 1.2MB per second data transfer.

**9221**   A series of CMOS-based mainframes from IBM introduced in 1992. These were rack-mounted, entry-level mainframes that were part of the ES/9000 line. The 9221s were not widely used. See *Parallel Enterprise Server*.

**9370**   A series of IBM entry-level mainframes introduced in 1986 that use the 370 architecture. In 1990, the Enterprise System models (ES/9370) were introduced, which used the MicroChannel bus and a 386 for I/O processing. A Model 14 biprocessor system added a second 386 for DOS and OS/2 applications with a high-speed link between the 386 and 370 processors.

**9660**   See *ISO 9660*.

**9672**   The model number designation for IBM's CMOS-based mainframes. See *Parallel Enterprise Server*.

**9-track**   Refers to magnetic tape that records 8-bit bytes plus parity on nine parallel tracks along the length of the tape. This is the common format for half-inch open reels. See *half-inch tape*.

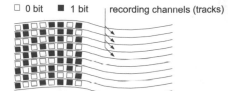

**9U**   See *Eurocard*.

**@ sign**   See *at sign*.

**.com**   (COMmercial)  A top-level Internet domain used by businesses mostly in the U.S. and Canada. See *Internet domain name* and *dot-com*.

**.edu**   (EDUcation)  A top-level Internet domain used by schools, colleges, universities and other educational groups mostly in the U.S. and Canada. See *Internet domain name*.

**.gov**   (GOVernment)  A top-level Internet domain used by governmental agencies in the U.S. See *Internet domain name*.

**.net**   (1) (NETwork)  A top-level Internet domain used by carriers, ISPs and other communications-oriented organizations. See *Internet domain name*.

**(2)** (.NET) A wide-reaching initiative from Microsoft that provides an operating environment for Web-based applications. Introduced in 2000, elements of .NET are expected over a period of several years. In Microsoft's ultimate vision, .NET will transform the Internet into a single computing experience. Applications will be hosted on the Internet and made available to the user via desktop and handheld devices that employ voice and handwriting recognition as optional interfaces.

.NET relies on HTTP, XML, SOAP and UDDI. Although HTTP and XML are fundamental elements of the Internet, SOAP provides a distributed object system that enables an application to call the services of other applications. UDDI provides the discovery mechanism that will enable applications to search for functions all over the world turning the Internet into a global processing system (see *HTTP, XML, SOAP* and *UDDI*).

.NET applications can run on intranets as well as public Internet sites, thus .NET is an all-inclusive Web-based software architecture for internal and external use. Microsoft browsers, applications and new versions of Windows will be .NET enabled.

.NET supports programming languages that are compiled into a Common Intermediate Language (CIL) which is executed on the fly or compiled into machine language by the Common Language Runtime (CLR) software in the target computer. This is similar to Java's intermediate bytecode, except that Java is one language, whereas .NET lets all programming languages be compiled into intermediate code. CLRs can also be developed to run under any operating system, not just Windows.

Microsoft has enhanced its programming languages to support the .NET platform (Visual Studio.NET, Visual Basic.NET, etc.). It also introduced the .NET-enabled C Sharp (C#) programming language. For backward compatibility, .NET supports existing Windows structures such as DLLs and COM objects. See *C#* and *CLI*.

**ASPs and ASPs**    One of the features of the .NET platform is ASP.NET, which is the .NET version of Microsoft's Active Server Page (ASP) technology. ASP pages are processed by the Web server and enable the development of dynamic, interactive sessions with the user. Since .NET is based on the Web, it is very appropriate for programs to be hosted by application service providers, another A-S-P acronym. Better know which ASP is which. See *ASP*.

**.NET SDK**    (**.NET S**oftware **D**evelopment **K**it) The developer's toolkit for Microsoft's .NET platform. It includes all the routines necessary to create and test .NET applications. See *.NET*.

**.org**    (**ORG**anization) A top-level Internet domain used by associations and non-profit organizations mostly in the U.S. and Canada. See *Internet domain name*.

**.tv**    See *dotTV*.

**.zip file**    See *ZIP file*.

**\**    See *backslash*.

## INTERNATIONAL CONTACT INFORMATION

**AUSTRALIA**
McGraw-Hill Book Company Australia Pty. Ltd.
TEL +61-2-9417-9899
FAX +61-2-9417-5687
http://www.mcgraw-hill.com.au
books-it_sydney@mcgraw-hill.com

**CANADA**
McGraw-Hill Ryerson Ltd.
TEL +905-430-5000
FAX +905-430-5020
http://www.mcgrawhill.ca

**GREECE, MIDDLE EAST,
NORTHERN AFRICA**
McGraw-Hill Hellas
TEL +30-1-656-0990-3-4
FAX +30-1-654-5525

**MEXICO (Also serving Latin America)**
McGraw-Hill Interamericana Editores S.A. de C.V.
TEL +525-117-1583
FAX +525-117-1589
http://www.mcgraw-hill.com.mx
fernando_castellanos@mcgraw-hill.com

**SINGAPORE (Serving Asia)**
McGraw-Hill Book Company
TEL +65-863-1580
FAX +65-862-3354
http://www.mcgraw-hill.com.sg
mghasia@mcgraw-hill.com

**SOUTH AFRICA**
McGraw-Hill South Africa
TEL +27-11-622-7512
FAX +27-11-622-9045
robyn_swanepoel@mcgraw-hill.com

**UNITED KINGDOM & EUROPE
(Excluding Southern Europe)**
McGraw-Hill Education Europe
TEL +44-1-628-502500
FAX +44-1-628-770224
http://www.mcgraw-hill.co.uk
computing_neurope@mcgraw-hill.com

**ALL OTHER INQUIRIES Contact:**
Osborne/McGraw-Hill
TEL +1-510-549-6600
FAX +1-510-883-7600
http://www.osborne.com
omg_international@mcgraw-hill.com

**About the CD**    The entire contents of *Computer Desktop Encyclopedia*, plus an additional 5,000 terms and 1,000 more pictures that would not fit into the physical book, are available on the enclosed CD-ROM. The contents of the CD-ROM are fully searchable by entries and by terms in the text.

**Getting Started**    The enclosed CD-ROM runs under Windows only (Windows 95, 98, ME, NT, 2000 and XP). Insert the CD into your CD-ROM drive and the installation program will automatically begin after a few seconds. Follow the onscreen instructions. The *Encyclopedia* takes takes 135MB of disk space.

If the installation program does not run automatically, double-click the My Computer icon on your desktop, and then double-click the CD-ROM drive icon where the name 9th_ed_cde appears. Then, double-click the Install icon, and the installation program will begin. Follow the onscreen instructions.

To run the program after installation, click *Computer Desktop Encyclopedia* on the Start menu. Click *Computer Desktop Encyclopedia* one more time. To find a definition, type the term into the Look Up box and press ENTER. If you have questions about how to use the software, press F1 or select Help | Contents from the menu bar to access the online user manual.

**Problems with the CD**    If you have followed the instructions above and the program will not work, you may have a defective CD or a defective CD-ROM drive. Be sure the CD is inserted correctly into the CD-ROM drive. Test the CD-ROM drive with other CDs to determine whether it works. If you need help or a replacement CD, call Hudson Software at 800-217-0059 for support.